MICROSOFT®

Office 2003

Advanced Concepts and Techniques

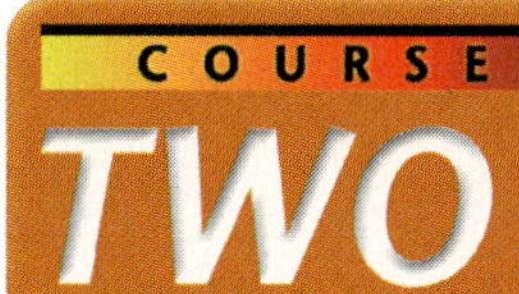

WORD 2003 EXCEL 2003 ACCESS 2003 POWERPOINT 2003 OUTLOOK 2003

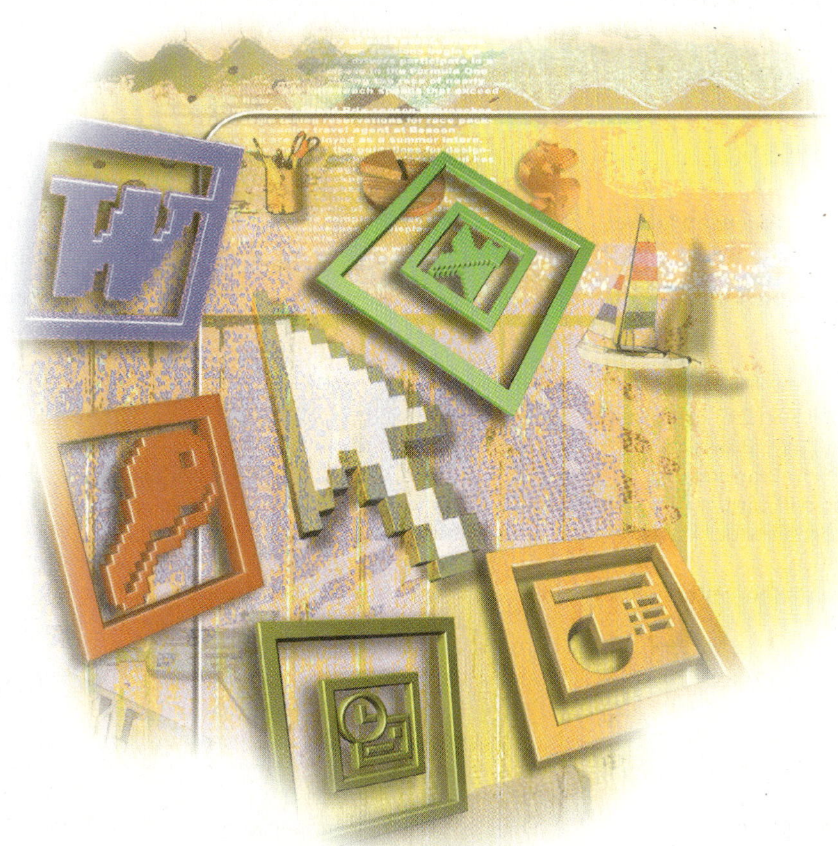

Gary B. Shelly
Thomas J. Cashman
Misty E. Vermaat

Contributing Authors
Mary Z. Last
Philip J. Pratt
James S. Quasney
Susan L. Sebok
Jeffrey J. Webb

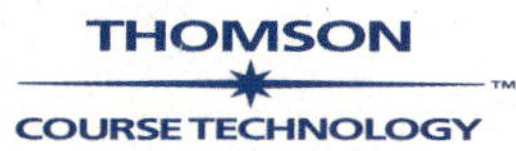

COURSE TECHNOLOGY
25 THOMSON PLACE
BOSTON MA 02210

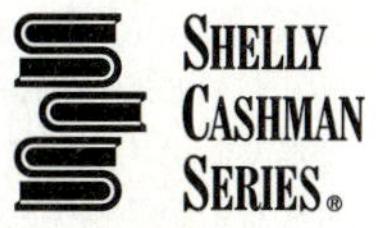

Australia • Canada • Denmark • Japan • Mexico • New Zealand • Philippines • Puerto Rico • Singapore
South Africa • Spain • United Kingdom • United States

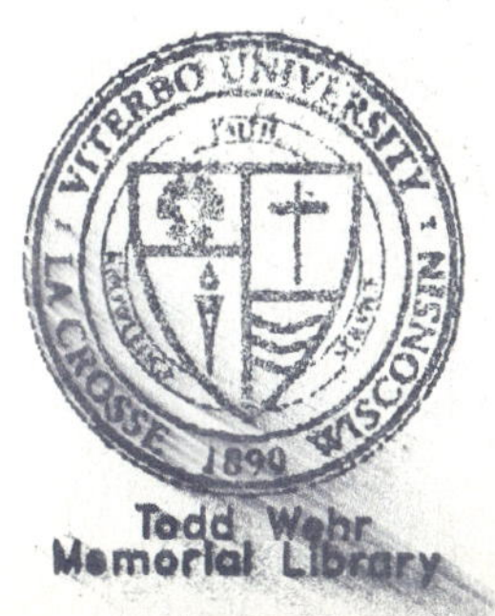

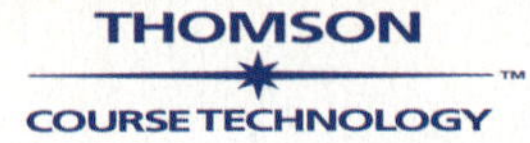

Microsoft Office 2003
Advanced Concepts and Techniques

Gary B. Shelly
Thomas J. Cashman
Misty E. Vermaat

Executive Editor:
Cheryl Costantini

Senior Product Manager:
Alexandra Arnold

Product Manager:
Erin Runyon

Associate Product Manager:
Reed Cotter

Editorial Assistant:
Selena Coppock

Print Buyer:
Laura Burns

Signing Representative:
Cheryl Costantini

Series Consulting Editor:
Jim Quasney

Director of Production:
Becky Herrington

Production Assistant:
Jennifer Quiambao

Development Editor:
Ginny Harvey

Copy Editors/Proofreaders:
Ginny Harvey
Nancy Lamm
Lyn Markowicz
Lori Silfen
Lisa Jedlicka
Kim Kosmatka
Ellana Russo

Interior Designer:
Becky Herrington

Cover Designers:
Ken Russo
Richard Herrera

Illustrators:
Richard Herrera
Andrew Bartel
Ken Russo

Compositors:
Jeanne Black
Andrew Bartel
Kellee LaVars
Kenny Tran
Michelle French

Indexer:
Cristina Haley

Printer:
Banta Menasha

Printed in the United States of America

1 2 3 4 5 6 7 8 9 10
BM 08 07 06 05 04

For more information, contact
Course Technology
25 Thomson Place
Boston, Massachusetts 02210

Or find us on the World Wide Web at:
www.course.com

ISBN 0-619-20025-1 (perfect bound)
ISBN 0-619-20026-X (hard cover/spiral bound)

PHOTO CREDITS: Microsoft PowerPoint 2003 *Project 1, page PPT 6* laptop computer, Courtesy of PhotoDisc, Inc.

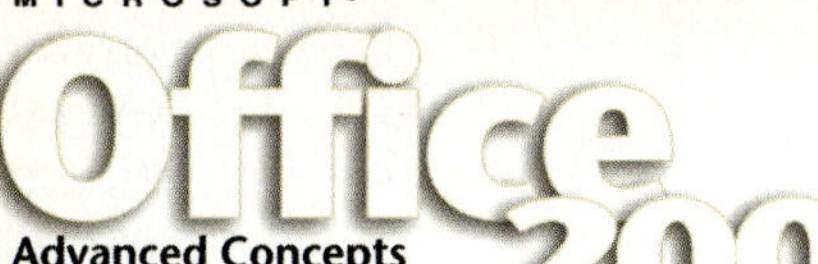

Advanced Concepts and Techniques

WORD 2003 EXCEL 2003 ACCESS 2003 POWERPOINT 2003 OUTLOOK 2003

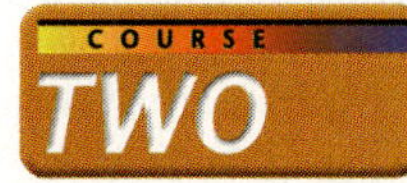

Contents

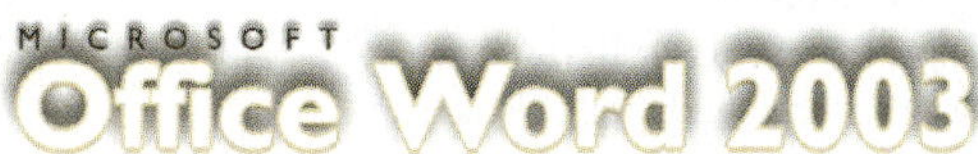

Project Four

Creating a Document with a Table, Chart, and Watermark

Project Five

Generating Form Letters, Mailing Labels, and Directories

Project Six

Creating a Professional Newsletter

Collaboration Feature

Using Word's Collaboration Tools

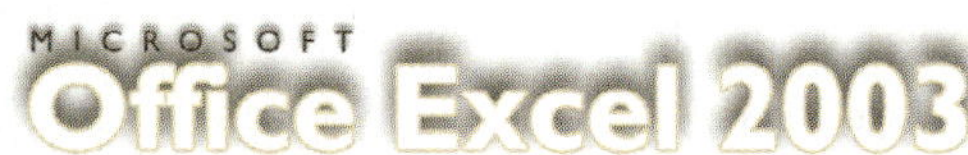

Project Four

Financial Functions, Data Tables, Amortization Schedules, and Hyperlinks

Project Five

Creating, Sorting, and Querying a List

Project Six

Creating Templates and Working with Multiple Worksheets and Workbooks

Integration Feature

Object Linking and Embedding (OLE) and Web Discussions

Microsoft Office Access 2003

Project Four

Reports, Forms, and Combo Boxes

Project Five

Enhancing Forms with OLE Fields, Hyperlinks, and Subforms

Project Six

Switchboards, PivotTables, and PivotCharts

Web Feature

Data Access Pages

MICROSOFT Office PowerPoint 2003

Project Three

Using Visuals to Enhance a Slide Show

Project Four

Modifying Visual Elements and Presentation Formats

Collaboration Feature

Delivering Presentations to and Collaborating with Workgroups

Microsoft Office Outlook 2003

Project Two

Schedule Management Using Outlook

Integration Case Studies

Appendix A

Microsoft Office Help System

Appendix B

Speech and Handwriting Recognition and Speech Playback

Appendix C

Publishing Office Web Pages to a Web Server

Appendix D

Changing Screen Resolution and Resetting the Word Toolbars and Menus

Appendix E

Microsoft Office Specialist Certification

Preface

The Shelly Cashman Series® offers the finest textbooks in computer education. We are proud of the fact that our series of Microsoft Office 4.3, Microsoft Office 95, Microsoft Office 97, Microsoft Office 2000, and Microsoft Office XP textbooks have been the most widely used books in education. With each new edition of our Office books, we have made significant improvements based on the software and comments made by the instructors and students. The *Microsoft Office 2003* books continue with the innovation, quality, and reliability that you have come to expect from the Shelly Cashman Series.

In this *Microsoft Office 2003* book, you will find an educationally sound, highly visual, and easy-to-follow pedagogy that combines a vastly improved step-by-step approach with corresponding screens. All projects and exercises in this book are designed to take full advantage of the Office 2003 enhancements. The popular Other Ways and More About features offer in-depth knowledge of the Office applications. The new Q&A feature offers students a way to solidify important application concepts. The Learn It Online page presents a wealth of additional exercises to ensure your students have all the reinforcement they need. The project material is developed to ensure that students will see the importance of learning how to use the Office applications for future coursework.

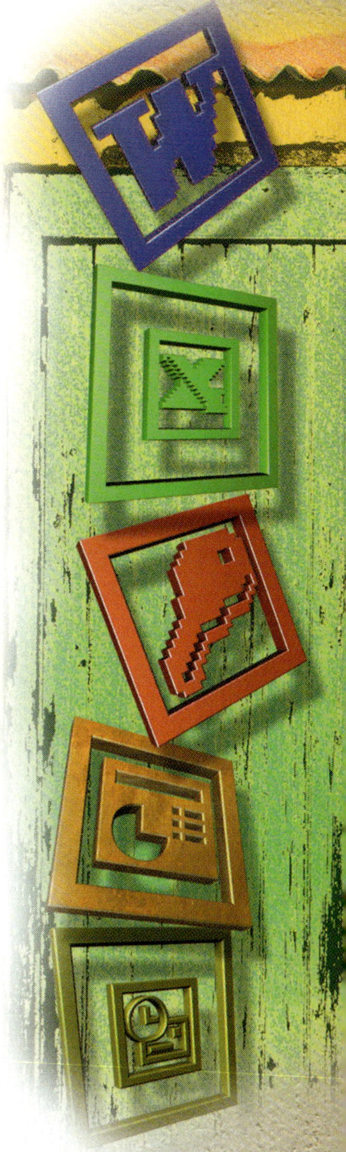

Objectives of This Textbook

Microsoft Office 2003: Advanced Concepts and Techniques is intended for a one-quarter or one semester advanced computer applications course. This book assumes that students are familiar with the fundamentals of Microsoft Windows XP, Microsoft Office Word 2003, Microsoft Office Excel 2003, Microsoft Office Access 2003, Microsoft Office PowerPoint 2003, and Microsoft Office Outlook 2003. The topics are covered in the companion textbook *Microsoft Office 2003: Introductory Concepts and Techniques*. The objectives of this book are:

- To extend the student's basic knowledge of and teach the fundamentals of Microsoft Office 2003
- To help students discover the underlying functionality of Microsoft Office 2003 so they can become more productive
- To expose students to practical examples of the computer as a useful tool
- To acquaint students with the proper procedures to create documents, worksheets, databases, Outlook-related files, and slide shows suitable for coursework, professional purposes, and personal use
- To help students demonstrate their proficiency with Microsoft Office 2003 by preparing them to pass the Microsoft Office Specialist certification specialist-level examinations for Word 2003, Excel 2003, Access 2003, PowerPoint 2003, and Outlook 2003
- To develop an exercise-oriented approach that allows learning by doing
- To encourage independent study, and help those who are working alone

Approved by Microsoft as Courseware for Microsoft Office Specialist Certification

Microsoft Office 2003: Advanced Concepts and Techniques, when used in combination with the companion textbook *Microsoft Office 2003: Introductory Concepts and Techniques* in a two-semester sequence, has been approved by Microsoft as courseware for Microsoft Office Specialist certification. After completing the projects and exercises in this book and its companion book, students will be prepared to take the specialist-level exams for the five basic Office applications.

By passing the certification exam for a Microsoft software application, students demonstrate their proficiency in that application to employers. This exam is offered at participating centers, participating corporations, and participating employment agencies. See Appendix E for additional information about obtaining Microsoft Office Specialist certification and for a table that includes the Word 2003, Excel 2003, Access 2003, PowerPoint 2003, and Outlook 2003 Microsoft Office Specialist skill sets and corresponding page numbers where a skill is discussed in the book, or visit the Web site microsoft.com/officespecialist.

The Shelly Cashman Series Microsoft Office Specialist Center (Figure 1) has links to valuable information on the certification program. The Web page (scsite.com/winoff2003/cert) includes links to general information on certification, choosing an application for certification, preparing for the certification exam, and taking and passing the certification exams.

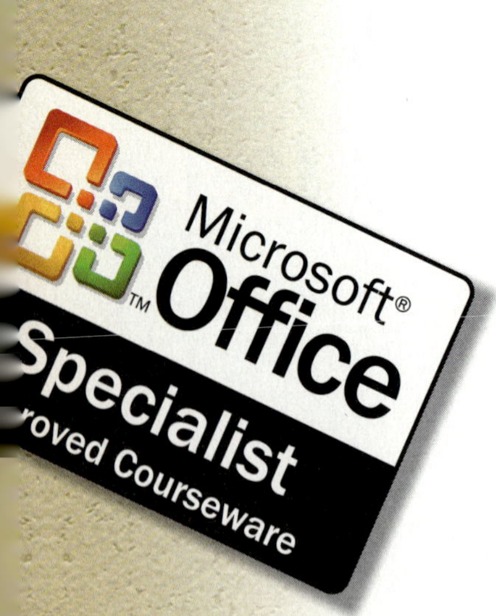

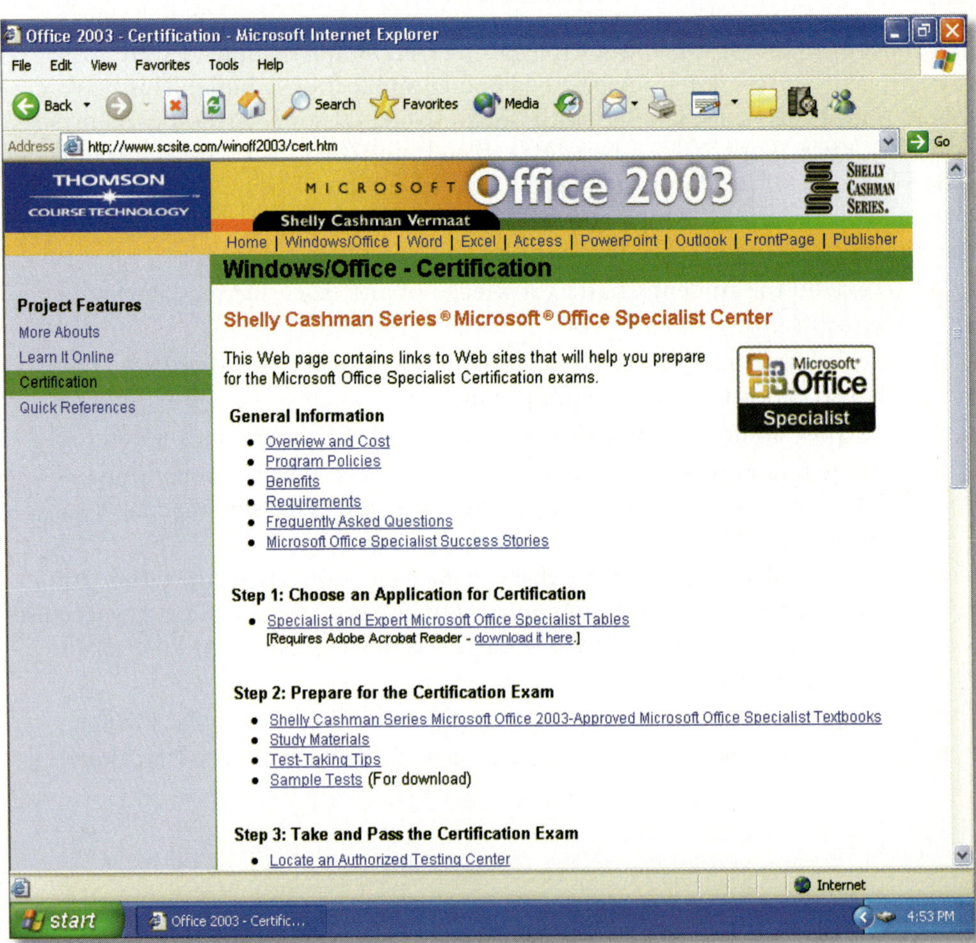

FIGURE 1

The Shelly Cashman Approach

Features of the Shelly Cashman Series *Microsoft Office 2003* books include:

- **Project Orientation:** Each project in the book presents a practical problem and complete solution in an easy-to-understand approach.
- **Step-by-Step, Screen-by-Screen Instructions:** Each of the tasks required to complete a project is identified throughout the project. Full-color screens with call outs accompany the steps.
- **Thoroughly Tested Projects:** Unparalleled quality is ensured because every screen in the book is produced by the author only after performing a step, and then each project must pass Course Technology's award-winning Quality Assurance program.
- **Other Ways Boxes and Quick Reference Summary:** The Other Ways boxes displayed at the end of most of the step-by-step sequences specify the other ways to do the task completed in the steps. Thus, the steps and the Other Ways box make a comprehensive reference unit.
- **More About and Q&A Features:** These marginal annotations provide background information, tips, and answers to common questions that complement the topics covered, adding depth and perspective to the learning process.
- **Integration of the World Wide Web:** The World Wide Web is integrated into the Office 2003 learning experience by (1) More About annotations that send students to Web sites for up-to-date information and alternative approaches to tasks; (2) a Microsoft Office Specialist Certification Web page so students can prepare for the certification examinations; (3) a Quick Reference Summary Web page that summarizes the ways to complete tasks (mouse, menu, shortcut menu, and keyboard); and (4) the Learn It Online page at the end of each project, which has project reinforcement exercises, learning games, and other types of student activities.

Other Ways

1. In Voice Command mode, say "Insert, Picture, New Drawing"

More About

Undoing Formats

If you started to assign formats to a range and then realize you made a mistake and want to start over, select the range, click Style on the Format menu, click Normal in the Style Name list, and then click the OK button.

Q&A

Q: How many ways can you format a cell?

A: You can format a cell using the (1) buttons on Formatting toolbar; (2) Cells command on the Format menu; (3) Format Cells command on shortcut menu; (4) format symbols; and (5) Format Painter button on the Standard toolbar.

Organization of This Textbook

Microsoft Office 2003: Advanced Concepts and Techniques consists of three projects each on Microsoft Office Word 2003, Microsoft Office Excel 2003, and Microsoft Office Access 2003, two projects on Microsoft Office PowerPoint 2003, four special features emphasizing Integration and Collaboration, one project on Microsoft Office Outlook 2003, three capstone Case Study exercises, five appendices, and a Quick Reference Summary. A short description of each follows.

Microsoft Office Word 2003

Project 4 – Creating a Document with a Table, Chart, and Watermark In Project 4, students work with a multi-page document that has a title page. Students learn how to border and shade paragraphs; change paragraph indentation; format characters using the Font dialog box; modify default font settings; clear formatting; insert clip art from the Web; center the contents of a page vertically; insert a section break; insert an existing Word document in an open document; create headers and footers different from previous headers and footers; change the starting page number in a section; edit and format a Word table; sum columns in a table; select and format nonadjacent text; chart a Word table; modify and format a chart; find a format; add picture bullets to a list; create and apply a character style; create a table using the Draw Table feature; change the direction and alignment of text in table cells; insert a text watermark; and reveal formatting.

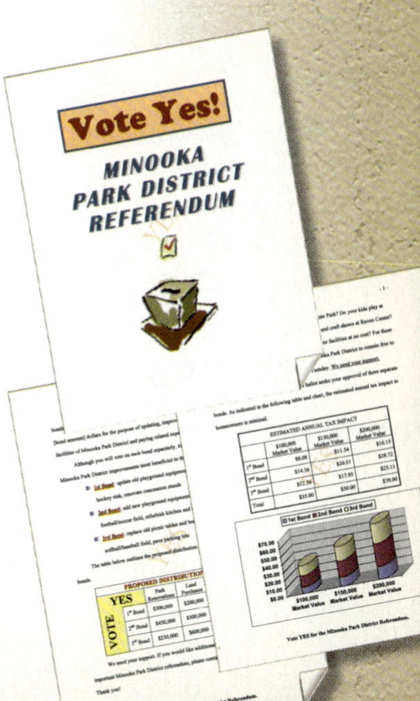

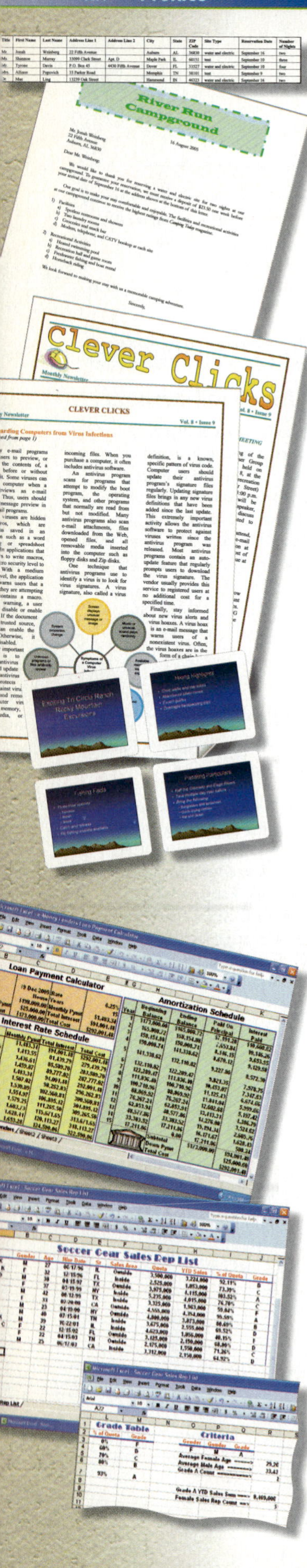

Project 5 – Generating Form Letters, Mailing Labels, Envelopes, and Directories In Project 5, students learn how to create and edit the main document for form letters, mailing labels, envelopes, and directories. Topics include using a letter template for the main document; inserting and formatting a drawing canvas; inserting and formatting an AutoShape; creating a folder while saving; creating and editing a data source; inserting a date field and editing its format; inserting and editing merge fields in a main document; using an IF field; creating an outline numbered list; applying a paragraph style; displaying and printing field codes; merging and printing the documents; selecting data records to merge and print; sorting data records and table contents; viewing merged data; modifying table properties; renaming a folder; formatting text as hidden; and printing a document in landscape orientation.

Project 6 – Creating a Professional Newsletter In Project 6, students learn how to use Word's desktop publishing features to create a newsletter. Topics include creating and formatting a WordArt drawing object; adding ruling lines; inserting a symbol; changing a graphic's wrapping style; flipping and brightening a graphic; formatting a document in multiple columns; justifying a paragraph; formatting a character as a drop cap; inserting a column break; placing a vertical rule between columns; displaying a document in full screen view; inserting, formatting, and positioning a text box; changing character spacing; shading a paragraph; using the Paste Special command; balancing columns; inserting and formatting a diagram; using the Format Painter button; adding a page border; highlighting text; animating text; changing background color and pattern; splitting a window; arranging open Word documents; and using reading layout view.

Collaboration Feature – Using Word's Collaboration Tools In the Collaboration feature, students create an outline, use Word's collaboration tools to review the outline, and then send the final outline to PowerPoint for use in a slide show. Collaboration tools presented include e-mailing a document for review; inserting and editing comments; tracking changes; reviewing tracked changes; viewing comments; and comparing and merging documents.

Microsoft Office Excel 2003

Project 4 – Financial Functions, Data Tables, Amortization Schedules, and Hyperlinks In Project 4, students use financial functions and learn more about analyzing data in a worksheet. Topics include applying the PMT function to determine a monthly payment; using the PV function to determine the amount due on a loan at the end of a year; adding a hyperlink to a Web page; using names to reference cells; protecting a worksheet; setting print options; conditional formatting; adding and modifying graphics; error checking; page setup; and analyzing data by creating a data table and an amortization schedule.

Project 5 – Creating, Sorting, and Querying a List In Project 5, students learn how to create, sort, and filter a list. Topics include data validation; using a data form to create and maintain a list; applying computational fields to a database; expanding the range of the list to include additional fields; creating subtotals; finding, extracting, and deleting records that pass a test; outlining a worksheet; applying database, COUNTIF, SUMIF, and lookup functions; and saving a workbook in different file formats.

Project 6 – Creating Templates and Working with Multiple Worksheets and Workbooks In Project 6, students learn to create a template and consolidate data into one worksheet. Topics include building and copying a template; using the ROUND function; working with multiple worksheets; using 3-D cell references, customized formats, and styles; using the Research task pane to find synonyms and do research; using WordArt; adding text boxes and arrows; adding notes to a cell; adding a header and footer; creating and modifying lines and objects; changing margins; finding and replacing data; searching for files on disk; creating a workspace, tiling; and consolidating data by linking workbooks.

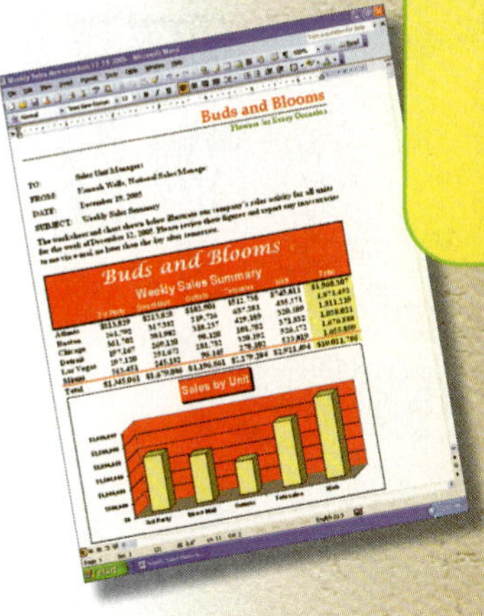

Integration Feature – Object-Linking and Embedding (OLE) and Web Discussions In the Integration feature, students are introduced to linking a worksheet to a Word document and Web discussions. Topics include an explanation of the differences among copying and pasting; copying and embedding; and copying and linking; opening multiple applications; linking a worksheet to a Word document; saving and printing a document with a linked worksheet; and editing a linked worksheet in a Word document. Finally, students are introduced to using the Web to discuss a document using a SharePoint server.

Microsoft Office Access 2003

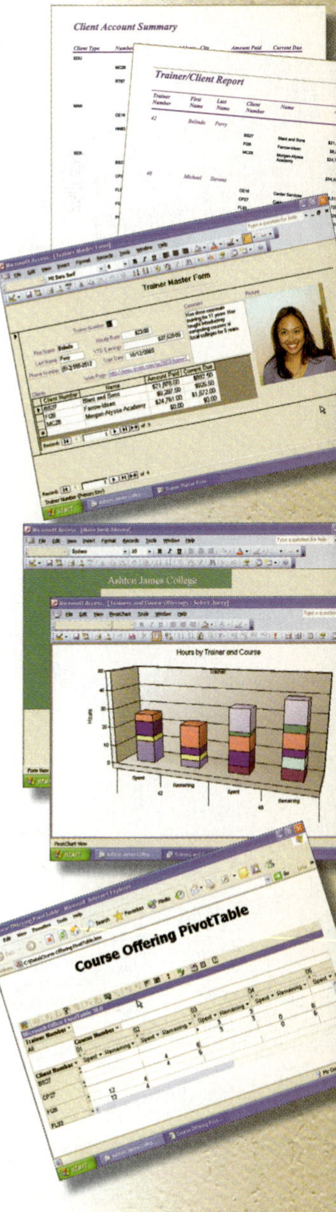

Project 4 – Reports, Forms, and Combo Boxes In Project 4, students learn to create custom reports and forms. Students learn how to change a variety of field properties such as font styles, formats, and colors. Topics include creating queries for reports; using the Report Wizard; modifying a report design; saving a report; sorting and grouping in a report; printing a report; creating a report with groups and subtotals; removing totals from a report; aligning controls; and changing the format of controls. Other topics include creating an initial form using the Form Wizard; modifying a form design; moving fields; and adding calculated fields and combo boxes.

Project 5 – Enhancing Forms with OLE Fields, Hyperlinks, and Subforms In Project 5, students learn to use date, memo, OLE, and hyperlink fields. Topics include incorporating these fields in the structure of a database; using the Input Mask Wizard; updating the data in these fields and changing table properties; creating a form that uses a subform to incorporate a one-to-many relationship between tables; manipulating subforms on a main form; incorporating date, memo, OLE, and hyperlink fields in forms; and incorporating various visual effects in forms. Students also learn to use the hyperlink fields to access Web pages and to use date and memo fields in a query.

Project 6 – Switchboards, PivotTables, and PivotCharts In Project 6, students create macros and learn how to create a switchboard system. Students also learn to create and use both PivotTables and PivotCharts. They also learn to create and present information in PivotTable view and PivotChart view. Topics include creating and running macros; creating a switchboard; creating switchboard pages and switchboard items; and using a switchboard.

Web Feature – Data Access Pages In the Web feature, students learn to create a data access page to enable users to access the data in a database via the Internet. They also learn how to create grouped data access pages, as well as how to create data access pages containing PivotTables and PivotCharts. Topics include creating a data access page using the Page Wizard; previewing a data access page from within Access; and using a data access page. Other topics include creating a grouped data access page in Design View; using a grouped data access page; creating a data access page containing a PivotTable; using a data access page containing a PivotTable; saving a PivotChart as a data access page; and using a data access page containing a PivotChart.

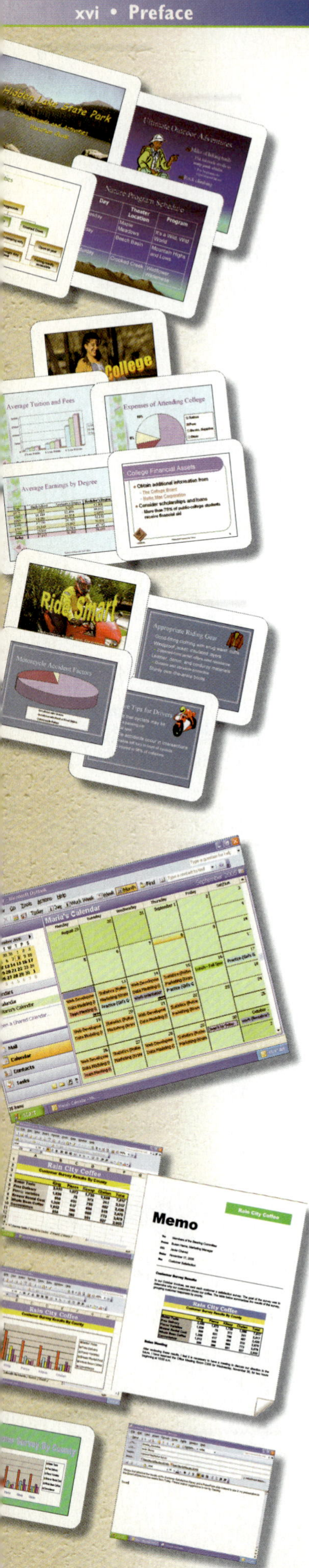

Microsoft Office PowerPoint 2003

Project 3 – Using Visuals to Enhance a Slide Show In Project 3, students create a presentation from a Microsoft Word outline and then enhance it with visuals. Topics include creating a slide background using a picture; modifying clips; deleting a slide; customizing bullets using the slide master; inserting and formatting a table; creating and formatting an organization chart; applying a new design template to a single slide; rearranging slides; adding animation schemes to selected slides, and printing slides as handouts.

Project 4 – Modifying Visual Elements and Presentation Formats In Project 4, students create a presentation using the AutoContent Wizard and then customize this slide show. Topics include adding a graphical heading using WordArt; modifying the presentation by changing the color scheme; adding information to the slide master footer; adding data from other sources; including an Excel chart and a Word table; finding and replacing text; adding hyperlinks and sound effects; using the Thesaurus; adding an action button and action setting; rehearsing presentation timings; running a slide show with hyperlinks; using the grid and guides to position objects; hiding slides; delivering and navigating a presentation using the Slide Show toolbar; printing speaker notes; and saving the presentation as a Rich Text Format outline.

Collaboration Feature – Delivering Presentations to and Collaborating with Workgroups In the Collaboration feature, students learn to use the Package for CD feature to save presentations along with the Microsoft Office PowerPoint Viewer. Topics include setting a up a review cycle to track, accept, and reject changes in a presentation; reviewing presentation comments; comparing and merging presentations; and scheduling online broadcasts.

Microsoft Office Outlook 2003

Project 2 – Schedule Management Using Outlook In Project 2, students discover the benefits of personal information management systems by using Outlook to create a schedule of classes, meetings, and extracurricular activities. Students learn how to enter both one-time and recurring appointments and events, send out meeting requests, assign tasks, and use Windows Messenger with Outlook. Topics include starting and quitting the Calendar folder; generating and managing, daily, weekly, and monthly schedules; printing and saving a calendar; creating, importing, and exporting personal subfolders; creating and assigning tasks; accepting a task assignment; printing tasks; inviting attendees to a meeting; accepting a meeting request; enabling instant messaging; sending an instant message; and sending a file with instant messaging.

Integration Case Studies

Following the five basic Office 2003 applications are three case studies on integration. In these case studies, students use the concepts and techniques presented in the projects and the Integration features in this book to integrate the Office 2003 applications. The first case study requires students to embed an existing Excel worksheet into a Word document and then embed a corresponding Excel chart into a PowerPoint presentation. The second case study requires students to embed an existing Access database as the data source in a Word form letter. The third case study requires student to create an Access database table and then convert the table to a Word document and an Excel worksheet. Student files are provided for the first and second case studies.

Appendices

The book includes five appendices. Appendix A presents an introduction to the Microsoft Office Help system. Appendix B describes how to use the Office speech and handwriting recognition and speech playback capabilities. Appendix C explains how to publish Web pages to a Web server. Appendix D shows how to change the screen resolution and reset the menus and toolbars. Appendix E introduces students to Microsoft Office Specialist certification.

Quick Reference Summary

In Office 2003, you can accomplish a task in a number of ways, such as using the mouse, menu, shortcut menu, and keyboard. The Quick Reference Summary at the back of the book provides a quick reference to each task presented.

End-of-Project Student Activities

A notable strength of the Shelly Cashman Series *Microsoft Office 2003* books is the extensive student activities at the end of each project. Well-structured student activities can make the difference between students merely participating in a class and students retaining the information they learn. The activities in the Shelly Cashman Series *Microsoft Office 2003* books include the following.

- **What You Should Know** A listing of the tasks completed within a project together with the pages on which the step-by-step, screen-by-screen explanations appear.
- **Learn It Online** Every project features a Learn It Online page that comprises twelve exercises. These exercises include True/False, Multiple Choice, Short Answer, Flash Cards, Practice Test, Learning Games, Tips and Tricks, Newsgroup usage, Expanding Your Horizons, Search Sleuth, Office Online Training, and Office Marketplace.
- **Apply Your Knowledge** This exercise usually requires students to open and manipulate a file on the Data Disk that parallels the activities learned in the project. To obtain a copy of the Data Disk, follow the instructions on the inside back cover of this textbook.
- **In the Lab** Three in-depth assignments per project require students to utilize the project concepts and techniques to solve problems on a computer.
- **Cases and Places** Five unique real-world case-study situations, including one small-group activity.

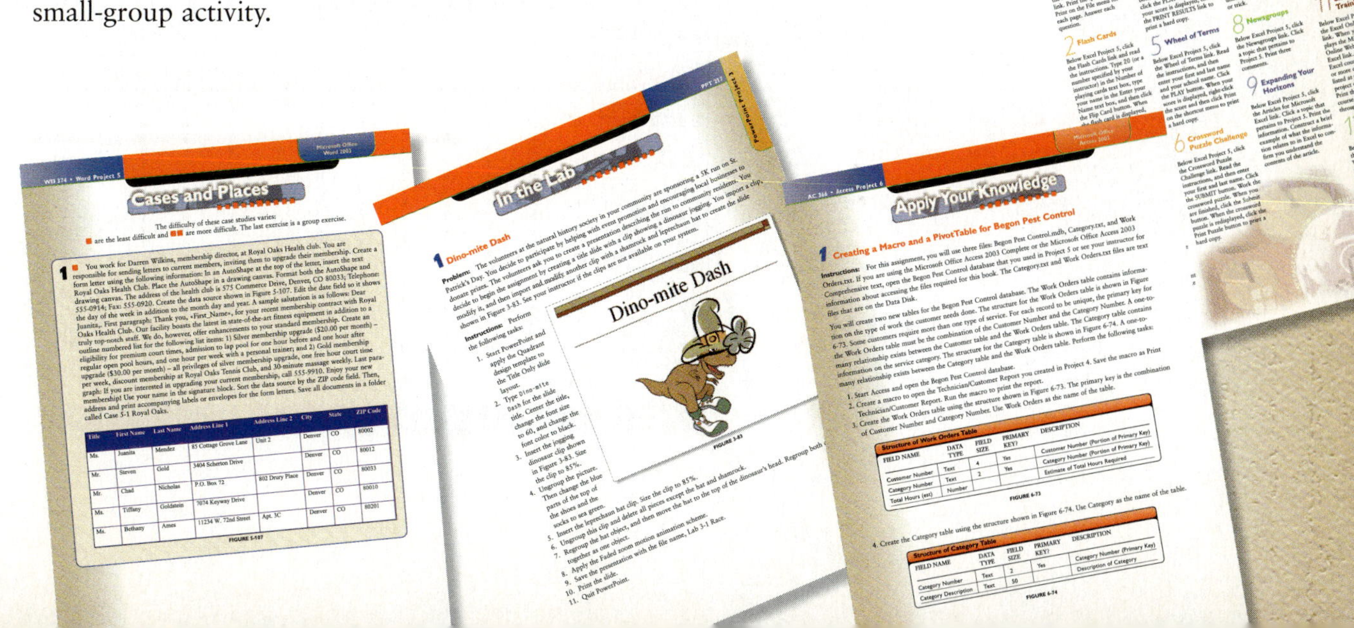

Instructor Resources CD-ROM

The Shelly Cashman Series is dedicated to providing you with all of the tools you need to make your class a success. Information on all supplementary materials is available through your Course Technology representative or by calling one of the following telephone numbers: Colleges and Universities, 1-800-648-7450; High Schools, 1-800-824-5179; Private Career Colleges, 1-800-347-7707; Canada, 1-800-268-2222; Corporations with IT Training Centers, 1-800-648-7450; and Government Agencies, Health-Care Organizations, and Correctional Facilities, 1-800-477-3692.

The Instructor Resources for this textbook include both teaching and testing aids. The contents of each item on the Instructor Resources CD-ROM (ISBN 0-619-20049-9) are described below.

INSTRUCTOR'S MANUAL The Instructor's Manual is made up of Microsoft Word files, which include detailed lesson plans with page number references, lecture notes, teaching tips, classroom activities, discussion topics, projects to assign, and transparency references. The transparencies are available through the Figure Files described below.

LECTURE SUCCESS SYSTEM The Lecture Success System consists of intermediate files that correspond to certain figures in the book, allowing you to step through the creation of an application in a project during a lecture without entering large amounts of data.

SYLLABUS Sample syllabi, which can be customized easily to a course, are included. The syllabi cover policies, class and lab assignments and exams, and procedural information.

FIGURE FILES Illustrations for every figure in the textbook are available in electronic form. Use this ancillary to present a slide show in lecture or to print transparencies for use in lecture with an overhead projector. If you have a personal computer and LCD device, this ancillary can be an effective tool for presenting lectures.

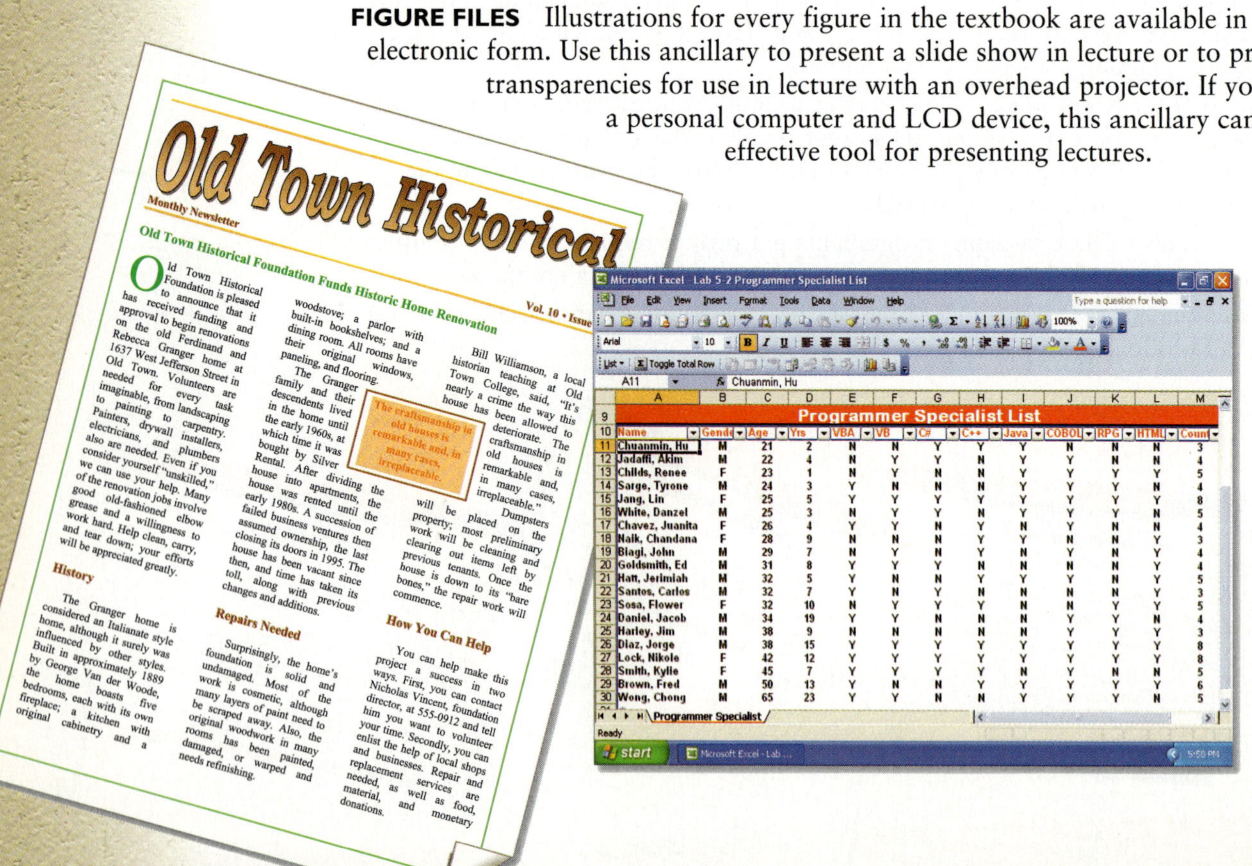

Old Town Historical

Monthly Newsletter

Vol. 10 • Issue

Old Town Historical Foundation Funds Historic Home Renovation

Old Town Historical Foundation is pleased to announce that it has received funding and approval to begin renovations on the old Ferdinand and Rebecca Granger home at 1637 West Jefferson Street in Old Town. Volunteers are needed for every task imaginable, from landscaping to painting to carpentry. Painters, drywall installers, electricians, and plumbers also are needed. Even if you consider yourself "unskilled," we can use your help. Many of the renovation jobs involve good old-fashioned elbow grease and a willingness to work hard. Help clean, carry, and tear down; your efforts will be appreciated greatly.

History

The Granger home is considered an Italianate style home, although it surely was influenced by other styles. Built in approximately 1889 by George Van der Woode, the home boasts five bedrooms, each with its own fireplace; a kitchen with original cabinetry and a woodstove; a parlor with built-in bookshelves; and a dining room. All rooms have their original windows, paneling, and flooring. The Granger family and their descendents lived in the home until the early 1960s, at which time it was bought by Silver Rental. After dividing the house into apartments, the house was rented until the early 1980s. A succession of failed business ventures then assumed ownership, the last closing its doors in 1995. The house has been vacant since then, and time has taken its toll, along with previous changes and additions.

Repairs Needed

Surprisingly, the home's foundation is solid and undamaged. Most of the work is cosmetic, although many layers of paint need to be scraped away. Also, the original woodwork in many rooms has been painted, damaged, or warped and needs refinishing.

Bill Williamson, a local historian teaching at Old Town College, said, "It's nearly a crime the way this house has been allowed to deteriorate. The craftsmanship in old houses is remarkable and, in many cases, irreplaceable."

The craftsmanship in old houses is remarkable and, in many cases, irreplaceable.

Dumpsters will be placed on the property; most preliminary work will be cleaning and clearing out items left by previous tenants. Once the house is down to its "bare bones," the repair work will commence.

How You Can Help

You can help make this project a success in two ways. First, you can contact Nicholas Vincent, foundation director, at 555-0912 and tell him you want to volunteer your time. Secondly, you can enlist the help of local shops and businesses. Repair and replacement services are needed, as well as food, material, and monetary donations.

Microsoft Excel - Lab 5-2 Programmer Specialist List

Programmer Specialist List

Name	Gende	Age	Yrs	VBA	VB	C#	C++	Java	COBOL	RPG	HTML	Count
Chuanmin, Hu	M	21	2	N	N	Y	Y	Y	N	N	N	3
Jadaffi, Akim	M	22	4	N	Y	Y	N	Y	Y	N	N	4
Childs, Renee	F	23	1	N	Y	N	N	Y	Y	Y	Y	5
Sarge, Tyrone	M	24	3	Y	N	N	N	Y	Y	Y	N	4
Jang, Lin	F	25	5	Y	Y	Y	Y	Y	Y	Y	Y	8
White, Danzel	M	25	3	N	Y	Y	N	Y	Y	Y	N	5
Chavez, Juanita	F	26	4	Y	Y	N	Y	N	Y	N	N	4
Naik, Chandana	F	28	9	N	N	N	Y	Y	N	N	Y	3
Biagi, John	M	29	7	N	Y	N	Y	N	Y	N	Y	4
Goldsmith, Ed	M	31	8	Y	Y	Y	N	N	N	N	Y	4
Hatt, Jerimiah	M	32	5	Y	N	N	Y	Y	Y	N	Y	5
Santos, Carlos	M	32	7	Y	N	Y	N	N	N	N	Y	3
Sosa, Flower	F	32	10	N	Y	Y	Y	N	N	Y	Y	5
Daniel, Jacob	M	34	19	Y	Y	N	N	N	Y	Y	N	4
Harley, Jim	M	38	9	N	N	N	N	N	Y	Y	Y	3
Diaz, Jorge	M	38	15	Y	Y	Y	Y	Y	Y	Y	Y	8
Lock, Nikole	F	42	12	Y	Y	Y	Y	Y	Y	Y	Y	8
Smith, Kylie	F	45	7	Y	Y	Y	Y	N	Y	N	N	5
Brown, Fred	M	50	13	Y	N	N	Y	Y	Y	Y	Y	6
Wong, Chong	M	65	23	Y	Y	N	N	Y	Y	Y	N	5

Programmer Specialist

POWERPOINT PRESENTATIONS PowerPoint Presentations is a multimedia lecture presentation system that provides slides for each project. Presentations are based on project objectives. Use this presentation system to present well-organized lectures that are both interesting and knowledge based. PowerPoint Presentations provides consistent coverage at schools that use multiple lecturers.

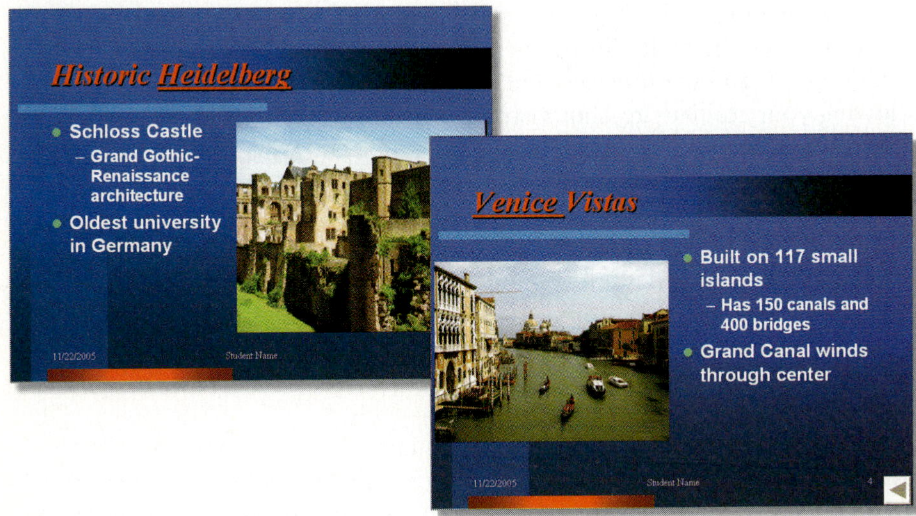

SOLUTIONS TO EXERCISES Solutions are included for the end-of-project exercises, as well as the Project Reinforcement exercises.

TEST BANK & TEST ENGINE The ExamView test bank includes 110 questions for every project (25 multiple-choice, 50 true/false, and 35 completion) with page number references, and when appropriate, figure references. A version of the test bank you can print also is included. The test bank comes with a copy of the test engine, ExamView, the ultimate tool for your objective-based testing needs. ExamView is a state-of-the-art test builder that is easy to use. ExamView enables you to create paper-, LAN-, or Web-based tests from test banks designed specifically for your Course Technology textbook. Utilize the ultra-efficient QuickTest Wizard to create tests in less than five minutes by taking advantage of Course Technology's question banks, or customize your own exams from scratch.

LAB TESTS/TEST OUT The Lab Tests/Test Out exercises parallel the In the Lab assignments and are supplied for the purpose of testing students in the laboratory on the material covered in the project or testing students out of the course.

DATA FILES FOR STUDENTS All the files that are required by students to complete the exercises are included. You can distribute the files on the Instructor Resources CD-ROM to your students over a network, or you can have them follow the instructions on the inside back cover of this book to obtain a copy of the Data Disk.

ADDITIONAL ACTIVITIES FOR STUDENTS These additional activities consist of Project Reinforcement Exercises, which are true/false, multiple choice, and short answer questions that help students gain confidence in the material learned.

SAM 2003

SAM 2003 helps you energize your class exams and training assignments by allowing students to learn and test important computer skills in an active, hands-on environment.

SAM 2003 ASSESSMENT With SAM 2003 Assessment, you create powerful interactive exams on critical applications such as Word, Excel, Access, PowerPoint, Windows, Outlook, and the Internet. The exams simulate the application environment, allowing your students to demonstrate their knowledge and think through the skill by performing real-world tasks. Build hands-on exams that allow students to work in the simulated application environment.

SAM 2003 TRAINING Invigorate your lesson plan with SAM 2003 Training. Using highly interactive text, graphics, and sound, SAM 2003 Training gives your students the flexibility to learn computer applications by choosing the training method that fits them best. Create customized training units that employ various approaches to teaching computer skills.

SAM 2003 ASSESSMENT AND TRAINING Designed to be used with the Shelly Cashman Series, SAM 2003 Assessment and Training includes built-in page references so students can create study guides that match the Shelly Cashman Series textbooks you use in class. Powerful administrative options allow you to schedule customized exams and assignments, secure your tests, and choose from more than one dozen reports to track testing and learning progress.

Online Content

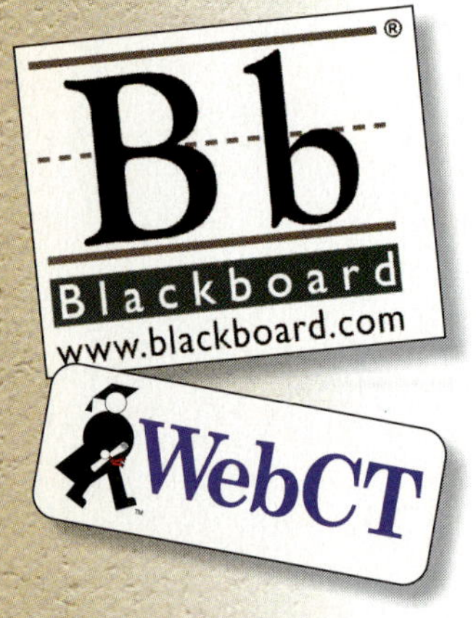

Course Technology offers textbook-based content for Blackboard, WebCT, and MyCourse 2.1

BLACKBOARD AND WEBCT As the leading provider of IT content for the Blackboard and WebCT platforms, Course Technology delivers rich content that enhances your textbook to give your students a unique learning experience. Course Technology has partnered with WebCT and Blackboard to deliver our market-leading content through these state-of-the-art online learning platforms. Course Technology offers customizable content in every subject area, from computer concepts to PC repair.

MYCOURSE 2.1 MyCourse 2.1 is Course Technology's powerful online course management and content delivery system. Completely maintained and hosted by Thomson, MyCourse 2.1 delivers an online learning environment that is completely secure and provides superior performance. MyCourse 2.1 allows nontechnical users to create, customize, and deliver World Wide Web-based courses; post content and assignments; manage student enrollment; administer exams; track results in the online gradebook; and more. With MyCourse 2.1, you easily can create a customized course that will enhance every learning experience.

Acknowledgments

The Shelly Cashman Series would not be the leading computer education series without the contributions of outstanding publishing professionals. First, and foremost, among them is Becky Herrington, director of production and book designer. She is the heart and soul of the Shelly Cashman Series, and it is only through her leadership, dedication, and tireless efforts that superior products are made possible.

Under Becky's direction, the following individuals made significant contributions to these books: Jennifer Quiambao, production assistant; Ken Russo, senior Web and graphic designer; Richard Herrera, cover designer; Kellee LaVars, Andrew Bartel, Phillip Hajjar, and Kenny Tran, graphic artists; Michelle French, Jeanne Black, Andrew Bartel, and Kellee LaVars, QuarkXPress compositors; Ginny Harvey, Nancy Lamm, Lisa Jedlicka, Lyn Markowicz, Kim Kosmatka, Lori Silfen, and Ellana Russo, copy editors and proofreaders; and Cristina Haley, indexer.

We also would like to thank Kristen Duerr, executive vice president and publisher; Cheryl Costantini, executive editor; Jim Quasney, series consulting editor; Alexandra Arnold, senior product manager; Erin Runyon, product manager; Marc Ouellette and Heather McKinstry, online product managers; Reed Cotter, associate product manager; and Selena Coppock, editorial assistant.

Gary B. Shelly
Thomas J. Cashman
Misty E. Vermaat

To the Student... Getting the Most Out of Your Book

Welcome to Microsoft Office 2003: Advanced Concepts and Techniques. You can save yourself a lot of time and gain a better understanding of the Office 2003 applications if you spend a few minutes reviewing the figures and callouts in this section.

1 Project Orientation

Each project presents a practical problem and shows the solution in the first figure of the project. The project orientation lets you see firsthand how problems are solved from start to finish using application software and computers.

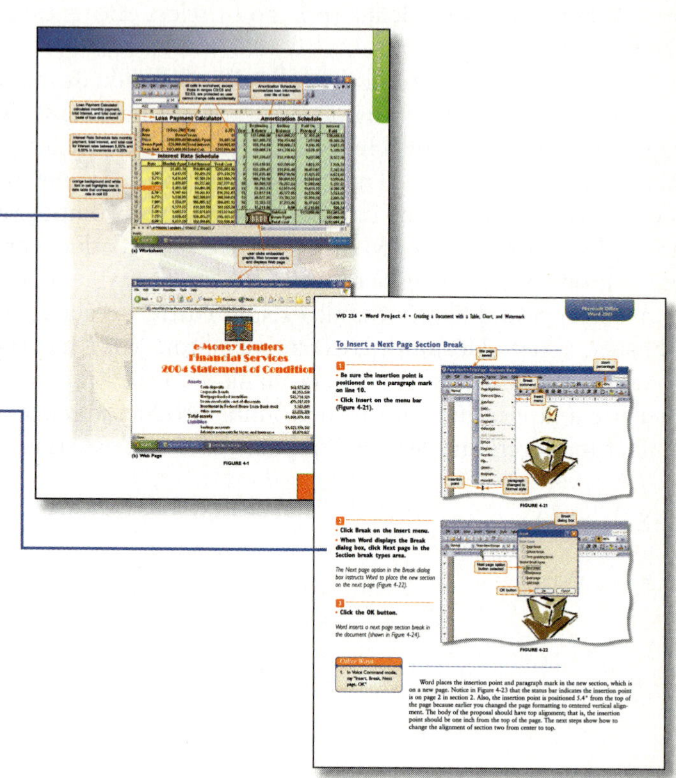

2 Consistent Step-by-Step, Screen-by-Screen Presentation

Project solutions are built using a step-by-step, screen-by-screen approach. This pedagogy allows you to build the solution on a computer as you read through the project. Generally, each step is followed by an italic explanation that indicates the result of the step.

3 More Than Just Step-by-Step

More About and Q&A annotations in the margins of the book and substantive text in the paragraphs provide background information, tips, and answers to common questions that complement the topics covered, adding depth and perspective. When you finish with this book, you will be ready to use the Office applications to solve problems on your own.

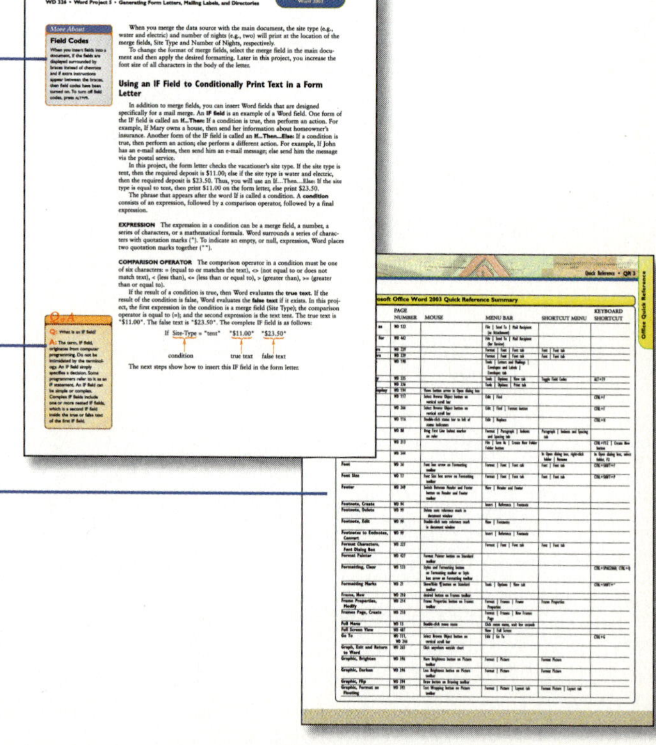

4 Other Ways Boxes and Quick Reference Summary

Other Ways boxes that follow many of the step sequences and a Quick Reference Summary at the back of the book explain the other ways to complete the task presented, such as using the mouse, menu, shortcut menu, and keyboard.

5 Emphasis on Getting Help When You Need It

The first project of each application and Appendix A show you how to use all the elements of the Office Help system. Being able to answer your own questions will increase your productivity and reduce your frustrations by minimizing the time it takes to learn how to complete a task.

6 Review

After you successfully step through a project, a section titled What You Should Know summarizes the project tasks with which you should be familiar. Terms you should know for test purposes are bold in the text.

7 Reinforcement and Extension

The Learn It Online page at the end of each project offers reinforcement in the form of review questions, learning games, and practice tests. Also included are Web-based exercises that require you to extend your learning beyond the book.

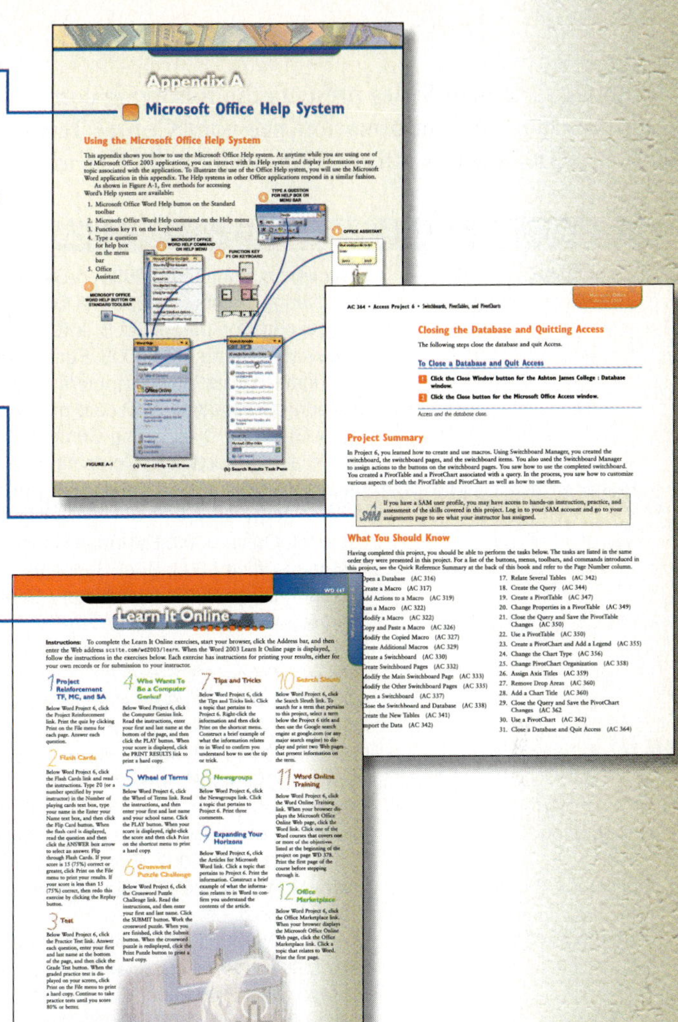

8 Laboratory Exercises

If you really want to learn how to use the applications, then you must design and implement solutions to problems on your own. Every project concludes with several carefully developed laboratory assignments that increase in complexity.

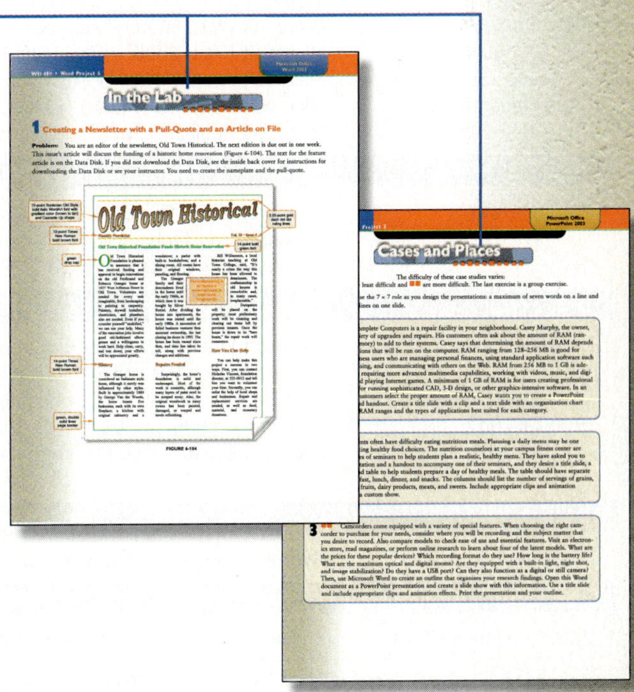

Shelly Cashman Series – Traditionally Bound Textbooks

The Shelly Cashman Series presents the following computer subjects in a variety of traditionally bound textbooks. For more information, see your Course Technology representative or call 1-800-648-7450. For Shelly Cashman Series information, visit Shelly Cashman Online at **scseries.com**

COMPUTERS	
Computers	Discovering Computers 2005: A Gateway to Information, Web Enhanced, Complete Edition Discovering Computers 2005: A Gateway to Information, Web Enhanced, Introductory Edition Discovering Computers 2005: A Gateway to Information, Web Enhanced, Brief Edition Discovering Computers 2005: Fundamentals Edition Teachers Discovering Computers: Integrating Technology in the Classroom 3e Exploring Computers: A Record of Discovery 4e Study Guide for Discovering Computers 2005: A Gateway to Information, Web Enhanced Essential Introduction to Computers 5e (40-page)
WINDOWS APPLICATIONS	
Microsoft Office	Microsoft Office 2003: Essential Concepts and Techniques (5 projects) Microsoft Office 2003: Brief Concepts and Techniques (9 projects) Microsoft Office 2003: Introductory Concepts and Techniques (15 projects) Microsoft Office 2003: Advanced Concepts and Techniques (12 projects) Microsoft Office 2003: Post Advanced Concepts and Techniques (11 projects) Microsoft Office XP: Essential Concepts and Techniques (5 projects) Microsoft Office XP: Brief Concepts and Techniques (9 projects) Microsoft Office XP: Introductory Concepts and Techniques, Windows XP Edition Microsoft Office XP: Introductory Concepts and Techniques, Enhanced Edition (15 projects)[1] Microsoft Office XP: Advanced Concepts and Techniques (11 projects) Microsoft Office XP: Post Advanced Concepts and Techniques (11 projects)
Integration	Integrating Microsoft Office XP Applications and the World Wide Web: Essential Concepts and Techniques
PIM	Microsoft Outlook 2002: Essential Concepts and Techniques
Microsoft Works	Microsoft Works 6: Complete Concepts and Techniques[2] • Microsoft Works 2000: Complete Concepts and Techniques[2]
Microsoft Windows	Microsoft Windows XP: Complete Concepts and Techniques[3] Microsoft Windows XP: Brief Concepts and Techniques Microsoft Windows 2000: Complete Concepts and Techniques (6 projects)[3] Microsoft Windows 2000: Brief Concepts and Techniques (2 projects) Microsoft Windows 98: Essential Concepts and Techniques (2 projects) Microsoft Windows 98: Complete Concepts and Techniques (6 projects)[3] Introduction to Microsoft Windows NT Workstation 4
Word Processing	Microsoft Word 2003[3] • Microsoft Word 2002[3]
Spreadsheets	Microsoft Excel 2003[3] • Microsoft Excel 2002[3]
Database	Microsoft Access 2003[3] • Microsoft Access 2002[3]
Presentation Graphics	Microsoft PowerPoint 2003[3] • Microsoft PowerPoint 2002[3]
Desktop Publishing	Microsoft Publisher 2003[2] • Microsoft Publisher 2002[2]
PROGRAMMING	
Programming	Microsoft Visual Basic.NET: Complete Concepts and Techniques[3] • Microsoft Visual Basic 6: Complete Concepts and Techniques[2] • Programming in QBasic • Java Programming 2e: Complete Concepts and Techniques[3] • Structured COBOL Programming 2e
INTERNET	
Browser	Microsoft Internet Explorer 6: Introductory Concepts and Techniques • Microsoft Internet Explorer 5: An Introduction • Netscape Navigator 6: An Introduction
Web Page Creation and Design	Web Design: Introductory Concepts and Techniques • HTML: Complete Concepts and Techniques 2e[3] Microsoft FrontPage 2003[3] • Microsoft FrontPage 2002[3] • Microsoft FrontPage 2002: Essential Concepts and Techniques • Java Programming: Complete Concepts and Techniques 2e[3] • JavaScript: Complete Concepts and Techniques 2e[2] • Macromedia Dreamweaver MX: Complete Concepts and Techniques[3]
SYSTEMS ANALYSIS	
Systems Analysis	Systems Analysis and Design 5e
DATA COMMUNICATIONS	
Data Communications	Business Data Communications: Introductory Concepts and Techniques 4e

[1]Available running under Windows XP or running under Windows 2000, [2]Also available as an Introductory Edition, which is a shortened version of the complete book, [3]Also available as an Introductory Edition, which is a shortened version of the complete book and also as a Comprehensive Edition, which is an extended version of the complete book

MICROSOFT Office Word 2003

Creating a Document with a Table, Chart, and Watermark

PROJECT

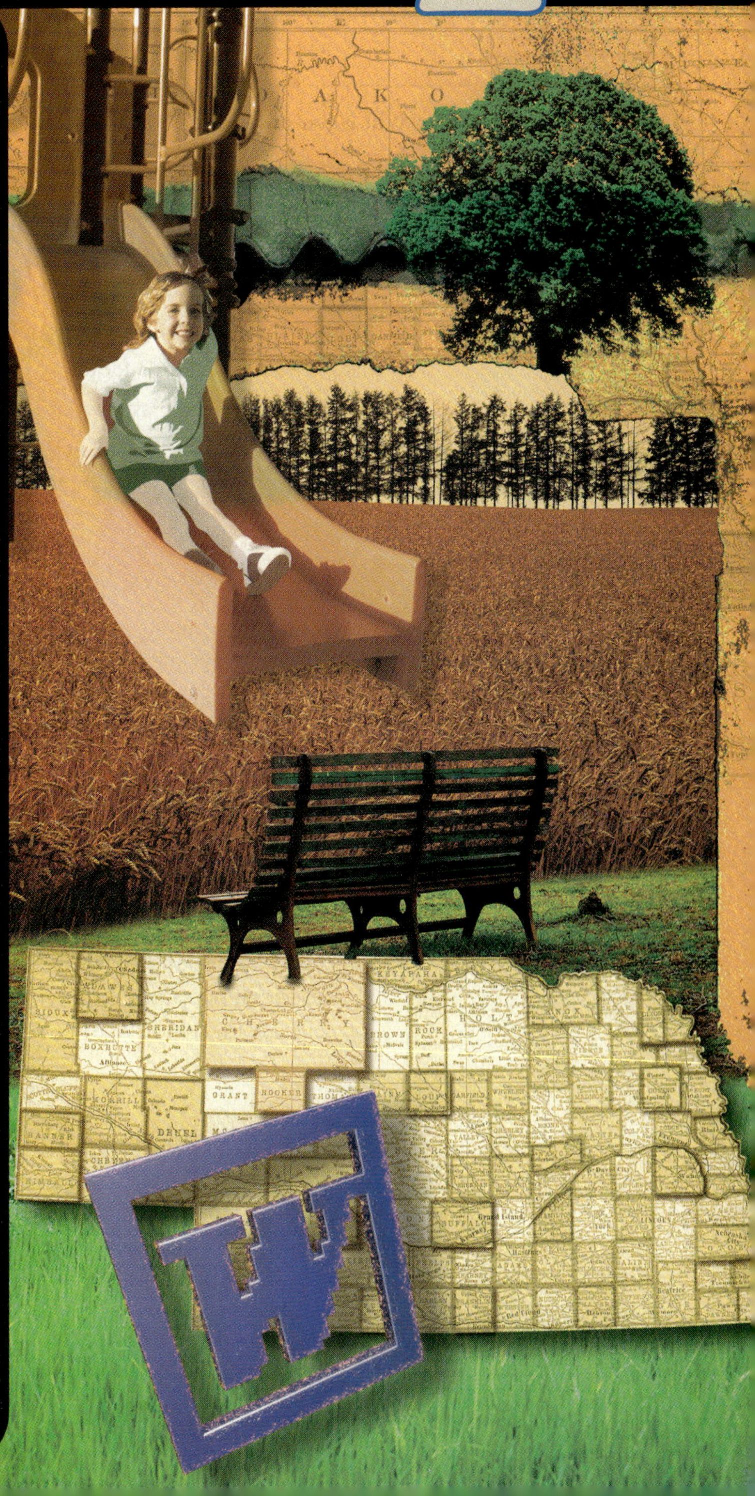

CASE PERSPECTIVE

The Minooka Park District provides facilities and services for the citizens of Minooka, Nebraska. For the past 55 years, residents have been enjoying these amenities at no cost. This will change if the bond referendum does not pass next month. The Minooka Park District needs community support to renovate parks, purchase land, and upgrade facilities. It plans to use the bond funds to update playground equipment, replace picnic tables and benches, refurbish concession stands, maintain kitchen and restroom facilities, pave parking lots, and develop an outdoor community skating/ice hockey rink and two playing fields.

Last year, the park district attempted to acquire similar bonds for park renovations and facility upgrades. Although the referendum did not pass, it was a close vote. Board members feel the referendum failed because they did not properly inform the community about the proposed use of funds from the bonds and the estimated tax impact to homeowners. This year, the board has a plan. To better educate community members about the referendum and persuade them to cast a yes vote, the board approved expenses for preparing and mailing a proposal to every Minooka homeowner. The park district director has asked you to design the proposal because she knows you are a marketing major with a minor in computer technology. You are thrilled to participate in this assignment. You will complete the proposal for her review within a week.

As you read through this project, you will learn how to use Word to create a proposal with a table, chart, and watermark.

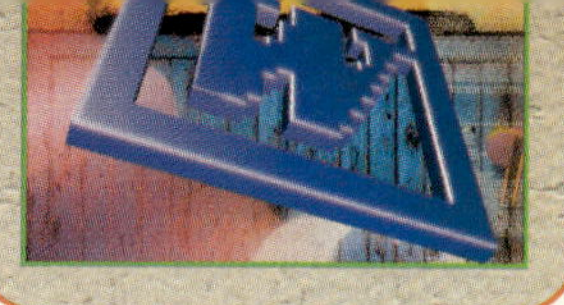

MICROSOFT
Office Word 2003

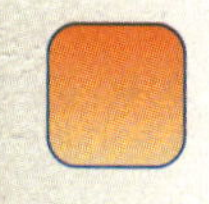

Creating a Document with a Table, Chart, and Watermark

PROJECT

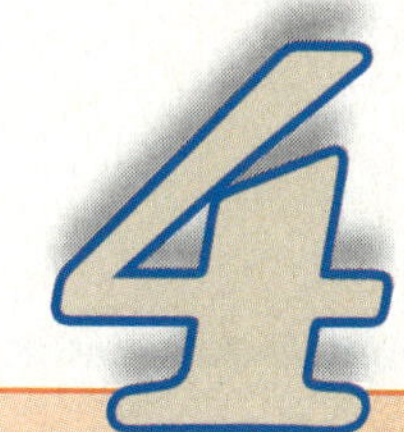

Objectives

You will have mastered the material in this project when you can:

- Add a border and shading to a paragraph
- Center page contents vertically on a page
- Insert a section break
- Insert a Word document into an open document
- Create and format a header and footer different from the previous header and footer
- Modify and format a Word table
- Sum columns in a table using the AutoSum button
- Select and format nonadjacent text
- Create a chart from a Word table and modify the chart in Microsoft Graph
- Add picture bullets to a list
- Create and apply a character style
- Use the Draw Table feature to create a table
- Insert a text watermark
- Reveal formatting

Introduction

Sometime during your professional life, you most likely will find yourself placed in a sales role. You might be selling a tangible product, such as vehicles or books, or a service, such as Web page design or interior decorating. Within an organization, you might be selling an idea, such as a benefits package to company employees or a budget plan to upper management. Instead of selling a product, you might be trying to persuade people to take an action, such as signing a petition, joining a club, or donating to a cause. To sell an item or persuade the public, you may find yourself writing a proposal. Proposals vary in length, style, and formality, but all are designed to elicit acceptance from the reader.

A proposal generally is one of three types: planning, research, or sales. A **planning proposal** offers solutions to a problem or improvement to a situation. A **research proposal** usually requests funding for a research project. A **sales proposal** sells an idea, a product, or a service.

Project Four — Sales Proposal

Project 4 uses Word to produce the sales proposal shown in Figure 4-1. The sales proposal is designed to persuade readers to cast a yes vote for the upcoming Minooka Park District bond referendum. The proposal has a colorful title page to attract the readers' attention. To add impact, the sales proposal has a watermark containing the words, YES, behind the text and uses tables and a chart to summarize data.

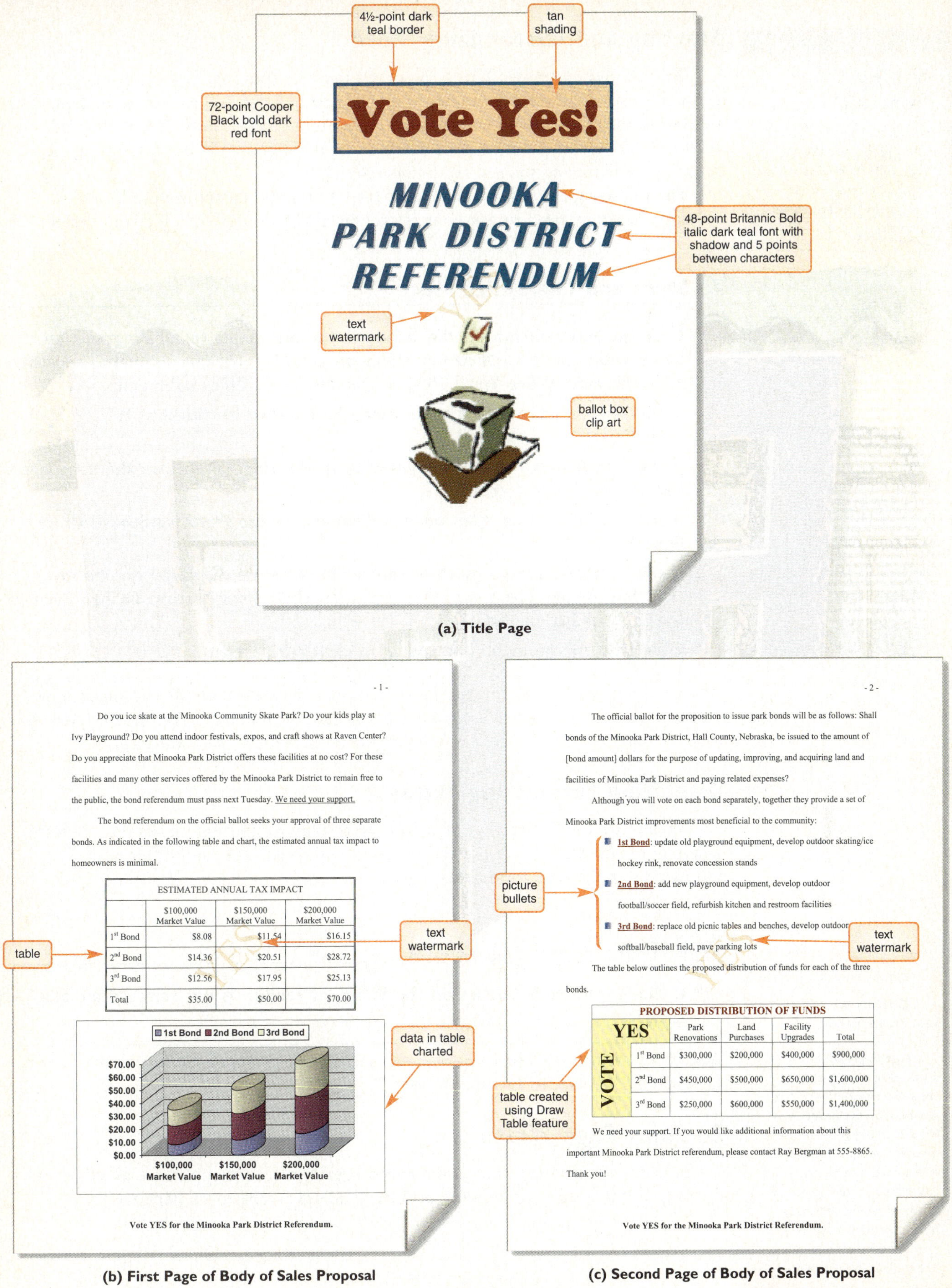

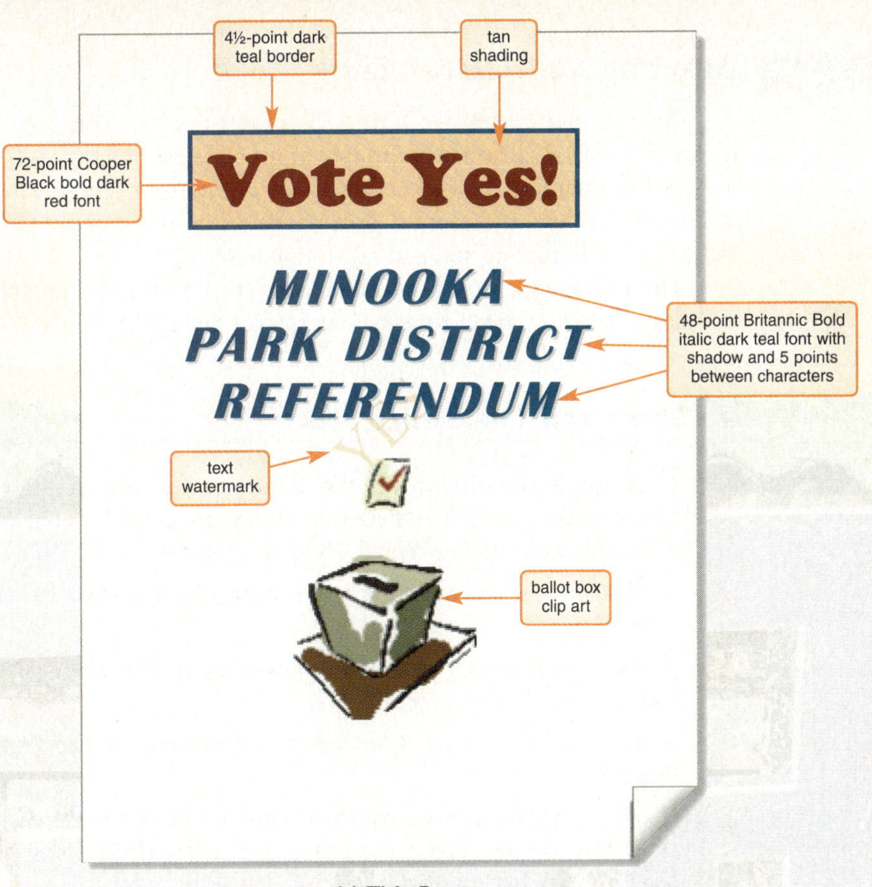

(a) Title Page

- 1 -

Do you ice skate at the Minooka Community Skate Park? Do your kids play at Ivy Playground? Do you attend indoor festivals, expos, and craft shows at Raven Center? Do you appreciate that Minooka Park District offers these facilities at no cost? For these facilities and many other services offered by the Minooka Park District to remain free to the public, the bond referendum must pass next Tuesday. We need your support.

The bond referendum on the official ballot seeks your approval of three separate bonds. As indicated in the following table and chart, the estimated annual tax impact to homeowners is minimal.

ESTIMATED ANNUAL TAX IMPACT			
	$100,000 Market Value	$150,000 Market Value	$200,000 Market Value
1st Bond	$8.08	$11.54	$16.15
2nd Bond	$14.36	$20.51	$28.72
3rd Bond	$12.56	$17.95	$25.13
Total	$35.00	$50.00	$70.00

1st Bond 2nd Bond 3rd Bond

$70.00 $60.00 $50.00 $40.00 $30.00 $20.00 $10.00 $0.00

$100,000 Market Value | $150,000 Market Value | $200,000 Market Value

Vote YES for the Minooka Park District Referendum.

table

text watermark

data in table charted

(b) First Page of Body of Sales Proposal

- 2 -

The official ballot for the proposition to issue park bonds will be as follows: Shall bonds of the Minooka Park District, Hall County, Nebraska, be issued to the amount of [bond amount] dollars for the purpose of updating, improving, and acquiring land and facilities of Minooka Park District and paying related expenses?

Although you will vote on each bond separately, together they provide a set of Minooka Park District improvements most beneficial to the community:

- 1st Bond: update old playground equipment, develop outdoor skating/ice hockey rink, renovate concession stands
- 2nd Bond: add new playground equipment, develop outdoor football/soccer field, refurbish kitchen and restroom facilities
- 3rd Bond: replace old picnic tables and benches, develop outdoor softball/baseball field, pave parking lots

The table below outlines the proposed distribution of funds for each of the three bonds.

PROPOSED DISTRIBUTION OF FUNDS						
YES		Park Renovations	Land Purchases	Facility Upgrades	Total
VOTE	1st Bond	$300,000	$200,000	$400,000	$900,000
	2nd Bond	$450,000	$500,000	$650,000	$1,600,000
	3rd Bond	$250,000	$600,000	$550,000	$1,400,000

We need your support. If you would like additional information about this important Minooka Park District referendum, please contact Ray Bergman at 555-8865. Thank you!

Vote YES for the Minooka Park District Referendum.

picture bullets

text watermark

table created using Draw Table feature

(c) Second Page of Body of Sales Proposal

FIGURE 4-1

More About

Writing Proposals

For more information about writing proposals, visit the Word 2003 More About Web page (scsite.com/wd2003/more) and then click Writing Proposals.

Starting and Customizing Word

To start and customize Word, Windows must be running. If you are stepping through this project on a computer and you want your screen to match the figures in this book, then you should change your computer's resolution to 800 × 600 and reset the toolbars and menus. For information about changing the resolution and resetting toolbars and menus, read Appendix D.

The following steps describe how to start Word and customize the Word window. You may need to ask your instructor how to start Word for your system.

To Start and Customize Word

1. **Click the Start button on the Windows taskbar, point to All Programs on the Start menu, point to Microsoft Office on the All Programs submenu, and then click Microsoft Office Word 2003 on the Microsoft Office submenu.**
2. **If the Word window is not maximized, double-click its title bar to maximize it.**
3. **If the Language bar appears, right-click it and then click Close the Language bar on the shortcut menu.**
4. **If the Getting Started task pane is displayed in the Word window, click its Close button.**
5. **If the Standard and Formatting toolbar buttons are displayed on one row, click the Toolbar Options button and then click Show Buttons on Two Rows in the Toolbar Options list.**
6. **Click View on the menu bar and then click Print Layout.**

Word starts and, after a few moments, displays an empty document in the Word window. You will use print layout view in this project because the proposal contains tables. Thus, the Print Layout View button on the horizontal scroll bar is selected (shown in Figure 4-2 on page WD 222).

Displaying Formatting Marks

As discussed in Project 1, it is helpful to display formatting marks that indicate where in the document you pressed the ENTER key, SPACEBAR, and other keys. The following step displays formatting marks.

Q&A

Q: Do all sales proposals have the same content?

A: A sales proposal may be solicited or unsolicited. If someone else requests that you develop the proposal, it is solicited. If you write the proposal because you recognize a need, the proposal is unsolicited. A sales proposal is successful if it addresses how its product or service meets the reader's needs better than the competition does.

To Display Formatting Marks

1. **If the Show/Hide ¶ button on the Standard toolbar is not selected already, click it.**

Word displays formatting marks in the document window, and the Show/Hide ¶ button on the Standard toolbar is selected (shown in Figure 4-2).

Zooming Page Width

In print layout view, many users **zoom page width** so they can see all edges of the page in the document window at once. The next steps zoom page width.

To Zoom Page Width

1. **Click the Zoom box arrow on the Standard toolbar.**
2. **Click Page Width in the Zoom list.**

Word computes the zoom percentage and displays it in the Zoom box (shown in Figure 4-2 on the next page). Your percentage may be different depending on your computer.

Creating a Title Page

A **title page** should attract a readers' attention. The title page of the sales proposal in Project 4 (Figure 4-1a on page WD 219) contains color, shading, an outside border, shadowed text, clip art, and a variety of fonts, font sizes, and font styles. The steps on the following pages discuss how to create this title page. The text watermark, which displays on all pages of the sales proposal, is created at the end of this project.

Formatting and Entering Characters

The first step in creating the title page is to enter the phrase, Vote Yes!, centered and using 72-point Cooper Black bold dark red font, as described below.

To Format Characters

1. **Click the Center button on the Formatting toolbar.**
2. **Click the Font box arrow on the Formatting toolbar. Scroll to and then click Cooper Black (or a similar font) in the list of available fonts.**
3. **Click the Font Size box arrow on the Formatting toolbar. Scroll to and then click 72.**
4. **Click the Bold button on the Formatting toolbar.**
5. **Click the Font Color button arrow on the Formatting toolbar and then click Dark Red on the color palette.**
6. **Type** `Vote Yes!`

Word enters the phrase, Vote Yes!, centered and using 72-point Cooper Black bold dark red font (shown in Figure 4-2).

Adding a Border and Shading to a Paragraph

The next step is to surround the phrase, Vote Yes!, with a 4½-point dark teal outside border and then shade inside the border in tan.

In Project 2, you added a bottom border to a paragraph using the Border button on the Formatting toolbar. When you click this button, Word applies the most recently defined border or the default border to the current paragraph. One method of specifying a different point size, color, shading, and placement of a border is to use the **Tables and Borders toolbar.**

To display the Tables and Borders toolbar, click the **Tables and Borders button** on the Standard toolbar. When you click the Tables and Borders button, Word displays the Tables and Borders toolbar in the Word window. Also, if your Word

Q&A

Q: What are the guidelines for a title page on a proposal?

A: Formal proposals often require a specific format for the title page. Beginning about 3 to 4 inches from the top margin, the following components are each centered and on a separate line: title; the word, For; reader's name, position, organization, and address; the word, by; your name, position, and organization; and the date the proposal was written.

More About

Borders

You can add a border to any edge of a paragraph. That is, borders may be added above or below a paragraph, to the left or right of a paragraph, or any combination of these sides. To add the most recently defined border, click the Border button on the Formatting toolbar. To change border specifications, use the Tables and Borders toolbar.

window is not already in print layout view, Word automatically switches to print layout view. The Tables and Borders button on the Standard toolbar remains selected until you close the Tables and Borders toolbar.

The following steps show how to add a 4½-point dark teal outside border around a paragraph using the Tables and Borders toolbar.

To Border a Paragraph

1

- **If the Tables and Borders toolbar is not displayed in the Word window, click the Tables and Borders button on the Standard toolbar.**
- **If the Tables and Borders toolbar is floating in the Word window, double-click the title bar of the Tables and Borders toolbar.**
- **With the insertion point on line 1, click the Line Weight box arrow on the Tables and Borders toolbar.**

Word displays a list of available line weights (Figure 4-2).

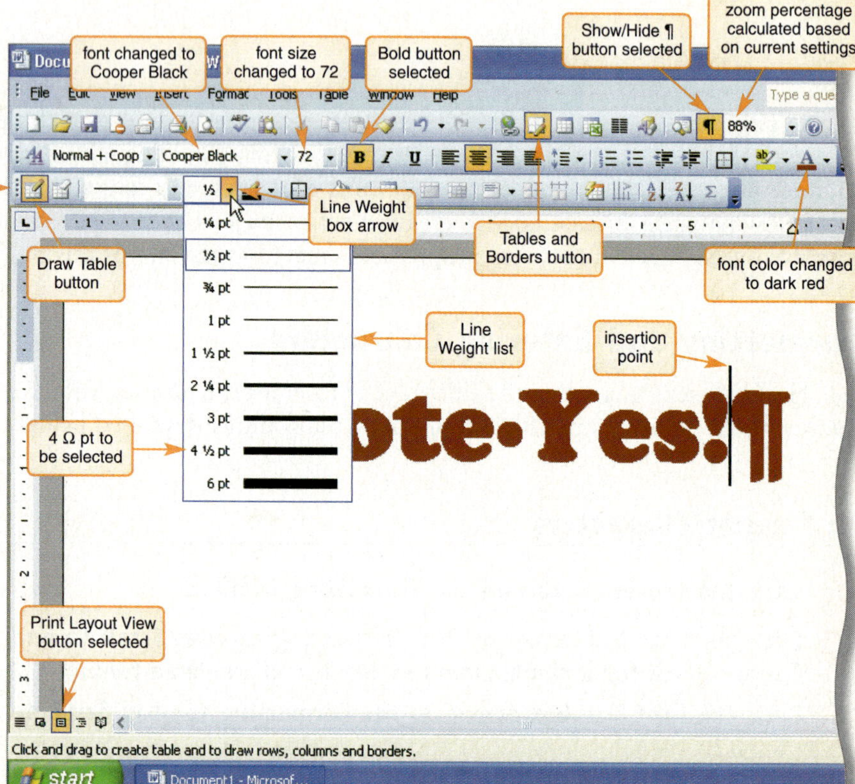

FIGURE 4-2

2

- **Click 4 ½ pt in the Line Weight list.**

Word changes the line weight to 4½ point.

3

- **Click the Border Color button arrow on the Tables and Borders toolbar.**

Word displays a color palette for border colors (Figure 4-3).

4

- **Click Dark Teal, which is the fifth color on the first row of the color palette.**

Word changes the color of the border to dark teal, as shown in the Line Style box and on the Border Color button.

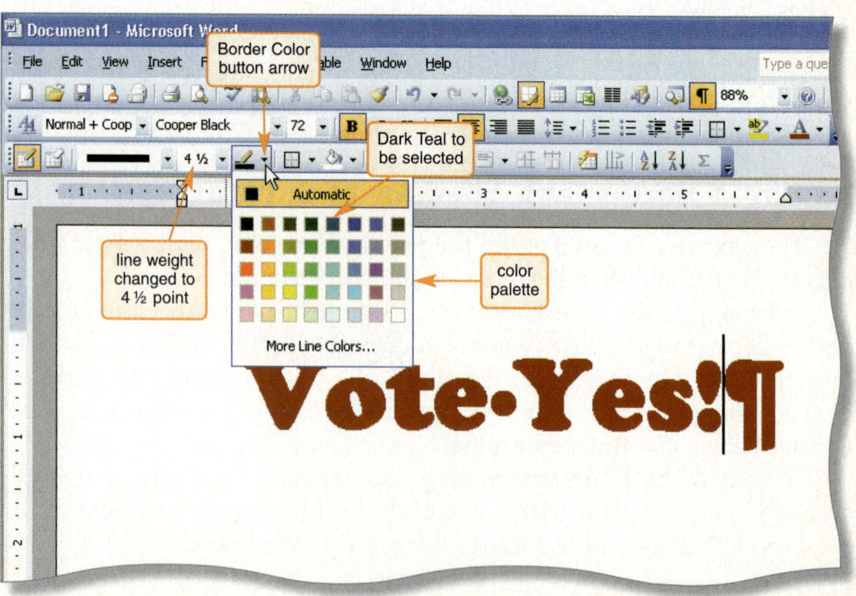

FIGURE 4-3

5

- **Click the Outside Border button on the Tables and Borders toolbar. (If your Border button does not show an outside border, click the Border button arrow on the Tables and Borders toolbar and then click Outside Border.)**

Word places a 4½-point dark teal outside border around the phrase, Vote Yes! (Figure 4-4).

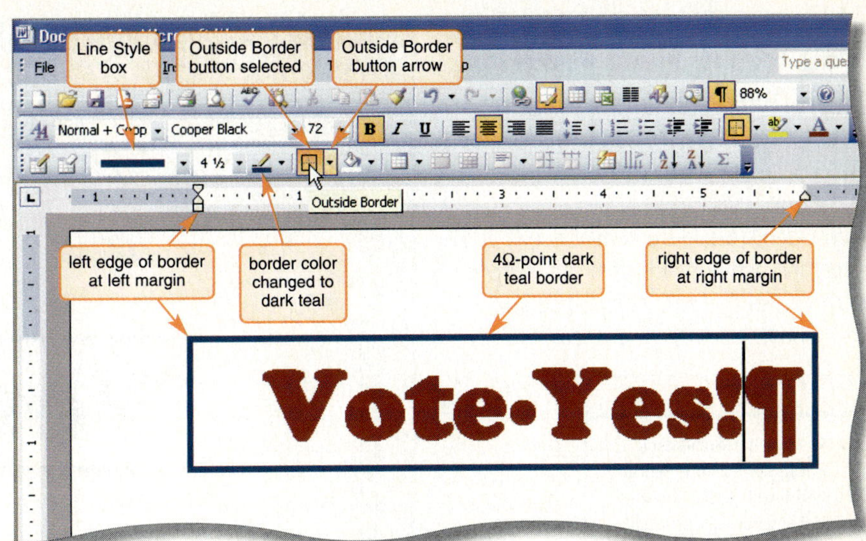

FIGURE 4-4

Other Ways

1. On Format menu click Borders and Shading, click Borders tab, click Box in Setting area, click desired style, color, and width, click OK button
2. With Tables and Borders toolbar displaying, in Voice Command mode, say "Line Weight, [select line weight], Border Color, [select color]"

Depending on the last position of the Tables and Borders toolbar, it may be floating or it may be docked. To dock a floating toolbar, double-click its title bar. Word docks the Tables and Borders toolbar above or below the Formatting toolbar. You can move the toolbar by dragging its move handle, which is the dotted vertical line at the left edge of the toolbar.

When the Draw Table button on the Tables and Borders toolbar is selected, the mouse pointer shape is a pencil — ready to draw a table. If you want to edit a document when the Tables and Borders toolbar is displayed, click the Draw Table button to deselect it.

As previously discussed, Word provides two Border buttons: one on the Formatting toolbar and one on the Tables and Borders toolbar. To place a border using the same settings as the most recently defined border, simply click the Border button on the Formatting toolbar. To change the size, color, or other settings of a border, use the Tables and Borders toolbar or the Borders and Shading dialog box.

Notice in Figure 4-4 that the border extends from the left margin to the right margin. If you want the border to start and end at a different location, you change the left and right paragraph indent. One way to change a paragraph indent is to drag the markers on the ruler, as shown in the following steps.

To Change Left and Right Paragraph Indent

1

- **Position the mouse pointer on the Left Indent marker on the ruler.**

The Left Indent marker is the small square at the 0" mark on the ruler (Figure 4-5).

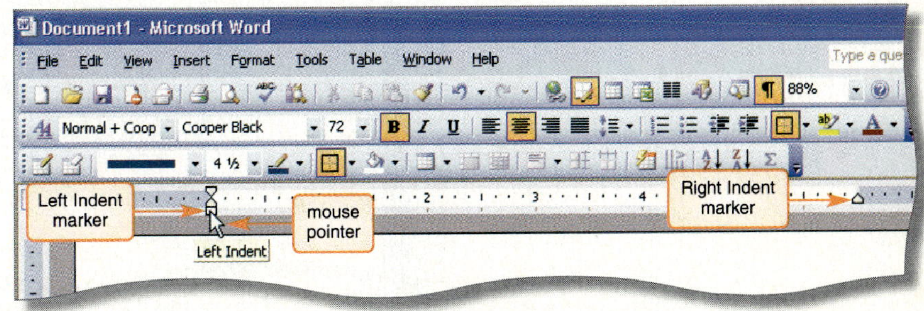

FIGURE 4-5

2

- **Drag the Left Indent marker to the .5" mark on the ruler.**
- **Drag the Right Indent marker to the 5.5" mark on the ruler.**

Word indents the left and right edges of the paragraph one-half inch from the margin, which causes the paragraph borders to move in one-half inch (Figure 4-6).

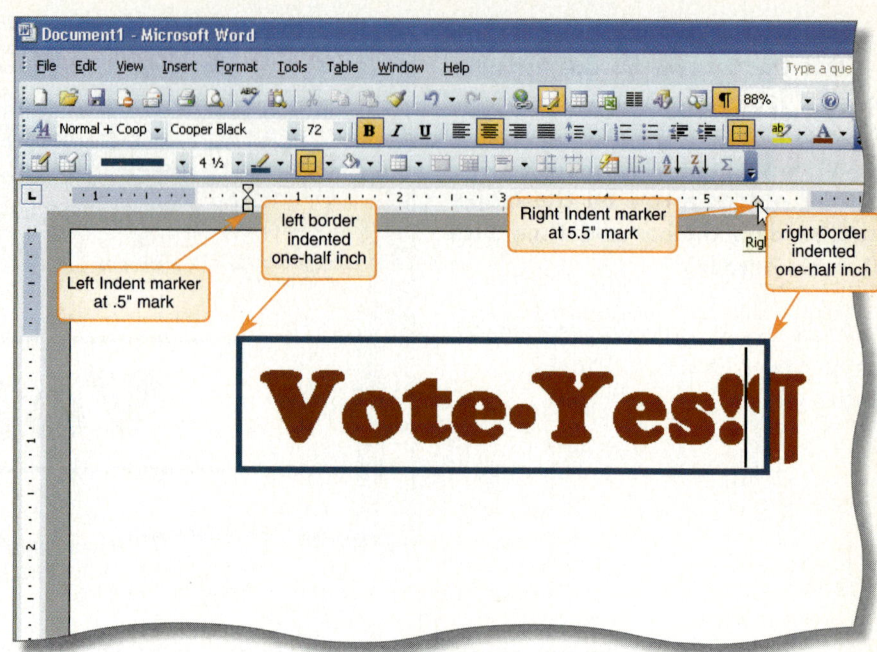

FIGURE 4-6

Other Ways

1. On Format menu click Paragraph, click Indents and Spacing tab, enter indentation values in Left and Right boxes, click OK button
2. Right-click paragraph, click Paragraph on shortcut menu, click Indents and Spacing tab, enter indentation values in Left and Right boxes, click OK button
3. In Voice Command mode, say "Format, Paragraph, Indents and Spacing, [enter indentation values in Left and Right boxes], OK"

The next step is to shade the paragraph containing the words, Vote Yes!, in the color tan. When you shade a paragraph, Word shades the rectangular area containing the paragraph from the left edge of the paragraph to the right edge. If the paragraph is surrounded by a border, Word shades inside the border.

The following steps show how to shade a paragraph.

To Shade a Paragraph

1

- **With the insertion point on line 1, click the Shading Color button arrow on the Tables and Borders toolbar.**

Word displays a color palette for shading (Figure 4-7).

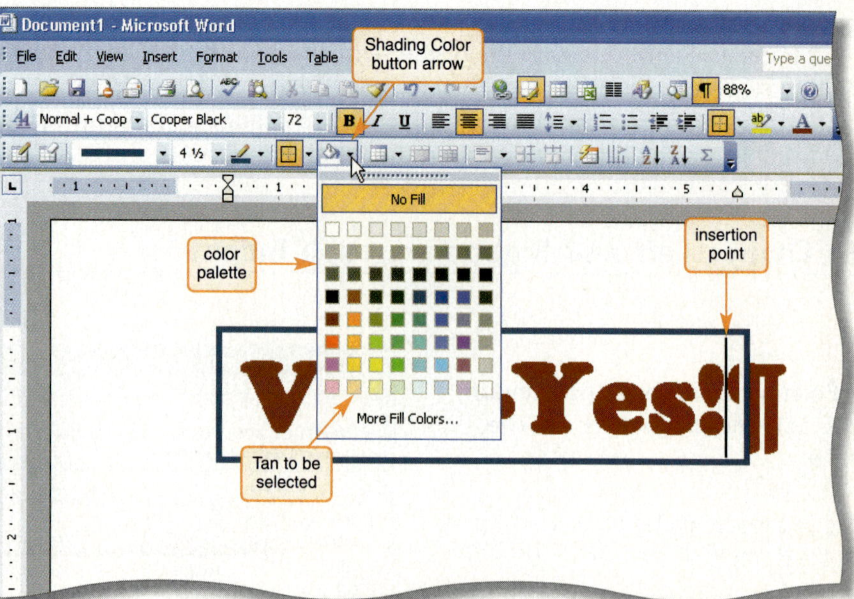

FIGURE 4-7

2

- **Click Tan, which is the second color on the bottom row of the color palette.**
- **Click the Tables and Borders button on the Standard toolbar to remove the Tables and Borders toolbar from the Word screen.**

Word shades the current paragraph tan (Figure 4-8). The Tables and Borders toolbar no longer is displayed on the screen.

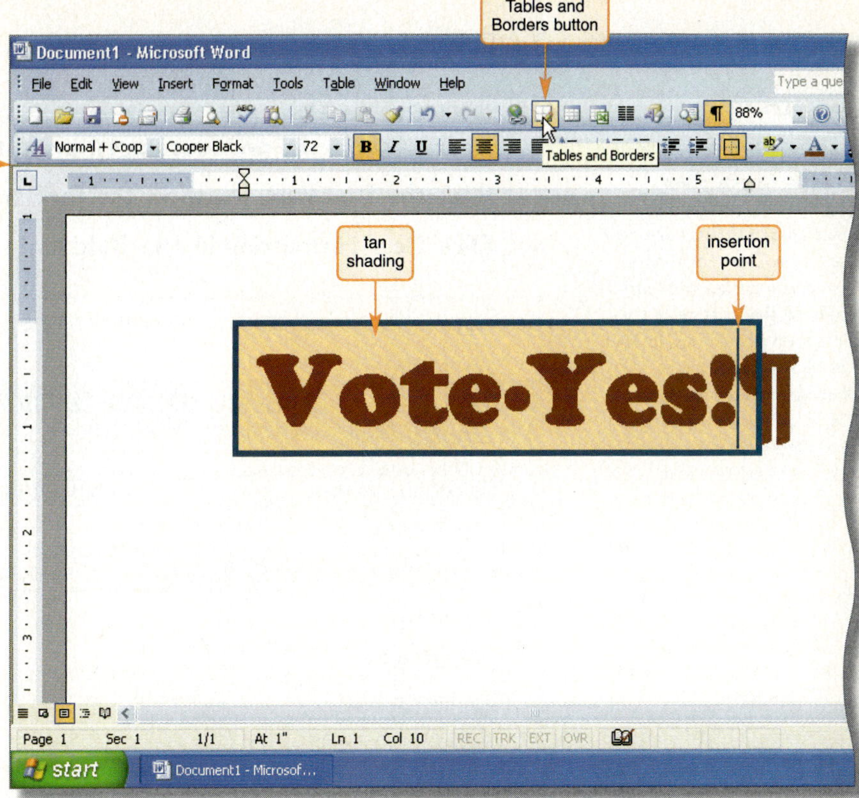

FIGURE 4-8

Other Ways

1. On Format menu click Borders and Shading, click Shading tab, click desired color in Fill area, click OK button
2. With Tables and Borders toolbar displaying, in Voice Command mode, say "Shading Color, [select color]"

The first line of the title page is entered and formatted. When you press the ENTER key to advance the insertion point to the next line on the title page, the border and shading also will be displayed on line 2 and the characters will be 72-point Cooper Black bold dark red font, because Word carries forward formatting each time you press the ENTER key. The paragraphs and characters on line 2 should not have the same formatting as line 1. Instead, they should be formatted using the Normal style.

Recall from Project 2 that the base style for a new Word document is the Normal style, which for a new installation of Word 2003 typically uses 12-point Times New Roman font for characters and single-spaced, left-aligned paragraphs (shown in Figure 4-10 on page WD 227). A previous project used the Styles and Formatting task pane to clear formatting, which returns the current paragraph to the Normal style. The steps on the next page clear formatting using the Style box on the Formatting toolbar.

More About

Removing Borders

If you wanted to remove a border from a paragraph, position the insertion point somewhere in the paragraph containing the border, click the Border button arrow on either the Formatting toolbar or on the Tables and Borders toolbar, and then click No Border on the border palette.

To Clear Formatting

1. **With the insertion point positioned at the end of line 1 (shown in Figure 4-8 on the previous page), press the ENTER key.**
2. **Click the Style box arrow on the Formatting toolbar (Figure 4-9).**
3. **Click Clear Formatting in the Style list.**

Word applies the Normal style to the location of the insertion point (shown in Figure 4-10).

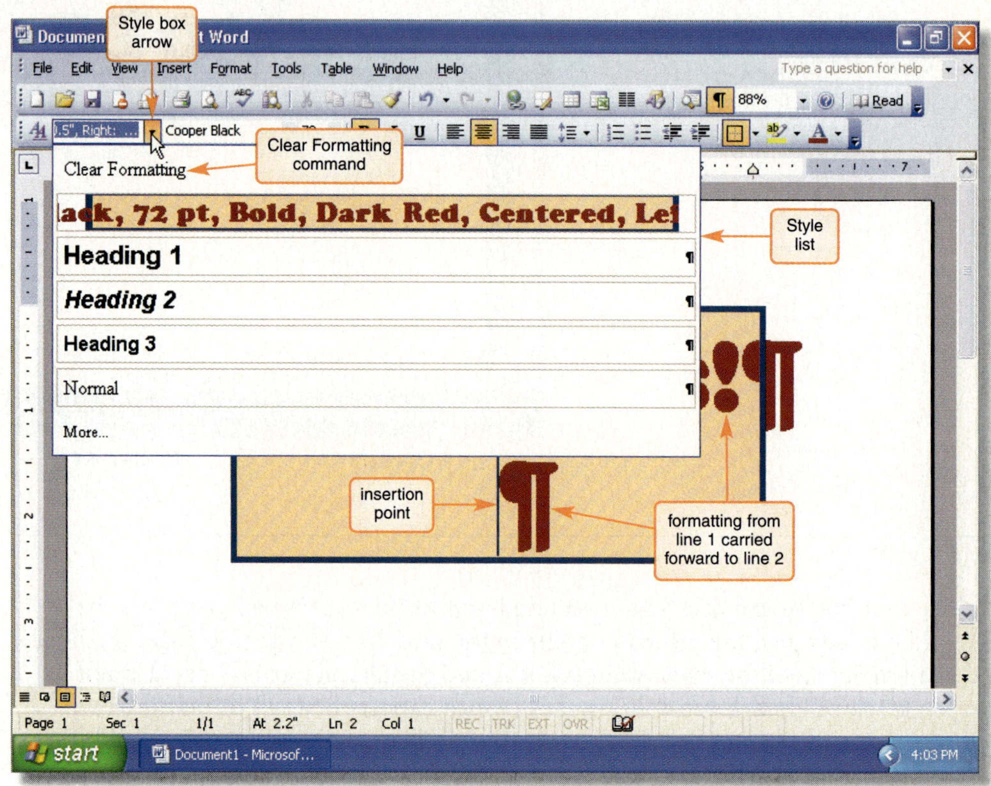

FIGURE 4-9

More About

Clearing Formatting

You can use the Clear Formatting command to clear formatting of text, tables, and lists. The Clear Formatting command applies the Normal style to the location of the insertion point. Thus, instead of clicking the Clear Formatting command in the Style list or in the Styles and Formatting task pane, you can click Normal in the Style list.

Depending on your installation of Word, the Normal style might be a different font or font size.

Formatting Characters Using the Font Dialog Box

The next step is to enter the text, MINOOKA PARK DISTRICT REFERENDUM, on the title page. This text is to be 48-point Britannic Bold italic dark teal font. Each letter in this text is to display a shadow. A **shadow** is a light gray duplicate image that appears on the lower-right edge of a character or object. Also, you want extra space between each character so the text spans across the width of the page.

You could use buttons on the Formatting toolbar to format much of the text. The shadow effect and expanded spacing, however, are applied using the Font dialog box. Thus, the next steps show how to apply all formats using the Font dialog box.

More About

Text Effects

For documents intended for online viewing, you can apply animated effects to text, such as moving rectangles or blinking lights. To do this, select the text, click Format on the menu bar, click Font, click the Text Effects tab, click the desired animation, and then click the OK button.

To Format Characters and Modify Character Spacing

1

- **With the insertion point positioned on line 2, press the ENTER key two times.**
- **Press CTRL+E to center the paragraph on line 4.**
- **Press the CAPS LOCK key. Type MINOOKA and then press the ENTER key.**
- **Type PARK DISTRICT and then press the ENTER key.**
- **Type REFERENDUM and then press the CAPS LOCK key.**
- **Drag through the three lines of text on lines 4 through 6 to select them. Right-click the selected text.**

Word displays a shortcut menu (Figure 4-10). The text in lines 4 through 6 of the document is selected.

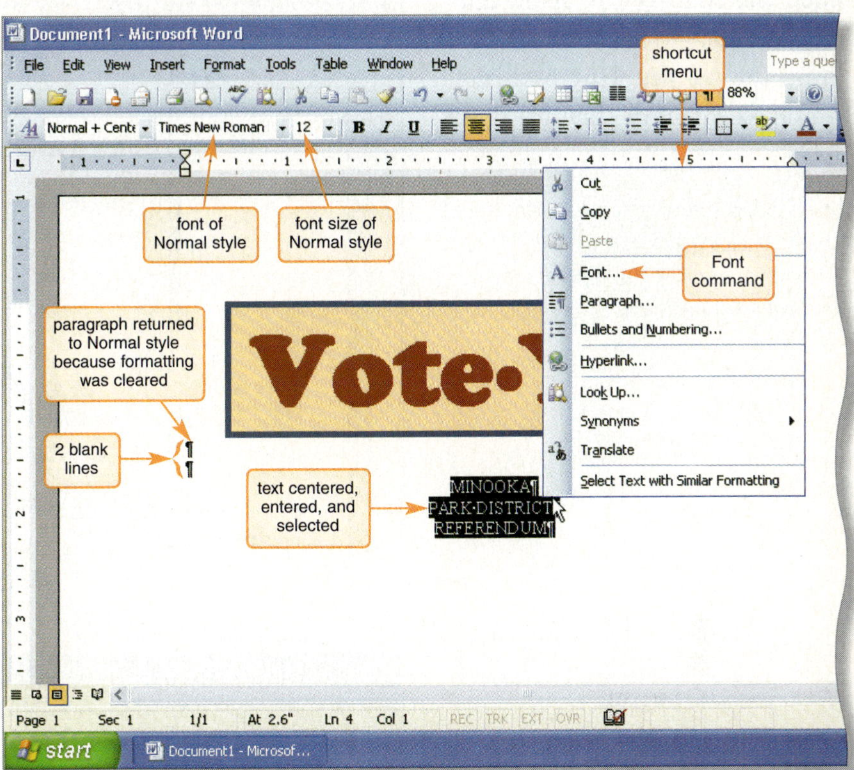

FIGURE 4-10

2

- **Click Font on the shortcut menu. When Word displays the Font dialog box, if necessary, click the Font tab.**
- **Scroll through the Font list and then click Britannic Bold (or a similar font).**
- **Click Italic in the Font style list.**
- **Scroll through the Size list and then click 48.**
- **Click the Font color box arrow and then click Dark Teal on the color palette.**
- **Click Shadow in the Effects area.**

Word displays the Font dialog box (Figure 4-11). The Preview area reflects the current selections.

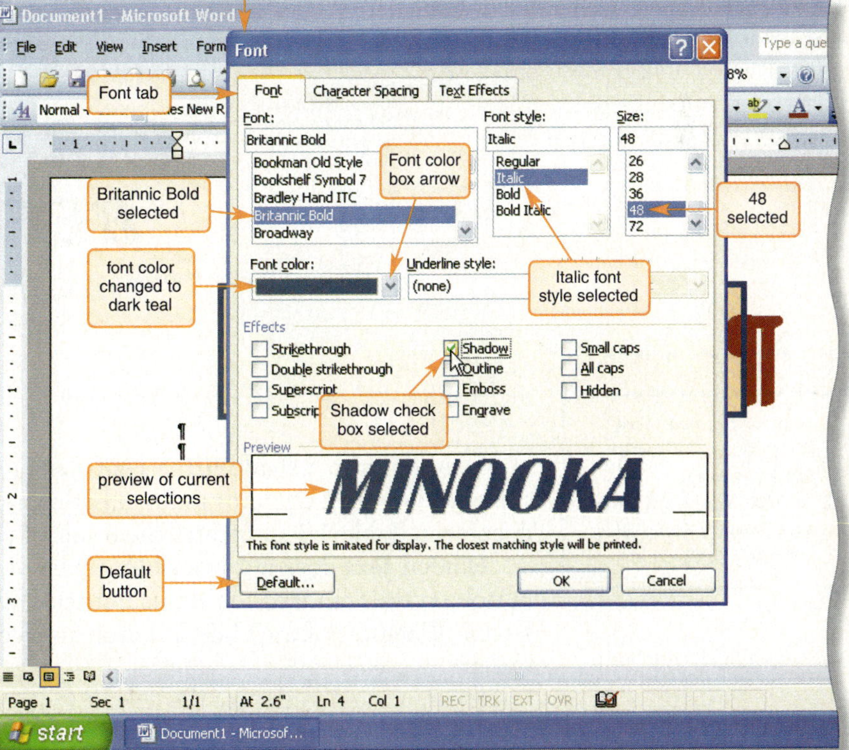

FIGURE 4-11

3

- **Click the Character Spacing tab.**
- **Click the Spacing box arrow and then click Expanded.**
- **Press the TAB key. Type 5 in the Spacing By box and then press the TAB key.**

Word displays the Character Spacing sheet in the Font dialog box (Figure 4-12). The Preview area displays the text with five points between each character.

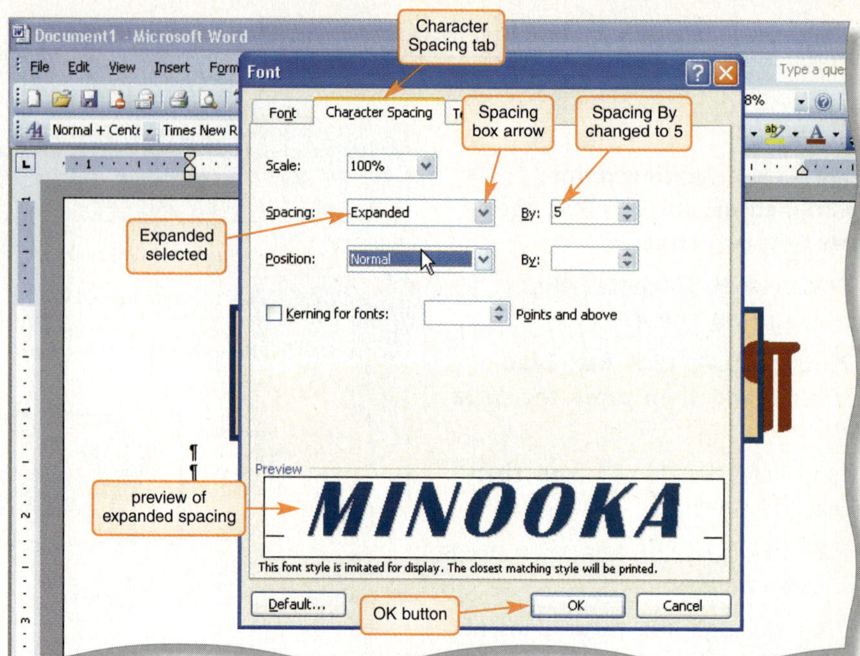

FIGURE 4-12

4

- **Click the OK button.**
- **Click at the end of line 6 to position the insertion point after the word, REFERENDUM.**

Word displays the characters in the text, MINOOKA PARK DISTRICT REFERENDUM, formatted to 48-point Britannic Bold italic dark teal font with a shadow and expanded by 5 points (Figure 4-13).

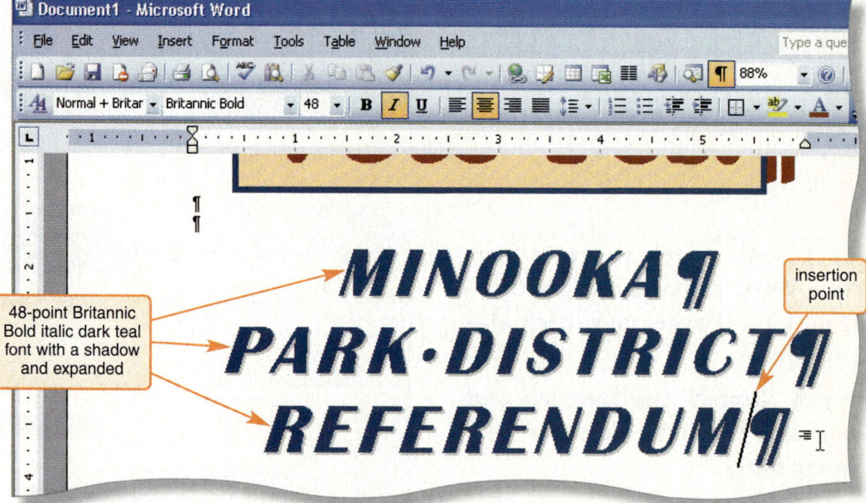

FIGURE 4-13

Other Ways

1. On Format menu click Font, [select formats], click OK button
2. In Voice Command mode, say "Format, Font, [select formats], OK"

In addition to a shadow, the Font sheet in the Font dialog box (Figure 4-11 on the previous page) contains many other character effects you can add to text in a document. Table 4-1 illustrates the result of each of these effects.

Hidden text does not print but is part of the document. When the Show/Hide ¶ button on the Standard toolbar is not selected, hidden text does not appear on the screen. When the Show/Hide ¶ button is selected, Word displays hidden text on the screen.

If you wanted to change the default font from 12-point Times New Roman to another font, font style, font size, font color, and/or font effects, you would use the Default button in the Font dialog box (Figure 4-11), as described in the next steps.

To Modify the Default Font Settings

1. Click Format on the menu bar and then click Font.
2. Make desired changes to the font in the Font dialog box.
3. Click the Default button.
4. When the Microsoft Word dialog box is displayed, click the Yes button.

Table 4-1 Character Effects Available in the Font Dialog Box

TYPE OF EFFECT	PLAIN TEXT	FORMATTED TEXT
Strikethrough	MINOOKA	~~MINOOKA~~
Double strikethrough	PARK DISTRICT	~~PARK DISTRICT~~
Superscript	1st	1st
Subscript	H2O	H_2O
Shadow	Referendum	Referendum
Outline	Referendum	Referendum
Emboss	Referendum	Referendum
Engrave	Referendum	Referendum
Small caps	Referendum	REFERENDUM
All caps	Referendum	REFERENDUM
Hidden	Referendum	

When you change the default font as described above, the current document and all future documents will use the new font settings. That is, if you quit Word, restart the computer, and restart Word, documents you create will use the new default font.

The insertion point currently is at the end of line 6 in the document window (Figure 4-13). When you press the ENTER key, the paragraph and character formatting will carry forward to line 7. You want to return formatting on line 7 to the Normal style. The following steps clear formatting below line 6.

To Clear Formatting

1. **With the insertion point positioned at the end of line 6 (shown in Figure 4-13), press the ENTER key.**
2. **Click the Style box arrow on the Formatting toolbar and then click Clear Formatting (shown in Figure 4-9 on page WD 226).**

Word applies the Normal style to the location of the insertion point, which is on line 7.

More About

Clip Art

For more information about clip art, visit the Word 2003 More About Web page (scsite.com/wd2003/more) and then click Clip Art.

Inserting Clip Art from the Web in a Word Document

As discussed in Project 1, Word 2003 includes a series of predefined graphics called **clip art** that you can insert in a Word document. This clip art is located in the **Clip Organizer**, which contains a collection of clip art, as well as photographs, sounds, and video clips.

To insert clip art, you use the Clip Art task pane. Word displays miniature clip art images, called **thumbnails**, in the Clip Art task pane. When the thumbnails appear in the Clip Art task pane, some display a small icon in their lower-left corner. Thumbnails with these icons link to clip art images that are not installed on your computer. For example, if you are connected to the Web while searching for clip art images, thumbnails from the Web appear in the Clip Art task pane with a small globe icon in their lower-left corner. Table 4-2 identifies various icons that may appear on a thumbnail in the Clip Art task pane.

If a thumbnail displays a small icon of a star ( ) in its lower-right corner, the clip art contains animation. These clip art images have the appearance of motion when displayed in some Web browsers.

Table 4-2 Icons on Thumbnails in Clip Art Task Pane

ICON	LOCATION OF CLIP
	CD-ROM or DVD-ROM
	Microsoft's Web site
	Web site partnering with Microsoft (free clip)
	Web site partnering with Microsoft (clip available for a fee)
	Unavailable clip

The following steps illustrate how to insert a clip art image from the Web in a Word document.

Note: The following steps assume your computer is connected to the Internet. If it is not, go directly to the shaded steps at the top of the next page.

To Insert Clip Art from the Web

1

- **With the insertion point on line 7, press the ENTER key twice.**
- **Press CTRL+E to center the insertion point.**
- **Click Insert on the menu bar, point to Picture, and then click Clip Art.**
- **If necessary, click the Results should be box arrow and then select All media file types.**
- **In the Clip Art task pane, drag through any text in the Search for text box. Type** `ballot box` **and then click the Go button.**
- **If necessary, scroll through the clips until the one shown in Figure 4-14 appears (or a similar clip).**

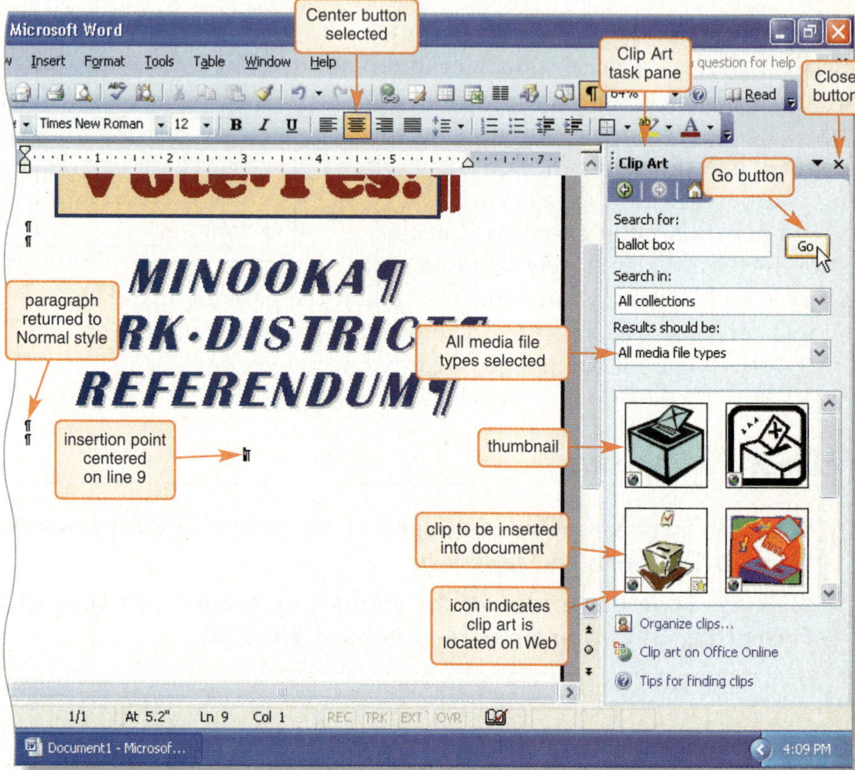

FIGURE 4-14

2

- **Click the clip to be inserted.**
- **Click the Close button on the Clip Art task pane title bar. If necessary, scroll to display the image in the document window.**

Word inserts the clip in the document at the location of the insertion point (Figure 4-15).

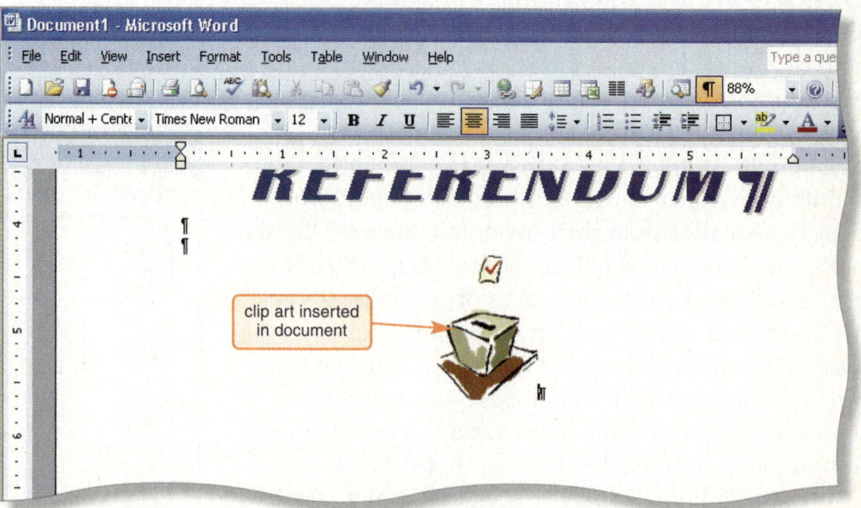

FIGURE 4-15

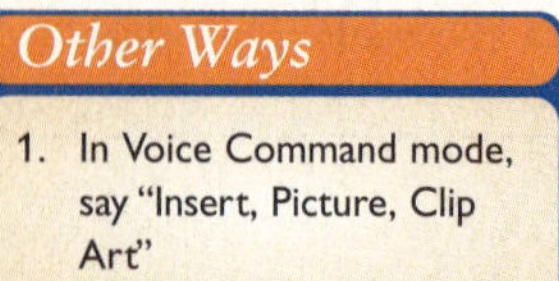

Other Ways

1. In Voice Command mode, say "Insert, Picture, Clip Art"

If you do not have access to the Web, you can insert the clip art file in the Word document from the Data Disk, as described in the following steps. If you did not download the Data Disk, see the inside back cover for instructions for downloading the Data Disk or see your instructor.

To Insert a Graphic File from the Data Disk

1. **With the insertion point on line 7, press the ENTER key twice. Press CTRL+E to center the insertion point.**
2. **Click Insert on the menu bar, point to Picture, and then click From File.**
3. **Insert the Data Disk into drive A. When Word displays the Insert Picture dialog box, click the Look in box arrow and then click 3½ Floppy (A:). Click the file name g1utss1r[1] and then click the Insert button.**

Word inserts the clip in your document at the location of the insertion point (shown in Figure 4-15).

The graphic of the ballot box is too small for the title page. The next step is to increase its size to about 250 percent, as described below.

More About

Inserting Graphics

If you have a file containing a graphic image, you can insert the file by following the shaded steps to the left. Graphic files Word can use include those with extensions or file types of .gif, .jpg, .png, .bmp, .wmf, .tif, and .eps. When you scan a photograph or other image and save it as a graphic file, you can select the file type for the saved graphic through the photo editing or illustration software. Word also can insert graphic files directly from a scanner or camera (through the Picture submenu).

To Resize a Graphic Using the Format Picture Dialog Box

1. **Double-click the graphic. When Word displays the Format Picture dialog box, if necessary, click the Size tab.**
2. **In the Scale area, double-click the number in the Height box to select it. Type** `250` **and then press the TAB key (Figure 4-16).**
3. **Click the OK button.**

Word resizes the graphic to 250 percent of its original size (shown in Figure 4-17 on the next page).

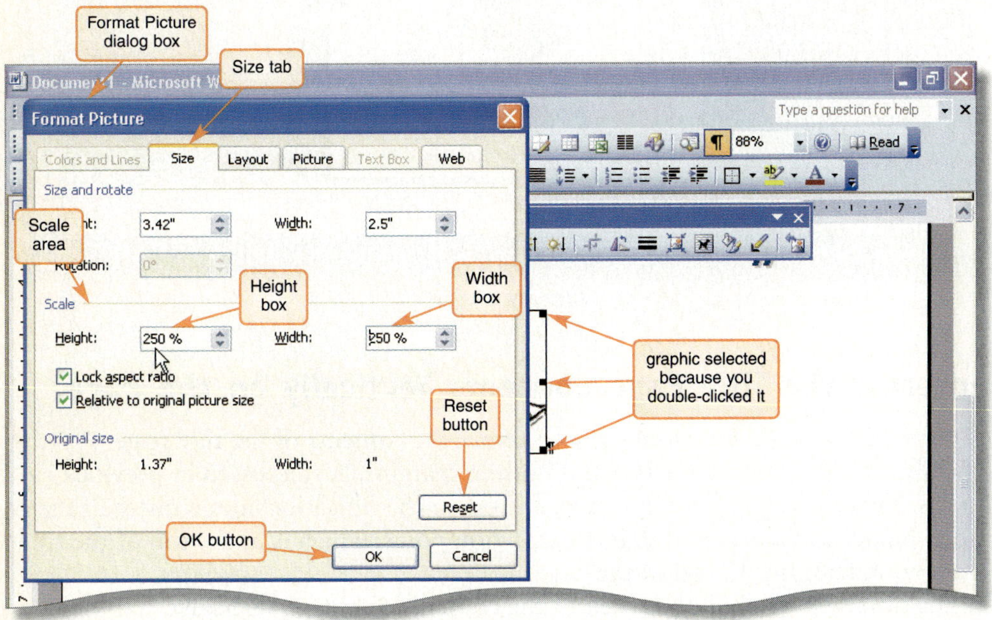

FIGURE 4-16

If you want a graphic to be an exact height and width, you can type the measurements in the Height and Width boxes in the Size and rotate area in the Size sheet in the Format Picture dialog box. If you want to return a graphic to its original size and start resizing it again, click the Reset button (Figure 4-16 on the previous page) in the Size sheet in the Format Picture dialog box.

To see the layout of the title page, the following steps display an entire page in the document window.

To Zoom Whole Page

1. **Click the Zoom box arrow on the Standard toolbar.**
2. **Click Whole Page in the Zoom list.**

Word displays the title page in reduced form so that the entire page is displayed in the document window (Figure 4-17).

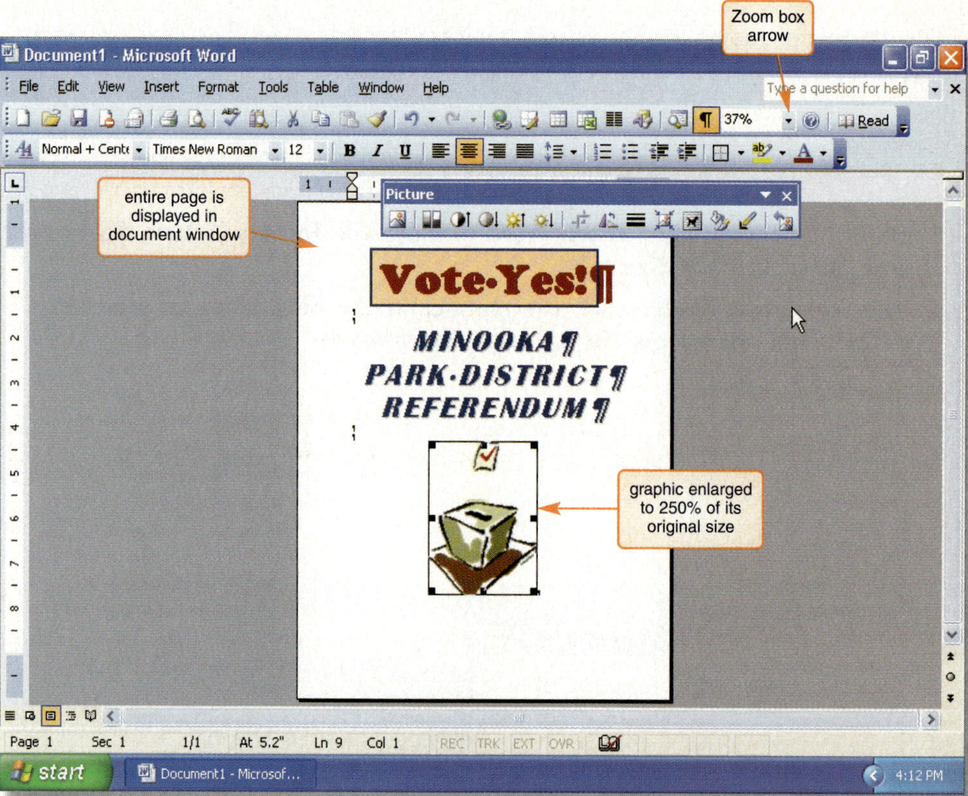

FIGURE 4-17

More About

Graphics

In addition to clip art, you can insert drawing objects such as shapes, lines, curves, arrows, flowchart symbols, stars, and diagrams into Word documents. To do this, display the Drawing toolbar by clicking the Drawing button on the Standard toolbar. Then, click the appropriate button on the Drawing toolbar and use the mouse to draw the object in the document window.

Centering the Title Page Contents Vertically on the Page

For visual appeal, you would like to center the contents of the title page vertically, that is, between the top and bottom margins. As discussed in previous projects, the default top margin in Word is one inch, which includes a one-half inch header. Notice in Figure 4-18 that the insertion point, which is at the top of the title page text, is 1" from the top of the page.

The next steps show how to center the contents of a page vertically.

More About

Centering Vertically

When you center a page vertically, Word does not change the size of the top and bottom margins. Instead, it changes the size of the header and footer areas to accommodate the extra spacing.

To Center Page Contents Vertically

1

- **Press CTRL+HOME to position the insertion point at the top of the document.**
- **Click File on the menu bar (Figure 4-18).**

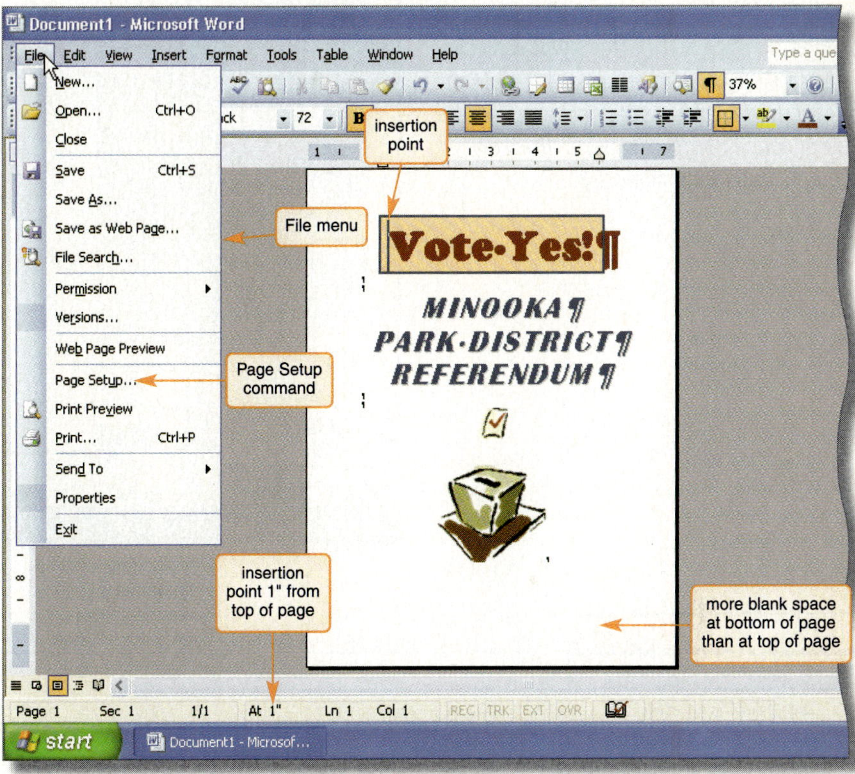

FIGURE 4-18

2

- **Click Page Setup on the File menu.**
- **When Word displays the Page Setup dialog box, if necessary, click the Layout tab.**
- **Click the Vertical alignment box arrow and then click Center.**

Word changes the vertical alignment to Center in the Page Setup dialog box (Figure 4-19).

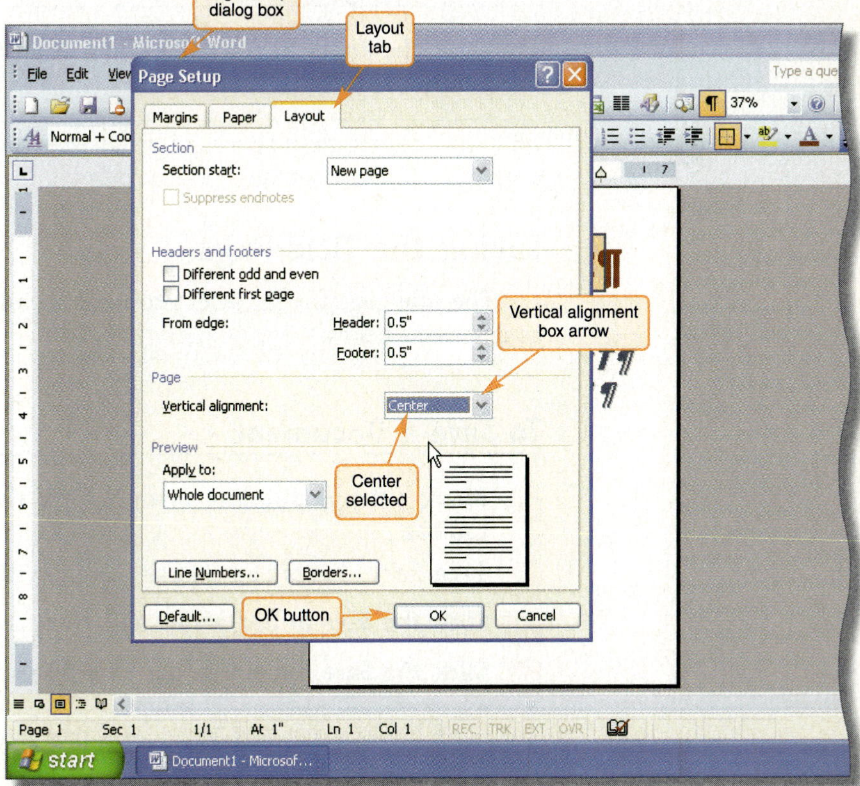

FIGURE 4-19

3

• **Click the OK button.**

Word centers the contents of the title page vertically (Figure 4-20). The status bar shows the insertion point now is 1.6" from the top of the document, which means the empty space above and below the page content totals approximately 3.2".

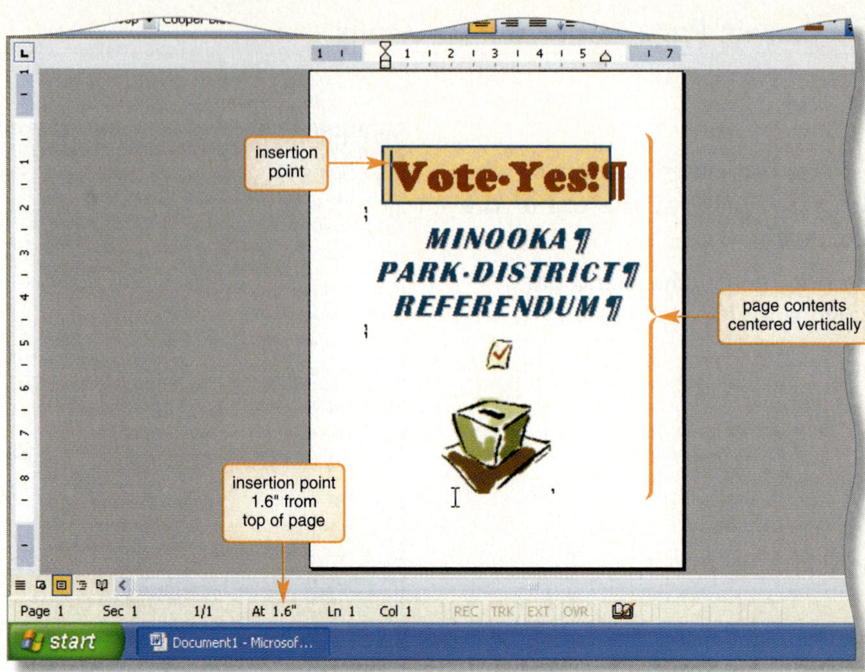

FIGURE 4-20

Other Ways

1. In Voice Command mode, say "File, Page Setup, Layout, Vertical alignment, Center, OK"

The following step changes the zoom back to page width.

To Zoom Page Width

1. **Click the Zoom box arrow on the Standard toolbar and then click Page Width.**

Word computes the zoom percentage and displays it in the Zoom box (shown in Figure 4-21 on page WD 236). Your percentage may be different depending on your computer.

Saving the Title Page

The title page for the sales proposal is complete. Thus, the next step is to save it, as described below.

To Save a Document

1. **Insert a floppy disk into drive A. Click the Save button on the Standard toolbar.**
2. **Type** `Park District Title Page` **in the File name box.**
3. **Click the Save in box arrow and then click 3½ Floppy (A:).**
4. **Click the Save button in the Save As dialog box.**

Word saves the document on a floppy disk in drive A with the file name, Park District Title Page (shown in Figure 4-21).

Inserting an Existing Document into an Open Document

Assume you already have prepared a draft of the body of the proposal and saved it with the file name, Park District Draft. You would like the draft to display on a separate page following the title page. Once the two documents are displayed on the screen together as one document, you save this active document with a new name so each of the original documents remains intact.

The inserted pages of the sales proposal are to use the Times New Roman font and be left-aligned. When you press the ENTER key at the bottom of the title page, the paragraph and character formatting will carry forward to the next line. Thus, you return formatting on the new line to the Normal style. The following steps describe how to clear formatting so the inserted pages use the Normal style.

Q&A

Q: What elements should a proposal contain?

A: All proposals should have an introduction, body, and conclusion. The introduction could contain the subject, purpose, statement of problem, need, background, or scope. The body may include available or required facilities, cost, feasibility, methods, timetable, materials, or equipment. The conclusion summarizes key points or requests some action.

To Clear Formatting

1. **Press CTRL+END to move the insertion point to the end of the title page. If necessary, scroll down to display the insertion point in the document window. Press the ENTER key.**
2. **Click the Style box arrow on the Formatting toolbar and then click Clear Formatting (shown in Figure 4-9 on page WD 226).**

Word applies the Normal style to the location of the insertion point, which now is on line 10 (shown in Figure 4-21 on the next page).

Inserting a Section Break

The body of the sales proposal requires page formatting different from that of the title page. Earlier in this project, you vertically centered the contents of the title page. The body of the proposal should have top alignment; that is, it should begin one inch from the top of the page.

Whenever you want to change page formatting for a portion of a document, you must create a new **section** in the document. Each section then may be formatted differently from the others. Thus, the title page formatted with centered vertical alignment must be in one section, and the body of the proposal formatted with top alignment must be in another section.

A Word document can be divided into any number of sections. All Word documents have at least one section. During the course of creating a document, if you need to change the top margin, bottom margin, page alignment, paper size, page orientation, page number position, or contents or position of headers, footers, or footnotes, you must create a new section.

When you create a new section, a **section break** is displayed on the screen as a double dotted line separated by the words, Section Break. Section breaks do not print. When you create a section break, you specify whether or not the new section should begin on a new page.

The body of the sales proposal is to be on a separate page following the title page. The steps on the next page show how to insert a section break that instructs Word to begin the new section on a new page in the document.

More About

Section Breaks

To see formatting associated with a section, double-click the section break notation to display the Layout sheet in the Page Setup dialog box. In this dialog box, you can click the Borders button to add a border to a section.

To Insert a Next Page Section Break

1

- **Be sure the insertion point is positioned on the paragraph mark on line 10.**
- **Click Insert on the menu bar (Figure 4-21).**

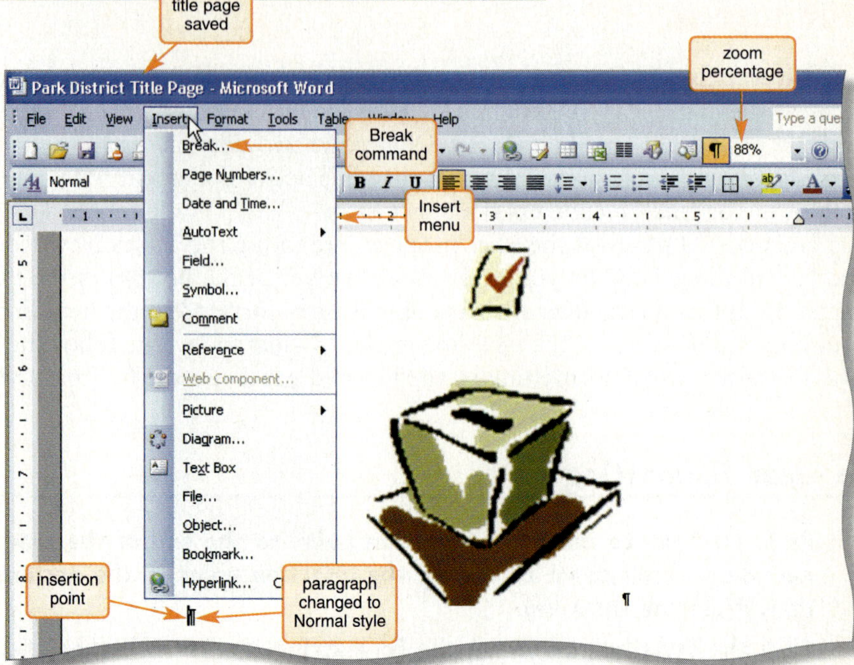

FIGURE 4-21

2

- **Click Break on the Insert menu.**
- **When Word displays the Break dialog box, click Next page in the Section break types area.**

The Next page option in the Break dialog box instructs Word to place the new section on the next page (Figure 4-22).

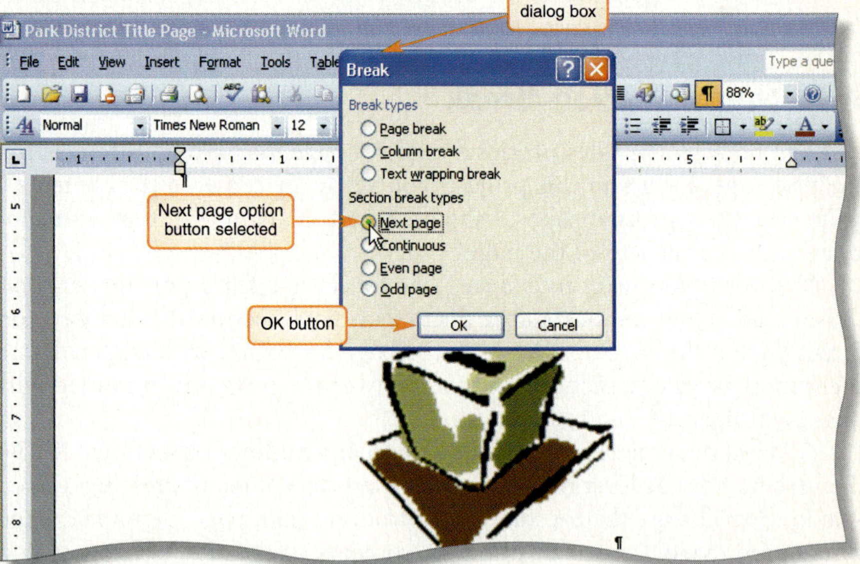

FIGURE 4-22

3

- **Click the OK button.**

Word inserts a next page section break in the document (shown in Figure 4-24).

Other Ways

1. In Voice Command mode, say "Insert, Break, Next page, OK"

Word places the insertion point and paragraph mark in the new section, which is on a new page. Notice in Figure 4-23 that the status bar indicates the insertion point is on page 2 in section 2. Also, the insertion point is positioned 5.4" from the top of the page because earlier you changed the page formatting to centered vertical alignment. The body of the proposal should have top alignment; that is, the insertion point should be one inch from the top of the page. The next steps show how to change the alignment of section two from center to top.

To Change Page Alignment of a Section

1

- **Be sure the insertion point is in section 2.**
- **Click File on the menu bar and then click Page Setup. When Word displays the Page Setup dialog box, if necessary, click the Layout tab.**
- **Click the Vertical alignment box arrow and then click Top.**

Word changes the vertical alignment to Top in the Page Setup dialog box (Figure 4-23).

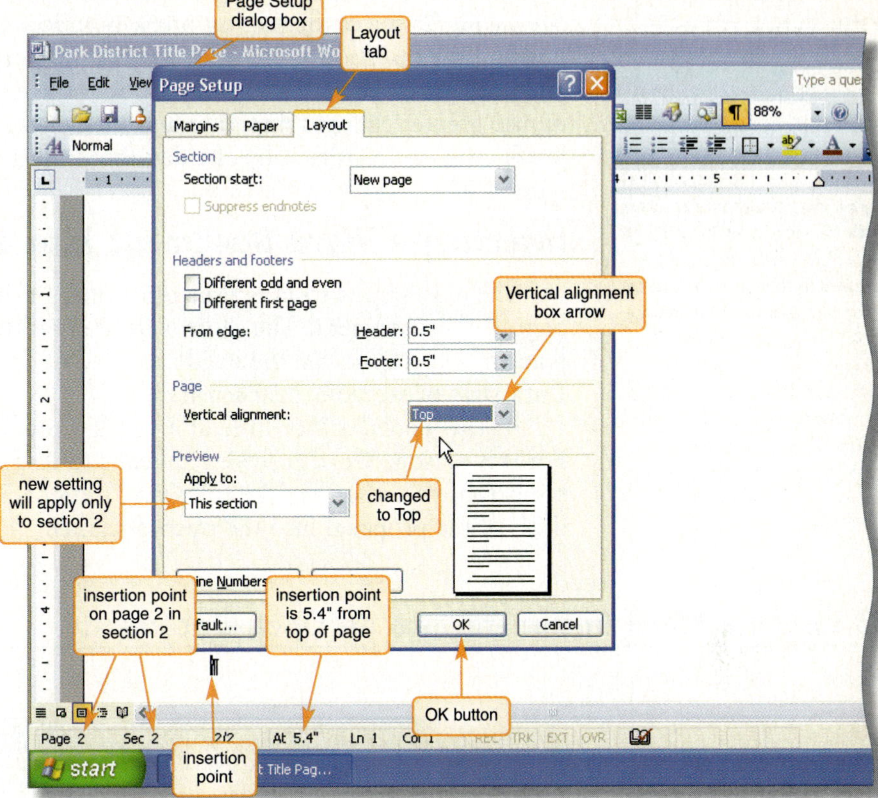

FIGURE 4-23

2

- **Click the OK button.**
- **Scroll up so Word displays the bottom of page 1 and the top of page 2 in the document window.**

Word changes the vertical alignment of section 2 to top (Figure 4-24). Notice the status bar indicates the insertion point now is positioned 1" from the top of the page, which is the top margin setting for section 2.

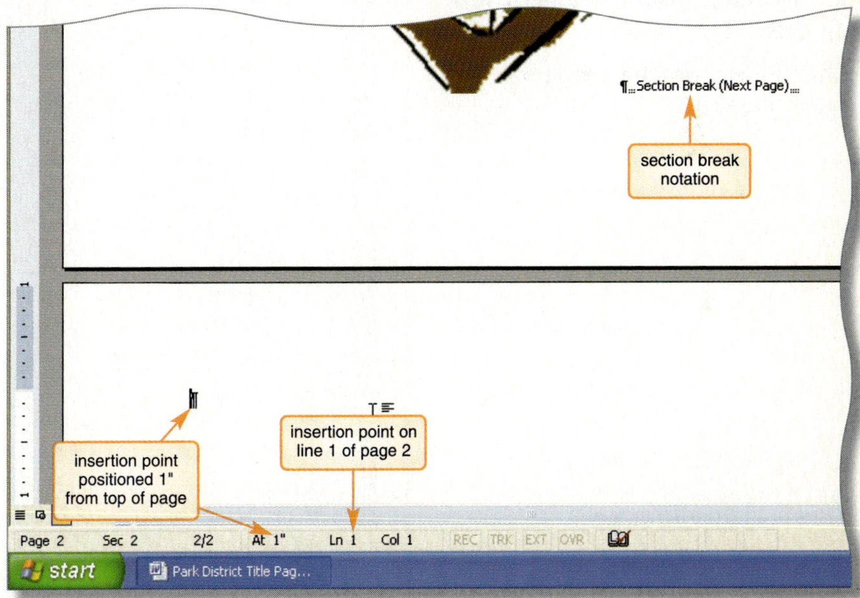

FIGURE 4-24

Other Ways

1. In Voice Command mode, say "File, Page Setup, Layout, Vertical alignment, Top, OK"

Word stores all section formatting in the section break. You can delete a section break and all associated section formatting using a variety of techniques: (1) select the section break notation, right-click the selection, and then click Cut on the shortcut menu; (2) select the section break notation and then press the DELETE key; or (3) position the insertion point immediately to the right of the section break notation and then press the BACKSPACE key. To select a section break, point to its left until the mouse pointer changes direction and then click. If you accidentally delete a section break, you can restore it by clicking the Undo button on the Standard toolbar.

More About

Opening Files

If you do not remember the exact file name you wish to open, you can substitute a special character, called a wildcard, for the character(s) you have forgotten. An asterisk (*) substitutes for zero to multiple characters, and a question mark (?) substitutes for one character. For example, typing `cat*` in the File name box will display file names such as catcher and cathedral. Typing `cat?` will display file names that are only four characters in length, such as cats or cat1.

Inserting a Word Document into an Open Document

The next step is to insert the draft of the sales proposal at the top of the second page of the document. The draft is located on the Data Disk. If you did not download the Data Disk, see the inside back cover for instructions for downloading the Data Disk or see your instructor.

If you created a Word file at an earlier time, you may have forgotten its name. For this reason, Word provides a means to display the contents of, or **preview**, any file before you insert it. The following steps show how to preview and then insert the draft of the proposal into the open document.

To Insert a Word Document into an Open Document

1

- **Be sure the insertion point is positioned on the paragraph mark at the top of section 2.**
- **If necessary, insert the Data Disk into drive A.**
- **Click Insert on the menu bar (Figure 4-25).**

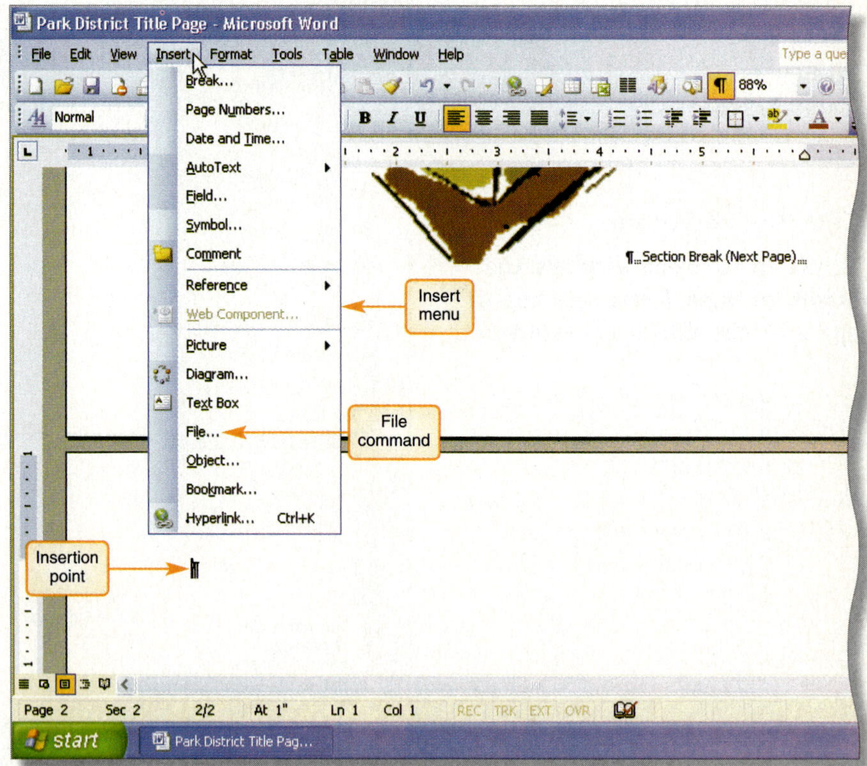

FIGURE 4-25

2

- **Click File on the Insert menu.**
- **When Word displays the Insert File dialog box, click the Look in box arrow and then click 3½ Floppy (A:).**
- **Click the Views button arrow and then click Preview.**
- **Click Park District Draft in the Name list.**

In the Insert File dialog box, the contents of the selected file (Park District Draft) are displayed on the right side of the dialog box (Figure 4-26).

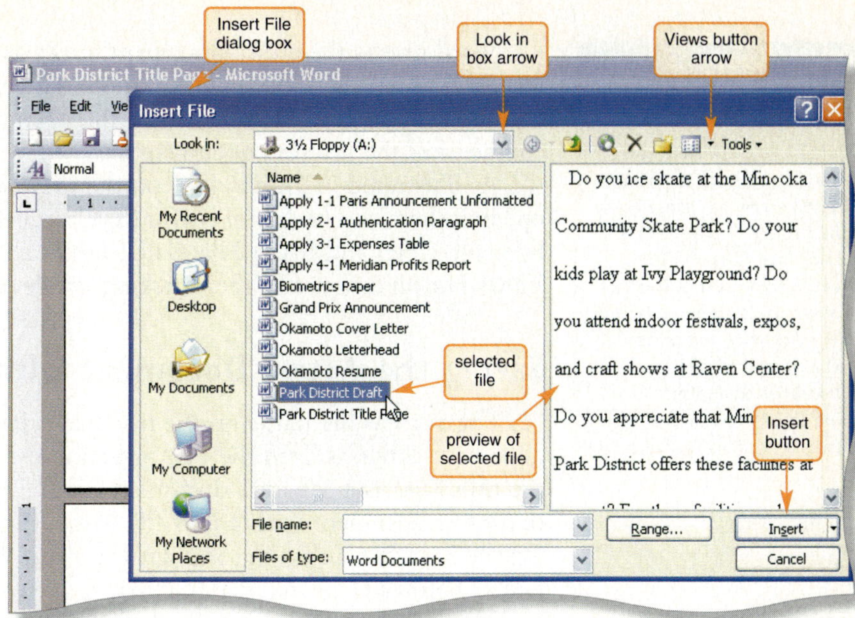

FIGURE 4-26

3

- **Click the Insert button in the dialog box.**

Word inserts the file, Park District Draft, into the open document at the location of the insertion point. The insertion point is at the end of the inserted document.

4

- **Press SHIFT+F5.**

*Word positions the insertion point on line 1 of page 2, which was its location prior to inserting the new Word document (Figure 4-27). Pressing **SHIFT+F5** instructs Word to place the insertion point at your last editing location.*

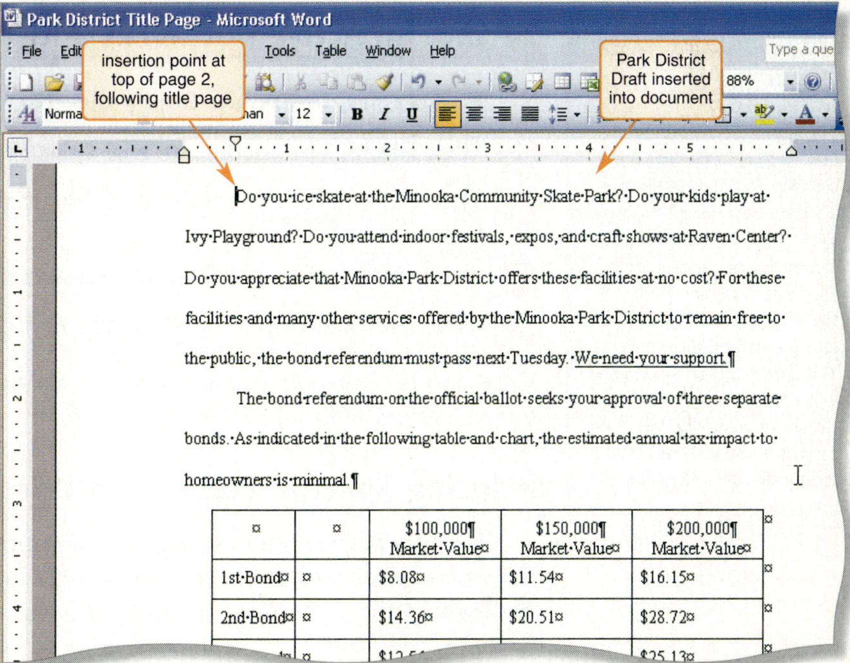

FIGURE 4-27

Other Ways

1. In Voice Command mode, say "Insert, File, [select file], Insert"

Word inserts the entire document at the location of the insertion point. If the insertion point, therefore, is positioned in the middle of the open document when you insert another Word document, the open document continues after the last character of the inserted document.

As illustrated in Figure 4-26 on the previous page, previewing files before opening them can be useful if you have forgotten the name of a file. For this reason, both the Open and Insert File dialog boxes allow you to preview files by clicking the Views button arrow and then clicking Preview.

More About

Files

In the Insert File and Open dialog boxes, click the Views button arrow to change how the files are displayed in the dialog box. Click the Tools button arrow and then click Delete to delete the selected file. Click the Tools button arrow and then click Properties to display information about the selected file.

Saving the Active Document with a New File Name

The current file name on the title bar is Park District Title Page, yet the active document contains both the title page and the draft of the sales proposal. To keep the title page as a separate document called Park District Title Page, you should save the active document with a new file name. If you save the active document by clicking the Save button on the Standard toolbar, Word will assign it the current file name. You want the active document to have a new file name.

The following steps describe how to save the active document with a new file name.

To Save an Active Document with a New File Name

1. **If necessary, insert the floppy disk containing your title page into drive A.**
2. **Click File on the menu bar and then click Save As.**
3. **Type** `Park District Proposal` **in the File name box. Do not press the ENTER key.**
4. **If necessary, click the Save in box arrow and then click 3½ Floppy (A:).**
5. **Click the Save button in the Save As dialog box.**

Word saves the document on a floppy disk in drive A with the file name, Park District Proposal (shown in Figure 4-28).

More About

File Types

Through the Save As dialog box, you also can change the file type. The default file type is Word document, which is a Word 2003 format. You also can save documents in other file types, including XML Document, Web Page, Document Template, Rich Text Format, Plain Text, several versions of Works, and earlier versions of Word. Use the File menu or press F12 to display the Save As dialog box.

Printing Specific Pages in a Document

The title page is the first page of the proposal. The body of the proposal spans the second and third pages. The next steps show how to print a hard copy of only the body of the proposal.

More About

Printing Pages

If you want to print from a certain page to the end of the document, enter the page number followed by a dash in the Pages text box. For example, 5- will print from page 5 to the end of the document. To print up to a certain page, put the dash first (e.g., -5 will print pages 1 through 5).

To Print Specific Pages in a Document

1

- **Ready the printer. Click File on the menu bar and then click Print.**
- **When Word displays the Print dialog box, click Pages in the Page range area.**
- **Type** 2-3 **in the Pages text box.**

The Print dialog box displays 2-3 in the Pages text box (Figure 4-28).

2

- **Click the OK button.**

Word prints the inserted draft of the sales proposal (shown in Figure 4-29a on the next page).

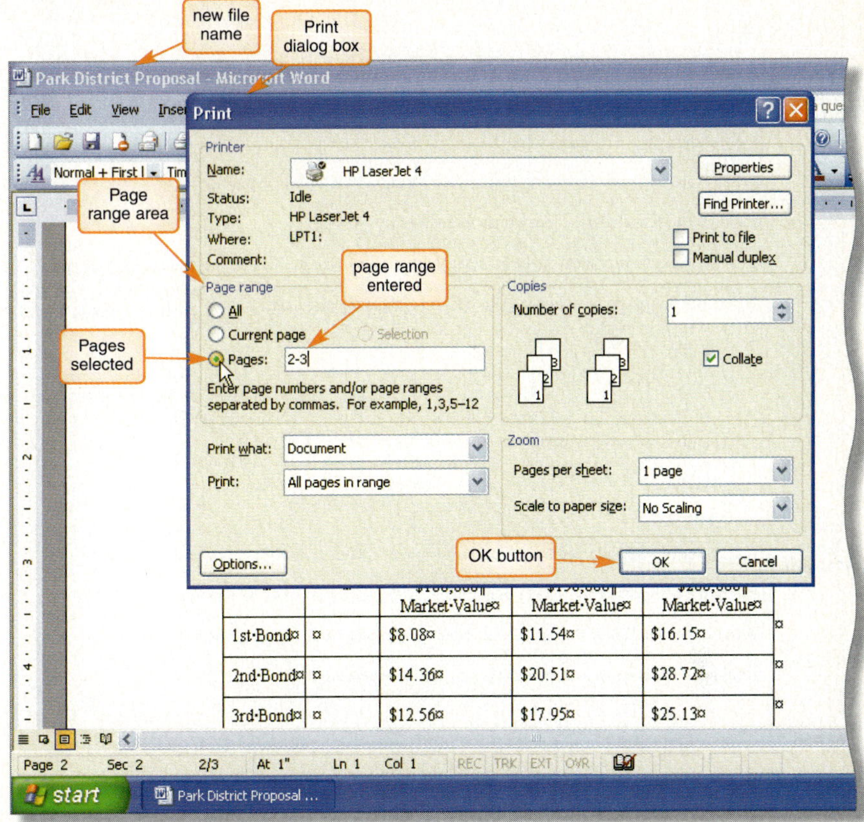

FIGURE 4-28

Other Ways

1. Press CTRL+P
2. In Voice Command mode, say "File, Print"

When you remove the document from the printer, review it carefully. Depending on your printer, wordwrap may occur in different locations from those shown in Figure 4-29a.

By adding a header and a footer, formatting and charting the table, changing the bullets to picture bullets, inserting another table into the document, and adding a watermark, you can make the body of the proposal more attention-grabbing. These enhancements to the body of the sales proposal are shown in Figure 4-29b on page WD 243.

The following pages illustrate how to change the document in Figure 4-29a so it looks like Figure 4-29b.

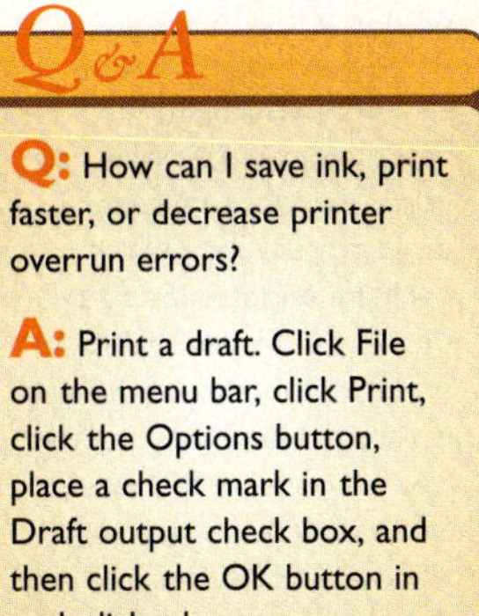

Q&A

Q: How can I save ink, print faster, or decrease printer overrun errors?

A: Print a draft. Click File on the menu bar, click Print, click the Options button, place a check mark in the Draft output check box, and then click the OK button in each dialog box.

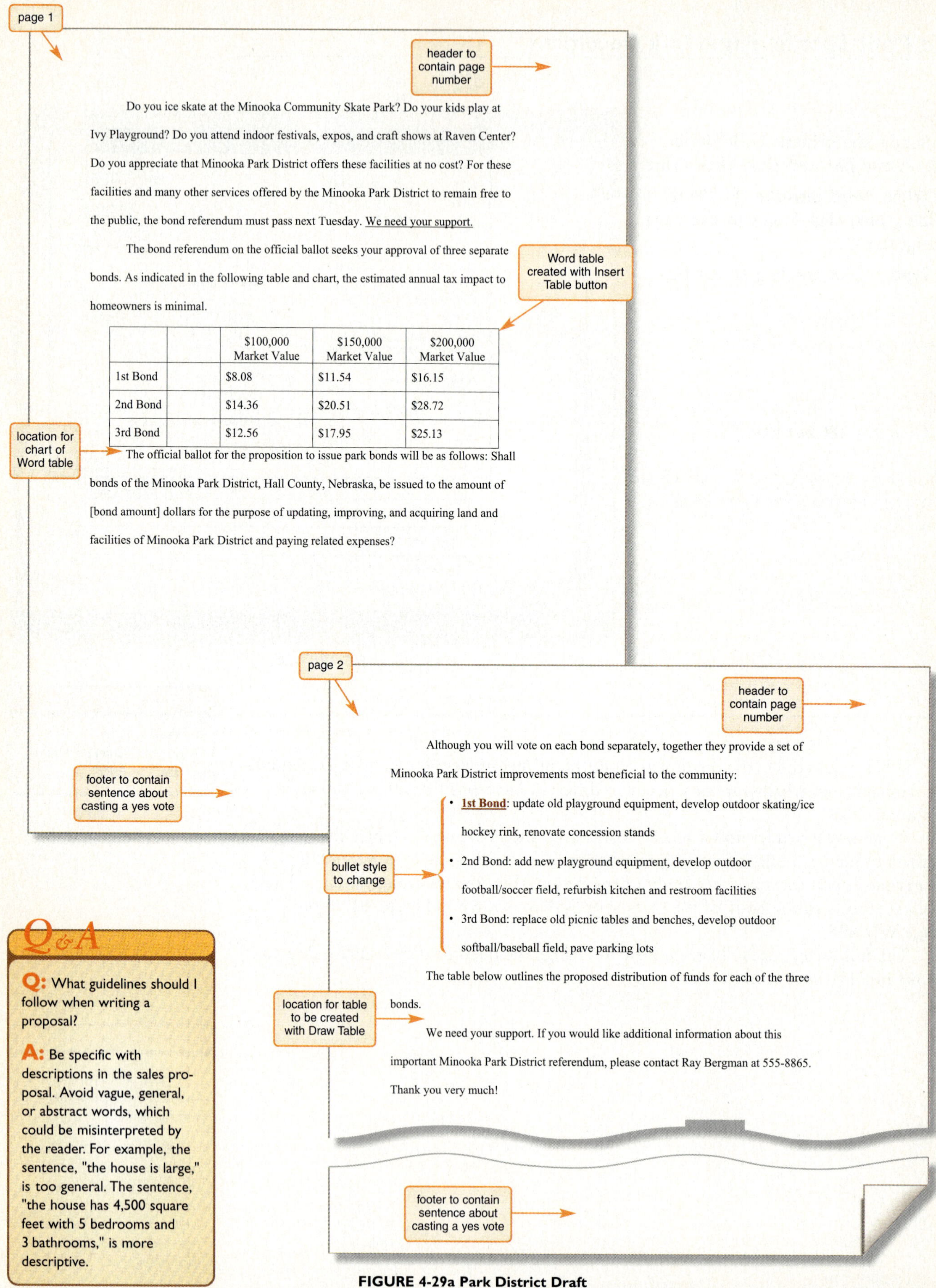
page 1
header to contain page number
Do you ice skate at the Minooka Community Skate Park? Do your kids play at Ivy Playground? Do you attend indoor festivals, expos, and craft shows at Raven Center? Do you appreciate that Minooka Park District offers these facilities at no cost? For these facilities and many other services offered by the Minooka Park District to remain free to the public, the bond referendum must pass next Tuesday. We need your support.
The bond referendum on the official ballot seeks your approval of three separate bonds. As indicated in the following table and chart, the estimated annual tax impact to homeowners is minimal.
Word table created with Insert Table button
$100,000 Market Value
$150,000 Market Value
$200,000 Market Value
1st Bond $8.08 $11.54 $16.15
2nd Bond $14.36 $20.51 $28.72
3rd Bond $12.56 $17.95 $25.13
location for chart of Word table
The official ballot for the proposition to issue park bonds will be as follows: Shall bonds of the Minooka Park District, Hall County, Nebraska, be issued to the amount of [bond amount] dollars for the purpose of updating, improving, and acquiring land and facilities of Minooka Park District and paying related expenses?
footer to contain sentence about casting a yes vote
page 2
header to contain page number
Although you will vote on each bond separately, together they provide a set of Minooka Park District improvements most beneficial to the community:
1st Bond: update old playground equipment, develop outdoor skating/ice hockey rink, renovate concession stands
2nd Bond: add new playground equipment, develop outdoor football/soccer field, refurbish kitchen and restroom facilities
3rd Bond: replace old picnic tables and benches, develop outdoor softball/baseball field, pave parking lots
bullet style to change
The table below outlines the proposed distribution of funds for each of the three bonds.
location for table to be created with Draw Table
We need your support. If you would like additional information about this important Minooka Park District referendum, please contact Ray Bergman at 555-8865. Thank you very much!
footer to contain sentence about casting a yes vote

FIGURE 4-29a Park District Draft

Q&A

Q: What guidelines should I follow when writing a proposal?

A: Be specific with descriptions in the sales proposal. Avoid vague, general, or abstract words, which could be misinterpreted by the reader. For example, the sentence, "the house is large," is too general. The sentence, "the house has 4,500 square feet with 5 bedrooms and 3 bathrooms," is more descriptive.

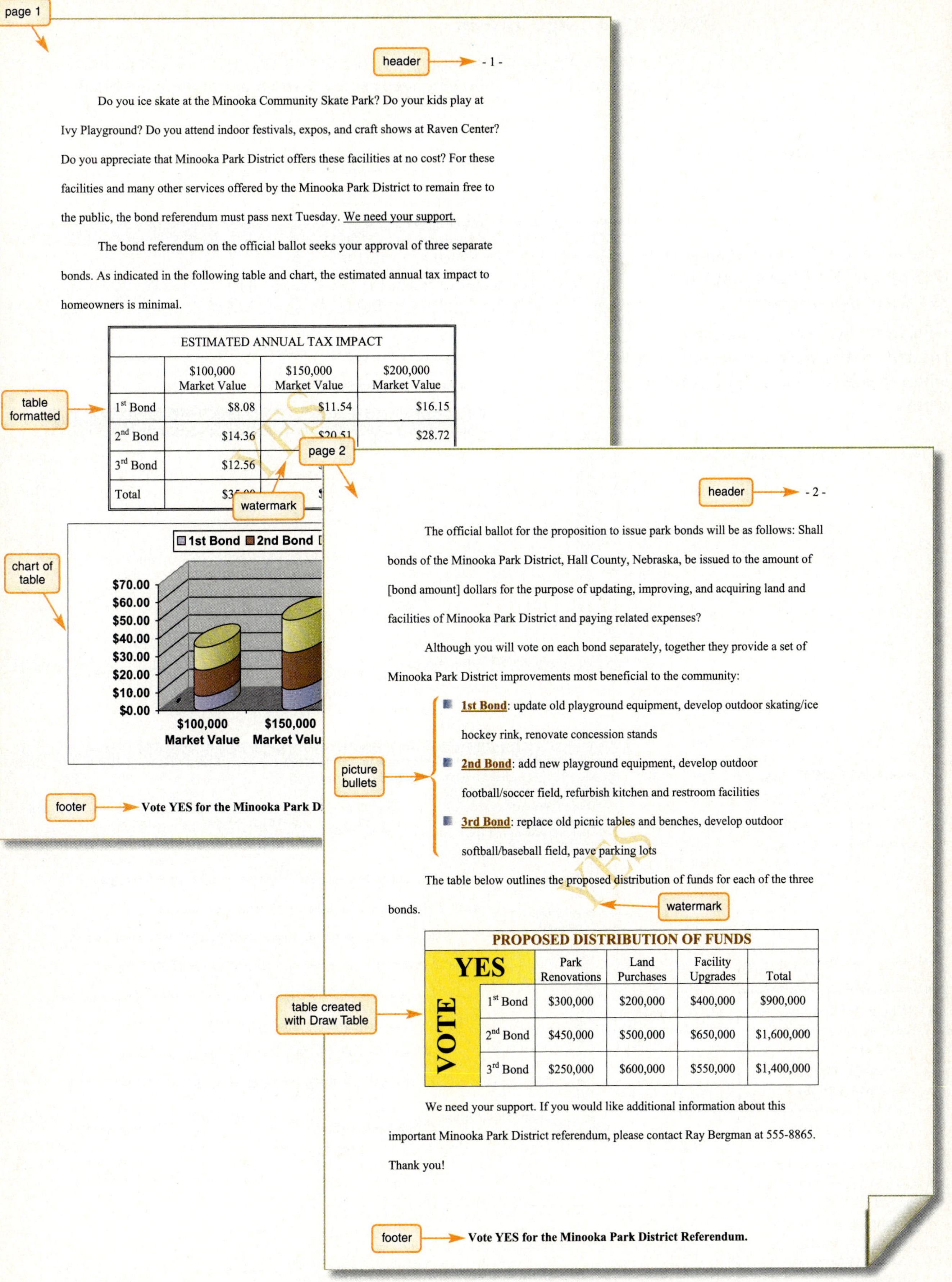
page 1
header
- 1 -
Do you ice skate at the Minooka Community Skate Park? Do your kids play at Ivy Playground? Do you attend indoor festivals, expos, and craft shows at Raven Center? Do you appreciate that Minooka Park District offers these facilities at no cost? For these facilities and many other services offered by the Minooka Park District to remain free to the public, the bond referendum must pass next Tuesday. We need your support.
The bond referendum on the official ballot seeks your approval of three separate bonds. As indicated in the following table and chart, the estimated annual tax impact to homeowners is minimal.
ESTIMATED ANNUAL TAX IMPACT
$100,000 Market Value
$150,000 Market Value
$200,000 Market Value
1st Bond $8.08 $11.54 $16.15
2nd Bond $14.36 $28.72
3rd Bond $12.56
Total
table formatted
watermark
chart of table
1st Bond
2nd Bond
$70.00
$60.00
$50.00
$40.00
$30.00
$20.00
$10.00
$0.00
$100,000 Market Value
$150,000
footer
page 2
header
- 2 -
The official ballot for the proposition to issue park bonds will be as follows: Shall bonds of the Minooka Park District, Hall County, Nebraska, be issued to the amount of [bond amount] dollars for the purpose of updating, improving, and acquiring land and facilities of Minooka Park District and paying related expenses?
Although you will vote on each bond separately, together they provide a set of Minooka Park District improvements most beneficial to the community:
1st Bond: update old playground equipment, develop outdoor skating/ice hockey rink, renovate concession stands
2nd Bond: add new playground equipment, develop outdoor football/soccer field, refurbish kitchen and restroom facilities
3rd Bond: replace old picnic tables and benches, develop outdoor softball/baseball field, pave parking lots
picture bullets
The table below outlines the proposed distribution of funds for each of the three bonds.
watermark
PROPOSED DISTRIBUTION OF FUNDS
YES
VOTE
Park Renovations
Land Purchases
Facility Upgrades
Total
1st Bond $300,000 $200,000 $400,000 $900,000
2nd Bond $450,000 $500,000 $650,000 $1,600,000
3rd Bond $250,000 $600,000 $550,000 $1,400,000
table created with Draw Table
We need your support. If you would like additional information about this important Minooka Park District referendum, please contact Ray Bergman at 555-8865. Thank you!
footer
Vote YES for the Minooka Park District Referendum.

FIGURE 4-29b Body of Sales Proposal with Enhancements

Deleting a Page Break

After reviewing the draft, you notice the document contains a page break below the third paragraph. The following steps show how to delete the page break.

To Delete a Page Break

1

- **Scroll to the bottom of page 2 to display the page break notation in the document window.**
- **Position the mouse pointer to the left of the page break and click when it changes to a right-pointing arrow.**

Word selects the page break notation (Figure 4-30).

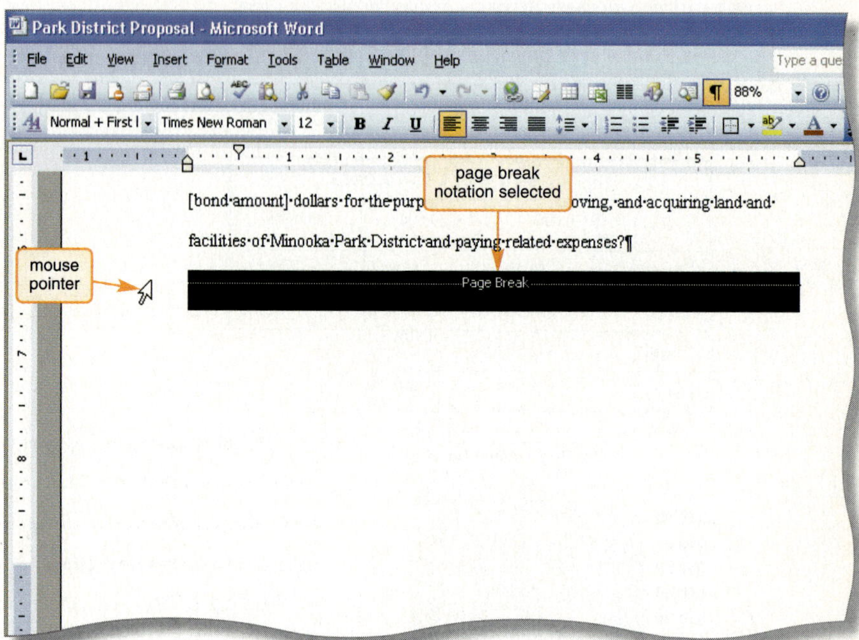
Park District Proposal - Microsoft Word
page break notation selected
mouse pointer
[bond·amount]·dollars·for·the·purp
oving,·and·acquiring·land·and·
facilities·of·Minooka·Park·District·and·paying·related·expenses?¶
Page Break

FIGURE 4-30

2

- **Press the DELETE key.**

Word removes the page break from the document (Figure 4-31).

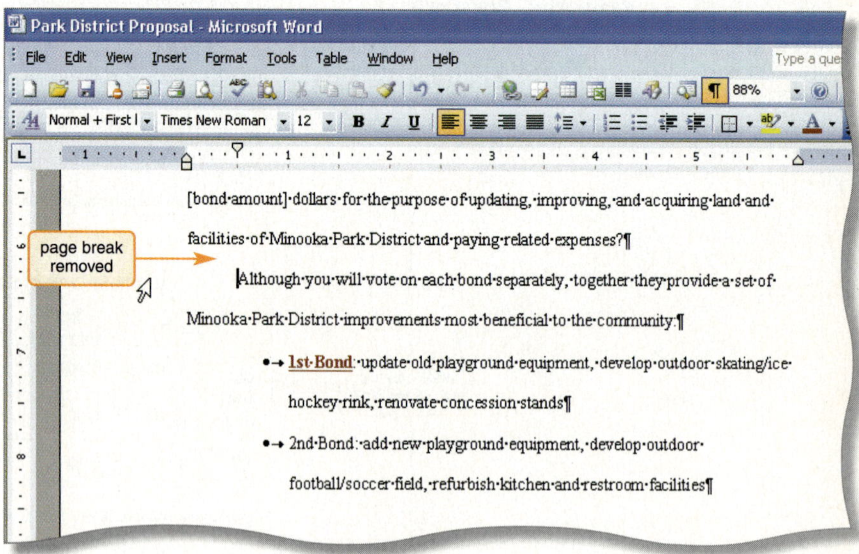
Park District Proposal - Microsoft Word
page break removed
[bond·amount]·dollars·for·the·purpose·of·updating,·improving,·and·acquiring·land·and·
facilities·of·Minooka·Park·District·and·paying·related·expenses?¶
Although·you·will·vote·on·each·bond·separately,·together·they·provide·a·set·of·
Minooka·Park·District·improvements·most·beneficial·to·the·community.¶
1st·Bond:·update·old·playground·equipment,·develop·outdoor·skating/ice·
hockey·rink,·renovate·concession·stands¶
2nd·Bond:·add·new·playground·equipment,·develop·outdoor·
football/soccer·field,·refurbish·kitchen·and·restroom·facilities¶

FIGURE 4-31

Other Ways

1. With page break notation selected, on Edit menu click Cut
2. With page break notation selected, right-click selected text and then click Cut on shortcut menu
3. With page break notation selected, press CTRL+X or BACKSPACE
4. With page break notation selected, in Voice Command mode, say "Delete"

Cutting Text

The last line of the document contains the phrase, Thank you very much! You decide to shorten it simply to say, Thank you! The following steps show how to cut the text from the document.

To Cut Text

1

- **Scroll to the bottom of the document.**
- **Drag through the words, very much.**

Word selects the text (Figure 4-32).

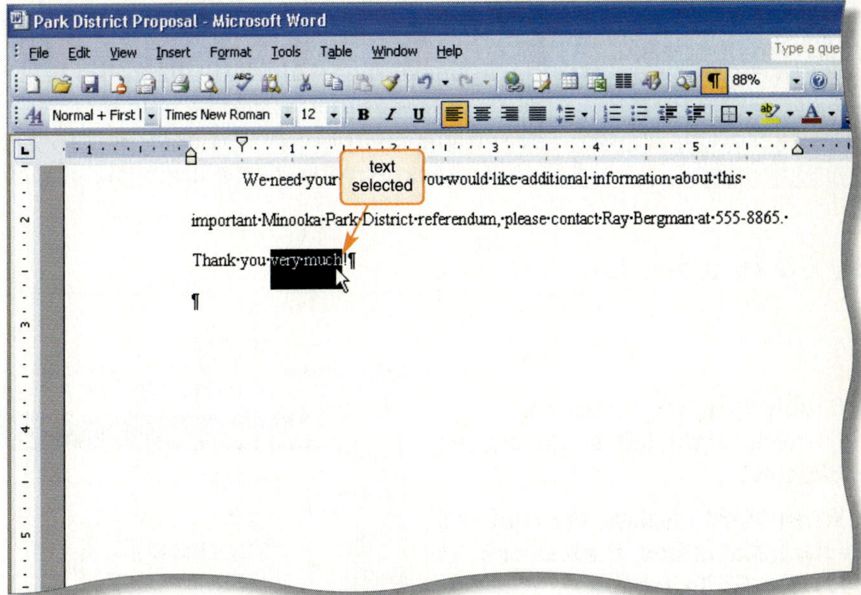

Park District Proposal - Microsoft Word
text selected
We·need·your
ou·would·like·additional·information·about·this·
important·Minooka·Park·District·referendum,·please·contact·Ray·Bergman·at·555-8865.·
Thank·you·very·much!¶

FIGURE 4-32

2

- **Click the Cut button on the Standard toolbar.**

Word removes the selected text from the document (Figure 4-33).

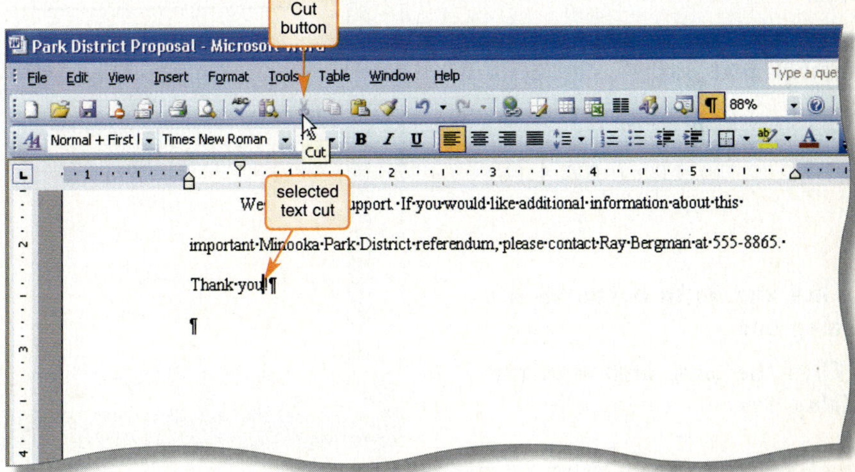

Cut button
Park District Proposal - Microsoft
Cut
selected text cut
upport.·If·you·would·like·additional·information·about·this·
important·Minooka·Park·District·referendum,·please·contact·Ray·Bergman·at·555-8865.·
Thank·you!¶

FIGURE 4-33

Other Ways

1. Right-click selected text and then click Cut on shortcut menu
2. Press CTRL+X
3. In Voice Command mode, say "Cut"

When you cut text or objects from a document, Word places the cut item(s) on the Clipboard. Recall from Project 3 that you can paste items on the Clipboard by clicking the Paste button on the Standard toolbar or by using the Clipboard task pane.

More About

Headers and Footers

If a portion of a header or footer does not print, it may be in a nonprintable area. Check the printer manual to see how close it can print to the edge of the paper. Then, click File on the menu bar, click Page Setup, click the Layout tab, adjust the From edge box to a value that is larger than the printer's minimum margin setting, and then click the OK button.

Creating Headers and Footers

As discussed in Project 2, a **header** is text that prints at the top of each page in the document. A **footer** is text that prints at the bottom of each page. In this proposal, you want the header and footer to display on each page in the body of the sales proposal. You do not want the header and footer on the title page. Recall that the title page and the body of the sales proposal are in two separate sections. Thus, the header and footer should not be in section 1, but they should be in section 2.

Creating a Header Different from a Previous Section Header

In this proposal, the header consists of the page number aligned at the right margin. This header should be only on the pages in section 2 of the document. Thus, be sure the insertion point is in section 2 when you create the header.

The next steps go to the beginning of section 2 in the document.

To Go To a Section

1

- **Double-click the status bar anywhere to the left of the status indicators.**
- **When Word displays the Find and Replace dialog box, if necessary, click the Go To tab.**
- **Click Section in the Go to what area.**
- **Type** 2 **in the Enter section number text box.**

Word displays the Go To sheet in the Find and Replace dialog box (Figure 4-34).

2

- **Click the Go To button in the dialog box.**
- **Click the Close button in the dialog box.**

Word displays the top of section 2 in the document window (shown in Figure 4-35).

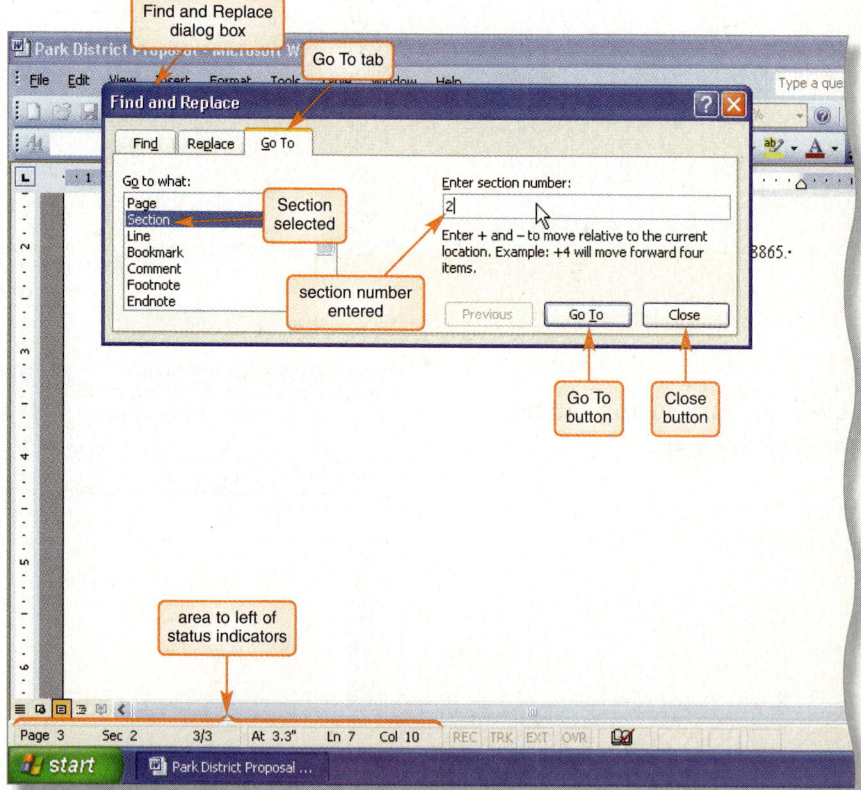

FIGURE 4-34

Other Ways

1. Click Select Browse Object button on vertical scroll bar, click Browse by Section
2. On Edit menu click Go To
3. Press CTRL+G
4. In Voice Command mode, say "Edit, Go To"

In addition to sections, you can go to pages, lines, bookmarks, comments, footnotes, and endnotes through the Go To sheet (Figure 4-34) in the Find dialog box.

The next steps show how to add a header only to the second section of the document so it does not appear on the title page but does appear on all pages in the body of the proposal.

To Create a Header Different from the Previous Section Header

1

- **Verify the insertion point is in section 2 by looking at the status bar.**
- **Click View on the menu bar and then click Header and Footer.**
- **Click the Align Right button on the Formatting toolbar.**

Word right-aligns the insertion point in the header area (Figure 4-35). The header area title displays, Header -Section 2-. Notice the label, Same as Previous, at the top of the header area, which indicates any text you type in this header will be copied to section 1. You do not want text you type to be in section 1.

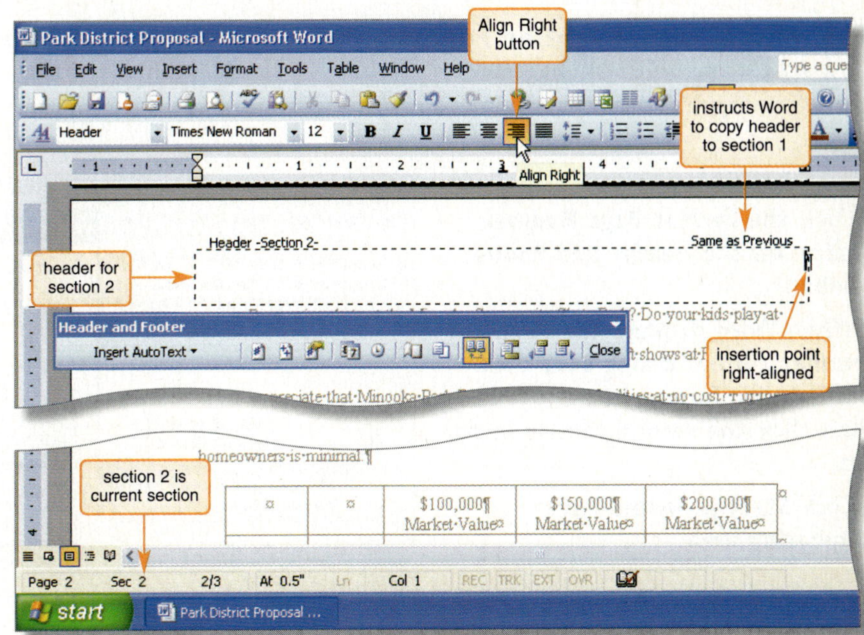

FIGURE 4-35

2

- **If the header area displays the label, Same as Previous, click the Link to Previous button on the Header and Footer toolbar to deselect the button.**
- **Click the Insert Page Number button on the Header and Footer toolbar.**

Word removes the Same as Previous label from the header area and inserts the page number at the location of the insertion point (Figure 4-36).

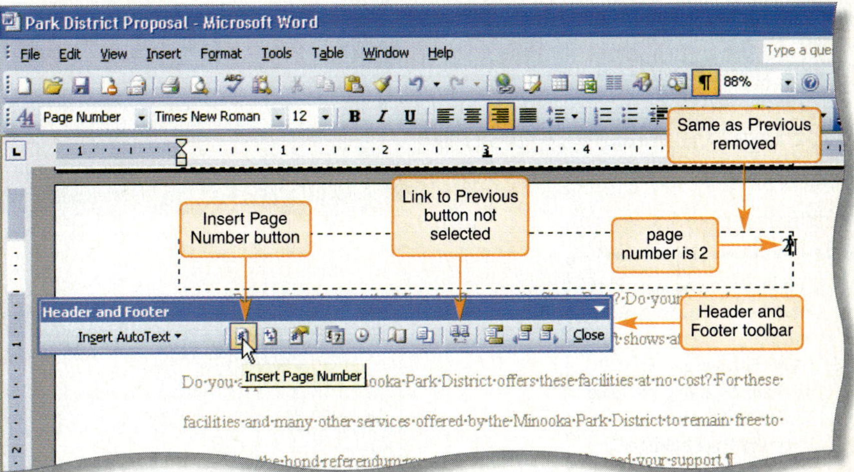

FIGURE 4-36

Other Ways

1. In Voice Command mode, say "View, Header and Footer, Link to Previous"

When the Link to Previous button is not selected on the Header and Footer toolbar, Word does not copy the typed header into the previous section. If you wanted the header typed in section 2 also to be in section 1, you would leave the Link to Previous button selected on the Header and Footer toolbar.

In Figure 4-36, the page number is 2 because Word begins numbering pages from the beginning of the document. You want to begin numbering the body of the sales proposal with a number 1. Thus, you need to instruct Word to begin numbering the pages in section 2 with the number 1.

The following steps show how to change the format of page numbers and how to page number differently in a section.

To Change Page Number Format and Page Number Differently in a Section

1

- **Click the Format Page Number button on the Header and Footer toolbar.**
- **When Word displays the Page Number Format dialog box, click the Number format box arrow and then click the second format in the list.**
- **Click Start at in the Page numbering area.**

By default, Word displays the number 1 in the Start at box in the Page Number Format dialog box (Figure 4-37).

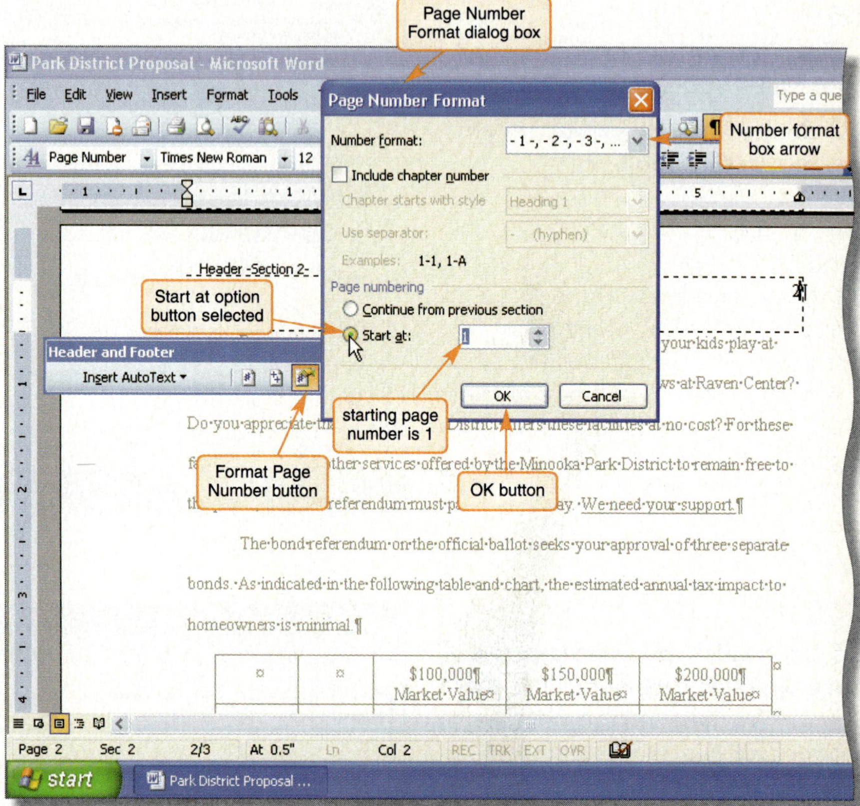

FIGURE 4-37

2

- **Click the OK button.**

Word changes the starting page number for section 2 to the number 1 (Figure 4-38).

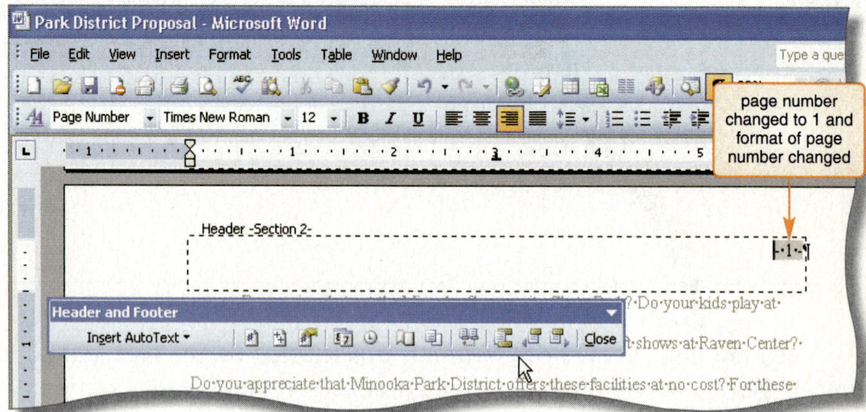

FIGURE 4-38

Other Ways

1. On Insert menu click Page Numbers, click Format button
2. With Header and Footer toolbar displaying, in Voice Command mode, say "Format Page Number"

More About

Page Numbers

If Word displays {PAGE} instead of the actual page number, press ALT+F9 to turn off field codes. If Word prints {PAGE} instead of the page number, click File on the menu bar, click Print, click the Options button, remove the check mark from the Field codes check box, and then click the OK button in each dialog box.

Creating a Footer Different from a Previous Section Footer

In this proposal, the footer consists of the following sentence: Vote YES for the Minooka Park District Referendum. This footer should be only on the pages in section 2 of the document. Thus, be sure the insertion point is in section 2 when you create the footer.

The following steps show how to add a footer only to the second section of the document.

To Create a Footer Different from the Previous Section Footer

1

- **Click the Switch Between Header and Footer button on the Header and Footer toolbar.**
- **If the footer area displays the label, Same as Previous, click the Link to Previous button on the Header and Footer toolbar to deselect the button.**
- **Click the Bold button on the Formatting toolbar.**
- **Click the Center button on the Formatting toolbar.**
- **Type** `Vote YES for the Minooka Park District Referendum.`

Word displays the text in the footer area (Figure 4-39). The footer area displays the title, Footer -Section 2-, at its left edge.

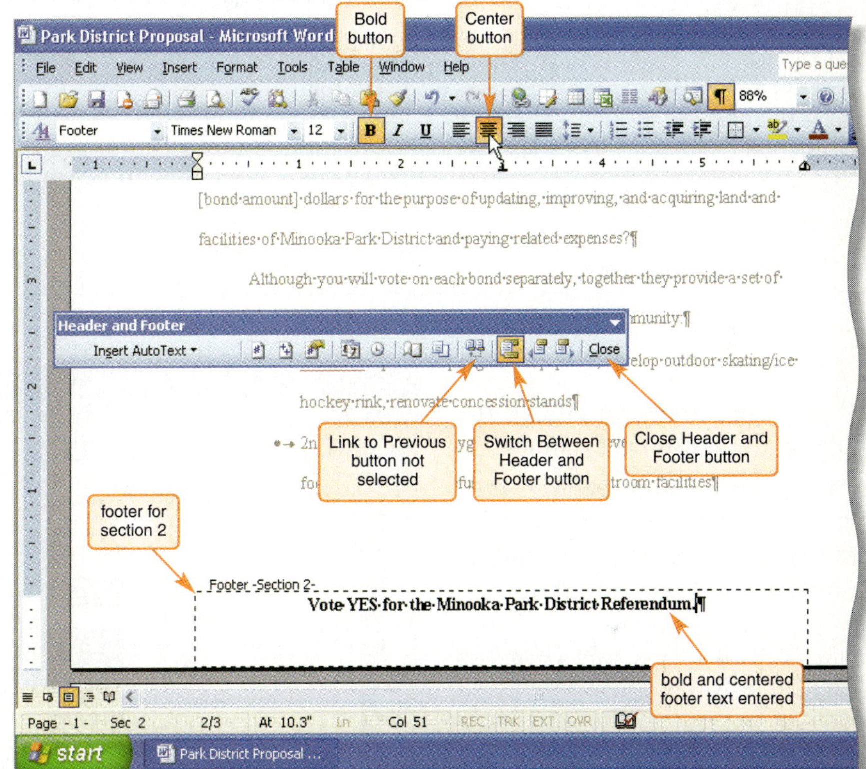

FIGURE 4-39

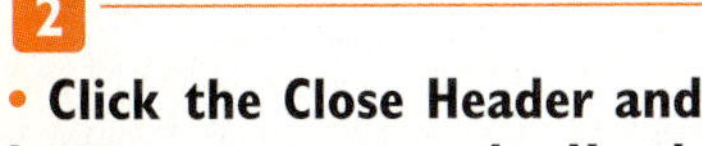

2

- **Click the Close Header and Footer button to remove the Header and Footer toolbar from the screen.**

Other Ways

1. With Header and Footer toolbar displaying, in Voice Command mode, say "Switch Between Header and Footer"

Notice you used the same technique as for the header. That is, the Link to Previous button on the Header and Footer toolbar is not selected. When this button is not selected, Word does not copy the typed footer into the previous section. If you wanted the footer typed in section 2 also to be in section 1, you would leave the Link to Previous button selected on the Header and Footer toolbar.

Formatting and Charting a Table

The sales proposal draft contains a Word table (shown in Figure 4-29a on page WD 242) that was created using the Insert Table button on the Standard toolbar. This table contains four rows and five columns. The first row identifies the market value of homes; the remaining rows show the estimated annual tax for each bond. The first column identifies the bond, and the remaining columns show the taxes for each home market value. The following pages explain how to modify the table, sum the contents of the table, format the table, chart the table's contents, modify the chart, and then format the chart.

Adding and Deleting Table Rows and Columns

The table needs several modifications. The blank column between the first and third columns should be deleted. A title should be added in a row at the top of the table, and a row that shows total dollar amounts needs to be added to the bottom of the table.

The following steps show how to delete a column from the middle of the table.

To Delete a Column

1

- **If necessary, scroll to display the table in the document window.**
- **Position the mouse pointer at the top of the column to be deleted and click when it changes to a downward pointing arrow.**

Word selects the entire column below the mouse pointer (Figure 4-40).

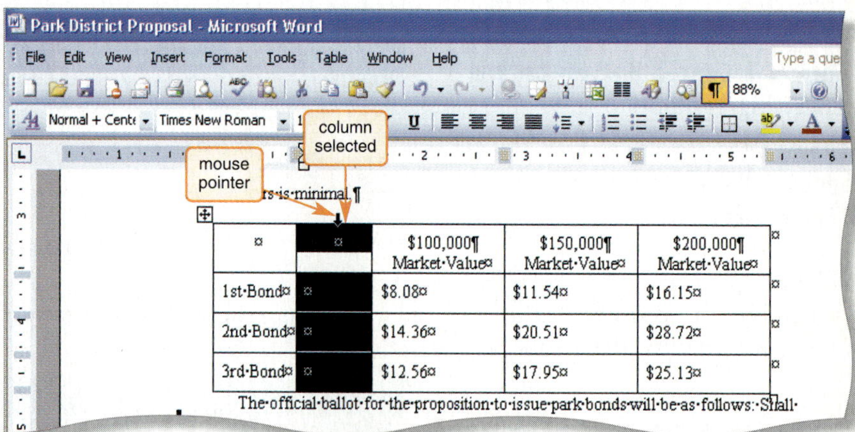

FIGURE 4-40

2

- **Right-click the selected column.**

Word displays a shortcut menu related to tables with a selected column(s) (Figure 4-41).

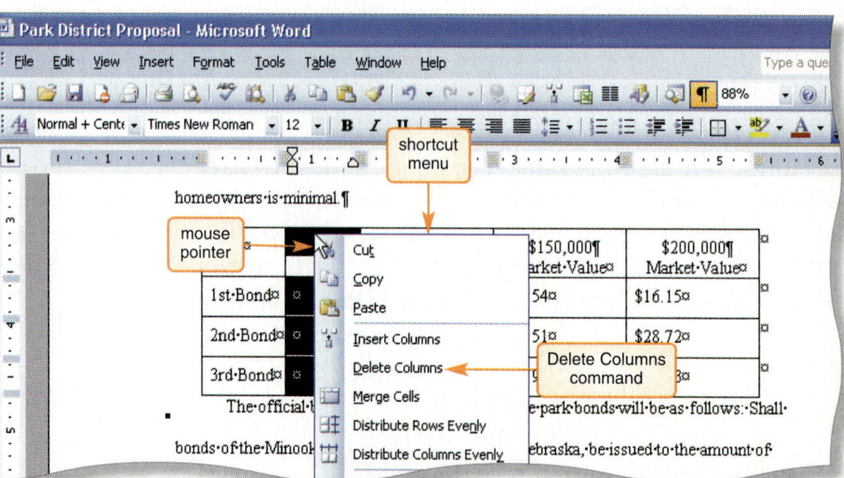

FIGURE 4-41

3

• **Click Delete Columns on the shortcut menu.**

Word deletes the selected column (Figure 4-42).

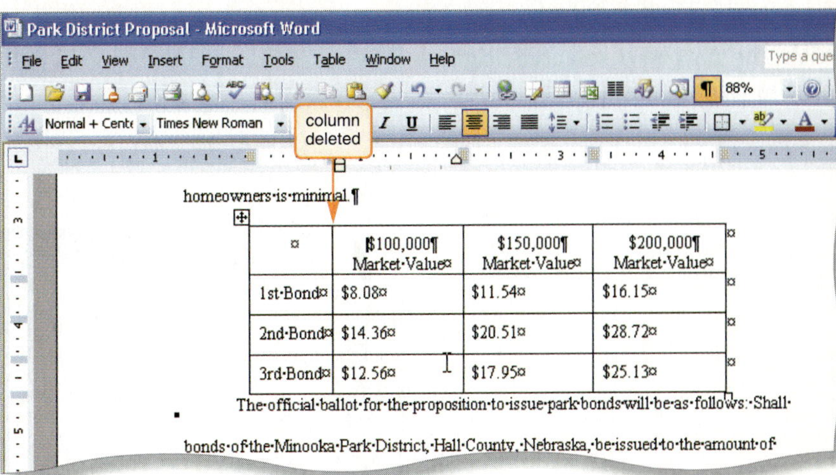

FIGURE 4-42

Other Ways

1. With the column selected, on Table menu point to Delete, click Columns
2. With the column selected, in Voice Command mode, say "Table, Delete, Columns"

If you want to **delete a row**, instead of a column, from a table, you would select the row(s) to delete and then click Delete Rows on the shortcut menu, or click Table on the menu bar, click Delete, and then click Rows.

The top row of the table is to contain the table title, which should be centered above the columns of the table. When you add a row, it will have one cell for each column, in this case, four cells. The title of the table, however, should be in a single cell that spans across all rows. Thus, the first step is to add a row to the top of the table and then merge its cells, as shown in the following steps.

To Add a Row and Merge Cells

1

• **Position the mouse pointer to the left of the first row of the table (the column headings) until it changes to a right-pointing arrow and then click to select the entire row.**

• **Right-click inside the selected row.**

Word displays a shortcut menu related to a table with a selected row(s) (Figure 4-43).

2

• **Click Insert Rows on the shortcut menu.**

Word adds a row above the selected row and selects the newly added row (shown in Figure 4-44 on the next page).

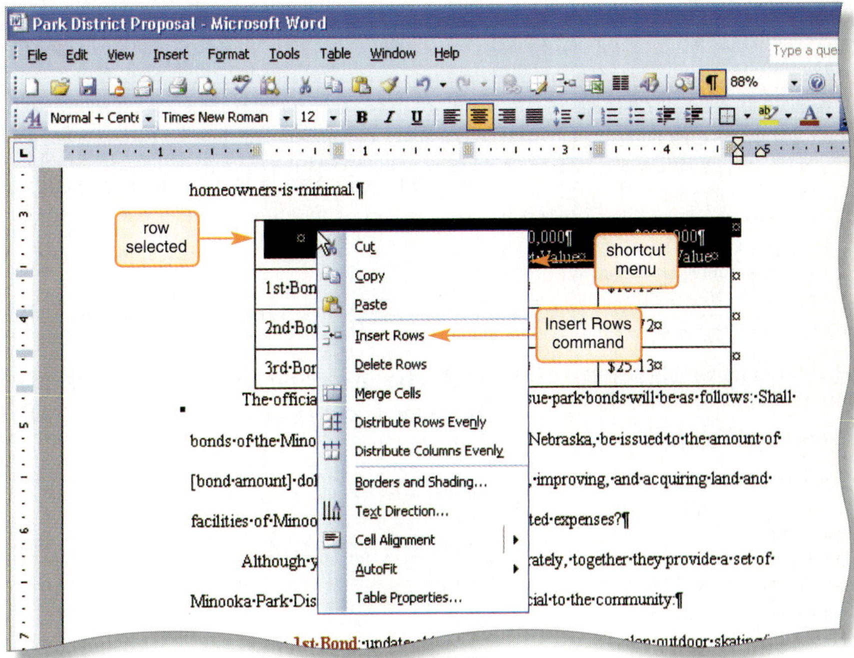

FIGURE 4-43

3

• **With the new row selected, right-click the added row (Figure 4-44).**

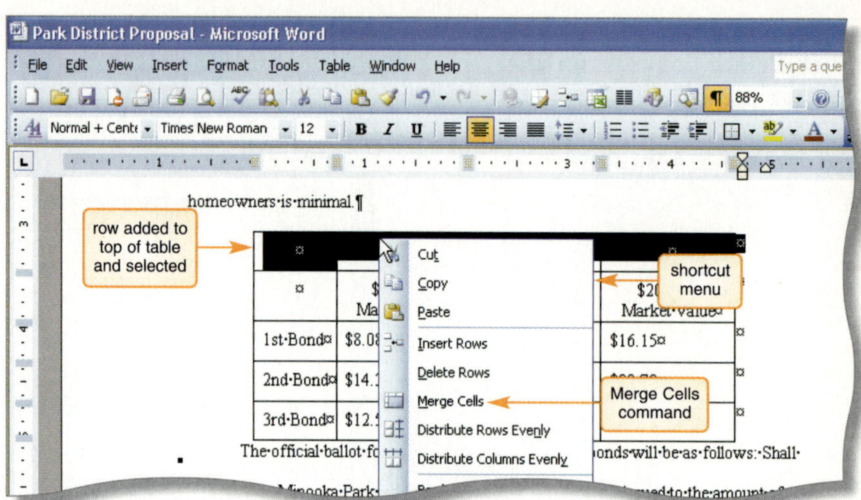

FIGURE 4-44

4

• **Click Merge Cells on the shortcut menu.**

• **Click inside the top row to remove the highlight.**

Word merges the four selected cells into a single cell (Figure 4-45). Text entered into this cell automatically will be centered.

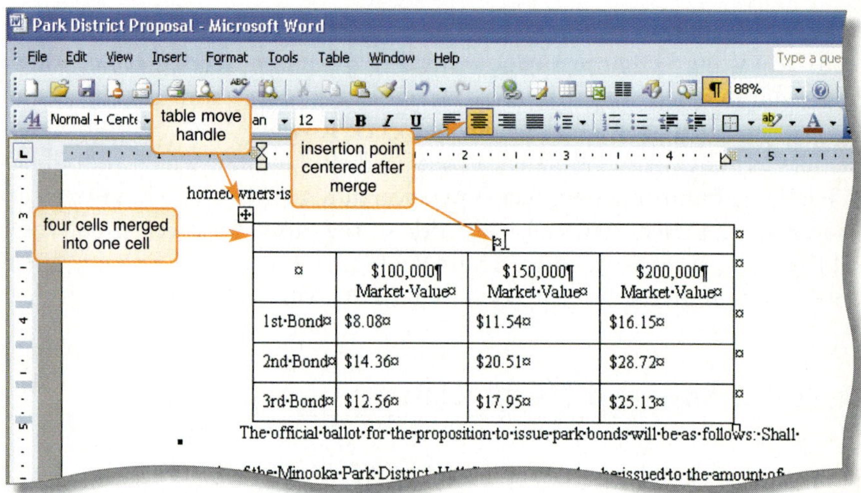

FIGURE 4-45

Other Ways

1. Click Merge Cells button on Tables and Borders toolbar
2. On Table menu click Merge Cells
3. In Voice Command mode, say "Table, Merge Cells"

More About

Moving Tables

To move a table to a new location, point to the upper-left corner of the table until the table move handle appears (a small box containing a four-headed arrow). Point to the table move handle and then drag it to move the entire table to a new location.

The next task is to add text into the merged cell, as described in the following steps.

To Enter and Format Text in a Table Cell

1 **With the insertion point in the cell at the top of the table, press the CAPS LOCK key. Type** ESTIMATED ANNUAL TAX IMPACT **and then press the CAPS LOCK key.**

2 **Press CTRL+5.**

Pressing ***CTRL+5*** *instructs Word to change the line spacing of the cell to 1.5 lines (shown in Figure 4-46).*

Instead of merging multiple cells into a single cell, sometimes you want to split a cell into more cells. To split cells, you would perform the following steps.

To Split Cells

1. Select the cell to split.
2. Right-click the selected cell and then click Split Cells on the shortcut menu; or click the Split Cells button on the Tables and Borders toolbar; or click Table on the menu bar and then click Split Cells.
3. When Word displays the Split Cells dialog box, enter the number of rows and columns into which you want the cell split.
4. Click the OK button.

The next step is to add a row to the bottom of the table that shows totals of the dollar amounts in the second, third, and fourth columns. As discussed in Project 3, to add a row to the end of a table, position the insertion point in the bottom-right corner cell and then press the TAB key, as described below.

To Add a Row to the End of a Table

1 **Position the insertion point at the end of the lower-right corner cell of the table (after the $25.13).**

2 **Press the TAB key to create a new row at the bottom of the table.**

3 **Type `Total` and then press the TAB key.**

Word adds a row to the bottom of the table (Figure 4-46). The first cell in the new row contains the word, Total. The remaining cells in the new row are empty.

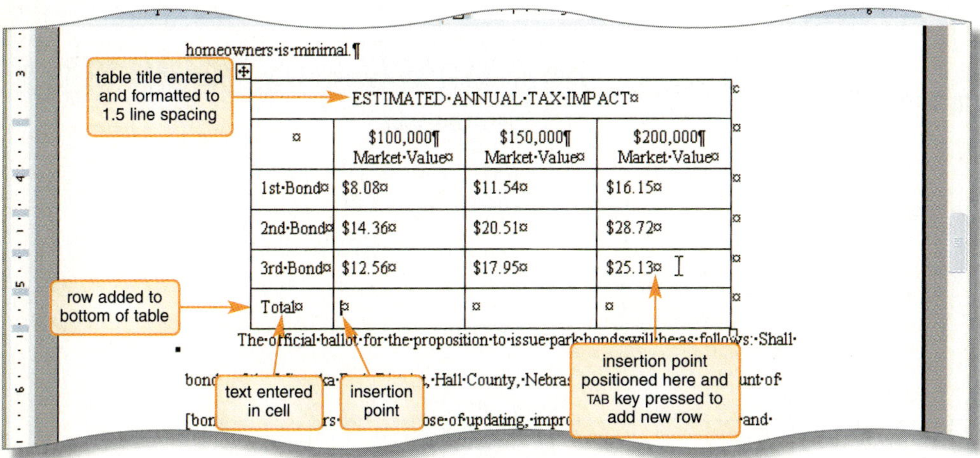

FIGURE 4-46

If you wanted to **add a column** in the middle of a table, you would select the column to the right of where the new column is to be inserted and then click the Insert Columns button on the Standard toolbar (the same button you click to insert a table); or click Insert Columns on the shortcut menu; or click Table on the menu bar, point to Insert, and then click Columns to the Left. To add a column to the right of a table, select the end-of-row marks at the right edge of the table, then click the Insert Columns button; or click Insert Columns on the shortcut menu; or click Table on the menu bar, point to Insert, and then click Columns to the Right.

More About

Table Columns

When the insertion point is in a table, the ruler displays column markers that indicate the beginning and ending of columns. A column boundary is the vertical gridline immediately to the right of a column in the table itself. To resize a column width, drag the column boundary in the table or the column marker on the ruler. Holding down the ALT key while dragging markers displays column width measurements.

Summing Table Contents

To quickly total a column or a row, Word provides an **AutoSum button** on the Tables and Borders toolbar. The following steps show how to sum columns in the table.

To Sum Columns in a Table

1

- **If the Tables and Borders toolbar is not displayed in the Word window, click the Tables and Borders button on the Standard toolbar.**
- **If the Draw Table button on the Tables and Borders toolbar is selected, click it to deselect it.**
- **With the insertion point in the cell to contain the sum (shown in Figure 4-46 on the previous page), click the AutoSum button on the Tables and Borders toolbar.**

Word places the sum of the numbers in the column in the current cell.

2

- **Press the TAB key. Click the AutoSum button on the Tables and Borders toolbar.**
- **Press the TAB key. Click the AutoSum button on the Tables and Borders toolbar.**

Word places a sum in each of the remaining columns (Figure 4-47).

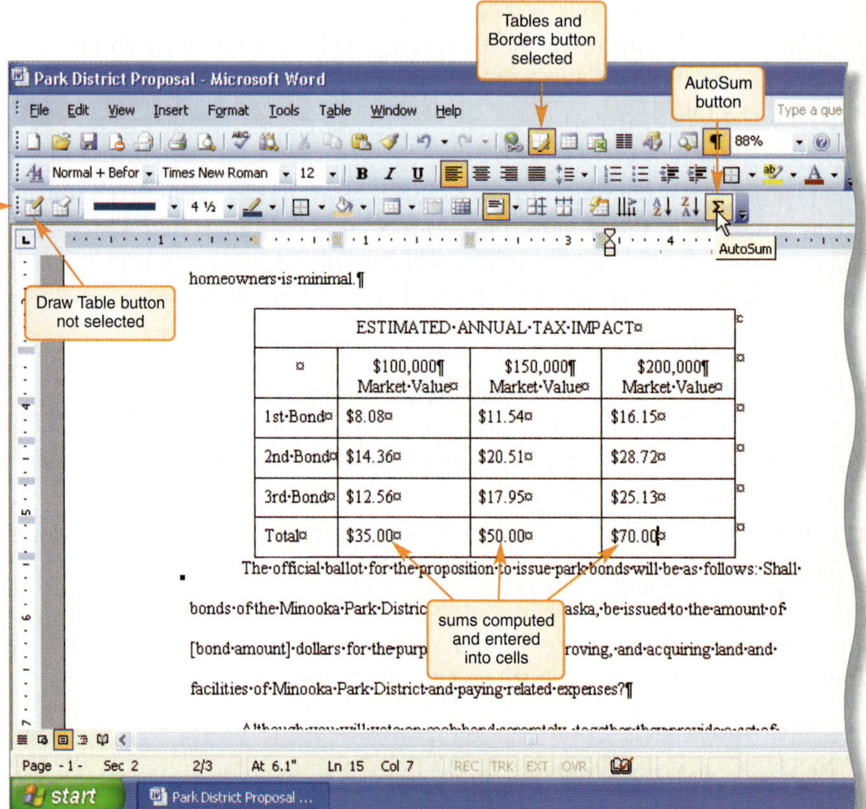

FIGURE 4-47

Other Ways

1. On Table menu click Formula, if necessary type =SUM(ABOVE) in Formula text box, click OK button
2. With Tables and Borders toolbar displayed, in Voice Command mode, say "AutoSum"

If you wanted to sum the contents of a row instead of a column, you would place the insertion point in the empty cell at the right of the row and then click the AutoSum button. Depending on the location of the insertion point, Word determines if it should sum a row or a column. If Word uses the wrong formula, you can change it. The formula for summing a column is =SUM(ABOVE), and the formula for summing a row is =SUM(LEFT). To change an existing formula, click Table on the menu bar and then click Formula. Make the change in the Formula dialog box and then click the OK button. You also use the Formula dialog box if you want to enter a formula into a cell other than summing a row or column.

Formatting a Table

The table in the document looks dull. Although you can format each row, column, and cell of a table individually, Word provides a Table AutoFormat feature that contains predefined styles for tables. The following steps show how to format the entire table using Table AutoFormat.

> *More About*
>
> **Table Borders**
>
> Instead of using AutoFormat, you can use buttons and boxes on the Tables and Borders toolbar to apply your own borders to a table.

To AutoFormat a Table

1

- **With the insertion point in the table, click the Table AutoFormat button on the Tables and Borders toolbar.**
- **When Word displays the Table AutoFormat dialog box, if necessary, scroll through the Table styles list and then click Table Elegant. Be sure all check boxes in the Apply special formats to area at the bottom of the dialog box contain check marks.**

Word displays a preview of the table style in the Table AutoFormat dialog box (Figure 4-48).

FIGURE 4-48

2

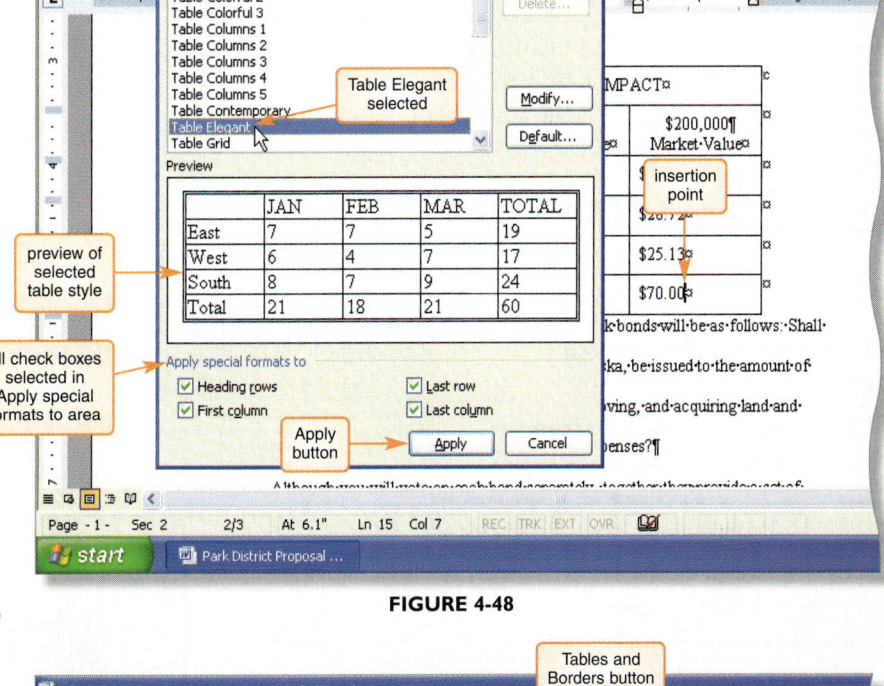

- **Click the Apply button in the dialog box.**
- **Click the Tables and Borders button on the Standard toolbar to remove the Tables and Borders toolbar from the screen.**

Word formats the table according to the Table Elegant style (Figure 4-49).

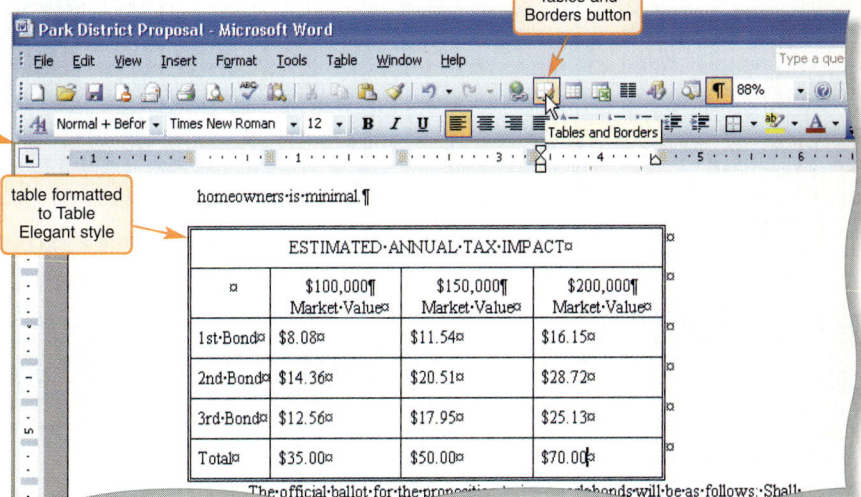

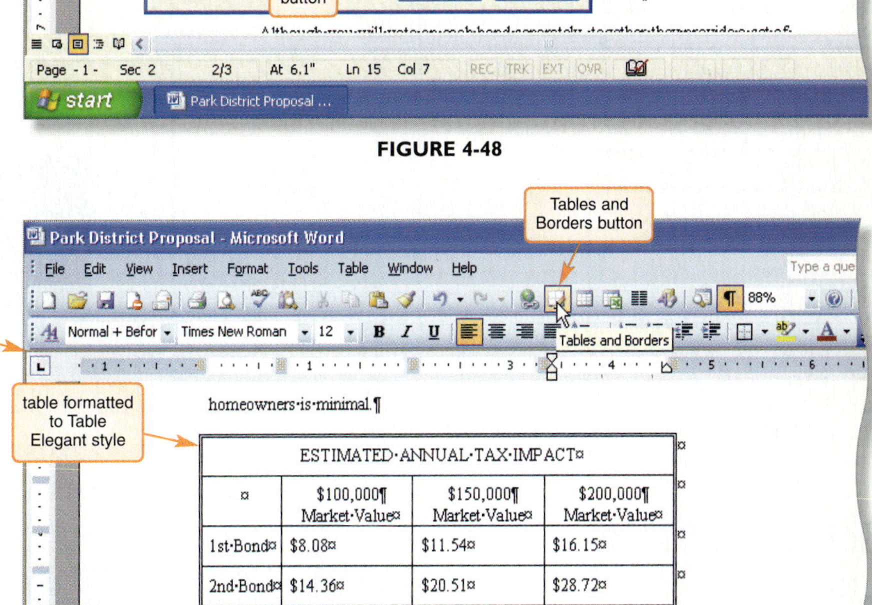

¤	$100,000¶ Market·Value¤	$150,000¶ Market·Value¤	$200,000¶ Market·Value¤
1st·Bond¤	$8.08¤	$11.54¤	$16.15¤
2nd·Bond¤	$14.36¤	$20.51¤	$28.72¤
3rd·Bond¤	$12.56¤	$17.95¤	$25.13¤
Total¤	$35.00¤	$50.00¤	$70.00¤

FIGURE 4-49

> *Other Ways*
>
> 1. In Styles and Formatting task pane, click Show box arrow and then click All styles, click desired table style in Pick formatting to apply area
> 2. On Table menu click Table AutoFormat, click desired table style, click Apply button

More About

Copying Tables

If you have two similar tables in a document, you can copy the first table and then modify the second one. To copy a table, point to the table move handle, press and hold the CTRL key, drag a copy of the table to a new location, and then release the CTRL key.

The next step is to center the table horizontally between the page margins, as described below.

To Center a Table

1. **Position the mouse pointer in the table to display the table move handle in the upper-left corner of the table. Position the mouse pointer on the table move handle and then click to select the table.**
2. **With the entire table selected, click the Center button on the Formatting toolbar.**
3. **Click anywhere to remove the selection in the table.**

Word centers the selected table (shown in Figure 4-50).

As with paragraphs, you can left-align, center, or right-align data in table cells. By default, the data you enter into the cells is left-aligned. You can change the alignment just as you would for a paragraph. If you want to change the alignment of multiple cells, first select the cells. The following step right-aligns the contents of all the cells that contain dollar amounts.

To Right-Align Cell Contents

1

- **Drag through the cells to right-align.**
- **Click the Align Right button on the Formatting toolbar.**

Word right-aligns the data in the selected cells (Figure 4-50).

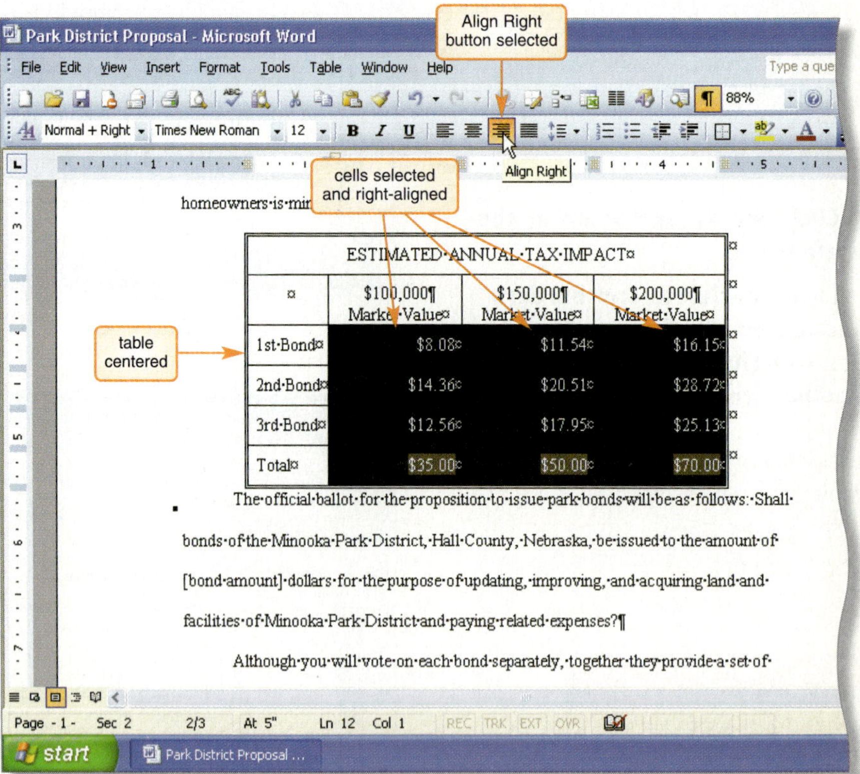
Park District Proposal - Microsoft Word
Align Right button selected
Align Right
cells selected and right-aligned
table centered
ESTIMATED ANNUAL TAX IMPACT
$100,000 Market Value
$150,000 Market Value
$200,000 Market Value
1st Bond
$8.08
$11.54
$16.15
2nd Bond
$14.36
$20.51
$28.72
3rd Bond
$12.56
$17.95
$25.13
Total
$35.00
$50.00
$70.00
The official ballot for the proposition to issue park bonds will be as follows: Shall bonds of the Minooka Park District, Hall County, Nebraska, be issued to the amount of [bond amount] dollars for the purpose of updating, improving, and acquiring land and facilities of Minooka Park District and paying related expenses?
Although you will vote on each bond separately, together they provide a set of

FIGURE 4-50

Other Ways

1. On Format menu click Paragraph, click Indents and Spacing tab, click Alignment box arrow, click Right, click OK button
2. Press CTRL+R
3. In Voice Command mode, say "Align Right"

More About

Deleting Table Contents

To delete the contents of a table and leave an empty table on the screen, select the table contents and then press the DELETE key.

Formatting Nonadjacent Characters

The next step is to change the ordinals in the first column of the table to be superscripts. That is, the 1st should display as 1st, the 2nd as 2nd, and so on. To do this, select the characters to be superscripted and then use the Font dialog box to apply this character effect to the selected text.

You want to select the st in 1st, the nd in 2nd, and the rd in 3rd. In Word, you can select several segments of text that are not next to each other, called **nonadjacent text** or **noncontiguous text**, by selecting the first segment of text and then pressing and holding down the CTRL key while selecting each additional segment of text.

The following steps show how to select nonadjacent text.

To Select Nonadjacent Text

1

- **Drag through the st in 1st.**

Word selects the st (Figure 4-51).

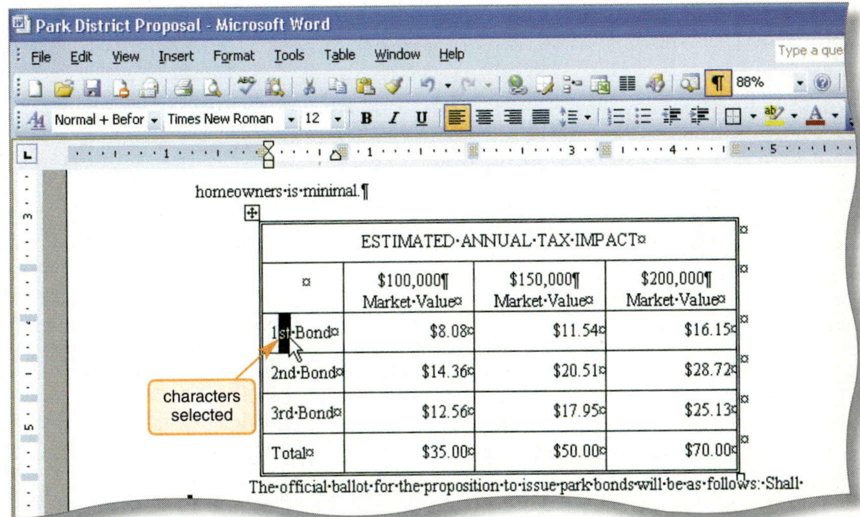

FIGURE 4-51

2

- **While holding down the CTRL key, drag through the nd in 2nd.**
- **While holding down the CTRL key, drag through the rd in 3rd. Release the CTRL key.**

Word selects the nonadjacent text (Figure 4-52).

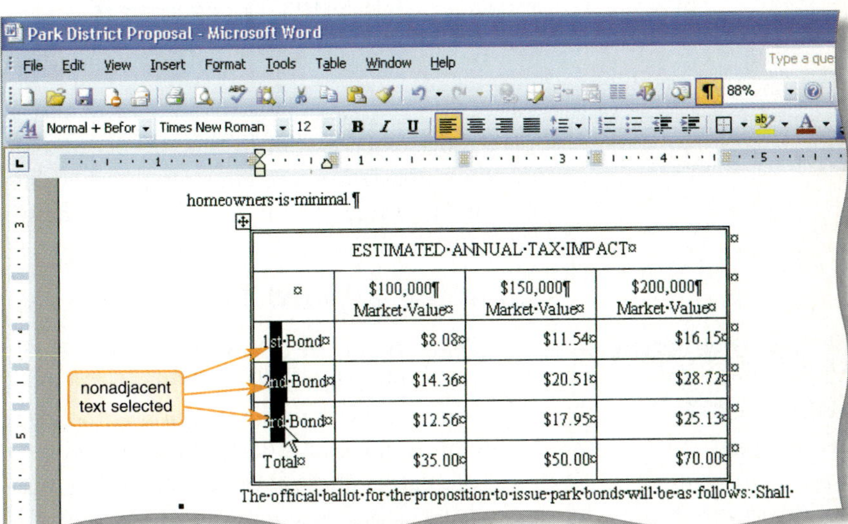

FIGURE 4-52

The next step is to apply the superscript character effect to the selected text, as described below.

To Superscript Selected Characters

1. **With the text selected, click Format on the menu bar and then click Font. When Word displays the Font dialog box, if necessary, click the Font tab.**
2. **Click Superscript in the Effects area to place a check mark in the check box (Figure 4-53).**
3. **Click the OK button. Click anywhere to remove the selections.**

Word superscripts the selected text (shown in Figure 4-54).

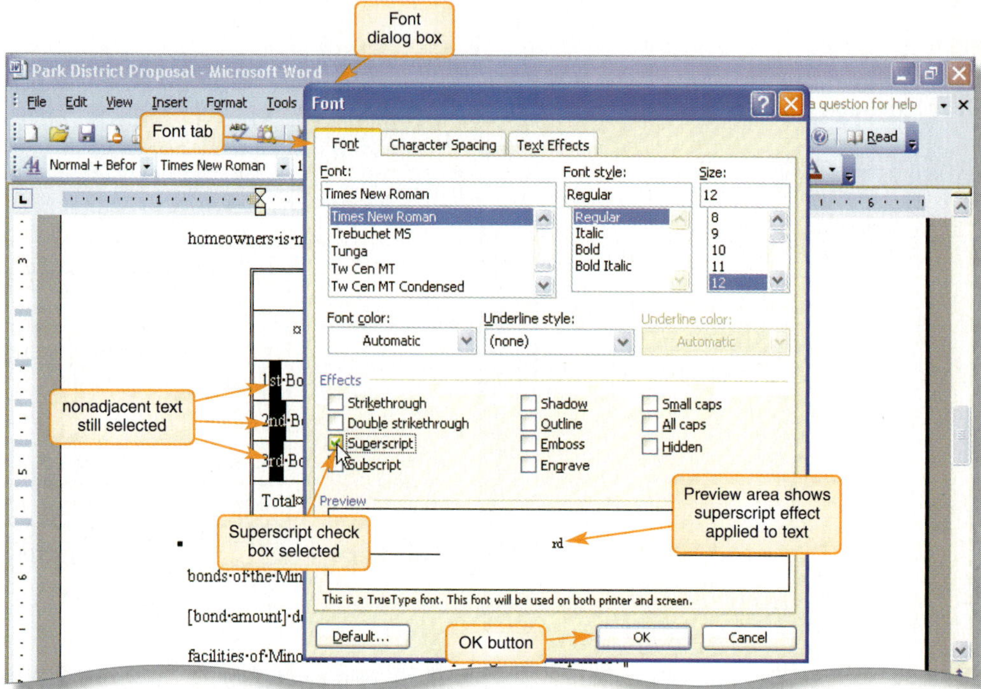

FIGURE 4-53

As discussed earlier in this project and shown in Figure 4-53, the Font sheet in the Font dialog box contains many other character effects you can add to text in a document. Table 4-1 on page WD 229 identified all of the available character effects.

Charting a Word Table

When you create a Word table, you easily can chart its data using an embedded charting application called **Microsoft Graph**. Graph has its own menus and commands because it is an application embedded in the Word program. Using Graph commands, you can modify the appearance of the chart once you create it.

To create a chart from a Word table, the first row and left column of the selected cells in the table must contain text labels, and the other cells in the selected cells must contain numbers. The table in the Park District Proposal meets these criteria.

More About

Word 2003 Features

For more information about the features and capabilities of Word 2003, visit the Word 2003 More About Web page (scsite.com/wd2003/more) and then click Features and Capabilities of Word 2003.

To chart a Word table, first select the rows and columns in the table to be charted. In this project, you do not want to chart the first row in the table that contains the title or the last row in the table that contains the totals. Thus, you will select the middle four rows in the table and then instruct Word to chart the selected cells, as shown in the following steps.

To Chart a Table

1

- **Point to the left of (outside) the second row in the table (the column headings) until the mouse pointer changes to a right-pointing arrow and then drag downward until the middle four rows in the table are selected.**

The rows to be charted are selected (Figure 4-54). Notice the first and last rows of the table are not selected.

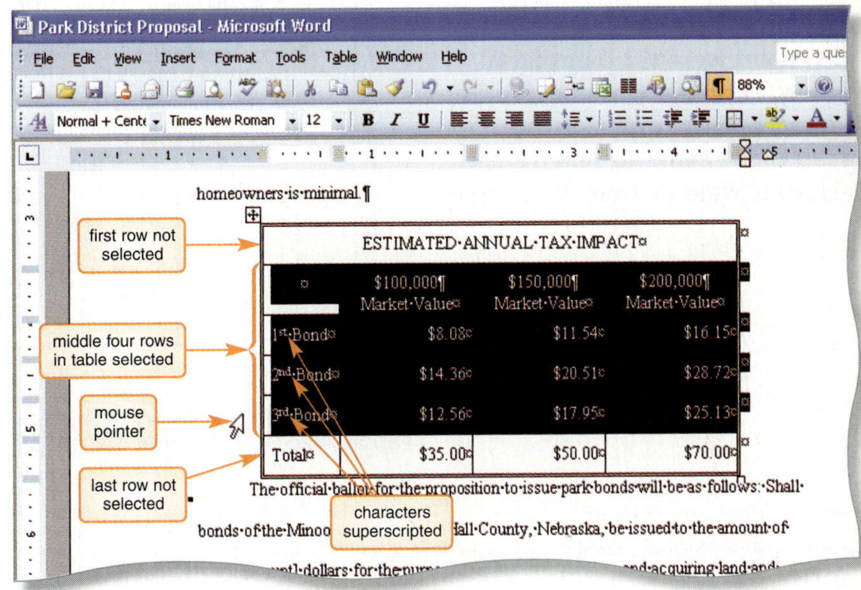

FIGURE 4-54

2

- **Click Insert on the menu bar and then point to Picture (Figure 4-55).**

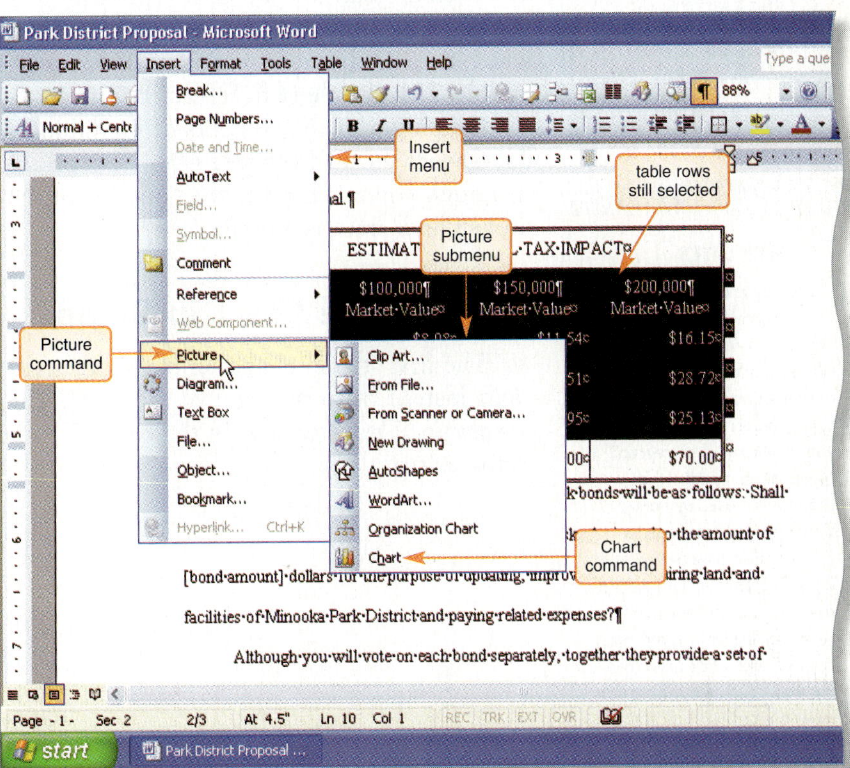

FIGURE 4-55

3

• **Click Chart on the Picture submenu.**

Word starts the Microsoft Graph program (Figure 4-56). Graph creates a chart of the selected rows in the table.

4

• **If Graph displays a Datasheet window, click the Close button in the upper-right corner of the Datasheet window to remove the Datasheet window from the screen.**

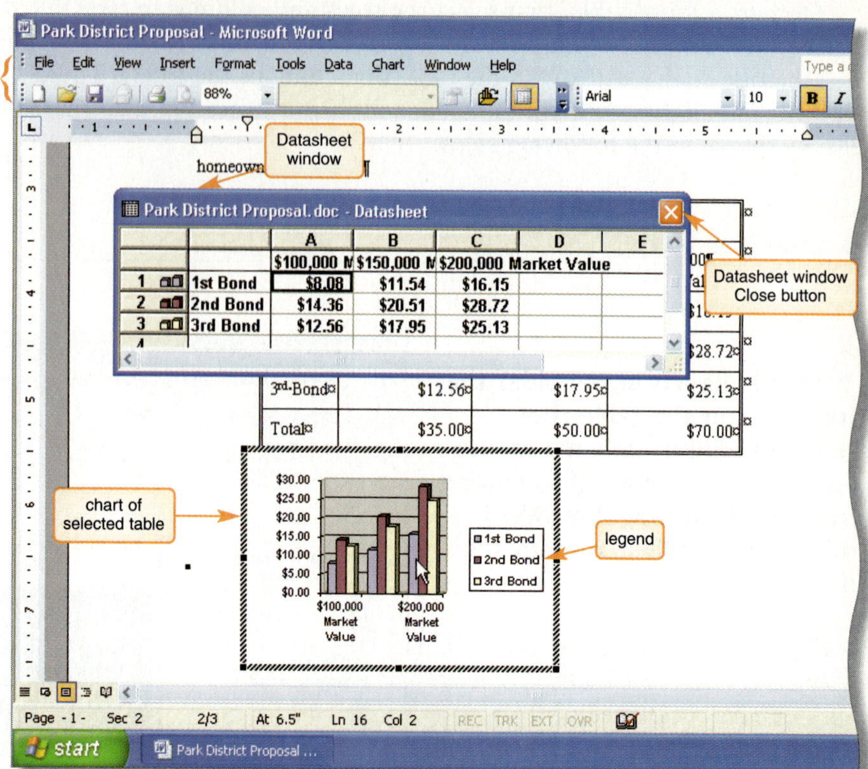

FIGURE 4-56

Other Ways

1. On Insert menu click Object, click Create New tab, click Microsoft Graph Chart in Object type list, click OK button
2. In Voice Command mode, say "Insert, Picture, Chart"

More About

Datasheets

A datasheet can contain up to 4,000 rows and 4,000 columns. When you modify values in a Word table, the datasheet values do not change automatically. Thus, you either need to regraph the table or update the datasheet values manually. Working in a datasheet is quite similar to working in an Excel worksheet. To insert a row or column, right-click a row heading or column heading and then click Insert on the shortcut menu. To enter data in a cell, click in the cell and then enter the data or text.

The menus on the menu bar and buttons on the toolbars change to Graph menus and toolbars because the Graph program is running inside the Word program. While you are working in Graph, you may inadvertently click somewhere outside the chart, which exits Graph and returns to Word menus and toolbars. If this occurs, simply double-click the chart to return to Graph.

Graph places the contents of the table into a **Datasheet window**, also called a **datasheet** (shown in Figure 4-56). Graph then charts the contents of the datasheet. Although you can modify the contents of the datasheet, it is not necessary in this project and, thus, is closed.

Changing the Chart in Graph

The first step in changing the chart is to move the legend so it displays above the chart instead of to the right of the chart. The **legend** is a box that identifies the colors assigned to categories in the chart. The next steps show how to move the legend in the chart.

To Move Legend Placement in a Chart

1

- **If necessary, scroll to display the chart in the document window.**
- **Right-click the legend in the chart.**

Word displays a shortcut menu related to legends (Figure 4-57).

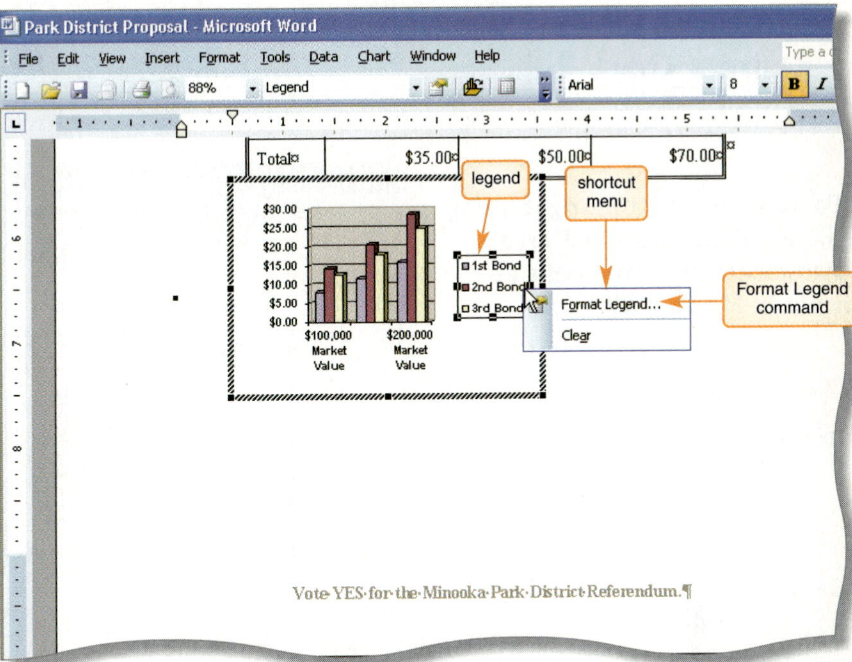

FIGURE 4-57

2

- **Click Format Legend on the shortcut menu.**
- **When Word displays the Format Legend dialog box, if necessary, click the Placement tab.**
- **Click Top in the Placement area.**

Graph displays the Format Legend dialog box (Figure 4-58).

3

- **Click the OK button.**

Graph places the legend above the chart (shown in Figure 4-59 on the next page).

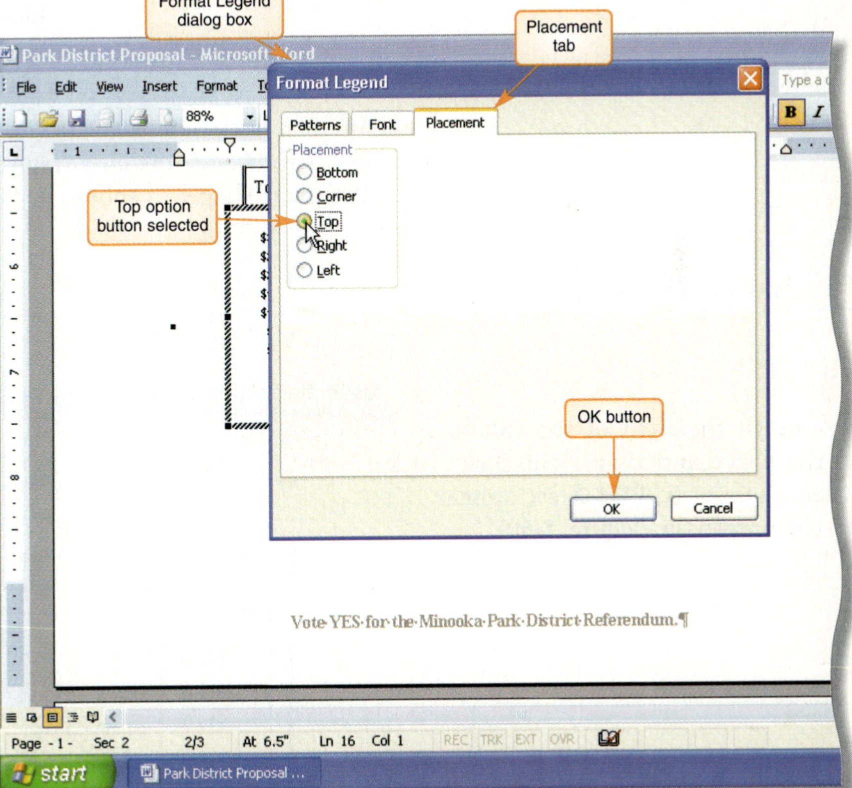

FIGURE 4-58

The next step is to resize the chart so it is bigger. You resize a chart the same way you resize any other graphical object. That is, you drag the chart's sizing handles, as shown in the following steps.

To Resize a Chart

1

• **Point to the bottom-right sizing handle on the chart and drag downward and to the right as shown in Figure 4-59.**

2

• **Release the mouse button.**

Graph resizes the chart (shown in Figure 4-60).

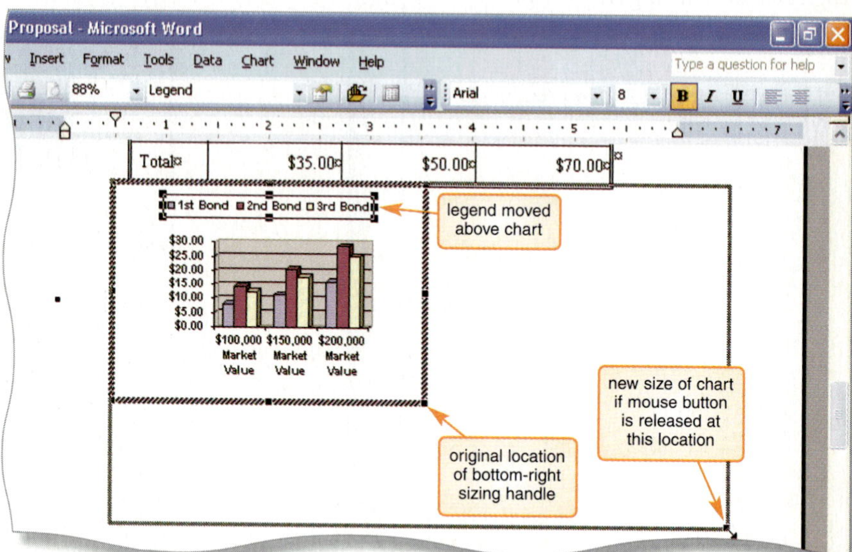

FIGURE 4-59

The next task is to change the chart type so the columns have a cylindrical shape instead of a rectangular shape, as shown in the following steps.

To Change the Chart Type

1

• **Point to the right of the columns in the chart and then right-click when the words, Plot Area, appear as the ScreenTip (Figure 4-60).**

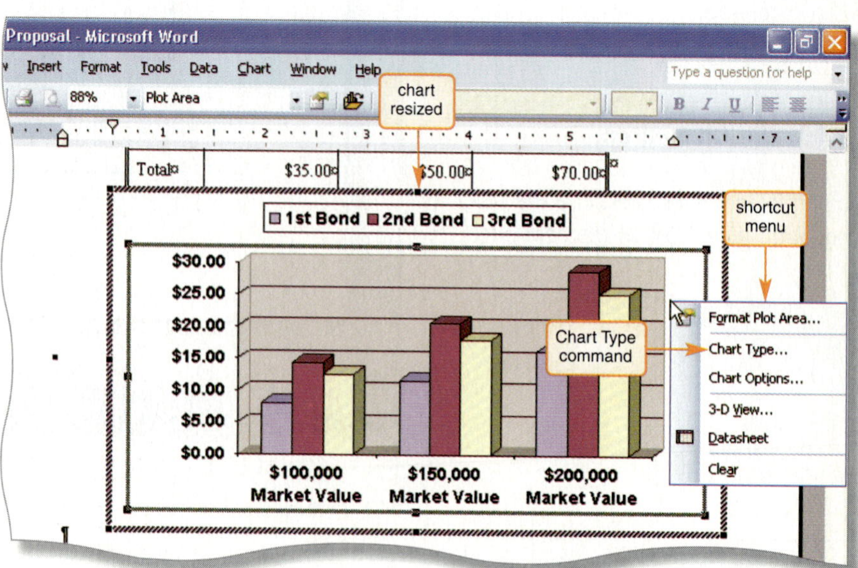

FIGURE 4-60

2

- **Click Chart Type on the shortcut menu.**
- **When Graph displays the Chart Type dialog box, if necessary, click the Standard Types tab.**
- **In the Chart type list, scroll to and then click Cylinder.**
- **In the Chart sub-type area, click the second graphic in the first row (Figure 4-61).**

3

- **Click the OK button.**

Graph changes the shape of the columns to a stacked column with a cylindrical shape (shown in Figure 4-62).

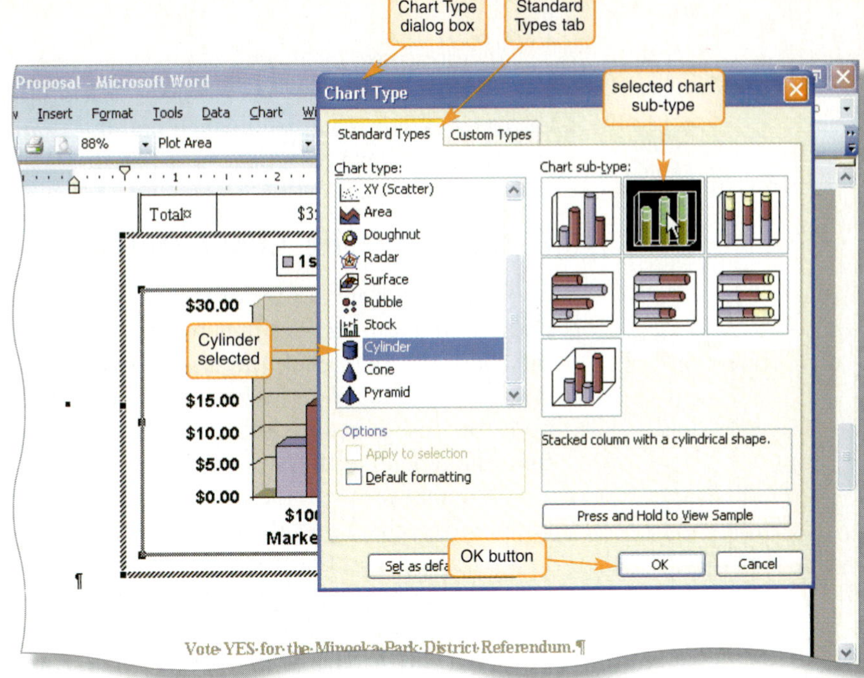

FIGURE 4-61

The modified chart is finished. The next step is to exit Graph and return to Word.

To Exit Graph and Return to Word

1

- **Click somewhere outside the chart. If necessary, scroll to display the chart in the document window.**

Word closes the Graph application (Figure 4-62). Word's menu bar and toolbars are redisplayed below the title bar.

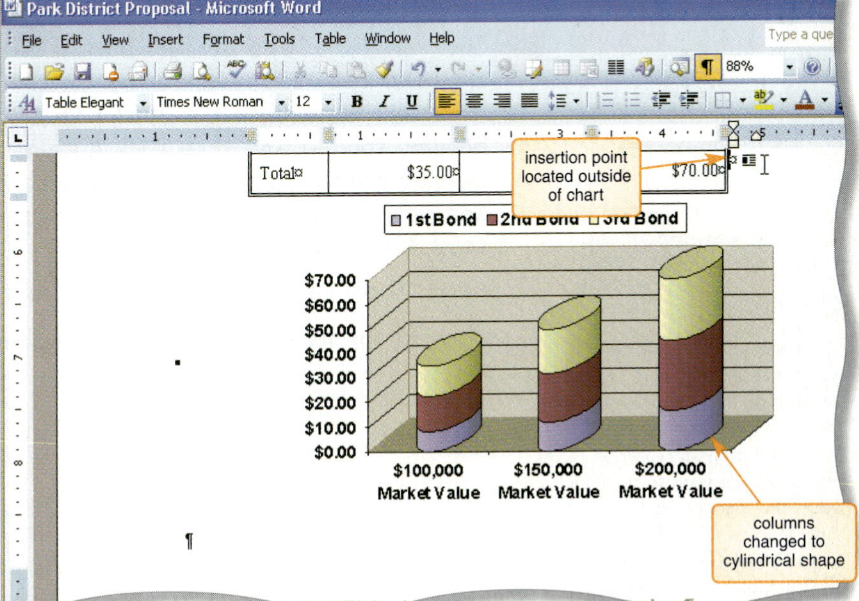

FIGURE 4-62

If you wanted to modify an existing chart in a document, you would double-click the chart to reopen the Microsoft Graph program. Then, you can make changes to the chart. When you are finished making changes to the chart, click anywhere outside the chart to return to Word.

Formatting the Chart Object in Word

The chart now is part of the paragraph below the table. Thus, you can apply any paragraph alignment settings to the chart. The chart should be centered. If you select the chart and then click the Center button on the Formatting toolbar, the chart will not be centered properly. Instead, it will be one-half inch to the right of the center point because first-line indent is set at one-half inch. Thus, you need to remove the first-line indent setting in order to center the paragraph (chart) properly.

You also want to add an outside border to the chart and insert a blank line between the chart and the table. Earlier in this project, you added an outside border to a paragraph on the title page. Its line weight was 4½ point, and its color was dark teal. You do not want this same border definition for the chart. Instead, you want a ½-point border in black.

The chart is part of the paragraph. To insert a blank line above a paragraph, position the insertion point in the paragraph and then press CTRL+0 (the numeral zero).

The following steps describe how to center, outline, and insert a blank line above the chart.

To Format a Chart Object

1. **Click anywhere in the chart to select it, so it displays sizing handles at its corner and middle locations.**
2. **Drag the First Line Indent marker to the 0" mark on the ruler. Click the Center button on the Formatting toolbar.**
3. **Click the Tables and Borders button on the Standard toolbar. If necessary, click the Line Weight box arrow on the Tables and Borders toolbar and then click ½ pt. Click the Border Color button arrow on the Tables and Borders toolbar and then click Automatic on the color palette. Click the Outside Border button on the Tables and Borders toolbar. Click the Tables and Borders button on the Standard toolbar to close the Tables and Borders toolbar.**
4. **Press CTRL+0 (the numeral zero) to insert a blank line above the chart.**
5. **Click to the right of the chart to deselect it.**

Word centers the chart between the left and right margins, places an outside border around the chart, and inserts a blank line above the chart (Figure 4-63).

More About

Charts

If you have an Excel chart or worksheet that you want to be displayed in a Word document, open the Excel workbook and display the chart or worksheet you want to copy. Select the chart or worksheet in Excel. Click the Copy button on Excel's Standard toolbar. Switch to the Word document. Click Edit on the menu bar, click Paste Special, click Paste, click Microsoft Office Excel Worksheet Object in the As list, and then click the OK button.

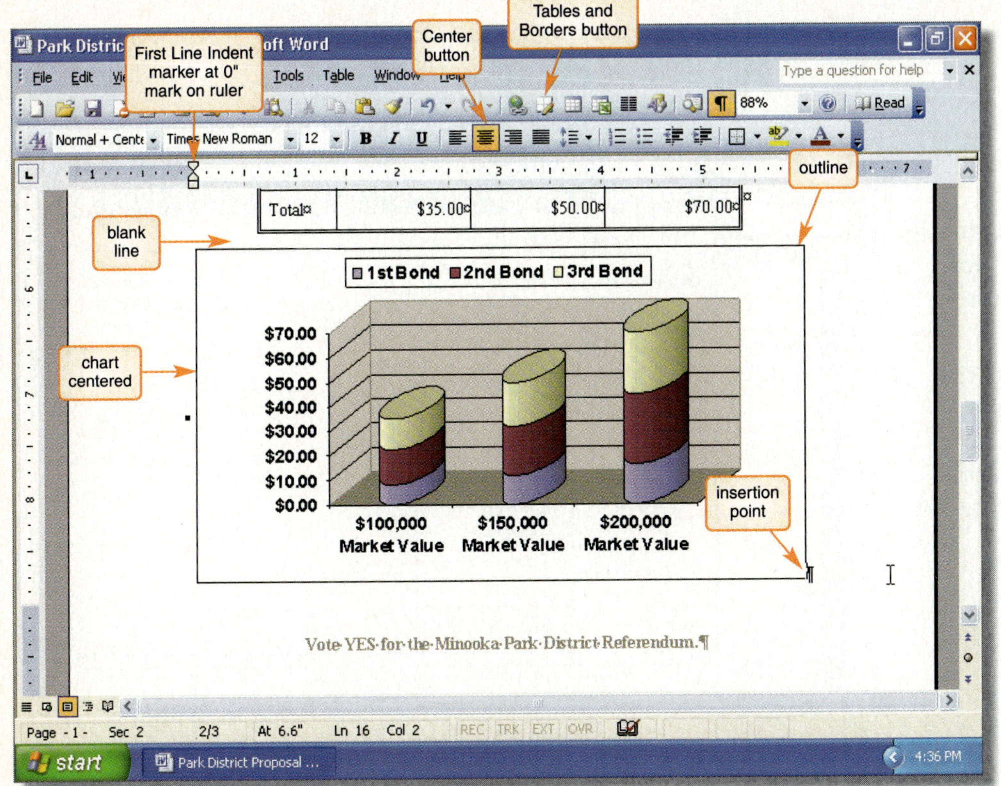

FIGURE 4-63

Working with Formats, Styles, and Bulleted Lists

In this document, the bond names at the beginning of each bulleted item and the bullet character in the bulleted list should be emphasized. The following pages illustrate each of these formatting changes.

Finding a Format

The second page of the body of the proposal has a bulleted list. The text at the beginning of each bulleted paragraph identifies a specific bond. The first bullet, identified with the text, 1st Bond, has been formatted as bold, underlined, and dark red. To find this text in the document, you could scroll through the document until it is displayed on the screen. A more efficient way is to find the bold, underlined, dark red format using the Find and Replace dialog box, as shown in the steps on the next page.

More About

Finding Special Characters

In addition to finding formats, you can use the Find and Replace dialog box to find special characters such as paragraph marks, page breaks, and line breaks. Click the Special button arrow in the Find and Replace dialog box and then click the special character in the list.

To Find a Format

1

- **Press CTRL+F to display the Find and Replace dialog box.**
- **If Word displays a More button in the Find and Replace dialog box, click it so it changes to a Less button.**
- **Click the Format button in the Find and Replace dialog box.**

Word displays the Format button menu above the Format button in the dialog box (Figure 4-64).

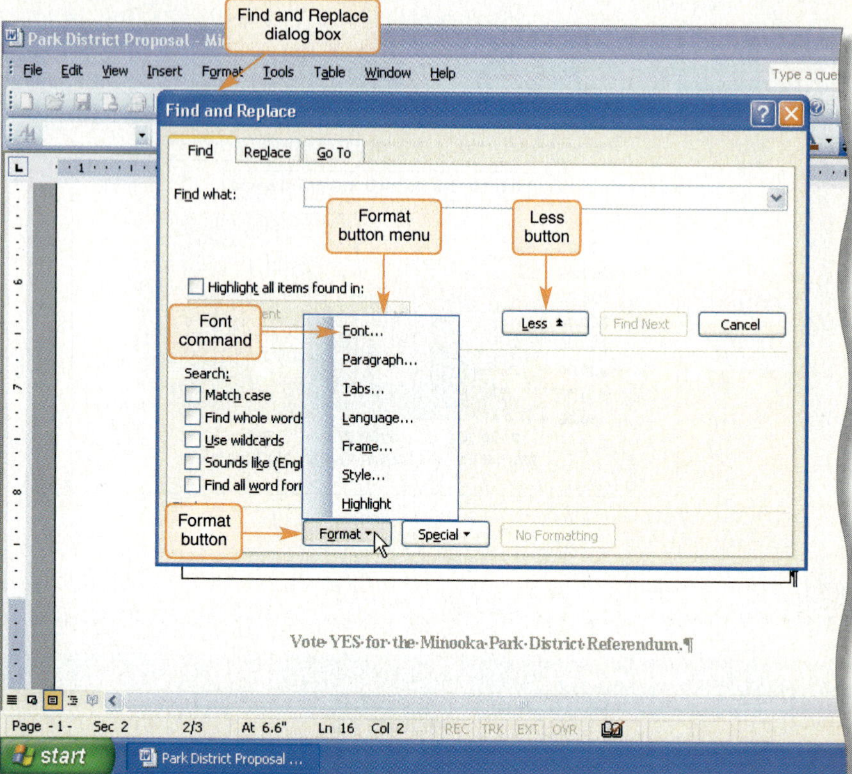

FIGURE 4-64

2

- **Click Font on the Format button menu in the Find and Replace dialog box.**
- **When Word displays the Find Font dialog box, click Bold in the Font style list.**
- **In the Find Font dialog box, click the Font color box arrow and then click Dark Red on the color palette.**
- **In the Find Font dialog box, click the Underline style box arrow and then click the first underline style in the list.**

The Preview area displays a sample of the selected font to find (Figure 4-65).

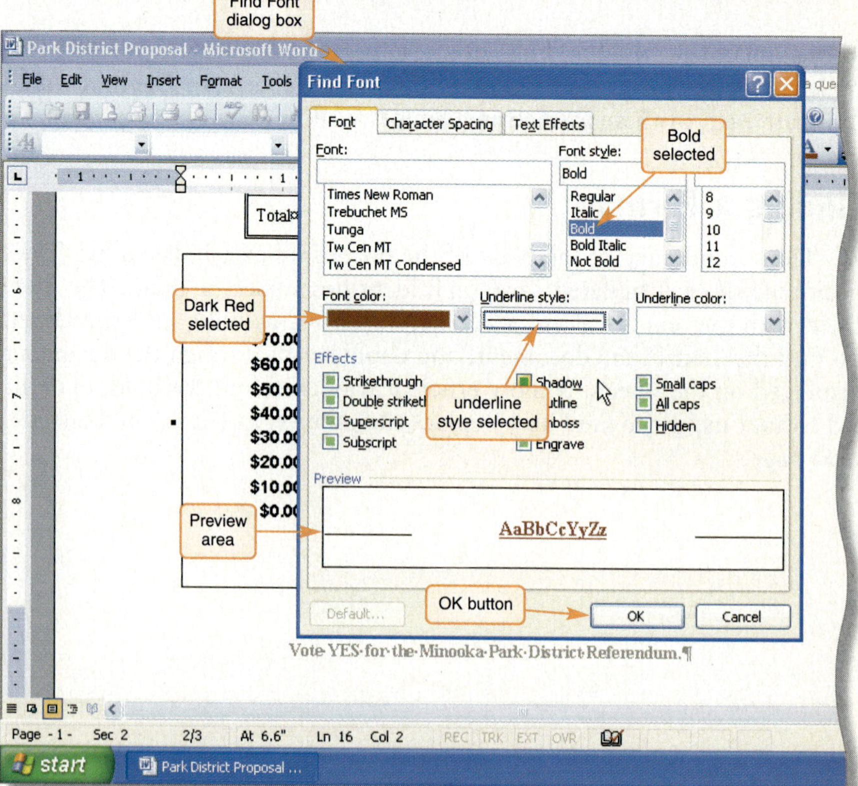

FIGURE 4-65

3

- **Click the OK button in the Find Font dialog box.**
- **When the Find and Replace dialog box is active again, click its Find Next button.**

Word locates and highlights the first occurrence of the specified format in the document (Figure 4-66).

4

- **Click the Cancel button in the Find and Replace dialog box.**

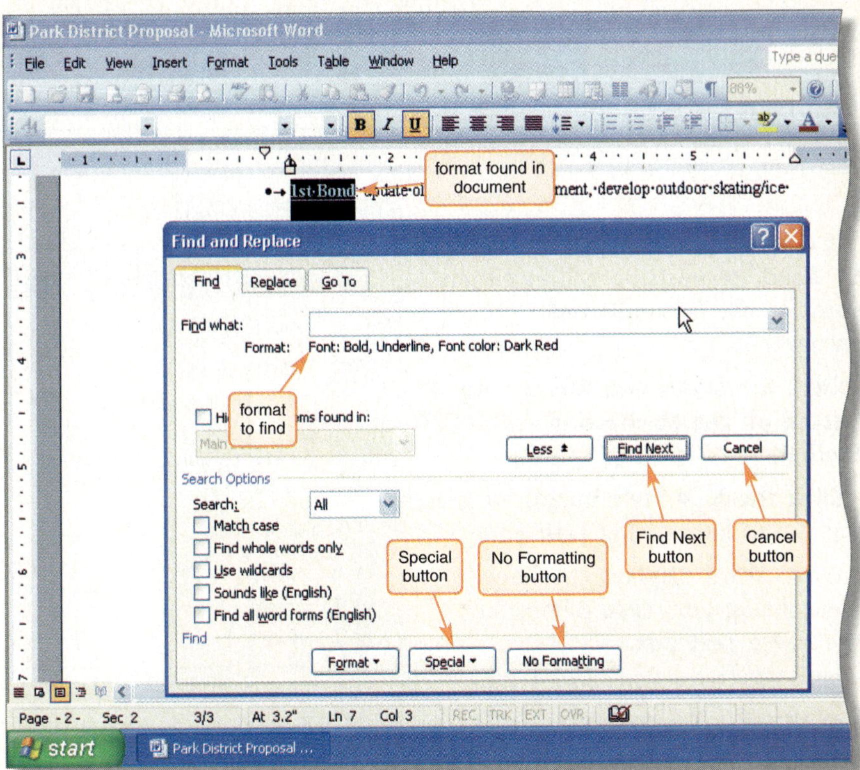

FIGURE 4-66

Other Ways

1. Click Select Browse Object button on vertical scroll bar, click Find on Select Browse Object menu
2. On Edit menu click Find
3. Press CTRL+F
4. In Voice Command mode, say "Edit, Find"

In addition to finding occurrences of text and formatting, you also can use the Find and Replace dialog box to find special characters such as paragraph marks, page breaks, and section breaks. For a complete list of special characters, click the Special button in the Find and Replace dialog box. To remove formatting specified in the Find and Replace dialog box, click the No Formatting button.

Creating and Applying a Character Style

In this project, the bond names at the beginning of the second and third bulleted paragraphs are to have the same character format as the bond name at the beginning of the first bulleted paragraph (bold, underlined, and dark red). As discussed in Project 1, **character formats** affect the way characters appear on the screen and in print. Character formats emphasize certain characters, words, and phrases to improve readability of a document.

You could select each of the bond names and then format them. A more efficient technique is to create a character style. If you decide to modify the formats of the bond names at a later time, you simply change the formats assigned to the style. All characters in the document based on that style will change automatically. Without a style, you would have to select all the bond names again and then change their format. Thus, creating a style saves time in the long run.

Recall that a **style** is a named group of formatting characteristics that you can apply to text. Whenever you create a document, Word formats the text using a particular style. The base style for a new Word document is the Normal style, which for a new installation of Word 2003 mostly likely uses 12-point Times New Roman font for characters. For the bulleted list, you also want the bond names to be bold, underlined, and dark red.

More About

Styles

If you want to create a new style that is based on text that you already have formatted, select the text and then display the Styles and Formatting task pane. When you click the New Style button, the formats of the selected text will display in the New Style dialog box.

The following steps show how to create a character style called Bonds.

To Create a Character Style

1

- **If necessary, click the bond name, 1st Bond, to position the insertion point in the first bulleted paragraph.**
- **Click the Styles and Formatting button on the Formatting toolbar.**
- **Click the New Style button in the Styles and Formatting task pane.**
- **When Word displays the New Style dialog box, type** Bonds **in the Name text box.**
- **Click the Style type box arrow and then click Character.**

The New Style dialog box displays formats assigned to the location of the insertion point (Figure 4-67).

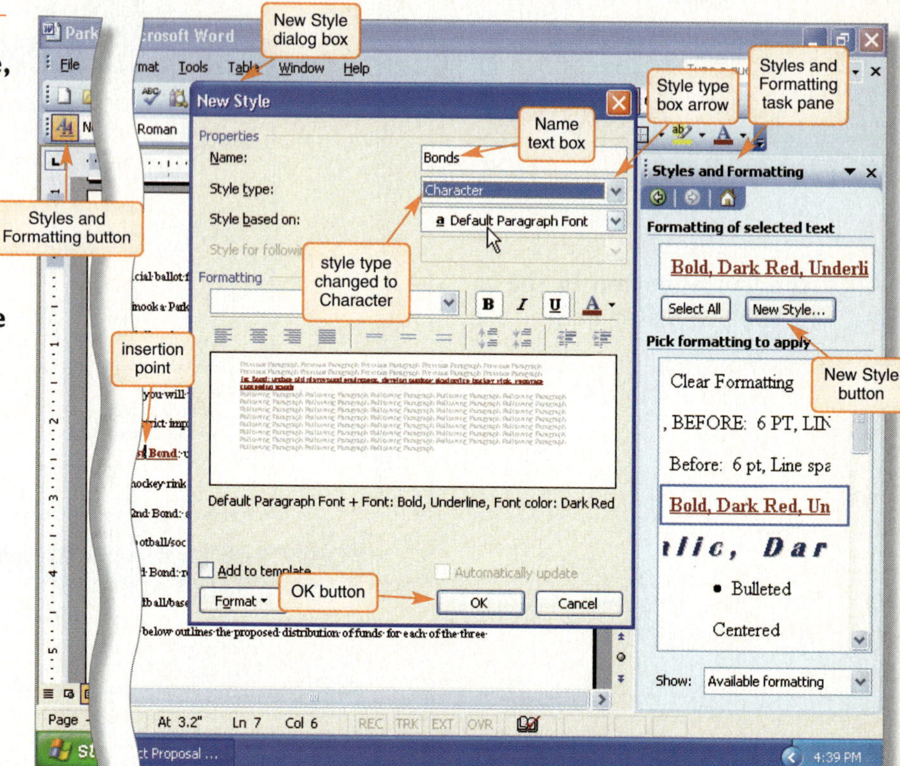

FIGURE 4-67

2

- **Click the OK button.**

Word inserts the new style, Bonds, alphabetically in the Pick formatting to apply area in the Styles and Formatting task pane (Figure 4-68).

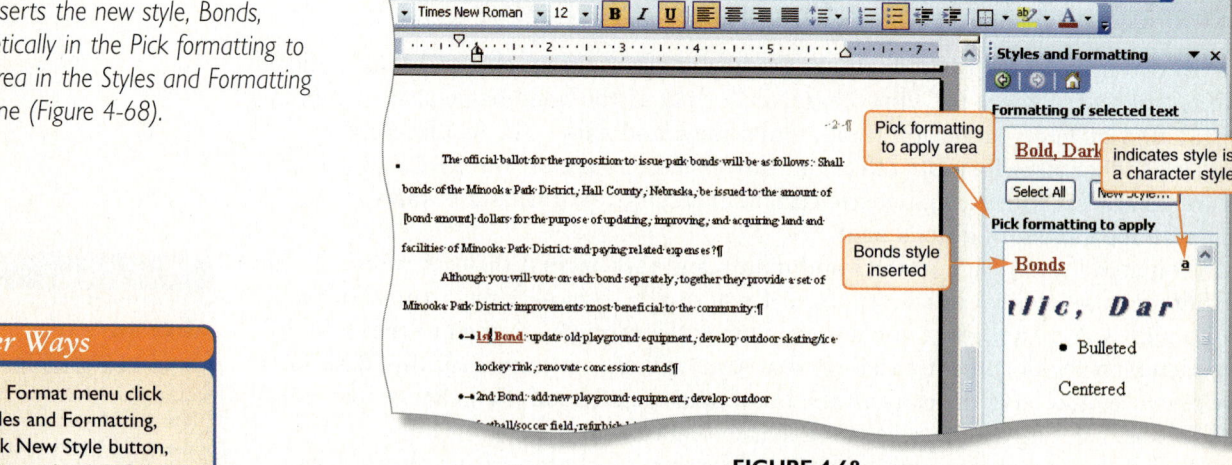

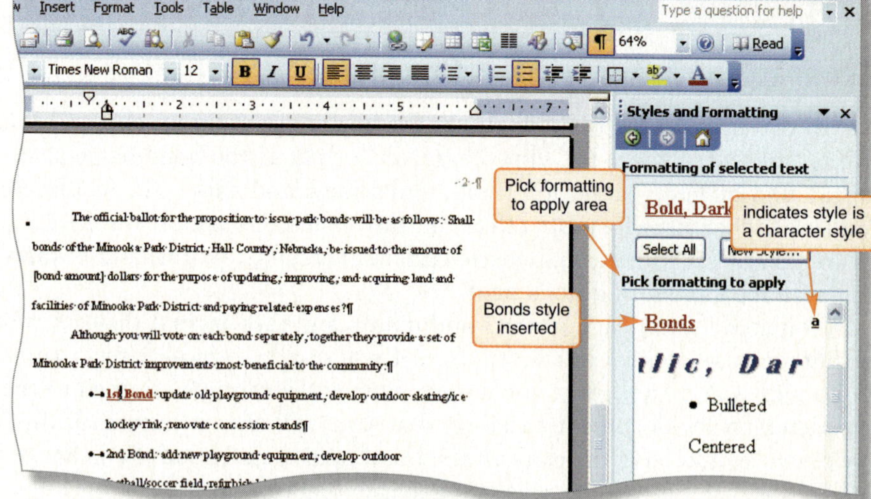

FIGURE 4-68

Other Ways

1. On Format menu click Styles and Formatting, click New Style button, define style, click OK button
2. In Voice Command mode, say "Styles and Formatting, New Style, [define style], OK"

The next step is to apply the style to the bond names in the bulleted list, as shown below.

To Apply a Character Style

1

- **Drag through the text, 2nd Bond, to select it.**
- **Press and hold down the CTRL key and then drag through the text, 3rd Bond, to select it also. Release the CTRL key.**

Word selects the nonadjacent text that is to be based on the Bonds style (Figure 4-69).

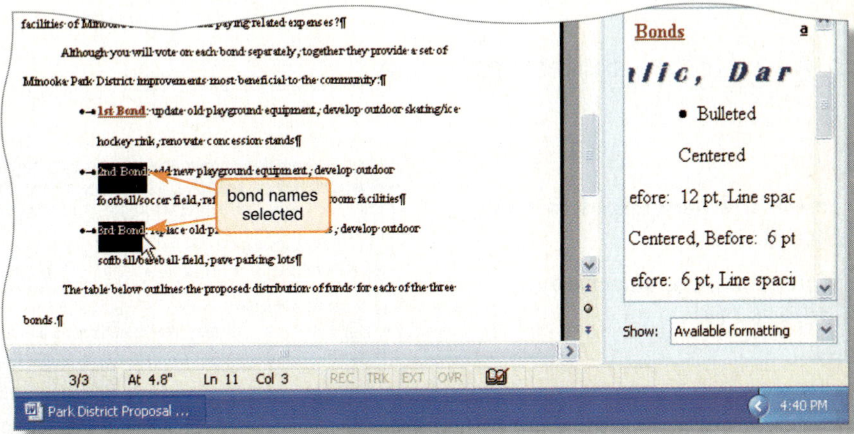

FIGURE 4-69

2

- **With the Styles and Formatting task pane displaying in the Word window, click Bonds in the Pick formatting to apply area.**
- **Click in the bulleted list to remove the selection.**

Word applies the character format, Bonds, to the selected bond names in the bulleted list (Figure 4-70).

3

- **Close the Styles and Formatting task pane by clicking its Close button.**

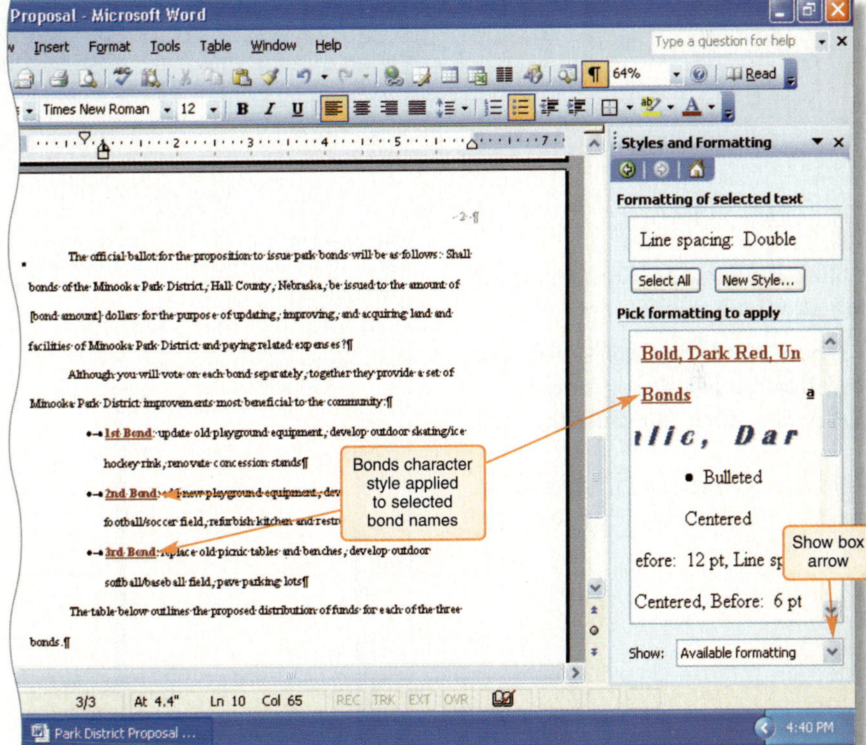

FIGURE 4-70

Other Ways

1. Click Style box arrow on Formatting toolbar and then click style name
2. In Voice Command mode, say "Style, [select style name]"

If a style you wish to use is not displayed in the Pick formatting to apply area of the Styles and Formatting task pane and you know the style exists, click the Show box arrow in the Styles and Formatting task pane and then click All styles.

Customizing Bullets in a List

The bulleted list uses default bullet characters (shown in Figure 4-71). To change the bullet symbol from a small, solid circle to the picture bullets shown in Figure 4-29b on page WD 243, use the Bullets and Numbering dialog box. The following steps show how to change the bullets in the list to picture bullets.

To Add Picture Bullets to a List

1

- **Select the paragraphs in the bulleted list.**
- **Right-click the selection (Figure 4-71).**

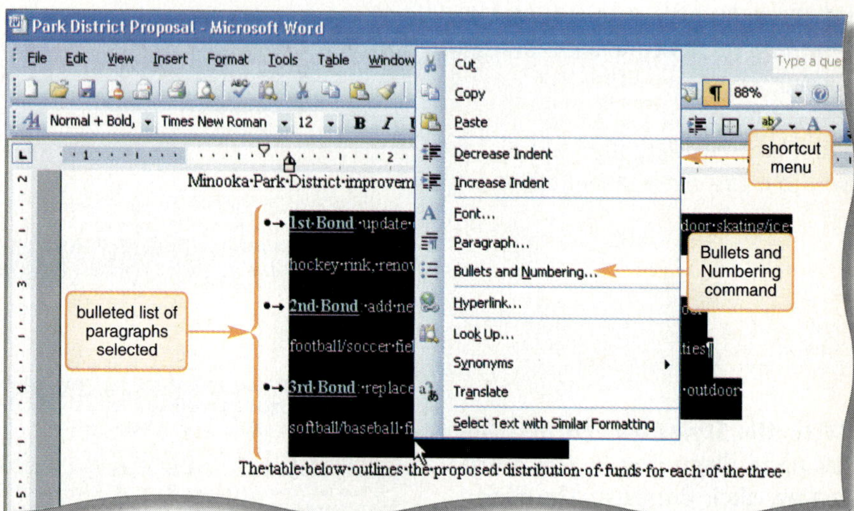

FIGURE 4-71

2

- **Click Bullets and Numbering on the shortcut menu.**
- **When Word displays the Bullets and Numbering dialog box, if necessary, click the Bulleted tab.**

Word displays several bullet styles in the Bullets and Numbering dialog box (Figure 4-72).

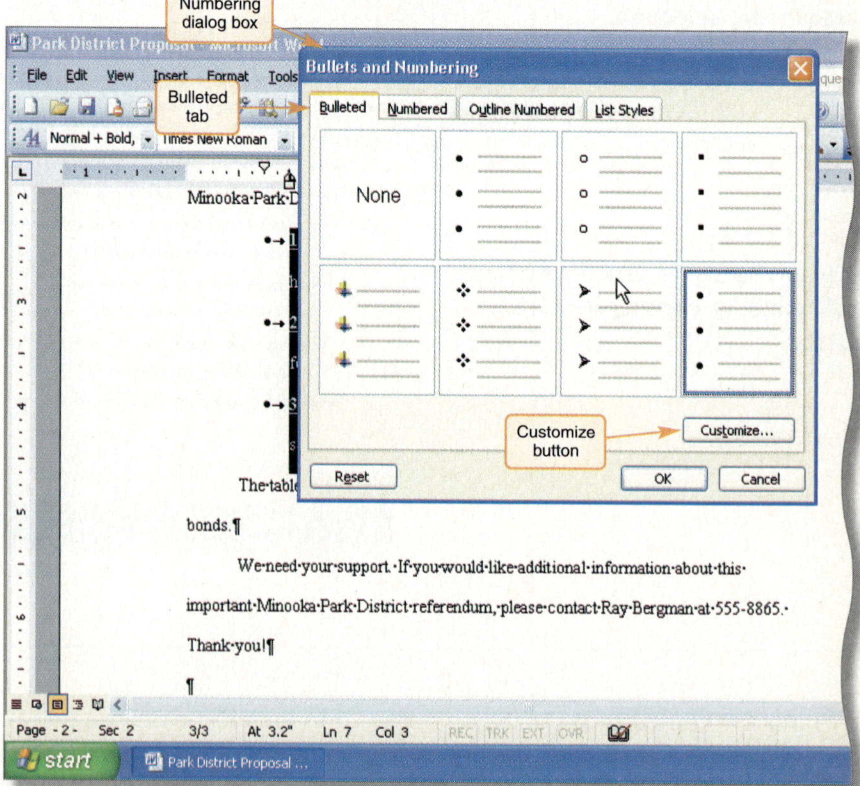

FIGURE 4-72

3

- **Click the Customize button in the Bullets and Numbering dialog box.**
- **When Word displays the Customize Bulleted List dialog box, click the Picture button.**
- **When Word displays the Picture Bullet dialog box, click the desired picture bullet (third row, second column).**

In the Picture Bullet dialog box, the selected picture bullet has a box around it, indicating it is selected (Figure 4-73).

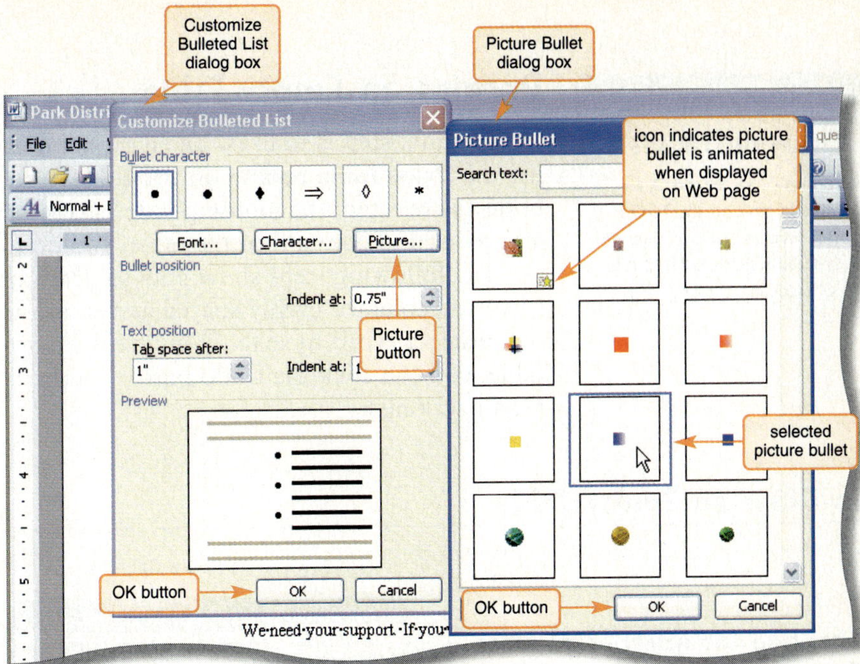

FIGURE 4-73

4

- **Click the OK button in the Picture Bullet dialog box.**
- **Click the OK button in the Customize Bulleted List dialog box.**
- **When the Word window is visible again, click in the selected list to remove the selection.**

Word changes the default bullets to picture bullets (Figure 4-74).

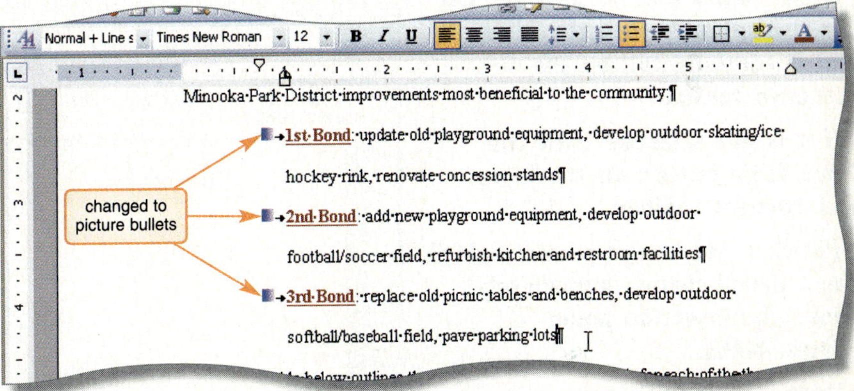

FIGURE 4-74

Other Ways

1. Select list, on Format menu click Bullets and Numbering, click Bulleted tab, click Customize button, click Picture button, click desired bullet style, click OK button, click OK button
2. Select list, in Voice Command mode, say "Format, Bullets and Numbering, Bullets, Customize, Picture, [select desired bullet style], OK, OK"

In addition to picture bullets, the Bullets and Numbering dialog box (Figure 4-72) provides a number of other bullet styles. To use one of these styles, simply click the desired style in the dialog box and then click the OK button.

Drawing a Table

The next step is to insert a table above the last paragraph of the proposal (Figure 4-29b on page WD 243). As previously discussed, a Word table is a collection of rows and columns; the intersection of a row and a column is called a cell. Cells are filled with data.

When you want to create a simple table, one with the same number of rows and columns, use the Insert Table button on the Standard toolbar to create the table. To create a more complex table, use Word's **Draw Table feature**. The table to be created at this point in the project is a complex table because it does not contain the same number of rows and columns. The following pages discuss how to use Word's Draw Table feature.

More About

Drawing Tables

To draw a table, the Draw Table button on the Tables and Borders toolbar must be selected (Figure 4-75). If it is not selected, click it.

Drawing an Empty Table

The first step is to draw an empty table in the document. To draw a table, you use the **Draw Table button** on the Tables and Borders toolbar. When the Draw Table button is selected, the mouse pointer shape changes to a pencil. To draw the boundary, rows, and columns of the table, you drag the pencil pointer on the screen.

The following steps show how to draw an empty table. Do not try to make the rows and columns evenly spaced as you draw them. After you draw the table, you will instruct Word to space them evenly. If you make a mistake while drawing the table, you can click the Undo button on the Standard toolbar to undo your most recent action(s).

To Draw an Empty Table

1

- **Position the insertion point at the beginning of the last paragraph.**
- **If the Tables and Borders toolbar is not displayed, click the Tables and Borders button on the Standard toolbar.**
- **If it is not selected, click the Draw Table button on the Tables and Borders toolbar.**
- **Position the mouse pointer, which has a pencil shape, immediately above the insertion point (Figure 4-75).**
- **Verify the insertion point is positioned exactly as shown in Figure 4-75.**

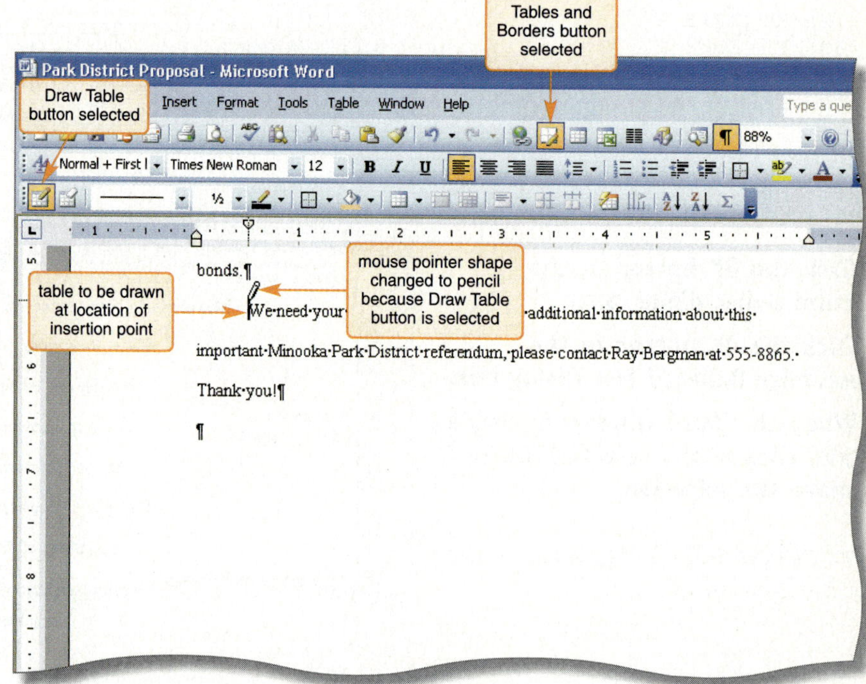

FIGURE 4-75

2

- **Drag the pencil pointer downward and to the right until the dotted rectangle is positioned similarly to the one shown in Figure 4-76.**

Word displays a dotted rectangle to indicate the proposed table's size (Figure 4-76).

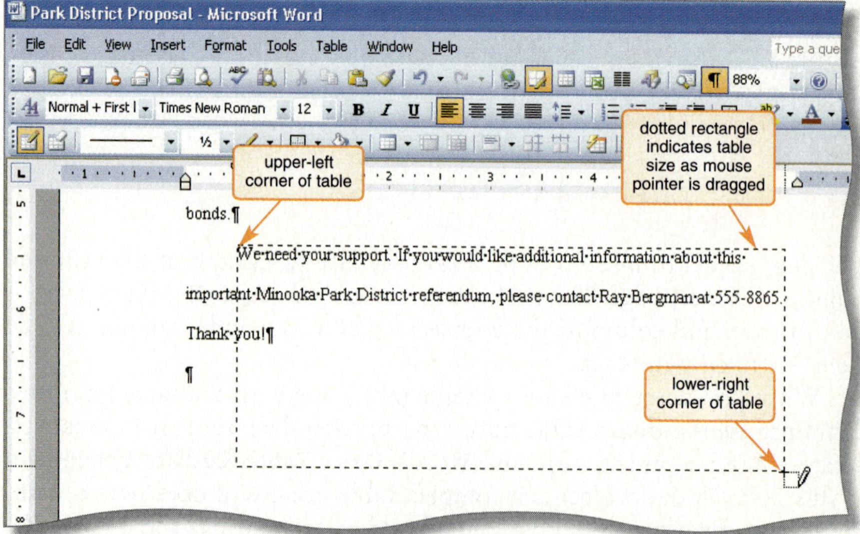

FIGURE 4-76

3

- Release the mouse button.
- If Word wraps the text around the table, right-click the table, click Table Properties on the shortcut menu, click the Table tab, click None in the Text wrapping area, and then click the OK button.
- If the table is not positioned as shown here, click the Undo button on the Standard toolbar and then repeat Step 2.
- Position the pencil pointer in the table as shown in Figure 4-77.

Word draws the table border (Figure 4-77).

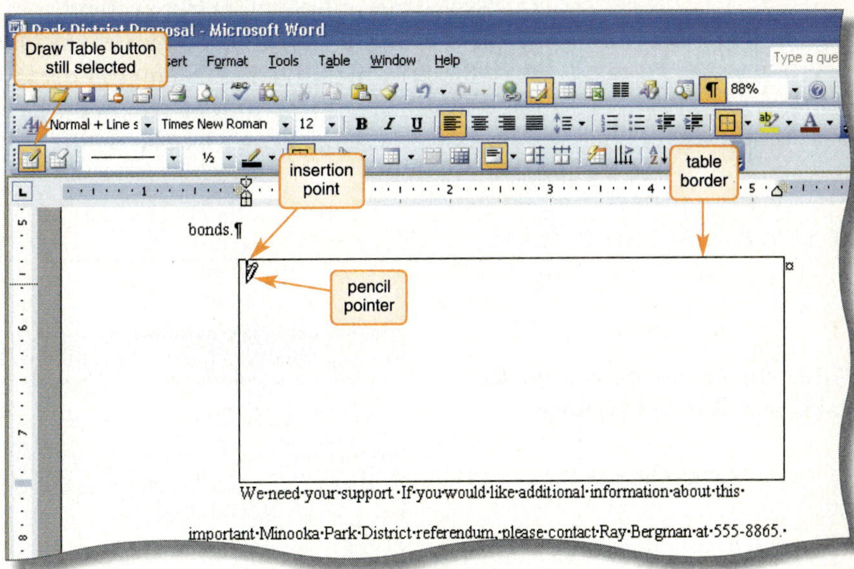

FIGURE 4-77

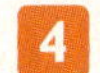

4

- Drag the pencil pointer to the right to draw a horizontal line.
- Drag the pencil pointer from left to right three more times to draw three more horizontal lines, as shown in Figure 4-78.
- Position the pencil pointer in the table as shown in Figure 4-78.

Word draws four horizontal lines, which form the rows in the table (Figure 4-78).

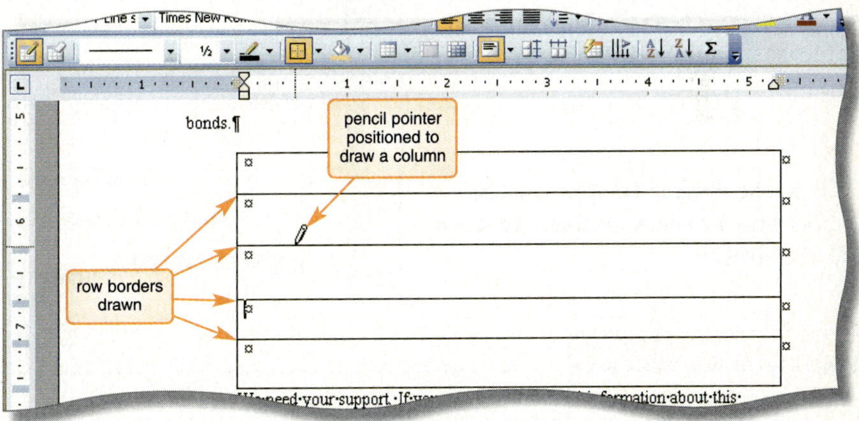

FIGURE 4-78

5

- Draw five vertical lines to form the column borders, similarly to those shown in Figure 4-79.

The empty table displays as shown in Figure 4-79.

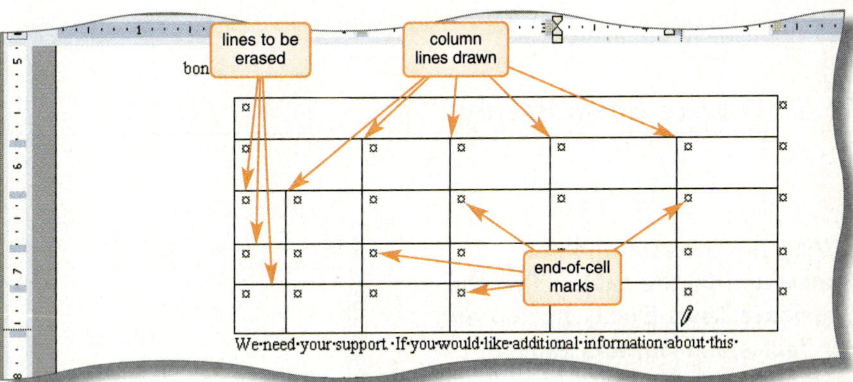

FIGURE 4-79

Other Ways

1. On Table menu click Draw Table, use pencil pointer to draw table
2. In Voice Command mode, say "Tables and Borders, [use pencil pointer to draw table]"

All Word tables that you draw have a one-half-point border, by default. To change this border, you can use the Tables and Borders toolbar, as described earlier in this project.

Notice the end-of-cell marks currently are left-aligned in each cell (Figure 4-79 on the previous page), which indicates the data will be left-aligned in the cells.

After drawing rows and columns in the table, you may want to remove a line. In this table, three lines need to be removed (shown in Figure 4-79). The following steps show how to use the **Eraser button** on the Tables and Borders toolbar to remove lines.

To Erase Lines in a Table

1

• **Click the Eraser button on the Tables and Borders toolbar.**

The mouse pointer shape changes to an eraser.

2

• **Drag the mouse pointer (eraser shape) through each line you wish to erase (Figure 4-80).**

3

• **Click the Eraser button on the Tables and Borders toolbar to turn off the eraser.**

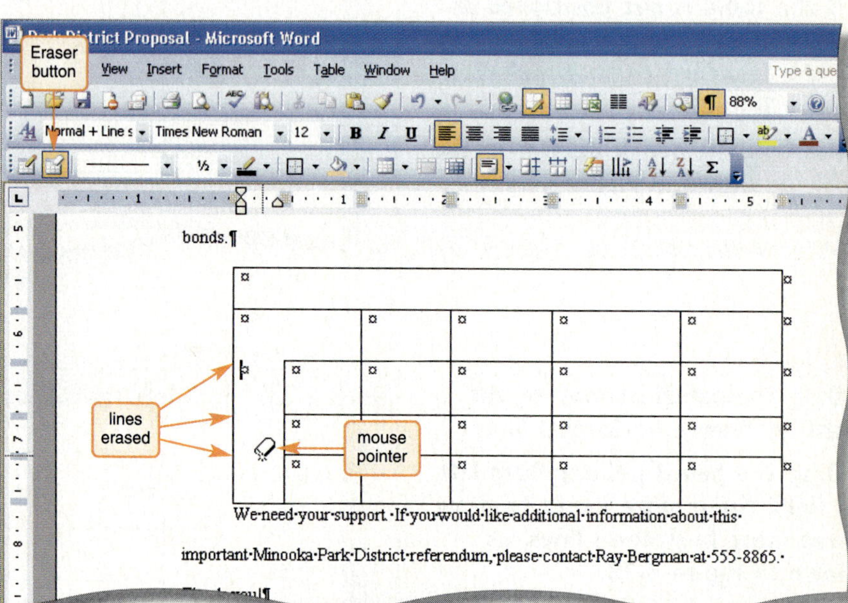
Eraser button
lines erased
mouse pointer
bonds.¶
We·need·your·support.·If·you·would·like·additional·information·about·this·
important·Minooka·Park·District·referendum,·please·contact·Ray·Bergman·at·555-8865.·

FIGURE 4-80

Other Ways

1. In Voice Command mode, say "Eraser, [erase lines]"

Because you drew the table borders with the mouse, some of the rows may be varying heights. The following step shows how to make the row spacing in the table even.

To Distribute Rows Evenly

1

• **With the insertion point somewhere in the table, click the Distribute Rows Evenly button on the Tables and Borders toolbar.**

Word makes the height of the rows uniform (Figure 4-81).

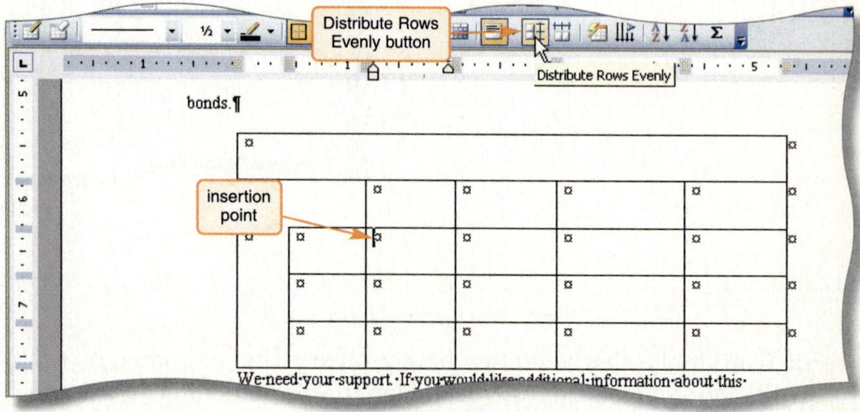
Distribute Rows Evenly button
Distribute Rows Evenly
bonds.¶
insertion point
We·need·your·support.·If·you·would·like·additional·information·about·this·

FIGURE 4-81

Other Ways

1. On Table menu point to AutoFit, click Distribute Rows Evenly on AutoFit submenu

You want the last four columns in the table to be the same width. Because you drew the borders of these columns, they may be varying widths. The following steps show how to evenly size these columns.

To Distribute Columns Evenly

1

- **Drag through the 16 cells shown in Figure 4-82 to select them.**
- **Click the Distribute Columns Evenly button on the Tables and Borders toolbar.**

Word applies uniform widths to the selected columns (Figure 4-82).

2

- **Click inside the table to remove the selection.**

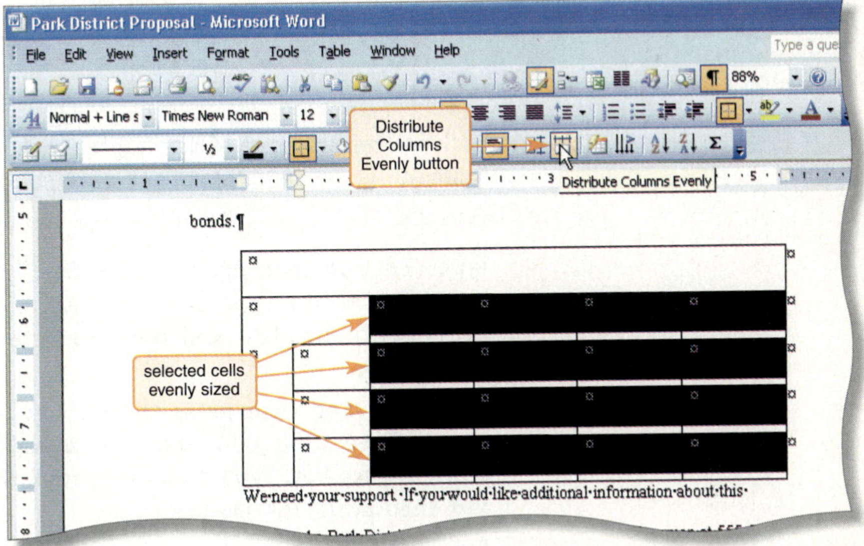

FIGURE 4-82

Other Ways

1. Select cells, on Table menu point to AutoFit, click Distribute Columns Evenly on AutoFit submenu
2. Drag row boundaries (borders) on table
3. Drag Table Column markers on horizontal ruler
4. In Voice Command mode, say "Distribute Columns Evenly"

Single-Space the Table Contents

You want the data you type within the cells to be single-spaced, instead of double-spaced. Thus, the following steps describe how to single-space the table cells.

To Single-Space Table Contents

1 **Position the mouse pointer in the table to display the table move handle in the upper-left corner of the table. Position the mouse pointer on the table move handle and then click to select the table.**

2 **With the entire table selected, press CTRL+1.**

3 **Click anywhere to remove the selection in the table.**

Word single-spaces the cells in the table. The size of the table does not change.

When you enter data that wraps within a cell, it will be single-spaced instead of double-spaced.

More About

Tables

If you do not want a page break to occur in the middle of a table, position the insertion point in the table, click Table on the menu bar, click Table Properties, click the Row tab, remove the check mark from the Allow row to break across pages check box, and then click the OK button.

Entering Data into the Table

The next step is to enter the data into the table. To advance from one column to the next, press the TAB key. To advance from one row to the next, also press the TAB key; do not press the ENTER key. Use the ENTER key only to begin a new paragraph within a cell.

More About

Nested Tables

You can create a table within a table, or a nested table, using the Drawing toolbar. To do this, click the Draw Table button on the Tables and Borders toolbar to display the pencil pointer. Draw the new table inside the current table. When you are finished, click the Draw Table button to turn off the pencil pointer.

Earlier in this project, the AutoSum button was used to enter row and column totals. The AutoSum button automatically inserts totals as dollars and cents, even when the numbers being summed are whole numbers. If you want the totals to display as whole numbers, you must edit the totals as you edit the contents of any other cell. In this case, because the numbers are easy to add up, you simply type the totals into the cells.

The following steps describe how to enter the data into this table (shown in Figure 4-83).

To Enter Data into a Table

1. **Click in the first cell of the table. Click the Center button on the Formatting toolbar.**
2. **Type** `PROPOSED DISTRIBUTION OF FUNDS` **and then press the TAB key.**
3. **Type** `YES` **and then press the TAB key. Type** `Park Renovations` **and then press the TAB key. Type** `Land Purchases` **and then press the TAB key. Type** `Facility Upgrades` **and then press the TAB key. Type** `Total` **and then press the TAB key.**
4. **Type** `VOTE` **and then press the TAB key. Type** `1st Bond` **and then press the TAB key. Type** `$300,000` **and then press the TAB key. Type** `$200,000` **and then press the TAB key. Type** `$400,000` **and then press the TAB key. Type** `$900,000` **and then press the TAB key twice.**
5. **Type** `2nd Bond` **and then press the TAB key. Type** `$450,000` **and then press the TAB key. Type** `$500,000` **and then press the TAB key. Type** `$650,000` **and then press the TAB key. Type** `$1,600,000` **and then press the TAB key twice.**
6. **Type** `3rd Bond` **and then press the TAB key. Type** `$250,000` **and then press the TAB key. Type** `$600,000` **and then press the TAB key. Type** `$550,000` **and then press the TAB key. Type** `$1,400,000` **as the last entry in the table.**

The table data is entered (shown in Figure 4-83). As you type an ordinal, such as 2nd, Word automatically formats it as a superscript (e.g., 2nd).

Formatting the Table

The data you enter in cells displays horizontally. You can rotate the text so it displays vertically. Changing the direction of text adds variety to your tables.

The following steps show how to display text in a table cell vertically.

To Vertically Display Text in a Cell

1

- **Select the cell containing the word, VOTE.**

The cell to be formatted is selected (Figure 4-83).

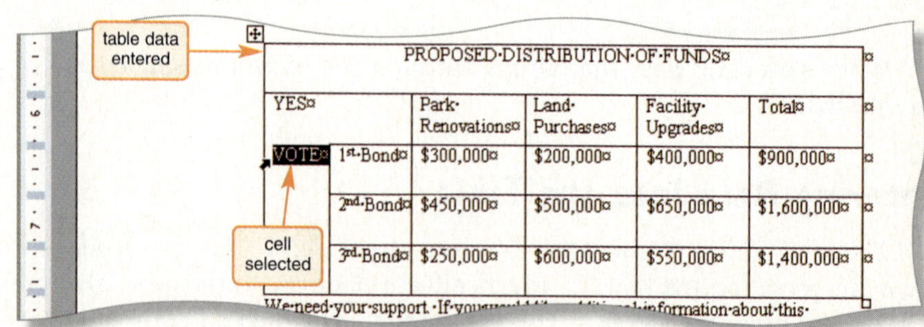

table data entered
PROPOSED·DISTRIBUTION·OF·FUNDS
YES
Park·Renovations
Land·Purchases
Facility·Upgrades
Total
VOTE
1st·Bond
$300,000
$200,000
$400,000
$900,000
2nd·Bond
$450,000
$500,000
$650,000
$1,600,000
cell selected
3rd·Bond
$250,000
$600,000
$550,000
$1,400,000

FIGURE 4-83

2

• **Click the Change Text Direction button on the Tables and Borders toolbar twice.**

Word displays the text vertically so that it reads from bottom to top (Figure 4-84).

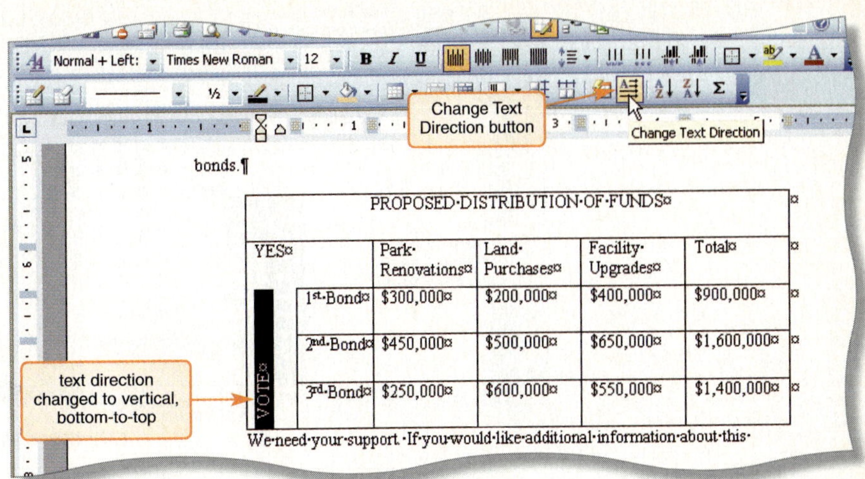

FIGURE 4-84

The first time you click the Change Text Direction button, Word displays the text vertically so it reads from top to bottom. The second time you click the Change Text Direction button, Word displays the text vertically so it reads from bottom to top (Figure 4-84). If you click the button a third time, the text would display horizontally again.

The words, VOTE YES, in the table are to be 26-point bold font and centered. The following steps describe how to format this text in the table.

To Format Table Text

1. **With the word VOTE selected, hold down the CTRL key and select the cell containing the word YES in the table. Release the CTRL key.**
2. **With both words, VOTE and YES, selected, click the Font Size box arrow on the Formatting toolbar and then click 26. Click the Bold button on the Formatting toolbar. Click the Center button on the Formatting toolbar.**

Word formats the table text (shown in Figure 4-85 on the next page).

The next step is to shade cells containing the words, VOTE and YES, in light yellow. The following steps describe how to shade selected cells.

To Shade Table Cells

1. **With the cells containing the words, VOTE and YES, selected, click the Shading Color button arrow on the Tables and Borders toolbar (Figure 4-85).**
2. **Click Light Yellow (third color in bottom row of color palette).**

Word shades the cells in light yellow (shown in Figure 4-86 on the next page).

More About

Shading

To remove shading from a cell(s), select the cell(s), click the Shading Color button arrow on the Tables and Borders toolbar, and then click No Fill on the palette.

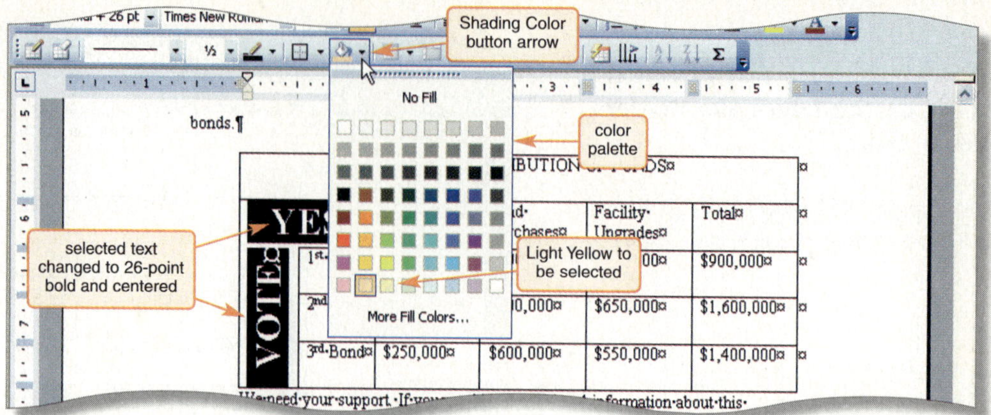

FIGURE 4-85

The title of the table should be 14-point Times New Roman bold dark red font. The following steps describe how to format the table title.

To Format the Table Title

1. **Drag through the table title, PROPOSED DISTRIBUTION OF FUNDS.**
2. **Click the Font Size button arrow on the Formatting toolbar and then click 14. Click the Bold button on the Formatting toolbar. Click the Font Color button arrow on the Formatting toolbar and then click Dark Red.**
3. **Click in the first row to remove the selection.**

Word formats the table title (shown in Figure 4-86).

Other Ways

1. On Table menu click Table Properties, click Row tab, enter row height in Specify height box, click OK button
2. Right-click row, click Table Properties on shortcut menu, click Row tab, enter row height in Specify height box, click OK button

The next step is to narrow the height of the row containing the table title. The steps below show how to change a row's height.

To Change Row Height

1

• **Point to the bottom border of the first row. When the mouse pointer changes to a double-headed arrow, drag up until the proposed row border looks like Figure 4-86.**

When you release the mouse button, Word will resize the row according to the location to which you dragged the row border.

2

• **Release the mouse button.**

Word resizes the row (shown in Figure 4-87).

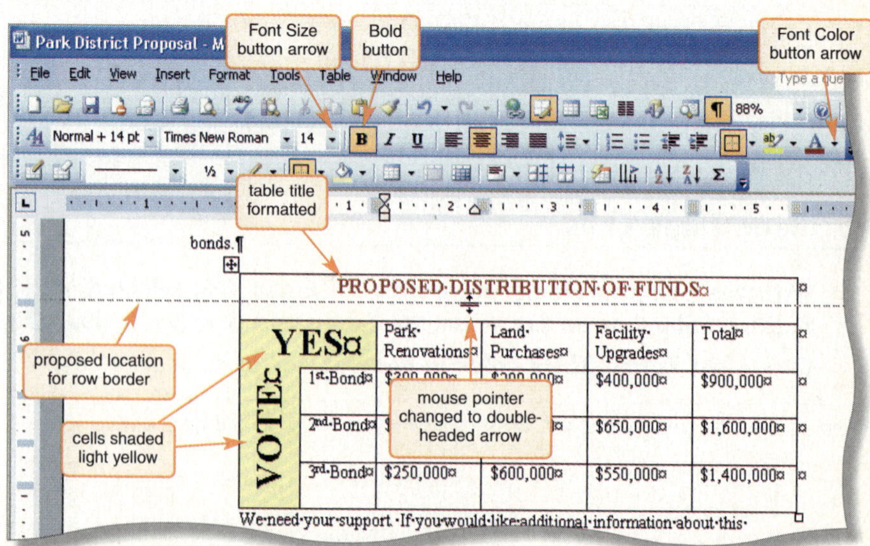

FIGURE 4-86

If you wanted to change the width of a column, you would drag the column border similarly to the way you dragged the row border in the previous steps.

The next step is to change the alignment of the data in the last three rows. In addition to aligning text horizontally in a cell (left, centered, or right) by clicking the appropriate button on the Formatting toolbar, you can center it vertically within a cell using the Align button arrow on the Tables and Borders toolbar. The following steps show how to align data in cells.

To Align Data in Cells

1

- **Select the cells in the bottom three rows of the table by dragging through them.**
- **Click the Align button arrow on the Tables and Borders toolbar.**

Word displays a list of cell alignment options (Figure 4-87).

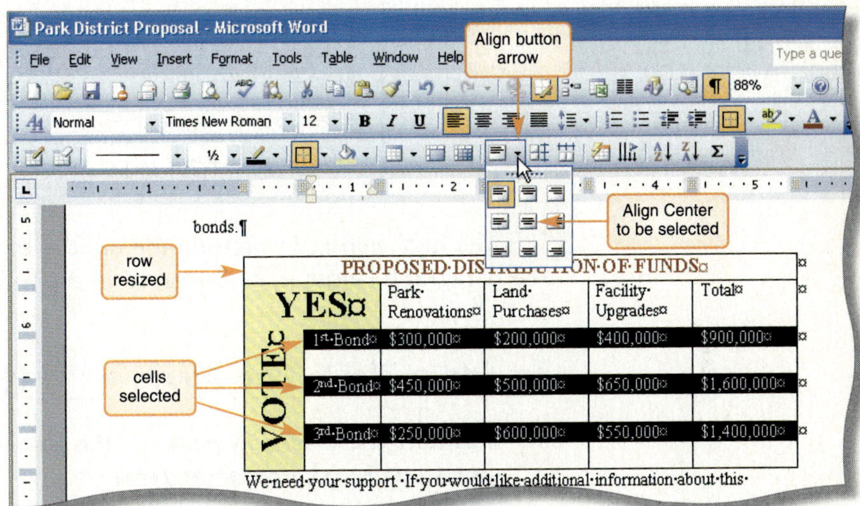

FIGURE 4-87

2

- **Click Align Center in the list.**

Word changes the alignment of the selected cells to center (Figure 4-88).

3

- **Select the four column headings by dragging through them.**
- **Click the Align button arrow on the Tables and Borders toolbar (Figure 4-88).**

4

- **Click Align Bottom Center in the list.**
- **Click the Tables and Borders button on the Standard toolbar to remove the toolbar from the screen.**

Word changes the alignment of selected cells to bottom center (shown in Figure 4-89 on the next page).

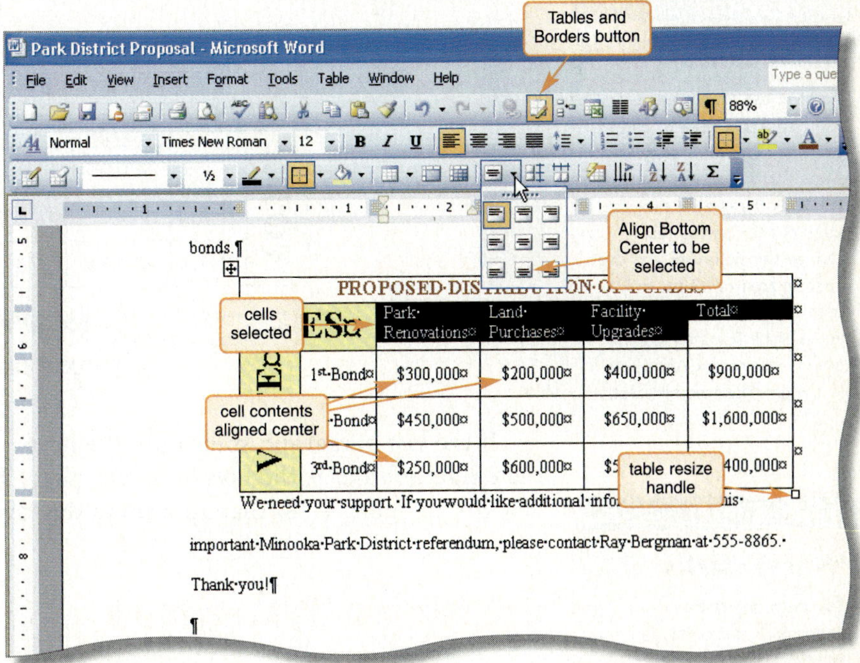

FIGURE 4-88

Other Ways

1. In Voice Command mode, say "Align, [select align option]"

Notice in Figure 4-88 on the previous page that when you click the Align button arrow on the Tables and Borders toolbar, Word provides several cell alignment options. Table 4-3 illustrates the various alignment options.

Table 4-3 Cell Alignment Options

Alignment	Example
Align Top Left	$300,000
Align Top Center	$300,000
Align Top Right	$300,000
Align Center Left	$300,000
Align Center	$300,000
Align Center Right	$300,000
Align Bottom Left	$300,000
Align Bottom Center	$300,000
Align Bottom Right	$300,000

The final step in formatting the table is to add a blank line between the table and the paragraph below it, as described in the following step.

To Add a Blank Line Above a Paragraph

1 **Position the insertion point in the last paragraph of the proposal and then press CTRL+0 (the numeral zero).**

*The shortcut key, **CTRL+0**, instructs Word to add a blank line above the paragraph (Figure 4-89).*

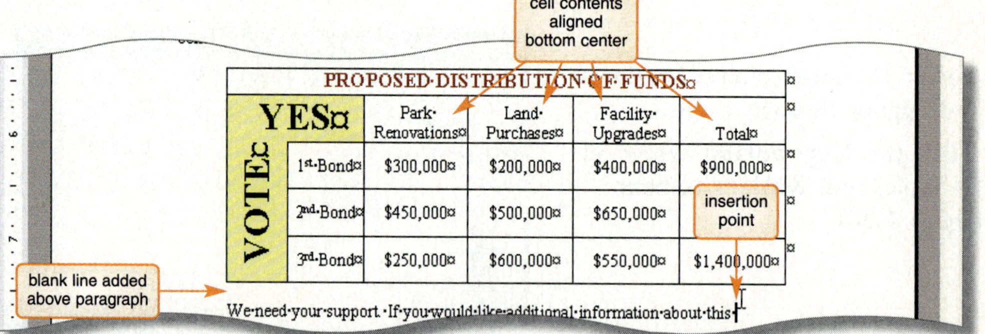

FIGURE 4-89

More About

Blank Lines

You can use menus instead of using shortcut keys to add a blank line above a paragraph. Click Format on the menu bar, click Paragraph, click the Indents and Spacing tab, change the Before box in the Spacing area to 12 pt, and then click the OK button. To add a blank line after a paragraph, change the After box in the Spacing area to 12 pt.

If the last paragraph spills onto the next page, you can make the table smaller so the paragraph fits at the bottom of the page. To do this, drag the table resize handle (shown in Figure 4-88) that appears in the lower-right corner of the table inward.

Creating a Watermark

A **watermark** is text or a graphic that is displayed on top of or behind the text in a document. For example, a catalog may print the words, Sold Out, on top of sold-out items. A product manager may want the word, Draft, to print behind his or her first draft of a five-year plan. Some companies use their logos or other graphics as watermarks on documents to add visual appeal to the document.

More About

Watermarks

To create a picture watermark, click Picture watermark in the Printed Watermark dialog box, click the Select Picture button, locate the picture, and then click the OK button in the Printed Watermark dialog box.

In this project, you would like the word, YES, to display on all pages of the proposal. The following steps show how to create this watermark.

To Create a Text Watermark

- **Click Format on the menu bar and then point to Background (Figure 4-90).**

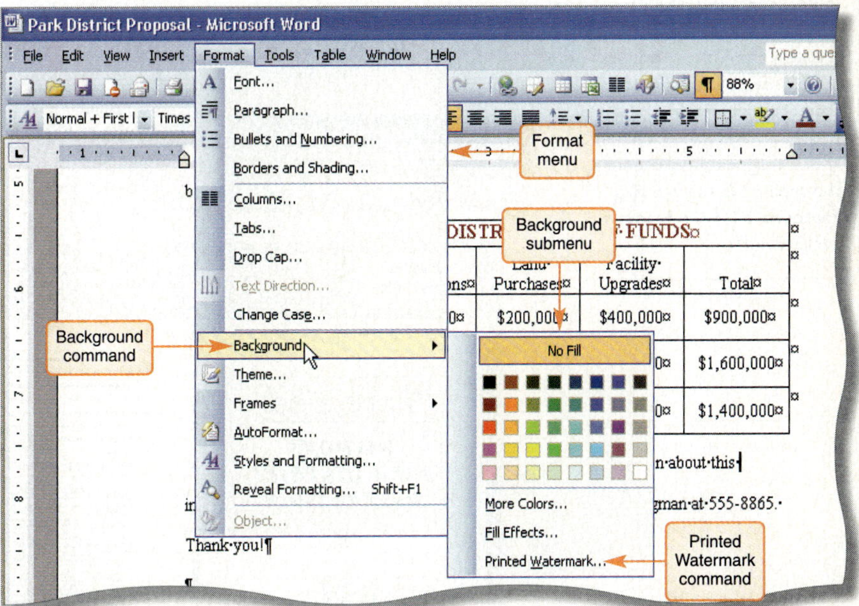

FIGURE 4-90

2

- **Click Printed Watermark on the Background submenu.**
- **When Word displays the Printed Watermark dialog box, click Text watermark.**
- **Drag through the text in the Text box to select it. Type** YES **in the Text box.**
- **Click the Size box arrow and then click 54.**
- **Click the Color box arrow and then click Tan on the color palette.**

In the Printed Watermark dialog box, the Semitransparent setting adjusts the brightness and contrast so the text is faded (Figure 4-91).

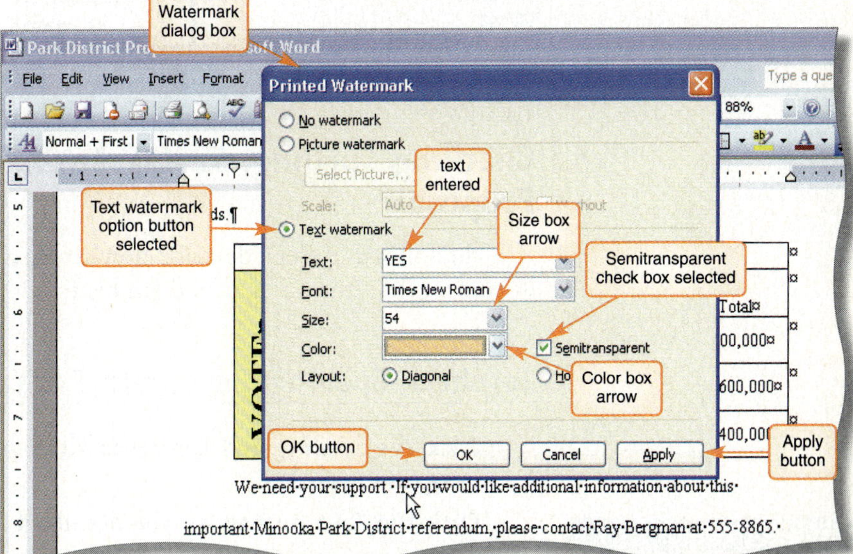

FIGURE 4-91

- **Click the Apply button.**

The Cancel button in the dialog box changes to a Close button.

4

- **Click the Close button in the dialog box.**

Word displays the watermark faded behind the text of the proposal (shown in Figure 4-92 on the next page).

Other Ways

1. In Voice Command mode, say "Format, Background, Printed Watermark, [enter settings], OK"

If you want to remove a watermark, click No watermark in the Printed Watermark dialog box (Figure 4-91). To see how the watermark looks in the entire document, print the document or view the document in print preview, as described in the steps on the next page.

Q&A

Q: How should I proofread the proposal?

A: Ask yourself these questions when proofreading the proposal: Is the subject original and specific? Is its purpose clear? Does the proposal provide specifics rather than generalizations? Is the product or service beneficial? Is the length appropriate for the subject? Is the wording appropriate for the reader's background?

To Print Preview a Document

1. **Click the Print Preview button on the Standard toolbar. If necessary, click the Multiple Pages button on the Print Preview toolbar and then click the third icon in the first row of the grid (1 × 3 Pages) to display all three pages of the proposal as shown in Figure 4-92.**
2. **When finished viewing the document, click the Close Preview button on the Print Preview toolbar.**

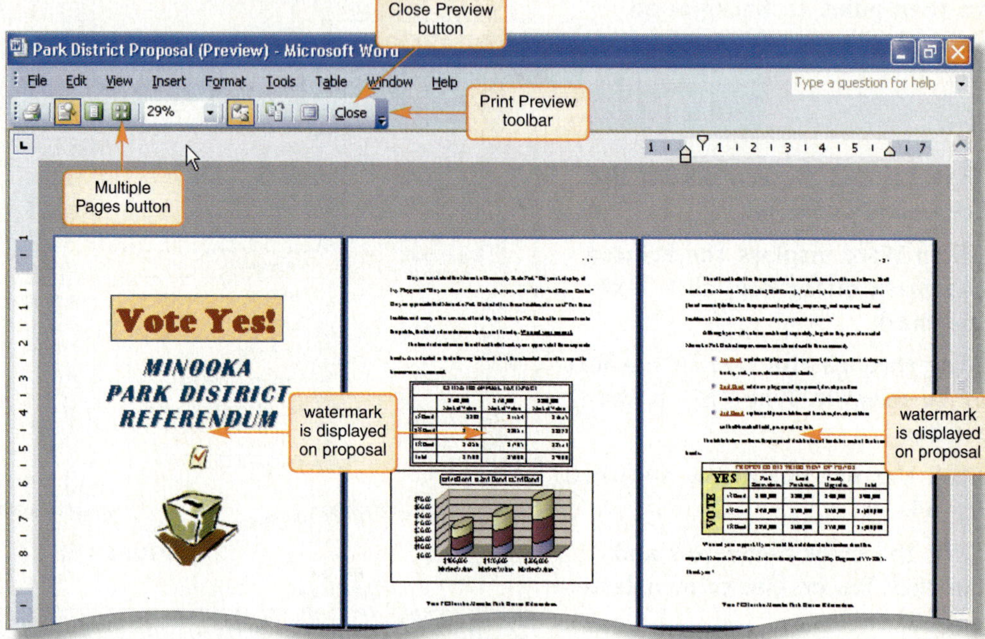

FIGURE 4-92

Checking Spelling, Saving Again, and Printing the Sales Proposal

The following steps describe how to check the spelling of the document, save the document, and then print the document.

To Check Spelling, Save, and Print the Document

1. **Click the Spelling and Grammar button on the Standard toolbar. Correct any misspelled words.**
2. **Click the Save button on the Standard toolbar.**
3. **Click the Print button on the Standard toolbar.**

The document prints as shown in Figure 4-1 on page WD 219.

More About

Reveal Formatting

To format selected text similarly to the text that surrounds it, select the text and then display the Reveal Formatting task pane. Point in the Selected text box, click the box arrow to its right, and then click Apply Formatting of Surrounding Text.

Revealing Formatting

Sometimes, when you review a document, you want to know what formats were applied to certain text items. For example, you may wonder what font, font size, font color, border size, border color, or shading color you used on the first line of the title page. To display formatting applied to text, use the **Reveal Formatting task pane**. The next steps illustrate how to reveal formatting.

To Reveal Formatting

1

- **Press CTRL+HOME and then verify that the insertion point in the first line of the document, Vote Yes!**
- **Click Format on the menu bar (Figure 4-93).**

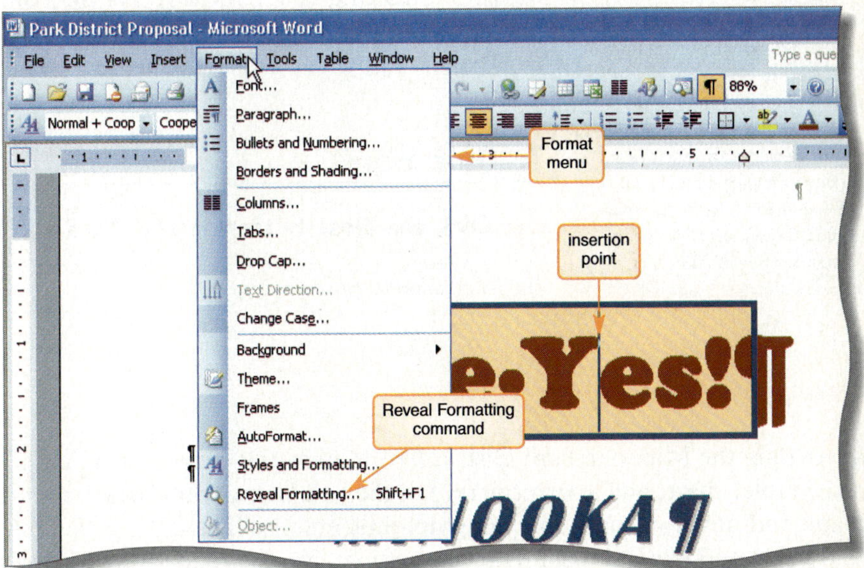

FIGURE 4-93

2

- **Click Reveal Formatting on the Format menu.**

Word displays the Reveal Formatting task pane (Figure 4-94). The Reveal Formatting task pane shows formatting applied to the location of the insertion point.

3

- **Click the Close button on the Reveal Formatting task pane to close the task pane.**

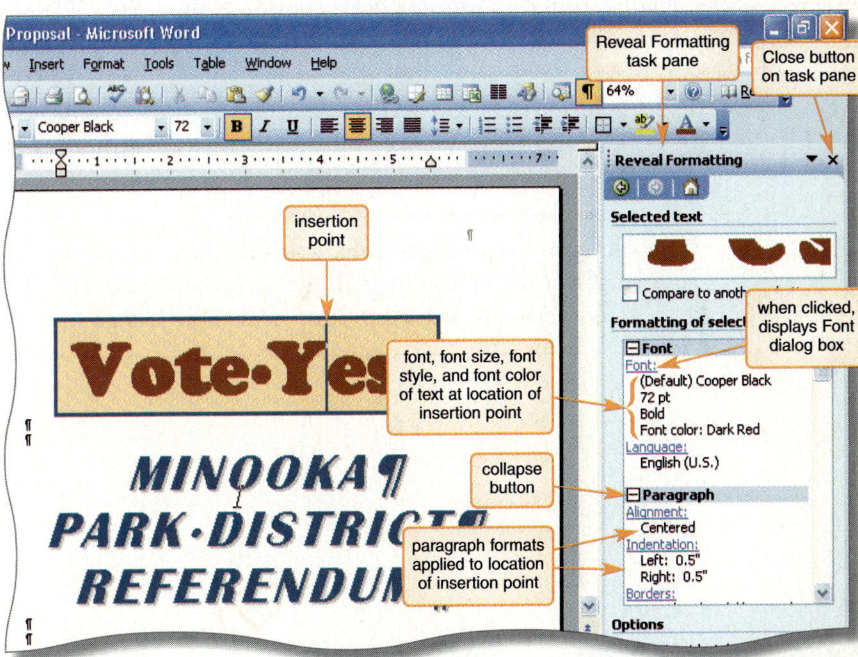

FIGURE 4-94

Other Ways

1. Press SHIFT+F1
2. In Voice Command mode, say "Format, Reveal Formatting"

When the Reveal Formatting task pane is displayed, you can click any text in the document window and the contents of the Reveal Formatting task pane changes to show formatting applied to the location of the insertion point. To display or hide items in the Formatting of selected text area of the Reveal Formatting task pane, click the expand (+) or collapse (-) buttons. For example, clicking the collapse button to the left of Paragraph hides the paragraph formats applied to the text.

More About

Certification

The Microsoft Office Specialist Certification program provides an opportunity for you to obtain a valuable industry credential - proof that you have the Word 2003 skills required by employers. For more information, see Appendix E or visit the Word 2003 Certification Web page (scsite.com/wd2003/cert).

If you want to change the format of text through the Reveal Formatting task pane, select the text and then click the blue underlined word in the Formatting of selected text area to display the linked dialog box. For example, clicking Font in the Reveal Formatting task pane displays the Font dialog box. As soon as you click the OK button in the dialog box, Word changes the format of the selected text.

Project 4 now is complete. The next step is to quit Word.

To Quit Word

1. **Click the Close button in the Word window.**

The Word window closes.

Project Summary

In creating the Minooka Park District Proposal in this project, you learned how to create a document with a title page, table, chart, and a watermark. On the title page, you learned how to add a border and shading to a paragraph and how to change the paragraph indentation. Then, the project showed how to add a shadow effect to characters and expand them by several points. You learned how to insert a graphic from the Web and center the contents of the title page vertically.

Next, you learned how to insert an existing Word document into the active document. The project showed how to insert a header and also a footer in the body of the proposal that was different from the title page header and footer. Then, you learned how to format an existing Word table and chart it using the embedded program, Microsoft Graph. Next, the project showed how to create a character style and add picture bullets to a list. Then, you learned how to use the Draw Table feature to create a complex table. Finally, the project showed how to add a text watermark to the document and how to reveal formatting of a document.

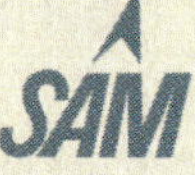

If you have a SAM user profile, you may have access to hands-on instruction, practice, and assessment of the skills covered in this project. Log in to your SAM account and go to your assignments page to see what your instructor has assigned.

More About

Quick Reference

For a table that lists how to complete the tasks covered in this book using the mouse, menu, shortcut menu, and keyboard, see the Quick Reference Summary at the back of this book, or visit the Word 2003 Quick Reference Web page (scsite.com/wd2003/qr).

What You Should Know

Having completed this project, you should be able to perform the tasks below. The tasks are listed in the same order they were presented in this project. For a list of the buttons, menus, toolbars, and commands introduced in this project, see the Quick Reference Summary at the back of this book and refer to the Page Number column.

1. Start and Customize Word (WD 220)
2. Display Formatting Marks (WD 220)
3. Zoom Page Width (WD 221, WD 234)
4. Format Characters (WD 221)
5. Border a Paragraph (WD 222)
6. Change Left and Right Paragraph Indent (WD 223)
7. Shade a Paragraph (WD 224)
8. Clear Formatting (WD 226, WD 229, WD 235)
9. Format Characters and Modify Character Spacing (WD 227)
10. Modify the Default Font Settings (WD 229)
11. Insert Clip Art from the Web (WD 230)
12. Insert a Graphic File from the Data Disk (WD 231)
13. Resize a Graphic Using the Format Picture Dialog Box (WD 231)
14. Zoom Whole Page (WD 232)
15. Center Page Contents Vertically (WD 232)
16. Save a Document (WD 234)
17. Insert a Next Page Section Break (WD 236)
18. Change Page Alignment of a Section (WD 237)
19. Insert a Word Document into an Open Document (WD 238)
20. Save an Active Document with a New File Name (WD 240)
21. Print Specific Pages in a Document (WD 241)
22. Delete a Page Break (WD 244)
23. Cut Text (WD 245)
24. Go To a Section (WD 246)
25. Create a Header Different from the Previous Section Header (WD 247)
26. Change Page Number Format and Page Number Differently in a Section (WD 248)
27. Create a Footer Different from the Previous Section Footer (WD 249)
28. Delete a Column (WD 250)
29. Add a Row and Merge Cells (WD 251)
30. Enter and Format Text in a Table Cell (WD 252)
31. Split Cells (WD 253)
32. Add a Row to the End of a Table (WD 253)
33. Sum Columns in a Table (WD 254)
34. AutoFormat a Table (WD 255)
35. Center a Table (WD 256)
36. Right-Align Cell Contents (WD 256)
37. Select Nonadjacent Text (WD 257)
38. Superscript Selected Characters (WD 258)
39. Chart a Table (WD 259)
40. Move Legend Placement in a Chart (WD 261)
41. Resize a Chart (WD 262)
42. Change the Chart Type (WD 262)
43. Exit Graph and Return to Word (WD 263)
44. Format a Chart Object (WD 264)
45. Find a Format (WD 266)
46. Create a Character Style (WD 268)
47. Apply a Character Style (WD 269)
48. Add Picture Bullets to a List (WD 270)
49. Draw an Empty Table (WD 272)
50. Erase Lines in a Table (WD 274)
51. Distribute Rows Evenly (WD 274)
52. Distribute Columns Evenly (WD 275)
53. Single-Space Table Contents (WD 275)
54. Enter Data into a Table (WD 276)
55. Vertically Display Text in a Cell (WD 276)
56. Format Table Text (WD 277)
57. Shade Table Cells (WD 277)
58. Format the Table Title (WD 278)
59. Change Row Height (WD 278)
60. Align Data in Cells (WD 279)
61. Add a Blank Line Above a Paragraph (WD 280)
62. Create a Text Watermark (WD 281)
63. Print Preview a Document (WD 282)
64. Check Spelling, Save, and Print the Document (WD 282)
65. Reveal Formatting (WD 283)
66. Quit Word (WD 284)

Learn It Online

Instructions: To complete the Learn It Online exercises, start your browser, click the Address bar, and then enter the Web address `scsite.com/wd2003/learn`. When the Word 2003 Learn It Online page is displayed, follow the instructions in the exercises below. Each exercise has instructions for printing your results, either for your own records or for submission to your instructor.

1 Project Reinforcement TF, MC, and SA

Below Word Project 4, click the Project Reinforcement link. Print the quiz by clicking Print on the File menu for each page. Answer each question.

2 Flash Cards

Below Word Project 4, click the Flash Cards link and read the instructions. Type 20 (or a number specified by your instructor) in the Number of playing cards text box, type your name in the Enter your Name text box, and then click the Flip Card button. When the flash card is displayed, read the question and then click the ANSWER box arrow to select an answer. Flip through Flash Cards. If your score is 15 (75%) correct or greater, click Print on the File menu to print your results. If your score is less than 15 (75%) correct, then redo this exercise by clicking the Replay button.

3 Practice Test

Below Word Project 4, click the Practice Test link. Answer each question, enter your first and last name at the bottom of the page, and then click the Grade Test button. When the graded practice test is displayed on your screen, click Print on the File menu to print a hard copy. Continue to take practice tests until you score 80% or better.

4 Who Wants To Be a Computer Genius?

Below Word Project 4, click the Computer Genius link. Read the instructions, enter your first and last name at the bottom of the page, and then click the PLAY button. When your score is displayed, click the PRINT RESULTS link to print a hard copy.

5 Wheel of Terms

Below Word Project 4, click the Wheel of Terms link. Read the instructions, and then enter your first and last name and your school name. Click the PLAY button. When your score is displayed, right-click the score and then click Print on the shortcut menu to print a hard copy.

6 Crossword Puzzle Challenge

Below Word Project 4, click the Crossword Puzzle Challenge link. Read the instructions, and then enter your first and last name. Click the SUBMIT button. Work the crossword puzzle. When you are finished, click the Submit button. When the crossword puzzle is redisplayed, click the Print Puzzle button to print a hard copy.

7 Tips and Tricks

Below Word Project 4, click the Tips and Tricks link. Click a topic that pertains to Project 4. Right-click the information and then click Print on the shortcut menu. Construct a brief example of what the information relates to in Word to confirm you understand how to use the tip or trick.

8 Newsgroups

Below Word Project 4, click the Newsgroups link. Click a topic that pertains to Project 4. Print three comments.

9 Expanding Your Horizons

Below Word Project 4, click the Articles for Microsoft Word link. Click a topic that pertains to Project 4. Print the information. Construct a brief example of what the information relates to in Word to confirm you understand the contents of the article.

10 Search Sleuth

Below Word Project 4, click the Search Sleuth link. To search for a term that pertains to this project, select a term below the Project 4 title and then use the Google search engine at google.com (or any major search engine) to display and print two Web pages that present information on the term.

11 Word Online Training

Below Word Project 4, click the Word Online Training link. When your browser displays the Microsoft Office Online Web page, click the Word link. Click one of the Word courses that covers one or more of the objectives listed at the beginning of the project on page WD 218. Print the first page of the course before stepping through it.

12 Office Marketplace

Below Word Project 4, click the Office Marketplace link. When your browser displays the Microsoft Office Online Web page, click the Office Marketplace link. Click a topic that relates to Word. Print the first page.

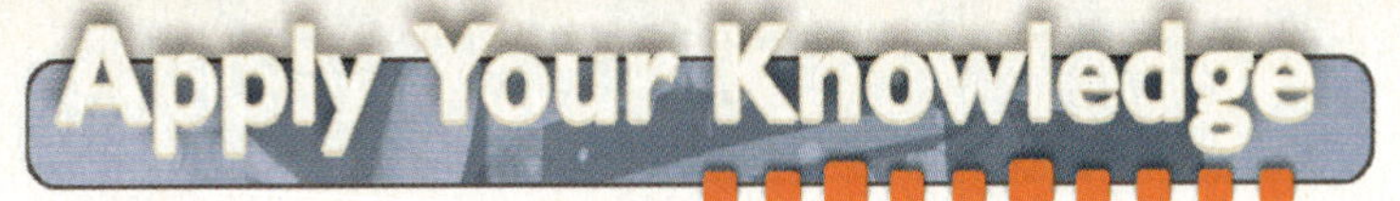

1 Working with Complex Tables

Instructions: Start Word. Open the document, Apply 4-1 Meridian Profits Report, on the Data Disk. If you did not download the Data Disk, see the inside back cover for instructions for downloading the Data Disk or see your instructor.

The document contains a table created with the Draw Table feature. You are to modify the table so it looks like Figure 4-95.

Meridian Sports Leagues					
Yearly Profits by Season					
		Concessions	Fund-raisers	Raffle	Total
Spring	Baseball	$2,504.35	$1,255.55	$1,480.00	**$5,239.90**
	Soccer	$1,753.87	$982.40	$1,199.00	**$3,935.27**
Fall	Football	$3,004.25	$2,125.83	$2,860.00	**$7,990.08**
	Soccer	$1,512.65	$876.07	$995.00	**$3,383.72**
Total Yearly Sales		**$8,775.12**	**$5,239.85**	**$6,534.00**	**$20,548.97**

FIGURE 4-95

Perform the following tasks.

1. Use the Split Cells command or the Split Cells button on the Tables and Borders toolbar to split the first row into two rows (one column). In the new cell below the company title, type `Yearly Profits by Season` as the subtitle.
2. Select the cell containing the title, Meridian Sports Leagues. Center it, bold it, change its font size to 28, and change its font color to brown. Shade the cell in the color light orange.
3. Select the row containing the subtitle, Yearly Profits by Season. Center and bold the subtitle. Change the font color to brown.
4. Select the cell containing the label, Total Yearly Sales, and the cell immediately to its right. Use the Merge Cells command or the Merge Cells button on the Tables and Borders toolbar to merge the two cells into a single cell. Bold the text in the cell. Center align the text in the cell.

(continued)

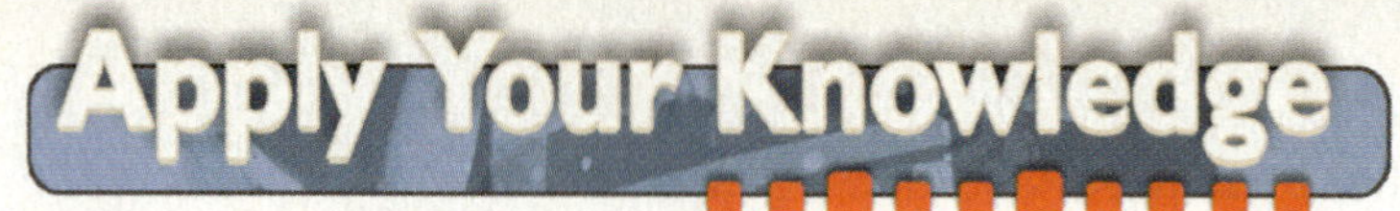

Working with Complex Tables *(continued)*

5. Select the cells containing the row headings, Spring and Fall. Use the Change Text Direction button on the Tables and Borders toolbar to position the text vertically from bottom to top. Change the alignment of these two cells to Align Center.
6. Click in the table to remove the selection. Drag the left edge of the table rightward to make the cells containing Spring and Fall narrower. The cell containing the words, Total Yearly Sales, should fit on one line (that is, it should not wrap).
7. Select the last four columns containing Concessions, Fund-raisers, Raffle, and Total. Use the Distribute Columns Evenly button on the Tables and Borders toolbar to make the columns the same widths.
8. Center the entire table across the width of the page.
9. Use the AutoSum button on the Tables and Borders toolbar to place totals in the bottom row for the concessions, fund-raisers, and raffle columns.
10. Use the AutoSum button on the Tables and Borders toolbar to place totals in the right column. Start in the bottom-right cell and work your way up the table. If your totals are incorrect, click Table on the menu bar, click Formula, be sure the formula is =SUM(LEFT) and then click the OK button.
11. Align center the cells containing the column headings, Concessions, Fund-raisers, Raffle, and Total.
12. Align center right the cells containing numbers.
13. Align center left the cells containing these labels: Baseball, Soccer, Football, Soccer, and Total Yearly Sales.
14. Select the rows below the subtitle, Yearly Profits by Season, and distribute the rows evenly.
15. Bold the numbers in the last row and also in the rightmost column.
16. Click File on the menu bar and then click Save As. Use the file name, Apply 4-1 Revised Meridian Profits Report.
17. Print the revised document.
18. Position the insertion point in the first row of the table. Display the Reveal Formatting task pane. On your printout, write down all the formatting assigned to this row.
19. Select the table and then clear formatting. Write down the purpose of the Clear Formatting command. Undo the clear formatting and then save the file again.

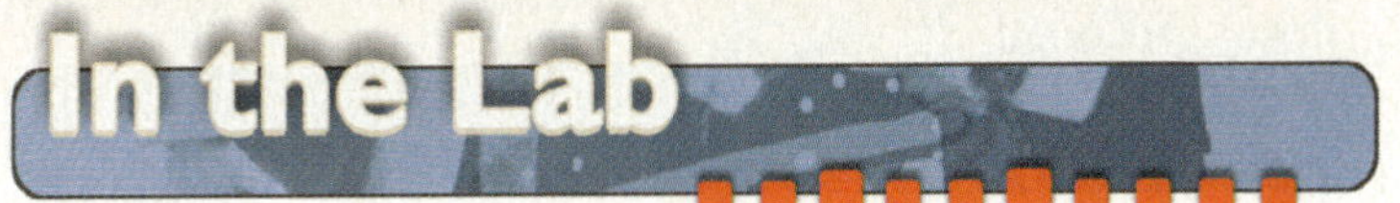

1 Creating a Proposal that Uses the Draw Table Feature

Problem: The owner of the Costume Barn has hired you to prepare a sales proposal describing the facility (Figures 4-96a and 4-96b on the next page), which will be mailed to all community residents.

Instructions:

1. Create the title page as shown in Figure 4-96a. Be sure to resize the clip art; change the fonts, font sizes, font colors, and font effects; and include the border, paragraph shading and indentation, and expanded character spacing, as indicated in the figure.
2. Center the contents of the title page vertically. Insert a next page section break. Clear formatting. Change the vertical alignment for the second section to top. Adjust line spacing to double.

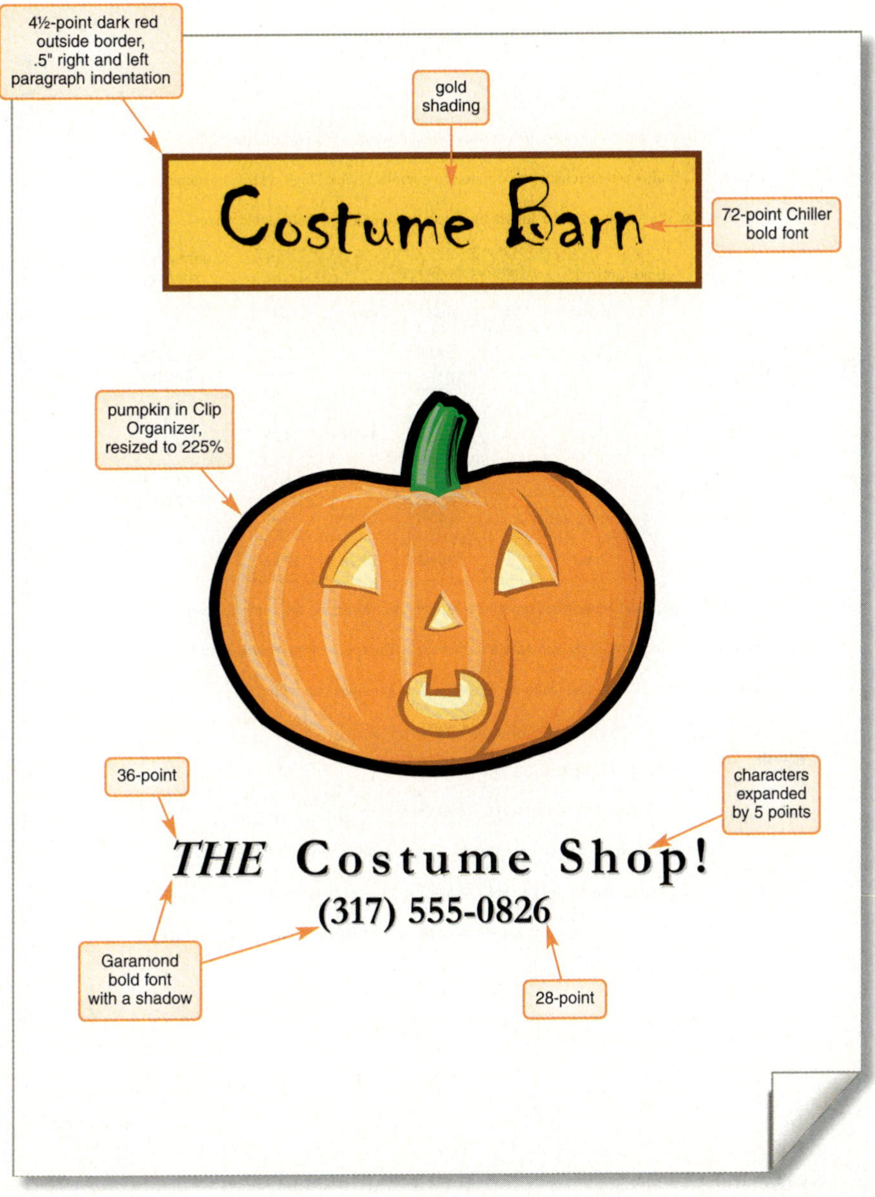

FIGURE 4-96a

(continued)

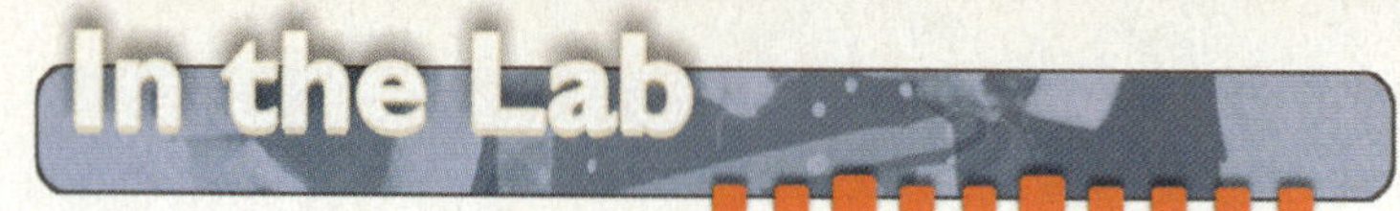

Creating a Proposal that Uses the Draw Table Feature *(continued)*

3. Type the body of the proposal as shown in Figure 4-96b.
   (a) Create the table with the Draw Table feature. Distribute rows evenly in the table. Center the table. Single-space the contents of the table. Bold and change the font color of text in the table as specified in the figure. Change the direction of the row titles, Vampire and Jester, and then align center the titles. Change the alignment of the title and column headings to align center; the second column to align center left; and the cells with numbers to align center right. Shade the table cells as specified in the figure.
   (b) The body of the proposal has a list with yellow picture bullets.
   (c) Create a character style of 12-point Arial brown bold characters. Apply the character style to the text in the bulleted list.
4. Check the spelling. Save the document with Lab 4-1 Costume Barn Proposal as the file name. View and print the document in print preview.

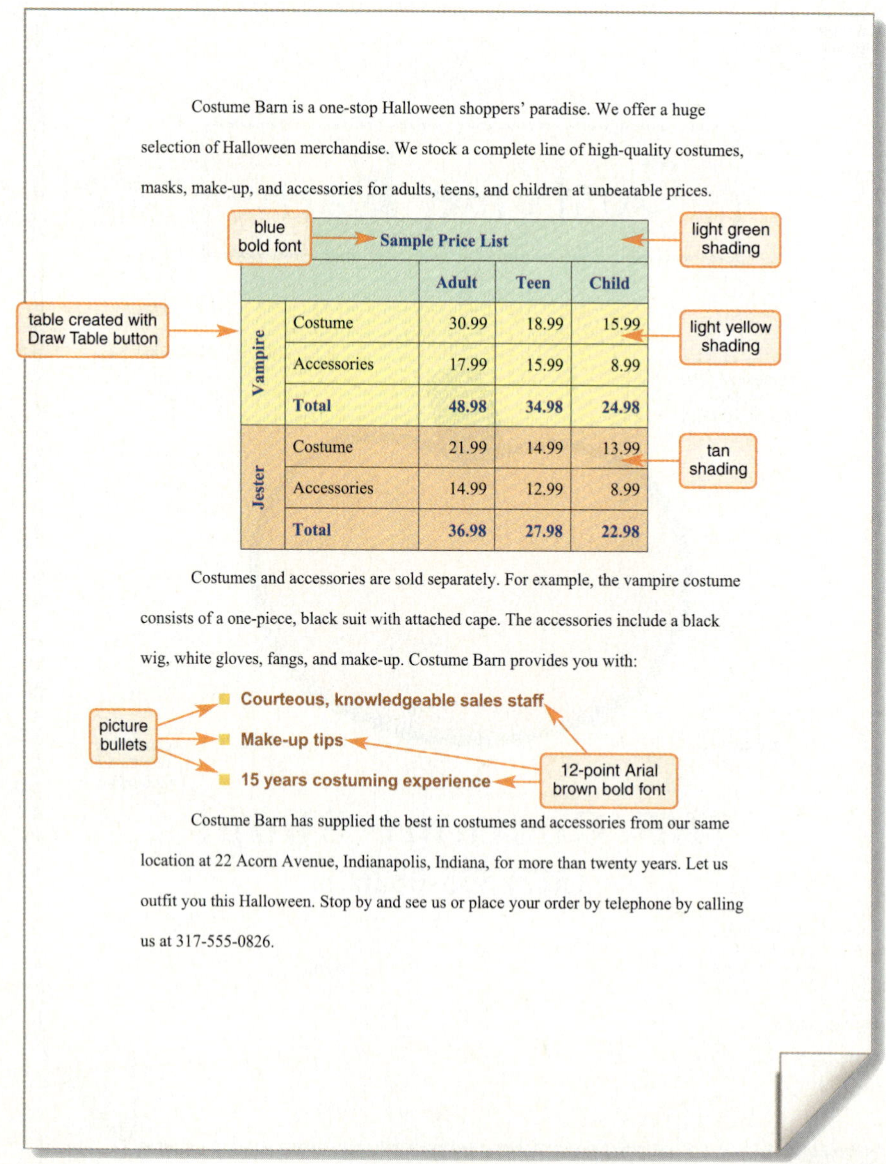

Costume Barn is a one-stop Halloween shoppers' paradise. We offer a huge selection of Halloween merchandise. We stock a complete line of high-quality costumes, masks, make-up, and accessories for adults, teens, and children at unbeatable prices.

Sample Price List				
		Adult	Teen	Child
Vampire	Costume	30.99	18.99	15.99
	Accessories	17.99	15.99	8.99
	Total	**48.98**	**34.98**	**24.98**
Jester	Costume	21.99	14.99	13.99
	Accessories	14.99	12.99	8.99
	Total	**36.98**	**27.98**	**22.98**

Costumes and accessories are sold separately. For example, the vampire costume consists of a one-piece, black suit with attached cape. The accessories include a black wig, white gloves, fangs, and make-up. Costume Barn provides you with:

- **Courteous, knowledgeable sales staff**
- **Make-up tips**
- **15 years costuming experience**

Costume Barn has supplied the best in costumes and accessories from our same location at 22 Acorn Avenue, Indianapolis, Indiana, for more than twenty years. Let us outfit you this Halloween. Stop by and see us or place your order by telephone by calling us at 317-555-0826.

FIGURE 4-96b

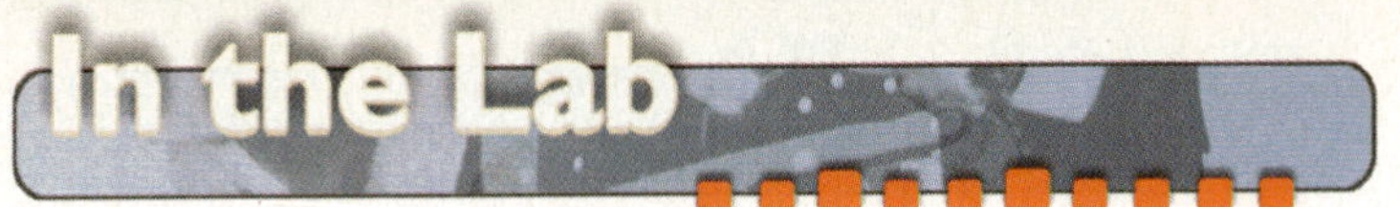

2 Creating a Proposal that Contains Clip Art from the Web and a Chart

Problem: Your neighbor owns Peerless Office Rentals and has hired you to create a sales proposal for her business. You develop the proposal shown in Figures 4-97a and 4-97b on the next page.

Instructions:

1. Create the title page as shown in Figure 4-97a. Be sure to resize the clip art; change the fonts, font sizes, font colors, and font effects; and include the borders, paragraph shading and indentation, and expanded character spacing, as indicated in the figure. Use the keyword, office buildings, to locate the clip art image, which is located on the Web. If you do not have access to the Web, you can insert the file (file name j0234930.wmf) from the Data Disk. If you did not download the Data Disk, see the inside back cover for instructions for downloading the Data Disk or see your instructor.
2. Center the contents of the title page vertically. Insert a next page section break. Clear formatting. Change the vertical alignment for the second section to top. Adjust line spacing to double.
3. Create the body of the proposal as shown in Figure 4-97b.
   (a) Use the Insert Table button to create the table. Use the Table AutoFormat dialog box to format the table as specified in the figure. Center the title, column headings, and numbers. Center the table between the page margins. Distribute the rows evenly.
   (b) Chart the table. Resize the chart so it is wider. Change the chart type to cylinder. Move the legend. Add a ½-point indigo outline around the chart. Insert a blank line above the chart.
   (c) Add picture bullets to the list at the end of the page. Create a character style of 12-point Trebuchet MS bold indigo characters. Apply the character style to the text in the bulleted list.

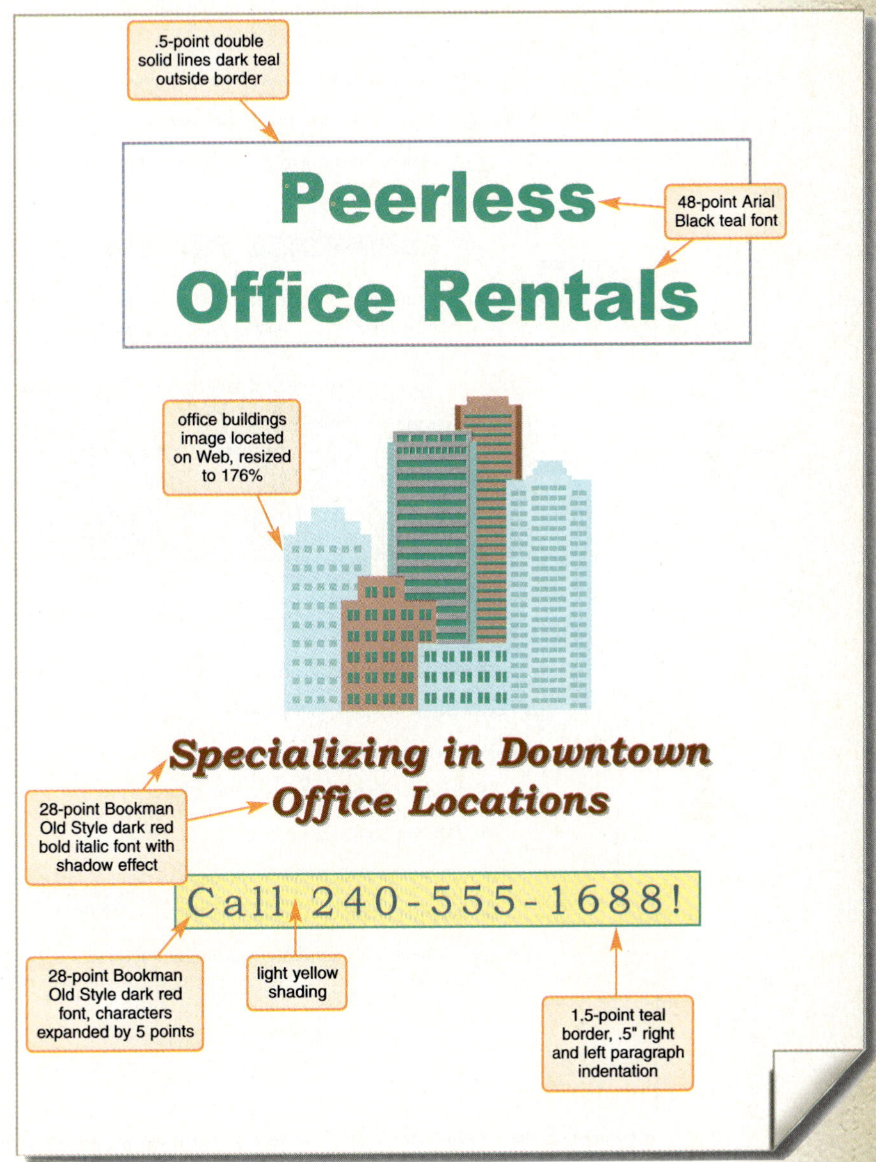

FIGURE 4-97a

(continued)

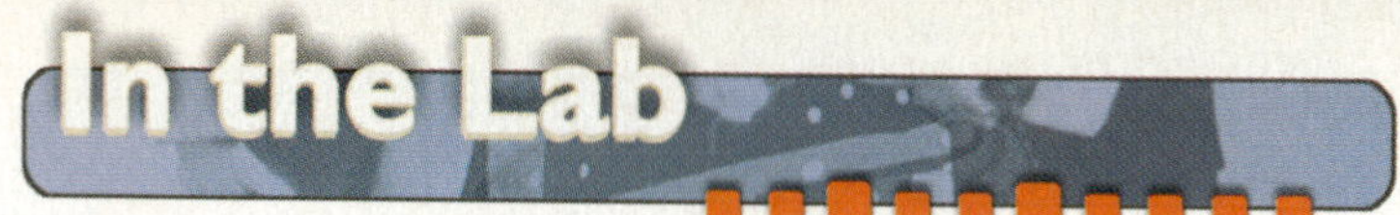

Creating a Proposal that Contains Clip Art from the Web and a Chart *(continued)*

4. Check the spelling. Save the document with Lab 4-2 Office Rentals Proposal as the file name. View and print the document in print preview.

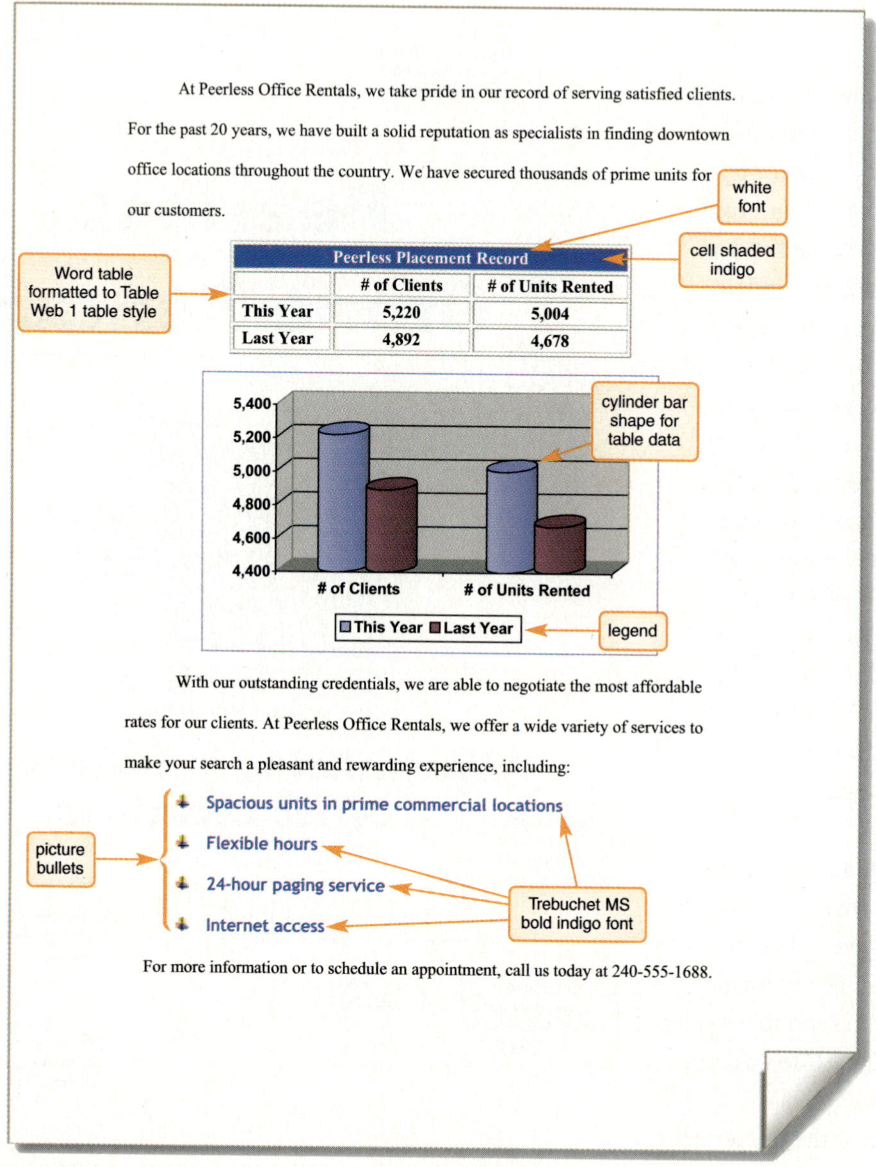

At Peerless Office Rentals, we take pride in our record of serving satisfied clients. For the past 20 years, we have built a solid reputation as specialists in finding downtown office locations throughout the country. We have secured thousands of prime units for our customers.

Peerless Placement Record		
	# of Clients	# of Units Rented
This Year	5,220	5,004
Last Year	4,892	4,678

With our outstanding credentials, we are able to negotiate the most affordable rates for our clients. At Peerless Office Rentals, we offer a wide variety of services to make your search a pleasant and rewarding experience, including:

- Spacious units in prime commercial locations
- Flexible hours
- 24-hour paging service
- Internet access

For more information or to schedule an appointment, call us today at 240-555-1688.

FIGURE 4-97b

3 Enhancing a Draft of a Proposal

Problem: You work for the transportation director at Centerton School Corporation. You create a title page (Figure 4-98a) for an informal sales proposal that your boss has drafted (Figure 4-98b on page WD 294) to be sent to the school board. You decide to add picture bullets, another table, a chart, and a watermark to the proposal.

This lab uses the Data Disk. If you did not download the Data Disk, see the inside back cover for instructions for downloading the Data Disk or see your instructor.

In the Lab

Instructions:

1. Create the title page as shown in Figure 4-98a. ***Hint:*** Use the Font dialog box to apply the decorative underline in color and the emboss and small caps effects.
2. Center the contents of the title page vertically. Insert a next page section break. Clear formatting. Insert the draft of the body of the proposal below the title page using the File command on the Insert menu. The draft is called Lab 4-3 Bus Route Draft on the Data Disk (shown in Figure 4-98b on the next page). Be sure to change the vertical alignment to top for section 2.
3. On the first page of the body of the draft, do the following:
   (a) Cut the first line of text in the draft.
   (b) Delete the page break at the bottom of the first page.
   (c) Below the second paragraph, use the Draw Table button to create a table that is similar to the one below at right. Format the table titles in bold, shade important cells, add a colorful border around the table, align data in the cells as shown, and expand the word, Total, by 10 points.
   (d) Change the style of bullet characters in the list to picture bullets.
   (e) Use the Find and Replace dialog box to find the format 14-point Britannic Bold dark red characters. Create a character style for this format. Apply the character style to the rest of the text in the bulleted list.
4. Change the formatting of the paragraph that follows the bulleted list in Step 3(d) to Keep lines together and Page break before. ***Hint:*** Use Help to search for the text, control pagination, to determine how to keep lines together and page break before a paragraph.
5. Set all paragraph formatting in the entire document so that no widows or orphans occur. ***Hint:*** Use Help to search for the text, control pagination, to determine how to control widows and orphans.

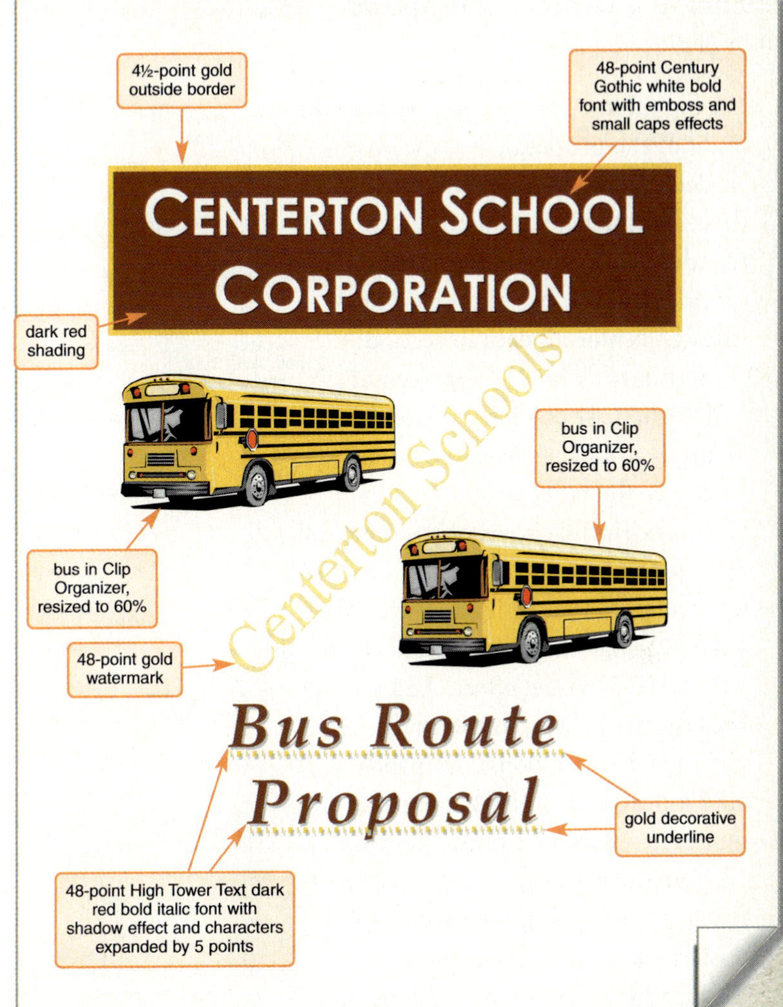

FIGURE 4-98a

CENTERTON SCHOOLS ENROLLMENT			
	School	Current Enrollment	Projected Enrollment
Bus 4 & 14	Pleasant Elementary	101	125
	North Elementary	85	100
Bus 8, 11, 17	Center Elementary	94	105
	West Elementary	80	120
	Total	360	450

(continued)

In the Lab

Enhancing a Draft of a Proposal

(continued)

6. On the table on the second page of the body of the proposal,
   (a) delete the duplicate row for Bus 8
   (b) delete the blank column
   (c) add a row to the table that totals the values in the two right columns
   (d) align center all data in second and third columns; align center left the first column of data
   (e) apply a table style to the table
   (f) center the table
7. Chart the first six rows of the table (all but the total row). Enlarge the chart so it is wider. Move the legend below the chart. Change the chart type to clustered bar with 3-D visual effect. Add the title, Breakdown by Bus, to the chart. ***Hint:*** Use the Chart Options command.
8. Add a header containing the page number to section 2 of the proposal. Change the starting page number to 1. Format the page number so it has dashes on each side (e.g., -1-).
9. Add a footer containing the words, Centerton Schools – Excellence, to section 2 of the proposal.
10. Create a text watermark on the proposal that contains the words, Centerton Schools, using 48-point gold font.
11. Modify the footer so it includes the words, A Tradition of, to the left of the word, Excellence.
12. Make any other formatting changes you feel would improve the document.
13. Save the active document with the file name, Lab 4-3 Bus Route Proposal.
14. View and print the document in print preview.
15. Position the insertion point in the first line of the title page. Display the Reveal Formatting task pane. On your printout, write down all formatting assigned to this paragraph.

printout of Bus Route Draft file
header to contain page number formatted as -1-
cut this text
****DRAFT – NEED TO FINISH****
Our school district has grown enormously over the last five years. Due to new neighborhoods being built each year, our enrollment has skyrocketed. Next year, a projected 75 to 100 new students will be placed in our schools. Most impacted are the elementary schools. Two additional buses need to be acquired to accommodate this influx of riders.
The following table shows current and projected enrollment for each of our four elementary schools, as well as the buses assigned:
location for table using Draw Table feature
Currently, five buses transport the students in our district each day, with pick-up and drop-off service provided for both morning and afternoon kindergarten students. These buses are crowded; most have three students in each seat. This situation, while within safety guidelines, is not ideal. Adding the two new buses will:
• Enhance student safety
character style to be created for this text and applied to rest of bulleted list text
• Increase student comfort
• Minimize driver distraction
• Accommodate future ridership increases
• Ensure students arrive on time
bullet style to be changed to picture bullets
The table below shows the current number of seats with two and three children assigned. These figures take into account the fact that some students walk to school and others have private transportation (family cars or day care vans).
remove page break
footer to contain words, Centerton Schools - A Tradition of Excellence
blank column to be removed
header to contain page number formatted as -2-

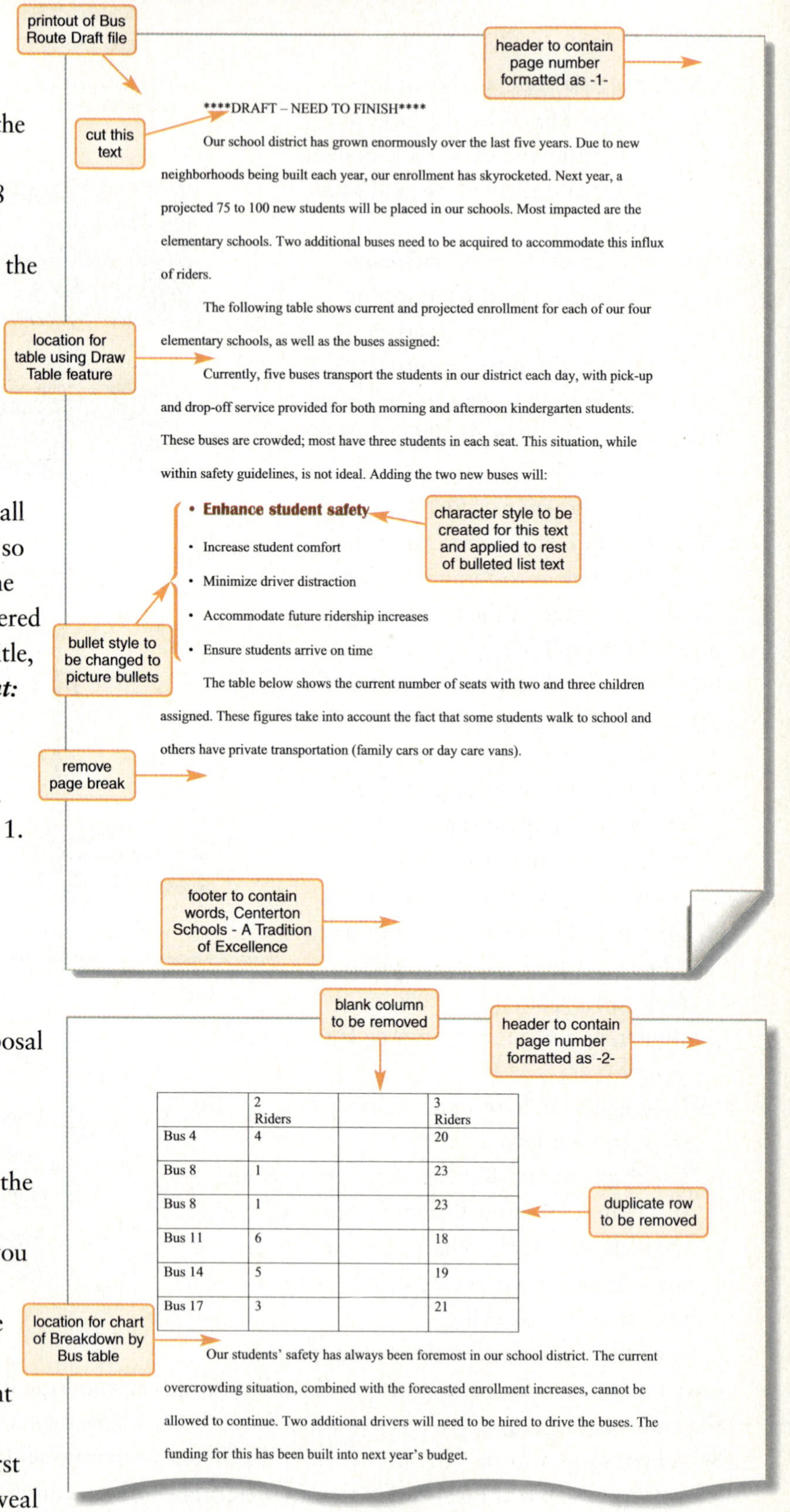

	2 Riders		3 Riders
Bus 4	4		20
Bus 8	1		23
Bus 8	1		23
Bus 11	6		18
Bus 14	5		19
Bus 17	3		21

duplicate row to be removed
location for chart of Breakdown by Bus table
Our students' safety has always been foremost in our school district. The current overcrowding situation, combined with the forecasted enrollment increases, cannot be allowed to continue. Two additional drivers will need to be hired to drive the buses. The funding for this has been built into next year's budget.

FIGURE 4-98b

Cases and Places

The difficulty of these case studies varies:
■ are the least difficult and ■■ are more difficult. The last exercise is a group exercise.

1 ■ As assistant to the owner of Happy Homes, you have been assigned the task of preparing a sales proposal that sells the business to prospective customers. The title page is to contain the name, Happy Homes, followed by an appropriate graphic, and then the slogan, A Clean House Is a Happy Home! The body of the proposal should contain the following: first paragraph — We know how busy you are. Between your job, family, and appointments, you barely have time for yourself, let alone the drudgery of cleaning your house. Let Happy Homes take care of your cleaning needs. We offer:, list with picture bullets — Bonded, licensed housekeepers; Light or heavy cleaning; Daily, weekly, or monthly service; Reasonable rates; next paragraph — We can clean your home and restore its sparkle, letting you devote your time to better projects. A sample price list follows:; the data for the table is shown in the table at right; paragraph below table — Standard service includes vacuuming; dusting; bathroom and kitchen cleaning; and floor mopping. Deluxe service provides additional services, including linen changes, window cleaning, and wall washing. We also perform one-time cleaning jobs, such as spring cleaning, pre-event cleaning, etc.; last paragraph – Whether you need us once a week or just once before your big party, call us to arrange an appointment time. Make your life easier and call Happy Homes today!

All prices weekly

SQUARE FEET	STANDARD SERVICE	DELUXE SERVICE
1000	$25.00	$40.00
1500	35.00	50.00
2000	50.00	75.00
3000	90.00	125.00

2 ■■ Your boss at Greenfield Lawns has asked you to design a sales proposal that sells his business. He plans to post the proposal around the community and mail to local residents and businesses. Create a proposal that discusses various types of lawn treatments (grub and pest control, weed control, seeding and sodding, aeration, and fertilizer and nutrients). The proposal also should discuss the preferred customer discount program that is tailored to the customer – as long as the customer commits to one year of lawn care by Greenfield Lawns. For example, the regular price of weed control is $55.00 and the preferred customer price is $42.25; regular price of grub and pest control is $48.00 and the preferred customer price is $31.95; regular price of fertilizer and nutrients is $43.00 and the preferred customer price is $30.00. Greenfield Lawns also has a 100 percent satisfaction guarantee. The company slogan is "A Greener Lawn – Guaranteed!" Place the company name, an appropriate graphic, and the company slogan on the title page. Be sure the body of the proposal includes the following items: a list with picture bullets, a table with totals, a chart, a watermark, a header with a formatted page number, and a footer.

Cases and Places

3 Your boss at RSM Industries has asked you to design a planning proposal that outlines a utility upgrade. Create a proposal using the following pertinent information. The plant is powered by an on-site power house, which provides and generates all utilities (steam, electricity, gas, water treating, and sewer). Excess needs of utilities are purchased from CTM Utilities. Lately, RSM is purchasing as much as it is generating. It needs to upgrade the following equipment to more effectively manage its energy needs: chillers, boilers, co-gen, turbines, automated controls, and water treating facility. The upgrade will allow RSM to combat rising utility costs. For example, current gas prices are $25,000, proposed prices with upgrade is $12,900; current electric prices are $19,998, proposed prices are $10,500; current water prices are $7,500, proposed prices are $4,500. Without the upgrade, RSM either will reduce its profit margin or pass the cost onto its customers. Place the company name, an appropriate graphic, and the name of the proposal on the title page. Be sure the body of the proposal includes the following items: a list with picture bullets, a table with totals, a chart, a watermark, a header with a formatted page number, and a footer.

4 As an assistant at Market Solutions, Inc., you have been asked to design a research proposal that outlines a computer system upgrade. Create a proposal that discusses that the current problems with employees and customers related to the existing computer system: complaints about late mailings, slow order processing, and poor inventory control. Upgrading will enable Market Solutions to network workstations, access the Internet, process orders faster, respond to customers quicker, maintain accurate inventory data, provide a Web site for customer inquiries, reduce redundant data, and increase customer satisfaction. Currently, 60 hours a week are spent on hardware maintenance, 25 hours on software queries, and 105 hours on customer queries. With the new system, these numbers reduce to 10, 5, and 10, respectively. The cost of this project will be negligible compared with the expected gain in benefits. Place the company name, an appropriate graphic, and the name of the proposal on the title page. Be sure the body of the proposal includes the following items: a list with picture bullets, a table with totals, a chart, a watermark, a header with a formatted page number, and a footer.

5 **Working Together** Your school provides several facilities and services such as registration, advising, cafeteria, day care, computer lab, career development, fitness center, library, bookstore, parking, and a tutoring center. Your team is to select an item from this list, or another facility or service that the group feels needs improvement at your school. The team is to develop a planning proposal that could be submitted to the Dean of Students. Visit the library or surf the Internet for guidelines about preparing a planning proposal. Team members can divide work as follows: create an appropriate title page, give details about the current situation, identify the problems, explain how the problems can be solved, identify any costs associated with the proposed solutions, and recommend a course(s) of action the school could take to improve the situation. Modify the default font settings to a font, font size, font style(s), font color, and effects to which the entire team agrees upon. Be sure the body of the proposal includes the following items: a list with picture bullets, a table, a chart, a header with a formatted page number, a footer, and a watermark.

MICROSOFT Office Word 2003

Generating Form Letters, Mailing Labels, and Directories

PROJECT 5

CASE PERSPECTIVE

Located in the popular destination of Gettysburg, Pennsylvania, River Run Campground is a favorite vacation spot for travelers from around the country. In addition to its scenic beauty, the main attraction is the historic battlefield of Gettysburg situated 15 minutes from the campground.

On Monday, you started working part-time for Tom and Deanna Rosatti, the campground's owners. The job allows you to meet many new people and obtain real-world computer experience. Your responsibilities include responding to e-mail questions, maintaining the campground Web site, and handling all correspondence.

The first day, you realize that you can simplify the correspondence procedures. Currently, each time a vacationer reserves a campsite, the owners type a confirmation letter. Instead of typing a separate letter for each reservation, you want to use Word to create a form letter because so much of the information is identical. To personalize each letter, you will need to create a separate file, called a data source, that contains the names and addresses of the guests as they make their reservations. Then, you will merge the guest data in the data source with the form letter so an individual letter prints for each guest. Each form letter should include the type of site, the deposit amount, and the arrival date. The deposit for a water and electric site is $23.50; tent sites require a deposit of $11.00.

As you read through this project, you will learn how to use Word to create and generate form letters, mailing labels, and a directory.

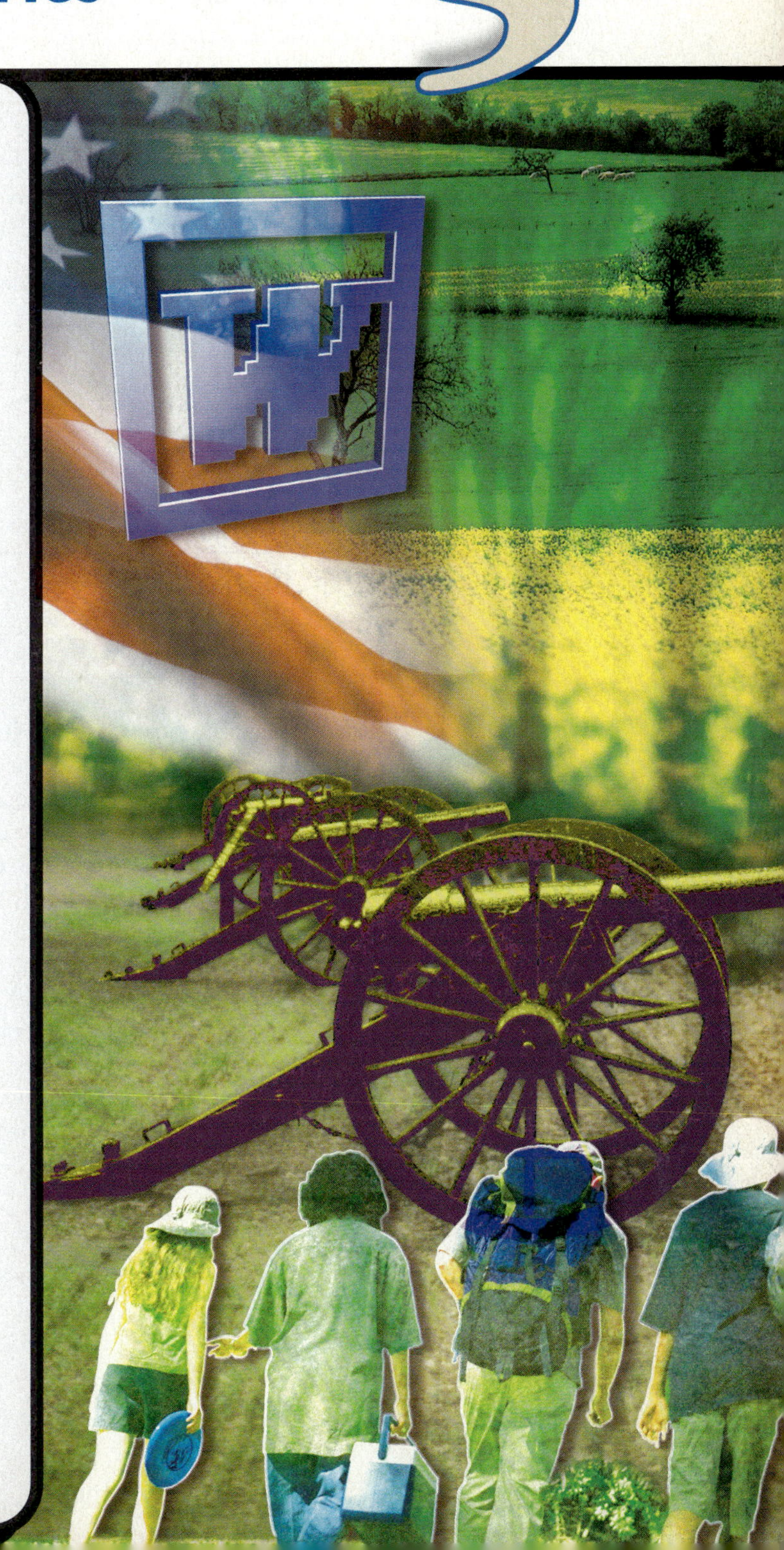

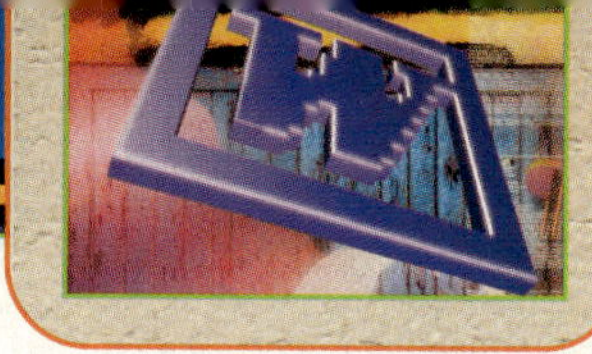

MICROSOFT Office Word 2003

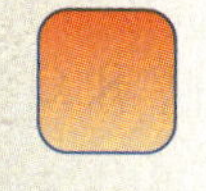

Generating Form Letters, Mailing Labels, and Directories

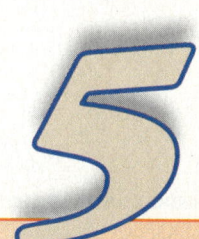

PROJECT 5

Objectives

You will have mastered the material in this project when you can:

- Explain the merge process
- Use the Mail Merge task pane and the Mail Merge toolbar
- Use a letter template
- Insert and format an AutoShape on a drawing canvas
- Create and edit a data source
- Insert and edit merge fields in a main document
- Use an IF field in a main document
- Create an outline numbered list
- Merge and print form letters
- Sort data records
- Address and print mailing labels and envelopes
- Merge all data records to a directory
- Change page orientation
- Modify table properties

Introduction

Individuals and business people are more likely to open and read a personalized letter than a letter addressed as Dear Sir, Dear Madam, or To Whom It May Concern. Typing individual personalized letters, though, can be a time-consuming task. Thus, Word provides the capability of creating a form letter, which is an easy way to generate mass mailings of personalized letters. The basic content of a group of form letters is similar. Items such as name, address, city, state, and ZIP code, however, vary from one letter to the next. With Word, you easily can address and print mailing labels or envelopes for the form letters.

Both business and personal correspondence regularly uses form letters to communicate via the postal service or e-mail with groups of people. **Business form letters** include announcements of sales to customers, confirmation letters (Figure 5-1), or notices of benefits to employees. **Personal form letters** include letters of application for a job or invitations to participate in a sweepstakes giveaway.

(a) Main Document for the Form Letter

(b) Data Source

Title	First Name	Last Name	Address Line 1	Address Line 2	City	State	ZIP Code	Site Type	Reservation Date	Number of Nights
Mr.	Jonah	Weinberg	22 Fifth Avenue		Auburn	AL	36830	water and electric	September 16	two
Ms.	Shannon	Murray	33099 Clark Street	Apt. D	Maple Park	IL	60151	tent	September 10	three
Mr.	Tyrone	Davis	P.O. Box 45	4430 Fifth Avenue	Dover	FL	33527	water and electric	September 10	four
Mrs.	Allison	Popovich	33 Parker Road		Memphis	TN	38101	tent	September 9	two
Dr.	Mae	Ling	13239 Oak Street		Hammond	IN	46323	water and electric	September 16	two

River
Camp
placeholder for address fields
16 August 2005
«AddressBlock»
placeholder for salutation fields
merge fields
IF field
«GreetingLine»
We would like to thank you for reserving a «Site_Type» site for «Number_of_Nights» nights at our campground. To guarantee your reservation, we must receive a deposit of « IF Site_Type = "tent" "$11.00" "$23.50" » one week before your arrival date of «Reservation_Date» at the address shown at the bottom of this letter.
Our goal is to make your stay comfortable and enjoyable. The facilities and recreational activities at our campground continue to receive the highest ratings from Camping Today magazine.
1) Facilities
a) Spotless restrooms and showers
b) Two laundry rooms
c) Groceries and snack bar
d) Modem, telephone, and CATV hookup at each site
2) Recreational Activities
a) Heated swimming pool
b) Recreation hall and game room
c) Freshwater fishing and boat rental
d) Horseback riding
outline numbered list
We look forward to making your stay with us a memorable cam
Sincerely,
Tom and Dea
Owners
form letter 1
campground name in banner shape
River Run Campground
vacationer name and address in first data record
16 August 2005
Mr. Jonah Weinberg
22 Fifth Avenue
Auburn, AL 36830
title and last name in first data record
Dear Mr. Weinberg:
We would like to thank you for reserving a water and electric site for two nights at our campground. To guarantee your reservation, we must receive a deposit of $23.50 one week before your arrival date of September 16 at the address shown at the bottom of this letter.
Our goal is to make your stay comfortable and enjoyable. The facilities and recreational activities at our campground continue to receive the highest ratings from Camping Today magazine.
deposit is $23.50 because site type is water and electric
1) Facilities
a) Spotless restrooms and showers
b) Two laundry rooms
c) Groceries and snack bar
d) Modem, telephone, and CATV hookup at each site
2) Recreational Activities
a) Heated swimming pool
b) Recreation hall and game room
c) Freshwater fishing and boat rental
d) Horseback riding
We look forward to making your stay with us a memorable camping adventure.
Sincerely,
Tom and Deanna Rosatti
Owners
13 KNOB ROAD • GETTYSBURG, PA • 17325
PHONE: 717-555-6543 • FAX: 717-555-6544
River Run
Campgrou
vacationer name and address in second data record
16 August 2005
Ms. Shannon Murray
33099 Clark Street
Apt. D
Maple Park, IL 60151
title and last name in second data record
Dear Ms. Murray:
We would like to thank you for reserving a tent site for three
guarantee your reservation, we must receive a deposit of $11.00 one
September 10 at the address shown at the bottom of this letter.
Our goal is to make your stay comfortable and enjoyable. The fac
at our campground continue to receive the highest ratings from Campi
deposit is $11.00 because site type is tent
1) Facilities
a) Spotless restrooms and showers
b) Two laundry rooms
c) Groceries and snack bar
d) Modem, telephone, and CATV hookup at each site
2) Recreational Activities
a) Heated swimming pool
b) Recreation hall and game room
c) Freshwater fishing and boat rental
d) Horseback riding
We look forward to making your stay with us a memorable camping adventure.
Sincerely,
form letter 2
form letter 3
form letter 4
form letter 5

(c) Form Letters

FIGURE 5-1

More About

Writing Letters

For more information about writing letters, visit the Word 2003 More About Web page (scsite.com/wd2003/more) and then click Writing Letters.

Project Five — Form Letters, Mailing Labels, and Directories

Project 5 illustrates how to create a business form letter and address and print corresponding mailing labels. The form letter is sent to future campground guests, confirming their reservation. Each form letter also identifies the type of site the vacationer reserved and specifies the deposit amount due. The type of site determines the deposit required.

The process of generating form letters involves creating a main document for the form letter and a data source, and then merging, or *blending*, the two together into a series of individual letters as shown in Figure 5-1 on the previous page.

Merging is the process of combining the contents of a data source with a main document. A **main document** contains the constant, or unchanging, text, punctuation, spaces, and graphics. In Figure 5-1a, the main document represents the portion of the form letter that repeats from one merged letter to the next. Conversely, the **data source** contains the variable, or changing, values for each letter. In Figure 5-1b, the data source contains five different vacationers. Thus, one form letter is generated for each vacationer listed in the data source.

Starting and Customizing Word

To start and customize Word, Windows must be running. If you are stepping through this project on a computer and you want your screen to match the figures in this book, then you should change your computer's resolution to 800 × 600 and reset the toolbars and menus. For information about changing the resolution and resetting toolbars and menus, read Appendix D.

The following steps describe how to start Word and customize the Word window. You may need to ask your instructor how to start Word for your system.

To Start and Customize Word

1. **Click the Start button on the Windows taskbar, point to All Programs on the Start menu, point to Microsoft Office on the All Programs submenu, and then click Microsoft Office Word 2003 on the Microsoft Office submenu.**
2. **If the Word window is not maximized, double-click its title bar to maximize it.**
3. **If the Language bar appears, right-click it and then click Close the Language bar on the shortcut menu.**
4. **If the Getting Started task pane is displayed in the Word window, click its Close button.**
5. **If the Standard and Formatting toolbar buttons are displayed on one row, click the Toolbar Options button and then click Show Buttons on Two Rows in the Toolbar Options list.**
6. **Click View on the menu bar and then click Print Layout.**

Word starts and, after a few moments, displays an empty document in the Word window. You use print layout view in this project because the letterhead contains a shape, and shapes are displayed properly only in print layout view. The Print Layout View button on the horizontal scroll bar is selected (shown in Figure 5-2 on page WD 302).

Displaying Formatting Marks

It is helpful to display formatting marks that indicate where in the document you pressed the ENTER key, SPACEBAR, and other keys. The following step describes how to display formatting marks.

To Display Formatting Marks

1. **If the Show/Hide ¶ button on the Standard toolbar is not selected already, click it.**

Word displays formatting marks in the document window, and the Show/Hide ¶ button on the Standard toolbar is selected (shown in Figure 5-2 on the next page).

> **More About**
>
> **Business Letter Software**
>
> For more information about business letter software, visit the Word 2003 More About Web page (scsite.com/wd2003/more) and then click Business Letter Software.

Zooming Page Width

In print layout view, many users **zoom page width** so they can see all edges of the page in the document window at once. The following steps zoom page width.

To Zoom Page Width

1. **Click the Zoom box arrow on the Standard toolbar (shown in Figure 5-2).**
2. **Click Page Width in the Zoom list.**

Word computes the zoom percentage and displays it in the Zoom box. Your percentage may be different depending on your computer.

Identifying the Main Document for Form Letters

Creating form letters requires merging a main document with a data source. To create form letters using Word's mail merge, you perform these tasks: (1) identify the main document, (2) create or specify the data source, (3) enter text, graphics, and fields into the main document for the form letter, and (4) merge the data source with the main document to generate and print the form letters. The following pages illustrate these tasks.

Word provides two methods of merging documents: the Mail Merge task pane and the Mail Merge toolbar. The **Mail Merge task pane** guides you through the process of merging. The **Mail Merge toolbar** provides buttons and boxes you use to merge documents. This project first illustrates the Mail Merge task pane and then later uses the Mail Merge toolbar.

> **More About**
>
> **Main Document Types**
>
> In addition to mass mailings through form letters and e-mail, you also can use Word to merge a main document to faxes. In order to create and distribute merged faxes, you must have a fax modem installed and also have the necessary fax software, such as Microsoft Fax, and a compatible e-mail program, such as Microsoft Outlook. Otherwise, the fax option will be unavailable (dimmed).

Identifying the Main Document

The first step in the mail merge process is to identify the type of document you are creating for the main document. Basic installations of Word support five types of main documents: letters, e-mail messages, envelopes, labels, and a directory. In this section, you are creating letters as the main document. Later in this project, you will specify labels and a directory as the main document.

When creating letters, such as the form letter in this project, you have three basic options: type the letter from scratch into a blank document window, as you did with the cover letter in Project 3; use the letter wizard and let Word format the letter based on your responses to the wizard; or use a letter template. As discussed in Project 3, a **template** is similar to a form with prewritten text; that is, Word prepares the requested document with text and/or formatting common to all documents of this nature. In the case of the letter template, Word prepares a letter with text and/or formatting common to all letters. Then, you customize the resulting letter by selecting and replacing prewritten text.

Word provides three styles of wizards and templates: Professional, Contemporary, and Elegant. The form letter in this project uses the Elegant Merge Letter template. The following steps show how to use a template as the main document for a form letter.

To Use a Template

1

- **Click File on the menu bar and then click New.**

Word displays the New Document task pane (Figure 5-2). You access templates through the Templates area in the task pane.

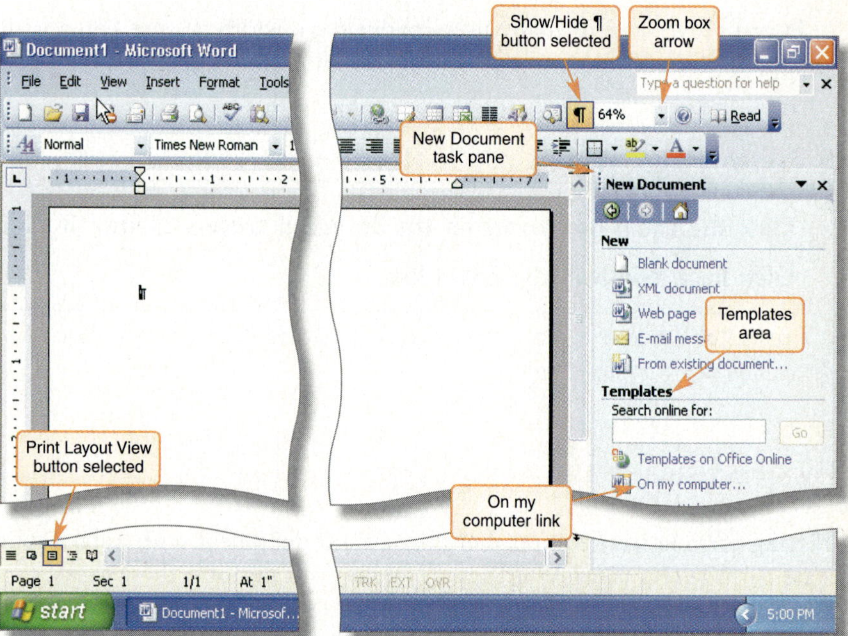

FIGURE 5-2

2

- **Click the On my computer link in the Templates area in the New Document task pane.**
- **When Word displays the Templates dialog box, click the Mail Merge tab.**
- **Click the Elegant Merge Letter icon.**

Word displays several template icons in the Mail Merge sheet in the Templates dialog box (Figure 5-3). If you click an icon, the Preview area shows a sample of the resulting document.

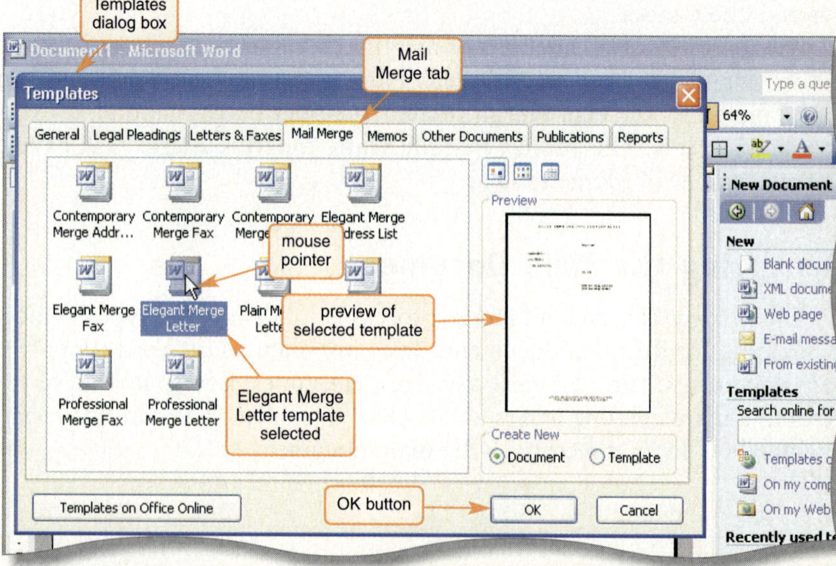

FIGURE 5-3

3

- **Click the OK button in the Templates dialog box.**

In the document window, Word displays a document that is based on the Elegant Merge Letter template (Figure 5-4). Word also opens the Mail Merge task pane at the right edge of the screen. Because you are not ready to continue with the merge process, you close the task pane.

4

- **Click the Close button in the upper-right corner of the Mail Merge task pane title bar.**
- **Click the Zoom box arrow and then click Page Width.**

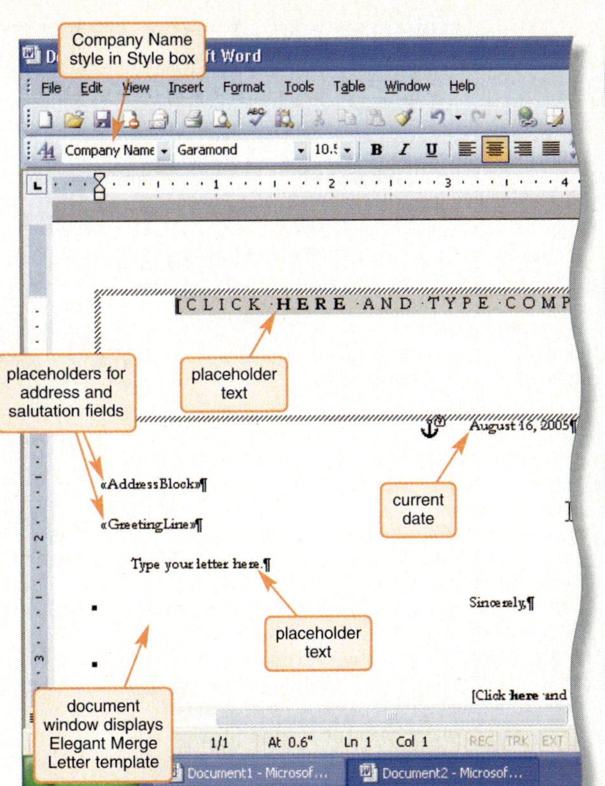

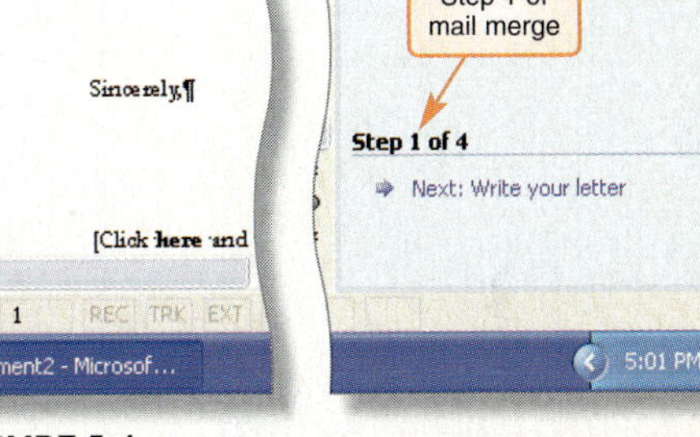

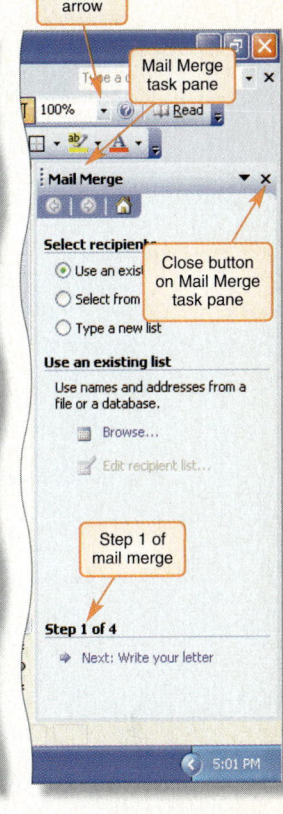

FIGURE 5-4

The letter template instructs Word to display the current date in the letter (Figure 5-4). More than likely, your date line will display a different date.

Recall from Project 3 that a template displays prewritten text, called **placeholder text**, that you select and replace to personalize the document. Figure 5-4 identifies some of the placeholder text created by the Elegant Merge Letter template.

Also recall that all business letters have common elements such as a date line, inside address, message, and signature block. The Elegant Merge Letter template uses formatting for a **modified block style** letter; that is, the date line, complimentary close, and signature block are slightly to the right of the center point, and all other letter components begin flush with the left margin.

In creating a letter from a template, Word uses styles to represent various elements of the letter. As discussed in previous projects, a style is a named group of formatting characteristics that you can apply to text. Figure 5-5 on the next page identifies the styles used by the Elegant Merge Letter template.

The Style box on the Formatting toolbar displays the name of the style associated with the location of the insertion point or the current selection (shown in Figure 5-4). When you modify the form letter, the style associated with the location of the insertion point will be applied to the text you type.

At this point, you closed the Mail Merge task pane because you want to create the letterhead for the letter. With the Mail Merge task pane closed, Word displays the document window larger on the screen. Later, this project shows how to redisplay the Mail Merge task pane to continue the Mail Merge process.

Other Ways

1. On Tools menu click Letters and Mailings, click Mail Merge, click Next: Starting document link, click Start from a template, click Select template link, click template name, click OK button
2. In Voice Command mode, say "File, New, On my computer, Mail Merge, [select template name], OK"

Q&A

Q: What elements should a business letter contain?

A: Business letters should contain the following items from top to bottom: date line, inside address, body or message, and signature block. Many business letters contain additional items such as a special mailing notation(s), attention line, salutation, subject line, complimentary close, reference initials, and enclosure notation.

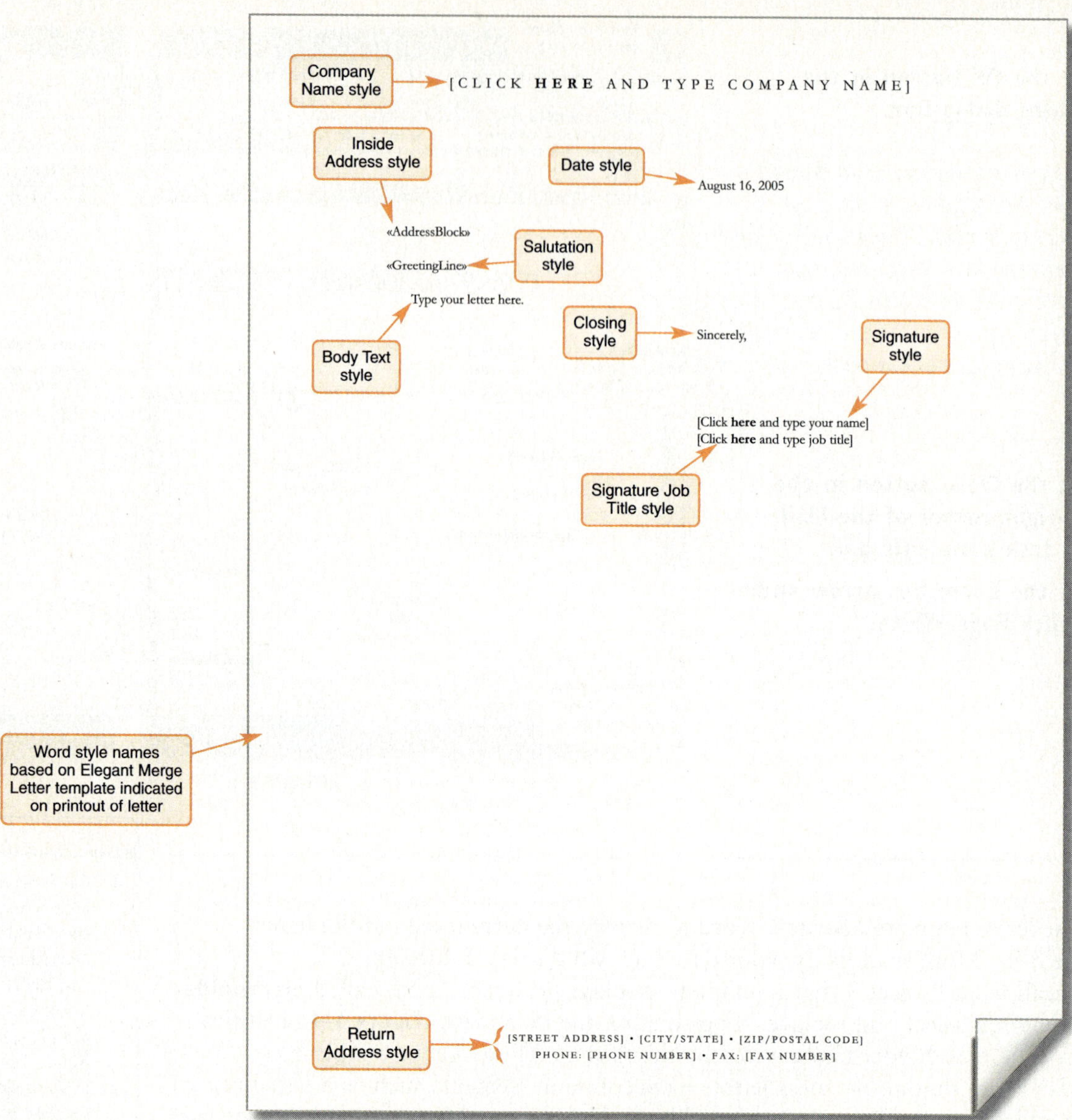

FIGURE 5-5

Working with AutoShapes and the Drawing Canvas

> *More About*
>
> **The Drawing Canvas**
>
> If you want the drawing canvas to be displayed automatically when you insert an AutoShape, click Tools on the menu bar, click Options, click the General tab, place a check mark in the Automatically create drawing canvas when inserting AutoShapes check box, and then click the OK button.

You can insert two types of graphics into a Word document: a picture and a drawing object. A **picture** is a graphic that was created in another program. Examples of pictures include scanned images, photographs, and clip art. A **drawing object** is a graphic that you create using Word.

Adding an AutoShape in a Drawing Canvas

In this project, the campground name is in a banner at the top of the form letter. A banner is a type of drawing object. This drawing object is in a drawing canvas. A **drawing canvas** is a container that helps you to resize and arrange shapes on the page. In this project, the banner is one color and the drawing canvas is another color. Also, the drawing canvas is surrounded with a border.

The following steps show how to insert a drawing canvas in a document and then format the drawing canvas.

To Insert a Drawing Canvas

1

- **Click the placeholder text, CLICK HERE AND TYPE COMPANY NAME, to select it.**
- **Click Insert on the menu bar and then point to Picture.**

Word selects the placeholder text (Figure 5-6). As soon as you instruct word to create a new drawing, it removes the selected placeholder text and inserts a drawing canvas in its place.

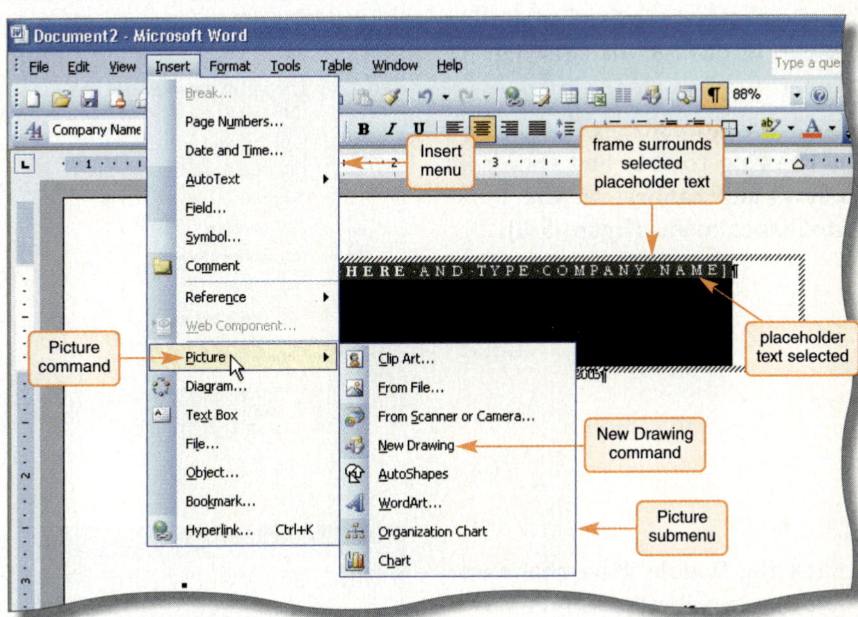

FIGURE 5-6

2

- **Click New Drawing on the Picture submenu.**

Word removes the selected placeholder text and inserts a drawing canvas at the location of the selection (Figure 5-7). When the drawing canvas is selected, Word automatically displays the Drawing Canvas toolbar.

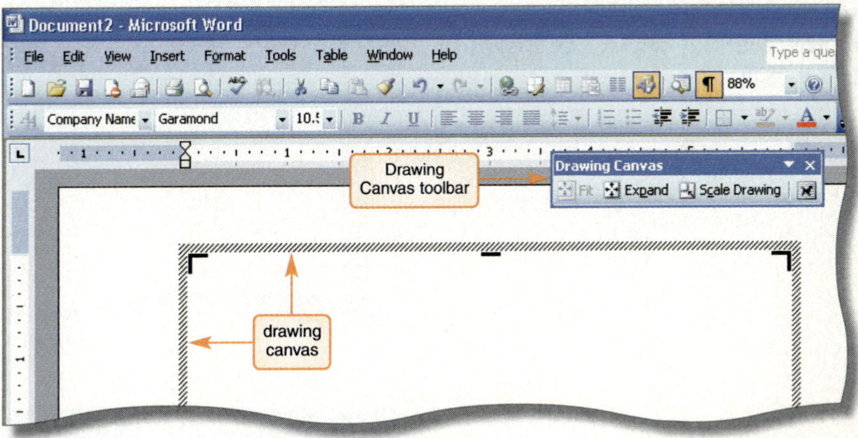

FIGURE 5-7

Other Ways

1. In Voice Command mode, say "Insert, Picture, New Drawing"

Notice in Figure 5-7 that the drawing canvas is surrounded by a patterned rectangle. This rectangle does not print; you use it to resize or move the drawing canvas and its contents.

The next step is to draw a banner AutoShape on the drawing canvas. An **AutoShape** is a shape that Word has predefined. Examples of AutoShapes include rectangles, circles, triangles, arrows, flowcharting symbols, stars, banners, and callouts. The steps on the next page show how to insert a banner AutoShape into a document.

To Insert an AutoShape

1

- **If the Drawing toolbar is not displayed on your screen, click the Drawing button on the Standard toolbar to display the Drawing toolbar.**
- **Click the AutoShapes button on the Drawing toolbar and then point to Stars and Banners on the AutoShapes menu (Figure 5-8).**

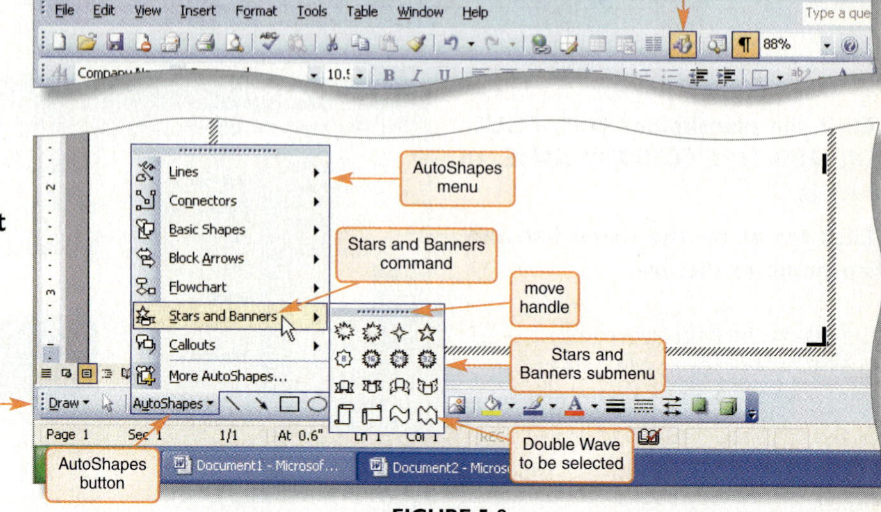

FIGURE 5-8

2

- **Click the Double Wave shape on the Stars and Banners submenu (bottom-right shape).**
- **Position the mouse pointer (a crosshair) in the upper-left corner of the drawing canvas, as shown in Figure 5-9.**

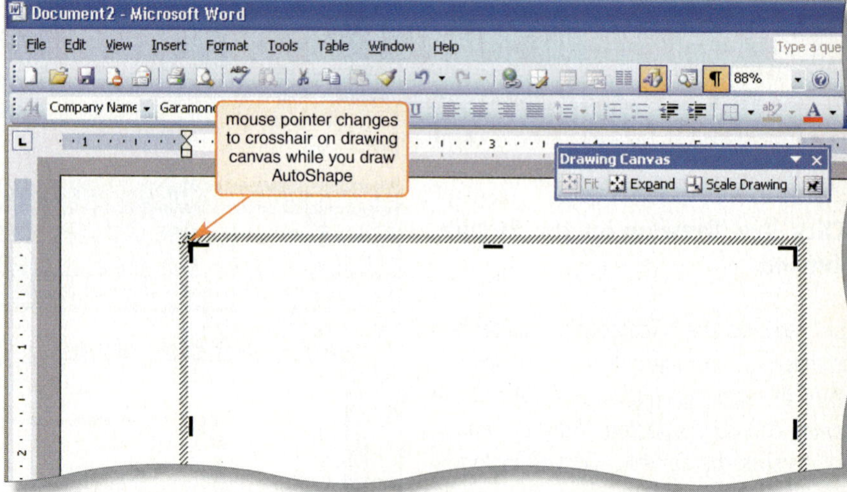

FIGURE 5-9

3

- **Drag the mouse to the right and downward to form a banner, as shown in Figure 5-10.**

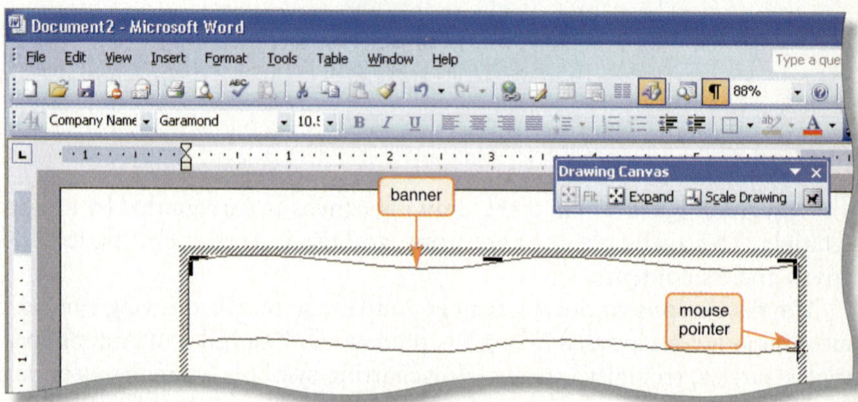

FIGURE 5-10

4

• **Release the mouse button. Once the shape is drawn, if you need to resize it, simply drag the sizing handles.**

Word places sizing handles at the middle and corner locations of the shape, allowing you to resize it if necessary (Figure 5-11).

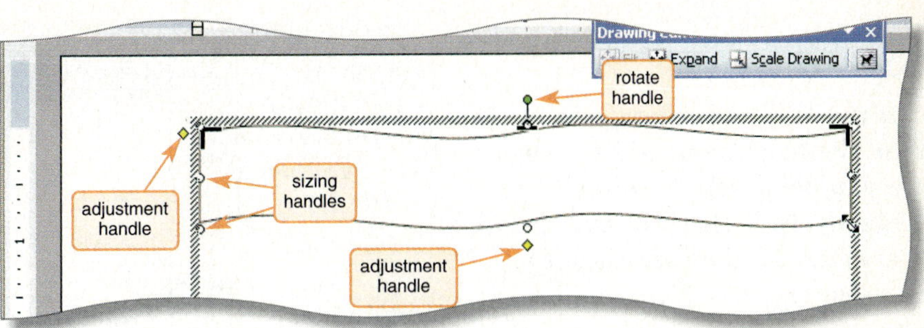

FIGURE 5-11

Other Ways

1. With Drawing toolbar displaying, in Voice Command mode, say "AutoShapes, Stars and Banners, [AutoShape name], [draw shape]"

Many objects, such as the banner AutoShape shown in Figure 5-11, have an adjustment handle(s) and a rotate handle. When you drag an object's **adjustment handle**, which is a yellow diamond, Word changes the object's shape. When you drag an object's **rotate handle**, which is a green circle, Word rotates the object in the direction you drag the mouse.

If, for some reason, you wanted to delete an AutoShape, you would click it to select it and then press the DELETE key or click the Cut button on the Standard toolbar.

More About

Submenus

Some submenus display a move handle at their top (shown in Figure 5-8). When you point to a submenu's move handle, the mouse pointer has a four-headed arrow attached to it. If you drag the move handle, Word converts the submenu to a floating toolbar. You later can close the floating toolbar by clicking its Close button.

Formatting an AutoShape

The next step is to color the inside of the banner light green and remove the line that surrounds the banner. You could use the Fill Color and Line Color buttons on the Drawing toolbar to change the fill color to light green and to remove the line, respectively. You also want to check the size of the banner. To fit the campground name properly in the banner, its width should be approximately six inches and its height approximately one inch. To check an object's size, you use the Format AutoShape dialog box. Thus, you will use the Format AutoShape dialog box for all formatting changes to the banner.

The following steps show how to format an AutoShape.

To Format an AutoShape

1

• **Position the mouse pointer inside the banner and then double-click when the mouse pointer has a four-headed arrow attached to it.**

• **When Word displays the Format AutoShape dialog box, if necessary, click the Colors and Lines tab.**

• **In the Fill area, click the Color box arrow and then click Light Green.**

• **In the Line area, click the Color box arrow and then click No Line.**

Word displays the Colors and Lines sheet in the Format AutoShape dialog box (Figure 5-12).

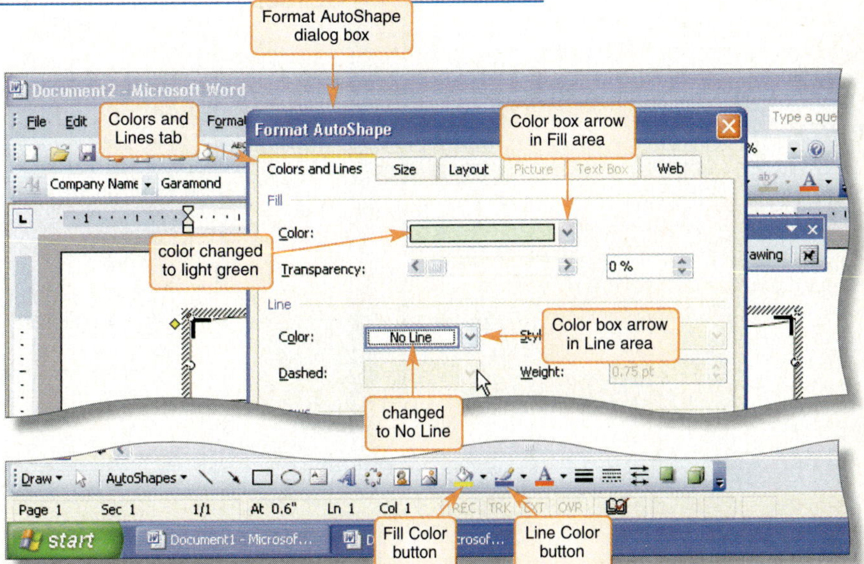

FIGURE 5-12

2

• **Click the Size tab.**

• **In the Size and rotate area, verify that the height and width values are approximately 1" and 6", respectively. If they are not, change the values so they are close to those in Figure 5-13.**

3

• **Click the OK button.**

Word fills the banner with light green and removes its line (shown in Figure 5-14).

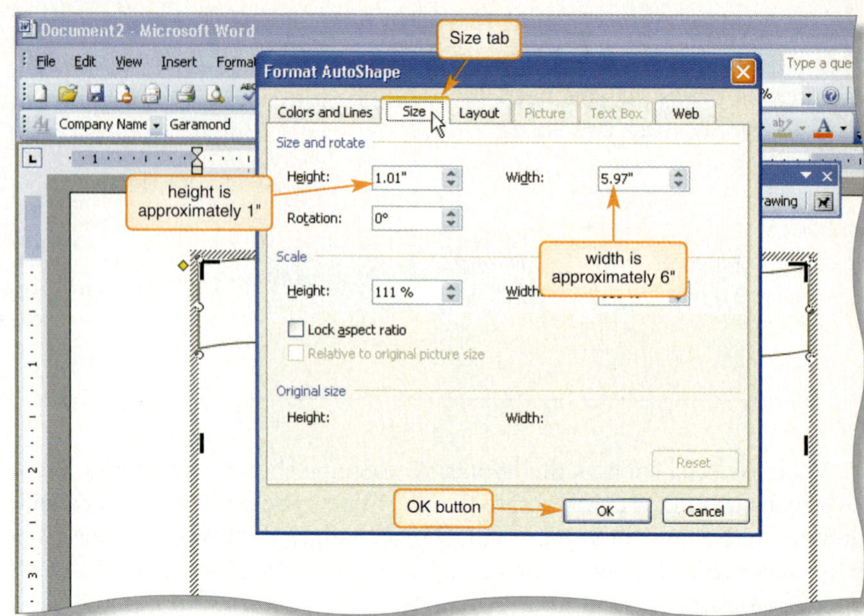

FIGURE 5-13

Other Ways

1. On Format menu click AutoShape
2. Right-click AutoShape, click Format AutoShape on shortcut menu
3. In Voice Command mode, say "Format, AutoShape"

The next step is to add the campground name inside the AutoShape. Thus, the following steps show how to add text to an AutoShape.

To Add Formatted Text to an AutoShape

1

• **Right-click the AutoShape.**

Word displays a shortcut menu (Figure 5-14).

2

• **Click Add Text on the shortcut menu.**

Word places an insertion point in the AutoShape.

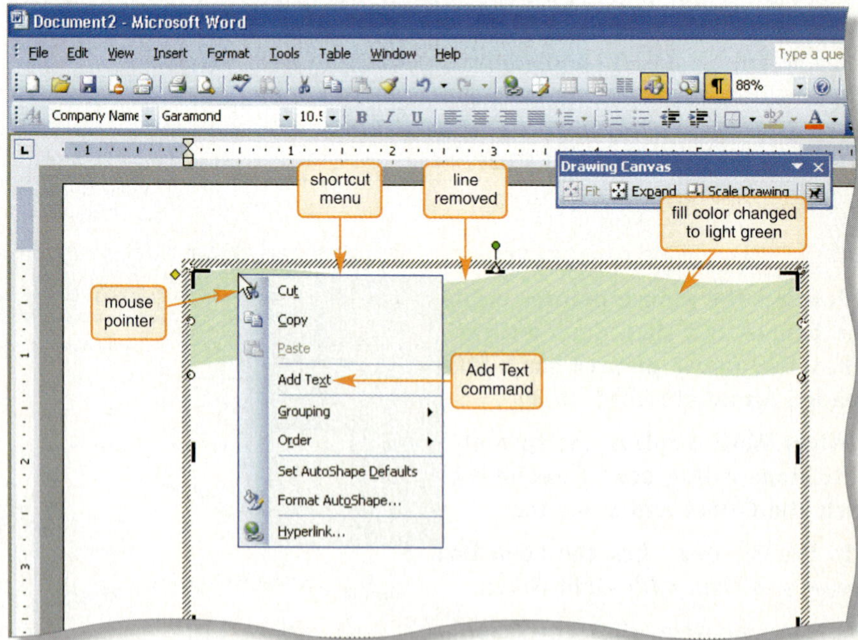

FIGURE 5-14

3

- **Click the Font box arrow on the Formatting toolbar, scroll to and then click Wide Latin (or a similar font).**
- **Click the Font Size box arrow on the Formatting toolbar and then click 20.**
- **Click the Bold button and then click the Center button on the Formatting toolbar.**
- **Click the Font Color button arrow on the Formatting toolbar and then click Green on the color palette.**
- **Type** `River Run` **and then press the ENTER key. Type** `Campground` **in the banner.**

Word formats and displays the campground name in the banner AutoShape (Figure 5-15). The Text Box toolbar also may appear on the screen.

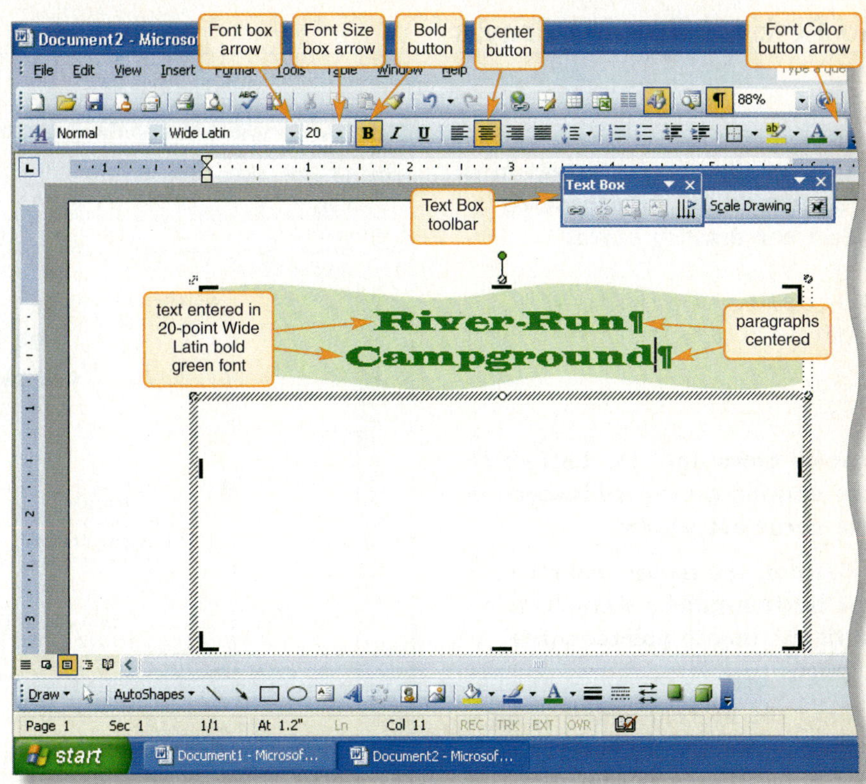

FIGURE 5-15

Other Ways

1. In Voice Command mode, say "Right Click, Add Text, [enter text]"

Resizing and Formatting the Drawing Canvas

Recall that the banner AutoShape was drawn on a drawing canvas. The height of the drawing canvas is about 3.5 inches, which is too big for this letter. You want the drawing canvas to touch the widest part of the wave in the AutoShape. Thus, you must resize the drawing canvas by dragging its bottom border up.

The steps on the next page show how to resize a drawing canvas.

More About

AutoShape Text and Drawing Canvas

To resize a text box to be as wide as its text, double-click an edge of the AutoShape, click the Text Box tab in the Format AutoShape dialog box, place a check mark in the Resize AutoShape to fit text check box, and then click the OK button. To make the drawing canvas larger and leave the AutoShape object the same size, click the Expand button on the Drawing Canvas toolbar. To make the drawing canvas fit tightly around the AutoShape, click the Fit button on the Drawing Canvas toolbar. To resize the drawing canvas and AutoShape object proportionately, click the Scale button on the Drawing Canvas toolbar and then drag the drawing canvas boundary.

To Resize a Drawing Canvas

1

- **Click in the drawing canvas in an area outside the AutoShape to select the drawing canvas.**

A selected drawing canvas has sizing handles at its corner and middle locations.

2

- **Scroll down until the bottom of the drawing canvas is displayed in the document window.**
- **Position the mouse pointer on the bottom-middle sizing handle until the mouse pointer shape changes to a T.**
- **Drag the bottom-middle sizing handle upward until the dotted line is positioned as shown in Figure 5-16.**

When you release the mouse, the bottom of the drawing canvas will be resized to the location of the dotted line.

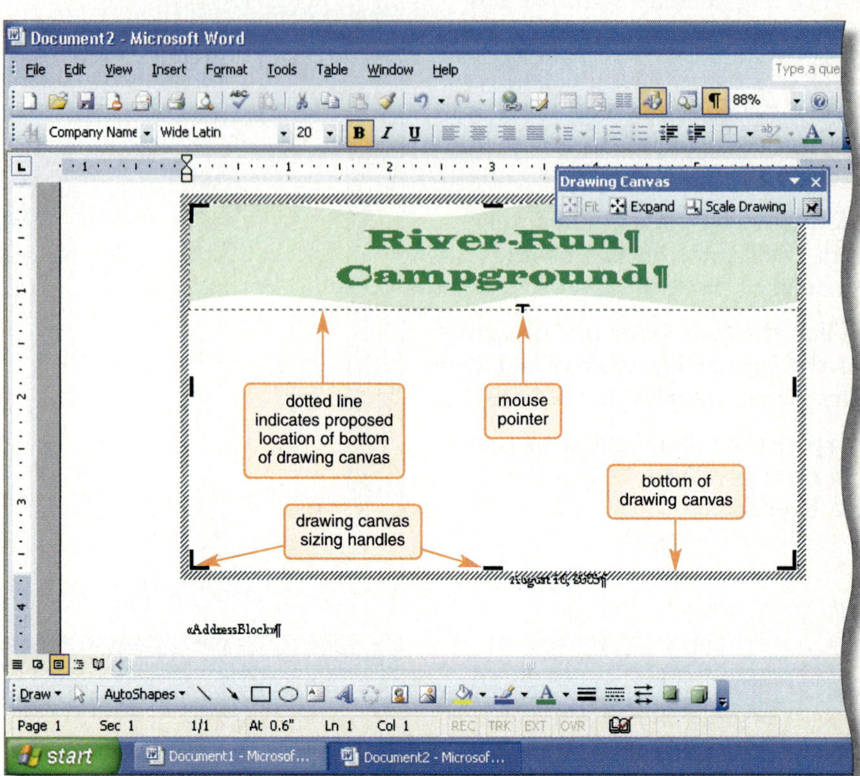

FIGURE 5-16

3

- **Release the mouse button.**
- **If the banner AutoShape is not centered properly inside the drawing canvas, click it and drag it to the desired location.**

Word resizes the drawing canvas (Figure 5-17).

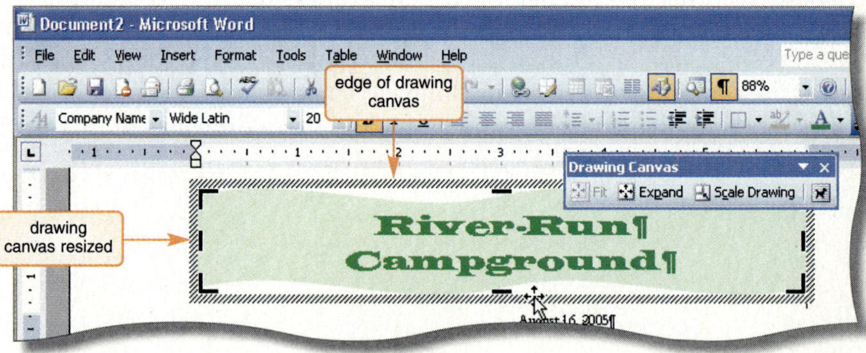

FIGURE 5-17

Other Ways

1. On Format menu click Drawing Canvas, click Size tab, enter height and width values in the Size and rotate area, click OK button

The next step is to fill the drawing canvas with a transparent (see-through) shade of pale blue. If you simply wanted to fill the drawing canvas, you would select it and then click the Fill Color button arrow on the Drawing toolbar. To make the fill color transparent, however, you must use the Format Drawing Canvas dialog box. You also want to change the line color and style, which requires you use the Format Drawing Canvas dialog box. The next steps show how to format the drawing canvas.

To Format a Drawing Canvas

1

- Point to an edge of the drawing canvas and double-click when the mouse pointer has a four-headed arrow attached to it.
- When Word displays the Format Drawing Canvas dialog box, if necessary, click the Colors and Lines tab.
- In the Fill area, click the Color box arrow and then click Pale Blue. Drag the Transparency slider until the Transparency box displays 50%.
- In the Line area, click the Color box arrow and then click Green on the color palette.
- Click the Dashed box arrow and then click the fifth line in the list.
- Click the Style box arrow and then click the next to last style in the list (Figure 5-18).

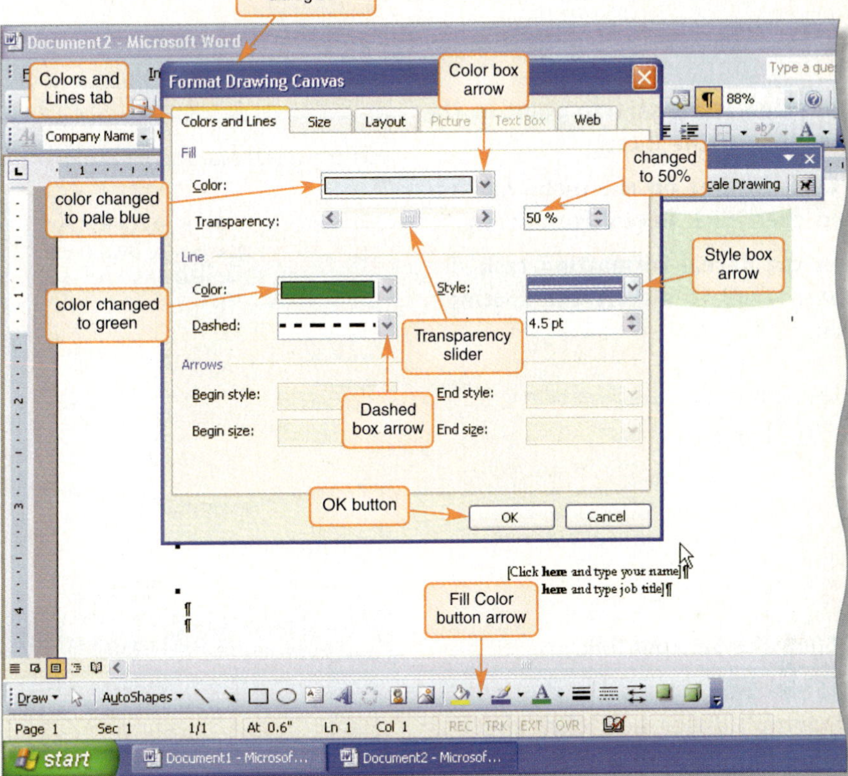

FIGURE 5-18

2

- Click the OK button.
- Click outside the drawing canvas to deselect it.
- Click the Drawing button on the Standard toolbar to remove the Drawing toolbar from the screen.

Word fills the drawing canvas with a transparent shade of pale blue and adds a dashed box around it (Figure 5-19).

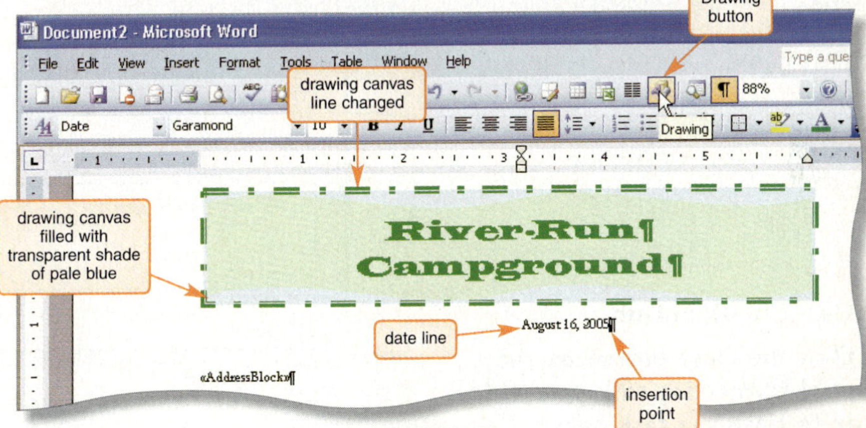

FIGURE 5-19

Other Ways

1. On Format menu click Drawing Canvas
2. Right-click edge of drawing canvas in area outside AutoShape, click Format Drawing Canvas on shortcut menu
3. In Voice Command mode, say "Format, Drawing Canvas"

Notice in Figure 5-19 that the bottom of the drawing canvas is too close to the top of the date. To be more readable, additional white space should be placed between the drawing canvas and the date. In a previous project, you pressed CTRL+0 (the numeral zero) to add one blank line, which is equal to 12 points, above a paragraph. In this project, you want 6 points above the date.

The steps on the next page show how to use the Reveal Formatting task pane to change paragraph formatting.

To Change Paragraph Formatting Using the Reveal Formatting Task Pane

1

- **Position the insertion point in the date line in the letter.**
- **Click Format on the menu bar and then click Reveal Formatting.**
- **In the Reveal Formatting task pane, scroll to display the Spacing link.**

Word displays the Reveal Formatting task pane (Figure 5-20).

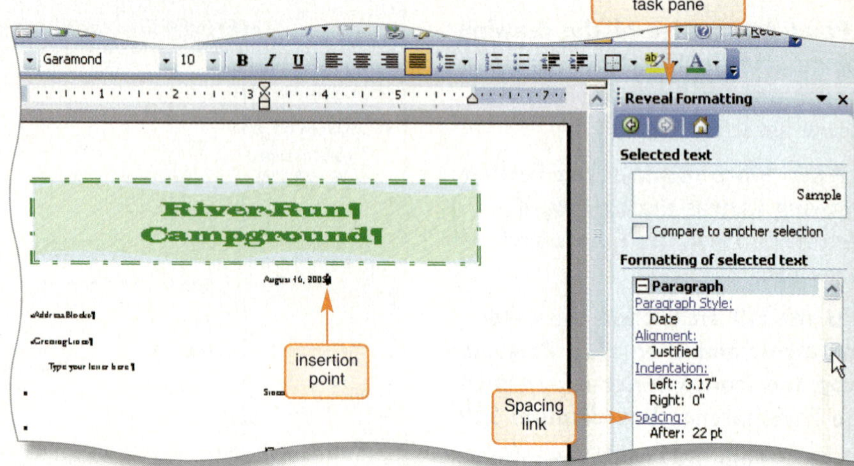

FIGURE 5-20

2

- **Click the Spacing link.**
- **In the Spacing area in the Paragraph dialog box, click the Before box up arrow.**

Word displays 6 pt in the Before box in the Paragraph dialog box (Figure 5-21).

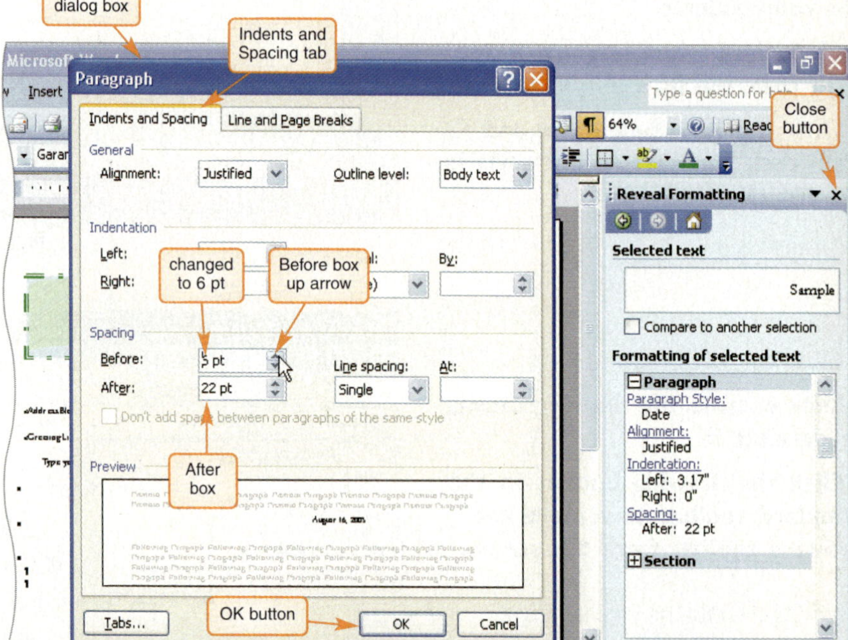

FIGURE 5-21

3

- **Click the OK button.**
- **Click the Close button on the Reveal Formatting task pane title bar to close the task pane.**

Word adds 6 points above the paragraph containing the date (Figure 5-22).

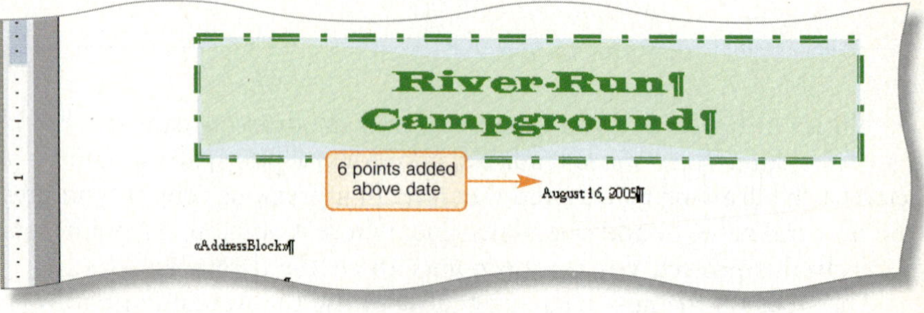

FIGURE 5-22

Other Ways

1. On Format menu click Paragraph
2. Right-click date line, click Paragraph on shortcut menu
3. In Voice Command mode, say "Format, Paragraph"

Through the Paragraph dialog box, you also can adjust the amount of space that is displayed after a paragraph by changing the value in the After box in the Spacing area (Figure 5-21).

Creating a Folder

You have performed several tasks to the form letter and should save it. You want to save this and all other documents created in this project in a folder called River Run. This folder does not exist, so you must create it. Rather than creating the folder in Windows, you can create folders in Word, which saves time.

The following steps show how to create a folder during the process of saving a document.

More About

Dialog Boxes

You can resize some dialog boxes, including the Save As dialog box and the Open dialog box. Simply point to the edge of the dialog box and drag when the mouse pointer shape changes to a double-headed arrow.

To Create a Folder while Saving

1

- **With a floppy disk in drive A, click the Save button on the Standard toolbar.**
- **When Word displays the Save As dialog box, type** `Campground Form Letter` **in the File name box. Do not press the ENTER key after typing the file name.**
- **If necessary, click the Save in box arrow and then click 3½ Floppy (A:).**
- **Click the Create New Folder button in the Save As dialog box.**
- **When Word displays the New Folder dialog box, type** `River Run` **(Figure 5-23).**

2

- **Click the OK button.**
- **Click the Save button in the Save As dialog box.**

Word saves the Campground Form Letter in the River Run folder on a disk in drive A.

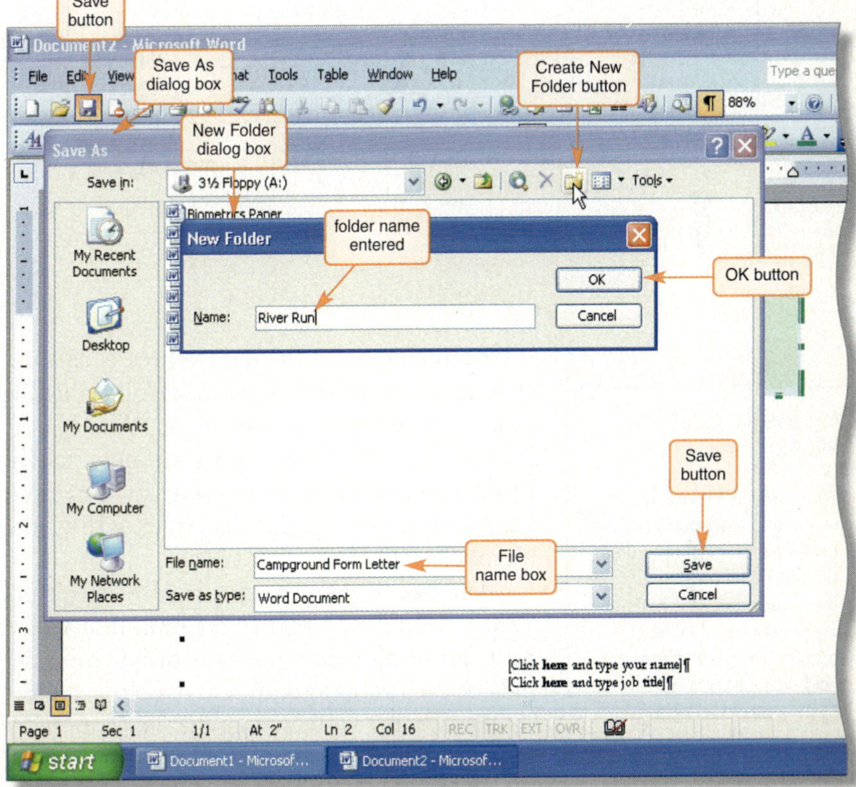

FIGURE 5-23

Other Ways

1. On File menu click Save As
2. Press CTRL+F12
3. In Voice Command mode, say "File, Save As"

Other dialog boxes, such as the Open and Insert File dialog boxes, also have a Create New Folder button, saving the time of using Windows to create a new folder for document storage.

Creating a Data Source

A data source is a file that contains the data that changes from one merged document to the next. As shown in Figure 5-24, a data source often is shown as a table that consists of a series of rows and columns. Each row is called a **record.** The first row of a data source is called the **header record** because it identifies the name of each column. Each row below the header row is called a **data record.** Data records contain the text that varies in each copy of the merged document. The data source for this project contains five data records. In this project, each data record identifies a different vacationer. Thus, five form letters will be generated from this data source.

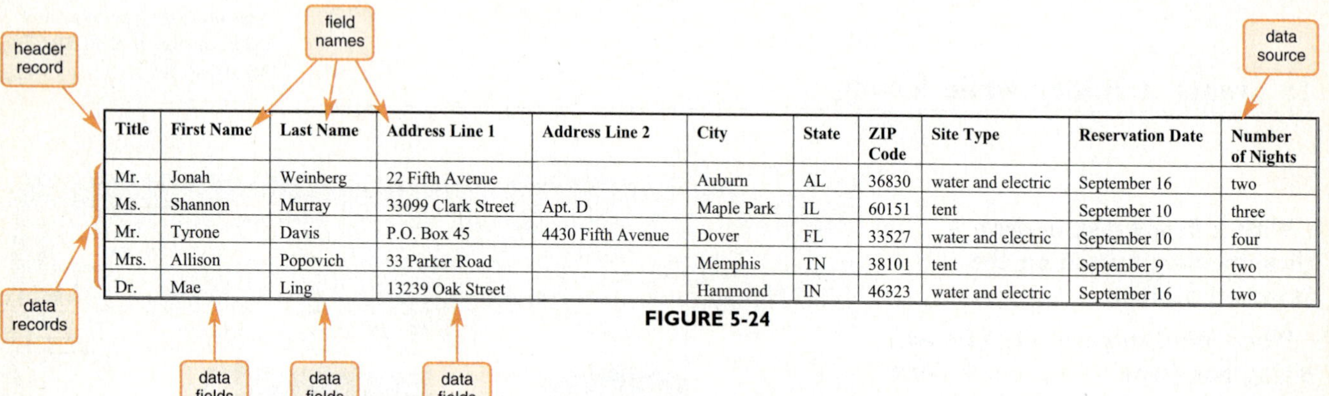

Title	First Name	Last Name	Address Line 1	Address Line 2	City	State	ZIP Code	Site Type	Reservation Date	Number of Nights
Mr.	Jonah	Weinberg	22 Fifth Avenue		Auburn	AL	36830	water and electric	September 16	two
Ms.	Shannon	Murray	33099 Clark Street	Apt. D	Maple Park	IL	60151	tent	September 10	three
Mr.	Tyrone	Davis	P.O. Box 45	4430 Fifth Avenue	Dover	FL	33527	water and electric	September 10	four
Mrs.	Allison	Popovich	33 Parker Road		Memphis	TN	38101	tent	September 9	two
Dr.	Mae	Ling	13239 Oak Street		Hammond	IN	46323	water and electric	September 16	two

FIGURE 5-24

> **Q&A**
>
> **Q:** What are fields and records?
>
> **A:** Field and record are terms that originate from the computer programming field. Do not be intimidated by these terms. A field is simply a column in a table, and a record is a row. Instead of field, some programmers identify a column of data as variable or attribute. All three terms (field, variable, and attribute) have the same meaning.

> ***More About***
>
> **Data Sources**
>
> A data source can be an Access database table, an Outlook contacts list, an Excel worksheet, or a Word table. If the necessary records already exist in one of these Office applications, you can instruct Word to use the existing file as the data source for the mail merge.

Each column in the data source is called a **data field.** A data field represents a group of similar data. Each data field must be identified uniquely with a name, called a **field name.** For example, First Name is the name of the field (column) that contains the first names of vacationers. In this project, the data source contains 11 data fields with the following field names: Title, First Name, Last Name, Address Line 1, Address Line 2, City, State, ZIP Code, Site Type, Reservation Date, and Number of Nights.

The first step in creating a data source is to decide which fields it will contain. That is, you must identify the data that will vary from one merged document to the next. For each field, you must decide on a field name. Field names must be unique; that is, no two field names may be the same.

Data sources often contain the same fields. For this reason, Word provides you with a list of 13 commonly used field names. This project uses eight of the 13 field names supplied by Word: Title, First Name, Last Name, Address Line 1, Address Line 2, City, State, and ZIP Code. The other five field names are deleted from the list supplied by Word. That is, this project deletes Company Name, Country, Home Phone, Work Phone, and E-mail Address. Then, three new field names (Site Type, Reservation Date, and Number of Nights) are added to the data source.

Fields may be listed in any order in the data source. That is, the order of fields has no effect on the order in which they will print in the main document.

The next steps show how to type a new data source for a mail merge.

To Type a New Data Source

1

• **Click Tools on the menu bar and then point to Letters and Mailings (Figure 5-25).**

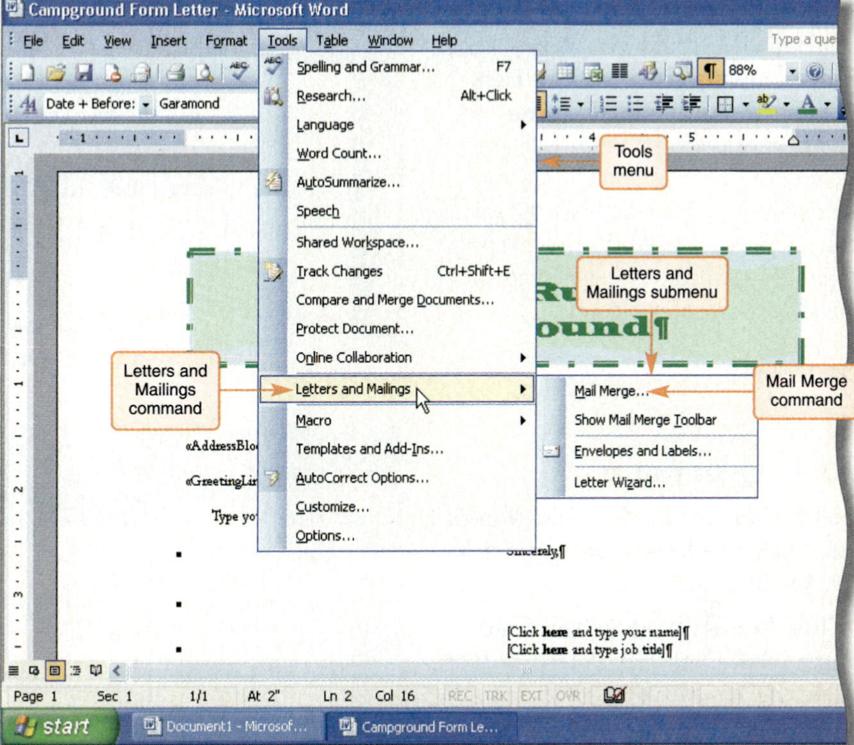

FIGURE 5-25

2

• **Click Mail Merge on the Letters and Mailings submenu.**

• **When Word displays the Mail Merge task pane, click Type a new list in the Select recipients area.**

When Word displays the Mail Merge task pane, it remembers where you left off in the merge process. You have three choices for the data source: use an existing list, select from Outlook contacts, or type a new list.

3

• **Click the Create link in the Mail Merge task pane.**

Word displays the New Address List dialog box with a list of commonly used field names (Figure 5-26). You can modify this list by clicking the Customize button.

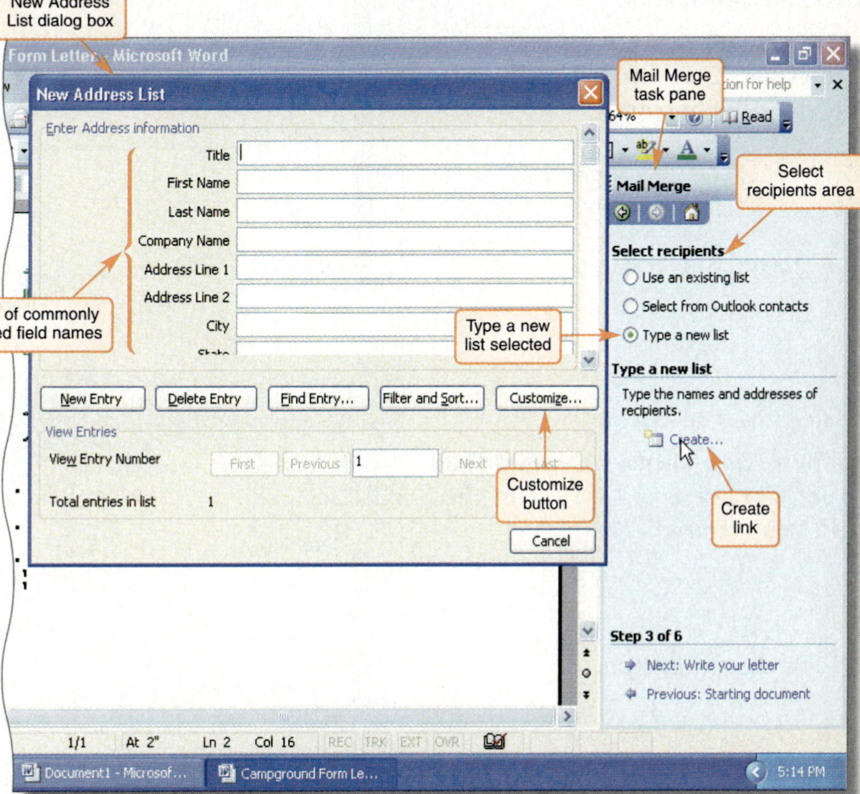

FIGURE 5-26

4

- **Click the Customize button in the New Address List dialog box.**
- **When Word displays the Customize Address List dialog box, click Company Name in the Field Names list and then click the Delete button.**

Word displays a dialog box asking if you are sure you want to delete the selected field (Figure 5-27). The field name, Company Name, is selected for removal.

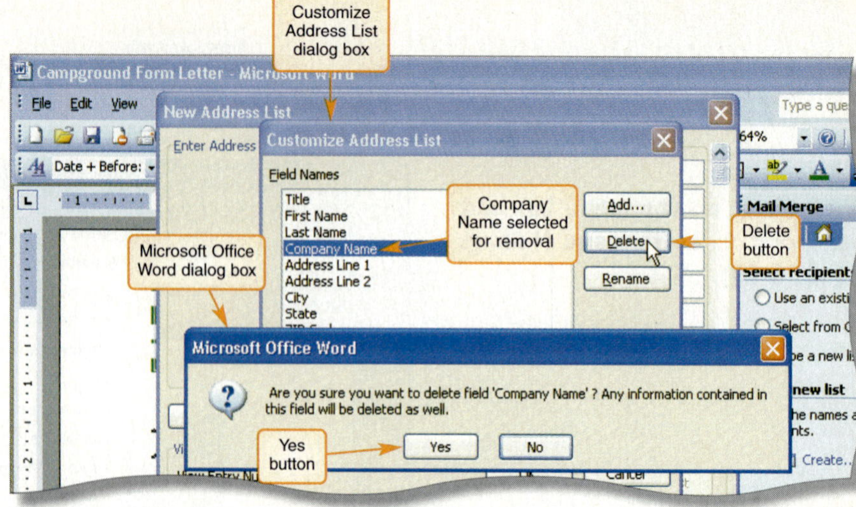

FIGURE 5-27

5

- **Click the Yes button.**
- **Click Country in the Field Names list. Click the Delete button. Click the Yes button.**
- **Click Home Phone in the Field Names list. Click the Delete button. Click the Yes button.**
- **Click Work Phone in the Field Names list. Click the Delete button. Click the Yes button.**
- **Click E-mail Address in the Field Names list. Click the Delete button. Click the Yes button.**

Word removes five field names from the list (Figure 5-28). The next step is to add the Site Type, Reservation Date, and Number of Nights field names to the list.

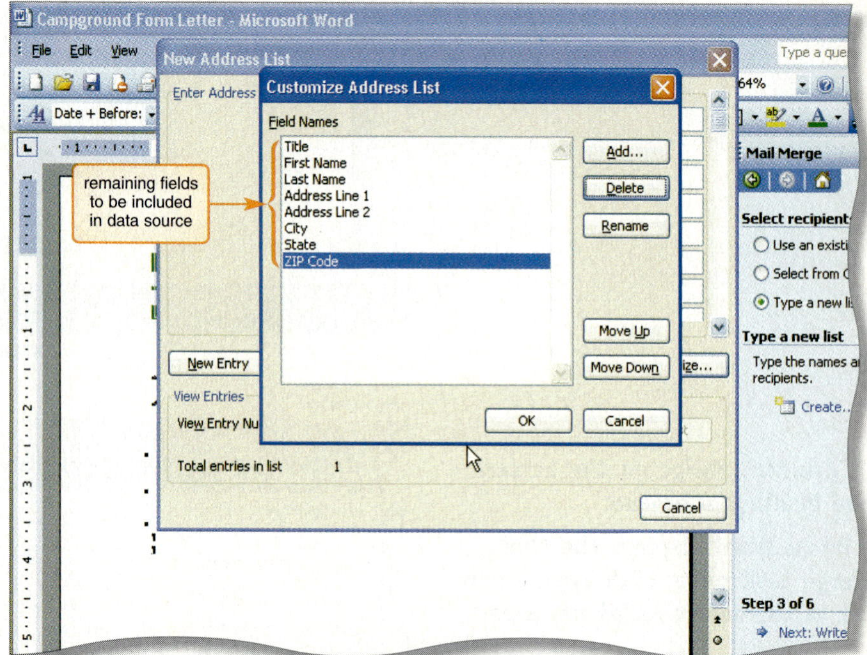

FIGURE 5-28

6

- **Click the Add button.**
- **When Word displays the Add Field dialog box, type** `Site Type` **in the text box (Figure 5-29).**

7

- **Click the OK button.**

Word adds the Site Type field name to the bottom of the Field Names list (shown in Figure 5-30).

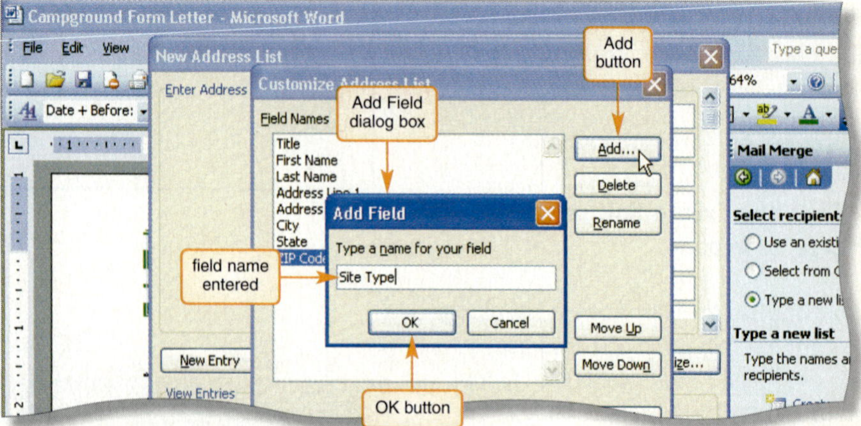

FIGURE 5-29

8

- **Click the Add button.**
- **When Word displays the Add Field dialog box, type** `Reservation Date` **in the text box and then click the OK button.**
- **Click the Add button.**
- **When Word displays the Add Field dialog box, type** `Number of Nights` **in the text box and then click the OK button.**

Word adds the Reservation Date and Number of Nights field names to the bottom of the Field Names list (Figure 5-30).

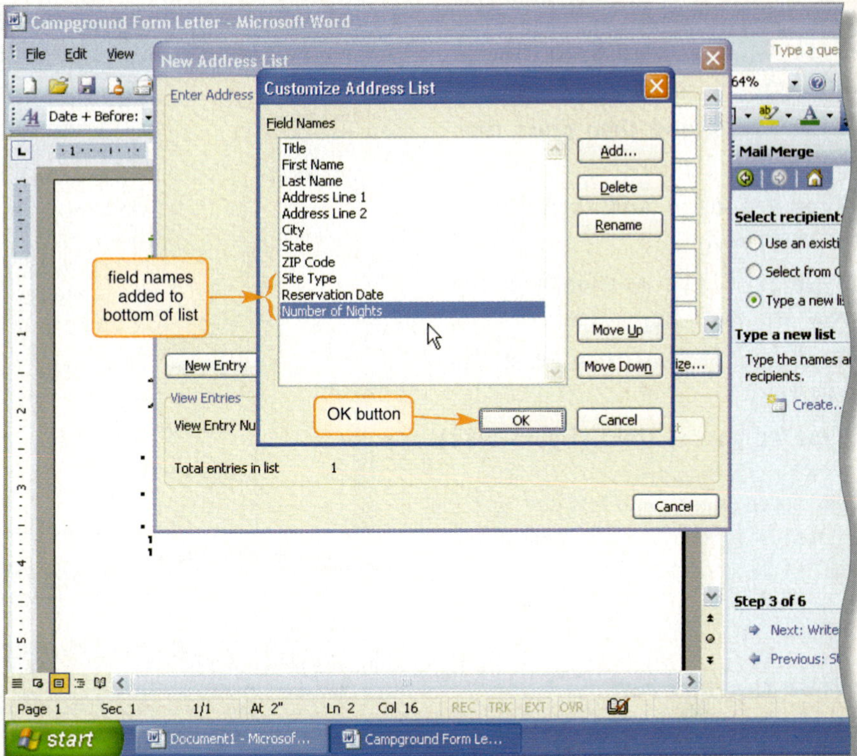

FIGURE 5-30

9

- **Click the OK button to close the Customize Address List dialog box.**
- **When the New Address List dialog box is active again, click the Title text box.**

Word displays the new list of field names in the Enter Address information area in the New Address List dialog box (Figure 5-31). The insertion point is displayed in the Title text box, ready for the first data record entry. Text entered in this dialog box becomes records in the data source.

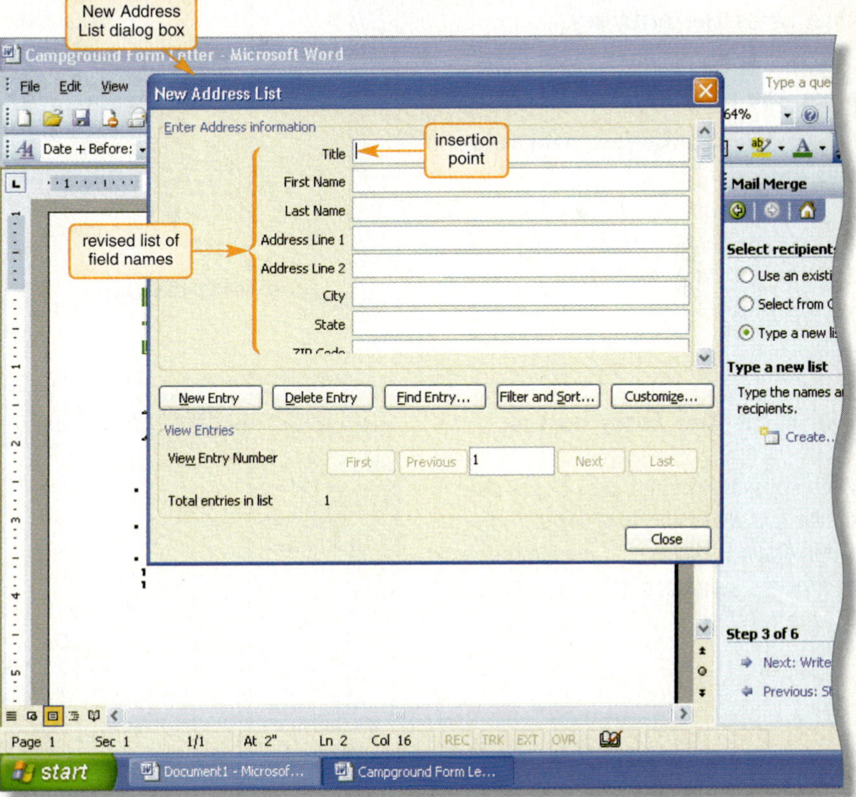

FIGURE 5-31

10

- **Type** `Mr.` **and then press the ENTER key.**
- **Type** `Jonah` **and then press the ENTER key.**
- **Type** `Weinberg` **and then press the ENTER key.**
- **Type** `22 Fifth Avenue` **and then press the ENTER key twice.**
- **Type** `Auburn` **and then press the ENTER key.**
- **Type** `AL` **as the state (Figure 5-32).**

If you notice an error in a text box, click the text box and then correct the error as you would in the document window.

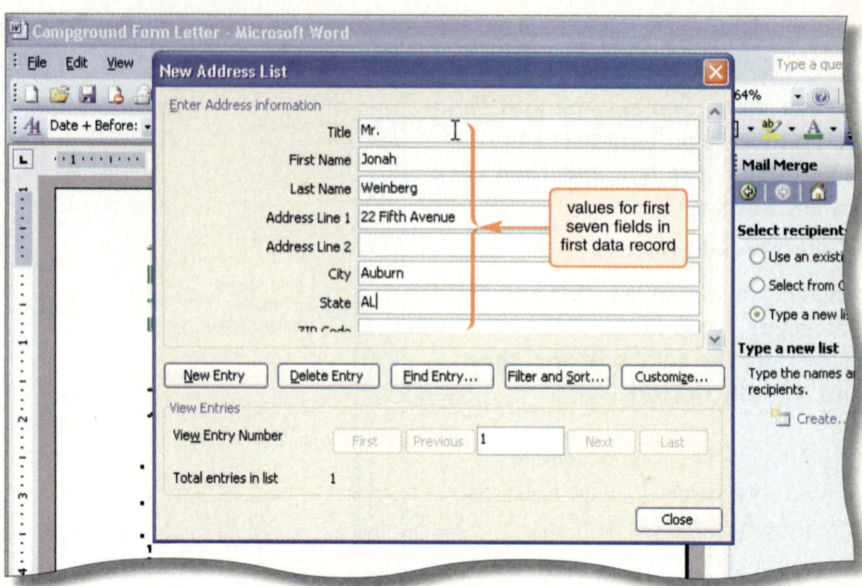

FIGURE 5-32

- **Press the ENTER key.**
- **Type** `36830` **and then press the ENTER key.**
- **Type** `water and electric` **and then press the ENTER key.**
- **Type** `September 16` **and then press the ENTER key.**
- **Type** `two` **as the last field value in this record.**

The first few fields scroll off the top of the dialog box to make room for the last three fields (Figure 5-33).

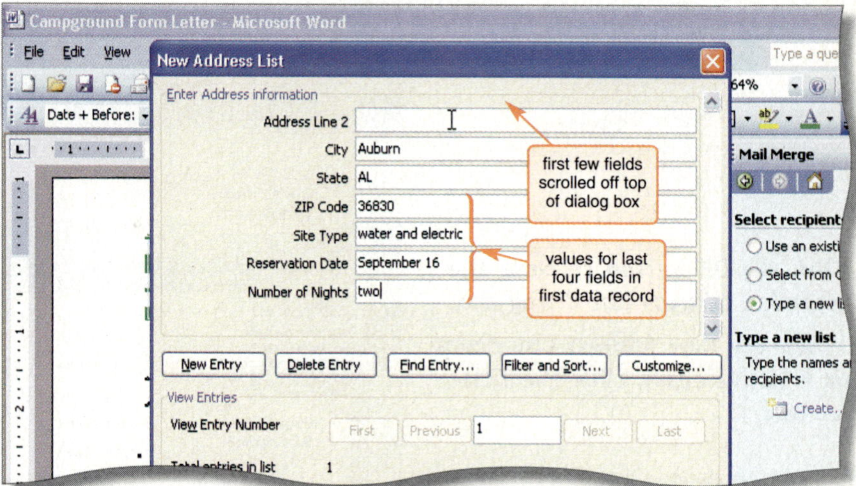

FIGURE 5-33

- **Click the New Entry button.**

Word adds the entered data to the data source and clears the text boxes in the Enter Address information area in preparation for the next data record to be entered (Figure 5-34).

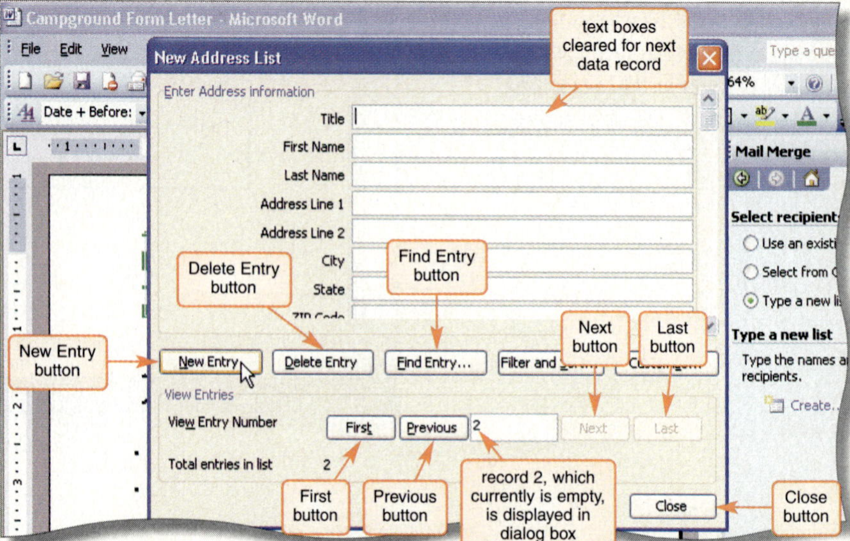

FIGURE 5-34

The next step is to enter the remaining four records into the New Address List dialog box, as described in the steps below.

To Enter More Records

1. **Type** Ms. **and then press the ENTER key. Type** Shannon **and then press the ENTER key. Type** Murray **and then press the ENTER key. Type** 33099 Clark Street **and then press the ENTER key. Type** Apt. D **and then press the ENTER key. Type** Maple Park **and then press the ENTER key. Type** IL **and then press the ENTER key. Type** 60151 **and then press the ENTER key. Type** tent **and then press the ENTER key. Type** September 10 **and then press the ENTER key. Type** three **and then click the New Entry button.**
2. **Type** Mr. **and then press the ENTER key. Type** Tyrone **and then press the ENTER key. Type** Davis **and then press the ENTER key. Type** P.O. Box 45 **and then press the ENTER key. Type** 4430 Fifth Avenue **and then press the ENTER key. Type** Dover **and then press the ENTER key. Type** FL **and then press the ENTER key. Type** 33527 **and then press the ENTER key. Type** water and electric **and then press the ENTER key. Type** September 10 **and then press the ENTER key. Type** four **and then click the New Entry button.**
3. **Type** Mrs. **and then press the ENTER key. Type** Allison **and then press the ENTER key. Type** Popovich **and then press the ENTER key. Type** 33 Parker Road **and then press the ENTER key twice. Type** Memphis **and then press the ENTER key. Type** TN **and then press the ENTER key. Type** 38101 **and then press the ENTER key. Type** tent **and then press the ENTER key. Type** September 9 **and then press the ENTER key. Type** two **and then click the New Entry button.**
4. **Type** Dr. **and then press the ENTER key. Type** Mae **and then press the ENTER key. Type** Ling **and then press the ENTER key. Type** 13239 Oak Street **and then press the ENTER key twice. Type** Hammond **and then press the ENTER key. Type** IN **and then press the ENTER key. Type** 46323 **and then press the ENTER key. Type** water and electric **and then press the ENTER key. Type** September 16 **and then press the ENTER key. Type** two **and then click the Close button (shown in Figure 5-34).**

The data records are entered in the data source.

When you click the Close button in the New Address List dialog box, Word displays a Save Address List dialog box so you can save the data source. The steps on the next page show how to save the data source in the River Run folder created earlier in this project.

Q&A

Q: How should I organize data in a data source?

A: Organize the items in a data source so it is reusable. For example, you may want to print a person's title, first name, middle initial, and last name (e.g., Mr. Roger A. Bannerman) in the inside address but only the title and last name in the salutation (Dear Mr. Bannerman). Thus, you should break the name into separate fields: title, first name, middle initial, and last name.

To Save the Data Source when Prompted by Word

1

- **When Word displays the Save Address List dialog box, type** `Camper List` **in the File name box.**
- **If necessary, change the drive to 3½ Floppy (A:) and then double-click the River Run folder.**

The data source for this project will be saved with the file name, Camper List (Figure 5-35). Word saves the data source as a Microsoft Office Address List, which is a Microsoft Access database file.

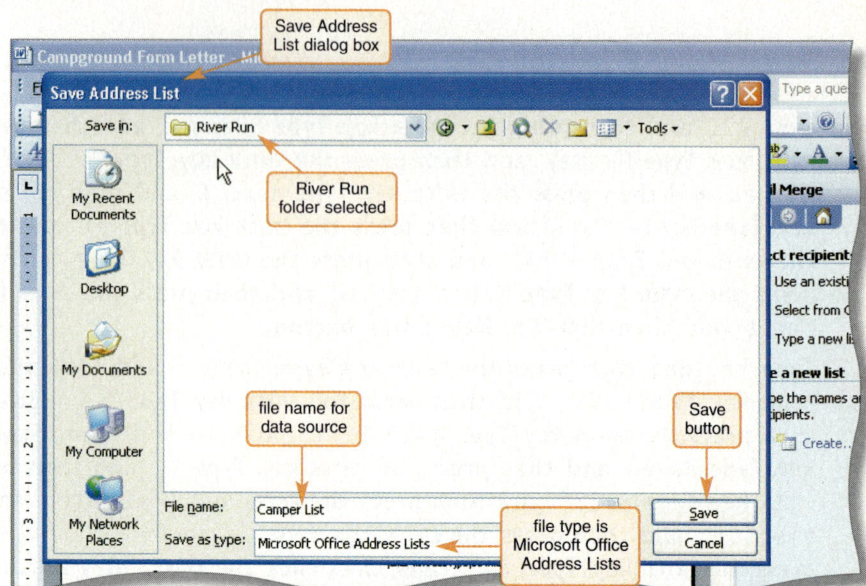

FIGURE 5-35

2

- **Click the Save button in the Save Address List dialog box.**

Word saves the data source in the River Run folder on the disk in drive A using the file name, Camper List, and then displays the Mail Merge Recipients dialog box (Figure 5-36).

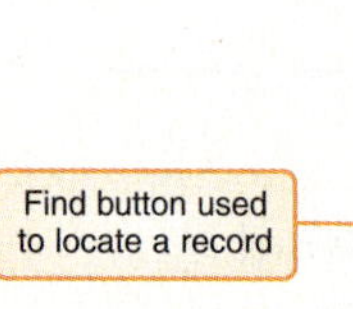

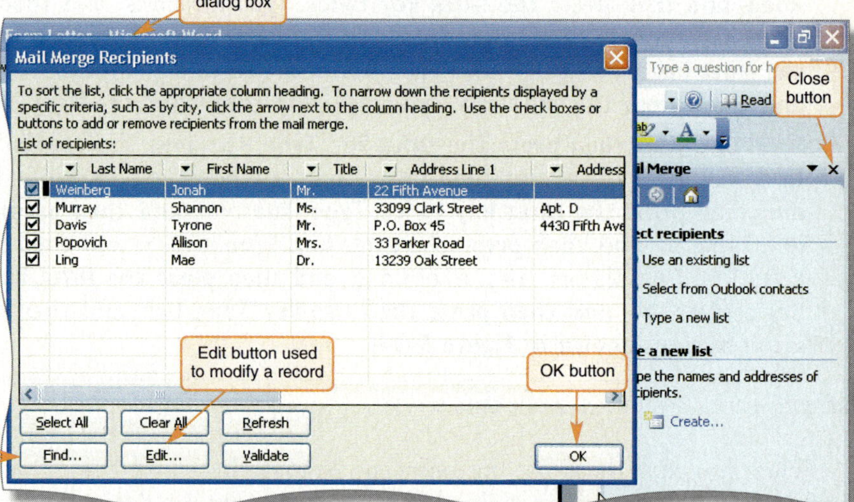

FIGURE 5-36

3

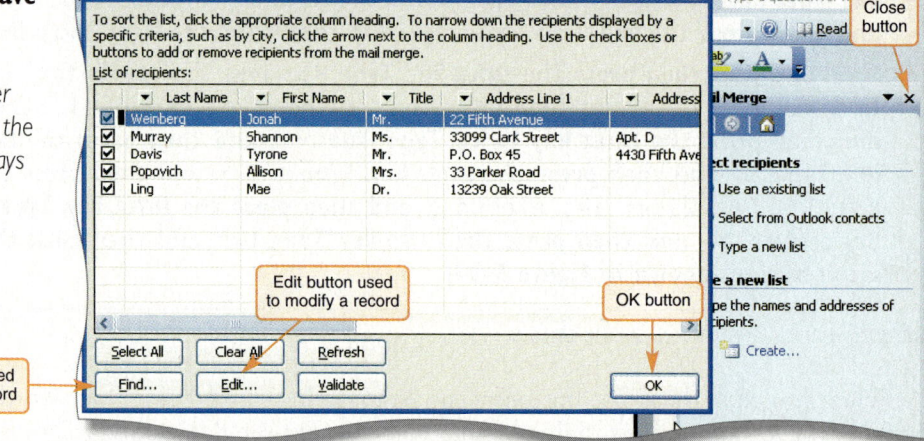

- **Click the OK button.**
- **Click the Close button on the Mail Merge task pane title bar.**
- **If the Mail Merge toolbar is not displayed on the screen, click Tools on the menu bar, point to Letters and Mailings, and then click Show Mail Merge Toolbar.**

Word displays the Mail Merge toolbar docked above or below the Formatting toolbar (Figure 5-37).

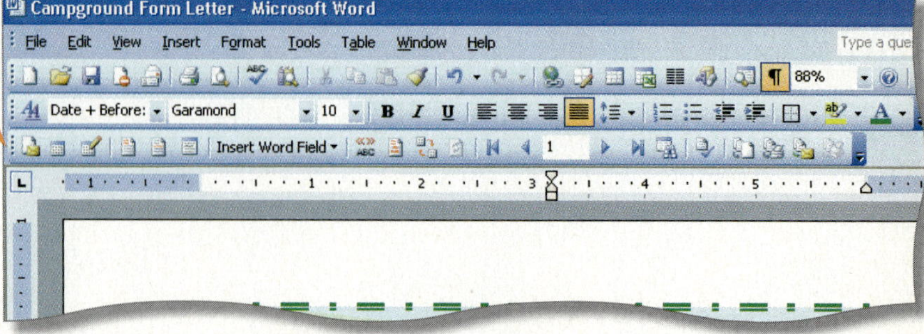

FIGURE 5-37

The Mail Merge task pane is closed because the next step is to enter the contents of the form letter, and the document window is larger if the task pane is closed.

If you are familiar with Microsoft Access, you can open the Camper List file in Access. You do not have to be familiar with Access, however, to continue with this mail merge process. Word simply stores a data source as an Access table because it is an efficient method of storing a data source.

More About

Saving Data Sources

Word, by default, saves a data source in the My Data Sources folder on your hard disk. Likewise, when you open a data source, Word initially looks in the My Data Sources folder for the file. The default file type for a new data source created in Word is called a Microsoft Office Address List. If you are familiar with Microsoft Access, you can open and view these file types in Access using the Microsoft Office Access file type.

Editing Records in the Data Source

The Mail Merge toolbar is displayed on the screen because you have identified a main document and a data source. Figure 5-38 identifies the buttons and boxes on the Mail Merge toolbar. These buttons and boxes are explained as they are used.

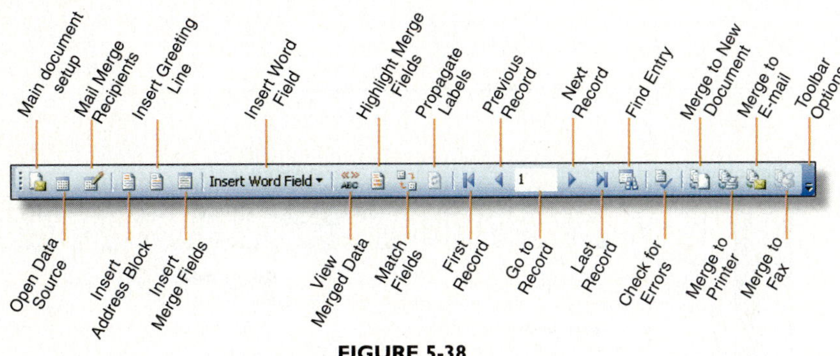

FIGURE 5-38

More About

Docked Toolbars

Word docks the Mail Merge toolbar at the top of the Word window. If you want to move the docked toolbar above or below the Standard and Formatting toolbars, drag the move handle on the Mail Merge toolbar to position the toolbar in a new location.

All of the data records have been entered into the data source and saved with the file name, Camper List. To add more data records to the data source, click the Mail Merge Recipients button on the Mail Merge toolbar to display the Mail Merge Recipients dialog box (shown in Figure 5-36). Click the Edit button in the Mail Merge Recipients dialog box to display the data records in a dialog box similar to the one shown in Figure 5-34 on page WD 318. Then add records as described in the previous steps.

To change an existing data record in the data source, display the data record by clicking the Mail Merge Recipients button on the Mail Merge toolbar to display the Mail Merge Recipients dialog box. Click the data record to change in the Mail Merge Recipients dialog box. If the list of data records is long, you can click the Find button to locate an item, such as the first name, quickly in the list. With the record to change selected, click the Edit button in the Mail Merge Recipients dialog box to display the selected data record in a dialog box similar to the one shown in Figure 5-34.

To delete a record, display it using the same procedure described in the previous paragraph. Then, click the Delete Entry button in the dialog box (Figure 5-34).

Composing the Main Document for the Form Letters

The next step is to enter and format the text and fields in the main document, which in this case is the form letter (shown in Figure 5-1a on page WD 299). The banner containing the campground name is complete. The steps on the following pages illustrate how to compose the rest of the main document for the form letter.

More About

Date Formats

Most business letters use the following date format: month day, year (August 16, 2005). Thus, Word uses this format as its default date format. Some people, however, prefer other date formats. This project demonstrates how to change the date format from this standard to another format.

Modifying a Field

In the elegant letter template, Word automatically displays the current computer date in the date line because the date actually is a field. Earlier in this project, you worked with data fields – the fields in the data source. A field, however, does not have to be associated with a data source. A **field** can be any placeholder for a value that changes. For example, when you print a document that contains a date field, Word always prints the current date on the document. If you want to update a field on the screen, for example if the date displayed is not the current computer date, click the field and then press the F9 key.

The date line at the top of the form letter displays the date August 16, 2005 in the form: month day, year. In this project, the date should be displayed as 16 August 2005, that is, in the form: day month year. To make this change, you edit the date field. The following steps show how to edit a field.

To Edit a Field

1

- **Right-click the field, in this case, the date field (Figure 5-39).**

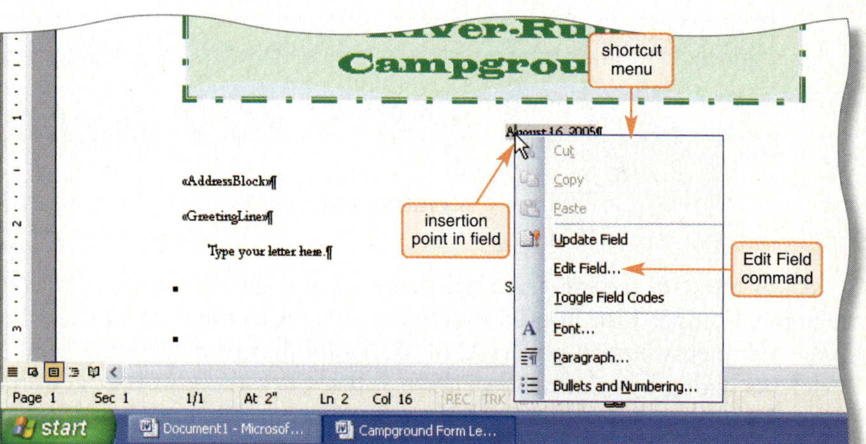

FIGURE 5-39

2

- **Click Edit Field on the shortcut menu.**
- **When Word displays the Field dialog box, click the desired format in the Date formats list (in this case, 16 August 2005).**

The Field dialog box shows a list of available formats for dates and times with the format d MMMM yyyy shown in the Date formats text box (Figure 5-40). Your screen probably will not show 16 August 2005; instead, it will display the current system date stored in your computer.

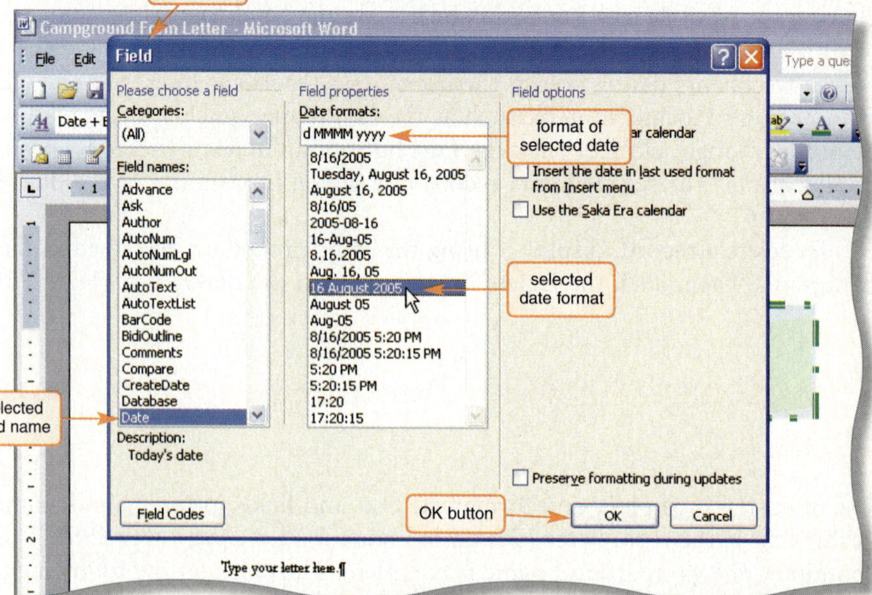

FIGURE 5-40

3

• **Click the OK button.**

Word displays the current date in the d MMMM yyyy format in the form letter (Figure 5-41).

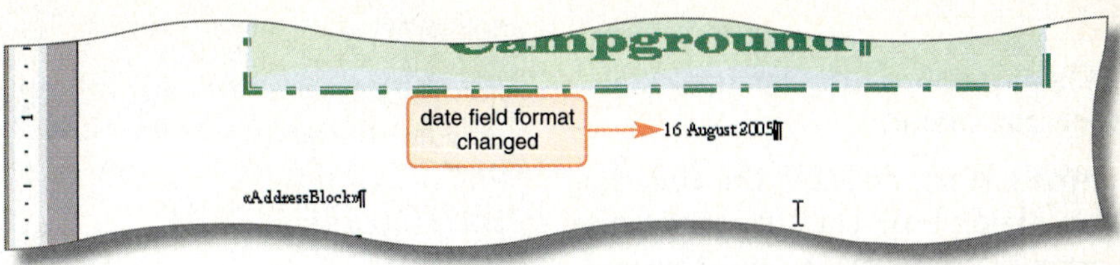

FIGURE 5-41

Other Ways

1. In Voice Command mode, say "Edit, Field, [select format], OK"

Inserting Merge Fields in the Main Document

In a letter, the inside address is below the date line, and the salutation is below the inside address. The contents of the inside address are located in the data source. That is, data in the data source is to be displayed in the main document.

Earlier, this project showed how to create the data source for this form letter. Recall that each field in the data source was assigned a field name. To link the data source to the main document, you insert these field names into the main document.

In the main document, these field names are called **merge fields** because they merge, or combine, the main document with the contents of the data source. When a merge field is inserted into the main document, Word surrounds the field name with merge field characters (shown in Figure 5-42). The **merge field characters**, which are chevrons, mark the beginning and ending of a merge field. Merge field characters are not on the keyboard; therefore, you cannot type them directly into the document. Word automatically displays them when a merge field is inserted into the main document.

Most letters contain an address and salutation. For this reason, Word provides an AddressBlock merge field and a GreetingLine merge field. The **AddressBlock merge field** contains several fields related to an address: title, first name, middle name, last name, suffix, company, street address 1, street address 2, city, state, and ZIP code. When Word is instructed to use the AddressBlock merge field, it automatically looks for any fields in the associated data source that are related to an address and then formats the address block properly when you merge the data source with the main document. For example, if your inside address does not use a middle name, suffix, or company, Word omits these items from the inside address and adjusts the spacing so the address prints correctly.

The **GreetingLine merge field** contains text and fields related to a salutation. The default greeting for the salutation is in the format, Dear Mr. Randall, followed by a comma. In this letter, you want a more formal ending to the salutation – a colon. The following steps show how to edit the GreetingLine merge field.

More About

Fields

Word, by default, shades a field in gray when the insertion point is in the field. The shading displays on the screen to help you identify fields; the shading does not print on a hard copy. To select an entire field, double-click it.

To Edit the GreetingLine Merge Field

1

• **If necessary, scroll down to display the GreetingLine merge field in the document window.**

• **Right-click the GreetingLine merge field (Figure 5-42).**

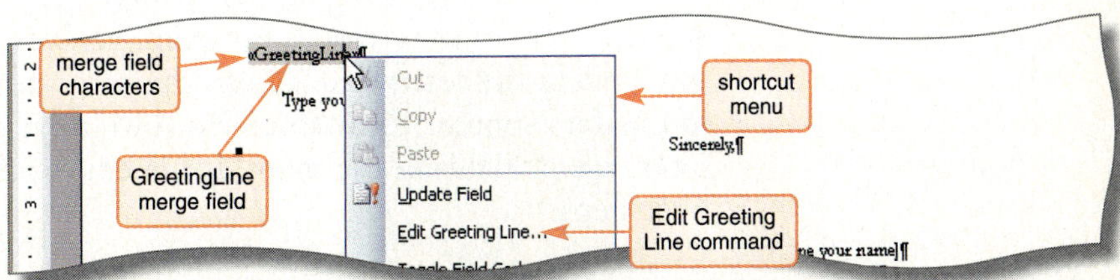

FIGURE 5-42

2

- **Click Edit Greeting Line on the shortcut menu.**
- **When Word displays the Greeting Line dialog box, click the right box arrow in the Greeting line format area and then click the colon (:).**

In the Greeting Line dialog box, the first box arrow displays a list of initial phrases in the greeting line; the second box arrow displays a list of formats for the name; the third box arrow displays a list of punctuation formats to end the salutation (Figure 5-43).

- **Click the OK button.**

Word modifies the format of the greeting line.

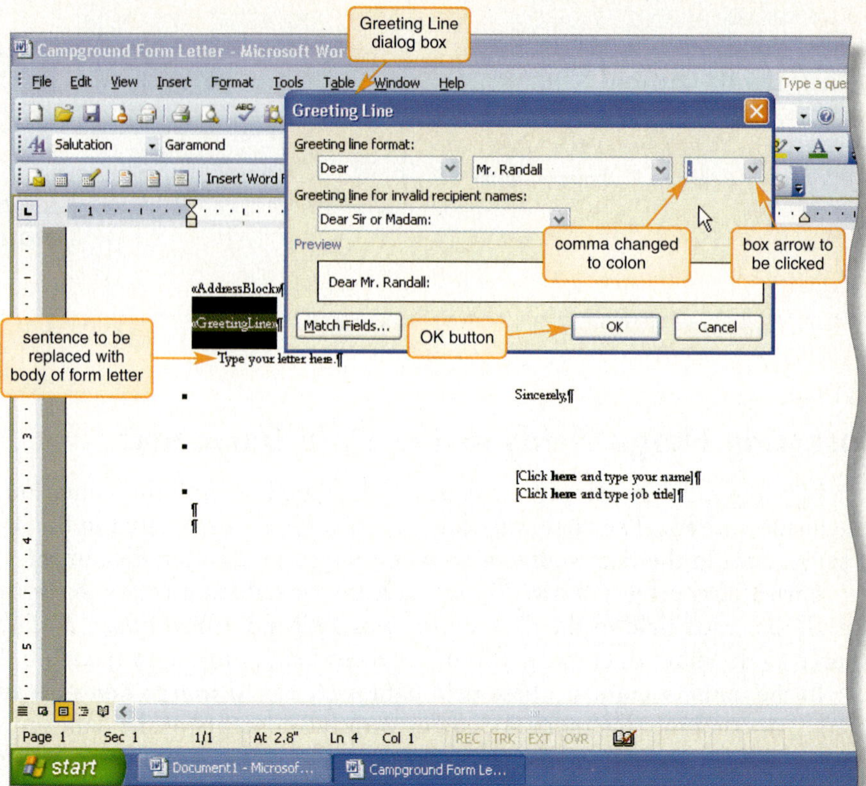

FIGURE 5-43

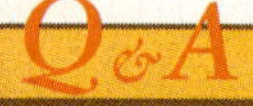

Q: What grammar and punctuation should I use in a salutation?

A: Formal business letters typically use a more formal salutation (e.g., Dear Ms. Cartright:). Less formal business letters may use a less formal salutation. Less formal salutations may address the reader by his or her first name. In this case, the salutation also may end with a comma instead of a colon (e.g., Dear Beth,).

You will not notice a change in the GreetingLine merge field at this time. The new format will be displayed when you merge the form letter to the data source later in this project.

The next step is to begin typing the body of the letter, which is to be located where Word has the placeholder text, Type your letter here (shown in Figure 5-43).

The following steps describe how to begin typing the body of the form letter.

To Begin Typing the Body of the Form Letter

1. **Triple-click the placeholder text containing the sentence, Type your letter here., to select it.**
2. **With the sentence selected, type** `We would like to thank you for reserving a` **and then press the SPACEBAR.**

The beginning of the first sentence below the GreetingLine merge field is entered (shown in Figure 5-44).

The first sentence in the first paragraph of the letter identifies the type of campsite the vacationer reserved, for example, water and electric, and the number of nights in the reservation. Both the site type and number of nights are data fields in the data source. To instruct Word to use data fields from the data source, you insert merge fields in the main document for the form letter, as shown in the next steps.

To Insert Merge Fields in the Main Document

1

- **With the insertion point positioned as shown in Figure 5-44, click the Insert Merge Fields button on the Mail Merge toolbar.**
- **When Word displays the Insert Merge Field dialog box, click Site Type in the Fields list.**

Word displays a list of field names in the data source file associated with this main document (Figure 5-44). The field you select will be inserted in the main document at the location of the insertion point.

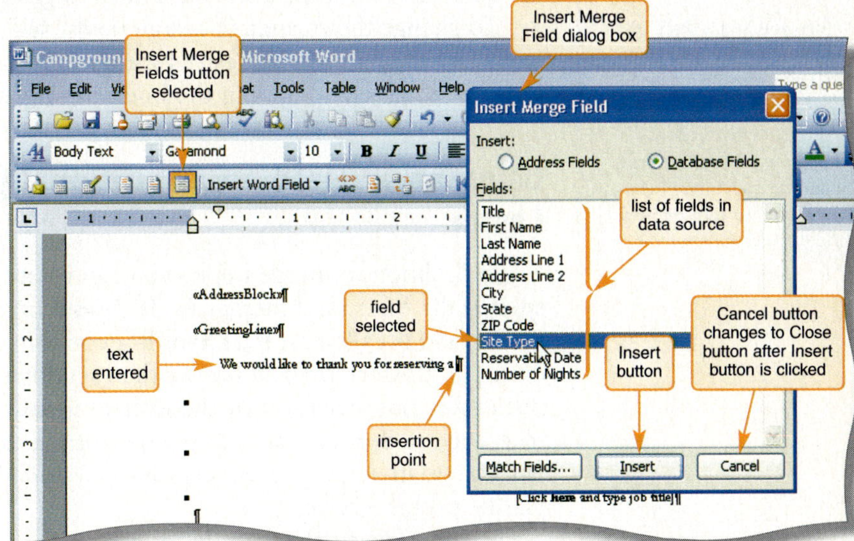

FIGURE 5-44

2

- **Click the Insert button in the dialog box.**
- **Click the Close button in the dialog box.**
- **Press the SPACEBAR. Type** `site for` **and then press the SPACEBAR.**
- **Click the Insert Merge Fields button on the Mail Merge toolbar, click Number of Nights in the Fields list, click the Insert button, and then click the Close button in the dialog box.**
- **Press the SPACEBAR and then type** `nights at our campground.`

Word displays the merge fields, Site Type and Number of Nights, surrounded by merge field characters in the main document (Figure 5-45).

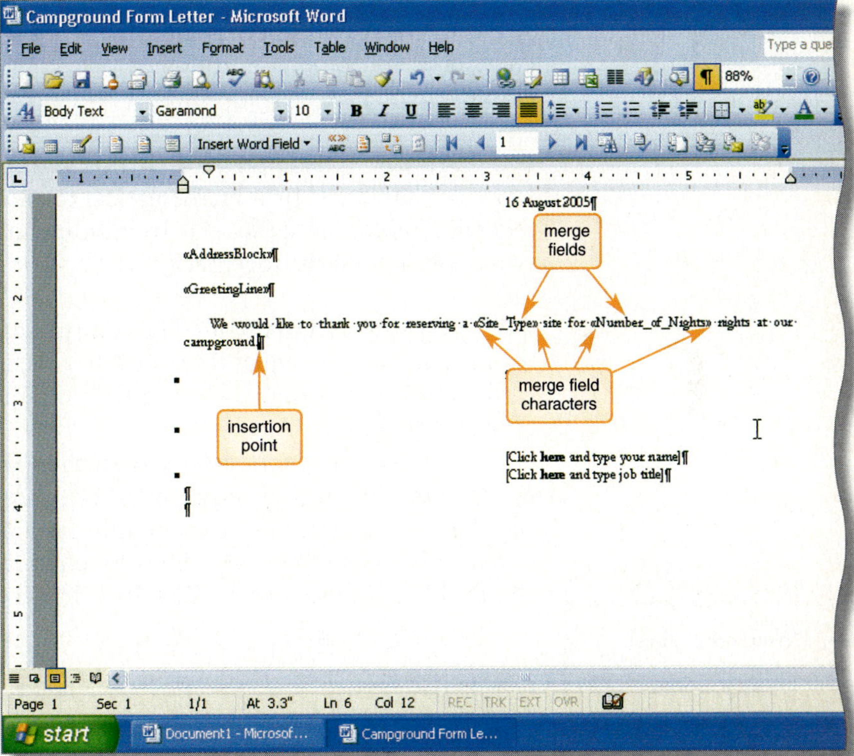

FIGURE 5-45

Other Ways

1. With Mail Merge toolbar displaying, in Voice Command mode, say "Insert Merge Fields, [select field], Insert, Close"

More About

Field Codes

When you insert fields into a document, if the fields are displayed surrounded by braces instead of chevrons and if extra instructions appear between the braces, then field codes have been turned on. To turn off field codes, press ALT+F9.

When you merge the data source with the main document, the site type (e.g., water and electric) and number of nights (e.g., two) will print at the location of the merge fields, Site Type and Number of Nights, respectively.

To change the format of merge fields, select the merge field in the main document and then apply the desired formatting. Later in this project, you increase the font size of all characters in the body of the letter.

Using an IF Field to Conditionally Print Text in a Form Letter

In addition to merge fields, you can insert Word fields that are designed specifically for a mail merge. An **IF field** is an example of a Word field. One form of the IF field is called an **If...Then:** If a condition is true, then perform an action. For example, If Mary owns a house, then send her information about homeowner's insurance. Another form of the IF field is called an **If...Then...Else:** If a condition is true, then perform an action; else perform a different action. For example, If John has an e-mail address, then send him an e-mail message; else send him the message via the postal service.

In this project, the form letter checks the vacationer's site type. If the site type is tent, then the required deposit is $11.00; else if the site type is water and electric, then the required deposit is $23.50. Thus, you will use an If...Then...Else: If the site type is equal to tent, then print $11.00 on the form letter, else print $23.50.

The phrase that appears after the word If is called a condition. A **condition** consists of an expression, followed by a comparison operator, followed by a final expression.

EXPRESSION The expression in a condition can be a merge field, a number, a series of characters, or a mathematical formula. Word surrounds a series of characters with quotation marks ("). To indicate an empty, or null, expression, Word places two quotation marks together ("").

COMPARISON OPERATOR The comparison operator in a condition must be one of six characters: = (equal to or matches the text), <> (not equal to or does not match text), < (less than), <= (less than or equal to), > (greater than), >= (greater than or equal to).

If the result of a condition is true, then Word evaluates the **true text**. If the result of the condition is false, Word evaluates the **false text** if it exists. In this project, the first expression in the condition is a merge field (Site Type); the comparison operator is equal to (=); and the second expression is the text tent. The true text is "$11.00". The false text is "$23.50". The complete IF field is as follows:

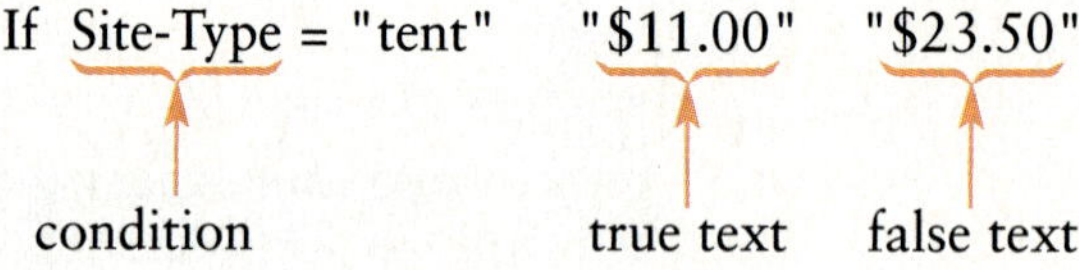

The next steps show how to insert this IF field in the form letter.

Q&A

Q: What is an IF field?

A: The term, IF field, originates from computer programming. Do not be intimidated by the terminology. An IF field simply specifies a decision. Some programmers refer to it as an IF statement. An IF field can be simple or complex. Complex IF fields include one or more nested IF fields, which is a second IF field inside the true or false text of the first IF field.

To Insert an IF Field in the Main Document

1

- **With the insertion point positioned as shown in Figure 5-45 on page WD 325, press the SPACEBAR. Type** `To guarantee your reservation, we must receive a deposit of` **and then press the SPACEBAR.**
- **Click the Insert Word Field button on the Mail Merge toolbar.**

A list of Word fields that may be inserted in the main document is displayed (Figure 5-46).

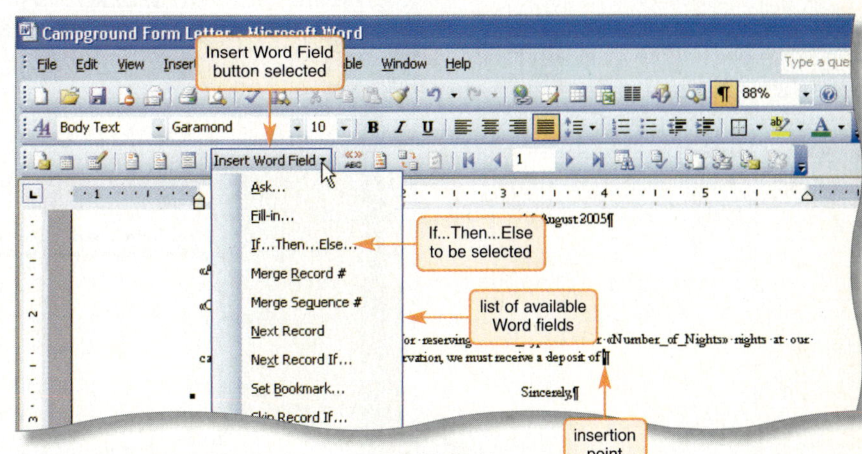

FIGURE 5-46

2

- **Click If...Then...Else in the list.**

Word displays the Insert Word Field: IF dialog box (Figure 5-47). You can specify the IF condition in the IF area of this dialog box.

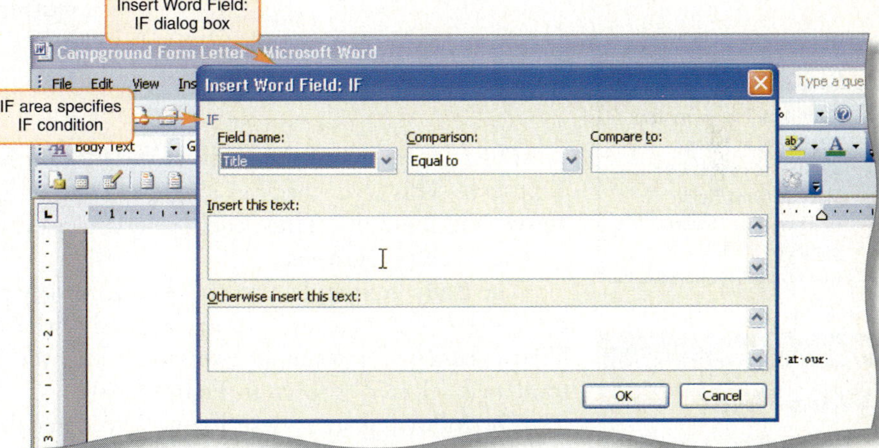

FIGURE 5-47

3

- **Click the Field name box arrow. Scroll through the list of fields and then click Site_Type.**
- **Click the Compare to text box. Type** `tent` **and then press the TAB key.**
- **Type** `$11.00` **and then press the TAB key.**
- **Type** `$23.50` **as the false text.**

The entries in the Insert Word Field: IF dialog box are complete (Figure 5-48).

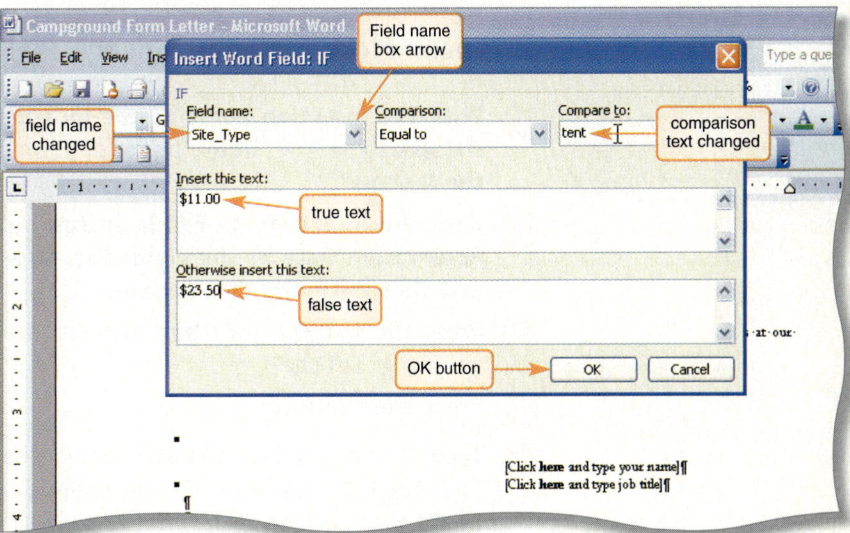

FIGURE 5-48

4

• **Click the OK button.**

Word displays $23.50 at the location of the insertion point in the main document because the first record in the data source has a site type of water and electric (Figure 5-49).

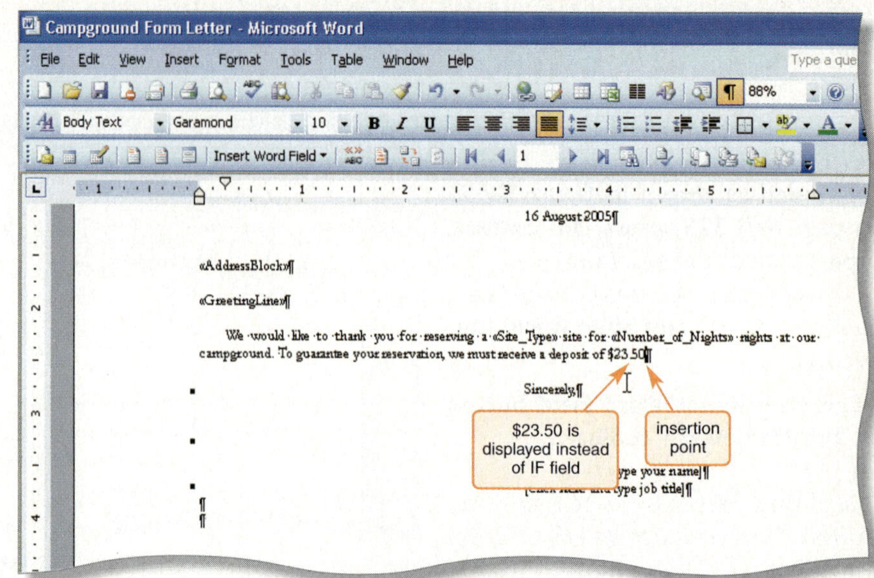
Campground Form Letter - Microsoft Word
16 August 2005¶
«AddressBlock»¶
«GreetingLine»¶
We would like to thank you for reserving a «Site_Type» site for «Number_of_Nights» nights at our campground. To guarantee your reservation, we must receive a deposit of $23.50¶
Sincerely,¶
$23.50 is displayed instead of IF field
insertion point

FIGURE 5-49

Other Ways

1. With Mail Merge toolbar displaying, in Voice Command mode, say "Insert Word Field, If...Then...Else, [enter condition], OK"

More About

Word Fields

In addition to the IF field, Word provides other fields that may be used in form letters. For example, the ASK and FILLIN fields prompt the user to enter data for each record in the data source. The SKIP RECORD IF field instructs the mail merge to not generate a form letter for a data record if a specific condition is met.

The paragraphs of the body of the Elegant Merge Letter template use the Body Text style. This style specifies single-spacing within paragraphs and double-spacing between paragraphs. Thus, each time you press the ENTER key, Word places a blank line between paragraphs.

The Body Text style also specifies to **justify** paragraphs, which means the left and right edges of the paragraphs are aligned with the left and right margins, respectively, like the edges of newspaper columns. Thus, the Justify button on the Formatting toolbar is selected (shown in Figure 5-50).

The following steps describe how to enter the remaining text in the current paragraph, which contains another merge field, and to enter another paragraph of text into the form letter.

To Enter More Text and Merge Fields

1. **With the insertion point at the location shown in Figure 5-49, press the SPACEBAR. Type** `one week before your arrival date of` **and then press the SPACEBAR.**
2. **Click the Insert Merge Fields button on the Mail Merge toolbar. Click Reservation Date in the Fields list. Click the Insert button in the dialog box and then click the Close button.**
3. **Press the SPACEBAR and then type** `at the address shown at the bottom of this letter.`
4. **Press the ENTER key.**
5. **Type** `Our goal is to make your stay comfortable and enjoyable. The facilities and recreational activities at our campground continue to receive the highest ratings from` *Camping Today* `magazine.` **Press the ENTER key.**

Word enters the text and merge field in the form letter (Figure 5-50).

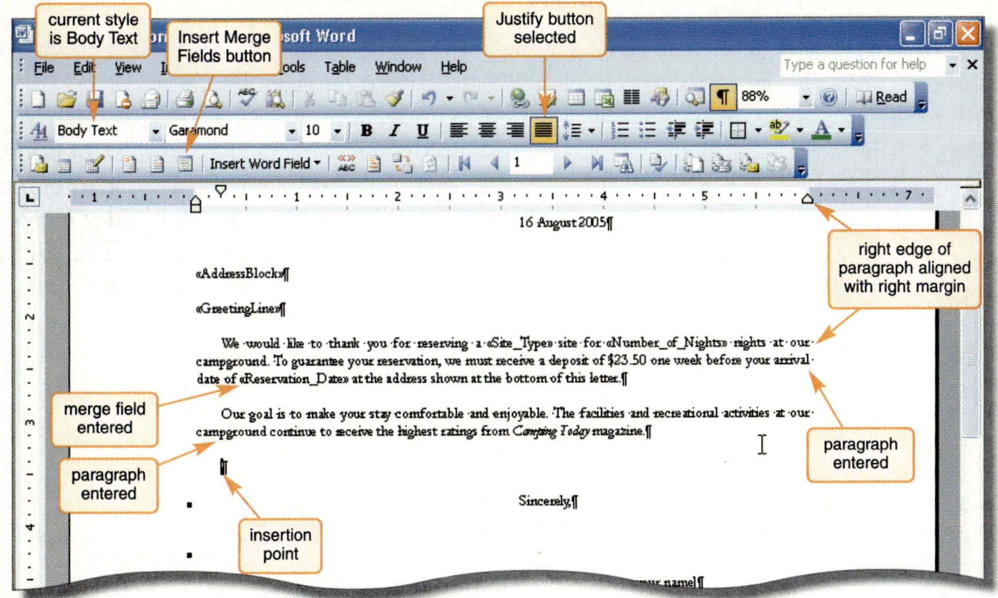

FIGURE 5-50

Creating an Outline Numbered List

The next step is to enter an outline numbered list in the form letter (shown in Figure 5-1a on page WD 299). An **outline numbered list** is a list that contains several levels of items, with each level displaying a different numeric, alphabetic, or bullet symbol.

To ensure that no existing formatting will affect the outline numbered list, the first step in creating the list is to clear formatting, which changes the paragraph from the Body Text style to the Normal style. The following steps show how to create an outline numbered list.

To Create an Outline Numbered List

1

- **If necessary, scroll down to display the insertion point in the document window.**
- **With the insertion point positioned as shown in Figure 5-50, click the Style box arrow on the Formatting toolbar and then click Clear Formatting.**
- **Click Format on the menu bar.**

Word clears formatting of the paragraph at the location of the insertion point (Figure 5-51). The Style box now displays Normal, instead of Body Text.

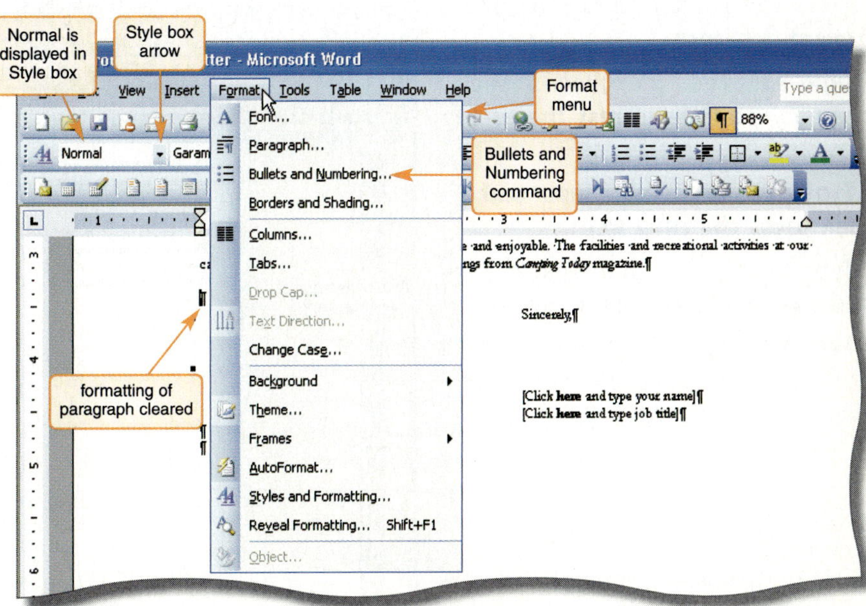

FIGURE 5-51

2

- **Click Bullets and Numbering on the Format menu.**
- **When Word displays the Bullets and Numbering dialog box, if necessary, click the Outline Numbered tab.**
- **Click the desired number or bullet style in the list (Figure 5-52).**

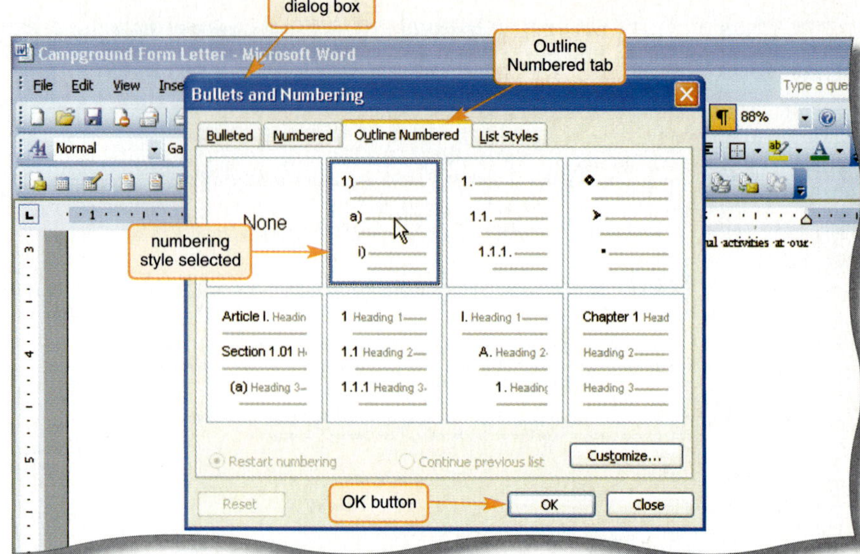

FIGURE 5-52

3

- **Click the OK button.**
- **Type** Facilities **and then press the ENTER key.**

Word places the number one, 1), on the first item in the list (Figure 5-53). The number two, 2), is displayed on the next line. This list item needs to be **demoted** *to a second-level list item, indented below the first list item.*

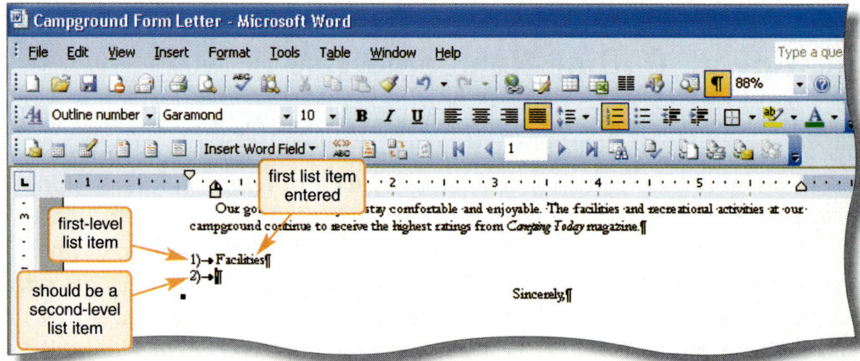

FIGURE 5-53

4

- **Press the TAB key to demote the current list item.**
- **Type** Spotless restrooms and showers **and then press the ENTER key.**
- **Type** Two laundry rooms **and then press the ENTER key.**
- **Type** Groceries and snack bar **and then press the ENTER key.**
- **Type** Modem, telephone, and CATV hookup at each site **and then press the ENTER key.**

The second level list items are entered (Figure 5-54). The letter e displays on the next line. This list item needs to be promoted to a first-level list item, aligned below the number one.

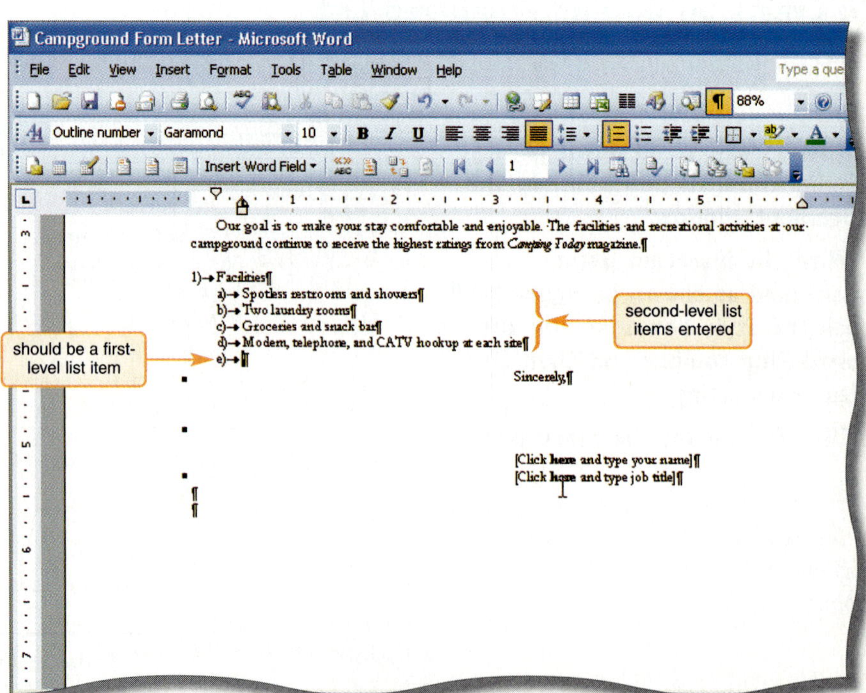

FIGURE 5-54

5

- **Press** SHIFT+TAB **to promote the current list item.**
- **Press** CTRL+0 **(the numeral zero) to add a blank line above the paragraph containing the number two list item.**
- **Type** `Recreational Activities` **and then press the** ENTER **key.**
- **Press the** TAB **key to demote the current list item.**
- **Press** CTRL+0 **(the numeral zero) to remove the blank line above the paragraph containing the letter a) list item.**

Recall that pressing CTRL+0 is a toggle that adds or removes a blank line above a paragraph (Figure 5-55).

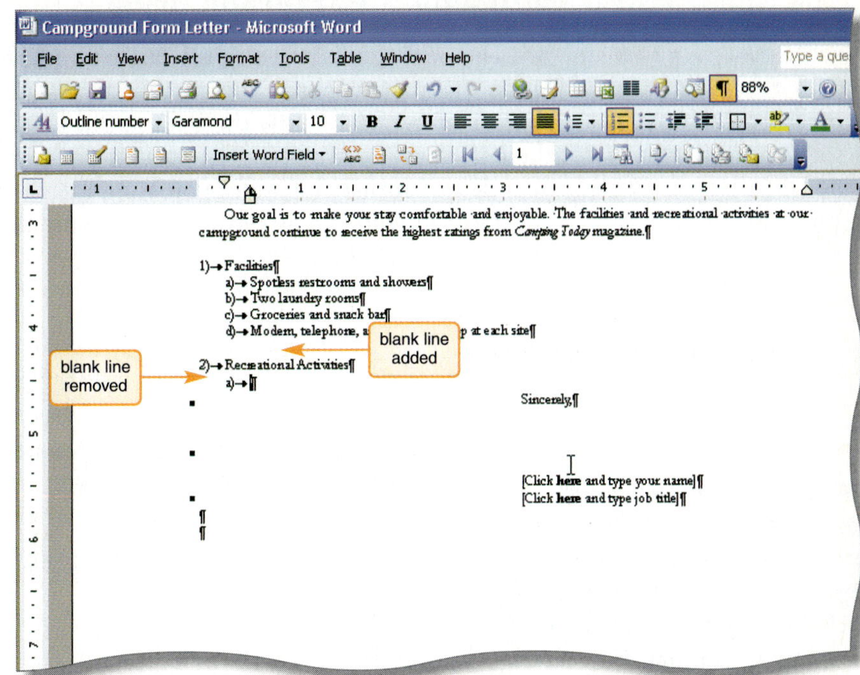

FIGURE 5-55

6

- **Type** `Heated swimming pool` **and then press the** ENTER **key.**
- **Type** `Recreation hall and game room` **and then press the** ENTER **key.**
- **Type** `Freshwater fishing and boat rental` **and then press the** ENTER **key.**
- **Type** `Horseback riding` **and then press the** ENTER **key twice.**

The outline numbered list is complete (Figure 5-56). Word removes the numbered list symbol from the current paragraph when you press the ENTER key twice at the end of a numbered or bulleted list.

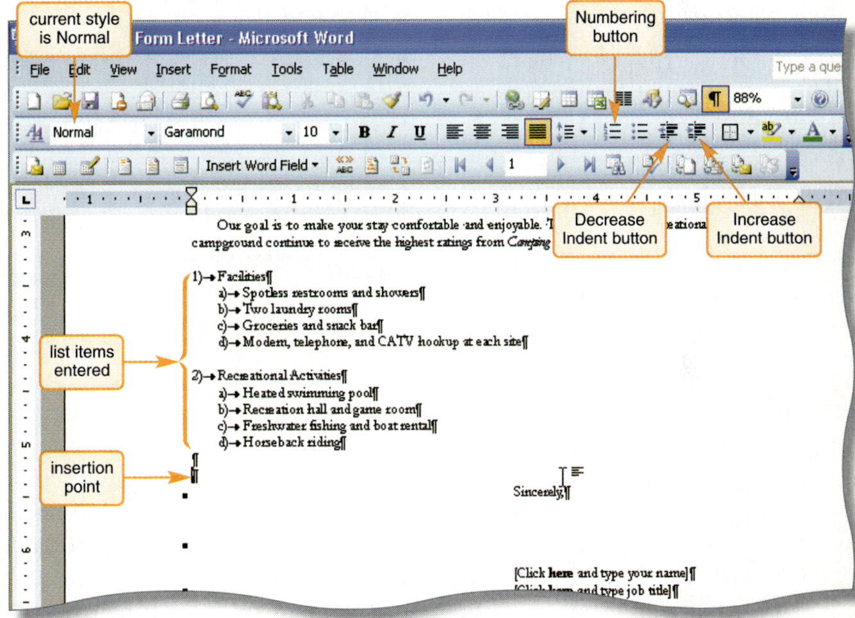

FIGURE 5-56

Other Ways

1. Right-click paragraph, click Bullets and Numbering on shortcut menu, click Outline Numbered tab, click numbering style, click OK button
2. In Voice Command mode, say "Format, Bullets and Numbering, Outline Numbered, [select numbering style], OK"

Instead of pressing the TAB key to demote a list item, you can click the Increase Indent button (Figure 5-56) on the Formatting toolbar. Likewise, you can click the Decrease Indent button on the Formatting toolbar to promote a list item – instead of pressing SHIFT+TAB.

As an alternative to pressing the ENTER key twice at the bottom of a list to stop Word from automatically numbering, you can click the Numbering button on the Formatting toolbar (Figure 5-56) to remove a number from a list item.

Applying a Paragraph Style

The next step is to enter the last paragraph of text into the body of the cover letter. The paragraphs in the cover letter use the Body Text style, which specifies spacing above and below the paragraph, first-line indents the paragraph, and justifies the text in the paragraph. The current paragraph is set to the Normal style because you cleared formatting before creating the outline numbered list.

The following steps show how to apply the Body Text paragraph style to the current paragraph.

To Apply a Paragraph Style

1

- **With the insertion point positioned two lines below the outline numbered list as shown in Figure 5-56 on the previous page, click the Style box arrow on the Formatting toolbar. If necessary, scroll until Body Text appears in the list.**

Word displays a list of styles associated with the current document (Figure 5-57).

2

- **Click Body Text.**

The entered paragraph will be formatted according to the Body Text paragraph style (shown in Figure 5-58).

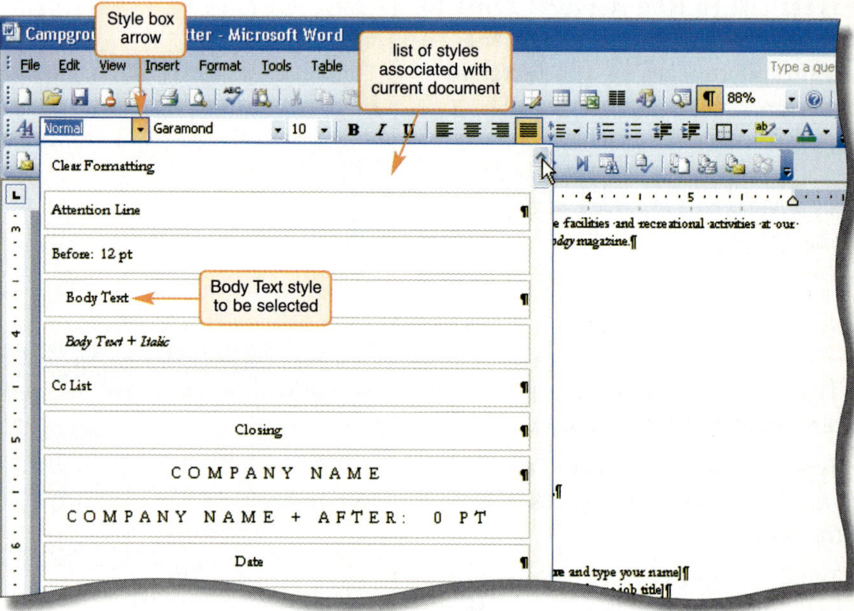

FIGURE 5-57

Other Ways

1. On Format menu click Styles and Formatting, click style name in Pick formatting to apply area
2. Click Styles and Formatting button on Formatting toolbar, click style name in Pick formatting to apply area
3. In Voice Command mode, say "Style, [select style]"

Many different styles are associated with a document. To view the complete list, click the Style box arrow on the Formatting toolbar or click the Styles and Formatting button on the Formatting toolbar (Figure 5-58) to display the Styles and Formatting task pane.

The following steps describe how to enter the text in the remainder of the letter.

To Enter More Text

1. **Type** `We look forward to making your stay with us a memorable camping adventure.`
2. **If necessary, scroll down to display the signature block. Click the placeholder text in the signature block, Click here and type your name, and then type** `Tom and Deanna Rosatti` **as the name.**
3. **Click the placeholder text in the signature block, Click here and type your job title, and then type** `Owners` **as the title.**

The body and signature block portions of the letter are complete (Figure 5-58).

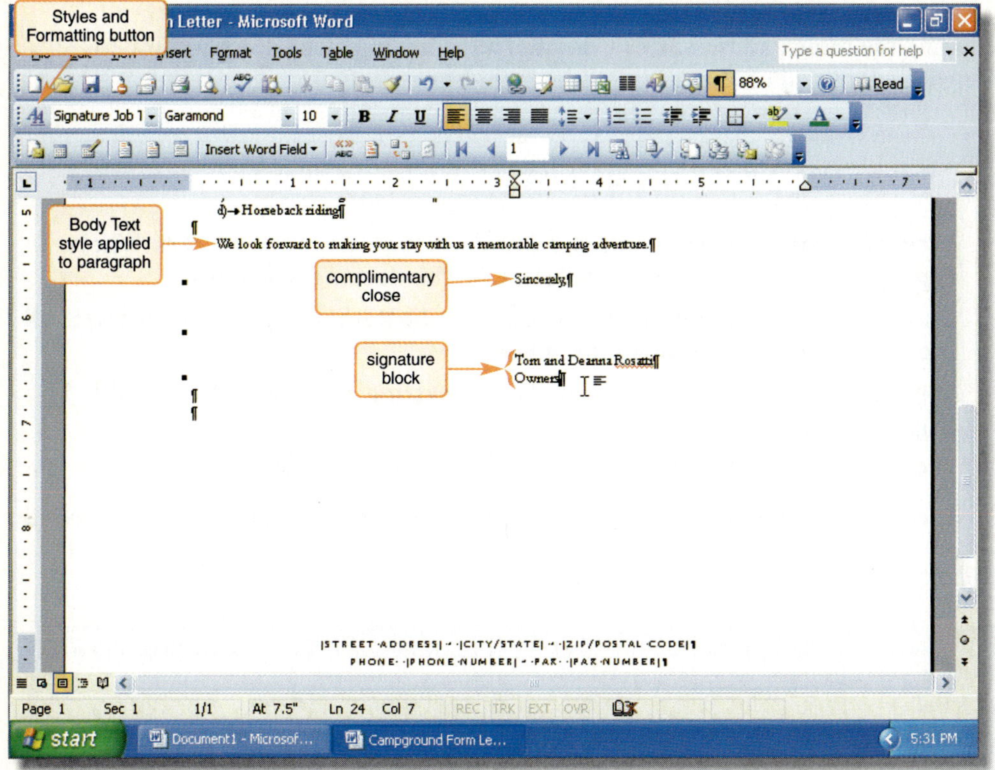

FIGURE 5-58

The return address at the bottom of the letter is formatted using the All Caps character effect (shown in Figure 5-5 on page WD 304). Thus, as you type characters, Word automatically converts them to capital letters. The following steps describe how to enter the return address at the bottom of the letter.

> *More About*
>
> **Character Effects**
>
> To apply other character effects, click Format on the menu bar, click Font, click the Font tab, click the desired effect in the Effects area, and then click the OK button.

To Select and Replace More Placeholder Text

1. **Scroll to the bottom of the letter to display the return address in the document window. Click the placeholder text, STREET ADDRESS. Type** `13 KNOB ROAD` **and then click the placeholder text, CITY/STATE.**
2. **Type** `GETTYSBURG, PA` **and then click the placeholder text, ZIP/POSTAL CODE.**
3. **Type** `17325` **and then click the placeholder text, PHONE NUMBER.**
4. **Type** `717-555-6543` **and then click the placeholder text, FAX NUMBER.**
5. **Type** `717-555-6544` **as the fax number.**

Word displays the return address at the bottom of the letter (Figure 5-59).

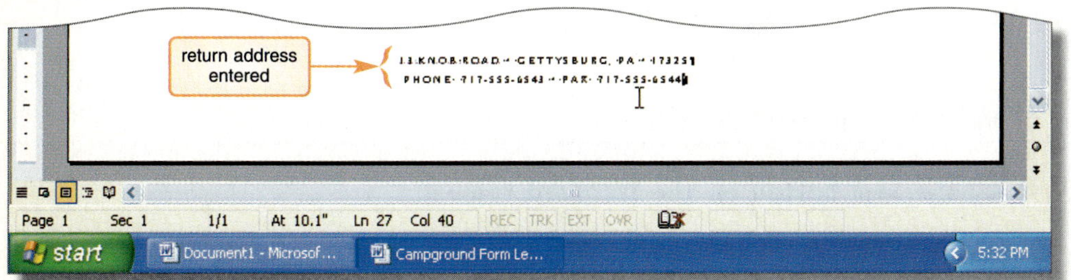

FIGURE 5-59

More About

Locking Fields

If you wanted to lock a field so that its field results cannot be changed, click the field and then press CTRL+F11. To subsequently unlock a field so that it may be updated, click the field and then press CTRL+SHIFT+F11.

The next step is to change the font size of characters below the letterhead, including the return address, to 11 point. The following steps describe how to change the font size of characters in the form letter.

To Change the Font Size of Text

1. **Click the Zoom box arrow on the Standard toolbar and then click Whole Page to display the entire form letter in the document window.**
2. **Drag from the date line down through the bottom of the letter to select all the text below the campground name.**
3. **Click the Font Size box arrow on the Formatting toolbar and then click 11 (Figure 5-60).**
4. **Click anywhere in the document to remove the selection.**
5. **Click the Zoom box arrow on the Standard toolbar and then click Page Width.**

Word changes the font size to 11.

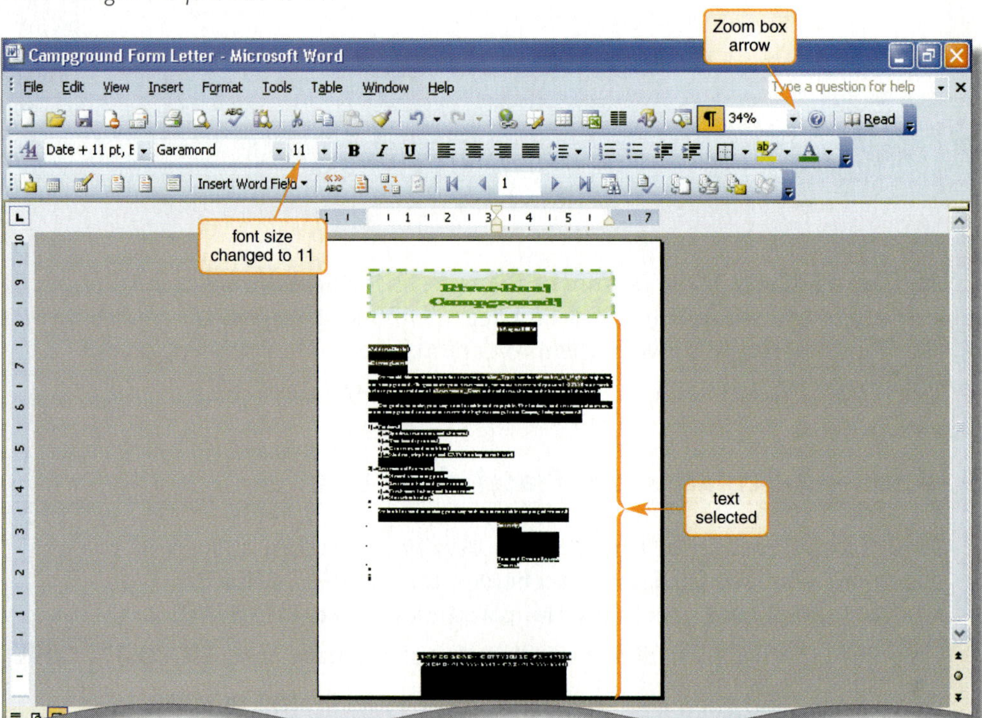

FIGURE 5-60

More About

Electronic Signatures

For more information about electronic signatures, visit the Word 2003 More About Web page (scsite.com/wd2003/more) and then click Electronic Signatures.

Saving the Document Again

The main document for the form letter now is complete. Thus, you should save it again, as described in the following step.

To Save a Document Again

1. **Click the Save button on the Standard toolbar.**

Word saves the main document for the form letter with the same name, Campground Form Letter, in the River Run folder.

Displaying Field Codes

The instructions in the IF field are not displayed in the document; instead, the field results are displayed. **Field results** represent the value to display after Word evaluates the instructions of the IF field. For example, Word displays the dollar amount, $23.50, in the document window (Figure 5-61) because the site type in the first data record is water and electric.

The instructions of an IF field are referred to as **field codes**, and the default for Word is field codes off. Thus, field codes do not print or show on the screen unless you turn them on. You use one procedure to show field codes on the screen and a different procedure to print them on a hard copy.

The following steps illustrate how to turn on a field code so you can see it on the screen. Most Word users turn on a field code only to verify its accuracy or to modify it. Field codes tend to clutter the screen. Thus, you should turn them off after viewing them.

More About

Main Documents

When you open a main document, Word attempts to open the associated data source file, too. If the data source is not in exactly the same location (i.e., drive and folder) as when it originally was saved, Word displays a dialog box indicating that it could not find the data source. When this occurs, click the Find Data Source button to display the Open Data Source dialog box, where you can locate the data source file.

To Display a Field Code

1

- **Scroll to and then right-click the dollar amount, $23.50.**

Word displays a shortcut menu (Figure 5-61).

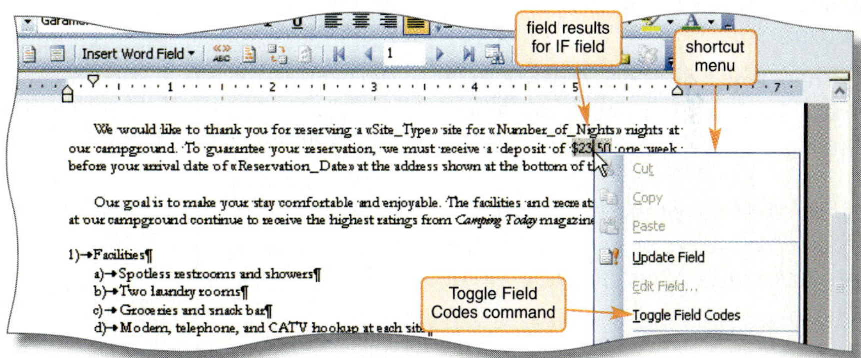

FIGURE 5-61

2

- **Click Toggle Field Codes on the shortcut menu.**

Word displays the field code instead of the field results, which means the instructions in the IF field are displayed (Figure 5-62). With field codes on, braces surround a field instead of chevrons.

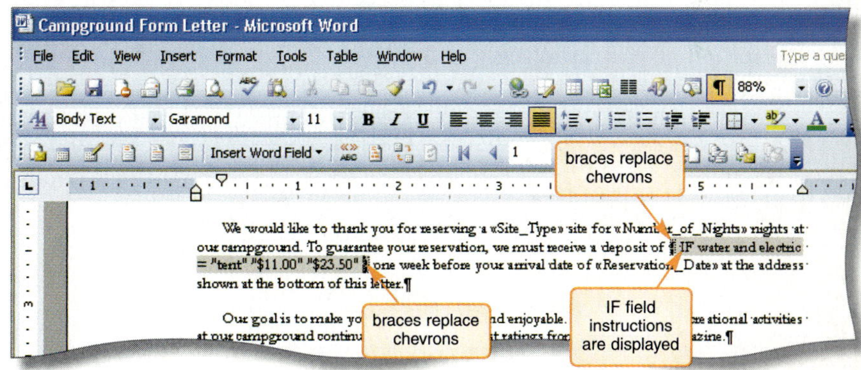

FIGURE 5-62

Other Ways

1. With insertion point in field, press SHIFT+F9
2. With insertion point in field, in Voice Command mode, say "Right-Click, Toggle Field Codes"

If you wanted all field codes in a document to be displayed on the screen, you would press **ALT+F9**. Then, to hide all the field codes, press ALT+F9 again.

Whether field codes are on or off on your screen has no effect on the merge process.

Printing Field Codes

When you merge or print a document, Word automatically converts field codes that show on the screen to field results. You may want to print the field codes version of the form letter, however, so you have a hard copy of the field codes for future reference. When you print field codes, you must remember to turn off the field codes option so that future documents print field results instead of field codes. For example, with field codes on, merged form letters will display field codes instead of data.

The following steps show how to print the field codes in the main document and then turn off the field codes print option for future printing.

To Print Field Codes in the Main Document

1

- **Click File on the menu bar and then click Print.**
- **When Word displays the Print dialog box, click the Options button.**
- **When Word displays another Print dialog box, place a check mark in the Field codes check box.**

Word displays a Print dialog box within another Print dialog box (Figure 5-63). The Field codes check box is selected.

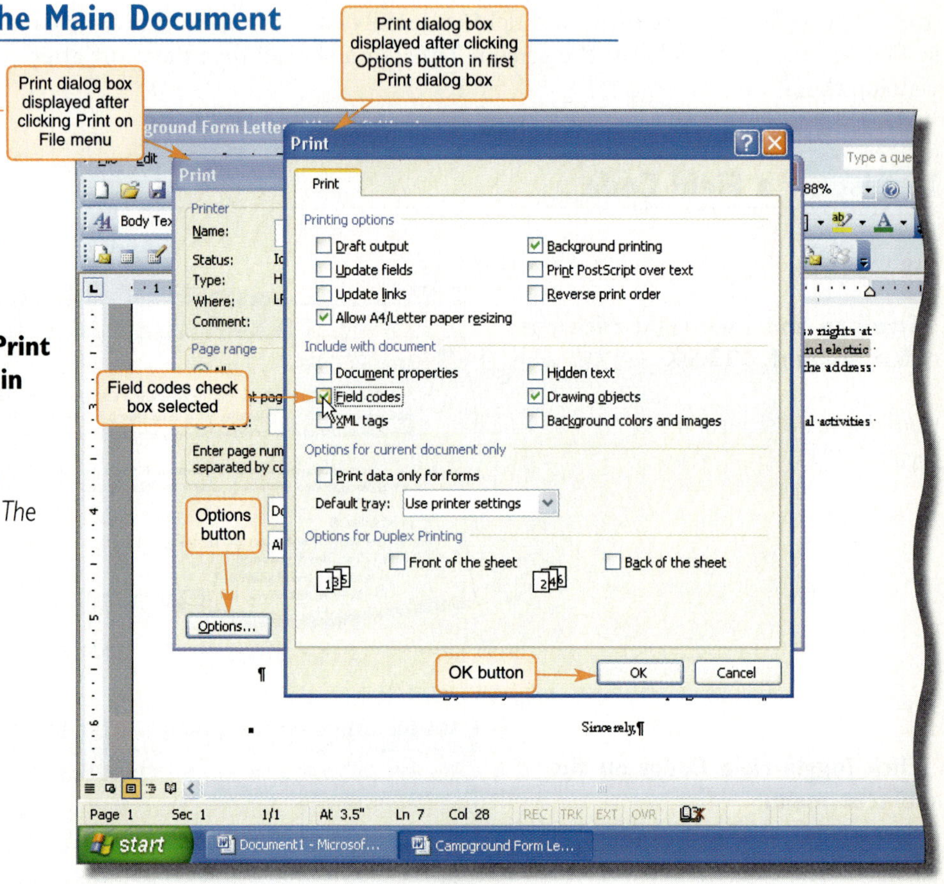

Print dialog box displayed after clicking Print on File menu

Print dialog box displayed after clicking Options button in first Print dialog box

Field codes check box selected

Options button

OK button

FIGURE 5-63

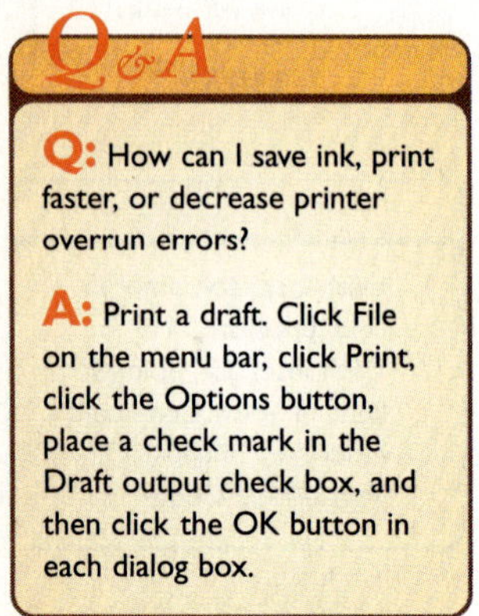
Q&A

Q: How can I save ink, print faster, or decrease printer overrun errors?

A: Print a draft. Click File on the menu bar, click Print, click the Options button, place a check mark in the Draft output check box, and then click the OK button in each dialog box.

2

- **Click the OK button.**
- **Click the OK button in the remaining Print dialog box.**

Word prints the main document with all field codes showing (Figure 5-64). Notice the contents of the letter are cluttered with many fields. Your printout also may show the banner at the top.

3

- **Click Tools on the menu bar and then click Options.**
- **When Word displays the Options dialog box, if necessary, click the Print tab.**
- **Click Field codes in the Include with document area to remove the check mark.**
- **Click the OK button.**

Word turns off field codes for printed documents.

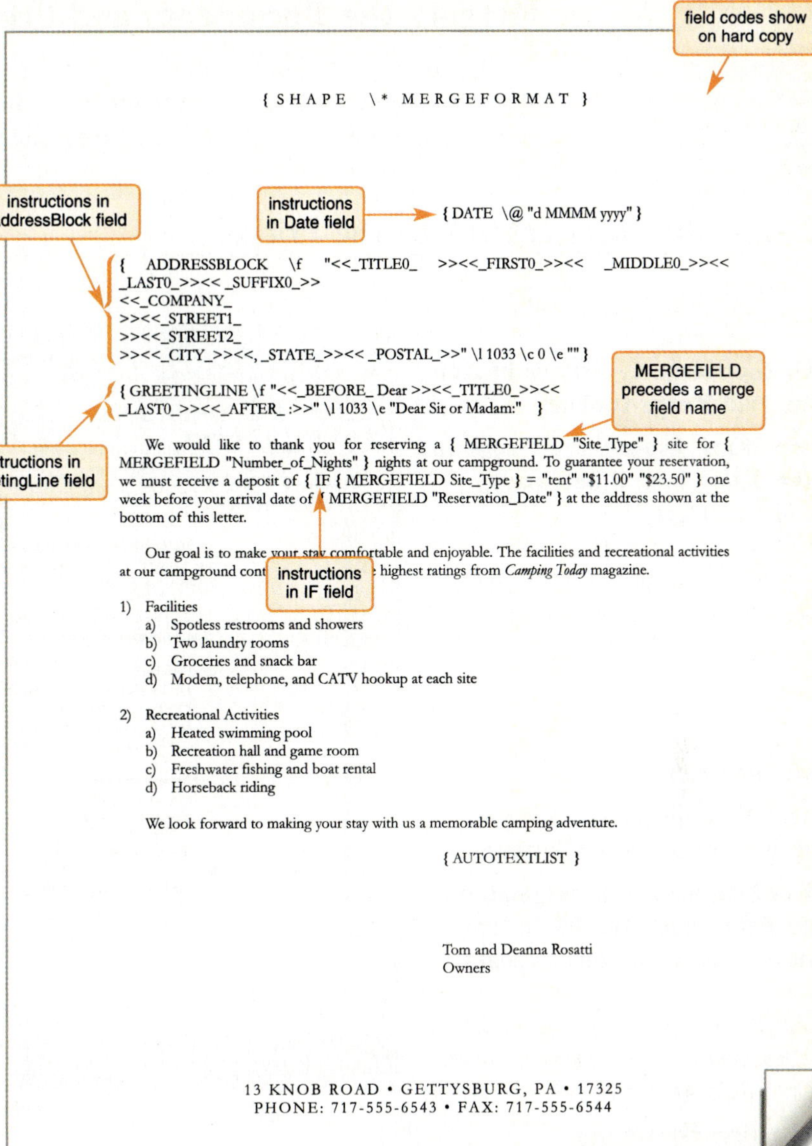

{ SHAPE * MERGEFORMAT }

{ DATE \@ "d MMMM yyyy" }

{ ADDRESSBLOCK \f "<<_TITLE0_ >><<_FIRST0_>><< _MIDDLE0_>><< _LAST0_>><< _SUFFIX0_>>
<<_COMPANY_
>><<_STREET1_
>><<_STREET2_
>><<_CITY_>><<, _STATE_>><< _POSTAL_>>" \l 1033 \c 0 \e "" }

{ GREETINGLINE \f "<<_BEFORE_ Dear >><<_TITLE0_>><< _LAST0_>><<_AFTER_ :>>" \l 1033 \e "Dear Sir or Madam:" }

We would like to thank you for reserving a { MERGEFIELD "Site_Type" } site for { MERGEFIELD "Number_of_Nights" } nights at our campground. To guarantee your reservation, we must receive a deposit of { IF { MERGEFIELD Site_Type } = "tent" "$11.00" "$23.50" } one week before your arrival date of { MERGEFIELD "Reservation_Date" } at the address shown at the bottom of this letter.

Our goal is to make your stay comfortable and enjoyable. The facilities and recreational activities at our campground cont[illegible] highest ratings from *Camping Today* magazine.

1) Facilities
   a) Spotless restrooms and showers
   b) Two laundry rooms
   c) Groceries and snack bar
   d) Modem, telephone, and CATV hookup at each site

2) Recreational Activities
   a) Heated swimming pool
   b) Recreation hall and game room
   c) Freshwater fishing and boat rental
   d) Horseback riding

We look forward to making your stay with us a memorable camping adventure.

{ AUTOTEXTLIST }

Tom and Deanna Rosatti
Owners

13 KNOB ROAD • GETTYSBURG, PA • 17325
PHONE: 717-555-6543 • FAX: 717-555-6544

FIGURE 5-64

Other Ways

1. On Tools menu click Options, click Print tab, click Field codes, click OK button, click Print button on Standard toolbar
2. In Voice Command mode, say "File, Print, Options, Field codes, OK, OK"

Merging the Documents and Printing the Letters

The data source and main document for the form letter are complete. The next step is to merge them to generate the individual form letters. The following steps show how to merge form letters, sending the merged letters to the printer.

To Merge the Form Letters to the Printer

1

- **Click the Merge to Printer button on the Mail Merge toolbar.**
- **When Word displays the Merge to Printer dialog box, if necessary, click All to select it.**

In the Merge to Printer dialog box, you indicate which data records should be merged (Figure 5-65).

2

- **Click the OK button.**
- **When Word displays the Print dialog box, click the OK button.**
- **If Word displays a message about locked fields, click the OK button whenever the dialog box appears.**

Word prints five separate letters, one for each vacationer in the data source (shown in Figure 5-1c on page WD 299).

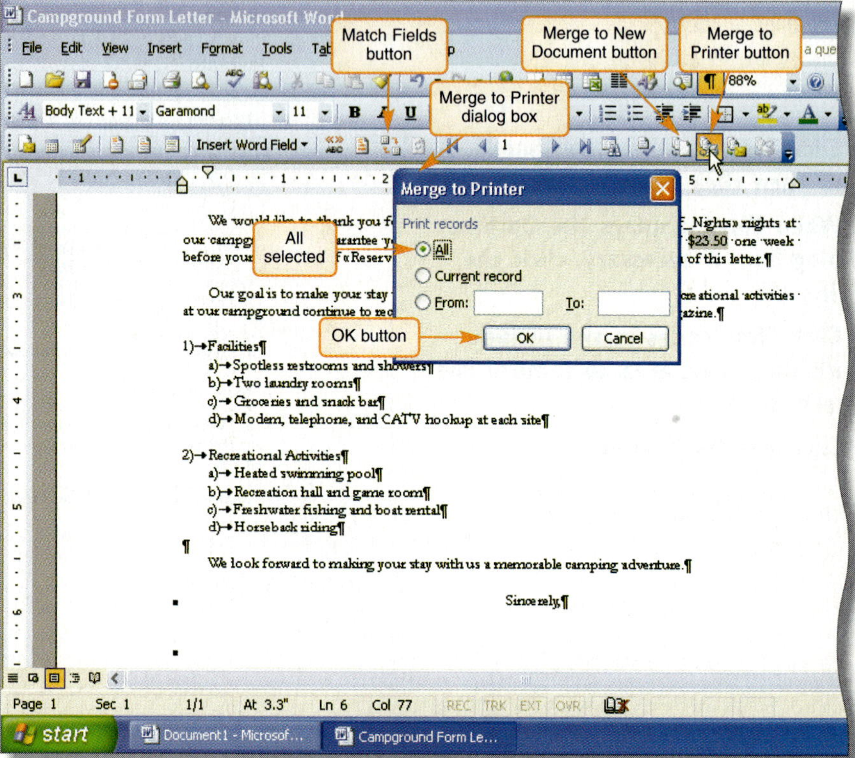

FIGURE 5-65

Other Ways

1. With Mail Merge toolbar displaying, in Voice Command mode, say "Merge to Printer, All, OK, OK"

The contents of the data source merge with the merge fields in the main document to generate the form letters. Word prints five form letters because the data source contains five records. The address lines suppress blanks. That is, vacationers without a second address line begin the city on the line immediately below the first address line. In addition, the deposit amount in each letter varies – depending on the type of campsite reserved.

If you notice errors in the printed form letters, edit the main document the same way you edit any other document. Then, save the changes and merge again. If the wrong field results print, Word may be mapping the fields incorrectly. To view fields, click the Match Fields button on the Mail Merge toolbar (Figure 5-65). Then, review the list of fields in the list. For example, the Last Name should map to the Last Name field in the data source. If it does not, click the box arrow to change the name of the data source field.

Instead of immediately printing the merged form letters, you could send them into a new document window by clicking the Merge to New Document button on the Mail Merge toolbar (shown in Figure 5-65). With this button, you view the merged form letters in a new document window on the screen to verify their accuracy before printing the letters. When you are finished viewing the merged form letters, you can print them by clicking the Print button on the Standard toolbar. In addition, you can save these merged form letters in a file. If you do not want to save the merged form letters, close the document window by clicking the Close button at the right edge of the menu bar. When the Microsoft Word dialog box is displayed asking if you want to save the document, click the No button.

Selecting Data Records to Merge and Print

Instead of merging and printing all of the records in the data source, you can choose which records will merge, based on a condition you specify. The dialog box in Figure 5-65 allows you to specify by record number which records to merge. Often you merge based on the contents of a specific field. For example, you may want to merge and print only those vacationers in the mailing list who are arriving on September 10.

The following steps show how to select records for a merge.

To Select Records to Merge

1

- **Click the Mail Merge Recipients button on the Mail Merge toolbar.**

Word displays the Mail Merge Recipients dialog box (Figure 5-66). You must scroll to the right to display the Reservation Date field in this dialog box.

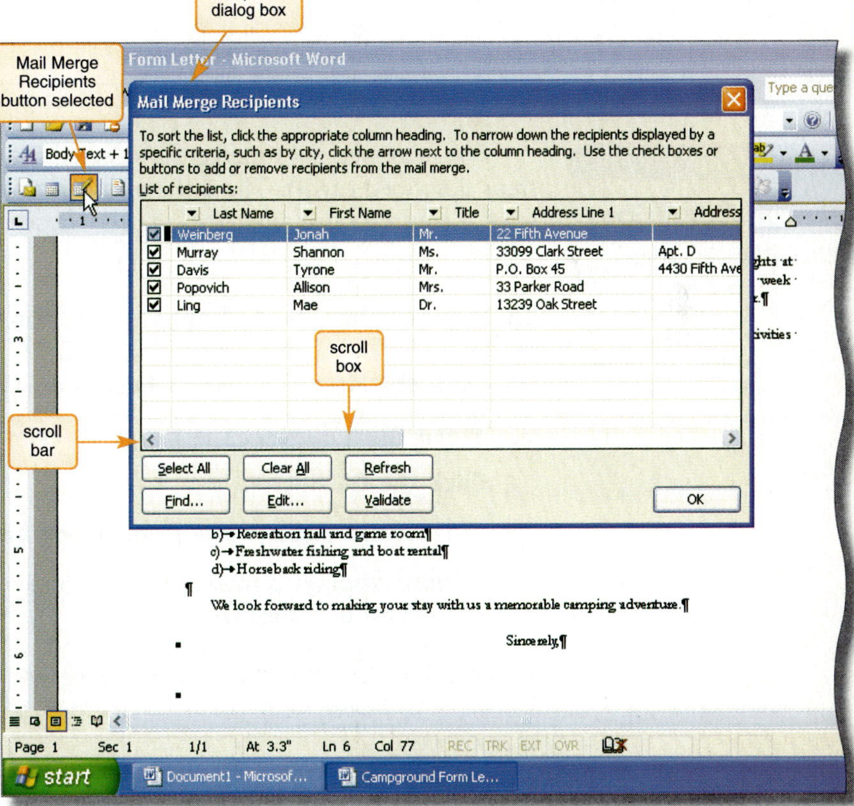

FIGURE 5-66

2

- **Drag the scroll box to the right edge of the scroll bar in the Mail Merge Recipients dialog box.**
- **Click the arrow to the left of the field name, Reservation Date.**

Word displays a list of selection criteria for the Reservation Date field (Figure 5-67).

3

- **Click September 10.**

Word reduces the number of data records that is displayed in the Mail Merge Recipients dialog box to two, because two vacationers have a reservation date of September 10.

4

- **Click the OK button to close the Mail Merge Recipients dialog box.**

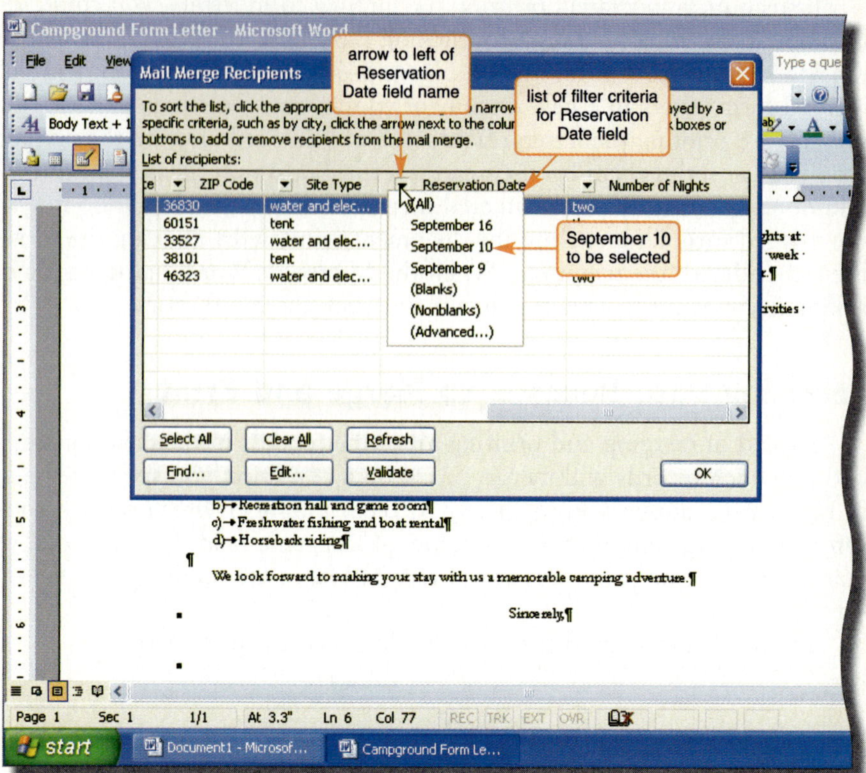

FIGURE 5-67

> ***More About***
>
> **Merge Conditions**
>
> When a field has a merge condition set, Word colors the arrow in blue that displays to the left of the field name. Thus, the arrow to the left of the Reservation Date field will be blue after you perform Step 3 in the steps above.

The next step is to merge the selected records. To do this, you follow the same steps described earlier. The difference is that Word will merge only those records that meet the criteria just specified, that is, those with a reservation date of September 10.

To Merge the Form Letters to the Printer

1. **Click the Merge to Printer button on the Mail Merge toolbar.**
2. **When Word displays the Merge to Printer dialog box, if necessary, click All.**
3. **Click the OK button.**
4. **When Word displays the Print dialog box, click the OK button.**
5. **If Word displays a message about locked fields, click the OK button whenever the dialog box appears.**

Word prints the form letters that match the specified condition: Reservation Date equal to September 10 (Figure 5-68). Two form letters print because two vacationers have a reservation date of September 10.

More About

Date Fields

The template used in this project contained a date field. To insert a date and/or time field into a Word document, click Insert on the menu bar, click Date and Time, select the desired date and/or time format, place a check mark in the Update automatically check box, and then click the OK button.

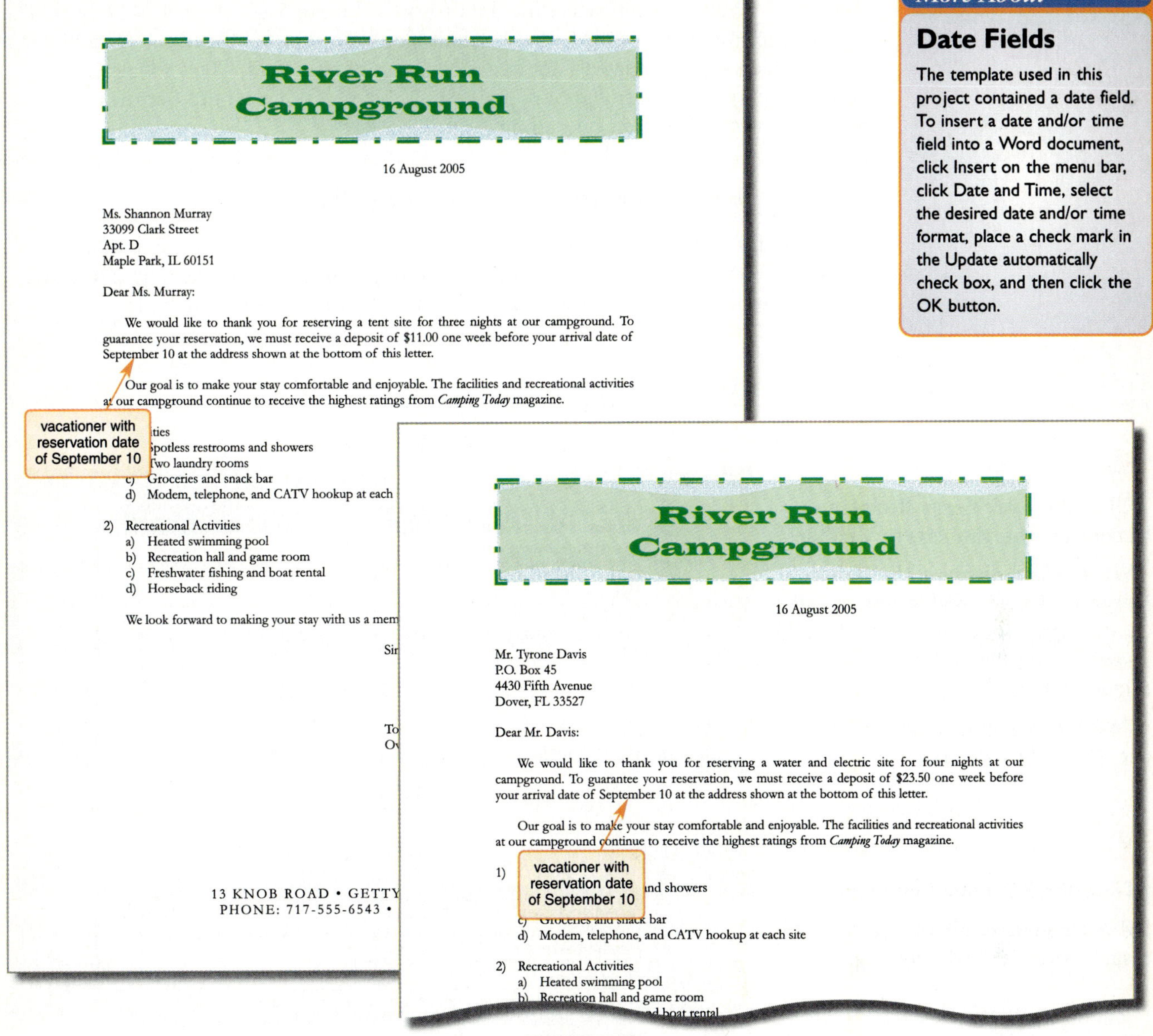
River Run Campground
16 August 2005
Ms. Shannon Murray
33099 Clark Street
Apt. D
Maple Park, IL 60151
Dear Ms. Murray:
We would like to thank you for reserving a tent site for three nights at our campground. To guarantee your reservation, we must receive a deposit of $11.00 one week before your arrival date of September 10 at the address shown at the bottom of this letter.
Our goal is to make your stay comfortable and enjoyable. The facilities and recreational activities at our campground continue to receive the highest ratings from Camping Today magazine.
vacationer with reservation date of September 10
Spotless restrooms and showers
Two laundry rooms
c) Groceries and snack bar
d) Modem, telephone, and CATV hookup at each
2) Recreational Activities
a) Heated swimming pool
b) Recreation hall and game room
c) Freshwater fishing and boat rental
d) Horseback riding
We look forward to making your stay with us a mem
13 KNOB ROAD • GETTY
PHONE: 717-555-6543 •
River Run Campground
16 August 2005
Mr. Tyrone Davis
P.O. Box 45
4430 Fifth Avenue
Dover, FL 33527
Dear Mr. Davis:
We would like to thank you for reserving a water and electric site for four nights at our campground. To guarantee your reservation, we must receive a deposit of $23.50 one week before your arrival date of September 10 at the address shown at the bottom of this letter.
Our goal is to make your stay comfortable and enjoyable. The facilities and recreational activities at our campground continue to receive the highest ratings from Camping Today magazine.
vacationer with reservation date of September 10
d) Modem, telephone, and CATV hookup at each site
2) Recreational Activities
a) Heated swimming pool
b) Recreation hall and game room

FIGURE 5-68

You should remove the merge condition so that future merges will not be restricted to vacationers with a September 10 reservation date.

To Remove a Merge Condition

1. **Click the Mail Merge Recipients button on the Mail Merge toolbar.**
2. **Scroll to the right of the dialog box and then click the arrow to the left of the field name, Reservation Date. Click (All) in the list.**
3. **Click the OK button.**

Word removes the specified condition.

In addition to selecting records based on values in a field, Word provides other choices by which you can select the data records (Figure 5-67 on page WD 340). The (Blanks) option selects records that contain blanks in that field, and the (Nonblanks) option selects records that do not contain blanks in that field. The (Advanced) option displays the Filter and Sort dialog box, which allows you to perform more advanced record selection operations.

Sorting Data Records to Merge and Print

If you mail the form letters using the U.S. Postal Service's bulk rate mailing service, the post office requires you to sort and group the form letters by ZIP code. Thus, the following steps show how to sort the data records by ZIP code.

To Sort the Data Records in a Data Source

1

- **Click the Mail Merge Recipients button on the Mail Merge toolbar.**
- **When Word displays the Mail Merge Recipients dialog box, scroll to the right until the ZIP Code field shows in the dialog box (Figure 5-69).**
- **Position the mouse pointer on the ZIP Code field name.**

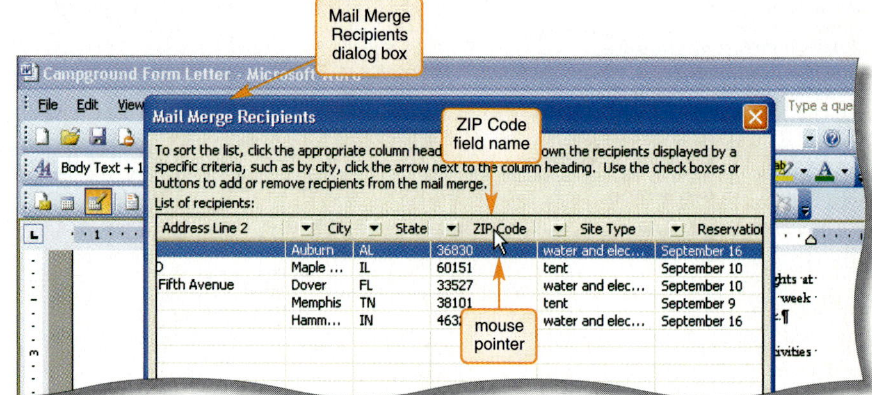

FIGURE 5-69

2

- **Click the ZIP Code field name.**
- **If necessary, scroll to the right to display the ZIP Code field again.**

The data records are sorted in ZIP code order (Figure 5-70). Future merged documents will print in ZIP code order.

3

- **Click the OK button in the Mail Merge Recipients dialog box.**

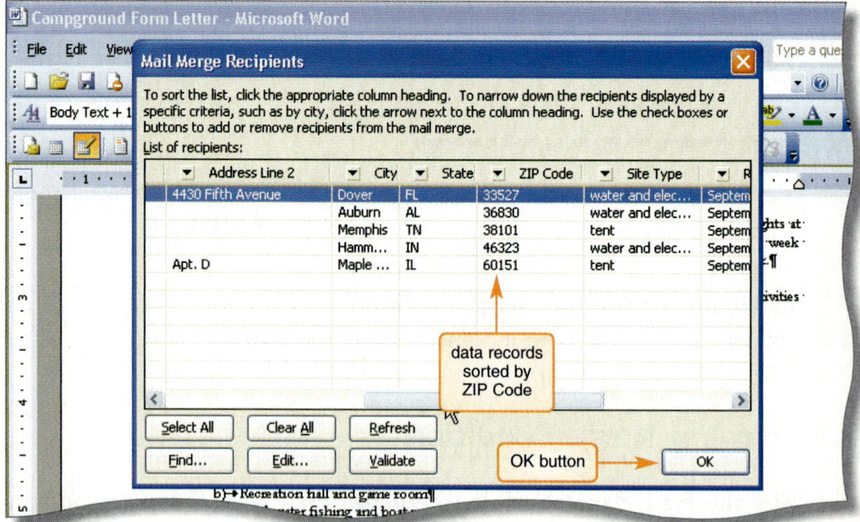

FIGURE 5-70

If you chose to merge the form letters again at this point, Word would print them in ZIP code order; that is, Tyrone Davis's letter would print first and Shannon Murray's letter would print last.

Viewing Merged Data

You can verify the order of the data records without printing them by using the **View Merged Data button** on the Mail Merge toolbar, as shown in the following steps.

To View Merged Data in the Main Document

1

- **If necessary, scroll up to display the AddressBlock merge field in the document window.**
- **Click the View Merged Data button on the Mail Merge toolbar.**

Word displays the contents of the first data record in the main document, instead of the merge fields (Figure 5-71). The View Merged Data button is selected.

2

- **Click the View Merged Data button on the Mail Merge toolbar again.**

Word displays the merge fields in the main document, instead of the field values.

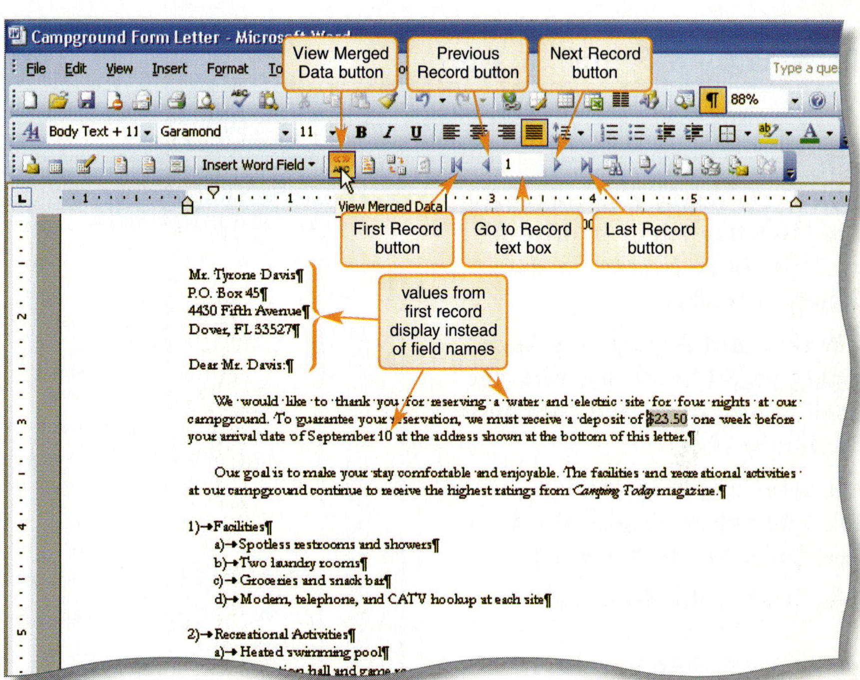

FIGURE 5-71

Other Ways

1. With Mail Merge toolbar displaying, in Voice Command mode, say "View Merged Data"

When you are viewing merged data in the main document (the View Merged Data button is selected), you can click the **Last Record button** (Figure 5-71) on the Mail Merge toolbar to display the values from the last record in the data source, the **First Record button** to display the values in record one, the **Next Record button** to display the values in the next consecutive record number, or the **Previous Record button** to display the values from the previous record number. You also can display a specific record by clicking the **Go to Record text box**, typing the record number you would like to be displayed in the main document, and then pressing the ENTER key.

The campground form letter is complete. Thus, the next step is to close the document as described below.

More About

Sorting Data Sources

When you sort a data source, the order of the data source does not change physically. Instead Word writes an instruction (called an SQL command) that is saved with the main document. When you open or use the main document, Word follows the SQL instruction to sort the records in the data source as specified.

To Close a Document

1. **Click File on the menu bar and then click Close.**
2. **When the Microsoft Office Word dialog box is displayed, click the Yes button to save the changes.**

Word saves the Campground Form Letter in the River Run folder on a disk in drive A.

Renaming a Folder

After reviewing folder names on a disk, you may decide to change a folder name. For example, you may want to change the folder name from River Run to Campground. Rather than renaming the folder in Windows, you can rename a folder through the Open, Save As, and Insert File dialog boxes in Word.

To rename a folder, you must be sure the folder is not in use. That is, all documents must be closed that are in the folder. The following steps show how to use the Open dialog box to rename the River Run folder.

To Rename a Folder in Word

1

- **With the floppy disk containing the River Run folder in drive A, click the Open button on the Standard toolbar.**
- **When Word displays the Open dialog box, if necessary, click the Look in box arrow and then click 3½ Floppy (A:).**
- **If necessary, click the Up One Level button to display the River Run folder in the Name list.**
- **Right-click the River Run folder.**

Word displays a shortcut menu (Figure 5-72).

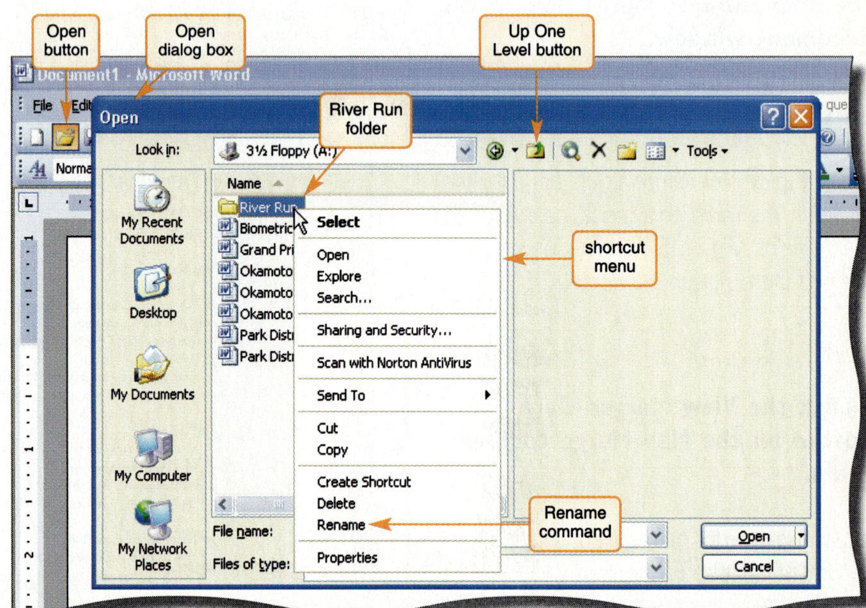

FIGURE 5-72

2

- **Click Rename on the shortcut menu.**
- **Type** `Campground` **as the new folder name (Figure 5-73).**

3

- **Press the ENTER key.**
- **Click the Cancel button in the dialog box.**

Word changes the name of the folder on the disk in drive A from River Run to Campground.

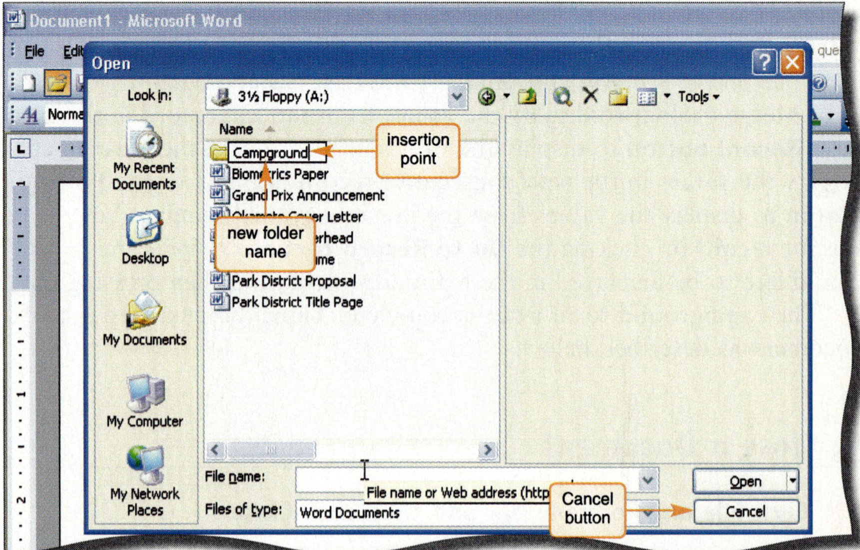

FIGURE 5-73

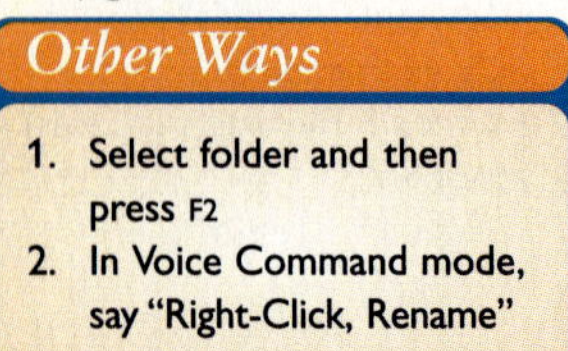

Other Ways

1. Select folder and then press F2
2. In Voice Command mode, say "Right-Click, Rename"

If a file in the folder is in use when you attempt to rename the folder, Word will display a dialog box indicating you cannot rename the folder at this time. If this occurs, simply close the open document and try to rename the folder again.

Addressing and Printing Mailing Labels

Now that you have merged and printed the form letters, the next step is to print addresses on mailing labels to be affixed to envelopes for the form letters. The mailing labels will use the same data source as the form letter, Camper List. The format and content of the mailing labels will be exactly the same as the inside address in the main document for the form letter. That is, the first line will contain the vacationer's title and first name followed by the last name. The second line will contain his or her street address, and so on. Thus, you will use the AddressBlock merge field in the mailing labels.

You follow the same basic steps to create the main document for the mailing labels as you did to create the main document for the form letters. The major difference is that the data source already exists because you created it earlier in this project.

To address mailing labels, you specify the type of labels you intend to use. Word will request the manufacturer's name, as well as a product number and name. You can obtain this information from the box of labels. For illustration purposes in addressing these labels, the manufacturer is Avery, and the product name is address labels, which has a product number of 5160.

The following steps illustrate how to address and print these mailing labels using an existing data source.

More About

Mailing Labels

Instead of addressing mailing labels from a data source, you can print a label(s) for a single address. Click Tools on the menu bar, point to Letters and Mailings, click Envelopes and Labels, click the Labels tab, type the name and address in the Address text box, click the Options button and select the label type, click the OK button, and then click the Print button in the Envelopes and Labels dialog box.

To Address and Print Mailing Labels Using an Existing Data Source

1

- **If necessary, open a new blank document.**
- **Click Tools on the menu bar, point to Letters and Mailings, and then click Mail Merge.**
- **When Word displays the Mail Merge task pane, click Labels in the Select document type area.**

Word displays Step 1 of the mail merge process in the Mail Merge task pane (Figure 5-74). In Step 1, you select a main document type.

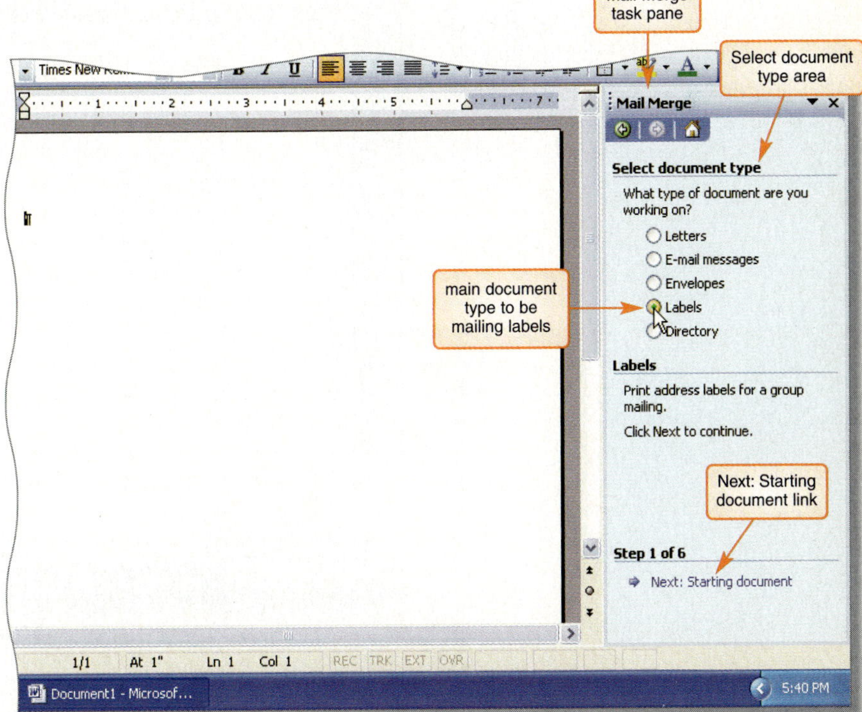

FIGURE 5-74

2

- **Click the Next: Starting document link.**
- **In the Mail Merge task pane, click the Label options link.**
- **When Word displays the Label Options dialog box, click the desired Avery product number in the Product number list (in this case, 5160 - Address).**

Step 2 of the mail merge process allows you to specify the label product information (Figure 5-75). If you have a dot matrix printer, your printer information will differ from this figure. The Product number list displays the product numbers for Avery mailing labels compatible with your printer.

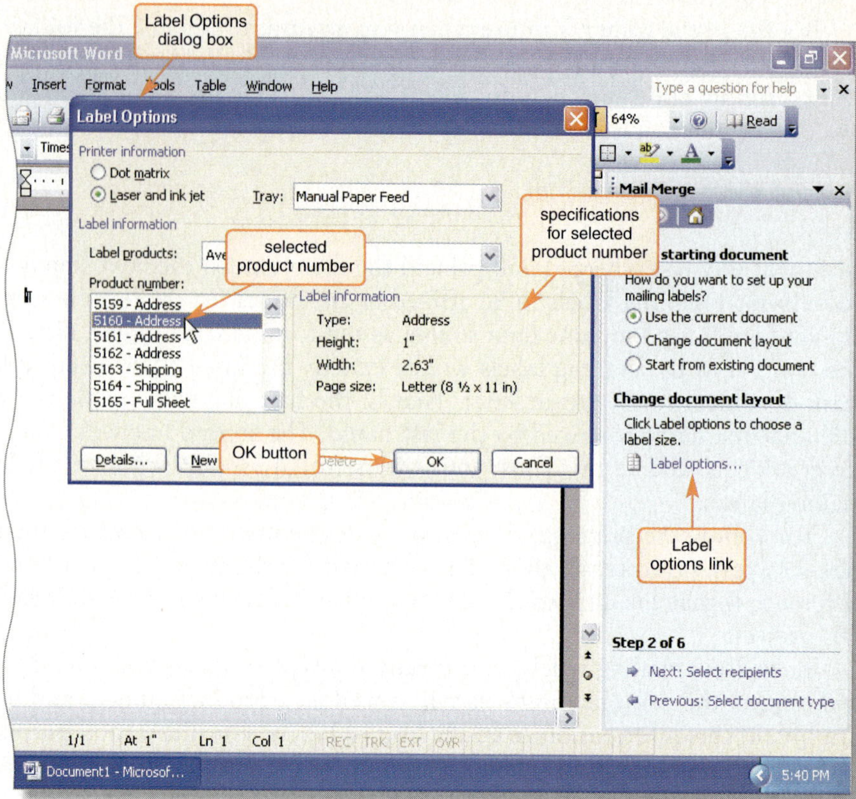

FIGURE 5-75

3

- **Click the OK button in the Label Options dialog box.**

Word displays the selected label layout in the main document (Figure 5-76). The next step is to select the data source. You will open and use the same data source you created for the form letters.

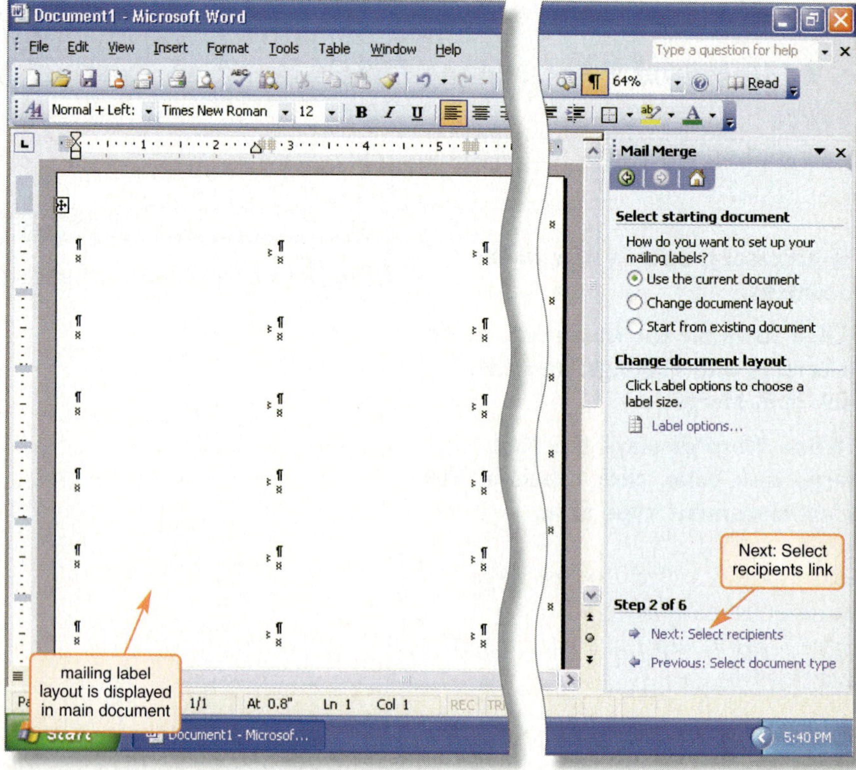

FIGURE 5-76

4

- **In the Mail Merge task pane, click the Next: Select recipients link (Figure 5-76) to display the next step of the mail merge process.**
- **In the Select recipients area, if necessary, click Use an existing list.**
- **In the Use an existing list area, click the Browse link.**
- **When Word displays the Select Data Source dialog box, if necessary, click the Look in box arrow, click 3½ Floppy (A:), and then double-click the Campground folder.**
- **Click the file name, Camper List.**

In the Select Data Source dialog box, you select the existing data source, Camper List, to address the mailing labels (Figure 5-77).

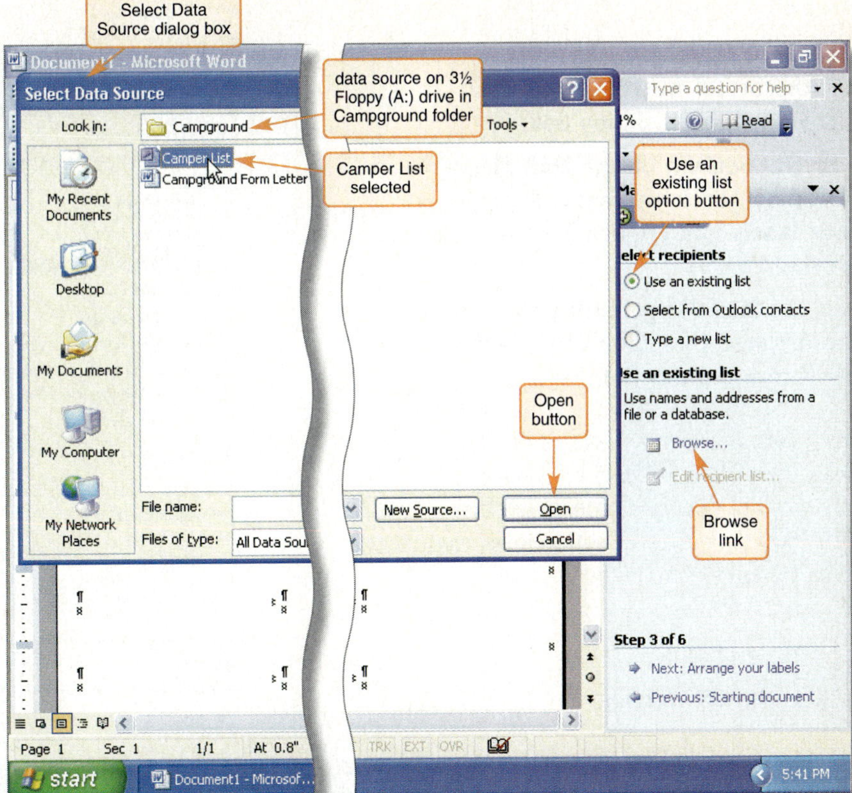

FIGURE 5-77

5

- **Click the Open button in the Select Data Source dialog box.**

Word displays the Mail Merge Recipients dialog box (Figure 5-78).

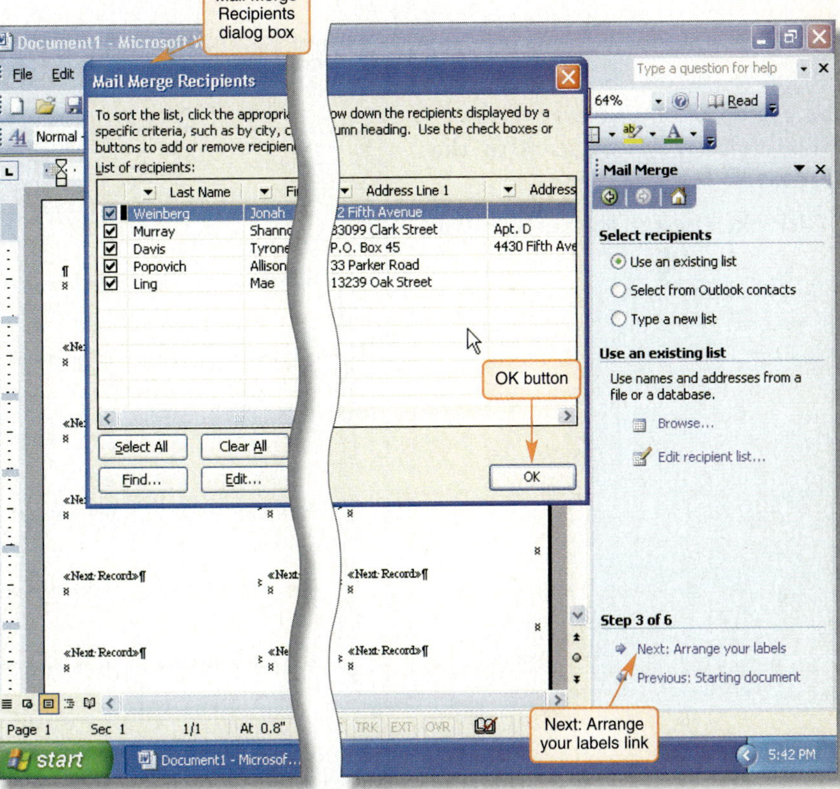

FIGURE 5-78

6

• **Click the OK button in the Mail Merge Recipients dialog box.**

• **At the bottom of the Mail Merge task pane, click the Next: Arrange your labels link (Figure 5-78 on the previous page).**

• **In the Mail Merge task pane, in the Arrange your labels area, click the Address block link.**

Word displays the Insert Address Block dialog box (Figure 5-79). Word automatically matches fields and suppresses blank lines. Thus, the address information will print according to the data in the data source.

7

• **Click the OK button.**

The next step is to copy the layout of the first label to the rest of the labels in the main document.

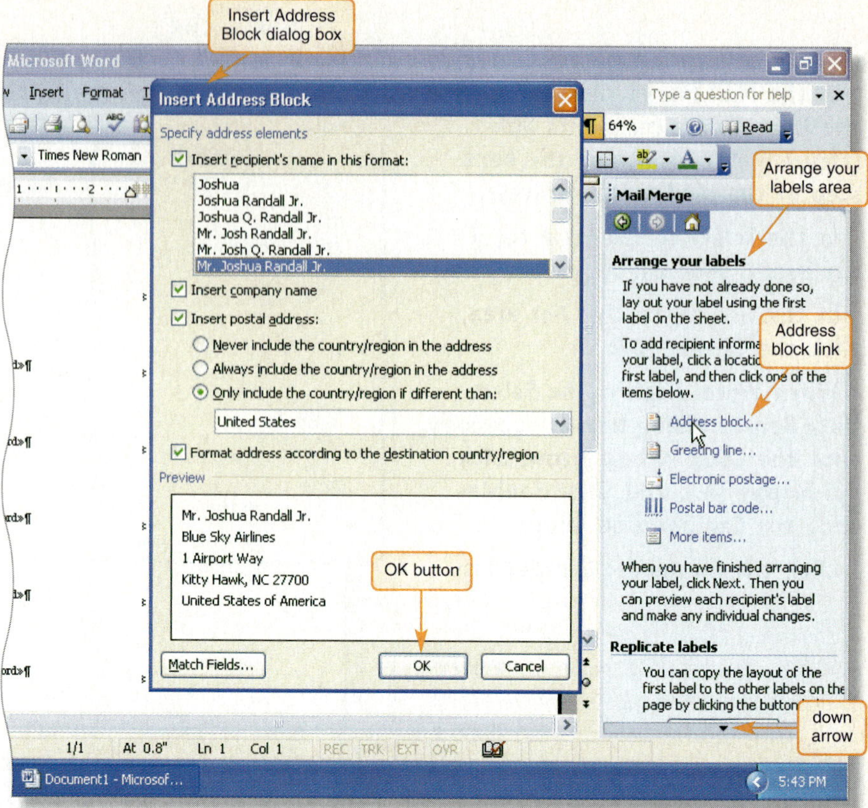

FIGURE 5-79

8

• **Point to the down arrow at the bottom of the Mail Merge task pane (Figure 5-79) to scroll to the bottom of the task pane.**

• **Click the Update all labels button.**

Word copies the layout of the first label to the remaining label layouts in the main document (Figure 5-80).

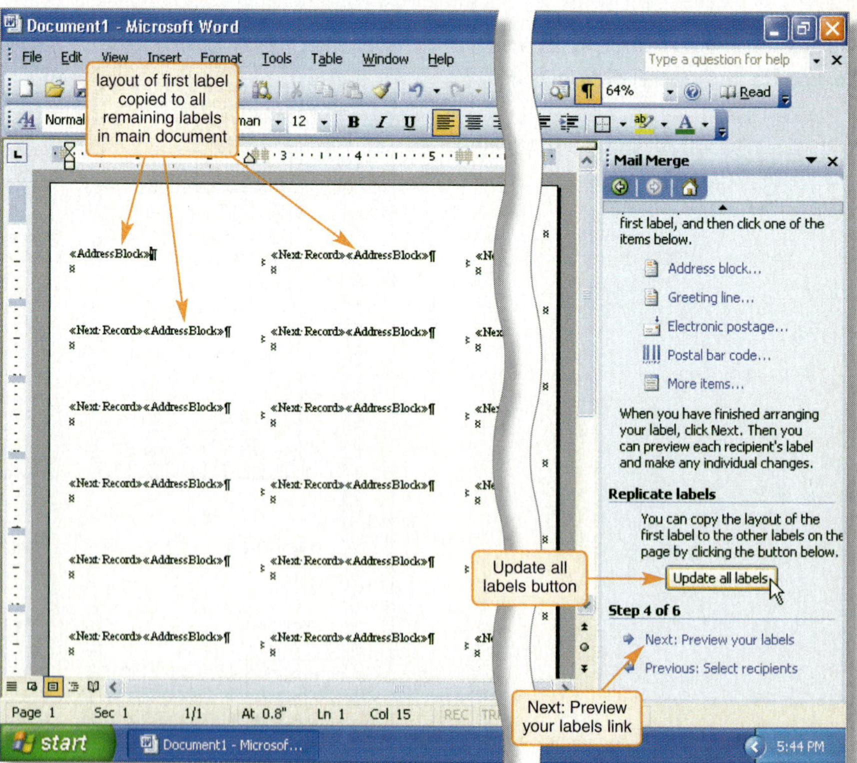

FIGURE 5-80

9

- **Click the Next: Preview your labels link at the bottom of the Mail Merge task pane.**

Word displays a preview of the mailing labels in the document window (Figure 5-81).

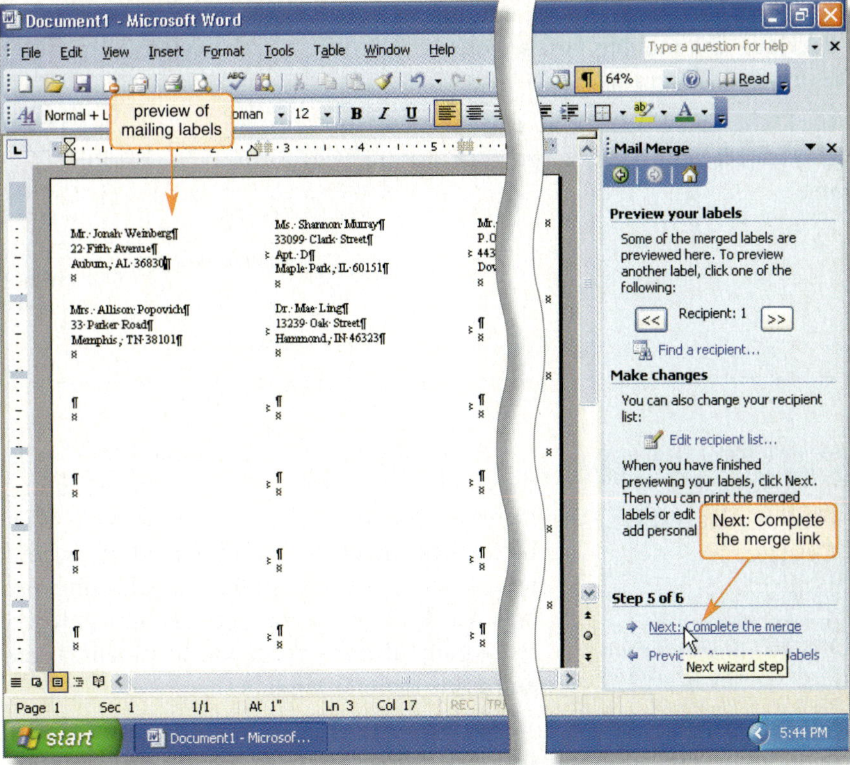

FIGURE 5-81

10

- **Click the Next: Complete the merge link at the bottom of the Mail Merge task pane.**
- **In the Mail Merge task pane, in the Merge area, click the Print link.**
- **If necessary, insert a sheet of blank mailing labels into the printer.**
- **When Word displays the Merge to Printer dialog box, if necessary, click All (Figure 5-82).**
- **Click the OK button.**
- **When the Print dialog box is displayed, click the OK button.**

The mailing labels print.

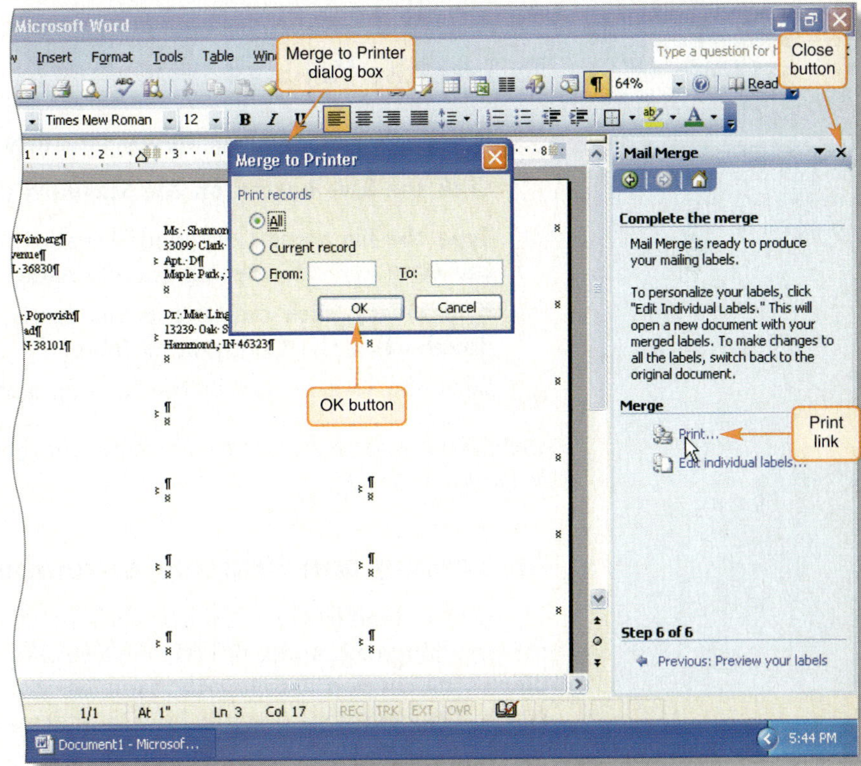

FIGURE 5-82

11

- **Retrieve the mailing labels from the printer (Figure 5-83).**
- **Click the Close button at the right edge of the Mail Merge task pane.**

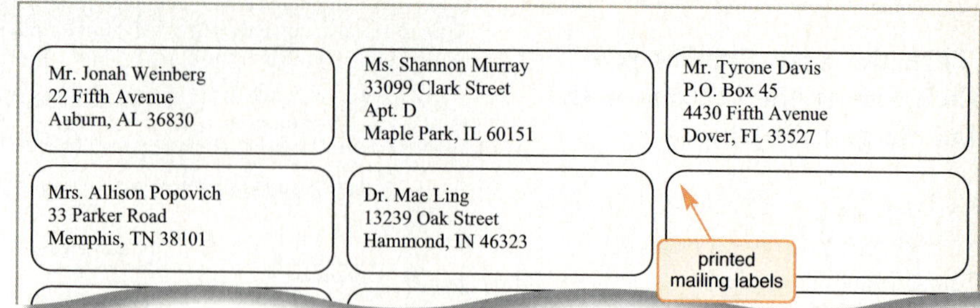

FIGURE 5-83

More About

Mailing Label Bar Codes

If your printer can print graphics, you can add a POSTNET (POSTal Numeric Encoding Technique) delivery-point bar code, usually referred to simply as a bar code, below the address on each mailing label or envelope. Using a bar code speeds up delivery by the U.S. Postal Service. The POSTNET bar code represents the addressee's ZIP code and first street address. To insert a bar code, click the Postal bar code link in the Mail Merge task pane (shown in Figure 5-79 on page WD 348).

As an alternative to using the Mail Merge task pane, you can use the buttons on the Mail Merge toolbar for the entire mailing label mail merge. Click the Main document setup button (Figure 5-38 on page WD 321) and then click Labels in the dialog box. Click the Open Data Source button to display the Select Data Source dialog box. Click the Insert Address Block button to display the Insert Address Block dialog box. Click the Propagate Labels button to copy the layout of the first label to the remaining labels in the main document. Click the Merge to Printer button to merge and print the mailing labels.

Saving the Mailing Labels

The following steps describe how to save the mailing labels.

To Save the Mailing Labels

1. **If necessary, insert your floppy disk into drive A.**
2. **Click the Save button on the Standard toolbar.**
3. **Type the file name** `Campground Labels` **in the File name box. Do not press the ENTER key after typing the file name.**
4. **If necessary, click the Save in box arrow, click 3½ Floppy (A:), and then double-click the Campground folder.**
5. **Click the Save button in the Save As dialog box.**

Word saves the document with the file name, Campground Labels, in the Campground folder on the floppy disk in drive A.

Addressing and Printing Envelopes

Instead of addressing mailing labels to affix to envelopes, your printer may have the capability of printing directly onto envelopes. To print the label information directly on envelopes, follow the same basic steps as you did to address the mailing labels. The next steps describe how to address envelopes using an existing data source.

Note: If your printer does not have the capability of printing envelopes, skip these steps and proceed to the next section titled, Merging All Data Records to a Directory. If you are in a laboratory environment, ask your instructor if you should perform these steps or skip them.

To Address and Print Envelopes Using an Existing Data Source

1. **Click the New Blank Document button on the Standard toolbar. Click Tools on the menu bar, point to Letters and Mailings, and then click Mail Merge.**
2. **In the Mail Merge task pane, in the Select document type area, click Envelopes. Click the Next: Starting document link.**
3. **In the Mail Merge task pane, click the Envelope options link. When Word displays the Envelope Options dialog box, select the envelope size and then click the OK button to create the envelope layout as the main document.**
4. **If your envelope does not have a pre-printed return address, position the insertion point in the upper-left corner of the envelope layout and then type a return address.**
5. **Click the paragraph mark in the middle of the envelope layout (Figure 5-84). Click the Next: Select recipients link at the bottom of the Mail Merge task pane.**
6. **In the Mail Merge task pane, in the Select recipients area, if necessary, click Use an existing list. In the Use an existing list area, click the Browse link. When Word displays the Select Data Source dialog box, if necessary, click the Look in box arrow, click 3½ Floppy (A:), and then double-click the Campground folder. Click the file name, Camper List. Click the Open button in the Select Data Source dialog box. Click the OK button in the Mail Merge Recipients dialog box. At the bottom of the Mail Merge task pane, click the Next: Arrange your envelope link.**
7. **In the Mail Merge task pane, in the Arrange your envelope area, click the Address block link. When Word displays the Insert Address Block dialog box, click the OK button.**
8. **Click the Next: Preview your envelopes link at the bottom of the Mail Merge task pane. Click the Next: Complete the merge link at the bottom of the Mail Merge task pane. In the Mail Merge task pane, in the Merge area, click the Print link. If necessary, insert blank envelopes into the printer. When Word displays the Merge to Printer dialog box, if necessary, click All. Click the OK button. When the Print dialog box displays, click the OK button to print the envelopes. Click the Close button in the Mail Merge task pane.**

More About

Data Sources

Word initially looks in the My Data Sources folder for a data source when it displays the Select Data Source dialog box. To find a data source in a different location, click the Look in box arrow, locate the file, and then click the Open button in the dialog box.

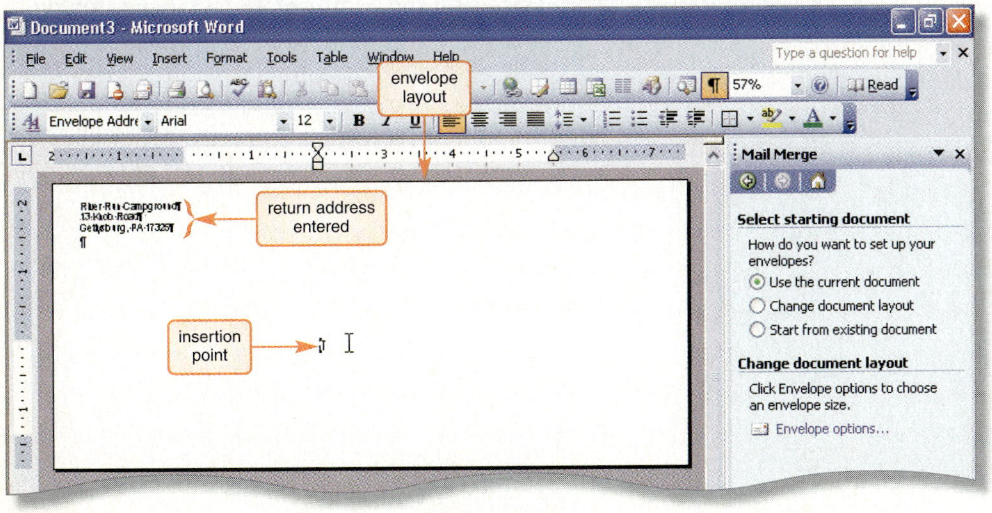

FIGURE 5-84

As an alternative to using the Mail Merge task pane, you can use the buttons on the Mail Merge toolbar for the entire envelope mail merge. Click the Main document setup button (Figure 5-38 on page WD 321) and then click Envelopes in the dialog box. Click the Open Data Source button to display the Select Data Source dialog box. Click the Insert Address Block button to display the Insert Address Block dialog box. Click the Merge to Printer button to merge and print the mailing labels.

The following steps describe how to save the envelopes.

To Save the Envelope

1. **If necessary, insert your floppy disk into drive A.**
2. **Click the Save button on the Standard toolbar.**
3. **Type the file name** `Campground Envelopes` **in the File name box. Do not press the ENTER key after typing the file name.**
4. **If necessary, click the Save in box arrow, click 3½ Floppy (A:), and then double-click the Campground folder.**
5. **Click the Save button in the Save As dialog box.**

Word saves the document with the file name, Campground Envelopes, in the Campground folder on the floppy disk in drive A.

Merging All Data Records to a Directory

You may want to print the data records in the data source. Recall that the data source is saved as a Microsoft Access database table. Thus, you cannot open the data source in Word. To view the data source, you click the Mail Merge Recipients button on the Mail Merge toolbar. The Mail Merge Recipients dialog box, however, does not have a Print button.

One way to print the contents of the data source is to merge all data records in the data source into a single document, called a **directory**, instead of merging to a separate document for each data record. The next steps show how to merge the data records in the data source into a directory. These steps illustrate the use of the buttons on the Mail Merge toolbar, instead of using the Mail Merge task pane, for the merge.

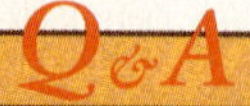

Q: How do I convert a mail merge main document into a regular Word document?

A: Open the main document. Click the Main document setup button on the Mail Merge toolbar, click Normal Word document in the Document type list, and then click the OK button.

To Merge to a Directory

1

- **Click the New Blank Document button on the Standard toolbar.**
- **If the Mail Merge toolbar is not displayed, click Tools on the menu bar, point to Letters and Mailings, and then click Show Mail Merge Toolbar.**
- **Click the Main document setup button on the Mail Merge toolbar.**
- **When Word displays the Main Document Type dialog box, click Directory.**

In the Main Document Type dialog box, you select the document type (Figure 5-85).

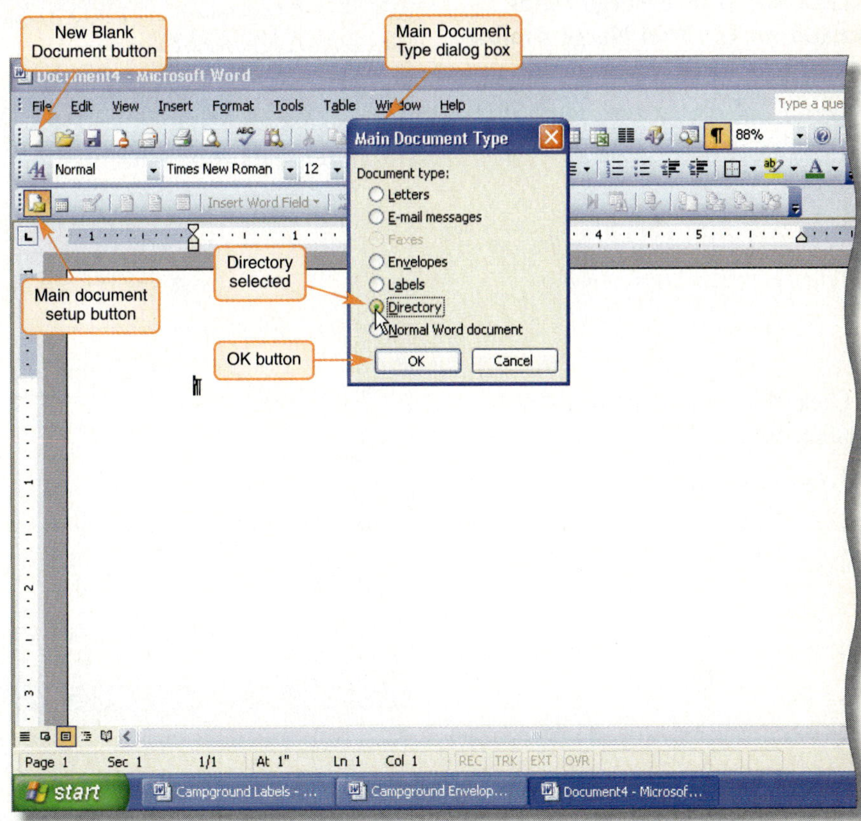

FIGURE 5-85

2

- **Click the OK button.**
- **Click the Open Data Source button on the Mail Merge toolbar.**
- **When Word displays the Select Data Source dialog box, if necessary, click the Look in box arrow, click 3½ Floppy (A:), and then double-click the Campground folder.**
- **Click the file name, Camper List.**

Word selects the data source, Camper List, in the Select Data Source dialog box (Figure 5-86).

3

- **Click the Open button in the Select Data Source dialog box.**

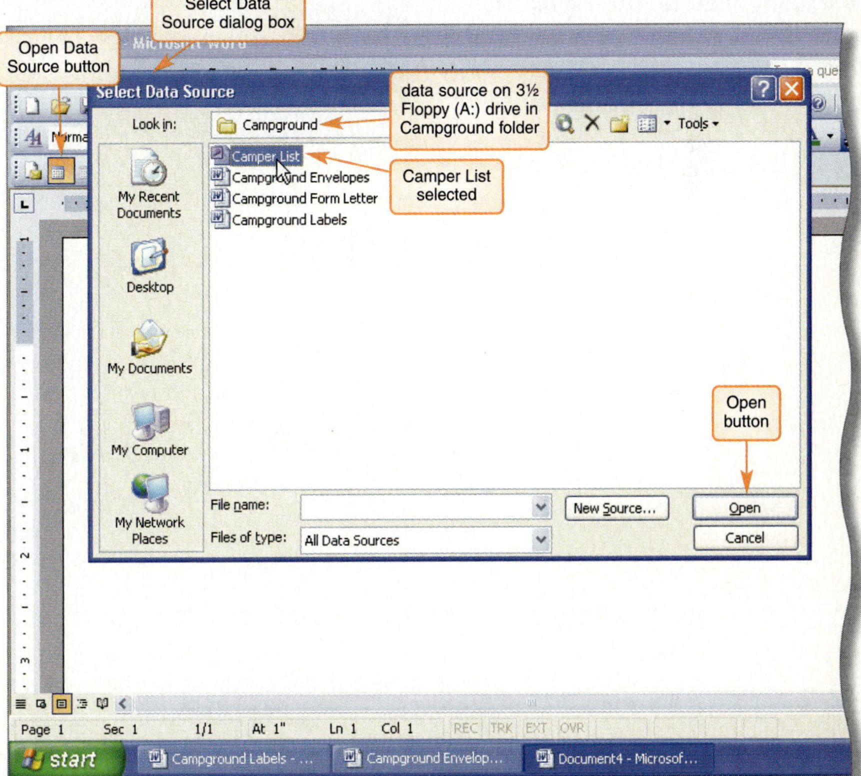

FIGURE 5-86

4

• **Click the Insert Merge Fields button on the Mail Merge toolbar.**

• **When Word displays the Insert Merge Field dialog box, click Title in the Fields list and then click the Insert button.**

Word inserts the field name in the document window (Figure 5-87).

5

• **Click the Close button in the dialog box.**

• **Press the ENTER key.**

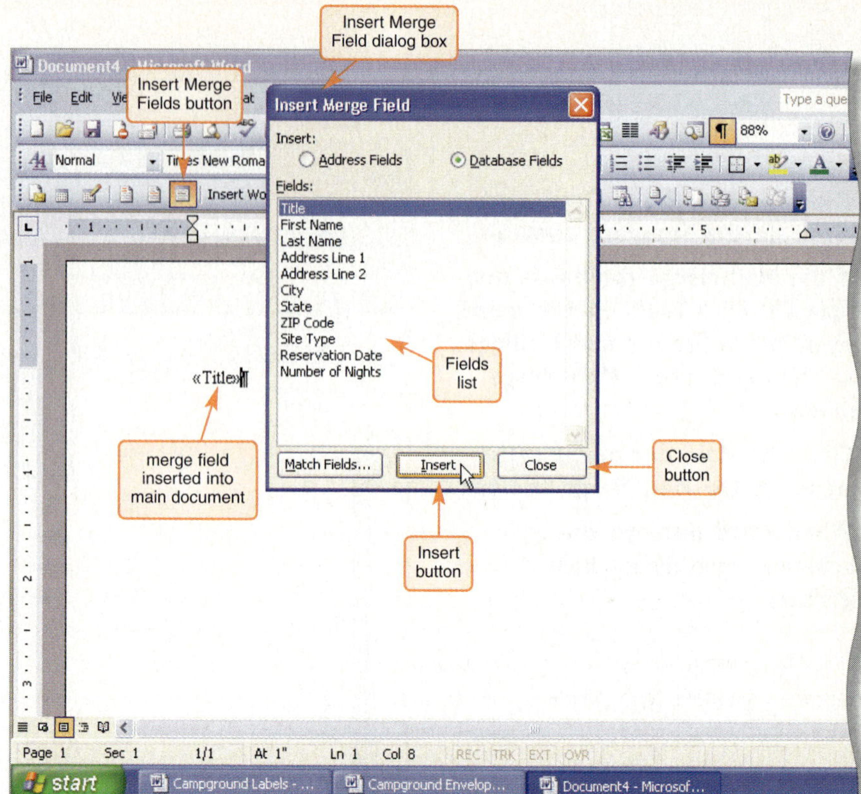

FIGURE 5-87

6

• **Repeat Steps 4 and 5 for each remaining field in the Fields list.**

Word displays the fields in the data source, each on a separate line in the document window (Figure 5-88).

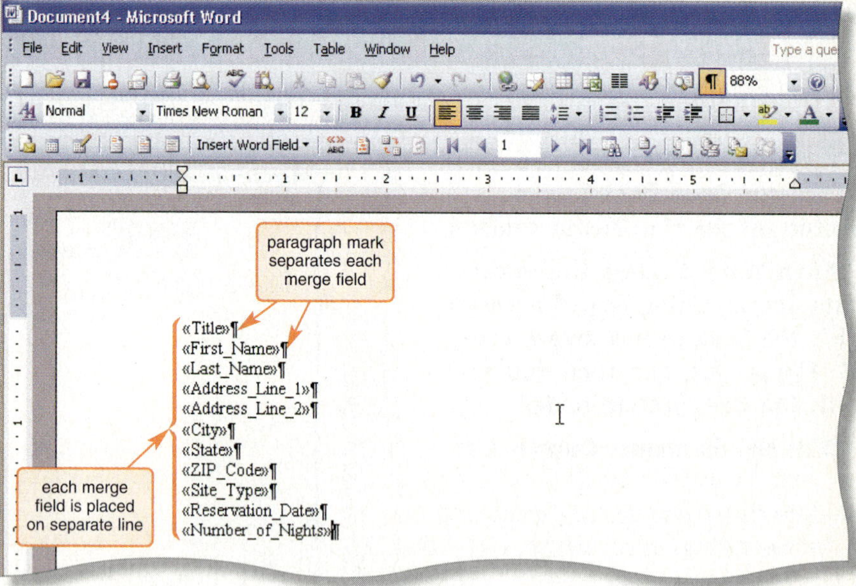

FIGURE 5-88

If you merge the records now, they will print in one long list, one record below the next. Instead of a long list, you want each data record to be in a single row and each merge field to be in a column. That is, you want the directory to be in a table form. The next steps show how to convert the text containing the merge fields to a table.

To Convert Text to a Table

1

- **Click Edit on the menu bar and then click Select All to select the entire document.**
- **Click Table on the menu bar and then point to Convert.**

Word selects all merge fields in the document (Figure 5-89).

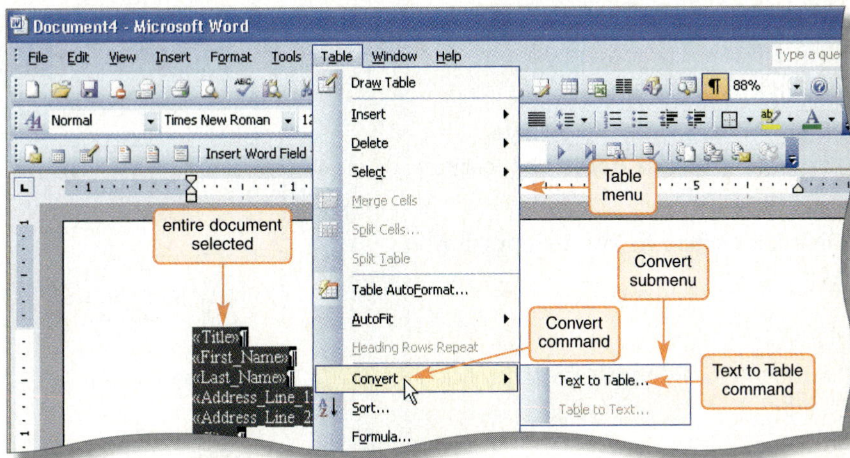

FIGURE 5-89

2

- **Click Text to Table on the Convert submenu.**
- **When Word displays the Convert Text to Table dialog box, type** 11 **in the Number of columns box.**

The resulting table should have 11 columns and 1 row (Figure 5-90). The one row will contain the merge field names.

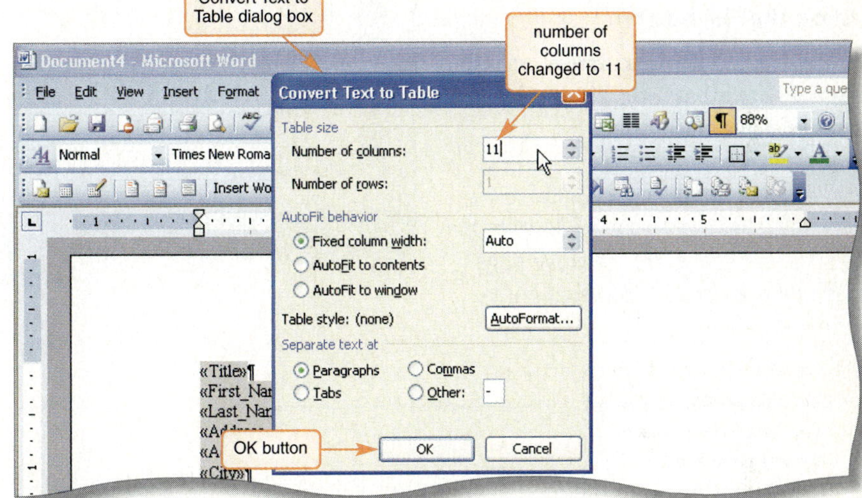

FIGURE 5-90

3

- **Click the OK button.**
- **If necessary, you can change column widths to match this figure.**

Word converts the text of the merge fields to a table (Figure 5-91). Each merge field is in its own column.

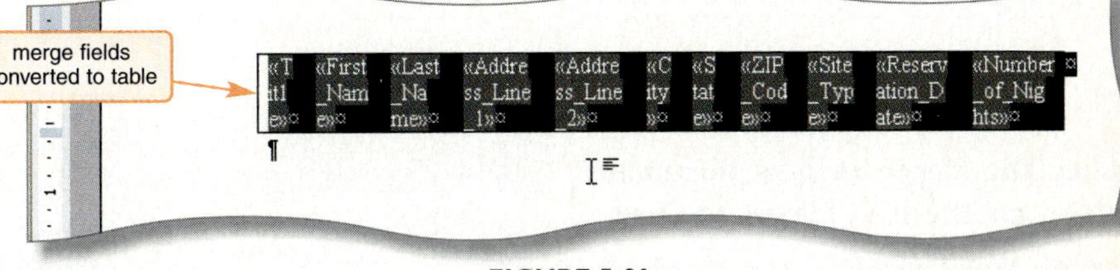

FIGURE 5-91

Other Ways

1. In Voice Command mode, say "Table, Convert, Text to Table, [enter number of columns], [enter number of rows], OK"

Notice in Figure 5-91 that the merge fields wrap in the first row and consume three lines in the document. This is because the table is too wide to fit on a piece of paper in **portrait orientation**; that is, with the short edge of the paper at the top. You can instruct Word to print a document in **landscape orientation** so the long edge of the paper is at the top. The steps on the next page show how to change the orientation of the document from portrait to landscape.

To Change Page Orientation

1

- **Click File on the menu bar and then click Page Setup.**
- **When Word displays the Page Setup dialog box, if necessary, click the Margins tab.**
- **Click Landscape in the Orientation area.**

In the Margins sheet, you can choose between Portrait and Landscape orientation (Figure 5-92).

2

- **Click the OK button.**
- **Click the Zoom box arrow on the Standard toolbar and then click Page Width.**

Word changes the print orientation to landscape (shown in Figure 5-93). With the zoom set to page width, the entire page in landscape orientation is displayed in the document window.

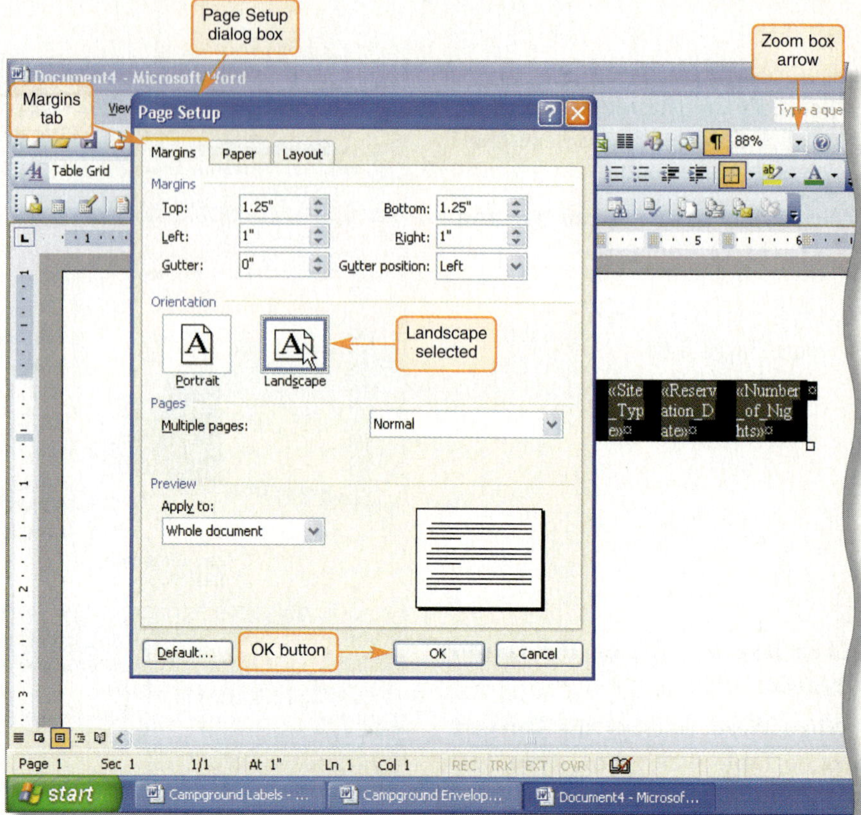

FIGURE 5-92

Other Ways

1. In Voice Command mode, say "File, Page Setup, Landscape, OK"

The next step is to merge the data records in the data source into the directory in a new document window, as described in the following steps.

To Merge to a New Document Window

1

- **Click the Merge to New Document button on the Mail Merge toolbar.**
- **When Word displays the Merge to New Document dialog box, if necessary, click All (Figure 5-93).**

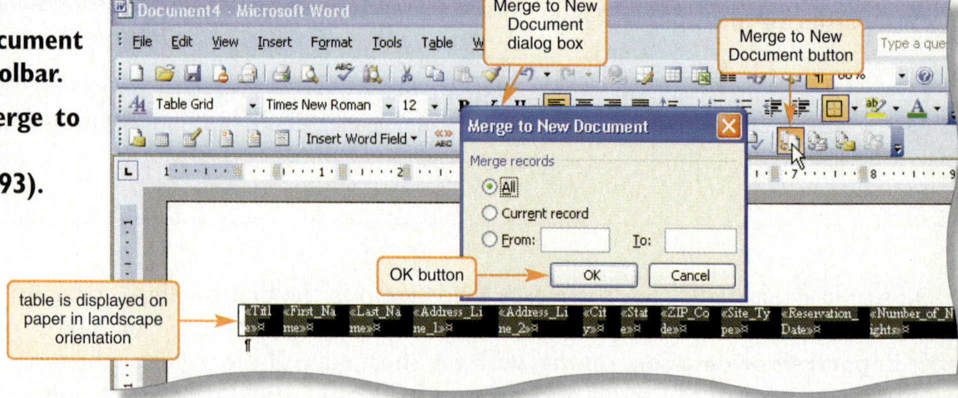

FIGURE 5-93

2

- **Click the OK button.**

Word merges the data records into a directory in a new document window (Figure 5-94).

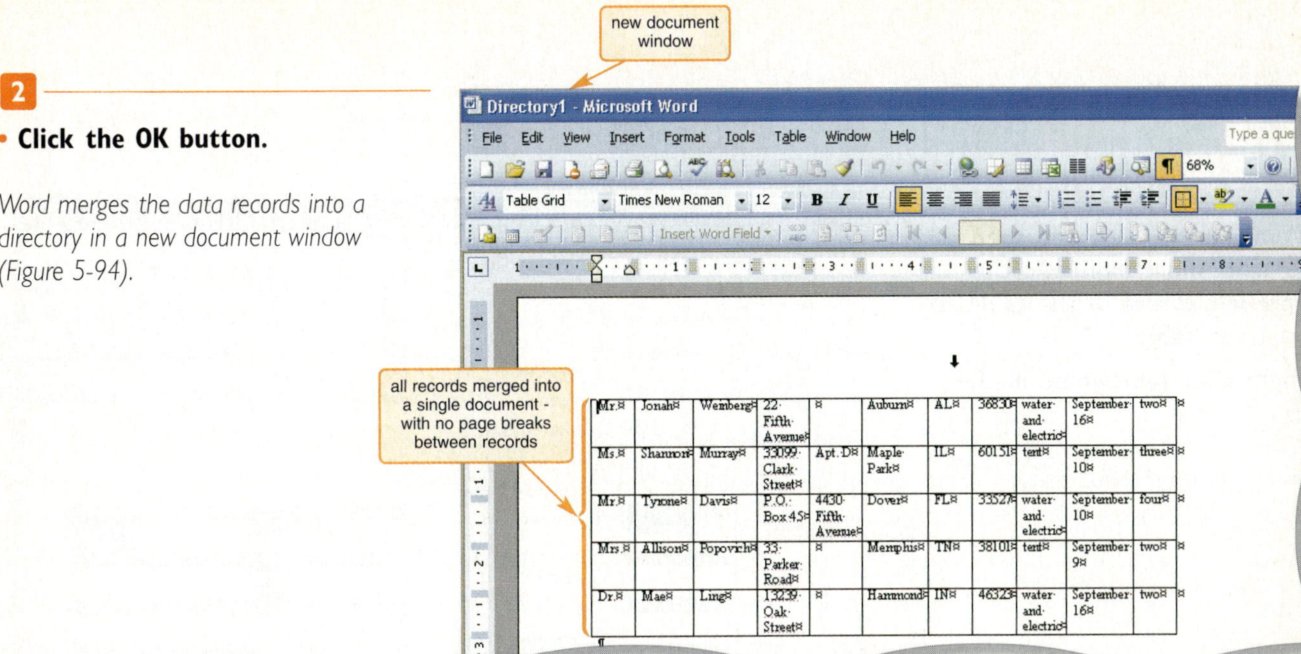

FIGURE 5-94

The table would be more descriptive if the field names were displayed in a row above the actual data. Thus, the following steps describe how to add a row to the top of a table and format it.

More About

Page Orientation

To change the page orientation for just part of a document, select the pages to be changed prior to displaying the Page Setup dialog box. With the pages selected, click the Apply to box arrow and then click Selected text in the Layout sheet of the Page Setup dialog box. Word inserts a section break before and after the selected pages.

To Modify and Format a Table

1. **Click in the upper-left cell of the table. Click Table on the menu bar, point to Insert, and then click Rows Above.**
2. **Click in the left cell of the new row. Type** `Title` **and then press the TAB key. Type** `First Name` **and then press the TAB key. Type** `Last Name` **and then press the TAB key. Type** `Address Line 1` **and then press the TAB key. Type** `Address Line 2` **and then press the TAB key. Type** `City` **and then press the TAB key. Type** `State` **and then press the TAB key. Type** `ZIP Code` **and then press the TAB key. Type** `Site Type` **and then press the TAB key. Type** `Reservation Date` **and then press the TAB key. Type** `Number of Nights` **as the last entry in the row.**
3. **Select this first row by pointing to the left of the new row and then clicking when the mouse pointer changes to a right-pointing arrow. Click the Bold button on the Formatting toolbar. Click anywhere in the document to remove the selection.**
4. **Double-click the border between the last two rows so the Reservation Dates are displayed on a single line. (You may have to double-click the border twice.)**

Word adds and formats a row at the top of the table (shown in Figure 5-95 on the next page).

The next step is to add a .05 inch margin at the top of each cell and place a .05 inch space between each cell in the table using the Table Properties dialog box. You also can center the table between the left and right margins in this dialog box, as shown in the steps on the next page.

To Modify Table Properties

1

- **Point in the table and then click the table move handle in the upper-left corner of the table to select the table.**
- **Right-click somewhere in the table.**

Word displays a shortcut menu (Figure 5-95).

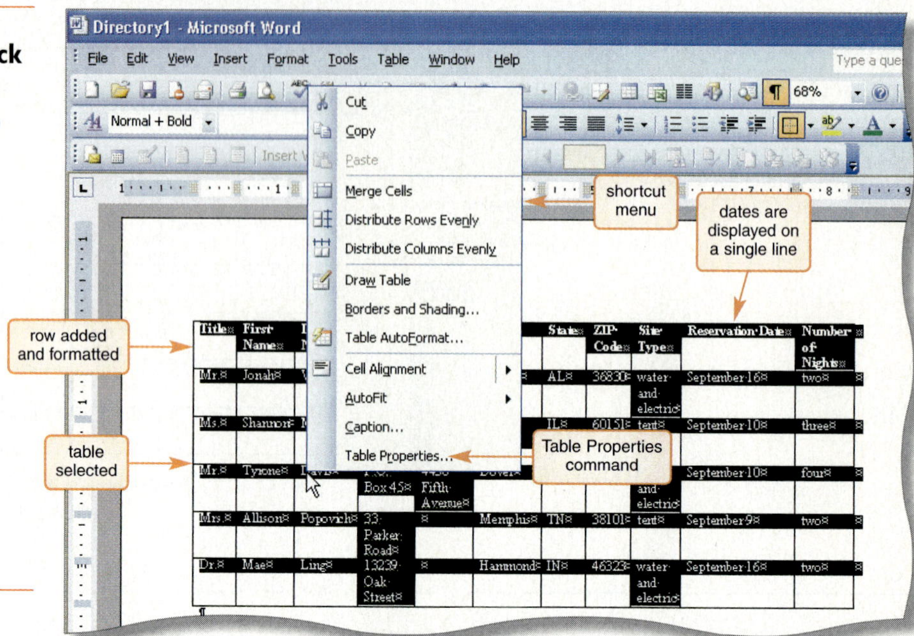

FIGURE 5-95

2

- **Click Table Properties on the shortcut menu.**
- **When Word displays the Table Properties dialog box, if necessary, click the Table tab.**
- **Click Center in the Alignment area.**
- **Click the Options button.**
- **When Word displays the Table Options dialog box, click the Top box up arrow until 0.05" is displayed in the Top box.**
- **Place a check mark in the Allow spacing between cells check box and then click the up arrow until 0.05" is displayed in this box also (Figure 5-96).**

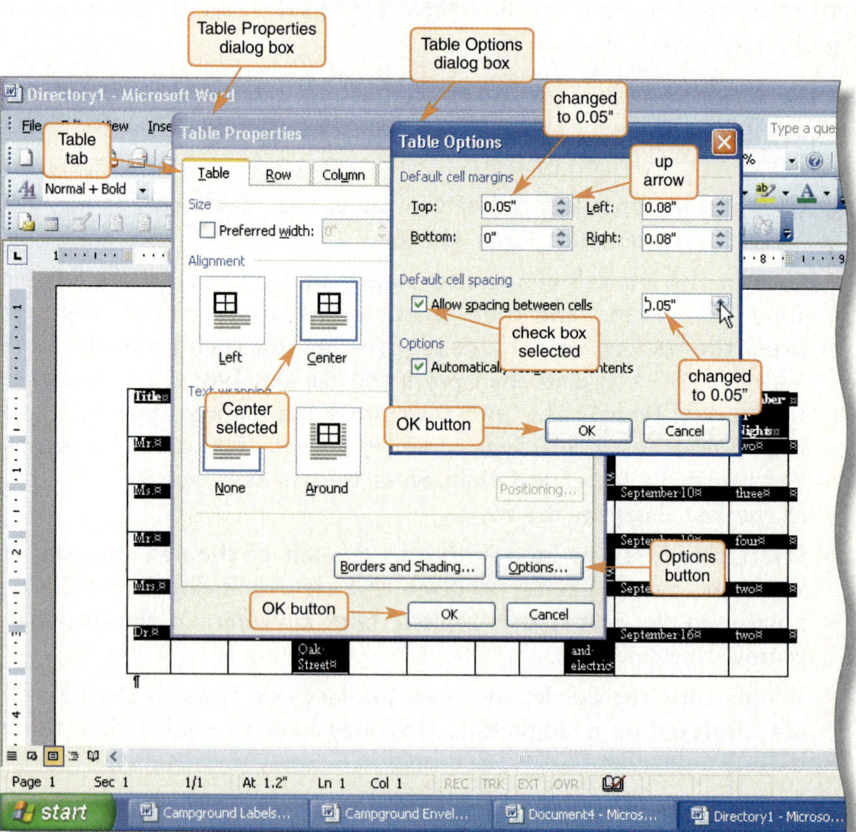

FIGURE 5-96

3

- **Click the OK button in both dialog boxes.**

Word modifies the table (shown in Figure 5-97).

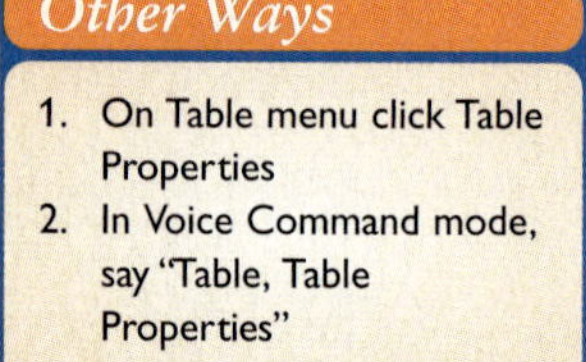

Other Ways

1. On Table menu click Table Properties
2. In Voice Command mode, say "Table, Table Properties"

The next step is to sort the table. You want its records to be displayed in order of reservation date. Within each reservation date, the records should be sorted by vacationer last name. The following steps show how to sort a table.

To Sort a Table

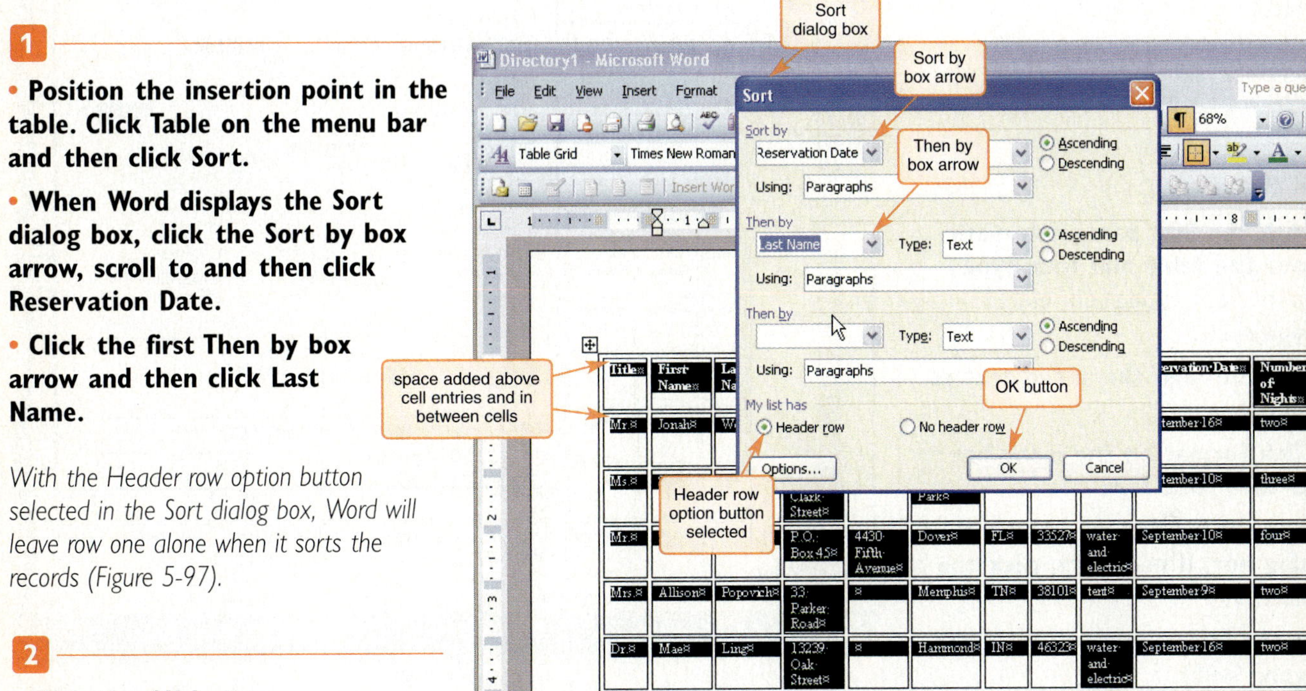

1

- **Position the insertion point in the table. Click Table on the menu bar and then click Sort.**
- **When Word displays the Sort dialog box, click the Sort by box arrow, scroll to and then click Reservation Date.**
- **Click the first Then by box arrow and then click Last Name.**

With the Header row option button selected in the Sort dialog box, Word will leave row one alone when it sorts the records (Figure 5-97).

2

- **Click the OK button.**
- **Click anywhere in the document to remove the highlight.**

Word sorts the records in the table in ascending Last Name order within ascending Reservation Date order (shown in Figure 5-99 on the next page).

FIGURE 5-97

Other Ways

1. In Voice Command mode, say "Table, Sort"

With the Last Name, ascending means alphabetical. With the Reservation Date, ascending means the earliest date is at the top of the list. If you were sorting a list of numbers in ascending order, it would put the smallest numbers first.

You may want to add a note to the top of this table, but do not want the note to print. To do this, you format the text as hidden. The steps on the next page show how to format text as hidden.

To Format Text as Hidden

1

- **Click in the top-left corner of the table and then press the ENTER key twice.**

Word places two paragraph marks above the table.

2

- **Click the first paragraph mark above the table and then type** `Table last updated on August 16.`
- **Drag through the added text to select it.**
- **Click Format on the menu bar and then click Font.**
- **When Word displays the Font dialog box, if necessary, click the Font tab.**
- **In the Effects area, click Hidden (Figure 5-98).**

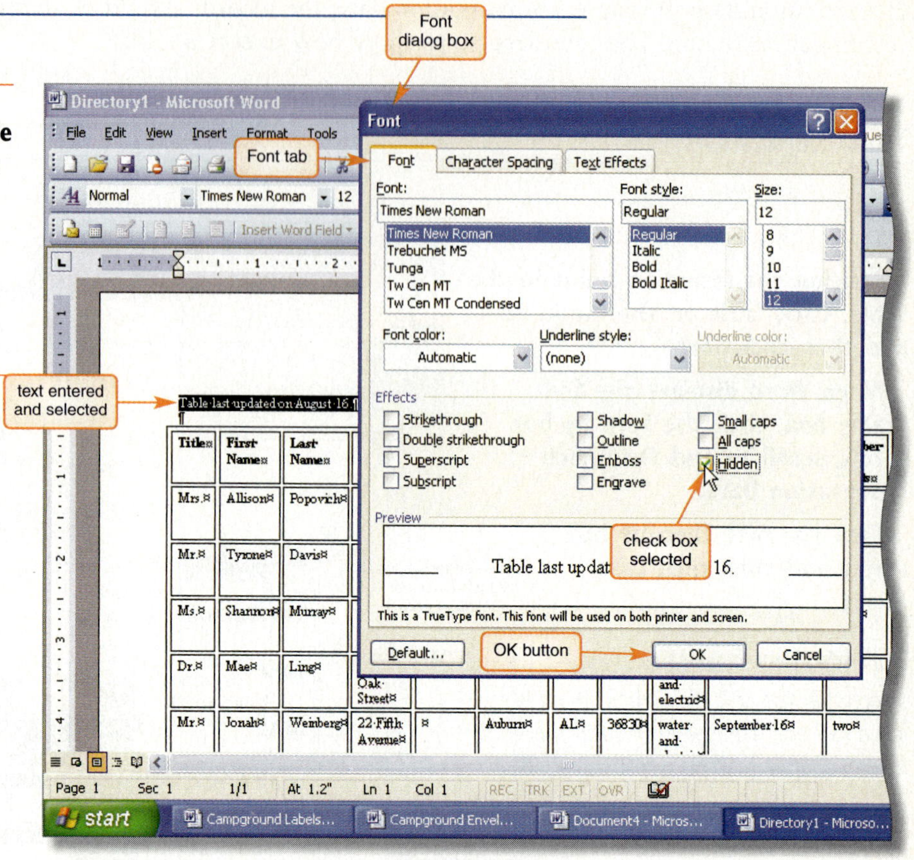

Font dialog box

Font tab

text entered

check box selected

OK button

FIGURE 5-98

- **Click the OK button.**
- **Click anywhere in the document to remove the highlight.**

Word places a dotted line below the text, which indicates it is hidden (Figure 5-99).

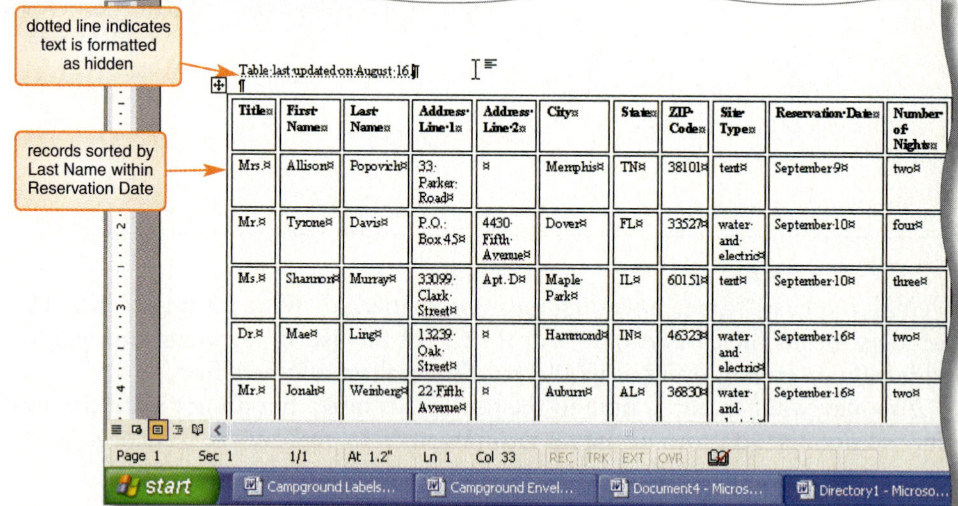

FIGURE 5-99

Other Ways

1. Right-click selected text, click Font on shortcut menu, click Font tab, click Hidden, click OK button
2. In Voice Command mode, say "Format, Font, Font, Hidden, OK"

Hidden text appears on the screen only when the Show/Hide ¶ button on the Standard toolbar is selected, as shown in the step on the next page.

To Hide Hidden Text

1

- **If the Show/Hide ¶ button on the Standard toolbar is selected, click it to deselect it.**

Word hides the hidden text (Figure 5-100).

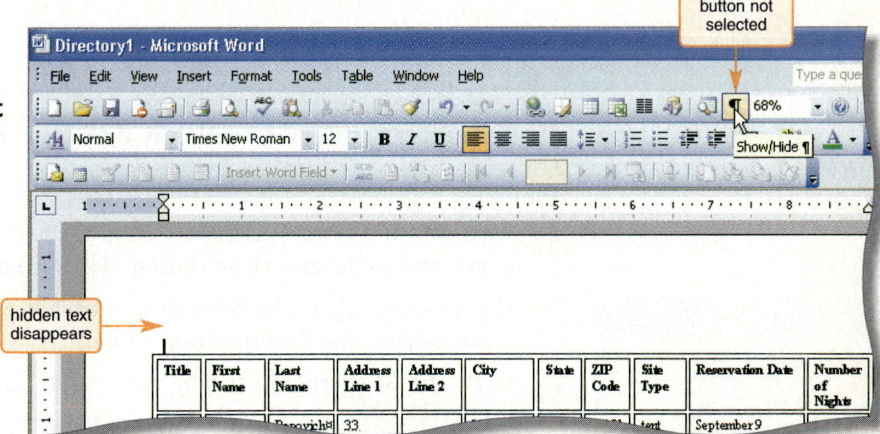

FIGURE 5-100

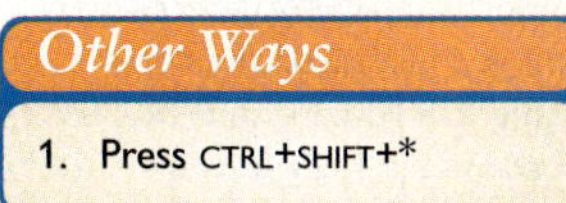

Other Ways

1. Press CTRL+SHIFT+*

To reveal the hidden text, simply click the Show/Hide ¶ button on the Standard toolbar to toggle it on.

The following step prints the directory.

To Print a Document

1 **Click the Print button on the Standard toolbar.**

Word prints the directory in landscape orientation (Figure 5-101). Notice that hidden text does not print on the hard copy.

directory in landscape orientation

hidden text does not print

Title	First Name	Last Name	Address Line 1	Address Line 2	City	State	Zip	Site Type	Reservation Date	Number of Nights
Mrs.	Allison	Popovich	33 Parker Road		Memphis	TN	38101	tent	September 9	two
Mr.	Tyrone	Davis	P.O. Box 45	4430 Fifth Avenue	Dover	FL	33527	water and electric	September 10	four
Ms.	Shannon	Murray	33099 Clark Street	Apt. D	Maple Park	IL	60151	tent	September 10	three
Dr.	Mae	Ling	13239 Oak Street		Hammond	IN	46323	water and electric	September 16	two
Mr.	Jonah	Weinberg	22 Fifth Avenue		Auburn	AL	36830	water and electric	September 16	two

FIGURE 5-101

As an alternative to merging to a directory and printing the results, if you are familiar with Microsoft Access, you can open and print the data source in Access.

Saving the Directory

The following steps save the directory.

To Save the Directory

1. **If necessary, insert your floppy disk into drive A.**
2. **Click the Save button on the Standard toolbar.**
3. **Type the file name** `Camper Directory` **in the File name text box. Do not press the ENTER key after typing the file name.**
4. **If necessary, click the Save in box arrow, click 3½ Floppy (A:), and then double-click the Campground folder.**
5. **Click the Save button in the Save As dialog box.**

Word saves the document with the file name, Camper Directory, in the Campground folder on the floppy disk on drive A.

> *More About*
>
> **Closing Form Letters**
>
> Word always asks if you want to save changes when you close a main document, even if you just saved the document. If you are sure that no additional changes were made to the document, click the No button; otherwise, click the Yes button - just to be safe.

Closing All Open Word Documents

More than one Word document currently is open: Campground Labels, Campground Envelopes, Document4, and Campground Directory. Instead of closing each file individually, you can close all open files at once, as shown in the following steps.

To Close All Open Word Documents

1

- **Press and hold the SHIFT key.**
- **While holding down the SHIFT key, click File on the menu bar. Release the SHIFT key.**

Word displays a Close All command, instead of a Close command, on the File menu because you pressed the SHIFT key when you clicked the menu name (Figure 5-102).

2

- **Click Close All.**
- **If a Microsoft Word dialog box is displayed, click the Yes button to save any changes made to the Campground Labels, Campground Envelopes, and Camper Directory files. For the Document4 file, click the No button.**

Word closes all open documents.

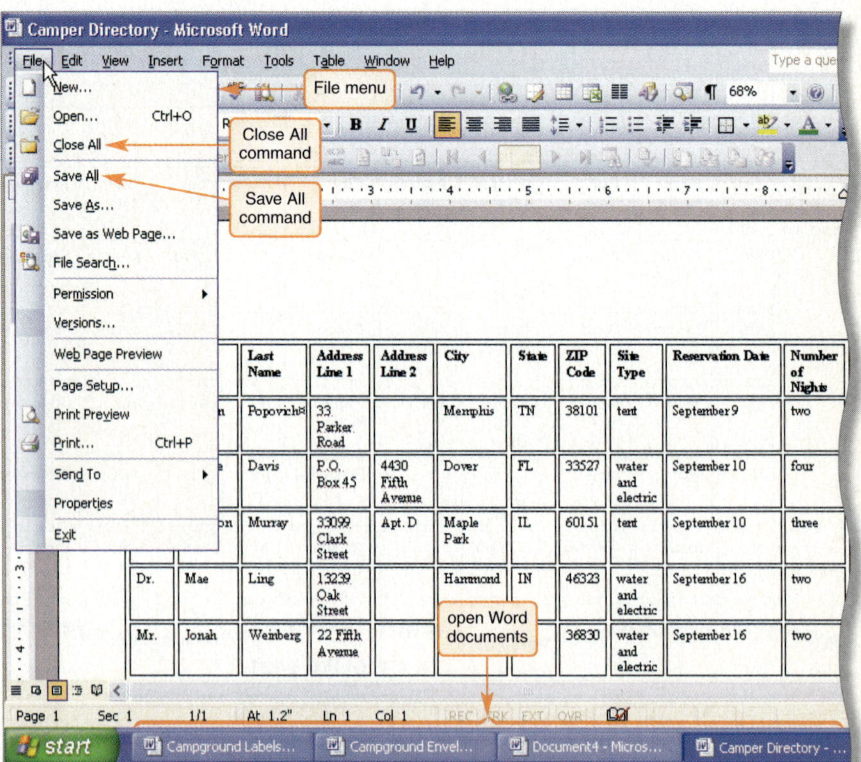

FIGURE 5-102

Notice the Save command also changes to a Save All command (Figure 5-102) when you SHIFT+click File on the menu bar. The **Save All command** saves all open documents at once.

Project 5 now is complete. The following step quits Word.

More About

Certification

The Microsoft Office Specialist Certification program provides an opportunity for you to obtain a valuable industry credential - proof that you have the Word 2003 skills required by employers. For more information, see Appendix E or visit the Word 2003 Certification Web page (scsite.com/wd2003/cert).

To Quit Word

1. **Click the Close button in the Word window.**

The Word window closes.

Project Summary

In Project 5, you learned how to create and print form letters and address corresponding mailing labels and envelopes. First, the project showed how to use a letter template to begin creating the main document for the form letter. Next, you learned how to insert and format an AutoShape on a drawing canvas. Then, the project showed how to create a data source. You learned how to enter text, merge fields, and an IF field into the main document for the form letter. The form letter also included an outline numbered list. You learned how to merge and print all the records in the data source, as well as only records that meet a certain criterion. You also learned how to sort the data source records.

The project illustrated how to address mailing labels and envelopes to accompany the form letters. Finally, you learned how merge all data records into a directory and print the resulting directory.

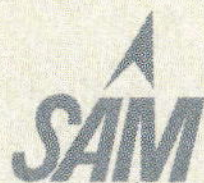

If you have a SAM user profile, you may have access to hands-on instruction, practice, and assessment of the skills covered in this project. Log in to your SAM account and go to your assignments page to see what your instructor has assigned.

What You Should Know

Having completed this project, you should be able to perform the tasks below. The tasks are listed in the same order they were presented in this project. For a list of the buttons, menus, toolbars, and commands introduced in this project, see the Quick Reference Summary at the back of this book and refer to the Page Number column.

1. Start and Customize Word (WD 300)
2. Display Formatting Marks (WD 301)
3. Zoom Page Width (WD 301)
4. Use a Template (WD 302)
5. Insert a Drawing Canvas (WD 305)
6. Insert an AutoShape (WD 306)
7. Format an AutoShape (WD 307)
8. Add Formatted Text to an AutoShape (WD 308)
9. Resize a Drawing Canvas (WD 310)
10. Format a Drawing Canvas (WD 311)
11. Change Paragraph Formatting Using the Reveal Formatting Task Pane (WD 312)
12. Create a Folder while Saving (WD 313)
13. Type a New Data Source (WD 315)
14. Enter More Records (WD 319)
15. Save the Data Source when Prompted by Word (WD 320)
16. Edit a Field (WD 322)
17. Edit the GreetingLine Merge Field (WD 323)
18. Begin Typing the Body of the Form Letter (WD 324)
19. Insert Merge Fields in the Main Document (WD 325)
20. Insert an IF Field in the Main Document (WD 327)
21. Enter More Text and Merge Fields (WD 328)

(continued)

What You Should Know *(continued)*

22. Create an Outline Numbered List (WD 329)
23. Apply a Paragraph Style (WD 332)
24. Enter More Text (WD 332)
25. Select and Replace More Placeholder Text (WD 333)
26. Change the Font Size of Text (WD 334)
27. Save a Document Again (WD 334)
28. Display a Field Code (WD 335)
29. Print Field Codes in the Main Document (WD 336)
30. Merge the Form Letters to the Printer (WD 338, WD 340)
31. Select Records to Merge (WD 339)
32. Remove a Merge Condition (WD 341)
33. Sort the Data Records in a Data Source (WD 342)
34. View Merged Data in the Main Document (WD 343)
35. Close a Document (WD 343)
36. Rename a Folder in Word (WD 344)
37. Address and Print Mailing Labels Using an Existing Data Source (WD 345)
38. Save the Mailing Labels (WD 350)
39. Address and Print Envelopes Using an Existing Data Source (WD 351)
40. Save the Envelope (WD 352)
41. Merge to a Directory (WD 353)
42. Convert Text to a Table (WD 355)
43. Change Page Orientation (WD 356)
44. Merge to a New Document Window (WD 356)
45. Modify and Format a Table (WD 357)
46. Modify Table Properties (WD 358)
47. Sort a Table (WD 359)
48. Format Text as Hidden (WD 360)
49. Hide Hidden Text (WD 361)
50. Print a Document (WD 361)
51. Save the Directory (WD 362)
52. Close All Open Word Documents (WD 362)
53. Quit Word (WD 363)

More About

Quick Reference

For a table that lists how to complete the tasks covered in this book using the mouse, menu, shortcut menu, and keyboard, see the Quick Reference Summary at the back of this book, or visit the Word 2003 Quick Reference Web page (scsite.com/wd2003/qr).

Learn It Online

Instructions: To complete the Learn It Online exercises, start your browser, click the Address bar, and then enter the Web address `scsite.com/wd2003/learn`. When the Word 2003 Learn It Online page is displayed, follow the instructions in the exercises below. Each exercise has instructions for printing your results, either for your own records or for submission to your instructor.

1 Project Reinforcement TF, MC, and SA

Below Word Project 5, click the Project Reinforcement link. Print the quiz by clicking Print on the File menu for each page. Answer each question.

2 Flash Cards

Below Word Project 5, click the Flash Cards link and read the instructions. Type 20 (or a number specified by your instructor) in the Number of playing cards text box, type your name in the Enter your Name text box, and then click the Flip Card button. When the flash card is displayed, read the question and then click the ANSWER box arrow to select an answer. Flip through Flash Cards. If your score is 15 (75%) correct or greater, click Print on the File menu to print your results. If your score is less than 15 (75%) correct, then redo this exercise by clicking the Replay button.

3 Practice Test

Below Word Project 5, click the Practice Test link. Answer each question, enter your first and last name at the bottom of the page, and then click the Grade Test button. When the graded practice test is displayed on your screen, click Print on the File menu to print a hard copy. Continue to take practice tests until you score 80% or better.

4 Who Wants To Be a Computer Genius?

Below Word Project 5, click the Computer Genius link. Read the instructions, enter your first and last name at the bottom of the page, and then click the PLAY button. When your score is displayed, click the PRINT RESULTS link to print a hard copy.

5 Wheel of Terms

Below Word Project 5, click the Wheel of Terms link. Read the instructions, and then enter your first and last name and your school name. Click the PLAY button. When your score is displayed, right-click the score and then click Print on the shortcut menu to print a hard copy.

6 Crossword Puzzle Challenge

Below Word Project 5, click the Crossword Puzzle Challenge link. Read the instructions, and then enter your first and last name. Click the SUBMIT button. Work the crossword puzzle. When you are finished, click the Submit button. When the crossword puzzle is redisplayed, click the Print Puzzle button to print a hard copy.

7 Tips and Tricks

Below Word Project 5, click the Tips and Tricks link. Click a topic that pertains to Project 5. Right-click the information and then click Print on the shortcut menu. Construct a brief example of what the information relates to in Word to confirm you understand how to use the tip or trick.

8 Newsgroups

Below Word Project 5, click the Newsgroups link. Click a topic that pertains to Project 5. Print three comments.

9 Expanding Your Horizons

Below Word Project 5, click the Articles for Microsoft Word link. Click a topic that pertains to Project 5. Print the information. Construct a brief example of what the information relates to in Word to confirm you understand the contents of the article.

10 Search Sleuth

Below Word Project 5, click the Search Sleuth link. To search for a term that pertains to this project, select a term below the Project 5 title and then use the Google search engine at google.com (or any major search engine) to display and print two Web pages that present information on the term.

11 Word Online Training

Below Word Project 5, click the Word Online Training link. When your browser displays the Microsoft Office Online Web page, click the Word link. Click one of the Word courses that covers one or more of the objectives listed at the beginning of the project on page WD 298. Print the first page of the course before stepping through it.

12 Office Marketplace

Below Word Project 5, click the Office Marketplace link. When your browser displays the Microsoft Office Online Web page, click the Office Marketplace link. Click a topic that relates to Word. Print the first page.

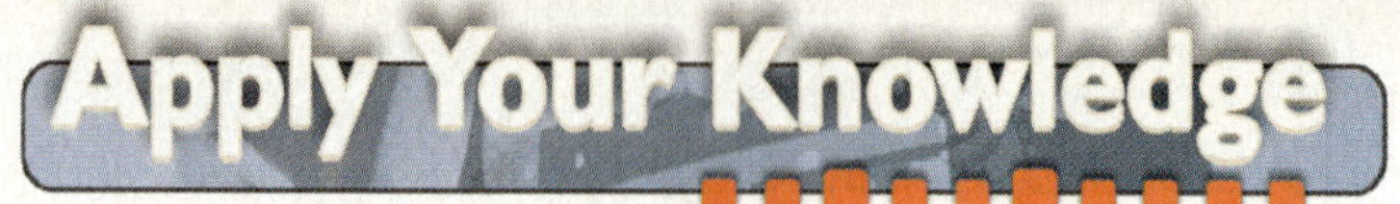

1 Working with a Form Letter

Instructions: Start Word. Open the document, Apply 5-1 Wellness Form Letter, on the Data Disk. If you did not download the Data Disk, see the inside back cover for instructions for downloading the Data Disk or see your instructor. When you open the main document, if Word displays a dialog box about an SQL command, click the Yes button. If Word prompts for the name of the data source, select Apply 5-1 Donor List on the Data Disk.

The document is a main document for the Child Wellness Council (Figure 5-103). You are to edit the date and greeting line fields, print the form letter with field codes displaying and then without field codes, add a record to the data source, and then merge the form letters to a file.

Perform the following tasks:

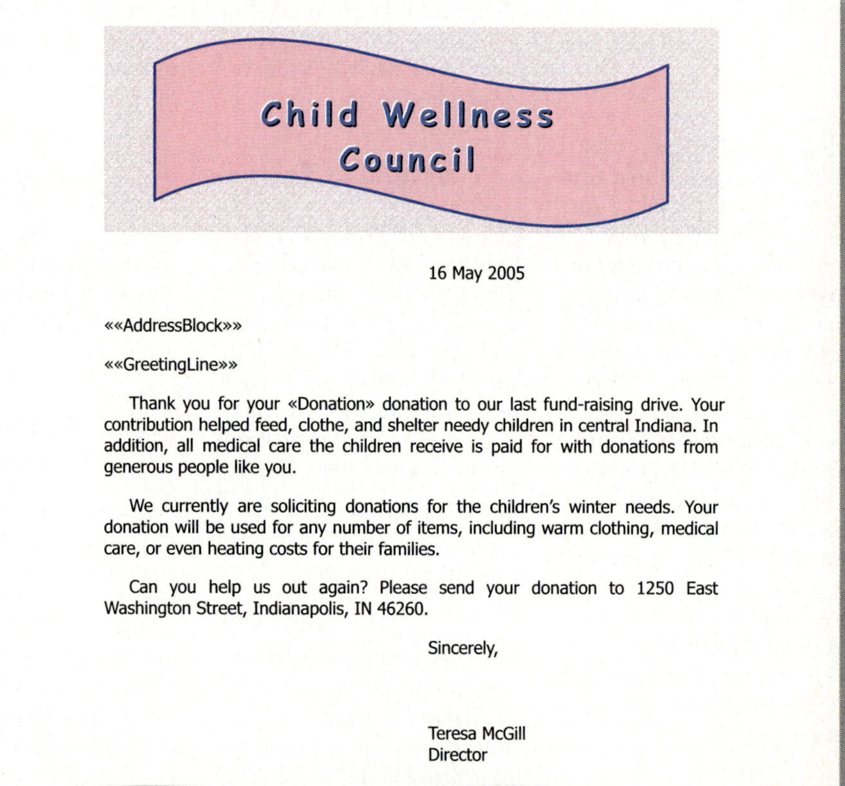
Child Wellness Council

16 May 2005

««AddressBlock»»

««GreetingLine»»

Thank you for your «Donation» donation to our last fund-raising drive. Your contribution helped feed, clothe, and shelter needy children in central Indiana. In addition, all medical care the children receive is paid for with donations from generous people like you.

We currently are soliciting donations for the children's winter needs. Your donation will be used for any number of items, including warm clothing, medical care, or even heating costs for their families.

Can you help us out again? Please send your donation to 1250 East Washington Street, Indianapolis, IN 46260.

Sincerely,

Teresa McGill
Director

FIGURE 5-103

1. Edit the date field so it is displayed in the format d MMMM yyyy.
2. Edit the GreetingLine merge field so the salutation ends with a colon (:).
3. Save the revised form letter with the name Apply 5-1 Wellness Form Letter Revised in a folder called Apply 5-1 Wellness Council. ***Hint:*** Create a folder while saving the document.
4. Print the form letter with field codes; that is, with the Field codes check box selected. Be sure to deselect the Field codes check box after printing the field codes version of the letter.
5. Add a record to the data source that contains your personal information. Type `North` in the Region field and `$75.00` in the Donation field. ***Hint***: Click the Edit button in the Mail Merge Recipients dialog box.
6. Sort the data source by the Last Name field.
7. Save the form letter again.
8. Merge the form letters to a new document. Save the new document with the name Apply 5-1 Merged Form Letters. Print the document containing the merged form letters.
9. Save all open documents using the Save All command.
10. Close all open documents using the Close All command.
11. Rename the Apply 5-1 Wellness Council folder to the name Apply 5-1 Child Wellness.

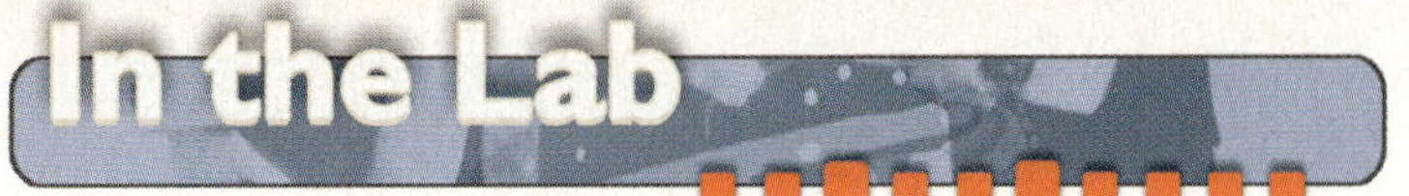

1 Creating a Form Letter, Data Source, Mailing Labels, and Directory

Problem: Ray Fleischner, the service manager at TLC Auto Care, has asked you to send a letter to customers that are due for a service call. You decide to use a form letter (Figure 5-104a).

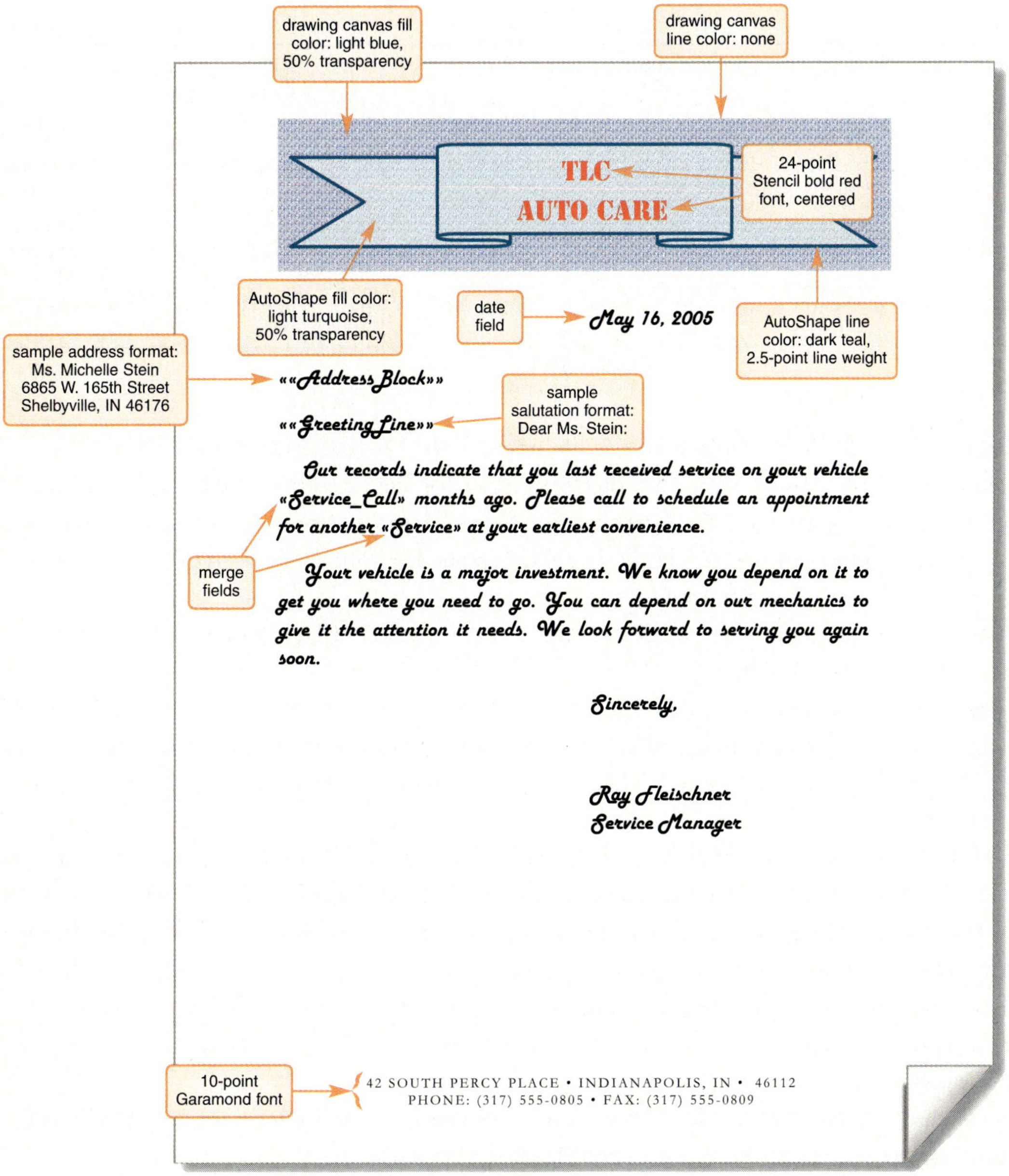

drawing canvas fill color: light blue, 50% transparency

drawing canvas line color: none

TLC
AUTO CARE

24-point Stencil bold red font, centered

AutoShape fill color: light turquoise, 50% transparency

date field

May 16, 2005

AutoShape line color: dark teal, 2.5-point line weight

sample address format:
Ms. Michelle Stein
6865 W. 165th Street
Shelbyville, IN 46176

««AddressBlock»»

sample salutation format:
Dear Ms. Stein:

««GreetingLine»»

Our records indicate that you last received service on your vehicle «Service_Call» months ago. Please call to schedule an appointment for another «Service» at your earliest convenience.

merge fields

Your vehicle is a major investment. We know you depend on it to get you where you need to go. You can depend on our mechanics to give it the attention it needs. We look forward to serving you again soon.

Sincerely,

Ray Fleischner
Service Manager

10-point Garamond font

42 SOUTH PERCY PLACE • INDIANAPOLIS, IN • 46112
PHONE: (317) 555-0805 • FAX: (317) 555-0809

FIGURE 5-104a

Instructions:

1. Use the Elegant Merge Letter template to create a form letter.
2. Insert the up ribbon AutoShape in place of the placeholder text at the top of the letterhead. Add text to and format the AutoShape as shown in Figure 5-104a.

(continued)

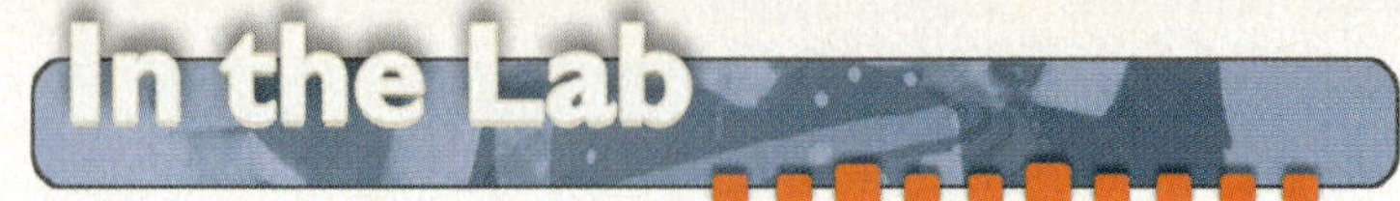

Creating a Form Letter, Data Source, Mailing Labels, and Directory *(continued)*

3. Use the Reveal Formatting task pane to insert 24 points above the date line.
4. Type a new data source using the data shown in Figure 5-104b. Delete field names not used, and add two field names: Service Call and Service. Save the data source with the file name, Lab 5-1 TLC Auto Care List, in a folder called Lab 5-1 TLC Auto. ***Hint***: You will need to create the folder while saving.

Title	First Name	Last Name	Address Line 1	Address Line 2	City	State	ZIP Code	Service Call	Service
Ms.	Michelle	Stein	6865 W. 165th Street		Shelbyville	IN	46176	six	tune-up
Mr.	Walter	Benjamin	9025 Wilson Court	Apt. 1E	Indianapolis	IN	46259	six	oil change
Mr.	Timothy	Jackson	2 East Penn Drive		Pittsboro	IN	46167	12	emission test
Ms.	Louella	Drake	33 Timmons Place	P.O. Box 12	Plainfield	IN	46168	12	emission test
Mr.	Adelbert	Ruiz	1722 East Lincoln Park Place		Carmel	IN	46033	six	tune-up

FIGURE 5-104b

5. Save the main document for the form letter with the file name, Lab 5-1 TLC Auto Care Form Letter, in the folder called Lab 5-1 TLC Auto. Compose the form letter for the main document as shown in Figure 5-104a on the previous page. Edit the GreetingLine field so it ends with a colon, instead of a comma. Insert the merge fields as shown in Figure 5-104a. Change the font of the body of the letter to 16-point Harrow Solid Italic, or a similar font.
6. Save the main document for the form letter again. Print the main document twice: once with field codes displaying and once without field codes.
7. Merge the form letters to the printer.
8. In a new document window, address mailing labels using the same data source you used for the form letters. Save the mailing labels with the name, Lab 5-1 TLC Auto Care Labels, in the Lab 5-1 TLC Auto folder. Print the mailing labels.
9. In a new document window, specify the main document type as a directory. Insert all merge fields into the document. Convert the list of fields to a Word table (the table will have 10 columns). Change the page layout to landscape orientation. Merge the directory layout to a new document window. Add a row to the top of the table and insert field names into the empty cells. Bold the first row. Resize the columns so the table looks like Figure 5-104b. Add 0.05" above each table cell using the Table Properties dialog box.
10. Insert your name as text above the table. Format your name as hidden text. Hide the text on the screen. Then, reveal the text on the screen.
11. Save the directory with the name, Lab 5-1 TLC Auto Care Directory, in the folder named Lab 5-1 TLC Auto. Print the directory (your name should not print because it is hidden).
12. Sort the table in the directory by the Last Name field. Print the sorted directory.
13. Save the directory again.
14. Close all open documents. Rename the folder from Lab 5-1 TLC Auto to Lab 5-1 TLC Auto Care.

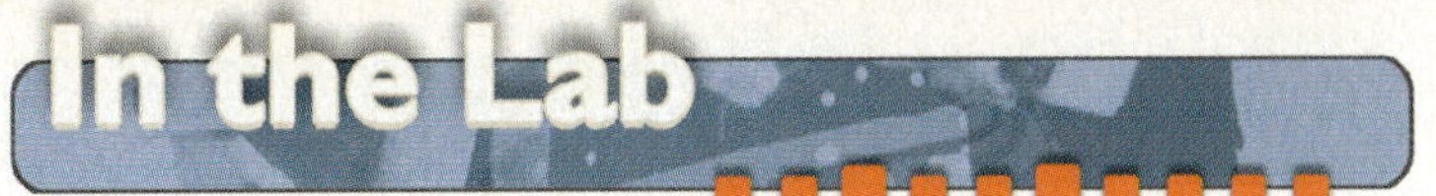

2 Creating a Form Letter with an IF Field and an Outline Numbered List

Problem: As the computer specialist at Global Choice Coffee Club, the owner has asked you to send a letter to new members, outlining the details of their membership. You have decided to use a form letter (Figure 5-105a). The contact telephone number will vary, depending if the new member resides in the west or the east sales zone.

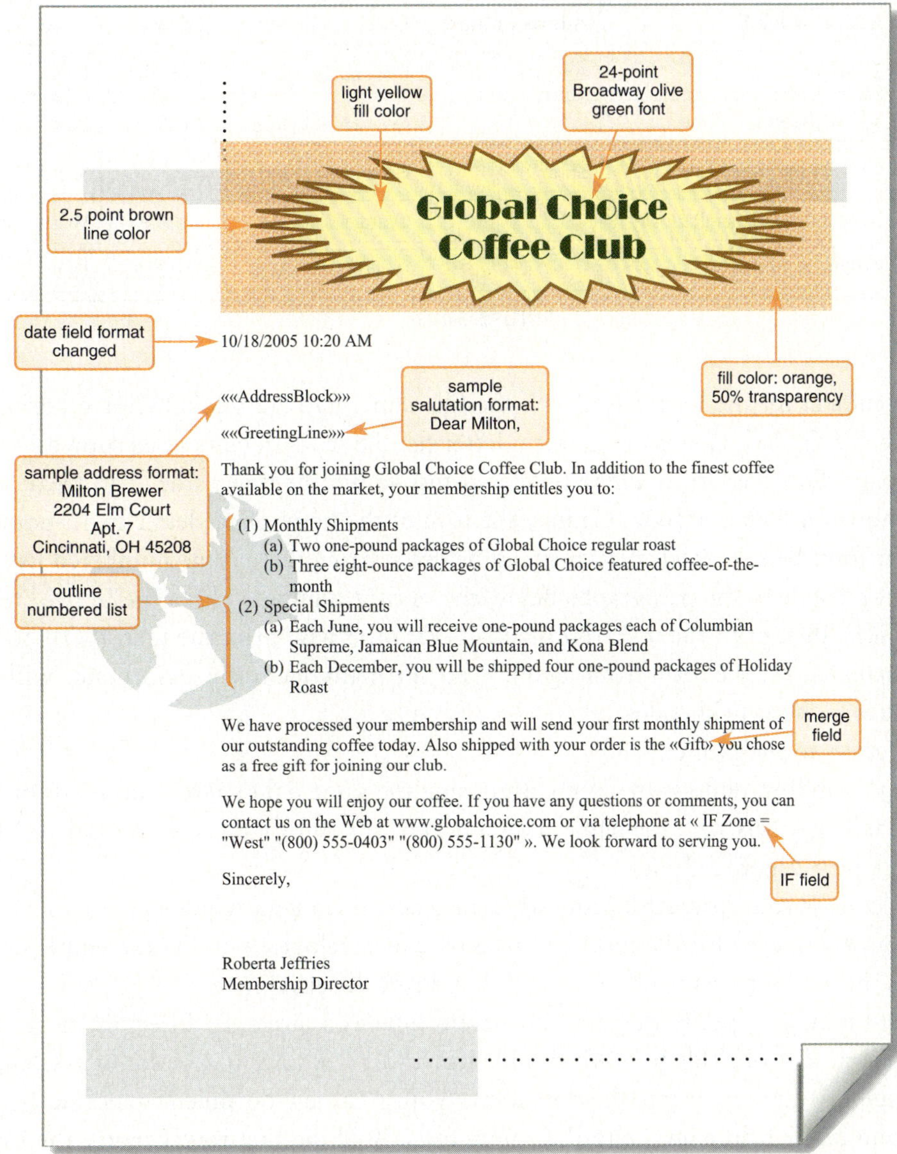

FIGURE 5-105a

Instructions:

1. Use the Contemporary Merge Letter template to create a form letter.
2. Insert a 32-point star AutoShape in place of the placeholder text at the top of the letterhead. Add text to and format the AutoShape as shown in Figure 5-105a.
3. Use the Reveal Formatting task pane to insert 6 points above the date line. Edit the date line field so it displays the date and time as shown in Figure 5-105a.

(continued)

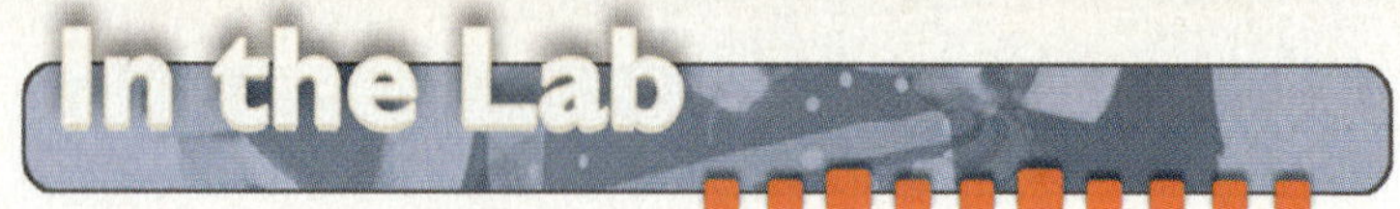

Creating a Form Letter with an IF Field and an Outline Numbered List *(continued)*

4. Type a new data source using the data shown in Figure 5-105b. Delete field names not used, and add two field names: Zone and Gift. Save the data source with the file name, Lab 5-2 Global Coffee Customer List, in a folder called Lab 5-2 Global. ***Hint:*** You will need to create the folder while saving.

First Name	Last Name	Address Line 1	Address Line 2	City	State	ZIP Code	Zone	Gift
Milton	Brewer	2204 Elm Court	Apt. 7	Cincinnati	OH	45208	East	carafe
Benjamin	Tu	54 Lacy Court		Ipswich	MA	01938	East	mug set
Elena	Gupta	99 E. 101st Place	Suite 9	Brea	CA	92821	West	carafe
Ronald	Hidalgo	7676 Independence Parkway		Orange	CA	92866	West	frothing pitcher
Adam	Rosen	8802 E. Schilling Avenue		Boston	MA	02219	East	mug set

FIGURE 5-105b

5. Save the main document for the form letter with the file name, Lab 5-2 Global Coffee Form Letter, in the folder named Lab 5-2 Global. Compose the form letter for the main document as shown in Figure 5-105a on the previous page. Edit the GreetingLine field so it just shows the first name (e.g., Dear Mike,). Insert the merge fields as shown in Figure 5-105a. Change the font of the body of the letter to 12-point Footlight MT Light, or a similar font. Be sure to clear formatting before starting the outline numbered list. Apply the Body Text paragraph style to the paragraphs below the outline numbered list. The IF field tests if Zone is equal to West; if it is, then print the text, (800) 555-0403; otherwise print the text, (800) 555-1130.
6. Save the main document for the form letter again. Print the main document twice: once with field codes displaying and once without field codes.
7. Merge the form letters to the printer.
8. In a new document window, address mailing labels using the same data source you used for the form letters. Save the mailing labels with the name, Lab 5-2 Global Coffee Labels, in the Lab 5-2 Global folder. Print the mailing labels (Figure 5-105c).
9. If your printer allows or your instructor requests it, in a new document window, address envelopes using the same data source you used for the form letters. Save the envelopes with the file name, Lab 5-2 Global Coffee Envelopes, in the folder named Lab 5-2 Global. Print the envelopes.
10. In a new document window, specify the main document type as a directory. Insert all merge fields into the document. Convert the list of fields to a Word table (the table will have nine columns). Change the page layout to landscape orientation. Merge the directory layout to a new document window. Add a row to the top of the table and insert field names into the empty cells. Bold the first row. Change the top, bottom, left, and right page margins to one-half inch (***Hint:*** Use the Page Setup dialog box). Resize the columns so the table looks like Figure 5-105b. Add 0.05" above and below each table cell using the Table Properties dialog box.

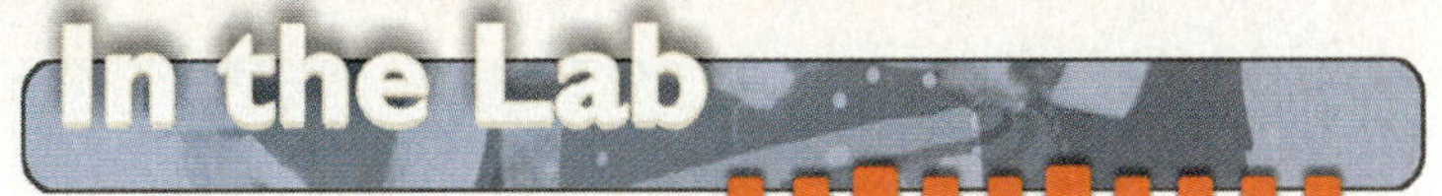

Milton Brewer 2204 Elm Court Apt. 7 Cincinnati, OH 45208	Benjamin Tu 54 Lacy Court Ipswich, MA 01938	Elena Gupta 99 E. 101st Place Suite 9 Brea, CA 92821
Ronald Hidalgo 7676 Independence Parkway Orange, CA 92866	Adam Rosen 8802 E. Schilling Avenue Boston, MA 02219	

FIGURE 5-105c

11. Insert your name as text above the table. Format your name as hidden text.
12. Save the directory with the name, Lab 5-2 Global Coffee Member Directory, in the folder named Lab 5-2 Global. Print the directory (your name should not print because it is hidden).
13. Sort the table in the directory by the Last Name field within the State field. Print the sorted directory.
14. Save the directory again.
15. Close all open documents. Rename the folder from Lab 5-2 Global to Lab 5-2 Global Coffee.

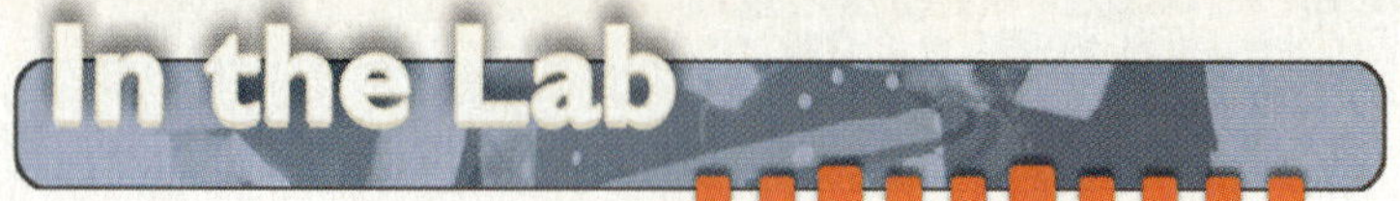

3 Designing a Data Source, Form Letter, and Mailing Labels from Sample Memos

Problem: The benefits director at CADdesign, Inc., would like to schedule an insurance benefits meeting. Two separate session times will be scheduled: salaried employees will meet on Thursday, October 6, and hourly employees will meet on Friday, October 7. Sample drafted memos for each type of employee are shown in Figure 5-106.

Instructions:

1. Decide which fields should be in the data source. Write the field names down on a piece of paper.
2. Use the Professional Memo template to create a form letter for the memorandums.

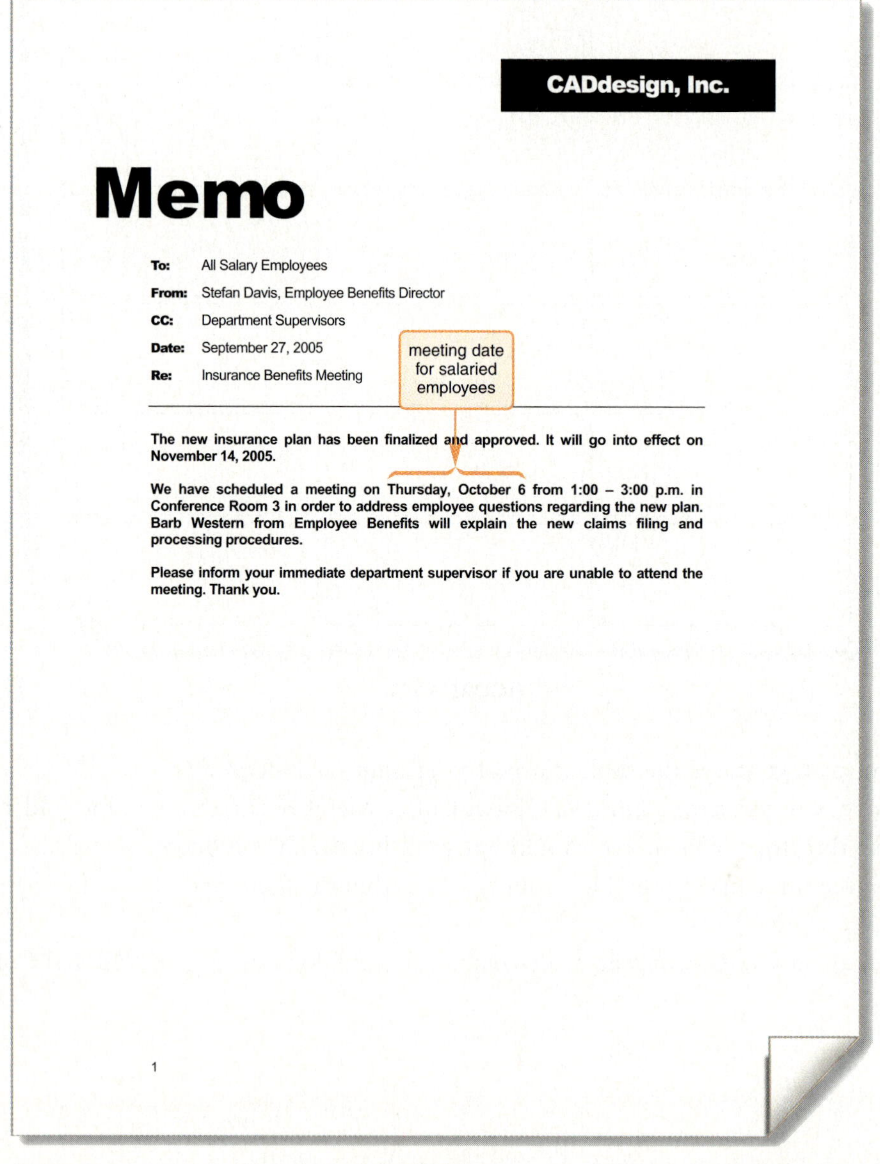

CADdesign, Inc.

Memo

To: All Salary Employees

From: Stefan Davis, Employee Benefits Director

CC: Department Supervisors

Date: September 27, 2005

Re: Insurance Benefits Meeting

The new insurance plan has been finalized and approved. It will go into effect on November 14, 2005.

We have scheduled a meeting on Thursday, October 6 from 1:00 – 3:00 p.m. in Conference Room 3 in order to address employee questions regarding the new plan. Barb Western from Employee Benefits will explain the new claims filing and processing procedures.

Please inform your immediate department supervisor if you are unable to attend the meeting. Thank you.

1

FIGURE 5-106a

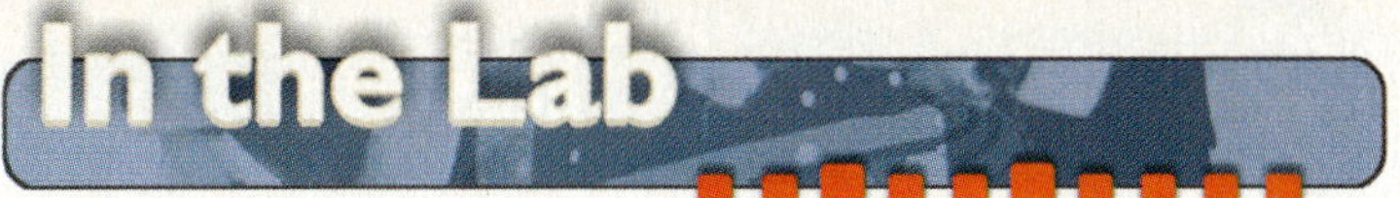

3. Create a data source containing two records that will generate the memos shown in Figure 5-106. Save the data source with the file name, Lab 5-3 CADdesign Data Source, in a folder named Lab 5-3 CADdesign.
4. Save the main document for the form letter with the file name, Lab 5-3 CADdesign Form Letter. Enter the text of the main document for the form letter shown in Figure 5-106. The IF field tests if Employee Type is equal to Salary; if it is, then print the text, Thursday, October 6; otherwise print the text, Friday, October 7. Resize the contents of the memorandum to 10-point Arial.
5. Print the main document twice, once with field codes displaying and once without field codes.
6. Merge and print the form letters.
7. Merge the data source to a directory. Convert it to a Word table. Add an attractive border to the table and apply any other formatting you feel necessary. Print the table. Save the file using the name Lab 5-3 CADdesign Directory.

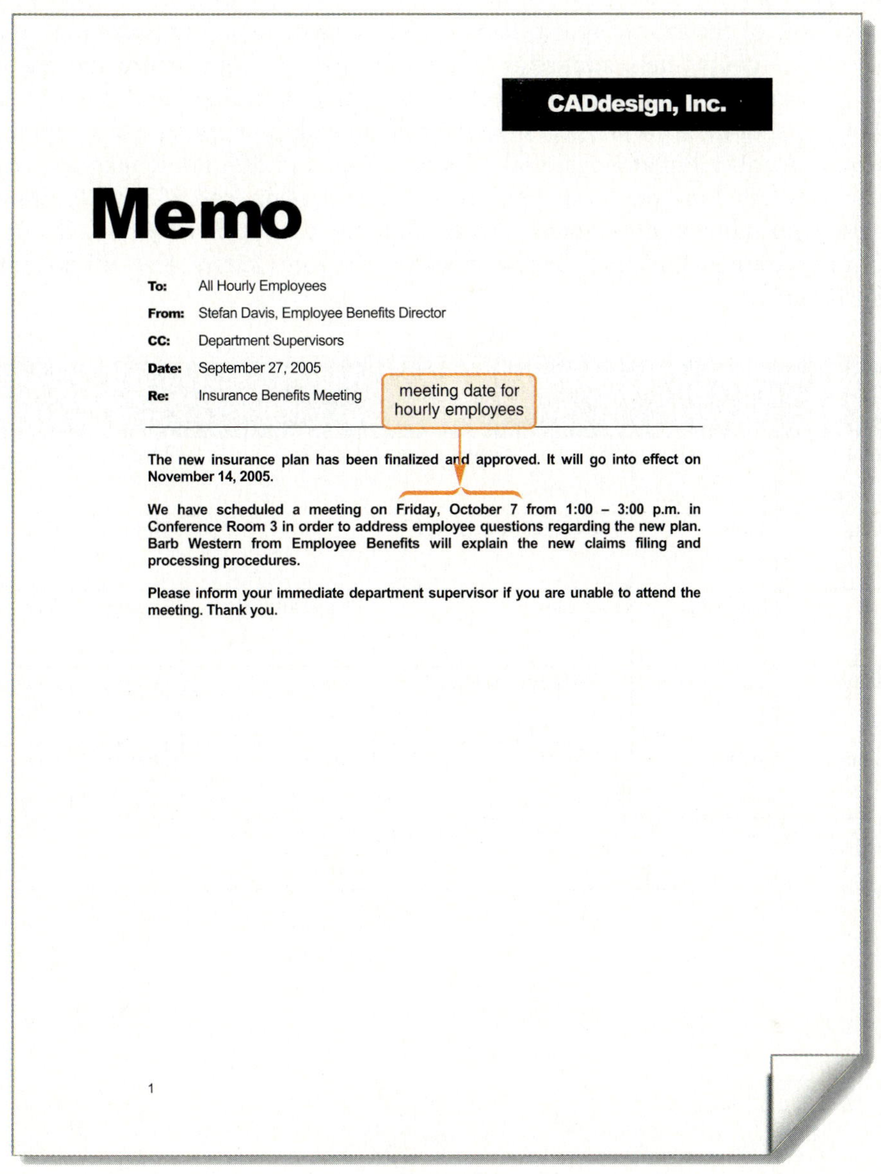
CADdesign, Inc.

Memo

To: All Hourly Employees

From: Stefan Davis, Employee Benefits Director

CC: Department Supervisors

Date: September 27, 2005

Re: Insurance Benefits Meeting

The new insurance plan has been finalized and approved. It will go into effect on November 14, 2005.

We have scheduled a meeting on Friday, October 7 from 1:00 – 3:00 p.m. in Conference Room 3 in order to address employee questions regarding the new plan. Barb Western from Employee Benefits will explain the new claims filing and processing procedures.

Please inform your immediate department supervisor if you are unable to attend the meeting. Thank you.

1

FIGURE 5-106b

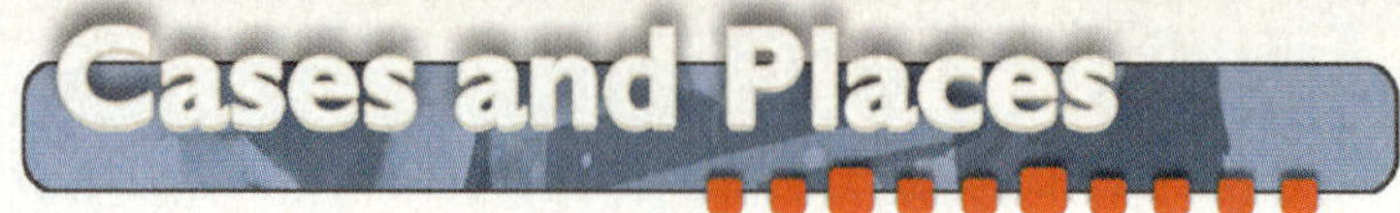

The difficulty of these case studies varies:
■ are the least difficult and ■■ are more difficult. The last exercise is a group exercise.

1 ■ You work for Darren Wilkins, membership director, at Royal Oaks Health club. You are responsible for sending letters to current members, inviting them to upgrade their membership. Create a form letter using the following information: In an AutoShape at the top of the letter, insert the text Royal Oaks Health Club. Place the AutoShape in a drawing canvas. Format both the AutoShape and drawing canvas. The address of the health club is 575 Commerce Drive, Denver, CO 80033; Telephone: 555-0914; Fax: 555-0920. Create the data source shown in Figure 5-107. Edit the date field so it shows the day of the week in addition to the month day and year. A sample salutation is as follows: Dear Juanita,. First paragraph: Thank you, «First_Name», for your recent membership contract with Royal Oaks Health Club. Our facility boasts the latest in state-of-the-art fitness equipment in addition to a truly top-notch staff. We do, however, offer enhancements to your standard membership. Create an outline numbered list for the following list items: 1) Silver membership upgrade ($20.00 per month) – eligibility for premium court times, admission to lap pool for one hour before and one hour after regular open pool hours, and one hour per week with a personal trainer; and 2) Gold membership upgrade ($30.00 per month) – all privileges of silver membership upgrade, one free hour court time per week, discount membership at Royal Oaks Tennis Club, and 30-minute massage weekly. Last paragraph: If you are interested in upgrading your current membership, call 555-9910. Enjoy your new membership! Use your name in the signature block. Sort the data source by the ZIP code field. Then, address and print accompanying labels or envelopes for the form letters. Save all documents in a folder called Case 5-1 Royal Oaks.

Title	First Name	Last Name	Address Line 1	Address Line 2	City	State	ZIP Code
Ms.	Juanita	Mendez	85 Cottage Grove Lane	Unit 2	Denver	CO	80002
Mr.	Steven	Gold	3404 Scherton Drive		Denver	CO	80012
Mr.	Chad	Nicholas	P.O. Box 72	802 Drury Place	Denver	CO	80033
Ms.	Tiffany	Goldstein	7074 Keyway Drive		Denver	CO	80010
Ms.	Bethany	Ames	11234 W. 72nd Street	Apt. 3C	Denver	CO	80201

FIGURE 5-107

Cases and Places

2 ■■ You currently are seeking an employment position in your field of study. You already have prepared a resume and would like to send it to a group of potential employers. You decide to design a cover letter to send along with the resume. Obtain a recent newspaper and cut out three classified advertisements pertaining to your field of study. Locate two job advertisements on the Internet. Create the cover letter for your resume as a form letter. Be sure the cover letter contains your name, address, and telephone number. The data source should contain the five potential employers' names, addresses, and position being sought. Use the information in the classified ads from newspapers and the Internet for the data source. Address accompanying labels or envelopes for the cover letters. Then, create a directory of the data source records. Save all documents in a folder called Case 5-2 Cover Letter. Use the concepts and techniques presented in this project to format the form letter and directory. Turn in the want ads with your printouts.

3 ■■ Your neighbor, Lynette Galens, owns a lawn care service, called Lynette's Lawn Care. She has asked you to assist her in preparing a form letter that thanks customers for their recent contracts with her business. Contracts include weekly care of mowing, watering, and weeding; and monthly care of fertilizing, edging, and pest/grub control. It also includes troubleshooting additional problems. Depending on the contract type, the customer contact person varies: Tammy at 555-1717 handles summer contracts; Sam at 555-1720 handles annual contracts. Create a form letter thanking customers, outlining contract services, outlining additional problems (you will need to research these), and informing them of their contact person (use an IF for this). Use an outline numbered list in the form letter. Place the business name at the top of the letter in an AutoShape in a drawing canvas. Obtain the names and addresses of five of your friends or family members and use them as records in the data source. Create a directory of the data source records. Address accompanying labels or envelopes for the form letters. Save all documents in a folder called Case 5-3 Lawn Care. Use the concepts and techniques presented in this project to format the form letter and directory.

4 ■■ You work part-time for Latisha Adams, credit manager, at American Fashions. One of your responsibilities is to inform applicants when their credit card is approved – and let them know the credit card will be mailed separately within a week. American Fashions assigns credit ratings of good or excellent. With a good rating, the letter includes a 15 percent off coupon to be used on their first credit purchase; with an excellent rating, they get a 25 percent off coupon. Be sure the top of the form letter has an AutoShape in a drawing canvas with appropriate text. Obtain the names and addresses of five of your classmates and use them as records in the data source. Create a directory of the data source records. Address accompanying labels or envelopes for the form letters. Save all documents in a folder called Case 5-4 American Fashions. Use the concepts and techniques presented in this project to format the form letter and directory.

Cases and Places

5 ■■ **Working Together** This team project investigates other types of data sources in form letters and other ways to merge. Select the Project 5 form letter, the Apply Your Knowledge form letter, or one of the assignments in this project as a starting point for the content of your form letter and data source. Team members are to create and merge form letters as follows:

1) One or more team members are to use Microsoft Office Excel to create a table and then use that table as the data source in the mail merge document. It may be necessary to use Help in Word and also Help in Excel to assist in the procedure for creating and saving a worksheet in the proper format for a mail merge;
2) One or more team members are to use Microsoft Office Outlook recipients as a data source in a mail merge document. It may be necessary to use Help in Word and also Help in Outlook;
3) One or more team members are to use Microsoft Office Access to view, format, and print the contents of a data source created in Word. It may be necessary to use Help in Access; and
4) One or more team members are to merge the contents of the data source to e-mail addresses. It may be necessary to use Help in Word.

Then, your team is to develop a PowerPoint slide show that outlines the steps required to complete these four tasks and present the results to your classmates.

MICROSOFT Office Word 2003

Creating a Professional Newsletter

PROJECT 6

CASE PERSPECTIVE

With a membership ranging from students to professionals, Clever Clicks User Group (CCUG) provides a means for novice to expert computer users to meet and converse. At the bimonthly meetings, CCUG members listen to a presentation by one or more industry experts and then network with each other in a casual setting. In addition to meetings, members communicate on CCUG's newsgroup, via instant messaging, and by e-mail. CCUG also distributes a monthly newsletter called *Clever Clicks* designed to provide computing tips and important user group information to all members.

As a member of CCUG, you are required to serve on one committee. This year, you chose the Publicity Committee. Your responsibility is to prepare the monthly newsletter. Each issue of *Clever Clicks* contains a feature article and announcements. This month's feature article will discuss how to safeguard computers from virus infections. You plan to create the article as a Word document. The article will discuss how computer viruses infect a computer and then present a variety of precautions users can take to protect their computers from viruses. The article also will have a diagram showing the symptoms of a computer virus infection. The announcements section will remind members about the upcoming user group meeting, inform them of a new CCUG member discount, and advise them of the topic of the next month's feature article.

Your task now is to design the newsletter so the feature article spans the first two columns of page 1 and then continues on page 2. The announcements should be located in the third column of page 1 of the newsletter. As you read through this project, you will learn how to use Word to create a newsletter.

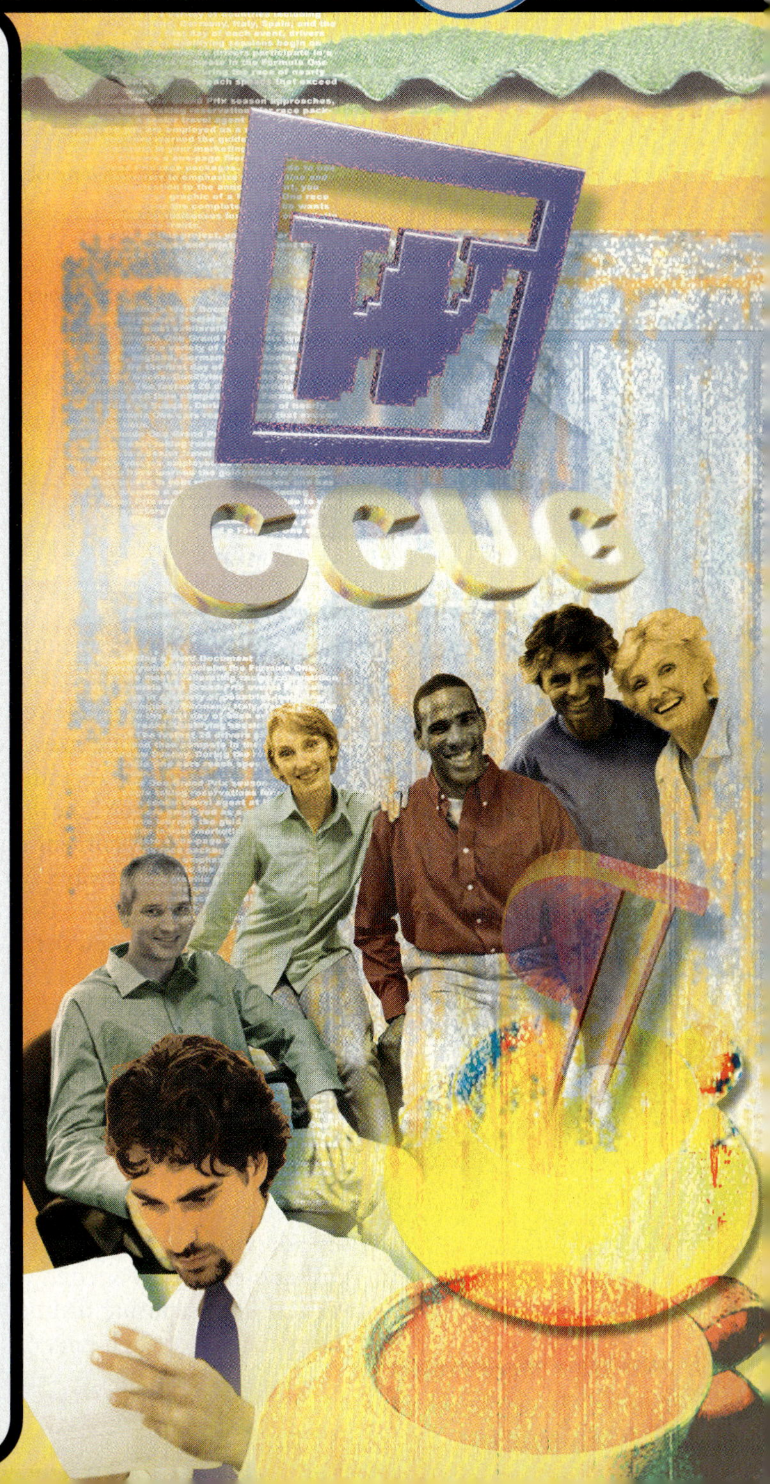

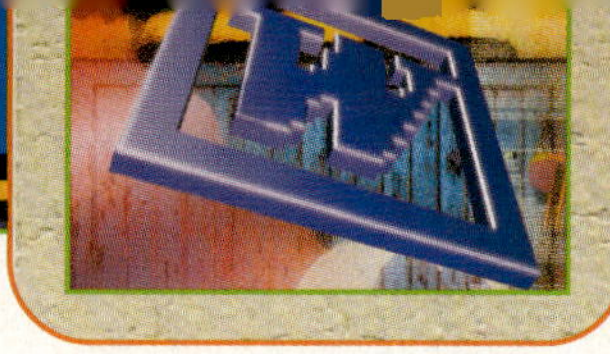

MICROSOFT Office Word 2003

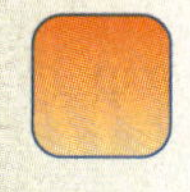

Creating a Professional Newsletter

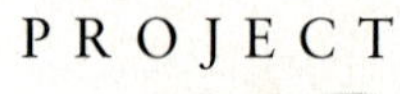

PROJECT

Objectives

You will have mastered the material in this project when you can:

- Create and format a WordArt drawing object
- Insert a symbol into a document
- Insert and format a floating graphic
- Format a document into multiple columns
- Format a character as a drop cap
- Insert a column break
- Place a vertical rule between columns
- Insert and format a text box
- Use the Paste Special command to link items in a document
- Balance columns
- Insert and format a diagram
- Use the Format Painter button
- Add a page border
- Enhance a document for online viewing

Introduction

Professional looking documents, such as newsletters and brochures, often are created using desktop publishing software. With desktop publishing software, you can divide a document into multiple columns, wrap text around diagrams and other objects, change fonts and font sizes, add color and lines, and so on, to create an attention-grabbing document. A traditionally held opinion of desktop publishing software, such as Adobe PageMaker or QuarkXpress, is that it enables you to open an existing word processing document and enhance it through formatting not provided in your word processing software. Word, however, provides many of the formatting features that you would find in a desktop publishing package. Thus, you can use Word to create eye-catching newsletters and brochures.

Project Six — Clever Clicks Newsletter

Project 6 uses Word to produce the newsletter shown in Figure 6-1. The newsletter is a monthly publication for members of Clever Clicks User Group (CCUG). Notice that it incorporates the desktop publishing features of Word. The body of each page of the newsletter is divided into three columns. A variety of fonts, font sizes, and colors add visual appeal to the document. The first page has text wrapped around a pull-quote, and the second page has text wrapped around a diagram. Horizontal and vertical lines separate distinct areas of the newsletter, including a page border around the perimeter of each page.

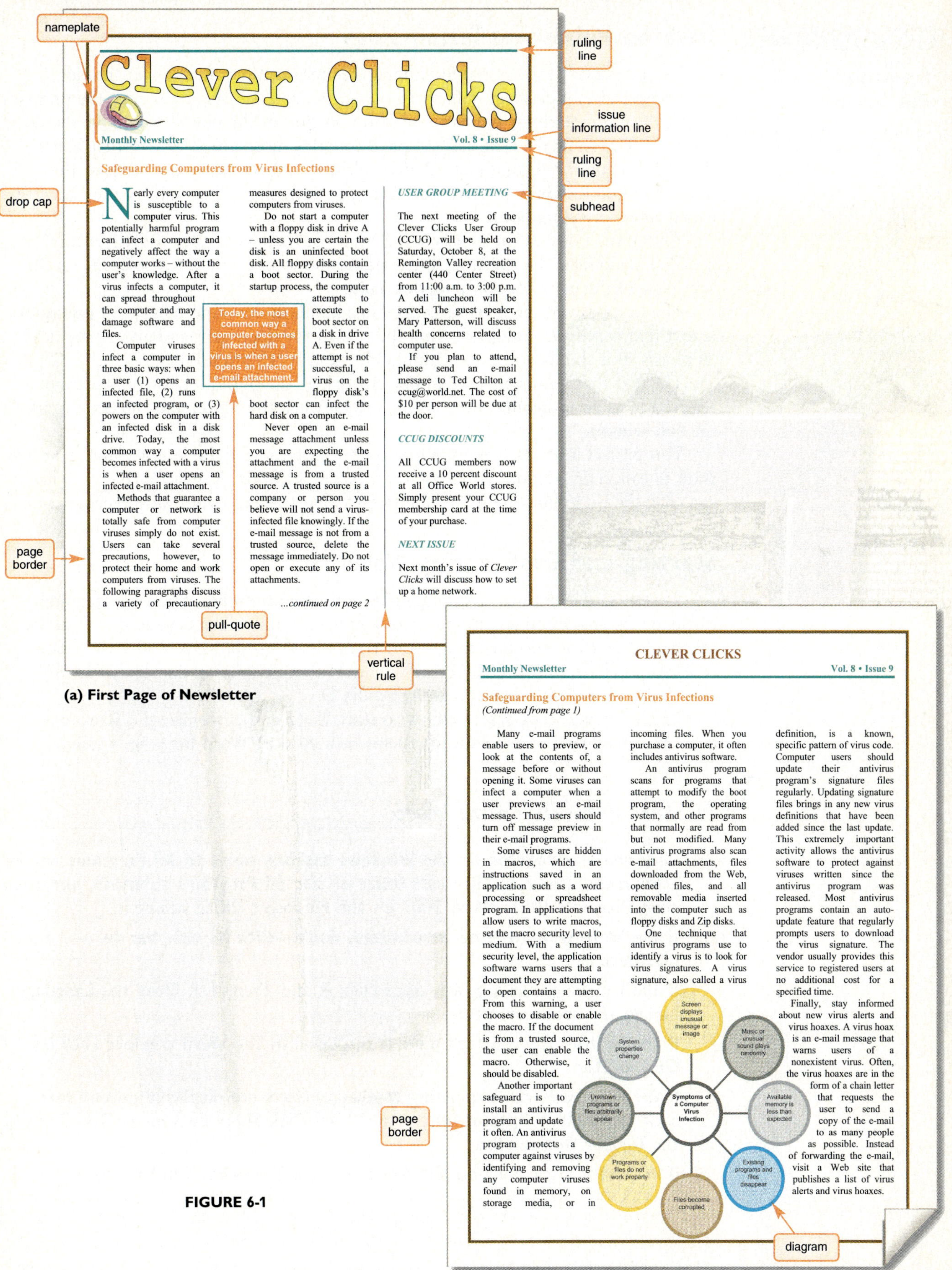

Clever Clicks

Monthly Newsletter — Vol. 8 • Issue 9

Safeguarding Computers from Virus Infections

Nearly every computer is susceptible to a computer virus. This potentially harmful program can infect a computer and negatively affect the way a computer works – without the user's knowledge. After a virus infects a computer, it can spread throughout the computer and may damage software and files.

Computer viruses infect a computer in three basic ways: when a user (1) opens an infected file, (2) runs an infected program, or (3) powers on the computer with an infected disk in a disk drive. Today, the most common way a computer becomes infected with a virus is when a user opens an infected e-mail attachment.

Methods that guarantee a computer or network is totally safe from computer viruses simply do not exist. Users can take several precautions, however, to protect their home and work computers from viruses. The following paragraphs discuss a variety of precautionary measures designed to protect computers from viruses.

Do not start a computer with a floppy disk in drive A – unless you are certain the disk is an uninfected boot disk. All floppy disks contain a boot sector. During the startup process, the computer attempts to execute the boot sector on a disk in drive A. Even if the attempt is not successful, a virus on the floppy disk's boot sector can infect the hard disk on a computer.

> Today, the most common way a computer becomes infected with a virus is when a user opens an infected e-mail attachment.

Never open an e-mail message attachment unless you are expecting the attachment and the e-mail message is from a trusted source. A trusted source is a company or person you believe will not send a virus-infected file knowingly. If the e-mail message is not from a trusted source, delete the message immediately. Do not open or execute any of its attachments.

...continued on page 2

USER GROUP MEETING

The next meeting of the Clever Clicks User Group (CCUG) will be held on Saturday, October 8, at the Remington Valley recreation center (440 Center Street) from 11:00 a.m. to 3:00 p.m. A deli luncheon will be served. The guest speaker, Mary Patterson, will discuss health concerns related to computer use.

If you plan to attend, please send an e-mail message to Ted Chilton at ccug@world.net. The cost of $10 per person will be due at the door.

CCUG DISCOUNTS

All CCUG members now receive a 10 percent discount at all Office World stores. Simply present your CCUG membership card at the time of your purchase.

NEXT ISSUE

Next month's issue of *Clever Clicks* will discuss how to set up a home network.

(a) First Page of Newsletter

CLEVER CLICKS

Monthly Newsletter — Vol. 8 • Issue 9

Safeguarding Computers from Virus Infections

(Continued from page 1)

Many e-mail programs enable users to preview, or look at the contents of, a message before or without opening it. Some viruses can infect a computer when a user previews an e-mail message. Thus, users should turn off message preview in their e-mail programs.

Some viruses are hidden in macros, which are instructions saved in an application such as a word processing or spreadsheet program. In applications that allow users to write macros, set the macro security level to medium. With a medium security level, the application software warns users that a document they are attempting to open contains a macro. From this warning, a user chooses to disable or enable the macro. If the document is from a trusted source, the user can enable the macro. Otherwise, it should be disabled.

Another important safeguard is to install an antivirus program and update it often. An antivirus program protects a computer against viruses by identifying and removing any computer viruses found in memory, on storage media, or in incoming files. When you purchase a computer, it often includes antivirus software.

An antivirus program scans for programs that attempt to modify the boot program, the operating system, and other programs that normally are read from but not modified. Many antivirus programs also scan e-mail attachments, files downloaded from the Web, opened files, and all removable media inserted into the computer such as floppy disks and Zip disks.

One technique that antivirus programs use to identify a virus is to look for virus signatures. A virus signature, also called a virus definition, is a known, specific pattern of virus code. Computer users should update their antivirus program's signature files regularly. Updating signature files brings in any new virus definitions that have been added since the last update. This extremely important activity allows the antivirus software to protect against viruses written since the antivirus program was released. Most antivirus programs contain an auto-update feature that regularly prompts users to download the virus signature. The vendor usually provides this service to registered users at no additional cost for a specified time.

Finally, stay informed about new virus alerts and virus hoaxes. A virus hoax is an e-mail message that warns users of a nonexistent virus. Often, the virus hoaxes are in the form of a chain letter that requests the user to send a copy of the e-mail to as many people as possible. Instead of forwarding the e-mail, visit a Web site that publishes a list of virus alerts and virus hoaxes.

Symptoms of a Computer Virus Infection: Screen displays unusual message or image; Music or unusual sound plays randomly; Available memory is less than expected; Existing programs and files disappear; Files become corrupted; Programs or files do not work properly; Unknown programs or files arbitrarily appear; System properties change

(b) Second Page of Newsletter

FIGURE 6-1

More About

Desktop Publishing

For more information about desktop publishing, visit the Word 2003 More About Web page (scsite.com/wd2003/more) and then click Desktop Publishing.

Desktop Publishing Terminology

As you create professional looking newsletters and brochures, you should understand several desktop publishing terms. In Project 6 (Figure 6-1 on the previous page), the **nameplate**, or **banner**, is the top portion of the newsletter above the three columns. The nameplate on the first page contains more graphical enhancements than the one on the second page. A nameplate usually contains the name of the newsletter and the **issue information line**. The horizontal lines in the nameplate are called **rules**, or **ruling lines**.

Within the body of the newsletter, a heading, such as USER GROUP MEETING, is called a **subhead**. The vertical line dividing the second and third columns on the first page of the newsletter is a **vertical rule**.

The first page of the newsletter contains a pull-quote (Figure 6-1a). A **pull-quote** is text that is *pulled*, or copied, from the text of the document and given graphical emphasis so it stands apart and commands the reader's attention.

The text that wraps around an object, such as the pull-quote or the diagram, is referred to as **wrap-around text**. The space between the object and the text is called the **run-around**.

This project involves several steps requiring you to drag the mouse. Thus, you may want to cancel an action if you drag to the wrong location. Remember that you always can click the Undo button on the Standard toolbar to cancel your most recent action.

Starting and Customizing Word

To start and customize Word, Windows must be running. If you are stepping through this project on a computer and you want your screen to match the figures in this book, then you should change your computer's resolution to 800 × 600 and reset the toolbars and menus. For information about changing the resolution and resetting toolbars and menus, read Appendix D.

The following steps describe how to start Word and customize the Word window. You may need to ask your instructor how to start Word for your system.

To Start and Customize Word

1. **Click the Start button on the Windows taskbar, point to All Programs on the Start menu, point to Microsoft Office on the All Programs submenu, and then click Microsoft Office Word 2003 on the Microsoft Office submenu.**
2. **If the Word window is not maximized, double-click its title bar to maximize it.**
3. **If the Language bar appears, right-click it and then click Close the Language bar on the shortcut menu.**
4. **If the Getting Started task pane is displayed in the Word window, click its Close button.**
5. **If the Standard and Formatting toolbar buttons are displayed on one row, click the Toolbar Options button and then click Show Buttons on Two Rows in the Toolbar Options list.**
6. **If necessary, click View on the menu bar and then click Print Layout.**

Word starts and, after a few moments, displays an empty document in the Word window. You use print layout view in this project because the newsletter contains columns and a diagram, and these display properly only in print layout view. The Print Layout View button on the horizontal scroll bar is selected (shown in Figure 6-2 on page WD 382).

Displaying Formatting Marks

It is helpful to display formatting marks that indicate where in the document you pressed the ENTER key, SPACEBAR, and other keys. The following step describes how to display formatting marks.

To Display Formatting Marks

1. **If the Show/Hide ¶ button on the Standard toolbar is not selected already, click it.**

Word displays formatting marks in the document window, and the Show/Hide ¶ button on the Standard toolbar is selected (shown in Figure 6-2 on the next page).

Zooming Page Width

In print layout view, many users zoom page width so they can see all edges of the page in the document window at once. The following steps zoom page width.

To Zoom Page Width

1. **Click the Zoom box arrow on the Standard toolbar.**
2. **Click Page Width in the Zoom list.**

Word computes the zoom percentage and displays it in the Zoom box (shown in Figure 6-2). Your percentage may be different depending on your computer.

Changing All Margin Settings

Word is preset to use standard 8.5-by-11-inch paper, with 1.25-inch left and right margins and 1-inch top and bottom margins. For the newsletter in this project, you want all margins (left, right, top, and bottom) to be .75 inches.

The following steps describe how to change margin settings.

To Change All Margin Settings

1. **Click File on the menu bar and then click Page Setup.**
2. **When Word displays the Page Setup dialog box, if necessary, click the Margins tab. Type** `.75` **in the Top box and then press the TAB key.**
3. **Type** `.75` **in the Bottom box and then press the TAB key.**
4. **Type** `.75` **in the Left box and then press the TAB key.**
5. **Type** `.75` **in the Right box (Figure 6-2).**
6. **Click the OK button to change the margin settings for this document.**

Depending on the printer you are using, you may need to set the margins differently for this project. In this case, Word displays a message when you attempt to print the newsletter.

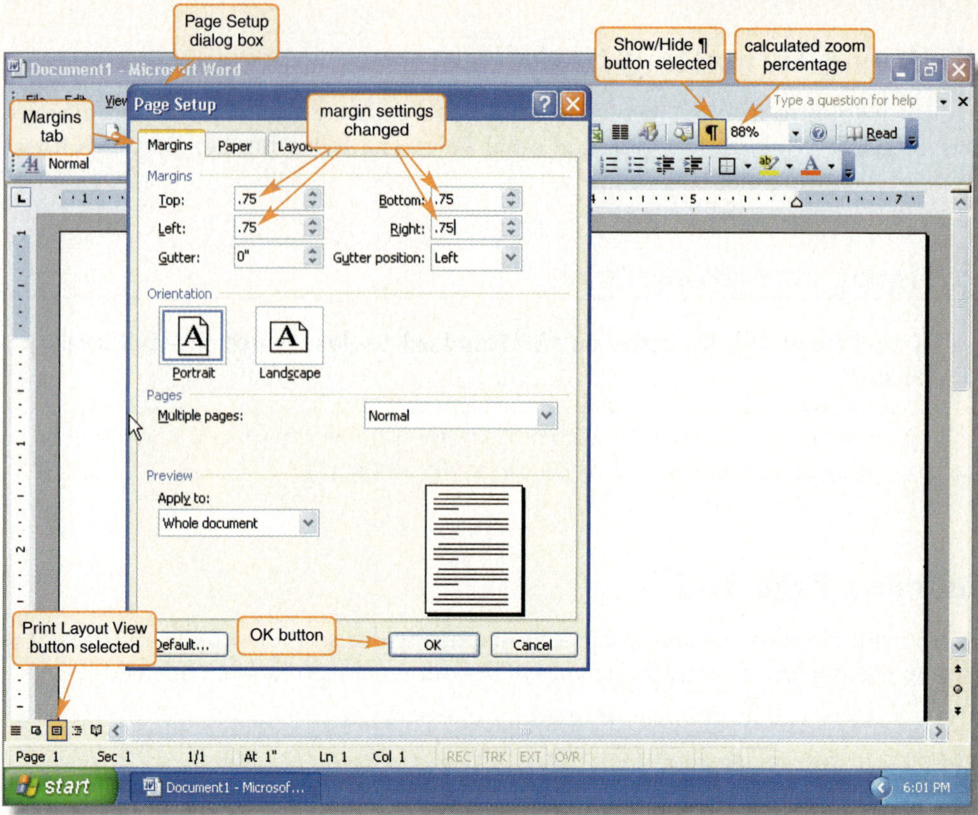

FIGURE 6-2

Creating the Nameplate

The nameplate on the first page of this newsletter consists of the information above the multiple columns (Figure 6-1a on page WD 379). In this project, the nameplate includes the newsletter title, Clever Clicks, the issue information line, and the title of the feature article. The steps on the following pages illustrate how to create the nameplate for the first page of the newsletter in this project.

Inserting a WordArt Drawing Object

In Project 5, you added an AutoShape drawing object to a document. Recall that a **drawing object** is a graphic you create using Word. You can create another type of drawing object, called **WordArt**, which enables you to create special effects such as shadowed, rotated, stretched, skewed, and wavy text.

On the first page of the newsletter in this project, the newsletter name, Clever Clicks, is a WordArt drawing object. The next steps show how to insert a WordArt drawing object.

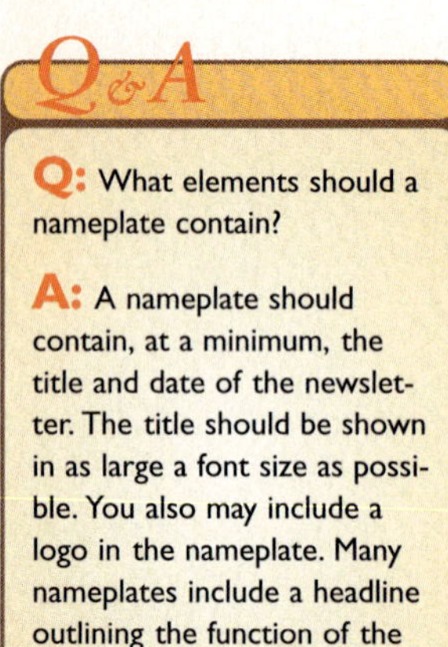

Q&A

Q: What elements should a nameplate contain?

A: A nameplate should contain, at a minimum, the title and date of the newsletter. The title should be shown in as large a font size as possible. You also may include a logo in the nameplate. Many nameplates include a headline outlining the function of the newsletter. Some nameplates also include a short table of contents.

To Insert a WordArt Drawing Object

- **If the Drawing toolbar is not displayed in the Word window, click the Drawing button on the Standard toolbar.**
- **Click the Insert WordArt button on the Drawing toolbar.**
- **When Word displays the WordArt Gallery dialog box, if necessary, click the style in the upper-left corner.**

Word displays the WordArt Gallery dialog box (Figure 6-3). You will add your own special text effects. Thus, you will use the default style in the WordArt Gallery.

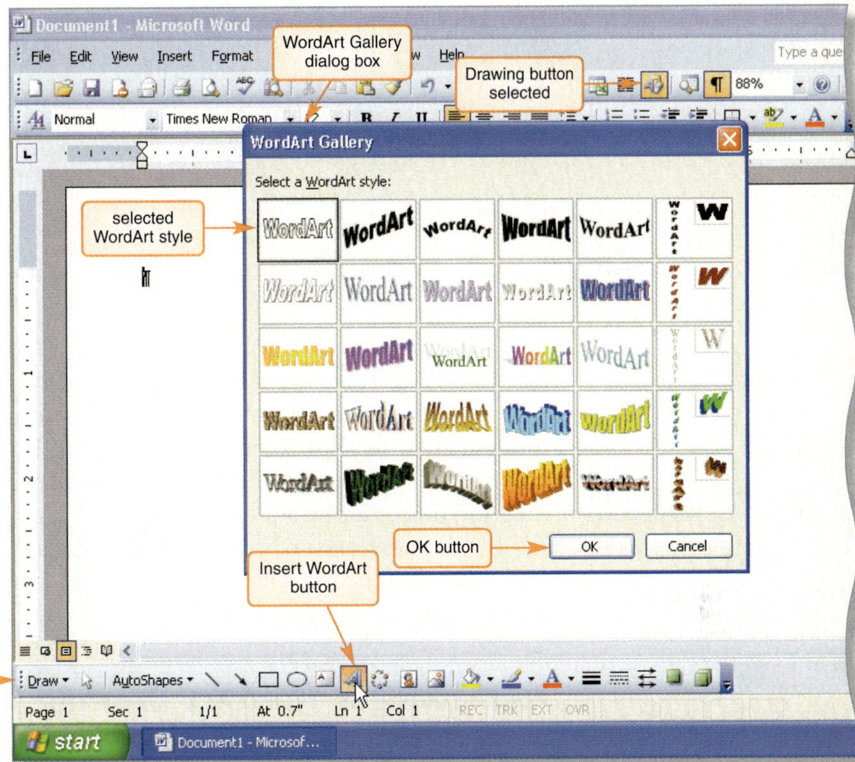

FIGURE 6-3

2

- **Click the OK button.**
- **When Word displays the Edit WordArt Text dialog box, type** `Clever Clicks` **in the Text text box.**
- **Click the Font box arrow in the dialog box. Scroll to and then click Courier New, or a similar font.**
- **Click the Size box arrow in the dialog box, scroll to and then click 72.**
- **Click the Bold button in the dialog box.**

In the Edit WordArt Text dialog box, you enter the WordArt text and change its font, font size, and font style (Figure 6-4).

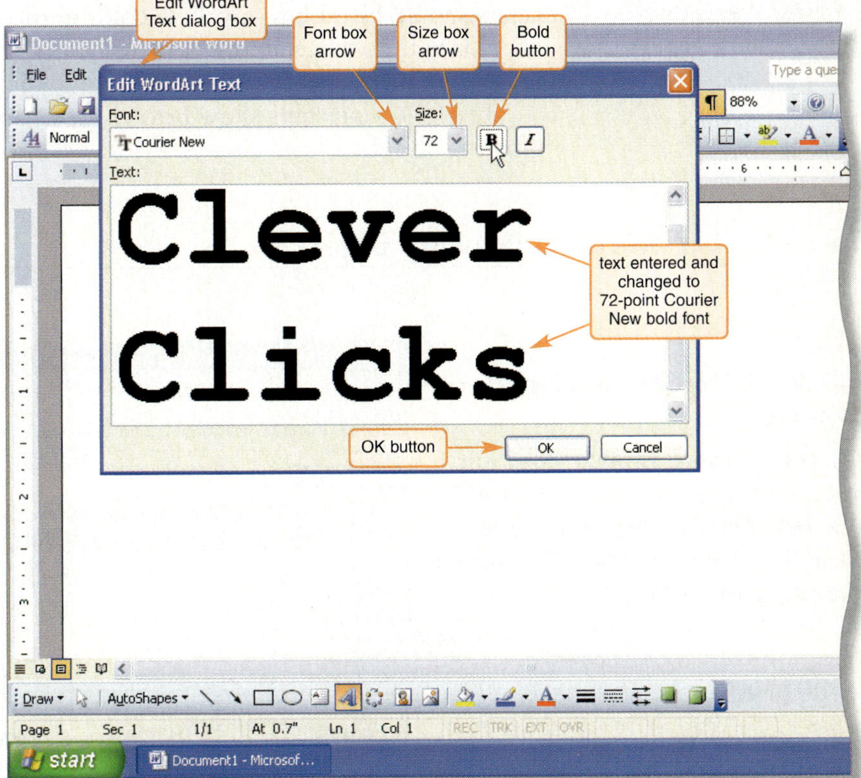

FIGURE 6-4

3

• **Click the OK button.**

A WordArt drawing object is displayed in the document window (Figure 6-5).

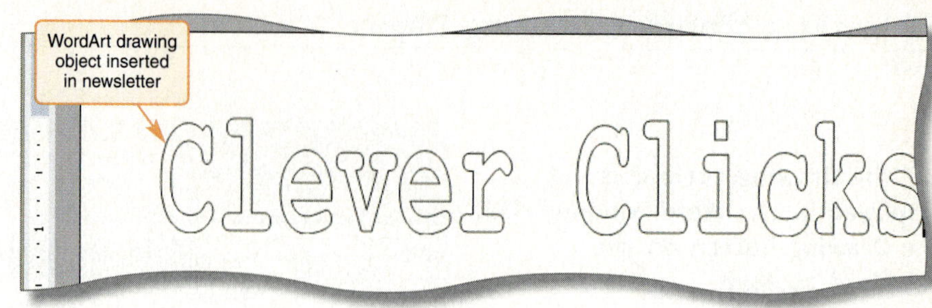

FIGURE 6-5

Other Ways

1. On Insert menu point to Picture, click WordArt on Picture submenu
2. In Voice Command mode, say "Insert, Picture, WordArt"

More About

WordArt Drawing Objects

Keep in mind that WordArt drawing objects are not treated as Word text. Thus, if you misspell the contents of a WordArt drawing object and then spell check the document, Word will not flag a misspelled word(s) in the WordArt drawing object.

To change the WordArt text, its font, its font size, or its font style, display the Edit WordArt Text dialog box (Figure 6-4 on the previous page) by clicking the Edit Text button on the WordArt toolbar (shown in Figure 6-6). To display the WordArt toolbar, click the WordArt drawing object. If the WordArt toolbar does not appear on your screen when you select the WordArt drawing object, right-click the WordArt drawing object and then click Show WordArt Toolbar on the shortcut menu.

If, for some reason, you wanted to delete the WordArt drawing object, you could right-click it and then click Cut on the shortcut menu, or click it and then press the DELETE key.

Formatting a WordArt Drawing Object

The next step is to change the size and color of the WordArt drawing object. It is to be slightly taller and display an orange to yellow to orange gradient color effect. **Gradient** colors blend into one another. Thus, an orange color at the top of the characters should blend into a yellow color in the middle of the characters, which will blend into the orange color again at the bottom of the characters. To make these formatting changes, use the Format WordArt dialog box.

The following steps show how to resize and change the color of the WordArt drawing object.

To Format a WordArt Drawing Object

1

• **Click the WordArt drawing object to select it.**

• **If the WordArt toolbar does not appear on the screen, right-click the WordArt drawing object and then click Show WordArt Toolbar on the shortcut menu.**

When a WordArt drawing object is selected, the WordArt toolbar is displayed in the Word window (Figure 6-6).

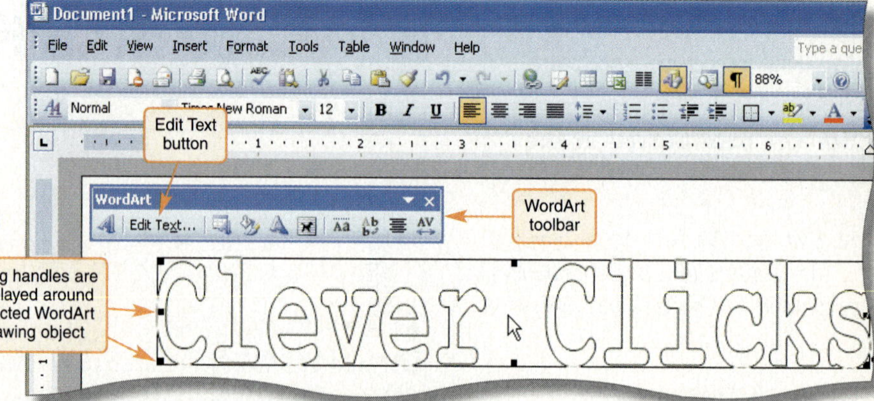

FIGURE 6-6

2

- **Click the Format WordArt button on the WordArt toolbar.**
- **When Word displays the Format WordArt dialog box, if necessary, click the Size tab.**
- **In the Size and rotate area, select the text in the Height box and then type `1.3` as the new height.**

Word displays the Size sheet in the Format WordArt dialog box (Figure 6-7).

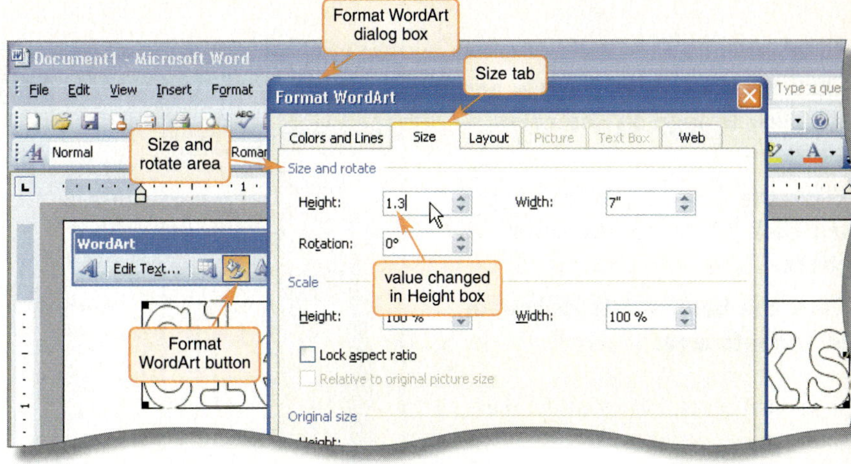

FIGURE 6-7

3

- **Click the Colors and Lines tab.**
- **In the Fill area, click the Color box arrow.**

Word displays the Colors and Lines sheet in the Format WordArt dialog box (Figure 6-8). You can add a gradient color effect through the Fill Effects button.

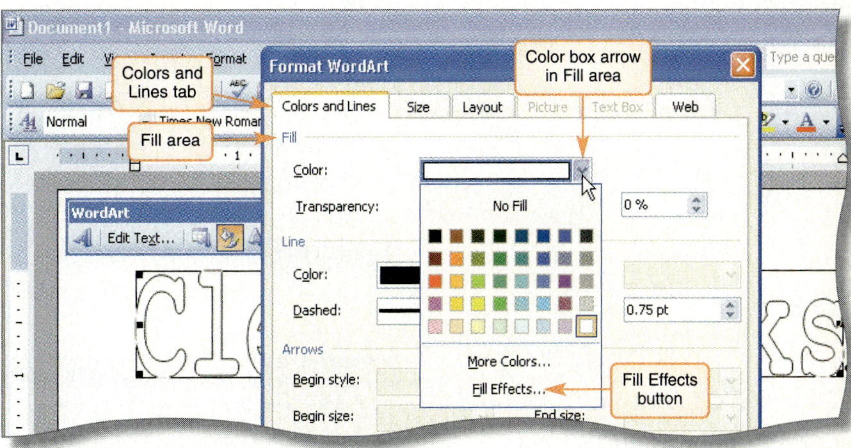

FIGURE 6-8

4

- **Click the Fill Effects button.**
- **When Word displays the Fill Effects dialog box, if necessary, click the Gradient tab.**
- **In the Colors area, click Two colors.**

When you select two colors for a drawing object, Word uses a gradient effect to blend them into one another (Figure 6-9).

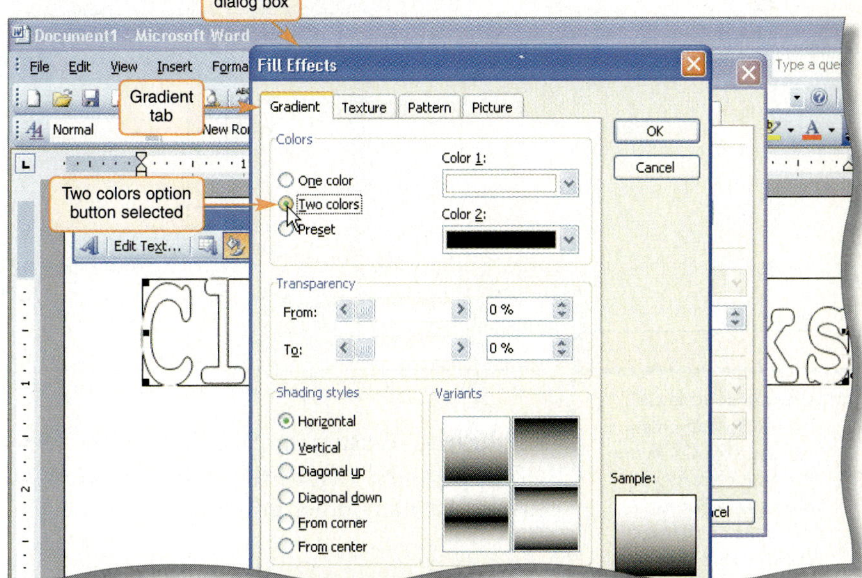

FIGURE 6-9

5

- **Click the Color 1 box arrow and then click Orange on the color palette.**
- **Click the Color 2 box arrow and then click Yellow on the color palette.**
- **Click the bottom-left variant in the Variants area.**

The selected colors and variant for the WordArt object are displayed in the Sample box (Figure 6-10). The default gradient shading style is horizontal, and the selected variant blends color 2 from the middle outward into color 1.

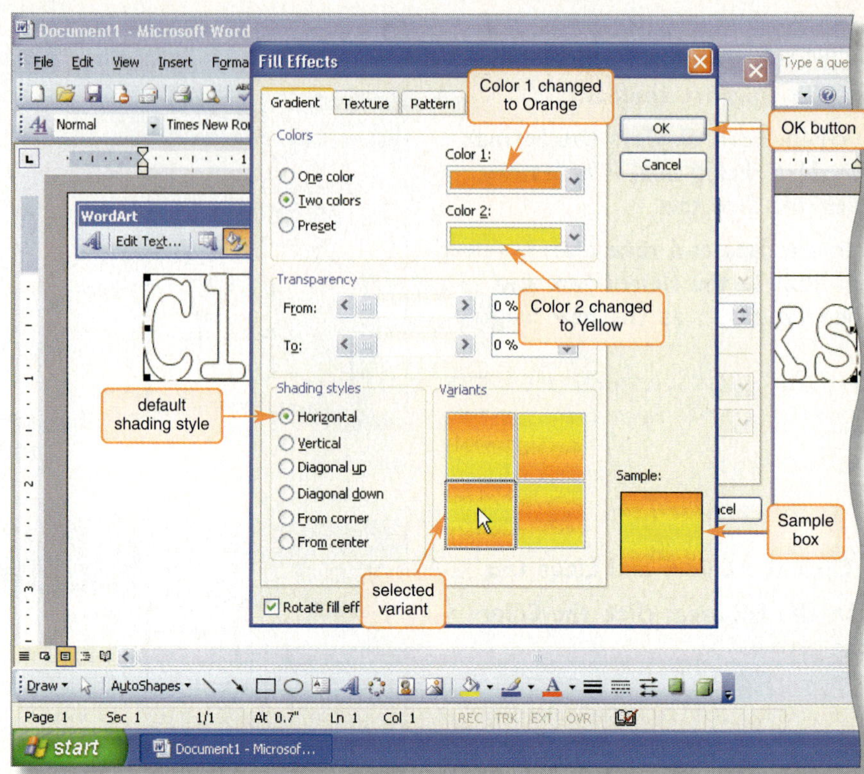

FIGURE 6-10

6

- **Click the OK button.**
- **Click the OK button in the Format WordArt dialog box.**

Word changes the colors of the WordArt object (Figure 6-11).

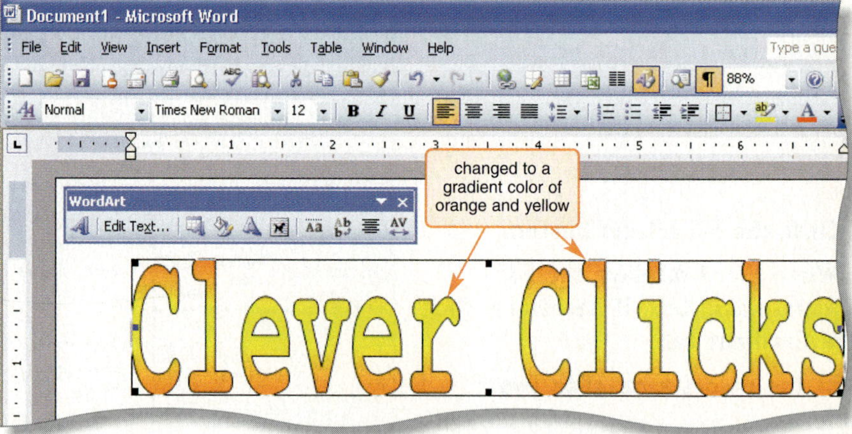

FIGURE 6-11

Other Ways

1. On Format menu click WordArt, change desired options, click OK button
2. Right-click WordArt object, click Format WordArt on shortcut menu, change desired options, click OK button
3. In Voice Command mode, say "Format, WordArt, [select options], OK"

Instead of using the Size sheet in the Format WordArt dialog box to change the size (width and height) of a WordArt drawing object, you can drag its sizing handles, just as with any other graphic.

Changing the WordArt Shape

Word provides a variety of shapes to make your WordArt drawing object more interesting. The next steps show how to change the WordArt drawing object to a cascade down shape.

To Change the Shape of a WordArt Drawing Object

1

- **Click the WordArt Shape button on the WordArt toolbar.**

Word displays a graphical list of available shapes (Figure 6-12). When you click a shape, the WordArt drawing object forms itself into the selected shape.

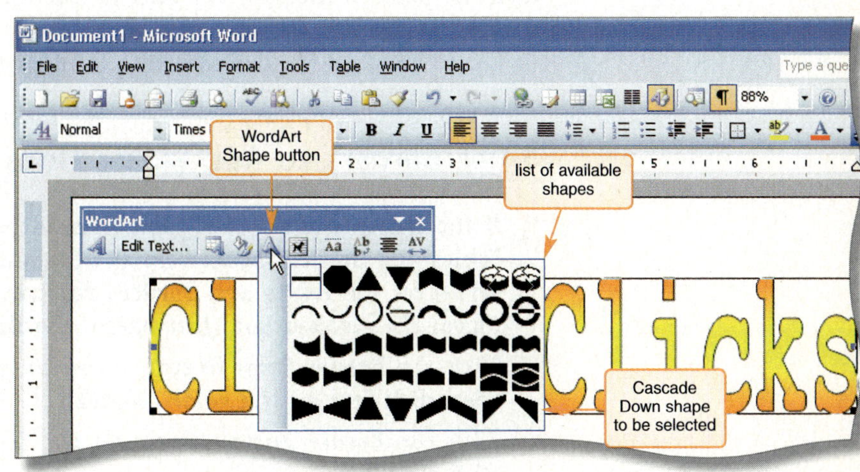

FIGURE 6-12

2

- **Click Cascade Down (the bottom-right shape) in the list of shapes.**
- **Click the paragraph mark to the right of the WordArt text.**

The newsletter title is displayed in a cascade down shape (Figure 6-13). The WordArt drawing object no longer is selected. Thus, the WordArt toolbar no longer appears in the Word window.

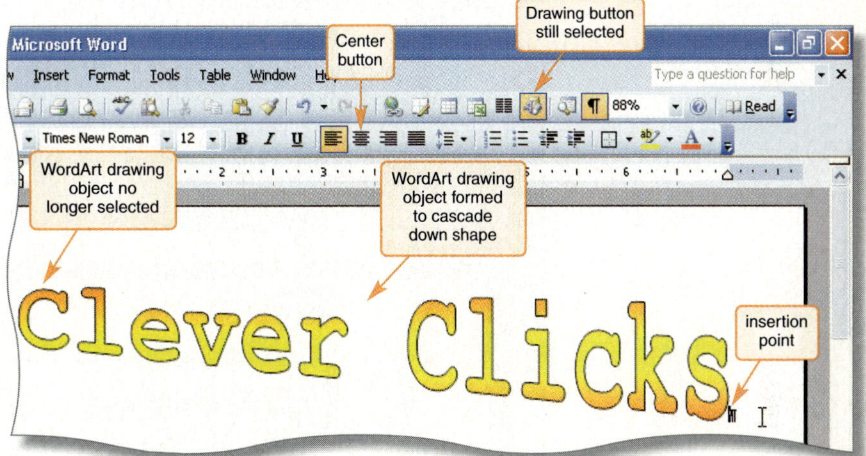

FIGURE 6-13

The Drawing toolbar still is displayed in the Word window because it will be used again later in this project.

The next step is to center the WordArt drawing object, as described below.

To Center the Newsletter Title

1 **Click the Center button on the Formatting toolbar.**

Word centers the WordArt drawing object between the left and right margins (shown in Figure 6-14 on the next page). Because the WordArt object extends from the left to the right margins, you may not notice a difference in its position after you click the Center button.

Adding Ruling Lines

In Word, you use borders to create ruling lines. As discussed in previous projects, Word can place borders on any edge of a paragraph(s), that is, the top, bottom, left, or right edges.

The following steps describe how to place ruling lines above the newsletter title.

To Use Borders to Add Ruling Lines

1. **If the Tables and Borders toolbar is not displayed on the screen, click the Tables and Borders button on the Standard toolbar. Click the Line Style box arrow on the Tables and Borders toolbar, scroll to and then click the diagonally stroked line (just below the double wavy lines) in the list.**
2. **Click the Border Color button arrow on the Tables and Borders toolbar and then click Teal on the color palette.**
3. **Click the Border button arrow on the Tables and Borders toolbar and then click Top Border.**

The newsletter title and Tables and Borders toolbar display as shown in Figure 6-14.

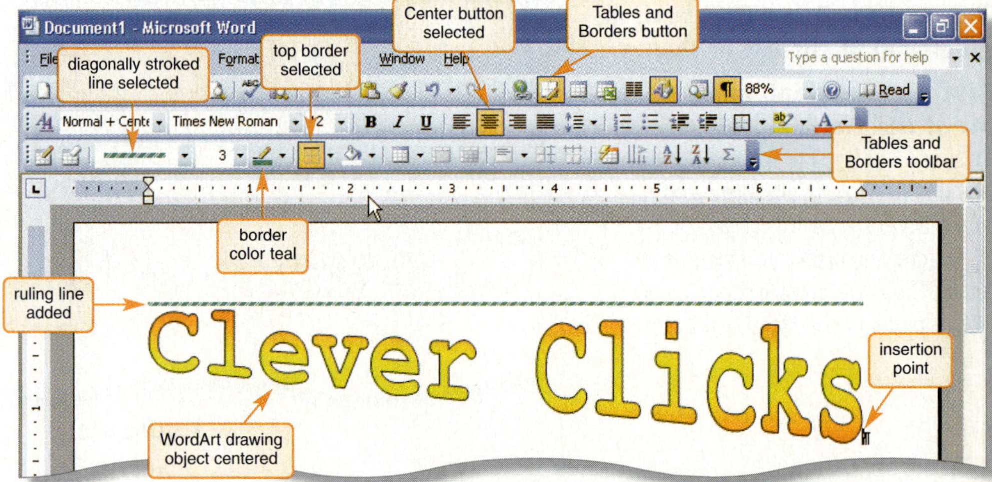

FIGURE 6-14

When you press the ENTER key at the end of the newsletter title to advance the insertion point to the next line, Word carries forward formatting. You do not want the paragraphs and characters on line 2 to have the same formatting as line 1. Instead, you clear formatting so the characters on line 2 use the Normal style.

The following steps describe how to clear formatting.

To Clear Formatting

1. **With the insertion point positioned at the end of line 1 (shown in Figure 6-14), press the ENTER key.**
2. **Click the Style box arrow on the Formatting toolbar (Figure 6-15).**
3. **Click Clear Formatting in the Style list.**

Word applies the Normal style to the location of the insertion point.

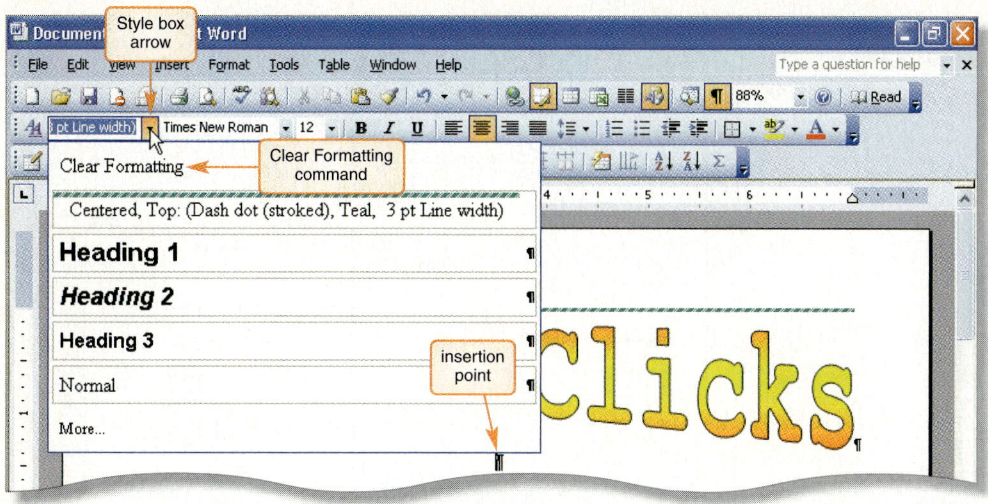

FIGURE 6-15

Depending on your installation of Word, the Normal style might be a different font or font size.

Inserting Symbols

The issue information line in this newsletter contains the text, Monthly Newsletter, at the left margin and the volume and issue number at the right margin (shown in Figure 6-1a on page WD 379). As discussed previously, a paragraph cannot be formatted as both left-aligned and right-aligned. To place text at the right margin of a left-aligned paragraph, you must set a tab stop at the right margin.

In this newsletter, between the volume number and issue number is a large round dot. This special symbol is not on the keyboard. You insert dots and other symbols, such as letters in the Greek alphabet and mathematical characters, using the Symbol dialog box.

The following steps explain how to enter the text in the issue information line. First, text is entered at the left margin and a right-aligned tab stop is set at the right margin. Then, text is entered at the right margin, with a dot symbol between the volume and issue numbers.

To Set a Right-Aligned Tab Stop

1. **Click the Bold button on the Formatting toolbar. Click the Font Color button arrow on the Formatting toolbar and then click Teal on the color palette. Type** `Monthly Newsletter` **on line 2 of the newsletter.**
2. **Click Format on the menu bar and then click Tabs. When Word displays the Tabs dialog box, type** `7` **in the Tab stop position text box and then click Right in the Alignment area. Click the Set button (Figure 6-16 on the next page).**
3. **Click the OK button.**

After clicking the OK button, Word places a right-aligned tab stop at the right margin (shown in Figure 6-17 on the next page).

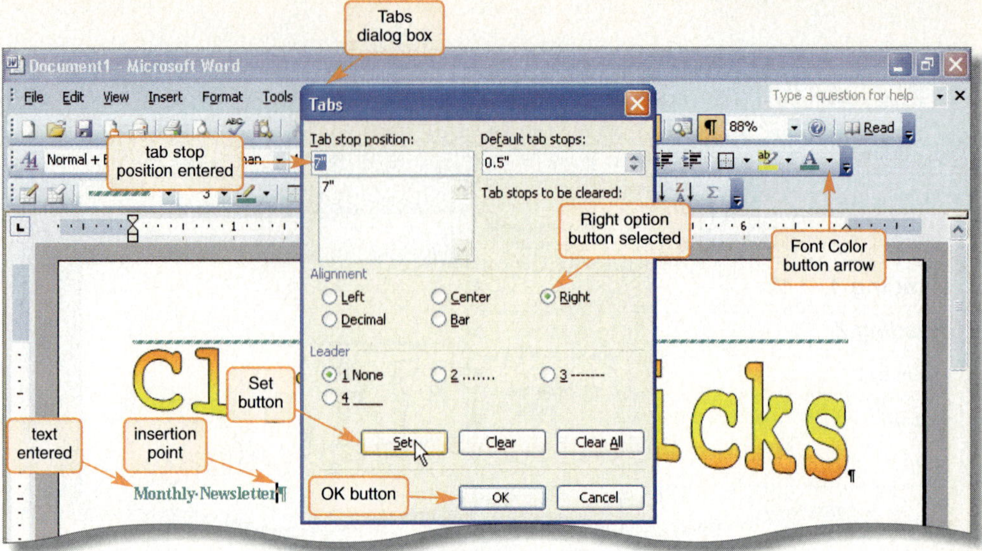

FIGURE 6-16

The next step is to insert a symbol in the middle of text, as shown below.

To Insert a Symbol

1

- **Press the TAB key. Type** `Vol. 8` **and then press the SPACEBAR.**
- **Click Insert on the menu bar.**

The volume number displays at the right margin (Figure 6-17). Notice the right tab marker is positioned directly on top of the right margin on the ruler.

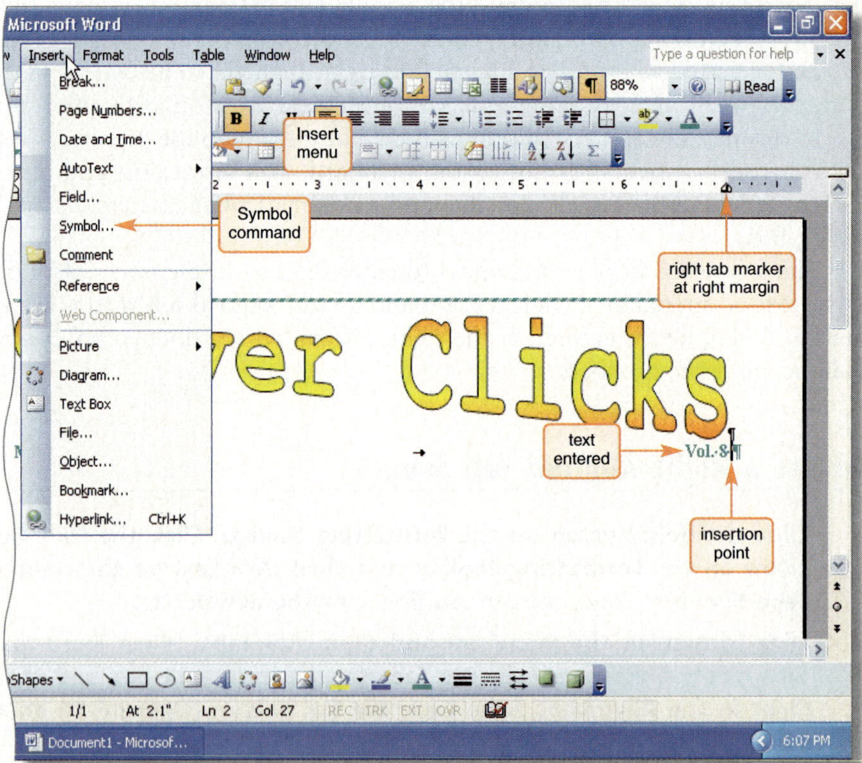

FIGURE 6-17

2

- **Click Symbol on the Insert menu.**
- **When Word displays the Symbol dialog box, if necessary, click the Symbols tab.**
- **In the Symbol dialog box, if necessary, click the Font box arrow, scroll to and then click Symbol.**
- **In the list of symbols, if necessary, scroll to and then click the dot symbol.**
- **Click the Insert button.**

As soon as you click the Insert button, the dot symbol is placed in the document to the left of the insertion point (Figure 6-18). At this point, you can insert additional symbols or close the Symbol dialog box.

3

- **Click the Close button in the Symbol dialog box.**

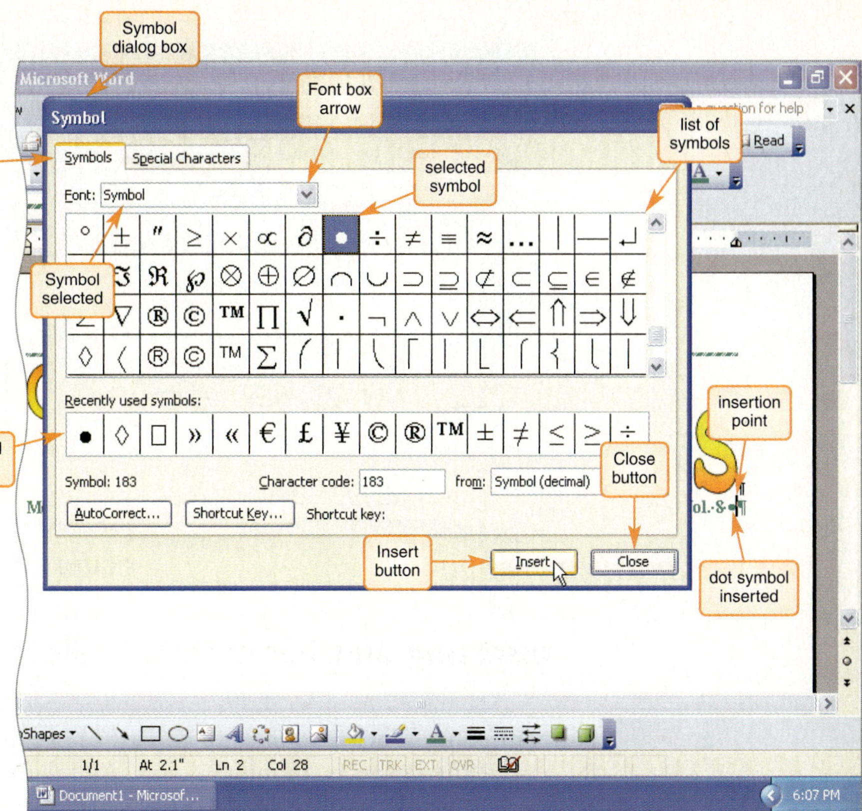

FIGURE 6-18

Other Ways

1. Press ALT+0 (zero) and then with the NUM LOCK key on, use numeric keypad to type ANSI character code for symbol
2. In Voice Command mode, say "Insert, Symbol, [select symbol], Insert, Close"

When you insert a symbol, Word places it in the Recently used symbols list in the Symbol dialog box (Figure 6-18).

You also can insert ANSI (American National Standards Institute) characters in a document by entering the ANSI code directly into the document. The **ANSI characters** are a predefined set of characters, including both characters on the keyboard and special characters, such as the dot symbol. To enter the ANSI code, make sure the NUM LOCK key on the numeric keypad is on. Press and hold the ALT key and then type the numeral zero followed by the ANSI code for the symbol. You must use the numeric keypad when entering the ANSI code. For a complete list of ANSI codes, see your Microsoft Windows documentation.

The next step is to finish entering text in the issue information line and then place a border immediately below the line, as described below.

More About

Inserting Special Characters

Through the Symbol dialog box, in addition to symbols you can insert special characters including a variety of dashes, hyphens, spaces, apostrophes, and quotation marks. Click Insert on the menu bar, click Symbol, click the Special Characters tab, click the desired character in the Character list, click the Insert button, and then click the Close button.

To Enter Text and Add a Border

1. **Press the SPACEBAR. Type** `Issue 9` **at the end of the issue information line.**
2. **Click the Border button arrow on the Tables and Borders toolbar and then click Bottom Border (Figure 6-19 on the next page).**
3. **Click the Tables and Borders button on the Standard toolbar to remove the Tables and Borders toolbar from the screen.**

The issue information line is complete. Word uses the previously defined line style (diagonal stroked line) and color (teal) for the bottom border.

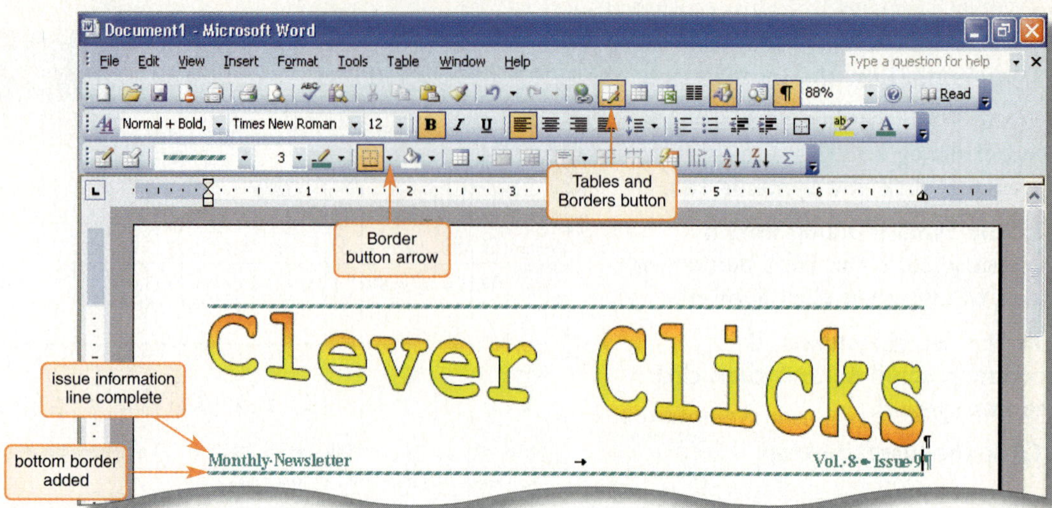

FIGURE 6-19

Inserting and Formatting a Floating Graphic

The next step is to insert a computer mouse clip art image from the Web into the nameplate. When you insert a clip art image in a paragraph in a document, Word inserts the image as an inline object. An **inline object** is an object that is part of a paragraph. With inline objects, you change the location of the object by setting paragraph options, such as centered, right-aligned, and so on.

In many cases, you want more flexibility in positioning graphics. That is, you want to position a graphic at a specific location in a document. To do this, the object must be floating. A **floating object** is an object that can be positioned at a specific location in a document or in a layer over or behind text in a document. You can position a floating object anywhere on the page.

In this project, for example, the computer mouse image is to be positioned at the left edge of the nameplate below the title of the newsletter. The following steps describe how to insert a clip art image and then change it from an inline object to a floating object.

Note: The following steps assume your computer is connected to the Internet. If it is not, go directly to the shaded steps on the opposite page that are titled To Insert a Graphic File from the Data Disk.

To Insert Clip Art from the Web

1. **Click Insert on the menu bar, point to Picture, and then click Clip Art on the Picture submenu.**
2. **In the Clip Art task pane, drag through any text in the Search for text box to select the text. Type** `computer hardware mouse` **and then press the ENTER key.**
3. **Scroll to and then click the clip that matches the one shown in Figure 6-20. (If the clip does not display in the task pane, click the Close button on the Clip Art task pane to close the task pane and then proceed to the shaded steps on the opposite page.)**
4. **Click the Close button on the Clip Art task pane title bar.**

Word inserts the computer mouse graphic at the location of the insertion point (Figure 6-20). The graphic is an inline object, that is, part of the current paragraph.

More About

Designing Newsletters

For more information about designing newsletters, visit the Word 2003 More About Web page (scsite.com/wd2003/more) and then click Designing Newsletters.

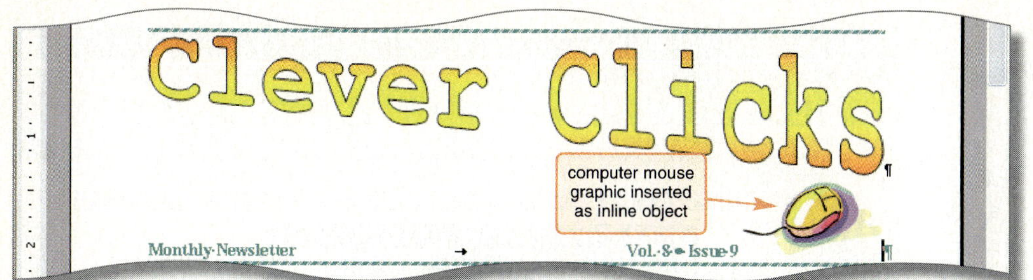

FIGURE 6-20

If you do not have access to the Web, you can insert the clip art file in the Word document from the Data Disk, as described in the following steps. If you did not download the Data Disk, see the inside back cover for instructions for downloading the Data Disk or see your instructor.

To Insert a Graphic File from the Data Disk

1. **Click Insert on the menu bar, point to Picture, and then click From File.**
2. **Insert the Data Disk into drive A. When the Insert Picture dialog box is displayed, click the Look in box arrow and then click 3½ Floppy (A:). Click the file name laq4py2r[1] and then click the Insert button.**

Word inserts the computer mouse graphic at the location of the insertion point (shown in Figure 6-20). The graphic is an inline object, that is, part of the current paragraph.

More About

Inserting Graphics

If you have a scanned image or photograph on disk that you would like to insert in a document, you would follow the steps to the left to insert the graphic file in the document.

Depending on the location of the insertion point, the computer mouse graphic may be in a different position.

The following steps show how to change the computer mouse graphic from inline to floating, which will enable you to move the graphic to any location on the page.

To Format a Graphic as Floating

1

- **In the document window, click the graphic to select it.**
- **If the Picture toolbar does not appear, right-click the graphic and then click Show Picture Toolbar on the shortcut menu.**
- **Click the Text Wrapping button on the Picture toolbar.**

Notice that a selected inline object has small squares as sizing handles (Figure 6-21).

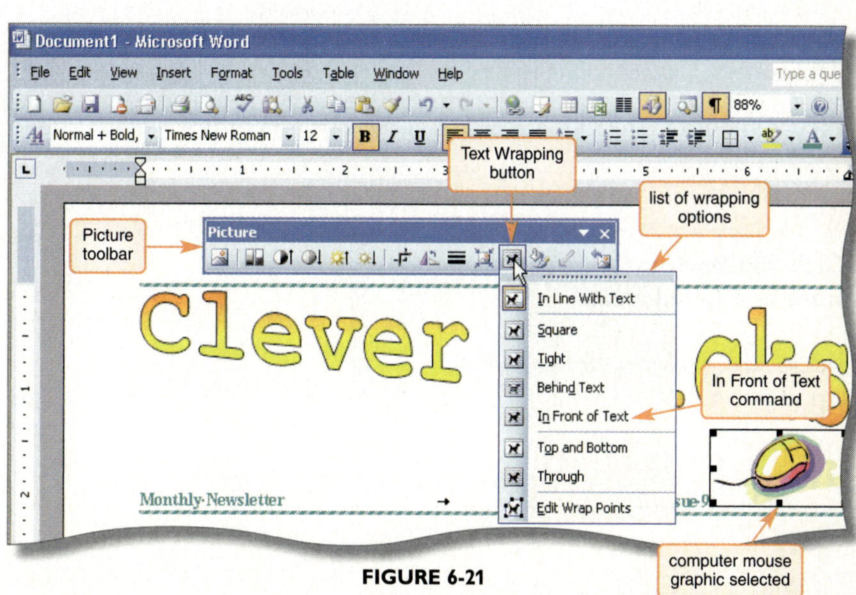

FIGURE 6-21

2

• **In the list of wrapping options, click In Front of Text.**

Word changes the format of the graphic from inline to floating (Figure 6-22). You can position a floating object anywhere in the document. The sizing handles on a floating object display as small circles.

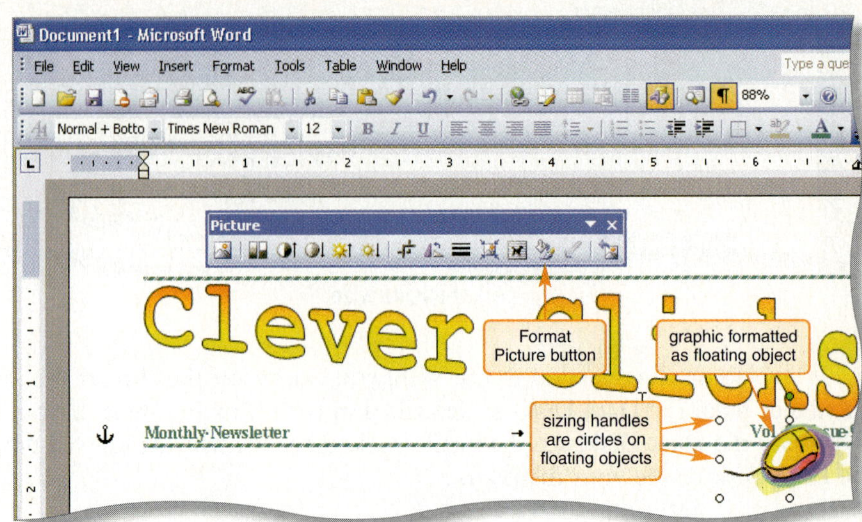

FIGURE 6-22

Other Ways

1. Click Format Picture button on Picture toolbar, click Layout tab, click In front of text, click OK button
2. On Format menu click Picture, click Layout tab, click In front of text, click OK button
3. In Voice Command mode, say "Format, Picture, Layout, In front of text, OK"

The next step is to flip the computer mouse graphic so the tail (cord) points toward the right instead of the left. The following steps show how to flip a graphic horizontally.

To Flip a Graphic

1

• **With the graphic still selected, click the Draw button on the Drawing toolbar.**

• **Point to Rotate or Flip on the Draw menu.**

Word displays the Draw menu above the Draw button (Figure 6-23). The Rotate or Flip submenu is displayed to the right of the Draw menu.

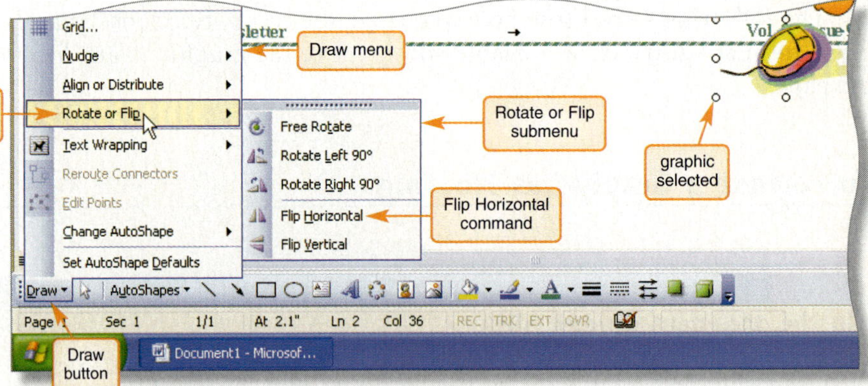

FIGURE 6-23

2

• **Click Flip Horizontal on the Rotate or Flip submenu.**

Word flips the graphic to display its mirror image (Figure 6-24).

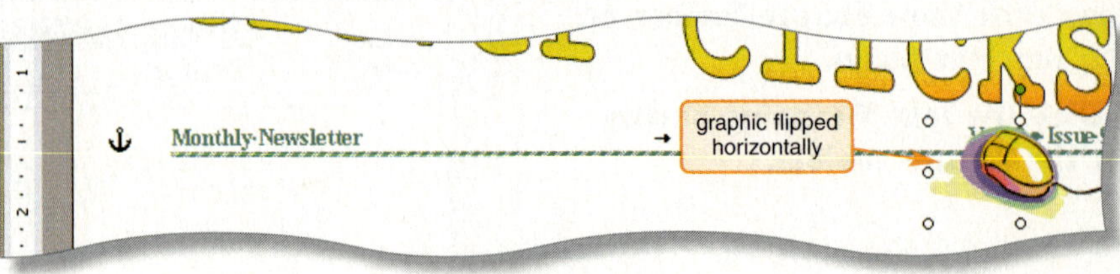

FIGURE 6-24

The next step is to move the computer mouse graphic to the left edge of the nameplate below the C in Clever. When you move an object, such as this graphic, Word automatically attaches it to an invisible set of horizontal and vertical lines, called the **drawing grid**. If you want to position an object at a precise spot, you must instruct Word to not use the drawing grid, as shown in the following steps.

To Not Use the Drawing Grid

- **Click the Draw button on the Drawing toolbar.**

Word displays the Draw menu above the Draw button (Figure 6-25).

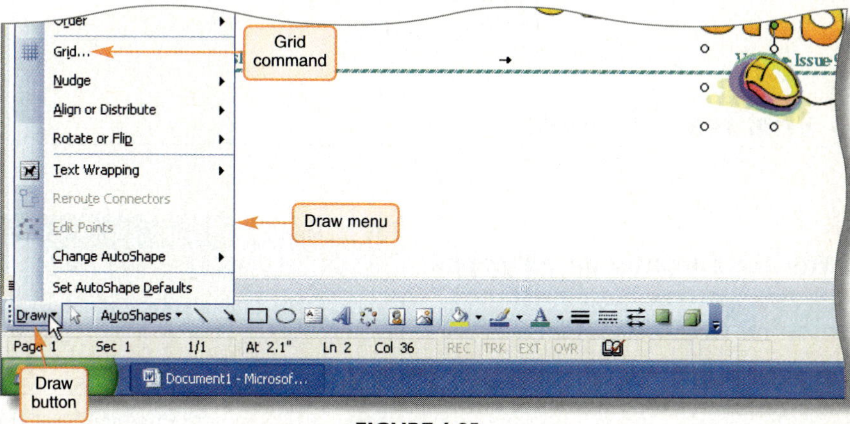

FIGURE 6-25

2

- **Click Grid on the Draw menu.**
- **When Word displays the Drawing Grid dialog box, if necessary, remove the check mark from the Snap objects to grid check box.**

The Drawing Grid dialog box allows you to specify many settings related to the drawing grid (Figure 6-26).

- **Click the OK button.**

When you drag objects in the document, Word will not attach them to the drawing grid.

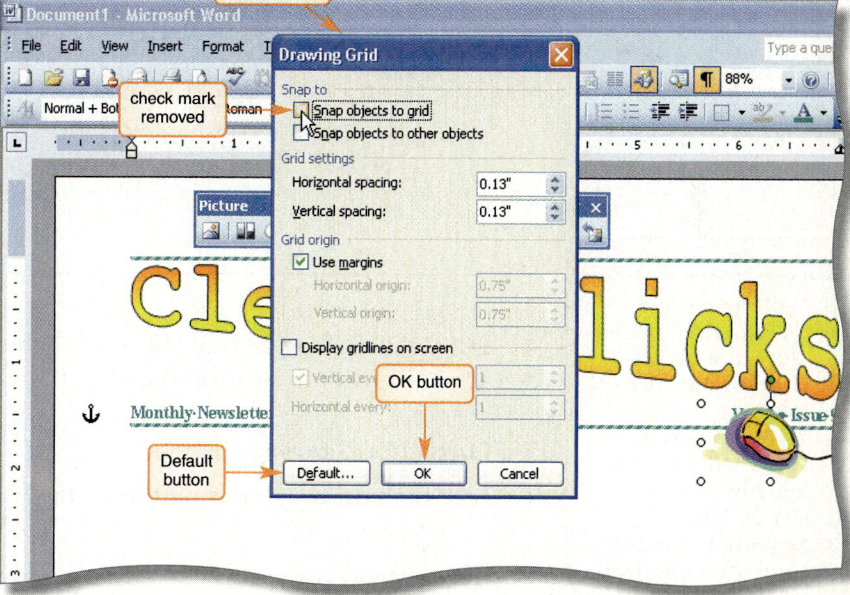

FIGURE 6-26

Other Ways

1. With Drawing toolbar displaying, in Voice Command mode, say "Draw, Grid, Snap objects to grid, OK"

If you wanted to restore the drawing grid to its default settings, you would click the Default button in the Drawing Grid dialog box and then click the Yes button in the Microsoft Word dialog box.

The next step is to move the computer mouse graphic to the left edge of the nameplate so its left edge is immediately below the letter C in Clever, as described on the next page.

To Move a Graphic

1 **Point to the middle of the graphic, and when the mouse pointer has a four-headed arrow attached to it, drag the graphic to the location shown in Figure 6-27.**

Word places the graphic at the exact location you desire.

The color on the computer mouse graphic is a bit dark. With Word, you can brighten or darken a graphic. The following step shows how to brighten the graphic in this project.

To Brighten a Graphic

1

- **With the computer mouse graphic selected, click the More Brightness button on the Picture toolbar four times.**

Word brightens the selected graphic (Figure 6-27). A brightened graphic has lighter colors.

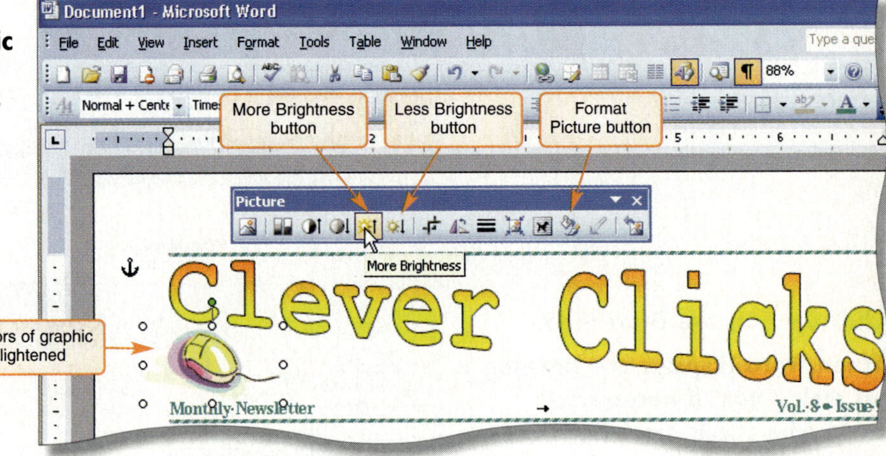

FIGURE 6-27

Other Ways

1. Click Format Picture button on Picture toolbar, click Picture tab, drag Brightness slider, click OK button
2. On Format menu click Picture, click Picture tab, drag Brightness slider, click OK button
3. Right-click graphic, click Format Picture on shortcut menu, click Picture tab, drag Brightness slider, click OK button
4. In Voice Command mode, say "Format, Picture, Picture, [adjust brightness], OK"

Instead of making a graphic's colors lighter, you can darken its colors. To darken a graphic, you would perform this step.

To Darken a Graphic

1. Click the Less Brightness button on the Picture toolbar.

If you wanted to return the brightness to its original settings, you would click the Format Picture button on the Picture toolbar, click the Picture tab, click the Reset button, and then click the OK button.

The next step is to enter the name of the feature article below the ruling line. To do this, you position the insertion point at the end of the issue information line (after the 9 in Issue 9) and then press the ENTER key. Recall that the issue information line has a bottom border. As mentioned earlier, when you press the ENTER key in a bordered paragraph, Word carries forward the border to the next paragraph. Thus, after you press the ENTER key, you should clear formatting to format the new paragraph to the Normal style.

The following steps describe how to clear formatting.

To Clear Formatting

1. **Click at the end of line 2 (the issue information line) so the insertion point is immediately after the 9 in Issue 9. Press the ENTER key.**
2. **With the insertion point on line 3, click the Style box arrow on the Formatting toolbar and then click Clear Formatting.**

Word applies the Normal style to the location of the insertion point.

One blank line below the bottom border is the name of the feature article, Safeguarding Computers from Virus Infections, in 14-point Times New Roman bold orange font. The following steps describe how to enter this text and then clear formatting on the line below the text.

To Format and Enter Text

1. **With the insertion point on line 3, press the ENTER key.**
2. **Click the Font Size box arrow on the Formatting toolbar and then click 14. Click the Bold button on the Formatting toolbar. Click the Font Color button arrow on the Formatting toolbar and then click Orange on the color palette.**
3. **Type** `Safeguarding Computers from Virus Infections` **and then press the ENTER key.**
4. **Click the Style box arrow on the Formatting toolbar and then click Clear Formatting.**

The article title is entered (Figure 6-28). The paragraph at the location of the insertion point is returned to the Normal style.

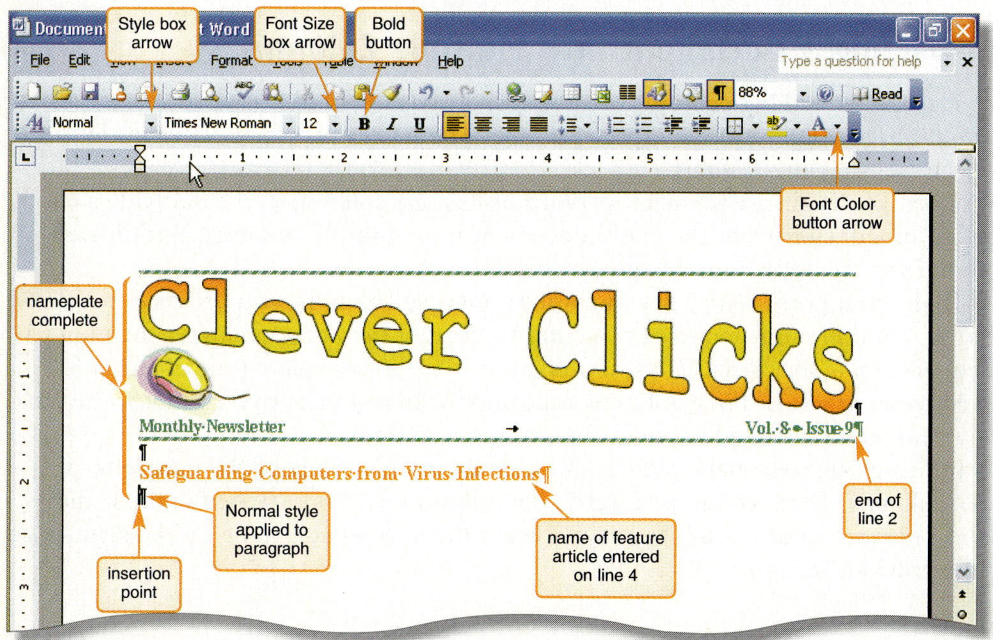

FIGURE 6-28

More About

Graphics

If you have multiple graphics in a single area on a page, you can group them together so they become one single object. To do this, select the first object by clicking it and then select each additional object by holding down the CTRL key while clicking it. With all objects selected, click the Draw button on the Drawing toolbar and then click Group on the Draw menu.

Saving the Newsletter

You have made several changes to this newsletter. Thus, you should save it, as described in the following steps.

To Save a Document

1. **Insert a floppy disk into drive A.**
2. **Click the Save button on the Standard toolbar.**
3. **Type** `Clever Clicks Newsletter` **in the File name box. Do not press the ENTER key.**
4. **Click the Save in box arrow and then click 3½ Floppy (A:).**
5. **Click the Save button in the Save As dialog box.**

Word saves the document on a floppy disk in drive A with the file name, Clever Clicks Newsletter (shown in Figure 6-29).

The nameplate for the newsletter is complete.

Formatting the First Page of the Body of the Newsletter

The next step is to format the first page of the body of the newsletter. The body of the newsletter in this project is divided into three columns (Figure 6-1a on page WD 379). The characters in the paragraphs are aligned on both the right and left edges — similar to newspaper columns. The first letter in the first paragraph is much larger than the rest of the characters in the paragraph. A vertical rule separates the second and third columns. The steps on the following pages illustrate how to format the first page of the body of the newsletter using these desktop publishing features.

Formatting a Document into Multiple Columns

The text in **snaking columns**, or newspaper-style columns, flows from the bottom of one column to the top of the next. The body of the newsletter in this project uses snaking columns.

When you begin a document in Word, it has one column. You can divide a portion of a document or the entire document into multiple columns. Within each column, you can type, modify, or format text.

To divide a portion of a document into multiple columns, you use section breaks. That is, Word requires that a new section be created each time you alter the number of columns in a document. Thus, if a document has a nameplate (one column) followed by an article of three columns followed by an article of two columns, then the document would be divided into a total of three sections.

In this project, the nameplate is one column and the body of the newsletter is three columns. Thus, you must insert a continuous section break below the nameplate. The term, continuous, means you want the new section to be on the same page as the previous section.

Q&A

Q: How many newspaper-style columns should be across a page?

A: Narrow columns generally are easier to read than wide ones. Columns, however, can be too narrow. Try to have between five and fifteen words per line. To do this, you may need to adjust the column width, the font size, or the leading. Leading is the line spacing, which can be adjusted through the Paragraph dialog box in Word.

The following steps show how to divide the body of the newsletter into three columns.

To Insert a Continuous Section Break

1

- **With the insertion point on line 5 (shown in Figure 6-28 on page WD 397), press the ENTER key. Scroll the document down a few lines.**
- **Click Insert on the menu bar and then click Break.**
- **When Word displays the Break dialog box, click Continuous in the Section break types area.**

In the Break dialog box, continuous means you want the new section on the same page as the previous section (Figure 6-29).

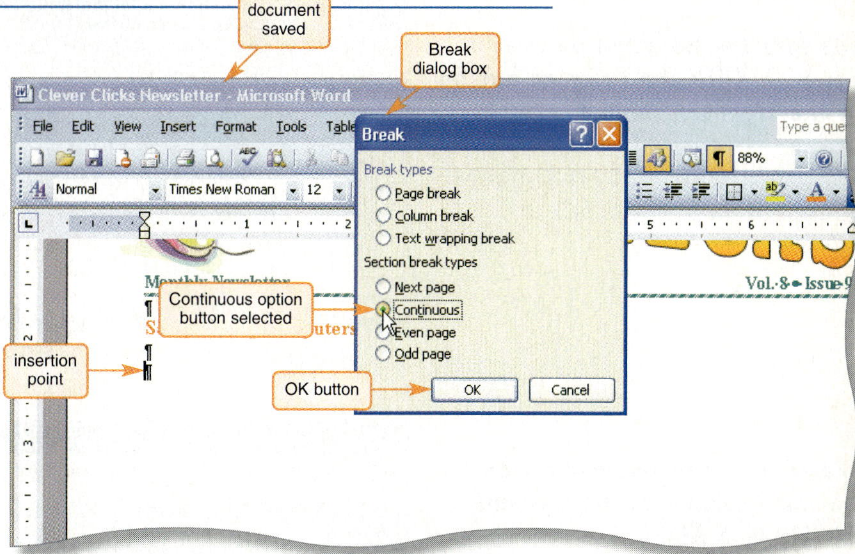

FIGURE 6-29

2

- **Click the OK button.**

Word inserts a continuous section break above the insertion point (Figure 6-30). The insertion point now is located in section 2.

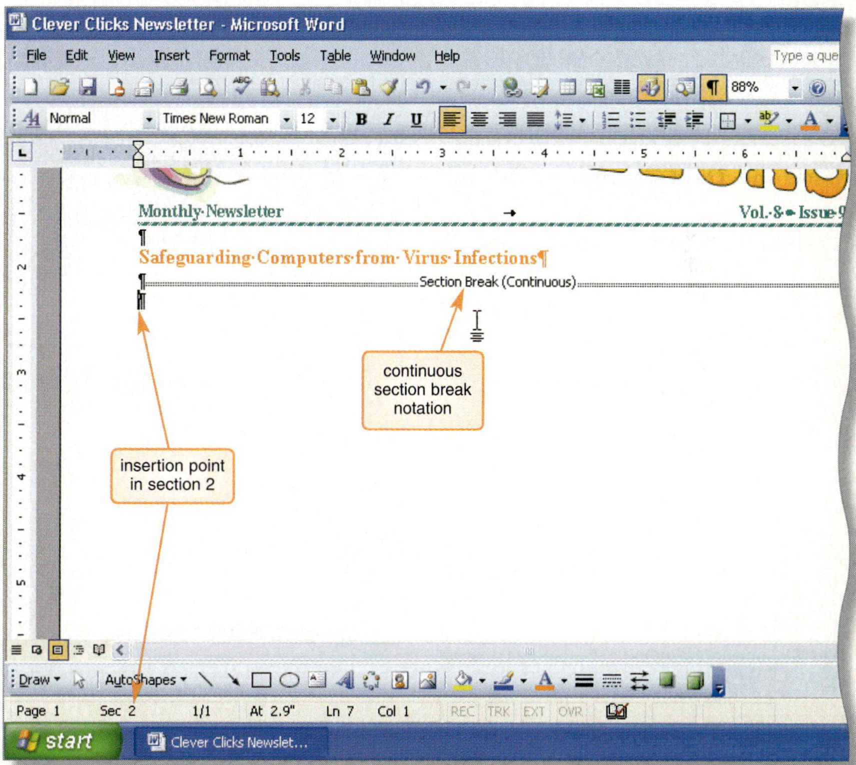

FIGURE 6-30

Other Ways

1. In Voice Command mode, say "Insert, Break, Continuous, OK"

The document now has two sections. The nameplate is in the first section, and the insertion point is in the second section. The second section is to be formatted to three columns. Thus, the steps on the next page show how to format the second section in the document to three columns.

To Change the Number of Columns

1

- **Be sure the insertion point is in section 2. Click the Columns button on the Standard toolbar.**

Word displays a columns list graphic below the Columns button (Figure 6-31).

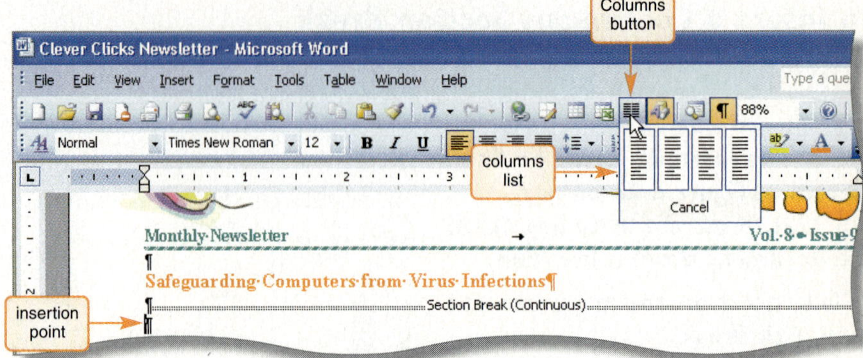

FIGURE 6-31

2

- **Position the mouse pointer on the third column in the columns list (Figure 6-32).**

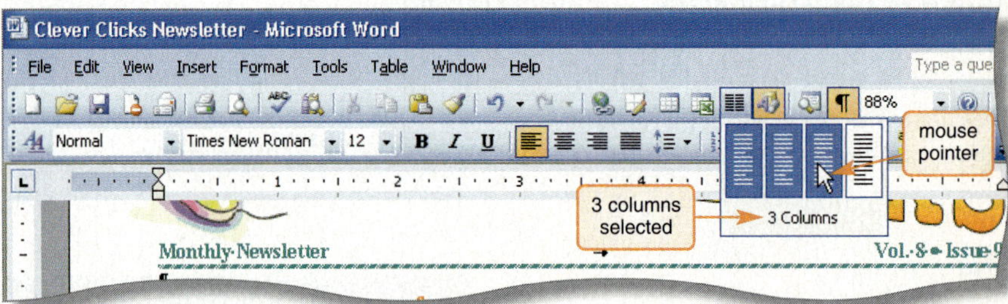

FIGURE 6-32

3

- **Click the third column in the list.**

Word divides the section containing the insertion point into three evenly sized and spaced columns (Figure 6-33). Notice that the ruler indicates the width of each column.

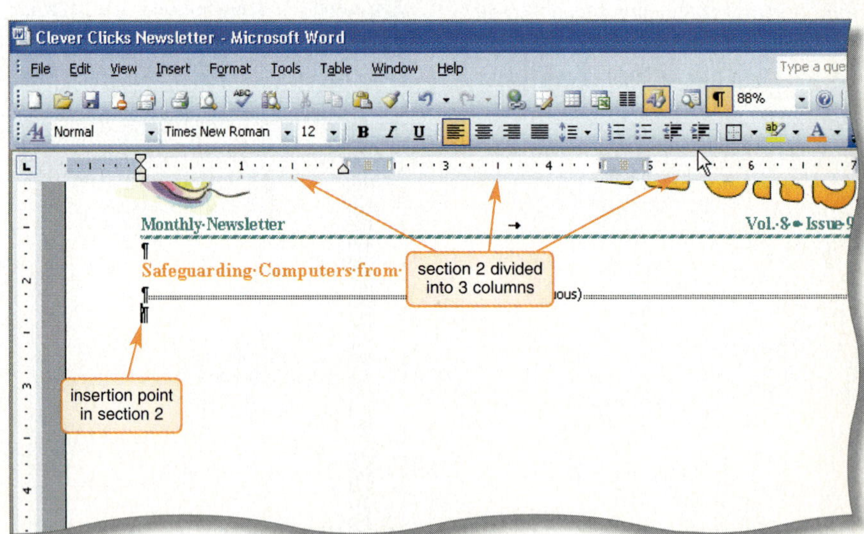

FIGURE 6-33

Other Ways

1. On Format menu click Columns, click desired number of columns in Presets area, click OK button
2. In Voice Command mode, say "Format, Columns, [select number of columns], OK"

When you use the Columns button to change the number of columns, Word creates columns of equal width. You can create columns of unequal width by clicking the Columns command on the Format menu.

Justifying a Paragraph

The text in the paragraphs of the body of the newsletter is **justified**, which means that the left and right margins are aligned, like the edges of newspaper columns. The following step shows how to enter the first paragraph of the feature article using justified alignment.

To Justify a Paragraph

1

- **Click the Justify button on the Formatting toolbar.**
- **Type the first paragraph of the feature article, as shown in Figure 6-34.**
- **Press the ENTER key.**

Word aligns both the left and right edges of the paragraph (Figure 6-34). Notice that Word places extra space between some words when text is justified.

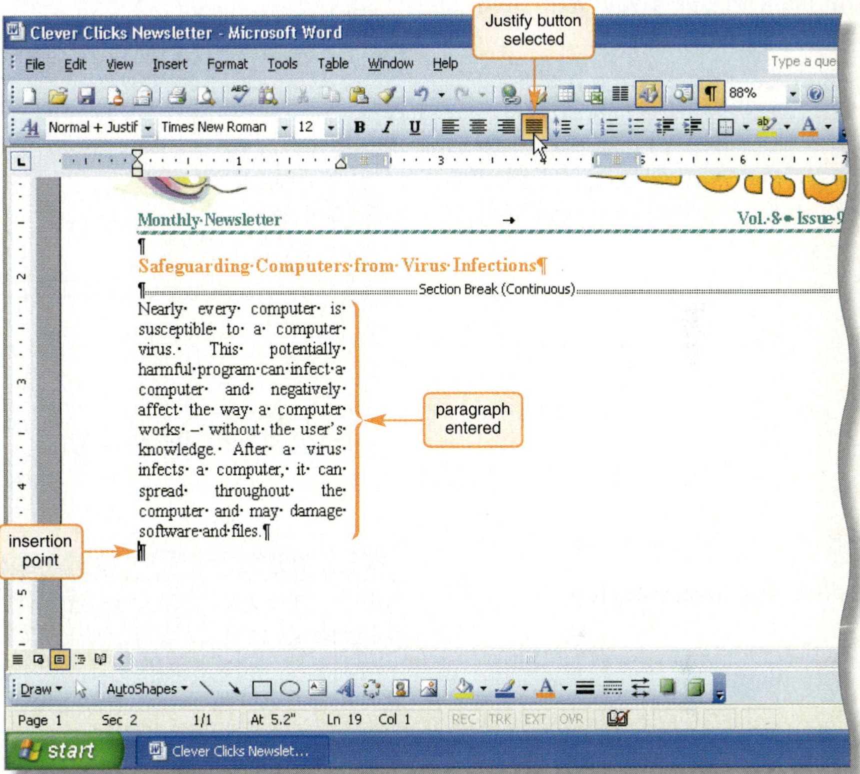

FIGURE 6-34

Other Ways

1. On Format menu click Paragraph, click Indents and Spacing tab, click Alignment box arrow, click Justified, click OK button
2. Press CTRL+J
3. In Voice Command mode, say "Justify"

Inserting the Remainder of the Feature Article

Instead of typing the rest of the feature article into the newsletter for this project, the next step is to insert a file named Computer Virus Article in the newsletter. This file, which contains the remainder of the feature article, is located on the Data Disk. If you did not download the Data Disk, see the inside back cover for instructions for downloading the Data Disk or see your instructor.

The steps on the next page show how to insert the Computer Virus Article file in the newsletter.

To Insert a File in the Newsletter

1

- **If necessary, insert the Data Disk into drive A. Click Insert on the menu bar and then click File.**
- **When Word displays the Insert File dialog box, if necessary, click the Look in box arrow and then click 3½ Floppy (A:).**
- **Click Computer Virus Article.**

The selected file in the Insert File dialog box will be inserted at the location of the insertion point in the document (Figure 6-35).

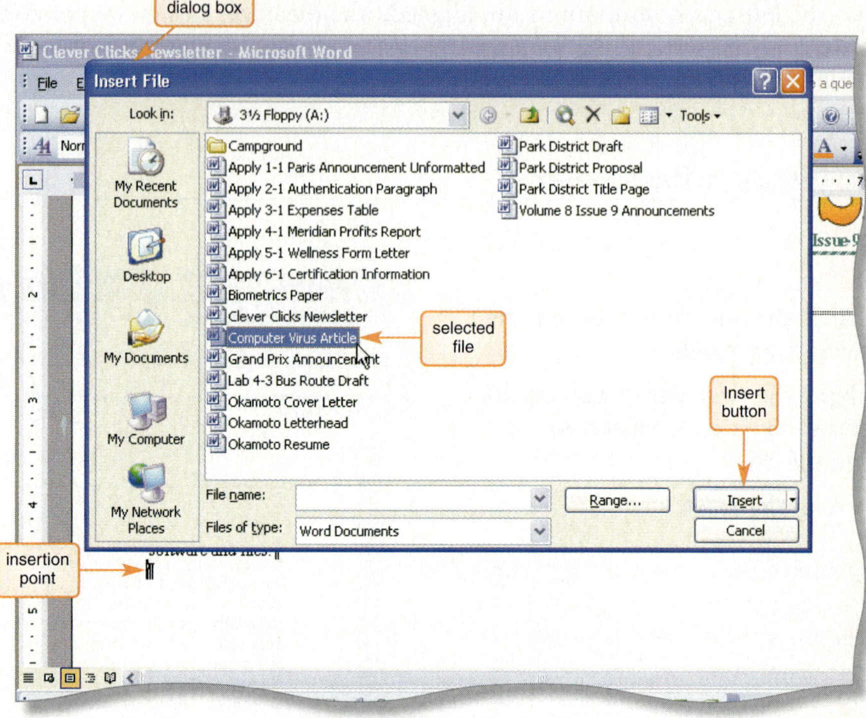

FIGURE 6-35

2

- **Click the Insert button.**

Word inserts the file, Computer Virus Article, in the file Clever Clicks Newsletter at the location of the insertion point (Figure 6-36). The text automatically is formatted into columns.

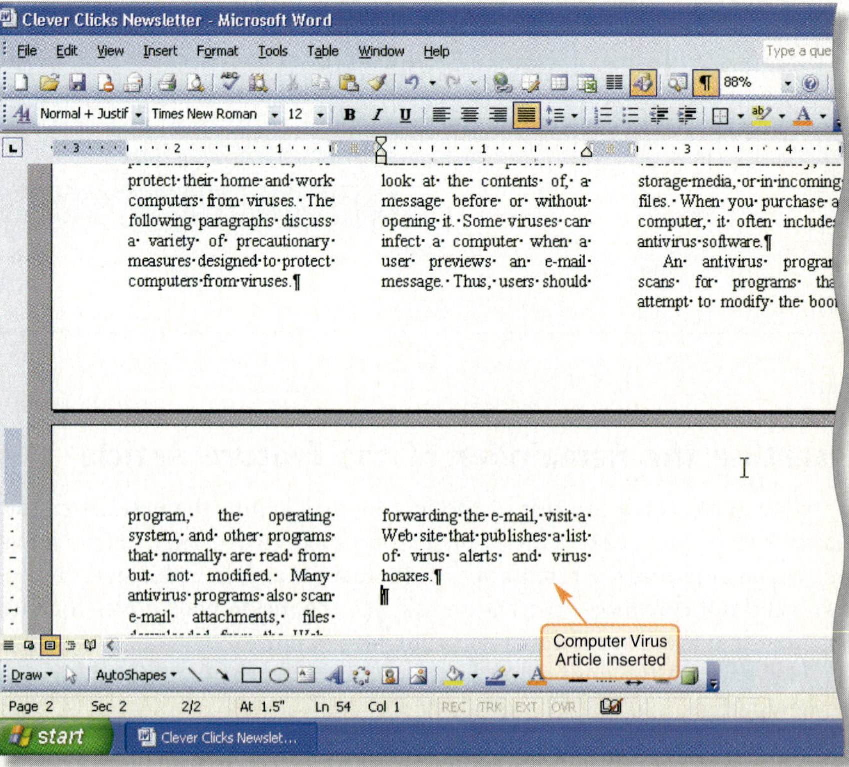

FIGURE 6-36

Other Ways

1. In Voice Command mode, say "Insert, File, [select file], Insert"

Formatting a Letter as a Drop Cap

You can format the first character in a paragraph to be a **drop cap**, which is a large, dropped capital letter. That is, a drop cap is larger than the rest of the characters in the paragraph. The text in the paragraph then wraps around the drop cap.

The following steps show how to create a drop cap in the first paragraph of the feature article in the newsletter.

To Format a Letter as a Drop Cap

1

- **Press CTRL+HOME to scroll to the top of the document. Scroll down and then click anywhere in the first paragraph of the feature article.**
- **Click Format on the menu bar.**

The insertion point is in the first paragraph of the feature article (Figure 6-37).

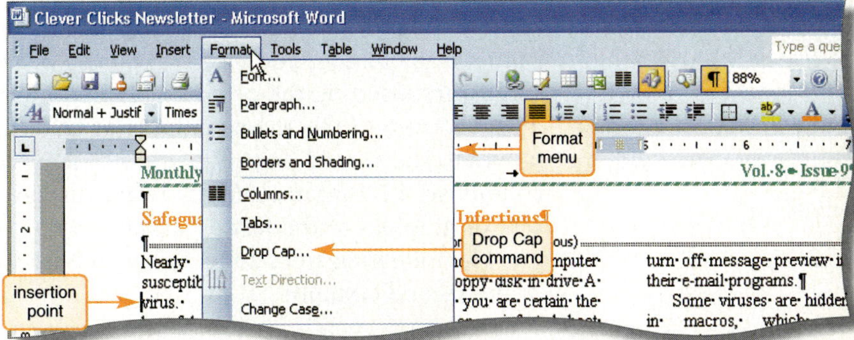

FIGURE 6-37

2

- **Click Drop Cap on the Format menu.**
- **When Word displays the Drop Cap dialog box, click Dropped in the Position area.**

Word displays the Drop Cap dialog box (Figure 6-38).

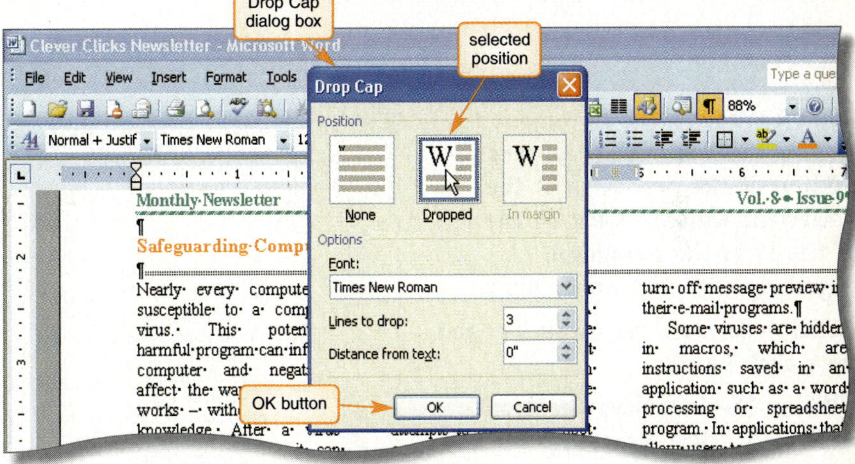

FIGURE 6-38

3

- **Click the OK button.**

Word drops the letter N in the word, Nearly, and wraps subsequent text around the drop cap (Figure 6-39).

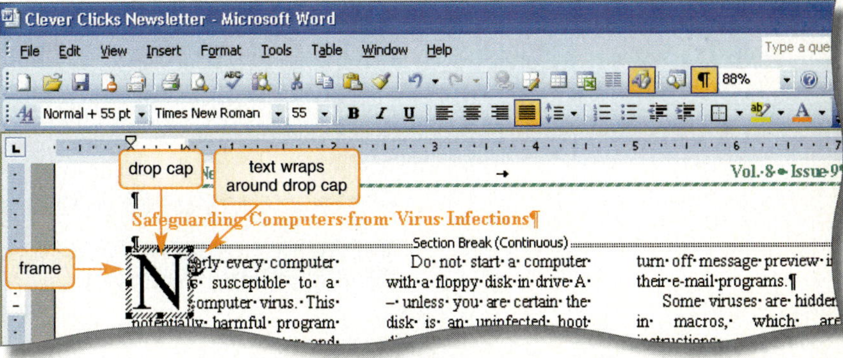

FIGURE 6-39

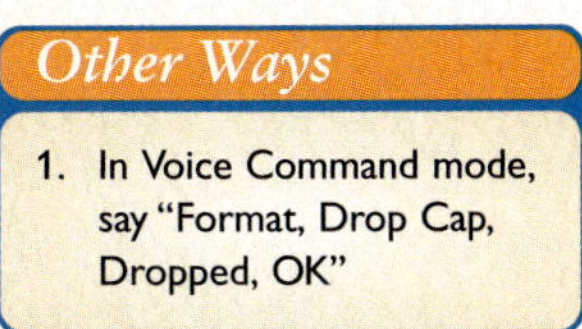

Other Ways

1. In Voice Command mode, say "Format, Drop Cap, Dropped, OK"

More About

Drop Caps

A drop cap often is used to mark the beginning of an article. To format the entire first word as a drop cap, select the word. An alternative to a drop cap is a stick-up cap, which extends into the left margin, instead of sinking into the first few lines of the text. To insert a stick-up cap, click In margin in the Drop Cap dialog box (Figure 6-38 on the previous page).

When you drop cap a letter, Word places a frame around it. A **frame** is a container for text that allows you to position the text anywhere on the page. As illustrated in the previous steps, Word can format a frame so that text wraps around it.

To remove the frame from displaying in the document window, simply click outside the frame to display the insertion point elsewhere in the document.

Inserting a Column Break

The next step is to insert a column break at the bottom of the second column. Notice in Figure 6-1a on page WD 379 that the third column on the first page of the newsletter is not a continuation of the feature article. The third column, instead, contains several member announcements. The feature article continues on the second page of the newsletter (Figure 6-1b). For the member announcements to be displayed in the third column, you insert a **column break** at the bottom of the second column.

Before inserting the column break, you first must insert a next page section break at the bottom of the second column so that the remainder of the feature article moves to the second page. Then, insert a column break at the bottom of the second column so the announcements always display in the third column, even if you add text or graphics to the feature article.

The following steps show how to insert a next page section break at the bottom of the second column.

To Insert a Next Page Section Break

1

- **Scroll through the document to display the bottom of the second column of the first page in the document window. Click to the left of the M in the paragraph beginning with the word, Many.**
- **Click Insert on the menu bar and then click Break.**
- **When Word displays the Break dialog box, click Next page in the Section break types area.**

The insertion point is to the left of the M in the word, Many (Figure 6-40).

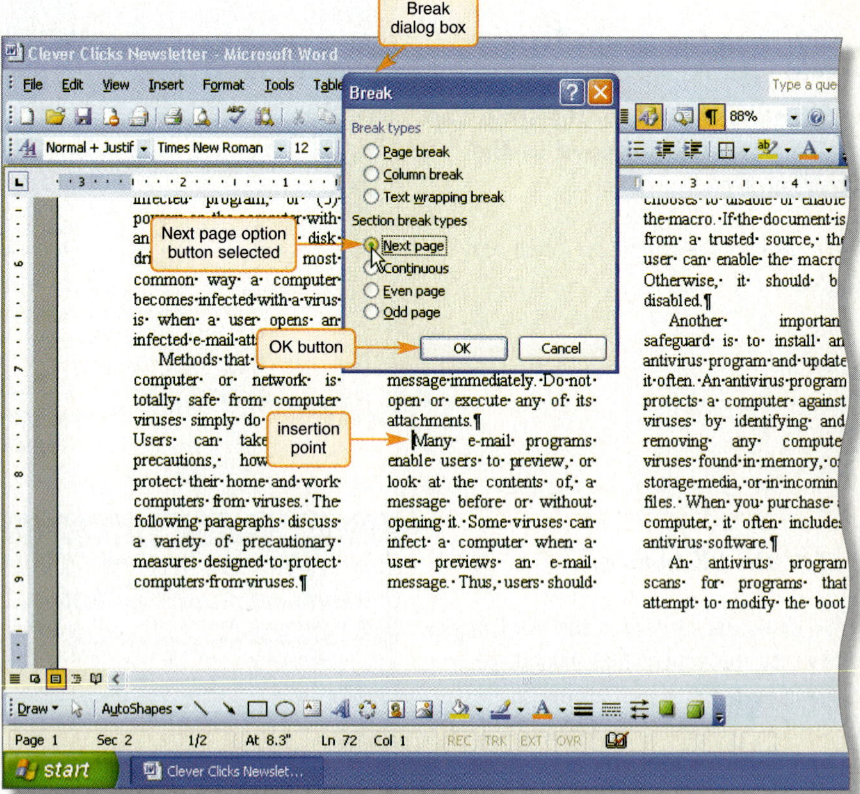

FIGURE 6-40

2

- **Click the OK button.**

Word inserts a section break at the location of the insertion point (Figure 6-41). The remainder of the article moves to page 2 of the document because a next page section break includes a page break. On page 1, the bottom of the second column and the entire third column are empty.

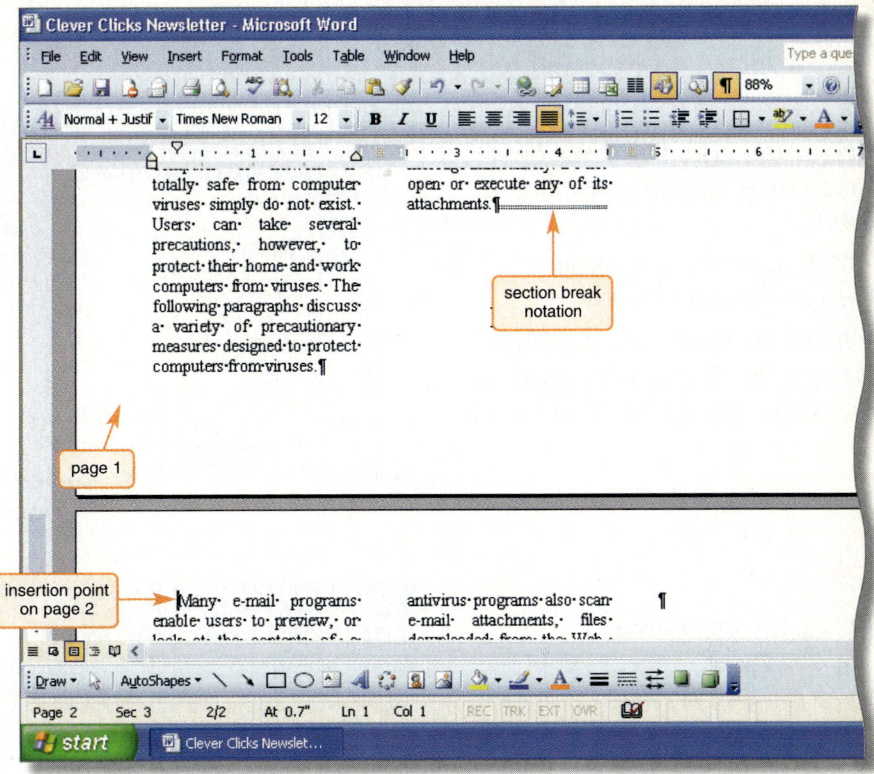

FIGURE 6-41

Other Ways

1. In Voice Command mode, say "Insert, Break, Next page, OK"

You want the member announcements to begin at the top of the third column, even though a small amount of room is available at the bottom of the second column. To move the insertion point to the top of the third column, you will insert a column break at the end of the text in the second column.

First, you add a note to the reader that the feature article continues on page 2, and then you insert a column break.

To Enter Text

1. **Scroll up to display the bottom of the second column of the first page of the newsletter and then position the insertion point between the paragraph mark and the section break notation.**
2. **Press the ENTER key three times. Press the UP ARROW key.**
3. **Press CTRL+R to right align the paragraph mark. Press CTRL+I to turn on italics. Type** `...continued on page 2` **and then press CTRL+I again to turn off italics.**

The continued message is entered at the bottom of the second column (shown in Figure 6-42 on the next page).

The steps on the next page show how to insert a column break below the continued message.

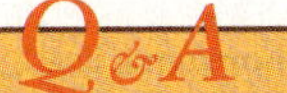

Q: Should multi-page articles contain jump lines?

A: An article that spans multiple pages should contain a jump or jump line, which informs the reader where to look for the rest of the article or story. The message on the first page is called a jump-to line, and a jump-from line marks the beginning of the continuation.

To Insert a Column Break

1

- **Press the ENTER key. Press CTRL+L to left-align the insertion point.**
- **Click Insert on the menu bar and then click Break.**
- **When Word displays the Break dialog box, click Column break in the Break types area (Figure 6-42).**

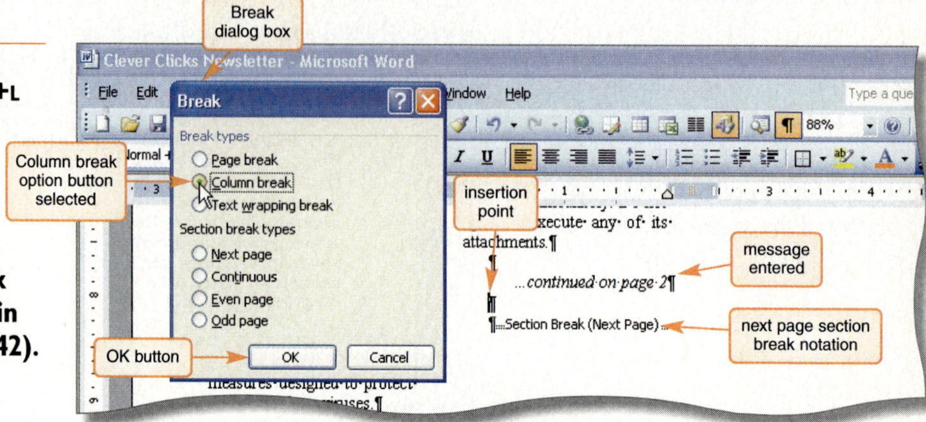

FIGURE 6-42

2

- **Click the OK button.**

Word inserts a column break at the bottom of the second column on page 1 and places the insertion point at the top of the third column (Figure 6-43).

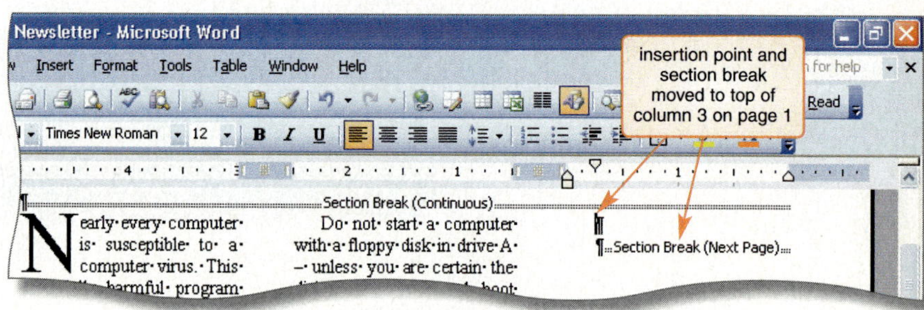

FIGURE 6-43

More About

Column Breaks

A column break is displayed on the screen with the words Column Break separated by a thinly dotted horizontal line. Figure 6-44 shows the column break notation at the bottom of the second column. To remove a column break, select it and then click the Cut button on the Standard toolbar or press the DELETE key.

The following step saves the newsletter again.

To Save a Document

1 **With the disk containing the newsletter file in drive A, click the Save button on the Standard toolbar.**

Word saves the document again with the file name, Clever Clicks Newsletter.

Inserting Text from a File, Viewing the Document, and Modifying the Inserted Text

To eliminate having to enter the entire third column of announcements into the newsletter, the next step in the project is to insert the file named Volume 8 Issue 9 Announcements in the third column of the newsletter. This file contains the three announcements: the first about a user group meeting, the second about member discounts, and the third about the topic of the next newsletter issue.

The Volume 8 Issue 9 Announcements file is located on the Data Disk. If you did not download the Data Disk, see the inside back cover for instructions for downloading the Data Disk or see your instructor.

The following steps describe how to insert a file in the newsletter.

To Insert a File in a Column of the Newsletter

1. **If necessary, insert the Data Disk into drive A. With the insertion point at the top of the third column, click Insert on the menu bar and then click File.**
2. **When Word displays the Insert File dialog box, if necessary, click the Look in box arrow and then click 3½ Floppy (A:). Click the file name, Volume 8 Issue 9 Announcements.**
3. **Click the Insert button.**

Word inserts the file, Volume 8 Issue 9 Announcements, in the third column of the newsletter (shown in Figure 6-45 on the next page).

Word provides a **full screen view** that places the current document in a window that fills the entire screen; that is, it removes the title bar, menu bar, toolbars, rulers, scroll bars, and taskbar. In full screen view, reading through a document is easier because more of the document is displayed. You scroll through a document in full screen view the same as when it is in the document window.

To see the announcements just inserted into the third column more easily, the next task is to switch to full screen view. The following steps show how to display a document in full screen view and then exit full screen view.

To Display a Document in Full Screen View

1

- **Click View on the menu bar.**

Word displays the View menu (Figure 6-44).

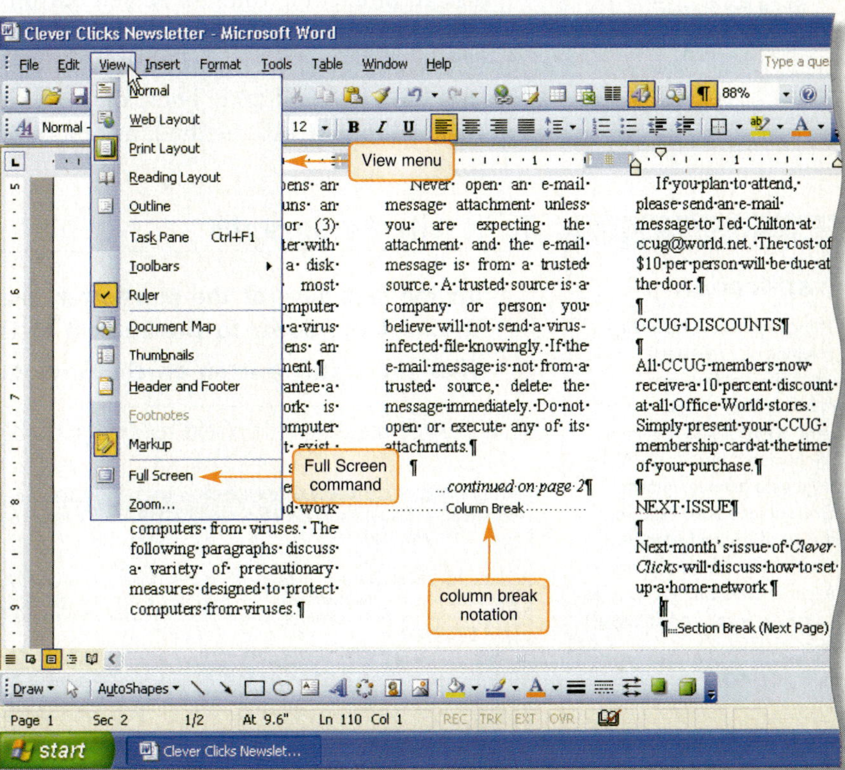

FIGURE 6-44

2

- **Click Full Screen on the View menu.**
- **Scroll through the document to display the announcements on the screen.**

Word displays the newsletter in full screen view (Figure 6-45). The newsletter fills the entire screen. The only toolbar on the screen is the Full Screen toolbar, which contains just the Close Full Screen button. You can scroll through the document in full screen view using the mouse or keyboard.

3

- **Click the Close Full Screen button on the Full Screen toolbar to return to print layout view.**

full screen view

Volume 8 Issue 9 Announcements file inserted in column 3

Nearly·every·computer·is· susceptible· to· a computer·virus.·This· potentially· harmful· program· can· infect· a· computer· and· negatively· affect· the· way· a· computer·works·—without·the· user's· knowledge.· After· a· virus· infects· a· computer,· it· can· spread· throughout· the· computer· and· may· damage· software·and·files.¶

Computer·viruses·infect·a· computer·in·three·basic·ways:· when· a· user· (1)· opens· an· infected· file,· (2)· runs· an· infected· program,· or· (3)· powers·on·the·computer·with· an· infected· disk· in· a· disk· drive.· Today,· the· most· common· way· a· computer· becomes·infected·with·a·virus· is· when· a· user· opens· an· infected·e-mail·attachment.¶

Methods·that· guarantee·a· computer· or· network· is· totally· safe· from· computer· viruses· simply· do· not· exist.· Users· can· take· several· precautions,· however,· to· protect· their· home· a... computers· from· viru... following· paragraph... a· variety· of· pre... measures· designed...

Do· not· start· a· computer· with·a·floppy·disk·in·drive·A· —·unless· you· are· certain· the· disk· is· an· uninfected· boot· disk.·All·floppy·disks·contain· a· boot· sector.· During· the· startup·process,·the·computer· attempts· to· execute· the· boot· sector· on· a· disk· in· drive· A.· Even· if· the· attempt· is· not· successful,· a· virus· on· the· floppy·disk's·boot·sector·can· infect· the· hard· disk· on· a· computer.¶

Never· open· an· e-mail· message· attachment· unless· you· are· expecting· the· attachment· and· the· e-mail· message· is· from· a· trusted· source.·A·trusted·source·is·a· company· or· person· you· believe·will·not·send·a·virus-infected·file·knowingly.·If·the· e-mail·message·is·not·from·a· trusted· source,· delete· the· message·immediately.·Do·not· open· or· execute· any· of· its· attachments.¶

¶

...continued·on·page·2¶

.........Column Break.........

USER·GROUP·MEETING¶

¶

The·next·meeting·of·the· Clever·Clicks·User·Group· (CCUG)·will·be·held·on· Saturday,·October·8,·at·the· Remington·Valley·recreation· center·(440·Center·Street)· from·11:00·a.m.·to·3:00·p.m.· A·deli·luncheon·will·be· served.·The·guest·speaker,· Mary·Patterson,·will·discuss· health·concerns·related·to· computer·use.¶

If·you·plan·to·attend,· please·send·an·e-mail· message·to·Ted·Chilton·at· ccug@world.net.·The·cost·of· $10·per·person·will·be·due·at· the·door.¶

¶

CCUG·DISCOUNTS¶

¶

All·CCUG·members·now· receive·a·10-percent·discount· at·all·Office·World·stores.· Simply·present·your·CCUG· membership·card·at·the·time· of·your·purchase.¶

¶

NEXT·ISSUE¶

¶

Next·month's·issue·of·*Clever· Clicks*·will·discuss·how·to·set· up·a·home·network.¶

Full Screen toolbar

Full Screen

Close Full Screen

Close Full Screen button

text is left-aligned instead of justified

FIGURE 6-45

Other Ways

1. In Voice Command mode, say "View, Full Screen, Close Full Screen"

Instead of clicking the Full Screen button on the Full Screen toolbar, you can press the ESCAPE key to exit full screen view.

While reviewing the document in full screen view, you notice that the last column does not have justified text. Thus, the next step is to change the formatting of the text from left-aligned to justified, as described below.

More About

Justification

The paragraphs within the columns of a newsletter very often are justified; that is, they are flush at both left and right margins. This alignment often causes rivers, which are large gaps between words. One solution is to rearrange the words or add additional words to minimize the rivers. Another solution, not quite as common, is to use left-aligned text.

To Justify Paragraphs

1 **On the first page of the newsletter, drag the mouse from the top of the third column down to the bottom of the third column.**

2 **Click the Justify button on the Formatting toolbar.**

Word changes the alignment of the selected paragraphs from left-aligned to justified (Figure 6-46).

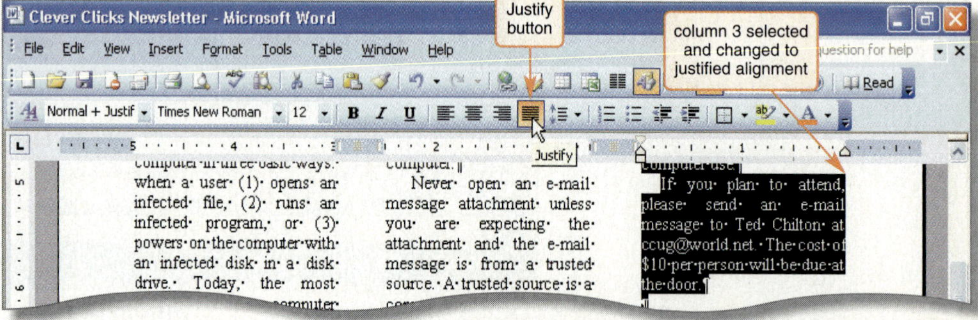

FIGURE 6-46

Adding a Vertical Rule between Columns

In newsletters, you often see a vertical rule separating columns. With Word, you can place a vertical rule between all columns by clicking the Columns command on the Format menu and then clicking the Line between check box.

In this project, you want a vertical rule between only the second and third columns. To do this, place a left border spaced several points from the text. A point is approximately 1/72 of an inch.

The following steps place a vertical rule between the second and third columns of the newsletter.

Q&A

Q: When should a vertical rule be used in a newsletter?

A: A vertical rule is used to guide the reader through the newsletter. If a multi-column newsletter contains a single article, place a vertical rule between every column. If different columns present different articles, place a vertical rule between each article.

To Place a Vertical Rule between Columns

1

- **With the third column of page 1 in the newsletter still selected, click Format on the menu bar.**

The entire third column of page 1 in the newsletter is selected (Figure 6-47).

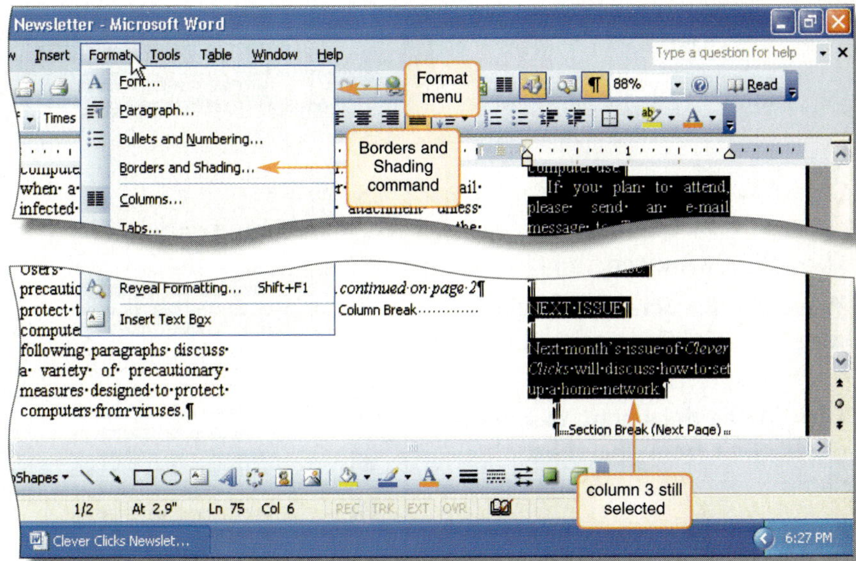

FIGURE 6-47

2

- **Click Borders and Shading on the Format menu.**
- **When Word displays the Borders and Shading dialog box, if necessary, click the Borders tab.**
- **Click the Left Border button in the Preview area.**

In the Borders and Shading dialog box, the border diagram graphically shows the selected borders (Figure 6-48).

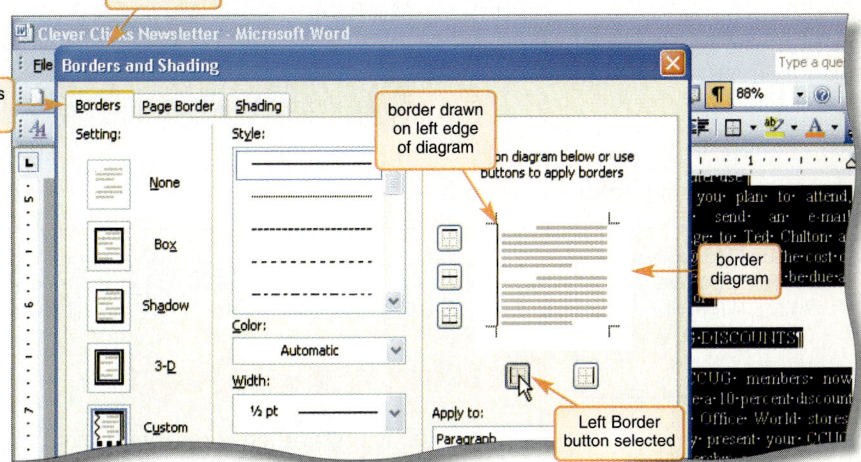

FIGURE 6-48

3

- **Click the Options button.**
- **When Word displays the Border and Shading Options dialog box, change the Left box to 15 pt.**

The Preview area shows the border positioned 15 points from the left edge of the paragraph (Figure 6-49).

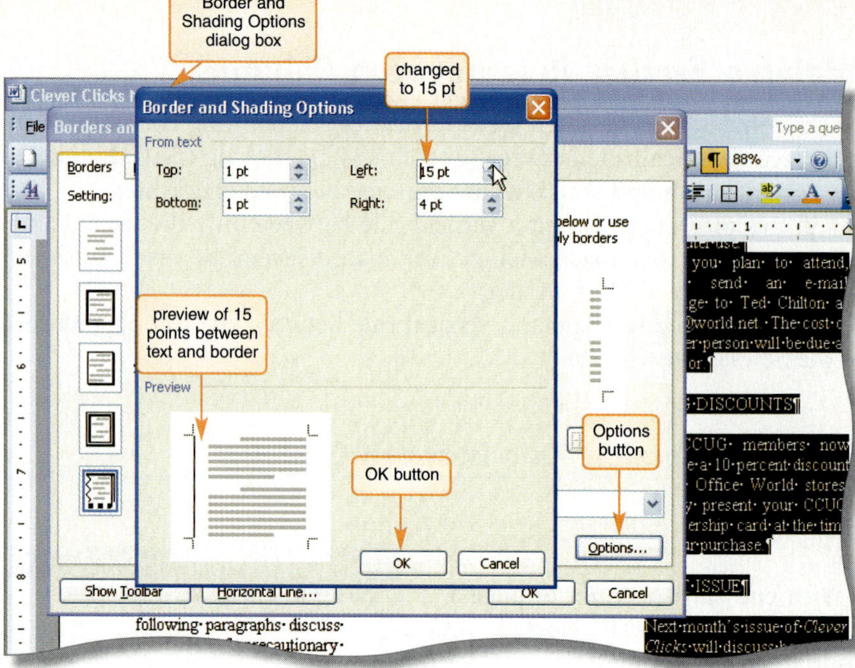

FIGURE 6-49

4

- **Click the OK button.**
- **When the Borders and Shading dialog box is visible again, click its OK button.**
- **Click in the document to remove the selection from the third column.**

Word draws a border positioned 15 points from the left edge of the text in the third column (Figure 6-50). The border is displayed as a vertical rule between the second and third columns of the newsletter.

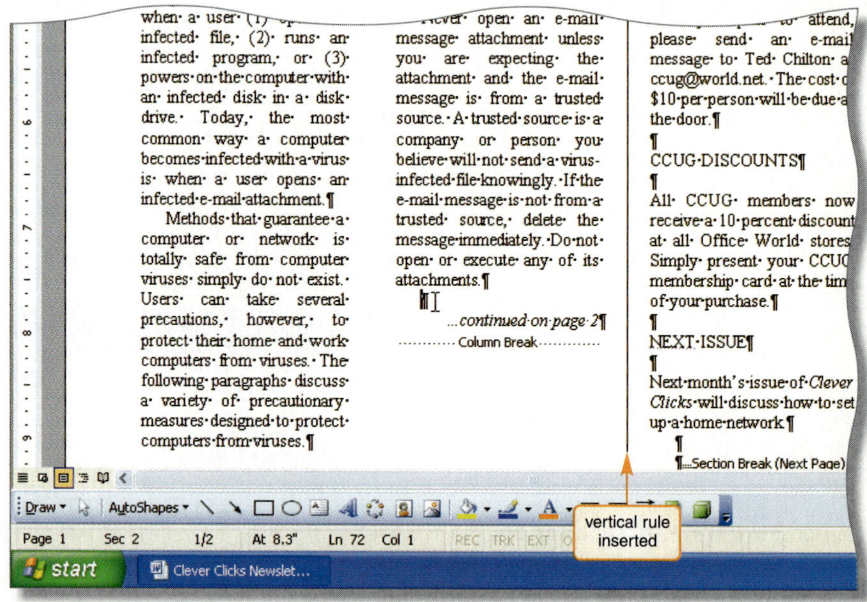

FIGURE 6-50

Other Ways

1. In Voice Command mode, say "Format, Borders and Shading, Left Border, Options, Left, [enter number], OK, OK"

Creating a Pull-Quote

A pull-quote is text pulled, or copied, from the text of the document and given graphical emphasis so it stands apart and commands the reader's attention. The newsletter in this project has a pull-quote on the first page between the first and second columns (Figure 6-1a on page WD 379).

To create a pull-quote, copy the text in the existing document to the Clipboard and then paste it into a column of the newsletter. To position the text between columns, place a text box around it. A **text box**, like a frame, is a container for text that allows you to position the text anywhere on the page. The difference between a text box and a frame is that a text box has more graphical formatting options than does a frame.

The steps on the following pages discuss how to create the pull-quote shown in Figure 6-1a on page WD 379.

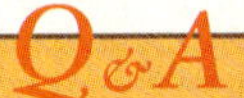

Q: What guidelines should I follow when using pull-quotes?

A: Because of their bold emphasis, pull-quotes should be used sparingly in a newsletter. Pull-quotes are useful for breaking the monotony of long columns of text. Typically, quotation marks are used only if you are quoting someone directly. If you use quotation marks, use curly (or smart) quotation marks instead of straight quotation marks.

Inserting a Text Box

The first step in creating the pull-quote is to copy the text to be used in the pull-quote and then insert a text box around it, as shown in the following steps.

To Insert a Text Box

1

- **Scroll to display the second paragraph in the newsletter and then select its last sentence: Today, the most common way a computer becomes infected with a virus is when a user opens an infected e-mail attachment.**
- **With the text selected, click the Copy button on the Standard toolbar.**

The text for the pull-quote is selected (Figure 6-51).

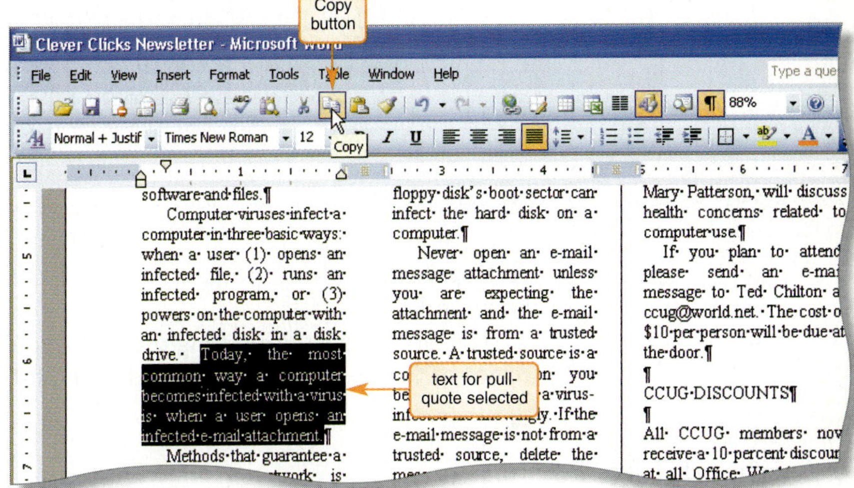

FIGURE 6-51

- **Click at the end of the paragraph that contains the selected sentence and then click the Paste button on the Standard toolbar to create a duplicate of the sentence at the end of the paragraph.**
- **Select the entire sentence to be in the pull-quote.**

The sentence to be in the text box is selected (Figure 6-52).

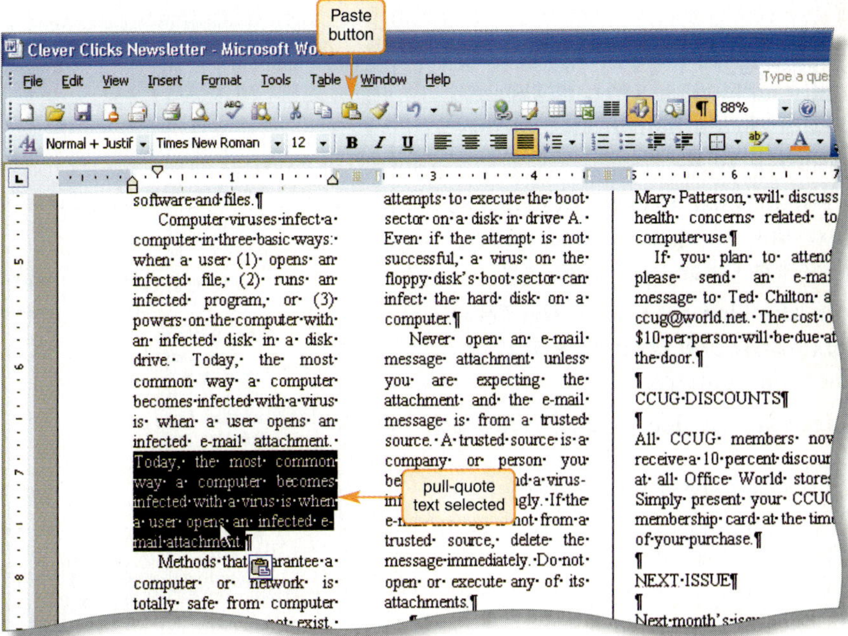

FIGURE 6-52

3

• **Click the Text Box button on the Drawing toolbar.**

Word places a text box around the pull-quote (Figure 6-53). The pull-quote now may be positioned anywhere on the page. The Text Box toolbar may appear on the screen when the text box is selected.

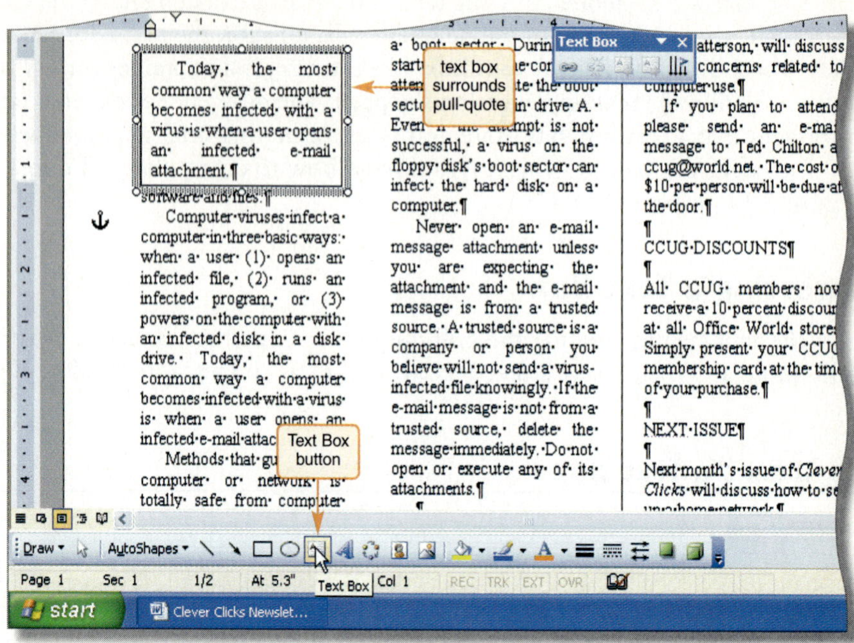

FIGURE 6-53

Other Ways

1. On Insert menu click Text Box
2. In Voice Command mode, say "Insert, Text Box"

Depending on your printer, the text in the text box may wrap differently than shown in Figure 6-53.

The next step in formatting the pull-quote is to change the color and increase the weight of the text box, as described in the following steps.

To Format a Text Box

1

• **Point to an edge of the text box and double-click when the mouse pointer has a four-headed arrow attached to it.**

• **When Word displays the Format Text Box dialog box, if necessary, click the Colors and Lines tab.**

• **In the Line area, click the Color box arrow and then click Teal on the color palette.**

• **Change the line weight to 1.5 pt.**

In the Colors and Lines sheet in the Format Text Box dialog box, you can modify characteristics of the fill color, lines, and arrows (Figure 6-54).

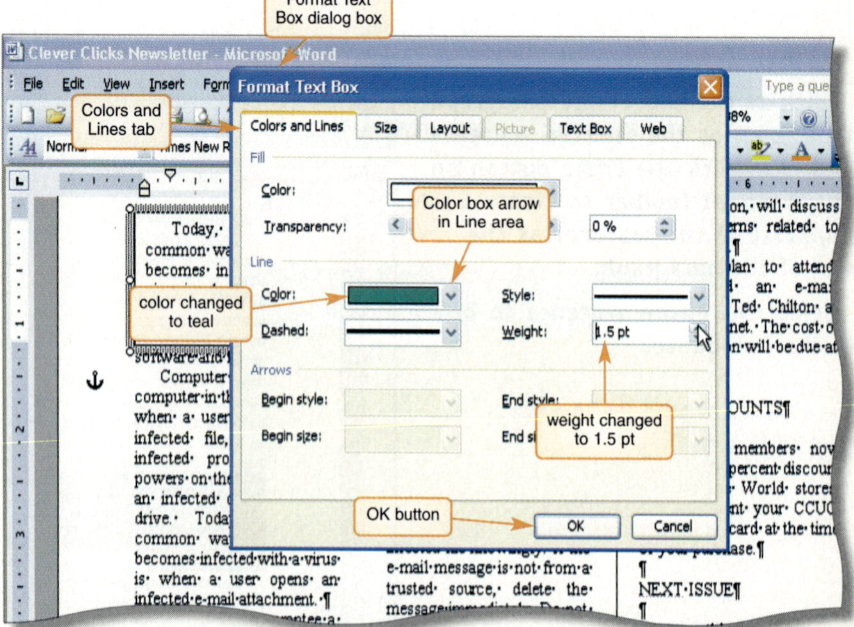

FIGURE 6-54

2

- **Click the OK button.**

Word formats the text box to a 1.5-point teal line (Figure 6-55).

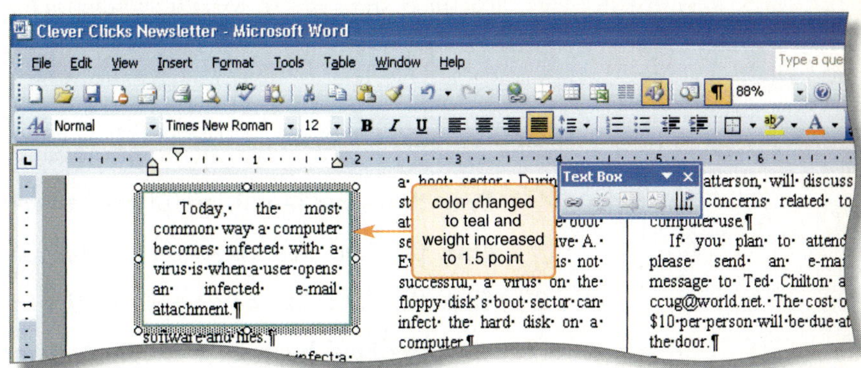

FIGURE 6-55

Other Ways

1. On Format menu click Text Box
2. Right-click edge of text box, click Format Text Box on shortcut menu
3. In Voice Command mode, say "Format, Text Box"

The next step in formatting the pull-quote is to shade the pull-quote paragraph orange, as shown in the following steps.

To Shade a Paragraph

1

- **Click in the pull-quote paragraph to position the insertion point in the pull-quote.**
- **Click Format on the menu bar and then click Borders and Shading.**
- **When Word displays the Borders and Shading dialog box, if necessary, click the Shading tab.**
- **In the Fill area, click Orange.**

Word displays the Shading sheet in the Borders and Shading dialog box (Figure 6-56).

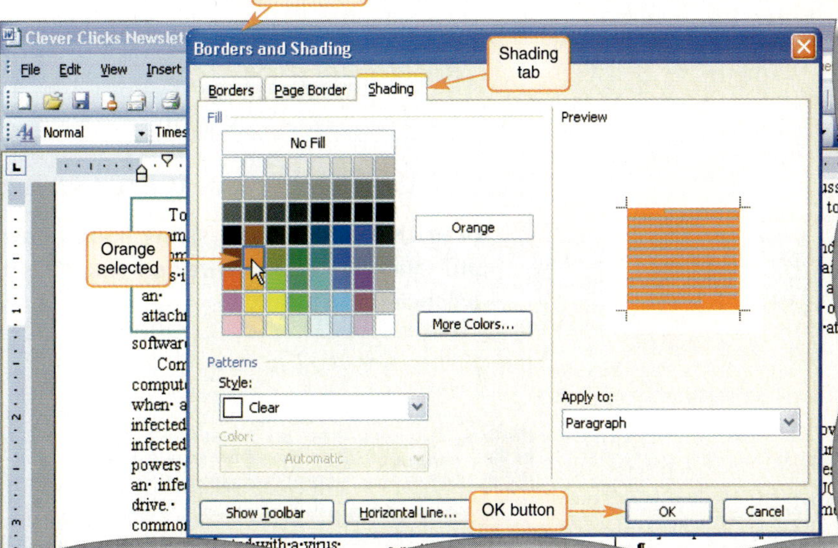

FIGURE 6-56

2

- **Click the OK button.**

Word shades the paragraph orange (Figure 6-57).

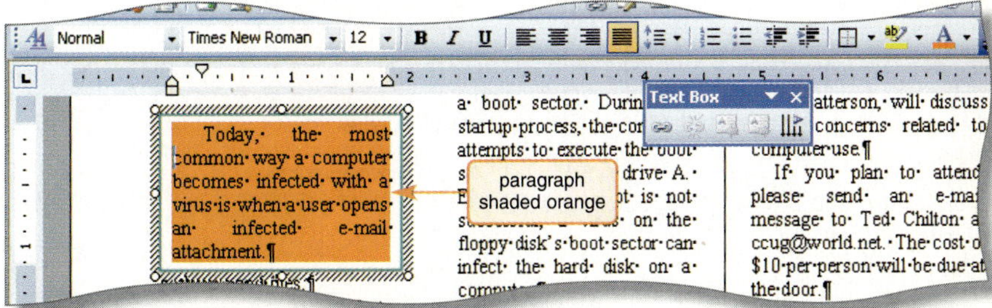

FIGURE 6-57

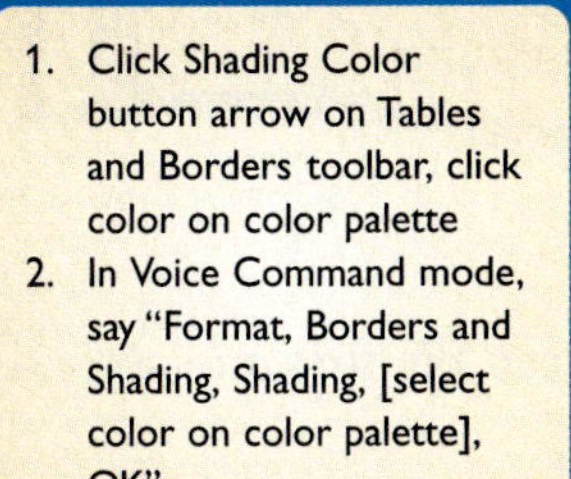

Other Ways

1. Click Shading Color button arrow on Tables and Borders toolbar, click color on color palette
2. In Voice Command mode, say "Format, Borders and Shading, Shading, [select color on color palette], OK"

The next steps are to format the characters and center the text in the pull-quote, as described below.

To Format Text

1. **Drag through the pull-quote text to select it.**
2. **Click the Font box arrow on the Formatting toolbar and then click Arial.**
3. **Click the Font Size box arrow on the Formatting toolbar and then click 11.**
4. **Click the Bold button on the Formatting toolbar.**
5. **Click the Center button on the Formatting toolbar.**
6. **Click the Font Color button arrow on the Formatting toolbar and then click White on the color palette.**
7. **Drag the First Line Indent marker to the 0" mark on the ruler.**
8. **Click inside the pull-quote text to remove the selection.**

Word formats the text in the pull-quote (shown in Figure 6-58).

The next step in formatting the pull-quote is to resize the text box. You resize a text box in the same way as any other object. That is, you drag its sizing handles, as described below.

To Resize a Text Box

1. **Click the edge of the text box to select it.**
2. **Drag the right-middle sizing handle inward about one-half inch to make the pull-quote a bit narrower so that the pull-quote text looks more balanced.**

The text box is resized (Figure 6-58).

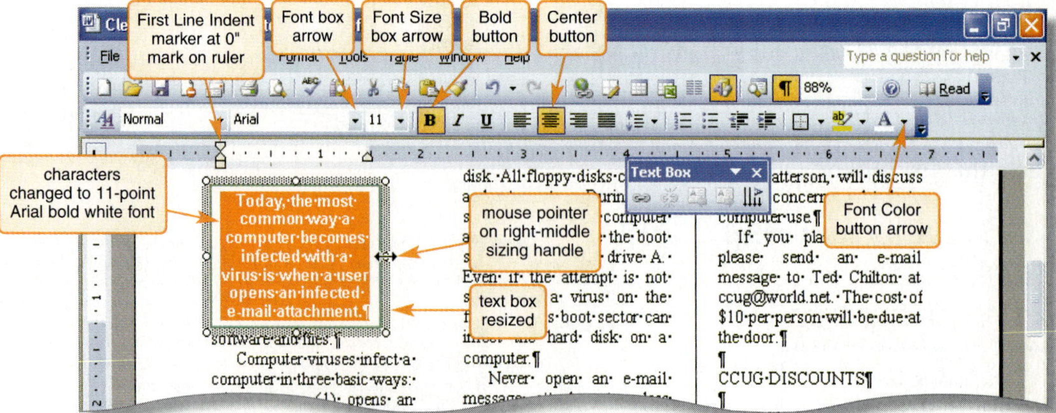

FIGURE 6-58

The final step is to position the pull-quote text box between the first and second columns of the newsletter, as shown next.

To Position a Text Box

1

- **With the text box still selected, drag the text box to its new location (Figure 6-59). You may need to drag the text box a couple of times to position it similarly to this figure.**
- **Click outside the text box to remove the selection.**

The pull-quote is complete (Figure 6-59). Depending on your printer, your wordwrap around the text box may occur in different locations.

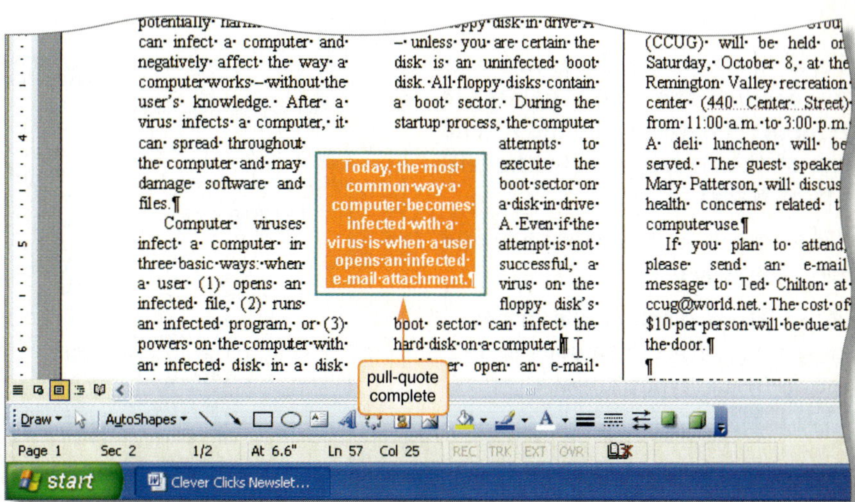

FIGURE 6-59

The following step saves the document again.

To Save a Document

1 **With the disk containing the newsletter file in drive A, click the Save button on the Standard toolbar.**

Word saves the document again with the file name, Clever Clicks Newsletter.

The first page of the newsletter is finished, with the exception of the page border and subhead colors, which will be added later in this project.

> *More About*
>
> **Moving Text Boxes**
>
> To move a text box using the keyboard, select the text box and then press the arrow keys on the keyboard. For example, each time you press the DOWN ARROW key, the selected text box moves down one line.

Formatting the Second Page of the Newsletter

The second page of the newsletter (Figure 6-1b on page WD 379) continues the feature article that began in the first two columns on the first page. The nameplate on the second page is simpler than the one on the first page of the newsletter. In addition to the text in the feature article, page two contains a diagram. The following pages illustrate how to format the second page of the newsletter in this project.

Changing Column Formatting

The document currently is formatted into three columns. The nameplate at the top of the second page, however, should be in a single column. The next step, then, is to change the number of columns at the top of the second page from three to one.

As discussed earlier in this project, Word requires a new section each time you change the number of columns in a document. Thus, you first must insert a continuous section break and then format the section to one column so the title can be entered on the second page of the newsletter, as shown in the steps on the next page.

To Change Column Formatting

1

- **Scroll through the document and then position the mouse pointer at the upper-left corner of the second page of the newsletter (to the left of M in Many).**
- **Click Insert on the menu bar and then click Break.**
- **When Word displays the Break dialog box, click Continuous in the Section break types area.**

A continuous section break will place the nameplate on the same physical page as the three columns of the continued feature article (Figure 6-60).

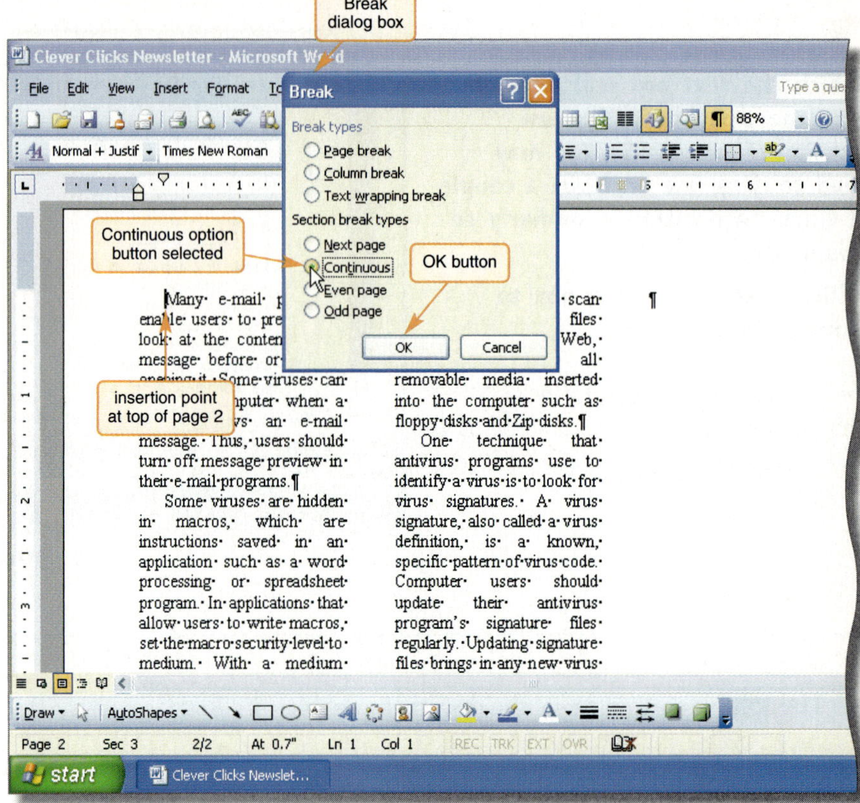

FIGURE 6-60

2

- **Click the OK button.**

Word inserts a continuous section break above the insertion point.

3

- **Press the UP ARROW key to position the insertion point in section 3 to the left of the section break notation.**
- **Click the Style box arrow and then click Clear Formatting to remove the paragraph formatting from the section break.**
- **Click the Columns button on the Standard toolbar.**
- **Position the mouse pointer on the first column in the columns list.**

Word displays the columns list (Figure 6-61).

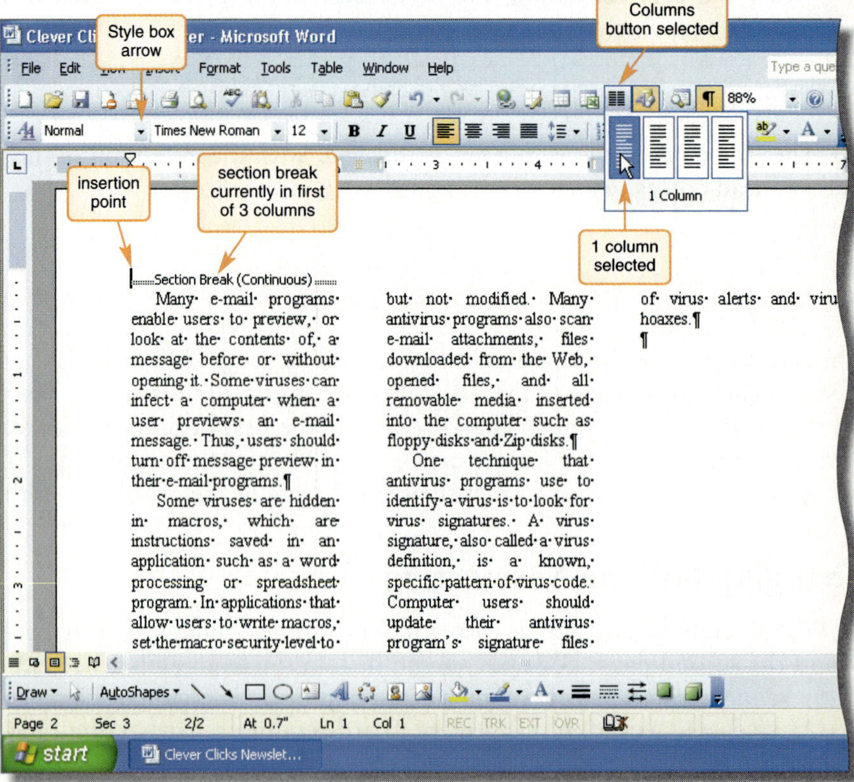

FIGURE 6-61

4

• **Click the first column in the columns list.**

Word formats the current section to one column (Figure 6-62). The section break now extends from the left margin to the right margin.

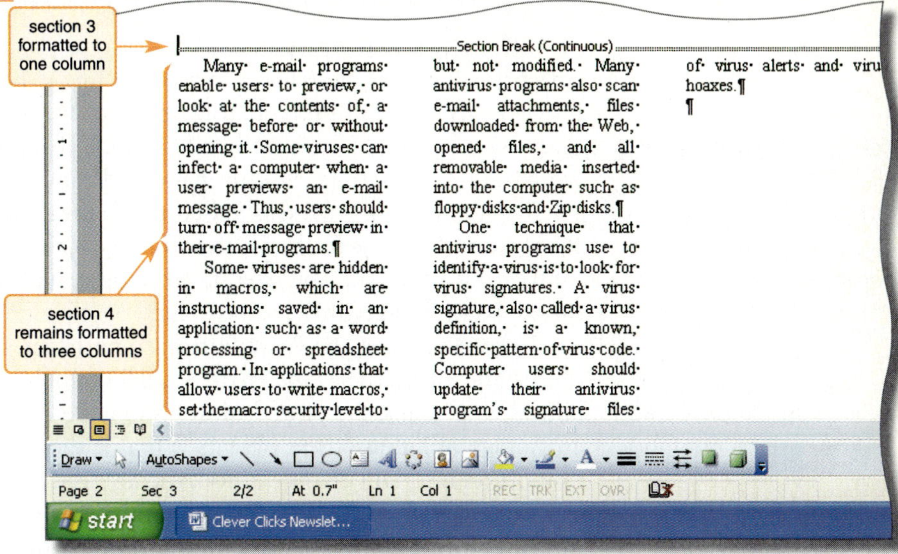

FIGURE 6-62

The following steps describe how to enter the newsletter title at the top of the second page in section 3.

To Format and Enter Text

1. **With the insertion point in section 3 to the left of the section break notation, press the ENTER key twice. Press the UP ARROW key.**
2. **Click the Font Size box arrow on the Formatting toolbar and then click 16. Click the Bold button on the Formatting toolbar. Click the Center button on the Formatting toolbar. Click the Font Color button arrow and then click Brown on the color palette.**
3. **Type** `CLEVER CLICKS` **and then press the ENTER key.**
4. **Click the Style box arrow on the Formatting toolbar and then click Clear Formatting.**

The title is formatted and entered at the top of the second page of the newsletter (Figure 6-63).

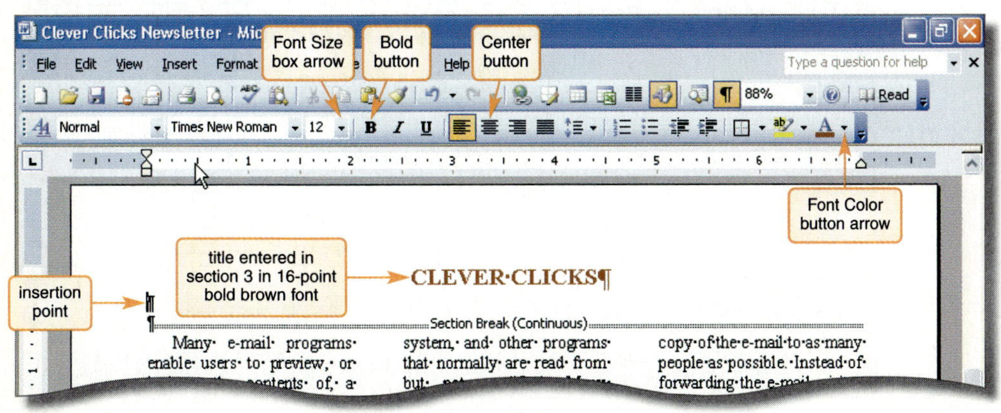

FIGURE 6-63

More About

Columns

If you already have typed text and would like it to be formatted in a different number of columns, select the text, click the Columns button on the Standard toolbar, and then click the number of columns desired in the columns list. Word automatically creates a new section for the newly formatted columns.

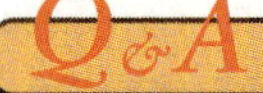

Q&A

Q: How should I design an inner page nameplate?

A: The top of the inner pages of the newsletter may or may not have a nameplate. If you choose to create one for your inner pages, it should not be the same as, or compete with, the one on the first page. Inner page nameplates usually contain only a portion of the nameplate from the first page of a newsletter.

Using the Paste Special Command to Link Text

The rest of the nameplate on the second page is identical to the nameplate on the first page. That is, the issue information line is below the newsletter title. A ruling line is below the issue information line. Then, the title of the feature article is one blank line below the bottom border. Thus, the next step is to copy these lines of text from the nameplate on the first page and then paste them on the second page.

The item being copied is called the **source object**. The item being pasted is called the **destination object**. Thus, the source object is the bottom part of the nameplate on the first page, and the destination object will be the bottom part of the nameplate on the second page of the newsletter.

Instead of using the Paste button to paste the source object to the destination object, this project uses the Paste Special command. The **Paste Special command** allows you to link the pasted (destination) object to the copied (source) object. The advantage of linking these objects is that if the source object ever changes, the destination object also will change automatically. That is, if you change the bottom part of the nameplate on page 1, the bottom part of the nameplate on page 2 also will change.

The following steps show how to link a copied item.

> *More About*
>
> **Links**
>
> If you wanted to modify the location of the source file in a link or remove a link while leaving the source text in the destination document, click the link, click Edit on the menu bar and then click Links to display the Links dialog box. Follow instructions in the dialog box to remove or modify the link.

To Link a Copied Item

1

- **Scroll up to display the top of page 1 in the document window.**
- **Drag through lines 2, 3, and 4 in the nameplate.**
- **Click the Copy button on the Standard toolbar.**

Word copies the second, third, and fourth lines on the first page of the newsletter to the Clipboard (Figure 6-64).

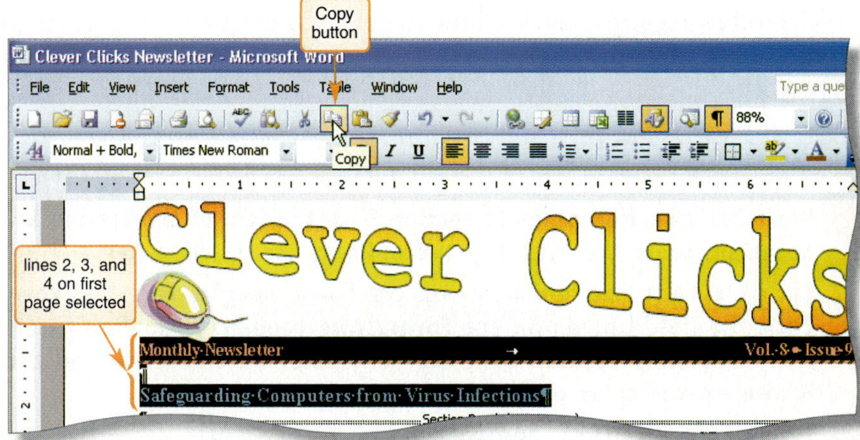

FIGURE 6-64

2

- **Press SHIFT+F5 to reposition the insertion point on line 2 of the second page of the newsletter.**
- **Click Edit on the menu bar.**

Recall that pressing SHIFT+F5 repositions the insertion point at your last editing location (Figure 6-65).

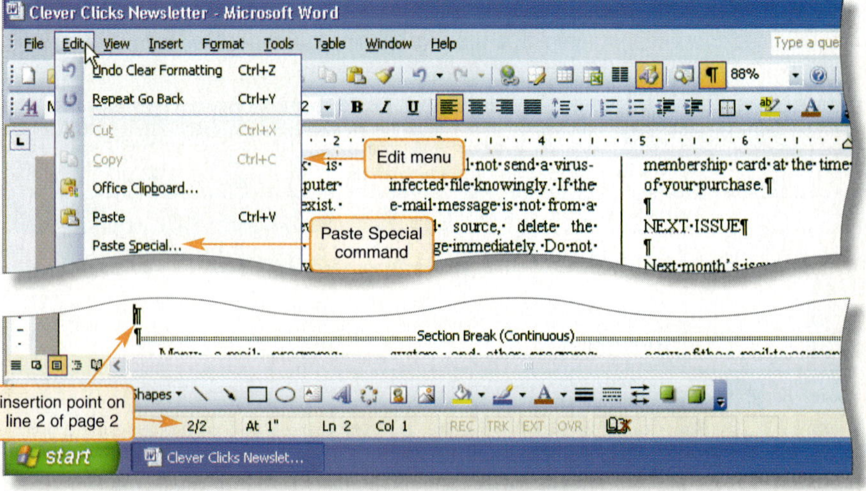

FIGURE 6-65

3

- **Click Paste Special on the Edit menu.**
- **When Word displays the Paste Special dialog box, click Paste link.**
- **Click Formatted Text (RTF) in the As list.**

In the Paste Special dialog box, the Formatted Text (RTF) option pastes the destination object using the same formatting as the source object (Figure 6-66).

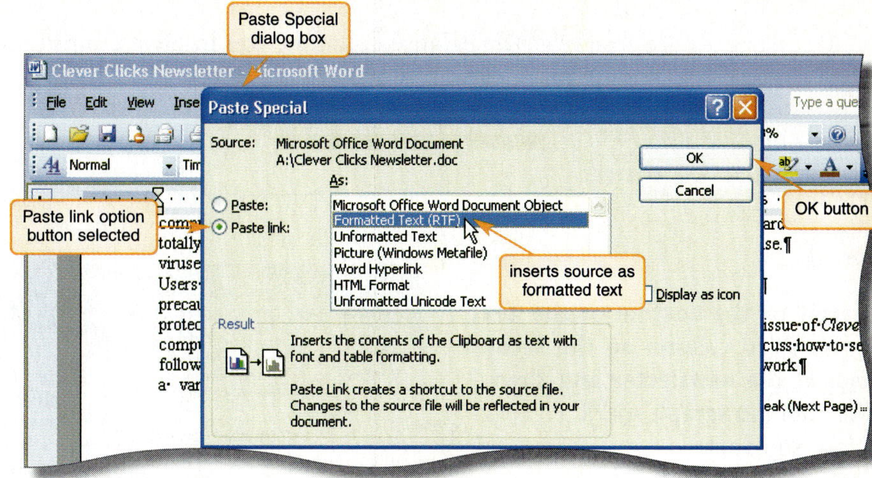

FIGURE 6-66

4

- **Click the OK button.**

Word pastes the copied object at the location of the insertion point (Figure 6-67).

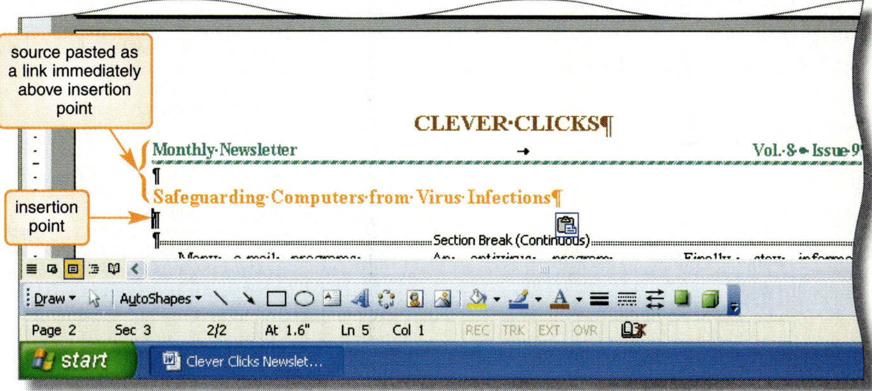

FIGURE 6-67

Other Ways

1. In Voice Command mode, say "Edit, Paste Special, Paste link, [select Formatted Text (RTF)], OK"

If a link, for some reason, is not updated automatically, click the link and then press the F9 key to update it manually. When you click in the link, it displays shaded in gray. This shading does not print; it helps you identify this item as a link.

The next step is to add a continued message immediately below the pasted link, as described below.

To Enter Text

1 **With the insertion point on the line immediately below the pasted link, press CTRL+I to turn on italics. Type** `(Continued from page 1)` **and then press CTRL+I to turn off italics.**

The continued message is entered below the pasted link (shown in Figure 6-68 on the next page).

Balancing Columns

Currently, the text on the second page of the newsletter completely fills up the first and second columns and spills into a portion of the third column. The text in the three columns is to consume the same amount of vertical space. That is, the three columns should be balanced.

To balance columns, you insert a continuous section break at the end of the text, as shown in the following steps.

To Balance Columns

1

- **Scroll to the bottom of the text in the third column on the second page of the newsletter and then click the paragraph mark below the text.**
- **Click Insert on the menu bar and then click Break.**
- **When Word displays the Break dialog box, click Continuous in the Section break types area.**

Word displays the Break dialog box (Figure 6-68).

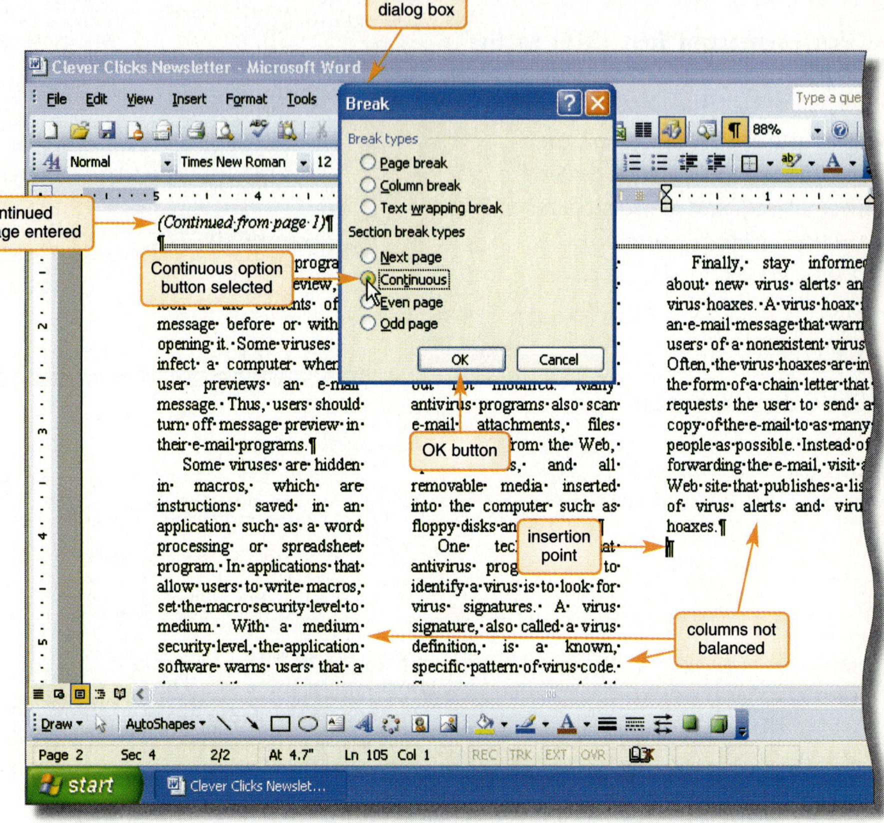

FIGURE 6-68

2

- **Click the OK button.**

Word inserts a continuous section break, which balances the columns on the second page of the newsletter (Figure 6-69).

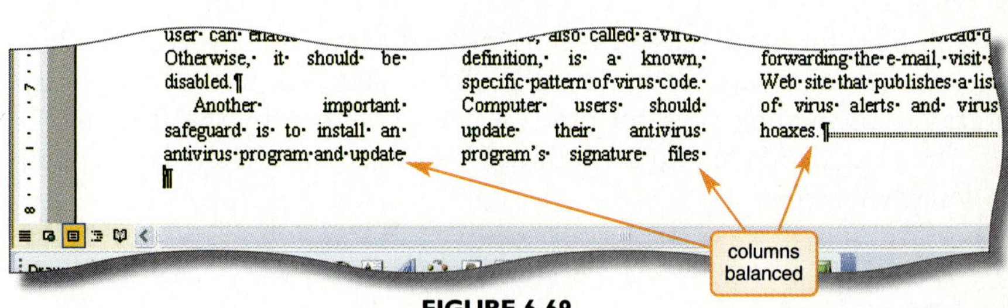

FIGURE 6-69

Other Ways

1. In Voice Command mode, say "Insert, Break, Continuous, OK"

The following step saves the document again.

To Save a Document

1 **With the disk containing the newsletter file in drive A, click the Save button on the Standard toolbar.**

Word saves the document again with the file name, Clever Clicks Newsletter.

Creating a Diagram

The next step is to insert a diagram between the second and third columns on the second page of the newsletter. In Word, you can insert an organization chart and five other types of diagrams in your documents: cycle, pyramid, radial, target, and Venn. Table 6-1 briefly describes the purpose of each of these diagrams.

Table 6-1 Word Diagrams

DIAGRAM TYPE	PURPOSE
Cycle	Shows a process with continuous steps that form a loop
Organization	Shows hierarchical relationships
Pyramid	Shows items that relate to one another
Radial	Shows elements that relate to a central item
Target	Shows steps toward a goal
Venn	Shows overlapping items

When working with these diagrams, it is best to insert the diagram in a single column layout so that you easily can see all its components. At this point in the newsletter, the number of columns is three. Thus, the next step is to open a new document window, which has one column, insert and format the diagram, and then copy it to the newsletter.

The newsletter in this project has a radial diagram on the second page that identifies various symptoms of a computer virus infection. The following steps show how to insert a radial diagram in a new document window.

Other Ways

1. On Insert menu click Diagram, [select diagram type], click OK button
2. In Voice Command mode, say "Insert, Diagram, [select diagram type], OK"

To Insert a Diagram

- **Click the New Blank Document button on the Standard toolbar.**
- **When Word displays a blank document window, click the Insert Diagram or Organization Chart button on the Drawing toolbar.**
- **When Word displays the Diagram Gallery dialog box, click the radial diagram.**

Word displays the Diagram Gallery dialog box in a new document window (Figure 6-70).

2

- **Click the OK button.**

Word inserts a radial diagram in the document window (shown in Figure 6-71 on the next page). The Diagram toolbar appears on the screen.

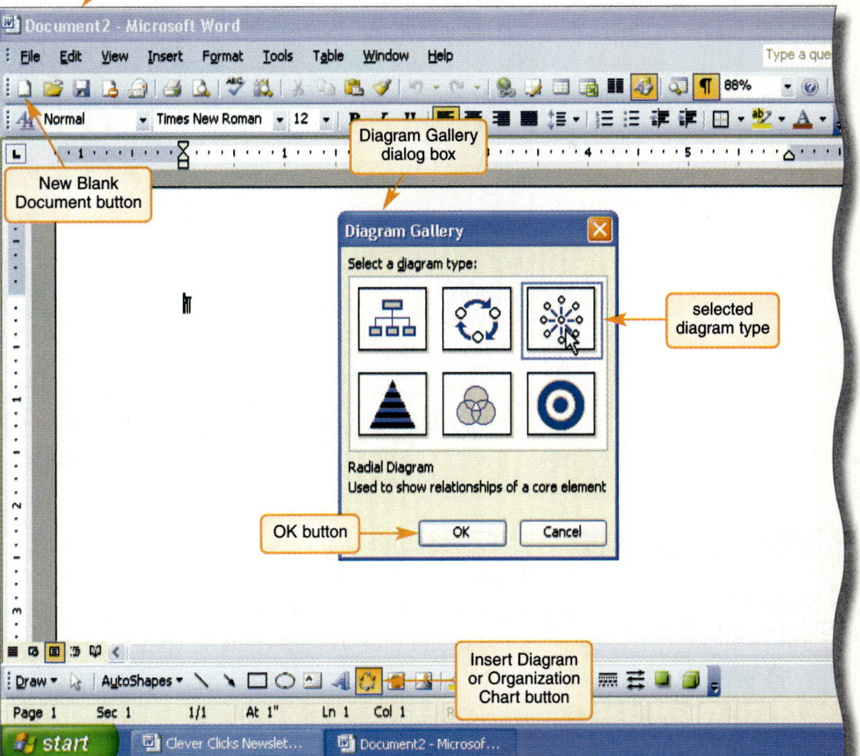

FIGURE 6-70

The entire radial diagram does not fit in the document window. Thus, the following steps change the zoom percentage so more of the radial diagram is displayed.

To Zoom to a Percentage

1. **Click the Zoom box arrow on the Standard toolbar.**
2. **Click 75% in the Zoom list.**
3. **If necessary, scroll up or down so the entire radial diagram is displayed in the document window.**

By changing the zoom percentage to 75%, more of the radial diagram shows in the document window (Figure 6-71).

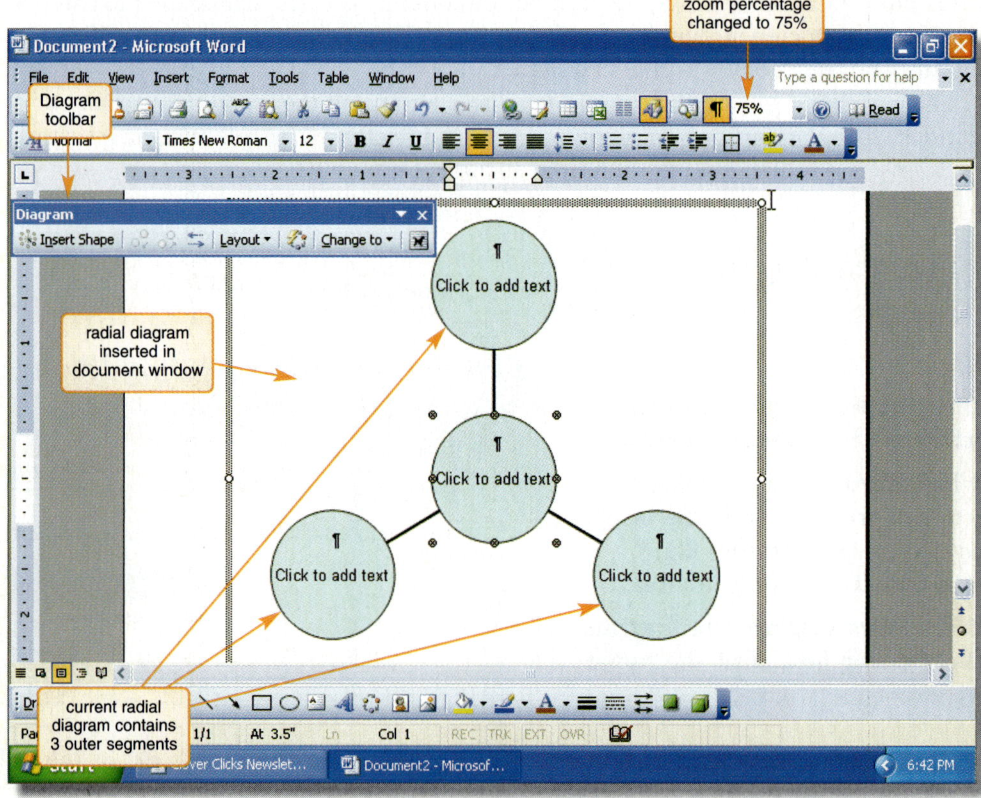

FIGURE 6-71

The radial diagram in this newsletter is to contain a total of eight segments (Figure 6-1b on page WD 379). The current radial diagram contains only three segments. Thus, the next task is to add five more segments to the diagram.

The next step shows how to add segments to a diagram.

More About

Diagram Segment Color

To change the fill color in a diagram segment, click the segment, click the Fill Color button arrow on the Drawing toolbar, and then click the desired color. To remove a fill color, click the Fill Color button arrow on the Drawing toolbar and then click No Fill on the color palette.

To Add Segments to a Diagram

1

- **With the diagram selected, click the Insert Shape button on the Diagram toolbar five times.**

Word adds five segments to the diagram (Figure 6-72).

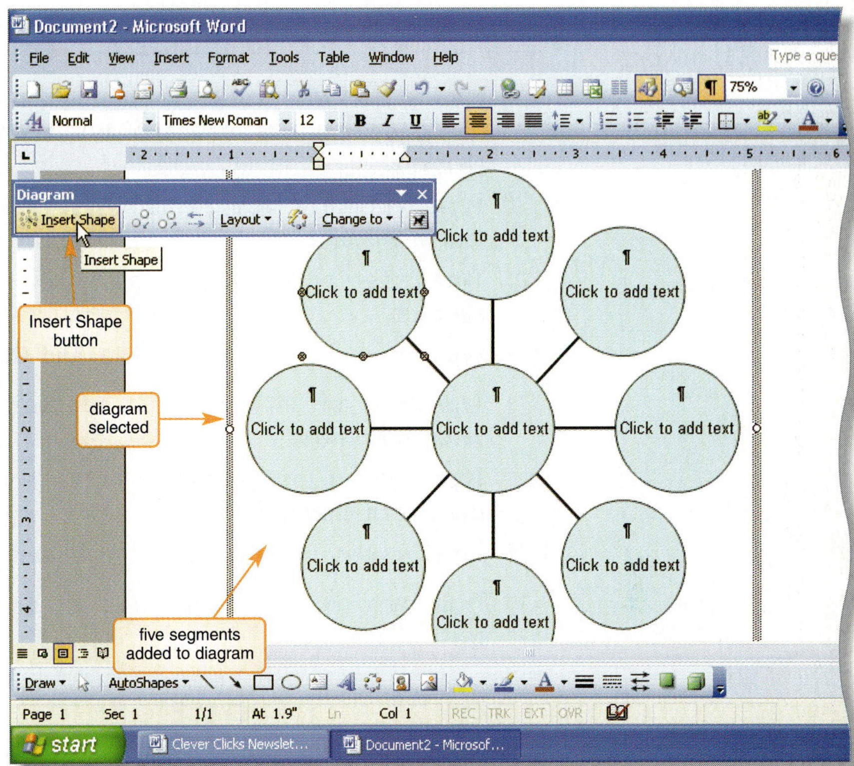

FIGURE 6-72

Other Ways

1. Right-click edge of outer element, click Insert Shape on shortcut menu
2. With Diagram toolbar displaying, in Voice Command mode, say "Insert Shape"

If you add too many elements (segments) to a diagram, you can remove an element(s). Simply click the edges of an element to select it and then click the Cut button on the Standard toolbar or press the DELETE key.

The next task is to add text to the elements of the diagram, as shown in the following step.

To Add Text to a Diagram

- **In the top element in the radial diagram, click the placeholder text, Click to add text.**
- **Type** `Screen displays unusual message or image` **as the element text.**

Word selects and adds text to the top element of the radial diagram (Figure 6-73).

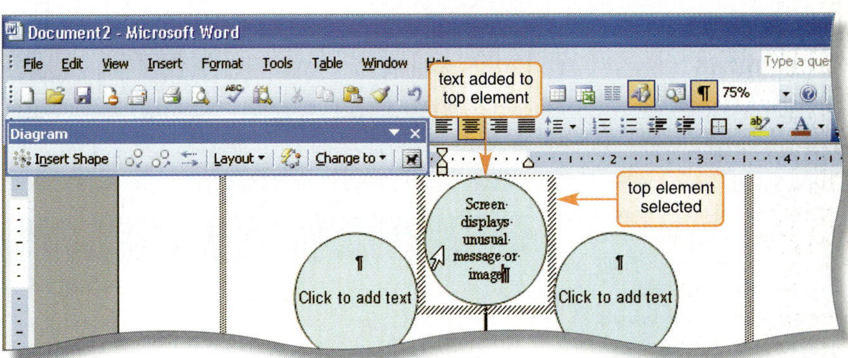

FIGURE 6-73

The following steps enter the text in the remaining elements of the radial diagram.

To Enter More Diagram Text

1. **Moving clockwise, click the placeholder text in the second element. Type** `Music or unusual sound plays randomly` **and then click the third element.**
2. **Type** `Available memory is less than expected` **and then click the fourth element.**
3. **Type** `Existing programs and files disappear` **and then click the fifth element.**
4. **Type** `Files become corrupted` **and then click the sixth element.**
5. **Type** `Programs or files do not work properly` **and then click the seventh element.**
6. **Type** `Unknown programs or files arbitrarily appear` **and then click the eighth element.**
7. **Type** `System properties change` **and then click the middle (core) element.**
8. **Type** `Symptoms of a Computer Virus Infection` **as the core element text.**

The text is added to the diagram (Figure 6-74).

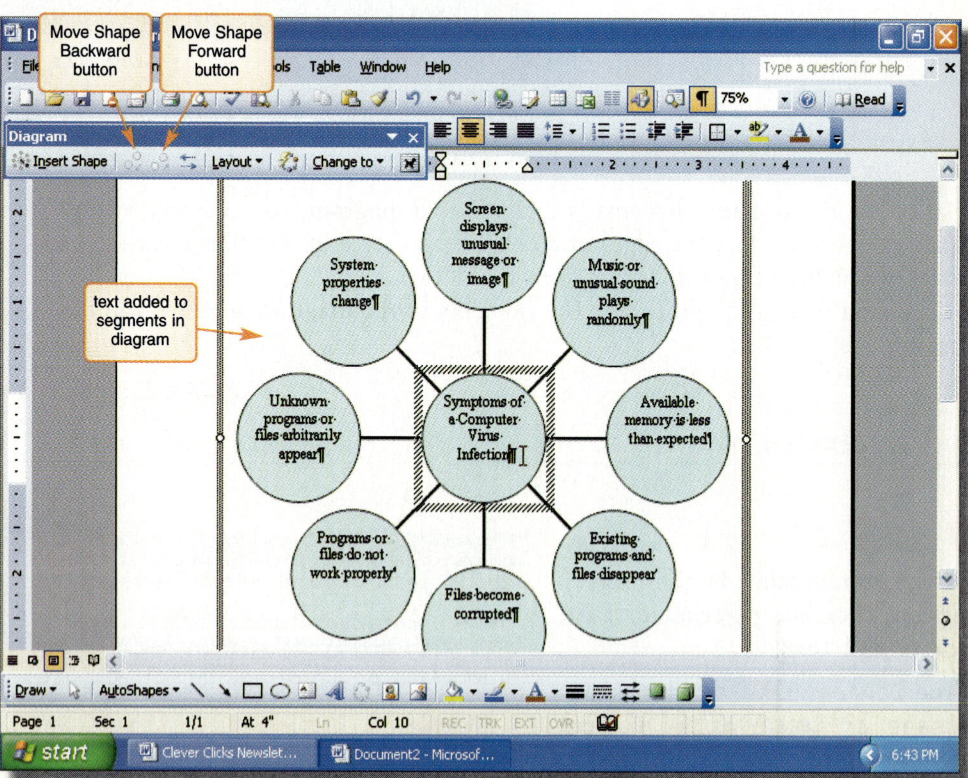

FIGURE 6-74

More About

Moving Diagram Segments

To move a segment of a diagram, select the segment and then click either the Move Shape Forward button or the Move Shape Backward button on the Diagram toolbar. For example, each time you click the Move Shape Forward button, the selected segment moves down one position in the diagram.

The next task is to format the diagram using one of the built-in AutoFormat styles, as shown in the following steps.

To AutoFormat a Diagram

1

- **Click the AutoFormat button on the Diagram toolbar.**
- **When Word displays the Diagram Style Gallery dialog box, click Thick Outline in the Select a Diagram Style list.**

The selected style in the Diagram Style Gallery dialog box will be applied to the diagram in the document window (Figure 6-75).

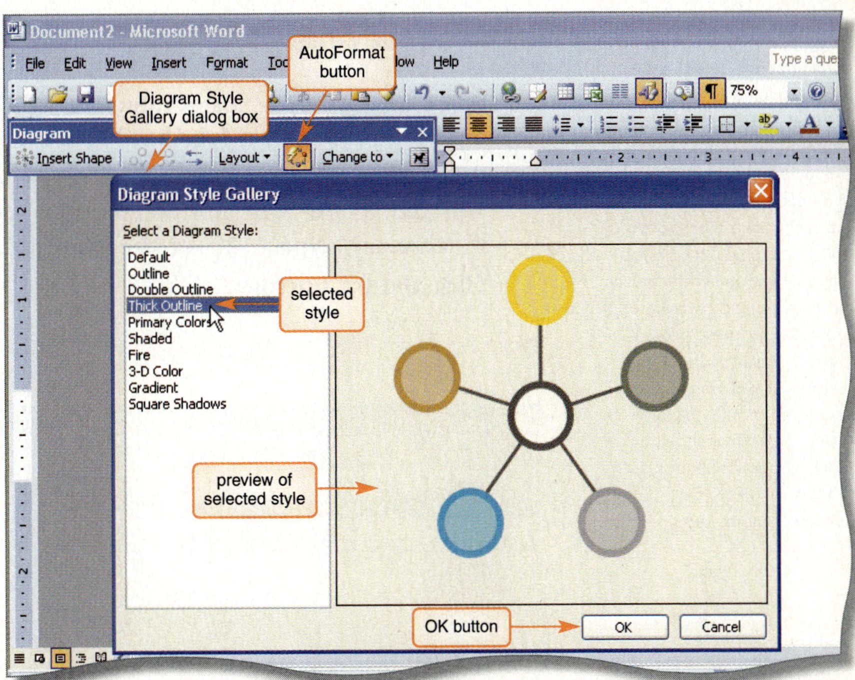

FIGURE 6-75

2

- **Click the OK button.**

Word applies the thick outline style to the diagram (Figure 6-76).

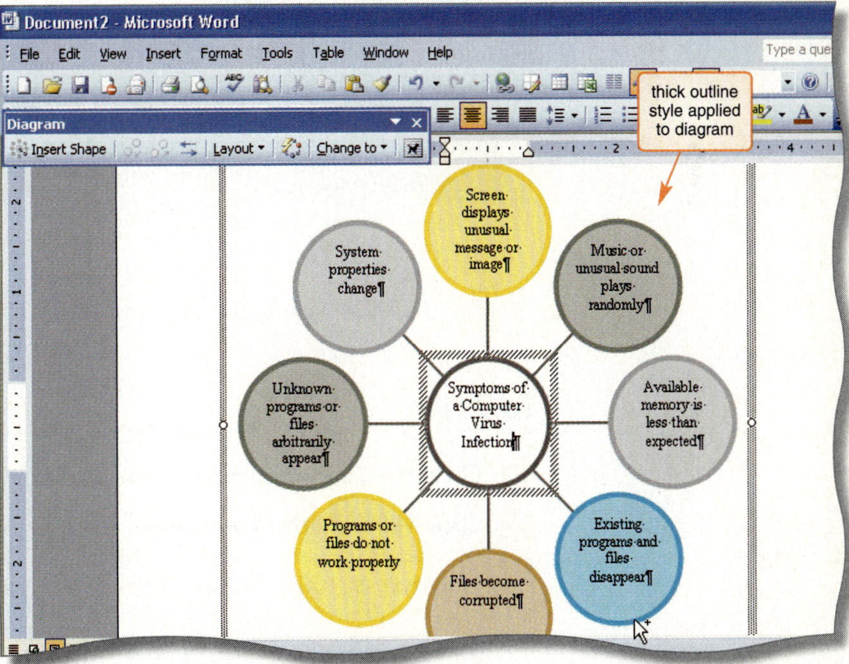

FIGURE 6-76

The next task is to reduce the size of the diagram so it will fit at the bottom of the second page of the newsletter. You resize a diagram the same as any other graphic object. That is, you can drag its sizing handles or enter exact measurements into the Format Diagram dialog box.

More About

Formatting Graphics

In the Format Diagram dialog box, when the Lock aspect ratio check box in the Scale area in the Size sheet contains a check mark, Word keeps the height and width percentage values the same to maintain the proportions of the graphic. Thus, if you type height and width values in the Size and rotate area that distort these proportions, Word readjusts your entries. If you want the percentages to differ, remove the check mark from the Lock aspect ratio check box so Word will allow the proportions to vary.

This diagram should be 4.25 inches tall and 4.25 inches wide. The following steps describe how to enter these measurements into the Format Diagram dialog box.

To Resize a Diagram

1. **Point to the frame surrounding the diagram and double-click when the mouse pointer has a four-headed arrow attached to it.**
2. **When Word displays the Format Diagram dialog box, if necessary, click the Size tab. In the Size and rotate area, type `4.25` in the Height box and then, if necessary, type `4.25` in the Width box.**
3. **Click the OK button.**

Word resizes the diagram (Figure 6-77).

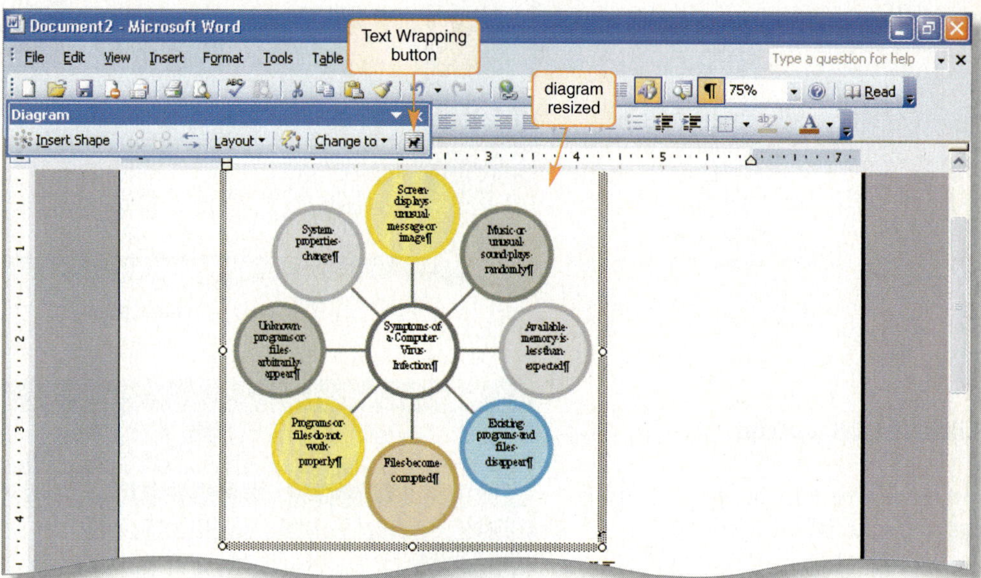

FIGURE 6-77

The diagram now is too small to read. The following steps zoom to 100%.

To Zoom to 100%

1. **Click the Zoom box arrow on the Standard toolbar.**
2. **Click 100% in the Zoom list.**

When you zoom to 100%, the text in the diagram is more readable (shown in Figure 6-78).

You want text in the newsletter to wrap around the diagram – fitting the form of the diagram. Thus, the next step is to change the graphic from inline to floating with a wrapping style of tight, as described in the next steps.

To Format a Graphic as Floating

1. **Click the frame around the diagram to select the diagram.**
2. **Click the Text Wrapping button on the Diagram toolbar and then click Tight.**

The diagram is formatted to a tight wrapping style, which means text will wrap tightly around the graphic. This format will become apparent when you copy the diagram into the newsletter.

Using the Format Painter Button

The next step is to reduce the font size of the text in each element of the AutoShape to 7.5 point, so the text fits completely in the elements. Instead of selecting each element one at a time and then changing its font size, you can format the text in the first element and then copy its formatting to the other elements. To copy formatting, use the Format Painter button on the Standard toolbar, as shown in the following steps.

> *More About*
>
> **Fonts**
>
> For more information about fonts, visit the Microsoft Word 2003 More About Web page (scsite.com/wd2003/more) and then click Fonts.

To Use the Format Painter Button

1

- **Triple-click the text in the top element of the radial diagram to select the text.**
- **If necessary, drag the Diagram toolbar off of the Formatting toolbar.**
- **Click the Font button arrow on the Formatting toolbar and then click Arial.**
- **Click the Font Size box arrow on the Formatting toolbar. Type** `7.5` **in the Font Size box and then press the ENTER key.**
- **Double-click the Format Painter button on the Standard toolbar.**
- **Moving clockwise, position the mouse pointer to the left of the text in the second element.**

The format painter copies the format of the selected text (Figure 6-78). When you double-click the Format Painter button, it remains selected until you click it again. This enables you to copy the format to multiple locations. Word attaches a paintbrush to the mouse pointer when the Format Painter button is selected.

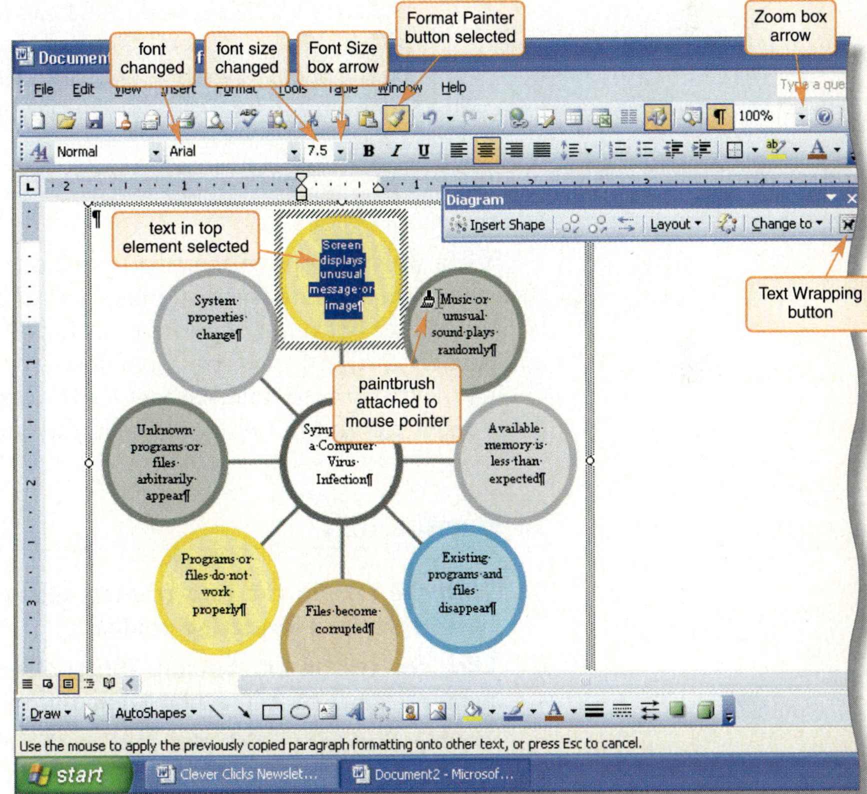

FIGURE 6-78

2

- **Select the text in the second element by triple-clicking the text.**
- **Triple-click the text in each of the remaining elements, including the core (center) element.**
- **Click the Format Painter button on the Standard toolbar to turn off the format painter.**

Word copies the 7.5-point Arial font to the text in the remaining elements (Figure 6-79).

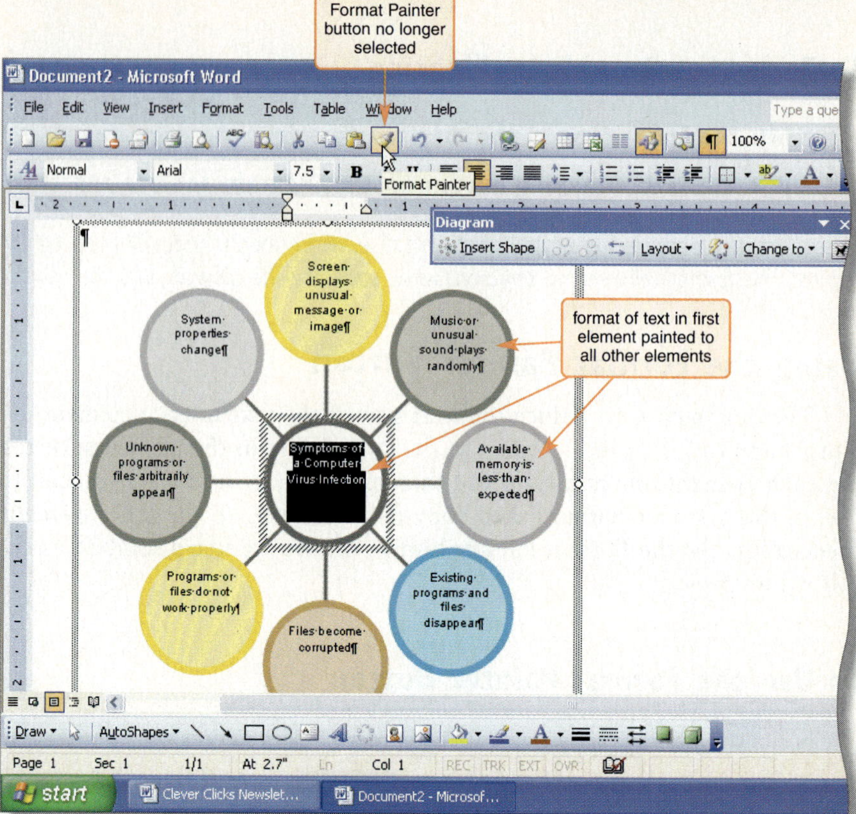

FIGURE 6-79

If you want to copy formatting to just one location in a document, you would click the Format Painter button, instead of double-clicking it. When you click the Format Painter button, it copies formatting to the next item you select and then immediately turns off the format painter.

The next step is to bold the text in the core (center) element and then add some space above the text in two elements in the diagram, as described below.

To Format Text

1. **With the text in the core (center) element still selected, click the Bold button on the Formatting toolbar.**
2. **Click the text in the bottom (fifth) element and then press CTRL+0 (the numeral zero) to add a blank line above the text.**
3. **Moving clockwise, click the text in the eighth element and then press CTRL+0.**

Word bolds the text in the core element and adds space above text in two other elements in the diagram (Figure 6-80). The bold format is difficult to see because the text is small. It will become apparent when you print the document.

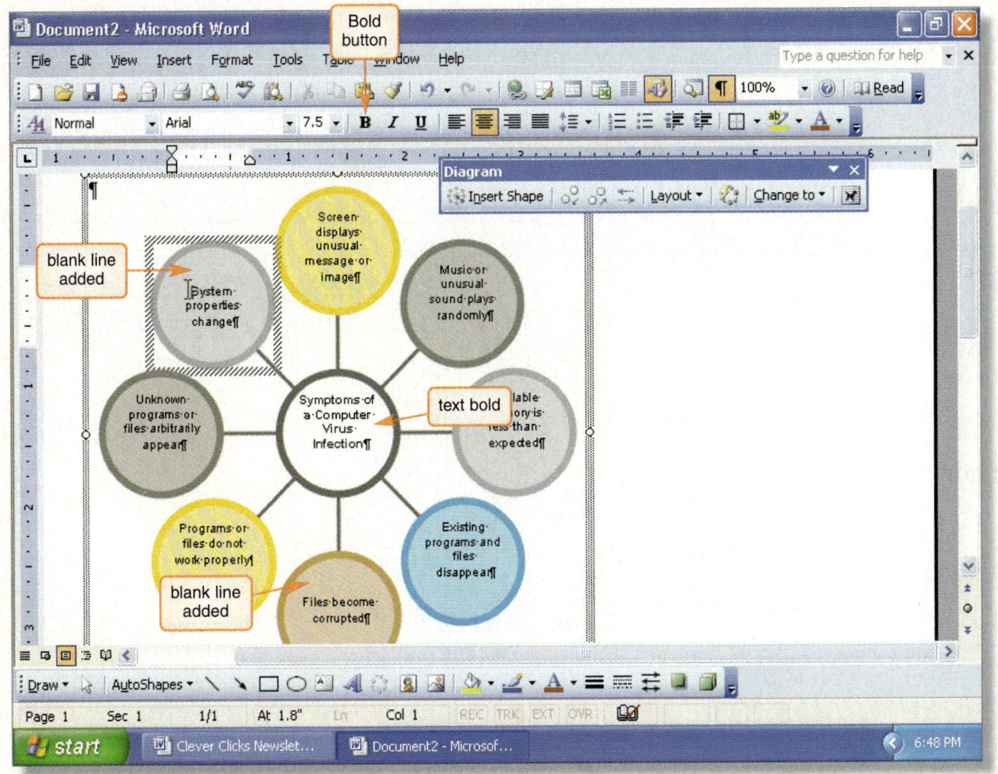

FIGURE 6-80

The next step is to save the diagram, as described below.

To Save a Document

1. **With the disk containing the newsletter in drive A, click the Save button on the Standard toolbar.**
2. **Type** `Computer Virus Symptoms Diagram` **in the File name box. Do not press the ENTER key.**
3. **If necessary, click the Save in box arrow and then click 3½ Floppy (A:).**
4. **Click the Save button in the Save As dialog box.**

Word saves the document on a floppy disk in drive A with the file name, Computer Virus Symptoms Diagram (shown in Figure 6-81 on the next page).

Copying, Pasting, and Positioning a Diagram

The diagram is finished. The next step is to copy it from this document window and then paste it in the newsletter. The steps on the next page show how to copy and paste the diagram in the second page of the newsletter.

More About

Go To

Recall that you can go to a certain page, section, line, or other object in a document through the Go To sheet in the Find and Replace dialog box. To display the Go To sheet, click Edit on the menu bar and then click Go To or press CTRL+G. In the Go to what list, click the item you want to go to, enter the item number (e.g., 2 for page 2), and then click the Go To button.

To Copy and Paste a Diagram

1

- **Click the frame around the diagram to select the diagram.**
- **Click the Copy button on the Standard toolbar (Figure 6-81).**

Word copies the diagram to the Clipboard.

2

- **Click File on the menu bar and then click Close.**

Word closes the file containing the diagram.

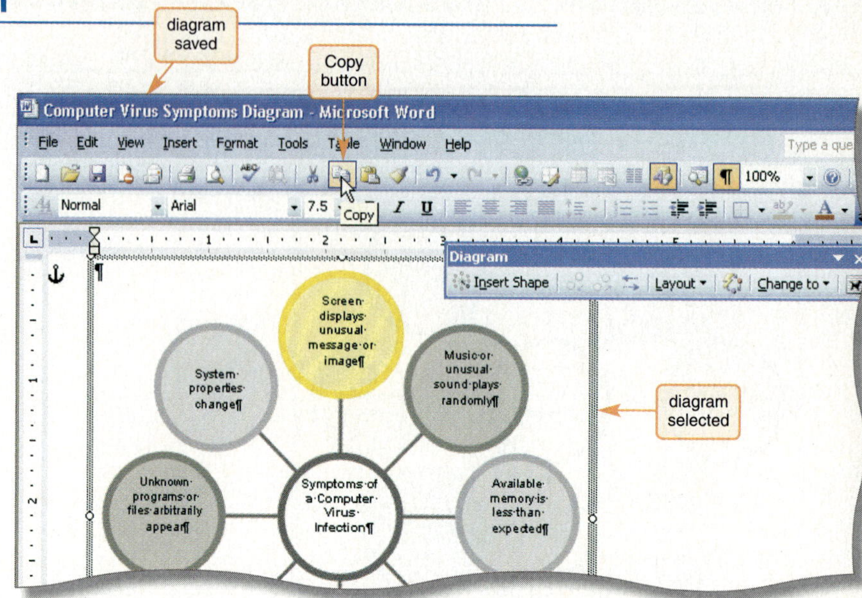

FIGURE 6-81

3

- **When Word redisplays the newsletter document window, right-click somewhere on page 2 in the feature article.**

Word displays a shortcut menu (Figure 6-82).

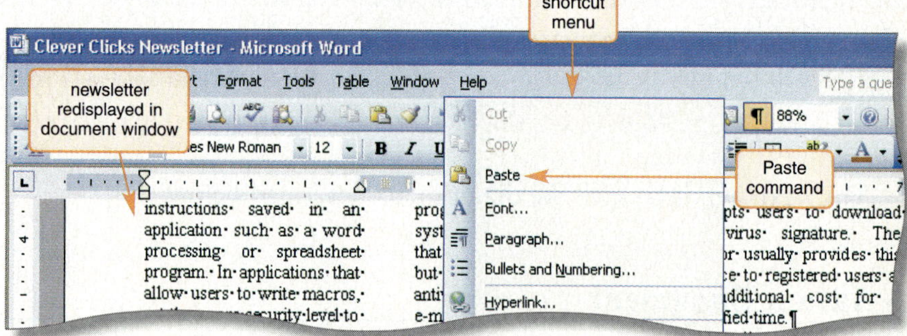

FIGURE 6-82

4

- **Click Paste on the shortcut menu.**

Word pastes the diagram from the Clipboard into the document (Figure 6-83). Your diagram may be pasted at a different location in the newsletter. The next step is to reposition the pasted diagram.

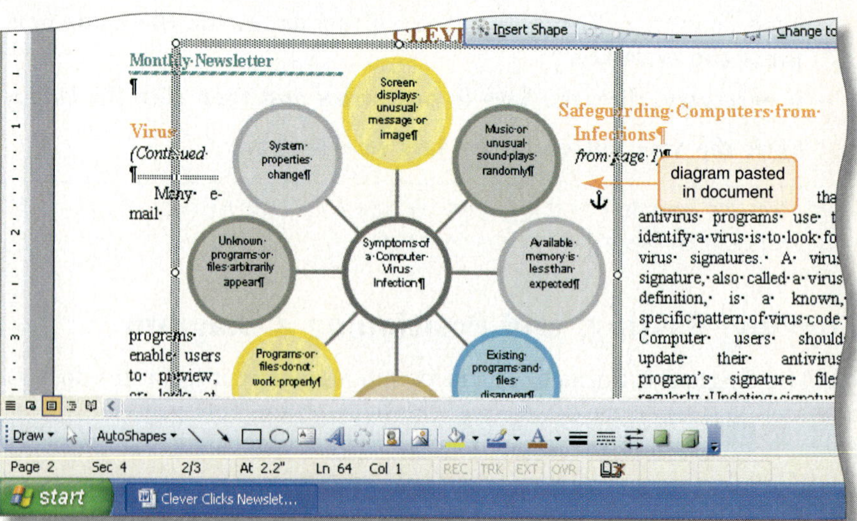

FIGURE 6-83

5

• **Point to the frame on the diagram and when the mouse has a four-headed arrow attached to it, drag the diagram to the desired location. You may have to drag the graphic a couple of times to position it similarly to Figure 6-84.**

Depending on the printer you are using, the wordwrap around the diagram may occur in different locations (Figure 6-84).

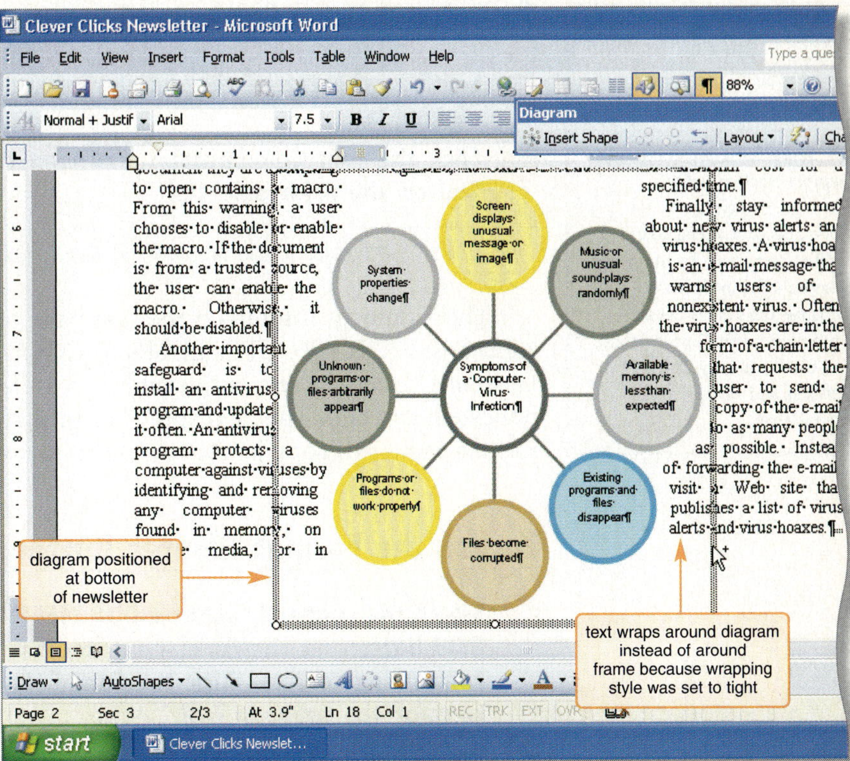

FIGURE 6-84

Notice in Figure 6-84 that the wrap-around text in the first and third columns wraps around the diagram, instead of the frame. This is because earlier you set the wrapping style to Tight. If you wanted the text to wrap around the frame in a square, you would set the wrapping style to Square.

The following step saves the document again.

To Save a Document

1 **With the disk containing the newsletter file in drive A, click the Save button on the Standard toolbar.**

Word saves the document again with the file name, Clever Clicks Newsletter.

> **Q&A**
>
> **Q:** How much space should be in the run-around?
>
> **A:** The run-around, which is the space between the diagram and the text, should be at least 1/8" and should be the same for all graphics in the newsletter. Adjust the run-around of a selected graphic by clicking the Format Picture button on the Picture toolbar, clicking the Layout tab, clicking the Advanced button, adjusting the Distance from text text boxes, and then clicking the OK button.

Enhancing the Newsletter with Color and a Page Border

Many of the characters and lines in the newsletter in this project are in color. The drop cap and the subheads in the announcements columns also should be in color. Lastly, a border should surround each page of the newsletter. The following pages illustrate these tasks.

The first step is to color the drop cap, as described on the next page.

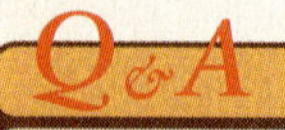

Q: Should I use color in a newsletter?

A: Yes, but avoid using light colors, such as yellow, orange, or light green for text, because these colors are difficult to read. If you do not have a color printer, still change the colors because the colors will print in shades of black and gray. These shades add variety to the newsletter.

To Color a Drop Cap

1. **Scroll to the top of the newsletter and then select the drop cap by double-clicking it.**
2. **Click the Font Color button arrow on the Formatting toolbar and then click Teal on the color palette.**

Word changes the color of the drop cap to teal (shown in Figure 6-1b on page WD 379).

The rightmost column on the first page of the newsletter contains three subheads: USER GROUP MEETING, CCUG DISCOUNTS, and NEXT ISSUE. Currently, all characters in the subheads are capitalized. They also should be bold, italicized, and teal. The next step is to format the first subhead and then use the format painter to copy its formatting to the other two subheads, as described below.

To Use the Format Painter Button

1. **Select the subhead, USER GROUP MEETING, by clicking to its left. Click the Bold button on the Formatting toolbar. Click the Italic button on the Formatting toolbar. Click the Font Color button on the Formatting toolbar to color the subhead Teal.**
2. **Double-click the Format Painter button on the Standard toolbar. Scroll through the newsletter to the next subhead, CCUG DISCOUNTS. Select the subhead by clicking to its left.**
3. **Scroll through the newsletter to the next subhead, NEXT ISSUE. Select the subhead by clicking to its left.**
4. **Click the Format Painter button on the Standard toolbar to turn off the format painter. Click outside the selection to remove the highlight.**

Word copies the bold, italic, teal font from the first subhead to the other two subheads (Figure 6-85).

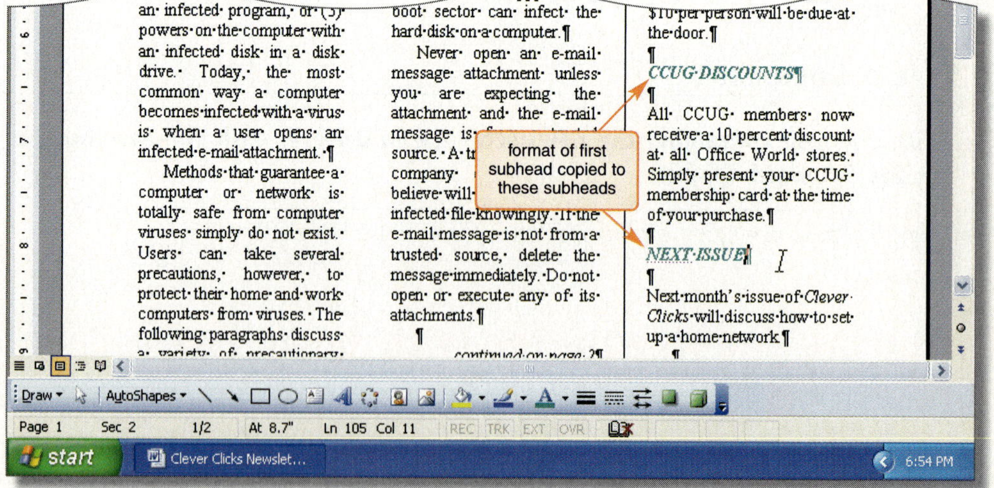

FIGURE 6-85

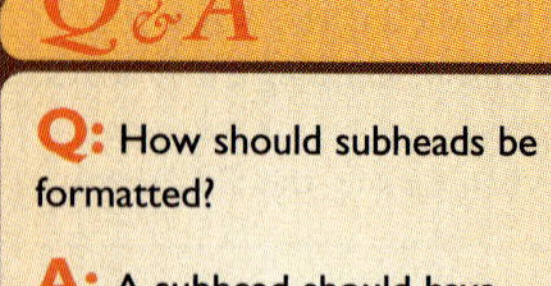

Q: How should subheads be formatted?

A: A subhead should have emphasis in the body of the newsletter, but it should not compete with the text in the nameplate. In general, subheads can be one or two points larger than the body text. Usually subheads are bold, especially if they are the same font size as the body text.

Adding a Page Border

In this and previous projects, you have added borders to the edges of a paragraph(s). In Word, you also can add a border around the perimeter of an entire page. Page borders add professionalism to documents.

In Word, page borders are positioned 24 points from the edge of the page. Many printers cannot print text and graphics that close to the edge of the page. To alleviate this problem, this project changes the border to be positioned from the edge of the text, instead of the edge of the page.

The following steps show how to add a light orange page border around the pages of the newsletter.

To Add a Page Border

1

- **Click Format on the menu bar and then click Borders and Shading.**
- **When Word displays the Borders and Shading dialog box, if necessary, click the Page Border tab.**
- **Click Box in the Setting area.**
- **Scroll through the Style list and click the style shown in Figure 6-86.**
- **Click the Color box arrow and then click Light Orange on the color palette.**
- **Click the Width box arrow and then click 2 ¼ pt.**

The page border is set to a 2¼-point light orange box in the Borders and Shading dialog box (Figure 6-86).

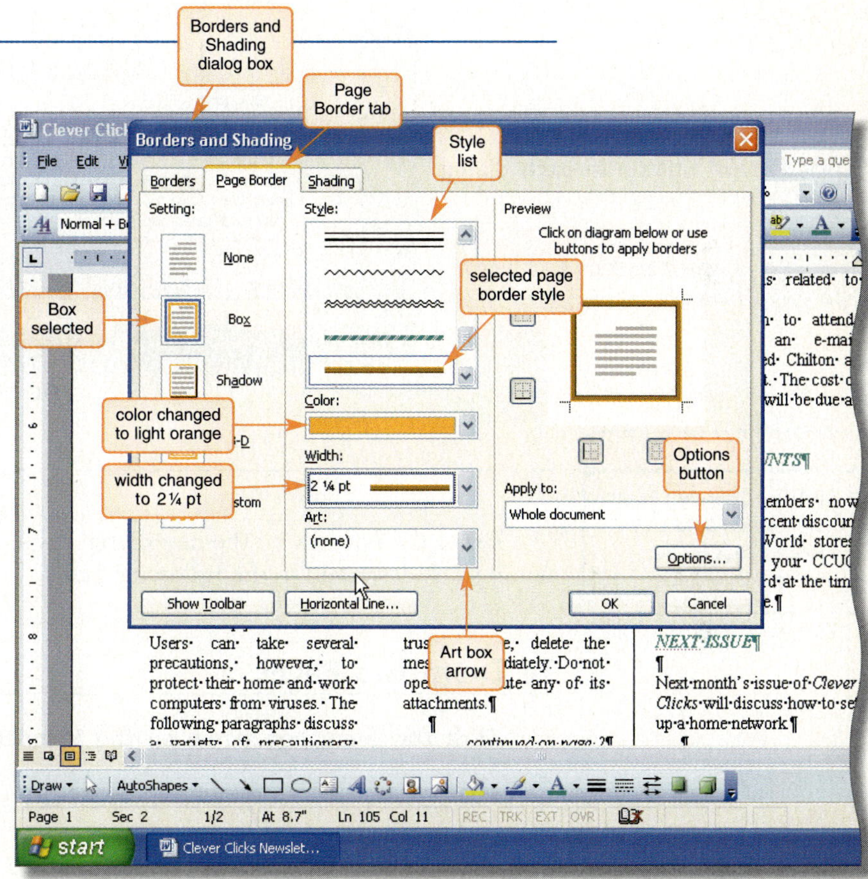

FIGURE 6-86

2

- **Click the Options button.**
- **When Word displays the Border and Shading Options dialog box, click the Measure from box arrow and then click Text.**
- **Change the Top box, Bottom box, Left box, and Right box to 15 pt.**

In the Borders and Shading Options dialog box, you specify the distance of the border from the edge of the page or from the text (Figure 6-87).

3

- **Click the OK button in each dialog box.**

Word places a page border on each page of the newsletter (shown in Figure 6-88).

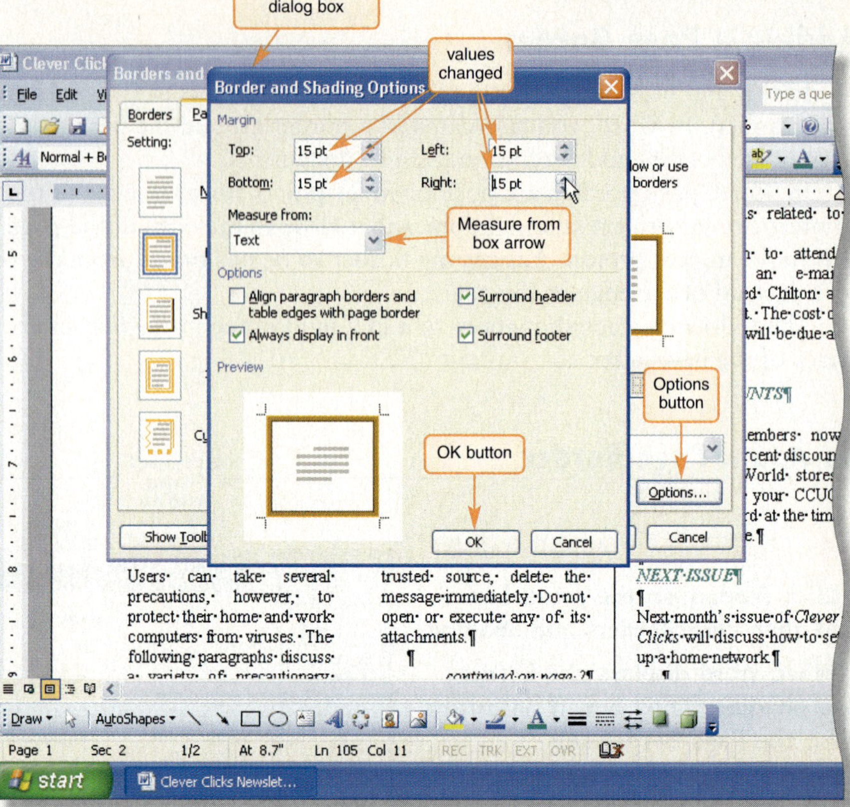

FIGURE 6-87

Other Ways

1. In Voice Command mode, say "Format, Borders and Shading, Page Border, [select settings], OK"

To see the borders on the newsletter, display both pages in the document window, as described in the following step.

To Zoom Two Pages

1 **Click the Zoom box arrow on the Standard toolbar and then click Two Pages.**

Word displays the pages of the newsletter in reduced form so that two pages display in the document window (Figure 6-88).

More About

Page Borders

To place an artistic border around a page, such as trees or balloons, click the Art box arrow in the Page Border sheet in the Borders and Shading dialog box (Figure 6-86 on the previous page), click the desired artistic border, and then click the OK button. To place a border around just a certain page in a document, you must place that page in a separate section and then instruct Word to place the border in just that section.

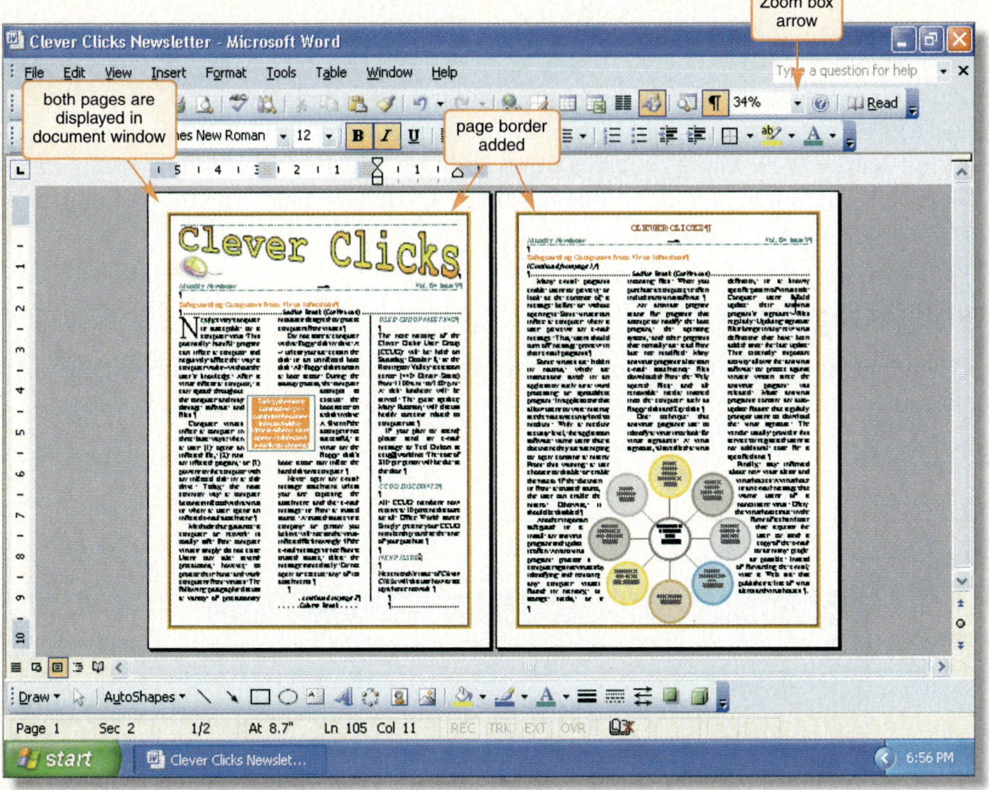

FIGURE 6-88

The following step returns the display to zoom page width.

To Zoom Page Width

1 **Click the Zoom box arrow on the Standard toolbar and then click Page Width.**

Word displays the page as wide as possible in the document window.

The newsletter now is complete. You should save the document again and print it, as described in the following series of steps.

To Save a Document

1 **With the disk containing the newsletter file in drive A, click the Save button on the Standard toolbar.**

Word saves the document again with the file name, Clever Clicks Newsletter.

To Print a Document

1 **Click the Print button on the Standard toolbar.**

The printed newsletter is shown in Figure 6-1 on page WD 379.

More About

Printing

If you want to save ink, print faster, or decrease printer overrun errors, print a draft. Click File on the menu bar, click Print, click the Options button, place a check mark in the Draft output check box, and then click the OK button in each dialog box.

Enhancing a Document for Online Viewing

Often, you will send documents to others online. For example, you may e-mail the Clever Clicks Newsletter instead of sending it via the postal service or you may publish it on the Web. Word provides some additional features for online documents. These include highlighted text, animated text, and backgrounds. The following pages illustrate each of these features.

> ***Other Ways***
>
> 1. In Voice Command mode, say "Highlight, [select text], Highlight"

Highlighting Text

Highlighting alerts a reader to online text's importance, much like a highlight marker does in a textbook. The following steps show how to highlight text yellow.

To Highlight Text

1

- **Scroll to display the feature article title, Safeguarding Computers from Virus Infections, on page 1.**
- **If the Highlight button on the Formatting toolbar displays yellow on its face, click the Highlight button; otherwise, click the Highlight button arrow and then click Yellow.**
- **Position the mouse pointer in the document window.**

The Highlight button is selected and displays yellow on its face (Figure 6-89). The mouse pointer is displayed as an I-beam with a highlighter attached to it when the Highlight button is selected.

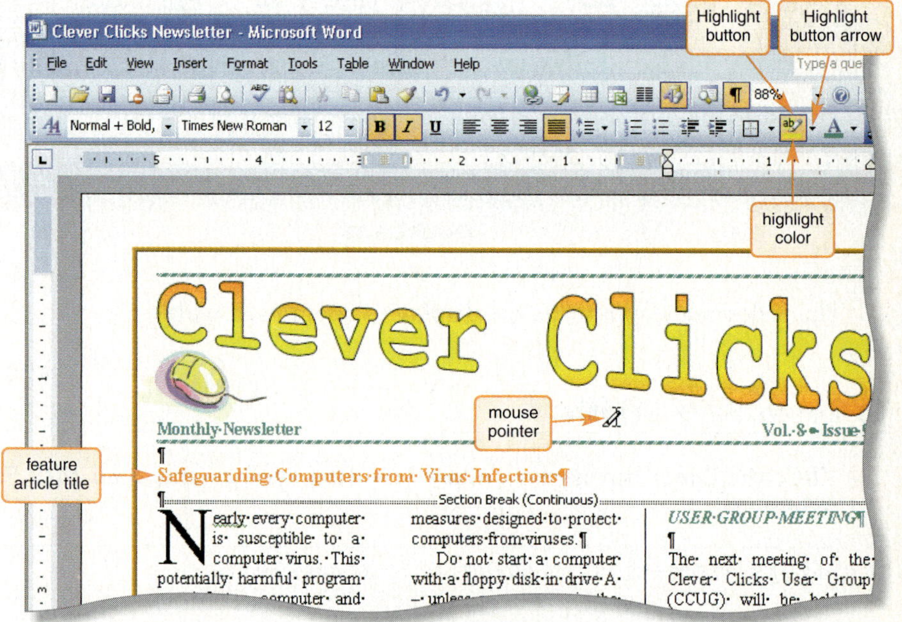

FIGURE 6-89

2

- **Drag through the feature article title, Safeguarding Computers from Virus Infections, to select it.**

Word highlights the selection yellow (Figure 6-90).

3

- **Click the Highlight button on the Formatting toolbar to turn off highlighting (shown in Figure 6-91).**

FIGURE 6-90

Word provides a variety of colors for highlighting text. If the Highlight button already displays your desired highlight color on its face, simply click the Highlight button to begin highlighting text. If you want to use a different highlight color, click the Highlight button arrow, select the desired highlight color, and then begin highlighting text.

If you wanted to remove a highlight, you would select the highlighted text, click the Highlight button arrow, and then click None.

If you scroll down to the second page of the newsletter, you will notice that the feature article title on the second page also is highlighted (shown in Figure 6-97 on page WD 440). Word automatically highlighted this text because earlier this project linked the nameplate on the second page to the nameplate on the first page. (In some instances, the highlight may not appear immediately.)

Animating Text

When you **animate text**, it has the appearance of motion. To animate text in Word, you select it and then apply one of the predefined text effects in the Text Effects sheet in the Font dialog box.

In this newsletter, you want to apply the Marching Black Ants text effect to the subhead USER GROUP MEETING. Once applied, the text has a moving black dashed rectangle around it.

The following steps show how to animate the words, USER GROUP MEETING, at the top of the announcements in the third column of the newsletter.

To Animate Text

1

- **Drag through the text to animate (in this case, USER GROUP MEETING).**
- **Right-click the selected text and then click Font on the shortcut menu.**
- **When Word displays the Font dialog box, if necessary, click the Text Effects tab.**
- **Click Marching Black Ants in the Animations list.**

The Preview area in the Font dialog box shows a sample of the selected animation (Figure 6-91).

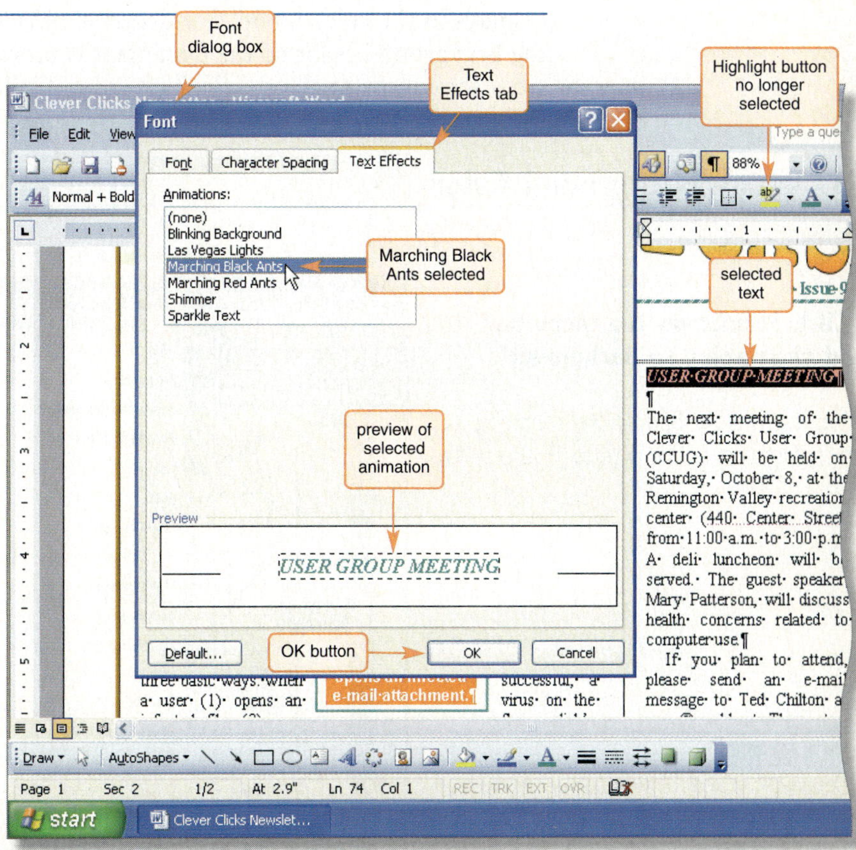

FIGURE 6-91

2

- **Click the OK button.**
- **Click outside the selected text.**

Word applies the selected animation to the text (Figure 6-92).

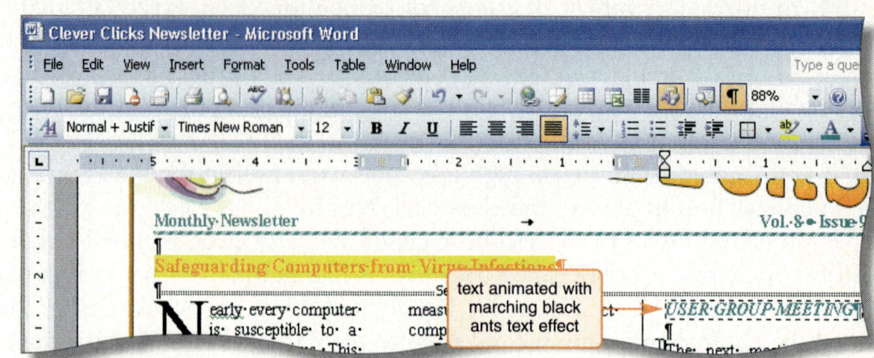

FIGURE 6-92

Other Ways

1. On Format menu click Font, click Text Effects tab, click desired animation, click OK button
2. In Voice Command mode, say "Format, Font, Text Effects, [select desired animation], OK"

If you wanted to remove animation from text, you would select the text, right-click the selection, click Font on the shortcut menu, click the Text Effects tab, click (none) in the Animations list, and then click the OK button.

If you print a document that contains animated text, the animations do not show on the hard copy; instead the text prints as regular text. Thus, animations are designed specifically for documents that will be viewed online.

Changing a Document's Background

In Word, the default background color is No Fill, which means the background displays in the color white. For documents viewed online, you may wish to change the background color so the document is more visually appealing. The following steps show how to change the background color of the newsletter to light turquoise.

To Change Background Color

1

- **Click Format on the menu bar and then point to Background.**

Word displays the Background submenu, which contains a color palette (Figure 6-93).

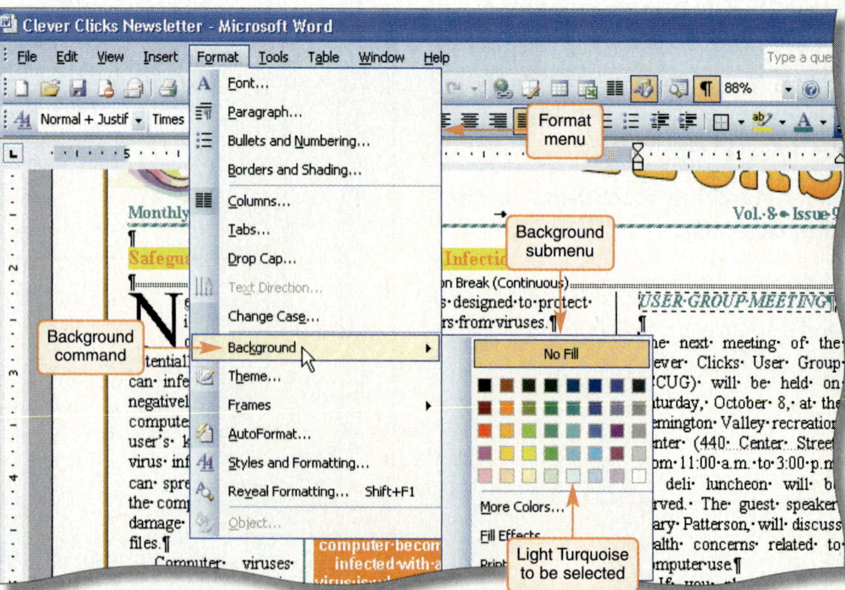

FIGURE 6-93

2

- **Click Light Turquoise on the color palette.**

Word changes the background color of the document to light turquoise (Figure 6-94).

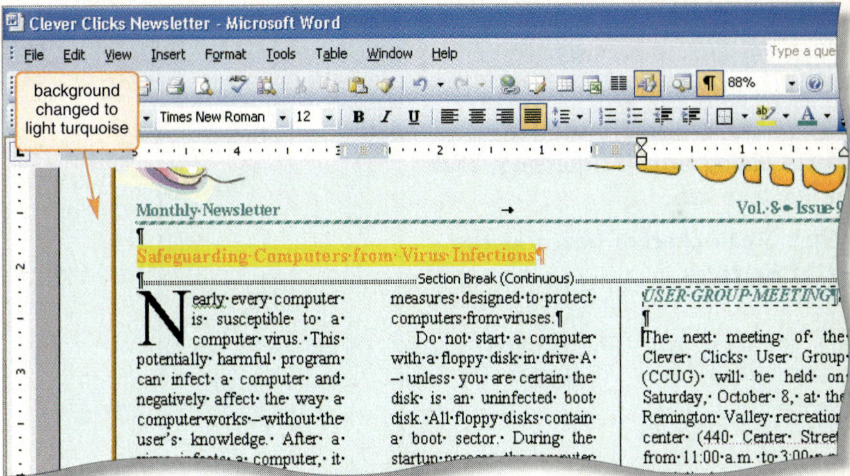

FIGURE 6-94

Other Ways

1. In Voice Command mode, say "Format, Background, [select color]"

When you change the background color of a document, Word places the solid color behind all text and graphics on the page. To soften the background, you can add patterns to the color. The following steps show how to add a pattern to the light turquoise background color.

To Add a Pattern Fill Effect to a Background

1

- **Click Format on the menu bar and then point to Background (Figure 6-95).**

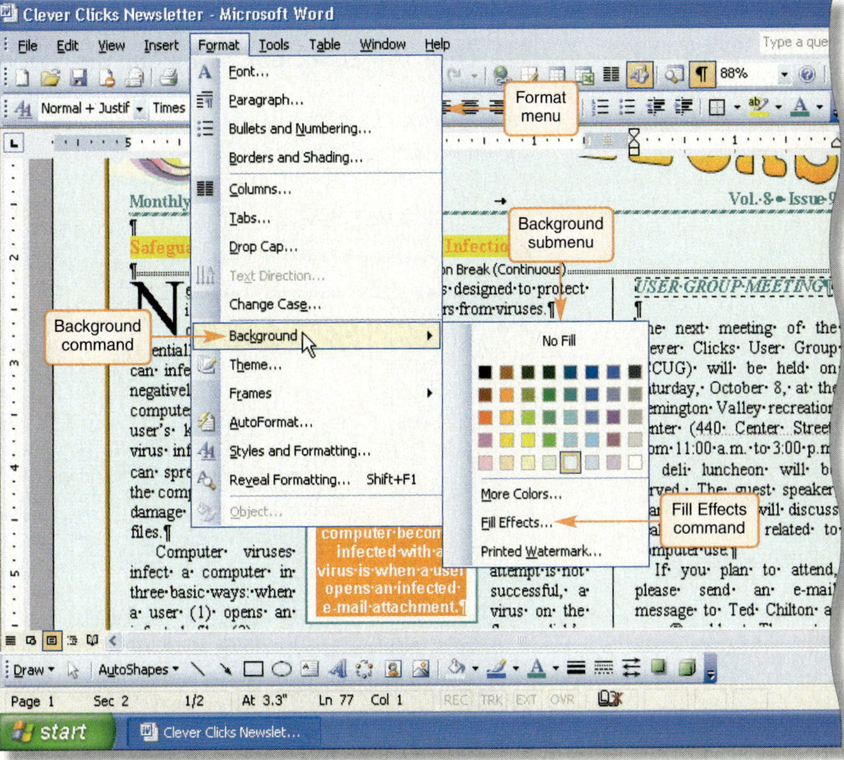

FIGURE 6-95

2

- **Click Fill Effects on the Background submenu.**
- **When Word displays the Fill Effects dialog box, if necessary, click the Pattern tab.**
- **Click Small checker board in the list of patterns.**

Word displays a sample of the selected pattern in the Fill Effects dialog box (Figure 6-96).

3

- **Click the OK button.**

Word applies the selected pattern to the document (shown in Figure 6-97).

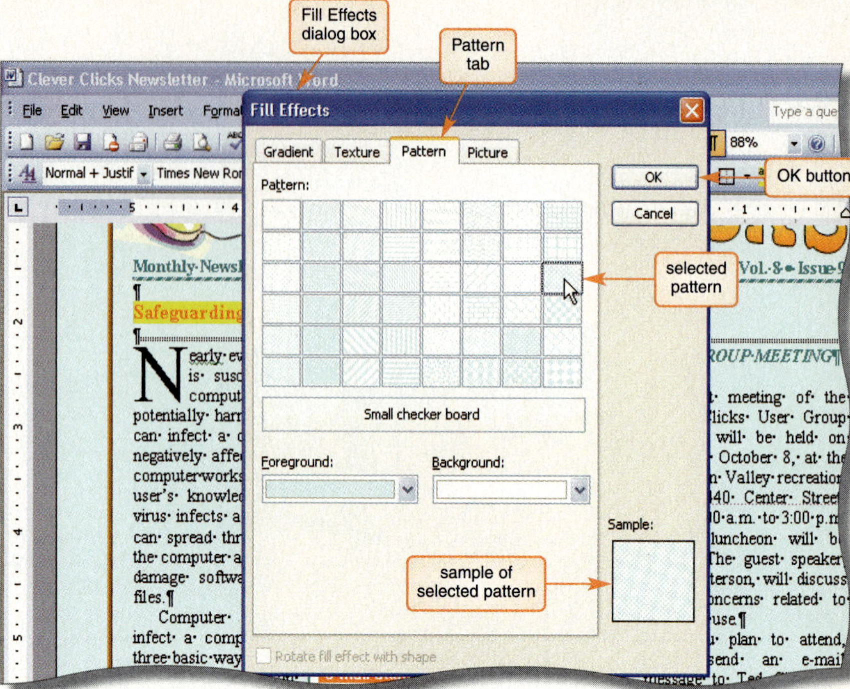

FIGURE 6-96

Other Ways

1. In Voice Command mode, say "Format, Background, Fill Effects, Pattern, [select pattern], OK"

To see the enhancements to the entire newsletter, display both pages in the document window, as described in the following step.

To Zoom Two Pages

1 **Click the Zoom box arrow on the Standard toolbar and then click Two Pages.**

Word displays the pages of the newsletter in reduced form so that two pages display in the document window (Figure 6-97).

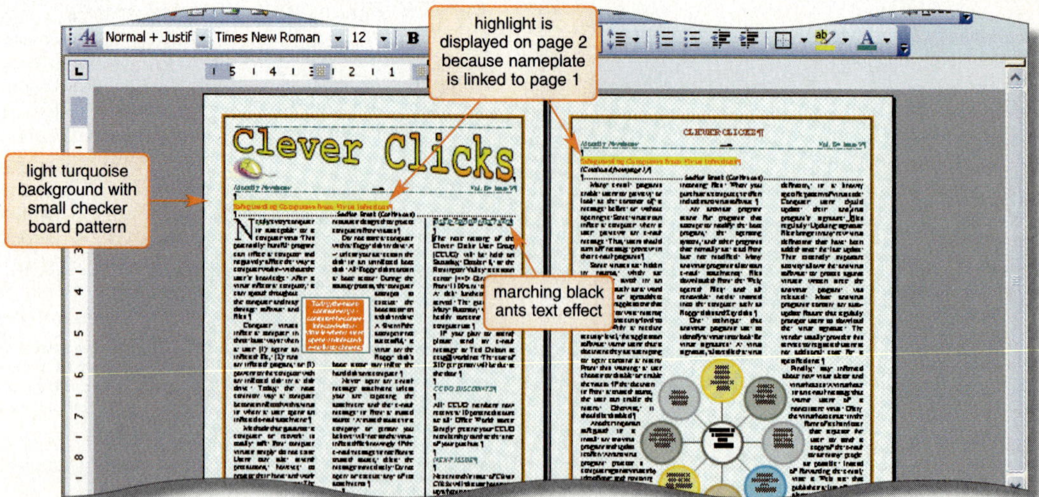

FIGURE 6-97

The following step returns the display to zoom page width.

To Zoom Page Width

1. **Click the Zoom box arrow on the Standard toolbar and then click Page Width.**

Word displays the page as wide as possible in the document window.

To keep the original newsletter intact, you should save the newsletter that was enhanced for online viewing with a new file name, as described in the following steps.

To Save a File with a New File Name

1. **Insert a floppy disk in drive A. Click File on the menu bar and then click Save As.**
2. **Type** `Clever Clicks Online Newsletter` **in the File name box. Do not press the ENTER key.**
3. **If necessary, click the Save in box arrow and then click 3½ Floppy (A:).**
4. **Click the Save button in the Save As dialog box.**

Word saves the document on a floppy disk in drive A with the file name, Clever Clicks Online Newsletter.

Splitting the Window and Arranging Open Windows

On some occasions, you may want to view two different portions of a document on the screen at the same time. For example, you may want to see the nameplate on the first page and the nameplate on the second page on the screen simultaneously.

Word allows you to split the window into two separate panes, each containing the current document and having its own scroll bar. This enables you to scroll to and view two different portions of the same document at the same time. The following steps show how to split the Word window.

To Split the Window

1

- **Position the mouse pointer on the split box at the top of the vertical scroll bar.**

*The mouse pointer changes to a **resize pointer**, which has two small horizontal lines each with a vertical arrow (Figure 6-98).*

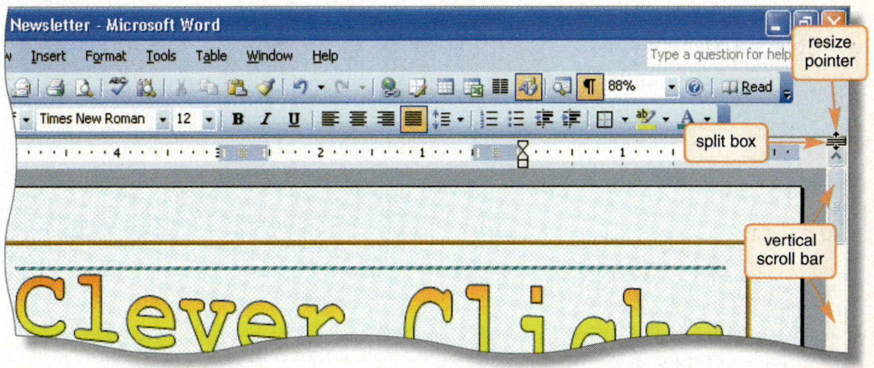

FIGURE 6-98

2

- **Drag the resize pointer about half-way down the screen.**

Word displays a split bar at the location of the resize pointer (Figure 6-99). The split bar will be positioned at the location you release the mouse.

3

- **Release the mouse button.**

Word places the current document in both the top and bottom panes.

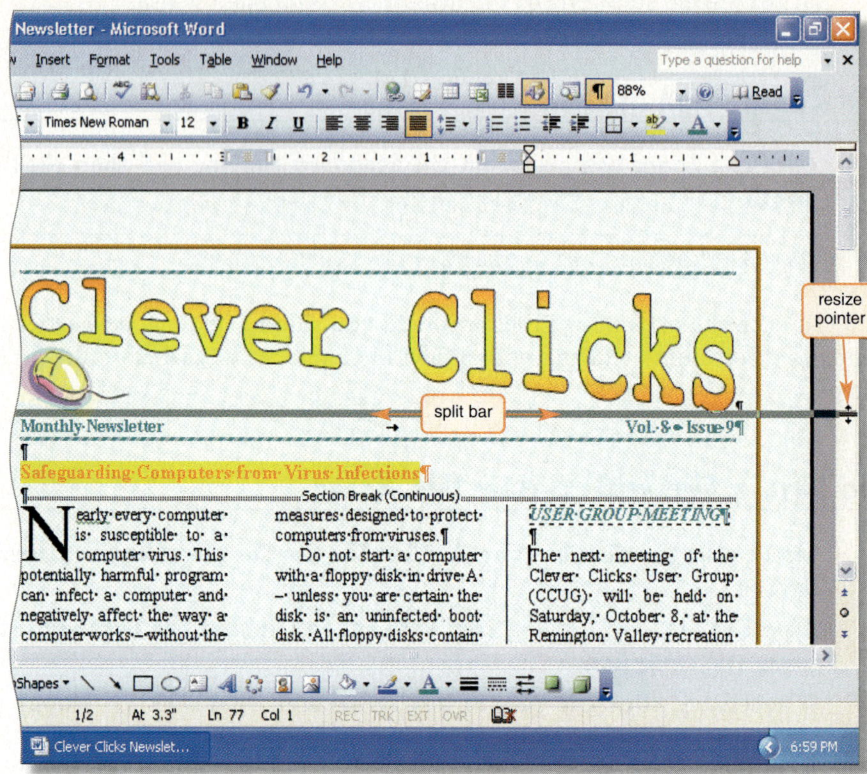

FIGURE 6-99

4

- **In the top pane, scroll to display the nameplate on page 1.**
- **In the bottom pane, scroll to display the nameplate on page 2.**

Word displays two separate parts of the same document on the screen simultaneously (Figure 6-100). The bottom pane does not show the background.

5

- **Double-click the split bar to return to a single Word window on the screen.**

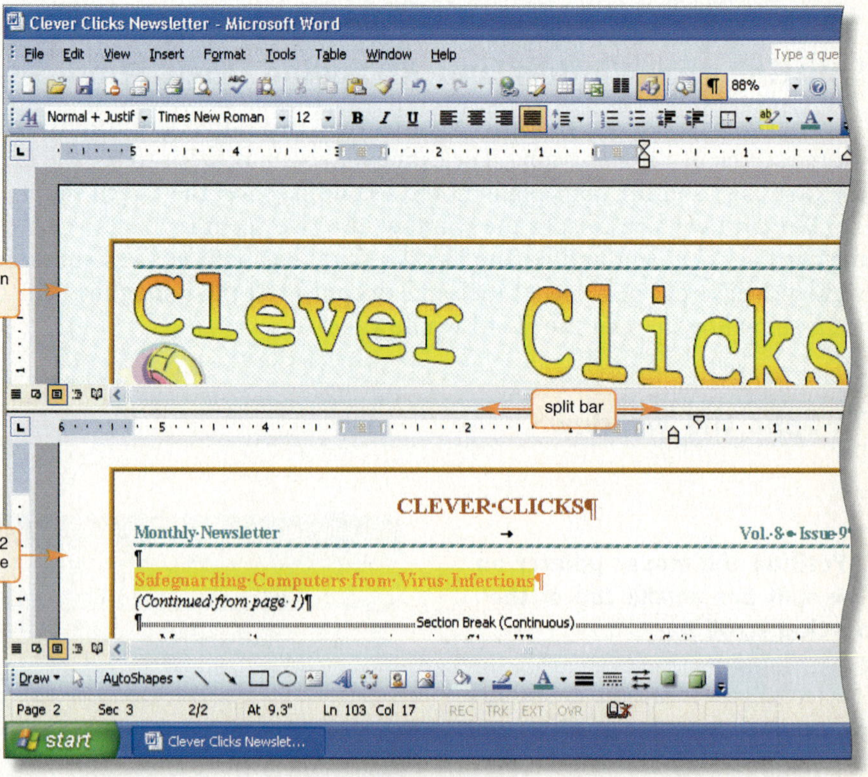

top of page 1 in upper pane

split bar

top of page 2 in lower pane

FIGURE 6-100

Other Ways

1. On Window menu click Split
2. In Voice Command mode, say "Window, Split"

Instead of double-clicking the split bar to return to a single Word window, you can click Window on the menu bar and then click Remove Split.

If you have multiple Word documents open and want to view all of them at the same time on the screen, you can instruct Word to arrange all the open documents on the screen from top to bottom.

More About

Splitting the Window

To move or copy text between parts of a long document, split the window into two panes. Display the text or graphics you want to move or copy in one pane and the destination for the text or graphics in the other pane, and then select and drag the text or graphics across the split bar.

To Arrange All Open Word Documents on the Screen

1. Click Window on the menu bar and then click Arrange All.

Word displays each open Word document on the screen.

To make one of the arranged documents fill the entire screen again, maximize the window by clicking its Maximize button or double-clicking its title bar.

If you have two documents that have similar content and you want to view and scroll through them at the same time, you can instruct Word to display them side by side.

To Display Two Documents Side by Side

1. Open the documents that you want to be displayed beside each other.
2. Click Window on the menu bar and then click Compare Side by Side with [file name].

*Word displays the **Compare Side by Side toolbar** on the screen. The two documents are beside each other, each in a separate window.*

You can scroll through each document as you do any other document. If you want to scroll through the two documents at the same time, click the Synchronous Scrolling button on the Compare Side by Side toolbar. To stop viewing the documents beside each other, click the Close Side by Side button on the Compare Side by Side toolbar.

Viewing a Document in Reading Layout

When you are finished with a document, you may want to proofread it. You could proofread a printout of the document or you could read it on the screen. If you prefer reading on the screen, Word provides a **reading layout view** that increases the readability and legibility of an onscreen document. Reading layout view is not WYSIWYG (what you see is what you get), which means the document in reading layout view does not represent how the document will look when it is printed.

The following steps show how to switch to reading layout view.

To Use Reading Layout View

1

• **Position the mouse pointer on the Read button on the Standard toolbar (Figure 6-101).**

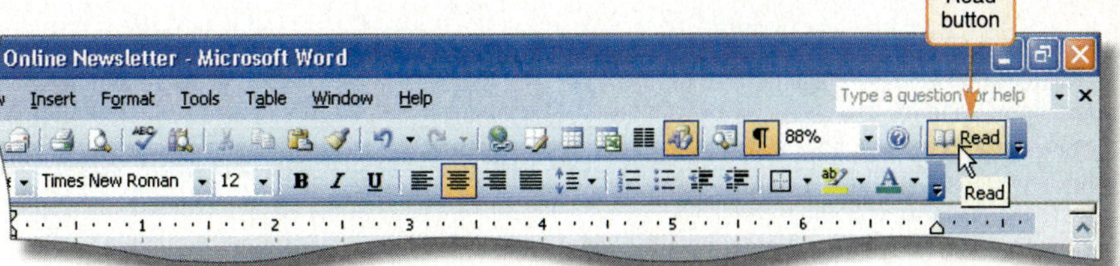

FIGURE 6-101

2

• **Click the Read button on the Standard toolbar.**

*Word switches to reading layout view (Figure 6-102). In reading layout view, Word hides all toolbars, except for the **Reading Layout toolbar** and the Reviewing toolbar.*

3

• **To close reading layout, click the Close button on the Reading Layout toolbar or press the ESCAPE key.**

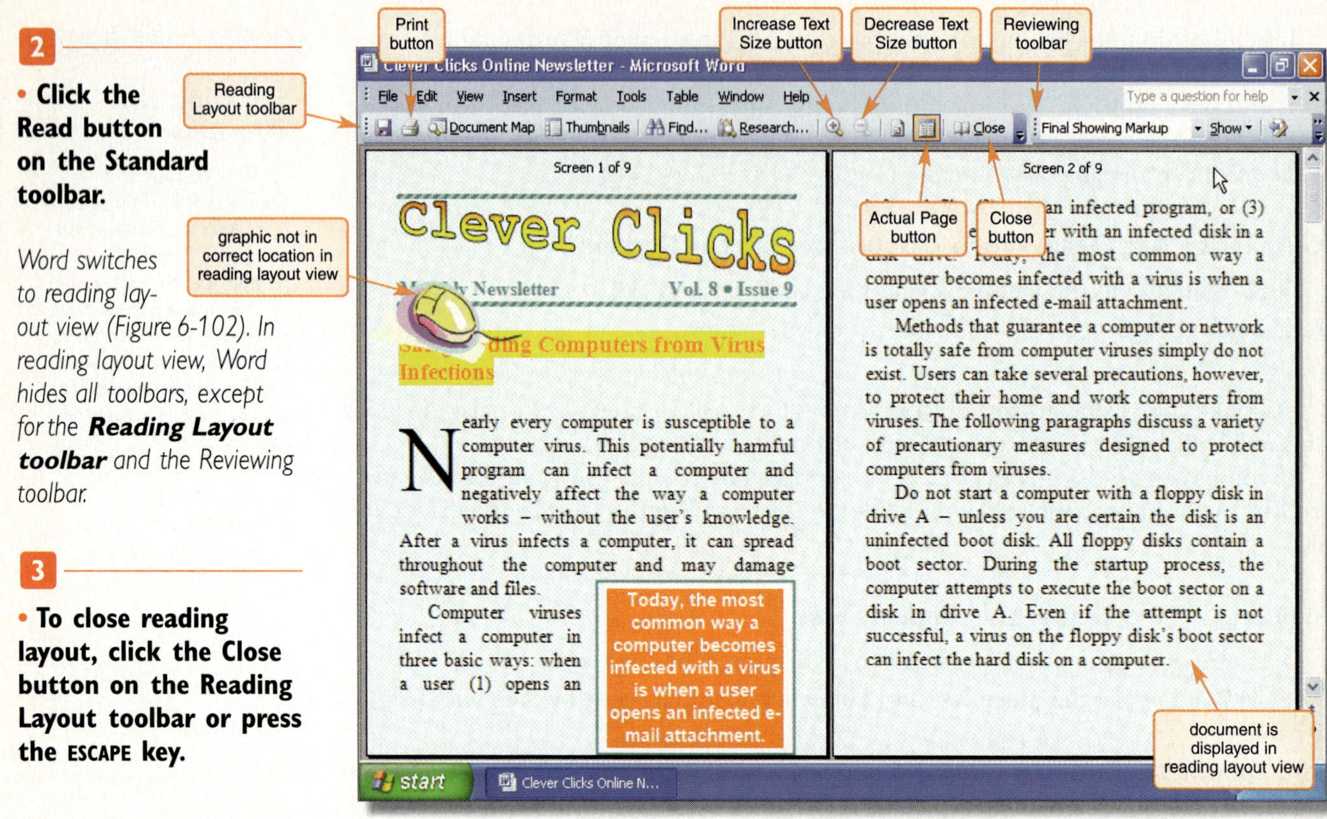

FIGURE 6-102

Other Ways

1. Click the Reading Layout view button on the horizontal scroll bar
2. On View menu, click Reading Layout
3. Press ALT+R
4. In Voice Command mode, say "Read"

Notice in reading layout view that the text is larger and easier to read. If you want to make the text on the screen even larger, click the Increase Text Size button on the Reading Layout toolbar. To make the text on the screen smaller, click the Decrease Text Size button on the Reading Layout toolbar. Adjusting text size in reading layout view does not change the font size of characters in the document.

In reading layout view, graphics and other elements do not display in their correct position because the view is designed for onscreen readability. To see the actual page layout, print the document by clicking the Print button on the Reading Layout toolbar or click the Actual Page button on the Reading Layout toolbar. To return to reading layout view, click the Actual Page button again.

You can edit the document in reading layout view the same way you edit a document in any other view. In reading layout view, Word displays the Reviewing toolbar so you can track changes as you edit the document. The Collaboration Feature that follows this project shows how to track changes using the Reviewing toolbar.

This project now is finished. The following step quits Word.

More About

Quick Reference

For a table that lists how to complete the tasks covered in this book using the mouse, menu, shortcut menu, and keyboard, see the Quick Reference Summary at the back of this book, or visit the Word 2003 Quick Reference Web page (scsite.com/wd2003/qr).

To Quit Word

1 **Click File on the menu bar and then click Exit.**

The Word window closes.

Project Summary

In creating the *Clever Clicks Newsletter* in this project, you learned how to create a professional looking newsletter using Word's desktop publishing features. First, the project discussed how to create a nameplate using a WordArt drawing object, borders for ruling lines, and a floating graphic. Next, you learned how to format the body of the newsletter into three columns and add a vertical rule between the second and third columns. You learned how to link one section of the document to another. The project showed how to create and format a pull-quote and also a diagram, and then how to move these graphical objects between columns. You learned how to use the Format Painter button and add a page border to the newsletter.

For documents that will be viewed online, the project showed how to highlight text, animate text, and add background colors and patterns. Finally, you learned how to split a document into two windows.

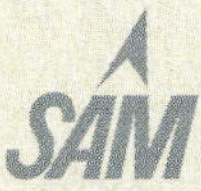

If you have a SAM user profile, you may have access to hands-on instruction, practice, and assessment of the skills covered in this project. Log in to your SAM account and go to your assignments page to see what your instructor has assigned.

What You Should Know

Having completed this project, you should be able to perform the tasks below. The tasks are listed in the same order they were presented in this project. For a list of the buttons, menus, toolbars, and commands introduced in this project, see the Quick Reference Summary at the back of this book and refer to the Page Number column.

1. Start and Customize Word (WD 380)
2. Display Formatting Marks (WD 381)
3. Zoom Page Width (WD 381, WD 435, WD 441)
4. Change All Margin Settings (WD 381)
5. Insert a WordArt Drawing Object (WD 383)
6. Format a WordArt Drawing Object (WD 384)
7. Change the Shape of a WordArt Drawing Object (WD 387)
8. Center the Newsletter Title (WD 387)
9. Use Borders to Add Ruling Lines (WD 388)
10. Clear Formatting (WD 388, WD 397)
11. Set a Right-Aligned Tab Stop (WD 389)
12. Insert a Symbol (WD 390)
13. Enter Text and Add a Border (WD 391)
14. Insert Clip Art from the Web (WD 392)
15. Insert a Graphic File from the Data Disk (WD 393)
16. Format a Graphic as Floating (WD 393)
17. Flip a Graphic (WD 394)
18. Not Use the Drawing Grid (WD 395)
19. Move a Graphic (WD 396)
20. Brighten a Graphic (WD 396)
21. Darken a Graphic (WD 396)
22. Format and Enter Text (WD 397, WD 417)
23. Save a Document (WD 398, WD 406, WD 415, WD 420, WD 429, WD 431, WD 435)
24. Insert a Continuous Section Break (WD 399)
25. Change the Number of Columns (WD 400)
26. Justify a Paragraph (WD 401)
27. Insert a File in the Newsletter (WD 402)
28. Format a Letter as a Drop Cap (WD 403)
29. Insert a Next Page Section Break (WD 404)
30. Enter Text (WD 405, WD 419)
31. Insert a Column Break (WD 406)
32. Insert a File in a Column of the Newsletter (WD 407)
33. Display a Document in Full Screen View (WD 407)
34. Justify Paragraphs (WD 408)
35. Place a Vertical Rule between Columns (WD 409)
36. Insert a Text Box (WD 411)
37. Format a Text Box (WD 412)
38. Shade a Paragraph (WD 413)
39. Format Text (WD 414, WD 428)

(continued)

What You Should Know *(continued)*

40. Resize a Text Box (WD 414)
41. Position a Text Box (WD 415)
42. Change Column Formatting (WD 416)
43. Link a Copied Item (WD 418)
44. Balance Columns (WD 420)
45. Insert a Diagram (WD 421)
46. Zoom to a Percentage (WD 422)
47. Add Segments to a Diagram (WD 423)
48. Add Text to a Diagram (WD 423)
49. Enter More Diagram Text (WD 424)
50. AutoFormat a Diagram (WD 425)
51. Resize a Diagram (WD 426)
52. Zoom to 100% (WD 426)
53. Format a Graphic as Floating (WD 427)
54. Use the Format Painter Button (WD 427, WD 432)
55. Copy and Paste a Diagram (WD 430)
56. Color a Drop Cap (WD 432)
57. Add a Page Border (WD 433)
58. Zoom Two Pages (WD 434, WD 440)
59. Print a Document (WD 435)
60. Highlight Text (WD 436)
61. Animate Text (WD 437)
62. Change Background Color (WD 438)
63. Add a Pattern Fill Effect to a Background (WD 439)
64. Save a File with a New File Name (WD 441)
65. Split the Window (WD 441)
66. Arrange All Open Word Documents on the Screen (WD 443)
67. Display Two Documents Side by Side (WD 443)
68. Use Reading Layout View (WD 443)
69. Quit Word (WD 444)

More About

Certification

The Microsoft Office Specialist Certification program provides an opportunity for you to obtain a valuable industry credential - proof that you have the Word 2003 skills required by employers. For more information, see Appendix E or visit the Word 2003 Certification Web page (scsite.com/wd2003/cert).

Learn It Online

Instructions: To complete the Learn It Online exercises, start your browser, click the Address bar, and then enter the Web address `scsite.com/wd2003/learn`. When the Word 2003 Learn It Online page is displayed, follow the instructions in the exercises below. Each exercise has instructions for printing your results, either for your own records or for submission to your instructor.

1 Project Reinforcement TF, MC, and SA

Below Word Project 6, click the Project Reinforcement link. Print the quiz by clicking Print on the File menu for each page. Answer each question.

2 Flash Cards

Below Word Project 6, click the Flash Cards link and read the instructions. Type 20 (or a number specified by your instructor) in the Number of playing cards text box, type your name in the Enter your Name text box, and then click the Flip Card button. When the flash card is displayed, read the question and then click the ANSWER box arrow to select an answer. Flip through Flash Cards. If your score is 15 (75%) correct or greater, click Print on the File menu to print your results. If your score is less than 15 (75%) correct, then redo this exercise by clicking the Replay button.

3 Test

Below Word Project 6, click the Practice Test link. Answer each question, enter your first and last name at the bottom of the page, and then click the Grade Test button. When the graded practice test is displayed on your screen, click Print on the File menu to print a hard copy. Continue to take practice tests until you score 80% or better.

4 Who Wants To Be a Computer Genius?

Below Word Project 6, click the Computer Genius link. Read the instructions, enter your first and last name at the bottom of the page, and then click the PLAY button. When your score is displayed, click the PRINT RESULTS link to print a hard copy.

5 Wheel of Terms

Below Word Project 6, click the Wheel of Terms link. Read the instructions, and then enter your first and last name and your school name. Click the PLAY button. When your score is displayed, right-click the score and then click Print on the shortcut menu to print a hard copy.

6 Crossword Puzzle Challenge

Below Word Project 6, click the Crossword Puzzle Challenge link. Read the instructions, and then enter your first and last name. Click the SUBMIT button. Work the crossword puzzle. When you are finished, click the Submit button. When the crossword puzzle is redisplayed, click the Print Puzzle button to print a hard copy.

7 Tips and Tricks

Below Word Project 6, click the Tips and Tricks link. Click a topic that pertains to Project 6. Right-click the information and then click Print on the shortcut menu. Construct a brief example of what the information relates to in Word to confirm you understand how to use the tip or trick.

8 Newsgroups

Below Word Project 6, click the Newsgroups link. Click a topic that pertains to Project 6. Print three comments.

9 Expanding Your Horizons

Below Word Project 6, click the Articles for Microsoft Word link. Click a topic that pertains to Project 6. Print the information. Construct a brief example of what the information relates to in Word to confirm you understand the contents of the article.

10 Search Sleuth

Below Word Project 6, click the Search Sleuth link. To search for a term that pertains to this project, select a term below the Project 6 title and then use the Google search engine at google.com (or any major search engine) to display and print two Web pages that present information on the term.

11 Word Online Training

Below Word Project 6, click the Word Online Training link. When your browser displays the Microsoft Office Online Web page, click the Word link. Click one of the Word courses that covers one or more of the objectives listed at the beginning of the project on page WD 378. Print the first page of the course before stepping through it.

12 Office Marketplace

Below Word Project 6, click the Office Marketplace link. When your browser displays the Microsoft Office Online Web page, click the Office Marketplace link. Click a topic that relates to Word. Print the first page.

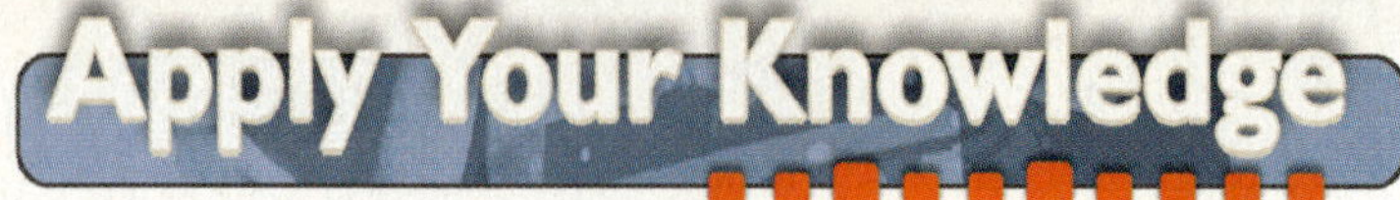

1 Enhancing a Document for Online Viewing

Instructions: Start Word. Open the document, Apply 6-1 Certification Information, on the Data Disk. If you did not download the Data Disk, see the inside back cover for instructions for downloading the Data Disk or see your instructor.

You are to modify the document for online viewing (Figure 6-103).

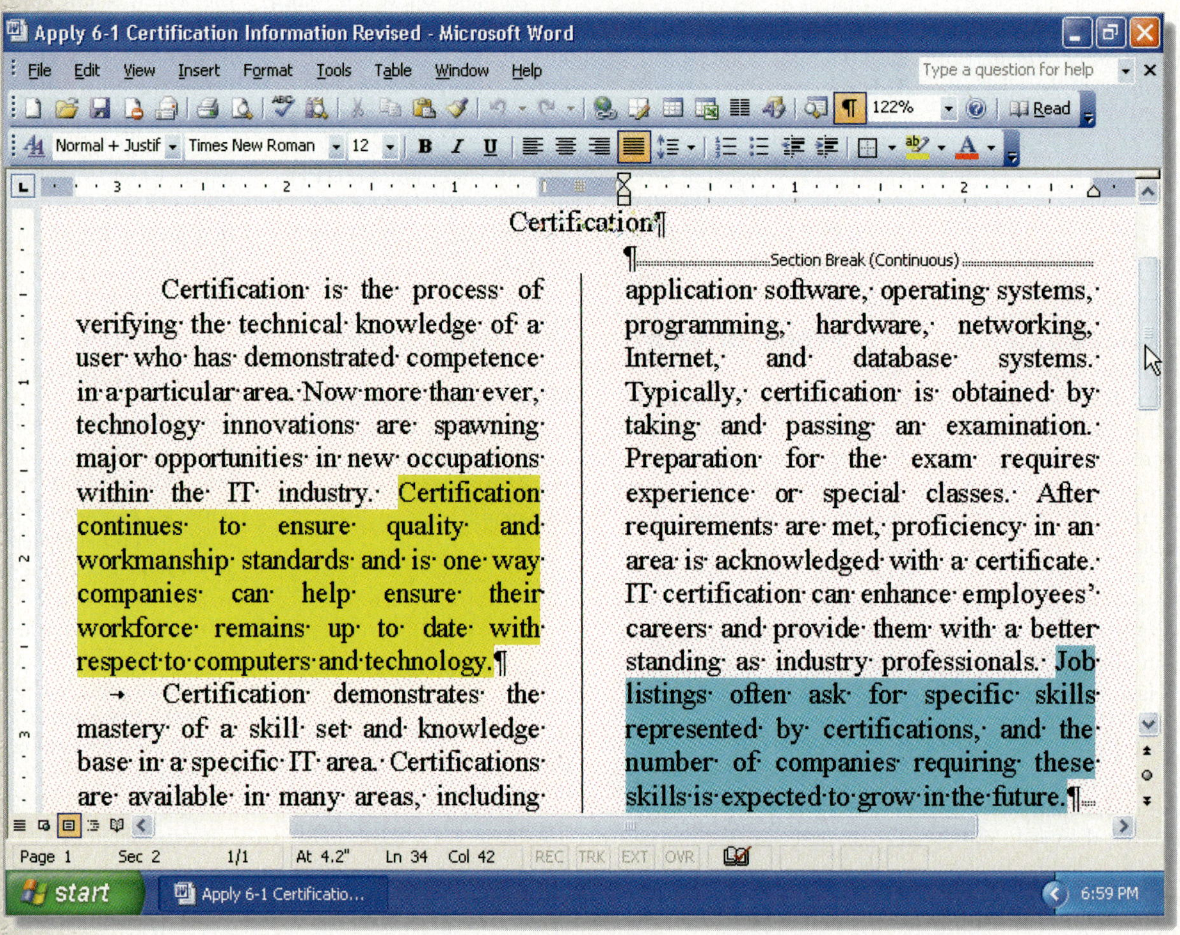

Apply 6-1 Certification Information Revised - Microsoft Word

Certification¶

Section Break (Continuous)

Certification is the process of verifying the technical knowledge of a user who has demonstrated competence in a particular area. Now more than ever, technology innovations are spawning major opportunities in new occupations within the IT industry. Certification continues to ensure quality and workmanship standards and is one way companies can help ensure their workforce remains up to date with respect to computers and technology.¶

Certification demonstrates the mastery of a skill set and knowledge base in a specific IT area. Certifications are available in many areas, including application software, operating systems, programming, hardware, networking, Internet, and database systems. Typically, certification is obtained by taking and passing an examination. Preparation for the exam requires experience or special classes. After requirements are met, proficiency in an area is acknowledged with a certificate. IT certification can enhance employees' careers and provide them with a better standing as industry professionals. Job listings often ask for specific skills represented by certifications, and the number of companies requiring these skills is expected to grow in the future.¶

Page 1 Sec 2 1/1 At 4.2" Ln 34 Col 42 REC TRK EXT OVR

start Apply 6-1 Certificatio... 6:59 PM

FIGURE 6-103

Apply Your Knowledge

Perform the following tasks:

1. For the two paragraphs below the title, change their alignment from left-aligned to justified.
2. Insert a continuous section break to the left of the first paragraph of text. In section 2, change the number of columns from one to two.
3. Balance the two columns by inserting a continuous section break at the end of the text.
4. Use the Columns dialog box (Format menu, Columns command) to draw a line between the two columns in section 2 of the document. ***Hint***: Be sure the insertion point is in section 2 before displaying the Columns dialog box.
5. Highlight the last sentence in the first paragraph in turquoise. Highlight the last sentence in the second paragraph in yellow.
6. Apply the Sparkle Text animation text effect to the title above the columns.
7. Change the background color of the document to rose.
8. Change the pattern fill effect of the background color to Small confetti.
9. Save the revised document with the name Apply 6-1 Certification Information Revised.
10. Print the document.
11. View the document in full screen view. In reading layout view, increase the text size and then decrease the text size. On the printout, write down how a document looks in full screen view. Close full screen view.
12. View the document in reading layout view. On the printout, write down how a document looks in reading layout view. Close reading layout view.
13. Split the window. Scroll through the document in the top window. Scroll through the document in the bottom window. Remove the split window. On the printout, write down the purpose of splitting a window.

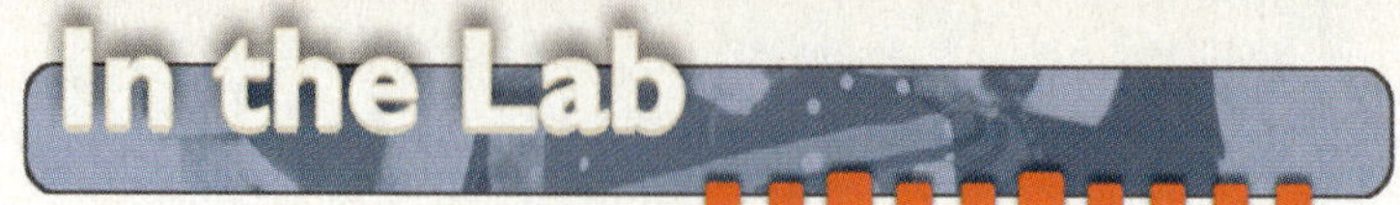

1 Creating a Newsletter with a Pull-Quote and an Article on File

Problem: You are an editor of the newsletter, Old Town Historical. The next edition is due out in one week. This issue's article will discuss the funding of a historic home renovation (Figure 6-104). The text for the feature article is on the Data Disk. If you did not download the Data Disk, see the inside back cover for instructions for downloading the Data Disk or see your instructor. You need to create the nameplate and the pull-quote.

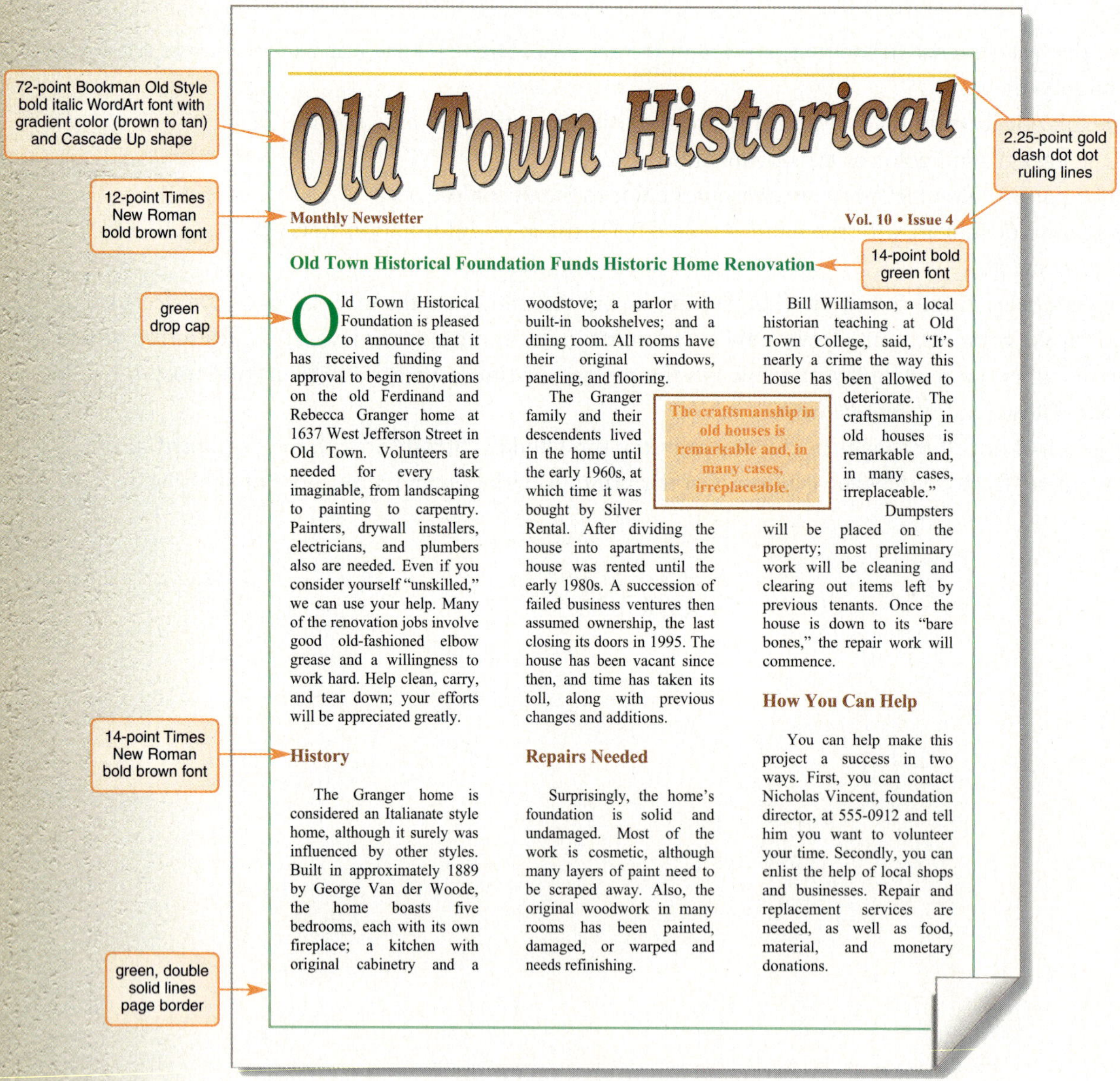

72-point Bookman Old Style bold italic WordArt font with gradient color (brown to tan) and Cascade Up shape

12-point Times New Roman bold brown font

green drop cap

14-point Times New Roman bold brown font

green, double solid lines page border

2.25-point gold dash dot dot ruling lines

14-point bold green font

Old Town Historical

Monthly Newsletter | Vol. 10 • Issue 4

Old Town Historical Foundation Funds Historic Home Renovation

Old Town Historical Foundation is pleased to announce that it has received funding and approval to begin renovations on the old Ferdinand and Rebecca Granger home at 1637 West Jefferson Street in Old Town. Volunteers are needed for every task imaginable, from landscaping to painting to carpentry. Painters, drywall installers, electricians, and plumbers also are needed. Even if you consider yourself "unskilled," we can use your help. Many of the renovation jobs involve good old-fashioned elbow grease and a willingness to work hard. Help clean, carry, and tear down; your efforts will be appreciated greatly.

History

The Granger home is considered an Italianate style home, although it surely was influenced by other styles. Built in approximately 1889 by George Van der Woode, the home boasts five bedrooms, each with its own fireplace; a kitchen with original cabinetry and a woodstove; a parlor with built-in bookshelves; and a dining room. All rooms have their original windows, paneling, and flooring.

The Granger family and their descendents lived in the home until the early 1960s, at which time it was bought by Silver Rental. After dividing the house into apartments, the house was rented until the early 1980s. A succession of failed business ventures then assumed ownership, the last closing its doors in 1995. The house has been vacant since then, and time has taken its toll, along with previous changes and additions.

Repairs Needed

Surprisingly, the home's foundation is solid and undamaged. Most of the work is cosmetic, although many layers of paint need to be scraped away. Also, the original woodwork in many rooms has been painted, damaged, or warped and needs refinishing.

Bill Williamson, a local historian teaching at Old Town College, said, "It's nearly a crime the way this house has been allowed to deteriorate. The craftsmanship in old houses is remarkable and, in many cases, irreplaceable."

> The craftsmanship in old houses is remarkable and, in many cases, irreplaceable.

Dumpsters will be placed on the property; most preliminary work will be cleaning and clearing out items left by previous tenants. Once the house is down to its "bare bones," the repair work will commence.

How You Can Help

You can help make this project a success in two ways. First, you can contact Nicholas Vincent, foundation director, at 555-0912 and tell him you want to volunteer your time. Secondly, you can enlist the help of local shops and businesses. Repair and replacement services are needed, as well as food, material, and monetary donations.

FIGURE 6-104

In the Lab

Instructions:

1. Change all margins to .75 inches. Depending on your printer, you may need different margin settings.
2. Create the nameplate using the formats identified in Figure 6-104. Insert the dot symbol between the volume and issue.
3. Create a continuous section break below the nameplate.
4. Format section 2 to three columns.
5. Insert the Lab 6-1 Home Renovation Article on the Data Disk into section 2 below the nameplate.
6. Format the newsletter according to Figure 6-104. Use the Format Painter button to copy formatting from the first subhead to remaining subheads.
7. Insert a continuous section break at the end of the document to balance the columns.
8. The text for the pull-quote is in the Repairs Needed section of the article. Copy the text and then insert it into a text box. Change the line color of the text box to brown, and the line weight to 1½ point. Format the characters in the pull-quote to bold orange font. Shade the paragraph tan. Resize the text box so it matches Figure 6-104. Position the text box as shown in Figure 6-104.
9. Add the page border as shown in the figure.
10. View the document in print preview. If it does not fit on a single page, click the Shrink to Fit button on the Print Preview toolbar or reduce the size of the WordArt object.
11. Save the document with Lab 6-1 Old Town Newsletter as the file name.
12. Print the newsletter.

2 Creating a Newsletter with a Diagram and an Article on File

Problem: You are responsible for the monthly preparation of Northside Newcomers, a newsletter for community members. The next edition welcomes those new to the community (Figure 6-105 on the next page). This article already has been prepared and is on the Data Disk. If you did not download the Data Disk, see the inside back cover for instructions for downloading the Data Disk or see your instructor. You need to create the nameplate and the diagram.

Instructions:

1. Change all margins to .75 inches. Depending on your printer, you may need different margin settings.
2. Create the nameplate using the formats identified in Figure 6-105. If necessary, resize the WordArt object. Insert the dot symbol between the volume and issue. Use the Clip Art task pane to locate the image shown, or use a similar graphic. Change its wrapping style to In front of text. Darken the graphic. If necessary, resize the graphic.
3. Create a continuous section break below the nameplate.
4. Format section 2 to three columns.
5. Insert the Lab 6-2 Northside Newcomers Article on the Data Disk into section 2 below the nameplate.
6. Format the newsletter according to Figure 6-105. Use the Format Painter button to format the subheads.
7. Insert a continuous section break at the end of the document to balance the columns.
8. Place a border to the left of the Next Month section.
9. Add the page border as shown in the figure.

(continued)

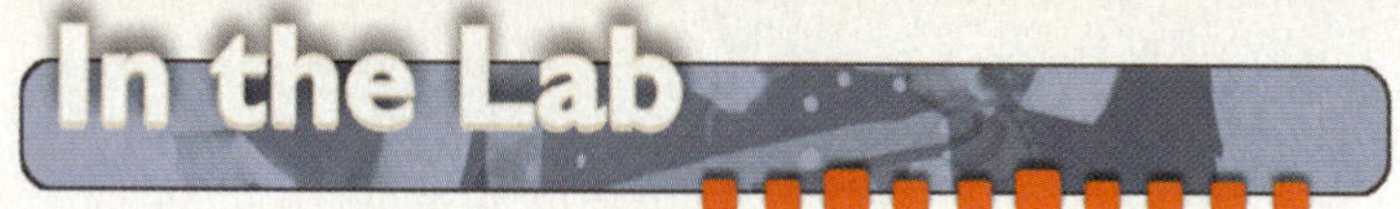

Creating a Newsletter with a Diagram and an Article on File *(continued)*

10. Create the pyramid diagram shown in Figure 6-105 in a separate document window. Change its height to 3.78 inches and its width to 3.39 inches. Remember to deselect the Lock aspect ratio check box. AutoFormat it to the square shadows style. Change its wrapping style to tight. Save the diagram with the file name Lab 6-2 Clubs Diagram. Copy and paste the diagram into the newsletter.
11. Save the document using Lab 6-2 Northside Newcomers Newsletter as the file name.
12. Arrange both documents (the diagram and the newsletter) on the screen. Scroll through both open windows. Maximize the newsletter window.
13. Switch to full screen view and read through the newsletter. Close full screen view.
14. Print the newsletter.

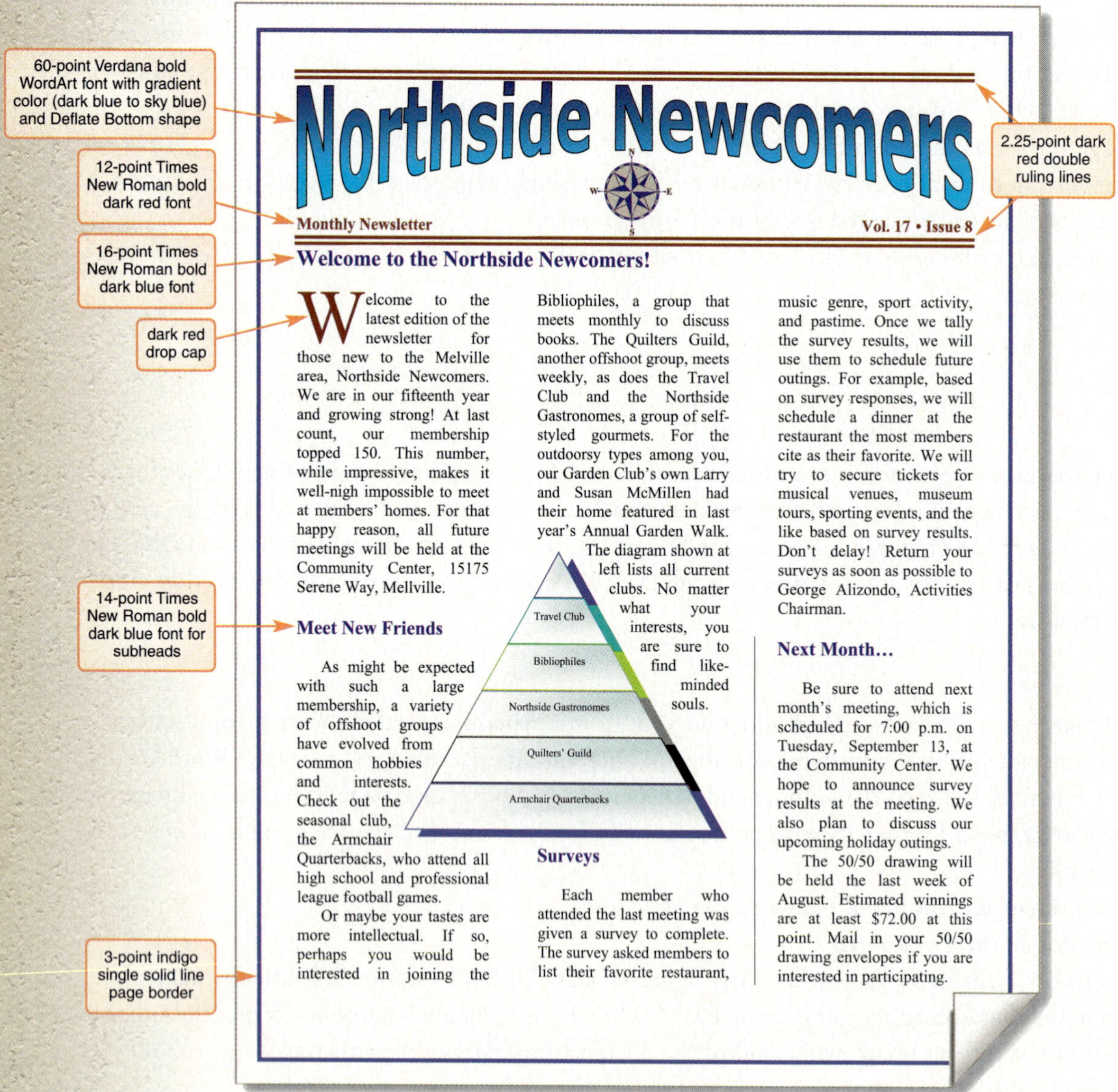

60-point Verdana bold WordArt font with gradient color (dark blue to sky blue) and Deflate Bottom shape

12-point Times New Roman bold dark red font

16-point Times New Roman bold dark blue font

dark red drop cap

14-point Times New Roman bold dark blue font for subheads

3-point indigo single solid line page border

2.25-point dark red double ruling lines

Northside Newcomers

Monthly Newsletter **Vol. 17 • Issue 8**

Welcome to the Northside Newcomers!

Welcome to the latest edition of the newsletter for those new to the Melville area, Northside Newcomers. We are in our fifteenth year and growing strong! At last count, our membership topped 150. This number, while impressive, makes it well-nigh impossible to meet at members' homes. For that happy reason, all future meetings will be held at the Community Center, 15175 Serene Way, Mellville.

Meet New Friends

As might be expected with such a large membership, a variety of offshoot groups have evolved from common hobbies and interests. Check out the seasonal club, the Armchair Quarterbacks, who attend all high school and professional league football games.

Or maybe your tastes are more intellectual. If so, perhaps you would be interested in joining the Bibliophiles, a group that meets monthly to discuss books. The Quilters Guild, another offshoot group, meets weekly, as does the Travel Club and the Northside Gastronomes, a group of self-styled gourmets. For the outdoorsy types among you, our Garden Club's own Larry and Susan McMillen had their home featured in last year's Annual Garden Walk.

Travel Club
Bibliophiles
Northside Gastronomes
Quilters' Guild
Armchair Quarterbacks

The diagram shown at left lists all current clubs. No matter what your interests, you are sure to find like-minded souls.

Surveys

Each member who attended the last meeting was given a survey to complete. The survey asked members to list their favorite restaurant, music genre, sport activity, and pastime. Once we tally the survey results, we will use them to schedule future outings. For example, based on survey responses, we will schedule a dinner at the restaurant the most members cite as their favorite. We will try to secure tickets for musical venues, museum tours, sporting events, and the like based on survey results. Don't delay! Return your surveys as soon as possible to George Alizondo, Activities Chairman.

Next Month…

Be sure to attend next month's meeting, which is scheduled for 7:00 p.m. on Tuesday, September 13, at the Community Center. We hope to announce survey results at the meeting. We also plan to discuss our upcoming holiday outings.

The 50/50 drawing will be held the last week of August. Estimated winnings are at least $72.00 at this point. Mail in your 50/50 drawing envelopes if you are interested in participating.

FIGURE 6-105

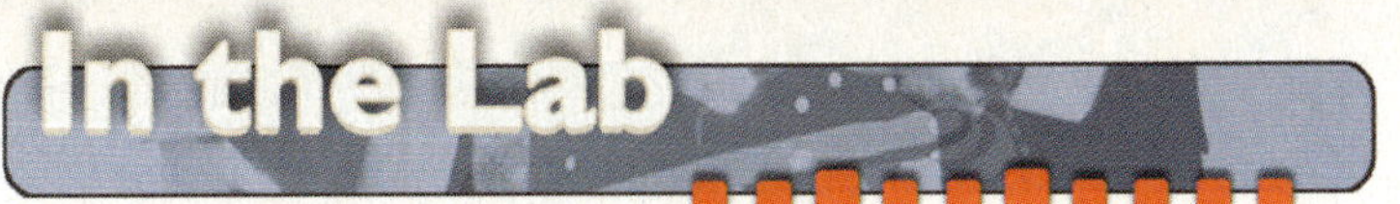

3 Creating a Newsletter from Scratch

Problem: You work part-time for Valley Vista Apartments, which publishes a newsletter for all tenants. Figure 6-106 shows the contents of the next issue.

Instructions:

1. Change all margins to .75 inches. Depending on your printer, you may need different margin settings.
2. Create the nameplate using the formats identified in Figure 6-106. ***Hint:*** Use the Shadow Style button on the Drawing toolbar to apply the shadow effect to the WordArt object in the nameplate. ***Hint:*** Use a tab leader character to fill the space in the middle of the issue information line. Insert the diamond symbol between the volume and issue.

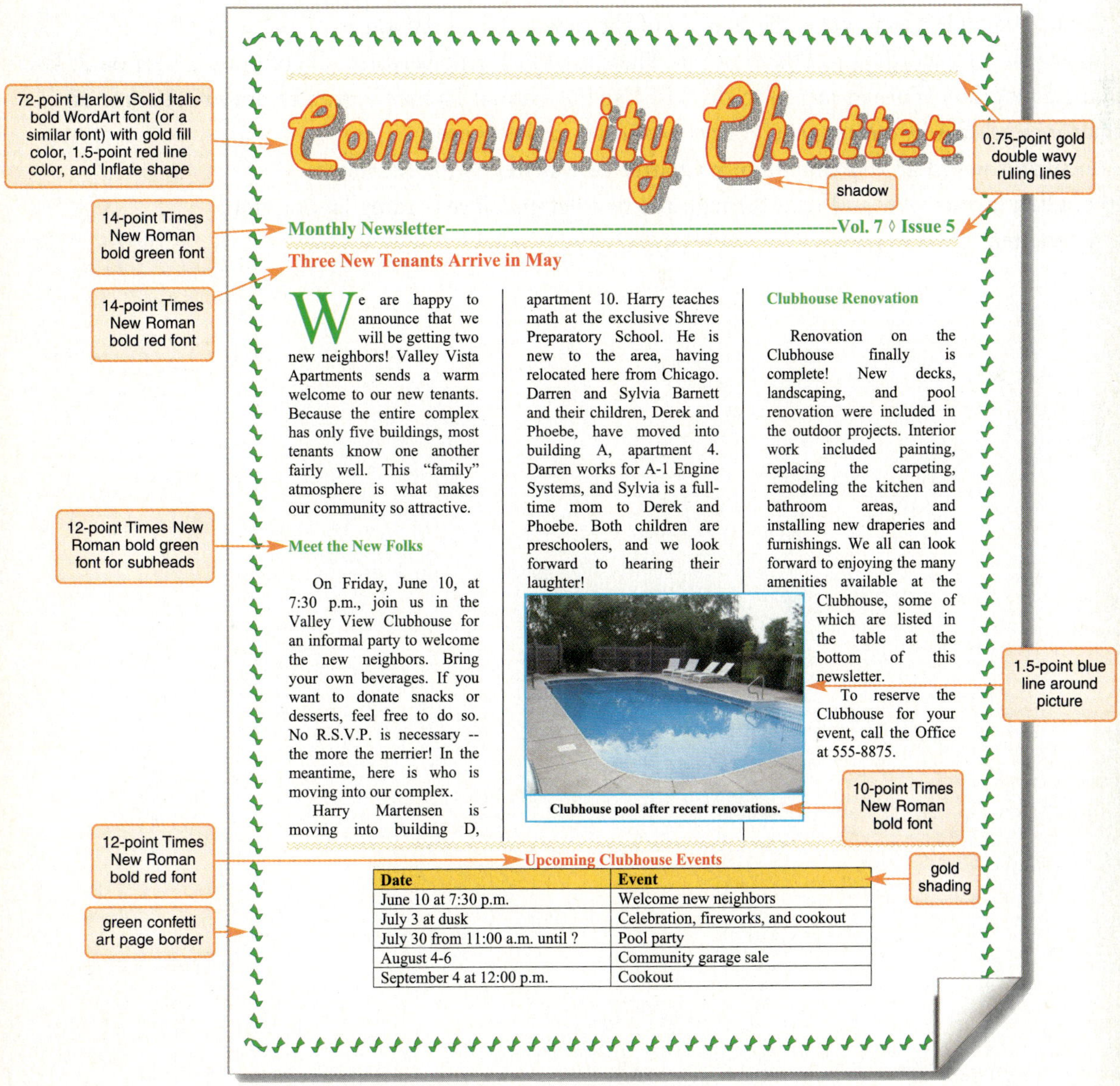

72-point Harlow Solid Italic bold WordArt font (or a similar font) with gold fill color, 1.5-point red line color, and Inflate shape

0.75-point gold double wavy ruling lines

shadow

14-point Times New Roman bold green font

14-point Times New Roman bold red font

12-point Times New Roman bold green font for subheads

1.5-point blue line around picture

10-point Times New Roman bold font

12-point Times New Roman bold red font

gold shading

green confetti art page border

Community Chatter

Monthly Newsletter--Vol. 7 ◊ Issue 5

Three New Tenants Arrive in May

We are happy to announce that we will be getting two new neighbors! Valley Vista Apartments sends a warm welcome to our new tenants. Because the entire complex has only five buildings, most tenants know one another fairly well. This "family" atmosphere is what makes our community so attractive.

Meet the New Folks

On Friday, June 10, at 7:30 p.m., join us in the Valley View Clubhouse for an informal party to welcome the new neighbors. Bring your own beverages. If you want to donate snacks or desserts, feel free to do so. No R.S.V.P. is necessary -- the more the merrier! In the meantime, here is who is moving into our complex.

Harry Martensen is moving into building D, apartment 10. Harry teaches math at the exclusive Shreve Preparatory School. He is new to the area, having relocated here from Chicago. Darren and Sylvia Barnett and their children, Derek and Phoebe, have moved into building A, apartment 4. Darren works for A-1 Engine Systems, and Sylvia is a full-time mom to Derek and Phoebe. Both children are preschoolers, and we look forward to hearing their laughter!

Clubhouse pool after recent renovations.

Clubhouse Renovation

Renovation on the Clubhouse finally is complete! New decks, landscaping, and pool renovation were included in the outdoor projects. Interior work included painting, replacing the carpeting, remodeling the kitchen and bathroom areas, and installing new draperies and furnishings. We all can look forward to enjoying the many amenities available at the Clubhouse, some of which are listed in the table at the bottom of this newsletter.

To reserve the Clubhouse for your event, call the Office at 555-8875.

Upcoming Clubhouse Events

Date	Event
June 10 at 7:30 p.m.	Welcome new neighbors
July 3 at dusk	Celebration, fireworks, and cookout
July 30 from 11:00 a.m. until ?	Pool party
August 4-6	Community garage sale
September 4 at 12:00 p.m.	Cookout

FIGURE 6-106

(continued)

Creating a Newsletter from Scratch *(continued)*

3. Create a continuous section break below the nameplate.
4. Format section 2 to three columns.
5. Enter the text into section 2 using justified paragraph formatting.
6. Insert the pool picture into the newsletter. The picture is called pool and is located on the Data Disk. If you did not download the Data Disk, see the inside back cover for instructions for downloading the Data Disk or see your instructor. ***Hint:*** Use Help to learn about inserting pictures. If necessary, resize the picture. Add a sky blue border around the picture. Add a text box below the picture as shown in Figure 6-106 on the previous page. Group the text box and the picture together. Be sure the newsletter text wraps around the picture and text box. ***Hint:*** Use Help to learn about grouping objects.
7. Compress the picture. ***Hint:*** Use Help to learn about compressing pictures.
8. Insert a continuous section break at the end of the third column in section 2. Format section 3 to one column. Create the table as shown at the bottom of the newsletter in section 3.
9. Format the newsletter according to Figure 6-106. Place a vertical rule between all columns in section 2. Use the Columns dialog box (Format menu) to do this. Use the Format Painter button to automate some of your formatting tasks. Add the art page border as shown in the figure.
10. Save the document with Lab 6-3 Community Chatter Newsletter as the file name.
11. Switch to reading layout view and read through the newsletter. Close reading layout view.
12. Print the newsletter.

Cases and Places

The difficulty of these case studies varies:
■ are the least difficult and ■■ are more difficult. The last exercise is a group exercise.

1 ■ As your final project in your computer concepts class, you have been assigned the task of creating page WD 447 in this textbook. The page contains many desktop publishing elements: nameplate in one column and text in four columns, balanced columns, and a variety of font sizes and font colors. Apply an animation text effect to the fill effect page title, Learn It Online. Highlight each exercise heading. Change the background color and pattern of the background color. Switch to full screen view and read through the document. Print the document. Change the exercise section from four to three columns. Switch to reading layout view and proofread the document. Print the revised document.

2 ■■ You work part-time at a local nature center. One of your responsibilities is to write articles for the Green Thumb Gazette, a one-page newsletter published by the nature center. Your assignment is to decide on a feature article for the next edition of the Green Thumb Gazette. The article can discuss any garden-related item such as planting or maintaining flowers or trees, controlling weeds or garden pests, cleaning out flower beds, using compost, protecting gardens in cold weather, gardening tips and tricks, etc. As a basis for the feature article, use personal experiences, the school library, the Internet, magazines, friends and family, or other resources. The newsletter should contain a clip art image or a picture with article text wrapping around the graphic. Adjust the lightness or darkness of the graphic as necessary. Enhance the newsletter with a drop cap, WordArt, color, ruling lines, and a page border.

3 ■■ Pennywise Press is a one-page newsletter that presents money-saving ideas and tips. As a part-time assistant at the village hall, one of your responsibilities is to write articles for Pennywise Press. One issue, for example, discussed the keys to smart shopping: buying in bulk, using coupons, stocking up on sale items, and resisting impulse buys. Your assignment is to decide on a feature article for the next edition of Pennywise Press. Select a money-saving topic with which you are familiar. As a basis for the feature article, use personal experiences, the school library, the Internet, magazines, friends and family, or other resources. The newsletter should contain a pull-quote taken from the article. Enhance the newsletter with a drop cap, WordArt, color, ruling lines, and a page border.

4 ■■ As an assistant in the admissions office at your school, you are responsible for writing the monthly newsletter, Frosh World. This newsletter is geared specifically for the school's college freshmen. Articles in the newsletter cover a wide range of topics such as campus life, school tours, clubs, study groups, tutoring, registering for classes, and upcoming events. Your assignment is to write the next edition of Frosh World. As a basis for the feature article, use personal experiences, friends and family, the school library, the Internet, magazines, or other resources. The newsletter should contain a diagram with the text wrapped around the diagram. Enhance the newsletter with a drop cap, WordArt, color, ruling lines, and a page border.

Cases and Places

5 ■■ **Working Together** The local newspaper has a two-page newsletter in its Wednesday edition each week that reviews current movies, live performances, books, restaurants, and local events. Your team is to design and write the next newsletter. The newsletter should have a feature article that contains the reviews and some announcements for community members. As a group, decide on the name of the newsletter and design the nameplate. Each team member independently is to see or rent a current movie, watch a live performance, read a book, dine at a local restaurant, or attend a local event and then write at least a three paragraph review. Then, the team should meet as a group to combine all the reviews into a single article. Before inserting the documents into a single file, arrange the open Word documents so you can see all of them on the screen at the same time. Once verified, insert each document into the newsletter in the appropriate location. The feature article should span both pages of the newsletter. Announcements should be on the first page of the newsletter. Use the Paste Special command to copy and then paste link some lines of the nameplate from page 1 to page 2. Split the window so you can verify that both nameplates were updated properly. Be sure the newsletter contains a drop cap, WordArt, color, shading, ruling lines, and a page border. Use an appropriate graphic, a diagram, and a pull-quote in the newsletter. Use the Go To sheet in the Find and Replace dialog box to move to specific pages in the newsletter. Proofread the document in reading layout view. Save the newsletter. Enhance the newsletter for online viewing: highlight text, animate text, change the background color, and add a pattern fill effect to the background color.

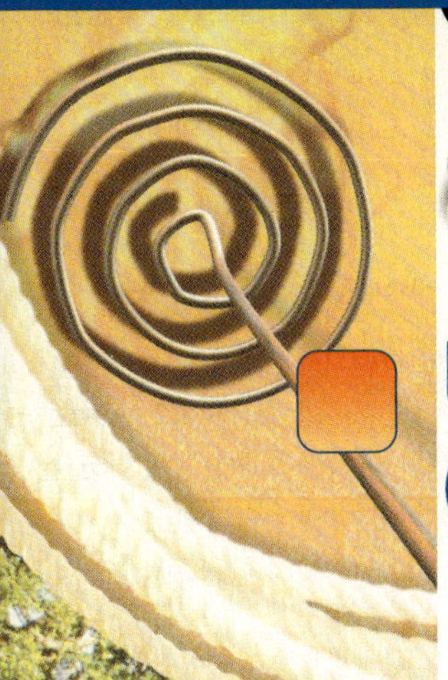

Microsoft Office Word 2003

Using Word's Collaboration Tools

CASE PERSPECTIVE

Nestled on 5,000 acres in the Colorado foothills, Tri-Circle Ranch has hosted Rocky Mountain excursions for the past decade. People from all walks of life thoroughly enjoy vacationing at this spectacular location where they see unspoiled wilderness, breathtaking snow-capped mountaintops, and a variety of wildlife including moose, antelope, coyote, fox, bighorn sheep, mule deer, elk, and water fowl. Expert guides lead the single-day, overnight, and week-long excursions. Daily activities consist of walking, hiking, backpacking, trout fishing, and rafting on the Colorado and Eagle Rivers.

As a part-time employee at Tri-Circle Ranch, you are responsible for all the company's computer work. Thus far, you have created a brochure, a fax cover sheet, several letters, mailing labels, a member newsletter, and a company Web page. Next week, your boss will be discussing Tri-Circle Ranch's Rocky Mountain excursions at a college fair. He has asked you to create an outline and corresponding slide show for his presentation. After creating the outline, you e-mail it to your boss for his review. He adds a couple of comments and incorporates some changes in the document and then e-mails it back to you. You review his comments and changes and then finalize the outline. Then, you send the final outline to Microsoft PowerPoint so your boss has an electronic slide show for his presentation. He is quite impressed!

As you read through this feature, you will learn how to create an outline, track changes in a document, and send an outline to PowerPoint.

Objectives

You will have mastered the material in this project when you can:

- Create an outline
- E-mail a document for review
- Insert comments
- Track changes
- Review tracked changes
- Send an outline to PowerPoint

Introduction

Word provides many tools that allow users to work with others, or **collaborate**, on a document. One set of collaboration tools allows you to track changes to a document and review the changes. That is, one computer user creates a document and another user(s) makes changes and inserts comments to the same document. Those changes then display on the screen with options that allow the originator (author) to accept or reject the changes and delete the comments. With another collaboration tool, you can compare and merge two documents to determine the differences between them.

As shown in Figure 1 on the next page, this feature illustrates how to track changes in Word and how to send a Word outline to PowerPoint for use in a slide show. Figure 1a shows the author's original outline. Figure 1b shows the reviewer's tracked changes and comments. Figure 1c shows the final outline, and Figure 1d shows the PowerPoint slide show created from the Word final outline.

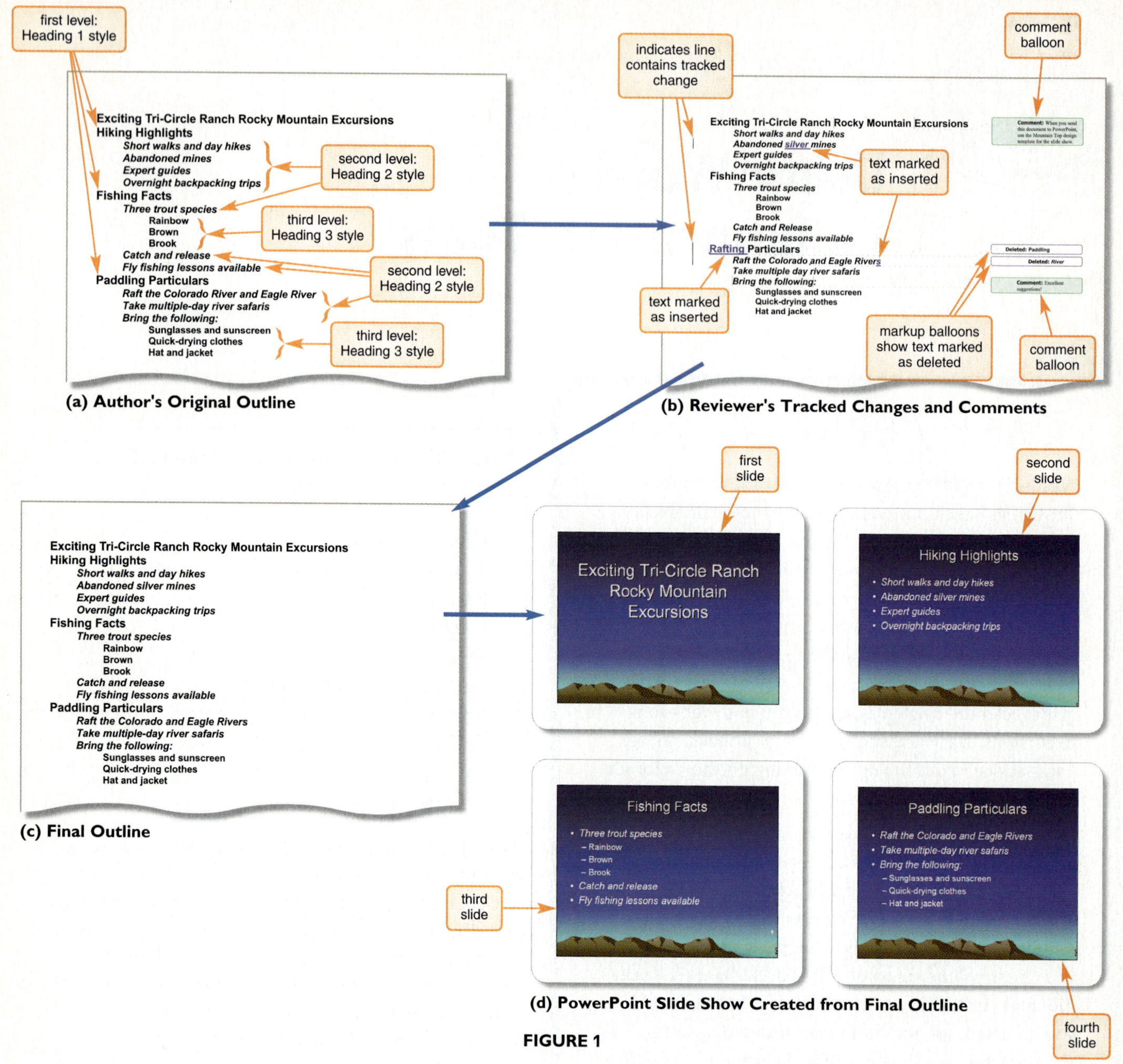

FIGURE 1

Creating an Outline

In an outline, the major (first level) headings are displayed at the left margin with each lower, or subordinate, level indented. The outline in this feature contains three major headings (shown in Figure 1a): Hiking Highlights, Fishing Facts, and Paddling Particulars.

To create an outline in Word, you use its built-in heading styles. When the document is displayed in **outline view**, Heading 1 style is displayed at the left margin, Heading 2 style is indented, Heading 3 style is indented further, and so on.

The following steps show how to create an outline. First, you switch to outline view. Then, you enter headings in the outline using heading styles.

To Enter Headings in an Outline

1

- **With Word started and a new document window open, click the Outline View button on the horizontal scroll bar.**
- **If your screen does not display the Outlining toolbar, click View on the menu bar, point to Toolbars, and then click Outlining.**
- **Type** `Exciting Tri-Circle Ranch Rocky Mountain Excursions` **and then press the ENTER key.**
- **Type** `Hiking Highlights` **and then press the ENTER key.**

Word switches to outline view, which shows an outline symbol to the left of each paragraph (Figure 2). The Outline Level box on the Outlining toolbar indicates the current heading is at the first level of the outline. The next heading entered is to be demoted to the second level.

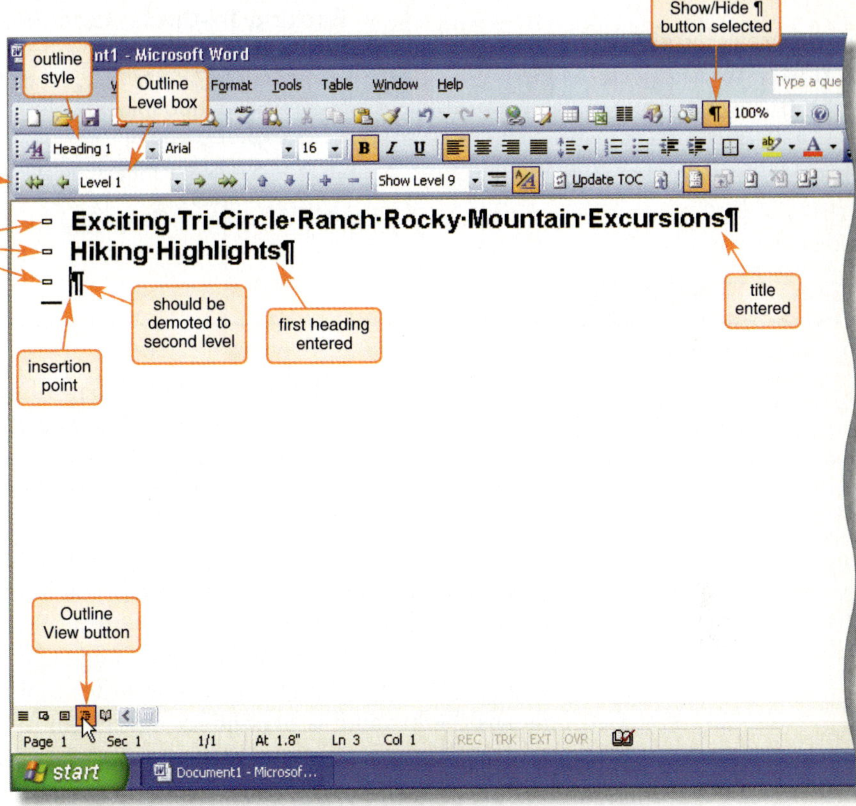

FIGURE 2

2

- **Press the TAB key.**

Word demotes the current paragraph to the second level, indented below the first heading.

3

- **Type** `Short walks and day hikes` **and then press the ENTER key.**
- **Type** `Abandoned mines` **and then press the ENTER key.**
- **Type** `Expert guides` **and then press the ENTER key.**
- **Type** `Overnight backpacking trips` **and then press the ENTER key.**

The Outline Level button on the Outlining toolbar shows Level 2 (Figure 3). The next item to be entered needs to be promoted to the first level.

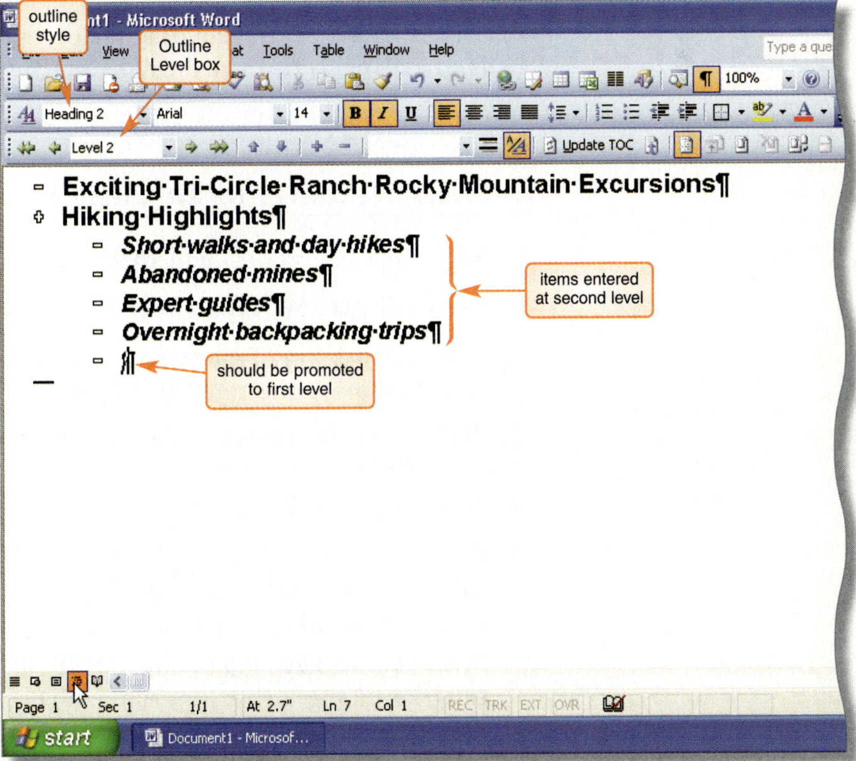

FIGURE 3

4

• **Press SHIFT+TAB.**

Word promotes the paragraph containing the insertion point to the first level (Figure 4).

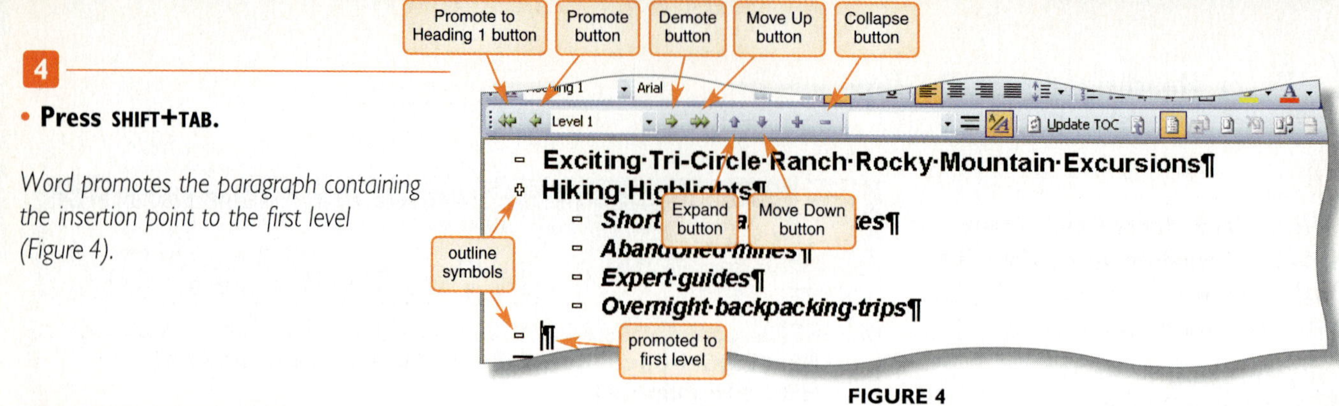

FIGURE 4

Other Ways

1. On View menu click Outline
2. In Voice Command mode, say "View, Outline"

The buttons and boxes on the left half of the Outlining toolbar allow you to promote and demote items in an outline and change an item's level. The buttons on the right half of the Outlining toolbar allow you to work with master and subdocuments.

Instead of pressing the TAB key to demote a paragraph, you can click the Demote button on the Outlining toolbar. Likewise, you can click the Promote button on the Outlining toolbar instead of pressing SHIFT+TAB to promote a paragraph. To promote a paragraph directly to the first level, you can click the Promote to Heading 1 button on the Outlining toolbar.

You use outline symbols to rearrange text or display and hide text. Notice in Figure 4 that the outline symbol is either a plus sign or a minus sign. A plus sign means the heading is **expanded**; that is, all lower-level headings are displayed on the screen. A minus sign means the heading has no lower levels or that the heading is **collapsed**; that is, lower-level headings are hidden from the screen. To expand a collapsed heading, double-click its outline symbol (the minus sign). To collapse an expanded heading, double-click its outline symbol (the plus sign).

If you wanted to rearrange headings in an outline, position the insertion point in the heading to be moved and then click the Move Up or Move Down button on the Outlining toolbar, or you can drag the outline symbol upward or downward.

The next step is to enter the remaining headings into the outline, as described below.

To Enter Headings in an Outline

1. **Type** `Fishing Facts` **and then press the ENTER key.**
2. **Press the TAB key. Type** `Three trout species` **and then press the ENTER key.**
3. **Press the TAB key. Type** `Rainbow` **and then press the ENTER key. Type** `Brown` **and then press the ENTER key. Type** `Brook` **and then press the ENTER key.**
4. **Press SHIFT+TAB. Type** `Catch and release` **and then press the ENTER key. Type** `Fly fishing lessons available` **and then press the ENTER key.**
5. **Press SHIFT+TAB. Type** `Paddling Particulars` **and then press the ENTER key.**
6. **Press the TAB key. Type** `Raft the Colorado River and Eagle River` **and then press the ENTER key. Type** `Take multiple-day river safaris` **and then press the ENTER key. Type** `Bring the following:` **and then press the ENTER key.**
7. **Press the TAB key. Type** `Sunglasses and sunscreen` **and then press the ENTER key. Type** `Quick-drying clothes` **and then press the ENTER key. Type** `Hat and jacket` **as the last heading in the outline.**

The outline headings are entered (Figure 5).

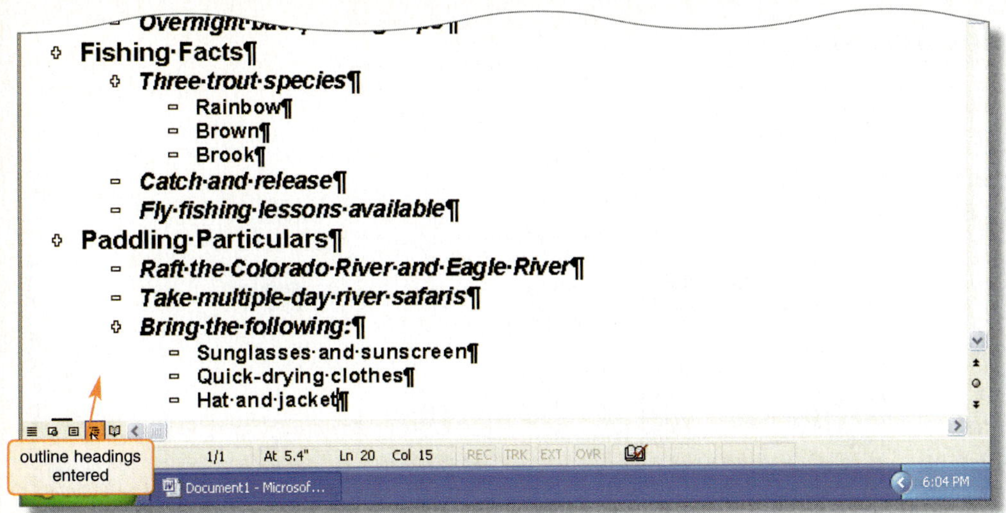

FIGURE 5

The following steps save the outline.

To Save a File

1. **With a floppy disk in drive A, click the Save button on the Standard toolbar.**
2. **Type** `Rocky Mountain Outline` **in the File name box. Do not press the ENTER key.**
3. **If necessary, click the Save in box arrow and then click 3½ Floppy (A:).**
4. **Click the Save button in the Save As dialog box.**

Word saves the document on a floppy disk in drive A with the file name, Rocky Mountain Outline.

Reviewing a Document

Reviewing a document is one of the collaboration tools provided in Word. After the originator (author) creates a document, reviewers make changes to the same document. For demonstration purposes, this project illustrates how both an originator and a reviewer work with a document.

E-Mailing a Document for Review

With the first draft of the outline complete, the next step in this feature is to e-mail the Rocky Mountain Outline document to another user for review. To e-mail a document for review, it should be displayed in the document window. A document sent for review becomes an attachment to the e-mail message. When the reviewer (recipient) opens the attached document in Word, the TRK indicator on the status bar is darkened, which means the document is ready to be reviewed.

The steps on the next page show how to e-mail a document for review.

To E-Mail a Document for Review

1

• **Click File on the menu bar and then point to Send To (Figure 6).**

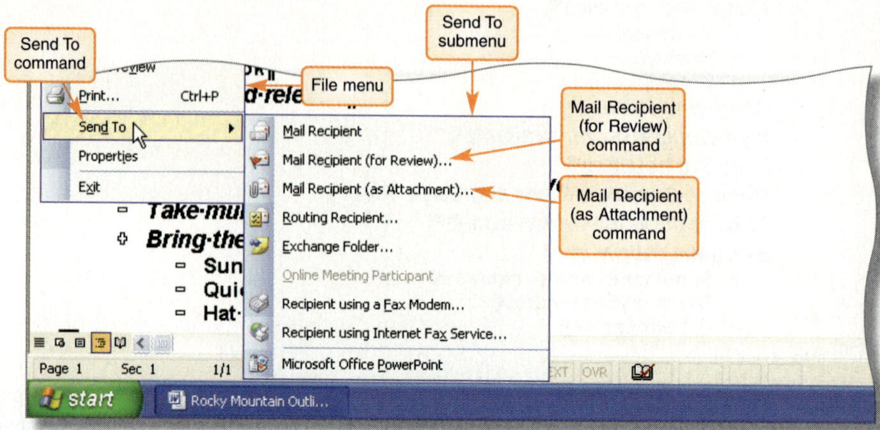

FIGURE 6

2

• **Click Mail Recipient (for Review).**

• **When Word opens the Please review 'Rocky Mountain Outline' window, type the recipient's e-mail address in the To text box (in this case, type your own e-mail address or an address provided by your instructor).**

Word automatically displays a message in the Subject text box and includes the Rocky Mountain Outline file as an attachment in the Please review 'Rocky Mountain Outline' window (Figure 7). The ***E-mail toolbar*** *is displayed below the menu bar.*

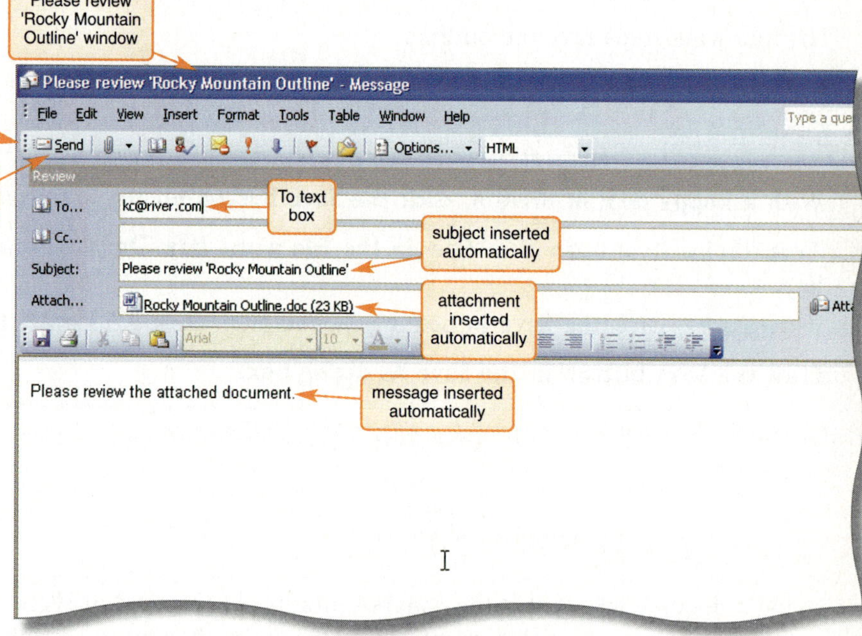

FIGURE 7

3

• **Click the Send button on the E-mail toolbar, if directed to do so by your instructor.**

Word sends the Rocky Mountain Outline document to the recipient named in the To text box.

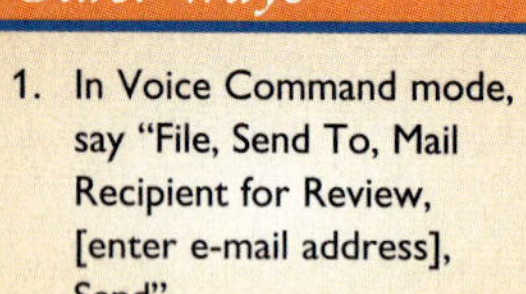

Other Ways

1. In Voice Command mode, say "File, Send To, Mail Recipient for Review, [enter e-mail address], Send"

When an e-mail recipient receives a document that has been sent to him or her for review, the subject line in the e-mail program shows the name of the attached file, and a paper clip denotes the attachment. The reviewer simply double-clicks the document attachment in the mail message to start the application and open the document. If Word opens the document in reading layout view, simply click View on the menu bar and then click Outline to switch to outline view.

Instead of sending a document for review, you can send an open document as an attachment (not for review) to an e-mail message from within Word.

To E-Mail an Open Document as an Attachment (not for review)

1. Click File on the menu bar, point to Send To, and then click Mail Recipient (as Attachment).
2. When Word displays the e-mail window with the document attached, type the recipient's e-mail address in the To text box.
3. Click the Send button on the E-mail toolbar.

If you wanted to cancel an e-mail operation, simply close the e-mail window.

Inserting, Viewing, and Editing Comments

After reading through the Rocky Mountain Outline document, your boss has a couple of comments. A **comment**, or annotation, is a note inserted in a document that does not affect the text of the document. Reviewers often use comments to communicate suggestions, tips, and other messages to the author of a document.

For example, your boss (Kyle Chambers) suggests using a mountain background in PowerPoint for the slide show of this outline. He also likes your list of items to bring on the rafting trips. Instead of writing his comments on a printout of the document, he plans to use Word to insert them. Then, you can delete the comments after viewing them.

The following steps show how a reviewer inserts a comment in a document.

Other Ways

1. On Insert menu click Comment
2. In Voice Command mode, say "Insert, Comment"

To Insert a Comment in the Reviewing Pane

1

- **If the Reviewing toolbar is not displayed in the Word window, click View on the menu bar, point to Toolbars, and then click Reviewing.**
- **Select the text on which you wish to comment (in this case, Rocky Mountain, in the first line in the outline).**
- **Click the Insert Comment button on the Reviewing toolbar.**

When you insert a comment and the Word window is in outline view, the Reviewing Pane is displayed at the bottom of the window (Figure 8). The Reviewing Pane button is selected on the Reviewing toolbar. ***Comment marks****, which look like parentheses, surround the selected text in the document window. The reviewer's initials and comment number are displayed immediately after the last comment mark and also in the Reviewing Pane.*

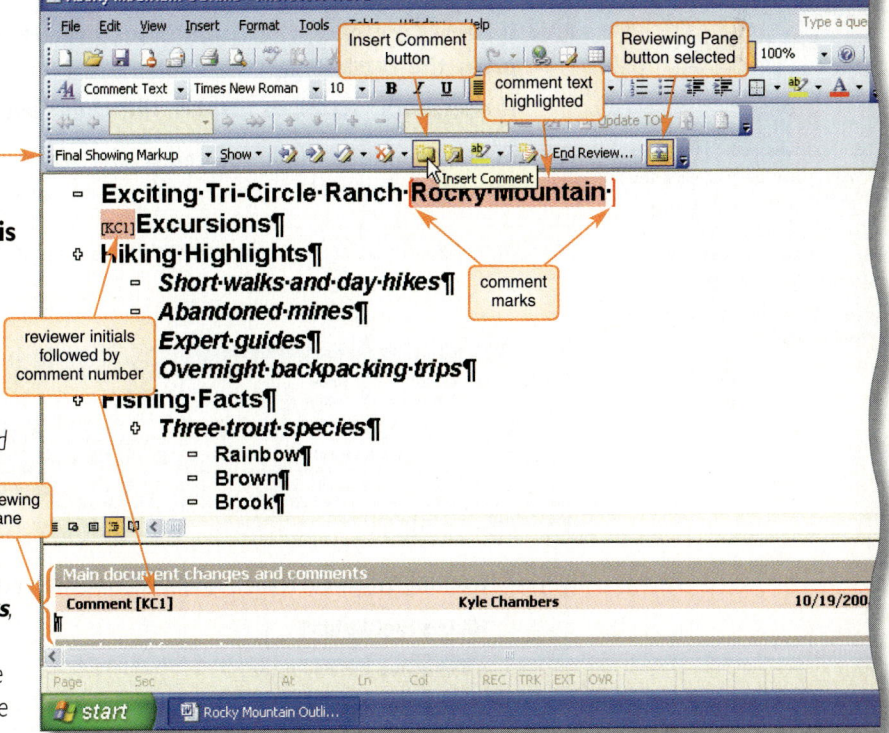

FIGURE 8

2

- **Type** `In PowerPoint, use a mountain background for the slide show.`

comment inserted

Word displays the comment in the Reviewing Pane (Figure 9).

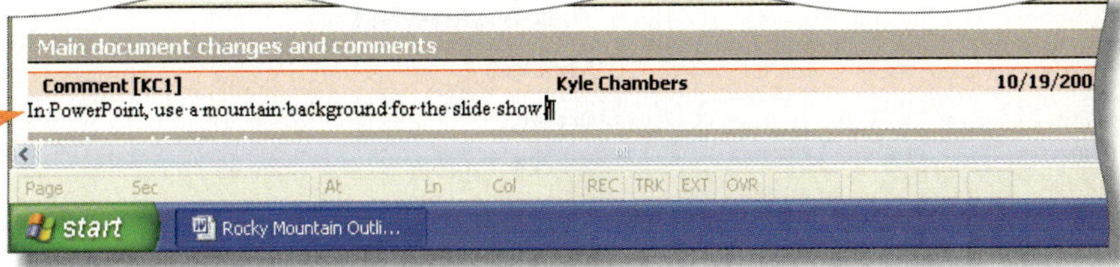

FIGURE 9

As with footnotes, if you point to the comment marks (parentheses) in the document window, Word displays the comment and the name of the comment's author above the comment mark as a ScreenTip.

Instead of selecting text on which you wish to comment (as shown in Step 1 on the previous page), you simply can click the location where you want to insert the comment. In this case, the comment marks (parentheses) display side by side at the location of the insertion point.

As an alternative to inserting comments in the Reviewing Pane, some users prefer to work with **comment balloons** that display to the right of the text in the document window. Comment balloons are not displayed in outline view or normal view; they are displayed only in print layout view, Web layout view, and reading layout view.

The following steps describe how to edit a comment when the Word window is in print layout view.

More About

Voice Comments

If your computer is equipped with a sound card and a microphone, you can record a voice comment in a document. Click the Insert Voice button on the Reviewing toolbar and then record the comment. If the Reviewing toolbar does not contain the Insert Voice button, click the Toolbar Options button at the right edge of the toolbar, point to Add or Remove Buttons, point to Reviewing, and then click Insert Voice on the submenu.

To Edit a Comment in a Comment Balloon

1. **Click the Reviewing Pane button on the Reviewing toolbar to remove the Reviewing Pane from the screen.**
2. **Click the Print Layout View button on the horizontal scroll bar.**
3. **If necessary, click the Zoom box to select its percentage. Type** `85` **and then press the ENTER key.**
4. **If necessary, scroll to display the comment balloon in the document window.**
5. **In the comment balloon, delete the word, In, at the beginning of the sentence. Type** `When you send this document to` **(Figure 10).**

Word modifies the contents of the comment in the comment balloon. The insertion point is positioned in the comment balloon.

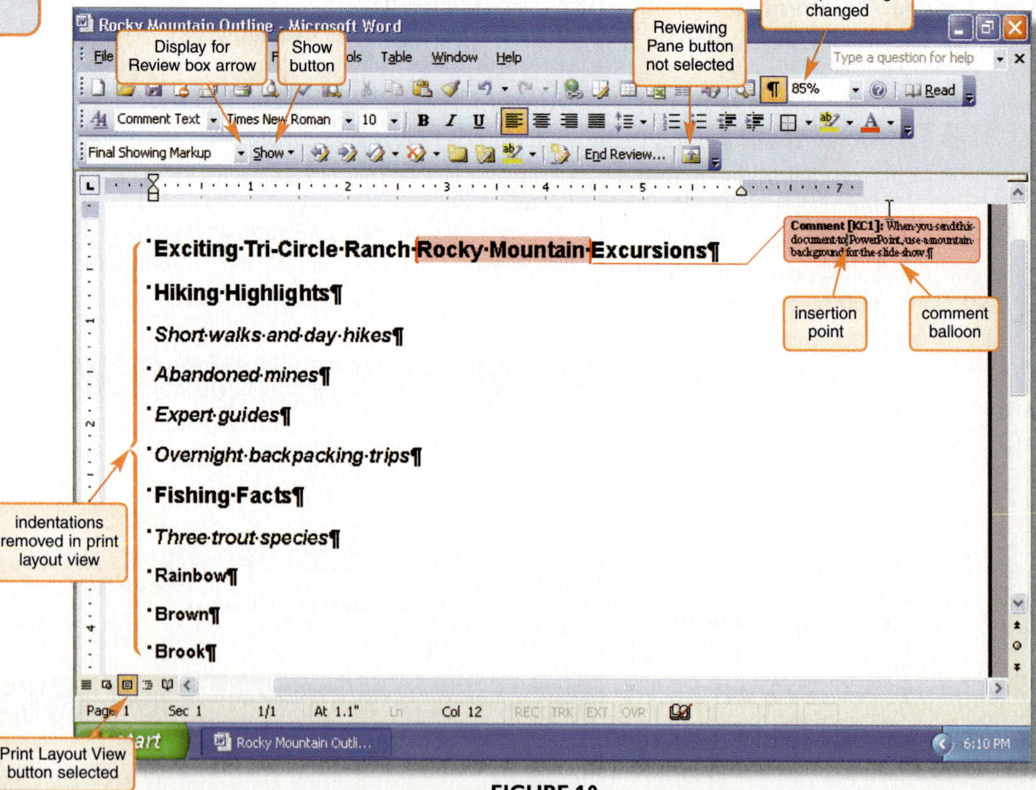

FIGURE 10

Notice in print layout view that Word removes the indentations for lower levels in the outline. That is, all text begins at the left margin. If you print the document while it is displayed in print layout view, it prints as shown on the screen – with all text at the left margin. To print the document so it looks like an outline, switch to outline view first and then print the document.

If comment marks do not appear on the screen, verify comments are showing by clicking the Show button on the Reviewing toolbar and then clicking Comments. Also, if necessary, click the Display for Review box arrow and then click Final Showing Markup. If comments still do not appear, click View on the menu bar and then click Markup.

Sometimes, Word cannot display the complete text of a comment in the comment balloon. If this occurs, simply display the Reviewing Pane to see the entire comment. The Reviewing Pane also is used to see comments in normal view and outline view, and to see items such as inserted or deleted graphics and text boxes. To display the Reviewing Pane, click the Reviewing Pane button on the Reviewing toolbar or right-click the TRK status indicator on the status bar and then click Reviewing Pane on the shortcut menu. To close the Reviewing Pane, click the Reviewing Pane button on the Reviewing toolbar again.

The next step is to insert another comment, as described below.

To Insert a Comment in a Comment Balloon

1. **If necessary, scroll down to display the text, Bring the following:, in the document window.**
2. **Select the text, Bring the following.**
3. **Click the Insert Comment button on the Reviewing toolbar.**
4. **In the comment balloon, type** `Excellent suggestions!`

Word inserts the comment in a comment balloon (Figure 11). Notice the number 2 follows the user initials in the comment balloon to indicate this is the second comment in the document.

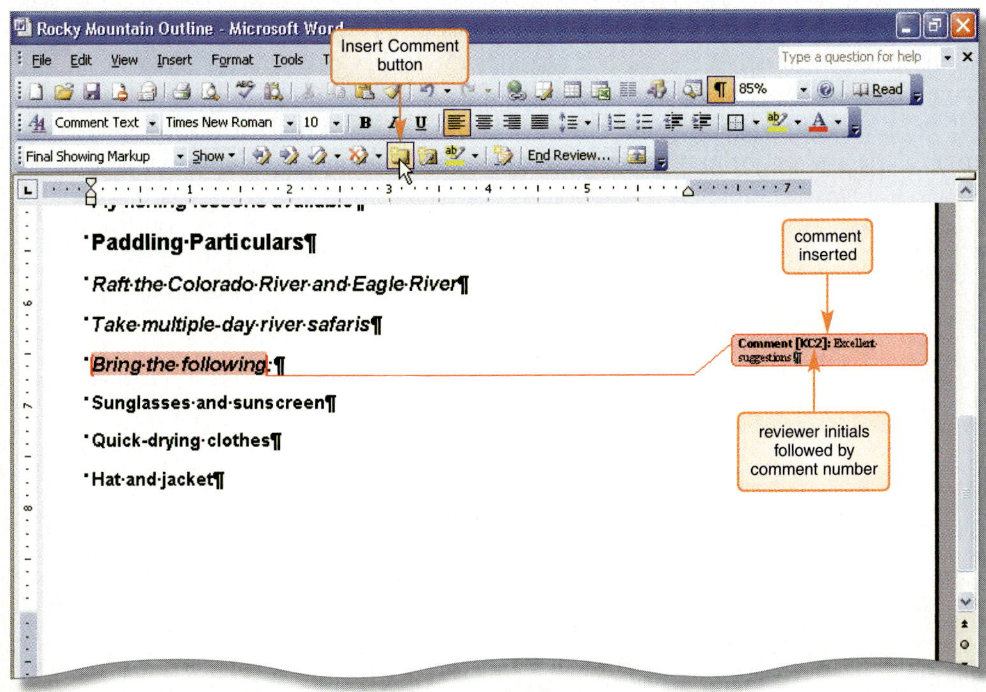

FIGURE 11

More About

Ink Comments

If you are using Word on a Tablet PC, then you can insert ink comments into a document. Click Insert on the menu bar and then click Ink Comment. Use the Tablet PC's digital pen to write the comment in the comment balloon. Word saves the handwritten comment with the document.

More About

Locating Comments

You can find a comment through the Go To dialog box. Click Edit on the menu bar and then click Go To or press CTRL+G to display the Go To dialog box. Click Comment in the Go to what list. Select the reviewer whose comments you wish to find and then click the Next button. You also can click the Select Browse Object button on the vertical scroll bar and then click Comment to scroll through comments.

You modify comments in a comment balloon by clicking inside the comment balloon and editing as you edit text in the document window.

If multiple users review the same document, each reviewer's comments are shaded in a different color to help you visually differentiate among multiple reviewers' comments.

Word uses predefined settings for the reviewer's name that are displayed in the ScreenTip and for the reviewer's initials that are displayed in the document window, the comment balloon, and the Reviewing Pane. If the reviewer's name or initials are not correct, you can modify them.

To Change Reviewer Information

1. Click Tools on the menu bar and then click Options.
2. When Word displays the Options dialog box, click the User Information tab and enter the correct name or initials in the respective text boxes.

When you print a document with comments, Word chooses the zoom percentage and page orientation to best display the comments in the printed document. If you want to print the comments only (without printing the document), click File on the menu bar, click Print, click the Print what box arrow, click List of markup, and then click the OK button. If you want to print the document without comments, click File on the menu bar, click Print, click the Print what box arrow, click Document, and then click the OK button.

Tracking Changes

Kyle has three suggested changes for the Rocky Mountain Outline document: (1) insert the word, silver, between Abandoned mines, (2) change the word, Paddling, to the word, Rafting, and (3) delete the word, River, after Colorado and then add the letter s to the end of the word River after Eagle.

To track changes in a document, you must turn on the change-tracking feature. When you edit a document that has the change-tracking feature enabled, Word marks all text or graphics that you insert, delete, or modify and calls the revisions a **markup**. Thus, an author can identify the changes a reviewer has made by looking at the markup in the document. The author also has the ability to accept or reject any change that a reviewer has made to a document.

The following pages illustrate how a reviewer tracks changes to a document and then how the author (originator) reviews the tracked changes made to the document.

More About

Tracked Changes

If you wanted to see a copy of the document before any tracked changes were made, click the Display for Review button arrow on the Reviewing toolbar and then click Original. To show the document as if all changes were accepted, click the Display for Review button arrow and then click Final. To redisplay the document with tracked changes, click the Display for Review button arrow on the Reviewing toolbar and then click Final Showing Markup.

To Track Changes

1

- **Press CTRL+HOME to position the insertion point at the beginning of the document.**
- **Double-click the TRK status indicator on the status bar.**
- **Position the insertion point immediately to the left of the word, mines, in the fourth paragraph.**
- **Type** `silver` **and then press the SPACEBAR.**

Word marks the inserted text, silver, as inserted (Figure 12). That is, it is displayed in color and underlined. When tracking changes is turned on, the characters in the TRK status indicator on the status bar appear darkened. Word places a ***changed line*** *(a vertical bar) at the left edge of each line that contains a tracked change.*

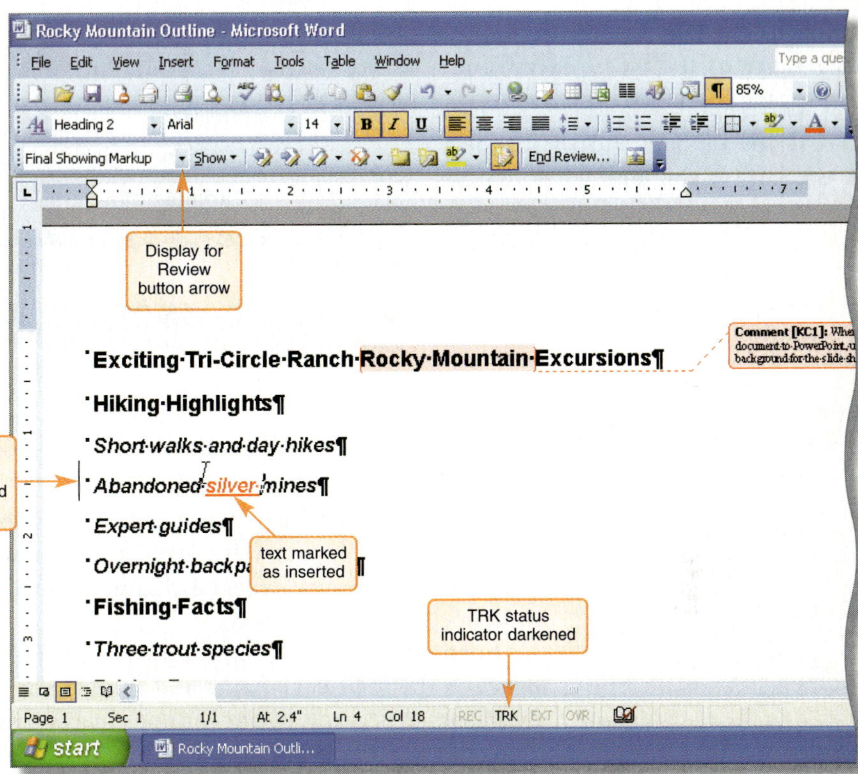

FIGURE 12

2

- **Scroll down and select the word, Paddling, in the third major heading of the outline by double-clicking it.**
- **Type** `Rafting` **as the replacement text.**
- **If necessary, click the right scroll arrow to display the markup balloon.**

Word marks the selected word, Paddling, as deleted, and marks the word, Rafting, as inserted (Figure 13). In print layout view, deleted text displays in a ***markup balloon****, and inserted text displays in the document in color and underlined.*

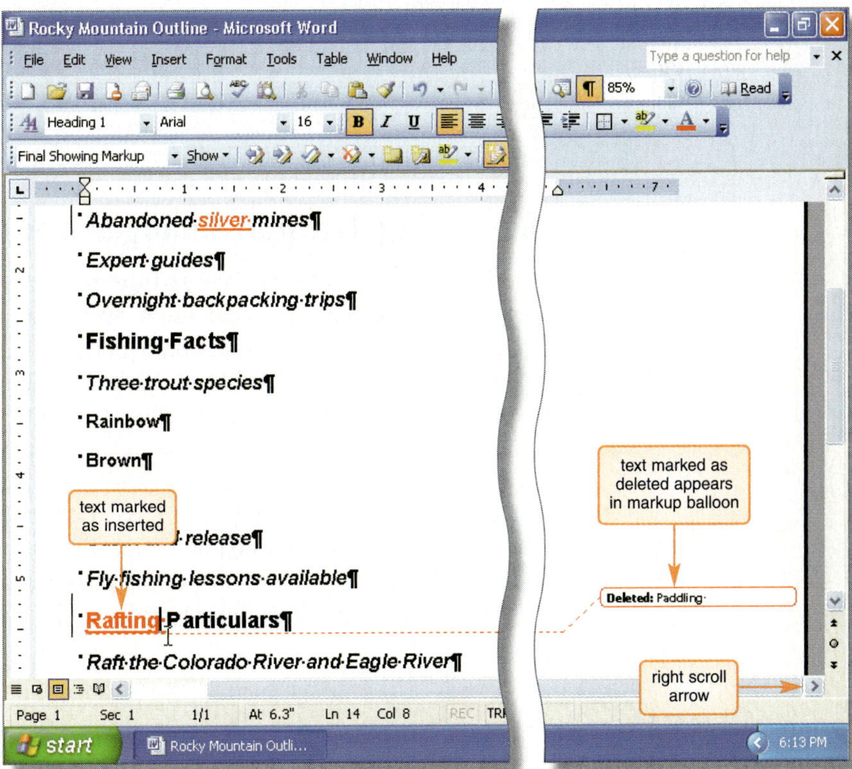

FIGURE 13

3

- **If necessary, scroll down to display the next line on the screen.**
- **In the next line, select the first occurrence of the word, River, and then press the DELETE key.**
- **Press the END key and then type s at the end of the line.**

The first occurrence of the word, River, is marked for deletion, and the second occurrence of the word River has been changed to Rivers (Figure 14).

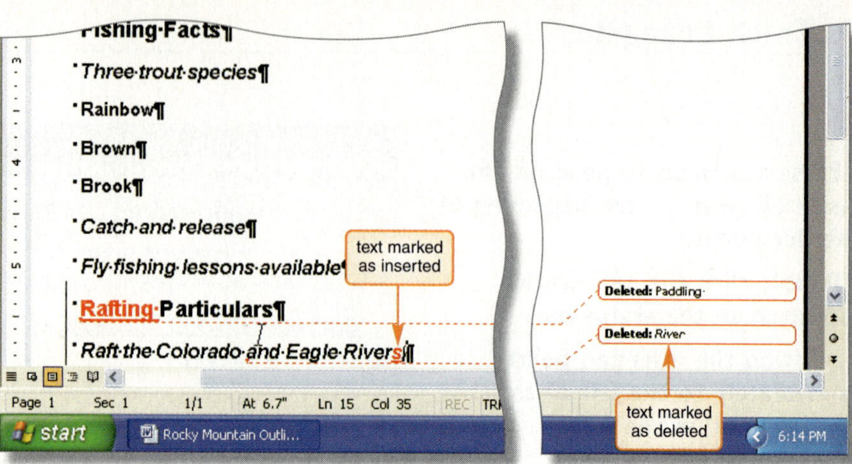

FIGURE 14

Other Ways

1. Click Track Changes button on Reviewing toolbar
2. On Tools menu click Track Changes
3. Press CTRL+SHIFT+E
4. In Voice Command mode, say "Tools, Track Changes"

Tracked changes, which are called **revision marks**, are displayed in markup balloons in print layout view, Web layout view, and reading layout view. In normal view and outline view, tracked changes display as strikethroughs for deleted text and underlined for inserted text.

In any view, if you point to a tracked change, Word displays a ScreenTip that identifies the reviewer's name and the type of change made by that reviewer. As with comments, Microsoft Word cannot always display the complete text of a tracked change in a markup balloon. Use the Reviewing Pane to view longer revisions.

The next step is to turn off the change-tracking feature, as described below.

To Stop Tracking Changes

1 **Double-click the TRK status indicator on the status bar.**

Word dims the characters in the TRK status indicator on the status bar (shown in Figure 15).

Reviewing Tracked Changes and Comments

Next, you would like to read the tracked changes and comments from Kyle. You could scroll through the document and point to each markup to read it, but you might overlook one or more changes using this technique. A more efficient method is to use the Reviewing toolbar to review the changes and comments one at a time, deciding whether to accept, modify, or delete them.

To do this, be sure the markups are displayed on the screen. Click the Show button on the Reviewing toolbar and verify that Comments, Insertions and Deletions, and Formatting each have a check mark beside them. Click the Display for Review box arrow and then click Final Showing Markup. If markups still are not displayed, click View on the menu bar and then click Markup.

The next steps show how to review the changes and comments from Kyle.

To Review Tracked Changes and View Comments

1

- **Press CTRL+HOME to position the insertion point at the beginning of the document.**
- **Click the Next button on the Reviewing toolbar.**
- **If necessary, click the right scroll arrow on the horizontal scroll bar so that the comment balloon is visible.**

The review of tracked changes and comments begins at the location of the insertion point, in this case, the top of the document (Figure 15). Word selects the comment and positions the insertion point in the comment balloon.

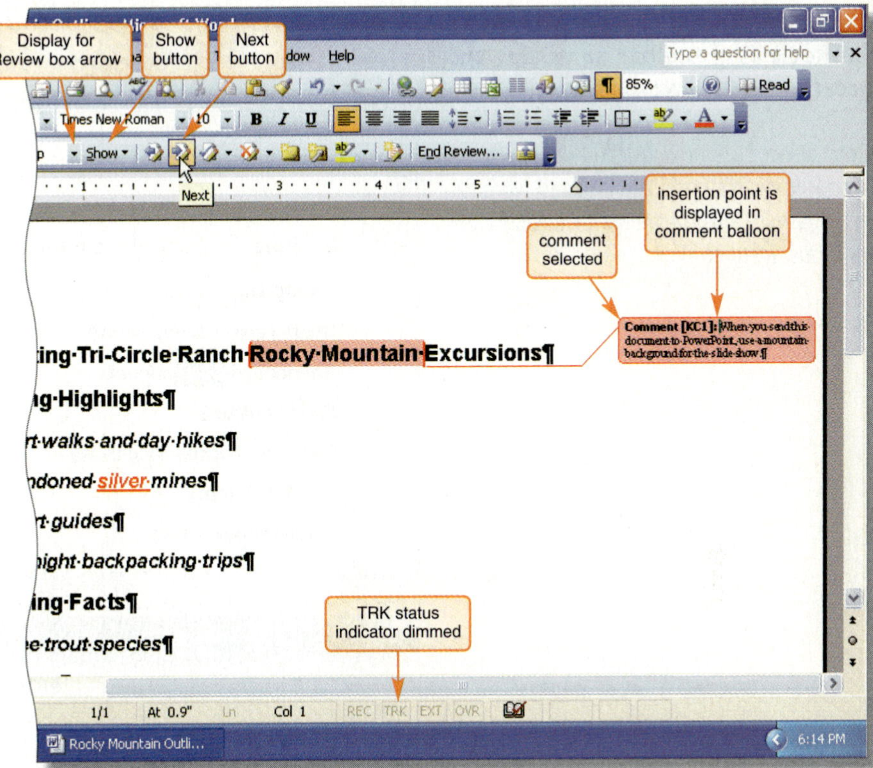

FIGURE 15

2

- **Read through the comment and then click the Reject Change/Delete Comment button on the Reviewing toolbar.**

Word deletes the comment balloon and the comment marks in the document (Figure 16).

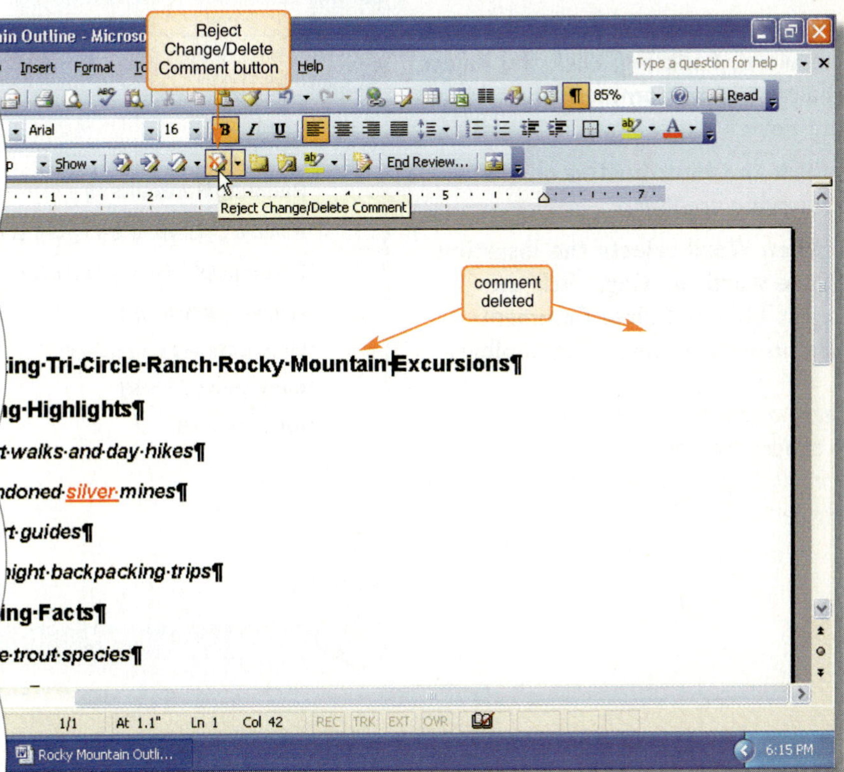

FIGURE 16

3

- **Click the Next button on the Reviewing toolbar again.**
- **Click the Accept Change button on the Reviewing toolbar to accept the insertion of the word, silver.**

Word selects the next tracked change or comment, in this case, the inserted word, silver (Figure 17). You agree with this change and, thus, instruct Word to accept it.

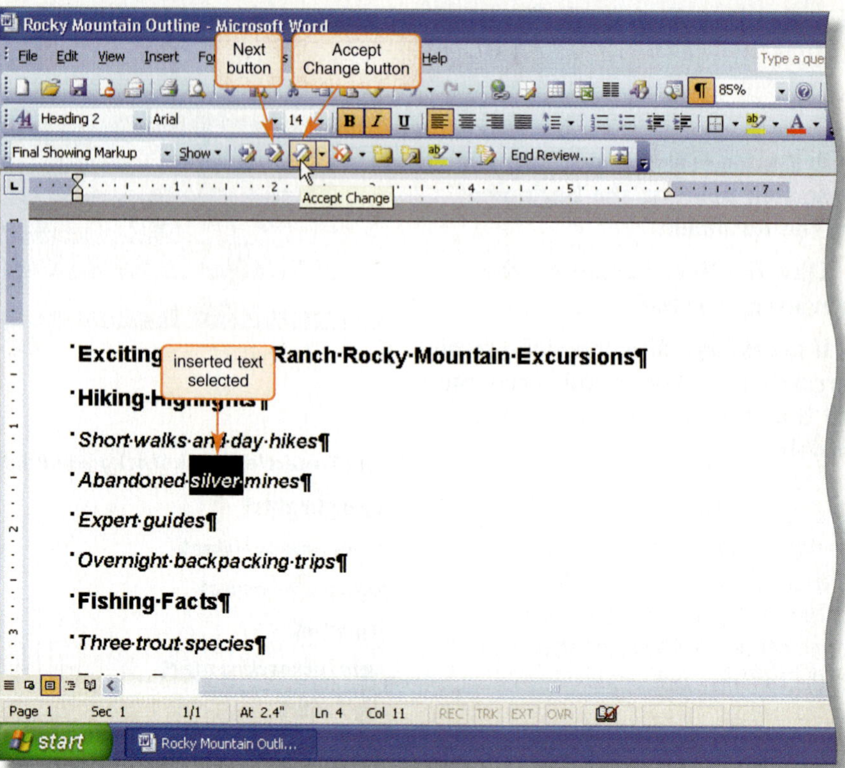

FIGURE 17

4

- **Click the Next button on the Reviewing toolbar.**
- **When Word selects the deletion of the word, Paddling, click the Reject Change/Delete Comment button on the Reviewing toolbar.**
- **Click the Next button on the Reviewing toolbar.**
- **When Word selects the insertion of the word, Rafting, click the Reject Change/Delete Comment button on the Reviewing toolbar.**

Because you do not agree with the change to replace the word, Paddling, with the word, Rafting, you instruct Word to reject it (Figure 18).

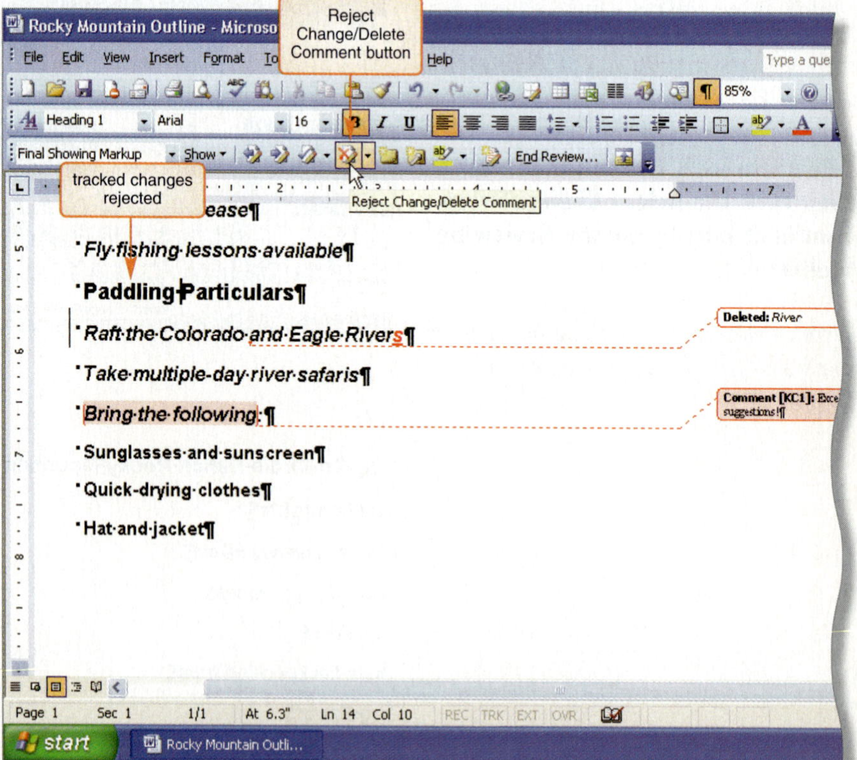

FIGURE 18

5

- **Click the Next button on the Reviewing toolbar.**
- **Click the Accept Change button to accept the deletion of the word, River.**
- **Click the Next button on the Reviewing toolbar.**
- **Click the Accept Change button to accept the insertion of the letter, s.**
- **Click the Next button on the Reviewing toolbar.**
- **Read through the selected comment and then click the Reject Change/Delete Comment button on the Reviewing toolbar to delete the comment.**

The review of tracked changes is complete (Figure 19).

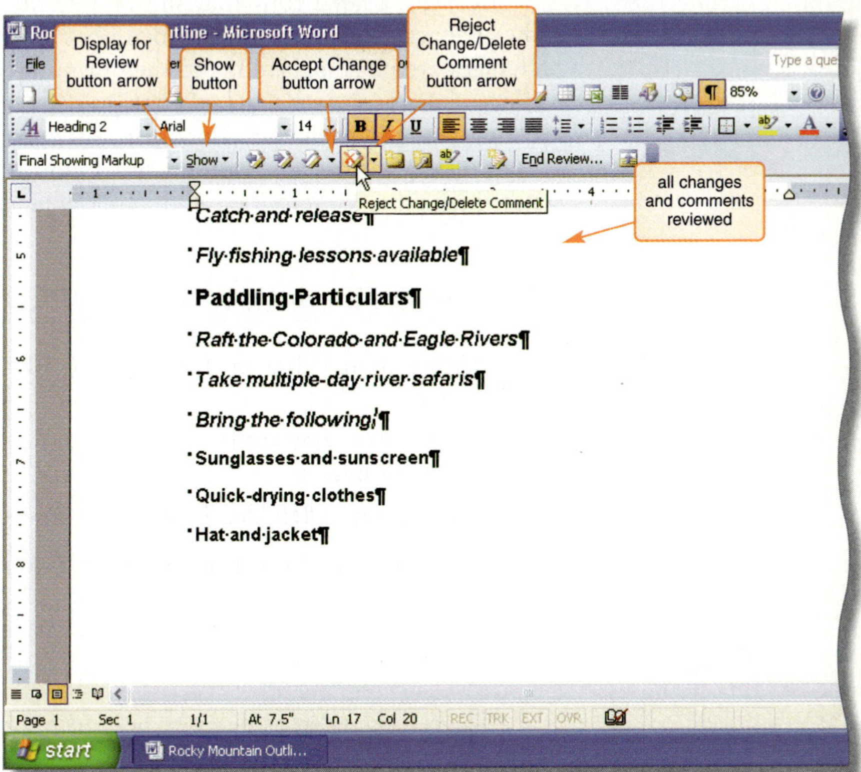

FIGURE 19

You also may accept or reject a change or comment by right-clicking it. On the shortcut menu, choices are displayed that allow you to accept or reject the changes and delete comments.

If you are certain you plan to accept all changes in a document containing tracked changes, you can accept all the changes at once by clicking the Accept Change button arrow on the Reviewing toolbar and then clicking Accept All Changes in Document. Likewise, you can click the Reject Change/Delete Comment button arrow on the Reviewing toolbar and then click Reject All Changes in Document or Delete All Comments in Document to reject all the changes or delete all the comments at once. If you click either of these commands by mistake, you can click the Undo button on the Standard toolbar to undo the action.

If you click the Next button and no tracked changes remain, Word displays a dialog box informing you the document contains no more changes. If this occurs, click the OK button.

To see how a document will look if you accept all the changes, without actually accepting them, click View on the menu bar and then click Markup, or click the Display for Review button arrow on the Reviewing toolbar and then click Final.

To show just a single reviewer's changes, click the Show button on the Reviewing toolbar, point to Reviewers, and then place a check mark beside the reviewer name whose changes you want the document to display. To hide a reviewer's changes, remove the check mark from beside the reviewer's name. Then, you can accept or reject changes and read and delete comments for one reviewer at a time.

More About

The Reviewing Toolbar

When you send a document for review, as shown on page WD 462, Word adds the End Review button to the Reviewing toolbar. After you have accepted/rejected all reviewer changes, you can click the End Review button to stop the reviewing process. Clicking the End Review button turns off tracking changes and removes the Reviewing toolbar from the Word window.

To print a hard copy that shows how the document will look if you accept all the changes, click View on the menu bar and then click Markup so the tracked changes are not displayed, and then print in the usual manner. To print a hard copy of the document with tracked changes, click the Print what box arrow in the Print dialog box and then click Document showing markup.

To keep the original outline intact, you should save the modified outline with a new file name, as described in the following steps.

To Save a File with a New File Name

1. **With a floppy disk in drive A, click File on the menu bar and then click Save As.**
2. **Type** `Rocky Mountain Outline Final` **in the File name box. Do not press the ENTER key.**
3. **If necessary, click the Save in box arrow and then click 3½ Floppy (A:).**
4. **Click the Save button in the Save As dialog box.**

Word saves the document on a floppy disk in drive A with the file name, Rocky Mountain Outline Final.

The following steps describe how to print the final outline.

More About

Printing Outlines

If you print the outline while in print layout view or normal view, Word does not indent levels of the outline. Instead, all levels print at the left margin. To print the outline with sublevels indented, switch to outline view first and then click the Print button.

To Print the Outline

1. **Click the Outline View button on the horizontal scroll bar to switch to outline view.**
2. **Click the Print button on the Standard toolbar.**

Word prints the outline as shown in Figure 1c on page WD 458.

Changing Review Settings

If you wanted to change the color and markings reviewers use for tracked changes or change how balloons are displayed, use the Track Options dialog box.

To Modify Reviewer Ink Colors and Balloon Options

1. Click Tools on the menu bar and then click Options.
2. When Word displays the Options dialog box, click the Track Changes tab.
3. To change how Word marks a change or the color a reviewer uses for changes, modify the settings in the Markup area in the dialog box. To change balloon options, modify settings in the Balloons area in the dialog box.
4. Click the OK button.

Other ways to display the Track Options dialog box include clicking the Show button on the Reviewing toolbar and then clicking Options, and right-clicking the TRK status indicator on the status bar and then clicking Options.

If you wanted to change the size or appearance of text in markup balloons, you would modify the Balloon Text style. The next steps describe how to modify the Balloon Text style.

To Modify the Balloon Text Style

1. Click the Styles and Formatting button on the Formatting toolbar.
2. In the Pick formatting to apply area in the Styles and Formatting task pane, scroll to Balloon Text. (If Balloon Text is not in the list, click the Show box arrow in the Styles and Formatting task pane, click Custom, place a check mark in the Balloon Text check box, and then click the OK button.)
3. Right-click Balloon Text and then click Modify on the shortcut menu.
4. Make desired changes to the Balloon Text style in the Modify Style dialog box and then click the OK button.

The size and appearance of text in comment balloons is controlled by the Comment Text style. To change the Comment Text style, follow the steps described above – replacing the occurrences of Balloon Text with Comment Text.

Comparing and Merging Documents

With Word, you can compare two documents to each other so you easily can identify any differences between the two files. Word displays the differences between the documents as tracked changes that you can review.

Assume you wanted to compare the original outline with the final outline so you easily can identify the changes made to the document. The following steps show how to compare and merge documents.

To Compare and Merge Documents

1

- **Be sure the Rocky Mountain Outline Final document is displayed on the screen and the disk that contains the original outline is in drive A.**
- **Click Tools on the menu bar (Figure 20).**

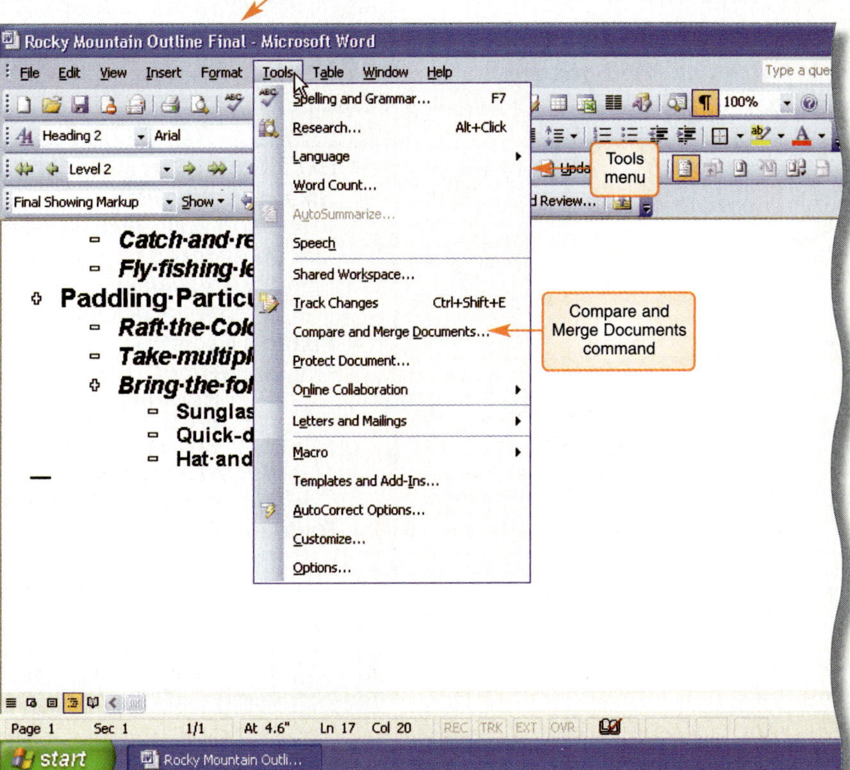

FIGURE 20

2

- **Click Compare and Merge Documents on the Tools menu.**
- **When Word displays the Compare and Merge Documents dialog box, if necessary, click the Look in box arrow and then click 3½ Floppy (A:). Click Rocky Mountain Outline in the list.**
- **Click the Merge button arrow.**

The Merge menu displays three commands: Merge, Merge into current document, and Merge into new document (Figure 21).

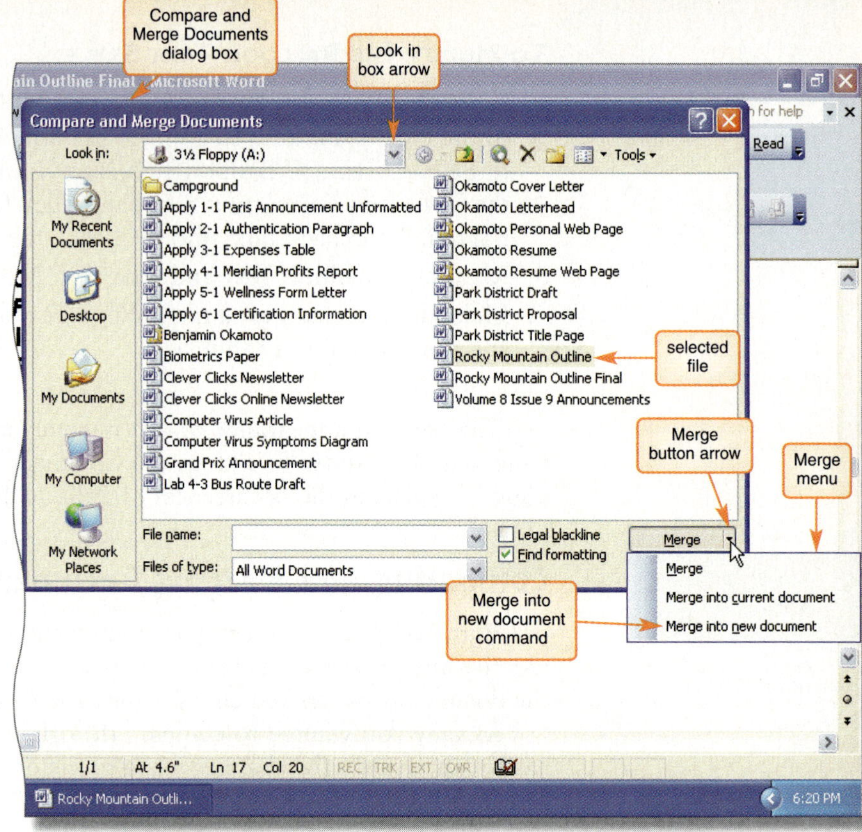

FIGURE 21

3

- **Click Merge into new document.**
- **If necessary, click the Outline View button on the horizontal scroll bar.**

Word displays the differences between the two documents as tracked changes (Figure 22).

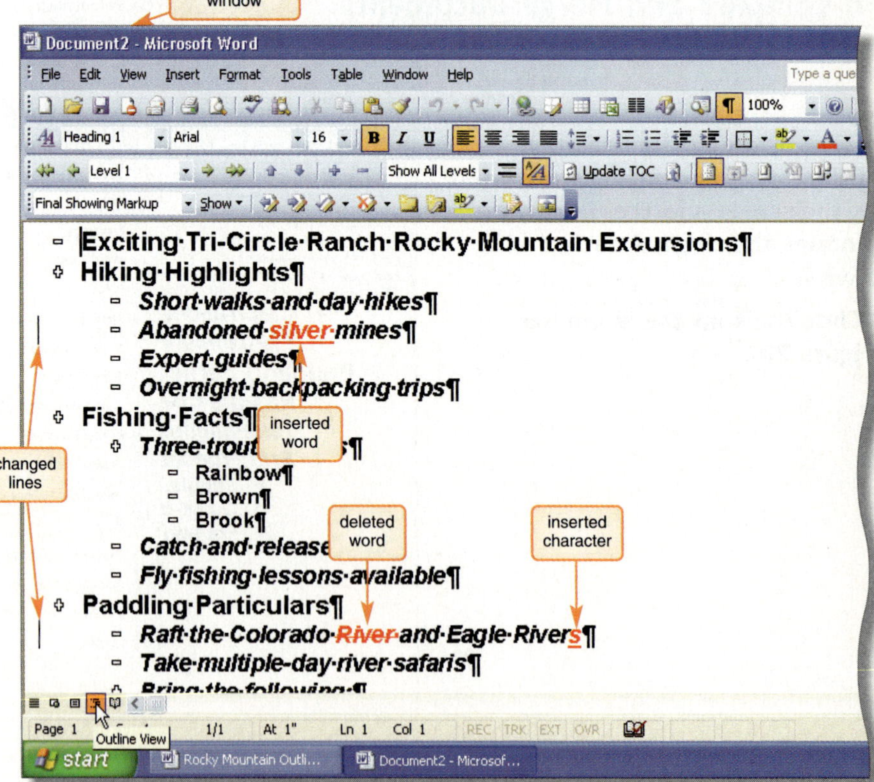

FIGURE 22

Other Ways

1. In Voice Command mode, say "Tools, Compare and Merge Documents"

Notice in Figure 22 that in outline view the deleted text is displayed as strikethrough text instead of in markup balloons. This is because markup balloons do not show on the screen in outline view or in normal view.

Word's Compare and Merge feature is useful if a reviewer does not remember to use the change-tracking feature while editing a document. That is, you can compare and merge the reviewer's document to your original document. Word tracks changes to display all differences between the two documents, which you later can accept or reject using the steps shown previously.

The following steps describe how to close the compared and merged document.

Q&A

Q: Other than for merging reviewer changes, why would I use the Compare and Merge command?

A: If you have two files in a folder that you believe to have the same content, you can be sure they are the same by using the Compare and Merge command to compare the two files. If no tracked changes are found, then the two documents are identical.

To Close a Document

1. **Click File on the menu bar and then click Close.**
2. **When Word displays a dialog box asking if you want to save changes, click the No button.**

Word closes the current document and redisplays the Rocky Mountain Outline Final document on the screen.

You now are finished tracking changes and reviewing tracked changes. Thus, you can hide the Reviewing toolbar, as described in the following steps.

To Hide the Reviewing Toolbar

1. **Right-click the Reviewing toolbar.**
2. **Click Reviewing on the shortcut menu.**

Word hides the Reviewing toolbar, which means it no longer is displayed in the Word window.

Sending an Outline to PowerPoint

Word has the capability of sending an outline to PowerPoint, which automatically creates a slide show from the outline. PowerPoint uses the heading styles (e.g., Heading 1, Heading 2, etc.) to set up the slides. Each Heading 1 begins on a new slide.

The steps on the next page show how to send a Word outline to PowerPoint.

More About

Certification

The Microsoft Office Specialist Certification program provides an opportunity for you to obtain a valuable industry credential - proof that you have the Word 2003 skills required by employers. For more information, see Appendix E or visit the Word 2003 Certification Web page (scsite.com/wd2003/cert).

To Send an Outline to PowerPoint

1

• **Click File on the menu bar and then point to Send To (Figure 23).**

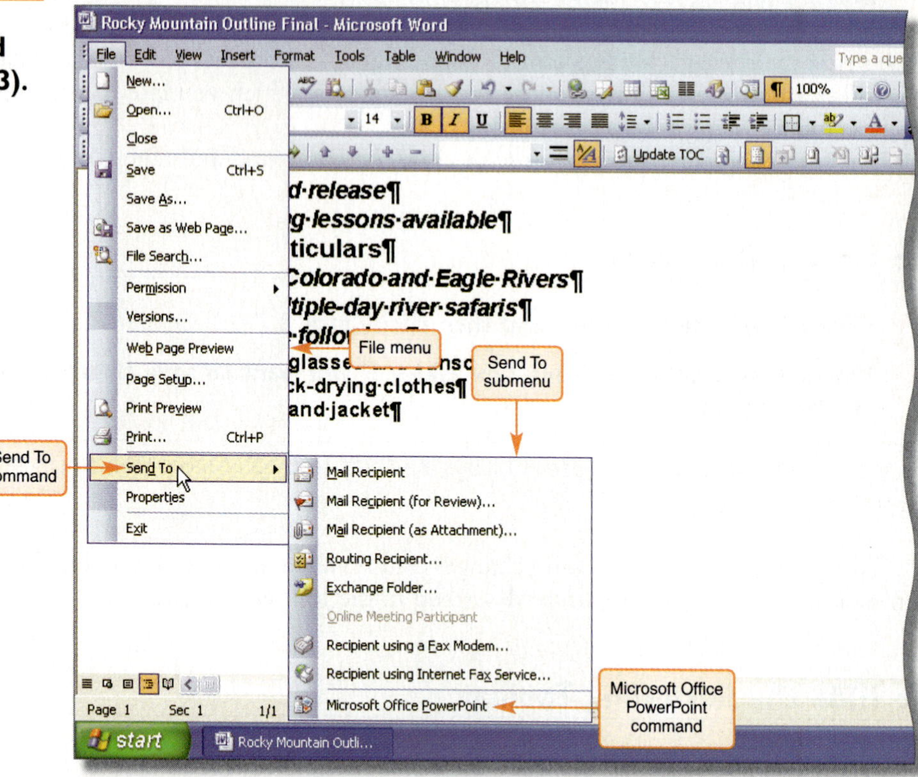

FIGURE 23

2

• **Click Microsoft Office PowerPoint on the Send To submenu.**

Word sends the outline to PowerPoint, which starts and then displays the slide show on the screen (Figure 24). The Word outline has four paragraphs formatted as Heading 1. Thus, the PowerPoint slide show contains four slides.

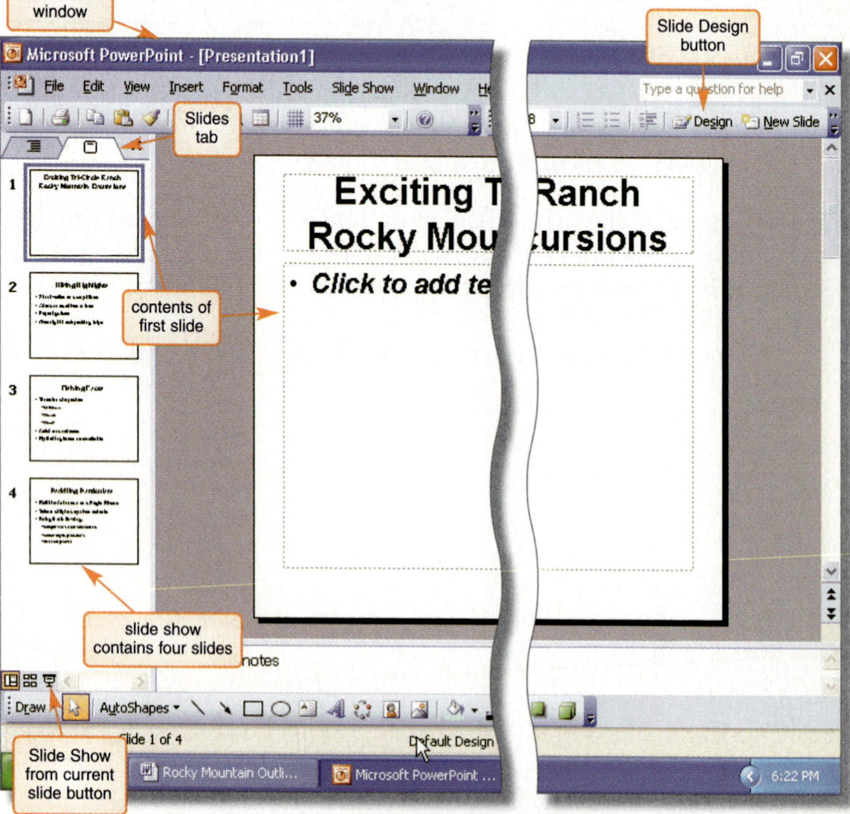

FIGURE 24

You can use PowerPoint to make a few adjustments to the slide show so it looks like Figure 1d on page WD 458. For example, the first slide should use the slide layout called Title Slide, and all slides should use the Mountain Top design template.

To Modify a PowerPoint Slide Show

1. **Right-click the first slide in the Slides tab and then click Slide Layout on the shortcut menu.**
2. **When PowerPoint displays the Slide Layout task pane, click the top-left text layout (called Title Slide) to apply the Title Slide layout to the first slide.**
3. **Click the Slide Design button on the Formatting toolbar.**
4. **When PowerPoint displays the Slide Design task pane, scroll through the list of designs until Mountain Top is displayed. Click Mountain Top.**

PowerPoint changes the layout of the first slide and applies the Mountain Top design to all slides (shown in Figure 1d).

To view the slide show in PowerPoint, click the Slide Show from current slide button in the lower-left corner of the PowerPoint window above the status bar. To move through the slide show one slide at a time, simply click anywhere on the displayed slide.

The following steps describe how to save the slide show in PowerPoint.

To Save the Slide Show

1. **With a floppy disk in drive A, click File on the menu bar and then click Save As.**
2. **Type** `Rocky Mountain Slide Show` **in the File name box. Do not press the ENTER key.**
3. **If necessary, click the Save in box arrow and then click 3½ Floppy (A:).**
4. **Click the Save button in the Save As dialog box.**

PowerPoint saves the slide show on a floppy disk in drive A with the file name, Rocky Mountain Slide Show.

More About

PowerPoint Slide Shows

When you save a slide show, PowerPoint appends the extension .ppt to the end of the file name. If your computer displays extensions for known file types, then this file will be displayed as Rocky Mountain Slide Show.ppt.

The outline and slide show are complete. The final tasks are to quit PowerPoint and Word.

To Quit PowerPoint and Word

1. **In PowerPoint, click File on the menu bar and then click Exit.**
2. **In Word, click File on the menu bar and then click Exit. If Word displays a dialog box about saving changes, click the No button.**

The PowerPoint and Word windows close.

Collaboration Feature Summary

In creating the outline for this feature, you learned how to work with Word's collaboration features and also how to send a Word outline to PowerPoint. First, you learned how to switch to outline view and then enter headings into the outline. Then, the feature showed how to e-mail a document for review, insert and edit comments, track changes, review tracked changes and view comments, and compare and merge documents. Finally, you learned how to send an outline to PowerPoint for use in a slide show.

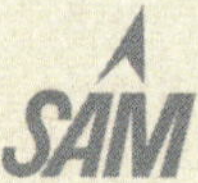

If you have a SAM user profile, you may have access to hands-on instruction, practice, and assessment of the skills covered in this project. Log in to your SAM account and go to your assignments page to see what your instructor has assigned.

What You Should Know

Having completed this feature, you should be able to perform the tasks below. The tasks are listed in the same order they were presented in this feature. For a list of the buttons, menus, toolbars, and commands introduced in this feature, see the Quick Reference Summary at the back of this book and refer to the Page Number column.

1. Enter Headings in an Outline (WD 459, WD 460)
2. Save a File (WD 461)
3. E-Mail a Document for Review (WD 462)
4. E-mail an Open Document as an Attachment (Not for Review) (WD 462)
5. Insert a Comment in the Reviewing Pane (WD 463)
6. Edit a Comment in a Comment Balloon (WD 464)
7. Insert a Comment in a Comment Balloon (WD 465)
8. Change Reviewer Information (WD 466)
9. Track Changes (WD 467)
10. Stop Tracking Changes (WD 468)
11. Review Tracked Changes and View Comments (WD 469)
12. Save a File with a New File Name (WD 472)
13. Print the Outline (WD 472)
14. Modify Reviewer Ink Colors and Balloon Options (WD 472)
15. Modify the Balloon Text Style (WD 473)
16. Compare and Merge Documents (WD 473)
17. Close a Document (WD 475)
18. Hide the Reviewing Toolbar (WD 475)
19. Send an Outline to PowerPoint (WD 476)
20. Modify a PowerPoint Slide Show (WD 477)
21. Save the Slide Show (WD 477)
22. Quit PowerPoint and Word (WD 477)

More About

Quick Reference

For a table that lists how to complete the tasks covered in this book using the mouse, menu, shortcut menu, and keyboard, see the Quick Reference Summary at the back of this book, or visit the Word 2003 Quick Reference Web page (scsite.com/wd2003/qr).

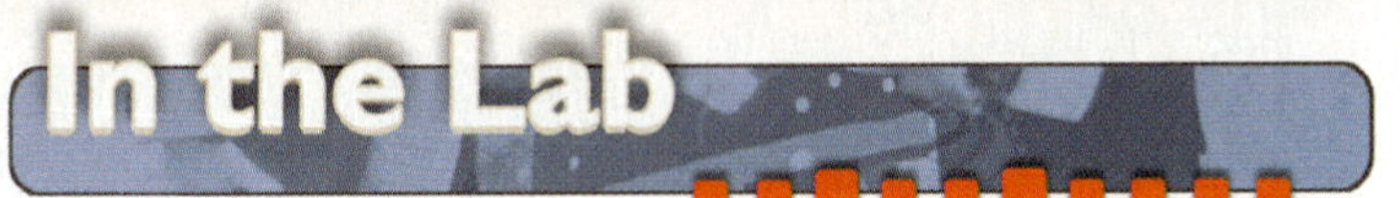

1 Creating an Outline and Sending It to PowerPoint

Problem: Fitness center employees present many classes on a variety of physical and emotional wellness topics. Carol O'Malley, coordinator at Mid-City College Fitness Center, has contacted you to help her prepare an outline and a presentation that will be delivered at community fairs and at the local shopping mall.

Instructions:

1. In Word, create the outline shown in Figure 25. Save the outline with the file name, Lab CF-1 Wellness Outline. Print the outline in outline view.
2. Send the Word outline to PowerPoint. In PowerPoint, change the first slide to the Title Slide layout and then apply an appropriate design template to the entire slide show. Save the slide show with the file name, Lab CF-1 Wellness Slide Show. View and then print the slide show.
3. If your instructor permits, send the outline to him or her as an e-mail attachment.

Enhance Your Wellness at Mid-City College Fitness Center
Mind/Body Programs
- ***Meditation***
  - **Various techniques**
  - **Practice time included**
- ***Stress Management Workshop***
  - **Relaxation strategies**
  - **Four-part series**

Lifestyle Programs
- ***CPR and First Aid***
  - **Certification and recertification**
  - **American Red Cross instructors**
- ***Smoking Cessation***
  - **Eight-session group program**
  - **Individual consultations**

Nutrition Programs
- ***Nutrition Connection***
  - **Semester-long program**
  - **Change your lifestyle to enhance your health**
  - **Achieve your weight-management goals**
  - **Increase your self-esteem**
- ***Dining Out: Eat and Be Healthy***

FIGURE 25

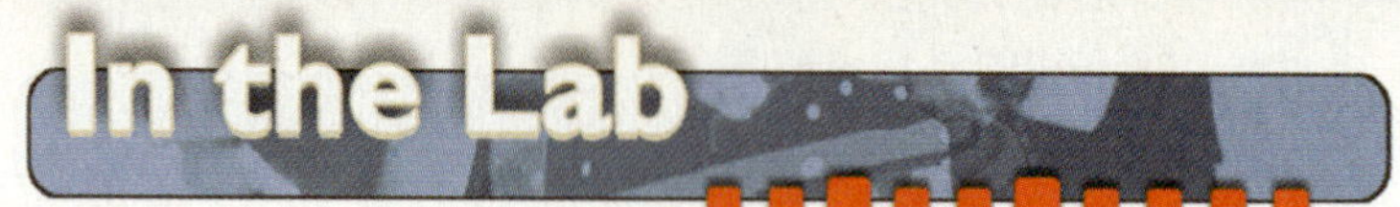

2 Working with Tracked Changes and Comments

Problem: As editor for the school newspaper, you review all articles before they are published. One section of the newspaper spotlights a student athlete of the month. For the next issue, the author has prepared an article about an outstanding athlete and sent it to you for review. When you review the article, you find several areas where you wish to make changes and offer suggestions. The document, named Lab CF-2 Spotlight Athlete First Draft, is located on the Data Disk. If you did not download the Data Disk, see the inside back cover for instructions for downloading the Data Disk or see your instructor.

Instructions:

1. Open the Lab CF-2 Spotlight Athlete First Draft file on the Data Disk.
2. Read (view) the comment and follow its instruction. Edit the comment so it includes a message that you completed the requested task.
3. Use Word's change-tracking feature to insert, delete, and replace text in the article. Make at least 10 changes to the article and insert at least three comments. Save the document with the file name, Lab CF-2 Spotlight Athlete Revision 1. Print the article with tracked changes showing and again without tracked changes showing.
4. Assume you are the author of the article and have received it back from the editor. Review the tracked changes and read the comments. Accept at least one-half of the changes, reject at least one of the changes, and delete all comments. Save the document with the file name, Lab CF-2 Spotlight Athlete Revision 2.
5. Compare and merge the original document with the revised document into a new document. Print the new document. Save the document with the file name, Lab CF-2 Spotlight Athlete Revision 3.
6. Obtain the revised article from another student in your class. Compare and merge your classmate's document into your document. Review all changes. Accept and reject the changes as you feel necessary. Save the document with the file name, Lab CF-2 Spotlight Athlete Revision 4. Print the revised document. If your instructor permits, e-mail the merged document for his or her review.

3 Modifying Tracking Changes Options

Problem: As editor for the Old Town Historical newsletter (shown in Figure 6-104 on page WD 450), you review all articles before they are published. For the next issue, the author has prepared an article about funding for a historic home renovation. The article, named Lab 6-1 Home Renovation Article, is located on the Data Disk. If you did not download the Data Disk, see the inside back cover for instructions for downloading the Data Disk or see your instructor. You are to review this article.

Instructions: After you open the file on the Data Disk, save it with the new name, Lab CF-3 Home Renovation Article Revised. Change your reviewer's ink colors for all markup options: insertions, deletions, formatting, changed lines, and comments. Change the balloon text style to 10-point Arial font. Change the balloon width to two inches. Make at least 10 changes to the article and insert at least three comments. Obtain the tracked changes documents from three other students in your class. Compare and merge the documents from these students into your document. Print this document with tracked changes showing. Hide all reviewer's changes, except for one. Accept and reject that reviewer's changes, as you deem appropriate. Show all remaining reviewer's changes. Accept and reject changes, as you deem appropriate. Save the final document. Print the final document. Turn in both the document with all reviewer's tracked changes and the final document.

MICROSOFT Office Excel 2003

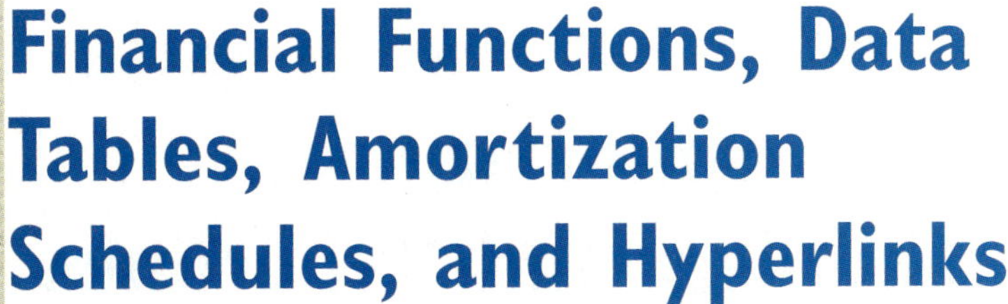

Financial Functions, Data Tables, Amortization Schedules, and Hyperlinks

PROJECT

CASE PERSPECTIVE

e-Money Lenders is a small online lending institution. The company has grown rapidly in the last decade, as consumers increasingly turn to the Web to gather financial and loan information. Ela Patel studied technology, business, and finance in college. Her friends were not surprised when she accepted a technical position with e-Money Lenders after graduation. Ela has been promoted several times since she joined the firm, most recently to the position of chief software engineer in charge of all programming and Web development.

Her major goal during these first few months is to computerize the loan department so loan officers can generate instant loan information when a customer calls to finalize an online loan. To help her achieve this goal, Ela has hired you as her technical consultant.

First, she asks you to create a workbook that will calculate loan payment information, display an amortization schedule, and display a table that shows loan payments for varying interest rates. She also wants loan officers to have the ability to print portions of the worksheet and display the e-Money Lenders Financial Services 2004 Statement of Condition using a Web browser.

Finally, to ensure that the loan officers do not delete the formulas in the worksheet, she has asked you to investigate the feasibility of protecting cells in the worksheet so they cannot be changed accidentally.

As you read through this project, you will learn how to create more complex worksheets using Excel's financial functions, data table commands, hyperlinks, and cell protection commands. You also will learn about some specialized printing techniques. Finally, you will learn how to hide and unhide sections of a workbook and use formula checking.

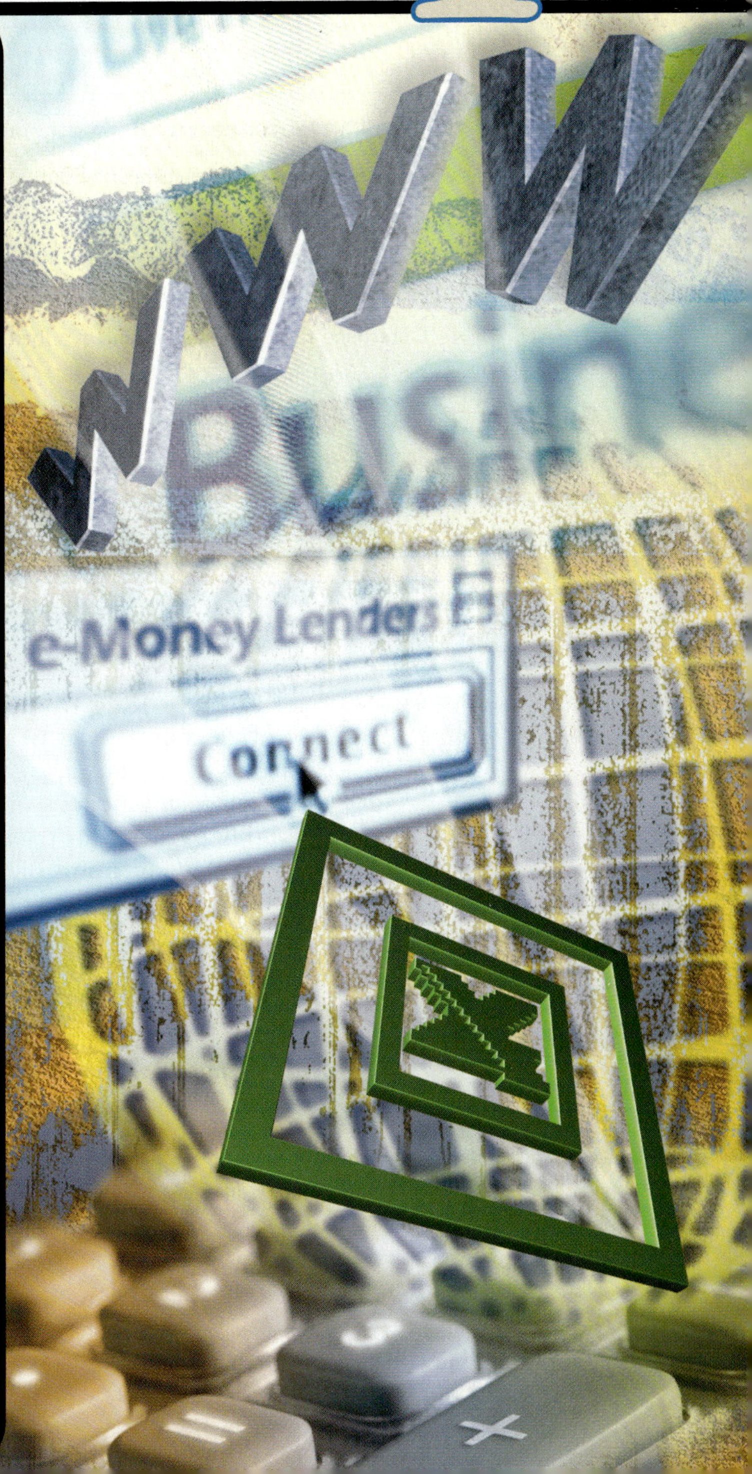

MICROSOFT Office Excel 2003

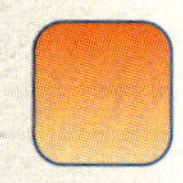

Financial Functions, Data Tables, Amortization Schedules, and Hyperlinks

PROJECT

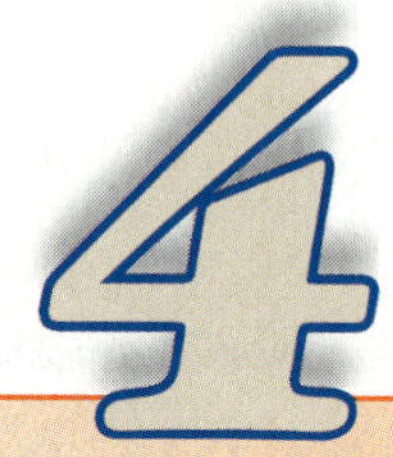

OBJECTIVES

You will have mastered the material in this project when you can:

- Control the color and thickness of outlines and borders
- Assign a name to a cell and refer to the cell in a formula using the assigned name
- Determine the monthly payment of a loan using the financial function PMT
- Use the financial functions PV (present value) and FV (future value)
- Create a data table to analyze data in a worksheet
- Add a pointer to a data table
- Create an amortization schedule
- Analyze worksheet data by changing values
- Add a hyperlink to a worksheet element
- Use names and the Set Print Area command to print sections of a worksheet
- Set print options
- Protect and unprotect cells in a worksheet
- Use the formula checking features of Excel
- Hide and unhide cell gridlines, rows, columns, sheets, and workbooks

Introduction

Two of the more powerful aspects of Excel are its wide array of functions and its capability of organizing answers to what-if questions. In this project, you will learn about financial functions such as the **PMT function**, which allows you to determine a monthly payment for a loan (cell E4 in Figure 4-1a), and the **PV function**, which allows you to determine the present value of an investment (column I in Figure 4-1a).

In earlier projects, you learned how to analyze data by using Excel's recalculation feature and goal seeking. This project introduces an additional what-if analysis tool, called data tables. You use a **data table** to automate data analyses and organize the answers returned by Excel. For example, the Interest Rate Schedule section on the lower left in Figure 4-1a is a data table used to determine the effect that the eleven different interest rates in column B have on the monthly payment, total interest, and total cost of a loan.

Another important loan analysis tool is the Amortization Schedule section (right side of Figure 4-1a). An **amortization schedule** shows the beginning and ending balances and the amount of payment that applies to the principal and interest over a period.

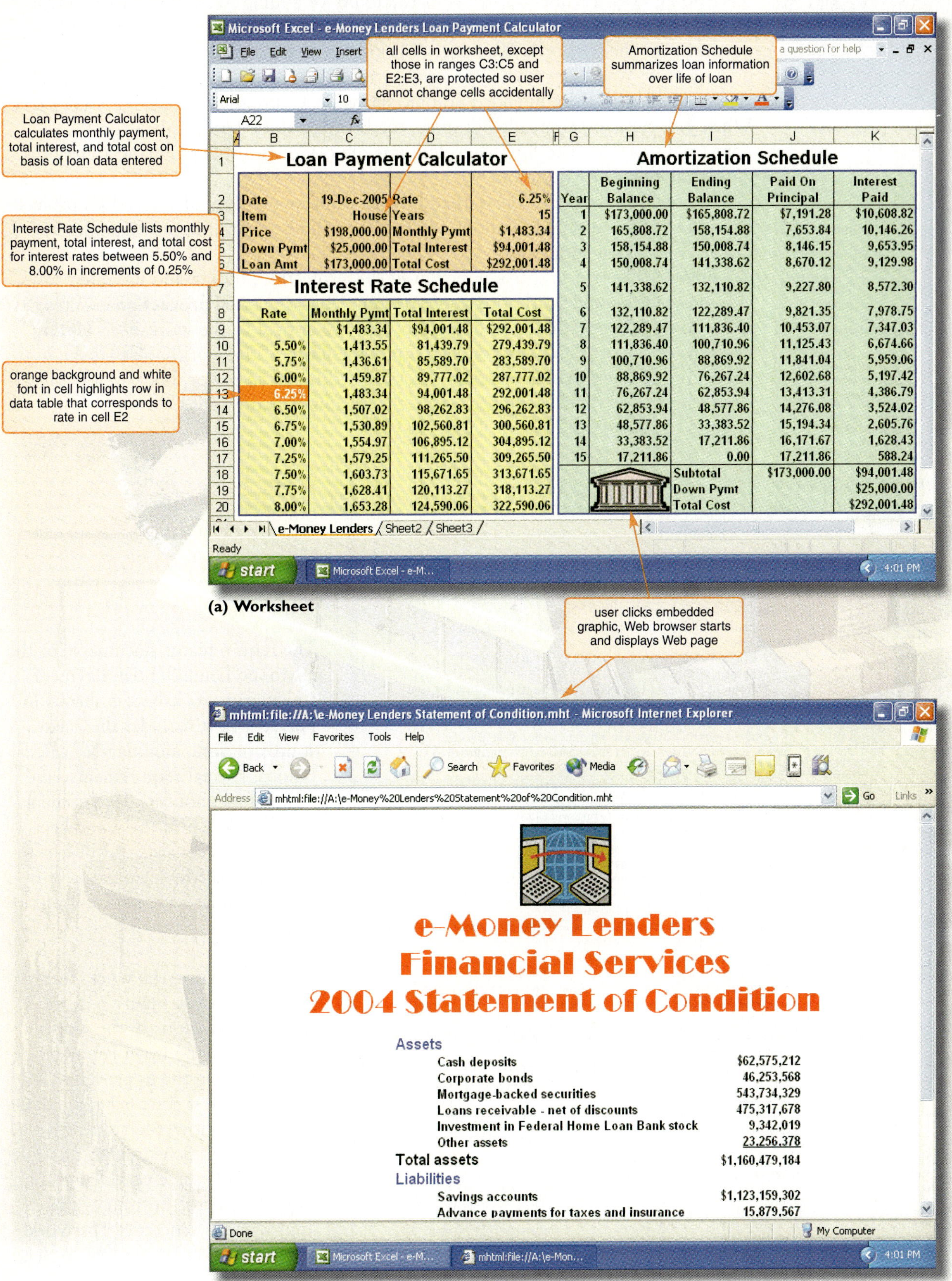

(a) Worksheet

(b) Web Page

FIGURE 4-1

More About

Good Worksheet Design

Do not create worksheets as if you are only going to use them once. Carefully design worksheets as if they will be on display and evaluated by your fellow workers. Smart worksheet design starts with visualizing the results you need. For additional information on good worksheet design, visit the Excel 2003 More About Web page (scsite.com/ex2003/more) and click Smart Spreadsheet Design.

Another key feature of Excel is its capability of adding hyperlinks to a worksheet. **Hyperlinks** are built-in links that indicate the file path and name to another Office document or the URL of a Web page. Clicking the hyperlink opens the Office document or Web page in the appropriate application. In this project, the hyperlink is associated with the embedded graphic shown in Figure 4-1a on the previous page. When you click the embedded graphic, the browser starts and displays the Web page (Figure 4-1b). The Web page contains the e-Money Lenders Financial Services 2004 Statement of Condition.

In previous projects, you learned how to print in a variety of ways. This project continues with a discussion about additional methods of printing using names and the Set Print Area command.

Finally, this project introduces you to cell protection; hiding and unhiding rows, columns, sheets, and workbooks; and formula checking. **Cell protection** ensures that users do not change values inadvertently that are critical to the worksheet. **Hiding** portions of a workbook lets you show only the parts of the workbook that the user needs to see. The **formula checker** checks the formulas in a workbook in a manner similar to the way the spell checker checks for misspelled words.

Project Four — e-Money Lenders Loan Payment Calculator

The requirements document for the e-Money Lenders Loan Payment Calculator worksheet is shown in Figure 4-2. It includes the needs, source of data, summary of calculations, special requirements, and other facts about its development.

The sketch of the worksheet (Figure 4-3) consists of titles, column and row headings, location of data values, calculations, and a general idea of the desired formatting.

As shown in the worksheet sketch shown in Figure 4-3, the four basic sections of the worksheet are (1) the Loan Payment Calculator on the upper-left side, (2) the Interest Rate Schedule data table on the lower-left side, (3) the Amortization Schedule on the right side, and (4) the embedded graphic hyperlink at the bottom of the amortization schedule. The worksheet will be created in this order.

REQUEST FOR NEW WORKBOOK

Date Submitted:	November 7, 2005
Submitted By:	Ela Patel
Worksheet Title:	Loan Payment Calculator
Needs:	An easy-to-read worksheet (Figure 4-3) that: 1. determines the monthly payment, total interest, and total cost for a loan; 2. shows a data table that answers what-if questions based on changing interest rates; 3. highlights the rate in the data table that matches the actual interest rate; 4. shows an amortization schedule that lists annual summaries; and 5. includes a hyperlink assigned to a graphic so that when you click the graphic, the e-Money Lenders 2004 Statement of Condition Web page appears.
Source of Data:	The data (item, price of the item, down payment, interest rate, and term of the loan in years) is determined by the loan officer and customer when they initially meet to review the loan. The Excel Table command creates the data table.
Calculations:	1. The following calculations must be made for each loan: a. Loan Amount = Price – Down Payment b. Monthly Payment = PMT function c. Total Interest = 12 × Years × Monthly Payment – Loan Amount d. Total Cost = Price + Total Interest 2. The amortization schedule involves the following calculations: a. Beginning Balance = Loan Amount b. Ending Balance = PV function or 0 c. Paid on Principal = Beginning Balance – Ending Balance d. Interest Paid = 12 × Monthly Payment – Paid on Principal or 0 e. Paid on Principal Subtotal = SUM function f. Interest Paid Subtotal = SUM function
Special Requirements:	1. Add a hyperlink to an HTML file containing the company's 2004 Statement of Condition. 2. Assign names to the ranges of the three major sections of the worksheet and the worksheet itself, so that the names can be used to print each section separately. 3. Protect the worksheet in such a way that the loan officers cannot enter data into wrong cells mistakenly.

Approvals

Approval Status:	X	Approved
		Rejected
Approved By:	Ela Patel, Chief Software Engineer	
Date:	November 10, 2005	
Assigned To:	J. Quasney, Spreadsheet Specialist	

FIGURE 4-2

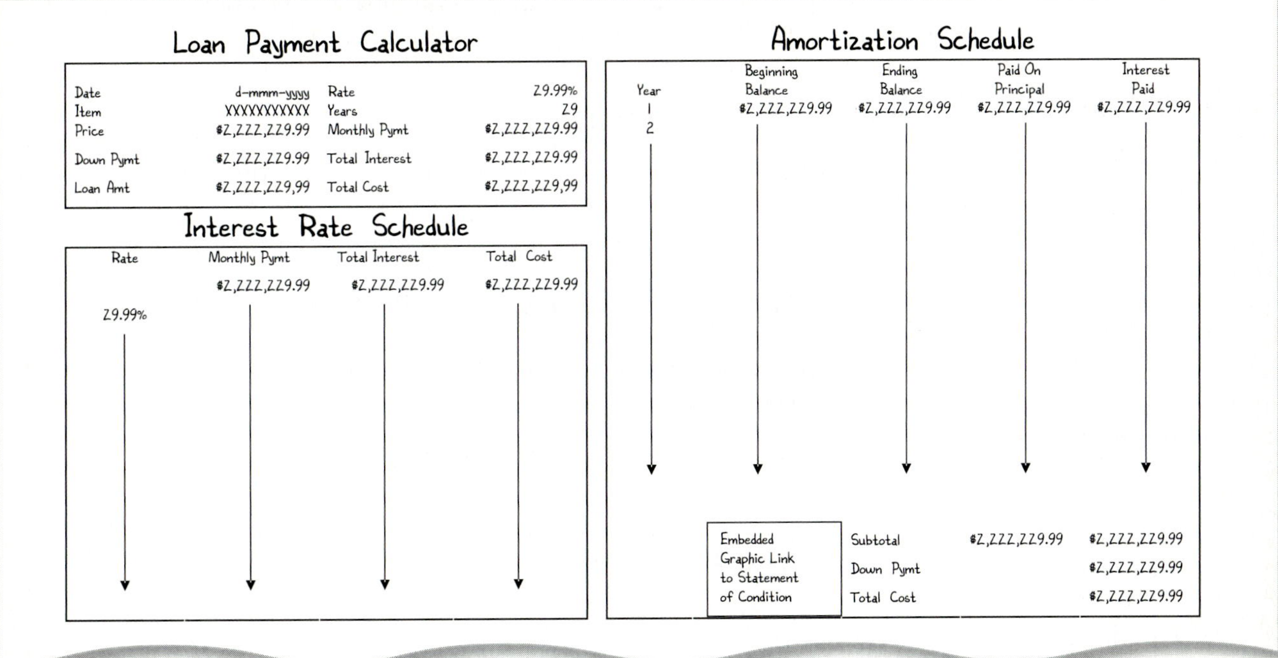

FIGURE 4-3

Starting and Customizing Excel

With the requirements document and sketch of the worksheet complete, the next step is to start and customize Excel. If you are stepping through this project on a computer and you want your screen to agree with the figures in this book, then you should change your computer's resolution to 800 × 600. To change the resolution on your computer, see Appendix D. The following steps start Excel and customize the Excel window.

> **Q&A**
>
> **Q:** Can more than one instance of Excel be running at the same time?
>
> **A:** Yes. Besides opening multiple workbooks in Excel, you can run multiple instances of Excel. Each instance of Excel will show as a button on the Windows taskbar. You also can have each workbook within an instance of Excel show as a button on the Windows taskbar by clicking Options on the Tools menu and then clicking Windows in Taskbar in the Show area on the View sheet of the Options dialog box.

To Start and Customize Excel

1. **Click the Start button on the Windows taskbar, point to All Programs on the Start menu, point to Microsoft Office on the All Programs submenu, and then click Microsoft Office Excel 2003 on the Microsoft Office submenu.**
2. **If the Excel window is not maximized, double-click its title bar to maximize the window.**
3. **If the Language bar appears, right-click it and then click Close the Language bar on the shortcut menu.**
4. **If the Getting Started task pane appears in the Excel window, click its Close button in the upper-right corner.**
5. **If the Standard and Formatting toolbars are positioned on the same row, click the Toolbar Options button and then click Show Buttons on Two Rows.**

Excel displays a blank workbook. The Standard and Formatting toolbars appear on two rows as shown at the top of Figure 4-4 on page EX 247.

If your toolbars appear differently than those shown in Figure 4-4, see Appendix D for additional information on resetting the toolbars and menus.

More About

Using the Mouse to Enter Arithmetic Operators

If you prefer to enter formulas using the mouse instead of the keyboard, then you can add arithmetic operator buttons to any toolbar. To add the arithmetic operator buttons, right-click a toolbar, click Customize, click the Commands tab, click Insert in the Categories list, and drag the arithmetic operator buttons to the desired toolbar one at a time.

Bolding the Entire Worksheet

The following steps show how to assign a bold format to the entire worksheet so that all entries will be emphasized.

To Bold the Font of the Entire Worksheet

1. **Click the Select All button immediately above row heading 1 and to the left of column heading A.**
2. **Click the Bold button on the Formatting toolbar.**

No immediate change takes place on the screen. As text and numbers are entered into the worksheet, however, Excel will display them in bold.

Entering the Section Title, Row Titles, and System Date, and Saving the Workbook

The next step is to enter the Loan Payment Calculator section title, row titles, and system date and then save the workbook. To make the worksheet easier to read, the width of column A will be decreased to 0.50 characters and used as a separator between the Loan Payment Calculator section and the row headings on the left. Using a column as a separator between sections on a worksheet is a common technique employed by spreadsheet specialists. The width of columns B through E will be increased so the intended values fit. The heights of rows 1 and 2, which contain the titles, will be increased so they stand out. The worksheet title also will be changed to 16-point Franklin Gothic Medium font.

The following steps show how to enter the section title, row titles, and system date and then save the workbook.

More About

Global Formatting

To assign formats to all the cells in all the worksheets in a workbook, click the Select All button, right-click a tab, and click Select All Sheets on the shortcut menu. Next, assign the formats. To deselect the sheets, hold down the SHIFT key and click the Sheet1 tab. You also can select a cell or a range of cells and then select all sheets to assign formats to that cell or a range of cells on all sheets in a workbook.

To Enter the Section Title, Row Titles, and System Date, and Save the Workbook

1. **Select cell B1. Enter** `Loan Payment Calculator` **as the section title. Select the range B1:E1. Click the Merge and Center button on the Formatting toolbar.**
2. **With cell B1 active, click the Font box arrow on the Formatting toolbar, scroll down in the Font list, and then click Franklin Gothic Medium (or a font of your choice). Click the Font Size box arrow on the Formatting toolbar and then click 16.**
3. **Position the mouse pointer on the bottom boundary of row heading 1. Drag down until the ScreenTip indicates Height: 21.75 (29 pixels). Position the mouse pointer on the bottom boundary of row heading 2. Drag down until the ScreenTip indicates Height: 27.00 (36 pixels).**
4. **Select cell B2 and then enter** `Date` **as the row title.**

5 With cell C2 selected, enter `=now()` to display the system date.

6 Right-click cell C2 and then click Format Cells on the shortcut menu. When Excel displays the Format Cells dialog box, click the Number tab, click Date in the Category list, scroll down in the Type list, and then click 14-Mar-2001. Click the OK button.

7 Enter the following row titles:

CELL	ENTRY	CELL	ENTRY
B3	Item	D2	Rate
B4	Price	D3	Years
B5	Down Pymt	D4	Monthly Pymt
B6	Loan Amt	D5	Total Interest
		D6	Total Cost

8 Position the mouse pointer on the right boundary of column heading A and then drag to the left until the ScreenTip indicates Width: 0.50 (6 pixels).

9 Position the mouse pointer on the right boundary of column heading B and then drag to the right until the ScreenTip indicates Width: 10.14 (76 pixels).

10 Click column heading C to select it and then drag through column headings D and E. Position the mouse pointer on the right boundary of column heading C and then drag until the ScreenTip indicates Width: 12.14 (90 pixels).

11 Double-click the Sheet1 tab and then enter `e-Money Lenders` as the sheet name. Right-click the tab and then click Tab Color. Click light orange (column 2, row 3) and then click the OK button.

12 Click the Save button on the Standard toolbar. Save the workbook using the file name `e-Money Lenders Loan Payment Calculator` on a floppy disk in drive A.

More About

Concatenation

You can concatenate text, numbers, or text and numbers from two or more cells into a single cell. The ampersand (&) is the concatenation operator. For example, if cell A1 = AB, cell A2 = CD, cell A3 = 25, and you assign cell A4 the formula =A1&A2&A3, then ABCD25 displays in cell A4.

Excel displays the Loan Payment Calculator section title, row titles, and system date as shown in Figure 4-4.

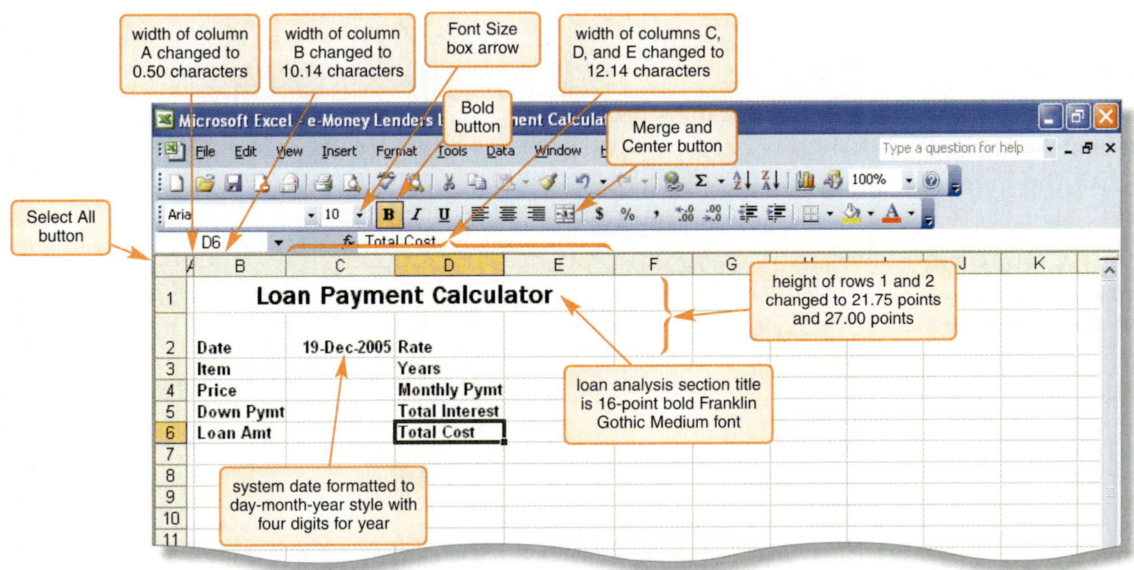

FIGURE 4-4

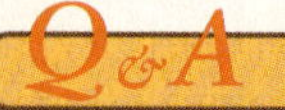

Q: Must the mouse pointer be within the selected range when you right-click for the shortcut menu to apply to it?

A: Excel requires that you point to the object (cell, range, toolbar) on the screen when you right-click to display the corresponding shortcut menu. For example, if you select the range G6:J14 and right-click with the mouse pointer on cell A1, then the shortcut menu pertains to cell A1 and not the selected range G6:J14.

Adding Custom Borders and a Background Color to a Range

In previous projects, you were introduced to outlining a range using the Borders button on the Formatting toolbar. The Borders button, however, does not allow you to select a color and offers only a limited border thickness selection. To control the color and thickness, Excel requires that you use the Border sheet in the Format Cells dialog box. The following steps add a thick blue border color and a tan background color to the Loan Payment Calculator section. Rather than using the Fill Color button to color the background of a range as was done in previous projects, the steps use the Patterns sheet in the Format Cells dialog box. To subdivide the row titles and numbers further, light borders also are added within the section as shown in Figure 4-1a on page EX 243.

To Add Custom Borders and a Background Color to a Range

1

- **Select the range B2:E6 and then right-click.**

Excel highlights the range and displays the shortcut menu (Figure 4-5).

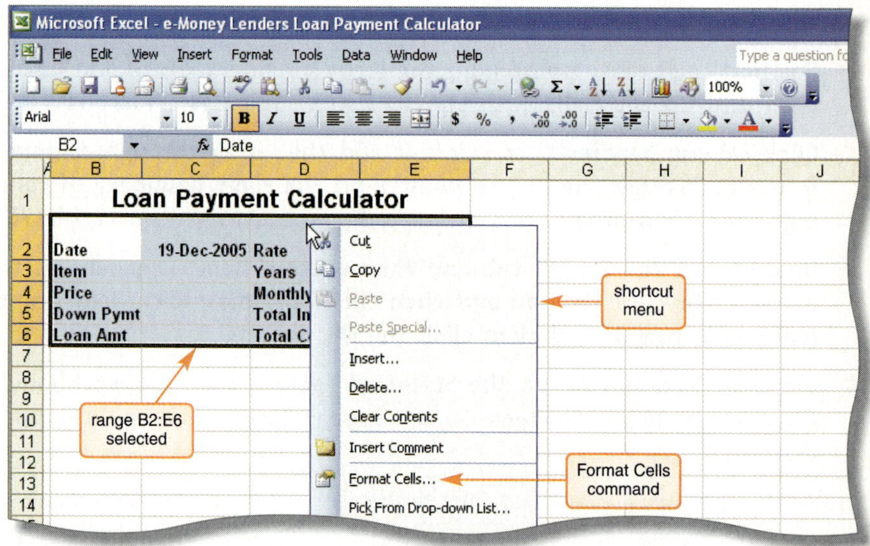

FIGURE 4-5

2

- **Click Format Cells on the shortcut menu.**
- **When Excel displays the Format Cells dialog box, click the Border tab.**
- **Click the Color box arrow, click Blue (column 6, row 2) on the Color palette, and then click the medium line style in the Style box (column 2, row 5).**
- **Click the Outline button in the Presets area.**

Excel previews the blue outline border in the Border area (Figure 4-6).

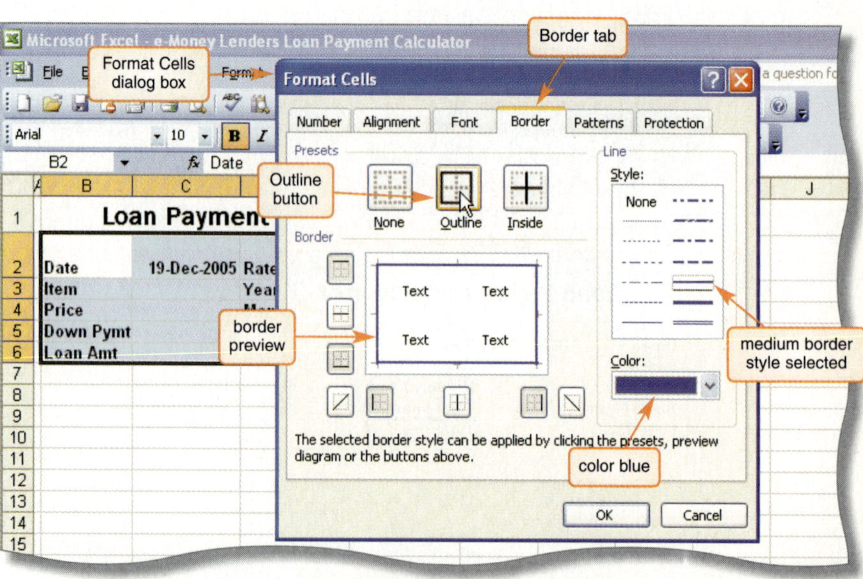

FIGURE 4-6

3

- **Click the Color box arrow and then click Automatic (row 1) on the Color palette.**
- **Click the light border in the Style box (column 1, row 7) and then click the Vertical Line button in the Border area.**

Excel previews the black vertical border in the Border area (Figure 4-7). Selecting Automatic on the Color palette sets the line color to black.

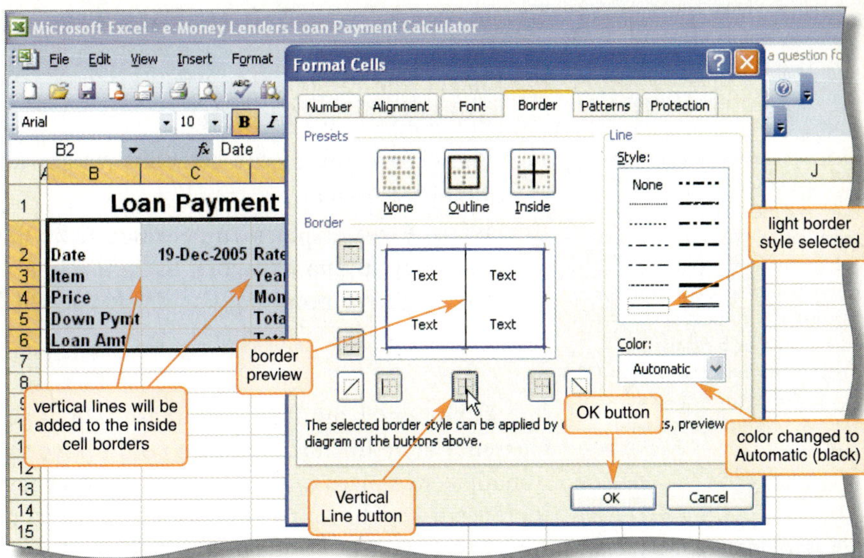

FIGURE 4-7

4

- **Click the Patterns tab and then click Tan (column 2, row 5) on the Color palette.**
- **Click the OK button and then select cell B8 to deselect the range B2:E6.**

Excel adds a blue outline with vertical borders to the right side of each column in the range B2:E6 (Figure 4-8). The background of the range B2:E6 is tan.

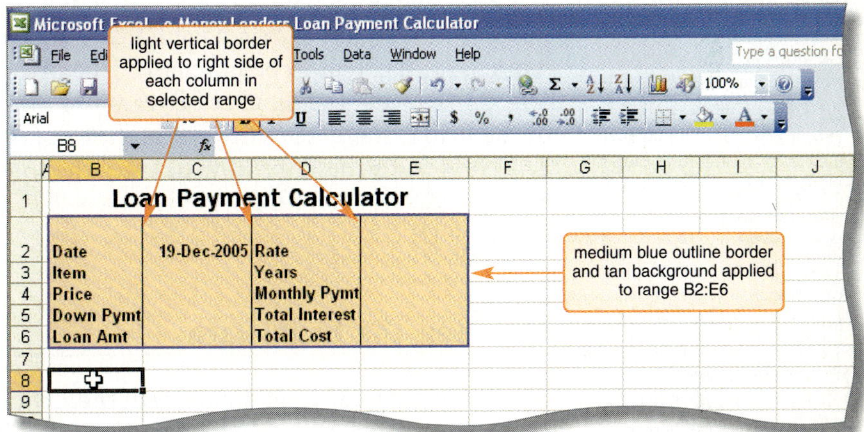

FIGURE 4-8

Other Ways

1. Select range, click Fill Color button arrow on Formatting toolbar, click color, click Borders button arrow on Formatting toolbar, click border
2. On Format menu click Cells, click Patterns tab, click color, click Border tab, click border
3. In Voice command mode, say "Format, Cells, Border, [select border], Patterns, [select color], OK"

As shown in Figure 4-7, you can add a variety of borders with different colors to a cell or range of cells to improve its appearance. It is important that you select border characteristics in the order specified in the steps; that is, (1) choose the color; (2) choose the border line style; and (3) choose the border type. If you attempt to do these steps in any other order, you may not end up with the desired borders.

Formatting Cells Before Entering Values

While usually you format cells after you enter values in cells, Excel also allows you to format cells before you enter the values. For example, at the beginning of this project, bold was applied to all the cells in the blank worksheet. The steps on the next page assign the Currency style format with a floating dollar sign to the ranges C4:C6 and E4:E6 before the values are entered.

More About

When to Format

Excel lets you format (1) before you enter data; (2) when you enter data, through the use of format symbols; (3) incrementally after entering sections of data; and (4) after you enter all the data. Spreadsheet specialists usually format a worksheet in increments as they build the worksheet, but occasions do exist where it makes sense to format cells before you enter any data.

To Format Cells Before Entering Values

1. **Select the range C4:C6. While holding down the CTRL key, select the nonadjacent range E4:E6.**
2. **Right-click one of the selected ranges and then click Format Cells on the shortcut menu.**
3. **When Excel displays the Format Cells dialog box, click the Number tab. Click Currency in the Category list and then click the second format, $1,234.10, in the Negative numbers list. Click the OK button.**

The ranges C4:C6 and E4:E6 are assigned the Currency style format with a floating dollar sign.

As you enter numbers into these cells, Excel will display the numbers using the Currency style format. You also could have selected the range B4:E6 rather than the nonadjacent ranges and assigned the Currency style format to this range, which includes text. The Currency style format has no impact on text in a cell.

More About

Entering Percents

When you format a cell to display percentages, Excel assumes that whatever you enter into that cell in the future will be a percentage. Thus, if you enter the number .5, Excel translates the value as 50%. A potential problem arises, however, when you start to enter numbers greater than or equal to one. For instance, if you enter the number 25, do you mean 25% or 2500%? If you want Excel to treat the number 25 as 25% instead of 2500% and Excel interprets the number 25 as 2500%, then click Options on the Tools menu. When the Options dialog box displays, click the Edit tab and make sure the Enable automatic percent entry check box is selected.

Entering the Loan Data

As shown in the Source of Data section of the Request for New Workbook document in Figure 4-2 on page EX 244, five items make up the loan data in the worksheet: the item to be purchased, the price of the item, the down payment, the interest rate, and the number of years until the loan is paid back (also called the term of the loan). These items are entered into cells C3 through C5 and cells E2 and E3. The steps below describe how to enter the following loan data: Item — House; Price — $198,000.00; Down Payment — $25,000.00; Interest Rate — 6.25%; and Years — 15.

To Enter the Loan Data

1. **Select cell C3. Type** `House` **and then click the Enter box in the formula bar. With cell C3 still active, click the Align Right button on the Formatting toolbar. Select cell C4 and then enter** `198000` **for the price of the house. Select cell C5 and then enter** `25000` **for the down payment.**
2. **Select cell E2. Enter** `6.25%` **for the interest rate. Select cell E3 and then enter** `15` **for the number of years.**

Excel displays the loan data in the worksheet as shown in Figure 4-9.

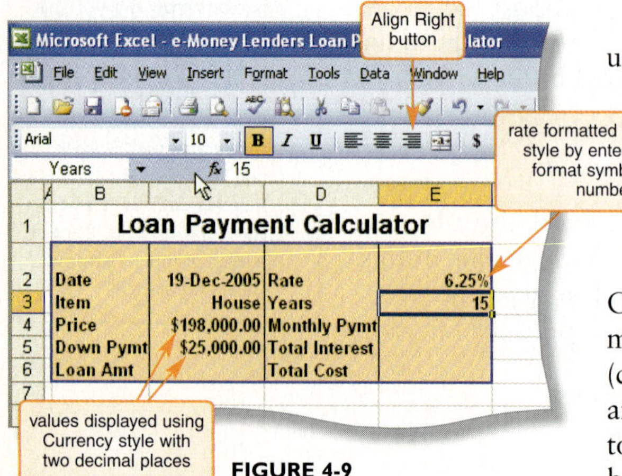

FIGURE 4-9

The values in cells C4 and C5 in Figure 4-9 are formatted using the Currency style with two decimal places, because this format was assigned to the cells prior to entering the values. Excel also automatically formats the interest rate in cell E2 to the Percent style with two decimal places, because the percent sign (%) was appended to 6.25 when it was entered.

Calculating the four remaining entries in the Loan Payment Calculator section of the worksheet — loan amount (cell C6), monthly payment (cell E4), total interest (cell E5), and total cost (cell E6) — requires formulas that reference cells C4, C5, C6, E2, and E3. The formulas will be entered referencing names assigned to cells, such as Price, rather than cell references, such as C4, because names are easier to remember than cell references.

Creating Cell Names Based on Row Titles

Worksheets often have column titles at the top of each column and row titles to the left of each row that describe the data within the worksheet. You can use these titles within formulas when you want to refer to the related data by name. A cell **name** is created from column and row titles through the use of the Name command on the Insert menu. You also can use the same command to define descriptive names that are not column titles or row titles to represent cells, ranges of cells, formulas, or constants.

Naming a cell that you plan to reference in a formula helps make the formula easier to read and remember. For example, the loan amount in cell C6 is equal to the price in cell C4 minus the down payment in cell C5. Therefore, according to what you learned in the earlier projects, you can enter the loan amount formula in cell C6 as =C4 – C5. By naming cells C4 and C5 using the corresponding row titles in cells B4 and B5, however, you can enter the loan amount formula as =Price – Down Pymt, which is clearer and easier to understand than =C4 – C5.

The following steps assign the row titles in the range B4:B6 to their adjacent cell in column C and assigns the row titles in the range D2:D6 to their adjacent cell in column E.

> *More About*
>
> **Cell References in Formulas**
>
> Are you tired of writing formulas that make no sense when you read them because of cell references? The Name command can help add clarity to your formulas by allowing you to assign names to cells. You then can use the names, such as Amount, rather than the cell reference, such as H10, in the formulas you create.

To Create Names Based on Row Titles

1

- **Select the range B4:C6.**
- **Click Insert on the menu bar and then point to Name on the Insert menu.**

Excel highlights the range B4:C6 and displays the Insert menu and Name submenu (Figure 4-10).

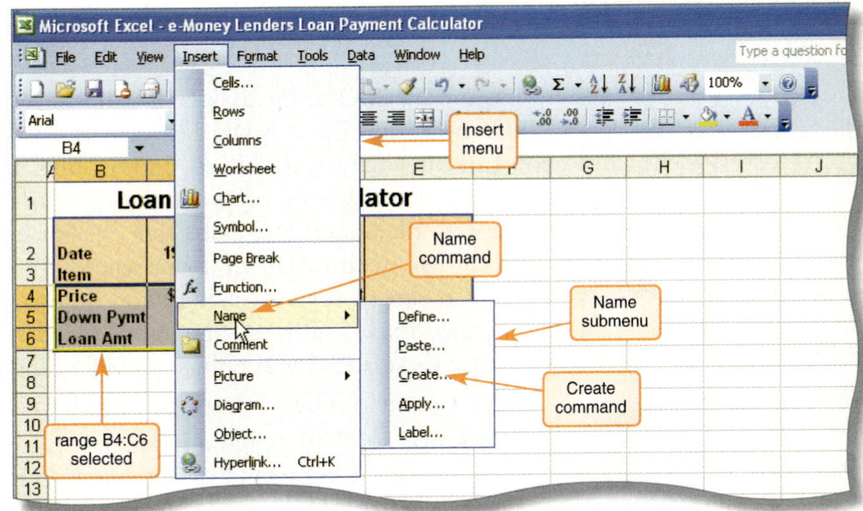

FIGURE 4-10

2

- **Click Create on the Name submenu.**

Excel displays the Create Names dialog box (Figure 4-11). Excel automatically selects the Left column check box in the Create names in area because the left column of the cells selected in Step 1 contains text.

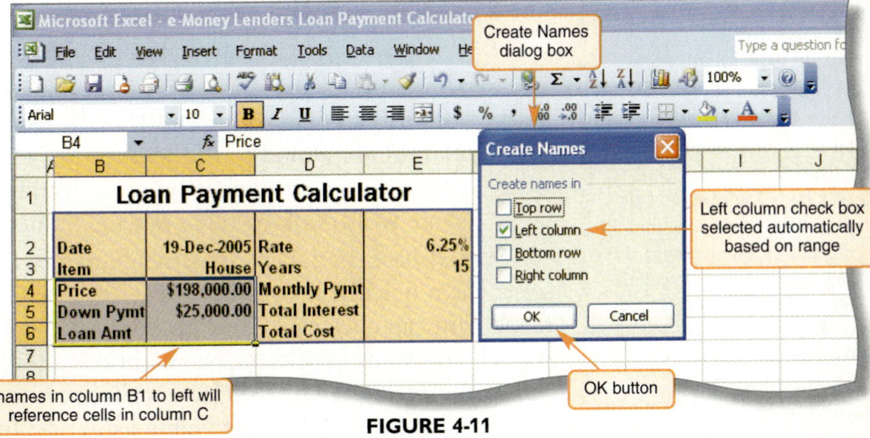

FIGURE 4-11

3

- **Click the OK button.**
- **Select the range D2:E6, click Insert on the menu bar, and then point to Name on the Insert menu.**
- **Click Create on the Name submenu and then click the OK button in the Create Names dialog box.**
- **Select cell B8 to deselect the range D2:E6 and then click the Name box arrow in the formula bar to view the names created.**

Excel displays the Name list with the names in the worksheet (Figure 4-12a). Figure 4-12b shows that the list of names also appears when you use the Go To command on the Edit menu.

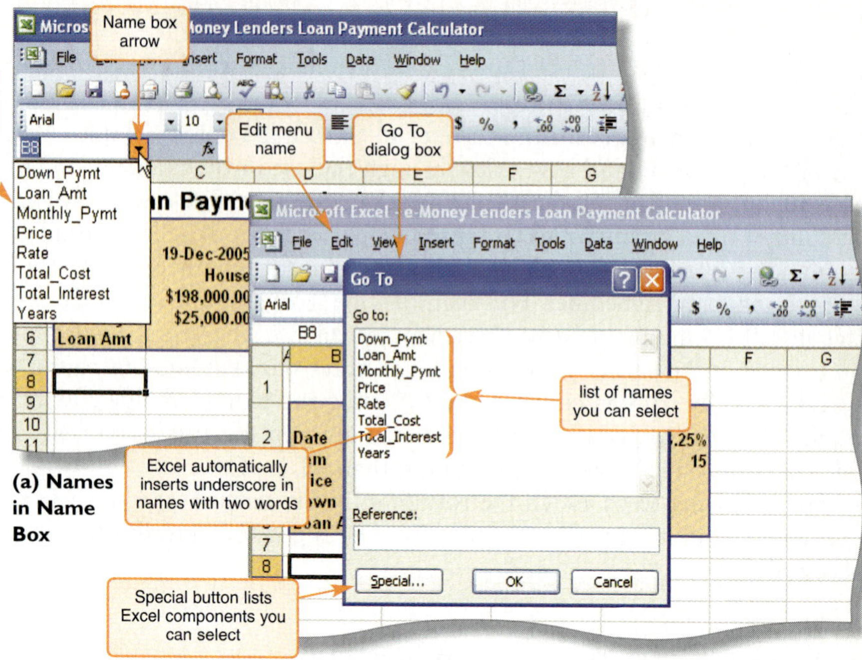

FIGURE 4-12

Other Ways

1. Select cell or range, type name in Name box, press ENTER key
2. Select cell or range, on Insert menu point to Names, click Define, [type name], click OK button
3. Select cell or range, in Voice Command mode, say "Insert, Name, Create, OK"

More About

Naming Cells

You can create row and column names at the same time if you have a worksheet with column titles and row titles. Simply select the column titles and row titles along with the cells to name. On the Insert menu, point to Name and then click Create on the Name submenu. In the Create Names dialog box, click both Top row and Left column and then click the OK button. After naming the cells, you can use the column title and row title separated by a space to refer to the intersecting cell (for example, =Boston Web+Dallas Telesales).

You now can use the assigned names in formulas to reference cells in the ranges C4:C6 or E2:E6. Excel is not case-sensitive with respect to names of cells. Hence, you can enter the names of cells in formulas in uppercase or lowercase letters. To use a name that is made up of two or more words in a formula, you should replace any space with the underscore character (_). For example, the name, Down Pymt, is written as down_pymt or Down_Pymt when you want to reference the adjacent cell C5.

If you enter a formula using Point mode and click a cell that has an assigned name, then Excel will insert the name of the cell rather than the cell reference. Consider these additional points regarding the assignment of names to cells:

1. A name can be a minimum of 1 character to a maximum of 255 characters.
2. If you want to assign a name that is not a text item in an adjacent cell, use the Define command on the Name submenu (Figure 4-10 on the previous page) or select the cell or range and then type the name in the Name box in the formula bar.
3. Names are absolute cell references. This is important to remember if you plan to copy formulas that contain names, rather than cell references.
4. Excel displays the names in alphabetical order in the Name list when you click the Name box arrow and in the Go To dialog box when you click Go To on the Edit menu (Figures 4-12a and 4-12b).
5. Names are **global** to the workbook. That is, a name assigned to a cell or cell range on one worksheet in a workbook can be used on other sheets in the same workbook to reference the name cell or range.

Spreadsheet specialists often assign names to a cell or range of cells so they can select them quickly. If you want to select a cell or range of cells using the assigned name, you can click the Name box arrow (Figure 4-12a) and then click the name of the cell you want to select. This method is similar to using the Go To command on the Edit menu or the F5 key to select a cell, but it is much quicker. When you select a name that references a range in the Name list, Excel highlights the range on the worksheet.

Determining the Loan Amount Using Names

To determine the loan amount in cell C6, subtract the down payment in cell C5 from the price in cell C4. As indicated earlier, this can be done by entering the formula =C4 – C5 or by entering the formula =price – down_pymt in cell C6. You also can use Point mode to enter the formula, as shown in the following steps.

To Enter the Loan Amount Formula Using Names

1

- **Select cell C6.**
- **Type = (equal sign), click cell C4, type - (minus sign), and then click cell C5.**

Excel displays the formula in cell C6 and in the formula bar using the names of the cells rather than the cell references (Figure 4-13).

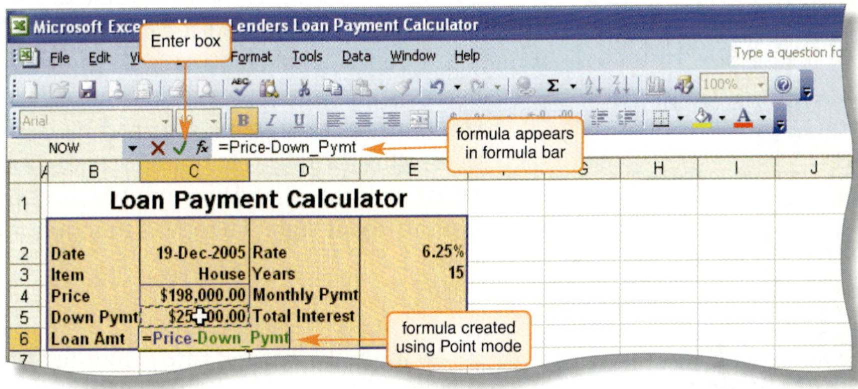

FIGURE 4-13

2

- **Click the Enter box.**

Excel assigns the formula =Price – Down_Pymt to cell C6. The result of the formula ($173,000.00) appears in cell C6 using the Currency style format assigned earlier (Figure 4-14). With cell C6 active, Excel displays the cell name Loan_Amt in the Name box, rather than C6.

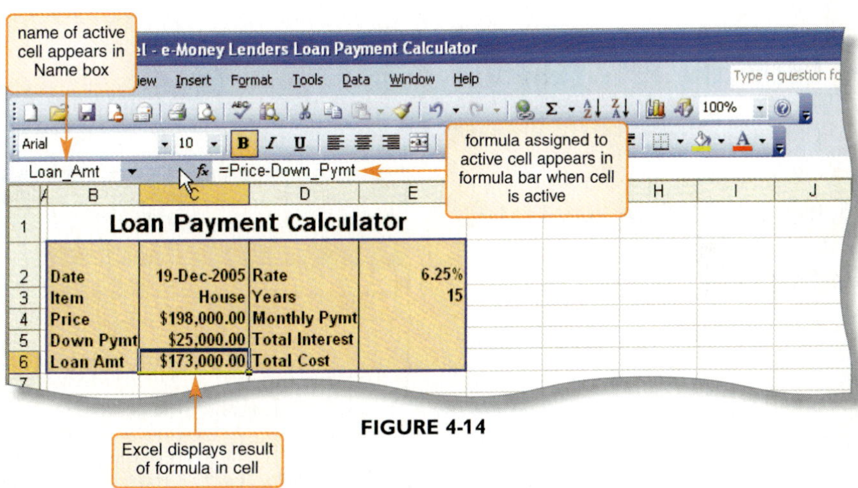

FIGURE 4-14

An alternative to assigning names is to use labels. A **label** is a row title or column title, similar to the adjacent names created earlier. Any row title or column title can be used in a formula to reference corresponding cells. The major difference between labels and names is that Excel considers labels to be relative references, while it considers names to be absolute references. This difference has implications you need to be aware of when you use labels in formulas that are copied. Other differences between labels and names include: (1) labels cannot be used on other worksheets in the workbook; (2) labels do not appear in the Name list or Go To dialog box (Figures 4-12a and 4-12b); and (3) you can use them without entering underscores in place of spaces.

It also is important to note that Excel does not recognize labels in formulas unless you activate label usage. To activate label usage, click Tools on the menu bar, click Options, click the Calculation tab, and select Accept labels in formulas. Any row title or column title then can be used in formulas to reference corresponding cells.

More About

Closing Parenthesis

Excel does not require you to enter the closing parenthesis when assigning a function to a cell, as shown in Figure 4-13 on the previous page. You must use the Enter box or ENTER key to complete the entry, however.

More About

Entering Interest Rates

An alternative to requiring the user to enter an interest rate in percent form, such as 7.75%, is to allow the user to enter the interest rate as a number without an appended percent sign (7.75) and then divide the interest rate by 1200, rather than 12.

Determining the Monthly Payment Using Names

The next step is to determine the monthly payment for the loan in cell E4. You can use Excel's **PMT function** to determine the monthly payment. The PMT function has three arguments — rate, payment, and loan amount. Its general form is:

=PMT(rate, periods, loan amount)

where rate is the interest rate per payment period, periods is the number of payments, and loan amount is the amount of the loan.

In the worksheet shown in Figure 4-14 on the previous page, Excel displays the annual interest rate in cell E2. Financial institutions, however, calculate interest on a monthly basis. Therefore, the rate value in the PMT function is rate / 12 (cell E2 divided by 12), rather than just rate (cell E2). The periods (or number of payments) in the PMT function is 12 * years (12 times cell E3) because there are 12 months, or 12 payments, per year.

Excel considers the value returned by the PMT function to be a debit and, therefore, returns a negative number as the monthly payment. To display the monthly payment as a positive number, begin the function with a negative sign instead of an equal sign. The PMT function for cell E4 is:

–PMT(rate / 12, 12 * years, loan_amt)

monthly interest rate   number of payments   loan amount

The following steps use the keyboard, rather than Point mode, to enter the PMT function to determine the monthly payment in cell E4.

To Enter the PMT Function

1

• **Select cell E4. Type** `-pmt(rate / 12, 12 * years, loan_amt` **as the function.**

Excel displays the PMT function in cell E4 and in the formula bar (Figure 4-15). The ScreenTip shows the general form of the PMT function. The arguments in brackets in the ScreenTip are optional and not required for the computation described here. Excel will add the closing parenthesis to the function automatically.

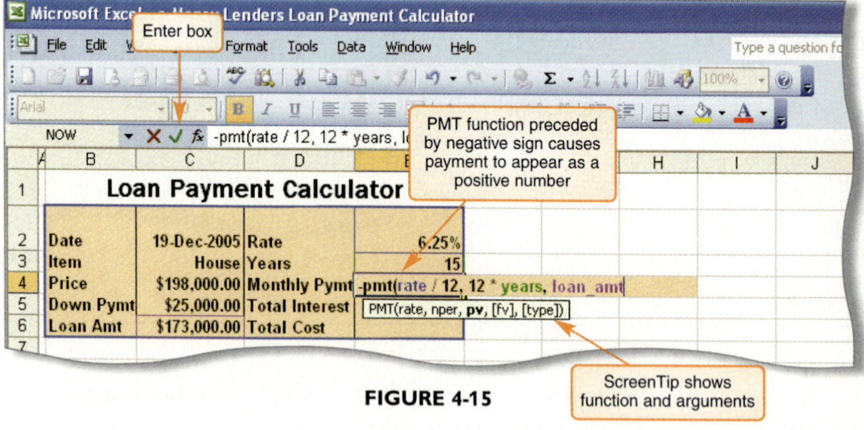

FIGURE 4-15

2

• **Click the Enter box in the formula bar.**

Excel displays the monthly payment $1,483.34 in cell E4, based on a loan amount of $173,000.00 (cell C6) with an annual interest rate of 6.25% (cell E2) for a term of 15 years (cell E3), as shown in Figure 4-16.

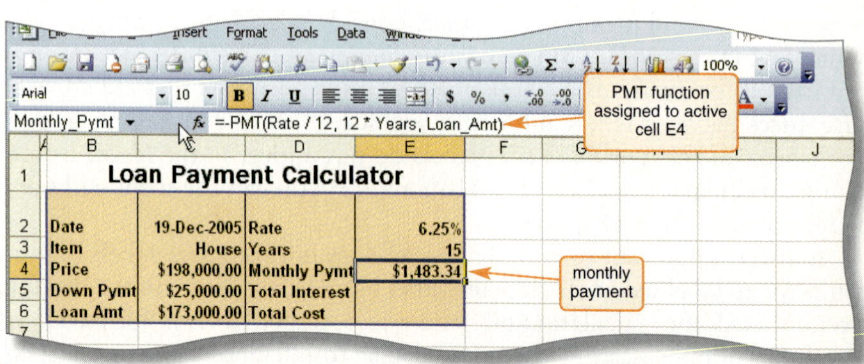

FIGURE 4-16

In addition to the PMT function, Excel provides more than 50 additional financial functions to help you solve the most complex finance problems. These functions save you from entering long, complicated formulas to obtain needed results. Table 4-1 summarizes three of the more frequently used financial functions.

Table 4-1 Financial Functions

FUNCTION	DESCRIPTION
FV (rate, periods, payment)	Returns the future value of an investment based on periodic, constant payments, and a constant interest rate.
PMT (rate, periods, loan amount)	Calculates the payment for a loan based on the loan amount, constant payments, and a constant interest rate.
PV (rate, periods, payment)	Returns the present value of an investment. The present value is the total amount that a series of future payments is worth now.

Determining the Total Interest and Total Cost Using Names

The next step is to determine the total interest the borrower will pay on the loan (the lending institution's gross profit on the loan) and the total cost the borrower will pay for the item being purchased. The total interest (cell E5) is equal to the number of payments times the monthly payment, less the loan amount:

=12 * years * monthly_pymt – loan_amt

The total cost of the item to be purchased (cell E6) is equal to the price plus the total interest:

=price + total_interest

The following steps enter formulas to determine the total interest and total cost using names.

More About

Range Finder

Remember to check all formulas carefully. You can double-click a cell with a 0formula and Excel will use Range Finder to highlight the cells that provide data to the formula. While Range Finder is active, you can drag the outlines from one cell to another to change the cells referenced in the formula.

To Determine the Total Interest and Total Cost

1. **Select cell E5. Use Point mode and the keyboard to enter the formula** `=12 * years * monthly_pymt – loan_amt` **to determine the total interest.**
2. **Select cell E6. Use Point mode and the keyboard to enter the formula** `=price + total_interest` **to determine the total cost.**
3. **Select cell B8 to deselect cell E6.**
4. **Click the Save button on the Standard toolbar to save the workbook using the file name e-Money Lenders Loan Payment Calculator.**

Excel displays a total interest (the lending institution's gross profit) of $94,001.48 in cell E5 and a total cost of $292,001.48 in cell E6, which is the total cost of the home to the borrower (Figure 4-17). Excel saves the workbook.

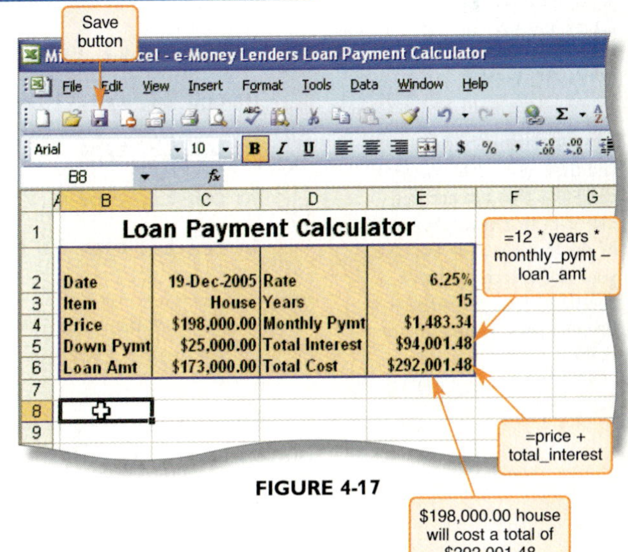

FIGURE 4-17

With the Loan Payment Calculator section of the worksheet complete, you can use it to determine the monthly payment, total interest, and total cost for any loan data.

Entering New Loan Data

Assume you want to purchase a Beetle GLX for $26,500.00. You have $4,350.00 for a down payment and you want the loan for a term of five years. e-Money Lenders currently is charging 7.75% interest for a five-year auto loan. The following steps show how to enter the new loan data.

To Enter New Loan Data

1. **Select cell C3. Type** `Beetle GLX` **and then press the DOWN ARROW key.**
2. **In cell C4, type** `26500` **and then press the DOWN ARROW key.**
3. **In cell C5, type** `4350` **and then select cell E2.**
4. **In cell E2, type** `7.75%` **and then press the DOWN ARROW key.**
5. **In cell E3, type** `5` **and then select cell B8.**

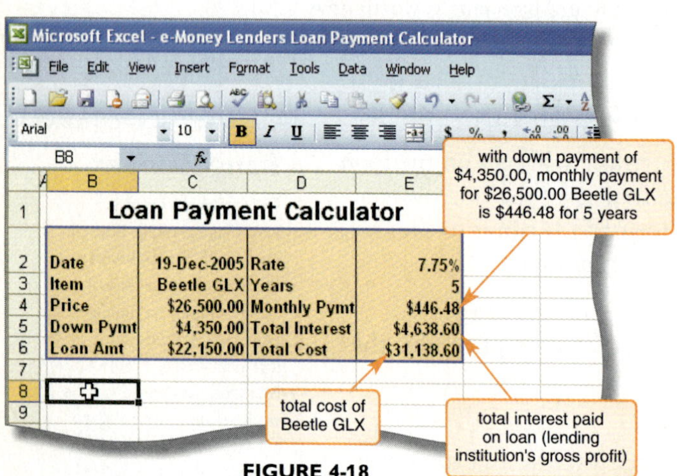

FIGURE 4-18

Excel instantaneously recalculates the loan information in cells C6, E4, E5, and E6 (Figure 4-18).

As you can see from Figure 4-18, the monthly payment for the Beetle GLX is $446.48. By paying for the car over a five-year period at an interest rate of 7.75%, you will pay total interest of $4,638.60 on the loan and pay a total cost of $31,138.60 for a $26,500.00 Beetle GLX.

Follow these steps to re-enter the original loan data.

To Enter the Original Loan Data

1. **Select cell C3. Type** `House` **and then press the DOWN ARROW key.**
2. **In cell C4, type** `198000` **and then press the DOWN ARROW key.**
3. **In cell C5, type** `25000` **and then select cell E2.**
4. **In cell E2, type** `6.25` **and then press the DOWN ARROW key.**
5. **In cell E3, type** `15` **and then select cell B8.**

Excel instantaneously recalculates all formulas in the worksheet each time you enter a value. Excel displays the original loan information as shown in Figure 4-17 on the previous page.

> *More About*
>
> **Testing a Worksheet**
>
> It is good practice to test the formulas in a worksheet over and over again until you are confident they are correct. Use data that tests the limits of the formulas. For example, you should enter negative numbers, zero, and large positive numbers to test the formulas.

An alternative to re-entering the original loan information is to click the Undo button on the Standard toolbar until the original loan data and information appears.

Using a Data Table to Analyze Worksheet Data

You already have seen that if you change a value in a cell, Excel immediately recalculates and displays the new results of any formulas that reference the cell directly or indirectly. But what if you want to compare the results of the formula for several different values? Writing down or trying to remember all the answers to the what-if questions would be unwieldy. If you use a data table, however, Excel will organize the answers in the worksheet for you automatically.

A **data table** is a range of cells that shows the answers generated by formulas in which different values have been substituted. Data tables are built in an unused area of the worksheet (in this case, the range B7:E20). Figure 4-19 illustrates the makeup of a one-input data table. With a **one-input data table**, you vary the value in one cell (in this worksheet, cell E2, the interest rate). Excel then calculates the results of one or more formulas and fills the data table with the results.

An alternative to a one-input table is a two-input data table. A **two-input data table** allows you to vary the values in two cells, but you can apply it to only one formula. A two-input data table example is illustrated in the In the Lab 1 exercise, Part 2 on page EX 298.

The interest rates that will be used to analyze the loan formulas in this project range from 5.50% to 8.00%, increasing in increments of 0.25%. The one-input data table shown in Figure 4-20 illustrates the impact of varying the interest rate on three formulas: the monthly payment (cell E4), total interest paid (cell E5), and the total cost of the item to be purchased (cell E6). The series of interest rates in column B are called **input values**.

> *More About*
>
> **Data Tables**
>
> Data tables have one purpose: to organize the answers to what-if questions. You can create two kinds of data tables. The first type involves changing one input value to see the resulting effect on one or more formulas. The second type involves changing two input values to see the resulting effect on one formula.

Entering the Data Table Titles and Column Titles

The first step in constructing the data table shown in Figure 4-20 is to enter the data table section title and column titles in the range B7:E8 and adjust the heights of rows 7 and 8.

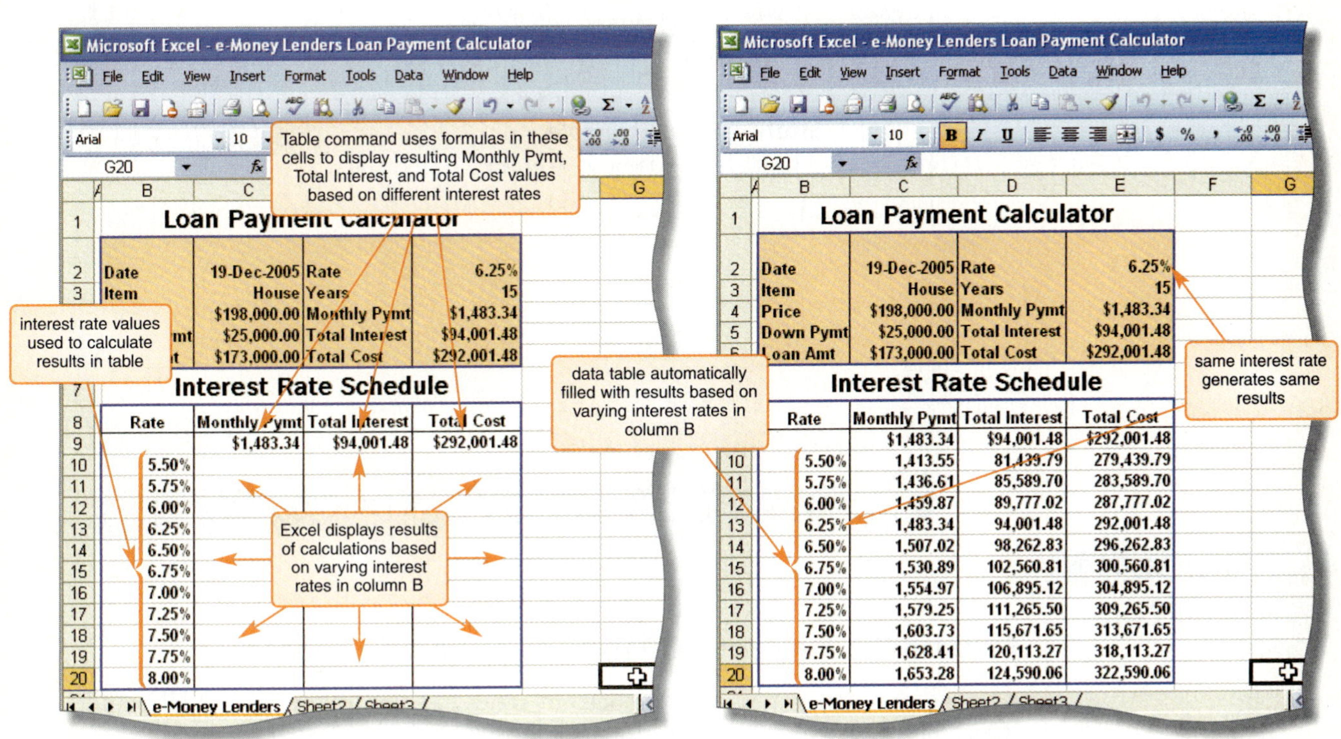

FIGURE 4-19

FIGURE 4-20

More About

Selecting Cells

If you double-click the top of the heavy black border surrounding an active cell, Excel will make the first non-blank cell in the column active. If you double-click the left side of the heavy black border surrounding the active cell, Excel will make the first non-blank cell in the row the active cell. This procedure works in the same fashion for the right border and the bottom border of the active cell.

To Enter the Data Table Title and Column Titles

1. **Select cell B7. Enter** `Interest Rate Schedule` **as the data table section title.**
2. **Select cell B1. Click the Format Painter button on the Standard toolbar. Select cell B7 to copy the format of cell B1.**
3. **Enter the column titles in the range B8:E8 as shown in Figure 4-21. Select the range B8:E8 and then click the Center button on the Formatting toolbar to center the column titles.**
4. **Position the mouse pointer on the bottom boundary of row heading 7. Drag down until the ScreenTip indicates Height: 21.75 (29 pixels). Position the mouse pointer on the bottom boundary of row heading 8. Drag down until the ScreenTip indicates Height: 16.50 (22 pixels). Click cell B10 to deselect the range B8:E8.**

Excel displays the data table title and column headings as shown in Figure 4-21.

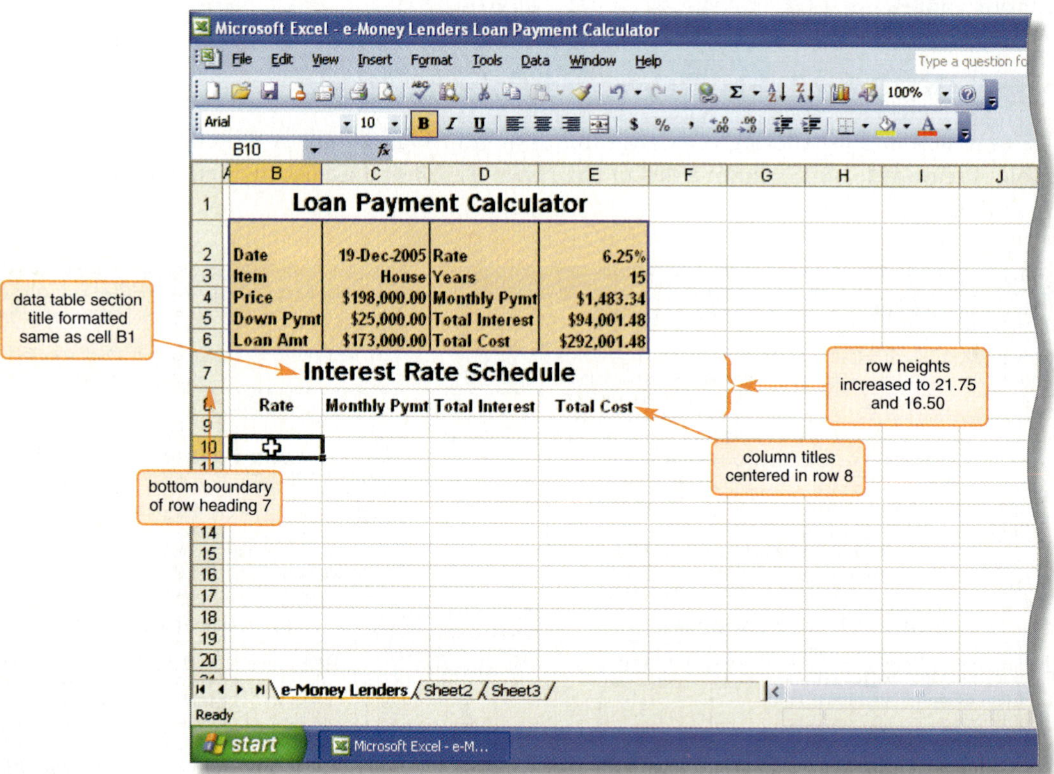

FIGURE 4-21

More About

Expanding Data Tables

The data table you see in Figure 4-20 on the previous page is relatively small. You can continue the series of percents to the bottom of the worksheet and insert additional formulas in columns to create as large a data table as you want.

Creating a Percent Series Using the Fill Handle

The next step is to create the percent series in column B using the fill handle. These percents will serve as the input data for the data table.

To Create a Percent Series Using the Fill Handle

1

- **With cell B10 selected, enter** 5.50% **as the first number in the series.**
- **Select cell B11 and then enter** 5.75% **as the second number in the series.**
- **Select the range B10:B11.**
- **Drag the fill handle through cell B20. Do not release the mouse button.**

Excel shades the border of the fill area (Figure 4-22). The ScreenTip, 8.00%, appears below the fill handle, indicating that the last value in the series in cell B20 will be 8.00%.

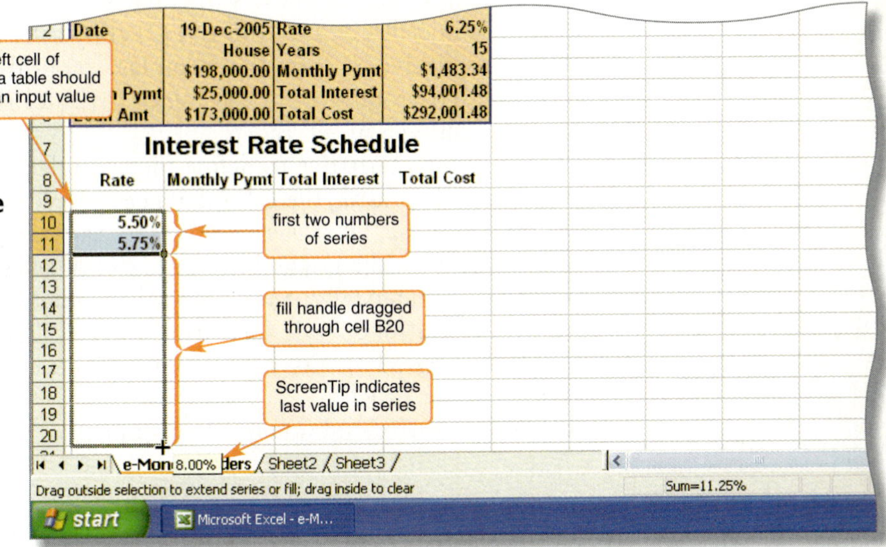

FIGURE 4-22

2

- **Release the mouse button. Click cell C9 to deselect the range B10:B20.**

Excel generates the percent series from 5.50% to 8.00% in the range B10:B20 (Figure 4-23). The series increases in increments of 0.25%. Excel displays the Auto Fill Options button to the right of the last cell filled.

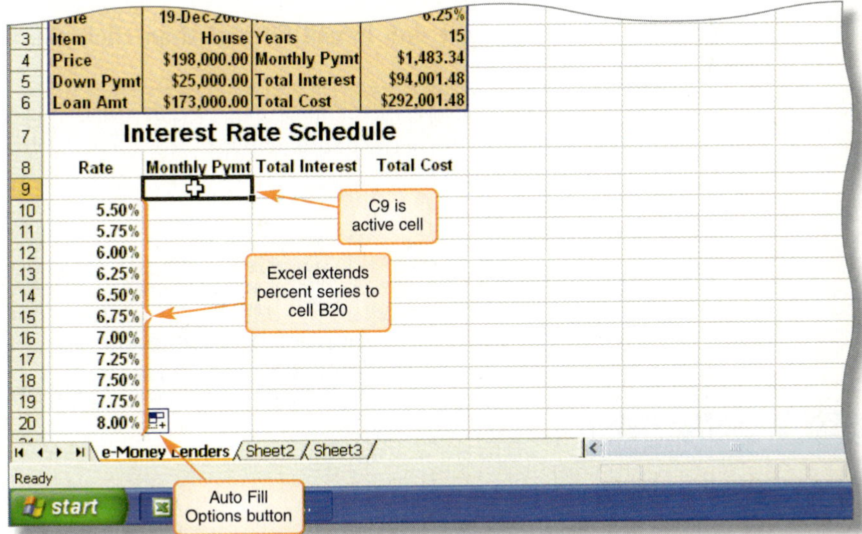

FIGURE 4-23

Other Ways

1. Right-drag fill handle in direction to fill, click Fill Series on shortcut menu
2. In Voice Command mode, say "Edit, Fill, Series, AutoFill, OK"

Excel will use the percents in column B to calculate the formulas to be evaluated and entered at the top of the data table in row 9. This series begins in cell B10, not cell B9, because the cell immediately to the left of the formulas in a one-input data table should not include an input value.

Entering the Formulas in the Data Table

The next step in creating the data table is to enter the three formulas in cells C9, D9, and E9. The three formulas are the same as the monthly payment formula in cell E4, the total interest formula in cell E5, and the total cost formula in cell E6. The number of formulas you place at the top of a one-input data table depends on the application. Some one-input data tables will have only one formula, while others might have several. In this case, three formulas are affected when the interest rate changes.

Excel provides four ways to enter these formulas in the data table: (1) retype the formulas in cells C9, D9, and E9; (2) copy cells E4, E5, and E6 to cells C9, D9, and E9, respectively; (3) enter the formulas =monthly_pymt in cell C9, =total_interest in cell D9, and =total_cost in cell E9; or (4) enter the formulas =e4 in cell C9, =e5 in cell D9, and =e6 in cell E9.

The best alternative to define the formulas in the data table is the fourth one, which involves using the cell references preceded by an equal sign. This is the best method because: (1) it is easier to enter the cell references; (2) if you change any of the formulas in the range E4:E6, the formulas at the top of the data table are updated automatically; and (3) Excel automatically assigns the format of the cell reference (Currency style format) to the cell. Using the names of the cells in formulas is nearly as good an alternative, but if you use cell names, Excel will not assign the format to the cells.

The following steps enter the formulas of the data table in row 9.

To Enter the Formulas in the Data Table

1. **With cell C9 active, type** =e4 **and then press the RIGHT ARROW key.**
2. **Type** =e5 **in cell D9 and then press the RIGHT ARROW key.**
3. **Type** =e6 **in cell E9 and then click the Enter box.**

Excel displays the results of the formulas in the range C9:E9 (Figure 4-24). Excel automatically assigns the Currency style format to cells C9 through E9 based on the formats assigned to cells E4 through E6.

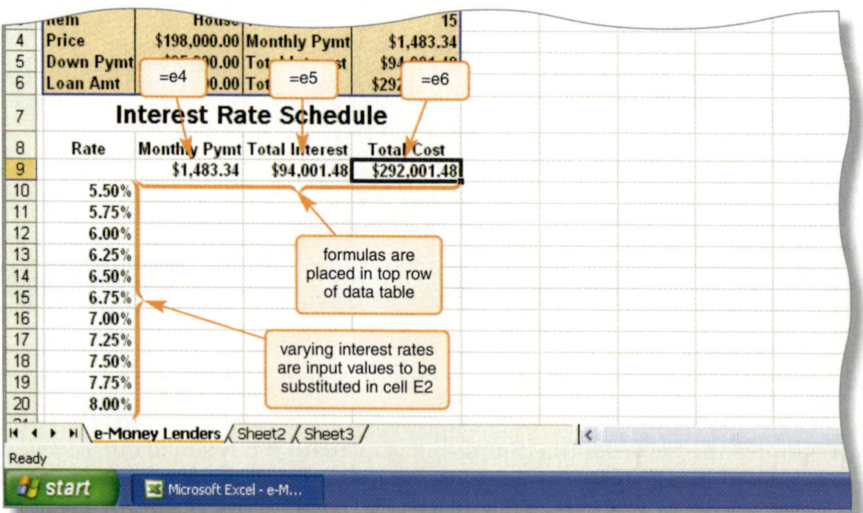

FIGURE 4-24

More About

Formulas in Data Tables

Any experienced Excel user will tell you that to enter the formulas at the top of the data table, you should enter the cell reference or name of the cell preceded by an equal sign (Figure 4-24). This ensures that if you change the original formula in the worksheet, Excel automatically will change the corresponding formula in the data table. If you use a cell reference, Excel also copies the format to the cell. If you use a name, Excel does not copy the format to the cell.

It is important to understand that the entries in the top row of the data table (row 9) refer to the formulas that the loan department wants to evaluate using the series of percentages in column B. Furthermore, recall that when you assign a formula to a cell, Excel applies the format of the first cell reference in the formula to the cell. Thus, Excel applies the Currency style format to cells C9, D9, and E9 because that is the format of cells E4, E5, and E6.

Defining the Data Table

After creating the interest rate series in column B and entering the formulas in row 9, the next step is to define the range B9:E20 as a data table. The Table command on the Data menu is used to define the range B4:E20 as a data table. Cell E2 is the input cell, which means it is the cell in which values from column B in the data table are substituted in the formulas in row 9.

To Define a Range as a Data Table

1

- **Select the range B9:E20.**
- **Click Data on the menu bar.**

Excel displays the Data menu (Figure 4-25). The range to be defined as the data table begins with the formulas in row 9. The section title and column headings in the range B7:E8 are not part of the data table, even though they identify the data table and columns in the table.

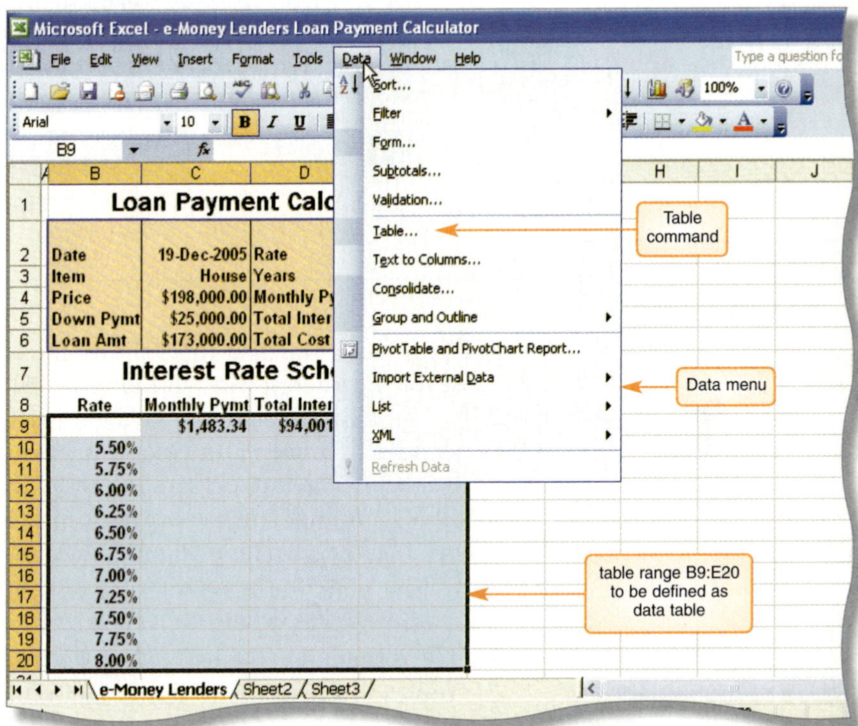

FIGURE 4-25

2

- **Click Table on the Data menu.**
- **When Excel displays the Table dialog box, click the Column input cell box, and then click cell E2 in the Loan Payment Calculator section.**

A marquee surrounds the selected cell E2, indicating it will be the input cell in which values from column B in the data table are substituted in the formulas in row 9. $E$2 appears in the Column input cell box in the Table dialog box (Figure 4-26).

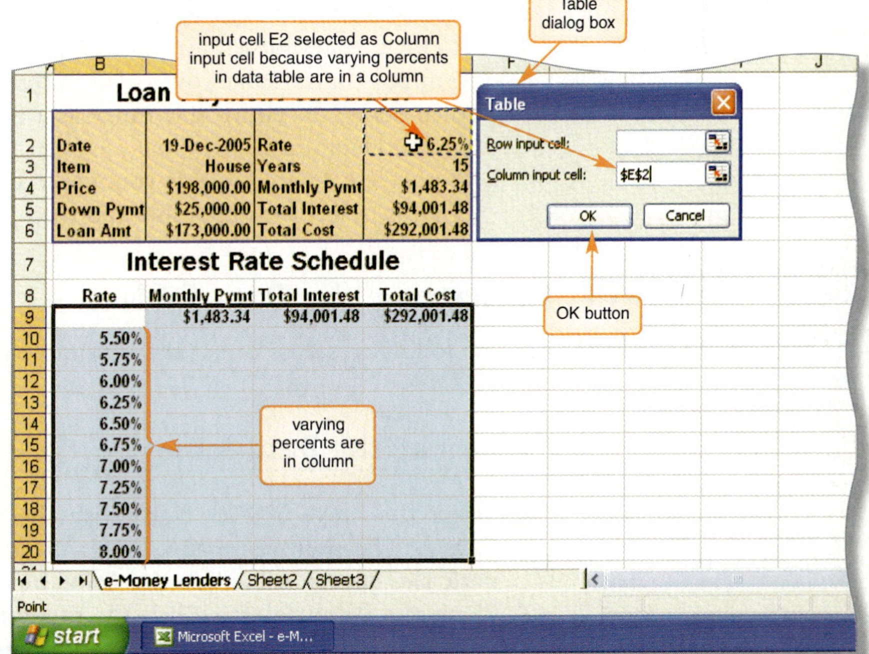

FIGURE 4-26

3

- **Click the OK button.**

Excel calculates the results of the three formulas in row 9 for each interest rate in column B and immediately fills columns C, D, and E of the data table (Figure 4-27). The resulting values for each interest rate are displayed in the corresponding rows.

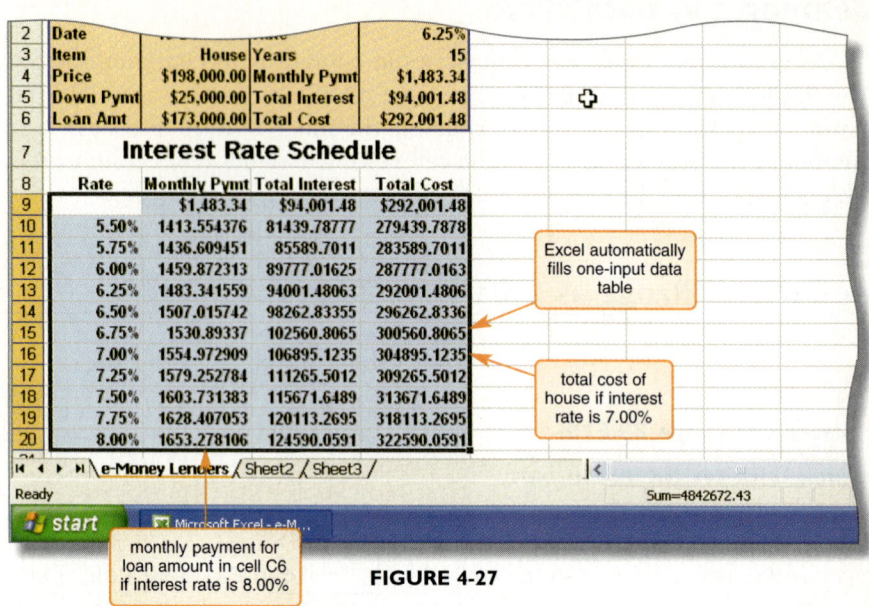

2	Date			6.25%
3	Item	House	Years	15
4	Price	$198,000.00	Monthly Pymt	$1,483.34
5	Down Pymt	$25,000.00	Total Interest	$94,001.48
6	Loan Amt	$173,000.00	Total Cost	$292,001.48
7	Interest Rate Schedule			
8	Rate	Monthly Pymt	Total Interest	Total Cost
9		$1,483.34	$94,001.48	$292,001.48
10	5.50%	1413.554376	81439.78777	279439.7878
11	5.75%	1436.609451	85589.7011	283589.7011
12	6.00%	1459.872313	89777.01625	287777.0163
13	6.25%	1483.341559	94001.48063	292001.4806
14	6.50%	1507.015742	98262.83355	296262.8336
15	6.75%	1530.89337	102560.8065	300560.8065
16	7.00%	1554.972909	106895.1235	304895.1235
17	7.25%	1579.252784	111265.5012	309265.5012
18	7.50%	1603.731383	115671.6489	313671.6489
19	7.75%	1628.407053	120113.2695	318113.2695
20	8.00%	1653.278106	124590.0591	322590.0591

FIGURE 4-27

Other Ways

1. Select data table range, in Voice Command mode, say "Data, Table, [select input cell], OK"

In Figure 4-27, the data table shows the monthly payment, total interest, and total cost for the interest rates in the range B10:B20. For example, if the interest rate is 6.25% (cell E2), the monthly payment is $1,483.34 (cell E4). If the interest rate is 8.00% (cell B20), however, the monthly payment is $1,653.28 rounded to the nearest cent (cell C20). If the interest rate is 7.00% (cell B16), then the total cost of the house is $304,895.12 rounded to the nearest cent (cell E16), rather than $292,001.48 (cell E6). Thus, a 0.75% increase from the interest rate of 6.25% to 7.00% results in a $12,893.64 increase in the total cost of the house.

The following list details important points you should know about data tables:

1. The formula(s) you are analyzing must include a cell reference to the input cell.
2. You can have as many active data tables in a worksheet as you want.
3. While only one value can vary in a one-input data table, the data table can analyze as many formulas as you want.
4. To include additional formulas in a one-input data table, enter them in adjacent cells in the same row as the current formulas (row 9 in Figure 4-27) and then define the entire new range as a data table by using the Table command on the Data menu.
5. You delete a data table as you would delete any other item on a worksheet. That is, select the data table and then press the DELETE key.

More About

Undoing Formats

If you started to assign formats to a range and then realize you made a mistake and want to start over, select the range, click Style on the Format menu, click Normal in the Style Name list box, and click the OK button.

Formatting the Data Table

The following steps format the data table to improve its readability.

To Format the Data Table

1 **Select the range B8:E20. Right-click the selected range and then click Format Cells on the shortcut menu. When Excel displays the Format Cells dialog box, click the Border tab, click the Color box arrow, and click Blue (column 6, row 2) on the Color palette. Click the medium line style in the Style area (column 2, row 5). Click the Outline button in the Presets area.**

2. **Click the Color box arrow. Click Automatic (row 1) on the Color palette. Click the light line style in the Style area (column 1, row 7). Click the Vertical Border button in the Border area.**

3. **Click the Patterns tab and then click Light Yellow (column 3, row 5). Click the OK button.**

4. **Select the range B8:E8. Click the Borders button on the Formatting toolbar to assign a light bottom border.**

5. **Select the range C10:E20 and right-click. Click Format Cells on the shortcut menu. When Excel displays the Format Cells dialog box, click the Number tab. Click Currency in the Category list, click the Symbol box arrow, click None, and then click the second format, 1,234.10, in the Negative numbers list. Click the OK button.**

6. **Click the Save button on the Standard toolbar to save the workbook using the file name e-Money Lenders Loan Payment Calculator.**

Excel displays the worksheet as shown in Figure 4-28.

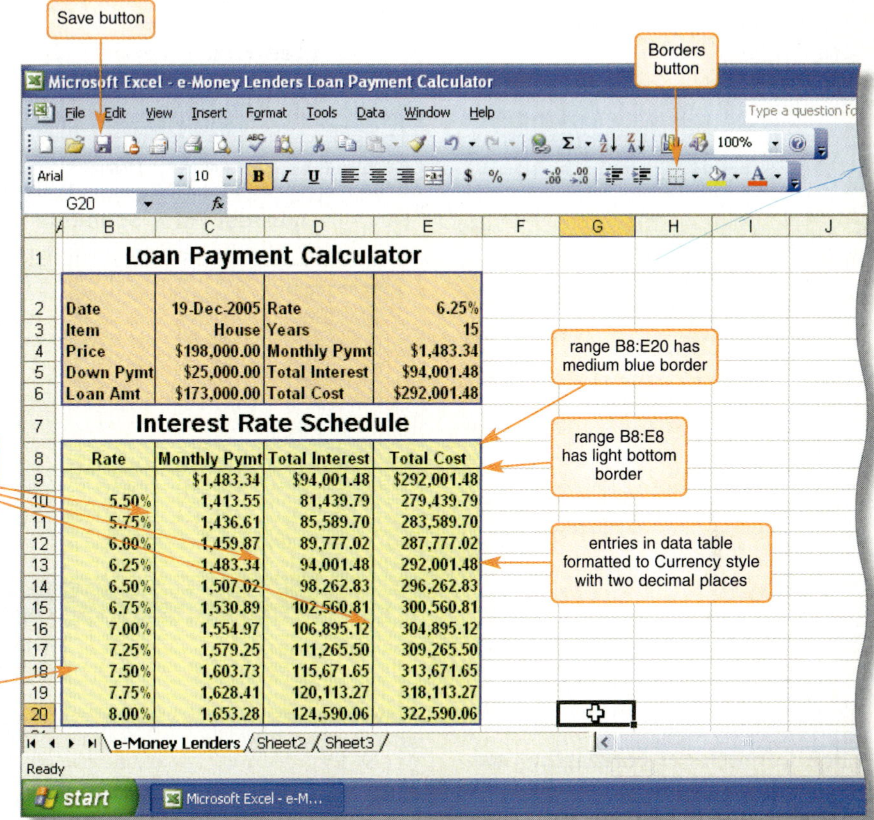

FIGURE 4-28

The data table is complete. Each time you enter new data into the Loan Payment Calculator section, Excel recalculates all formulas, including the formulas in the data table.

Adding a Pointer to the Data Table Using Conditional Formatting

If the interest rate in cell E2 is between 5.50% and 8.00% and its decimal portion is a multiple of 0.25 (such as 6.25%), then one of the rows in the data table agrees exactly with the monthly payment, interest paid, and total cost in the range E4:E6. For example, in Figure 4-28, row 13 (6.25%) in the data table agrees with the results in the range E4:E6, because the interest rate in cell B13 is the same as the interest rate in cell E2. Analysts often look for the row in the data table that agrees with the input cell results. To make this row stand out you can add formatting that serves as a pointer to a row. To add a pointer, you can use conditional formatting to make the cell in column B that agrees with the input cell (cell E2) stand out, as shown in the steps on the next page.

More About

Conditional Formatting

You can add up to three different conditions to a cell or range of cells. After adding the first condition, click the Add button in the Conditional Formatting dialog box to add a second or third condition. If more than one condition is true for a cell, then Excel applies the formats of each condition, beginning with the first.

To Add a Pointer to the Data Table

1

- **Select the range B10:B20.**
- **Click Format on the menu bar.**

Excel displays the Format menu (Figure 4-29).

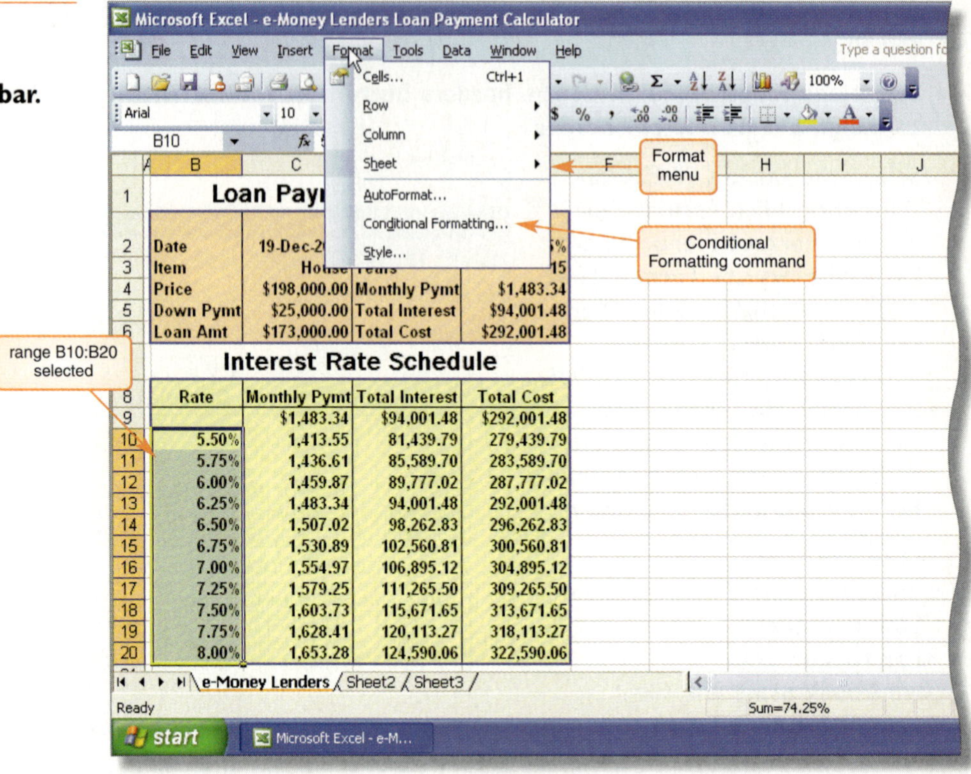

FIGURE 4-29

2

- **Click Conditional Formatting on the Format menu.**
- **When Excel displays the Conditional Formatting dialog box, if necessary, click Cell Value Is in the left list and then click equal to in the middle list.**
- **Type =$E$2 in the right box.**
- **Click the Format button, click the Patterns tab, and then click Orange (column 2, row 2) on the Color palette.**
- **Click the Font tab, click the Color box arrow, and then click White (column 8, row 5) on the Color palette.**
- **Click Bold in the Font Style list. Click the OK button in the Format Cells dialog box.**

Excel displays the Conditional Formatting dialog box as shown in Figure 4-30.

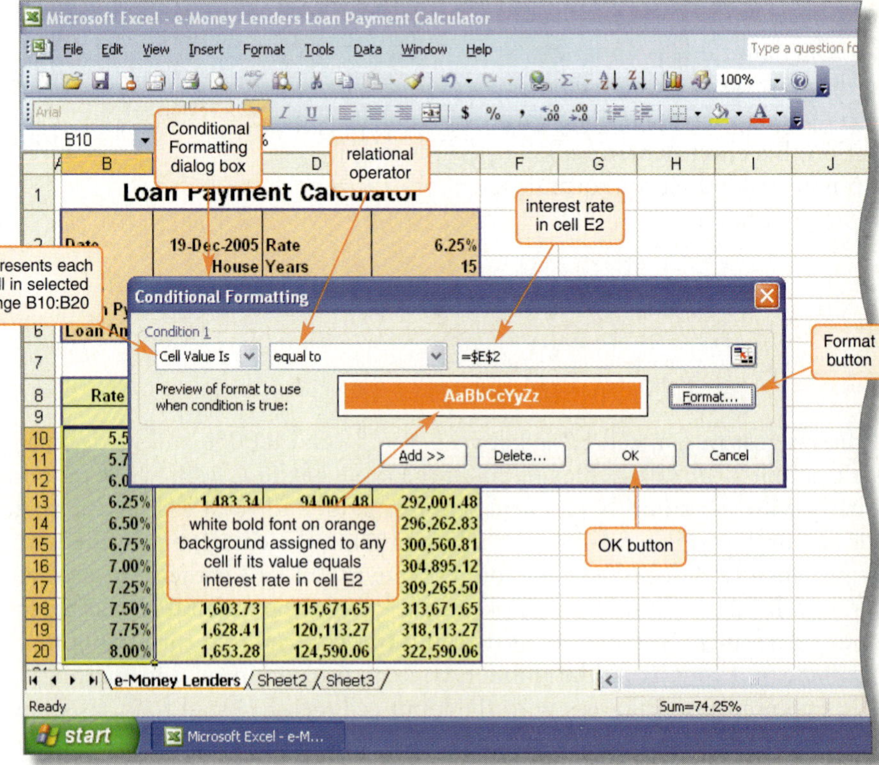

FIGURE 4-30

3

• **Click the OK button in the Conditional Formatting dialog box. Click cell G20 to deselect the range B10:B20.**

Cell B13 in the data table, which contains the value, 6.25%, appears with white bold font on an orange background, because the value 6.25% is the same as the interest rate value in cell E2 (Figure 4-31).

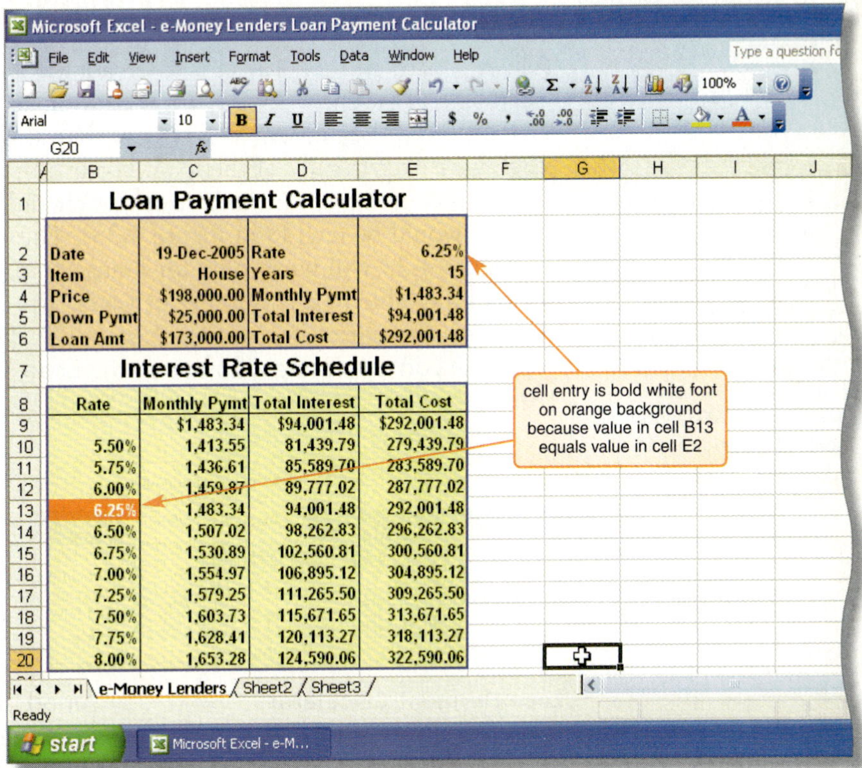

FIGURE 4-31

4

• **Select cell E2 and then enter** 7.75 **as the interest rate.**

Excel immediately displays cell B19 with a white bold font on an orange background and displays cell B13 with black bold font on a white background (Figure 4-32). Thus, the white bold font on an orange background serves as a pointer in the data table to indicate the row that agrees with the input cell (cell E2).

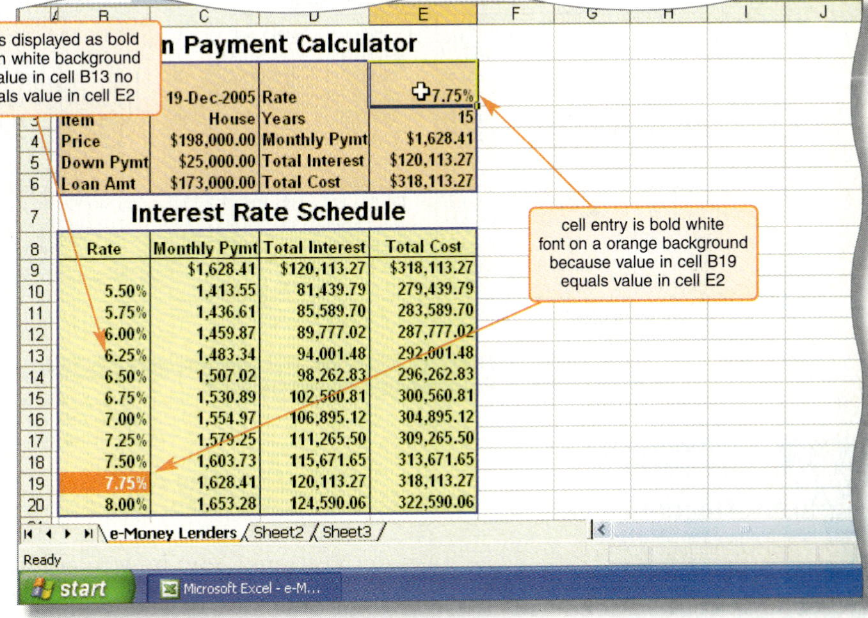

FIGURE 4-32

5

• **Enter** 6.25 **in cell E2 to return the Loan Payment Calculator section and Interest Rate Schedule section to their original states as shown in Figure 4-31.**

Other Ways

1. Press ALT+O, D
2. In Voice Command mode, say "Format, Conditional Formatting"

When the loan officer using this worksheet enters a different percent in cell E2, the pointer will move or disappear. It will disappear whenever the interest rate in cell E2 is outside the range of the data table or its decimal portion is not a multiple of 0.25, such as when the interest rate is 8.25% or 5.80%.

Creating an Amortization Schedule

The next step in this project is to create the Amortization Schedule section on the right side of Figure 4-33. An **amortization schedule** shows the beginning and ending balances and the amount of payment that applies to the principal and interest for each year over the life of the loan. For example, if a customer wanted to pay off the loan after six years, the Amortization Schedule section tells the loan officer what the payoff would be (cell I8 in Figure 4-33). The Amortization Schedule section shown in Figure 4-33 will work only for loans of up to 15 years. You could, however, extend the table to any number of years. The Amortization Schedule section also contains summaries in rows 18, 19, and 20. These summaries should agree exactly with the corresponding amounts in the Loan Payment Calculator section in the range B1:E6.

> *More About*
>
> **Amortization Schedules**
>
> Hundreds of Web sites offer amortization schedules. To find these Web sites, use a search engine, such as Google at google.com and search using the keywords, amortization schedule. For an example of a Web site that determines an amortization schedule, visit the Excel 2003 More About Web page (scsite.com/ex2003/more) and click Amortization Schedule.

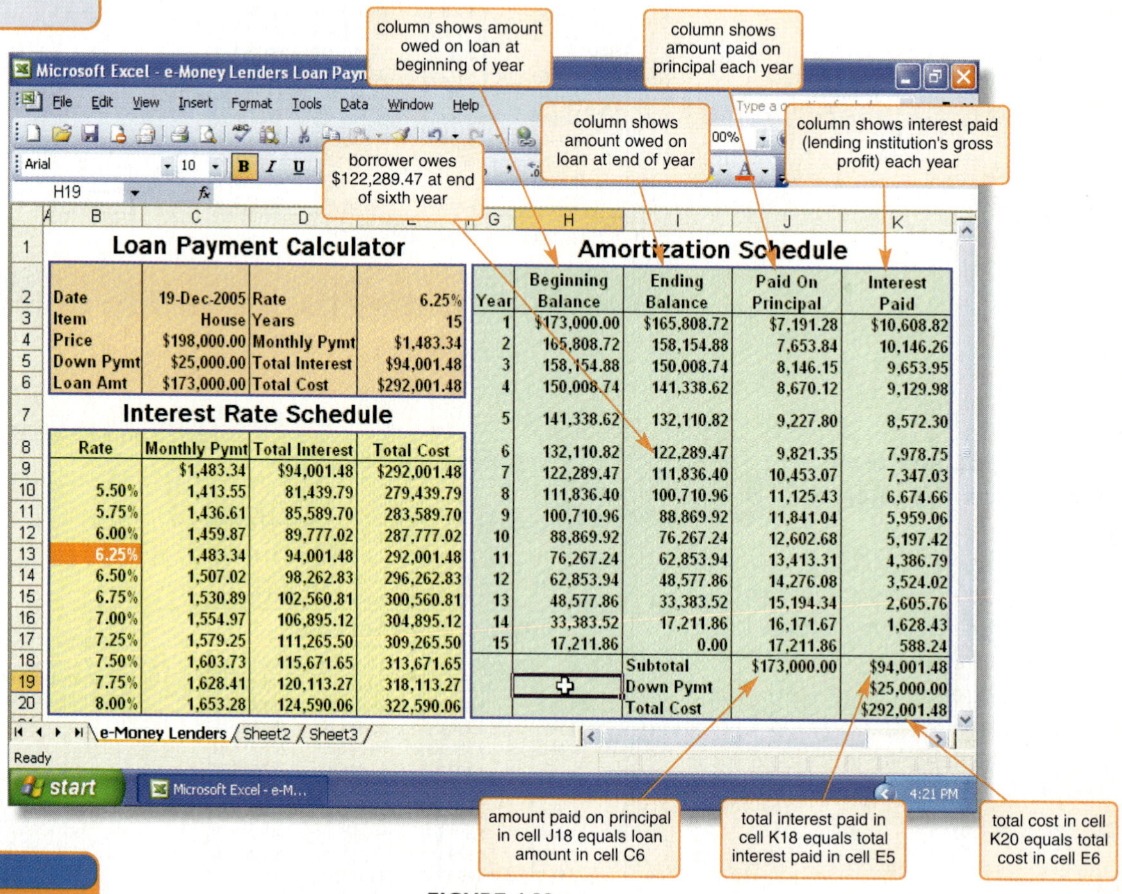

FIGURE 4-33

The following sections show how to construct the Amortization Schedule section shown in Figure 4-33.

> *More About*
>
> **Column Borders**
>
> In this project, columns A and F are used as column borders to divide sections of the worksheet from one another, as well as from the row headings. A column border is an unused column with a significantly reduced width. You also can use row borders to separate sections of a worksheet.

Changing Column Widths and Entering the Titles

The first step in creating the Amortization Schedule section is to adjust the column widths and enter the Amortization Schedule section title and column titles, as shown in the following steps.

To Change Column Widths and Enter Titles

1. **Position the mouse pointer on the right boundary of column heading F and then drag to the left until the ScreenTip shows Width: 0.50 (6 pixels).**
2. **Position the mouse pointer on the right boundary of column heading G and then drag to the left until the ScreenTip shows Width: 4.00 (33 pixels).**
3. **Drag through column headings H through K to select them. Position the mouse pointer on the right boundary of column heading K and then drag to the right until the ScreenTip shows Width: 12.14 (90 pixels).**
4. **Select cell G1. Type** `Amortization Schedule` **as the section title. Press the ENTER key.**
5. **Select cell B1. Click the Format Painter button on the Standard toolbar. Click cell G1 to copy the format of cell B1. Click the Merge and Center button on the Formatting toolbar to split cell G1. Select the range G1:K1 and then click the Merge and Center button on the Formatting toolbar.**
6. **Enter the column titles in the range G2:K2 as shown in Figure 4-34. Where appropriate, press ALT+ENTER to enter the titles on two lines. Select the range G2:K2 and then click the Center button on the Formatting toolbar. Select cell G3.**

Excel displays the section title and column headings as shown in Figure 4-34.

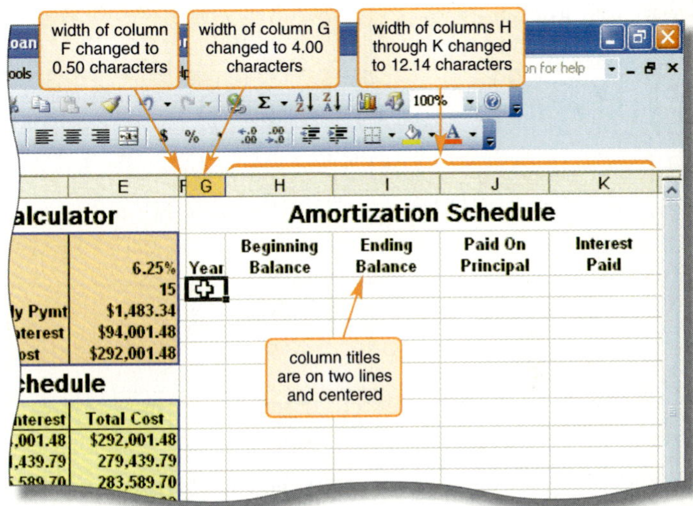

FIGURE 4-34

Creating a Series of Integers Using the Fill Handle

The next step is to create a series of numbers, using the fill handle, that represent the years during the life of the loan. The series begins with 1 (year 1) and ends with 15 (year 15).

To Create a Series of Integers Using the Fill Handle

1. **With cell G3 active, enter** `1` **as the initial year. Select cell G4 and then enter** `2` **to represent the next year.**
2. **Select the range G3:G4 and then point to the fill handle. Drag the fill handle through cell G17.**

Excel creates the series of integers 1 through 15 in the range G3:G17 (Figure 4-35).

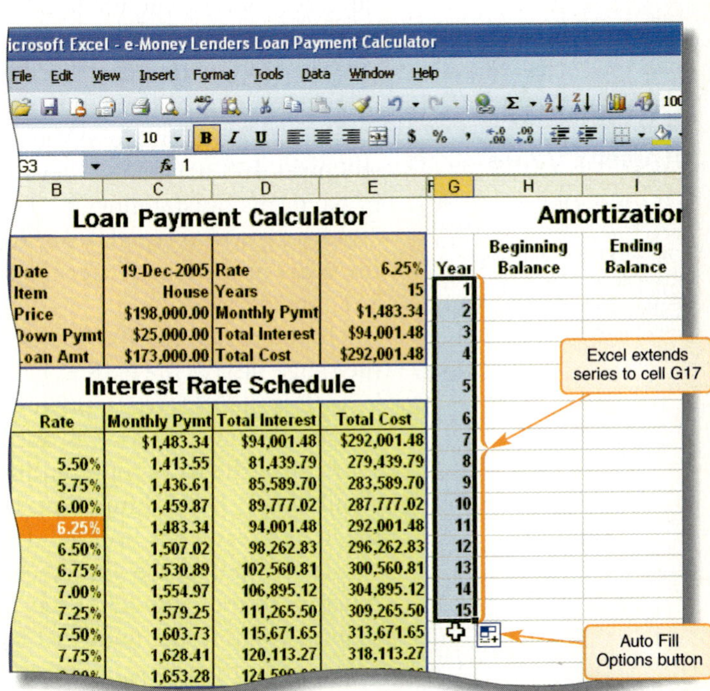

FIGURE 4-35

More About

Annuities

For additional information on annuities, visit the Excel 2003 More About Web page (scsite.com/ex2003/more) and click Annuities.

As you will learn in the next section, the series of integers in the range G3:G17 plays an important role in determining the ending balance and interest paid in the amortization schedule.

Entering the Formulas in the Amortization Schedule

The next step is to enter the four formulas that form the basis of the amortization schedule in row 3. Later, these formulas will be copied through row 17. The formulas are summarized in Table 4-2.

Table 4-2 Formulas for the Amortization Schedule

CELL	DESCRIPTION	FORMULA	COMMENT
H3	Beginning Balance	=C6	The beginning balance (the balance at the end of a year) is the initial loan amount in cell C6.
I3	Ending Balance	=PV($E$2 /12, 12 * ($E$3 – G3), –$E$4)	The ending balance (the balance at the end of a year) is equal to the present value of the payments paid over the remaining life of the loan.
J3	Paid on Principal	=H3 – I3	The amount paid on the principal at the end of the year is equal to the beginning balance (cell H3) less the ending balance (cell I3).
K3	Interest Paid	=12 * $E$4 – J3	The interest paid during the year is equal to 12 times the monthly payment (cell E4) less the amount paid on the principal (cell J3).

Of the four formulas in Table 4-2, the most difficult to understand is the PV function that will be assigned to cell I3. The **PV function** returns the present value of an annuity. An **annuity** is a series of fixed payments (such as the monthly payment in cell E4) made at the end of a fixed number of periods (months) at a fixed interest rate. You can use the PV function to determine how much the borrower of the loan still owes at the end of each year.

More About

Present Value

For additional information on the present value of an investment, visit the Excel 2003 More About Web page (scsite.com/ex2003/more) and click Present Value.

The PV function can determine the ending balance after the first year (cell I3) by using a term equal to the number of months for which the borrower still must make payments. For example, if the loan is for 15 years (180 months), then the borrower still owes 168 payments after the first year (180 months – 12 months). The number of payments outstanding can be determined from the formula 12 * (E3 – G3) or 12 * (15 – 1), which equals 168. Recall that column G contains integers that represent the years of the loan. After the second year, the number of payments remaining is 156, and so on.

If you assign the PV function as shown in Table 4-2 to cell I3 and then copy it to the range I4:I17, the ending balances for each year will display properly. If the loan is for less than 15 years, however, then the ending balances displayed for the years beyond the time the loan is due are invalid. For example, if a loan is taken out for 5 years, then the rows representing years 6 through 15 in the amortization schedule should be 0. The PV function, however, will display negative numbers even though the loan already has been paid off.

To avoid this, the worksheet should include a formula that assigns the PV function to the range I3:I17 as long as the corresponding year in column G is less than or equal to the number of years in cell E3. If the corresponding year in column G is greater than the number of years in cell E3, then the ending balance for that year and the remaining years should be 0. The following IF function causes the value of the PV function or 0 to display in cell I3 depending on whether the corresponding value in column G is less than or equal to the number of years in cell E3. Recall that the dollar signs within the cell references indicate the cell reference is absolute and, therefore, will not change as you copy the function downward.

```
=IF(G3 <= $E$3, PV($E$2 /12, 12 * ($E$3 – G3), –$E$4), 0)
```

logical test — value if true — value if false

In the above formula, the logical test determines if the year in column G is less than or equal to the term of the loan in cell E3. If the logical test is true, then the IF function assigns the PV function to the cell. If the logical test is false, then the IF function assigns zero (0) to the cell.

The PV function in the IF function includes absolute cell references (cell references with dollar signs) to ensure that the references to cells in column E do not change when the IF function later is copied down the column.

The following steps enter the four formulas shown in Table 4-2 into row 3. Row 3 represents year 1 of the loan.

To Enter the Formulas in the Amortization Schedule

1

- **Select cell H3 and then enter** `=c6` **as the beginning balance of the loan.**
- **Select cell I3 and then type** `=if(g3 <= $e$3, pv($e$2 / 12, 12 * ($e$3 – g3), –$e$4), 0)` **as the entry.**

Excel displays the loan amount in cell H3 as the first year's beginning balance using the same format as in cell C6. The IF function appears in cell I3 and in the formula bar (Figure 4-36).

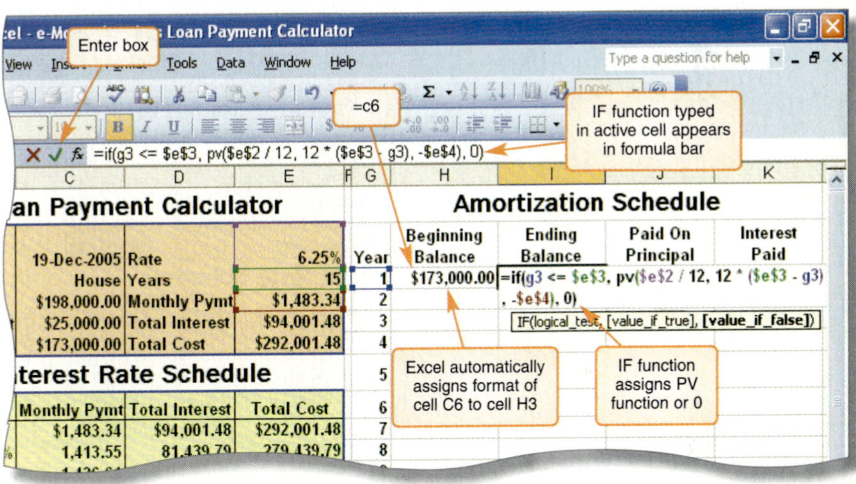

FIGURE 4-36

2

- **Click the Enter box in the formula bar.**

Excel evaluates the IF function in cell I3 and displays the result of the PV function (165808.7195) because the value in cell G3 (1) is less than or equal to the term of the loan in cell E3 (15). With cell I3 active, Excel also displays the formula in the formula bar (Figure 4-37). If the borrower wanted to pay off the loan after one year, the cost would be $165,808.72.

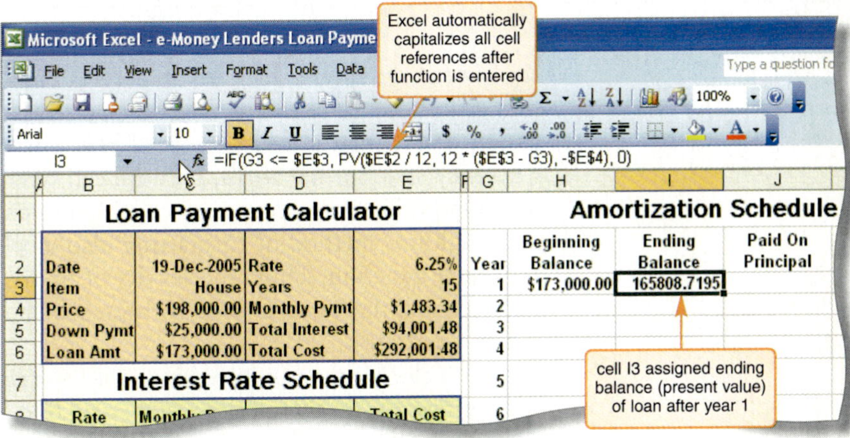

FIGURE 4-37

3

- **Select cell J3. Type** =h3 – i3 **and then press the RIGHT ARROW key.**
- **Type** =if(h3 > 0, 12 * e4 – j3, 0) **in cell K3.**

Excel displays the amount paid on the principal after 1 year ($7,191.28) in cell J3, using the same format as in cell H3. Excel also displays the IF function in cell K3 and in the formula bar (Figure 4-38).

FIGURE 4-38

4

- **Click the Enter box in the formula bar.**

Excel displays the interest paid after 1 year (10608.81825) in cell K3 (Figure 4-39). Thus, the lending institution's gross profit for the first year of the loan is $10,608.82.

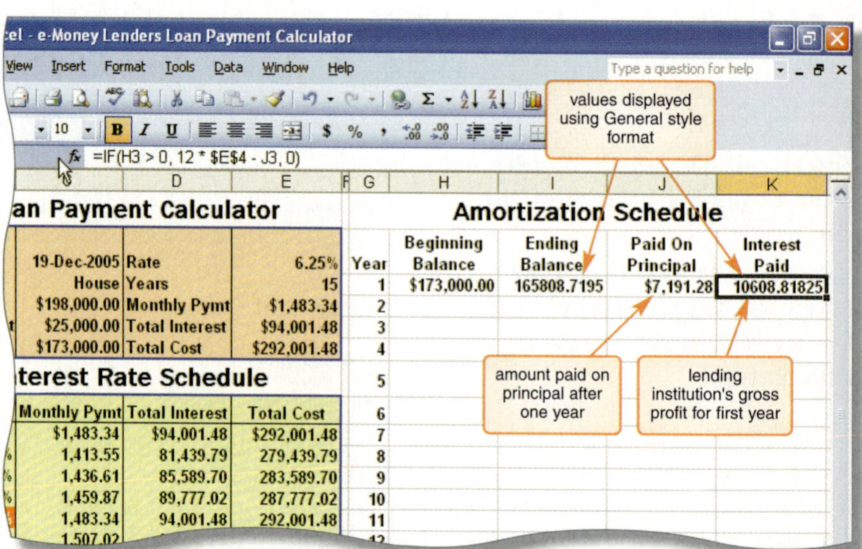

FIGURE 4-39

When you enter a formula in a cell, Excel assigns the cell the same format as the first cell reference in the formula. For example, when you enter =c6 in cell H3, Excel assigns the format in cell C6 to cell H3. The same applies to cell J3. Excel assigns the Currency style format to J3, because cell reference H3 is the first cell reference in the formula (=H3 – I3) assigned to cell J3, and cell H3 has a Currency style format. Although this method of formatting also works for most functions, it does not work for the IF function. Thus, the results of the IF functions in cells I3 and K3 are displayed using the General style format, which is the format of all cells when you open a new workbook.

With the formulas entered into the first row, the next step is to copy them to the remaining rows in the amortization schedule. The required copying is straightforward, except for the beginning balance column. To obtain the next year's beginning balance (cell H4), you have to use last year's ending balance (cell I3). After cell I3 is copied to cell H4, then H4 can be copied to the range H5:H17.

To Copy the Formulas to Fill the Amortization Schedule

1

- **Select the range I3:K3 and then drag the fill handle down through row 17.**

The formulas in cells I3, J3, and K3 are copied to the range I4:K17 (Figure 4-40). Many of the numbers displayed are incorrect because most of the cells in column H do not contain beginning balances. Excel displays the Auto Fill Options button below and to the right of the destination area.

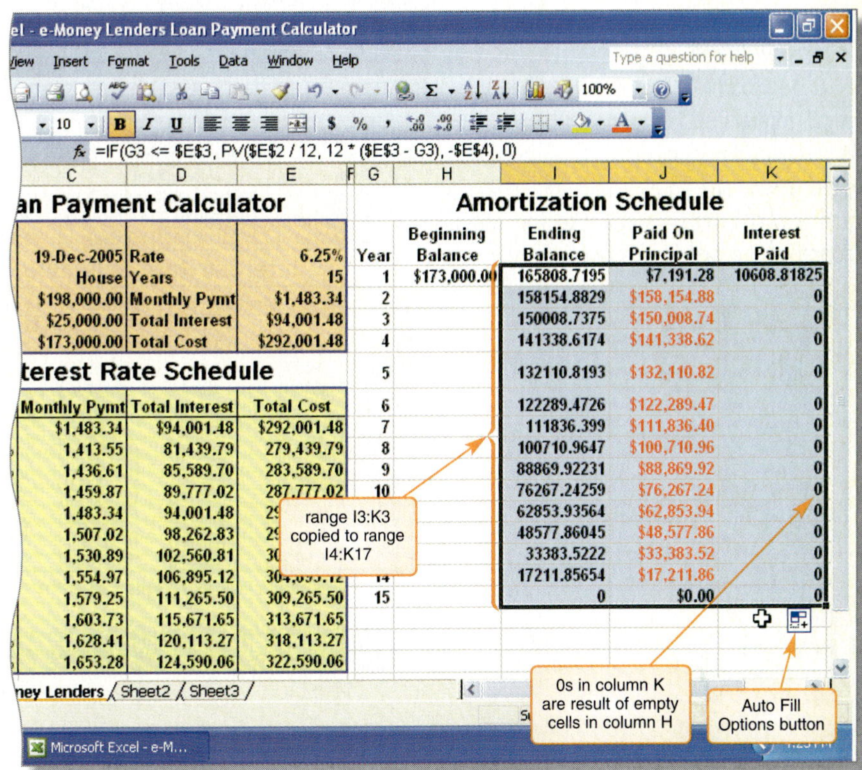

FIGURE 4-40

2

- **Select cell H4, type =i3 as the cell entry, and then click the Enter box in the formula bar.**

Excel displays the ending balance for year 1(165808.7195) as the beginning balance for year 2 in cell H4 (Figure 4-41).

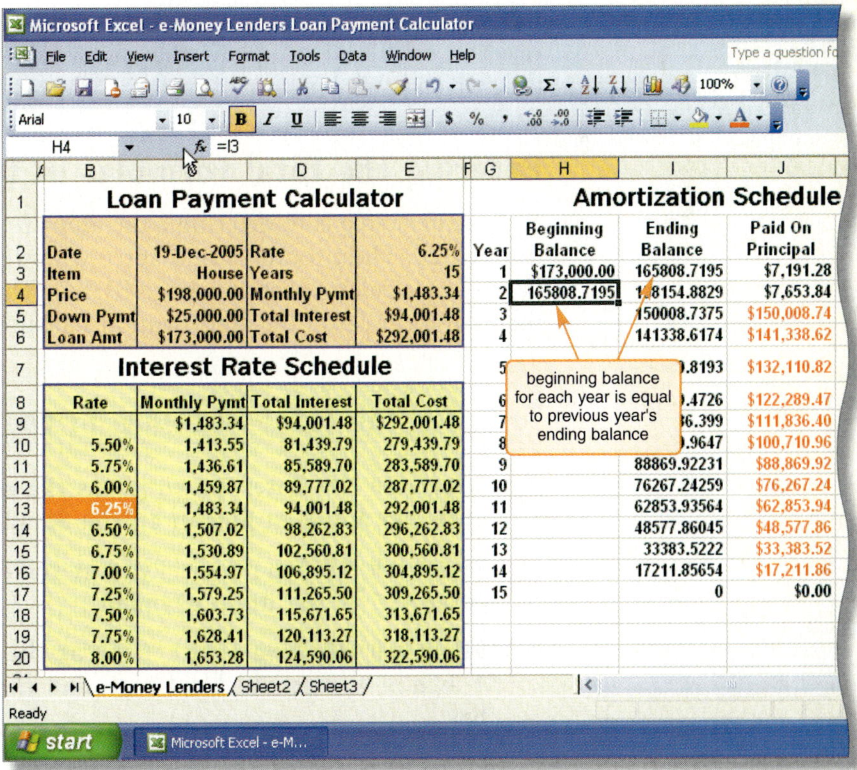

FIGURE 4-41

• **With cell H4 active, drag the fill handle down through row 17.**

The formula in cell H4 (=I3) is copied to the range H5:H17 (Figure 4-42). Because the cell reference I3 is relative, Excel adjusts the row portion of the cell reference as it is copied downward. Thus, each new beginning balance in column H is equal to the ending balance of the previous year.

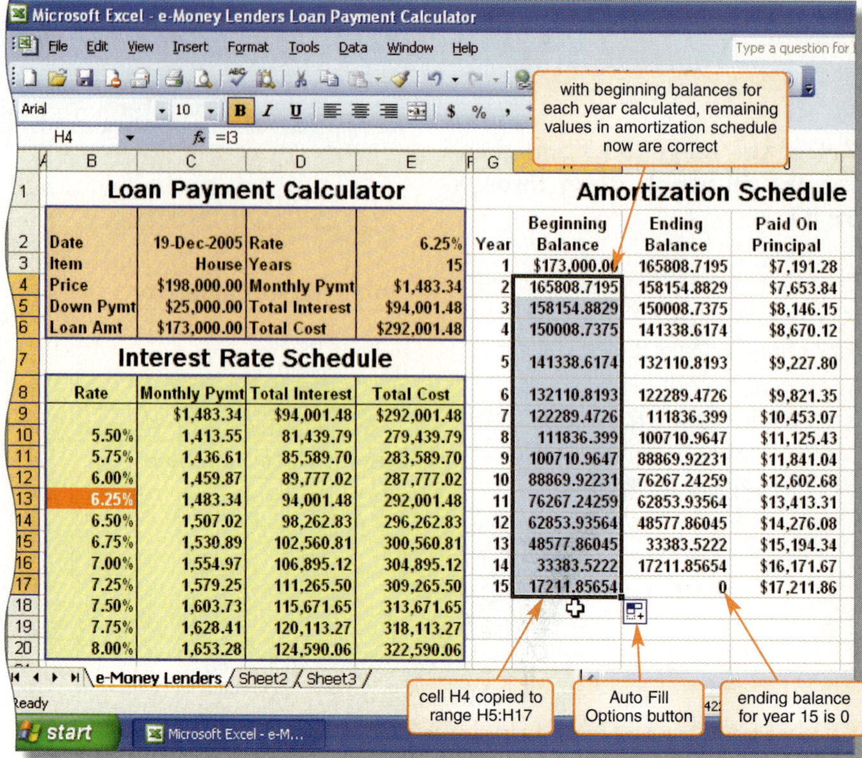

FIGURE 4-42

The numbers that Excel displays in the Amortization Schedule section in Figure 4-42 are now correct, although they need to be formatted to make them easier to read. Cell I17 shows that at the end of the fifteenth year, the ending balance is 0, which is what it should be for a 15-year loan.

Entering the Total Formulas in the Amortization Schedule

The next step is to determine the amortization schedule totals in rows 18 through 20. These totals should agree with the corresponding totals in the Loan Payment Calculator section (range B1:E6). The following steps show how to enter the total formulas in the amortization schedule.

To Enter the Total Formulas in the Amortization Schedule

1. **Select cell I18. Enter** `Subtotal` **as the row title. Select the range J18:K18. Click the AutoSum button on the Standard toolbar.**

2. **Select cell I19. Type** `Down Pymt` **as the row title. Select cell K19 and then enter** `=c5` **as the down payment.**

3. **Select cell I20. Type** `Total Cost` **as the row title. Select cell K20, type** `=j18 + k18 + k19` **as the total cost, and then click the Enter box in the formula bar.**

The amortization schedule totals are displayed in rows 18 through 20 as shown in Figure 4-43.

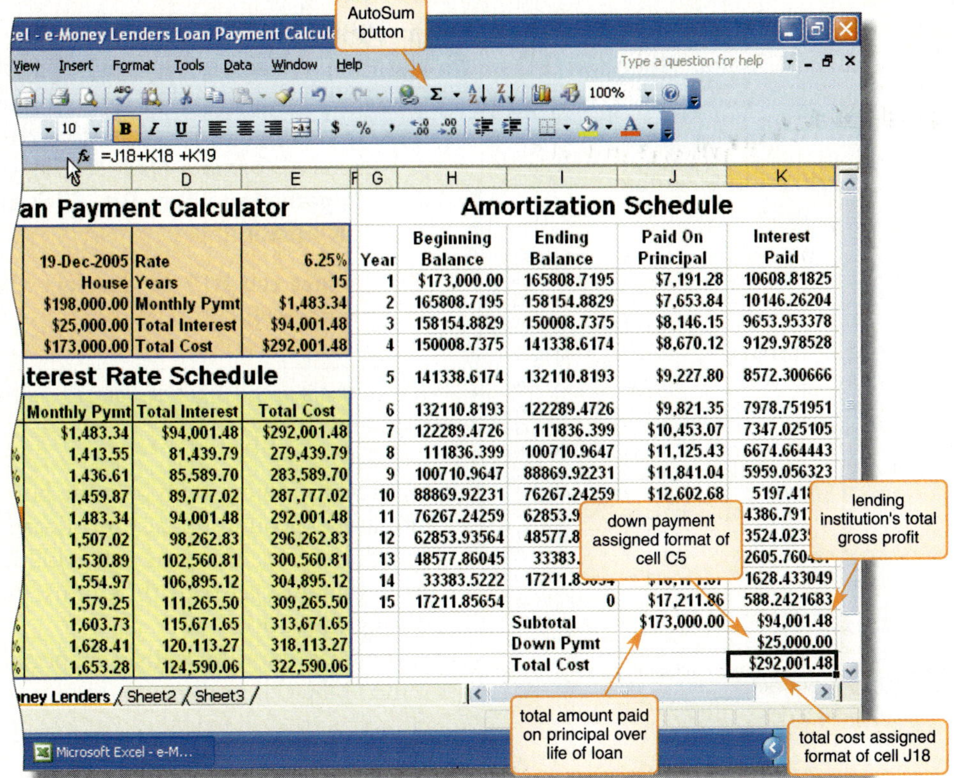

FIGURE 4-43

The formula assigned to cell K20 (=j18 + k18 + k19) sums the total amount paid on the principal (cell J18), the total interest paid (cell K18), and the down payment (cell K19). Excel assigns cell J18 the same format as cell J3, because cell J3 is the first cell reference in =SUM(J3:J17). Furthermore, because cell J18 was selected first when the range J18:K18 was selected to determine the sum, Excel assigned cell K18 the same format it assigned to cell J18. Finally, cell K19 was assigned the Currency style format, because cell K19 was assigned the formula =c5, and cell C5 has a Currency style format. For the same reason, the value in cell K20 appears in Currency style format.

More About

Round-Off Errors

If you manually add the numbers in column K (range K3:K17) and compare it to the sum in cell K18, you will notice that the total interest paid is $0.01 off. This round-off error is due to the fact that some of the numbers involved in the computations have additional decimal places that do not appear in the cells. You can use the ROUND function on the formula entered into cell K3 to ensure the total is exactly correct. For information on the ROUND function, click the Insert Function box in the formula bar, click Math & Trig in the Or select a category list, scroll down in the Select a function list, and then click ROUND.

Formatting New Loan Data

The final step in creating the amortization schedule is to format it so it is easier to read. The formatting is divided into two parts: (1) formatting the numbers and (2) adding borders and background.

When the beginning balance formula (=c6) was entered earlier into cell H3, Excel automatically copied the Currency style format along with the value from cell C6 to cell H3. The following steps use the Format Painter button to copy the Currency style format from cell H3 to the range I3:K3. Then the Comma Style button on the Formatting toolbar will be used to assign the Comma style format to the range H4:K17.

To Format the Numbers in the Amortization Schedule

1 **Select cell H3. Click the Format Painter button on the Standard toolbar. Drag through the range I3:K3 to assign the Currency style format to the numbers.**

2. **Select the range H4:K17 and then right-click. Click Format Cells on the shortcut menu. When Excel displays the Format Cells dialog box, click the Number tab. Click Currency in the Category list, click the Symbol box arrow, click None, and then click the second format, 1,234.10, in the Negative numbers list. Click the OK button.**

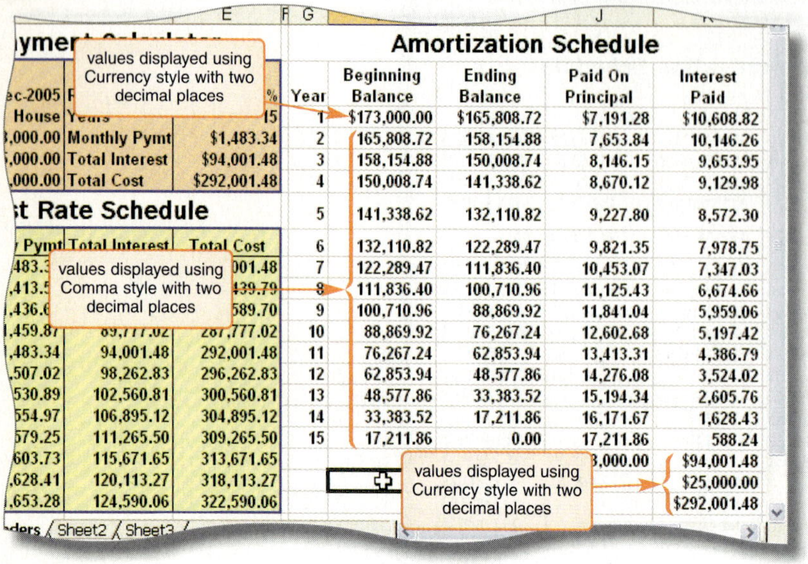

3. **Select cell H19 to deselect the range H4:K17.**

The numbers in the amortization schedule are displayed as shown in Figure 4-44.

Amortization Schedule

Year	Beginning Balance	Ending Balance	Paid On Principal	Interest Paid
1	$173,000.00	$165,808.72	$7,191.28	$10,608.82
2	165,808.72	158,154.88	7,653.84	10,146.26
3	158,154.88	150,008.74	8,146.15	9,653.95
4	150,008.74	141,338.62	8,670.12	9,129.98
5	141,338.62	132,110.82	9,227.80	8,572.30
6	132,110.82	122,289.47	9,821.35	7,978.75
7	122,289.47	111,836.40	10,453.07	7,347.03
8	111,836.40	100,710.96	11,125.43	6,674.66
9	100,710.96	88,869.92	11,841.04	5,959.06
10	88,869.92	76,267.24	12,602.68	5,197.42
11	76,267.24	62,853.94	13,413.31	4,386.79
12	62,853.94	48,577.86	14,276.08	3,524.02
13	48,577.86	33,383.52	15,194.34	2,605.76
14	33,383.52	17,211.86	16,171.67	1,628.43
15	17,211.86	0.00	17,211.86	588.24
				$94,001.48
				$25,000.00
				$292,001.48

FIGURE 4-44

The following steps add the borders and a background to the amortization schedule and remove the cell gridlines from the worksheet. Although useful during the process of creating a worksheet, many spreadsheet specialists remove the cell gridlines to reduce the clutter on the screen.

To Add Borders and a Background to the Amortization Schedule and Hide Cell Gridlines

1. **Select the range G2:K20. Right-click the selected range and then click Format Cells on the shortcut menu. When Excel displays the Format Cells dialog box, click the Border tab.**

2. **Click the Color box arrow. Click Blue (column 6, row 2) on the Color palette. Click the medium line style in the Style area (column 2, row 5). Click the Outline button in the Presets area.**

3. **Click the Color box arrow. Click Automatic (row 1) on the Color palette. Click the light line style in the Style area (column 1, row 7). Click the vertical line button in the Border area.**

4. **Click the Patterns tab and then click Light Green (column 4, row 5). Click the OK button.**

5. **Select the range G2:K2. Click the Borders button on the Formatting toolbar to assign the range a light bottom border.**

6. **Select the range G17:K17 and then click the Borders button on the Formatting toolbar to assign the range a light bottom border. Select cell H19.**

7. **Click Tools on the menu bar and then click Options. When Excel displays the Options dialog box, click the View tab, click Gridlines in the Window options area to deselect it, and then click the OK button.**

8. **Click the Save button on the Standard toolbar to save the workbook using the file name, e-Money Lenders Loan Payment Calculator.**

Excel displays the worksheet as shown in Figure 4-45. The Amortization Schedule section of the worksheet is now complete.

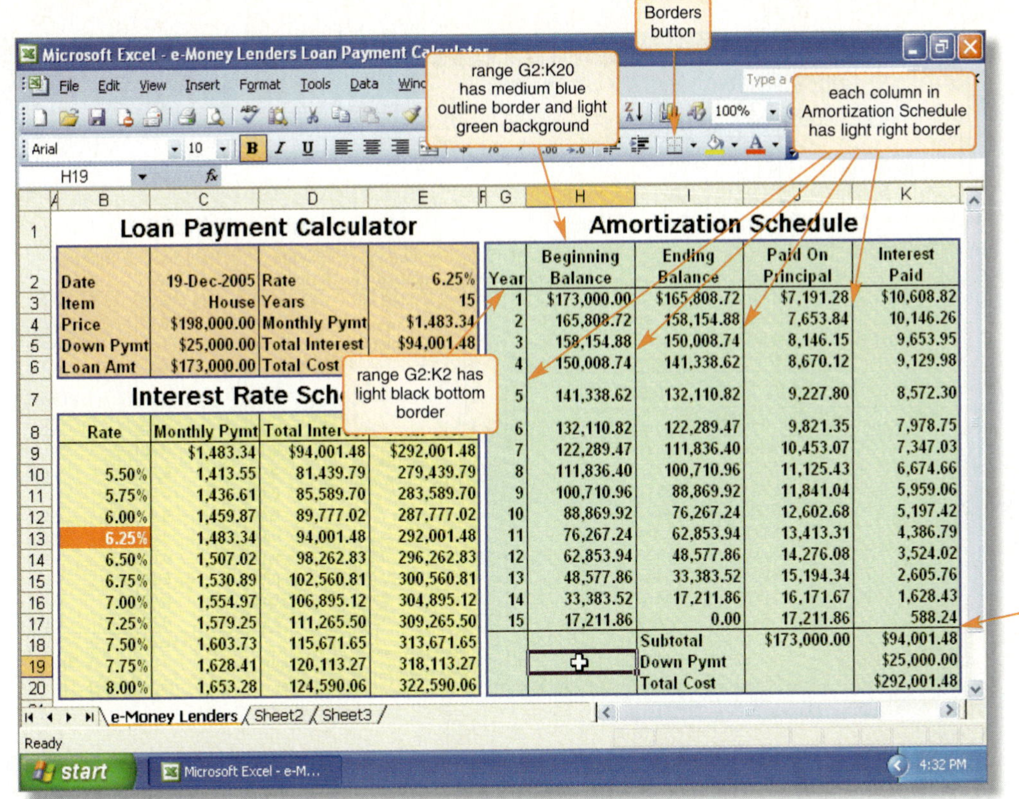

FIGURE 4-45

Entering New Loan Data

With the Loan Payment Calculator, Interest Rate Schedule, and Amortization Schedule sections of the worksheet complete, you can use them to generate new loan information. For example, assume you want to purchase a 24-foot boat for $32,550.00. You have $5,000.00 for a down payment and want the loan for 5 years. e-Money Lenders currently is charging 7.75% interest for a 5-year loan.

The following steps show how to enter the new loan data.

To Enter New Loan Data

1. **Select cell C3. Type** `24' Boat` **and then press the DOWN ARROW key.**
2. **In cell C4, type** `32550` **and then press the DOWN ARROW key.**
3. **In cell C5, type** `5000` **as the down payment.**
4. **Select cell E2, type** `7.75` **and then press the DOWN ARROW key.**
5. **In cell E3, type** `5` **and then press the DOWN ARROW key. Select cell H19.**

Excel automatically recalculates the loan information in cells C6, E4, E5, E6, the data table in the range B7:E20, and the amortization schedule in the range G1:K20 (Figure 4-46 on the next page).

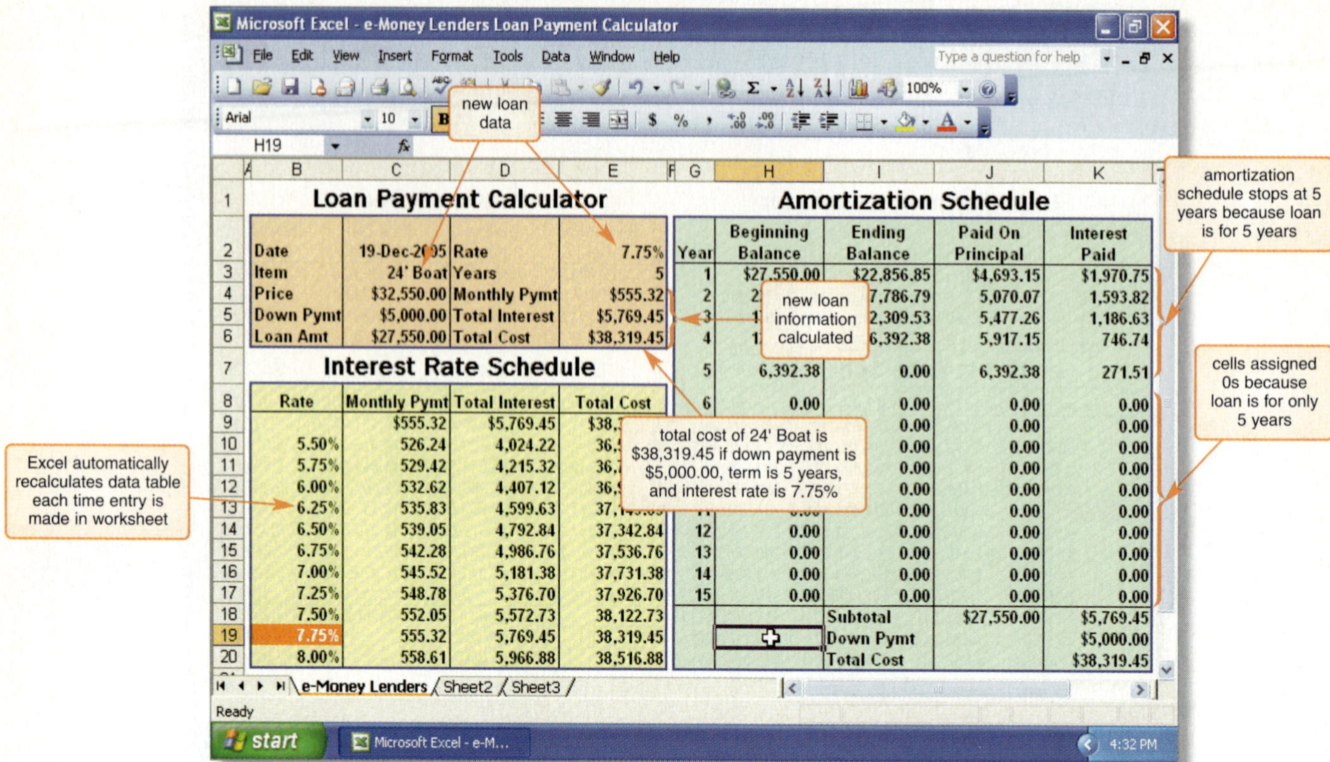

FIGURE 4-46

As shown in Figure 4-46, the monthly payment for the 24-foot boat is $555.32 (cell E4). The total interest is $5,769.45 (cell E5) and the total cost for the boat is $38,319.45 (cell E6). Because the term of the loan is for 5 years, the rows for years 6 through 15 in the Amortization Schedule section display 0.00.

The following steps enter the original loan data.

To Enter the Original Loan Data

1. **Select cell C3. Type** House **and then press the DOWN ARROW key.**
2. **In cell C4, type** 198000 **and then press the DOWN ARROW key.**
3. **In cell C5, type** 25000 **as the down payment.**
4. **Select cell E2, type** 6.25 **and then press the DOWN ARROW key.**
5. **In cell E3, type** 15 **and then click the Enter box in the formula bar or press the ENTER key. Select cell H19.**

Excel automatically recalculates the loan information, the data table, and the amortization schedule.

Adding a Hyperlink to the Worksheet

With Excel, you easily can create hyperlinks (Figure 4-1a on page EX 243) to other files on your personal computer, your intranet, or the Web. The destination file (or hyperlinked file) can be any Office document or Web page, as shown in Figure 4-1b. Two primary worksheet elements exist to which you can assign a hyperlink:

1. Text — Enter text in a cell and make the text a hyperlink; text hyperlinks display in the color blue and are underlined.
2. Embedded graphic — Draw or insert a graphic, such as clip art, and then make the graphic a hyperlink.

The Hyperlink command on the shortcut menu is used to assign the hyperlink to the worksheet element, either text or an embedded graphic.

Assigning a Hyperlink to an Embedded Graphic

The following steps show how to assign a hyperlink to an embedded graphic. The destination file is a Web page that contains the e-Money Lenders 2004 Statement of Condition. The destination file, e-Money Lenders Statement of Condition.mht, is located on the Data Disk. If you do not have a copy of the Data Disk, see the inside back cover of this book.

To Assign a Hyperlink to an Embedded Graphic

1

- **With the Data Disk in drive A, click Insert on the menu bar and then point to Picture.**

Excel displays the Insert menu and Picture submenu display (Figure 4-47).

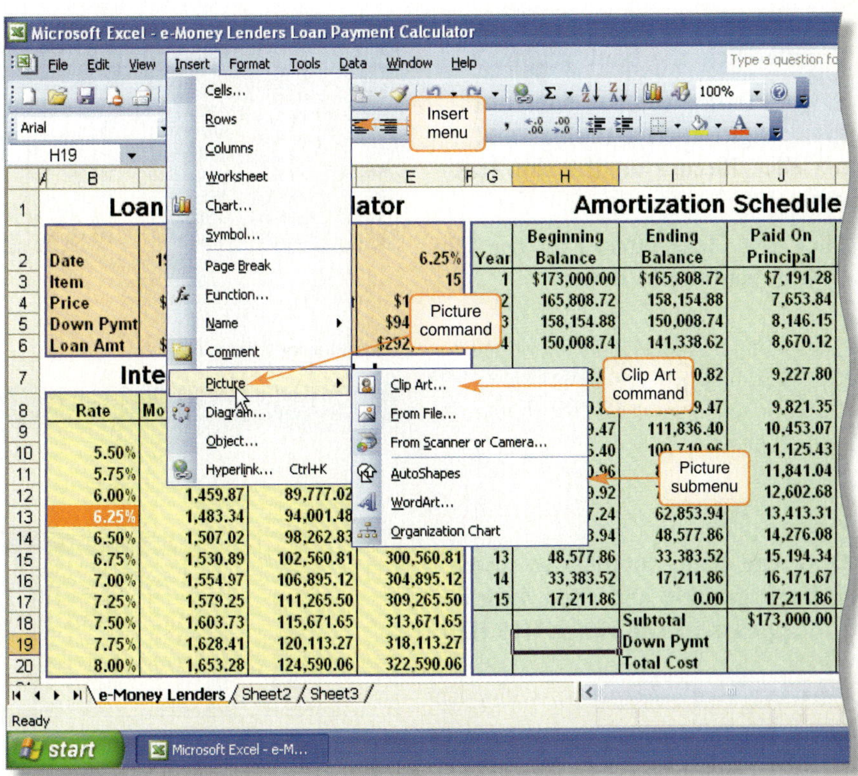

FIGURE 4-47

2

- **Click Clip Art on the Picture submenu.**
- **When Excel displays the Clip Art task pane, click the Search for text box, type** bank **as the search keyword, select Selected media file types from the Results should be list, and then click the Go button.**
- **When Excel displays the results of the search in the Clip Art task pane, scroll down to view the graphics. Scroll back to the top so the bank graphic shown in Figure 4-48 appears.**

Excel displays the Clip Art task pane as shown in Figure 4-48. The results of the search appear in the lower portion of the task pane.

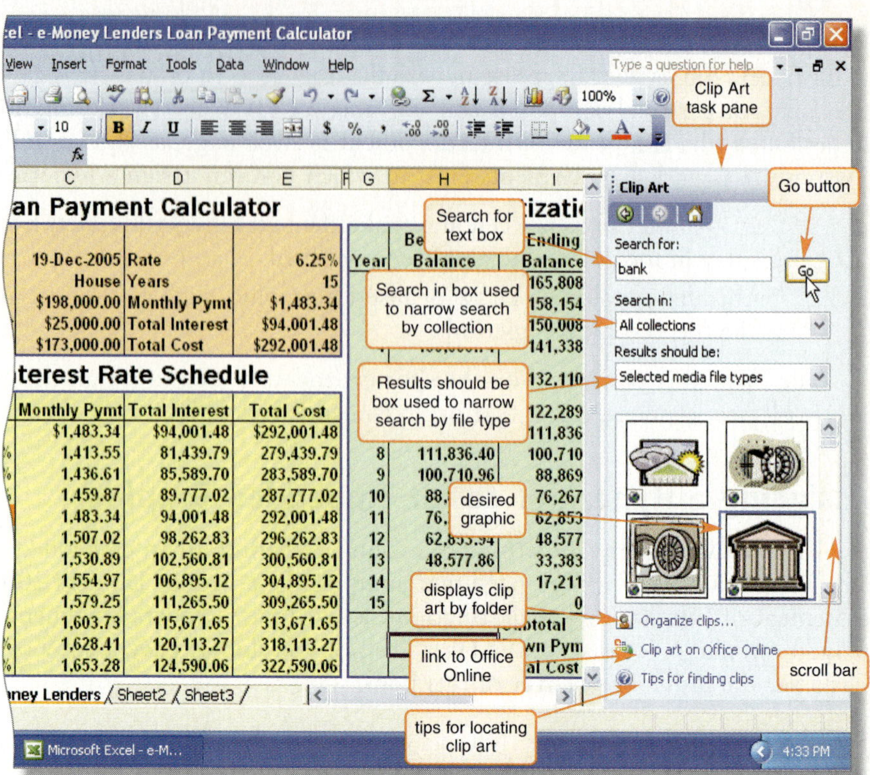

FIGURE 4-48

3

- **Double-click the bank graphic.**
- **If the Picture toolbar does not appear, right-click a toolbar and then click Picture on the shortcut menu.**
- **Click the Close button on the Clip Art task pane title bar.**

Excel embeds the bank graphic below the data in the worksheet and closes the Clip Art task pane (Figure 4-49). The Picture toolbar appears.

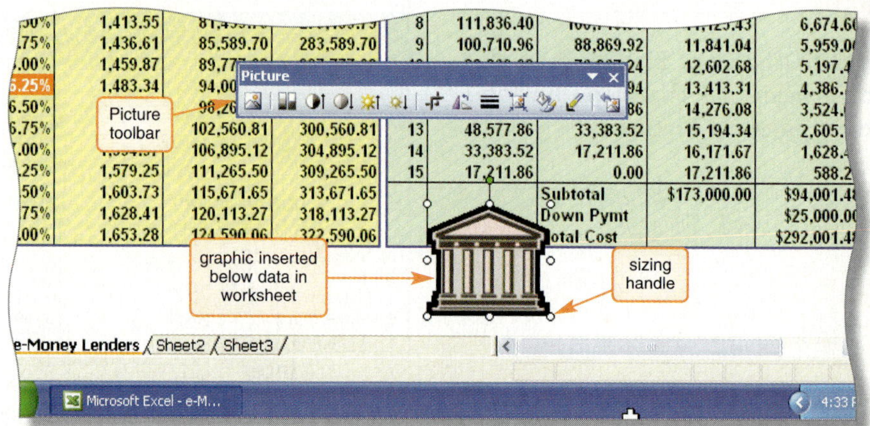

FIGURE 4-49

4

- **Drag the sizing handles to resize the bank graphic and then drag it so it appears in the range H18:H20.**

Excel displays the bank graphic as shown in Figure 4-50.

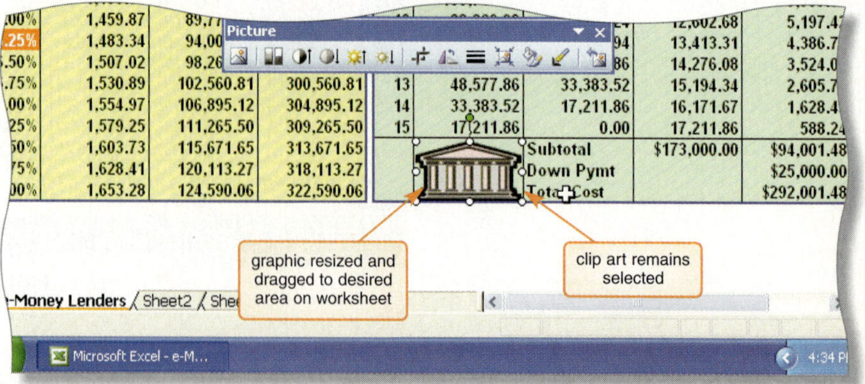

FIGURE 4-50

5

- **With the graphic selected, right-click it.**

Excel displays a shortcut menu (Figure 4-51).

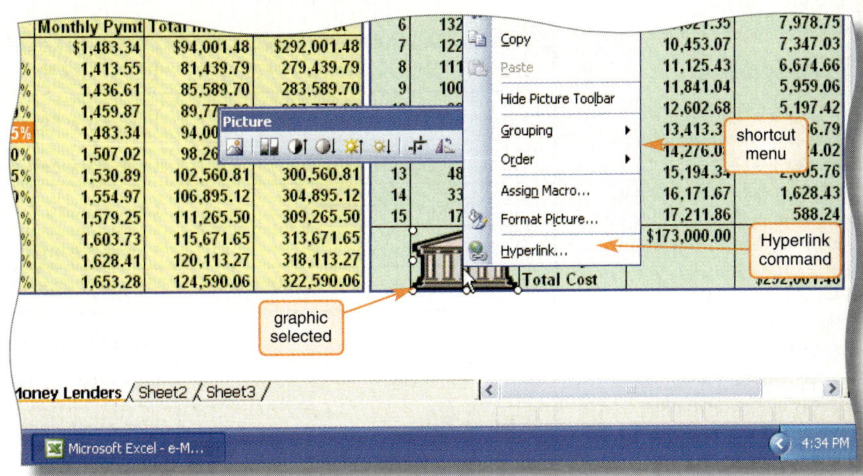

FIGURE 4-51

6

- **Click Hyperlink on the shortcut menu.**
- **When Excel displays the Insert Hyperlink dialog box, click the Look in box arrow, click 3½ Floppy (A:) in the Look in list, and then click the file name e-Money Lenders Statement of Condition.**

Excel displays the Insert Hyperlink dialog box as shown in Figure 4-52.

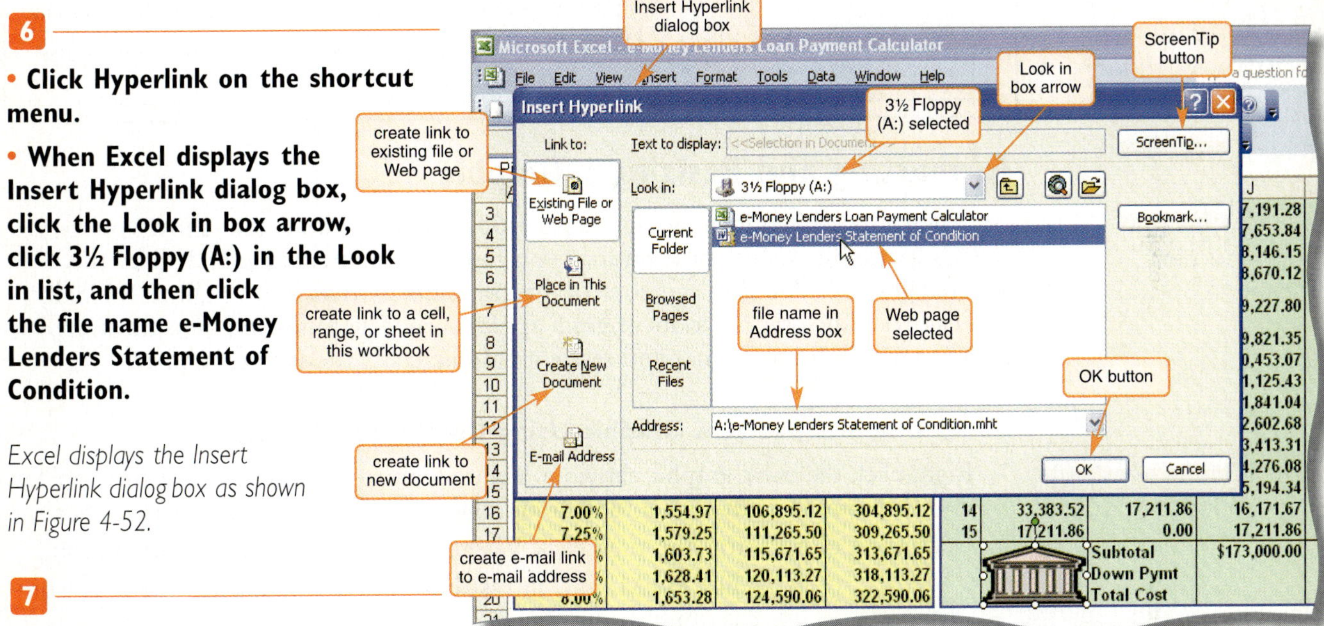

FIGURE 4-52

7

- **Click the OK button.**
- **If a Microsoft Office Excel dialog box displays, click the Yes button.**
- **Select cell J19 to deselect the graphic.**
- **Click the Save button on the Standard toolbar to save the workbook using the file name e-Money Lenders Loan Payment Calculator.**

Excel assigns the hyperlink, a:\e-Money Lenders Statement of Condition.mht, to the bank graphic. Excel saves the workbook using the file name e-Money Lenders Loan Payment Calculator.

Other Ways

1. Click Insert Hyperlink button on Standard toolbar
2. On Insert menu click Hyperlink
3. Press CTRL+K
4. In Voice Command mode, say "Insert Hyperlink"

To assign a hyperlink, you also can select the bank graphic and then click the Insert Hyperlink button on the Standard toolbar. To edit the hyperlink, right-click the bank graphic to display the shortcut menu and then click Edit Hyperlink.

Table 4-3 on the next page describes buttons in the Insert Hyperlink dialog box that can be used to create different types of hyperlinks.

More About

Hyperlinks

The hyperlink capability in Excel is quite powerful and extends well beyond linking to Web pages. For example, as shown in the Insert Hyperlink dialog box in Figure 4-52 on the previous page, you can create a hyperlink to any Office file, including a Word document, Excel workbook, Access database, or PowerPoint presentation. Excel even lets you create a hyperlink to a specific part or location in an Office file.

Table 4-3 Summary of Buttons in the Insert Hyperlink Dialog Box

BUTTONS IN LINK TO AREA	FUNCTION
Existing File or Web Page	Link to a file or Web page
Place in This Document	Link to a cell reference or defined name in the workbook
Create New Document	Link to and create new document
E-mail Address	Link to e-mail address to send an e-mail
BUTTONS IN LOOK IN AREA	**FUNCTION**
Current Folder	List files in current folder
Browsed Pages	List Web pages visited in browser
Recent Files	List most recent files used
OTHER BUTTONS	**FUNCTION**
ScreenTip	Lets you customize the message that appears in the ScreenTip when the mouse pointer points to the hyperlink
Bookmark	Lets you choose a bookmark at which to start the display of the selected file

Formatting and Resizing a Graphic

The Picture toolbar shown in Figure 4-53 includes buttons that allow you to modify a graphic. Using these buttons you can crop, rotate, scale, and resize the selected graphic. You also can control the graphic's contrast and brightness. Finally, you can reset the graphic to its original appearance. The following steps illustrate Excel's capabilities to format and resize a graphic using the Picture toolbar.

To Format and Resize a Graphic Using the Picture Toolbar

1. Right-click the bank graphic shown in Figure 4-54 to select it. If the Picture toolbar does not appear, right-click a toolbar and then click Picture on the shortcut menu.
2. Click the Color button and then click Washout. Click the Reset Picture button.
3. Click the More Contrast button five times. Click the Less Contrast button five times.
4. Click the More Brightness button five times. Click the Less Brightness button five times.
5. Click the Crop button, and then drag the border halfway in towards the middle. Click the Reset Picture button.
6. Click the Rotate Left 90° button four times.
7. Click the Format Picture button. When the Format Picture dialog box appears, click the Color and Lines tab. Select Red as the fill color. Click the OK button. Click the Reset Picture button.
8. Click the Set Transparent Color button and then click the bank graphic so the background is transparent. Click the Reset Picture button.
9. Resize the bank graphic so it appears as shown in Figure 4-54.

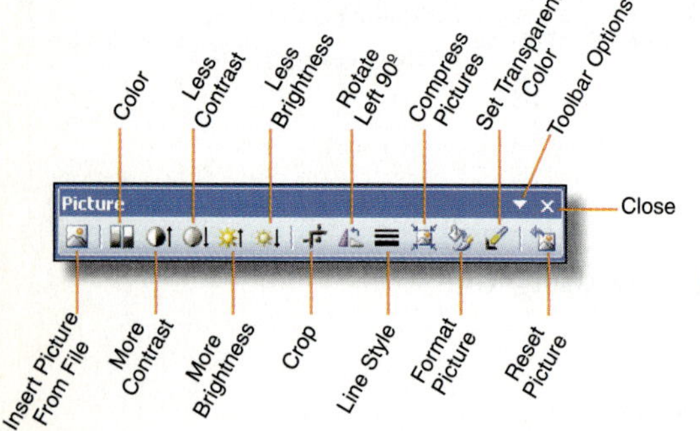

FIGURE 4-53

Displaying and Printing a Hyperlinked File

The next step is to display and print the hyperlinked file by clicking the bank graphic on the worksheet and using the Print command in the browser. Once you assign a hyperlink to an element on a worksheet, you can position the mouse pointer on the element to display the hyperlink's ScreenTip. Clicking the bank graphic causes the hyperlinked file to display, as shown in the following steps.

To Display and Print a Hyperlinked File

1

- **With the Data Disk in drive A, point to the bank graphic on the worksheet.**

The mouse pointer changes to a hand. A ScreenTip appears indicating the destination file to which the graphic is hyperlinked (Figure 4-54).

FIGURE 4-54

2

- **Click the bank graphic.**

The browser displays the Web page as shown in Figure 4-55.

3

- **Click File on the menu bar and then click Print in the browser window.**
- **When the Print dialog box appears, click the Print button.**
- **Click the Back button to return to Excel.**

The hyperlinked file prints on the printer. The browser is closed and the worksheet appears in the active window.

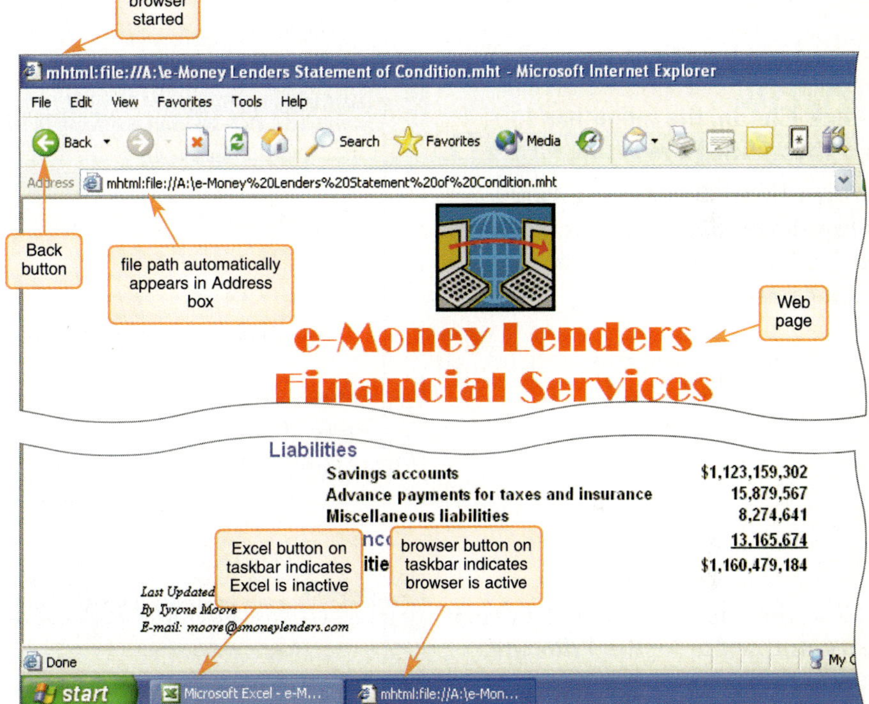

FIGURE 4-55

If the hyperlinked file is not displayed when the hyperlink is clicked, make sure the correct file was selected from the list in the Insert Hyperlink dialog box (Figure 4-52 on page EX 279).

Printing Sections of the Worksheet

In Project 2, you learned to print a section of a worksheet by selecting it and using the Selection option in the Print dialog box (see page EX 117). If you find yourself continually selecting the same range in a worksheet to print, you can set a specific

More About

Personalized ScreenTips

You can add a personalized ScreenTip to a hyperlink by clicking the ScreenTip button in the Insert Hyperlink dialog box (Figure 4-52 on page EX 279). If you add a personalized ScreenTip, it appears in place of the file path of the when you point to the hyperlink (Figure 4-54 on the previous page).

range to print each time you print the worksheet by using the Set Print Area command on the Print Area submenu. You display the Print Area submenu by pointing to the Print Area command on the File menu. When you set a range to print using the Set Print Area command, Excel will continue to print only that range until you clear it using the Clear Print command on the Print Area submenu or set a new print area.

Setting Up a Worksheet to Print

This section describes print options available on the Sheet sheet in the Page Setup dialog box (Figure 4-56b). These print options pertain to the way the worksheet will appear in the printed copy. One of the more important print options is the capability of printing in black and white. Printing in black and white not only speeds up the printing process, but also saves ink. This is especially true if you have a color printer and need only a black and white printed copy of the worksheet. The following steps show how to ensure any printed copy fits on one page and prints in black and white.

To Set Up a Worksheet to Print

1

- **Click File on the menu bar and then click Page Setup.**
- **When Excel displays the Page Setup dialog box, click the Page tab and then click Fit to in the Scaling area.**

Excel displays the Page sheet as shown in Figure 4-56a.

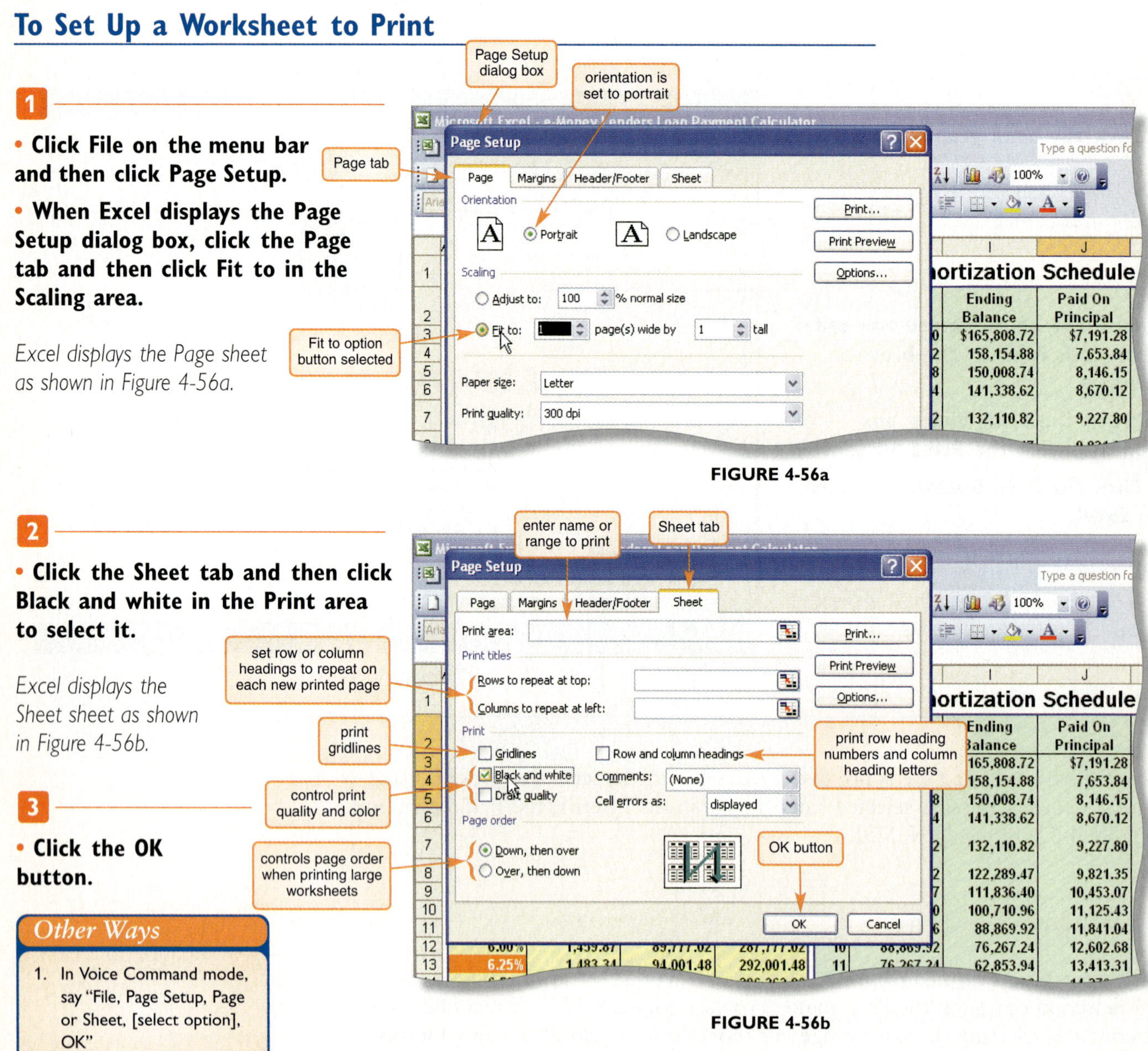

FIGURE 4-56a

2

- **Click the Sheet tab and then click Black and white in the Print area to select it.**

Excel displays the Sheet sheet as shown in Figure 4-56b.

3

- **Click the OK button.**

FIGURE 4-56b

Other Ways

1. In Voice Command mode, say "File, Page Setup, Page or Sheet, [select option], OK"

Table 4-4 summarizes the print options available in the Sheet sheet in the Page Setup dialog box.

Table 4-4 Print Options Available Using the Sheet Sheet in the Page Setup Dialog Box

PRINT OPTION	DESCRIPTION
Print area text box	Excel prints from cell A1 to the last occupied cell in a worksheet unless you instruct it to print a selected area. You can select a range to print with the mouse, or you can enter a range or name of a range in the Print area text box. Nonadjacent ranges will print on a separate page.
Print titles area	This area is used to instruct Excel to print row titles and column titles on each printed page of a worksheet. You must specify a range, even if you are designating one column (e.g., 1:4 means the first four rows).
Gridlines check box	A check mark in this check box instructs Excel to print gridlines.
Black and white check box	A check mark in this check box speeds up printing and saves colored ink if you have colors in a worksheet and a color printer.
Draft quality check box	A check mark in this check box speeds up printing by ignoring formatting and not printing most graphics.
Row and column headings check box	A check mark in this check box instructs Excel to include the column heading letters (A, B, C, etc.) and row heading numbers (1, 2, 3, etc.) in the printout.
Comments	Indicates where comments are to be displayed on the printout.
Cell errors as	Indicates how errors in cells should be displayed on the printout.
Page order area	Determines the order in which multipage worksheets will print.

Printing a Section of a Worksheet Using the Set Print Area Command

The following steps show how to print only the Loan Payment Calculator section by setting the print area to the range B1:E6.

To Set the Print Area

1

• **Select the range B1:E6, click File on the menu bar, and then point to Print Area.**

Excel displays the File menu and Print Area submenu (Figure 4-57). The range B1:E6 is selected.

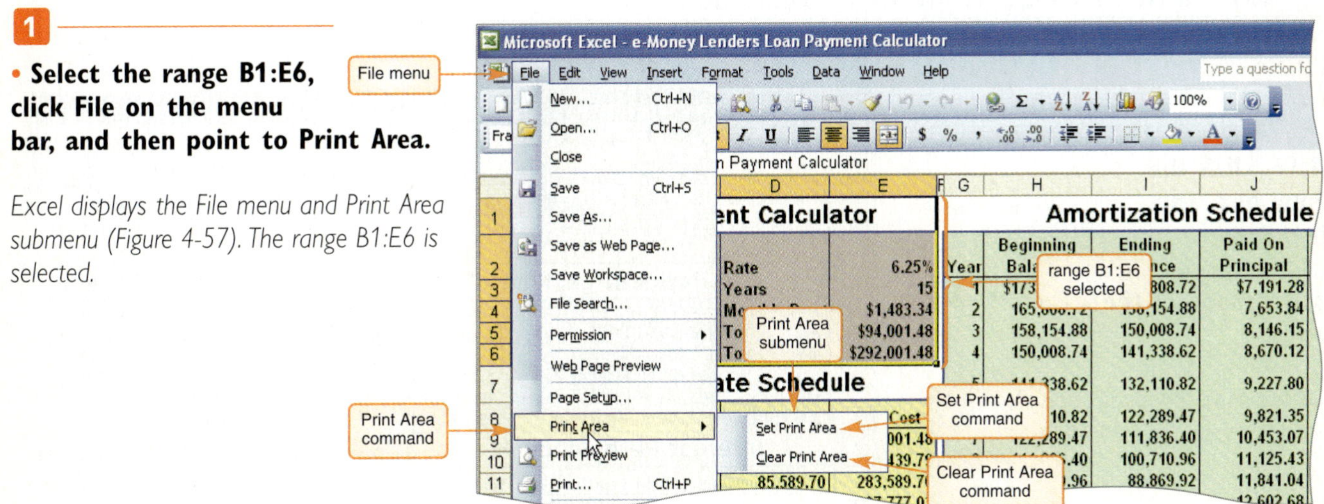

FIGURE 4-57

- **Click Set Print Area on the Print Area submenu.**
- **Click the Print button on the Standard toolbar.**
- **Click Clear Print Area on the Print Area submenu (Figure 4-57 on the previous page) to reset the print area to the entire worksheet.**

Excel prints the range B1:E6 (Figure 4-58).

Loan Payment Calculator

Date	29-Jul-2003	Rate	6.25%
Item	House	Years	15
Price	$198,000.00	Monthly Pymt	$1,483.34
Down Pymt	$25,000.00	Total Interest	$94,001.48
Loan Amt	$173,000.00	Total Cost	$292,001.48

range B1:E6 prints

FIGURE 4-58

Other Ways

1. Press ALT+F, T, S
2. In Voice Command mode, say "File, Print Area, Set Print Area; or Clear Print Area"

Once you set a print area, Excel will continue to print the specified range, rather than the entire worksheet. If you save the workbook with the print area set, then Excel will remember the settings the next time you open the workbook and print only the specified range. To remove the print area so that the entire worksheet prints, click Clear Print Area on the Print Area submenu as described at the end of Step 2.

Naming Print Areas

With some spreadsheet applications, you will want to print several different areas of a worksheet, depending on the request. Rather than using the Set Print Area command or manually selecting the range each time you want to print, you can name the ranges using the Name box in the formula bar. You then can use one of the names to select an area before using the Set Print Area command or Selection option button. The following steps name the Loan Payment Calculator section, the Interest Rate Schedule section, the Amortization Schedule section, and the entire worksheet and then print each section using the Selection option button in the Print dialog box.

To Name and Print Sections of a Worksheet

1

- **If necessary, select the range B1:E6, click the Name box, and then type** `Loan_Payment` **as the name of the range.**

Excel displays the name Loan_Payment in the Name box (Figure 4-59).

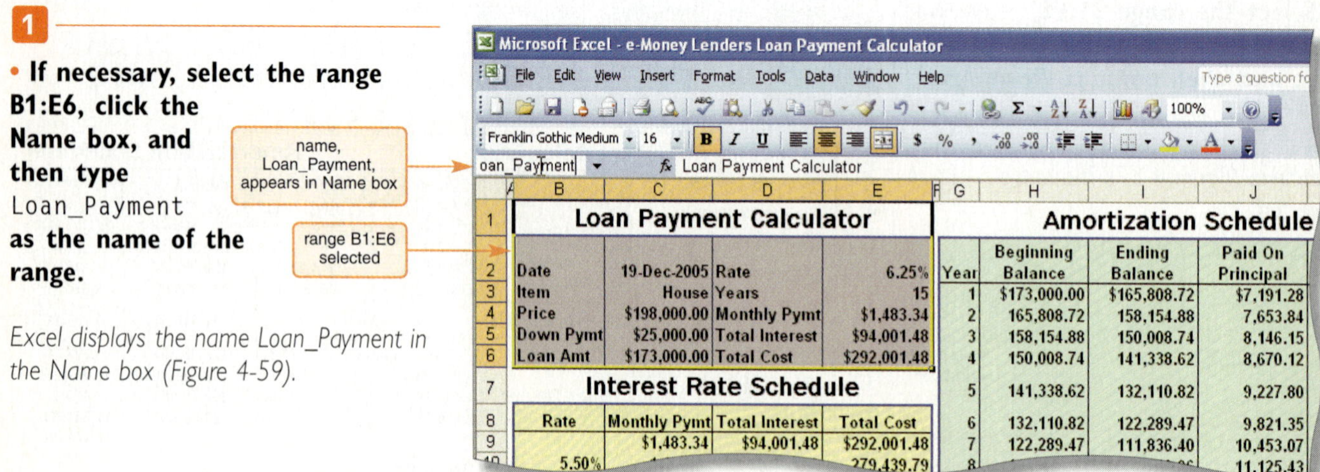

FIGURE 4-59

2

- **Press the ENTER key.**
- **Select the range B7:E20, click the Name box, type** `Interest_Schedule` **as the name of the range, and then press the ENTER key.**
- **Select the range G1:K20, click the Name box, type** `Amortization_Schedule` **as the name of the range, and then press the ENTER key.**
- **Select the range B1:K20, click the Name box, type** `All_Sections` **as the name of the range, and then press the ENTER key.**
- **Select any cell on the worksheet and then click the Name box arrow in the formula bar.**

Excel displays the new names in the Name list (Figure 4-60).

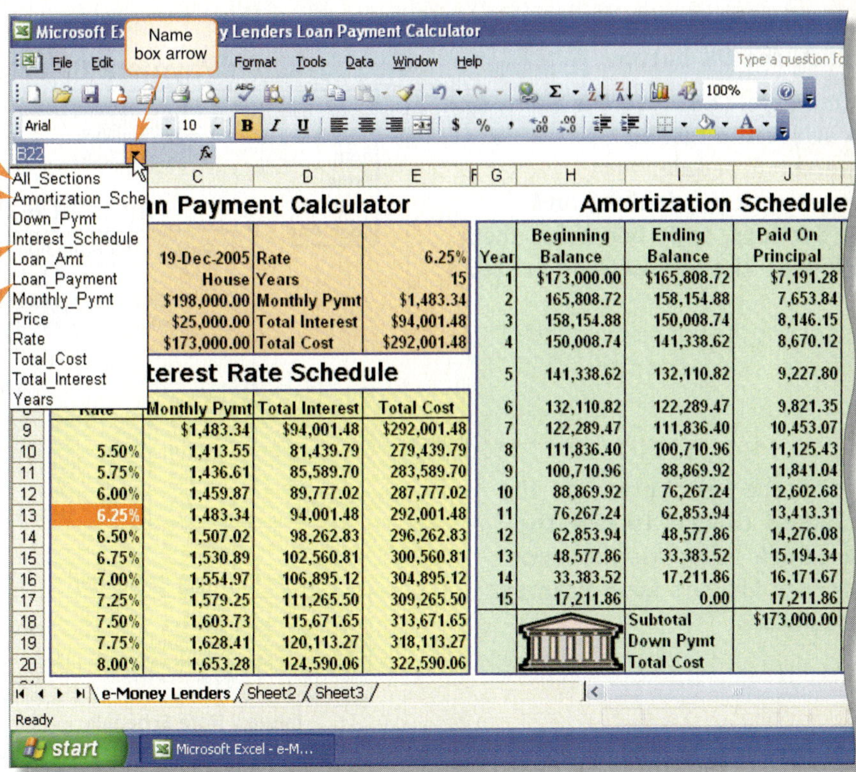

FIGURE 4-60

3

- **Click Loan_Payment in the Name list.**
- **Click File on the menu bar and then click Print.**
- **When Excel displays the Print dialog box, click Selection in the Print what area.**

The range named Loan_Payment is selected. Excel displays the Print dialog box as shown in Figure 4-61.

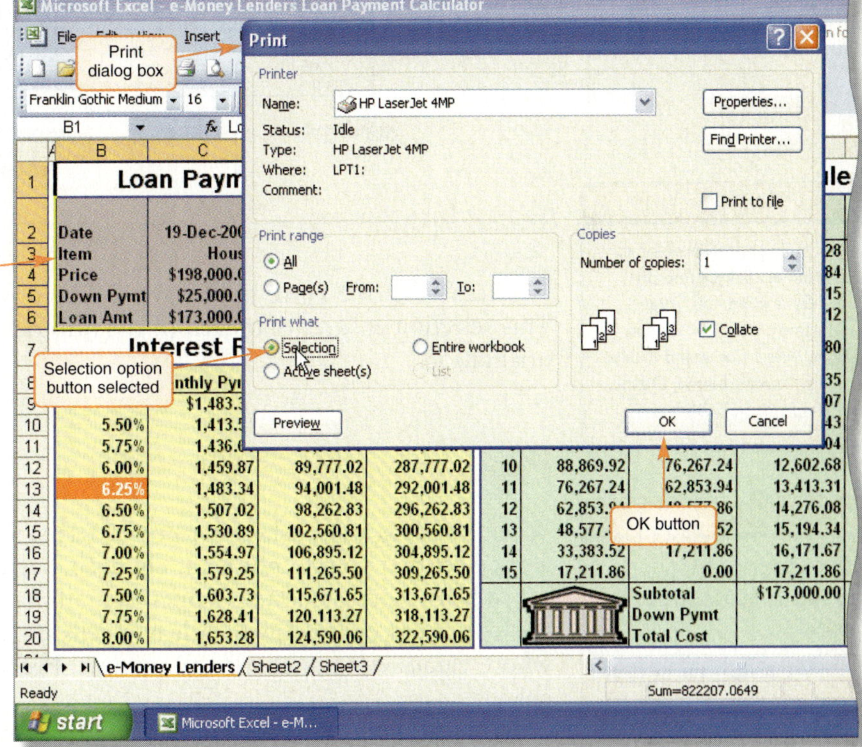

FIGURE 4-61

4

- **Click the OK button.**
- **One at a time, use the Name box to select the names Interest_Schedule, Amortization_Schedule, and All_Sections, and then print them following the instructions in Step 3.**

Excel prints the four sections of the worksheet as shown in Figure 4-62.

5

- **Click the Save button on the Standard toolbar to save the workbook using the file name e-Money Lenders Loan Payment Calculator.**

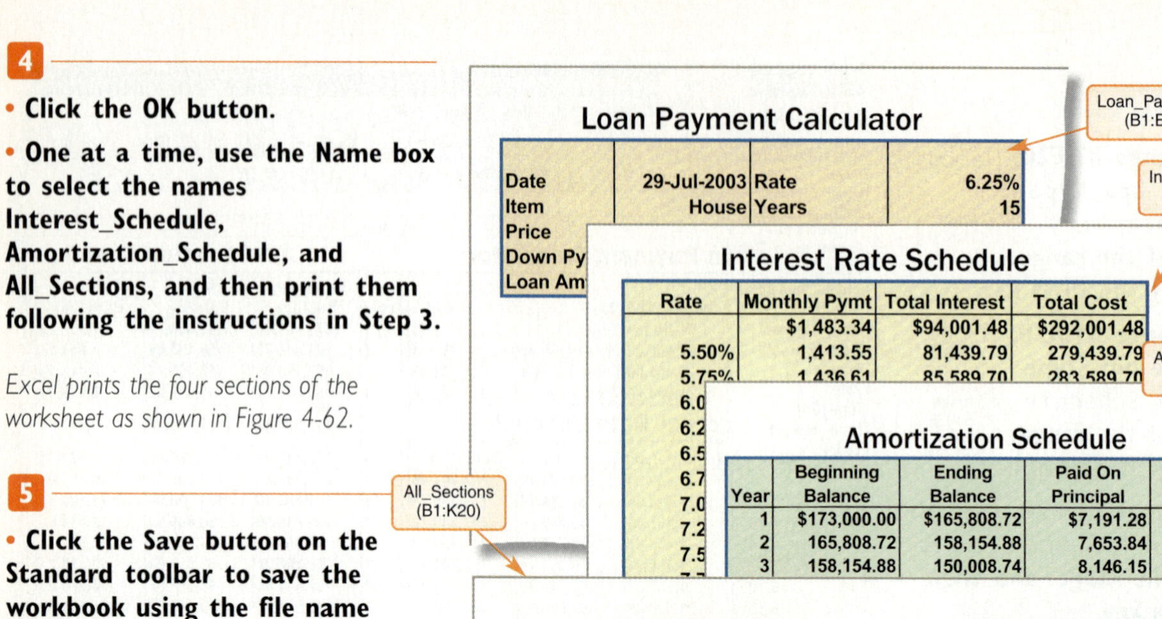

Loan Payment Calculator

Date	29-Jul-2003	Rate	6.25%
Item	House	Years	15
Price	$198,000.00	Monthly Pymt	$1,483.34
Down Pymt	$25,000.00	Total Interest	$94,001.48
Loan Amt	$173,000.00	Total Cost	$292,001.48

Interest Rate Schedule

Rate	Monthly Pymt	Total Interest	Total Cost
	$1,483.34	$94,001.48	$292,001.48
5.50%	1,413.55	81,439.79	279,439.79
5.75%	1,436.61	85,589.70	283,589.70
6.00%	1,459.87	89,777.02	287,777.02
6.25%	1,483.34	94,001.48	292,001.48
6.50%	1,507.02	98,262.83	296,262.83
6.75%	1,530.89	102,560.81	300,560.81
7.00%	1,554.97	106,895.12	304,895.12
7.25%	1,579.25	111,265.50	309,265.50
7.50%	1,603.73	115,671.65	313,671.65
7.75%	1,628.41	120,113.27	318,113.27
8.00%	1,653.28	124,590.06	322,590.06

Amortization Schedule

Year	Beginning Balance	Ending Balance	Paid On Principal	Interest Paid
1	$173,000.00	$165,808.72	$7,191.28	$10,608.82
2	165,808.72	158,154.88	7,653.84	10,146.26
3	158,154.88	150,008.74	8,146.15	9,653.95
4	150,008.74	141,338.62	8,670.12	9,129.98
5	141,338.62	132,110.82	9,227.80	8,572.30
6	132,110.82	122,289.47	9,821.35	7,978.75
7	122,289.47	111,836.40	10,453.07	7,347.03
8	111,836.40	100,710.96	11,125.43	6,674.66
9	100,710.96	88,869.92	11,841.04	5,959.06
10	88,869.92	76,267.24	12,602.68	5,197.42
11	76,267.24	62,853.94	13,413.31	4,386.79
12	62,853.94	48,577.86	14,276.08	3,524.02
13	48,577.86	33,383.52	15,194.34	2,605.76
14	33,383.52	17,211.86	16,171.67	1,628.43
15	17,211.86	0.00	17,211.86	588.24
		Subtotal	$173,000.00	$94,001.48
		Down Pymt		$25,000.00
		Total Cost		$292,001.48

FIGURE 4-62

Other Ways

1. On Insert menu point to Name, click Define on Name submenu, [type name], click OK button
2. In Voice Command mode, say "Insert, Name, Define, [type name], OK"

Q&A

Q: Can a name be assigned to two or more nonadjacent ranges?

A: Yes. A name can be assigned to two or more nonadjacent ranges. After selecting the first range, hold down the CTRL key and drag through the additional ranges of cells to select them before entering the name in the Name box.

Recall that the Fit to option was selected earlier (Figure 4-56a on page EX 282). This selection ensures that each of the printouts fits across the page in portrait orientation.

Protecting the Worksheet

When building a worksheet for novice users, you should protect the cells in the worksheet that you do not want changed, such as cells that contain text or formulas.

When you create a new worksheet, all the cells are assigned a locked status, but the lock is not engaged, which leaves cells unprotected. **Unprotected cells** are cells whose values you can change at anytime. **Protected cells** are cells that you cannot change.

You should protect cells only after the worksheet has been tested fully and the correct results appear. Protecting a worksheet is a two-step process:

1. Select the cells you want to leave unprotected and then change their cell protection settings to an unlocked status.
2. Protect the entire worksheet.

At first glance, these steps may appear to be backwards. Once you protect the entire worksheet, however, you cannot change anything, including the locked status of individual cells.

In the loan payment calculator worksheet (Figure 4-63), the user should be able to make changes to only five cells: the item in cell C3; the price in cell C4; the down payment in cell C5; the interest rate in cell E2; and the years in cell E3. These cells must remain unprotected so that users can enter the correct data. The remaining cells and the embedded bank graphic in the worksheet should be protected so that the user cannot change them.

The following steps show how to protect the loan payment calculator worksheet.

To Protect a Worksheet

1

- **Select the range C3:C5.**
- **Hold down the CTRL key and then select the nonadjacent range E2:E3.**
- **Right-click one of the selected ranges.**

Excel displays the shortcut menu (Figure 4-63).

FIGURE 4-63

2

- **Click Format Cells on the shortcut menu.**
- **When Excel displays the Format Cells dialog box, click the Protection tab, and then click Locked to remove the check mark.**

Excel displays the Protection sheet in the Format Cells dialog box with the check mark removed from the Locked check box (Figure 4-64). This means the selected cells (C3:C5 and E2:E3) will not be protected when the Protect command is invoked later.

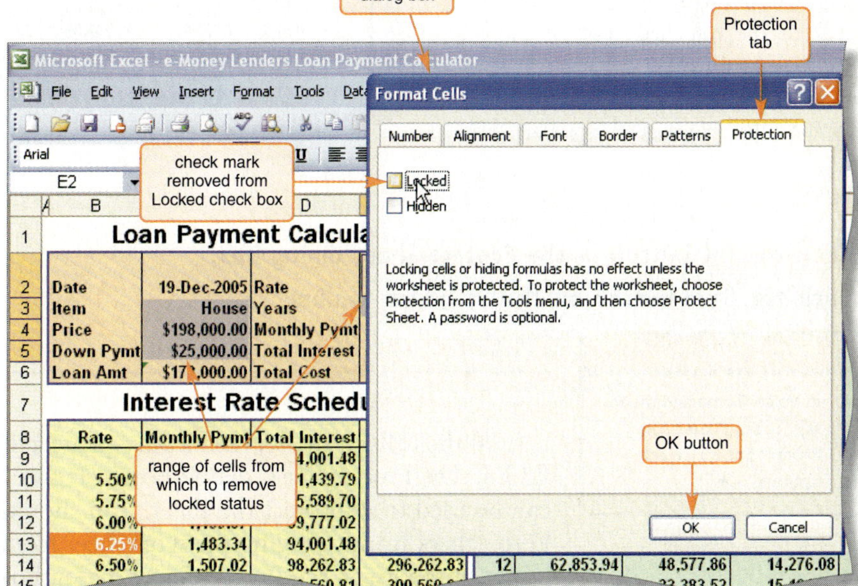

FIGURE 4-64

3

- **Click the OK button and then select cell J19 to deselect the ranges C3:C5 and E2:E3.**
- **Click Tools on the menu bar and then point to Protection.**

Excel displays the Tools menu and Protection submenu (Figure 4-65).

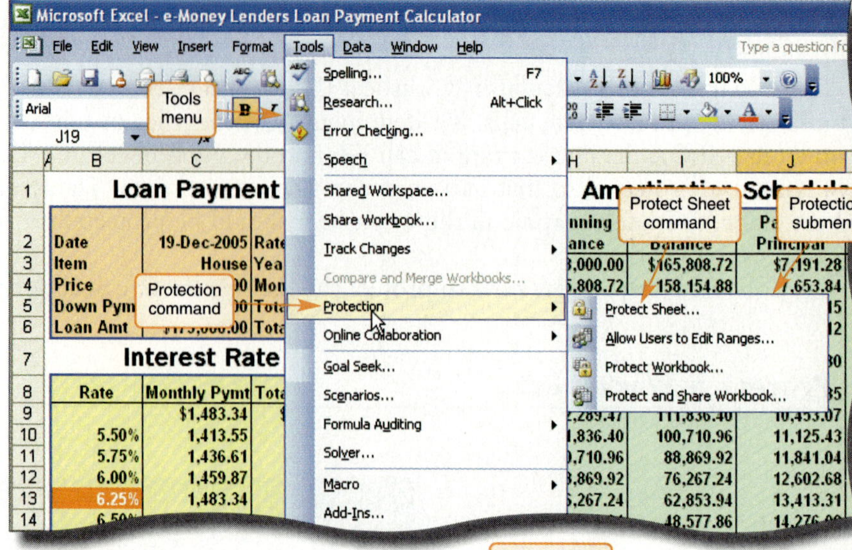

FIGURE 4-65

4

- **Click Protect Sheet on the Protection submenu.**
- **When Excel displays the Protect Sheet dialog box, make sure the Protect worksheet and contents of locked cells check box at the top of the dialog box and the first two check boxes in the list contain check marks.**

Excel displays the Protect Sheet dialog box (Figure 4-66). All three check boxes are selected, thus protecting the worksheet from changes to contents (except the cells left unlocked). The two check boxes in the list allow the user to select any cell on the worksheet, but the user can change only unlocked cells.

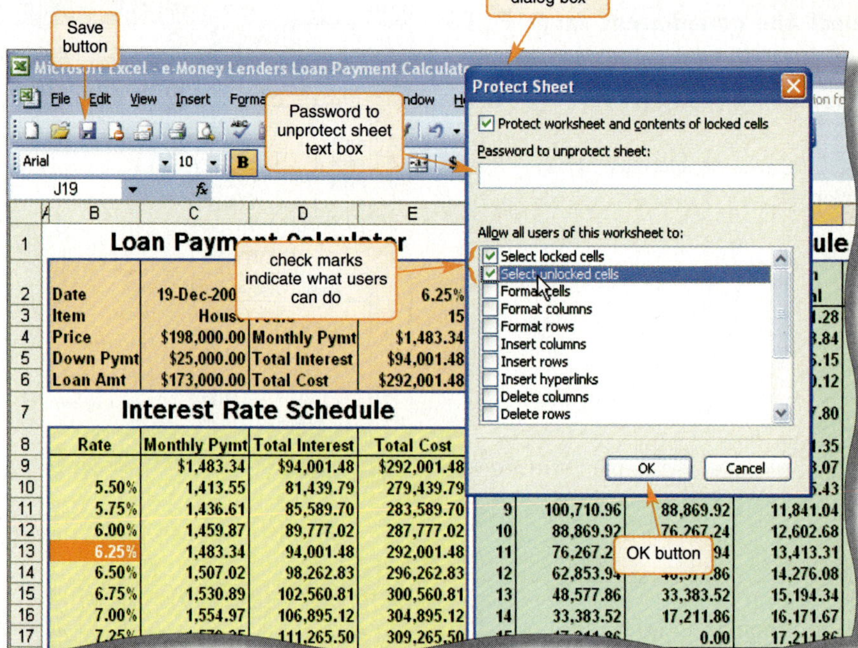

FIGURE 4-66

5

- **Click the OK button in the Protect Sheet dialog box.**
- **Click the Save button on the Standard toolbar.**

Other Ways

1. In Voice Command mode, say "Tools, Protection, Protect Sheet, [select options], OK"

All the cells in the worksheet are protected, except for the ranges C3:C5 and E2:E3. The Protect Sheet dialog box in Figure 4-66 lets you enter a password that can be used to unprotect the sheet. You should create a **password** when you want to keep others from changing the worksheet from protected to unprotected. The check boxes in the list in the Protect Sheet dialog box also give you the option to modify the protection so that the user can make certain changes, such as formatting cells or inserting hyperlinks.

If you want to protect more than one sheet in a workbook, select each sheet before you begin the protection process or click Protect Workbook on the Protection submenu, instead of clicking Protect Sheet (Figure 4-65).

If you want to unlock cells for specific users, you can use the Allow Users to Edit Ranges command on the Protection submenu. For additional information about unlocking cells for specific users, enter `protect worksheet` in the Type a question for help box on the right side of the menu bar.

When this workbook is put into production, users will be able to enter data in only the unprotected cells. If they try to change any protected cell, such as the monthly payment in cell E4, Excel displays a dialog box with an error message as shown in Figure 4-67. An alternative to displaying this dialog box is to remove the check mark from the Select unlocked cells check box in the Protect Sheet dialog box (Figure 4-66). With the check mark removed, the user cannot select a locked cell.

To unprotect the worksheet so that you can change all cells in the worksheet, unprotect the document by clicking Tools on the menu bar, pointing to Protection on the Tools menu, and then clicking Unprotect Sheet on the Protection submenu.

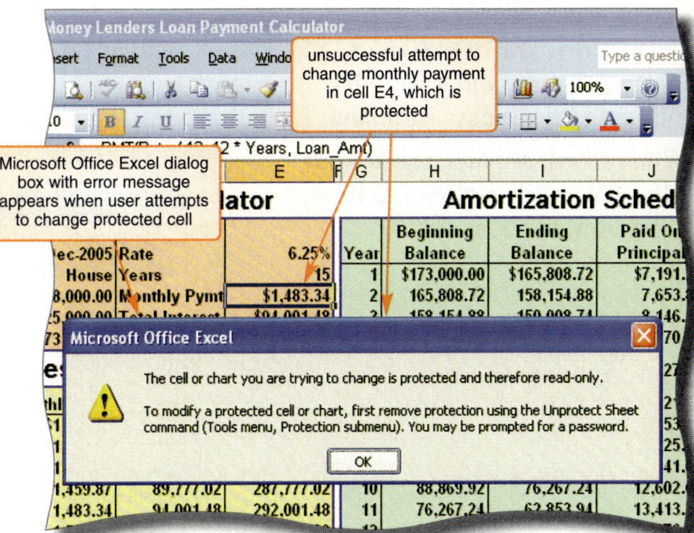

FIGURE 4-67

Hiding and Unhiding Rows, Columns, and Sheets

You can hide rows, columns, and sheets that contain sensitive data. Rows, columns, and sheets are hidden by first selecting one or more of them and then using the Hide command on the Row, Column, and Sheet submenus that are available on the Format menu (Figure 4-68). Later, you can use the Unhide command on the same submenus to unhide hidden rows, columns, and sheets. You also learned earlier in Project 2 (pages EX 109 and EX 111) that you can use the mouse and keyboard to hide and unhide rows and columns.

The following steps show how to hide and then unhide a sheet. The same steps can be used to hide and unhide rows and columns, except that you would first unprotect the worksheet and then select the rows or columns, rather than the sheet.

More About

Using Protected Worksheets

You can move from one unprotected cell to another unprotected cell in a worksheet by using the TAB and SHIFT+TAB keys. This is especially useful when the cells are not adjacent to one another.

To Hide and Unhide a Sheet

1

- **If the e-Money Lenders sheet is not active, click its tab.**
- **Click Format on the menu bar and then point to Sheet.**

Excel displays the Format menu and Sheet submenu (Figure 4-68).

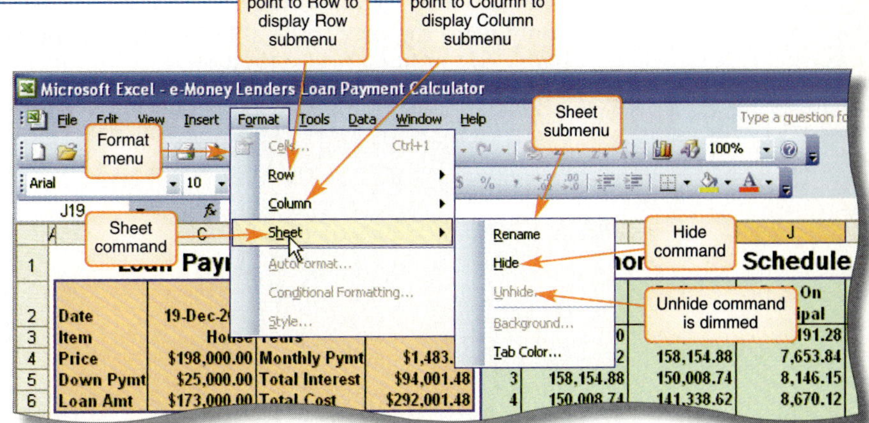

FIGURE 4-68

2

• **Click Hide on the Sheet submenu.**

Excel hides the e-Money Lenders sheet.

3

• **Click Format on the menu bar, point to Sheets, and then click Unhide on the Sheets submenu.**

• **When Excel displays the Unhide dialog box, click e-Money Lenders in the Unhide sheet list.**

Excel displays the Unhide dialog box with the name of the hidden sheet, e-Money Lenders (Figure 4-69).

4

• **Click the OK button.**

Excel unhides the e-Money Lenders sheet and displays it as shown in Figure 4-68 on the previous page.

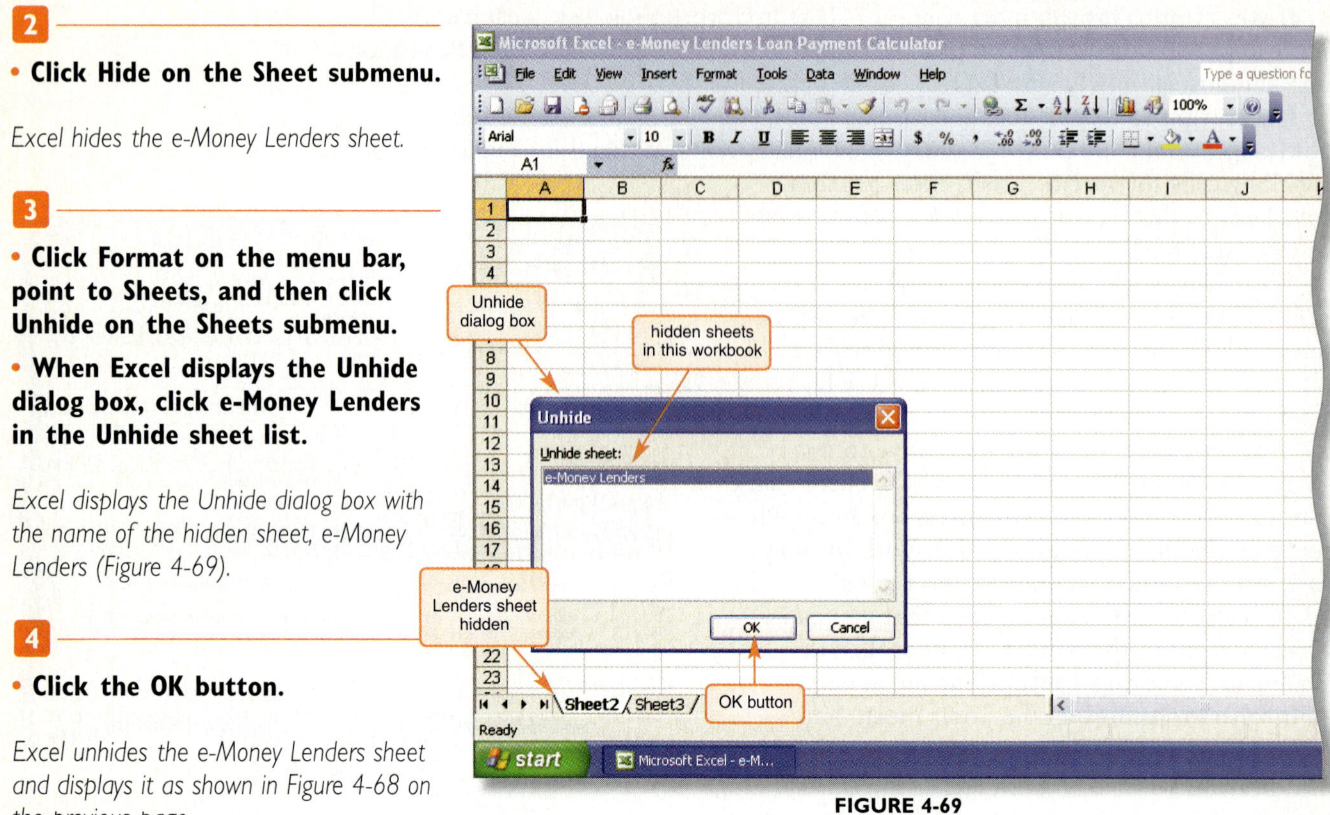

FIGURE 4-69

Hiding sheets in a workbook is not uncommon when working with complex workbooks that have one sheet with the results the user needs to see and one or more sheets with essential data that is unimportant to the user, and thus hidden from view. The fact that a sheet is hidden does not mean the data and formulas on the hidden sheets are unavailable for use on other sheets in the workbook. This same logic applies to hidden rows and columns.

Hiding and Unhiding Workbooks

You hide an entire workbook by using the Hide command on the Window menu. Some users employ this command when they leave a workbook up on an unattended computer and do not want others to be able to see the workbook. The Hide command is also useful when you have several workbooks opened simultaneously and only want the user to be able to view one of them. The following steps show how to hide and unhide a workbook.

To Hide and Unhide a Workbook

1

- **Click Window on the menu bar.**

Excel displays the Window menu (Figure 4-70).

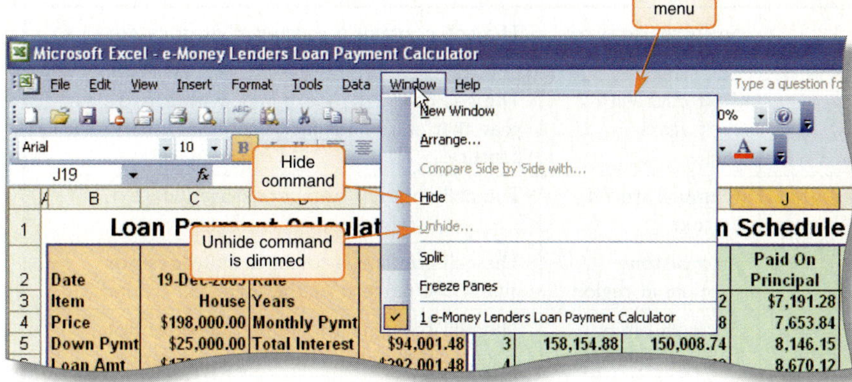

FIGURE 4-70

2

- **Click Hide on the Window menu.**

Excel hides the e-Money Lenders Loan Payment Calculator workbook.

3

- **Click Window on the menu bar and then click Unhide.**
- **When Excel displays the Unhide dialog box, if necessary, click e-Money Lenders Loan Payment Calculator in the Unhide workbook list.**

Excel displays the Unhide dialog box with the name of the hidden workbook, e-Money Lenders Loan Payment Calculator (Figure 4-71).

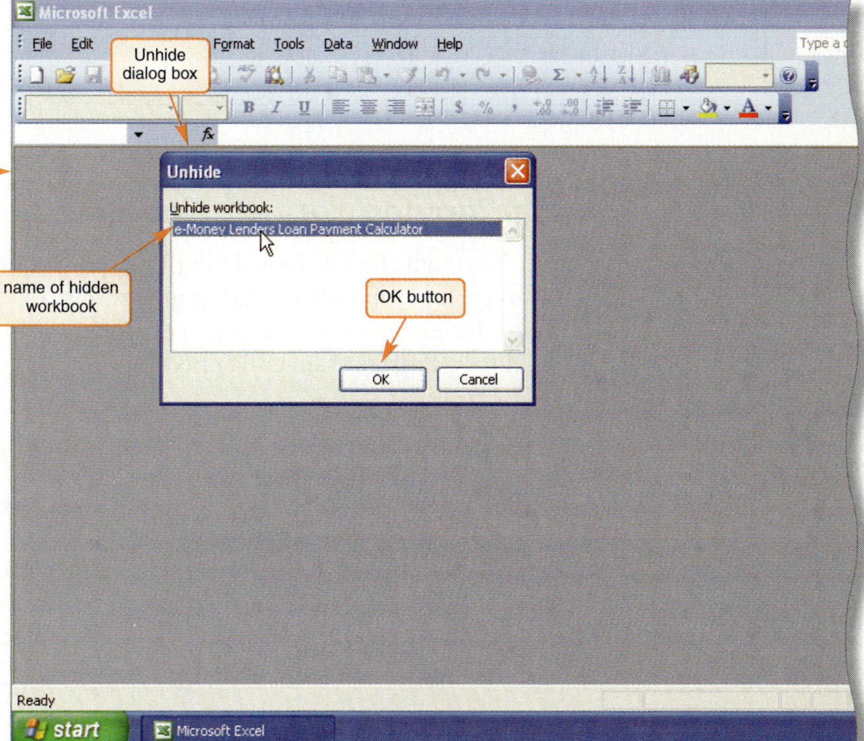

FIGURE 4-71

4

- **Click the OK button.**

Excel unhides the e-Money Lenders Loan Payment Calculator workbook and displays it as shown in Figure 4-70.

You can hide most window elements in order to display more rows of worksheet data. These window elements include the Microsoft Windows taskbar and the Excel title bar, toolbars, formula bar, and status bar. The Excel window elements can be hidden by using the Full Screen command on the View menu. These elements only remain hidden as long as the workbook is open. They redisplay when you close the workbook and open it again.

Table 4-5 Formula Checking Rules

RULE	NAME OF RULE	DESCRIPTION
1	Evaluates to error value	The cell contains a formula that does not use the expected syntax, arguments, or data types.
2	Text date with 2 digit years	The cell contains a text date with a two-digit year that can be misinterpreted as the wrong century.
3	Number stored as text	The cell contains numbers stored as text.
4	Inconsistent formula in region	The cell contains a formula that does not match the pattern of the formulas around it.
5	Formula omits cells in region	The cell contains a formula that does not include a correct cell or range reference.
6	Unlocked cells containing formulas	The cell with a formula is unlocked in a protected worksheet.
7	Formulas referring to empty cells	The cells referred to in a formula are empty.
8	List data validation error	The cell has a data validation error.

Formula Checking

Similar to the spell checker, Excel has a **formula checker** that checks formulas in a worksheet for rule violations. You invoke the formula checker by clicking the Error Checking command on the Tools menu. Each time Excel encounters a cell with a formula that violates one of its rules, it displays a dialog box containing information about the formula and a suggestion on how to fix the formula. Table 4-5 lists Excel's formula checking rules. You can choose which rules you want Excel to use by enabling and disabling them on the Error Checking sheet in the Options dialog box shown in Figure 4-72.

Background Formula Checking

Through the Options dialog box, you can enable background formula checking. **Background formula checking** means that Excel continually will review the workbook for errors in formulas as you create or manipulate it. The following steps enable background formula checking.

To Enable Background Formula Checking

1. **Click Tools on the menu bar, click Options, and then click the Error Checking tab in the Options dialog box.**
2. **If necessary, click Enable background error checking in the Settings area to select it.**
3. **Click any check box in the Rules area that does not contain a check mark.**
4. **Click the OK button.**

Following Step 3, the Error Checking sheet in the Options dialog box appears as shown in Figure 4-72.

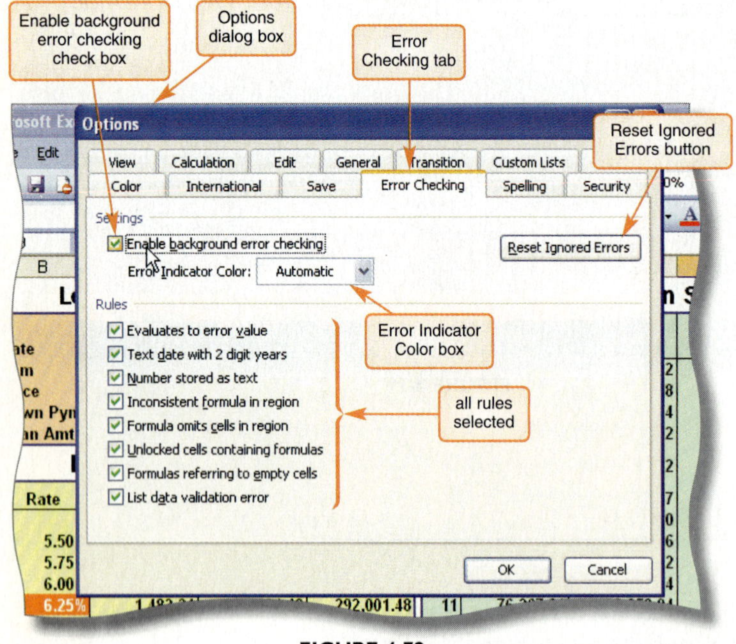

FIGURE 4-72

You can decide which rules you want the background formula checker to highlight by adding and removing check marks from the check boxes in the Rules area on the Error Checking sheet (Figure 4-72). If you add or remove check marks, then you should click the Reset Ignored Errors button to reset error checking.

When a formula fails to pass one of the rules and background formula checking is enabled, then Excel displays a small green triangle in the upper-left corner of the cell assigned the formula in question.

Assume for example, that background formula checking is enabled and that cell E4, which contains the PMT function in the e-Money Lenders workbook, is unlocked. Because rule 6 in Table 4-5 stipulates that a cell containing a formula must be locked, Excel displays a green triangle in the upper-left corner of cell E4.

When you select the cell with the green triangle, a Trace Error button appears next to the cell. If you click the Trace Error button, Excel displays the Trace Error menu (Figure 4-73). The first item in the menu identifies the error (Unprotected Formula). The remainder of the menu lists commands from which you can choose. The first command locks the cell. Invoking the Lock Cell command fixes the problem so that the formula no longer violates the rule. The Error Checking Options command instructs Excel to display the Options dialog box with the Error Checking sheet active, as shown in Figure 4-72.

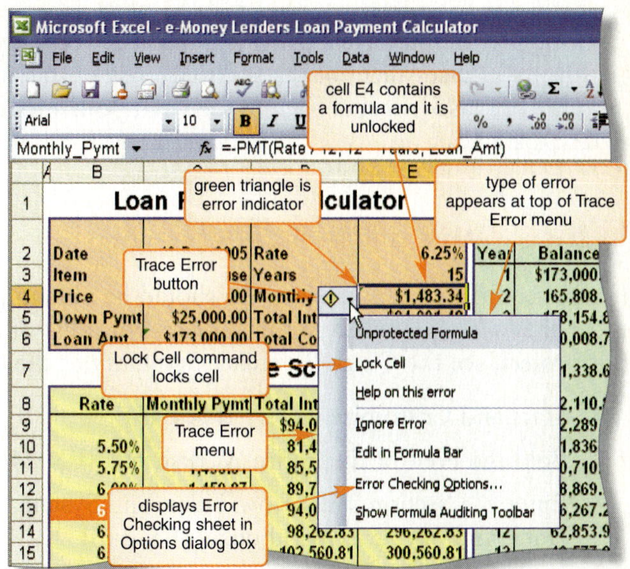

FIGURE 4-73

The background formula checker can become annoying when you are creating certain types of worksheets that may violate the formula rules until referenced cells contain data. It is not unusual to end up with green triangles in cells throughout your worksheet. If this is the case, then disable background formula error checking by removing the check mark from the Enable background error checking check box (Figure 4-72) and use the Error Checking command on the Tools menu to check your worksheet once you have finished creating it.

It is strongly recommended that you use background formula checking or the Error Checking command on the Tools menu during the testing phase to ensure the formulas in your workbook do not violate the rules listed in Table 4-5.

More About

Closing Files

If you have multiple workbooks opened, you can close them all at the same time by holding down the SHIFT key when you click File on the menu bar. The Close command changes to the Close All command. When you click the Close All command, Excel closes all open workbooks.

Quitting Excel

To quit Excel, follow the steps below.

To Quit Excel

1. **Click the Close button on the right side of the title bar.**
2. **If Excel displays a Microsoft Office Excel dialog box, click the No button.**

Project Summary

In this project, you learned how to use names, rather than cell references, to enter formulas. You learned how to develop professional-looking worksheets using borders, background colors, and other formatting. You learned how to use financial functions, such as the PMT and PV functions. You also learned how to analyze data by creating a data table and amortization schedule. This project explained how to add a hyperlink to a worksheet. You learned how to set print options and print sections of a worksheet using names and the Set Print Area command. You learned how to protect a worksheet or workbook. Finally, you learned how to hide and unhide rows, columns, sheets, and workbooks, and how to check formulas for rule violations.

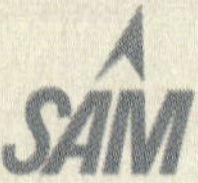

If you have a SAM user profile, you may have access to hands-on instruction, practice, and assessment of the skills covered in this project. Log in to your SAM account and go to your assignments page to see what your instructor has assigned.

What You Should Know

Having completed this project, you should be able to perform the tasks below. The tasks are listed in the same order they were presented in this project. For a list of the buttons, menus, toolbars, and commands introduced in this project, see the Quick Reference Summary at the back of this book and refer to the Page Number column.

1. Start and Customize Excel (EX 245)
2. Bold the Font of the Entire Worksheet (EX 246)
3. Enter the Section Title, Row Titles, and System Date, and Save the Workbook (EX 246)
4. Add Custom Borders and a Background Color to a Range (EX 248)
5. Format Cells Before Entering Values (EX 250)
6. Enter the Loan Data (EX 250)
7. Create Names Based on Row Titles (EX 251)
8. Enter the Loan Amount Formula Using Names (EX 253)
9. Enter the PMT Function (EX 254)
10. Determine the Total Interest and Total Cost (EX 255)
11. Enter New Loan Data (EX 256 and EX 275)
12. Enter the Original Loan Data (EX 256 and EX 276)
13. Enter the Data Table Title and Column Titles (EX 258)
14. Create a Percent Series Using the Fill Handle (EX 259)
15. Enter the Formulas in the Data Table (EX 260)
16. Define a Range as a Data Table (EX 261)
17. Format the Data Table (EX 262)
18. Add a Pointer to the Data Table (EX 264)
19. Change Column Widths and Enter Titles (EX 267)
20. Create a Series of Integers Using the Fill Handle (EX 267)
21. Enter the Formulas in the Amortization Schedule (EX 269)
22. Copy the Formulas to Fill the Amortization Schedule (EX 271)
23. Enter the Total Formulas in the Amortization Schedule (EX 272)
24. Format the Numbers in the Amortization Schedule (EX 273)
25. Add Borders and a Background to the Amortization Schedule and Hide Cell Gridlines (EX 274)
26. Assign a Hyperlink to an Embedded Graphic (EX 277)
27. Format and Resize a Graphic Using the Picture Toolbar (EX 280)
28. Display and Print a Hyperlinked File (EX 281)
29. Set Up a Worksheet to Print (EX 282)
30. Set the Print Area (EX 283)
31. Name and Print Sections of a Worksheet (EX 284)
32. Protect a Worksheet (EX 287)
33. Hide and Unhide a Sheet (EX 289)
34. Hide and Unhide a Workbook (EX 291)
35. Enable Background Formula Checking (EX 292)
36. Quit Excel (EX 293)

More About

The Quick Reference

For more information, see the Quick Reference Summary at the back of this book, or visit the Excel 2003 Quick Reference Web page (scsite.com/ex2003/qr).

More About

Microsoft Certification

The Microsoft Office Specialist Certification program provides an opportunity for you to obtain a valuable industry credential — proof that you have the Excel skills required by employers. For more information, see Appendix E, or visit the Excel 2003 Certification Web page (scsite.com/ex2003/cert).

Learn It Online

Instructions: To complete the Learn It Online exercises, start your browser, click the Address bar, and then enter the Web address `scsite.com/ex2003/learn`. When the Excel 2003 Learn It Online page is displayed, follow the instructions in the exercises below. Each exercise has instructions for printing your results, either for your own records or for submission to your instructor.

1 Project Reinforcement TF, MC, and SA

Below Excel Project 4, click the Project Reinforcement link. Print the quiz by clicking Print on the File menu for each page. Answer each question.

2 Flash Cards

Below Excel Project 4, click the Flash Cards link and read the instructions. Type 20 (or a number specified by your instructor) in the Number of playing cards text box, type your name in the Enter your Name text box, and then click the Flip Card button. When the flash card is displayed, read the question and then click the ANSWER box arrow to select an answer. Flip through Flash Cards. If your score is 15 (75%) correct or greater, click Print on the File menu to print your results. If your score is less than 15 (75%) correct, then redo this exercise by clicking the Replay button.

3 Practice Test

Below Excel Project 4, click the Practice Test link. Answer each question, enter your first and last name at the bottom of the page, and then click the Grade Test button. When the graded practice test is displayed on your screen, click Print on the File menu to print a hard copy. Continue to take practice tests until you score 80% or better.

4 Who Wants To Be a Computer Genius?

Below Excel Project 4, click the Computer Genius link. Read the instructions, enter your first and last name at the bottom of the page, and then click the PLAY button. When your score is displayed, click the PRINT RESULTS link to print a hard copy.

5 Wheel of Terms

Below Excel Project 4, click the Wheel of Terms link. Read the instructions, and then enter your first and last name and your school name. Click the PLAY button. When your score is displayed, right-click the score and then click Print on the shortcut menu to print a hard copy.

6 Crossword Puzzle Challenge

Below Excel Project 4, click the Crossword Puzzle Challenge link. Read the instructions, and then enter your first and last name. Click the SUBMIT button. Work the crossword puzzle. When you are finished, click the Submit button. When the crossword puzzle is redisplayed, click the Print Puzzle button to print a hard copy.

7 Tips and Tricks

Below Excel Project 4, click the Tips and Tricks link. Click a topic that pertains to Project 4. Right-click the information and then click Print on the shortcut menu. Construct a brief example of what the information relates to in Excel to confirm you understand how to use the tip or trick.

8 Newsgroups

Below Excel Project 4, click the Newsgroups link. Click a topic that pertains to Project 4. Print three comments.

9 Expanding Your Horizons

Below Excel Project 4, click the Articles for Microsoft Excel link. Click a topic that pertains to Project 4. Print the information. Construct a brief example of what the information relates to in Excel to confirm you understand the contents of the article.

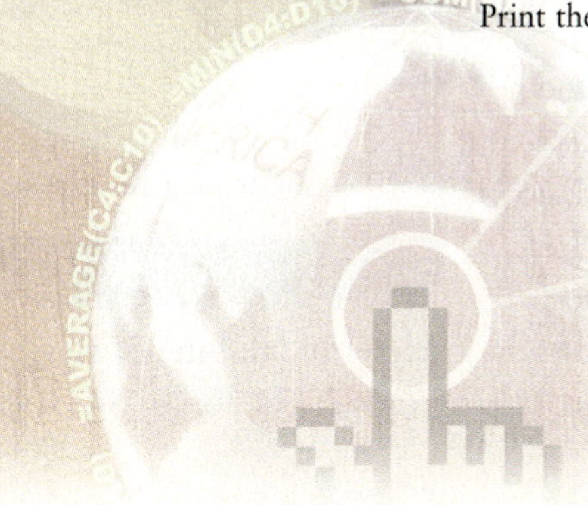

10 Search Sleuth

Below Excel Project 4, click the Search Sleuth link. To search for a term that pertains to this project, select a term below the Project 4 title and then use the Google search engine at google.com (or any major search engine) to display and print two Web pages that present information on the term.

11 Excel Online Training

Below Excel Project 4, click the Excel Online Training link. When your browser displays the Microsoft Office Online Web page, click the Excel link. Click one of the Excel courses that covers one or more of the objectives listed at the beginning of the project on page EX 242. Print the first page of the course before stepping through it.

12 Office Marketplace

Below Excel Project 4, click the Office Marketplace link. When your browser displays the Microsoft Office Online Web page, click the Office Marketplace link. Click a topic that relates to Excel. Print the first page.

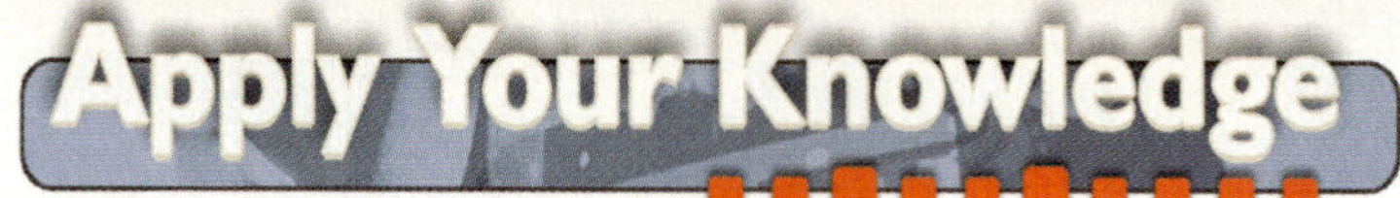

1 Determining the Monthly Loan Payment

Instructions: Perform the following tasks.

1. Start Excel. Open the workbook Apply 4-1 Determine the Monthly Loan Payment from the Data Disk.
2. Use the Name command on the Insert menu to create names for cells in the range C4:C9 using the row titles in the range B4:B9.
3. Enter the formulas shown in Table 4-6.
4. Use the Table command on the Data menu to define the range E4:H19 as a one-input data table. Use cell C6 (interest rate) as the column input cell. Format the data table so that it appears as shown in Figure 4-74.
5. Add your name, course, computer laboratory assignment number (Apply Your Knowledge 4-1), date, and instructor name in column B beginning in cell B14.
6. Use the Page Setup command to select the Fit to and Black and white options. Use the Set Print Area command to select the range B2:C9 and then use the Print button on the Standard toolbar to print. Use the Clear Print Area command to clear the print area. Name the following ranges: B2:C9 – Calculator; E2:H19 – Rate_Schedule; and B1:H19 – All_Sections. Print each range by selecting the name in the Name box and using the Selection option in the Print dialog box.
7. Unlock the range C3:C7. Protect the worksheet so that the user can select only unlocked cells.
8. Press CTRL+` and print the formulas version in landscape. Press CTRL+` to display the values version.
9. Hide and then unhide the Monthly Loan Payment sheet. Hide and then unhide the workbook. Unprotect the worksheet and then hide columns E through H. Print the worksheet. Select columns D and I and unhide the hidden columns. Hide rows 11 through 19. Print the worksheet. Select rows 10 and 20 and unhide rows 11 through 19. Protect the worksheet.
10. Save the workbook using the file name, Apply 4-1 Determine the Monthly Loan Payment Answer.
11. Determine the monthly payment and print the worksheet for each data set: (a) Item = Condo; Price = $313,000.00; Down Payment = $65,000.00; Interest Rate = 7.75%; Years = 15; (b) Item = Motorcycle; Price = $22,000.00; Down Payment = $0.00; Interest Rate = 6.60%; Years = 5. You should get the following monthly payment results: (a) $2,334.36; (b) $431.49.

Table 4-6 Data Table Formulas

CELL	FORMULA
C8	=Price – Down_Payment
C9	PMT(Interest_Rate/12, 12 * Years, Loan_Amount)
F4	=C9
G4	+12 * C7 * C9 + C5
H4	=G4 – C4

FIGURE 4-74

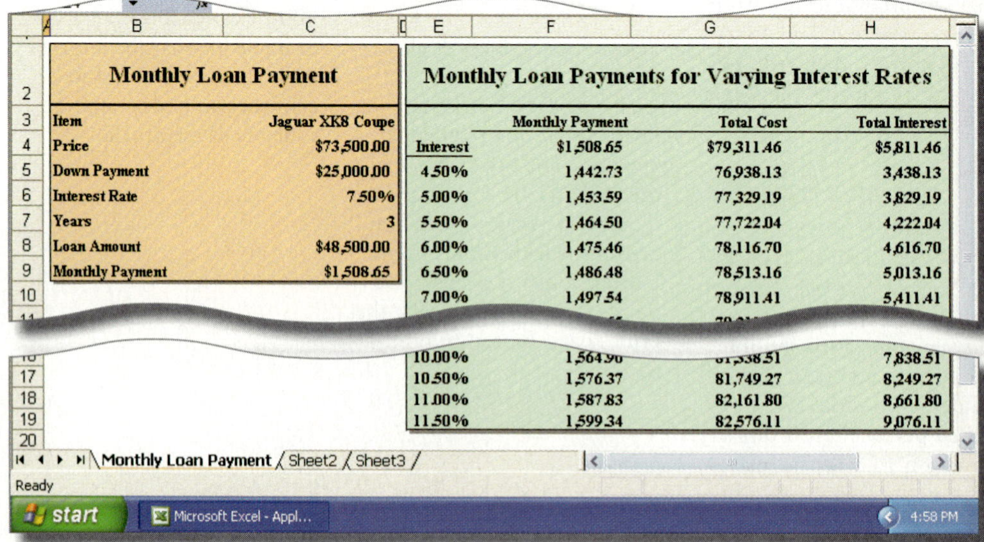

In the Lab

1 401(k) Planning Sheet

Problem: The chairperson of the Benefits committee has asked you to develop a 401(k) planning worksheet that will allow each current and prospective employee to see the effect (dollar accumulation) of investing a percent of his or her monthly salary over a period of years (Figure 4-75). The plan calls for the company to match an employee's investment, dollar for dollar, up to 4%. Thus, if an employee invests 6% of his or her annual salary, then the company matches the first 4%. If an employee invests only 2% of his or her annual salary, then the company matches the entire 2%. The chairperson wants a one-input data table to show the future value of the investment for different periods.

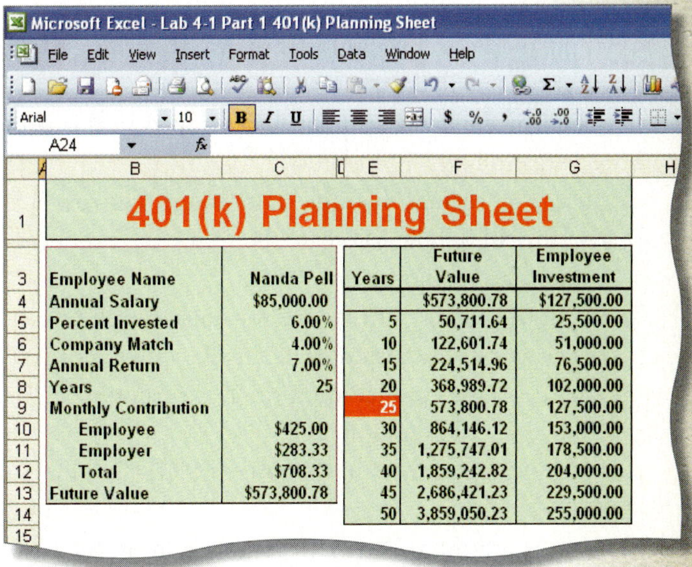

Microsoft Excel - Lab 4-1 Part 1 401(k) Planning Sheet

401(k) Planning Sheet

	B	C	E	F	G
3	Employee Name	Nanda Pell	Years	Future Value	Employee Investment
4	Annual Salary	$85,000.00		$573,800.78	$127,500.00
5	Percent Invested	6.00%	5	50,711.64	25,500.00
6	Company Match	4.00%	10	122,601.74	51,000.00
7	Annual Return	7.00%	15	224,514.96	76,500.00
8	Years	25	20	368,989.72	102,000.00
9	Monthly Contribution		25	573,800.78	127,500.00
10	Employee	$425.00	30	864,146.12	153,000.00
11	Employer	$283.33	35	1,275,747.01	178,500.00
12	Total	$708.33	40	1,859,242.82	204,000.00
13	Future Value	$573,800.78	45	2,686,421.23	229,500.00
14			50	3,859,050.23	255,000.00

FIGURE 4-75

Instructions Part 1: With a blank worksheet on the screen, perform the following tasks.

1. Change the font of the entire worksheet to bold. Change the column widths to the following: A and D = 0.50; B = 20.00; C, F, and G = 13.00. Change the row heights to the following: 1 = 36.00; 2 = 0.50; and 3 = 26.25. Turn off gridlines.
2. In cell B1, enter `401(k) Planning Sheet` as the worksheet title. Change the font in cell B1 to 26-point red. Merge and center cell B1 across columns B through G. Draw a medium black border around cell B1.
3. Enter the row titles in column B, beginning in cell B3 as shown in Figure 4-75. Add the data in Table 4-7 to column C. Use the dollar and percent signs to format the numbers in the range C4:C7.
4. Use the Create command on the Name submenu (Insert menu) to assign the row titles in column B (range B3:B13) to the adjacent cells in column C. Use these names to enter the following formulas in the range C10:C13. Step 4e formats the displayed results of the formulas.
   a. Employee Monthly Contribution (cell C10) = Annual_Salary * Percent_Invested / 12
   b. Employer Monthly Contribution (cell C11) = IF(Percent_Invested < Company_Match, Percent_Invested * Annual_Salary / 12, Company_Match * Annual_Salary / 12)
   c. Total Monthly Contribution (cell C12) = SUM(C10:C11)
   d. Future Value (cell C13) = –FV(Annual_Return/12, 12 * Years, Total)
   e. If necessary, use the Format Painter button on the Standard toolbar to assign the Currency style format in cell C4 to the range C10:C13.

Table 4-7 401(k) Planning Sheet Employee Data

ROW TITLE	ITEM
Employee Name	Nanda Pell
Annual Salary	$85,000.00
Percent Invested	6.00%
Company Match	4.00%
Annual Return	7.00%
Years	25

(continued)

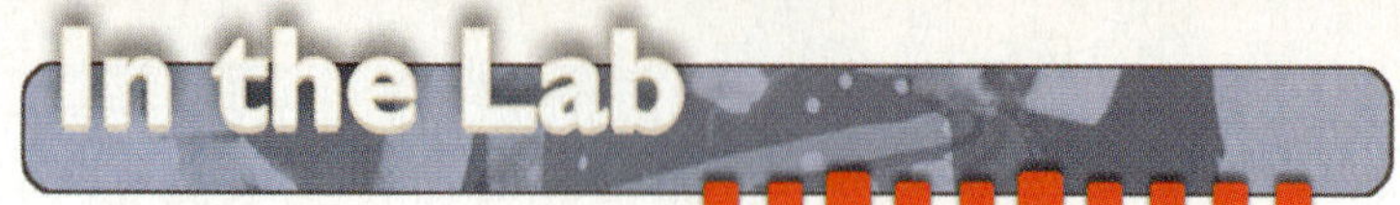

401(k) Planning Sheet *(continued)*

The **Future Value function** (**FV**) in Step 4d returns to the cell the future value of the investment. The **future value** of an investment is its value at some point in the future based on a series of payments of equal amounts made over a number of periods earning a constant rate of return.

5. Add borders to the range B3:C13 as shown in Figure 4-75 on the previous page.
6. Use the concepts and techniques developed in this project to add the data table in Figure 4-75 to the range E3:G14 as follows.
   a. Enter and format the table column titles in row 3.
   b. Use the fill handle to create the series of years beginning with 5 and ending with 50 in increments of 5 in column E, beginning in cell E5.
   c. In cell F4, enter `=C13` as the formula. In cell G4, enter `=12 * C10 * C18` as the formula (using cell references in the formulas means Excel will copy the formats).
   d. Use the Table command on the Data menu to define the range E4:G14 as a one-input data table. Use cell C8 as the column input cell.
   e. Format the numbers in the range F5:G14 to the Comma style format. Underline rows 3 and 4 as shown in Figure 4-75.
7. Use the Conditional Formatting command on the Format menu to add a red pointer that shows the row that equals the years in cell C8 to the Years column in the data table. Add the light green background color as shown in Figure 4-75.
8. Add your name, course, computer laboratory assignment number (Lab 4-1), date, and instructor name in column B beginning in cell B17.
9. Spell check and formula check the worksheet.
10. Use the Page Setup command to select the Fit to and Black and white options.
11. Print the worksheet. Print the formulas version.
12. Unlock the cells in the range C3:C8. Protect the worksheet. Allow users to select only unlocked cells.
13. Save the workbook using the file name Lab 4-1 Part 1 401(k) Planning Sheet.
14. Hide and then unhide the 401(k) Planning Sheet sheet. Hide and then unhide the Workbook. Unprotect the worksheet and then hide columns D through G. Print the worksheet. Select columns C and H and unhide the hidden columns. Hide rows 1 and 2. Print the worksheet. Select rows 3 and unhide rows 1 and 2.
15. Close the workbook without saving changes. Open the workbook Lab 4-1 Part 1 401(k) Planning Sheet. Determine the future value for the data in Table 4-8. Print the worksheet for each data set. The following Future Value results should display in cell C13: Data Set 1 = $650,948.47; Data Set 2 = $1,309,683.88; and Data Set 3 = $476,970.65. Close Excel without saving the workbook.

Instructions Part 2: The chairperson of the Benefits committee has requested that you include a two-input data table (Figure 4-76) on the worksheet created in Part 1 that shows the future value that results from varying the employee investment (cell C5) and company match (cell C6). Complete the following tasks to create the two-input data table.

Table 4-8 Future Value Data

	DATA SET 1	DATA SET 2	DATA SET 3
Employee Name	Kareem Jones	Juanita Chavez	Al Jones
Annual Salary	$95,000.00	$182,500.00	$74,500.00
Percent Invested	6.5%	8%	4.5%
Company Match	2.5%	3.5%	2%
Annual Return	5.5%	6.5%	4%
Years	30	25	40

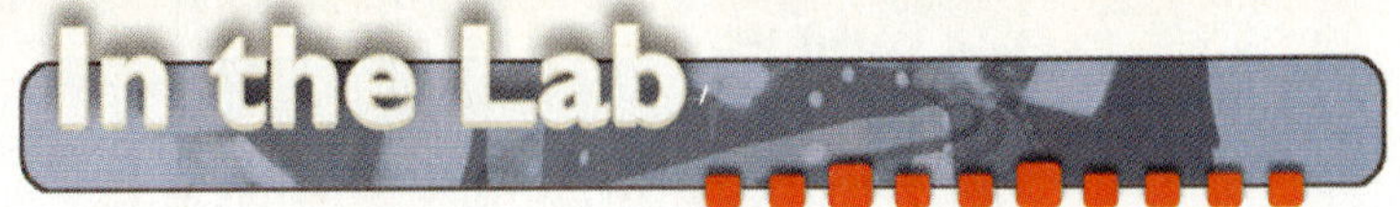

In the Lab

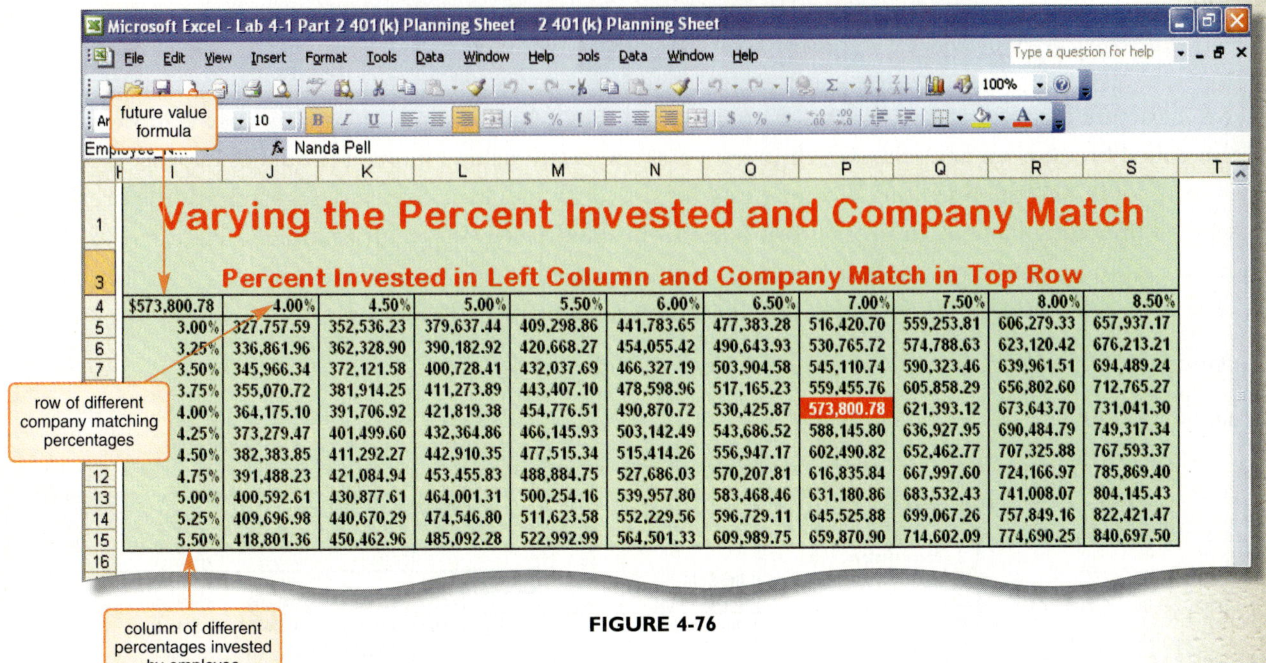

Varying the Percent Invested and Company Match

Percent Invested in Left Column and Company Match in Top Row

$573,800.78	4.00%	4.50%	5.00%	5.50%	6.00%	6.50%	7.00%	7.50%	8.00%	8.50%
3.00%	327,757.59	352,536.23	379,637.44	409,298.86	441,783.65	477,383.28	516,420.70	559,253.81	606,279.33	657,937.17
3.25%	336,861.96	362,328.90	390,182.92	420,668.27	454,055.42	490,643.93	530,765.72	574,788.63	623,120.42	676,213.21
3.50%	345,966.34	372,121.58	400,728.41	432,037.69	466,327.19	503,904.58	545,110.74	590,323.46	639,961.51	694,489.24
3.75%	355,070.72	381,914.25	411,273.89	443,407.10	478,598.96	517,165.23	559,455.76	605,858.29	656,802.60	712,765.27
4.00%	364,175.10	391,706.92	421,819.38	454,776.51	490,870.72	530,425.87	573,800.78	621,393.12	673,643.70	731,041.30
4.25%	373,279.47	401,499.60	432,364.86	466,145.93	503,142.49	543,686.52	588,145.80	636,927.95	690,484.79	749,317.34
4.50%	382,383.85	411,292.27	442,910.35	477,515.34	515,414.26	556,947.17	602,490.82	652,462.77	707,325.88	767,593.37
4.75%	391,488.23	421,084.94	453,455.83	488,884.75	527,686.03	570,207.81	616,835.84	667,997.60	724,166.97	785,869.40
5.00%	400,592.61	430,877.61	464,001.31	500,254.16	539,957.80	583,468.46	631,180.86	683,532.43	741,008.07	804,145.43
5.25%	409,696.98	440,670.29	474,546.80	511,623.58	552,229.56	596,729.11	645,525.88	699,067.26	757,849.16	822,421.47
5.50%	418,801.36	450,462.96	485,092.28	522,992.99	564,501.33	609,989.75	659,870.90	714,602.09	774,690.25	840,697.50

FIGURE 4-76

1. If necessary, open the workbook created in Part 1 of this exercise. Unprotect the worksheet.
2. Enter the data table title and subtitle as shown in cells I1 and I3 in Figure 4-76. Change the width of column H to 0.50 characters. Merge and center the titles over columns I through S. Format the titles as shown.
3. Enter `=C13` in cell I4. For a two-input data table, the formula you are analyzing must be assigned to the upper-left cell in the range of the data table.
4. Use the fill handle to create two lists of percents (a) 3.00% through 5.50%, in increments of 0.25% in the range I5:I15; and (b) 4.00% through 8.50% in increments of 0.50% in the range J4:S4.
5. Select the range I4:S15. Click Table on the Data menu. When Excel displays the Table dialog box, enter `c5` in the Row input cell box and `c6` in the Column input cell box.
6. Format the two-input data table as shown in Figure 4-76.
7. Use conditional formatting to change the format of the cell in the two-input data table that is equal to the future value in cell C13 to white bold font on a red background.
8. Protect the worksheet so that the user can select only unlocked cells.
9. Change the print orientation to landscape. Print the worksheet using the Fit to option. Print the formulas version of the worksheet.
10. Save the workbook using the file name Lab 4-1 Part 2 401(k) Planning Sheet.

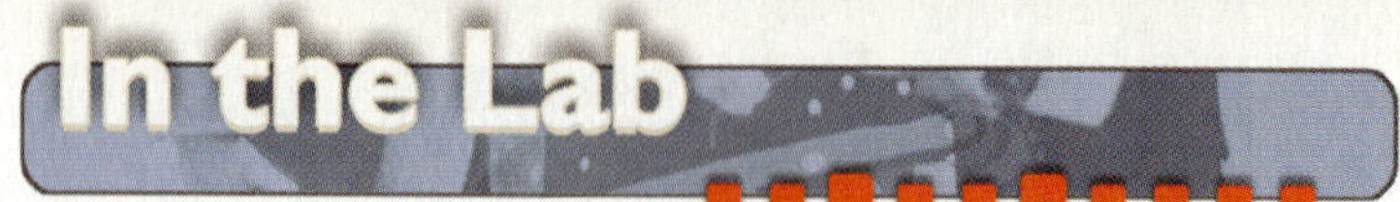

2 Quarterly Income Statement and Break-Even Analysis

Problem: You are a consultant to Celine's Scooter Supply Ltd. Your area of expertise is **cost-volume-profit** or **CVP** (also called **break-even analysis**), which investigates the relationship among a product's expenses (cost), its volume (units sold), and the operating income (gross profit). Any money a company earns above the break-even point is called operating income, or gross profit (row 13 in the Break-Even Analysis table in Figure 4-77). You have been asked to prepare a quarterly income statement and a data table that shows revenue, expenses, and income for units sold between 400,000 and 800,000 in increments of 25,000.

Instructions: With a blank worksheet on the screen, perform the following tasks.

1. Change the font of the entire worksheet to bold. Change the column widths to the following: A = 21.00; B = 26.00; C = 13.71; D = 0.50; E = 7.14; and F through H = 11.14. Change the heights of rows 1 and 2 to 18.00. Name the sheet tab Break-Even Analysis and color the tab green (column 4, row 2 on the Tab Color palette).
2. Enter the worksheet titles: `Celine's Scooter Supply Ltd.` in cell A1; and `Quarterly Income Statement` in cell A2. Change the font in cells A1 and A2 to 16-point Arial Rounded MT Bold. One at a time, merge and center cells A1 and A2 across columns A through C. Change the background color of cells A1 and A2 to green (column 4, row 2 on the Fill Color palette). Change the font color to white (column 8, row 5 on the Font Color palette). Add a thick border to the range A1:A2.
3. Enter the row titles in columns A and B as shown in Figure 4-77. Change the row titles in column A to 12-point Arial Rounded MT Bold green. Add the data shown in Table 4-9 in column C. Use the dollar sign ($) and comma symbol (,) to format the numbers in column C as you enter them.

Celine's Scooter Supply Ltd.
Quarterly Income Statement

Row	A	B	C
3	Revenue		
4		Units Sold	625,000
5		Price per Unit	$21.00
6		Total Revenue	$13,125,000
7	Fixed Expenses		
8		Administrative	$2,250,000
9		Leasing	800,000
10		Marketing	500,000
11		Salary and Benefits	1,100,000
12		Total Fixed Expenses	$4,650,000
13	Variable Expenses		
14		Material Cost per Unit	$4.00
15		Total Material Cost	$2,500,000
16		Manufacturing Cost per Unit	$9.00
17		Total Manufacturing Cost	$5,625,000
18		Total Variable Expenses	$8,125,000
19	Summary		
20		Total Expenses	$12,775,000
21		Operating Income	$350,000

Break-Even Analysis

Units	Revenue	Expenses	Income
	$13,125,000	$12,775,000	$350,000
400,000	8,400,000	9,850,000	(1,450,000)
425,000	8,925,000	10,175,000	(1,250,000)
450,000	9,450,000	10,500,000	(1,050,000)
475,000	9,975,000	10,825,000	(850,000)
500,000	10,500,000	11,150,000	(650,000)
525,000	11,025,000	11,475,000	(450,000)
550,000	11,550,000	11,800,000	(250,000)
575,000	12,075,000	12,125,000	(50,000)
600,000	12,600,000	12,450,000	150,000
625,000	13,125,000	12,775,000	350,000
650,000	13,650,000	13,100,000	550,000
675,000	14,175,000	13,425,000	750,000
700,000	14,700,000	13,750,000	950,000
725,000	15,225,000	14,075,000	1,150,000
750,000	15,750,000	14,400,000	1,350,000
775,000	16,275,000	14,725,000	1,550,000
800,000	16,800,000	15,050,000	1,750,000

FIGURE 4-77

Table 4-9 Annual Income Data

TITLE	CELL	ITEM
Units Sold	C4	625,000
Price per Unit	C5	$21
Administrative	C8	$2,250,000
Leasing	C9	$800,000
Marketing	C10	$500,000
Salary and Benefits	C11	$1,100,000
Material Cost per Unit	C14	$4
Manufacturing Cost per Unit	C16	$9

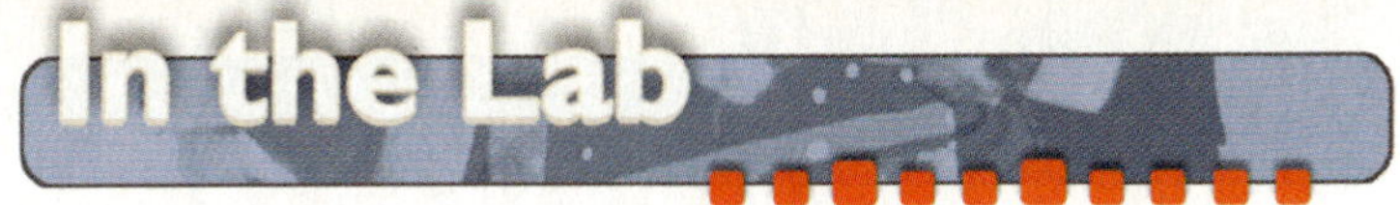

4. Use the Create command on the Name submenu to assign the row titles in column B in the range B4:B21 to the adjacent cells in column C. Use these names to enter the following formulas in column C:
   a. Total Revenue (cell C6) = Units Sold * Price per Unit (or =C4 * C5)
   b. Total Fixed Expenses (cell C12) = SUM(C8:C11)
   c. Total Material Cost (cell C15) = Units Sold * Material Cost per Unit (or =C4 * C14)
   d. Total Manufacturing Cost (cell C17) = Units Sold * Manufacturing Cost per Unit (or =C4 * C16)
   e. Total Variable Expenses (cell C18) = Total Material Cost + Total Manufacturing Cost (or =C15 + C17)
   f. Total Expenses (cell C20) = Total Fixed Expenses + Total Variable Expenses (or =C12 + C18)
   g. Operating Income (cell C21) = Total Revenue – Total Expenses (or =C6 – C20)
5. If necessary, use the Format Painter button on the Standard toolbar to assign the Currency style format in cell C8 to the unformatted dollar amounts in column C.
6. Add a thick black bottom border to the ranges B5:C5, B11:C11, and B17:C17 as shown in Figure 4-77.
7. Use the concepts and techniques presented in this project to add the data table to the range E1:H21 as follows:
   a. Add the data table titles and format them as shown in Figure 4-77.
   b. Create the series in column E from 400,000 to 800,000 in increments of 25,000, beginning in cell E5.
   c. Enter the formula `=c6` in cell F4. Enter the formula `=c20` in cell G4. Enter the formula `=c21` in cell H4. If necessary, adjust the column widths.
   d. Use the Table command on the Data menu to define the range E4:H21 as a one-input data table. Use cell C4 (units sold) as the column input cell.
   e. Use the Format Cells command on the shortcut menu to format the range F5:H21 to the Comma style format with no decimal places and negative numbers in red with parentheses. Add a medium red outline border and light black vertical borders to the range E1:H21.
8. Spell check and formula check the worksheet. Add your name, course, computer laboratory assignment number (Lab 4-2), date, and instructor name in column A beginning in cell A24.
9. Use the Page Setup command to select the Fit to and Black and white options. Hide the gridlines.
10. Unlock the following cells: C4, C5, C14, and C16. Protect the workbook so the user can select only unlocked cells.
11. Save the workbook using the file name Lab 4-2 Celine's Scooter Supply Ltd Quarterly Income.
12. Print the worksheet. Print the formulas version.
13. Determine the operating income for the data sets in Table 4-10. Print the worksheet for each data set. You should get the following Operating Income results in cell C21: Data Set 1 = $4,100,000; Data Set 2 = $1,590,000; and Data Set 3 = $635,000.

Table 4-10 Operating Income Data

TITLE	CELL	DATA SET 1	DATA SET 2	DATA SET 3
Units Sold	C4	875,000	640,000	755,000
Price per Unit	C5	$22.50	$21.00	$20.50
Material Cost per Unit	C14	$3.25	$3.75	$10.00
Manufacturing Cost per Unit	C16	$4.75	$7.50	$3.50

14. Hide and then unhide the Break-Even Analysis sheet. Hide and then unhide the workbook. Unprotect the worksheet and then hide columns D through H. Print the worksheet. Select columns C and I and unhide the hidden columns. Hide rows 7 through 21. Print the worksheet. Select rows 4 and 21 and unhide rows 7 and 21. Do not save the workbook.

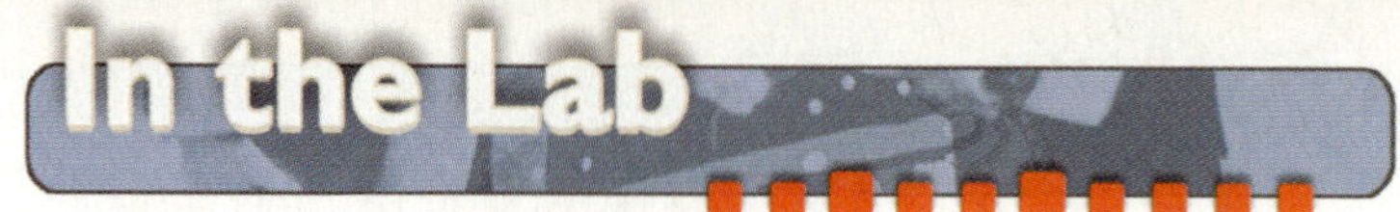

3 Loan Analysis and Amortization Schedule

Problem: Each student in your course is assigned a real-world project that involves working with a local company. For your project, you are working with the Internet Bank of Chicago, a division of WeSavU National Bank. The manager of the Internet Bank of Chicago has asked you to create the loan analysis worksheet shown in Figure 4-78. She also wants a hyperlink added to the worksheet that displays the WeSavU National Bank 2004 Statement of Condition Web page. Finally, she wants you to demonstrate the goal seeking capabilities of Excel.

Instructions: Do the following:

1. Bold the entire worksheet and change all the columns to a width of 15.00. Change column A to a width of 0.50.
2. Enter the worksheet title in cell B1 and change its font to 20-point Franklin Gothic Heavy red (or a font of your choice). Enter the worksheet subtitle in cell B2 and change its font to 12-point Franklin Gothic Medium red (or a font of your choice). One at a time, merge and center cells B1 and B2 across columns B through F.
3. Use the Create command on the Name submenu to assign the row titles in the ranges B3:B5 and E3:E5 to the adjacent cells in ranges C3:C5 and F3:F5.
4. Enter `237500` (price) in cell C3, `32250` (down payment) in cell C4, `5.25%` (interest rate) in cell F3, and `30` (years) in cell F4. Determine the loan amount by entering the formula `=Price – Down_Pymt` in cell C5. Determine the monthly payment by entering the PMT function `–PMT(Rate / 12, 12 * Years, Loan_Amount)` in cell F5.
5. Create the amortization schedule in the range B6:F36 by assigning the formulas and functions to the cells indicated in Table 4-11. Use names when appropriate.

	B	C	D	E	F
1	**Internet Bank of Chicago**				
2	A Subsidiary of WeSavU National Bank				
3	Price	237,500.00		Rate	5.25%
4	Down Pymt	32,250.00		Years	30
5	Loan Amount	205,250.00		Monthly Pymt	1,133.40
6	Year	Beginning Balance	Ending Balance	Paid On Principal	Interest Paid
7	1	$205,250.00	$202,355.87	$2,894.13	$10,706.64
8	2	202,355.87	199,306.08	3,049.79	10,550.99
9	3	199,306.08	196,092.27	3,213.81	10,386.97
10	4	196,092.27	192,705.62	3,386.65	10,214.12
11	5	192,705.62	189,136.82	3,568.79	10,031.98
12	6		185,376.09		9,840.05
		59,696.31		10,722.27	
33	27	48,974.30	37,675.36	11,298.94	2,301.84
34	28	37,675.36	25,768.75	11,906.61	1,694.16
35	29	25,768.75	13,221.77	12,546.97	1,053.80
36	30	13,221.77	0.00	13,221.77	379.00
37			Subtotal	205,250.00	202,773.32
38			Down Pymt		32,250.00
39			Total Cost		440,273.32
40					

Amortization Schedule / Sheet2 / Sheet3 — Ready — start — Microsoft Excel - Lab ...

FIGURE 4-78

6. Enter the total titles in the range D37:D39 as shown in Figure 4-78.
7. Insert the piggy bank graphic shown in the range D3:D5. Assign the Web page a:\WeSavU National Bank.mht to the graphic. Display and print the Web page. You must have the Data Disk in drive A to display the Web page.
8. Change the tab name and color as shown in Figure 4-78.
9. Add your name, course, laboratory assignment number (Lab 4-3), date, and instructor name in column B beginning in cell B40.
10. Spell check and formula check the worksheet. Use Range Finder (double-click cell) to check all formulas listed in Table 4-11.
11. Hide gridlines. Use the Page Setup command to select the Fit to and Black and white options.

In the Lab

12. Unlock the cells in the ranges C3:C4 and F3:F4. Protect the worksheet so that users can select any cell in the worksheet, but can change only the unlocked cells.
13. Save the workbook using the file name Lab 4-3 Internet Bank of Chicago Loan Calculator.
14. Print the worksheet. Print the formulas version.
15. Use Excel's goal seeking capabilities to determine the down payment required for the loan data in Figure 4-78 if the monthly payment is set to $1,000.00. The down payment that results for a monthly payment of $1,000.00 is $56,407.41. Print the worksheet with the new monthly payment of $1,000.00. Close the workbook without saving changes.
16. Hide and then unhide the Loan Payment Calculator sheet. Hide and then unhide the workbook. Unprotect the worksheet and then hide columns D through F. Print the worksheet. Select columns C and G and unhide the hidden columns. Hide rows 6 through 39. Print the worksheet. Select rows 5 and 40 and unhide rows 6 and 39. Do not save the workbook.
17. Modify the piggy graphic following the steps outlined on page EX 280.

Table 4-11 Cell Assignments

CELL	FORMULA OR FUNCTION
C7	=C5
D7	=IF(B7 <= $F$4, PV($F$3 / 12, 12 * ($F$4 – B7), –$F$5),0)
E7	=C7 – D7
F7	=IF(C7 > 0, 12 * $F$5 – E7, 0)
C8	=D7
E37	=SUM(E7:E36)
F37	=SUM(F7:F36)
F38	=C4
F39	=E37 + F37 + F38

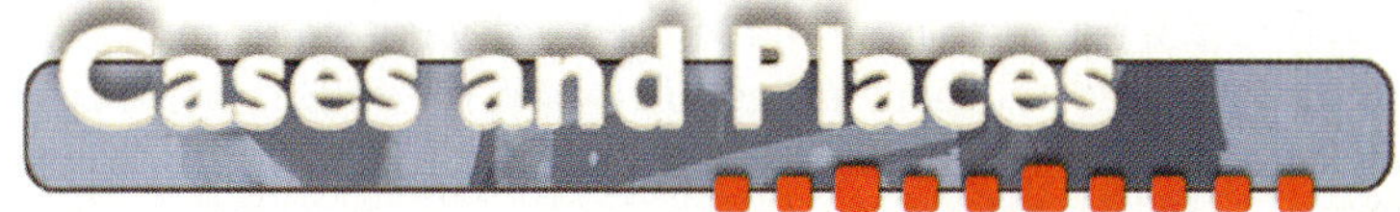

The difficulty of these case studies varies:
■ are the least difficult and ■■ are more difficult. The last exercise is a group exercise.

1 ■ Audrey Holsum, president of Holsum Construction, recently purchased a new forklift. Audrey wants a worksheet that uses the financial function SLN to show the forklift's **straight-line depreciation** and a formula to determine the annual rate of depreciation. Straight-line depreciation is based on an asset's initial cost, how long it can be used (called useful life), and the price at which it eventually can be sold (called salvage value). Audrey has supplied the following information:

Cost = $96,345; Salvage = $25,000; Life = 6 years; and Annual Rate of Depreciation = SLN / Cost.

Audrey is not sure how much she will be able to sell the forklift for in 6 years. Create a data table that shows straight-line depreciation and annual rate of depreciation for salvage from $20,000 to $29,000 in $500 increments. Use Excel Help to learn more about the SLN function. Protect the worksheet.

Cases and Places

2 ■ You can calculate the number of units you must sell to break even (break-even point) if you know the fixed expenses, the price per unit, and the expense (cost) per unit. You are a part-time consultant and have been hired by Mid-Teens to create a data table that analyzes the break-even point for prices between $1.00 and $7.25 in increments of $0.25. The following formula determines the break-even point:

Break-Even Point = Fixed Expenses / (Price per Unit – Expense per Unit)

Assume Fixed Expenses = $1,000,000; Price per Unit = $3.50; and Expense per Unit = $2.55.

Enter the data and formula into a worksheet and then create the data table. Use the Price per Unit as the input cell and the break-even value as the result. For a price per unit of $3.25, the data table should show a break-even point of 1,428,571 units. Protect the worksheet.

3 ■■ Aunt Alice and Uncle Bud's dream for their one-year-old son, Evan Samuel, is that one day he will attend their alma mater, Butler University. For the next 15 years, they plan to make monthly payment deposits to a long-term savings account at a local bank. The account pays 4.75% annual interest, compounded monthly. Create a worksheet for Aunt Alice and Uncle Bud that uses a financial function to show the future value (FV) of their investment and a formula to determine the percentage of the college's tuition saved. Aunt Alice and Uncle Bud have supplied the following information:

Out of State Annual Tuition = $45,000; Rate (per month) = 4.25% / 12; Nper (number of monthly payments) = 15 * 12; Pmt (payment per period) = $375; and percentage of Tuition Saved = FV / Tuition for four years.

Aunt Alice and Uncle Bud are not sure how much they will be able to save each month. Create a data table that shows the future value and percentage of tuition saved for monthly payments from $275 to $875, in $50 increments. Insert a graphic file and assign it a hyperlink to WeSavU National Bank.mht on the Data Disk. Protect the worksheet.

4 ■■ Your cousin Cecelia and her husband Pedro have decided to save for the down payment on a home, after living with your parents for years. Cecelia's nephew, Julio, who works for the local electric company, promises them he can get them an annual interest rate of 6.35% on their savings through a special company program. Pedro would like you to create a worksheet that determines how much they have to save each month so that in eight years the value of the account is $50,000. Hint: Use the FV function with a monthly savings of $250. Then use the Goal Seek command to determine the monthly savings amount. The Goal Seek command should yield a result of $401.04 per month savings to reach their goal of $50,000 in eight years. Protect the worksheet.

5 ■■ **Working Together** Churchill University is offering its faculty a generous retirement package. Professor Norman Smith has accepted the proposal, but before moving to his retirement home in Naples, Florida, he wants to settle his account with the school credit union. Professor Smith has five years remaining on a six-year car loan, with an interest rate of 8.25% and a monthly payment of $525.00. The credit union is willing to accept the present value (PV) of the loan as a payoff. Develop an amortization schedule that shows how much Professor Smith must pay at the end of each of the six years. As a team, use the Excel Help system to learn more about present value. Then, design and create a worksheet that includes the beginning and ending balance, the amount paid on the principal, and the interest paid for years two through six. Because he has paid for the first year already, determine only the ending balance (present value) for year one. Hand in the worksheet and a one-page paper on one of the following topics: (1) error checking; (2) elements you can protect in a workbook; or (3) present value.

Creating, Sorting, and Querying a List

PROJECT 5

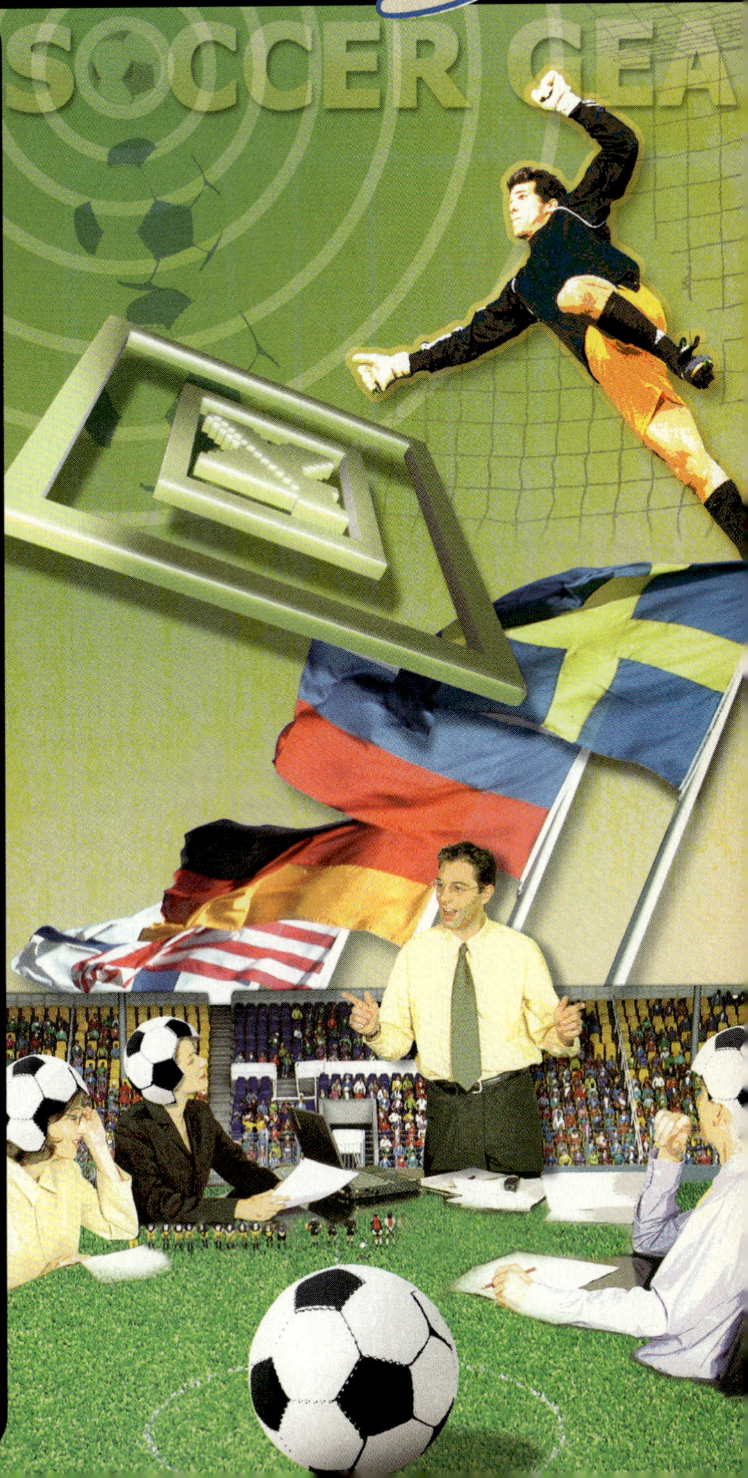

CASE PERSPECTIVE

Soccer Gear is a national corporation that offers the most complete line of soccer equipment in the world. To remain competitive, Soccer Gear has purchased notebook computers and Office 2003 for each of its managers. At a recent sales meeting, the managers learned how to take advantage of their new equipment and software.

Evan Samuels, one of eight sales managers for Soccer Gear, oversees 12 sales representatives spread equally among six states: California, Florida, Illinois, New York, Tennessee, and Texas. Evan has decided to use Excel to create, maintain, and query a list containing data about the Soccer Gear sales representatives (Figure 5-1a on page EX 307) whom he manages.

Using what he learned during the seminar at the sales meeting and by searching Excel Help, Evan discovered that an Excel list can hold both data and formulas and that he can generate meaningful statistics from the list using Excel database functions (Figure 5-1b). Furthermore, he learned that Excel has a lookup function that can be used to grade the performance of sales reps based on the percentage of quota met. Finally, he wants to convert the list to different file formats so that other applications can be used to open and manipulate the list. Evan has assigned you the challenge of creating the Excel list. In addition to creating the list, he wants you to demonstrate how to generate meaningful information from the list by sorting, querying, determining subtotals, and outlining using Excel's powerful list capabilities.

As you read through this project, you will learn how to create, maintain, and query a list using Excel. You also will learn how to save the workbook in different file formats.

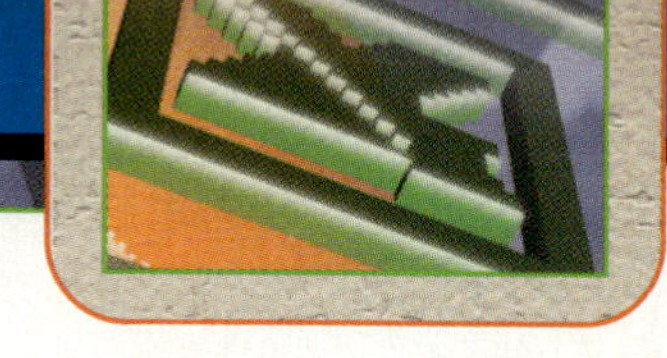

MICROSOFT Office Excel 2003

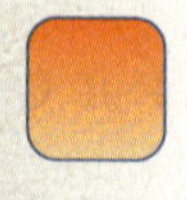

Creating, Sorting, and Querying a List

PROJECT

Objectives

You will have mastered the material in this project when you can:

- Create and manipulate a list
- Delete sheets in a workbook
- Validate data
- Add computational fields to a list
- Use the VLOOKUP function to look up a value in a table
- Use the Toggle Total Row in a list
- Print a list
- Use a data form to display, add, and delete records and change field values in a list
- Sort a list on one field or multiple fields
- Display automatic subtotals
- Use Group and Outline features to hide and unhide data
- Query a list
- Apply database functions, the SUMIF function, and the COUNTIF function to generate information from a list
- Save a workbook in different file formats

Introduction

A **list**, also called a **database**, is an organized collection of data. For example, a list of friends, a list of students registered for a class, a club membership roster, and an instructor's grade book are lists. In these cases, the data related to a person is called a **record**, and the data items that make up a record are called **fields**. For example, in a list of sales reps, each sales rep would have a separate record; each record might include several fields, such as name, age, hire date, state, and quota. A record in a list also can include fields that contain formulas and functions. A field that contains formulas or functions is called a **computational field**. A computational field displays results based on other fields in the list.

A worksheet's row-and-column structure can be used to organize and store a list (Figure 5-1a). Each row of a worksheet can store a record and each column can store a field. Additionally, a row of column headings at the top of the worksheet can store field names that identify each field. Excel's built-in data validation features help ensure data integrity of the data entered in the list.

After you enter a list onto a worksheet, you can use Excel to (1) add and delete records; (2) change the values of fields in records; (3) sort the records so Excel displays them in a different order; (4) determine subtotals for numeric fields; (5) display records that meet comparison criteria; and (6) analyze data using database functions. This project illustrates all six of these list capabilities.

The VLOOKUP function will be used to determine the grades in column J in Figure 5-1a, based on the grade table in columns L and M in Figure 5-1b. The DAVERAGE function will be used to find the average age of female and male sales reps in the list (range O4:R5 in Figure 5-1b). The DCOUNT function will be used to count the number of sales reps that received a grade of A (range O6:R6 in Figure 5-1b). These two functions require that a **criteria area** (range O1:Q3) be set up to tell Excel what items to average and count. Finally, the SUMIF and COUNTIF functions will be used to sum selectively the sales of sales reps that received a grade of A and count the number of female sales reps in the list (range O8:R9 in Figure 5-1b).

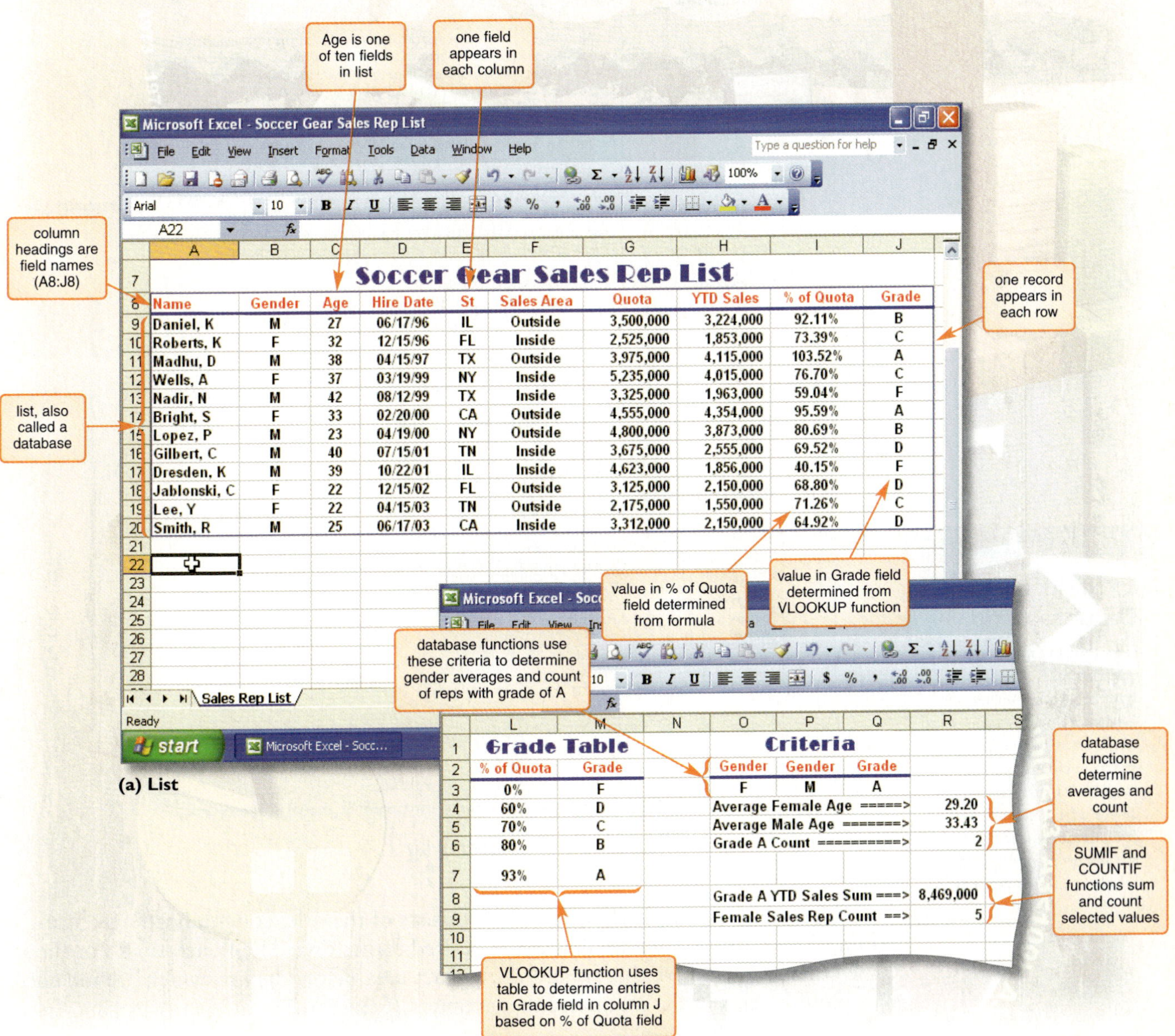

Name	Gender	Age	Hire Date	St	Sales Area	Quota	YTD Sales	% of Quota	Grade
Daniel, K	M	27	06/17/96	IL	Outside	3,500,000	3,224,000	92.11%	B
Roberts, K	F	32	12/15/96	FL	Inside	2,525,000	1,853,000	73.39%	C
Madhu, D	M	38	04/15/97	TX	Outside	3,975,000	4,115,000	103.52%	A
Wells, A	F	37	03/19/99	NY	Inside	5,235,000	4,015,000	76.70%	C
Nadir, N	M	42	08/12/99	TX	Inside	3,325,000	1,963,000	59.04%	F
Bright, S	F	33	02/20/00	CA	Outside	4,555,000	4,354,000	95.59%	A
Lopez, P	M	23	04/19/00	NY	Outside	4,800,000	3,873,000	80.69%	B
Gilbert, C	M	40	07/15/01	TN	Inside	3,675,000	2,555,000	69.52%	D
Dresden, K	M	39	10/22/01	IL	Inside	4,623,000	1,856,000	40.15%	F
Jablonski, C	F	22	12/15/02	FL	Outside	3,125,000	2,150,000	68.80%	D
Lee, Y	F	22	04/15/03	TN	Outside	2,175,000	1,550,000	71.26%	C
Smith, R	M	25	06/17/03	CA	Inside	3,312,000	2,150,000	64.92%	D

(a) List

% of Quota	Grade
0%	F
60%	D
70%	C
80%	B
93%	A

Gender	Gender	Grade
F	M	A

Average Female Age =====>	29.20
Average Male Age =======>	33.43
Grade A Count ==========>	2
Grade A YTD Sales Sum ===>	8,469,000
Female Sales Rep Count ==>	5

(b) Grade Table, Criteria, and Statistics

FIGURE 5-1

Project Five — Soccer Gear Sales Rep List

The requirements document for the Soccer Gear Sales Rep list is shown in Figure 5-2. It includes the needs, source of data, calculations, special requirements, and other facts about its development. Table 5-1 on page EX 310 describes the field names, columns, types of data, and column widths to use when creating the list.

REQUEST FOR NEW WORKBOOK

Date Submitted:	August 1, 2005
Submitted By:	Evan Samuels
Worksheet Title:	Soccer Gear Sales Rep List
Needs:	Create a sales representative list (Figure 5-3a) that can be sorted, queried, maintained, and printed to obtain meaningful information. Using the data in the list, compute statistics that include the average female age, average male age, grade A count, sum of YTD Sales for those with grade A, and the count of the female sales reps as shown in Figure 5-3b. The list field names, columns, types of data, and column widths are described in Table 5-1. Because Evan will use the list online as he travels among the offices, it is important that it be readable and that the list is visible on the screen. Therefore, some of the column widths listed in Table 5-1 are determined from the field names and not the maximum length of the data. The last two fields (located in columns I and J) use a formula and function to determine values based on data within each sales representative record.
Source of Data:	Evan will supply the sales representative data required for the list.
Calculations:	Include the following calculations: 1. % of Quota field in list = YTD Sales / Quota 2. Grade field in list = VLOOKUP function that uses the Grade table in Figure 5-3b 3. Average Female Age = AVERAGE function that uses the Criteria table in Figure 5-3b 4. Average Male Age = AVERAGE function that uses the Criteria table in Figure 5-3b 5. Grade A Count = DCOUNT function that uses the Criteria table in Figure 5-3b 6. Grade A YTD Sales Sum = SUMIF function 7. Female Sales Rep Count = COUNTIF function
Special Requirements:	1. Delete unused sheets. 2. A Criteria area will be created above the list, in rows 1 through 6, to store criteria for use in a query. An Extract area will be created below the list, beginnning in row 24, to receive records that meet a criteria. 3. Save the list as a CSV (Comma delimited) file.

Approvals

Approval Status:	X	Approved
		Rejected
Approved By:	Evan Samuels	
Date:	August 5, 2005	
Assigned To:	J. Quasney, Spreadsheet Specialist	

FIGURE 5-2

More About

Excel as a Database Tool

Even though Excel is not a true database management system, such as Access or Oracle, it does give you many of the same basic capabilities. For example, in Excel you can create a list; add, change, and delete data in the list; use computational fields; sort data in the list; query the list; and create forms and reports.

The sketch of the list (Figure 5-3a) consists of the title, column headings, location of data values, and an idea of the desired formatting. The sketch does not show the criteria area above the list and the extract area below the list, which are included as requirements in the requirements document (Figure 5-2).

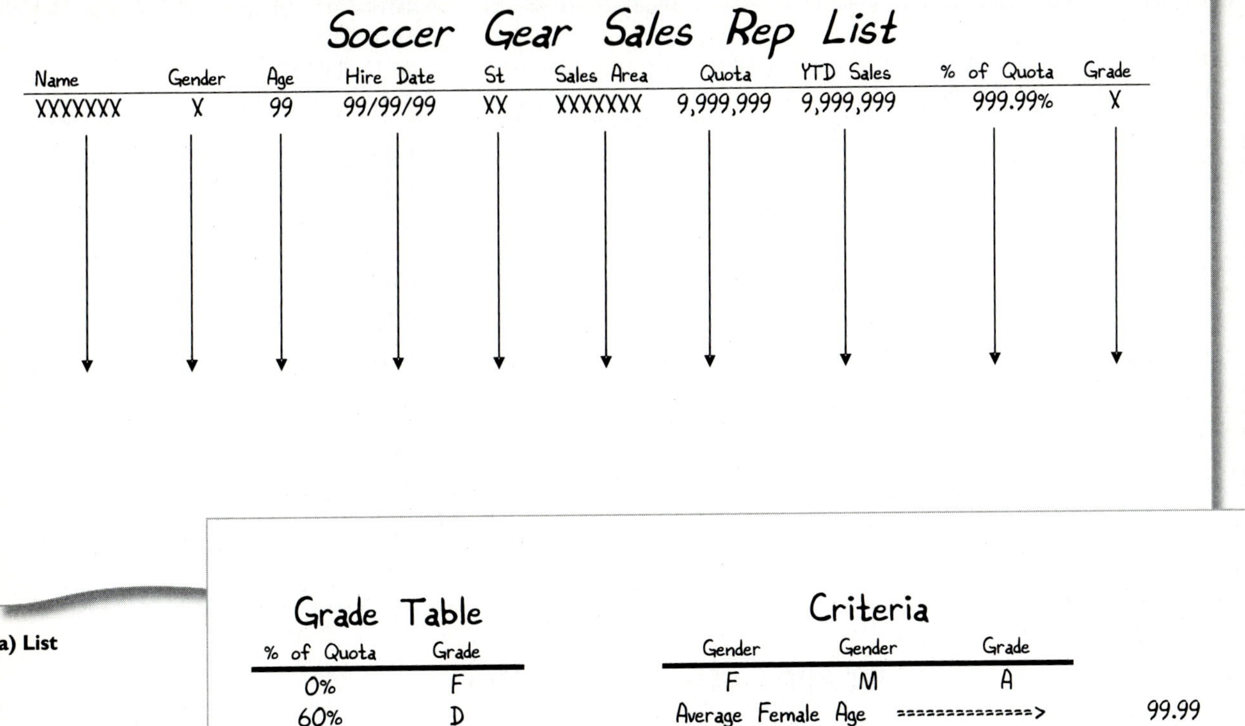

Soccer Gear Sales Rep List
Name
Gender
Age
Hire Date
St
Sales Area
Quota
YTD Sales
% of Quota
Grade
XXXXXXX
X
99
99/99/99
XX
XXXXXXX
9,999,999
9,999,999
999.99%
X

(a) List

Grade Table

% of Quota	Grade
0%	F
60%	D
70%	C
80%	B
93%	A

Criteria

Gender	Gender	Grade
F	M	A

Average Female Age ===============>	99.99
Average Male Age ==============>	99.99
Grade A Count ================>	99
Grade A YTD Sales Sum =========>	99,999,999
Female Sales Rep Count===========>	99

(b) Grade Table, Criteria, and Statistics

FIGURE 5-3

The general layout of the grade table, criteria area, and required statistics are shown in Figure 5-3b.

The list and its accompanying statistics will be created and manipulated in this sequence: (1) create the list; (2) determine list totals; (3) sort, query, and determine subtotals; (4) add the criteria area above the list and the extract area below the list; and (5) add the criteria area for the database functions in columns O through Q, apply the database functions, and finally apply the SUMIF and COUNTIF functions.

Table 5-1 Column Information for Soccer Gear Sales Rep List

COLUMN HEADINGS (FIELD NAMES)	COLUMN IN WORKSHEET	TYPE OF DATA	COLUMN WIDTH	DESCRIPTION AS IT PERTAINS TO A SALES REP
Name	A	Text	11.29	Last name and first initial
Gender	B	Text	9.00	Male or female
Age	C	Numeric	6.00	Age in years
Hire Date	D	Date	11.00	Date hired
St	E	Text	5.00	Sales territory
Sales Area	F	Text	12.00	Inside or outside sales
Quota	G	Numeric	12.00	Annual sales quota
YTD Sales	H	Numeric	12.14	Year-to-date sales
% of Quota	I	YTD Sales / Quota	12.00	Percent of annual quota met
Grade	J	VLOOKUP function	9.00	Grade indicates how much of quota has been met

Starting and Customizing Excel

With the requirements document and sketch of the worksheet complete, the next step is to start and customize Excel. If you are stepping through this project on a computer and you want your screen to agree with the figures in this book, then you should change your computer's resolution to 800 × 600. For information on changing the resolution on your computer, see Appendix D. The following steps start Excel and customize the Excel window.

To Start and Customize Excel

1. **Click the Start button on the Windows taskbar, point to All Programs on the Start menu, point to Microsoft Office on the All Programs submenu, and then click Microsoft Office Excel 2003 on the Microsoft Office submenu.**
2. **If the Excel window is not maximized, double-click its title bar to maximize it.**
3. **If the Language bar appears, right-click it and then click Close the Language bar on the shortcut menu.**
4. **If the Getting Started task pane appears in the Excel window, click its Close button in the upper-right corner.**
5. **If the Standard and Formatting toolbars are positioned on the same row, click the Toolbar Options button and then click Show Buttons on Two Rows.**

Excel displays the Standard and Formatting toolbars on two rows, as shown in Figure 5-1a on page EX 307.

If your toolbars display differently than those shown in Figure 5-1a, see Appendix D for additional information on resetting the toolbars and menus.

More About

Starting Excel

If you plan to open an existing workbook, you can start Excel and open the workbook at the same time by double-clicking the workbook file name in Windows Explorer.

Creating a List

One way to create a list in Excel is to follow these five steps: (1) enter the column headings (field names); (2) define a range as a list using the Create List command; (3) format the insert row immediately below the column headings; (4) set up data validation using the Validation command; and (5) enter records into the list using a data form. The following pages illustrate the process of creating the Soccer Gear Sales Rep list using these five steps.

Entering the Column Headings for a List

The following steps change the column widths to those specified in Table 5-1, enter the list title, change the height of row 8 to 15 points to emphasize this row, and enter and format the column headings. These steps also change the name of Sheet1 to Sales Rep List, delete the unused sheets in the workbook, and save the workbook using the file name Soccer Gear Sales Rep List.

Although Excel does not require a list title to be entered, it is a good practice to include one on the worksheet to show where the list begins. With Excel, you usually enter the list several rows below the first row in the worksheet. These blank rows later will be used as a criteria area to store criteria for use in a query.

More About

Setting Up a List

When creating a list, leave several rows empty above the list on the worksheet to set up a criteria area for querying the list. Some spreadsheet specialists also leave several columns empty to the left of the list, beginning with column A, for additional worksheet activities. A range of blank rows or columns on the side of a list is called a moat of cells.

Note: The majority of tasks involved in entering and formatting the list title and column headings of a list are similar to what you have done in previous projects. Thus, if you plan to complete this project on your computer and want to skip the set of steps below, open the workbook Soccer Gear Sales Rep List from the Data Disk.

To Enter the Column Headings for a List

1. **Use the mouse to change the column widths as follows: A = 11.29, B = 9.00, C = 6.00, D = 11.00, E = 5.00, F = 12.00, G = 12.00, H = 12.14, I = 12.00, and J = 9.00.**
2. **Enter** `Soccer Gear Sales Rep List` **as the list title in cell A7.**
3. **With cell A7 selected, click the Font box arrow on the Formatting toolbar and then click Broadway (or a font of your choice) in the Font list. Click the Font Size box arrow on the Formatting toolbar and then click 18 in the Font Size list. Click the Font Color button arrow on the Formatting toolbar and then click Blue (column 6, row 2) on the Font Color palette.**
4. **Select the range A7:H7. Right-click the selected range and then click Format Cells on the shortcut menu. When Excel displays the Format Cells dialog box, click the Alignment tab, click the Horizontal box arrow in the Text Alignment area, click Center Across Selection in the Horizontal list, and then click the OK button.**
5. **Enter the column headings in row 8 as shown in Figure 5-4 on the next page. Center the column headings in the range B8:H8. Change the height of row 8 to 15.00 points.**

(continued)

6. **Select the range A8:H8, click the Bold button on the Formatting toolbar, click the Font Color button arrow on the Formatting toolbar, and then click Red (column 1, row 3) on the Font Color palette. Right-click the selected range and then click Format Cells on the shortcut menu. Click the Border tab, click the Color box arrow in the Line area, click Blue (column 6, row 2) on the Color palette, click the heavy border style in the Style box (column 2, row 6), click the Underline button on the left side of the Border area, and then click the OK button.**

7. **Select the range A7:H7. Right-click the selection, click Format Cells, click the Alignment tab, click the Horizontal box arrow, select Center Across Selection in the Horizontal list, and then click the OK button.**

8. **Double-click the Sheet1 tab at the bottom of the screen. Type** `Sales Rep List` **as the sheet name. Press the ENTER key. Right-click the tab, click Tab Color on the shortcut menu, click Blue (column 6, row 2), and then click the OK button.**

9. **Click the Sheet2 tab, hold down the CTRL key, and then click the Sheet3 tab. Right-click the selected sheet tabs and then click Delete on the shortcut menu.**

10. **With a floppy disk in drive A, click the Save button on the Standard toolbar. When Excel displays the Save As dialog box, type** `Soccer Gear Sales Rep List` **in the File name text box. If necessary, click 3½ Floppy (A:) in the Save in list and then click the Save button in the Save As dialog box.**

Excel saves the workbook on the floppy disk in drive A using the file name, Soccer Gear Sales Rep List, and displays the worksheet as shown in Figure 5-4.

More About

About Extending Formats

When you are entering a column or row list, the Extend List Format feature of Excel automatically formats new entries added to the end of a list to match the format of the rest of the list. For the formats to be extended properly, the format must appear in at least three of the five last rows (or columns) preceding the new row (or column). To toggle this feature off, click Options on the Tools menu, click the Edit tab, click Extend list formats and formulas to remove the check mark, and then click the OK button.

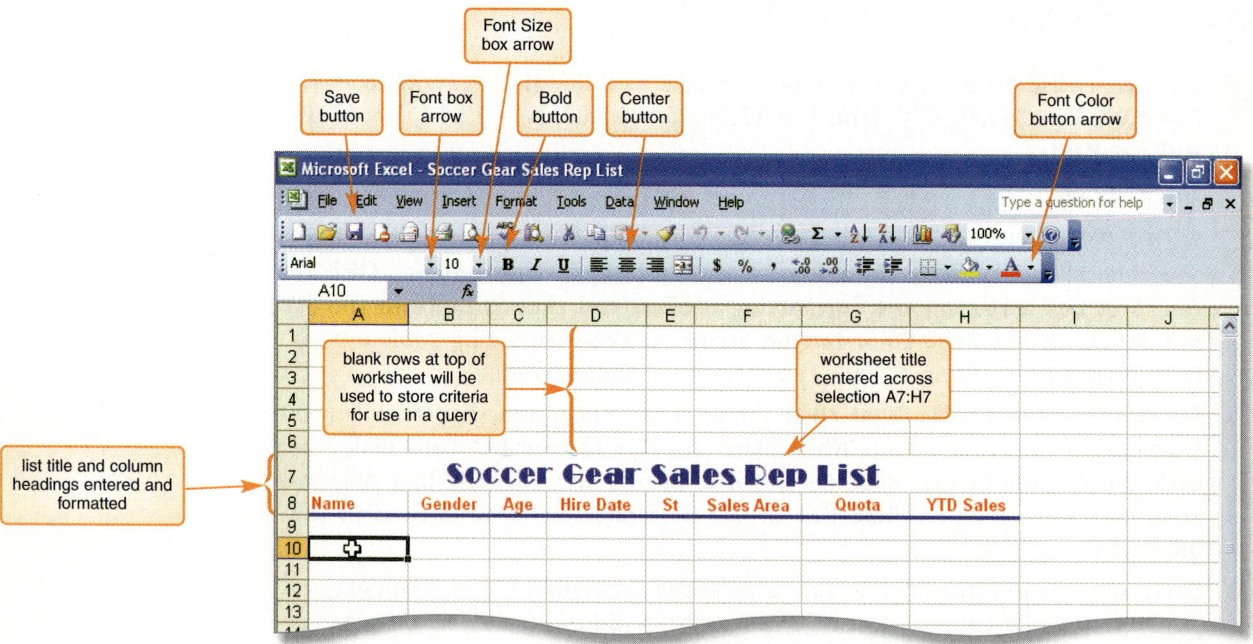

FIGURE 5-4

Compare the column headings in row 8 in Figure 5-4 with Figure 5-3a on page EX 309. In Figure 5-4, the two computational fields, % of Quota and Grade, are not included in columns I and J. These two fields will be added after the data is entered for the 12 sales reps. With Excel, computational fields that depend on data in the list usually are entered after the data has been entered.

In Step 4 on page EX 311, the Center Across Selection horizontal alignment was used to center the list title in row 7 horizontally across the range A7:H7. In earlier projects, the Center and Merge button on the Formatting toolbar was used to center text across a range. The major difference between the Center Across Selection horizontal alignment and the Merge and Center button is that, unlike the Merge and Center button, the Center Across Selection horizontal alignment does not merge the selected cell range into one cell.

Q&A

Q: When do you center and merge and when do you center across a selection?

A: You center and merge when you want to treat the range of cells over which you center as a single cell. You center across a selection when you want the selected range of cells to be independent of one another. With most workbooks, it makes little difference whether you center using one technique or the other. Thus, most spreadsheet specialists use the center and merge technique because the procedure is available as a button on the Formatting toolbar.

Defining a Range as a List

The following steps define the range A8:H8 as a list. Excel allows you to enter data in a range either before defining it as a list or after defining it as a list. This project uses the latter procedure because it offers additional tools that help ensure data integrity, such as data forms and data validation. These tools will be discussed shortly.

To Define a Range as a List

1

- **Select the range A8:H8.**
- **Click Data on the menu bar and then point to List on the Data menu.**

Excel displays the Data menu and List submenu (Figure 5-5).

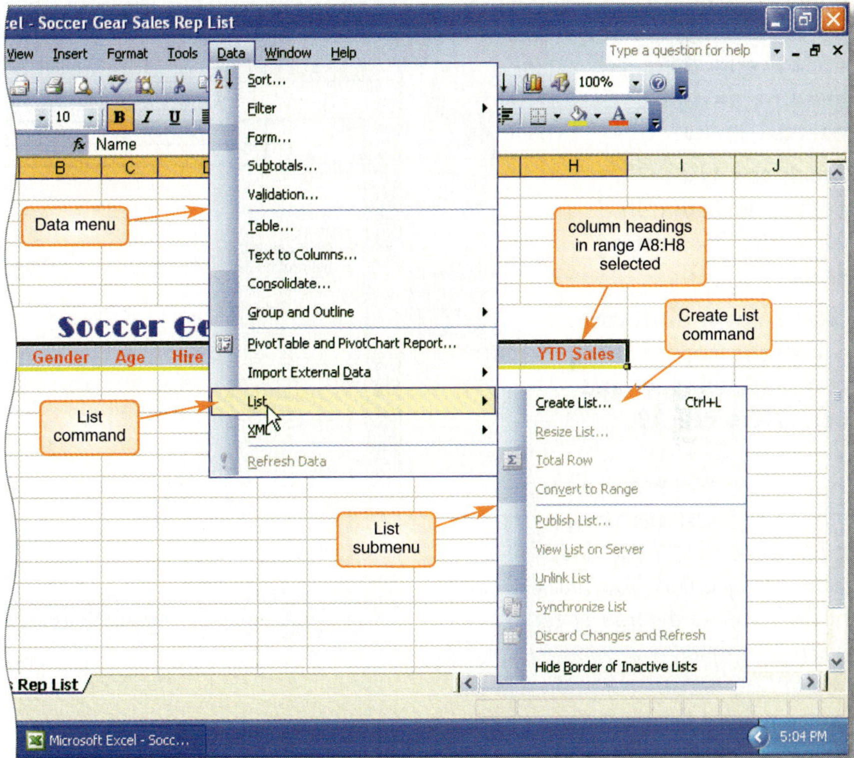

FIGURE 5-5

2

- **Click Create List on the List submenu.**
- **When Excel displays the Create List dialog box, click the My list has headers check box.**

Excel displays the Create List dialog box as shown in Figure 5-6. Because the range A8:H8 was selected before invoking the Create List command, Excel automatically selects this range for the Where is the data for your list box. The My list has headers check box is selected.

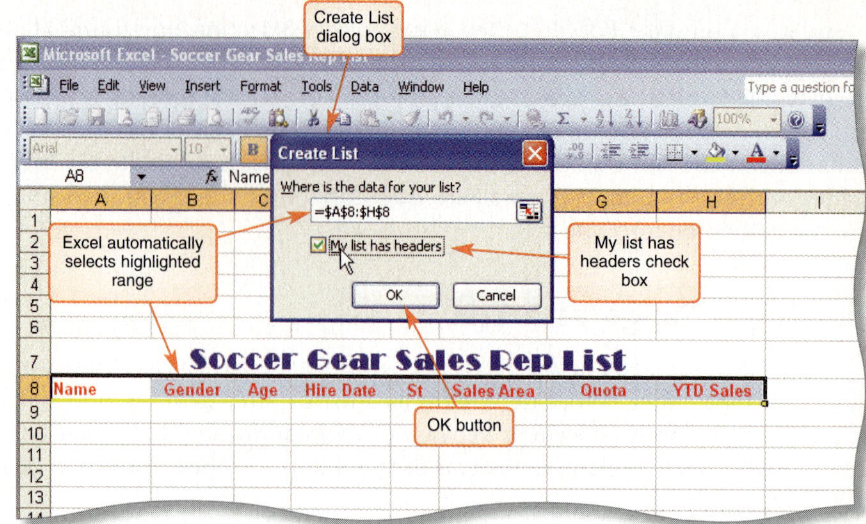

FIGURE 5-6

3

- **Click the OK button.**
- **If Excel does not display the List toolbar automatically, right-click any toolbar at the top of the Excel window and then click List on the shortcut menu.**
- **Dock the List toolbar immediately below the Formatting toolbar.**
- **Scroll down until row 7 is at the top of the worksheet window and then select cell A9.**

Excel creates a list from the selected column headings and the corresponding cells in the row below it (Figure 5-7). The list is surrounded by a dark blue outline. Down arrows appear to the right of each column heading. The empty row below the column headings with the asterisk in the leftmost column is called the insert row.

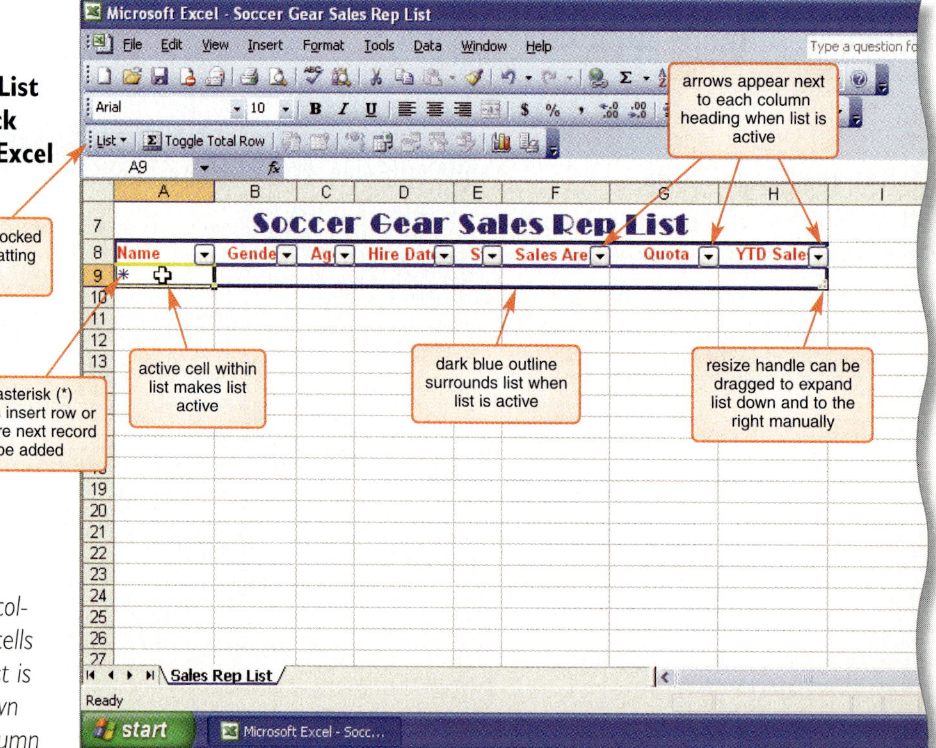

FIGURE 5-7

Other Ways

1. Select range, press ALT+D, I, C
2. Select range, type Database in Name box
3. Select range, in Voice command mode, say "Data, List, Create List"

As shown in Figure 5-7, when a list is active in Excel, Excel adds several visual elements to the range of the list to make it easy to identify and modify. You make a list active by selecting a cell in the list. You make a list inactive by selecting a cell outside the list.

When a list is active, Excel adds the following visual elements:

1. A down arrow appears next to each column heading; each arrow can be used to sort and query the data in the list.
2. The dark blue outline border distinguishes the range from the rest of the worksheet.
3. An empty row, called the **insert row**, appears below the column headings. It contains an asterisk in the leftmost cell. Each time a record is added to the list, the insert row moves down one row.
4. The **resize handle** found in the lower right corner of the list can be used to increase or decrease the range associated with the list manually.
5. The List toolbar is displayed, unless the user has closed it.

When a list is inactive, Excel removes the visual elements listed above, but does draw a light blue outline around the list so it remains recognizable.

More About

Lists

To change an active list back to a normal range of cells, select the range, click the List command on the Data menu, and then click the Convert to Range command on the List submenu (Figure 5-5 on page EX 313).

Formatting the Insert Row in an Empty List

If the list contains no data, as in Figure 5-7, then Excel sets the format of the cells in the insert row to the default. That is, if you assigned any formats to the insert row before it became part of a list, then those formats are lost when the list is created. For this reason, if you create an empty list and want the records to be formatted, you must format the insert row after you create the list as shown in the following steps.

To Format the Insert Row in an Empty List

1. **Select the range A9:H9 and then click the Bold button on the Formatting toolbar.**
2. **Select the range B9:H9 and then click the Center button on the Formatting toolbar.**
3. **Right-click cell D9. Click Format Cells on the shortcut menu. When Excel displays the Format Cells dialog box, click the Number tab, click Date in the Category list, click 03/14/01 in the Type list, and then click the OK button.**
4. **Select the range G9:H9 and then click the Comma Style button on the Formatting toolbar. Click the Decrease Decimal button on the Formatting toolbar twice so columns G and H will display whole numbers.**

No visible changes appear on the worksheet, because the list contains no records. As records are entered into the list, the assigned formats will apply.

Data Validation

Excel has built-in **data validation** features to ensure that the data you enter into a cell or range of cells is within limits. For example, the cells in the Gender column in Figure 5-7 should be either an M for male or F for female. Any entry other than M or F is invalid and should not be allowed. The steps on the next page show how to use the Validation command on the Data menu to ensure that Excel will accept only an entry of M or F in the Gender column.

More About

Garbage In Garbage Out (GIGO)

In information processing, Garbage In Garbage Out, or GIGO (pronounced gee-go), is used to describe the output of inaccurate information that results from the input of invalid data.

To Validate Data

1

- **Select cell B9, the cell in the insert row below the Gender column heading in cell B8.**
- **Click Data on the menu bar.**

Excel displays the Data menu (Figure 5-8).

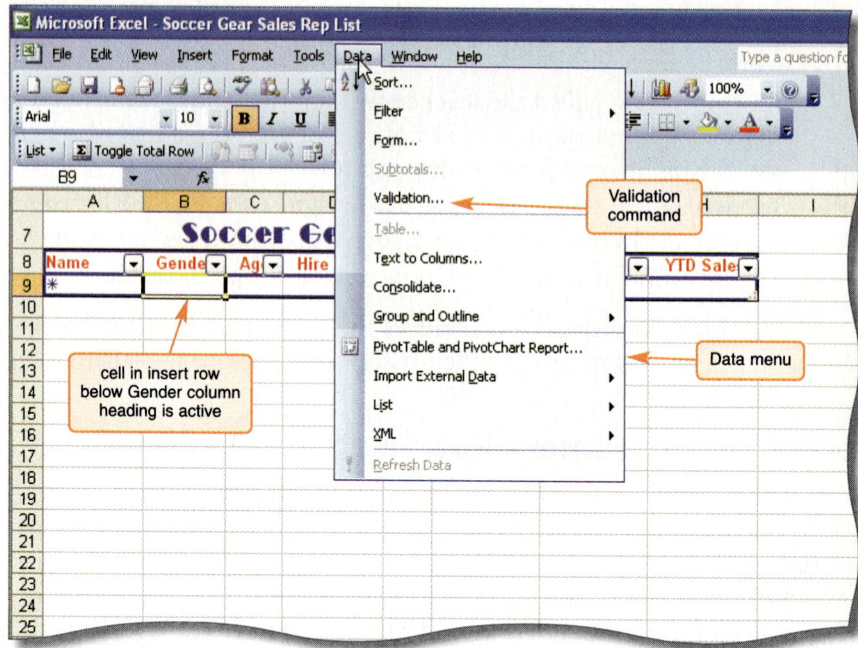

FIGURE 5-8

2

- **Click Validation on the Data menu.**
- **When Excel displays the Data Validation dialog box, click the Settings tab, click the Allow box arrow, and then click List in the Allow list.**
- **Type** F,M **in the Source box.**
- **Click the In-cell dropdown check box to clear it.**

Excel displays the Sheet tab in the Data Validation dialog box as shown in Figure 5-9.

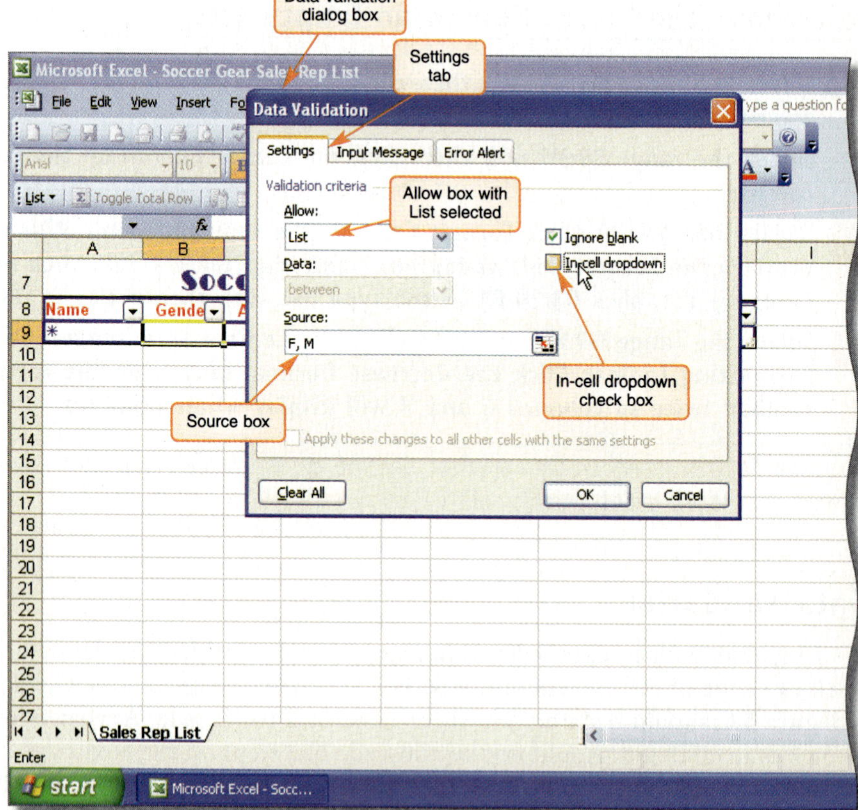

FIGURE 5-9

3

- **Click the Error Alert tab.**
- **If necessary, click Show error alert after invalid data is entered.**
- **Click the Style box arrow and then click Stop in the Style list.**
- **Type** `Gender Invalid` **in the Title box.**
- **Type** `Gender code must be an F or M.` **in the Error message box.**

Excel displays the Error Alert tab in the Data Validation dialog box as shown in Figure 5-10.

4

- **Click the OK button.**

No immediate changes appear on the worksheet. If, however, you try to enter any value other than F or M in cell B9, Excel rejects the data and displays the Gender Invalid dialog box created in Step 3.

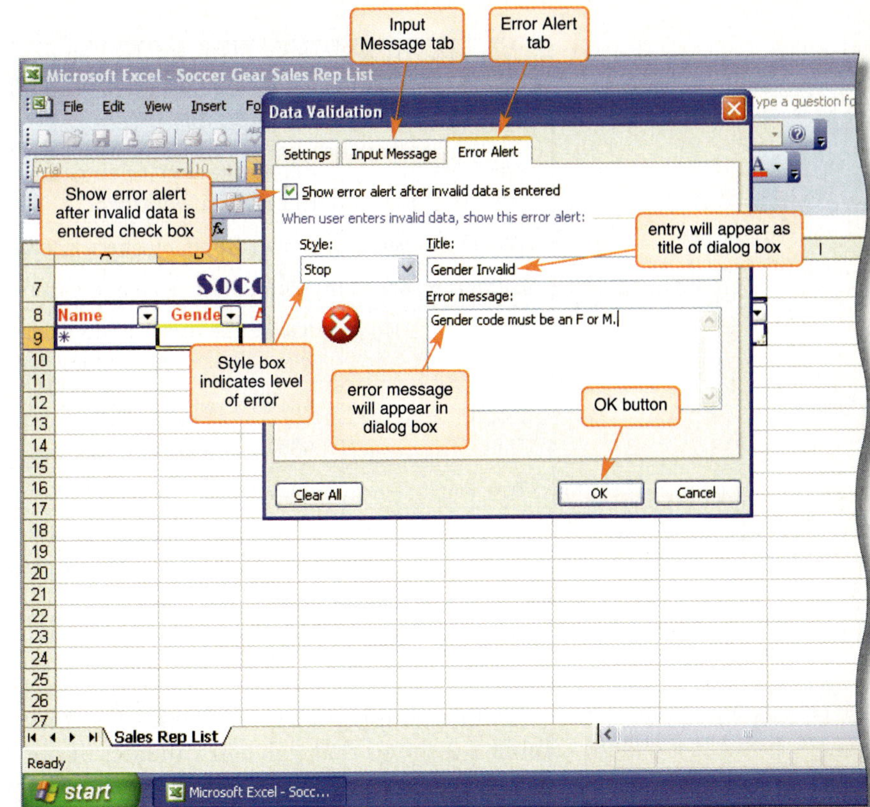

FIGURE 5-10

Other Ways

1. Press ALT+D, L
2. In Voice Command mode, say "Data, Validation"

The Style box in the Error Alert sheet shown in Figure 5-10 sets the level of error. Valid entries include Stop, Warning, and Information. Figure 5-11 shows the Gender Invalid dialog box that Excel displays when a user enters a value other than F or M into a cell in the Gender column in the list. The Retry button leaves the invalid value in the cell for you to change. The Cancel button removes the invalid value.

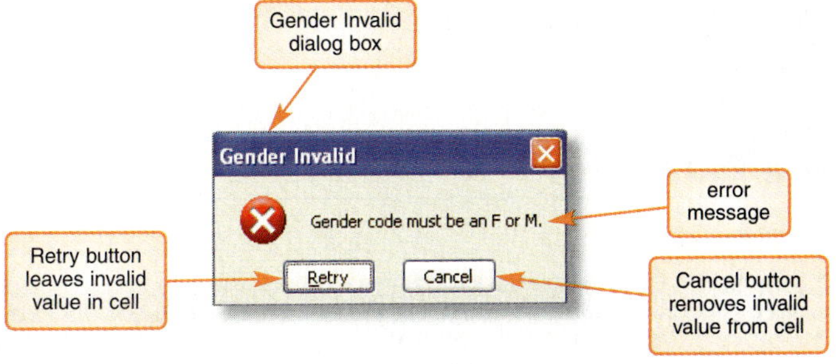

FIGURE 5-11

Excel's built-in data validation features are powerful and easy to use. The different data validation criteria allowed by Excel and summarized in Table 5-2 on the next page can be selected in the Allow list in the Settings sheet in the Data Validation dialog box (Figure 5-9).

More About

Validation

Data validation rules can be mandatory or cautionary. If the rule is mandatory (a Stop), then Excel rejects the cell entry via a dialog box (Figure 5-11) and gives you a chance to correct it. If the rule is cautionary (a Warning), then Excel displays a dialog box to warn you of the invalid entry and then gives you a chance to redo the cell entry or leave it as entered.

Table 5-2 Types of Data Validation Criteria Allowed

ALLOWS	DESCRIPTION
Any value	Allows the user to enter anything in the cell. Any value is the default for all cells in a worksheet.
Whole number	Allows whole numbers in a specific range.
Decimal number	Allows decimal numbers in a specific range.
List	Allows the user to enter only an item from a list. Useful when working with codes, such as M for male and F for female.
Date	Allows a range of dates.
Time	Allows a range of times.
Text length	Allows a certain length of text.
Custom	Allows you to specify a formula that will validate the data entered by the user. For example, the formula <3 would require the cell entry to be less than 3.

Q: Does Excel ever ignore data validation?

A: Yes. Excel ignores data validation when you paste data from the Office Clipboard or use the mouse to copy by dragging.

Although this project only validates the values entered into the Gender column, Table 5-2 shows that you can validate, in one way or another, all of the columns in the Soccer Gear Sales Rep List. For example, you can validate the data entered in the Age column by establishing limits for a whole number between 18 and 65. Or, you can validate the data entered in the Hire Date column to ensure the user enters a date between 1960 and 2005.

Entering Records into a List Using a Data Form

The next step is to use a data form to enter the sales reps' records into the list. A **data form** is an Excel dialog box that lists the field names in the list and provides corresponding boxes in which you enter the values for each field. If you are stepping through this project on a computer and inadvertently make a mistake and notice it after you enter the record into the list, then correct it later after you enter all the records. As indicated earlier, the computational fields in columns I and J will be added after the data is in the list.

To Enter Records into a List Using a Data Form

1

- **If necessary, select cell A9 to activate the list.**
- **Click Data on the menu bar.**

Excel displays the Data menu (Figure 5-12).

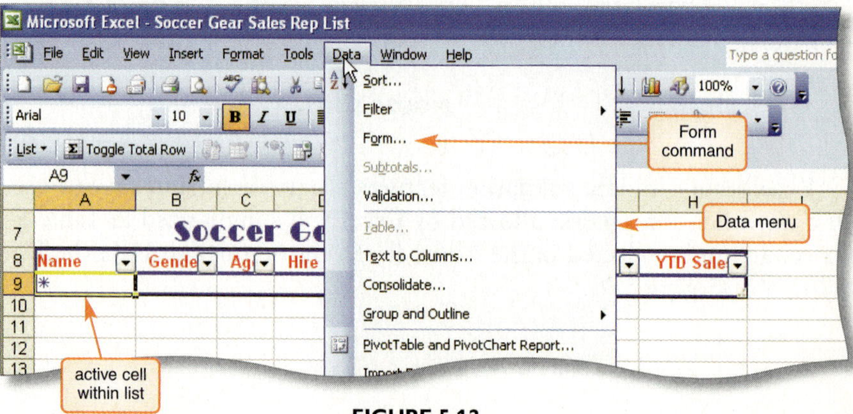

FIGURE 5-12

2

- **Click Form on the Data menu.**

Excel displays the data form (Figure 5-13) with the sheet name Sales Rep List on the title bar. The data form automatically includes the column heading names and corresponding text boxes for entering the field values. Excel selects the column heading names in the range A8:H8 because they comprise the top row in the list.

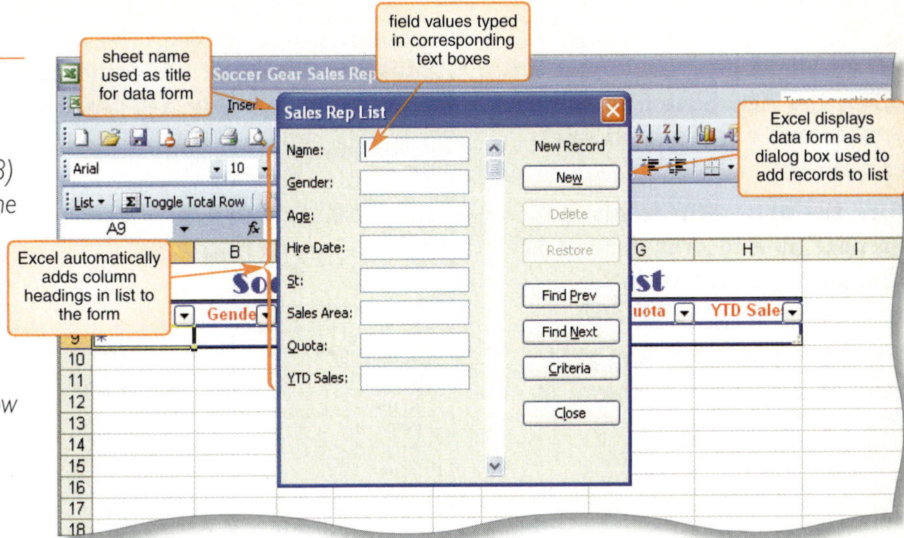

FIGURE 5-13

3

- **Enter the first sales rep's record into the data form as shown in Figure 5-14.**
- **Use the mouse or the TAB key to move the insertion point down to the next text box.**
- **If you make a mistake, use the mouse or the SHIFT+TAB keys to move the insertion point to the previous text box in the data form and then edit the entry.**

The data form shows the first sales rep's record (Figure 5-14).

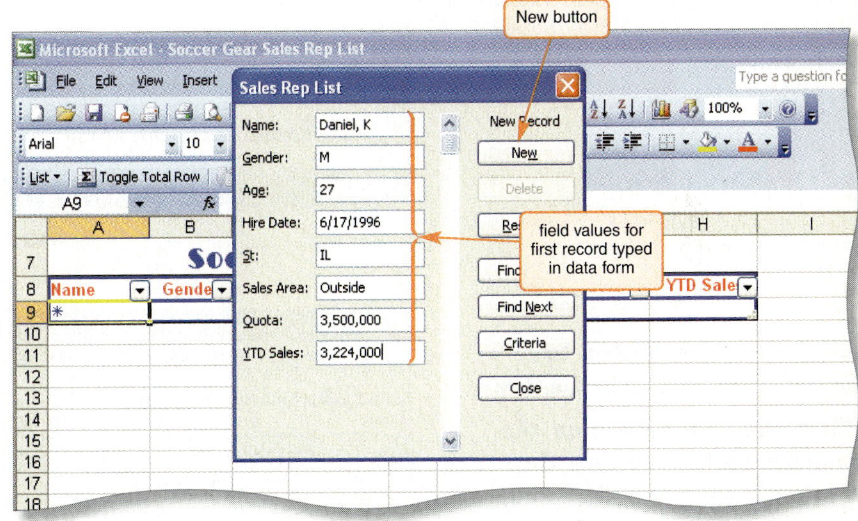

FIGURE 5-14

4

- **Click the New button in the data form.**
- **Type the second sales rep's record into the data form as shown in Figure 5-15.**

Excel adds the first sales rep's record to row 9 in the list range and then moves the insert row down one row to row 10. The data form shows the second sales rep's record (Figure 5-15).

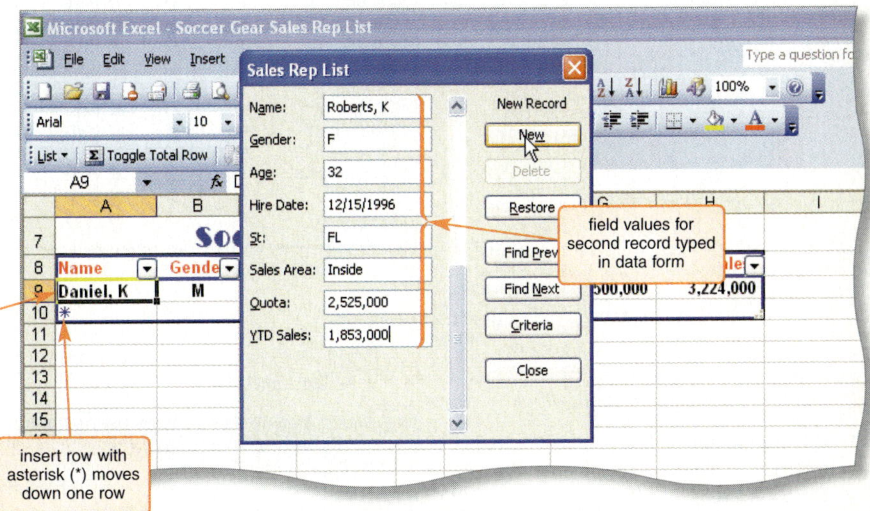

FIGURE 5-15

5

- **Click the New button in the data form to enter the second sales rep's record.**
- **Use the data form to enter the next nine records in rows 11 through 19, as shown in Figure 5-1a on page EX 307.**
- **Type the last sales rep's record into the data form as shown in Figure 5-16.**

Excel enters the sales rep's records into the list range as shown in Figure 5-16. The data form shows the last record.

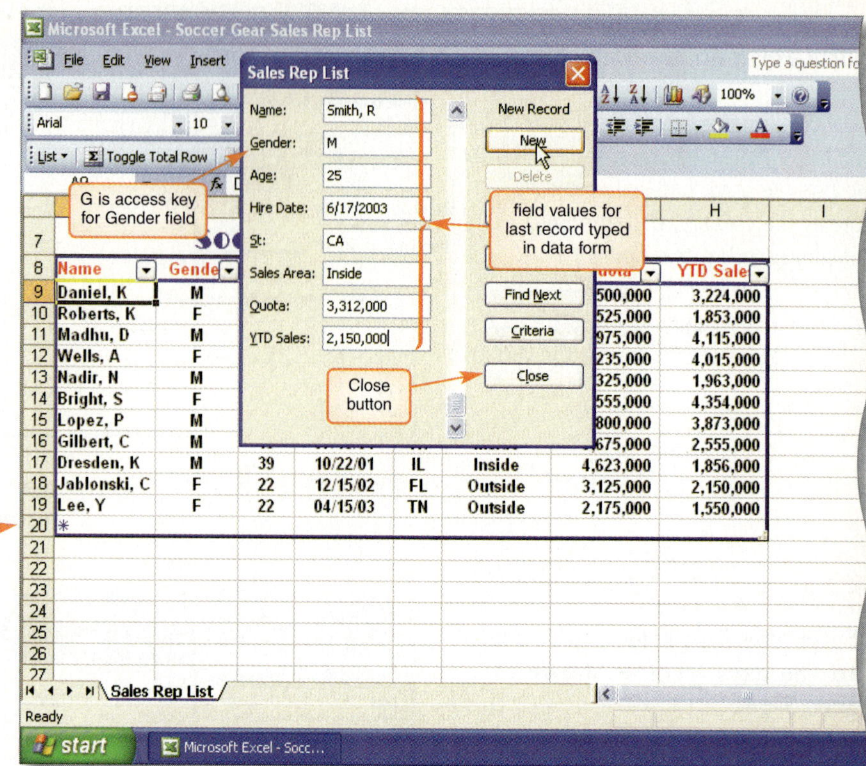

FIGURE 5-16

6

- **Click the Close button to complete the last record entry.**
- **Click the Save button on the Standard toolbar to save the workbook using the file name, Soccer Gear Sales Rep List.**

Excel enters the last sales rep record in row 20 of the list, closes the data form, and saves the workbook (Figure 5-17).

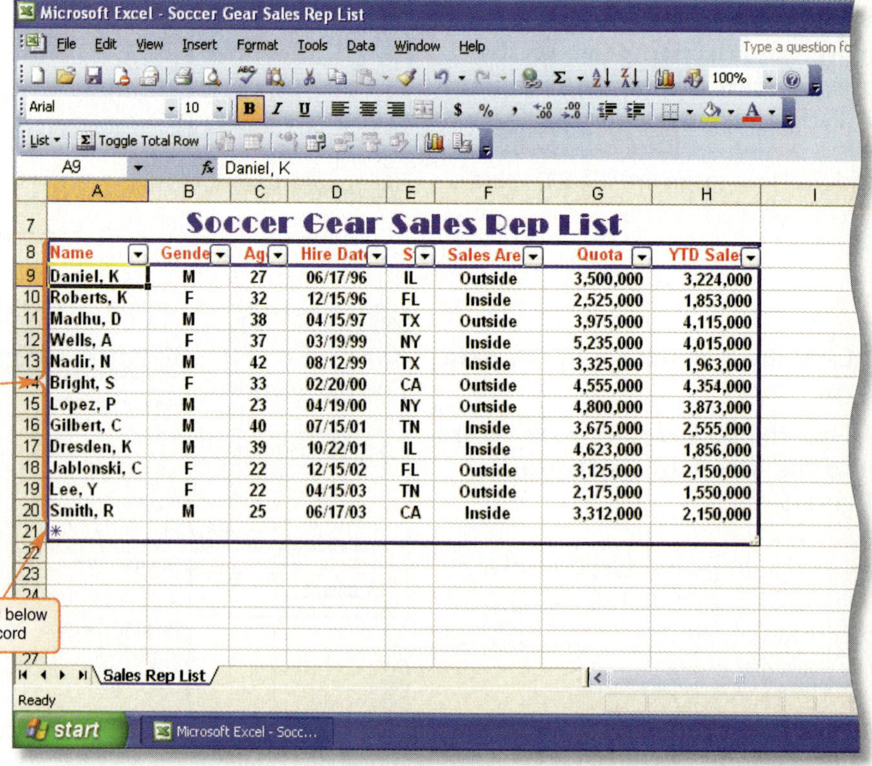

FIGURE 5-17

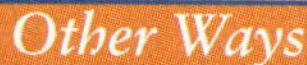

Other Ways

1. Click List button on List toolbar, click Form on List button menu
2. Press ALT+D, O
3. In Voice Command mode, say "Data, Form"

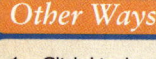

If you entered an incorrect Gender code while entering the sales rep's records, then Excel should have displayed the dialog box in Figure 5-11 on page EX 317. After you click the Retry or Cancel button in the error message dialog box, Excel requires you to re-enter all values up to and including the value in error. For example, if you made a mistake entering a Gender code in the data form, Excel displays the Gender Invalid dialog box. After you click the Retry or Cancel button in the Gender Invalid dialog box, you must re-enter the name of the sales rep as well as the Gender code. You do not have to re-enter the values following the Gender field in the data form.

Instead of using a data form, the sales rep's records could have been entered in columns and rows, just as you would enter data into any worksheet. Using a data form, however, is considered to be a more accurate and reliable method of data entry.

Moving from Field to Field in a Data Form

You can move from field to field in a data form using the TAB key to move the insertion point to the next text box or the SHIFT+TAB keys to move the insertion point to the previous text box. Alternatively, you can hold down the ALT key and press the key that corresponds to the underlined letter in the name of the field to which you want to move. An underlined letter in a field name is called an **access key**. Thus, to select the Gender field in the data form in Figure 5-16, you would hold down the ALT key and then press the G key (ALT+G), because G is the access key for the Gender field.

More About

The Watchdog

Excel always is watching what you are doing. If you manually enter the data into a list, Excel will enter data automatically for you, based on the data entered into the column. For example, in the Sales Area column in Figure 5-19 on the next page, if you type the letter I in cell F21, Excel will display Inside in the cell. To toggle this feature off, click Options on the Tools menu, click the Edit tab, click Enable AutoComplete for cell values to remove the check mark, and then click the OK button. You also can right-click an empty cell under a list of items in a column and click the Pick From List command on the shortcut menu. Excel will display a list of items in the column; clicking an item in the list will assign it to the selected cell.

Adding Computational Fields to the List

The next step is to add the computational fields % of Quota in column I and Grade in column J. The first computational field involves dividing the YTD Sales in column H by the Quota in column G. The second computational field involves a table lookup to determine a grade based upon the % of Quota in column I.

Adding New Fields to a List

Adding new fields to a list in a worksheet illustrates another of Excel's powerful list capabilities. As shown in the steps on the next page, if you add a new column heading in a column adjacent to the current column headings in the list, then Excel automatically adds the adjacent column to the list's range.

The first step in adding the two new fields is to enter and format the two column headings, or field names, in cells I8 and J8, enter the first % of Quota formula in cell I9, and then format the two cells immediately below the new column headings. The formula for the % of Quota in cell I9 is YTD Sales / Quota or =H9 / G9. After the formula is entered in cell I9, the formula must be copied to the range I10:I20.

To Add New Fields to a List

1

- **Select cell I8, type** `% of Quota`**, click cell J8, type** `Grade`**, click cell H8, click the Format Painter button on the Standard toolbar, and then drag through the range I8:J8.**
- **Select cell I9, enter** `=h9 / g9` **as the formula, click the Percent Style button on the Formatting toolbar, and then click the Increase Decimal button on the Formatting toolbar twice.**
- **Select the range I9:J9, click the Bold button on the Formatting toolbar, and then click the Center button on the Formatting toolbar.**

Excel displays the new field names in cells I8 and J8 and the formatted result of the % of Quota formula in cell I9 (Figure 5-18).

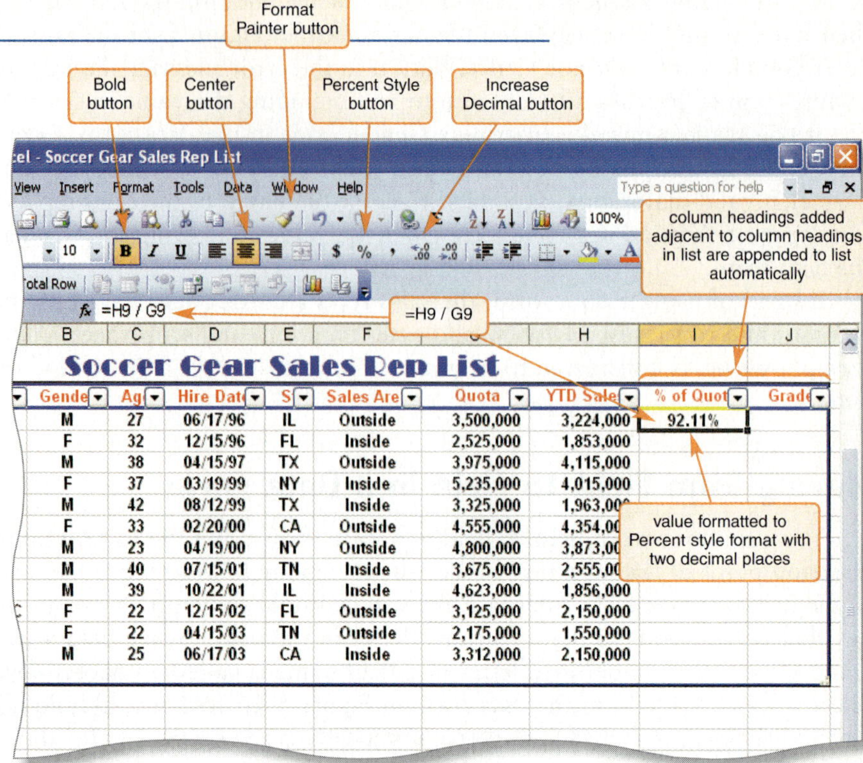

FIGURE 5-18

2

- **Select the range A7:J7, right-click the selected range, click Format Cells on the shortcut menu, click the Alignment tab, click the Horizontal box arrow, click Center Across Selection, and then click the OK button.**
- **Click cell I9 and then drag the fill handle down through cell I20.**

Excel centers the list title across columns A through J and displays the % of Quota for each sales rep (Figure 5-19).

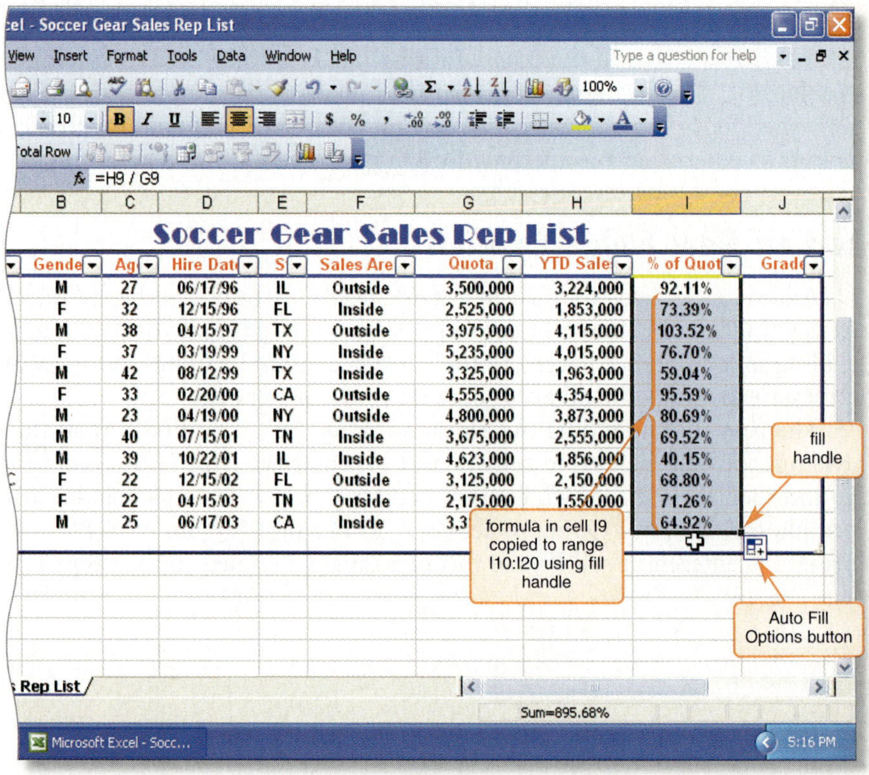

FIGURE 5-19

Other Ways

1. Drag resize handle in lower-right corner of list
2. Click List button on List toolbar, click Resize List

The entries in the % of Quota column give the user an immediate evaluation of where each sales rep's YTD Sales stand in relation to their annual quota. Many people, however, dislike numbers as an evaluation tool. Most prefer simple letter grades, which, when used properly, can group the sales reps in the same way an instructor groups students by letter grades. Excel contains functions that allow you to assign letter grades based on a table, as explained in the next section.

More About

Lookup Functions

Lookup functions are powerful, useful, and interesting in the way they work. For additional information on lookup functions, enter `vlookup` in the Type a question for help box on the menu bar.

Using Excel's VLOOKUP Function to Determine Letter Grades

Excel has several lookup functions that are useful for looking up values in tables, such as tax tables, discount tables, parts tables, and grade tables. The two most widely used lookup functions are the HLOOKUP and VLOOKUP functions. Both functions look up a value in a table and return a corresponding value from the table to the cell assigned the function. The **HLOOKUP function** is used when the table direction is horizontal, or across the worksheet. The **VLOOKUP function** is used when a table direction is vertical, or down the worksheet. The VLOOKUP function is by far the most often used because most tables are vertical, as is the table in this project.

The grading scale in this project (Table 5-3) is similar to one that your instructor uses to determine your letter grade. As shown in Table 5-3, any score greater than or equal to 93% equates to a letter grade of A. Scores greater than or equal to 80 and less than 93 are assigned a letter grade of B, and so on.

Table 5-3 Typical Grade Table

% OF QUOTA	GRADE
93% and higher	A
80% to 92%	B
70% to 79%	C
60% to 69%	D
0 to 59%	F

The VLOOKUP function requires that the table indicate only the lowest score for a letter grade. Furthermore, the table entries must be in sequence from lowest score to highest score. Thus, the entries in Table 5-3 must be re-sequenced for use with the VLOOKUP function so they appear as shown in Table 5-4.

The general form of the VLOOKUP function is:

=VLOOKUP(lookup_value, table_array, col_index_num)

The VLOOKUP function searches the leftmost column of the **table array**. The leftmost column of the table_array is called the **table arguments**. In this example, the table arguments are made up of percentages (see Table 5-4). The VLOOKUP function uses the % of Quota value (called the lookup_value) in the record of a sales rep to search the leftmost column of the table array for a particular value and then returns the corresponding **table value** from the column indicated by the col_index_num value. In this example, the the grades are in the second or rightmost column.

Table 5-4 Typical Grade Table Modified for VLOOKUP Function

% OF QUOTA	GRADE
0	F
60%	D
70%	C
80%	B
93%	A

For the VLOOKUP function to work correctly, the table arguments must be in ascending sequence, because the VLOOKUP function will return a table value based on the lookup_value being less than or equal to the table arguments. Thus, if the % of Quota value is 76.70% (fourth record in list), then the VLOOKUP function returns a grade of C, because 76.70% is greater than or equal to 70% and less than 80%.

The steps on the next page create the grade table in the range L1:M7.

To Create a Lookup Table

1. Select column headings L and M. Point to the boundary on the right side of the column M heading above row 1 and then drag to the right until the ScreenTip indicates, Width: 11.00 (82 pixels).
2. Select cell L1 and then enter `Grade Table` as the table title.
3. With cell L1 selected, click the Font box arrow on the Formatting toolbar and then click Broadway (or a font of your choice) in the Font list. Click the Font Size box arrow on the Formatting toolbar and then click 14 in the Font Size list. Click the Bold button on the Formatting toolbar. Click the Font Color button arrow on the Formatting toolbar and then click Blue (column 6, row 2) on the Font Color palette. Drag through cell M1 and then click the Merge and Center button on the Formatting toolbar.
4. Select the range I8:J8. While holding down the CTRL key, point to the border of the range I8:J8 and drag to the range L2:M2 to copy the column headings, % of Quota and Grade.
5. Enter the table entries in Table 5-4 on the previous page in the range L3:M7. Select the range L3:M7, click the Bold button on the Formatting toolbar, and then click the Center button on the Formatting toolbar. Select cell J9 to deselect the range L3:M7.

Excel displays the grade table as shown in Figure 5-20.

More About

The VLOOKUP Function

A score that is outside the range of the table causes the VLOOKUP function to return an error message (#N/A) to the cell. For example, any % of Quota score less than zero in column I of Figure 5-19 on page EX 322 would result in the error message #N/A being assigned to the corresponding cell.

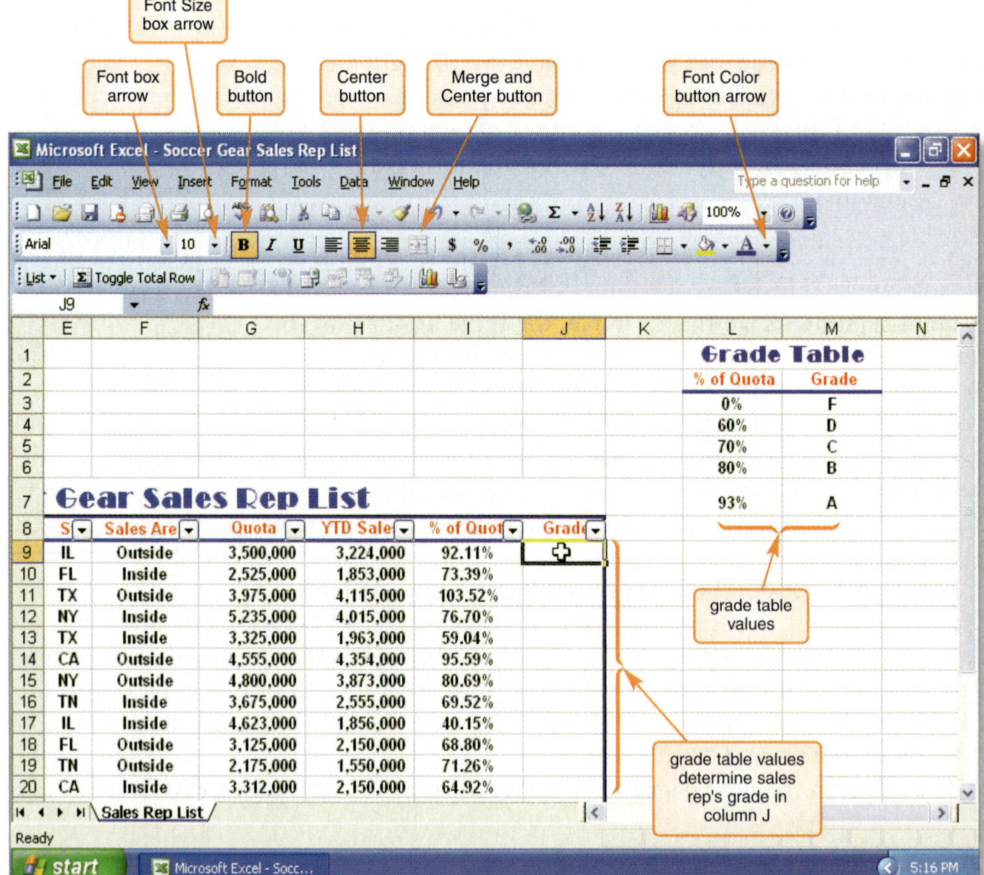

FIGURE 5-20

The following steps show how to use the VLOOKUP function and the grade table to determine the letter grade for each sales rep based on the sales rep's % of Quota value.

To Use the VLOOKUP Function to Determine Letter Grades

1

- **With cell J9 selected, type** `=vlookup (i9, $1$3:$m$7, 2` **as the cell entry.**

Excel displays the VLOOKUP function in the cell and in the formula bar (Figure 5-21). In this case, cell i9 is the lookup_value; l3:m7 is the table_array; and 2 is the col_index_num in the table_array.

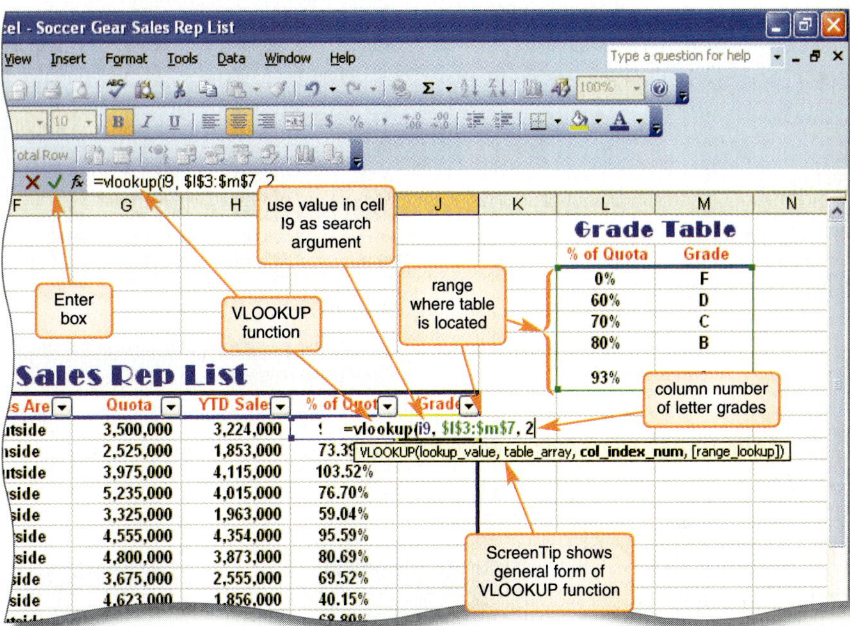

FIGURE 5-21

2

- **Click the Enter box.**

The VLOOKUP function returns a grade of B to cell J9 for a % of Quota value of 92.11% in cell I9 (Figure 5-22).

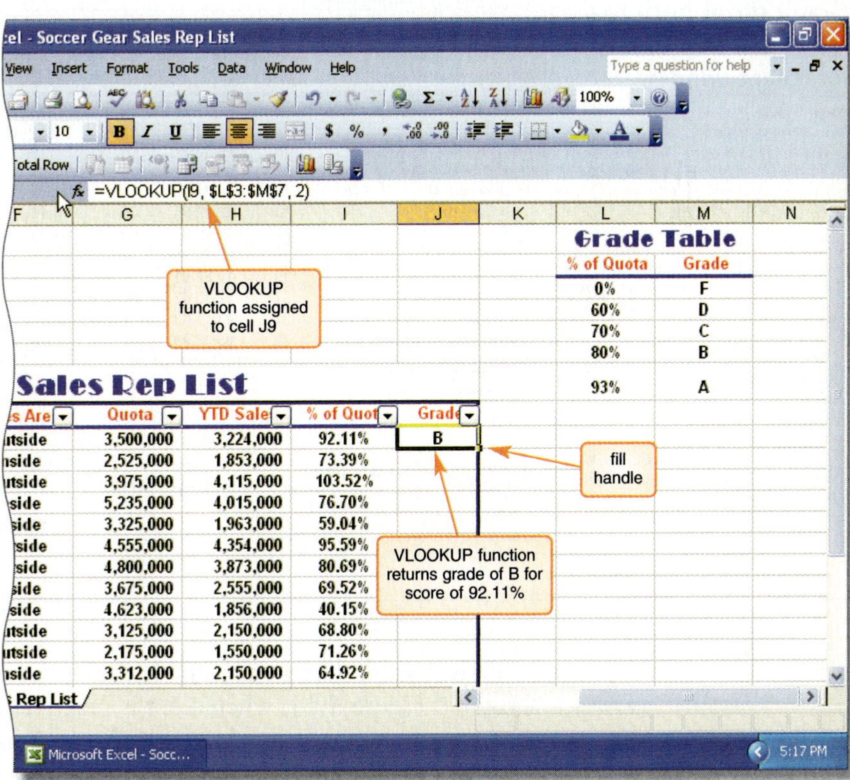

FIGURE 5-22

3

• **With cell J9 selected, drag the fill handle through cell J20 to copy the function to the range J10:J20.**

The VLOOKUP function uses the grade table in columns L and M to look up the letter grades for the corresponding % of Quota values in column I (Figure 5-23). The VLOOKUP function then returns the grades to column J.

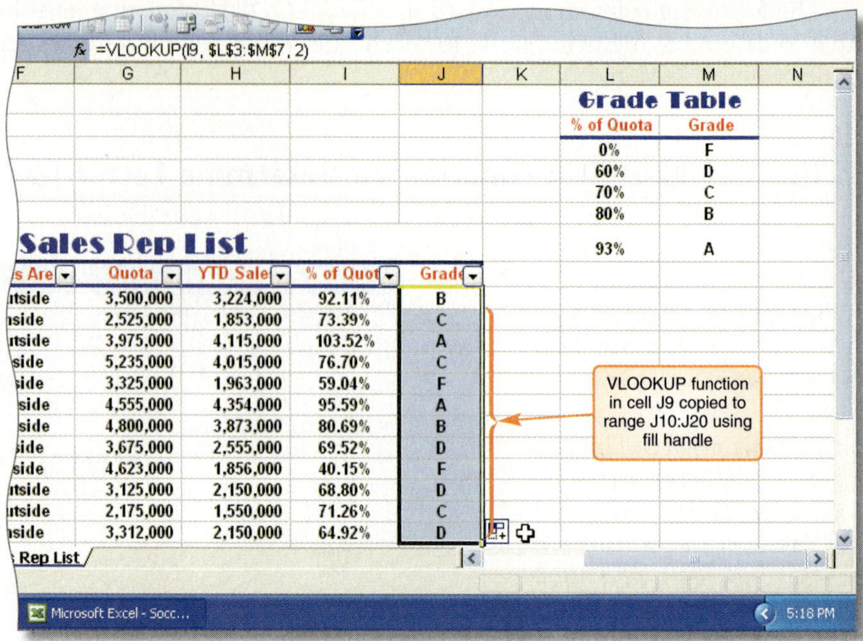

FIGURE 5-23

4

• **Select cell A22 to deselect the range J9:J20.**

• **Scroll down until row 7 is at the top of the worksheet window.**

The entries for the Soccer Gear Sales Rep list are complete (Figure 5-24).

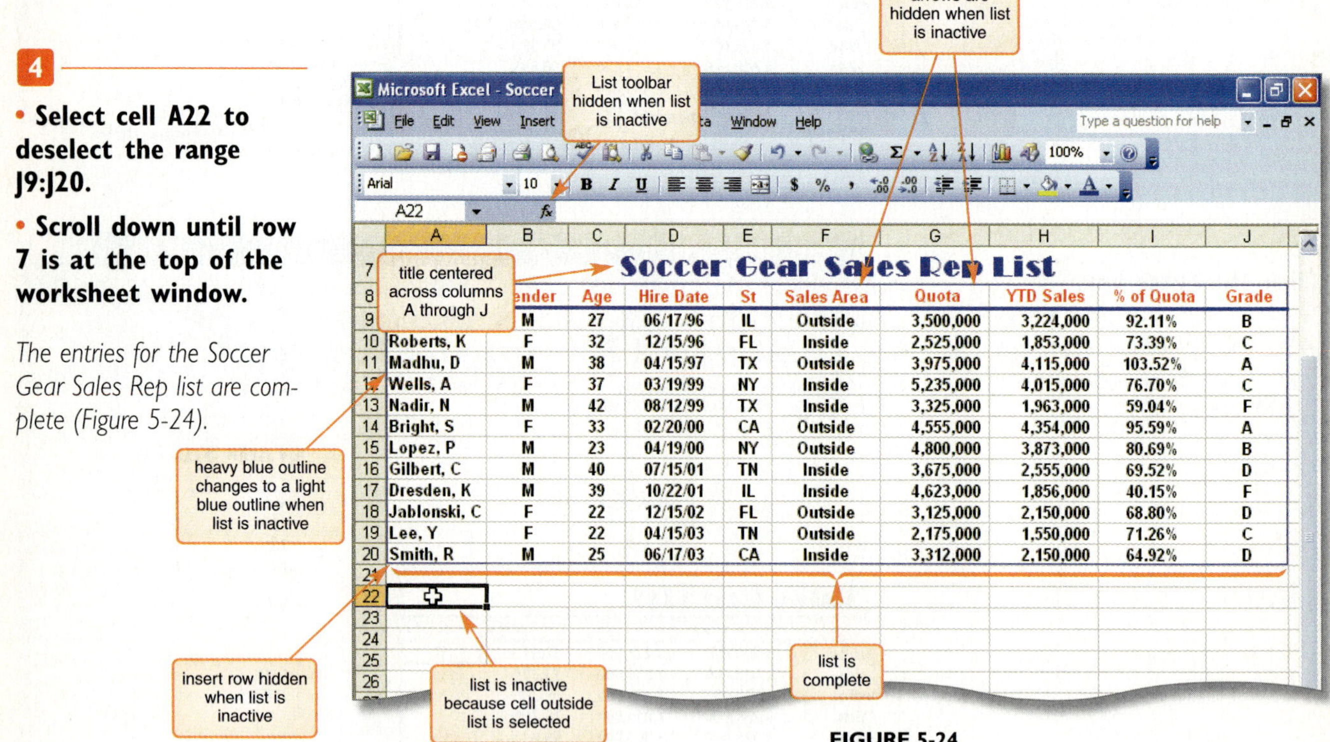

FIGURE 5-24

When you select a cell outside the list as in Step 4, the list becomes inactive. As shown in Figure 5-24, when a list is inactive, Excel hides the List toolbar, changes the heavy blue border outlining the list to a light blue outline border, hides the arrows to the right of the column headings, and hides the insert row. If you select a cell within the list as in Figure 5-23, then the list becomes active and Excel shows the List toolbar, displays the arrows next to the column headings, shows the insert row, and draws a heavy blue outline around the list.

As shown in Figure 5-24, any % of Quota value below 60 in column I returns a grade of F in column J. The eighth record (Gilbert in row 16) receives a grade of D because its % of Quota value is 69.52%. A % of Quota value of 70% is required to move up to the next letter grade. The next to the last record (Lee in row 19) receives a grade of C because her % of Quota value is 71.26%, which is equal to or greater than 70% and less than 80%.

From column J in Figure 5-24, you can see that the VLOOKUP function is not searching for a table argument that matches the lookup_value exactly. The VLOOKUP function begins the search at the top of the table and works downward. As soon as it finds the first table argument greater than the lookup_value, it returns the previous table value. For example, when it searches the table with the fourth record (Wells in row 12), it determines the % of Quota is less than 80% in the first column in the grade table and returns the grade of C from the second column in the grade table, which actually corresponds to 70% in the table. The letter grade of F is returned for any value greater than or equal to 0 (zero) and less than 60. A score less than 0 returns an error message (#N/A) to the cell assigned the VLOOKUP function.

It is most important that you use absolute cell references ($) for the table_array ($L$3:$M$7) in the VLOOKUP function (see the entry in the formula bar shown in Figure 5-22 on page EX 325) or Excel will adjust the cell references when you copy the function down through column L in Step 3. This will cause unexpected results in column J.

Other Ways

1. Click Insert Function box in formula bar, click Or select a category box arrow, click Lookup & Reference, click VLOOKUP in Select a function list
2. Click AutoSum button arrow on Standard toolbar, click More Functions, click Or select a category box arrow, click Lookup & Reference, click VLOOKUP in Select a function list
3. On Insert menu click Function, click Or select a category box arrow, click Lookup & Reference, click VLOOKUP in Select a function list
4. In Voice command mode, say "Insert Function", [select Lookup & Reference category], say "Vlookup, OK"

Guidelines for Creating a List in Excel

When you create a list in Excel, you should follow some basic guidelines, as listed in Table 5-5.

Table 5-5 Guidelines for Creating a List in Excel

LIST SIZE AND WORKBOOK LOCATION

1. Do not enter more than one list per worksheet.
2. Maintain at least one blank row between a list and other worksheet entries.
3. A list can have a maximum of 256 fields and 65,536 records on a worksheet.
4. If you name the list, name it Database.

COLUMN HEADINGS (FIELD NAMES)

1. Place column headings (field names) in the first row of the list.
2. Do not use blank rows or rows with dashes to separate the column headings (field names) from the data.
3. Apply a different format to the column headings and the data. For example, bold the column headings and format the data below the column headings using a regular style.
4. Column headings (field names) can be up to 32,767 characters in length. The column headings should be meaningful.

CONTENTS OF LIST

1. Each column should have similar data. For example, Hire Date should be in the same column for all sales reps.
2. Format the data to improve readability, but do not vary the format of the data in a column.

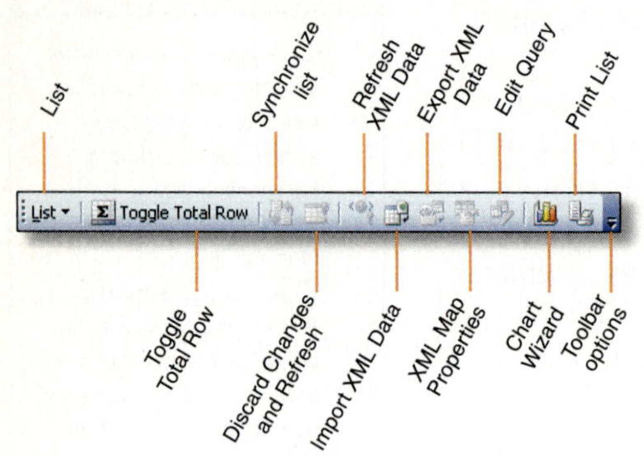

FIGURE 5-25

The List Toolbar

Earlier in this project when the list was created, the List toolbar was docked below the Formatting toolbar at the top of the Excel window. Excel displays this toolbar whenever a list is active, unless you choose to hide the toolbar. This section explores the use of the List toolbar, which includes several buttons that simplify working with lists. Figure 5-25 identifies the buttons on the List toolbar. Some of the buttons, such as those related to XML, are beyond the scope of this project. For this project, the most useful buttons on the List toolbar are the List, Toggle Total Row, and Print List buttons.

The List Button

The List button on the List toolbar displays a menu of commands (Figure 5-26) that primarily are used to maintain the list. For example, the Insert command is used to add rows or columns to the list. The Delete command is used to delete rows or columns from the list. The Sort command is used to sort the list. Sorting is discussed later in this project. The Form command on the List button menu causes Excel to display the data form. This is the same form used earlier to add records to the list.

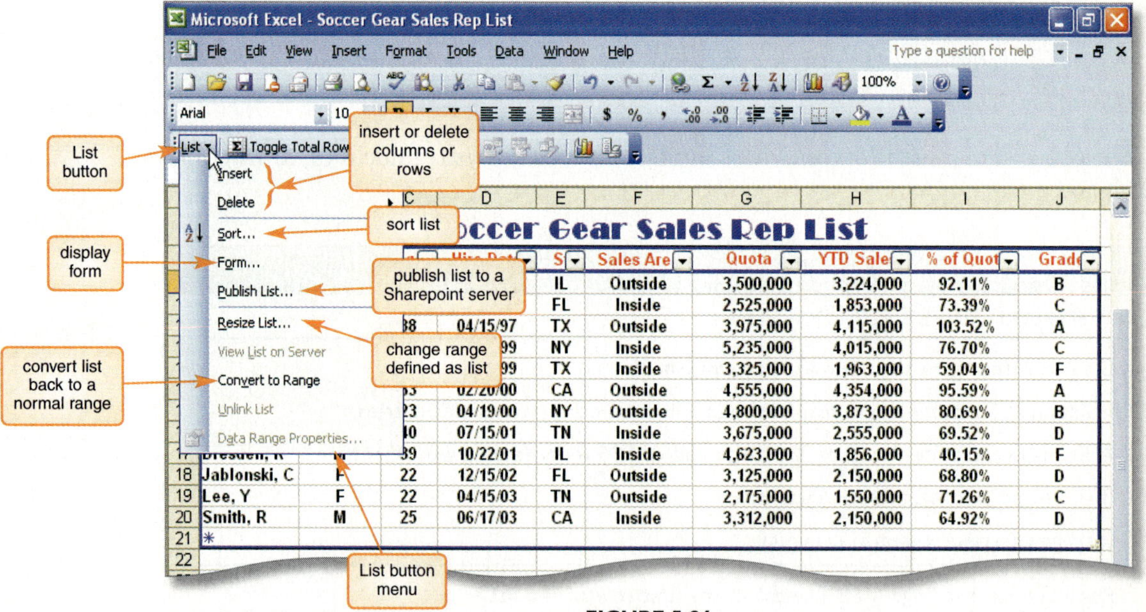

FIGURE 5-26

The Publish List command on the List button menu in Figure 5-26 is used to publish the list to a Sharepoint server (see the feature following Project 6 in this book for an example of publishing to a Sharepoint server). The Resize List command resizes the list by changing the range defined as a list. The Convert to Range command converts the list back to a normal range in the worksheet.

The Toggle Total Row Button

A very useful button on the List toolbar is the Toggle Total Row button. When you click this button, Excel adds a row below the insert row called the **total row**. When you click the button again, Excel hides the total row. Within the total row, it sums the values in the rightmost column of the list, if the values are numeric. If the values in the rightmost column of the list are text, then Excel counts the number of records. For example, in Figure 5-27, the 12 in cell J22 on the right side of the total row is a count of the number of sales rep records. Excel provides additional computations for the total row as shown in the following steps.

To Use the Toggle Total Row Button

1

- **Select cell A9 to make the list active. Click the Toggle Total button on the List toolbar.**

Excel adds the total row to the list and displays the record count in the rightmost column of the list (Figure 5-27). If a numeric column, such as Quota, had been on the far right, then Excel would have displayed the sum of the numbers.

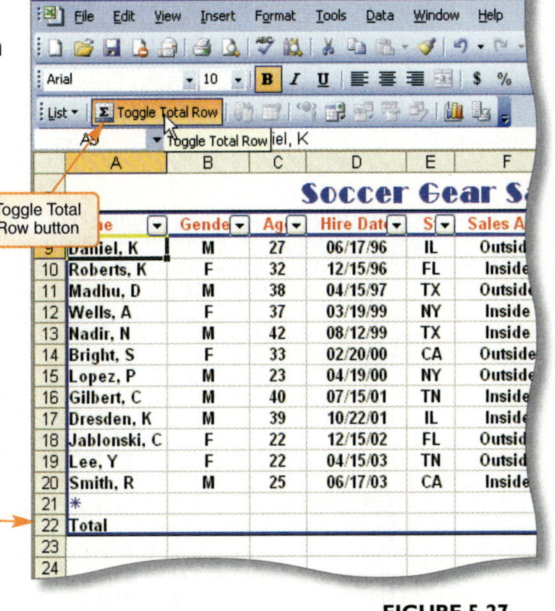

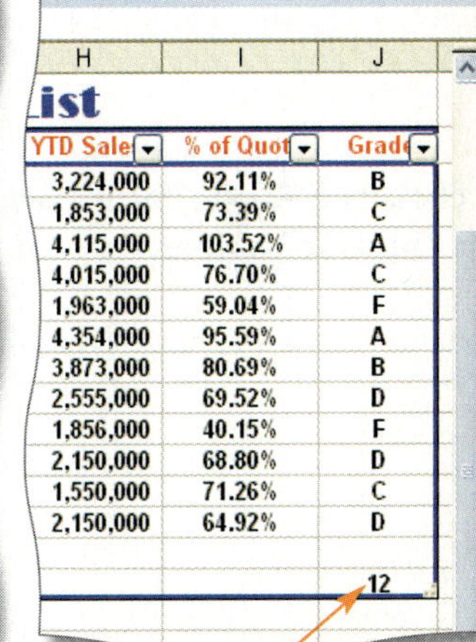

FIGURE 5-27

2

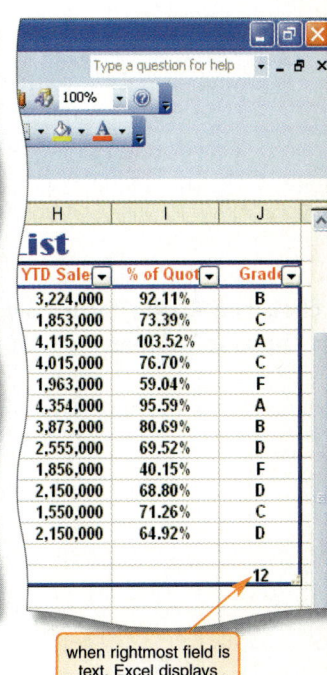

- **Select cell H22.**
- **When Excel displays an arrow on the right side of the cell, click the arrow.**

Excel displays a list of available statistical functions (Figure 5-28).

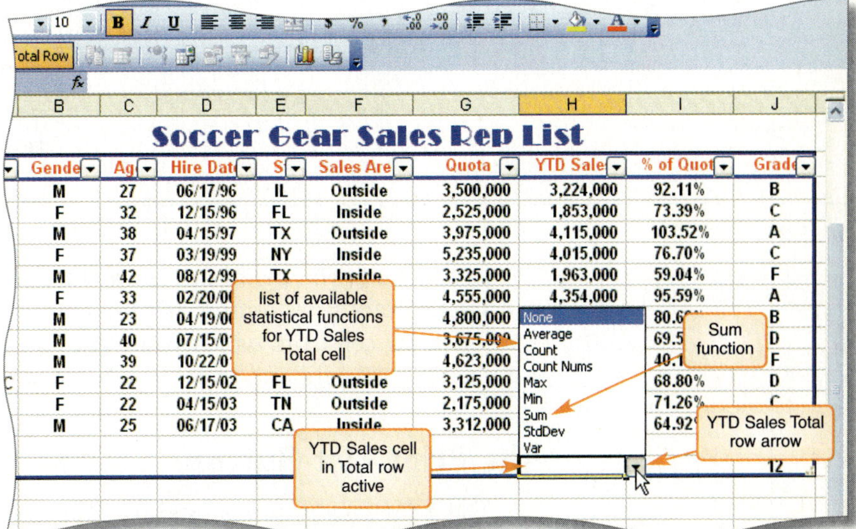

FIGURE 5-28

3

- **Click Sum in the list.**
- **Select cell G22, click the arrow on the right side of the cell, and then click Sum in the list.**
- **Select cell C22, click the arrow on the right side of the cell, and then click Average in the list.**
- **Select cell A9.**

Excel displays the four totals in row 22 (Figure 5-29).

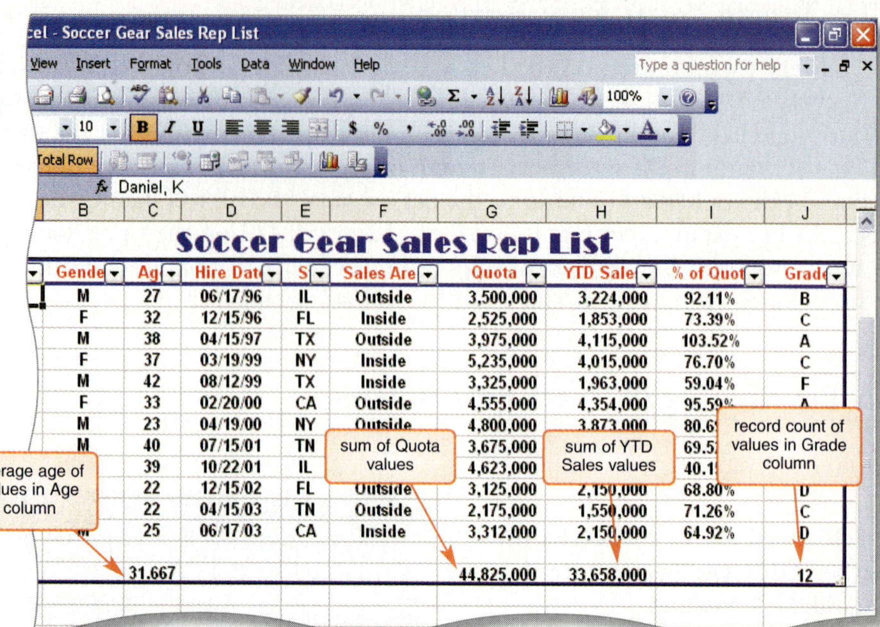

FIGURE 5-29

4

- **Click the Toggle Total Row button on the List toolbar.**

Excel hides the total row (Figure 5-30).

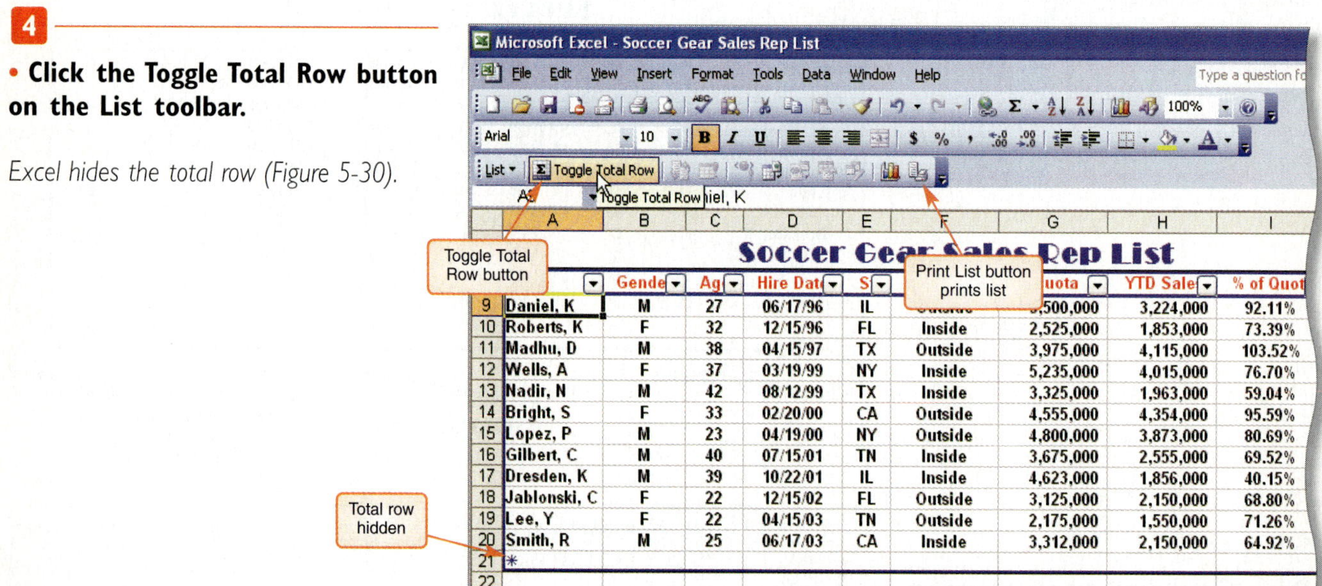

FIGURE 5-30

At any time, you again can show the total row with the four totals by clicking the Toggle Total Row button. If you want to remove one of the totals from the total line, click the cell from which you want to remove the total, click the arrow on the right side of the cell, and then click None in the list.

The Print List Button

The Print List button is used to print the list. If the total row is visible, then it prints it as part of the list. The following steps show how to toggle on the total row, print the list, and then toggle off the total row.

To Use the Print List Button

1. **With the list active, click the Toggle Total Row button to show the total row.**
2. **Click the Print List button on the List toolbar.**
3. **Click the Toggle Total Row button to hide the total row.**

Excel prints the list as shown in Figure 5-31.

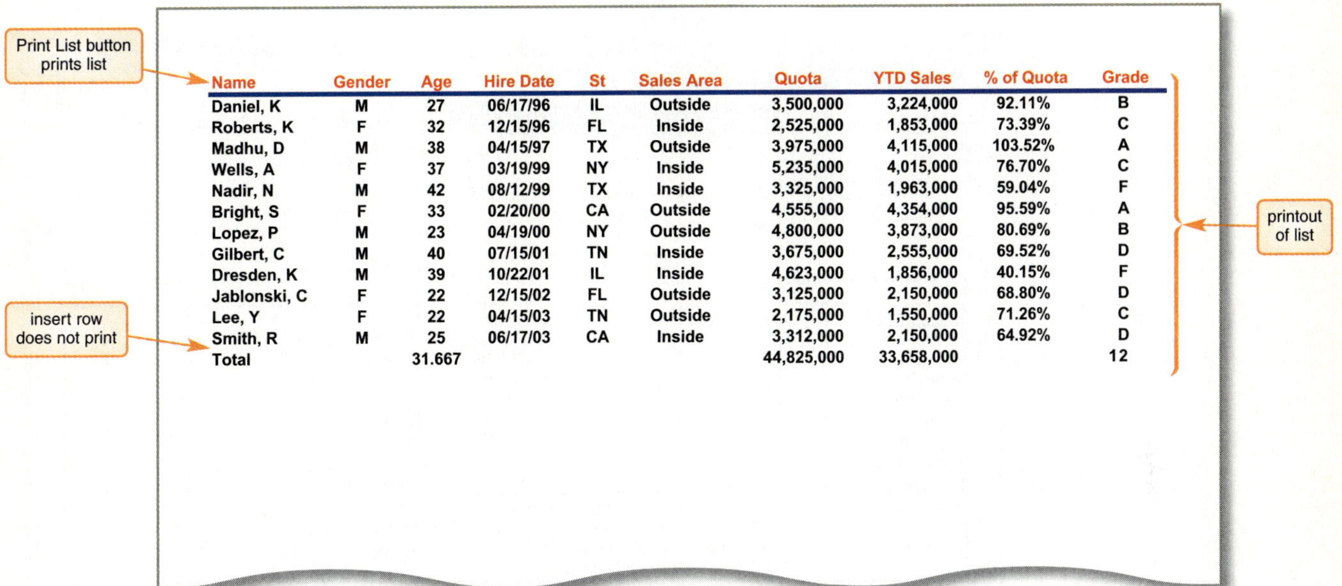

Name	Gender	Age	Hire Date	St	Sales Area	Quota	YTD Sales	% of Quota	Grade
Daniel, K	M	27	06/17/96	IL	Outside	3,500,000	3,224,000	92.11%	B
Roberts, K	F	32	12/15/96	FL	Inside	2,525,000	1,853,000	73.39%	C
Madhu, D	M	38	04/15/97	TX	Outside	3,975,000	4,115,000	103.52%	A
Wells, A	F	37	03/19/99	NY	Inside	5,235,000	4,015,000	76.70%	C
Nadir, N	M	42	08/12/99	TX	Inside	3,325,000	1,963,000	59.04%	F
Bright, S	F	33	02/20/00	CA	Outside	4,555,000	4,354,000	95.59%	A
Lopez, P	M	23	04/19/00	NY	Outside	4,800,000	3,873,000	80.69%	B
Gilbert, C	M	40	07/15/01	TN	Inside	3,675,000	2,555,000	69.52%	D
Dresden, K	M	39	10/22/01	IL	Inside	4,623,000	1,856,000	40.15%	F
Jablonski, C	F	22	12/15/02	FL	Outside	3,125,000	2,150,000	68.80%	D
Lee, Y	F	22	04/15/03	TN	Outside	2,175,000	1,550,000	71.26%	C
Smith, R	M	25	06/17/03	CA	Inside	3,312,000	2,150,000	64.92%	D
Total		31.667				44,825,000	33,658,000		12

FIGURE 5-31

When the list is active, you also can print the list by selecting a cell within the list and then clicking the Print button on the Standard toolbar or clicking the Print command on the File menu. If you select a cell outside the list to make the list inactive and then use the Print button or Print command, then Excel will print the entire worksheet, which would include the list and any additional entries, such as the list title in row 7.

Note that Excel does not print the insert row when it prints the list. The total row prints immediately after the last record as shown in Figure 5-31. If the total row is hidden, then it does not print as part of the list.

> *More About*
>
> **Sensitive Information in a List**
>
> If you have a list with one or more columns of sensitive information, such as salary information, you can hide the columns by selecting them and then pressing CTRL+0. Next, password protect the worksheet. To view the hidden columns, unprotect the worksheet, select the two adjacent columns, and then press CTRL+SHIFT+RIGHT PARENTHESIS.

Using a Data Form to View Records and Change Data

At any time while the list on the worksheet is active, you can use the Form command on the Data menu to display records, add new records, delete records, and change the data in records. When a data form initially is opened, Excel displays the first record in the list. The steps on the next page show how to display the sixth record in the list using a data form.

To View a Record Using a Data Form

1. **With the list active, click the List button on the List toolbar and then click Form on the List button menu (Figure 5-26 on page EX 328).**
2. **When Excel displays the data form, click the Find Next button until the sixth record in the list appears on the data form.**

Excel displays the sixth record in the list on the data form (Figure 5-32).

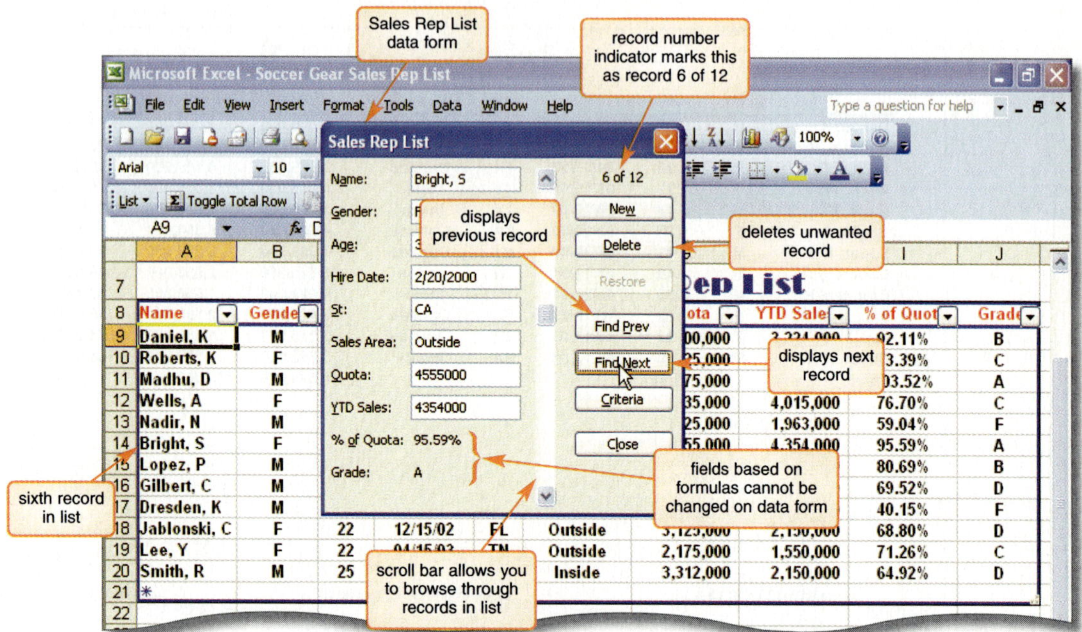

FIGURE 5-32

Each time you click the Find Next button, Excel advances to the next record in the list. You also can press the ENTER key or the DOWN ARROW key to advance to the next record. To go back to a previous record, you can use the Find Prev button, the SHIFT+ENTER keys, or the UP ARROW key. You also can use the vertical scroll bar in the middle of the data form to browse through and move among records.

To change data in a record using a data form, you first must display it on the data form. Next, you select the fields to change. Finally, you use the DOWN ARROW key or the ENTER key to confirm or enter the field changes. If you change field values on a data form and then select the Find Next button to move to the next record without entering the field changes, Excel will not make these changes.

To add a new record, click the New button in the data form. Excel will display a blank data form. Next, the data is entered for the record and then the New button on the data form is clicked. Excel automatically adds the new record to the bottom of the list and increases the size of the range assigned to the list. To delete a record, you first display it on a data form and then click the Delete button. Excel automatically moves all records below the deleted record up one row and appropriately redefines the range assigned to the list.

Sorting a List

The data in a list is easier to work with and more meaningful if the records are arranged sequentially based on one or more fields. Arranging records in a specific sequence is called **sorting**. Data is in **ascending sequence** if it is in order from lowest to highest, earliest to most recent, or alphabetically from A to Z. For example, the records in the Soccer Gear Sales Rep list were entered in order from the earliest hire date to the most recent hire date. Thus, the list shown in Figure 5-33 is sorted in ascending sequence by hire date. Data is in **descending sequence** if it is sorted from highest to lowest, most recent to earliest, or alphabetically from Z to A.

You can sort data in a list using one of the following techniques:

1. Select a cell in the field on which to sort and then click the Sort Ascending button or Sort Descending button on the Standard toolbar.
2. With the list active, click the column heading arrow in the column on which to sort and then click Sort Ascending or Sort Descending in the list.
3. Use the Sort command on the Data menu.
4. Use the Sort command on the List button menu.

The first two sort techniques usually are used when you want to sort on one field. The last two sort techniques are used when you want to sort on multiple fields. The field or fields you select to sort the records are called **sort keys**.

> **More About**
>
> **Sorting**
>
> Excel uses the following order of priority: numbers from smallest to largest positive, (space), special characters, text, (blanks). For example, the sort order is: 0 1 2 3 4 5 6 7 8 9 (space) ! " # $ % & ( ) * , . / : ; ? @ [\ ] ^ _ ` { | } ~ + < = > A B C D E F G H I J K L M N O P Q R S T U V W X Y Z (blanks).

> **More About**
>
> **Sorting Hidden Columns and Rows**
>
> When you sort rows, the data in hidden rows is not sorted, but the data in hidden columns is sorted. It is recommended that you unhide any hidden rows and columns before you sort.

Sorting a List in Ascending Sequence by Name Using the Sort Ascending Button

The following example shows how to sort the list in ascending sequence by name using the Sort Ascending button on the Standard toolbar.

To Sort a List in Ascending Sequence by Name Using the Sort Ascending Button

1

- **Select cell A9 and then point to the Sort Ascending button on the Standard toolbar (Figure 5-33).**

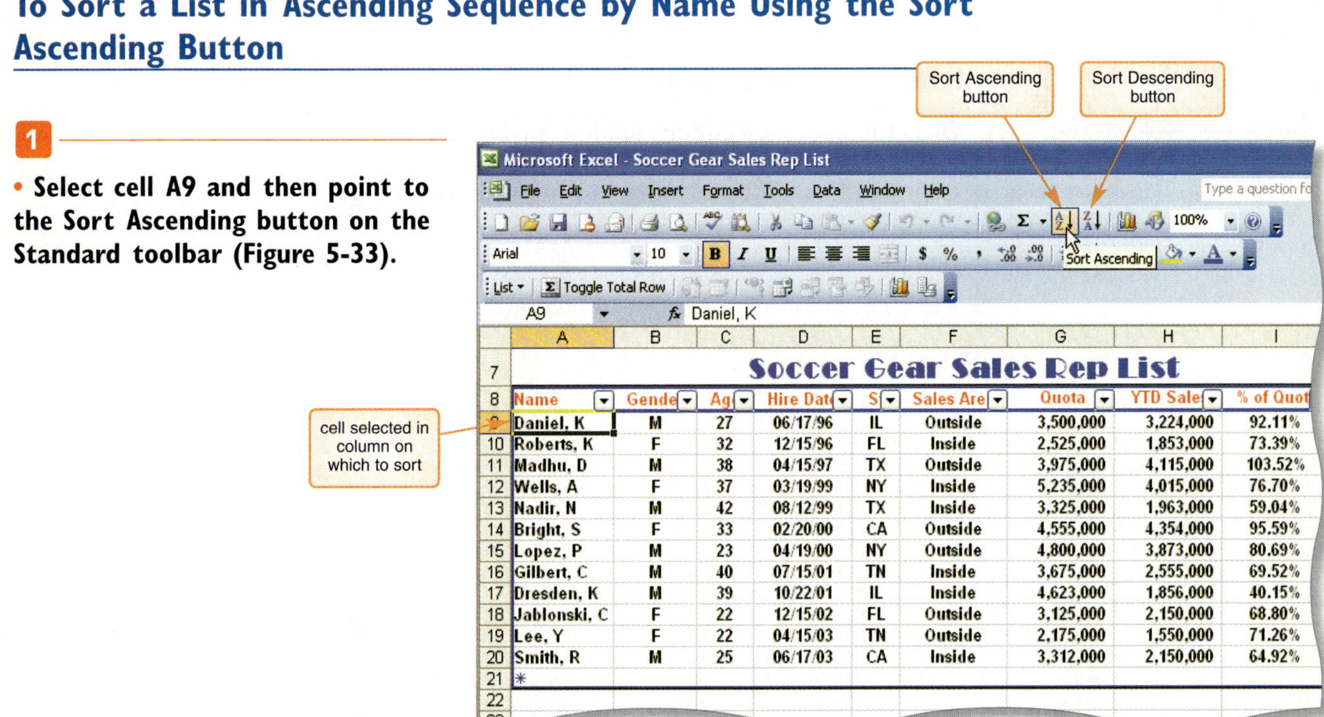

FIGURE 5-33

2

- **Click the Sort Ascending button.**

Excel sorts the sales rep list in ascending sequence by name (Figure 5-34).

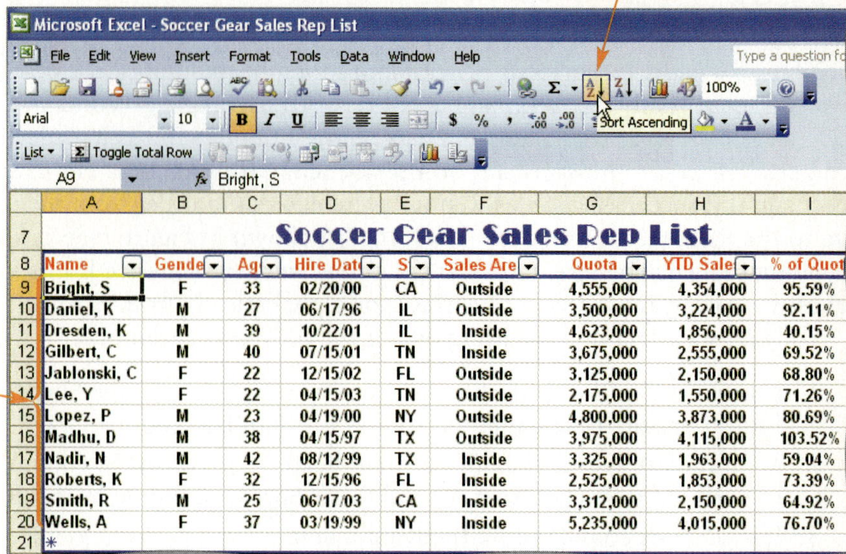

Name	Gender	Age	Hire Date	State	Sales Area	Quota	YTD Sales	% of Quota
Bright, S	F	33	02/20/00	CA	Outside	4,555,000	4,354,000	95.59%
Daniel, K	M	27	06/17/96	IL	Outside	3,500,000	3,224,000	92.11%
Dresden, K	M	39	10/22/01	IL	Inside	4,623,000	1,856,000	40.15%
Gilbert, C	M	40	07/15/01	TN	Inside	3,675,000	2,555,000	69.52%
Jablonski, C	F	22	12/15/02	FL	Outside	3,125,000	2,150,000	68.80%
Lee, Y	F	22	04/15/03	TN	Outside	2,175,000	1,550,000	71.26%
Lopez, P	M	23	04/19/00	NY	Outside	4,800,000	3,873,000	80.69%
Madhu, D	M	38	04/15/97	TX	Outside	3,975,000	4,115,000	103.52%
Nadir, N	M	42	08/12/99	TX	Inside	3,325,000	1,963,000	59.04%
Roberts, K	F	32	12/15/96	FL	Inside	2,525,000	1,853,000	73.39%
Smith, R	M	25	06/17/03	CA	Inside	3,312,000	2,150,000	64.92%
Wells, A	F	37	03/19/99	NY	Inside	5,235,000	4,015,000	76.70%

FIGURE 5-34

Other Ways

1. On Data menu click Sort, select field in Sort by list, click Ascending, click OK button
2. Click column heading arrow of field on which to sort, click Sort Ascending
3. Click List button on List toolbar, click Sort, select field in Sort by list, click Ascending, click OK button
4. Press ALT+D, S
5. Click cell in column on which to sort, in Voice Command mode, say "Sort Ascending"

Sorting a List in Descending Sequence by Name Using the Sort Descending Button

The following steps show how to sort the records in descending sequence by name.

To Sort a List in Descending Sequence by Name Using the Sort Descending Button

1 **If necessary, select cell A9.**

2 **Click the Sort Descending button on the Standard toolbar.**

Excel sorts the sales rep list in descending sequence by name (Figure 5-35).

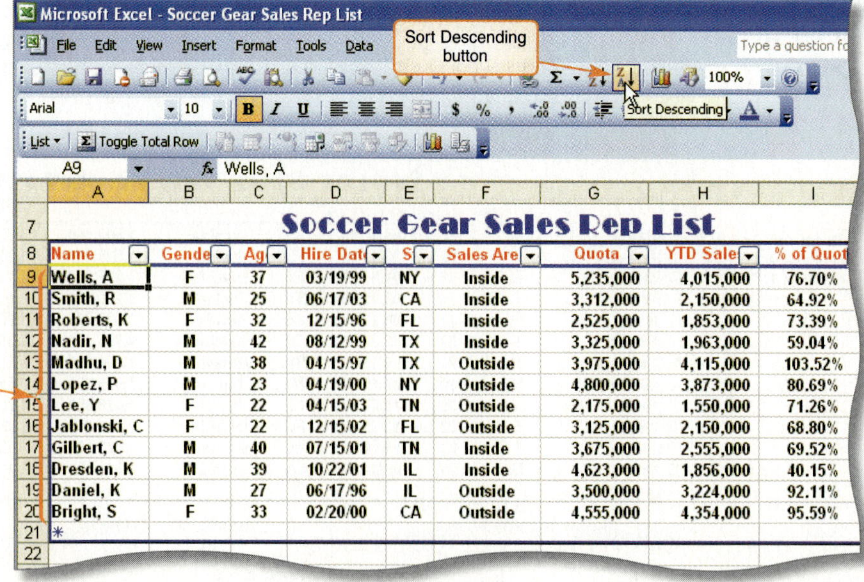

Name	Gender	Age	Hire Date	State	Sales Area	Quota	YTD Sales	% of Quota
Wells, A	F	37	03/19/99	NY	Inside	5,235,000	4,015,000	76.70%
Smith, R	M	25	06/17/03	CA	Inside	3,312,000	2,150,000	64.92%
Roberts, K	F	32	12/15/96	FL	Inside	2,525,000	1,853,000	73.39%
Nadir, N	M	42	08/12/99	TX	Inside	3,325,000	1,963,000	59.04%
Madhu, D	M	38	04/15/97	TX	Outside	3,975,000	4,115,000	103.52%
Lopez, P	M	23	04/19/00	NY	Outside	4,800,000	3,873,000	80.69%
Lee, Y	F	22	04/15/03	TN	Outside	2,175,000	1,550,000	71.26%
Jablonski, C	F	22	12/15/02	FL	Outside	3,125,000	2,150,000	68.80%
Gilbert, C	M	40	07/15/01	TN	Inside	3,675,000	2,555,000	69.52%
Dresden, K	M	39	10/22/01	IL	Inside	4,623,000	1,856,000	40.15%
Daniel, K	M	27	06/17/96	IL	Outside	3,500,000	3,224,000	92.11%
Bright, S	F	33	02/20/00	CA	Outside	4,555,000	4,354,000	95.59%

FIGURE 5-35

Sorting a List Using the Sort Command on a Column Heading List

When you design a list, it is good practice to include a field that you can use as a sort key to return the list to its original order. In the case of the Soccer Gear Sales Rep list, the records were entered in ascending sequence by hire date (column D). The following steps show how to return the records back to their original order in ascending sequence by hire date using the Sort Ascending command on a column heading list — in this case, the Hire Date list.

More About

Space on the Standard Toolbar

If you want to add a button to the Standard toolbar and have no space left, you can delete the Sort Descending button. To perform a descending sort, you instead can hold down the SHIFT key and then click the Sort Ascending button on the Standard toolbar.

To Sort a List Using the Sort Command on a Column Heading List

- **Click the Hire Date arrow as shown in Figure 5-36.**
- **Click Sort Ascending in the Hire Date list.**

Excel sorts the Soccer Gear Sales Rep list in ascending sequence by hire date. The list is again in its original order (Figure 5-33 on page EX 333).

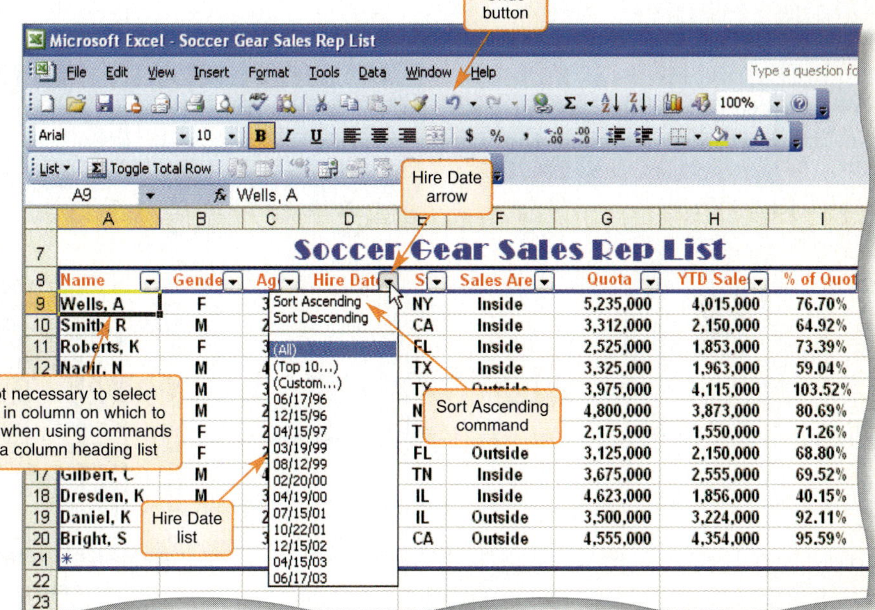

FIGURE 5-36

Other Ways

1. On Data menu click Sort, select field in Sort by list, click Ascending, click OK button
2. Select cell in column on which to sort, click Sort Ascending button on Standard toolbar
3. Click List button on List toolbar, click Sort, select field in Sort by list, click Ascending, click OK button
4. Press ALT+D, S
5. Click cell in column on which to sort, in Voice Command mode, say "Sort Ascending"

You also can undo a sort operation by performing one of the following actions: (1) click the Undo button on the Standard toolbar; or (2) click the Undo Sort command on the Edit menu. If you have sorted the list more than once, you can click the Undo button multiple times to undo the previous sorts.

Sorting a List on Multiple Fields Using the Sort Command on the List Button Menu

Excel allows you to sort on a maximum of three fields in a single sort operation. For instance, the sort example that follows uses the Sort command on the List button menu to sort the Soccer Gear Sales Rep list by quota (column G) within gender (column B) within sales area (column F). The Sales Area and Gender fields will be sorted in ascending sequence; the Quota field will be sorted in descending sequence.

More About

Sort Options

You can sort left to right across rows by clicking the Options button (Figure 5-38) and then clicking Sort left to right in the Orientation area. You also can click Case sensitive to sort lowercase letters ahead of the same capital letters for an ascending sort.

The phrase, sort by quota within gender within sales area, means that the records in the list first are arranged in ascending sequence by sales area (Inside and Outside). Within sales area, the records are arranged in ascending sequence by gender (M or F). Within gender, the records are arranged in descending sequence by the sales rep's quota. In this case, Sales Area is the **major sort key** (Sort by field), Gender is the **intermediate sort key** (first Then by field), and Quota is the **minor sort key** (second Then by field). Sorting a list on multiple fields is illustrated below.

To Sort a List on Multiple Fields Using the Sort Command on the List Button Menu

1

- **With a cell in the list active, click the List button on the List toolbar.**

Excel displays the List button menu (Figure 5-37).

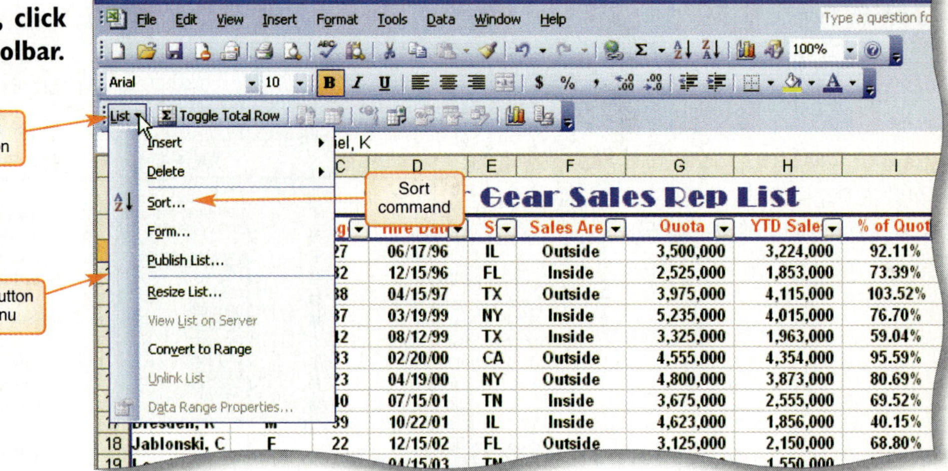

FIGURE 5-37

2

- **Click the Sort command on the List button menu.**
- **When Excel displays the Sort dialog box, click the Sort by box arrow.**

Excel selects the entire list, and displays the Sort dialog box. The Sort by list includes the field names in the list (Figure 5-38).

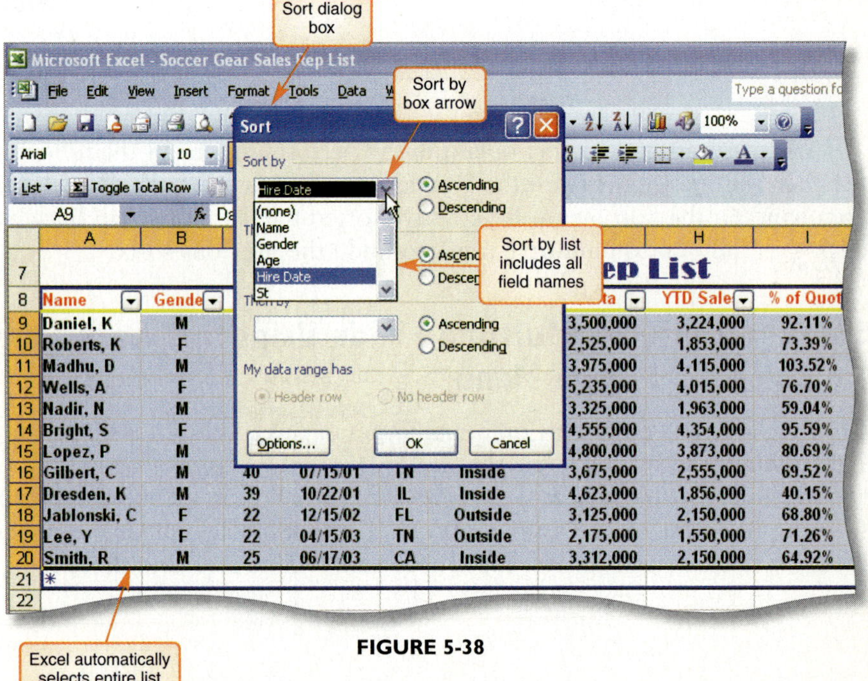

FIGURE 5-38

3

- **Scroll down the list and then click Sales Area. Click the first Then by box arrow and then click Gender.**
- **Click the second Then by box arrow and then click Quota.**
- **Click Descending in the second Then by area.**

Excel displays the Sort dialog box as shown in Figure 5-39. The list will be sorted by quota within gender within sales area.

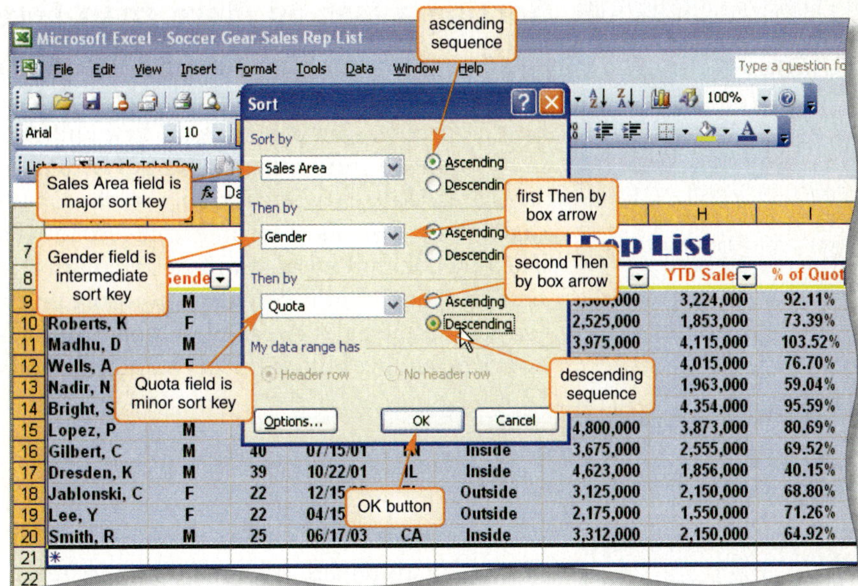

FIGURE 5-39

4

- **Click the OK button.**

Excel sorts the Soccer Gear Sales Rep list by quota within gender within sales area as shown in Figure 5-40.

5

- **After viewing the sorted list, click the Hire Date arrow and then click Sort Ascending in the Hire Date list to sort the list into its original sequence.**

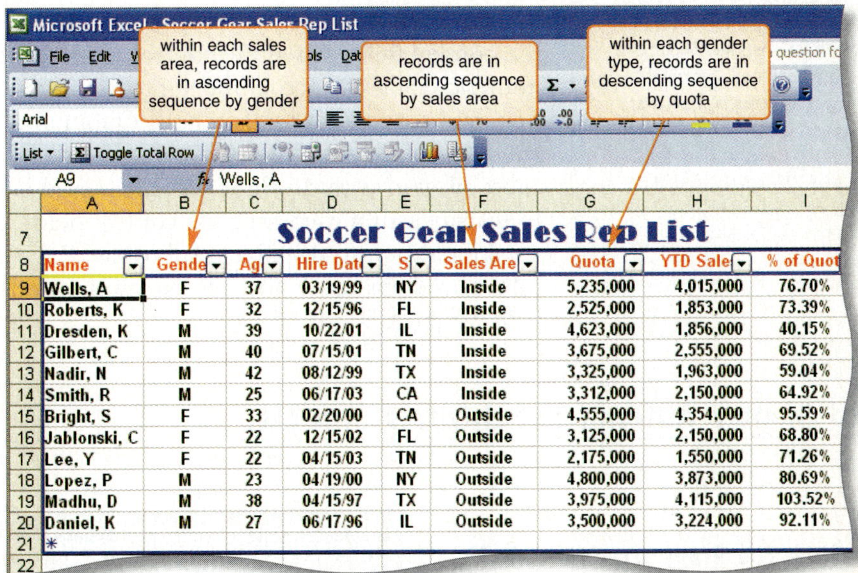

FIGURE 5-40

Other Ways

1. Click minor field column heading arrow, click Sort Descending, click intermediate field column heading arrow, click Sort Ascending, click major field column heading arrow, click Sort Ascending
2. Press ALT+D, S

As shown in Figure 5-40, Excel sorts the records in ascending sequence by sales area in column F. Within each sales area, the records are in ascending sequence by gender in column B. Finally, within gender, the records are sorted in descending sequence by the quotas in column G. Remember, if you make a mistake in a sort operation, you can return the records to their original order by clicking the Undo button on the Standard toolbar or by sorting the list by hire date.

Because Excel sorts the list using the current order of the records, the previous example could have been completed by sorting on one field at a time using the Sort buttons on the Standard toolbar or the Sort commands in the column heading lists, beginning with the minor sort key Quota.

More About

Sorting

Some spreadsheet specialists use the fill handle to create a series in an additional field in the list that is used only to reorder the records into their original sequence.

Sorting a List on More than Three Fields

To sort on more than three fields, you must sort the list two or more times. The most recent sort takes precedence. Hence, if you plan to sort on four fields, you sort on the three least important keys first and then sort on the major key. For example, if you want to sort on name (Name) within grade (Grade) within state (St) within sales area (Sales Area), click Sort on the Data menu. When Excel displays the Sort dialog box, you first sort on Name (second Then by column) within Grade (first Then by column) within St (Sort by column) and then click the OK button. After the first sort operation is complete, you sort on the Sales Area field by clicking one of the cells in the Sales Area column and then clicking the Sort Ascending button or Sort Descending button on the Standard toolbar.

Displaying Automatic Subtotals in a List

More About

Sort Algorithms

Numerous sort algorithms are used with computers, such as the Insertion sort, Selection sort, Bubble sort, Shaker sort, and Shell Sort. For additional information on sort algorithms, visit the Excel 2003 More About Web page (scsite.com/ex2003/more) and click Sort Algorithms.

Displaying **automatic subtotals** is a powerful tool for summarizing data in a list. To display automatic subtotals, Excel requires that you sort the list on the field on which the subtotals should be based and then use the Subtotals command on the Data menu. When Excel displays the Subtotal dialog box, you select the subtotal function you want to use.

The field on which you sort prior to invoking the Subtotals command is called the **control field.** When the control field changes, Excel displays a subtotal for the numeric fields selected in the Subtotal dialog box. For example, if you sort on the St field and request subtotals for the Quota and YTD Sales fields, then Excel recalculates the subtotal and grand total each time the St field changes. The most common subtotal used with the Subtotals command is the SUM function, which causes Excel to display a sum each time the control field changes.

In addition to displaying subtotals, Excel also creates an outline for the list. The following steps show how to display subtotals for the Quota field and YTD Sales field by state.

To Display Automatic Subtotals in a List

1

- **Click the State arrow in cell E8 and then click Sort Ascending in the State list.**
- **Select cell A7 to make the list inactive.**
- **Click Data on the menu bar.**

Excel sorts the list in ascending sequence by state and displays the Data menu (Figure 5-41).

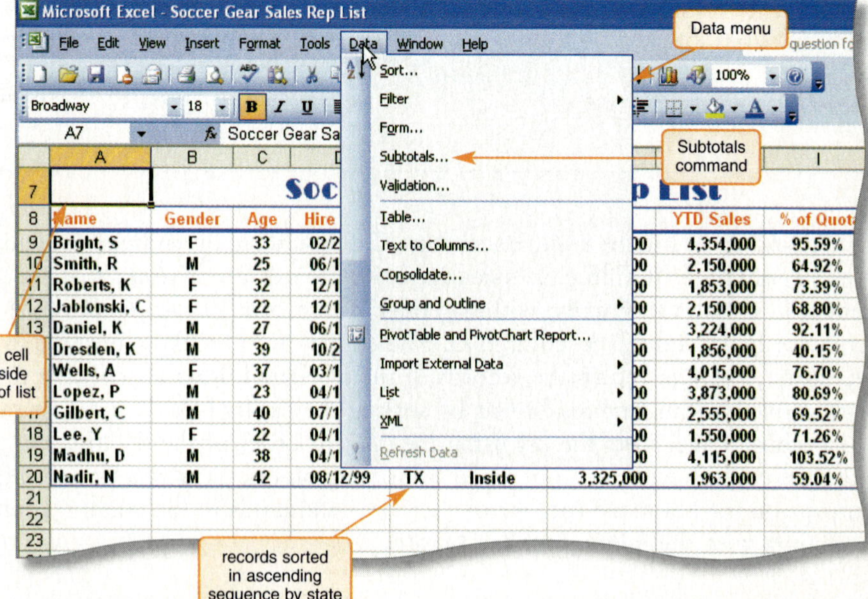

FIGURE 5-41

2

- **Click Subtotals on the Data menu.**
- **When Excel displays the Subtotal dialog box, click the At each change in box arrow and then click St.**
- **If necessary, select Sum in the Use function list.**
- **In the Add subtotal to list, click Grade to clear it and then click Quota and YTD Sales to select them.**

Excel displays the Subtotal dialog box (Figure 5-42). The At each change in box contains the St field. The Use function box contains Sum. In the Add subtotal to box, Quota and YTD Sales are the only selected fields.

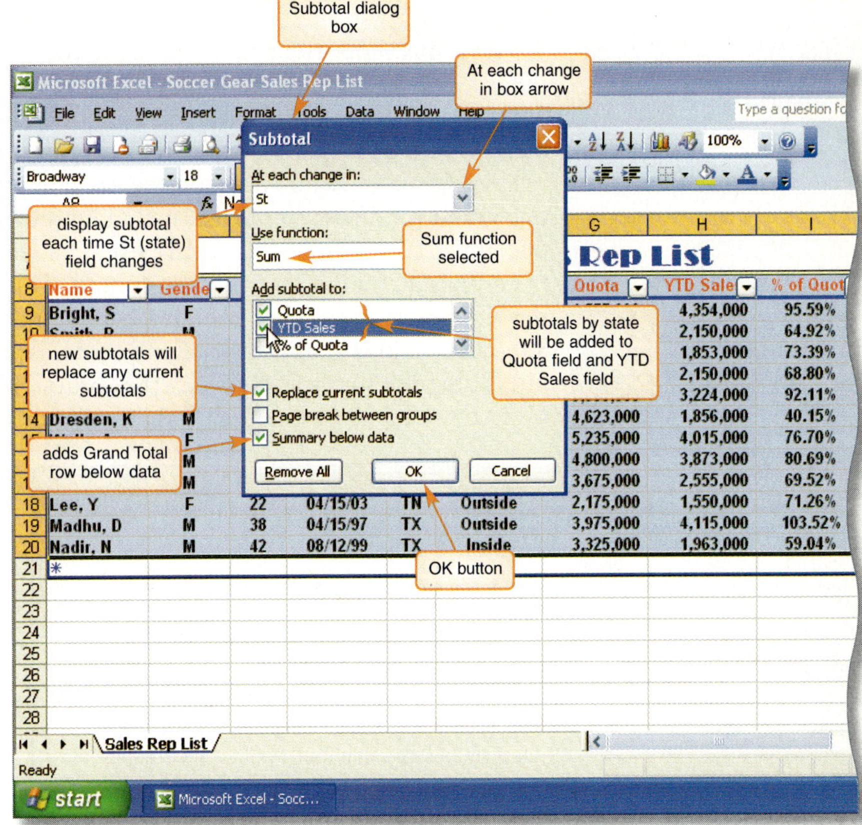

FIGURE 5-42

3

- **Click the OK button.**

Excel inserts seven new rows in the Soccer Gear Sales Rep list. Six of the new rows contain Quota and YTD Sales subtotals for each state (Figure 5-43). The seventh new row displays grand totals for the Quota and YTD Sales fields. Excel also outlines the list, which causes the Grade column (column J) to be outside the window.

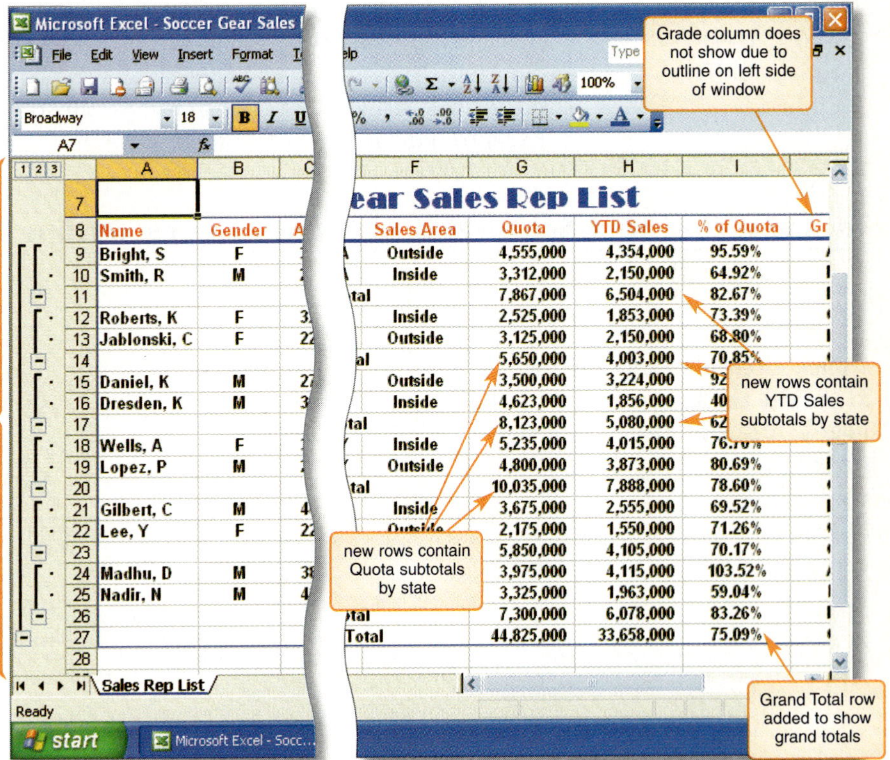

FIGURE 5-43

Other Ways

1. Press ALT+D, B
2. In Voice Command mode, say "[click cell in column to sort], Sort Ascending, Data, Subtotals, [select subtotal characteristics], OK"

> *More About*
>
> **Outlining**
>
> When you hide data using the outline feature, you can chart the resulting rows and columns as if they were adjacent to one another. Thus, in Figure 5-45 you can sort the quotas by state as an adjacent range, even though they are not in adjacent rows when Excel displays the worksheet without outlines.

It is most important that you make the list inactive by selecting a cell outside of the list, as was done in Step 1 on page EX 338, before attempting to invoke the Subtotals command. If the list is active, then the Subtotals command on the Data menu is dimmed (not available).

As shown in Figure 5-43 on the previous page, Excel adds six subtotal rows and one grand total row to the list, including one subtotal for each different state and one grand total row for the entire list. The names for each subtotal row are derived from the state names and appear in bold. Thus, the text, CA Total, in cell E11 identifies the subtotal row that contains Quota and YTD Sales totals for California. The Subotals command also instructs Excel to compute any formulas used on the detail lines using the totals and display the values on the toal lines. For example, I11 and G11 show the % of Quota and the grade for the entire state, respectively.

In Figure 5-42 on the previous page, the Use function box contains Sum, which instructs Excel to sum the fields selected in the Add subtotal to list. Additional functions, including complex subtotal functions, are available by clicking the Use function box arrow. The frequently used subtotal functions are listed in Table 5-6.

Table 5-6 Frequently Used Subtotal Functions

SUBTOTAL FUNCTION	DESCRIPTION
Sum	Sums the numbers in a column
Count	Counts the number of entries in a column
Average	Determines the average of numbers in a column
Max	Determines the maximum value in a column
Min	Determines the minimum value in a column

Zooming Out on a Subtotaled List and Using the Outline Feature

The following steps show how to use the Zoom box on the Standard toolbar to reduce the magnification of the worksheet so that all columns in the list appear in the worksheet window. The steps also illustrate how to use the outline features of Excel to hide and unhide data and totals.

To Zoom Out on a Subtotaled List and Use the Outline Feature

- **Click the Zoom box on the Standard toolbar, type** 90 **as the new value, and then press the ENTER key.**

Excel reduces the magnification of the worksheet so that all columns in the list appear (Figure 5-44).

with worksheet zoomed to 90%, all columns are displayed

Soccer Gear Sales Rep List

	Gender	Age	Hire Date	St	Sales Area	Quota	YTD Sales	% of Quota	Grade
ıt, S	F	33	02/20/00	CA	Outside	4,555,000	4,354,000	95.59%	A
h, R	M	25	06/17/03	CA	Inside	3,312,000	2,150,000	64.92%	D
				CA Total		7,867,000	6,504,000	82.67%	B
ts, K	F	32	12/15/96	FL	Inside	2,525,000	1,853,000	73.39%	C
ıski, C	F	22	12/15/02	FL	Outside	3,125,000	2,150,000	68.80%	D
				FL Total		5,650,000	4,003,000	70.85%	C
, K	M	27	06/17/96	IL	Outside	3,500,000	3,224,000	92.11%	B
en, K	M	39	10/22/01	IL	Inside	4,623,000	1,856,000	40.15%	F
				IL Total		8,123,000	5,080,000	62.54%	D
, A	F	37	03/19/99	NY	Inside	5,235,000	4,015,000	76.70%	C
z, P	M	23	04/19/00	NY	Outside	4,800,000	3,873,000	80.69%	B
				NY Total		10,		78.60%	C
rt, C	M	40	07/15/01	TN	Inside	3,		69.52%	D
	F	22	04/15/03	TN	Outside	2,		71.26%	C
				TN Total		5,		70.17%	C
, D	M	38	04/15/97	TX	Outside	3,975,000	4,115,000	103.52%	A
N	M	42	08/12/99	TX	Inside	3,325,000	1,963,000	59.04%	F
				TX Total		7,300,000	6,078,000	83.26%	B
				Grand Total		44,825,000	33,658,000	75.09%	C

sales reps as a group have attained 75.09% of quota

Grand Total row

FIGURE 5-44

2

- **Click the row level symbol 2 on the left side of the window.**

Excel hides all detail rows and displays only the subtotal and grand total rows (Figure 5-45).

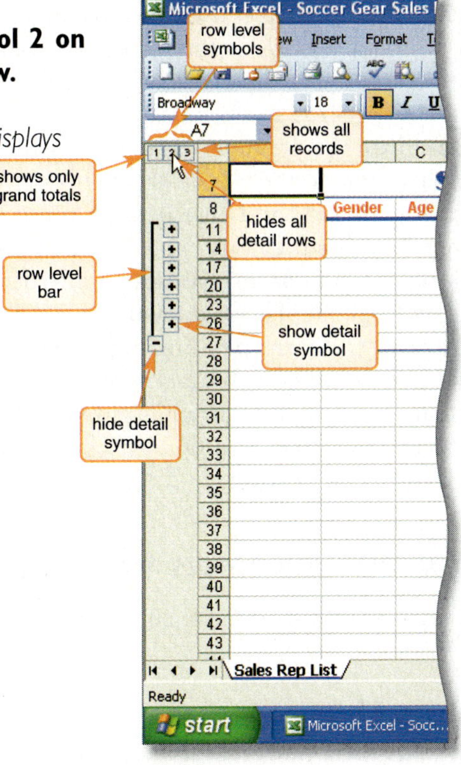

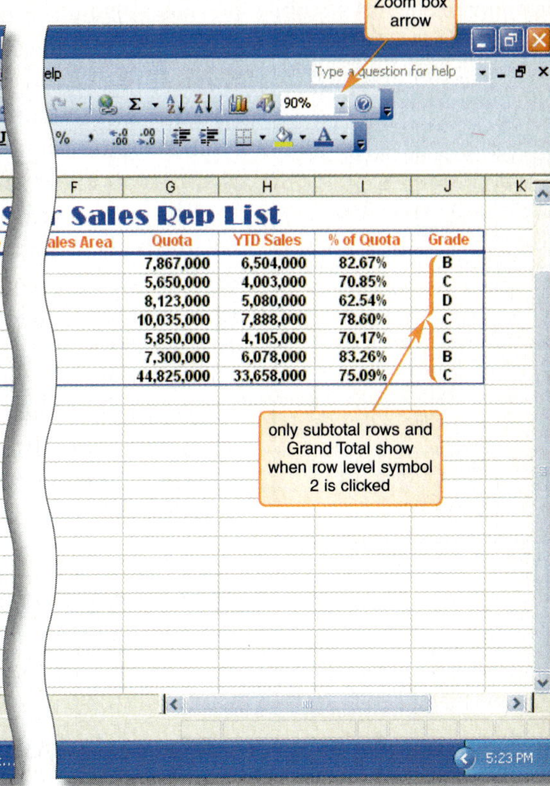

FIGURE 5-45

3

- **Click each of the lower three show detail symbols (+) on the left side of the window (Figure 5-45).**

Excel displays the detail records for NY, TN, and TX (Figure 5-46). The show detail symbols change to hide detail symbols.

4

- **Click the row level symbol 3 on the left side of the window to show all detail rows.**
- **Click the Zoom box arrow on the Standard toolbar and then click 100% in the Zoom list.**

Excel displays the worksheet at 100% magnification, with all detail rows showing (Figure 5-43 on page EX 339).

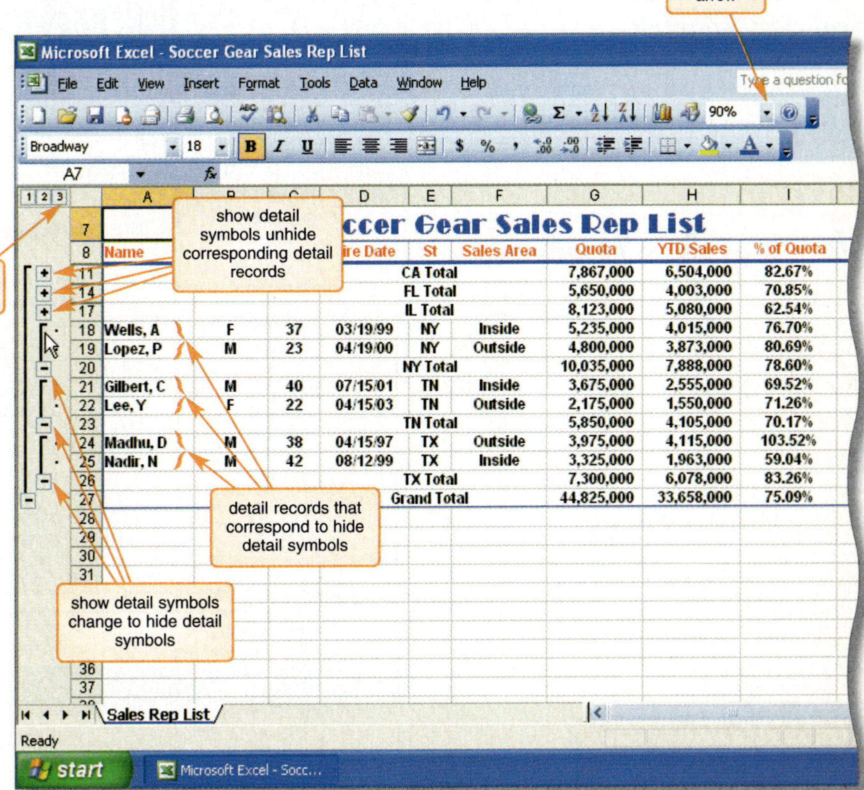

FIGURE 5-46

Other Ways

1. To group and outline, on Data menu point to Group and Outline, click Group on the Group and Outline submenu
2. To group and outline, press ALT+D, G, G
3. To zoom, on View menu click Zoom, click magnification, click OK button
4. To zoom, press ALT+V, Z, select magnification, press ENTER key
5. To group and outline, in Voice Command mode, say "Data, Group and Outline, Group"

By utilizing the **outlining features** of Excel, you quickly can hide and show detail rows. As described in Step 2 on the previous page, you can click the **row level symbols** to expand or collapse rows in the worksheet. Row level symbol 1, immediately below the Name box, hides all rows except the Grand Total row. Row level symbol 2 hides the detail records so the subtotal rows and Grand Total row appear as shown in Figure 5-45 on the previous page. Row level symbol 3 shows all rows.

The minus and plus signs to the left on the row level bar in Figure 5-45 are called the show detail symbol (+) and hide detail symbol (-). Clicking a **show detail symbol** (+), as in Step 3 on the previous page, instructs Excel to display the hidden detail records. Clicking the **hide detail symbol** (-) instructs Excel to hide the detail records within the row level bar. The **row level bar** indicates which detail records will be hidden if you click the corresponding hide detail symbol.

You do not have to invoke the Subtotals command to outline a worksheet. You can outline a worksheet by using the Group and Outline command on the Data menu. Usually, however, the Group and Outline command is only useful when you already have total lines in a worksheet.

Removing Automatic Subtotals from a List

The following steps show how remove subtotals from a list.

To Remove Automatic Subtotals from a List

1

• **Click Data on the menu bar and then click Subtotals.**

Excel selects the list and displays the Subtotal dialog box (Figure 5-47).

2

• **Click the Remove All button.**

Excel removes all subtotal and total rows and the outline from the list so it appears as shown previously in Figure 5-40 on page EX 337.

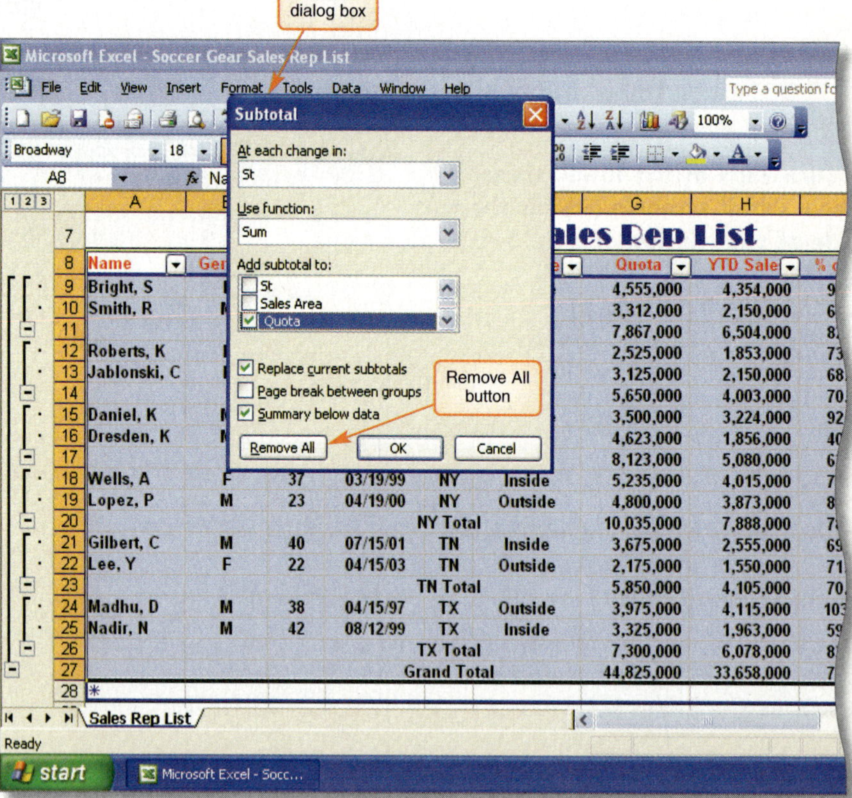

FIGURE 5-47

Other Ways

1. Press ALT+D, B, ALT+R
2. In Voice Command mode, say "Data, Subtotals, Remove All"

As shown in the previous sections, Excel makes it easy to add and remove subtotals from a list. Thus, you quickly can generate the type of information that users need from a list to help them make decisions about a company's direction.

The following steps sort the Soccer Gear Sales Rep list into its original sort order, sorted in ascending sequence by hire date.

To Sort a List into Its Original Order Using a Column Heading List

1. **Select cell A9 (or any cell in the list) to make the list active.**
2. **Click the Hire Date arrow and then click Sort Ascending in the Hire Date list.**

The records in the Soccer Gear Sales Rep list are sorted in ascending sequence by hire date.

More About

Outlining

The Group and Outline command on the Data menu is especially useful with large worksheets where the user can get lost in the sea of numbers. Outlining allows the user to hide the detail records to reduce the complexity of the worksheet.

Finding Records Using a Data Form

Finding records that pass a test that comprises certain conditions is called **querying** the list. You can use a data form to find and view records that meet certain conditions, or comparison criteria. **Comparison criteria** are one or more conditions that include the field names and entries in the corresponding boxes in a data form. For example, using comparison criteria entered in a data form, you can instruct Excel to find and display only those records that pass the test:

Gender = M AND Age > 38 AND Sales Area = Inside AND YTD Sales < 2,600,000

The same relational operators (=, <, >, >=, <=, and <>) used to formulate conditions in IF functions are used to enter comparison criteria in a data form.

For Excel to display a record in the data form, the record must pass all four parts of the test. Finding records that pass a test is useful for viewing specific records, as well as maintaining the list. When a record that passes the test shows in the data form, its fields can be changed or the record can be deleted from the list.

To find records in the list that pass a test that comprises comparison criteria, use the Find Prev and Find Next buttons together with the Criteria button in the data form. The steps on the next page illustrate how to use a data form to find records that pass the test using the comparison criteria described above.

Q&A

Q: How do companies with which you do not do business get your name in their contact list?

A: In many cases, a company's customer or contact list constitutes a major portion of its assets. Many companies sell their lists to non-competing companies, sometimes for millions of dollars. In fact, some companies' entire business involves creating and selling lists of names. Consequently, if one company has your name in its contact list, chances are good that several other companies do, too.

To Find Records Using a Data Form

1

- **Select cell A9 to activate the list.**
- **Click Data on the menu bar and then click Form.**

Excel displays the first record in the Soccer Gear Sales Rep list in the data form (Figure 5-48).

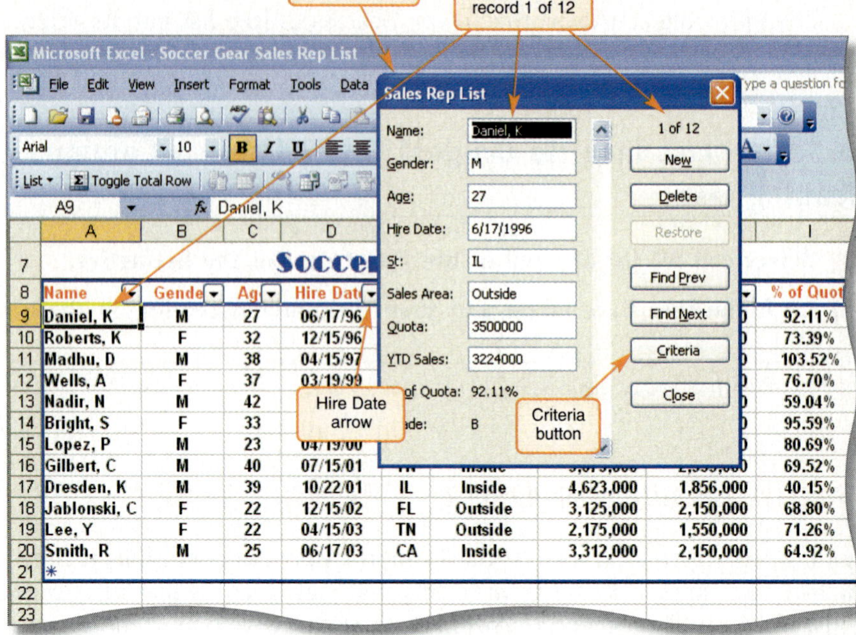

FIGURE 5-48

2

- **Click the Criteria button in the data form.**

Excel clears the field values in the data form and displays a data form with blank text boxes for all fields, including the computational fields.

3

- **Type `M` in the Gender text box, `>38` in the Age text box, `Inside` in the Sales Area text box, and `<2,600,000` in the YTD Sales text box.**

Excel displays the data form with the comparison criteria entered as shown in Figure 5-49.

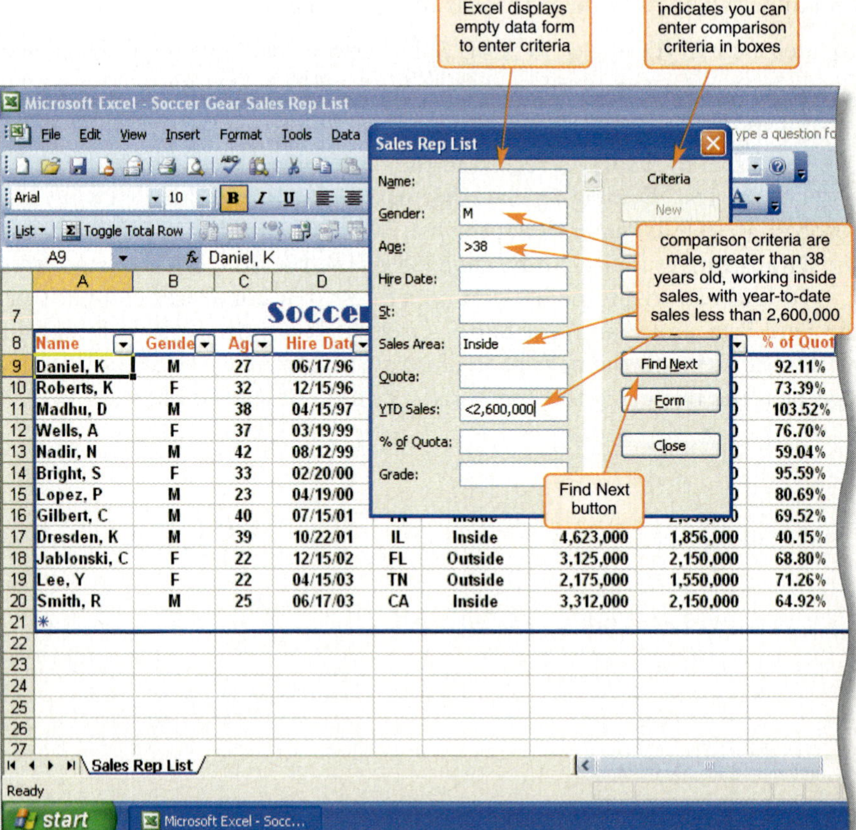

FIGURE 5-49

4

• **Click the Find Next button.**

Excel immediately displays the fifth record in the list because it is the first record that meets the comparison criteria (Figure 5-50). Nadir is a 42-year-old male, who is an Inside sales rep and has YTD sales of 1,963,000. The first four records in the list failed to meet one or more of the four criteria.

5

• **Click the Find Next and Find Prev buttons to view the remaining records in the list that pass the test (Gilbert and Dresden).**

Click the Close button in the data form.

FIGURE 5-50

Other Ways

1. Press ALT+D, O
2. In Voice Command mode, say "Data, Form, Criteria, [enter criteria], Find Next"

Three records in the list pass the test: record 5 (Nadir in row 13), record 8 (Gilbert in row 16), and record 9 (Dresden in row 17). Each time you click the Find Next button, Excel displays the next record that passes the test. Each time you click the Find Prev button, Excel displays the previous record that passed the test. If you click the Find Next button and the record does not change, then no subsequent records in the list meet the criteria.

In Figure 5-49, no blank characters appear between the relational operators and the values. Leading or trailing blank characters have a significant impact on text comparisons. Also note that Excel is not **case-sensitive**. That is, Excel considers uppercase and lowercase characters in a comparison criterion to be the same. For example, if a lowercase letter m is entered as the comparison criteria for Gender, Excel considers it to be the same as uppercase letter M.

Using Wildcard Characters in Comparison Criteria

If you are querying on text fields, you can use **wildcard characters** to find records that contain certain characters in a field. Excel has two wildcard characters, the question mark (?) and the asterisk (*). The **question mark (?)** represents any single character in the same position as the question mark. For example, if the comparison criteria for Name is =Jabl?nski, then any last name must have the following to pass the test: Jabl as the first four characters, any fifth character, and the letters nski as the last three characters. In this list, only Jablonski, C (record 10 in row 18) passes the test.

An **asterisk (*)** can be used in a comparison criteria to represent any number of characters in the same position as the asterisk. L*, *z, S*h, are examples of valid text entries with the asterisk wildcard character. For example, if the comparison criteria entered for the Name field is L*, then any record with a name that begins with the letter L will pass the test. Lopez, P (record 7 in row 15) and Lee, Y (record 11 in

More About

Wildcard Characters

If you want to search for a wildcard character (* or ?), precede the wildcard character with a tilde (~). For example, the criteria, mo10~?, finds mo10? and mo~*10 finds mo*10.

row 19) pass the test (see Figure 5-50 on the previous page). Querying the Name field with *R as the comparison criteria means any records with names that end with the letter R pass the test. Only Smith, R (record 12 in row 20) passes the test. Querying the Name field with G*C means any records with a name that begins with the letters G and ends with the letter C pass the test. Only Gilbert, C (record 8 in row 16) passes the test.

Using Computed Criteria

Using **computed criteria** to query a list involves using a formula as a comparison criteria. For example, using the computed criterion > Quota / 100000 in the Age field in a data form finds all records whose Age field is greater than the corresponding Quota field divided by 100000.

More About

About Protected Worksheets

The Sort, Subtotals, and AutoFilter commands are unavailable if the worksheet or workbook is protected, unless you selected them in the Allows users of this worksheet to list in the Protect Sheet dialog box when you protect the worksheet or workbook.

Querying a List Using AutoFilter

An alternative to using a data form to find records in a list that meet comparison criteria is to use the column heading arrows. The AutoFilter command on the Filter submenu, which is accessible through the Data menu, places the arrows to the right of the column headings in a list. Thus, the query technique that uses the column heading arrows is called **AutoFilter**.

When you first create a list, Excel automatically enables AutoFilter; the column heading arrows thus appear to the right of the column headings whenever the list is active. You can hide the arrows so they do not show when the list is active by invoking the AutoFilter command.

Whereas the data form displays only one record at a time, AutoFilter displays all records that meet the criteria as a subset of the list by hiding records that do not pass the test. Clicking a column heading arrow causes Excel to display, among other commands, a list of all the items in the field (column). If you select an item from the column heading list, Excel immediately hides records that do not contain the item. The item you select from the list is called the **filter criterion**. If you select a filter criterion from a second column heading while the first is still active, then Excel displays a subset of the first subset. The process of filtering activity based on one or more filter criteria is called a **query**.

The following steps show how to query the Soccer Gear Sales Rep list using AutoFilter, so that the list displays only those records that pass the following test:

Gender = F AND Sales Area = Inside

To Query a List Using AutoFilter

1

- **With the list active, click the arrow to the right of Gender in cell B8.**

Excel displays the Gender list (Figure 5-51). The first five entries in the Gender list — Sort Ascending, Sort Descending, (All), (Top 10...), and (Custom...) — are found in every column heading list. When you first create a list, the filter criterion for each field in the list is set to All, so that Excel displays all records.

Microsoft Excel - Soccer Gear Sales Rep List

clicking Gender arrow causes Excel to display Gender list

Soccer Gear Sales Rep List

	Name	Gender	Age	Hire Date	State	Sales Area	Quota	YTD Sales	% of Quota
9	Daniel		27	06/17/96	IL	Outside	3,500,000	3,224,000	92.11%
10	Robert		32	12/15/96	FL	Inside	2,525,000	1,853,000	73.39%
11	Madhu		38	04/15/97	TX	Outside	3,975,000	4,115,000	103.52%
12	Wells,		37	03/19/99	NY	Inside	5,235,000	4,015,000	76.70%
13	Nadir,		42	08/12/99	TX	Inside	3,325,000	1,963,000	59.04%
14	Bright,		33	02/20/00	CA	Outside	4,555,000	4,354,000	95.59%

Sort Ascending
Sort Descending
(All)
(Top 10...)
(Custom...)
F
M

Gender list includes sort commands, entries in field, and other useful query commands

FIGURE 5-51

2

- **Click F in the Gender list.**
- **Click the Sales Area arrow in row 8.**

Excel hides all records representing males, so that only records representing females appear (Figure 5-52). Excel displays the Sales Area list.

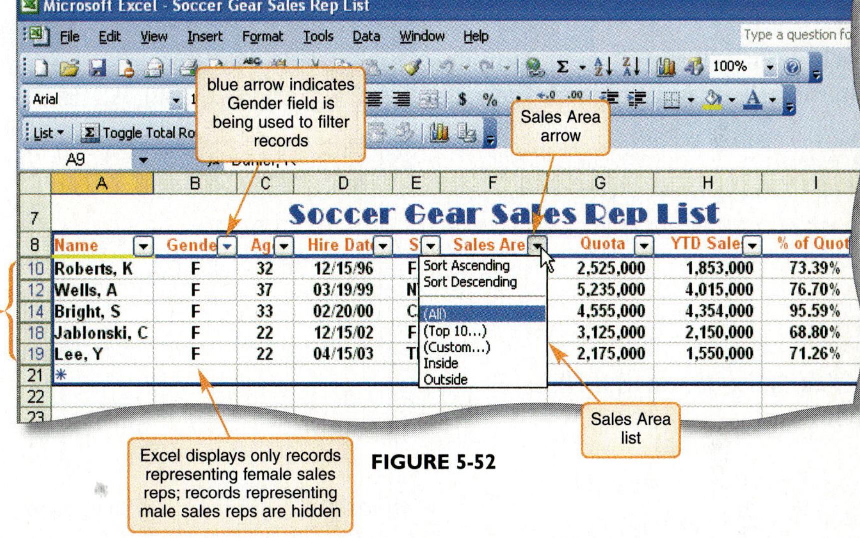

FIGURE 5-52

3

- **Click Inside in the Sales Area list.**

Excel hides all records representing females who are not inside sales reps. As shown in Figure 5-53, only two records pass the filter criteria Gender = F AND Sales Area = Inside. Excel displays row headings 10 and 12 in blue to indicate that the two rows are the result of a filtering process.

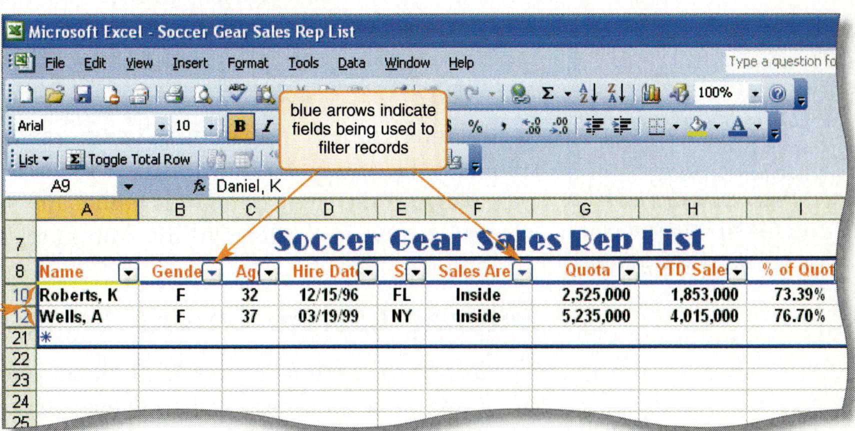

FIGURE 5-53

When you select a second filter criterion, Excel adds it to the first. Hence, in the previous steps, each record must pass two tests to appear as part of the final subset of the list. Other important points regarding AutoFilter include the following:

1. When AutoFilter is enabled and records are hidden, Excel displays the column heading arrows used to establish the filter and the row headings of the selected records in blue.
2. If the list is active and the column heading arrows do not show, then you must manually enable AutoFilter by clicking AutoFilter on the Filter submenu. The Filter command is on the Data menu (Figure 5-54).
3. To remove a filter criterion for a single field, select the All option from the column heading list for that field.

Showing All Records in a List

The following steps illustrate how to show all records in the list following a query.

To Show All Records in a List

1

• **With the list active, click Data on the menu bar and point to Filter.**

Excel displays the Data menu and Filter submenu (Figure 5-54). The check mark to the left of the AutoFilter command indicates AutoFilter is active.

2

• **Click Show All on the Filter submenu.**

Excel displays all of the records in the Soccer Gear Sales Rep list.

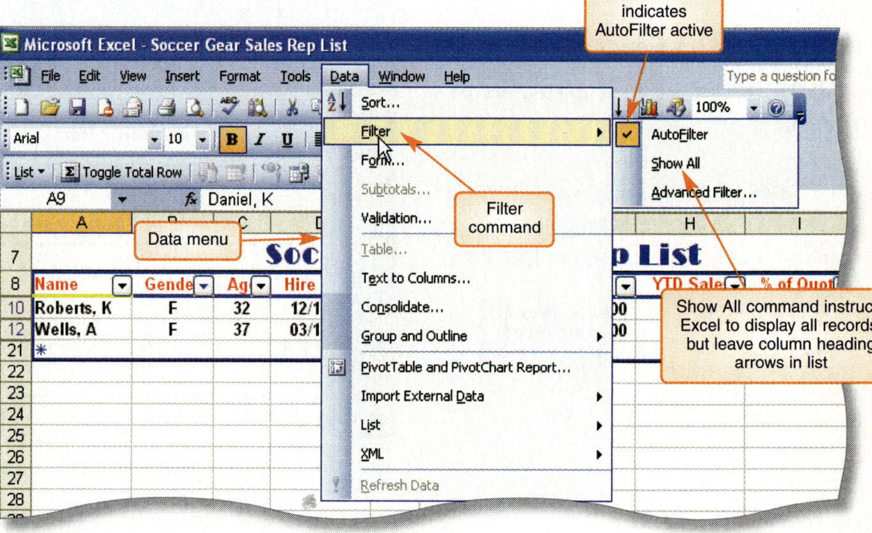

FIGURE 5-54

Other Ways

1. Press ALT+D, F, S
2. Click each blue column heading arrow, click All in column heading list
3. In Voice Command mode, say "Data, Filter, Show All"

An alternative to the Show All command is the AutoFilter command on the Filter submenu (Figure 5-54). Both instruct Excel to show all records in the list. The difference between the two commands is that the Show All command leaves the column heading arrows in the list and the AutoFilter command hides them.

Entering Custom Criteria Using AutoFilter

One of the options available in all column heading lists is (Custom...). The (Custom...) option allows you to enter custom criteria, such as multiple options or ranges of numbers. The following steps show how to enter custom criteria to show records in the list that represent sales reps whose ages are between 30 to 40 inclusive — that is, they are greater than or equal to 30 and less than or equal to 40 ($30 \leq \text{Age} \leq 40$).

To Enter Custom Criteria Using AutoFilter

1

- **With the list active, click the Age arrow in cell C8.**

Excel displays the Age list (Figure 5-55).

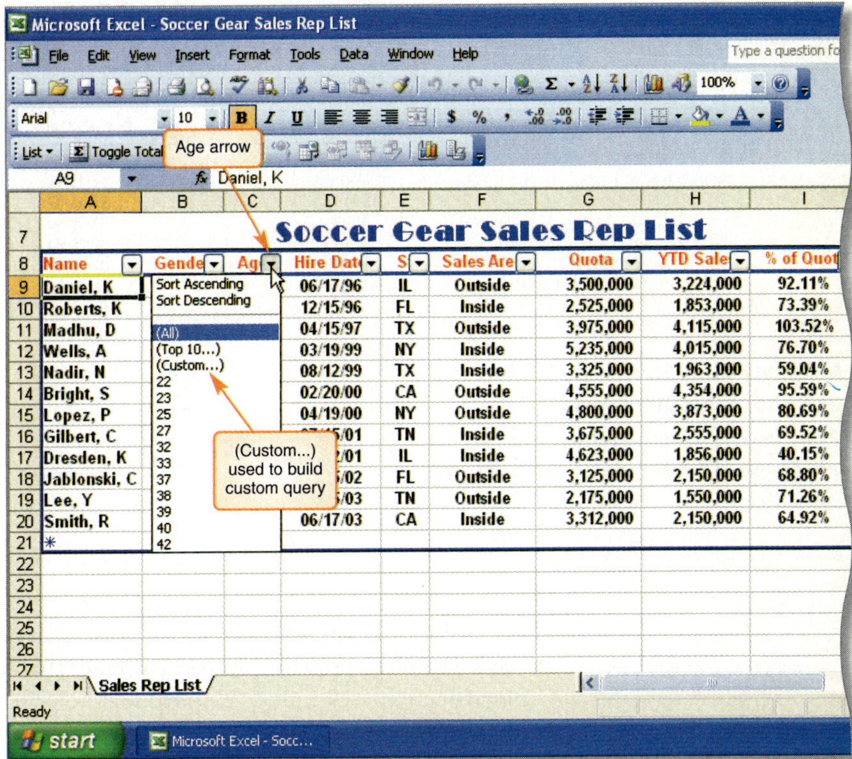

FIGURE 5-55

2

- **Click (Custom...) in the Age list.**
- **When Excel displays the Custom AutoFilter dialog box, click the top left box arrow, click is greater than or equal to in the list, and then type** 30 **in the top right box.**
- **Click the bottom left box arrow, click is less than or equal to in the list, and then type** 40 **in the bottom right box.**

Excel displays the Custom AutoFilter dialog box (Figure 5-56). The And option button is selected by default.

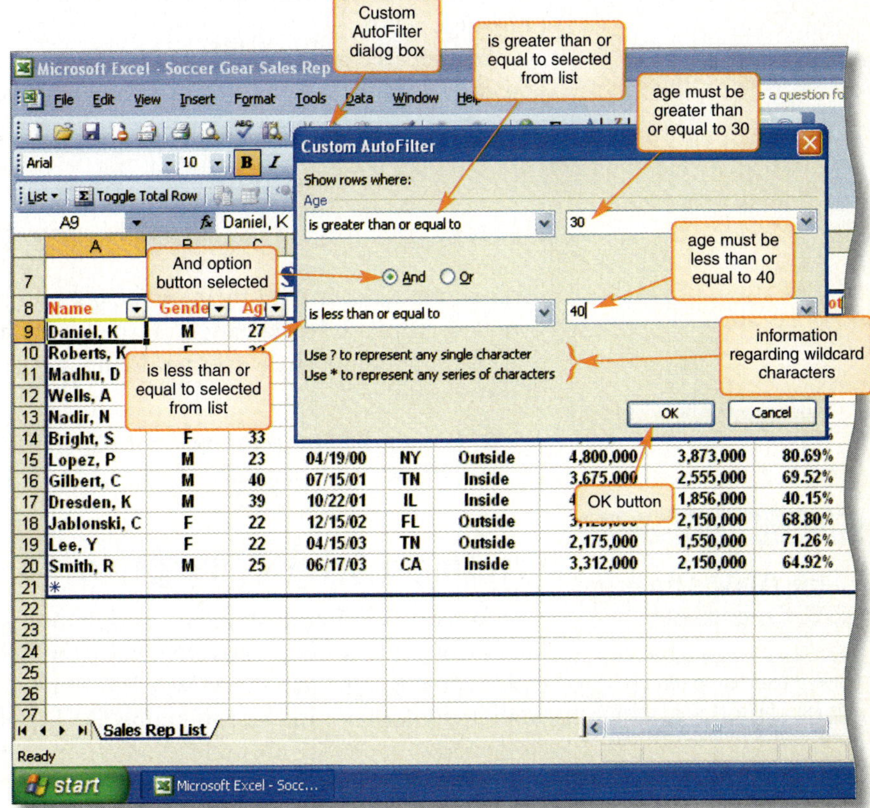

FIGURE 5-56

3

• **Click the OK button in the Custom AutoFilter dialog box.**

Excel displays the records in the list that represent sales reps whose ages are between 30 and 40 inclusive (Figure 5-57). Records that represent sales reps whose ages are not between 30 and 40 inclusive are hidden.

records representing sales reps whose ages are greater than or equal to 30 AND less than or equal to 40

blue arrow indicates Age field used to filter records

4

• **After viewing the records that meet the custom criteria, point to Filter on the Data menu, and then click Show All to display all records in the list.**

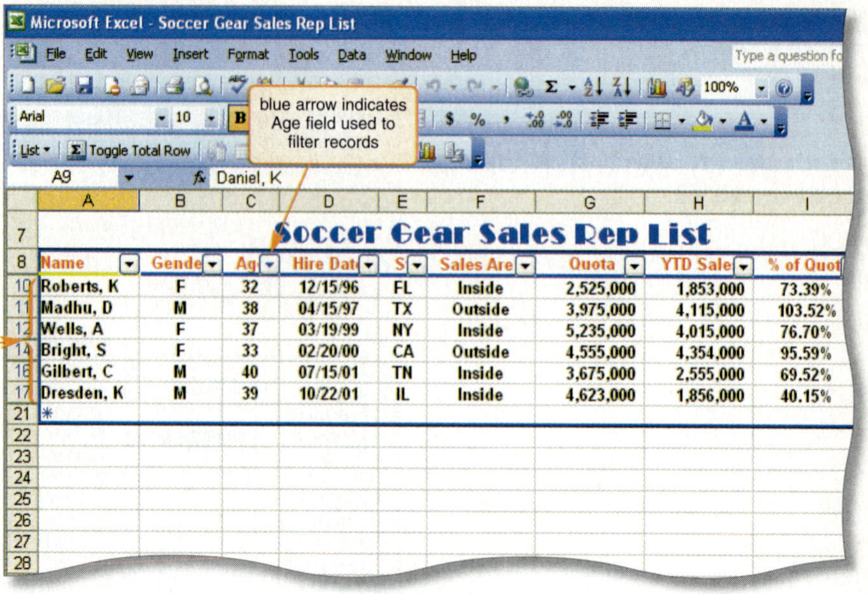

FIGURE 5-57

As shown in Figure 5-56 on the previous page, you can click the And option button or the Or option button to select the AND or the OR operator. The **AND operator** indicates that both parts of the criteria must be true; the **OR operator** indicates that only one of the two must be true. Use the AND operator when the custom criteria is continuous over a range of values, such as Age between 30 AND 40 inclusive ($30 \leq Age \leq 40$). Use the OR operator when the custom criteria is not continuous, such as Age less than or equal to 30 OR greater than or equal to 40 ($30 \leq Age \geq 40$).

As indicated at the bottom of the Custom AutoFilter dialog box in Figure 5-56, you can use wildcard characters to build custom criteria just as you can with data forms.

Using a Criteria Range on the Worksheet

Rather than using a data form or the column heading arrows to establish criteria, you can set up a **criteria range** on the worksheet and use it to manipulate records that pass the comparison criteria. Using a criteria range on the worksheet involves two steps:

1. Create the criteria range and name it Criteria.
2. Use the Advanced Filter command on the Filter submenu.

More About

The AND and OR Operators

AND means each and every one of the comparison criteria must be true. OR means only one of the comparison criteria must be true.

Creating a Criteria Range on the Worksheet

To set up a criteria range, first copy the column headings in the list to another area of the worksheet. If possible, copy the field names to rows above the list, in case the list is expanded downward or to the right in the future. Next, enter the comparison criteria in the row immediately below the field names you just copied to the criteria range. Then use the Name Box in the formula bar to name the criteria range Criteria.

The following steps show how to create a criteria range in the range A2:J3 to find records that pass the test:

Gender = M AND Age > 35 AND Grade > C

A grade greater than or equal to C alphabetically means that only sales reps with grades of D and F pass the test.

To Create a Criteria Range on the Worksheet

1

- **Select the range A7:J8 and then click the Copy button on the Standard toolbar.**
- **Click cell A1 and then press the ENTER key to copy the contents on the Office Clipboard to the destination area A1:J2.**

2

- **Change the title to** `Criteria Area` **in cell A1, enter** `M` **in cell B3, enter** `>35` **in cell C3, and then enter** `>C` **in cell J3.**
- **Select the range A2:J3, click the Name box in the formula bar, type** `Criteria` **as the range name, press the ENTER key, and then click cell J3.**

Excel displays the worksheet as shown in Figure 5-58. Excel assigns the name Criteria to the range A2:J3.

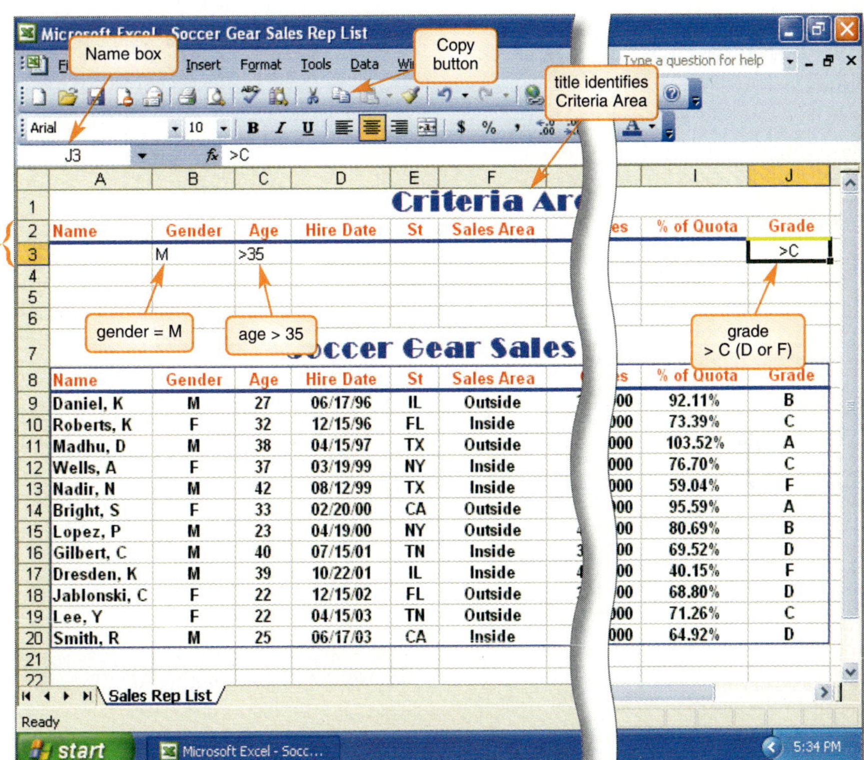

FIGURE 5-58

When setting up a criteria range, remember the following important points:

1. To ensure the column headings in the criteria range are spelled exactly the same as the column headings in the list, copy and paste the column headings in the list to the criteria range as shown in the previous set of steps.
2. The criteria range is independent of the criteria set up in a data form.
3. You can print the criteria range by clicking Criteria in the Name box list and then printing the selection.

Query a List Using the Advanced Filter Command

Using the Advanced Filter command is similar to using the AutoFilter query technique, except that it does not filter records based on comparison criteria you select from a list. Instead, the Advanced Filter command uses the comparison criteria set up in a criteria range (A2:J3) on the worksheet.

The following steps show how to use the Advanced Filter command to query a list and show only the records that pass the test established in the criteria range in Figure 5-58 on the previous page (Gender = M AND Age > 35 AND Grade > C).

To Query a List Using the Advanced Filter Command

1

- **Select cell A9 to activate the list.**
- **Click Data on the menu bar and then point to Filter on the Data menu.**

Excel displays the Data menu and Filter submenu (Figure 5-59).

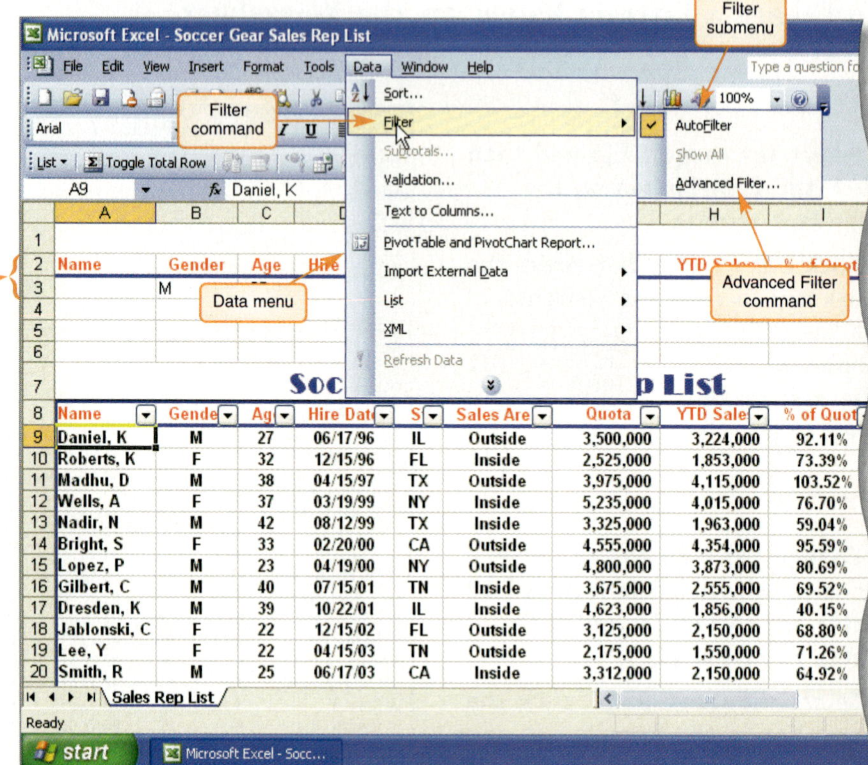

FIGURE 5-59

2

- **Click Advanced Filter on the Filter submenu.**

Excel displays the Advanced Filter dialog box (Figure 5-60). In the Action area, the Filter the list, in-place option button is selected automatically. Excel automatically selects the list (range $A$8:$J$20) in the List range box. Excel also automatically selects the criteria range ($A$2:$J$3) in the Criteria range box, because the name Criteria was assigned to the range A2:J3 earlier.

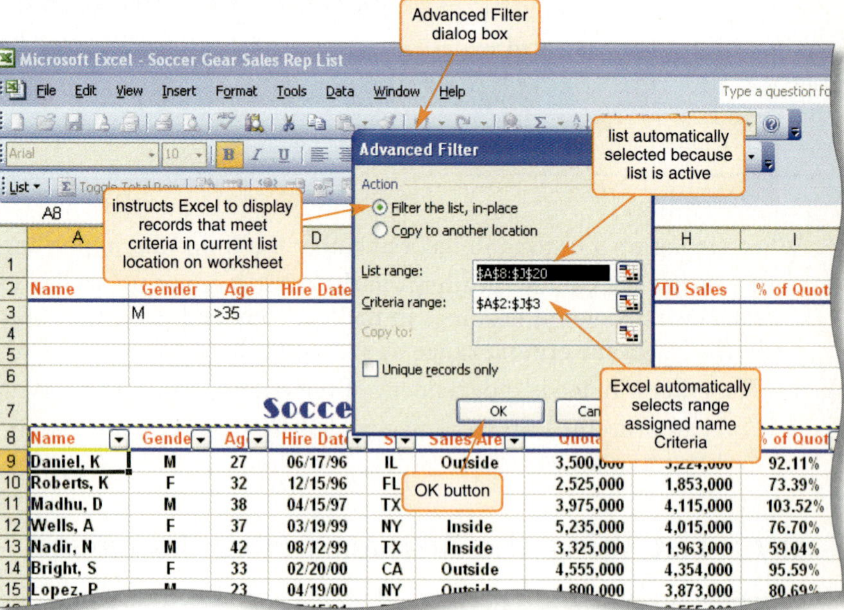

FIGURE 5-60

3

- **Click the OK button in the Advanced Filter dialog box.**

Excel hides all records that do not meet the comparison criteria, showing only three records in the list on the worksheet (Figure 5-61). Nadir, Gilbert, and Dresden are the only three sales reps that are male, are older than 35, and have a grade of D or F.

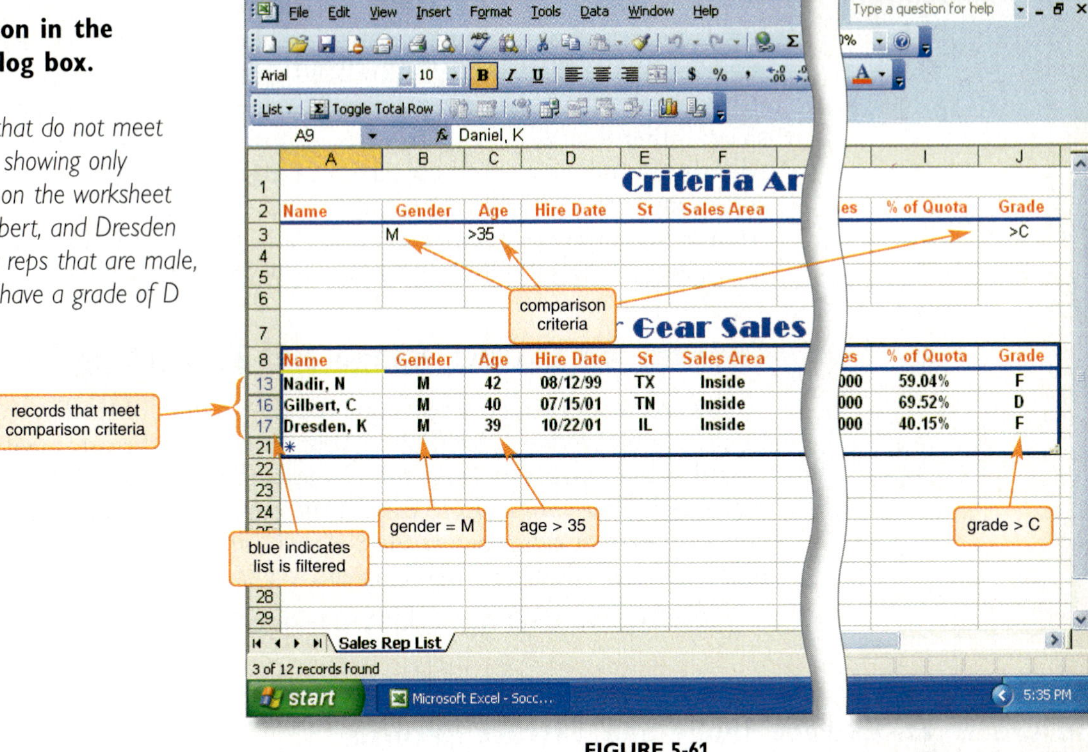

FIGURE 5-61

Other Ways

1. Press ALT+D, F, A
2. In Voice Command mode, say "Data, Filter, Advanced Filter, [select options], OK"

Like the AutoFilter query technique, the Advanced Filter command displays a subset of the list. The primary difference between the two is that the Advanced Filter command allows you to create more complex comparison criteria, because the criteria range can be as many rows long as necessary, allowing for many sets of comparison criteria. The following steps illustrate how to show all records in the list.

To Show All Records in a List

1 **Click Data on the menu bar and then point to Filter.**

2 **Click Show All on the Filter submenu.**

Excel displays all records in the Soccer Gear Sales Rep list.

When the Advanced Filter command is invoked, Excel disables the AutoFilter command, thus hiding the column heading arrows in the active list as shown in Figure 5-61.

Extracting Records

If you click the Copy to another location option button in the Action area of the Advanced Filter dialog box (Figure 5-60 on page EX 352), Excel copies the records that meet the comparison criteria in the criteria range to another part of the worksheet, rather than displaying them as a subset of the list. The location where the records are copied is called the **extract range**. Creating an extract range requires steps similar to those used to create a criteria range earlier in the project. Once the records that meet the comparison criteria in the criteria range are extracted (copied to the extract range), you can create a new list or manipulate the extracted records.

Creating an Extract Range and Extracting Records

To create an extract range, copy the field names of the list and then paste them to an area on the worksheet, preferably well below the list range. Next, name the pasted range Extract by using the Name box in the formula bar. Finally, use the Advanced Filter command to extract the records. The following steps show how to create an extract range below the Soccer Gear Sales Rep list and then extract records that meet the following criteria, as entered earlier in the Criteria range:

Gender = M AND Age > 35 AND Grade > C

To Create an Extract Range and Extract Records

1

- **Select range A7:J8, click the Copy button on the Standard toolbar, select cell A24, and then press the ENTER key to copy the contents on the Office Clipboard to the destination area A24:J25.**
- **Select cell A24 and then type** `Extract Area` **as the title.**
- **Select the range A25:J25, type the name** `Extract` **in the Name box in the formula bar, and then press the ENTER key.**
- **Select cell A9 to activate the list, click Data on the menu bar and then point to Filter.**

Excel displays the Data menu and the Filter submenu (Figure 5-62).

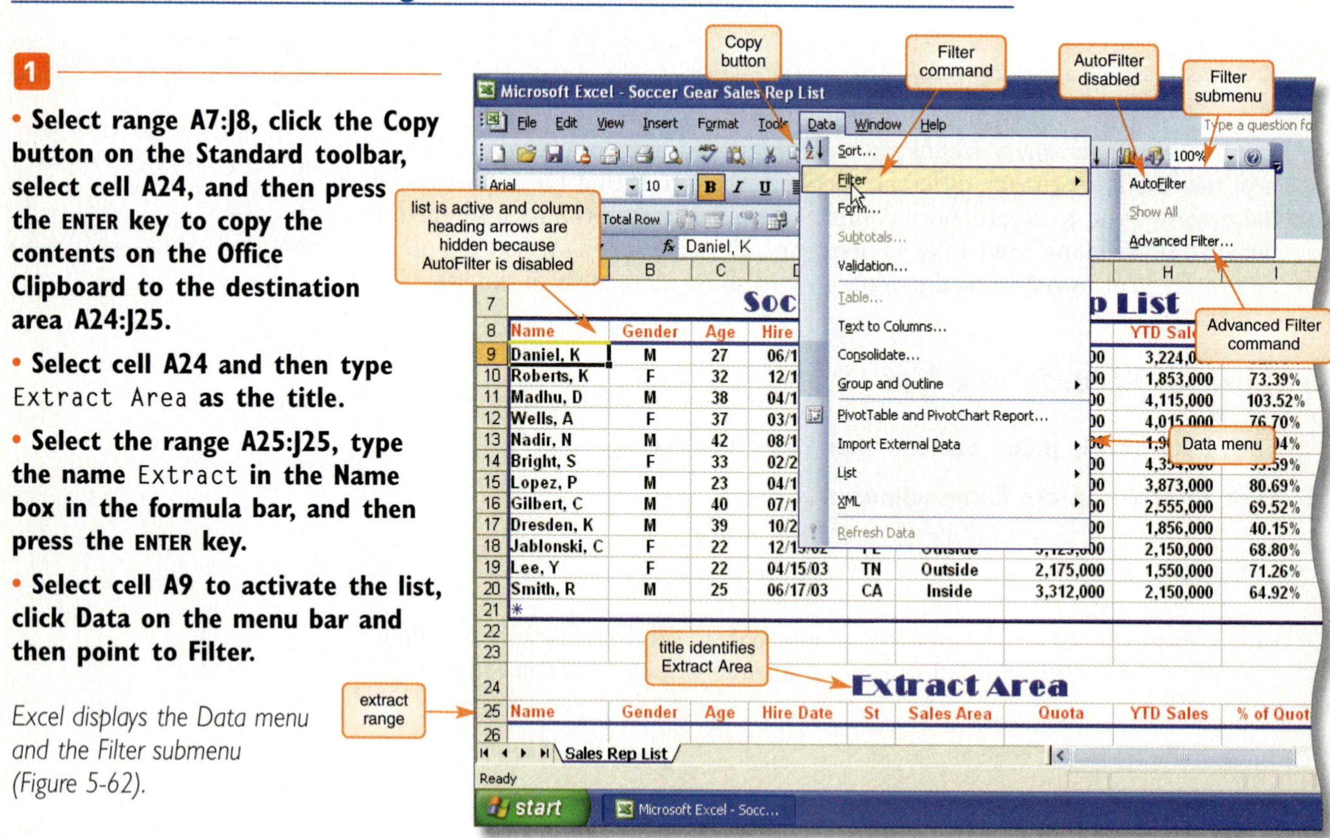

FIGURE 5-62

2

- **Click Advanced Filter on the Filter submenu.**
- **When Excel displays the Advanced Filter dialog box, click Copy to another location in the Action area.**

Excel displays the Advanced Filter dialog box (Figure 5-63). Excel automatically assigns the list range A8:J20 to the List range box. Excel automatically assigns the range named Criteria ($A$2:$J$3) to the Criteria range box and the range named Extract ($A$25:$J$25) to the Copy to box because they were named Criteria and Extract, respectively.

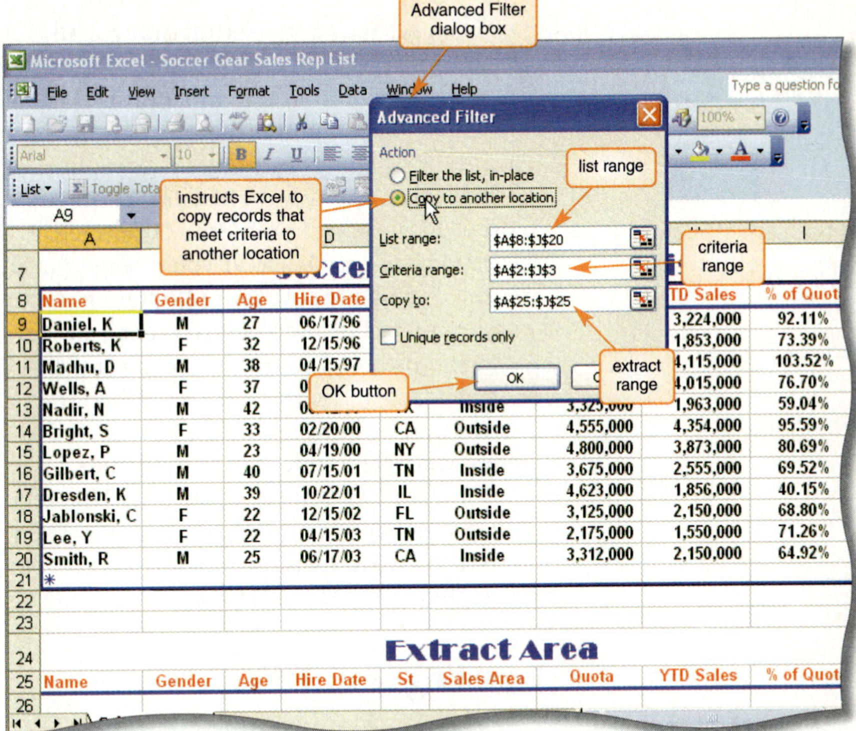

FIGURE 5-63

3

- **Click the OK button.**

Excel copies any records that meet the comparison criteria in the criteria range from the list to the extract range (Figure 5-64).

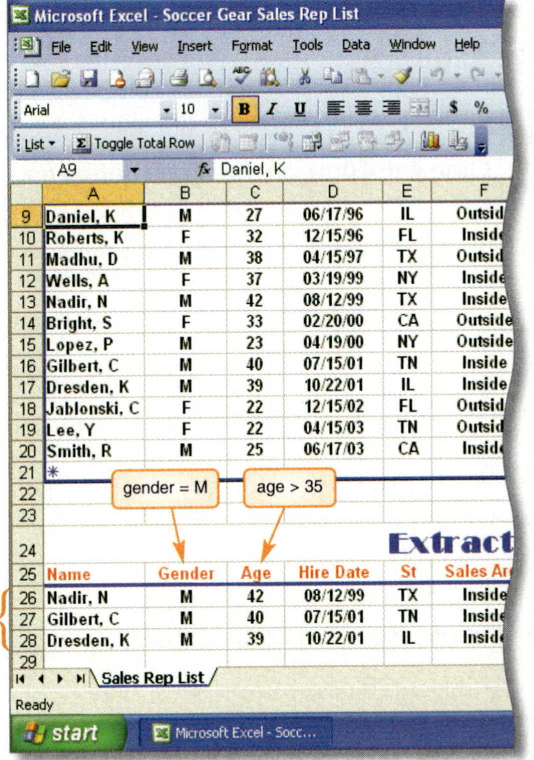

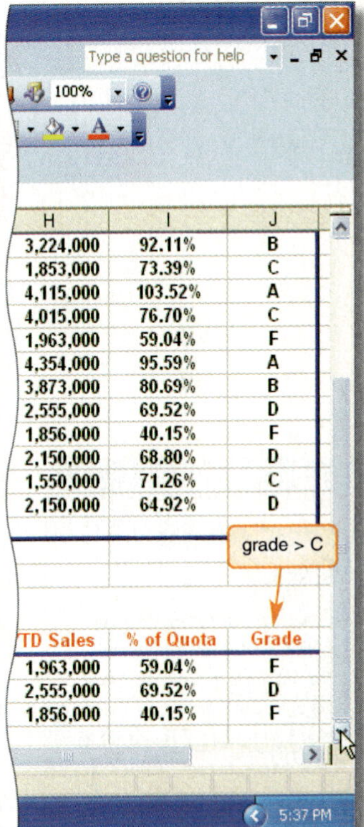

FIGURE 5-64

Other Ways

1. Press ALT+D, F, A
2. In Voice Command mode, say "Data, Filter, Advanced Filter, [select options], OK"

When setting up the extract range, all of the column headings do not have to be copied in the list to the proposed extract range. Instead, copy only those column headings you want, in any order. You also can type the column headings rather than copy them, although this method is not recommended because it increase the likelihood of misspellings or other typographical errors.

Each time the Advanced Filter command is invoked and then the Copy to another location option button is selected, Excel clears cells below the field names in the extract range. Hence, if you change the comparison criteria in the criteria range and then invoke the Advanced Filter command a second time, Excel clears the previously extracted records before it copies a new set of records that pass the new test.

In the previous example, the extract range was defined as a single row containing the field names (range A25:J25). When the extract range is defined as just one row (the column headings), any number of records can be extracted from the list. Excel will expand the extract range to include all rows below the first row (row 25) to the bottom of the worksheet, if needed. The alternative is to define an extract range with a fixed number of rows. If you define a fixed-sized extract range, however, and if more records are extracted than rows are available, Excel displays a dialog box with a error message indicating the extract range is full.

Enabling AutoFilter

As indicated earlier, when the Advanced Filter command is invoked, Excel disables AutoFilter, thus hiding the column heading arrows in an active list. The following steps show how to enable AutoFilter.

To Enable AutoFilter

1. **Click Data on the menu bar and then point to Filter.**
2. **Click AutoFilter on the Filter submenu.**

Excel enables AutoFilter and displays the column heading arrows in the list when the list is active.

To disable AutoFilter, follow the same set of steps.

More About

The Criteria Area

When you add items in multiple rows to a criteria area, you must redefine the range of the name Criteria before you use it. To redefine the name Criteria, point to Name on the Insert menu and then click Define on the Name submenu. When Excel displays the Define Name dialog box, select Criteria in the Names in workbook list and then click the Delete button. Next, select the new Criteria area and name it Criteria using the Name box.

More About the Criteria Range

The comparison criteria in the criteria range determine the records that will pass the test when the Advanced Filter command is invoked. This section describes examples of different comparison criteria.

A Blank Row in the Criteria Range

If the criteria range contains a blank row, it means that no comparison criteria have been defined. Thus, all records in the list pass the test. For example, the blank row in the criteria range shown in Figure 5-65 means that all records will pass the test.

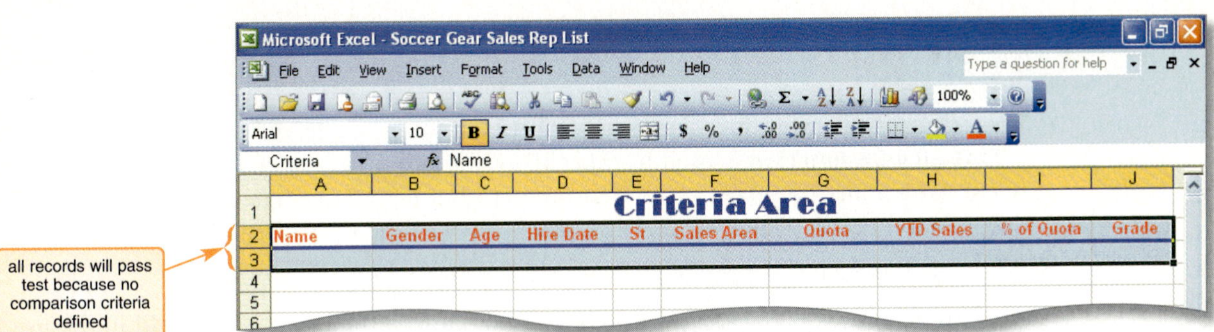

FIGURE 5-65

Using Multiple Comparison Criteria with the Same Field

If the criteria range contains two or more entries below the same field name, then records that pass either comparison criterion pass the test. For example, based on the criteria range shown in Figure 5-66, all records that represent sales reps with a St value of IL OR TX will pass the test.

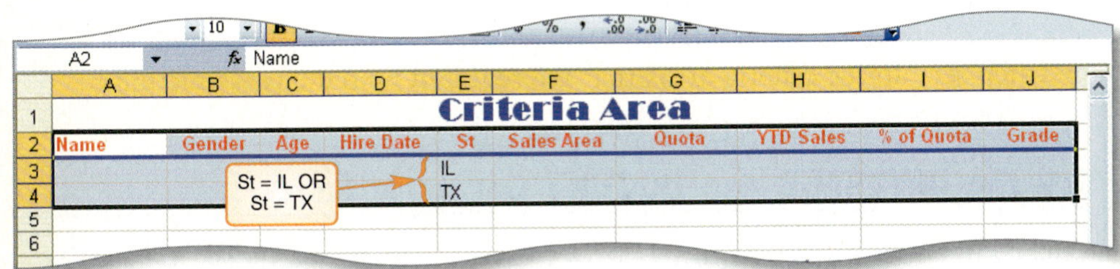

FIGURE 5-66

If an AND operator applies to the same field name (Age > 50 AND Age < 55), then you must duplicate the field name (Age) in the criteria range. That is, add the field name Age in cell K2 to the right of Grade and then adjust the range assigned to the name Criteria by using the Name command on the Insert menu.

Comparison Criteria in Different Rows and Below Different Fields

When the comparison criteria below different field names are in the same row, then records pass the test only if they pass all the comparison criteria. If the comparison criteria for the field names are in different rows, then the records must pass only one of the tests. For example, in the criteria range shown in Figure 5-67, female sales reps OR outside sales reps pass the test.

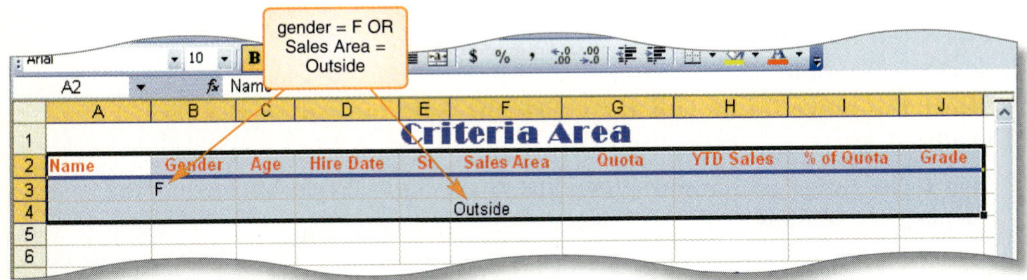

FIGURE 5-67

Using Database Functions

Excel has 12 **database functions** that can be used to evaluate numeric data in a list. One of the functions is called the DAVERAGE function. As the name implies, the **DAVERAGE function** is used to find the average of numbers in a list field that pass a test. This function serves as an alternative to finding an average using the Subtotals command on the Data menu. The general form of the DAVERAGE function is:

=DAVERAGE(list range, "field name", criteria range)

where list range is the range of the list, field name is the name of the field in the list, and criteria range is the comparison criteria or test to pass.

Another often used list function is the DCOUNT function. The **DCOUNT function** will count the number of numeric entries in a list field that pass a test. The general form of the DCOUNT function is:

=DCOUNT(list range, "field name", criteria range)

where list range is the range of the list, field name is the name of the field in the list, and criteria range is the comparison criteria or test to pass.

The following steps use the DAVERAGE function to find the average age of female sales reps and the average age of male sales reps in the list. The DCOUNT function is used to count the number of sales reps records that have a grade of A. The first step sets up the criteria areas that are required by these two functions.

To Use the DAVERAGE and DCOUNT Database Functions

1. **Select cell O1 and then enter** `Criteria` **as the criteria area title. Select cell L1, click the Format Painter button on the Standard toolbar, and then select cell O1.**
2. **Select cell O2 and then enter** `Gender` **as the field name. Select cell P2 and enter** `Gender` **as the field name. Select cell Q2 and then enter** `Grade` **as the field name. Select cell L2. Click the Format Painter button on the Standard toolbar. Drag through the range O2:Q2.**
3. **Enter** `F` **in cell O3 as the Gender code for female sales reps. Enter** `M` **in cell P3 as the Gender code for male sales reps. Enter** `A` **in cell Q3 as the Grade value. Select M3, click the Format Painter button on the Formatting toolbar, and then drag through the range O3:Q3.**
4. **Enter** `Average Female Age = = = = = >` **in cell O4. Enter** `Average Male Age = = = = = = =>` **in cell O5. Enter** `Grade A Count = = = = = = = = = = >` **in cell O6.**
5. **Select cell R4 and then enter** `=daverage(a8:j20, "Age", o2:o3)` **as the database function.**
6. **Select cell R5 and then enter** `=daverage(a8:j20, "Age", p2:p3)` **as the database function.**
7. **Select cell R6 and then enter** `=dcount(a8:j20, "Age", q2:q3)` **as the database function.**
8. **Select the range O4:R6 and then click the Bold button on the Formatting toolbar.**
9. **Select the range R4:R5 and then click the Comma Style button on the Formatting toolbar.**

Excel computes and displays the average age of the female sales reps in the list (29.20) in cell R4, the average age of the male sales reps in the list (33.43) in cell R5, and a count of the sales reps that have a grade of A (2) in cell R6 (Figure 5-68).

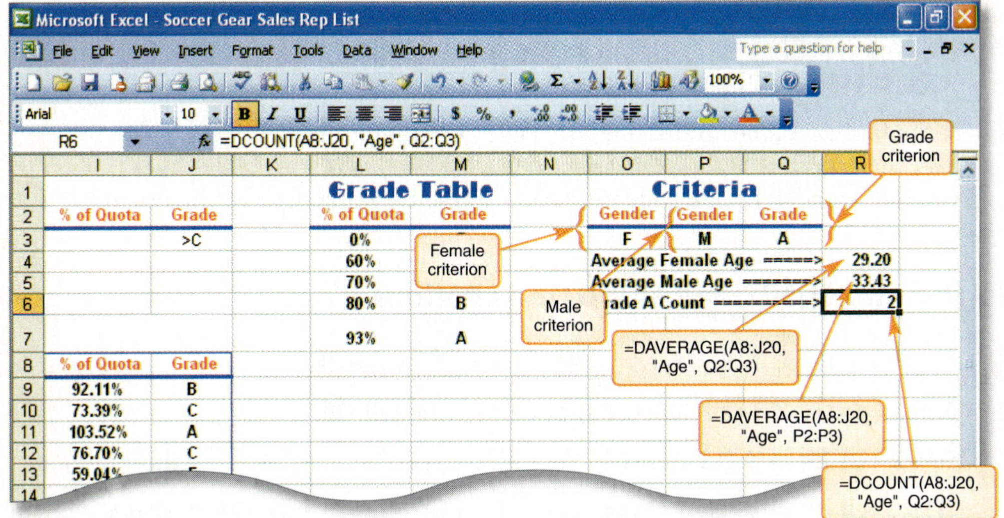

FIGURE 5-68

In Figure 5-68, the first value in the DCOUNT function, A8:J20, refers to the list range defined earlier in this project (range A8:J20). Instead of using the cell range, you can name the list using the Name box in the formula bar and then use the list name as the first argument in the database functions. Database is the name most often assigned to a list. If the list were named Database, then the DCOUNT function would be entered as:

```
=DCOUNT(Database, "Age", Q2:Q3)
```

The second value, "Age", identifies the field on which to compute the average. Excel requires that you surround the field name Age with quotation marks unless the field has been assigned a name through the Name box in the formula bar.

The third value, Q2:Q3, is the criteria range for the grade count. In the case of the DCOUNT function, it is required that you select a numeric field to count.

Other list functions that are similar to the functions described in previous projects include the DMAX, DMIN, and DSUM functions. For a complete list of the database functions available for use with a list, click the Insert Function box in the formula bar. When Excel displays the Insert Function dialog box, select Database in the Or select a category list. The Select a function box displays the database functions. If you click a database function name, Excel displays a description of the function above the OK button in the Insert Function dialog box.

More About

Database Functions

Database functions are useful when working with lists of data, such as the one in this project. Remembering the function arguments and their order within parentheses is not easy, however. Thus, it is recommended that you use the Insert Function button in the formula bar to assign a database function to your worksheet.

Using the SUMIF and COUNTIF Functions

The SUMIF and COUNTIF functions are useful when you want to sum values in a range or count values in a range only if they meet criteria. The range need not be a list. For example, assume you want to sum the YTD sales of the sales reps that have a grade of A. Or, assume you want to count the number of female sales reps. The first question can be answered by using the SUMIF function as follows:

=SUMIF(J9:J20,"A",H9:H20)

where the first argument J9:J20 is the range containing the numbers to add, the second argument "A" is the criteria, and the third argument H9:H20 is the range containing the cells with which to compare the criteria.

The second question can be answered by using the COUNTIF function as follows:

=COUNTIF(B9:B20,"F")

where the first argument B9:B20 is the range containing the cells with which to compare the criteria.

The following steps enter identifiers and these two functions in the range Q8:T9.

To Use the SUMIF and COUNTIF Functions

1. **Enter** `Grade A YTD Sales Sum ===>` **in cell O8.**
2. **Enter** `Female Sales Rep Count ==>` **in cell O9.**
3. **Select cell R8 and then enter** `=SUMIF(j9:j20,"A",h9:h20)` **as the function.**
4. **Select cell R9 and then enter** `=COUNTIF(b9:b20,"F")` **as the function.**
5. **Select the range O8:R9 and then click the Bold button on the Formatting toolbar.**
6. **Select cell R8, click the Comma Style button on the Formatting toolbar, and then click the Decrease Decimal button on the Formatting toolbar twice.**
7. **Double-click the right border of column heading R to change the width of column R to best fit.**

Excel computes and displays the sum of the YTD Sales for those sales reps that have a grade of A and the count of female sales reps (Figure 5-69).

More About

The Quick Reference

For more information, see the Quick Reference Summary at the back of this book, or visit the Excel 2003 Quick Reference Web page (scsite.com/ex2003/qr).

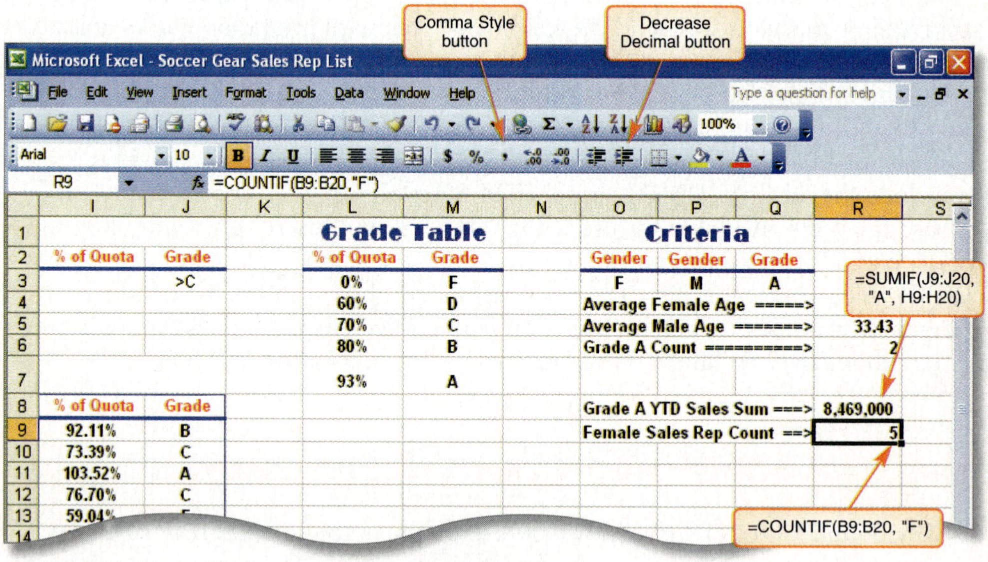

FIGURE 5-69

The COUNTIF, SUMIF, and database functions will work on any range. The difference between using these functions on a range and list is that if the function references a list, then Excel automatically adjusts the first argument as a list grows or shrinks. The same cannot be said if the function's first argument is a range reference that is not defined as a list.

Printing the Worksheet and Saving the Workbook

To print the worksheet on one page and save the workbook, follow the steps below.

> ***More About***
>
> **Printing**
>
> To print individual sections of the worksheet, click the Name box, click the name of the section (Criteria or Extract) you want to print, and then click Print on the File menu. When Excel displays the Print dialog box, click Selection in the Print what area and then click the OK button.

To Print the Worksheet and Save the Workbook

1. **Select any cell outside the list.**
2. **Click File on the menu bar and then click Page Setup. Click the Page tab.**
3. **Click Landscape in the Orientation area. Click Fit to in the Scaling area.**
4. **Click the Print button. When the Print dialog box appears, click the OK button.**
5. **Click the Save button on the Standard toolbar to save the workbook using the file name, Soccer Gear Sales Rep List.**

Excel prints the worksheet on one page in landscape orientation (Figure 5-70). Excel saves the workbook using the file name Soccer Gear Sales Rep List.

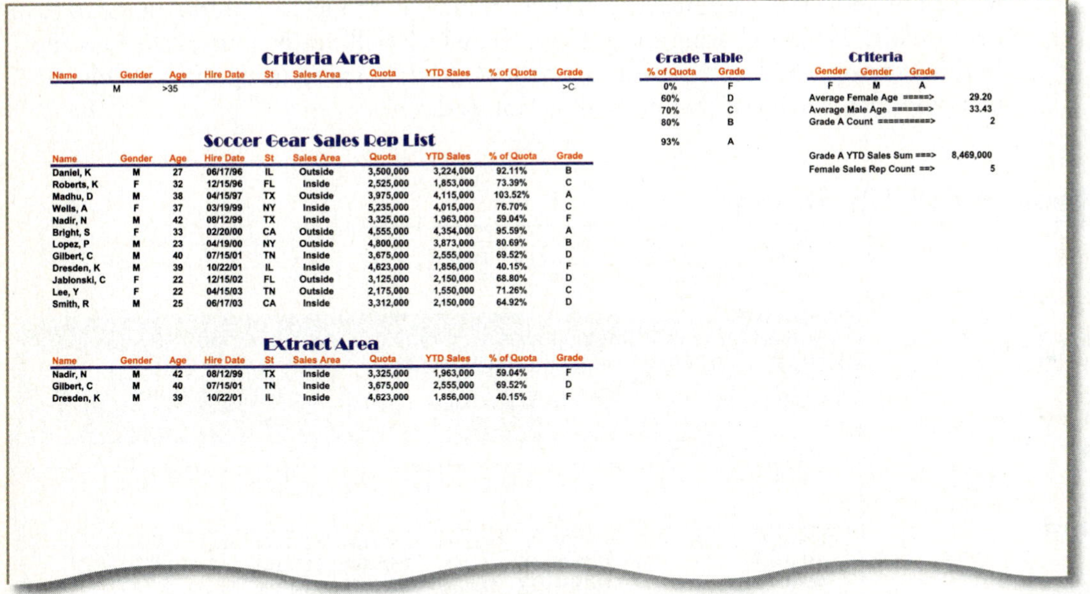

Criteria Area

Name	Gender	Age	Hire Date	St	Sales Area	Quota	YTD Sales	% of Quota	Grade
	M	>35							>C

Soccer Gear Sales Rep List

Name	Gender	Age	Hire Date	St	Sales Area	Quota	YTD Sales	% of Quota	Grade
Daniel, K	M	27	06/17/96	IL	Outside	3,500,000	3,224,000	92.11%	B
Roberts, K	F	32	12/15/96	FL	Inside	2,525,000	1,853,000	73.39%	C
Madhu, D	M	38	04/15/97	TX	Outside	3,975,000	4,115,000	103.52%	A
Wells, A	F	37	03/19/99	NY	Inside	5,235,000	4,015,000	76.70%	C
Nadir, N	M	42	08/12/99	TX	Inside	3,325,000	1,963,000	59.04%	F
Bright, S	F	33	02/20/00	CA	Outside	4,555,000	4,354,000	95.59%	A
Lopez, P	M	23	04/19/00	NY	Outside	4,800,000	3,873,000	80.69%	B
Gilbert, C	M	40	07/15/01	TN	Inside	3,675,000	2,555,000	69.52%	D
Dresden, K	M	39	10/22/01	IL	Inside	4,623,000	1,856,000	40.15%	F
Jablonski, C	F	22	12/15/02	FL	Outside	3,125,000	2,150,000	68.80%	D
Lee, Y	F	22	04/15/03	TN	Outside	2,175,000	1,550,000	71.26%	C
Smith, R	M	25	06/17/03	CA	Inside	3,312,000	2,150,000	64.92%	D

Extract Area

Name	Gender	Age	Hire Date	St	Sales Area	Quota	YTD Sales	% of Quota	Grade
Nadir, N	M	42	08/12/99	TX	Inside	3,325,000	1,963,000	59.04%	F
Gilbert, C	M	40	07/15/01	TN	Inside	3,675,000	2,555,000	69.52%	D
Dresden, K	M	39	10/22/01	IL	Inside	4,623,000	1,856,000	40.15%	F

Grade Table

% of Quota	Grade
0%	F
60%	D
70%	C
80%	B
93%	A

Criteria

Gender	Gender	Grade
F	M	A

Average Female Age =====>	29.20
Average Male Age =======>	33.43
Grade A Count ==========>	2
Grade A YTD Sales Sum ===>	8,469,000
Female Sales Rep Count ==>	5

FIGURE 5-70

Saving a Workbook in Different File Formats

Excel workbooks usually are saved in a file format called **Microsoft Excel Workbook**. A file saved in the Microsoft Excel Workbook file format has a file extension of **xls**. A **file extension**, which usually is three characters in length, is used by Windows to classify files by application. By default, you do not see the file extensions when you use the Save As or Open dialog boxes, but the file extensions are appended to the file name and separated by a period. Excel allows you to save a workbook in more than 30 different file formats, so that the data can be transferred to other applications easily. Table 5-7 on the next page summarizes the more popular file formats available in Excel via the Save as type box in the Save As dialog box.

More About

Microsoft Certification

The Microsoft Office Specialist Certification program provides an opportunity for you to obtain a valuable industry credential — proof that you have the Excel skills required by employers. For more information, see Appendix E, or visit the Excel 2003 Certification Web page (scsite.com/ex2003/cert).

Table 5-7 Popular File Formats Available with the Save As Command in Excel

FILE FORMATS	EXTENSION
Microsoft Excel Workbook	xls
XML Spreadsheet	xml
XML Data	xml
Single File Web Page	mht
Web Page	htm
Template	xlt
Text (Tab delimited)	txt
Unicode Text	txt
CSV (Comma delimited)	csv
Formatted Text (Space delimited)	prn

The following steps show how to save the list (range A8:I20) in the Soccer Gear Sales Rep List workbook in a CSV (Comma delimited) file format so that the file can be read by most applications. The Grade column is not included in the range to save because it is computed using the grade table, which will not be part of the new file. In this example, the list is copied to a new workbook, saved using the CSV file format, and then displayed and printed in Notepad.

To Save a Workbook in CSV File Format

1

- **Select the list in the range A8:I20.**
- **Click the Copy button on the Standard toolbar.**
- **Click the New button on the Standard toolbar.**
- **With cell A1 selected in the new workbook, click the Paste button on the Standard toolbar.**
- **Click the Select All button, point to the right border of the column A heading, and double-click to set all column widths to best fit.**
- **Select cell A15.**

Excel displays the Soccer Gear Sales Rep list as shown in Figure 5-71.

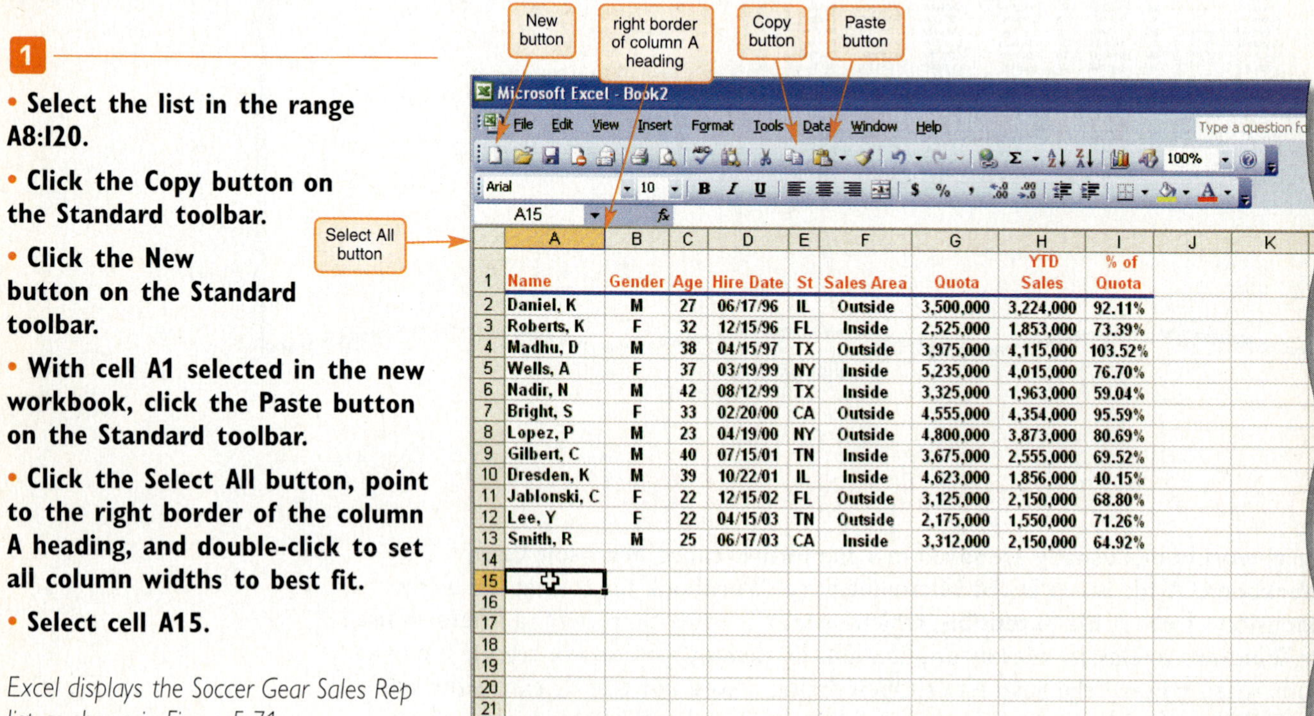

FIGURE 5-71

2

- **With a floppy disk in drive A, click the Save button on the Standard toolbar.**
- **When Excel displays the Save As dialog box, type** `Soccer Gear Sales Rep List CSV` **in the File name text box.**
- **Click the Save as type box arrow and then scroll down and click CSV (Comma delimited) in the Save as type list as shown in Figure 5-72.**
- **If necessary, click 3½ Floppy (A:) in the Save in list, click the Save button in the Save As dialog box, and then click the OK button and the Yes button in the Microsoft Office Excel dialog boxes when they appear.**
- **Click the workbook Close button on the right side of the Excel title bar.**

Excel saves the workbook on the floppy disk in drive A as a CSV (Comma delimited) file using the file name, Soccer Gear Sales Rep List CSV.csv.

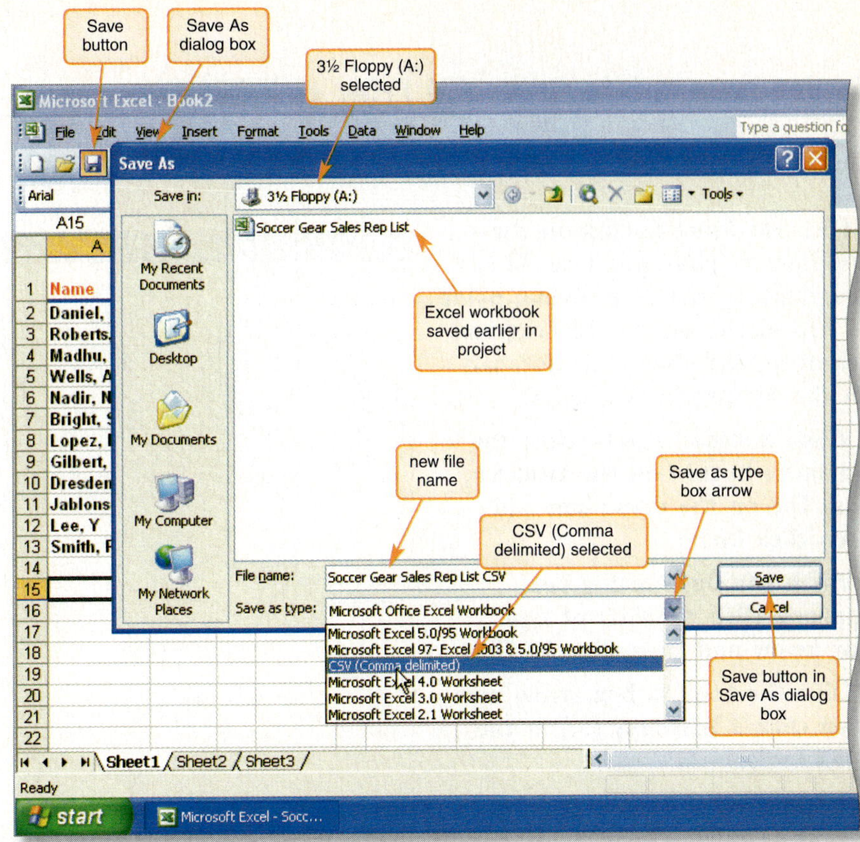

FIGURE 5-72

Other Ways

1. On File menu click Save As, type file name, select file type, select drive or folder, click Save button in Save As dialog box
2. Right-click workbook Control-menu icon on menu bar, click Save As on shortcut menu, type file name, select file type, select drive or folder, click Save button in Save As dialog box
3. Press CTRL+S, type file name, select file type, select drive or folder, click Save button in Save As dialog box
4. In Voice Command mode, say "File, Save As", [type desired file name, select file type], say "Save"

If you open the Soccer Gear Sales Rep List CSV in Excel, it will place the fields from the CSV file in the same cells as shown in Figure 5-71, but without some of the formatting. The steps on the next page show how to use Notepad to open and print the CSV file.

To Use Notepad to Open and Print the CSV File

1

- **Click the Start button on the Windows taskbar, point to All Programs on the Start menu, point to Accessories on the All Programs submenu, and then click Notepad on the Accessories submenu.**
- **When Notepad starts, click the Maximize button on the title bar, click File on the menu bar, and then click Open.**
- **When the Open dialog box appears, click the Files of type box arrow and then click All Files.**
- **Click the Look in box arrow and then click 3 ½ Floppy (A:) in the Look in list.**
- **Double-click Soccer Gear Sales Rep List CSV.**

Notepad displays the Soccer Gear Sales Rep List CSV file (Figure 5-73).

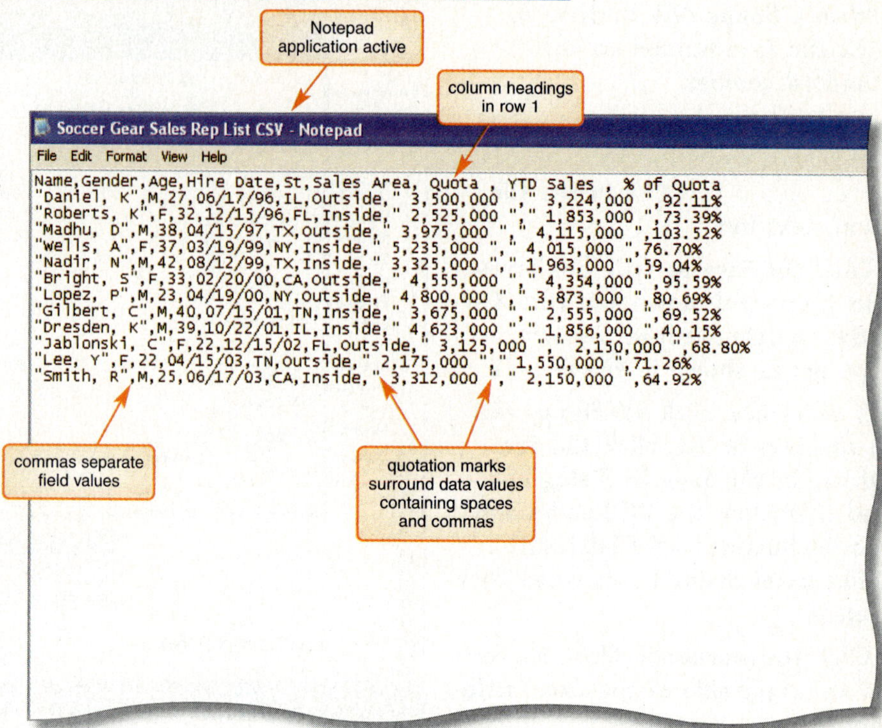


```
Name,Gender,Age,Hire Date,St,Sales Area, Quota , YTD Sales , % of Quota
"Daniel, K",M,27,06/17/96,IL,Outside," 3,500,000 "," 3,224,000 ",92.11%
"Roberts, K",F,32,12/15/96,FL,Inside," 2,525,000 "," 1,853,000 ",73.39%
"Madhu, D",M,38,04/15/97,TX,Outside," 3,975,000 "," 4,115,000 ",103.52%
"Wells, A",F,37,03/19/99,NY,Inside," 5,235,000 "," 4,015,000 ",76.70%
"Nadir, N",M,42,08/12/99,TX,Inside," 3,325,000 "," 1,963,000 ",59.04%
"Bright, S",F,33,02/20/00,CA,Outside," 4,555,000 "," 4,354,000 ",95.59%
"Lopez, P",M,23,04/19/00,NY,Outside," 4,800,000 "," 3,873,000 ",80.69%
"Gilbert, C",M,40,07/15/01,TN,Inside," 3,675,000 "," 2,555,000 ",69.52%
"Dresden, K",M,39,10/22/01,IL,Inside," 4,623,000 "," 1,856,000 ",40.15%
"Jablonski, C",F,22,12/15/02,FL,Outside," 3,125,000 "," 2,150,000 ",68.80%
"Lee, Y",F,22,04/15/03,TN,Outside," 2,175,000 "," 1,550,000 ",71.26%
"Smith, R",M,25,06/17/03,CA,Inside," 3,312,000 "," 2,150,000 ",64.92%
```

FIGURE 5-73

2

- **Click File on the menu bar and then click Print.**
- **When the Print dialog box appears, click the Print button.**
- **Click the Close button on the right side of the Notepad title bar.**

Notepad prints the CSV version of the Soccer Gear Sales Rep list (Figure 5-74).

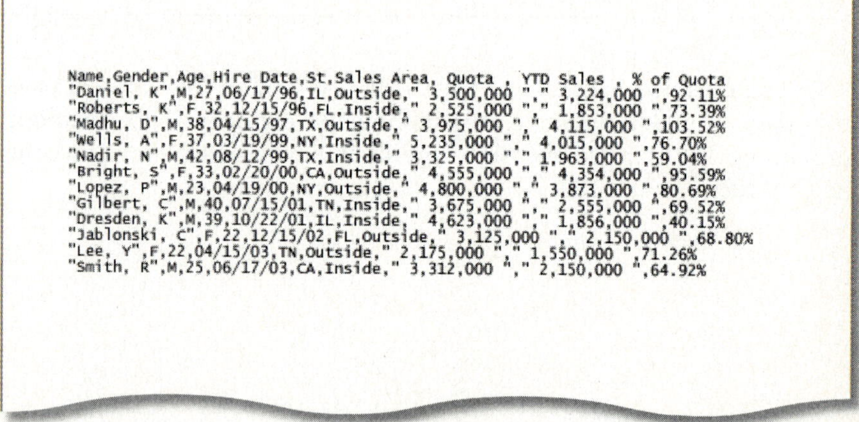

```
Name,Gender,Age,Hire Date,St,Sales Area, Quota , YTD Sales , % of Quota
"Daniel, K",M,27,06/17/96,IL,Outside," 3,500,000 "," 3,224,000 ",92.11%
"Roberts, K",F,32,12/15/96,FL,Inside," 2,525,000 "," 1,853,000 ",73.39%
"Madhu, D",M,38,04/15/97,TX,Outside," 3,975,000 "," 4,115,000 ",103.52%
"Wells, A",F,37,03/19/99,NY,Inside," 5,235,000 "," 4,015,000 ",76.70%
"Nadir, N",M,42,08/12/99,TX,Inside," 3,325,000 "," 1,963,000 ",59.04%
"Bright, S",F,33,02/20/00,CA,Outside," 4,555,000 "," 4,354,000 ",95.59%
"Lopez, P",M,23,04/19/00,NY,Outside," 4,800,000 "," 3,873,000 ",80.69%
"Gilbert, C",M,40,07/15/01,TN,Inside," 3,675,000 "," 2,555,000 ",69.52%
"Dresden, K",M,39,10/22/01,IL,Inside," 4,623,000 "," 1,856,000 ",40.15%
"Jablonski, C",F,22,12/15/02,FL,Outside," 3,125,000 "," 2,150,000 ",68.80%
"Lee, Y",F,22,04/15/03,TN,Outside," 2,175,000 "," 1,550,000 ",71.26%
"Smith, R",M,25,06/17/03,CA,Inside," 3,312,000 "," 2,150,000 ",64.92%
```

FIGURE 5-74

Figure 5-73 shows the contents of the Soccer Gear Sales Rep List CSV file. The column headings are on the first line, separated by commas. Each record is on a separate line. Commas separate the fields in each record; quotation marks surround any fields with data containing spaces or commas. Data saved in this format can be read by most applications, including Excel.

Quitting Excel

To quit Excel, complete the following steps.

To Quit Excel

1. **Click the Close button on the right side of the title bar.**
2. **If the Microsoft Office Excel dialog box is displayed, click the No button.**

Project Summary

In this project, you learned how to create, sort, and filter a list (also called a database). Creating a list involves entering and formatting the column headings, defining the column headings as a list, formatting the insert row, and then adding, changing, and deleting records in the list using a data form. You learned about the List toolbar, which has several useful buttons, including the Toggle Total Row button that lets you display a total row. Sorting a list can be achieved using the column heading arrow and column heading list, the Sort Ascending and Sort Descending buttons on the Standard toolbar, or the Sort command on the List button menu.

After a list is sorted, you can use the Subtotals command on the Data menu to generate subtotals that Excel displays within the list range. Filtering a list involves displaying a subset of the list or copying (extracting) records that pass a test. The database functions, the lookup function, and the SUMIF and COUNTIF functions are useful for generating statistics.

Finally, this project explained that Excel can save a workbook in more than 30 different file formats, so that the data can be transferred to other applications easily. The project then stepped you through saving an Excel workbook in a CSV file format, so that that list can be read by other applications, such as Notepad.

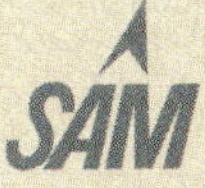

If you have a SAM user profile, you may have access to hands-on instruction, practice, and assessment of the skills covered in this project. Log in to your SAM account and go to your assignments page to see what your instructor has assigned.

What You Should Know

Having completed this project, you should be able to perform the tasks below. The tasks are listed in the same order they were presented in this project. For a list of the buttons, menus, toolbars, and commands introduced in this project, see the Quick Reference Summary at the back of this book and refer to the Page Number column.

1. Start and Customize Excel (EX 310)
2. Enter the Column Headings for a List (EX 311)
3. Define a Range as a List (EX 313)
4. Format the Insert Row in an Empty List (EX 315)
5. Validate Data (EX 316)
6. Enter Records into a List Using a Data Form (EX 318)
7. Add New Fields to a List (EX 322)
8. Create a Lookup Table (EX 324)
9. Use the VLOOKUP Function to Determine Letter Grades (EX 325)
10. Use the Toggle Total Row Button (EX 329)
11. Use the Print List Button (EX 331)
12. View a Record Using a Data Form (EX 332)
13. Sort a List in Ascending Sequence by Name Using the Sort Ascending Button (EX 333)
14. Sort a List in Descending Sequence by Name Using the Sort Descending Button (EX 334)
15. Sort a List Using the Sort Command on a Column Heading List (EX 335)
16. Sort a List on Multiple Fields Using the Sort Command on the List Button Menu (EX 336)
17. Display Automatic Subtotals in a List (EX 338)
18. Zoom Out on a Subtotaled List and Use the Outline Feature (EX 340)
19. Remove Automatic Subtotals from a List (EX 342)
20. Sort a List into Its Original Order Using a Column Heading List (EX 343)
21. Find Records Using a Data Form (EX 344)
22. Query a List Using AutoFilter (EX 347)
23. Show All Records in a List (EX 348, EX 353)
24. Enter Custom Criteria Using AutoFilter (EX 349)
25. Create a Criteria Range on the Worksheet (EX 351)
26. Query a List Using the Advanced Filter Command (EX 352)
27. Create an Extract Range and Extract Records (EX 354)
28. Enable AutoFilter (EX 356)
29. Use the DAVERAGE and DCOUNT Database Functions (EX 358)
30. Use the SUMIF and COUNTIF Functions (EX 360)
31. Print the Worksheet and Save the Workbook (EX 361)
32. Save a Workbook in CSV File Format (EX 362)
33. Use Notepad to Open and Print the CSV File (EX 364)
34. Quit Excel (EX 365)

Learn It Online

Instructions: To complete the Learn It Online exercises, start your browser, click the Address bar, and then enter the Web address `scsite.com/ex2003/learn`. When the Excel 2003 Learn It Online page is displayed, follow the instructions in the exercises below. Each exercise has instructions for printing your results, either for your own records or for submission to your instructor.

1 Project Reinforcement TF, MC, and SA

Below Excel Project 5, click the Project Reinforcement link. Print the quiz by clicking Print on the File menu for each page. Answer each question.

2 Flash Cards

Below Excel Project 5, click the Flash Cards link and read the instructions. Type 20 (or a number specified by your instructor) in the Number of playing cards text box, type your name in the Enter your Name text box, and then click the Flip Card button. When the flash card is displayed, read the question and then click the ANSWER box arrow to select an answer. Flip through Flash Cards. If your score is 15 (75%) correct or greater, click Print on the File menu to print your results. If your score is less than 15 (75%) correct, then redo this exercise by clicking the Replay button.

3 Practice Test

Below Excel Project 5, click the Practice Test link. Answer each question, enter your first and last name at the bottom of the page, and then click the Grade Test button. When the graded practice test is displayed on your screen, click Print on the File menu to print a hard copy. Continue to take practice tests until you score 80% or better.

4 Who Wants To Be a Computer Genius?

Below Excel Project 5, click the Computer Genius link. Read the instructions, enter your first and last name at the bottom of the page, and then click the PLAY button. When your score is displayed, click the PRINT RESULTS link to print a hard copy.

5 Wheel of Terms

Below Excel Project 5, click the Wheel of Terms link. Read the instructions, and then enter your first and last name and your school name. Click the PLAY button. When your score is displayed, right-click the score and then click Print on the shortcut menu to print a hard copy.

6 Crossword Puzzle Challenge

Below Excel Project 5, click the Crossword Puzzle Challenge link. Read the instructions, and then enter your first and last name. Click the SUBMIT button. Work the crossword puzzle. When you are finished, click the Submit button. When the crossword puzzle is redisplayed, click the Print Puzzle button to print a hard copy.

7 Tips and Tricks

Below Excel Project 5, click the Tips and Tricks link. Click a topic that pertains to Project 5. Right-click the information and then click Print on the shortcut menu. Construct a brief example of what the information relates to in Excel to confirm you understand how to use the tip or trick.

8 Newsgroups

Below Excel Project 5, click the Newsgroups link. Click a topic that pertains to Project 5. Print three comments.

9 Expanding Your Horizons

Below Excel Project 5, click the Articles for Microsoft Excel link. Click a topic that pertains to Project 5. Print the information. Construct a brief example of what the information relates to in Excel to confirm you understand the contents of the article.

10 Search Sleuth

Below Excel Project 5, click the Search Sleuth link. To search for a term that pertains to this project, select a term below the Project 5 title and then use the Google search engine at google.com (or any major search engine) to display and print two Web pages that present information on the term.

11 Excel Online Training

Below Excel Project 5, click the Excel Online Training link. When your browser displays the Microsoft Office Online Web page, click the Excel link. Click one of the Excel courses that covers one or more of the objectives listed at the beginning of the project on page EX 306. Print the first page of the course before stepping through it.

12 Office Marketplace

Below Excel Project 5, click the Office Marketplace link. When your browser displays the Microsoft Office Online Web page, click the Office Marketplace link. Click a topic that relates to Excel. Print the first page.

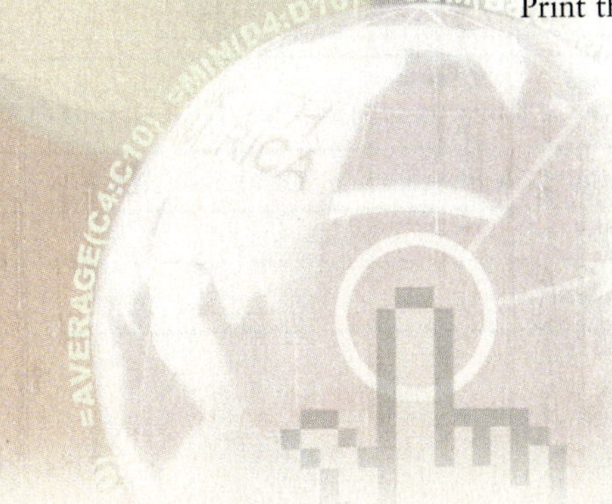

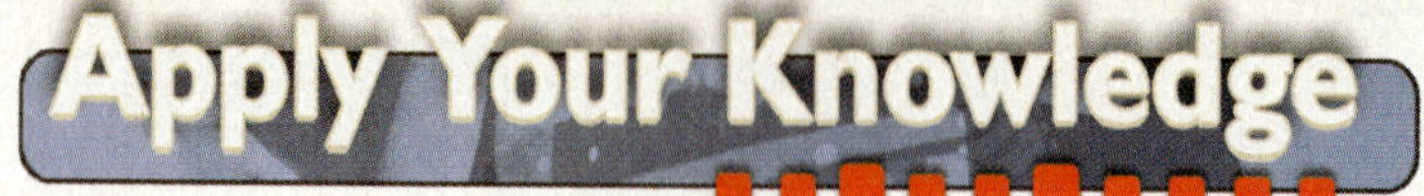

1 Querying a List

Instructions: Assume that the figures that accompany each of the following six problems make up the criteria range for the Union Employee List shown in Figure 5-75. Fill in the comparison criteria to select records from the list to solve each of these six problems. So that you understand better what is required for this assignment, the answer is given for the first problem. You can open the workbook, Apply 5-1 Union Employee List, from the Data Disk and use the Filter command to verify your answers.

Union Employee List

	Employee	Gender	Age	Dept	Trade	Seniority
12	James, Rita	F	50	5	Electrician	9
13	Gonzalez, Rosa	F	30	7	Electrician	7
14	Mount, Tiger	M	38	6	Welder	14
15	Alamo, Jean	F	37	5	Carpenter	17
16	Iesa, Imaad	M	34	7	Carpenter	15
17	Texan, Ebony	M	21	5	Welder	6
18	Nowinski, Donna	F	47	6	Welder	25
19	Sanchez, Chitra	F	23	7	Electrician	9
20	Charu, Aisha	F	50	5	Carpenter	0
21	Garcia, Jose	M	20	6	Welder	0
22	Akita, Aya	F	37	7	Carpenter	17

Union Employee List / Sheet2 / Sheet3

Ready

start | Microsoft Excel - Appl...

FIGURE 5-75

1. Select records that represent females who are less than 45 years old.

EMPLOYEE	GENDER	AGE	DEPT	TRADE	SENIORITY
	F	<45			

2. Select records that represent a Welder or Carpenter.

EMPLOYEE	GENDER	AGE	DEPT	TRADE	SENIORITY

3. Select records that represent female members whose last names begin with the letter A and who work in department 7.

EMPLOYEE	GENDER	AGE	DEPT	TRADE	SENIORITY

4. Select records that represent male members who are at least 31 years old and have at least 10 years of seniority.

EMPLOYEE	GENDER	AGE	DEPT	TRADE	SENIORITY

5. Select records that represent male employees who work in department 6 or have at least 10 years of seniority.

EMPLOYEE	GENDER	AGE	DEPT	TRADE	SENIORITY

6. Select records that represent employees who are at least 37 years old and work in departments 6 or 7.

EMPLOYEE	GENDER	AGE	DEPT	TRADE	SENIORITY

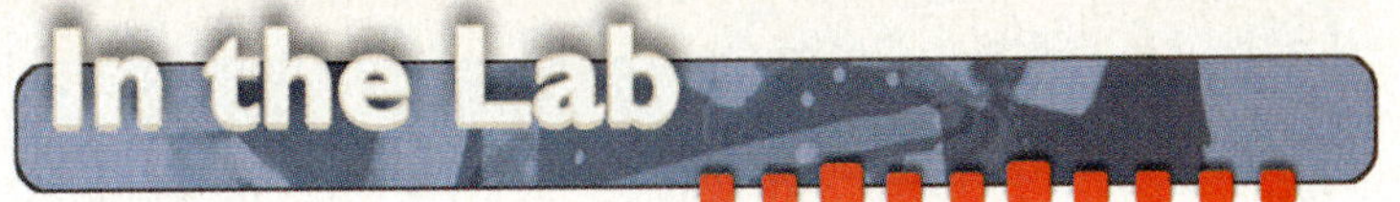

1 Creating, Filtering, and Sorting a List and Determining Subtotals

Problem: You are employed by Apothecary Sales, a company that supplies pharmaceutical products. The national sales force is divided into districts within divisions within regions. The three regions are the Eastern region (1), Midwest region (2), and Western region (3). The director of the Information Systems department has asked you to create a sales rep list (Figure 5-76), run queries against the list, generate various sorted reports, and generate subtotal information.

Instructions Part 1: Create the list shown in Figure 5-76 using the techniques learned in this project. Enter and format the list title and field names in rows 6 and 7. Change the Sheet1 tab name and delete Sheet2 and Sheet3. Use the List command to create a list from the range A7:J8. Format the insert row and then use a data form to enter the data in rows 8 through 20. Use the List toolbar to toggle on the total row. Show the record count in the Gender column, the average age in the Age column, and sums in the Sales and Quota columns as shown in Figure 5-76. Enter your name, course number, laboratory assignment (Lab 5-1), date, and instructor name in the range A32:A36. Use the Page Setup command to change the orientation to Landscape. Print the list. Save the workbook using the file name Lab 5-1 Apothecary Sales Rep List.

Microsoft Excel - Lab 5-1 Apothecary Sales Rep List

Apothecary Sales Rep List

	Region	Div	Dist	Rep	Lname	Fname	Gender	Age	Sales	Quota
8	2	B	2	101	Knight	Tonya	F	31	2,167,301	3,000,000
9	1	A	2	108	Li	Chang	M	25	4,544,023	5,000,000
10	3	B	2	120	Law	Sam	F	58	4,893,014	5,000,000
11	1	B	2	207	Free	Lucy	F	32	3,718,292	4,000,000
12	1	B	2	208	Great	Jim	M	37	989,483	2,000,000
13	2	A	3	210	May	Rodney	M	23	2,565,942	3,000,000
14	1	B	1	212	Lempke	Pat	M	56	5,560,345	6,000,000
15	3	B	2	298	Patel	Gandhi	M	29	2,109,583	2,000,000
16	2	B	2	299	Fenner	John	M	32	3,693,219	5,000,000
17	3	A	3	312	Penny	Josh	M	32	2,210,459	3,000,000
18	1	A	1	313	George	Doreen	F	35	8,300,845	10,000,000
19	3	A	1	406	Lopes	Pedro	M	45	6,921,032	5,000,000
20	3	A	1	432	Wheatly	Jane	F	65	1,034,054	2,000,000
21	*									
22	Total						13	38.462	48,707,592	55,000,000

FIGURE 5-76

Instructions Part 2: Step through each query exercise in Table 5-8 on the next page and print the results for each in landscape orientation. To complete a filter exercise, use the AutoFilter technique. If the arrows are not showing to the right of the column headings when the list is active, then invoke the AutoFilter command. Select the appropriate arrow(s) and option(s) in the lists. Use the (Custom...) option for field names that do not contain appropriate selections. Following each query, select All for each column heading with a blue arrow. You should end up with the following number of records for Filters 1 through 12: 1 = 2; 2 = 2; 3 = 3; 4 = 8; 5 = 6; 6 = 3; 7 = 0; 8 = 4; 9 = 5; 10 = 2; 11 = 1; and 12 = 13. When you are finished querying the list, close the workbook without saving changes.

(continued)

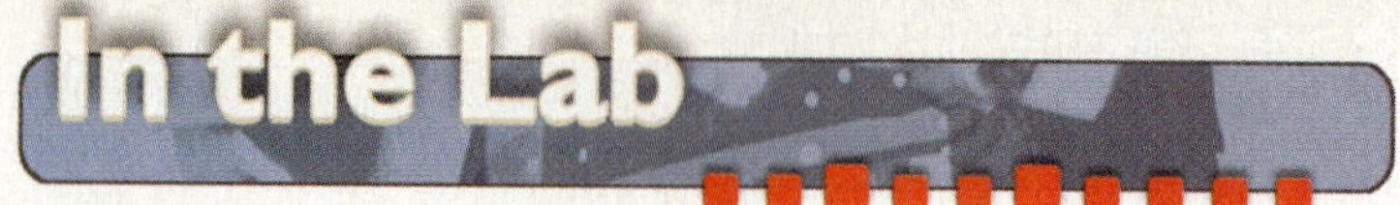

Creating, Filtering, and Sorting a List and Determining Subtotals *(continued)*

Table 5-8 Apothecary Sales Rep List Filter Criteria

FILTER	REGION	DIV	DIST	REP	LNAME	FNAME	GENDER	AGE	SALES	QUOTA
1	1	A								
2	2	B	2							
3					Ends with letter e					
4							M			
5								>30 and < 40		
6			2							>4,000,000
7						Begins with L	M			
8							M			>=5,000,000
9							M	>29		
10								>50	>3,500,000	
11	1						F	<39	<3,000,000	
12	All	All	All	All	All	All	All	All	All	All

Instructions Part 3: Open the workbook Lab 5-1 Apothecary Sales Rep List created in Part 1. Sort the list according to the following six sort problems. Print the list for each sort problem in landscape orientation using the Fit to option. Begin problems 2 through 6 by sorting on the Rep field to sort the list back into its original order.

1. Sort the list in descending sequence by region.
2. Sort the list by district within division within region. All three sort keys are to be in ascending sequence.
3. Sort the list by division within region. Both sort keys are to be in descending sequence.
4. Sort the list by representative number within district within division within region. All four sort keys are to be in ascending sequence.
5. Sort the list in descending sequence by sales.
6. Sort the list by district within division within region. All three sort keys are to be in descending sequence.
7. Hide columns I and J by selecting them and pressing CTRL+0 (zero). Print the list. Select columns H and K. Press CTRL+SHIFT+RIGHT PARENTHESIS to display the hidden columns. Close the Lab 5-1 Apothecary Sales Rep List workbook without saving changes.

Instructions Part 4: Open the Lab 5-1 Apothecary Sales Rep List workbook created in Part 1. Toggle off the total row. Sort the list by district within division within region. Select ascending sequence for all three sort keys. Select a cell immediately above the list. Use the Subtotals command on the Data menu to generate subtotals for sales by region. Print the list. Click row level symbol 1 and print the list. Click row level symbol 2 and print the list. Click row level symbol 3. Remove all subtotals. Close the workbook without saving changes.

Instructions Part 5: Open the Lab 5-1 Apothecary Sales Rep List workbook created in Part 1. Copy the list (range A7:J20) to a new workbook. Save the new workbook in a CSV (Comma delimited) file format using the file name Lab 5-1 Apothecary Sales Rep List CSV. Close the workbook. Start Notepad and open the CSV file. Print the CSV file. Close Notepad. Open the CSV file in Excel. Close Excel.

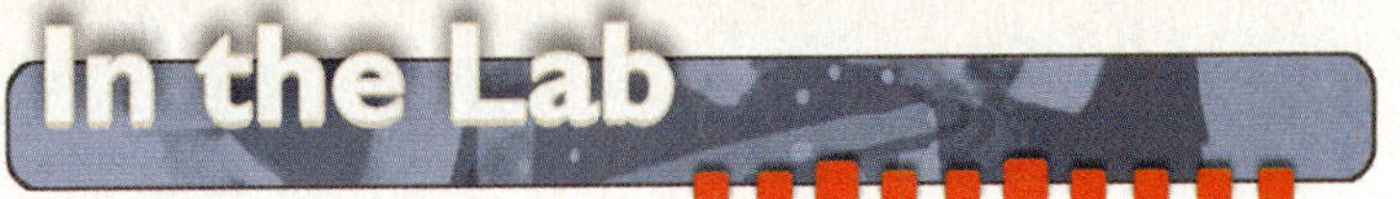

2 Sorting, Finding, and Advanced Filtering

Problem: Programmer Temps, Inc. specializes in supplying consultants to companies in need of programmers. The company uses a list (Figure 5-77) that shows whether an employee is knowledgeable in a programming language.

The president, Rosalyn Chavez, has asked you to sort, query, and determine some statistics from the list. Carefully label each required printout by using the part number and step. If a step results in multiple printouts, label them a, b, c, and so on.

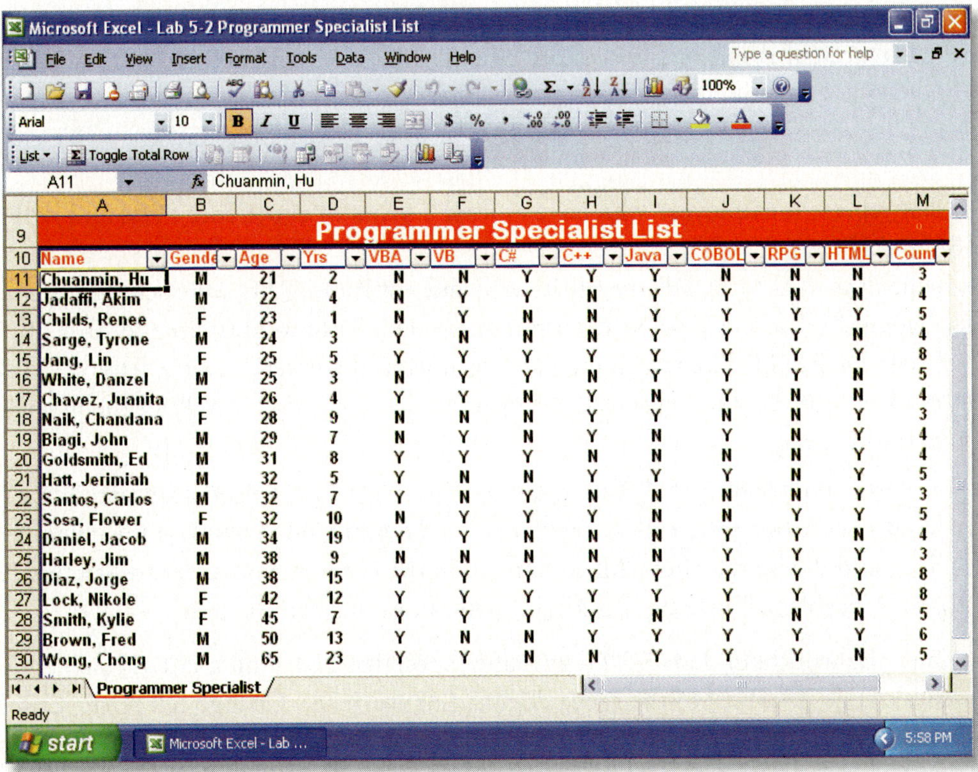

Programmer Specialist List

	Name	Gende	Age	Yrs	VBA	VB	C#	C++	Java	COBOL	RPG	HTML	Count
11	Chuanmin, Hu	M	21	2	N	N	Y	Y	Y	N	N	N	3
12	Jadaffi, Akim	M	22	4	N	Y	Y	N	Y	Y	N	N	4
13	Childs, Renee	F	23	1	N	Y	N	N	Y	Y	Y	Y	5
14	Sarge, Tyrone	M	24	3	Y	N	N	N	Y	Y	Y	N	4
15	Jang, Lin	F	25	5	Y	Y	Y	Y	Y	Y	Y	Y	8
16	White, Danzel	M	25	3	N	Y	Y	N	Y	Y	Y	N	5
17	Chavez, Juanita	F	26	4	Y	Y	N	Y	N	Y	N	N	4
18	Naik, Chandana	F	28	9	N	N	N	Y	Y	N	N	Y	3
19	Biagi, John	M	29	7	N	Y	N	Y	N	Y	N	Y	4
20	Goldsmith, Ed	M	31	8	Y	Y	Y	N	N	N	N	Y	4
21	Hatt, Jerimiah	M	32	5	Y	N	N	Y	Y	Y	N	Y	5
22	Santos, Carlos	M	32	7	Y	N	Y	N	N	N	N	Y	3
23	Sosa, Flower	F	32	10	N	Y	Y	Y	N	N	Y	Y	5
24	Daniel, Jacob	M	34	19	Y	Y	N	N	N	Y	Y	N	4
25	Harley, Jim	M	38	9	N	N	N	N	N	Y	Y	Y	3
26	Diaz, Jorge	M	38	15	Y	Y	Y	Y	Y	Y	Y	Y	8
27	Lock, Nikole	F	42	12	Y	Y	Y	Y	Y	Y	Y	Y	8
28	Smith, Kylie	F	45	7	Y	Y	Y	Y	N	Y	N	N	5
29	Brown, Fred	M	50	13	Y	N	N	Y	Y	Y	Y	Y	6
30	Wong, Chong	M	65	23	Y	Y	N	N	Y	Y	Y	N	5

FIGURE 5-77

Instructions Part 1: Start Excel and perform the following tasks.

1. Open the workbook Lab 5-2 Programmer Specialist List from the Data Disk.
2. Complete the following tasks:
   a. Sort the records in the list into descending sequence by name. Chong Wong should appear first in the list. John Biagi should appear last. Print the list. Undo the sort.
   b. Sort the records in the list by age within gender. Select descending sequence for the age and ascending sequence for gender. Kylie Smith should be the first record. Print the list. Undo the sort.
   c. Sort the list by Java within C++ within C# within VB. Apply sort descending for all four fields. Sort the list first on Java, then C++, then C#, and finally VB. Those who are proficient in all four programming languages will rise to the top of the list. Lin Jang should be the first record. Print the list. Close the workbook without saving it.

(continued)

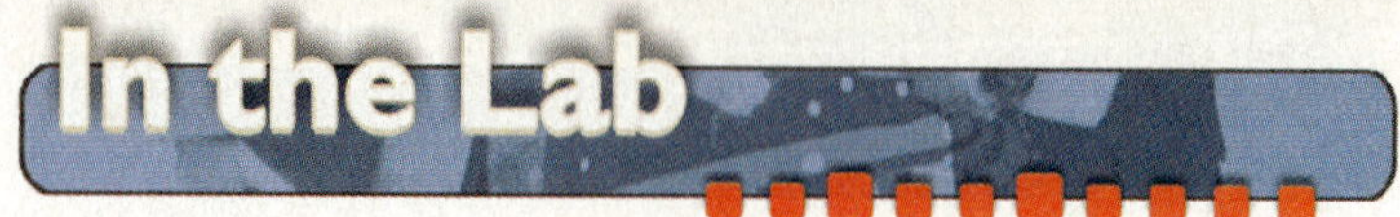

Sorting, Finding, and Advanced Filtering *(continued)*

Instructions Part 2: Open the workbook Lab 5-2 Programmer Specialist List (Figure 5-77 on the previous page). Select a cell within the list. Use the Form command on the List button menu (or Data menu) to display a data form. Use the Criteria button in the data form to enter the comparison criteria for the tasks below. Use the Find Next and Find Prev buttons in the data form to find the records that pass the comparison criteria. Write down and submit the names of the employees who pass the comparison criteria for items a through d. Close the data form after each query and then reopen it by invoking the Form command. You should end up with the following number of records for items a through d: a = 8; b = 5; c = 2; and d = 7.

a. Find all records that represent specialists who are male and are proficient in Java.
b. Find all records that represent employees with more than 9 years of experience (Yrs) and who are certified in VB and RPG.
c. Find all records that represent female employees who are at least 30 years old and are proficient in COBOL.
d. Find all records that represent employees who have at least 5 years of experience (Yrs) and who are proficient in VBA and HTML.
e. Close and then reopen the data form. All specialists who did not know RPG were sent to a seminar on the programming language. Use the Find Next button in the data form to locate the records of these employees and change the RPG field entry in the data form from the letter N to the letter Y. Make sure you press the ENTER key or press the DOWN ARROW key after changing the letter. Print the list. Close the list without saving the changes.

Instructions Part 3: Open the workbook Lab 5-2 Programmer Specialist List. Select a cell within the list. If the column heading arrows do not appear, then click AutoFilter on the Filter submenu. Use the column heading arrows to redo Part 2 a, b, c, and d. Use the Show All command on the Filter submenu before starting items b, c, and d. Print the list for each problem. Close the workbook without saving the changes.

Instructions Part 4: Open the workbook Lab 5-2 Programmer Specialist List. Add a criteria range by copying the list title and field names (range A9:M10) to the range A1:M2 (Figure 5-78). Change cell A1 to Criteria Area and then color the title area as shown in Figure 5-78. Use the Name box in the formula bar to name the criteria range (A2:M3) Criteria.

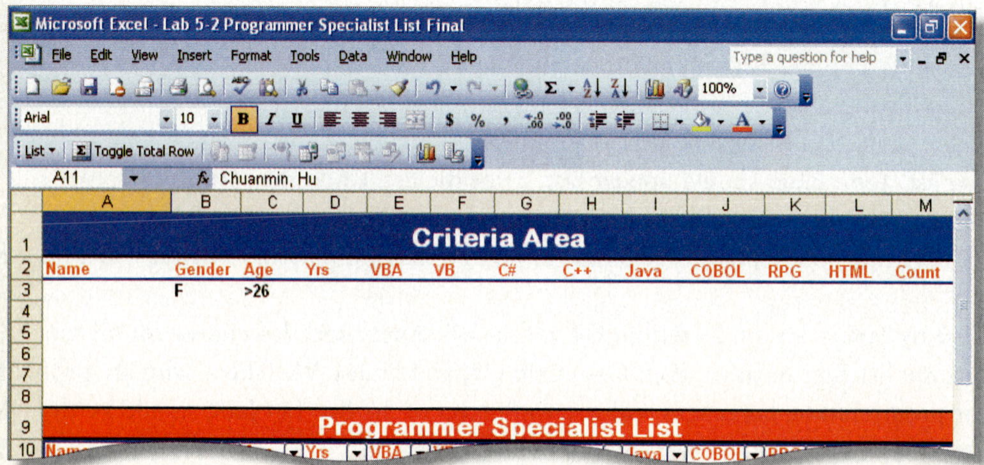

FIGURE 5-78

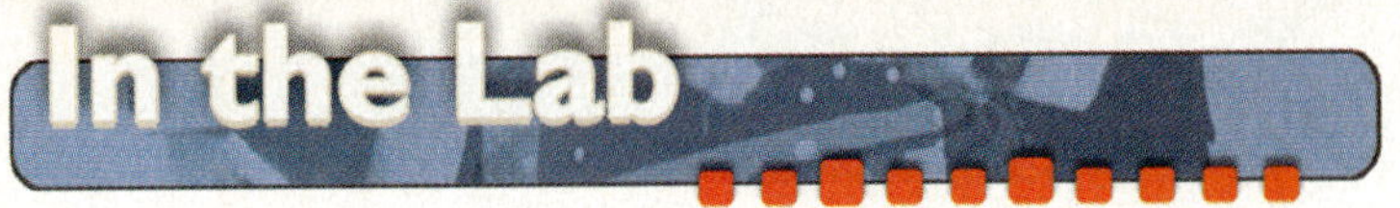

Add an extract range by copying the list title and field names (range A9:M10) to the range A35:M36 (Figure 5-79). Change cell A35 to Extract Area and then color the title area as shown in Figure 5-79. Use the Name box in the formula bar to name the extract range (range A36:M36) Extract.

Microsoft Excel - Lab 5-2 Programmer Specialist List Final

A11 — Chuanmin, Hu

	A	B	C	D	E	F	G	H	I	J	K	L	M
35	Extract Area												
36	Name	Gender	Age	Yrs	VBA	VB	C#	C++	Java	COBOL	RPG	HTML	Count
37	Naik, Chandana	F	28	9	N	N	N	Y	Y	N	N	Y	3
38	Sosa, Flower	F	32	10	N	Y	Y	Y	N	N	Y	Y	5
39	Lock, Nikole	F	42	12	Y	Y	Y	Y	Y	Y	Y	Y	8
40	Smith, Kylie	F	45	7	Y	Y	Y	Y	N	Y	N	N	5
41													
42													

FIGURE 5-79

Enter your name, course, laboratory assignment (Lab 5-2), date, and instructor name in the range P15:P19. With the list active, use the Advanced Filter command on the Filter submenu to extract records that pass the tests listed below in a through e. Print the entire worksheet using landscape orientation and the Fit to option for each extract.

a. Extract the records that represent employees who are female and older than 26 (Figure 5-78). You should extract four records (Figure 5-79).
b. Extract the records that represent female employees who are proficient in VB, but not in COBOL. You should extract one record.
c. Extract the records that represent female employees who are at least 30 years old and are proficient in at least five programming languages. The field Count in column M uses the COUNTIF function to count the number of Ys in a record. A count of 4 means the record represents a specialist with expertise in four areas. You should extract three records.
d. Extract the records that represent employees whose last name begins with the letter C. You should extract three records.
e. Extract the records that represent employees who are proficient in three programming languages or fewer. You should extract 4 records.
f. Save the workbook using the file name Lab 5-2 Programmer Specialist List Final. Close the workbook.

Instructions Part 5: Open the workbook Lab 5-2 Programmer Specialist List Final created in Part 4. If you did not complete Part 4, then open the Lab 5-2 Programmer Specialist List from the Data Disk.

Scroll to the right to display cell G1 in the upper-left corner of the window. Enter the criteria in the range O1:Q3 as shown in Figure 5-80 on the next page. Enter the row titles in cells O5:O10 as shown in Figure 5-80.

Use the database function DAVERAGE and the appropriate criteria in the range O2:Q3 to determine the average age of the males and females in the range. Use the list function DCOUNT and the appropriate criteria in the range O2:Q3 to determine the record count of those who are proficient in HTML. The DCOUNT function requires that you choose a numeric field in the list to count, such as Age.

(continued)

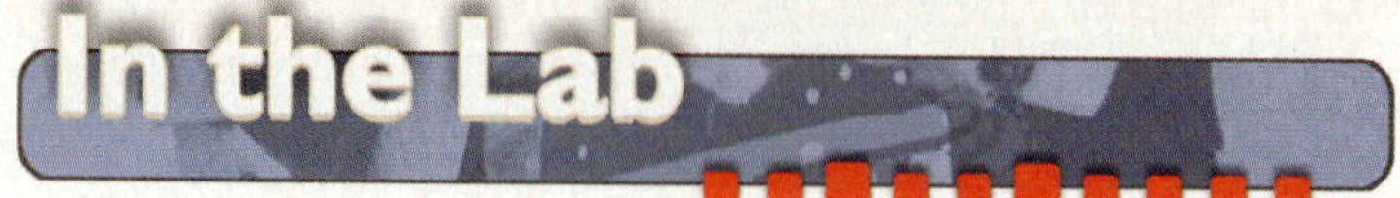

Sorting, Finding, and Advanced Filtering *(continued)*

Use the SUMIF function to determine the RPG Y Sum Count in cell R9. That is, sum the Count field for all records containing a Y in the RPG column. Use the COUNTIF function to determine the COBOL N Count in cell R10.

Print the worksheet in landscape orientation using the Fit to option. Save the workbook using the file name Lab 5-2 Programmer Specialist List Final.

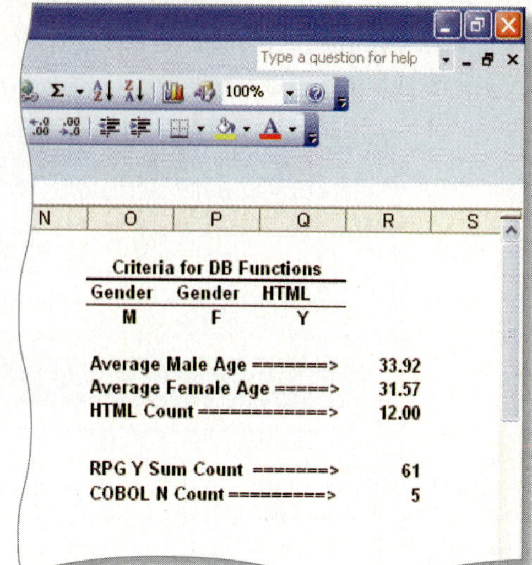

FIGURE 5-80

3 Creating a List with a Lookup Function

Problem: You are a member of the Enviro Student Club, a club for young adults interested in protecting the environment. The president has asked for a volunteer to create a list of the club's members (Figure 5-81). You decide it is a great opportunity to show your Excel skills. Besides including a member's GPA in the list, the president also would like a GPA letter grade assigned to each member based on the GPA value in column G.

Instructions Part 1: Perform the following tasks to create the list shown in the range A7:H17 in Figure 5-81.

1. Enter the title in cell A6 and the column headings in row 7. Format the titles and column widths as shown in Figure 5-81. Define the range A7:G7 as list. Assign appropriate formats to the insert row. Rename the Sheet1 tab and delete Sheet2 and Sheet3.
2. Use the Form command on the Data menu to enter the data shown in the range A8:G17.
3. Enter the Grade table in the range J6:K20. In cell H8, enter the function `=vlookup(g8, $j$8:$k$20, 2)` to determine the letter grade that corresponds to the GPA in cell G8. Copy the function in cell H8 to the range H9:H17.

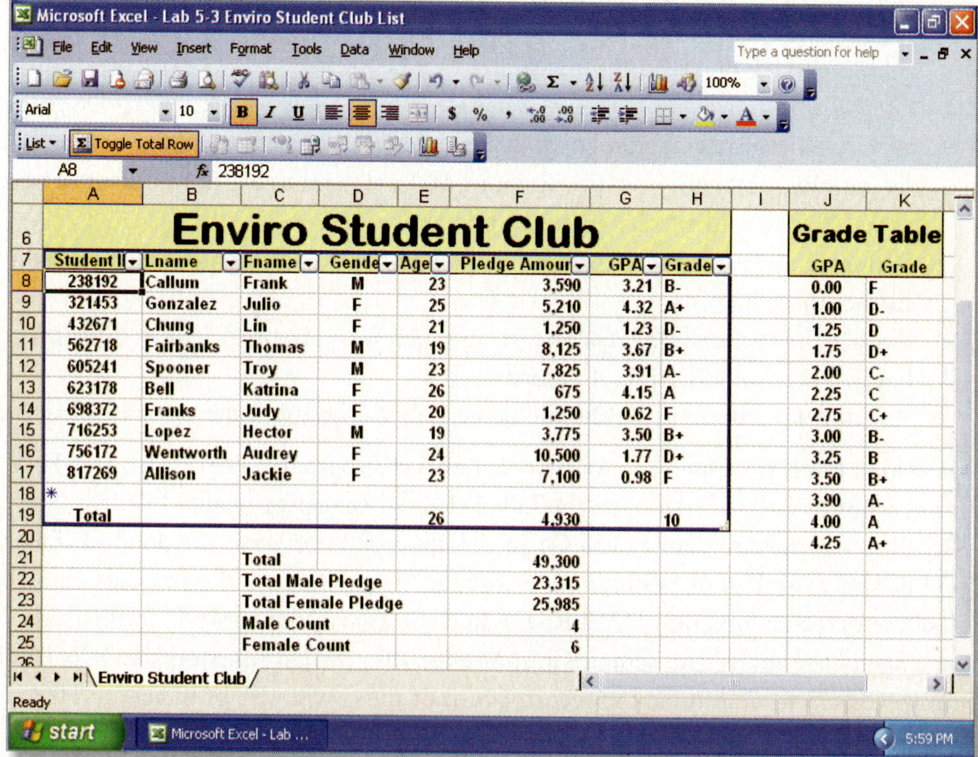

Student ID	Lname	Fname	Gender	Age	Pledge Amount	GPA	Grade
238192	Callum	Frank	M	23	3,590	3.21	B-
321453	Gonzalez	Julio	F	25	5,210	4.32	A+
432671	Chung	Lin	F	21	1,250	1.23	D-
562718	Fairbanks	Thomas	M	19	8,125	3.67	B+
605241	Spooner	Troy	M	23	7,825	3.91	A-
623178	Bell	Katrina	F	26	675	4.15	A
698372	Franks	Judy	F	20	1,250	0.62	F
716253	Lopez	Hector	M	19	3,775	3.50	B+
756172	Wentworth	Audrey	F	24	10,500	1.77	D+
817269	Allison	Jackie	F	23	7,100	0.98	F
Total				26	4,930	10	

Total	49,300
Total Male Pledge	23,315
Total Female Pledge	25,985
Male Count	4
Female Count	6

GPA	Grade
0.00	F
1.00	D-
1.25	D
1.75	D+
2.00	C-
2.25	C
2.75	C+
3.00	B-
3.25	B
3.50	B+
3.90	A-
4.00	A
4.25	A+

FIGURE 5-81

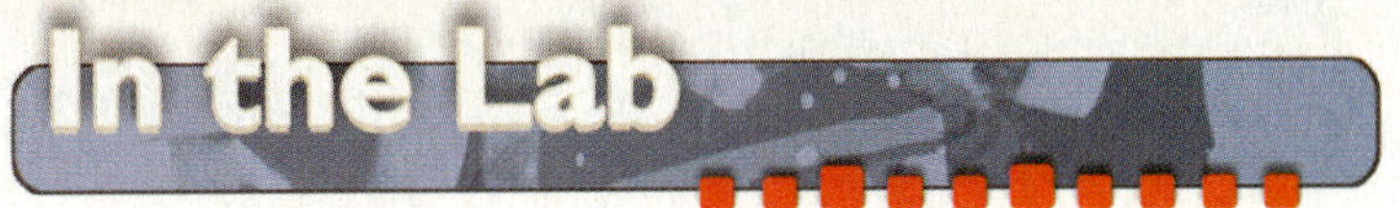

4. Use the Toggle Row Total button on the List toolbar to determine the average age, average pledge amount, and the record count in the Grade column.
5. Enter the total row headings in the range C21:C25. Use the SUM, SUMIF and COUNTIF functions to determine the totals in the range F21:F25.
6. Enter your name, course number, laboratory assignment (Lab 5-3), date, and instructor name in the range H22:H26.
7. Save the workbook using the file name Lab 5-3 Enviro Student Club List. Print the worksheet in landscape orientation. At the bottom of the printout, explain why the dollar signs ($) are necessary in the VLOOKUP function in Step 3.

Instructions Part 2: Open the workbook Lab 5-3 Enviro Student Club List and perform the following tasks:

1. Hide columns G and H by clicking column heading G, dragging through column heading H to select both columns, and then pressing CTRL+0 (zero). Print the list with columns G and H hidden. Unhide columns G and H by clicking column heading F, dragging through column heading I to select the columns adjacent to the hidden columns, and then pressing CTRL+SHIFT+RIGHT PARENTHESIS.
2. Hide rows 12 through 16 by clicking row heading 12, dragging through row heading 16 to select rows 12 through 16, and then pressing CTRL+9. Print the list with rows 15 through 20 hidden. Unhide rows 15 through 20 by clicking row heading 14, dragging through row heading 21 to select the rows adjacent to the hidden rows, and then pressing CTRL+SHIFT+LEFT PARENTHESIS.

Close the workbook without saving changes.

Instructions Part 3: Open the workbook Lab 5-3 Enviro Student Club List. Use a data form to change the following GPAs: 432671 = 3.75; 698372 = 2.10; 817269 = 1.10. Close the data form. The three members' grades should appear as B+, C-, and D-, respectively. Print the list. Close the workbook without saving changes.

Instructions Part 4: Open the workbook Lab 5-3 Enviro Student Club List. Use the Criteria button and the Find Next and Find Prev buttons in the data form to display records that meet the following criteria. Print the list and then write down the Student IDs of the records that pass the tests on the printout.

1. Gender = F; GPA > 3.50 (Two records pass the test.)
2. Age > 23 (Three records pass the test.)
3. Gender = M; Age < 21 (Two records pass the test.)

Close the workbook without saving the changes.

Instructions Part 5: Open the workbook Lab 5-3 Enviro Student Club List. Sort the list as follows. Print the list after each sort. After completing the third sort, close the workbook without saving the changes.

1. Sort the list in ascending sequence by the Pledge Amount.
2. Sort the list by GPA within Gender. Use descending sequence for both fields.
3. Sort the list by Age within Gender. Use ascending sequence for both fields.

Instructions Part 6: Open the workbook Lab 5-3 Enviro Student Club List. Use the concepts and techniques presented in this project to set up a Criteria area above the list, set up an Extract area below the Grade table, and complete the following extractions. Extract the records that meet the three criteria sets in Part 4 above. Print the list for each criteria set. Extract the records that meet the following criteria: 21 < Age < 25. It is necessary that you add a second field called Age to the immediate right of the Criteria range and redefine the Criteria range to include the new field. Four records pass the final test. Select a cell outside the list and print the workbook in landscape orientation. Save the workbook with the last criteria range using the file name Lab 5-3 Enviro Student Club List Final.

Cases and Places

The difficulty of these case studies varies:
■ are the least difficult and ■■ are more difficult. The last exercise is a group exercise.

1 ■ Create an inventory list from the data in Table 5-9. Also include an Amount field and a Priority field. Both are computational fields. Amount equals Inventory times Price. Create a Priority Code table in the range J1:K7 using the data shown in Table 5-10. Use the VLOOKUP function to determine the priority to assign to each record. Print the worksheet in landscape orientation using the Fit to option. Save the workbook.

Table 5-9 Allied Sports Inventory List

PART NO	DESCRIPTION	INVENTORY	PRICE
UT67	Trunks	88	7.50
QG56	Hip Pads	37	52.65
DE34	Shoulder Pads	225	83.20
AD34	Helmet	893	92.00
AG19	Jersey	345	17.35
WR45	Wrist Band	210	3.25
QW23	Football	24	190.55
QH78	Go Cart	135	180.25
DF13	Racquet	225	24.30
SD45	Tennis Ball	987	0.75
FD13	Soccer Ball	213	16.75

Table 5-10 Priority Codes

INVENTORY	PRIORITY
0	1
100	2
200	3
300	4
400	5

2 ■ Open the list created in Cases and Places Exercise 1. Complete the following three sorts, print each sorted version of the list, and then undo the sorts in preparation for the next sort: (a) sort the list in descending sequence by inventory; (b) sort the list by amount (ascending) within priority code (descending); and (c) sort the list in ascending sequence by priority code. With the list sorted by priority, toggle off the total row, and then use the Subtotals command to determine subtotals for each priority code. Print the list with the subtotals. Save the workbook with the subtotals.

3 ■■ Open the list created in Cases and Places Exercise 1. Filter (query) the list using the column heading arrows. Make sure you show all records before each query. Print the list for each of the following queries: (1) priority code equal to 3, (2) inventory greater than 75 and less than 400, (3) priority code equals 1 and inventory greater than 30, and (4) price greater than 7.00. The number of records that show in the queries are: (1) 4, (2) 7, (3) 2, and (4) 9.

4 ■■ **Working Together:** Have your group design a form that students in the class can fill out. Ask for the following information: (1) last initial and first initial, (2) gender, (3) age, (4) college start date, (5) resident state, (6) major, (7) credit hours required for degree, (8) credit hours towards degree, (9) % of degree completed (computational field), (10) approximate GPA, and (11) letter grade based on GPA (1 = D, 2 = C, 3 = B, and 4 = A). Use the concepts and techniques introduced in this project to design and create a list from the data collected along with a grade field that corresponds to the GPA. Also, run sorts, determine subtotals, and use the database, COUNTIF, and SUMIF functions to generate statistics.

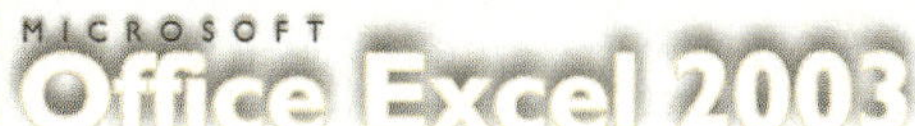

Creating Templates and Working with Multiple Worksheets and Workbooks

PROJECT

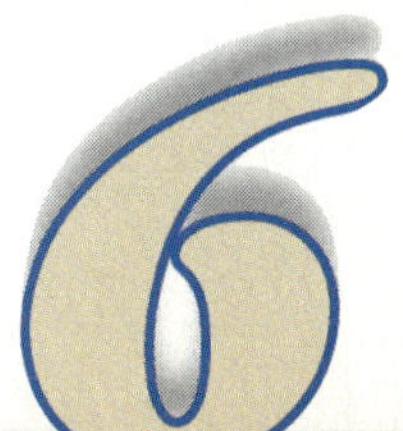

CASE PERSPECTIVE

Adelle Cheramie is an amateur photographer with interests in cameras and camera equipment. In her senior year in college, Adelle took an elective Small Business course in which she learned how to start, run, and market a small business. As part of the required work, she did a research paper on eBay's Web-based revenue model, which allows anyone to trade practically anything over the Web.

Shortly after graduation, Adelle started her own camera supply company, Awesome Images, which sells a variety of digital cameras over the World Wide Web. The company maintains its inventory at three store locations in Cleveland, Lexington, and San Diego. The company's sales model is unique in that customers sign up on the Web to purchase a camera over a two-week period. The price continues to decrease as more customers buy the camera. At the end of the two weeks, a final price is determined.

A major competitor recently sent the chief financial officer, Frances Kaczka, a letter of intent to purchase the company. As part of due diligence, the competitor has requested that Frances supply a report that shows the total gross profit potential based on the month-end inventory.

Frances has asked you to consolidate the inventory data from the three stores (Figures 6-1a, 6-1b, and 6-1c) on one worksheet (Figure 6-1d) and to create a chart that compares the profit potentials of the digital cameras in stock by company (Figure 6-1e).

As you read through this project, you will learn about creating and using templates, advanced formatting techniques, the Research tool, 3-D cell references, and drawing techniques. You then will learn how to set up a workbook for printing, apply research techniques, organize workbooks on disk, and consolidate data by linking workbooks.

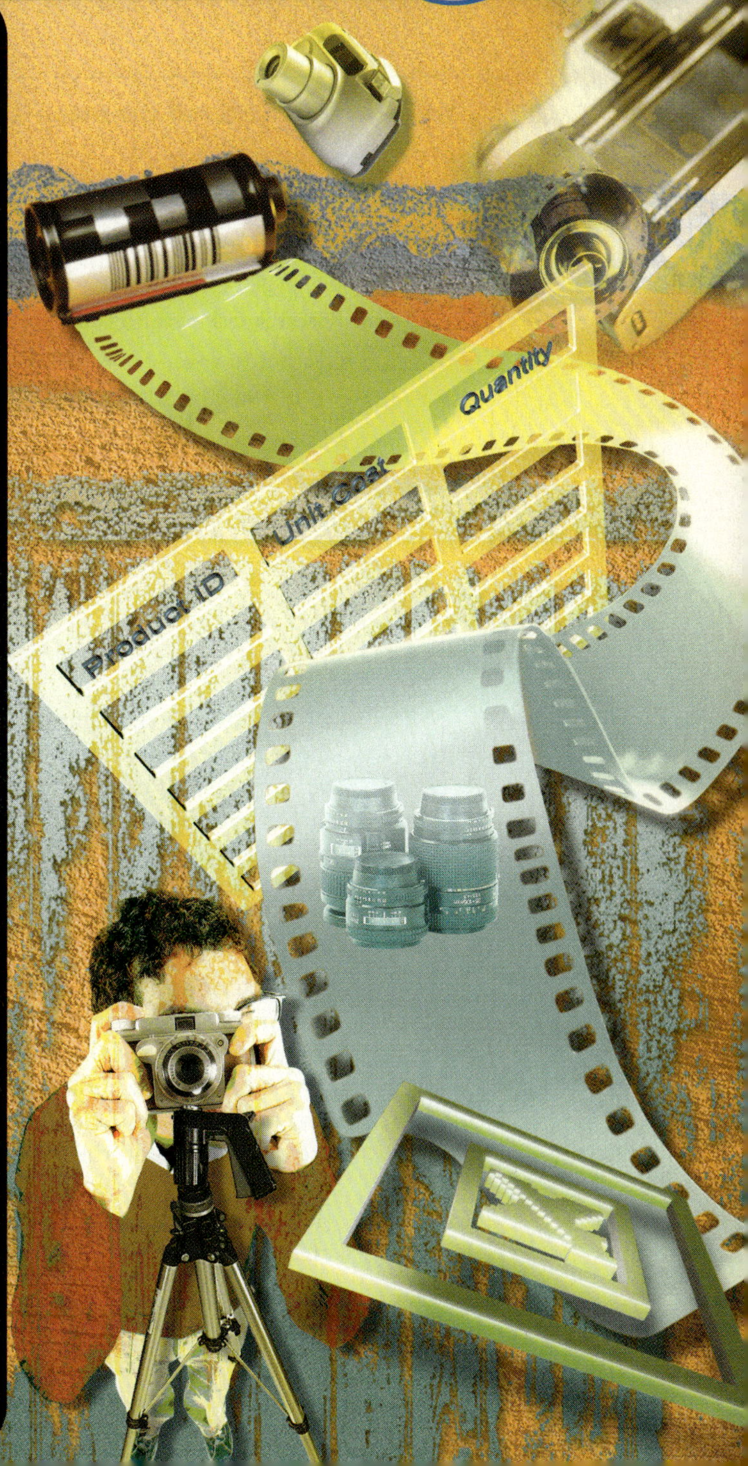

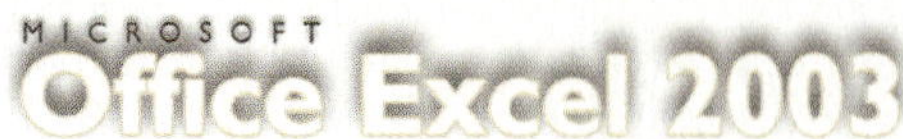

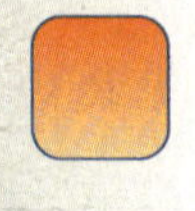

Creating Templates and Working with Multiple Worksheets and Workbooks

PROJECT

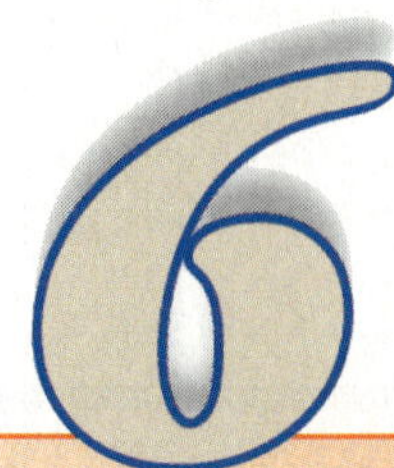

Objectives

You will have mastered the material in this project when you can:

- Create and use a template
- Use the ROUND function
- Utilize custom format codes
- Define, apply, and remove a style
- Use the Research task pane to find a synonym
- Add a worksheet to a workbook
- Create formulas that use 3-D cell references
- Draw a 3-D Cylinder chart
- Use WordArt to create a title and create and modify lines and objects
- Assign comments to cells
- Use the Research task pane to research a topic
- Add a header or footer, change margins, and insert a page break
- Use the Find and Replace commands
- Search for files and create and use a workspace file
- Consolidate data by linking workbooks

Introduction

Many business applications, such as the profit potential workbook requested in the Case Perspective on the previous page, require data from several worksheets to be summarized on one worksheet. In the case of Awesome Images, data comes from three different store locations. If you enter each store location's inventory data on a worksheet in a workbook, you can click the sheet tabs at the bottom of the Excel window to move from worksheet to worksheet, or store to store. On a fourth worksheet, you then can enter formulas that reference cells on the other worksheets, which allows you to summarize worksheet data. The process of summarizing data included on multiple worksheets on one worksheet is called **consolidation**.

Another important concept presented in this project is the use of a template. A **template** is a special workbook you can create and then use as a pattern to create new, similar workbooks or worksheets. A template usually consists of a general format (worksheet title, column and row titles, and numeric format) and formulas that are common to all the worksheets. For example, in the Awesome Images workbook, the worksheets for each of the three stores and the company worksheet are identical (Figure 6-1), except for the data and the worksheet subtitle. One efficient way to create the workbook is first to create a template, save the template, and then copy the template to a workbook as many times as necessary.

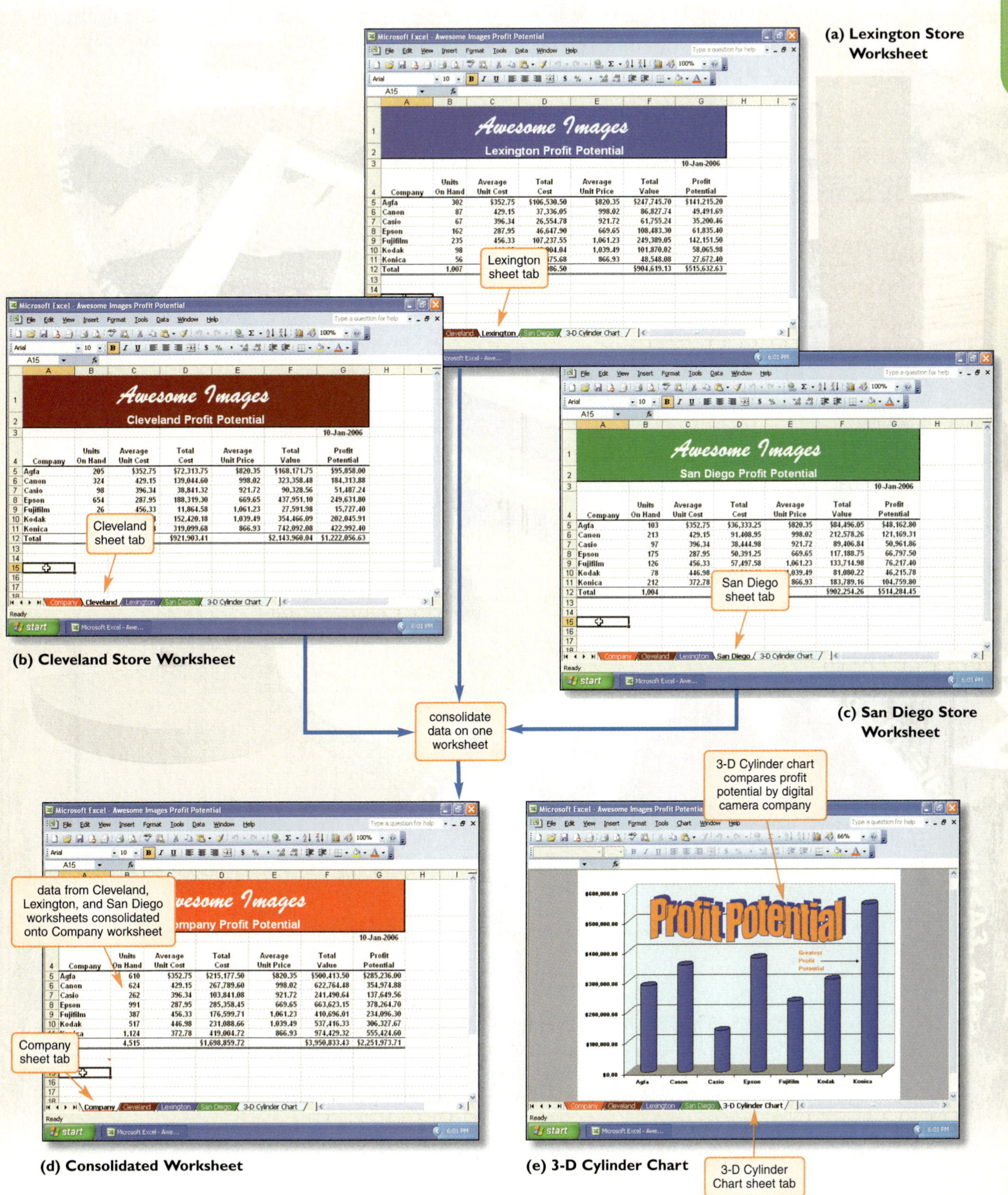

(a) Lexington Store Worksheet

(b) Cleveland Store Worksheet

(c) San Diego Store Worksheet

(d) Consolidated Worksheet

(e) 3-D Cylinder Chart

FIGURE 6-1

Project Six — Awesome Images Profit Potential

The requirements document for the Awesome Images Profit Potential workbook is shown in Figure 6-2. It includes the needs, source of data, summary of calculations, chart requirements, special requirements, and other facts about its development.

More About

Workbook Survival

For workbooks to be successful and survive their expected lifecycle in a business environment, they must be well documented and easy to understand. You document a workbook by adding comments to cells that contain complex formulas or to cells containing content that may not be understood easily. The documentation also should take into consideration those who will maintain the workbook after you leave. You create easy to understand workbooks by reviewing alternative designs prior to creating the workbook. The more time you spend documenting and designing a workbook, the easier it will be for users and spreadsheet maintenance specialists to understand.

REQUEST FOR NEW WORKBOOK

Date Submitted:	January 4, 2006
Submitted By:	Frances Kaczka
Worksheet Title:	Awesome Images Profit Potential
Needs:	The needs are as follows: 1. A template (Figure 6-3a) that can be used to create similar worksheets. 2. A workbook containing three worksheets for the three store locations and one worksheet to consolidate the company data. 3. A chart (Figure 6-3b) that compares the profit potential of the different digital cameras in inventory, by company or brand. The chart should be placed on a separate sheet.
Source of Data:	The data will be collected and organized by the chief financial officer, Frances Kaczka.
Calculations:	Include the following formulas in the template for each camera: 1. Total Cost = Units On Hand * Average Unit Cost 2. Average Unit Price = Average Unit Cost / (1 – .57) 3. Total Value = Units On Hand * Average Unit Price 4. Profit Potential = Total Value – Total Cost 5. Use the SUM function to determine totals. 6. After using the template to create the multiple-worksheet workbook, use the SUM function to determine the units on hand totals on the Company sheet in the workbook. **Note:** Use dummy data in the template to verify the formulas. Round the Average Unit Price to the nearest penny.
Chart Requirements:	Include a chart sheet with a 3-D Cylinder chart that compares the profit potential for each of the digital camera brands listed on the Company sheet. Use a Text Box to create a callout to highlight the cylinder representing the camera with the greatest profit potential.
Special Requirements:	Research and incorporate a digital camera sales forecast in a comment. Investigate a way Awesome Images can consolidate data from multiple workbooks into another workbook.

Approvals

Approval Status:	X	Approved
		Rejected
Approved By:	Adelle Cheramie	
Date:	January 6, 2006	
Assigned To:	J. Quasney, Spreadsheet Specialist	

FIGURE 6-2

The sketch of the template (Figure 6-3a) consists of titles, column and row headings, location of data values, and a general idea of the desired formatting. The sketch of the 3-D Cylinder chart (Figure 6-3b) consists of a chart title, which will be added using WordArt, and a callout that emphasizes the cylinder representing the greatest profit potential.

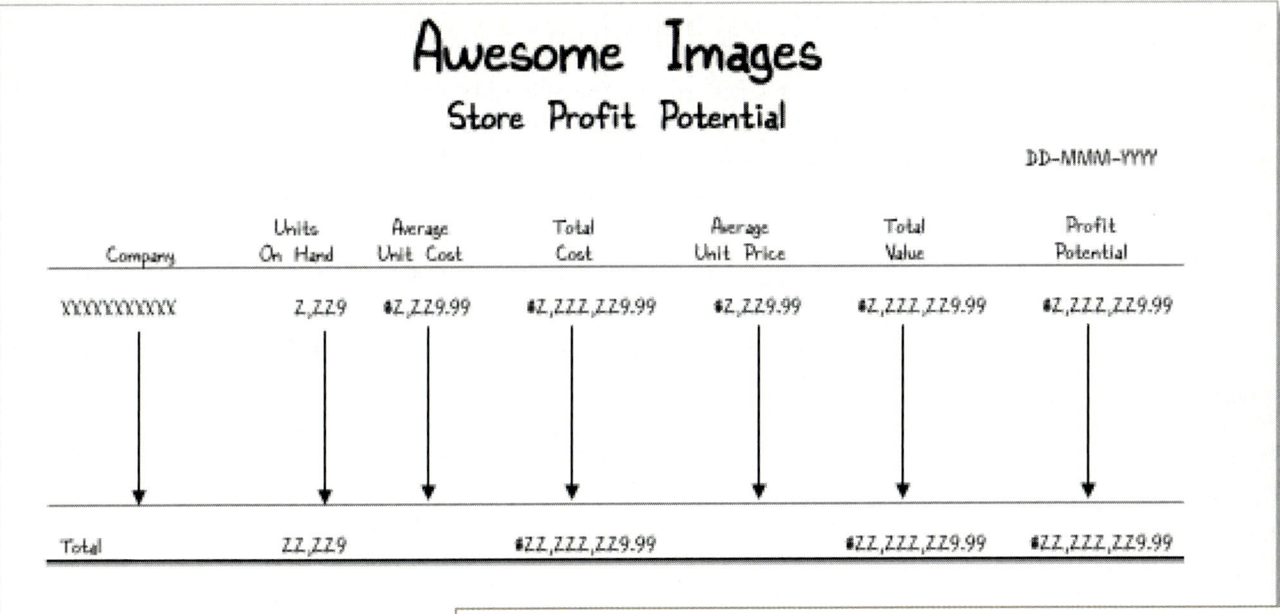

(a) Sketch of Template

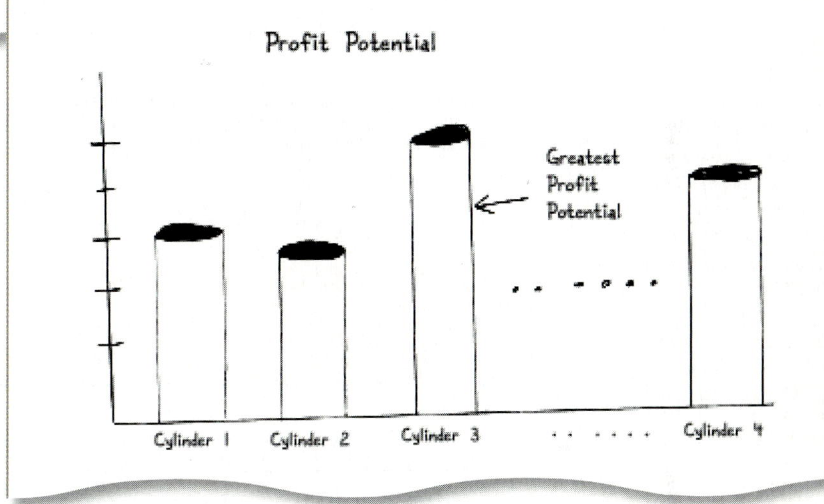

(b) Sketch of 3-D Cylinder Chart

FIGURE 6-3

After the template is created using dummy data and the required formulas (Figure 6-4 on the next page) and then saved on disk, it will be copied to a workbook made up of four worksheets. Actual data for the three store locations then will replace the dummy data on the three store worksheets. The data from the three store worksheets then will be consolidated on the company worksheet.

Starting and Customizing Excel

With the requirements document and sketch of the worksheet and chart complete, the next step is to start and customize Excel. If you are stepping through this project on a computer and you want your screen to agree with the figures in this book, then you should change your computer's resolution to 800 × 600. For information on changing the resolution on your computer, see Appendix D. The steps on the next page start Excel and customize the Excel window.

More About

Templates

Templates are most helpful when you need to create several similar or identical workbooks. They help reduce work and ensure consistency. Templates can contain: (1) text and graphics, such as a company name and logo; (2) formats and page layouts; and (3) formulas or macros.

To Start and Customize Excel

1 **Click the Start button on the Windows taskbar, point to All Programs on the Start menu, point to Microsoft Office on the All Programs submenu, and then click Microsoft Office Excel 2003 on the Microsoft Office submenu.**

2 **If the Excel window is not maximized, double-click its title bar to maximize it.**

3 **If the Language bar appears, right-click it and then click Close the Language bar on the shortcut menu.**

4 **If the Getting Started task pane appears in the Excel window, click its Close button in the upper-right corner.**

5 **If the Standard and Formatting toolbars are positioned on the same row, click the Toolbar Options button and then click Show Buttons on Two Rows.**

Excel displays a blank workbook. The Standard and Formatting toolbars appear on two rows as shown at the top of Figure 6-4.

> *More About*
>
> **Built-In Templates**
>
> A set of templates that provides solutions to common business problems is available with Excel. To view the templates, click New on the File menu, click On my computer in the New Workbook task pane, and then click the Spreadsheet Solutions tab in the Templates dialog box. Many more templates that solve a wide range of problems are available at Microsoft Office Online. To view the online templates, click the Templates on Office Online button in the New Workbook task pane.

If your toolbars appear differently than those shown in Figure 6-4, see Appendix D for additional information on resetting the toolbars and menus.

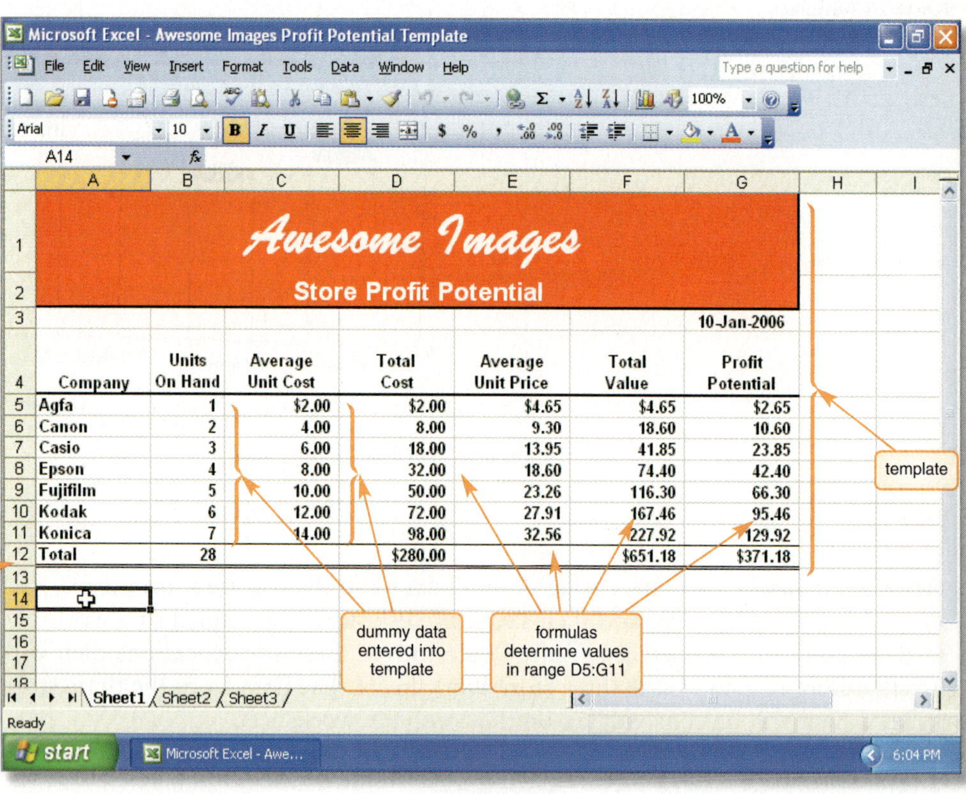

FIGURE 6-4

Creating the Template

The first step in building the workbook is to create and save a template that contains the titles, column and row headings, formulas, and formats used on each of the sheets.

After the template is saved on disk, it can be used every time a similar workbook is developed. Because templates help speed and simplify their work, many Excel users create a template for each application on which they work. Templates can be simple — possibly using a special font or worksheet title — or more complex — perhaps utilizing specific formulas and format styles, such as the template for the Awesome Images Profit Potential workbook.

Creating a template, as shown in Figure 6-4, follows the same basic steps used to create a workbook. The only difference between developing a workbook and a template is the file type used to save the template.

Bolding the Font and Adjusting the Row Heights and Column Widths of the Template

The first step in this project is to change the font style of the entire template to bold and adjust the height of row 4 to 39.00 points and column widths as follows: columns A and C through G = 13.00 characters; and column B = 8.14 characters.

To Bold the Font and Adjust the Row Heights and Column Widths of the Template

1. **Click the Select All button immediately above row heading 1 and to the left of column heading A and then click the Bold button on the Formatting toolbar. Select cell A1 to deselect the worksheet.**
2. **Drag the button boundary of row heading 4 down until the ScreenTip, Height 39.00 (52 pixels), appears.**
3. **Drag the right boundary of column heading A to the right until the ScreenTip, Width: 13.00 (97 pixels), appears.**
4. **Drag the right boundary of column heading B to the left until the ScreenTip, Width: 8.14 (62 pixels), appears.**
5. **Click column heading C, drag through to column heading G, and then drag the right boundary of column heading G right until the ScreenTip, Width: 13.00 (97 pixels), appears. Select cell A1 to deselect columns C through G.**

Excel assigns the bold font style to all cells in the worksheet. Columns A and C through G have a width of 13.00 characters and column B has a width of 8.14 characters. Row 4 has a height of 39.00 points.

More About

About Selecting a Range of Cells

You can select any range of cells with entries surrounded by blank cells by clicking a cell in the range and pressing CTRL+SHIFT+ASTERISK (*).

Entering the Title, Subtitle, and Row Titles in the Template

The following steps enter the titles in cells A1 and A2 and the row titles in column A.

To Enter the Title, Subtitle, and Row Titles in the Template

1. **Type** `Awesome Images` **in cell A1 and then press the DOWN ARROW key. Type** `Store Profit Potential` **in cell A2 and then press the DOWN ARROW key twice to make cell A4 active.**
2. **Type** `Manufacturer` **and then press the DOWN ARROW key.**

(continued)

3 **With cell A5 active, enter the remaining row titles in column A as shown in Figure 6-5.**

Excel displays the template title and row titles in column A as shown in Figure 6-5.

> *More About*
>
> **Displaying Future Dates**
>
> You can display a future date, such as tomorrow's date, in a cell by adding a number to the NOW or TODAY function. For example, =NOW() + 1 displays tomorrow's date in a cell and =NOW()+14 displays a date two weeks in the future. =NOW() - 1 displays yesterday's date.

Notice that, in the sketch of the template in Figure 6-3a and in Figure 6-4, cell A4 has the column heading Company, rather than the column heading Manufacturer as shown in Figure 6-5. Later in this project, the Research button on the Standard toolbar will be used to change the word Manufacturer to the synonym Company.

Entering Column Titles and the System Date in the Template

The next step is to enter the column titles in row 4 and the system date in cell G3.

To Enter Column Titles and the System Date in the Template

1 **Select cell B4. Type** `Units` **and then press ALT+ENTER. Type** `On Hand` **and then press the RIGHT ARROW key.**

2 **Type** `Average` **and then press ALT+ENTER. Type** `Unit Cost` **and then press the RIGHT ARROW key.**

3 **With cell D4 active, enter the remaining column titles in row 4 as shown in Figure 6-5.**

4 **Select cell G3. Type** `=now()` **and then press the ENTER key. Right-click cell G3 and then click Format Cells on the shortcut menu. When Excel displays the Format Cells dialog box, click Date in the Category list and then double-click 3/14/01 13:30 in the Type list. Select cell A14 to deselect cell G3.**

Excel displays the column titles and system date as shown in Figure 6-5. The format assigned to the system date in cell G3 is temporary. For now, it ensures that the system date will appear properly, rather than as a series of number signs (#). The system date will be assigned a permanent format later in this project.

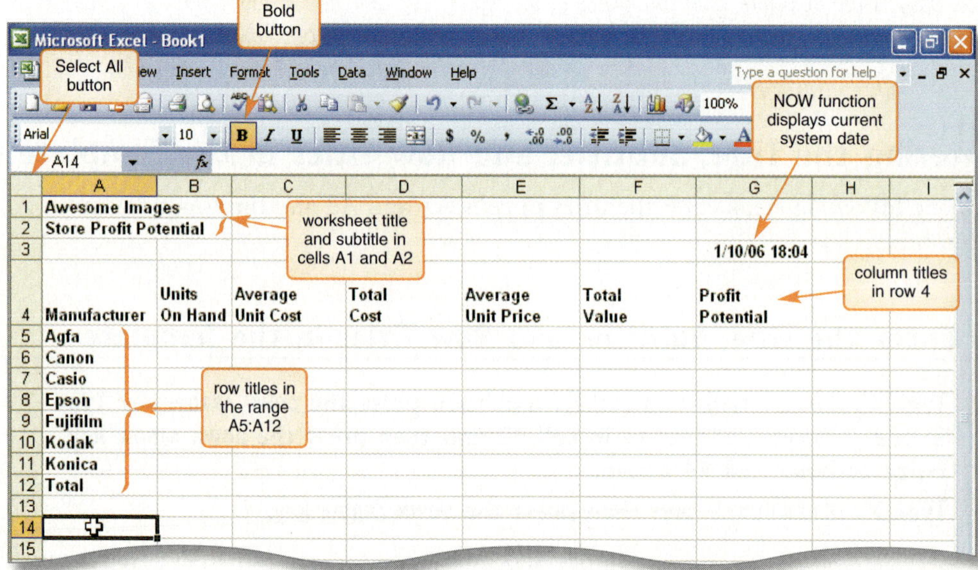

FIGURE 6-5

Entering Dummy Data in the Template

When a template is created, **dummy data** — that is, sample data used in place of actual data to verify the formulas in the template — should be used in place of actual data to verify the formulas in the template. Selecting simple numbers such as 1, 2, and 3 allows you to check quickly to see if the formulas are generating the proper results. In templates with more complex formulas, you may want to use numbers that test the extreme boundaries of valid data. While creating the Awesome Images Template in Project 6, dummy data is used for the units on hand values in the range B5:B11 and the average unit cost values in the range C5:C11.

The dummy data is entered by using the fill handle to create a series of numbers in columns B and C. The series in column B begins with 1 and increments by 1; the series in column C begins with 2 and increments by 2. Recall that you must enter the first two numbers in a series so that Excel can determine the increment amount. If the cell to the right of the start value is empty and you want to increment by 1, however, you can create a series by entering only one number as shown in the following steps. The following steps enter dummy data in the template, by using the fill handle to create a series.

> *More About*
>
> **Dummy Numbers**
>
> As you develop more sophisticated workbooks, it will become increasingly important that you create good test data to ensure your workbooks are error-free. The more you test a workbook, the more confident you will be in the results generated. Always take the time to select test data that tests the limits of the formulas.

To Enter Dummy Data in the Template Using the Fill Handle

1

- **Select cell B5.**
- **Type** 1 **and then press the ENTER key.**
- **Select the range B5:C5.**
- **Drag the fill handle through cells B11 and C11. Do not release the mouse button.**

Excel surrounds the range B5:C11 with a gray border and displays a ScreenTip showing that it will assign cell B11 the series stop value of 7.

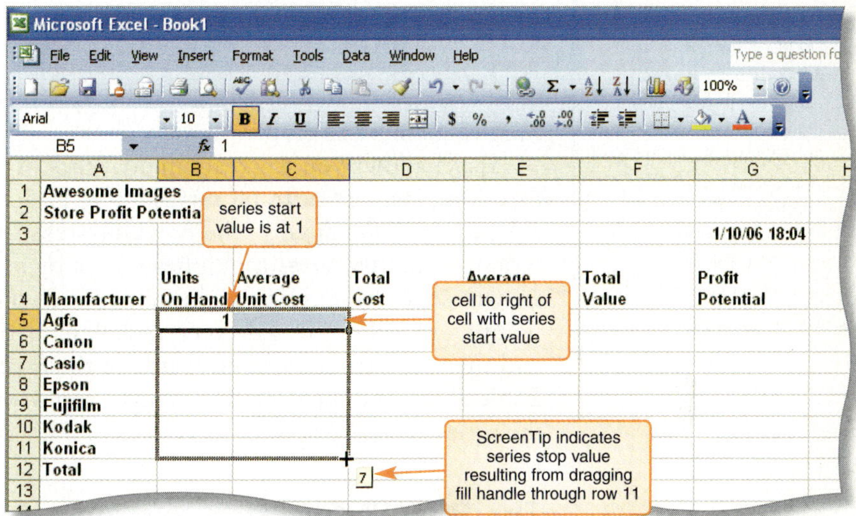

FIGURE 6-6

2

- **Release the mouse button.**

Excel creates the series 1 through 7 in increments of 1 in the range B5:B11 (Figure 6-7).

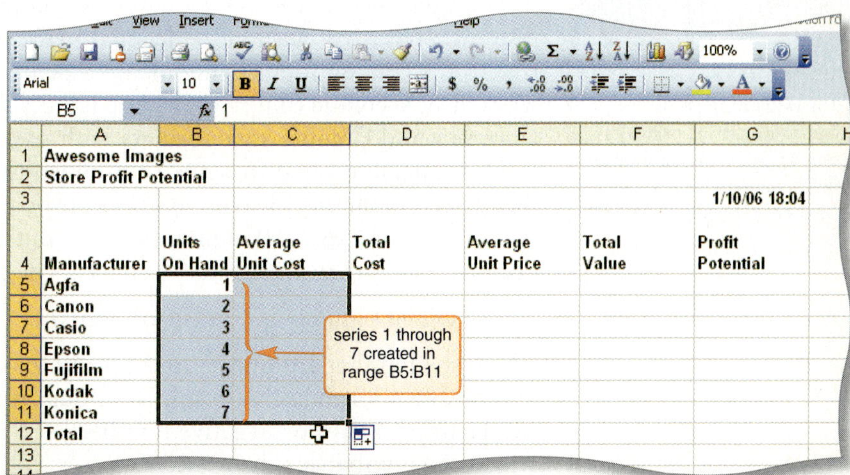

FIGURE 6-7

3

- **Select cell C5. Type** 2 **and then press the DOWN ARROW key.**
- **Type** 4 **and then press the ENTER key.**
- **Select the range C5:C6. Drag the fill handle through cell C11.**

Excel creates the series 2 through 14 in increments of 2 in the range C5:C11 (Figure 6-8).

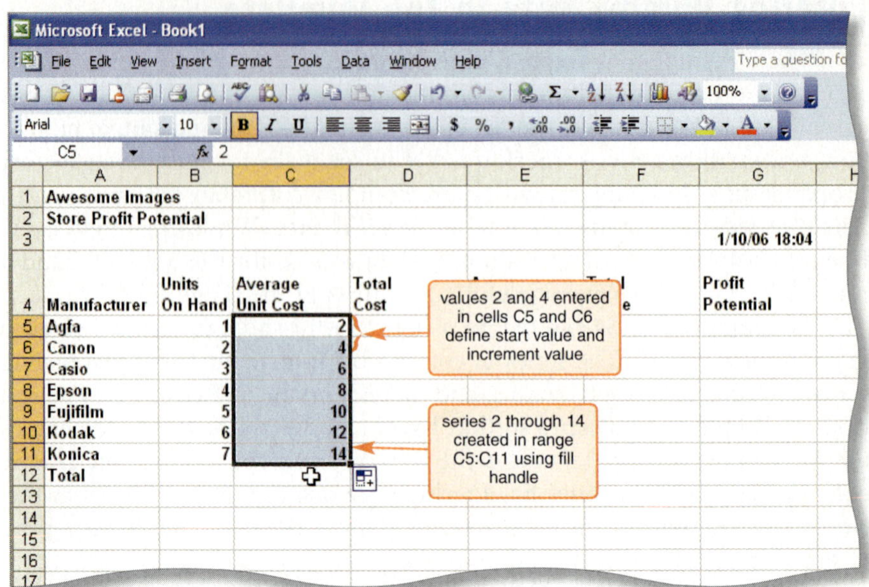

FIGURE 6-8

Other Ways

1. Enter first number, while holding down CTRL key drag through range
2. Enter start value, select range, on Edit menu point to Fill, click Series, enter parameters, click OK button
3. In Voice Command mode, say "Edit, Fill, Series, [enter parameters], OK"

If you create a linear series by selecting the cell to the right of the start value as demonstrated in Steps 1 and 2 on the previous page, then the cell to the right of the start value must be empty.

Excel allows you to create many types of series, including a **date series** (Jan, Feb, Mar, etc.), an **auto fill series** (1, 1, 1, etc.), and a **linear series** (1, 2, 3, etc. or 2, 4, 6, etc.) as created in the previous steps. A fourth type of series is a growth series. A **growth series** multiplies values by a constant factor. You can create a growth series by entering an initial value in the first cell, selecting the range to fill, pointing to Fill on the Edit menu, clicking Series, clicking Growth in the type area, and then entering a constant factor in the Step value box. For example, if you enter 2 in cell D5 and then create a growth series with a step value of 2, Excel will create the series 2, 4, 8, 16, 32, 64, 128, 256, 512, 1024, 2048 in the range D5:D15.

The ROUND Function and Entering Formulas in the Template

More About

Accuracy

The result of an arithmetic operation, such as multiplication or division, is accurate to the factor with the least number of decimal places.

The next step is to enter the four formulas for the first digital camera manufacturer (Agfa) in the range D5:G5. When you multiply or divide decimal numbers that result in an answer with more decimal places than the format allows, you run the risk of the column totals being off by a penny or so. For example, as shown in the worksheet sketch in Figure 6-3a on page EX 381, columns C through G use the Currency and Comma style formats with two decimal places. And yet, the formulas used to calculate values for these columns result in several additional decimal places that Excel maintains for computation purposes. For this reason, it is recommended that you use the **ROUND function** on formulas that potentially can result in more decimal places than the format displays. The general form of the ROUND function is

=ROUND (number, number of digits)

where the number argument can be a number, a cell reference that contains a number, or a formula that results in a number; and the number of digits argument can be any positive or negative number used to determine the number of places to which the number will be rounded.

The following is true about the ROUND function:

1. If the number of digits argument is greater than 0 (zero), then the number is rounded to the specified number of digits to the right of the decimal point.
2. If the number of digits argument is equal to 0 (zero), then the number is rounded to the nearest integer.
3. If the number of digits argument is less than 0 (zero), then the number is rounded to the specified number of digits to the left of the decimal point.

Table 6-1 shows the four formulas to enter in the template in the range D5:G5. The ROUND function is used to round the value resulting from the formula assigned to cell E5 to two decimal places.

Table 6-1 Formulas Used to Determine Profit Potential

CELL	DESCRIPTION	FORMULA	ENTRY
D5	Total Cost	Units On Hand x Average Unit Cost	=B5 * C5
E5	Average Unit Price	ROUND(Average Unit Cost / (1–.65), 2)	=ROUND(C5 / (1–.57), 2)
F5	Total Value	Units On Hand x Average Unit Price	=B5 * E5
G5	Profit Potential	Total Value – Total Cost	=F5 – D5

The most difficult formula to understand in Table 6-1 is the one that determines the average unit price, which also is called the average selling price. To make a net profit, companies must sell their merchandise for more than the unit cost of the merchandise plus the company's operating expenses (taxes, rent, upkeep, and so forth).

To determine what selling price to set for an item, companies often first establish a desired margin and then determine a selling price. Most companies look for a margin of 50% to 75%. Awesome Images, for example, tries to make a margin of 57% on each of its digital cameras. The formula for the average unit price in Table 6-1 helps the company determine the price at which to sell an item so that it ends up with a 57% margin. For example, if an item costs Awesome Images $2.00 (the unit cost), then the company must sell it for $4.65 [$2.00 / (1–.57)] to make a 57% margin. Of this $4.65, $2.00 goes to pay the unit cost of the item; the other $2.65 is the gross profit potential (57% x $4.65 = $2.65).

The steps on the next page use Point mode to enter the four formulas in Table 6-1 in the range D5:G5. After the formulas are entered for the Agfa digital cameras in row 5, the formulas will be copied for the remaining six digital cameras. The AutoSum button then is use to determine the totals in row 12.

More About

Fractions

The forward slash (/) has multiple uses. For example, dates often are entered using the backslash. In formulas, the backslash represents division. What about fractions? To enter a fraction, such as ½, type .5 or 0 1/2 (i.e., type zero, followed by a space, followed by the number 1, followed by a slash, followed by the number 2). If you type 1/2, Excel will store the value in the cell as the date January 2.

Q&A

Q: What changes Excel from Enter mode or Edit mode to Point mode?

A: Typing the EQUAL SIGN (=) followed by clicking a cell or clicking the Insert Function box on the formula bar, selecting a function, and then clicking a cell. You know you are in Point mode when the word Point appears on the left side of the status bar at the bottom of the Excel window.

To Enter Formulas Using Point Mode and Determine Totals in the Template

1

• **Select cell D5, type = to start the formula, click cell B5, type * (asterisk), click cell C5, and then click the Enter box in the formula bar.**

*Excel displays the formula =B5*C5 in the formula bar and the value 2 (1 x 2) as the total cost in cell D5 (Figure 6-9).*

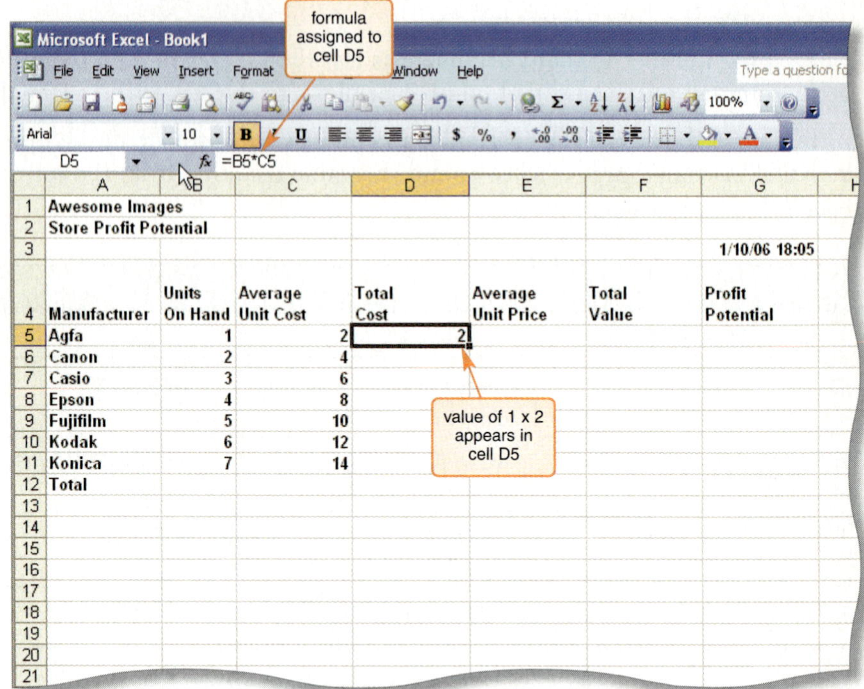

FIGURE 6-9

2

• **Select cell E5, type** `=round(c5 / (1 - .57), 2)`**, and then click the Enter box in the formula bar.**

Excel displays the formula =ROUND(C5 /(1 – 0.57), 2) in the formula bar and the value 4.65 (4.651162791 rounded to two decimal places) as the average unit price in cell E5 (Figure 6-10).

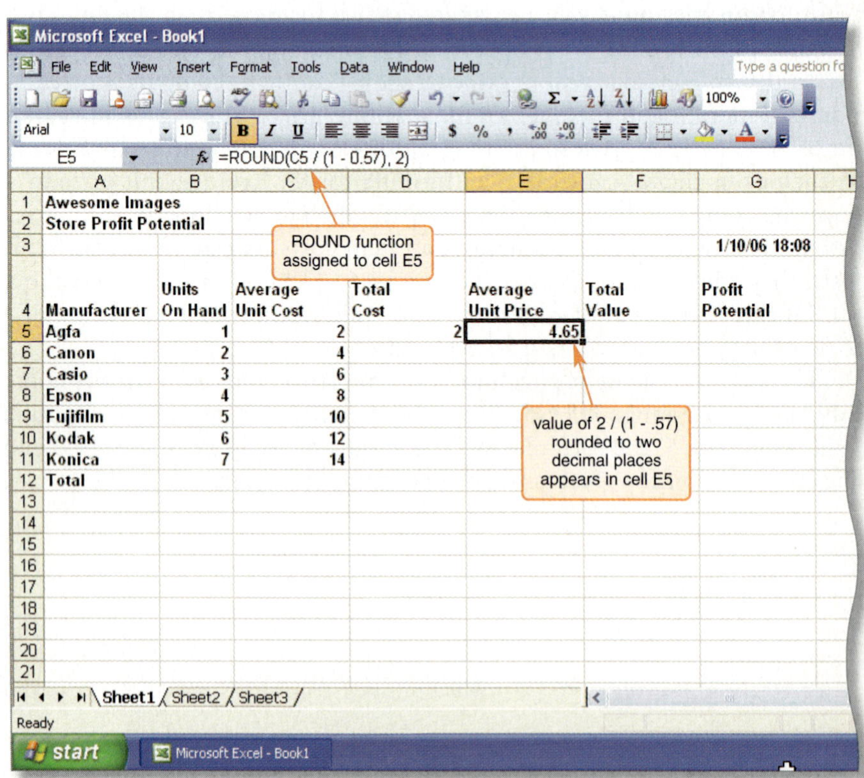

FIGURE 6-10

3

• **Select cell F5, type = to start the formula, click cell B5, type * (asterisk), click cell E5, and then click the Enter box in the formula bar.**

*Excel displays the formula =B5*E5 in the formula bar and the value 4.65 (1 x 4.65) as the total value in cell F5 (Figure 6-11).*

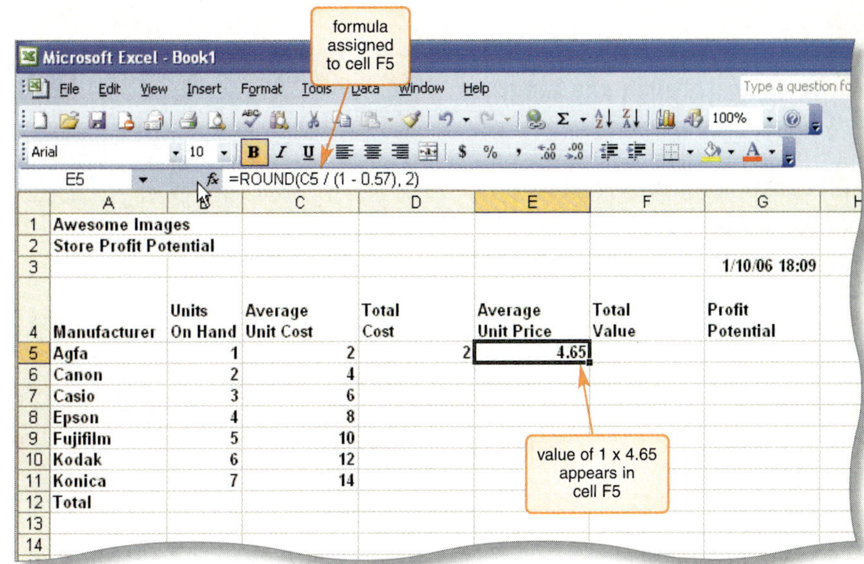

FIGURE 6-11

4

• **Select cell G5, type = to start the formula, click cell F5, type - (minus sign), click cell D5, and then click the Enter box in the formula bar.**

Excel displays the formula =F5 – D5 in the formula bar and the value 2.65 (4.65 – 2) as the profit potential in cell G5 (Figure 6-12).

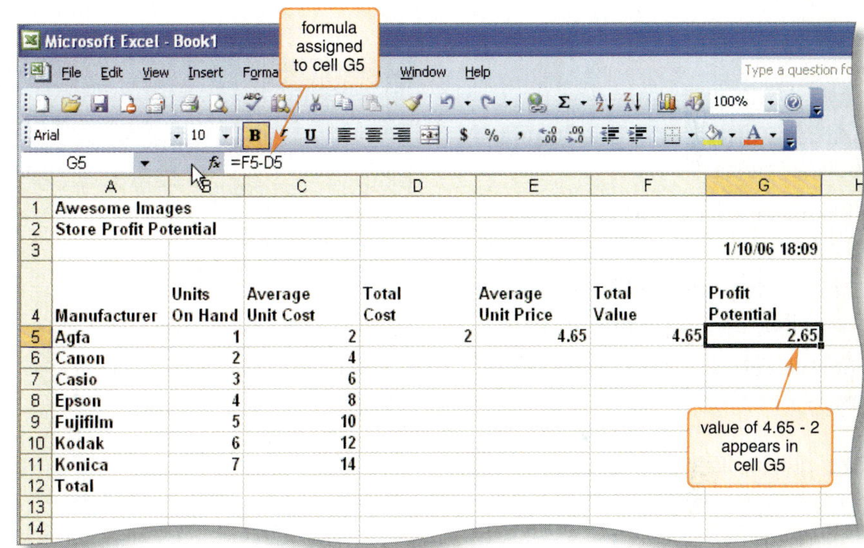

FIGURE 6-12

5

• **Select the range D5:G5 and then point to the fill handle.**

The range D5:G5 is selected and the mouse pointer changes to a cross hair when positioned on the fill handle (Figure 6-13).

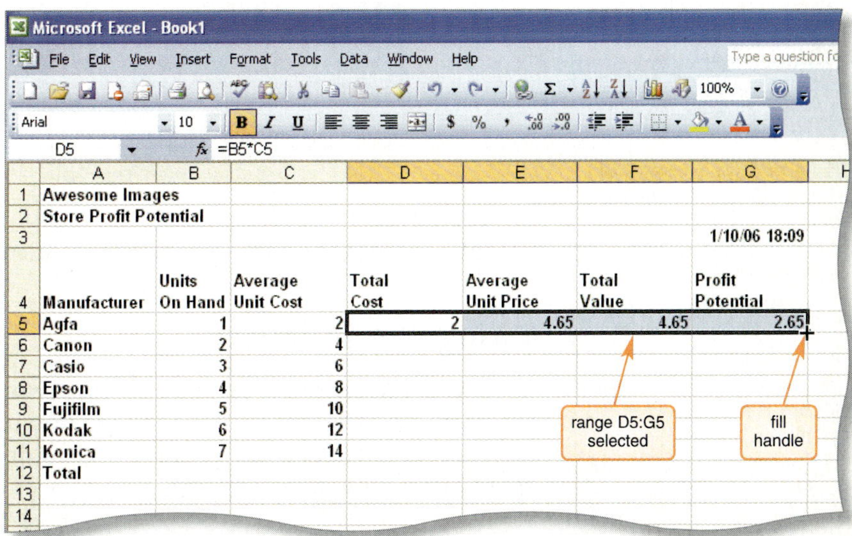

FIGURE 6-13

6

- **Drag down through the range D6:G11.**

Excel copies the formulas in the range D5:G5 to the range D6:G11. Excel automatically adjusts the cell references so each formula references the data in the row to which it is copied (Figure 6-14).

Microsoft Excel - Book1

D5 =B5*C5

	A	B	C	D	E	F	G
1	Awesome Images						
2	Store Profit Potential						
3							1/10/06 18:10
4	Manufacturer	Units On Hand	Average Unit Cost	Total Cost	Average Unit Price	Total Value	Profit Potential
5	Agfa	1	2	2	4.65	4.65	2.65
6	Canon	2	4	8	9.3	18.6	10.6
7	Casio	3	6	18	13.95	41.85	23.85
8	Epson	4	8	32	18.6	74.4	42.4
9	Fujifilm	5	10	50	23.26	116.3	66.3
10	Kodak	6	12	72	27.91	167.46	95.46
11	Konica	7	14	98	32.56	227.92	129.92
12	Total						

formulas in range D5:G5 copied to range D6:G11

FIGURE 6-14

7

- **Select cell B12, and then click the AutoSum button on the Standard toolbar twice.**
- **Select cell D12 and then click the AutoSum button twice.**
- **Select the range F12:G12 and then click the AutoSum button.**
- **Select cell A14 to deselect the range F12:G12.**

Excel displays the totals for columns B, D, F, and G in row 12 (Figure 6-15).

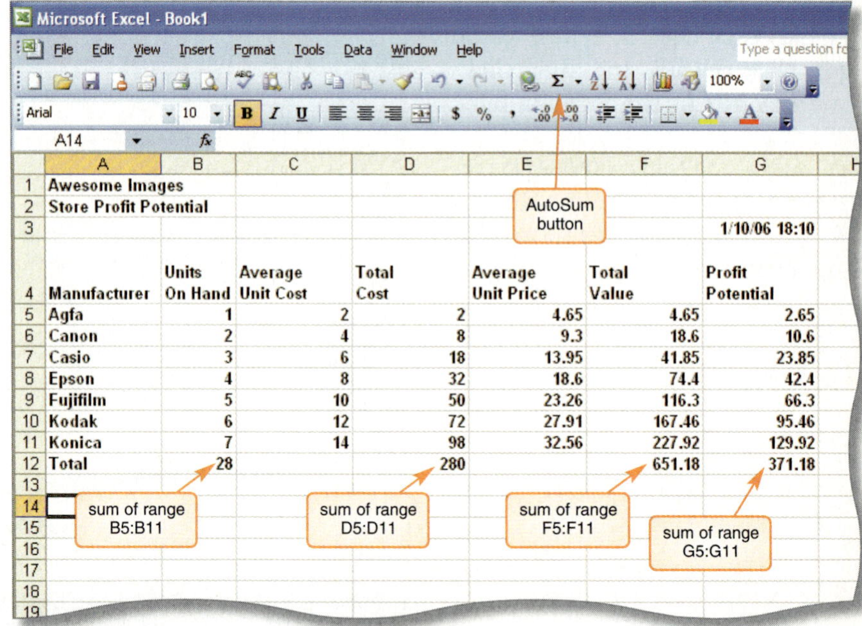

FIGURE 6-15

More About

File Extensions

If the MS-DOS extension .xlt or .xls shows in your title bar following the file name, it means that the option to omit the MS-DOS extension is not selected on the View sheet in the Options dialog box in Windows Explorer. You display the Options dialog box in Windows Explorer by clicking View on the menu bar, and then clicking Options.

The formulas for the template are complete. The values Excel generates from the formulas are based on the dummy data entered earlier in columns B and C.

Saving the Template

Saving a template is just like saving a workbook, except that the file type Template is selected in the Save as type box in the Save As dialog box. The following steps save the template on a floppy disk in drive A using the file name Awesome Images Profit Potential Template.

To Save the Template

1

- **With a floppy disk in drive A, click the Save button on the Standard toolbar.**
- **When Excel displays the Save As dialog box, type** `Awesome Images Profit Potential Template` **in the File name text box.**
- **Click the Save as type box arrow and then click Template in the list.**
- **Click the Save in box arrow and then click 3½ Floppy (A:).**

Excel displays the Save As dialog box as shown in Figure 6-16.

2

- **Click the Save button in the Save As dialog box.**

Excel saves the template on the floppy disk in drive A. The file name Awesome Images Profit Potential Template appears on the title bar as shown in Figure 6-17 on the next page.

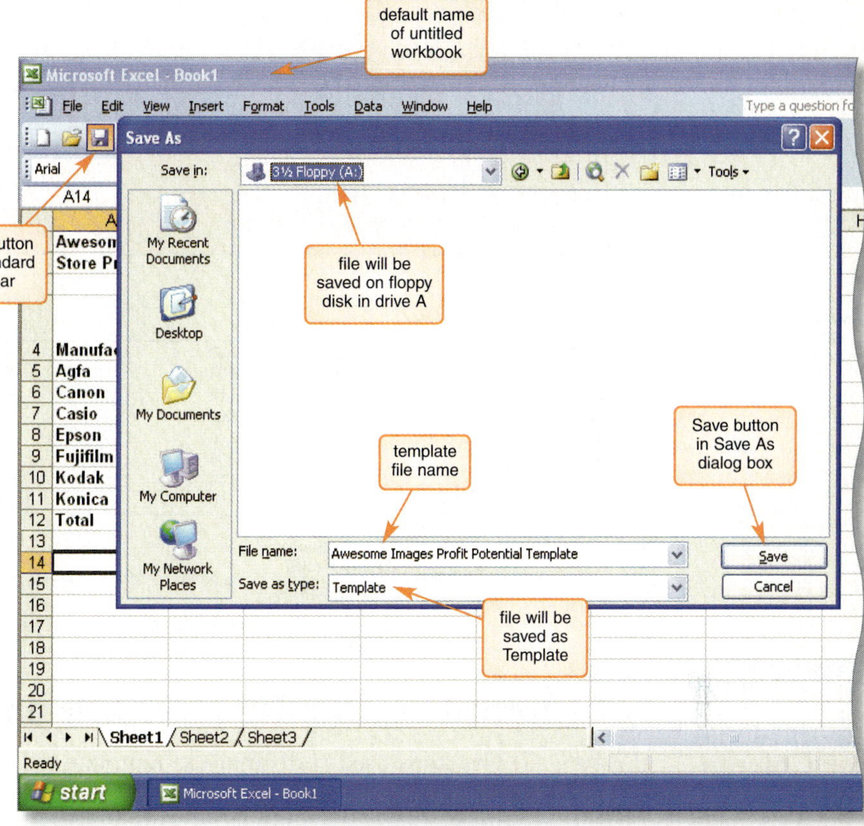

FIGURE 6-16

Other Ways

1. On File menu click Save As, type file name, select Template in Save as type box, select drive or folder, click Save button in Save As dialog box
2. Press CTRL+S, type file name, select Template in Save as type box, select drive or folder, click Save button in Save As dialog box
3. In Voice Command mode, say "File, Save As, [type file name, select Template in Save as type box, select drive or folder], Save"

When the file type Template is chosen in the Save as type box, Excel automatically changes the contents of the Save in box to the Templates folder created when Office 2003 was installed. In a **production environment** — that is, when you are creating a template for a business, school, or personal application — the template typically would be saved to the Templates folder, not the floppy disk in drive A.

Formatting the Template

The next step is to format the template so it appears as shown in Figure 6-17 on the next page. The following list summarizes the steps required to format the template.

1. Format the titles in cells A1 and A2.
2. Format the column titles and add borders to rows 4 and 12.
3. Assign the Currency style format with a floating dollar sign to the nonadjacent ranges C5:G5 and D12:G12.
4. Assign a Custom style format to the range C6:G11.
5. Assign a Comma style format to the range B5:B12.
6. Create a format style and assign it to the date in cell G3.

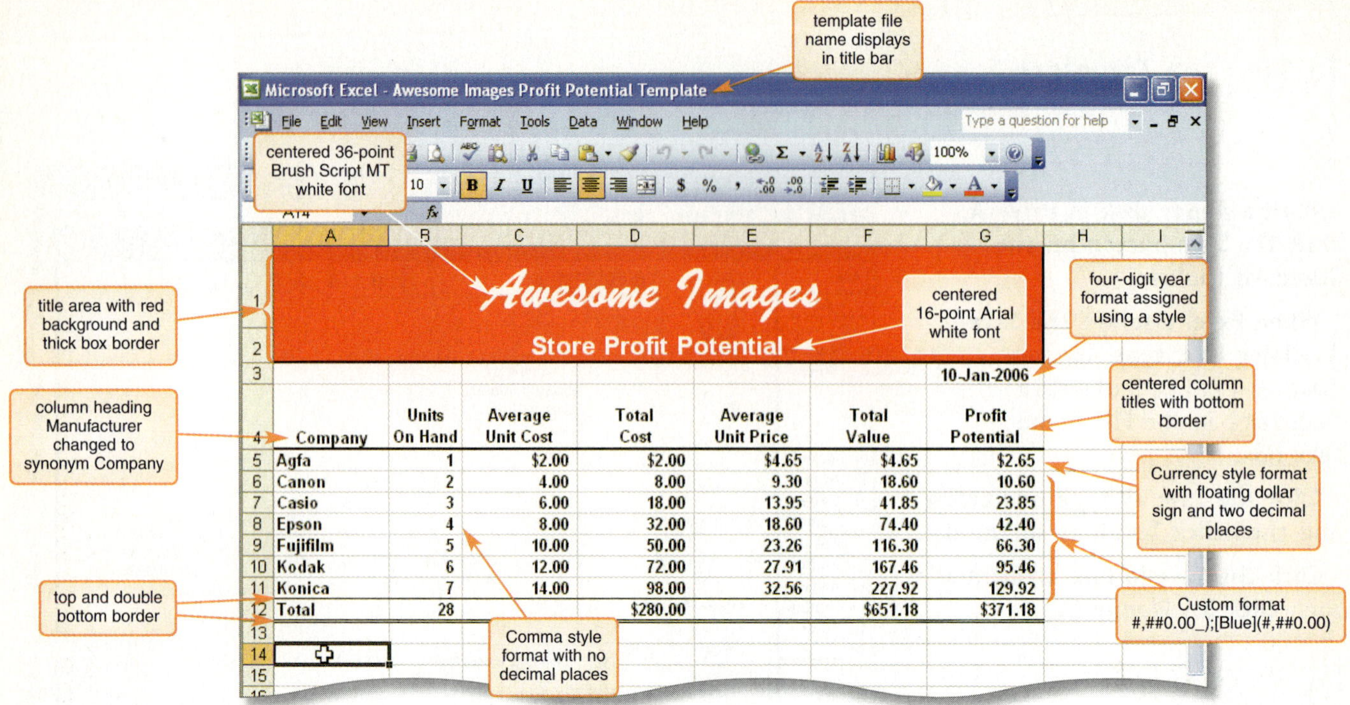

FIGURE 6-17

More About

Summing a Row or Column

You can reference an entire column or an entire row in a function argument by listing only the column or only the row. For example, =sum(a:a) sums all the values in all the cells in column A, and =sum(1:1) sums all the values in all the cells in row 1. You can verify this by entering =sum(a:a) in cell C1 and then begin entering numbers in a few of the cells in column A. Excel will respond by showing the sum of the numbers in cell C1.

Formatting the Template Title and Subtitle

The steps used to format the template title and subtitle include changing cell A1 to 36-point Brush Script MT font (or a similar font); changing cell A2 to 16-point Arial font; centering both titles across columns A through G; changing the title background color to red and the title font to white; and drawing a thick box border around the title area.

To Format the Template Title and Subtitle

1. **Select cell A1, click the Font box arrow on the Formatting toolbar, scroll down and then click Brush Script MT (or a similar font) in the list. Click the Font Size box arrow on the Formatting toolbar and then click 36 in the Font Size list. Select the range A1:G1. Click the Merge and Center button on the Formatting toolbar.**
2. **Select cell A2, click the Font Size box arrow on the Formatting toolbar, and then click 16 in the Font Size list. Select the range A2:G2. Click the Merge and Center button on the Formatting toolbar.**
3. **Select the range A1:A2, click the Fill Color button arrow on the Formatting toolbar, and then click Red (column 1, row 3) on the Fill Color palette.**
4. **Click the Font Color button arrow on the Formatting toolbar and then click White (column 8, row 5) on the Font Color palette.**
5. **Click the Borders button arrow on the Formatting toolbar and then click Thick Box Border (column 4, row 3) on the Borders palette.**
6. **Select cell A14 to deselect the range A1:A2.**

Excel displays the template title area as shown in Figure 6-18.

More About

Copying

To copy the contents of a cell to the cell directly below it, click in the target cell and press CTRL+D.

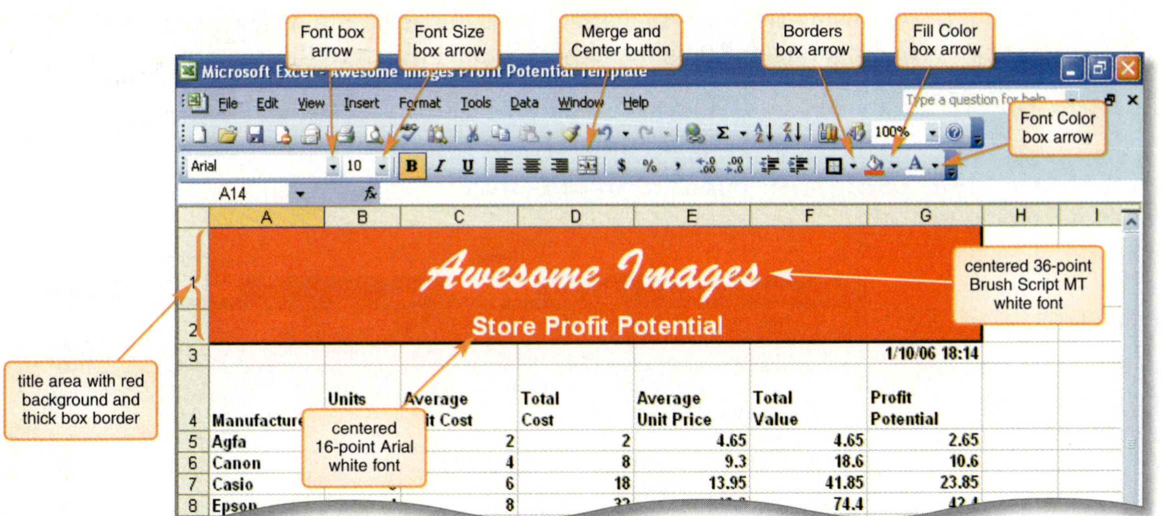

FIGURE 6-18

When you increase the font size, Excel automatically increases the heights of rows 1 and 2 so the tallest letter will appear properly in the cells.

Formatting the Column Titles and Total Row

The next step involves centering and underlining the column titles and drawing a top and double bottom border on the Total row in row 12.

To Format the Column Titles and Total Row

1. **Select the range A4:G4, click the Center button on the Formatting toolbar, click the Borders button arrow on the Formatting toolbar, and then click Bottom Border (column 2, row 1) on the Borders palette.**
2. **Select the range A12:G12, click the Borders button arrow on the Formatting toolbar, and then click Top and Double Bottom Border (column 4, row 2) on the Borders palette.**

Excel displays the column titles and Total row (row 12) as shown in Figure 6-19 on the next page.

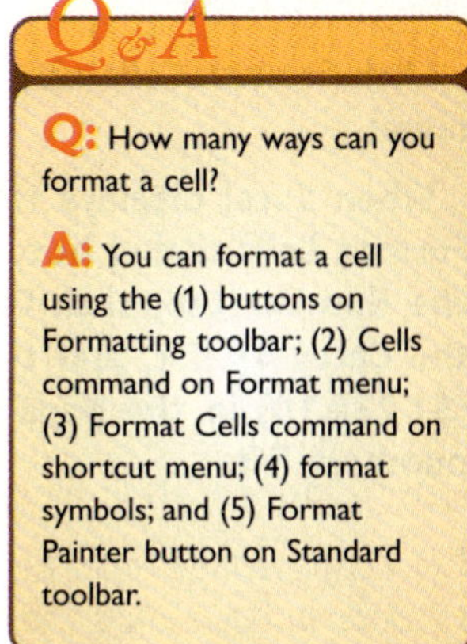

Q: How many ways can you format a cell?

A: You can format a cell using the (1) buttons on Formatting toolbar; (2) Cells command on Format menu; (3) Format Cells command on shortcut menu; (4) format symbols; and (5) Format Painter button on Standard toolbar.

Applying Number Formats Using the Format Dialog Box

As shown in Figure 6-17, the template for this project follows the **standard accounting format** for a table of numbers; that is, it contains floating dollar signs in the first row of numbers (row 5) and the totals row (row 12). Recall that while a fixed dollar sign always appears in the same position in a cell (regardless of the number of significant digits), a floating dollar sign always appears immediately to the left of the first significant digit in the cell. To assign a fixed dollar sign to rows 5 and 12, select the range and then click the Currency button on the Formatting toolbar. Assigning a floating dollar sign, by contrast, requires you to select the desired format in the Format Cells dialog box.

The following steps use the Format Cells dialog box to assign a Currency style with a floating dollar sign and two decimal places to the ranges C5:G5 and D12:G12.

To Assign a Currency Style Using the Format Dialog Box

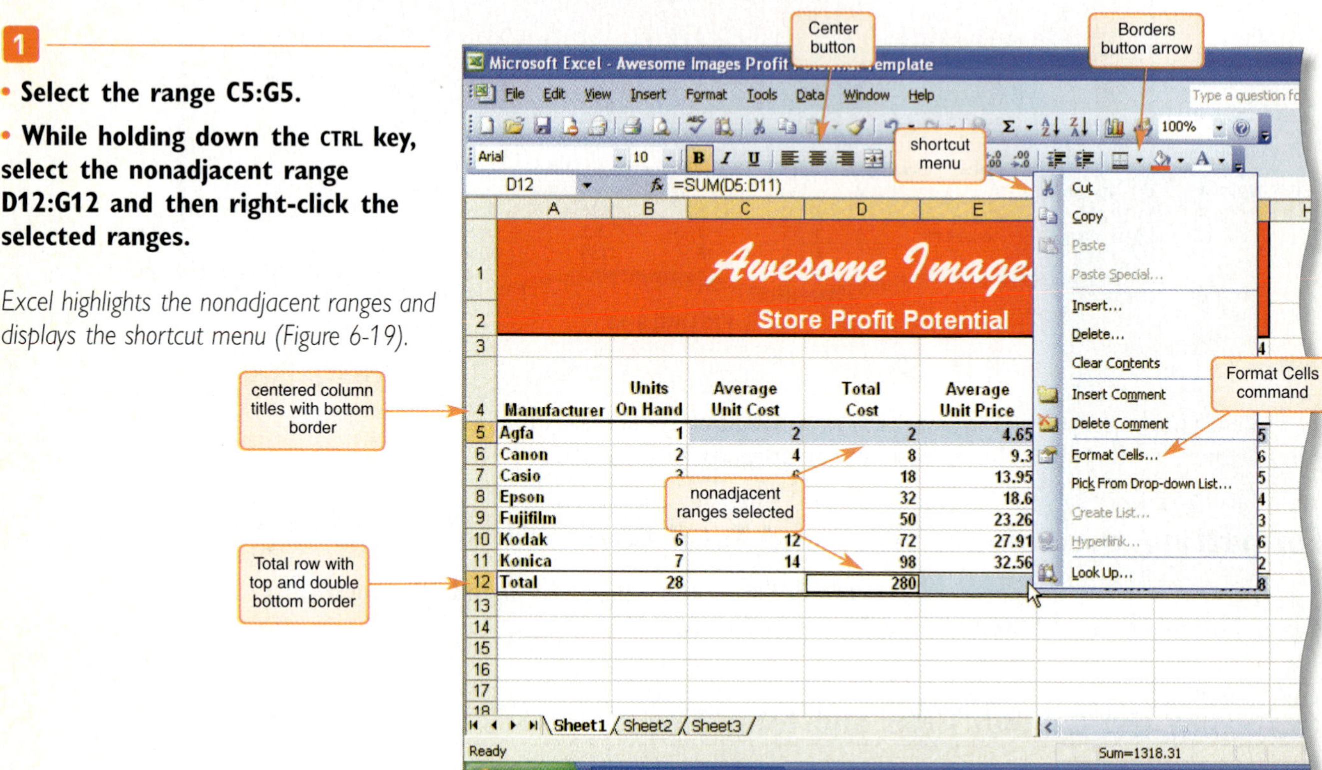

1

- **Select the range C5:G5.**
- **While holding down the CTRL key, select the nonadjacent range D12:G12 and then right-click the selected ranges.**

Excel highlights the nonadjacent ranges and displays the shortcut menu (Figure 6-19).

FIGURE 6-19

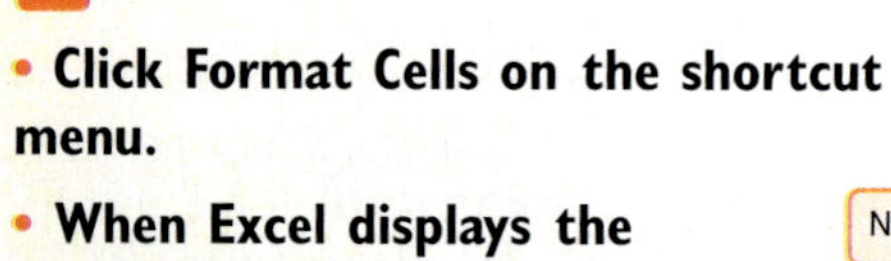

2

- **Click Format Cells on the shortcut menu.**
- **When Excel displays the Format Cells dialog box, click the Number tab, click Currency in the Category list, and then click ($1,234.10) in the Negative numbers list.**

Excel displays the Format Cells dialog box as shown in Figure 6-20. The selected format will apply a Currency style with a floating dollar sign and two decimal places to the selected ranges.

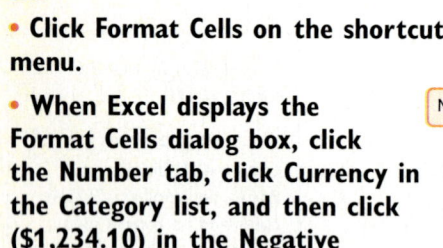

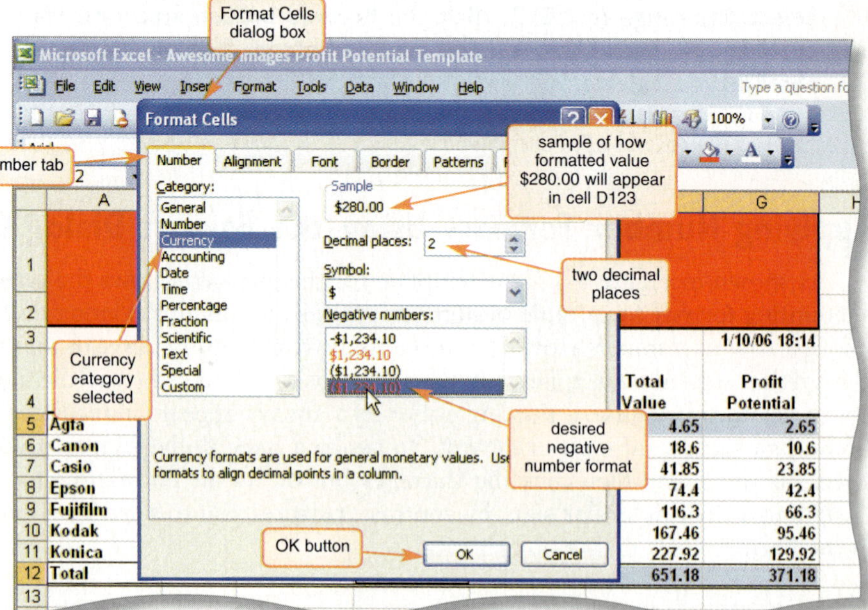

FIGURE 6-20

3

- **Click the OK button and then select cell A14 to deselect the nonadjacent ranges.**

Excel assigns the Currency style with a floating dollar sign and two decimal places to the ranges C5:G5 and D12:G12 (Figure 6-21).

FIGURE 6-21

Other Ways

1. On Format menu click Cells, click Number tab, select format, click OK button
2. Press CTRL+1, click Number tab, select format, click OK button
3. In Voice Command mode, say "Format, Cells, Number, [select format], OK"

Creating and Assigning a Custom Format Code

Excel assigns a format code to every format style listed in the Category list in the Number sheet in the Format Cells dialog box. As shown in Table 6-2 on the next page, a **format code** is a series of format symbols that defines how a cell entry assigned a format will appear. To view the entire list of format codes that come with Excel, select Custom in the Category list (Figure 6-20).

Before creating custom format codes or modifying an existing custom format code, you should understand their makeup. As shown below, a format code can have up to four sections: positive numbers, negative numbers, zeros, and text. Each section is divided by a semicolon.

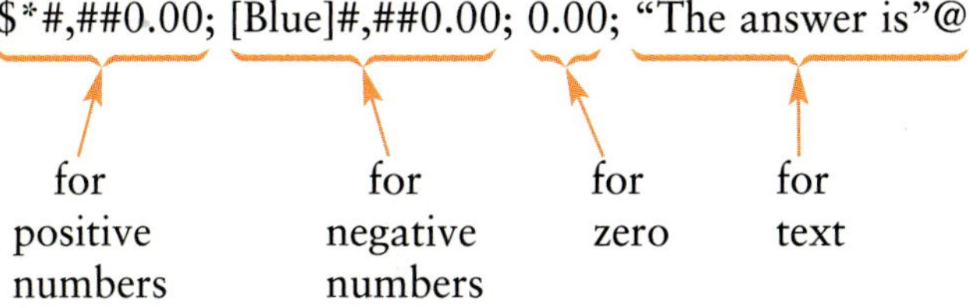

More About

Creating Customized Formats

Each format symbol within the format code has special meaning. Table 6-2 on the next page summarizes the more frequently used format symbols and their meanings. For additional information on creating format codes, type `create a custom number format` in the Type a question for help box and then scroll down in the Search Results task pane and click Create or delete a custom number format.

Table 6-2 Format Symbols in Format Codes

FORMAT SYMBOL	EXAMPLE OF SYMBOL	DESCRIPTION
# (number sign)	###.##	Serves as a digit placeholder. If the value in a cell has more digits to the right of the decimal point than number signs in the format, Excel rounds the number. Extra digits to the left of the decimal point are displayed.
0 (zero)	0.00	Functions like a number sign (#), except that if the number is less than 1, Excel displays a 0 in the ones place.
. (period)	#0.00	Ensures Excel will display a decimal point in the number. The placement of period symbols determines how many digits appear to the left and right of the decimal point.
% (percent)	0.00%	Displays numbers as percentages of 100. Excel multiplies the value of the cell by 100 and displays a percent sign after the number.
, (comma)	#,##0.00	Displays a comma as a thousands separator.
( )	#0.00;(#0.00)	Displays parentheses around negative numbers.
$ or + or –	$#,##0.00; ($#,##0.00)	Displays a floating sign ($, +, or –).
* (asterisk)	$*##0.00	Displays a fixed sign ($, +, or –) to the left in the cell followed by spaces until the first significant digit.
[color]	#.##;[Red]#.##	Displays the characters in the cell in the designated color. In the example, positive numbers appear in the default color, and negative numbers appear in red.
" " (quotation marks)	$0.00 "Surplus"; $-0.00 "Shortage"	Displays text along with numbers entered in a cell.
_ (underscore)	#,##0.00_)	Skips the width of the character that follows the underscore.

A format code need not have all four sections. For most applications, a format code will have only a positive section and possibly a negative section.

The next step is to create and assign a custom format code to the range C6:G11. To assign a custom format code, you select the Custom category in the Category list in the Format Cells dialog box, select a format code close to the one to be created, and then modify or customize the selected format code. The following steps show how to create and assign a custom format code.

More About

The Format Painter Button

The Format Painter button is on the Standard toolbar by default. Because of the button's function, you would think that Microsoft would have placed it on the Formatting toolbar. If you feel the same way about it, then hold down the ALT key and drag the Format Painter button from the Standard toolbar to the Formatting toolbar.

To Create and Assign a Custom Format Code and a Comma Style Format

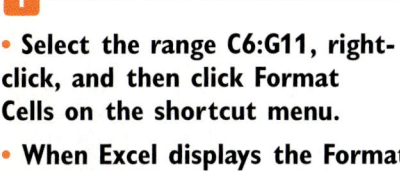

1

- **Select the range C6:G11, right-click, and then click Format Cells on the shortcut menu.**
- **When Excel displays the Format Cells dialog box, if necessary, click the Number tab, and then click Custom in the Category list.**
- **Scroll down and then click #,##0.00_);[Red](#,##0.00) in the Type list.**
- **In the Type text box, change the word Red to Blue.**

Excel displays the Format Cells dialog box as shown in Figure 6-22. The Custom format has been modified to show negative numbers in blue. In the Sample area, Excel displays a sample of the custom format assigned to the first number in the selected range.

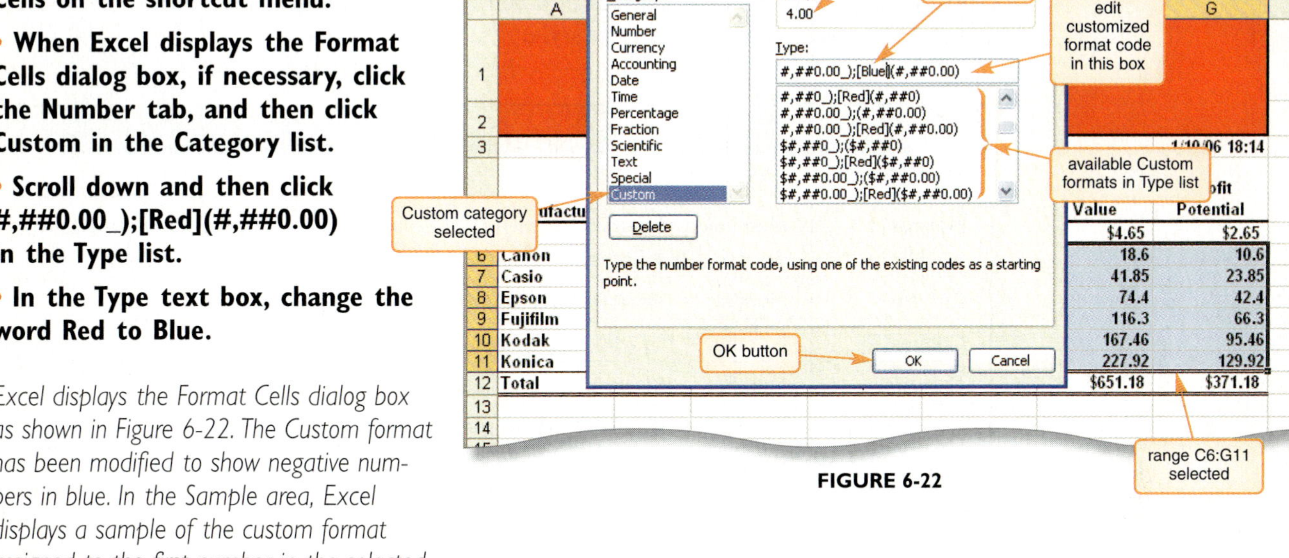

FIGURE 6-22

2

- **Click the OK button.**
- **Select the range B5:B12, click the Comma Style button on the Formatting toolbar, and then click the Decrease Decimal button on the Formatting toolbar twice.**
- **Select cell A14.**

Excel displays the numbers in the range C6:G11 using the custom format code created in Step 1 and the numbers in the range B5:B12 using the Comma style format with no decimal places (Figure 6-23). When numbers with more than three whole-number digits are entered into the range B5:B12, the numbers will appear with a comma as the thousands separator.

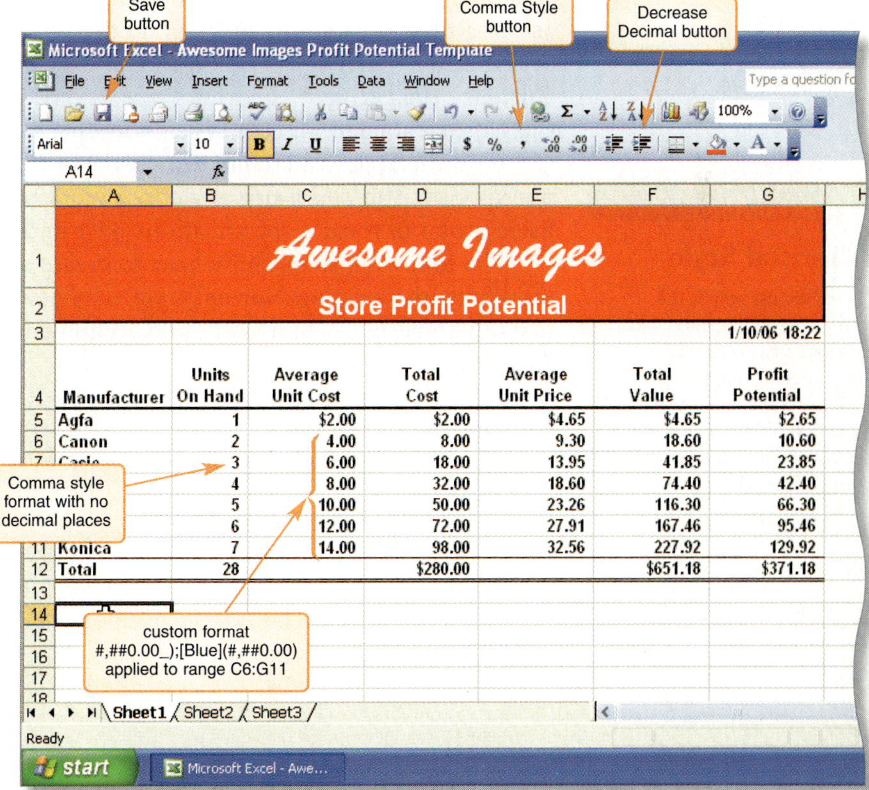

FIGURE 6-23

When you create a new custom format code, Excel adds it to the bottom of the Type list in the Number sheet in the Format Cells dialog box to make it available for future use.

Creating a New Style

A **style** is a group of format specifications that are assigned to a style name. Excel makes several styles available with all workbooks, as described in Table 6-3. You can apply these existing styles to a cell or cells in a worksheet, modify an existing style, or create an entirely new style.

Table 6-3 Styles Available with All Workbooks

STYLE NAME	DESCRIPTION
Normal	Number = General; Alignment = General, Bottom Aligned; Font = Arial 10; Border = No Borders; Patterns = No Shading; Protection = Locked
Comma	Number = (*#,##0.00);_(*(#,##0.00);_(*"-"_);_(@_)
Comma(0)	Number = (*#,##0_);_(*(#,##0);_(*"-"_);_(@_)
Currency	Number = ($#,##0.00_);_($*(#,##0.00);_($*"-"??_);_(@_)
Currency(0)	Number = ($#,##0_);_($*(#,##0);_($*"-"_);_(@_)
Percent	Number = 0%

Using the Style command on the Format menu, you can create and then assign a style to a cell, a range of cells, a worksheet, or a workbook in the same way you assign a format using the buttons on the Formatting toolbar. In fact, the Comma Style button, Currency Style button, and Percent Style button assign the Comma, Currency, and Percent styles in Table 6-3, respectively. Excel automatically assigns the Normal style to all cells when you open a new workbook.

With the Style command, you also can delete styles and merge styles from other workbooks. You add a new style to a workbook or merge styles when you plan to use a group of format specifications over and over.

The following steps show how to create a new style called Four-Digit Year by modifying the existing Normal style. The new style will include the following formats: Number = 14-Mar-2001 and Alignment = Horizontal Center and Bottom Aligned.

After the Four-Digit Year style is created, it will be assigned to cell G3, which contains the system date.

More About

Normal Style

The Normal style is the format style that Excel initially assigns to all cells in a workbook. If you change the Normal style, Excel applies the new format specifications to all cells that are not assigned another style.

To Create a New Style

1

- **Click Format on the menu bar.**

Excel displays the Format menu as shown in Figure 6-24.

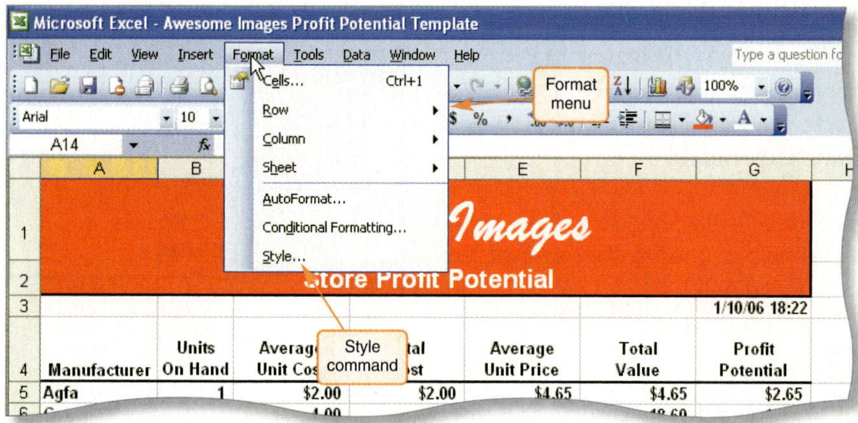

FIGURE 6-24

2

- **Click Style.**
- **When Excel displays the Style dialog box, drag through Normal in the Style name box and then type** `Four-Digit Year` **as the new style name.**

Excel displays the Style dialog box with the new style name Four-Digit Year (Figure 6-25).

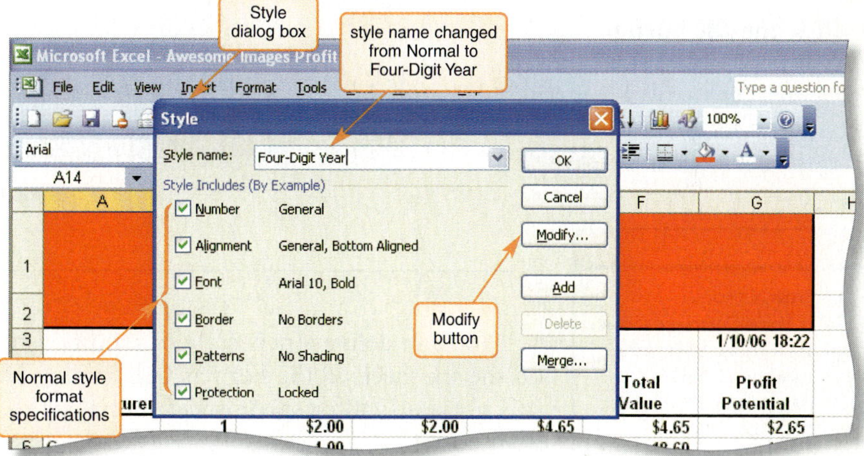

FIGURE 6-25

3

- **Click the Modify button.**
- **When Excel displays the Format Cells dialog box, if necessary, click the Number tab, click Date in the Category list, and then click 14-Mar-2001 in the Type list.**

Excel displays the Format Cells dialog box as shown in Figure 6-26. The Format Cells dialog box contains a tab for each check box in the Style dialog box.

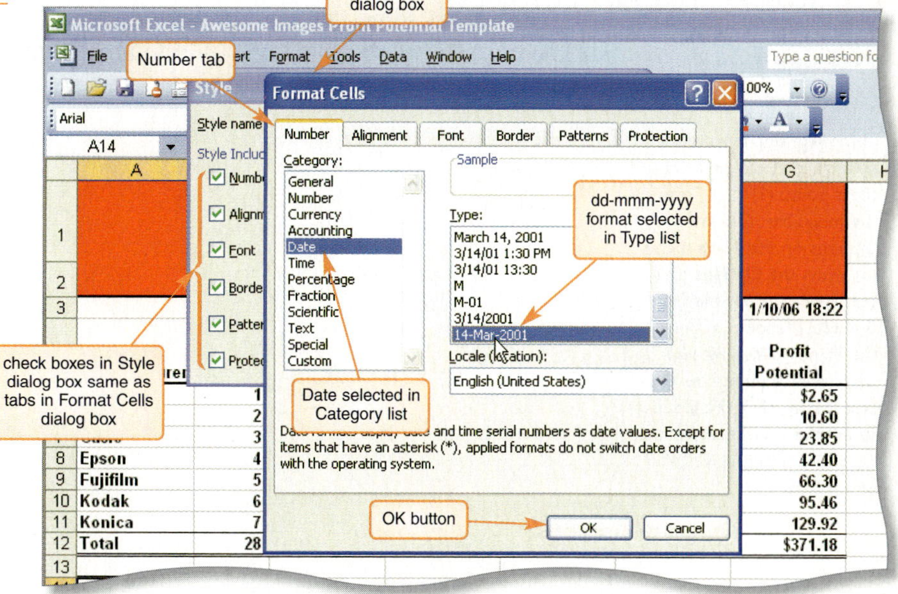

FIGURE 6-26

4

- **Click the Alignment tab, click the Horizontal box arrow, click Center, and then click the OK button.**
- **When the Style dialog box becomes active, click Font, Border, Patterns, and Protection to clear the check boxes.**

Excel displays the Style dialog box with the formats assigned to the Four-Digit Year style (Figure 6-27).

5

- **Click the Add button to add the new style to the list of styles available with this template.**
- **Click the OK button.**

Excel adds the new Four-Digit Year style to the list of styles available with the Awesome Images Profit Potential Template file.

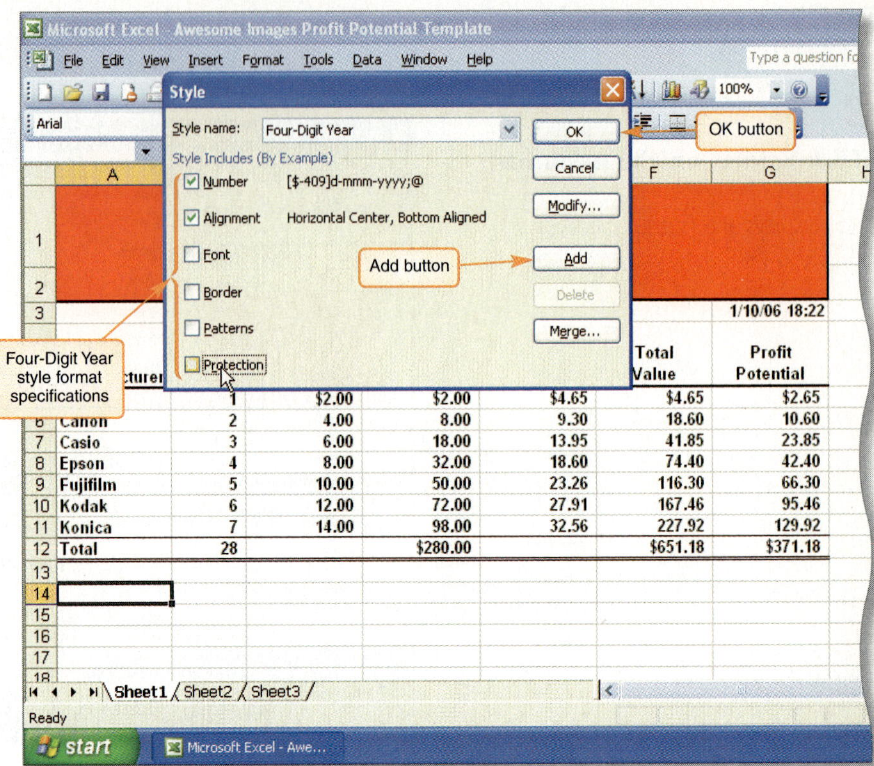

FIGURE 6-27

Other Ways

1. Press ALT+O, S
2. In Voice Command mode, say "Format, Style, [select style name], Modify, [select desired formats], OK, Add, OK"

More About

Changing the Default Font Settings

To change the default font settings for Excel, follow these steps: (1) click Tools on the menu bar; (2) click Options on the Tools menu; (3) when the Options dialog box appears, click the General tab; (4) select a font in the Standard font list and then select a point size in the Size list; (5) click the OK button; (6) restart Excel for the new font default settings to take effect.

You can define a new style or modify a current style using any format available on the six sheets in the Format Cells dialog box (Figure 6-26 on the previous page). It is not unusual for spreadsheet specialists to create several styles for use in a workbook.

Applying a Style

In earlier steps, cell G3 was assigned the system date using the now() function. The next step is to assign cell G3 the Four-Digit Year style, which centers the contents of the cell and assigns it the date format dd-mmm-yyyy.

To Apply a Style

1

- **Select cell G3, click Format on the menu bar, and then click Style.**
- **When Excel displays the Style dialog box, click the Style name box arrow and then click Four-Digit Year in the list.**

Excel displays the Style dialog box (Figure 6-28).

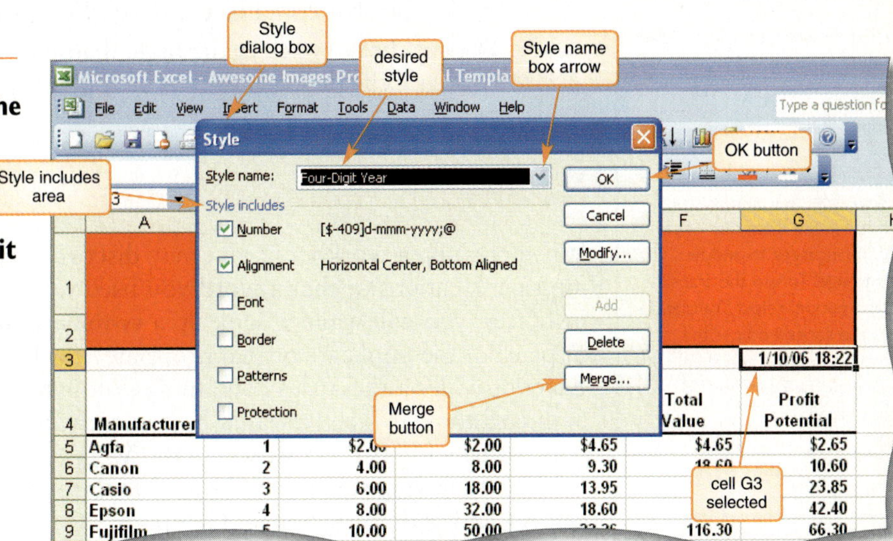

FIGURE 6-28

2

- **Click the OK button.**

Excel assigns the Four-Digit Year style to cell G3 (Figure 6-29).

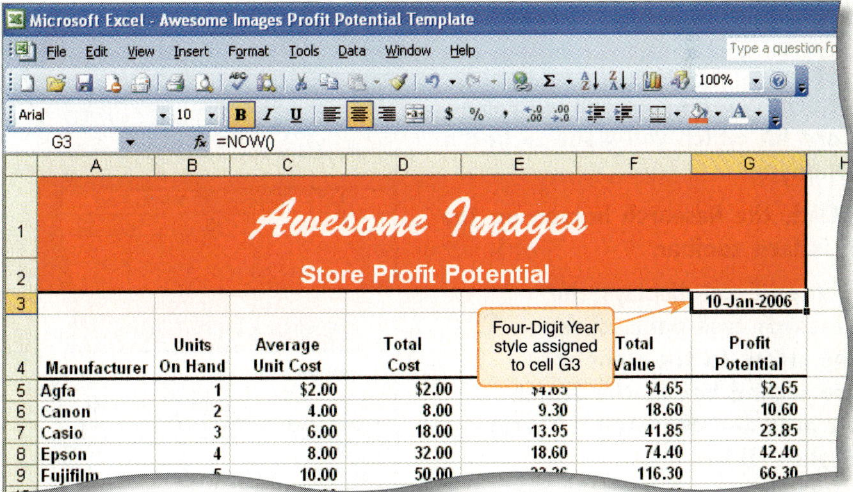

FIGURE 6-29

Other Ways

1. Press ALT+O, S
2. In Voice Command mode, say "Format, Style, [select style name], OK"

Keep in mind the following additional points concerning styles:

1. A style only affects the format of a cell or range of cells if the corresponding check box is selected in the Style includes area of the Style dialog box (Figure 6-28). For example, if the Font check box is not selected in the Style dialog box, then the cell assigned the style maintains the font format it had before the style was assigned.
2. If you assign two different styles to a range of cells, Excel adds the second style to the first, rather than replacing it.
3. Do not delete the default styles that come with Excel because some of the buttons on the toolbars are dependent on them.

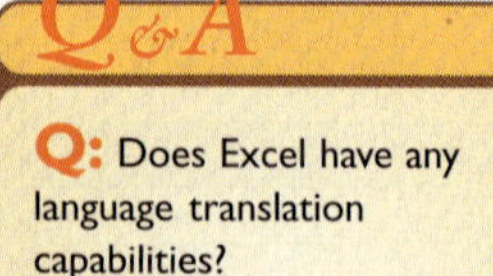

Q: Does Excel have any language translation capabilities?

A: Yes. You can use the Research task pane to translate a word from one of several languages to another language. To use the translation option, select Translation in the second box in the Search for area and then choose the From and To languages.

4. You can merge styles from another workbook into the active workbook by using the Merge button in the Style dialog box. You must, however, open the workbook that contains the desired styles before you use the Merge button.
5. The six check boxes in the Style dialog box are identical to the six tabs in the Format Cells dialog box (Figure 6-26 on page EX 399).

Finding a Synonym Using the Research Task Pane

When creating a workbook, you may discover that you used the same word in multiple locations or that a word you used was not quite appropriate. In these instances, you will want to look up a **synonym**, or word similar in meaning, to use in place of the duplicate or inappropriate word. A **thesaurus** is a book of synonyms. Excel provides a thesaurus containing synonyms via the Research button on the Standard toolbar. The Research button activates the Research task pane, which lets you search various thesauruses on the Web.

The following steps show how to replace the column heading Manufacturer in cell A4 and with the synonym Company.

To Find a Synonym Using the Research Task Pane

1

- **Select cell A4, the cell with the word for which you want to find a synonym.**
- **Click the Research button on the Standard toolbar.**
- **When Excel displays the Research task pane, click the arrow to the right of the second box in the Search for area and then select Thesaurus: English (U.S.).**
- **When Excel displays the results of the search in the Research task pane, point to the synonym company, and then click the arrow to the right of it.**

When Excel first displays the Research task pane, the contents of the active cell A4, Manufacturer, are placed in the first Search for box automatically. After selecting Thesaurus: English (U.S.) in the second Search for box, Excel activates the search and returns a list of synonyms.

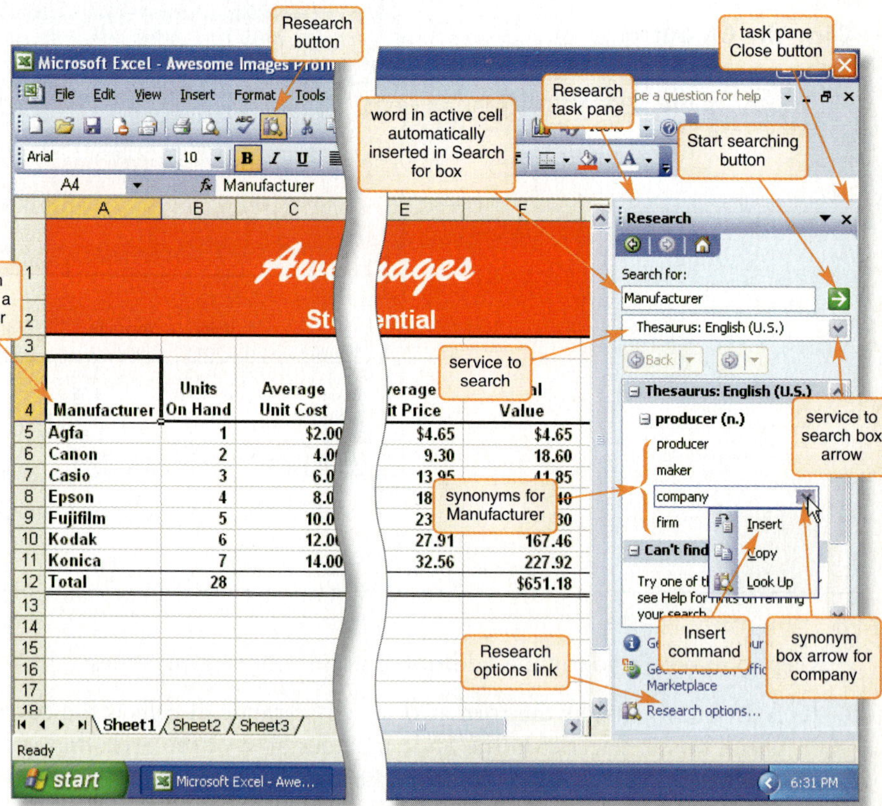

FIGURE 6-30

2

- **Click Insert in the synonym list.**
- **When Excel replaces the word Manufacturer in cell A4 with the word company, if necessary, double-click cell A4 and then type an uppercase C to replace the lowercase c in company.**
- **Click the Close button on the Research task pane title bar and then select cell A14.**

Excel replaces the word Manufacturer in cell A4 with the synonym Company (Figure 6-31).

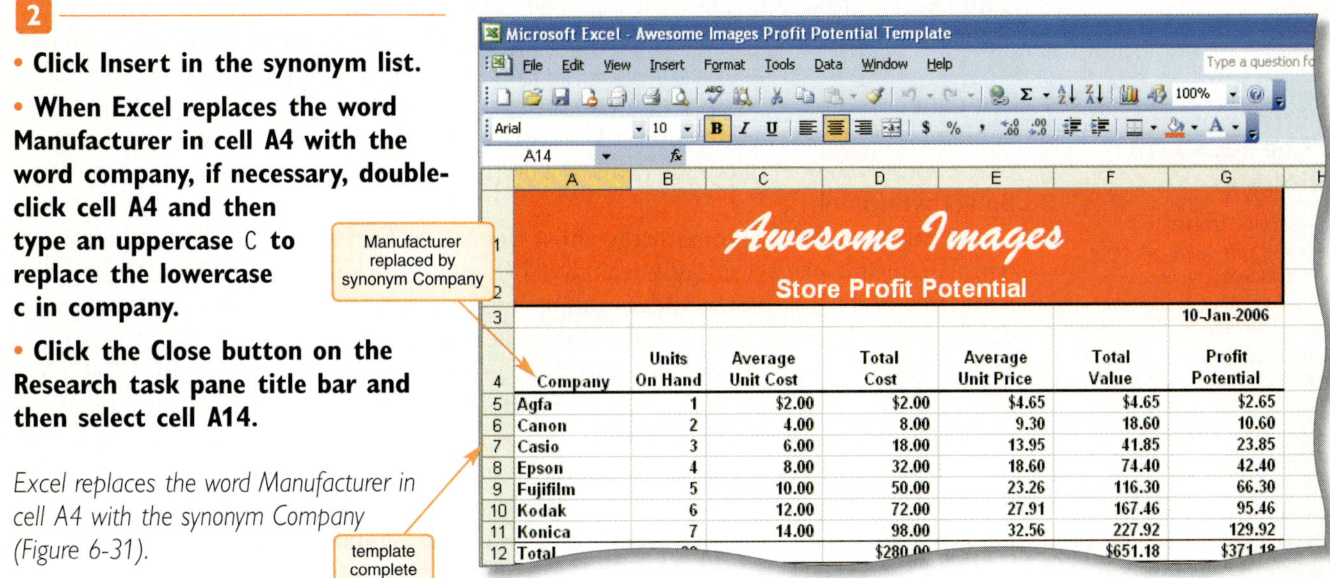

FIGURE 6-31

Other Ways

1. On Tools menu click Research
2. Hold down ALT key, click cell containing word to look up
3. In Voice Command mode, say "Tools, Research"

The Research task pane has access to several thesauruses, in which you can look up synonyms for various meanings of a word. You can continue the search by invoking the Look Up command in the synonym list (Figure 6-30). The results of a synonym search often will include an **antonym**, or word with an opposite meaning, as well.

If you manually change the word in the Search for box in the Research task pane, then you will have to click the Start searching button to the right of the Search for box.

Spell Checking, Saving, and Printing the Template

With the formatting complete, the next step is to spell check the template, save it, and then print it.

To Spell Check, Save, and Print the Template

1. **Select cell A1. Click the Spelling button on the Standard toolbar. Change any misspelled words.**
2. **Click the Save button on the Standard toolbar.**
3. **Click the Print button on the Standard toolbar.**
4. **Click the Close Window button on the right side of the menu bar.**

Excel spell checks the template, saves it using the file name, Awesome Images Profit Potential Template, prints it, and closes the template.

Using Templates

Before using the template to create the Awesome Images Profit Potential workbook, you should be aware of how templates are used and their importance. If you click the New command on the File menu, the New Workbook task pane appears on the

More About

The XLSTART Folder

You could replace your default workbook template (Book) with the new template you create; the new template then becomes the basis for all new workbooks. All you need to do is give the template the name Book.xlt and save it in the XLSTART folder. (The XLSTART folder is in different places on different systems; use the Search feature of Windows to locate where it is on your system.)

right side of the screen (Figure 6-32). The New Workbook task pane includes an On my computer link, which you can click to view a list of Excel templates available on your computer. Clicking the On my computer link causes Excel to display the Templates dialog box shown in Figure 6-32. The Templates dialog box includes a default workbook template icon titled Workbook. The template associated with this icon contains the defaults that you see whenever you start Excel and it displays the Book1 workbook.

Recall that Excel automatically chose Templates as the Save in folder when the template in this project initially was saved (Figure 6-16 on page EX 391). Saving templates in the Templates folder, rather than in another folder, is the standard procedure in the business world. If the Awesome Images Profit Potential template created in this project had been saved in the Templates folder, then the template would appear in the Templates dialog box in Figure 6-32. The template then could have been selected to start a new workbook.

When you select a template from the Templates dialog box to create a new workbook, Excel names the new workbook using the template name with an appended digit 1 (for example, Template1). This is similar to what Excel does when you first start Excel and it assigns the name Book1 to the workbook.

Excel provides additional workbook templates, which you can access by clicking the Spreadsheet Solutions tab shown in Figure 6-32. Additional workbook templates also are available on the Web. To access the templates on the Web, click the Templates on Office Online button in the Templates dialog box or the Templates home page link in the New Workbook task pane (Figure 6-32).

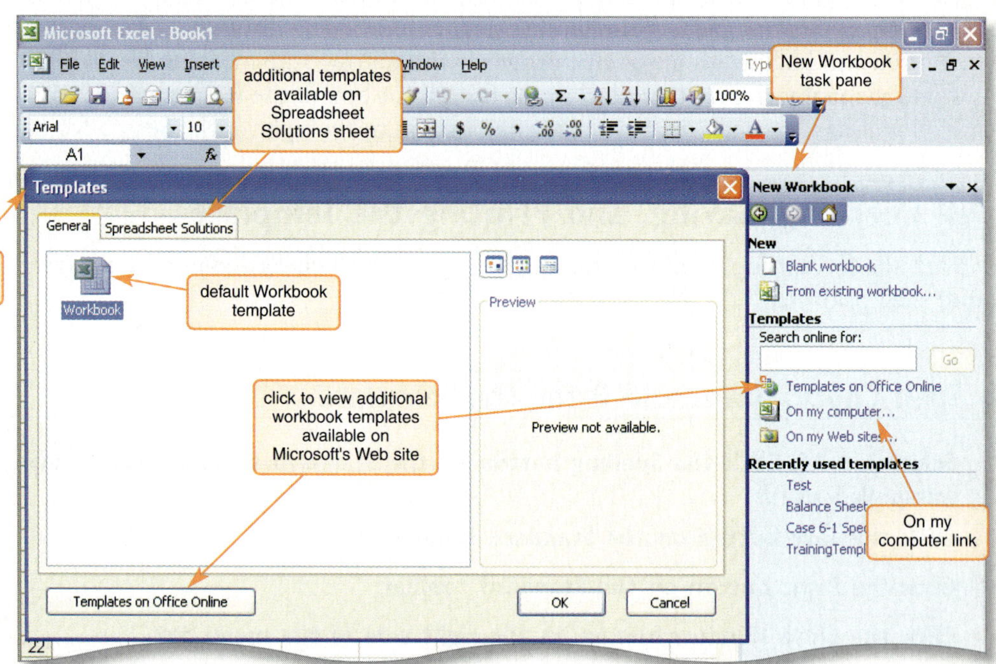

FIGURE 6-32

More About

Opening a Workbook at Startup

You can instruct Windows to open a workbook (or template) automatically when you turn on your computer by adding the workbook (or template) to the Startup folder. Use Windows Explorer to copy the file to the Startup folder. The Startup folder is on the All Programs submenu.

Creating a Workbook from a Template

With the template created, the next step is to use it to create the Awesome Images Profit Potential workbook shown in Figure 6-1 on page EX 379. The following steps open the Awesome Images Profit Potential template and save it as a workbook.

To Open a Template and Save It as a Workbook

1

- **With Excel active, click the Open button on the Standard toolbar.**
- **When Excel displays the Open dialog box, click the Look in box arrow and then click 3½ Floppy (A:).**
- **Click the file name Awesome Images Profit Potential Template.**

Excel displays the Open dialog box as shown in Figure 6-33.

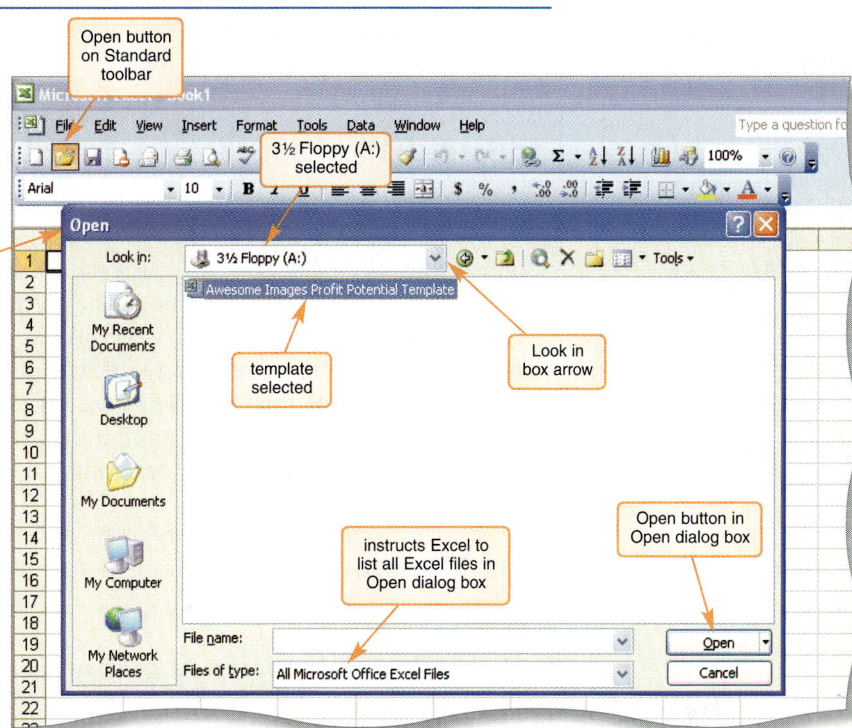

FIGURE 6-33

2

- **Click the Open button in the Open dialog box.**
- **When Excel displays the Awesome Images Profit Potential Template, click Save As on the File menu.**
- **When the Save As dialog box appears, type** `Awesome Images Profit Potential` **in the File name box.**
- **Click the Save as type box arrow and then click Microsoft Excel Workbook.**
- **Click the Save in box arrow and then click 3½ Floppy (A:).**

Excel displays the Save As dialog box as shown in Figure 6-34.

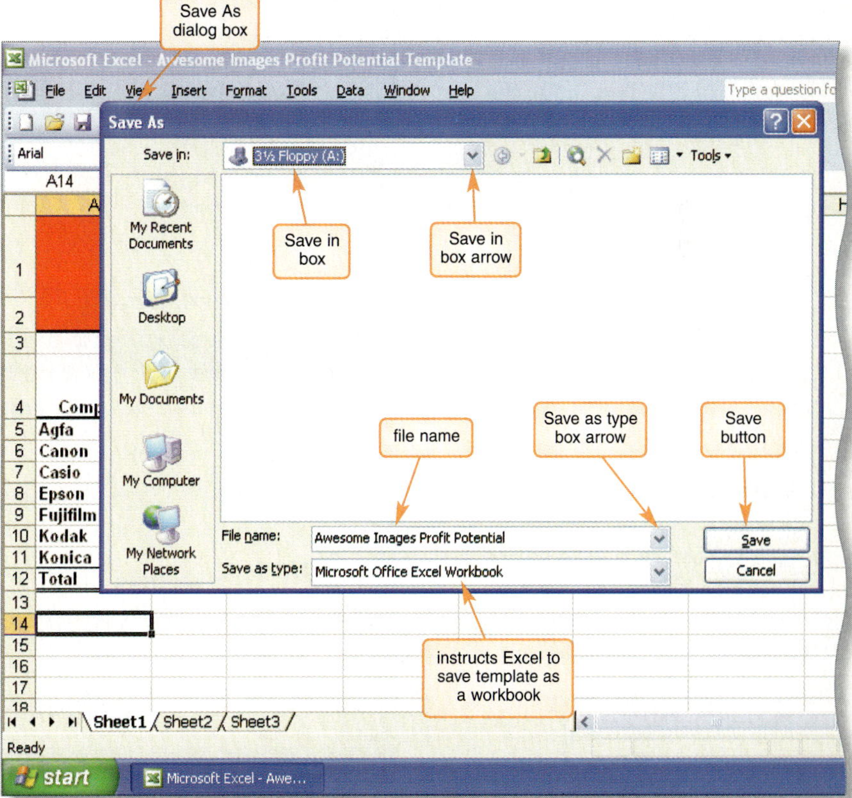

FIGURE 6-34

3

- **Click the Save button in the Save As dialog box.**

Excel saves the template as a workbook and displays the workbook on the screen.

More About

Default Number of Worksheets

To change the default number of worksheets in a workbook, follow these steps: (1) click Tools on the menu bar; (2) click Options on the Tools menu; (3) when the Options dialog box appears, click the General tab; (4) enter a number between 1 and 255 in the Sheets in new workbook box; and (5) click the OK button. The next time you start Excel or open a new workbook, the new default number of worksheets will appear.

In a production environment in which templates are saved to the Templates folder, Excel automatically selects Microsoft Excel workbook as the file type when you attempt to save a template as a workbook, as well as appending the digit 1 to the template name as described earlier.

Adding a Worksheet to a Workbook

A workbook contains three worksheets by default. You can have a maximum of 255 worksheets in a workbook. The Awesome Images Profit Potential workbook requires four worksheets — one for each of the three stores and one for the company totals. Thus, a worksheet must be added to the workbook.

When you add a worksheet, Excel places the new worksheet tab to the left of the active tab. To keep the worksheet with the dummy data shown in Figure 6-31 on top — that is, to keep its tab (Sheet1) to the far left — spreadsheet specialists often add a new worksheet between Sheet1 and Sheet2, rather than to the left of Sheet1. The following steps select Sheet2 before adding a worksheet to the workbook.

To Add a Worksheet to a Workbook

1

• **Click the Sheet2 tab at the bottom of the window and then click Insert on the menu bar.**

Excel displays the blank Sheet2 and the Insert menu (Figure 6-35).

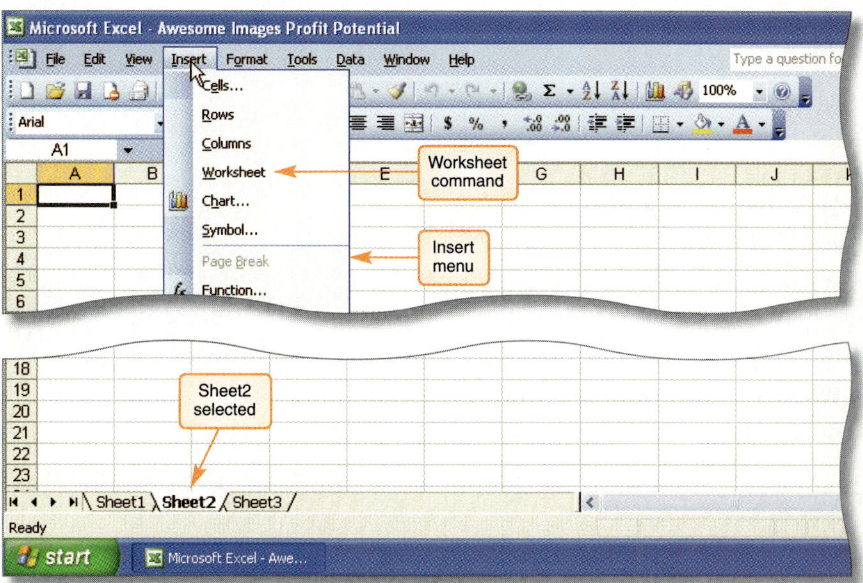

FIGURE 6-35

2

• **Click Worksheet.**

Excel adds a fourth worksheet named Sheet4 between Sheet1 and Sheet2 (Figure 6-36). Recall that Sheet1 contains the dummy data from the template.

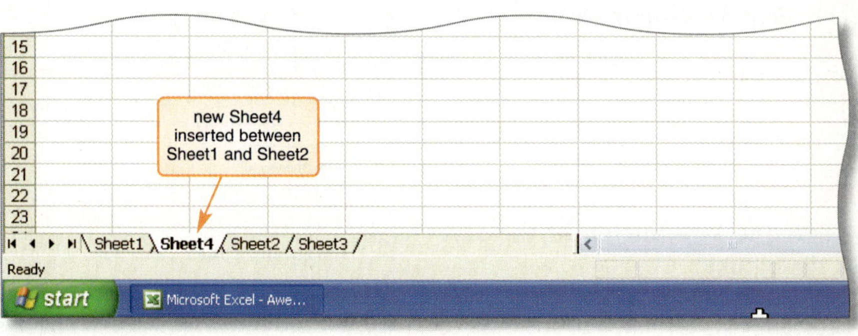

FIGURE 6-36

Other Ways

1. Right-click tab, click Insert on shortcut menu
2. Press ALT+I, W
3. In Voice Command mode, say "Insert, Worksheet"

An alternative to adding worksheets is to change the default number of worksheets before you open a new workbook. To change the default number of worksheets in a blank workbook, click Options on the Tools menu, click the General tab, and then change the number in the Sheets in new workbook box. Recall from Project 4 that you can delete a worksheet by right-clicking the sheet tab of the worksheet you want to delete and then clicking Delete on the shortcut menu.

> *More About*
>
> **Adding a Worksheet by Copying It**
>
> You can add a worksheet by copying an existing one and pasting it into the same workbook. You copy a worksheet by right-clicking its tab and clicking the Move or Copy command. A dialog box appears after you invoke the command, which offers a choice of where you want to paste the worksheet into the workbook.

Copying the Contents of a Worksheet to Other Worksheets in a Workbook

With four worksheets in the workbook, the next step is to copy the contents of Sheet1 to Sheet4, Sheet2, and Sheet3. Sheet1 eventually will be used as the Company worksheet with the consolidated data. Sheet4, Sheet2, and Sheet3 will be used for the three store worksheets.

To Copy the Contents of a Worksheet to Other Worksheets in a Workbook

1

- **Click the Sheet1 tab.**
- **Click the Select All button and then click the Copy button on the Standard toolbar.**

Excel highlights the entire Sheet1 sheet (Figure 6-37) and displays a marquee around it to indicate what was copied on the Office Clipboard.

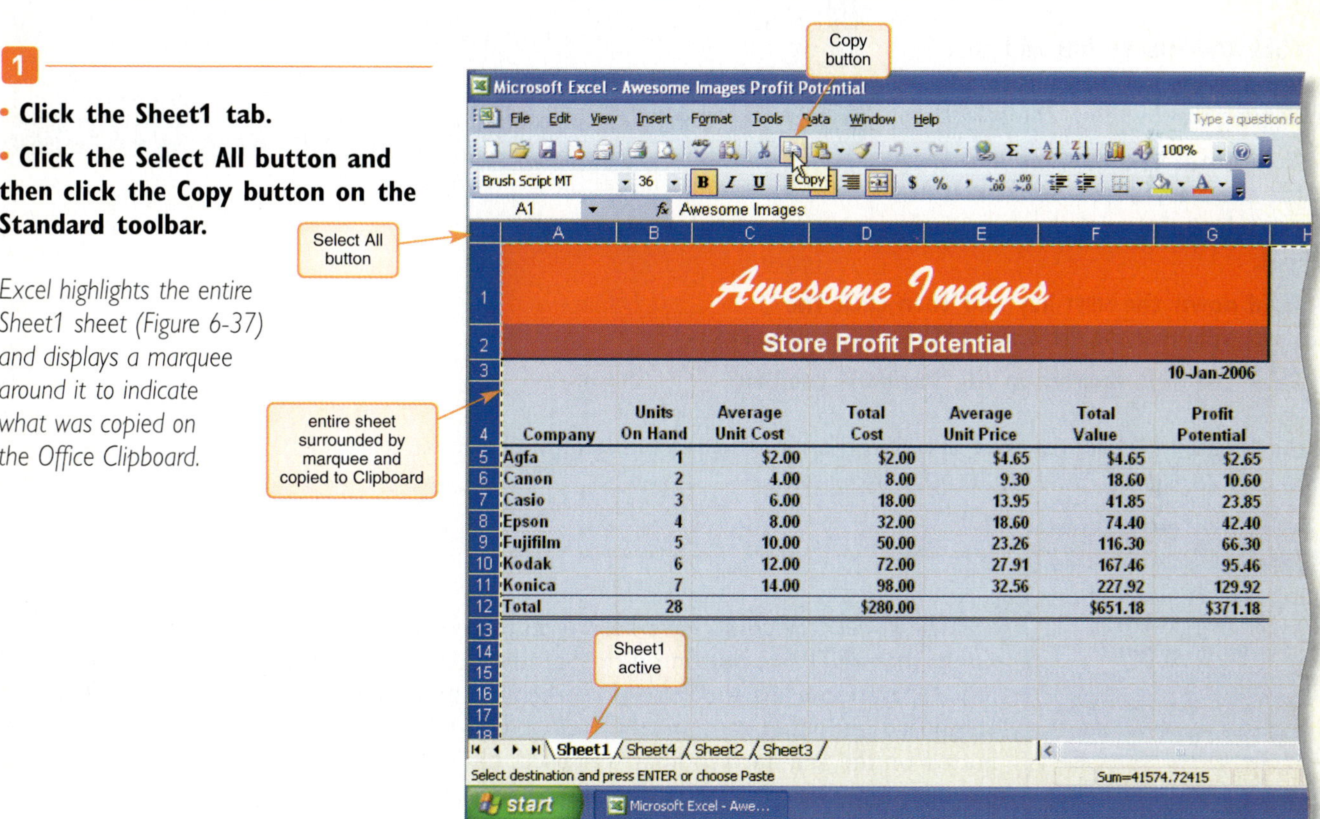

FIGURE 6-37

2

- **Click the Sheet4 tab.**
- **While holding down the SHIFT key, click the Sheet3 tab so all three blank worksheets in the workbook are selected.**
- **Click the Paste button on the Standard toolbar.**

Excel copies the data on the Office Clipboard to Sheet4, Sheet2, and Sheet3. Because multiple worksheets are selected, the term [Group] follows the template name on the title bar (Figure 6-38).

Paste button

[Group] indicates multiple worksheets are selected

contents of Sheet4 after copy and paste operation

Sheet4, Sheet2, and Sheet3 selected

FIGURE 6-38

3

- **Click the Sheet1 tab and then press the ESC key to remove the marquee surrounding the selection.**
- **Hold down the SHIFT key and then click the Sheet3 tab. Select cell A14 to deselect the worksheet on each sheet.**
- **Hold down the SHIFT key and then click the Sheet1 tab to deselect Sheet4, Sheet2, and Sheet3.**
- **Click the Save button on the Standard toolbar.**

Excel creates four identical worksheets in the workbook and saves it using the file name Awesome Images Profit Potential. Sheet1 is the active worksheet.

Other Ways

1. Select source area, on Edit menu click Copy, select worksheets, on Edit menu click Paste
2. Right-click source area, click Copy on shortcut menu, select worksheets, click Paste on shortcut menu
3. Select source area, press CTRL+C, select worksheets, press CTRL+V
4. In Voice Command mode, [select source area], say "Copy", [select worksheets], say "Paste"

The ENTER key could have been used to complete the paste operation in Step 2, rather than the Paste button on the Standard toolbar. Recall, that if you complete a paste operation using the ENTER key, then the marquee disappears and the Office Clipboard no longer contains the copied data following the action. Because the Paste button on the Standard toolbar was used, the ESC key was used in Step 3 to clear the marquee and Office Clipboard of the copied data.

Drilling an Entry through Worksheets

The next step is to replace the dummy numbers in the range C5:C11 with the average unit cost for each type of digital camera (Table 6-4). The average unit costs for each category are identical on all four sheets. For example, the average unit cost for the Agfa digital camera in cell C5 is $352.75 on all four sheets. To speed data entry, Excel allows you to enter a number once and drill it through worksheets so it is entered in the same cell on all the selected worksheets. This technique is referred to as **drilling an entry**. The following steps drill the seven average unit cost entries in Table 6-4 through all four worksheets in the range C5:C11.

Table 6-4 Average Unit Cost Entries

COMPANY	AVERAGE UNIT COST
Agfa	352.75
Canon	429.15
Casio	396.34
Epson	287.95
Fujifilm	456.33
Kodak	446.98
Konica	372.78

More About

Drilling an Entry

Besides drilling a number down through a workbook, you can drill a format, a function, or a formula down through a workbook.

To Drill an Entry through Worksheets

1

- **With Sheet1 active, hold down the SHIFT key and then click the Sheet3 tab.**
- **Select cell C5, type** `352.75` **and then press the DOWN ARROW key.**
- **Enter the six remaining average unit costs in Table 6-4 in the range C6:C11.**

All four tabs at the bottom of the window are selected. The word Sheet1 on the first tab is bold, indicating it is the active sheet. Excel displays the average unit cost entries as shown in Figure 6-39.

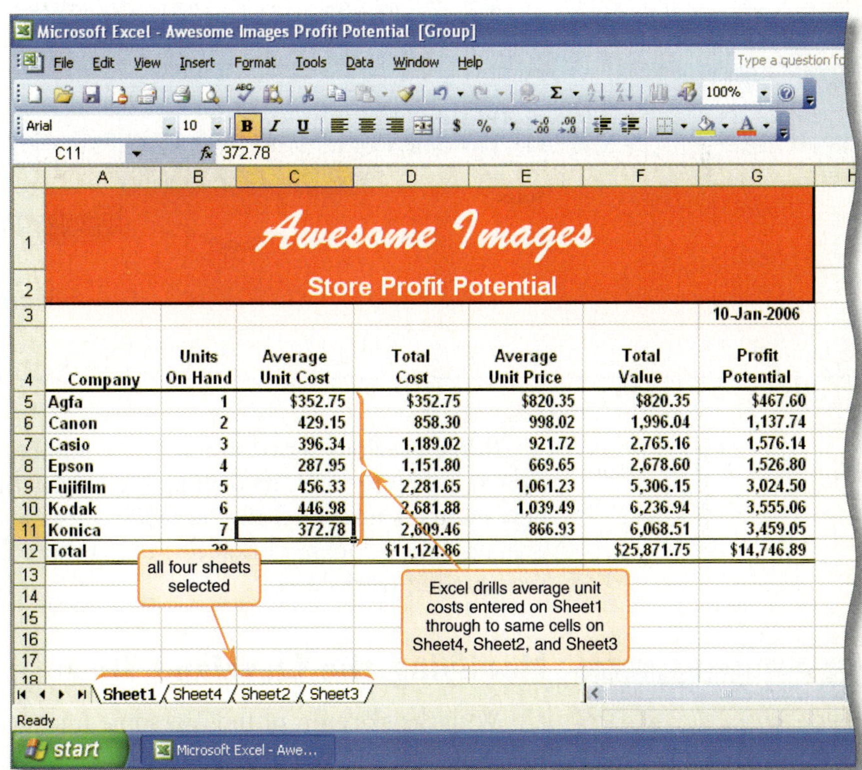

FIGURE 6-39

2

- **Hold down the SHIFT key and then click the Sheet1 tab to deselect Sheet4, Sheet2, and Sheet3.**
- **One at a time, click the Sheet4 tab, the Sheet2 tab, and the Sheet3 tab.**

The four sheets are identical (Figure 6-40).

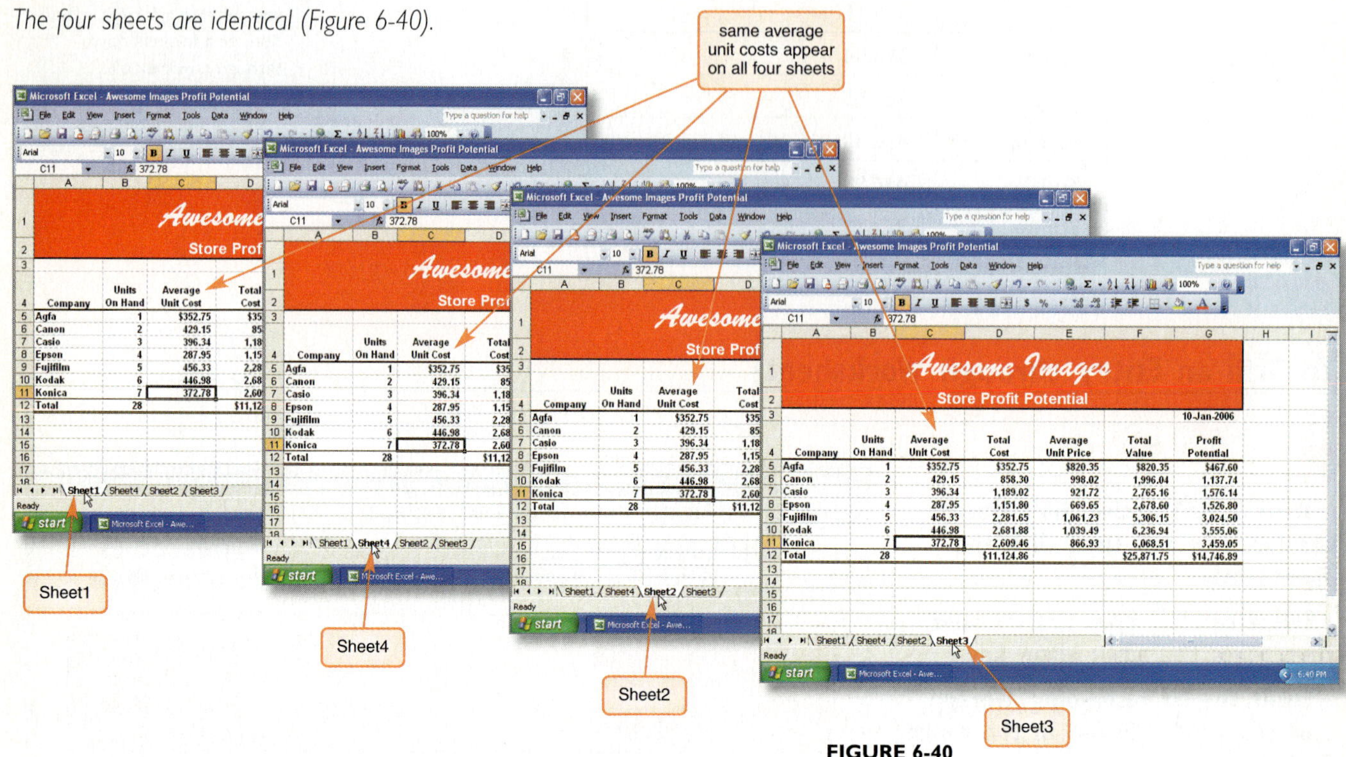

FIGURE 6-40

In the previous set of steps, 7 new numbers were entered on one worksheet. As shown in Figure 6-39, by drilling the entries through the four other worksheets, 28 new numbers now appear, 7 on each of the four worksheets. Excel's capability of drilling data through worksheets thus is an efficient way to enter data that is common among worksheets.

> *More About*
>
> **The Keyboard Shortcuts**
>
> Prefer to use the keyboard over the mouse? If you prefer the keyboard and want a list of shortcuts, then enter the phrase `keyboard shortcuts` in the Type a question for help box.

Modifying the Cleveland Sheet

With the skeleton of the Awesome Images Profit Potential workbook created, the next step is to modify the individual sheets. The following steps modify the Cleveland sheet by changing the sheet name, tab color, worksheet subtitle; changing the color of the title area; and entering the units on hand values in column B.

To Modify the Cleveland Sheet

1 **Double-click the Sheet4 tab, type** `Cleveland`**, and then press the ENTER key. Right-click the Cleveland tab, click Tab Color on the shortcut menu, click Dark Red (column 1, row 2) on the Color palette, and then click the OK button.**

2 **Double-click cell A2, drag through the word Store, and then type** `Cleveland` **to change the worksheet subtitle.**

3 **Select the range A1:A2, click the Fill Color button arrow on the Formatting toolbar, and then click Dark Red (column 1, row 2) on the Fill Color palette.**

4 **Enter the data listed in Table 6-5 in the range B5:B11.**

5 **Click the Save button on the Standard toolbar.**

Excel displays the Cleveland sheet as shown in Figure 6-41.

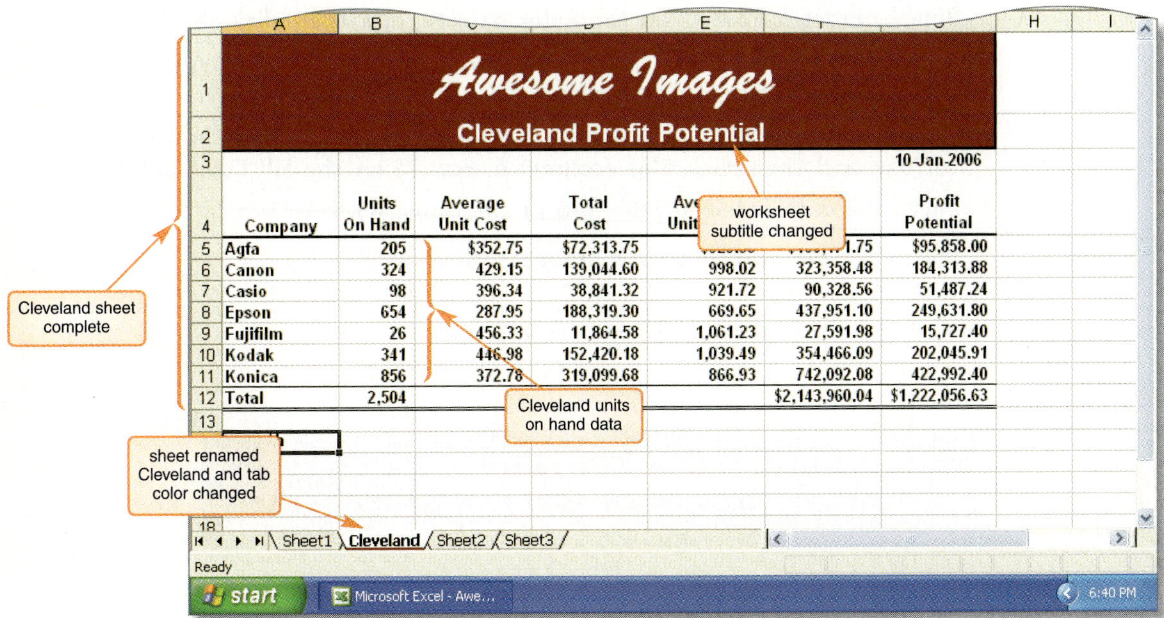

FIGURE 6-41

Table 6-5 Cleveland Units On Hand

CELL	UNITS ON HAND
B5	205
B6	324
B7	98
B8	654
B9	26
B10	341
B11	856

Excel immediately recalculates the formulas on the Cleveland worksheet as each new units on hand value is entered.

Modifying the Lexington Sheet

The following steps modify the Lexington sheet.

To Modify the Lexington Sheet

1. **Double-click the Sheet2 tab, type** `Lexington` **and then press the ENTER key. Right-click the Lexington tab, click Tab Color on the shortcut menu, click Blue (column 6, row 2) on the Color palette, and then click the OK button.**
2. **Double-click cell A2, drag through the word Store and then type** `Lexington` **to change the worksheet subtitle.**
3. **Select the range A1:A2, click the Fill Color button arrow on the Formatting toolbar, and then click Blue (column 6, row 2) on the Fill Color palette.**
4. **Enter the data listed in Table 6-6 in the range B5:B11.**
5. **Click the Save button on the Standard toolbar.**

Excel displays the Lexington sheet as shown in Figure 6-42.

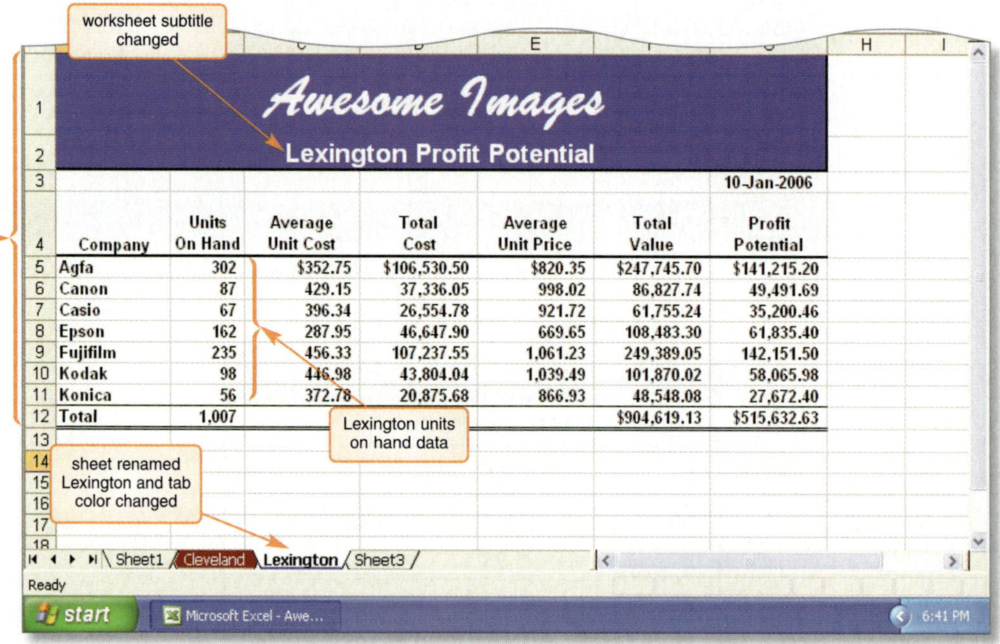

FIGURE 6-42

Table 6-6 Lexington Units On Hand

CELL	UNITS ON HAND
B5	302
B6	87
B7	67
B8	162
B9	235
B10	98
B11	56

More About

Importing Data

Costs, such as those entered into the range C5:C11, often are maintained in another workbook, a file, or a database. If the costs are maintained elsewhere, ways exist to link to a workbook or import data from a file or database into a workbook. Linking to a workbook is discussed later in this project. For information on importing data, see the Get External Data command on the Data menu.

Modifying the San Diego Sheet

As with the Cleveland and Lexington sheets, the sheet name, tab color, worksheet subtitle, data, and background colors must be changed on the San Diego sheet. The following steps modify the San Diego sheet.

To Modify the San Diego Sheet

1. **Double click the Sheet3 tab, type** `San Diego` **and then press the ENTER key. Right-click the San Diego tab, click Tab Color on the shortcut menu, click Green (column 4, row 2) on the Color palette, and then click the OK button.**
2. **Double-click cell A2, drag through the word Store and then type** `San Diego` **to change the worksheet subtitle.**
3. **Select the range A1:A2, click the Fill Color button arrow on the Formatting toolbar, and then click Green (column 4, row 2) on the Fill Color palette.**
4. **Enter the data in Table 6-7 in the range B5:B11.**
5. **Click the Save button on the Standard toolbar.**

Excel displays the San Diego sheet as shown in Figure 6-43.

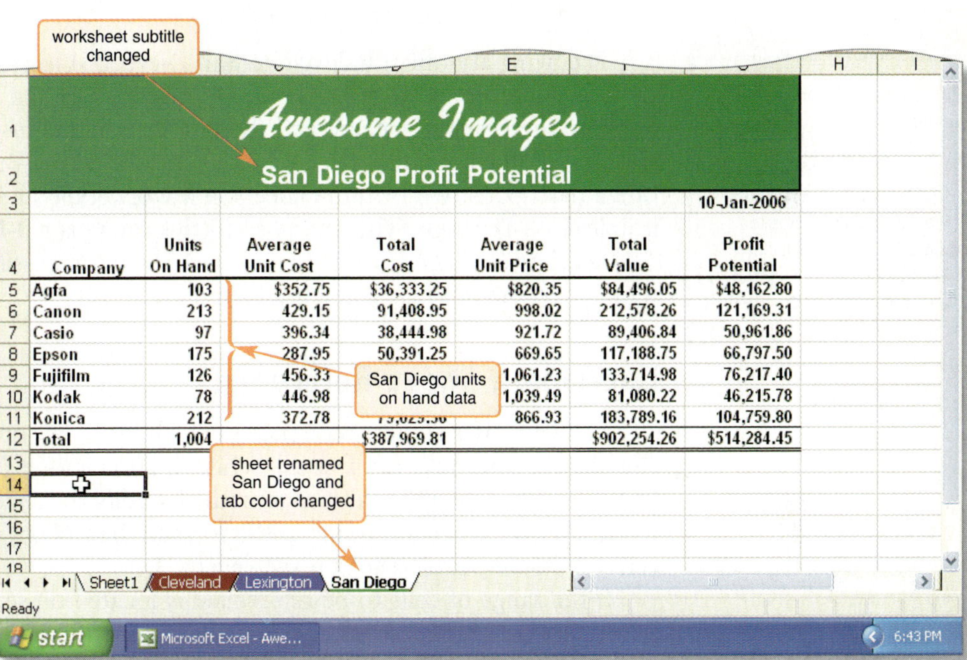

FIGURE 6-43

Table 6-7 San Diego Units On Hand

CELL	UNITS ON HAND
B5	103
B6	213
B7	97
B8	175
B9	126
B10	78
B11	212

With the three store sheets complete, the next step is to modify Sheet1, which will serve as the consolidation worksheet containing totals of the data on the Cleveland, Lexington, and San Diego sheets. Because this sheet contains totals of the data, you need to understand how to reference cells in other sheets in a workbook before modifying Sheet1.

Referencing Cells in Other Sheets in a Workbook

To reference cells in other sheets in a workbook, you use the sheet name, which serves as the **sheet reference**, and the cell reference. For example, you refer to cell B5 on the Cleveland sheet as shown below.

=Cleveland!B5

Using this method, you can sum cell B5 on the three store sheets by selecting cell B5 on the Sheet1 sheet and then entering:

= Cleveland!B5 + Lexington!B5 + San Diego!B5

A much quicker way to total the three cells is to use the SUM function as follows:

=SUM(Cleveland:San Diego!B5)

The SUM argument (Cleveland:San Diego!B5) instructs Excel to sum cell B5 on each of the three sheets (Cleveland, Lexington, and San Diego). The colon (:) between the first sheet name and the last sheet name instructs Excel to include these sheets and all sheets in between, just as it does with a range of cells on a sheet. A range that spans two or more sheets in a workbook such as Cleveland:San Diego!B5 is called a **3-D range**. The reference to this range is a **3-D reference**.

A sheet reference such as San Diego! always is absolute. Thus, the sheet reference remains constant when you copy formulas.

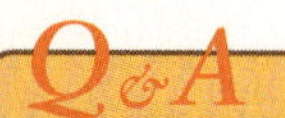

Q: What is a circular reference?

A: A circular reference is a formula that depends on its own value. The most common type is a formula that contains a reference to the same cell in which the formula resides.

Entering a Sheet Reference

You can enter a sheet reference in a cell by typing the sheet reference or by clicking the appropriate sheet tab while in Point mode. When you click the sheet tab, Excel activates the sheet and automatically adds the sheet name and an exclamation point after the insertion point in the formula bar. Next, select or drag through the cells you want to reference on the sheet.

If the range of cells to be referenced is located on several worksheets (as when selecting a 3-D range), click the first sheet tab and then select the cell or drag through the range of cells. Next, while holding down the SHIFT key, click the sheet tab of the last sheet you want to reference. Excel will include the cell(s) on the first sheet, the last sheet, and any sheets in between.

Modifying the Company Sheet

This section modifies the Company sheet by changing the sheet name, tab color, subtitle and then entering the SUM function in each cell in the range B5:B11. The SUM functions will determine the total units on hand at the three stores, by camera company. Cell B5 on the Company sheet, for instance, will contain the sum of the Agfa digital camera units on hand in cells Cleveland!B5, Lexington!B5, and San Diego!B5. Before determining the totals, the following steps change the sheet name from Sheet1 to Company, color the tab, and change the worksheet subtitle to Company Profit Potential.

To Modify the Company Sheet

1. **Double-click the Sheet1 sheet tab, type** `Company` **and then press the ENTER key. Right-click the Company tab, click Tab Color on the shortcut menu, click Red (column 1, row 3) on the Color palette, and then click the OK button.**

2. **Double-click cell A2, drag through the word Store, and then type** `Company` **as the worksheet subtitle. Press the ENTER key.**

Excel changes the name of Sheet1 to Company and changes the tab color to red. The worksheet subtitle appears as Company Profit Potential (Figure 6-44).

The following steps enter the 3-D references used to determine the total units on hand for each of the seven digital camera companies. In these steps, the Formulas command on the Paste button menu on the Standard toolbar is used to complete the paste operation. When the Formulas command is used, the paste operation pastes only the formulas, leaving the formats of the destination area unchanged.

To Enter and Copy 3-D References Using the Paste Button Menu

1.

• **Select cell B5 and then click the AutoSum button on the Standard toolbar.**

Excel displays the SUM function and ScreenTip (Figure 6-44). The SUM function has no arguments within the parentheses because text data is above and to the right of cell B5.

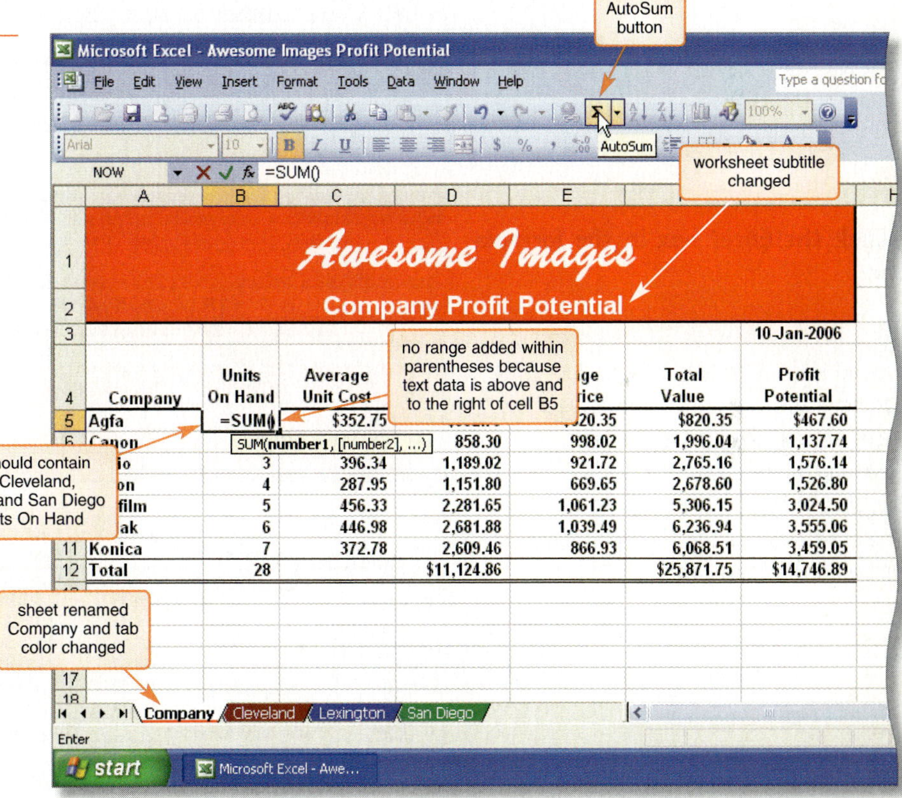

FIGURE 6-44

2

• **Click the Cleveland tab and then click cell B5. While holding down the SHIFT key, click the San Diego tab.**

Excel surrounds cell Cleveland!B5 with a marquee (Figure 6-45). All four sheet tabs are selected and the Cleveland tab appears in bold because it is the active sheet. The SUM function in cell Company!B5 appears in the formula bar.

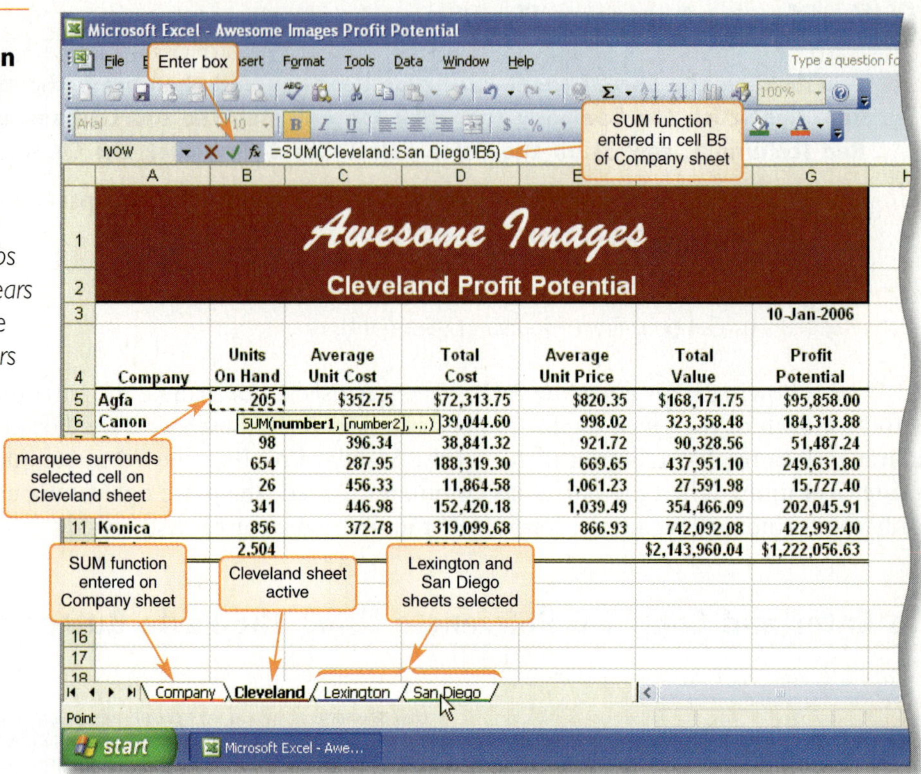

FIGURE 6-45

3

• **Click the Enter box in the formula bar.**

The SUM function with 3-D references is entered in cell Company!B5 and the Company sheet becomes the active sheet. Excel displays the sum of the cells Cleveland!B5, Lexington!B5, and San Diego!B5 in cell B5 of the Company sheet. Excel also displays the SUM function in the formula bar (Figure 6-46).

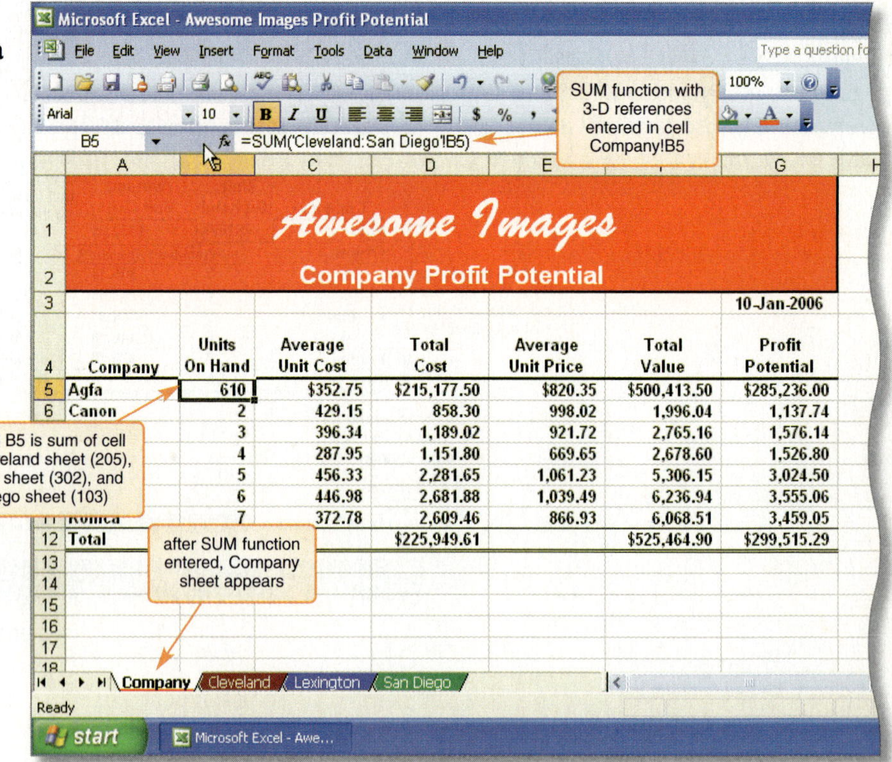

FIGURE 6-46

4

• **With cell B5 active, click the Copy button on the Standard toolbar (Figure 6-47).**

The SUM function and the formats assigned to cell B5 are copied on the Office Clipboard. A marquee surrounds the source area, cell B5.

Copy button

Microsoft Excel - Awesome Images Profit Potential

B5 =SUM('Cleveland:San Diego'!B5)

Awesome Images

Company Profit Potential

10-Jan-2006

	Company	Units On Hand	Average Unit Cost	Total Cost	Average Unit Price	Total Value	Profit Potential
5	Agfa	610	$352.75	$215,177.50	$820.35	$500,413.50	$285,236.00
6	Canon	624	429.15	267,789.60	998.02	622,764.48	354,974.88
7	Casio	262	396.34	103,841.08	921.72	241,490.64	137,649.56
8		991	287.95	285,358.45	669.65	663,623.15	378,264.70
9		387	456.33	176,599.71	1,061.23	410,696.01	234,096.30
10		517	446.98	231,088.66	1,039.49	537,416.33	306,327.67
11	Konica	1,124	372.78	419,004.72	866.93	974,429.32	555,424.60
12	Total	4,515		$1,698,859.72		$3,950,833.43	$2,251,973.71

marquee surrounds source area

Company / Cleveland / Lexington / San Diego

Select destination and press ENTER or choose Paste

FIGURE 6-47

5

• **Select the range B6:B11 and then click the Paste button arrow on the Standard toolbar.**

Excel highlights the range B6:B11 and displays the Paste button menu (Figure 6-48.)

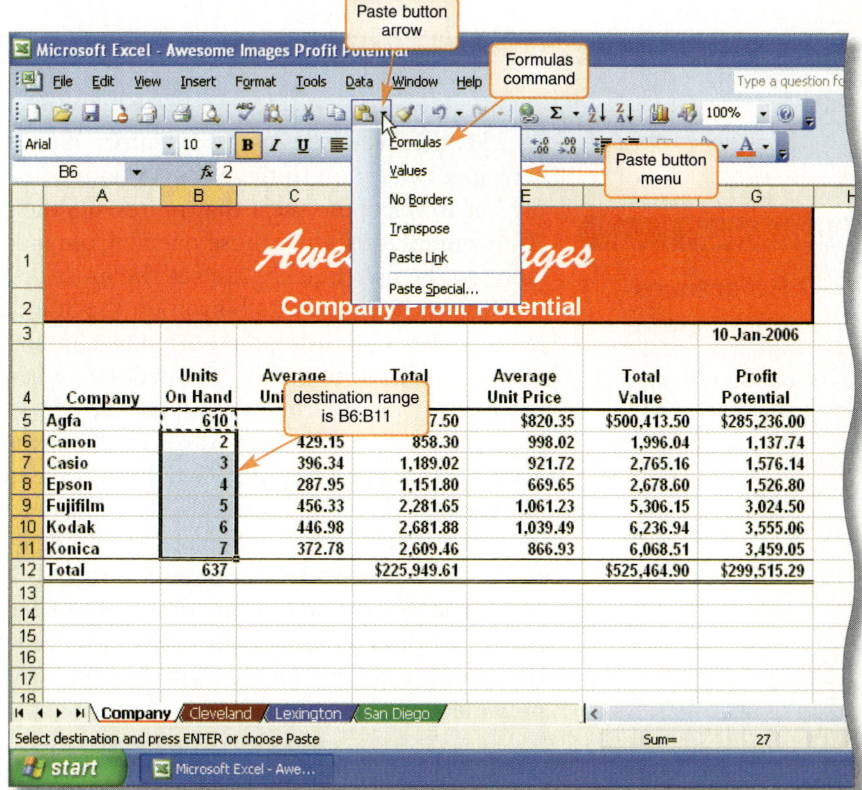

FIGURE 6-48

6

- **Click Formulas on the Paste button menu.**
- **Press the ESC key to clear the marquee surrounding cell B5 and then select cell A14 to deselect the range B6:B11.**
- **Click the Save button on the Standard toolbar to save the Awesome Images Profit Potential workbook.**

Excel copies the SUM function in cell B5 to the range B6:B11 (Figure 6-49) and automatically adjusts the cell references in the SUM function to reference the corresponding cells on the three sheets in the workbook. The units on hand for each brand of digital camera are tabulated in the range B5:B11. The Company worksheet with the consolidated data is complete and the workbook is saved.

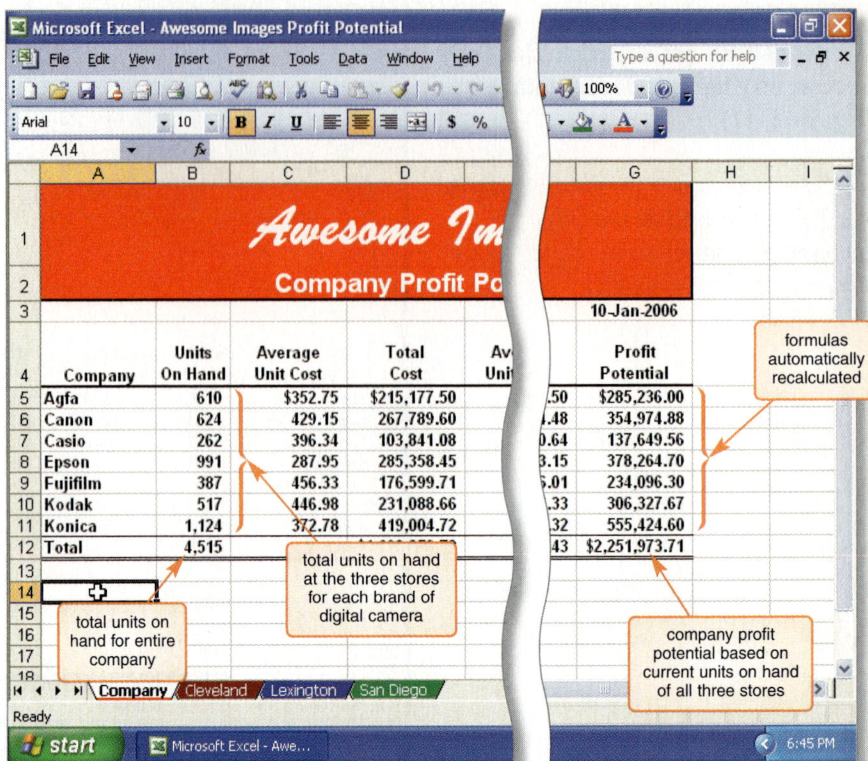

FIGURE 6-49

More About

3-D References

If you are summing numbers on noncontiguous sheets, hold down the CTRL key rather than the SHIFT key when selecting the sheets.

As shown in cell G12 in Figure 6-49, Awesome Images has a profit potential of $2,251,973.71, based on the inventory data submitted by the three stores. If a store calls in a correction to the units on hand value for any digital camera, the user simply has to select the sheet that represents the store and then enter the correct value. All formulas, including those on the Company sheet, will be recalculated immediately, so the user quickly can see the most up-to-date company-wide profit potential.

If you click the Paste button on the Standard toolbar to complete the paste operation, rather than using the Formulas command as shown in Figure 6-48, then any formats assigned to cell B5 also will be copied to the range B6:B11. Completing the paste operation by using the fill handle or by pressing the ENTER key also will copy any formats from the source area to the destination area. When you use the Formulas command on the Paste button menu, Excel copies the SUM function, but not the format, assigned to cell B5. In this example, the format assigned to cell B5 is the same as the format assigned to the range B6:B11, so it does not matter if you use the Paste button or the Formulas command. In many cases, however, the formats of the source area and destination area differ; the Paste button menu thus is a useful option to complete the copy and paste operation. Table 6-8 summarizes the commands available on the Paste button menu, as shown in Figure 6-48 on the previous page.

Table 6-8 Paste Button Menu Commands

COMMAND	DESCRIPTION
Formulas	Pastes the formulas from the source area, but not the formats.
Values	Pastes the value of the formula from the source area, but not the formulas or formats.
No Borders	Pastes the formula and all formats from the source area, except for borders.
Transpose	Pastes the formula and formats from the source area, but transposes the columns and rows. For example, if you are summing numbers in a column in the source area, then Excel will sum numbers in a row in the destination area.
Paste Link	Pastes the cell reference of the source area in the destination area.
Paste Special	Displays the Paste Special dialog box that allows you to choose what you want pasted from the source area to the destination area.

Drawing the 3-D Cylinder Chart

The **3-D Cylinder chart** is similar to a 3-D Bar chart in that it can be used to show trends or illustrate comparisons among items. The 3-D Cylinder chart in Figure 6-50, for example, compares the total profit potential of the different brands of digital cameras in inventory. WordArt is used to draw the curved chart title, Profit Potential. A text box and arrow are used to highlight the digital camera brand with the greatest profit potential.

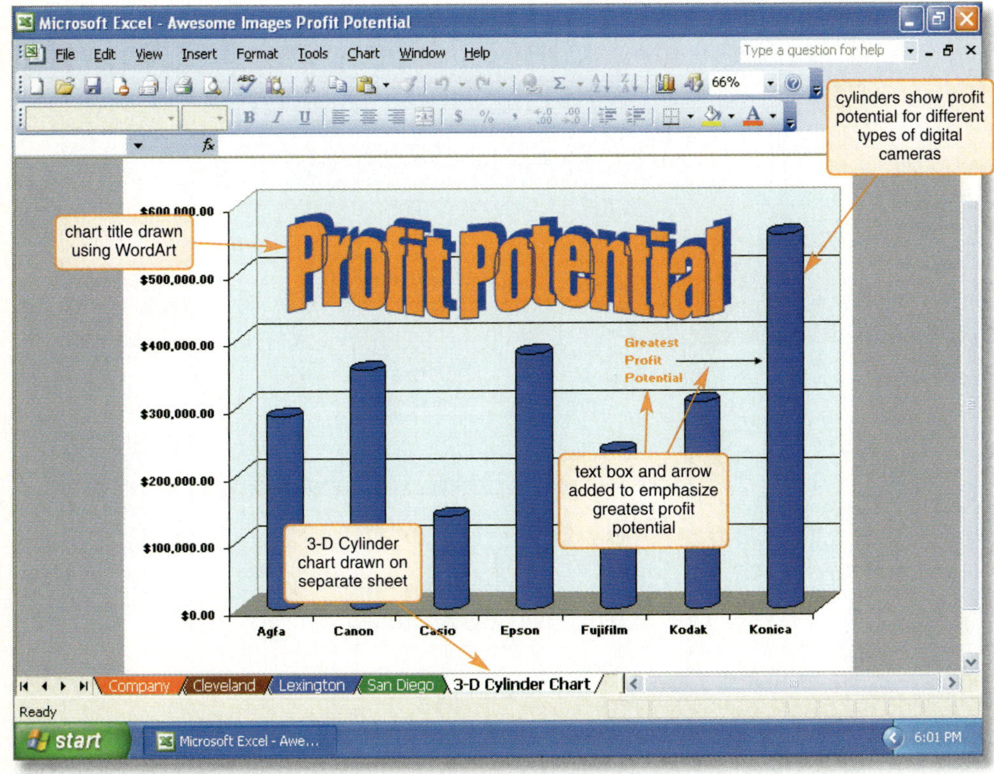

FIGURE 6-50

More About

User-Defined Charts

To create a user-defined chart, create a chart on a worksheet and customize it. Click the chart and then on the Chart menu click Type. Click the Custom Types tab, click User-defined, click Add, type a name in the Name box and a description in the Description box, and then click the OK button. Once you create a user-defined chart, you can click the Set as Default chart button in the Chart Type dialog box to set the user-defined chart as the default chart.

To Draw the 3-D Cylinder Chart

1

- **With the Company sheet active, select the range A5:A11.**
- **Hold down the CTRL key and then select the range G5:G11.**
- **Click the Chart Wizard button on the Standard toolbar.**
- **When Excel displays the Chart Wizard - Step 1 of 4 - Chart Type dialog box, click Cylinder in the Chart type list and then click Column with a cylindrical shape (column 1, row 1) in the Chart sub-type area.**

Excel displays the Chart Wizard - Step 1 of 4 - Chart Type dialog box as shown in Figure 6-51. The nonadjacent ranges A5:A11 and G5:G11 are selected on the Company sheet.

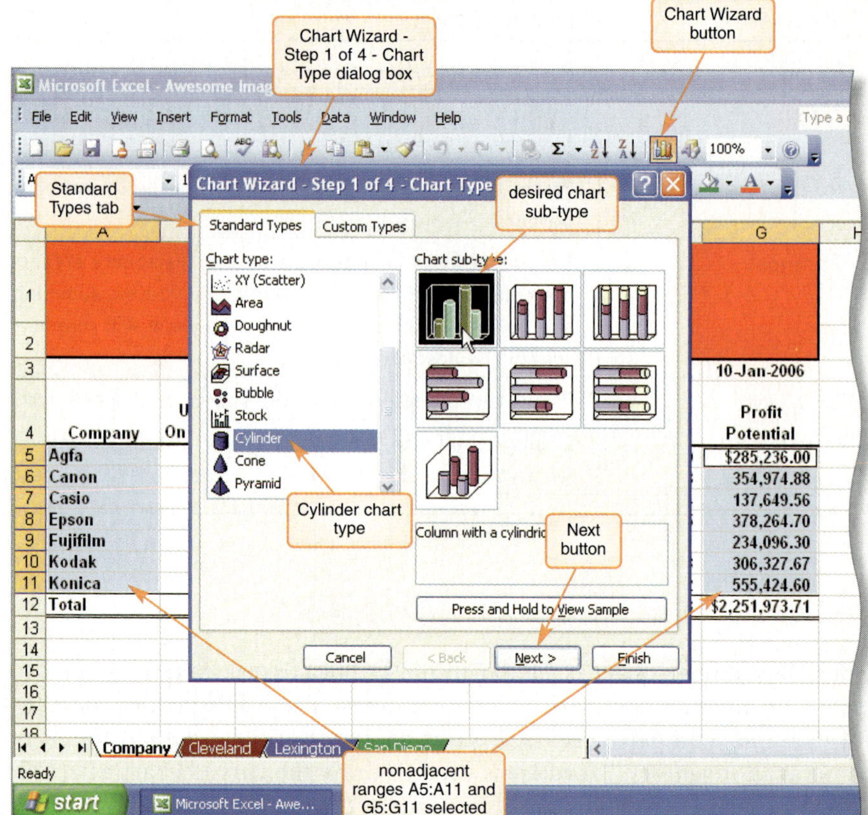

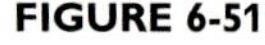
FIGURE 6-51

2

- **Click the Next button.**

Excel displays the Chart Wizard - Step 2 of 4 - Chart Source Data dialog box with a sample of the 3-D Cylinder chart and the data range selection (Figure 6-52). A marquee surrounds the data range on the Company sheet. Because the range is down the sheet, Excel automatically determines the data range is in columns.

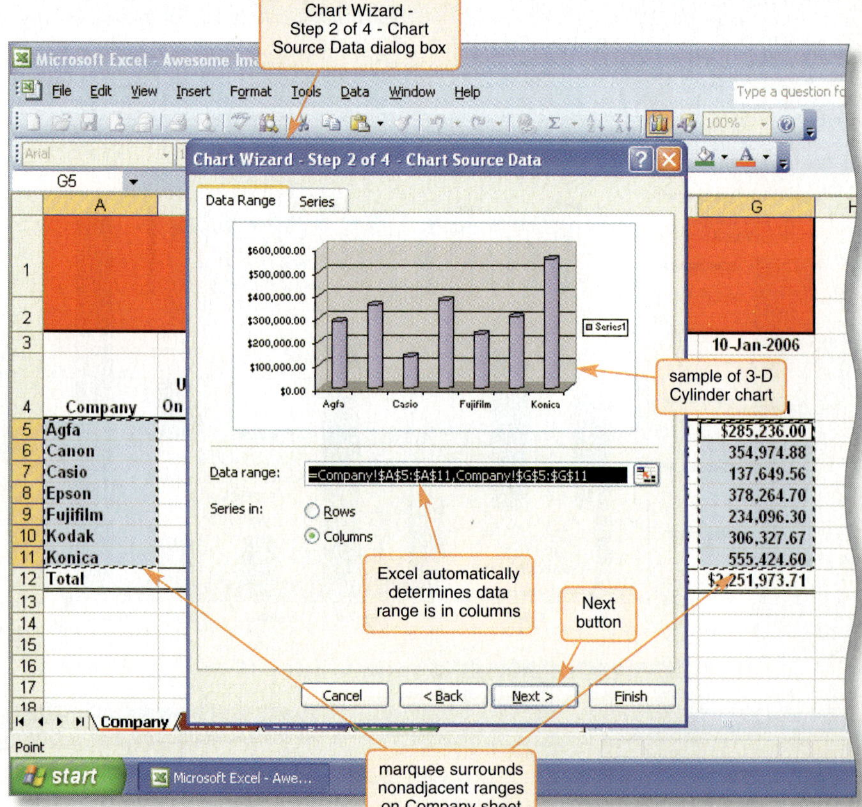

FIGURE 6-52

3

- **Click the Next button.**
- **When Excel displays the Chart Wizard - Step 3 of 4 - Chart Options dialog box, click the Legend tab and then click Show legend to deselect it so Excel does not display the legend with the chart.**

Excel displays the Chart Wizard - Step 3 of 4 - Chart Options dialog box (Figure 6-53). Excel redraws the sample of the chart without the legend.

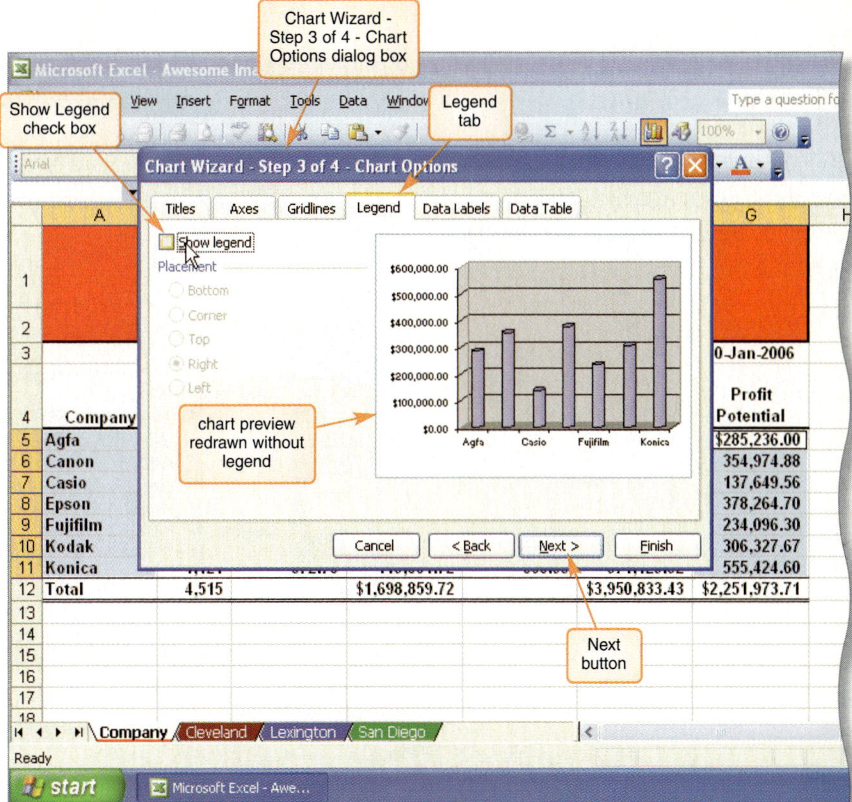

FIGURE 6-53

4

- **Click the Next button.**
- **When Excel displays the Chart Wizard - Step 4 of 4 - Chart Location dialog box, click As new sheet.**

Excel displays the Chart Wizard - Step 4 of 4 - Chart Location dialog box (Figure 6-54). Because the As new sheet option button is selected, the chart will be drawn on a separate chart sheet.

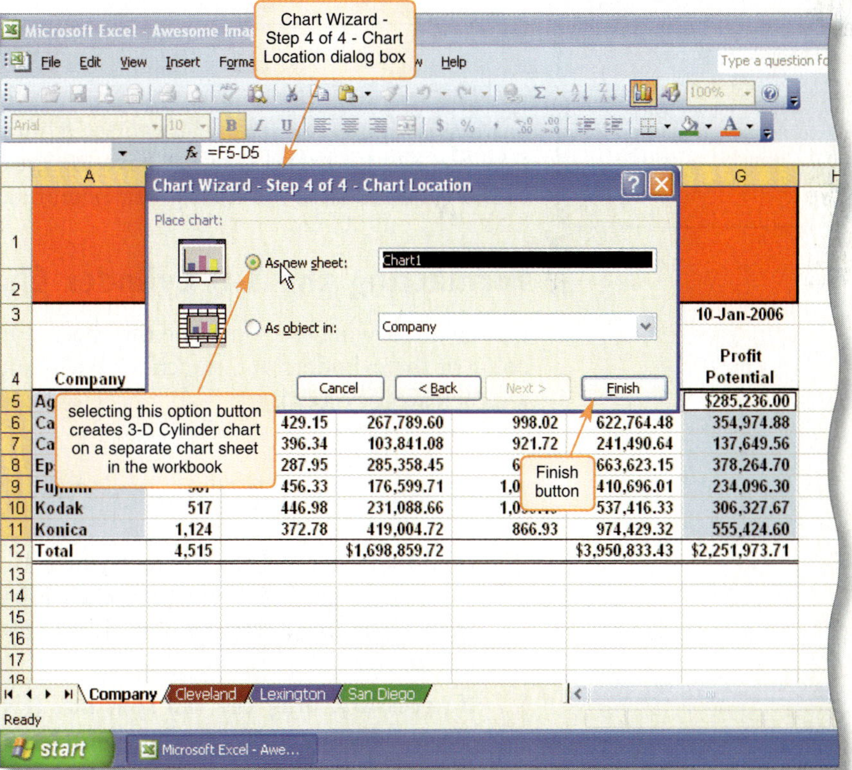

FIGURE 6-54

5

• **Click the Finish button.**

Excel draws the 3-D Cylinder chart. The chart sheet, which is named Chart1, is inserted as the first sheet in the workbook (Figure 6-55).

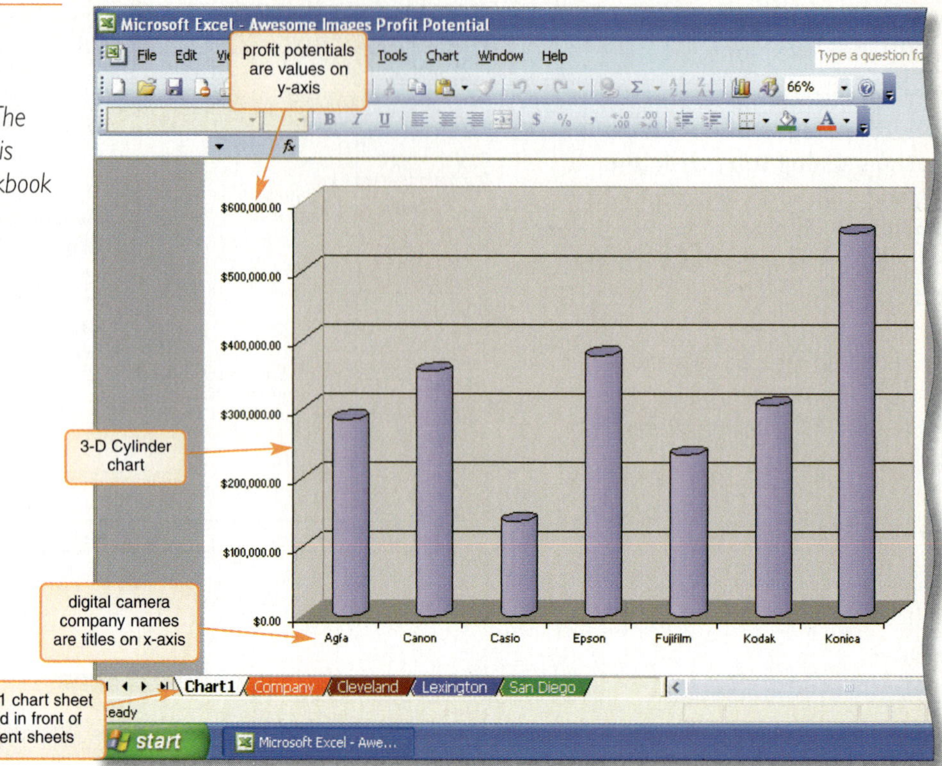

FIGURE 6-55

Other Ways

1. Select range, on Insert menu click Chart
2. Select range, press F11
3. Select range, in Voice Command mode, say "Chart Wizard"

The 3-D Cylinder chart compares the profit potential of the seven different brands of digital cameras. You can see from the chart that, of the cameras in inventory, the Konica brand cameras have the greatest profit potential and the Casio brand cameras have the least profit potential.

Formatting the 3-D Cylinder Chart

The following steps rename the sheet, color the tab, move the sheet, change the color of the cylinders and the chart walls, and format the y-axis (values axis) and x-axis (category axis).

To Format the 3-D Cylinder Chart

1 **Double-click the Chart1 tab, type** `3-D Cylinder Chart` **and then press the ENTER key. Right-click the tab, click Tab Color on the shortcut menu, and then click Light Turquoise (column 5, row 5) on the Color palette. Click the OK button.**

2 **If necessary, drag the tab split box (Figure 6-56) to the right to ensure all five tabs show. Drag the 3-D Cylinder Chart sheet tab to the right of the San Diego sheet tab.**

3. **Click the chart walls behind the cylinders, click the Fill Color button arrow on the Formatting toolbar, and then click Light Turquoise (column 5, row 5) on the Fill Color palette. Click one of the cylinders to select all the cylinders, click the Fill Color button arrow on the Formatting toolbar, and then click Blue (column 6, row 2) on the Fill Color palette.**

4. **Click the x-axis and then click the Bold button on the Formatting toolbar. Click the y-axis and then click the Bold button on the Formatting toolbar. Click outside the chart area.**

Excel displays the 3-D Cylinder chart as shown in Figure 6-56.

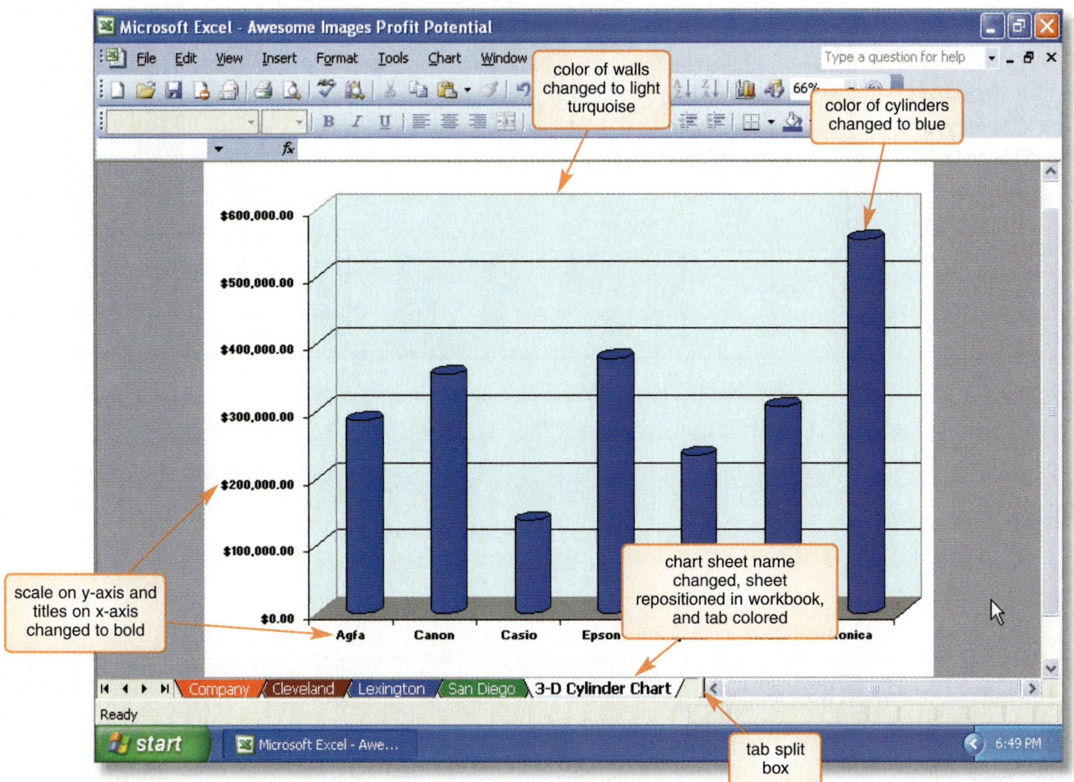

FIGURE 6-56

Adding a Chart Title Using the WordArt Tool

Earlier, you learned how to add a chart title by using the Chart Wizard and how to format it using the Formatting toolbar. You also can create a chart title using the WordArt tool. The **WordArt tool** allows you to create shadowed, skewed, rotated, and stretched text on a chart sheet or worksheet and apply other special text formatting effects. The WordArt text added to a worksheet is called an **object**. The steps on the next page show how to add a chart title using the WordArt tool.

To Add a Chart Title Using the WordArt Tool

1

- **With the 3-D Cylinder Chart sheet active, click the Drawing button on the Standard toolbar.**
- **When Excel displays the Drawing toolbar, dock it at the bottom of the screen, if necessary.**
- **Click the Insert WordArt button on the Drawing toolbar.**
- **When Excel displays the WordArt Gallery dialog box, click the style in column 4, row 4 of the Select a WordArt style area.**

Excel displays the Drawing toolbar and the WordArt Gallery as shown in Figure 6-57.

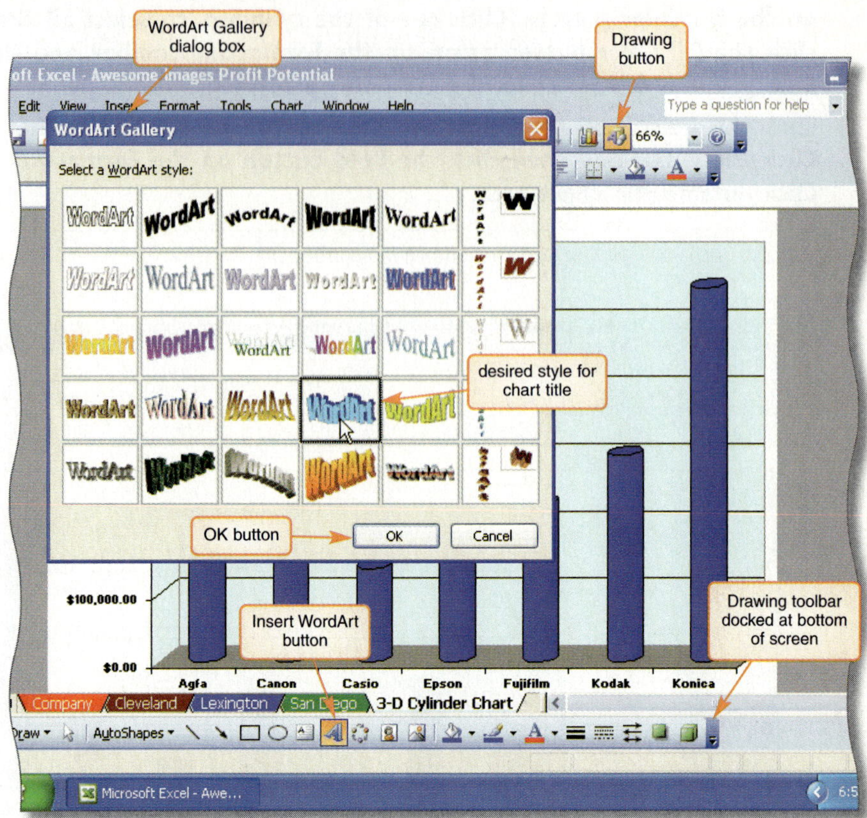

FIGURE 6-57

2

- **Click the OK button.**
- **When Excel displays the Edit WordArt Text dialog box, type** `Profit Potential` **as the title of the 3-D Cylinder chart.**

Excel displays the Edit WordArt Text dialog box as shown in Figure 6-58. Profit Potential will be the chart title. The default font and font size will be used.

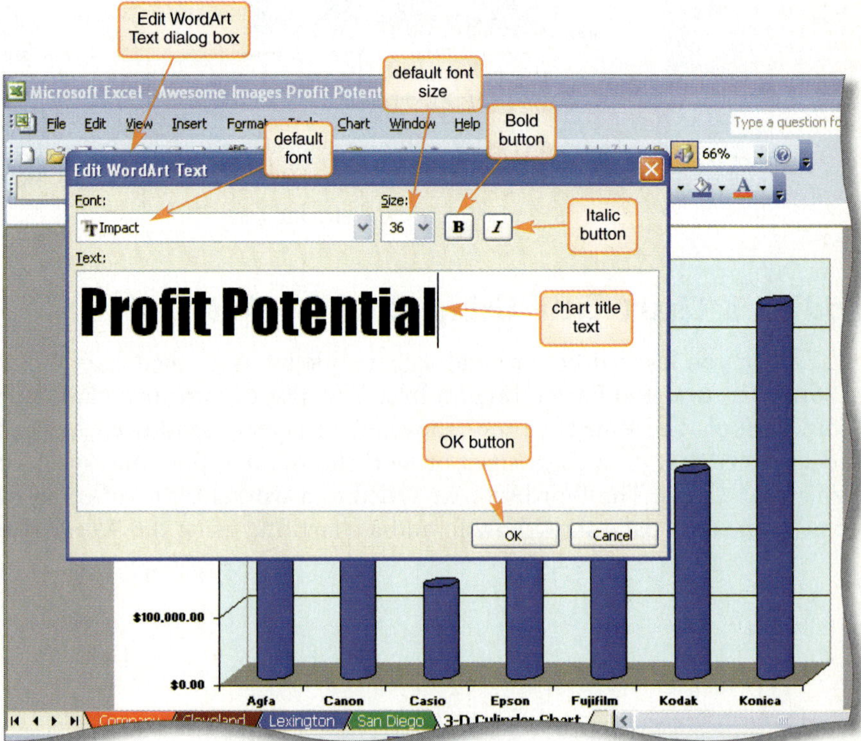

FIGURE 6-58

3

• **Click the OK button.**

The WordArt object Profit Potential appears in the middle of the chart sheet (Figure 6-59). Excel displays the WordArt toolbar.

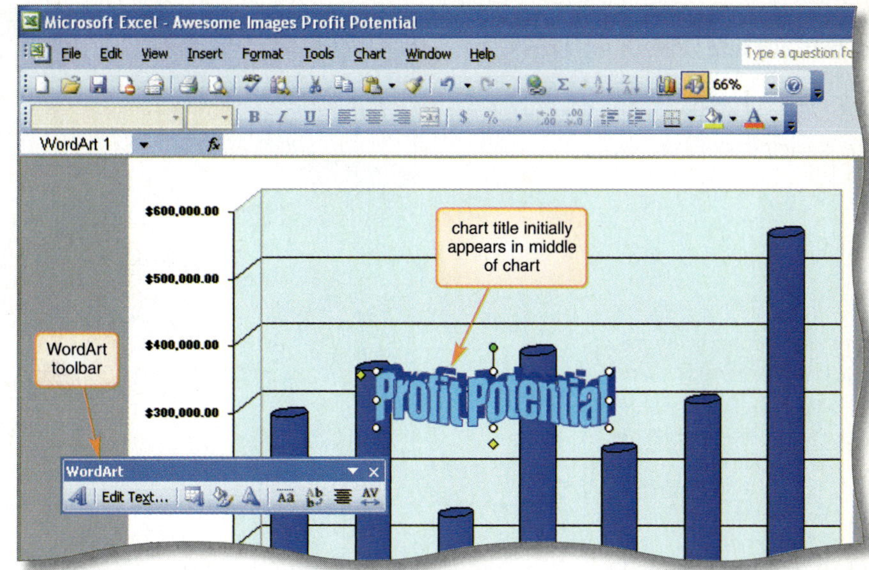

FIGURE 6-59

4

• **Point to the center of the WordArt object, drag it above the cylinders in the chart, and then drag the sizing handles to resize it as shown in Figure 6-60.**

The sizing handles (small circles) surrounding the WordArt object indicate it is selected.

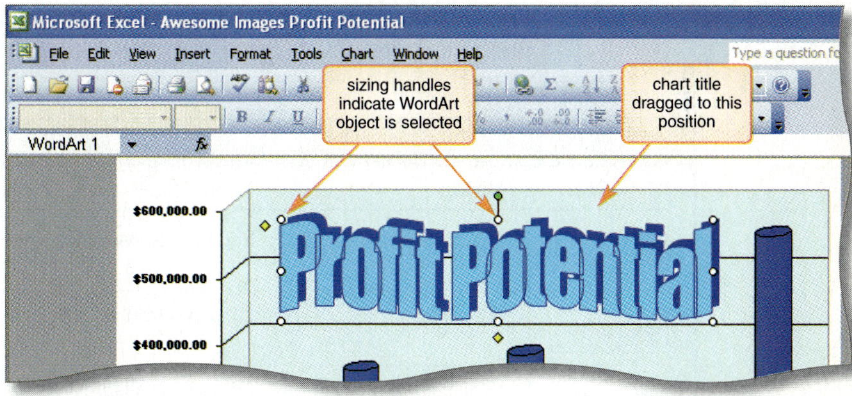

FIGURE 6-60

5

• **With the WordArt object selected, click the Fill Color button arrow on the Formatting toolbar and then click Orange (column 2, row 2) on the Fill Color palette.**

Excel changes the color of the WordArt object to orange (Figure 6-61). Even though the title consists of text, the chart title is an object. Thus, the Fill Color button, not the Font Color button, is used to change the color of the object.

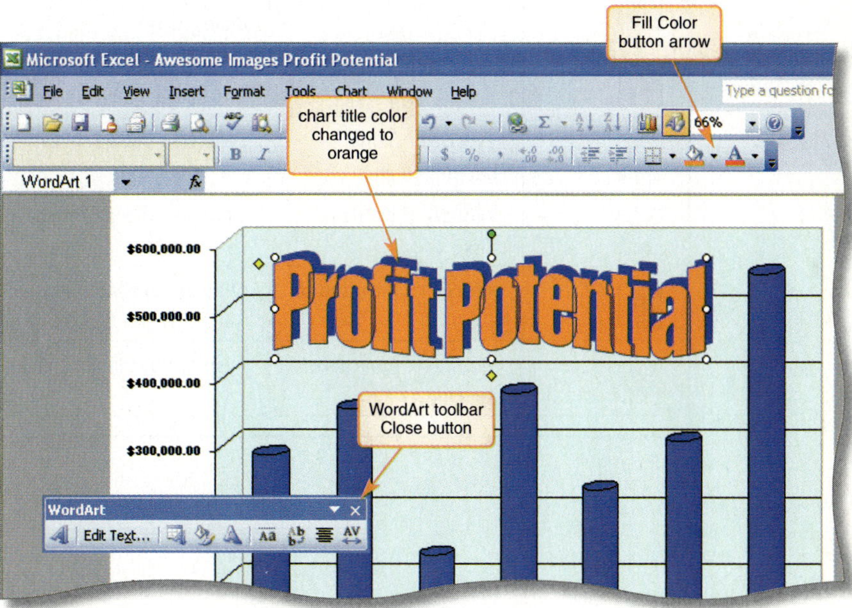

FIGURE 6-61

6

• **Click outside the chart area.**

Excel hides the WordArt toolbar. The chart title is complete (Figure 6-62).

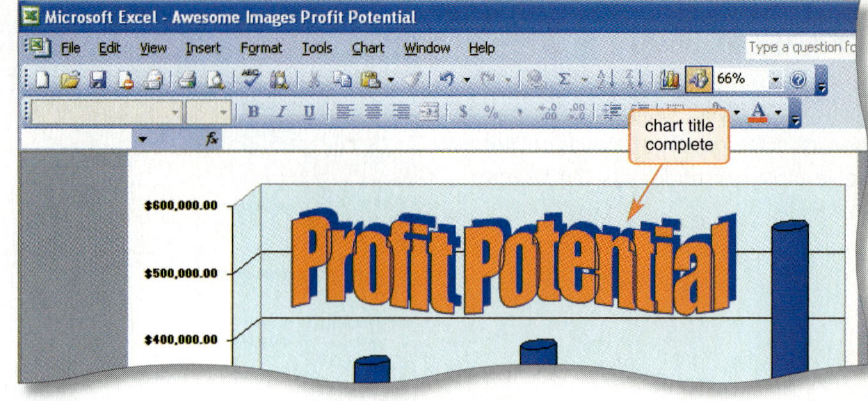

FIGURE 6-62

Other Ways

1. On Insert menu, point to Picture, click WordArt on Picture submenu
2. To format object, click Format WordArt on WordArt toolbar
3. In Voice Command mode, say "Insert, Picture, WordArt"

After you add a WordArt object to your workbook, you can use the WordArt toolbar (Figure 6-61) to edit it. Any time you select the WordArt object, Excel should display the WordArt toolbar. If it fails to appear, right-click any toolbar and click WordArt on the shortcut menu. The buttons on the WordArt toolbar and their functions are described in Table 6-9.

Table 6-9 Buttons on the WordArt Toolbar

BUTTON	NAME	FUNCTION
	Insert WordArt	Starts the WordArt tool
Edit Text...	Edit Text	Displays text editing options in Edit WordArt Text dialog box
	WordArt Gallery	Displays available WordArt styles in the WordArt Gallery dialog box
	Format WordArt	Displays available formatting options in the Format WordArt dialog box
	WordArt Shape	Changes the shape of an object
	WordArt Same Letter Heights	Switches between the same and different letter heights in an object
	WordArt Vertical Text	Changes the orientation of the WordArt object from horizontal to vertical
	WordArt Alignment	Displays available alignment options for the WordArt object
	WordArt Character Spacing	Displays available character spacing options for the WordArt object

Adding a Text Box and an Arrow to the Chart

A text box and an arrow can be used to **annotate** (call out or highlight) other objects or elements in a worksheet or chart. For example, in a worksheet, you may want to annotate a particular cell or group of cells by adding a text box and arrow. In a chart, you may want to emphasize a column or slice of a Pie chart.

A **text box** is a rectangular area of variable size in which you can add text. You use the sizing handles to resize a text box in the same manner you resize an embedded chart or a WordArt object. If the text box has the same color as the background, then the text appears as if it was written freehand, because the box itself does not show. An **arrow** allows you to connect an object, such as a text box, to an item that you want to annotate.

The following steps add the text box and arrow indicated in the sketch of the chart in Figure 6-3b on page EX 381 and also shown in Figure 6-50 on page EX 419.

More About

Drawing Objects

To draw multiple objects, such as text boxes and arrows, double-click the corresponding button. The button will stay recessed, allowing you to draw more objects, until you click the corresponding button. If you need a series of identical objects, create one object, then use the Copy and Paste buttons.

To Add a Text Box and an Arrow to the Chart

1

- **Click the Text Box button on the Drawing toolbar, point to the upper-left corner of the planned text box location, and then drag the cross hair to the lower-right corner (Figure 6-63).**
- **With the insertion point active in the text box, type** `Greatest Profit Potential` **as the text.**
- **Drag through the text, click the Font Size box arrow on the Formatting toolbar, click 12 in the Font Size list, click the Bold button on the Formatting toolbar, click the Font Color button arrow on the Formatting toolbar, and then click Orange (column 2, row 2) on the Font Color palette.**

Excel displays the text box as shown in Figure 6-63.

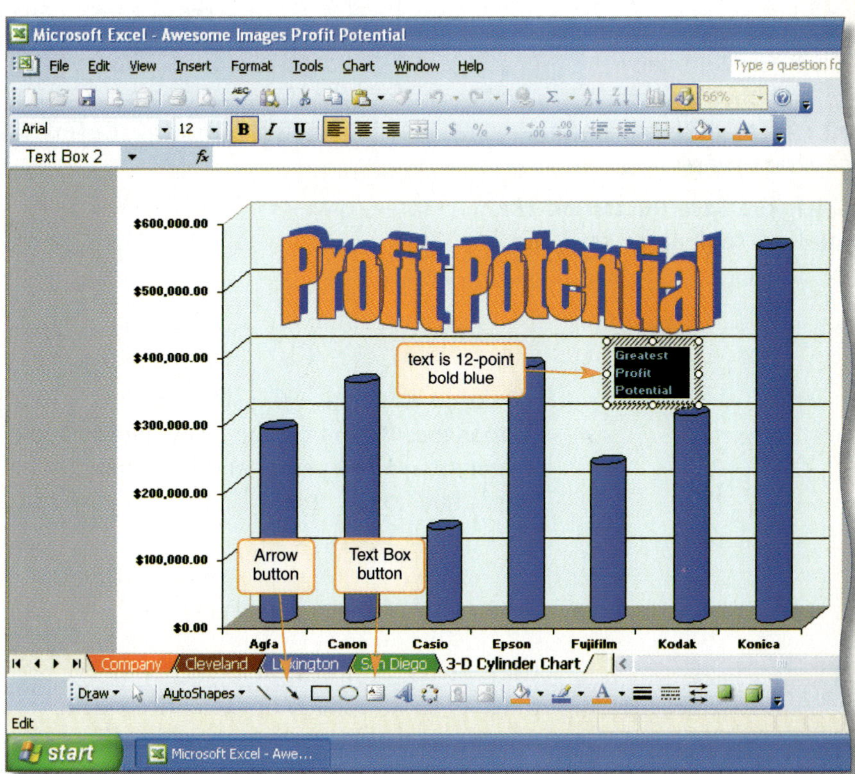

FIGURE 6-63

2

• **Click the Arrow button on the Drawing toolbar, point immediately to the left of the letter t in Profit in the text box, and then drag the arrow to the cylinder representing Konica.**

• **Click the Drawing button on the Standard toolbar to hide the Drawing toolbar and then click outside the chart area.**

The text box with an arrow points to the cylinder representing Konica (Figure 6-64). Excel hides the Drawing toolbar. The 3-D Cylinder chart is complete.

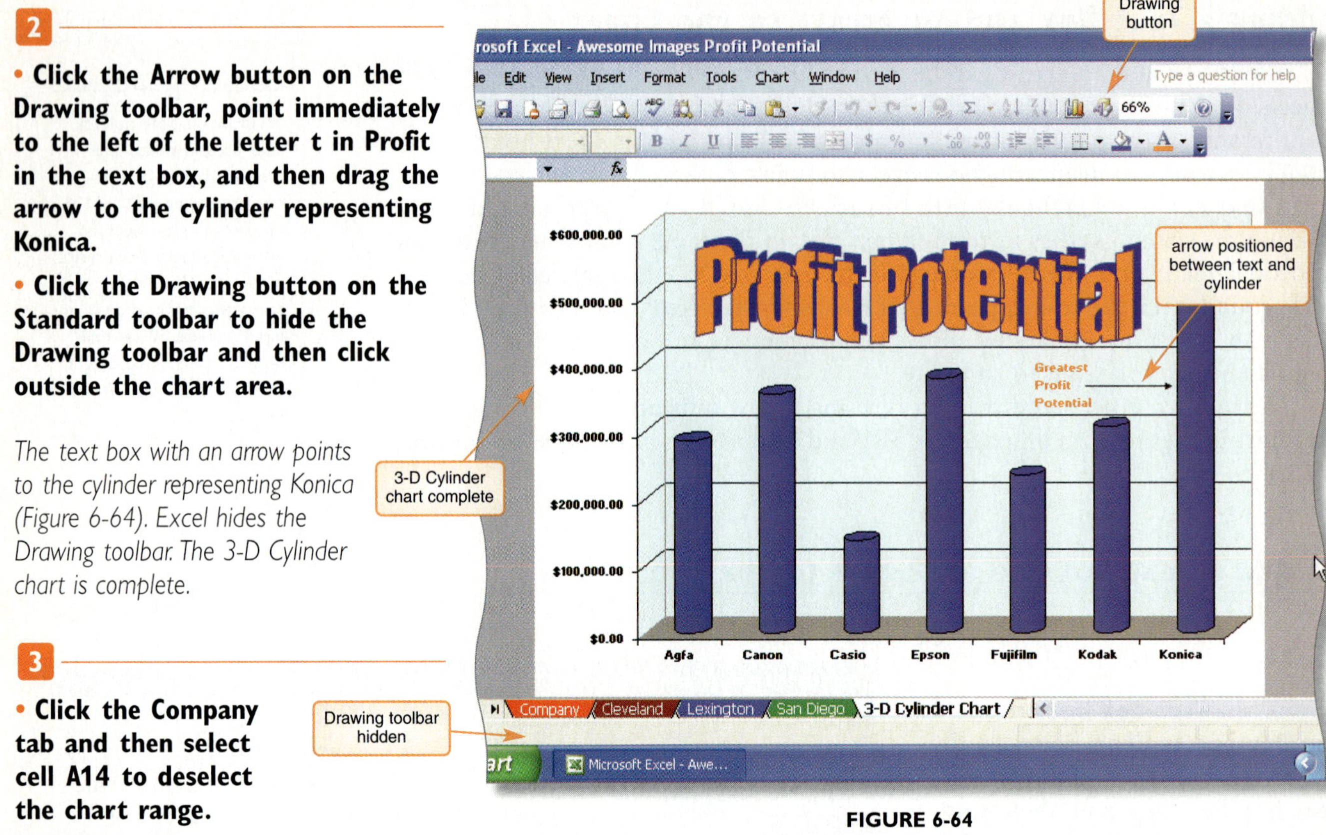

FIGURE 6-64

3

• **Click the Company tab and then select cell A14 to deselect the chart range.**

• **Click the Save button on the Standard toolbar to save the workbook.**

As an alternative to using text boxes to add annotations, you can use the AutoShapes button on the Drawing toolbar to draw more artistic callouts, such as flowchart symbols, stars and banners, and balloons similar to those used to display words in a comic book.

Assigning a Comment to a Cell

Comments, or **notes**, in a workbook are used to describe the function of a cell, a range of cells, a sheet, or the entire workbook. Typically, comments are used to identify entries that might otherwise be difficult to understand or to provide overall workbook comments. In general, a workbook comment should include the following:

1. Worksheet title
2. Author's name
3. Date created
4. Date last modified (use N/A if it has not been modified)
5. Template(s) used, if any
6. A short description of the purpose of the worksheet

You can assign comments to any cell in the worksheet using the Comment command on the Insert menu or the Insert Comment command on the shortcut menu. Once a comment is assigned to a cell, pointing to the cell causes Excel to display the comment in a comment box.

More About

Comments

More often than not, spreadsheet specialists are asked to support the workbooks they create by means of internal comments. Comments are used to identify workbooks and clarify parts of a workbook that otherwise would be difficult fore others to understand.

The following steps assign a workbook comment to cell A14 on the Company sheet.

To Assign a Comment to a Cell

1

- **Right-click cell A14 on the Company sheet.**

Excel displays the shortcut menu (Figure 6-65).

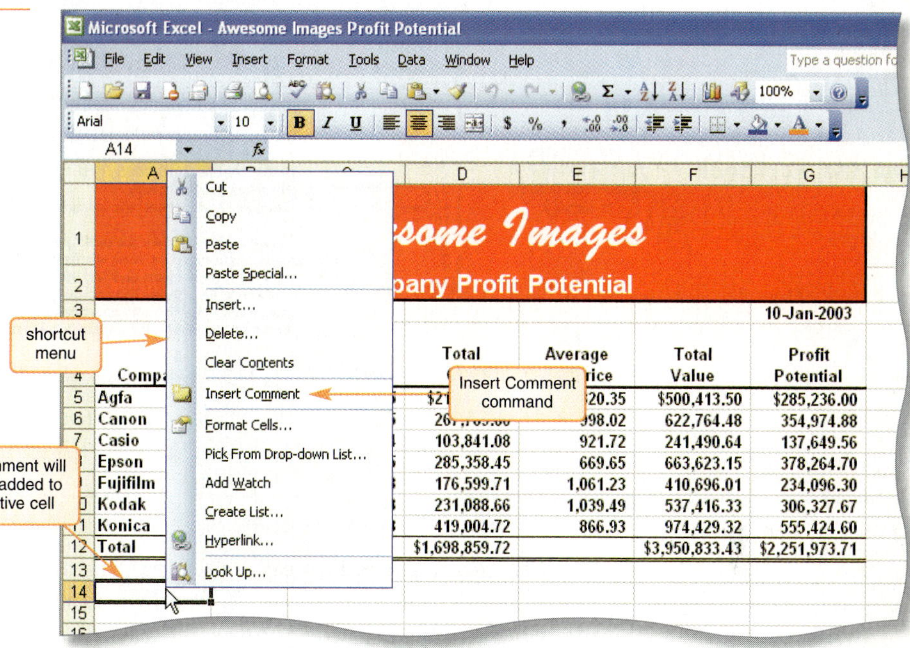

FIGURE 6-65

2

- **Click Insert Comment on the shortcut menu.**
- **When Excel displays the comment box, drag the lower-right handle to increase the size of the comment box and then enter the comment text shown in the comment box in Figure 6-66.**
- **Select the comment text, click the Bold button on the Standard toolbar, and then click after the last period in the comment.**

Excel adds a small red triangle, called a comment indicator, to cell A14 (Figure 6-66). A small black arrow attached to the comment box points to the comment indicator.

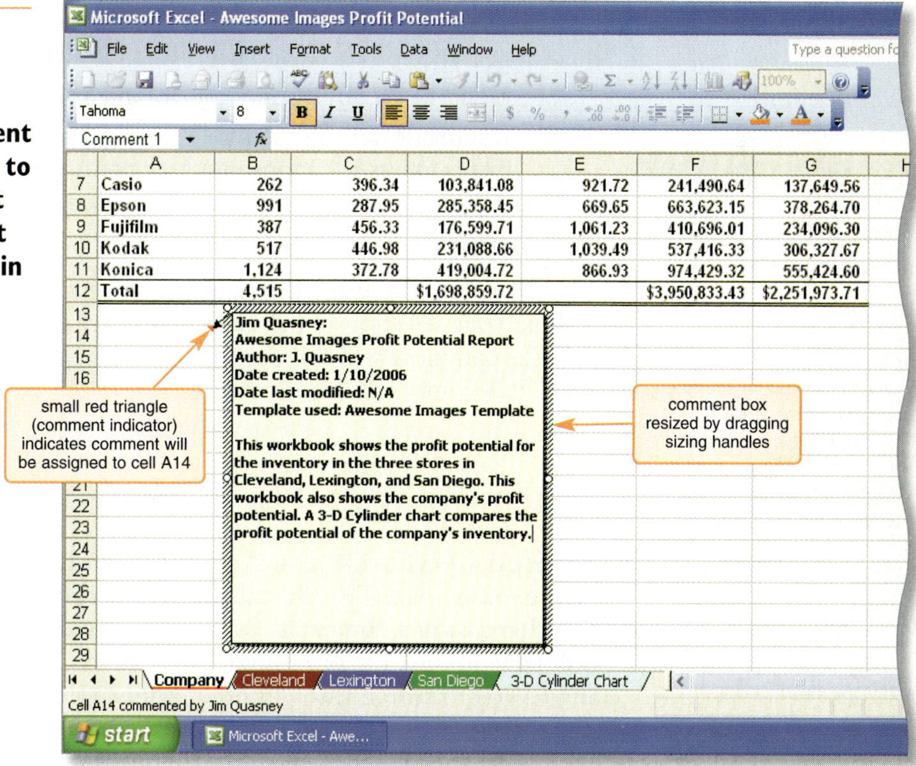

FIGURE 6-66

3

• **Select cell A17 and then point to cell A14.**

Excel displays the comment box (Figure 6-67).

4

• **Click the Save button on the Standard toolbar to save the workbook.**

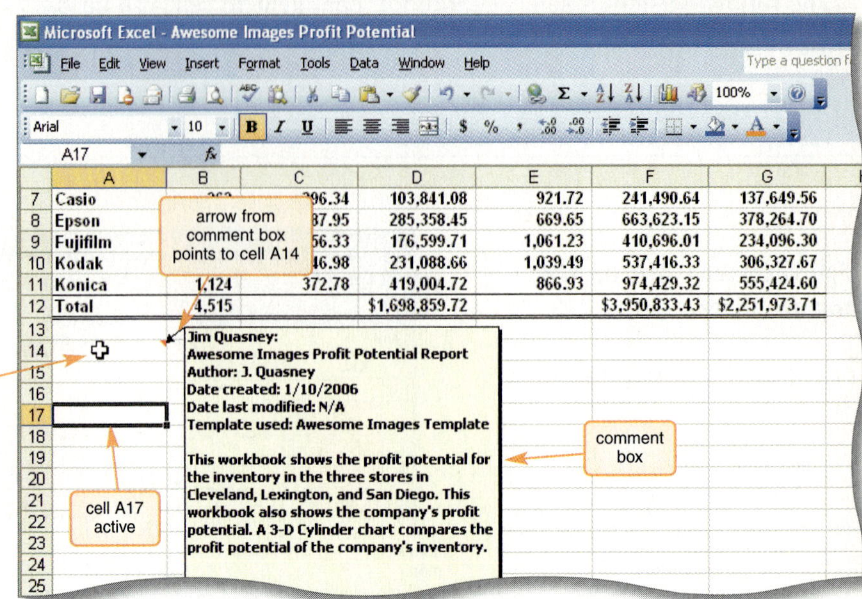

FIGURE 6-67

Other Ways

1. On the Insert menu click Comment
2. Press ALT+I, M
3. In Voice Command mode, say "Insert, Comment"

The **comment indicator** in the upper-right corner of cell A14 indicates the cell has a comment assigned to it. To read the comment, point to the cell and Excel displays the comment in the comment box. To edit the comment, right-click the cell and then click Edit Comment on the shortcut menu, or select the cell and then press SHIFT+F2. To delete the comment, right-click the cell and then click Delete Comment on the shortcut menu.

If you incorporate comments in a worksheet, you have three options regarding their appearance on the worksheet:

1. None — do not display the comment indicator or comment
2. Comment indicator only — display the comment indicator, but not the comment, unless the mouse pointer points to cell
3. Comment & indicator — display both the comment indicator and comment at all times

You select one of the three options by clicking Options on the Tools menu and making your selection in the Comments area in the View sheet. If you choose None, then the comment will not appear when you point to the cell with the comment. Thus, it becomes a hidden comment.

More About

Printing Comments

You can print comments assigned to cells as follows: click File on the menu bar, click Page Setup on the File menu, click the Sheet tab, click the Comments arrow, and click where you want the comments printed in relation to the worksheet printout.

Researching a Topic Using the Research Task Pane

The Special Requirements section of the Request for New Workbook document in Figure 6-2 on page EX 380 calls for researching and incorporating a digital camera sales forecast in a comment. Earlier, this project showed how to use the Research task pane to look up a synonym in an online thesaurus. The Research task pane also allows you to search through other online references, include the Microsoft Encarta English dictionary, bilingual dictionaries, the Microsoft Encarta Encyclopedia (with a Web connection), and Web sites that provide information such as stock quotes, news articles, and company profiles.

The following steps show how to use the Research task pane to look up a digital camera sales forecast on the Web and then copy the forecast into the comment assigned to cell A14.

To Research a Topic Using the Research Task Pane

1

- **Click the Research button on the Standard toolbar.**
- **When Excel displays the Research task pane, type** `digital camera shipments` **in the Search for box 1.**
- **Click the Search for box 2 arrow and then click All Research Sites.**
- **When Excel displays the search results in the Research task pane, scroll down, click one of the article titles, and then point to the Preview Article link. (If none of the articles in the list contains appropriate information, then scroll up to the top and click the Next button.)**

Excel displays the search results for the phrase digital shipment in the Research task pane (Figure 6-68).

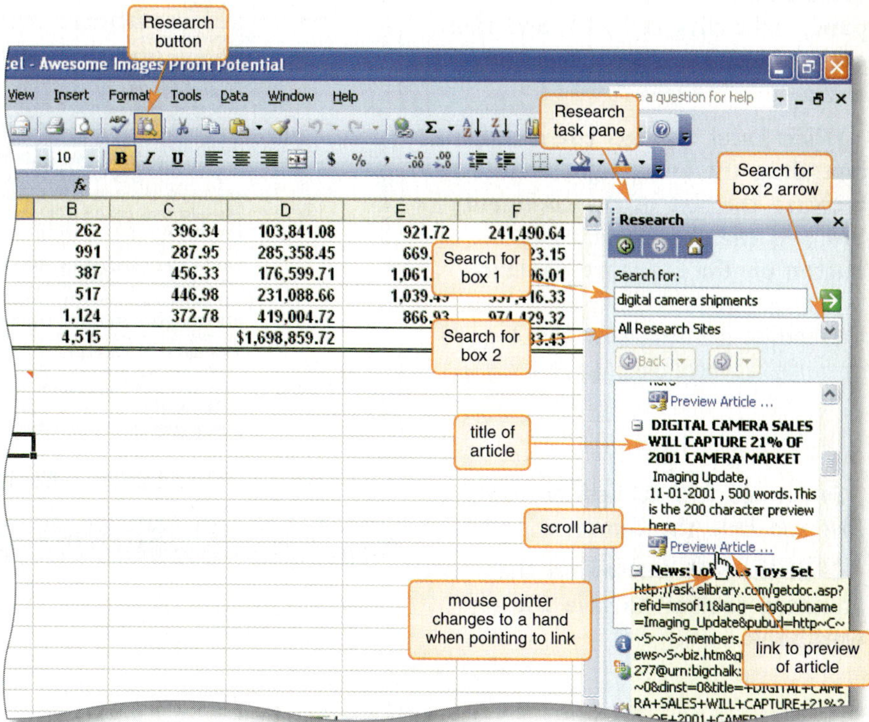

FIGURE 6-68

2

- **Click the Preview Article link.**
- **When the browser displays the article preview, select a portion of the article to copy and then right-click.**

The browser displays a preview of the article. The desired portion of the article is selected and the shortcut menu appears (Figure 6-69).

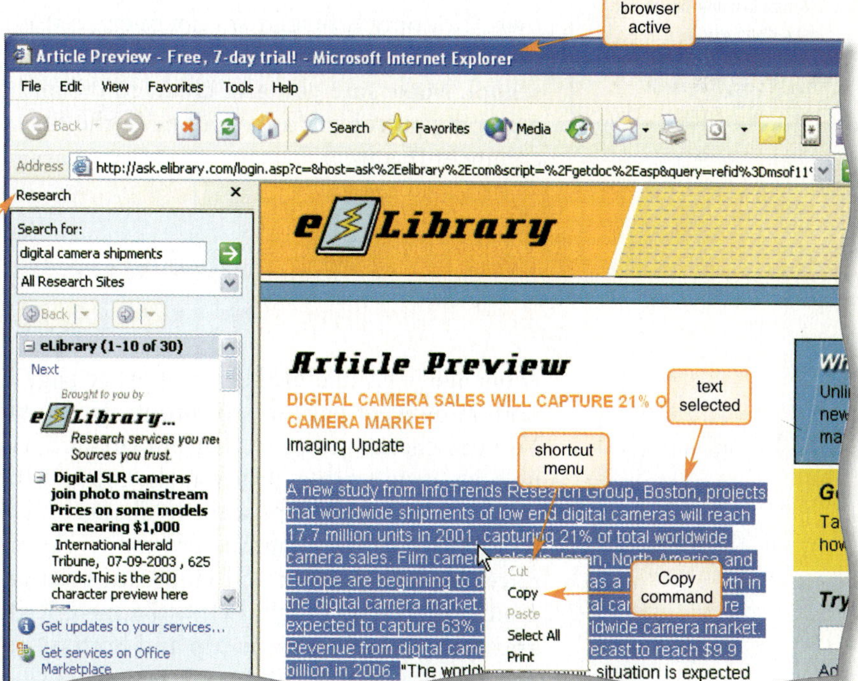

FIGURE 6-69

3

- **Click Copy on the shortcut menu and then click the Close button on the browser's title bar.**
- **When Excel reappears, click the Close button in the Research task pane, right-click cell A14, and then click Edit Comment on the shortcut menu.**
- **When Excel displays the comment box, drag the lower-right handle to increase the size of the comment box and then click the Paste button on the Standard toolbar.**

Excel pastes the text copied from the article in the comment area (Figure 6-70).

4

- **Select cell A19 to deselect cell A14 and hide the comment.**
- **Click the Save button on the Standard toolbar to save the workbook.**

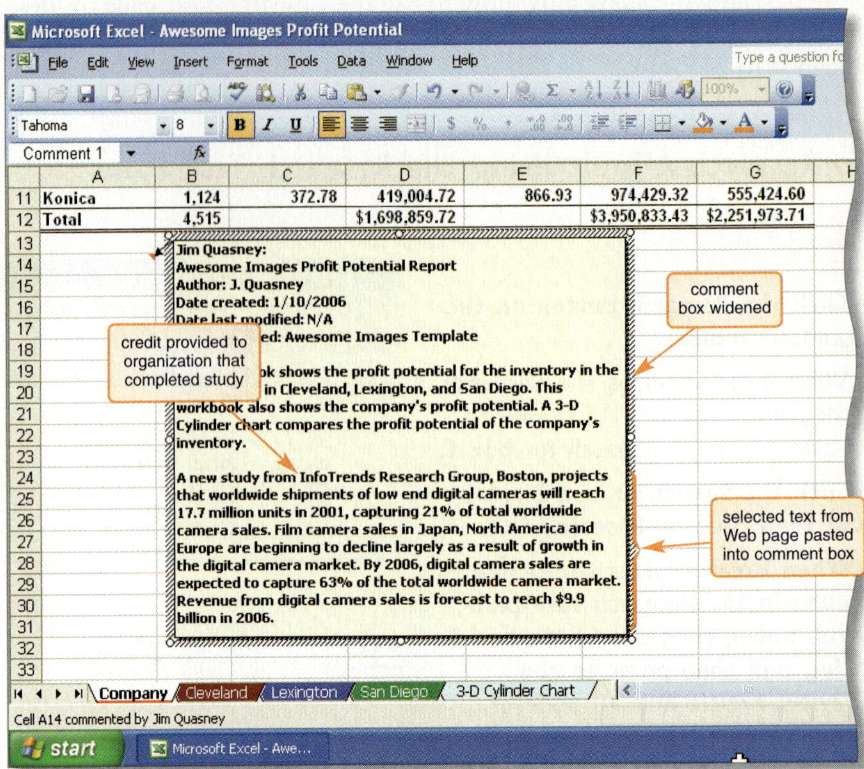

FIGURE 6-70

> *Other Ways*
>
> 1. On Tools menu click Research
> 2. While holding down ALT key, click word
> 3. In Voice Command mode, say "Tools, Research"

When using material found using the Research task pane or any other online reference, be very careful not to **plagiarize**, or copy other's work and use it as your own. Not only is plagiarism unethical, but it is considered an academic crime that can result in severe punishments such as failing a course or being expelled from school. Make sure you give credit to the author or organization that produced the material you copied, as was done in the first sentence of the material pasted in the comment (Figure 6-70).

Adding a Header, Changing the Margins, and Printing the Workbook

A **header** is printed at the top of every page in a printout. A **footer** is printed at the bottom of every page in a printout. By default, both the header and footer are blank. You can change either so that information, such as the workbook author, date, page number, or tab name, prints at the top or bottom of each page.

Sometimes, you will want to change the **margins** to increase or decrease the white space surrounding the printed worksheet or chart. The default margins in Excel for both portrait and landscape orientation are set to the following: Top = 1 inch; Bottom = 1 inch; Left = .75 inch; Right = .75 inch. The header and footer are set at .5 inch from the top and bottom, respectively. You also can center a printout horizontally and vertically.

Changing the header and footer and changing the margins are all part of **page setup**, which defines the appearance and format of a printed worksheet. To change page setup characteristics, select the desired sheet(s) and then click the Page Setup command on the File menu. Remember to select all the sheets you want to modify before you change the headers, footers, or margins, because the page setup characteristics will change only for selected sheets. The headers and footers for chart sheets must be assigned separately from worksheets.

As you modify the page setup, remember that Excel does not copy page setup characteristics when one sheet is copied to another. Thus, even if you assigned page setup characteristics to the template before copying it to the Awesome Images Profit Potential workbook, the page setup characteristics would not copy to the new sheet. The following steps use the Page Setup dialog box to change the headers and margins and center the printout horizontally.

To Add a Header, Change Margins, and Center the Printout Horizontally

1

- **With the Company sheet active, scroll to the top of the document.**
- **While holding down the SHIFT key, click the San Diego sheet tab.**
- **Click File on the menu bar.**

Excel displays the File menu (Figure 6-71). The four worksheet tabs at the bottom of the window are selected. The 3-D Cylinder Chart sheet is not selected because page setup for chart sheets must be handled independently.

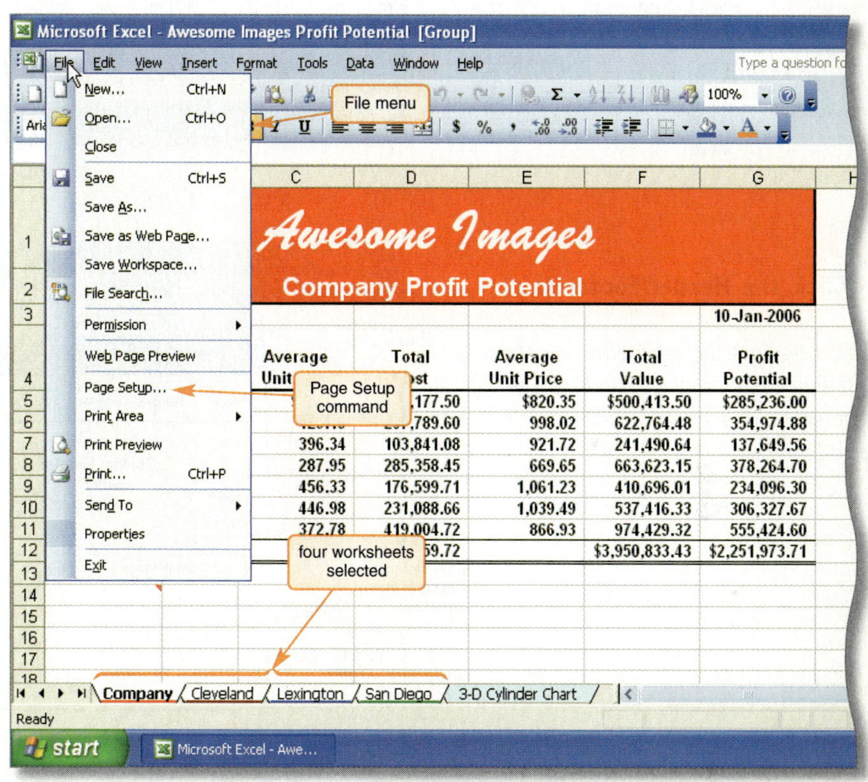

FIGURE 6-71

2

- **Click Page Setup.**
- **When Excel displays the Page Setup dialog box, if necessary, click the Margins tab.**
- **Click the Top box and then type** `1.5` **to change the top margin to 1.5 inch.**
- **Enter** `.5` **in both the Left box and Right box to change the left and right margins to .5 inch.**
- **Click Horizontally in the Center on page area to center the worksheet on the page horizontally.**

Excel displays the Margins sheet in the Page Setup dialog box as shown in Figure 6-72. Excel allows you to use the up and down arrows next to the boxes to change margins in increments of .25 inch, in addition to typing the new margin values.

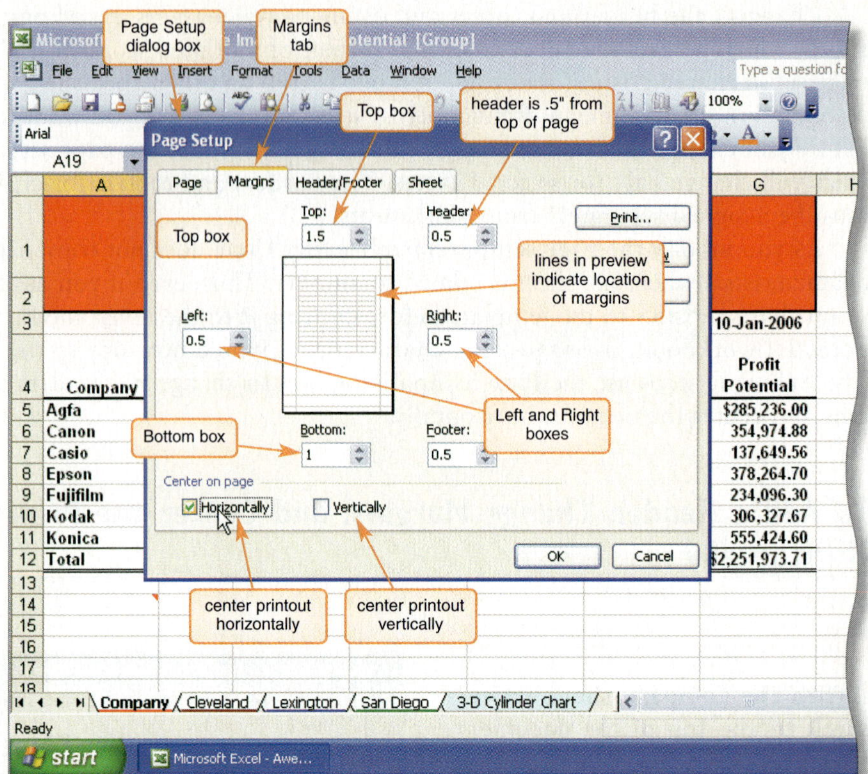

FIGURE 6-72

3

- **Click the Header/Footer tab.**

Excel displays the Header/Footer sheet in the Page Setup dialog box (Figure 6-73). The entry (none) indicates that the headers and footers are blank.

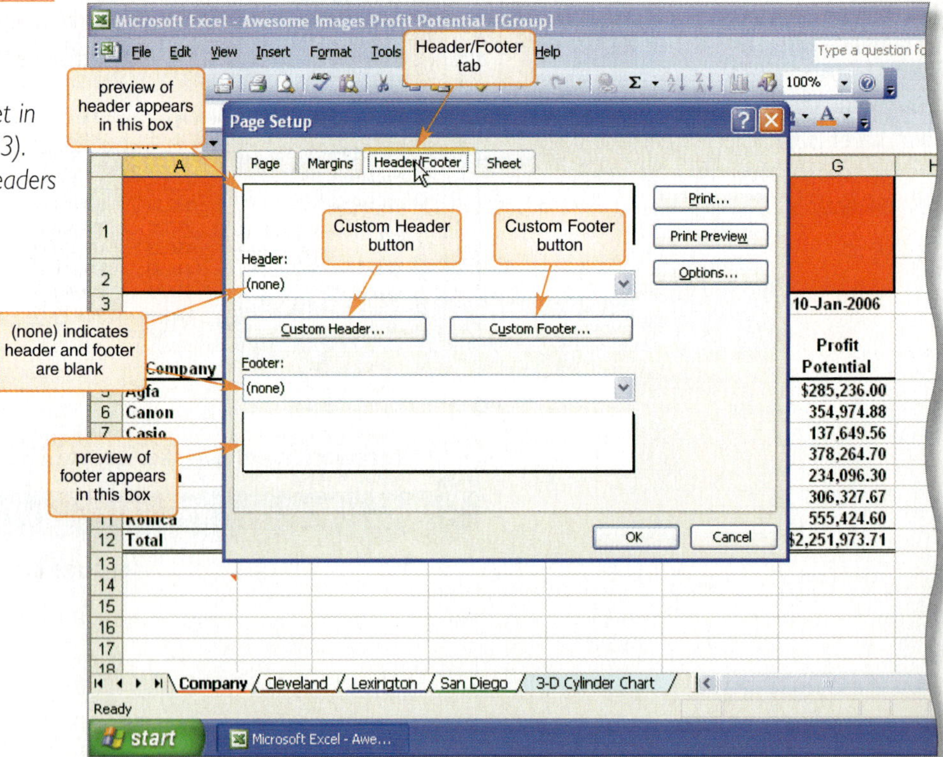

FIGURE 6-73

4

- **Click the Custom Header button.**
- **When Excel displays the Header dialog box, click the Left section text box, type** `J. Quasney` **(or your name if you are stepping through the project on a computer), press the ENTER key, and then type** `Profit Potential`.
- **Click the Center section text box and then click the Tab button.**
- **Click the Right section text box, type** `Page`**, press the SPACEBAR, click the Page Number button, press the SPACEBAR, type** `of`**, press the SPACEBAR, and then click the Total Pages button.**

Excel displays the Header dialog box with the new header (Figure 6-74). Clicking the Tab button instructs Excel to insert the sheet name that appears on the sheet tab as part of the header.

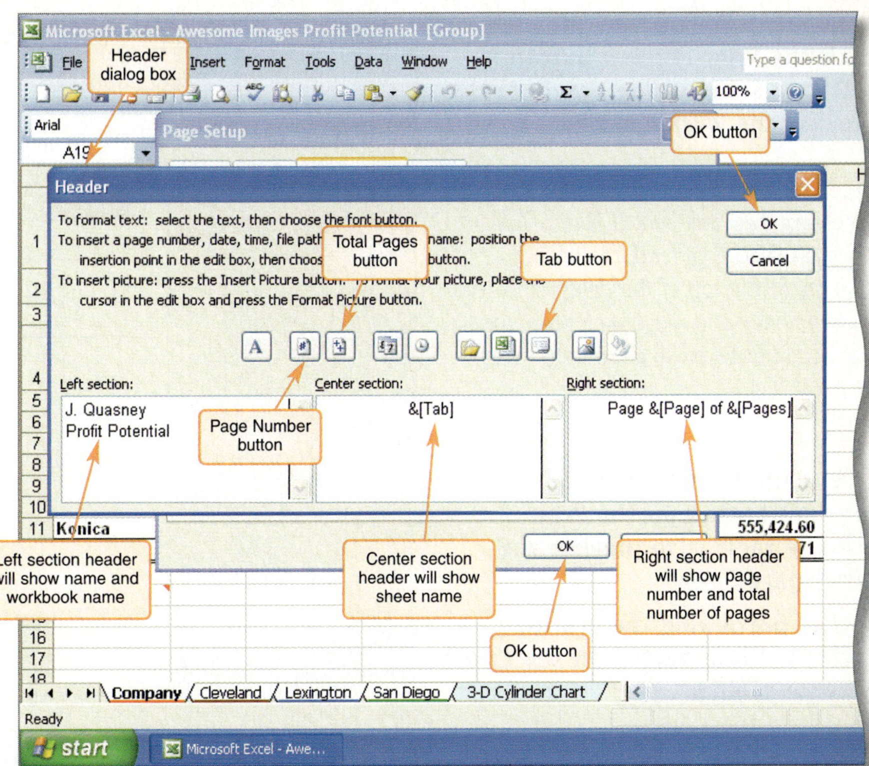

FIGURE 6-74

**5**

- **Click the OK button.**

Excel displays a preview of the header in the Header/Footer sheet in the Page Setup dialog box as shown in Figure 6-75.

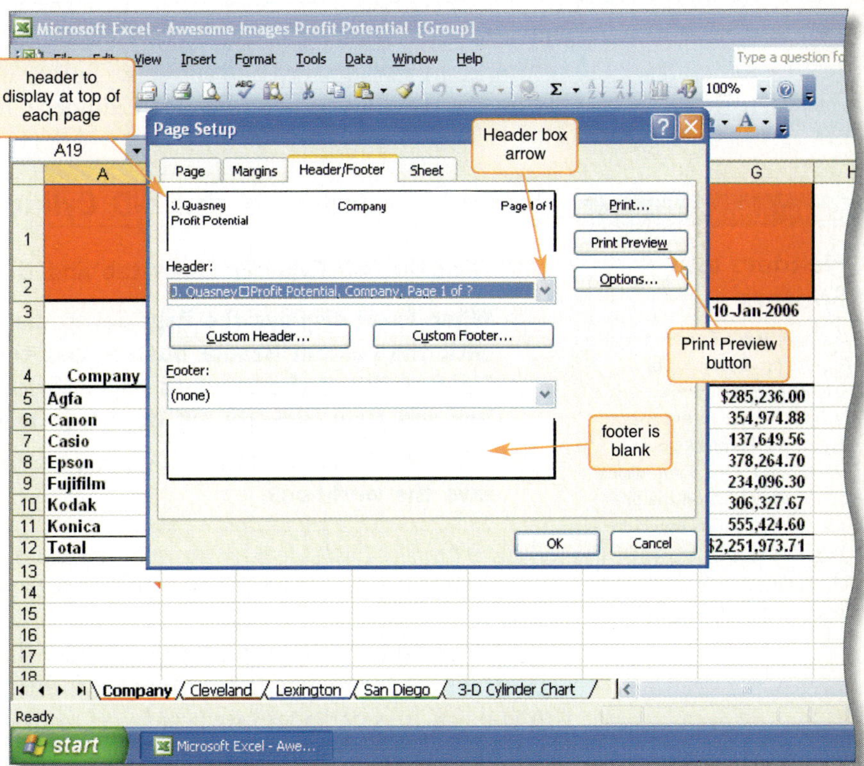

FIGURE 6-75

6

Click the Print Preview button in the Page Setup dialog box to preview the workbook.

Excel displays a preview of how the Company sheet will print (Figure 6-76). Although difficult to read, the header appears at the top of the page. While the mouse pointer is a magnifying glass, the page can be clicked to get a better view.

7

- **Click the Next button and Previous button on the Print Preview toolbar to preview the other pages.**
- **After previewing the printout, click the Close button on the Print Preview toolbar.**

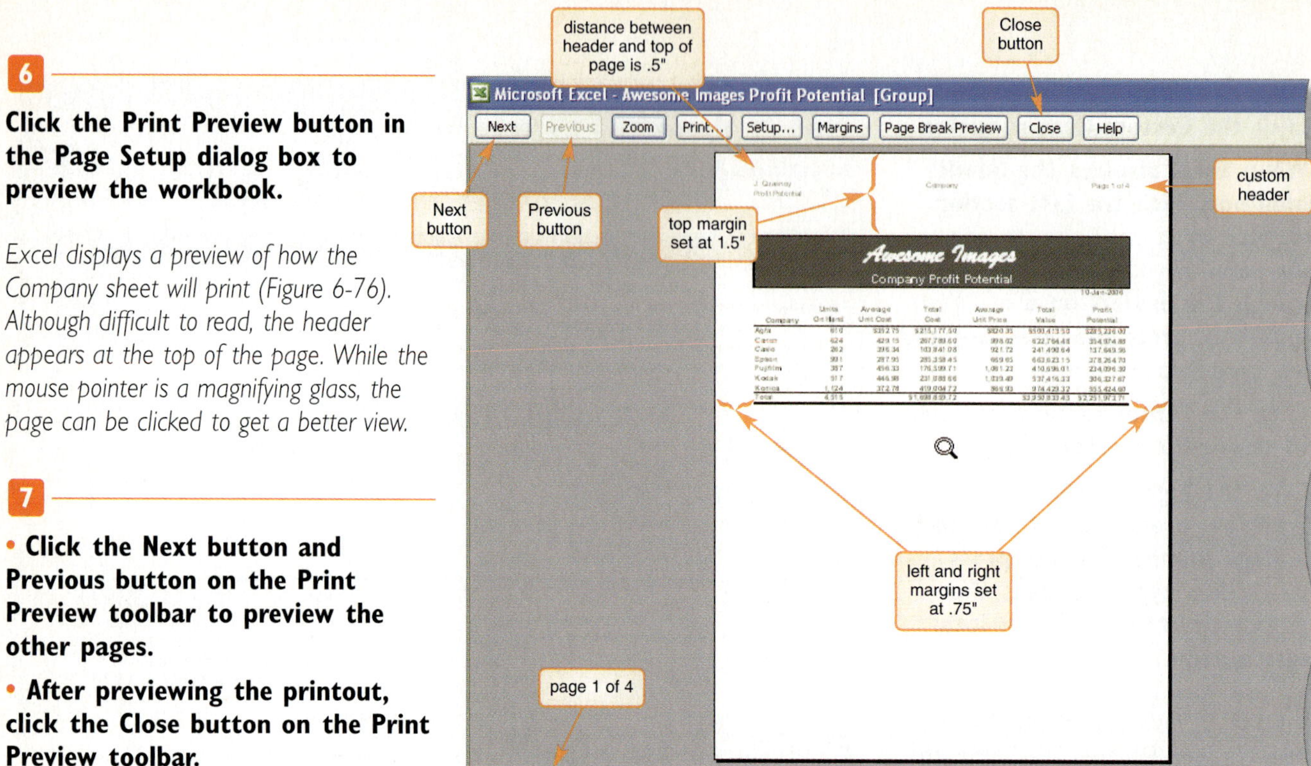

FIGURE 6-76

The following steps add the same header applied to the four worksheets in Step 4 on the previous page to the 3-D Cylinder Chart sheet.

To Add a Header to the 3-D Cylinder Chart Sheet

1. **Click the 3-D Cylinder Chart tab and then on the File menu, click Page Setup.**
2. **When Excel displays the Page Setup dialog box, click the Header/Footer tab, click the Custom Header button, and then enter the header shown in Figure 6-75 on the previous page. Click the OK button in the Header dialog box and then click the OK button in the Page Setup dialog box.**
3. **Click the Company tab. Click the Save button on the Standard toolbar to save the workbook.**

The 3-D Cylinder Chart sheet has the same header as the four worksheets. The Awesome Images Profit Potential workbook is saved with the new page setup settings.

More About

Headers and Footers

You can turn off headers and footers for a printout by selecting (none) in the Header list and in the Footer list on the Header/Footer sheet in the Page Setup dialog box (Figure 6-75 on the previous page). This is especially helpful when printing charts for slides.

When you click a button in the Header dialog box (Figure 6-74 on the previous page), Excel enters a code (similar to a format code) into the active header section. A code such as &[Page] instructs Excel to insert the page number. Table 6-10 summarizes the buttons in the Header or Footer dialog box, along with their codes and their functions.

Table 6-10 Buttons in the Header or Footer Dialog Box

BUTTON	NAME	CODE	FUNCTION
	Font	None	Displays the Font dialog box
	Page	&[Page]	Inserts a page number
	Number of Pages	&[Pages]	Inserts total number of pages
	Date	&[Date]	Inserts the system date
	Time	&[Time]	Inserts the system time
	Path	&[Path]&[File]	Inserts the path and file name
	File	&[File]	Inserts the file name of the workbook
	Tab	&[Tab]	Inserts the sheet name as it appears on the sheet tab
	Picture	&[Picture]	Inserts a picture
	Format Picture	None	Displays the Format Picture dialog box

Printing All Worksheets in a Workbook

The following steps print all five sheets in the workbook by selecting all the sheets before clicking the Print button on the Standard toolbar.

To Print All Worksheets in a Workbook

1. **Ready the printer.**
2. **Click the Company sheet tab. While holding down the SHIFT key, click the 3-D Cylinder Chart tab.**
3. **Click the Print button on the Standard toolbar.**
4. **Hold down the SHIFT key and then click the Company sheet tab to deselect all sheets but the Company sheet.**

Excel prints the workbook as shown in Figures 6-77a and 6-77b on the next page. Excel automatically prints the chart sheet in Landscape orientation.

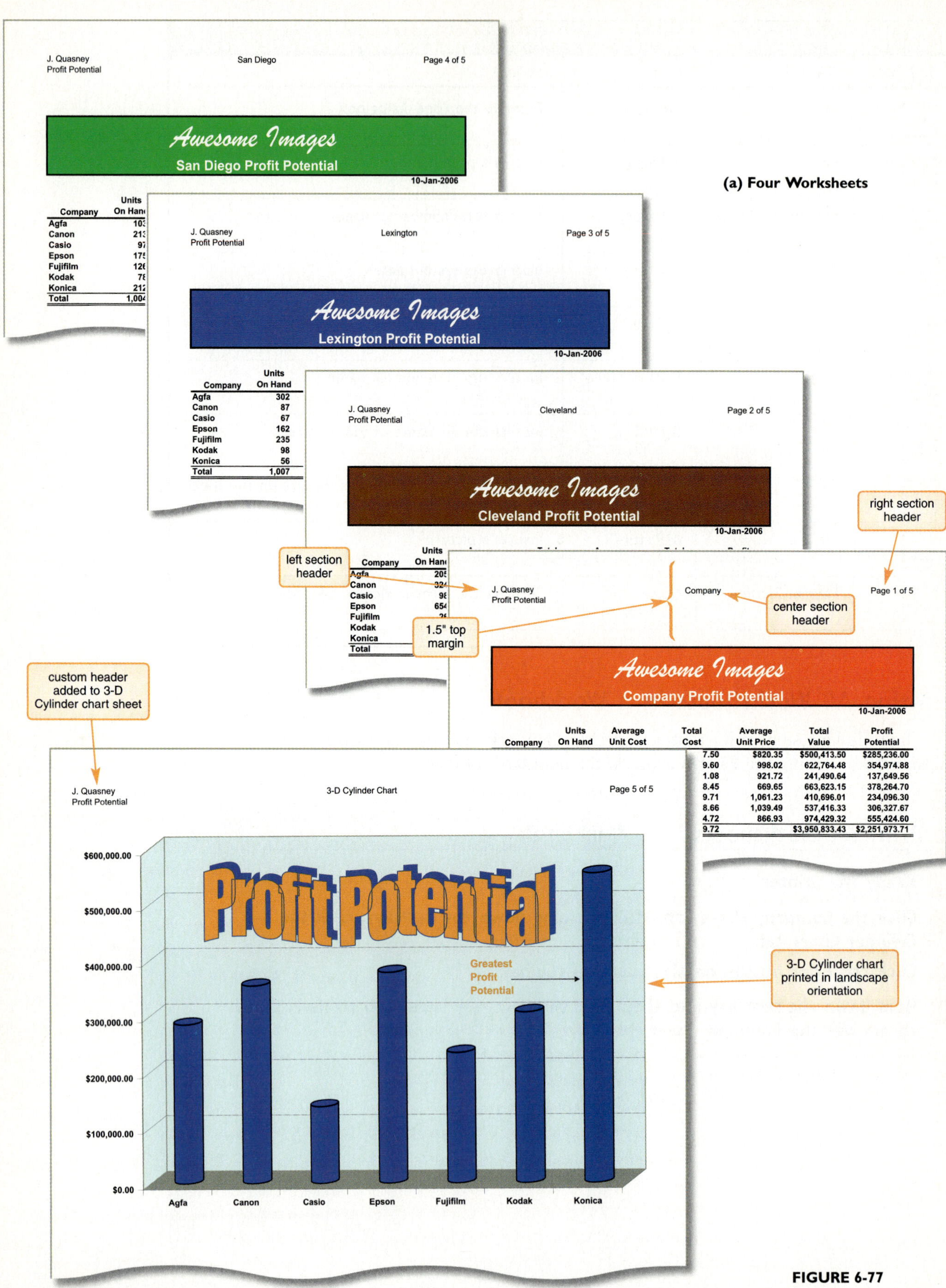

(a) Four Worksheets

(b) 3-D Cylinder Chart

FIGURE 6-77

Printing Nonadjacent Worksheets in a Workbook

In some situations, nonadjacent sheets in a workbook may need to be printed. To select nonadjacent sheets, select the first sheet and then hold down the CTRL key and click the nonadjacent sheets. The following steps show how to print the nonadjacent Company, Lexington, and 3-D Cylinder Chart sheets.

To Print Nonadjacent Sheets in a Workbook

1. **With the Company sheet active, hold down the CTRL key, click the Lexington sheet tab, and then click the 3-D Cylinder Chart tab.**
2. **Click the Print button on the Standard toolbar.**
3. **Hold down the SHIFT key and click the Company sheet tab to deselect the Lexington and 3-D Cylinder Chart sheets.**

Excel prints the Company sheet, Lexington sheet, and 3-D Cylinder Chart sheet, as shown in Figures 6-77a and 6-77b.

Beginning Excel users sometimes have difficulty trying to select and deselect sheets. Table 6-11 summarizes how to select and deselect sheets.

Table 6-11 Summary of How to Select and Deselect Sheets

TASK	HOW TO CARRY OUT THE TASK
Select adjacent sheets	Select the first sheet by clicking its tab and then hold down the SHIFT key and click the sheet tab at the other end of the list of adjacent sheet tabs.
Select nonadjacent sheets	Select the first sheet by clicking its tab and then hold down the CTRL key and click the sheet tabs of the remaining sheets you want to select.
Multiple sheets selected and you want to select a sheet that is selected, but not active (sheet tab name not in bold)	Click the sheet tab you want to select.
Multiple sheets selected and you want to select the active sheet (sheet tab name in bold)	Hold down the SHIFT key and then click the sheet tab of the active sheet.

Inserting and Removing Page Breaks

When you print a worksheet or use the Page Setup command, Excel inserts **page breaks** that show the boundaries of what will print on each page. These page breaks are based upon the margins selected in the Margins sheet in the Page Setup dialog box and the type of printer you are using. If the Page breaks option is selected, then Excel displays dotted lines on the worksheet to show the boundaries of each page. For example, the dotted line in Figure 6-78 on the next page shows the right boundary of the first page. If the dotted line does not show on your screen, then click Options on the Tools menu. When Excel displays the Options dialog box, click the View tab (Figure 6-81 on page EX 441). In the View sheet, click Page breaks in the Window options area and then click the OK button.

More About

Page Break Preview

You can get a better view of page breaks by clicking the Print Preview button on the Standard toolbar and then clicking the Page Break Preview button at the top of the Preview window.

You can insert both horizontal and vertical page breaks in a worksheet. Manual page breaks are useful if you have a worksheet that is several pages long and you want certain parts of the worksheet to print on separate pages. For example, say you had a worksheet that comprised 10 departments in sequence and each department had many rows of information. If you wanted each department to begin on a new page, then inserting page breaks would satisfy the requirement.

To insert a horizontal page break, you select a cell in column A or an entire row that you want to print on the next page and then click the Page Break command on the Insert menu. To insert a vertical page break, you select a cell in row 1 or an entire column that you want to print on the next page and then click the Page Break command on the Insert menu. Excel displays a dotted line to indicate the beginning of a new page. To remove a page break, you select the cell in the row immediately below or to the right of the dotted line that indicates the page break you want to remove and then click the Remove Page Break command on the Insert menu.

If you select a cell outside row 1 or column A and click the Page Break command on the Insert menu, then Excel inserts both a horizontal and vertical page break as shown in the following steps.

To Insert and Remove a Page Break

1

- **Select cell B12 and then click Insert on the menu bar.**

Excel displays the Insert menu (Figure 6-78). The current vertical page break shows as a dotted line between columns G and H.

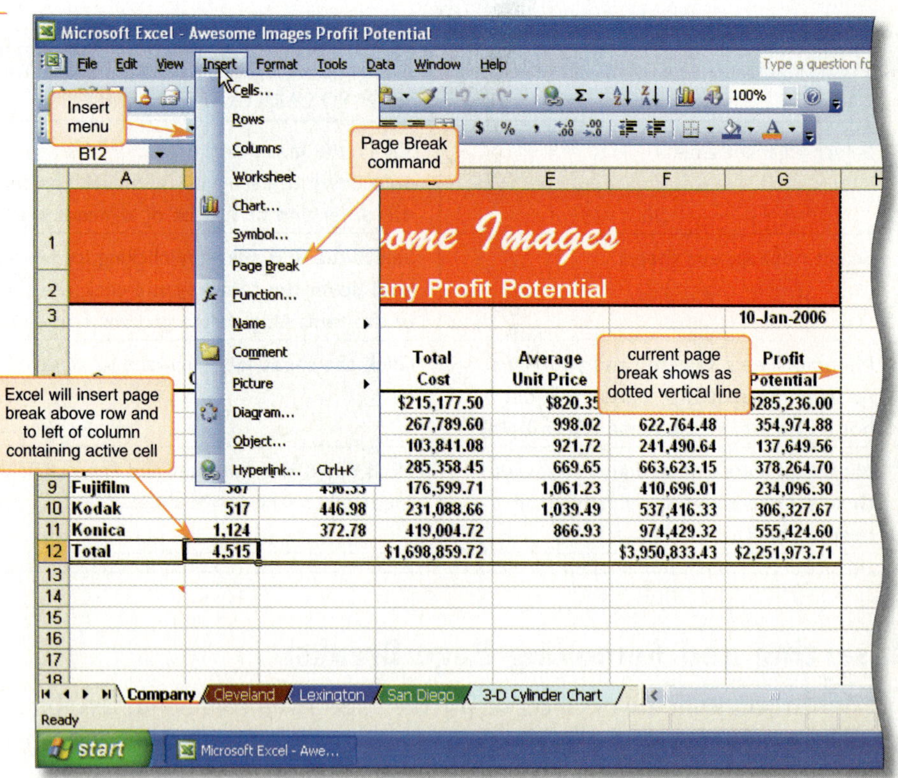

FIGURE 6-78

2

• **Click Page Break.**

Excel inserts a dotted line above row 12 indicating a horizontal page break and inserts a dotted line to the left of column B indicating a vertical page break (Figure 6-79). Excel moves the original page break on the right border of column G (Figure 6-78) to the right border of column I, so that it no longer appears on the screen.

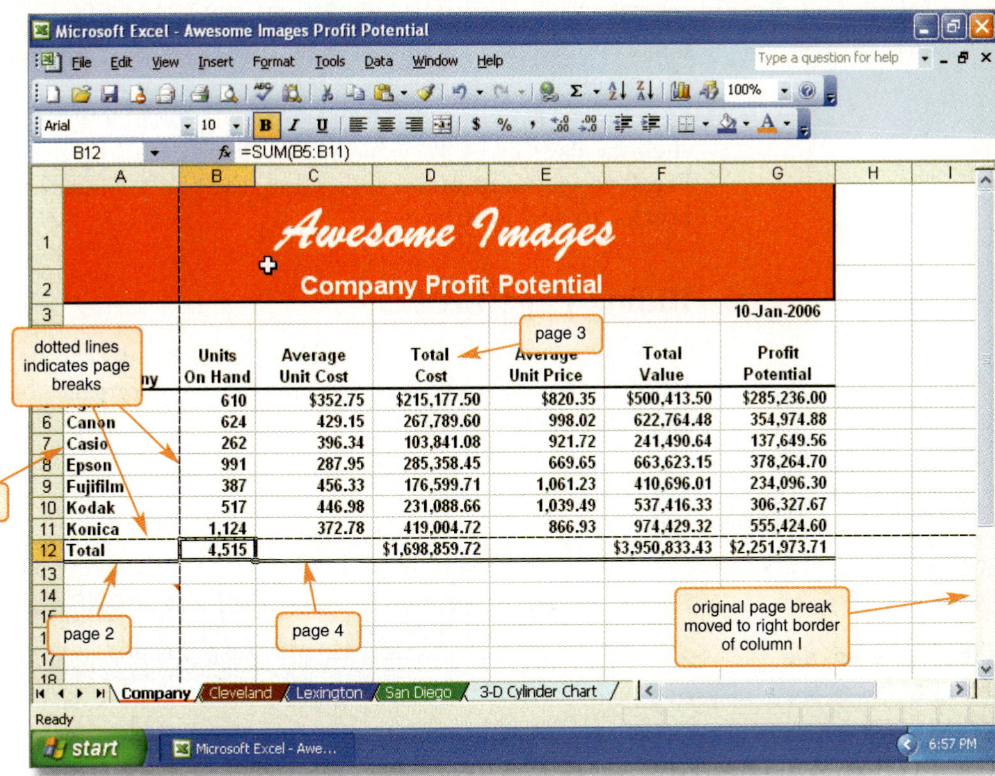

FIGURE 6-79

3

• **With cell B12 active, click Insert on the menu bar.**

Excel displays the Insert menu (Figure 6-80).

4

• **Click Remove Page Break to remove the page breaks.**

Excel removes the page breaks at the intersection of cell B12 and reinserts the page break on the right border of column G.

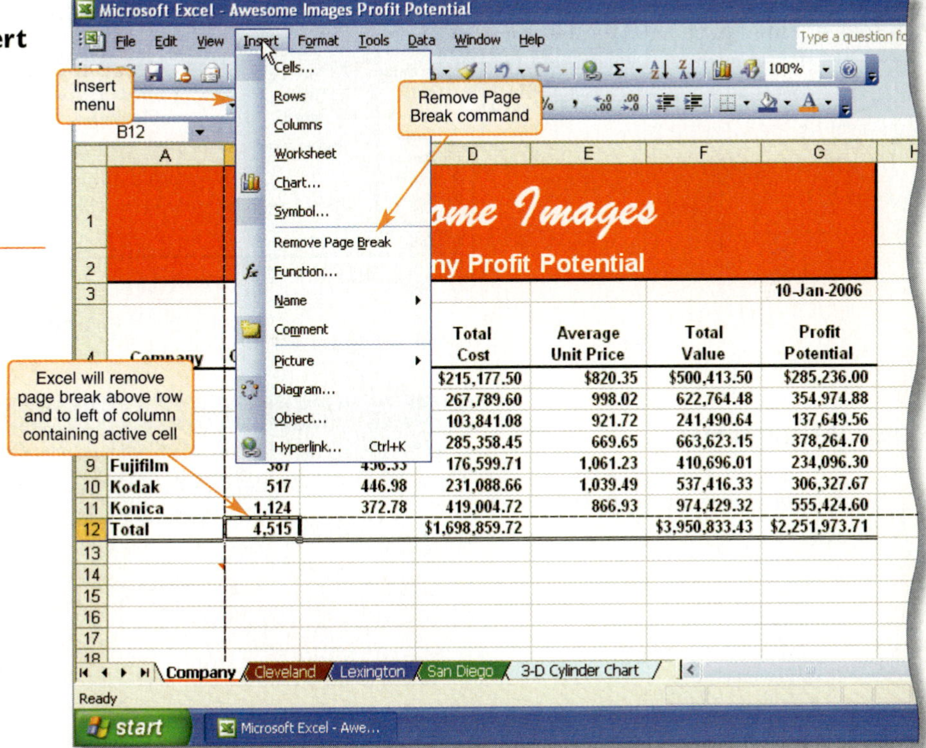

FIGURE 6-80

Other Ways

1. Click Print Preview button on Standard toolbar, click Page Break Preview button, click OK button, drag page breaks
2. Select cell, press ALT+I, B
3. Select cell in row, in Voice Command mode, say "Insert, Page Break"

The Page Break command on the Insert menu changes to Remove Page Break when you select a cell immediately below a page break symbol.

An alternative to using the Page Break command on the Insert menu to insert page breaks is to click the Print Preview button on the Standard toolbar and then click the Page Break Preview button (Figure 6-76 on page EX 436). When the Page Break preview appears, you can drag the blue boundaries, which represent page breaks, to new locations.

Hiding Page Breaks

When working with a workbook, page breaks can be an unnecessary distraction, especially to users who have no interest in where pages break. The following steps show how to hide the dotted lines that represent page breaks.

To Hide Page Breaks

1

- **Click Tools on the menu bar and then click Options.**
- **When Excel displays the Options dialog box, click the View tab.**
- **Click Page breaks in the Window options area to clear the check box.**

Excel displays the View sheet in the Options dialog box (Figure 6-81).

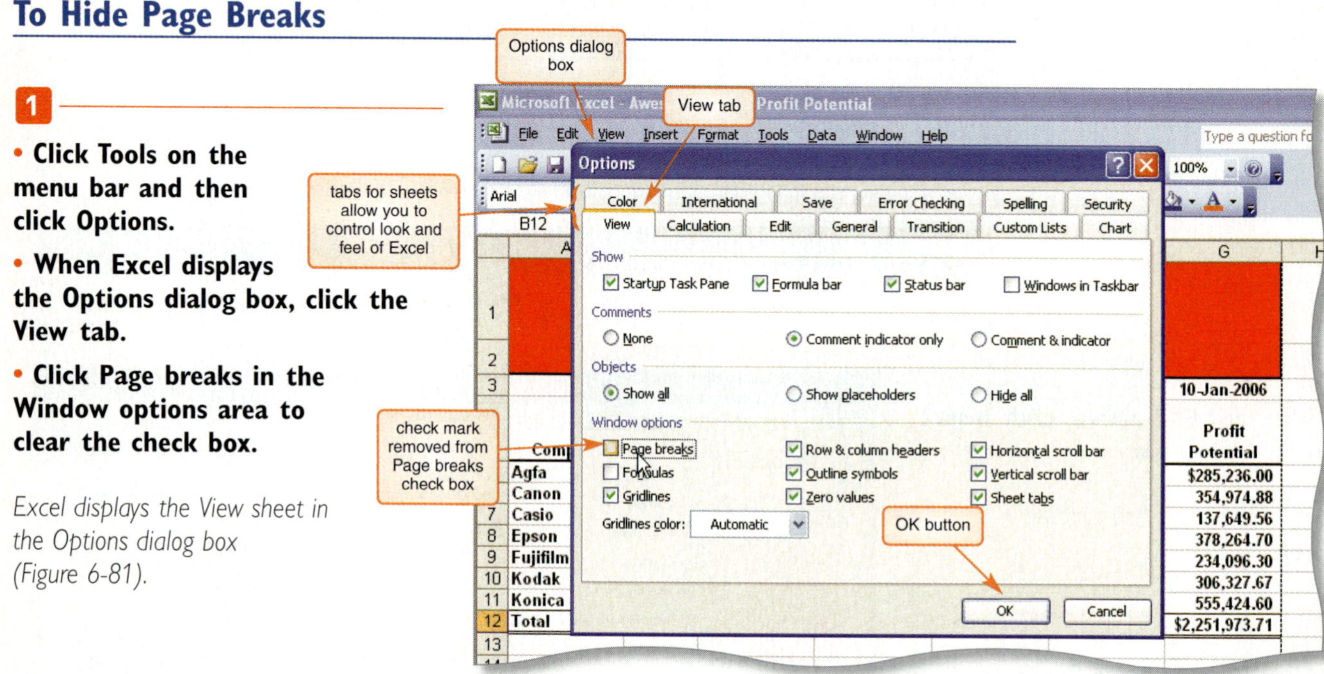

FIGURE 6-81

2

- **Click the OK button.**

Excel hides page breaks as shown in Figure 6-82.

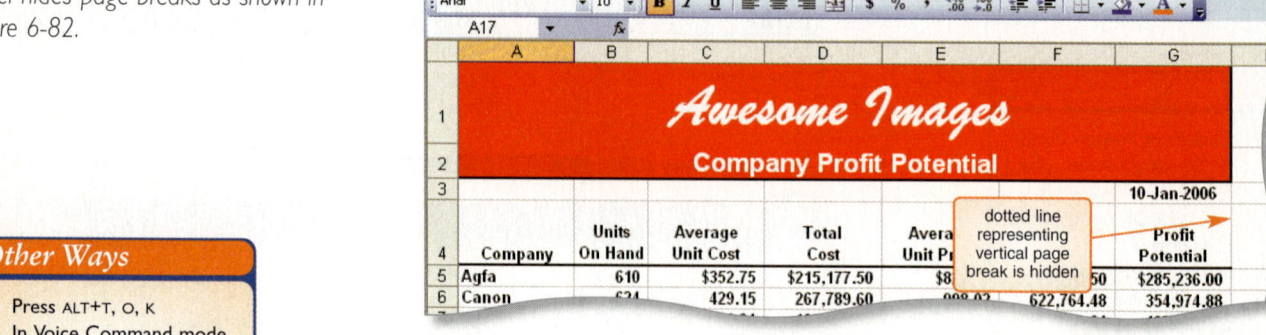

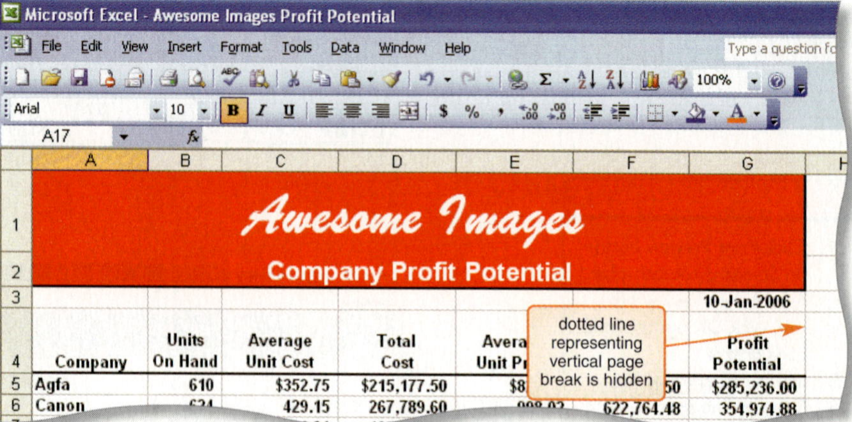

FIGURE 6-82

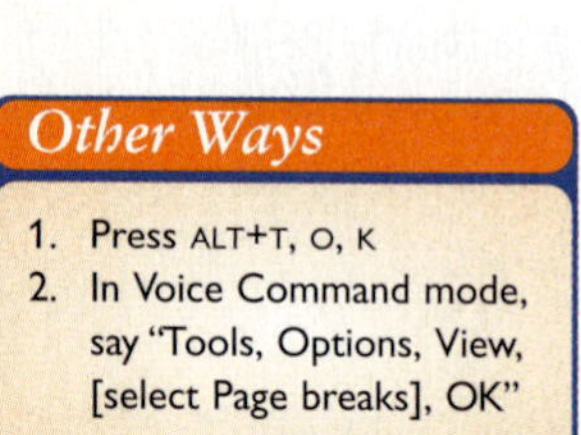

Other Ways

1. Press ALT+T, O, K
2. In Voice Command mode, say "Tools, Options, View, [select Page breaks], OK"

The Options dialog box (Figure 6-81) provides additional options that will change the look and feel of Excel. Many of the changes are machine-dependent. That is, these options will affect only the computer on which they are changed.

The Find and Replace Commands

A **string** can be a single character, a word, or a phrase in a cell on a worksheet. The Find command on the Edit menu is used to locate a string. The Replace command on the Edit menu is used to locate one string and then replace it with another string. The Find and Replace commands are not available for a chart sheet.

Both the Find and Replace commands cause the Find and Replace dialog box to display. The Find and Replace dialog box has two variations. One version displays minimal options, while the other version displays all of the available options. When you invoke the Find or Replace command, Excel displays the dialog box variation that was used the last time either command was invoked.

The Find Command

The following steps show how to locate the string, Konica, in the four worksheets: Company, Cleveland, Lexington, and San Diego. The Find and Replace dialog box that displays all the options will be used to customize the search to include the entire workbook and to use the match case and match entire cell contents options. **Match case** means that the search is case-sensitive and the cell contents must match the word exactly the way it is typed. **Match entire cell contents** means that the string cannot be part of another word or phrase and must be unique in the cell. Unlike the Spelling command, which starts the spell checker at the active cell and works downward, the Find and Replace commands always begin at cell A1, regardless of the location of the active cell.

More About

The Find Command

If you want to search only a specified range of a worksheet, then select the range before invoking the Find command. The range can consist of adjacent cells or non-adjacent cells.

To Find a String

1

- **With the Company sheet active, click Edit on the menu bar.**

Excel displays the Edit menu (Figure 6-83).

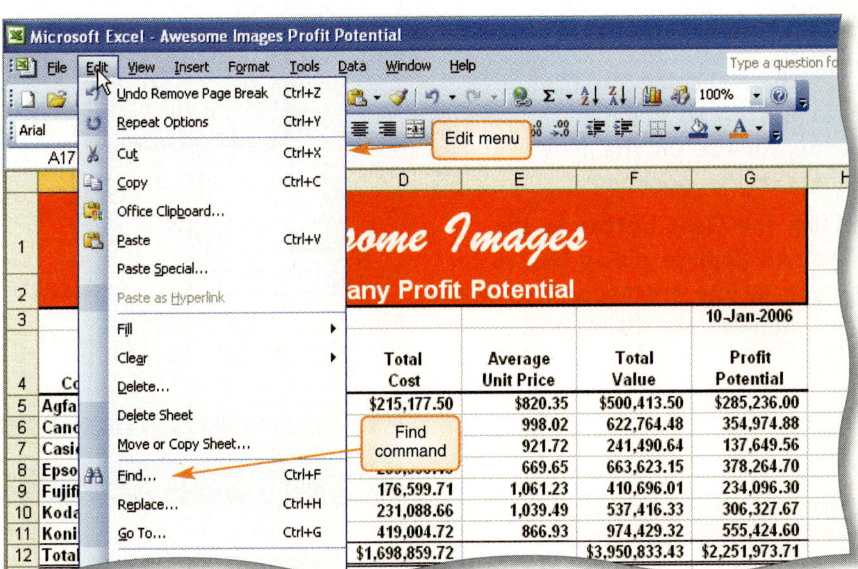

FIGURE 6-83

2

- **Click Find.**
- **When Excel displays the Find and Replace dialog box, click the Options button so that it appears as shown in Figure 6-84.**
- **Type** `Konica` **in the Find what text box, click the Within box arrow, select Workbook, and then click Match case and Match entire cell contents.**

Excel displays the Find and Replace dialog box as shown in Figure 6-84. The two greater than signs pointing to the left on the Options button indicate that the more comprehensive Find and Replace dialog box is active.

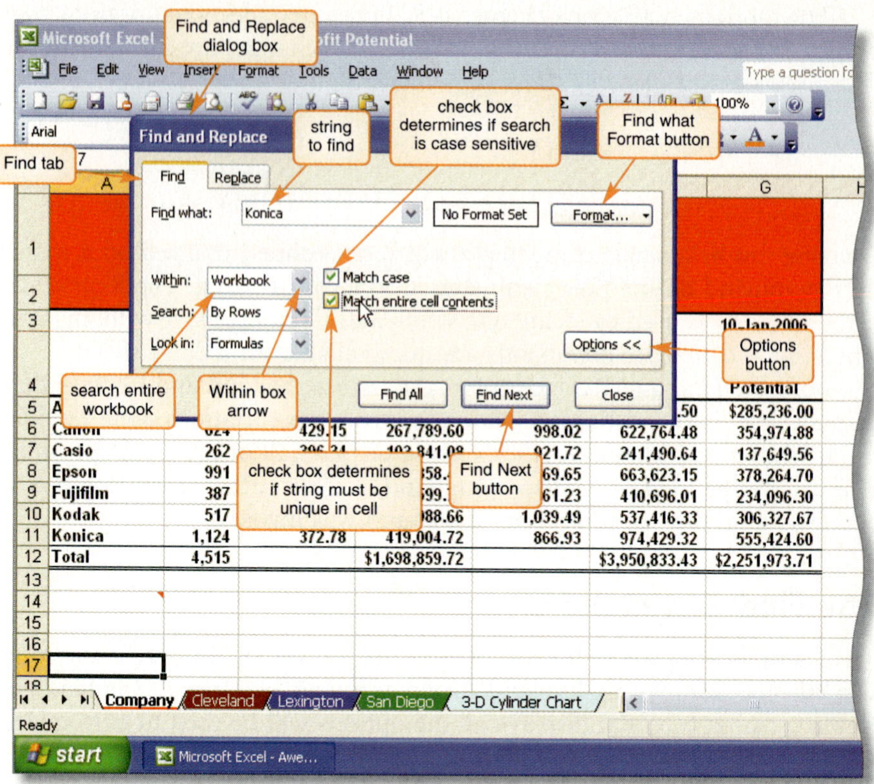

FIGURE 6-84

3

- **Click the Find Next button.**

Excel begins the search at cell A1 on the Company sheet and makes cell A11 the active cell (Figure 6-85) because it is the first cell to match the search string.

4

- **Continue clicking the Find Next button to find the string, Konica, on the other sheets in the workbook.**
- **Click the Close button in the Find and Replace dialog box to terminate the process and close the Find and Replace dialog box.**

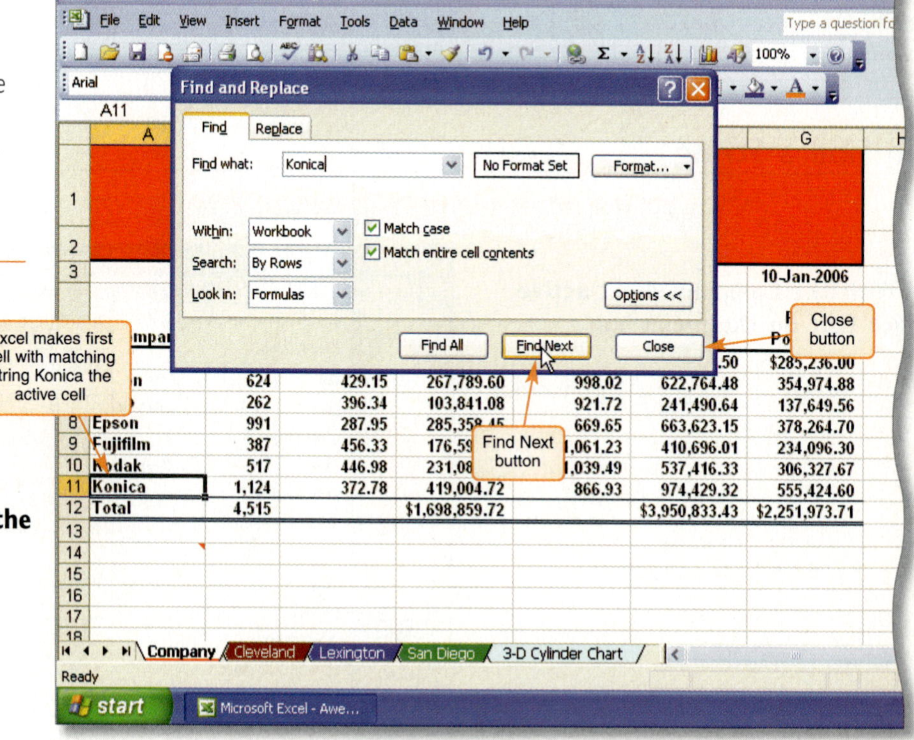

FIGURE 6-85

Other Ways

1. Press CTRL+F
2. In Voice Command mode, say "Edit, Find"

The Format button in the Find and Replace dialog box in Figure 6-84 allows you to fine-tune the search by adding formats, such as bold, font style, and font size, to the string. The Within box options include Sheet and Workbook. The Search box indicates whether the search will be done vertically through rows or horizontally across columns. The Look in box allows you to select Values, Formulas, or Comments. If you select Values, Excel will look for the search string only in cells that do not have formulas. If you select Formulas, Excel will look in all cells. If you select Comments, Excel will look only in comments. If you select the Match case check box, Excel will locate only cells in which the string is in the same case. For example, konica is not the same as Konica. If you select the Match entire cell contents check box, Excel will locate only the cells that contain the string and no other characters. For example, Excel will find a cell entry of Konica, but not Konica Cameras.

If the Find command does not find the string for which you are searching, Excel displays a dialog box indicating it has searched the selected worksheets and cannot find the data for which you are looking.

The Replace Command

The Replace command is used to replace the found search string with a new string. You can use the Find Next and Replace buttons to find and replace a string one occurrence at a time, or you can use the Replace All button to replace the string in all locations at once. The following steps show how use the Replace All button to replace the string Konica with the string Konica XL formatted as red italic font.

To Replace a String with Another String

1

- **With the Company sheet active, click Edit on the menu bar and then click Replace.**
- **When Excel displays the Find and Replace dialog box, type** `Konica` **in the Find what text box and** `Konica XL` **in the Replace with text box.**
- **Click the Replace with Format button. When Excel displays the Replace Format dialog box, click the Font tab, click the Color box arrow, click Red (column 1, row 3), click Italic in the Font style list, and then click the OK button.**
- **Click the Within box arrow and then click Workbook.**
- **Click Match case and Match entire cell contents to select them.**

Excel displays the Find and Replace dialog box as shown in Figure 6-86.

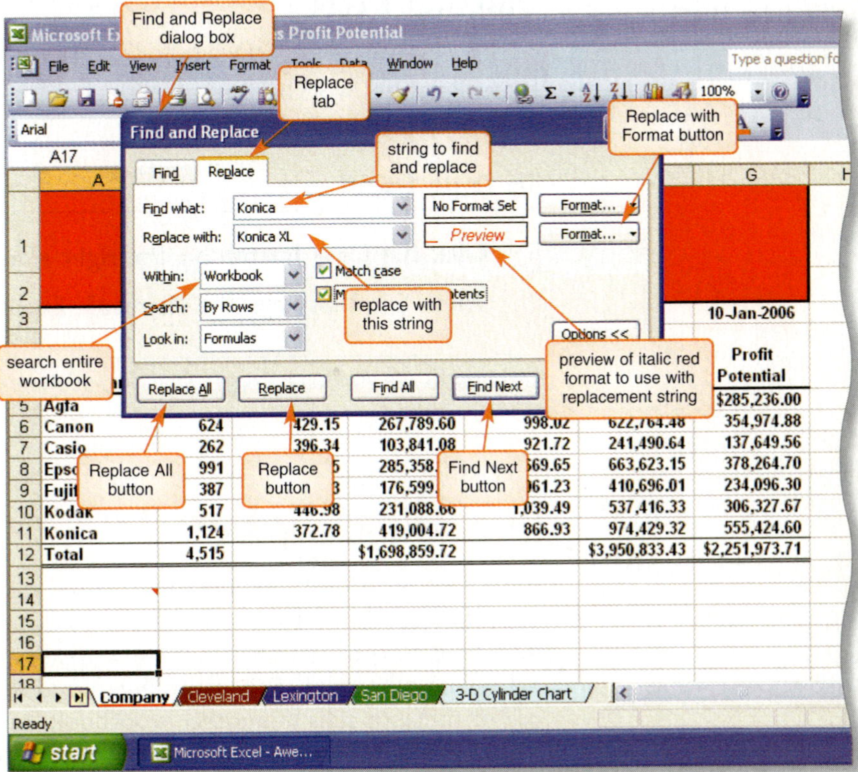

FIGURE 6-86

2

- **Click the Replace All button.**

Excel replaces the string, Konica, with the replacement string Konica XL (cell A11) throughout the four worksheets in the workbook. The replacement string is formatted as red italic font. Excel does not replace the string Konica on the 3-D Cylinder Chart sheet. Excel displays the Microsoft Office Excel dialog box indicating four replacements were made (Figure 6-87).

3

- **Click the OK button in the Microsoft Office Excel dialog box.**
- **Click the Close button in the Find and Replace dialog box.**

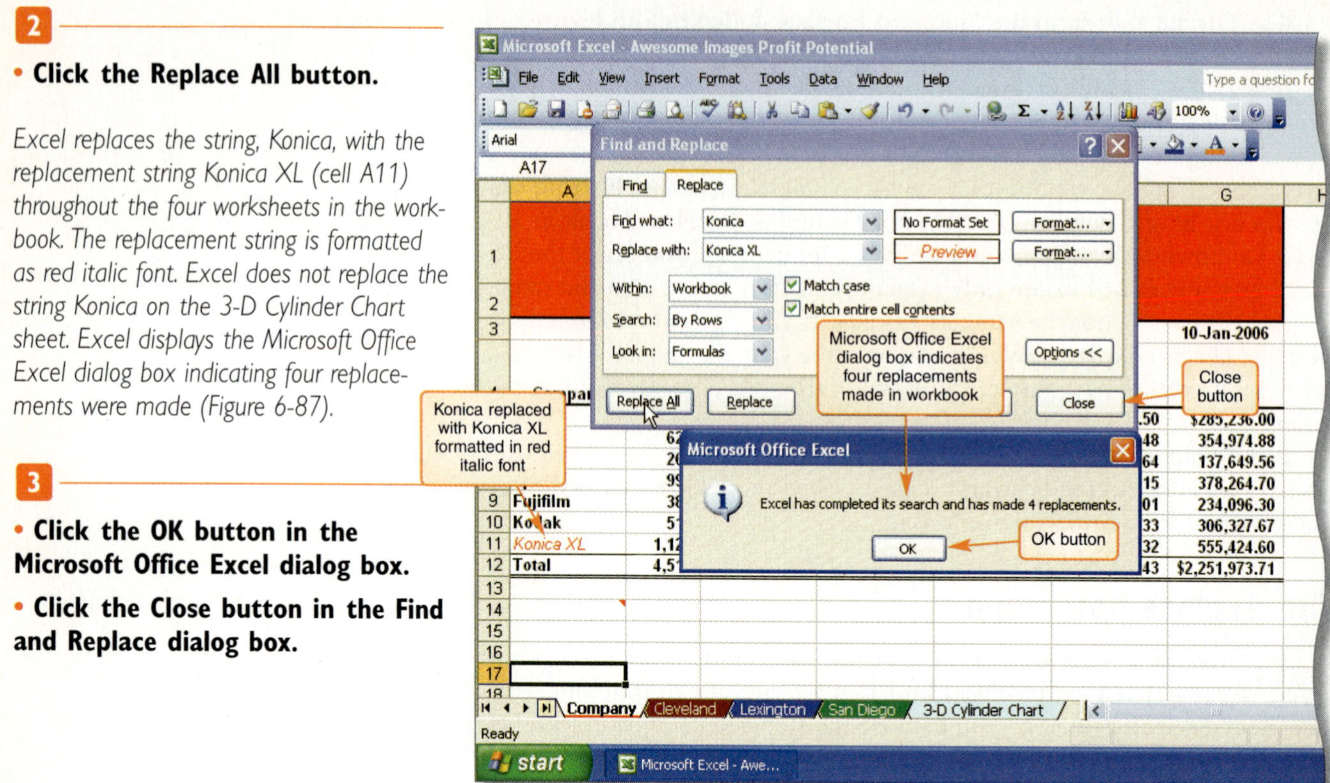

FIGURE 6-87

Other Ways

1. Press CTRL+H
2. In Voice Command mode, say "Edit, Replace"

Quitting Excel

The following steps quit Excel without saving changes to the Awesome Images Profit Potential workbook.

To Quit Excel

1 **Click the Close button on the right side of the Excel title bar.**

2 **When Excel displays the Microsoft Excel dialog box, click the No button.**

Excel closes the Awesome Images Profit Potential workbook without saving changes. The Excel window closes.

Consolidating Data by Linking Workbooks

Earlier in this project, the data from three worksheets were consolidated onto another worksheet in the same workbook using 3-D references. An alternative to this method is to consolidate data from worksheets in other workbooks. Consolidating data from other workbooks also is referred to as linking. A **link** is a reference to a cell or range of cells in another workbook. In this case, the 3-D reference also includes a workbook name. For example, the following 3-D reference pertains to cell B5 on the Cleveland sheet in the workbook AWI Cleveland Profit Potential located on drive A.

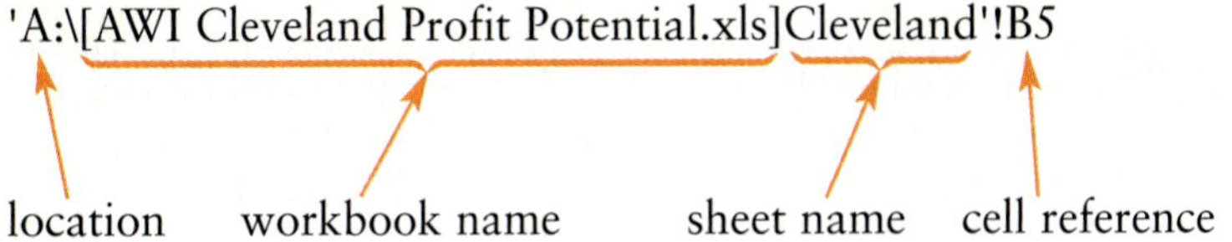

The single quotation marks surrounding the location, workbook name, and sheet name are required if any of the three names contain spaces. If the workbook you are referring to is in the same folder as the active workbook, the location (A:\) is not necessary. The brackets surrounding the workbook name are required.

To illustrate linking cells between workbooks, the Company, Cleveland, Lexington, and San Diego worksheets from the workbook created earlier in this project are on the Data Disk in separate workbooks as described in Table 6-12. In the workbook names in Table 6-12, the AWI stands for Awesome Images. The store workbooks contain the store data, but the AWI Company workbook does not include any consolidated data. The consolidation of data from the three store workbooks into the AWI Company Profit Potential workbook will be completed later in this section.

The remaining sections of this project demonstrate how to search for the four workbooks in Table 6-12 on drive A, how to create a Workspace from the four workbooks, and finally how to link the three store workbooks to consolidate the data into the AWI Company Profit Potential workbook.

More About

Consolidation

You also can consolidate data across different workbooks using the Consolidate command on the Data menu, rather than entering formulas. For more information on the Consolidate command, enter `consolidate` in the Type a question for help box on the menu bar, and then click the Consolidate data link in the Search Results task pane.

Table 6-12 Workbook Names

WORKSHEET IN AWESOME IMAGES PROFIT POTENTIAL WORKBOOK	SAVED ON THE DATA DISK USING THE WORKBOOK NAME
Company	AWI Company Profit Potential
Cleveland	AWI Cleveland Profit Potential
Lexington	AWI Lexington Profit Potential
San Diego	AWI San Diego Profit Potential

Searching for and Opening Workbooks

Excel has a powerful search tool that you can use to locate workbooks (or any file) stored on disk. You start the search tool by invoking the File Search command on the File menu, which opens the Basic File Search task pane. If you view files on the Data Disk, then you would see the four workbooks listed in the right column of Table 6-12. The following steps, however, show how to search for workbooks when you cannot remember exactly the name of the file or its location. In this example, the string AWI (the first three characters in the workbook names) will be used to locate the workbooks. The located workbooks then are opened and **arranged** so that each one appears in its own window.

To Search for and Open Workbooks

1

- **Start Excel following the steps on page EX 382 and then click File on the menu bar.**

Excel starts, opens Book1, and displays the File menu (Figure 6-88).

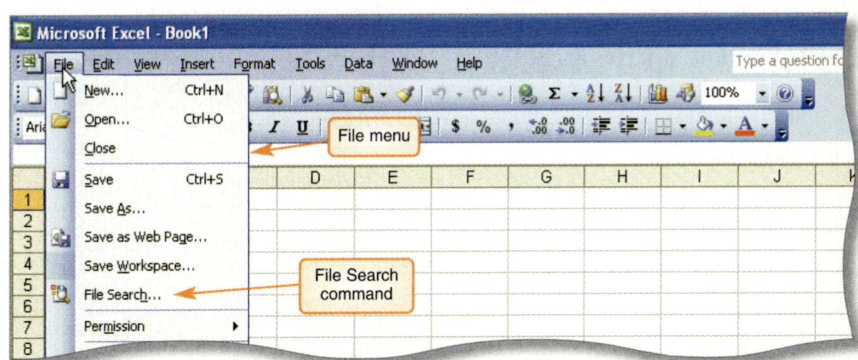

FIGURE 6-88

2

- **Click the File Search command.**
- **When Excel displays the Basic File Search task pane, type AWI in the Search text text box.**
- **Click the Search in box arrow.**
- **If necessary, click the plus sign to the left of Everywhere, click the plus sign to the left of My Computer, click 3½ Floppy (A:) to select it, and then click any other folder that has a check mark to clear it.**

Excel displays the Basic File Search task pane on the right side of the screen as shown in Figure 6-89.

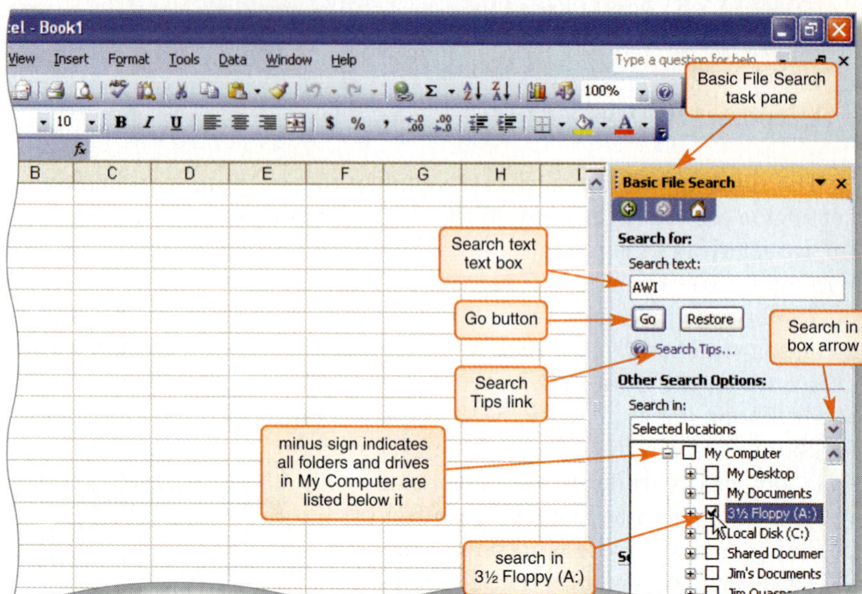

FIGURE 6-89

3

- **Click the Search in box arrow to close the Search in list.**
- **Click the Go button in the Basic File Search task pane.**

Excel displays the Search Results task pane (Figure 6-90), listing the four workbooks described earlier in Table 6-12.

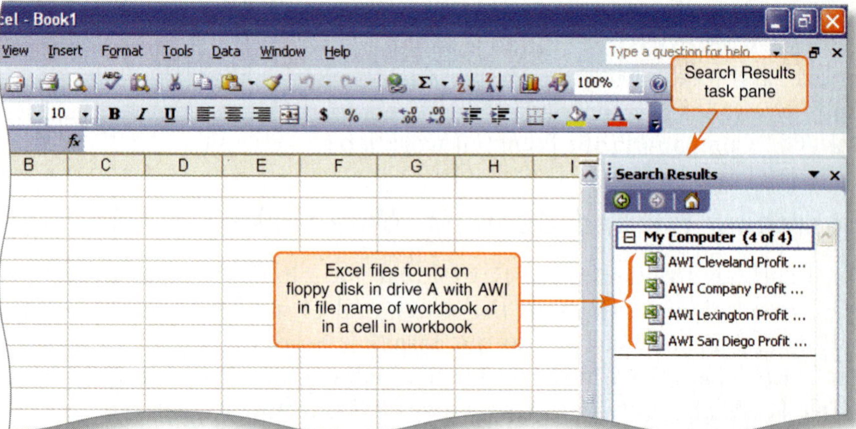

FIGURE 6-90

4

- **In the Search Results task pane, click each of the three store workbook names one at a time and then click the company workbook name to open them.**
- **Click Window on the menu bar.**

Excel opens the four workbooks. The names of the four workbooks appear on the Window menu with a check mark to the right of the active workbook (Figure 6-91).

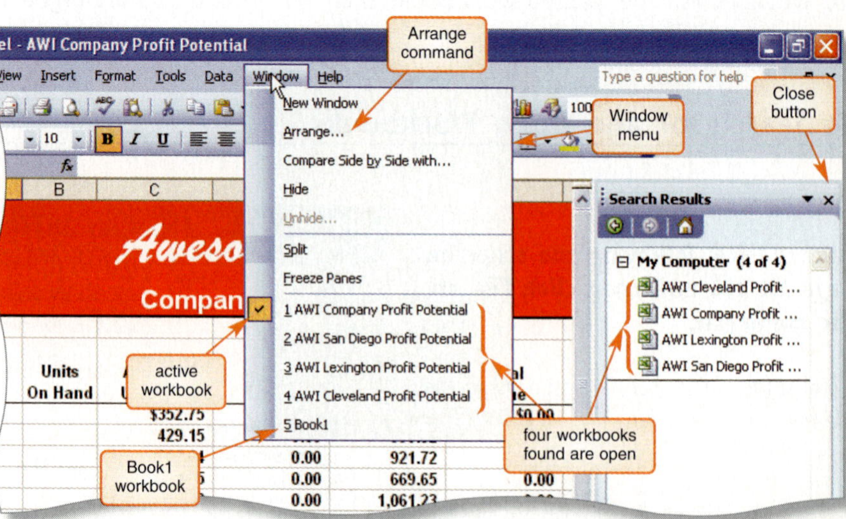

FIGURE 6-91

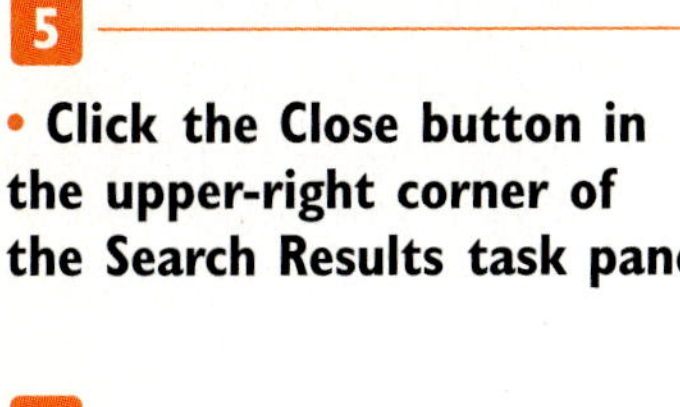

5

- **Click the Close button in the upper-right corner of the Search Results task pane.**

6

- **Click Window on the menu bar and then click Book1.**
- **Click Window on the menu bar and then click Arrange.**
- **When Excel displays the Arrange Windows dialog box, click Vertical, and then, if necessary, click the Windows of active workbook check box to clear it.**

Excel displays Book1 and the Arrange Windows dialog box as shown in Figure 6-92.

Book1
Arrange Windows dialog box
Vertical option button
Windows of active workbook check box
ways to arrange workbooks in Excel window
OK button

FIGURE 6-92

7

- **Click the OK button in the Arrange Windows dialog box.**

Excel displays the five opened workbooks as shown in Figure 6-93.

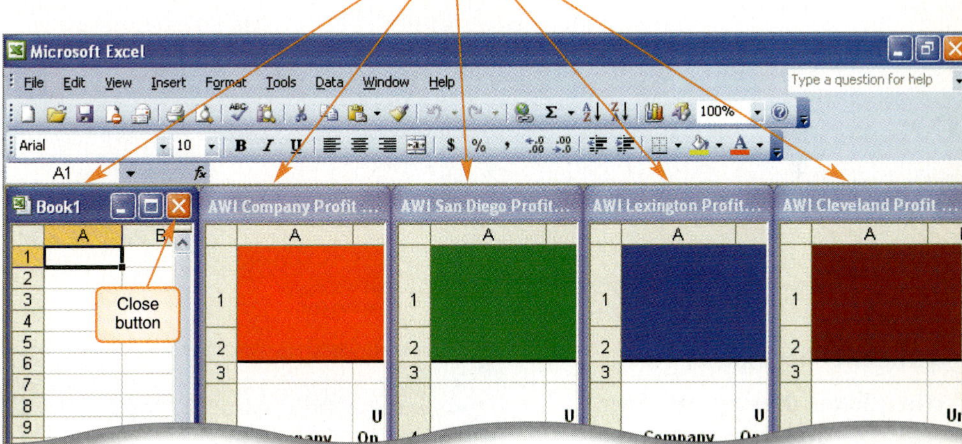

FIGURE 6-93

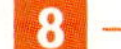

8

- **Click the Close button on the right side of the Book1 title bar.**
- **Double-click the AWI Company Profit Potential title bar to maximize it and hide the other opened workbooks.**

Other Ways

1. Press ALT+F, H
2. In Voice Command mode, say "File, File Search"

The Basic File Search task pane includes an Advanced Search link and a Search Tips link. Clicking the Advanced Search link allows you to add conditions to customize the file search. Clicking the Search Tips link displays additional information on advanced searching.

As shown in Figure 6-92, multiple opened workbooks can be arranged in four ways. The option name in the Arrange Windows dialog box identifies the resulting window's configuration. You can modify any of the arranged workbooks by clicking within its window to activate it. To return to showing one workbook, double-click its title bar as described in step 8.

More About

Searching for Files

The key to finding the file you are searching for is to be as specific as you can with the search text and file location. The search text can be in the file name, in the file, or in other file properties. You also can use the wildcard characters asterisk (*) and question mark (?) in the same fashion discussed in the previous project. Excel also will return files with similar words.

Creating a Workspace File

If you plan to consolidate data from other workbooks, it is recommended that you first bind the workbooks together using a workspace file. A **workspace file** saves information about all the workbooks that are open. The workspace file does not contain the actual workbooks; rather, it stores information required to open the files associated with the workspace file, including file names, which file was active at the time of the save, and other display settings. To create a workspace file, click the Save Workspace command on the File menu. After you create and save a workspace file, you can open all of the associated files by opening the workspace. The following steps show how to create a workspace file from the files opened in the previous set of steps.

To Create a Workspace File

1

- **With the four AWI workbooks opened and the Company Profit Potential workbook active, click File on the menu bar.**

Excel displays the AWI Company Profit Potential workbook and the File menu (Figure 6-94).

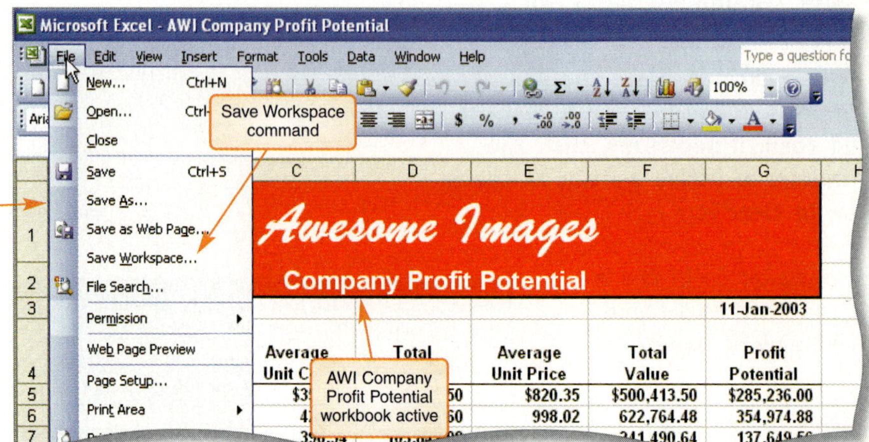

FIGURE 6-94

2

- **Click Save Workspace.**
- **When Excel displays the Save Workspace dialog box, type** `Awesome Images Workspace` **in the File name box, click the Save in box arrow, and then click 3½ Floppy (A:).**

Excel displays the Save Workspace dialog box (Figure 6-95), which is identical to the Save As dialog box used in previous projects, except for the name of the dialog box. Excel automatically chooses Workspaces as the file type in the Save as type box.

3

- **Click the Save button in the Save Workspace dialog box.**
- **Click the Close button on the title bar to quit Excel.**

Excel saves the file names of the workbooks open, of the workbooks displaying, and other display settings. The Excel window closes.

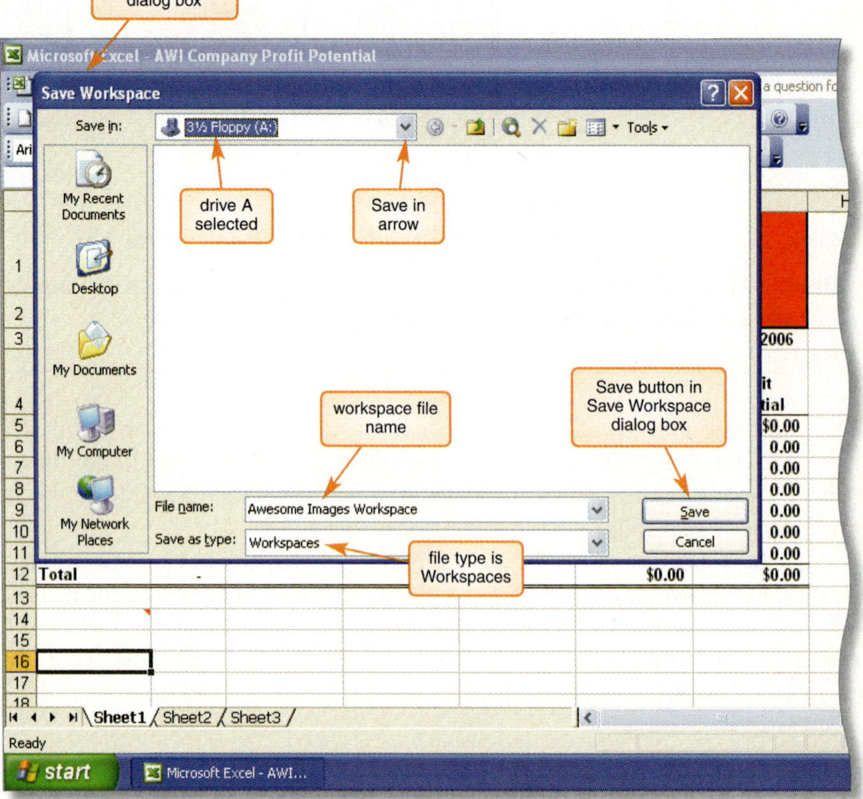

FIGURE 6-95

After the workspace is saved to disk, you can open the workbooks one at a time as you did in the past, or you can open all of the associated workbooks by opening the workspace. When you invoke the Open command, workspace file names appear in the Open dialog box, the same as any workbook file name.

More About

Workspace Files

A workspace file saves display information about open workbooks, such as window sizes, print areas, screen magnification, and display settings. Workspace files do not contain the workbooks themselves.

Consolidating Data by Linking Workbooks

The following steps show how to open the workspace file Awesome Images Workspace and consolidate the data from the three store workbooks into the AWI Company Profit Potential workbook.

To Consolidate Data by Linking Workbooks

1. **Start Excel as described on page EX 382. Click the Open button on the Standard toolbar. When Excel displays the Open dialog box, click the Look in box arrow and then click 3½ Floppy (A:). Double-click Awesome Images Workspace to open the four workbooks saved in the workspace. Make AWI Company Profit Potential the active worksheet. If necessary, double-click the AWI Company Profit Potential window title bar to maximize it.**
2. **Select cell B5. Click the AutoSum button on the Standard toolbar. Click Window on the menu bar and then click AWI Cleveland Profit Potential. Click cell B5. Delete the dollar signs ($) in the reference to cell B5 in the formula bar. Click immediately after B5 in the formula bar and then press the COMMA key.**
3. **Click Window on the menu bar and then click AWI Lexington Profit Potential. Select cell B5. Delete the dollar signs ($) in the reference to cell B5 in the formula bar. Click immediately after B5 in the formula bar and then press the COMMA key.**
4. **Click Window on the menu bar and then click AWI San Diego Profit Potential. Select cell B5. Delete the dollar signs ($) in the reference to cell B5 in the formula bar. Click the Enter box.**
5. **With cell B5 active in the AWI Company Profit Potential workbook, drag the cell's fill handle through cell B11. Select cell B5.**
6. **Click the Save button on the Standard toolbar. If Excel displays a dialog box, select Overwrite changes. Click the OK button. Click the Print button on the Standard toolbar.**

Excel displays the consolidated profit potential for Awesome Images as shown in Figure 6-96. Excel saves and prints the workbook.

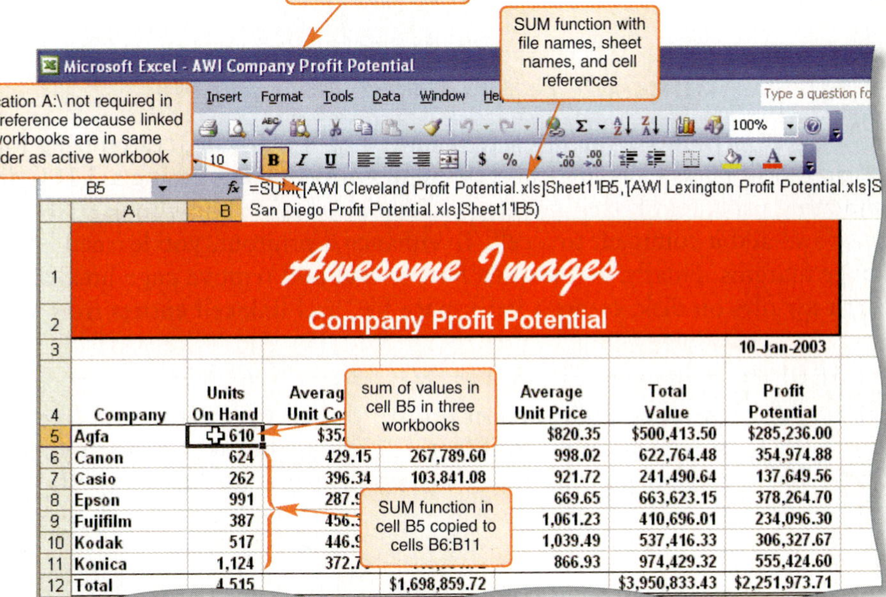

FIGURE 6-96

More About

The Quick Reference

For more information, see the Quick Reference Summary at the back of this book, or visit the Excel 2003 Quick Reference Web page (scsite.com/ex2003/qr).

As you link workbooks, remember that the cell reference inserted by Excel each time you click a cell in a workbook is an absolute cell reference ($B$5). You must edit the formula and change these to relative cell references because the SUM function later is copied to the range B6:B11. If the cell references are left as absolute, then the copied function always would refer to cell B5 in the three workbooks no matter where you copy the SUM function.

Updating Links

Later, if you open the AWI Company Profit Potential workbook by itself, also called the **dependent workbook**, Excel will ask you whether you want to update the links. The linked workbooks are called the **source workbooks**. If the source workbooks are not open, Excel will display a dialog box that will give you the option to update the links. If you choose to update the links, Excel reads the data in the source workbooks on disk and recalculates formulas in the dependent workbook, but it does not open the source workbooks.

If the three source workbooks are open along with the dependent workbook as in the previous set of steps, Excel automatically updates the links (recalculates) in the AWI Company Profit Potential workbook when a value changes in any one of the source workbooks.

More About

Microsoft Certification

The Microsoft Office Specialist Certification program provides an opportunity for you to obtain a valuable industry credential — proof that you have the Excel skills required by employers. For more information, see Appendix E, or visit the Excel 2003 Certification Web page (scsite.com/ex2003/cert).

Closing All Workbooks at One Time and Quitting Excel

To close all four workbooks at one time and quit Excel, complete the following steps.

To Close All Workbooks at One Time and Quit Excel

1. **Hold down the SHIFT key, click File on the menu bar, and then click the Close All command.**
2. **If Excel displays the Microsoft Excel dialog box, click the No button.**
3. **Click the Close button on the right side of the Excel title bar.**

Project Summary

This project introduced you to creating and using a template, customizing formats, creating styles, using the Research task pane, changing chart types, drawing and enhancing a 3-D Cylinder chart using WordArt, and annotating using text boxes and arrows. You also learned how to use 3-D references to reference cells in other sheets and add a comment to a cell. To enhance a printout, you learned how to add a header and footer and to change margins. Finally, you learned how to add and remove page breaks, use the Find and Replace commands, search for files on disk, create a workspace file, and link cell entries from external workbooks.

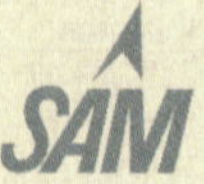

If you have a SAM user profile, you may have access to hands-on instruction, practice, and assessment of the skills covered in this project. Log in to your SAM account and go to your assignments page to see what your instructor has assigned.

What You Should Know

Having completed this project, you should be able to perform the tasks below. The tasks are listed in the same order they were presented in this project. For a list of the buttons, menus, toolbars, and commands introduced in this project, see the Quick Reference Summary at the back of this book and refer to the Page Number column.

1. Start and Customize Excel (EX 382)
2. Bold the Font and Adjust the Row Heights and Column Widths of the Template (EX 383)
3. Enter the Title, Subtitle, and Row Titles in the Template (EX 383)
4. Enter Column Titles and the System Date in the Template (EX 384)
5. Enter Dummy Data in the Template Using the Fill Handle (EX 385)
6. Enter Formulas Using Point Mode and Determine Totals in the Template (EX 388)
7. Save the Template (EX 391)
8. Format the Template Title and Subtitle (EX 392)
9. Format the Column Titles and Total Row (EX 393)
10. Assign a Currency Style Using the Format Dialog Box (EX 394)
11. Create and Assign a Custom Format Code and a Comma Style Format (EX 397)
12. Create a New Style (EX 399)
13. Apply a Style (EX 401)
14. Find a Synonym Using the Research Task Pane (EX 402)
15. Spell Check, Save, and Print the Template (EX 403)
16. Open a Template and Save It as a Workbook (EX 405)
17. Add a Worksheet to a Workbook (EX 406)
18. Copy the Contents of a Worksheet to Other Worksheets in a Workbook (EX 407)
19. Drill an Entry through Worksheets (EX 409)
20. Modify the Cleveland Sheet (EX 410)
21. Modify the Lexington Sheet (EX 412)
22. Modify the San Diego Sheet (EX 413)
23. Modify the Company Sheet (EX 415)
24. Enter and Copy 3-D References Using the Paste Button Menu (EX 415)
25. Draw the 3-D Cylinder Chart (EX 420)
26. Format the 3-D Cylinder Chart (EX 422)
27. Add a Chart Title Using the WordArt Tool (EX 424)
28. Add a Text Box and an Arrow to the Chart (EX 427)
29. Assign a Comment to a Cell (EX 429)
30. Research a Topic Using the Research Task Pane (EX 431)
31. Add a Header, change the Margins and Center the Printout Horizontally (EX 433)
32. Add a Header to the 3-D Cylinder Chart Sheet (EX 436)
33. Print All Worksheets in a Workbook (EX 437)
34. Print Nonadjacent Sheets in a Workbook (EX 439)
35. Insert and Remove a Page Break (EX 440)
36. Hide Page Breaks (EX 442)
37. Find a String (EX 443)
38. Replace a String with Another String (EX 445)
39. Quit Excel (EX 446)
40. Search for and Open Workbooks (EX 447)
41. Create a Workspace File (EX 450)
42. Consolidate Data by Linking Workbooks (EX 451)
43. Close all Workbooks at One Time and Quit Excel (EX 452)

Learn It Online

Instructions: To complete the Learn It Online exercises, start your browser, click the Address bar, and then enter the Web address `scsite.com/ex2003/learn`. When the Excel 2003 Learn It Online page is displayed, follow the instructions in the exercises below. Each exercise has instructions for printing your results, either for your own records or for submission to your instructor.

1 Project Reinforcement TF, MC, and SA

Below Excel Project 6, click the Project Reinforcement link. Print the quiz by clicking Print on the File menu for each page. Answer each question.

2 Flash Cards

Below Excel Project 6, click the Flash Cards link and read the instructions. Type 20 (or a number specified by your instructor) in the Number of playing cards text box, type your name in the Enter your Name text box, and then click the Flip Card button. When the flash card is displayed, read the question and then click the ANSWER box arrow to select an answer. Flip through Flash Cards. If your score is 15 (75%) correct or greater, click Print on the File menu to print your results. If your score is less than 15 (75%) correct, then redo this exercise by clicking the Replay button.

3 Practice Test

Below Excel Project 6, click the Practice Test link. Answer each question, enter your first and last name at the bottom of the page, and then click the Grade Test button. When the graded practice test is displayed on your screen, click Print on the File menu to print a hard copy. Continue to take practice tests until you score 80% or better.

4 Who Wants To Be a Computer Genius?

Below Excel Project 6, click the Computer Genius link. Read the instructions, enter your first and last name at the bottom of the page, and then click the PLAY button. When your score is displayed, click the PRINT RESULTS link to print a hard copy.

5 Wheel of Terms

Below Excel Project 6, click the Wheel of Terms link. Read the instructions, and then enter your first and last name and your school name. Click the PLAY button. When your score is displayed, right-click the score and then click Print on the shortcut menu to print a hard copy.

6 Crossword Puzzle Challenge

Below Excel Project 6, click the Crossword Puzzle Challenge link. Read the instructions, and then enter your first and last name. Click the SUBMIT button. Work the crossword puzzle. When you are finished, click the Submit button. When the crossword puzzle is redisplayed, click the Print Puzzle button to print a hard copy.

7 Tips and Tricks

Below Excel Project 6, click the Tips and Tricks link. Click a topic that pertains to Project 6. Right-click the information and then click Print on the shortcut menu. Construct a brief example of what the information relates to in Excel to confirm you understand how to use the tip or trick.

8 Newsgroups

Below Excel Project 6, click the Newsgroups link. Click a topic that pertains to Project 6. Print three comments.

9 Expanding Your Horizons

Below Excel Project 6, click the Articles for Microsoft Excel link. Click a topic that pertains to Project 6. Print the information. Construct a brief example of what the information relates to in Excel to confirm you understand the contents of the article.

10 Search Sleuth

Below Excel Project 6, click the Search Sleuth link. To search for a term that pertains to this project, select a term below the Project 6 title and then use the Google search engine at google.com (or any major search engine) to display and print two Web pages that present information on the term.

11 Excel Online Training

Below Excel Project 6, click the Excel Online Training link. When your browser displays the Microsoft Office Online Web page, click the Excel link. Click one of the Excel courses that covers one or more of the objectives listed at the beginning of the project on page EX 378. Print the first page of the course before stepping through it.

12 Office Marketplace

Below Excel Project 6, click the Office Marketplace link. When your browser displays the Microsoft Office Online Web page, click the Office Marketplace link. Click a topic that relates to Excel. Print the first page.

Apply Your Knowledge

1 Consolidating Data in a Workbook

Instructions Part 1: Follow the steps below to consolidate the four quarterly payroll worksheets on the Annual Totals worksheet in the workbook Apply 6-1 Annual Payroll (Figure 6-97). At the conclusion of the Part 1 instructions, the Annual Totals worksheet should display as shown in the lower screen in Figure 6-95.

1. Open the workbook Apply 6-1 Annual Payroll on the Data Disk. One by one, click the first four tabs and review the quarterly payroll totals. Click the Annual Totals tab.
2. Determine the quarterly totals by using the SUM function and 3-D references to sum the hours worked in cell B20. Copy cell B20 to the range B20:C23. Copy only the formulas using the Formulas command on the Paste button menu.
3. Save the workbook using the file name, Apply 6-1 Annual Payroll 1.
4. Select all five worksheets. Use the Page Setup command on the File menu to add a header that includes your name and course number in the Left section, the computer laboratory exercise number (Apply 6-1) in the Center section, and the system date and your instructor's name in the Right section. Add the page number and total number of pages to the footer. Center all worksheets horizontally on the page and print without gridlines. Preview and print the five worksheets. Click the Annual Totals tab to select the sheet. Save the workbook with the new page setup using the same file name as in step 3.
5. Use the Research button and the English (U.S.) thesaurus to find a synonym for the word Gross. Write down five synonyms and one antonym for Gross on page 1 of the printout from step 4. Use the Replace command to replace the word Gross on all five worksheets with one of the synonyms.

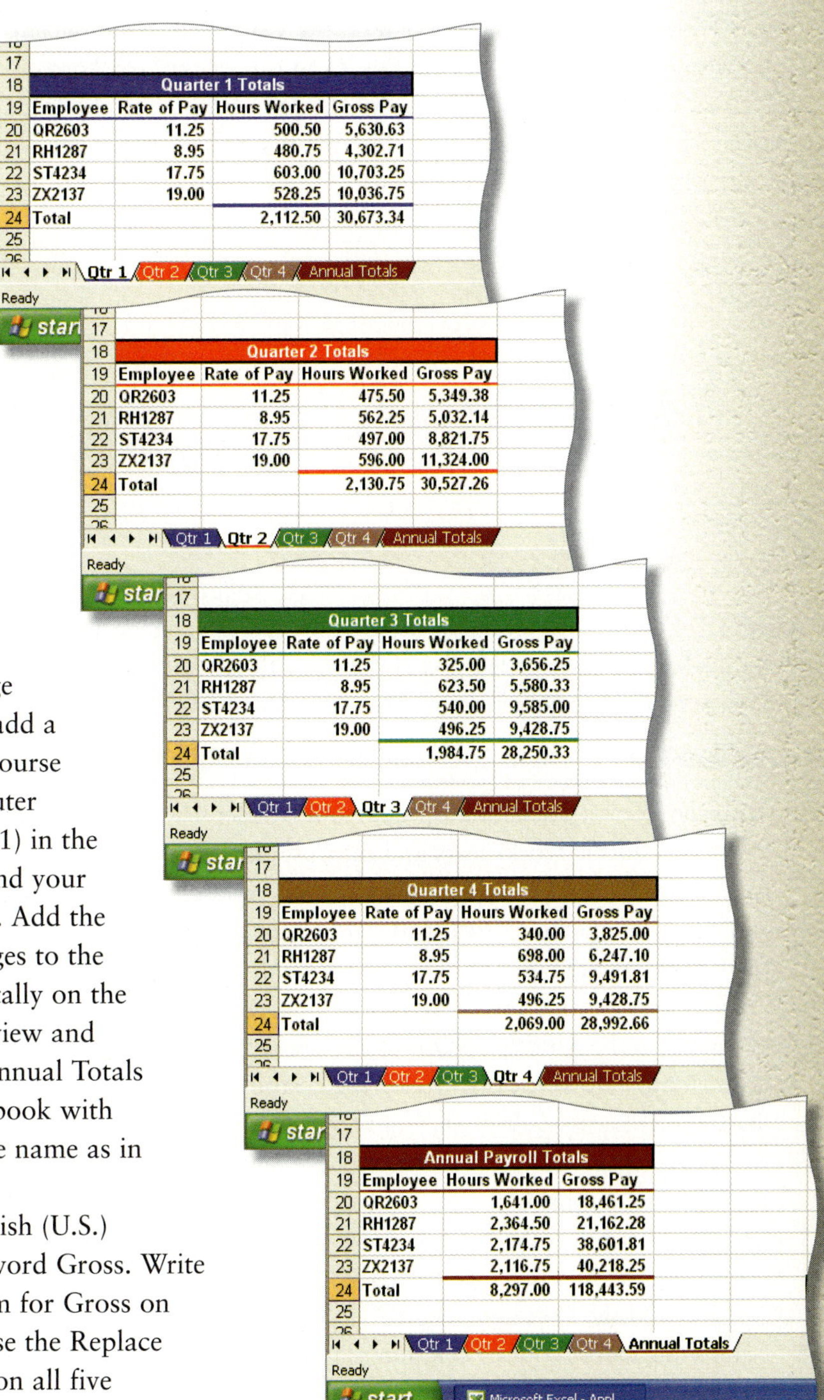

FIGURE 6-97

(continued)

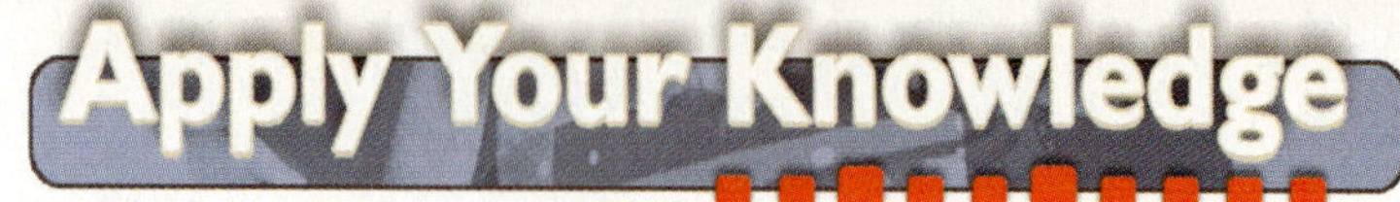

Consolidating Data in a Workbook *(continued)*

Instructions Part 2: If Excel is active, quit Excel and then start Excel. Use the File Search command on the File menu to find all Excel workbooks on drive A (on the Data Disk) that include the string Emp. Open the five files, close any other files, make the Apply 6-1 Co Emp workbook the active workbook, and then save a workspace file on drive A using the file name Apply 6-1 Emp Workspace. Close all files. Open the workspace file Apply 6-1 Emp Workspace and maximize the workbook window. Consolidate the data in the four quarterly payroll workbooks into the range B20:C23 in the workbook Apply 6-1 Co Emp. Save the workbook using the same name. Close all files. Open Apply 6-1 Qtr 1 Emp from the Data Disk and change the hours worked for employee ST4234 to 300. Save and close the workbook. Open the workspace Apply 6-1 Emp Workspace. The gross pay total in cell C24 on the Annual Totals worksheet should be $113,065.34 with the change made to Apply 6-1 Qtr 1 Emp. Print the five workbooks.

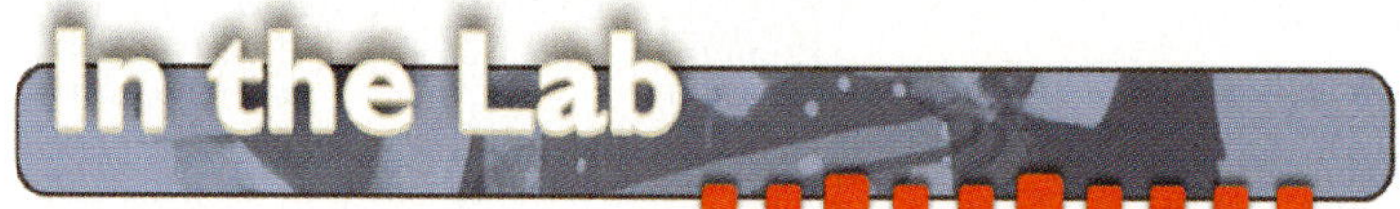

1 Creating a Template and Style

Problem: You recently obtained a part-time job at Jogger's Wear as a salesperson. Once you were on the job, your immediate supervisor learned about your Excel skills and she asked you to create a template (Figure 6-98) for management to use when they create new Excel workbooks.

Instructions Part 1: Start Excel and perform the following steps to create a template.

1. With the Book1 workbook opened, add a Sheet 4 worksheet and then move the sheet so it is the far right tab. Select all the worksheets and then use the Select All button to change the font of all cells to 12-point Arial bold. Increase all row heights to 16.50. Select Sheet1, change the name from Sheet1 to Jogger's Wear, and then change the tab color to red.
2. Use the Style command on the Format menu to create the format style called Comma (4) as shown in Figure 6-98. Display the Comma style, change the name in the Style name box from Comma to Comma (4), and use the Modify button to change the decimal places to 4 and the font to Arial Bold 12. Align cells horizontally and vertically. Create the custom format $#,##0.00);[Red]($#,##0.00) and then assign it to all the cells on Sheets 2 through 4 in the workbook.
3. Add a comment to cell A8 to identify the template and its purpose, as shown in Figure 6-98. Include your name as the author.
4. Use WordArt to create the title shown in the range A1:H6. Use the style in column 4, row 1 of the WordArt Gallery dialog box. Change the color of the title to red. Add a thick dashed red bottom border to the range A6:H6. Add the subtitle in cell F7.
5. Enter your name, course, computer laboratory assignment (Lab 6-1), date, time, and instructor's name as the header. Add a page number as the footer.

In the Lab

6. Use the Save As command to save the template, selecting Template in the Save as type list. Make sure you save the template on the Data Disk in drive A and not in the computer's template folder. Save the template using the file name, Lab 6-1 Jogger's Wear Template.

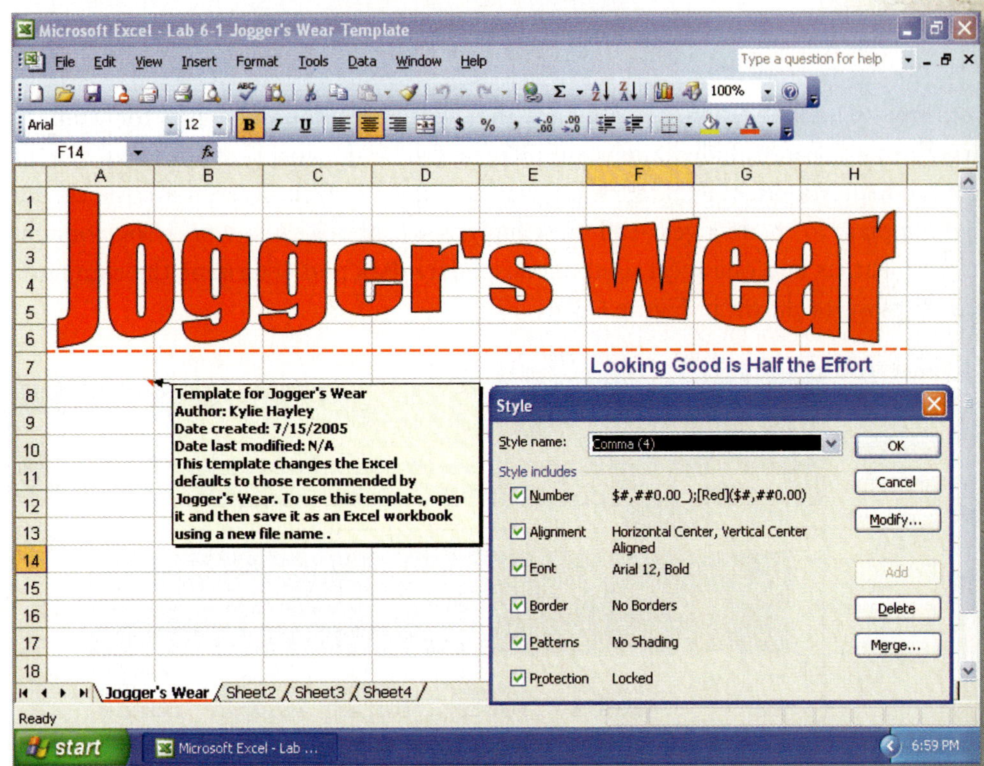

FIGURE 6-98

7. Print the template and comment. To print the comment, click the Sheet tab in the Page Setup dialog box. Click the Comments box arrow and then click At end of sheet. The comment will print on a separate sheet. After the comment prints, deselect printing the comment by clicking the Comment box arrow in the Sheet tab in the Page Setup dialog box and then clicking (None).
8. Close the template and then reopen it. Save the template as a workbook using the file name Lab 6-1 Jogger's Wear. Use the Research button on the Standard toolbar to find two synonyms for any three words in the workbook. Use the Research button to add a statement about jogging from the Web to the bottom of the comment in cell A8. Cite the reference in the comment. Save the workbook. Print the workbook along with the comment. Close the workbook. Write the three words you selected earlier and their corresponding synonyms at the top of the printout below the header.

Instructions Part 2: Do the following:

1. Change the default font settings for Excel to 16-point Lucida Handwriting by following the steps outlined in the More About on page EX 400. Make sure you restart Excel for the default font settings to take effect.
2. Change the default number of worksheets from three to five by following the steps outlined in the More About on page EX 406.
3. Open a new workbook. Hold down the SHIFT key and then click the Sheet5 tab.
4. Enter your name, course, computer laboratory assignment (Lab 6-1 Part 2), and instructor's name in the range A1:A4.
5. Hold down the SHIFT key and click the Sheet1 tab. Enter the tab name (Sheet1) in cell A5. Do the same for the remaining four sheets using their tab names.
6. Click the Sheet1 tab. Hold down the SHIFT key and then click the Sheet5 tab. Print all five worksheets. Close the workbook without saving changes.
7. Change the default font settings for Excel to 10-point Arial by following the steps outlined in the More About on page EX 400. Make sure you restart Excel for the default font settings to take effect.

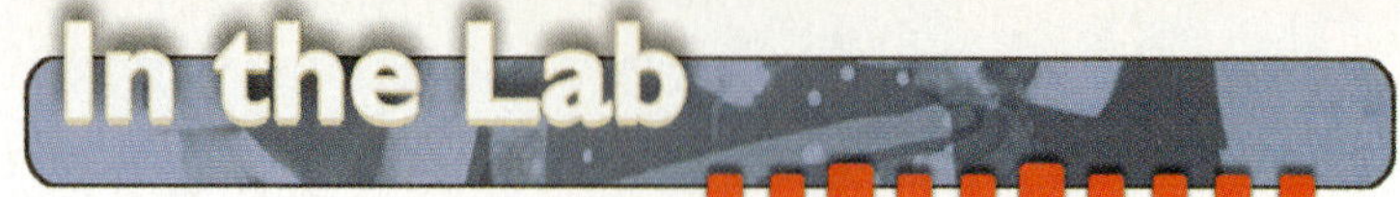

2 Using a Template to Create a Multiple-Sheet Workbook

Problem: The Web Salon is a company that specializes in unique gifts for women. The company has outlets in three cities — Boston, Indianapolis, and Phoenix — and a corporate office in Cincinnati. All of the outlets sell their products via direct mail, telesales, walk-in, and the Web. Every year, the corporate officers in Cincinnati use a template to create a year-end sales analysis workbook. The workbook contains four sheets, one for each of the three outlets and one sheet used to consolidate data and determine the company totals. The Consolidated sheet displays as shown in Figure 6-99.

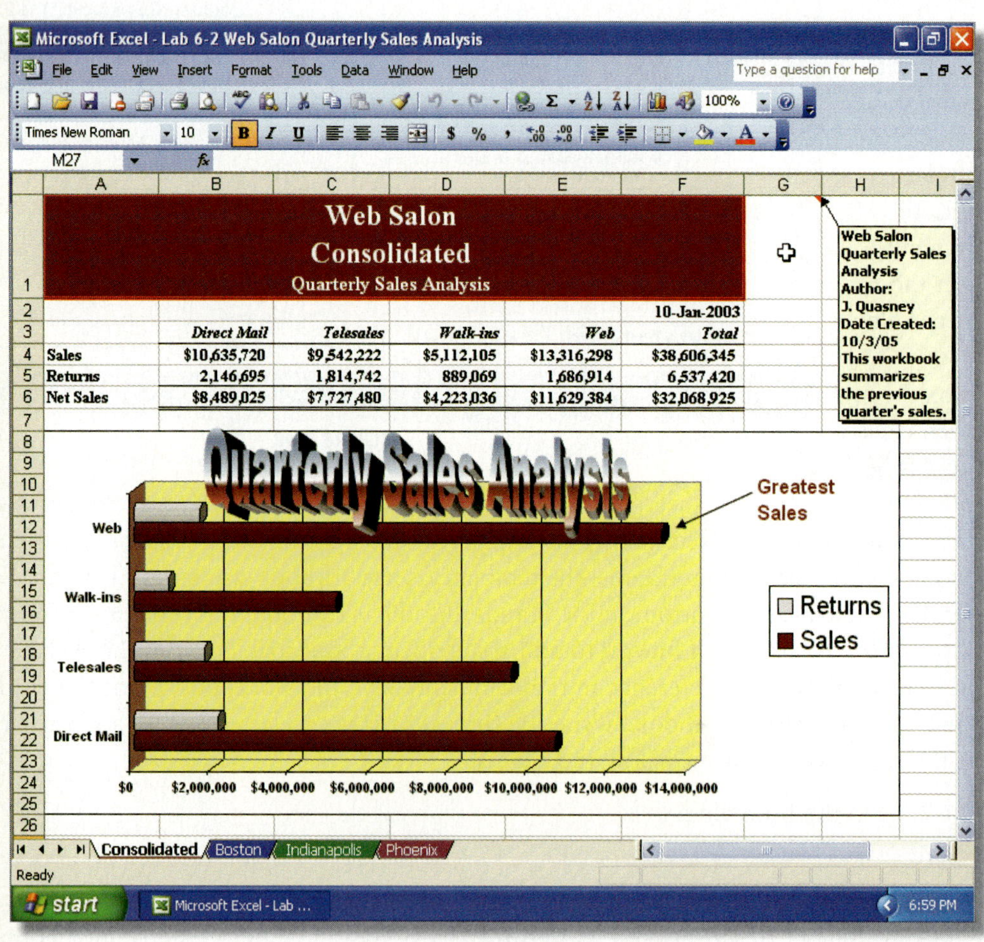

FIGURE 6-99

The template used to create the quarterly sales analysis workbook is on the Data Disk. Rebecca Smart, the company's accountant, has asked you to use the template to create the year-end sales analysis workbook.

Instructions Part 1: Perform the following tasks.

1. Open the template, Lab 6-2 Web Salon Quarterly Sales Analysis Template, on the Data Disk. Save the template as a workbook using the file name Lab 6-2 Web Salon Quarterly Sales Analysis. Make sure Microsoft Excel Workbook is selected in the Save as type list.

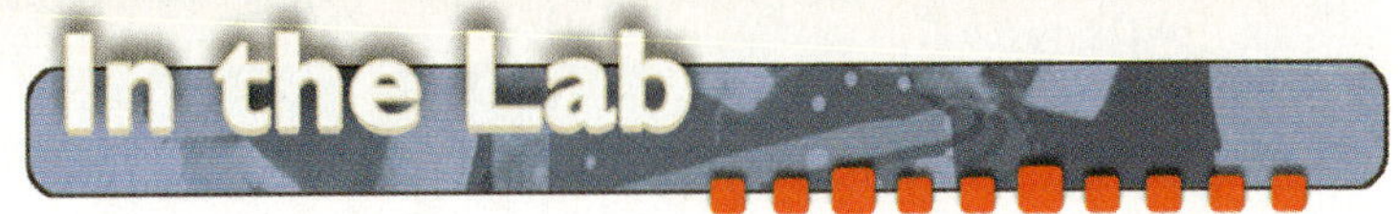

2. Add a worksheet to the workbook between Sheet1 and Sheet2 and then paste the contents of Sheet1 to the three empty sheets. Save the workbook.
3. From left to right, rename the sheet tabs Company, Boston, Indianapolis, and Phoenix. Color the tabs as shown in Figure 6-99. On each of the three city worksheets, change the subtitle in cell A2 to match the tab name. Use the title Consolidated in cell A2 of the Consolidated worksheet. Change the background color for each title area in the range A1:F1 to match the tab color. Enter the data in Table 6-13 into the three city sheets.
4. On the Consolidated worksheet, use the SUM function, 3-D references, and copy and paste capabilities of Excel to total the corresponding cells on the three outlet worksheets. First, compute the sum in cell B4 and then compute the sum in cell B5. Copy the range B4:B5 to the range C4:E5. The Consolidated worksheet should resemble the top of Figure 6-99. Save the workbook.

Table 6-13 Web Salon Sales Data

		BOSTON	INDIANAPOLIS	PHOENIX
Direct Mail	Sales	6153961	2918928	1562831
	Returns	856125	673281	617289
Telesales	Sales	3251698	3145261	3145263
	Returns	623918	671541	519283
Walk-ins	Sales	2198196	2156981	756928
	Returns	231476	426112	231481
Web	Sales	6415283	3718279	3182736
	Returns	845918	417829	423167

5. Create an embedded Cylinder chart in the range A8:H25 on the Consolidated worksheet by charting the range A3:E5. Select the Bar with a cylindrical shape type chart. Do not include a chart title. Reduce the font size of the labels on both axes to 8-point bold. Use the chart colors shown in Figure 6-99. Use the WordArt button on the Drawing toolbar to add the chart title (column 5, row 5 in the WordArt Gallery). Add the text box and arrow as shown in Figure 6-99. Save the workbook.
6. Add the comment shown in cell G1 in Figure 6-99.
7. Select all four sheets. Change the header to include your name, course, computer laboratory exercise (Lab 6-2), date, and instructor's name. Change the footer to include the page number and total pages. Change the left and right margins to .5.
8. Preview and then print the entire workbook, including the comment. Save the workbook with the new page setup characteristics. Print the worksheets in landscape orientation and use the Black and white option.

Instructions Part 2: With the workbook created in Part 1 open, complete the following corrections that were sent in to the main office from the outlets: (a) Boston Walk-in Sales 3,225,150; (b) Indianapolis Web Returns 525,175; (c) Phoenix Direct Mail Sales 1,250,575. The Consolidated Total Net Sales in cell F6 should equal $32,676,277. Place a page break above row 7 on the Consolidated worksheet. Hide page breaks. Print all the worksheets. Do not print the comment. Close the workbook without saving changes.

Instructions Part 3: Select all the worksheets in the Lab 6-2 Web Salon Quarterly Sales Analysis workbook and do the following:

1. Select cell A1 on the Consolidated worksheet. Use the Find command and the Find All button in the Find and Replace dialog box to list all occurrences of the word Sales in the workbook. You should find 16 occurrences of the word Sales. Click each occurrence.

(continued)

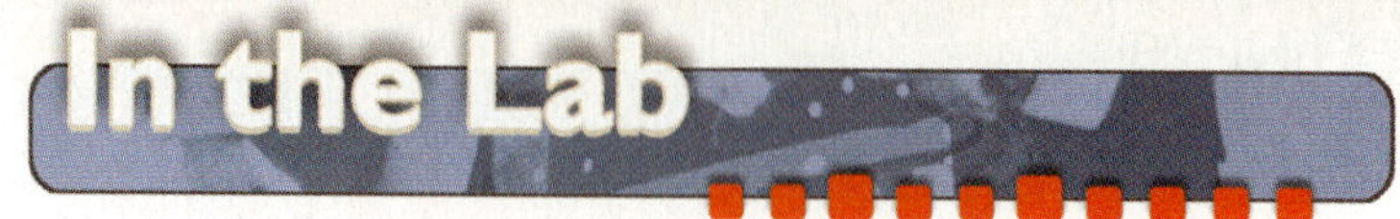

Using a Template to Create a Multiple-Sheet Workbook *(continued)*

2. Click Match entire cell contents in the Find dialog box. (If necessary, click the Options button to display the desired check box.) Use the Find command to find all occurrences of the word Sales. You should find four occurrences.
3. Use the Find command to find all occurrences of the word sales in italics. Deselect the Match entire cell contents check box.
4. Use the Replace command to replace the word, Web, with the acronym, WWW, on all four sheets. Print all four sheets. Do not save the workbook.

3 Returning Real-Time Stock Quotes to the Stock Portfolio Worksheet

Problem: You belong to the Golden Stock club, which has been investing in the stock market for the past several years. As secretary of the club, you maintain a summary of the club's stock market investments in an Excel workbook (Figure 6-100a). Each day you go through the Business section of the newspaper and manually update the current prices in column G to determine the value of the club's equities. You recently heard about the Web query capabilities of Excel and have decided to use them to update the club's stock portfolio automatically.

Instructions: Perform the following steps to have Web queries automatically update the current price in column G and the major indices in the range B12:B15 of Figure 6-100a.

1. Start Excel and open the workbook Lab 6-3 Stock Portfolio Basics on the Data Disk. After reviewing the worksheet, you should notice that it lacks current prices in column G and the major indices in the range B12:B15.
2. Click Sheet2 and then select cell A1. Select Data on the menu bar, point to Import External Data, and then click Import Data on the Import External Data submenu. When Excel displays the Select Data Source dialog box, double-click MSN Money Central Investor Stock Quotes. When Excel displays the Import Data dialog box, click the OK button. When the Enter Parameter Value dialog box appears, click the Portfolio tab at the bottom of the screen and drag through the range B3:B10. Click the Use this value/reference for future refreshes check box to select it. The Enter Parameter Value dialog box should display as shown in Figure 6-100b. Click the OK button. The Web query should return a worksheet with real-time stock quotes to the Stock Quotes worksheet similar to the one shown in Figure 6-100c. Rename the Sheet2 tab Stock Quotes.
3. Click the Portfolio tab. Click cell G3. Type = (equal sign). Click the Stock Quotes tab. Click cell D4 (the last price for Boeing). Press the ENTER key. Use the fill handle to copy cell G3 on the Portfolio sheet to the range G4:G10. You now should have current prices for the stock portfolio that are the same as the last prices on the Stock Quotes worksheet in column D. Select cell A16 and then save the workbook using the file name, Lab 6-3 Golden Stock Club Portfolio.
4. Click Sheet3 and then select cell A1. Click Data on the menu bar, point to Import External Data, and then click Import Data on the Import External Data submenu. When Excel displays the Select Data Source dialog box, double-click MSN Money Central Investor Major Indices. When the Import Data dialog box appears, click the OK button. Rename the Sheet3 tab Major Indices. The worksheet should be similar to the one shown in Figure 6-100d.

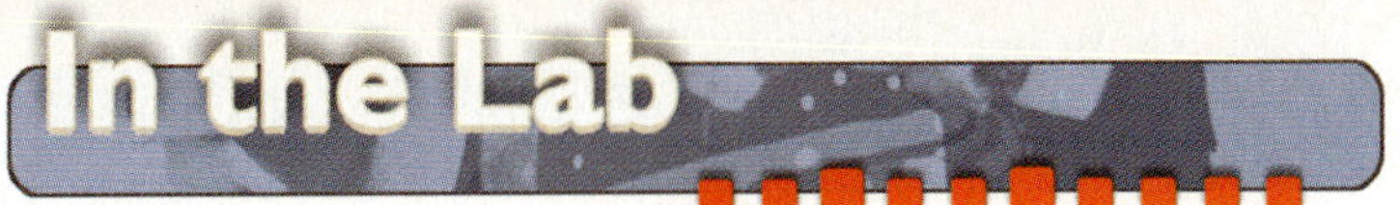

(a) Portfolio Worksheet

Microsoft Excel - Lab 6-3 Golden Stock Club Portfolio

Golden Stock Club Portfolio

Stock	Symbol	Date Acquired	Shares	Initial Price	Initial Cost	Current Price	Current Value	Gain/Loss	% Gain/Lost
Boeing	BA	02/12/01	300	$29.50	$8,850.00	$35.75	$10,725.00	$1,875.00	21.19%
IBM	IBM	12/21/99	500	82.00	41,000.00	83.95	41,975.00	975.00	2.38%
Intel	INTC	09/13/02	325	18.90	6,142.50	22.14	7,195.50	1,053.00	17.14%
Microsoft	MSFT	06/12/02	700	21.40	14,980.00	24.99	17,493.00	2,513.00	16.78%
SBC Comm	SBC	12/14/01	2,000	35.00	70,000.00	26.02	52,040.00	-17,960.00	-25.66%
Oracle	ORCL	12/01/99	500	6.25	3,125.00	13.33	6,665.00	3,540.00	113.28%
Pfizer	PFE	06/12/02	500	26.75	13,375.00	33.52	16,760.00	3,385.00	25.31%
Wal-Mart	WMT	07/14/99	950	29.15	27,692.50	55.03	52,278.50	24,586.00	88.78%
Total					$185,165.00		$205,132.00	$19,967.00	10.78%

Index	Value
Dow Jones	9196.55
Nasdaq	1653.62
Russell 2000	456.74
DJ Trans	2505.29

Portfolio | Stock Quotes | Major Indices

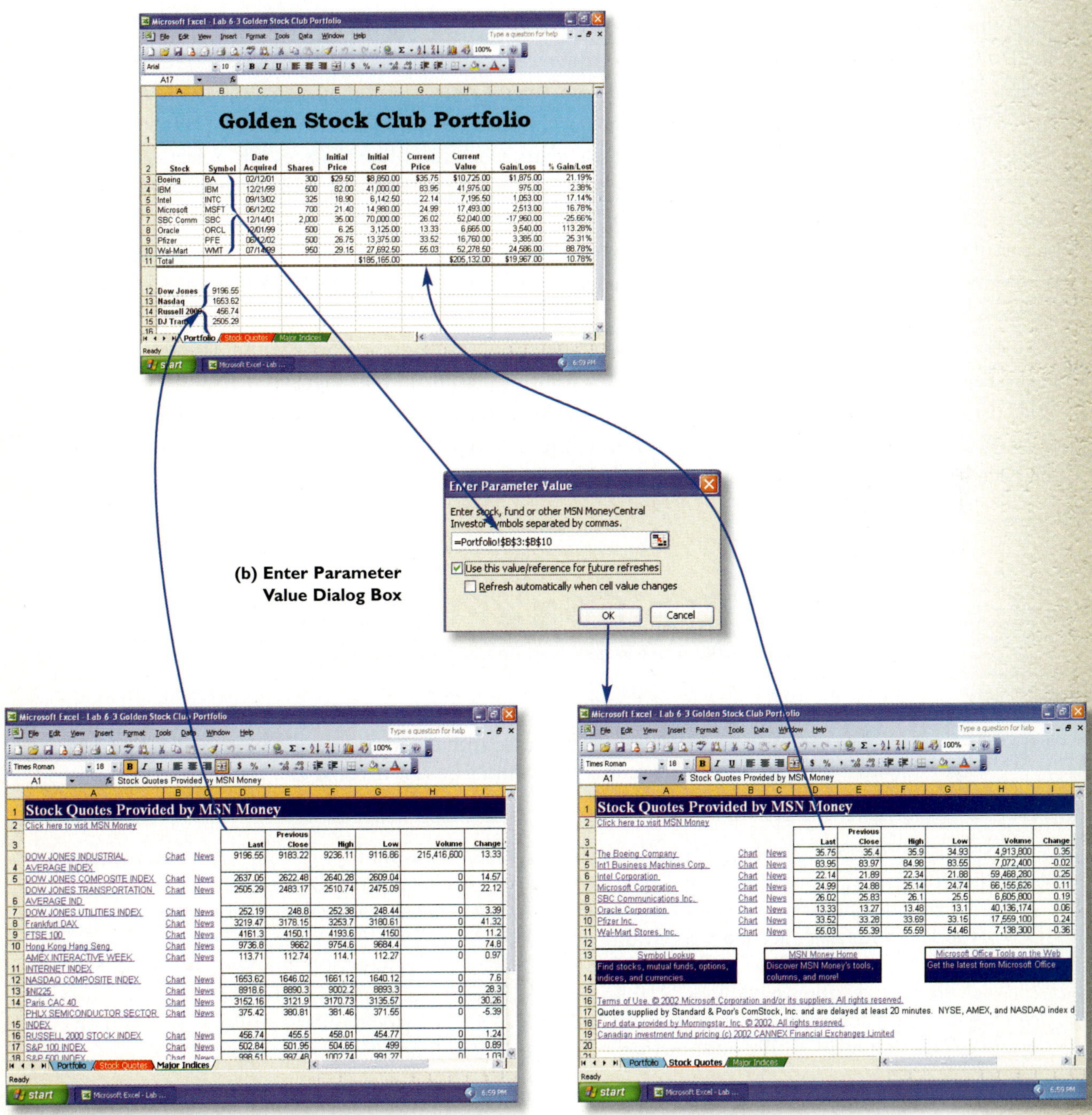

(b) Enter Parameter Value Dialog Box

Enter Parameter Value

Enter stock, fund or other MSN MoneyCentral Investor symbols separated by commas.

=Portfolio!$B$3:$B$10

☑ Use this value/reference for future refreshes

☐ Refresh automatically when cell value changes

OK | Cancel

(c) Real-Time Stock Quotes

Microsoft Excel - Lab 6-3 Golden Stock Club Portfolio

Stock Quotes Provided by MSN Money

Click here to visit MSN Money

			Last	Previous Close	High	Low	Volume	Change
The Boeing Company	Chart	News	35.75	35.4	35.9	34.93	4,913,800	0.35
Int'l Business Machines Corp.	Chart	News	83.95	83.97	84.98	83.55	7,072,400	-0.02
Intel Corporation	Chart	News	22.14	21.89	22.34	21.88	59,468,280	0.25
Microsoft Corporation	Chart	News	24.99	24.88	25.14	24.74	66,155,626	0.11
SBC Communications Inc.	Chart	News	26.02	25.83	26.1	25.5	6,605,800	0.19
Oracle Corporation	Chart	News	13.33	13.27	13.48	13.1	40,136,174	0.06
Pfizer Inc.	Chart	News	33.52	33.28	33.69	33.15	17,559,100	0.24
Wal-Mart Stores, Inc.	Chart	News	55.03	55.39	55.59	54.46	7,138,300	-0.36

Symbol Lookup — Find stocks, mutual funds, options, indices, and currencies.

MSN Money Home — Discover MSN Money's tools, columns, and more!

Microsoft Office Tools on the Web — Get the latest from Microsoft Office

Terms of Use. © 2002 Microsoft Corporation and/or its suppliers. All rights reserved.

Quotes supplied by Standard & Poor's ComStock, Inc. and are delayed at least 20 minutes. NYSE, AMEX, and NASDAQ index d

Fund data provided by Morningstar, Inc. © 2002. All rights reserved.

Canadian investment fund pricing (c) 2002 CANNEX Financial Exchanges Limited

(d) Major Indices

Microsoft Excel - Lab 6-3 Golden Stock Club Portfolio

Stock Quotes Provided by MSN Money

Click here to visit MSN Money

			Last	Previous Close	High	Low	Volume	Change
DOW JONES INDUSTRIAL AVERAGE INDEX	Chart	News	9196.55	9183.22	9236.11	9116.86	215,416,600	13.33
DOW JONES COMPOSITE INDEX	Chart	News	2637.05	2622.48	2640.28	2609.04	0	14.57
DOW JONES TRANSPORTATION AVERAGE IND	Chart	News	2505.29	2483.17	2510.74	2475.09	0	22.12
DOW JONES UTILITIES INDEX	Chart	News	252.19	248.8	252.38	248.44	0	3.39
Frankfurt DAX	Chart	News	3219.47	3178.15	3253.7	3180.61	0	41.32
FTSE 100	Chart	News	4161.3	4150.1	4193.6	4150	0	11.2
Hong Kong Hang Seng	Chart	News	9736.8	9662	9754.6	9684.4	0	74.8
AMEX INTERACTIVE WEEK INTERNET INDEX	Chart	News	113.71	112.74	114.1	112.27	0	0.97
NASDAQ COMPOSITE INDEX	Chart	News	1653.62	1646.02	1661.12	1640.12	0	7.6
$NI225	Chart	News	8918.6	8890.3	9002.2	8893.3	0	28.3
Paris CAC 40	Chart	News	3152.16	3121.9	3170.73	3135.57	0	30.26
PHLX SEMICONDUCTOR SECTOR INDEX	Chart	News	375.42	380.81	381.46	371.55	0	-5.39
RUSSELL 2000 STOCK INDEX	Chart	News	456.74	455.5	458.01	454.77	0	1.24
S&P 100 INDEX	Chart	News	502.84	501.95	504.65	499	0	0.89
S&P 500 INDEX	Chart	News	998.51	997.48	1002.74	991.27	0	1.03

FIGURE 6-100

(continued)

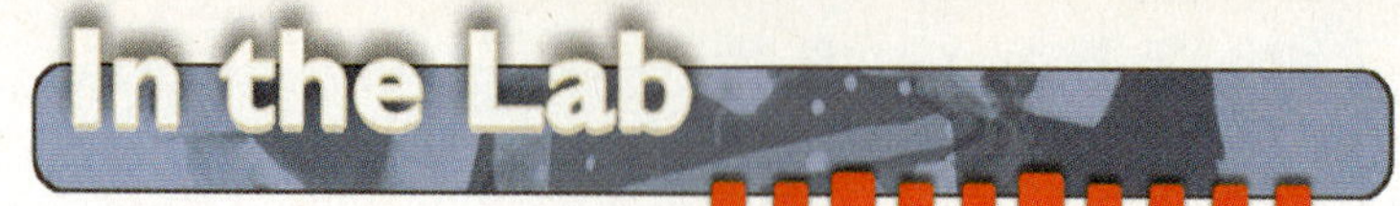

Returning Real-Time Stock Quotes to the Stock Portfolio Worksheet *(continued)*

5. Click the Portfolio tab. Select cell B12. Type = (equal sign). Click the Major Indices tab. Select cell D4 (the last Dow Jones Industrial Index). Press the ENTER key. Select cell B13. Type = (equal sign). Click the Major Indices tab. Select cell D12 (the last NASDAQ Combined Composite Index). Press the ENTER key. Select cell B14. Type = (equal sign). Click the Major Indices tab. Select cell D16 (the last Russell 2000 Stock Index). Press the ENTER key. Select cell B15. Type = (equal sign). Click the Major Indices tab. Select cell D6 (the last Dow Jones Transportation Index). Press the ENTER key. Select cell A16 and then save the workbook using the file name, Lab 6-3 Golden Stock Club Portfolio.
6. Select all three worksheets. Use the Page Setup command on the File menu to enter your name, course, computer laboratory assignment (Lab 6-3), date, and instructor name as the header. Add a page number as the footer. Change the top margin to 1.5 inches.
7. Print the three worksheets using the Black and white option in landscape orientation. Use the Fit to option in the Page sheet in the Page Setup dialog box to print the sheets on one page.
8. With the Portfolio worksheet active, click View on the menu bar, point to Toolbars, and then click External Data on the Toolbars submenu. If necessary, drag the External Data toolbar to the lower-right corner. Click the Refresh All button on the External Data toolbar. Print the three worksheets.

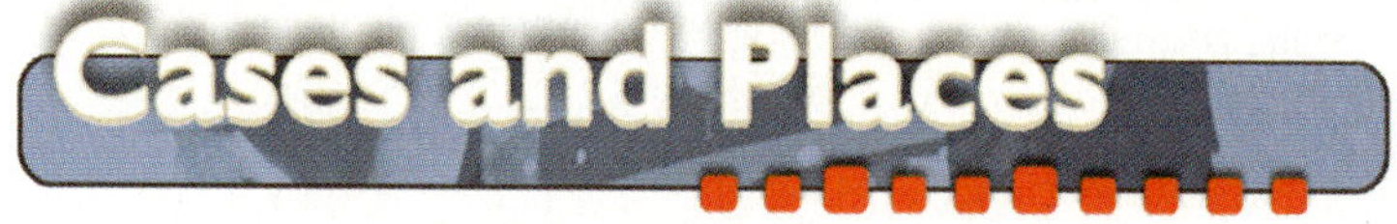

The difficulty of these case studies varies:
■ are the least difficult and ■■ are more difficult. The last exercise is a group exercise.

1 ■ Specialty Toys, Inc. is a Paris-based company that sells high-end toys globally. After launching its Web site five years ago, the company has attracted so many clients from Germany that the owners opened a shop in Munich. The Paris and Munich shops' assets last year, respectively, were: cash $675,436 and $425,375; accounts receivable $357,019 and $235,000; marketable securities $567,340 and $196,500; inventory $967,345 and $275,000; and equipment $89,500 and $45,500. The liabilities for each store were: notes payable $1,250,456 and $256,000; accounts payable $125,375 and $198,450; and income tax payable $67,500 and $132,000. The stockholders' equity was: common stock $971,170 and $435,000 and retained earnings $242,139 and $155,925.

Use the concepts and techniques presented in this project to design a template as a balance worksheet to reflect the figures above. Include totals for assets, liabilities, stockholders' equity, and liabilities and stockholders' equity. Use the template to create a balance worksheet for the Paris store, the Munich store, and the consolidated balance worksheet for the corporation.

Cases and Places

2 J.D. Fault, the local high school tennis coach, has jotted down notes on three players (Table 6-14) based on a recent match. Create a template that Coach Fault can use to evaluate her players. Include each statistic, the percentage of winners (winner / total shots) and the percentage of errors (errors / total shots), rounded to the nearest ten-thousandths place. Also include what Coach Fault calls the *success rate* (percentage of winners – percentage of errors). Use the template to develop a worksheet for each player and the team. Summarize the results on a team worksheet. Compute the percentages on the Team worksheet in a manner similar to the player's worksheets. Add appropriate comments, headers, footers, and margins.

Table 6-14 Summary of Player Statistics

Rachel Rally	Total Shots	Winners	Errors
Forehand	235	76	38
Backhand	278	68	36
Volley	30	3	18
Service	175	87	25
Service Return	198	56	35
Lenny Love	**Total Shots**	**Winners**	**Errors**
Forehand	275	98	43
Backhand	175	65	25
Volley	56	38	17
Service	145	45	0
Service Return	135	60	14
Hillary Forehand	**Total Shots**	**Winners**	**Errors**
Forehand	225	24	23
Backhand	169	13	26
Volley	135	94	4
Service	92	53	13
Service Return	187	60	34

3 Tupelo's Public Safety store comprises three departments — Fire, Police, and Streets & Sanitation. The departments have submitted figures comparing this year's budget with next year's budget in four categories (Table 6-15). Develop a template that can be used to prepare each department's budget and the Public Safety store's consolidated total budget within one workbook. Include this year's budget, next year's budget, and the variance [(next year's budget – this year's budget) / this year's budget] for each expenditure. Indicate totals where appropriate. Create an embedded chart on the Public Safety store's worksheet comparing the store's expenditures this year and next.

Table 6-15 Tupelo's Public Safety Store Expenditures

	Fire		Police		Streets and Sanitation	
	Next Year	This Year	Next Year	This Year	Next Year	This Year
Equipment	98000	115000	35250	30275	215375	222670
Maintenance	78500	65250	17500	16000	104500	100500
Miscellaneous	38210	36675	39340	32500	37500	22800
Salaries and Benefits	125580	115450	215000	210000	175000	165750

Cases and Places

4 The owner of Specialties for Everyone needs a worksheet representation of the business year-to-year sales data summarized in Table 6-16. Create a worksheet for each year and one for the totals, adding a column for quarter totals and a row for item totals. Include the percentage of annual growth (2002 – 2001) / 2001 on the Company Totals worksheet. Include an out-of-state sales count, which shows the number of sales made over the Web. Add an embedded 3-D Pie chart to the Company Totals worksheet that shows the sales contribution of each quarter to the two-year sales total. Include an appropriate header identifying yourself and the workbook. Print the worksheets centered on the page in landscape orientation with page numbers. Add a comment to one of the cells on the company worksheet that includes a cited quote from an article obtained from the Web. Create and apply a style to the column headings that include center aligned and 12-point Arial Rounded MT Bold red, bold italic font.

Table 6-16 Specialties for Everyone Year-to-Year Sales Data

	Qtr	Consumable	Non-Consumable	Out of State
2005	1	515757	223019	5065
	2	600125	256010	7509
	3	725813	275019	10256
	4	852900	370135	15913
2004	1	235198	123018	560
	2	312780	178193	725
	3	324800	192345	1356
	4	412513	201871	2004

5 **Working Together** Complete the exercise outlined in Cases and Places 3 using separate workbooks for each department, rather than a single workbook. As a team, create an appropriate template. Assign each member of the team one or more of the four required workbooks to build using the template. After the workbooks have been created, use the concepts and techniques presented in this project to consolidate the data by creating a workspace and linking the workbooks. Test the linkage to the store workbook by changing values in the department workbooks.

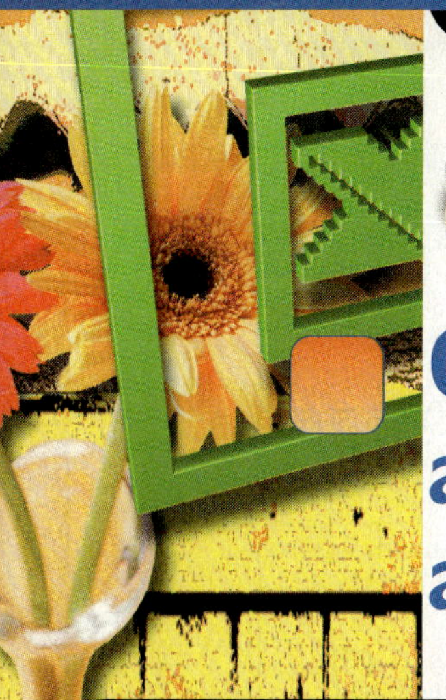

MICROSOFT Office Excel 2003

Object Linking and Embedding (OLE) and Web Discussions

CASE PERSPECTIVE

Hannah Wells is the national sales manager for Buds and Blooms, a company that sells flower arrangements nationwide. The company has five sales units: 3rd Party, Telesales, Direct Mail, Outlets, and the Web. Each sales unit has a manager who reports directly to Hannah.

Every Monday morning, Hannah sends a memorandum that summarizes the previous week's sales by sales unit by office to the sales unit managers. She uses Word to produce the memorandum, which includes a table of the previous week's sales.

Hannah recently learned of the object linking and embedding (OLE) capabilities of Microsoft Office and wants to use them to create the basic memorandum (Figure 1a on the next page) using Word and maintain the previous week's sales on an Excel worksheet (Figure 1b on the next page). Every Monday morning, she envisions sending out the Word document with the updated worksheet at the bottom (Figure 1c on the next page). By linking the Excel worksheet to the Word document, Hannah can update the worksheet each week, modify the date in the memorandum, and then print and distribute a hard copy of the memorandum to the sales unit managers. She also wants to publish the memorandum to the Web, so that the field sales representatives can comment on the memorandum using a discussion server.

Hannah has asked you to handle the details of linking the Excel worksheet to the memorandum created in Word and then publishing the Word document to a discussion server.

As you read through this Integration Feature, you will learn how to use object linking and embedding to copy objects between applications and how to use a discussion server.

Objectives

You will have mastered the material in this project when you can:

- Differentiate among the three methods of copying objects between applications
- Link an Excel worksheet and chart to a Word document
- Edit a linked Excel workbook
- Save and access an Office document using a discussion server

Introduction

With Microsoft Office, you can copy parts of documents or entire documents, called **objects**, from one application into another application. For example, you can copy a worksheet created in Excel and paste it as an object into a document created in Word. In this case, the workbook in Excel is called the **source document** (copied from), and the document in Word is called the **destination document** (copied to). Copying objects among applications can be accomplished in three ways: (1) copy and paste; (2) copy and embed; and (3) copy and link.

All of the Microsoft Office applications allow you to use these three methods to copy objects among applications. The first method uses the Copy and Paste buttons. The latter two methods use the Paste Special command on the Edit menu and are referred to as **object linking and embedding**, or **OLE**. Table 1 on page EX 467 summarizes the differences among the three methods.

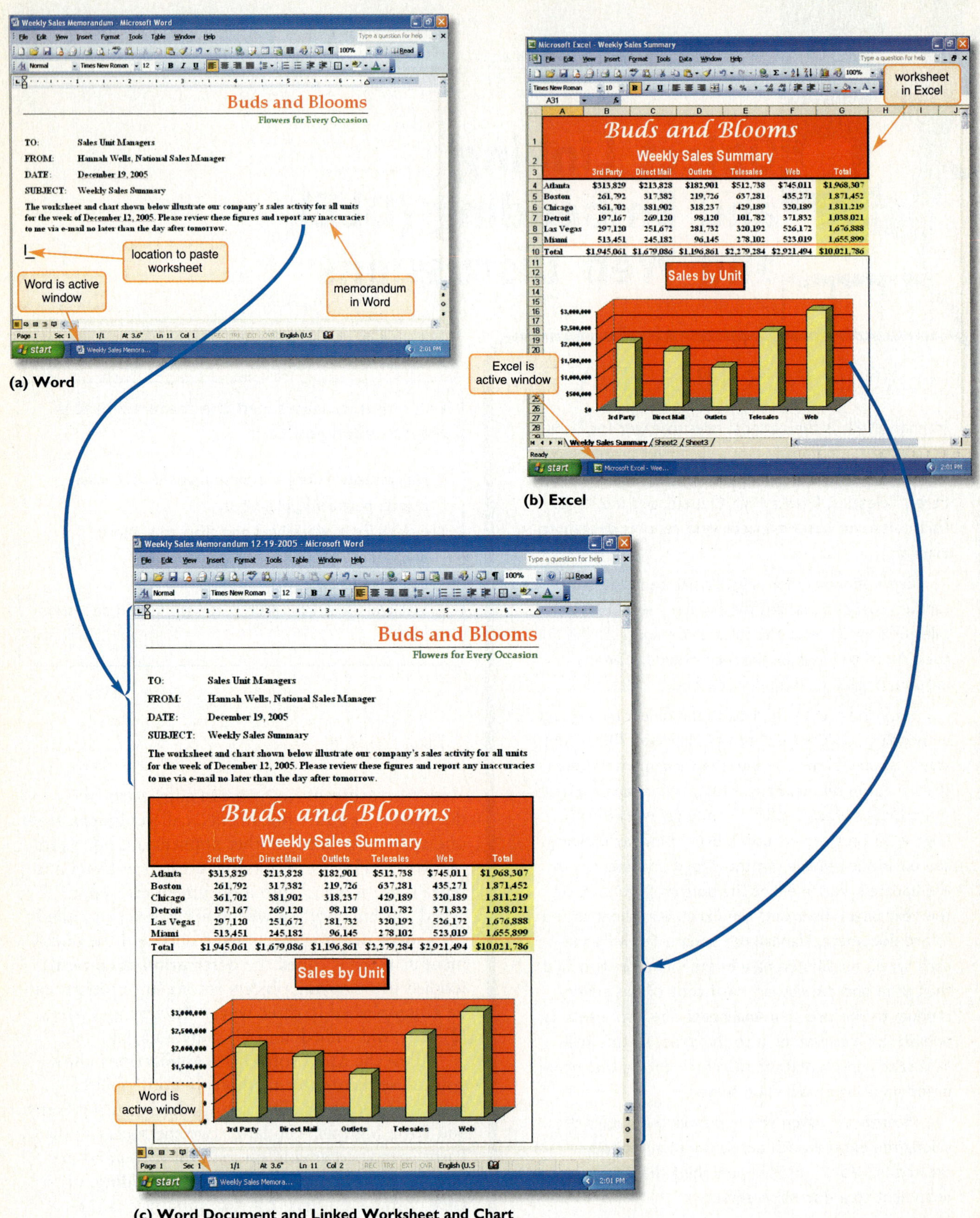

(a) Word

(b) Excel

(c) Word Document and Linked Worksheet and Chart

FIGURE 1

Table 1 Three Methods of Copying Objects among Applications

METHOD	CHARACTERISTICS
Copy and paste	The source document becomes part of the destination document. The object may be edited, but the editing features are limited to those in the destination application. An Excel worksheet pasted to a Word document becomes a Word table. If changes are made to values in the Word table, any original Excel formulas are not recalculated.
Copy and embed	The source document becomes part of the destination document. The object may be edited in the destination application using source editing features. An Excel worksheet embedded in a Word document remains a worksheet in Word. If changes are made to values on the worksheet with Word active, Excel formulas will be recalculated, but the changes are not updated on the Excel worksheet in the workbook saved on disk. If Excel is used to change values on the worksheet, the changes will not show in the Word document the next time it is opened.
Copy and link	The source document does not become part of the destination document, even though it appears to be part of it. Rather, a link is established between the two documents so that when the Word document is opened, the Excel worksheet appears as part of it. When an attempt is made to edit a linked worksheet in Word, the system activates Excel. If the worksheet is changed in Excel, the changes will show in the Word document the next time it is opened.

Copy and link is the preferred method to use when an object is likely to change and those changes should be reflected in the source document. For example, by linking all or part of a worksheet (the object) to a memorandum (the source document), the latest changes to the worksheet will appear in the memorandum each time it is opened in Word. The copy and link method also should be used if the object is large, such as a video clip or sound clip.

More About

Scrap

You can store objects, such as worksheets and pictures, on the desktop, rather than using the Office Clipboard. When you use this technique, the objects are called scrap. To accomplish this task, part of the desktop must be visible behind the window of the source application. Next, point to a border of the object in the source application and right-drag it onto the desktop. When the shortcut menu displays, click Create Scrap Here. Once the object is placed on the desktop, Windows displays it as an icon. Next, activate the destination document and then drag the icon from the desktop to the destination document and drop it where you want it inserted. To delete scrap from the desktop, right-click the scrap icon and then click Delete on the shortcut menu.

Opening a Word Document and an Excel Workbook

The first step in linking the Excel worksheet and chart to the Word document is to open both the document in Word and the workbook in Excel as shown in the steps on the next page.

To Open a Word Document and an Excel Workbook

1

- **Insert the Data Disk in drive A, click the Start button on the Windows taskbar, point to All Programs on the Start menu, and then click Open Office Document on the All Programs submenu.**
- **When Windows displays the Open Office Document dialog box, click the Look in box arrow, click 3½ Floppy (A:), and then double-click the Word file name, Weekly Sales Memorandum, in the list.**
- **If necessary, click the Normal View button in the lower-left corner of the screen.**
- **Click the blank line at the bottom of the document.**

The Word window is opened and Word displays the Weekly Sales Memorandum in Normal view (Figure 2).

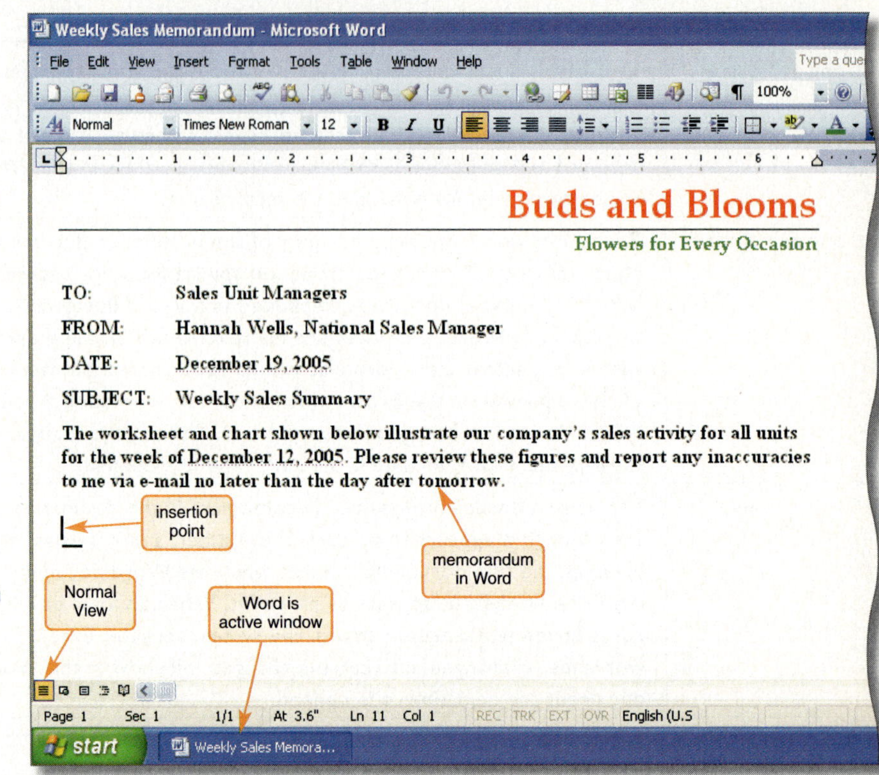

Weekly Sales Memorandum - Microsoft Word
Buds and Blooms
Flowers for Every Occasion
TO: Sales Unit Managers
FROM: Hannah Wells, National Sales Manager
DATE: December 19, 2005
SUBJECT: Weekly Sales Summary
The worksheet and chart shown below illustrate our company's sales activity for all units for the week of December 12, 2005. Please review these figures and report any inaccuracies to me via e-mail no later than the day after tomorrow.
insertion point
memorandum in Word
Normal View
Word is active window
Page 1 Sec 1 1/1 At 3.6" Ln 11 Col 1
start
Weekly Sales Memora...

FIGURE 2

2

- **Click the Start button on the Windows taskbar, point to All Programs on the Start menu, and then click Open Office Document on the All Programs submenu.**
- **When Windows displays the Open Office Document dialog box, click the Look in box arrow, click 3½ Floppy (A:), and then double-click the Excel file name, Weekly Sales Summary, in the list.**

The Excel window is opened and Excel displays the Weekly Sales Summary workbook (Figure 3). At this point, Word is inactive. Excel is the active window, as shown on the Windows taskbar.

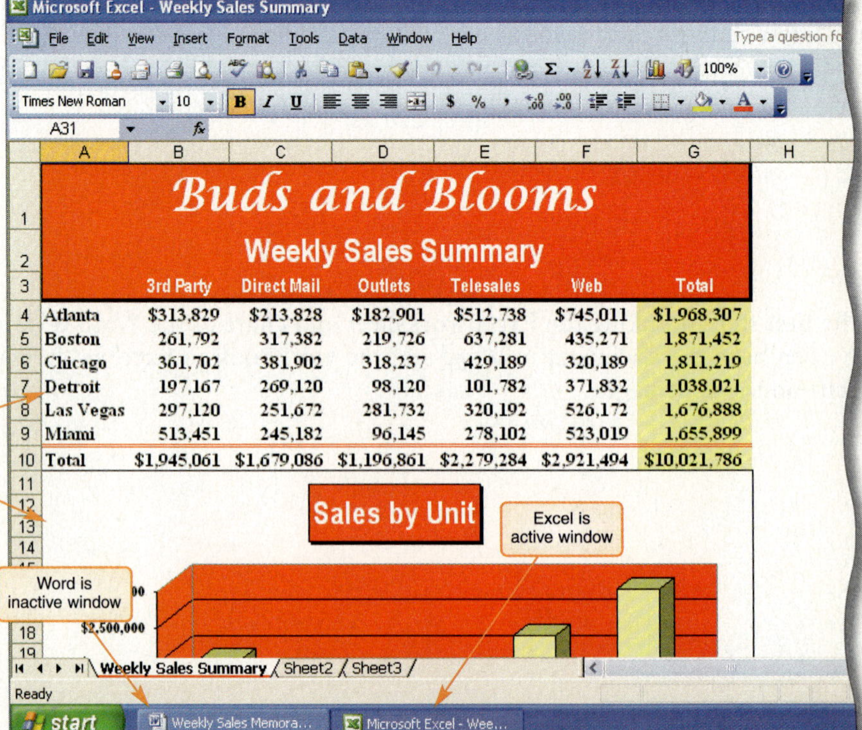

	3rd Party	Direct Mail	Outlets	Telesales	Web	Total
Atlanta	$313,829	$213,828	$182,901	$512,738	$745,011	$1,968,307
Boston	261,792	317,382	219,726	637,281	435,271	1,871,452
Chicago	361,702	381,902	318,237	429,189	320,189	1,811,219
Detroit	197,167	269,120	98,120	101,782	371,832	1,038,021
Las Vegas	297,120	251,672	281,732	320,192	526,172	1,676,888
Miami	513,451	245,182	96,145	278,102	523,019	1,655,899
Total	$1,945,061	$1,679,086	$1,196,861	$2,279,284	$2,921,494	$10,021,786

FIGURE 3

With both Word and Excel open, clicking the appropriate program button on the Windows taskbar switches between the applications.

Linking an Excel Worksheet and Chart to a Word Document

With both applications running, the next step is to link the worksheet and chart (range A1:G28) on the Weekly Sales Summary sheet in the Excel workbook to the Word document as shown in the following steps.

To Link an Excel Worksheet and Chart to a Word Document

1

- **With the Excel window active, select the range A1:G28 on the Weekly Sales Summary sheet.**
- **Click the Copy button to copy the selected range to the Office Clipboard.**

Excel displays a marquee around the range A1:G28 on the Weekly Sales Summary sheet (Figure 4), indicating the range A1:G28 is available on the Office Clipboard for pasting purposes.

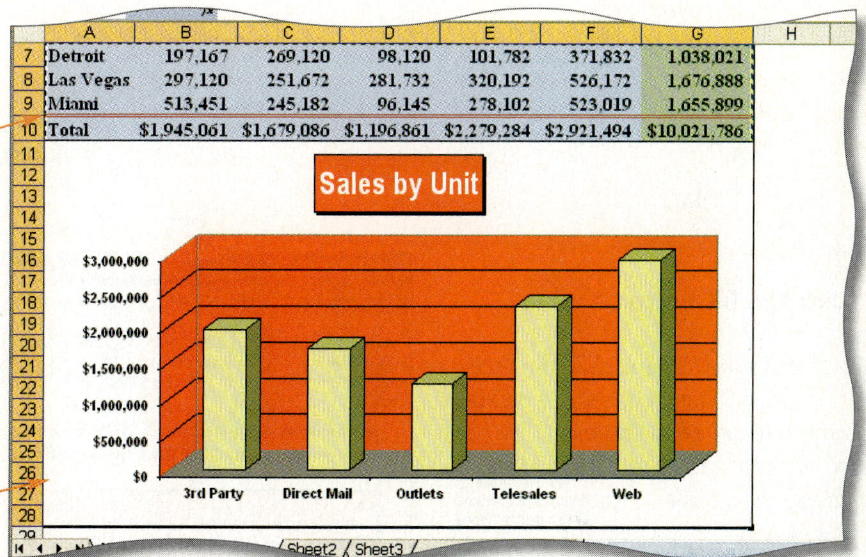

FIGURE 4

2

- **Click the Weekly Sales Memorandum program button on the Windows taskbar to activate the Word window.**
- **Click Edit on the menu bar.**

Word becomes active and displays the Weekly Sales Memorandum document and the Edit menu (Figure 5). The insertion point is positioned at the bottom of the document.

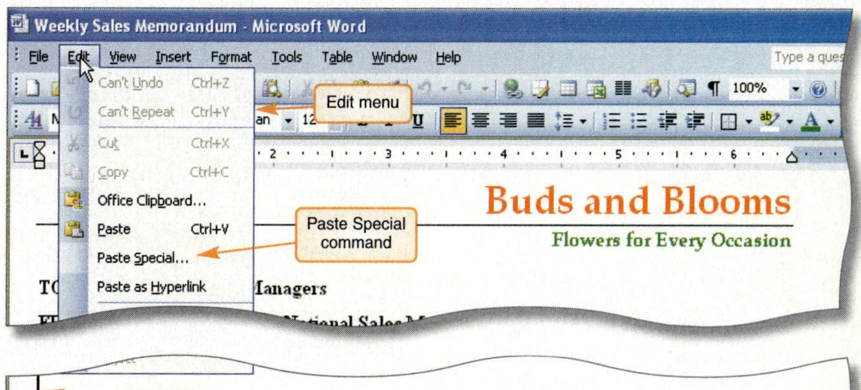

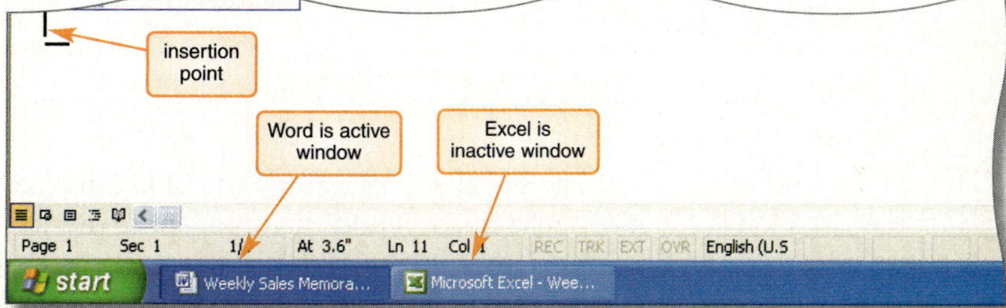

FIGURE 5

3

- **Click Paste Special on the Edit menu.**
- **When the Paste Special dialog box appears, click Paste link in the Source area, and then click Microsoft Office Excel Worksheet Object in the As list.**

Word displays the Paste Special dialog box as shown in Figure 6.

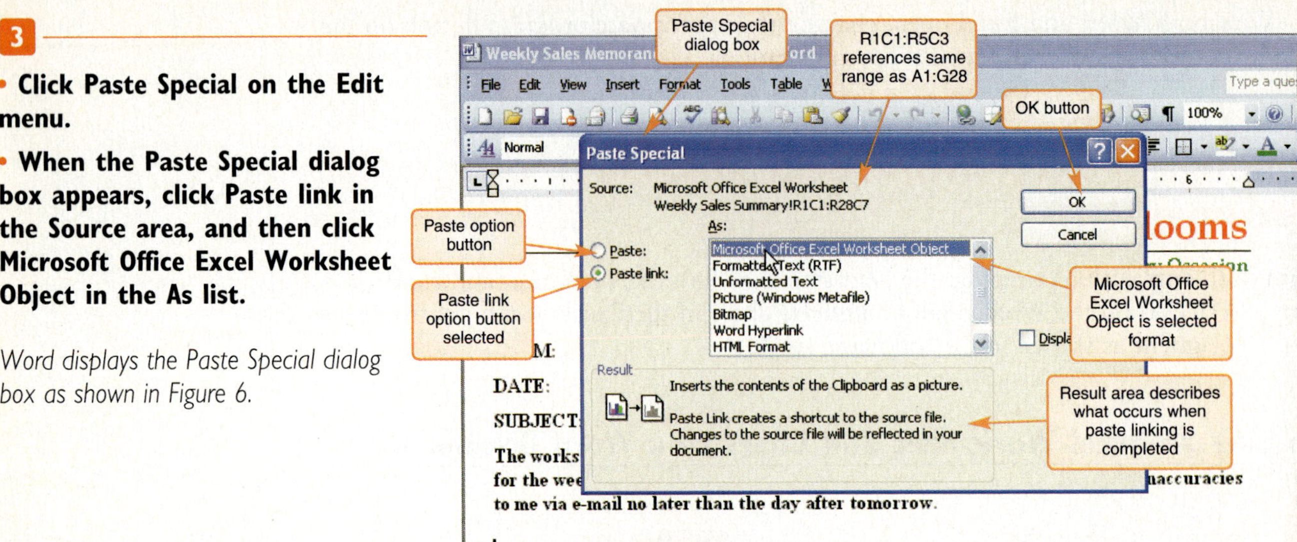

FIGURE 6

4

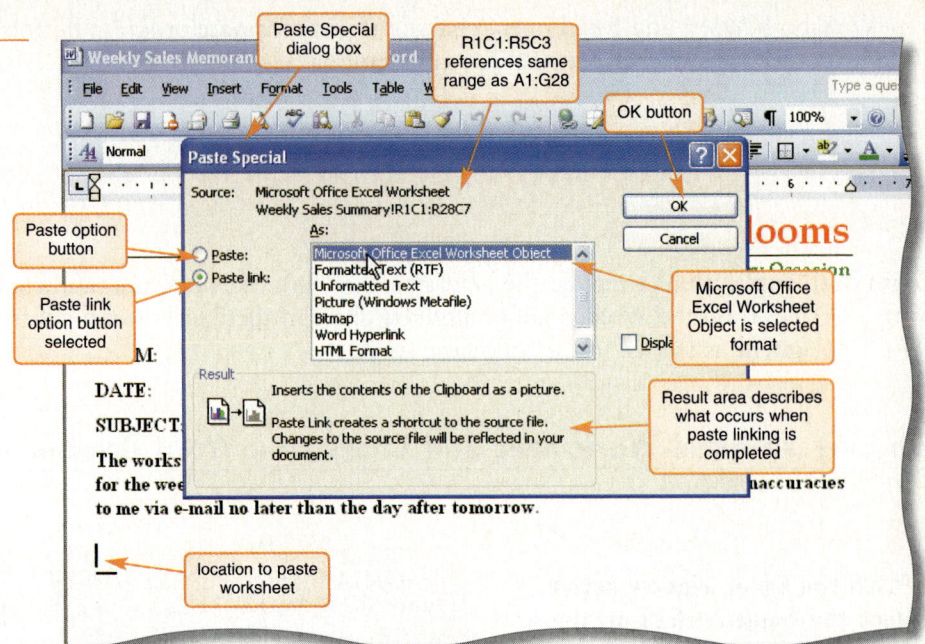

- **Click the OK button.**

Word pastes the range A1:G28 from the Weekly Sales Summary sheet in the Excel workbook to the Word document, beginning at the location of the insertion point (Figure 7).

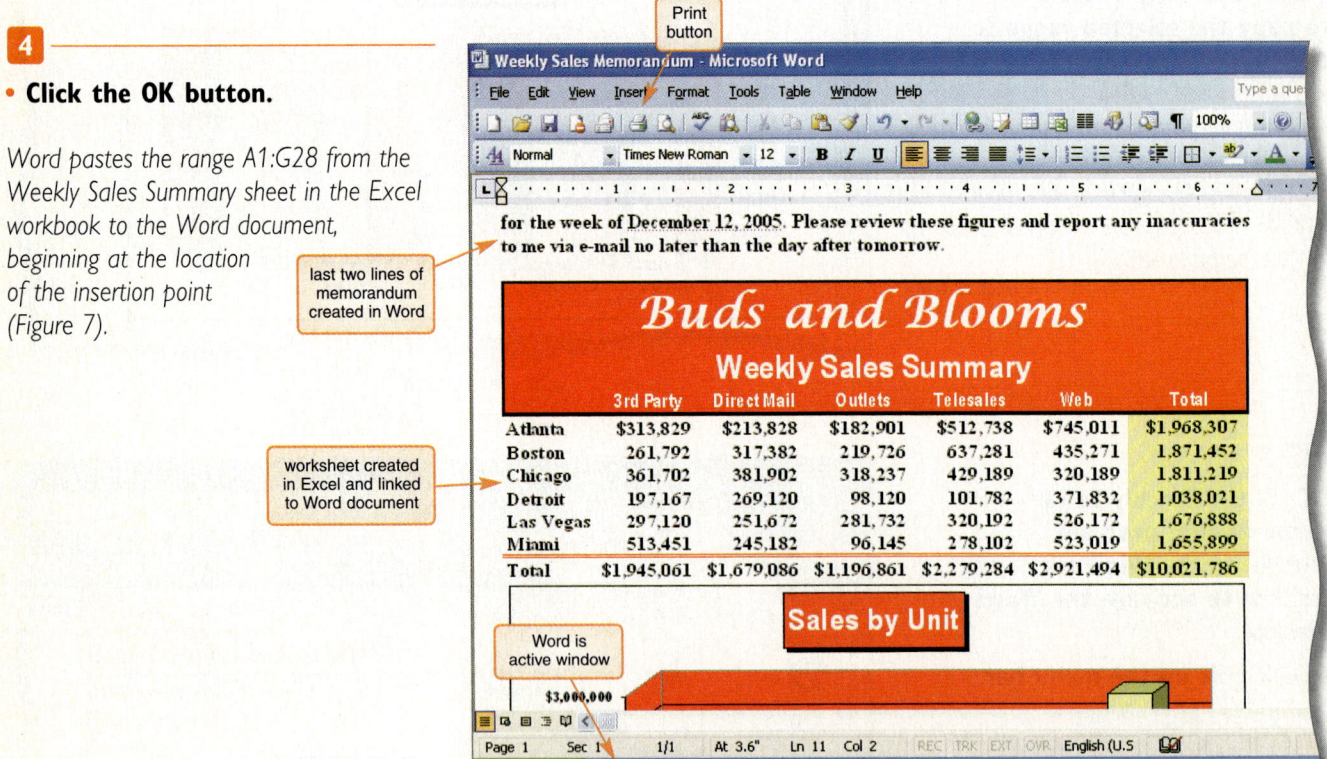

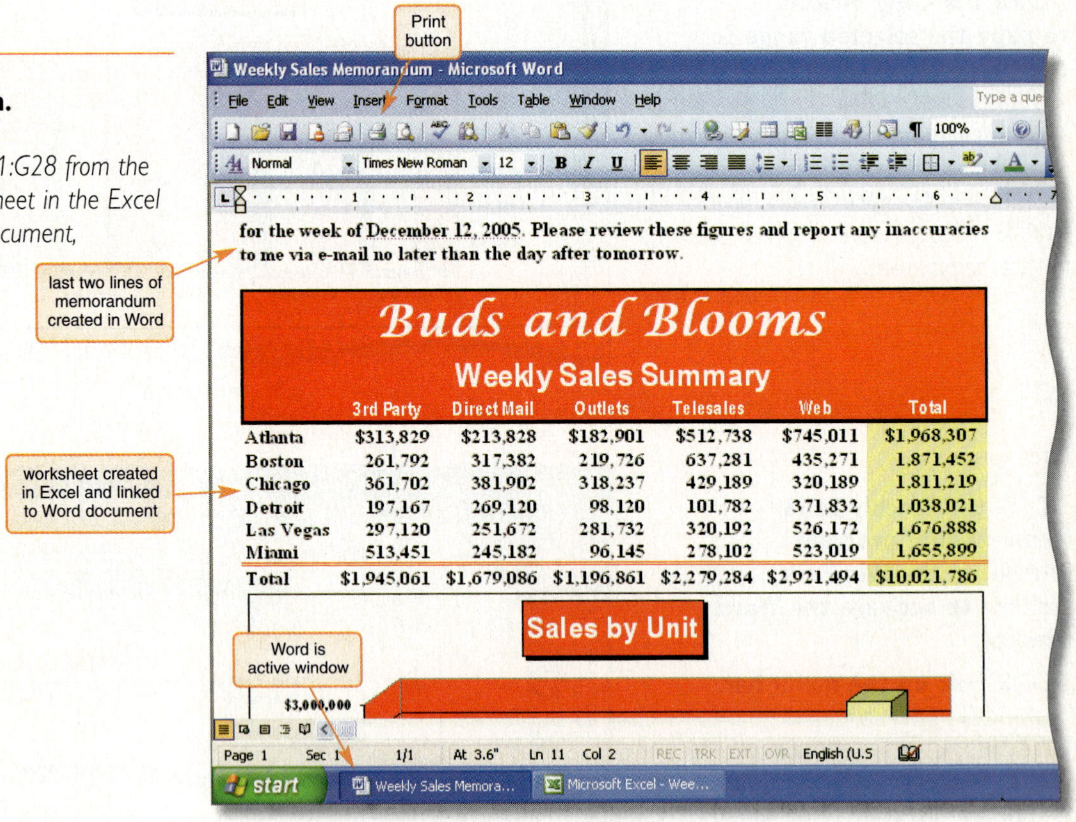

Print button

last two lines of memorandum created in Word

worksheet created in Excel and linked to Word document

Word is active window

for the week of December 12, 2005. Please review these figures and report any inaccuracies to me via e-mail no later than the day after tomorrow.

Buds and Blooms

Weekly Sales Summary

	3rd Party	Direct Mail	Outlets	Telesales	Web	Total
Atlanta	$313,829	$213,828	$182,901	$512,738	$745,011	$1,968,307
Boston	261,792	317,382	219,726	637,281	435,271	1,871,452
Chicago	361,702	381,902	318,237	429,189	320,189	1,811,219
Detroit	197,167	269,120	98,120	101,782	371,832	1,038,021
Las Vegas	297,120	251,672	281,732	320,192	526,172	1,676,888
Miami	513,451	245,182	96,145	278,102	523,019	1,655,899
Total	$1,945,061	$1,679,086	$1,196,861	$2,279,284	$2,921,494	$10,021,786

Sales by Unit

FIGURE 7

The Excel worksheet now is linked to the Word document. If the Word document is saved and then reopened, the worksheet and chart object will appear just as it does in Figure 7. To delete the worksheet and chart, select the worksheet and chart object and then press the DELETE key.

Printing and Saving the Word Document with the Linked Worksheet and Chart

The following steps print and then save the Word document with the linked worksheet and chart.

> **More About**
>
> **Printing**
>
> Because the memo and linked worksheet are colorful, they will require additional time and ink in order to print. To speed up printing and save ink, select the Black and White option on the Sheet tab in the Page Setup dialog box.

To Print and Save the Word Document with the Linked Worksheet and Chart

1

- **With the Word window active, click the Print button on the Standard toolbar.**

The memorandum with the linked worksheet and chart prints as one document (Figure 8).

2

- **Click File on the menu bar and then click Save As.**
- **Type** `Weekly Sales Memorandum 12-19-2005` **in the File name text box.**
- **Click the Save button.**

Word saves the document on the Data Disk in drive A using the file name, Weekly Sales Memorandum 12-19-2005.doc.

3

- **Right-click the Excel program button on the Windows taskbar and then click Close on the shortcut menu.**
- **When Excel displays the Microsoft Excel dialog box, click the No button.**
- **Right-click the Word program button on the Windows taskbar and then click Close on the shortcut menu.**

Buds and Blooms

Flowers for Every Occasion

TO: Sales Unit Managers

FROM: Hannah Wells, National Sales Manager

DATE: December 19, 2005

SUBJECT: Weekly Sales Summary

The worksheet and chart shown below illustrate our company's sales activity for all units for the week of December 12, 2005. Please review these figures and report any inaccuracies to me via e-mail no later than the day after tomorrow.

Buds and Blooms

Weekly Sales Summary

	3rd Party	Direct Mail	Outlets	Telesales	Web	Total
Atlanta	$313,829	$213,828	$182,901	$512,738	$745,011	$1,968,307
Boston	261,792	317,382	219,726	637,281	435,271	1,871,452
Chicago	361,702	381,902	318,237	429,189	320,189	1,811,219
Detroit	197,167	269,120	98,120	101,782	371,832	1,038,021
Las Vegas	297,120	251,672	281,732	320,192	526,172	1,676,888
Miami	513,451	245,182	96,145	278,102	523,019	1,655,899
Total	$1,945,061	$1,679,086	$1,196,861	$2,279,284	$2,921,494	$10,021,786

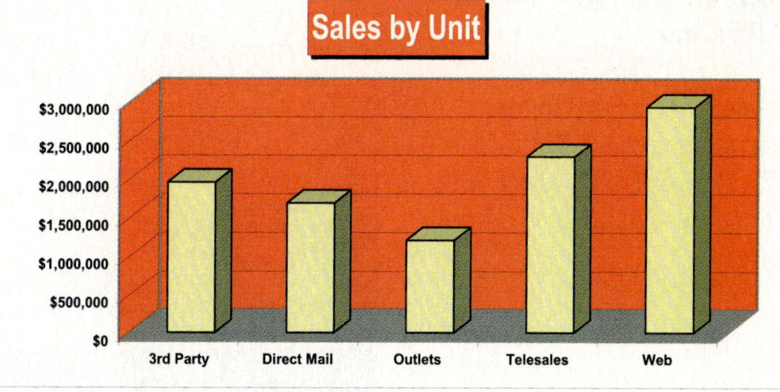

FIGURE 8

More About

Opening a File

You can open a copy of a workbook, rather than the workbook itself, by clicking the arrow to the right of the Open button in the Open dialog box and selecting the Open as Copy command.

If you start Word and then reopen the Weekly Sales Memorandum 12-19-2005 document, the linked object (worksheet and chart) will appear in the document even though Excel is not running. Because Word supports object linking and embedding (OLE), it is capable of displaying the linked portion of the Excel workbook without Excel running.

After the Weekly Sales Memorandum 12-19-2005 document is open, you can double-click the worksheet or chart to edit the data in the linked worksheet. Another alternative is to open the Excel workbook, update the data, and then open the Word document to view the updates.

Editing the Linked Worksheet

This section shows how to edit the data in the linked worksheet using Excel. The following steps change the amount sold by the Telesales unit in Detroit (cell E7) from $101,782 to $500,000.

To Edit the Linked Worksheet

1

- **Start Excel and open the Weekly Sales Summary workbook located on the Data Disk in drive A.**
- **When Excel displays the Weekly Sales Summary workbook, click cell E7 and then enter** 500000 **as the new value for the Telesales unit in Detroit.**
- **Click the Save button on the Standard toolbar and then click the Close button on the right side of the Excel title bar.**

Excel recalculates all formulas in the workbook and redraws the 3-D Bar chart (Figure 9). Excel saves the workbook with the new data on the Data Disk in drive A and then closes.

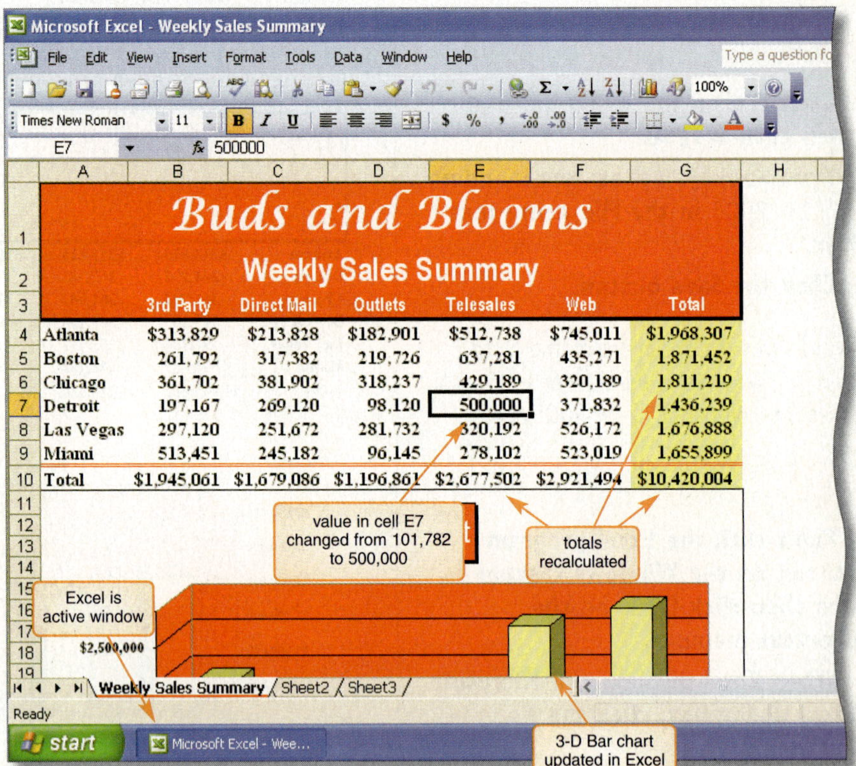

FIGURE 9

2

- **Start Word and open the Weekly Sales Memorandum 12-19-2005 document located on the Data Disk in drive A.**
- **When the Microsoft Office Word dialog box appears, click the Yes button to update links.**

Word displays the Weekly Sales Memorandum 12-19-2005 document. The weekly sales amount for the Telesales unit in Detroit, which was 101,782, now is 500,000. The 3-D Bar chart is updated and new totals appear in row 10 and column G (Figure 10).

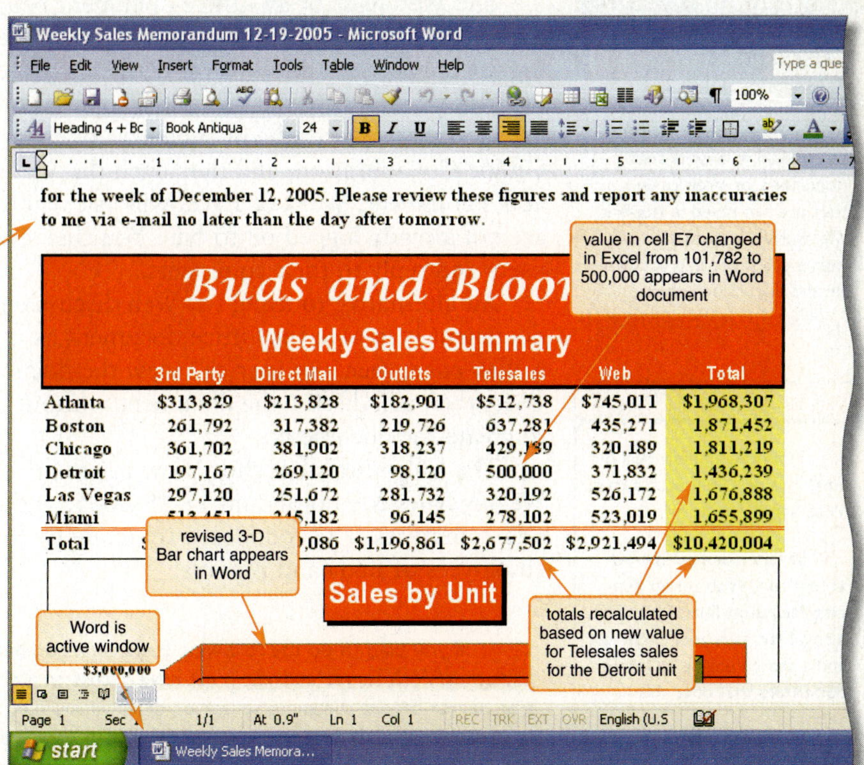

FIGURE 10

3

- **Click the Close button on the right side of the Word title bar.**
- **When the Microsoft Office Word dialog box displays, click the No button.**

As indicated earlier, to make a change to the worksheet data while the Word document containing the linked data appears on the screen, double-click the worksheet or chart. Double-clicking a linked object causes Windows to activate the application in which the linked object was created. You then can edit the object and return to the destination application. Any changes made to the object will appear in the destination document.

More About

Quick Reference

For more information, see the Quick Reference Summary at the back of this book, or visit the Excel 2003 Quick Reference Web page (scsite.com/ex2003/qr).

Saving the Word Document as a Web Page and Using a Discussion Server

The Office applications and Internet Explorer include a **collaborative feature** that allows you and your colleagues to comment on documents online. This feature, called the **Web discussions feature**, allows users to attach comments to a Web page or any Office document. This is especially useful in companies that have teams working on projects. The comments that users attach are stored in a database on a discussion server. A **discussion server** is a server that is running Microsoft's SharePoint Portal Server software.

More About

Discussion Servers

When discussion comments are posted to a workbook, document, or Web page, they are not saved in the files themselves. Instead, the comments are saved in a database on the discussion server.

Q&A

Q: How can an individual or small business gain access to a Web server?

A: Several companies offer access to a Web server running Microsoft SharePoint for a small fee. Use your browser and a search engine to locate companies that offer this service.

The Web page or an Office document being discussed does not have to reside on a discussion server; it can be stored on any Web server. (See Appendix C about saving documents on a Web server.) One way to discuss a Word or Excel document with other users is to save the document on a Web server and then open the document on the Web server. After the document is opened, click Tools on the menu bar, point to Online Collaboration, and then click the Web Discussions command. If you try to add a comment, Word or Excel will ask you to log on to a discussion server if you are not already logged on to one. You then can read the comments entered by other users and reply to their comments.

An alternative to using the Web discussions feature to comment on an Office document is to save the Office document as a Web page. If you save the document as a Web page, then any user can view the document as a Web page using a browser. Users then can discuss the document without a need for the Office application used to create the document.

The following steps show how to create a Web page from the Word document, Weekly Sales Memorandum 12-19-2005, and then use the Web discussions feature to add comments. The comments are made by Rosa Sanchez and Tanya Johnson, employees of Buds and Blooms.

Note: If you plan to do the following steps on a computer, then you must have rights to save a Web page on a Web server and you must have access to a discussion server. The Web server and discussion server can be the same server or different servers. In the following example, the Web server, jquasney1.sbsbeta.iponet.net, is a fictitious Web server and discussion server. See your instructor for details regarding access to a Web server and discussion server.

To Save the Word Document as a Web Page and Use the Web Discussions Feature to Enter a Comment

1

- **If necessary, insert the Data Disk in drive A. Start Word and then open the Word document, Weekly Sales Memorandum 12-19-2005, on the Data Disk.**
- **Click File on the menu bar.**

Word starts, opens the document Weekly Sales Memorandum 12-19-2005, and displays the File menu (Figure 11).

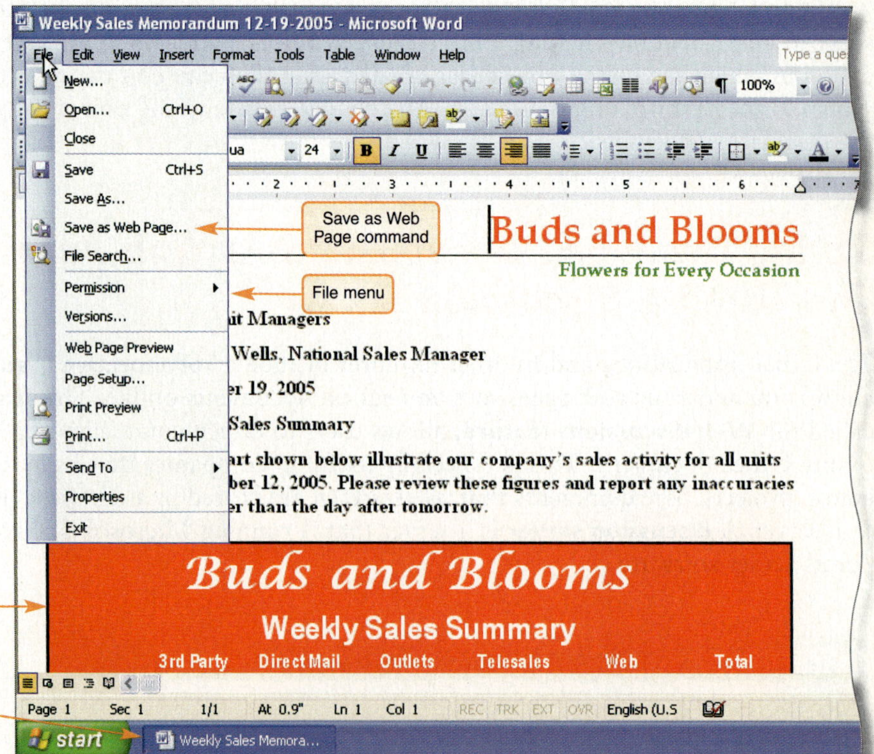

FIGURE 11

2

- **Click Save as Web Page on the File menu.**
- **When Word displays the Save As dialog box, click the Save as type box arrow, and then click Single File Web Page.**
- **Click the My Network Places button in the lower-left corner of the Save As dialog box.**
- **Double-click a Web server you have rights to use.**
- **Click the folder to which you plan to save the Web page.**

Excel displays the Save A dialog box as shown in Figure 12.

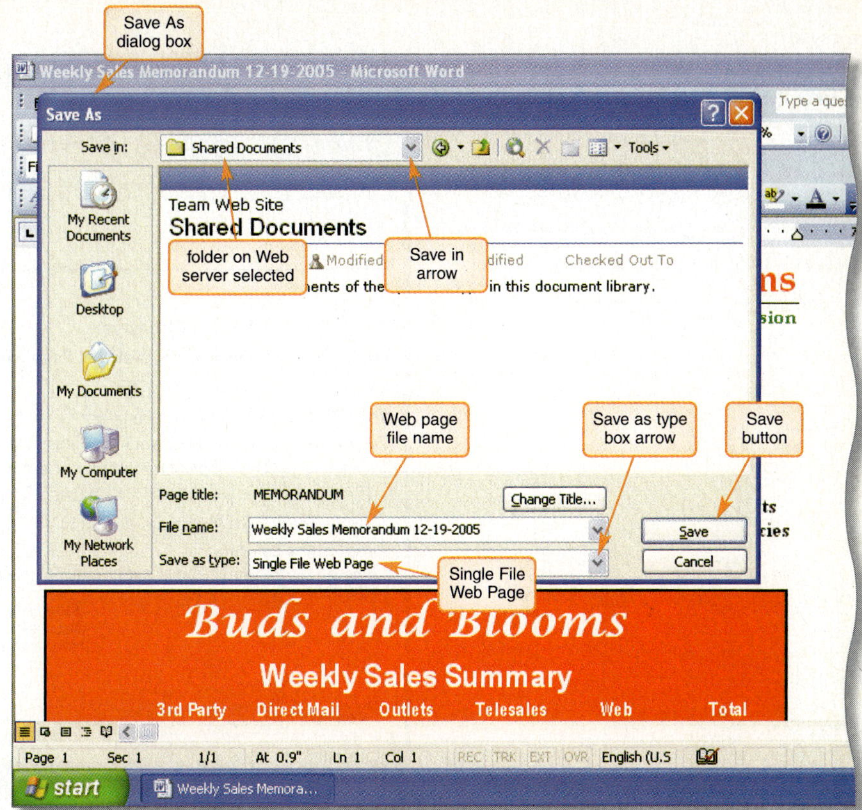

FIGURE 12

3

- **Click the Save button in the Save As dialog box and then click the Close button on the right side of the Word title bar.**
- **View the Web page Weekly Sales Memorandum 12-19-2005.mht in the browser.**
- **Click the Discuss button on the Standard Buttons toolbar.**
- **When the browser displays the Web Discussions toolbar, click the Insert Discussion about this Document button on the Web Discussions toolbar.**
- **When the browser displays the Enter Discussion Text dialog box, enter the discussion subject and discussion text as shown in Figure 13.**

The browser displays the Enter Discussion Text dialog box as shown in Figure 13.

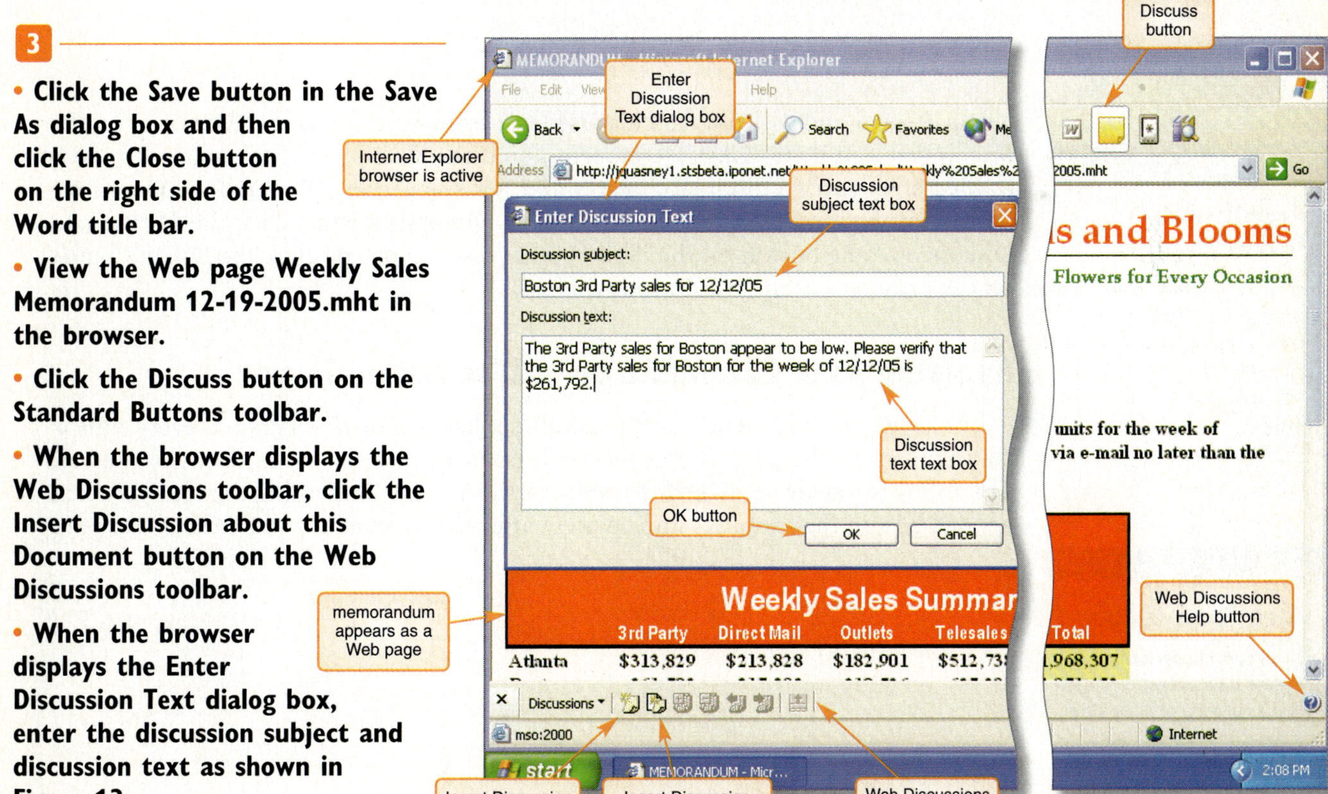

FIGURE 13

• **Click the OK button.**

The browser displays a Discussion pane at the bottom of the browser window (Figure 14). The comment entered in Step 3 appears in the Discussions pane.

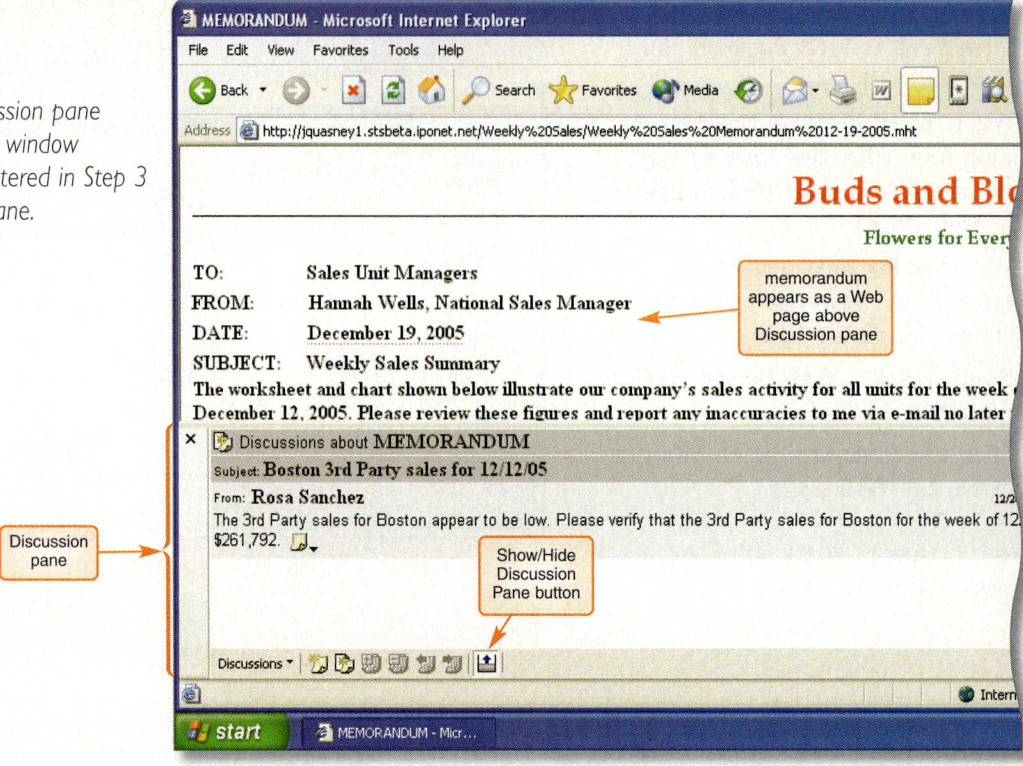

FIGURE 14

In Steps 3 and 4, Rosa Sanchez used her browser to view the Web page on the Web server and then makes a comment about the Web page. The comment is added to the database on a discussion server and is displayed in a **Discussion pane** at the bottom of the browser window. To hide the Discussion pane, click the Show/Hide Discussion Pane button on the Web Discussions toolbar or click the Discuss button on the browser's Standard Buttons toolbar.

More About

SharePoint Portal Server

For more information on Microsoft SharePoint Portal Server software, visit the Excel 2003 More About Web page (scsite.com/ex2003/more) and click SharePoint.

Replying to a Comment on a Discussion Server

Once Rosa's comment is in the database, her comment will show every time a colleague views the same Web page while connected to the same discussion server. The following steps show how to reply to Rosa's comment using the Show a menu of actions button that appears immediately after the comment in the Discussion pane.

More About

Web Discussions

For additional information on Web discussions, click the Type a question for help box on the menu bar and type `Web discussions`.

To Reply to a Comment on a Discussion Server

1

- **With the comment in the Discussion pane as shown in Figure 15, click the Show a menu of actions button that appears after the comment.**

The shortcut menu appears as shown in Figure 15.

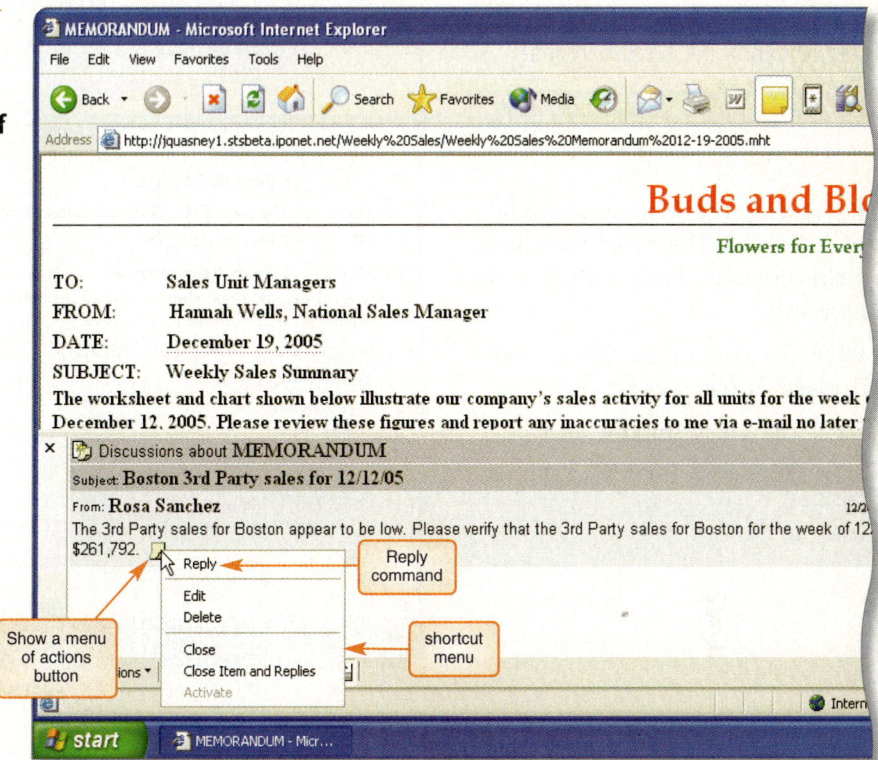

FIGURE 15

2

- **Click Reply on the shortcut menu.**
- **When the browser displays the Enter Discussion Text dialog box, enter the discussion text as shown in Figure 16.**

The browser displays the Enter Discussion Text dialog box as shown in Figure 16.

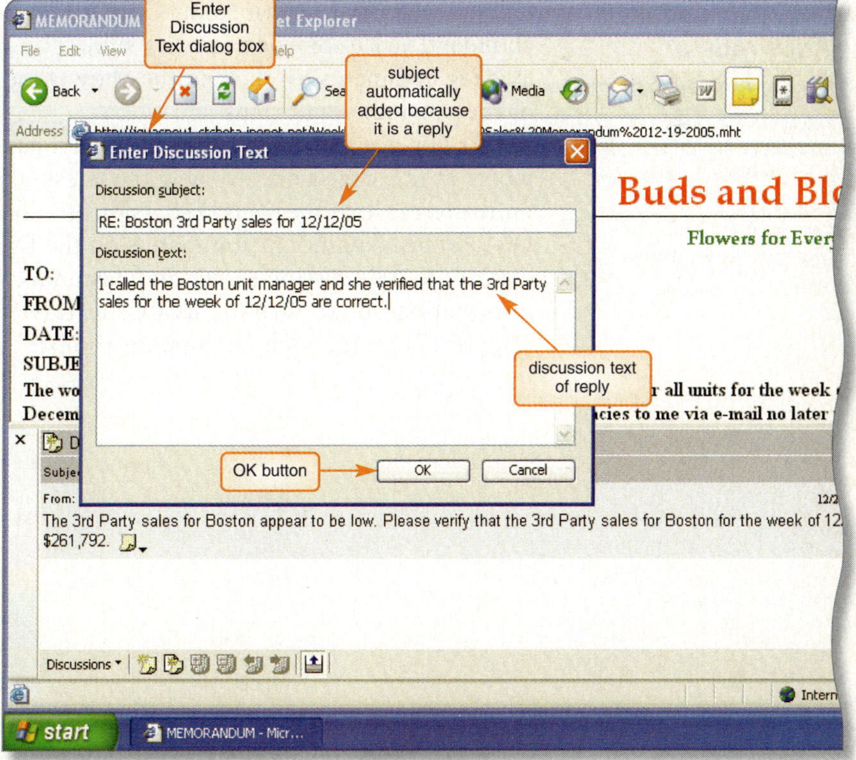

FIGURE 16

3

• **Click the OK button.**

The reply to the first comment appears at the bottom of the Discussion pane (Figure 17).

4

• **Right-click the Discussion pane and then click the Print command on the shortcut menu to print the comments.**

• **Click the Discuss button on the Standard Buttons toolbar.**

• **Click the Close button on the right side of the browser's title bar.**

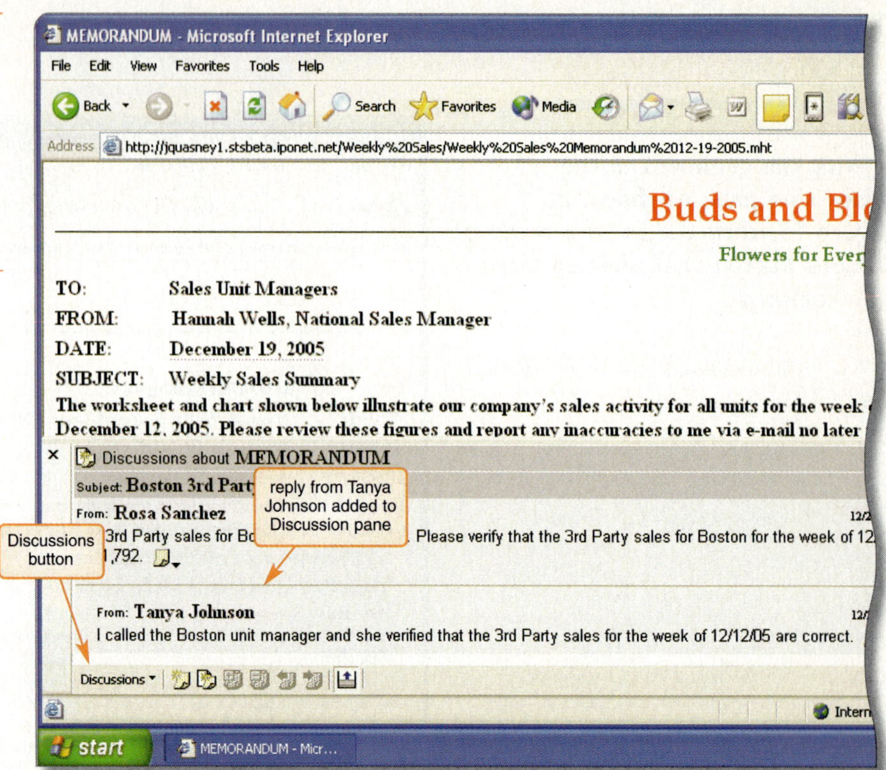

FIGURE 17

More About

Accessing a Discussion Server

To gain temporary access to a discussion server, visit the Excel 2003 More About Web page (scsite.com/ex2003/more.htm) and click Discussion Server Access.

The shortcut menu shown in Figure 15 on the previous page allows you to reply to, edit, and delete a comment. Only the author of a comment can delete and edit a comment. Once someone enters a subject and comment, colleagues usually reply to existing comments by clicking the Show a menu of actions button as shown in Step 1 of the previous set of steps.

As you are working in the Discussion pane, other users might be entering comments at the same time. To view the latest comments, click the Discussions button on the left side of the Web Discussions toolbar (Figure 17) and then click Refresh Discussions. Additional commands on the Discussions button menu allow you to connect to a discussion server and customize the Discussion pane. For additional information on the Web discussions feature, click the Web Discussions Help button (Figure 17) on the Web Discussions toolbar.

Integration Feature Summary

This Integration Feature introduced you to Object Linking and Embedding (OLE). OLE allows you to bring together data and information that have been created in different applications. When you link an object to a document and save it, a link to the object is saved with the document. You edit a linked object by double-clicking it. The system activates the application and then opens the file containing the linked object. If you change any part of the object and then return to the destination document, the updated object will appear. Finally, this Integration Feature introduced you to publishing an Office document to a Web server and then using a discussion server to allow a team to make comments about a document.

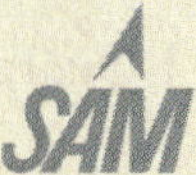

If you have a SAM user profile, you may have access to hands-on instruction, practice, and assessment of the skills covered in this project. Log in to your SAM account and go to your assignments page to see what your instructor has assigned.

What You Should Know

Having completed this project, you should be able to perform the tasks below. The tasks are listed in the same order they were presented in this project. For a list of the buttons, menus, toolbars, and commands introduced in this project, see the Quick Reference Summary at the back of this book and refer to the Page Number column.

1. Open a Word Document and an Excel Workbook (EX 468)
2. Link an Excel Worksheet and Chart to a Word Document (EX 469)
3. Print and Save the Word Document with the Linked Worksheet and Chart (EX 471)
4. Edit the Linked Worksheet (EX 472)
5. Save the Word Document as a Web Page and Use the Web Discussions Feature to Enter a Comment (EX 474)
6. Reply to a Comment on a Discussion Server (EX 477)

More About

Microsoft Certification

The Microsoft Office Specialist Certification program provides an opportunity for you to obtain a valuable industry credential — proof that you have the Excel skills required by employers. For more information, see Appendix E, or visit the Excel 2003 Certification Web page (scsite.com/ex2003/cert).

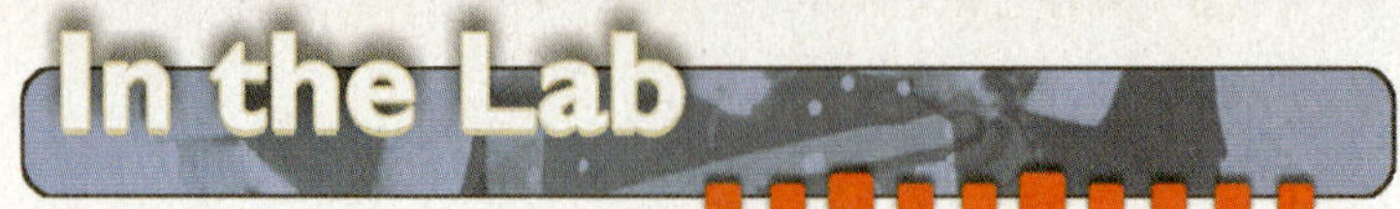

1 Linking a Sales Summary Worksheet to an Annual Sales Memo

Problem: Kelly Waters, the Vice President of Sales at Plasma City, Inc., wants to send out a year-end memo with the previous year's sales by quarter to the sales force. The memo was created in Word. The quarterly sales information is on an Excel worksheet. You have been asked to link the worksheet to the Word document.

Instructions Part 1: Perform the following tasks.

1. Open the document Lab IF-1 Annual Sales Memorandum and then open the workbook Lab IF-1 Quarterly Sales Summary located on the Data Disk.
2. Link the range A1:F24 in the Lab IF-1 Quarterly Sales Summary workbook to the bottom of the Lab IF-1 Annual Sales Memorandum document.
3. Print and then save the document as Lab IF-1 Annual Sales Memorandum 1-9-06.
4. Close the document and workbook without saving changes.
5. Start Word and open the Annual Sales Memorandum 1-9-06 document. Double-click the worksheet in the document and use the keyboard to increase each of the four quarter sales by $300,000 manually. The total sales in cell F4 should be $22,831,323. Activate Word and then print the Annual Sales Memorandum 1-9-06 document with the new values. Close the document and workbook without saving changes.

Instructions Part 2: If you have access to a Web server and discussion server, save the document Lab IF-1 Annual Sales Memorandum 1-9-06 as a single file Web page. Use Internet Explorer to view the page. Click the Discuss button on the Standard Buttons toolbar, add a comment, and then reply to the comment. Print the comments. Close the browser. Close the document without saving changes.

2 Linking an Annual Sales Memo to a Sales Summary Workbook

Problem: Kelly Waters, the Vice President of Sales at Plasma City, Inc., has asked you to link the year-end memo to the Excel workbook with the quarterly sales information, rather than linking the Excel worksheet to the year-end memo, as was done in the previous exercise.

Instructions Part 1: Perform the following tasks.

1. One at a time, open the document Lab IF-1 Annual Sales Memorandum and the workbook Lab IF-1 Quarterly Sales Summary located on the Data Disk.
2. With the Excel window active, insert 20 rows above row 1 and then select cell A1. Activate Word and then copy the entire document. Link the Word document at the top of the Quarterly Sales Analysis worksheet in the Lab IF-1 Quarterly Sales Summary workbook. To link, click Paste link in the Paste Special dialog box, select Microsoft Word Document Object in the As list, and then click the OK button.
3. Print and then save the workbook as Lab IF-2 Quarterly Sales Summary with Memo 1-9-06. Close the document and workbook without saving changes.

Instructions Part 2: If you have access to a Web server and discussion server, save the workbook Lab IF-2 Quarterly Sales Summary with Memo 1-9-06 as a single file Web page. Use Internet Explorer to view the page. Click the Discuss button on the Standard Buttons toolbar, add a comment, and then reply to the comment. Print the comments. Close the browser. Close the document without saving changes.

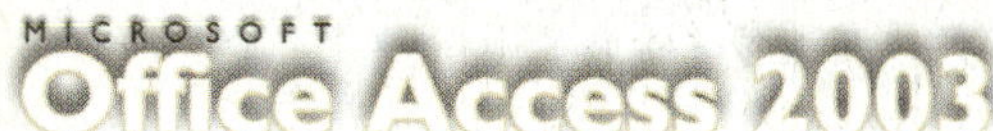

Reports, Forms, and Combo Boxes

PROJECT 4

CASE PERSPECTIVE

Dr. Gernaey and his colleagues at Ashton James College have realized several benefits from using the database of clients and trainers. AJC hopes to realize additional benefits using two custom reports that meet their specific needs. The first report is organized by client type and includes subtotals of both the amount paid and current due amounts for the clients of that type. In addition, it includes grand totals of both of these amounts. The second report groups the clients by trainer number. Similarly to the first report, the second report includes subtotals of the amount paid and current due amounts after each group, and displays grand totals at the end.

AJC also wants to improve the data entry process by using a custom form. The form will have a title with the fields arranged in two columns. It will include the total amount, which will be calculated automatically by adding the amount paid and current due amounts. To assist users in entering the correct client type, users should be able to select from a list of possible client types. To assist users in entering the correct trainer number, users should be able to select from a list of existing trainers. Your task is to help the administration in accomplishing these goals.

As you read through this project, you will learn how to use the Access Report and Form Wizards as well as the various design windows to create custom reports and forms.

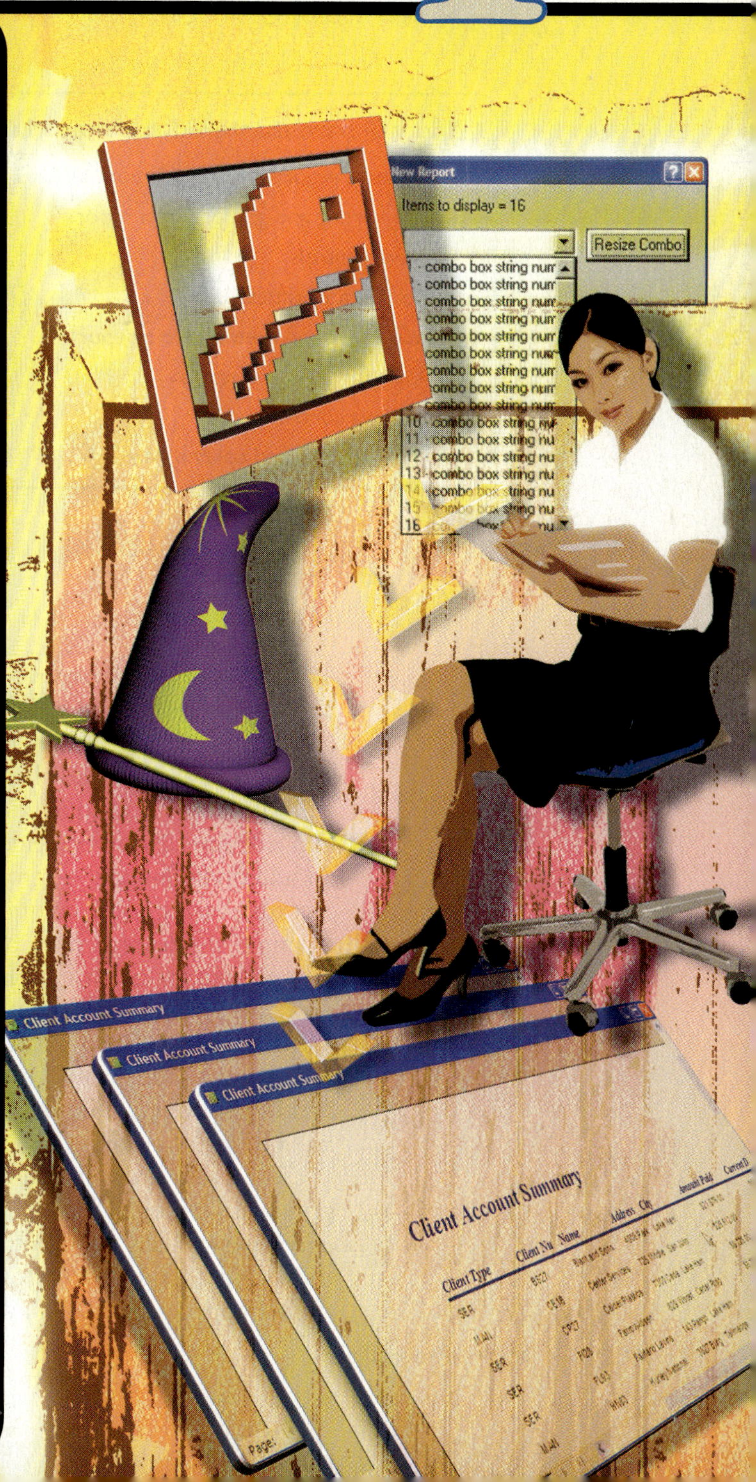

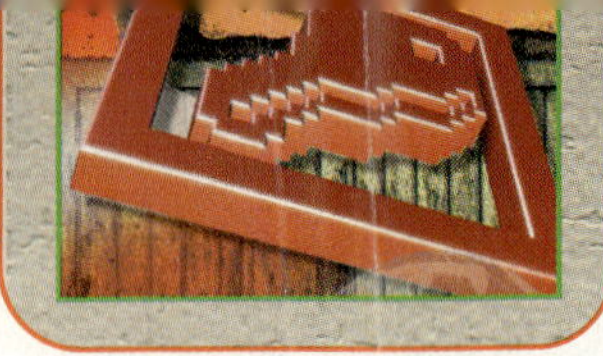

Microsoft Office Access 2003

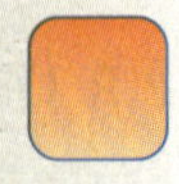

Reports, Forms, and Combo Boxes

PROJECT

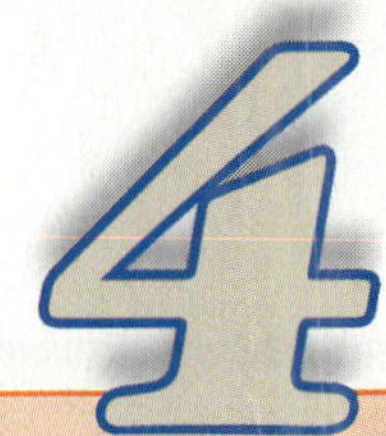

OBJECTIVES

You will have mastered the material in this project when you can:

- Create a report using the Report Wizard
- Use sorting and grouping in a report
- Move controls
- Change properties
- Add totals and subtotals to a report
- Align and format controls
- Remove controls
- Change labels and column headings
- Use multiple tables in a report
- Remove unwanted controls
- Understand report design considerations
- Use the Form Wizard to create a form
- Add a calculated field, combo box, and title to a form
- Understand form design considerations

Introduction

This project creates two reports and a form. The first report is shown in Figure 4-1. This report includes the client type, number, name, address, city, state, amount paid, and current due for each client. It is similar to the one produced by clicking the Print button on the toolbar. It has some significant differences, however.

Not all fields are included. The Client table includes a State field, a Zip Code field, and a Trainer Number field, none of which are included in this report. It also contains an additional feature — grouping. **Grouping** means creating separate collections of records sharing some common characteristic. In the report shown in Figure 4-1, for example, the records have been grouped by client type. There are three separate groups: one for client type EDU, one for client type MAN, and one for client type SER. The appropriate client type appears before each group, and the total of the amount paid and current due amounts for the clients in the group (called a **subtotal**) appears after the group. At the end of the report is a grand total of the amount paid and current due amounts for all groups. Finally, the words, Subtotal and Grand Total, are a different color.

The second report is shown in Figure 4-2. Like the report in Figure 4-1, the data is grouped, although this time it is grouped by trainer number. This report, however, encompasses data from both the Trainer table and the Client table. Not only does the trainer number appear before each group, but the first name and last name of the trainer appear as well. In addition, the column headings have been split over two lines.

Client Account Summary

Client Type	Number	Name	Address	City	Amount Paid	Current Due
EDU						
	MC28	Morgan-Alyssa Academy	923 Williams	Crumville	$24,761.00	$1,572.00
	RT67	Richards-Trent	382 Alder	Lake Hammond	$0.00	$0.00
				Subtotal:	$24,761.00	$1,572.00
MAN						
	CE16	Center Services	725 Mitchell	San Julio	$26,512.00	$2,672.00
	HN83	Hurley National	3827 Burgess	Tallmadge	$0.00	$0.00
				Subtotal:	$26,512.00	$2,672.00
SER						
	BS27	Blant and Sons	4806 Park	Lake Hammond	$21,876.00	$892.50
	CP27	Calder Plastics	7300 Cedar	Lake Hammond	$8,725.00	$0.00
	FL93	Fairland Lawns	143 Pangborn	Lake Hammond	$21,625.00	$0.00
	FI28	Farrow-Idsen	829 Wooster	Cedar Ridge	$8,287.50	$925.50
	PS82	PRIM Staffing	72 Crestview	San Julio	$11,682.25	$2,827.50
				Subtotal:	$72,195.75	$4,645.50
			Grand Total:		$123,468.75	$8,889.50

FIGURE 4-1

Trainer/Client Report

Trainer Number	First Name	Last Name	Client Number	Name	Amount Paid	Current Due
42	Belinda	Perry				
			BS27	Blant and Sons	$21,876.00	$892.50
			FI28	Farrow-Idsen	$8,287.50	$925.50
			MC28	Morgan-Alyssa Academy	$24,761.00	$1,572.00
					$54,924.50	*$3,390.00*
48	Michael	Stevens				
			CE16	Center Services	$26,512.00	$2,672.00
			CP27	Calder Plastics	$8,725.00	$0.00
			FL93	Fairland Lawns	$21,625.00	$0.00
			HN83	Hurley National	$0.00	$0.00
					$56,862.00	*$2,672.00*
53	Manuel	Gonzalez				
			PS82	PRIM Staffing	$11,682.25	$2,827.50
					$11,682.25	*$2,827.50*
67	Marty	Danville				
			RT67	Richards-Trent	$0.00	$0.00
					$0.00	*$0.00*
					$123,468.75	*$8,889.50*

FIGURE 4-2

The **custom form** to be created is shown in Figure 4-3a. Although similar to the form created in Project 1, it offers some distinct advantages. Some of the differences are merely aesthetic. The form has a title and the fields have been rearranged in two columns. In addition, two other major differences are present. This form displays the total amount and will calculate it automatically by adding the amount paid and current due amounts. Second, to assist users in entering the correct client type and trainer, the form contains **combo boxes**, which are boxes that allow you to select entries from a list. An arrow appears in the Client Type field, for example. Clicking the arrow causes a list of the possible client types to appear as shown in the figure. You then either can type the desired client type or simply click it in the list.

An arrow also appears in the Trainer Number field. Clicking the arrow in this field causes a list of the trainers in the Trainer table to appear as shown in Figure 4-3b. You then either can type the desired trainer number or click the desired trainer.

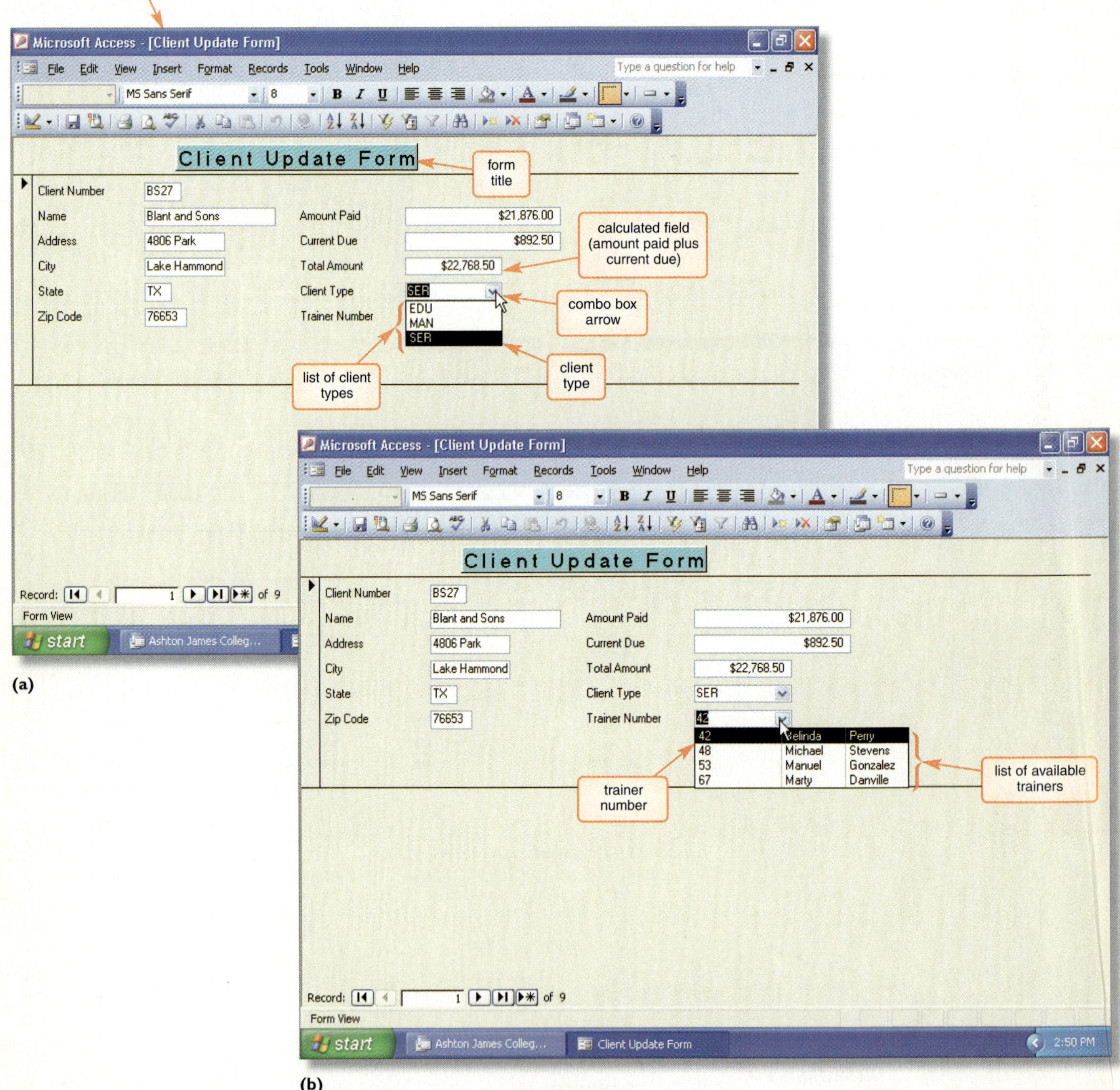

(a)

(b)

FIGURE 4-3

Project Four — Reports, Forms, and Combo Boxes

The steps in this project show how to create reports for the Ashton James College database. The steps also illustrate how to create a custom data-entry form for the database.

Note: When you create forms and reports, you can increase the size of a database substantially. A database containing pictures, for example, can get very large, too large for a diskette. Because these projects illustrate adding pictures to tables as well as to forms and reports, the Ashton James College database is located on disk C. The steps in these projects assume the database is located in a folder called Data on disk C and the pictures (bmp files) are located in a folder called Pictures on disk C. You will use these pictures in Project 5. You are encouraged to copy both your databases and your pictures to disk C, to a network disk, or to a Zip disk. If you cannot do so, you will be instructed which steps to skip in these projects.

More About

The Access Help System

Need Help? It is no further than the Type a question for help box on the menu bar in the upper-right corner of the window. Click the box that contains the text, Type a question for help (Figure 4-3), type `help`, and then press the ENTER key. Access responds with a list of topics you can click to learn about obtaining help on any Access-related topic. To find out what is new in Access 2003, type `what is new in Access` in the Type a question for help box.

Opening the Database

Before you can create the reports and the form, you must open the database. If you are stepping through this project on a computer and you want your screen to match the figures in this book, then you should change your computer's resolution to 800 x 600. For more information on how to change the resolution on your computer, see Appendix D. The following steps, which start Access and open the database, assume that the database is located in a folder called Data on disk C. If your database is located anywhere else, you will need to make the appropriate adjustments in the steps.

To Open a Database

1. **Click the Start button on the Windows taskbar, point to All Programs on the Start menu, point to Microsoft Office on the All Programs submenu, and then click Office Access 2003 on the Microsoft Office submenu.**
2. **If the Access window is not maximized, double-click its title bar to maximize it.**
3. **If the Language bar appears, right-click it and then click Close the Language bar on the shortcut menu.**
4. **Click Open on the Database toolbar, and then click Local Disk (C:) in the Look in box. Double-click the Data folder, and then make sure the Ashton James College database is selected.**
5. **Click the Open button in the Open dialog box. If a Security Warning dialog box appears, click the Open button.**

The database opens and the Ashton James College : Database window appears.

More About

Creating a Report

There are two alternatives to using the Report Wizard to create reports. You can use AutoReport to create a very simple report that includes all fields and records in the table or query. Design view also allows you to create a report from scratch.

Report Creation

The simplest way to create a report design is to use the Report Wizard. For some reports, the Report Wizard can produce exactly the desired report. For others, however, you first must use the Report Wizard to produce a report that is as close as possible to the desired report. Then, use the Report window to modify the report and transform it into the correct report. In either case, once the report is created and saved, you can print it at anytime. Access will use the current data in the database for the report, formatting and arranging it in exactly the way you specified when the report was created.

Creating a Report

Next, you will create a report using the Report Wizard. Access leads you through a series of choices and questions and then creates the report automatically. The following steps illustrate how to create a report.

To Create a Report Using the Report Wizard

1

- **If necessary, in the Database window, click Tables on the Objects bar and then click Client.**
- **Click the New Object button arrow on the Database toolbar.**

The list of available objects appears (Figure 4-4).

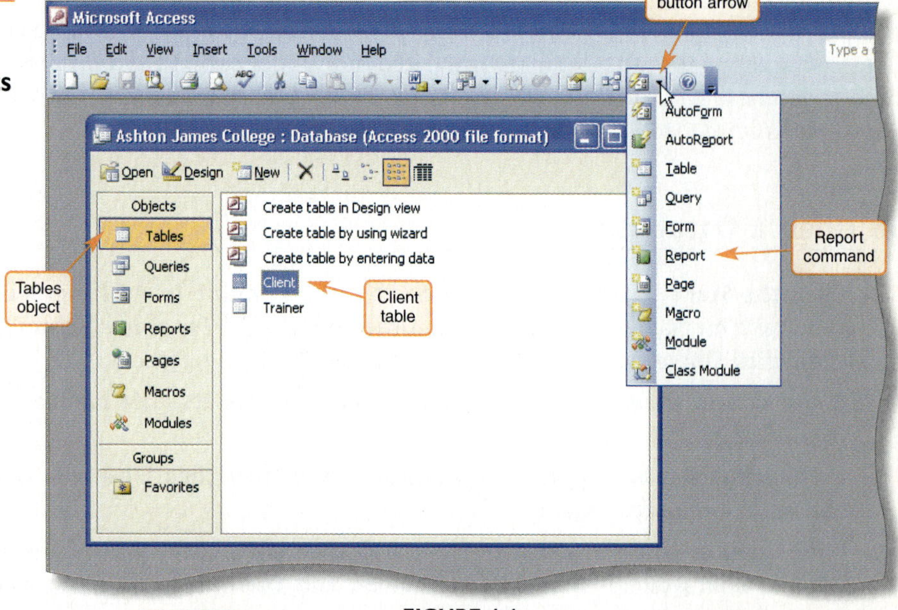

FIGURE 4-4

2

- **Click Report.**

Access displays the New Report dialog box. The Client table is selected (Figure 4-5).

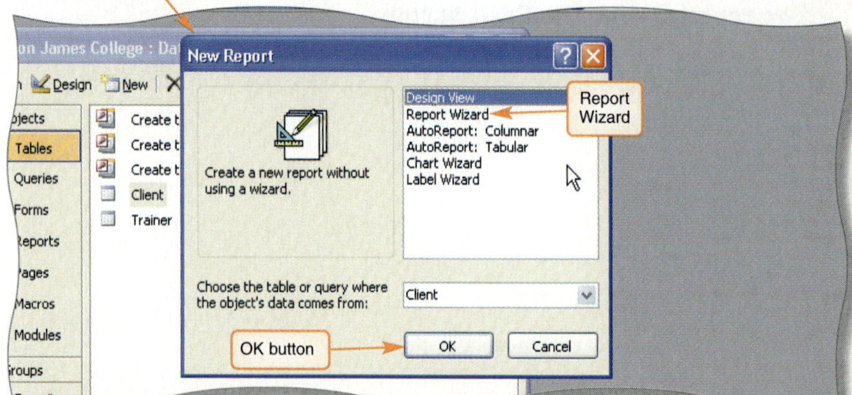

FIGURE 4-5

3

• **Click Report Wizard and then click the OK button.**

The Report Wizard dialog box appears, requesting the fields for the report (Figure 4-6). To add the selected field to the list of fields on the report, use the Add Field button. To add all fields, use the Add All Fields button.

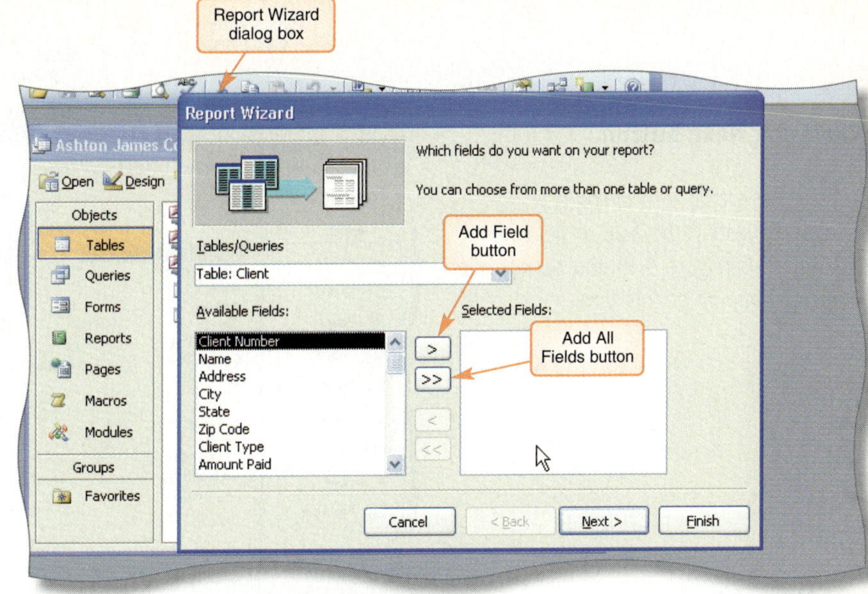

FIGURE 4-6

4

• **Click the Client Type field and then click the Add Field button.**

The Client Type field is selected (Figure 4-7).

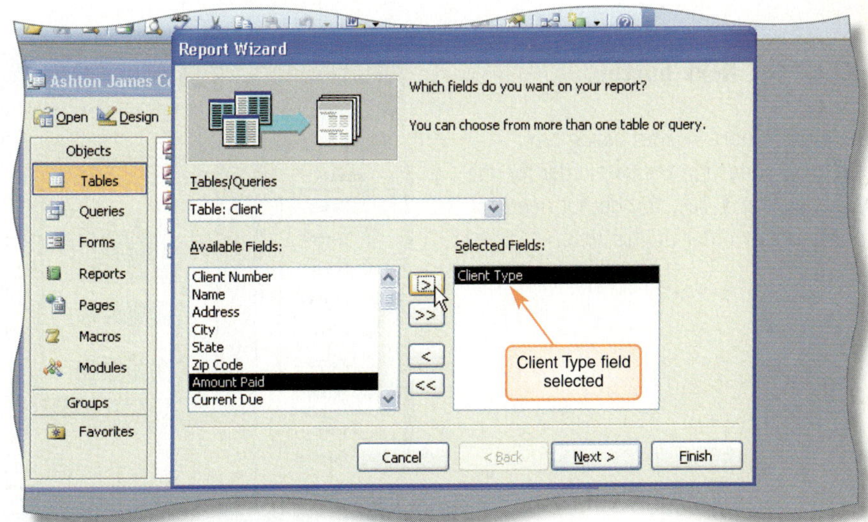

FIGURE 4-7

5

• **Using the same technique, select the Client Number, Name, Address, City, Amount Paid, and Current Due fields.**

The fields are selected (Figure 4-8).

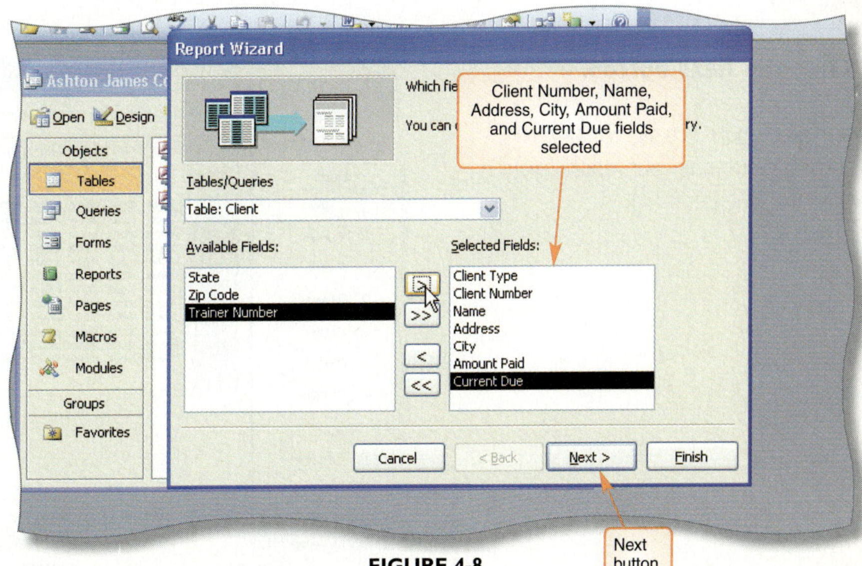

FIGURE 4-8

6

• **Click the Next button.**

The next Report Wizard dialog box appears, requesting the field or fields for grouping levels (Figure 4-9). You do not need to specify grouping at this time.

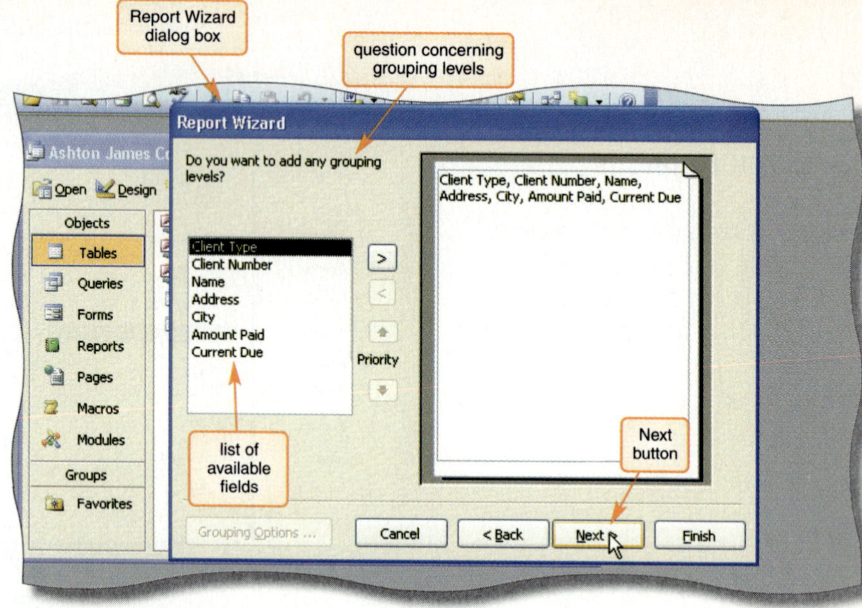

FIGURE 4-9

7

• **Click the Next button.**

The next Report Wizard dialog box appears, requesting the sort order for the report (Figure 4-10). You do not need to specify a sort order at this time.

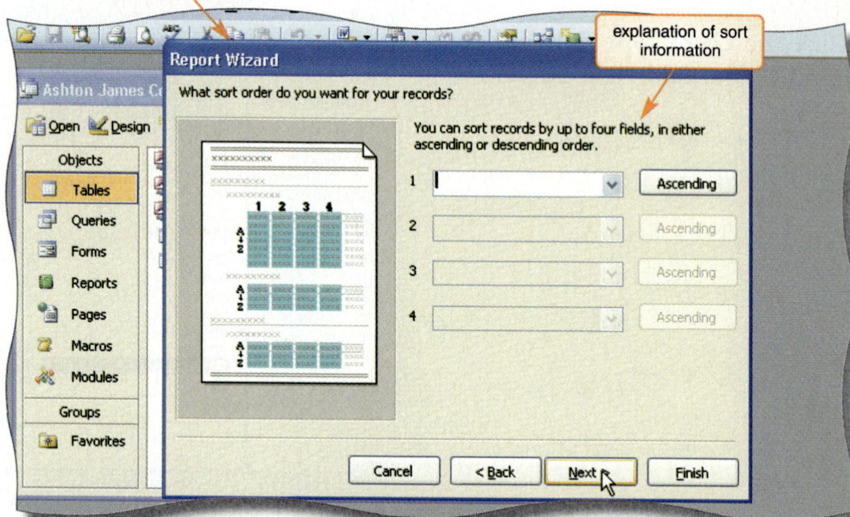

FIGURE 4-10

8

• **Click the Next button.**

The next Report Wizard dialog box appears, requesting your report layout preference (Figure 4-11).

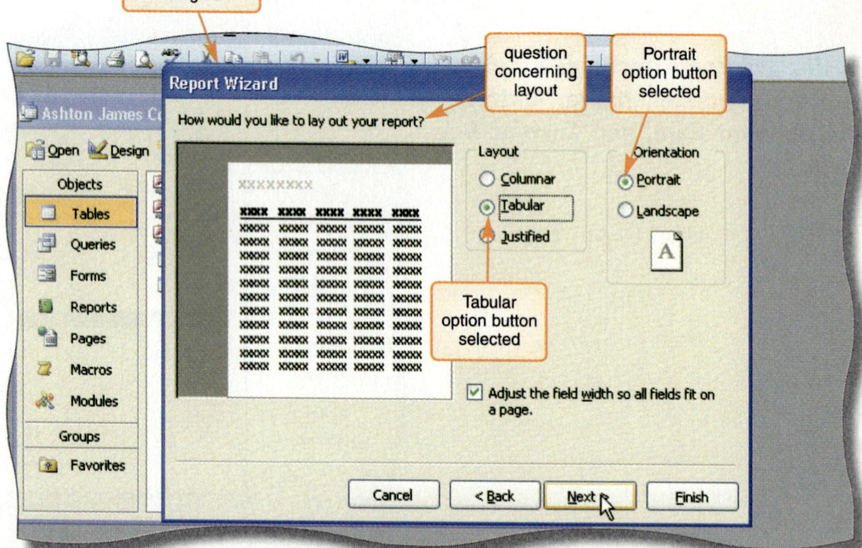

FIGURE 4-11

9

• **Be sure the options selected in the Report Wizard dialog box on your screen match those shown in Figure 4-11, and then click the Next button.**

• **If Corporate is not already selected, click Corporate to select it.**

The next Report Wizard dialog box appears, requesting a style for the report (Figure 4-12). The Corporate style is selected.

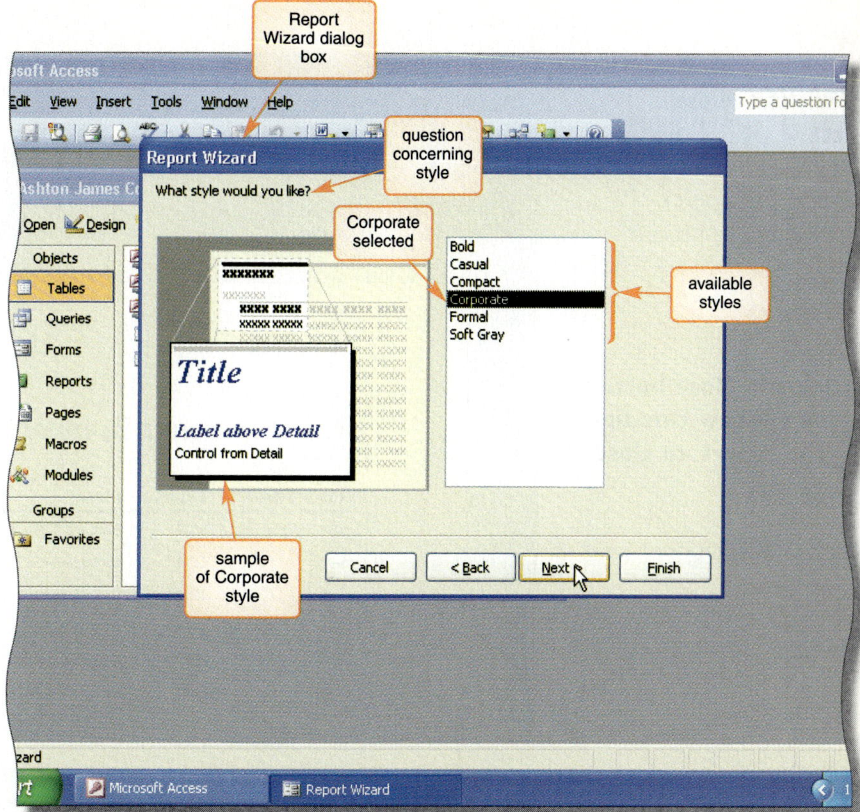

FIGURE 4-12

10

• **Click the Next button and then type** `Client Account Summary` **as the report title.**

The next Report Wizard dialog box appears, requesting a title for the report (Figure 4-13). Client Account Summary is entered as the title.

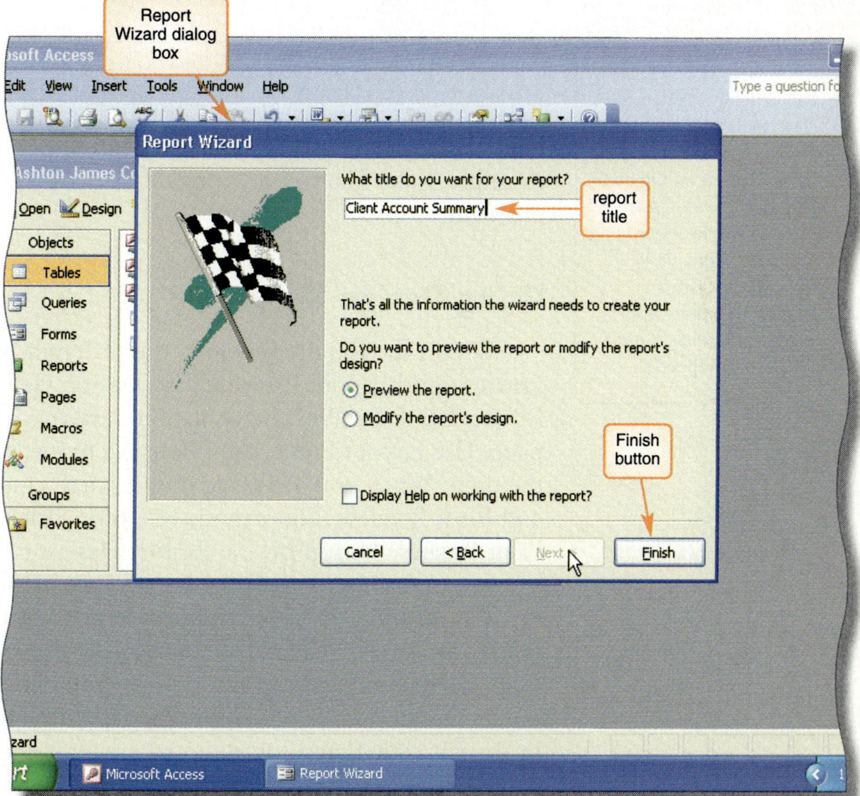

FIGURE 4-13

11

• **Click the Finish button.**

The report design is complete and appears in Print Preview (Figure 4-14).

12

• **Click the Close button in the window containing the report to close the report.**

The report no longer appears.

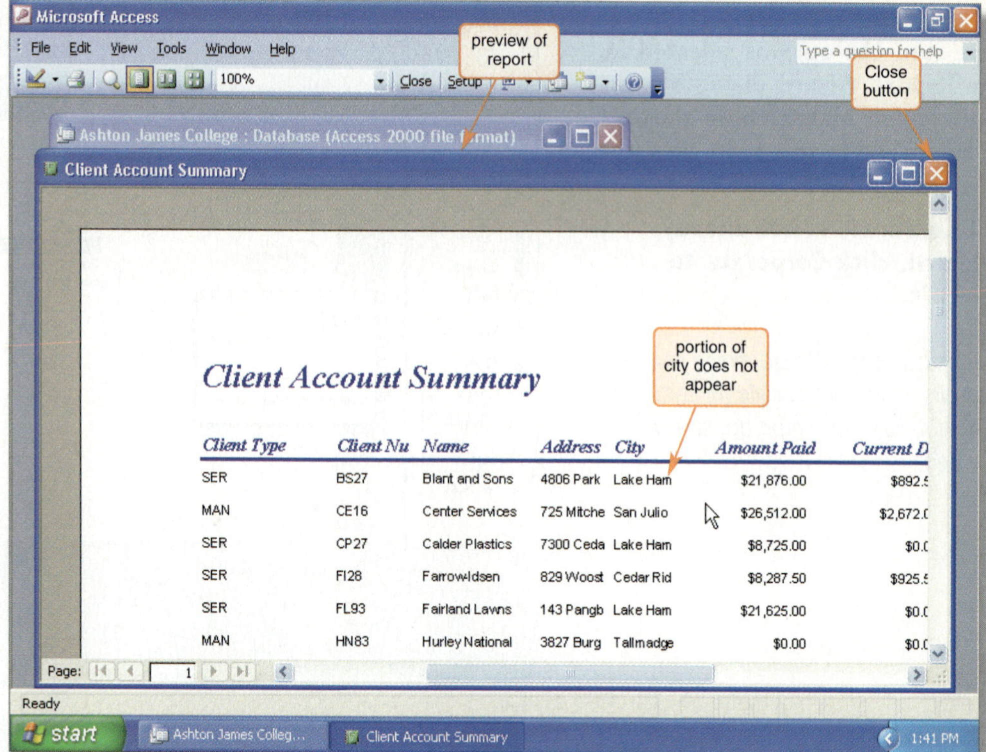

FIGURE 4-14

Other Ways

1. Click Reports on Objects bar, click New button, click Report Wizard to create report
2. Click Reports on Objects bar, double-click Create report by using wizard
3. On Insert menu click Report, click Report Wizard to create report
4. In Voice Command mode, say "Insert, Report"

Because of the insufficient amount of space allowed in the report shown in Figure 4-14, some of the data does not appear completely. In the City field, for example, Lake Hammond appears as Lake Ham. You will need to correct this problem.

Using Design View

Within the Report window, the different possible views are Design view, Print Preview, and Layout Preview. Use Design view to modify the design (layout) of the report. Use Print Preview to see the report with actual data as it will appear on every page. Use Layout Preview to view the report's layout, which includes just a sample of the data. When you are designing reports, the two most useful views are Design view and Print Preview. You can move from Design view to Print Preview by using the Print Preview button on the Report Design toolbar. To return to Design view after previewing a report, click the button labeled Close on the Print Preview toolbar.

Within Print Preview, you can switch between viewing an entire page and viewing a portion of a page. To do so, click somewhere within the report. When pointing within the report, the mouse pointer will change shape to a magnifying glass.

In Design view, you can modify the design of the report. A toolbox is available in Design view that allows you to create special objects for the report. The toolbox also can obscure a portion of the report, however. You can use the Toolbox button on the Report Design toolbar to remove it and then return it to the screen when needed. Because you use the toolbox frequently when modifying report and form designs, it is desirable to leave it on the screen, however. You can move the toolbar to different positions on the screen using a process referred to as **docking**. The bottom of the screen usually is a good position for it.

The following steps illustrate how to open the report in Design view, remove a field list that is not needed, and dock the toolbox.

To Move to Design View and Dock the Toolbox

1

- **Click the Reports object in the Database window, right-click Client Account Summary, and then click Design View on the shortcut menu.**
- **If necessary, maximize the window.**

The report appears in Design view (Figure 4-15). A field list may appear. The toolbox also may appear.

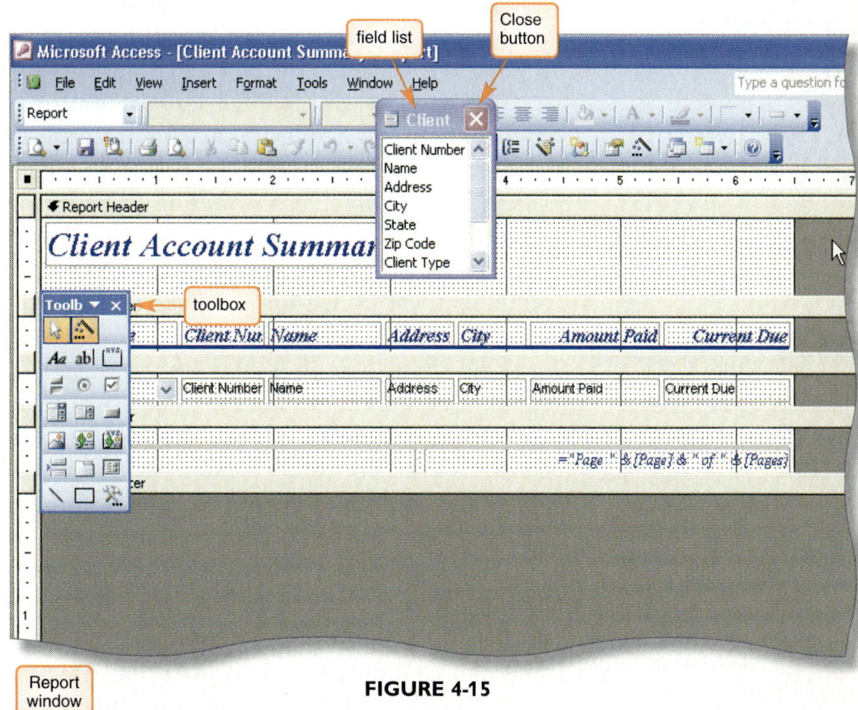

FIGURE 4-15

2

- **If a field list appears, click its Close button to remove the field list from the screen.**
- **If necessary, click the Toolbox button on the Report Design toolbar to display the toolbox.**
- **If the toolbox is not docked at the bottom of the screen, dock it there by dragging its title bar to the bottom of the screen.**

The field list no longer appears, the toolbox is docked at the bottom of the screen, and the window is maximized (Figure 4-16).

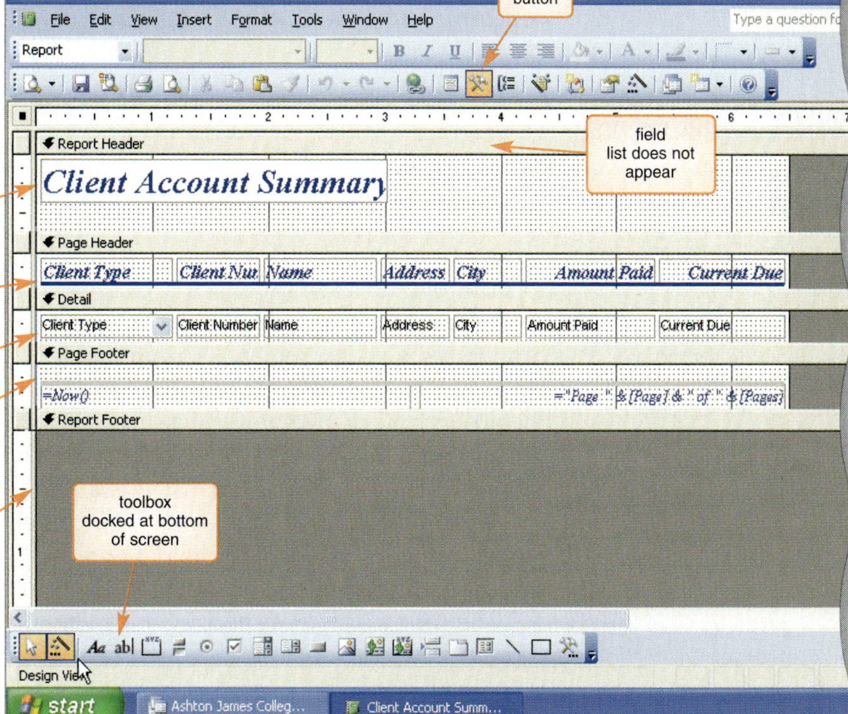

FIGURE 4-16

More About

Report Sections

Another common term for the sections in a report is band. The term, band-oriented applied to a report tool means that the tool is very similar to the report design feature in Access; that is, you design a report by simply modifying the contents of the various sections (bands).

More About

Using Queries for Reports

The records in the report will appear in the specified order if you have sorted the data in the query. You also can enter criteria in the query, in which case only records that satisfy the criteria will be included in the report. Reports based on queries open faster than those based on tables.

More About

Grouping in a Report

To force each group to begin on a new page of the report, change the value of the ForceNewPage property for the Group Header section from None to Before Section. The ForceNewPage property does not apply to Page Header or Page Footer sections.

Report Sections

Each portion of the report is described in what is termed a **section**. The sections are labeled on the screen (see Figure 4-16 on the previous page). Notice the following sections: Report Header section, Page Header section, Detail section, Page Footer section, and Report Footer section.

The contents of the **Report Header section** print once at the beginning of the report. The contents of the **Report Footer section** print once at the end of the report. The contents of the **Page Header section** print once at the top of each page, and the contents of the **Page Footer section** print once at the bottom of each page. The contents of the **Detail section** print once for each record in the table.

The various rectangles appearing in Figure 4-16 (Client Account Summary, Client Type, Name, and so on) are called **controls**. All the information on a report or form is contained in the controls. The control containing Client Account Summary displays the report title; that is, it displays the words, Client Account Summary. The control in the Page Header section containing Name displays the word, Name.

The controls in the Detail section display the contents of the corresponding fields. The control containing Name, for example, will display the client's name. The controls in the Page Header section serve as captions for the data. The Client Type control in this section, for example, will display the words, Client Type, immediately above the column of client types, thus making it clear to anyone reading the report that the items in the column are, in fact, client types.

To move, resize, delete, or modify a control, click it. Small squares called sizing handles appear around the border of the control. To move a control, point to the border of the control away from any sizing handle. The mouse pointer shape will change to a hand. You then can drag the control to move it. To resize a control, point to one of the sizing handles. The mouse pointer shape will change to a double-pointing arrow. You then can drag the handle to resize the control. To delete the control, press the DELETE key. Clicking a second time produces an insertion point in the control in order to modify its contents.

Sorting and Grouping

Grouping arranges the records in your report into separate collections of records that share a common characteristic. In the report shown in Figure 4-1 on page AC 195, for example, the records are grouped by client type. Three separate groups are formed, one for each type.

In grouping, reports often include two additional types of sections: a group header and a group footer. A **group header** is printed before the records in a particular group are printed, and a **group footer** is printed after the group. In Figure 4-1, the group header indicates the client type. The group footer includes the total of the amount paid and current due amounts for the clients assigned to that trainer. Such a total is called a subtotal, because it is a subset of the overall total.

Within the records in a group, you can choose to further sort the records. In the report in Figure 4-1, for example, the records in each group are sorted by name. You specify both sorting and grouping in the Sorting and Grouping dialog box.

The following steps specify both sorting and grouping for the report.

To Use Sorting and Grouping

1

- **Click the Sorting and Grouping button on the Report Design toolbar.**

The Sorting and Grouping dialog box appears (Figure 4-17).

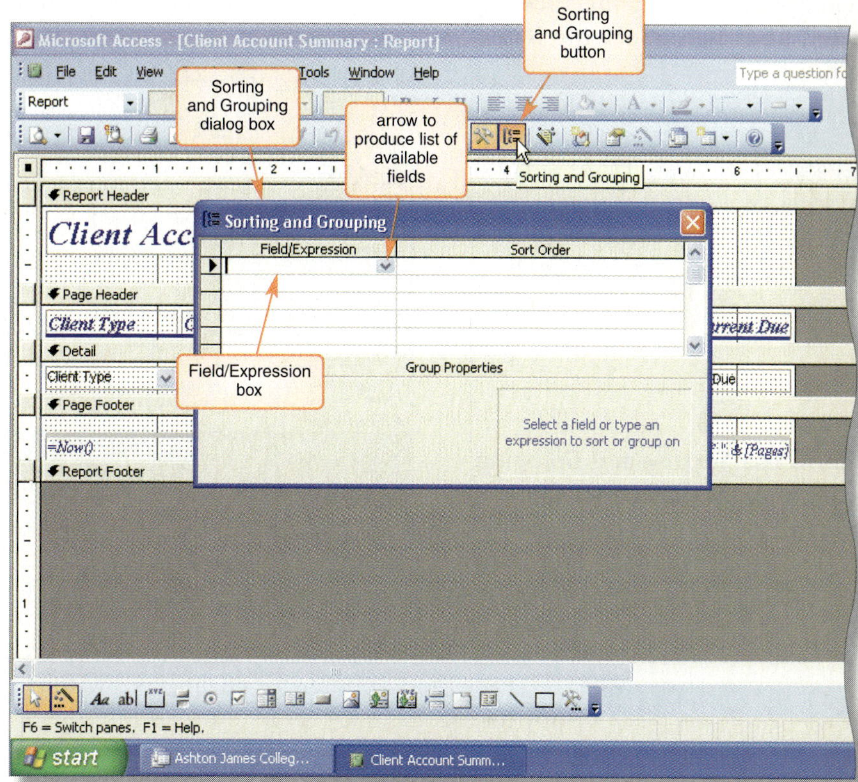

FIGURE 4-17

2

- **Click the down arrow in the Field/Expression box, and then click the Client Type field in the list.**
- **Click the Group Header property box, click the Group Header box arrow, and then click Yes.**
- **Click the Group Footer property box, click the Group Footer box arrow, and then click Yes.**
- **Click the Keep Together property box, click the Keep Together box arrow, and then click With First Detail.**

The Client Type field is selected (Figure 4-18). Because the Group Header and Group Footer properties are changed from No to Yes, the Client Type Header and Client Type Footer sections now are included.

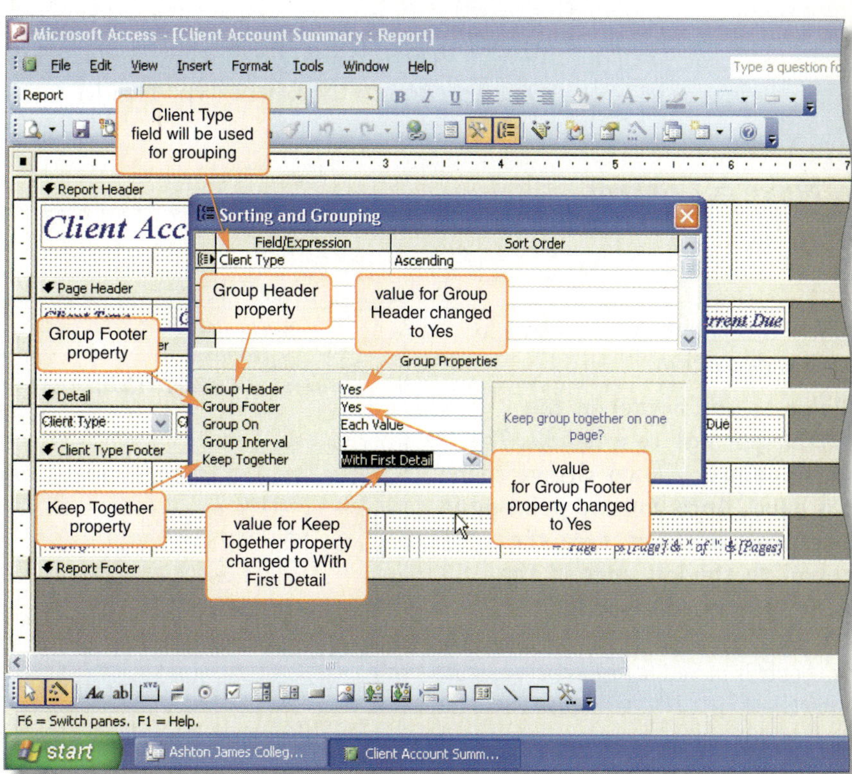

FIGURE 4-18

3

• **Click the second row in the Field/Expression column, click the arrow, and then select the Name field.**

The Name field is selected (Figure 4-19). This ensures that within all the clients with the same client type, the records will be sorted by Name. No header or footer will be included, because both the Group Header and Group Footer properties still are set to No.

4

• **Close the Sorting and Grouping dialog box by clicking its Close button.**

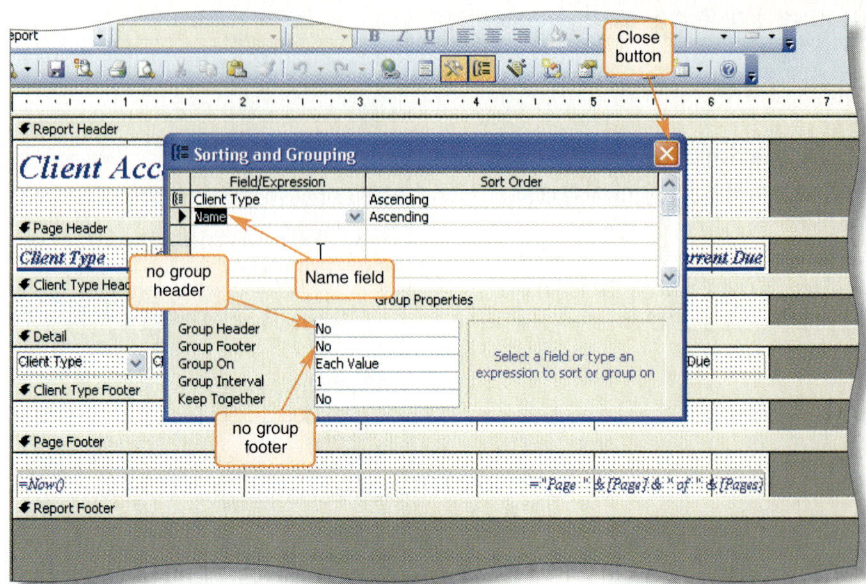

FIGURE 4-19

The records in the report now will be grouped by client type. There will be both a header and a footer for client type. Within each group, the records will be sorted by name.

Moving a Control

To move a control, select it, and then point to the border of the control but away from any sizing handle. The mouse pointer then will be a hand. Drag the control to move it. The following step shows how to move the Client Type control from the Detail section to the Client Type Header section.

To Move a Control

1

• **Click the Client Type control in the Detail section.**

• **Point to the border of the control, but not to a handle. The mouse pointer should change shape to a hand. Once you are pointing in the correct position, drag the control to the left edge of the Client Type Header section.**

The control is moved from the Detail section to the Client Type Header section (Figure 4-20).

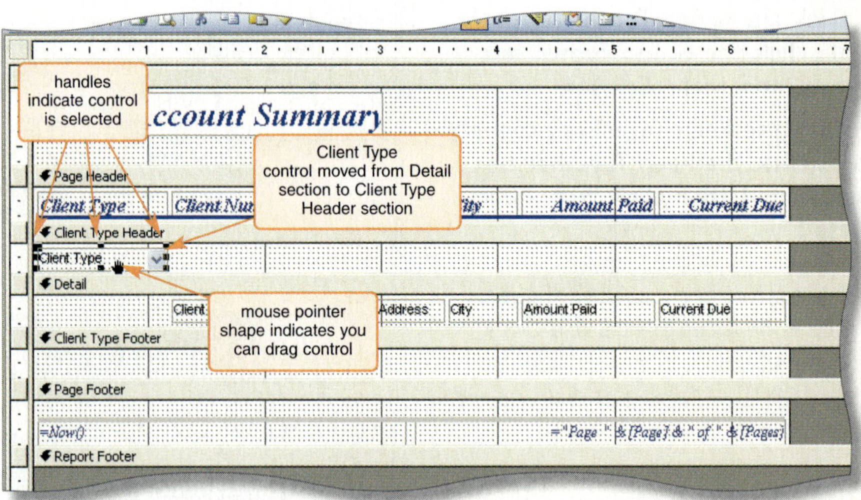

FIGURE 4-20

Changing Properties

Some of the changes you may make will involve using the property sheet for the control to be changed. The **property sheet** for each control is a list of properties that can be modified. By using the property sheet, you can change one or more of the control's properties.

The problem of the missing data in the report shown in Figure 4-14 on page AC 202 can be corrected in several ways.

1. Move the controls to allow more space in between. Then, drag the appropriate handles on the controls that need to be expanded to enlarge them.
2. Use the Font Size property to select a smaller font size. This will allow more data to print in the same space.
3. Use the Can Grow property. By changing the value of this property from No to Yes, the data can be spread over two lines, thus allowing all the data to print. The city of Lake Hammond, for example, will have Lake on one line and Hammond on the next line. Access will split data at natural break points, such as commas, spaces, and hyphens.

The first approach will work, but it can be cumbersome. The second approach also works but makes the report more difficult to read. The third approach, changing the Can Grow property, is the simplest method to use and generally produces a very readable report. The following steps show how to change the Can Grow property for the Detail section.

Q&A

Q: If you were asked to change some characteristic of a control on a report or a form that you had not seen before, such as the border style, how would you approach the problem?

A: You certainly can use help to find the process for making such a change. A quicker way, however, is to right-click the control, click Properties on the shortcut menu, and then scroll down the list of properties until you find one that relates to the characteristic you want to change. For the border style, for example, there is a Border Style property. If you click it and then click the arrow that appears, you will see all the available border styles and then can select one. If the property does not have a drop-down list, press the F1 key to display help specific to that property.

To Change the Can Grow Property

1

- **Right-click below the section selector for the Detail section.**

The shortcut menu appears (Figure 4-21). (If your shortcut menu looks different, you right-clicked the wrong place and will have to repeat the step.) All the controls in the Detail section are selected.

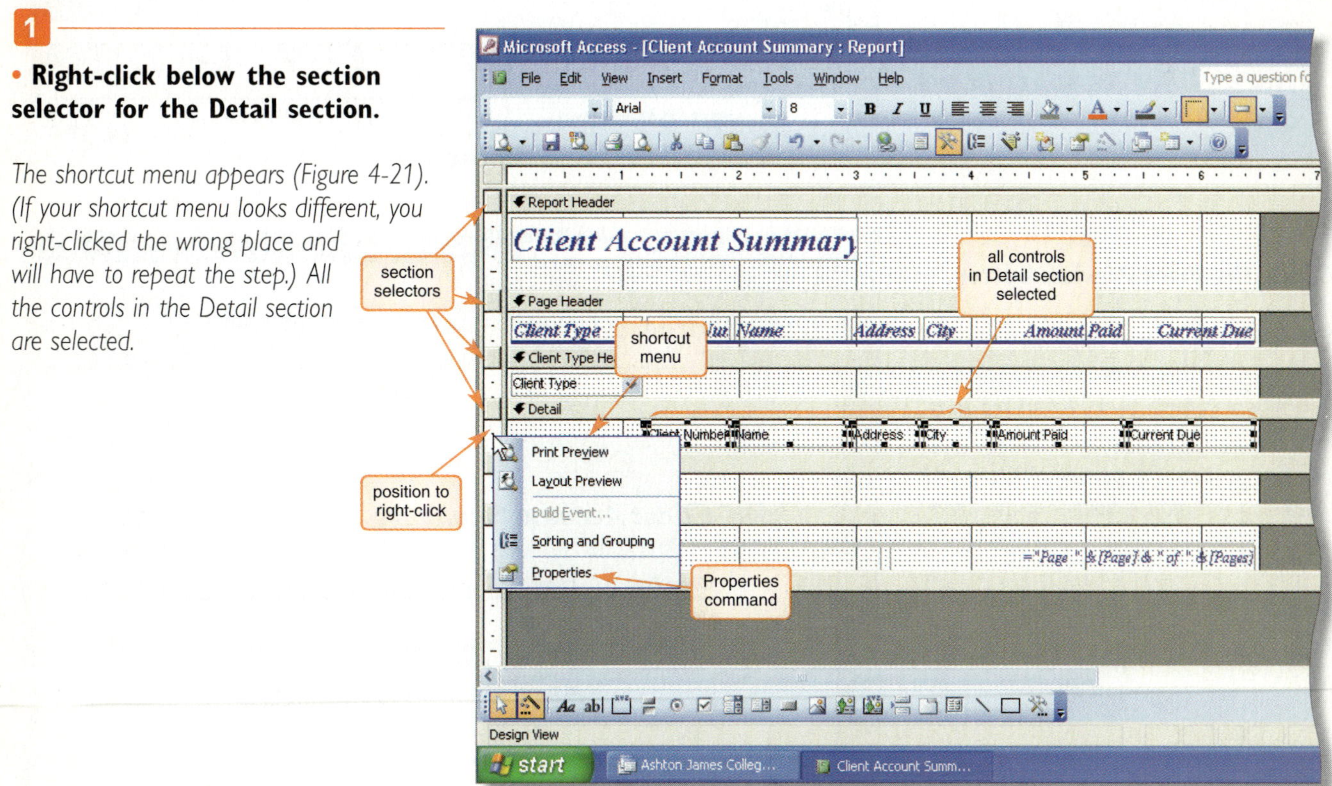

FIGURE 4-21

2

- **Click Properties and then, if necessary, click the All tab to ensure that all available properties appear.**
- **Click the Can Grow property, click the Can Grow property box arrow, and then click Yes in the list that appears.**

The Multiple selection property sheet appears (Figure 4-22). All the properties appear in the All sheet. The value for the Can Grow property has been changed to Yes for all fields in the Detail section.

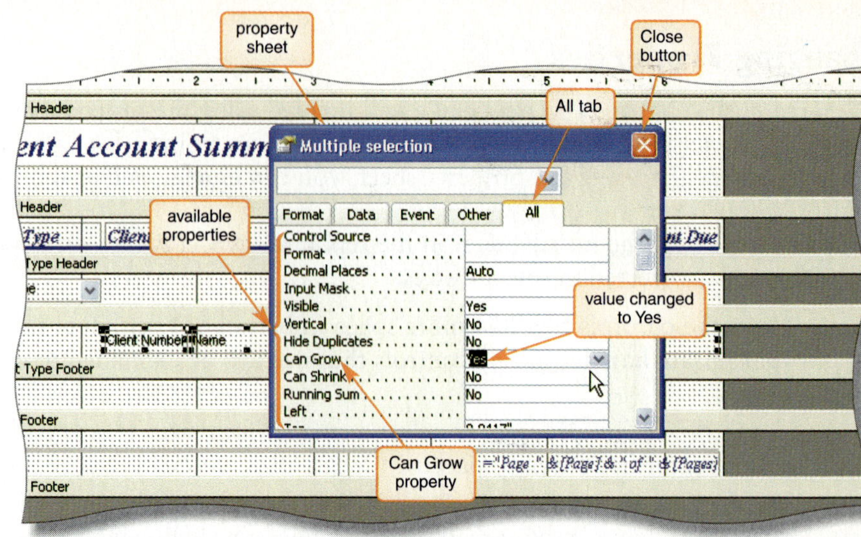

FIGURE 4-22

3

- **Close the property sheet by clicking its Close button.**

The property sheet no longer appears (Figure 4-23).

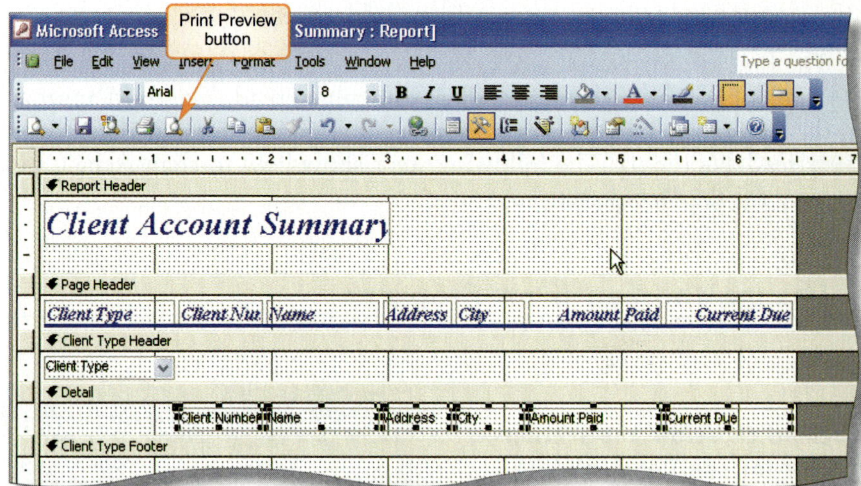

FIGURE 4-23

4

- **Click the Print Preview button.**

A portion of the report appears (Figure 4-24). The addresses and cities now appear completely by extending to a second line. (If your computer shows an entire page, click the portion of the report containing the mouse pointer in the figure.)

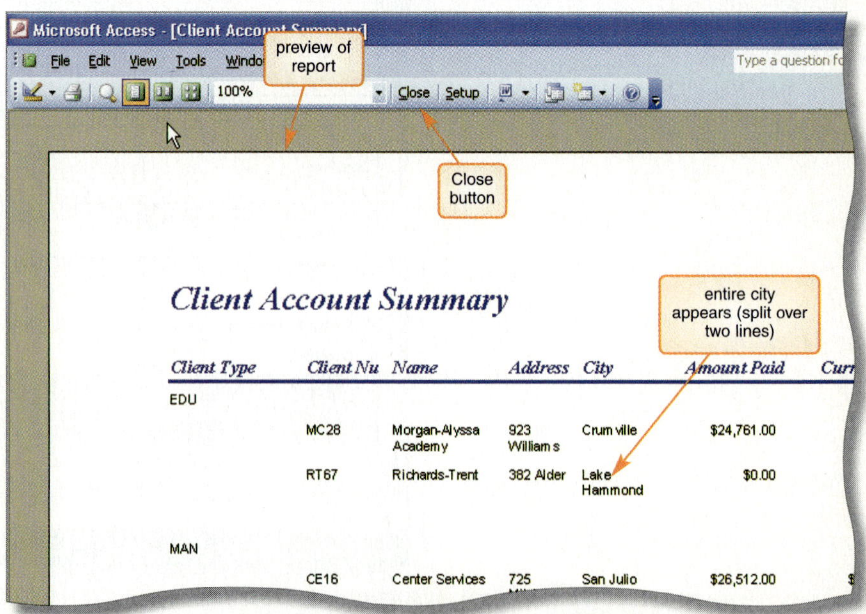

FIGURE 4-24

Adding Totals and Subtotals

To add totals or other statistics to a footer, add a **text box**. A text box is a control that displays data. In the text box, enter an expression that performs the appropriate calculation. You can use any of the aggregate functions: COUNT, SUM, AVG (average), MAX (largest value), MIN (smallest value), STDEV (standard deviation), VAR (variance), FIRST, and LAST. To use a function, type an equal (=) sign, followed by the function name. You then include a set of parentheses containing the item for which you want to perform the calculation. If the item name contains spaces, such as Amount Paid, you must enclose it in square brackets. For example, to calculate the sum of the amount paid values, the expression would be =SUM([Amount Paid]).

Access will perform the calculation for the appropriate collection of records. If you enter this expression in the Client Type Footer section, Access only will calculate the total for clients with the given client type; that is, it will calculate the appropriate subtotal. If you enter the expression in the Report Footer section, Access will calculate the total for all clients.

The following steps illustrate how to add the total of amount paid and current due to both the Client Type Footer section and the Report Footer section. The steps also label the totals in the Client Type Footer section as subtotals and the totals in the Report Footer section as grand totals.

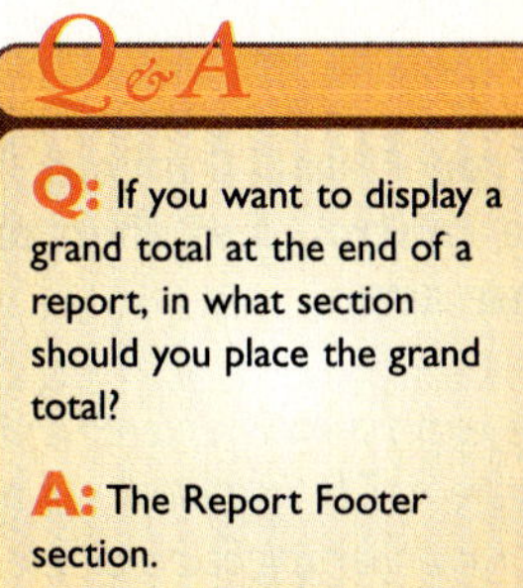

To Add Totals and Subtotals

1

- **Click the Close button on the toolbar to return to Design view.**
- **Click the Text Box tool in the toolbox, and then point to the position shown in Figure 4-25.**

The mouse pointer shape indicates you are placing a text box.

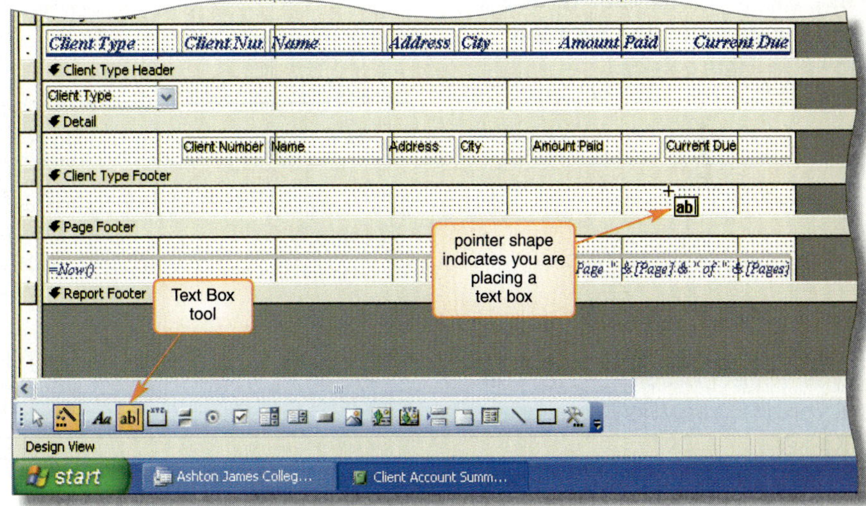

FIGURE 4-25

2

- **Click the position shown in Figure 4-25.**

Access adds a control to the Client Type Footer section (Figure 4-26). The label for the control is Text19: (yours might be different).

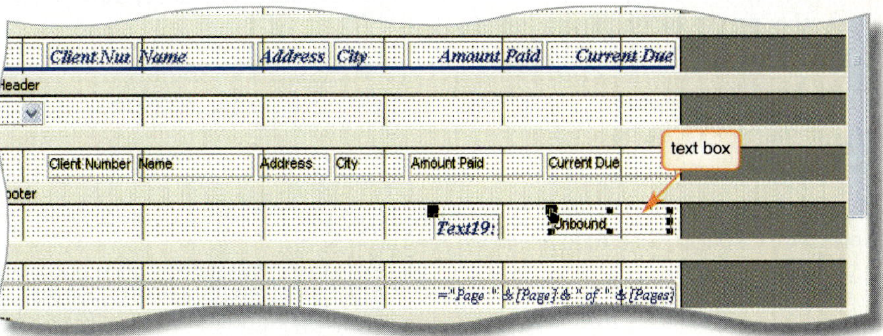

FIGURE 4-26

3

• **Type** =Sum([Current Due]) **in the control, and then press the ENTER KEY.**

The expression is entered in the text box (Figure 4-27). The label still reads Text19. Your number might be different.

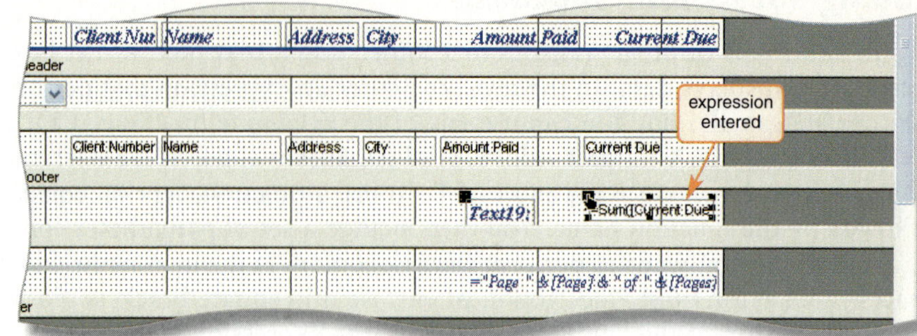

FIGURE 4-27

4

• **Click the label to select it, and then press the DELETE key to delete the label.**

The label is removed from the design (Figure 4-28).

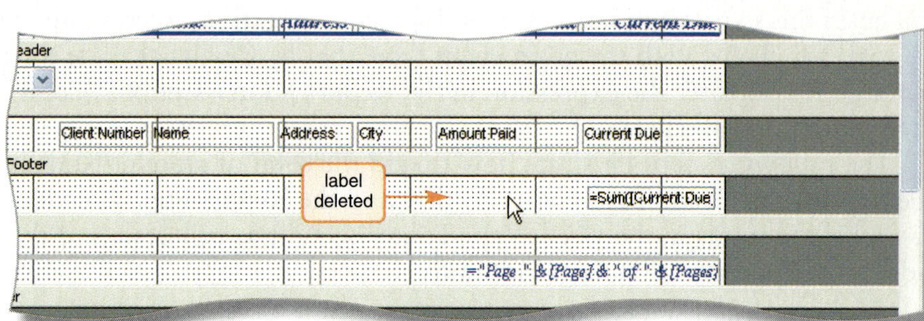

FIGURE 4-28

5

• **Use the Text Box tool to add a second control in the position shown in Figure 4-29.**

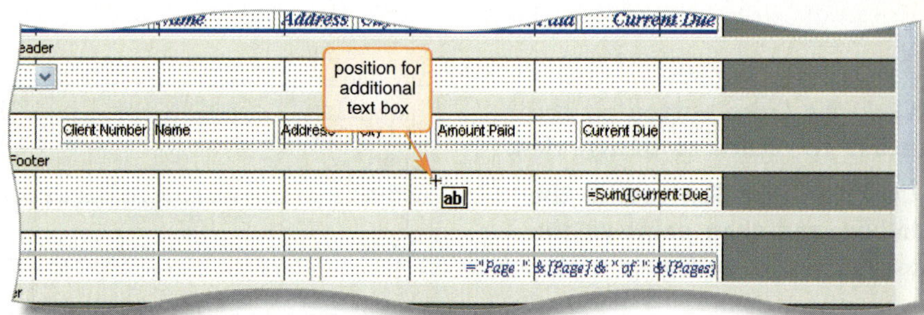

FIGURE 4-29

6

• **Type** =Sum([Amount Paid]) **in the control, and then press the ENTER KEY.**

• **Click the label to select it.**

• **Click the label a second time to produce an insertion point.**

• **Use the DELETE or BACKSPACE key to delete the Text19 (your number might be different).**

• **Type** Subtotal **as the label.**

The expression is entered in the text box (Figure 4-30). The label has been changed to Subtotal:.

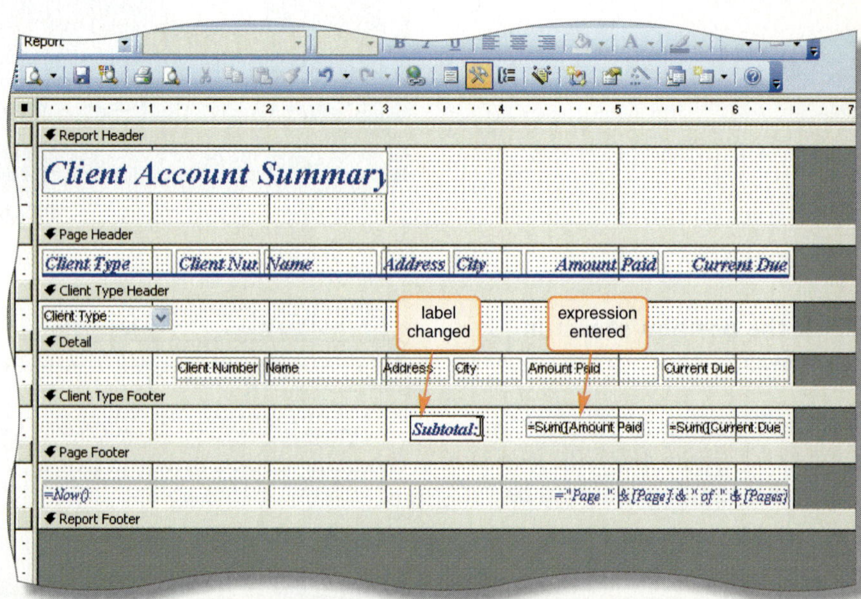

FIGURE 4-30

7

- **Click outside the label to deselect the label.**
- **Click the label a second time to select it.**
- **Move the label to the position shown in Figure 4-31 by dragging the Move handle in the upper-left corner.**

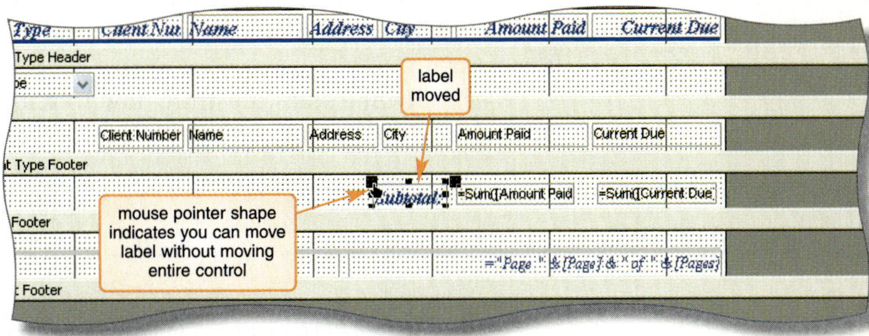

FIGURE 4-31

8

- **Use the techniques in Steps 1 through 7 above to add the controls in the Report Footer section shown in Figure 4-32. The only difference is that the label reads Grand Total: rather than Subtotal:. The expressions in both labels are the same as the expressions you entered earlier. That is, the expression for the control in the Current Due column is =Sum([Current Due]), and the expression in the Amount Paid column is =Sum([Amount Paid]).**

The controls are added to the Report Footer section. When you place the text box controls in the Report Footer section, Access automatically will enlarge the size of the section to accommodate the controls.

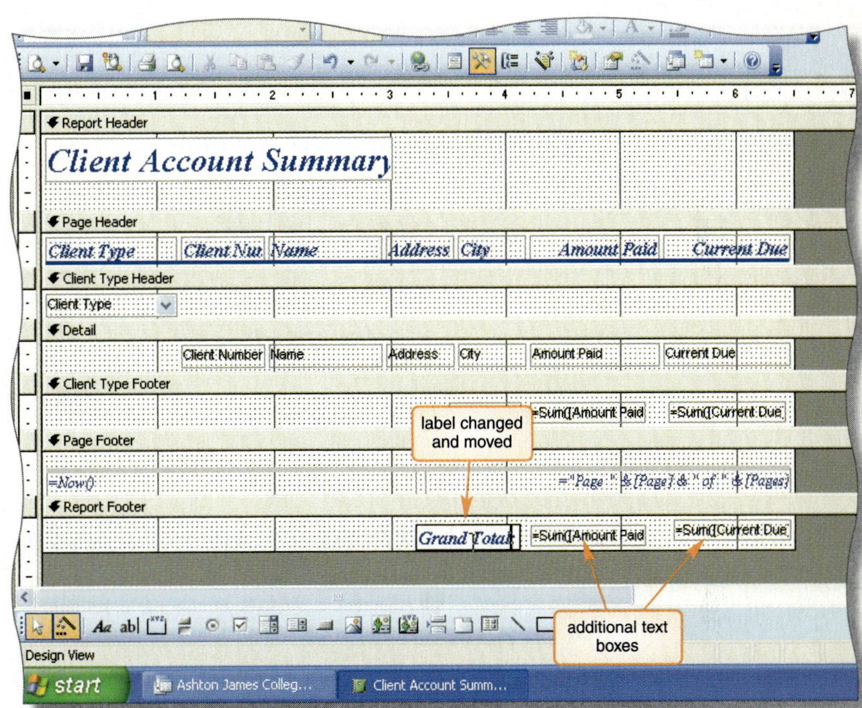

FIGURE 4-32

The report now contains totals and subtotals.

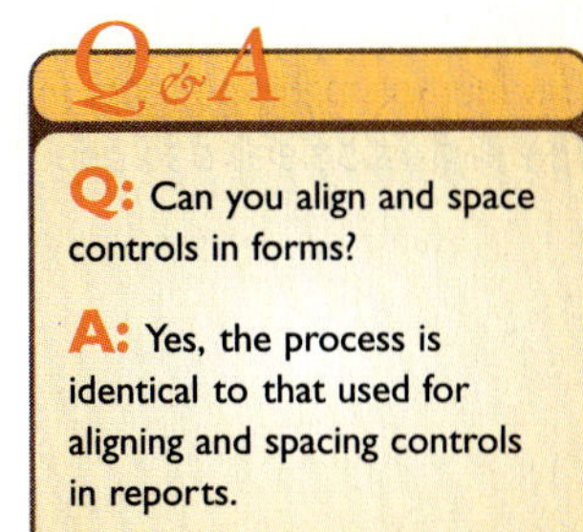

Q: Can you align and space controls in forms?

A: Yes, the process is identical to that used for aligning and spacing controls in reports.

Aligning Controls

There are cases where several controls should be aligned in some fashion. For example, the controls may be aligned so their right edges are even with each other. In another case, controls may be aligned so their top edges are even. To ensure that a collection of controls is aligned properly with each other, select all of the affected controls, and then use the Align command on the format menu.

There are two ways to select multiple controls. One way is to use a ruler. If you click a position on the horizontal ruler, you will select all the controls for which a portion of the control is under that position on the ruler. Similarly, if you click a position on the vertical ruler, you will select all the controls for which a portion of the control is to the right of that position on the ruler.

The second way to select multiple controls is to select the first control by clicking it. Then, select all the other controls by holding down the SHIFT key while clicking the control.

The following steps illustrate how to select multiple controls and then align them appropriately.

To Align Controls

1

- **Click the horizontal ruler above the Current Due controls.**

The Current Due controls in the Page Header, Detail, Client Type Footer, and Report Footer sections are selected (Figure 4-33). The control that includes the page number also is selected.

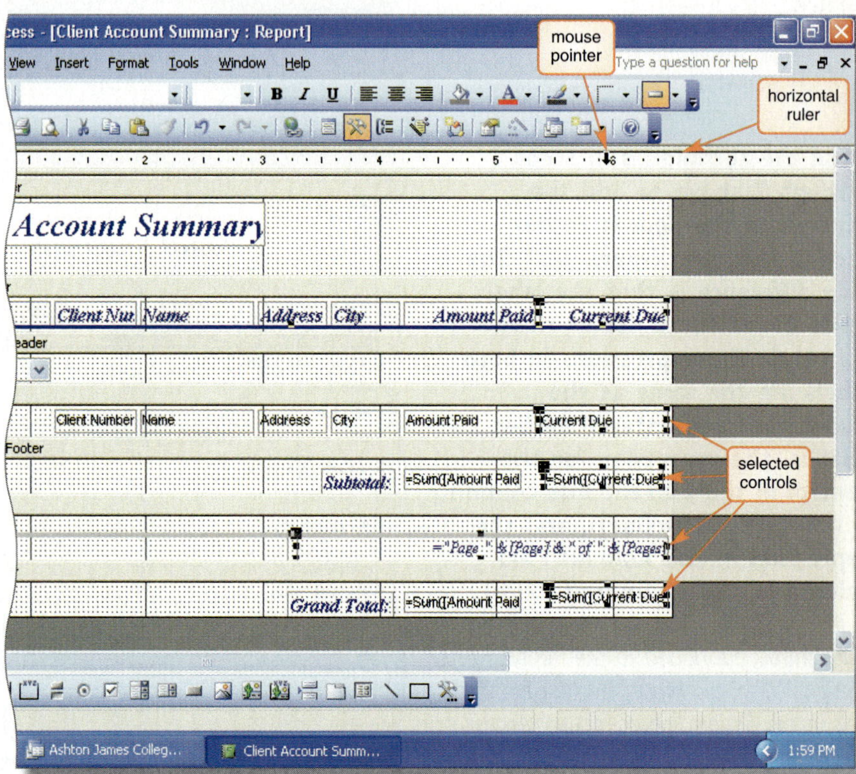

FIGURE 4-33

2

- **Click Format on the menu bar and then point to Align.**

The Format menu appears (Figure 4-34). The Align submenu also appears.

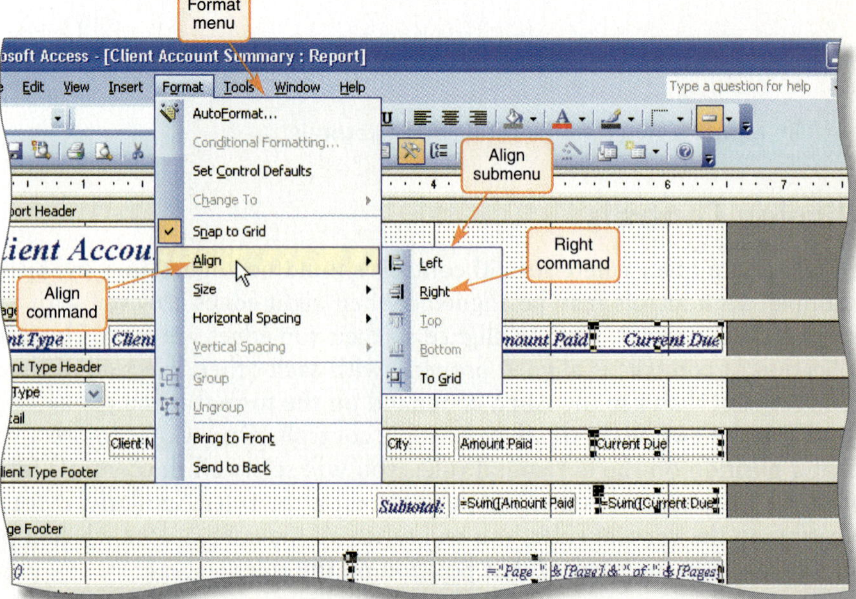

FIGURE 4-34

3

- **Click Right on the Align submenu.**
- **Click the Amount Paid control in the Page Header section to select it.**
- **Press and hold down the SHIFT key and then click the Amount Paid controls in the Detail, Client Type Footer, and Report Footer sections to select them.**
- **Click Format on the menu bar and then point to Align.**

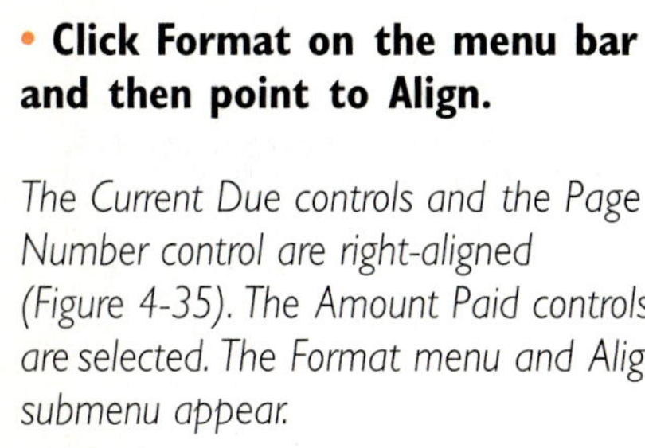

The Current Due controls and the Page Number control are right-aligned (Figure 4-35). The Amount Paid controls are selected. The Format menu and Align submenu appear.

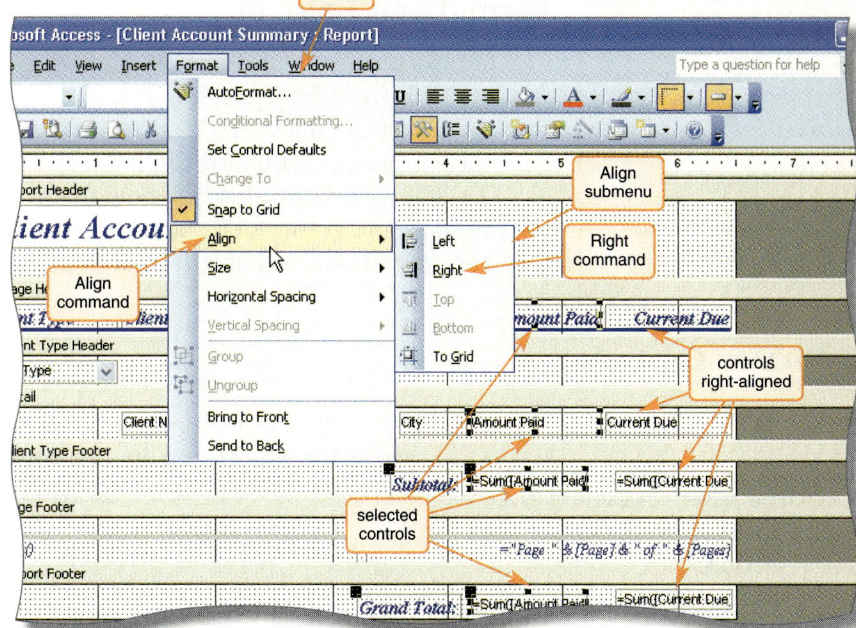

FIGURE 4-35

4

- **Click Right on the Align submenu.**
- **Click the left ruler below the section selector for the Client Type Footer section.**
- **Click Format on the menu bar and then point to Align.**

All the controls in the Client Type Footer section are selected (Figure 4-36). The Format menu and Align submenu appear.

5

- **Click Top on the Align submenu.**
- **Use the same technique to top-align the controls in the Report Footer section.**

All the controls in the Client Type Footer and Report Footer sections are top-aligned.

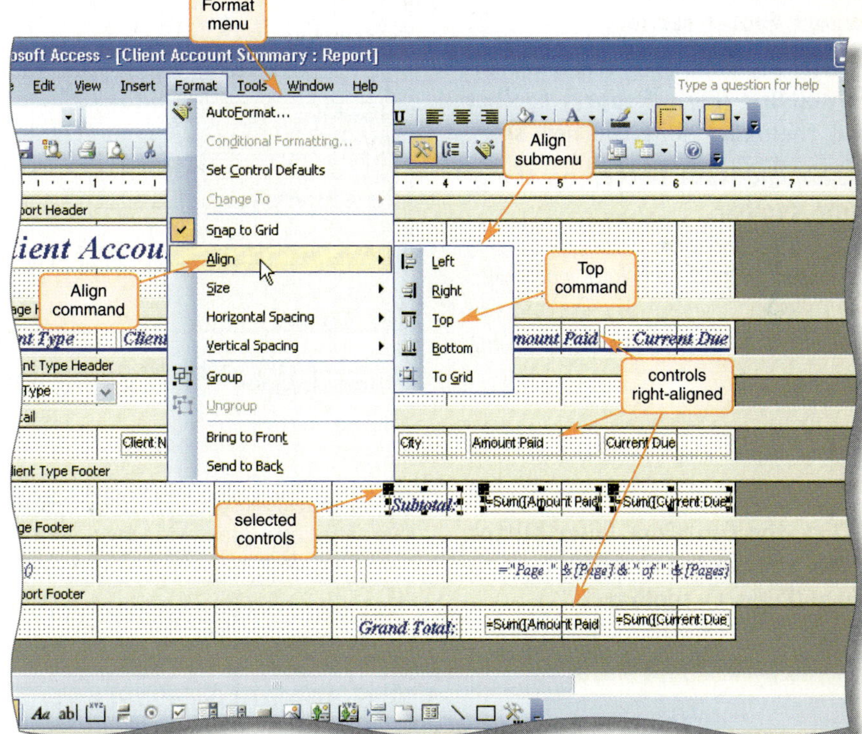

FIGURE 4-36

The controls are all aligned properly. You can use this technique to align any collection of controls.

Other Ways

1. Right-click any selected control, point to Align on shortcut menu, click Right on Align submenu
2. Right-click any selected control, point to Align on shortcut menu, click Top on Align submenu

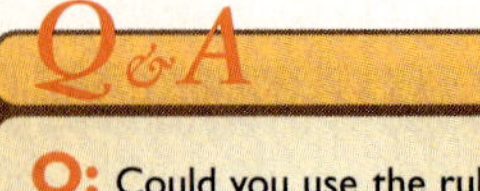

Q: Could you use the ruler to select the Amount Paid controls?

A: No, clicking the ruler in any position that would select the Amount Paid controls also would select the Page Number control.

Formatting Controls

You can change the format of controls in a variety of ways. You can change the font, the font size, and the color. You also can change the way data in the control is displayed. You can make any of these changes using the control's property sheet. For some of the changes, you also can use a button on the Formatting toolbar.

The following steps illustrate how to change the font and color of the labels for the subtotals and grand totals, and remove italics as well as to change the controls so they appear with the currency format (dollars and cents).

To Format Controls

- **Click the label containing the word, Subtotal, in the Client Type Footer section.**
- **Press and hold down the SHIFT key and then click the label containing the words, Grand Total, in the Report Footer section.**
- **Click the Font Size arrow on the Formatting (Form/Report) toolbar and then click 8 as the new size.**
- **Click the Italic button on the same toolbar.**

The Subtotal and Grand Total labels are both selected (Figure 4-37). The font size is changed to 8, and the labels are no longer in italics.

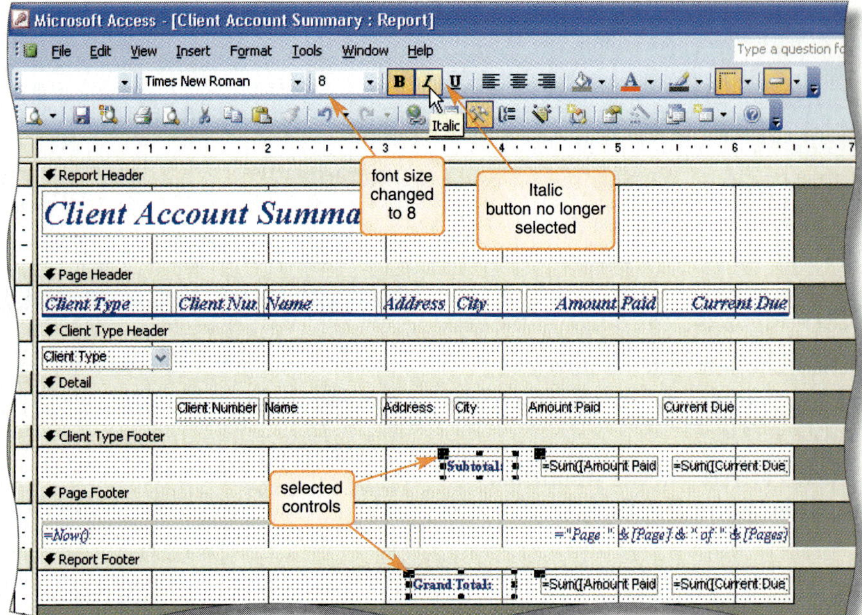

FIGURE 4-37

2

- **Click the Font/Fore Color button arrow on the Formatting (Form/Report) toolbar.**

The color palette appears (Figure 4-38).

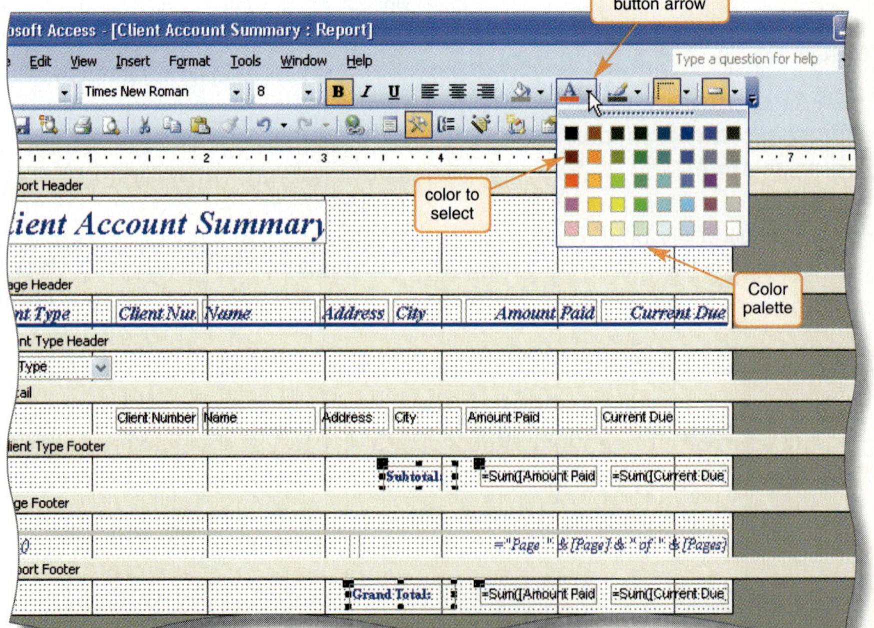

FIGURE 4-38

3

- **Click the color in the second row and first column.**
- **Click the control for the sum of Amount Paid in the Client Type Footer section.**
- **Press and hold down the SHIFT key and click the control for the sum of Amount Paid in the Report Footer section, the control for the sum of Current Due in the Client Type Footer section, and the control for the sum of Current Due in the Report Footer section.**
- **Right-click any of the selected controls.**

The controls are selected and the shortcut menu for the selected controls appears (Figure 4-39).

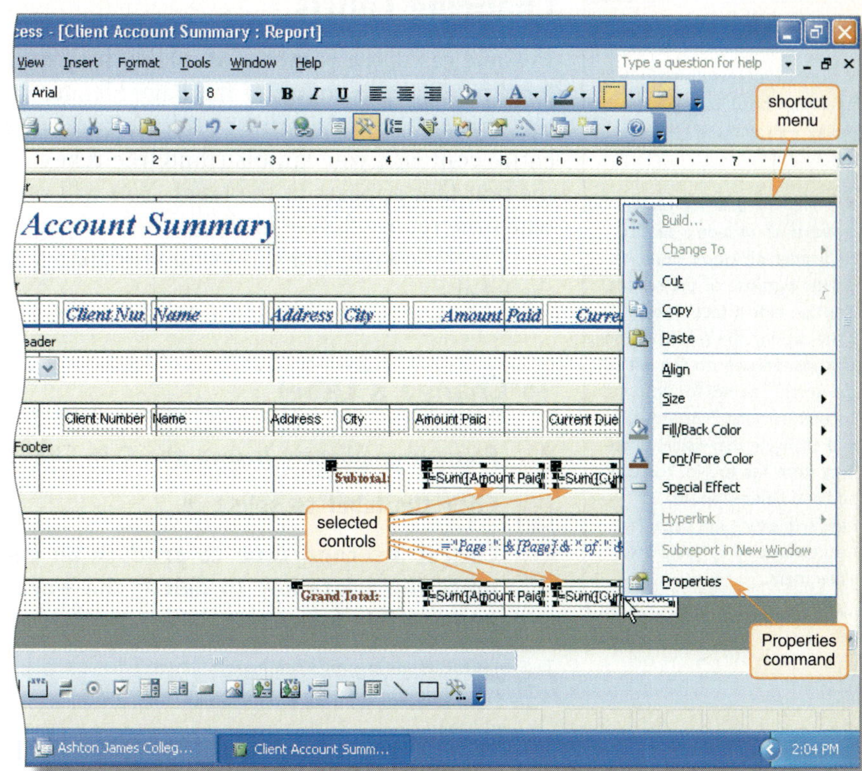

FIGURE 4-39

4

- **Click Properties on the shortcut menu.**
- **Click the Format tab to display only the Format properties, click the Format property box, click the Format property box arrow, and then select Currency.**

The Multiple selection property sheet appears and the Currency format is selected (Figure 4-40).

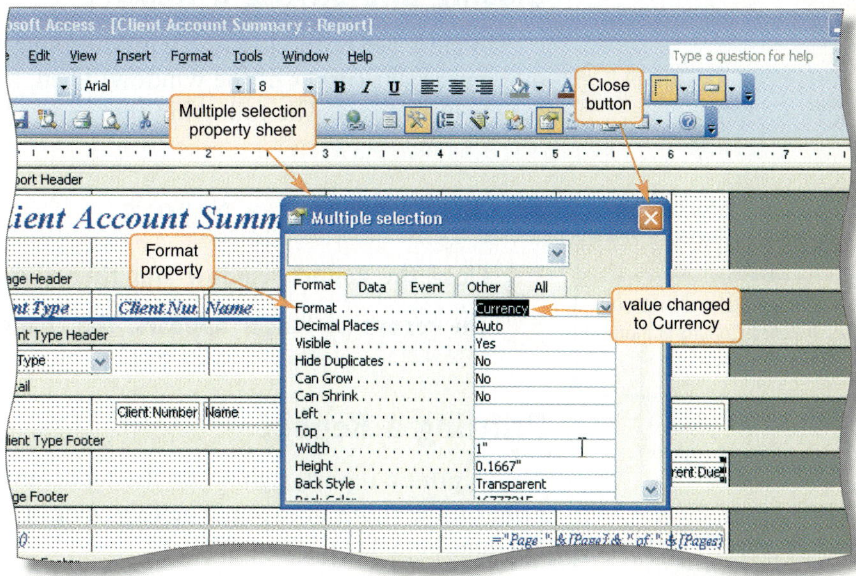

FIGURE 4-40

5

- **Close the property sheet by clicking its Close button.**

The format changes now are complete. The steps illustrated using one of the tabs, in this case the Format tab, in the property sheet. You also can use the All tab to display all the properties and then scroll down to find the one you want. If you know the type of property you are looking for and then click the tab for that type of property, you will have a shorter list to scroll through. By clicking the Format tab, for example, only properties that relate to formatting will appear.

Changing Labels

In some cases, the contents of a label may not display completely. For example, the label for Client Number in the Page Header section displays only Client Nu. There are several ways to fix this problem. You can enlarge the size of a label to display the entire contents, you can distribute the text over two lines, or you can delete some of the text that appears in the label. You will see how to distribute text over two lines when the report shown in Figure 4-2 on page AC 195 is created later in this project.

The following step shows how to change a label by deleting text that appears in the label.

Q&A

Q: Must a report always have page headers and footers as well as report headers and footers?

A: No, the decision on whether to include a particular header or footer depends on the purpose of the report. You can hide a section by right-clicking the selector (the box immediately to the left of the section name) for the section, clicking Properties, and changing the Visible property from Yes to No. You can add and delete report header/footers and page header/footers by using the View menu.

To Change a Label

1. **Point immediately before the C in Client Nu label in the Page Header section.**
2. **Click the label to select it.**
3. **Click it a second time to produce an insertion point before the C, repeatedly press the delete key to delete the word, Client, and the space that immediately follows.**

The label is changed to Number.

The changes to the report now are complete and it should look like the report shown in Figure 4-1 on page AC 195.

Closing and Saving a Report

To close a report, close the window using the window's Close Window button in the upper-right corner of the window. Then, indicate whether or not you want to save your changes. The following step shows how to close and save the report.

To Close and Save a Report

1. **Close the Report window and then click the Yes button to save the report.**
2. **The report no longer appears. The changes are saved.**

Other Ways

1. On File menu click Close
2. In Voice Command mode, say "File, Close"

Printing a Report

To print a report, right-click the report in the Database window, and then click Print on the shortcut menu. The following steps illustrate how to print the Client Account Summary.

To Print a Report

1. **If necessary, click the Reports object in the Database window and then right-click Client Account Summary.**
2. **Click Print on the shortcut menu.**

The report prints. It should look like the report shown in Figure 4-1 on page AC 195.

Other Ways

1. Click Reports object, select report, click Print button on Database toolbar
2. Click Reports object, select report, on File menu click Print
3. Click Reports object, select report, press CTRL+P
4. In Voice Command mode, say "Reports, [file name], Print"

Using Multiple Tables in a Report

You are not restricted to a single table when you create a report. You can use multiple related tables. The report in Figure 4-2 on page AC 195, for example, incorporates data from both the Trainer and Client tables.

Creating a Report Involving Multiple Tables

As you did when you created the first report, you will use the Report Wizard to create the second report. This time, however, you will select fields from two tables. To do so, you will select the first table (for example, Trainer) and then select the fields from this table you would like to include. Next, you will select the second table (for example, Client) and then select the fields from the second table. You will use the wizard to group, sort, and include totals and subtotals. The following steps show how to create a report that incorporates data from both the Trainer and Client tables.

Q&A

Q: Is there more than one way to use the Report Wizard to create a report containing two tables?

A: Yes, you can create a report using one of the tables. Select all the fields needed from this table, select the other table, and then select the fields from the other table. You also can first create a query that joins the two tables, and then base the report on the query.

To Create a Report that Involves Multiple Tables

1

- **In the Database window, click the Tables object and then click Trainer.**
- **Click the New Object button arrow on the Database toolbar.**

The list of available objects appears (Figure 4-41).

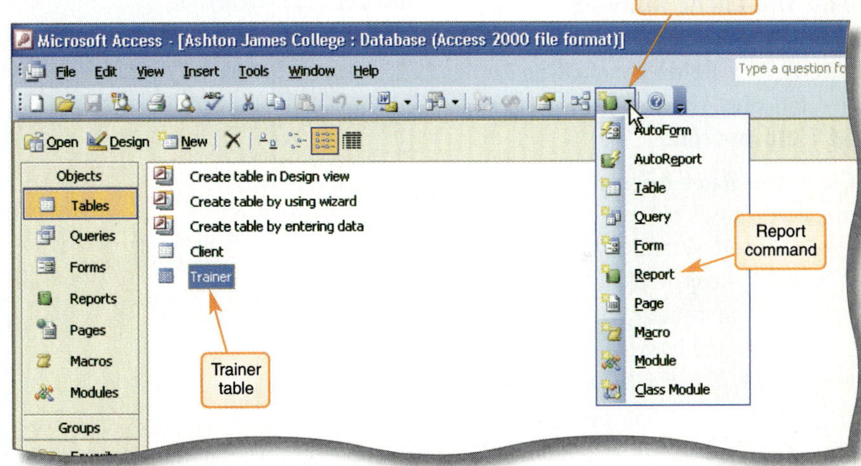

FIGURE 4-41

2

- **Click Report, click Report Wizard, and then click the OK button.**

The Report Wizard dialog box appears, requesting the fields for the report (Figure 4-42). Fields from the Trainer table appear. The Trainer Number field is selected.

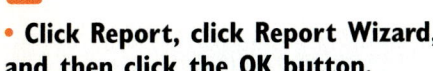

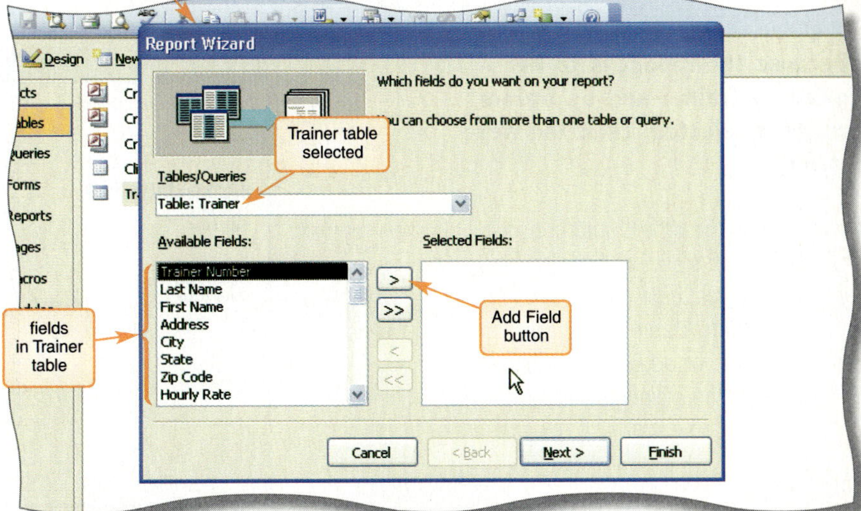

FIGURE 4-42

3

- **Click the Add Field button to add the Trainer Number field.**
- **Add the First Name field by clicking it and then clicking the Add Field button.**
- **Add the Last Name field in the same manner.**
- **Click the Tables/Queries arrow, and then click Table: Client in the Tables/Queries list box.**

The Trainer Number, First Name, and Last Name fields are selected (Figure 4-43). The fields from the Client table appear in the Available Fields box.

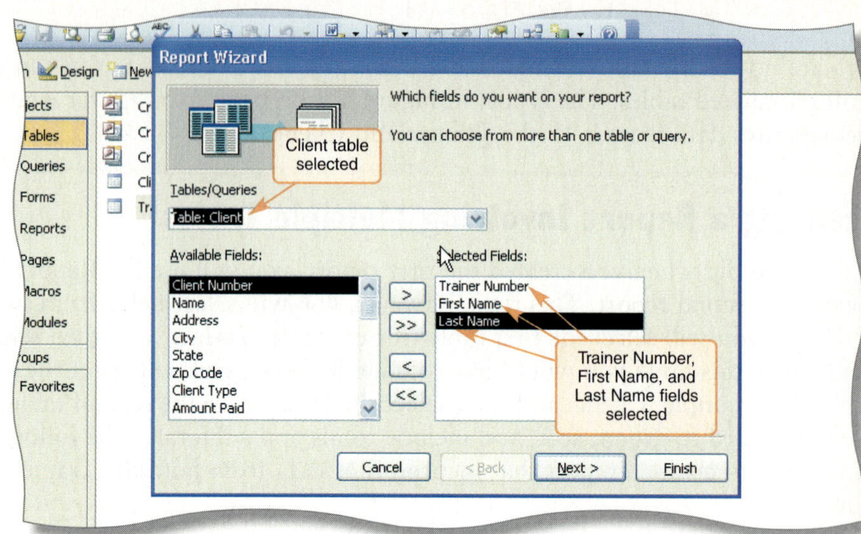

FIGURE 4-43

4

- **Add the Client Number, Name, Amount Paid, and Current Due fields by clicking the field and then clicking the Add Field button.**
- **Click the Next button.**

The next Report Wizard dialog box appears (Figure 4-44). Because the Trainer and Client tables are related, the wizard is asking you to indicate how the data is to be viewed; that is, the way the report is to be organized. The report may be organized by Trainer or by Client.

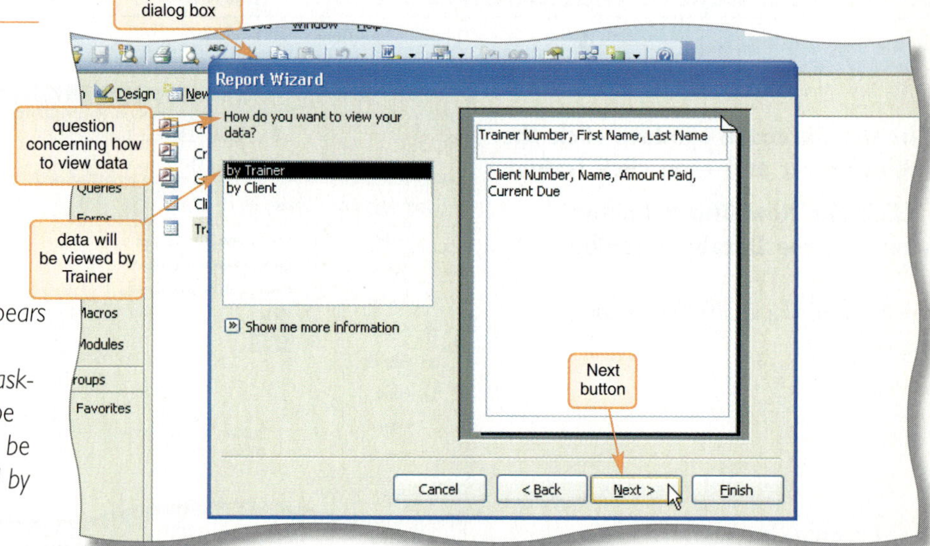

FIGURE 4-44

5

- **Because the report is to be viewed by Trainer and by Trainer already is selected, click the Next button.**

Access groups the report automatically by Trainer Number, which is the primary key of the Trainer table (Figure 4-45). The next Report Wizard dialog box appears, asking for additional grouping levels other than the Trainer Number.

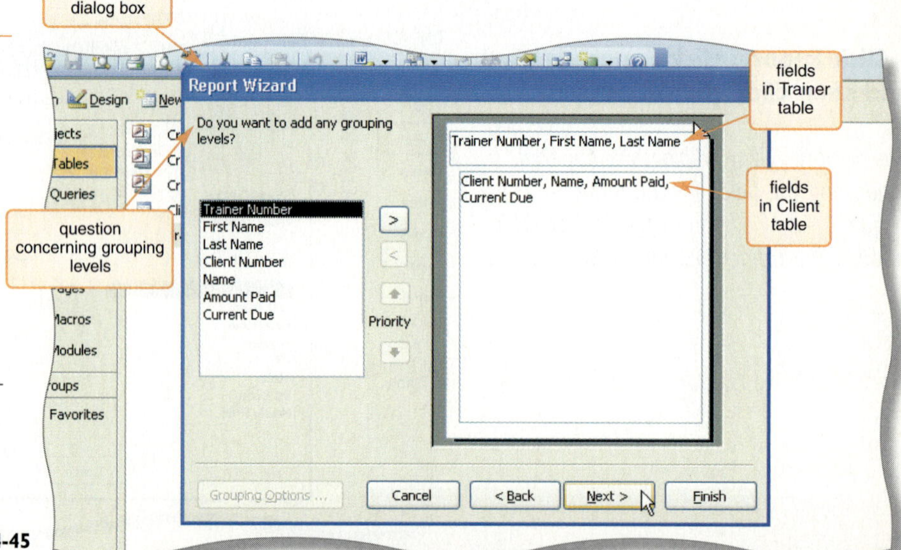

FIGURE 4-45

6

- **Because no additional grouping levels are required, click the Next button.**
- **Click the box arrow in the text box labeled 1 and then click the Client Number field in the list.**

The next Report Wizard dialog box appears, requesting the sort order for detail records in the report; that is, the way in which records will be sorted within each of the groups (Figure 4-46). The Client Number field is selected for the sort order, indicating that within the group of clients of any trainer, the clients will be sorted by client number.

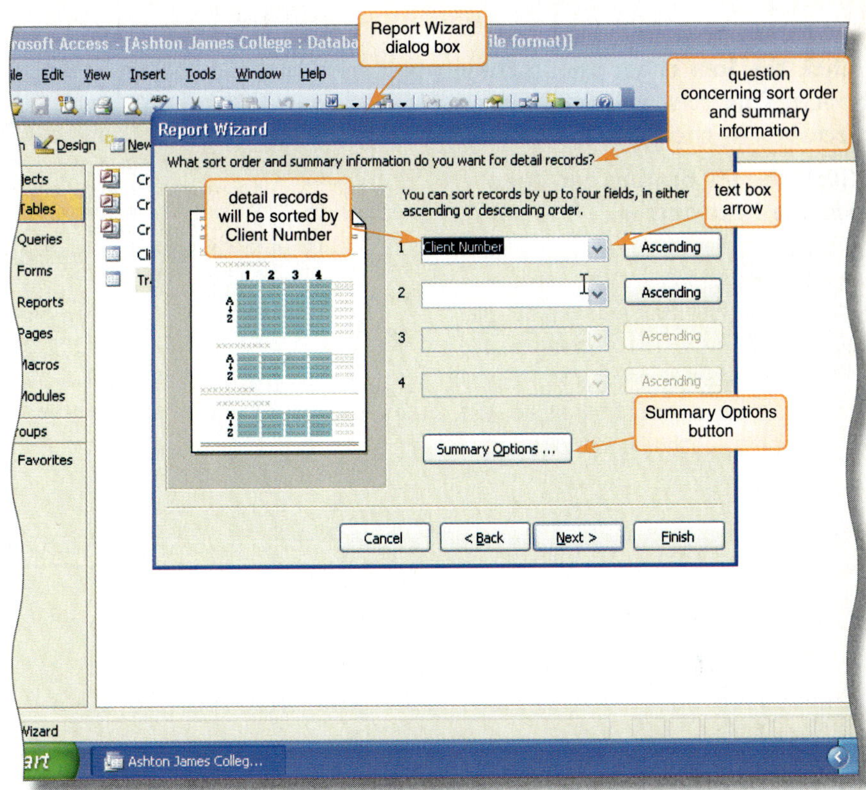

FIGURE 4-46

7

- **Click the Summary Options button.**

The Summary Options dialog box appears (Figure 4-47). This dialog box allows you to indicate any statistics you want calculated in the report by clicking the appropriate check box.

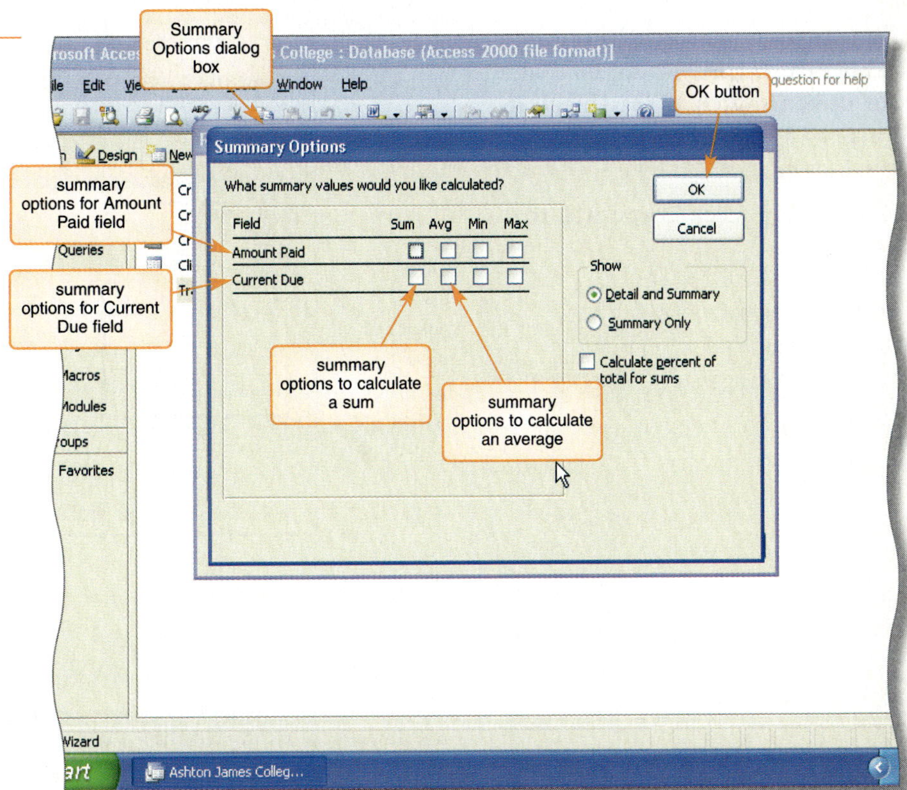

FIGURE 4-47

8

- **Click the Sum check box in the Amount Paid row and the Sum check box in the Current Due row.**
- **Click the OK button, and then click the Next button.**

The next Report Wizard dialog box appears, requesting your report layout preference (Figure 4-48). The Stepped layout, which is the correct one, already is selected. To see the effect of any of the others, click the appropriate option button.

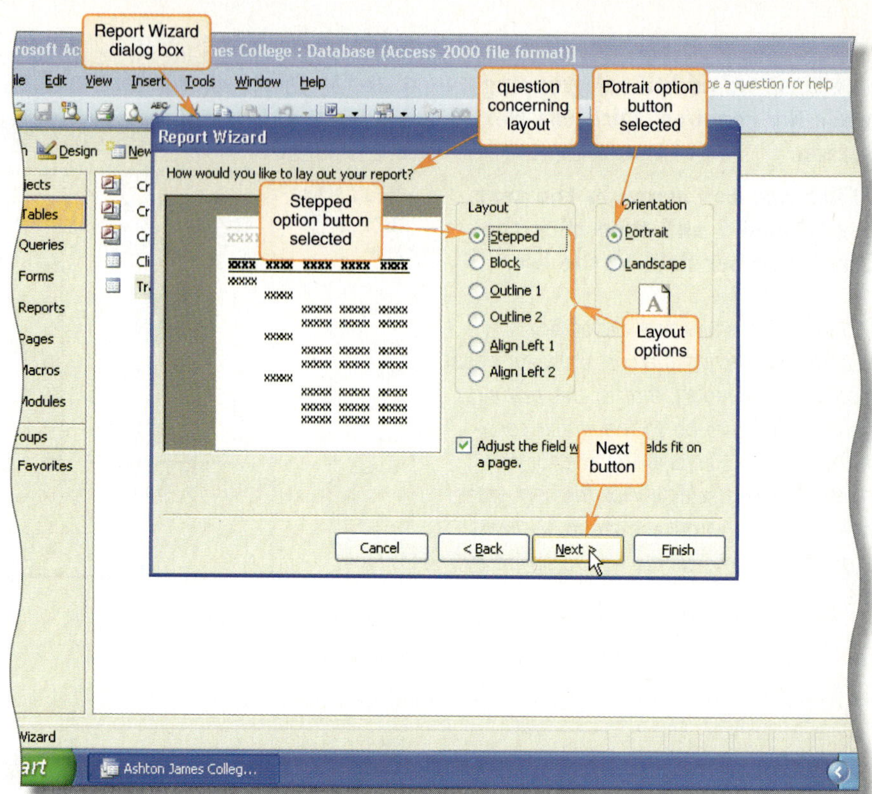

FIGURE 4-48

9

- **Be sure the options selected in the Report Wizard dialog box on your screen match those shown in Figure 4-48, and then click the Next button.**
- **If necessary, click Corporate to select it.**

The next Report Wizard dialog box appears, requesting a style for the report. The Corporate style is selected (Figure 4-49).

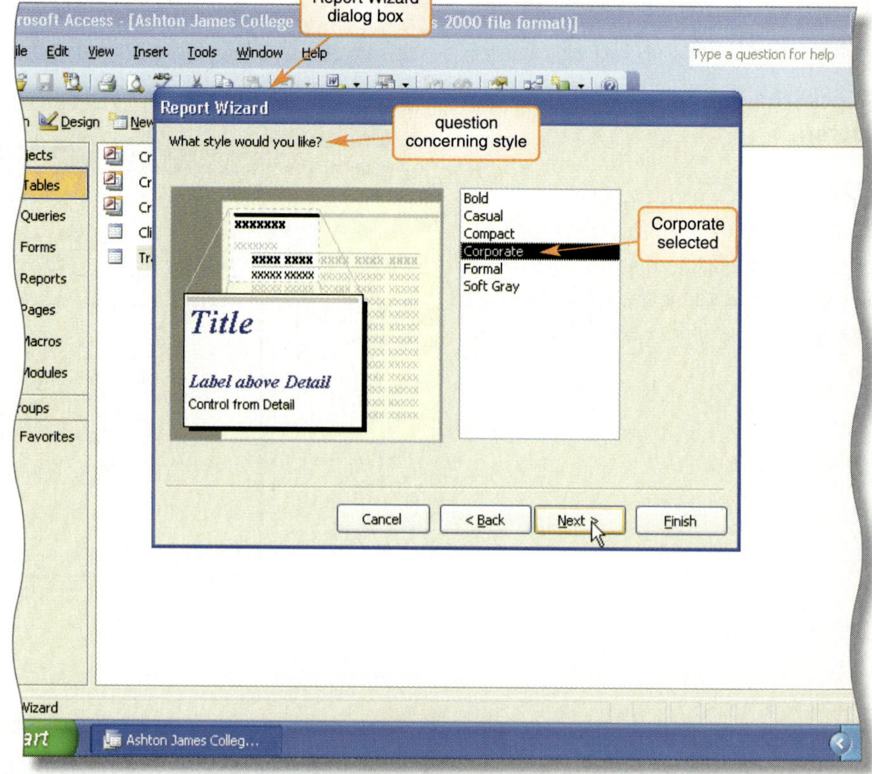

FIGURE 4-49

10

• **Click the Next button, and then type** `Trainer/Client Report` **as the report title.**

The next Report Wizard dialog box appears, requesting a title for the report (Figure 4-50). Trainer/Client Report is typed as the title.

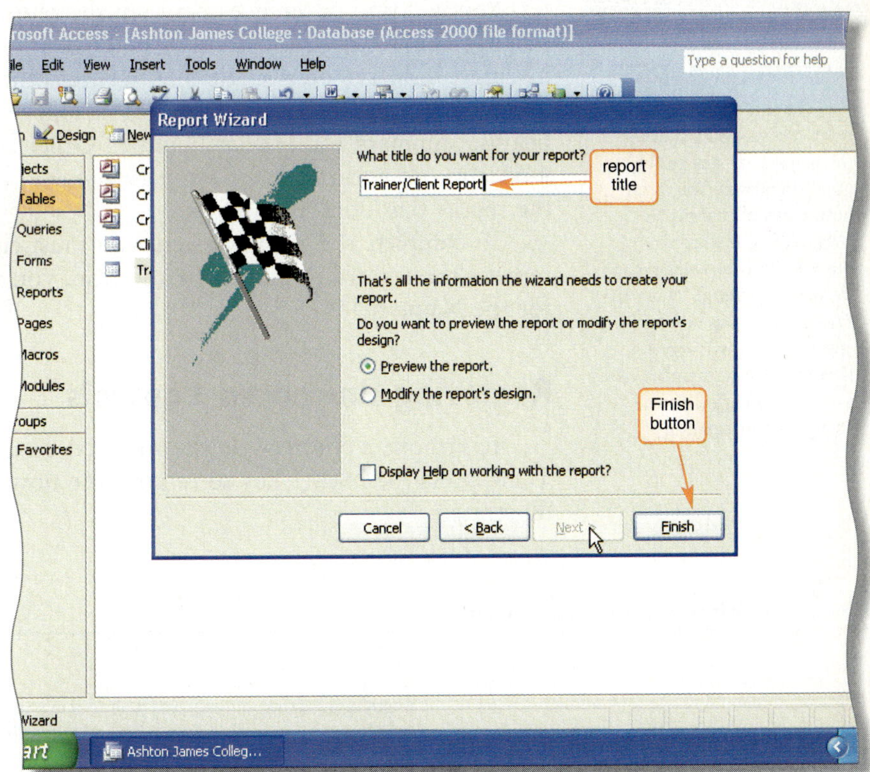

FIGURE 4-50

11

• **Click the Finish button.**

The report design is complete and appears in the Print Preview window (Figure 4-51).

12

• **Close the report by clicking the Close Window button for the window containing the report.**

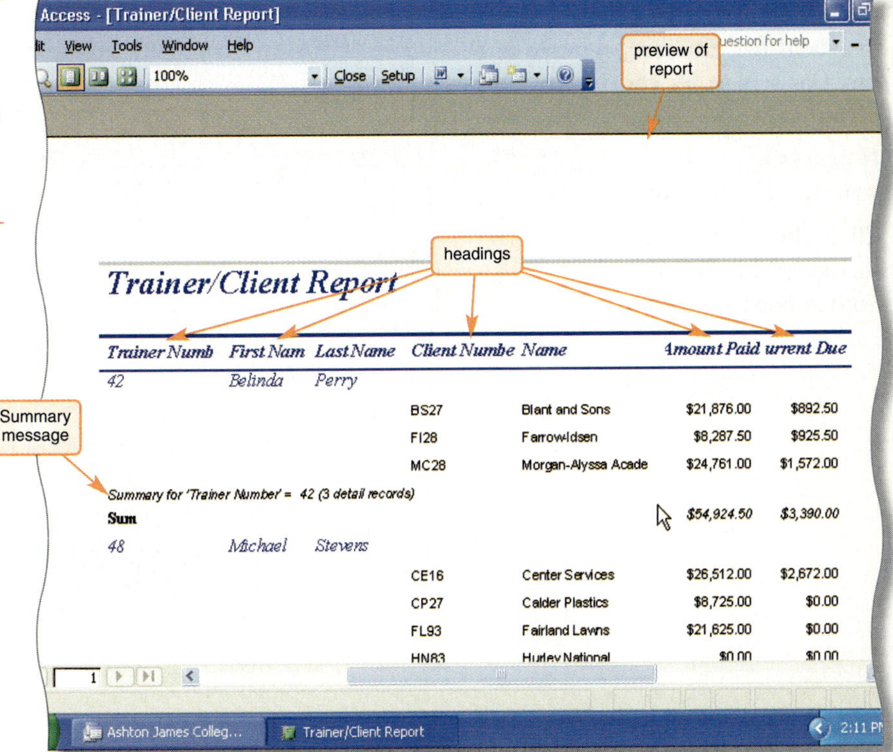

FIGURE 4-51

More About

Printing a Report

If a report is too wide for the printed page, you can adjust the margins or change the page orientation. You make both types of changes by right-clicking the report in the Print Preview window and clicking Page Setup. When the Page Setup dialog box appears, use the Margins sheet to change the margins and use the Page sheet to change the orientation.

You will find differences between the report shown in Figure 4-51 on the previous page and the one illustrated in Figure 4-2 on page AC 195. The column headings in Figure 4-51 are on a single line, whereas they extend over two lines in the report in Figure 4-2. In addition, the report in Figure 4-2 does not contain the message that begins, Summary for Trainer Number. Other messages found on the report in Figure 4-51 also are not on the report in Figure 4-2, but they are included in a portion of the report that does not appear.

To complete the report design, you must change the column headings and remove these extra messages. In addition, you will change the Can Grow property for the Name field.

Removing Unwanted Controls

To remove a control you do not need, first click the control to select it. Then, press the DELETE key to remove the unwanted control as the following steps illustrate.

To Remove Unwanted Controls

1

- **Be sure the Reports object is selected in the Database window, right-click Trainer/Client Report, and then click Design View on the shortcut menu.**
- **If a field list appears, remove it from the screen by clicking its Close button.**
- **If necessary, maximize the window.**
- **Click the control at the top of the Trainer Number Footer section.**

The report appears in Design view (Figure 4-52). The control is selected.

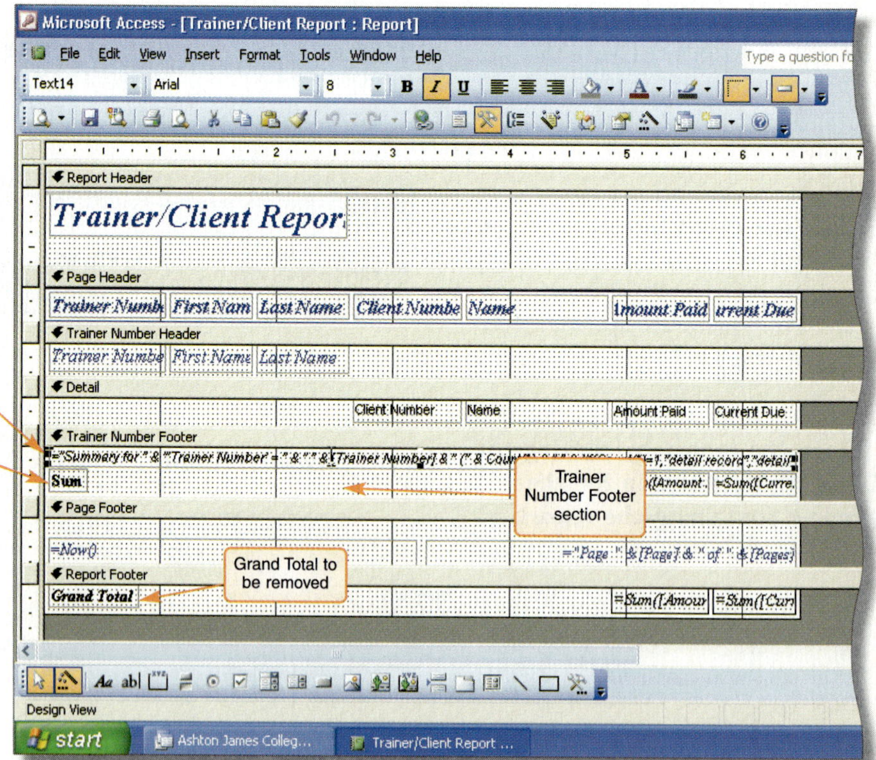

FIGURE 4-52

2

- **Press the DELETE key to delete it.**
- **Click the control that reads SUM, then press the delete key to delete the control.**
- **Click the control that reads Grand Total, then press the delete key to delete the control.**

The controls have been removed (Figure 4-54).

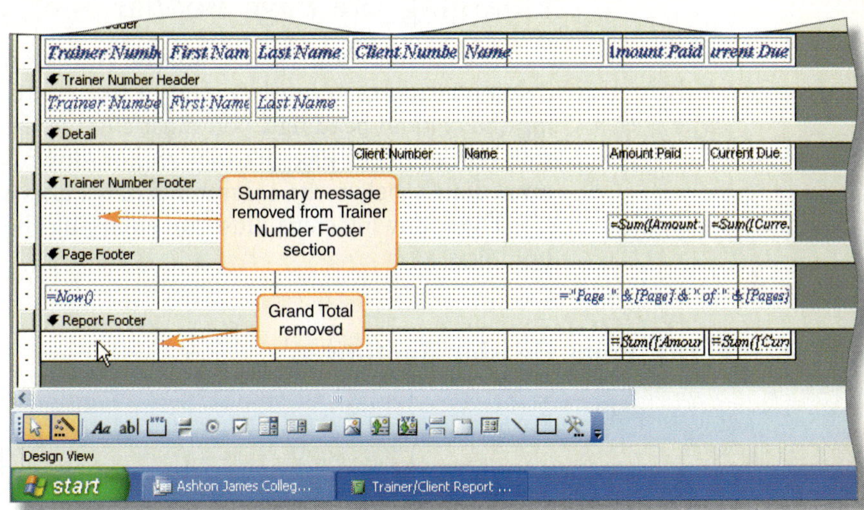

FIGURE 4-53

Changing a Property

Just as in the previous report, there is missing data in the Detail section of the report. The following steps select all the controls in the Detail section and change the Can Grow property for the controls.

> **More About**
>
> **Enlarging Controls**
>
> If you want to make a slight adjustment to a control, it often is easier to hold down the SHIFT key and use the appropriate arrow key.

To Change a Property

1

- **Right-click below the section selector for the Detail section.**
- **Click Properties and then, if necessary, click the Format tab.**
- **Click the Can Grow property, click the Can Grow property box arrow, and then click Yes in the list that appears.**

The Multiple selection property sheet appears (Figure 4-54). The value for the Can Grow property has been changed to Yes for all fields in the Detail section.

2

- **Close the property sheet by clicking its Close button.**

The property sheet no longer appears.

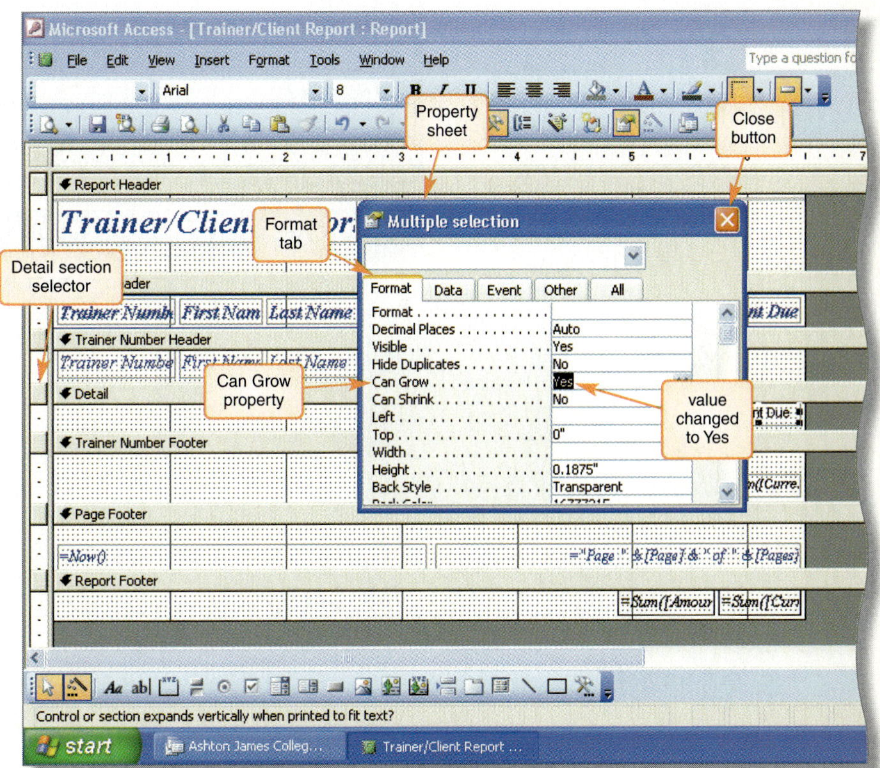

FIGURE 4-54

Enlarging the Page Header Section

The current Page Header section is not large enough to encompass the desired column headings because several of them extend over two lines. Thus, before changing the column headings, you must enlarge the Page Header. To do so, drag the bottom border of the Page Header section down. A bold line in the Page Header section immediately below the column headings also must be dragged down.

The following steps illustrate enlarging the Page Header section and moving the bold line.

To Enlarge the Page Header Section

1

- **Point to the bottom border of the Page Header section. The mouse pointer shape changes to a two-headed vertical arrow with a crossbar.**
- **Drag the mouse pointer down to enlarge the size of the Page Header section.**

The section is enlarged (Figure 4-55).

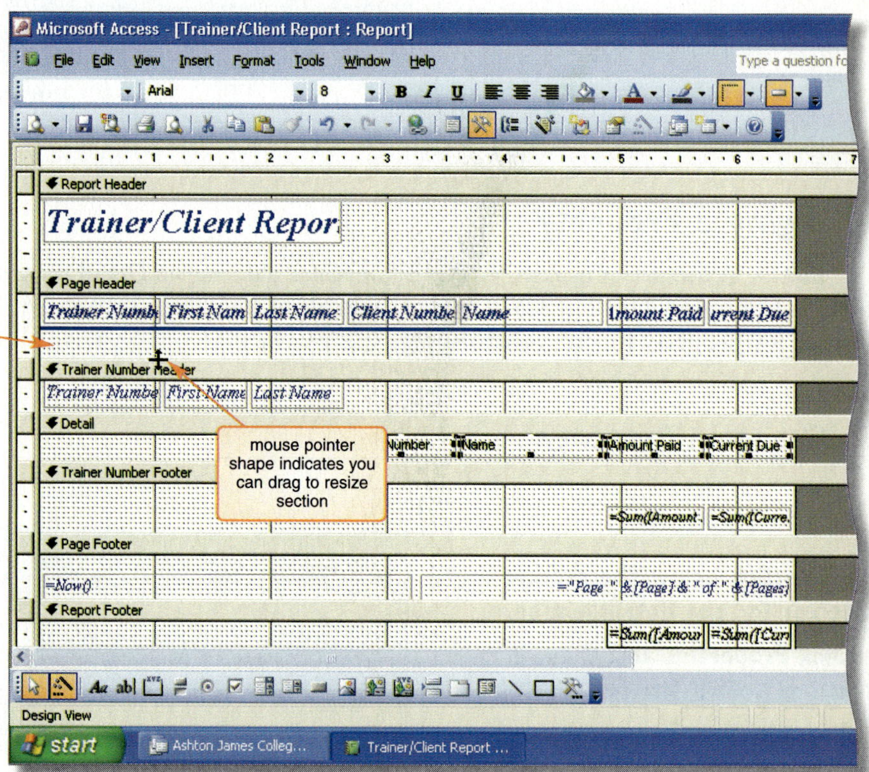

FIGURE 4-55

2

• **Click the bold line underneath the column headings in the Page Header section, and then drag the bold line down to the bottom of the Page Header section. The mouse pointer is displayed as a hand when you drag the line.**

The bold line is moved (Figure 4-56).

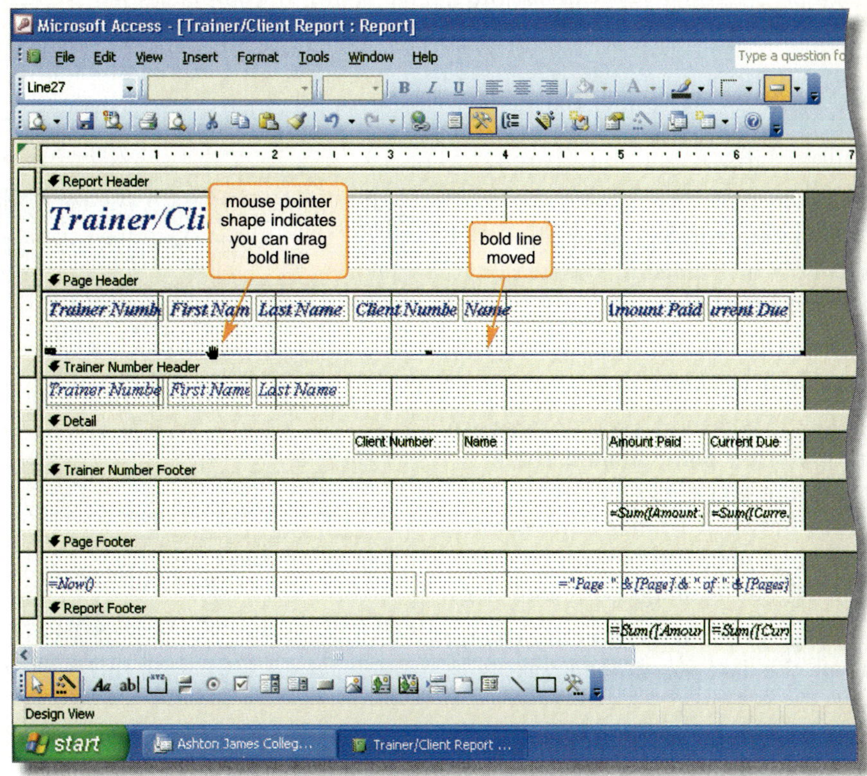

FIGURE 4-56

The page heading now is enlarged appropriately so the column headings can be changed.

Changing Column Headings

To change a column heading, point to the position where you would like to display an insertion point. Click once to select the heading. Handles will appear around the border of the heading after clicking. Then, click a second time to display the insertion point. Then, you can make the desired changes. To delete a character, press the DELETE key to delete the character following the insertion point, or press the BACKSPACE key to delete the character preceding the insertion point. To insert a new character, simply type the character. To move the portion following the insertion point to a second line, press SHIFT+ENTER.

If you click the second time too rapidly, Access will assume you have double-clicked the heading. Double-clicking a control is another way to produce the control's property sheet. If this happens, simply close the property sheet and begin the process again.

More About

Report Design

Proper report design is critical because users judge the value of information based on the way it is presented. Many organizations have formal rules governing the design of printed documents. For more information on report design, visit the Microsoft Access 2003 More About Web page (scsite.com/ac2003/more) and click Report Design.

The following step shows how to change the column headings.

To Change the Column Headings

- Point immediately after the second r in Trainer in the heading for the first field.
- Click the column heading for the first field to select it.
- Click it a second time to produce an insertion point behind the r, press the DELETE key to delete the space between Trainer and Number, and then press SHIFT+ENTER to extend the headings over two lines.
- Using the same technique, change all of the two word headings.

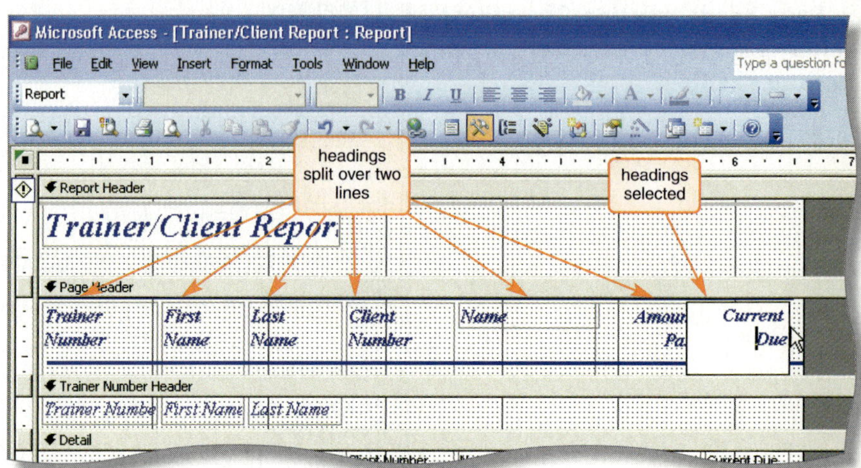

FIGURE 4-57

The headings are split over two lines (Figure 4-57).

Previewing a Report

To see what the report looks like with actual data, preview the report by clicking the Print Preview button on the Report Design toolbar as illustrated in the following step.

Other Ways

1. Click View button arrow on Report Design toolbar, click Print Preview
2. On View menu click Print Preview
3. In Voice Command mode, say "Print Preview"

To Preview a Report

1 **Click the Print Preview button on the Report Design toolbar. If the entire width of the report does not appear, click anywhere within the report.**

A preview of the report appears. The extra messages have been removed. The column headings have been changed and now extend over two lines. The name for Morgan-Alyssa Academy extends over two lines.

More About

Previewing a Report

You can view two pages at the same time when previewing a report by clicking the Two Pages button on the toolbar. You can view multiple pages by clicking Multiple Pages on the toolbar, and then clicking the number of pages to view.

Closing and Saving a Report

To close a report, close the window containing the report. Then, indicate whether you want to save your changes. The following step shows how to close and save the report.

To Close and Save a Report

1 **Click the Close Window button for the window containing the report to close the window. Click the Yes button to save the design of the report.**

Access displays the Database window. The changes are saved.

Printing a Report

To print the report, right-click the report name in the Database window, and then click Print on the shortcut menu as the following step illustrates.

To Print a Report

1 **Be sure the Reports object is selected in the Database window. Right-click Trainer/Client Report and then click Print on the shortcut menu.**

The report prints. It should look like the report shown in Figure 4-2 on page AC 195.

More About

Modifying Form Properties

You can modify many of the properties associated with a form. To modify a form property, right-click the form selector (the box in the upper-left corner of the form) and click Properties. For example, to change the default view to continuous form, right-click the form selector, click Properties, click the Default View property, and then click Continuous Form. Other property changes, such as changing the caption for a form are done similarly. For example, you could change the caption for the form from Client Update Form to AJC Client Update Form by clicking the Caption property and entering the new caption name.

Report Design Considerations

When designing and creating reports, keep in mind the following guidelines.

1. The purpose of any report is to provide specific information. Ask yourself if the report conveys this information effectively. Are the meanings of the rows and columns in the report clear? Are the column captions easily understood? Are all abbreviations used in the report clear to those looking at the report?
2. Be sure to allow sufficient white space between groups. If you feel the amount is insufficient, add more space by enlarging the group footer.
3. You can use different fonts and sizes by changing the appropriate properties. It is important not to overuse them, however. Consistently using several different fonts and sizes often gives a cluttered and amateurish look to the report.
4. Be consistent when creating reports. Once you have decided on a general style, stick with it.

Creating and Using Custom Forms

Thus far, you have used a form to add new records to a table and change existing records. When you did, you created a basic form using the AutoForm command. Although the form did provide some assistance in the task, the form was not particularly pleasing. The standard form stacked fields on top of each other at the left side of the screen. This section covers custom forms that you can use in place of the basic form created by the AutoForm command. To create such a form, first use the Form Wizard to create a basic form. Then, modify the design of this form, transforming it into the one you want.

More About

Creating Forms

There are two alternatives to using the Form Wizard to create forms. You can use AutoForm to create a very simple form that includes all fields in the table or query. You also can use Design view to create a form totally from scratch.

Beginning the Form Creation

To create a form, select a table for the form and then use the New Object button. Next, use the Form Wizard to create the form. The Form Wizard will lead you through a series of choices and questions. Access then will create the form automatically.

The steps on the next page show how to create an initial form. This form later will be modified to produce the form shown in Figure 4-3 on page AC 196.

To Begin Creating a Form

1

- **Make sure the Tables object is selected and then click Client.**
- **Click the New Object button arrow, click Form, and then click Form Wizard. Click the OK button.**

The Form Wizard dialog box appears (Figure 4-58). The Client Number field is selected.

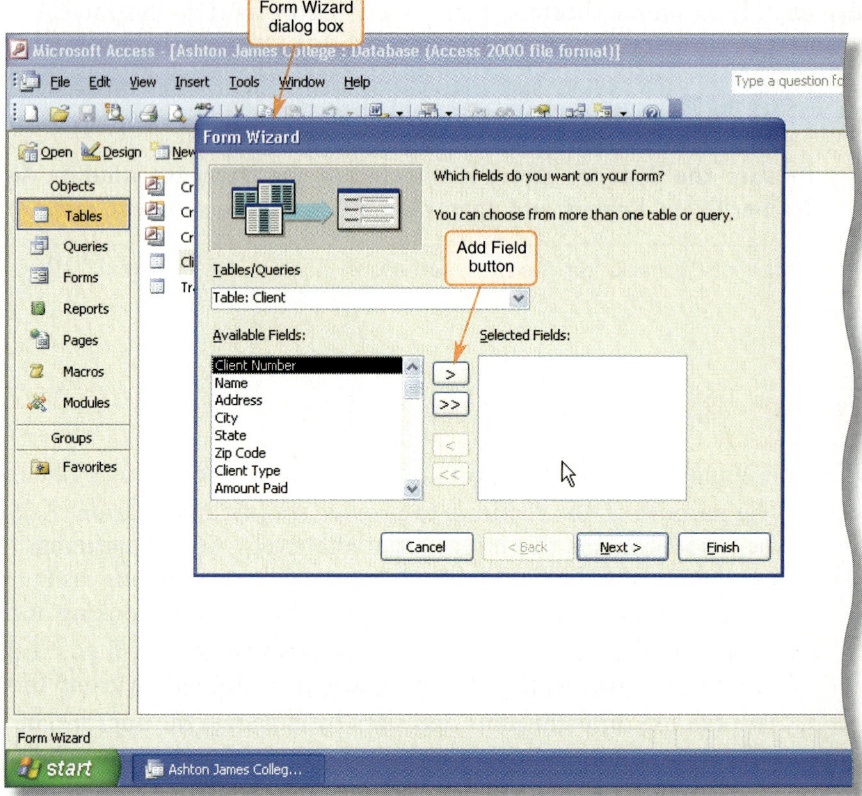

FIGURE 4-58

2

- **Use the Add Field button to add all the fields except the Client Type and Trainer Number fields.**
- **Click the Next button.**
- **When asked for a layout, be sure Columnar is selected, and then click the Next button again.**

The Form Wizard dialog box appears, requesting a form style (Figure 4-59).

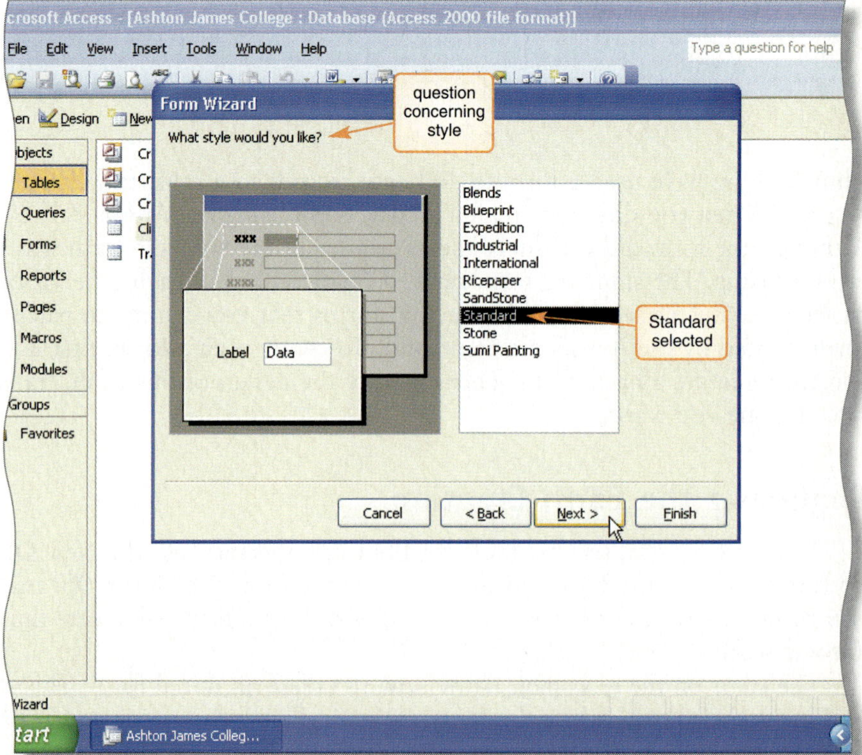

FIGURE 4-59

3

- **Be sure Standard is selected, click the Next button, and then type** Client Update Form **as the title for the form.**
- **Click the Finish button to complete and display the form.**

Access displays the Client Update Form in Form view (Figure 4-60).

4

- **Click the Close Window button for the Client Update Form window to close the form.**

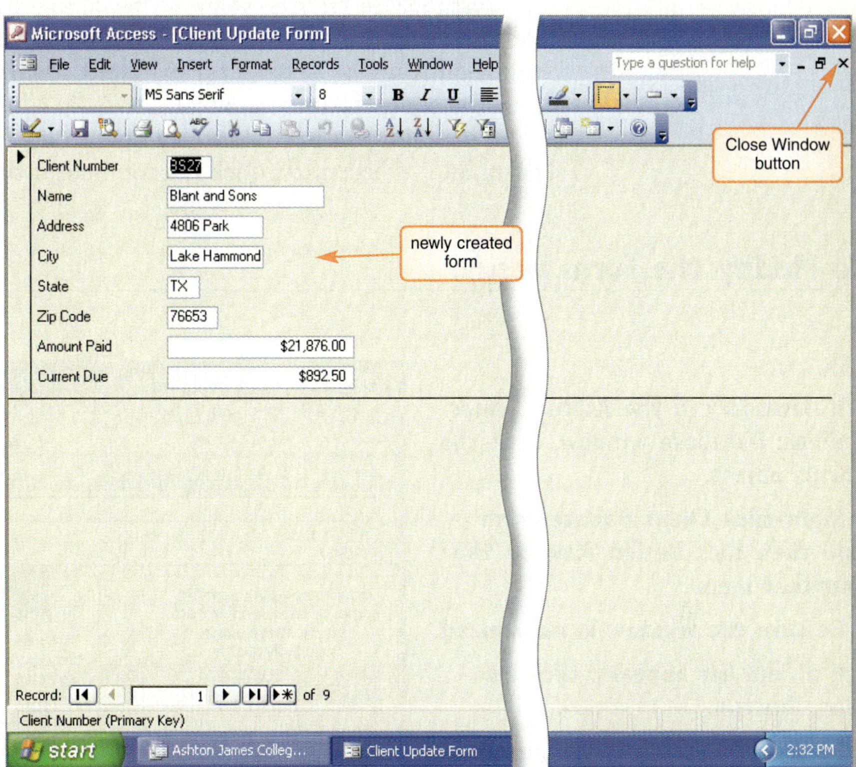

FIGURE 4-60

Other Ways

1. Click Forms on Objects bar, click New button, click Form Wizard
2. Click Forms on Objects bar, double-click Create form by using wizard
3. On Insert menu click Form, click Form Wizard
4. In Voice Command mode, say "Forms, New," click Form Wizard

Modifying the Form Design

To modify the design of an existing form, open the form in Design view. The modifications can include moving fields, adding new fields, and changing field characteristics. In addition, you can add special features, such as combo boxes and titles and change the colors used.

Just as with reports, the various items on a form are called controls. The three types are bound controls, unbound controls, and calculated controls. **Bound controls** are used to display data that comes from the database, such as the client number and name. Bound controls have attached labels that typically display the name of the field that furnishes the data for the control. The **attached label** for the Client Number field, for example, is the portion of the screen immediately to the left of the field. It contains the words, Client Number.

Unbound controls are not associated with data from the database and are used to display such things as the form's title. Finally, **calculated controls** are used to display data that is calculated from other data in the database, such as the Total Amount, which is calculated by adding the amount paid and current due amounts.

To move, resize, delete, or modify a control, click it. Clicking a second time produces an insertion point in the control to let you modify its contents. When a control is selected, handles appear around the border of the control and, if appropriate, around the attached label. If you point to the border of the control, but away from any handle, the pointer shape will change to a hand. You then can drag the control to move it. If an attached label appears, it will move along with the control. If you wish to move the control or the attached label separately, drag the large handle in the upper-left corner of the control or label. To resize the control, drag one of the sizing handles; and to delete it, press the DELETE key.

Just as with reports, some of the changes you wish to make to a control will involve using the property sheet for the control. You will use the property sheet of the Total Amount control, for example, to change the format that Access uses to display the contents of the control.

The following steps illustrate how to modify the design of the Client Update Form and, if necessary, dock the toolbox at the bottom of the screen.

To Modify the Form Design

1

- **If necessary in the Ashton James College: Database window, click the Forms object.**
- **Right-click Client Update Form and then click Design View on the shortcut menu.**
- **Be sure the window is maximized.**
- **If a field list appears, click its Close button.**
- **Be sure the toolbox appears and is docked at the bottom of the screen.**
- **Click the control for the Amount Paid field, and then move the mouse pointer until the shape changes to a hand. (You will need to point to the border of the control but away from any handle.)**

Move handles appear, indicating the field is selected (Figure 4-61). The shape of the mouse pointer changes to a hand.

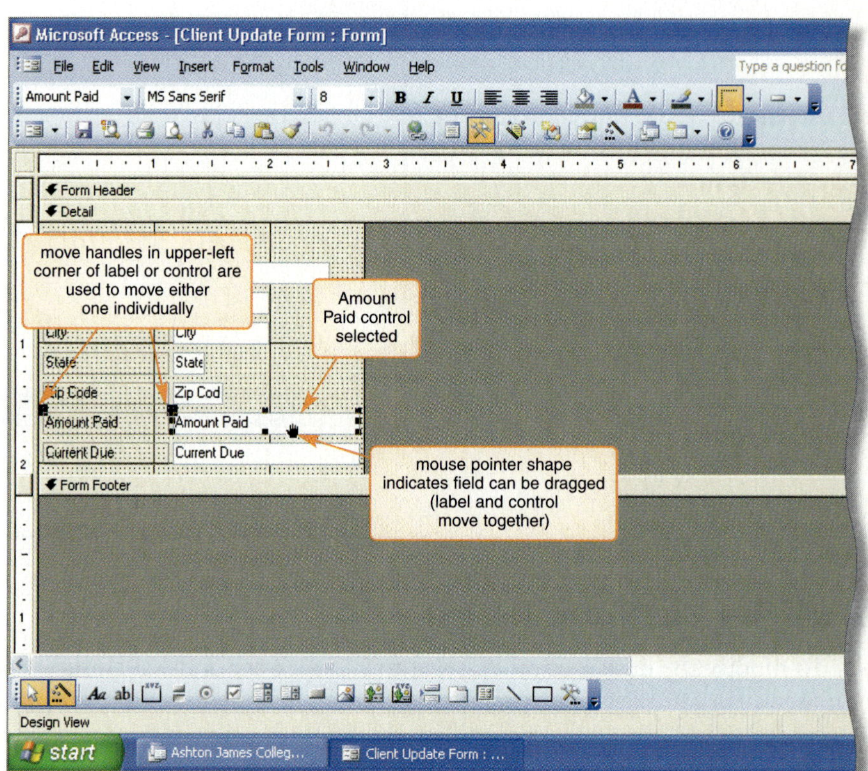

FIGURE 4-61

2

- **Drag the Amount Paid field to the approximate position shown in Figure 4-62.**

The form expands automatically in size to accommodate the new position for the field.

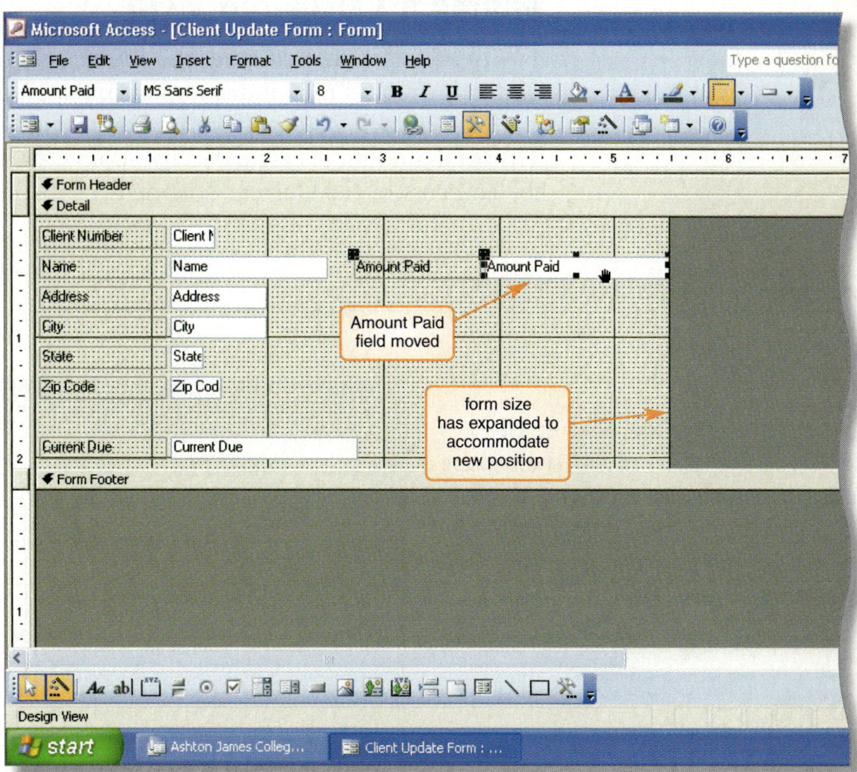

FIGURE 4-62

3

- **Use the same steps to move the Current Due field to the position shown in Figure 4-63.**

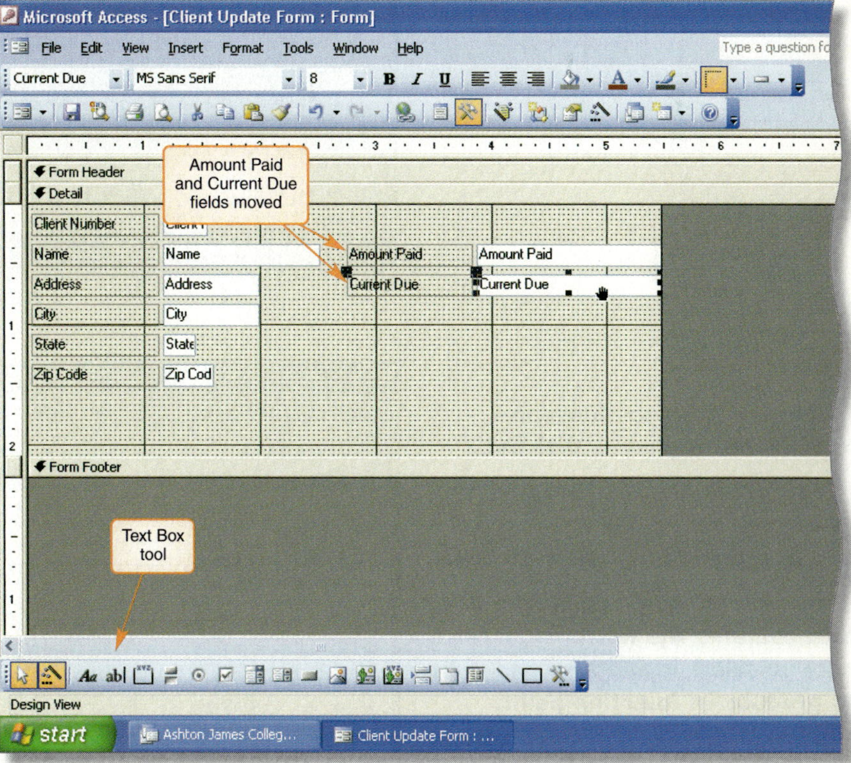

FIGURE 4-63

Adding a Calculated Field

To add a calculated field, use the Text Box tool in the toolbox. Place the text box on the form, and then indicate the contents of the field.

The following steps illustrate how to add the Total Amount field to the form. The total amount is calculated by adding the contents of the Amount Paid field and the contents of the Current Due field.

To Add a Calculated Field

1

- **Click the Text Box tool in the toolbox, and then move the mouse pointer, which has changed shape to a small plus symbol accompanied by a text box, to the position shown in Figure 4-64.**

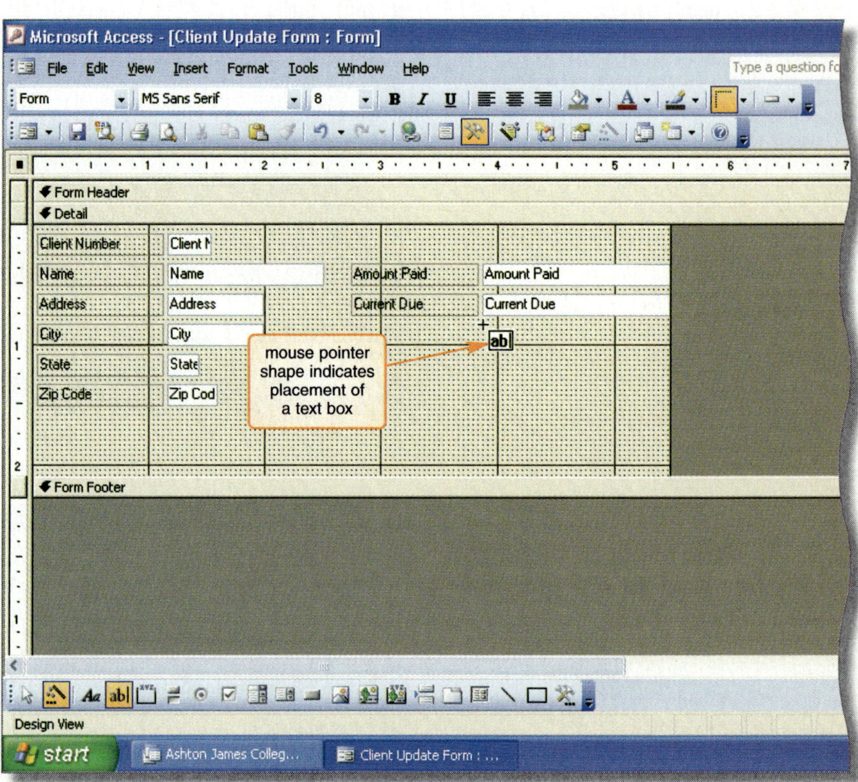

FIGURE 4-64

2

- **Click the position shown in Figure 4-64 to place a text box.**
- **Click inside the text box and type** `=[Amount Paid]+[Current Due]` **as the expression in the text box.**
- **Click the attached label (the box that contains the word, Text) twice, once to select it and a second time to produce an insertion point.**
- **Use the DELETE key or the BACKSPACE key to delete the current entry.**
- **Type** `Total Amount` **as the new entry.**

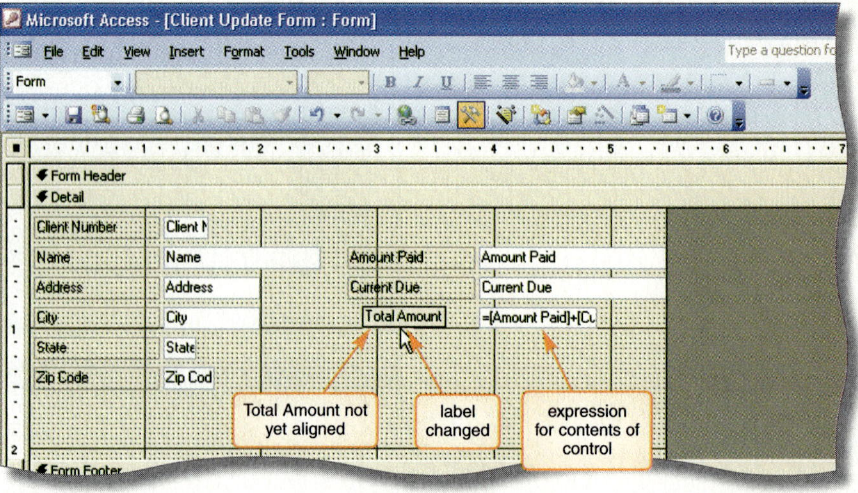

FIGURE 4-65

The expression for the field has been entered and the label has been changed to Total Amount (Figure 4-65).

3

- **Click outside the Total Amount control to deselect it, and then click the control to select it once more. Handles will appear around the control.**
- **Move the label portion so its left edge lines up with the labels for the Amount Paid and Current Due fields by dragging the move handle in its upper-left corner.**

The label is moved (Figure 4-66). The mouse pointer has assumed the pointing finger shape.

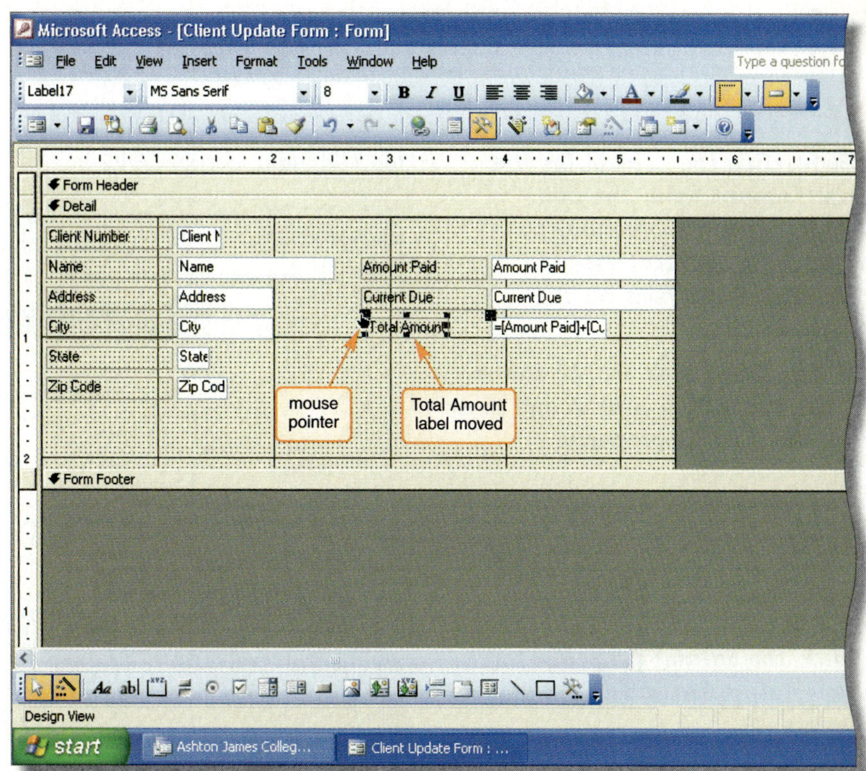

FIGURE 4-66

The control is added to the form. The expression and label are correct and the control is in the correct position.

Changing the Format of a Field

Access automatically formats fields from the database appropriately because it knows their data types. Usually, you will find the formats assigned by Access to be acceptable. For calculated fields, such as Total Amount, however, Access just assigns a general format. The value will not display automatically with two decimal places and a dollar sign.

To change to a special format, such as Currency, which displays the number with a dollar sign and two decimal places, requires using the field's property sheet to change the Format property. The steps on the next page change the format for the Total Amount field to Currency.

More About

Adding a Calculated Control

You can receive assistance in entering the expression for a calculated control you are adding by using the Expression Builder. To do so, click the Control Source property on the control's property sheet and then click the Build button. The Expression Builder dialog box then will open.

To Change the Format of a Field

1

- **Right-click the control for the Total Amount field (the box containing the expression) to produce its shortcut menu, and then click Properties on the shortcut menu.**
- **If necessary, click the All tab so all the properties appear, and then click the Format property.**

Access displays the property sheet for the field (Figure 4-67).

2

- **Click the Format property box arrow to produce a list of available formats.**
- **Scroll down so Currency appears and then click Currency.**
- **Close the property sheet by clicking its Close button.**

The property sheet no longer appears.

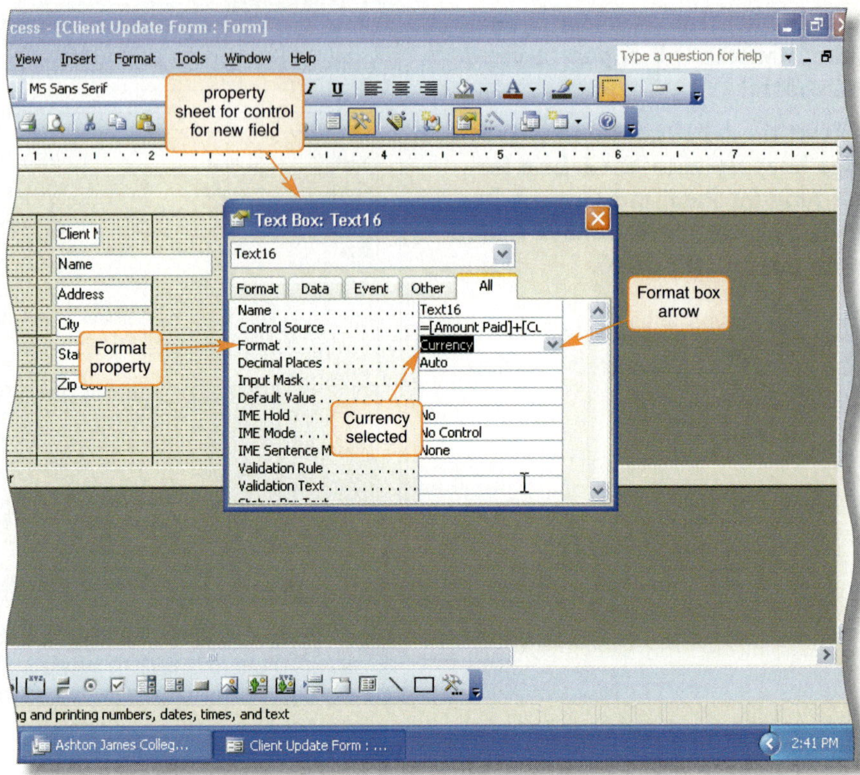

FIGURE 4-67

The values in the Total Amount field will appear in Currency format, which includes a dollar sign and two decimal places.

Combo Boxes

When entering a value for the client type, there are only three legitimate values: EDU, MAN, and SER. When entering a trainer number, the value must match the number of a trainer currently in the Trainer table. To assist the users in entering this data, the form will contain combo boxes. With a combo box, the user can type the data, if that is convenient. Alternatively, the user can click the combo box arrow to display a list of possible values and then select an item from the list.

To place a combo box in the form, use the Combo Box tool in the toolbox. If the Control Wizards tool in the toolbox is selected, you can use a wizard to guide you through the process of creating the combo box. The following steps show how to place a combo box that selects values from a list for the Client Type field on the form.

To Place a Combo Box that Selects Values from a List

1

- **If necessary, click the Control Wizards tool in the toolbox to select it.**
- **Click the Combo Box tool in the toolbox, and then move the mouse pointer, whose shape has changed to a small plus symbol accompanied by a combo box, to the position shown in Figure 4-68.**

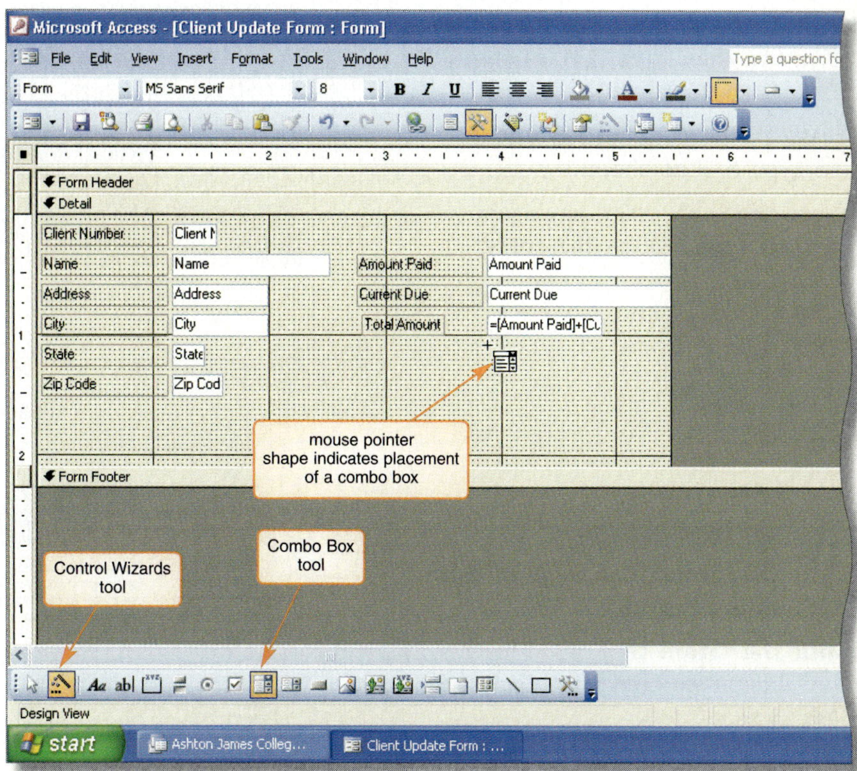

FIGURE 4-68

2

- **Click the position shown in Figure 4-68 to place a combo box.**
- **If necessary, click the "I will type in the values that I want." option button to select it.**

The Combo Box Wizard dialog box appears, requesting that you indicate how the combo box is to receive values for the list (Figure 4-69). The "I will type in the values that I want." option button is selected.

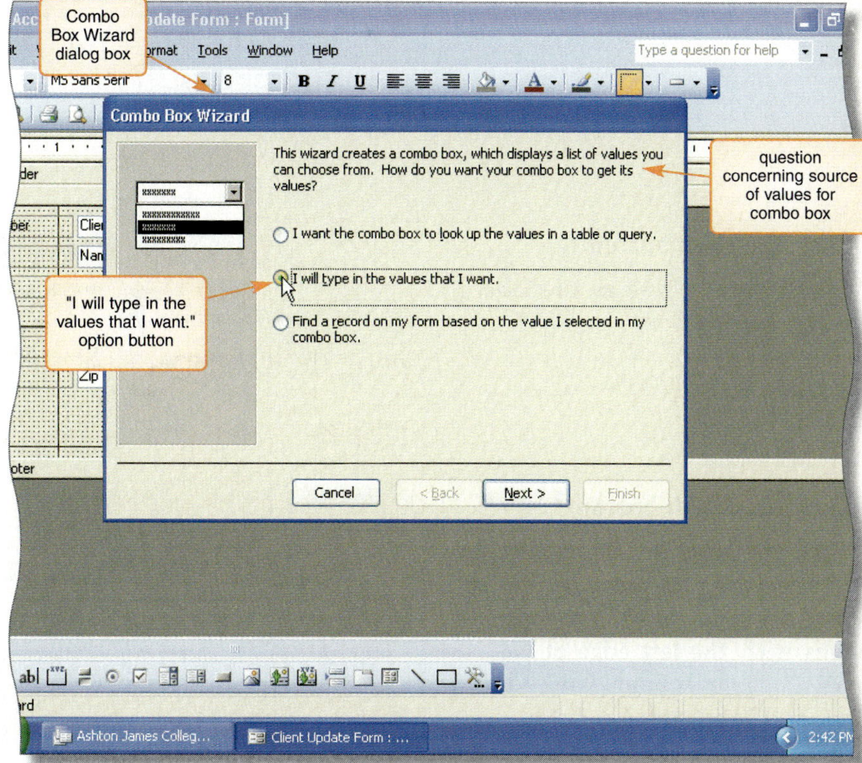

FIGURE 4-69

3

- **Click the Next button in the Combo Box Wizard dialog box, click the first row of the table (under Col1), and then type** EDU **as the entry.**
- **Press the DOWN ARROW key and then type** MAN **as the entry.**
- **Press the DOWN ARROW key again and then type** SER **as the entry.**

The list of values for the combo box is entered (Figure 4-70).

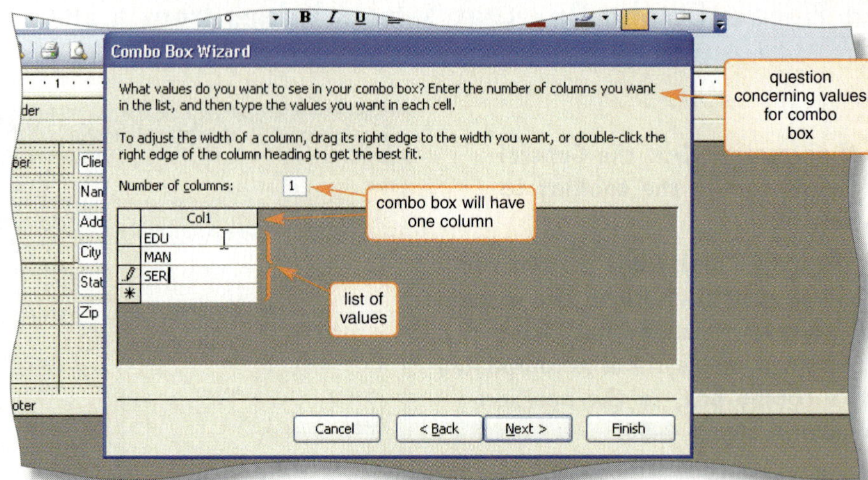

FIGURE 4-70

4

- **Click the Next button.**
- **Click the "Store that value in this field:" option button.**
- **Click the "Store that value in this field:" box arrow and then click Client Type.**

The "Store that value in this field:" option button is selected, and the Client Type field is selected (Figure 4-71).

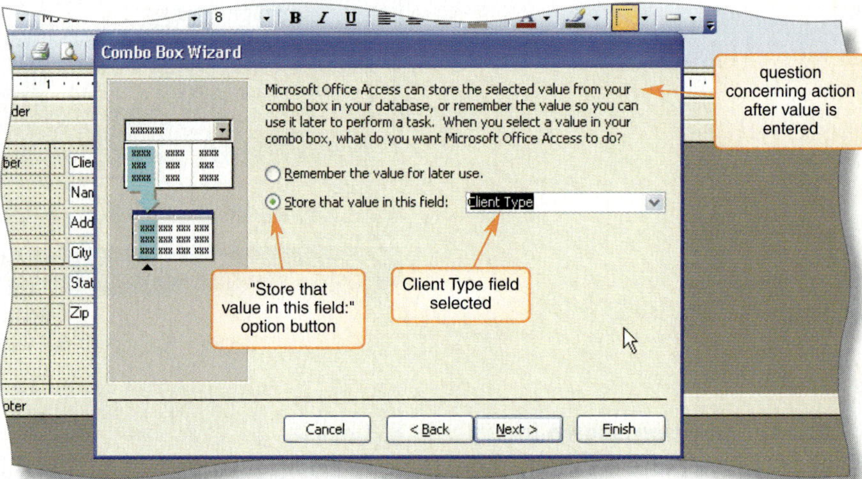

FIGURE 4-71

5

- **Click the Next button.**
- **Type** Client Type **as the label for the combo box.**

The label is entered (Figure 4-72).

6

- **Click the Finish button.**
- **Click the label for the combo box, and then drag its move handle to move the label so its left edge aligns with the left edge of the labels for the Amount Paid, Current Due, and Total Amount fields.**

The combo box is placed on the form.

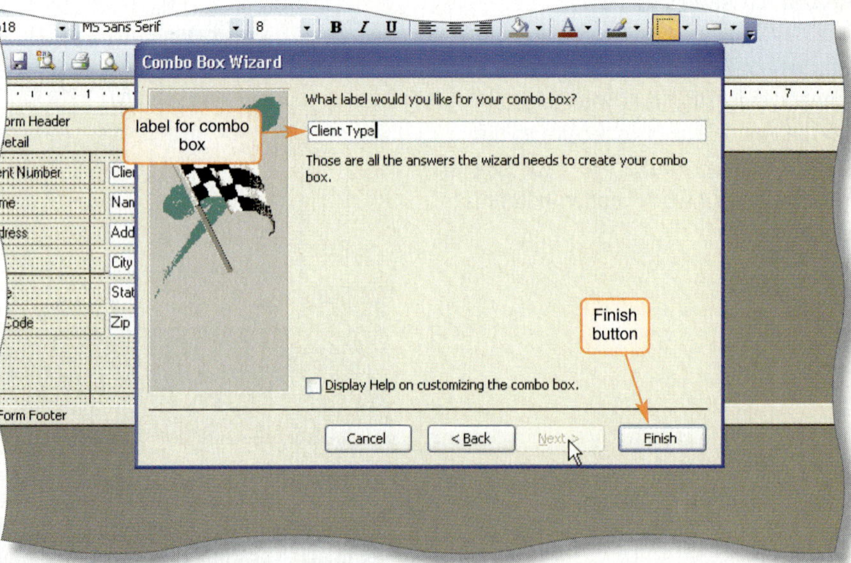

FIGURE 4-72

The steps for placing a combo box to select values from a table are similar to those for placing a combo box to select values from a list. The only difference is the source of the data. The following steps show how to place a combo box that selects values from a related table for the Trainer Number field on the form.

To Place a Combo Box that Selects Values from a Related Table

1

- **With the Control Wizards tool in the toolbox selected, click the Combo Box tool in the toolbox, and then move the mouse pointer, whose shape has changed to a small plus symbol accompanied by a combo box, to the position shown in Figure 4-73.**

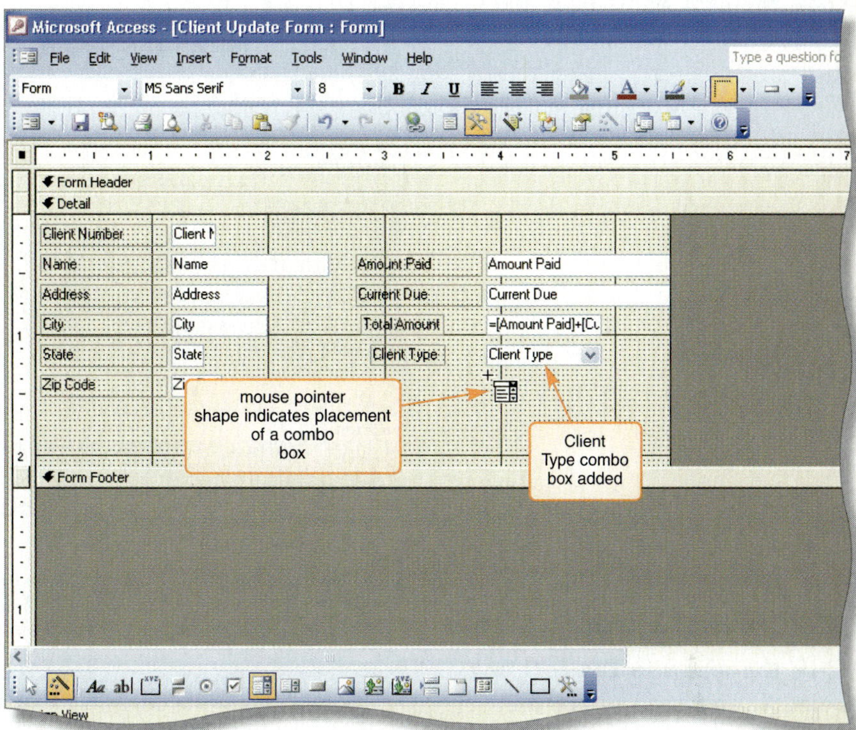

FIGURE 4-73

2

- **Click the position shown in Figure 4-73 to place a combo box.**
- **In the Combo Box Wizard dialog box, click the "I want the combo box to look up the values in a table or query." option button if it is not already selected.**
- **Click the Next button and then click Table: Trainer.**

The Trainer table is selected as the table to provide values for the combo box (Figure 4-74).

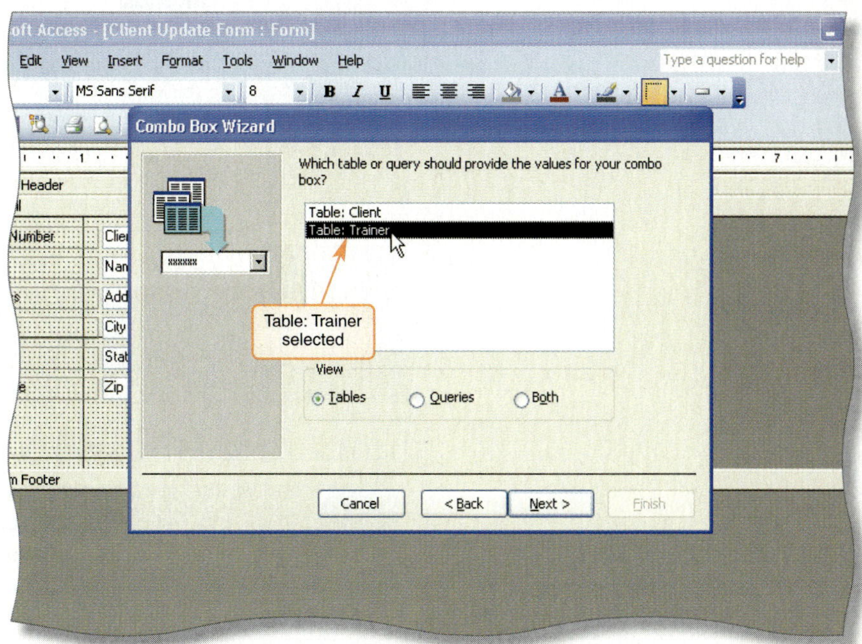

FIGURE 4-74

3

- **Click the Next button.**
- **Click the Add Field button to add the Trainer Number as a field in the combo box.**
- **Click the First Name field and then click the Add Field button.**
- **Click the Last Name field and then click the Add Field button.**

The Trainer Number, First Name, and Last Name fields are selected for the combo box (Figure 4-75).

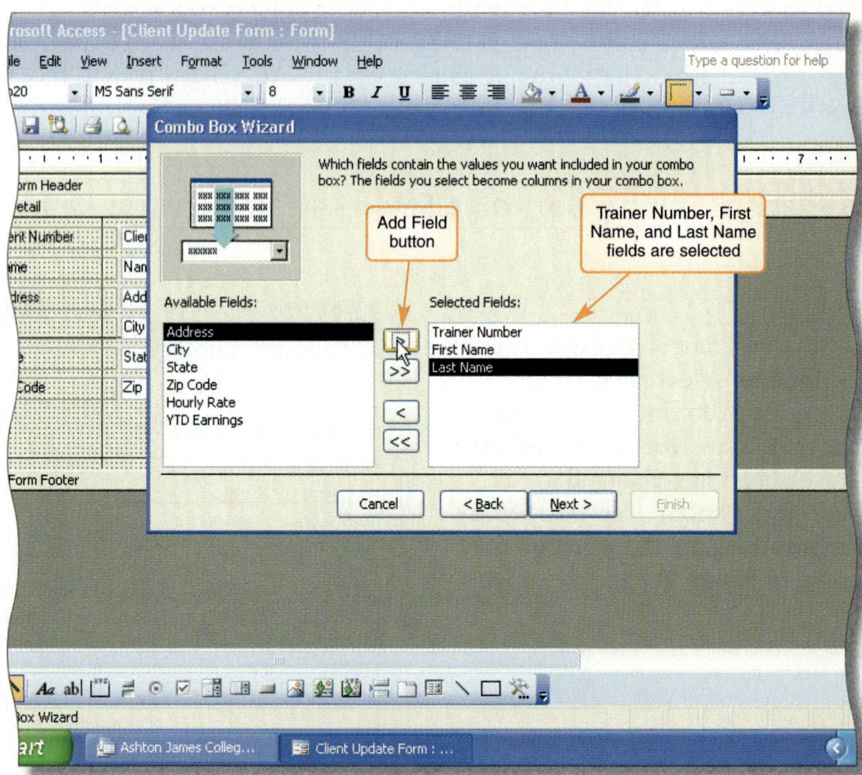

FIGURE 4-75

4

- **Click the Next button.**
- **Click the arrow in the text box labeled 1, and then select the Trainer Number field.**

The rows within the combo box will be sorted by trainer number (Figure 4-76).

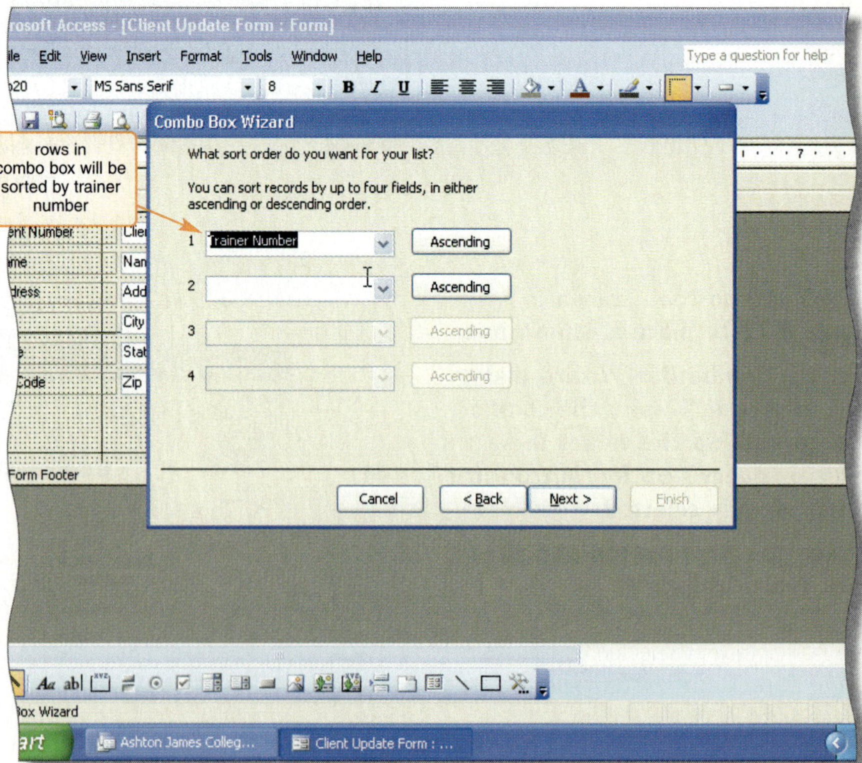

FIGURE 4-76

5

- **Click the Next button.**

The next Combo Box Wizard dialog box appears (Figure 4-77). You can use this dialog box to change the sizes of the fields. You also can use it to indicate whether the key field, in this case the Trainer Number field, should be hidden.

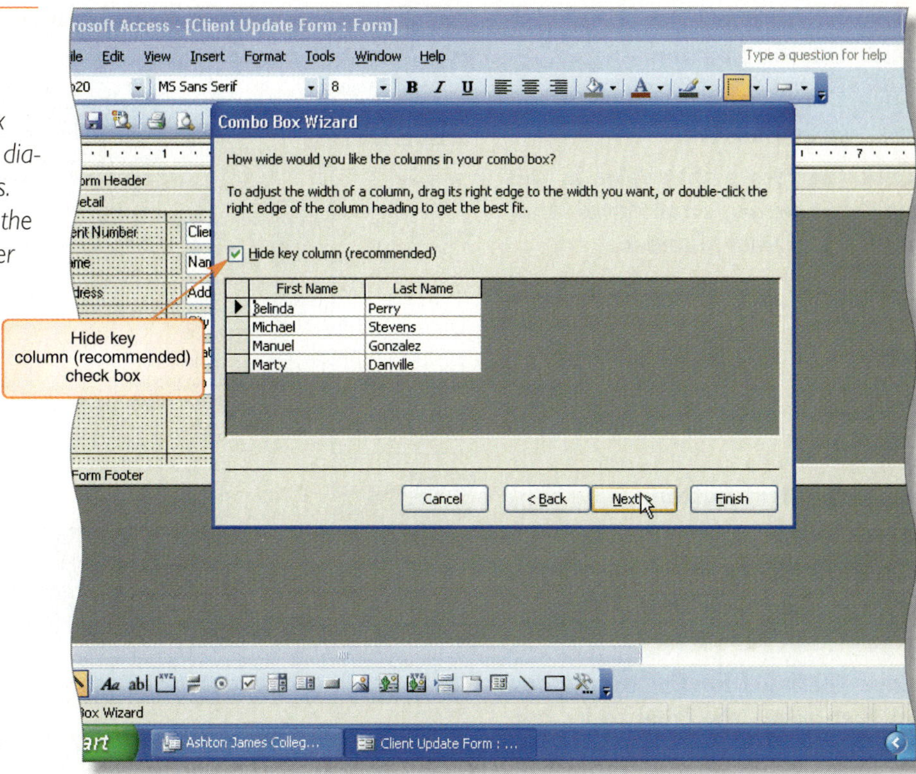

FIGURE 4-77

6

- **Click the "Hide key column (recommended)" check box to remove the check mark to ensure the Trainer Number field appears along with the First Name and Last Name fields.**
- **Resize each column to best fit the data by double-clicking the right-hand border of the column heading.**
- **Click the Next button.**

The Combo Box Wizard dialog box appears, asking you to choose a field that uniquely identifies a row in the combo box (Figure 4-78). The Trainer Number field, which is the correct field, is already selected.

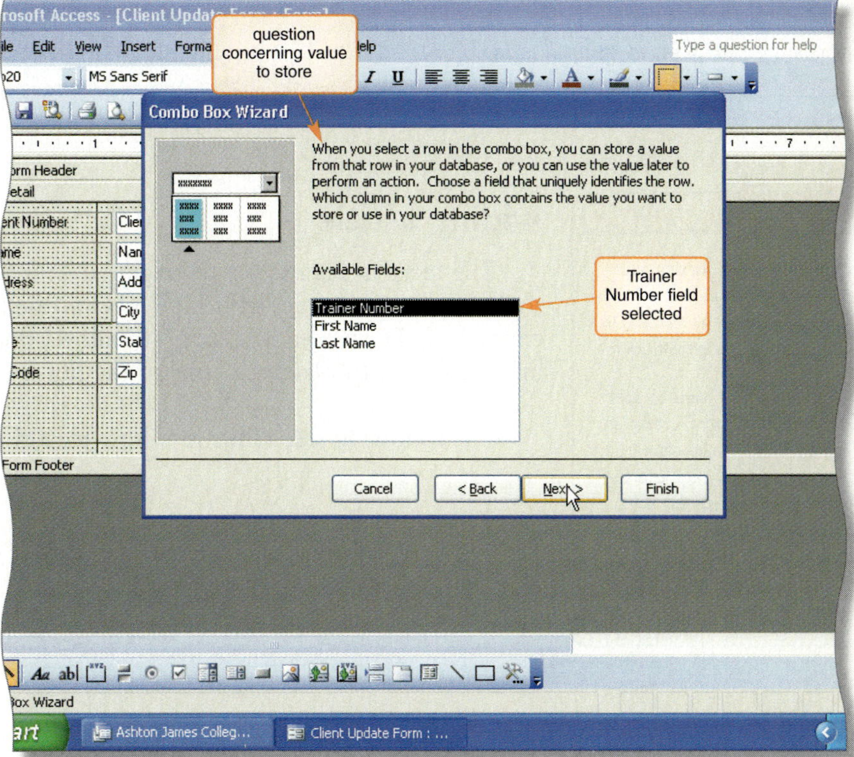

FIGURE 4-78

7

- **Click the Next button.**
- **Click the "Store that value in this field:" option button.**
- **Click the "Store that value in this field:" box arrow, scroll down, and then click Trainer Number.**

The Trainer Number field is selected as the field in which to store the value (Figure 4-79).

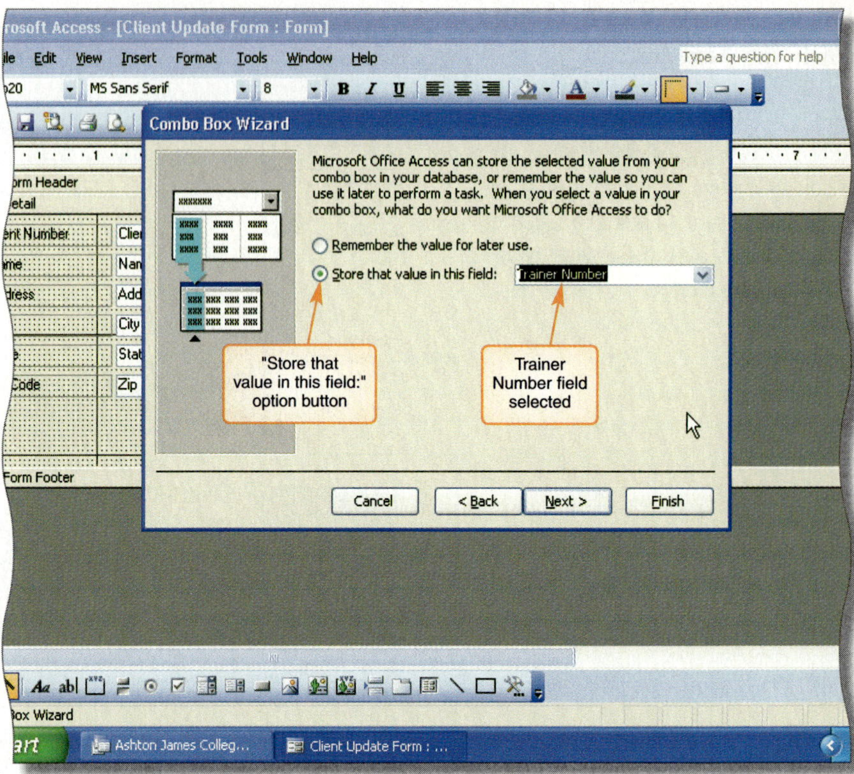

FIGURE 4-79

8

- **Click the Next button.**
- **Be sure `Trainer Number` is entered as the label for the combo box, and then click the Finish button.**
- **Click the label for the combo box, and then move the label so its left edge aligns with the left edge of the Amount Paid, Current Due, Total Amount, and Client Type fields.**

The combo box is placed on the form.

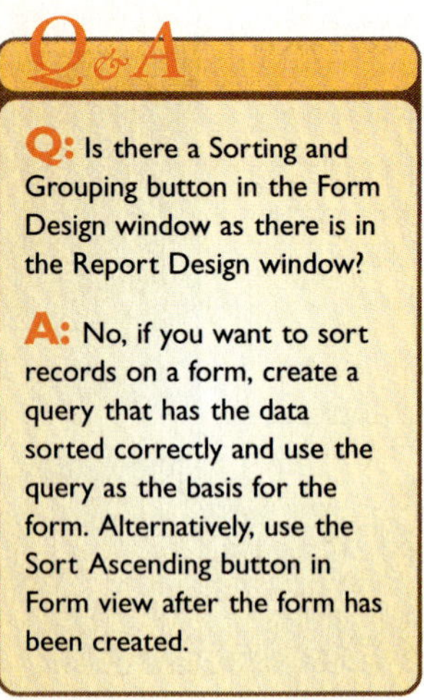

Q&A

Q: Is there a Sorting and Grouping button in the Form Design window as there is in the Report Design window?

A: No, if you want to sort records on a form, create a query that has the data sorted correctly and use the query as the basis for the form. Alternatively, use the Sort Ascending button in Form view after the form has been created.

Adding a Title

The form in Figure 4-3 on page AC 196 contains a title, Client Update Form, that appears in a large, light blue label at the top of the form. To add a title, first expand the Form Header section to allow room for the title. Next, use the Label tool in the toolbox to place the label in the Form Header section. Finally, type the title in the label.

The following steps illustrate how to add a title to the form.

To Add a Title

1

- **Point to the bottom border of the Form Header section. The mouse pointer changes shape to a two-headed vertical arrow with a crossbar.**
- **Drag the bottom border of the Form Header section to resize the Form Header section to the approximate size shown in Figure 4-80.**
- **Click the Label tool in the toolbox and then move the mouse pointer, whose shape has changed to a small plus symbol accompanied by a label, to the approximate position shown in the figure.**

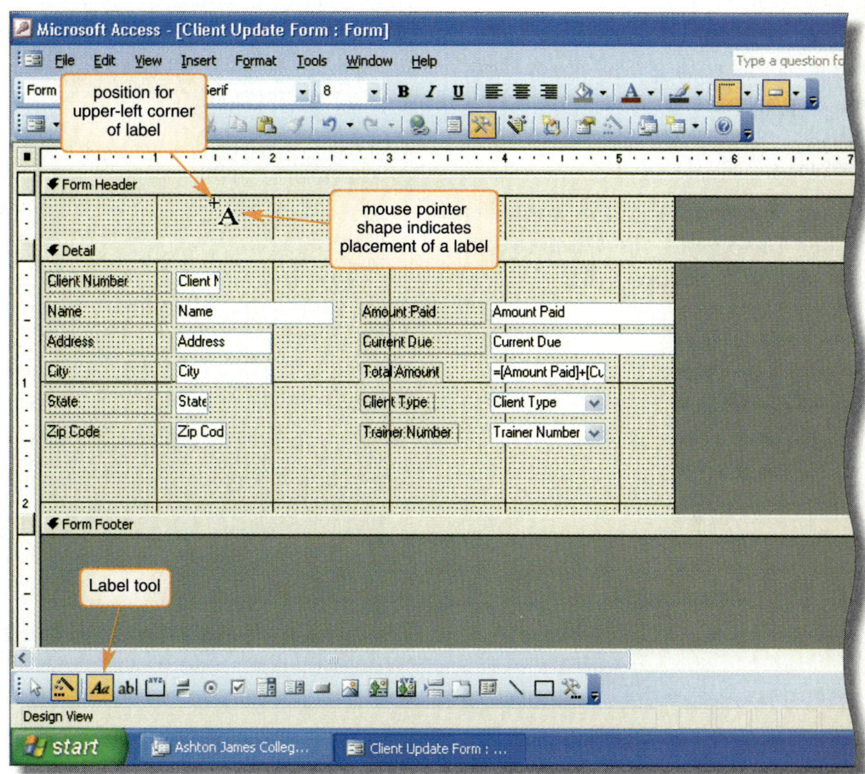

FIGURE 4-80

2

- **Click the mouse pointer in the position in the figure, and then type `Client Update Form` as the contents of the label.**

The label has been placed (Figure 4-81).

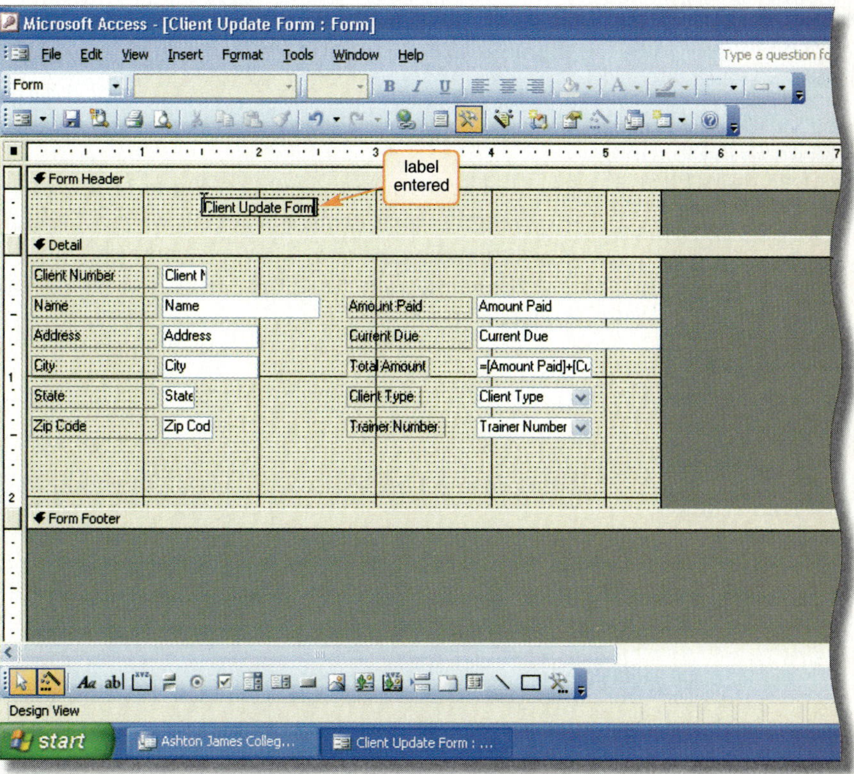

FIGURE 4-81

- Click outside the label to deselect it.
- Click the label to select it once again. (Deselecting and reselecting are required to produce the handles around the border of the control.)
- Drag the handle in the lower-right corner to expand the label to the size shown in Figure 4-82.

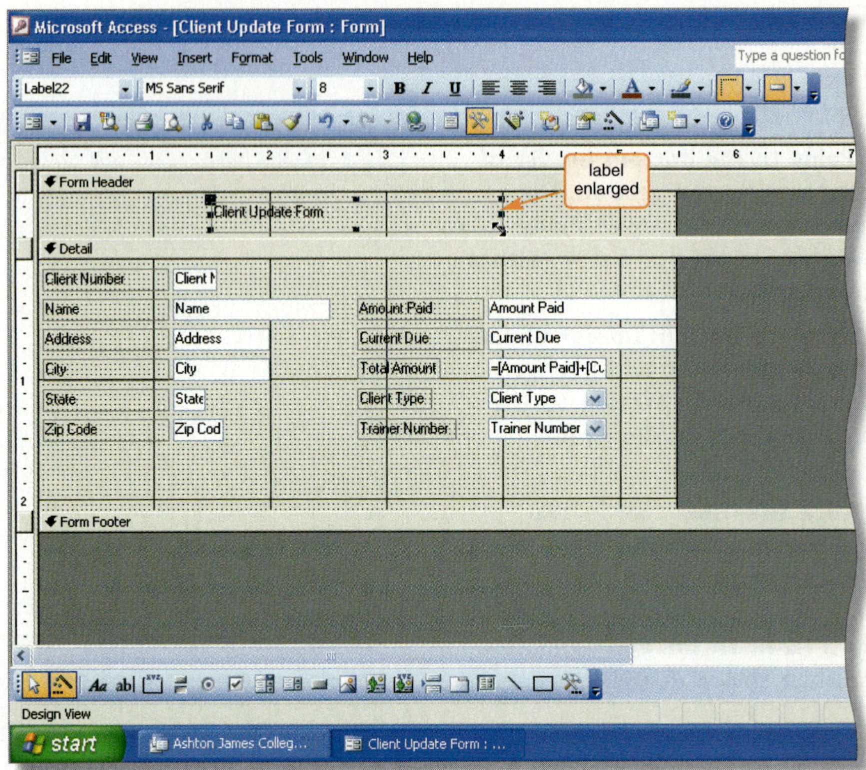

FIGURE 4-82

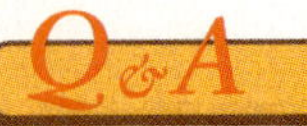

Q: Can you print a form that displays data?

A: Yes, you can print a form that displays data by opening the form, clicking File on the menu bar, and then clicking Print. When the Print dialog box appears, click the appropriate Print Range option button. Click the OK button.

The title currently is much too small for the rectangle, but you can correct that by changing the font size. Changing the font size is just one of the enhancements you can make to the title.

Enhancing a Title

The form now contains a title. You can enhance the appearance of the title by changing various properties of the label containing the title. The following steps change the color of the label, make the label appear to be raised from the screen, change the font size of the title, and change the alignment of the title within the label.

To Enhance a Title

1

- **Right-click the label containing the title.**

The shortcut menu for the label is displayed (Figure 4-83).

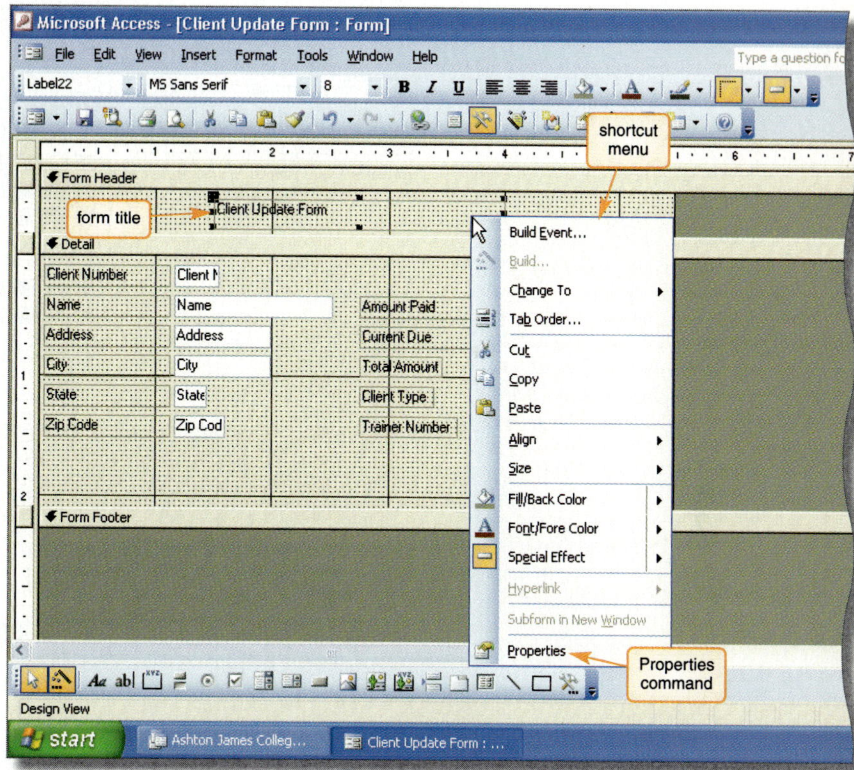

FIGURE 4-83

2

- **Click Properties.**
- **If necessary, click the All tab in the property sheet.**
- **Click the down scroll arrow to display the Back Color property and then click Back Color.**

Access displays the property sheet for the label (Figure 4-84). The insertion point is displayed in the Back Color property and the Build button appears.

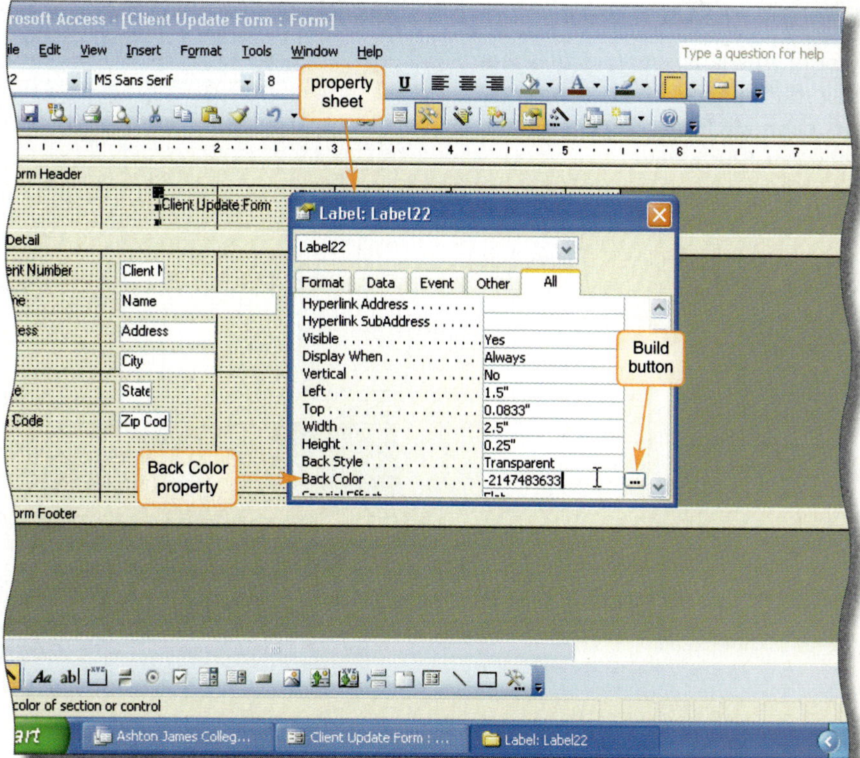

FIGURE 4-84

3

- **Click the Build button.**

The Color palette appears (Figure 4-85).

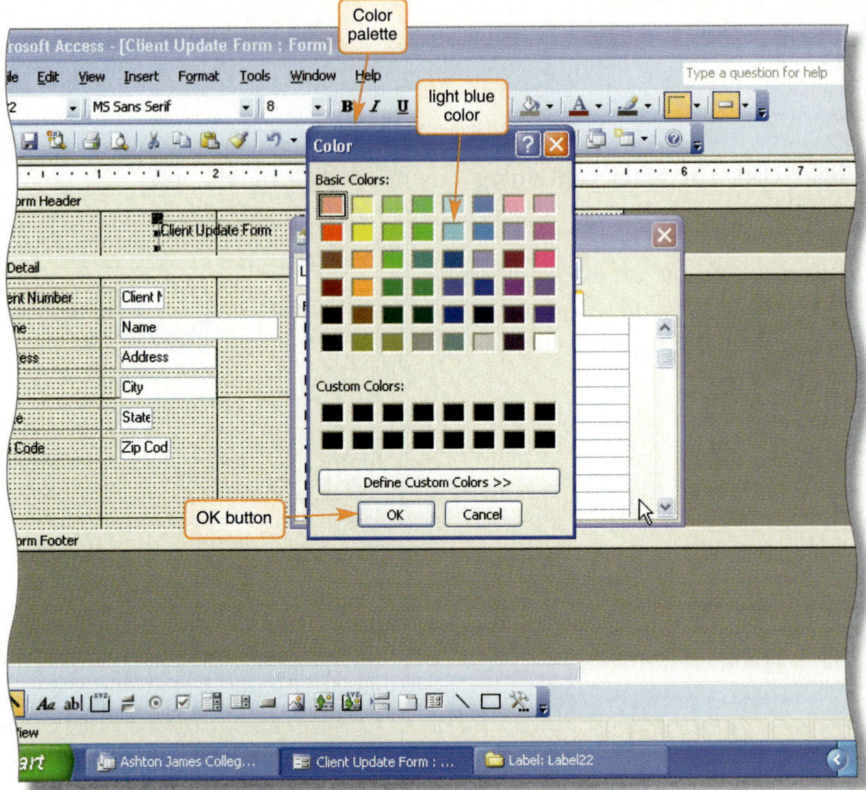

FIGURE 4-85

4

- **Click the color light blue in the second row and fifth column, and then click the OK button.**
- **Scroll down the property sheet, click the Special Effect property, and then click the Special Effect property box arrow.**

The list of available values for the Special Effect property is displayed (Figure 4-86).

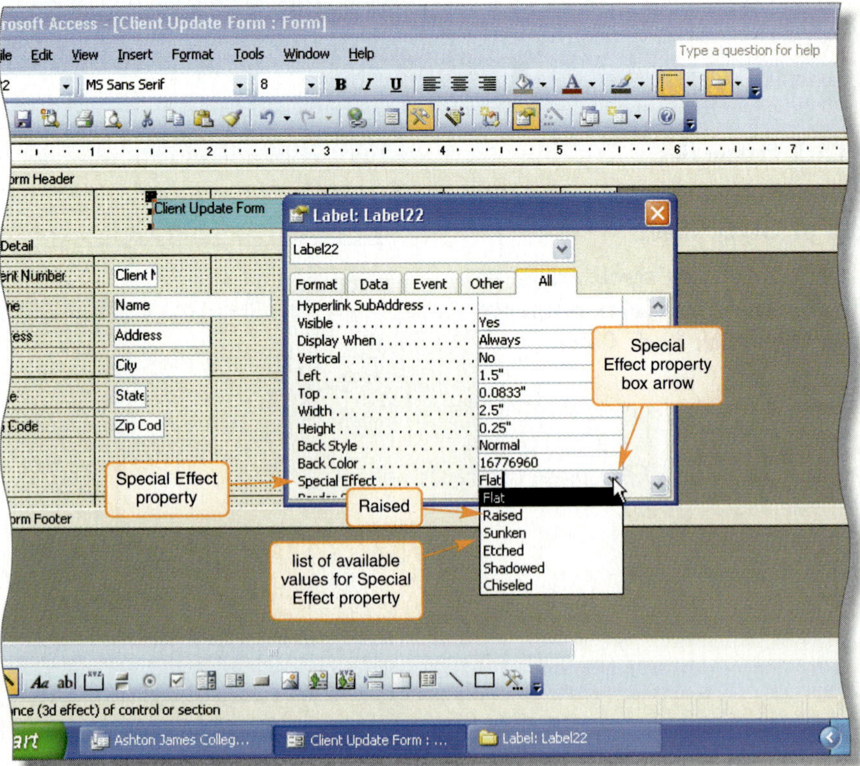

FIGURE 4-86

5

- **Click Raised.**
- **Scroll down the property sheet and then click the Font Size property.**
- **Click the Font Size property box arrow.**
- **Click 14 in the list of font sizes.**
- **Scroll down and then click the Text Align property.**
- **Click the Text Align property box arrow.**

The list of available values for the Text Align property appears (Figure 4-87).

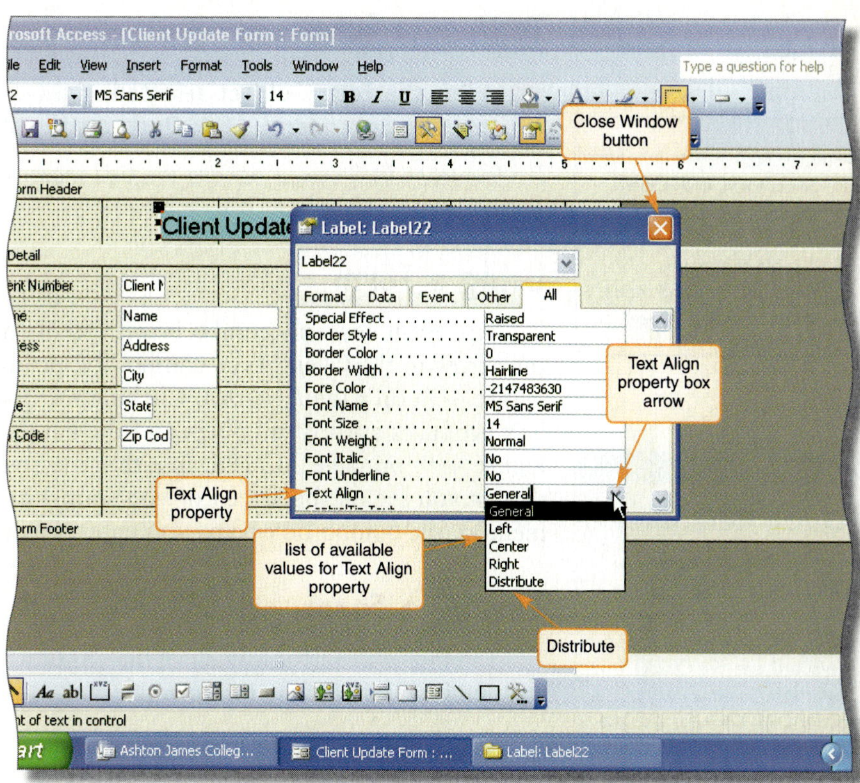

FIGURE 4-87

6

- **Click Distribute.**
- **Close the property sheet by clicking its Close button.**
- **If necessary, use the sizing handles to resize the label so the entire title is displayed.**
- **Click outside the label to deselect it.**

The enhancements to the title now are complete.

More About

Microsoft Certification

The Microsoft Office Specialist Certification program provides an opportunity for you to obtain a valuable industry credential - proof that you have the Access 2003 skills required by employers. For more information, see Appendix E, or visit the Microsoft Access 2003 Certification Web page (scsite.com/ac2003/cert).

Saving and Closing a Form

To close a form, close the window using the window's Close Window button. Then, indicate whether you want to save your changes. The following step shows how to close and save the form.

To Close and Save a Form

1 **Click the window's Close Window button to close the window, and then click the Yes button to save the design of the form.**

Access displays the Database window. The changes are saved.

Other Ways

1. On File menu click Close
2. In Voice Command mode, say "File, Close"

Opening a Form

To open a form, use the Open command on the shortcut menu. The form will appear and can be used to examine and update data. The step on the next page illustrates how to open the Client Update Form.

To Open a Form

1 With the Forms object selected, right-click the Client Update Form to display the shortcut menu. Click Open on the shortcut menu.

The form appears. It should look like the form shown in Figure 4-3 on page AC 196.

Other Ways

1. Select form, click Open button on Database toolbar
2. Double-click form
3. In Voice Command mode, select form, say "Open"

Using a Form

This form contains combo boxes. To use a combo box, click the arrow. Clicking the arrow in the Client Type combo box produces a list of client types (see Figure 4-3a on page AC 196). Clicking the arrow in the Trainer Number combo box produces a list of numbers and the names of available trainers as shown in Figure 4-3b on page AC 196. In either case, you can type the appropriate value from the list you see on the screen or you simply can click the value in the list. With either method, the combo box helps you enter the correct value.

More About

Quick Reference

For a table that lists how to complete tasks covered in this book using the mouse, menu, shortcut menu, and keyboard, see the Quick Reference Summary at the back of this book, or visit the Microsoft Access 2003 Quick Reference Web page (scsite.com/ac2003/qr).

Closing a Form

To close a form, simply close the window containing the form. The following step shows how to close the form.

To Close a Form

1 Click the Close Window button for the Form window.

Form Design Considerations

As you design and create custom forms, keep in mind the following guidelines.

1. Remember that someone using your form may be looking at the form for several hours at a time. Forms that are cluttered or contain too many different effects (colors, fonts, frame styles, and so on) can become very hard on the eyes.
2. Place the fields in logical groupings. Fields that relate to each other should be close to one another on the form.
3. If the data that a user will enter comes from a paper form, make the screen form resemble the paper form as closely as possible.

More About

Form Design

Forms should be appealing visually and present data logically and clearly. Properly designed forms improve both the speed and accuracy of data entry. For more information on form design, visit the Microsoft Access 2003 More About Web page (scsite.com/ac2003/more) and click Form Design.

Closing the Database and Quitting Access

The following steps close the database and quit Access.

To Close a Database and Quit Access

1 Click the Close Window button for the Ashton James College : Database window.

2 Click the Close button for the Microsoft Access window.

Access and the database close.

Project Summary

In Project 4, you used wizards to create two reports and a form, which you then modified in Design view. To create the reports, you learned the purpose of the various sections and how to modify their contents. You used sorting and grouping in a report and saw how to add totals and subtotals. Then, you created and used a custom form. Steps and techniques were presented showing you how to move controls, create new controls, add combo boxes, and add a title. You changed the characteristics of various objects in the form. You also learned general principles to help you design effective reports and forms.

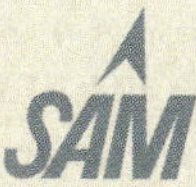

If you have a SAM user profile, you may have access to hands-on instruction, practice, and assessment of the skills covered in this project. Log in to your SAM account and go to your assignments page to see what your instructor has assigned.

What You Should Know

Having completed this project, you should be able to perform the tasks below. The tasks are listed in the same order they were presented in this project. For a list of the buttons, menus, toolbars, and commands introduced in this project, see the Quick Reference Summary at the back of this book and refer to the Page Number column.

1. Open a Database (AC 197)
2. Create a Report Using the Report Wizard (AC 198)
3. Move to Design View and Dock the Toolbox (AC 203)
4. Use Sorting and Grouping (AC 205)
5. Move a Control (AC 206)
6. Change the Can Grow Property (AC 207)
7. Add Totals and Subtotals (AC 209)
8. Align Controls (AC 212)
9. Format Controls (AC 214)
10. Change a Label (AC 216)
11. Close and Save a Report (AC 216, AC 226)
12. Print a Report (AC 216)
13. Create a Report that Involves Multiple Tables (AC 217)
14. Remove Unwanted Controls (AC 222)
15. Change a Property (AC 223)
16. Enlarge the Page Header Section (AC 224)
17. Change the Column Headings (AC 226)
18. Preview a Report (AC 226)
19. Close and Save a Report (AC 226)
20. Print a Report (AC 227)
21. Begin Creating a Form (AC 228)
22. Modify the Form Design (AC 230)
23. Add a Calculated Field (AC 232)
24. Change the Format of a Field (AC 234)
25. Place a Combo Box that Selects Values from a List (AC 235)
26. Place a Combo Box that Selects Values from a Related Table (AC 237)
27. Add a Title (AC 241)
28. Enhance a Title (AC 243)
29. Close and Save a Form (AC 245)
30. Open a Form (AC 246)
31. Close a Form (AC 246)
32. Close a Database and Quit Access (AC 246)

Learn It Online

Instructions: To complete the Learn It Online exercises, start your browser, click the Address bar, and then enter the Web address scsite.com/ac2003/learn. When the Access 2003 Learn It Online page is displayed, follow the instructions in the exercises below. Each exercise has instructions for printing your results, either for your own records or for submission to your instructor.

1 Project Reinforcement TF, MC, and SA

Below Access Project 4, click the Project Reinforcement link. Print the quiz by clicking Print on the File menu for each page. Answer each question.

2 Flash Cards

Below Access Project 4, click the Flash Cards link and read the instructions. Type 20 (or a number specified by your instructor) in the Number of playing cards text box, type your name in the Enter your Name text box, and then click the Flip Card button. When the flash card is displayed, read the question and then click the ANSWER box arrow to select an answer. Flip through Flash Cards. If your score is 15 (75%) correct or greater, click Print on the File menu to print your results. If your score is less than 15 (75%) correct, then redo this exercise by clicking the Replay button.

3 Test

Below Access Project 4, click the Practice Test link. Answer each question, enter your first and last name at the bottom of the page, and then click the Grade Test button. When the graded practice test is displayed on your screen, click Print on the File menu to print a hard copy. Continue to take practice tests until you score 80% or better.

4 Who Wants To Be a Computer Genius?

Below Access Project 4, click the Computer Genius link. Read the instructions, enter your first and last name at the bottom of the page, and then click the PLAY button. When your score is displayed, click the PRINT RESULTS link to print a hard copy.

5 Wheel of Terms

Below Access Project 4, click the Wheel of Terms link. Read the instructions, and then enter your first and last name and your school name. Click the PLAY button. When your score is displayed, right-click the score and then click Print on the shortcut menu to print a hard copy.

6 Crossword Puzzle Challenge

Below Access Project 4, click the Crossword Puzzle Challenge link. Read the instructions, and then enter your first and last name. Click the SUBMIT button. Work the crossword puzzle. When you are finished, click the Submit button. When the crossword puzzle is redisplayed, click the Print Puzzle button to print a hard copy.

7 Tips and Tricks

Below Access Project 4, click the Tips and Tricks link. Click a topic that pertains to Project 4. Right-click the information and then click Print on the shortcut menu. Construct a brief example of what the information relates to in Access to confirm you understand how to use the tip or trick.

8 Newsgroups

Below Access Project 4, click the Newsgroups link. Click a topic that pertains to Project 4. Print three comments.

9 Expanding Your Horizons

Below Access Project 4, click the Articles for Microsoft Access link. Click a topic that pertains to Project 4. Print the information. Construct a brief example of what the information relates to in Access to confirm you understand the contents of the article.

10 Search Sleuth

Below Access Project 4, click the Search Sleuth link. To search for a term that pertains to this project, select a term below the Project 4 title and then use the Google search engine at google.com (or any major search engine) to display and print two Web pages that present information on the term.

11 Access Online Training

Below Access Project 4, click the Access Online Training link. When your browser displays the Microsoft Office Online Web page, click the Access link. Click one of the Access courses that covers one or more of the objectives listed at the beginning of the project on page AC 194 . Print the first page of the course before stepping through it.

12 Office Marketplace

Below Access Project 4, click the Office Marketplace link. When your browser displays the Microsoft Office Online Web page, click the Office Marketplace link. Click a topic that relates to Access. Print the first page.

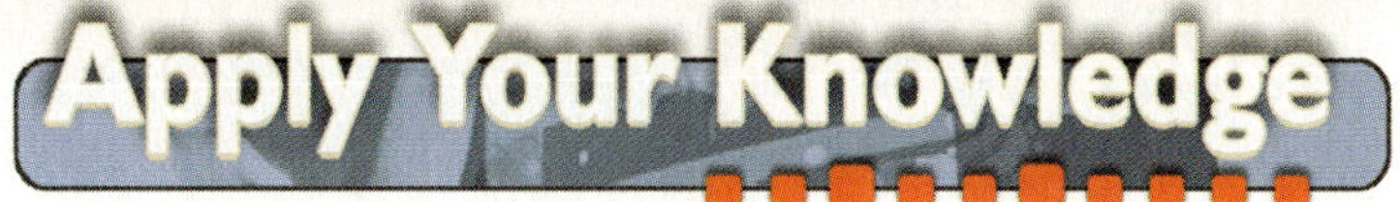

1 Presenting Data in the Begon Pest Control Database

Instructions: Start Access. If you are using the Microsoft Office Access 2003 Complete or the Microsoft Office Access 2003 Comprehensive text, open the Begon Pest Control database that you used in Project 3. Otherwise, see the inside back cover for instructions for downloading the Data Disk or see your instructor for information about accessing the files required for this book. Perform the following tasks:

1. Create the report shown in Figure 4-88.
2. Print the report.
3. Using the Form Wizard, create a form for the Customer table. Include all fields except Technician Number on the form. Use Customer Update Form as the title for the form.
4. Modify the form in the Design window to create the form shown in Figure 4-89. The form includes a combo box for the Technician Number field.
5. Print the form. To print the form, open the form, click File on the menu bar, and then click Print. Click Selected Record(s) as the Print Range. Click the OK button.

Technician/Customer Report

Technician Number	*First Name*	*Last Name*	*Customer Number*	*Name*	*Balance*
203	*Miguel*	*Estevez*			
			AT23	Atlas Repair	$335.00
			MC10	Moss Carpet	$398.00
					$733.00
210	*Rachel*	*Hillsdale*			
			AZ01	AZ Auto	$300.00
			BL35	Blanton Shoes	$290.00
			HI25	Hill Crafts	$334.00
			SE05	Servete Manufacturing	$343.00
					$1,267.00
214	*Chou*	*Liu*			
			CJ45	C Joe Diner	$0.00
			KL50	Klean n Dri	$365.00
			PV83	Prime Video	$0.00
					$365.00
					$2,365.00

FIGURE 4-88

Microsoft Access - [Customer Update Form]

File Edit View Insert Format Records Tools Window Help | Type a question for help

MS Sans Serif | 8

Customer Update Form

Customer Number	AT23		
Name	Atlas Repair	Balance	$335.00
Address	220 Beard	Technician Number	203
City	Kady		
State	TN		
Zip Code	42514		

FIGURE 4-89

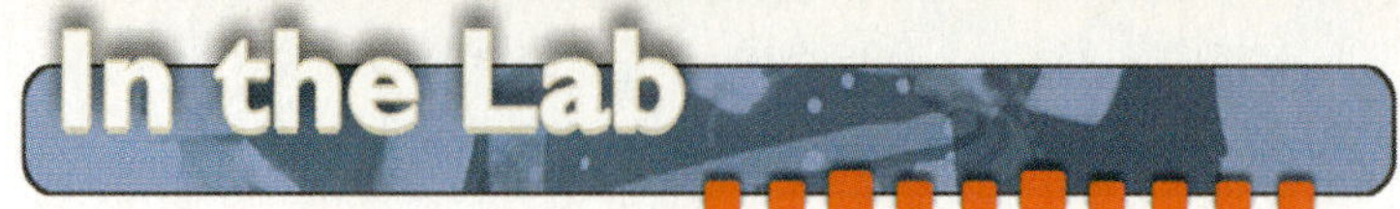

1 Presenting Data in the Birds2U Database

Problem: The management of Birds2U already has realized the benefits from the database of products and suppliers that you created. The management now would like to prepare reports and forms from the database.

Instructions: If you are using the Microsoft Office Access 2003 Complete or the Microsoft Office Access 2003 Comprehensive text, open the Birds2U database that you used in Project 3. Otherwise, see the inside back cover for instructions for downloading the Data Disk or see your instructor for information about accessing the files required for this book. Perform the following tasks:

1. Create the On Hand Value Report shown in Figure 4-90 for the Item table. The report is sorted by Description. On Hand Value is the result of multiplying On Hand by Cost.

On Hand Value Report

Item Code	*Description*	*On Hand*	*Cost*	*On Hand Value*
BO22	Barn Owl House	2	$97.50	$195.00
BA35	Bat House	14	$43.50	$609.00
BE19	Bee Box	7	$39.80	$278.60
BB01	Bird Bath	2	$82.10	$164.20
BL06	Bluebird House	9	$14.35	$129.15
BS10	Bunny Sprinkler	4	$41.95	$167.80
BU24	Butterfly Box	6	$36.10	$216.60
FS11	Froggie Sprinkler	5	$41.95	$209.75
GF12	Globe Feeder	12	$14.80	$177.60
HF01	Hummingbird Feeder	5	$11.35	$56.75
LM05	Leaf Mister	3	$29.95	$89.85
PM05	Purple Martin House	3	$67.10	$201.30
WF10	Window Feeder	10	$14.25	$142.50

FIGURE 4-90

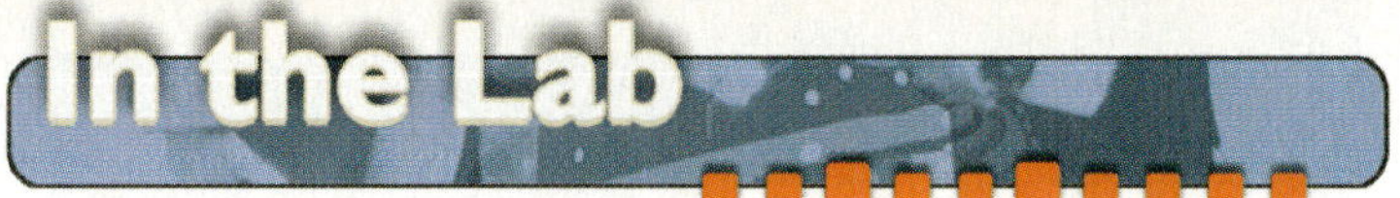

2. Print the report.
3. Create the Supplier/Item report shown in Figure 4-91. Profit is the difference between Selling Price and Cost.
4. Print the report.
5. Create the form shown in Figure 4-92. On Hand Value is a calculated control and is the result of multiplying On Hand by Cost. Include a combo box for Supplier Code.
6. Print the form. To print the form, open the form, click File on the menu bar, and then click Print. Click Selected Record(s) as the Print Range. Click the OK button.

Supplier/Item Report

Supplier Code	*Name*	*Item Code*	*Description*	*Selling Price*	*Cost*	*Profit*
05	*All Birds Supply*					
		GF12	Globe Feeder	$16.25	$14.80	$1.45
		HF01	Hummingbird Feeder	$14.25	$11.35	$2.90
		WF10	Window Feeder	$15.95	$14.25	$1.70
13	*Bird Casa Ltd*					
		BB01	Bird Bath	$86.25	$82.10	$4.15
		BL06	Bluebird House	$15.99	$14.35	$1.64
		PM05	Purple Martin House	$69.95	$67.10	$2.85
17	*Lawn Fixtures*					
		BS10	Bunny Sprinkler	$50.00	$41.95	$8.05
		FS11	Froggie Sprinkler	$50.00	$41.95	$8.05
		LM05	Leaf Mister	$34.75	$29.95	$4.80
21	*Natural Woods*					
		BA35	Bat House	$45.50	$43.50	$2.00
		BE19	Bee Box	$42.50	$39.80	$2.70
		BO22	Barn Owl House	$107.75	$97.50	$10.25
		BU24	Butterfly Box	$37.75	$36.10	$1.65

FIGURE 4-91

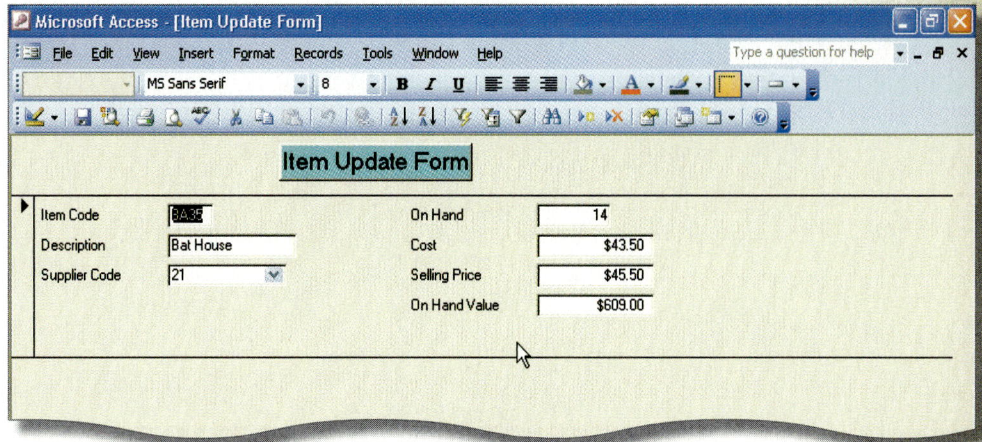

FIGURE 4-92

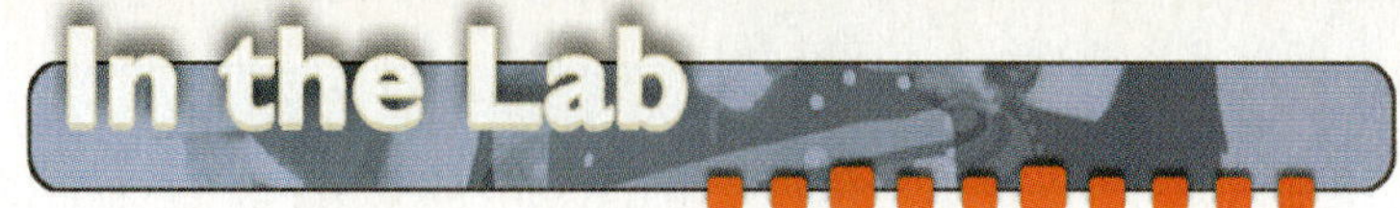

2 Presenting Data in the Babbage Bookkeeping Database

Problem: Babbage Bookkeeping already has realized several benefits from the database you created. The company now would like to prepare reports and forms from the database.

Instructions: If you are using the Microsoft Office Access 2003 Complete or the Microsoft Office Access 2003 Comprehensive text, open the Babbage Bookkeeping database that you used in Project 3. Otherwise, see the inside back cover for instructions for downloading the Data Disk or see your instructor for information about accessing the files required for this book. Perform the following tasks:

1. Create the Client Income Report shown in Figure 4-93 for the Client table. Group the report by Client Type and sort the records within Client Type by Name.

Client Income Report

Client Type	*Client Number*	*Name*	*Address*	*City*	*Balance*
MAN					
	B26	Blake-Scripps	557 Maum	Grant City	$229.50
	S56	SeeSaw Industries	31 Liatris	Portage	$362.50
				Subtotal:	$592.00
RET					
	A54	Afton Mills	612 Revere	Grant City	$315.50
	A62	Atlas Suppliers	227 Dandelion	Empeer	$525.00
	C21	Crompton Meat Market	72 Main	Empeer	$0.00
	D76	Dege Grocery	446 Linton	Portage	$485.75
	H21	Hill Shoes	247 Fulton	Grant City	$228.50
	M26	Mohr Crafts	665 Maum	Empeer	$312.50
				Subtotal:	$1,867.25
SER					
	G56	Grand Cleaners	337 Abelard	Empeer	$265.00
	L50	Lou's Salon	124 Fulton	Grant City	$125.00
	T45	Tate Repair	824 Revere	Grant City	$254.00
				Subtotal:	$644.00
				Grand Total:	$3,103.25

FIGURE 4-93

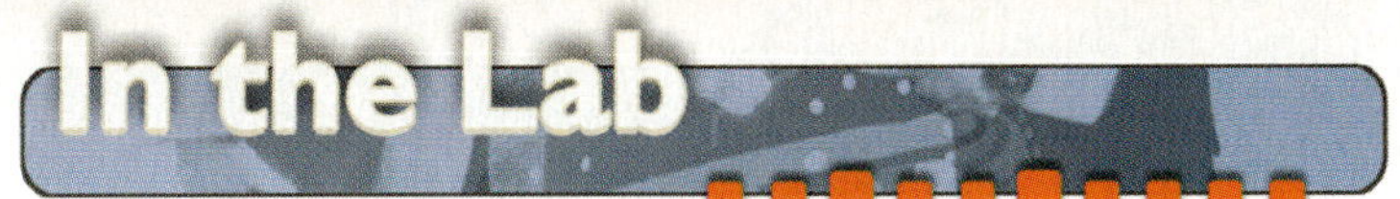

2. Print the report.
3. Create the Bookkeeper/Client report shown in Figure 4-94. Preview the report to check page margins and orientation. Adjust as necessary.
4. Print the report.
5. Create the form shown in Figure 4-95. Client Type and Bookkeeper Number are combo boxes.
6. Print the form. To print the form, open the form, click File on the menu bar, and then click Print. Click Selected Record(s) as the Print Range. Click the OK button.

Bookkeeper/Client Report

Bookkeeper Number	*First Name*	*Last Name*	*Client Number*	*Name*	*Balance*
22	*Johanna*	*Lewes*			
			A54	Afton Mills	$315.50
			G56	Grand Cleaners	$265.00
			M26	Mohr Crafts	$312.50
				Average Balance	*$297.67*
24	*Mario*	*Rodriguez*			
			A62	Atlas Suppliers	$525.00
			B26	Blake-Scripps	$229.50
			C21	Crompton Meat Market	$0.00
			H21	Hill Shoes	$228.50
			T45	Tate Repair	$254.00
				Average Balance	*$247.40*
34	*Choi*	*Wong*			
			D76	Dege Grocery	$485.75
			L50	Lou's Salon	$125.00
			S56	SeeSaw Industries	$362.50
				Average Balance	*$324.42*

FIGURE 4-94

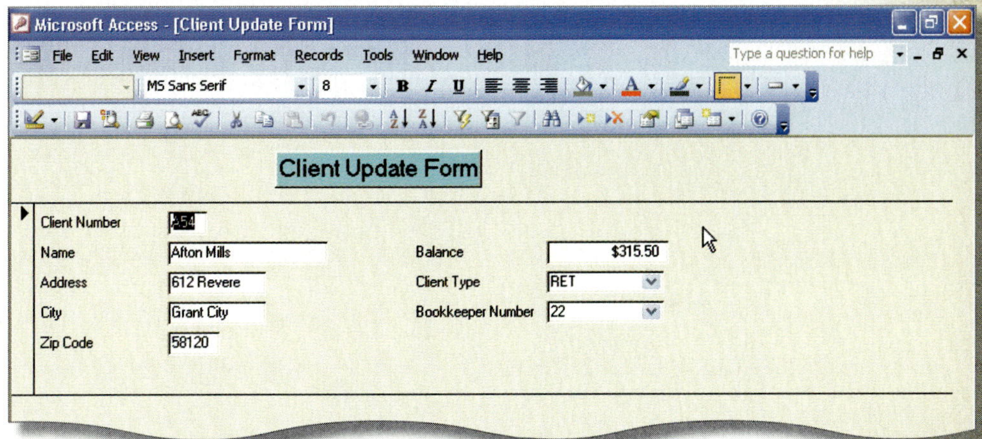

FIGURE 4-95

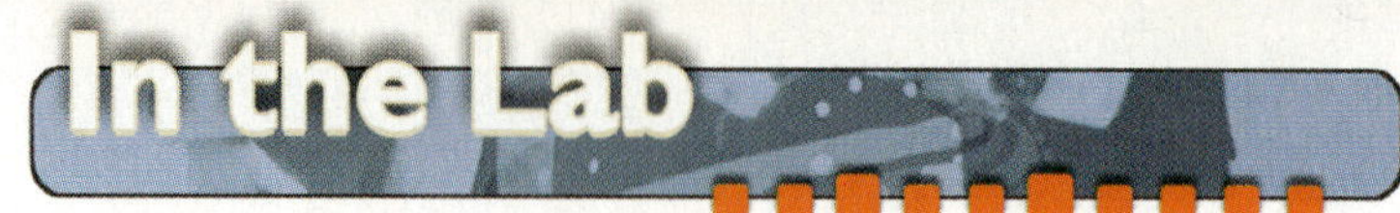

3 Presenting Data in the City Guide Database

Problem: The chamber of commerce already has realized several benefits from the database you created. The company now would like to prepare reports and forms from the database.

Instructions: If you are using the Microsoft Office Access 2003 Complete or the Microsoft Office Access 2003 Comprehensive text, open the City Guide database that you used in Project 3. Otherwise, see the inside back cover for instructions for downloading the Data Disk or see your instructor for information about accessing the files required for this book. Perform the following tasks:

Instructions Part 1: Create two reports for the chamber of commerce. The first report should be similar to the Client Account Summary report shown in Figure 4-1 on page AC 195. Group the report by Advertiser Type, sort the records within Advertiser Type by Name. The report also should include the address, amount paid, and balance fields. Provide subtotals and a grand total for the Balance and Amount Paid fields. Be sure to align controls appropriately. The second report should be similar to the Trainer/Client Report shown in Figure 4-2 on page AC 195 with the records grouped by Ad Rep Number.

Instructions Part 2: Create a form for the chamber of commerce that is similar to the form shown in Figures 4-3a and 4-3b on page AC 196. Total Amount is the sum of Balance and Amount Paid. Advertiser Type and Ad Rep Number should be combo boxes. Check the alignment and spacing of all controls. Adjust as necessary. Change the Default view for the form to Continuous Forms and the caption for the form to City Guide Advertiser Update Form. Sort the data by Name and print the form.

Cases and Places

The difficulty of these case studies varies:
■ are the least difficult and ■■ are more difficult. The last exercise is a group exercise.

1 ■ If you are using the Microsoft Office Access 2003 Complete or the Microsoft Office Access 2003 Comprehensive text, use the College Dog Walkers database that you used in Project 3. Otherwise, see the inside back cover for instructions for downloading the Data Disk or see your instructor for information about accessing the files required for this book. Use this database and create a form for the Customer table that is similar to that shown in Figure 4-89 on page AC 249.

2 ■ If you are using the Microsoft Office Access 2003 Complete or the Microsoft Office Access 2003 Comprehensive text, use the InPerson Fitness Company database that you used in Project 3. Otherwise, see the inside back cover for instructions for downloading the Data Disk or see your instructor for information about accessing the files required for this book. The InPerson Fitness Company needs a custom report and a custom form. Create a report for the company that is similar to the Trainer/Client Report shown in Figure 4-2 on page AC 195. Create a form for the company that is similar to the form shown in Figures 4-3a and 4-3b on page AC 196. Total Amount is the sum of Balance and Amount Paid.

3 ■■ If you are using the Microsoft Office Access 2003 Complete or the Microsoft Office Access 2003 Comprehensive text, use the Regional Books database that you used in Project 3. Otherwise, see the inside back cover for instructions for downloading the Data Disk or see your instructor for information about accessing the files required for this book. The bookstore owner would like a report that lists books by book type (used or new) with the average price for each type as well as the overall average price for all books. Create a report similar to that shown in Figure 4-1 on page AC 195 that groups books by book type. Within each book type, the records should be sorted by title. The report also should include the book code, units on hand, and price. Create a form similar to that shown in Figure 4-92 on page AC 251. Use a calculated control called Inventory Value that is the result of multiplying units on hand by price. Book type and Publisher code should be combo boxes.

4 ■■ If you are using the Microsoft Office Access 2003 Complete or the Microsoft Office Access 2003 Comprehensive text, use the Campus Housing database that you used in Project 3. Otherwise, see the inside back cover for instructions for downloading the Data Disk or see your instructor for information about accessing the files required for this book. The campus housing office would like an easy way to enter new rentals into the database. Create a custom form for the campus housing office that meets their needs. The form should include combo boxes for bedrooms, bathrooms, lease term, and owner code. Create a report for the campus housing office that lists all rentals grouped by owner. Do not include any subtotals or totals in the report.

Cases and Places

5 ■■ **Working Together** The Report and Form Wizards offer several different styles. Each member of the team should pick a different style and create the report shown in Figure 4-2 on page AC 195 and the form shown in Figure 4-3 on page AC 196 using the chosen styles. Compare the styles and as a team vote on which one you prefer. The project gave some general guidelines for designing reports and forms. Use the Internet to find more information about form design guidelines; for example, there are certain fonts that you should not use for a title and certain colors that are harder for individuals to see. Then, as a group, create a form that illustrates poor design features. Include a short write-up that explains what design principles were violated. Be sure to cite your references. Turn in each of the reports and forms that your team created using different styles. Also, turn in the poorly-designed form and the write-up.

Copy the Ashton James College database and rename the database as Team Name_AJC. For example, if your team is Team 1, then name the database Team 1_AJC. View the Trainer/Client Report in Layout view. Print the report. Change the page orientation for the report to landscape and adjust the page margins so that report is centered (approximately) on the page. Print the report in landscape orientation. Hide the report footer for the report and print the report. Unhide the report footer and hide the page header. Print the report. As a team discuss the changes that you made. Include a short write-up that summarizes the team's comments on the changes to the report. Turn in each of the modified reports and the short write-up.

MICROSOFT
Office Access 2003

Enhancing Forms with OLE Fields, Hyperlinks, and Subforms

PROJECT 5

CASE PERSPECTIVE

Ashton James College uses its database to keep records about clients and trainers. After several months, however, the administration has found that it needs to maintain additional data on its trainers. AJC needs to store the start date of each trainer in the database. The administration wants the database to contain a comment about each trainer as well as the trainer's picture. Additionally, each trainer now has a page on the Web, and the administration requires easy access to this page from the database. The administration wants to add the Phone Number field to the Trainer table. They also want to type only the digits in the telephone number and then have Access format the number appropriately. If the user enters 5125554625, for example, Access will format the number as (512) 555-4625.

After the proposed fields have been added to the database, they want a form created that incorporates some of the new fields with some of the existing fields. The administration wants the form to include the client number, name, amount paid, and current due amount for the clients of each trainer. Then, they would like to see multiple clients on the screen at the same time. The database should provide the capability of scrolling through all the clients of a trainer and of accessing the trainer's Web page directly from the form. The administration requires queries that use the Start Date and Comment fields.

As you read through this project, you will learn how to make the changes required by Ashton James College.

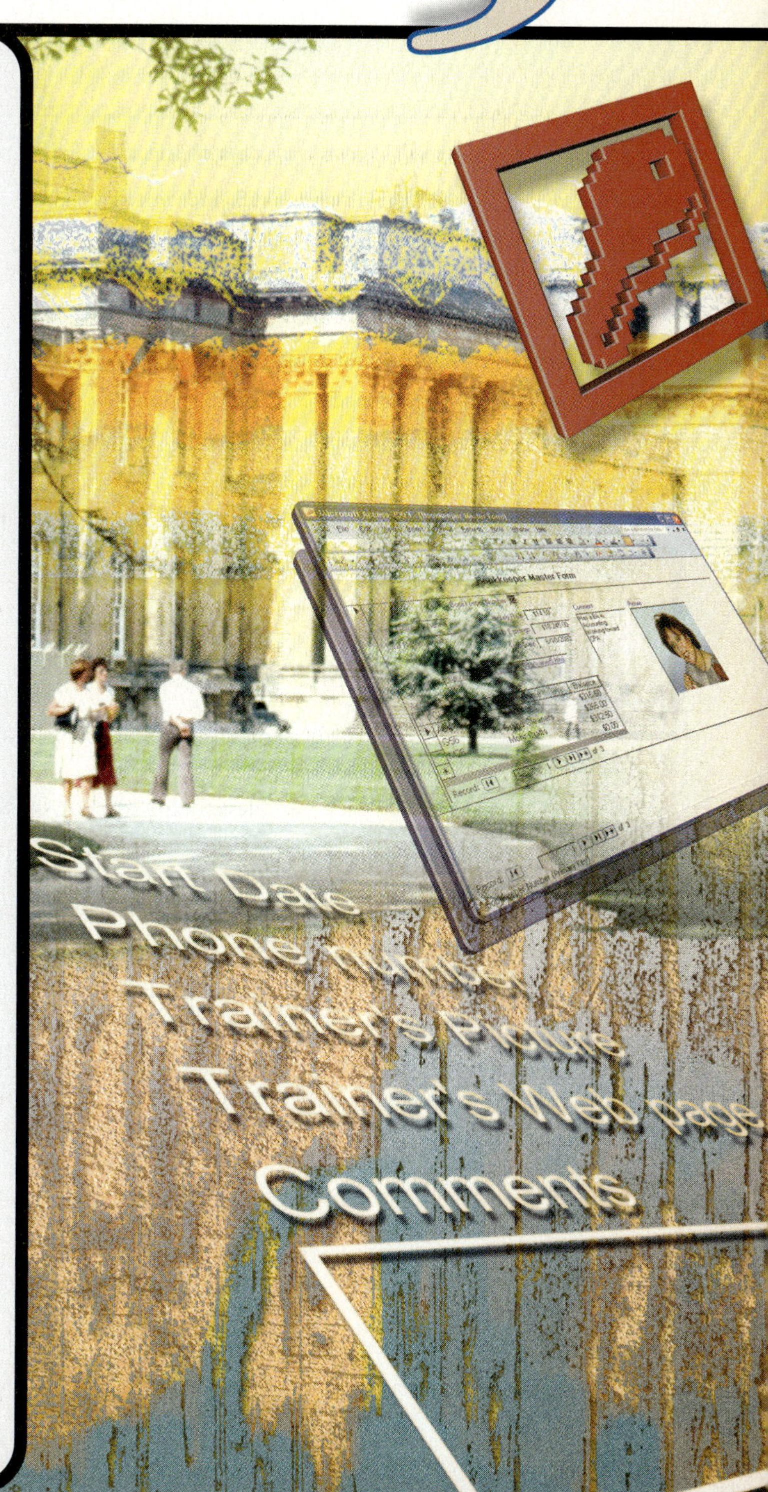

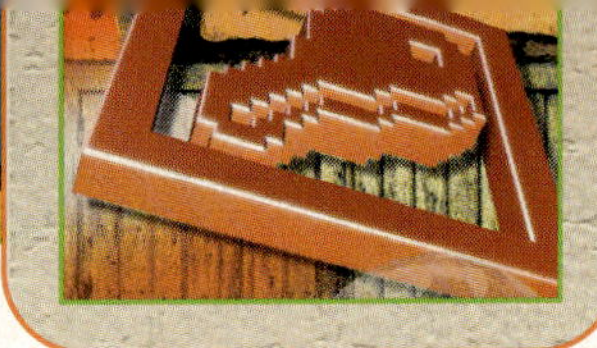

MICROSOFT Office Access 2003

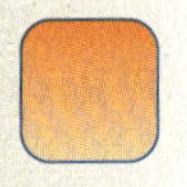

Enhancing Forms with OLE Fields, Hyperlinks, and Subforms

PROJECT

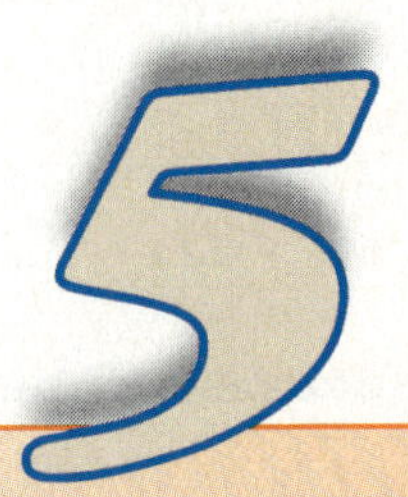

Objectives

You will have mastered the material in this project when you can:

- Use date, memo, OLE, and hyperlink fields
- Use the Input Mask wizard
- Update fields and enter data
- Change row and column size
- Create a form with a subform using the Form wizard
- Modify a subform design
- Modify a form design
- Move and resize fields and labels
- Change label alignment and size
- Change the size mode of a picture
- Change special effects and colors of labels
- Add a form title and fine-tune the form
- Change tab stops and tab order
- Use the form to view data and Web pages
- Use Date and Memo fields in a query
- View object dependencies

Introduction

This project creates the form shown in Figure 5-1. The form incorporates the following new features:

- New fields appear on the form. These include the date the trainer started working at the college and the trainer's telephone number.
- The Comment field allows the administration to store notes concerning the trainer. The Comment entry can be as long as the administration desires.
- The Picture field holds a photograph of the trainer.
- The Web Page field enables the user to access the Trainer's Web page directly from the database.
- The form shows data concerning the trainer, and information about the trainer's clients. The clients are displayed in a table on the form.

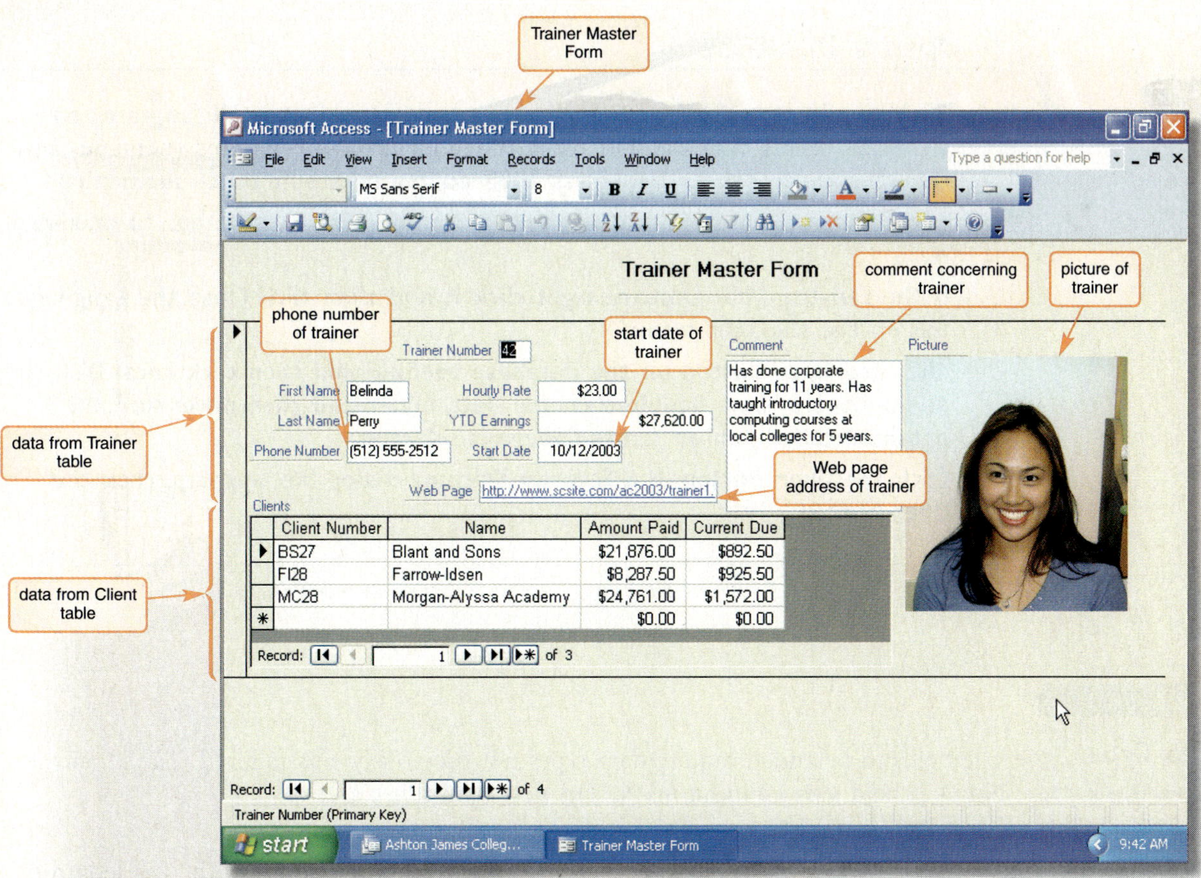

FIGURE 5-1

Project Five — Enhancing the Ashton James College Forms

The steps in this project create the form required by the administration of Ashton James College. Before creating the form, the structure of the Trainer table must be changed to include the four new fields: Start Date, Comment, Picture, and Web Page. Each of these new fields uses a data type not encountered previously. The Phone Number field must be added and steps taken to ensure that the telephone numbers are entered in an appropriate format. The appropriate data must be entered in these new fields. The manner in which this is achieved depends on the data type. After entering data in the fields, the form including the table of client data is created. Finally, queries are created to obtain the answer to two important questions that reference the new fields.

Opening the Database

If you are stepping through this project on a computer and you want your screen to match the figures in this book, then you should change your computer's resolution to 800 x 600. For more information on how to change the resolution on your computer, see Appendix D. Before modifying the Trainer table and creating the form, you must open the database. The steps on the next page illustrate how to start Access and open the database. These steps assume that the database is located in a folder called Data on disk C. (See the note in Project 4 on page AC 197.) If your database is located anywhere else, you will need to adjust the appropriate steps.

More About

The Access Help System

Need Help? It is no further than the Type a question for help box on the menu bar in the upper-right corner of the window. Click the box that contains the text, Type a question for help (Figure 5-1), type `help`, and then press the ENTER key. Access responds with a list of topics you can click to learn about obtaining help on any Access-related topic. To find out what is new in Access 2003, type `what is new in Access` in the Type a question for help box.

To Open a Database

1. **Click the Start button on the Windows taskbar, point to All Programs on the Start menu, point to Microsoft Office on the All Programs submenu, and then click Microsoft Office Access 2003 on the Microsoft Office submenu.**
2. **If the Access window is not maximized, double-click its title bar to maximize it.**
3. **If the Language bar appears, right-click it and then click Close the Language bar on the shortcut menu.**
4. **Click the Open button on the Database toolbar, and then click Local Disk (C:) in the Look in box. Double-click the Data folder and then make sure the database called Ashton James College is selected.**
5. **Click the Open button. If a Security Warning dialog box appears, click the Open button.**

The database opens and the Ashton James College : Database window appears.

More About

OLE Data Type

A field with a data type of OLE can store data such as Word documents, Excel worksheets, pictures, sounds, and other types of binary data created in other programs. For more information, visit the Access 2003 More About Web page (scsite.com/ac2003/more), and then click OLE Fields.

Special Fields

The fields to be added require data types not previously encountered. The Phone Number field uses an input mask. The new data types are:

1. **Date** (**D**) — The field contains only valid dates.
2. **Memo** (**M**) — The field contains text that is variable in length. The length of the text stored in memo fields virtually is unlimited.
3. **OLE** (**O**) — The field contains objects created by other applications that support **OLE** (**Object Linking and Embedding**) as a server. Object Linking and Embedding is a feature of Microsoft Windows that creates a special relationship between Microsoft Access and the application that created the object. When you edit the object, Microsoft Access returns automatically to the application that created the object.
4. **Hyperlink** (**H**) — The field contains links to other Office documents or to Web pages. If the link is to a Web page, the field will contain the address of the Web page.

Q&A

Q: Why use Date as a data type for date fields? Why not simply use Text?

A: If you use Date, the computer will ensure that only legitimate dates are entered in the field. In addition, you can use date arithmetic. For example, you could subtract one date from another to find how many days there are between the two dates. You also can use dates in criteria.

Adding Fields to a Table

You add the new fields to the Trainer table by modifying the design of the table and inserting the fields at the appropriate position in the table structure. The following steps illustrate how to add the Start Date, Comment, Picture, and Web Page fields to the Trainer table.

To Add Fields to a Table

1

- **If necessary, click Tables on the Objects bar.**
- **Right-click Trainer.**

The shortcut menu for the Trainer table appears (Figure 5-2).

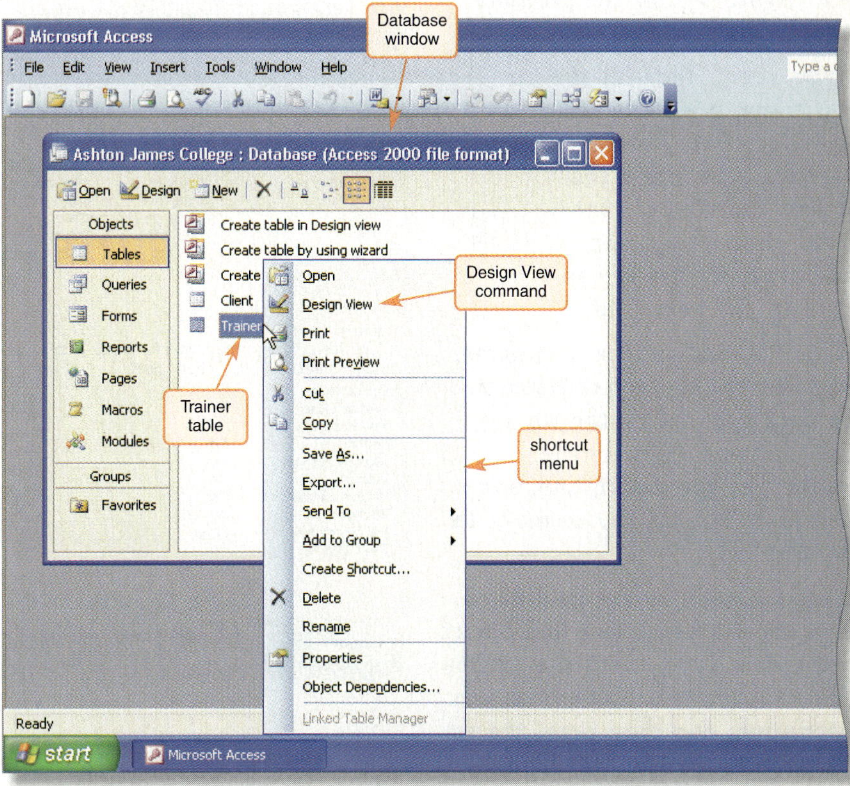

FIGURE 5-2

2

- **Click Design View on the shortcut menu, and then maximize the Microsoft Access – [Trainer : Table] window by double-clicking its title bar.**

The Microsoft Access – [Trainer : Table] window appears (Figure 5-3).

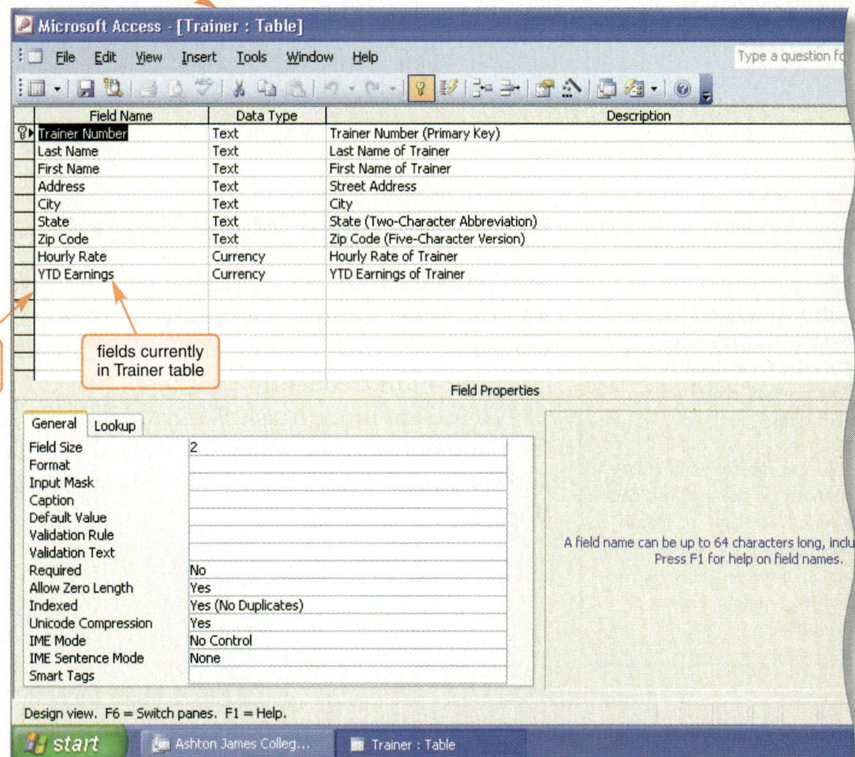

FIGURE 5-3

3

- **Click the position for the new field (Figure 5-3 on the previous page).**
- **Type** `Start Date` **as the field name, press the TAB key, select Date/Time as the data type, press the TAB key, type** `Start Date` **as the description, and then press the TAB key to move to the next field.**
- **Type** `Comment` **as the field name, press the TAB key, select Memo as the data type, press the TAB key, type** `Comment Concerning Trainer` **as the description, and then press the TAB key to move to the next field.**
- **Type** `Picture` **as the field name, press the TAB key, select OLE Object as the data type, press the TAB key, type** `Picture of Trainer` **as the description, and then press the TAB key to move to the next field.**
- **Type** `Web Page` **as the field name, press the TAB key, select Hyperlink as the data type, press the TAB key, and then type** `Address of Trainer's Web Page` **as the description.**

The new fields are entered (Figure 5-4).

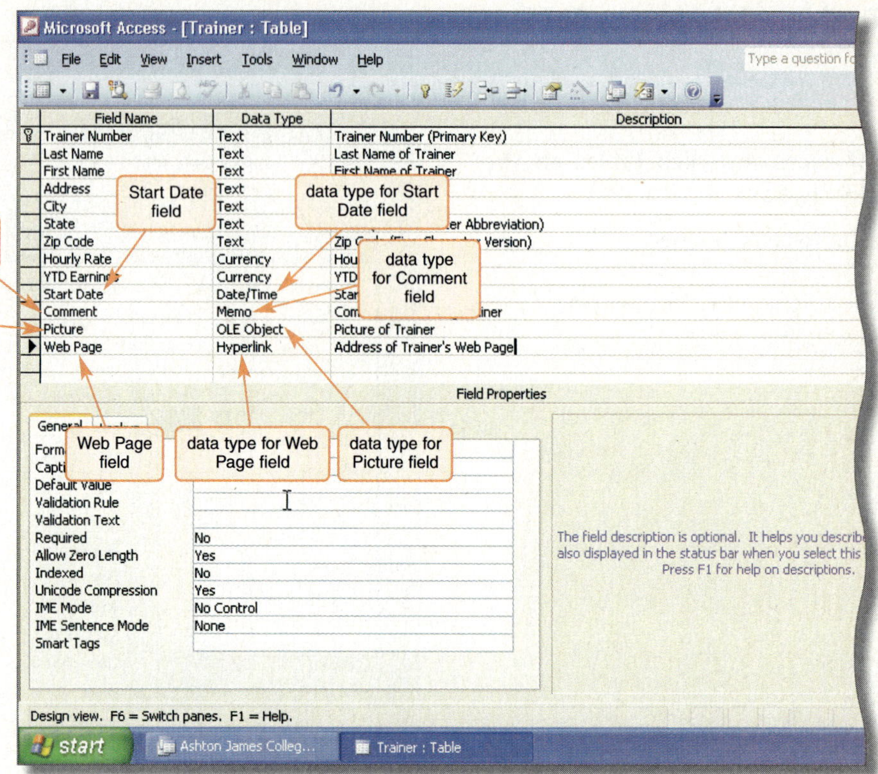

FIGURE 5-4

> **Q&A**
>
> **Q:** Can you sort on fields with data types of Date/Time, Memo, OLE Object, or Hyperlink? On fields of which type can you create a single-field index?
>
> **A:** You can sort and create an index on fields whose data type is Date/Time or Memo. You neither can sort nor create an index on fields whose data type is OLE Object or Hyperlink.

Using the Input Mask Wizard

An **input mask** specifies how the data is to be entered and how it will appear. You can enter an input mask directly or you can use the Input Mask Wizard. The wizard assists you in the creation of the input mask by allowing you to select from a list of the most frequently used input masks.

To use the Input Mask Wizard, select the Input Mask property and then select the Build button. The following steps illustrate how to add the Phone Number field and then specify how the telephone number is to appear by using the Input Mask Wizard.

To Use the Input Mask Wizard

1

- **Click the row selector for the Hourly Rate field, and then press the INSERT key to insert a blank row.**
- **Click the Field Name column for the new field.**
- **Type** `Phone Number` **as the field name and then press the TAB key.**
- **Select the Text data type by pressing the TAB key.**
- **Type** `Phone Number` **as the description.**
- **Click the Input Mask property box.**

The data is entered for the field and the Build button appears (Figure 5-5).

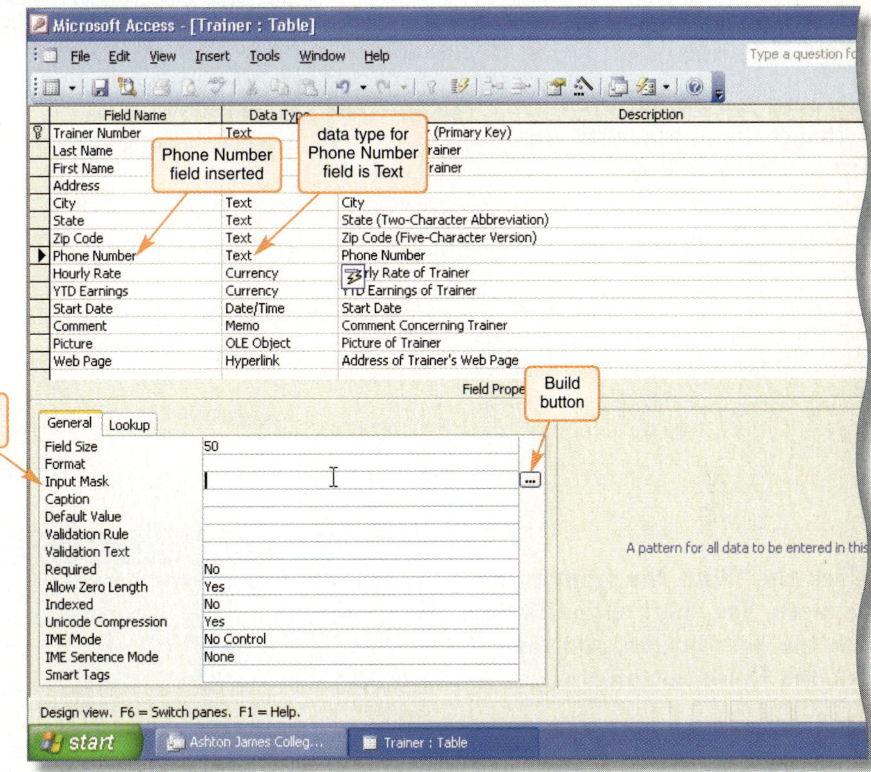

FIGURE 5-5

2

- **Click the Build button.**
- **If a dialog box appears asking you to save the table, click the Yes button. (If a dialog box displays a message that the Input Mask Wizard is not installed, check with your instructor before proceeding with the following steps.)**
- **Ensure that Phone Number is selected.**

The Input Mask Wizard dialog box displays several common input masks (Figure 5-6). Your list may be different. The Phone Number input mask is highlighted.

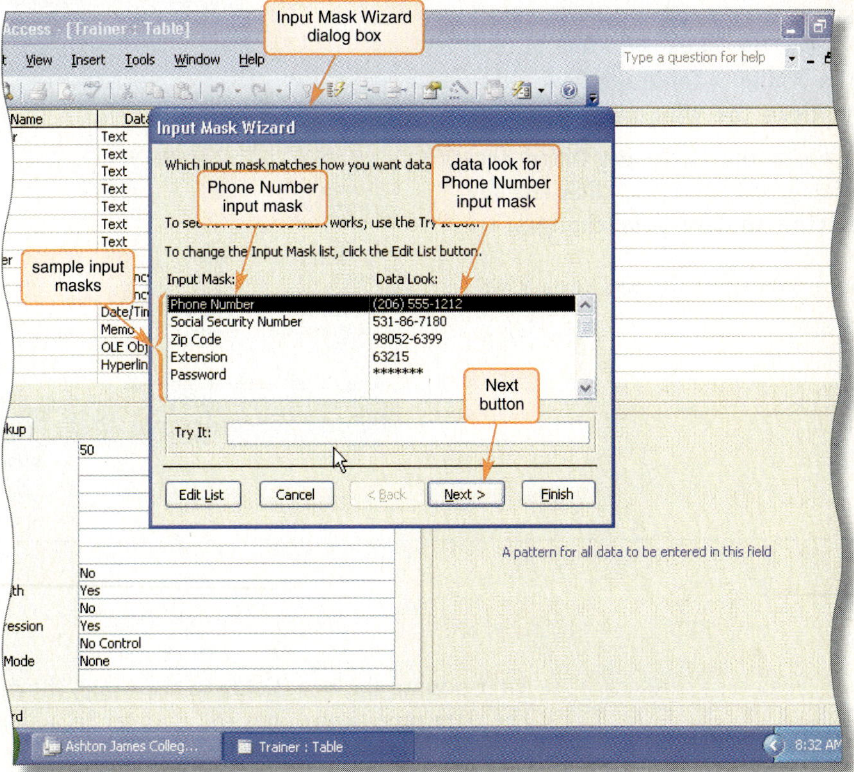

FIGURE 5-6

3

- **Click the Next button.**
- **You then are given the opportunity to change the input mask.**
- **Because you do not need to change the mask, click the Next button a second time.**

The Input Mask Wizard dialog box displays options for storing the data (Figure 5-7). Options allow Access to store the symbols in the mask (the parentheses and the hyphen) in the database or not. Your dialog box may display different numbers in the examples.

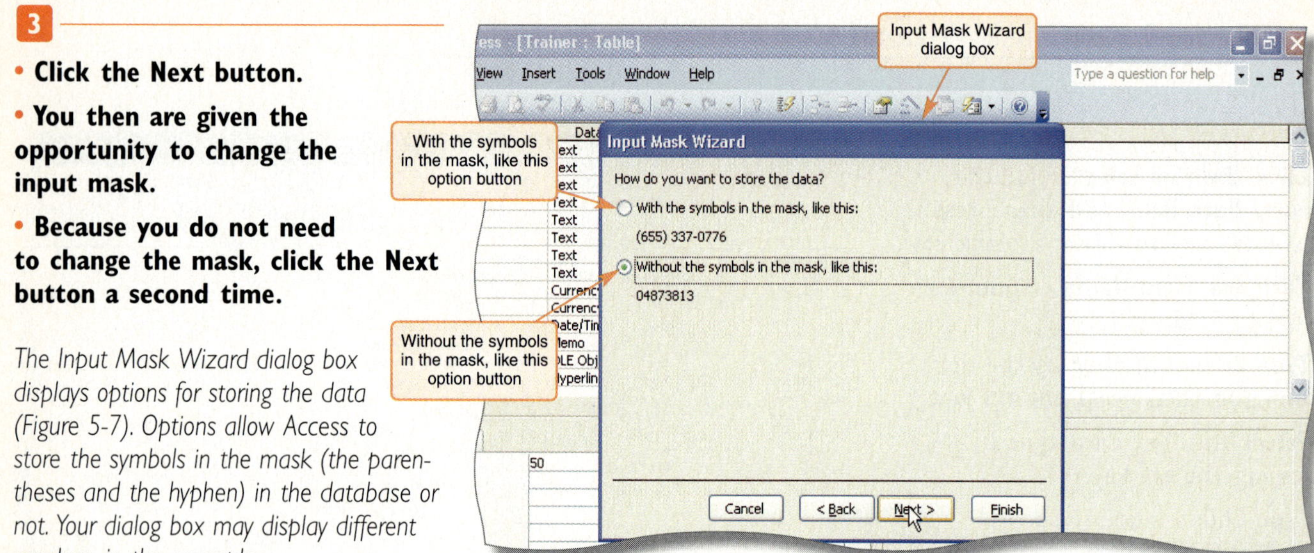

FIGURE 5-7

4

- **Click the "With the symbols in the mask, like this" option button, click the Next button, and then click the Finish button.**

The Input Mask property box displays the input mask (Figure 5-8).

5

- **Click the Close Window button on the Trainer : Table window title bar to close the window.**
- **When the Microsoft Office Access dialog box appears, click the Yes button to save your changes.**

Access saves the changes to the table design.

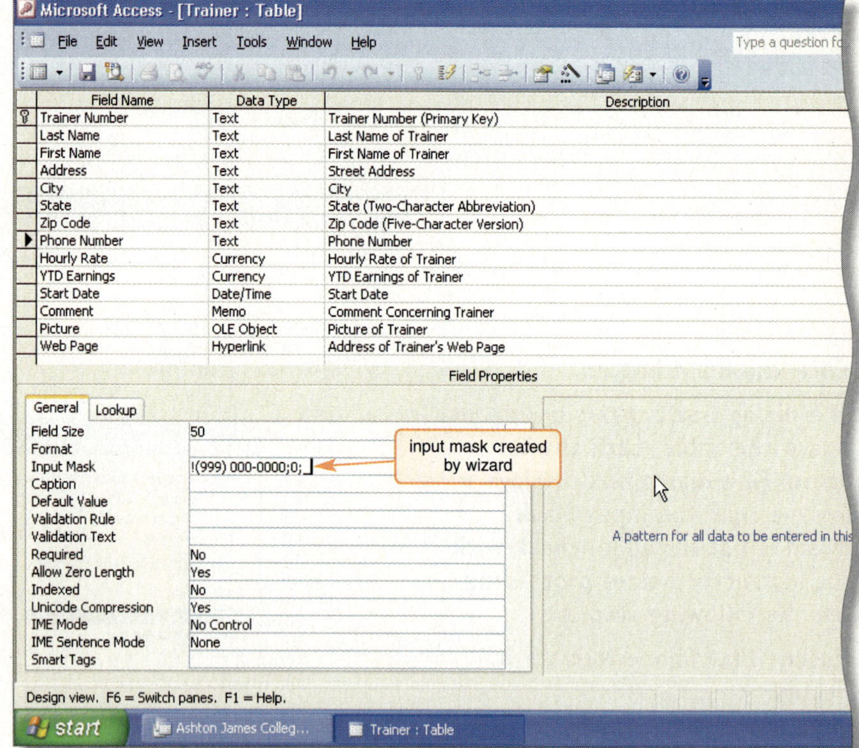

FIGURE 5-8

Updating the New Fields

After adding the new fields to the table, the next task is to enter data into the fields. The data type determines the manner in which this is accomplished. The following sections cover the methods for updating fields with an input mask, date fields, memo fields, OLE fields, and Hyperlink fields.

Entering Data Using an Input Mask

When entering data in a field that has an input mask, Access will insert the appropriate special characters in the proper positions. This means Access will insert the parentheses around the area code, the space following the second parenthesis, and the hyphen in the Phone Number field automatically. The following steps show how to use the input mask to add the telephone numbers.

To Enter Data Using an Input Mask

1

- **If necessary, click the Tables object on the Objects bar, right-click Trainer, and then click Open on the shortcut menu.**
- **Make sure the window is maximized.**
- **Tab to the Phone Number field on the first record.**

Access displays the table in Datasheet view (Figure 5-9). The insertion point is in the Phone Number field on the first record. The parentheses and hyphen do not appear yet. If you click the field, the parentheses and hyphen may appear.

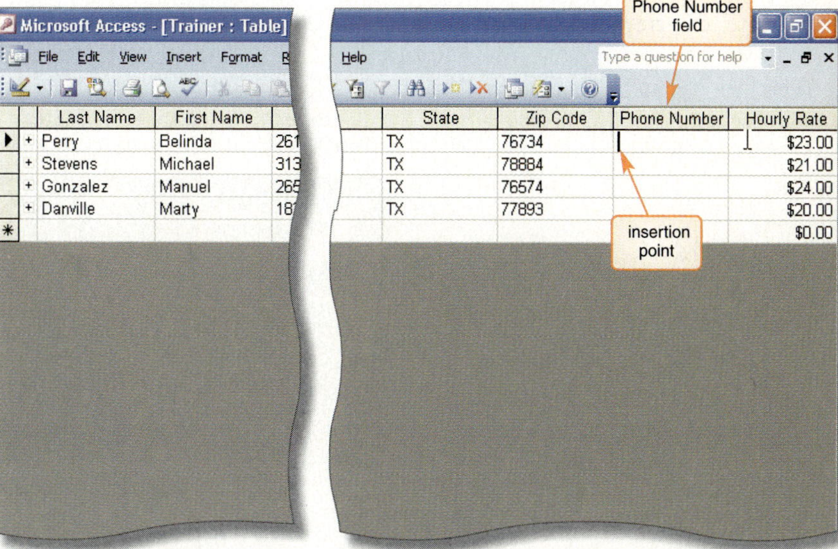

FIGURE 5-9

2

- **Type** `5125552512` **as the telephone number.**

Access inserts the data in its proper location and displays the telephone number with the appropriate symbols (Figure 5-10). The symbols appear as soon as you begin typing the number.

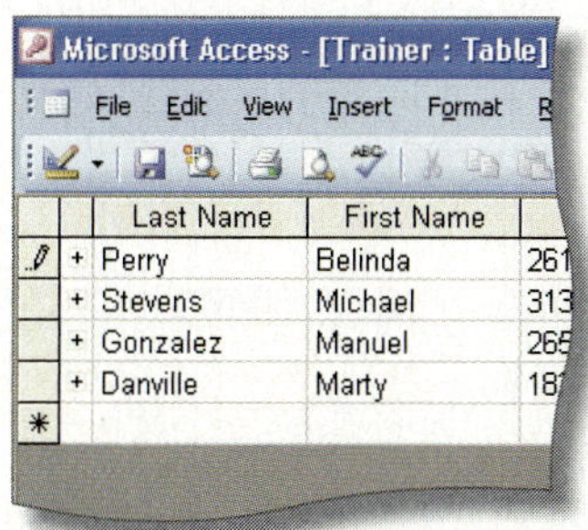

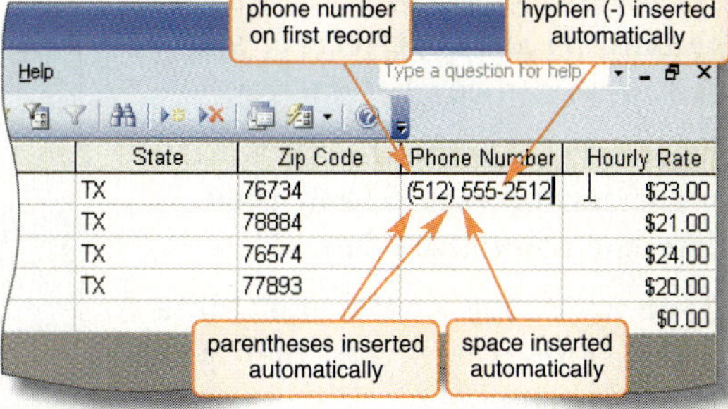

FIGURE 5-10

3

- **Use the same technique to enter the remaining telephone numbers as shown in Figure 5-11.**

The telephone numbers are entered.

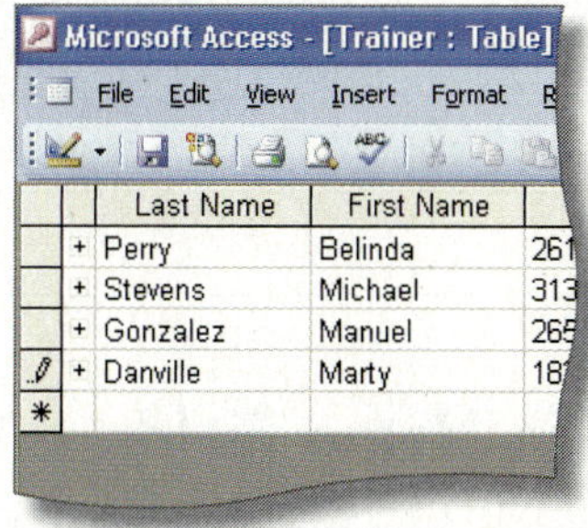

FIGURE 5-11

all phone numbers entered

Entering Data in Date Fields

To enter data in date fields, simply type the dates and include slashes (/). The following steps show how to add the Start Dates for the trainers using Datasheet view.

To Enter Data in Date Fields

1

- **Repeatedly click the right scroll arrow until the new fields appear.**

The fields have shifted to the left (Figure 5-12).

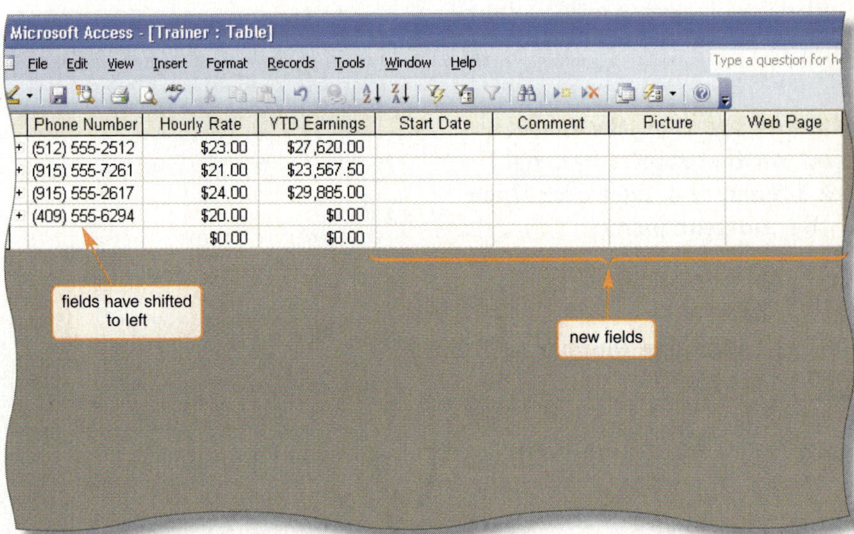

FIGURE 5-12

2

- **Click the Start Date field on the first record, type** 10/12/2003 **as the date on the first record, and then press the DOWN ARROW key.**
- **Type** 5/5/2003 **as the start date on the second record, and then press the DOWN ARROW key.**
- **Type** 2/5/2002 **as the start date on the third record, and then press the DOWN ARROW key.**
- **Type** 8/12/2005 **as the start date on the fourth record.**

The dates are entered (Figure 5-13).

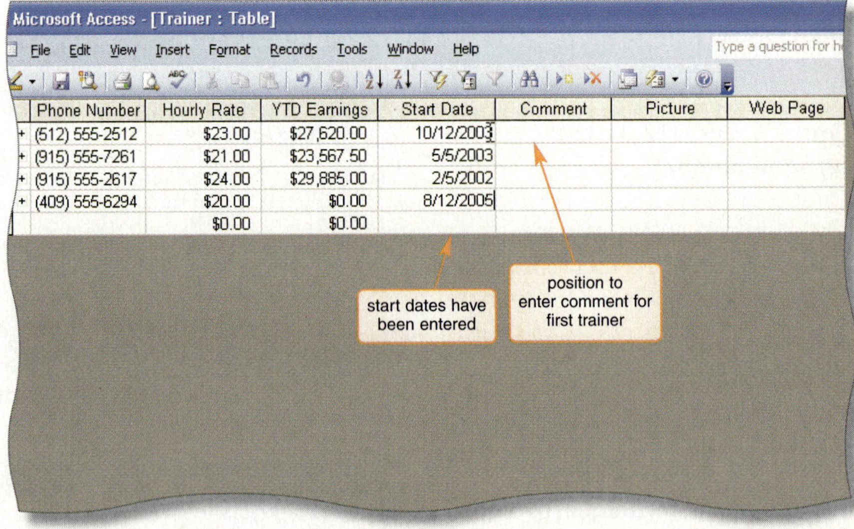

FIGURE 5-13

Entering Data in Memo Fields

To update a memo field, simply type the data in the field. With the current row and column spacing on the screen, only a small portion of the memo will appear. To correct this problem, you will change the spacing later to allow more room for the memo. The following steps show how to enter each trainer's comment.

To Enter Data in Memo Fields

1

- **If necessary, click the right scroll arrow so the Comment field appears.**
- **Click the Comment field on the first record, and then type** Has done corporate training for 11 years. Has taught introductory computing courses at local colleges for 5 years. **as the entry.**

The last portion of the comment appears (Figure 5-14).

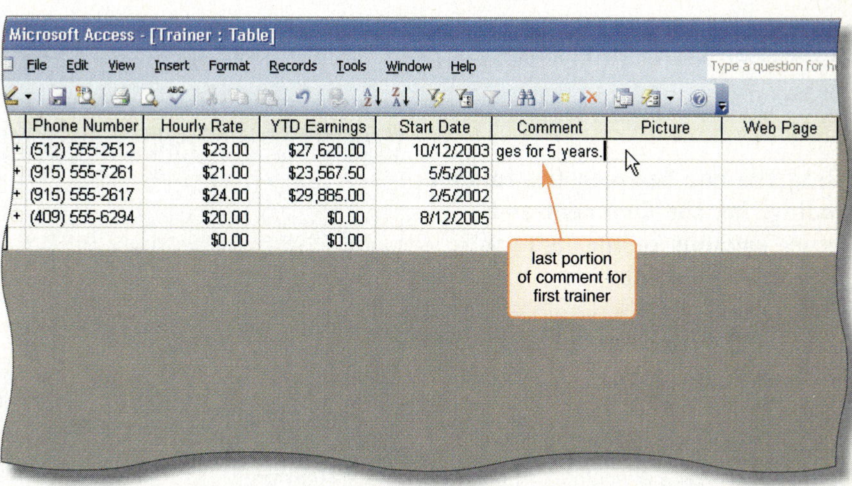

FIGURE 5-14

2

- **Click the Comment field on the second record, and then type** In previous position, was head of training at Information Technology department for large company. Specialist in database design and development. **as the entry.**

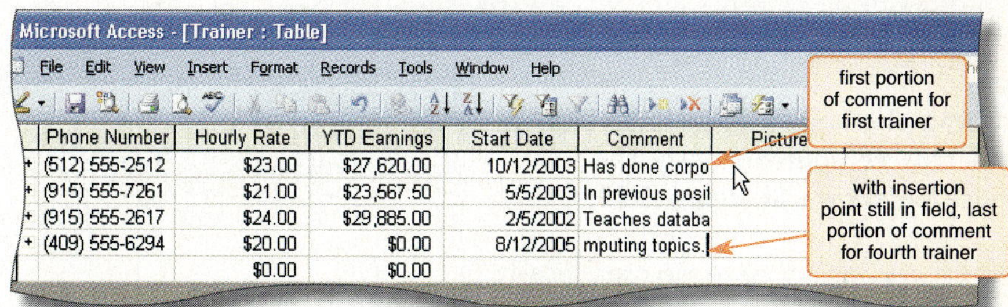

FIGURE 5-15

3

- **Click the Comment field on the third record, and then type** Teaches database courses at local college and gives database seminars to area industries. **as the entry.**

4

- **Click the Comment field on the fourth record, and then type** New trainer. Was active in tutoring other students in computing topics. **as the entry.**

All the comments are entered (Figure 5-15). The first portion of the comments for the first three trainers appears. Because the insertion point still is in the field for the fourth trainer, only the last portion of the comment appears.

Other Ways

1. In Dictation mode, say "[specific text for each comment]"

Changing the Row and Column Size

Only a small portion of the comments appears in the datasheet. To allow more of the information to appear, you can expand the size of the rows and the columns. You can change the size of a column by using the field selector. The **field selector** is the bar containing the field name. To change the size of a row, you use a record's **record selector**, which is the small box at the beginning of each record.

The following steps describe how to resize the column containing the Comment field and the rows of the table so a larger portion of the Comment field text will appear.

To Change the Row and Column Size

1

- **Drag the line between the column headings for the Comment and Picture columns to the right to resize the Comment column to the approximate size shown in Figure 5-16.**

The mouse pointer changes to a two-headed arrow with a horizontal bar, indicating you can drag the line to resize the column.

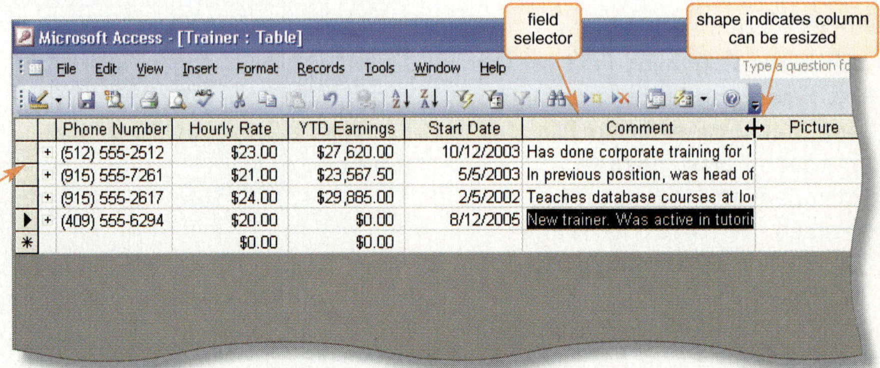

FIGURE 5-16

2

- **Drag the lower edge of the record selector to approximately the position shown in Figure 5-17.**

All the rows are resized at the same time. The comments now appear in their entirety. The last row has a different appearance from the other three because it still is selected.

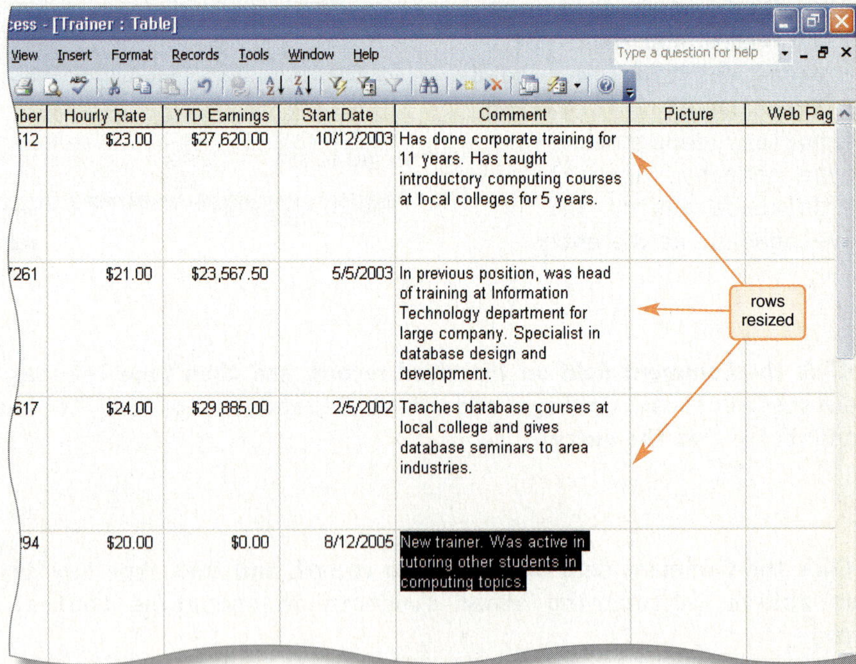

FIGURE 5-17

Other Ways

1. Right-click record selector, click Row Height to change row spacing
2. Right-click field selector, click Column Width to change column size
3. In Voice Command mode, say "Format, Row Height" to change row spacing
4. In Voice Command mode, say "Format, Column Width" to change column size

Entering Data in OLE Fields

To insert data into an OLE field, you use the Insert Object command on the OLE field's shortcut menu. The Insert Object command presents a list of the various types of objects that can be inserted. Access then opens the corresponding application to create the object, for example, Microsoft Drawing. If the object already is created and stored in a file, as is the case in this project, you simply insert it directly from the file.

The following steps illustrate how to insert pictures into the Picture field. The steps assume that the pictures are located in a folder called Pictures on disk C. If your pictures are located elsewhere, you will need to make the appropriate changes.

Note: Because this project illustrates adding pictures to a table, the Ashton James College database is located in a folder called Data on disk C. If your database is on a floppy disk (drive A), copy your database to disk C or to a network disk, or skip the steps in this section so your database will not become too large for your disk.

To Enter Data in OLE Fields

1

- **Ensure the Picture field appears on your screen, and then right-click the Picture field on the first record.**

The shortcut menu for the Picture field appears (Figure 5-18).

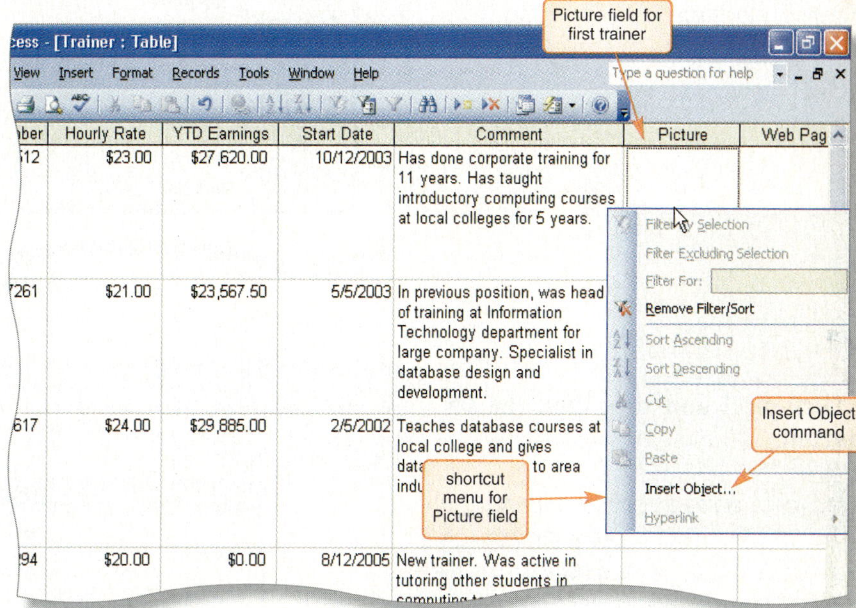

FIGURE 5-18

2

- **Click Insert Object.**

The Microsoft Office Access dialog box displays the Object Type list (Figure 5-19). Your list may be different.

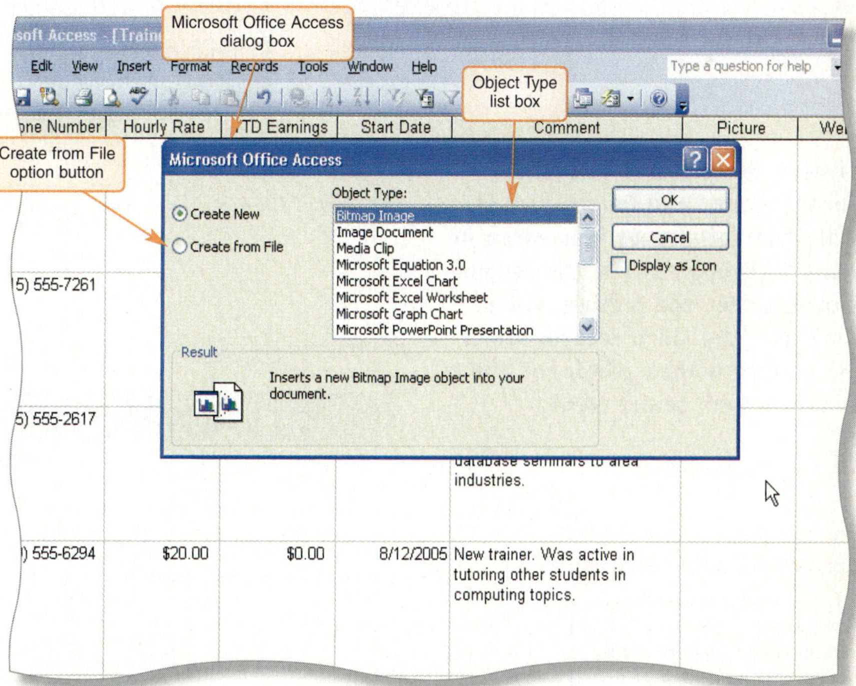

FIGURE 5-19

3

- **Click the Create from File option button, and then click the Browse button.**
- **Navigate to the Pictures folder in the Look in box. (If your pictures are located elsewhere, navigate to the folder where they are located instead of the Pictures folder.)**

The Browse dialog box appears (Figure 5-20). If you do not have the pictures, you will need to locate the folder in which yours are stored.

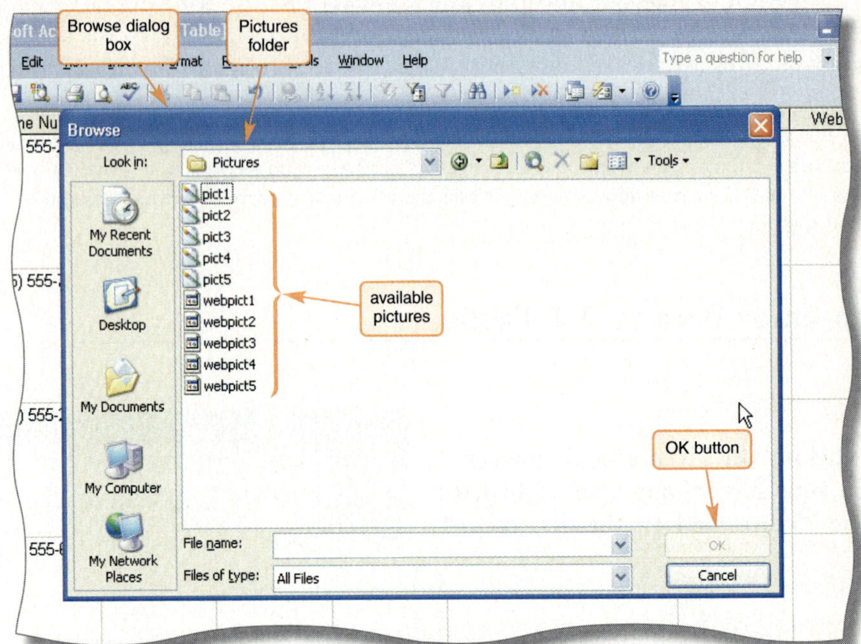

FIGURE 5-20

4

- **Click pict1 and then click the OK button.**

The Browse dialog box closes and the Microsoft Office Access dialog box appears (Figure 5-21). The File text box displays the name of the selected picture.

5

- **Click the OK button.**

6

- **Insert the pictures into the second, third, and fourth records using the techniques illustrated in Steps 1 through 5. For the second record, select the picture named pict2. For the third record, select the picture named pict3. For the fourth record, select pict4.**

The pictures are inserted.

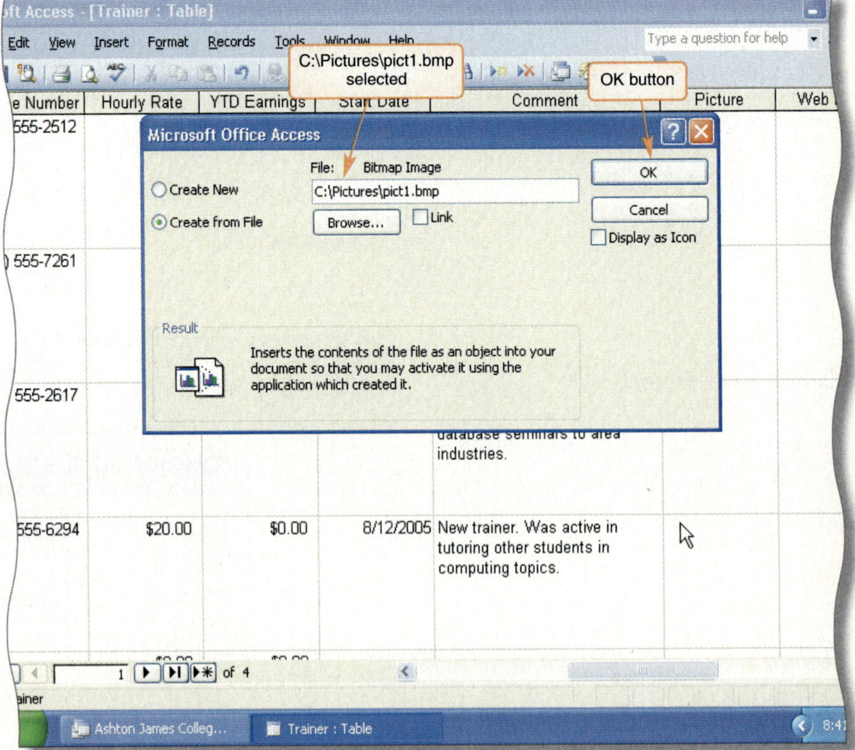

FIGURE 5-21

Other Ways

1. On Insert menu click Object
2. In Voice Command mode, say "Insert, Object"

The entries in the Picture field all should be Bitmap images (BMP). If you see the word Package instead of Bitmap image, there is a problem either with the graphics filters that are installed or with the file associations for BMP files. In that case, you can use a slightly different technique to add the pictures. After right-clicking the Picture field, and clicking Insert Object, *do not* click the Create from File button. Instead, select the Paintbrush Picture object type from the list, select the Paste From command on the Edit menu of the Paintbrush window, select the desired BMP file, and then select the Exit command from the File menu to return to the datasheet. The entry in the Picture field then will be Bitmap image as it should.

More About

Updating OLE Fields

OLE fields can occupy a great deal of space. To save space in your database, you can convert a picture from Bitmap Image to Picture (Device Independent Bitmap). To make the conversion, right-click the field, click Bitmap Image Object, click Convert, and then double-click Picture.

Entering Data in Hyperlink Fields

To insert data into a Hyperlink field, you will use the Hyperlink command on the Hyperlink field's shortcut menu. You then edit the hyperlink. You can enter the Web page address for the appropriate Web page or specify a file that contains the document to which you want to link.

The following steps show how to insert the addresses of the trainers' Web pages.

To Enter Data in Hyperlink Fields

1

• **Be sure the Web Page field appears, right-click the Web Page field on the first record, and then point to Hyperlink on the shortcut menu.**

The shortcut menu for the Web Page field is displayed (Figure 5-22). The Hyperlink submenu also appears.

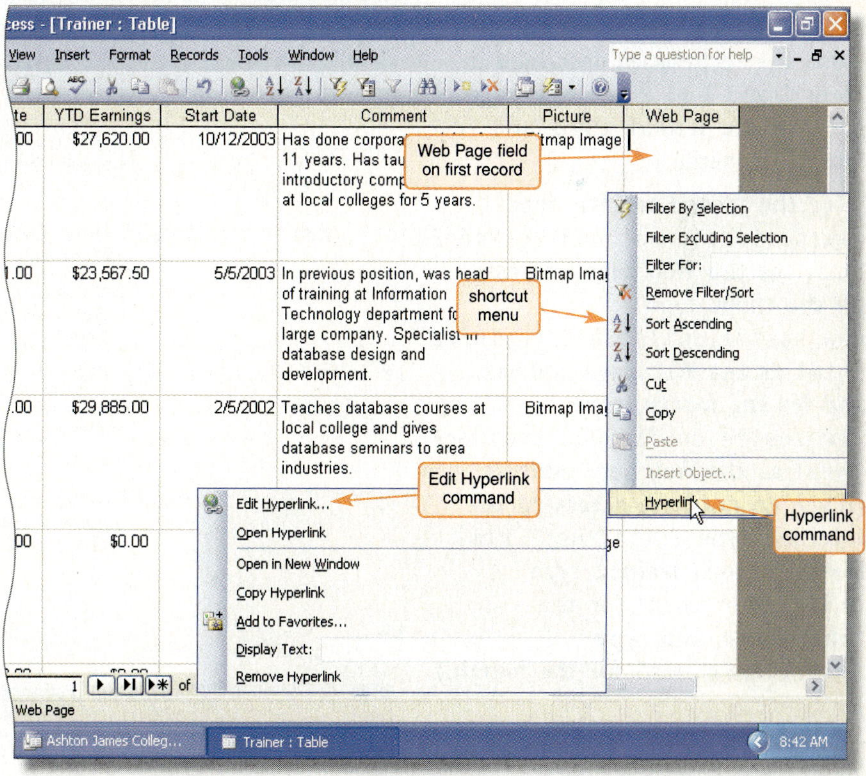

FIGURE 5-22

2

- **Click Edit Hyperlink.**
- **Type** `www.scsite.com/ac2003/trainer1.html` **in the Address text box. (If you do not have access to the Internet, type** `a:\trainer1.html` **in the Address text box instead of www.scsite.com/ac2003/trainer1.html as the Web page address.)**

The Insert Hyperlink dialog box displays the contents of the current folder in the list box. Your current folder list will be different or a browsed pages list may appear instead of the current folder (Figure 5-23).

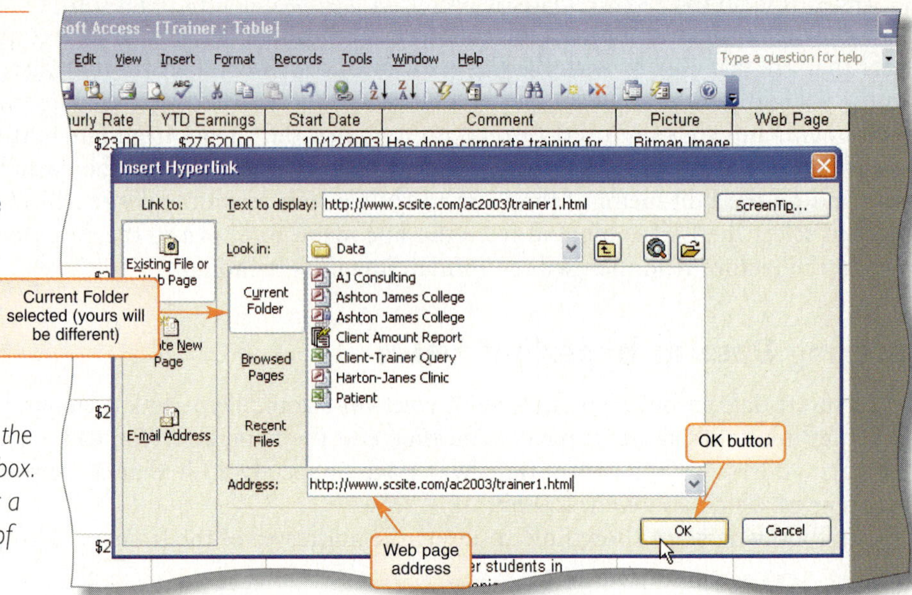

FIGURE 5-23

3

- **Click the OK button.**
- **Use the techniques described in Steps 1 and 2 to enter Web page data for the second, third, and fourth trainers.**
- **For the second trainer, type** `www.scsite.com/ac2003/trainer2.html` **as the Web page address; for the third, type** `www.scsite.com/ac2003/trainer3.html` **as the Web page address; and for the fourth, type** `www.scsite.com/ac2003/trainer4.html` **as the Web page address. (If you do not have access to the Internet, type** `a:\trainer2.html` **for the second trainer, type** `a:\trainer3.html` **for the third trainer, and type** `a:\trainer4.html` **for the fourth.)**

The Web page data is entered (Figure 5-24).

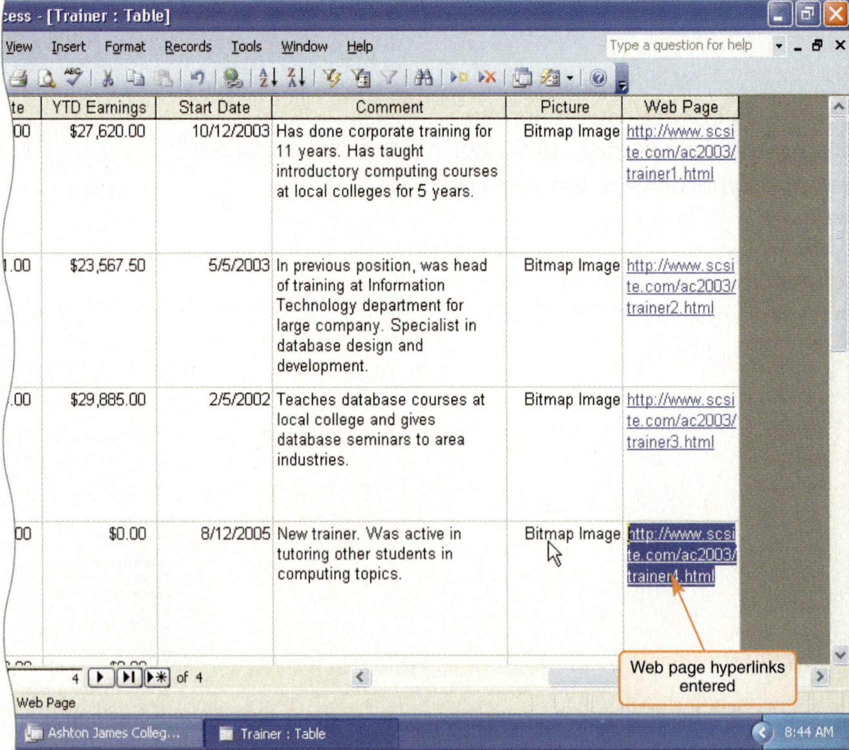

FIGURE 5-24

Other Ways

1. On Insert menu click Hyperlink
2. In Voice Command mode, say "Insert, Hyperlink"

Saving the Table Properties

The row and column spacing are table properties. When changing any table properties, the changes apply only as long as the table is active *unless they are saved*. If they are saved, they will apply every time the table is opened. To save them, simply close the table. If any properties have changed, you will be asked if you want to save the changes. By answering Yes, you can save the changes.

The following steps illustrate how to close the table and save the properties that have been changed.

To Close the Table and Save the Properties

1

- **Close the table by clicking its Close Window button.**

The Microsoft Office Access dialog box appears (Figure 5-25).

2

- **Click the Yes button to save the table properties.**

The properties are saved.

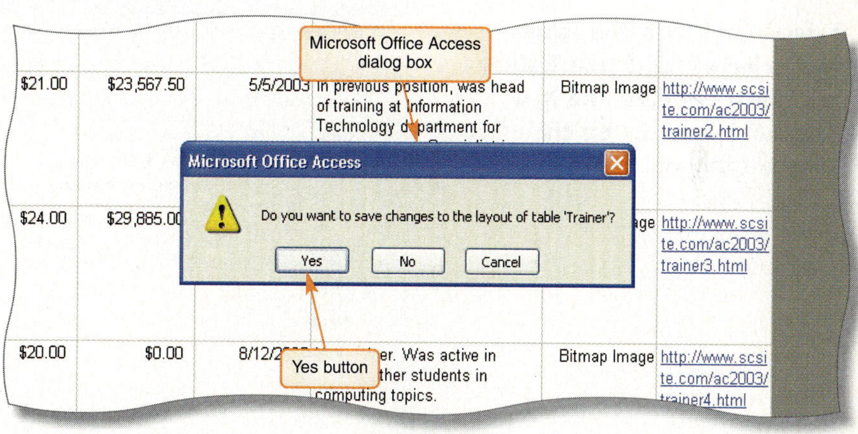

FIGURE 5-25

Although the pictures do not appear on the screen, you can view them at anytime. To view the picture of a particular trainer, right-click the Picture field for the trainer. Click Bitmap Image Object on the shortcut menu, and then click Open. The picture will appear. Once you have finished viewing the picture, close the window containing the picture by clicking its Close button. You also can view the Web page for a trainer, by clicking the trainer's Web Page field.

> *More About*
>
> **Changing the Row and Column Size**
>
> To undo changes to the row height, right-click the row selector, click Row Height on the shortcut menu, and then click the Standard Height check box in the Row Height dialog box. To undo changes to the column width, right-click the field selector, click Column Width on the shortcut menu, and then click the Standard Width check box in the Column Width dialog box.

Advanced Form Techniques

The form in this project includes data from both the Trainer and Client tables. The form will display data concerning one trainer. It also will display data concerning the many clients to which the trainer is assigned. Formally, the relationship between trainers and clients is called a **one-to-many relationship** (*one* trainer services *many* clients).

To include the data for the many clients of a trainer on the form, the client data must appear in a **subform**, which is a form that is contained within another form. The form in which the subform is contained is called the main form. Thus, the **main form** will contain trainer data, and the subform will contain client data.

Creating a Form with a Subform

No special action is required to create a form with a subform if you use the Form Wizard. You must, however, have created previously a one-to-many relationship between the two tables. The Form Wizard will create both the form and subform automatically once you have selected the tables and indicated the general organization of your data. The following steps show how to use the wizard to create the form and subform.

To Create a Form with a Subform Using the Form Wizard

1

- **If necessary, with the Tables object selected, click the Trainer table, and then click the New Object button arrow on the Database toolbar.**

The list of available objects is displayed (Figure 5-26).

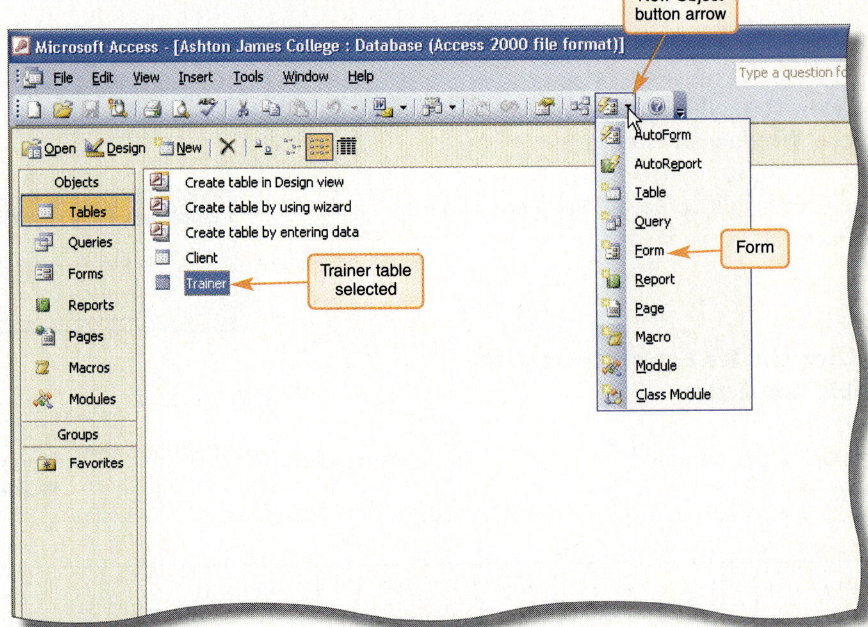

FIGURE 5-26

2

- **Click Form.**

Access displays the New Form dialog box (Figure 5-27).

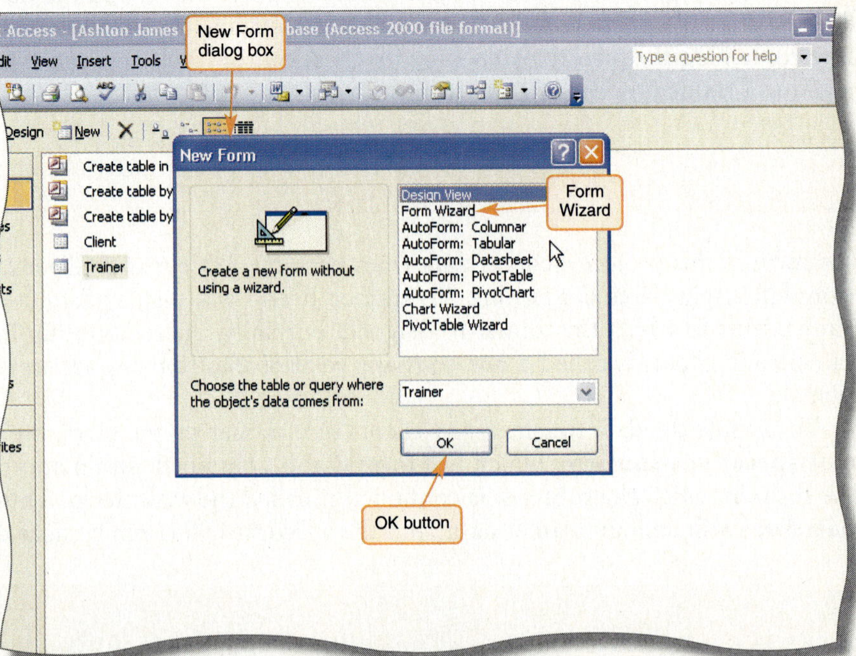

FIGURE 5-27

3

- **Click Form Wizard and then click the OK button.**
- **With the Trainer Number field selected in the Available Fields box, click the Add Field button.**
- **Select the First Name, Last Name, Phone Number, Hourly Rate, YTD Earnings, Start Date, Web Page, Comment, and Picture fields by clicking the field and then clicking the Add Field button.**
- **Click the Table/Queries box arrow.**

The fields from the Trainer table are selected for the form (Figure 5-28). The list of available tables and queries appears.

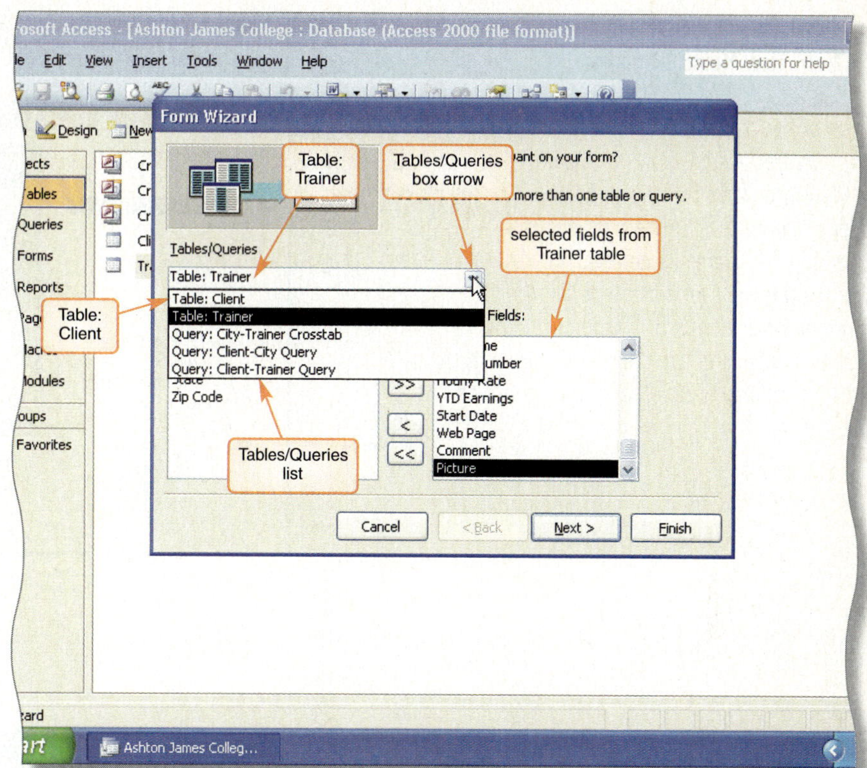

FIGURE 5-28

4

- **Click Table: Client and then select the Client Number, Name, Amount Paid, and Current Due fields.**

The fields are selected (Figure 5-29).

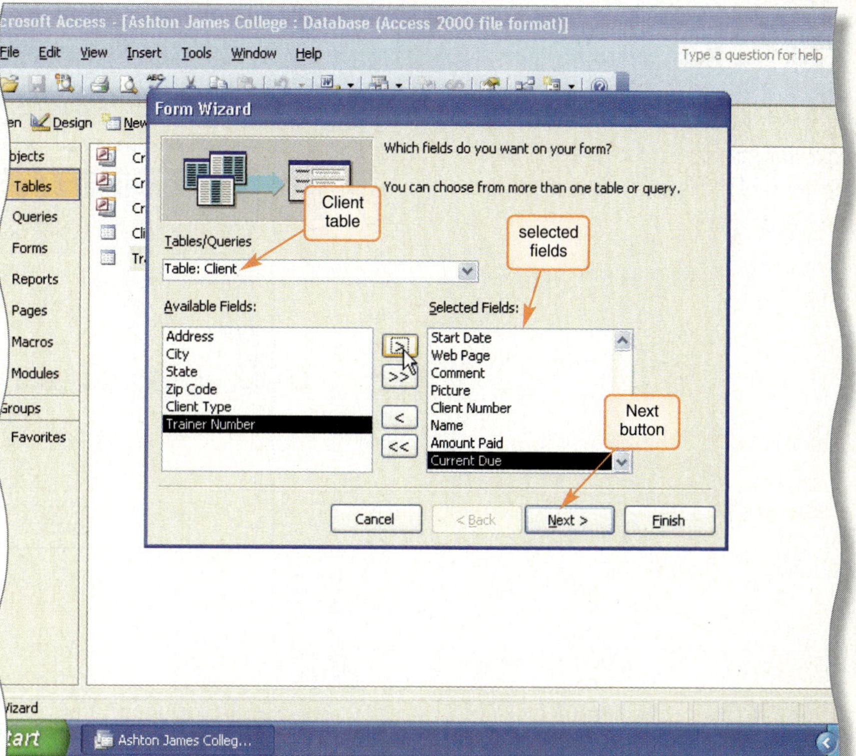

FIGURE 5-29

5

• **Click the Next button.**

The Form Wizard dialog box appears, requesting how you want to view the data: by Trainer or by Client (Figure 5-30). The highlighted selection, by Trainer, is correct. The box on the right indicates visually that the main organization is by Trainer, with the Trainer fields listed at the top. Contained within the form is a subform that contains client data.

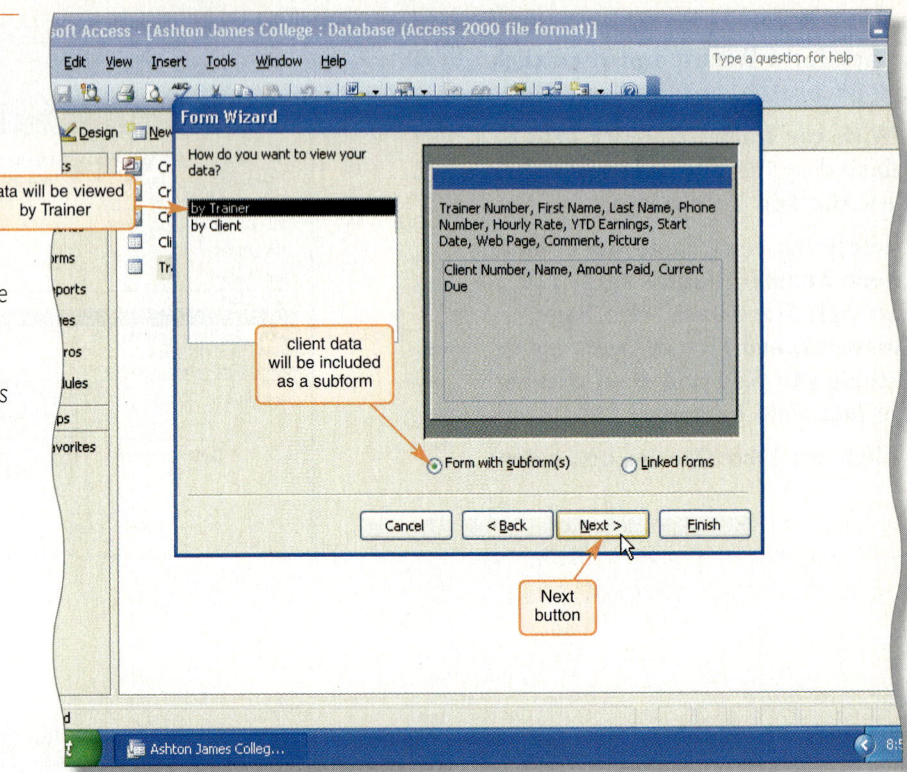

FIGURE 5-30

6

• **Click the Next button.**

Access displays the Form Wizard dialog box requesting the layout for the subform (Figure 5-31). This subform is to appear in Datasheet view.

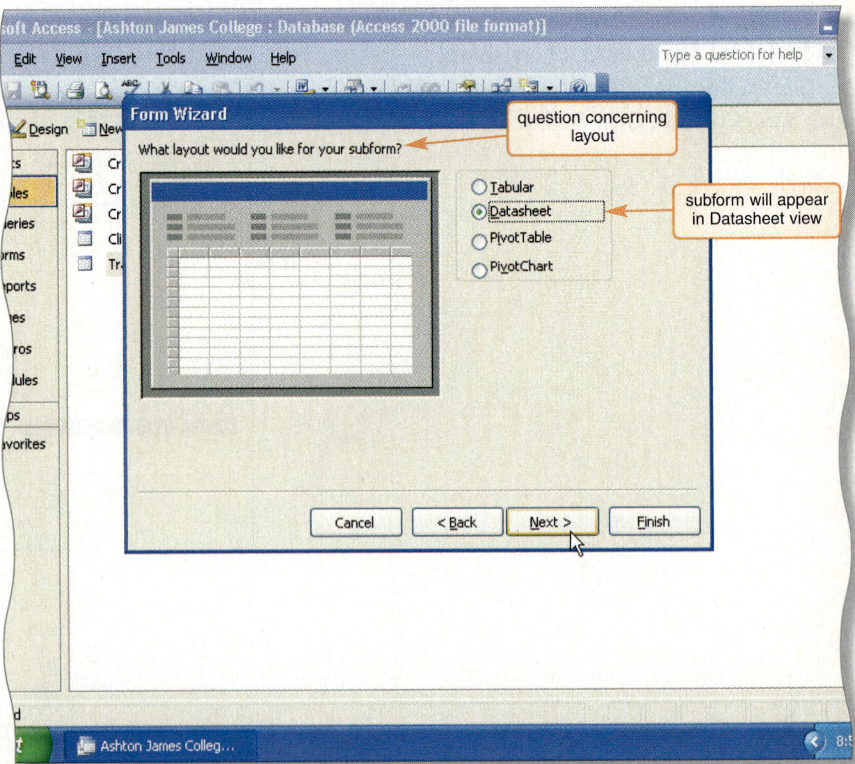

FIGURE 5-31

7

- **Be sure Datasheet is selected and then click the Next button.**
- **Ensure Standard style is selected.**

The Form Wizard dialog box requests a style for the report, and Standard is selected (Figure 5-32).

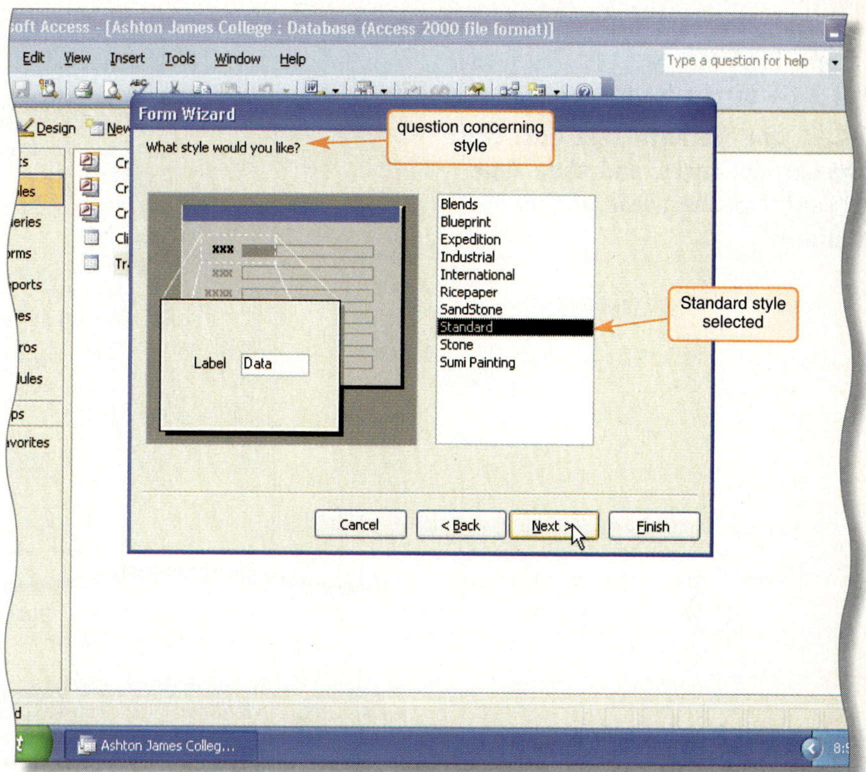

FIGURE 5-32

8

- **Click the Next button.**

The Form Wizard dialog box allows you to change the titles of the form and subform (Figure 5-33).

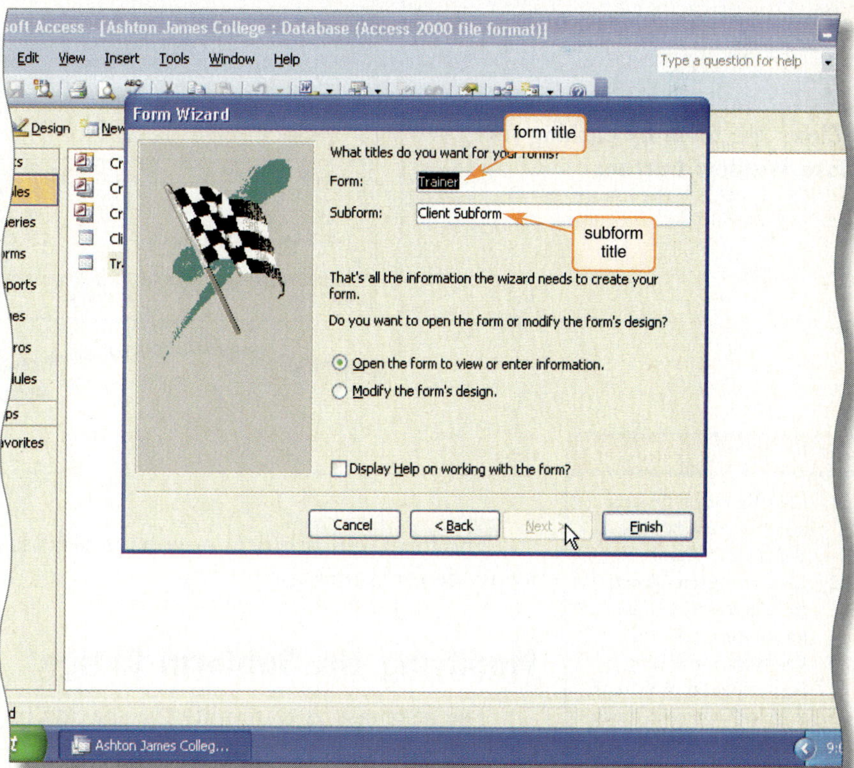

FIGURE 5-33

9

- **Type** `Trainer Master Form` **as the title of the form.**
- **Click the Subform text box, erase the current entry, and then type** `Clients` **as the name of the subform.**

The titles are changed (Figure 5-34).

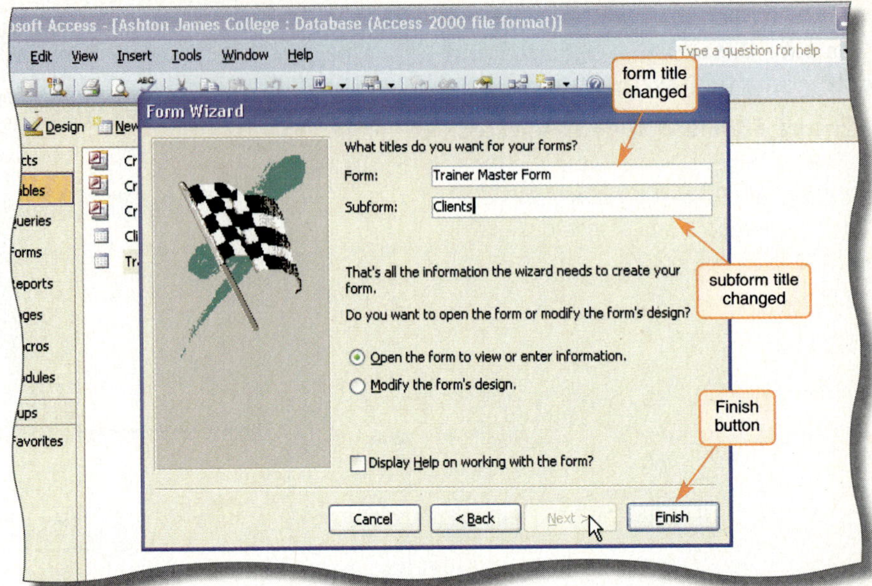

FIGURE 5-34

10

- **Click the Finish button.**

Access displays the form (Figure 5-35). Your form layout may differ slightly. You will modify the layout in the following sections.

11

- **Close the form by clicking its Close Window button.**

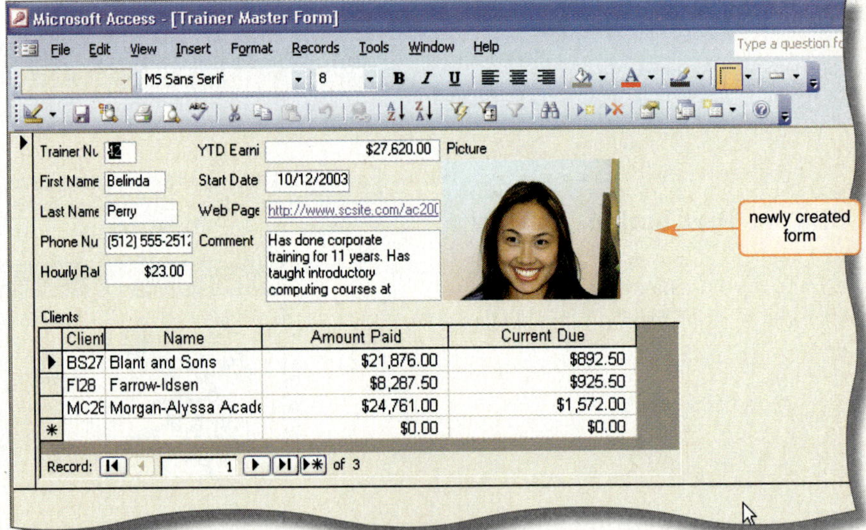

FIGURE 5-35

Other Ways

1. Click Forms on Objects bar, click New button, click Form Wizard
2. Click Forms on Objects bar, double-click Create form by using wizard
3. On Insert menu click Form, click Form Wizard
4. In Voice Command mode, say "Insert, Form, Form Wizard"

The form and subform now have been saved as part of the database and are available for future use.

Modifying the Subform Design

The next task is to modify the spacing of the columns in the subform. The columns are much wider than needed. You can correct these problems by opening the subform in Design view. When the design of the subform appears, you then can convert it to Datasheet view. At this point, you can resize each column.

The following steps illustrate how to modify the subform design to improve the column spacing.

To Modify the Subform Design

1

- **With the Forms object selected, right-click Clients.**

The shortcut menu for the subform appears (Figure 5-36).

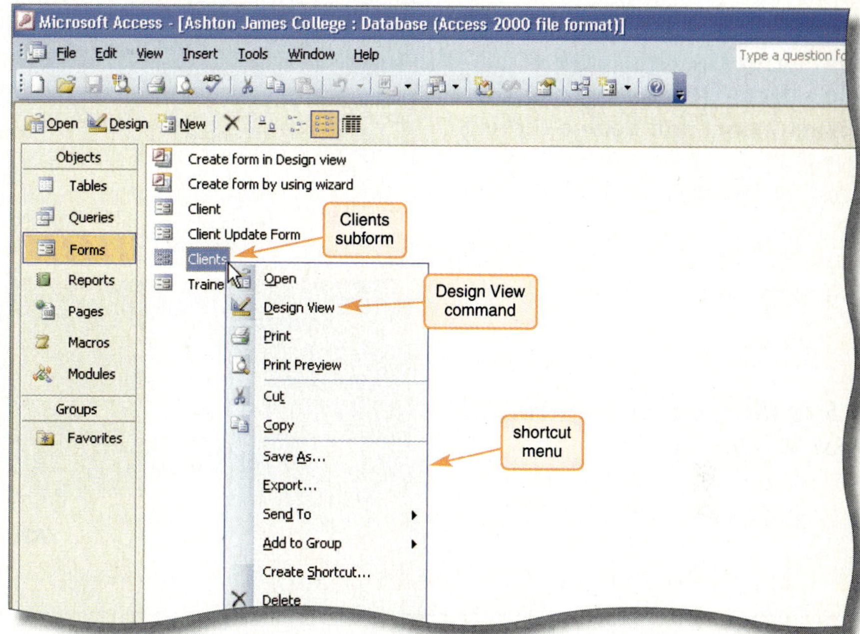

FIGURE 5-36

2

- **Click Design View on the shortcut menu.**

Access displays the form design for the subform (Figure 5-37).

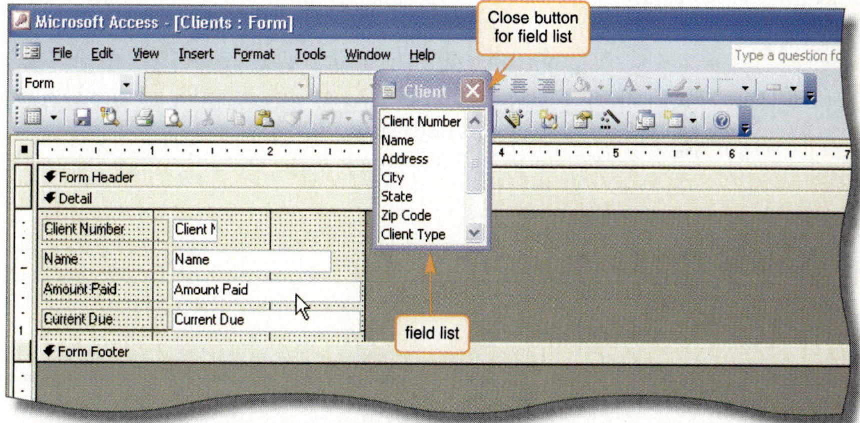

FIGURE 5-37

3

- **If the field list appears, click its Close button.**
- **Click the View button arrow on the Form Design toolbar.**

The View list appears (Figure 5-38).

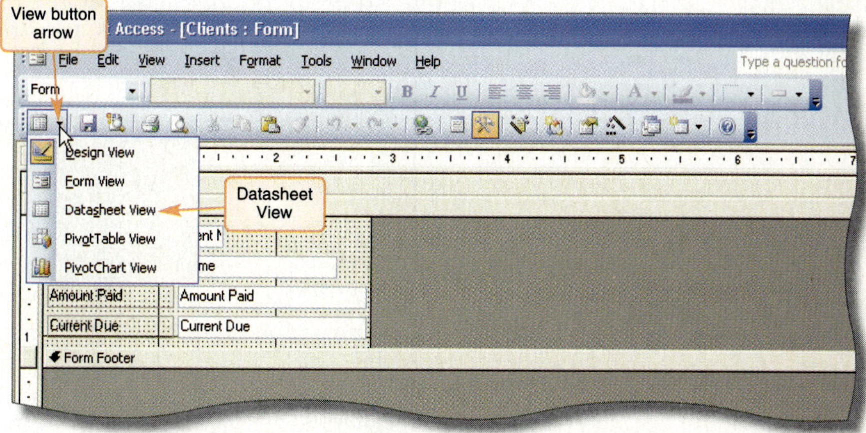

FIGURE 5-38

4

- **Click Datasheet View to display the subform in Datasheet view.**
- **Resize each of the columns by pointing to the right edge of the field selector (to the right of the column name) and double-clicking.**

Access displays the subform in Datasheet view (Figure 5-39). The columns have been resized. You also can resize each column by dragging the right edge of the field selector.

5

- **Close the subform by clicking its Close Window button.**

The changes are made and saved.

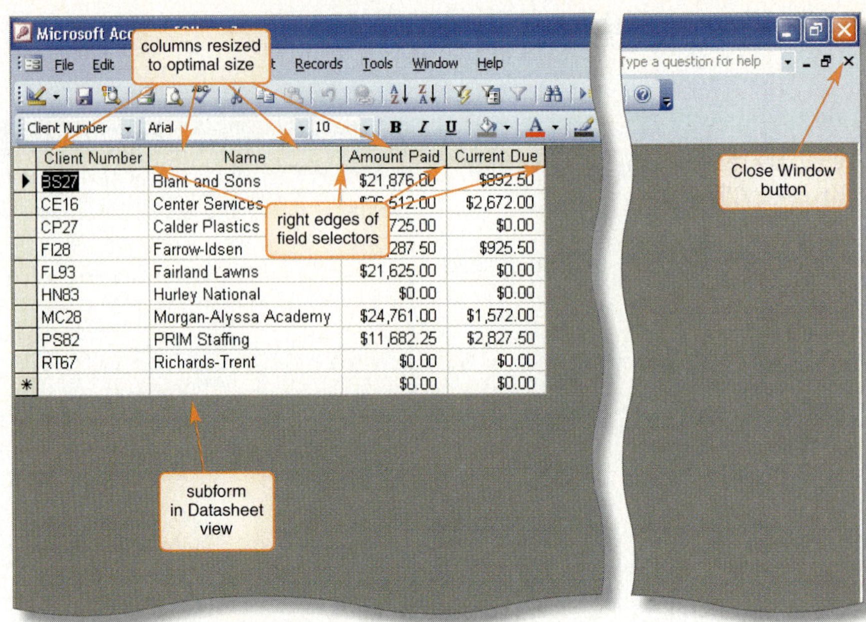

FIGURE 5-39

Modifying the Form Design

The next step is to make several changes to the form. Various objects need to be moved or resized. The properties of the picture need to be adjusted so the entire picture appears. The appearance of the labels needs to be changed and a title needs to be added to the form.

The following steps show how to begin the modification of the form design.

To Modify the Form Design

1

- **Right-click Trainer Master Form.**

The shortcut menu for the form appears (Figure 5-40).

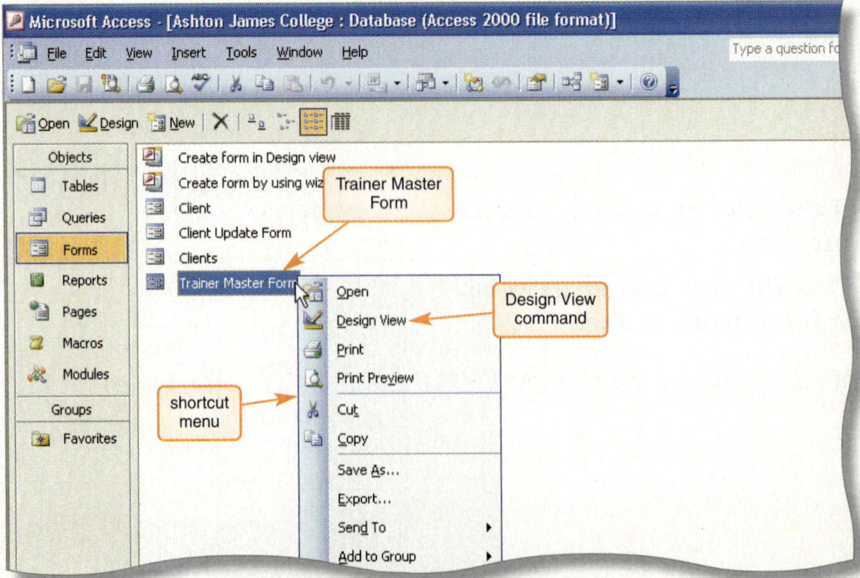

FIGURE 5-40

2

- **Click Design View on the shortcut menu.**
- **Be sure the window is maximized.**
- **If the toolbox does not appear, click the Toolbox button on the toolbar.**
- **Make sure the toolbox is docked at the bottom of the screen. If it is not, drag its title bar to the bottom of the screen to dock it there.**

The form appears in Design view (Figure 5-41). The toolbox is docked at the bottom of the screen.

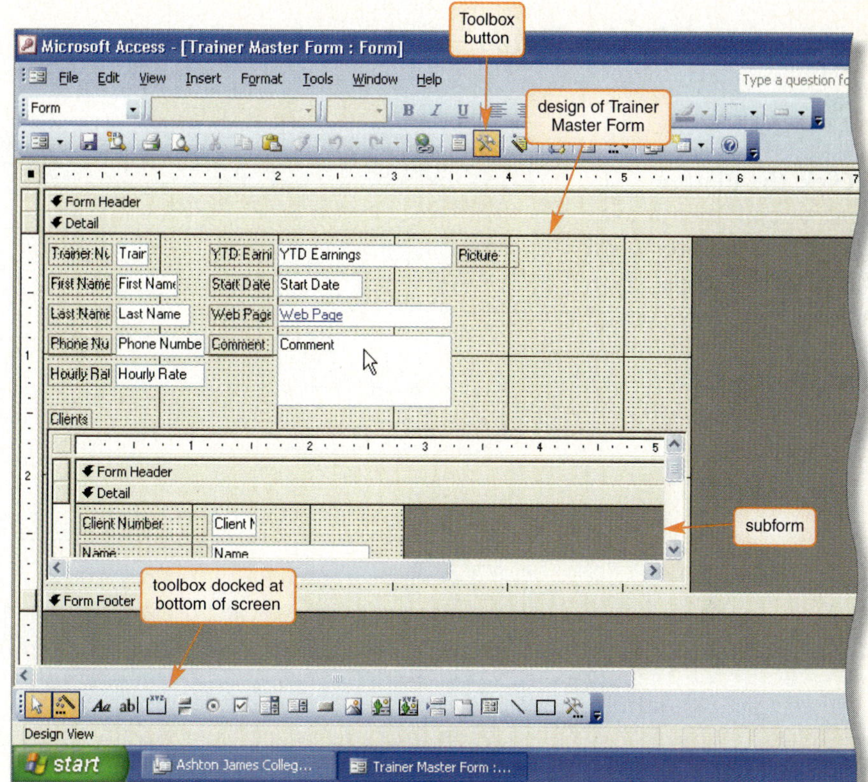

FIGURE 5-41

Your form layout may differ slightly. In the following sections, you will modify the form to match that shown in Figure 5-3 on page AC 261.

Moving and Resizing Fields

Fields on this form can be moved or resized just as they were in the form created in the previous project. First, select the field. To move it, move the mouse pointer to the boundary of the field so it becomes a hand, and then drag the field. To resize a field, drag the appropriate sizing handle. The steps on the next page show how to move certain fields on the form and resize the fields appropriately.

More About

Subforms

When you create forms with subforms, the tables for the main form and the subform must be related. The relationship must have been set previously in the Relationships window. To see if your tables are related, click the Relationships button. Relationships between tables display as lines connecting the tables.

To Move and Resize Fields

1

- **Click the Picture control and then move the mouse pointer until the shape changes to a hand.**

The Picture control is selected and sizing handles appear (Figure 5-42).

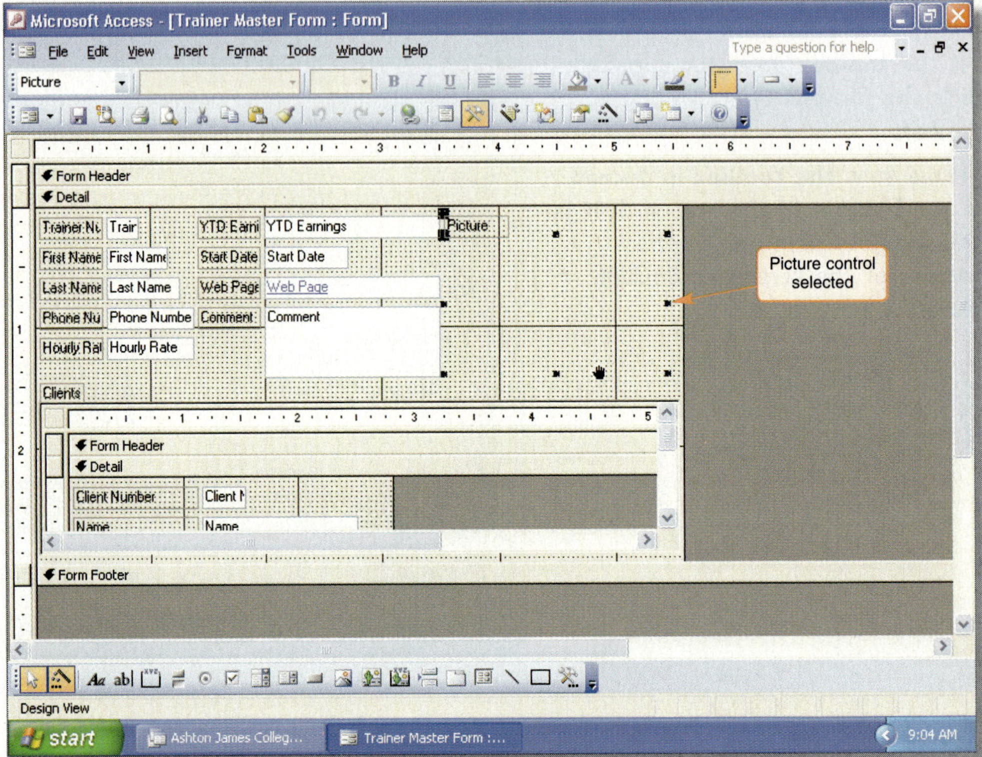

FIGURE 5-42

2

- **Drag the Picture control to approximately the position shown in Figure 5-43.**

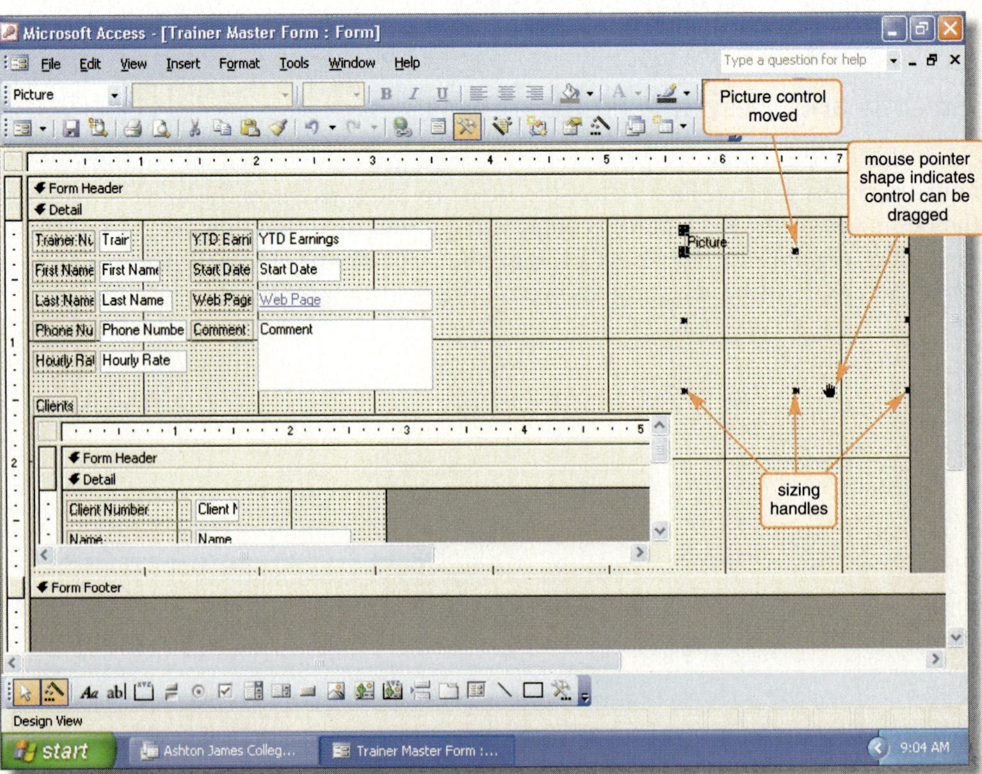

FIGURE 5-43

3

• **Drag the lower sizing handle to approximately the position shown in Figure 5-44.**

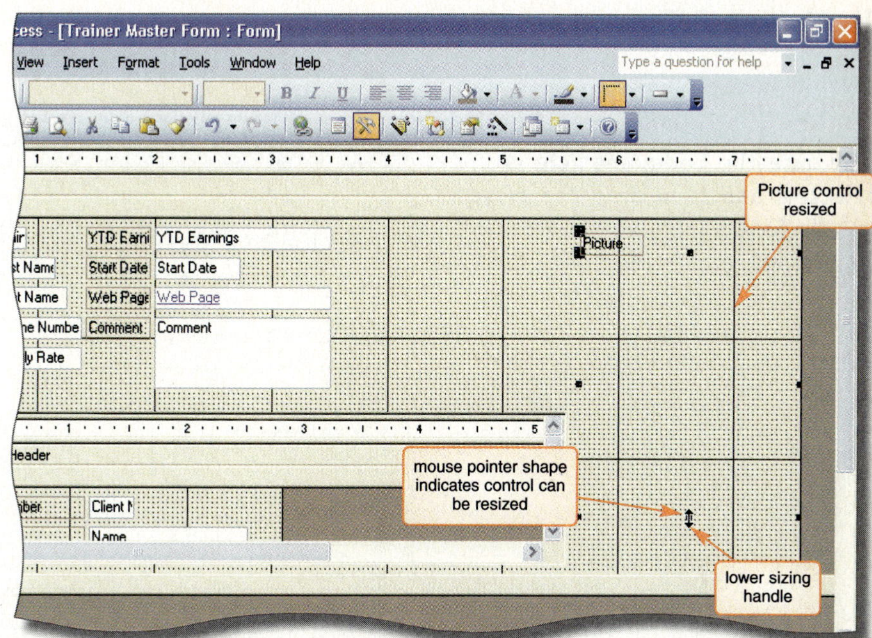

FIGURE 5-44

4

• **Move and resize the Comment control to the approximate position and size shown in Figure 5-45.**

The Comment and Picture controls now are the correct size and in the correct position.

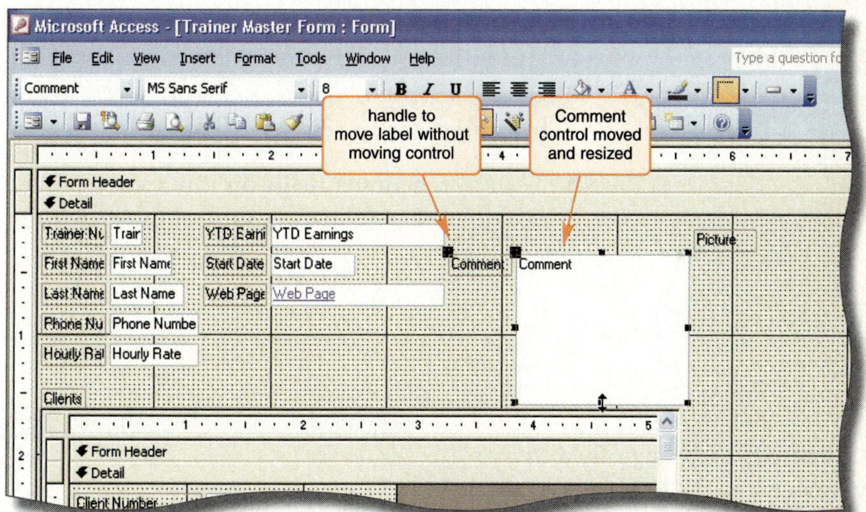

FIGURE 5-45

Moving Labels

To move a label independently from the field with which the label is associated, point to the large, move handle in the upper-left corner of the label. The shape of the mouse pointer changes to a hand with a pointing finger. By dragging this move handle, you will move the label without moving the associated field. The step on the next page illustrates how to move the label of the Comment field without moving the field itself.

To Move a Label

1

- **Be sure the Comment field is selected, and then drag the move handle for its label to the position shown in Figure 5-46.**

The label is moved. The shape of the mouse pointer is a hand with a pointing finger.

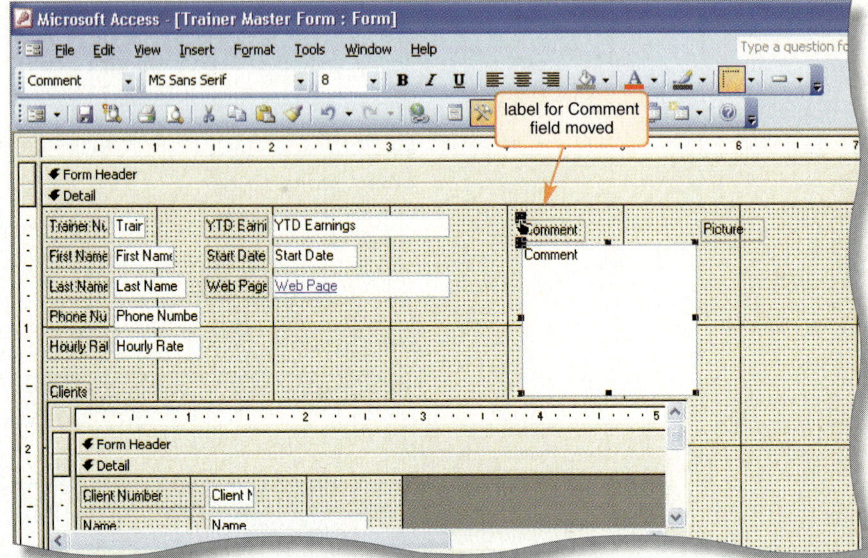

FIGURE 5-46

Moving Remaining Fields

The remaining fields on this form also need to be moved into appropriate positions. The following steps show how to move these fields on the form.

To Move Fields

1

- **Click the Web Page field, move the mouse pointer until the shape changes to a hand, and then drag the field to the position shown in Figure 5-47.**

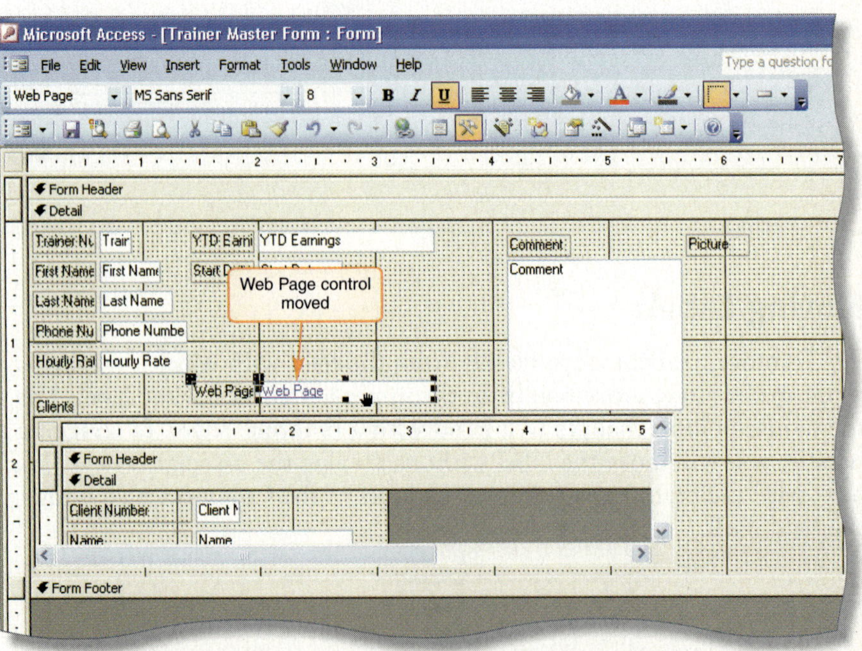

FIGURE 5-47

2

• **Drag the Hourly Rate, YTD Earnings, Start Date, First Name, Last Name, Phone Number, and Trainer Number fields to the positions shown in Figure 5-48.**

The fields now are in the correct positions.

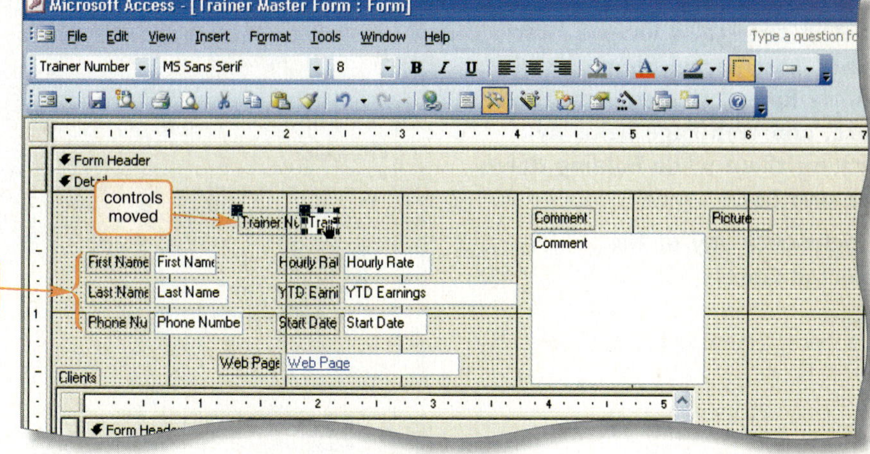

FIGURE 5-48

Changing Label Alignment

The labels for the Trainer Number, First Name, Last Name, Phone Number, Hourly Rate, YTD Earnings, Start Date, and Web Page fields illustrated in Figure 5-1 on page AC 259 are right-aligned; that is, within the controls, the labels are all aligned with the right margins. Because the labels currently are left-aligned, the alignment needs to be changed. To change the alignment, use the property sheet. In the property sheet, you can select the appropriate alignment.

In some cases, you will want to make the same change to several objects, perhaps to several labels at one time. Instead of making the changes individually, you can select all the objects at once, and then make a single change. The following steps illustrate how to change the alignment of the labels.

More About

Selecting Multiple Controls

To select all the controls in a given column or row, you can use the rulers. To select all the controls in a column, click the horizontal ruler above the column. To select all the controls in a row, click the vertical ruler to the left of the row.

To Change Label Alignment

1

• **Click the label for the Trainer Number field to select it.**

The label for the Trainer Number field is selected (Figure 5-49).

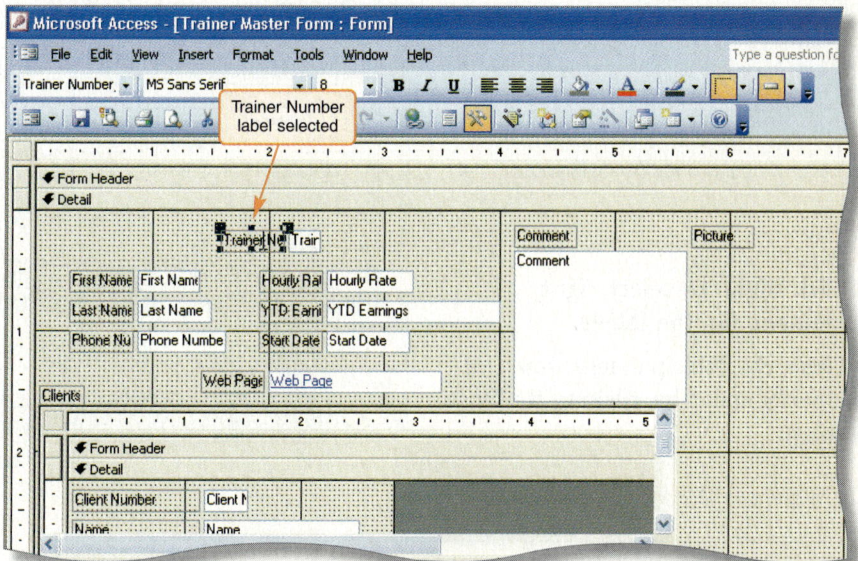

FIGURE 5-49

2

- **Select the labels for the First Name, Last Name, Phone Number, Hourly Rate, YTD Earnings, Start Date, and Web Page fields by clicking them while holding down the SHIFT key.**
- **Right-click any of the selected labels.**

The shortcut menu appears (Figure 5-50).

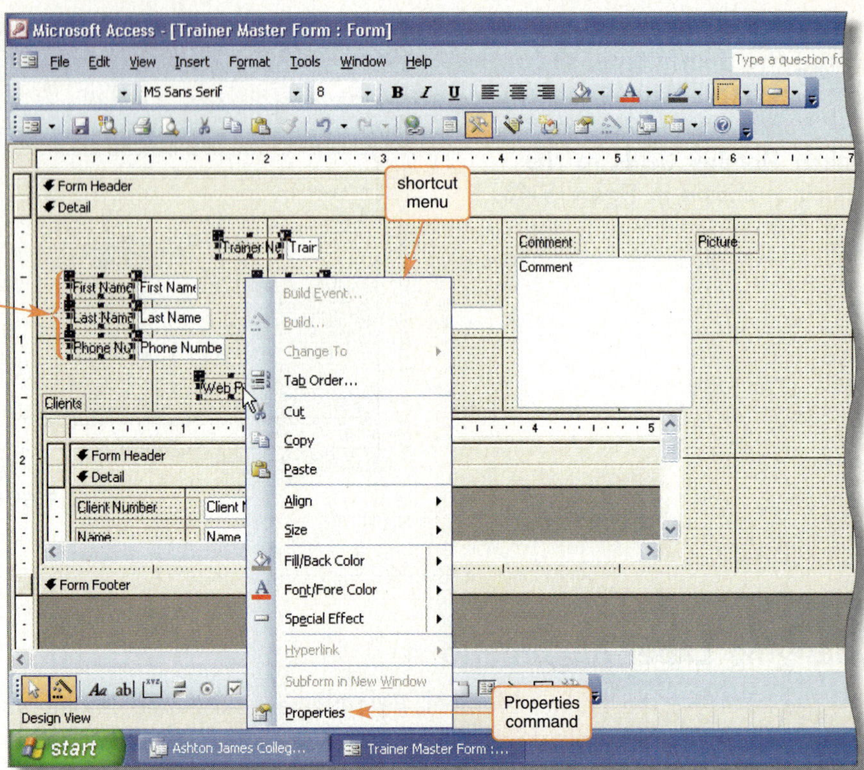

FIGURE 5-50

3

- **Click Properties, click the All tab if it is not selected already, and then click the down scroll arrow to display the Text Align property.**
- **Click Text Align and then click the Text Align property box arrow.**

Access displays the Multiple selection property sheet (Figure 5-51). Text Align property is selected and the list of available options for the Text Align property appears. Depending on where you clicked in the property box, the General property may be highlighted.

4

- **Click Right to select right alignment for the labels.**
- **Close the Multiple selection property sheet by clicking its Close button.**

The alignment is changed.

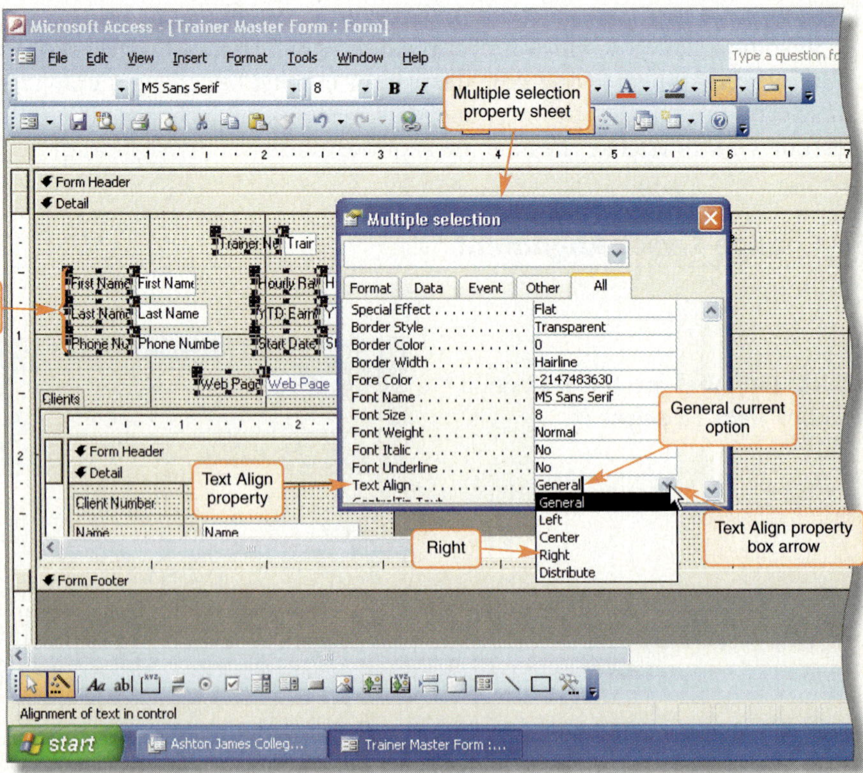

FIGURE 5-51

Resizing the Labels

To resize a label to optimum size, select the label, and then double-click an appropriate sizing handle. The following steps illustrate how to resize the label for the Trainer Number, First Name, Last Name, Phone Number, Hourly Rate, YTD Earnings, Start Date, and Web Page fields. You can resize them individually, but it is easier, however, to make sure the labels are all selected and then resize one of the labels. Access will automatically resize all the others as demonstrated in the following steps.

To Resize a Label

1

- **With all the labels selected, point to the handle on the left edge of the Trainer Number label (Figure 5-52).**

2

- **Double-click the middle sizing handle on the left edge of the Trainer Number label to resize all the labels.**

All the labels now have the optimal size.

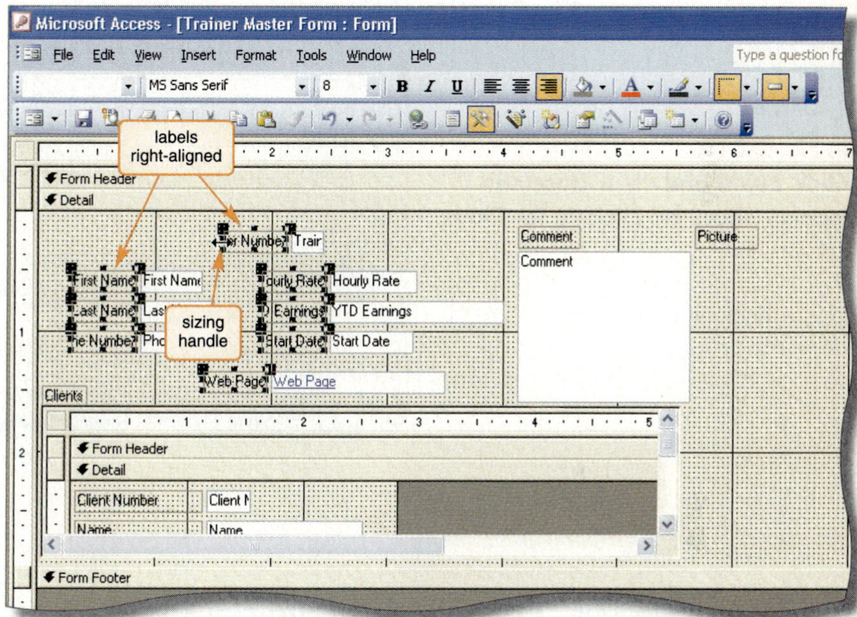

FIGURE 5-52

Changing the Size Mode

The portion of a picture that appears as well as the way it appears is determined by the **size mode**. The possible size modes are as follows:

1. **Clip** — Displays only the portion of the picture that will fit in the space allocated to it.
2. **Stretch** — Expands or shrinks the picture to fit the precise space allocated on the screen. For photographs, usually this is not a good choice, because fitting a photograph to the allocated space can distort the image, giving it a stretched appearance.
3. **Zoom** — Does the best job of fitting the picture to the allocated space without changing the look of the picture. The entire picture will appear and be proportioned correctly. Some white space may be visible either above or to the right of the picture, however.

Currently, the size mode is Clip, and that is the reason only a portion of the picture may appear. To see the whole picture, use the property sheet for the picture to change the size mode to Zoom as shown in the steps on the next page.

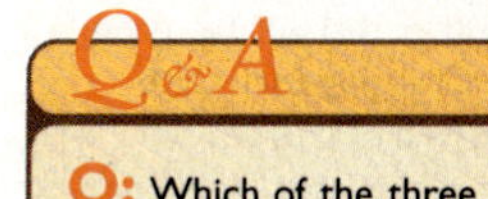

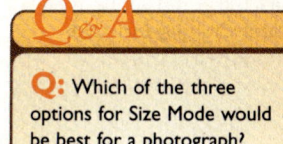

Q: Which of the three options for Size Mode would be best for a photograph?

A: Clip is not appropriate, because it can cut off part of the photograph. Stretch usually is not a good choice, because fitting a photograph to the allocated space can distort the image, giving it a stretched appearance. In general, the best choice is Zoom.

To Change the Size Mode

1

- **Right-click the Picture control to produce its shortcut menu, and then click Properties on the shortcut menu.**
- **Click the Size Mode property, and then click the Size Mode property box arrow.**

The Bound Object Frame: Picture property sheet displays the list of Size Mode property options (Figure 5-53).

2

- **Click Zoom and then close the property sheet by clicking its Close button.**

The Size Mode property is changed. The form now will display the entire picture.

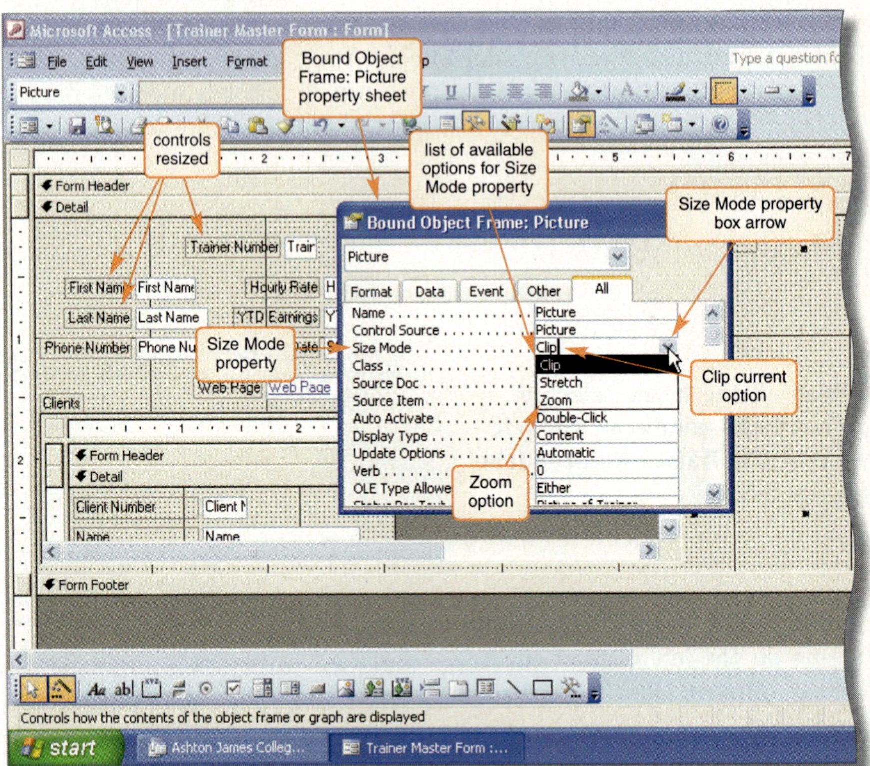

FIGURE 5-53

> **More About**
>
> **Colors of Labels**
>
> There are two different colors you can change for many objects, including labels. Changing Fore Color (foreground) changes the color of the letters that appear in the label. Changing Back Color (background) changes the color of the label itself.

Changing the Special Effects and Colors of Labels

Access allows you to change a variety of the characteristics of the labels in the form. You can change the border style and color, the background color, the font, and the font size. You also can give the label special effects, such as raised or sunken. The following steps illustrate how to change the special effects and colors (characteristics) of a label.

To Change Special Effects and Colors of Labels

1

- **Click the Trainer Number label to select it.**
- **Select each of the remaining labels by holding down the SHIFT key while clicking the label. Be sure to include the Clients label for the subform.**
- **Right-click one of the selected labels.**

All labels are selected (Figure 5-54). The shortcut menu appears.

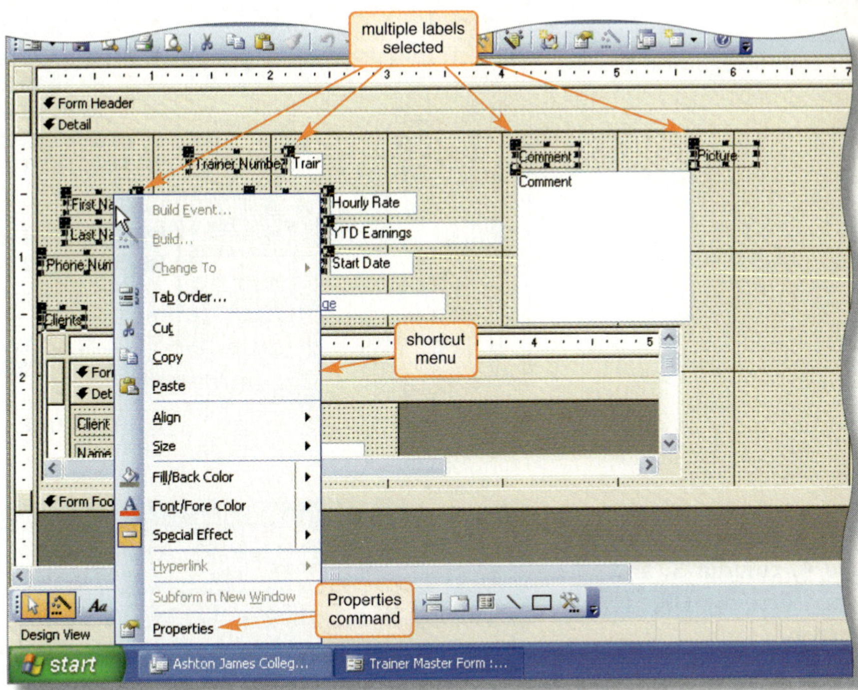

FIGURE 5-54

2

- **Click Properties on the shortcut menu.**
- **Click the Special Effect property, and then click the Special Effect property box arrow.**

The Multiple selection property sheet displays the list of options for the Special Effect property (Figure 5-55). The Flat Special Effect property is highlighted.

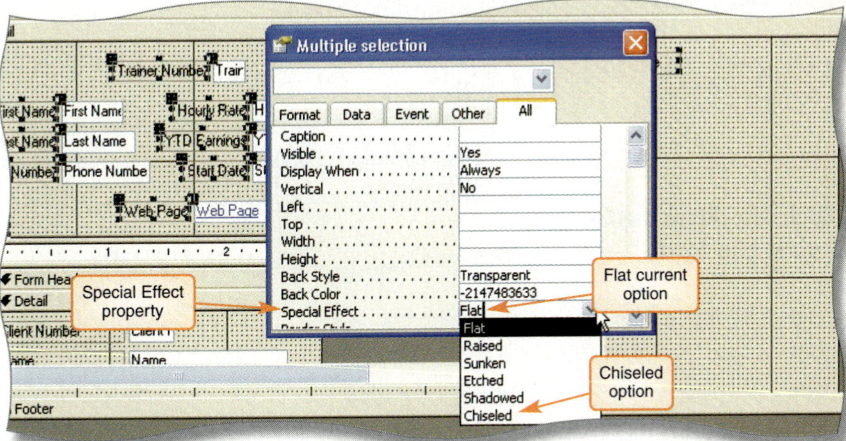

FIGURE 5-55

3

- **Click Chiseled.**
- **If necessary, click the down scroll arrow until the Fore Color property appears, and then click the Fore Color property.**

The Fore Color property is selected (Figure 5-56).

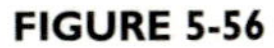

FIGURE 5-56

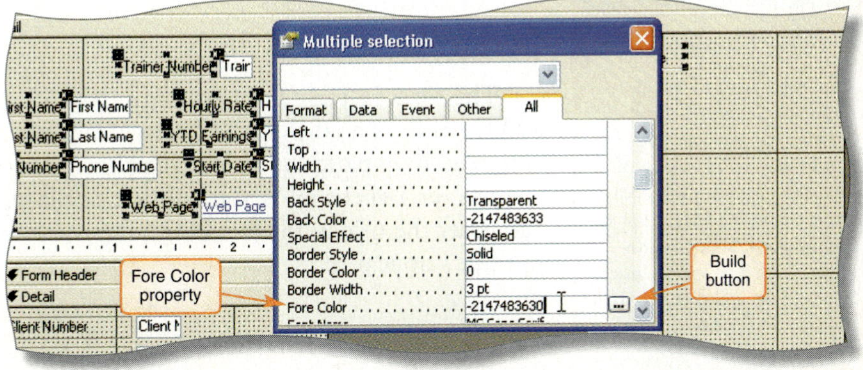

4

• **Click the Build button.**

The Color dialog box appears (Figure 5-57).

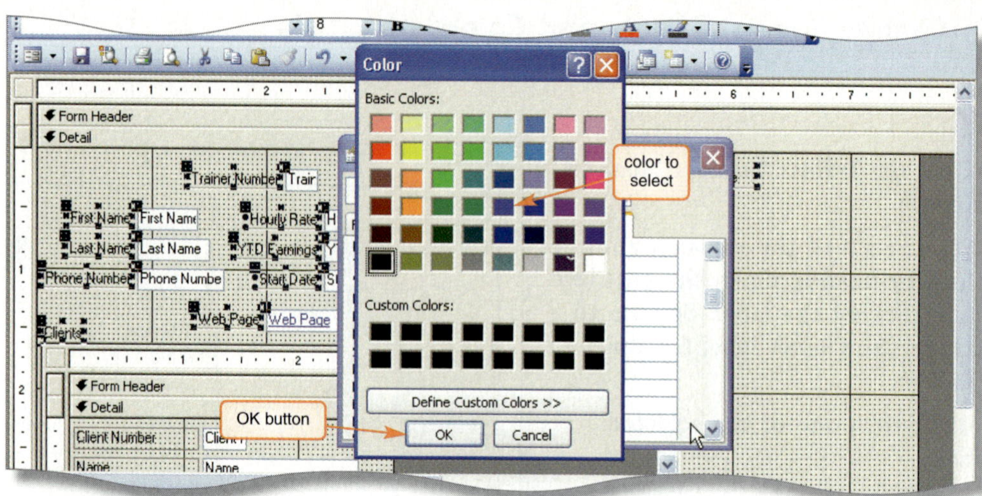

FIGURE 5-57

5

• **Click the color blue in row 4, column 5, and then click the OK button.**

• **Close the Multiple selection property sheet by clicking its Close button.**

The changes to the labels are complete.

6

• **Click the View button to view the form.**

The form appears (Figure 5-58).

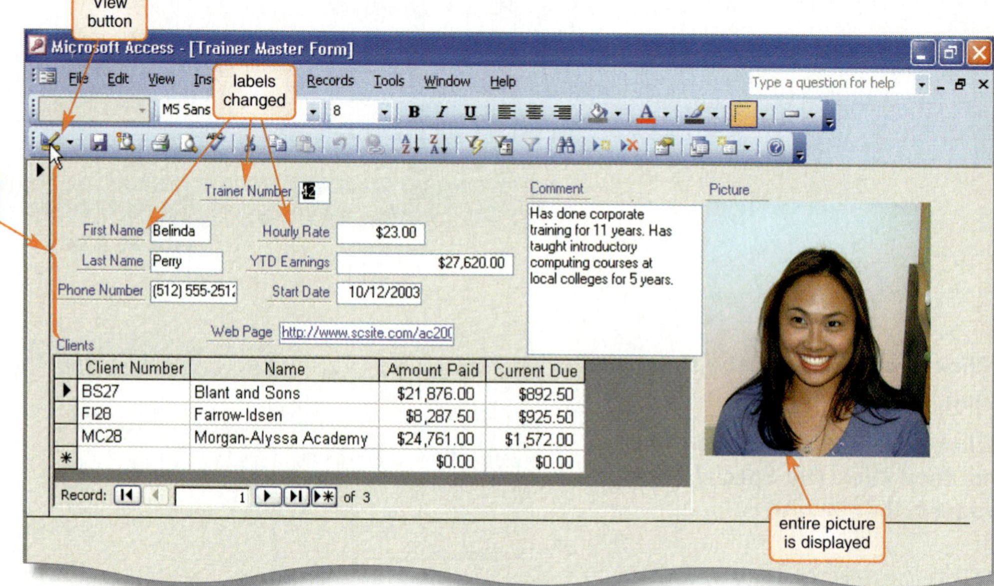

FIGURE 5-58

The fields have been moved, and the appearance of the labels has been changed. The form displays the picture correctly.

> *More About*
>
> **Form Headers**
>
> You might wish to add more than just a title to a form header. For example, you might wish to add a picture such as a company logo. To do so, click the Image tool in the toolbox, click the position where you want to place the picture, and then select the picture to insert.

Adding a Form Title

The form in Figure 5-1 on page AC 259 includes a title. To add a title to a form, add the title as a label in the Form Header section. To accomplish this task, first you will need to expand the size of the form header to accommodate the title. Then, you can use the Label tool in the toolbox to place the label. After placing the label, you can enter the title in the label. Finally, you can change various properties to improve the title's appearance.

The following steps show how to place a title on the form.

To Add a Form Title

1

- **Click the View button to return to Design view.**
- **Resize the Form Header section by dragging down the line separating the Form Header section from the Detail section to the approximate position shown in Figure 5-59.**

The shape of the mouse pointer changes to a two-headed vertical arrow with a horizontal crossbar, indicating you can drag the line to resize the Form Header section.

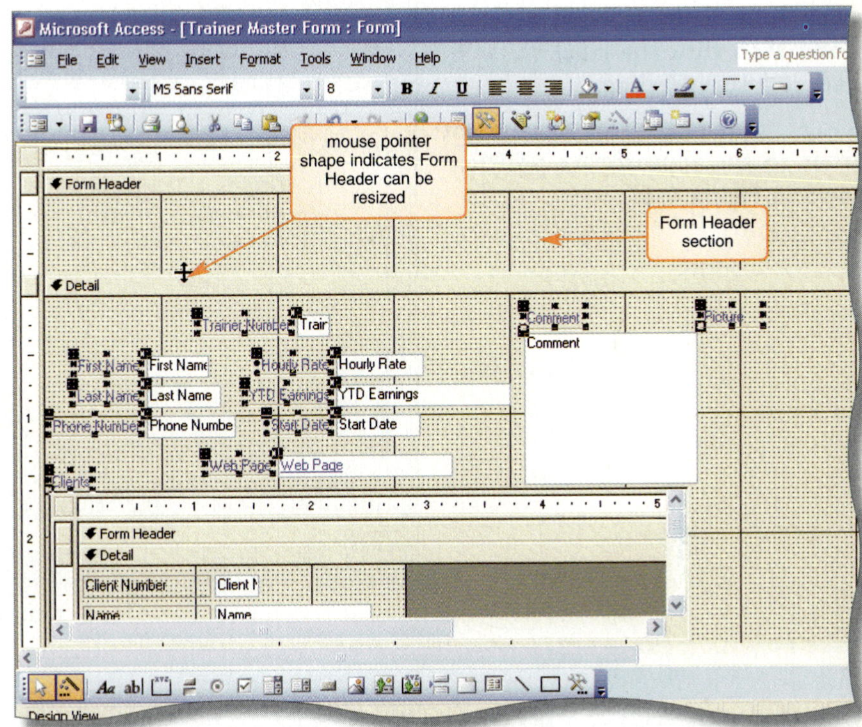

FIGURE 5-59

2

- **Click the Label tool in the toolbox, and then position the mouse pointer as shown in Figure 5-60. The shape of the mouse pointer has changed, indicating you are placing a label.**

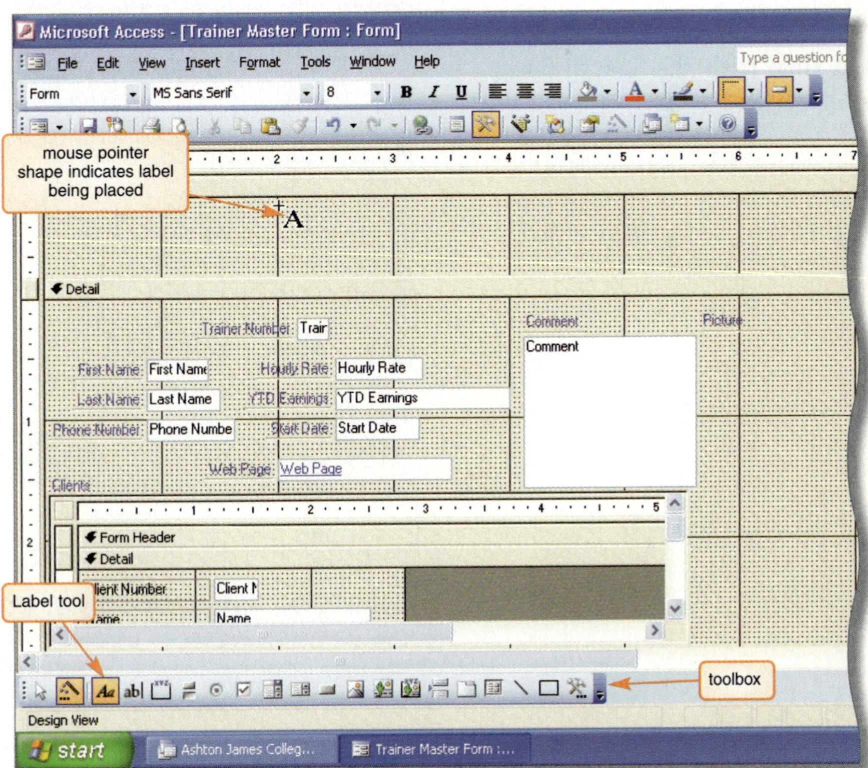

FIGURE 5-60

3

- **Click the position shown in Figure 5-60 on the previous page, and then type** `Trainer Master Form` **as the title.**
- **Click outside the label to deselect it, and then click the label to select it a second time.**
- **Drag the handle in the lower-right corner to the approximate position shown in Figure 5-61.**

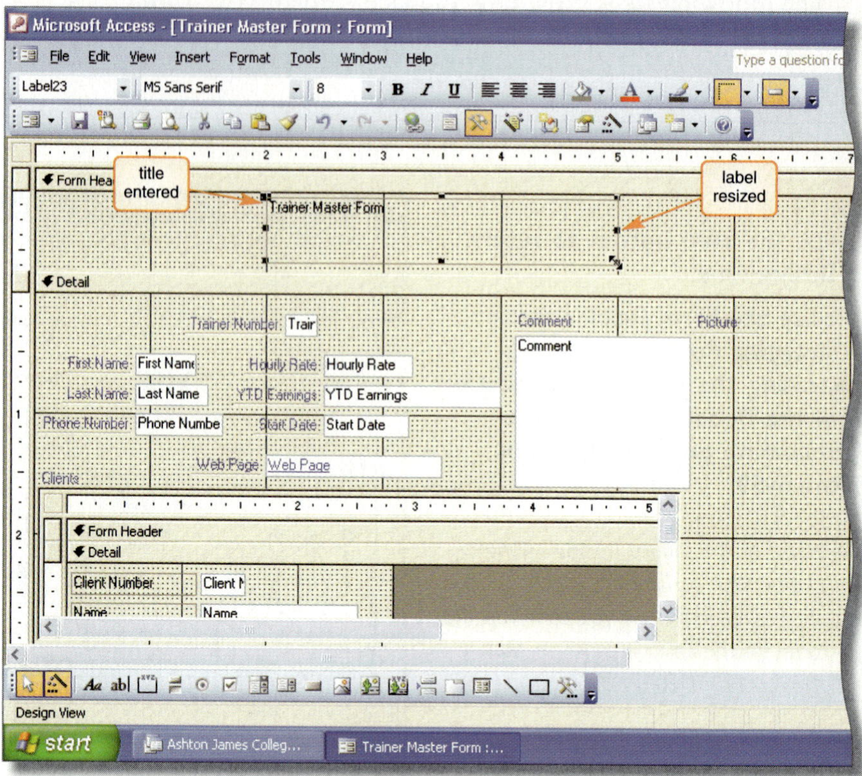

FIGURE 5-61

4

- **Right-click the label and then click Properties on the shortcut menu.**
- **Click the Special Effect property, and then click the Special Effect property box arrow.**

The property sheet displays the list of options for the Special Effect property (Figure 5-62). The Flat Special Effect property is highlighted.

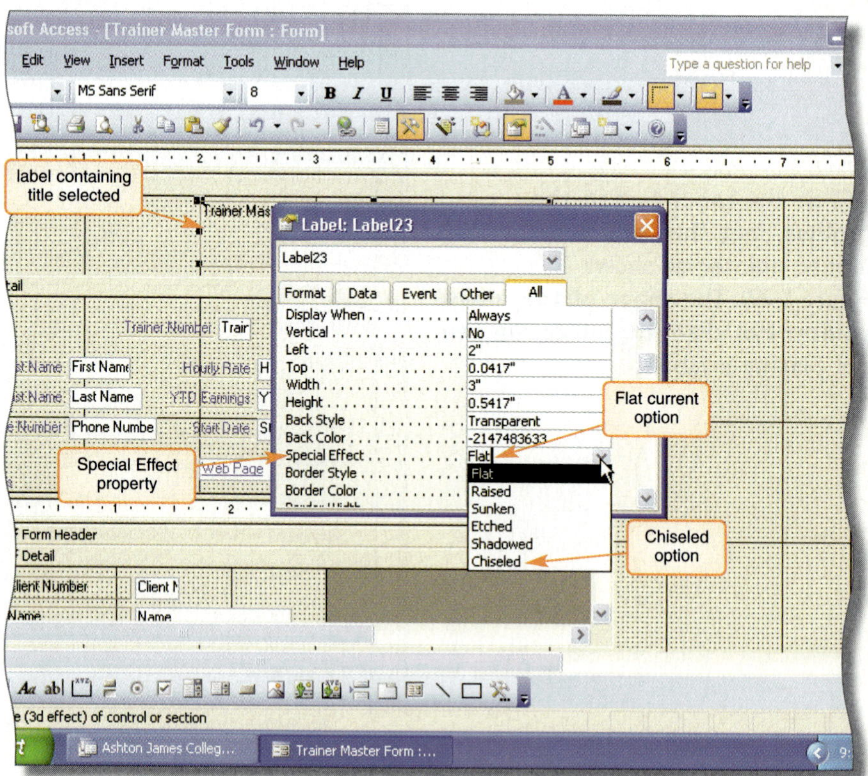

FIGURE 5-62

5

- **Click Chiseled.**
- **Click the down scroll arrow to display the Font Size property.**
- **Click the Font Size property, click the Font Size property box arrow, and then click 12.**
- **If necessary, click the down scroll arrow to display the Font Weight property.**
- **Click the Font Weight property, click the Font Weight property box arrow, and then click Bold.**
- **Close the property sheet by clicking its Close button.**
- **Resize the label to fit the title, and then move the label so it is centered over the form.**

The form header is complete (Figure 5-63).

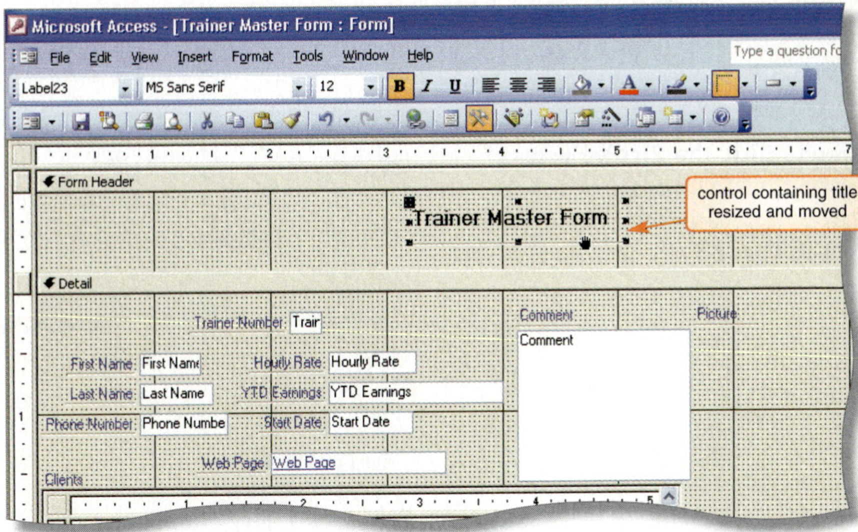

FIGURE 5-63

Fine-Tuning the Form

Once the form is complete, you should fine-tune it; that is, you should make any minor adjustments necessary to make the form look better. If you look at the form in Figure 5-58 on page AC 290, for example, you see that you need to expand the width of the Phone Number control so the entire telephone number appears. You might want to expand the Web Page control so the text box displays more of the Web page address. The following steps show how to fine-tune the form by increasing the size of these two controls.

To Fine-Tune the Form

1. **Click the Phone Number control, and then drag the right sizing handle to the right to expand the control.**
2. **Click the View button to display the form, examine the Phone Number control to see if it is the size you want, and then click the View button to return to the form design.**
3. **If the Phone Number control is not the desired size, repeat Steps 1 and 2 until it is.**
4. **Using the techniques shown in Steps 1 through 3, resize the Web Page control to the size you want.**

The fine-tuning process now is complete.

Changing Tab Stops

If users repeatedly press the TAB key to move through the controls on the form, they should bypass the Picture control, because they typically would not change the picture. In order to force this to happen, change the Tab Stop property for the control as illustrated in the steps on the next page.

To Change a Tab Stop

1

- **Right-click the Picture control.**

The shortcut menu for the Picture control appears (Figure 5-64).

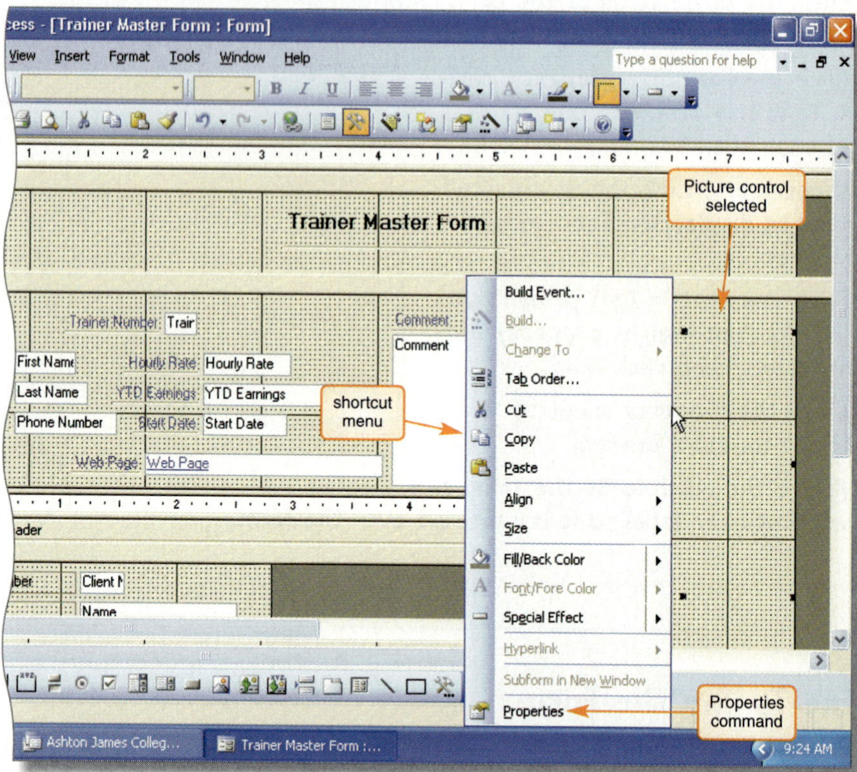

FIGURE 5-64

2

- **Click Properties on the shortcut menu. Make sure the All tab is selected, click the down scroll arrow until the Tab Stop property appears, click the Tab Stop property, click the Tab Stop property box arrow, and then click No.**

The value for the Tab Stop property is changed to No (Figure 5-65).

- **Close the property sheet.**
- **With this change, tabbing through the controls on the form will bypass the picture.**

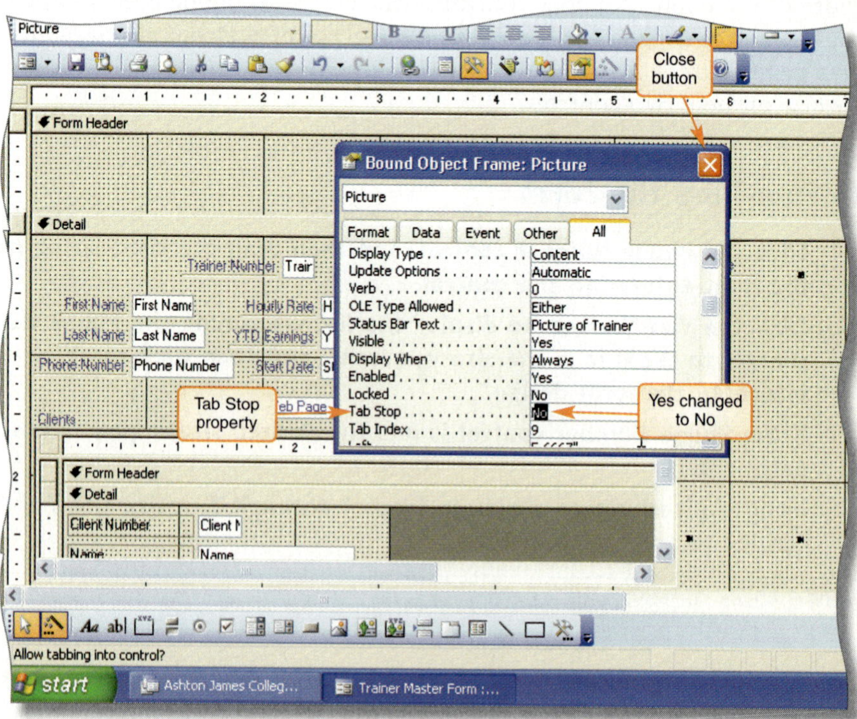

FIGURE 5-65

Changing the Tab Order

Users can repeatedly press the TAB key to move through the fields on a form. Access determines the order in which the fields are encountered in this process. In the default order for this form, the Comment field would come after the Web Page field. With the way the fields are positioned on the form, it would be better for the Comment field to come first. To change the tab order, that is, the order in which fields are encountered when tabbing through a form, use the Tab Order command on the View menu. When the Tab Order dialog box appears, you can change the tab order.

The following steps show how to change the tab order so the Comment field comes before the Web Page field.

More About

Microsoft Certification

The Microsoft Office Specialist Certification program provides an opportunity for you to obtain a valuable industry credential — proof that you have the Access 2003 skills required by employers. For more information, see Appendix E, or visit the Access 2003 Certification Web page (scsite.com/ac2003/cert).

To Change the Tab Order

1

- **Click View on the menu bar.**

The View menu appears (Figure 5-66).

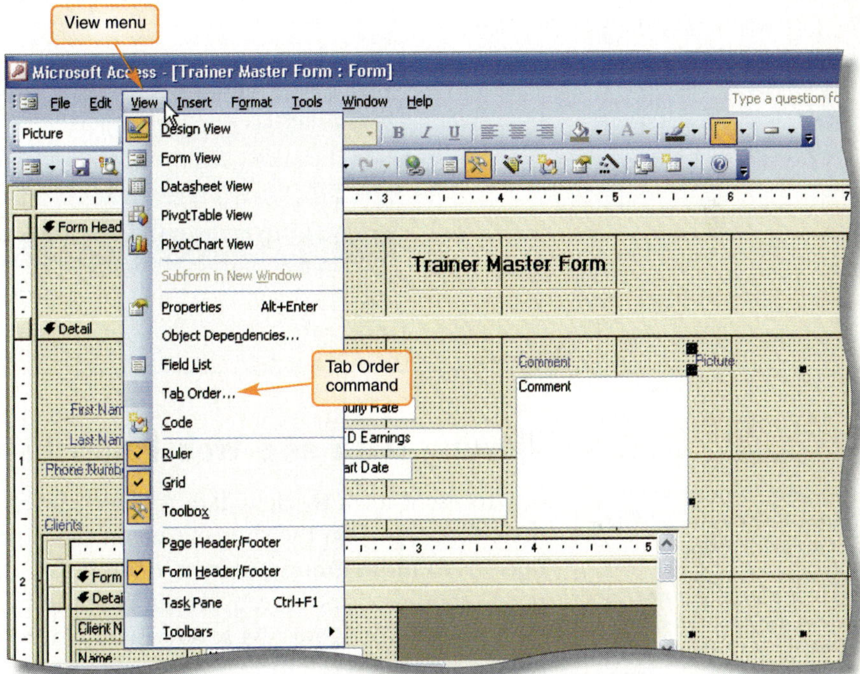

FIGURE 5-66

2

- **Click Tab Order on the View menu, and then click the Comment row to select it.**

The Comment field is selected (Figure 5-67).

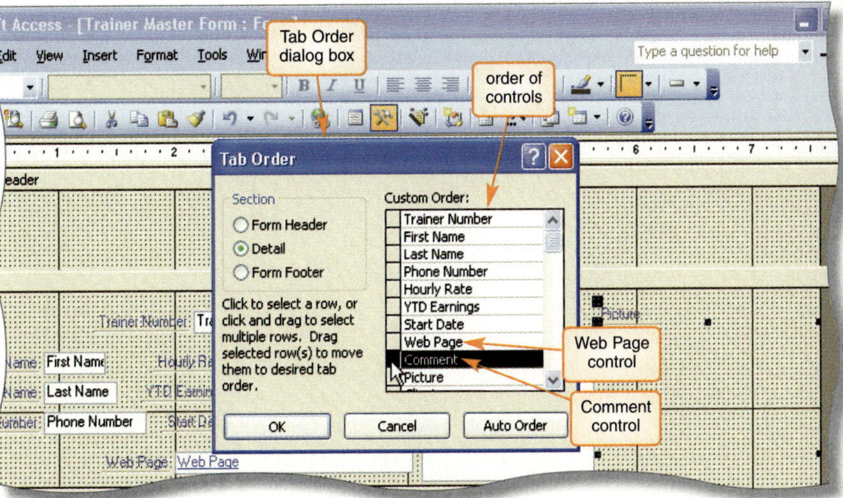

FIGURE 5-67

3

- **Drag the Comment field above the Web Page field.**

The order is changed (Figure 5-68).

4

- **Click OK.**
- **Close the window containing the form.**
- **When asked if you want to save the changes to the design of the form, click Yes.**

The tab order now is changed. The form is closed and all the changes have been saved.

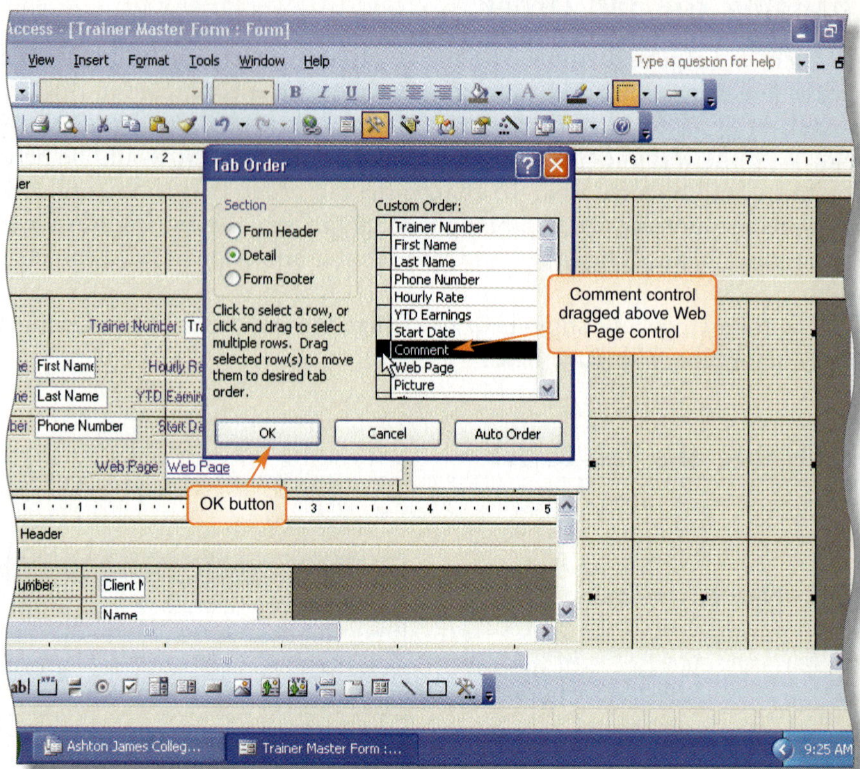

FIGURE 5-68

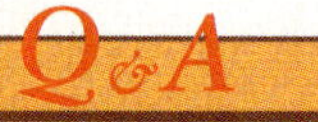

Q: Why does the form in Figure 5-69 contain two sets of navigation buttons?

A: One set of buttons allows navigation between trainers. The subform contains another set of navigation buttons that allow navigation between the clients of the trainer who appears on the screen.

Viewing Data and Web Pages Using the Form

To use a form to view data, right-click the form in the Database window, and then click Open on the shortcut menu that appears. You then can use the navigation buttons to move among trainers or to move among the clients of the trainer currently shown on the screen. By clicking the trainer's Web Page field, you can display the trainer's Web page. As soon as you close the window containing the Web page, Access returns to the form.

The following steps illustrate how to display data using the form.

To Use the Form to View Data and Web Pages

1

- **If necessary, click Forms on the Objects bar.**
- **Right-click Trainer Master Form and then click Open on the shortcut menu.**
- **Be sure the window containing the form is maximized.**

The form displays the data from the first record (Figure 5-69).

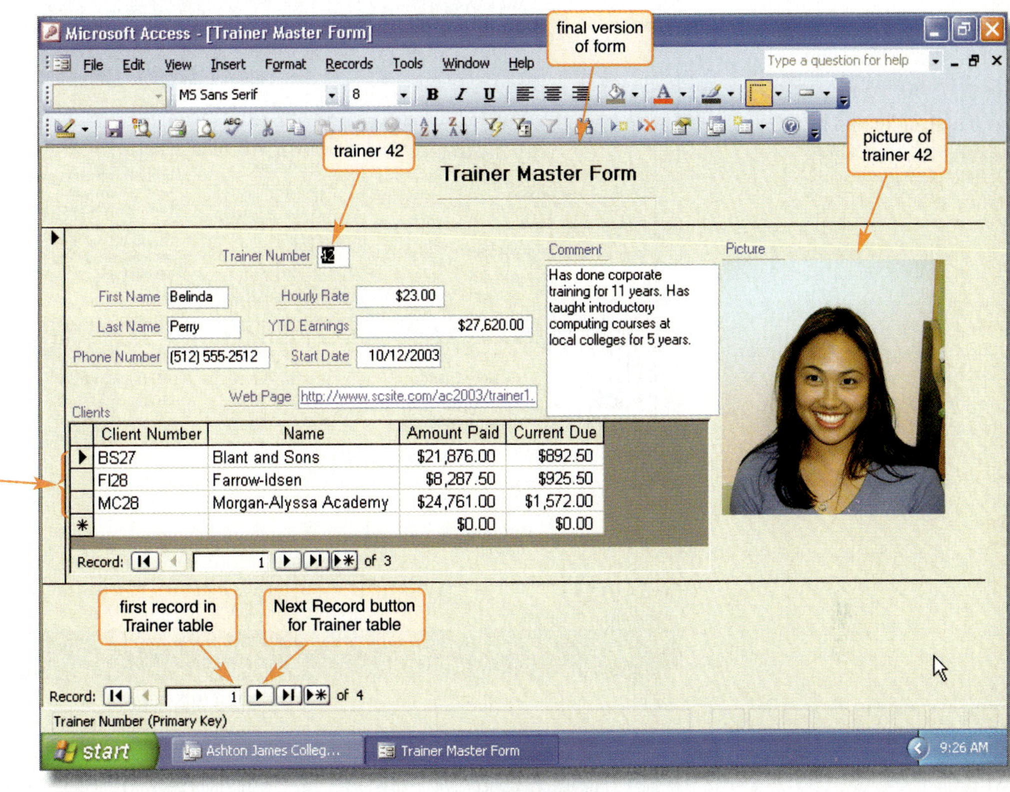

FIGURE 5-69

2

- **Click the Next Record button to move to the second trainer.**

The data from the second record appears (Figure 5-70). If more clients were included than would fit in the subform at a single time, Access would automatically add a vertical scroll bar to the Clients subform. You either can use a scroll bar or the navigation buttons to move among clients.

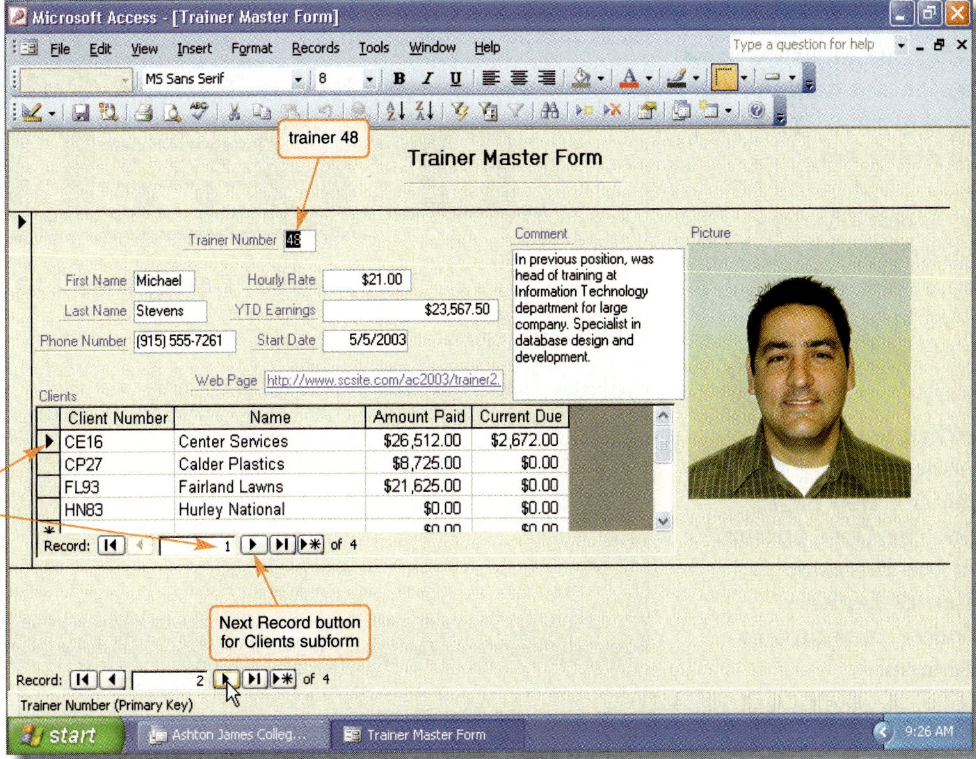

FIGURE 5-70

3

• **Click the subform's Next Record button twice.**

The data from the third client of trainer 48 is selected (Figure 5-71).

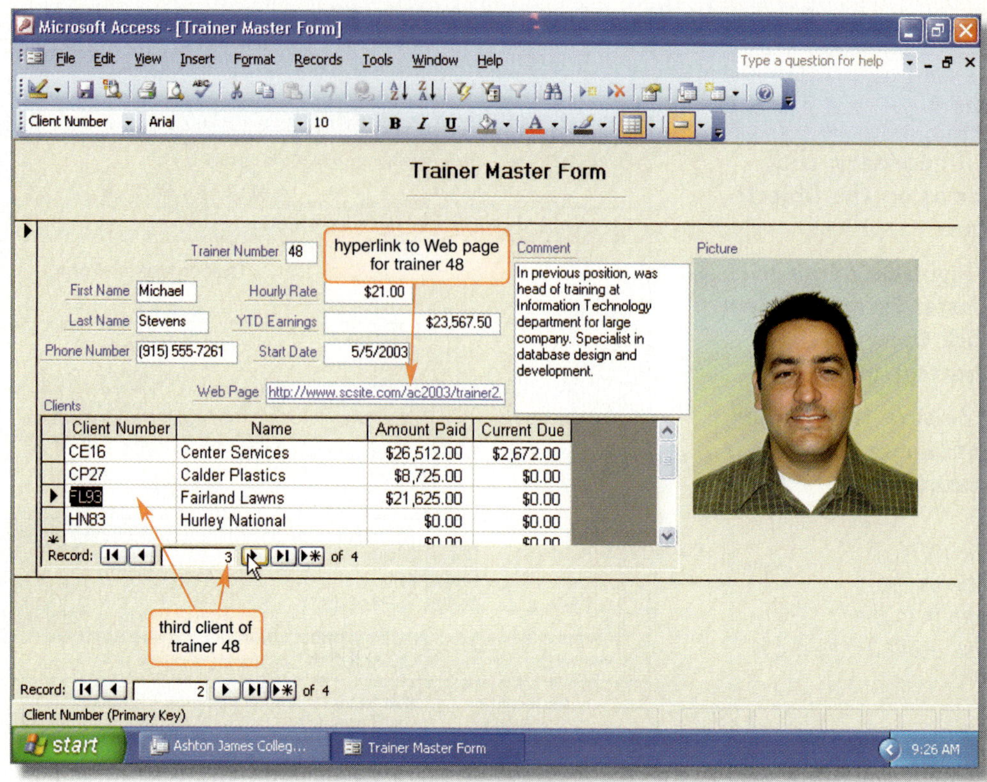

FIGURE 5-71

4

• **Click the Web Page control.**

• **If Access displays a dialog box in either this step or the next, follow the directions given in the dialog box.**

The trainer's Web page appears in the Microsoft Internet Explorer window (Figure 5-72).

Trainer 2 for Ashton James College - Microsoft Internet Explorer

Web page of trainer 48

http://www.scsite.com/ac2003/trainer2.html

Ashton James College

Corporate Computer Training

Meet the Trainer

Michael Stevens moved to our area from the Midwest where he was Director of Training for Information Technology at a major furniture corporation. He has designed industrial databases and has a special interest in database design and development. Michael teaches a special topics course on data warehousing at AJC.

FIGURE 5-72

5

• **When you have finished viewing the trainer's Web page, click the Close button for the Microsoft Internet Explorer window to return to the form.**

• **Click the Close Window button to close the form.**

The form no longer appears.

The previous steps illustrated the way you work with a main form and subform, as well as how to use a hyperlink (the Web Page control in this form). Clicking the navigation buttons for the main form moves to a different trainer. Clicking the navigation buttons for the subform moves to a different client of the trainer whose photograph appears in the main form. Clicking a hyperlink moves to the corresponding document or Web page. The following are other actions you can take within the form:

1. To move from the last field in the main form to the first field in the subform, press the TAB key. To move back to the last field in the main form, press CTRL+SHIFT+TAB.
2. To move from the last field in the subform to the first field in the next record's main form, press CTRL+TAB.
3. To switch from the main form to the subform using the mouse, click anywhere in the subform. To switch back to the main form, click any control in the main form. Clicking the background of the main form will not cause the switch to occur.

More About

Quick Reference

For a table that lists how to complete tasks covered in this book using the mouse, menu, shortcut menu, and keyboard, see the Quick Reference Summary at the back of this book, or visit the Access 2003 Quick Reference Web page (scsite.com/ac2003/qr).

More About

Date Fields in Queries: Using Date()

To test for the current date in a query, type `Date()` in the Criteria row of the appropriate column. Typing <Date() in the Criteria row for Start Date, for example, finds those trainers who started anytime before the date on which you run the query.

Viewing Object Dependencies

In Access, you can view information on dependencies between database objects. Viewing a list of objects that use a specific object helps in the maintenance of a database and avoids errors when changes are made to the objects involved in the dependency. For example, the Trainer Master Form depends on data from the Client table and the Trainer table. The form also depends on the Clients subform. The Object Dependencies command allows you to see the dependencies for any given object or to see what objects depend on the object. The following steps illustrate how to view object dependencies for the Trainer Master Form.

To View Object Dependencies

1. **If necessary, click Forms on the Objects bar and then click the Trainer Master Form.**
2. **Click View on the menu bar and then click Object Dependencies.**
3. **When the Microsoft Access dialog box appears stating that Access must update dependency information, click OK.**
4. **Click the "Objects that I depend on" option button.**

Access displays the Object Dependencies task pane and lists all the objects on which the Trainer Master Form depends.

More About

Date Fields in Queries: Using Expressions

Expressions have a special meaning in date fields in queries. Numbers that appear in expressions represent numbers of days. The expression <Date()+30 for Start Date finds trainers who started anytime up to 30 days before the day on which you run the query.

Using Date and Memo Fields in a Query

To use date fields in queries, you simply type the dates including the slashes. To search for records with a specific date, you must type the date. You also can use comparison operators. To find all the trainers whose start date is prior to January 1, 2003, for example, you type `<1/1/2003` as the criterion.

You also can use memo fields in queries. Typically, you will want to find all the records on which the memo field contains a specific word or phrase. To do so, you use wildcards. For example, to find all the trainers who have the word, database, somewhere in the Comment field, you type `*database*` as the criterion.

The steps on the next page illustrate how to create and run queries that use date and memo fields.

To Use Date and Memo Fields in a Query

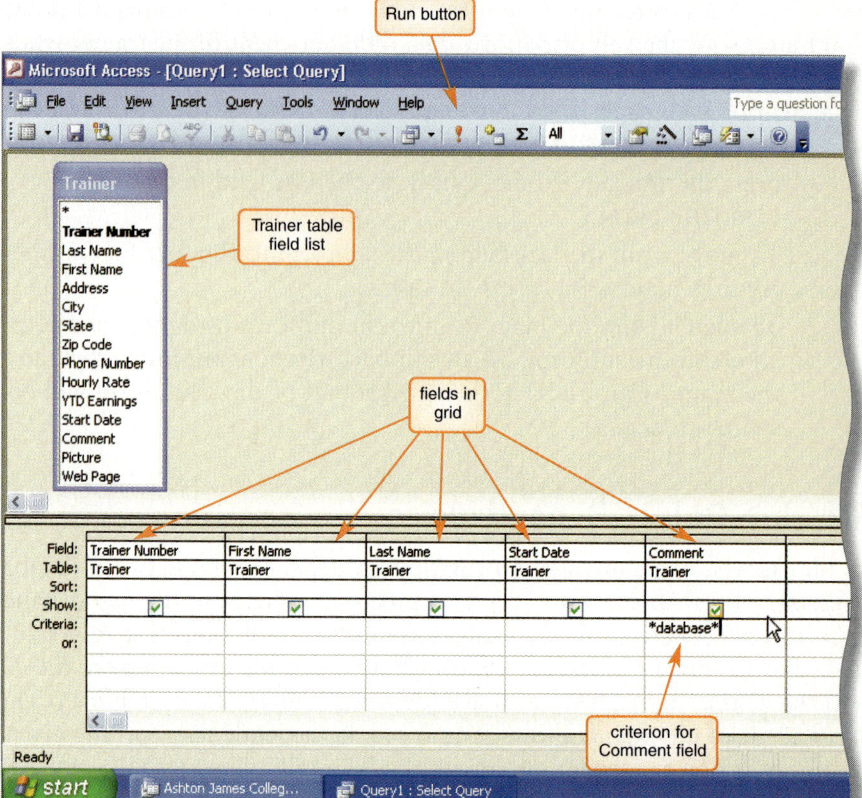

FIGURE 5-73

1

- **In the Database window, click Tables on the Objects bar, and then, if necessary, select the Trainer table.**
- **Click the New Object button arrow on the Database toolbar.**
- **Click Query.**
- **Be sure Design View is highlighted, and then click the OK button.**
- **Be sure the Microsoft Access [Query1 : Select Query] window is maximized.**
- **Resize the upper and lower panes and the Trainer field list so all fields in the Trainer table appear.**
- **Double-click the Trainer Number, First Name, Last Name, Start Date, and Comment fields to include them in the query.**
- **Click the Criteria row under the Comment field and then type** `*database*` **as the criterion.**

The criterion is entered (Figure 5-73).

2

- **Click the Run button on the Query Design toolbar to run the query.**

The results appear in Datasheet view (Figure 5-74). Two records are included. Both records have the word, database, contained within the comment.

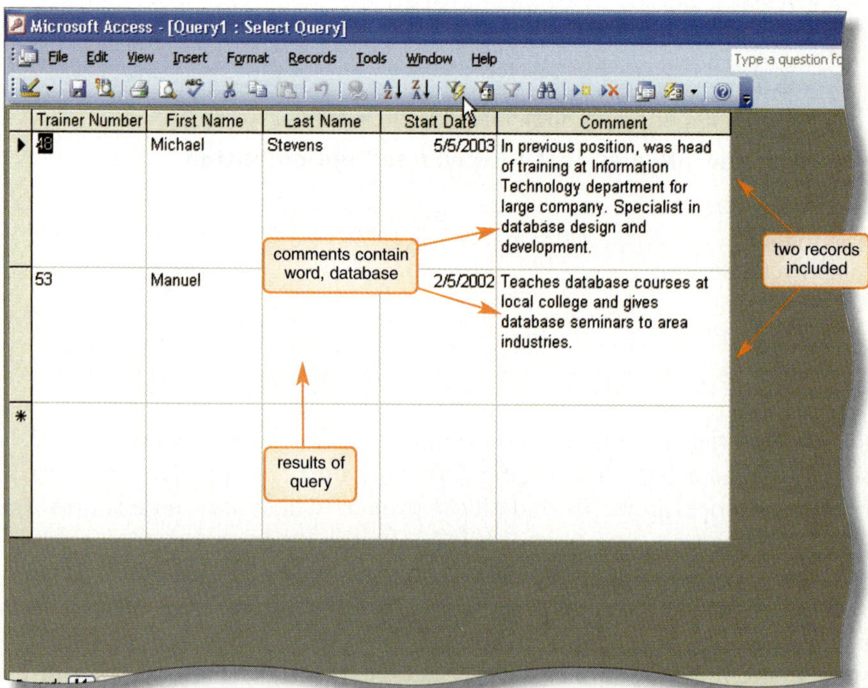

FIGURE 5-74

3

- **Click the View button to return to the Select Query window.**
- **Click the Criteria row under the Start Date field, and then type** <1/1/2003 **as the criterion.**

*The criterion for the Start Date field is entered (Figure 5-75). Access automatically adds the LIKE operator and quotation marks to criteria that use the * wildcard.*

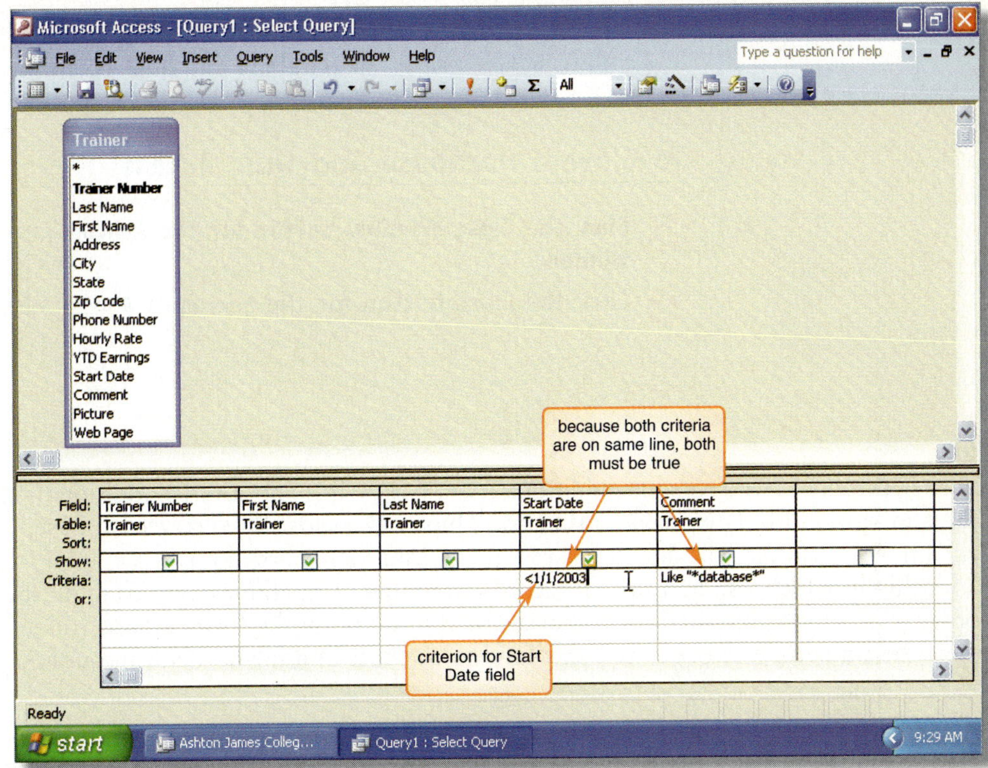

FIGURE 5-75

4

- **Click the Run button to run the query.**

The result contains only a single row, because only one trainer was hired before January 1, 2003 and has a comment entry that contains the word, database (Figure 5-76).

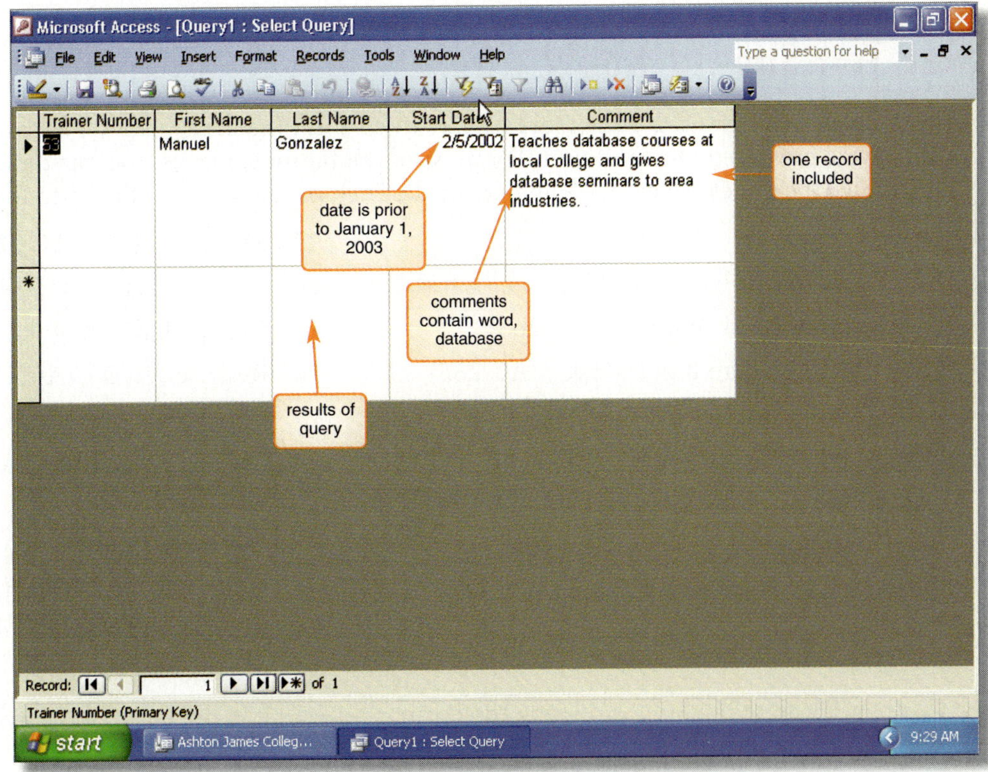

FIGURE 5-76

5

- **Close the Select Query window by clicking its Close Window button.**
- **When asked if you want to save the query, click the No button.**

The results of the query are removed from the screen and the Database window again appears.

Closing the Database and Quitting Access

The following steps close the database and quit Access.

To Close a Database and Quit Access

1. **Click the Close Window button for the Ashton James College : Database window.**
2. **Click the Close button for the Microsoft Access window.**

Project Summary

Project 5 introduced you to some additional data types. To maintain the additional data, you learned how to create and work with date, memo, OLE, and Hyperlink fields. You created and used an input mask. You also learned how to use the new data types in a form. You then learned how to build a form on a one-to-many relationship in which you had several records from one of the tables appearing on the screen at the same time in order to create the required form. You learned how to use the form to view trainer and client data as well as to view the trainer's Web page. You saw how to use date and memo fields in queries.

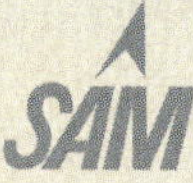

If you have a SAM user profile, you may have access to hands-on instruction, practice, and assessment of the skills covered in this project. Log in to your SAM account and go to your assignments page to see what your instructor has assigned.

What You Should Know

Having completed this project, you should be able to perform the tasks below. The tasks are listed in the same order they were presented in this project. For a list of the buttons, menus, toolbars, and commands introduced in this project, see the Quick Reference Summary at the back of this book and refer to the Page Number column.

1. Open a Database (AC 260)
2. Add Fields to a Table (AC 261)
3. Use the Input Mask Wizard (AC 263)
4. Enter Data Using an Input Mask (AC 265)
5. Enter Data in Date Fields (AC 266)
6. Enter Data in Memo Fields (AC 267)
7. Change the Row and Column Size (AC 268)
8. Enter Data in OLE Fields (AC 269)
9. Enter Data in Hyperlink Fields (AC 271)
10. Close the Table and Save the Properties (AC 273)
11. Create a Form with a Subform Using the Form Wizard (AC 274)
12. Modify the Subform Design (AC 279)
13. Modify the Form Design (AC 280)
14. Move and Resize Fields (AC 282)
15. Move a Label (AC 284)
16. Move Fields (AC 284)
17. Change Label Alignment (AC 285)
18. Resize a Label (AC 287)
19. Change the Size Mode (AC 288)
20. Change Special Effects and Colors of Labels (AC 289)
21. Add a Form Title (AC 291)
22. Fine-Tune the Form (AC 293)
23. Change a Tab Stop (AC 294)
24. Change the Tab Order (AC 295)
25. Use the Form to View Data and Web Pages (AC 297)
26. View Object Dependencies (AC 299)
27. Use Date and Memo Fields in a Query (AC 300)
28. Close a Database and Quit Access (AC 302)

Learn It Online

Instructions: To complete the Learn It Online exercises, start your browser, click the Address bar, and then enter the Web address `scsite.com/ac2003/learn`. When the Access 2003 Learn It Online page is displayed, follow the instructions in the exercises below. Each exercise has instructions for printing your results, either for your own records or for submission to your instructor.

1 Project Reinforcement TF, MC, and SA

Below Access Project 5, click the Project Reinforcement link. Print the quiz by clicking Print on the File menu for each page. Answer each question.

2 Flash Cards

Below Access Project 5, click the Flash Cards link and read the instructions. Type 20 (or a number specified by your instructor) in the Number of playing cards text box, type your name in the Enter your Name text box, and then click the Flip Card button. When the flash card is displayed, read the question and then click the ANSWER box arrow to select an answer. Flip through Flash Cards. If your score is 15 (75%) correct or greater, click Print on the File menu to print your results. If your score is less than 15 (75%) correct, then redo this exercise by clicking the Replay button.

3 Practice

Below Access Project 5, click the Practice Test link. Answer each question, enter your first and last name at the bottom of the page, and then click the Grade Test button. When the graded practice test is displayed on your screen, click Print on the File menu to print a hard copy. Continue to take practice tests until you score 80% or better.

4 Who Wants To Be a Computer Genius?

Below Access Project 5, click the Computer Genius link. Read the instructions, enter your first and last name at the bottom of the page, and then click the PLAY button. When your score is displayed, click the PRINT RESULTS link to print a hard copy.

5 Wheel of Terms

Below Access Project 5, click the Wheel of Terms link. Read the instructions, and then enter your first and last name and your school name. Click the PLAY button. When your score is displayed, right-click the score and then click Print on the shortcut menu to print a hard copy.

6 Crossword Puzzle Challenge

Below Access Project 5, click the Crossword Puzzle Challenge link. Read the instructions, and then enter your first and last name. Click the SUBMIT button. Work the crossword puzzle. When you are finished, click the Submit button. When the crossword puzzle is redisplayed, click the Print Puzzle button to print a hard copy.

7 Tips and Tricks

Below Access Project 5, click the Tips and Tricks link. Click a topic that pertains to Project 5. Right-click the information and then click Print on the shortcut menu. Construct a brief example of what the information relates to in Access to confirm you understand how to use the tip or trick.

8 Newsgroups

Below Access Project 5, click the Newsgroups link. Click a topic that pertains to Project 5. Print three comments.

9 Expanding Your Horizons

Below Access Project 5, click the Articles for Microsoft Access link. Click a topic that pertains to Project 5. Print the information. Construct a brief example of what the information relates to in Access to confirm you understand the contents of the article.

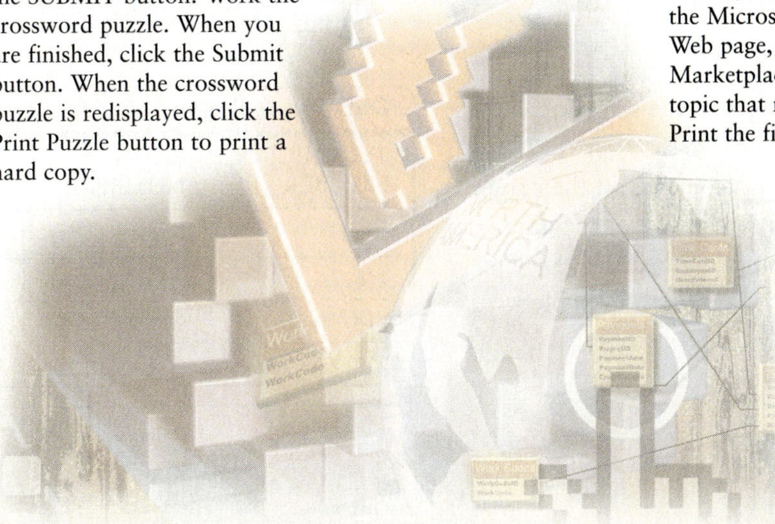

10 Search Sleuth

Below Access Project 5, click the Search Sleuth link. To search for a term that pertains to this project, select a term below the Project 5 title and then use the Google search engine at google.com (or any major search engine) to display and print two Web pages that present information on the term.

11 Access Online Training

Below Access Project 5, click the Access Online Training link. When your browser displays the Microsoft Office Online Web page, click the Access link. Click one of the Access courses that covers one or more of the objectives listed at the beginning of the project on page AC 258. Print the first page of the course before stepping through it.

12 Office Marketplace

Below Access Project 5, click the Office Marketplace link. When your browser displays the Microsoft Office Online Web page, click the Office Marketplace link. Click a topic that relates to Access. Print the first page.

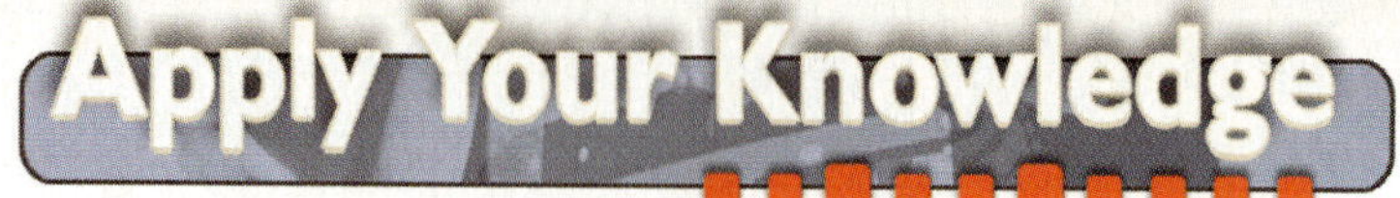

1 Enhancing the Begon Pest Control Database

Instructions: Start Access. If you are using the Microsoft Office Access 2003 Complete or the Microsoft Office Access 2003 Comprehensive text, open the Begon Pest Control database that you used in Project 4. Otherwise, see your instructor for information on accessing the files required for this book. Perform the following tasks:

1. Add the fields, Phone Number, Start Date, and Picture to the Technician table structure as shown in Figure 5-77. Create an input mask for the Phone Number field. Use the same input mask type that you used for the Trainer table in this project.

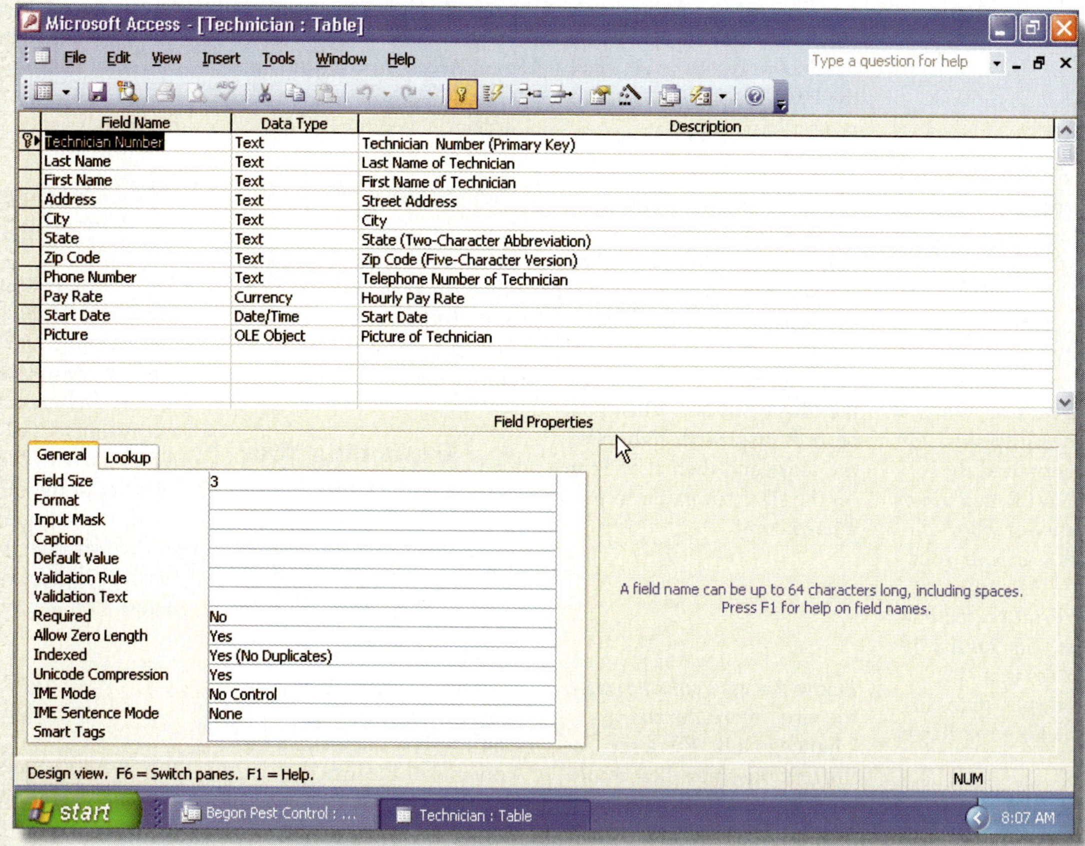

FIGURE 5-77

2. Save the changes to the structure.
3. Add the data shown in Figure 5-78 to the Technician table. Adjust the column width to best fit the size of the data.
4. Print and then close the table. Save the changes to the layout of the table.

Data for Technician Table

TECHNICIAN NUMBER	PHONE NUMBER	START DATE	PICTURE
203	901-555-6667	11/12/2003	pict2
210	865-555-2112	12/02/2004	pict1
214	901-555-3223	10/16/2004	pict4
220	865-555-5445	01/06/2005	pict5

FIGURE 5-78

Apply Your Knowledge

5. Query the Technician table to find all technicians who started after January 1, 2005. Display the Technician Number, First Name, Last Name, and Pay Rate. Print the results. Do not save the query.
6. Use the Form Wizard to create a form with a subform for the Technician table. Include the Technician Number, First Name, Last Name, Phone Number, Pay Rate, Start Date, and Picture fields from the Technician table. Include the Customer Number, Name, and Balance fields from the Customer table. Users should not be able to tab through the Picture control.
7. Modify the form design to create the form shown in Figure 5-79.

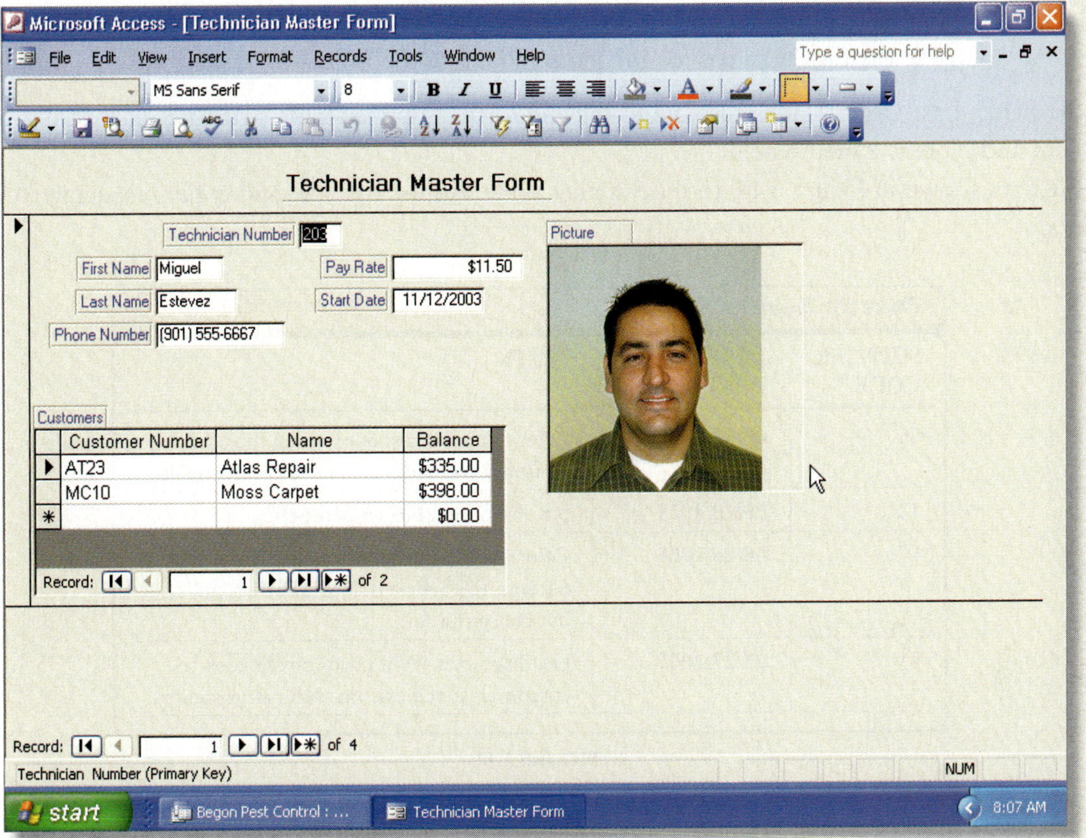

FIGURE 5-79

8. Print the form. To print the form, open the form, click File on the menu bar, click Print, and then click Selected Record(s) as the Print Range. Click the OK button.

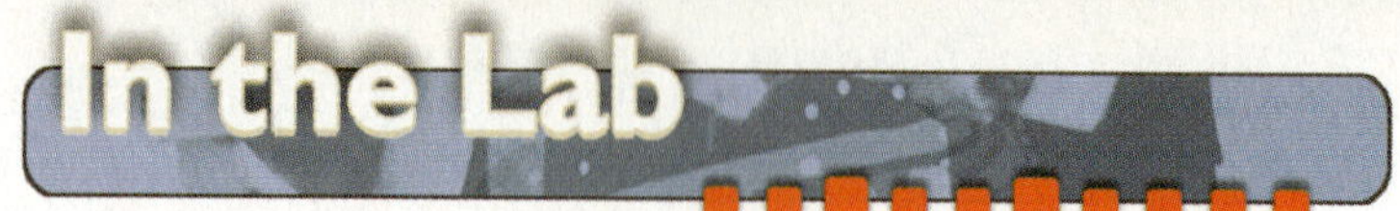

1 Enhancing the Birds2U Database

Problem: The management of Birds2U has found that the Birds2U database needs to maintain additional data on suppliers. Management needs to know the last date an order was placed with a supplier and would like to store some notes about each supplier's policies. Birds2U requires a form that displays information about the supplier as well as the items that are purchased from the supplier.

Instructions: If you are using the Microsoft Office Access 2003 Complete or the Microsoft Office Access 2003 Comprehensive text, open the Birds2U database that you used in Project 4. Otherwise, see your instructor for information on accessing the files required for this book. Perform the following tasks:

1. Add the fields, Last Order Date and Note to the end of the Supplier table structure. Last Order Date is a date field and Note is a memo field.
2. Add the data shown in Figure 5-80 to the Supplier table. Adjust the row and column spacing to best fit the data.

Data for Supplier Table

SUPPLIER CODE	LAST ORDER DATE	NOTE
05	07/10/2005	Offers volume discount when more than 12 items are ordered. Has a return policy.
13	08/18/2005	No discounts. No return policy.
17	08/25/2005	Offers volume discount when more than 6 items are ordered. Has a return policy but charges a fee.
21	07/27/2005	No discounts. Will make birdhouses to customer specifications. No return policy.

FIGURE 5-80

3. Print the table. Save the changes to the table layout.
4. Create the form shown in Figure 5-81 for the Supplier table. Use Supplier Master Form as the name of the form and Items as the name of the subform.

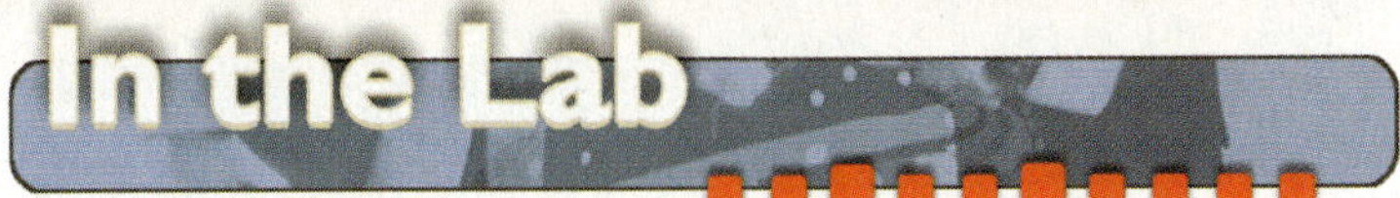

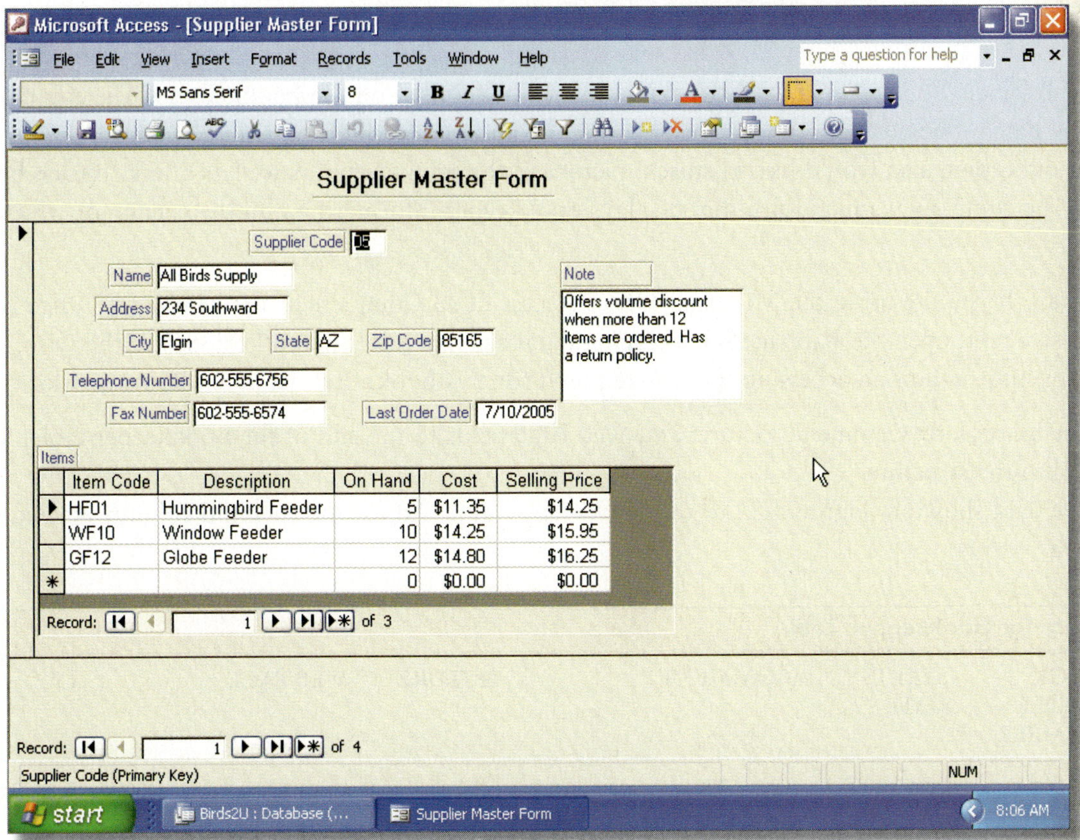

FIGURE 5-81

5. Print the form. To print the form, open the form, click File on the menu bar, click Print, and then click Selected Record(s) as the Print Range. Click the OK button.
6. Query the Supplier table to find all suppliers that accept returns. Include the Supplier Code and Name in the query. Print the results. Do not save the query.

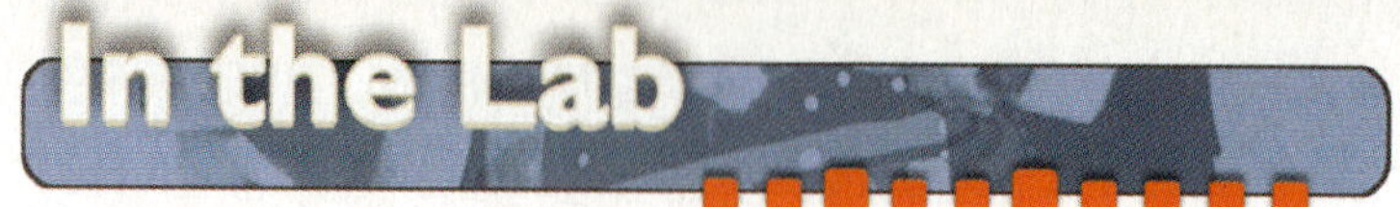

2 Enhancing the Babbage Bookkeeping Database

Problem: Babbage Bookkeeping needs to maintain additional data on the bookkeepers. The company needs to maintain the date a bookkeeper started as well as some notes concerning the bookkeeper's training and abilities. Babbage Bookkeeping also would like to store a picture of the bookkeeper as well as a link to each bookkeeper's Web page. The company wants a form that displays bookkeeper information and the clients for which they are responsible.

Instructions: If you are using the Microsoft Office Access 2003 Complete or the Microsoft Office Access 2003 Comprehensive text, open the Babbage Bookkeeping database that you used in Project 4. Otherwise, see your instructor for information on accessing the files required for this book. Perform the following tasks:

1. Add the Start Date, Comment, Picture, and Web Page fields to the end of the Bookkeeper table. Save the changes to the structure.
2. Add the data shown in Figure 5-82 to the Bookkeeper table. Adjust the row and column spacing to best fit the data.

Data for Bookkeeper Table

BOOK KEEPER NUMBER	START DATE	COMMENT	PICTURE	WEB PAGE
22	06/10/2003	Has a BA in Accounting. Working toward CPA.	pict5	www.scsite.com/ac2003/trainer5.html
24	01/15/2004	Has an AA in Accounting.	pict3	www.scsite.com/ac2003/trainer3.html
34	09/09/2003	Has an AA in Records Management. Working toward BA.	pict1	www.scsite.com/ac2003/trainer1.html

FIGURE 5-82

3. Print the table. Save the changes to the layout of the table.
4. Create the form shown in Figure 5-83 for the Bookkeeper table. Use Bookkeeper Master Form as the name of the form and Accounts as the name of the subform. Change the tab order so users tab to the Web Page field before the Comment field. Users should not be able to tab through the Picture control.

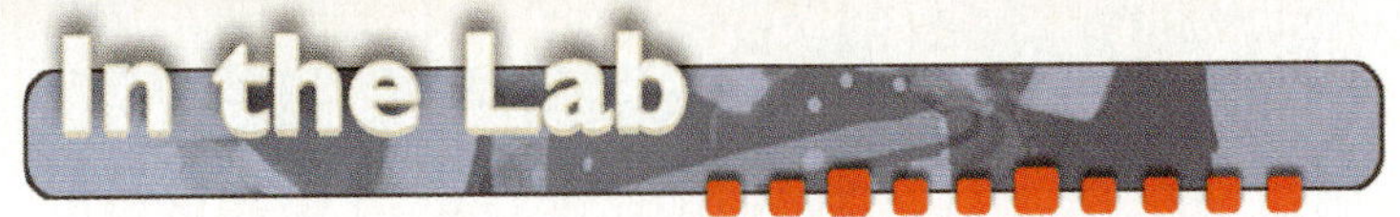

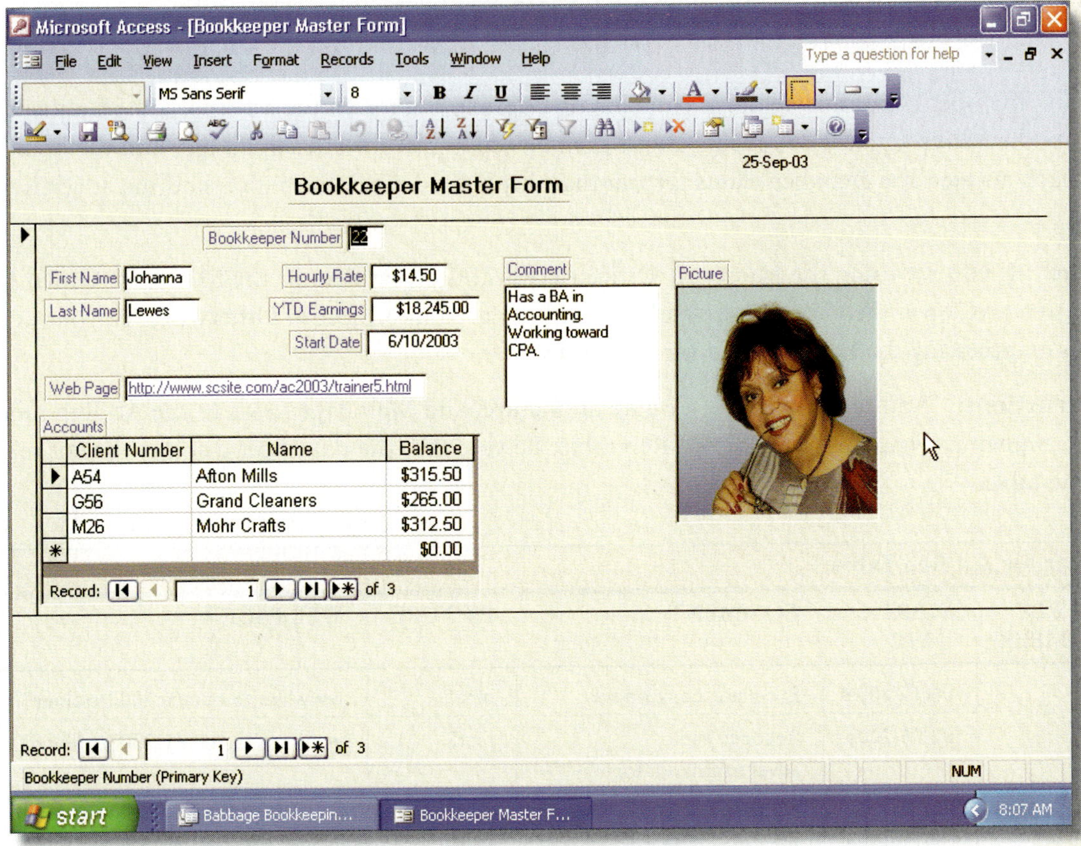

FIGURE 5-83

5. Add the current date to the form. ***Hint:*** Use Microsoft Office Access Help to solve this problem.
6. Print the form. To print the form, open the form, click File on the menu bar, and then click Print. Click Selected Record(s) as the Print Range. Click the OK button.
7. Query the Bookkeeper table to find all bookkeepers that have an AA degree and started during 2003. Include the Bookkeeper Number, First Name, Last Name, Hourly Rate, and YTD Earnings in the query. Print the query results. Do not save the query.

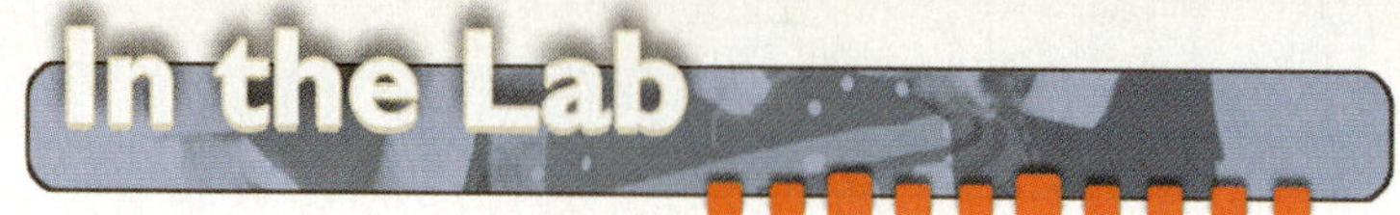

3 Enhancing the City Guide Database

Problem: The chamber of commerce needs to maintain additional data on the ad reps. The chamber needs to store the date the ad rep started, comments about each ad rep, a picture of each ad rep, and the Web page address of each ad rep. The chamber wants a form that displays ad rep information and the advertisers they represent.

Instructions: If you are using the Microsoft Office Access 2003 Complete or the Microsoft Office Access 2003 Comprehensive text, open the City Guide database that you used in Project 4. Otherwise, see your instructor for information on accessing the files required for this book.

Part 1 Instructions: Add the Start Date, Comment, Picture, and Web Page fields to the Ad Rep table and then add the data shown in Figure 5-84 to the Ad Rep table. Be sure that the datasheet displays the entire comment and print the table.

Data for Ad Rep Table

AD REP NUMBER	START DATE	COMMENT	PICTURE	WEB PAGE
21	06/12/2004	Excellent copy editor	pict1	www.scsite.com/ac2003/trainer1.html
29	02/06/2005	Records radio advertisements for chamber	pict2	www.scsite.com/ac2003/trainer2.html
32	09/21/2004	Also works as a freelance journalist	pict5	www.scsite.com/ac2003/trainer5.html

FIGURE 5-84

Part 2 Instructions: Create a form for the Ad Rep table that is similar in design to the form shown in Figure 5-1 on page AC 259. Include all fields from the Ad Rep table except the Address, State, and Zip Code fields. Include the Advertiser Number, Name, Balance, and Amount Paid fields from the Advertiser table. Print the form for ad rep 29.

Part 3 Instructions: Find all ad reps that also work as freelance journalists. Include the Ad Rep Number, First Name, and Last Name in the query result. Find all ad reps that started after 2004. Include the Ad Rep Number, First Name, Last Name, Comm Rate, and Commission in the query result.

Cases and Places

The difficulty of these case studies varies:
■ are the least difficult and ■■ are more difficult. The last exercise is a group exercise.

1 ■ Use the College Dog Walkers database that you used in Project 4 for this assignment or see your instructor for information on accessing the files required for this book. Add a Picture field and a Web Page field to the Walker table and add pictures and hyperlinks for all dog walkers. Update the two fields by using appropriate pictures and hyperlinks from the Data Disk. Create a form for the Walker table that is similar in design to the form shown in Figure 5-1 on page AC 259. Include all fields from the Walker table. Include the Customer Number, First Name, Last Name, Per Walk Amount, and Balance fields from the Customer table.

2 ■ Use the InPerson Fitness Company database that you used in Project 4 for this assignment or see your instructor for information on accessing the files required for this book. Add a Start Date, Comment, Picture, and Web Page field to the Trainer table. Add the data shown in Figure 5-85 to the Trainer table. Create a form for the Trainer table that is similar in design to the form shown in Figure 5-1 on page AC 259. Include all fields from the Trainer table. Include the Client Number, First Name, Last Name, Amount Paid, and Balance fields from the Client table. Query the Trainer table to find all trainers that have a degree in recreation management.

Data for Trainer Table

TRAINER NUMBER	START DATE	COMMENT	PICTURE	WEB PAGE
203	2/5/2005	Working toward a degree in physical therapy. Member of volunteer fire department.	pict1	www.scsite.com/ac2003/trainer1.html
205	3/14/2004	Has a degree in Recreation Management. Runs marathons.	pict3	www.scsite.com/ac2003/trainer3.html
207	6/2/2005	Coaches high school tennis.	pict4	www.scsite.com/ac2003/trainer4.html

FIGURE 5-85

Cases and Places

3 Use the Regional Books database that you used in Project 4 for this assignment or see your instructor for information on accessing the files required for this book. Regional Books needs to store additional information on publishers. Add the fields and data shown in Figure 5-86 to the Publisher table. Query the database to find all publishers that will fill single orders. Create a Publisher Master Form for the Publisher table. Include all fields in the Book table except the Book Type and Publisher Code. Be sure to include a form header with a title and change the special effects and colors of the labels.

Data for Publisher Table

PUBLISHER CODE	ORDER DATE	NOTE
BB	7/21/2005	Will fill single orders and special requests.
PB	7/30/2005	Will fill single orders on an emergency basis only. Ships twice a week.
SI	7/15/2005	Has minimum order requirement of 20 books. Ships weekly.
VN	8/25/2005	Will fill single orders and special requests. Ships daily.

FIGURE 5-86

4 Use the Campus Housing database that you used in Project 4 for this assignment or see your instructor for information on accessing the files required for this book. Add a Phone Number, Picture, and Web Page field to the Owner table. The Phone Number field should use the same input mask as that shown in the project. Create your own data for the Phone Number field. Update the Picture and Web Page fields by using appropriate pictures and hyperlinks from the Data Disk. Create a form that contains a subform for the Owner table. The subform should display all the fields from the Rental table except Owner Code. Be sure to include a form header with a title and the current date. Change the special effects and colors of the labels.

5 **Working Together** Copy the Regional Books database and rename the database to your team name. For example, if your team is Team 1, then name the database Team 1 Books. As a team, enhance this Books database by adding a summary description for each book. Make up your own summaries. Add a field to the Publisher table that will store the publisher's Web page. Make up your own Web pages for the publisher or use existing Web pages. For example, use the Course Technology Web page for one of the publisher's Web pages. Modify the Publisher Master Form to include the Web Page field. Determine the object dependencies for all forms and queries in the database. Write a short report that explains what you found and why it is useful information.

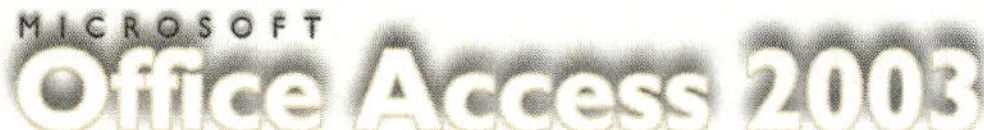

Switchboards, PivotTables, and PivotCharts

PROJECT

CASE PERSPECTIVE

The tables, forms, and reports created for Ashton James College are a real benefit for the administration. Although, it is not difficult to use a form or a table, or to print or preview a report, users do have to remember some specific steps. To view client data using a form, for example, they need to first select the Forms object and then open the desired form. To view the same client data in Datasheet view, they need to remember to select the Tables object, after which they must open the correct table. If they want a window maximized, they must take the correct action to maximize it. AJC has heard about switchboard systems that enable users to click a button or two to open any form or table, preview any report, or print any report. The administration would like such a switchboard system because they believe this will improve the user-friendliness of the system, thereby improving employee satisfaction.

The administration also wants to summarize their data in additional ways. While they use the crosstab queries created previously, they want the ability to make changes to the way the data is summarized and presented on the screen. Presenting the query results as PivotTables addresses these needs. Presenting the results as PivotCharts gives the same flexibility in a graphical format. Your task is to help the administration accomplish these goals.

As you read through this project, you will learn how to create the switchboard, a PivotTable, and a PivotChart for Ashton James College.

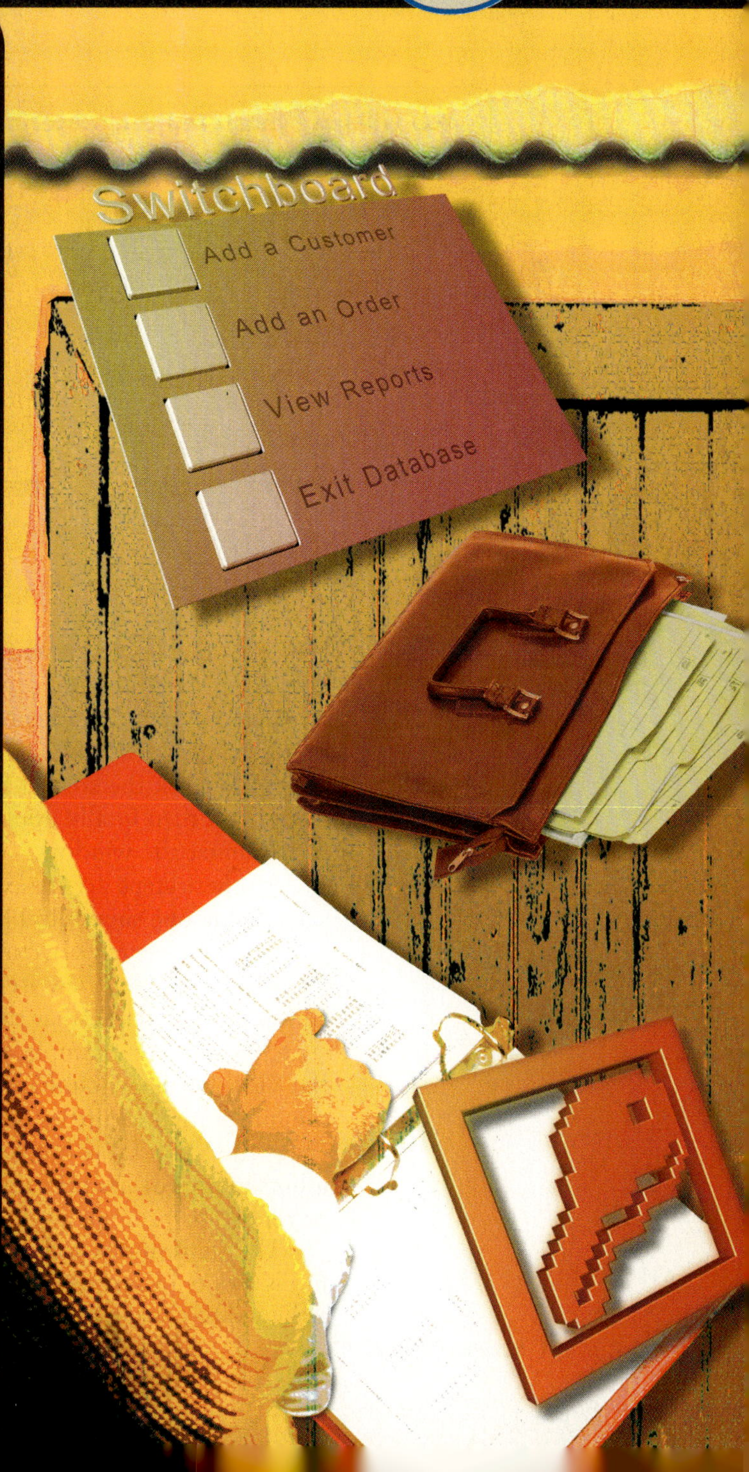

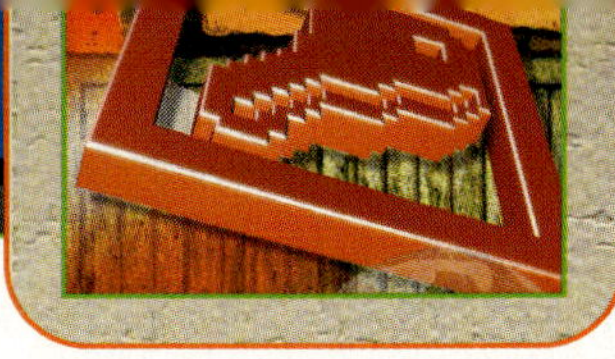

MICROSOFT Office Access 2003

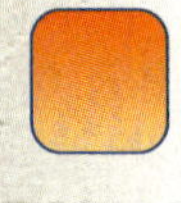

Switchboards, PivotTables, and PivotCharts

PROJECT

OBJECTIVES

You will have mastered the material in this project when you can:

- Create, add actions to, run, copy, and modify macros
- Create a switchboard and switchboard pages
- Modify switchboard pages
- Use a switchboard
- Import data and create a query
- Create a PivotTable
- Change properties in a PivotTable
- Use a PivotTable
- Create a PivotChart and add a legend
- Change the chart type and organization of a PivotChart
- Remove drop areas in a PivotChart
- Assign axis titles and a chart title in a PivotChart
- Use a PivotChart

Introduction

Previous projects illustrated how to create tables, forms, and reports. Each time a user needs to utilize any of these, however, the user needs to follow a correct series of steps. To open the Client Update Form in a maximized window, for example, requires that a user click Forms on the Objects bar in the Database window, and then right-click the correct form. Next, the user must click Open on the shortcut menu, and then finally double-click the title bar for the window containing the form to maximize the window.

All these steps are unnecessary if the database includes a switchboard system, such as the one shown in Figure 6-1a. A **switchboard** is a form that includes buttons to perform a variety of actions. In this system, the user just clicks a button — View Form, View Table, View Report, Print Report, or Exit Application — to indicate the action to be taken. Other than Exit Application, clicking a button leads to another switchboard. For example, when a user clicks the View Form button, Access displays the View Form switchboard as shown in Figure 6-1b. On this form, the user clicks the button that identifies the form he or she wants to view. Similarly, when the user clicks the View Table button, Access displays a switchboard on which the user clicks a button to indicate the table he or she wants to view. Thus, viewing any form, table, or report, or printing any report requires clicking only two buttons.

The steps in this project show how to create the switchboard system represented in Figures 6-1a and 6-1b. Before doing so, **macros**, which are collections of actions designed to carry out specific tasks, such as opening a form and maximizing the

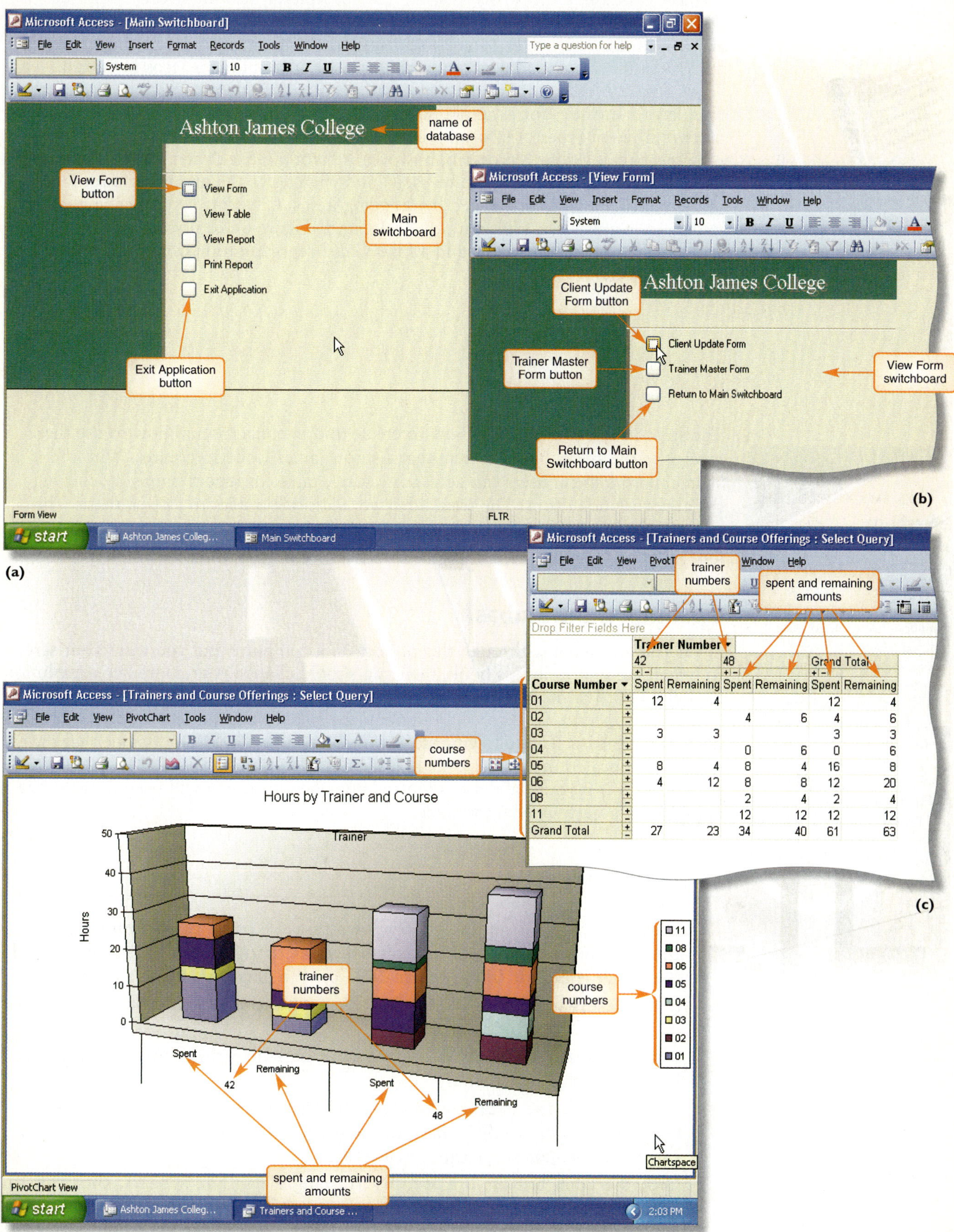
Microsoft Access - [Main Switchboard]
Ashton James College
name of database
View Form button
View Form
View Table
View Report
Print Report
Exit Application
Main switchboard
Exit Application button
(a)
Microsoft Access - [View Form]
Client Update Form button
Client Update Form
Trainer Master Form button
Trainer Master Form
Return to Main Switchboard
View Form switchboard
Return to Main Switchboard button
(b)
Microsoft Access - [Trainers and Course Offerings : Select Query]
trainer numbers
spent and remaining amounts
Drop Filter Fields Here
Trainer Number
Course Number
Grand Total
(c)
Hours by Trainer and Course
Hours
Trainer
Spent
Remaining
42
48
course numbers
trainer numbers
spent and remaining amounts
Chartspace
PivotChart View
(d)

FIGURE 6-1

window containing the form, must be created. Macros are run directly from the Database window. When a macro is run, Access will execute the various steps, called **actions**, in the macro. The switchboard system also uses macros. Clicking certain buttons in the switchboard system will cause the appropriate macros to be run.

Project 2 illustrated the steps for creating a crosstab query, which is a query that calculates a statistic (for example, sum, average, or count) for data that is grouped by two different types of information. A PivotTable is similar (Figure 6-1c on the previous page). Unlike a crosstab, however, a PivotTable is dynamic. In a PivotTable, different levels of detail are shown easily and changes to the organization or layout of the table can be accomplished by dragging items. Checking or unchecking values in drop-down lists can filter data. A PivotChart (Figure 6-1d) presents similar data graphically. Both a PivotTable and a PivotChart representation of a query are created in this project.

Project Six — Switchboards, PivotTables, and PivotCharts

The steps in this project show how to create and test macros and how to use these macros in the switchboard system that Ashton James College requires. With the switchboard system, users can access any form, table, or report simply by clicking the appropriate buttons. The steps add two additional tables to the database. The steps also create a query incorporating this new data, and then use the data in this query to create both a PivotTable and a PivotChart.

More About

The Access Help System

Need Help? It is no further than the Type a question for help box on the menu bar in the upper-right corner of the window. Click the box that contains the text, Type a question for help (Figure 6-1a on the previous page), type `help`, and then press the ENTER key. Access responds with a list of topics you can click to learn about obtaining help on any Access-related topic. To find out what is new in Access, type `what is new in Access` in the Type a question for help box.

Opening the Database

If you are stepping through this project on a computer and you want your screen to match the figures in this book, then you should change your computer's resolution to 800 x 600. For more information on how to change the resolution on your computer, see Appendix D. Before carrying out the steps in this project, first you must open the database. The following steps, which open the database, assume that the database is located in a folder called Data on disk C. (See the note in Project 4 on page AC 197.) If your database is located anywhere else, you will need to make the appropriate adjustments in the steps.

To Open a Database

1. **Click the Start button on the Windows taskbar, point to All Programs on the Start menu, point to Microsoft Office on the All Programs submenu, and then click Microsoft Office Access 2003 on the Microsoft Office submenu.**
2. **If the Access window is not maximized, double-click its title bar to maximize it.**
3. **If the Language bar appears, right-click it and then click Close the Language bar on the shortcut menu.**
4. **Click Open on the Database toolbar, and then click Local Disk (C:) in the Look in box. Double-click the Data folder, and then make sure the database called Ashton James College is selected.**
5. **Click the Open button. If a Security Warning dialog box appears, click the Open button.**

The database opens and the Ashton James College : Database window appears.

Creating and Using Macros

A macro consists of a series of actions that Access performs when the macro is run; therefore, you will need to specify the actions when you create the macro. The actions are entered in a special window called a Macro window. Once a macro is created, you can run it from the Database window by right-clicking the macro and then clicking Run on the shortcut menu. Macros also can be associated with items on switchboards. When you click the corresponding button on the switchboard, Access will run the macro. Whether a macro is run from the Database window or from a switchboard, the effect is the same: Access will execute the actions in the macro in the order in which they are entered.

In this project, you will learn how to create macros to open forms and maximize the windows; open tables in Datasheet view; open reports in preview windows; and print reports. As you enter actions, you will select them from a list box. The names of the actions are self-explanatory. The action to open a form, for example, is OpenForm. Thus, it is not necessary to memorize the specific actions that are available.

The following steps demonstrate how to create a macro.

To Create a Macro

1

- **Click the Macros object.**

The list of previously created macros appears (Figure 6-2). Currently, no macros exist.

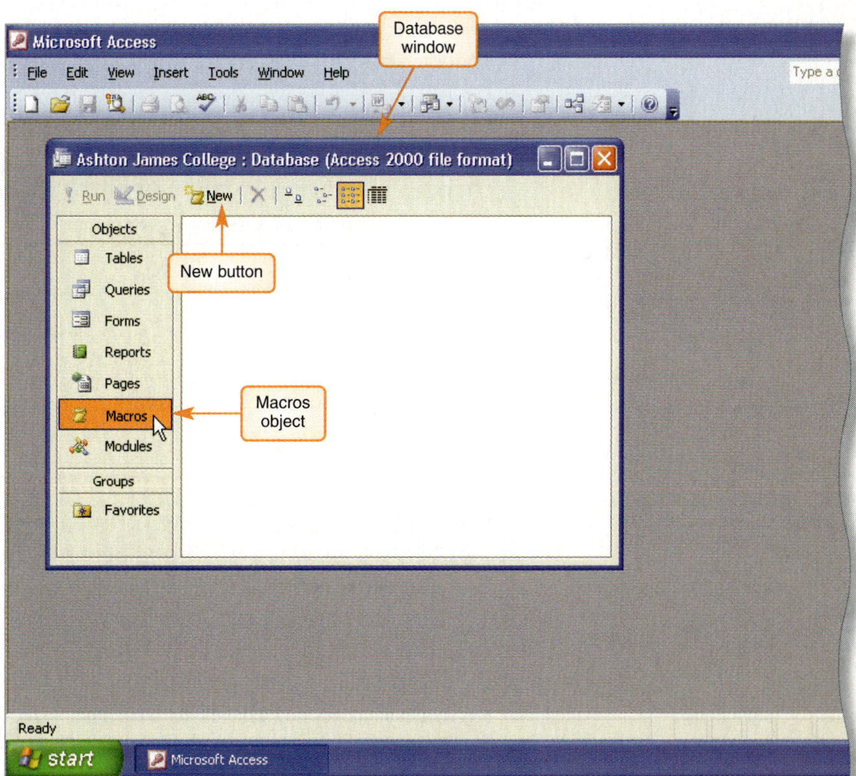

FIGURE 6-2

2

- **Click the New button.**
- **If necessary, maximize the window by double-clicking its title bar.**

The Microsoft Access – [Macro1: Macro] window appears (Figure 6-3).

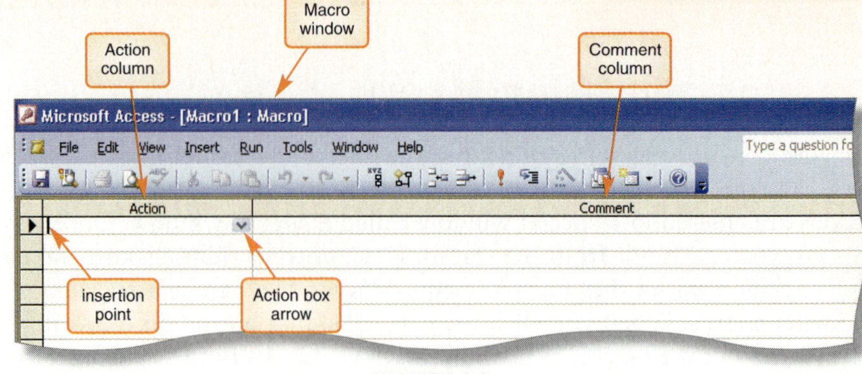

FIGURE 6-3

Other Ways

1. Click New Object button arrow on Database window toolbar, click Macro
2. On Insert menu click Macro
3. In Voice Command mode, say "Macros, New"

The Macro Window

The first column in the Macro window is the Action column. You enter the actions you want the macro to perform in this column (Figure 6-3). To enter an action, click the arrow in the Action column and then select the action from the list that appears. Many actions require additional information, called the **arguments** of the action. If you select such an action, the arguments will appear in the lower portion of the Macro window and you can make any necessary changes to them.

The second column in the Macro window is the Comment column. In this column, you enter **comments**, which are brief descriptions of the corresponding action's purpose. The actions, the arguments requiring changes, and the comments for the first macro you will create are shown in Table 6-1.

Table 6-1 Specifications for First Macro

ACTION	ARGUMENT TO CHANGE	NEW VALUE FOR ARGUMENT	COMMENT
Echo	Echo On	No	Turn echo off to avoid screen flicker
Hourglass			Turn on hourglass
OpenForm	Form Name	Client Update Form	Open Client Update Form
Hourglass	Hourglass On	No	Turn off hourglass
Echo			Turn echo on

The macro begins by turning off the echo. This will eliminate the screen flicker that can be present when a form is being opened. The second action changes the shape of the mouse pointer to an hourglass to indicate that some process is taking place. The third action opens the form called Client Update Form. The fourth action turns off the hourglass, and the fifth action turns the echo back on so the Client Update Form will appear.

Turning on and off the echo and the hourglass are not absolutely necessary. On computers with faster processors, you may not notice a difference between running a macro that includes these actions and one that does not. For computers with slower processors, however, these actions can make a noticeable difference, so they are included here.

Adding Actions to a Macro

To continue creating this macro, enter the actions. For each action, enter the action and comment in the appropriate text boxes, and then make the necessary changes to any arguments. The following steps show how to add the actions to, and save, the macro.

To Add Actions to a Macro

1

- **Click the box arrow in the first row of the Action column to display a list of available actions.**
- **Scroll down until Echo appears.**

The list of available actions appears (Figure 6-4).

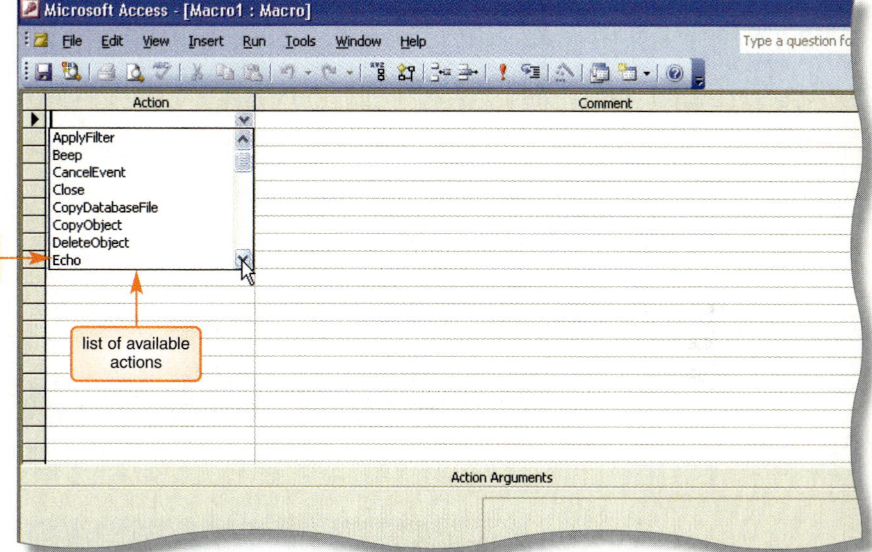

FIGURE 6-4

2

- **Click Echo.**
- **Press the F6 key to move to the Action Arguments for the Echo action.**
- **Click the Echo On box arrow.**

The arguments for the Echo action appear (Figure 6-5). The list of values for the Echo On argument appears.

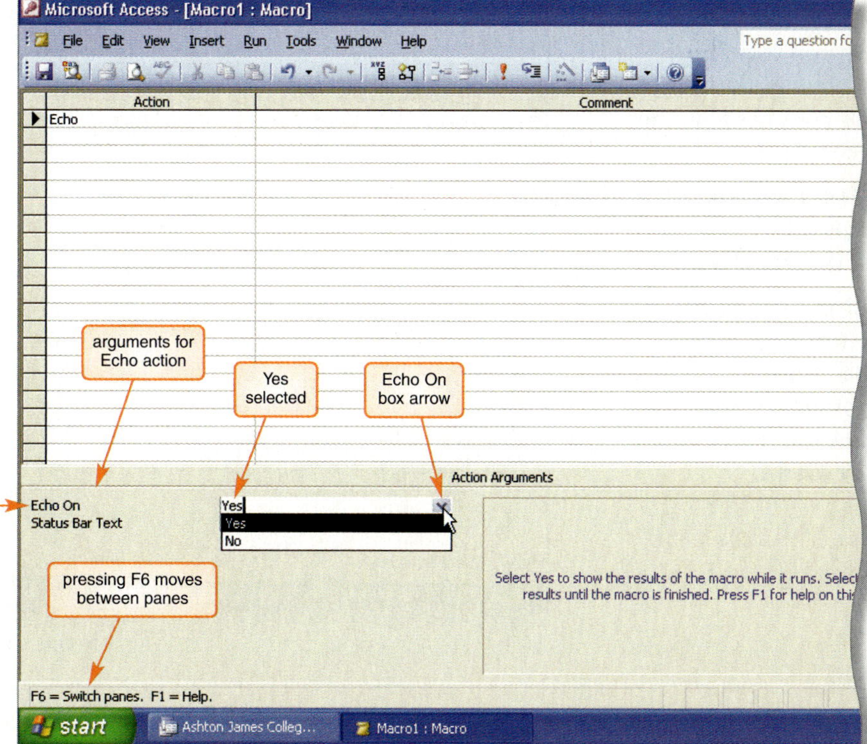

FIGURE 6-5

3

- **Click No.**
- **Press the F6 key to move back to Echo in the Action column, and then press the TAB key.**
- **Type** `Turn echo off to avoid screen flicker` **in the Comment column, and then press the TAB key.**

The first action and comment are entered (Figure 6-6). The insertion point has moved to the second row.

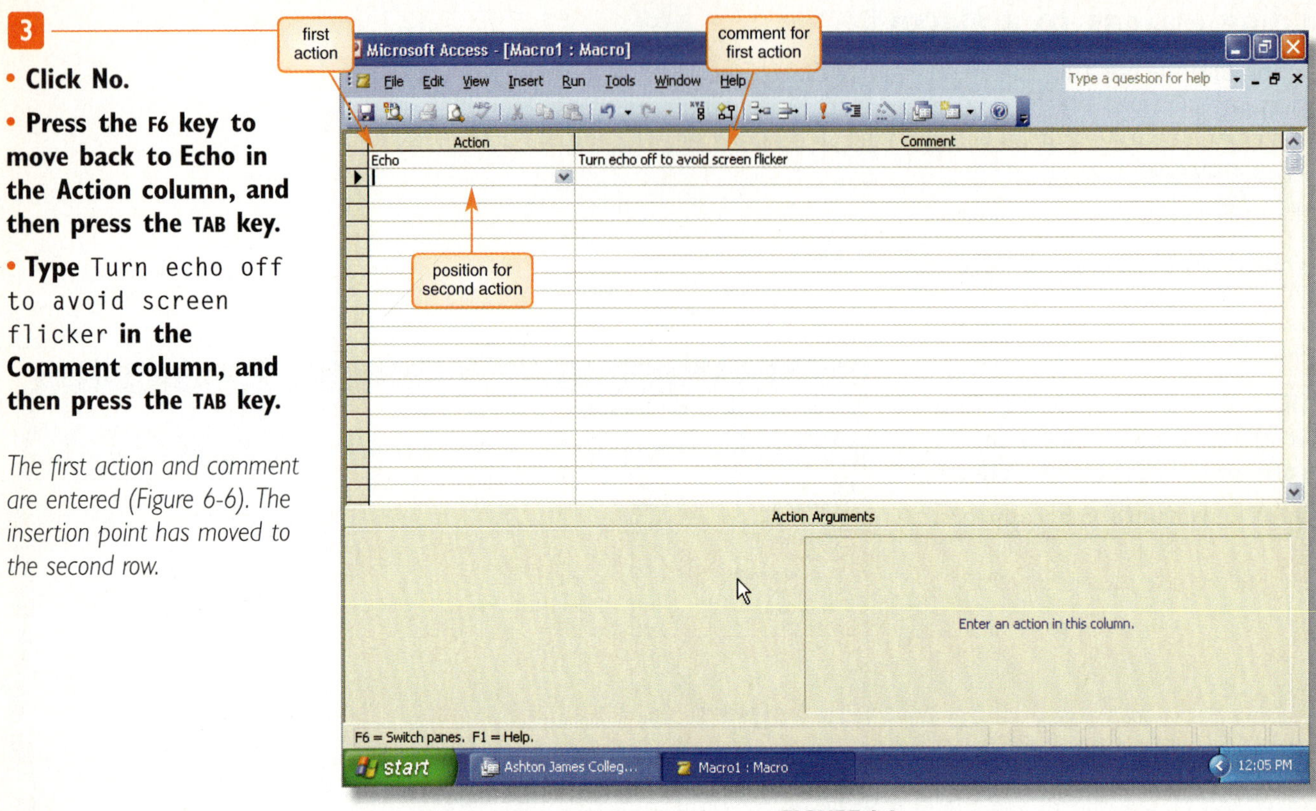

FIGURE 6-6

4

- **Select Hourglass as the action in the second row.**
- **Press the TAB key and then type** `Turn on hourglass` **as the comment in the second row.**
- **Press the TAB key and then select OpenForm as the third action.**
- **Press the F6 key to move to the Action Arguments, and then click the Form Name box arrow.**

A list of available forms appears (Figure 6-7).

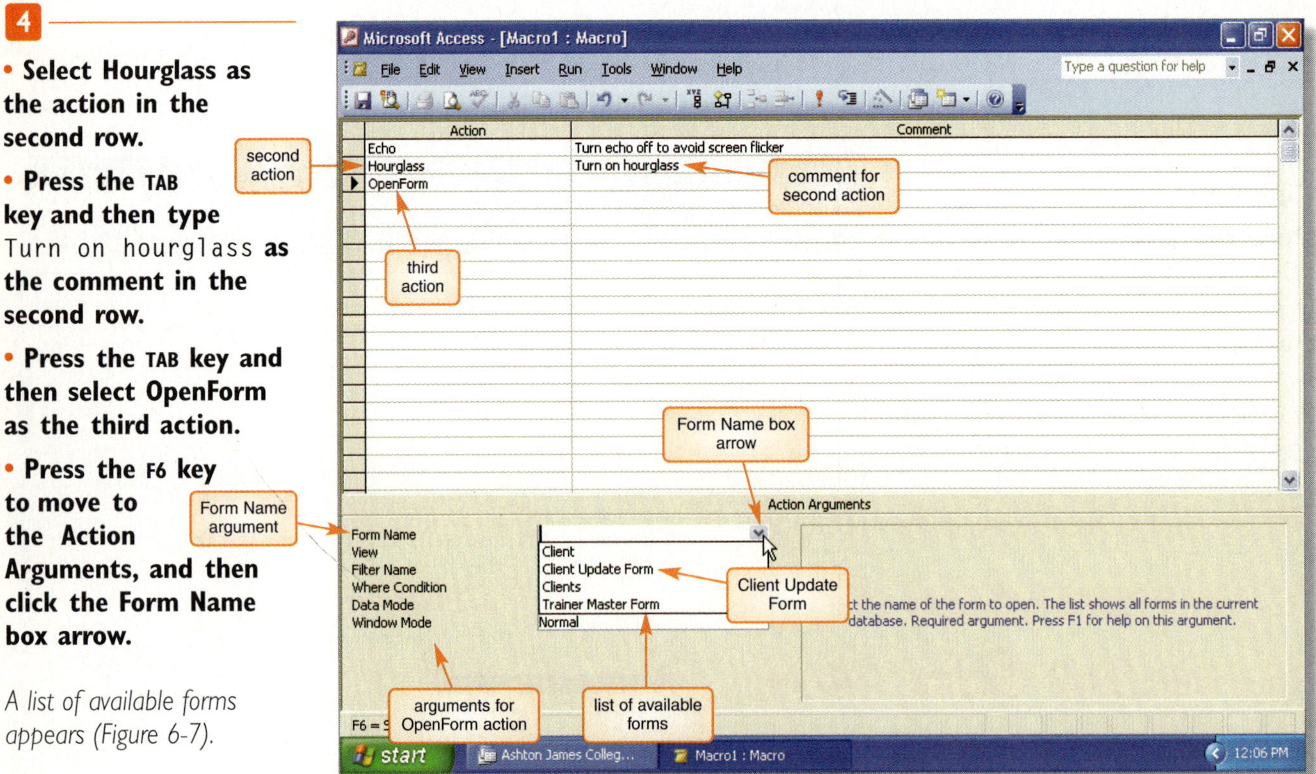

FIGURE 6-7

5

- **Click Client Update Form, press the F6 key, press the TAB key, and then type** `Open Client Update Form` **as the comment.**
- **Select Hourglass as the fourth action.**
- **Change the Hourglass On argument to No, and then type** `Turn off hourglass` **as the comment.**
- **Select Echo as the fifth action, and then type** `Turn echo on` **as the comment.**

The actions and comments are entered (Figure 6-8).

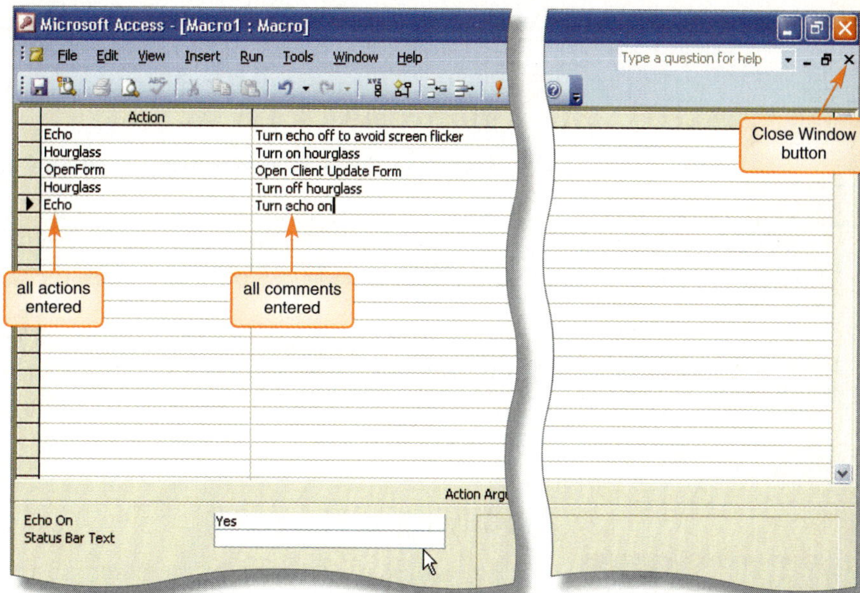

FIGURE 6-8

- **Click the Close Window button to close the macro, click the Yes button to save the macro, type** `Open Client Update Form` **as the name of the macro.**

The Save As dialog box appears (Figure 6-9).

- **Click the OK button.**

The actions and comments have been added to the macro, and the macro is saved.

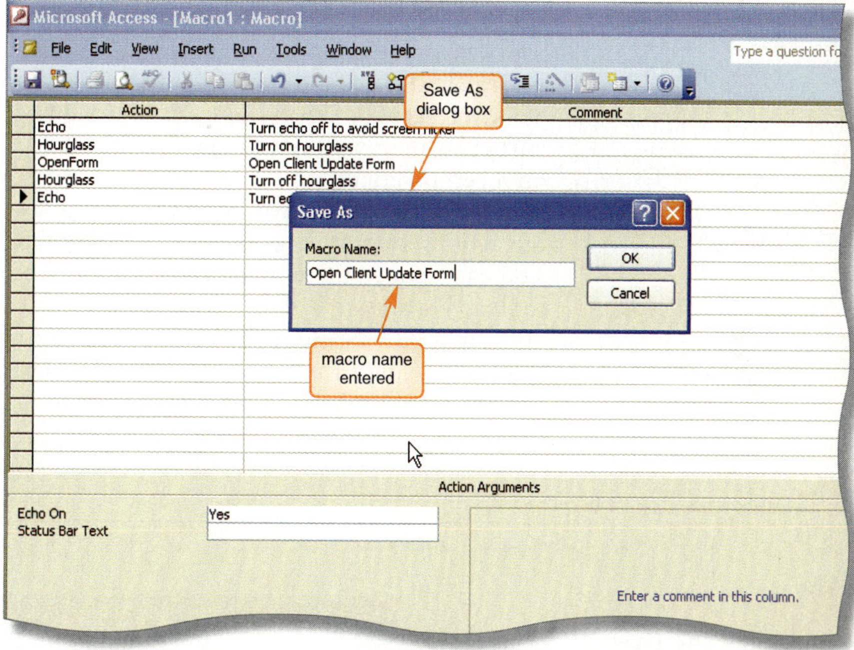

FIGURE 6-9

Running a Macro

To run a macro, select the Macros object in the Database window, right-click the macro, and then select Run on the shortcut menu. The actions in the macro will execute. The steps on the next page illustrate how to run the macro that was just created.

Other Ways

1. On Insert menu click Macro
2. Click New Object button arrow, click Macro
3. In Voice Command mode, say "Macros, New"

To Run a Macro

1 **Right-click the Open Client Update Form macro and then click Run on the shortcut menu.**

2 **Click the Close Window button on the Client Update Form window title bar.**

The macro runs and displays the Client Update Form. The window containing the form is maximized because the previous windows were maximized. The form no longer appears.

Other Ways

1. Click Macros on Objects bar, click macro name, click Run button
2. Click Macros on Objects bar, double-click macro name
3. In Voice Command mode, say "Macros, [click macro name], Run"

If previous windows had not been maximized, the window containing the form also would not be maximized. In order to ensure that the window containing the form is maximized automatically, you can include the Maximize action in your macro.

Modifying a Macro

To modify a macro, select the macro in the Database window, select Design View on the shortcut menu, and then make the necessary changes. To insert a new action, click the position for the action, or press the INSERT key to insert a new blank row if the new action is to be placed between two actions. Enter the new action, change the values for any necessary arguments, and then enter a comment.

When modifying a macro, two additional columns may appear: the Macro Name column and the Condition column. It is possible to group multiple macros into a single macro group. When doing so, the Macro Name column is used to identify the particular macro within the group. It also is possible to have an action be contingent on a certain condition being true. If so, the condition is entered in the Condition column. Because the macros you are creating are not combined into a macro group and the actions are not dependent on any conditions, you will not need these columns. You can remove these unneeded columns from the screen by clicking the appropriate toolbar buttons.

The following steps show how to modify the macro just created, adding a new step to maximize the form automatically. The steps remove both the Macro Name and the Condition column from the screen.

More About

Inserting an Action

If you inadvertently press the DELETE key instead of the INSERT key when you are inserting a new line in a macro, you will delete the selected action from the macro. To return the deleted action to the macro, click the Undo button on the toolbar.

To Modify a Macro

1

- **Right-click the Open Client Update Form macro.**

The shortcut menu appears (Figure 6-10).

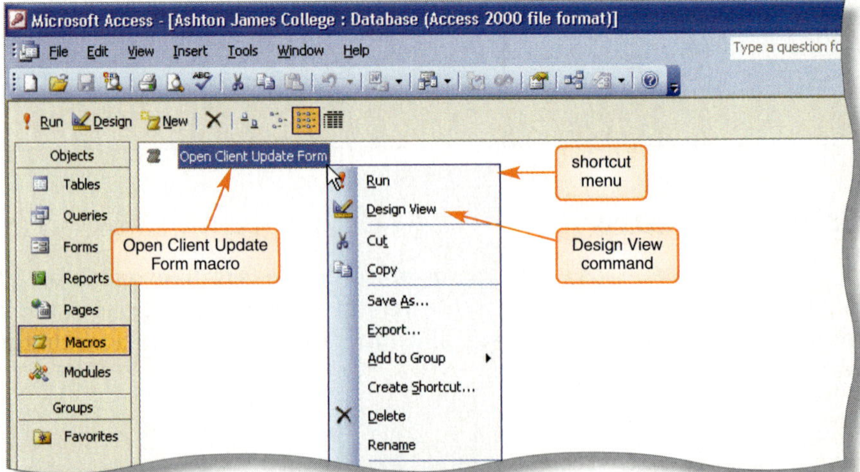

FIGURE 6-10

2

• **Click Design View.**

The macro appears in Design view (Figure 6-11). The Macro Name and Condition columns may be included.

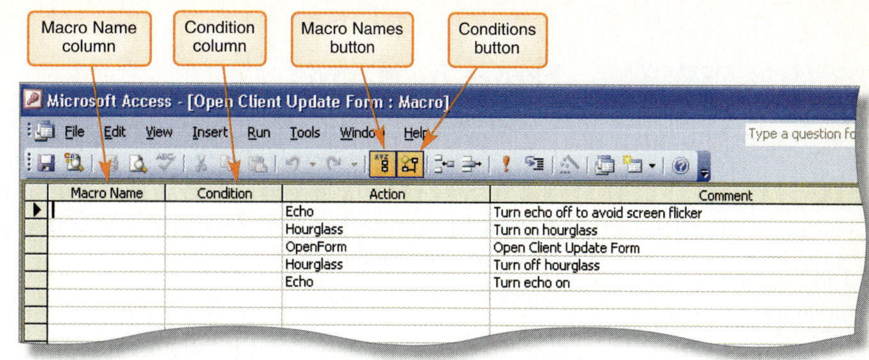

FIGURE 6-11

3

• **If the Macro Name column appears, click the Macro Names button on the Macro Design toolbar to remove the Macro Name column.**

• **If the Condition column appears, click the Conditions button on the Macro Design toolbar to remove the Condition column.**

The Microsoft Access - [Open Client Update Form : Macro] window appears (Figure 6-12). The Macro Name and Condition columns do not appear.

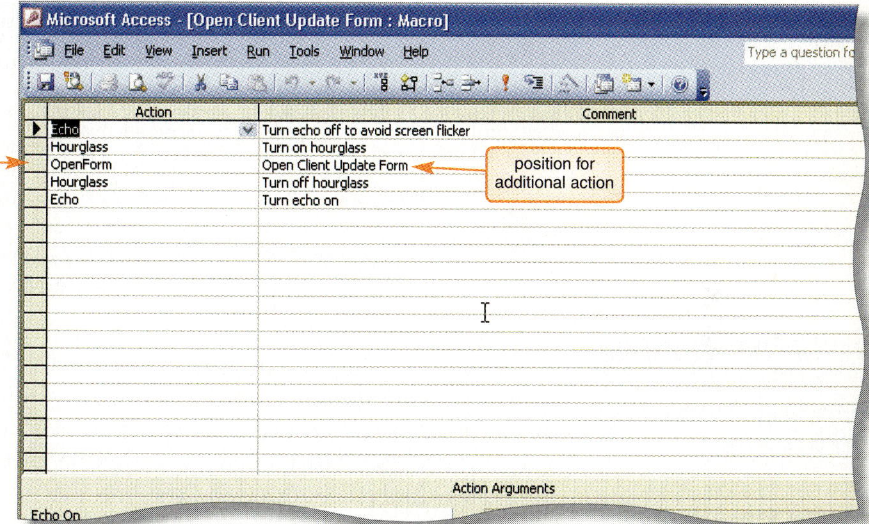

FIGURE 6-12

4

• **Click the row selector on the row containing the OpenForm action to select the row, and then press the INSERT key to insert a new row.**

• **Click the Action column arrow on the new row, select Maximize as the action, and then type** `Maximize the window` **as the comment.**

The new action is entered (Figure 6-13).

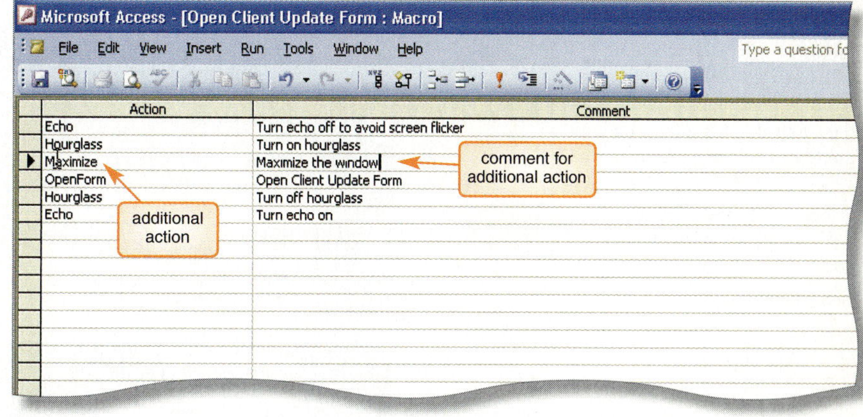

FIGURE 6-13

5

• **Click the Close Window button, and then click the Yes button to save the changes.**

The macro has been changed and saved.

Other Ways

1. Click Macros on Objects bar, click Macro name, click Design on Macro Design toolbar
2. In Voice Command mode, say "Macros, [click macro name], Design"

The next time the macro is run, the form not only will be opened, but the window containing the form also will be maximized automatically.

More About

Errors in Macros

The order of the actions in a macro may be incorrect. You can move an action by clicking the row selector to the left of the action name to highlight the row. Then click the highlighted row again and drag it to the correct location.

Errors in Macros

Macros can contain errors. For example, if you type the name of the form in the Form Name argument of the OpenForm action instead of selecting it from the list, you may type it incorrectly. Access then will not be able to execute the desired action. In that case, a Microsoft Access dialog box will appear, indicating the error and solution as shown in Figure 6-14.

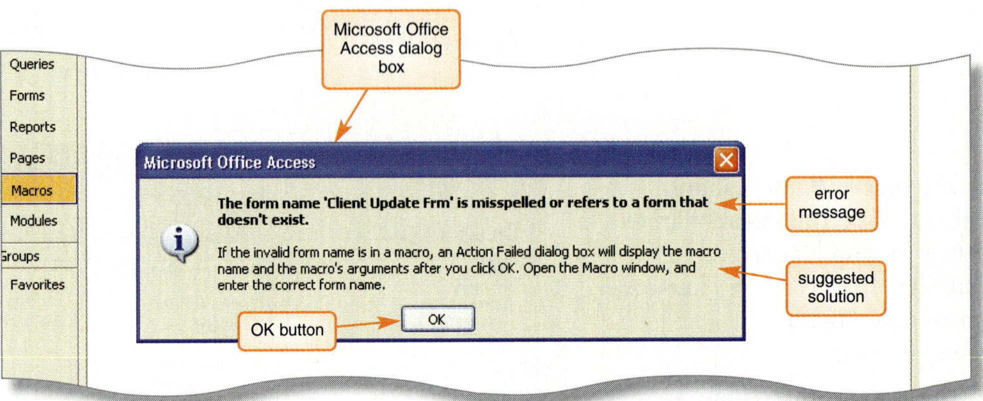

FIGURE 6-14

More About

Finding Problems in Macros

You can single step (run a macro one action at a time) through a macro to observe the results of each action and identify any action that causes an error or produces unexpected results. To single step through a macro, open the macro in Design view, click the Single Step button, and then click the Run button on the Macro Design toolbar. When the Macro Single Step dialog box appears, click the Step button to run the macro one action at a time.

If such a dialog box appears, click the OK button. The Action Failed dialog box then appears (Figure 6-15). The dialog box indicates the macro that was being run, the action that Access was attempting to execute, and the arguments for the action. This information tells you which action needs to be corrected. To make the correction, click the Halt button, and then modify the design of the macro.

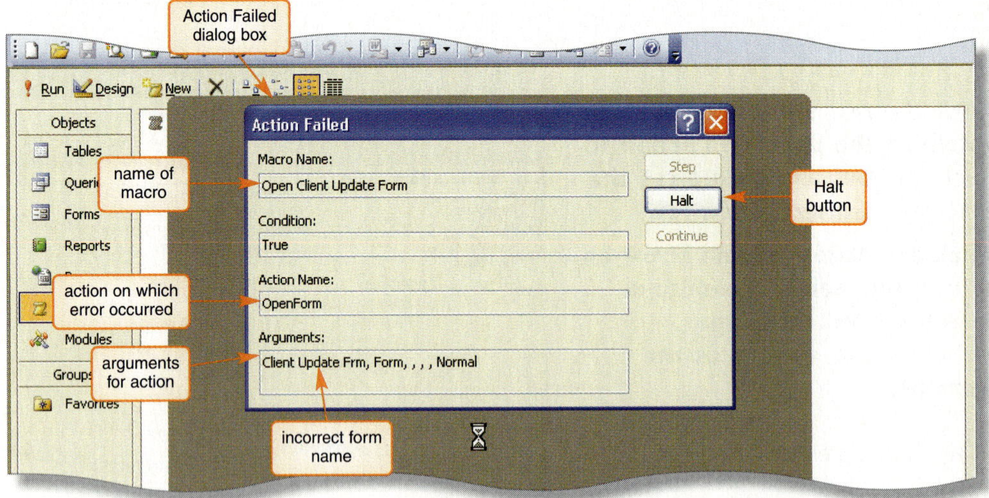

FIGURE 6-15

Additional Macros

The additional macros to be created are shown in Table 6-2. The first column gives the name of the macro, and the second column indicates the actions for the macro. The third column contains the values of those arguments that may need to be changed, and the fourth column contains the comments. (Any arguments not listed can be left as they are.)

Table 6-2 Specifications for Additional Macros

MACRO NAME	ACTION	ARGUMENT(S)	COMMENT
Open Trainer Master Form	Echo	Echo On: No	Turn echo off to avoid screen flicker
	Hourglass	Hourglass On: Yes	Turn on hourglass
	Maximize		Maximize the window
	OpenForm	Form Name: Trainer Master Form	Open Trainer Master Form
	Hourglass	Hourglass On: No	Turn off hourglass
	Echo	Echo On: Yes	Turn echo on
Open Client Table	OpenTable	Table Name: Client	Open Client Table
		View: Datasheet	
	Maximize		Maximize the window
Open Trainer Table	OpenTable	Table Name: Trainer	Open Trainer Table
		View: Datasheet	
	Maximize		Maximize the window
Preview Client Amount Report	OpenReport	Report Name: Client Amount Report	Preview Client Amount Report
		View: Print Preview	
	Maximize		Maximize the window
Print Client Amount Report	OpenReport	Report Name: Client Amount Report	Print Client Amount Report
		View: Print	
Preview Client Account Summary	OpenReport	Report Name: Client Account Summary	Preview Client Account Summary
		View: Print Preview	
	Maximize		Maximize the window
Print Client Account Summary	OpenReport	Report Name: Client Account Summary	Print Client Account Summary
		View: Print	
Preview Trainer/Client Report	OpenReport	Report Name: Trainer/Client Report	Preview Trainer/Client Report
		View: Print Preview	
	Maximize		Maximize the window
Print Trainer/Client Report	OpenReport	Report Name: Trainer/Client Report	Print Trainer/Client Report
		View: Print	

Copying a Macro

When you want to create a new macro, you often find there is an existing macro that is very similar to the one you wish to create. If this is the case, it often is simpler to use a copy of the existing macro and modify it instead of creating a new macro from scratch. The Open Trainer Master Form macro, for example, is very similar to the existing Open Client Update Form macro. Thus, you can make a copy of the Open Client Update Form macro, call it Open Trainer Master Form, and then modify it to the new requirements by changing only the portion that differs from the original macro.

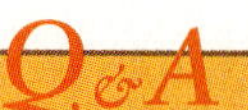

Q: One way to construct a new macro from an existing macro is to use Copy and Paste. Are there any other ways?

A: Yes, open the existing macro. Click File on the menu bar, click Save As on the File menu, and then type the name of the new macro. Make the appropriate changes to the new macro.

To make a copy of a macro, you use the clipboard. First, copy the existing macro to the clipboard and then paste the contents of the clipboard. At that point, assign the new name to the macro.

These same techniques will work for other objects as well. If you want to create a new report that is similar to an existing report, for example, use the clipboard to make a copy of the original report, paste the contents, rename it, and then modify the copied report in whatever way you wish.

The following steps illustrate how to use the clipboard to copy and paste the Open Client Update Form macro.

To Copy and Paste a Macro

1

- **Ensure the Macros object is selected, and right-click the Open Client Update Form macro.**

The shortcut menu for the Open Client Update Form macro appears (Figure 6-16).

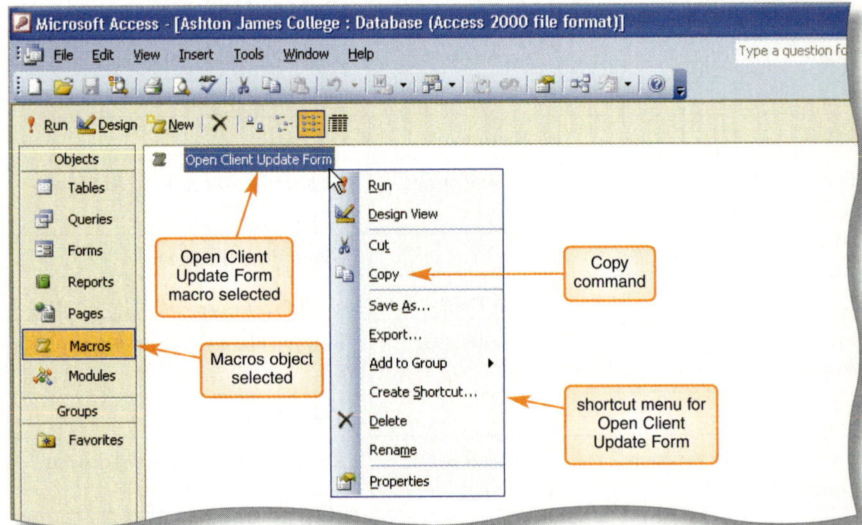

FIGURE 6-16

2

- **Click Copy to copy the macro to the clipboard.**
- **Right-click any open area of the Database window.**

The shortcut menu appears (Figure 6-17).

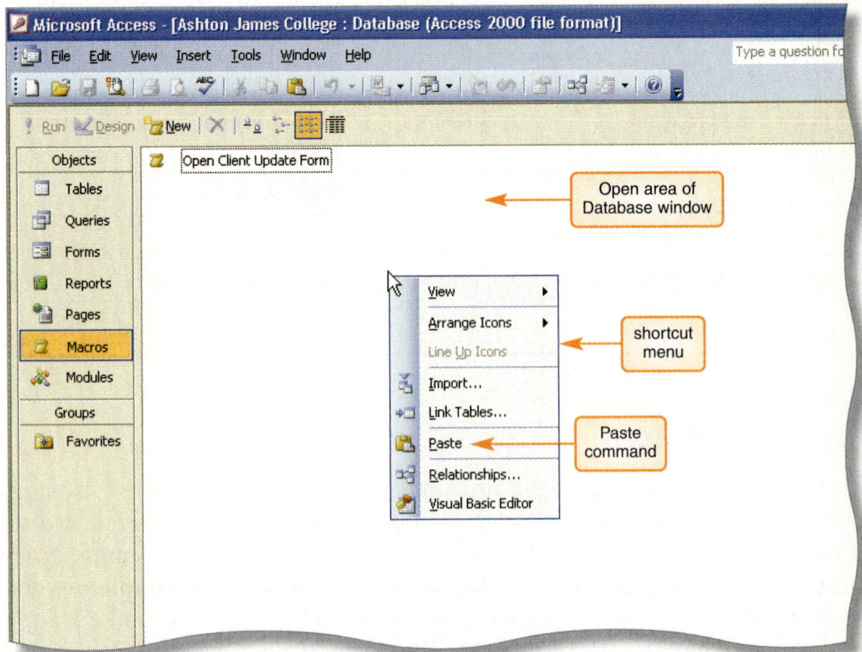

FIGURE 6-17

3

• **Click Paste, type** `Open Trainer Master Form` **in the Macro Name text box in the Paste As dialog box.**

The Paste As dialog box appears, and the new macro name is entered in the text box (Figure 6-18).

4

• **Click the OK button.**

The new macro is copied and saved.

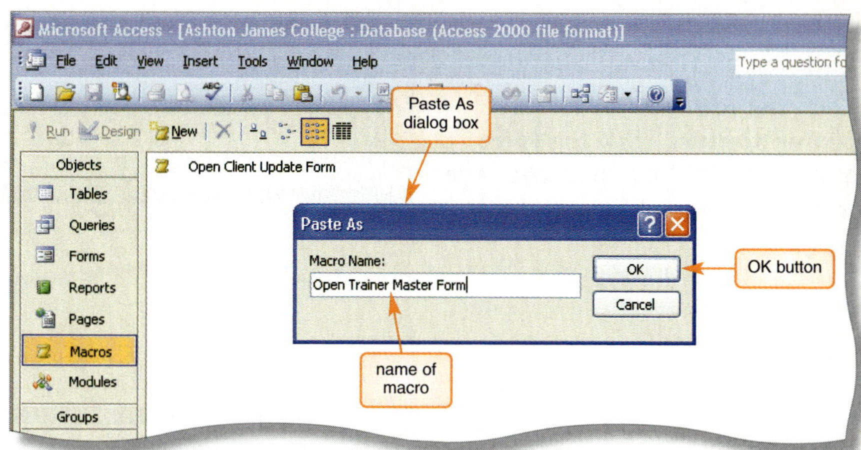

FIGURE 6-18

Modifying the Copied Macro

Once you have copied the macro, you can modify the copy to make any needed changes. The following steps show how to modify the macro just copied by changing the Form Name argument for the OpenForm action to Trainer Master Form.

To Modify the Copied Macro

1

• **Right-click the Open Trainer Master Form macro.**

The shortcut menu for the macro appears (Figure 6-19).

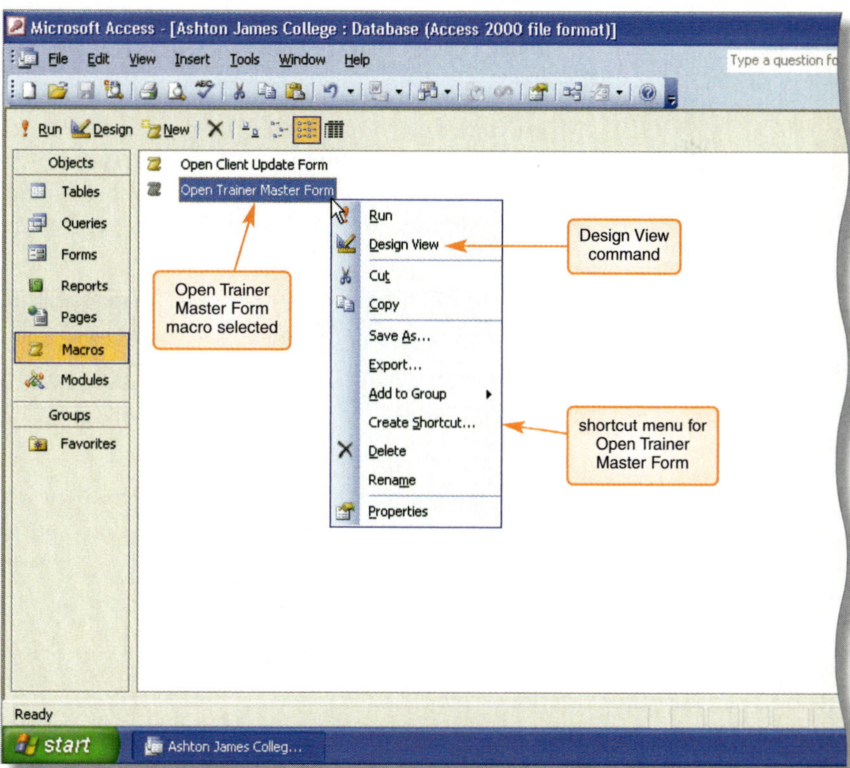

FIGURE 6-19

2

- **Click Design View.**
- **Click the row selector for the OpenForm action, click the Form Name argument, and then click the Form Name box arrow.**

The macro appears in Design view. The OpenForm action is selected, and the list of available forms appears (Figure 6-20).

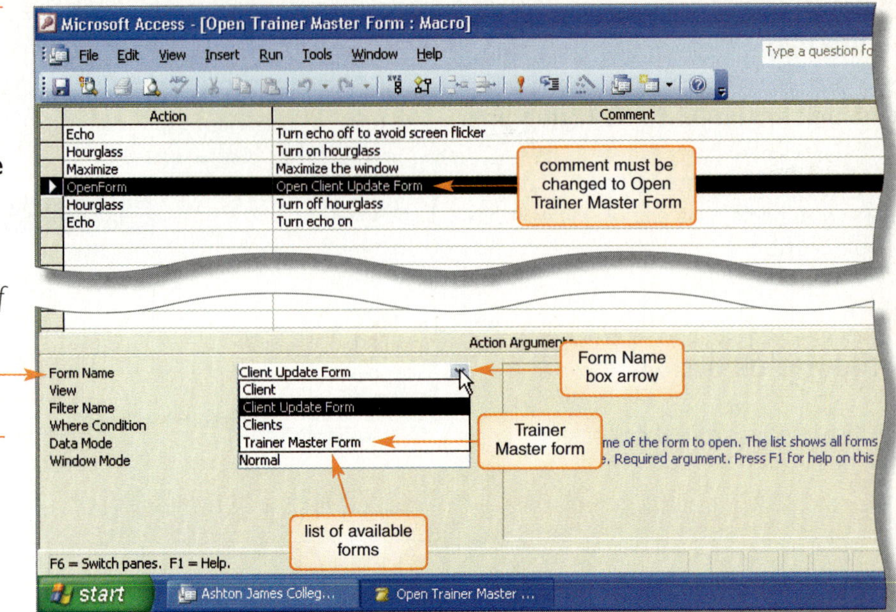

FIGURE 6-20

3

- **Click Trainer Master Form to change the Form Name argument.**
- **Click the Comment text box for the OpenForm action, delete the comment, and then type** `Open Trainer Master Form` **as the new comment.**
- **Click the Close Window button for the Open Trainer Master Form : Macro window, and then click the Yes button to save the changes.**

The changes to the macro have been saved.

Macro Arguments

Some macros require a change to more than one argument. For example, to create a macro to preview or print a report requires a change to both the Report Name and the View arguments. In Figure 6-21, the OpenReport action displays Client Account Summary in the Report Name argument text box and Print Preview is highlighted in the View argument text box.

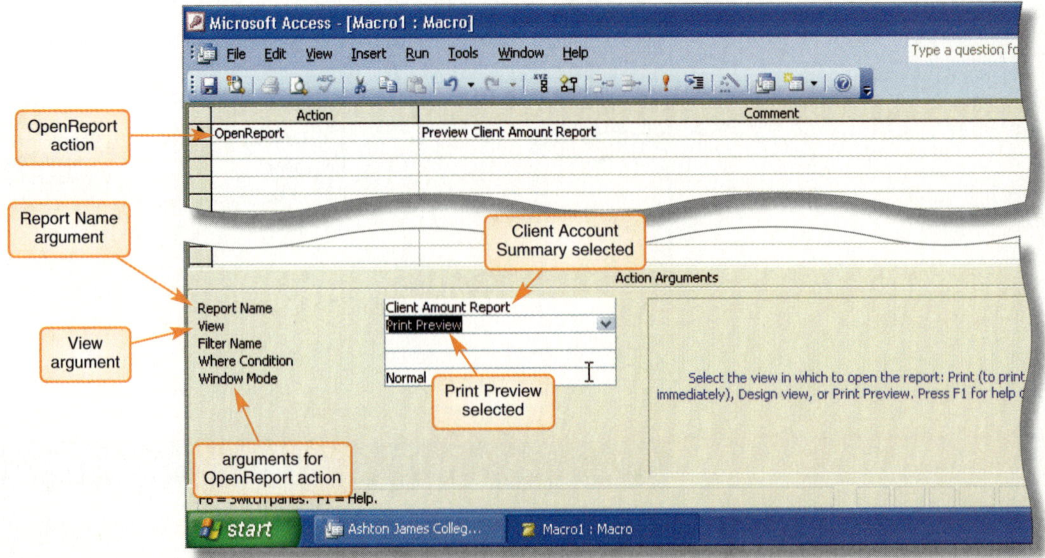

FIGURE 6-21

Creating Additional Macros

You can create additional macros using the same steps you used to create the first macro. You copy an existing macro and then modify the copied macro as needed. The following step shows how to create the additional macros illustrated in Table 6-2 on page AC 325.

To Create Additional Macros

1. **Using the same techniques used to create the Open Client Update Form macro (page AC 319), create each of the macros described in Table 6-2.**

The Open Client Table, Open Trainer Table, Preview Client Amount Report, Print Client Amount Report, Preview Client Account Summary, Print Client Account Summary, Preview Trainer/Client Report, and Print Trainer/Client Report macros are created.

Running the Macros

To run any of the other macros just as you ran the first macro, select the appropriate macro in the Database window and then select Run on the shortcut menu. The appropriate actions then are carried out. Running the Preview Client Amount Report macro, for example, displays the Client Amount Report in a maximized preview window.

More About

Running a Macro

You can run a macro from any window within Access. To do so, click Macro on the Tools menu, click Run Macro, and then select the macro from the Macro Name list.

Opening Databases Containing Macros

When a database contains macros, there is a chance a computer virus can attach to a macro. To protect against these types of macro viruses, Microsoft Access has a macro level security feature. Various levels of macro security are available, for example: high, medium, and low. If the macro level security is medium or higher, Access displays a Security Warning dialog box when a user attempts to open a database containing macros. If the database comes from a trusted source and you are sure that it does not contain any macro viruses, click Open in the Security Warning dialog box to open the database.

Creating and Using a Switchboard

A switchboard (see Figures 6-1a and 6-1b on page AC 315) is a special type of form. It contains buttons you can click to perform a variety of actions. Buttons on the Main switchboard can lead to other switchboards. Clicking the View Form button, for example, causes Access to display the View Form switchboard. Buttons also can be used to open forms or tables. Clicking the Client Update Form button on the View Form switchboard opens the Client Update Form. Still other buttons cause reports to appear in a preview window or print reports.

More About

Application Systems

An application system is simply an easy-to-use collection of forms, reports, and queries designed to satisfy the needs of some specific user or group of users, such as the users at Ashton James College. A switchboard system is one type of application system that has found widespread acceptance in the Windows environment. For more information about application systems, visit the Access 2003 More About Web page (scsite.com/ac2003/more) and click Application Systems.

Creating a Switchboard

To create a switchboard, you use the Database Utilities command on the Tools menu and then select Switchboard Manager, which is an Access tool that allows you to create, edit, and delete switchboard forms for an application. If you have not previously created a switchboard, you will be asked if you wish to create one. The steps on the next page illustrate how to create a switchboard for the Ashton James College database.

To Create a Switchboard

1

- **With the Database window appearing, click Tools on the menu bar, and point to Database Utilities on the Tools menu.**

The Tools menu appears (Figure 6-22). The Database Utilities submenu also appears.

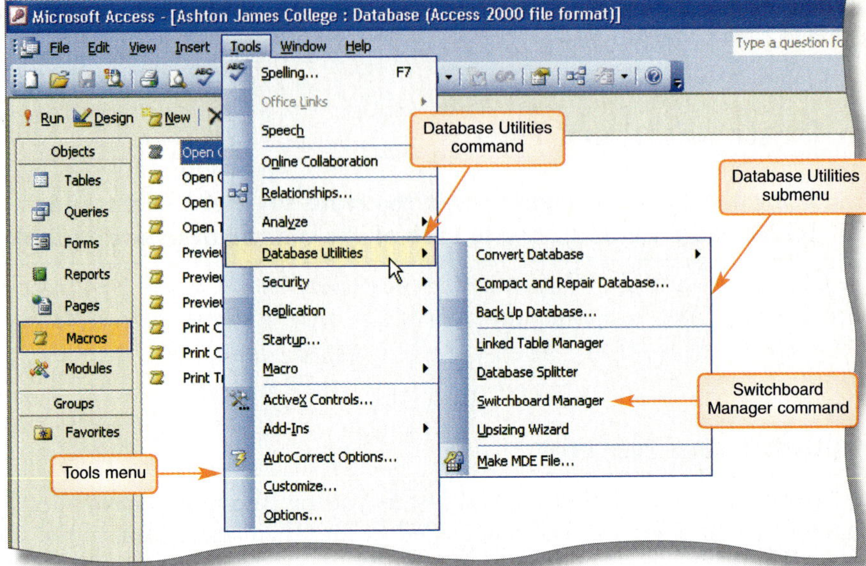

FIGURE 6-22

2

- **Click Switchboard Manager.**

The Switchboard Manager dialog box displays a message indicating that no switchboard currently exists for this database and asks whether to create one (Figure 6-23).

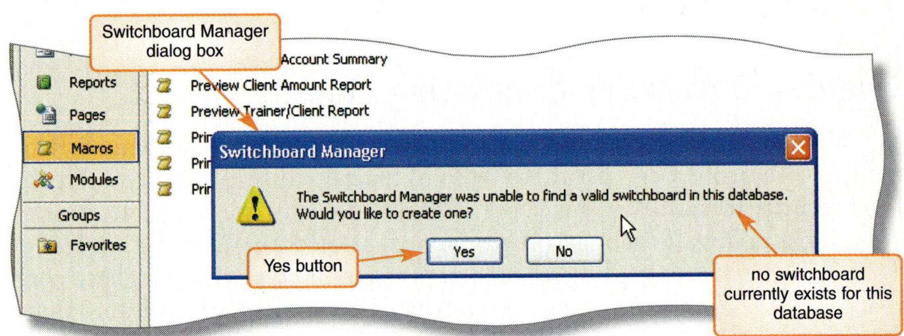

FIGURE 6-23

3

- **Click the Yes button to create a new switchboard.**

The Switchboard Manager dialog box appears and indicates there is only the Main Switchboard (Default) at this time (Figure 6-24).

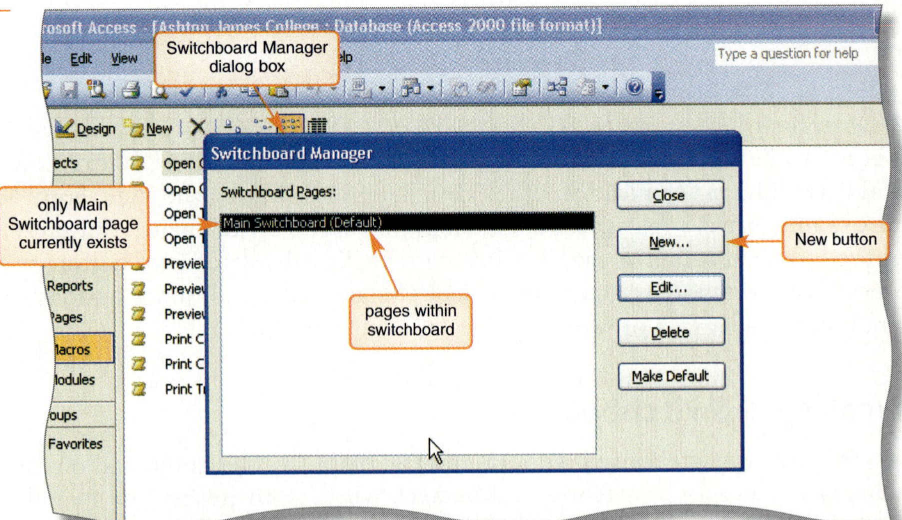

FIGURE 6-24

Creating Switchboard Pages

The next step in creating the switchboard system is to create the individual switchboards within the system. These individual switchboards are called the **switchboard pages.** The switchboard pages to be created are listed in the first column of Table 6-3. You do not have to create the Main Switchboard page because Access has created it automatically (Figure 6-24). To create each of the other pages, use the New button in the Switchboard Manager dialog box, and then enter the name of the page.

Table 6-3 Specifications for Switchboard Pages and Items

SWITCHBOARD PAGE	SWITCHBOARD ITEM	COMMAND	ARGUMENT
Main Switchboard	View Form	Go to Switchboard	Switchboard: View Form
	View Table	Go to Switchboard	Switchboard: View Table
	View Report	Go to Switchboard	Switchboard: View Report
	Print Report	Go to Switchboard	Switchboard: Print Report
	Exit Application	Exit Application	None
View Form	Client Update Form	Run Macro	Macro: Open Client Update Form
	Trainer Master Form	Run Macro	Macro: Open Trainer Master Form
	Return to Main Switchboard	Go to Switchboard	Switchboard: Main Switchboard
View Table	Client Table	Run Macro	Macro: Open Client Table
	Trainer Table	Run Macro	Macro: Open Trainer Table
	Return to Main Switchboard	Go to Switchboard	Switchboard: Main Switchboard
View Report	View Client Amount Report	Run Macro	Macro: Preview Client Amount Report
	View Client Account Summary	Run Macro	Macro: Preview Client Account Summary
	View Trainer/Client Report	Run Macro	Macro: Preview Trainer/Client Report
	Return to Main Switchboard	Go to Switchboard	Switchboard: Main Switchboard
Print Report	Print Client Amount Report	Run Macro	Macro: Print Client Amount Report
	Print Client Account Summary	Run Macro	Macro: Print Client Account Summary
	Print Trainer/Client Report	Run Macro	Macro: Print Trainer/Client Report
	Return to Main Switchboard	Go to Switchboard	Switchboard: Main Switchboard

The steps on the next page show how to create the switchboard pages.

To Create Switchboard Pages

1

- **Click the New button in the Switchboard Manager dialog box.**
- **Type `View Form` as the name of the new switchboard page.**

The Create New dialog box appears (Figure 6-25). The name of the new page is entered in the Switchboard Page Name text box.

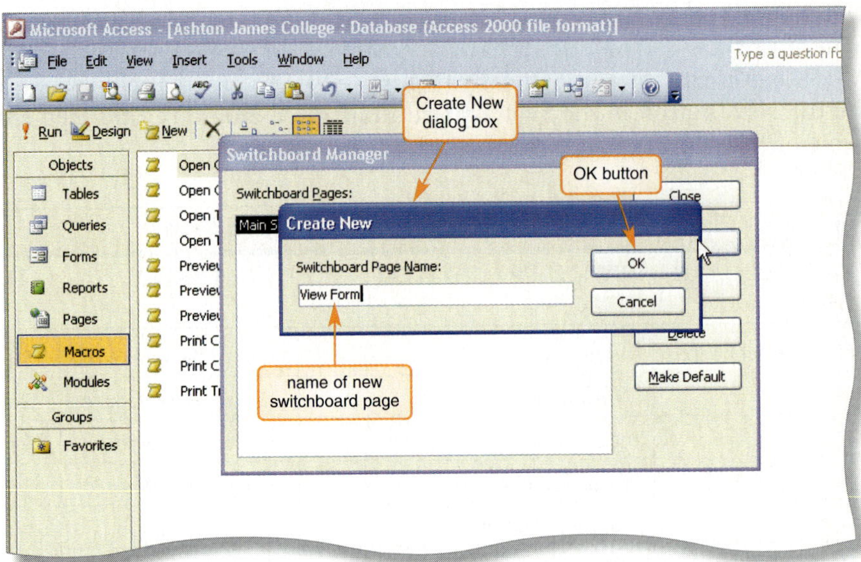

FIGURE 6-25

2

- **Click the OK button to create the View Form switchboard page.**
- **Use the same technique to create the View Table, View Report, and Print Report switchboard pages.**

The Switchboard Manager dialog box displays the newly created switchboard pages in alphabetical order (Figure 6-26).

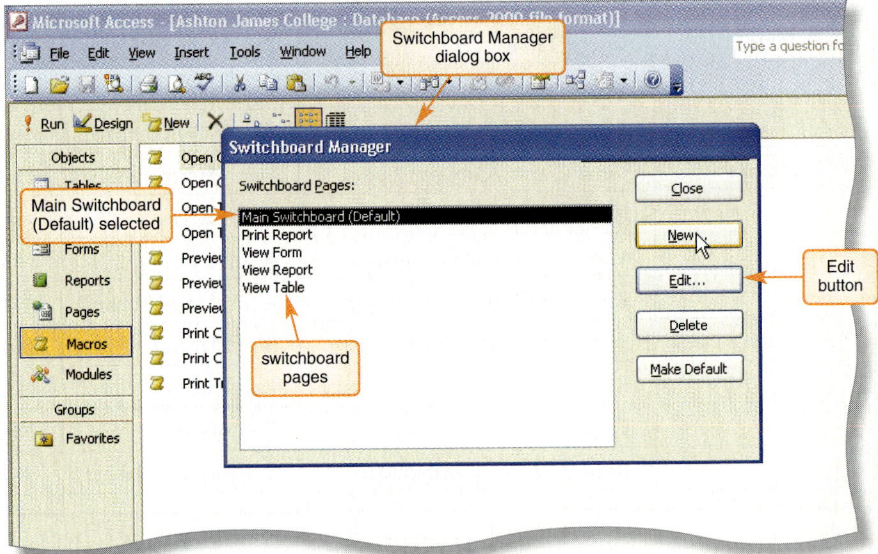

FIGURE 6-26

The switchboard pages now exist. Currently, there are no actions associated with the pages.

Modifying Switchboard Pages

You can modify a switchboard page by using the following procedure. Select the page in the Switchboard Manager dialog box, click the Edit button, and then add new items to the page, move existing items to a different position in the list of items, or delete items. For each item, you can indicate the command to be executed when the item is selected.

The following steps illustrate how to modify the Main Switchboard page.

To Modify the Main Switchboard Page

1

- **With the Main Switchboard (Default) page selected, click the Edit button.**

The Edit Switchboard Page dialog box appears (Figure 6-27).

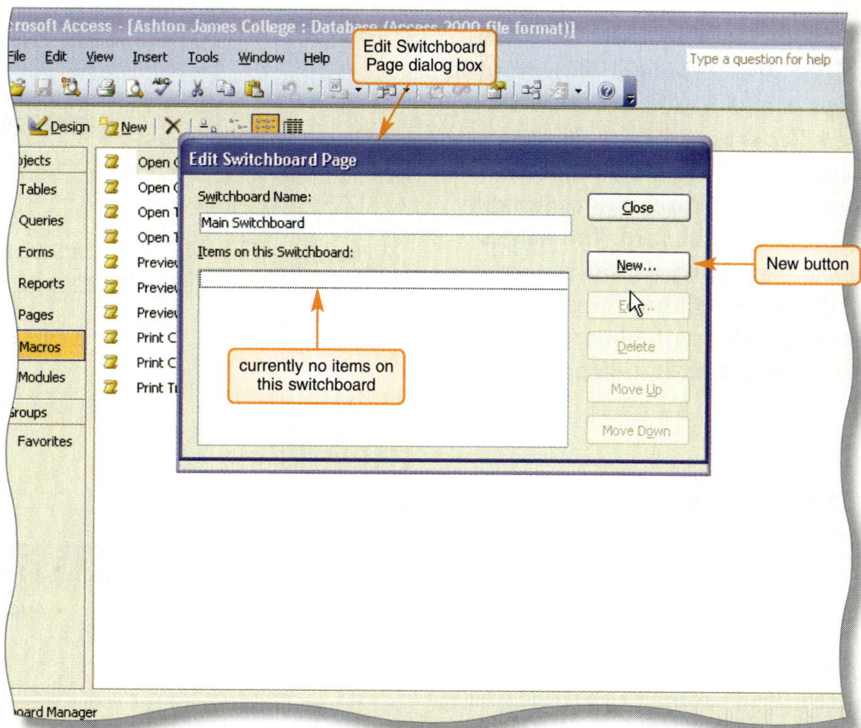

FIGURE 6-27

2

- **Click the New button, type `View Form` as the text, and then click the Switchboard box arrow.**

The Edit Switchboard Item dialog box appears (Figure 6-28). The text is entered, the command is Go to Switchboard, and the list of available switchboards appears.

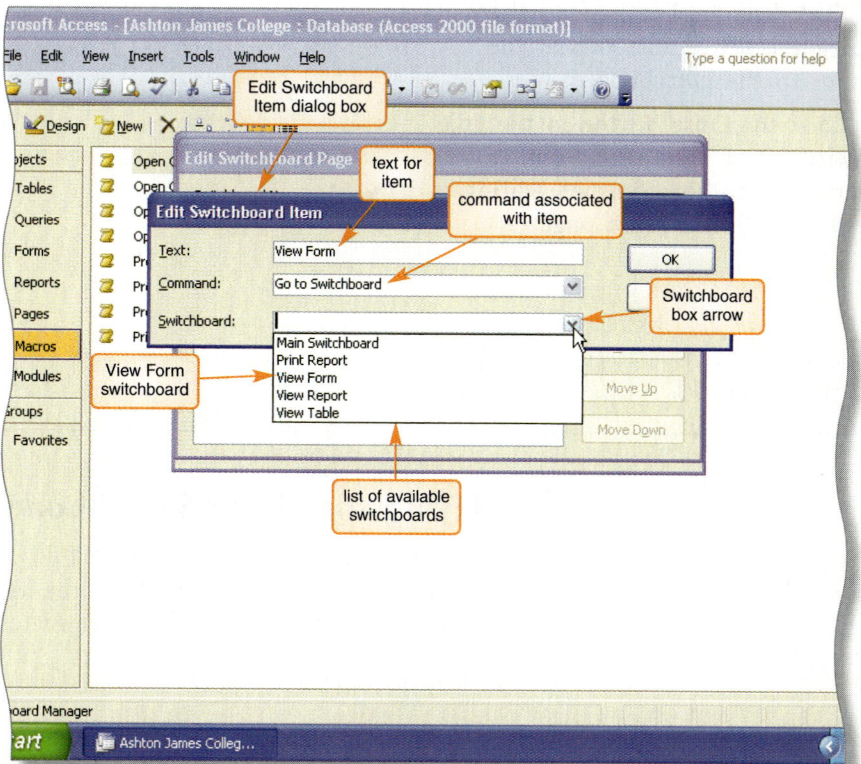

FIGURE 6-28

3

• **Click View Form and then click the OK button to add the item to the switchboard.**

4

• **Using the technique illustrated in Steps 2 and 3, add the View Table, View Report, and Print Report items to the Main Switchboard page. In each case, the command is Go to Switchboard. The names of the switchboards are the same as the name of the items. For example, the switchboard for the View Table item is called View Table.**

5

• **Click the New button, type** `Exit Application` **as the text, and click the Command box arrow.**

The Edit Switchboard Item dialog box appears (Figure 6-29). The text is entered and the list of available commands appears.

6

• **Click Exit Application and then click the OK button to add the item to the switchboard.**

• **Click the Close button in the Edit Switchboard Page dialog box to indicate you have finished editing the Main Switchboard page.**

The Main Switchboard page now is complete. The Edit Switchboard Page dialog box closes, and the Switchboard Manager dialog box appears.

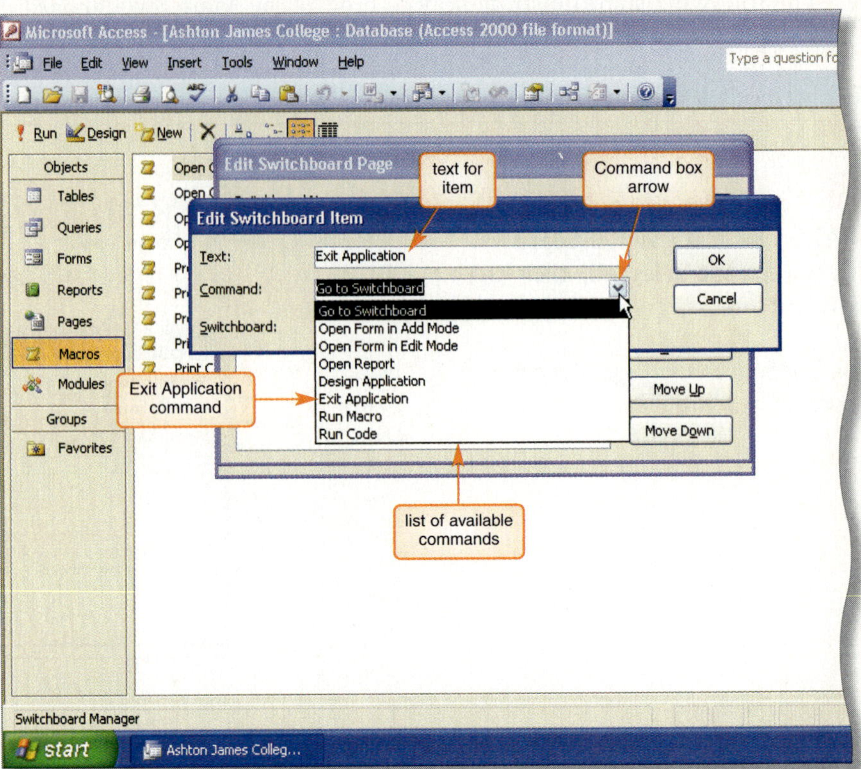

FIGURE 6-29

Modifying the Other Switchboard Pages

The other switchboard pages from Table 6-3 on page AC 331 are modified in exactly the same manner you modified the Main Switchboard page. The following steps illustrate how to modify the other switchboard pages.

To Modify the Other Switchboard Pages

1

- **Click the View Form switchboard page.**

The View Form page is selected (Figure 6-30).

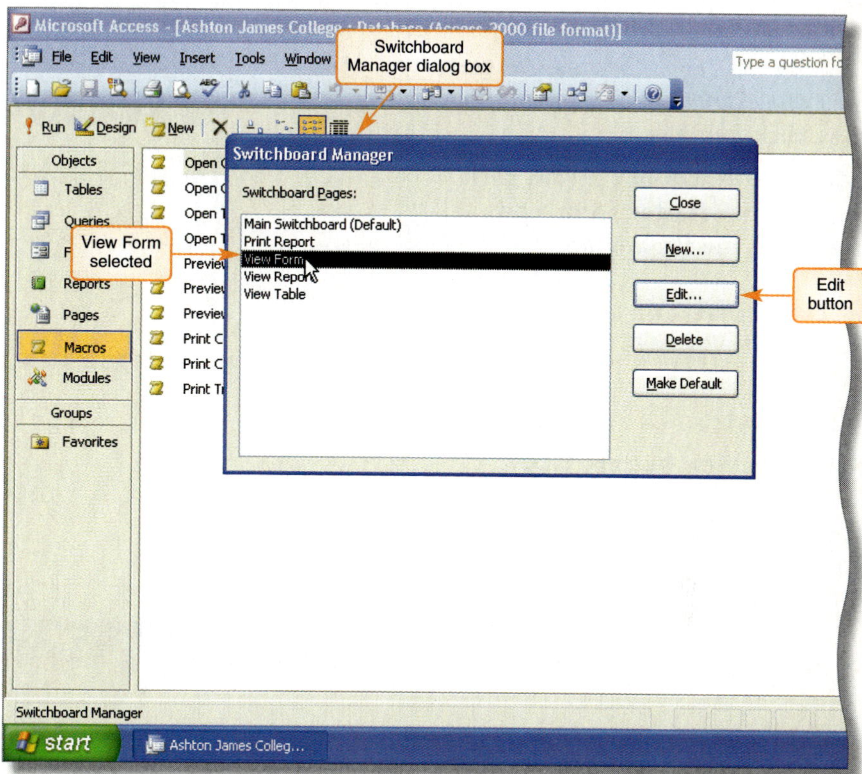

FIGURE 6-30

2

- **Click the Edit button, click the New button to add a new item, type** `Client Update Form` **as the text, click the Command box arrow, and then click Run Macro.**
- **Click the Macro box arrow.**

The Edit Switchboard Item dialog box appears (Figure 6-31). The text is entered and the command selected. The list of available macros appears.

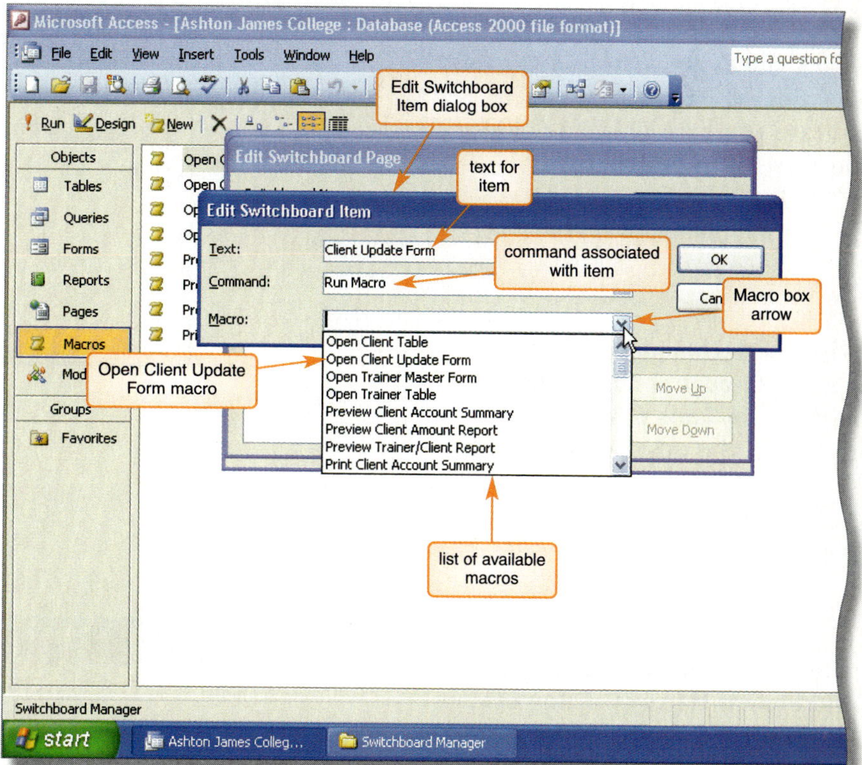

FIGURE 6-31

3

- **Click Open Client Update Form, and then click the OK button.**
- **Click the New button, type** `Trainer Master Form` **as the text, click the Command box arrow, and then click Run Macro.**
- **Click the Macro box arrow, click Open Trainer Master Form, and then click the OK button.**

The Client Update Form and Trainer Master Form items are added to the switchboard.

4

- **Click the New button, type** `Return to Main Switchboard` **as the text, and click the Switchboard box arrow.**

The text is entered and the list of available switchboards appears (Figure 6-32).

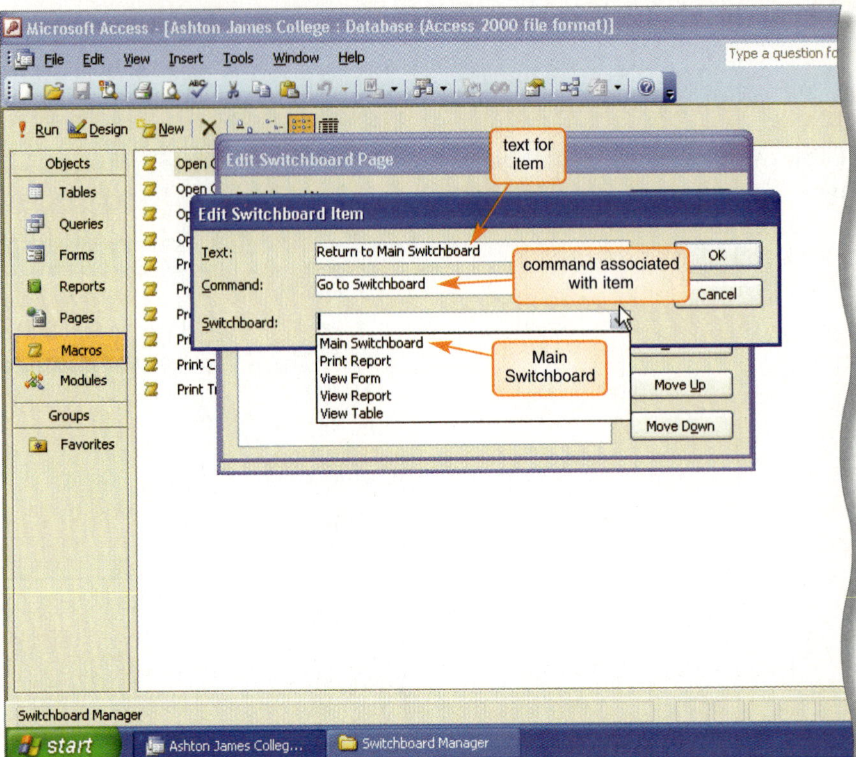

FIGURE 6-32

5

- **Click Main Switchboard in the list of available switchboards, and then click the OK button.**
- **Click the Close button in the Edit Switchboard Page dialog box to indicate you have finished editing the View Form switchboard.**

The View Form switchboard is complete.

6

- **Use the techniques illustrated in Steps 1 through 5 to add the items indicated in Table 6-3 on page AC 331 to the other switchboards.**

The Switchboard Manager dialog box appears (Figure 6-33).

7

- **Click the Close button in the Switchboard Manager dialog box.**

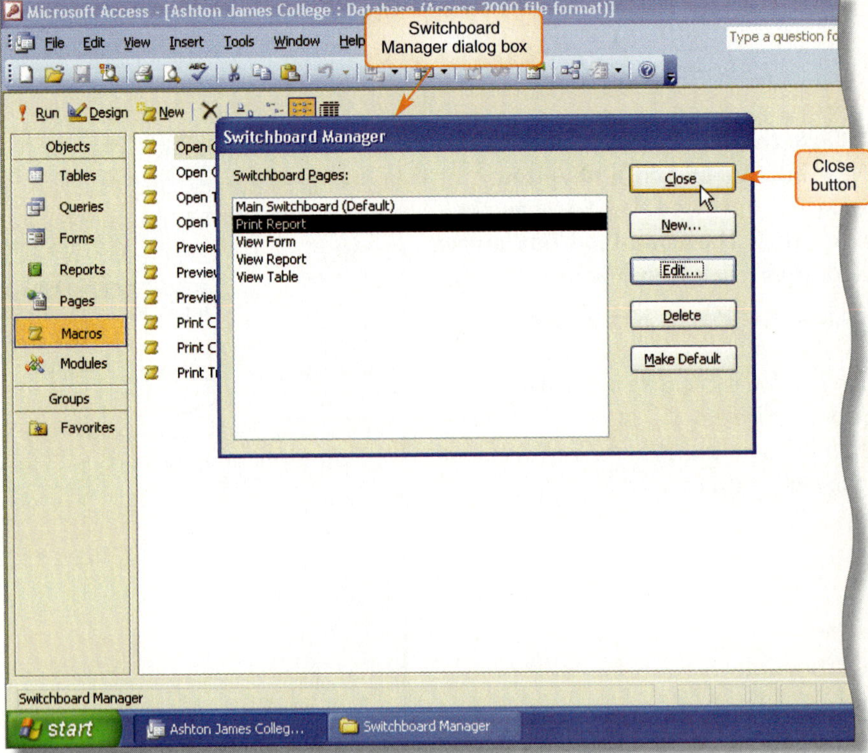

FIGURE 6-33

The switchboard is complete and ready for use. Access has created a form called Switchboard that you will run to use the switchboard. It also has created a table called Switchboard Items. *Do not modify this table.* Switchboard Manager uses this table to keep track of the various switchboard pages and items.

Q&A

Q: If the switchboard is a form, can I modify the switchboard by opening it in Design view?

A: Yes, but you should use the Switchboard Manager. If you make changes to the switchboard in Design view, the corresponding Switchboard Items table will not be updated and your switchboard may not function correctly.

Opening a Switchboard

To use the switchboard, select the Forms object, select the switchboard, and then click Open on the shortcut menu. The Main Switchboard then will appear. To take any action, click the appropriate buttons. When you have finished, click the Exit Application button. The switchboard will be removed from the screen, and the database will be closed. The following steps illustrate opening a switchboard system for use.

To Open a Switchboard

1

- **Click the Forms object and then right-click Switchboard.**

The shortcut menu for the Switchboard appears (Figure 6-34).

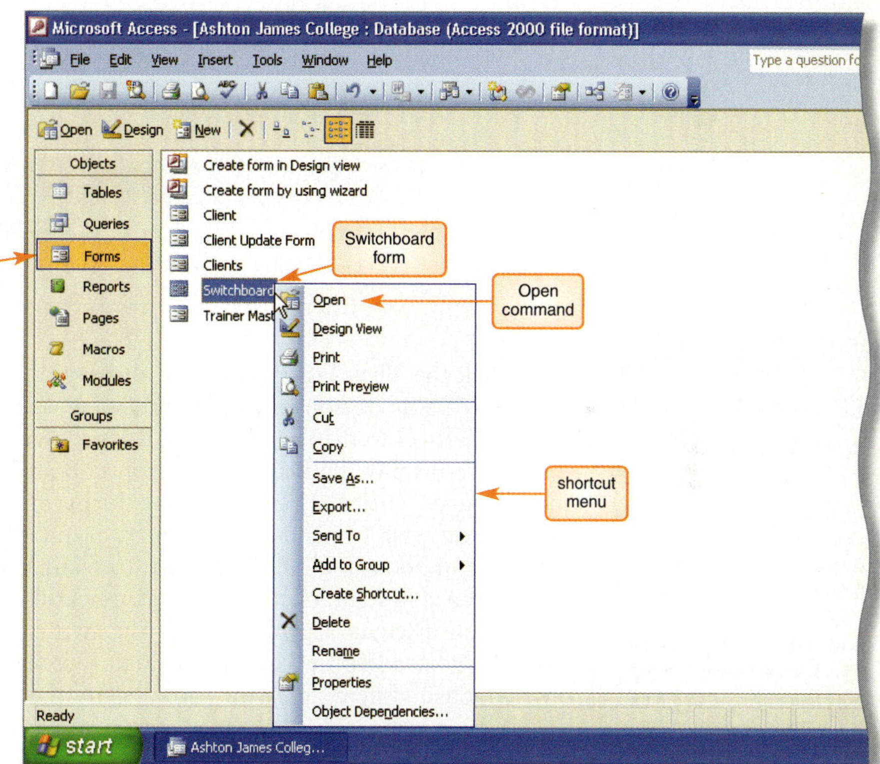

FIGURE 6-34

2

• **Click Open.**

The Main Switchboard appears (Figure 6-35).

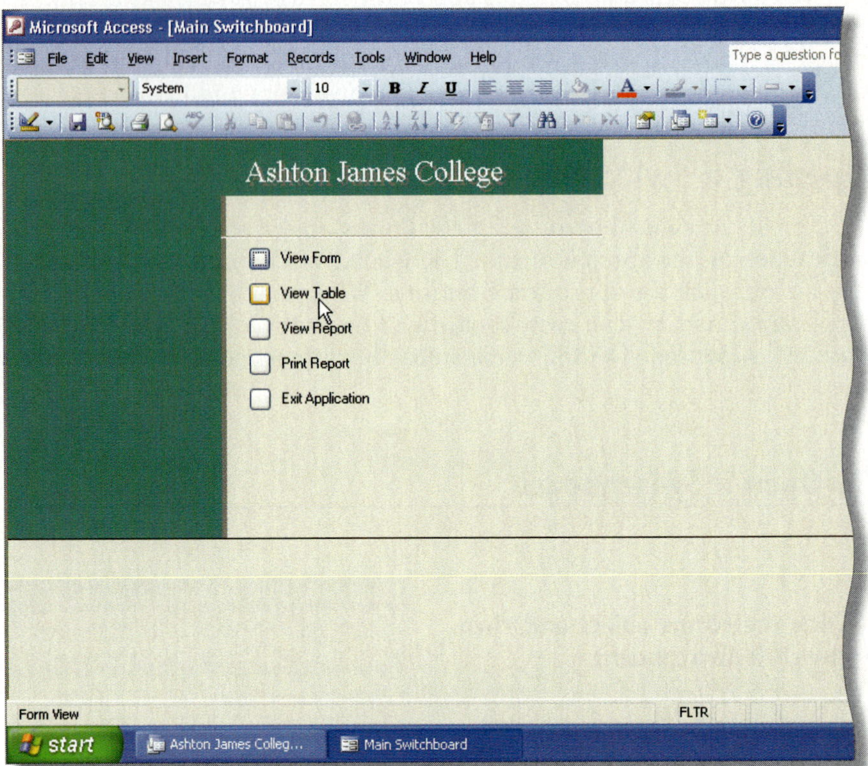

FIGURE 6-35

More About

Displaying Switchboards

It is possible to have the switchboard display automatically when the database is opened. To do so, point to Database Utilities on the Tools menu and then click Switchboard Manager. In the Switchboard Manager dialog box, select the switchboard you want to use as the default switchboard and then click Make Default.

Click the View Form button to display the View Form switchboard page. Click the View Table button to display the View Table switchboard page. Click the View Report button to display the View Report switchboard page. Click the Print Report button to display the Print Report switchboard page. On each of the other switchboard pages, click the button for the form, table, or report you wish to view, or the report you wish to print. To return from one of the other switchboard pages to the Main Switchboard, click the Return to Main Switchboard button. To leave the switchboard system, click the Exit Application button.

If you discover a problem with the switchboard, click Tools on the menu bar, click Database Utilities, and then click Switchboard Manager. You can modify the switchboard system using the same techniques you used to create it.

Closing the Switchboard and Database

To close the switchboard and the database, click the Exit Application button. The following step shows how to close the switchboard.

To Close the Switchboard and Database

1 **Click the Exit Application button.**

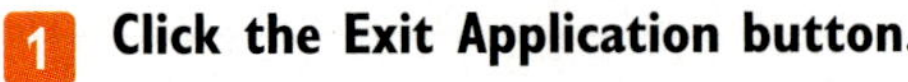

The switchboard is removed from the screen. The database closes.

Additional Tables

Before examining PivotTables and PivotCharts, you need to create the two additional tables. The first table, Course, is shown in Figures 6-36a and 6-36b. This table contains the specific courses that the trainers at Ashton James College offer to their customers. Each course has a number and a description. The table also includes the total hours for which the course usually is offered and the increments, that is, the standard time blocks in which the course usually is offered. The first row, for example, indicates that course 01 is called Integrating MS Office Programs. It typically is offered in 4 hour increments for a total of 16 hours.

Q&A

Q: Can I delete a switchboard?

A: Yes. To delete a switchboard, point to Database Utilities on the Tools menu and then click Switchboard Manager. In the Switchboard Manager dialog box, select the switchboard you want to delete and then click Delete.

Structure of Course Table

FIELD NAME	DATA TYPE	FIELD SIZE	PRIMARY KEY?	DESCRIPTION
Course Number	Text	2	Yes	Course Number (Primary Key)
Course Description	Text	50		Description of Course
Hours	Number			Hours for Typical Offering
Increments	Number			Number of Hours in Typical Session

(a)

Course Table

COURSE NUMBER	COURSE DESCRIPTION	HOURS	INCREMENTS
01	Integrating MS Office Programs	16	4
02	Long Documents with Word	8	4
03	Creating Forms with Word	6	6
04	Newsletters and Graphics with Word	6	6
05	Creating Custom Access Reports	12	4
06	Introduction to Computers	16	4
07	Preventing Pain and Injury at Your Computer	4	2
08	Importing, Exporting, and Linking Data	6	3
09	Presentation Authoring Using PowerPoint	16	4
10	Access Database Projects (ADP)	12	4
11	Excel Programming	24	4

(b)

FIGURE 6-36

The second table, Course Offerings, is shown in Figures 6-37a and 6-37b on the next page. Figure 6-37a, the structure, indicates that the table contains a client number, a course number, the total number of hours for which the course is scheduled, and the number of hours already spent in the course.

Structure of Course Offerings Table

FIELD NAME	DATA TYPE	FIELD SIZE	PRIMARY KEY?	DESCRIPTION
Client Number	Text	4	Yes	Client Number (Portion of Primary Key)
Course Number	Text	2	Yes	Course Number (Portion of Primary Key)
Total Hours	Number	-		Estimate of Total Number of Hours
Hours Spent	Number	-		Hours Already Spent

(a)

Course Offerings Table

CLIENT NUMBER	COURSE NUMBER	TOTAL HOURS	HOURS SPENT
BS27	06	16	4
BS27	03	6	3
CP27	04	6	0
CP27	02	10	4
FI28	01	16	12
FI28	05	12	8
FL93	06	16	8
HN83	05	12	8
HN83	08	6	2
HN83	11	24	12

(b)

FIGURE 6-37

Figure 6-37b gives the data. For example, the first record shows that client number BS27 currently has scheduled course 06 (Introduction to Computers). The course is scheduled for 16 hours, of which they have already spent 4 hours in class.

If you examine the data in Figure 6-37b, you see that the Client Number field cannot be the primary key. The first two records, for example, both have a client number of BS27. The Course Number field also cannot be the primary key. The first and seventh records, for example, both have course number 06. Rather, the primary key is the combination of both of these fields.

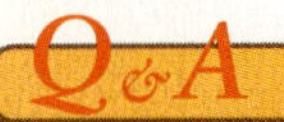

Q: What kind of relationship exists between the Client table and the Course table?

A: If the primary key of the Course Offerings table contains the primary keys for both the Client table and Course table, there is a many-to-many relationship between clients and courses. A client can take many courses and a course can be offered to many clients.

Creating the New Tables

The steps to create the new tables are similar to those you have used in creating other tables. The only difference is the way you specify a primary key consisting of more than one field. First, you select both fields that make up the primary key by clicking the row selector for the first field, and then holding down the SHIFT key while clicking the row selector for the second field. Once the fields are selected, you can use the Primary Key button to indicate that the primary key consists of both fields.

The following steps show how to create the tables.

To Create the New Tables

1

- **Click Open on the Database toolbar, and then click Local Disk (C:) in the Look in box. Click the Data folder, and then make sure the database called Ashton James College is selected.**
- **Click the Open button.**
- **If the Security Warning dialog box appears, click the Open button.**
- **Click the Tables object.**
- **Click the New button on the Database window toolbar, click Design View, and then click the OK button.**
- **Maximize the window.**
- **Enter the information for the fields in the Course table as indicated in Figure 6-36a on page AC 339.**
- **Close the window containing the table by clicking its Close Window button.**
- **Click the Yes button to save the changes.**
- **Type** `Course` **as the name of the table, and then click the OK button.**
- **Click the New button on the Database window toolbar, click Design View, and then click the OK button.**
- **Enter the information for the fields in the Course Offerings table as indicated in Figure 6-37a.**
- **Click the row selector for the Client Number field.**
- **Hold down the SHIFT key and then click the row selector for the Course Number field so both fields are selected.**
- **Click the Primary Key button on the toolbar.**

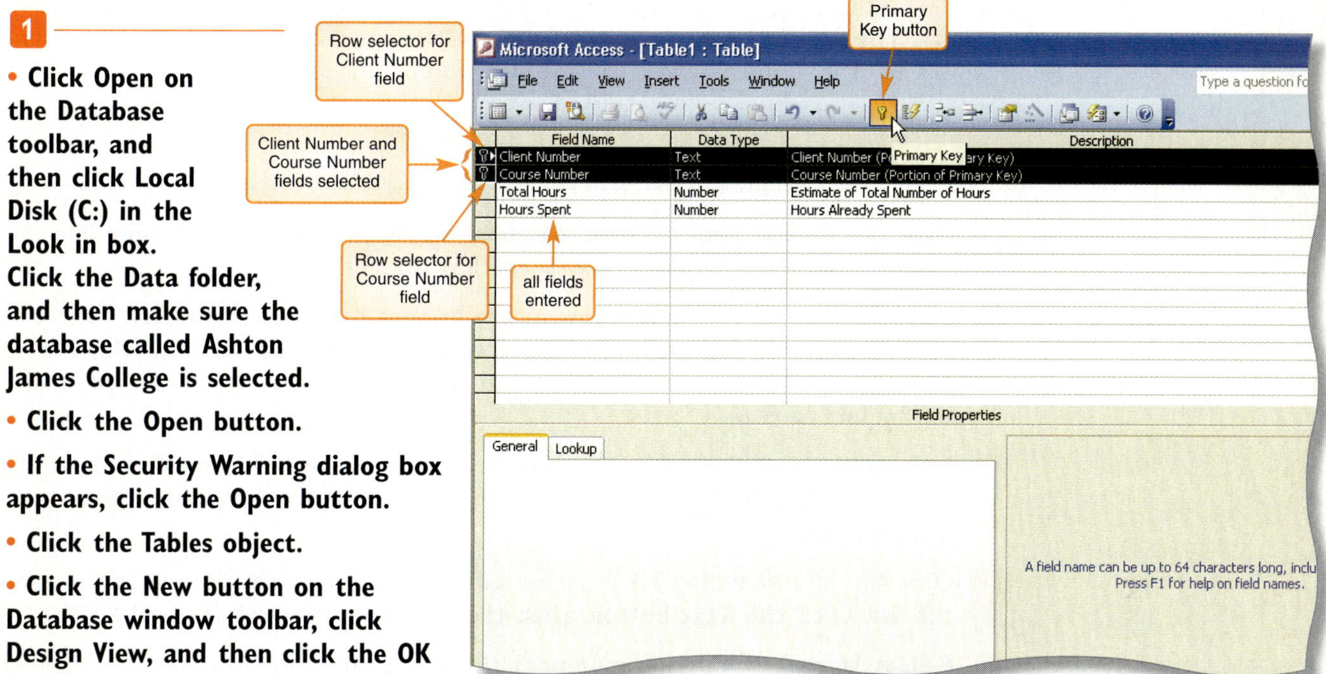

FIGURE 6-38

The primary key consists of both the Client Number and Course Number fields (Figure 6-38).

2

- **Close the window by clicking its Close Window button.**
- **Click the Yes button to save the table.**
- **Type** `Course Offerings` **as the name of the table, and then click the OK button to save the table.**

The tables now are created.

Importing the Data

Now that the tables have been created, you need to add data to them. You either could enter the data, or if the data is already in electronic form, you could import the data. The data for the Course and Course Offerings tables are on your Data Disk as text files. The following steps show how to import the data.

To Import the Data

1 **With the Ashton James College database open, click File on the menu bar, point to Get External Data, and then click Import.**

2 **Click the Files of type box arrow in the Import dialog box and then click Text Files. Select the location of the files to be imported (for example, the folder called Data on disk C). Make sure the Course text file is selected. Click the Import button.**

3 **Make sure the Delimited option button is selected and click the Next button. Click First Row Contains Field Names check box and then click the Next button again.**

4 **Click the In an Existing Table option button and select the Course table from the list. Click the Next button, click the Finish button, and then click OK.**

5 **Repeat Steps 1 through 4 to import the Course Offerings text file.**

The data for the Course and Course Offerings tables are imported.

More About

Editing Relationships

You can modify existing relationships between tables to change the relationships options such as cascading the update and cascading the delete. To do so, close any open tables in the database and then click the Relationships button on the toolbar. When the Relationships window appears, double-click the relationship line for the relationship you want to edit and then set relationship options.

Relating Several Tables

Now that the tables have been created they need to be related to the existing tables. The Client and Course Offerings tables are related through the Client Number fields in both. The Course and Course Offerings tables are related through the Course Number fields in both. The following steps illustrate the process of relating the tables.

To Relate Several Tables

1 **Close any open datasheet on the screen by clicking its Close button. Click the Relationships button on the toolbar. Right-click in the Relationships window and then click Show Table on the shortcut menu. Click the Course Offerings table, click the Add button, click the Course table, click the Add button again, and then click the Close button.**

2 **Drag the Client Number field from the Client table to the Course Offerings table. Click the Enforce Referential Integrity check box in the Edit Relationships dialog box and then click the Create button.**

3 **Drag the Course Number field from the Course table to the Course Offerings table. Click Enforce Referential Integrity check box and then click the Create button.**

4 **Drag the Course and Course Offerings tables to the positions shown in Figure 6-39. Click the Close Window button and then click the Yes button to save the changes.**

The relationships are created.

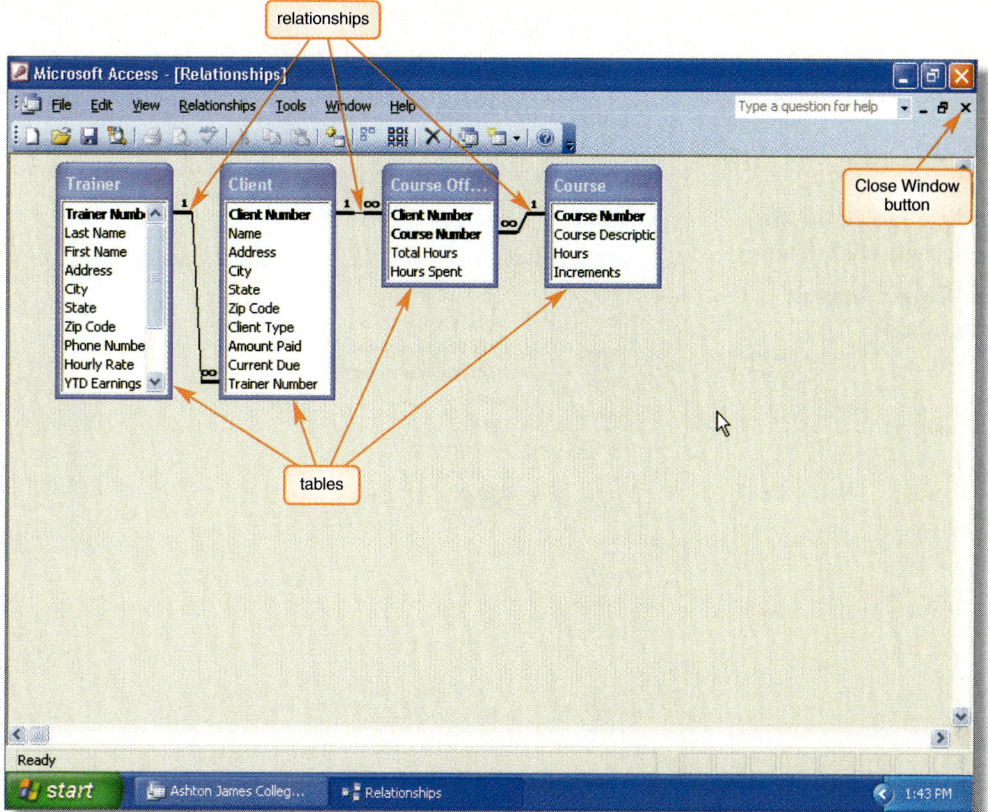

FIGURE 6-39

PivotTables and PivotCharts

There are two alternatives to viewing data in Datasheet view or Form view. **PivotTable view** presents data as a **PivotTable**, that is, an interactive table that summarizes or analyzes data. In a PivotTable, you can show different levels of detail easily as well as change the organization or layout of the table by dragging items. You also can filter data by checking or unchecking values in drop-down lists. PivotChart view presents data as a **PivotChart**, that is, a graphical representation of the data. In a PivotChart, just as in a PivotTable, you can show different levels of detail or change the layout by dragging items. You also can filter data by checking or unchecking values in drop-down lists. You can change the type of chart that appears as well as customize the chart by adding axis titles, a chart title, and a legend. In this section, you will create a PivotTable and a PivotChart. Both the PivotTable and the PivotChart are based on a query.

More About

PivotTables

You do not need to create a query to view fields in PivotTable view. To display data in a table in PivotTable view, open the table in Datasheet view, click the View button arrow on the Table Datasheet toolbar, and then click PivotTable View in the list.

Creating a Query

Because the PivotTable and PivotChart you will create will be based on a query, you first must create the query. The steps on the next page show how to create the necessary query.

To Create the Query

1

- **If necessary, click Tables on the Objects bar, and then click Trainer.**
- **Click the New Object button arrow on the Database toolbar.**

The list of available objects appears (Figure 6-40).

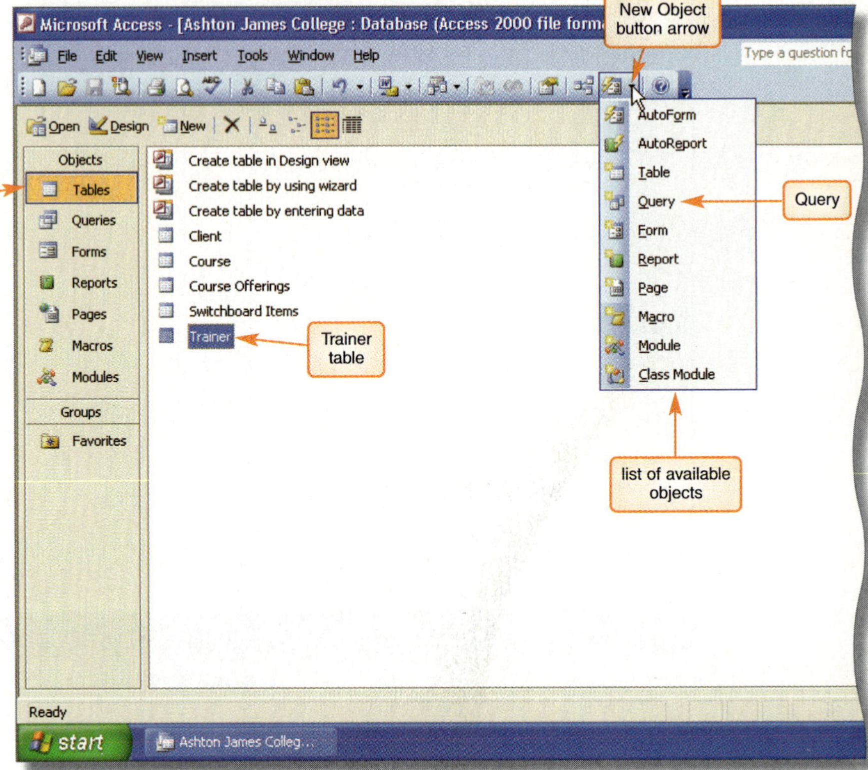

FIGURE 6-40

2

- **Click Query.**
- **Be sure Design View is selected, and then click the OK button.**
- **Be sure the Query1 : Select Query window is maximized.**
- **Resize the upper and lower panes and the Trainer field list so all the fields in the Trainer table appear.**
- **Right-click any open area in the upper pane, click Show Table on the shortcut menu, click the Client table, click the Add button, click the Course Offerings table, click the Add button, and then click the Close button in the Show Table dialog box.**
- **Resize the Client and Course Offering field lists so all the fields appear.**

The Trainer, Client, and Course Offering tables are included (Figure 6-41).

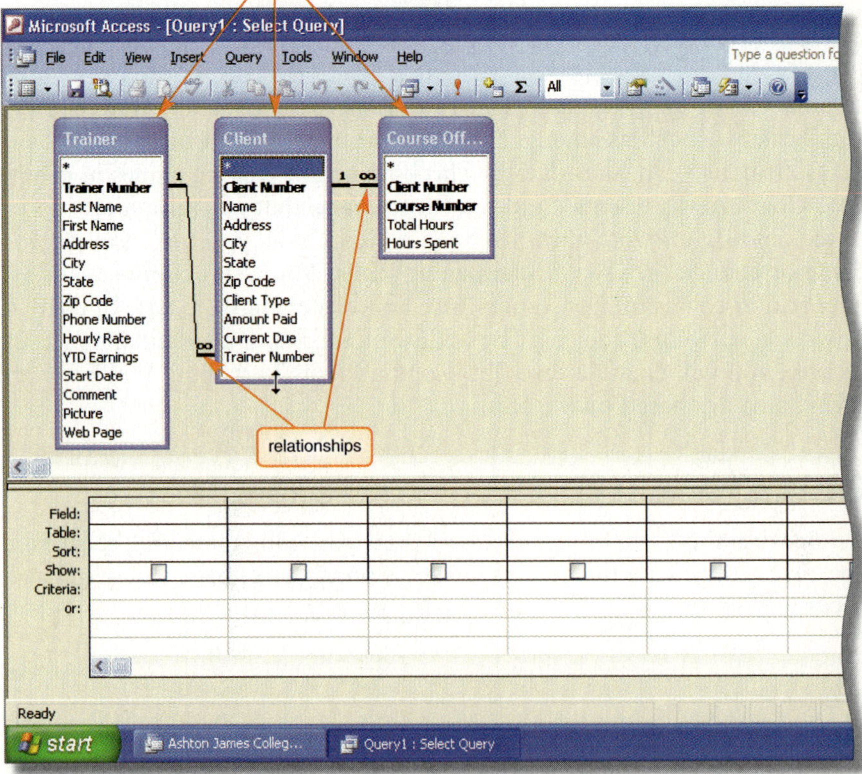

FIGURE 6-41

3

- **Double-click the Trainer Number field from the Trainer table and the Client Number field from the Client table.**
- **Double-click the Course Number and Hours Spent fields from the Course Offerings table.**
- **Right-click the Field row in the first open column.**

The fields are selected. The shortcut menu appears (Figure 6-42).

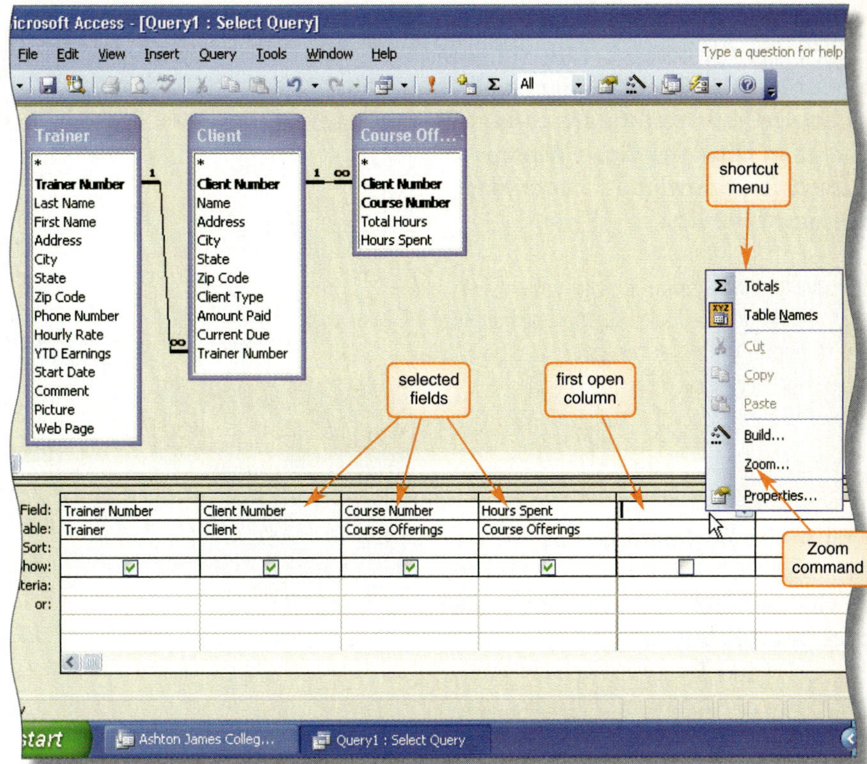

FIGURE 6-42

4

- **Click Zoom on the shortcut menu, type** `Hours Remaining:[Total Hours]-[Hours Spent]` **in the Zoom dialog box.**

The expression for Hours Remaining is entered (Figure 6-43).

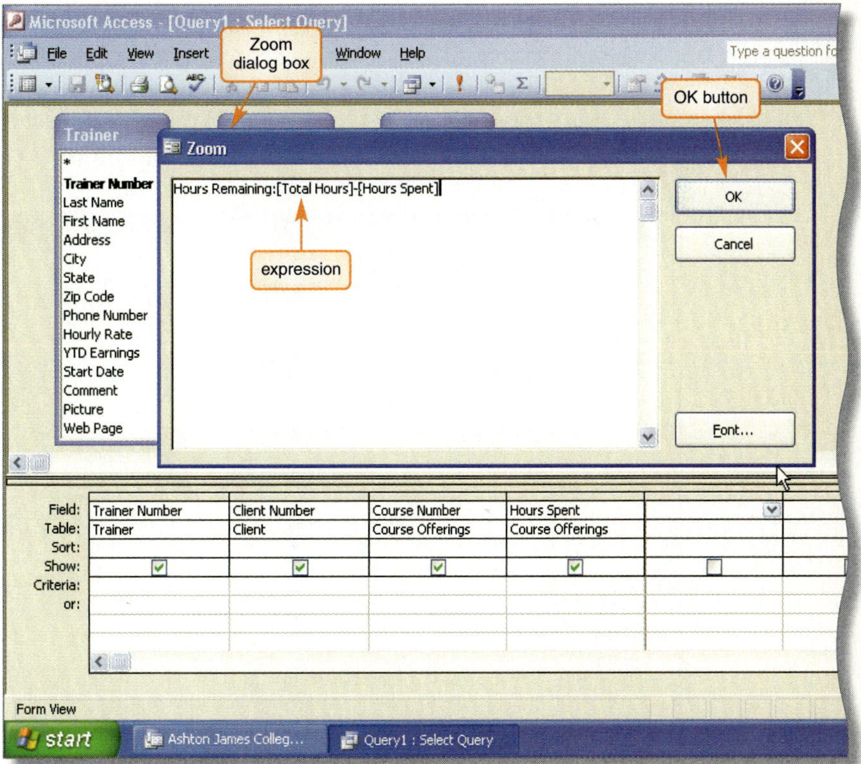

FIGURE 6-43

5

• **Click the OK button, click the Run button on the Query Design toolbar to ensure your results are correct, and then click the Close Window button for the window containing the query results.**

The query results appear (Figure 6-44). (If your results do not look like the ones shown in the figure, return to the query design and make any necessary changes, before attempting to close and save the query.)

6

• **Click the Yes button, type** `Trainers and Course Offerings` **as the name of the query, and then click the OK button.**

The query is saved and available for use.

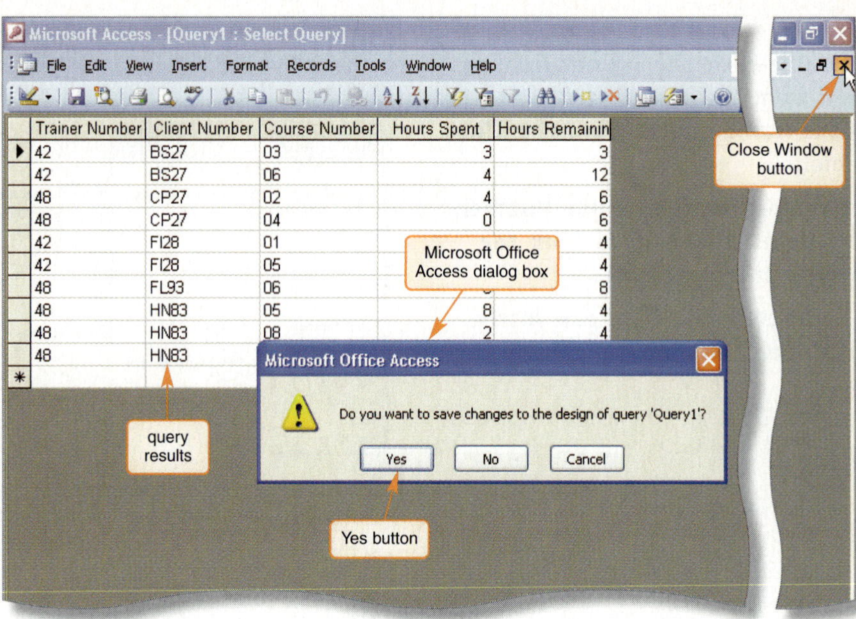

FIGURE 6-44

PivotTables

Figure 6-45 shows a sample PivotTable. The rows in the table represent the courses. The columns represent the trainer numbers. Each column is subdivided into the total of the hours spent and the total of the hours remaining for work orders for those clients assigned to the trainer. The last column shows the grand total for the items in each row. The last row shows the grand total for items in each column.

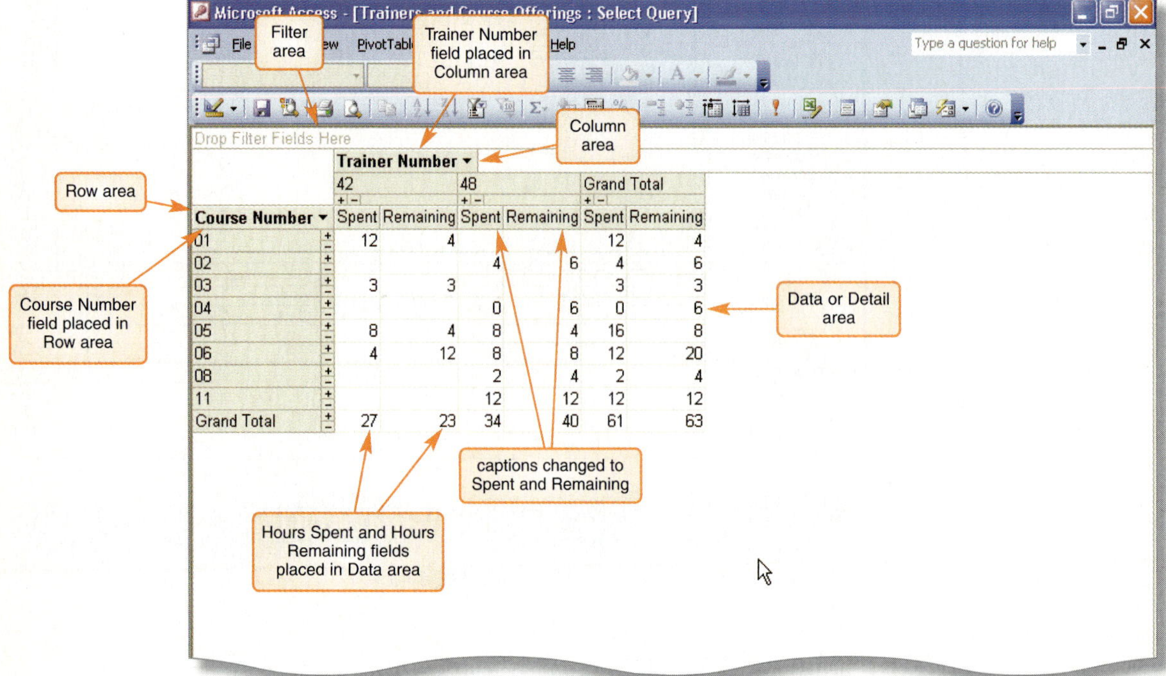

FIGURE 6-45

To create the PivotTable, you place fields in predefined areas of the table called **drop areas**. In the PivotTable in Figure 6-45, the Course Number field has been placed in the Row area, for example. The drop areas are listed and described in Table 6-4.

Table 6-4 PivotTable Drop Areas

AREA	PURPOSE
Row	Data from fields in this area will appear as rows in the table.
Column	Data from fields in this area will appear as columns in the table.
Filter	Data from fields in this area will not appear in the table but can be used to restrict the data that appears.
Detail	Data from fields in this area will appear in the detail portion (the body) of the table.
Data	Summary data (for example, a sum) from fields in this area will appear in the detail portion (the body) of the table. Individual values will not appear.

The following steps show how to create a PivotTable using the PivotTable view of the Trainers and Course Offerings query and how to place fields in appropriate drop areas.

To Create a PivotTable

1

- **Click Queries on the Objects bar, right-click the Trainers and Course Offerings query, and then click Open on the shortcut menu. If necessary, maximize the window.**
- **Click the View button arrow.**

The query appears in Datasheet view (Figure 6-46). The list of available views appears.

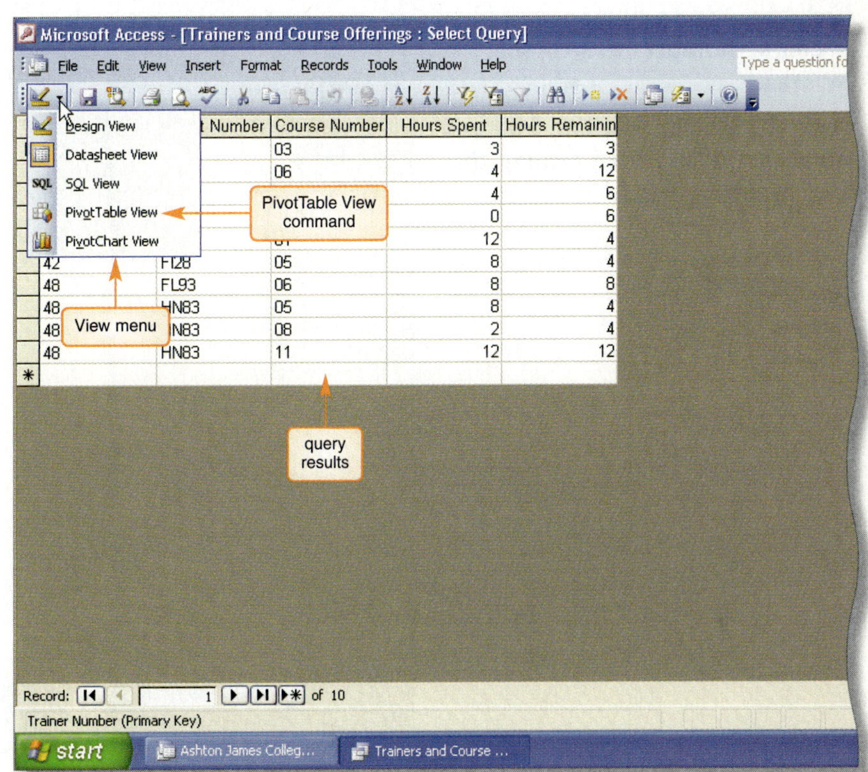

FIGURE 6-46

2

- **Click PivotTable View.**
- **If the PivotTable Field List does not appear, click the Field List button on the PivotTable toolbar to display the field list.**
- **Click Course Number in the field list, and then ensure Row Area appears next to the Add to button.**

The PivotTable appears (Figure 6-47). Course Number is selected in the field list and Row Area is selected.

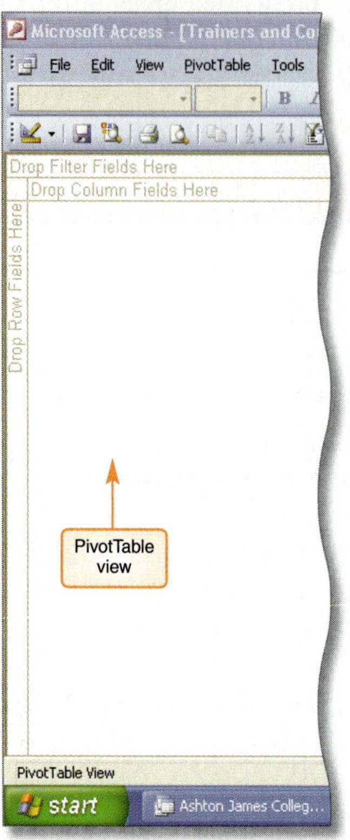

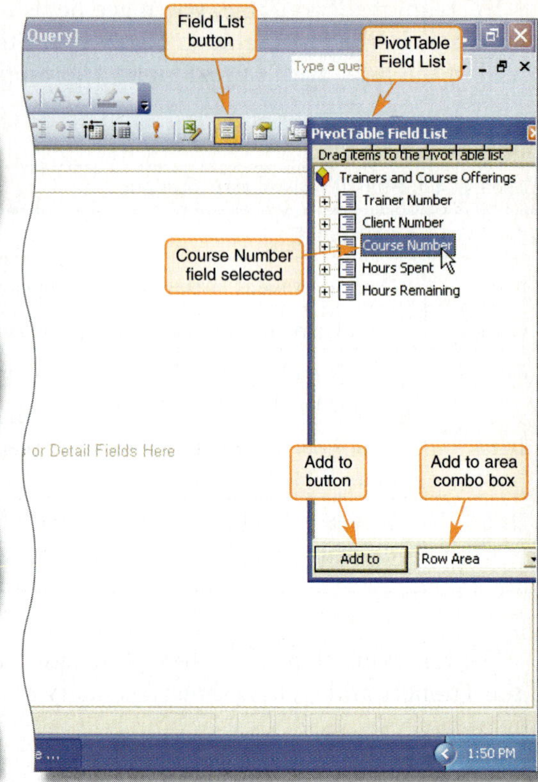

FIGURE 6-47

3

- **Click the Add to button to add the Course Number field to the Row area.**
- **Click the Trainer Number field and then click the arrow to display the list of available areas.**

The list of available areas appears (Figure 6-48). The Trainer Number field is selected.

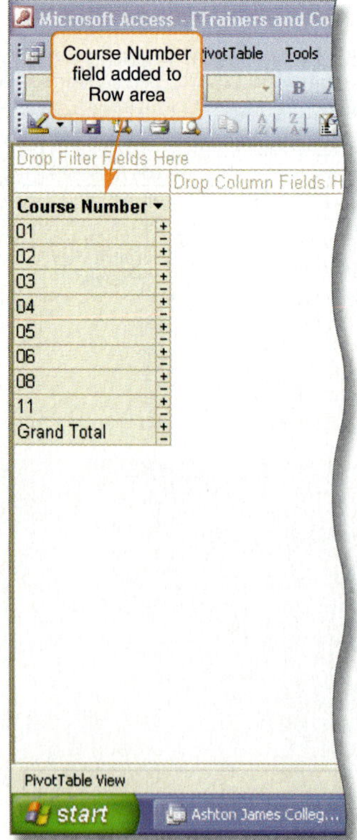

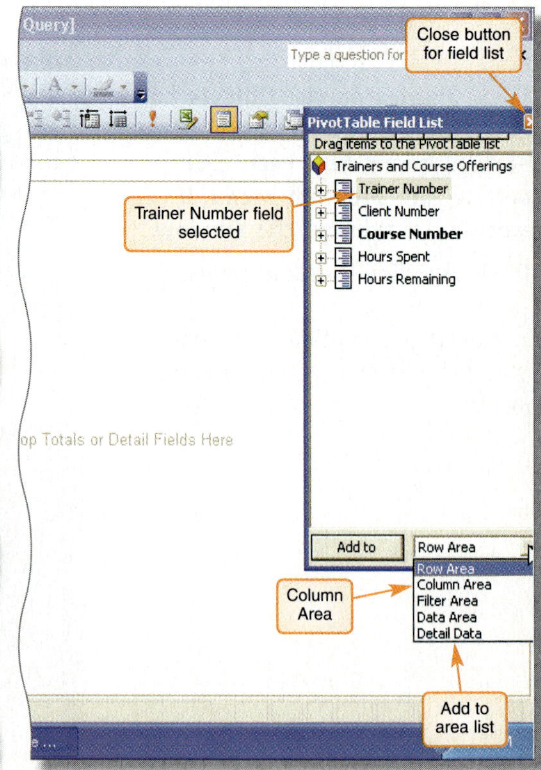

FIGURE 6-48

4

- **Click Column Area and then click the Add to button to add the Trainer Number field to the Column area.**
- **Click Hours Spent, click the arrow to display the list of available areas, click Data Area, and then click the Add to button to add the Hours Spent field to the Data area.**
- **Use the same technique to add the Hours Remaining field to the Data area. Close the PivotTable Field List by clicking its Close button.**

The fields have been added to appropriate areas of the PivotTable (Figure 6-49).

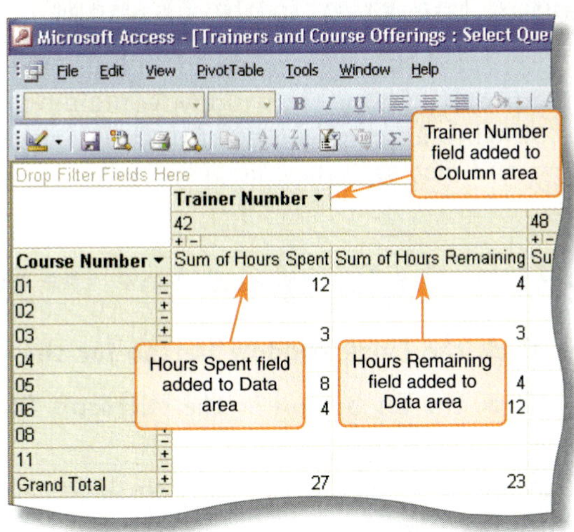

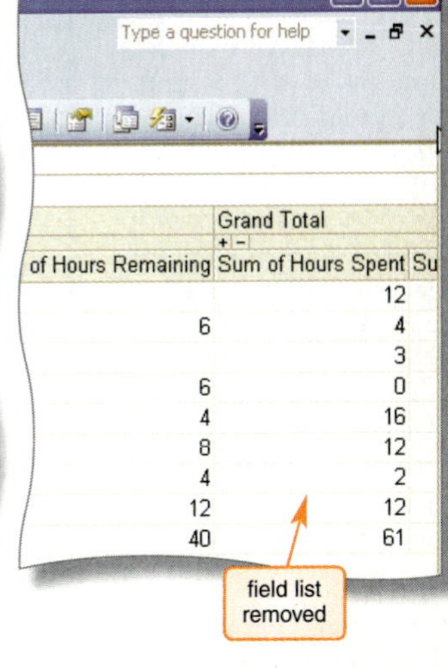

FIGURE 6-49

Other Ways

1. On View menu click PivotTable View
2. In Voice Command mode, say "View, PivotTable View"

Changing Properties in a PivotTable

You can use the property sheet for the objects in a PivotTable to change characteristics of the objects. The following steps show how to use the appropriate property sheet to change the caption for Sum of Hours Spent to Spent and for Sum of Hours Remaining to Remaining in order to reduce the size of the columns in the PivotTable.

To Change Properties in a PivotTable

1

- **Right-click the Sum of Hours Spent box, and then click Properties on the shortcut menu.**
- **Click the Captions tab in the property sheet.**

The property sheet and the Caption property appear (Figure 6-50).

2

- **Delete the current entry in the Caption property box, type** Spent **as the new value for the Caption property, and then close the property sheet.**
- **Use the same technique to change the caption for the Sum of Hours Remaining box to Remaining.**

The captions are changed.

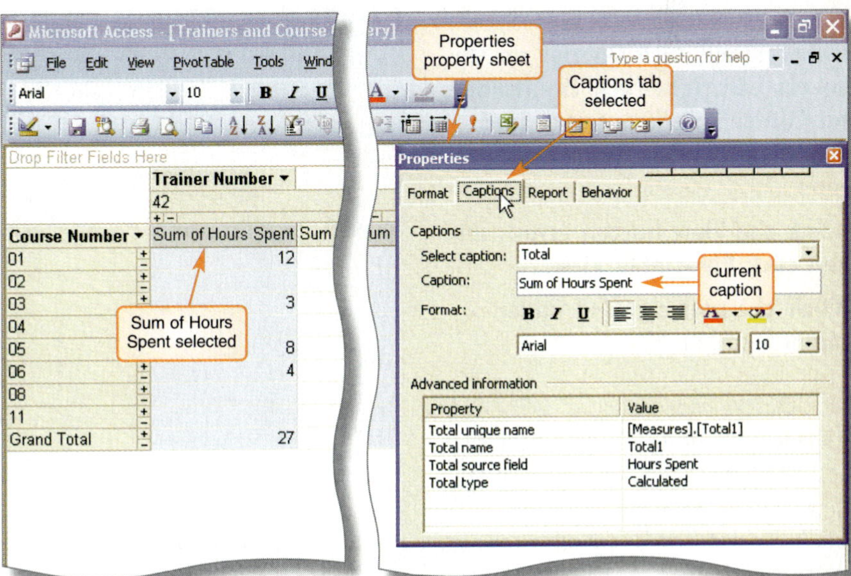

FIGURE 6-50

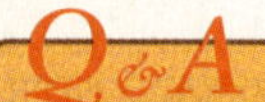

Q: In addition to changing captions, what other types of formatting changes can you make to a PivotTable?

A: You can format row, column, total, or detail areas as well as drop areas by aligning text in cells, and by changing the text's font, font size, and font color. You can bold, italicize, and underline text. You can change the format of numbers. You can change the background color for cells.

Saving the PivotTable Changes

To save the changes to the PivotTable view of the query, you save the query. You can do so, by closing the window containing the PivotTable and then clicking the Yes button when asked if you want to save your changes. The following steps close the query and then save the changes.

To Close the Query and Save the PivotTable Changes

1. **Click the Close Window button for the window containing the PivotTable.**
2. **Click the Yes button in the Microsoft Office Access dialog box.**

The changes to the layout of the query are saved. In particular, the changes to the PivotTable view of the query are saved.

Using a PivotTable

To use a PivotTable, you must open it. If the PivotTable is associated with a query, this would involve opening the query and then switching to PivotTable view. You then can click appropriate plus (+) or minus (-) signs to hide or show data. You also can click appropriate arrows and then check or uncheck the various items that appear to restrict the data that appears. You can drag items from one location to another to change the layout of the PivotTable. The following steps illustrate how to use the PivotTable view of the Trainers and Course Offerings query.

To Use a PivotTable

1

- **If necessary, click Queries on the Objects bar, right-click the Trainers and Course Offerings query, and then click Open on the shortcut menu.**
- **Click the View button arrow, and then click PivotTable View.**
- **Click the plus sign (+) under trainer number 42.**

The PivotTable appears (Figure 6-51). Data for trainer number 42 is hidden, that is, it does not appear. The column heading for trainer number 42 is changed to No Details. The captions for the other columns are changed to Spent and Remaining. By clicking the appropriate plus sign, you also can hide the data for course numbers or the Grand Total data.

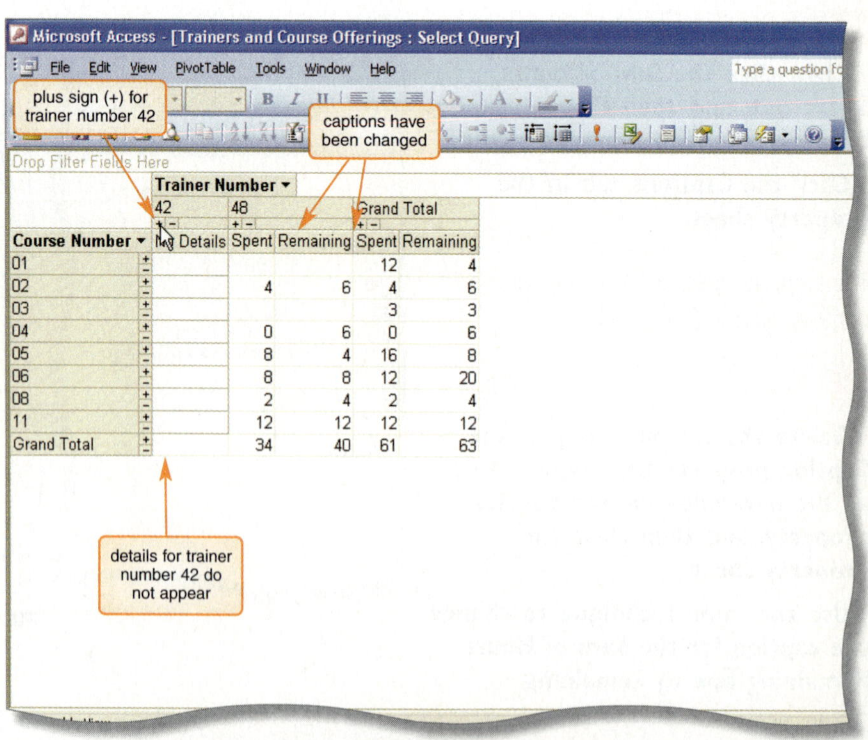

Course Number	42 No Details	48 Spent	48 Remaining	Grand Total Spent	Grand Total Remaining
01				12	4
02		4	6	4	6
03				3	3
04		0	6	0	6
05		8	4	16	8
06		8	8	12	20
08		2	4	2	4
11		12	12	12	12
Grand Total		34	40	61	63

FIGURE 6-51

2

- **Click the minus sign (-) under trainer number 42 to again display data for trainer number 42.**
- **Click the Trainer Number arrow.**

The list of available trainer numbers appears (Figure 6-52). Removing a check mark on a trainer number causes that trainer to be hidden, that is, the trainer number will not appear.

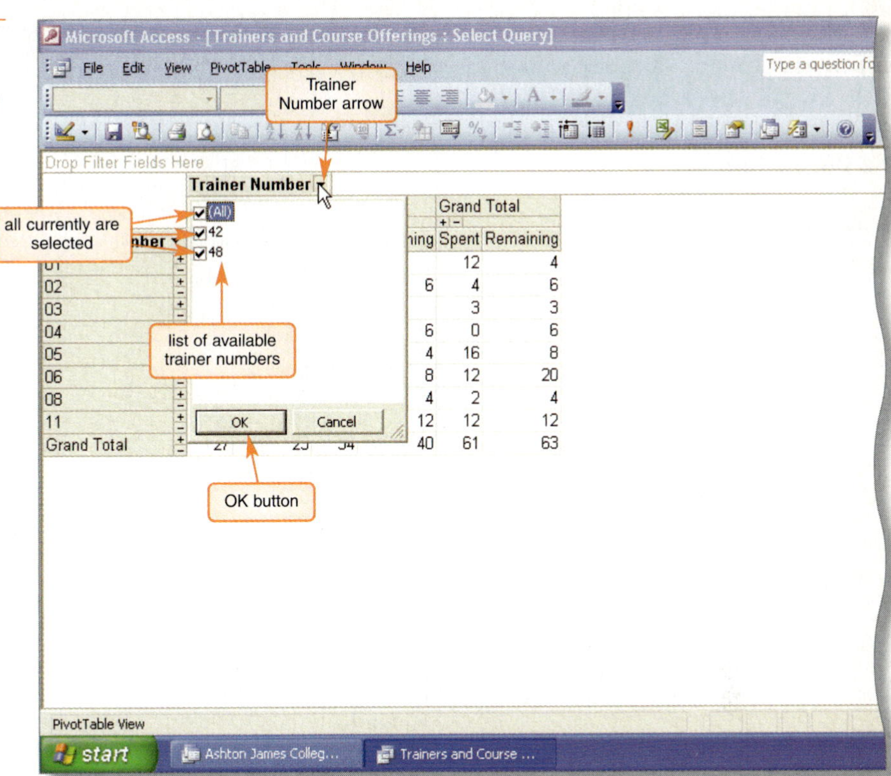

FIGURE 6-52

3

- **Click the Check box for trainer number 42 to remove the check mark, and then click the OK button.**

Trainer number 42 does not appear (Figure 6-53).

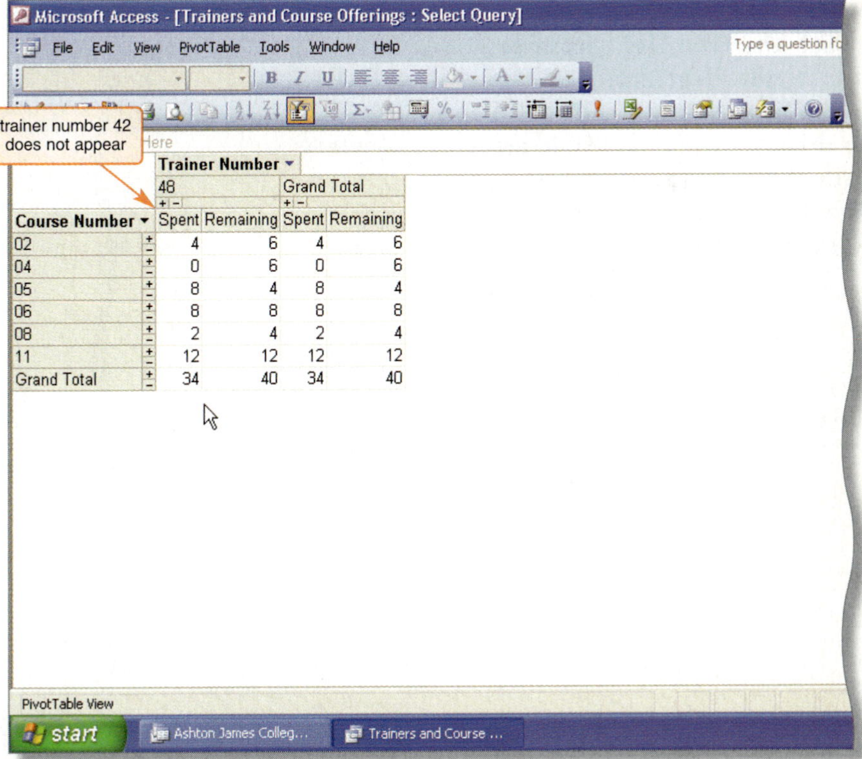

Course Number	48 Spent	48 Remaining	Grand Total Spent	Grand Total Remaining
02	4	6	4	6
04	0	6	0	6
05	8	4	8	4
06	8	8	8	8
08	2	4	2	4
11	12	12	12	12
Grand Total	34	40	34	40

FIGURE 6-53

4

- **Click the Trainer Number arrow, click the All check box to display all trainer numbers, and then click the OK button.**

All trainer numbers appear (Figure 6-54).

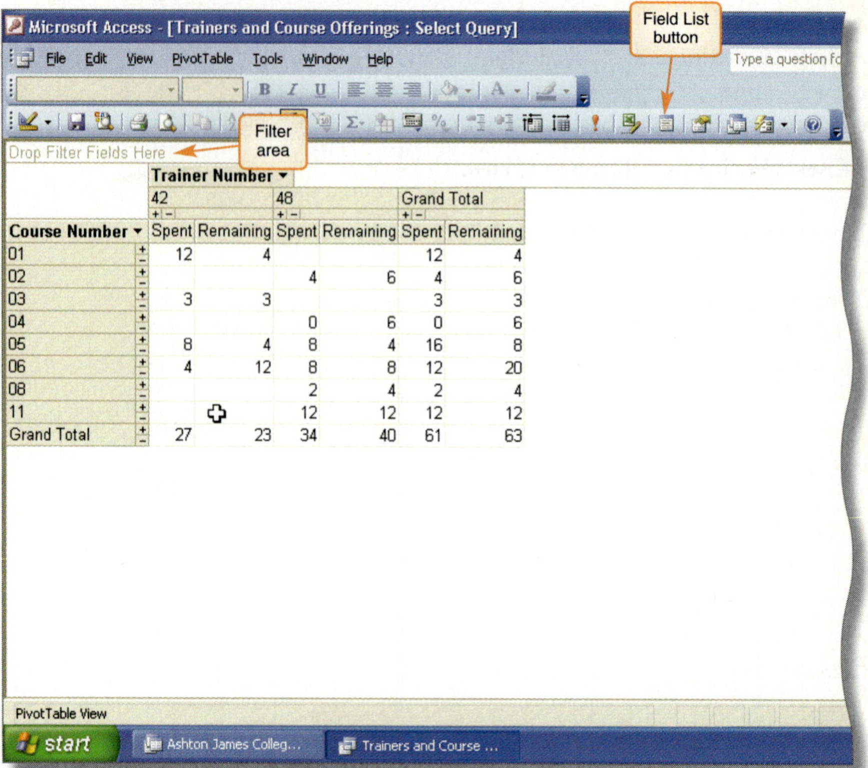

FIGURE 6-54

5

- **Click the Field List button to display the PivotTable Field List. Click Client Number, click the arrow to display a list of available areas, click Filter Area, and then click the Add to button to add the Client Number field to the Filter area.**
- **Click the Client Number arrow.**

The Client Number field is added to the Filter area (Figure 6-55). The list of client numbers used in the query appears.

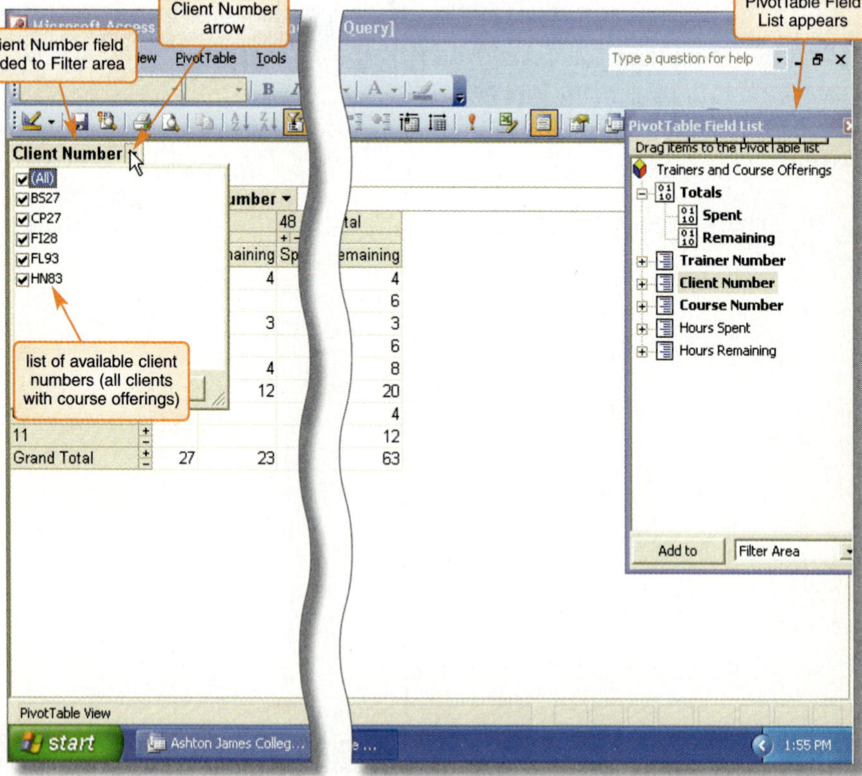

FIGURE 6-55

6

• **Click the check boxes in front of clients BS27 and CP27 to remove the check marks, and then click the OK button.**

The data appearing in the PivotTable is changed (Figure 6-56). The amounts for clients BS27 or CP27 do not appear.

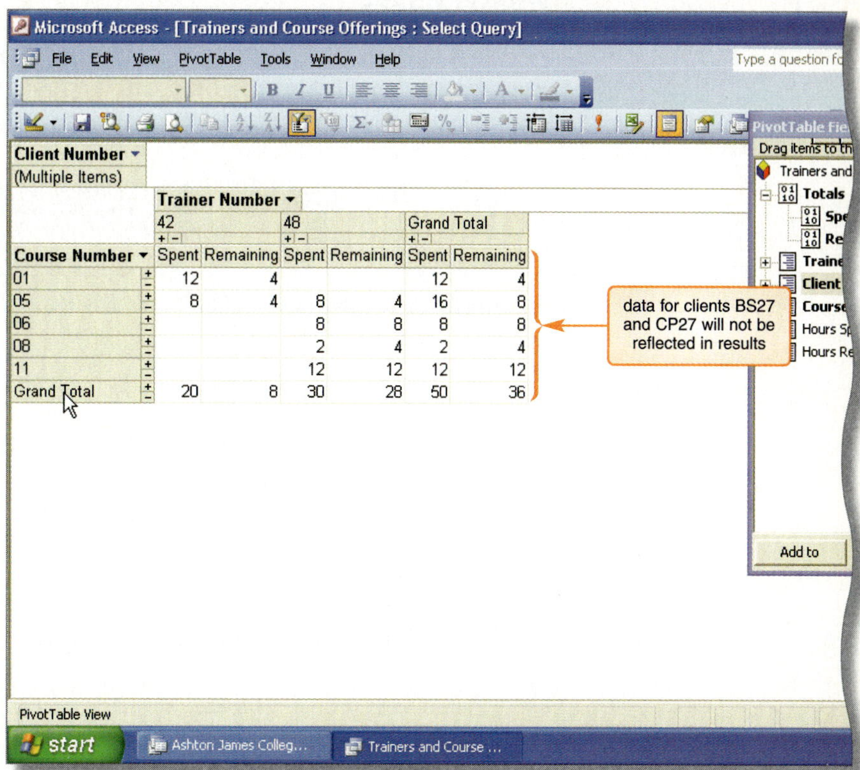

FIGURE 6-56

7

• **Click the Client Number arrow, click the All check box, and then click the OK button to display data for all clients.**

• **Drag the Trainer Number field from the Column area to the Row area, and then drag Course Number field from the Row area to the Column area.**

The rows and columns in the PivotTable are reversed (Figure 6-57).

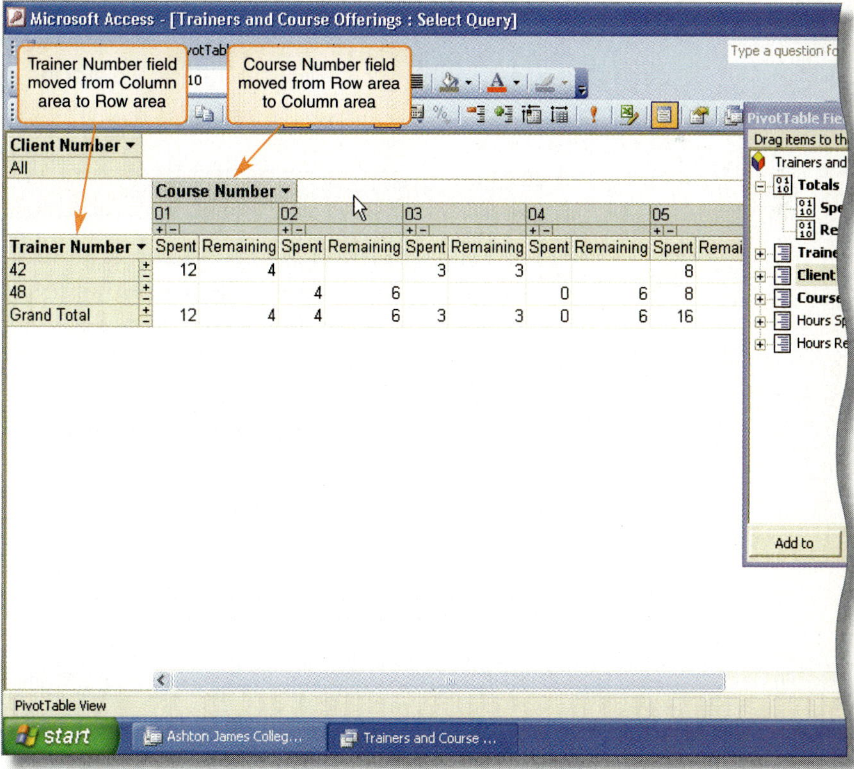

FIGURE 6-57

8

• **Click the Close Window button for the window containing the PivotTable.**

• **Click the No button when asked if you want to save your changes.**

The PivotTable is closed. The changes are not saved. The next time you open the PivotTable, the changes you just made will not be reflected.

PivotCharts

You can create a PivotChart from scratch by placing fields in appropriate drop areas just as you did when you created a PivotTable. The drop areas are shown in Figure 6-58. Their purpose is described in Table 6-5.

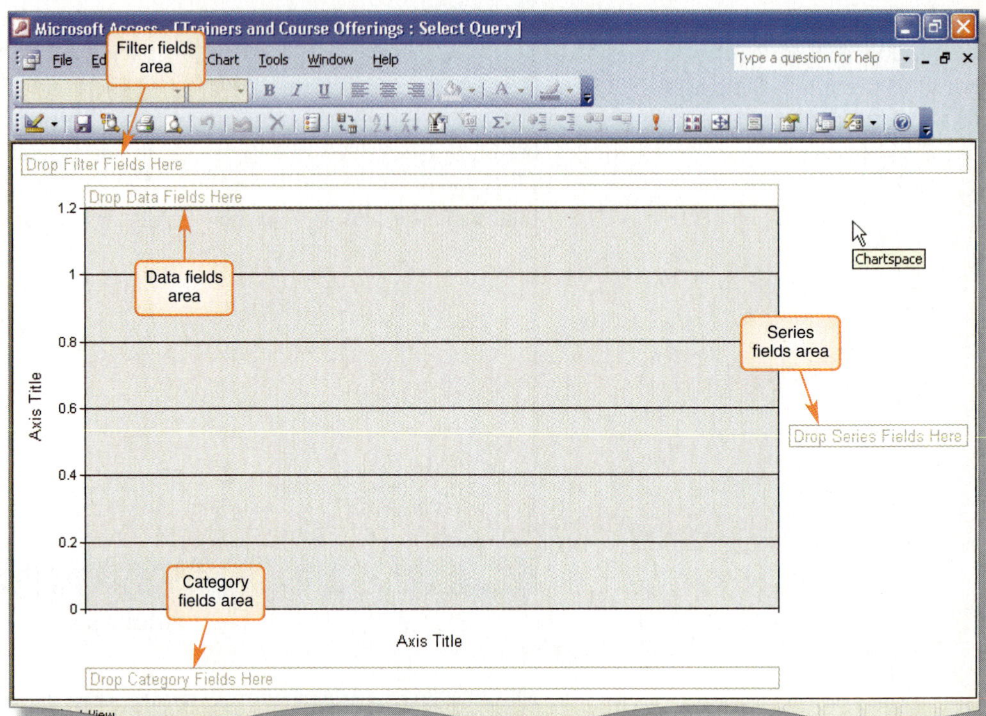

FIGURE 6-58

Table 6-5 PivotChart Drop Areas

AREA	PURPOSE
Series	Data from fields in this area will appear as data series, which are represented by colored data markers such as bars. Related markers constitute a series and are assigned a specific color. The names and colors appear in the chart legend.
Category	Data from fields in this area will appear as categories, that is, related groups of data. Category labels appear across the x-axis (horizontal) of the chart provided the graph type selected has such an axis.
Filter	Data from fields in this area will not appear in the chart but can be used to restrict the data that appears.
Data	Data from fields in this area will be summarized within the chart.

If you are using the PivotChart view of a table or query and already have modified the PivotTable view, much of this work already is done. The same information is used wherever possible. You can, of course, modify any aspect of this information. You can remove fields from drop areas by clicking the field name and then pressing the DELETE key. You can add fields to drop areas just as you did with the PivotTable. You also can make other changes, including adding a legend, changing the chart type, changing captions, and adding titles.

The following steps show how to create a PivotChart using PivotChart view of the Trainers and Course Offerings query and then add a legend.

To Create a PivotChart and Add a Legend

1

- **If necessary, click Queries on the Objects bar, right-click the Trainers and Course Offerings query, and then click Open on the shortcut menu.**
- **Click the View button arrow, and then click PivotChart View.**
- **If the Chart Field List appears, close the field list by clicking its Close button.**

The PivotChart appears (Figure 6-59). It represents the same data specified in the PivotTable.

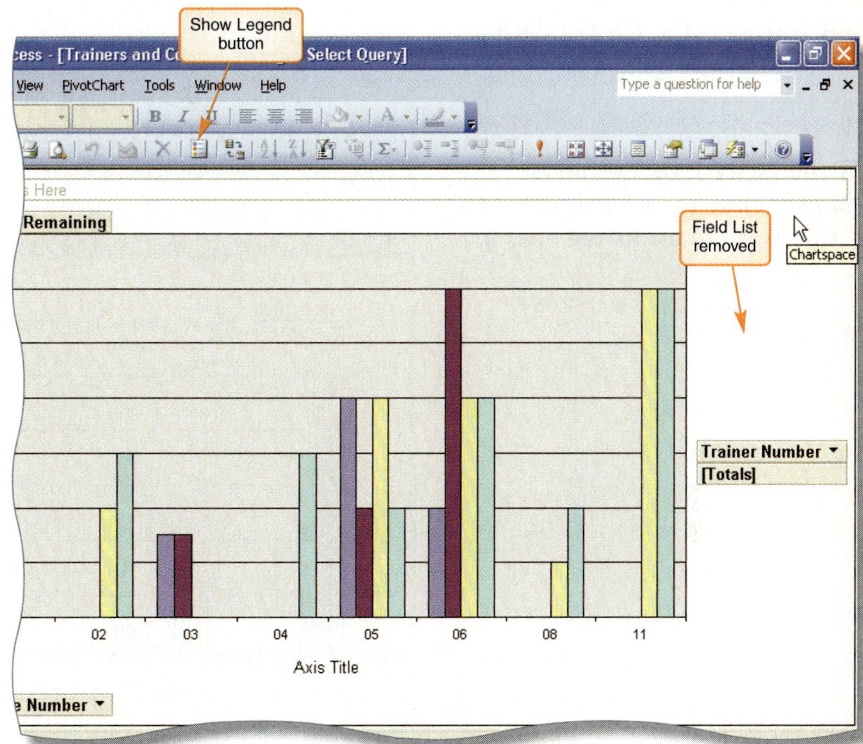

FIGURE 6-59

2

- **Click the Show Legend button.**

A legend appears (Figure 6-60).

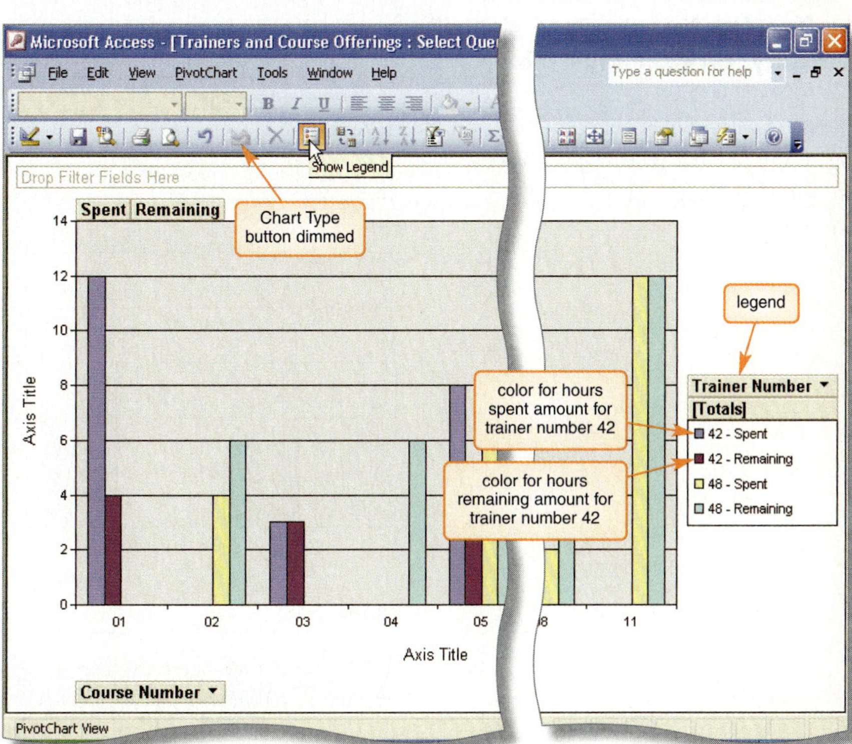

FIGURE 6-60

Changing the Chart Type

Several types of charts are available. To change the chart type, use the Chart Type button, and then select the desired chart type. The following steps illustrate how to change the chart type to 3D Stacked Column.

To Change the Chart Type

1

• **If the Chart Type button is dimmed, click the Chartspace (that is, the white space in the chart).**

The Chart Type button is available (Figure 6-61).

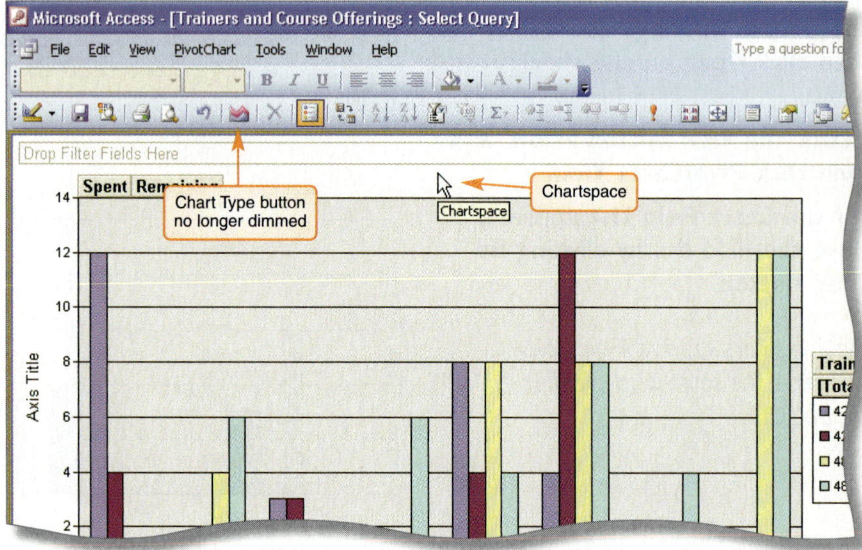

FIGURE 6-61

2

• **Click the Chart Type button on the PivotChart toolbar, and then, if necessary, click the Type tab.**

The list of graph types appears (Figure 6-62). (Your graph types may be arranged differently). The Type tab is selected.

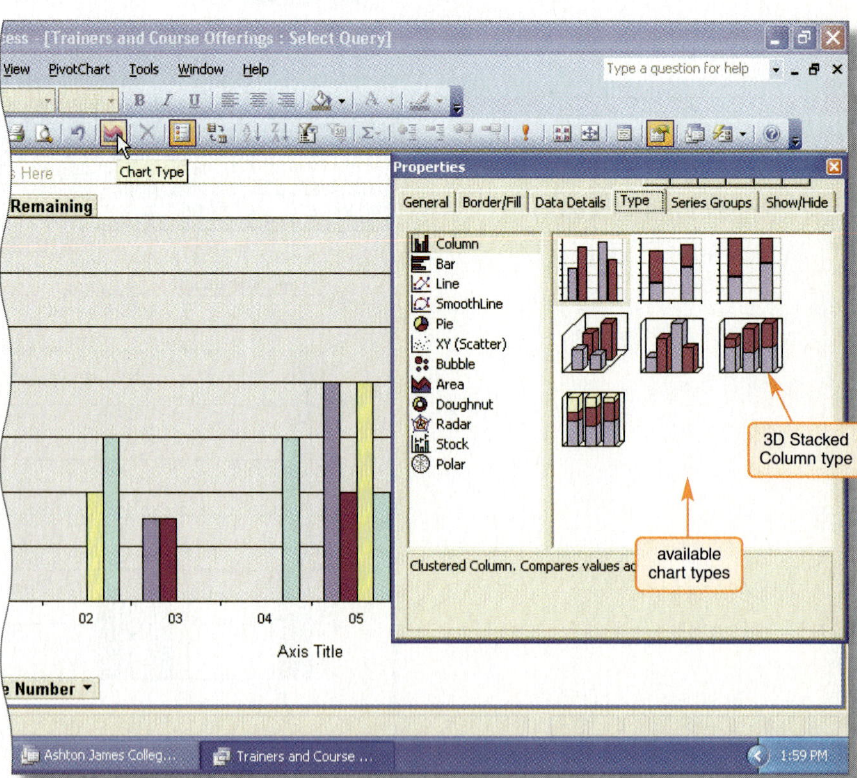

FIGURE 6-62

3

- **Click the 3D Stacked Column type, and then close the Properties window.**

The chart type is changed to 3D Stacked Column (Figure 6-63).

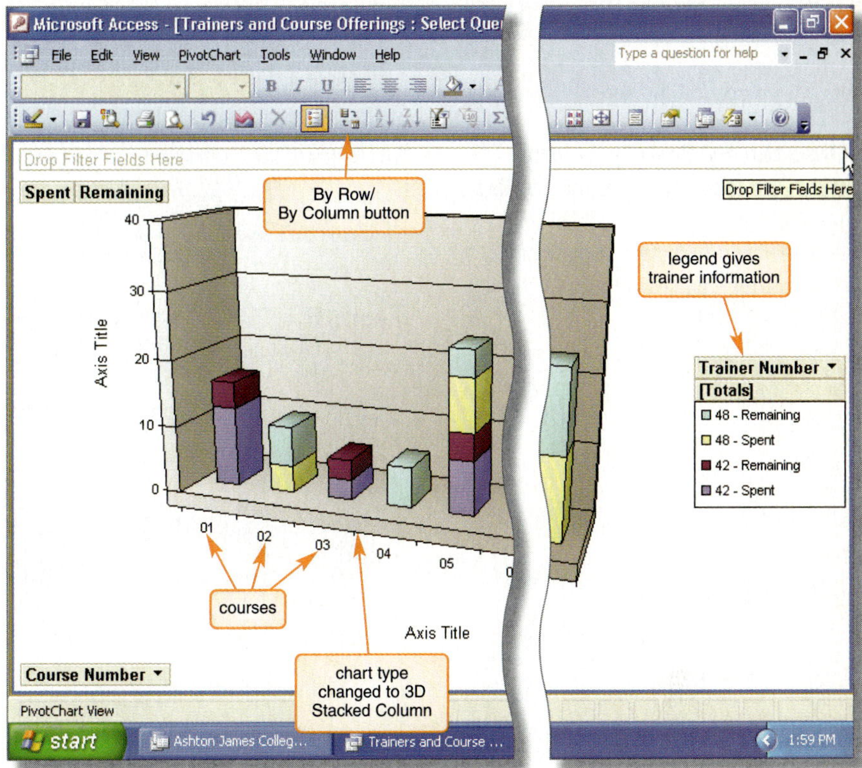

FIGURE 6-63

Changing PivotChart Organization

The chart in Figure 6-63 has the Course numbers along the horizontal axis and trainer numbers in the legend. The heights of the bars represent the total number of hours for each course. Within a bar, the colors represent the trainer and whether the amount represents hours remaining or hours spent (see legend). To change the orientation, you can click the By Row/By Column button. The step on the next page shows how to change the orientation so the trainer numbers appear along the horizontal axis and the courses appear in the legend.

More About

PivotCharts

You do not need to create a query to view fields in PivotChart view. To display data in a table in PivotChart view, open the table in Datasheet view, click the View button arrow on the Table Datasheet toolbar, and then click PivotChart View in the list.

To Change PivotChart Organization

1

• **Click the By Row/By Column button on the PivotChart toolbar.**

The trainer numbers now appear along the x-axis and the courses appear in the legend (Figure 6-64).

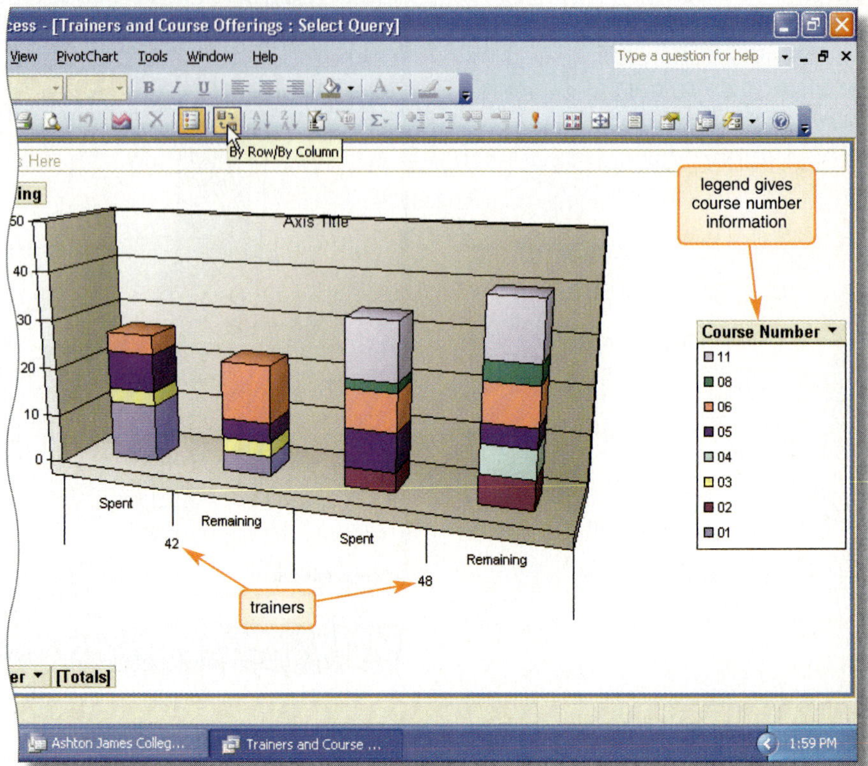

FIGURE 6-64

Assigning Axis Titles

You can assign titles to an axis by right-clicking the Axis Title box for the axis you want to change, selecting Properties on the shortcut menu, and then changing the Caption property to the title you want to assign. The following steps illustrate how to change the two axis titles to Hours and Trainer.

To Assign Axis Titles

1

- **Right-click the axis title to the left of the chart, and then click Properties on the shortcut menu.**
- **Click the Format tab in the Properties window, and then click the Caption box.**
- **Use the BACKSPACE or DELETE key to delete the old caption.**
- **Type** `Hours` **as the new caption.**

The Properties property sheet appears (Figure 6-65). Your font properties may be different. The caption is changed to Hours.

2

- **Close the property sheet to complete the change of the axis title.**
- **Use the same technique to change the other axis title to Trainer.**

The axis titles are changed.

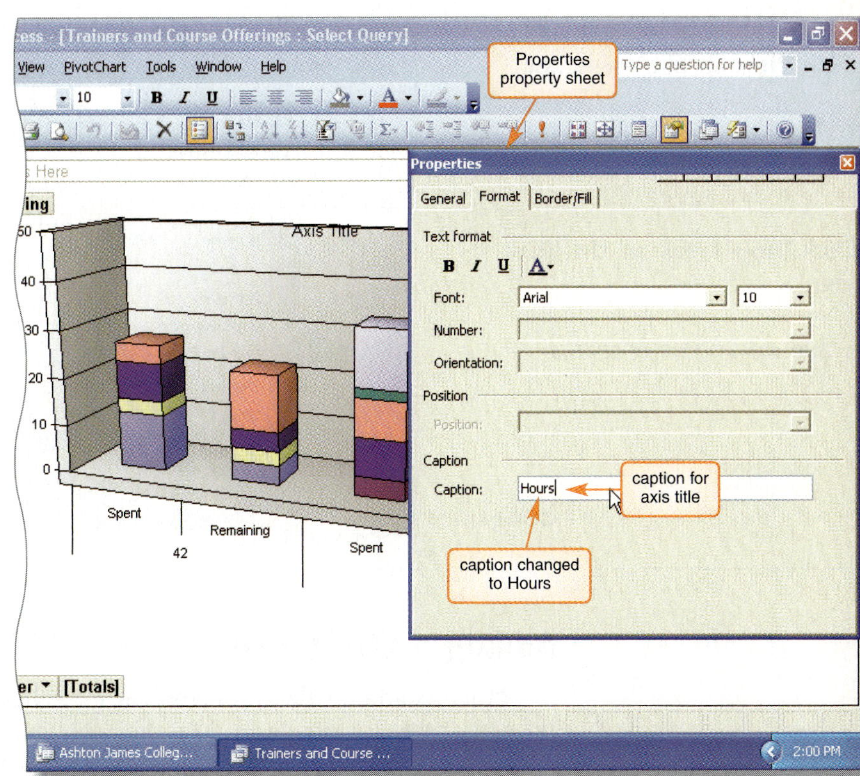

FIGURE 6-65

Removing Drop Areas

You can remove the drop areas from the PivotChart to give the chart a cleaner look. To do so, use the Drop Areas command on the View menu. If you later need to use the drop areas to perform some task, you can return them to the screen by using the Drop Areas command on the View menu a second time. The steps on the next page show how to remove the drop areas.

> *More About*
>
> **Microsoft Certification**
>
> The Microsoft Office Specialist Certification program provides an opportunity for you to obtain a valuable industry credential — proof that you have the Access 2003 skills required by employers. For more information, see Appendix E, or visit the Access 2003 Certification Web page (scsite.com/ac2003/cert).

To Remove Drop Areas

1

- **Click View on the menu bar.**

The View menu appears (Figure 6-66).

2

- **Click Drop Areas on the View menu.**

The drop areas no longer appear.

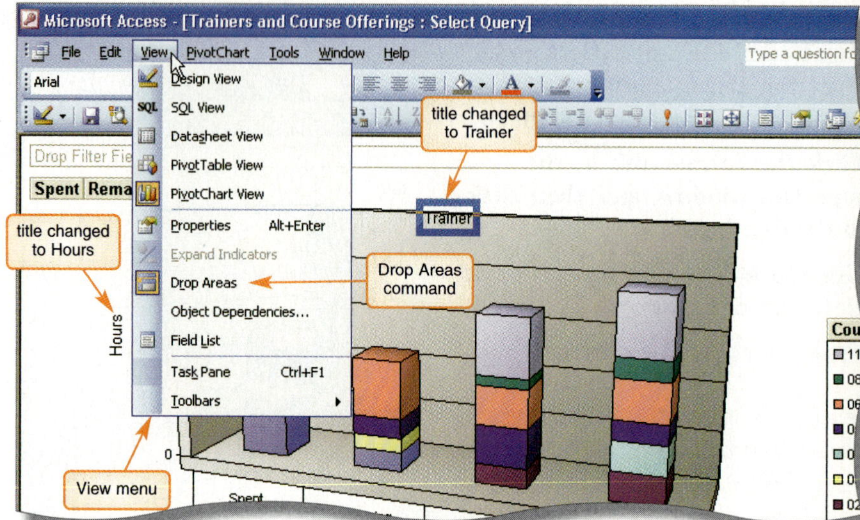

FIGURE 6-66

Adding a Chart Title

You can add a title to a PivotChart by clicking the Add Title button in the property sheet for the chart. You then can change the Caption property for the newly added title to assign the title of your choice. The following steps illustrate how to add a title to the PivotChart and then change the title's Caption property to Hours by Trainer and Course.

To Add a Chart Title

1

- **Right-click anywhere in the Chartspace (the white space) of the PivotChart, click Properties on the shortcut menu, and then, if necessary, click the General tab.**
- **Click the Add Title button.**

The property sheet appears (Figure 6-67). The General tab is selected. The chart now includes a title.

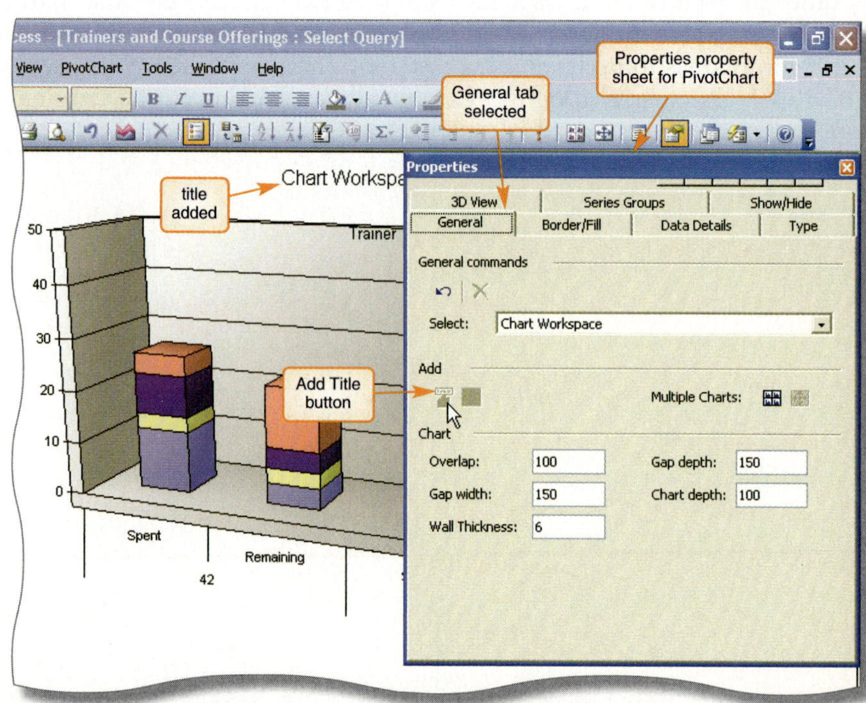

FIGURE 6-67

2

- **Close the Properties property sheet, right-click the newly added title, and then click Properties on the shortcut menu.**
- **When the Properties property sheet appears, click the Format tab.**
- **Click the Caption box, and then use the BACKSPACE or DELETE key to erase the old caption.**
- **Type** `Hours by Trainer and Course` **as the new caption.**

The property sheet appears (Figure 6-68). The caption is changed.

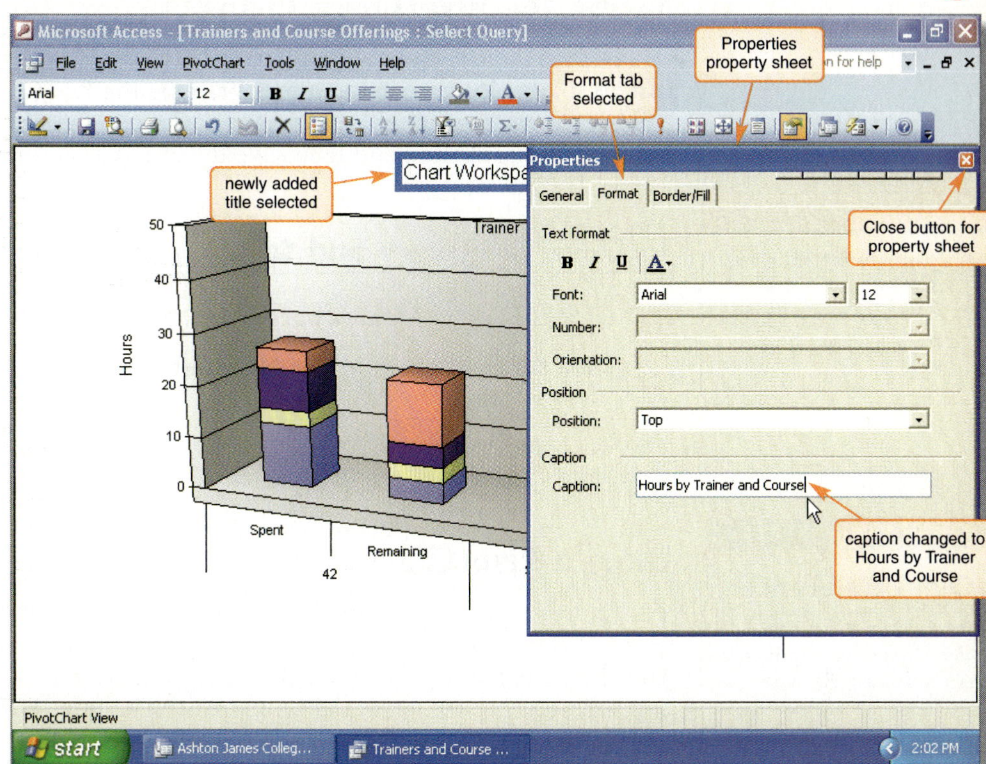

FIGURE 6-68

3

- **Close the property sheet by clicking its Close button.**

The chart has the desired title (Figure 6-69).

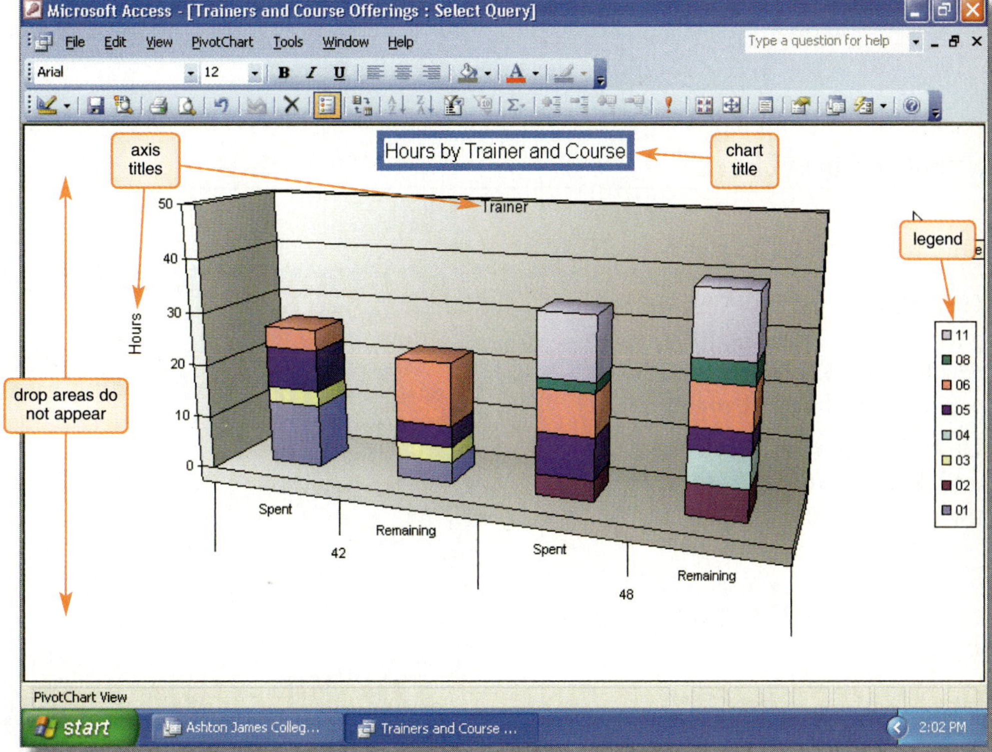

FIGURE 6-69

Saving the PivotChart Changes

To save the changes to the PivotChart view of the query, you save the query. You can do so, by closing the window containing the PivotChart and then clicking the Yes button when asked if you want to save your changes. The following steps show how to close the query and then save the changes.

Other Ways

1. Click View button arrow, click PivotChart View
2. In Voice Command mode, say "View, PivotChart View"

To Close the Query and Save the PivotChart Changes

1 **Click the Close Window button for the window containing the PivotChart.**

2 **Click the Yes button in the Microsoft Office Access dialog box.**

The changes to the layout of the query are saved. In particular, the changes to the PivotChart view of the query are saved.

More About

Quick Reference

For a table that lists how to complete the tasks covered in this book using the mouse, menu, shortcut menu, and keyboard, see the Quick Reference Summary at the back of this book, or visit the Access 2003 Quick Reference Web page (scsite.com/ac2003/qr).

Using a PivotChart

To use a PivotChart, you first must open it. If the PivotChart is associated with a query, this would involve opening the query and then switching to PivotChart view. You then can check or uncheck the various items that appear to restrict the data that appears. In order to do so, the drop areas must appear. If they do not, use the Drop Areas command on the View menu to display them. You then can click the arrows. You also can drag fields to the drop areas.

You can make the same types of changes you made when you first created the PivotChart. You can change the chart type. You can change the orientation by clicking the By Row/By Column button. You can add or remove a legend. You can change titles. The following steps show how to use the PivotChart view of the Trainers and Course Offerings query.

To Use a PivotChart

1

- **Click Queries on the Objects bar, right-click the Trainers and Course Offerings query, and then click Open on the shortcut menu.**
- **Click the View button arrow, and then click PivotChart View. Click View on the menu bar.**

The PivotChart and View menu appear (Figure 6-70). The drop areas currently do not appear.

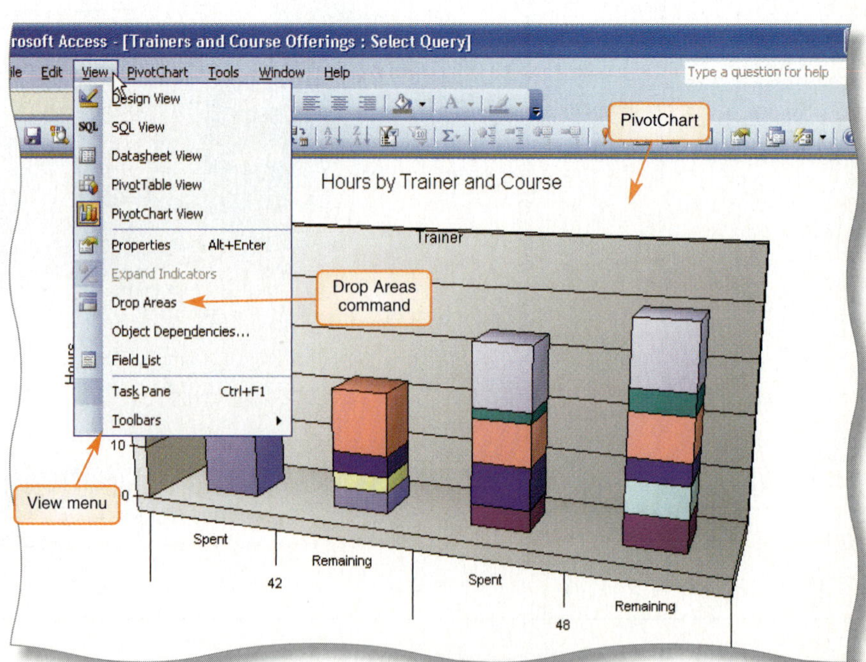

FIGURE 6-70

2

• **Click Drop Areas on the View menu, and then click the Trainer Number arrow.**

The list of available trainers appears (Figure 6-71).

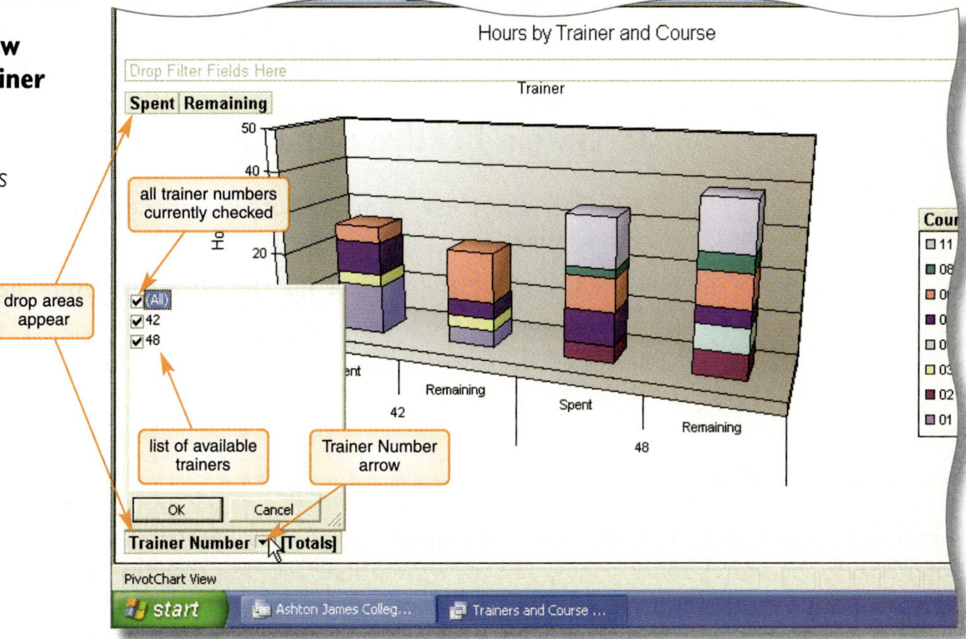

FIGURE 6-71

3

• **Click the check box for trainer number 42 to remove the check mark, and then click the OK button.**

Trainer number 42 no longer appears on the PivotChart (Figure 6-72).

4

• **Click the Close Window button for the window containing the PivotChart.**

• **Click the No button when asked if you want to save your changes.**

The PivotChart is closed. The changes are not saved. The next time you open the PivotChart, the changes you just made will not be reflected.

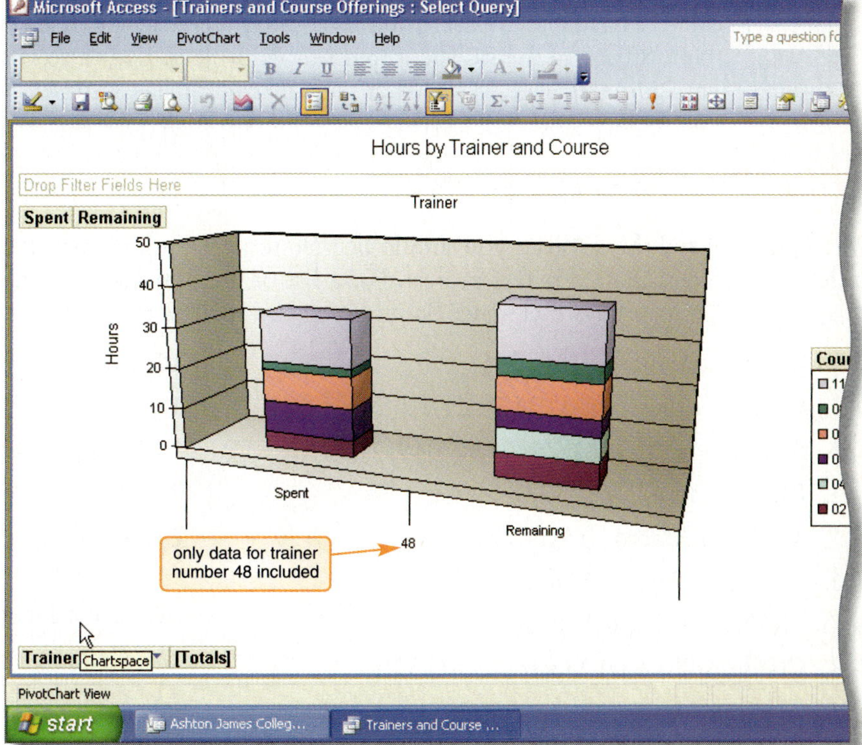

FIGURE 6-72

Closing the Database and Quitting Access

The following steps close the database and quit Access.

To Close a Database and Quit Access

1. **Click the Close Window button for the Ashton James College : Database window.**
2. **Click the Close button for the Microsoft Office Access window.**

Access and the database close.

Project Summary

In Project 6, you learned how to create and use macros. Using Switchboard Manager, you created the switchboard, the switchboard pages, and the switchboard items. You also used the Switchboard Manager to assign actions to the buttons on the switchboard pages. You saw how to use the completed switchboard. You created a PivotTable and a PivotChart associated with a query. In the process, you saw how to customize various aspects of both the PivotTable and PivotChart as well as how to use them.

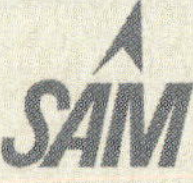

If you have a SAM user profile, you may have access to hands-on instruction, practice, and assessment of the skills covered in this project. Log in to your SAM account and go to your assignments page to see what your instructor has assigned.

What You Should Know

Having completed this project, you should be able to perform the tasks below. The tasks are listed in the same order they were presented in this project. For a list of the buttons, menus, toolbars, and commands introduced in this project, see the Quick Reference Summary at the back of this book and refer to the Page Number column.

1. Open a Database (AC 316)
2. Create a Macro (AC 317)
3. Add Actions to a Macro (AC 319)
4. Run a Macro (AC 322)
5. Modify a Macro (AC 322)
6. Copy and Paste a Macro (AC 326)
7. Modify the Copied Macro (AC 327)
8. Create Additional Macros (AC 329)
9. Create a Switchboard (AC 330)
10. Create Switchboard Pages (AC 332)
11. Modify the Main Switchboard Page (AC 333)
12. Modify the Other Switchboard Pages (AC 335)
13. Open a Switchboard (AC 337)
14. Close the Switchboard and Database (AC 338)
15. Create the New Tables (AC 341)
16. Import the Data (AC 342)
17. Relate Several Tables (AC 342)
18. Create the Query (AC 344)
19. Create a PivotTable (AC 347)
20. Change Properties in a PivotTable (AC 349)
21. Close the Query and Save the PivotTable Changes (AC 350)
22. Use a PivotTable (AC 350)
23. Create a PivotChart and Add a Legend (AC 355)
24. Change the Chart Type (AC 356)
25. Change PivotChart Organization (AC 358)
26. Assign Axis Titles (AC 359)
27. Remove Drop Areas (AC 360)
28. Add a Chart Title (AC 360)
29. Close the Query and Save the PivotChart Changes (AC 362)
30. Use a PivotChart (AC 362)
31. Close a Database and Quit Access (AC 364)

Learn It Online

Instructions: To complete the Learn It Online exercises, start your browser, click the Address bar, and then enter the Web address scsite.com/ac2003/learn. When the Access 2003 Learn It Online page is displayed, follow the instructions in the exercises below. Each exercise has instructions for printing your results, either for your own records or for submission to your instructor.

1 Project Reinforcement TF, MC, and SA

Below Access Project 6, click the Project Reinforcement link. Print the quiz by clicking Print on the File menu for each page. Answer each question.

2 Flash Cards

Below Access Project 6, click the Flash Cards link and read the instructions. Type 20 (or a number specified by your instructor) in the Number of playing cards text box, type your name in the Enter your Name text box, and then click the Flip Card button. When the flash card is displayed, read the question and then click the ANSWER box arrow to select an answer. Flip through Flash Cards. If your score is 15 (75%) correct or greater, click Print on the File menu to print your results. If your score is less than 15 (75%) correct, then redo this exercise by clicking the Replay button.

3 Practice Test

Below Access Project 6, click the Practice Test link. Answer each question, enter your first and last name at the bottom of the page, and then click the Grade Test button. When the graded practice test is displayed on your screen, click Print on the File menu to print a hard copy. Continue to take practice tests until you score 80% or better.

4 Who Wants To Be a Computer Genius?

Below Access Project 6, click the Computer Genius link. Read the instructions, enter your first and last name at the bottom of the page, and then click the PLAY button. When your score is displayed, click the PRINT RESULTS link to print a hard copy.

5 Wheel of Terms

Below Access Project 6, click the Wheel of Terms link. Read the instructions, and then enter your first and last name and your school name. Click the PLAY button. When your score is displayed, right-click the score and then click Print on the shortcut menu to print a hard copy.

6 Crossword Puzzle Challenge

Below Access Project 6, click the Crossword Puzzle Challenge link. Read the instructions, and then enter your first and last name. Click the SUBMIT button. Work the crossword puzzle. When you are finished, click the Submit button. When the crossword puzzle is redisplayed, click the Print Puzzle button to print a hard copy.

7 Tips and Tricks

Below Access Project 6, click the Tips and Tricks link. Click a topic that pertains to Project 6. Right-click the information and then click Print on the shortcut menu. Construct a brief example of what the information relates to in Access to confirm you understand how to use the tip or trick.

8 Newsgroups

Below Access Project 6, click the Newsgroups link. Click a topic that pertains to Project 6. Print three comments.

9 Expanding Your Horizons

Below Access Project 6, click the Articles for Microsoft Access link. Click a topic that pertains to Project 6. Print the information. Construct a brief example of what the information relates to in Access to confirm you understand the contents of the article.

10 Search Sleuth

Below Access Project 6, click the Search Sleuth link. To search for a term that pertains to this project, select a term below the Project 6 title and then use the Google search engine at google.com (or any major search engine) to display and print two Web pages that present information on the term.

11 Access Online Training

Below Access Project 6, click the Access Online Training link. When your browser displays the Microsoft Office Online Web page, click the Access link. Click one of the Access courses that covers one or more of the objectives listed at the beginning of the project on page AC 314. Print the first page of the course before stepping through it.

12 Office Marketplace

Below Access Project 6, click the Office Marketplace link. When your browser displays the Microsoft Office Online Web page, click the Office Marketplace link. Click a topic that relates to Access. Print the first page.

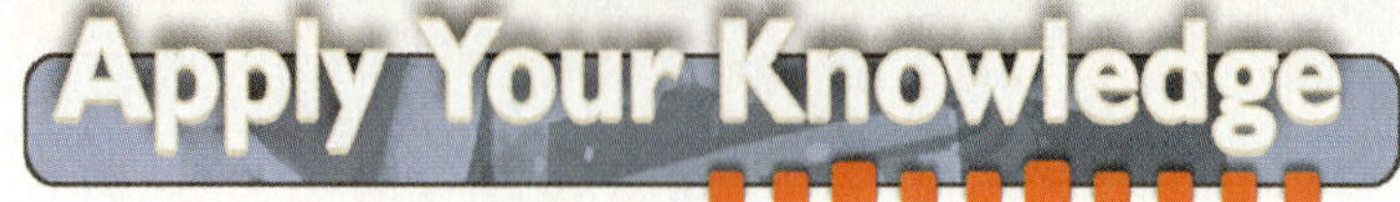

1 Creating a Macro and a PivotTable for Begon Pest Control

Instructions: For this assignment, you will use three files: Begon Pest Control.mdb, Category.txt, and Work Orders.txt. If you are using the Microsoft Office Access 2003 Complete or the Microsoft Office Access 2003 Comprehensive text, open the Begon Pest Control database that you used in Project 5 or see your instructor for information about accessing the files required for this book. The Category.txt and Work Orders.txt files are text files that are on the Data Disk.

You will create two new tables for the Begon Pest Control database. The Work Orders table contains information on the type of work the customer needs done. The structure for the Work Orders table is shown in Figure 6-73. Some customers require more than one type of service. For each record to be unique, the primary key for the Work Orders table must be the combination of the Customer Number and the Category Number. A one-to-many relationship exists between the Customer table and the Work Orders table. The Category table contains information on the service category. The structure for the Category table is shown in Figure 6-74. A one-to-many relationship exists between the Category table and the Work Orders table. Perform the following tasks:

1. Start Access and open the Begon Pest Control database.
2. Create a macro to open the Technician/Customer Report you created in Project 4. Save the macro as Print Technician/Customer Report. Run the macro to print the report.
3. Create the Work Orders table using the structure shown in Figure 6-73. The primary key is the combination of Customer Number and Category Number. Use Work Orders as the name of the table.

Structure of Work Orders Table

FIELD NAME	DATA TYPE	FIELD SIZE	PRIMARY KEY?	DESCRIPTION
Customer Number	Text	4	Yes	Customer Number (Portion of Primary Key)
Category Number	Text	2	Yes	Category Number (Portion of Primary Key)
Total Hours (est)	Number			Estimate of Total Hours Required

FIGURE 6-73

4. Create the Category table using the structure shown in Figure 6-74. Use Category as the name of the table.

Structure of Category Table

FIELD NAME	DATA TYPE	FIELD SIZE	PRIMARY KEY?	DESCRIPTION
Category Number	Text	2	Yes	Category Number (Primary Key)
Category Description	Text	50		Description of Category

FIGURE 6-74

Apply Your Knowledge

5. Import the Work Orders text file into the Work Orders table and then import the Category text file into the Category table. For each table, be sure to check the First Row Contains Column Headings box. The data is in delimited format with each field separated by tabs.
6. Open the Relationships window and establish a one-to-many relationship between the Category table and the Work Orders table and between the Customer table and the Work Orders table. Print the Relationships window by making sure the Relationships window is open, clicking File on the menu bar, and then clicking Print Relationships. When Access displays the Print Preview window, click the Print button on the Print Preview toolbar. Do not save the report.
7. Create a query for the Work Orders table. Include all fields in the query and save the query as Customers and Categories.
8. Open the Customers and Categories query and switch to PivotTable view. Create the PivotTable shown in Figure 6-75. Save the changes to the layout of the query. Print the PivotTable.

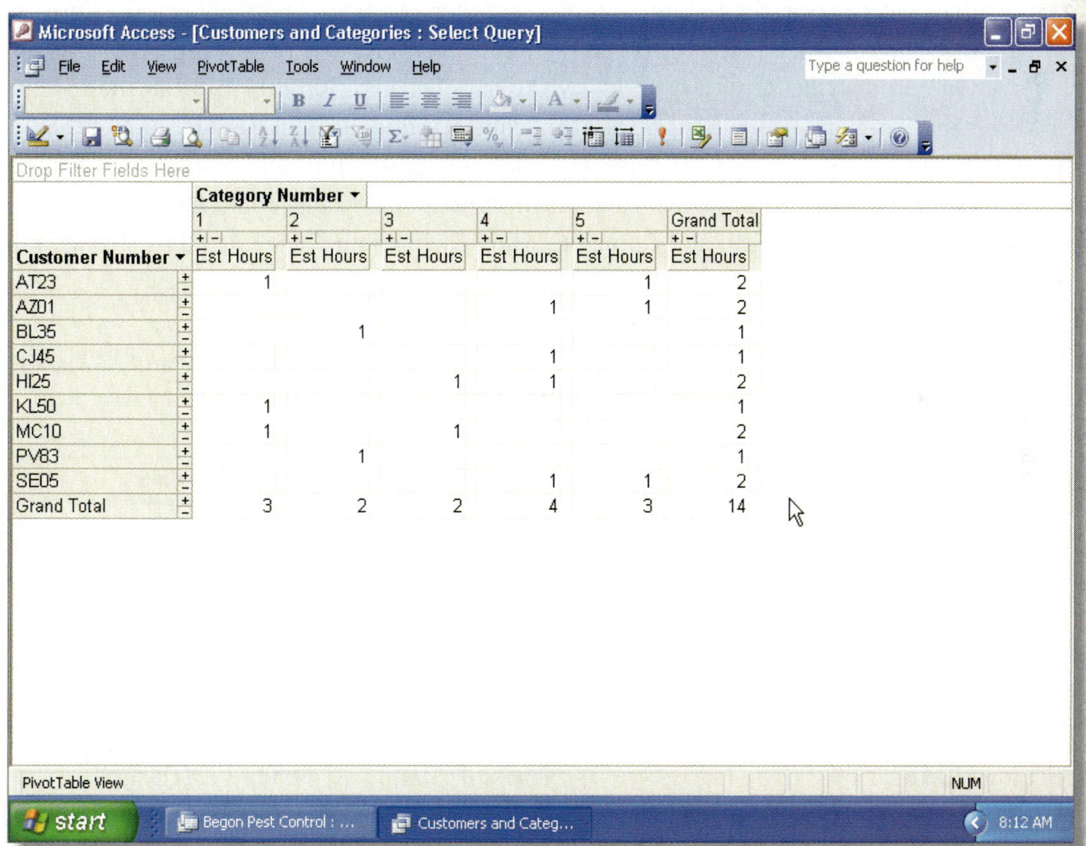

Customer Number	1 Est Hours	2 Est Hours	3 Est Hours	4 Est Hours	5 Est Hours	Grand Total Est Hours
AT23	1				1	2
AZ01				1	1	2
BL35		1				1
CJ45				1		1
HI25			1	1		2
KL50	1					1
MC10	1		1			2
PV83		1				1
SE05				1	1	2
Grand Total	3	2	2	4	3	14

FIGURE 6-75

9. Hide the details for category number 4 and print the PivotTable again. Do not save the changes to the layout of the query.

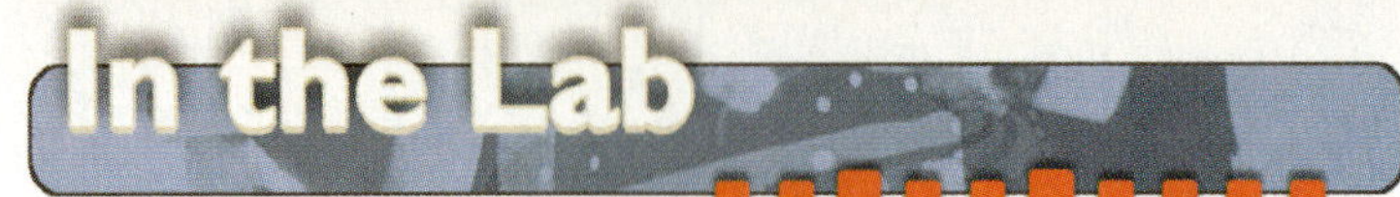

1 Creating Macros, a Switchboard, a PivotTable, and a PivotChart for the Birds2U Database

Problem: The management of Birds2U would like an easy way to access the various tables, forms, and reports, by simply clicking a button or two. This would make the database much easier to maintain and update. Management also needs to track items that are being reordered from suppliers. Management must know when an item was ordered and how many were ordered. Birds2U may place an order with a supplier one day and then find it needs to order more of the same item before the original order is filled.

Instructions: If you are using the Microsoft Office Access 2003 Complete or the Microsoft Office Access 2003 Comprehensive text, open the Birds2U database that you used in Project 5 or see your instructor for information about accessing the files required in this book. Perform the following tasks:

1. Create macros that will perform the following tasks: (a) Open the Item Update Form, (b) Open the Supplier Master Form, (c) Open the Item Table, (d) Open the Supplier Table, (e) Preview the Inventory Report, (f) Preview the On Hand Value Report, (g) Preview the Supplier/Item Report, (h) Print the Inventory Report, (i) Print the On Hand Value Report, and (j) Print the Supplier/Item Report.
2. Create a switchboard for the Birds2U database. Use the same design for your switchboard pages as the one illustrated in this project. For example, the View Form switchboard page should have three choices: Item Update Form, Supplier Master Form, and Return to Main Switchboard. Include all the forms, tables, and reports for which you created macros in Step 1.
3. Run the switchboard and correct any errors.
4. Create a table in which to store the item reorder information using the structure shown in Figure 6-76. Use Reorder as the name of the table. Add the data shown in Figure 6-76 to the Reorder table. Print the table.

Structure of Reorder Table

FIELD NAME	DATA TYPE	FIELD SIZE	PRIMARY KEY?	DESCRIPTION
Item Code	Text	4	Yes	Item Code (Portion of Primary Key)
Date Ordered	Date/Time (Change Format property to Short Date)		Yes	Date Item Ordered (Portion of Primary Key)
Number Ordered	Number			Number of Items Ordered

Reorder table

ITEM CODE	DATE ORDERED	NUMBER ORDERED
BB01	7/15/2005	3
BB01	7/27/2005	1
BO22	8/1/2005	2
BO22	8/9/2005	2
BS10	8/25/2005	2
LM05	8/1/2005	4
LM05	8/15/2005	2
PM05	8/18/2005	2

FIGURE 6-76

5. Add the Reorder table to the Relationships window and establish a one-to-many relationship between the Item table and the Reorder table. Print the Relationships window by making sure the Relationships window is open, clicking File on the menu bar, and then clicking Print Relationships. When Access displays the Print Preview window, click the Print button on the Print Preview toolbar. Do not save the report.

In the Lab

6. Create a query that joins the Reorder table, Item table, and Supplier table. Include the item code from the Reorder table, the supplier code and number on hand from the Item table, and the number ordered from the Reorder table in the design grid. Run the query and save the query as Supplier and Number of Items.
7. Open the Supplier and Number of Items query and switch to PivotTable view. Create the PivotTable shown in Figure 6-77. Print the PivotTable.

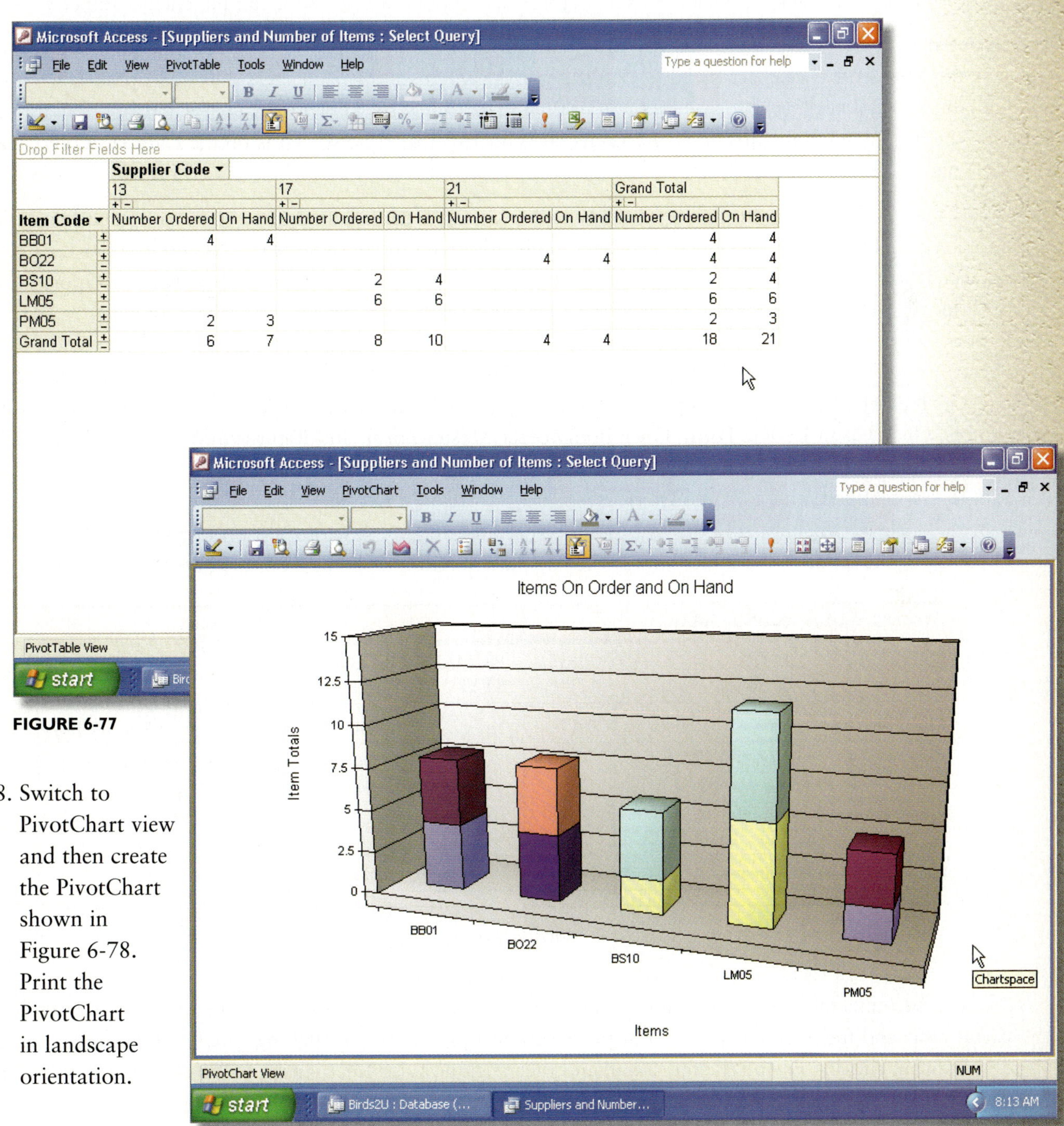

Microsoft Access - [Suppliers and Number of Items : Select Query]

Drop Filter Fields Here

Supplier Code	13		17		21		Grand Total	
Item Code	Number Ordered	On Hand	Number Ordered	On Hand	Number Ordered	On Hand	Number Ordered	On Hand
BB01	4	4					4	4
BO22					4	4	4	4
BS10			2	4			2	4
LM05			6	6			6	6
PM05	2	3					2	3
Grand Total	6	7	8	10	4	4	18	21

FIGURE 6-77

8. Switch to PivotChart view and then create the PivotChart shown in Figure 6-78. Print the PivotChart in landscape orientation.

FIGURE 6-78

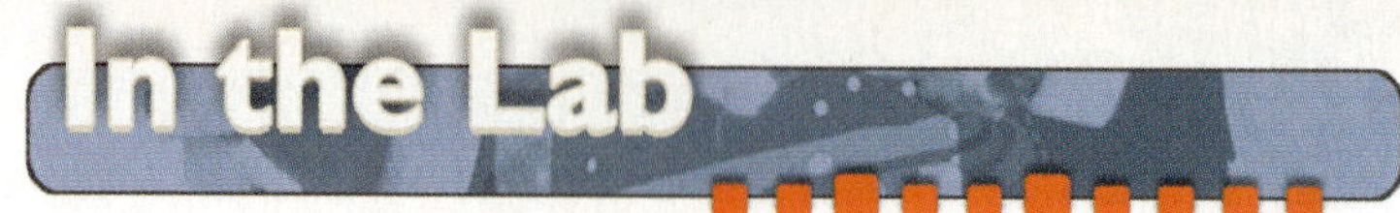

2 Creating Macros, a Switchboard, a PivotTable, and a PivotChart for the Babbage Bookkeeping Database

Problem: Babbage Bookkeeping would like an easy way to access the various tables, forms, and reports by simply clicking a button or two. This would make the database much easier to maintain and update. The company also needs to keep track of when bookkeeping services were performed so it can bill clients properly.

Instructions: For this assignment, you will use two files: Babbage Bookkeeping.mdb and Accounts.xls. If you are using the Microsoft Office Access 2003 Complete or the Microsoft Office Access 2003 Comprehensive text, use the Babbage Bookkeeping database that you used in Project 5 or see your instructor for information about accessing the files required for this book. Accounts.xls is an Excel workbook that is on the Data Disk. Perform the following tasks:

1. Create macros that will perform the following tasks: (a) Open the Client Update Form, (b) Open the Bookkeeper Master Form, (c) Open the Client Table, (d) Open the Bookkeeper Table, (e) Preview the Balance Due Report, (f) Preview the Client Income Report, (g) Preview the Bookkeeper/Client Report, (h) Print the Balance Due Report, (i) Print the Client Income Report, and (j) Print the Bookkeeper/Client Report.
2. Create a switchboard for the Babbage Bookkeeping database. Use the same design for your switchboard pages as the one illustrated in this project. For example, the View Form switchboard page should have three choices: Open Client Update Form, Open Bookkeeper Master Form, and Return to Main Switchboard. Include all the forms, tables, and reports for which you created macros in Step 1.
3. Run the switchboard and correct any errors.
4. Create a table in which to store the account information using the structure shown in Figure 6-79. Use Accounts as the name of the table. Import the Accounts workbook to the Accounts table. Print the table.

Structure of Accounts Table

FIELD NAME	DATA TYPE	FIELD SIZE	PRIMARY KEY?	DESCRIPTION
Client Number	Text	3	Yes	Client Number (Portion of Primary Key)
Service Date	Date/Time (Change the Format property to Short Date)		Yes	Date that Bookkeeping was Performed (Portion of Primary Key)
Hours Worked	Number			Number of Hours Worked

FIGURE 6-79

5. Add the Accounts table to the Relationships window and establish a one-to-many relationship between the Client table and the Accounts table. Print the Relationships window by making sure the Relationships window is open, clicking File on the menu bar, and then clicking Print Relationships. When Access displays the Print Preview window, click the Print button on the Print Preview toolbar. Do not save the report.

In the Lab

6. Create a query that joins the Accounts, Bookkeeper, and Client tables. Include the client number, service date, and hours worked fields from the Accounts table in the design grid. Calculate the current due amount (hours worked * hourly rate). Run the query and save the query as Total Current Due by Client.

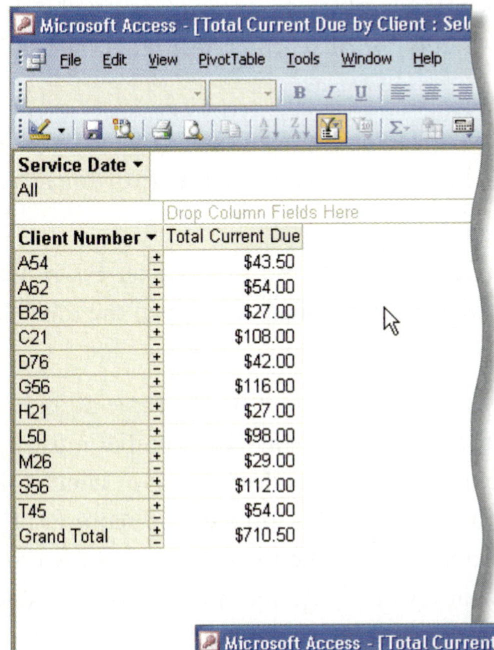

FIGURE 6-80

7. Open the Total Current Due by Client query and switch to PivotTable view. Create the PivotTable shown in Figure 6-80. Print the PivotTable.
8. Filter the PivotTable to show only current due amounts for service dates between 8/22/2005 and 8/26/2005. Print the PivotTable and then redisplay all current due amounts.
9. Switch to PivotChart view and then create the PivotChart shown in Figure 6-81. Print the PivotChart in landscape orientation.

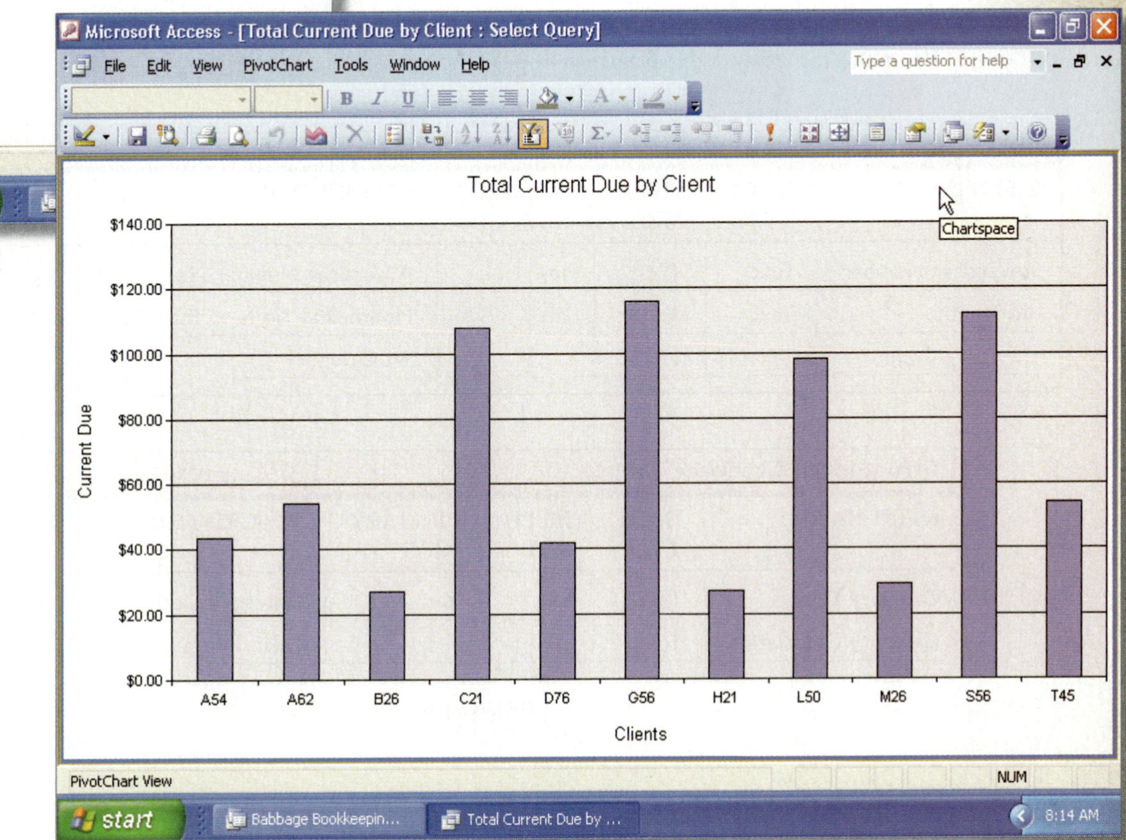

FIGURE 6-81

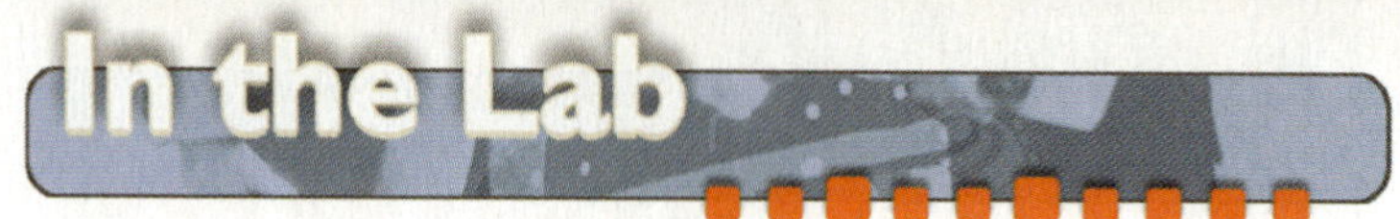

3 Creating Macros, a Switchboard, and a PivotTable for the City Guide Database

Problem: The chamber of commerce wants an easy way to access various tables, forms, and reports by simply clicking a button or two. The chamber also needs to track active accounts for the current year and wants the ability to change easily the way data is summarized and presented.

Instructions: If you are using the Microsoft Office Access 2003 Complete or the Microsoft Office Access 2003 Comprehensive text, open the City Guide database that you used in Project 5 or see your instructor for information about accessing the files required for this book.

Part 1 Instructions: Create macros to open the Advertiser Update Form and the Ad Rep Master Form. Create macros to preview and to print all the reports in the City Guide database. Create macros to open the tables in the database. Create a switchboard that uses these macros.

Part 2 Instructions: Advertisers contract with the chamber to advertise for one month. The same ad may run for several months or be replaced monthly with an ad of a different size or design. The chamber must track the active accounts for the current year and must be able to query the database for information on which advertisers currently have ads they want to appear in the newcomer's guide. To track this information requires two tables: an Active Accounts table and a Category table. Create these two tables using the structures shown in Figure 6-82. Import the Active Accounts text file into the Active Accounts table and the Ad Categories text file into the Category table. These text files are on your Data Disk. Then, update the relationships for the City Guide database. Print the tables and the Relationships window.

Structure of Active Accounts Table

FIELD NAME	DATA TYPE	FIELD SIZE	PRIMARY KEY?	DESCRIPTION
Advertiser Number	Text	4	Yes	Advertiser Number (Portion of Primary Key)
Ad Month	Text	3	Yes	Month that Ad is to Run (Portion of Primary Key)
Category Code	Text	1		Ad Category

Structure of Category Table

FIELD NAME	DATA TYPE	FIELD SIZE	PRIMARY KEY?	DESCRIPTION
Category Code	Text	1	Yes	Category Code (Primary Key)
Category Description	Text	50		Description of Ad Category

FIGURE 6-82

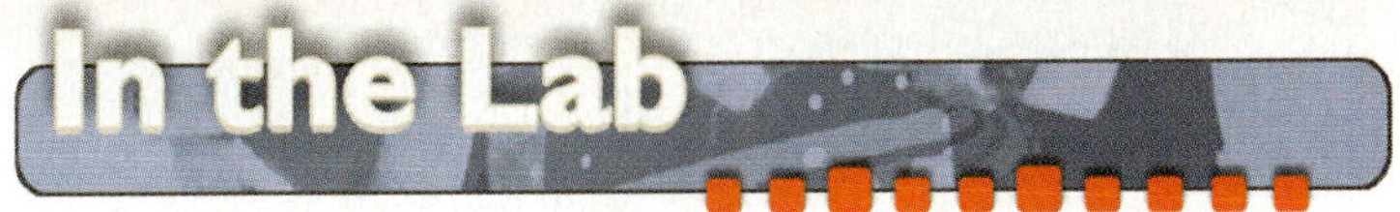

Part 3 Instructions: The chamber would like to actively track amount paid and balance amounts by advertiser and ad rep. Create a query for the Advertiser table that includes the advertiser number, ad rep number, advertiser type, amount paid, and balance, and then create the PivotTable shown in Figure 6-83. The chamber wants the ability to filter the data by advertiser type.

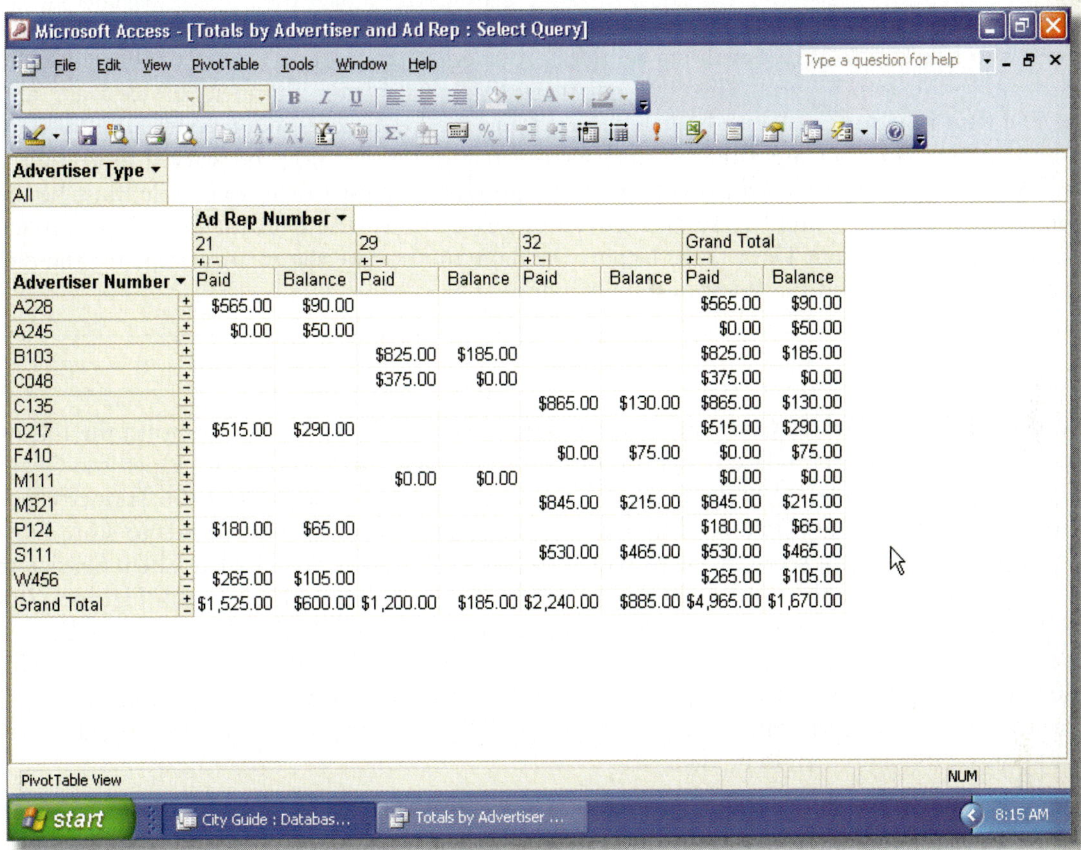

Advertiser Number	21 Paid	21 Balance	29 Paid	29 Balance	32 Paid	32 Balance	Grand Total Paid	Grand Total Balance
A228	$565.00	$90.00					$565.00	$90.00
A245	$0.00	$50.00					$0.00	$50.00
B103			$825.00	$185.00			$825.00	$185.00
C048			$375.00	$0.00			$375.00	$0.00
C135					$865.00	$130.00	$865.00	$130.00
D217	$515.00	$290.00					$515.00	$290.00
F410					$0.00	$75.00	$0.00	$75.00
M111			$0.00	$0.00			$0.00	$0.00
M321					$845.00	$215.00	$845.00	$215.00
P124	$180.00	$65.00					$180.00	$65.00
S111					$530.00	$465.00	$530.00	$465.00
W456	$265.00	$105.00					$265.00	$105.00
Grand Total	$1,525.00	$600.00	$1,200.00	$185.00	$2,240.00	$885.00	$4,965.00	$1,670.00

FIGURE 6-83

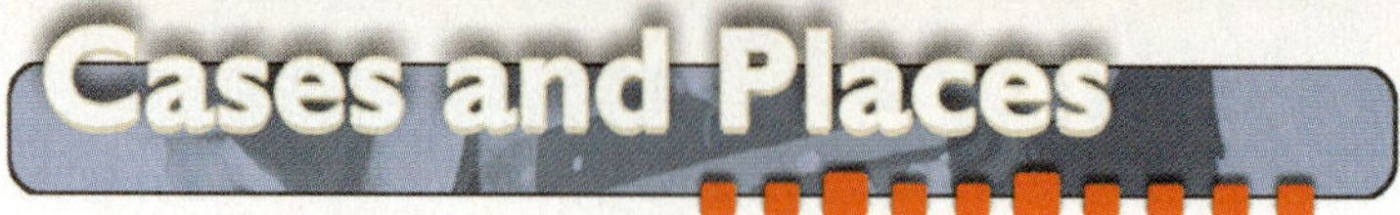

The difficulty of these case studies varies:
■ are the least difficult and ■■ are more difficult. The last exercise is a group exercise.

1 ■ Use the College Dog Walkers database that you used in Project 5 for this assignment or see your instructor for information about accessing the files required for this book. Create macros to open the Customer Update Form, the Walker Master Form, the Customer table, and the Walker table. The business needs to keep track of dog-walking services provided to customers. Create a table called Service in which to store this information. The table has three fields: Customer Number, Service Date, and Service Time. The data type for Customer Number is Text and the field size is 4. The data type for Service Date and Service Time is Date/Time. Several customers require that dogs be walked more than once a day. Therefore, for each record to be unique, the primary key for the Service table must be the combination of customer number, service date, and service time. The data for the Service table is in the Services workbook on your Data Disk. Import the data and update the relationships for the database. Print the Service table and the Relationships window.

2 ■ Use the InPerson Fitness Company database and create macros that will perform the following tasks: (a) Open the Client Update Form, (b) Open the Trainer Master Form, (c) Open the Client table, (d) Open the Trainer table, (e) Preview the Trainer/Client Report, and (f) Print the Trainer/Client Report. Create and run a switchboard that uses these macros. The company needs to store information on when personal training services are provided to clients. Create a table called Client Service in which to store this data. The table has the same structure as the Accounts table shown in Figure 6-79 on page AC 370. Change the field size for the Client Number field to four (4). The data for the Client Service table is in the Client Service text file on your Data Disk. Import the data and update the relationships for the database. Print the Client Service table and the Relationships window. Edit the relationship between the Client table and the Client Service table. When a client is deleted, the related records in the Client Service table also should be deleted.

Cases and Places

3 Use the Regional Books database that you used in Project 5 for this assignment or see your instructor for information about accessing the files required in this book. Create macros to open all forms and tables in the database. Create macros to preview and to print all reports in the database. Create and run a switchboard that uses these macros. The owner of the bookstore has several customers who have purchased books on the layaway plan. He wants to add data on these customers and the books they are buying to the database. Because a customer can purchase more than one book, the primary key for the Book Order table is the combination of Customer Number and Book Code fields. The structures for the Book Order and Customer tables are shown in Figure 6-84. The data for these tables is in the Books workbook on your Data Disk. Update the Regional Books database to include these tables and establish the necessary relationships.

Structure of Book Order Table

FIELD NAME	DATA TYPE	FIELD SIZE	PRIMARY KEY?	DESCRIPTION
Book Code	Text	4	Yes	Book Code (Portion of Primary Key)
Customer Number	Text	3	Yes	Customer Ordering Book (Portion of Primary Key)
Order Date	Date/Time			Date Ordered

Structure of Customer Table

FIELD NAME	DATA TYPE	FIELD SIZE	PRIMARY KEY?	DESCRIPTION
Customer Number	Text	3	Yes	Customer Number (Primary Key)
Last Name	Text	15		Customer Last Name
First Name	Text	15		Customer First Name
Address	Text	15		Address
Phone Number	Text	8		Customer Phone Number (999-9999 version)

FIGURE 6-84

Cases and Places

4 ■■ Use the Campus Housing database that you used in Project 5 for this assignment or see your instructor for information about accessing the files required in this book. Create macros to open all forms and tables in the database. Create macros to preview and to print all reports in the database. Create and run a switchboard that uses these macros. The Housing office would like to store information on potential renters, that is, individuals interested in renting off-campus housing. Because these potential renters can show an interest in more than one rental unit, the primary key for the Property table is the combination of Renter Number and Rental Code. The structure for the Renter table is the same as the Customer table shown in Figure 6-84 on the previous page. Replace Customer with Renter. The Property table contains only the Renter Number and Rental Code fields. Be sure the data types and field size match those in the Renter and Rentals tables, respectively. The data for these tables is in the Property and Renter text files on your Data Disk. Update the Campus Housing database to include these tables and establish the necessary relationships.

5 ■■ **Working Together** As a team, research the differences between a crosstab query and a PivotTable. Modify one of the crosstab queries created previously. What type of modifications are possible to a crosstab query? How difficult is it to make the changes? Discuss when a crosstab is appropriate and when a PivotTable is appropriate and write a short paper that explains these differences. Create a PivotTable for one of the databases described in Cases and Places. The team must have a specific purpose in mind for the PivotTable. Also create a PivotChart for the same database. Write a paragraph that explains how the PivotTable and the PivotChart will help database users.

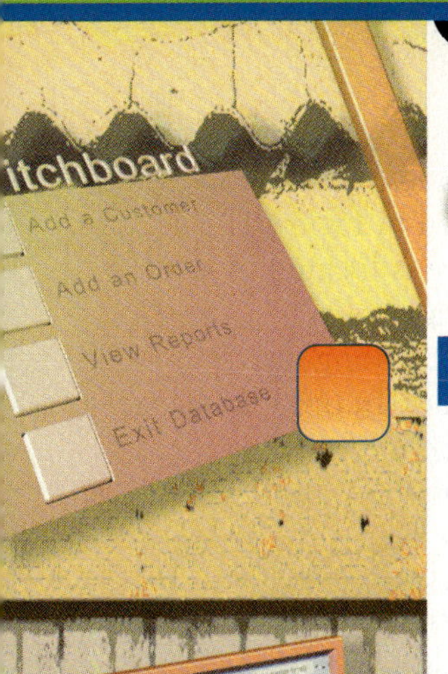

MICROSOFT
Office Access 2003

Data Access Pages

CASE PERSPECTIVE

Dr. Guernay and his colleagues at Ashton James College are pleased with all the database work that has been done for them thus far. The administration appreciates the ease with which the database can be modified to include additional fields and tables. The administration also likes the ease with which they can query the database. The default values, validation rules, validation text, and the relationships are useful in ensuring the database contains only valid data. They also find the reports, forms, and switchboard to be useful. Because they have found the forms particularly useful, they would like to use a Web page that would be similar to a form in order to view and/or update client data over the Internet. The administration would like to develop a sample of such a Web page, called a data access page, which they then would review. If they determine that it satisfies their needs, they have other requests for data to be accessible over the Web. The first request is to make a list of trainers available over the web. When viewing this data, they would like the option of displaying all the clients for one or more of the trainers appearing on the data access page. In addition, they have found both the PivotTable and the PivotChart to be very useful and would like to be able to view such a PivotTable and PivotChart over the Web. The administration would like to place both a PivotTable and a PivotChart on data access pages. Your task is to help the administration in accomplishing these goals.

As you read through this project, you will learn how to use the Page Wizard as well as the Design window to create data access pages.

Objectives

You will have mastered the material in this Web Feature when you can:

- Create a data access page using the wizard
- Create a grouped data access page in Design view
- Create a PivotTable in a data access page
- Save a PivotChart to a data access page

Introduction

Microsoft Access supports data access pages. A **data access page** is an HTML document that can be bound directly to data in the database. The fact that it is an HTML document implies that it can be run in the Internet Explorer browser. The fact that it is bound directly to the database means that it can access data in the database directly.

Data Access Pages

Figure 1 on the next page shows a sample data access page run in the Internet Explorer browser. Notice that it is similar to a form. Although running in the browser, the data access page is displaying data in the Ashton James College database. Furthermore, the page can be used to update this data. You can use it to change the contents of existing records, to delete records, and to add new records.

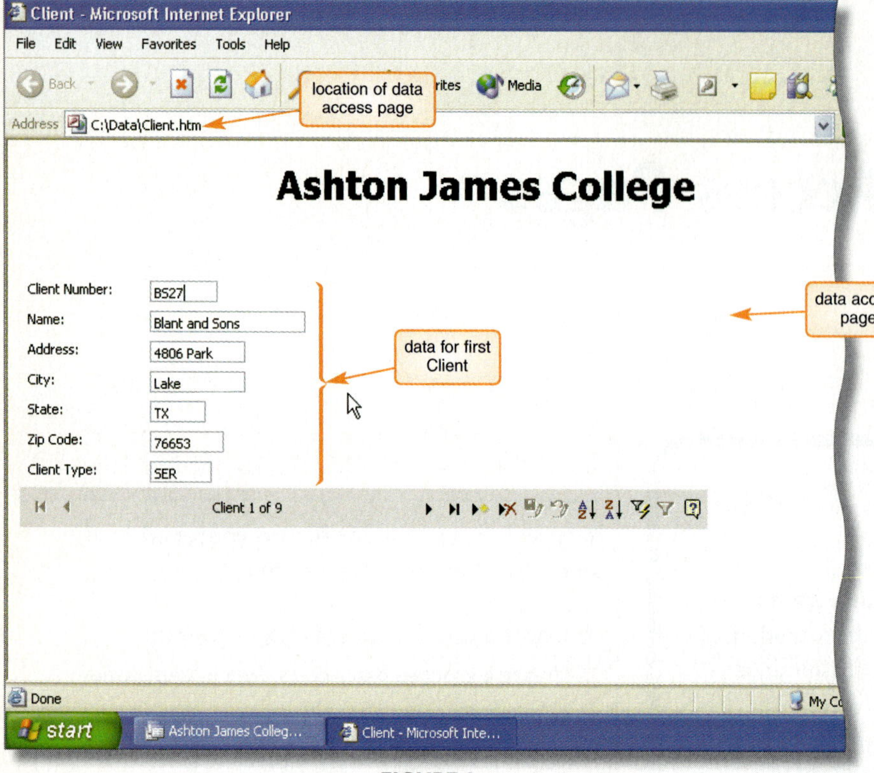

FIGURE 1

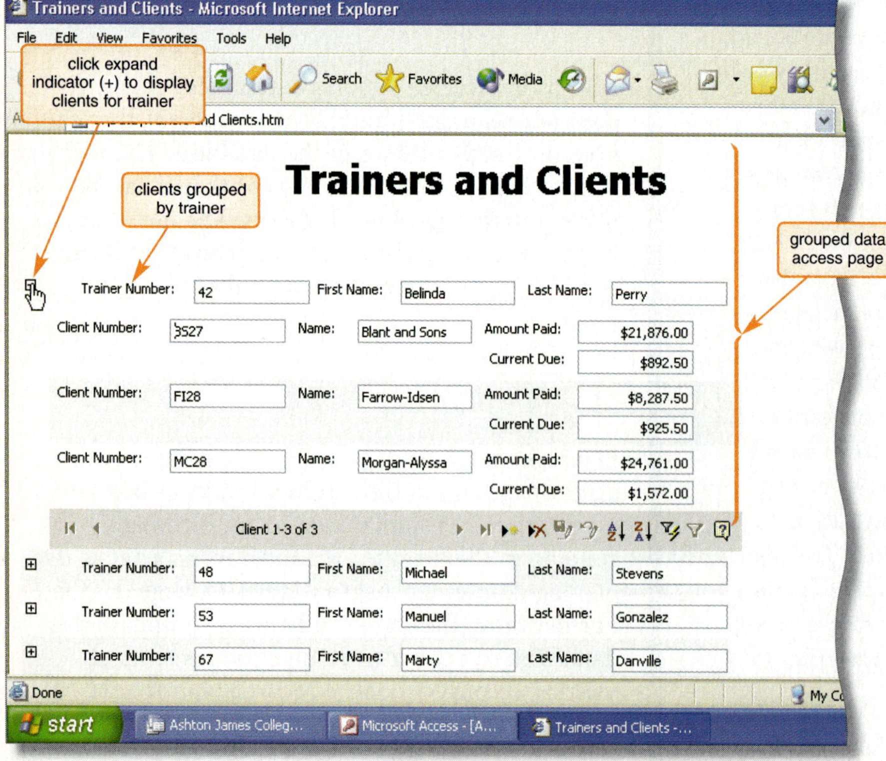

FIGURE 2

In this project, you will learn how to create the data access page shown in Figure 1. This data access page is located in a folder called Data on disk C. The database it is accessing also is located in this folder. In order to use this page on the Internet, both the page and the database would need to be located on some server that would be available to the Internet. The address entered in the browser would be changed to reflect the true location of the page.

You also will learn how to create the data access pages shown in Figures 2, 3, and 4. Figure 2 shows a grouped data access page. The data is grouped by trainer number. Clicking the expand indicator (+) in front of a trainer displays all the clients associated with that trainer. When the clients associated with a trainer appear, the plus sign changes to a minus sign (-). Clicking the minus sign will hide the clients associated with the trainer.

The data access page in Figure 3 contains a PivotTable. The Trainer Number field is in the filter area and can be used to restrict the data reflected in the PivotTable to only clients associated with certain trainers. The Client Number field is in the row area. The Course Number field is in the column area. The Hours Spent and Hours Remaining fields are in the detail area with their captions changed to Spent and Remaining, respectively. Sums of both the Hours Spent and Hours Remaining also are included in the PivotTable.

The data access page in Figure 4 contains a PivotChart. The PivotChart is a 3D Stacked Column chart. The bar heights represent total hours. The x-axis (horizontal axis) shows the trainer numbers subdivided into hours spent and hours remaining.

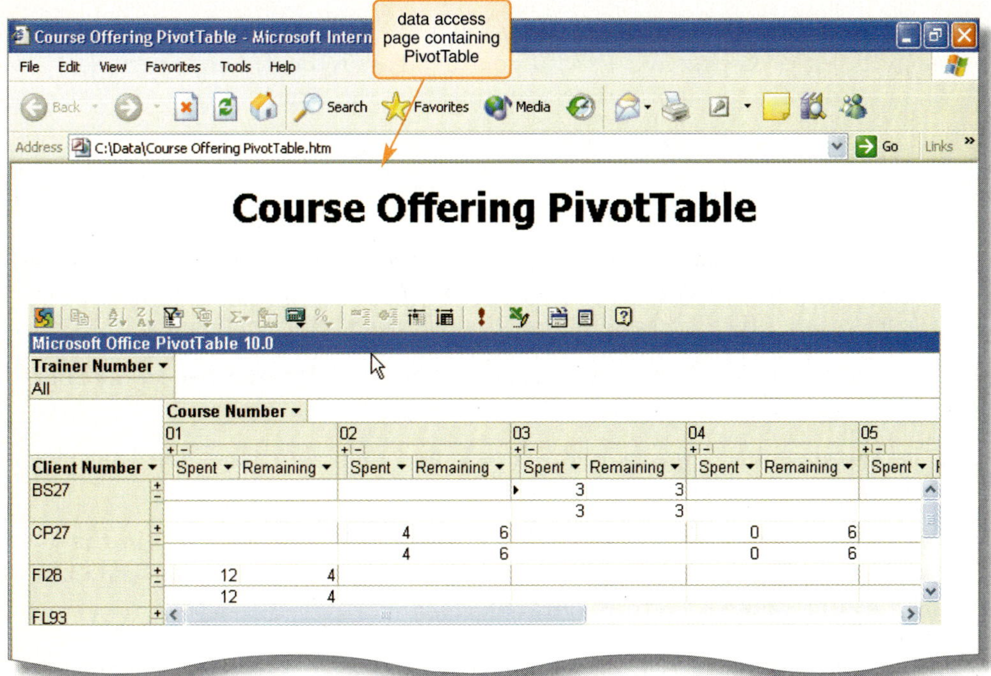

FIGURE 3

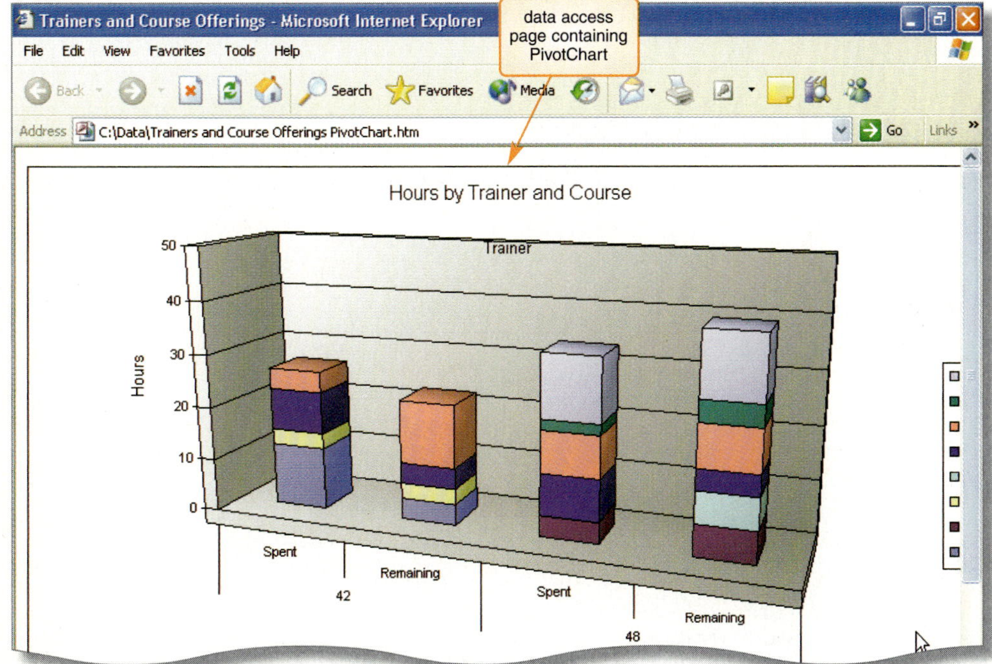

FIGURE 4

Opening the Database

If you are stepping through this project on a computer and want your screen to match the figures in this book, then you should change your computer's resolution to 800 x 600. For more information on how to change the resolution on your computer, see Appendix D. Before carrying out the steps in this project, first you must open the database. The steps on the next page, which start Access and open the

More About

The Access Help System

Need Help? It is no further than the Type a question for help box on the menu bar in the upper-right corner of the window. Click the box that contains the text, Type a question for help (Figure 5), type `help`, and then press the ENTER key. Access responds with a list of topics you can click to learn about obtaining help on any Access-related topic. To find out what is new in Access 2003, type `what is new in Access` in the Type a question for help box.

database, assume that the database is located in a folder called Data on disk C. (See the note in Project 4 on page AC 197.) If your database is located anywhere else, you will need to make the appropriate adjustments in the steps.

To Open a Database

1. **Click the Start button on the Windows taskbar, point to All Programs on the Start menu, point to Microsoft Office on the All Programs submenu, and then click Microsoft Office Access 2003 on the Microsoft Office submenu.**
2. **If the Access window is not maximized, double-click its title bar to maximize it.**
3. **If the Language bar appears, right-click it and then click Close the Language bar on the shortcut menu.**
4. **Click Open on the Database toolbar, and then click Local Disk (C:) in the Look in box. Double-click the Data folder, and then make sure the database called Ashton James College is selected.**
5. **Click the Open button.**
6. **If the Security Warning dialog box appears, click the Open button.**

The database opens and the Ashton James College : Database window appears.

Creating a Data Access Page

To create a data access page, use the Page Wizard as shown in the following steps.

To Create a Data Access Page Using the Page Wizard

1

- **With the Client table selected, click the New Object button arrow on the Database toolbar.**
- **Click Page and then click Page Wizard.**
- **Click the OK button.**

The Page Wizard dialog box displays the fields in the Client table in the list of available fields. The Client Number field currently is selected (Figure 5).

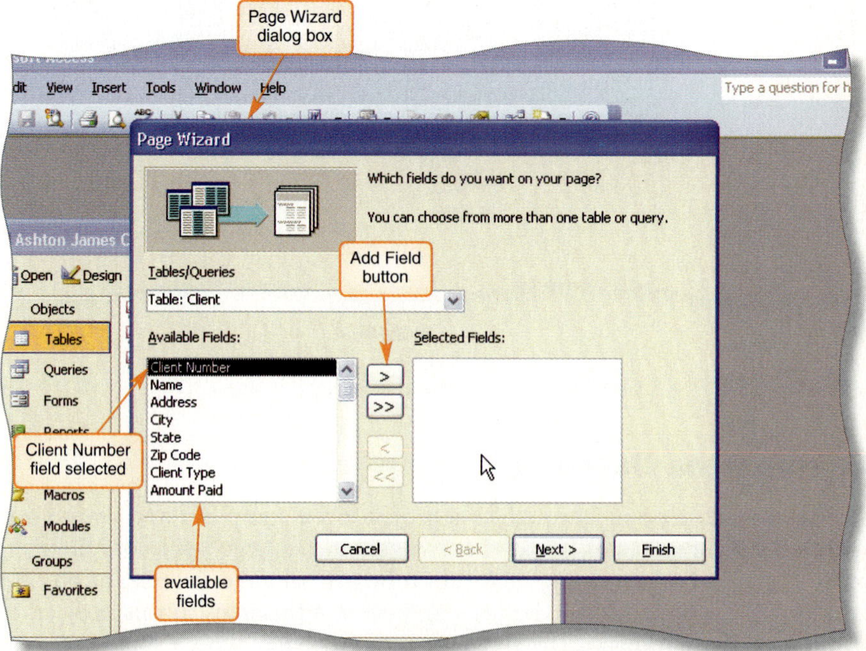

FIGURE 5

2

- **Click the Add Field button to add the Client Number field to the list of selected fields.**
- **Click the Add Field button six more times to add the Name, Address, City, State, Zip Code, and Client Type fields.**

The Client Number, Name, Address, City, State, Zip Code, and Client Type fields are selected (Figure 6).

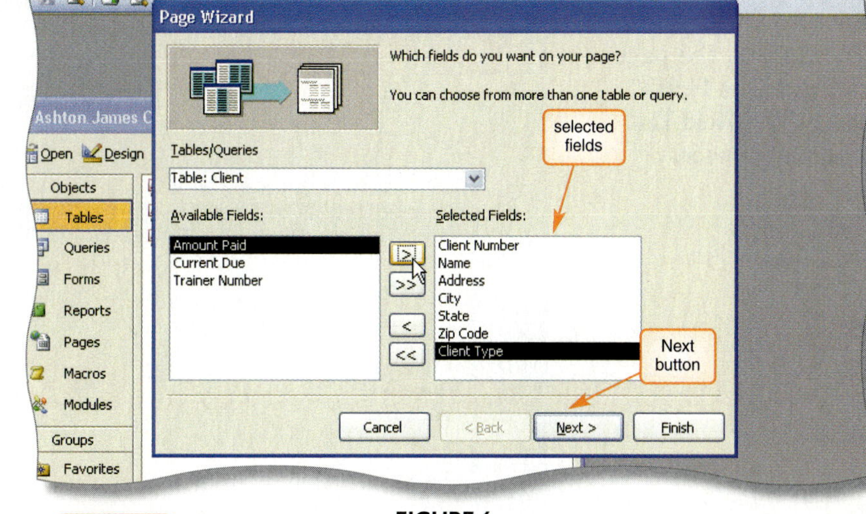

FIGURE 6

3

- **Click the Next button.**

The Page Wizard dialog box appears asking if you want to add any grouping levels (Figure 7).

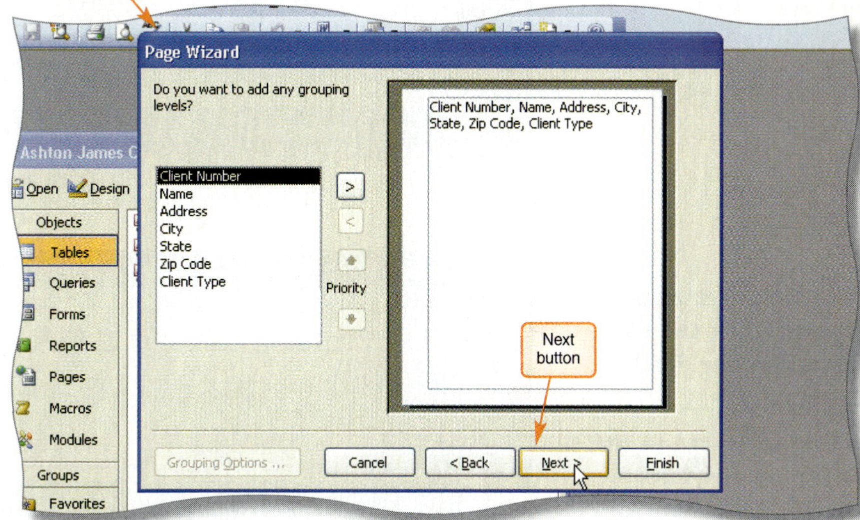

FIGURE 7

4

- **Because you do not need any grouping levels, click the Next button.**
- **Click the Next button a second time, because you do not need to make any changes on the following screen, which enables you to specify a special sort order.**

The Page Wizard dialog box appears asking what title you want for your page (Figure 8).

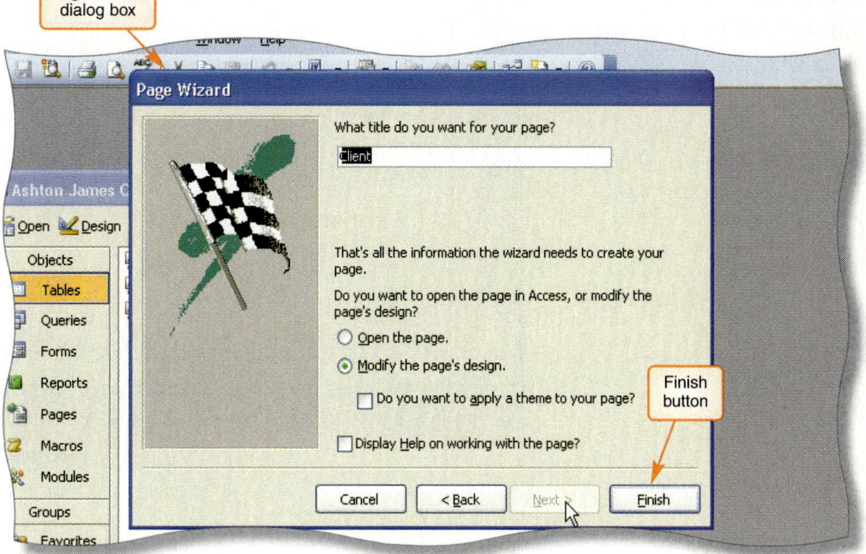

FIGURE 8

5

- **Because Client is acceptable as the page title, click the Finish button. The Field List pane may appear.**

The Client data access page appears (Figure 9).

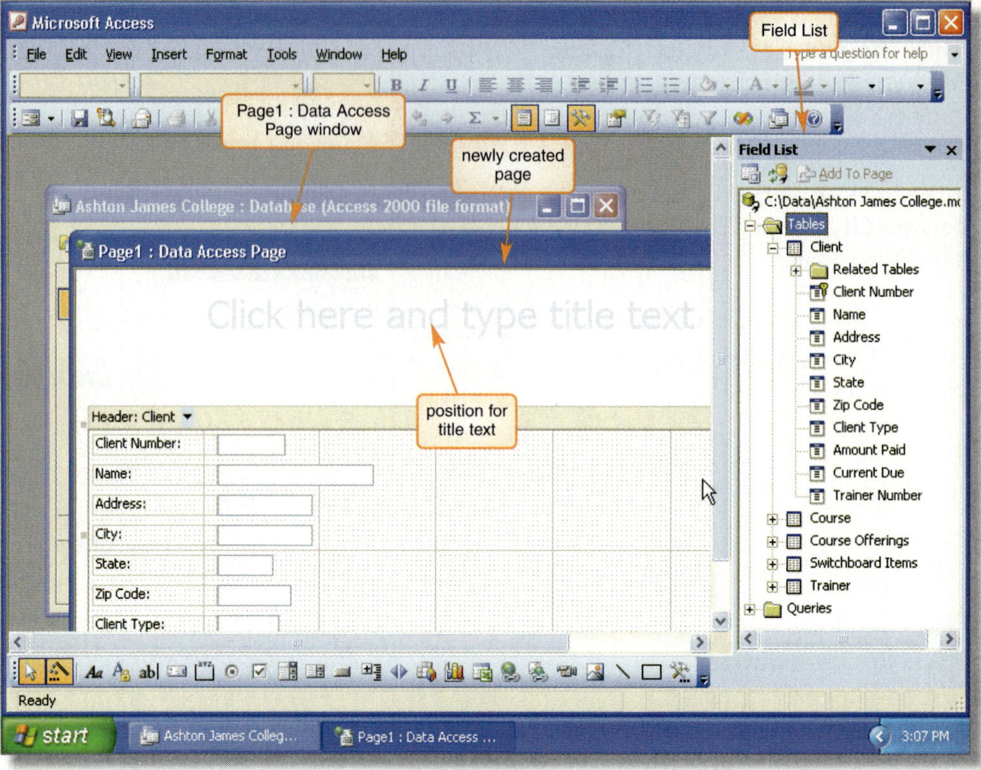

FIGURE 9

6

- **If a Field List pane appears, click the Close button for the Field List pane.**
- **Click anywhere in the portion of the screen labeled "Click here and type title text," and then type** `Ashton James College` **as the title text.**

The data access page appears (Figure 10). The title is changed to Ashton James College.

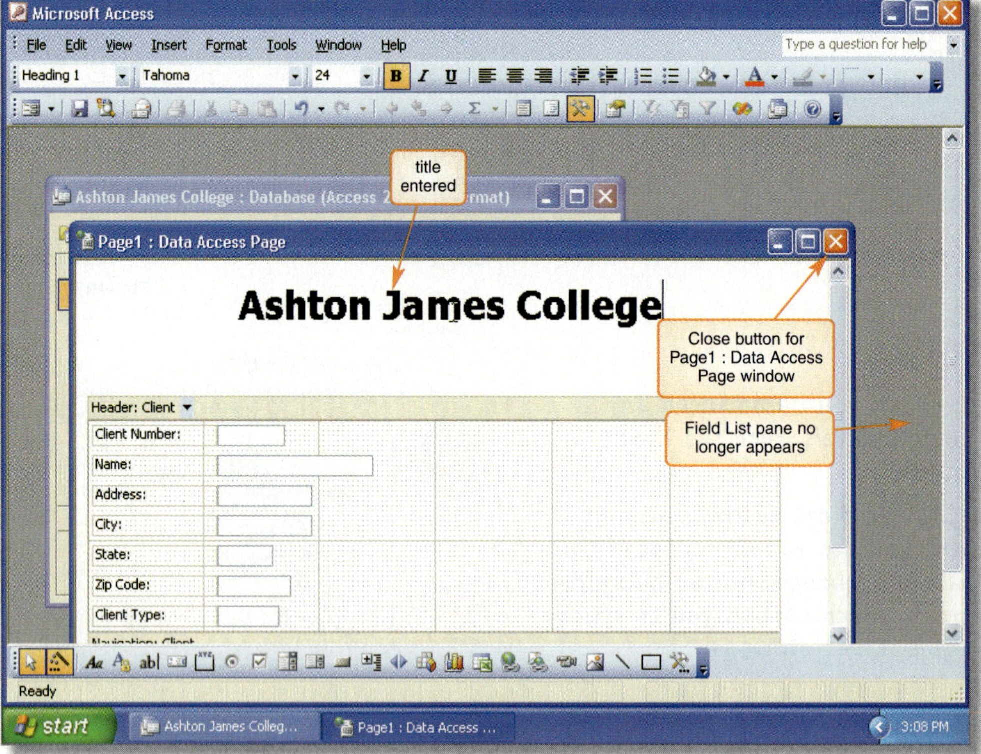

FIGURE 10

7

- **Click the Close button for the Page1 : Data Access Page window to close the window, and then click the Yes button in the Microsoft Office Access dialog box to indicate you want to save your changes.**
- **When the Save As Data Access Page dialog box appears, be sure the Data folder (or whatever folder contains your database) is selected and that the file name is Client.**

The Save As Data Access Page dialog box appears (Figure 11).

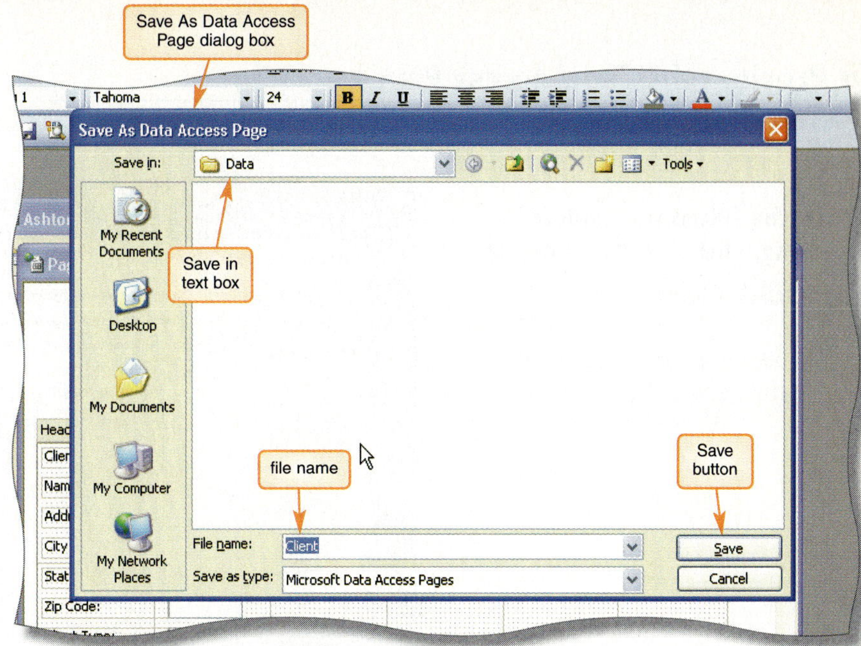

FIGURE 11

8

- **Click the Save button.**
- **If you see a message similar to the one in Figure 12, click the OK button, because the file location you specified is acceptable. [This message indicates that you will need to specify a UNC (Universal Naming Convention) address, rather than the file location you have specified if you want the page to be accessible over a network.]**

The data access page is created.

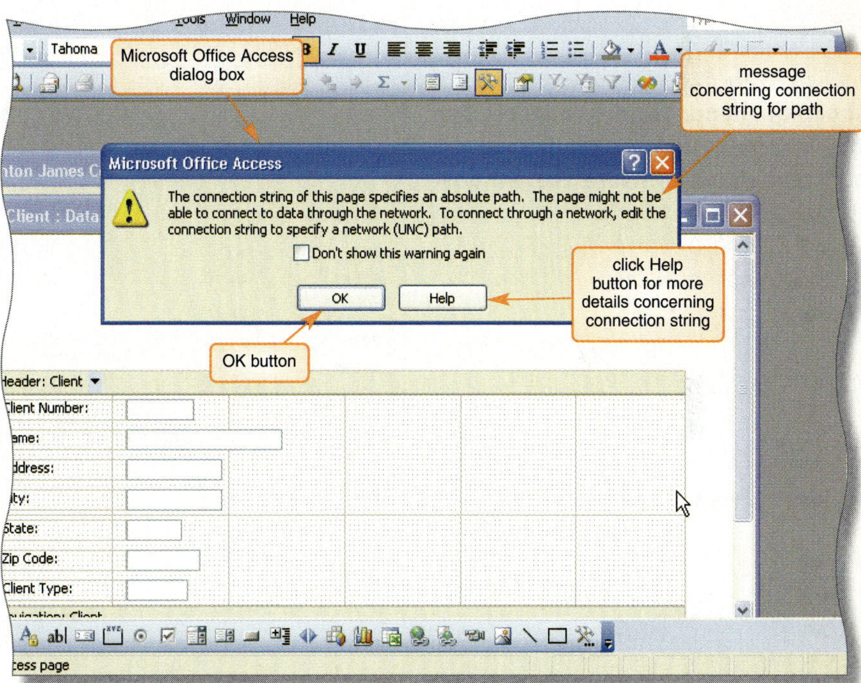

FIGURE 12

Previewing the Data Access Page

If you are connected to the Internet, you can view the data access page in the browser. To do this, you use the Web Page Preview command. When not connected to the Internet, you may not be able to view the data access page using the Web Page Preview command. You still can view the data access page, however, by using the Open command. The steps on the next page illustrate how to preview the data access page that was just created.

To Preview the Data Access Page

1

- **With the Database window appearing, click the Pages object.**
- **Right-click Client.**

The shortcut menu for the Client data access page appears (Figure 13).

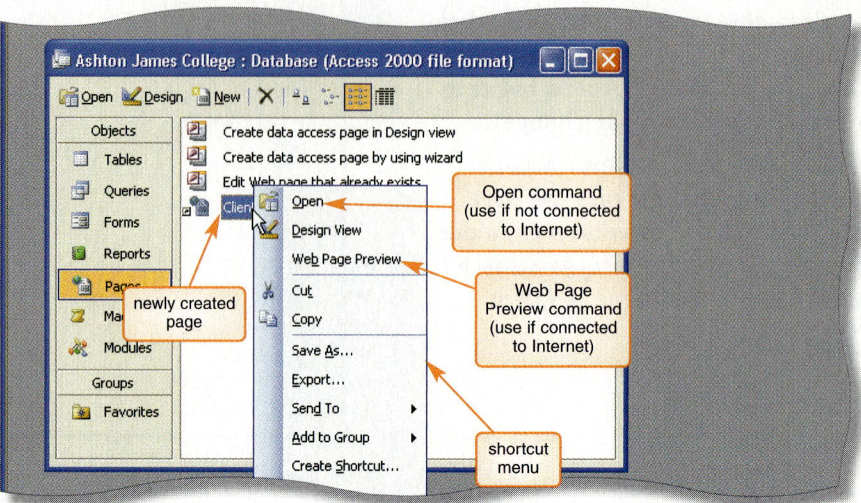

FIGURE 13

2

- **Click Web Page Preview on the shortcut menu. (If not connected to the Internet, click Open on the shortcut menu.) Ensure the window is maximized.**

The page appears within Internet Explorer (Figure 14). If you used the Open command, your screen will look slightly different.

3

- **Close Internet Explorer.**

The page no longer appears.

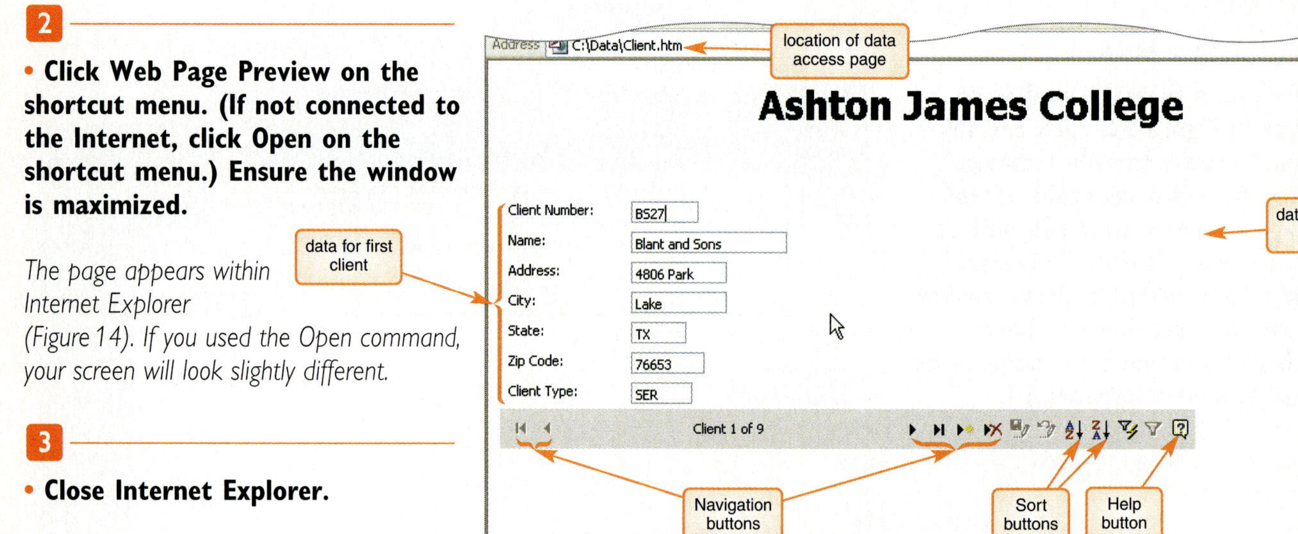

FIGURE 14

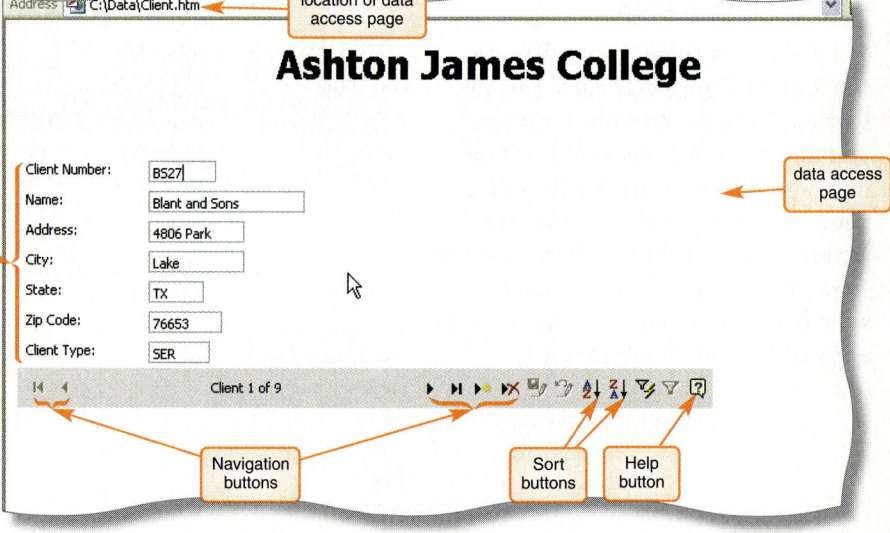

Using the Data Access Page

To use the data access page, start Internet Explorer, type the location of the data access page (for example: c:\data\client.htm, if you created the page in the Data folder on disk C), and then press the ENTER key. The page then will appear and look similar to the one in Figure 14.

You can use the navigation buttons, the Sort buttons, and the Filter buttons just as you do when viewing a datasheet or a form in Access. You can get help on the way you use the page by clicking the Help button (Figure 14). A book icon indicates subtopics are available. Double-clicking the icon displays the subtopics. A question mark icon indicates that information on the topic will appear when you click the question mark. In Figure 15, for example, the subtopics for both Getting

Started and Getting Help appear. The question mark in front of "Get Help using a data access page" has been clicked so the information on that topic appears. In addition, the window has been maximized, which makes it easier to read the help information.

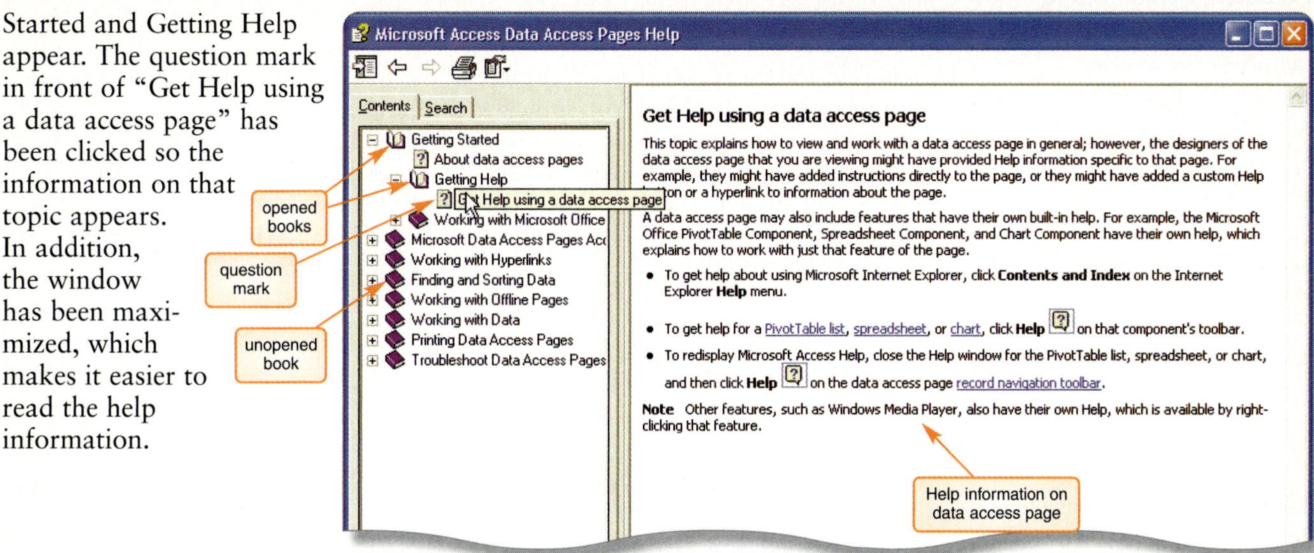

FIGURE 15

Grouped Data Access Pages

You can group records on a data access page that have some common characteristic. For example, you could group clients by trainer number, as in the data access page shown in Figure 2 on page AC 378. Thus, the clients of trainer 42 form one group, the clients of trainer 48 form a second, and the clients of trainer 53 form a third. In the data access page, you can show or hide any of these groups.

To create such a data access page, you can use a wizard. When you do, the wizard will give you an opportunity to specify grouping levels. You also can group in a data access page you are creating in Design view. The following steps show how to create a data access page in Design view.

To Create a Data Access Page in Design View

1. **Click Pages on the Objects bar and then click the New button.**
2. **Be sure Design View is selected in the New Data Access Page dialog box, and then click the OK button.**
3. **When a message appears indicating that you will not be able to open this data access page in Design view in Access 2000 or Access 2002, click the OK button.**
4. **If a field list does not appear, click the Field List button on the Page Design toolbar to display a field list.**
5. **Maximize the window containing the data access page by clicking its title bar.**

The data access page appears in a maximized window (Figure 16). A field list appears.

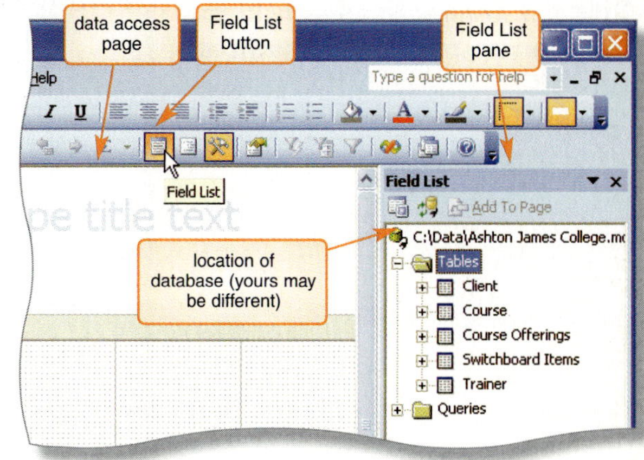

FIGURE 16

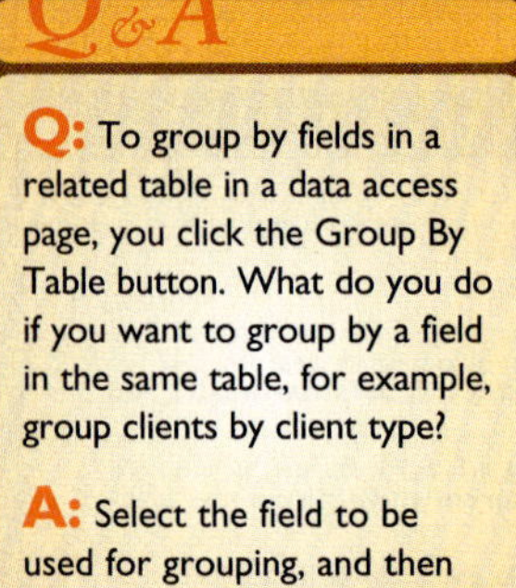

Q: To group by fields in a related table in a data access page, you click the Group By Table button. What do you do if you want to group by a field in the same table, for example, group clients by client type?

A: Select the field to be used for grouping, and then click the Promote button.

Adding the Fields and Grouping

To group in a data access page, you include the fields by dragging them from a field list to the desired position. You indicate grouping by using the Group by Table button on the Page Design toolbar. For example, to indicate grouping by the Trainer table, you first will select the Trainer Number field, and then click the Group by Table button. This will add a section for Trainer above a section for Client. Trainer fields will be in the Trainer section and Client fields will be in the Client section. The following steps illustrate how to add the fields and specify grouping.

To Add the Fields and Grouping

1

- **Click the plus sign in front of Client in the field list.**
- **When the Client fields appear, click the plus sign in front of Related tables, and then click the plus sign in front of the Trainer table listed in the Related Tables section.**

The fields in the Trainer table appear (Figure 17).

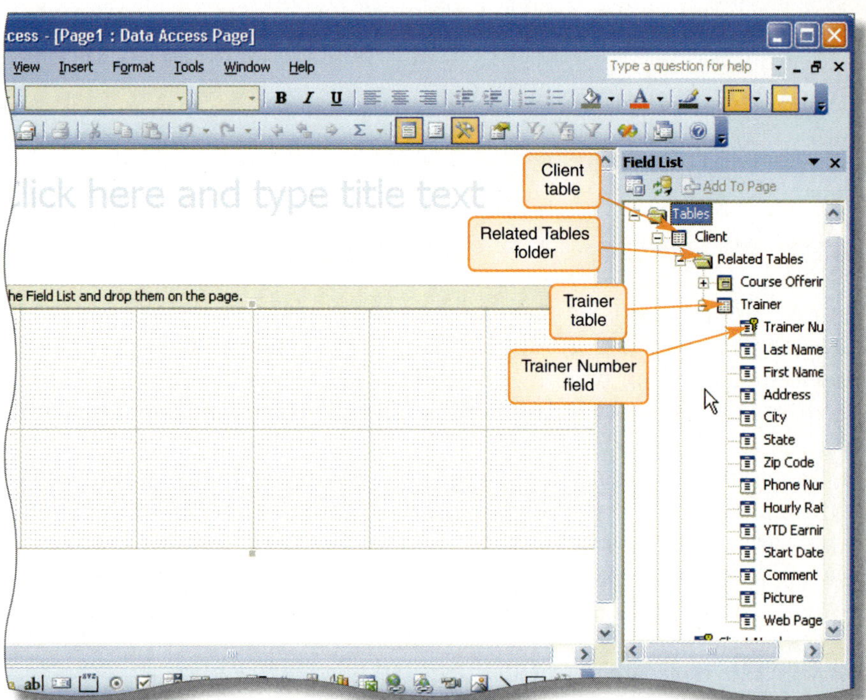

FIGURE 17

2

- **Drag the Trainer Number field to the approximate position shown in Figure 18.**

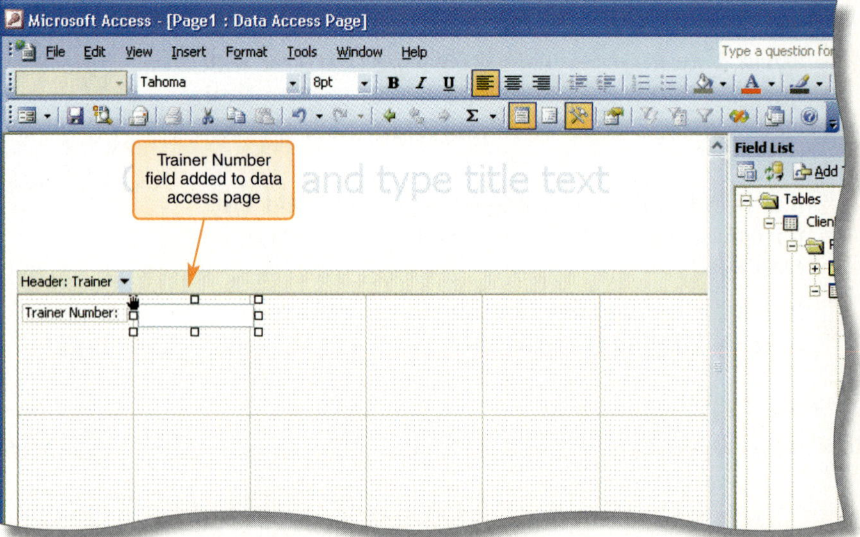

FIGURE 18

3

• **Drag the First Name and Last Name fields to the approximate positions shown in Figure 19.**

• **Drag the labels for the First Name and Last Name fields to the positions shown in the figure.**

• **Click the minus sign (-) in front of the Trainer table so the fields no longer appear, and then drag the Client Number field to the position shown in the figure.**

• **When the Layout Wizard dialog box appears, click the OK button and then click the Trainer Number field to select it.**

The First Name, Last Name, and Client Number fields are added. The Trainer Number field is selected.

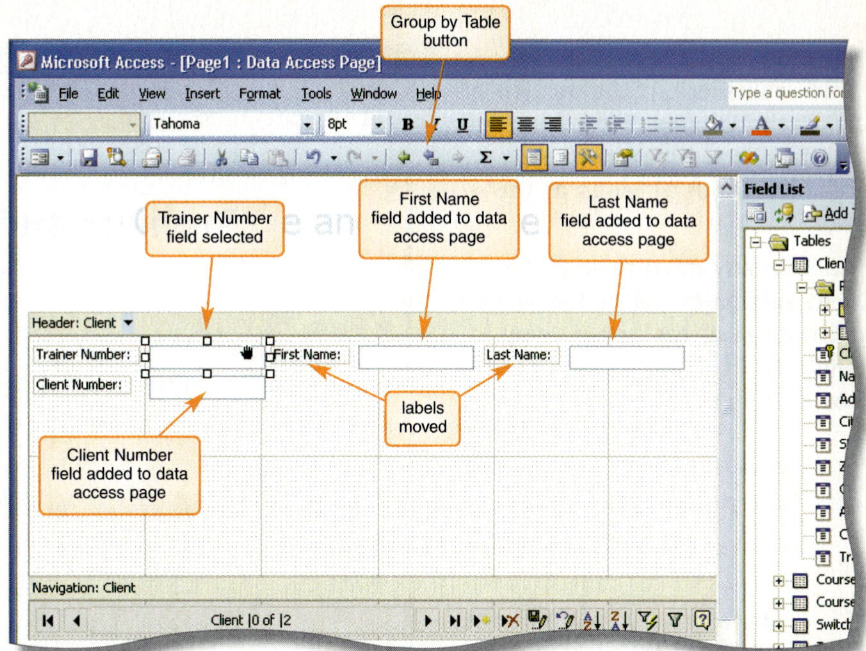

FIGURE 19

4

• **Click the Group by Table button.**

The data is grouped by trainer (Figure 20). A header for the Trainer table is added above the header for the Client table.

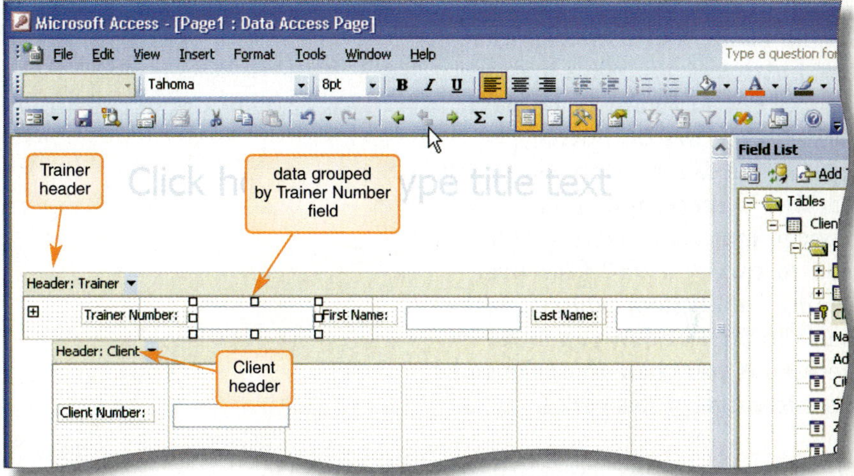

FIGURE 20

5

• **Drag the Client Number field to the approximate position shown in Figure 21.**

• **Drag the Name, Amount Paid, and Current Due fields from the field list to the approximate positions shown in the figure.**

• **Drag the labels to the positions shown in the figure.**

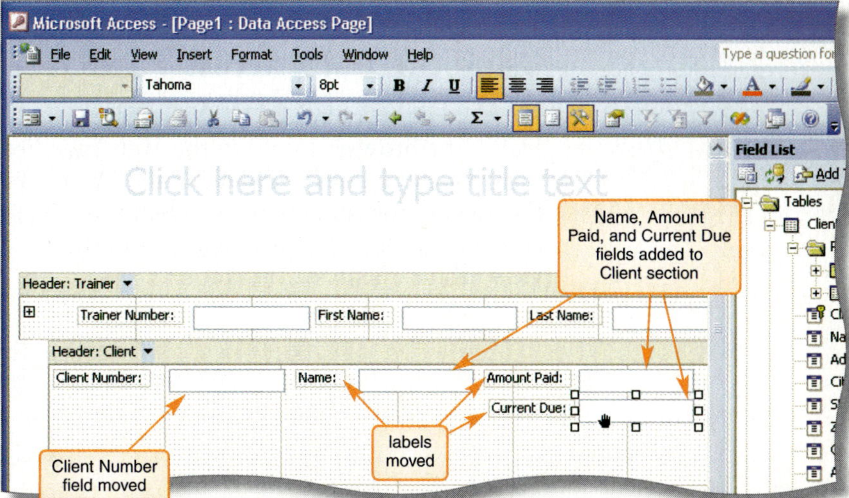

FIGURE 21

6

- Click anywhere in the portion of the screen labeled "Click here and type title text," and then type `Trainers and Clients` as the title.
- Click in any open area of the Client section to select the section, and then drag the lower sizing handle to the approximate position shown in Figure 22.

The title is added and the Client section is resized.

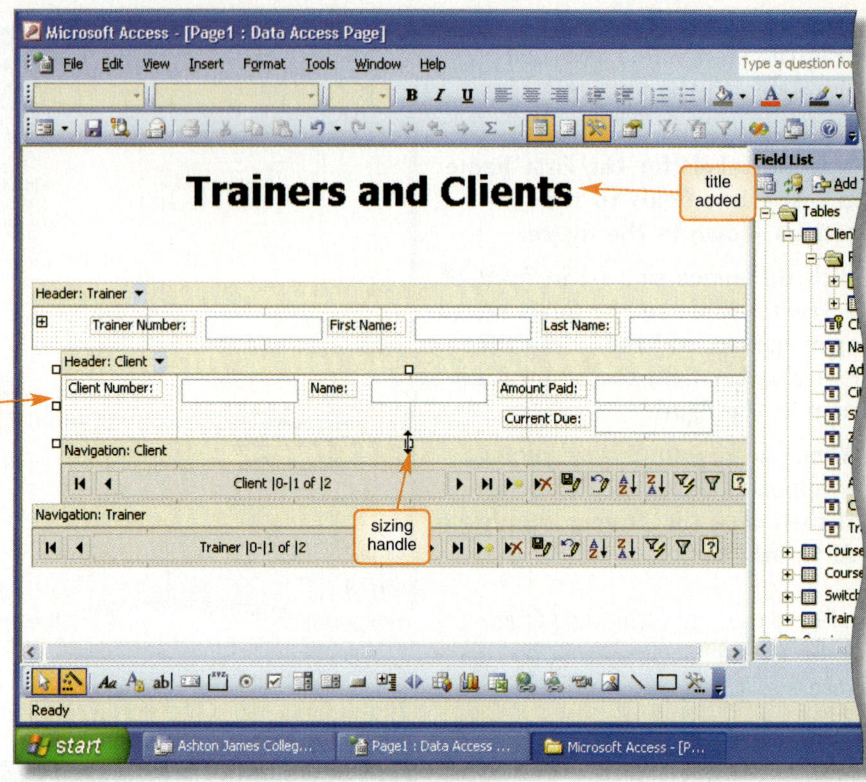

FIGURE 22

7

- Close the window containing the data access page by clicking its Close Window button.
- Click the Yes button when asked if you want to save your changes, type `Trainers and Clients` as the file name, and then click the Save button. If you see a message like the one in Figure 12 on page AC 383, click the OK button, because the file location you specified is acceptable. [This message indicates that you will need to specify a UNC (Universal Naming Convention) address, rather than the file location you have specified if you want the page to be accessible over a network.]

The grouped data access page is created.

Using the Data Access Page

If you are connected to the Internet, you can preview what the page will look like in the browser by using the Web Page Preview command. You also can simply open the data access page using the Open command. In either case, you work with the page in the same manner. The following steps show how to preview the data access page that was just created and then click the plus sign in front of trainer 30 to view all the clients of the trainer.

To Use the Data Access Page

1

- **With the Database window appearing, be sure the Pages object is selected, right-click Trainers and Clients, and then click Web Page Preview on the shortcut menu.**

The data access page appears (Figure 23). Clients currently do not appear.

2

- **Click the plus sign in front of trainer number 42.**

The clients of trainer 42 appear underneath trainer 42 as shown in Figure 2 on page AC 378.

3

- **Close the browser window containing the data access page by clicking its Close button.**

The page no longer appears.

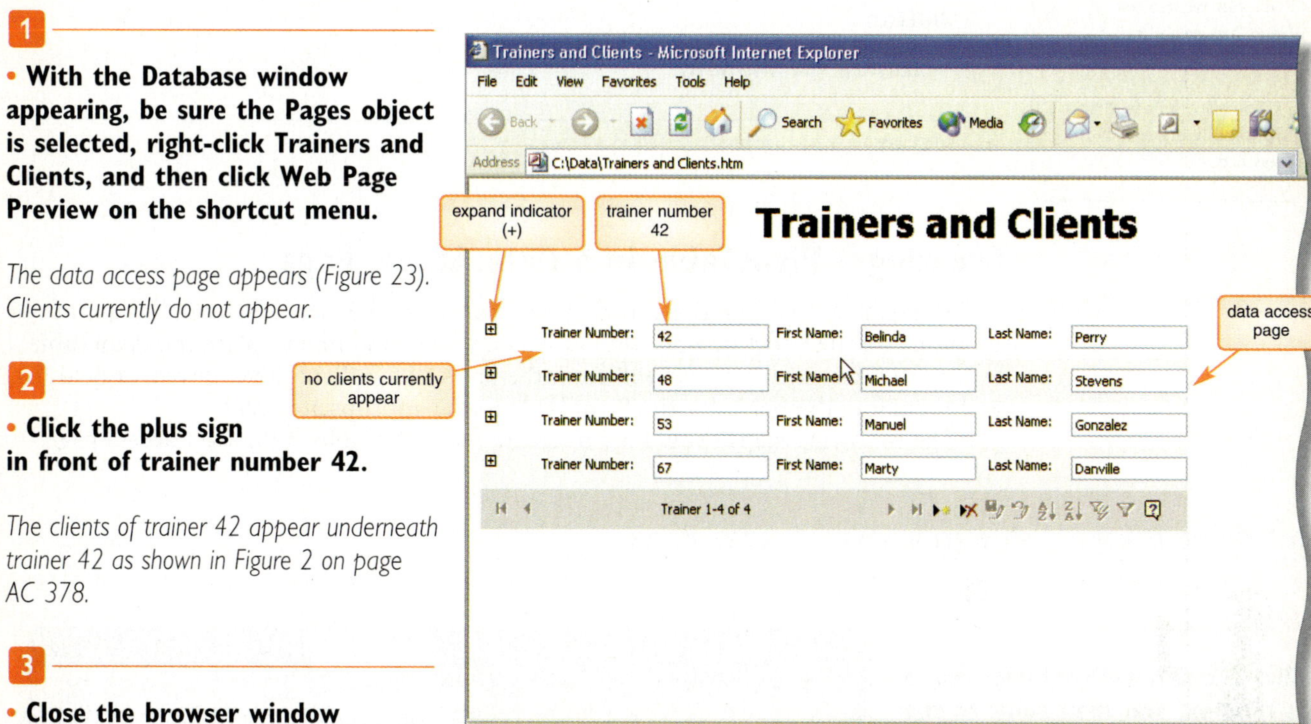

FIGURE 23

PivotTables in Data Access Pages

There are two ways to create a PivotTable in a data access page. You can create a PivotTable view of a table or query and then save the PivotTable as a data access page. Alternatively, you can create a data access page in Design view, place a PivotTable on the data access page, and then place the desired fields in appropriate areas of the PivotTable as you did when you created a PivotTable in Project 6. For the second approach, you first must create a data access page in Design view as illustrated in the following steps.

More About

Publishing to the Internet: Saving Other Objects

You also can publish other objects such as reports and datasheets to the Internet. To publish a datasheet or report to the Internet, save the object as a Web page in HTML format. To do so, select the name of the object in the Database window, click File on the menu bar, and then click Export. In the Save As Type box, click HTML documents.

To Create a Data Access Page in Design View

1. **If necessary, click Pages on the Objects bar and then click the New button.**
2. **Be sure Design View is selected in the New Data Access Page dialog box, and then click the OK button.**
3. **When a message appears indicating that you will not be able to open this data access page in Design view in Access 2000 or Access 2002, click the OK button.**
4. **If a field list appears, click the Field List button on the Page Design toolbar to remove the field list.**

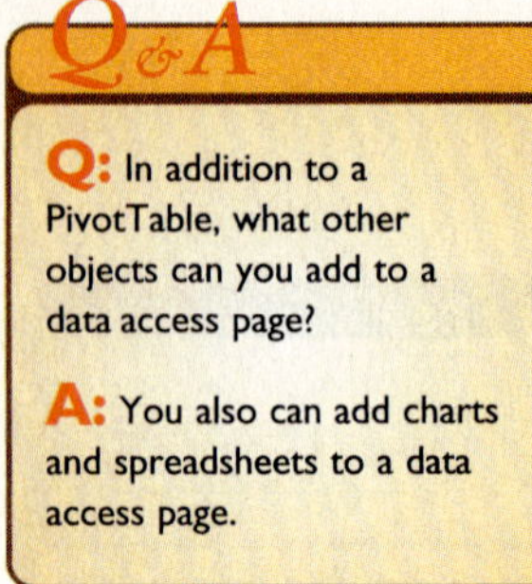

Q: In addition to a PivotTable, what other objects can you add to a data access page?

A: You also can add charts and spreadsheets to a data access page.

5 **If the toolbox does not appear, click the Toolbox button on the Page Design toolbar. Be sure the toolbox is docked at the bottom of the screen. If it is not, drag its title bar to the bottom of the screen and release the left mouse button.**

6 **Maximize the window.**

The data access page appears in Design view.

Creating a PivotTable in a Data Access Page

To create a PivotTable in a data access page, use the Office PivotTable tool in the toolbox and then click the position at which you would like to place the PivotTable. Select the table or query that will form the basis of the PivotTable, display a field list, and then drag the fields for the PivotTable to the appropriate areas.

The following steps show how to create the PivotTable in the data access page.

To Create a PivotTable in a Data Access Page

1

- **Click the Office PivotTable tool in the toolbox, and then point to the approximate position shown in Figure 24.**

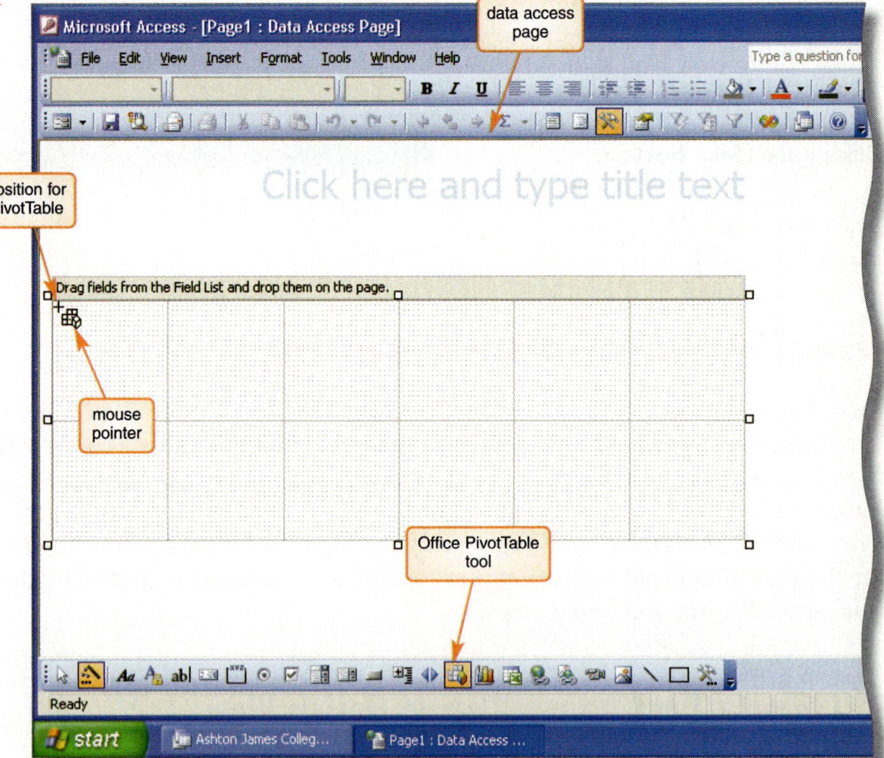

FIGURE 24

2

- **Click the position shown in Figure 24 to place the PivotTable. A field list may reappear.**
- **If a field list reappears, close it by clicking its Close button.**
- **Right-click the PivotTable and then click Commands and Options on the shortcut menu.**
- **If necessary, click the "Data member, table, view, or cube name" option button, click the arrow, and then select the Trainers and Course Offerings query.**
- **Click the Close button in the Commands and Options dialog box.**
- **Resize the PivotTable to the approximate size shown in Figure 25 by dragging its lower-right sizing handle.**

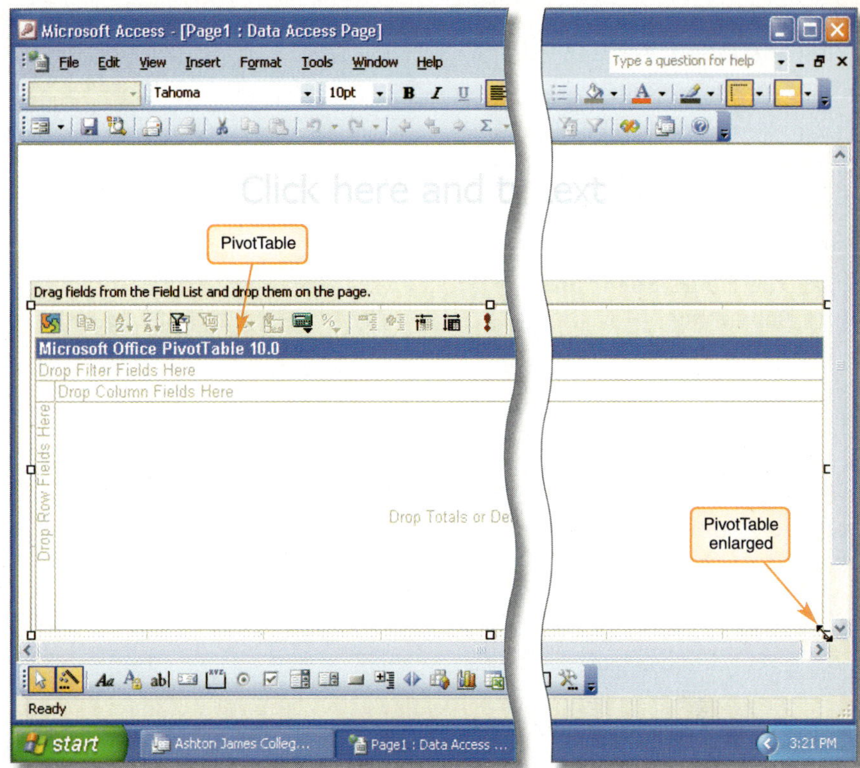

FIGURE 25

3

- **Right-click the PivotTable, and then click Field List on the shortcut menu to display the PivotTable Field List pane.**
- **If the field list does not appear in the position shown in Figure 26, move it to the indicated position by dragging its title bar.**

The PivotTable Field List pane appears. It contains only the Trainers and Course Offerings query, the query you identified for the PivotTable.

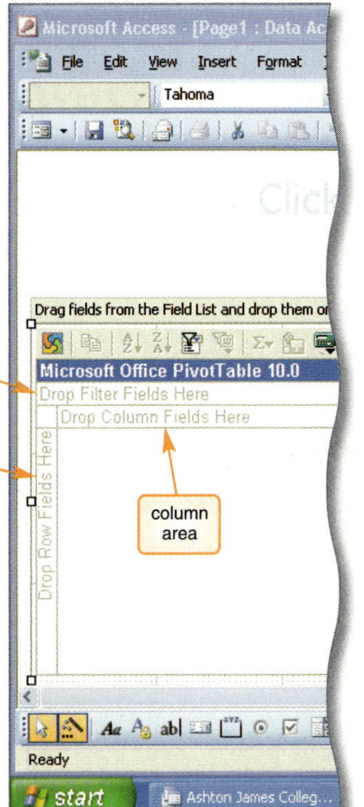

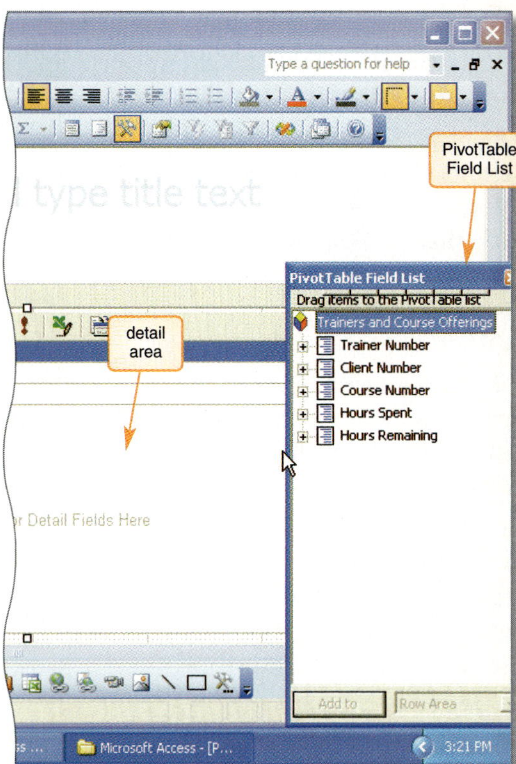

FIGURE 26

4

- **Drag the Client Number field to the row area.**
- **Drag the Course Number field to the column area.**
- **Drag the Trainer Number field to the filter area.**
- **Drag the Hours Spent and Hours Remaining fields to the detail area.**
- **The Hours Remaining field should be to the right of the Hours Spent field in the detail area. If it is not, drag the Hours Remaining field to the right of the Hours Spent field.**

The Client Number field is added to the row area (Figure 27). The Course Number field is added to the column area. The Trainer Number field is added to the filter area. The Hours Spent and Hours Remaining fields are added to the detail area.

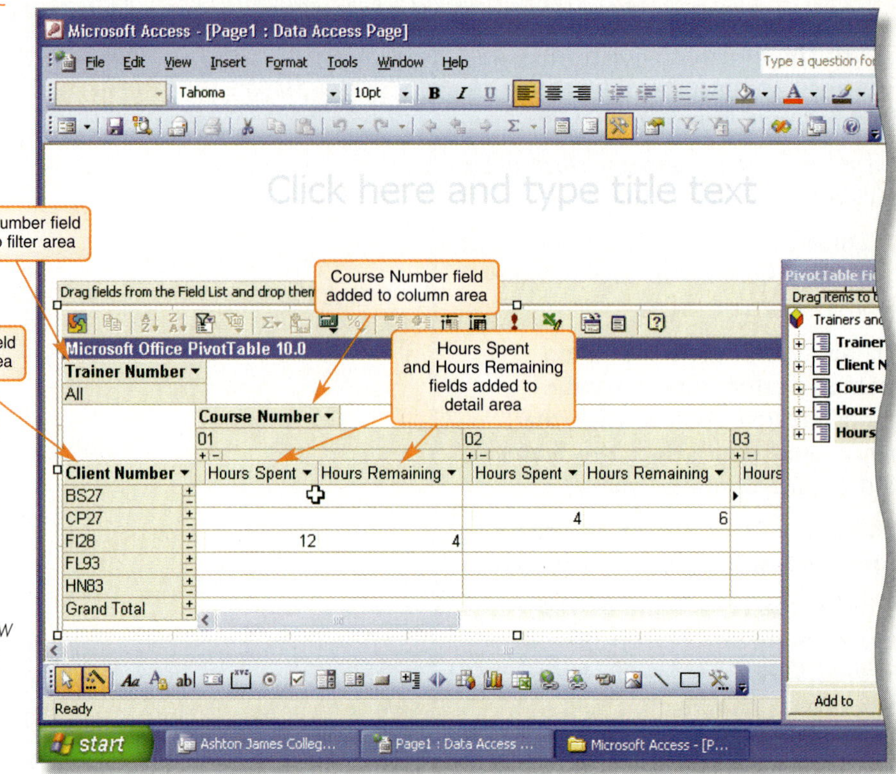

FIGURE 27

5

- **Close the PivotTable Field List pane by clicking its Close button.**
- **Right-click the Hours Spent field, click Commands and Options on the shortcut menu, click the Captions tab, erase the current caption, and type** `Spent` **as the new caption.**
- **Using the same technique, change the caption for Hours Remaining to Remaining.**
- **Click anywhere in the portion of the screen labeled "Click here and type title text," and then type** `Course Offering PivotTable` **as the title.**

The caption for the Hours Spent field is changed to Spent (Figure 28). The caption for the Hours Remaining field is changed to Remaining. The title is changed to Course Offering PivotTable.

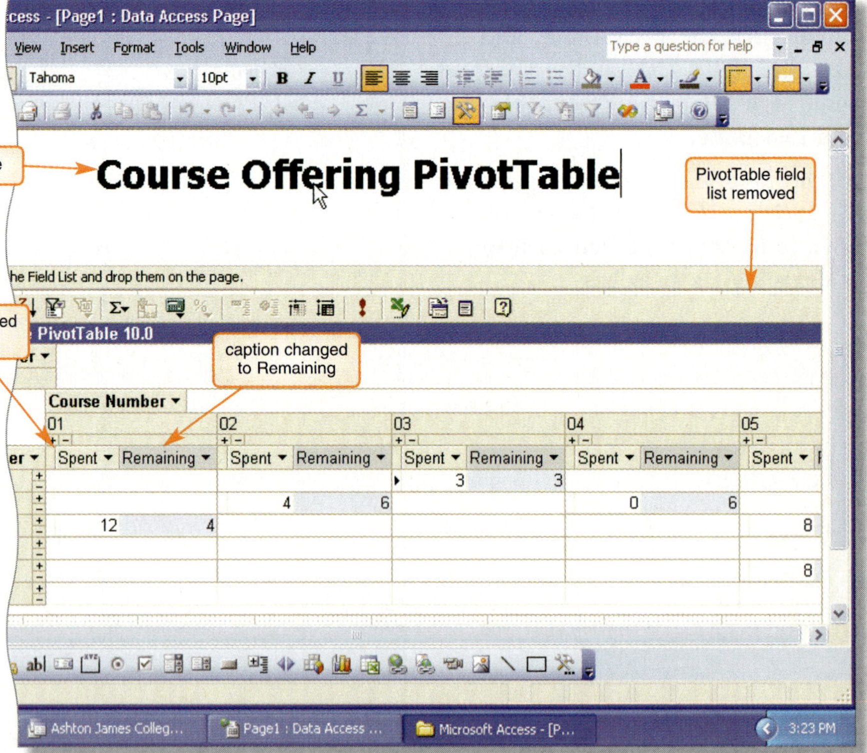

FIGURE 28

6

- **Click the Spent field, and then click the AutoCalc button on the PivotTable toolbar.**

The AutoCalc menu appears (Figure 29).

7

- **Click Sum on the AutoCalc menu.**
- **Click the Remaining field, click the AutoCalc button on the PivotTable toolbar, and then click Sum.**
- **Close the window containing the data access page by clicking its Close Window button.**
- **Click the Yes button when asked if you want to save your changes, type** `Course Offering PivotTable` **as the field name, and then click the Save button.**
- **If you see a message like the one in Figure 12 on page AC 383, click the OK button, because the file location you specified is acceptable.**

The data access page containing the PivotTable is created.

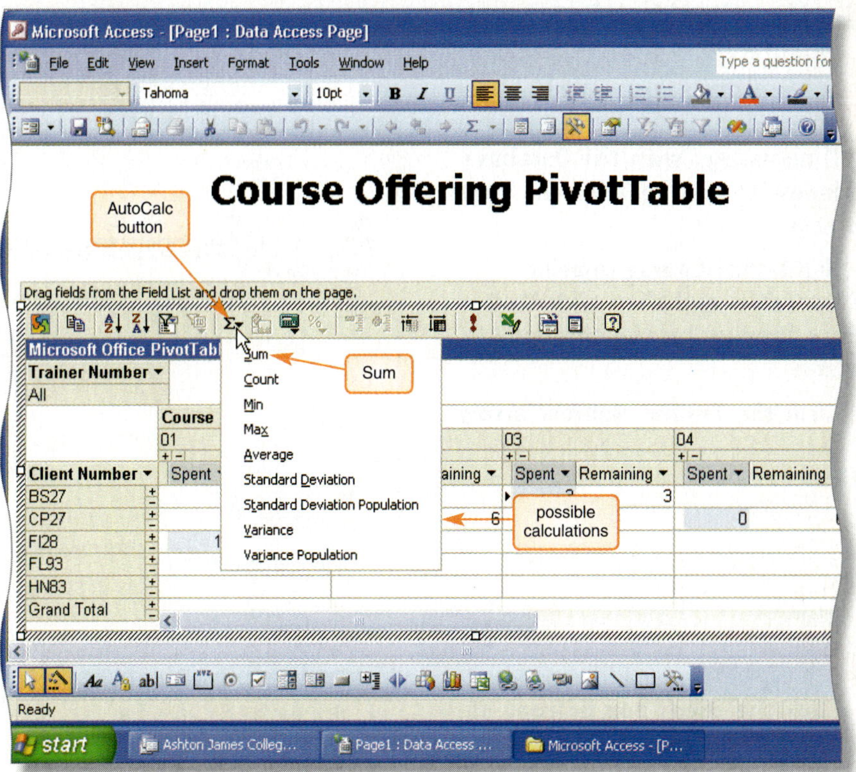

FIGURE 29

Using the PivotTable

You use the PivotTable in the data access page in a similar manner to the way you use PivotTable view for a table or query. You can click appropriate plus or minus signs to hide or show relevant data. You can restrict the data that will be reflected in the PivotTable by clicking an appropriate down arrow and then checking or unchecking items in the list that appears. You also can drag the fields to different locations in the PivotTable to change its organization. The steps on the next page illustrate how to open the data access page, and then restrict the data reflected in the table so clients of trainer 42 are not included.

More About

Microsoft Certification

The Microsoft Office Specialist Certification program provides an opportunity for you to obtain a valuable industry credential — proof that you have the Access 2003 skills required by employers. For more information, see Appendix E, or visit the Access 2003 Certification Web page (scsite.com/ac2003/cert).

To Use the PivotTable

1

- **If necessary, with the Database window appearing, click the Pages object.**
- **Right-click Course Offering PivotTable, and then click Web Page Preview on the shortcut menu.**
- **Click the Trainer Number arrow.**

The data access page appears (Figure 30). The list of trainers also appears.

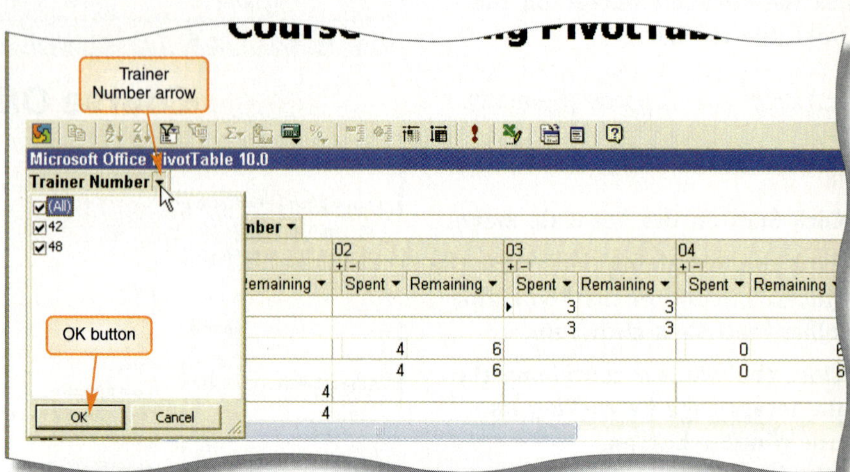

FIGURE 30

2

- **Click the check box in front of trainer 42 to remove the check mark, and then click the OK button.**

The data for clients of trainer 42 no longer is represented in the PivotTable (Figure 31).

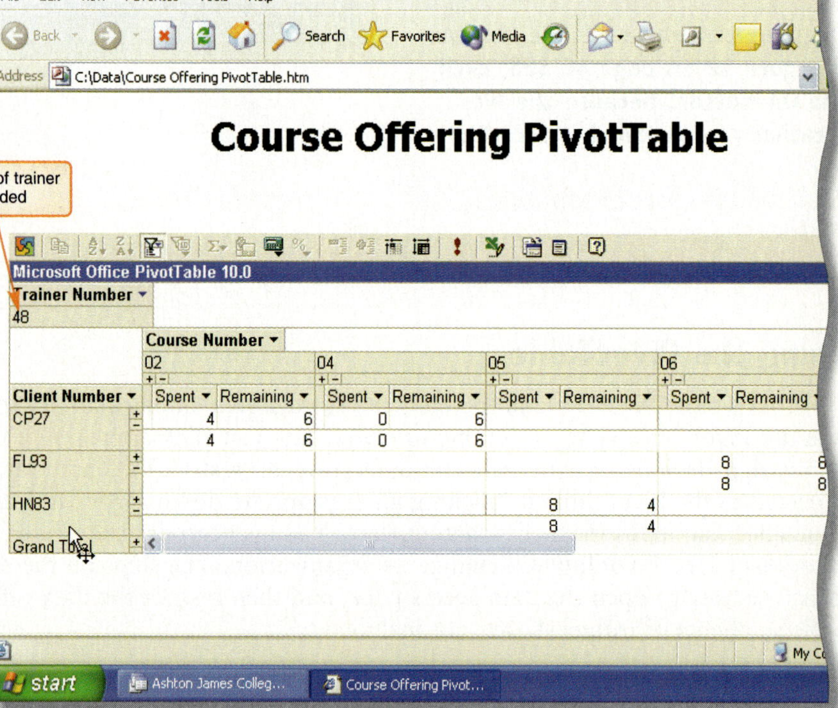

FIGURE 31

3

- **Close the browser window containing the data access page by clicking its Close Window button.**

The page no longer appears.

Saving a PivotChart to a Data Access Page

You can create a PivotChart on a data access page by first creating the PivotChart as the PivotChart view of a table or query and then saving the PivotChart as a data access page. The following steps show how to save the PivotChart view of the Trainers and Course Offerings query created in Project 6 as a data access page.

To Save a PivotChart to a Data Access Page

1

- **Click Queries on the Objects bar, right-click the Trainers and Course Offerings query, and then click Open on the shortcut menu.**
- **Click the View button arrow, and then click PivotChart View on the View menu.**
- **With the PivotChart appearing, click File on the menu bar, and then click Save As on the View menu.**
- **Change the name from Trainers and Course Offerings to** `Trainers and Course Offerings PivotChart`**, click the arrow in the As text box, and then select Data Access Page.**

The PivotChart and the Save As dialog box appear (Figure 32).

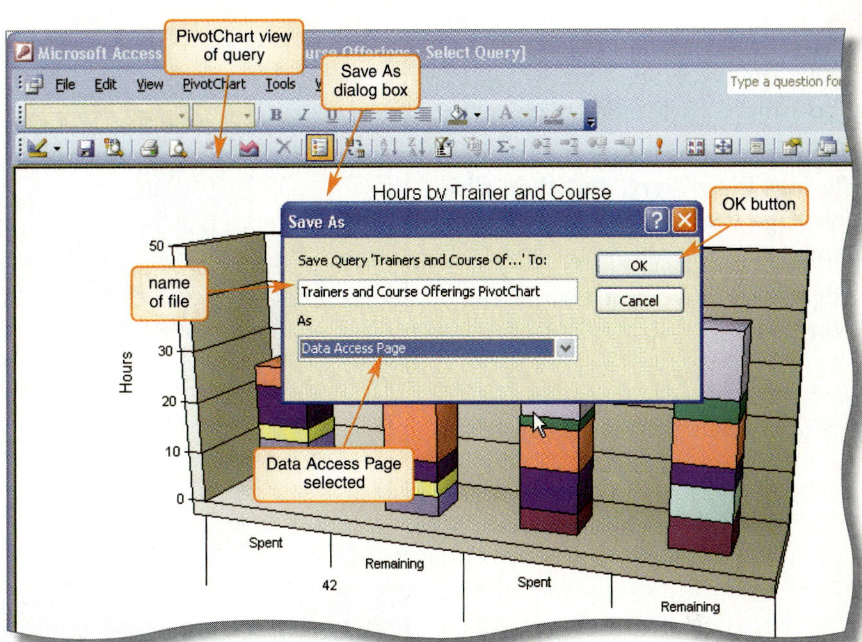

FIGURE 32

2

- **Click the OK button in the Save As dialog box, be sure the file name is Trainers and Course Offerings PivotChart, and then click the OK button in the New Data Access Page dialog box.**

The data access page containing the PivotChart is created.

3

- **Click the Close Window button twice, once to close the data access page and once to close the PivotChart view of the query.**
- **If asked if you want to save the changes to the layout of the Trainers and Course Offerings query, click the No button.**

The window is closed. Changes to the query layout are not saved.

Using the Data Access Page

You use the PivotChart in the data access page in a similar manner to the way you use the PivotChart view of a table or query. You can display the drop areas and then use them to restrict the data that will be reflected in the PivotChart. You also can display the PivotChart toolbar and use it to change the chart type, to change the chart organization, to show or hide a legend, and so on. The steps on the next page show how to open the data access page when you are connected to the Internet, display a field list, display the drop areas, place the Client Number field in the filter fields area, and then use the Client Number control to restrict the clients whose data is reflected in the PivotChart.

More About

Quick Reference

For a table that lists how to complete the tasks covered in this book using the mouse, menu, shortcut menu, and keyboard, see the Quick Reference Summary at the back of this book, or visit the Access 2003 Quick Reference Web page (scsite.com/ac2003/qr).

To Use the Data Access Page

1

- **With the Database window appearing, click the Pages object.**
- **Right-click Trainers and Course Offerings PivotChart, and then click Web Page Preview on the shortcut menu.**
- **Right-click any open area of the PivotChart.**

The PivotChart appears (Figure 33). The shortcut menu for the PivotChart appears.

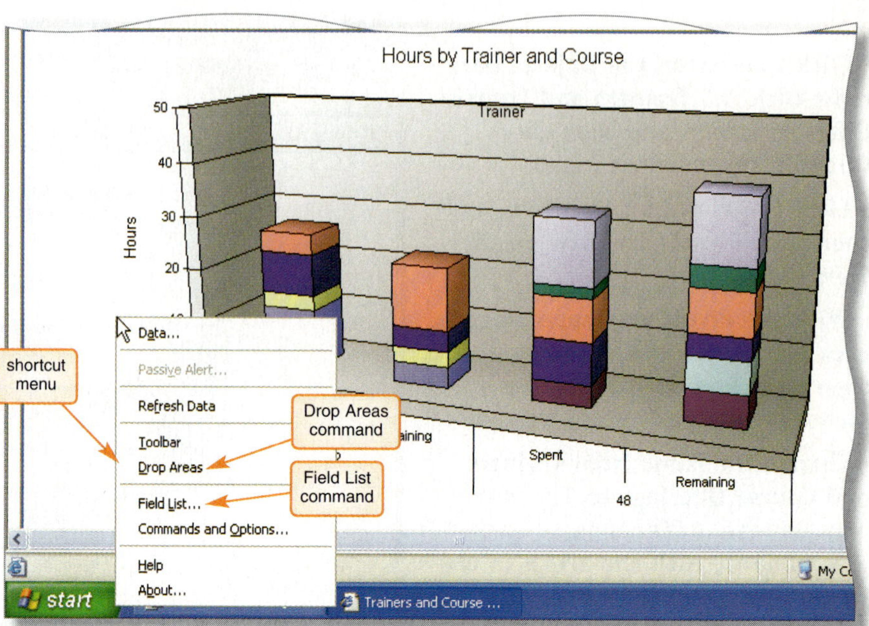

FIGURE 33

2

- **Click Field List on the shortcut menu to display a field list.**
- **Right-click any open area of the PivotChart, and then click Drop Areas on the shortcut menu.**
- **Drag the Client Number field to the filter fields.**
- **Click the Client Number arrow, and then remove the check marks from Client FI28 and Client FL93.**
- **Click the OK button.**

The PivotChart appears (Figure 34). Only course offerings for clients BS27, CP27, and HN83 are reflected in the chart.

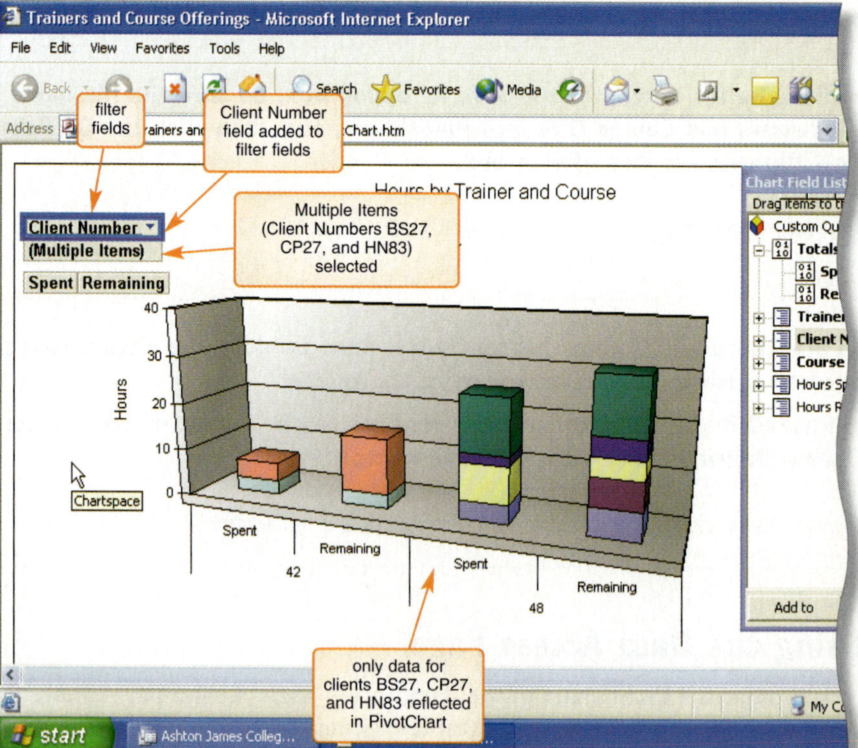

FIGURE 34

3

- **Close the browser window containing the data access page by clicking its Close Window button.**

The page no longer appears.

Closing the Database and Quitting Access

The following steps close the database and quit Access.

To Close a Database and Quit Access

1. **Click the Close Window button for the Ashton James College : Database window.**
2. **Click the Close button for the Microsoft Access 2003 window.**

Web Feature Summary

In this Web Feature, you learned how to create a data access page for the Client table in the Ashton James College database. To do so, you used the Page Wizard. You then saw how to preview the data access page from within Access. You learned how to create and use a grouped data access page that grouped clients by trainer. You also saw how to create a data access page in Design view, and then created a PivotTable in the data access page. The feature also illustrated how to save a PivotChart that was created earlier as a data access page. You also saw how to use each of the data access pages that were created.

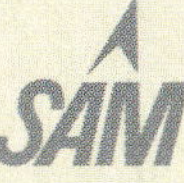

If you have a SAM user profile, you may have access to hands-on instruction, practice, and assessment of the skills covered in this project. Log in to your SAM account and go to your assignments page to see what your instructor has assigned.

What You Should Know

Having completed this Web Feature, you should be able to perform the tasks listed below. The tasks are listed in the same order they were presented in this feature. For a list of the buttons, menus, toolbars, and commands introduced in this Web Feature, see the Quick Reference Summary at the back of this book and refer to the Page Number column.

1. Open a Database (AC 380)
2. Create a Data Access Page Using the Page Wizard (AC 380)
3. Preview the Data Access Page (AC 384)
4. Create a Data Access Page in Design View (AC 385)
5. Add the Fields and Grouping (AC 386)
6. Use the Data Access Page (AC 389)
7. Create a Data Access Page in Design View (AC 389)
8. Create a PivotTable in a Data Access Page (AC 390)
9. Use the PivotTable (AC 394)
10. Save a PivotChart to a Data Access Page (AC 395)
11. Use the Data Access Page (AC 396)
12. Close a Database and Quit Access (AC 397)

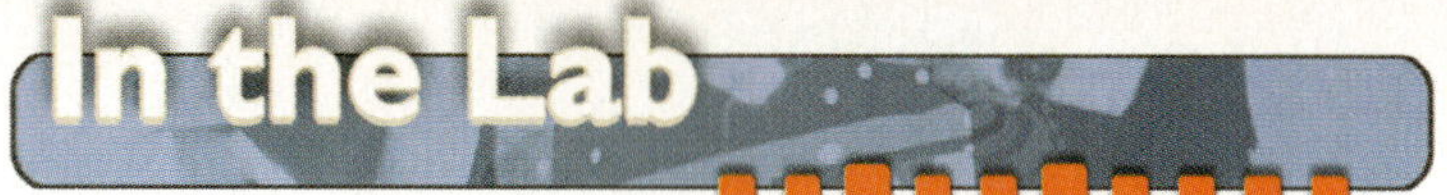

1 Creating Data Access Pages for Begon Pest Control

Problem: Begon Pest Control would like to create Web pages that would allow them to view and/or update customer data over the Internet. The company also would like to make a list of technicians available over the Web. When viewing this data, the company would like the option of displaying all the customers for one or more of the technicians appearing on the data access page.

Instructions: Start Access. Open the Begon Pest Control database that you used in Project 6 or see the inside back cover of this book for instructions for downloading the Data Disk or see your instructor for information about accessing the files required for this book. Perform the following tasks:

1. Use the Page Wizard to create the data access page for the Customer table shown in Figure 35.

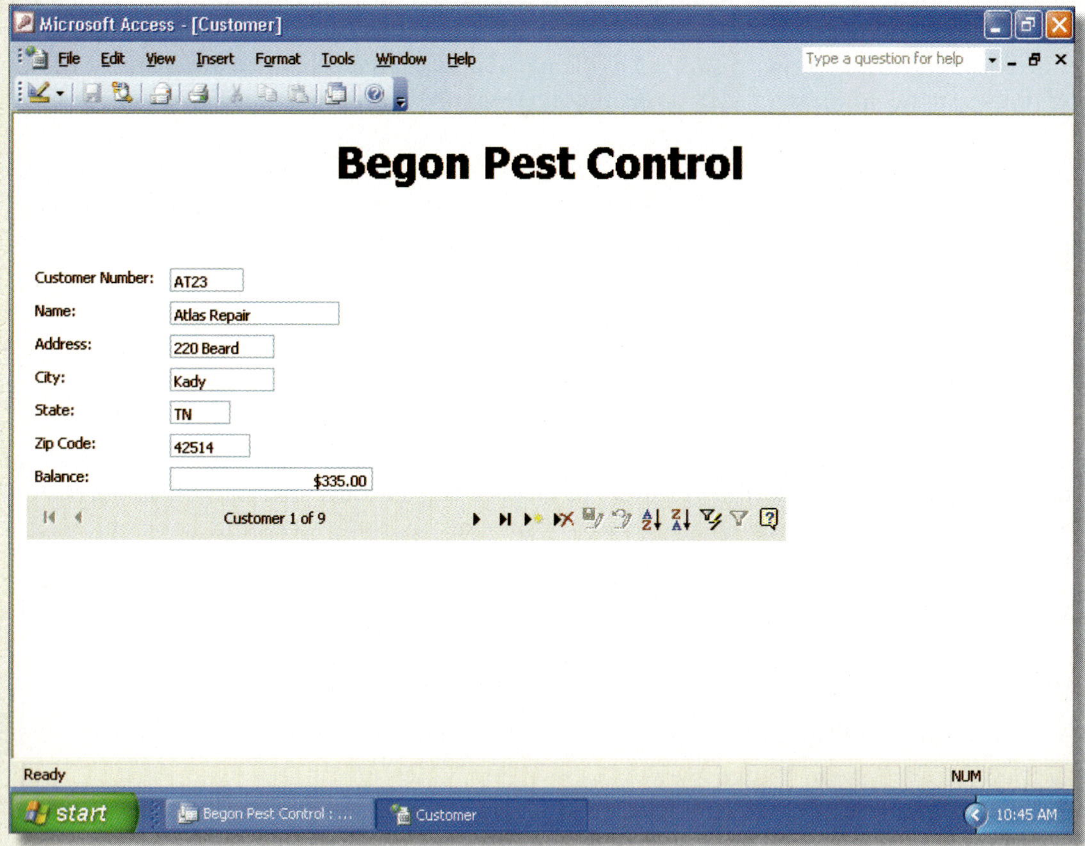

FIGURE 35

2. Print the data access page for customer BL35. To print the page, open the page, click File on the menu bar, and then click Print.
3. Create the grouped data access page shown in Figure 36. The page groups customers by technicians.

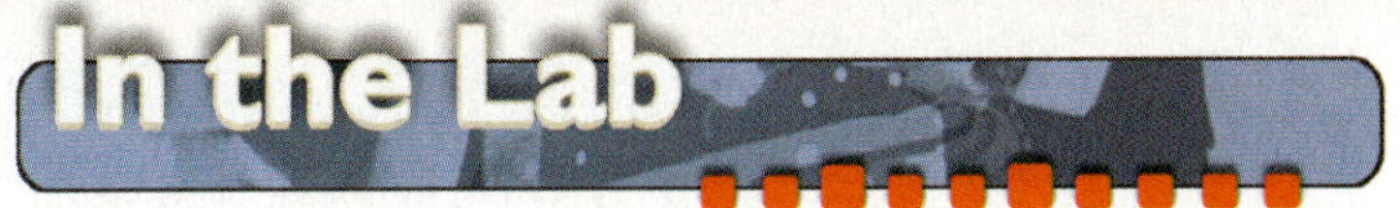

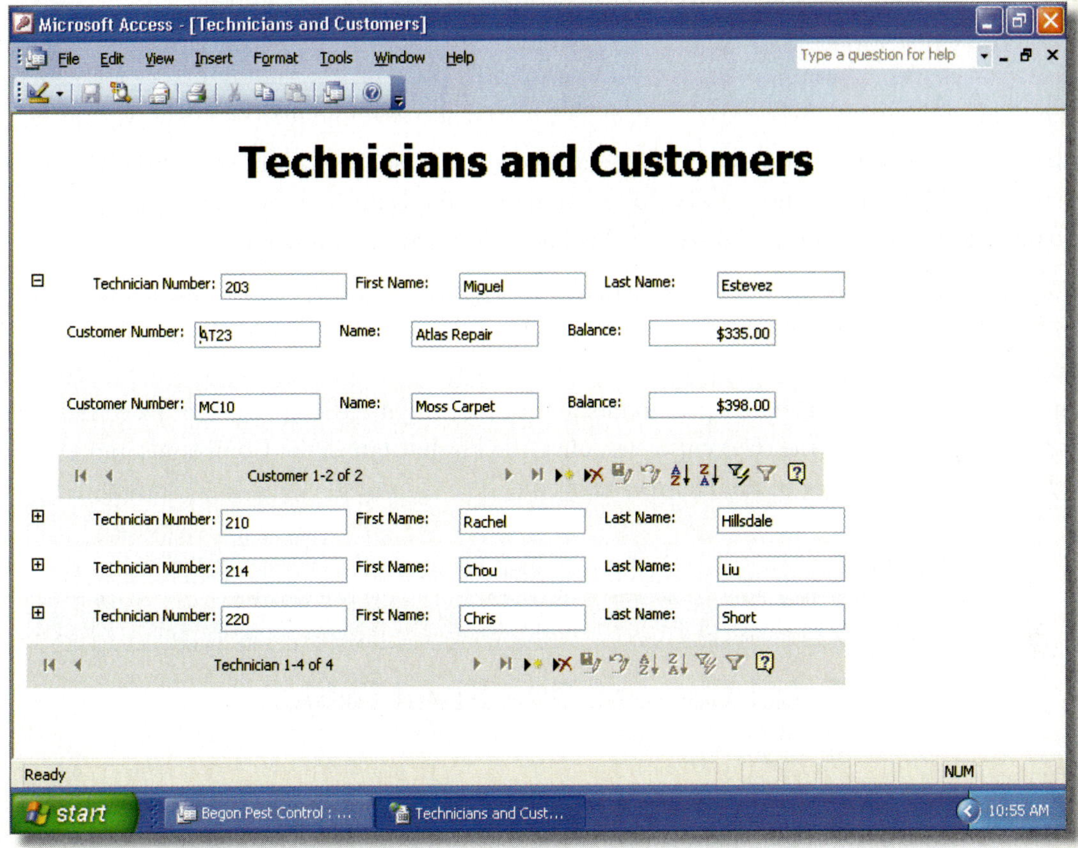

FIGURE 36

4. Open the data access page and then click the First Name field. Click the Sort Ascending button to sort the records in order by first name.
5. Print the data access page.
6. Sort the records in order by technician number and then click the plus sign in front of technician 210. Print the data access page.

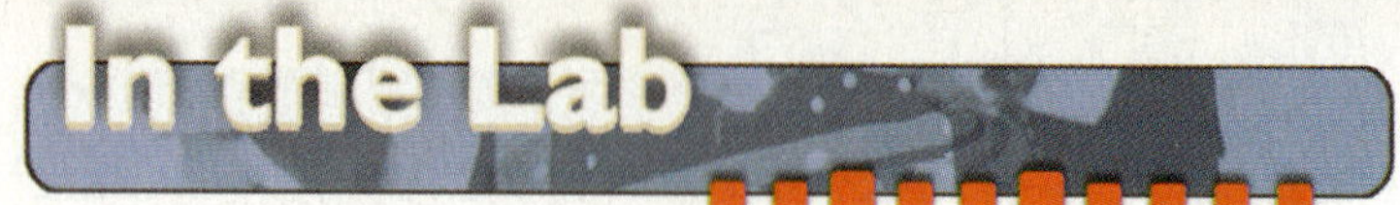

2 Creating Data Access Pages for Babbage Bookkeeping

Problem: Babbage Bookkeeping would like to be able to view PivotTables and PivotCharts over the Web.

Instructions: Start Access. Open the Babbage Bookkeeping database that you used in Project 6 or see the inside back cover of this book for instructions for downloading the Data Disk or see your instructor for information about accessing the files required for this book. Perform the following tasks:

1. Open the Total Current Due by Client query that was created previously in Design view.
2. Add the Bookkeeper Number field from the Client table to the query and save the query.
3. Create the data access page shown in Figure 37. The PivotTable uses the modified Total Current Due by Client query. To display current due amounts as currency, right-click the Current Due field, click Commands and Options on the shortcut menu, click the Format tab in the Commands and Options dialog box, and then select Currency in the Number text box.

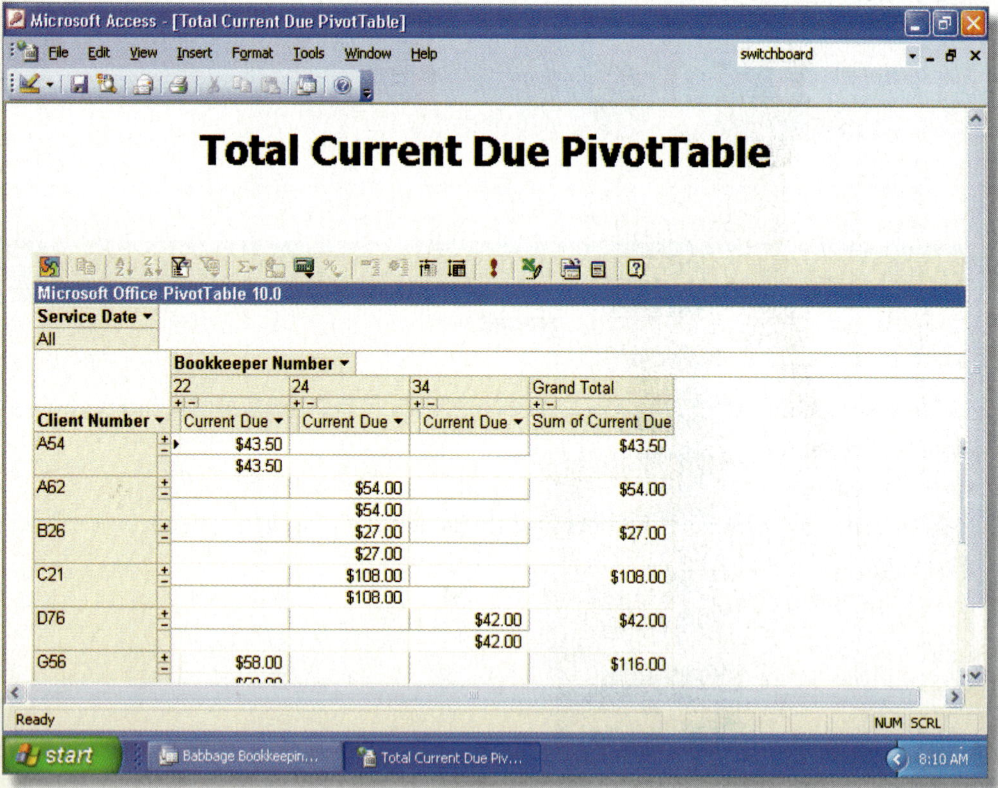

FIGURE 37

4. Save the data access page as Total Current Due PivotTable.
5. Open the data access page and filter the PivotTable to show only current due amounts for service dates between 8/22/2005 and 8/26/2005. Print the PivotTable.
6. Remove the filter to redisplay all service dates. Hide the details for each client number. Print the PivotTable.
7. Open the modified Total Current Due by Client query and then display the query in PivotChart View.
8. Save the PivotChart as a data access page with the name, Total Current Due by Client PivotChart.
9. Print the PivotChart in landscape orientation.

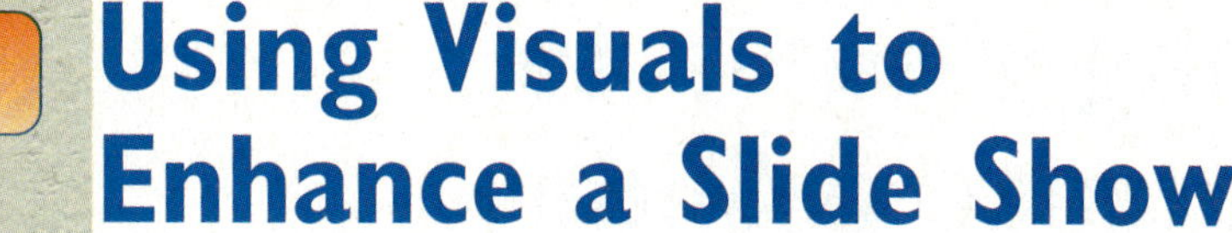

Using Visuals to Enhance a Slide Show

PROJECT 3

CASE PERSPECTIVE

Vacationers are turning toward campgrounds instead of hotel rooms. In an effort to travel to destinations near home, save money, and bond with family and friends, travelers are finding that camping is a pleasurable alternative to costly resorts and airfares.

Whether the campground is located in state parks or private land, the areas have been swamped since the mid-1990s with requests for campsite activity reservations. Choice areas often are booked for the entire season, so vacation planners need to begin their search for the ideal spot early and earnestly. Computers enter into the camping picture, too, for handheld global positioning system receivers can survey hiking trail terrain and elevation and the campsite reservations can be made via the Internet.

The rangers at Hidden Lake State Park also are experiencing an upturn in camping activity. In an effort to assist camping planners, they want to create a PowerPoint presentation that describes the three campgrounds in the park. The presentation also could list the outdoor activities available, including hiking, rock climbing, and fly fishing. Each campground has an amphitheater where lectures are held three times weekly. Wally Freeman, the campground director of activities, has asked you to help with the marketing efforts. He knows you have extensive computer experience and wants you to develop a PowerPoint slide show that promotes Hidden Lake and describes its campgrounds, activities, and programs. He has asked you to use a variety of visuals, including clip art, a table, and an organization chart. You agree to create the presentation.

As you read through this project, you will learn how to use PowerPoint to add clip art and animation to increase the presentation's visual interest.

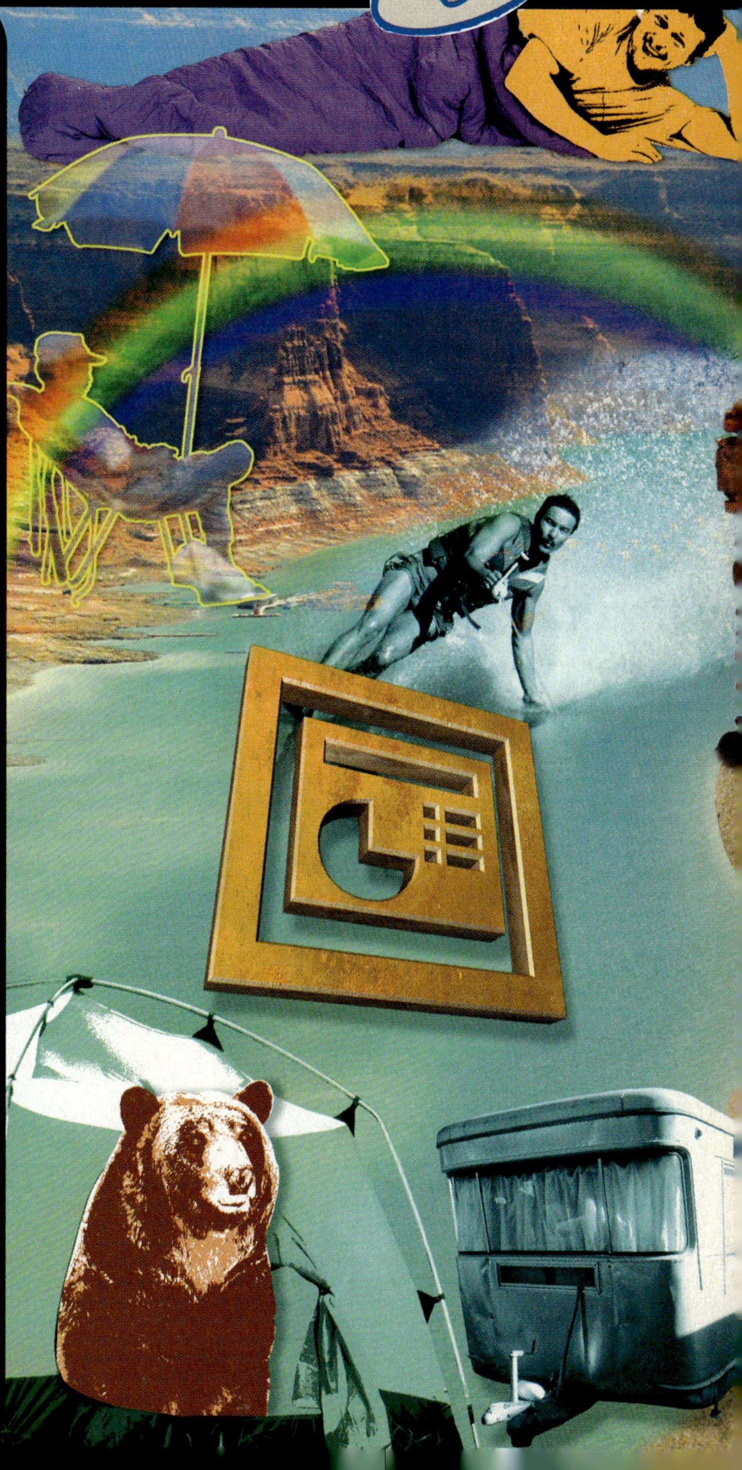

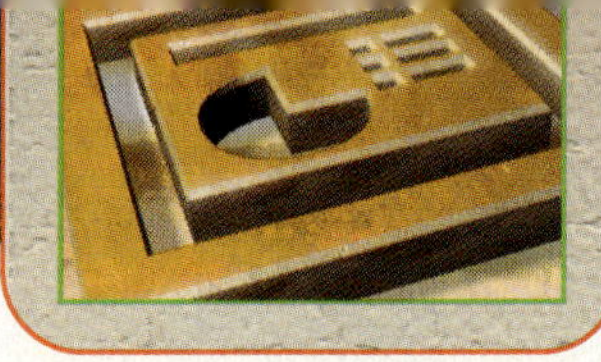

MICROSOFT Office PowerPoint 2003

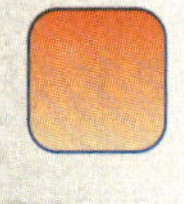

Using Visuals to Enhance a Slide Show

PROJECT

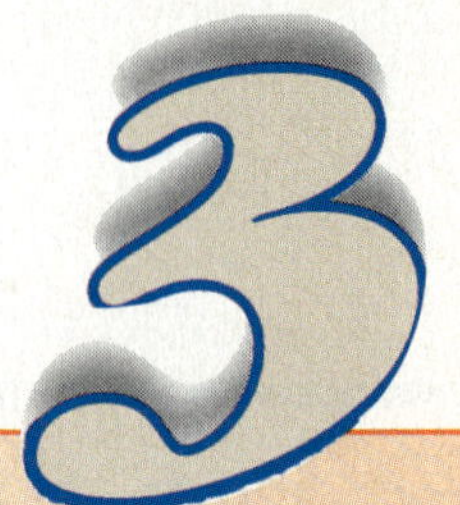

Objectives

You will have mastered the material in this project when you can:

- Create presentations using visuals
- Open a Microsoft Word outline as a presentation
- Add a picture to create a custom background
- Format text-based content
- Insert and modify a clip
- Customize bullets using the slide master
- Insert and format a table
- Create and format an organization chart
- Apply a new design template to a single slide
- Rearrange slides
- Add an animation scheme to selected slides
- Print slides as handouts

Introduction

Bulleted lists and simple graphics are the starting point for most presentations, but they can become boring. Advanced PowerPoint users want exciting presentations — something to impress their audiences. With PowerPoint, it is easy to develop impressive presentations by modifying slide backgrounds, customizing bullets, embedding organization charts and tables, and creating new graphics.

One problem you may experience when developing a presentation is finding the proper graphic to convey your message. One way to overcome this obstacle is to modify clip art from the Microsoft Clip Organizer. Another solution is to create a table and an organization chart.

This project introduces several techniques to make your presentations more exciting.

Project Three — Hidden Lake Camping and Outdoor Activities

Project 3 expands on PowerPoint's basic presentation features by importing existing files and embedding objects. This project creates a presentation that is used to promote the camping and nature activities at Hidden Lake State Park (Figures 3-1a through 3-1d). The project begins by building the presentation from an outline created in Microsoft Word. Then, several objects are inserted to customize the presentation. These objects include customized bullets, an organization chart, a table, and clip art.

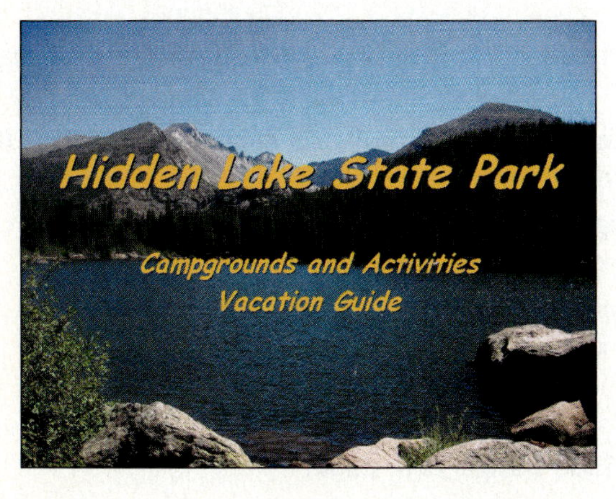

(a) Slide 1

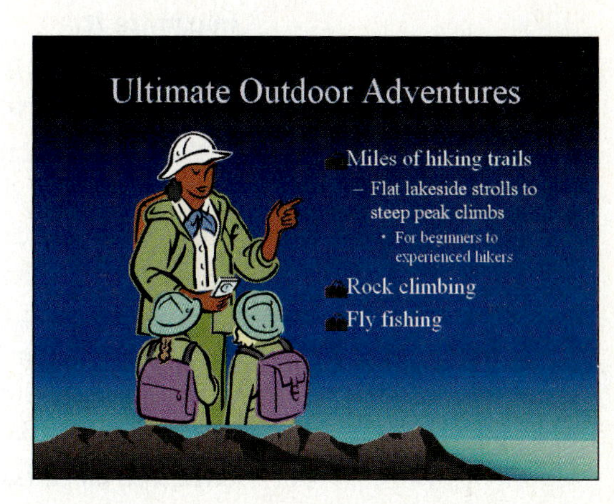

(b) Slide 2

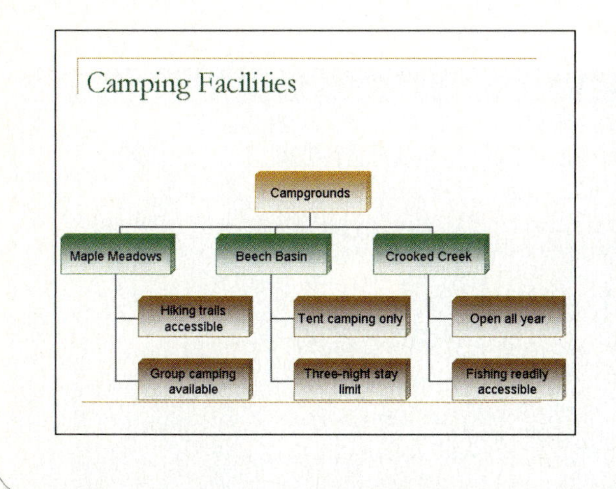

(c) Slide 3

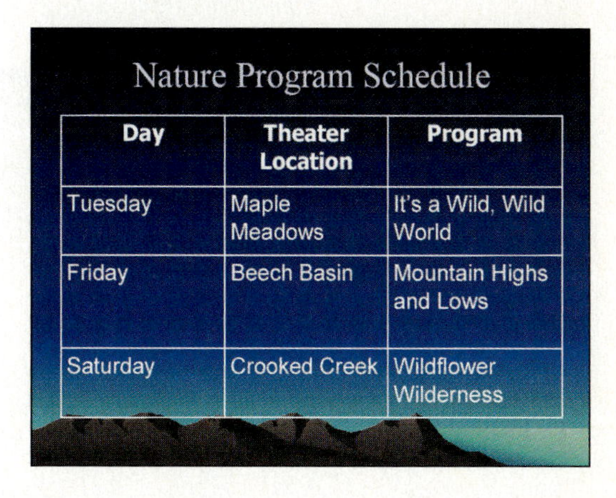

(d) Slide 4

FIGURE 3-1

Starting and Customizing a New Presentation

In Projects 1 and 2, you started a presentation document, chose layouts, applied a design template, and reset your toolbars. You need to repeat the same steps to begin this project. The steps on the next page show how to start and customize a new presentation and change to the Outline tab. See your instructor if the Mountain Top template is not available on your system.

To Start and Customize a New Presentation and Change to the Outline Tab

1. **Click the Start button on the Windows taskbar, point to All Programs on the Start menu, point to Microsoft Office on the All Programs submenu, and then click Microsoft Office PowerPoint 2003 on the Microsoft Office submenu.**
2. **If the PowerPoint window is not maximized, double-click its title bar to maximize it.**
3. **If the Language bar appears, right-click it and then click Close the Language bar on the shortcut menu.**
4. **If the Getting Started task pane appears in the PowerPoint window, click its Close button in the upper-right corner.**
5. **If the Standard and Formatting toolbars are positioned on the same row, click the Toolbar Options button and then click Show Buttons on Two Rows.**
6. **Click the Slide Design button on the Formatting toolbar. When the Slide Design task pane is displayed, click the down scroll arrow in the Apply a design template list, and then click the Mountain Top template in the Available For Use area.**
7. **Click the Close button in the Slide Design task pane.**
8. **Click the Outline tab in the tabs pane.**

The PowerPoint window with the Standard and Formatting toolbars on two rows appears as shown in Figure 3-2. PowerPoint displays the Title Slide slide layout and the Mountain Top template on Slide 1 in normal view.

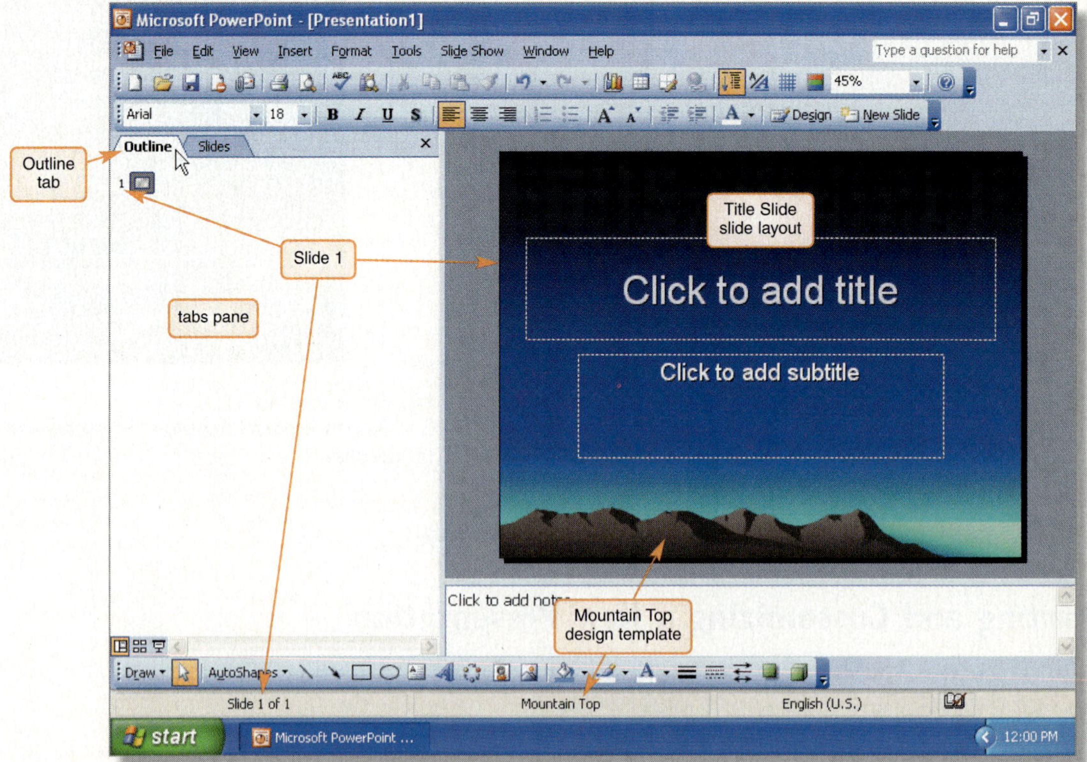

FIGURE 3-2

Importing Text Created in Another Application

In your classes, you may be asked to make an oral presentation. For example, in your English composition class, your instructor may require you to summarize verbally a research paper you wrote. You can use a PowerPoint presentation to help you construct and deliver your presentation.

PowerPoint can use text created in other programs to create a new slide show. This text may have originated in Microsoft Word or another word processing program, or it may have appeared on a Web page. Microsoft Word files use the file extension **.doc** in their file names. Text originating in other word processing programs should be saved in Rich Text Format (.rtf) or plain text format (.txt), and Web page documents should have an HTML extension (.htm).

An outline created in Microsoft Word or another word processing program works well as a shell for a PowerPoint presentation. Instead of typing text in PowerPoint, as you did in Projects 1 and 2, you can import this outline; add visual elements such as clip art, photos, graphical bullets, and animation schemes; and ultimately create an impressive slide show. If you did not create an outline to help you write your word processing document, you can create one by saving your paper with a new file name, removing all text except the topic headings, and then saving the file again.

The advantage of using an outline saved as a Microsoft Word or Rich Text Format document is that PowerPoint uses the heading styles in the document and creates an outline structure. For example, a Heading 1 style becomes a slide title, and a Heading 2 style becomes the first level of body text. If the document does not have any heading styles and has text styled as Normal, PowerPoint creates a slide title from each paragraph.

A file saved in Rich Text Format in Microsoft Word is saved with minimal formatting. This **Rich Text Format**, which has the file extension **.rtf**, does not contain heading styles, so PowerPoint uses the tabs at the beginning of paragraphs to define the outline structure.

To create a presentation using an existing outline, select **Slides from Outline** on the Insert menu. PowerPoint opens the Insert Outline dialog box, displays All Outlines in the Files of type box, and displays a list of outlines. Next, you select the file that contains the outline. PowerPoint then creates a presentation using your outline. Each major heading in your outline becomes a slide title, and subheadings become a bulleted list.

More About

File Conversion

PowerPoint uses converters to open Microsoft Office files automatically. These converters are installed when PowerPoint is installed. If PowerPoint recognizes the file extension, such as .doc or .xls, it converts the file to the correct format. If PowerPoint does not recognize the file extension, you can run Office Setup to add additional converters.

Opening a Microsoft Word Outline as a Presentation

The next step in this project is to import an outline created in Microsoft Word. PowerPoint can produce slides based on an outline created in Microsoft Word or another word processing program if the outline was saved in a format that PowerPoint can recognize. The outline you import in this project was saved as a file with an .rtf extension.

Importing an outline into PowerPoint requires two steps. First, you must tell PowerPoint you are opening an existing document. Then, to open the outline, you need to select the proper file in the Insert Outline dialog box. The steps on the next page open a Microsoft Word outline as a presentation.

More About

Sending Outlines to Word

While you can open Microsoft Word outlines in PowerPoint, you also can send your PowerPoint outline to Word and then use the text to create handouts and other documents. To perform this action, click File on the menu bar, point to Send To, click Microsoft Office Word, and then click Outline only.

To Open a Microsoft Word Outline as a Presentation

1

- **Insert your Data Disk into drive A.**
- **Click Insert on the menu bar and then point to Slides from Outline.**

The Insert menu is displayed (Figure 3-3). You want to open the outline created in Microsoft Word and saved on your Data Disk.

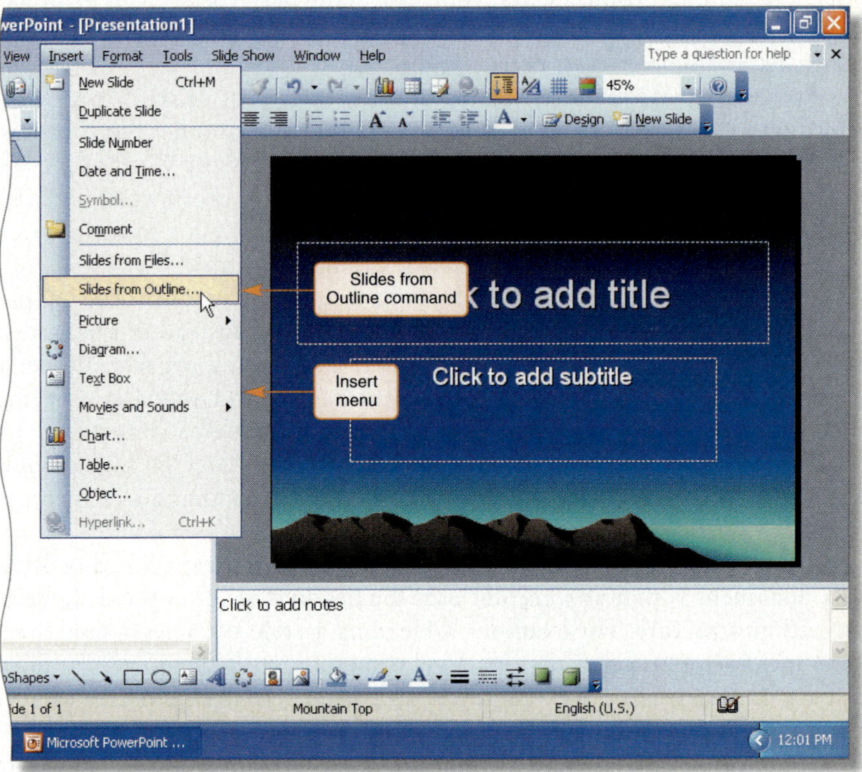

FIGURE 3-3

2

- **Click Slides from Outline.**
- **Click the Look in box arrow and then click 3½ Floppy (A:).**
- **Click Hidden Lake Outline in the Look in list.**

The Insert Outline dialog box is displayed (Figure 3-4). A list displays the outline files that PowerPoint can open. Your list may be different depending on the files stored on your floppy disk.

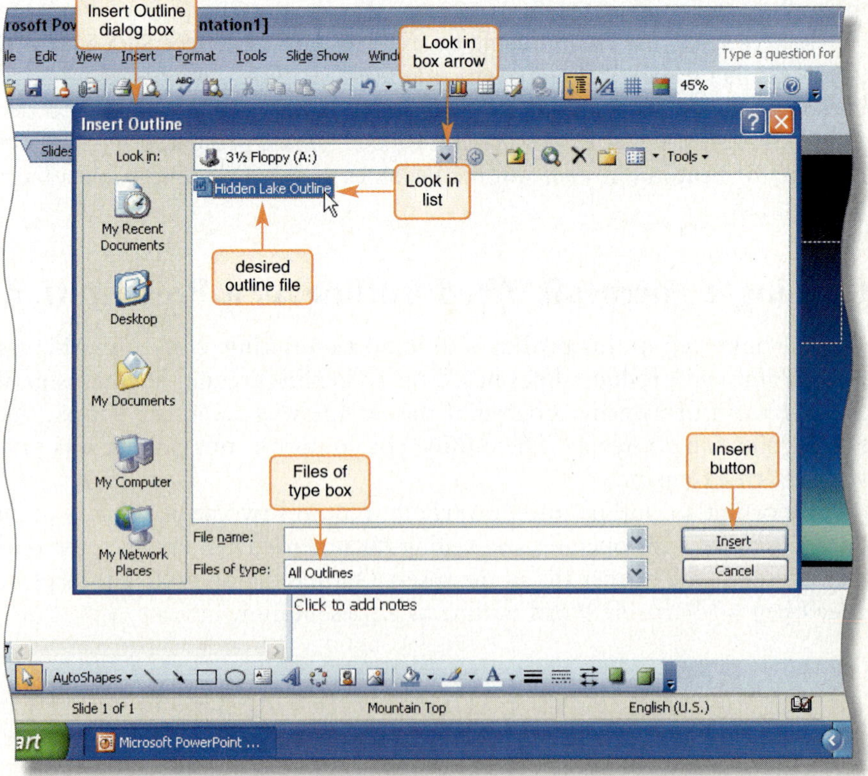

FIGURE 3-4

3

• **Click the Insert button.**

PowerPoint opens the Hidden Lake Outline and creates Slides 2 through 5 (Figure 3-5). The outline is displayed in the tabs pane, and Slide 2 is displayed in the slide pane. The outline text on Slides 2 and 3 is displayed bulleted, indicating the slide layout is a bulleted list.

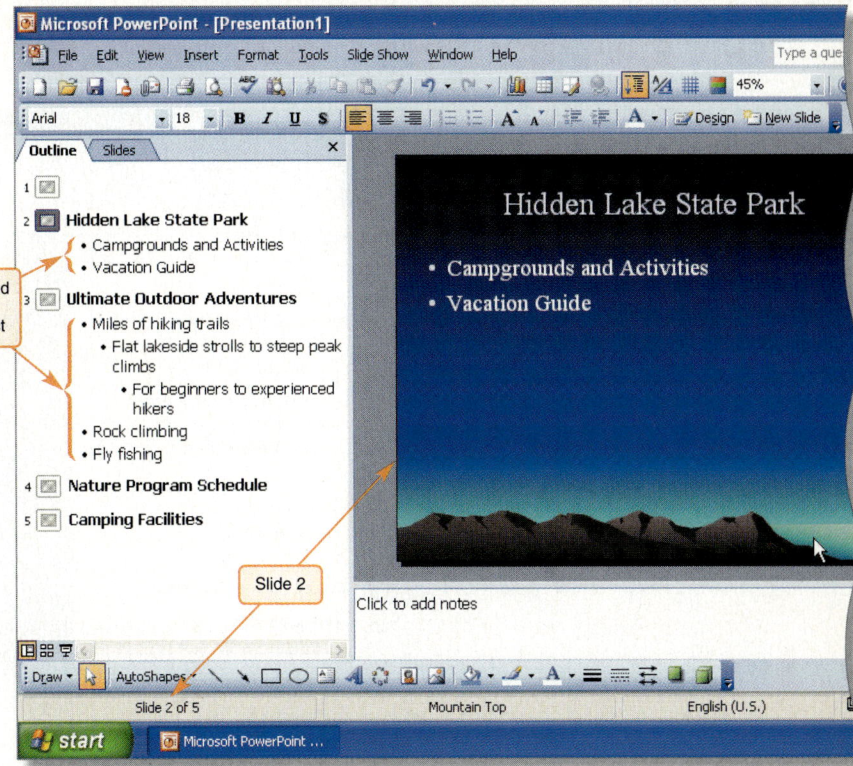

FIGURE 3-5

Other Ways

1. In Microsoft Word, open desired document, on File menu point to Send To, click Microsoft PowerPoint
2. Press ALT+I, press L, press ENTER
3. In Voice Command mode, say "Insert, Slides from Outline, Insert"

Imported outlines can contain up to nine outline levels, whereas PowerPoint outlines are limited to six levels (one for the title text and five for body paragraph text). When you import an outline, all text in outline levels six through nine is treated as a fifth-level paragraph.

Deleting a Slide

PowerPoint added Slides 2 through 5 when you imported the Microsoft Word outline. Slide 1 is blank and should be deleted. The steps on the next page delete Slide 1.

To Delete a Slide

1

• **Click the Slide 1 slide icon on the Outline tab.**

The Slide 1 slide icon is selected, and Slide 1 is displayed (Figure 3-6).

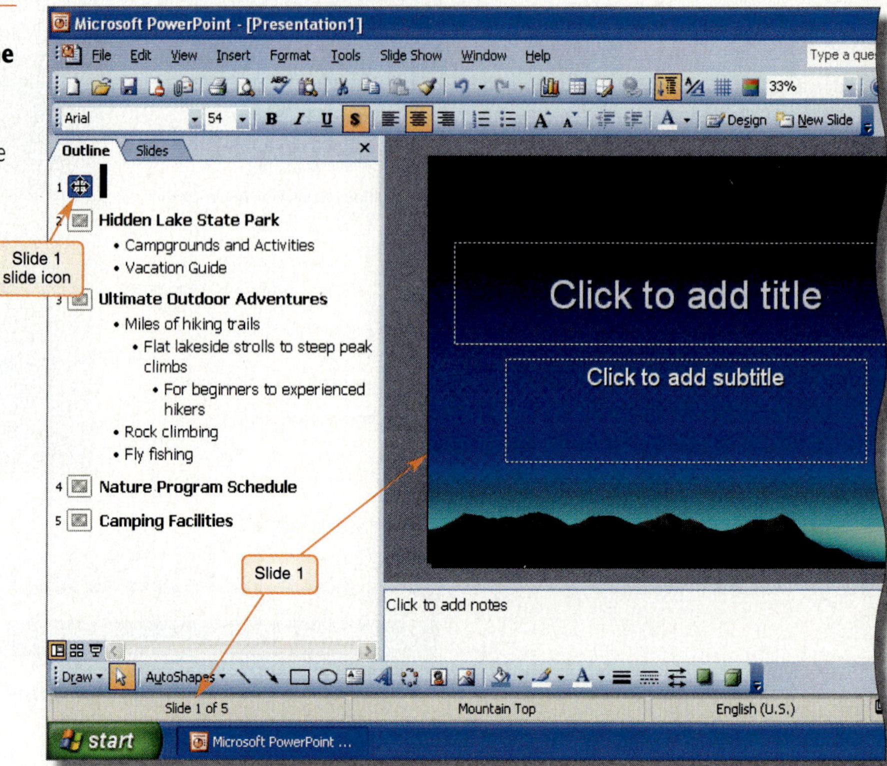

FIGURE 3-6

2

• **Click Edit on the menu bar and then point to Delete Slide (Figure 3-7).**

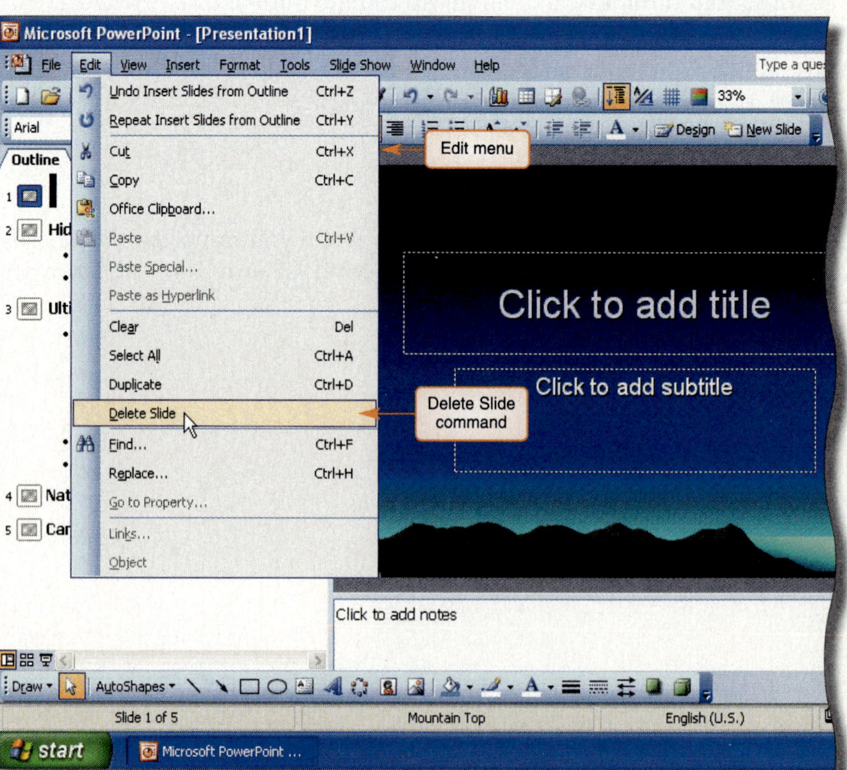

FIGURE 3-7

3

• **Click Delete Slide.**

The blank Slide 1 is deleted and is replaced with the original Slide 2 (Figure 3-8).

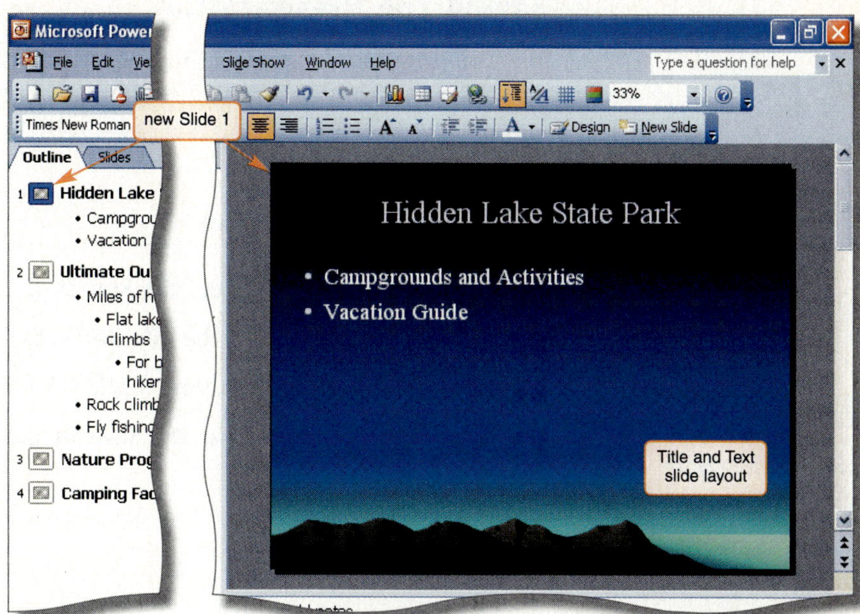

FIGURE 3-8

Other Ways

1. Click Slide 1 slide icon, press DELETE
2. Right-click Slide 1 slide icon, click Delete Slide on shortcut menu
3. Press ALT+E, press D
4. In Voice Command mode, say "Edit, Delete Slide"

The current slides in the presentation have the Title and Text slide layout. The following steps show how to apply the Title Slide layout to Slide 1.

Changing the Slide 1 Layout to Title Slide

When you started the new presentation, PowerPoint created Slide 1 and applied the Title Slide slide layout. Now that the original Slide 2 is the new Slide 1, you want to apply the Title Slide slide layout to introduce the presentation. The following steps change the Slide 1 slide layout.

To Change the Slide Layout to Title Slide

1 **Click Format on the menu bar and then click Slide Layout.**

2 **Click the Title Slide slide layout located in the Text Layouts area in the Slide Layout task pane.**

3 **Click the Close button in the Slide Layout task pane.**

Slide 1 has the desired Title Slide slide layout (Figure 3-9).

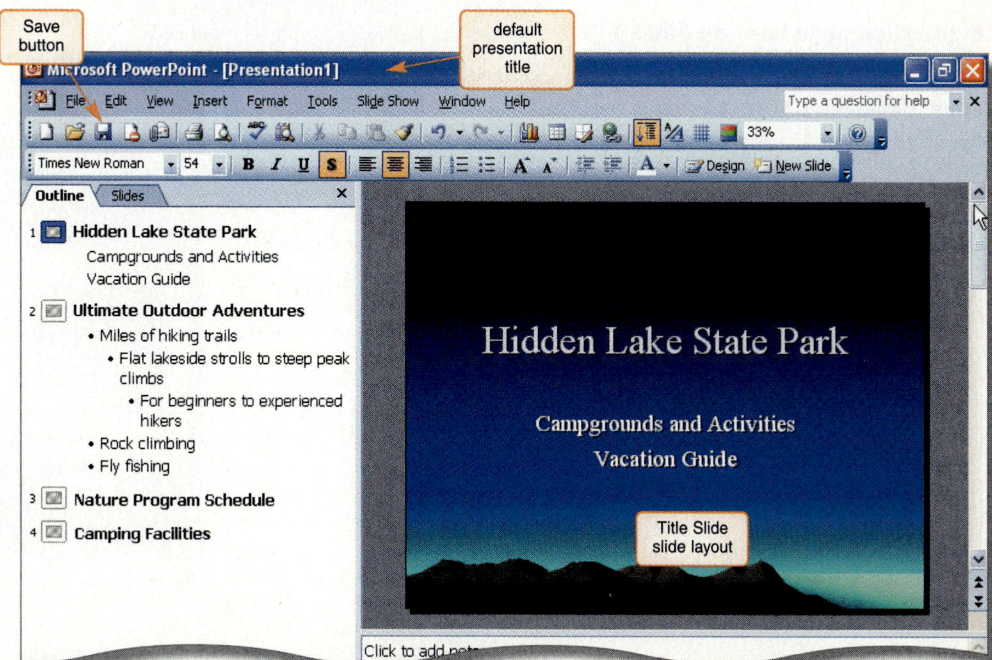

FIGURE 3-9

Saving the Presentation

You now should save the presentation because you applied a design template, created a presentation from an outline file, deleted a slide, and applied a new slide layout. The following steps summarize how to save a presentation.

To Save a Presentation

1. **Click the Save button on the Standard toolbar.**
2. **Type** `Hidden Lake` **in the File name text box.**
3. **Click the Save in box arrow. Click 3½ Floppy (A:) in the Save in list.**
4. **Click the Save button in the Save As dialog box.**

The presentation is saved on the floppy disk in drive A with the file name Hidden Lake. This file name is displayed on the title bar.

> *More About*
>
> **Reducing File Size**
>
> Pictures can increase a presentation's file size dramatically. To decrease the size, use PowerPoint's Compress Pictures feature by selecting the picture and then clicking the Compress Picture button on the Picture toolbar. Recommended resolutions are 96 dpi for presentations posted to the Internet and 200 dpi for presentations that are printed.

Adding a Picture to Create a Custom Background

To generate audience interest in a presentation, you can add pictures. The next step is to insert a picture of Hidden Lake to create a custom background. This picture is stored on the Data Disk. See the inside back cover of this book for instructions for downloading the Data Disk or see your instructor for information about accessing the files required for this book. The following steps add this picture to the Slide 1 background.

To Add a Picture to Create a Custom Background

1

- **Right-click anywhere on Slide 1 except the title text placeholder.**
- **Click Background on the shortcut menu.**

The Background dialog box is displayed (Figure 3-10).

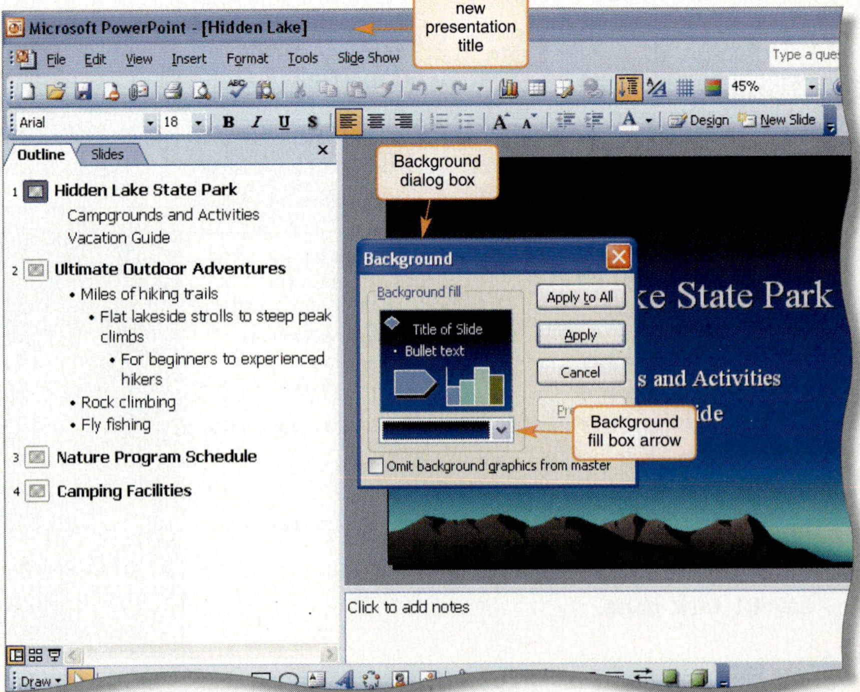

FIGURE 3-10

2

- **Click the Background fill box arrow in the Background dialog box.**
- **Point to Fill Effects on the menu.**

The Background fill menu containing commands and options for filling the slide background is displayed (Figure 3-11). The current background fill color is light purple, which is the Mountain Top design template default. The eight colors in the top row are for the Mountain Top color scheme. Fill Effects is highlighted.

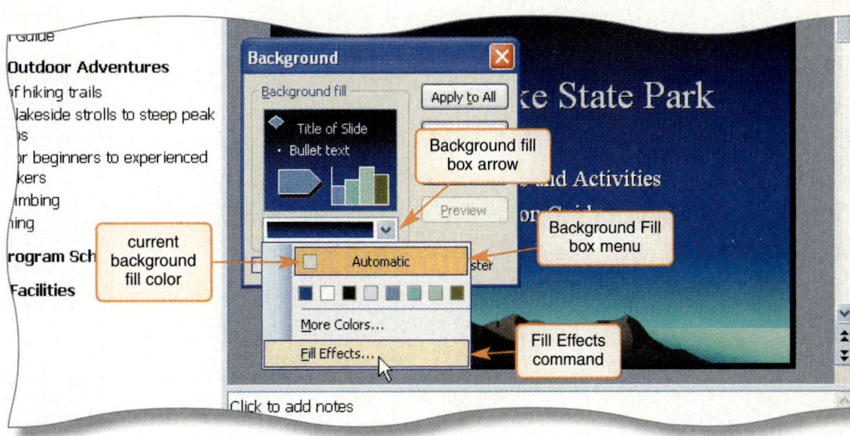

FIGURE 3-11

3

- **Click Fill Effects.**
- **If necessary, when the Fill Effects dialog box is displayed, click the Picture tab.**

The Fill Effects dialog box is displayed (Figure 3-12).

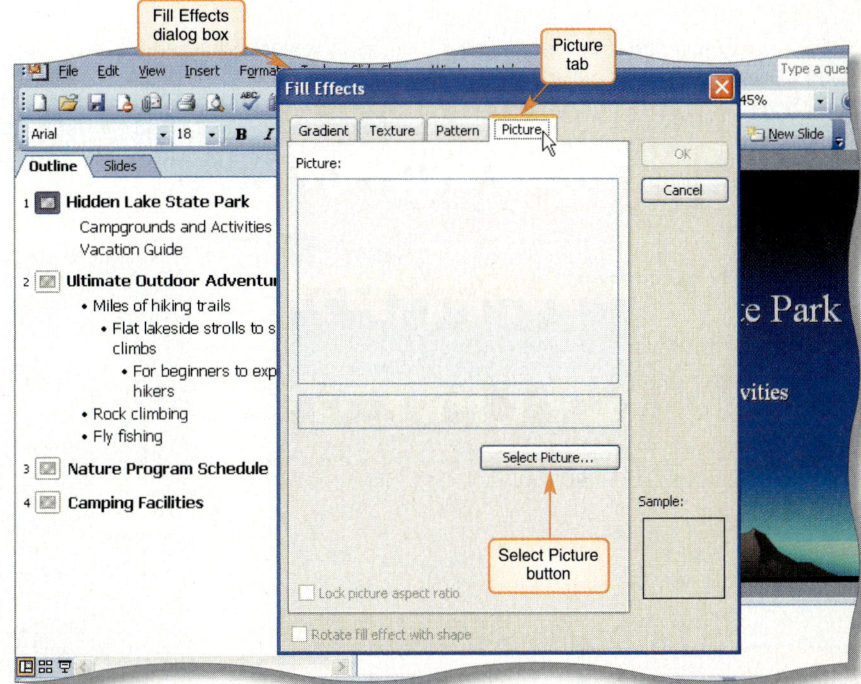

FIGURE 3-12

4

- **Click the Select Picture button.**
- **When the Select Picture dialog box is displayed, click the Look in box arrow and then click 3½ Floppy (A:).**
- **Click the Hidden Lake thumbnail.**

The Select Picture dialog box is displayed (Figure 3-13). The selected file, Hidden Lake, is displayed in the Preview box.

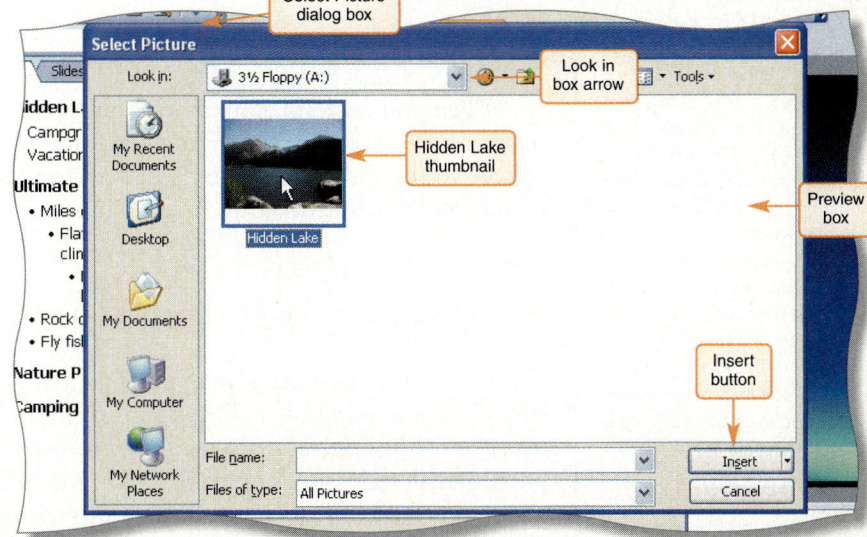

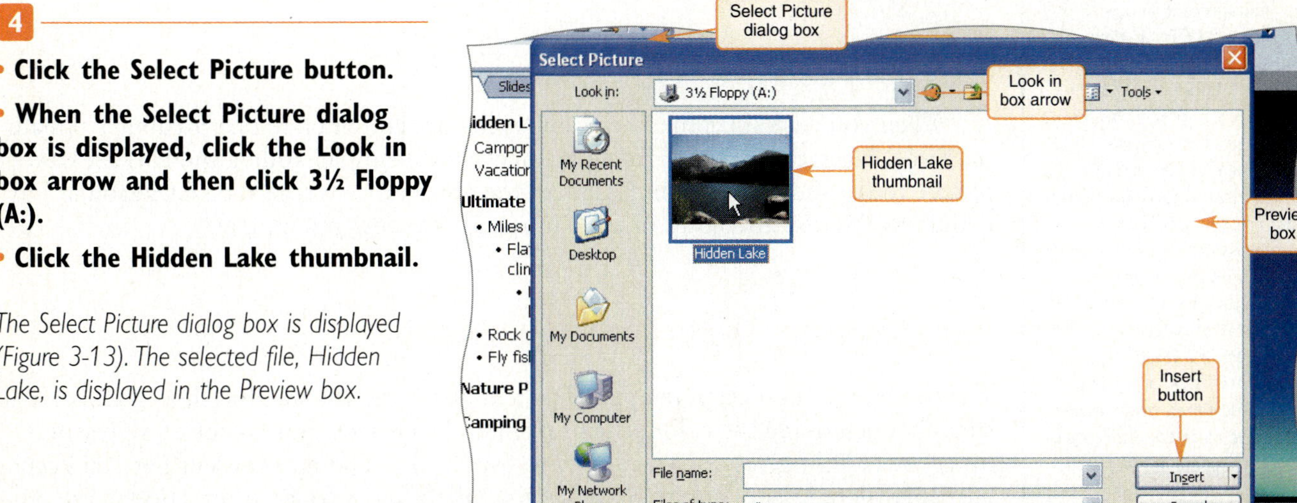

FIGURE 3-13

5

- **Click the Insert button.**
- **When the picture is displayed in the Fill Effects dialog box, click the OK button.**
- **When the Background dialog box is displayed, click the Omit background graphics from master check box.**

The Background dialog box displays the Hidden Lake picture in the Background fill area (Figure 3-14). You do not want the mountains that are part of the Mountain Top design template to display, so you click the Omit background graphics from master box to have only the Hidden Lake photograph and outline text display on Slide 1.

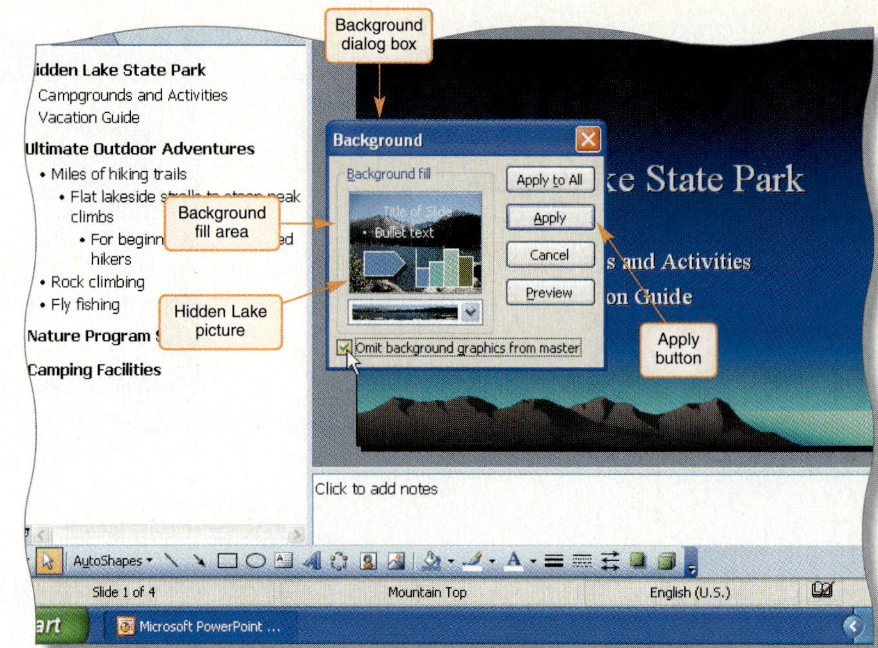

FIGURE 3-14

6

- **Click the Apply button.**

The Hidden Lake picture is displayed as the Slide 1 background (Figure 3-15). You could add the picture to Slide 1 or to all slides in the presentation. The Mountain Top design template text attributes are displayed on the slide.

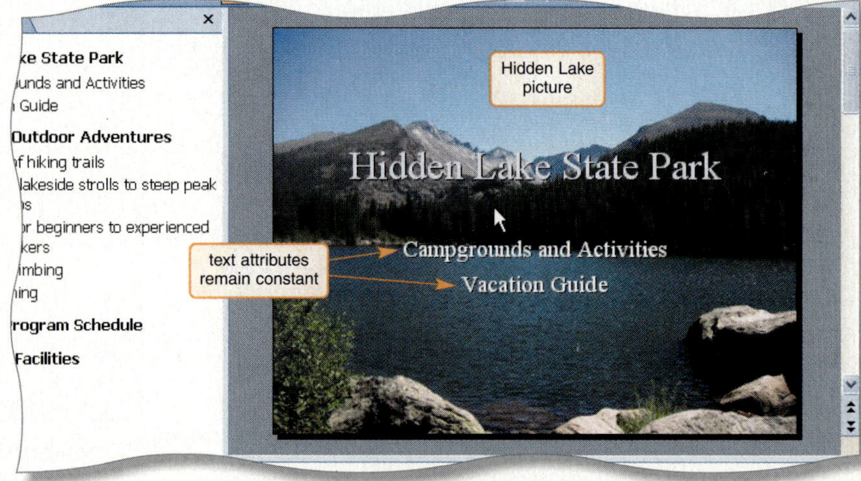

FIGURE 3-15

Other Ways

1. On Format menu click Background, click Background fill box arrow, click Fill Effects, click Select Picture button, click Look in box arrow, click 3½ Floppy (A:), click desired picture, click Insert button, click OK button, click Apply button
2. Press ALT+O, press K, press DOWN ARROW, press F, if necessary press LEFT ARROW, press ALT+L, press ALT+I, press arrow key to select 3½ Floppy (A:), press ENTER, press TAB three times, press arrow keys to select desired picture, press ALT+S, press ENTER, press ENTER
3. In Voice Command mode, say "Format, Background"

When you customize the background, the design template text attributes remain the same, but the slide background changes. For example, adding the Hidden Lake picture to the slide background changes the appearance of the slide background but maintains the text attributes of the Mountain Top design template.

Formatting Text-Based Content

The Mountain Top design template has text attributes for the title slide and each text slide that determine the color scheme, font and font size, and layout of a presentation. PowerPoint gives you the ability to format the slide text content but still keep a particular design template by changing the font and the font's color, effects, size, and style. In Project 1 you changed the font style and size. In the next section, you will change the font and font color.

Changing the Font and Font Attributes

Text font attributes include styles (regular, bold, italic, and bold italic), size, effects, and color. PowerPoint allows you to use one or more text attributes on a slide. The following steps add emphasis to the title text by changing the font, font style, and font color.

To Change the Title Slide Font and Font Attributes

1

- **Position the mouse pointer before the word, Hidden, in Slide 1 on the Outline tab.**
- **Click and then drag through the title slide title and subtitle text.**

PowerPoint highlights the title and subtitle text paragraphs (Figure 3-16).

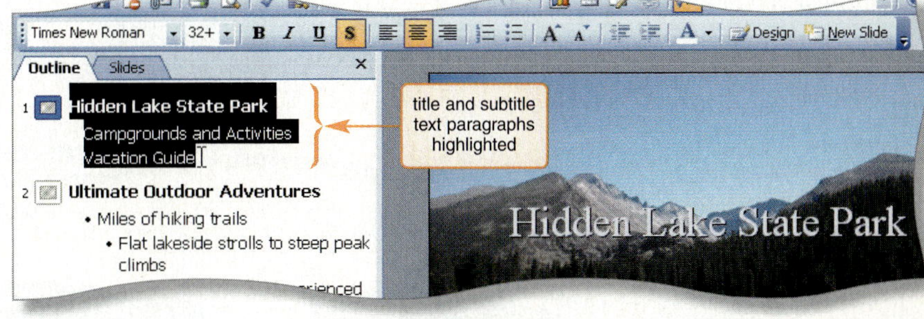

FIGURE 3-16

2

- **Right-click the highlighted text and then click Font on the shortcut menu.**

The Font dialog box is displayed (Figure 3-17). Times New Roman is the default font for the Mountain Top slide template.

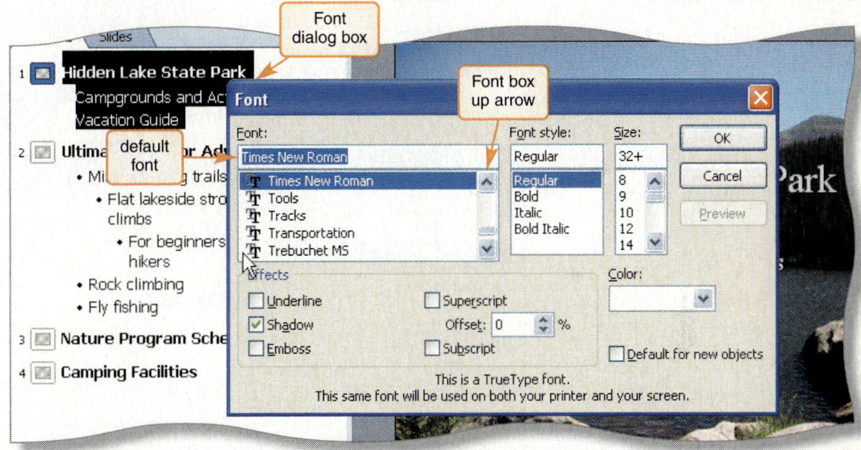

FIGURE 3-17

3

- **Click the Font box up arrow.**
- **Scroll up the list until the font name, Comic Sans MS, is displayed in the Font list.**
- **Click Comic Sans MS.**

Comic Sans is the new title slide font.

4

- **Click Bold Italic in the Font style list.**

The title slide text will display with bold and italic attributes (Figure 3-18).

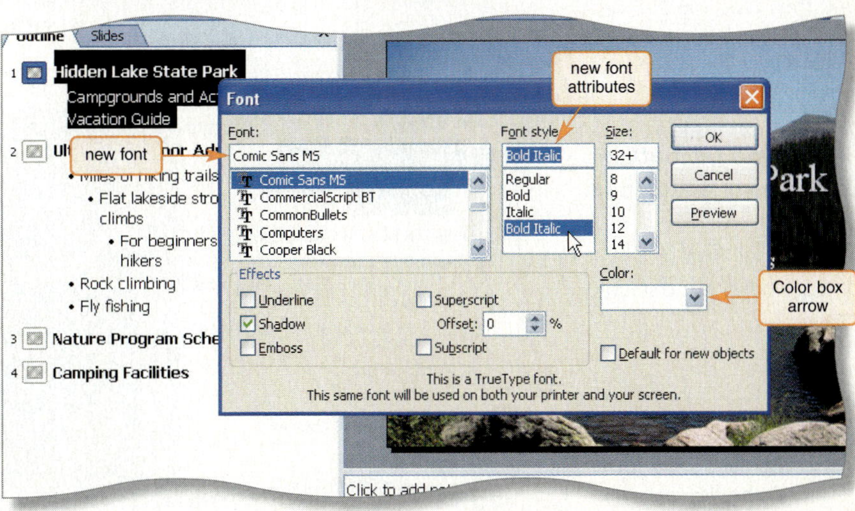

FIGURE 3-18

5

- **Click the Color box arrow.**
- **Click More Colors in the Color list.**
- **If necessary, click the Standard tab in the Colors dialog box.**
- **Click the color, gold, on the Standard tab (row 11, color 4).**

Light purple is the default title text font color in the Mountain Top color scheme (Figure 3-19). The color, gold, is not part of the Mountain Top color scheme. You also can mix your own color by clicking the Custom tab.

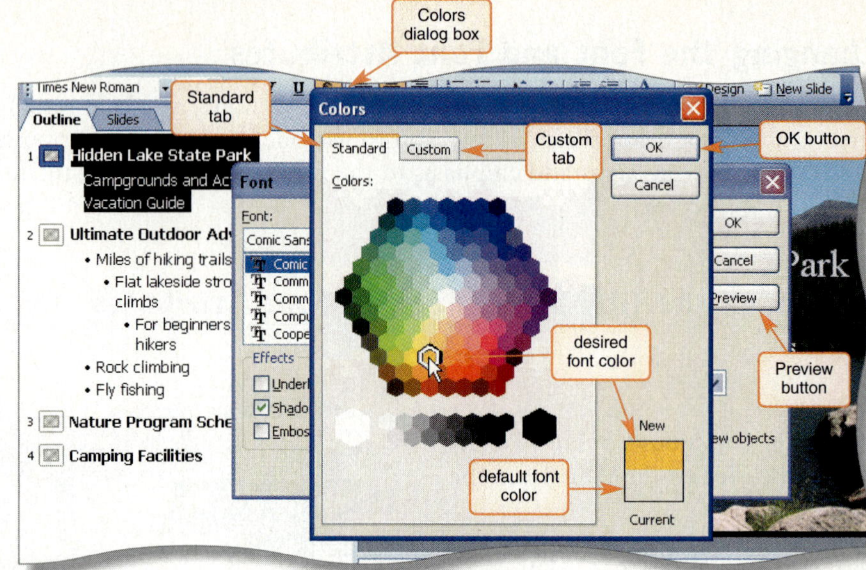

FIGURE 3-19

6

- **Click the OK button in the Colors dialog box.**

7

- **Click the Preview button in the Font dialog box.**

The text on Slide 1 is displayed with the Comic Sans MS font with bold italic and gold font attributes (Figure 3-20). If the Font dialog box is displayed over the slide, click the Font dialog box title bar and then drag the box to a new location.

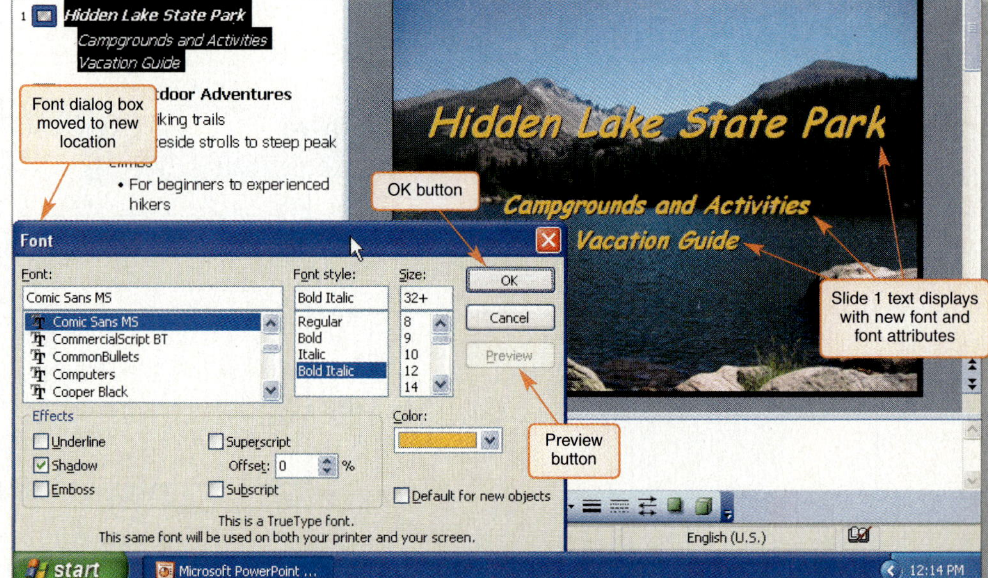

FIGURE 3-20

8

- **Click the OK button in the Font dialog box.**

The modified Slide 1 font and attributes are displayed (Figure 3-21).

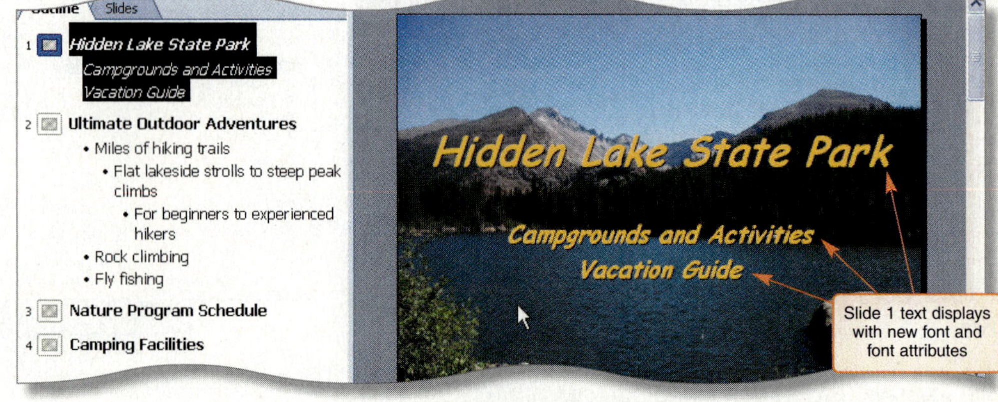

FIGURE 3-21

Other Ways

1. Click Font Color arrow on Formatting toolbar
2. On Format menu click Font, click Color down arrow

To remove the bold and italic styles from text, select the text and then click the Italic and Bold buttons. As a result, the Italic and Bold buttons are not selected, and the text does not have the bold italic font attributes.

Inserting and Modifying Clips

A **clip art picture** is composed of many objects grouped together to form one object. PowerPoint allows you to modify and enhance the clip by disassembling it into the objects. **Disassembling** a clip art picture, also called **ungrouping**, separates one object into multiple objects. Once ungrouped, you can manipulate the individual objects as needed to form a new object. When you ungroup a clip art picture in PowerPoint, it becomes a **drawing object** and loses its link to the Microsoft Clip Organizer. In addition to clips, other drawing objects are curves, lines, AutoShapes, and WordArt.

Objects usually are saved in one of two **graphic formats**: vector or bitmap. A **vector graphic** is a piece of art that has been created by a drawing program such as CorelDRAW or Adobe Illustrator. The clip art pictures used in this project are vector graphic objects and are created as a collection of lines. Vector graphic files store data either as picture descriptions or as calculations. These files describe a picture mathematically as a set of instructions for creating the objects in the picture. These mathematical descriptions determine the position, length, and direction in which the lines are drawn. These calculations allow the drawing program to re-create the picture on the screen as necessary. Because vector graphic objects are described mathematically, they also can be layered, rotated, and magnified with relative ease. Vector graphics also are known as **object-oriented pictures**. Clip art pictures in the Microsoft Clip Organizer that have the file extension of **.wmf** are examples of vector files. Vector files can be ungrouped and manipulated by their component objects. You will ungroup the hiking clips used on Slide 2 in this project.

PowerPoint allows you to insert vector files because it uses **graphic filters** to convert the various graphic formats into a format PowerPoint can use. These filters are installed with the initial PowerPoint installation or can be added later by running the Setup program.

A **bitmap graphic** is the other major format used to store objects. These art pieces are composed of a series of small dots, called pixels, which form shapes and lines. A **pixel**, short for **picture element**, is one dot in a grid. A picture that is produced on the computer screen or on paper by a printer is composed of thousands of these dots. Just as a bit is the smallest unit of information a computer can process, a pixel is the smallest element that can display or that print hardware and software can manipulate in creating letters, numbers, or graphics.

Bitmap graphics are created by digital cameras or in paint programs such as Microsoft Paint. Bitmap graphics also can be produced from **digitizing** art, pictures, or photographs by passing the artwork through a scanner. A **scanner** is a hardware device that converts lines and shading into combinations of the binary digits 0 and 1 by sensing different intensities of light and dark. The scanner shines a beam of light on the picture being scanned. The beam passes back and forth across the picture, sending a digitized signal to the computer's memory. A **digitized signal** is the conversion of input, such as the lines in a drawing, into a series of discrete units represented by the binary digits 0 and 1. **Scanned pictures** are bitmap pictures and have jagged edges. The jagged edges are caused by the individual pixels that create the picture. Bitmap graphics also are known as **raster images**. Pictures in the Microsoft Clip Organizer that have the file extensions of **.jpg** (Joint Photographic Experts Group), **.bmp** (Windows Bitmap), **.gif** (Graphics Interchange Format), and **.png** (Portable Network Graphics) are examples of bitmap graphic files.

More About

Modifying and Using Art

If you change a clip, be certain you have the legal right to do so. For example, corporate logos are designed using specific colors and shapes and often cannot be altered. In addition, you cannot use photographs and illustrations to damage people's reputations by representing them falsely. For example, you cannot insert a photograph of a former boyfriend or girlfriend in a slide that gives information about students who have been arrested on campus for committing criminal acts.

Q&A

Q: Can I Import Macintosh PICT Files?

A: Yes. PowerPoint uses the Macintosh PICT graphics filter (Pictim32.flt) to convert Macintosh files. You should rename these files using the .pct extension so Microsoft Office for Windows recognizes the files as PICT graphics.

More About

Cropping Pictures

Use the Crop command to cut unwanted areas from any picture except an animated GIF picture. Select the picture, click the Crop button on the Picture toolbar, position the cropping tool over a center cropping handle, and then drag the handle inward. Click the Crop button again to turn off the cropping command.

Bitmap files cannot be ungrouped and converted to smaller PowerPoint object groups. They can be manipulated, however, in an imaging program such as Microsoft Photo Editor. This program allows you to rotate or flip the pictures and then insert them in your slides.

Slide 2 contains a modified version of three people: an adult leader and two child hikers. This clip is from the Microsoft Clip Organizer. You may want to modify a clip art picture for various reasons. Many times you cannot find a clip art picture that precisely illustrates your topic. For example, you want a picture of a man and woman shaking hands, but the only available clip art picture has two men and a woman shaking hands.

Occasionally you may want to remove or change a portion of a clip art picture or you might want to combine two or more clip art pictures. For example, you can use one clip art picture for the background and another picture as the foreground. Still other times, you may want to combine a clip art picture with another type of object. The types of objects you can combine with a clip art picture depend on the software installed on your computer. The **Object type list** in the Insert Object dialog box identifies the types of objects you can combine with a clip art picture. In this presentation, the picture with three people hiking contains a background that is not required to display on the slide, so you will ungroup the clip art picture and remove the background.

Modifying the clip on Slide 2 requires several steps. First, you display Slide 2 and change the slide layout. Then, you insert the hiking picture into the slide. In the next step, you scale the picture to increase its size. Finally, you ungroup the clip, change the color of the backpacks and hats, and then regroup the component objects. The following steps explain in detail how to insert, scale, ungroup, modify, and regroup a clip art image.

Changing the Slide 2 Layout to Title, Content and Text

For aesthetic reasons, you want the bulleted list to display on the right side of the slide. The following steps change the slide layout.

To Change the Slide Layout to Title, Content and Text

1. **Click the Next Slide button to display Slide 2.**
2. **Click Format on the menu bar and then click Slide Layout.**
3. **Scroll down and then click the Title, Content and Text slide layout in the Text and Content Layouts area in the Slide Layout task pane.**
4. **Click the Close button in the Slide Layout task pane.**
5. **Click the Slides tab in the tabs pane.**

Slide 2 has the desired Title, Content and Text slide layout (Figure 3-22). The slide thumbnails display in the tabs pane.

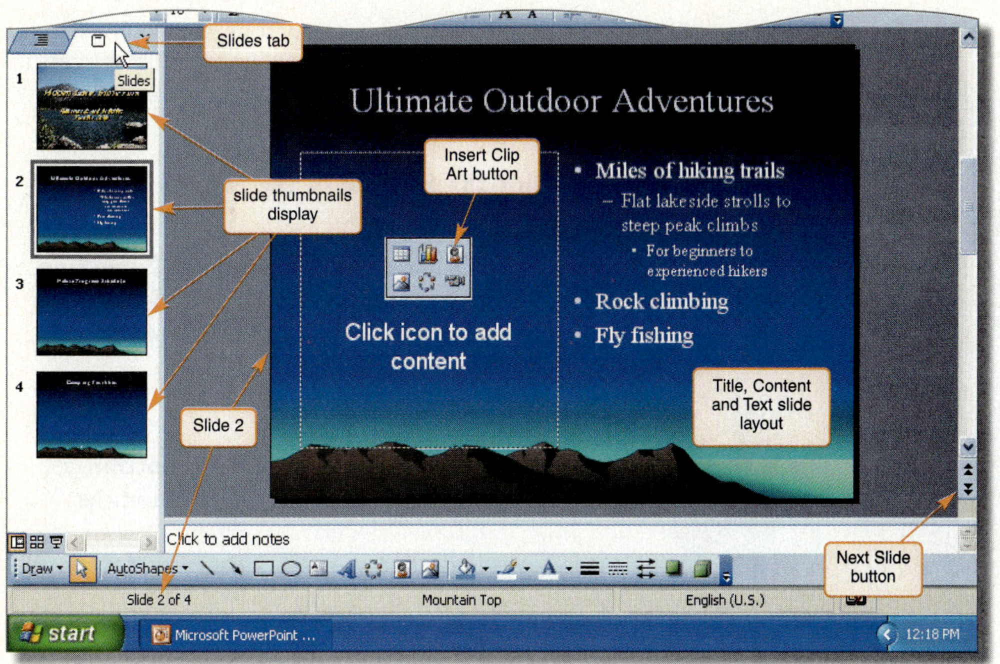

FIGURE 3-22

Inserting a Clip into a Content Placeholder

The first step in modifying a clip is to insert the picture into a slide. You insert the hiking clip from the Microsoft Clip Organizer. In later steps, you modify the clip.

The following steps explain how to insert the clip of the three hikers. See your instructor if this clip is not available on your system.

To Insert a Clip into a Content Placeholder

1. **Click the Insert Clip Art button in the content placeholder (row 1, column 3).**
2. **Type** `backpackers` **in the Search text text box and then click the Go button.**
3. **If necessary, scroll down the list to display the desired clip shown in Figure 3-1b on page PPT 163, click the clip to select it, and then click the OK button.**

The selected clip is inserted into the content placeholder on Slide 2 (Figure 3-23). If the desired clip does not display on your system, see your instructor.

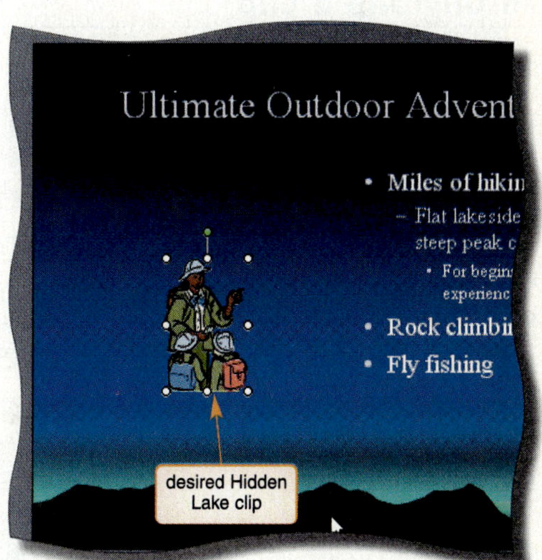

FIGURE 3-23

Sizing and Moving Clips

With the hiking clip inserted on Slide 2, the next step is to increase its size. The steps on the next page size and move the clip.

To Size and Move a Clip

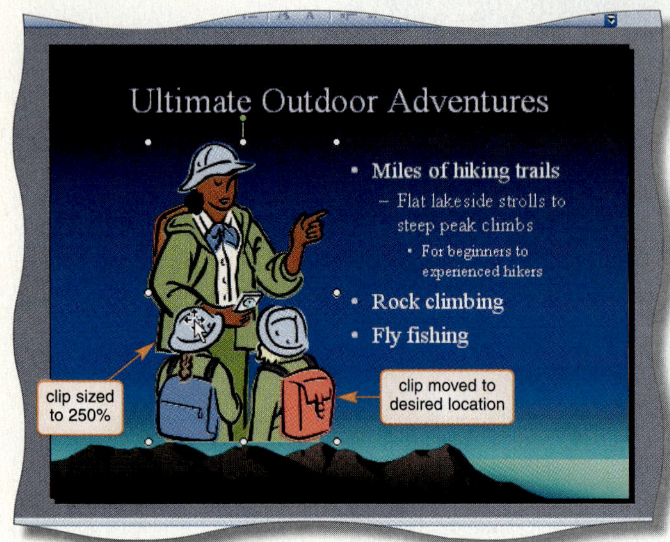

FIGURE 3-24

1. **Right-click the clip and then click Format Picture on the shortcut menu.**
2. **Click the Size tab in the Format Picture dialog box.**
3. **Click and hold down the mouse button on the Height box up arrow in the Scale area until 250 % is displayed and then release the mouse button.**
4. **Click the OK button.**
5. **Drag the hiking clip up so the bottom of the clip is on the top of the mountains.**

The hiking clip art picture increases in size and is displayed in the desired location (Figure 3-24).

Ungrouping a Clip

The next step is to ungroup the hiking clip on Slide 2. When you **ungroup** a clip art picture, PowerPoint breaks it into its component objects. A clip may be composed of a few individual objects or several complex groups of objects. These groups can be ungrouped repeatedly until they decompose into individual objects.

The following steps ungroup a clip.

To Ungroup a Clip

1

- **With the hiking clip selected, right-click the clip.**
- **Point to Grouping on the shortcut menu, and then point to Ungroup on the Grouping submenu.**

Sizing handles indicate the clip is selected (Figure 3-25).

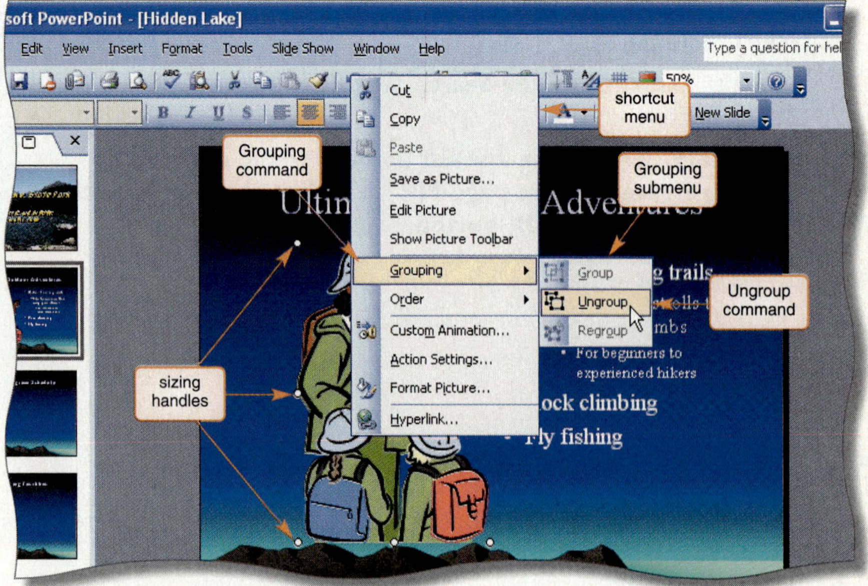

FIGURE 3-25

2

- **Click Ungroup.**
- **Click the Yes button in the Microsoft PowerPoint dialog box.**

The message in the Microsoft PowerPoint dialog box explains that this clip is an imported picture. Converting it to a Microsoft Office drawing permanently discards any embedded data or linking information it contains.

3

- **Right-click the clip, point to Grouping on the shortcut menu, and then click Ungroup.**

The clip now displays as many objects, and sizing handles display around the ungrouped objects (Figure 3-26).

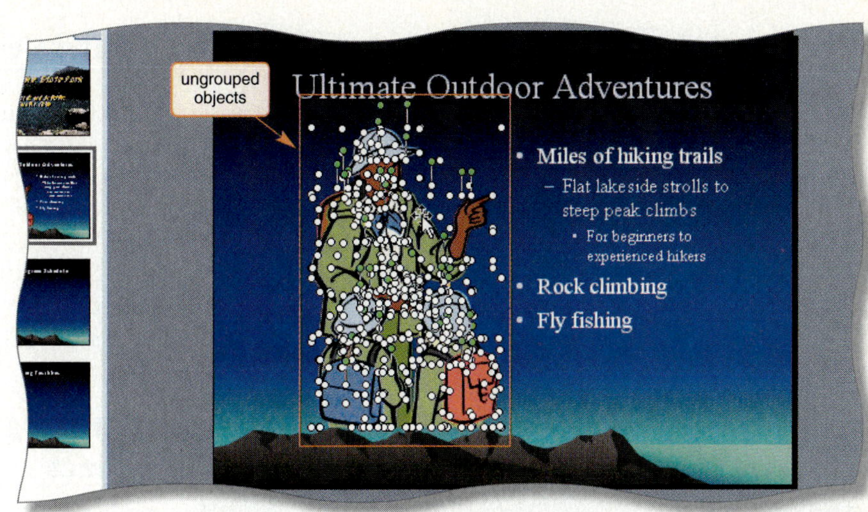

FIGURE 3-26

Other Ways

1. On Draw menu click Ungroup
2. In Voice Command mode, say "Draw, Ungroup"

Because a clip art picture is a collection of complex groups of objects, you may need to ungroup a complex object into less complex objects before being able to modify a specific object. When you ungroup a clip and click the Yes button in the Microsoft PowerPoint dialog box (Step 2 above), PowerPoint converts the clip to a PowerPoint object. Recall that a PowerPoint object is an object not associated with a supplementary application.

If for some reason you decide not to ungroup the clip art picture, click the No button in the Microsoft PowerPoint dialog box. Clicking the No button terminates the Ungroup command, and the clip art picture is displayed on the slide as a clip art picture.

Recall that a clip art picture is an object imported from the Microsoft Clip Organizer. Disassembling imported, embedded, or linked objects eliminates the embedding data or linking information the object contains that ties it back to its original source. Use caution when objects are not completely regrouped. Dragging or scaling affects only the selected object, not the entire collection of objects. To **regroup** the individual objects, select all the objects, click the Draw button on the Drawing toolbar, and then click Group.

More About

Adding Pictures to Notes

If you want to see your pictures on your printed notes, you can add the images to these pages. Click Notes Page on the View menu and then add the picture or object. Then click the Normal View button at the lower-left corner of the Microsoft PowerPoint window to return to normal view.

Deselecting Clip Art Objects

All of the ungrouped objects in Figure 3-26 are selected. Before you can manipulate an individual object, you must deselect all selected objects to remove the selection rectangles, and then you must select the object you want to manipulate. For example, on this slide, you will change the colors of the hats and backpacks. The step on the next page explains how to deselect objects.

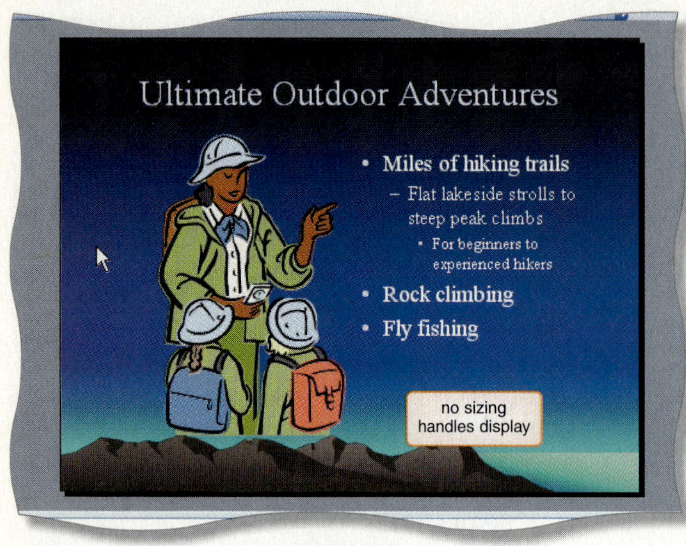

FIGURE 3-27

To Deselect Clip Art Objects

1 **Click outside the clip area.**

Slide 2 displays without the sizing handles around the objects (Figure 3-27).

The hiking clip now is ungrouped into many objects. The next section explains how to change the color of objects.

Changing the Color of a PowerPoint Object

Now that the hiking picture is ungrouped, you can change the color of the objects. The clip is composed of hundreds of objects, so you must exercise care when selecting the correct object to modify. If sizing handles are displayed around the incorrect object, click outside of the clip art and then retry. The following steps change the color of the hikers' hats.

To Change the Color of a PowerPoint Object

- **Click the adult hiker's hat.**

Sizing handles display around the hat (Figure 3-28). If you inadvertently select a different area, click outside of the clip and retry.

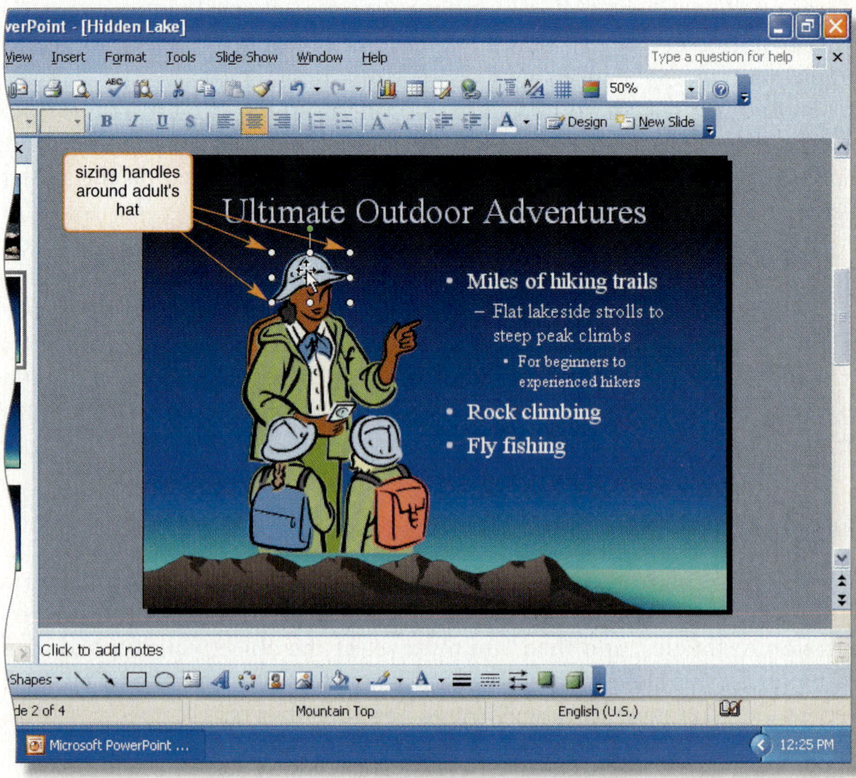

FIGURE 3-28

2

- **Right-click the hat and then point to Format AutoShape on the shortcut menu.**

The shortcut menu displays (Figure 3-29).

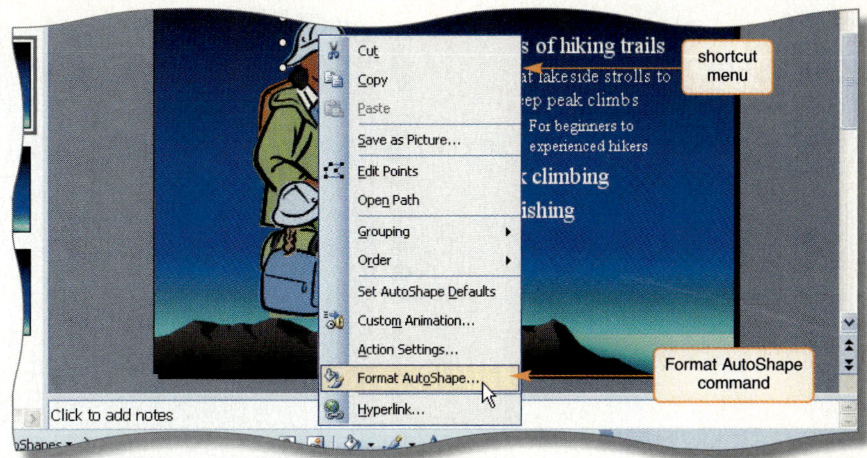

FIGURE 3-29

3

- **Click Format AutoShape.**
- **When the Format AutoShape dialog box displays, click the Colors and Lines tab, and then click the Color box arrow in the Fill area.**

The Format AutoShape dialog box displays (Figure 3-30). The blue hat color is displayed in the Automatic area. The colors displayed in the row directly below the Automatic area are the default colors associated with the Mountain Top design template.

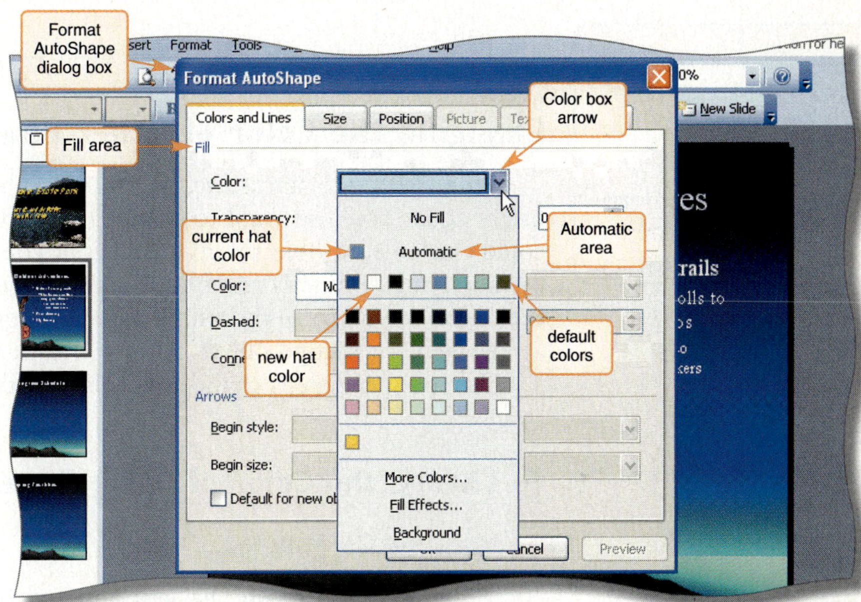

FIGURE 3-30

4

- **Click the color, white, in the row of colors directly below the Automatic area (row 1, column 2).**

White is the default text and lines color for the Mountain Top design template (Figure 3-31). The white color displays in the Color box in the Format AutoShape dialog box.

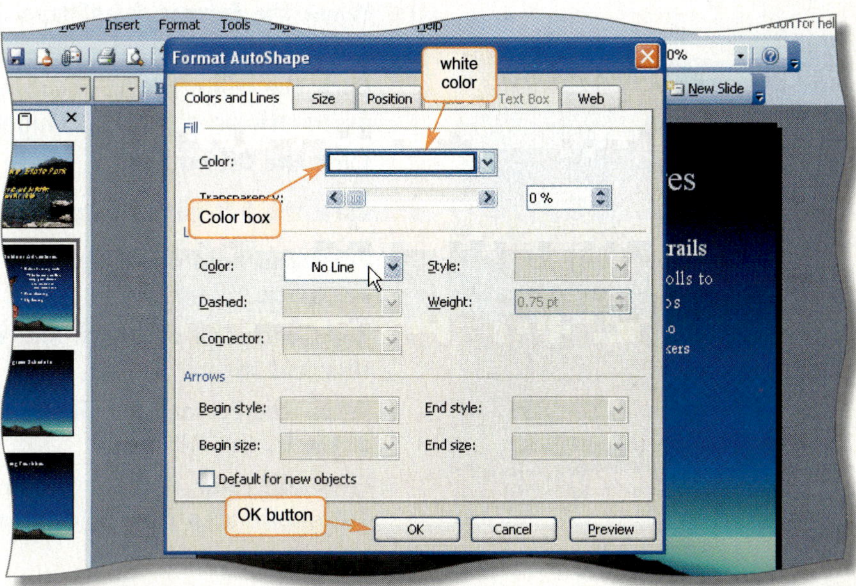

FIGURE 3-31

5

• **Click the OK button.**

The Format AutoShape dialog box closes, and the adult's hat is white (Figure 3-32).

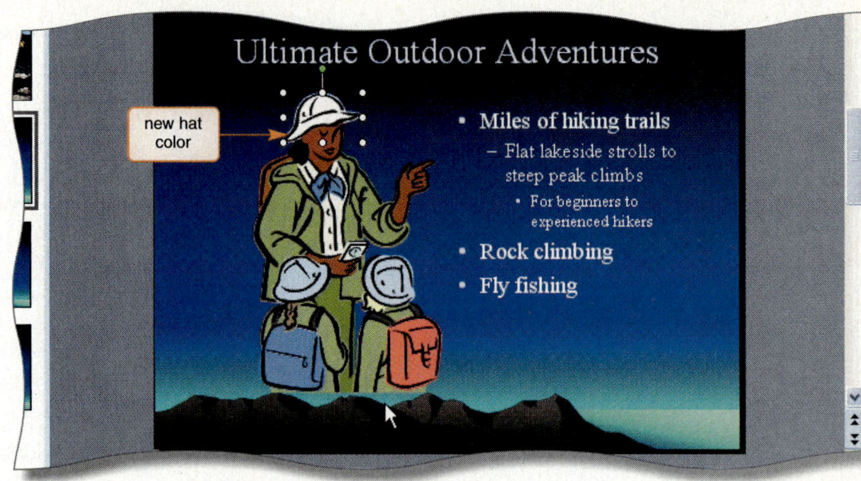

FIGURE 3-32

Other Ways

1. On Format menu click AutoShape
2. Press ALT+O, press O, press ALT+C
3. In Voice Command mode, say "Format, AutoShape, Color"

Changing the Color of Other PowerPoint Objects

With the adult's hat white, you want to change the color of the girls' hats to bright aqua. You also want to change the color of their backpacks to pink. You could change each object individually, but you can perform this task more efficiently by modifying both hats and both backpacks simultaneously using the **SHIFT+click technique**. To perform the SHIFT+click technique, press and hold down the SHIFT key as you click the second object. After you click the second object, release the SHIFT key.

The following steps change the colors of the girls' hats and backpacks.

To Change the Color of Other PowerPoint Objects

1. **Click the left girl's hat.**
2. **Press and hold down the SHIFT key and then click the right girl's hat.**
3. **Right-click one hat and then click Format AutoShape on the shortcut menu.**
4. **When the Format AutoShape dialog box displays, click the Color box arrow in the Fill area.**
5. **Click the color, bright aqua, in the row of colors directly below the Automatic area (row 1, column 7).**
6. **Click the OK button.**
7. **Click the left girl's backpack.**
8. **Press and hold down the SHIFT key and then click the right girl's backpack.**
9. **Right-click one backpack and then click Format AutoShape on the shortcut menu.**
10. **When the Format AutoShape dialog box displays, click the Color box arrow in the Fill area.**
11. **Click the color, pink, in the first column of colors directly below the Automatic area (row 5, column 1).**
12. **Click the OK button.**

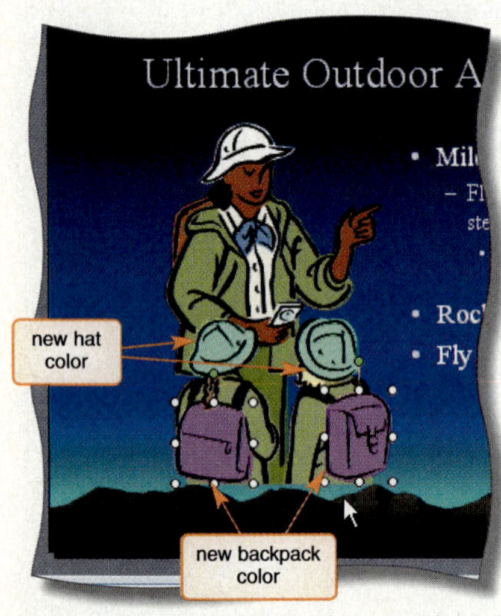

FIGURE 3-33

The PowerPoint object displays with the girls' bright aqua hats and pink backpacks (Figure 3-33).

Regrouping Objects

All of the ungrouped objects in the hikers' picture must be regrouped so they are not accidentally moved or manipulated. The following steps regroup these objects.

To Regroup Objects

1

- **Click outside the lower-right corner of the clip and then drag diagonally to the upper-left corner of the clip above the woman's hat.**

A dotted-line rectangle is displayed around the hiking clip as you drag (Figure 3-34). You want to group the objects within this area. The mouse pointer should be a block arrow only, not an arrow overlaying a double two-headed arrow.

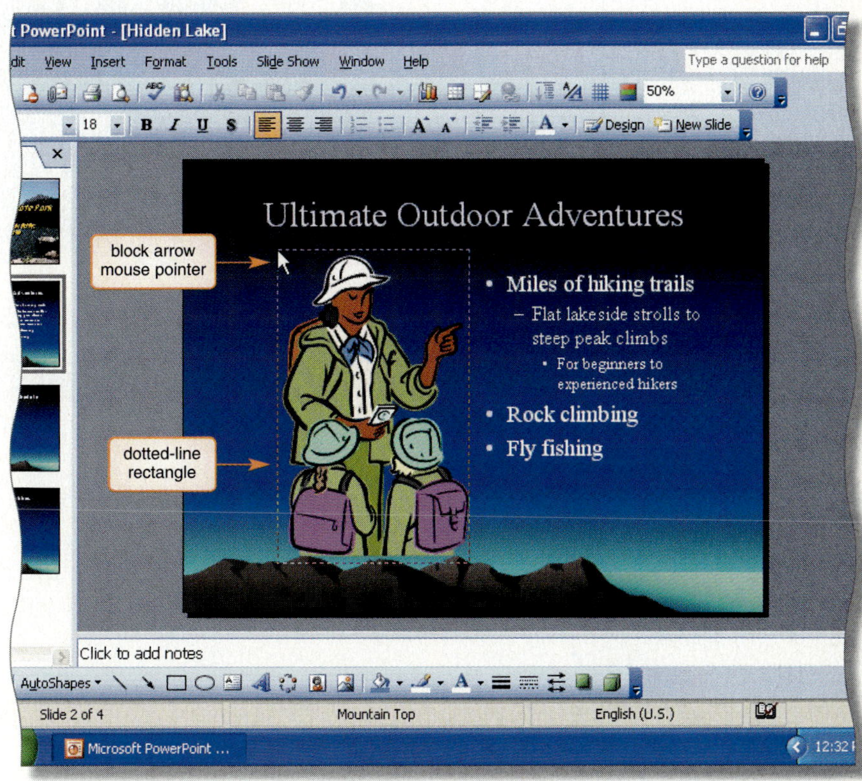

FIGURE 3-34

2

- **Release the mouse button.**
- **Click the Draw button on the Drawing toolbar and then point to Regroup on the Draw menu.**

Sizing handles display on all the selected components of the hiking clip (Figure 3-35).

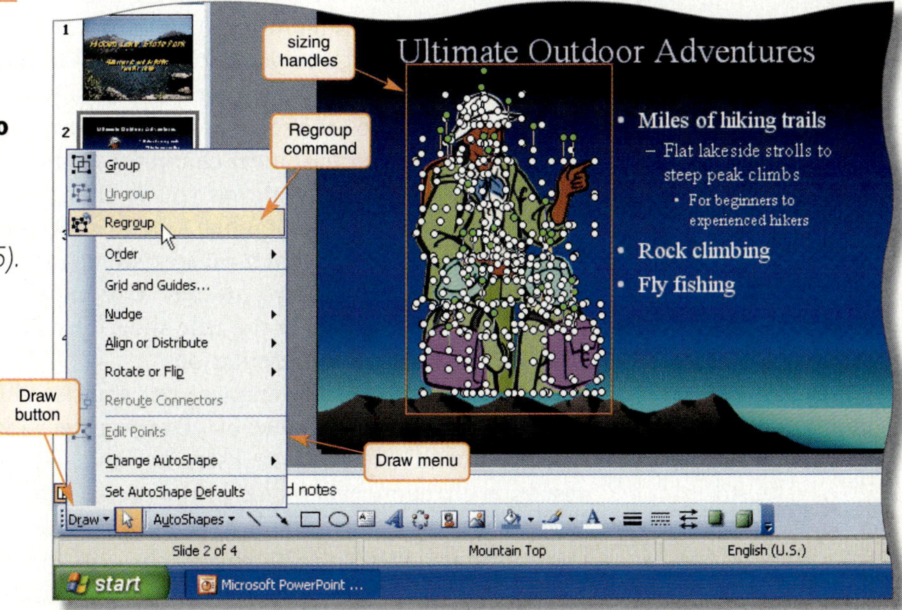

FIGURE 3-35

3

• **Click Regroup.**

The eight sizing handles displaying around the entire clip indicate the object is regrouped (Figure 3-36).

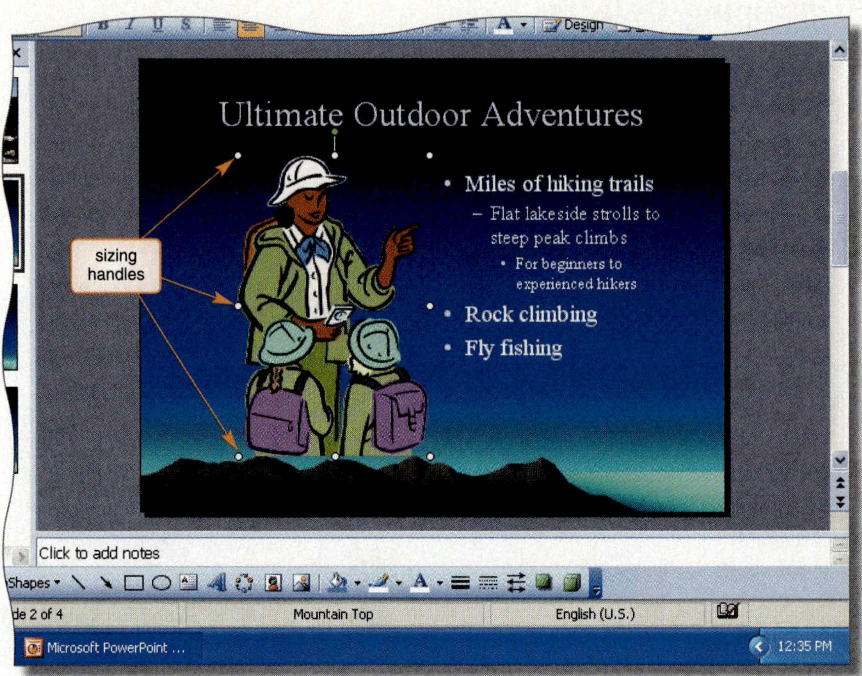

FIGURE 3-36

Other Ways

1. On Drawing toolbar click Draw button, click Regroup
2. In Voice Command mode, say "Draw, Regroup"

All the components of the hiking picture now are grouped into one object. The next change you want to make to Slide 2 is to modify bullets in the list.

Customizing Graphical Bullets Using the Slide Master

More About

Bullets

Use a numbered list to add emphasis to your presentation. When necessary, numbers can show ordered steps or sequences. To add numbering, select the lines of text you want numbered and then click the Numbering button on the Formatting toolbar.

PowerPoint allows you to change the appearance of bullets in a slide show. Slide 2's Title, Content and Text slide layout uses the default bullet styles determined by the Mountain Top design template. You may want to change these characters, however, to add visual interest and variety to your slide show.

The Mountain Top design template uses white dots for the first-level paragraphs and white dashes for the second-level paragraphs. Changing the solid white round bullet to a mountain graphical character would enhance the visual nature of your presentation. PowerPoint allows you to change the bullet style for a single list or throughout a presentation. When several slides need to be changed, you should change the slide master. Each **master** stores information about the design template's appearance. Slides have two masters: title master and slide master. The **title master** controls the appearance of the title slide. The **slide master** controls the appearance of the other slides in a presentation.

If you select a design template but want to change one of its components, you can override that component by changing the slide master. The slide master components frequently changed are listed in Table 3-1. Any change to the slide master results in changing every slide in the presentation, except the title slide. For example, if you change the level-2 bullet on the slide master, each slide (except the title slide) changes that bullet. In this project, you will change the bullet style on the slide master to reflect the change throughout the presentation, so the new symbol will display in the bulleted list on Slide 2.

Bullet styles have three components: character, size, and color. A **bullet character** can be a predefined style, a variety of fonts and characters displayed in the Symbol dialog box, or a picture from the Clip Organizer. **Bullet size** is measured as a percentage of the text size and can range from 25 to 400 percent. **Bullet color** is based on the eight colors in the design template's color scheme. Additional standard and custom colors also are available.

To emphasize the nature message in the slide show, you want to change the bullet style in the first-level paragraphs from a solid round bullet to the mountain symbol and from white to brown. You will make these changes on the slide master.

Table 3-1 Summary of Slide Master Components

COMPONENT	DESCRIPTION
Background items	Any object other than the title object or text object. Typical items include borders and graphics such as a company logo, page number, date, and time.
Color scheme	A coordinated set of eight colors designed to complement each other. Color schemes consist of background color, line and text color, shadow color, title text color, object fill color, and three different accent colors.
Date	Inserts the special symbol used to print the date the presentation was printed.
Font	Defines the appearance and shape of letters, numbers, and special characters.
Size	Specifies the size of the characters on the screen in a measurement system called points.
Slide number	Inserts the special symbol used to print the slide number.
Style	Font styles include regular, bold, italic, and bold italic. Effects include underline, shadow, emboss, superscript, and subscript. Effects can be applied to most fonts.
Text alignment	Position of text in a paragraph is left-aligned, right-aligned, centered, or justified. Justified text is spaced proportionally across the object.
Time	Inserts the special symbol used to print the time the presentation was printed.

Displaying the Slide Master

To change all first-level bullets throughout the presentation, the bullet should be changed on the slide master. The following steps display the slide master.

To Display the Slide Master

1

• **Click View on the menu bar, point to Master, and then point to Slide Master on the Master submenu.**

The View menu and Master submenu display (Figure 3-37). Each PowerPoint component — slides (both title and text), audience handouts, and notes pages — has a master that controls its appearance.

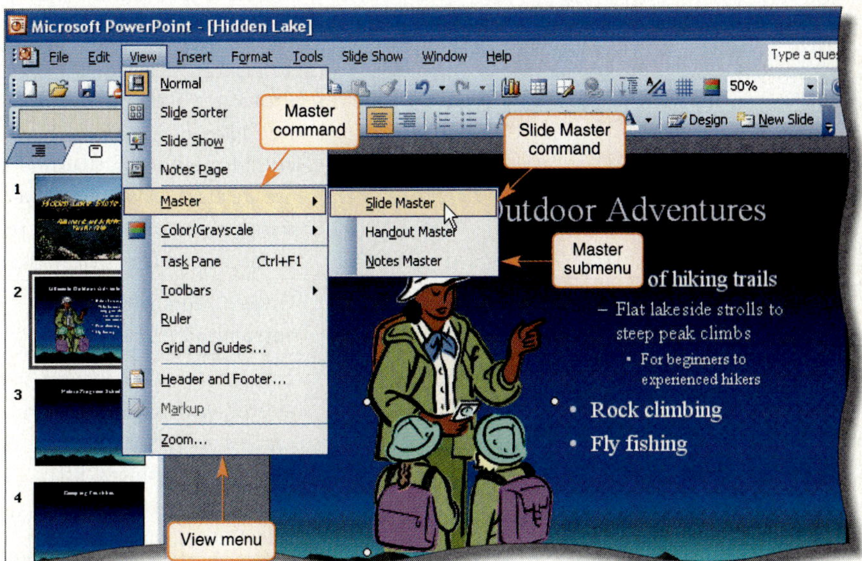

FIGURE 3-37

2

• **Click the Slide Master command.**

The Mountain Top slide master and Slide Master View toolbar display (Figure 3-38). The Mountain Top Title Master slide thumbnail and Mountain Top Slide Master slide thumbnail display on the left edge of the screen. The Mountain Top Slide Master slide thumbnail is selected.

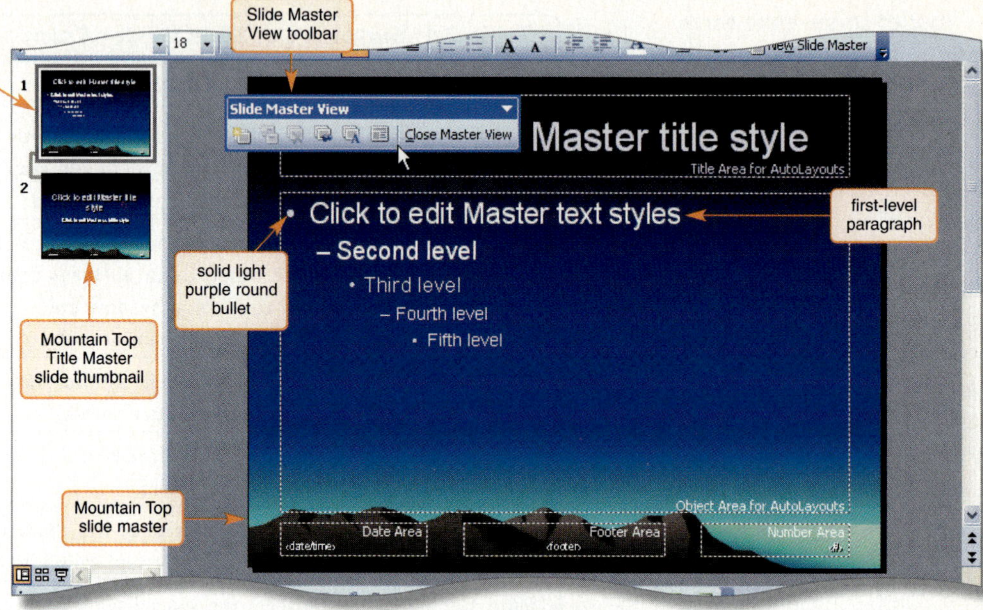

FIGURE 3-38

Other Ways

1. Press and hold down SHIFT, click Slide Master View button
2. In Voice Command mode, say "View, Master, Slide Master"

The **Slide Master View toolbar** contains buttons that are useful when inserting multiple slide masters or title masters in a slide show. Table 3-2 describes the buttons on the Slide Master View toolbar. You will use some of these buttons in Project 4.

Once the slide master is displayed, any changes to the components are reflected throughout the slide show except on the title slide. In Figure 3-38, the text styles and bullets for the five paragraph levels and for the title are shown. The first-level paragraph has a solid light purple round bullet, the Arial font, a font size of 32, and it is left-aligned. These slide master text attributes are modified in a manner similar to changing attributes on an individual slide.

Table 3-2 Buttons on the Slide Master View Toolbar

BUTTON	BUTTON NAME	DESCRIPTION
	Insert New Slide Master	Adds multiple slide masters to a slide show.
	Insert New Title Master	Adds multiple title masters to a slide show.
	Delete Master	Deletes a slide master from a slide show. When a slide master is deleted, the title master is deleted automatically.
	Preserve Master	Protects a slide master so it is not deleted automatically when all slides following that master are deleted or when another design template is applied to all slides that follow that master.
	Rename Master	Gives a slide master a customized name.
	Master Layout	Displays the elements on the master, such as the title and subtitle text, header and footer placeholders, lists, pictures, tables, charts, AutoShapes, and movies.
Close Master View	Close Master View	Hides the Slide Master View toolbar.

Changing a Bullet Character on the Slide Master

The first bullet style change replaces the solid light purple round bullet with the mountain symbol. The following steps change the level-1 bullet character.

To Change a Bullet Character on the Slide Master

1

- **On the slide master, click the paragraph, Click to edit Master text styles.**
- **Click Format on the menu bar.**

The Format menu is displayed (Figure 3-39).

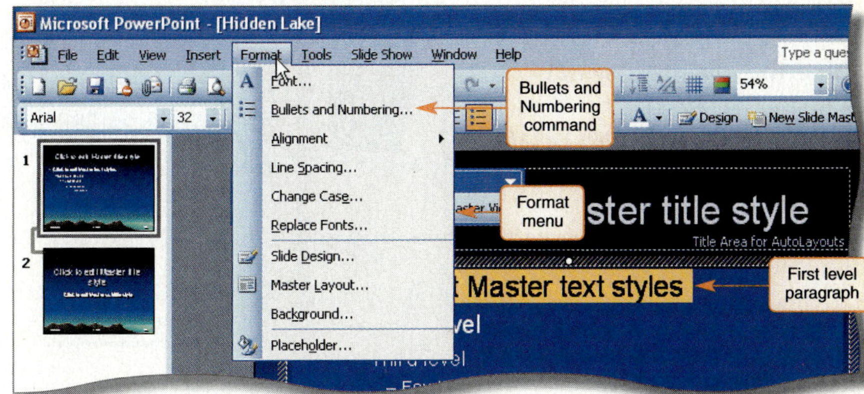

FIGURE 3-39

2

- **Click Bullets and Numbering on the Format menu.**
- **If necessary, click the Bulleted tab when the Bullets and Numbering dialog box is displayed.**

The Bullets and Numbering dialog box is displayed (Figure 3-40). The Bulleted tab has a variety of bullets and the options of no bullets or custom bullets.

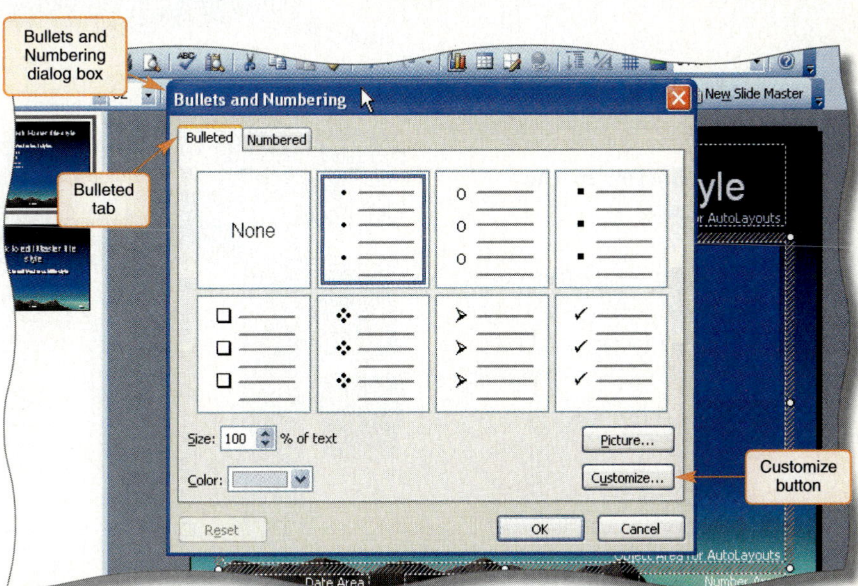

FIGURE 3-40

3

- **Click the Customize button in the Bullets and Numbering dialog box.**
- **Click the Font box arrow in the Symbol dialog box.**

The round bullet symbol is selected in the Symbol dialog box because it is the default level-1 bullet style for the Mountain Top design template (Figure 3-41). The round bullet is part of the General Punctuation subset of symbols for the Arial font.

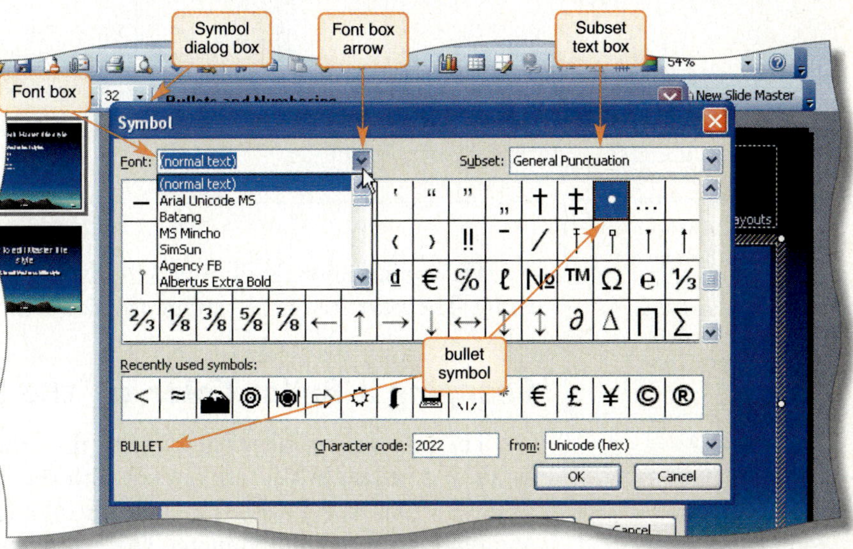

FIGURE 3-41

4

- **Scroll through the list until Webdings is displayed.**
- **Click Webdings.**
- **Click the mountain symbol.**

The symbols for the Webdings font are displayed, and the mountain symbol is selected (Figure 3-42). You may have to scroll through the symbols to locate the mountain symbol. Your list of available fonts may differ depending on the type of printer you are using and the fonts that are installed on your system. Any Webdings symbol can be used as a bullet.

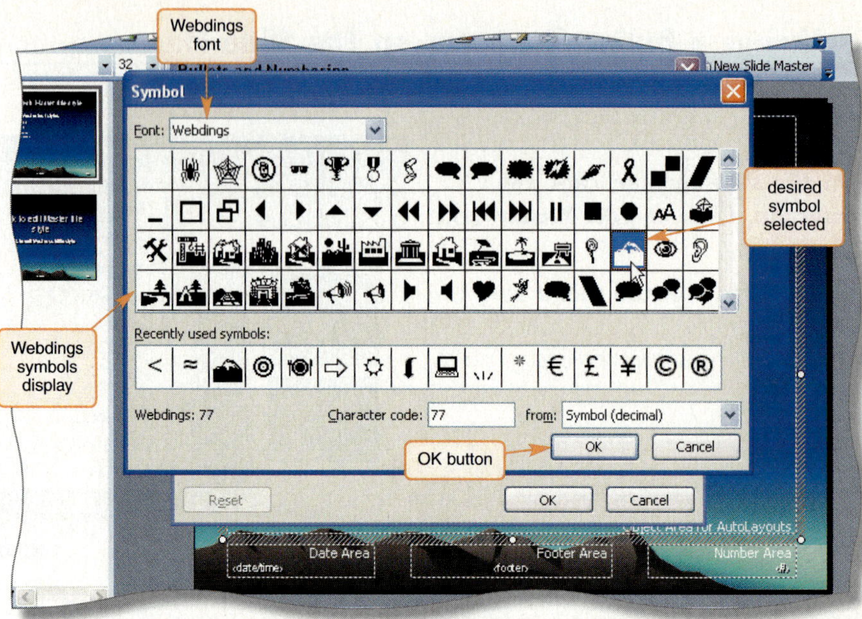

FIGURE 3-42

5

- **Click the OK button in the Symbol dialog box.**

The Bullets and Numbering dialog box is displayed (Figure 3-43). PowerPoint applies the mountain symbol to the first-level paragraph, which you will see when the dialog box closes.

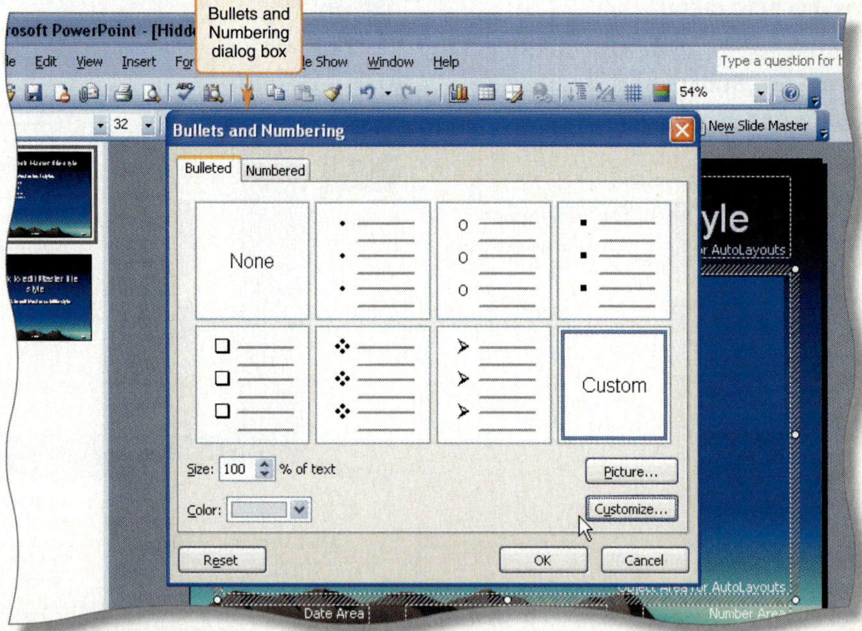

FIGURE 3-43

Other Ways

1. Right-click first-level paragraph, click Bullets and Numbering on shortcut menu, click Customize button
2. Press ALT+O, press B, press ALT+U
3. In Voice Command mode, say "Format, Bullets and Numbering, Customize"

The mountain symbol now will display as the level-1 bullet throughout the slide show. The next step is to change the color of the mountain bullet.

Changing a Bullet Color on the Slide Master

The new white bullet blends with the other bullets. To add contrast to the symbol, a brown bullet works well with the blue background and brown mountains at the bottom of the slide. The color brown is one of the eight default colors of the Mountain Top design template. The following steps change the level-1 bullet color.

To Change a Bullet Color on the Slide Master

1

- **With the Bullets and Numbering dialog box displaying, click the Color box arrow.**

The color light purple is displayed in the Color box and is selected in the row of available colors because it is the default bullet color in the Mountain Top design template (Figure 3-44).

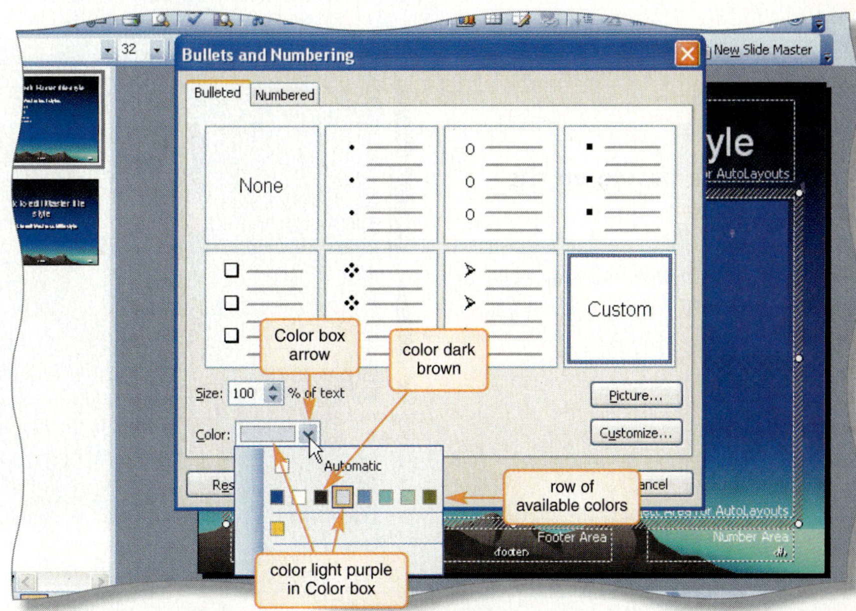

FIGURE 3-44

2

- **Click the color dark brown in the row of available colors (row 1, column 3).**

The color dark brown is displayed in the Color box (Figure 3-45).

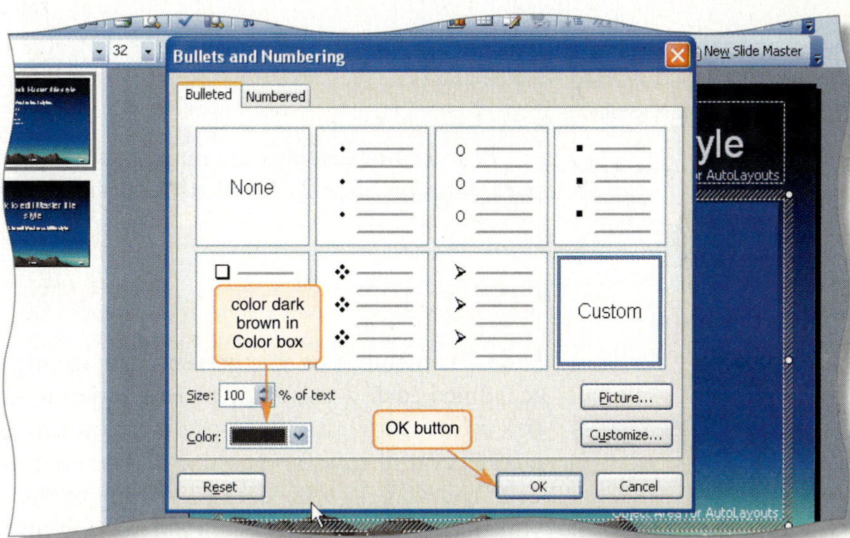

FIGURE 3-45

3

- **Click the OK button.**
- **Point to the Close Master View button on the Slide Master View toolbar.**

The dark brown mountain custom bullet is displayed in the level-1 paragraph (Figure 3-46). All changes to the slide master are complete. After closing the slide master view, the presentation returns to normal view.

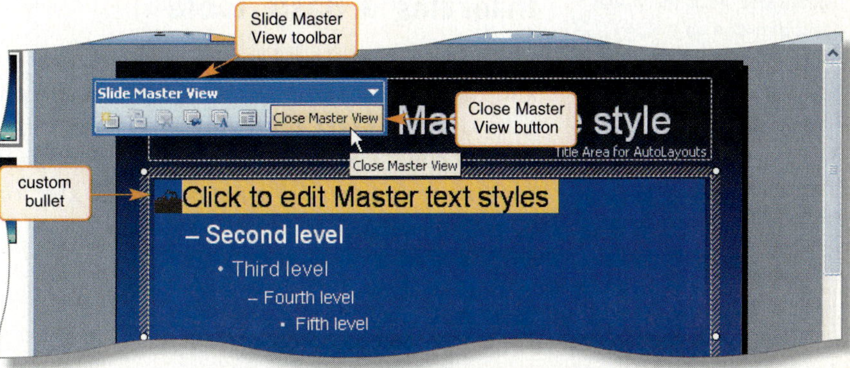

FIGURE 3-46

4

• **Click the Close Master View button.**

Slide 2 is complete (Figure 3-47).

5

• **Click the Save button on the Standard toolbar.**

PowerPoint saves the file. You may need to insert a new disk or save the file to your hard drive.

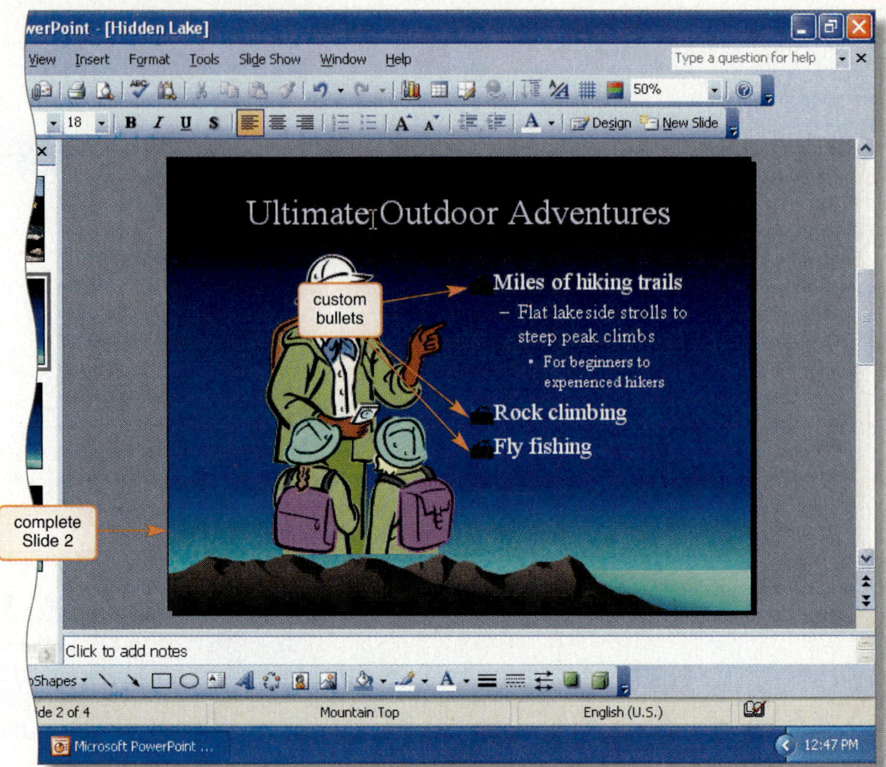

FIGURE 3-47

> *Other Ways*
>
> 1. In Voice Command mode, say, "Color"

PowerPoint displays the new brown bullet symbol in front of each level-1 paragraph on Slide 2. The next section describes how to add a table to a slide.

Creating a Table on a Slide

Slide 3 is included in this presentation to inform campers of the three programs scheduled each week at the three Hidden Lake State Park campgrounds. To make this information visually appealing, you can arrange the figures in a table. A **table** is a collection of rows and columns. The intersection of a row and a column is called a **cell**. You fill cells with data pertaining to the Hidden Lake nature programs. Then you format the table by changing the column heading alignment, font style, and size.

> *More About*
>
> **Slide Space**
>
> Do not be afraid to leave some blank space on a slide. The absence of text, called white space, helps the viewer focus attention on the presenter. It also gives your text and visual elements, such as a table, some breathing room.

Inserting a Basic Table

PowerPoint provides two major methods of creating a table. If the table is basic and has the same number of rows in each column, such as the one for this presentation, use the **Insert Table button** on the Standard toolbar and specify the number of desired rows and columns. If the table is more complex, use the **Tables and Borders toolbar** to draw and format the table. The following steps insert a basic table.

To Insert a Basic Table

1

- **Click the Next Slide button to display Slide 3.**
- **Click the Insert Table button on the Standard toolbar.**
- **Point to the upper-left square in the grid.**

Slide 3 displays the slide title and a text placeholder. The first square is dark blue, meaning it is selected. The message at the bottom of the grid states that the table has one row and one column (Figure 3-48).

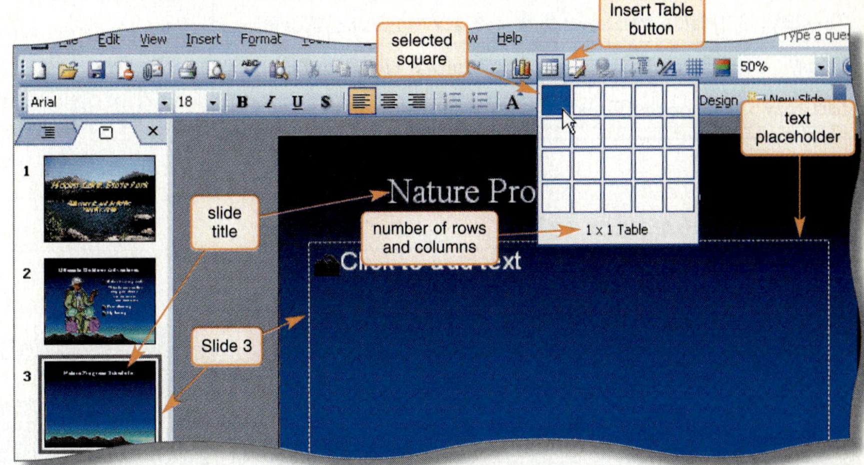

FIGURE 3-48

2

- **Move the mouse pointer two squares to the right so the first three squares in the grid are selected.**
- **Move the mouse pointer down to select four rows in the grid.**

Four rows and three columns are selected, as indicated by the dark blue squares and the message at the bottom of the grid (Figure 3-49).

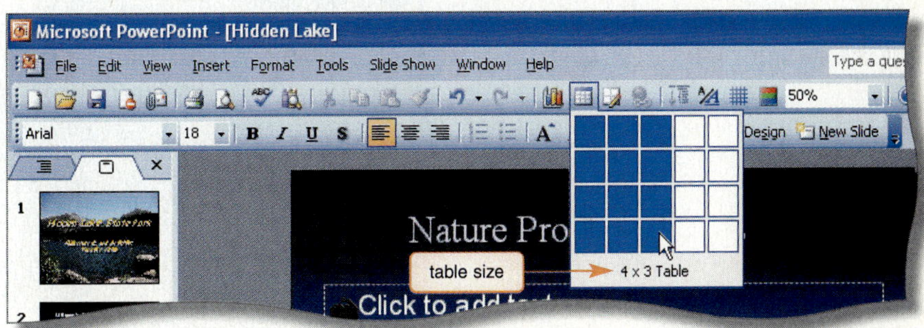

FIGURE 3-49

3

- **Click the selected square at the bottom-right corner of the grid.**
- **Click the Close button on the Tables and Borders toolbar.**

PowerPoint displays a table with four rows and three columns. The insertion point is in the upper-left cell, which is selected (Figure 3-50).

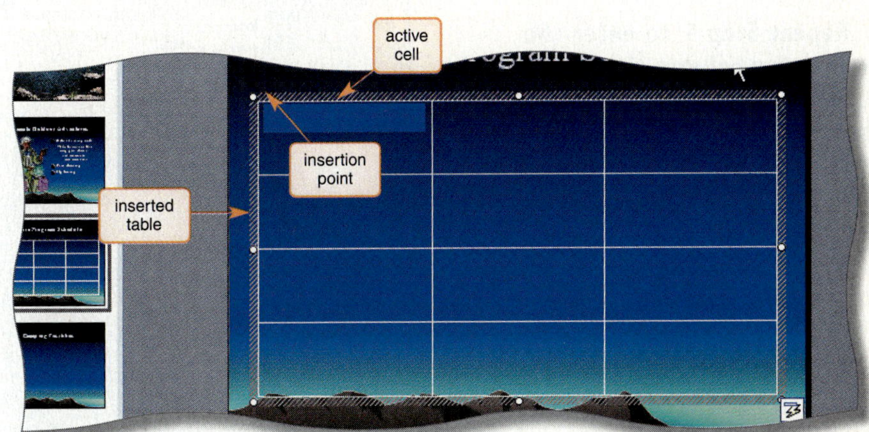

FIGURE 3-50

Other Ways

1. On Insert menu click Table, type desired number of rows and columns, click OK button
2. Press ALT+I, press B, type desired number of columns, press TAB, type desired number of rows, press ENTER

Table 3-3 Nature Program Schedule Data

Day	Theater Location	Program
Tuesday	Maple Meadows	It's a Wild, Wild World
Friday	Beech Basin	Mountain Highs and Lows
Saturday	Crooked Creek	Wildflower Wilderness

Entering Data in a Table

The table on Slide 3 consists of three columns: one for the day of the week, one for the location of the theater, and one for the program name. A **heading** identifies each column. The days, locations, and programs are summarized in Table 3-3.

The following steps enter data in the table.

To Enter Data in a Table

1

• **Type** Day **and then press the RIGHT ARROW key.**

The first column title, Day, is displayed in the top-left cell. The middle cell in the first row is the active cell (Figure 3-51). You also can press the TAB key to advance to the next cell.

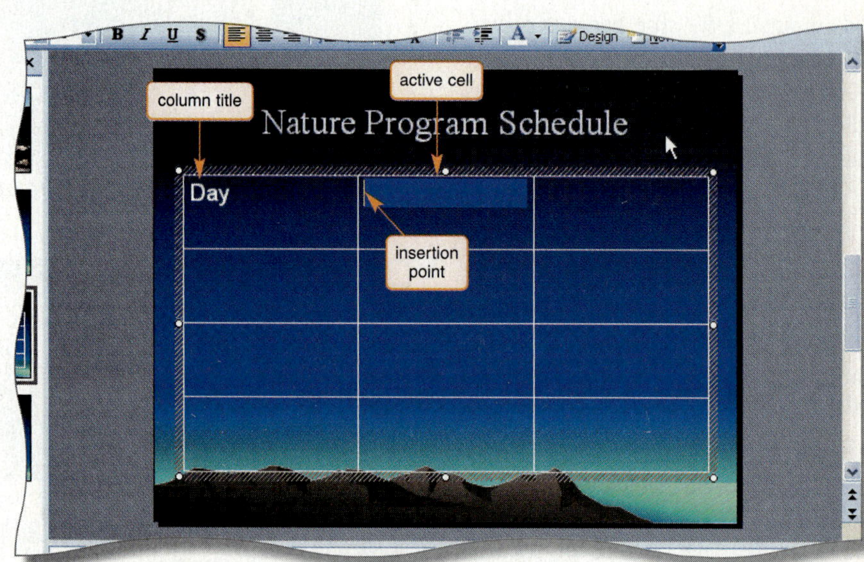

FIGURE 3-51

2

• **Repeat Step 1 to enter the remaining column titles and for the other table cells by using Table 3-3 as a guide.**

The three days of the week and the corresponding theater locations and programs display (Figure 3-52). All entries are left-aligned and display in 28-point Arial font.

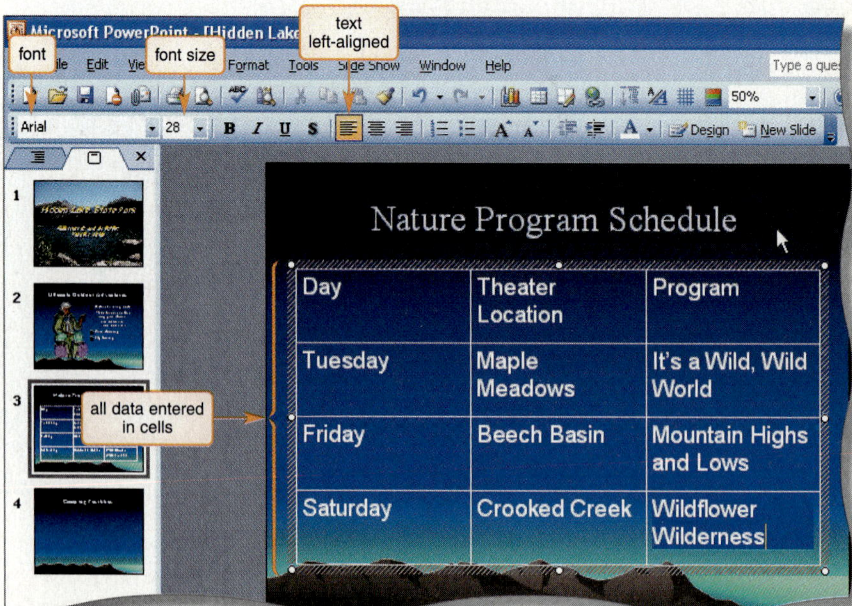

FIGURE 3-52

The next step is to format the table. You **format** the table to emphasize certain entries and to make it easier to read and understand. In this project, you will change the column heading alignment and font style and size. The process required to format the table is explained in the remainder of this section. Although the format procedures will be carried out in a particular manner, you should be aware that you can make these format changes in any order.

> *More About*
>
> **Embedding Tables**
>
> If the data in your table changes frequently, consider using an embedded table. This table can be created in another Microsoft Office program, such as Word or Excel, and then added to a PowerPoint slide. Once embedded, the table becomes part of the original file. When the information changes in the original file, it also changes in your PowerPoint table.

Formatting a Table Cell

You format an entry in a cell to emphasize it or to make it stand out from the rest of the table. The following steps bold and center the column headings and then increase the font size.

To Format a Table Cell

1

- **Click the top-left cell, Day.**
- **Press and hold the SHIFT key and then click the top-right cell, Program.**
- **Release the SHIFT key.**

The three column headings, Day, Theater Location, and Program, are selected (Figure 3-53).

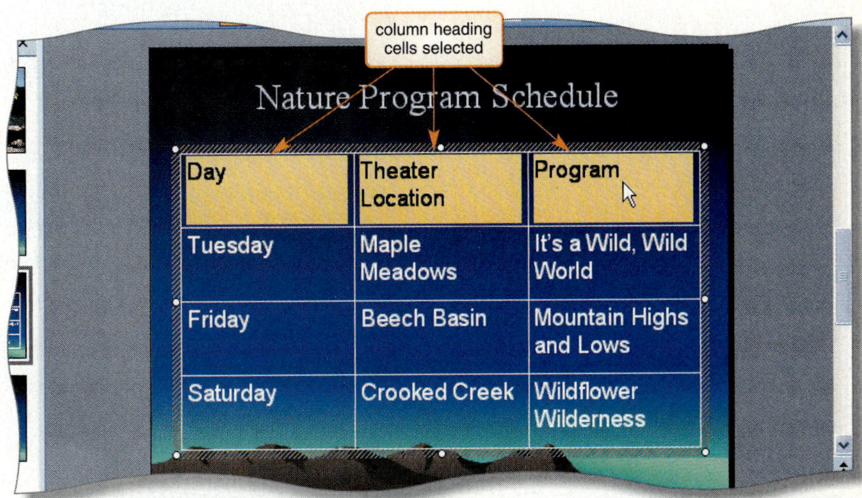

FIGURE 3-53

2

- **Click the Font box arrow on the Formatting toolbar.**
- **Scroll down and then click Times New Roman.**

The text in the heading cells is displayed in 28-point Times New Roman font (Figure 3-54).

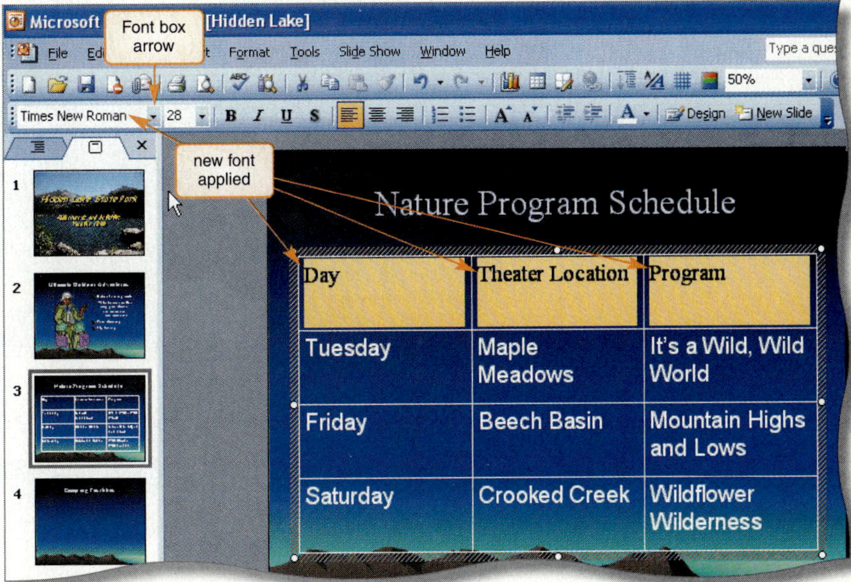

FIGURE 3-54

3

- **Click the Bold button on the Formatting toolbar.**

The text is displayed in bold and is left-aligned in the cells (Figure 3-55).

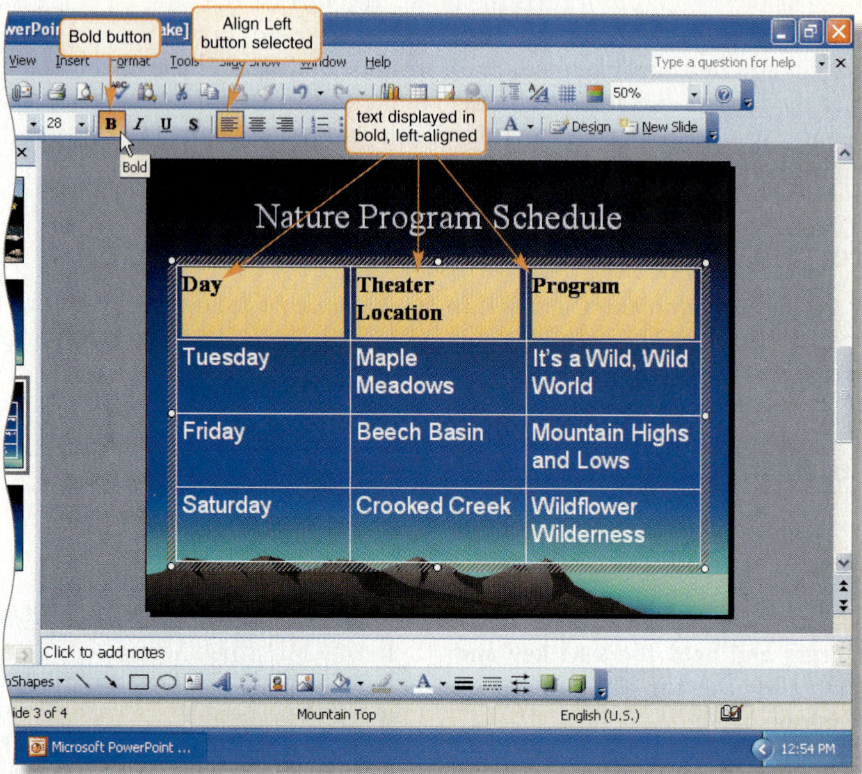

FIGURE 3-55

4

- **Click the Center button on the Formatting toolbar.**

The text is centered in the cells (Figure 3-56).

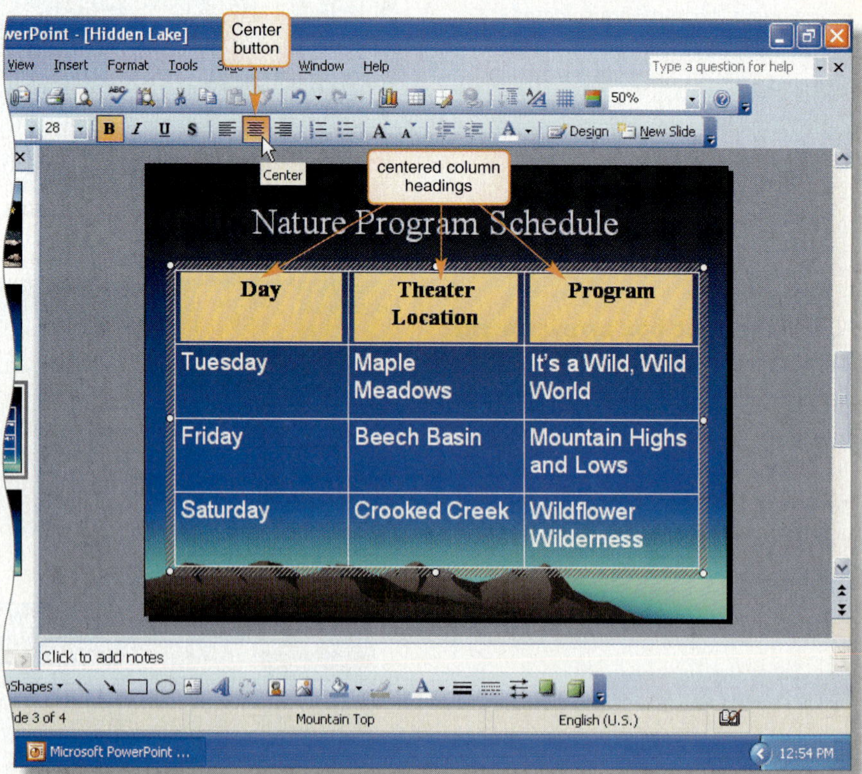

FIGURE 3-56

5

• **Click the Increase Font Size button on the Formatting toolbar twice.**

The text is enlarged to a font size of 36 point (Figure 3-57).

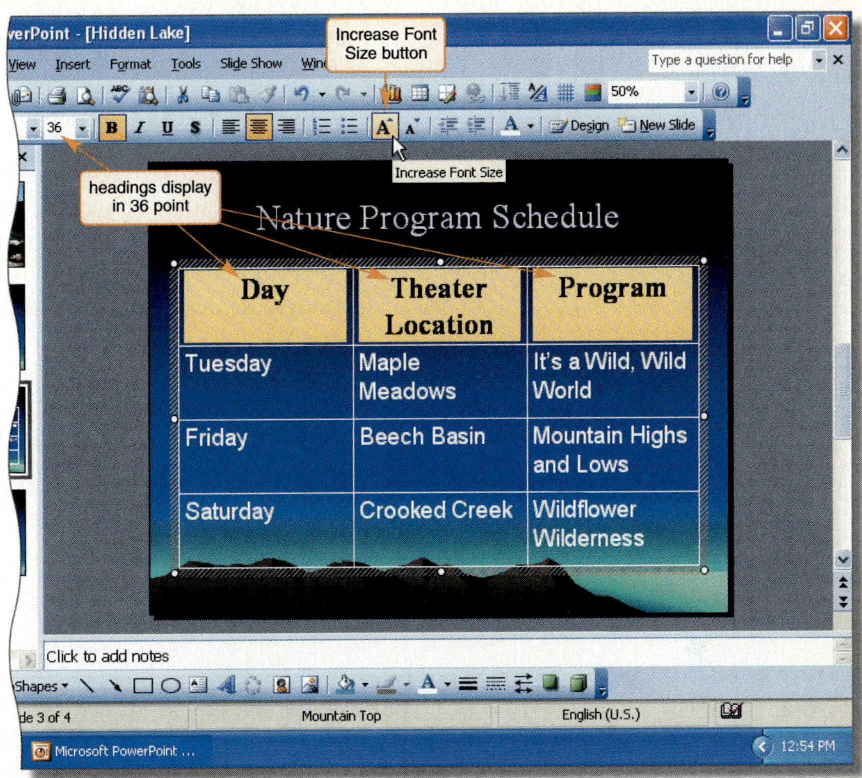

FIGURE 3-57

You can change the font type, style, or size at any time while the table is selected. Some PowerPoint users prefer to change font and cell alignments before they enter any data. Others change the font and alignment while they are building the table or after they have entered all the data.

Slide 3 now is complete. Again, because you have made some significant changes to the presentation, save the slide show by clicking the Save button on the Standard toolbar. The next section shows how to create an organization chart that describes the three campgrounds at Hidden Lake.

Creating an Organization Chart

Slide 4 contains a chart that elaborates on the campgrounds available at Hidden Lake, as shown in Figure 3-58. This type of chart is called an **organization chart**, which is a hierarchical collection of elements depicting various functions or responsibilities that contribute to an organization or to a collective function. Typically, you would use an organization chart to show the structure of people or departments within an organization, hence the name, organization chart.

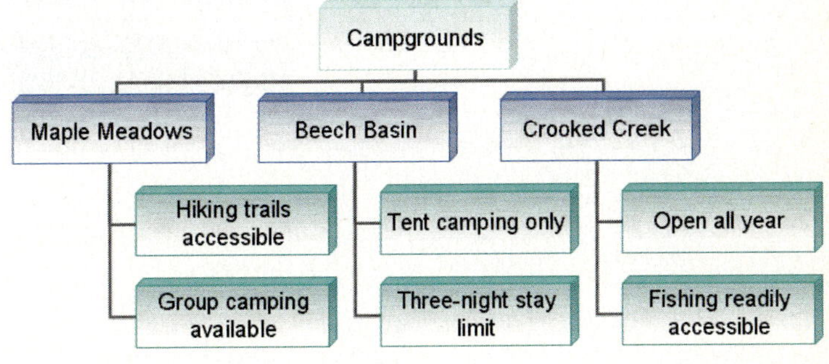

FIGURE 3-58

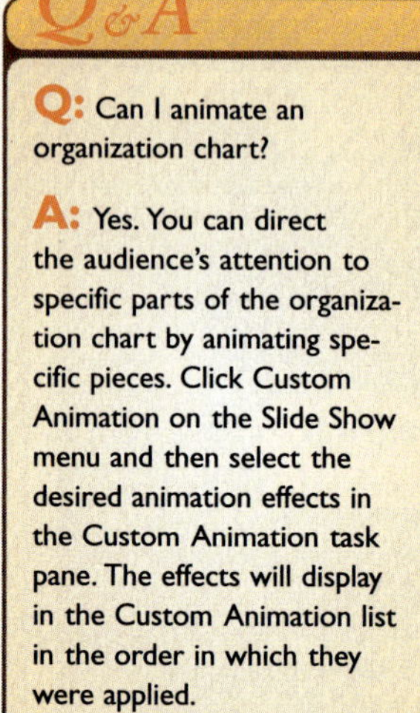

Q&A

Q: Can I animate an organization chart?

A: Yes. You can direct the audience's attention to specific parts of the organization chart by animating specific pieces. Click Custom Animation on the Slide Show menu and then select the desired animation effects in the Custom Animation task pane. The effects will display in the Custom Animation list in the order in which they were applied.

Organization charts are used in a variety of ways to depict relationships. For example, a company uses an organization chart to describe the relationships between the company's departments. In the information sciences, often organization charts show the decomposition of a process or program. When used in this manner, the chart is called a **hierarchy chart**.

Creating an organization chart requires several steps. First, you display the slide that will contain the organization chart and then select the Organization Chart diagram from the Diagram Gallery. Then you enter and format the contents of the shapes in the organization chart.

The following steps create the organization chart for this project.

Displaying the Next Slide and the Organization Chart Diagram

The following steps display Slide 4 and the organization chart diagram.

To Display the Next Slide and the Organization Chart Diagram

1

- **Click the Next Slide button to display Slide 4.**
- **Click the Insert Diagram or Organization Chart button on the Drawing toolbar.**

Slide 4 displays the slide title, a text placeholder, and the Diagram Gallery dialog box (Figure 3-59). The Organization Chart diagram type is selected. The other diagram types are Cycle Diagram, Radial Diagram, Pyramid Diagram, Venn Diagram, and Target Diagram.

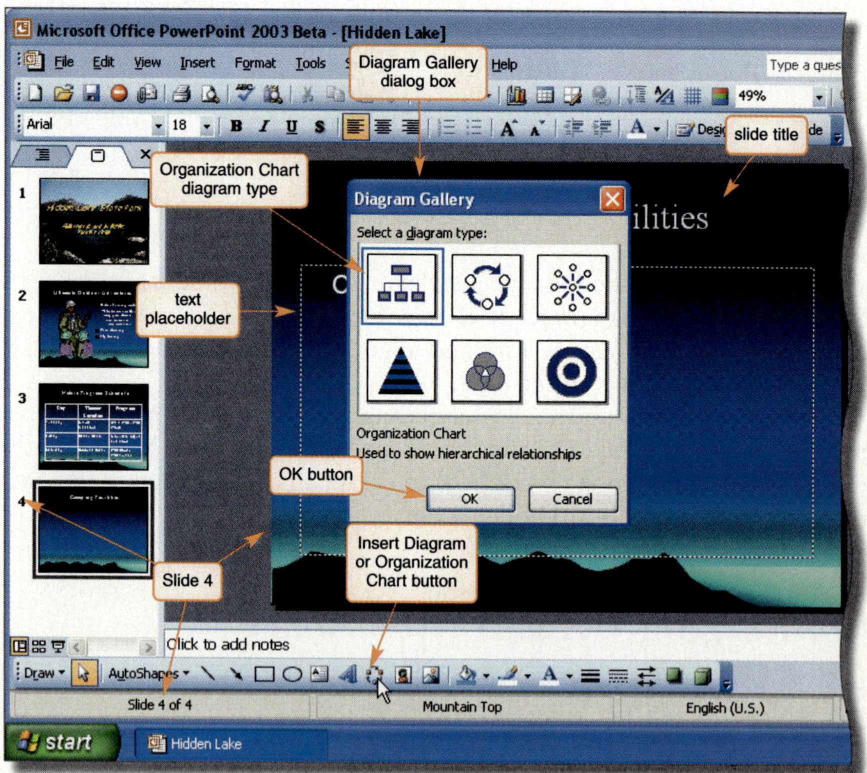

FIGURE 3-59

2

- **Click the OK button.**

A sample organization chart and the Organization Chart toolbar display (Figure 3-60). The organization chart is composed of four shapes connected by lines. The top shape, called the superior shape, is selected automatically.

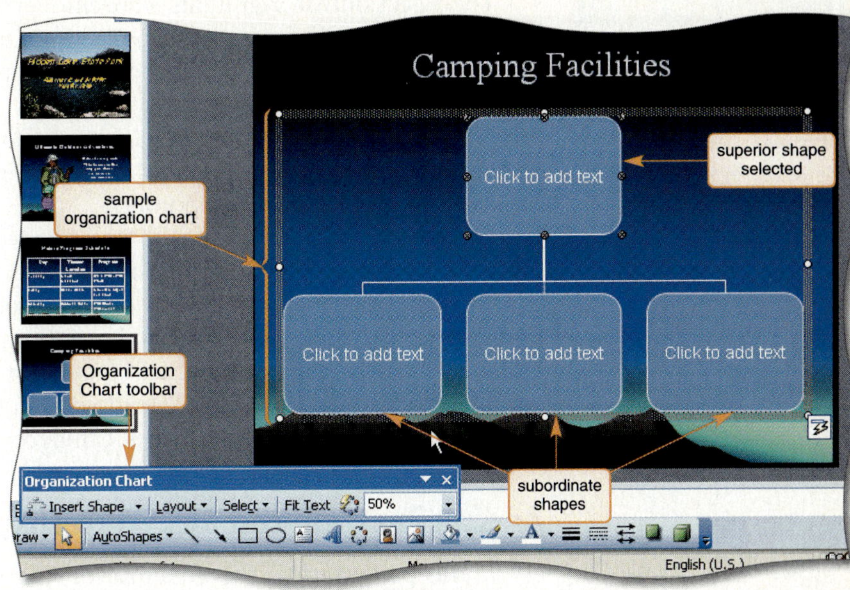

FIGURE 3-60

Other Ways

1. On Insert menu point to Picture, click Organization Chart on Picture submenu
2. On Insert menu click Diagram, click OK button
3. In Voice Command mode, say "Insert, Picture, Organization Chart"

PowerPoint displays a sample organization chart to help create the chart. The sample is located in a work area called the **canvas** and is composed of one **superior shape**, located at the top of the chart, and three **subordinate shapes**. Lines to one or more subordinates connect a superior shape, also called a manager. A subordinate shape is located at a lower level than its manager and has only one manager. When a lower-level subordinate shape is added to a higher-level subordinate shape, the higher-level subordinate shape becomes the manager of the lower-level subordinate shape. A whole section of an organization chart is referred to as a **branch**, or an appendage, of the chart.

The Organization Chart toolbar (Figure 3-61) contains buttons to help you create and design your chart. The Insert Shape button allows you to add three different shapes to your chart: subordinate, coworker, and assistant. Three subordinate shapes are displayed by default in the sample organization chart. A **coworker shape** is located next to another shape and is connected to the same superior shape. An **assistant shape** is located below another shape and is connected to any other shape with an elbow connector.

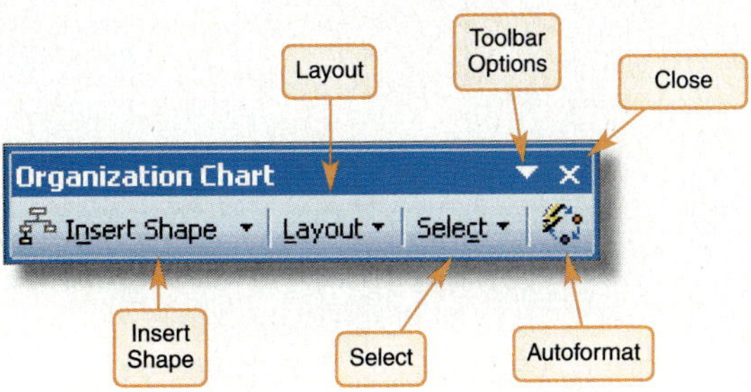

FIGURE 3-61

The Layout button changes the location of the lines connecting the subordinate branches. Layout options include Standard, Both Hanging, Left Hanging, and Right Hanging. It also has options to change the size of the entire organization chart by shrinking, expanding, or scaling.

More About

Organization Chart Shapes

To create a unique look, change the superior, assistant, subordinate, or coworker shapes, or the lines and connectors. AutoShapes include stars, banners, callouts, flowcharting symbols, and basic shapes, such as a heart, lightning bolt, sun, and moon.

The Select button highlights a specific level or branch in the chart. It also allows you to select all assistants or all connecting lines. Once these areas are selected, you easily can change their visual elements, such as text color, fill colors, line style, or line color.

The Autoformat button allows you to add a preset design scheme by selecting a style from the Organization Chart Style Gallery. These designs have a variety of colors, background shades, and borders.

Hidden Lake State Park has three campgrounds: Maple Meadows, Beech Basin, and Crooked Creek. Each campground varies in the type of camping allowed and nearby activities. As a result, your organization chart will consist of three shapes immediately below the manager and two shapes immediately below each subordinate manager. These organization chart layouts for each activity are identical, so you create the structure for the Maple Meadows campground and then repeat the steps for the Beech Basin and Crooked Creek campgrounds.

Adding Text to the Superior Shape

In this presentation, the organization chart is used to describe the three Hidden Lake campgrounds. The topmost shape, called the superior, identifies the purpose of this organization chart: Campgrounds. Recall that when you inserted the Organization Chart diagram, the superior shape is selected. The following step explains how to create the title for this shape.

To Add Text to the Superior Shape

1

- **Type** `Campgrounds` **in the superior shape.**

Campgrounds is displayed in the superior shape (Figure 3-62).

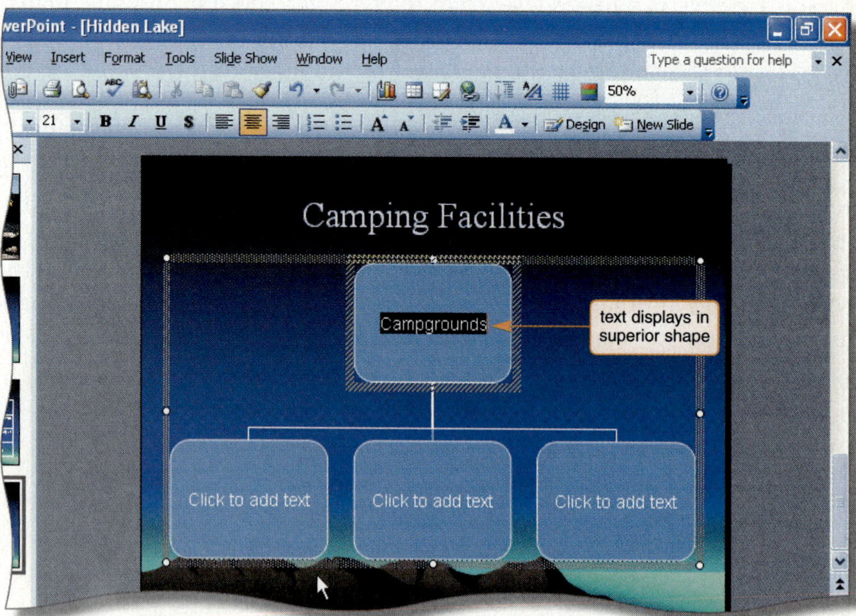

FIGURE 3-62

The text for the superior shape is entered. The next steps are to add text to the three subordinate shapes and then insert and add text to the subordinate and coworker shapes.

Adding Text to the Subordinate Shapes

The process of adding text to a subordinate shape is the same as adding text to the superior shape except that first you must select the subordinate shape. The following steps explain how to add text to subordinate shapes.

To Add Text to the Subordinate Shapes

1

- **Click the left subordinate shape.**
- **Type** `Maple Meadows` **in the shape.**

Maple Meadows is displayed as the text for the left subordinate shape (Figure 3-63).

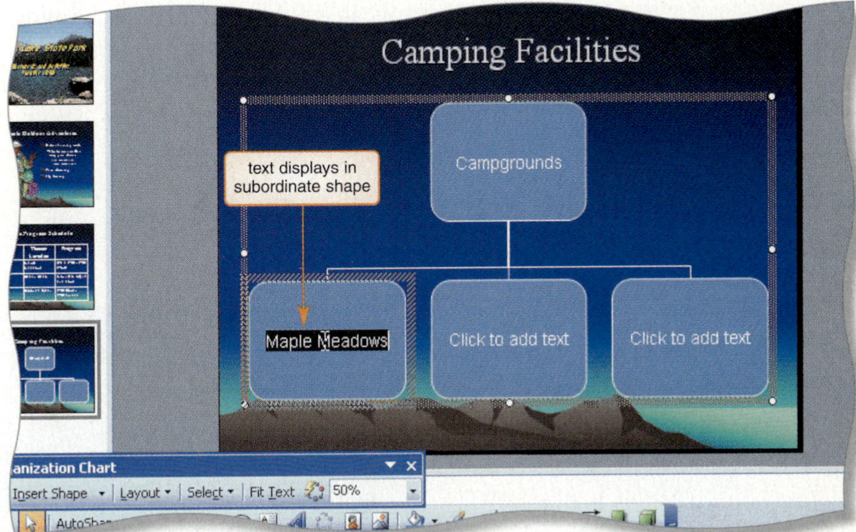

FIGURE 3-63

2

- **Click the middle subordinate shape.**
- **Type** `Beech Basin` **in the shape.**

Beech Basin is displayed as the text for the middle subordinate shape.

3

- **Click the right subordinate shape.**
- **Type** `Crooked Creek` **in the shape.**

Crooked Creek is displayed as the text for the right subordinate shape (Figure 3-64).

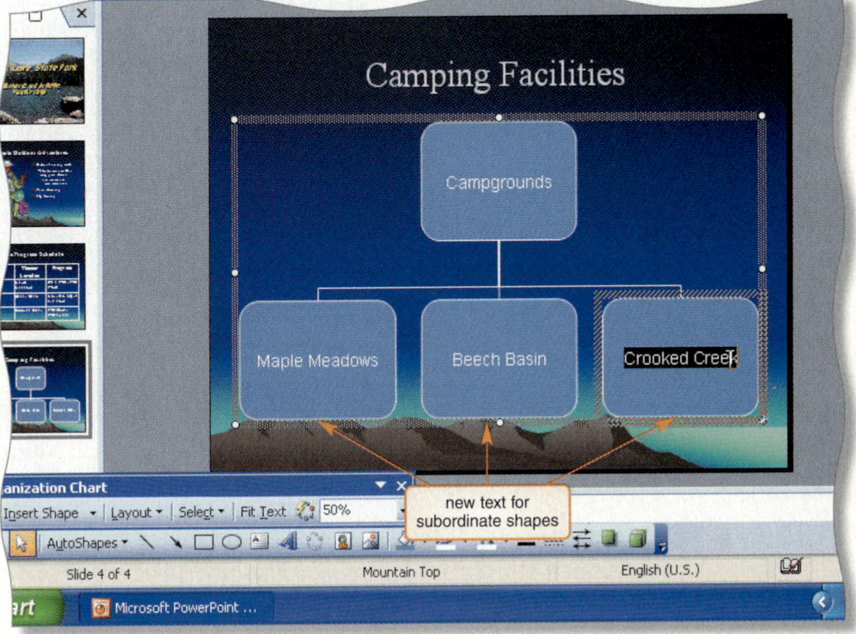

FIGURE 3-64

Inserting Subordinate and Coworker Shapes

> *More About*
>
> **Choosing Colors**
>
> More than eight percent of males have color perception difficulties, with the most common problem being distinguishing red and green. For more information about this color deficiency, visit the Microsoft PowerPoint 2003 More About Web page (scsite.com/ppt2003/more) and click Colors.

You can add three types of shapes to the organization chart: subordinate, coworker, and assistant. Because each of the three Hidden Lake campgrounds has two qualities, you need to add two subordinate shapes to each of the campgrounds.

To add a single subordinate shape to the chart, click the Insert Shape button on the Organization Chart toolbar. The subordinate shape is the default shape. To add a coworker or assistant shape, click the Insert Shape button arrow and then click the desired shape.

In this organization chart, the two features of the Maple Meadows campground — hiking trails accessible and group camping available — are subordinate to the Maple Meadows shape. These two features are coworkers because they both are connected to the same manager. The following steps explain how to use the Insert Shape button to add these two shapes below the Maple Meadows shape.

To Insert Subordinate and Coworker Shapes

1

- **Click the Maple Meadows shape.**
- **Click the Insert Shape button on the Organization Chart toolbar.**

The Maple Meadows shape is selected and the new subordinate shape is displayed (Figure 3-65).

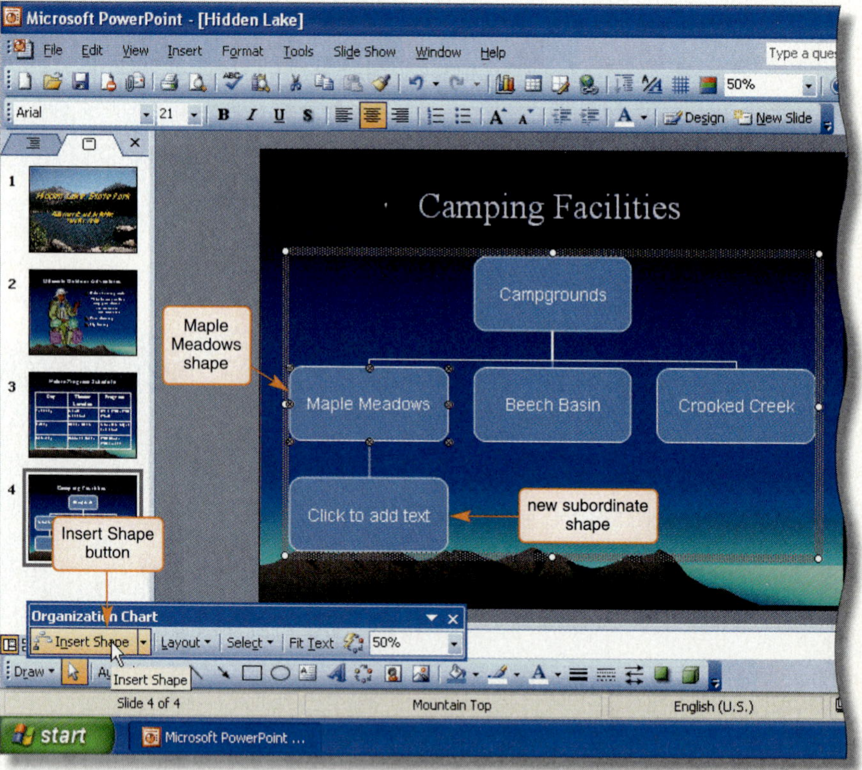

FIGURE 3-65

2

- **Click the new subordinate shape.**
- **Click the Insert Shape button arrow on the Organization Chart toolbar.**

The new subordinate shape is selected below the Maple Meadows shape. Maple Meadows now is the manager to the new subordinate shapes. Three possible shapes display on the Insert Shape menu (Figure 3-66).

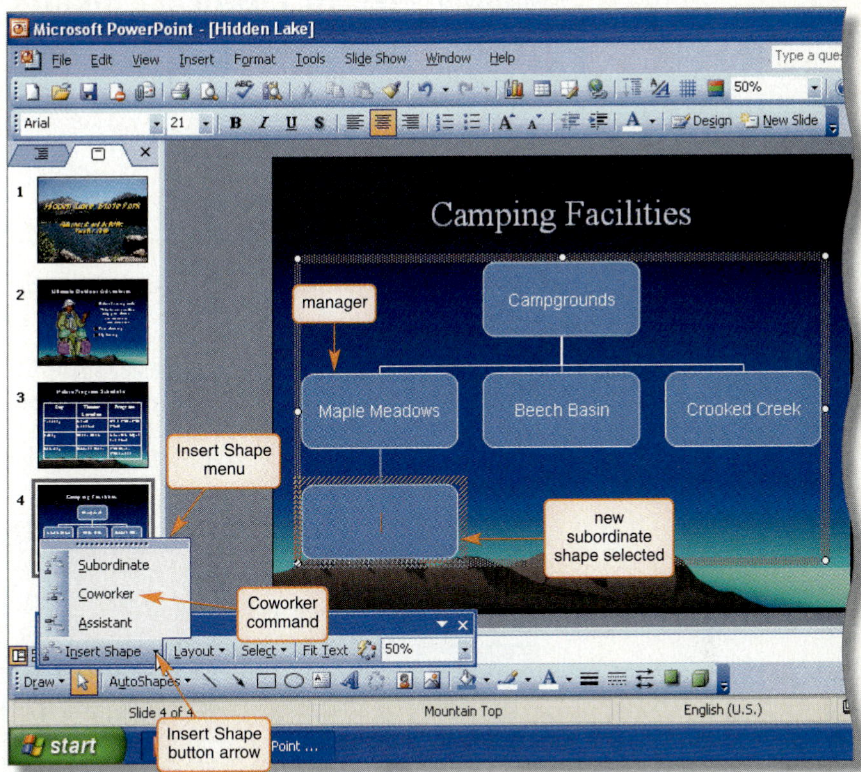

FIGURE 3-66

3

- **Click Coworker on the Insert Shape menu.**

A new coworker shape is added to the right of the subordinate shape (Figure 3-67).

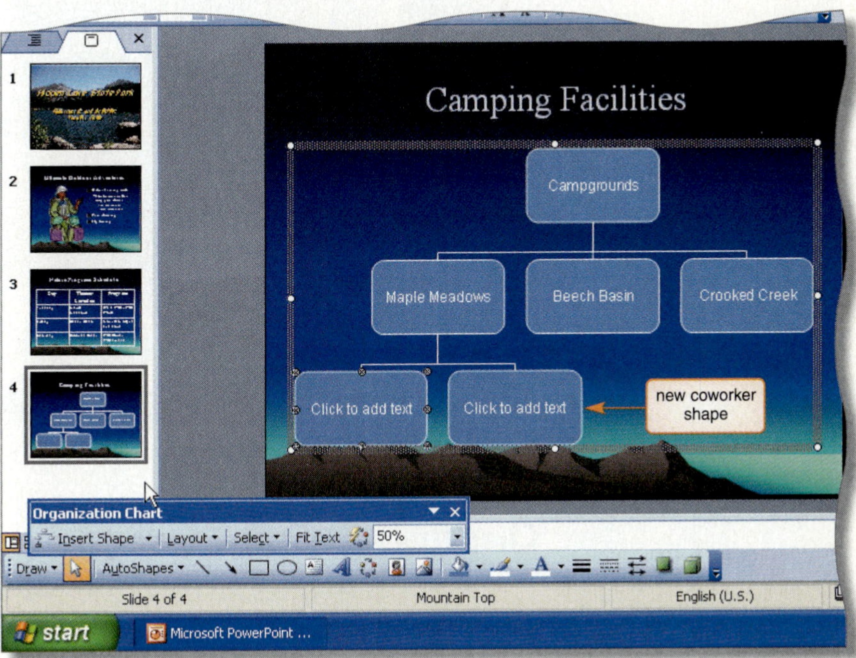

FIGURE 3-67

Other Ways

1. Press ALT+N, press DOWN ARROW, press C
2. In Voice Command mode, say "Insert Shape, Coworker"

The basic structure of the left side of the organization chart is complete. You now will add text to the coworker shapes in the chart.

Adding Text to Coworker Shapes

The next step in creating the organization chart is to add text to the two new shapes that are subordinate to the Maple Meadows shape. The following steps summarize adding text to each coworker shape.

To Add Text to Coworker Shapes

1. **If necessary, click the left coworker shape. Type** `Hiking trails` **and then press the ENTER key. Type** `accessible` **in the shape.**
2. **Click the right coworker shape. Type** `Group camping` **and then press the ENTER key. Type** `available` **in the shape.**

Both coworker shapes contain text related to the Maple Meadows campground (Figure 3-68).

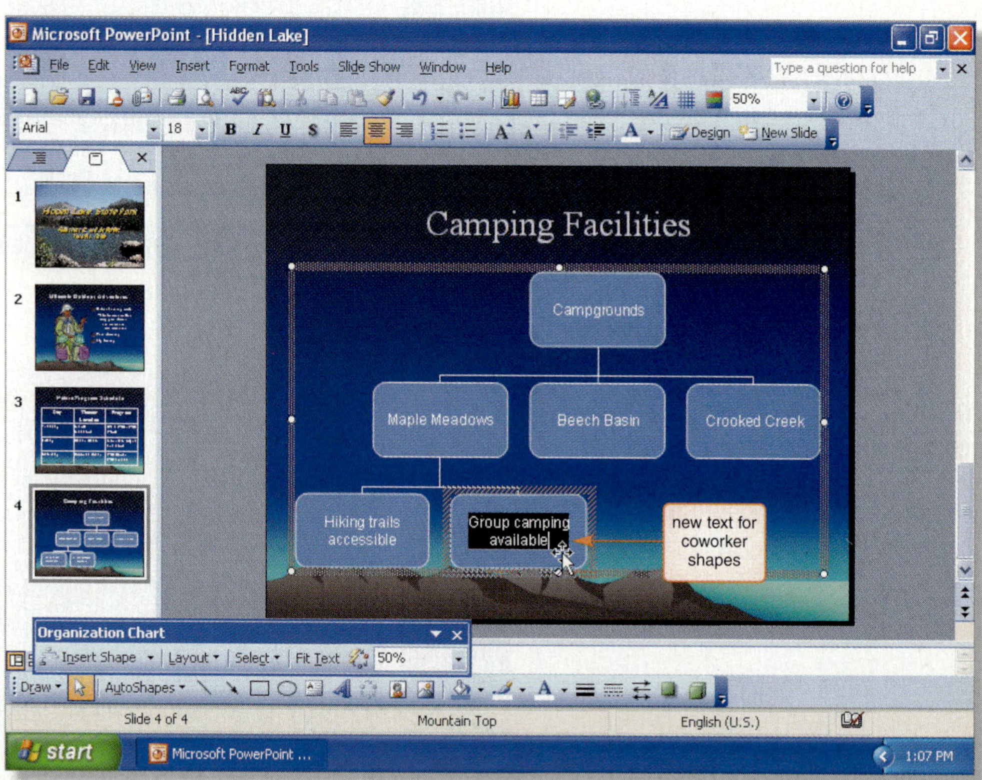

FIGURE 3-68

> **More About**
>
> **Layouts**
>
> An effective presentation has objects, text, and graphics placed in appropriate locations. You can find many resources, tips, and articles on making clear and interesting presentations on the Internet. For more information about presentation design resources, visit the Microsoft PowerPoint 2003 More About Web page (scsite.com/ppt2003/more) and click Layouts.

Changing the Shape Layout

Now that the shapes for the Maple Meadows branch are labeled, you want to change the way the organization chart looks. With the addition of each new shape, the chart expanded horizontally, which is the default layout. Before you add the Beech Basin campground qualities, you will change the layout of the coworker shapes from Standard to Right Hanging. To change the layout, you must select the most superior shape of the branch to which you want to apply the new layout. The following steps change the shape layout.

To Change the Shape Layout

1

- **Click the Maple Meadows shape.**
- **Click the Layout button on the Organization Chart toolbar.**

The default Standard style is selected, which is indicated by the selected icon (Figure 3-69). The Maple Meadows shape is the superior shape of the coworker shapes.

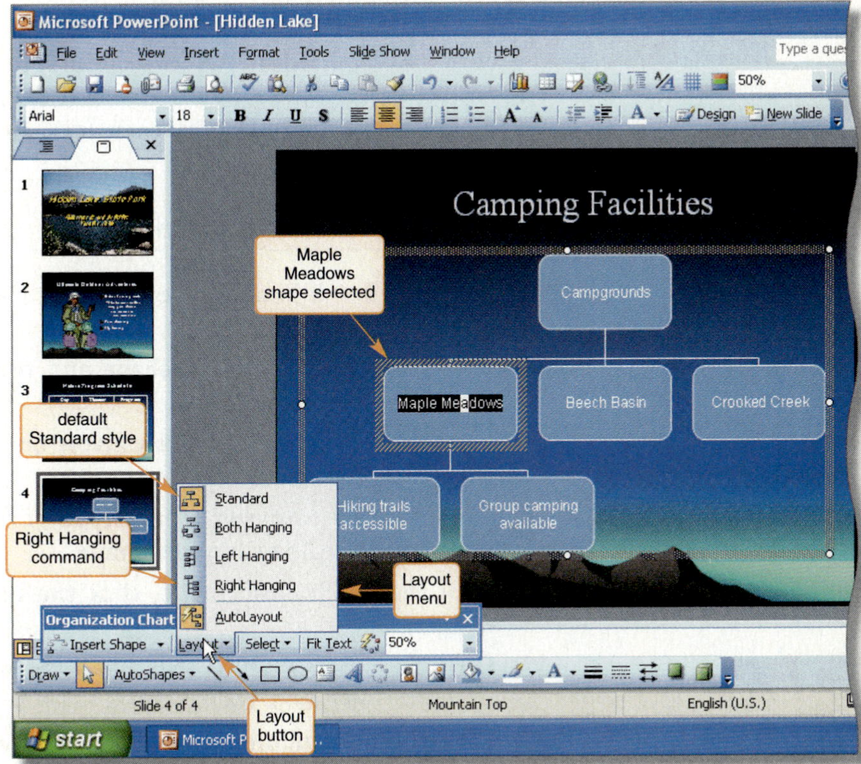

FIGURE 3-69

2

- **Click Right Hanging on the Layout menu.**

The organization chart displays the two coworker shapes vertically below the Maple Meadows shape (Figure 3-70).

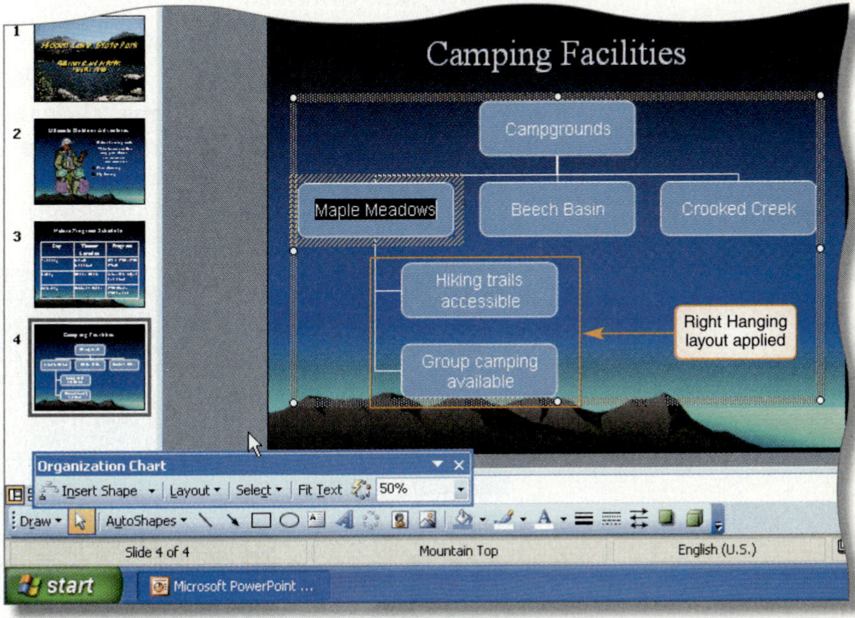

FIGURE 3-70

Other Ways

1. Press ALT+L, press R
2. In Voice Command mode, say "Layout, Right Hanging"

If you select an incorrect style or want to return to the previous style, click the Undo Change Layout command on the Edit menu or press CTRL+Z.

Inserting Additional Subordinate and Coworker Shapes

With the Maple Meadows campground features added to the organization chart, you need to create the Beech Basin and Crooked Creek components of the chart. The following steps add four shapes, enter text, and change the layout.

To Insert Additional Subordinate and Coworker Shapes

1. **Click the Beech Basin shape and then click the Insert Shape button on the Organization Chart toolbar.**
2. **Click the new subordinate shape and then type** `Tent camping only` **in the shape.**
3. **Click the Insert Shape button arrow on the Organization Chart toolbar and then click Coworker.**
4. **Click the new coworker shape, type** `Three-night stay` **and then press the ENTER key. Type** `limit` **in the shape.**
5. **Click the Beech Basin shape, click the Layout button, and then click Right Hanging.**
6. **Click the Crooked Creek shape and then click the Insert Shape button on the Organization Chart toolbar.**
7. **Click the new subordinate shape and then type** `Open all year` **in the shape.**
8. **Click the Insert Shape button arrow on the Organization Chart toolbar and then click Coworker.**
9. **Click the new coworker shape, type** `Fishing readily` **and then press the ENTER key. Type** `accessible` **in the shape.**
10. **Click the Crooked Creek shape, click the Layout button on the Organization Chart toolbar, and then click Right Hanging.**

Four shapes contain text related to the campground facilities at Hidden Lake (Figure 3-71).

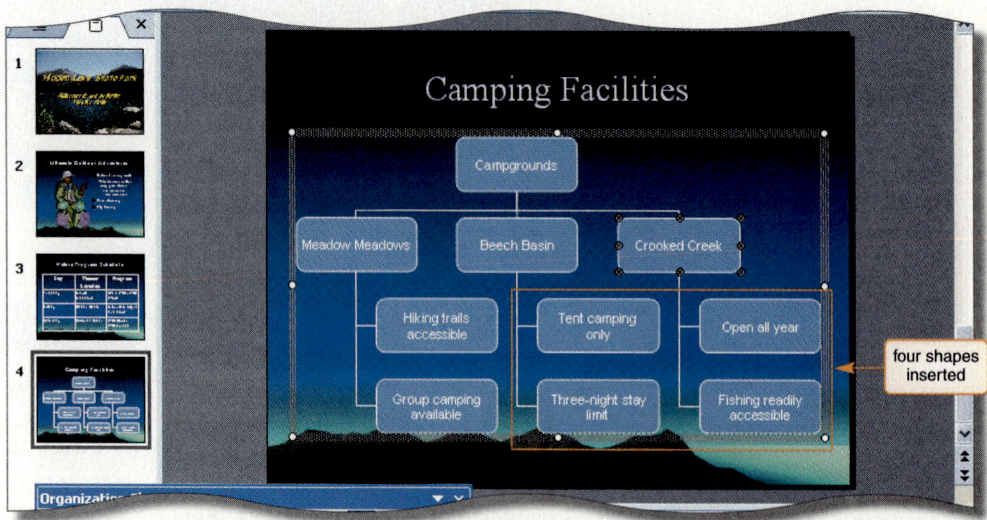

FIGURE 3-71

All the desired text now is displayed on the organization chart. The next section explains how to change the organization chart style.

More About

Background Colors

The most popular background color is blue. Used in more than 90 percent of business presentations, this color connotes serenity, reflection, and proficiency.

Changing the Preset Design Scheme

To format the organization chart so it looks like the chart shown in Figure 3-58 on page PPT 195, select a diagram style in the Organization Chart Style Gallery. The **Organization Chart Style Gallery** contains a variety of styles that use assorted colors, border styles, and shadow effects. The following steps describe how to change the default design scheme.

To Change the Preset Design Scheme

1

- **Point to the Autoformat button on the Organization Chart toolbar (Figure 3-72).**

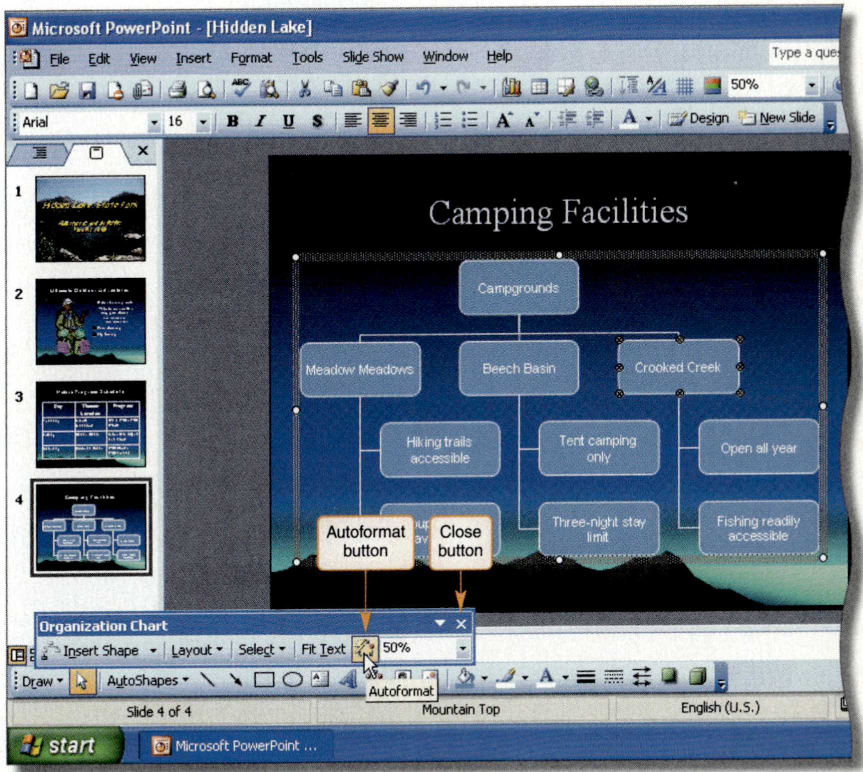

FIGURE 3-72

2

• **Click the Autoformat button and then click the 3-D Color diagram style in the Diagram Style list.**

Diagram Style names display in the list. When you click a name, PowerPoint previews that style (Figure 3-73).

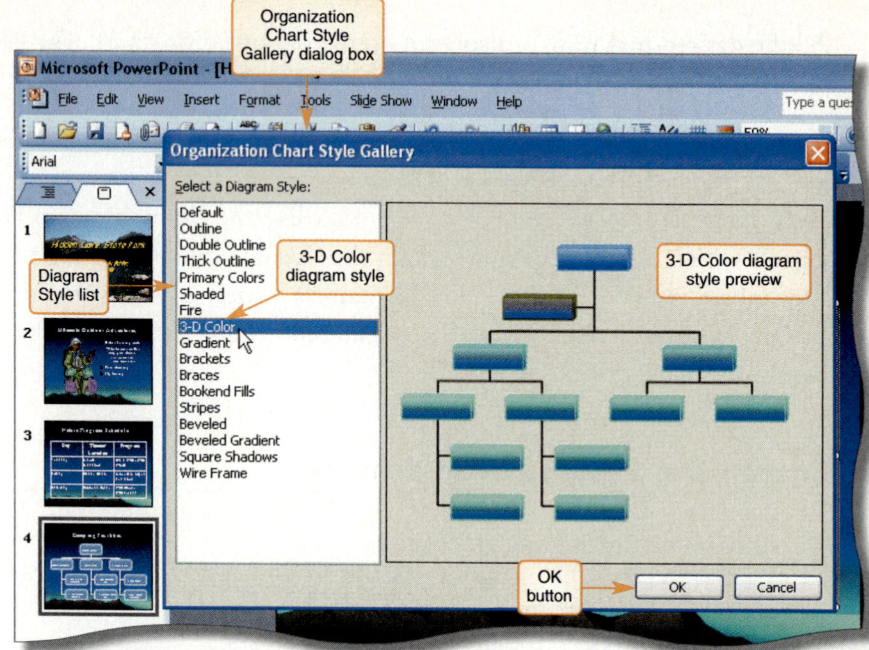

FIGURE 3-73

3

• **Click the OK button in the Organization Chart Style Gallery dialog box.**

• **Click the Close button on the Organization Chart toolbar.**

PowerPoint applies the 3-D Color diagram style to all the shapes and lines in the chart (Figure 3-74).

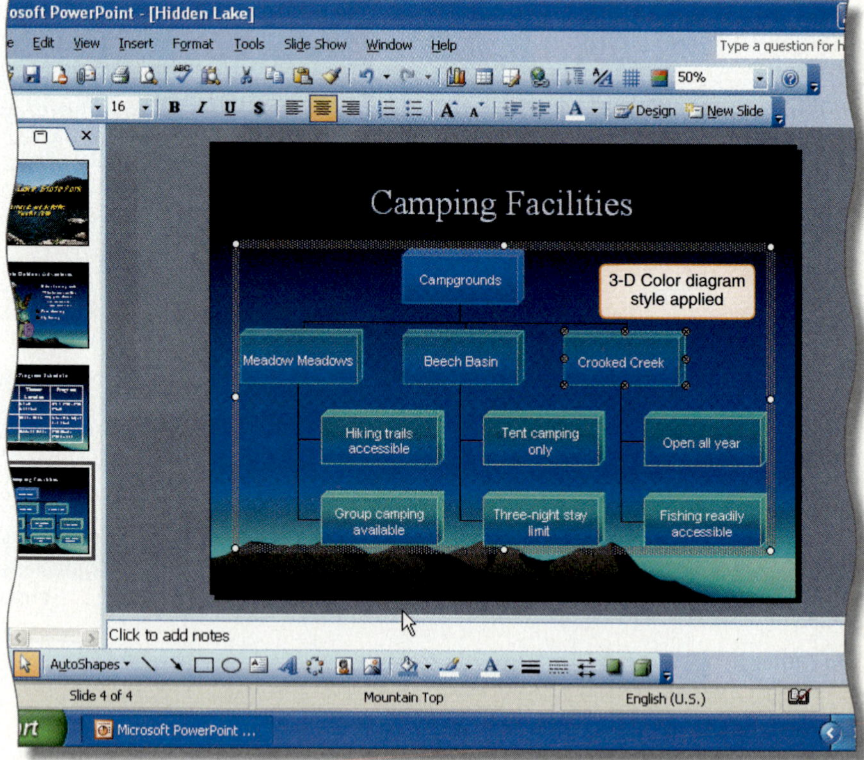

FIGURE 3-74

Other Ways

1. Press SHIFT+ALT+C, press RIGHT ARROW, press ENTER, press DOWN ARROW or UP ARROW to scroll through styles, press ENTER
2. In Voice Command mode, say "Autoformat, 3-D Color, Apply"

Scaling an Organization Chart

The organization chart on Slide 4 would be easier to read if it were enlarged. **Scaling** allows you to enlarge or reduce an object by very precise amounts while retaining the object's original proportions.

The following steps scale an organization chart object.

To Scale an Organization Chart

1. **Right-click a blank area of the chart placeholder and then right-click Format Organization Chart on the shortcut menu.**
2. **Click the Size tab. In the Scale area, double-click 100 in the Height text box. Type** `110` **as the entry.**
3. **Click the OK button.**
4. **Use the UP and LEFT ARROW keys to move the organization chart to the desired location on the slide.**

The organization chart is scaled to 110 percent of its original size (Figure 3-75). If necessary, adjust the chart size by repeating Steps 1–4 with a different percentage or by dragging a corner sizing handle.

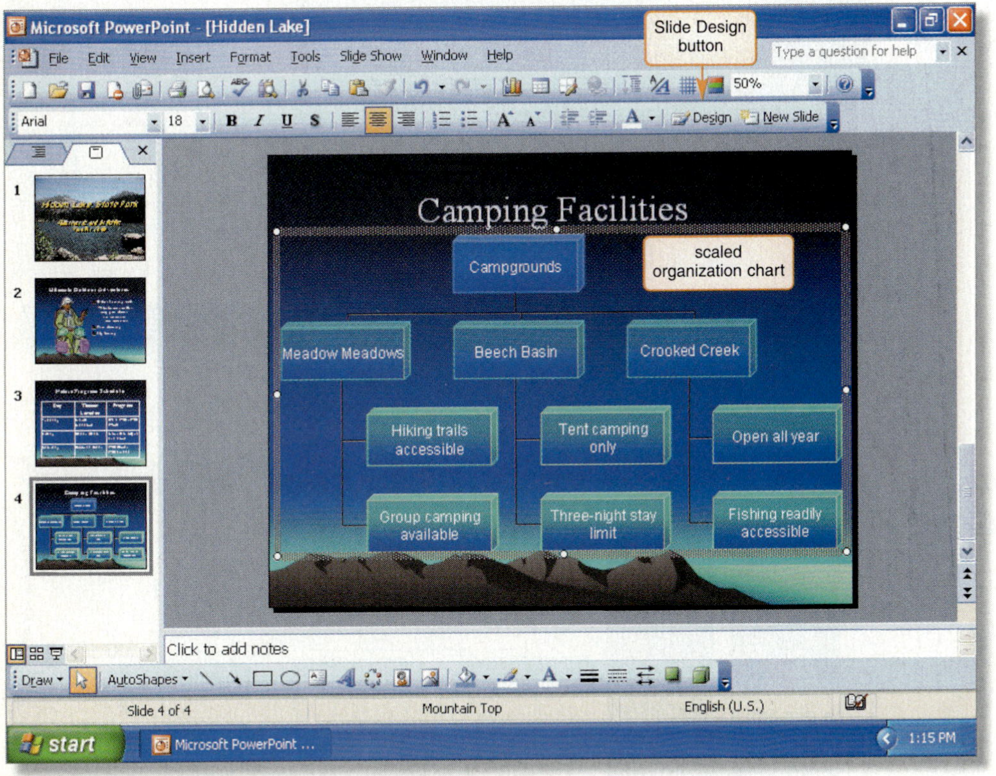

FIGURE 3-75

Applying a New Design Template

You can see that the information in the organization chart will display more prominently if the slide has a different background. One method of changing the look of an individual slide is to change the design template. The steps on the next page change the design template on Slide 4 from Mountain Top to Quadrant.

More About

The PowerPoint Help System

Need Help? It is no further away than the Type a question for help box on the menu bar in the upper-right corner of the window. Click the box that contains the text, Type a question for help (Figure 3-75), type `help`, and then press the ENTER key. PowerPoint responds with a list of topics you can click to learn about obtaining help on any PowerPoint-related topic. To find out what is new in PowerPoint 2003, type `what is new in PowerPoint` in the Type a question for help box.

To Apply a New Design Template to a Single Slide

1

- **With Slide 4 displaying, click the Slide Design button on the Formatting toolbar.**
- **When the Slide Design task pane is displayed, click the down scroll arrow in the Apply a design template list until the Edge template is displayed in the Available For Use area.**
- **Click the button arrow on the right side of the Edge template.**

The Edge template menu is displayed with options for applying the template to all slides, the selected slide, or to view a larger preview (Figure 3-76).

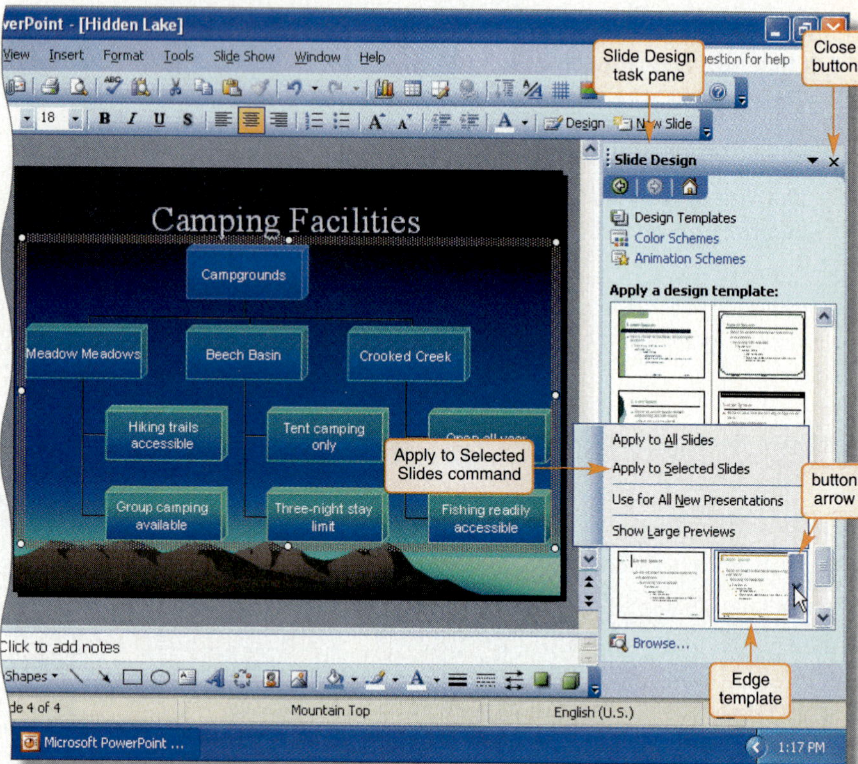

FIGURE 3-76

2

- **Click Apply to Selected Slides.**
- **Click the Close button in the Slide Design task pane.**

PowerPoint applies the Edge template to only Slide 4 (Figure 3-77).

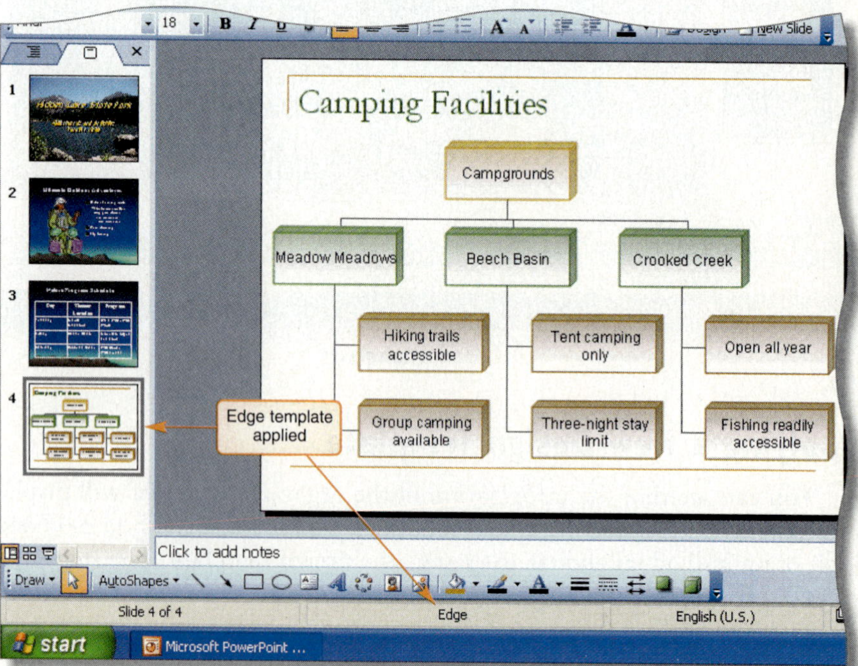

FIGURE 3-77

Slide 4 now is complete. The next section describes how to change the order of individual slides.

Rearranging Slides

The Slide 4 organization chart should display before the Slide 3 table in a slide show. Changing slide order is an easy process. The following steps rearrange Slides 3 and 4.

To Rearrange Slides

1

- **Click the Slide 3 slide thumbnail in the tabs pane.**

The Slide 3 slide thumbnail is selected (Figure 3-78).

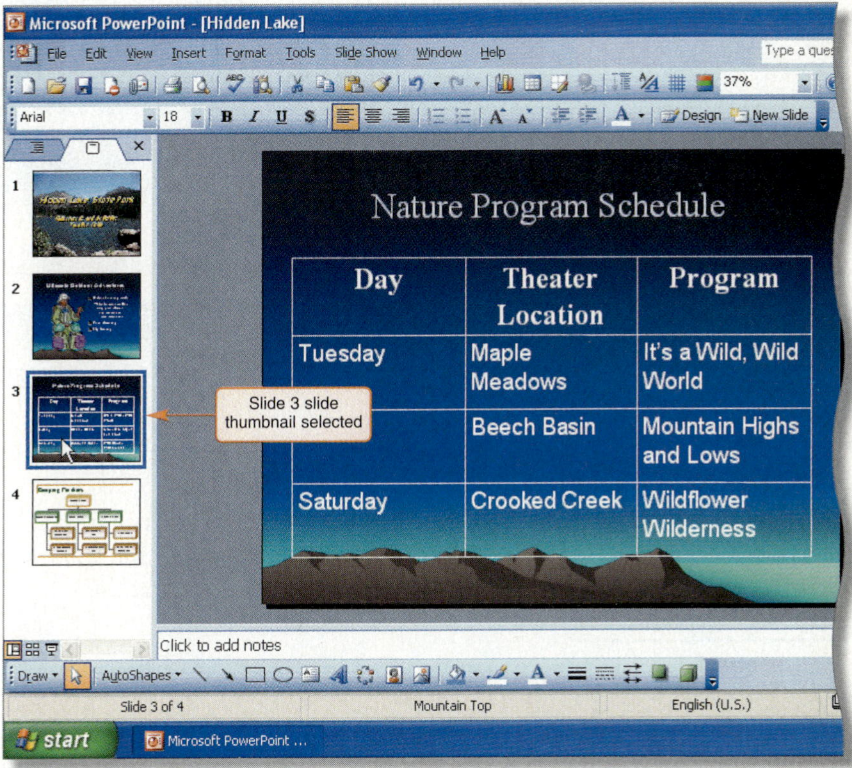

FIGURE 3-78

2

• **Drag the Slide 3 slide thumbnail below the Slide 4 slide thumbnail.**

The slide with the organization chart is displayed above the slide with the table (Figure 3-79). When you are dragging the slide thumbnail, a line indicates the new location of the selected slide.

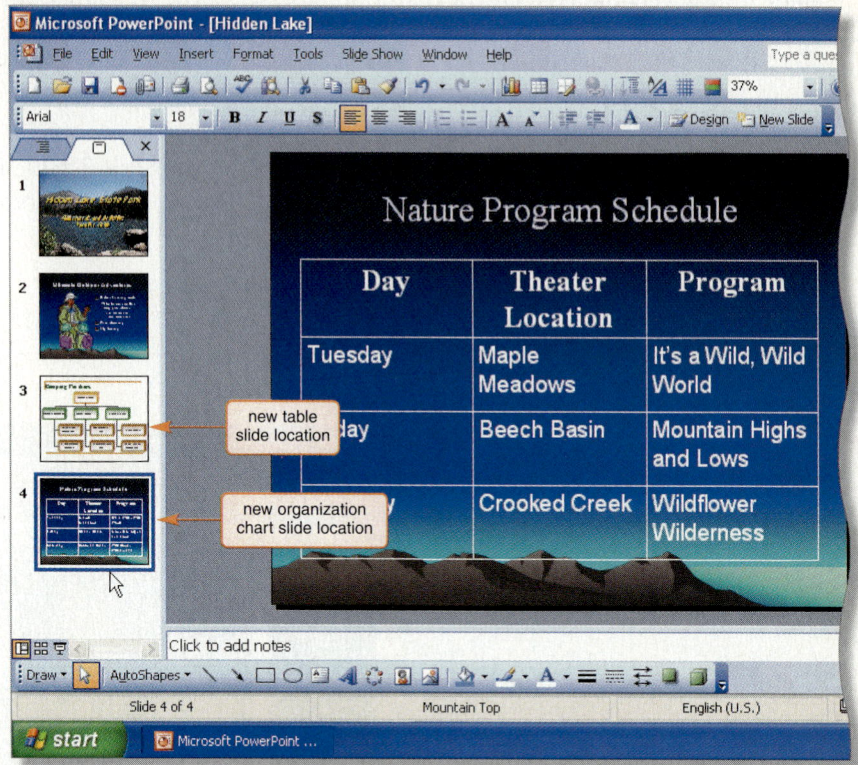

FIGURE 3-79

Other Ways

1. On Outline tab select slide icon, drag icon to new location
2. In slide sorter view select slide thumbnail, drag thumbnail to new location

The order of Slides 3 and 4 is changed. If you want to change the order of multiple consecutive slides, press the SHIFT key before clicking each slide icon or slide thumbnail. Save the presentation.

Adding an Animation Scheme to Selected Slides

The final step in preparing the Hidden Lake presentation is to add an animation scheme to Slides 1, 2, and 4. The following steps add the Rise Up animation scheme to these three slides.

Other Ways

1. In slide sorter view, select slides to add transitions, right-click selected slide, click Animation Schemes on shortcut menu, click desired animation, click Close button
2. Select slides to add transitions, on Slide Show menu click Animation Schemes, click desired animation, click Close button

To Add an Animation Scheme to Selected Slides

1 **If necessary, click the Slide 4 thumbnail to select it. Press and hold down the CTRL key and then click the Slide 2 and Slide 1 slide thumbnails. Release the CTRL key.**

2 **Click Slide Show on the menu bar and then click Animation Schemes.**

3 **Scroll down the Apply to selected slides list and then click Rise Up in the Moderate category.**

4 **Click the Close button in the Slide Design task pane.**

The Rise Up animation scheme is applied to Slides 1, 2, and 4 in the Hidden Lake presentation (Figure 3-80).

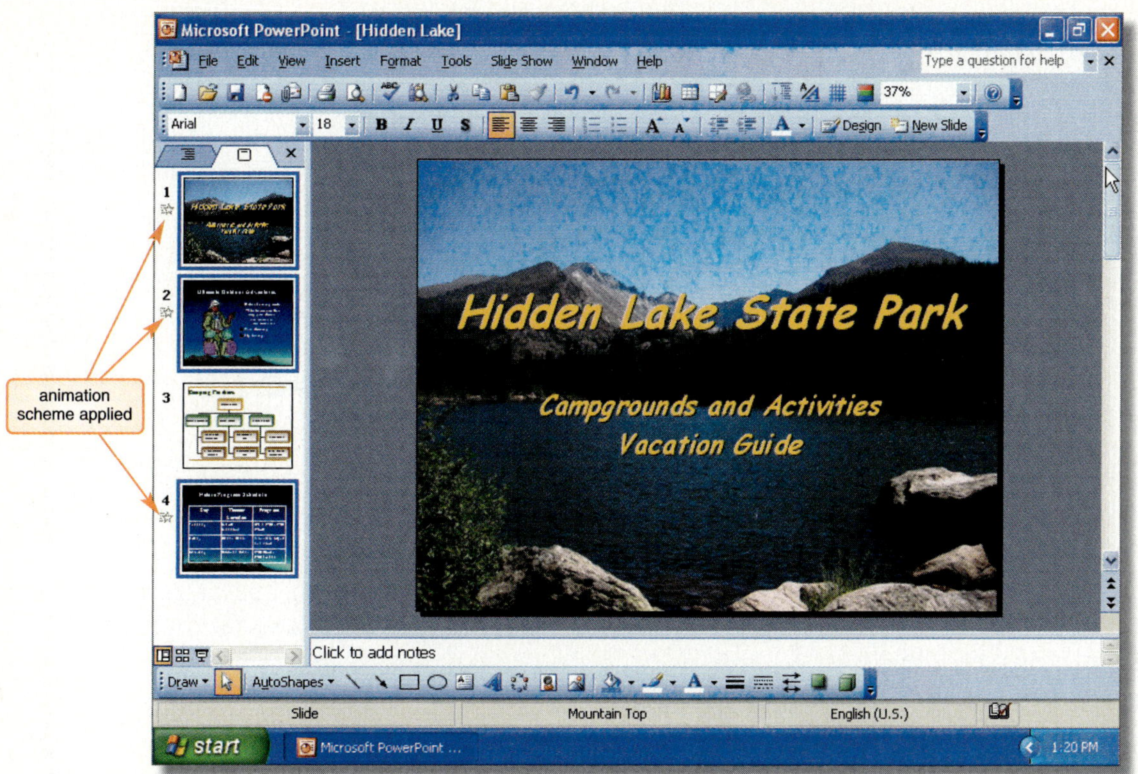

FIGURE 3-80

Printing Slides as Handouts

The following steps print the presentation slides as handouts, four slides per page.

To Print Slides as Handouts

1. **Ready the printer.**
2. **Click File on the menu bar and then click Print.**
3. **Click the Print what box arrow and then click Handouts in the list.**
4. **Click the Slides per page box arrow in the Handouts area and then click 4 in the list. Verify the Horizontal option button is selected. If it is not selected, then click to select it.**
5. **If Grayscale is not displayed in the Color/grayscale box, click the Color/grayscale arrow and then click Grayscale.**
6. **Click the OK button.**

The handout prints as shown in Figure 3-81 on the next page.

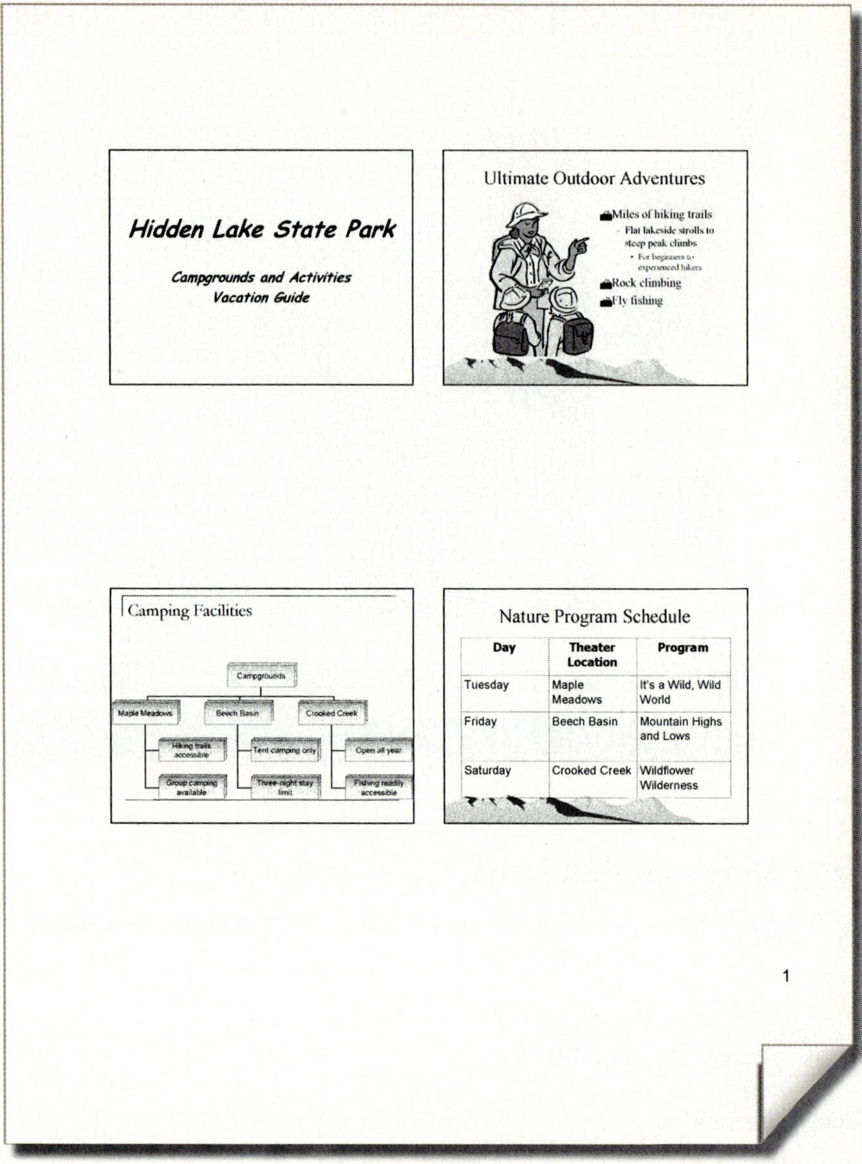

FIGURE 3-81

More About

Presenting a Slide Show

If you are displaying your slide show on a projection system or external monitor, you need to match the resolutions of your computer and the projector. To do this, open the Display Properties dialog box for your computer and then click the Settings tab. In the Screen resolution box, move the slider to adjust the resolution. If you are uncertain of the resolution, try 800 × 600 pixels. When you are using two monitors, you can display your slide show on one monitor and view your notes, outline, and slides on the second monitor.

Creating and Presenting a Custom Show

A **custom show** is a presentation within a presentation. You can group slides in an existing presentation so that you can show that section of a presentation to a particular audience. To create a custom show, you would follow these steps.

To Create a Custom Show

1. **Click Slide Show on the menu bar and then click Custom Shows.**
2. **When the Custom Shows dialog box is displayed, click the New button.**
3. **In the Slides in presentation area, select a slide you want to include in the custom show. To select multiple slides, hold down the CTRL key as you click the slide titles.**
4. **Click the Add button.**

5 **Type a name in the Slide show name text box.**

6 **Click the OK button.**

If you decide to add or remove slides from a custom show, you can click the Edit button in the Custom Shows dialog box, add or remove the desired slide, and then click the OK button. Once the custom show has been finalized, you can display these slides rather than the entire presentation. To present the custom show, you would follow these steps.

To Present a Custom Show

1 **Click Slide Show on the menu bar and then click Set Up Show.**

2 **When the Set Up Show dialog box is displayed, click the Custom show option button in the Show Slides area, click the Custom show arrow, and then select the show you want to display.**

3 **Click the OK button.**

4 **Start the slide show.**

More About

Custom Shows

If you decide you no longer need a custom show, you can remove it. To remove a custom show, click Slide Show on the menu bar and then click Custom Shows. When the Custom Shows dialog box is displayed, click the name of the custom show you want to remove and then click the Remove button. Click the Close button.

Running the Slide Show, Saving, and Quitting PowerPoint

With the slide show complete, click the Slide Show button and run the presentation to ensure that you are satisfied with the slide content and animation scheme.

If you made any changes to your presentation since your last save, you should save it again before quitting PowerPoint. The following steps save changes to the presentation and quit PowerPoint.

To Save Changes and Quit PowerPoint

1 **Click the Close button on the Microsoft PowerPoint window title bar.**

2 **If prompted, click the Yes button in the Microsoft PowerPoint dialog box.**

PowerPoint saves any changes made to the presentation since the last save and then quits PowerPoint.

Project Summary

Project 3 introduced you to several methods of enhancing a presentation with visuals. You began the project by creating the presentation from an outline that was created in Word. Then, when you created Slide 2, you learned how to ungroup and customize clip art. You also learned how to change the bullet character on the slide master. You learned to create and format a table on Slide 3. Slide 4 introduced you to creating an organization chart and applying a design template to a single slide and changing the order of slides in the presentation. Finally, you printed your presentation slides as handouts.

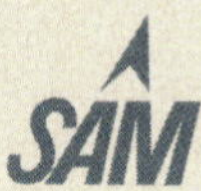

If you have a SAM user profile, you may have access to hands-on instruction, practice, and assessment of the skills covered in this project. Log in to your SAM account and go to your assignments page to see what your instructor has assigned.

What You Should Know

Having completed this project, you should be able to perform the tasks below. For a list of the buttons, menus, toolbars, and commands introduced in this project, see the Quick Reference Summary at the back of this book and refer to the Page Number column.

Learn It Online

Instructions: To complete the Learn It Online exercises, start your browser, click the Address bar, and then enter the Web address `scsite.com/ppt2003/learn`. When the PowerPoint 2003 Learn It Online page is displayed, follow the instructions in the exercises below. Each exercise has instructions for printing your results, either for your own records or for submission to your instructor.

1 Project Reinforcement TF, MC, and SA

Below PowerPoint Project 3, click the Project Reinforcement link. Print the quiz by clicking Print on the File menu for each page. Answer each question.

2 Flash Cards

Below PowerPoint Project 3, click the Flash Cards link and read the instructions. Type 20 (or a number specified by your instructor) in the Number of playing cards text box, type your name in the Enter your Name text box, and then click the Flip Card button. When the flash card is displayed, read the question and then click the ANSWER box arrow to select an answer. Flip through Flash Cards. If your score is 15 (75%) correct or greater, click Print on the File menu to print your results. If your score is less than 15 (75%) correct, then redo this exercise by clicking the Replay button.

3 Practice Test

Below PowerPoint Project 3, click the Practice Test link. Answer each question, enter your first and last name at the bottom of the page, and then click the Grade Test button. When the graded practice test is displayed on your screen, click Print on the File menu to print a hard copy. Continue to take practice tests until you score 80% or better.

4 Who Wants To Be a Computer Genius?

Below PowerPoint Project 3, click the Computer Genius link. Read the instructions, enter your first and last name at the bottom of the page, and then click the PLAY button. When your score is displayed, click the PRINT RESULTS link to print a hard copy.

5 Wheel of Terms

Below PowerPoint Project 3, click the Wheel of Terms link. Read the instructions, and then enter your first and last name and your school name. Click the PLAY button. When your score is displayed, right-click the score and then click Print on the shortcut menu to print a hard copy.

6 Crossword Puzzle Challenge

Below PowerPoint Project 3, click the Crossword Puzzle Challenge link. Read the instructions, and then enter your first and last name. Click the SUBMIT button. Work the crossword puzzle. When you are finished, click the Submit button. When the crossword puzzle is redisplayed, click the Print Puzzle button to print a hard copy.

7 Tips and Tricks

Below PowerPoint Project 3, click the Tips and Tricks link. Click a topic that pertains to Project 3. Right-click the information and then click Print on the shortcut menu. Construct a brief example of what the information relates to in PowerPoint to confirm you understand how to use the tip or trick.

8 Newsgroups

Below PowerPoint Project 3, click the Newsgroups link. Click a topic that pertains to Project 3. Print three comments.

9 Expanding Your Horizons

Below PowerPoint Project 3, click the Articles for Microsoft PowerPoint link. Click a topic that pertains to Project 3. Print the information. Construct a brief example of what the information relates to in PowerPoint to confirm you understand the contents of the article.

10 Search Sleuth

Below PowerPoint Project 3, click the Search Sleuth link. To search for a term that pertains to this project, select a term below the Project 3 title and then use the Google search engine at google.com (or any major search engine) to display and print two Web pages that present information on the term.

11 Word Online Training

Below PowerPoint Project 3, click the PowerPoint Online Training link. When your browser displays the Microsoft Office Online Web page, click the PowerPoint link. Click one of the PowerPoint courses that covers one or more of the objectives listed at the beginning of the project on page PPT 162. Print the first page of the course before stepping through it.

12 Office Marketplace

Below PowerPoint Project 3, click the Office Marketplace link. When your browser displays the Microsoft Office Online Web page, click the Office Marketplace link. Click a topic that relates to PowerPoint. Print the first page.

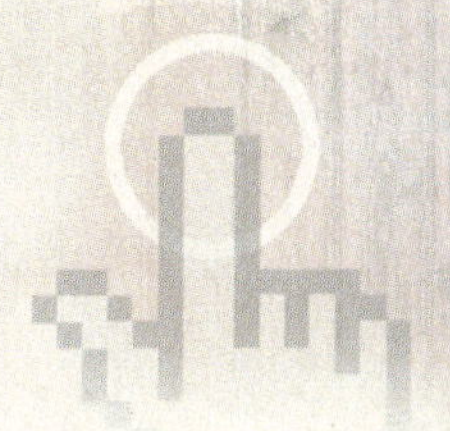

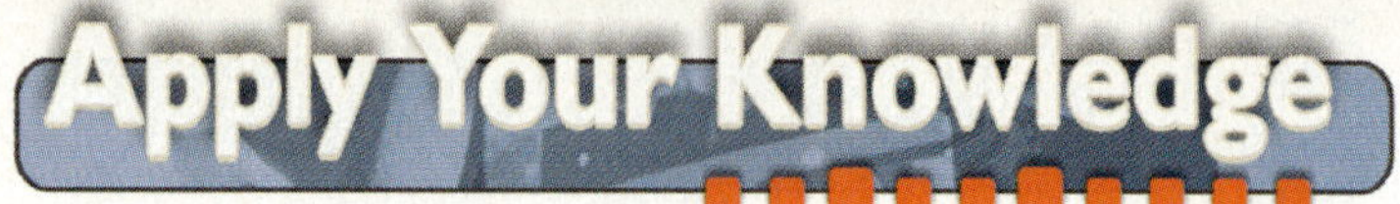

1 Computer Security

Instructions: Start PowerPoint. Open the outline, Apply 3-1 Security Risks, from the Data Disk. See the inside back cover of this book for instructions for downloading the Data Disk or see your instructor for information on accessing the clips and files required for this book. The outline gives three specific methods for safeguarding a computer. Make the following changes to the slides so they appear as shown in Figure 3-82.

Apply the Glass Layers design template. Delete the blank Slide 1. Change the slide layout for Slide 1 to Title Slide (Figure 3-82a).

On Slide 1, insert the computer inoculation clip. Size the clip to 43%. Ungroup the clip and change the man's shirt to red. Regroup the clip. On Slide 2, insert the computer clip shown in Figure 3-82b. Size the clip to 295%. Ungroup the clip and delete the flames from the right and top. Regroup the clip.

Change the first-level paragraph bullets on the slide master to the computer symbol located in the Wingdings font. Change the bullet color to red.

Apply the Zoom animation scheme in the Moderate category list to both slides. Save the presentation with the file name, Apply 3-1 Computer Security. Print the slides as a handout with both slides on one page. Hand in the hard copy to your instructor.

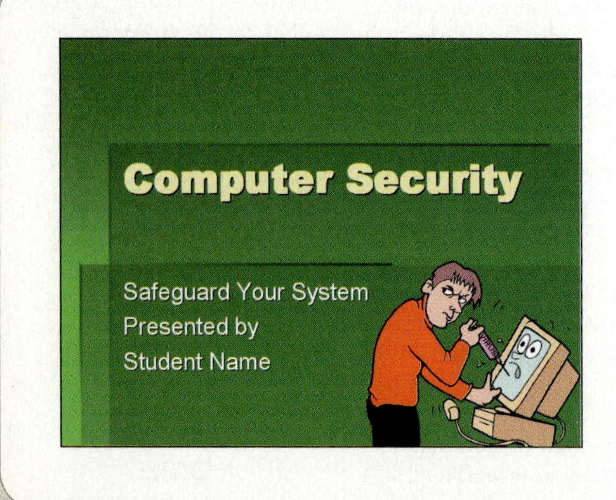

(a) Slide 1

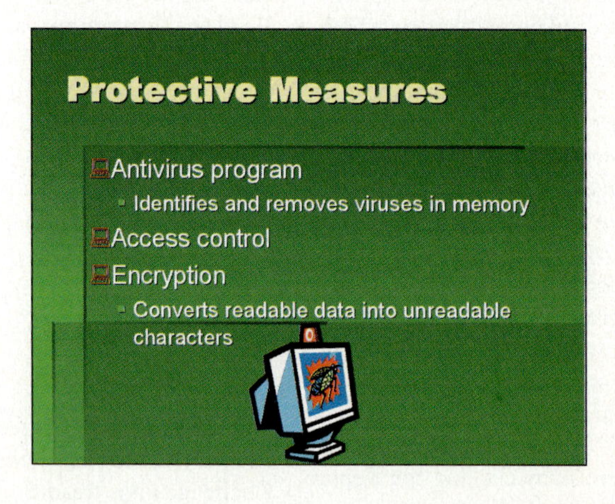

(b) Slide 2

FIGURE 3-82

In the Lab

1 Dino-mite Dash

Problem: The volunteers at the natural history society in your community are sponsoring a 5K run on St. Patrick's Day. You decide to participate by helping with event promotion and encouraging local businesses to donate prizes. The volunteers ask you to create a presentation describing the run to community residents. You decide to begin the assignment by creating a title slide with a clip showing a dinosaur jogging. You import a clip, modify it, and then import and modify another clip with a shamrock and leprechaun hat to create the slide shown in Figure 3-83. See your instructor if the clips are not available on your system.

Instructions: Perform the following tasks:

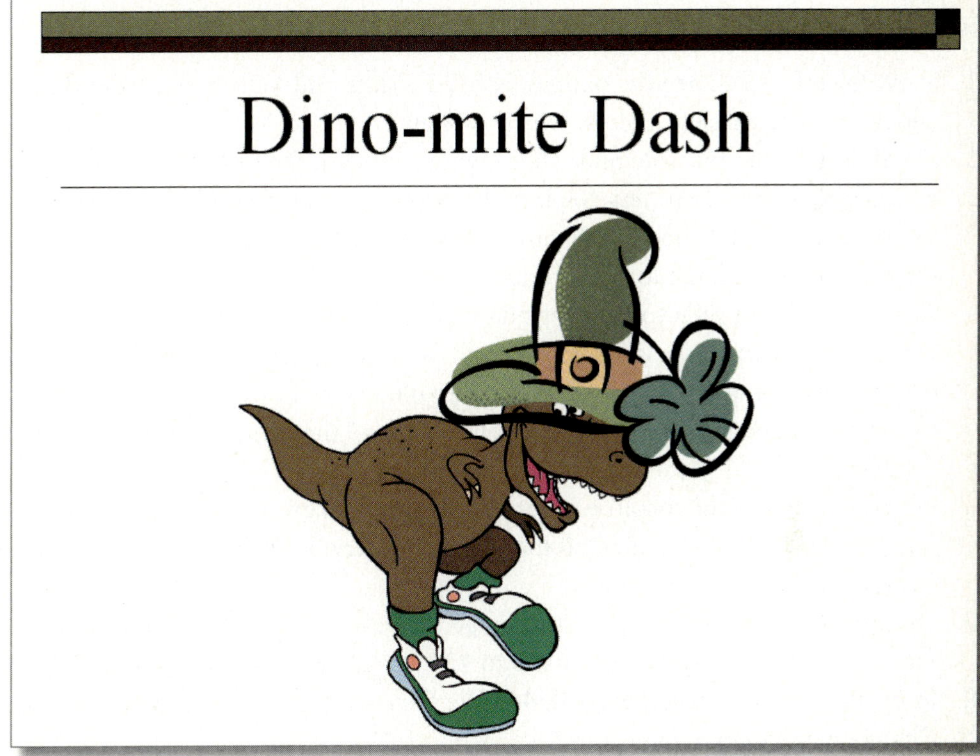

FIGURE 3-83

1. Start PowerPoint and apply the Quadrant design template to the Title Only slide layout.
2. Type `Dino-mite Dash` for the slide title. Center the title, change the font size to 60, and change the font color to black.
3. Insert the jogging dinosaur clip shown in Figure 3-83. Size the clip to 85%.
4. Ungroup the picture. Then change the blue parts of the top of the shoes and the socks to sea green.
5. Insert the leprechaun hat clip. Size the clip to 85%.
6. Ungroup this clip and delete all pieces except the hat and shamrock.
7. Regroup the hat object, and then move the hat to the top of the dinosaur's head. Regroup both clips together as one object.
8. Apply the Faded zoom motion animation scheme.
9. Save the presentation with the file name, Lab 3-1 Race.
10. Print the slide.
11. Quit PowerPoint.

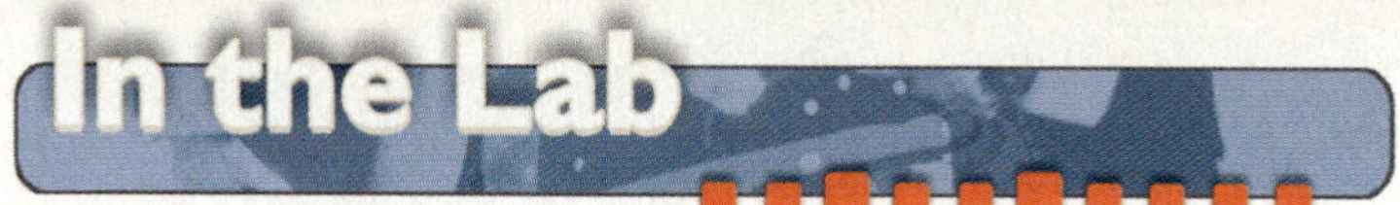

2 Fruit and Vegetable Nutrition

Problem: Nutritionists are discovering the increased health benefits of eating fruits and vegetables. The vitamins, antioxidants, minerals, and fiber that occur naturally in these foods can help prevent disease and help increase the quality of life. Five servings are recommended each day, but the average adult eats only three servings daily. In an effort to urge students to have a healthier diet, nutritionists at your campus fitness center have asked you to help them create a presentation describing fruit and vegetable nutrition facts. They want you to include one table listing the serving size and calories of three fruits and another listing the serving size and calories of three vegetables. Create the presentation shown in Figures 3-84a, 3-84b, 3-84c, and 3-84d.

Instructions: Perform the following tasks:

1. Start PowerPoint. Open the outline, Lab 3-2 Fruits and Vegetables, from the Data Disk. Apply the Ripple design template. Delete Slide 1, which is blank.
2. On Slide 1, apply the Title Slide slide layout. Increase the title font size to 80 point, italicize the text, and change the font color to red. Replace the nutritionist's name with your name.
3. Insert the apple clip shown in Figure 3-84a and size it to 250%. Ungroup the clip and then delete the brown border from the top. Regroup the clip.
4. View the slides in slide sorter view and then move Slide 2 so that it displays after Slide 4.
5. On Slide 2, insert the oranges photograph as a background. Create the table shown in Figure 3-84b. Format the table by changing all the text to Baskerville Old Face or a similar font if your system does not have this font. Change the font color to bright blue. Change the column headings to 40 point. Center and bold these headings.
6. On Slide 3, insert the tomatoes photograph as a background. Create the table shown in Figure 3-84c. Format the table by changing all the text to Baskerville Old Face. Change the column headings to 40 point. Center and bold these headings.
7. On Slide 4, use the slide master to change the first-level bullet to the fork, plate, and knife shown in Figure 3-84d. Increase the bullet size to 125% of text. Change the bullet color to red.
8. Insert the clip shown in Figure 3-84d. Size the clip to 200% and then delete the person from the clip. Change the placemat color to red.
9. Apply the Title arc animation scheme to Slides 1 and 4.
10. Save the presentation with the file name, Lab 3-2 Five a Day.
11. Create a custom show using Slides 1 and 4. Name the custom show Fruits and Vegetables 2. Run both the custom and full slide shows. Save the file again.
12. Print handouts with two slides on one page. Quit PowerPoint.

In the Lab

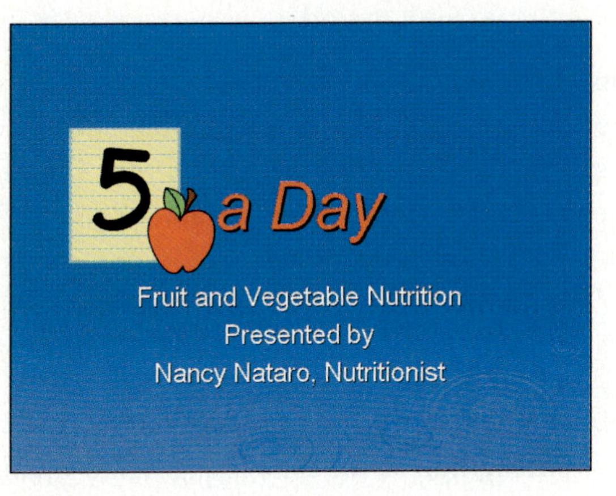

(a) Slide 1

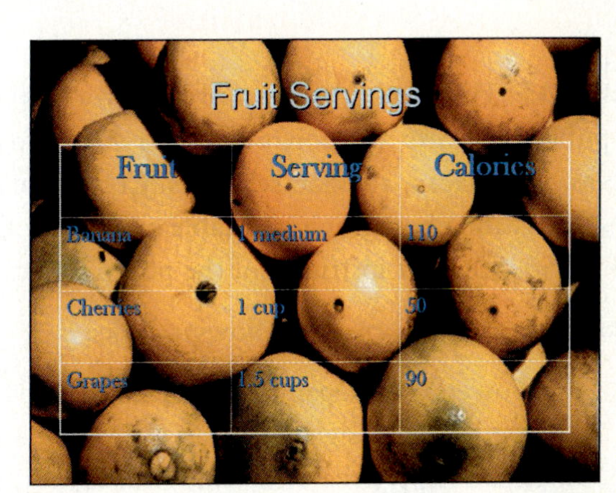

(b) Slide 2

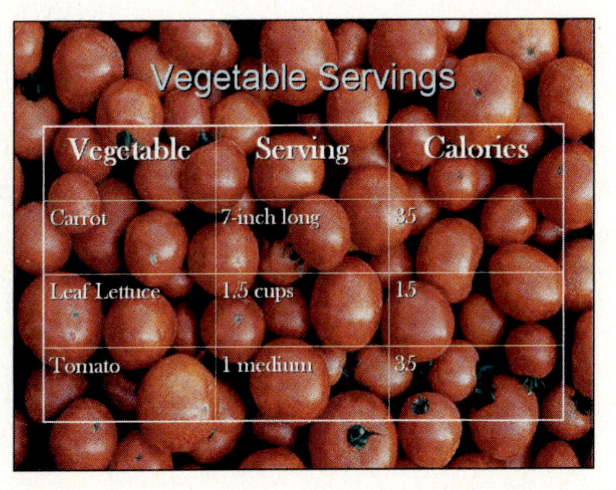

(c) Slide 3

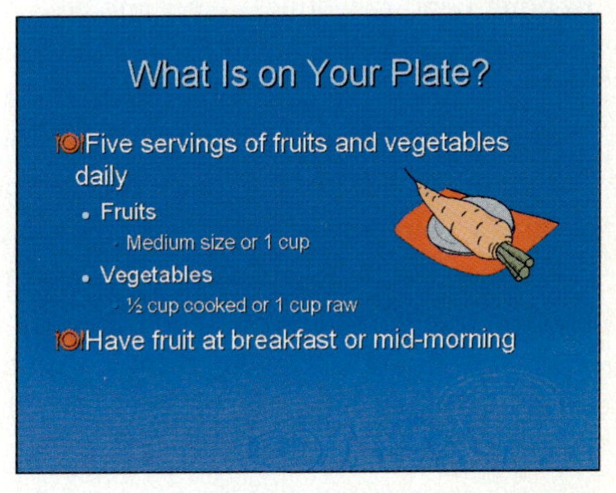

(d) Slide 4

FIGURE 3-84

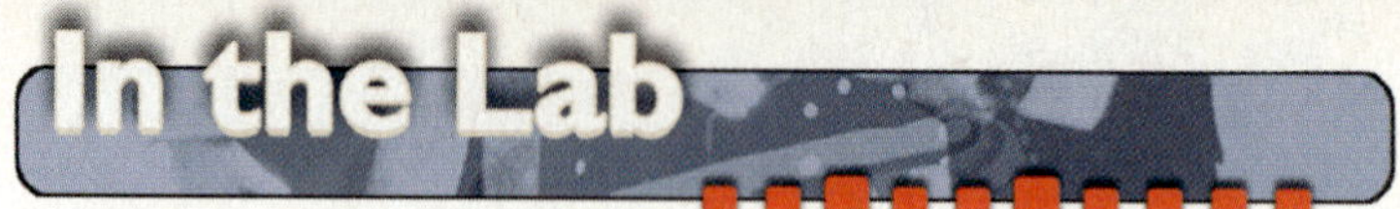

3 Westwood Wolf Exhibit

Problem: The zoo in the town of Westwood is refurbishing its wolf exhibit. You have been asked to help with the publicity efforts and donations. You decide to develop a presentation that includes information about the wolves, wolf packs, and zoo seminars. Create the presentation starting with the Wolf outline on your Data Disk. Then insert the photograph and table and create the organization chart shown in Figures 3-85a, 3-85b, 3-85c, and 3-85d. See your instructor if the photo and clip art are not available on your system.

Instructions: Perform the following tasks:

1. Start PowerPoint. Open the outline, Lab 3-3 Wolf Outline, on your Data Disk.
2. Apply the Edge design template. Delete Slide 1, which is blank.
3. On Slide 1, apply the Title Slide slide layout. Insert the Wolf photograph as the slide background. Change the title and subtitle text font color to white. Right-align the title and subtitle text. Replace the director's name with your name.
4. View the slides in slide sorter view and then change the order of Slides 2 and 3.
5. On Slide 2, insert the table shown in Figure 3-85b. Format the table by changing the column headings to 38-point Century Gothic. Center and bold the headings.
6. On Slide 3, create the organization chart shown in Figure 3-85c. Apply the Shaded diagram style. Scale the chart to 115% or to another size so that the chart fills the slide.
7. On Slide 4, use the slide master to change the first-level bullets to the sun symbol shown in Figure 3-85d that is part of the Webdings font. Change the bullet color to dark green. Change the second-level bullets to the arrow symbol that is part of the Wingdings 3 font. Change the bullet color to brown.
8. On Slide 4, insert the wolf clip shown in Figure 3-85d. Size the clip to 135%. Ungroup this clip and delete the blue background. Regroup the clip.
9. Apply the Unfold animation scheme to Slides 1 and 4.
10. Create a custom show using Slides 1, 3, and 4. Name the custom show Wolf 2. Run both the full and custom shows.
11. Save the presentation with the file name, Lab 3-3 Wolf Exhibit. Print the presentation and then quit PowerPoint.

In the Lab

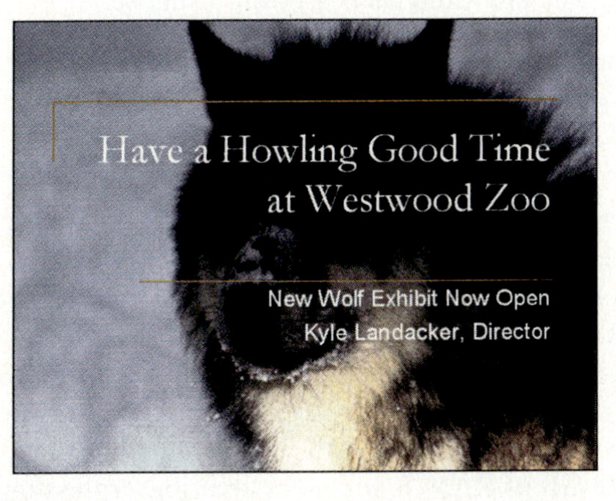

(a) Slide 1

Westwood Zoo Wolf Seminars

Date	Program
March 22	Photographing the Animals
June 8	Anatomy and Physiology
September 15	Folklore and History

(b) Slide 2

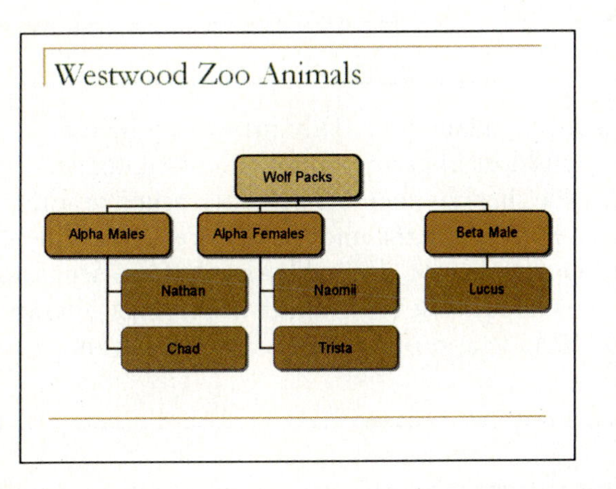

(c) Slide 3

Westwood Zoo Wolf Exhibition

- Five animals on display
  - Two acquired from Wyoming
- Fed twice weekly
  - Mondays and Fridays at noon
- Adult wolves weigh more than 100 pounds
- Howling is method of communicating

(d) Slide 4

FIGURE 3-

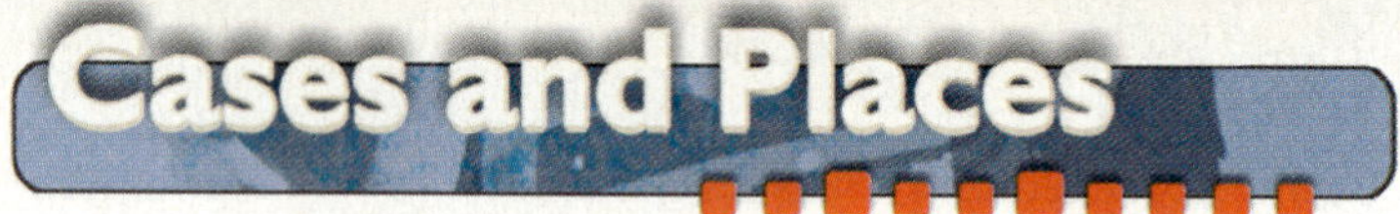

The difficulty of these case studies varies:
■ are the least difficult and ■■ are more difficult. The last exercise is a group exercise.

Note: Remember to use the 7 × 7 rule as you design the presentations: a maximum of seven words on a line and a maximum of seven lines on one slide.

1 ■ Casey's Complete Computers is a repair facility in your neighborhood. Casey Murphy, the owner, performs a variety of upgrades and repairs. His customers often ask about the amount of RAM (random access memory) to add to their systems. Casey says that determining the amount of RAM depends on the applications that will be run on the computer. RAM ranging from 128–256 MB is good for home and business users who are managing personal finances, using standard application software such as word processing, and communicating with others on the Web. RAM from 256 MB to 1 GB is adequate for users requiring more advanced multimedia capabilities, working with videos, music, and digital imaging, and playing Internet games. A minimum of 1 GB of RAM is for users creating professional Web sites and for running sophisticated CAD, 3-D design, or other graphics-intensive software. In an effort to help customers select the proper amount of RAM, Casey wants you to create a PowerPoint presentation and handout. Create a title slide with a clip and a text slide with an organization chart describing the RAM ranges and the types of applications best suited for each category.

2 ■ Busy students often have difficulty eating nutritious meals. Planning a daily menu may be one method of making healthy food choices. The nutrition counselors at your campus fitness center are planning a series of seminars to help students plan a realistic, healthy menu. They have asked you to create a presentation and a handout to accompany one of their seminars, and they desire a title slide, a bulleted list, and table to help students prepare a day of healthy meals. The table should have separate rows for breakfast, lunch, dinner, and snacks. The columns should list the number of servings of grains, vegetables and fruits, dairy products, meats, and sweets. Include appropriate clips and animation effects. Create a custom show.

3 ■■ Camcorders come equipped with a variety of special features. When choosing the right camcorder to purchase for your needs, consider where you will be recording and the subject matter that you desire to record. Also compare models to check ease of use and essential features. Visit an electronics store, read magazines, or perform online research to learn about four of the latest models. What are the prices for these popular devices? Which recording format do they use? How long is the battery life? What are the maximum optical and digital zooms? Are they equipped with a built-in light, night shot, and image stabilization? Do they have a USB port? Can they also function as a digital or still camera? Then, use Microsoft Word to create an outline that organizes your research findings. Open this Word document as a PowerPoint presentation and create a slide show with this information. Use a title slide and include appropriate clips and animation effects. Print the presentation and your outline.

Cases and Places

4 Many students are scheduling massage therapy treatments to relieve the stress they encounter and to improve circulation. The fitness center at your school offers four different massages, each designed for a specific purpose. Jessica Cantero, the Fitness Center director, has asked you to prepare a PowerPoint presentation, and she gives you the data shown in Table 3-4. Select a design template and create a slide show using this data. Introduce the presentation with a title slide. For Slide 2, list information promoting massage therapy treatment benefits. Use the row headings in Table 3-4 to create Slides 3 through 6. Modify the slide layouts using the slide master. Choose appropriate clip art and animation effects. Display the presentation title in the outline header and your name in the outline footer. Print the slides and the presentation outline.

Table 3-4 Massage Therapy Treatment Data

TREATMENT	BENEFIT	COST
Stone Massage Therapy	Heat penetrates deep into muscle tissue	1 hour - $65
Sports Massage	Reduces chance of injury	½ hour - $40
Shiatsu	Strengthens immune system	1 hour - $55
Reflexology	Stimulates body's natural ability to heal itself	½ hour - $45

5 **Working Together** Discussing eating habits with a nutrition counselor is one of the first steps people can make toward enhancing their diets. These counselors generally are available in a variety of locations, including fitness centers and clinics. Have each member of your team visit or telephone several local nutrition counselors to gather information about:

1) Healthy eating during the holidays
2) Essential vitamins for males
3) Essential vitamins for females
4) Special diets for marathon runners
5) Tips for effective weight loss

After coordinating the data, create a presentation with at least one slide describing specific nutrition advice. Introduce the presentation with a title slide. Include clip art and animation effects. Create a custom show. As a group, critique each slide. Hand in a hard copy of the final presentation.

MICROSOFT
Office PowerPoint 2003

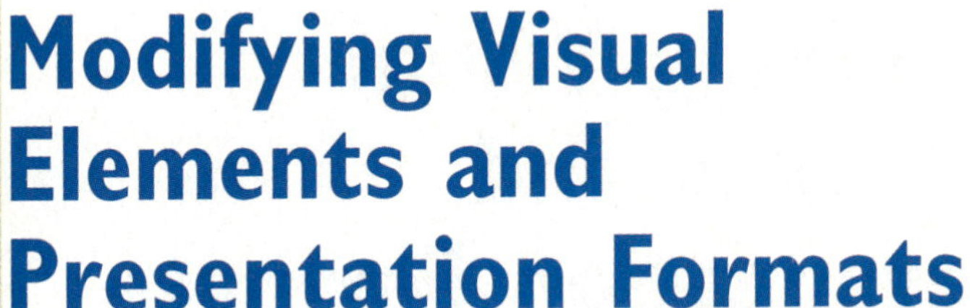

Modifying Visual Elements and Presentation Formats

PROJECT 4

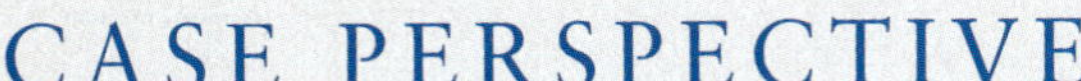

CASE PERSPECTIVE

College costs are rising dramatically. In recent years, higher education expenses have increased nearly twice as quickly as the inflation rate. Depending on the type of college chosen, students can expect their tuition bills and fees to be more than $1,000 higher than the previous year's total. Almost one-half of students attend two-year public colleges, where the average tuition can be less than $2,000 for a full-time class load. Tuition at a four-year private school can exceed $18,000, and the total bill can add to more than $40,000.

When planning a budget for college, students need to consider expenses for tuition, fees, books and supplies, and other miscellaneous costs. Of these expenses, tuition is the largest, amounting to nearly two-thirds of the total college bill. Room and board averages another $7,000.

Despite the high costs of higher education, the expense generally pays for itself. The U.S. Census Bureau reports that students earning a bachelor's degree earn, on average, more than 80 percent more than high school graduates. During a lifetime, this additional income can amount to more than $1 million.

Financial aid counselors at Eastwood State College assist prospective and current students prepare for college expenses. The director, Melissa Jackson, wants to offer a seminar for groups of students and community residents regarding paying for a college education. She has asked you to help with this project by developing a PowerPoint presentation. You recommend using a variety of graphics to help the audience visualize the monetary aspects of college.

As you read through this project, you will learn how to use PowerPoint to add these visual elements, including charts and tables.

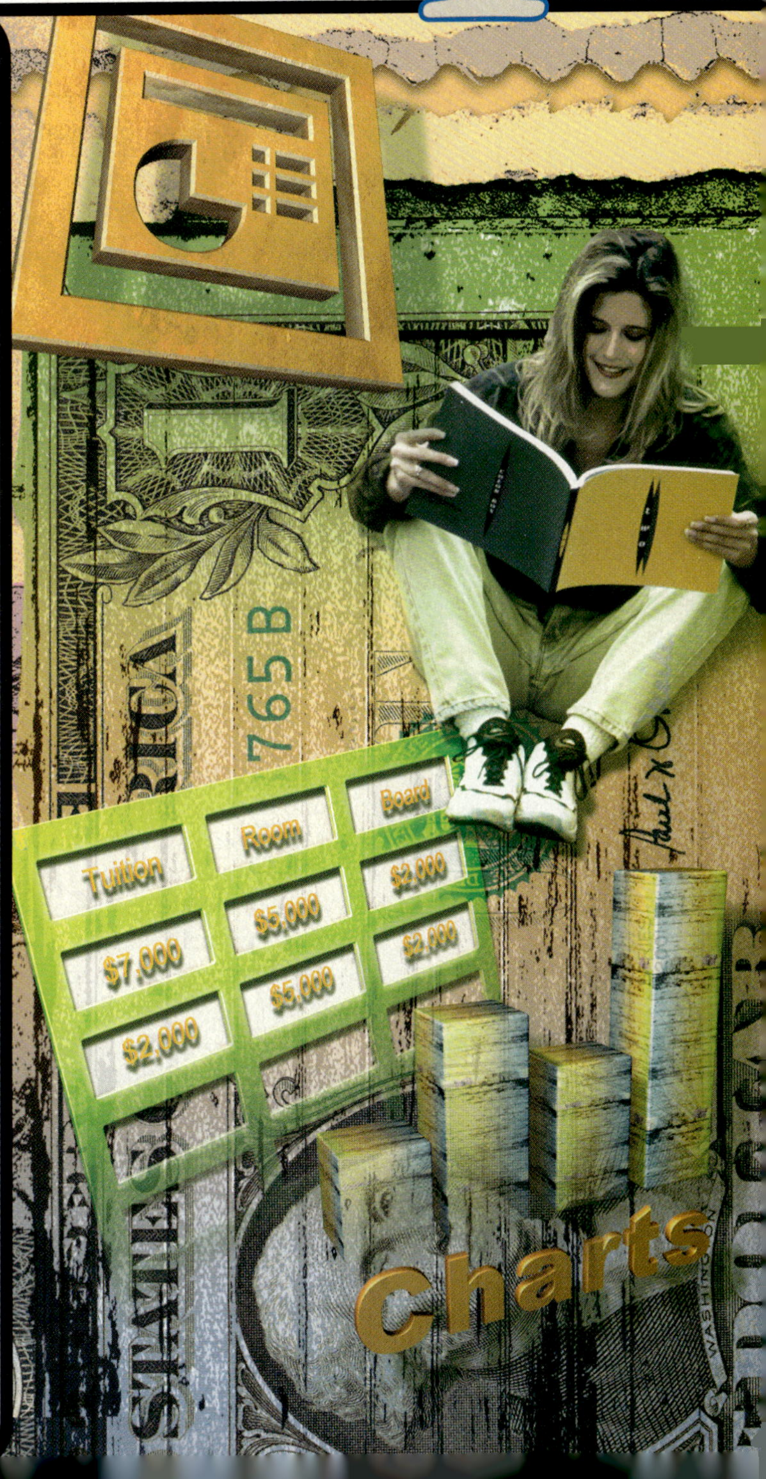

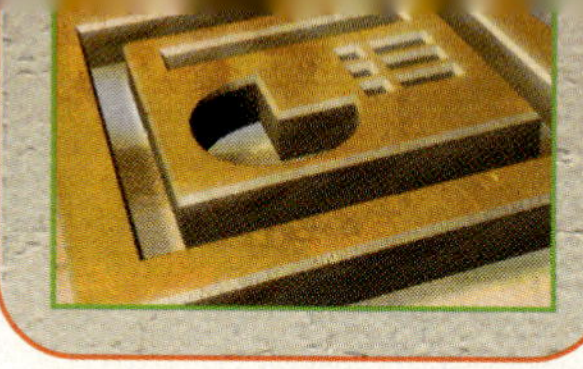

MICROSOFT
Office PowerPoint 2003

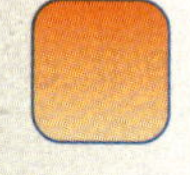

Modifying Visual Elements and Presentation Formats

PROJECT

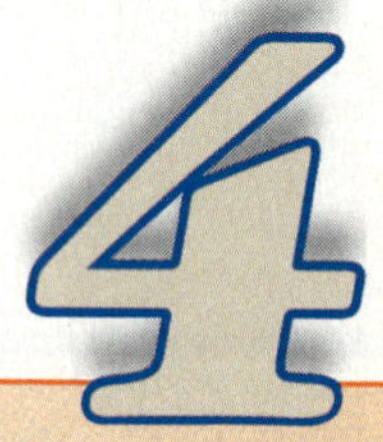

OBJECTIVES

You will have mastered the material in this project when you can:

- Create a presentation using the AutoContent Wizard
- Create and scale a WordArt element and add it to a slide
- Add sound effects and hyperlinks to slides
- Insert a chart, an Excel chart, and a Word table
- Revise and customize individual slides
- Use the Thesaurus
- Modify a presentation template by changing the color scheme
- Add information to the slide master Footer Area
- Add an action button and action setting
- Apply transition effects to a presentation
- Rehearse presentation timings and run a slide show with hyperlinks
- Print speaker notes and save slide presentations as Rich Text Format outlines

Introduction

"Variety's the very spice of life that gives it all its flavour," according to the British poet William Cowper. A PowerPoint presentation shows variety by selecting design templates, appropriate colors, and slide layouts for specific audiences. The beginning of a PowerPoint slide show sets the tone, announces the topic, and generates interest.

All this variety may result in confusion when starting to compose a presentation. Microsoft designers recognize this undertaking and have developed the AutoContent Wizard to help begin a presentation. This wizard creates up to 12 slides with suggested content about specific topics, such as selling a new product or reporting the status of a project. Based on the user's responses to questions about the presentation type, style, and options, the wizard selects a design template and creates slides with varying layouts and content that can be modified to fit the audience's needs.

Project Four — College Finances

Project 4 customizes the slide show generated by the AutoContent Wizard. You will add a graphical heading and change the background on Slide 1 to call attention to the college finances slide show topic. You also will add data from other sources, including an Excel chart and a Word table, and insert visual elements to create the slide show shown in Figures 4-1a through 4-1e.

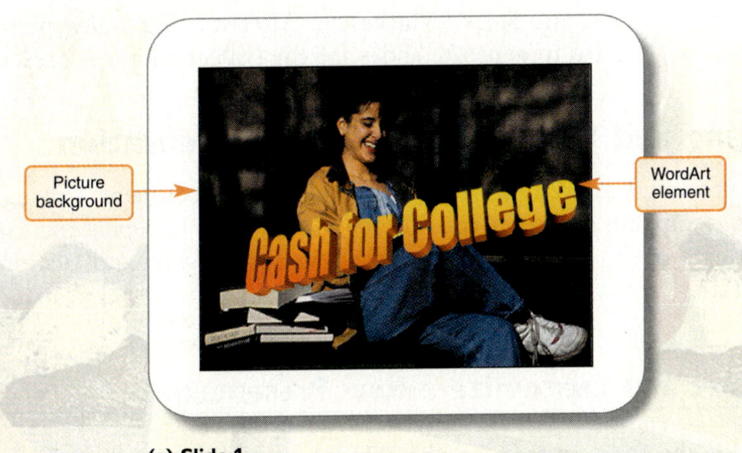

(a) Slide 1

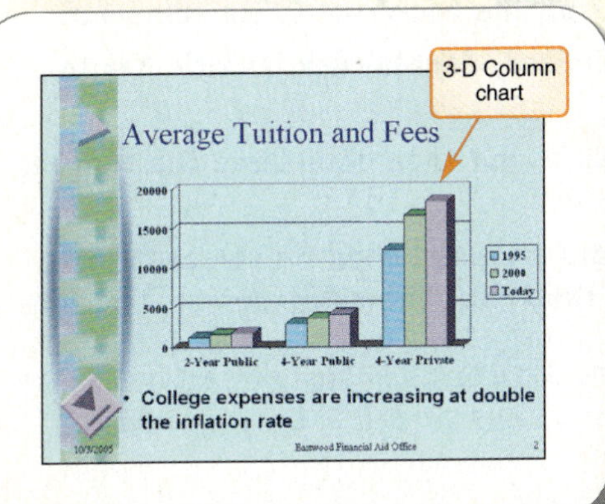

(b) Slide 2

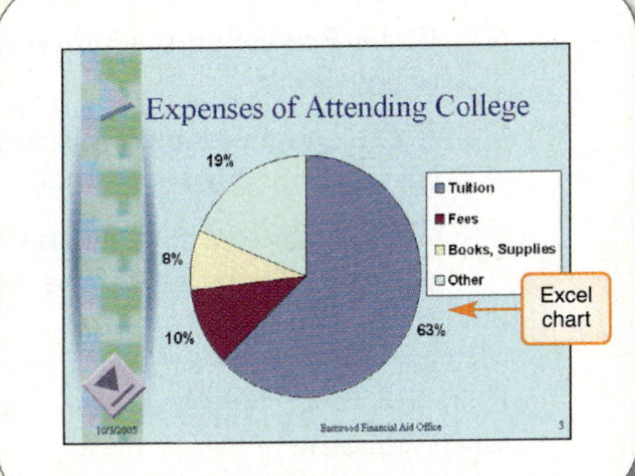

(c) Slide 3

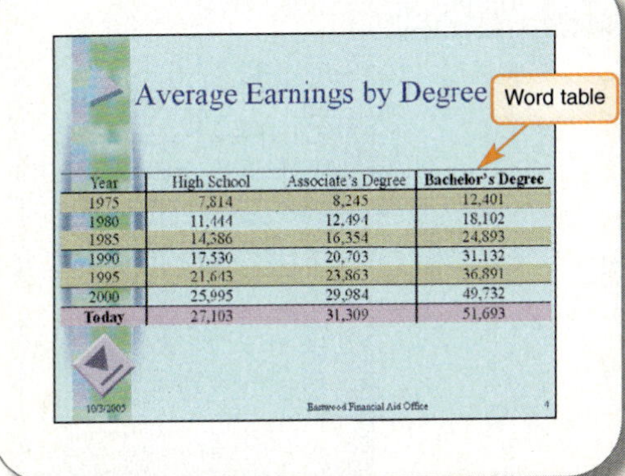

Year	High School	Associate's Degree	**Bachelor's Degree**
1975	7,814	8,245	12,401
1980	11,444	12,494	18,102
1985	14,386	16,354	24,893
1990	17,530	20,703	31,132
1995	21,643	23,863	36,891
2000	25,995	29,984	49,732
Today	27,103	31,309	51,693

(d) Slide 4

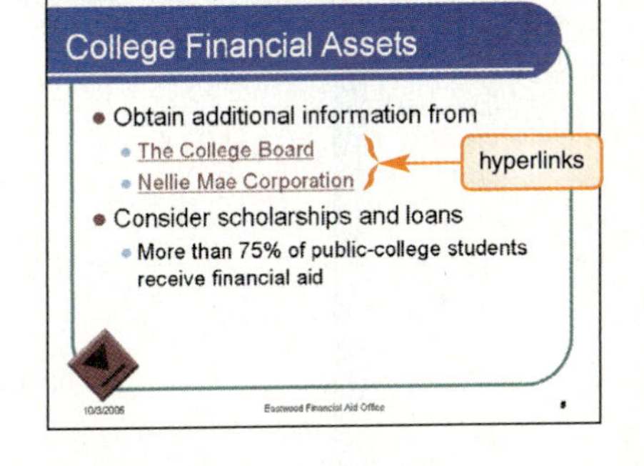

College Financial Assets
• Obtain additional information from
• The College Board
• Nellie Mae Corporation
hyperlinks
• Consider scholarships and loans
• More than 75% of public-college students receive financial aid

(e) Slide 5

FIGURE 4-1

More About

Presentation Design

The key to a successful presentation is organization, and the AutoContent Wizard can help organize your ideas. As you review the 18 presentations, formulate the context of your slide show and decide which topic best fits your slide show plan. Then, select the slides that support your major topic and eliminate the slides that are not relevant.

Starting a New Presentation Using the AutoContent Wizard

Beginning the college finances slide show is made easier by using the AutoContent Wizard. This feature helps you get started by supplying organization and ideas for the slides. The 18 presentations are organized in five categories: All, General, Corporate, Projects, and Sales / Marketing. After starting a new presentation, use the AutoContent Wizard to generate slides for the college finances presentation.

Starting and Customizing a New Presentation

In Projects 1 and 2, you started a presentation document, chose layouts, applied a design template, and reset your toolbars. You need to repeat the same steps to begin this project. The following steps show how to start and customize a new presentation.

To Start and Customize a New Presentation

1. **Click the Start button on the Windows taskbar, point to All Programs on the Start menu, point to Microsoft Office on the All Programs submenu, and then click Microsoft Office PowerPoint 2003 on the Microsoft Office submenu.**
2. **If the PowerPoint window is not maximized, double-click its title bar to maximize it.**
3. **If the Language bar appears, right-click it and then click Close the Language bar on the shortcut menu.**
4. **If the Standard and Formatting toolbars are positioned on the same row, click the Toolbar Options button and then click Show Buttons on Two Rows.**

The PowerPoint window with the Standard and Formatting toolbars on two rows appears as shown in Figure 4-2. PowerPoint displays the Title Slide slide layout and the Default Design template on Slide 1 in normal view.

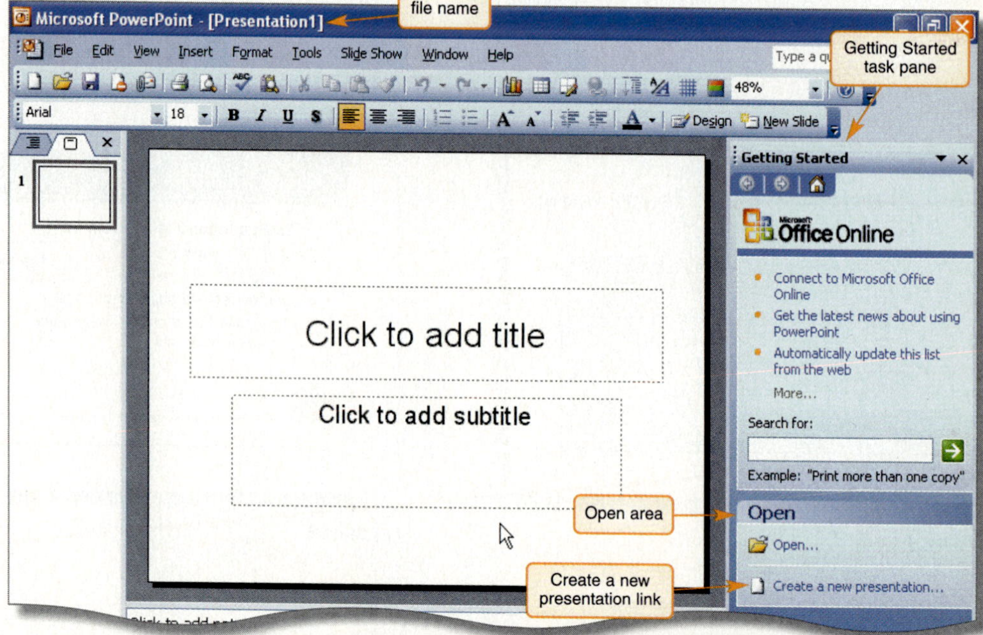

FIGURE 4-2

Using the AutoContent Wizard

With the presentation created, you can use the AutoContent Wizard to generate content. Because the topic of your slide show involves marketing a college finances seminar, the **Marketing Plan presentation** that is part of the Sales / Marketing presentation type creates useful ideas to begin developing the presentation. The wizard also will create a footer that is displayed at the bottom of each slide. The following steps use the AutoContent Wizard.

To Use the AutoContent Wizard

1

- **Click the Create a new presentation link in the Open area of the Getting Started task pane.**

The New Presentation task pane is displayed (Figure 4-3).

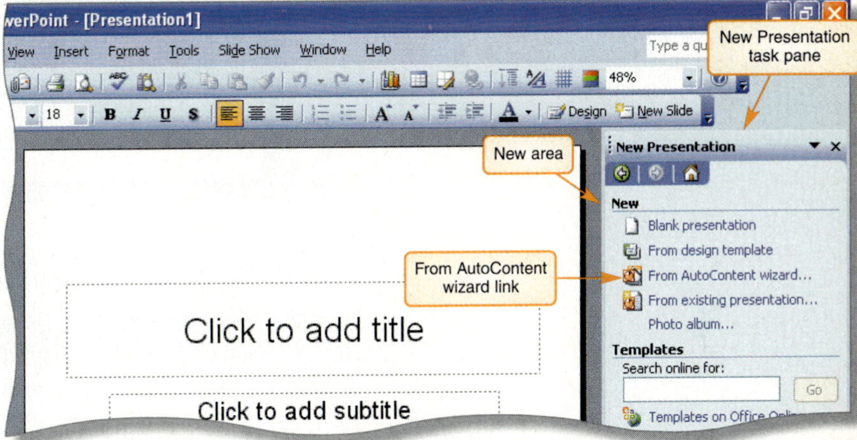

FIGURE 4-3

2

- **Click From AutoContent wizard.**
- **If the Office Assistant is displayed, right-click the Office Assistant and then click Hide on the shortcut menu.**

PowerPoint opens the AutoContent Wizard dialog box and displays the Start panel, describing the function of the AutoContent Wizard (Figure 4-4).

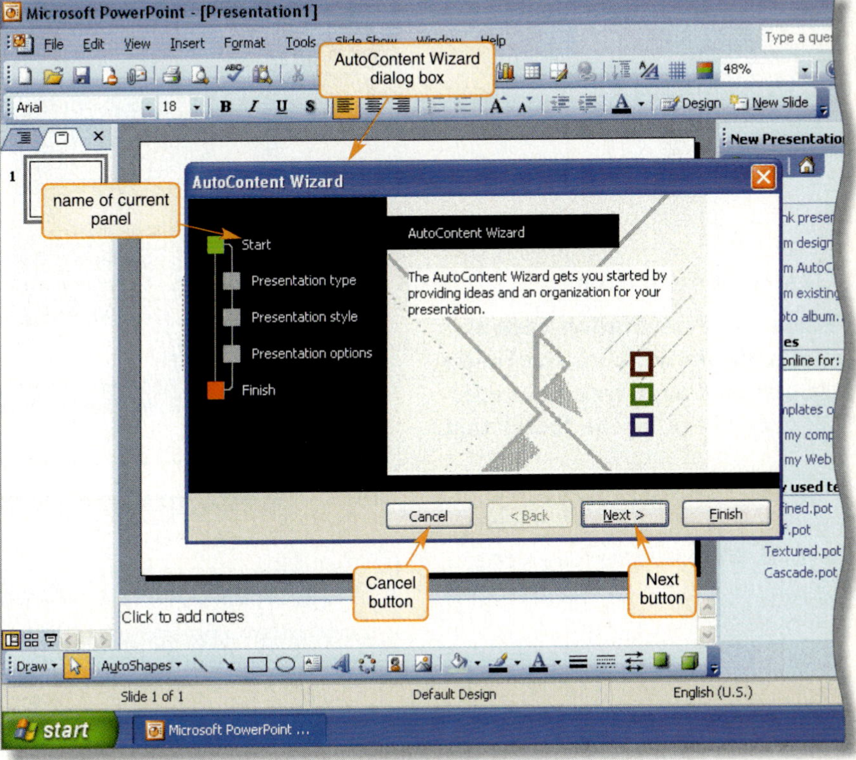

FIGURE 4-4

3

- **Click the Next button.**
- **When the Presentation type panel is displayed, click the Sales / Marketing button.**
- **Click the Marketing Plan presentation type.**

The 24 presentations are grouped in five categories (Figure 4-5). General is the default category. The names of the presentations within the Sales / Marketing category display in a list. You can click the Back button to review previous panels.

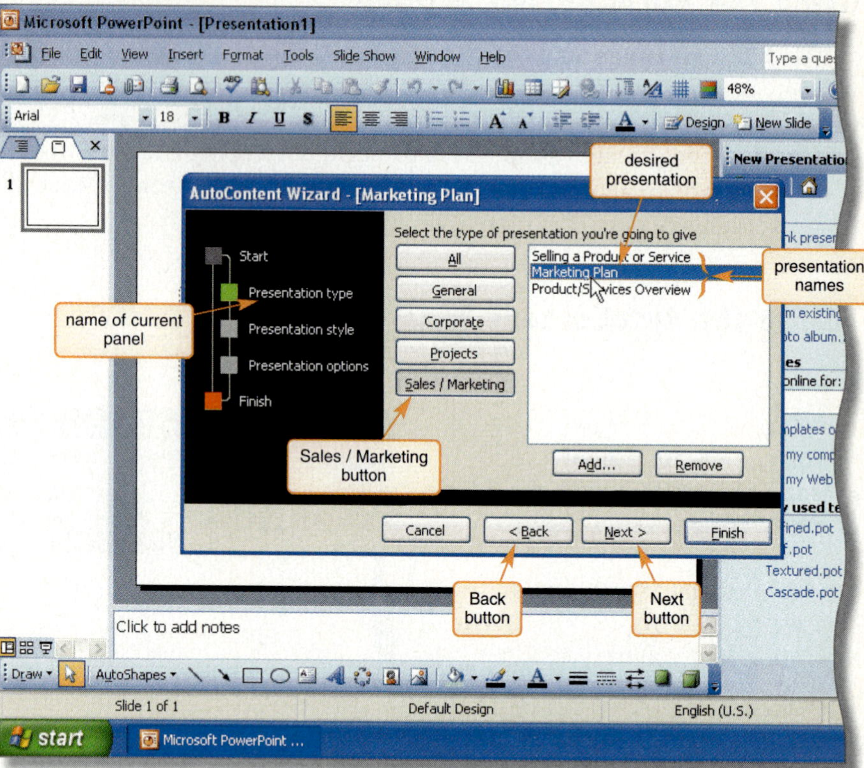

FIGURE 4-5

4

- **Click the Next button.**

The Presentation style panel is displayed. PowerPoint defaults to developing an on-screen presentation. You could select alternate outputs, such as a Web presentation, overheads, or slides.

5

- **Click the Next button.**
- **When the Presentation options panel is displayed, click the Footer text box and then type** `Eastwood State College` **as the footer text.**

The AutoContent Wizard creates a footer that will display at the bottom of each slide. The footer will contain the current date, the slide number, and the text you typed (Figure 4-6).

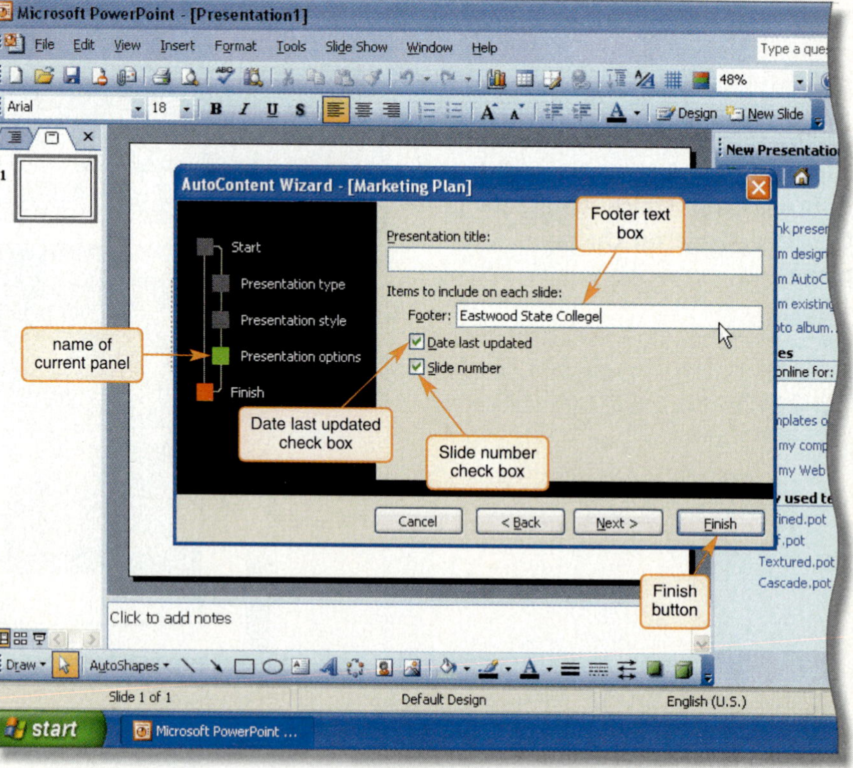

FIGURE 4-6

6

- **Click the Next button.**

The Finish panel displays a message that the AutoContent Wizard has all the necessary information to develop the slides.

7

- **Click the Finish button.**

PowerPoint closes the AutoContent Wizard and displays Slide 1 in the presentation (Figure 4-7). Melissa Jackson's name is displayed because her name was entered as the software user when PowerPoint was installed on the system for this project; a different name will display on your slide. The footer displays the current date, the Eastwood State College text, and the slide number. The AutoContent Wizard created a new presentation, so Presentation2 is displayed as the presentation title in the PowerPoint window.

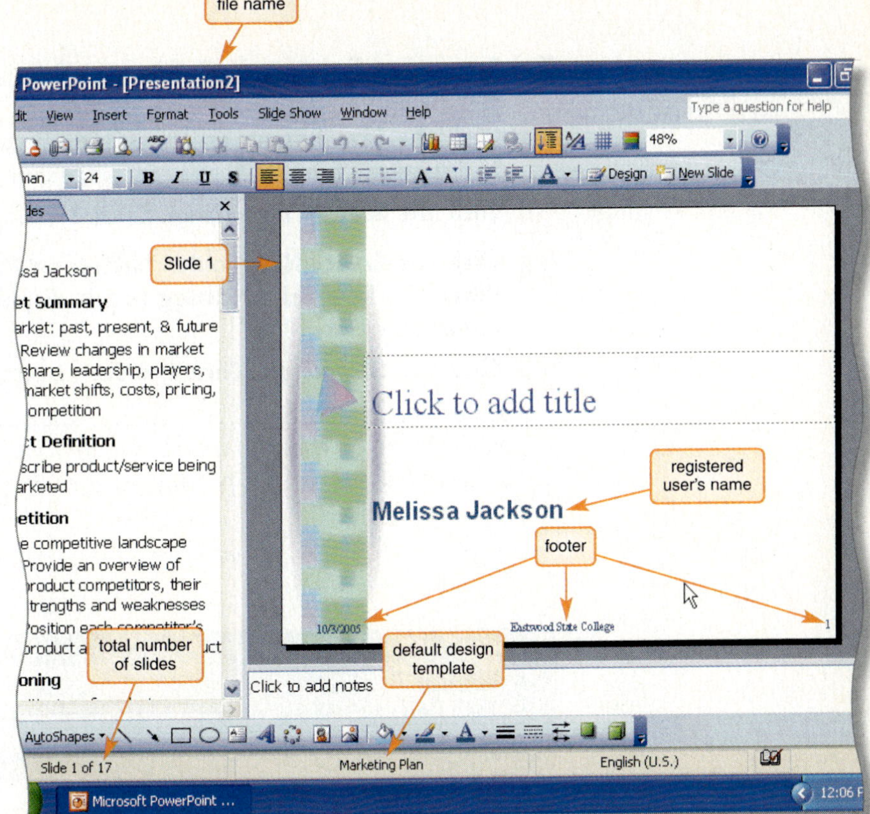

FIGURE 4-7

Other Ways

1. In Voice Command mode, say "View, Task Pane, From AutoContent Wizard, Next, [click Sales / Marketing], [click Marketing Plan], Next, [type footer], Next, Finish"

The AutoContent Wizard developed seventeen slides in the Marketing Plan theme. You will modify these slides to fit the college finances topic by changing the presentation color scheme, changing the slide backgrounds, adding a bitmap graphic, creating a WordArt element, inserting an Excel chart and a Word table, and adding a chart, hyperlinks, sound, and transitions.

Creating a Folder and Saving a Presentation

You now should create a folder and save the presentation. The steps on the next page create a folder and save the presentation.

To Create a Folder and Save a Presentation

1. **Click the Save button on the Standard toolbar. When the Save As dialog box is displayed, type** `College Finances` **in the File name text box.**
2. **Click the Save in box arrow. Click 3½ Floppy (A:) in the Save in list.**
3. **Click the Create New Folder button on the toolbar in the Save As dialog box. When the New Folder dialog box is displayed, type** `Cash for College` **in the Name text box.**
4. **Click the OK button. Click the Save button in the Save As dialog box.**

The presentation is saved in the Cash for College folder on the floppy disk in drive A with the file name College Finances. This file name is displayed on the title bar (Figure 4-8).

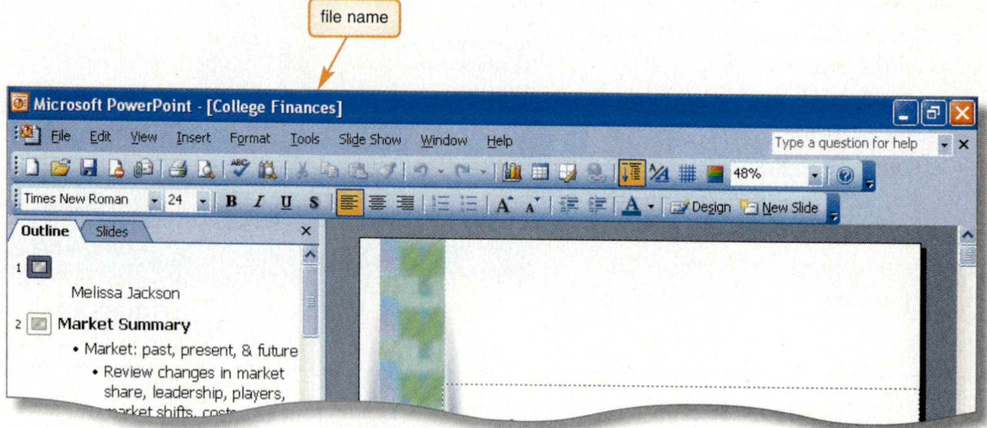

FIGURE 4-8

Adding a Picture to Create a Custom Background

To add variety to the presentation, you can insert a photograph to a slide background. As in Project 3, you decide to add a photograph to the Slide 1 background. This photograph is stored on the Data Disk. See the inside back cover of this book for instructions for downloading the Data Disk or see your instructor for information about accessing the files required for this book. The following steps add this picture to the Slide 1 background.

> **Q&A**
>
> **Q:** Which backgrounds do viewers prefer?
>
> **A:** Photographs. Audience members prefer color photographs as backgrounds compared with line art and black-and-white objects, according to some researchers. The line art, however, may be more effective in conveying the desired message. To learn more about designing backgrounds, visit the PowerPoint 2003 More About Web page (`scsite.com/ppt2003/more`) and click Backgrounds.

To Add a Picture to Create a Custom Background

1. **Right-click anywhere on Slide 1 except the title text placeholder. Click Background on the shortcut menu. When the Background dialog box is displayed, click the Background fill box arrow.**
2. **Click Fill Effects on the menu. When the Fill Effects dialog box is displayed, click the Picture tab and then click the Select Picture button.**
3. **When the Select Picture dialog box is displayed, click the Look in box arrow and then click 3½ Floppy (A:). Click the Student thumbnail.**
4. **Click the Insert button. When the picture is displayed in the Fill Effects dialog box, click the OK button.**

5 **Click Omit background graphics from master.**

6 **Click the Apply button.**

Slide 1 displays the Student picture as the slide background (Figure 4-9). The Marketing Plan design template text attributes display on the slide. The vertical stripe on the left side of the slide does not display because you clicked the Omit background graphics from master check box.

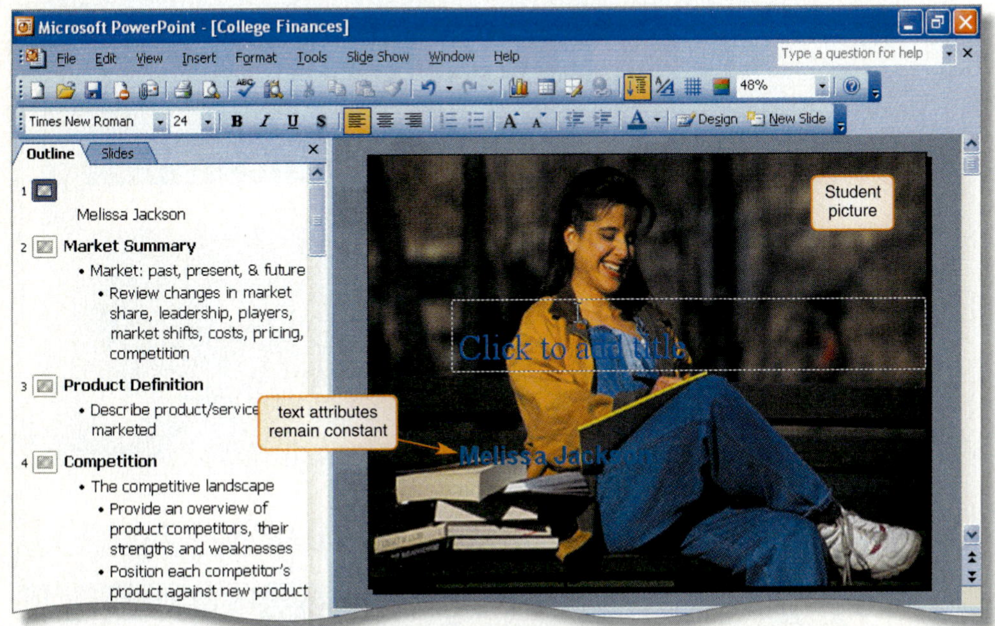

FIGURE 4-9

Creating a WordArt Element and Adding It to a Slide

The Student picture on Slide 1 is intended to generate interest in the presentation. Another method of attracting viewers is by using a **WordArt element**, which is text that has been altered with special effects. PowerPoint supplies 30 predefined WordArt styles that vary in shape and color.

Creating and adding the Cash for College WordArt element shown in Figure 4-1a on page PPT 227 requires several steps. First, you delete the title text placeholder because you are going to use the WordArt element as the presentation title. Then, you create the WordArt object. Finally, you position and size the element on the title slide. The next several sections explain how to create the WordArt element and then add it to Slide 1.

Deleting the Title and Subtitle Text Placeholders

The Cash for College WordArt object will display in the middle of Slide 1 as a substitution for title text. You need to delete the title text and subtitle text placeholders because you are not going to use them in this presentation. The steps on the next page delete the title and subtitle text placeholders.

More About

Shadows

Many WordArt elements have shadows that add interest. You can change the position of these shadows by selecting the WordArt object, clicking the Shadow Style button on the Drawing toolbar, and then clicking the Shadow Settings command. When the Shadow Settings toolbar is displayed, click one of the four Nudge Shadow buttons to change the shadow effect. The shadow moves one point each time you click a Nudge Shadow button.

To Delete the Title and Subtitle Text Placeholders

1

- **Click the title text placeholder's selection rectangle.**

The mouse pointer changes to a four-headed arrow (Figure 4-10).

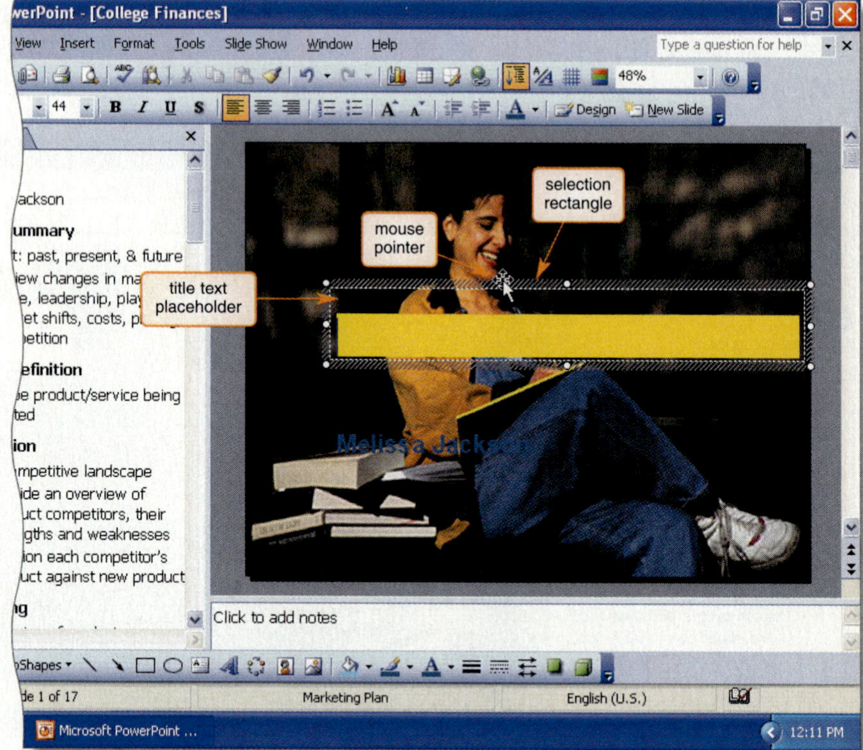

FIGURE 4-10

2

- **Right-click the selection rectangle.**
- **Point to Cut on the shortcut menu (Figure 4-11).**

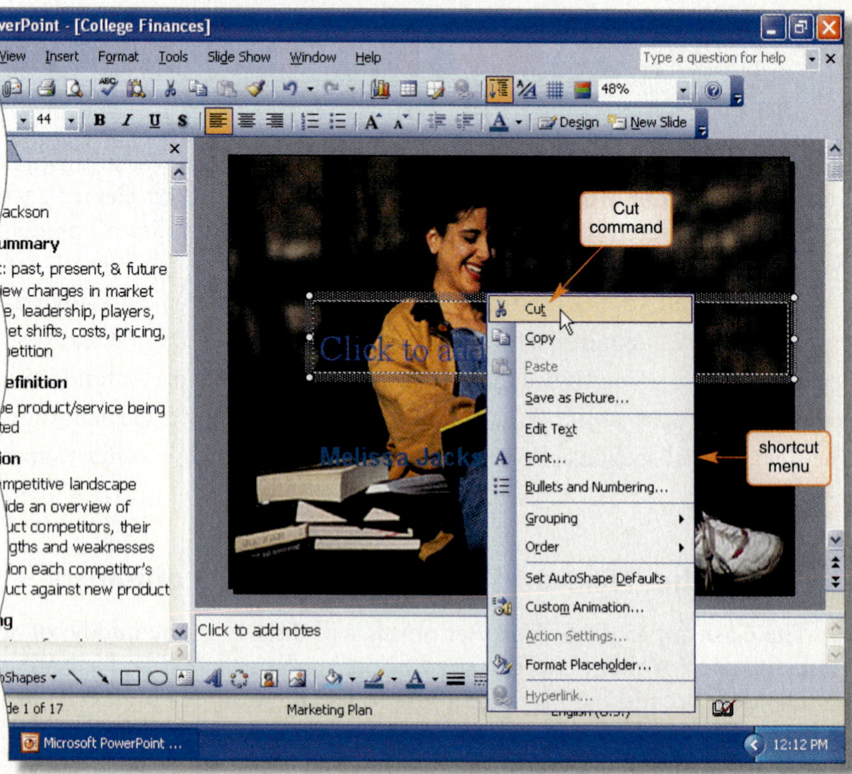

FIGURE 4-11

3

- **Click Cut.**
- **Click the subtitle text placeholder and then click the placeholder's selection rectangle.**

The mouse pointer changes to a four-headed arrow (Figure 4-12). Slide 1 is displayed without the title text placeholder.

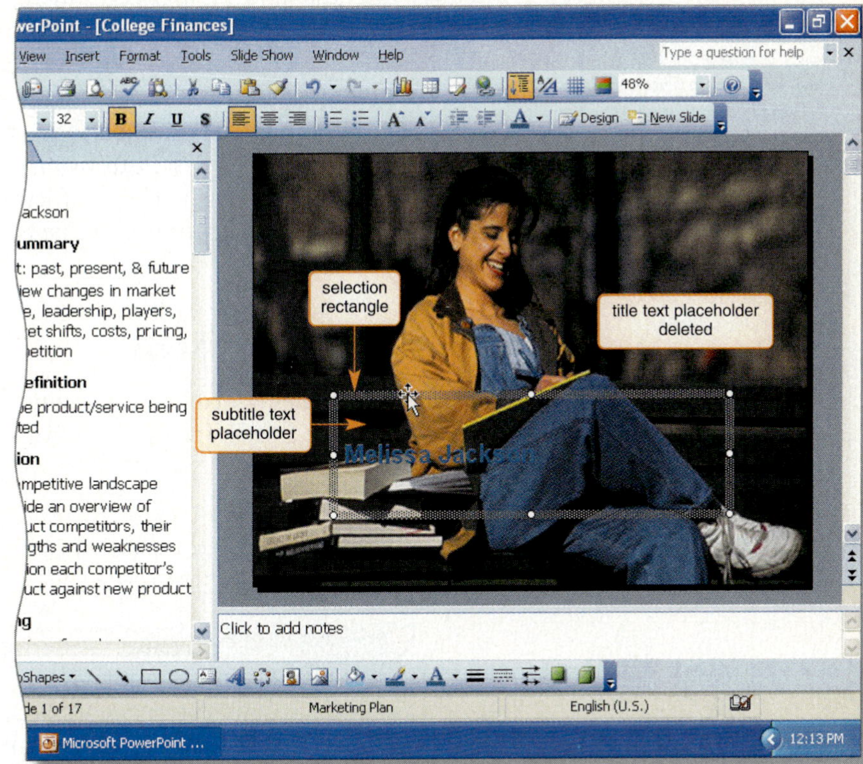

FIGURE 4-12

4

- **Right-click the selection rectangle.**
- **Click Cut.**
- **Press the DELETE key.**

Slide 1 is displayed without the subtitle text placeholder (Figure 4-13).

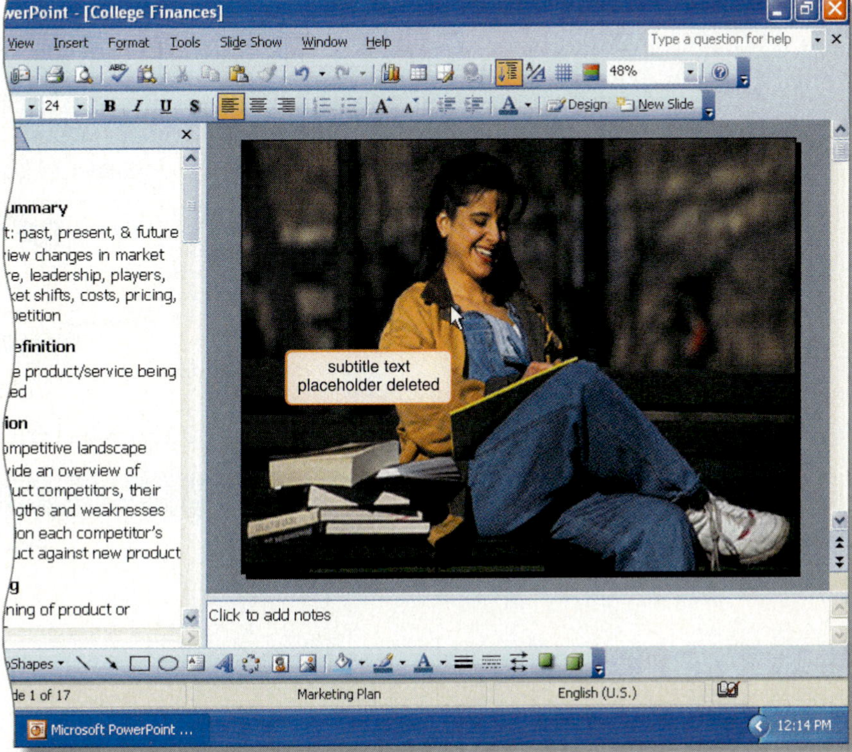

FIGURE 4-13

Other Ways

1. Click title text placeholder selection rectangle, click Cut button on Standard toolbar
2. Click title text placeholder selection rectangle, on Edit menu click Cut
3. Click title text placeholder selection rectangle, press CTRL+X
4. In Voice Command mode, say "Edit, Cut"

With the title and subtitle text placeholders deleted, you can create the WordArt element. The Cash for College title on Slide 1, shown in Figure 4-1a on page PPT 227, contains letters that have been altered with special text effects. Using WordArt, first you will select a letter style for this text. Then, you will type the name of the presentation and select a unique shape for its layout, although many other predefined shapes could be used. Buttons on the WordArt toolbar allow you to rotate, slant, curve, and alter the shape of letters. WordArt also can be used in the other Microsoft Office applications. The next several sections explain how to create the text WordArt element.

Selecting a WordArt Style

PowerPoint supplies WordArt styles with a variety of shapes and colors. The following steps select a style for the Cash for College text.

To Select a WordArt Style

1

- **Click the Insert WordArt button on the Drawing toolbar.**
- **When the WordArt Gallery dialog box is displayed, click the WordArt style in row 5, column 4.**

The WordArt Gallery dialog box is displayed (Figure 4-14).

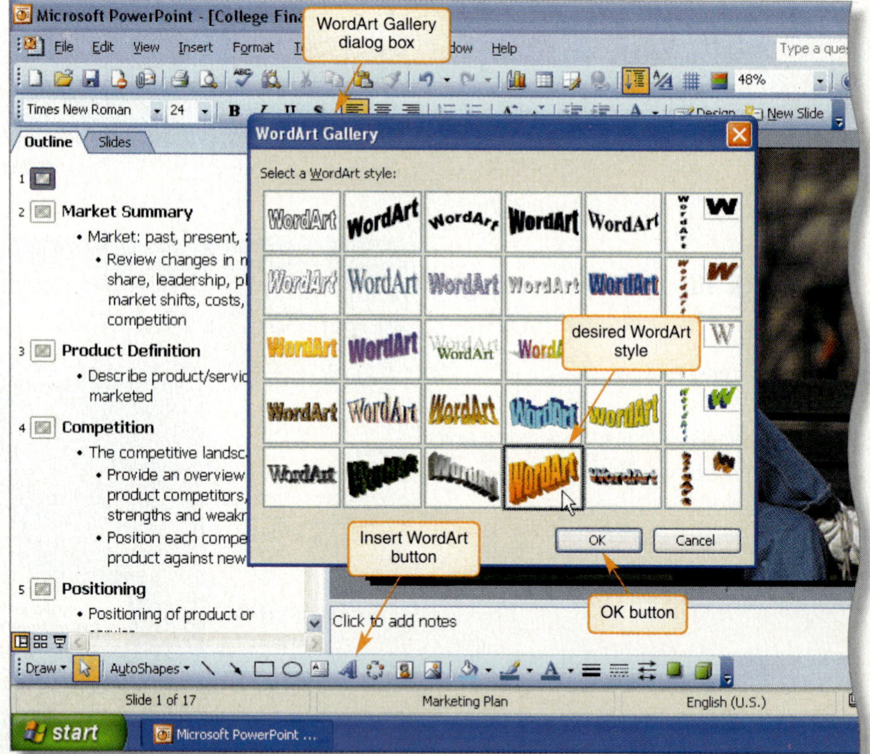

FIGURE 4-14

2

• **Click the OK button.**

The Edit WordArt Text dialog box is displayed (Figure 4-15). The default text, Your Text Here, in the Text text box is selected.

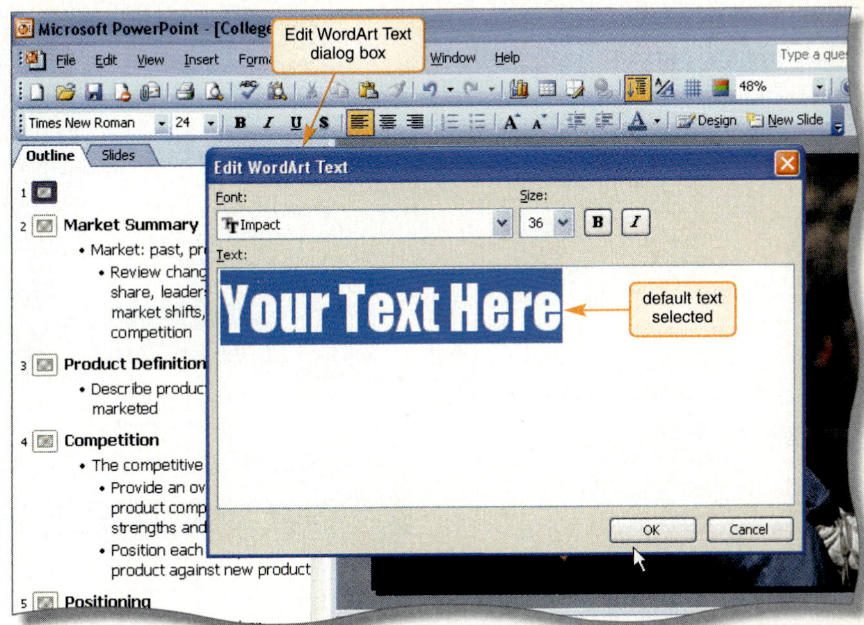

FIGURE 4-15

Other Ways

1. On Insert menu point to Picture, click WordArt, click desired style, click OK
2. Press ALT+I, press P, press W, press arrow keys to select desired style, press ENTER
3. In Voice Command mode, say "Insert, Picture, WordArt, [click desired style], OK"

Entering the WordArt Text

To create a text element, you must enter text in the Edit WordArt Text dialog box. By default, the words, Your Text Here, in the Text text box are selected. When you type the text for your title object, it replaces the selected text. When you want to start a new line, press the ENTER key. The following steps enter the text for the Cash for College heading.

To Enter the WordArt Text

1

• **If necessary, select the text in the Edit WordArt Text dialog box.**

• **Type** `Cash for College` **in the Text text box.**

The text is displayed in the Text text box in the Edit WordArt Text dialog box (Figure 4-16). The default font is Impact, and the font size is 36.

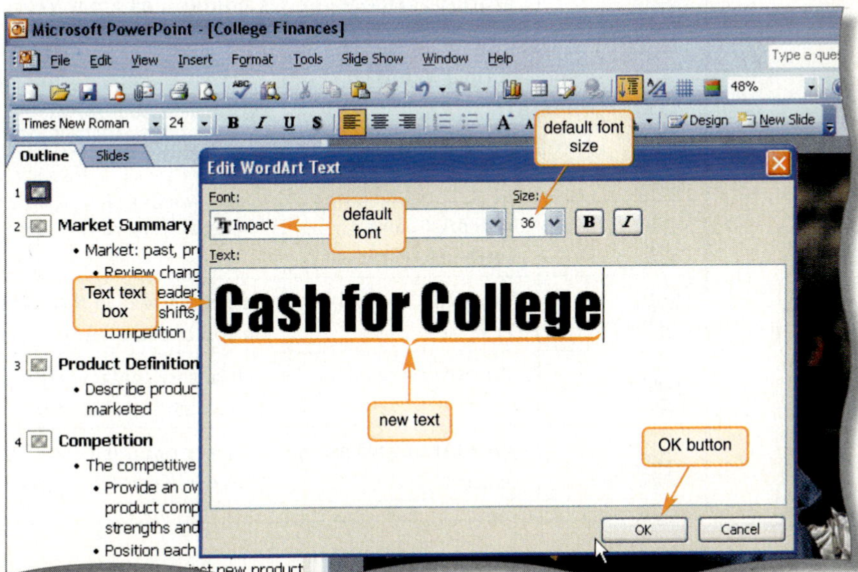

FIGURE 4-16

2

- **Click the OK button.**
- **If necessary, display the WordArt toolbar by right-clicking a toolbar and then clicking WordArt.**

The Cash for College text is displayed (Figure 4-17). The WordArt toolbar is displayed in the same location and with the same shape as it displayed the last time it was used. You can move the WordArt toolbar by dragging its title bar.

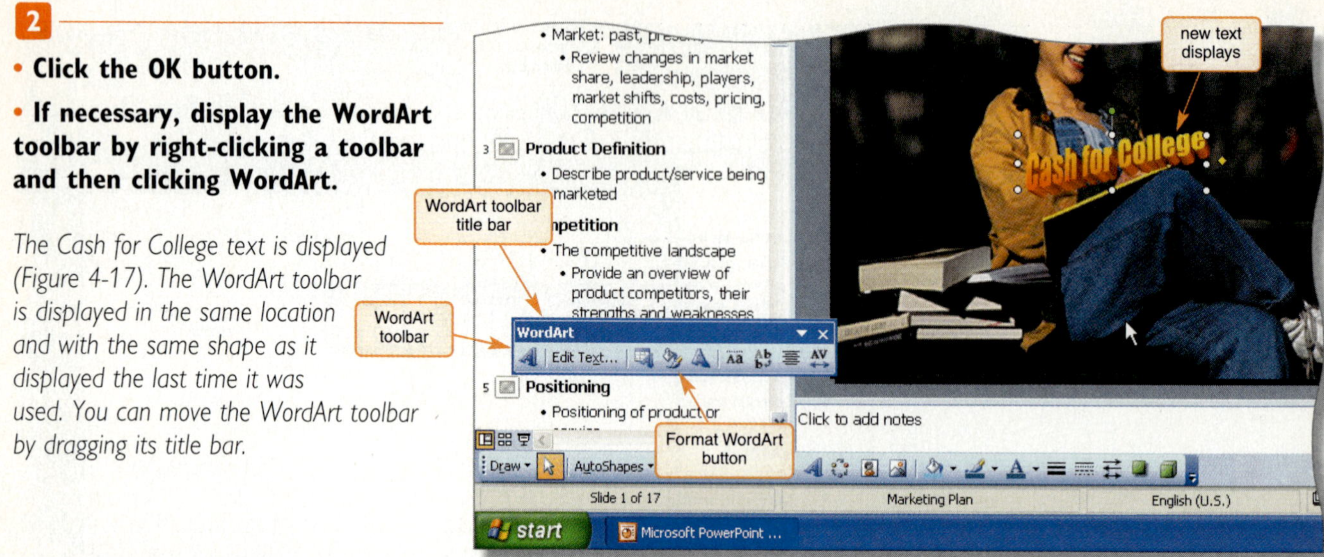

FIGURE 4-17

Other Ways

1. Type text, press ENTER
2. In Dictation mode, say "Cash for College"

The WordArt toolbar contains buttons that allow you to change an object's appearance. For example, you can rotate the letters, change the character spacing and alignment, scale the size, and add different fill and line colors. Table 4-1 explains the purpose of each button on the WordArt toolbar.

Table 4-1 WordArt Toolbar Button Functions

BUTTON	NAME	FUNCTION
	Insert WordArt	Creates a WordArt element
Edit Text...	Edit Text	Changes the text characters, font, and font size
	WordArt Gallery	Chooses a different WordArt style for the selected WordArt object
	Format WordArt	Formats the color, lines, size, pattern, position, and other properties of the selected object
	WordArt Shape	Modifies the text into one of 40 shapes
Aa	WordArt Same Letter Heights	Makes all letters the same height, regardless of case
Ab	WordArt Vertical Text	Stacks the text in the selected WordArt object vertically — one letter on top of the other — for reading from top to bottom
	WordArt Alignment	Left-aligns, centers, right-aligns, word-justifies, letter-justifies, or stretch-justifies text
AV	WordArt Character Spacing	Displays options (Very Tight, Tight, Normal, Loose, Very Loose, Custom, Kern Character Pairs) for adjusting spacing between text

The next section explains how to shape the WordArt text.

Changing the WordArt Height and Width

WordArt objects actually are drawing objects, not text. Consequently, WordArt objects can be modified in various ways, including changing their height, width, line style, fill color, and shadows. Unlike text, however, they neither can display in outline view nor be spell checked. In this project, you will increase the height and width of the WordArt object. The Size tab in the Format WordArt dialog box contains two areas used to change an object's size. The first, the **Size and rotate area**, allows you to enlarge or reduce an object, and the rotate area allows you to turn an object around its axis. The second, the **Scale area**, allows you to change an object's size while maintaining its height-to-width ratio, or **aspect ratio**. If you want to retain the object's original settings, you click the Reset button in the **Original size area**. The following steps change the height and width of the WordArt object.

More About

Saving a Slide as a Graphic

You can insert a PowerPoint slide into another file or into a Web page. To save a slide as a graphic, display the slide, click Save As on the File menu, and then click Windows Metafile or GIF Graphics Interchange Format in the Save as type box.

To Change the WordArt Height and Width

1

- **Click the Format WordArt button on the WordArt toolbar.**
- **If necessary, click the Size tab in the Format WordArt dialog box.**
- **Click Lock aspect ratio.**

The Size sheet is displayed in the Format WordArt dialog box (Figure 4-18). The Cash for College text currently is .96 inches high and 3.38 inches wide.

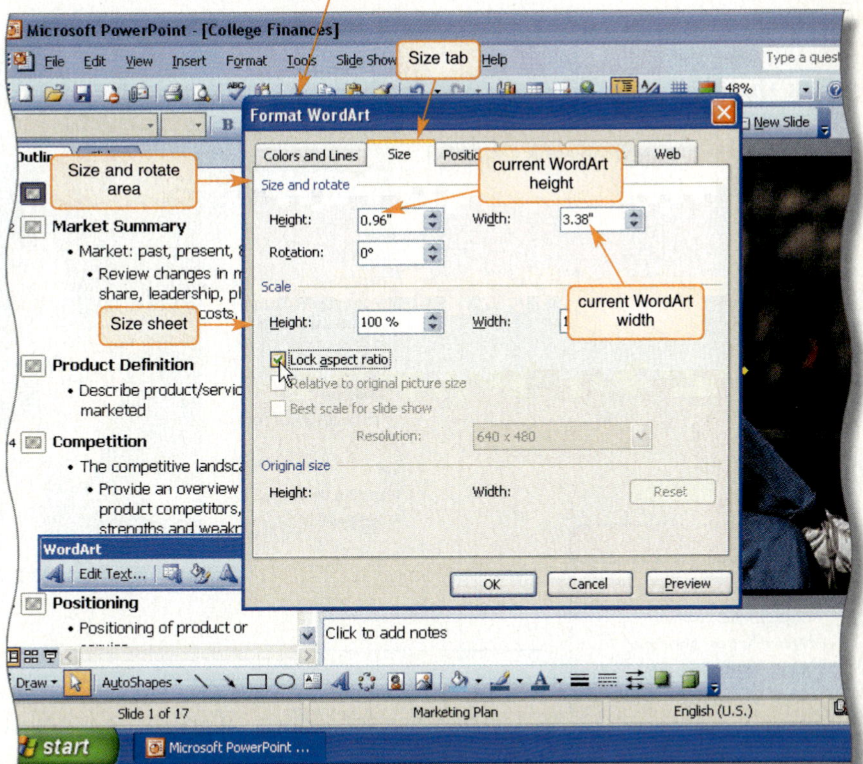

FIGURE 4-18

2

- **Triple-click the Height text box in the Size and rotate area.**
- **Type** 2.5 **in the Height text box.**

The Height text box displays the new entry (Figure 4-19). The width will change proportionally when you click the OK button.

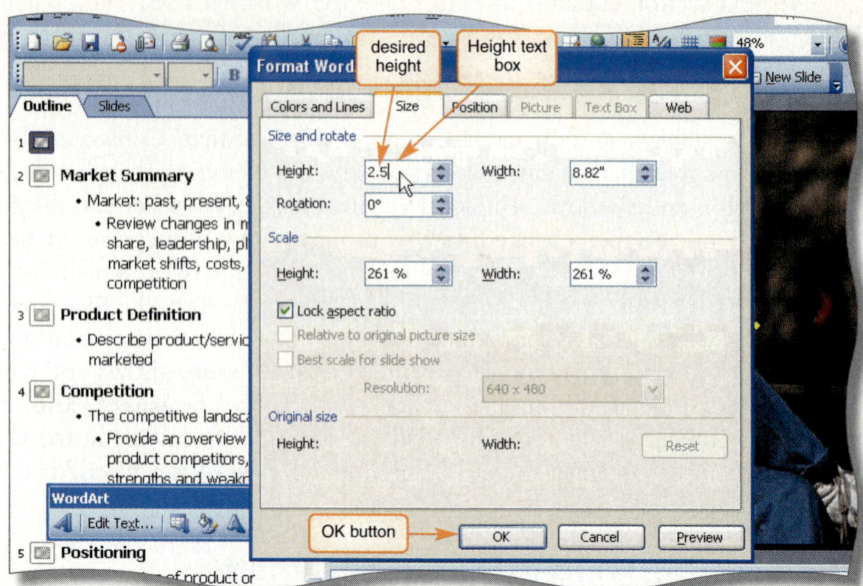

FIGURE 4-19

3

- **Click the OK button.**

The resized WordArt text object is displayed (Figure 4-20).

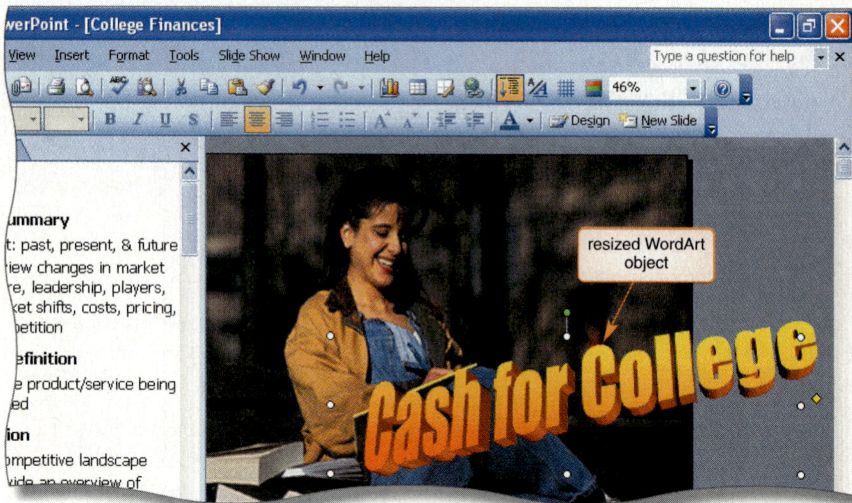

FIGURE 4-20

Other Ways

1. Right-click WordArt object, click Format WordArt on shortcut menu, click Size tab, triple-click Height text box in Size and rotate area, type new value, triple-click Width text box in Size and rotate area, type new value, click OK button
2. Press ALT+O, press O, press ALT+E, enter percent, press ALT+D, type new value, press ENTER
3. In Voice Command mode, say "Format, WordArt, Size, Height, [type new value], Width, [type appropriate percent], OK"

The Cash for College WordArt text object is created. The next step is to display it in a precise location on the slide. The grids and guides help you align objects in exact locations on slides.

Displaying Grids and Guides and Positioning a WordArt Object

In this project, you use the PowerPoint grid and guides to help position the WordArt object on Slide 1. The **grid** is a set of intersecting lines, and the **guides** are two straight dotted lines, one horizontal and one vertical. When an object is close to a guide, its corner or its center (whichever is closer) **snaps**, or attaches itself, to the guide. You can drag a guide to a new location to meet your alignment requirements.

When you point to a guide and then press and hold the mouse button, PowerPoint displays a box containing the exact position of the guide on the slide in inches. The center of a slide is 0.00 on both the vertical and the horizontal guides. An arrow displays below the guide position to indicate the vertical guide is either left or right of center. An arrow displays to the right of the guide position to indicate the horizontal guide is either above or below center. The following steps display the grid and guides and position the Cash for College WordArt text object on Slide 1.

To Display the Grid and Guides and Position the WordArt Object

1

- **With Slide 1 selected, right-click anywhere on the slide except the WordArt text object.**
- **Point to Grid and Guides on the shortcut menu (Figure 4-21).**

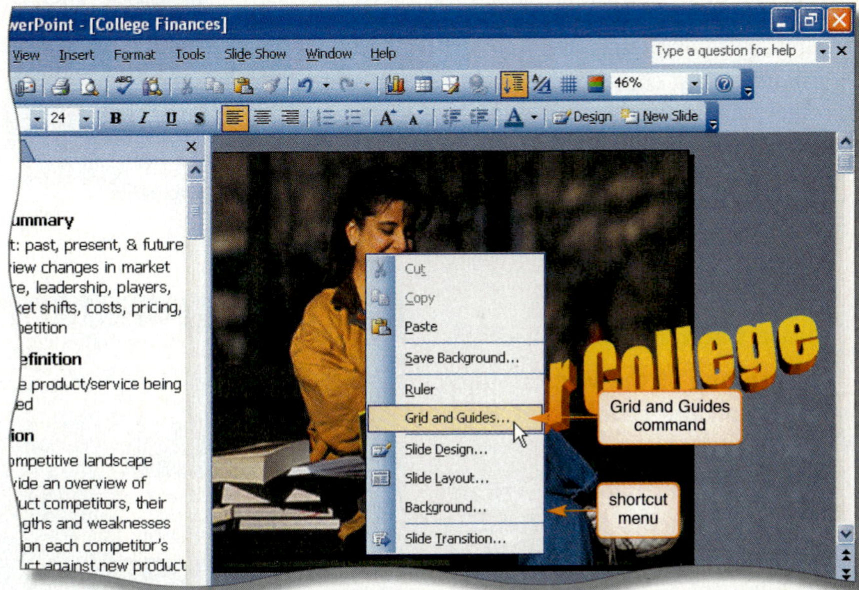

FIGURE 4-21

2

- **Click Grid and Guides.**
- **When the Grid and Guides dialog box displays, click the Spacing box arrow in the Grid settings area and then click 1/10".**
- **Click Display grid on screen in the Grid settings area.**
- **Click Display drawing guides on screen in the Guide settings area.**

Once you click 1/10" in the Grid settings area, the value changes to 0.1. The Snap object to grid check box indicates the action buttons and other objects will snap to the drawing guides that display on the screen (Figure 4-22).

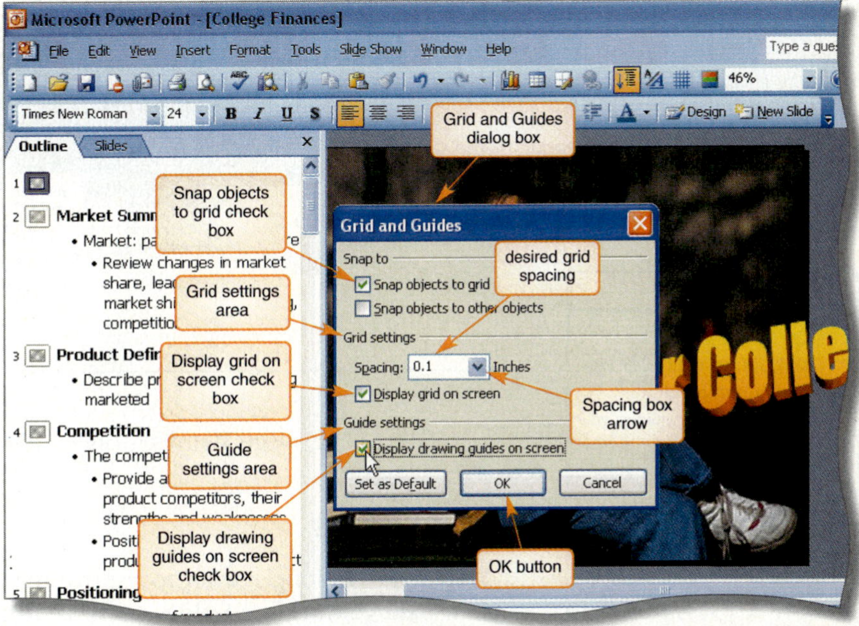

FIGURE 4-22

3

- **Click the OK button.**
- **Point to one of the horizontal guides anywhere on the slide except the WordArt text object.**
- **Click and then drag the horizontal guide to .60 inches above center. Do not release the mouse button.**

The grid and the horizontal and vertical guides display (Figure 4-23). While holding down the mouse button, a ScreenTip displays indicating the position of the horizontal guide. This guide will be used to position the top-left edge of the WordArt text object.

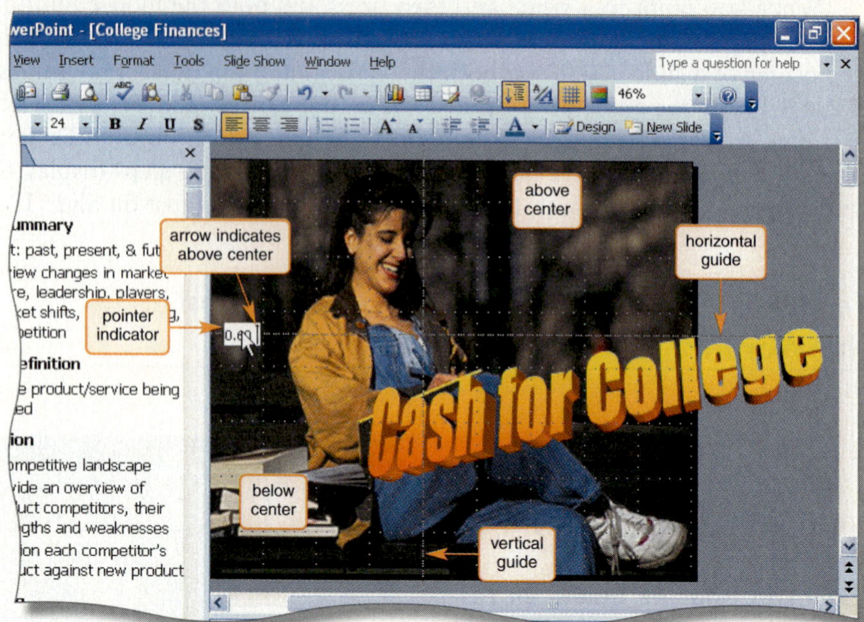

FIGURE 4-23

4

- **Release the mouse button.**
- **Point to one of the vertical guides anywhere on the slide except the WordArt text object.**
- **Click and then drag the vertical guide to 4.50 inches left of center.**
- **Drag the WordArt text object until the upper-left sizing handle snaps to the intersection of the vertical and horizontal guides.**

The WordArt text object is positioned correctly (Figure 4-24). The top of the WordArt text object aligns with the horizontal guide, and the left edge of the object aligns with the vertical guide.

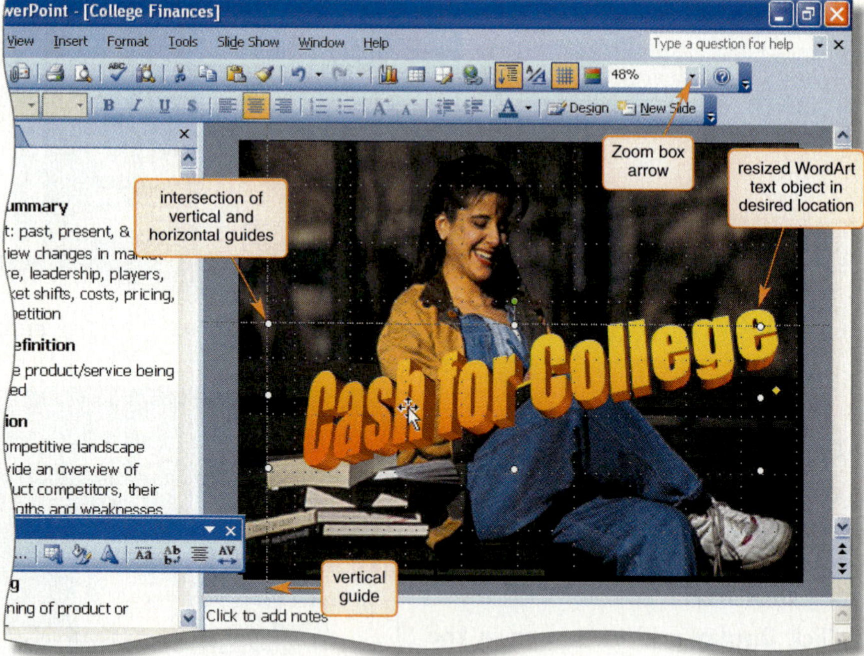

FIGURE 4-24

Other Ways

1. On View menu click Grid and Guides, click Display grid on screen, click Display drawing guides on screen
2. Press ALT+V, press I, press I
3. In Voice Command mode, say "View, Grid and Guides, Display grid on screen, Display drawing guides on screen"

The Cash for College WordArt object displays in the desired location.

Hiding Guides

When you no longer want to control the exact placement of objects on the slide, you can **hide guides.** The following steps hide guides.

To Hide Guides

1. **Right-click Slide 1 anywhere except the WordArt text object. Click Grid and Guides on the shortcut menu.**
2. **When the Grid and Guides dialog box displays, click Display grid on screen in the Grid settings area.**
3. **Click Display drawing guides on screen in the Guide settings area.**
4. **Click the OK button.**

The guides are hidden.

Adding a Sound Effect

The final modification to the title slide is adding music to play when Slide 1 is displayed during a slide show. Using a **sound effect** calls attention to areas of interest or importance to which a presenter may want to call attention. PowerPoint allows you to add sounds and music to a presentation. These sounds can be from the Microsoft Clip Organizer, files you have stored on your computer, a CD, and the Internet. To hear the sound effects, you need speakers and a sound card on your system. During the slide show, the sound clip, Marketing Music, should play when Slide 1 is displayed. This clip is available on the Microsoft Office Clip Art and Media Web site and is on your Data Disk. Marketing Music is a **Musical Instrument Digital Interface** (**MIDI**) file, which uses a standard format to encode and communicate music and sound between computers, music synthesizers, and instruments. The following steps add the music to Slide 1.

Q&A

Q: I cannot hear the sound effects. Why?

A: Your computer needs speakers and a sound card to play music and sounds. To see what multimedia hardware is installed on your system and which settings are in use, check the Sounds and Audio Devices folder settings in the Control Panel window. To learn more about sound files, visit the PowerPoint 2003 More About Web page (scsite.com/ppt2003/more) and click Sound.

To Add a Sound Effect

1

- **Click Insert on the menu bar and then point to Movies and Sounds.**
- **Point to Sound from File on the Movies and Sounds submenu.**

The Insert menu and Movies and Sounds submenu display (Figure 4-25).

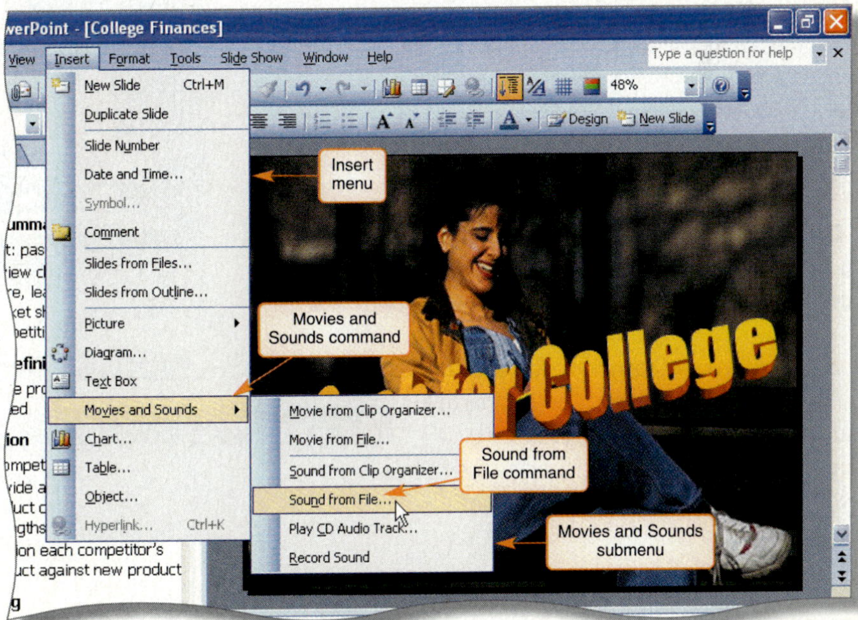

FIGURE 4-25

2

- **Click Sound from File.**
- **If necessary, when the Insert Sound dialog box is displayed, click the Look in box arrow and then click 3½ Floppy (A:).**
- **Click Marketing Music.**

The Marketing Music file in the Insert Sound dialog box is displayed (Figure 4-26). Your list of file names may vary.

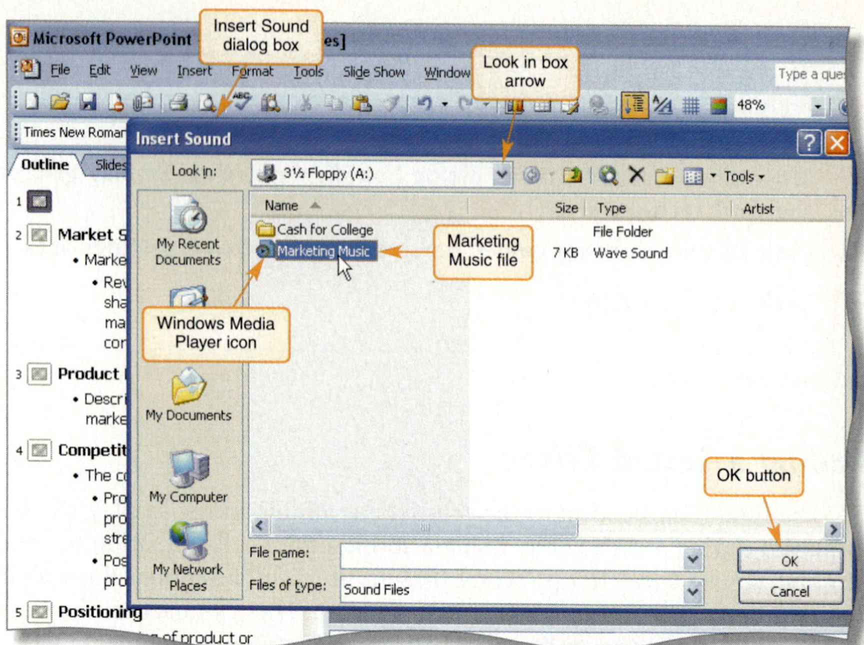

FIGURE 4-26

3

- **Click the OK button.**
- **When the Microsoft Office PowerPoint dialog box is displayed, click the Automatically button.**

The speaker icon indicates the sound is added to Slide 1. Clicking the Automatically button instructs PowerPoint to play the Marketing Music sound file automatically when the slide show starts. Clicking the When Clicked button tells PowerPoint to play the sound when you click Slide 1.

4

- **Drag the speaker icon off the slide to the lower-right corner of the screen.**

You cannot hide the speaker icon, but you can drag it off the slide because it is set to play automatically during the slide show (Figure 4-27). If you had not selected the automatic option, you would have to click the speaker icon to play the sound effect.

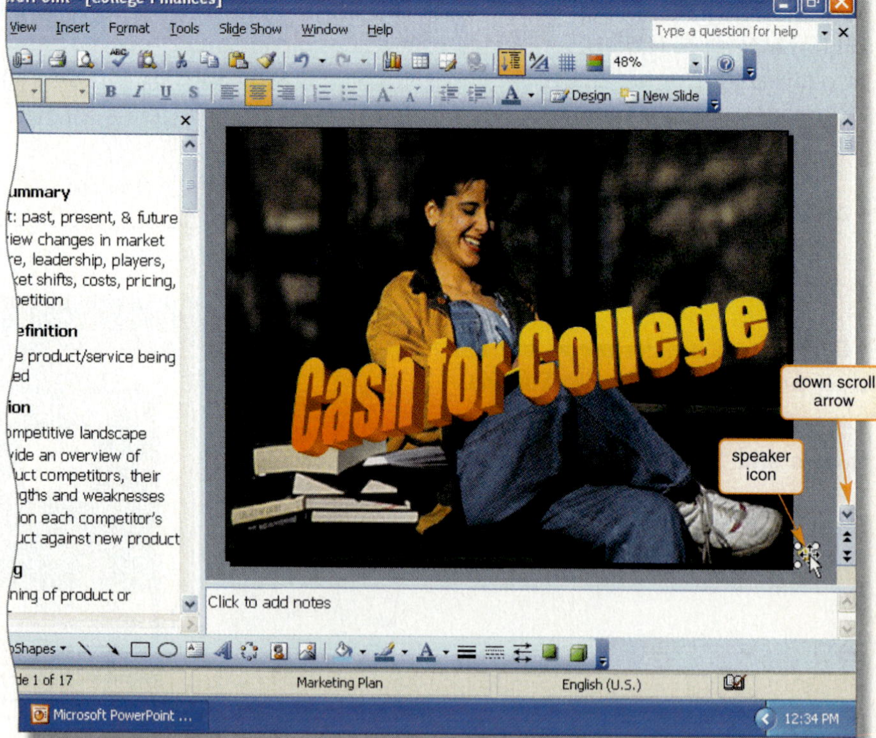

FIGURE 4-27

Deleting Slides

The financing college presentation will have five slides. You will add a chart on Slide 3, an Excel chart on Slide 5, a Word table on Slide 7, and resource information on Slide 8. Slides 2, 4, 6, and 9 through 17 are not needed in this presentation. One quick method of deleting multiple adjacent slides is to use the SHIFT+click technique. You used this technique in Project 3 to select multiple clip art objects before changing their colors. One quick method of deleting multiple slides that are not consecutive is to use the **CTRL+click technique**. You perform the CTRL+click technique by pressing and holding down the CTRL key as you click the desired slides to delete. In this project, the SHIFT+click technique can be used to delete Slides 9 through 17 and the CTRL+click technique can be used to delete Slides 2, 4, and 6. The slides can be deleted when viewing the tabs pane in normal view or when using slide sorter view. This presentation consists of 17 slides, so it is easier and more efficient to use slide sorter view because many slide thumbnails are visible simultaneously in this view. The following steps delete the slides.

Other Ways

1. On Insert menu point to Movies and Sounds, click Sound from File, click Look in box arrow, click 3½ Floppy (A), click desired file, click OK button, click Automatically button
2. Press ALT+I, press V, press N, press ALT+I, press UP ARROW key to select 3½ Floppy (A:), press ENTER, press TAB key three times, press arrow keys to select desired file, press ENTER, press ENTER
3. In Voice Command mode, say "Insert, Movies and Sounds, Sound from File, [click desired file], OK, Automatically"

To Delete Slides

1. **Click the Slide Sorter View button at the lower left of the PowerPoint window.**
2. **Click the Slide 9 thumbnail. Click the down scroll arrow until Slide 17 is displayed. Press and hold down the SHIFT key and then click slide 17.**
3. **Press the DELETE key.**
4. **Click the Slide 2 thumbnail. Press and hold down the CTRL key and then click Slides 4 and 6.**
5. **Press the DELETE key.**
6. **Click the Normal View button at the lower left of the PowerPoint window.**

Slides 2, 4, 6, and 9 through 17 are deleted (Figure 4-28). The presentation now is composed of five slides.

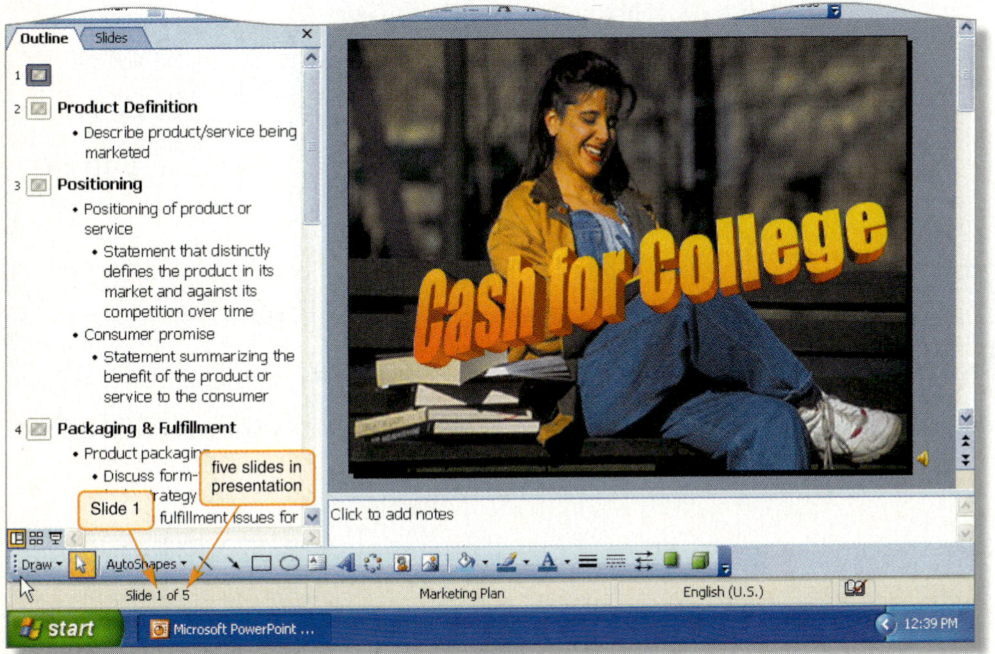

FIGURE 4-28

You now should save the presentation again because you inserted a picture to create a custom background, deleted the title and subtitle text placeholders and replaced them with a WordArt object, and deleted several slides.

The next steps will change the content and graphics on individual slides.

Adding a Chart to a Slide

More About

Automatic File Recovery

PowerPoint saves a copy of your presentation every 10 minutes by default. To change this save interval, click the Options command on the Tools menu and then click the Save tab. Click the Save AutoRecover info every check box, and then specify in the minutes box how frequently you want PowerPoint to save your file.

Financial aid counselors at Eastwood State College have surveyed neighboring institutions to determine the tuition and fees charges. The chart on Slide 2 shows the average total tuition and fees expenses for full-time students attending area two-year and four-year public colleges and four-year private colleges. The findings denote that students at public community colleges generally spend less than $2,000 yearly for their education, and students at four-year public schools spend twice that amount. In contrast, students at nearby private colleges are incurring approximately $18,000 in tuition and fees expenses. The costs at all three types of colleges have increased steadily during the past decade. You will build the chart on Slide 2, shown in Figure 4-29, directly within the PowerPoint presentation using the supplementary application called **Microsoft Graph**, which is installed automatically with PowerPoint.

When you start to create this tuition and fees chart, Microsoft Graph opens and displays a chart and associated data. The default Microsoft Graph chart style is a **3-D Column chart.** This style compares values across categories and across series. The 3-D Column chart is appropriate when comparing two or more items in specified intervals, such as in this Slide 2 chart depicting how college students have faced rising costs from 1995 to the present.

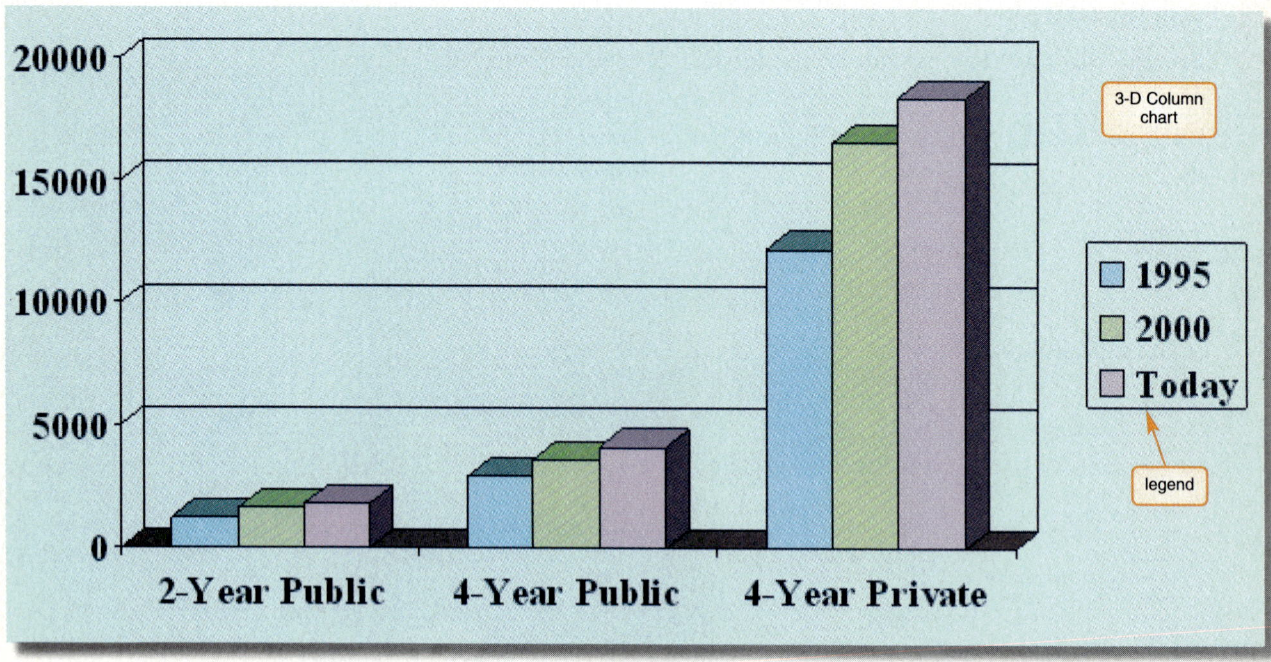

FIGURE 4-29

The figures for the chart are entered in a corresponding **datasheet**, which is a rectangular grid containing columns (vertical) and rows (horizontal). Column letters display above the grid to identify particular **columns**, and row numbers display on the left side of the grid to identify particular **rows. Cells** are the intersections of rows and columns, and they are the locations for the chart data and text labels. For example, cell A1 is the intersection of column A and row 1. Numeric and text data are entered in the **active cell**, which is the one cell surrounded by a heavy border. You will replace the sample data in the datasheet by typing entries in the cells, but you also can import data from a text file or Lotus 1-2-3 file, import a Microsoft Excel worksheet or chart, or paste data obtained in another program.

> *More About*
>
> **AutoNumber Bullets**
>
> PowerPoint's AutoNumber feature adds numbers to the beginning of each slide paragraph. To use this feature on all slides, display the slide master. Then, remove any bullets by pressing the BACKSPACE key. Type 1. (the number 1 and a period) or I) (the Roman numeral one and a closing parenthesis). When you press the ENTER key, PowerPoint will add the next consecutive number or Roman numeral.

Displaying the Next Slide and Editing the Title and Bulleted List Text

Before you create the 3-D Column chart, you first must display Slide 2 and edit the text generated by the AutoContent Wizard. The following steps describe these tasks.

To Display the Next Slide and Edit the Title and Bulleted List Text

1. **Click the Next Slide button to display Slide 2. Triple-click the title text, Product Definition. Type** `Average Tuition and Fees` **in the title text placeholder.**
2. **Triple-click the first first-level paragraph in the text placeholder.**
3. **Type** `College expenses are increasing at double the inflation rate` **as the new text.**

Slide 2 is displayed with the edited text (Figure 4-30).

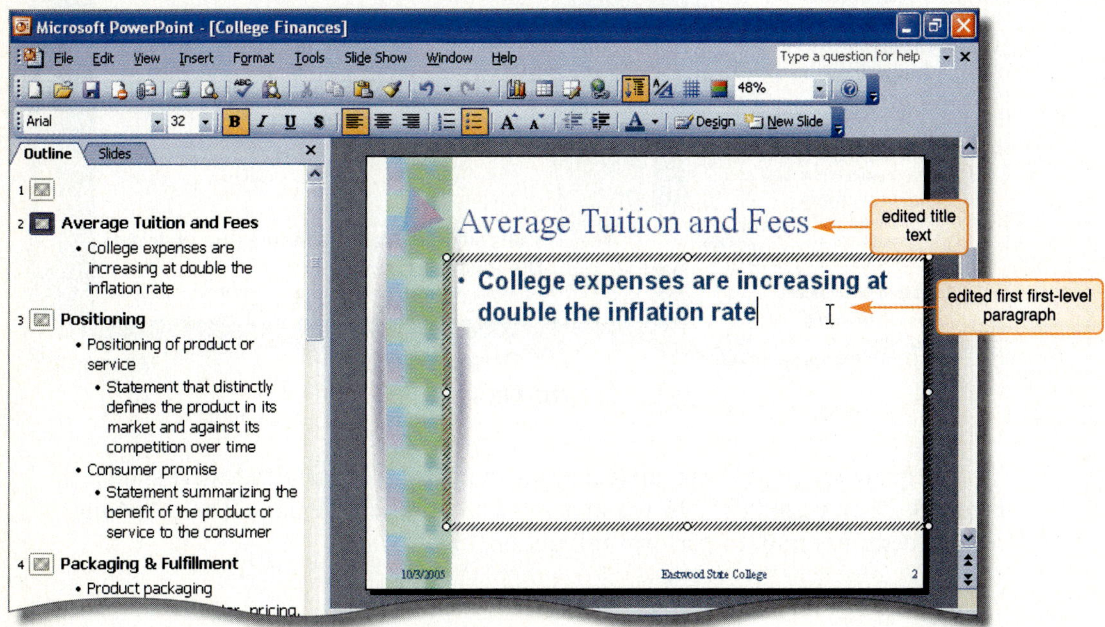

FIGURE 4-30

Changing the Slide Layout and Positioning the Text Placeholder

The next steps require changing the layout so the chart is displayed above the text placeholder and then positioning the text placeholder above the footer. The following steps describe this procedure.

To Change the Slide Layout and Position the Text Placeholder

1. **Click Format on the menu bar and then click Slide Layout.**
2. **Click the Title and Content over Text slide layout in the Text and Content Layouts area in the Slide Layout task pane.**
3. **Click the Close button in the Slide Layout task pane.**
4. **Click the text placeholder border. Drag the middle sizing handle on the bottom edge of the text placeholder up until it is below the paragraph.**
5. **Drag the text placeholder down until it is displayed above the footer text. If the AutoFit Options smart tag is displayed, click it and then click Stop Fitting Text to This Placeholder.**

Slide 2 has the desired Title and Content over Text slide layout. The text placeholder is displayed in the desired position (Figure 4-31).

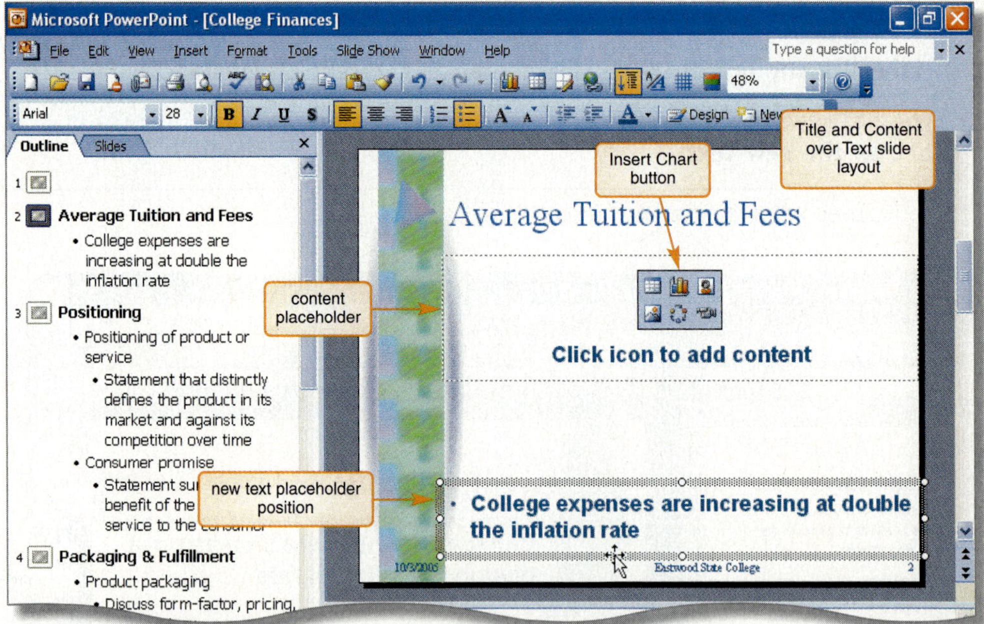

FIGURE 4-31

Adequate space has been allocated for the chart. Creating the chart shown in Figure 4-29 on page PPT 246 requires replacing the sample data. The following section describes how to perform this action.

Inserting a Chart and Replacing the Sample Data

Microsoft Graph provides sample data to create the default chart. You need to change these figures to the numbers representing the costs at area two-year public, four-year public, and four-year private colleges in 1995, in 2000, and today. Table 4-2 summarizes the survey data. Each column represents the tuition and fees at these higher education institutions in three specific years. The numbers are entered into rows 1 through 3, and the titles are entered above the data rows in columns A, B, and C. The legend titles are entered in the first column. The chart **legend** identifies each bar in the chart. In this case, the aqua bar identifies the 1st quarter results, the pink bar identifies the 2nd quarter, and the purple bar identifies the 3rd quarter. The sample data is displayed in four columns; the tuition and fees chart requires only three categories: two-year public, four-year public, and four-year private. You therefore need to delete one column of sample data. The following steps describe how to replace the sample data.

Q&A

Q: Can I add more rows and columns to the datasheet?

A: Yes. The Microsoft Graph sample datasheet displays five rows and six columns. To display additional rows and columns, click the scroll boxes and scroll arrows. Drag the window corner in the lower-right corner of the datasheet to increase the datasheet size.

Table 4-2 Tuition and Fees Survey Data

	2-Year Public	4-Year Public	4-Year Private
1995	1234	2901	12224
2000	1624	3592	16542
Today	1802	4125	18352

To Insert a Chart and Replace the Sample Data

1

- **Click the Insert Chart button in the content placeholder.**
- **Right-click the letter D at the top of column D in the datasheet and then point to Clear Contents on the shortcut menu.**

Microsoft Graph displays the sample datasheet and chart (Figure 4-32). The cells in column D are selected.

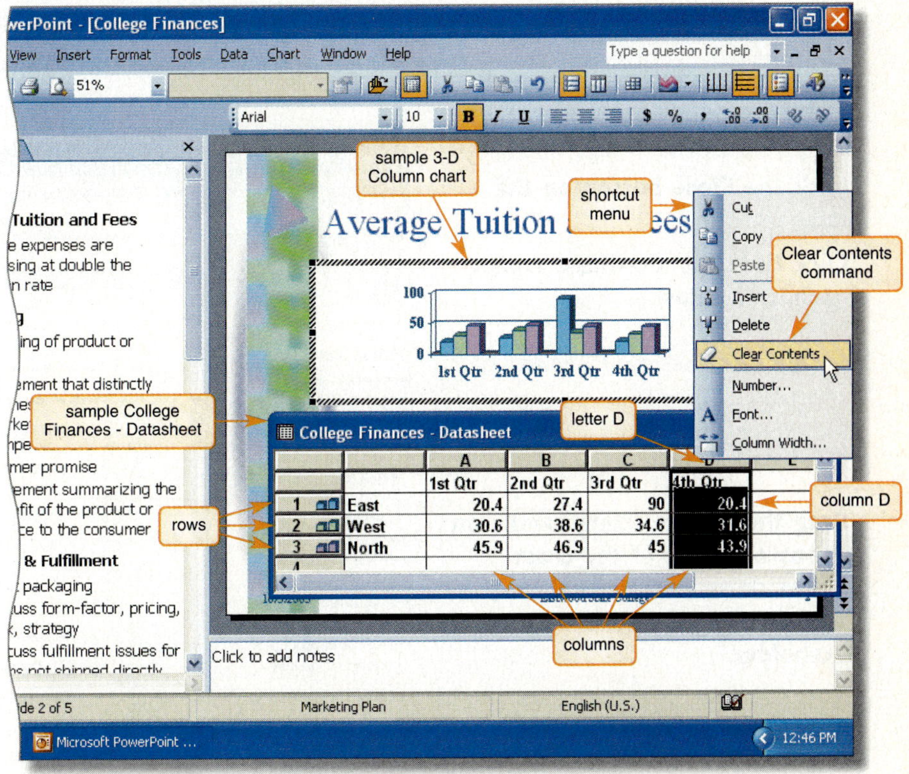

FIGURE 4-32

2

- **Click Clear Contents.**
- **Click cell A1, which is the intersection of column A and row 1.**

Cell A1 is selected (Figure 4-33). The mouse pointer changes to a block plus sign.

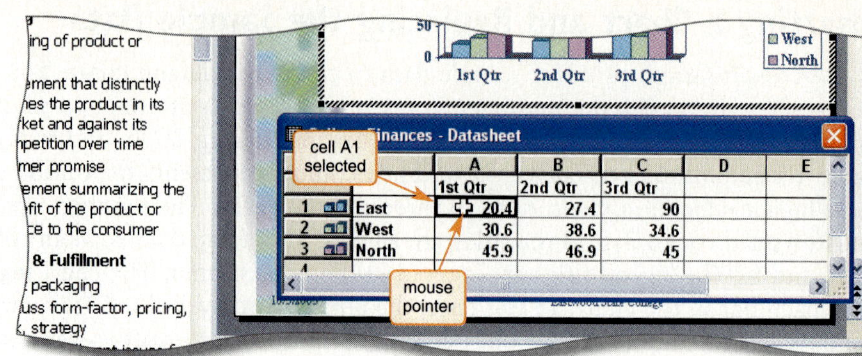

FIGURE 4-33

3

- **Type** 1234 **in cell A1 and then press the RIGHT ARROW key.**
- **Enter the remaining figures and data labels by using Table 4-2 on the previous page as a guide.**

As you type these figures and data labels in the datasheet, they modify the chart (Figure 4-34).

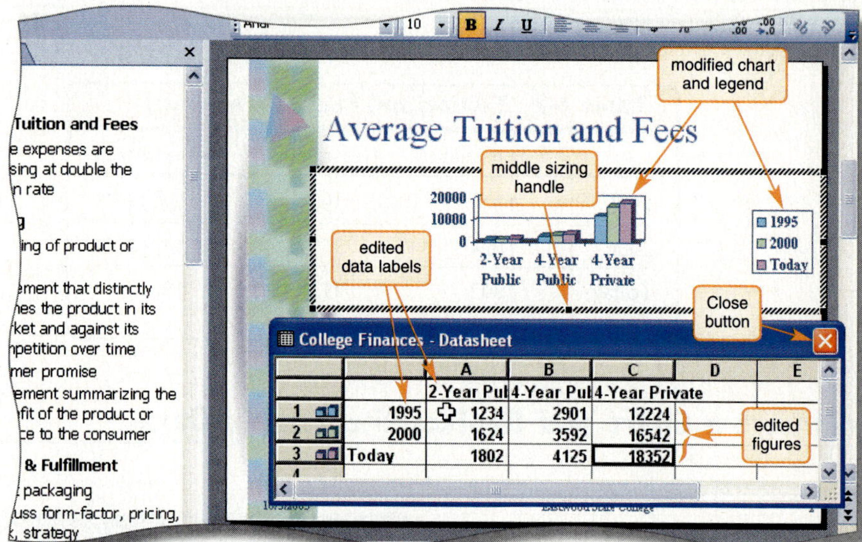

FIGURE 4-34

4

- **Click the Close button on the datasheet.**
- **Click the slide anywhere except the chart window.**

The datasheet closes and the revised chart and legend display.

5

- **Drag the middle sizing handle on the bottom edge of the chart window down until it is above the bulleted paragraph in the text placeholder.**

The chart and legend display in the desired location on Slide 2 (Figure 4-35).

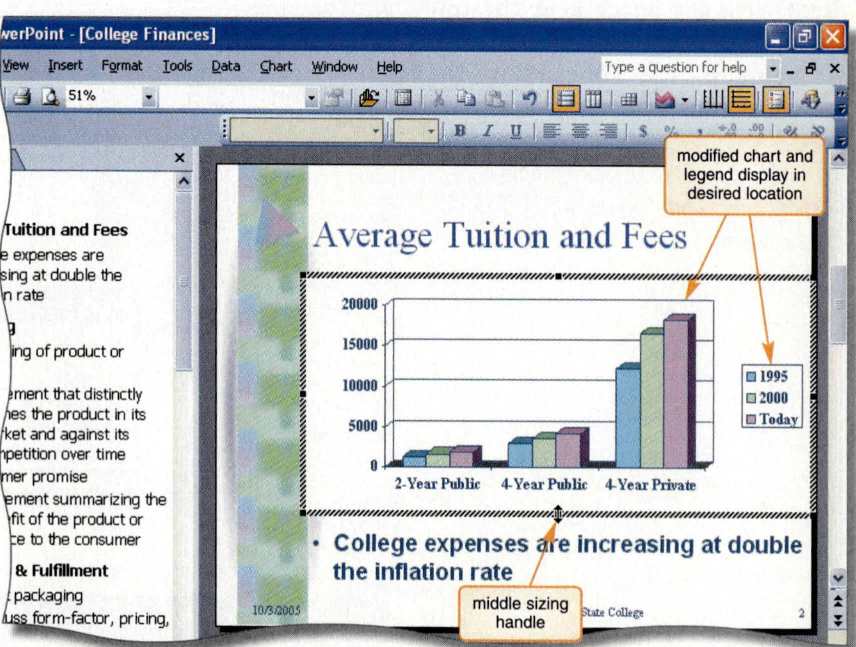

FIGURE 4-35

The tuition and fees data has been entered in the Microsoft Graph datasheet. The three categories surveyed — two-year public, four-year public, and four-year private — display. Slide 2 is complete. You should save the presentation by clicking the Save button on the Standard toolbar.

The next slide in the presentation also will have a chart. Unlike the chart you just created using Microsoft Graph, this chart was created in Microsoft Excel. You will insert this chart into Slide 3. This graphic depicts the percentages of the four categories of college expenses: tuition, fees, books and supplies, and other.

Other Ways

1. On Insert menu click Chart, click column D, on Edit menu point to Clear, click All, enter data, on View menu click Datasheet
2. Press ALT+I, press H, click column D, press ALT+E, press A, press A, enter data, press ALT+V, press D
3. In Voice Command mode, say "Insert, Chart, [click column D], Edit, Clear, All, [enter data], View, Datasheet"

Inserting an Excel Chart

Tuition accounts for nearly two-thirds of Eastwood State College students' academic expenses. Fees are another 10 percent of the bill, and books and supplies are 8 percent. Miscellaneous fees comprise the remaining 20 percent of the total expenses. The proportion of these expenses should be of interest to students and community residents attending the seminar, and a chart created in Microsoft Excel can depict these percentages. A **Clustered Bar chart** compares values across categories. Similarly, the college expenses chart shown in Figure 4-36 illustrates the proportion of tuition, fees, books and supplies, and other expenses.

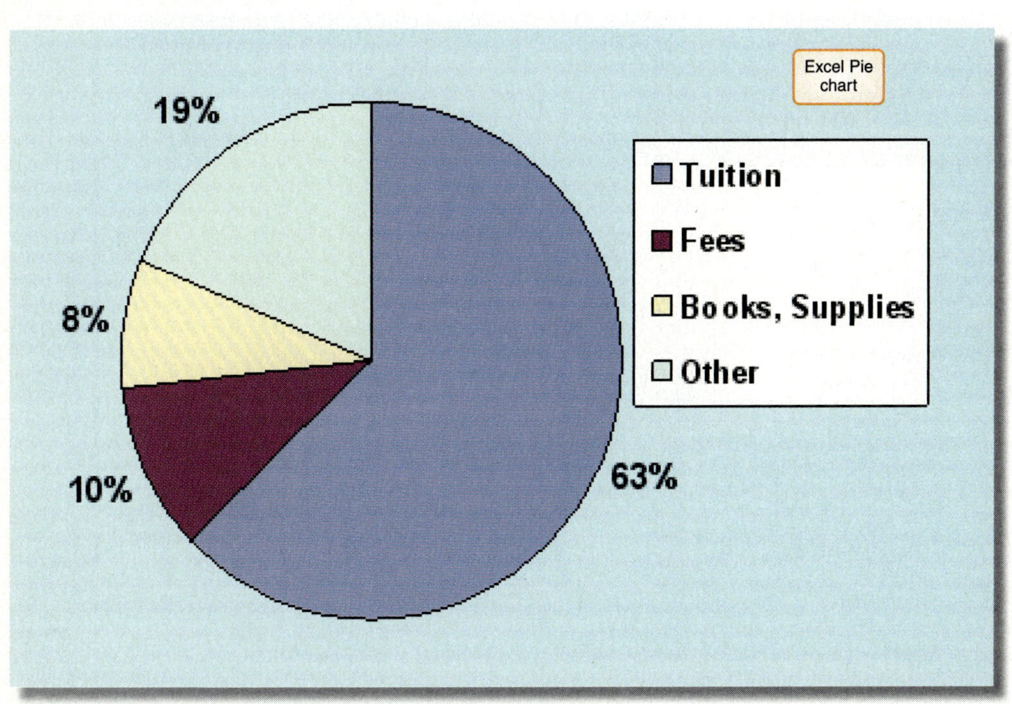

FIGURE 4-36

PowerPoint allows you to insert, or **embed**, many types of objects into a presentation. You inserted clips into slides in Projects 2 and 3, and you will embed a Microsoft Word table into Slide 4. Other objects you can embed include video clips, Microsoft PhotoDraw pictures, and Adobe Acrobat documents.

More About

Formatting Chart Text

You can format the font used for the legend and axes. To format the legend, right-click the legend, click Format Legend on the shortcut menu, click the Font tab, and then select Font attributes, such as font style, size, color, and effects. To format the axes, right-click on an axis, click Format Axis on the shortcut menu, click the Font tab, and then make the selections.

Displaying the Next Slide, Editing the Title Text, and Deleting the Text Placeholder

Before you insert the Excel chart from the Data Disk, you need to display the next slide, change the title text, and delete the text placeholder. The following steps describe how to display the slide, enter a title, and delete the text placeholder.

To Display the Next Slide, Edit the Title Text, and Delete the Text Placeholder

1. **Click the Next Slide button to display Slide 3.**
2. **Double-click the title text, Positioning. Type** `Costs of Attending College` **in the title text placeholder.**
3. **Click in the text placeholder. Click the text placeholder selection rectangle.**
4. **Press the DELETE key twice.**

Slide 3 is displayed with the new title text and deleted text placeholder (Figure 4-37).

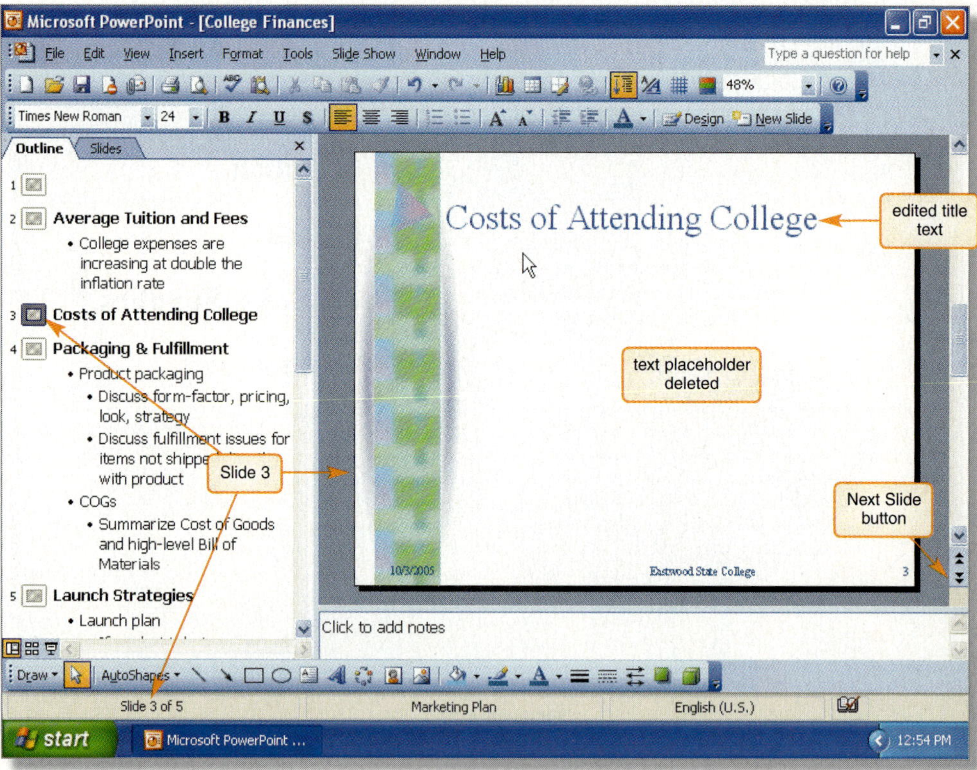

FIGURE 4-37

The slide title and a blank area for the Excel chart now are displayed in Slide 3. The next section explains how to insert this Excel chart.

Inserting an Excel Chart

The Clustered Bar chart on the Data Disk shows the proportion of expenses incurred while attending college. The following steps embed this chart.

To Insert an Excel Chart

1

- **Click Insert on the menu bar and then point to Object.**

The Insert menu is displayed (Figure 4-38). You want to insert the chart created in Microsoft Excel and saved on your Data Disk.

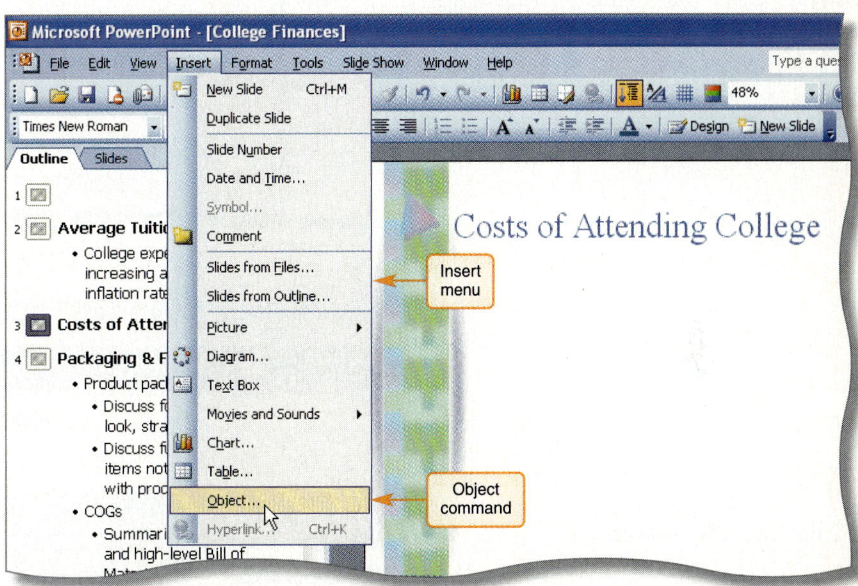

FIGURE 4-38

2

- **Click Object.**
- **When the Insert Object dialog box is displayed, click Create from file.**

The Insert Object dialog box is displayed (Figure 4-39). The Create from file option allows you to select an object created in another application or in PowerPoint.

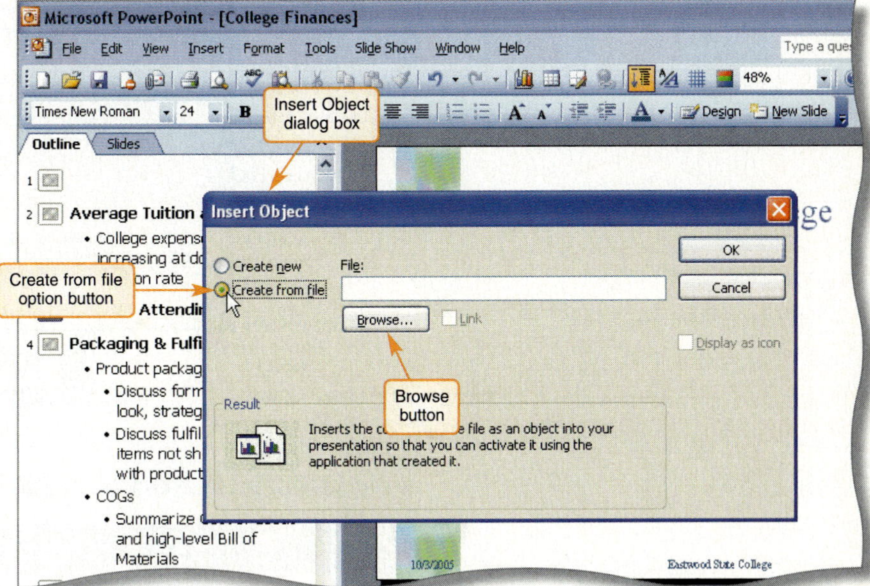

FIGURE 4-39

3

- **Click the Browse button.**
- **When the Browse dialog box is displayed, click the Look in box arrow and then click 3½ Floppy (A:).**
- **Click College Expenses in the Look in list.**

The Browse dialog box shows the files on the Data Disk (Figure 4-40). Your list of file names may vary. College Expenses is the Excel file you will insert into Slide 3.

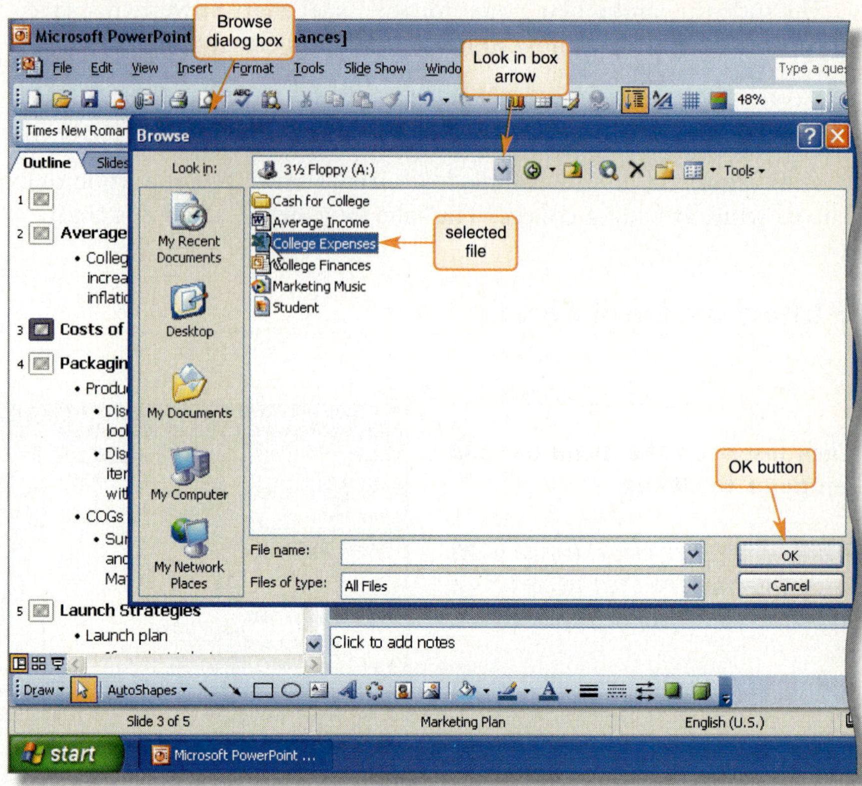

FIGURE 4-40

4

- **Click the OK button.**

The Insert Object dialog box now appears with A:\College Expenses.xls in the File text box (Figure 4-41). The .xls extension indicates the file is a Microsoft Excel file.

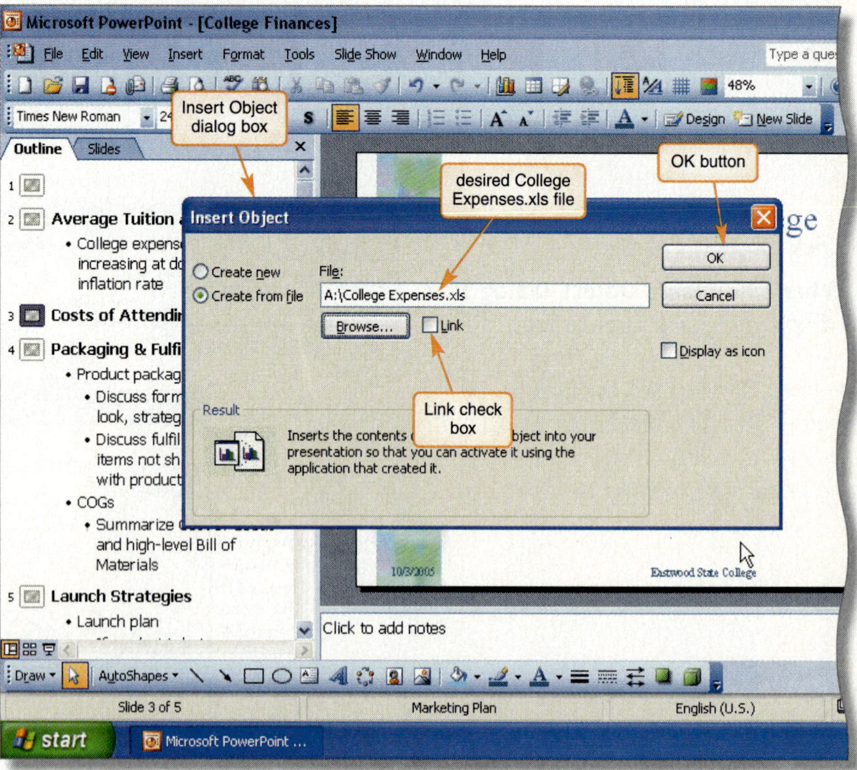

FIGURE 4-41

5

- **When the Insert Object dialog box is redisplayed, click the OK button.**

Slide 3 includes the College Expenses chart (Figure 4-42).

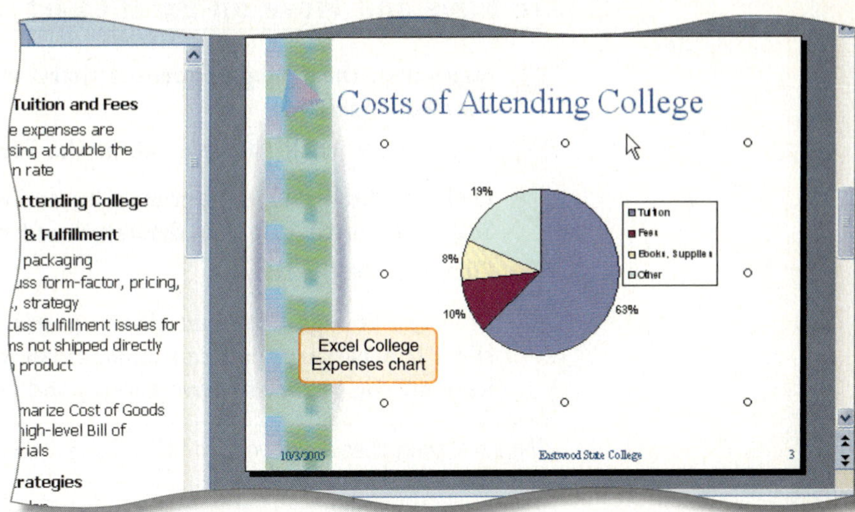

FIGURE 4-42

Other Ways

1. On Insert menu click Object, click Create from file, type file name, click OK button
2. Press ALT+I, press O, press ALT+F, type file name, click OK button
3. In Voice Command mode, say "Insert, Object, Create from file, [type file name], OK"

When you click the Create from file option button in the Insert Object dialog box, the dialog box changes. The File box replaces the Object type box. Another change to the dialog box is the addition of the Link check box. If the **Link check box** is selected, the object is inserted as a linked, instead of an embedded, object. Similar to an embedded object, a **linked object** also is created in another application; however, the linked object maintains a connection to its source. If the original object is changed, the linked object on the slide also changes. The linked object is stored in the **source file**, the file in which the object was created.

For example, the Excel chart you embedded into the slide is stored on the Data Disk. If you were to link rather than embed the College Expenses file, then every time the College Expenses file changes in Excel, the changes would display on the chart in Slide 3. Your PowerPoint presentation would store a representation of the original College Expenses file and information about its location. If you later moved or deleted the source file, the link would be broken, and the object would not be available. Consequently, if you make a presentation on a computer other than the one on which the presentation was created and the presentation contains a linked object, be certain to include a copy of the source files. The source files must be stored in the exact location as originally specified when you linked them to your presentation.

When you select a source file from the Browse dialog box, PowerPoint associates the file with a specific application, which is based on the file extension. For example, if you select a source file with the file extension **.doc**, PowerPoint recognizes the file as a Microsoft Word file. Additionally, if you select a source file with the file extension **.xls**, PowerPoint recognizes the file as a Microsoft Excel file.

Q&A

Q: Can I edit an Excel chart?

A: Yes. If you want to change the chart that you imported into your slide, double-click the chart, use the Excel tools and menus to modify the chart, and then click outside the chart to return to PowerPoint.

Scaling and Moving an Excel Chart

Sufficient space exists on Slide 3 to enlarge the chart. The steps on the next page scale the chart object.

To Scale and Move an Excel Chart

1. **Right-click the College Expenses chart and then click Format Object on the shortcut menu.**
2. **If necessary, click the Size tab in the Format Object dialog box.**
3. **Click and hold down the mouse button on the Height box up arrow in the Scale area until 110 % is displayed and then release the mouse button.**
4. **Click the OK button.**
5. **Drag the College Expenses chart up and to the left so it is centered on the slide. If necessary, you can make small adjustments by pressing the arrow keys on the keyboard that correspond to the direction in which to move.**

The Excel chart is enlarged and moved to the desired position (Figure 4-43).

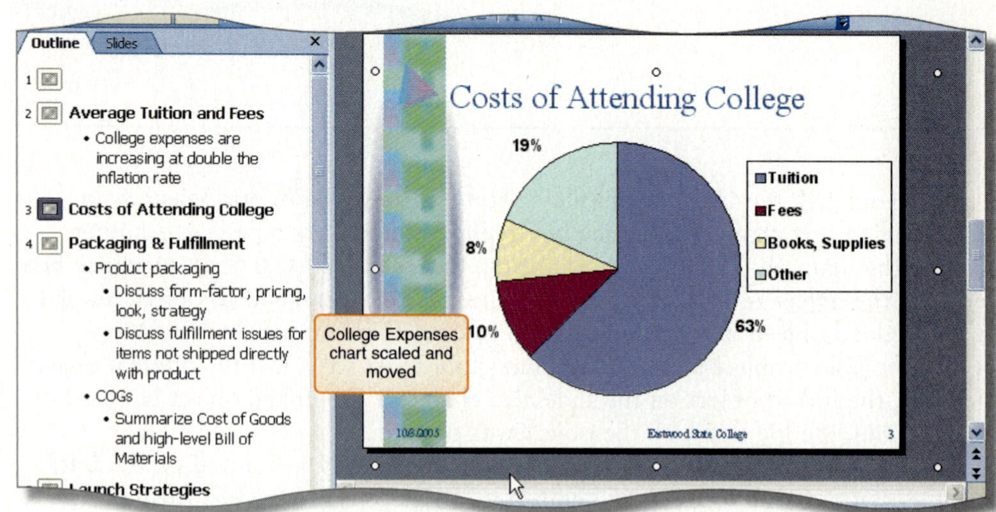

FIGURE 4-43

Other Ways

1. On Format menu click Object, click Size tab, click Scale Height box up arrow to display desired height, click OK button
2. Press ALT+O, press O, if necessary press RIGHT ARROW key, press ALT+H, press UP ARROW key to display desired height, press ENTER
3. In Voice Command mode, say "Format, Object, Height, [type height], OK"

Slide 3 now is complete. Again, because you have changed the presentation significantly, save the slide show by clicking the Save button on the Standard toolbar. The next slide also will have a graphic, and it will show the average salary Eastwood State College community residents have earned since 1975 based on the amount of education they have completed.

Adding a Table from Word

The College Finances presentation now shows how community members' salaries have increased since 1975 based on their education levels. Figure 4-44 shows a Microsoft Word table that lists the yearly income earned by high school graduates, community residents who have earned only an associate's degree, and residents with a bachelor's degree. Eastwood State College administrators have been tracking these numbers since 1975. The Average Income file was created using Microsoft Word and enhanced with Word's Table AutoFormat feature. PowerPoint allows you to embed this table into a presentation. The same steps used to insert the Excel College Expenses chart into a slide are used to insert a Microsoft Word table. In the following sections, you will display the next slide, edit the title text, and insert the Word table from the Data Disk.

Year	High School	Associate's Degree	**Bachelor's Degree**
1975	7,814	8,245	12,401
1980	11,444	12,494	18,102
1985	14,386	16,354	24,893
1990	17,530	20,703	31,132
1995	21,643	23,863	36,891
2000	25,995	29,984	49,732
Today	27,103	31,309	51,693

Word Average Income table

FIGURE 4-44

Displaying the Next Slide, Editing the Title Text, and Changing the Slide Layout

Before you insert the Word table, you need to display the next slide, edit the slide title text, and change the slide layout.

To Display the Next Slide, Edit the Title Text, and Change the Slide Layout

1. **Click the Next Slide button to display Slide 4.**
2. **Triple-click the title text, Packaging & Fulfillment. Type** `Average Income by Degree` **in the title text placeholder.**
3. **Click in the text placeholder. Click the text placeholder selection rectangle.**
4. **Press the DELETE key twice.**

Slide 4 has a new title and the desired Title Only slide layout (Figure 4-45).

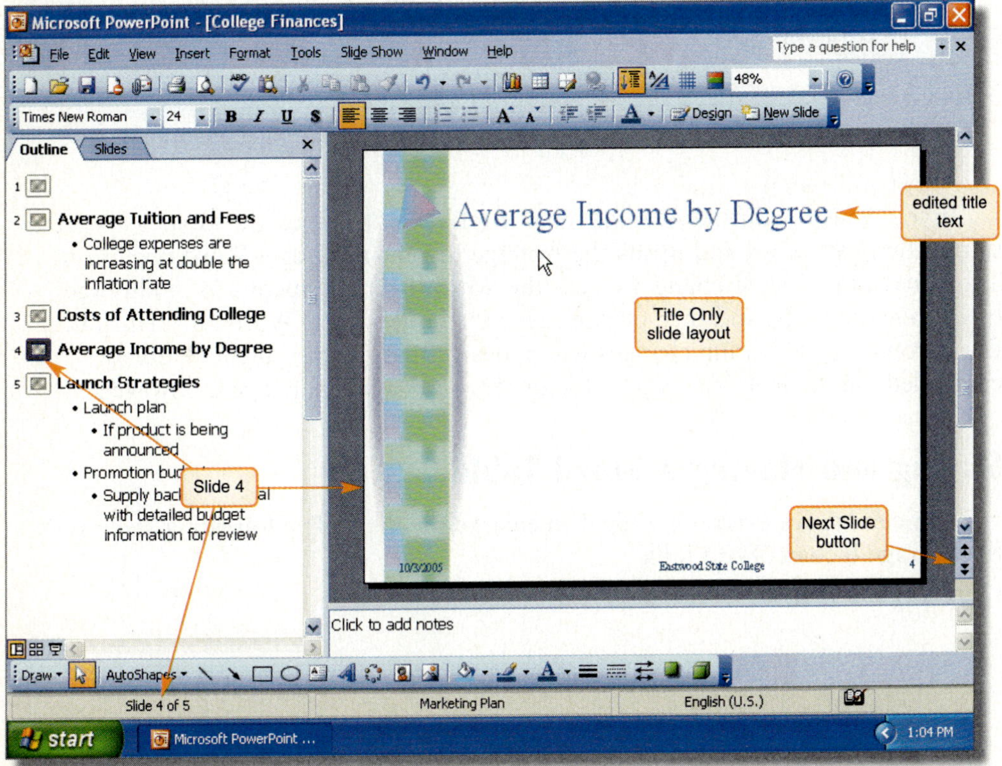

FIGURE 4-45

Inserting a Word Table

Slide 4 now appears with the slide title and a blank area for the Average Income table. The following steps explain how to insert this Word table, which has the file name Average Income.doc.

To Insert a Word Table

1. **Click Insert on the menu bar and then click Object.**
2. **When the Insert Object dialog box is displayed, click Create from file. Click the Browse button.**
3. **When the Browse dialog box is displayed, click the Look in box arrow and then click 3½ Floppy (A:). Click Average Income in the Look in list. Click the OK button.**
4. **When the Insert Object dialog box is displayed, click the OK button.**

Slide 4 appears with the Average Income table (Figure 4-46).

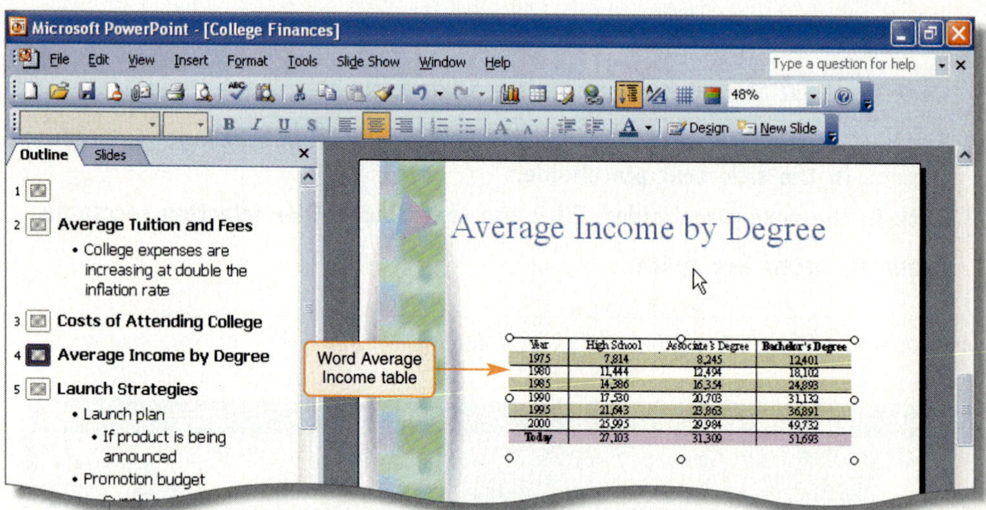

FIGURE 4-46

> **Other Ways**
>
> 1. Press ALT+I, press O, press ALT+F, type file name, press ENTER
> 2. In Voice Command mode, say, "Insert, Object, Create from file, [type file name], OK"

If you want to edit the Average Income table, double-click the table. This action starts Microsoft Word and opens the Average Income table as a Word document. Then, make the desired changes or use the Word tools and menus to modify the table, save the table, and then click outside the table to quit Word and return to PowerPoint. These editing changes will appear in the Average Income table embedded into Slide 4. The source file in Word remains unchanged, however.

Scaling and Moving a Word Table

Sufficient space exists on Slide 4 to enlarge the table. The following steps scale the Average Income Word table.

To Scale and Move a Word Table

1. **Right-click the Average Income table and then click Format Object on the shortcut menu.**
2. **If necessary, click the Size tab in the Format Object dialog box.**
3. **Click and hold down the mouse button on the Height box up arrow in the Scale area until 160 % is displayed and then release the mouse button.**
4. **Click the OK button.**
5. **Drag the Average Income table up and to the left so it is centered on the slide. If necessary, you can make small adjustments by pressing the arrow keys on the keyboard that correspond to the direction in which to move.**

The Average Income table is enlarged and moved to the desired position (Figure 4-47).

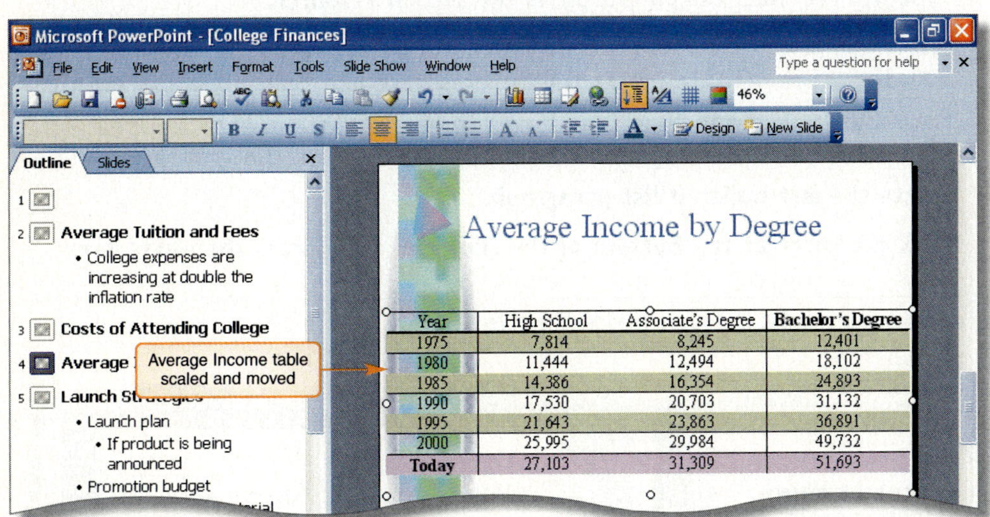

Year	High School	Associate's Degree	Bachelor's Degree
1975	7,814	8,245	12,401
1980	11,444	12,494	18,102
1985	14,386	16,354	24,893
1990	17,530	20,703	31,132
1995	21,643	23,863	36,891
2000	25,995	29,984	49,732
Today	27,103	31,309	51,693

FIGURE 4-47

Slide 4 is complete, so you should save the slide show by clicking the Save button on the Standard toolbar. The College Finances presentation informs Eastwood State College seminar attendees viewing the slide show about the need to save for the various college expenses. The final slide in the presentation will give information on locating additional information on financial topics.

Other Ways

1. On Format menu click Object, if necessary click Size tab, click Scale Height box up arrow to display desired height, click OK button
2. Press ALT+O, press O, if necessary press RIGHT ARROW KEY, press ALT+H, press UP ARROW key to display desired height, press ENTER
3. In Voice Command mode, say "Format, Object, Height, [type height], OK"

Adding Hyperlinks

Slide 5 in the College Finances slide show presents resources for additional information. Eastwood State College audience members can refer to these sources to learn more about the topics presented in the slide show or to obtain specific information that would benefit them personally.

Part of this slide will contain hyperlinks. A **hyperlink**, also called a **link**, is a connection from one slide to a Web page, another slide, a custom show consisting of specific slides in a presentation, or a file. Hyperlinks can be text or an object, such as a picture, graph, shape, or WordArt. On Slide 5, the text hyperlinks will be **absolute links** because they will specify the exact location of a page on the World Wide Web. This location is encoded as a **Uniform Resource Locator** (**URL**), also called a **Web address**. The following sections explain how to create the hyperlinks.

Displaying the Next Slide and Editing the Text

Before you create the hyperlinks to the World Wide Web, you need to display the next slide and edit the slide text.

To Display the Next Slide and Edit the Text

1. **Click the Next Slide button to display Slide 5.**
2. **Triple-click the title text, Launch Strategies. Type** `College Financial Assets` **in the title text placeholder.**
3. **Triple-click the first bullet text paragraph in the text placeholder. Type** `Obtain additional information from` **and then press the ENTER key.**
4. **Press the TAB key. Type** `The College Board` **and then press the ENTER key.**
5. **Type** `Nellie Mae Corporation` **as the second resource.**
6. **Select and then delete the second first-level paragraph. Type** `Consider scholarships and loans` **as the bulleted text and then press the ENTER key.**
7. **Press the TAB key and then type** `More than 75% of public-college students receive financial aid` **but do not press the ENTER key.**
8. **Delete the last bulleted list paragraph.**
9. **Click the chart at the bottom of the slide and then press the DELETE key.**

The edited bulleted list is displayed in Slide 5 (Figure 4-48).

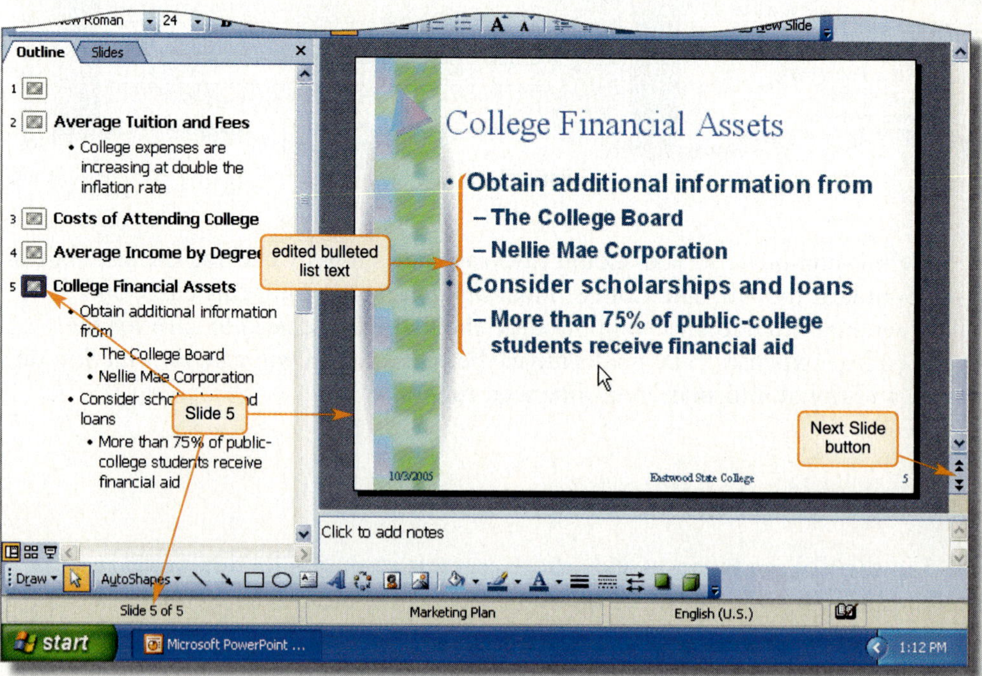

FIGURE 4-48

All editing changes are complete. The next step is to create hyperlinks for the two second-level paragraphs to receive additional information.

Other Ways

1. In Dictation mode, say "Obtain additional information from, New Line, Tab, The College Board, New Line, Nellie Mae Corporation, New Line, [press BACKSPACE], Consider scholarships and loans, New Line, Tab, More than 75% of public-college students receive financial aid"

Adding a Hyperlink to a Slide

Each of the first two second-level paragraphs will be a hyperlink to an organization's Web page. If you are connected to the Internet when you run your presentation, you can click a hyperlink, and your default Web browser will access the URL you specified. The following steps describe how to create the first hyperlink.

To Add a Hyperlink to a Slide

1

- **Triple-click the first second-level paragraph, The College Board.**
- **Click the Insert Hyperlink button on the Standard toolbar.**

The Insert Hyperlink dialog box is displayed (Figure 4-49). The first second-level paragraph is selected.

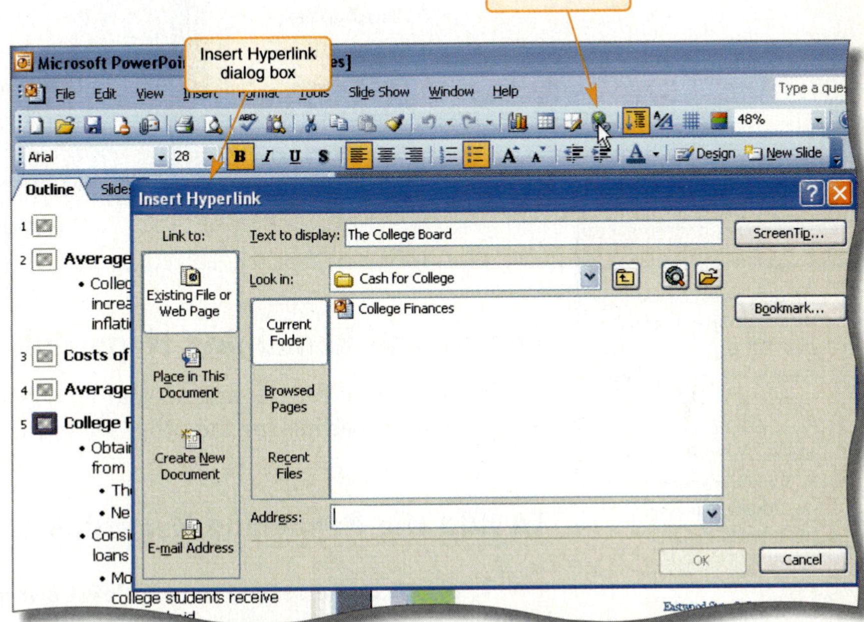

FIGURE 4-49

2

- **If necessary, click the Existing File or Web Page button on the Link to bar.**
- **Type** `www.collegeboard.com` **in the Address text box.**

The URL for The College Board hyperlink text is http://www.collegeboard.com (Figure 4-50). PowerPoint automatically appends the http:// to the URL.

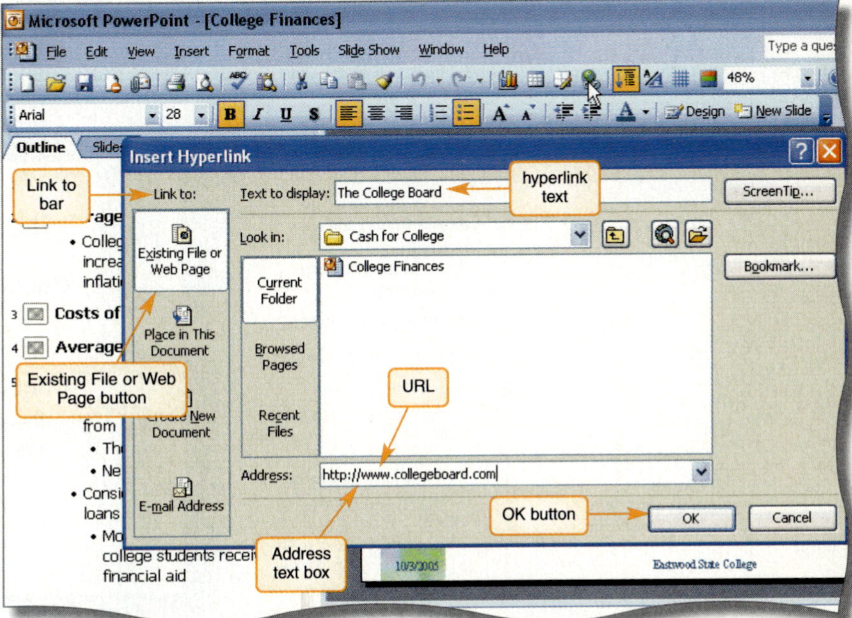

FIGURE 4-50

3

• **Click the OK button.**

• **Click Slide 5 anywhere except the text placeholder.**

The College Board hyperlink text is underlined and has the font color light purple (Figure 4-51).

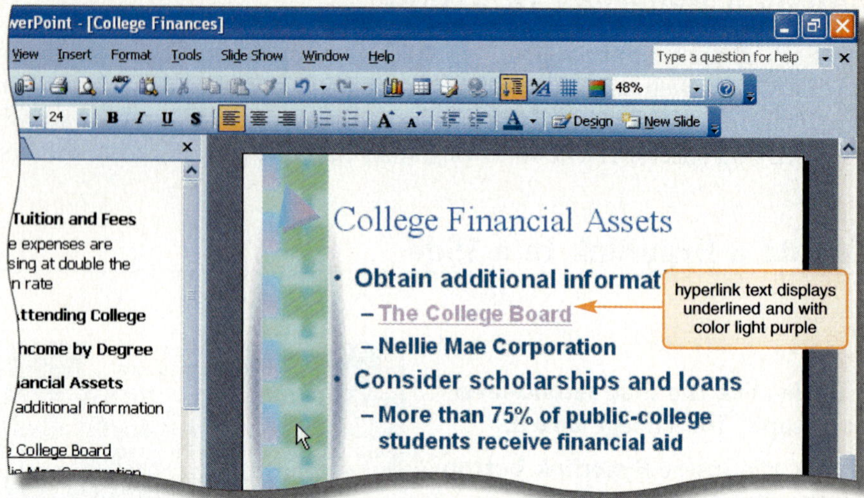

FIGURE 4-51

Other Ways

1. On Insert menu click Hyperlink, type address, click OK button
2. Press ALT+I, press I, press ENTER
3. Press CTRL+K, type address, press ENTER
4. In Voice Command mode, say "Insert Hyperlink, [type address], OK"

Adding the Remaining Hyperlink to the Slide

The hyperlink for the first second-level paragraph is complete. The next task is to create the hyperlink for the other second-level paragraph on Slide 5.

To Add the Remaining Hyperlink to a Slide

1. **Triple-click the second second-level paragraph, Nellie Mae Corporation.**
2. **Click the Insert Hyperlink button and then type** `www.nelliemae.org` **in the Address text box. Click the OK button.**
3. **Click Slide 5 anywhere except the text placeholder.**

The hyperlink for the second second-level paragraph is added (Figure 4-52).

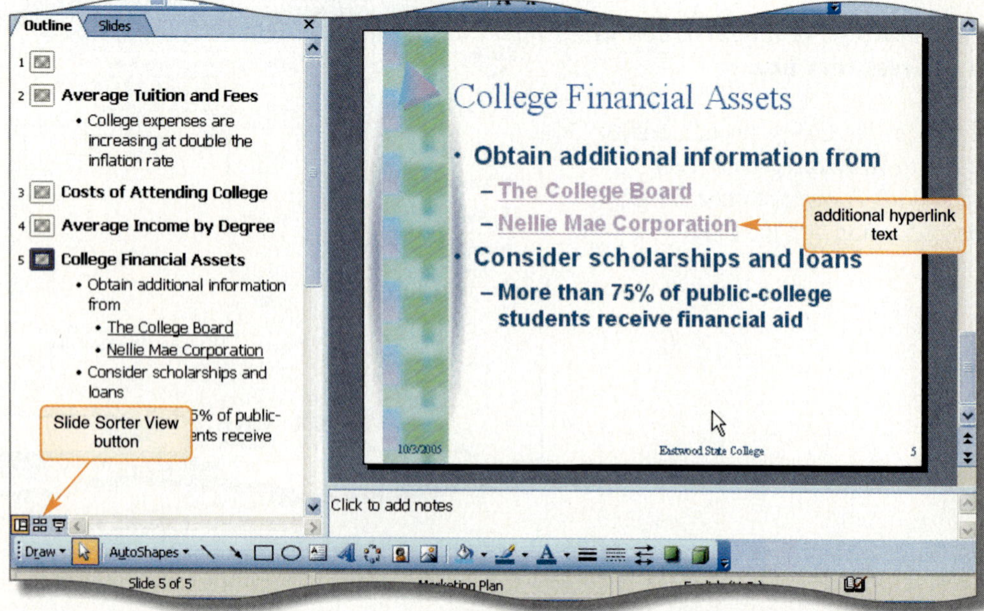

FIGURE 4-52

When you point to a hyperlink, the pointer becomes the shape of a hand to indicate it is something you can click. Hyperlinked text displays underlined and in a color that is part of the color scheme. Pictures, shapes, and objects also can serve as hyperlinks.

Hyperlinks are active only when you run the presentation, not when you are creating it in normal or slide sorter view. If you are connected to the Internet when you run the presentation, you will click each of the two second-level paragraphs. Your browser will display the corresponding Web page for each paragraph.

More About

Removing Hyperlinks

If you decide you no longer want a hyperlink in your presentation but you want to keep the text or object that represents the hyperlink, right-click the text or object and then click Remove Hyperlink on the shortcut menu. If you want to delete the hyperlink and the corresponding text or object, select the text or object and then press the DELETE key.

Revising and Customizing Individual Slides

The text for all five slides in the College Finances presentation has been entered. Once you complete a slide show, you might decide to change elements. PowerPoint provides several tools to assist you with making changes. The following pages discuss these tools.

Hiding Slides

Slides 2, 3, and 4 present technical information in graphical form. Depending on the audience's needs and the time constraints, you may decide not to display Slide 5 because it is a supporting slide. A supporting slide provides detailed information to supplement another slide in the presentation. For example, in a presentation to academic deans about the increase in student enrollment, one slide displays a graph representing the current year's enrollment and the previous three years' enrollment figures. A supporting slide might display a table showing each department's enrollment figures for every year in the graph.

When running a slide show, you may not want to display the supporting slide. You would want to display it when time permits and when you want to show the audience more details about a topic. You should insert the supporting slide after the slide you anticipate may warrant more detail. Then, you use the Hide Slide command to hide the supporting slide. The Hide Slide command hides the supporting slide from the audience during the normal running of a slide show. When you want to display the supporting hidden slide, press the H key. No visible indicator displays to show that a hidden slide exists. You must be aware of the content of the presentation to know where the supporting slide is located.

Slide 5 is a slide that supports information presented in the entire presentation. If time permits, or if the audience requires more information, you can display Slide 5. As the presenter, you decide whether to show Slide 5. You hide a slide in slide sorter view so you can see the slashed square surrounding the slide number, which indicates a slide is hidden. The steps on the next page hide Slide 5.

More About

Closing Slides

When you have created your final slide, review all the slides in slide sorter view to see if each slide fits the slide show theme. Some PowerPoint experts recommend starting to design a slide show by developing the closing slide first. Knowing how you want the slide show to end helps you focus on reaching this conclusion. You can create each slide in the presentation with this goal in mind. To learn more about developing presentations, visit the PowerPoint 2003 More About Web page (`scsite.com/ppt2003/more`) and click Developing.

To Hide a Slide

1

- **Click the Slide Sorter View button at the lower left of the PowerPoint window.**
- **Right-click Slide 5 and then point to Hide Slide on the shortcut menu.**

The shortcut menu is displayed in Slide Sorter view (Figure 4-53).

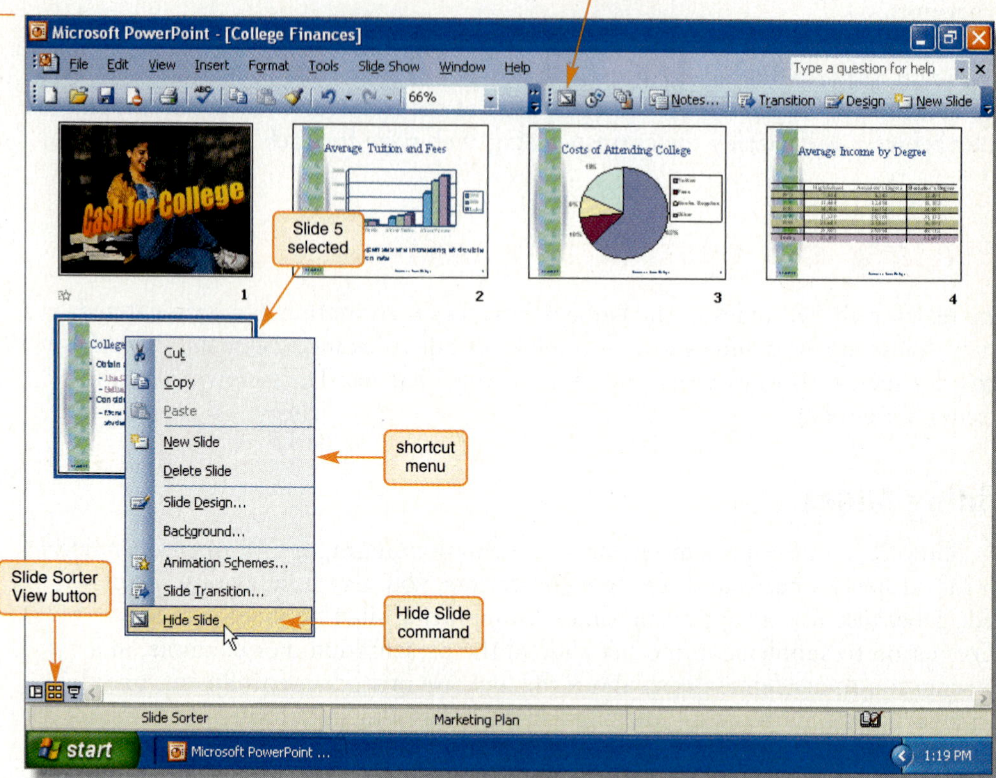

FIGURE 4-53

2

- **Click Hide Slide.**

A square with a slash surrounds the slide number to indicate Slide 5 is a hidden slide (Figure 4-54). The Hide Slide button is selected on the Slide Sorter toolbar.

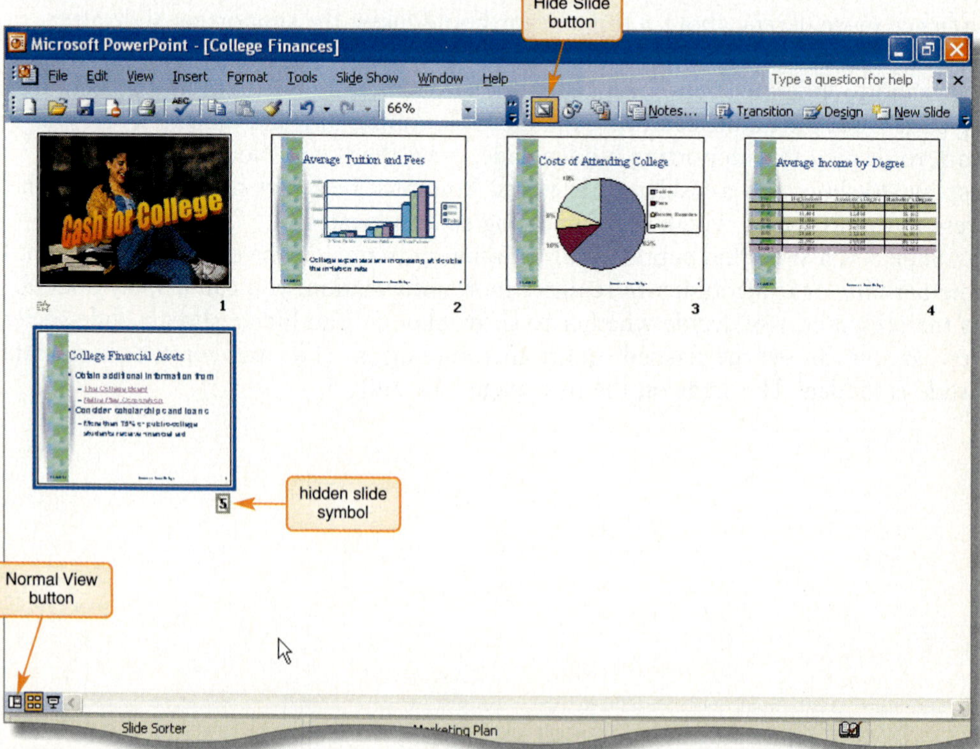

FIGURE 4-54

The Hide Slide button is a toggle — it either hides or displays a slide. The button also applies or removes a square with a slash surrounding the slide number. When you no longer want to hide a slide, change view to slide sorter view, right-click the slide, and then click Hide Slide on the shortcut menu. This action removes the square with the slash surrounding the slide number.

An alternative to hiding a slide in slide sorter view is to hide a slide in normal view. In this view, however, no visible indication is given that the slide is hidden. To hide a slide in normal view, display the slide you want to hide, click Slide Show on the menu bar, and then click Hide Slide.

When you run your presentation, the hidden slide does not display unless you press the H key when the slide preceding the hidden slide is displaying. For example, Slide 5 does not display unless you press the H key when Slide 4 is displayed in slide show view. You continue your presentation by clicking the mouse or pressing any of the keys associated with running a slide show. You skip the hidden slide by clicking the mouse and advancing to the next slide.

Other Ways

1. Click Hide Slide button on Slide Sorter toolbar
2. On Slide Show menu click Hide Slide
3. Press ALT+D, press H
4. In Voice Command mode, say "Slide Show, Hide Slide"

Finding Text

If you want to find a particular word on a slide, you can use PowerPoint's Find feature, which automatically locates each occurrence of a word or phrase. To search for a word, you would follow these steps.

To Find Text

1. **Click Edit on the menu bar and then click Find on the Edit menu.**
2. **Type the text to locate in the Find what text box and then click the Find Next button. To find the next occurrence of the text, click the Find Next button.**

Other Ways

1. Press CTRL+F
2. Press ALT+E, press F
3. In Voice Command mode, say "Edit, Find"

Finding and Replacing Text

If you want to change all occurrences of a particular word or phrase throughout the slide show, you can use PowerPoint's Find and Replace feature. This function locates each desired word or phrase and then replaces it with specified text. To find and replace a word or phrase, you would follow these steps.

To Find and Replace Text

1. **Click Edit on the menu bar and then click Replace on the Edit menu.**
2. **Type the text to locate in the Find what text box. Type the replacement text in the Replace with box. Click the Find Next button.**
3. **To replace all occurrences of the word or phrase, click the Replace All button.**

You occasionally might want to replace only certain occurrences of the word or phrase, not all of them. To instruct PowerPoint to confirm each change, click the Find Next button in the Replace dialog box instead of the Replace all button. When PowerPoint locates an occurrence of the text, it pauses and waits for you to click either the Replace button or the Find Next button. Clicking the Replace button changes the text; clicking the Find Next button instructs PowerPoint to disregard the replacement and look for the next occurrence of the Find what text.

If you accidentally replace the wrong text, you can undo a replacement by clicking the Undo button on the Standard toolbar. If you used the Replace All button, Word undoes all replacements. If you used the Replace button, Word undoes only the most recent replacement.

Other Ways

1. On Edit menu click Find, type Find what text, click Replace button, type Replace with text
2. Press CTRL+H
3. Press ALT+E, press E
4. In Voice Command mode, say "Edit, Replace"

Using the Thesaurus

When reviewing your slide show, you may decide that a particular word does not express the exact usage you intended or that you used the same word on multiple slides. In these cases, you could find a **synonym**, or word similar in meaning, to replace the inappropriate or duplicate word. PowerPoint provides a **thesaurus**, which is a list of synonyms, to help you find a replacement word.

In this project, you want to find synonyms to replace the word, Costs, on Slide 3 and the word, Income, on Slide 4. The following steps locate appropriate synonyms.

To Find a Word and Use the Thesaurus

1

- **Click the Normal View button at the lower left of the PowerPoint window.**
- **Click Edit on the menu bar and then click Find.**
- **When the Find dialog box is displayed, type** `Costs` **in the Find what box.**

PowerPoint displays the Find dialog box (Figure 4-55).

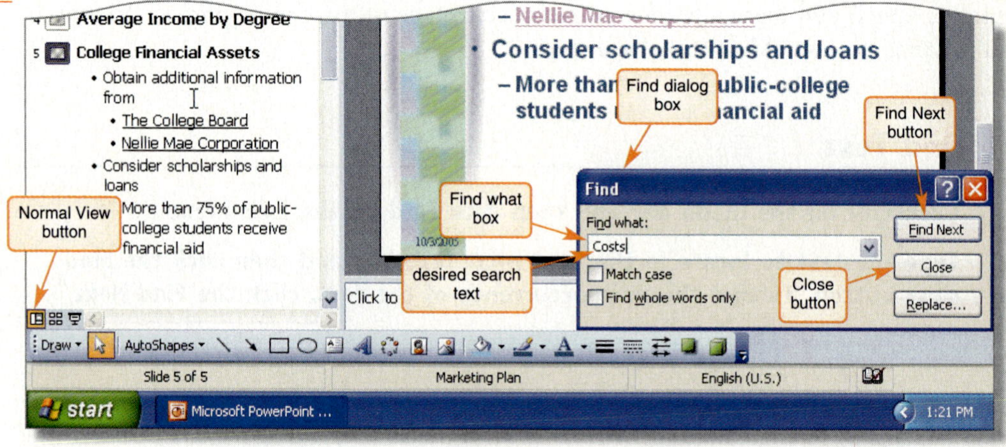

FIGURE 4-55

2

- **Click the Find Next button.**
- **Click the Close button in the Find dialog box.**

Slide 3 is displayed and the word, Costs, is selected (Figure 4-56).

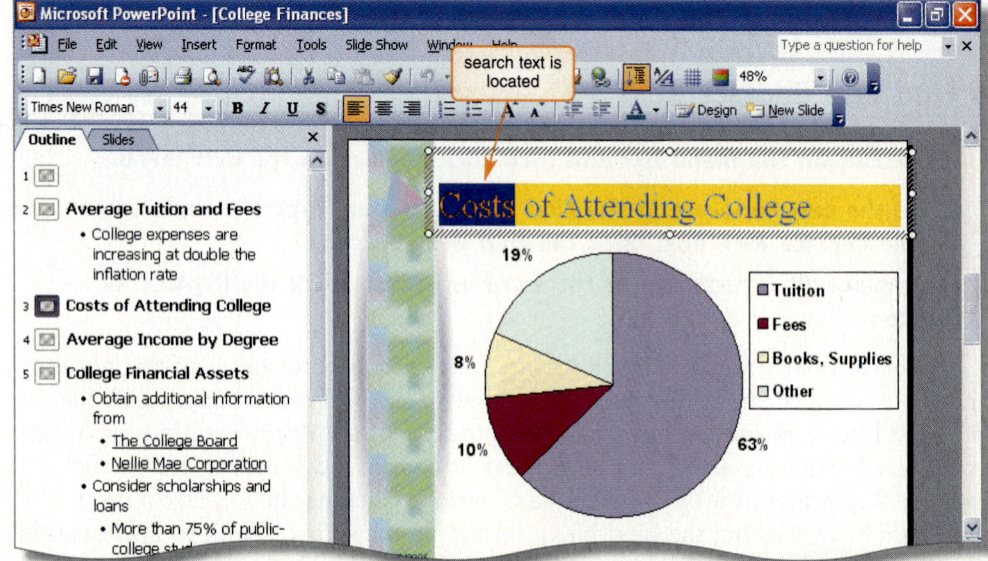

FIGURE 4-56

3

- **Click Tools on the menu bar and then point to Thesaurus.**

The Tools menu is displayed (Figure 4-57).

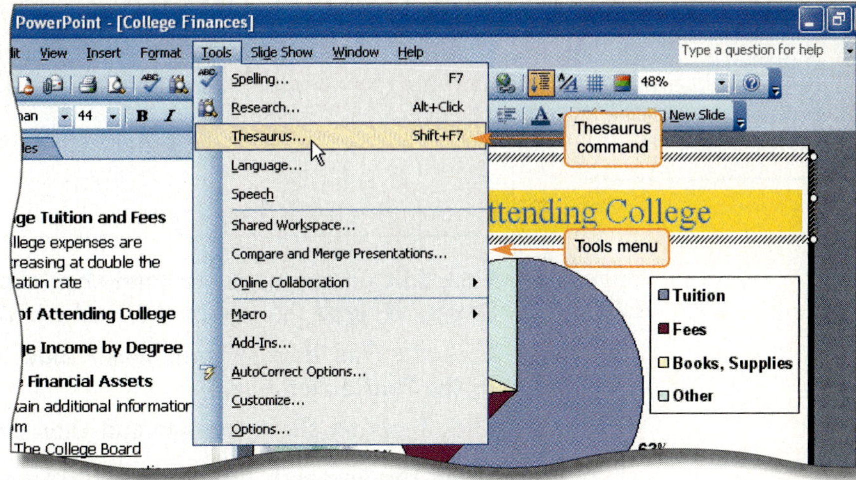

FIGURE 4-57

4

- **Click Thesaurus.**
- **When the Research task pane is displayed, point to the word, expenses, in the Thesaurus list and then click the arrow to the right of that word.**
- **Point to Insert.**

A list of synonyms for the word, Costs, displays in the Thesaurus area of the Research task pane (Figure 4-58).

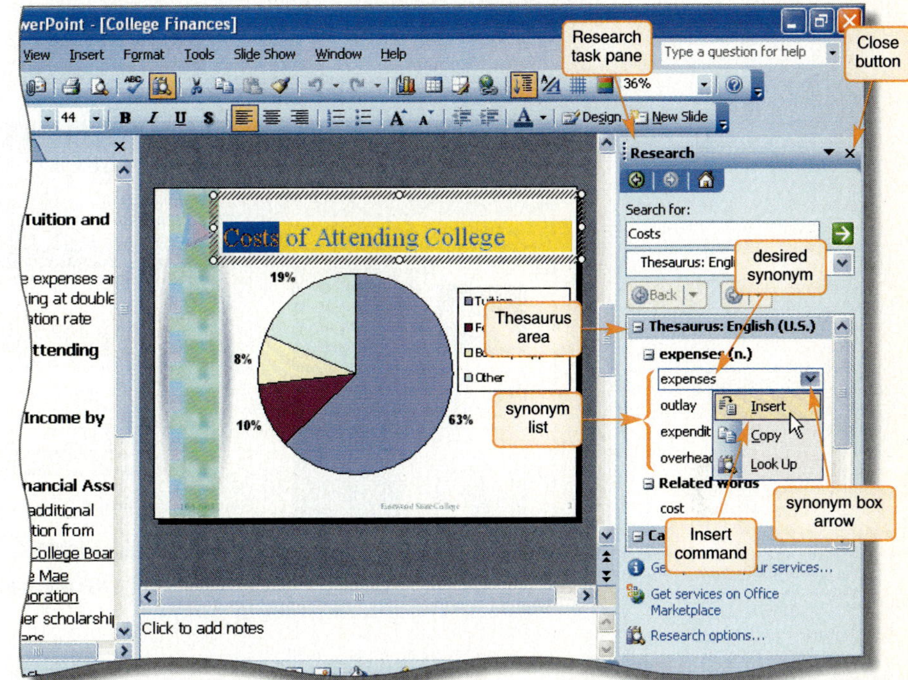

FIGURE 4-58

5

- **Click Insert.**
- **Click the Close button in the Research task pane.**

The word, Costs, is replaced by the synonym, Expenses, on Slide 3 (Figure 4-59).

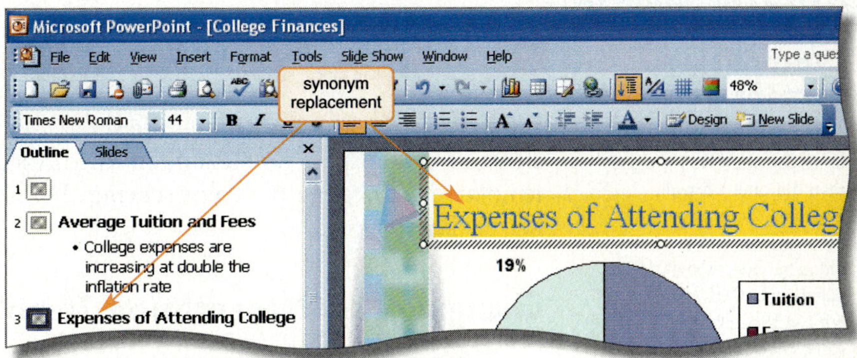

FIGURE 4-59

Other Ways

1. Press SHIFT+F7
2. Press ALT+T, press T
3. In Voice Command mode, say "Tools, Thesaurus"

Finding a Second Synonym

Now that you have found a synonym for the word, Costs, you want to find a synonym for the word, Income, on Slide 4. The following steps replace that word with the synonym, Earnings.

To Find a Second Synonym

1. **Click Edit on the menu bar and then click Find. When the Find dialog box is displayed, type** `Income` **in the Find what box.**
2. **Click the Find Next button. When Slide 4 is displayed, click the Close button in the Find dialog box.**
3. **Click Tools on the menu bar and then click Thesaurus.**
4. **When the Research task pane is displayed, point to the word, earnings, and then click the arrow to the right of that word. Click Insert.**
5. **Click the Close button in the Research task pane.**

The word, Income, is replaced by the synonym, Earnings, on Slide 4 (Figure 4-60).

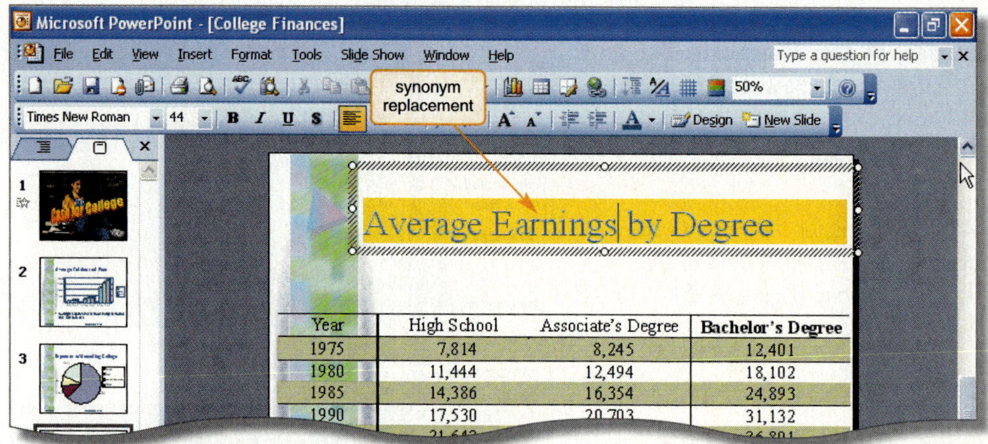

FIGURE 4-60

Using these steps, you revised individual slides. In the following section, you now will add variety to the entire presentation by changing the color scheme and using the title and slide masters to modify the footer text and add action buttons.

More About

Customizing Buttons

Customize your toolbars by using buttons that are larger than the ones normally displayed. To enlarge the buttons, click Tools on the menu bar and then click Customize. Click the Options tab and then click the Large icons check box. This setting will affect all Microsoft Office programs.

Customizing Entire Presentation Elements

With the basic elements of the slide show created, you need to modify two default elements that display on all slides in the presentation. First, you will modify the template by changing the color scheme. Then, you will add information to the slide master Footer Area.

Changing the Presentation Template Color Scheme

The first modification to make is to change the color scheme throughout the presentation. The **color scheme** of each slide template consists of eight balanced colors you can apply to all slides, an individual slide, notes pages, or audience handouts. A color scheme consists of colors for a background, text and lines, shadows, title text, fills, accent, accent and hyperlink, and accent and followed hyperlink. Table 4-3 explains the components of a color scheme.

Table 4-3 Color Scheme Components

COMPONENT	DESCRIPTION
Background color	The background color is the fundamental color of a PowerPoint slide. For example, if the background color is black, you can place any other color on top of it, but the fundamental color remains black. The black background shows everywhere you do not add color or other objects.
Text and lines color	The text and lines color contrasts with the background color of the slide. Together with the background color, the text and lines color sets the tone for a presentation. For example, a gray background with a black text and lines color sets a dramatic tone. In contrast, a red background with a yellow text and lines color sets a vibrant tone.
Title text color	The title text color contrasts with the background color in a manner similar to the text and lines color. Title text is displayed in the title text placeholder on a slide.
Shadow color	The shadow color is applied when you color an object. This color usually is a darker shade of the background color.
Fill color	The fill color contrasts with both the background color and the text and lines color. The fill color is used for graphs and charts.
Accent colors	Accent colors are designed as colors for secondary features on a slide. Additionally, accent colors are used as colors on graphs.

The following steps change the color scheme for the template from a white background and blue letters to a blue background with purple title text.

To Change the Presentation Template Color Scheme

1

- **Click the Slide Design button on the Formatting toolbar.**
- **Point to Color Schemes in the Slide Design task pane.**

The Slide Design task pane is displayed (Figure 4-61).

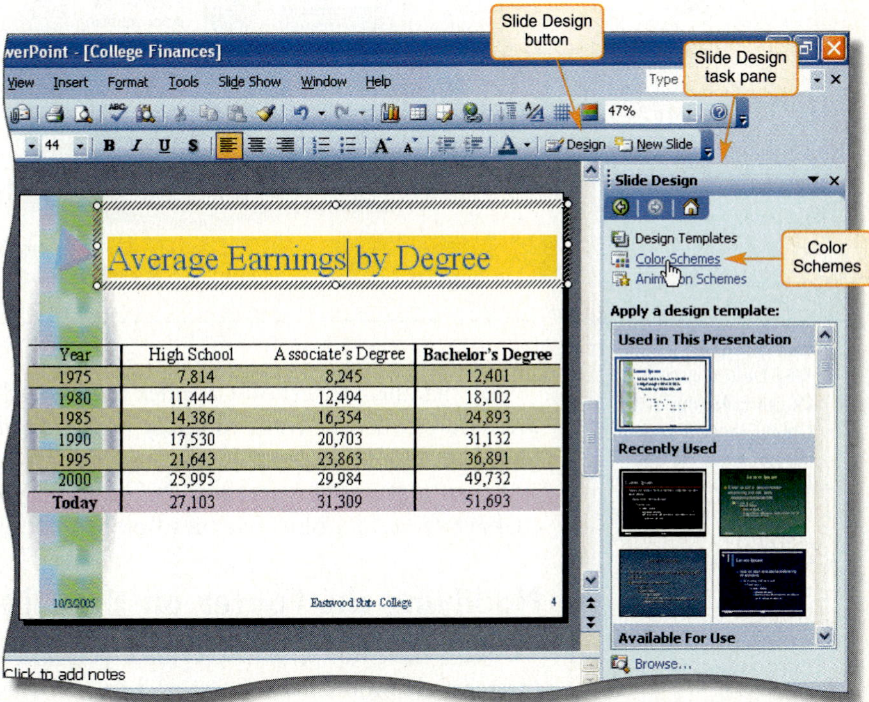

FIGURE 4-61

2

- **Click Color Schemes.**
- **Click the top-right color scheme template.**

Three color schemes are available (Figure 4-62). The top-right color scheme is selected and will be applied to all slides in the presentation.

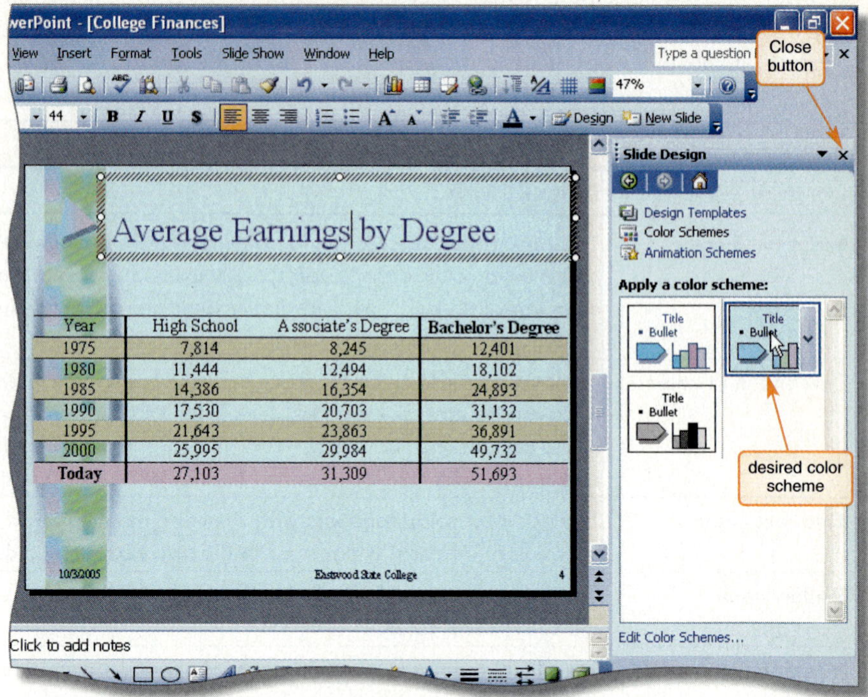

FIGURE 4-62

3

- **Click the Close button in the Slide Design task pane title bar.**

Slide 4 is displayed with the new color scheme (Figure 4-63). Slide thumbnails of the slides in the presentation display in the tabs pane.

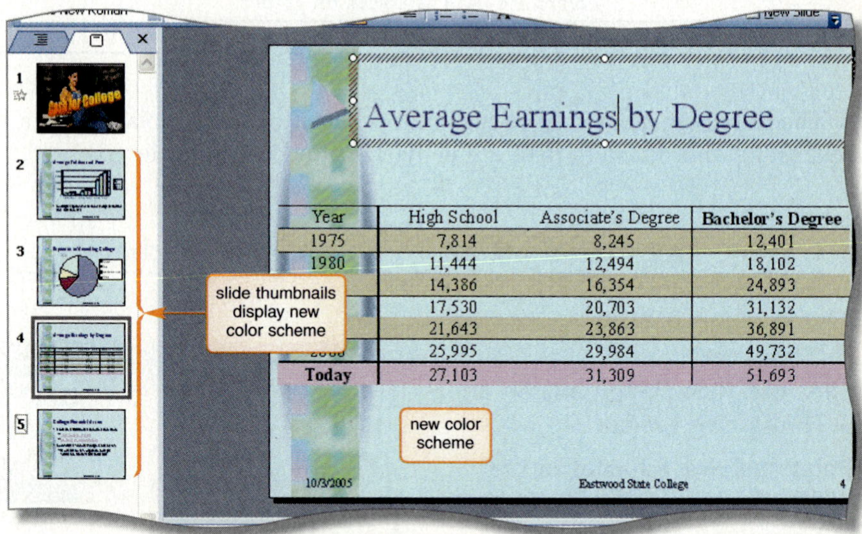

FIGURE 4-63

Other Ways

1. On Format menu click Slide Design, in Slide Design task pane click Color Schemes, click desired color scheme
2. Press ALT+O, press D, press DOWN ARROW key, press ENTER, press arrow keys until desired color selected, press ENTER
3. In Voice Command mode, say "Format, Slide Design, Color Schemes"

By default, PowerPoint applies the desired color scheme to all slides in the presentation. If you want to apply it to individual slides or want to see a larger template thumbnail, you would click the arrow button of the selected color scheme and then make your selections. In addition, you can edit the current color scheme by clicking the Edit Color Schemes link at the bottom of the task pane.

Modifying the Footer on the Slide Master

With the color scheme changed, you now can revise the text on the slide master slide footer from Eastwood State College to Eastwood Financial Aid Office.

One method of making this change is to modify the footer on the slide master. In Project 3, you modified the slide master when you customized bullets. In this project, you will display the slide master to add information to the Footer Area of that slide. The following steps modify the slide master footer.

To Modify the Footer on the Slide Master

1

- **Click View on the menu bar, point to Master, and then click Slide Master on the Master submenu.**

The Marketing Plan Title Master and Slide Master View toolbar display (Figure 4-64). The title master and slide master slide thumbnails display on the left edge of the screen. The slide master thumbnail is selected.

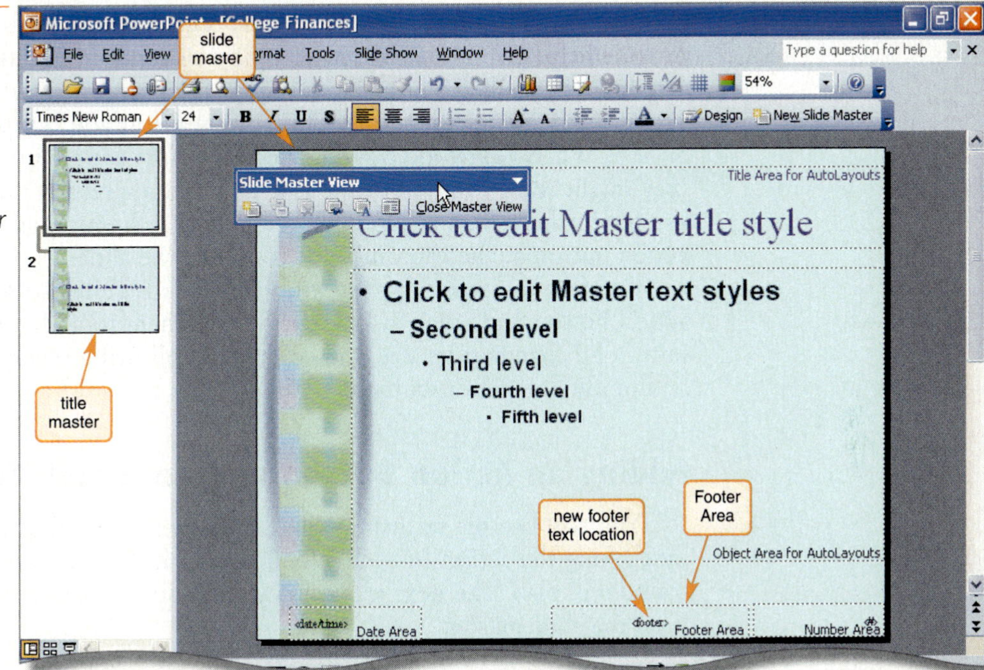

FIGURE 4-64

2

- **If necessary, click the Marketing Plan Slide master thumbnail on the left slide of the screen.**
- **Click the word, <footer>, in the Footer Area on the slide master.**
- **Type** `Eastwood Financial Aid Office` **in the footer text box.**

The Marketing Plan title master and slide master slide thumbnails display (Figure 4-65). The new footer text is displayed in the slide master Footer Area.

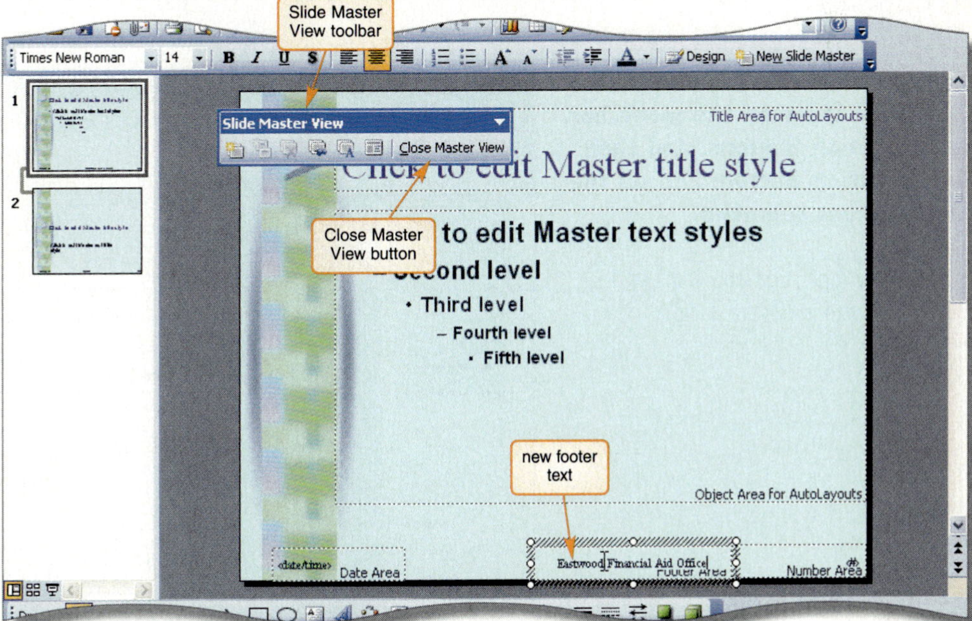

FIGURE 4-65

Other Ways

1. Press and hold down SHIFT key, click Normal View button, click Footer Area, type footer text
2. Press ALT+V, press M, press S, type footer text
3. In Voice Command mode, say "View, Master, Slide Master, [type footer text]"

You have made a color scheme change on all five slides in the presentation and a footer change on the title slide in the presentation. The next steps will add an action button to the slide master.

Adding an Action Button on the Slide Master

With the footer changed on the title master, you now can add variety to your presentation by placing an action button on the slide master. An **action button** is a built-in 3-D button that can perform specific tasks such as display the next slide, provide help, give information, and play a sound. In addition, the action button can activate a hyperlink that allows users to jump to a specific slide in the presentation.

In this presentation, you will associate the action button with a hyperlink to Slide 5. When Eastwood State College speakers are lecturing about college costs, they might want to jump to the last slide in the presentation and then access a Web site for further information. One method of jumping easily to Slide 5 is to click the action button at the bottom-right corner of the slide.

Creating the action button and hyperlink requires several steps. First, add an action button and create a link to Slide 5. Then, to add variety, modify the action button by changing its size and color. The following sections describe how to add and modify an action button.

Adding an Action Button and an Action Setting

You will be able to display Slide 5 easily at any point in the presentation simply by clicking the action button. When you click the action button, a cash register sound will play. The next section describes how to create the action button and place it on the slide master.

To Add an Action Button and an Action Setting

1

• **Click Slide Show on the menu bar, point to Action Buttons, and then point to Action Button: End on the Action Buttons submenu.**

The Action Buttons submenu displays 12 built-in 3-D buttons (Figure 4-66).

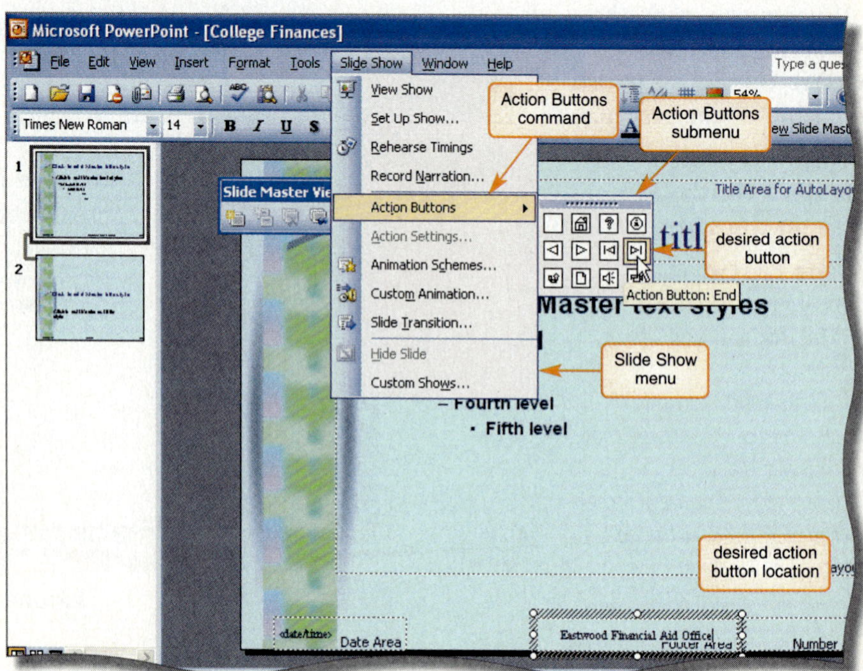

FIGURE 4-66

2

- **Click Action Button: End.**
- **Click the bottom-right corner of the slide master.**
- **If necessary, when the Action Settings dialog box is displayed, click the Mouse Click tab.**

The Action Settings dialog box is displayed (Figure 4-67) with the action button placed on Slide 2. Hyperlink to is the default Action on click. Last Slide displays in the Hyperlink to list box because the End action button is selected. The hyperlink can be established in other locations in the slide show or elsewhere.

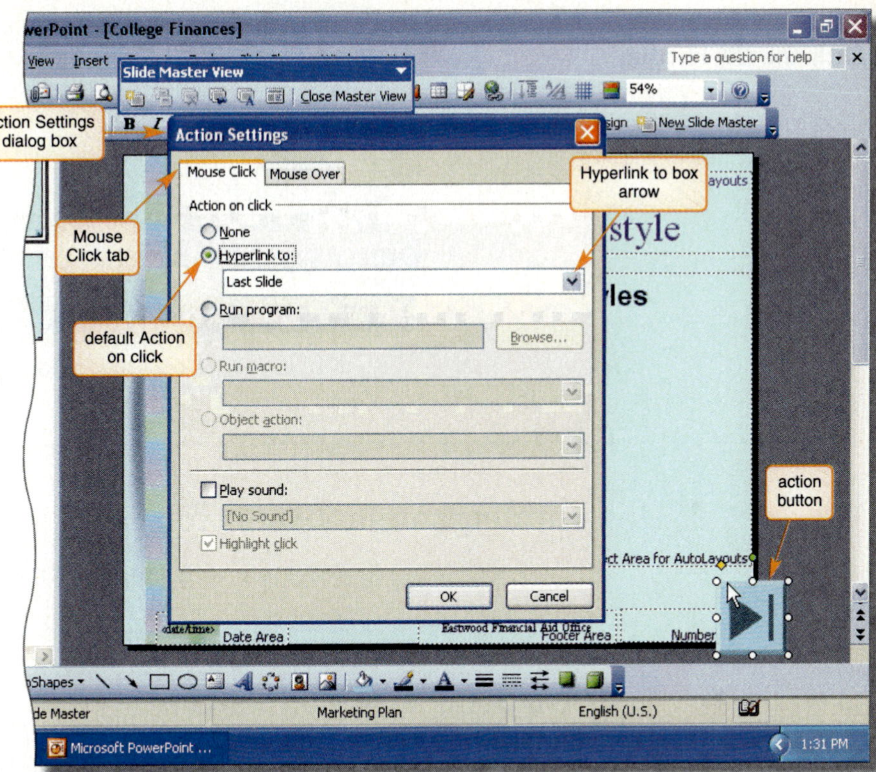

FIGURE 4-67

3

- **Click Play sound.**
- **Click the Play sound box arrow, click the down scroll arrow, and then click Cash Register.**

A check mark displays in the Play sound check box, and the Cash Register sound is selected (Figure 4-68). The Play sound list displays sounds that can play when you click the action button. You may have to install the Sound Effects feature to enable this sound function; if a Microsoft Office PowerPoint dialog box is displayed asking if you want to install the Sound Effects feature, click the Yes button.

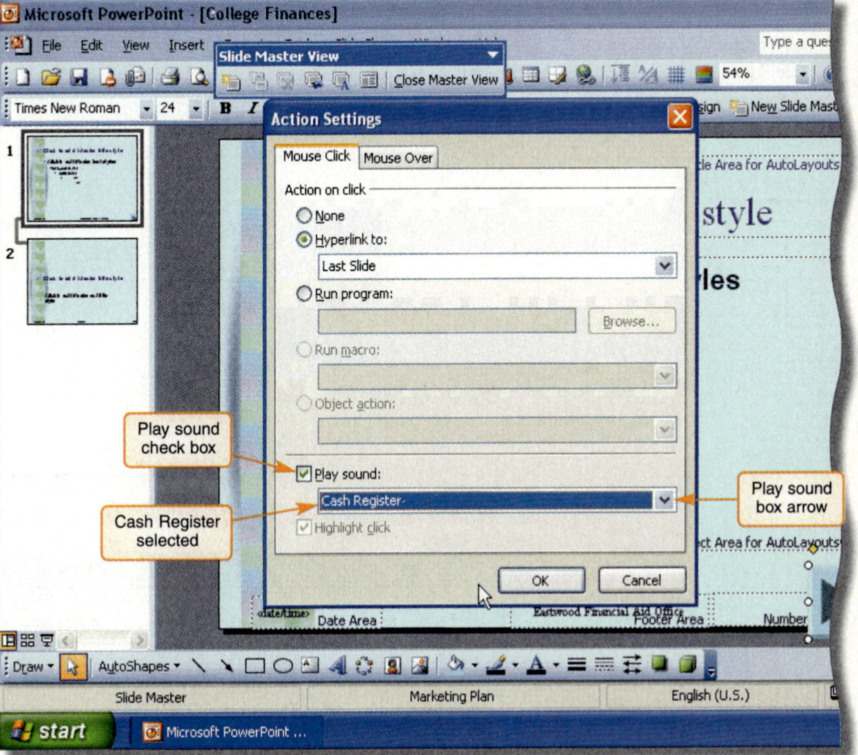

FIGURE 4-68

4

• **Click the OK button.**

The action button is highlighted on the slide master as indicated by the sizing handles (Figure 4-69).

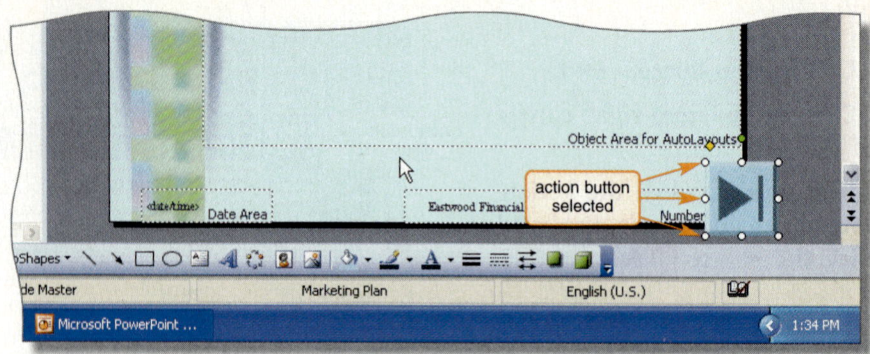

FIGURE 4-69

Scaling an Action Button

The size of the action button can be decreased. The following steps scale the action button.

Other Ways

1. On Format menu click AutoShape, click Size tab, click Lock aspect ratio
2. Press ALT+ O, press O, RIGHT ARROW
3. In Voice Command mode, say "Format, AutoShape, Size, Lock aspect ratio"

To Scale an Action Button

1. **With the slide master displaying, right-click the action button and then click Format AutoShape on the shortcut menu.**
2. **If necessary, click the Size tab. Click Lock aspect ratio in the Scale area and then triple-click the Height text box in the Scale area. Type** 80 **in the Height box.**
3. **Click the OK button.**

The action button is resized to 80 percent of its original size (Figure 4-70).

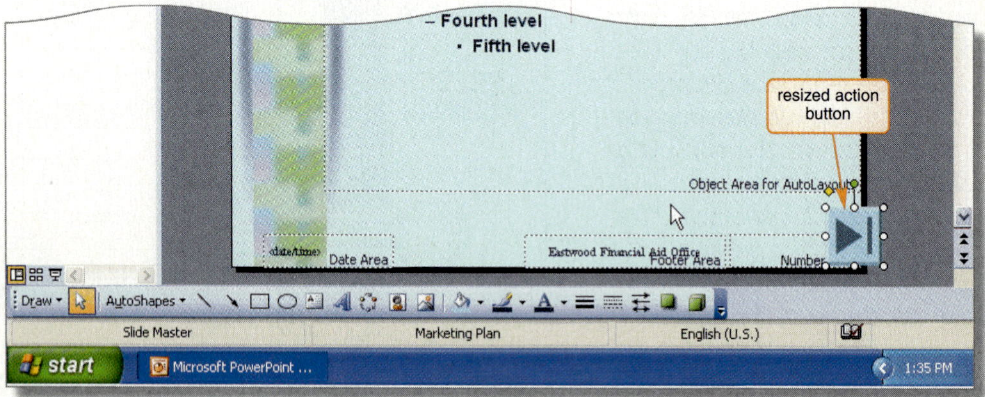

FIGURE 4-70

Adding a Fill Color to the Action Button

To better identify the action button from the slide background, you can add fill color. **Fill color** is the interior color of a selected object. The following steps add fill color to the action button on the slide master.

To Add a Fill Color to the Action Button

1

- **With the action button selected on the slide master, click the Fill Color button arrow on the Drawing toolbar.**

The Fill Color palette is displayed (Figure 4-71). Automatic is selected, indicating that medium blue is the current default fill color based on the Marketing Plan design template color scheme. Light purple is the default Follow Accent and Hyperlink Scheme Color.

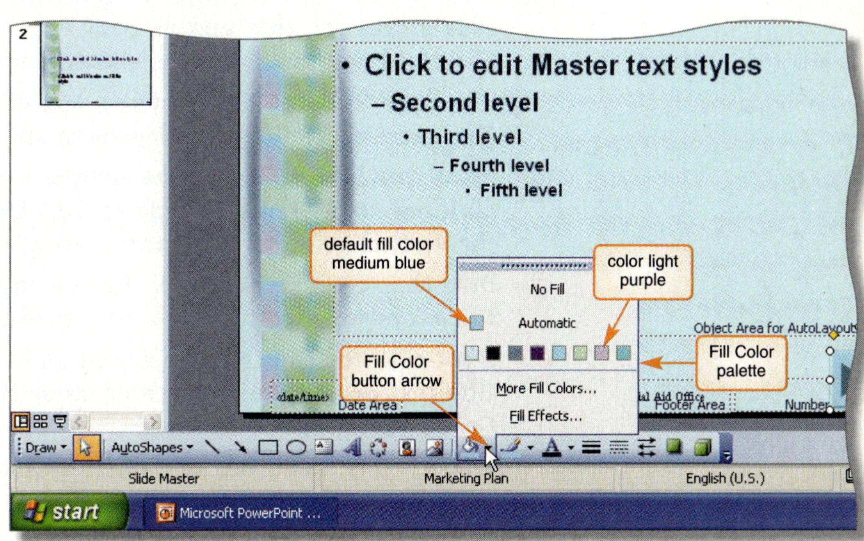

FIGURE 4-71

2

- **Click the color light purple (row 1, column 7).**

The action button displays filled with the color light purple (Figure 4-72).

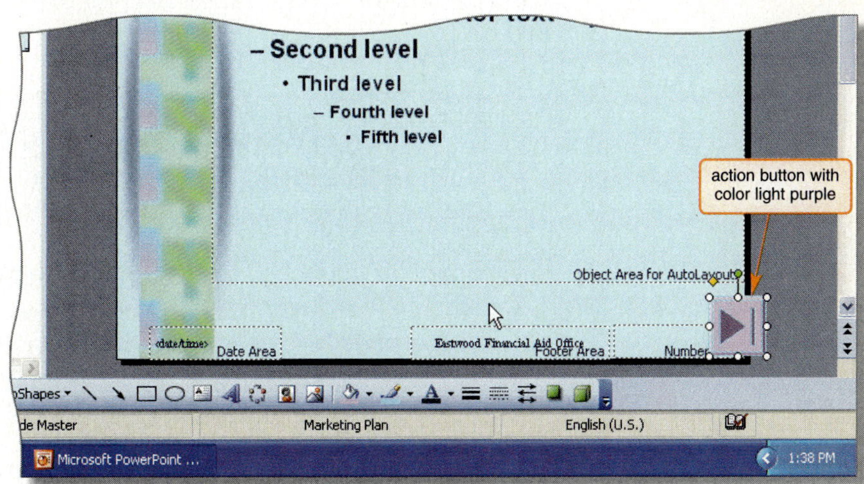

FIGURE 4-72

Other Ways

1. On Format menu click AutoShape, click Colors tab and Lines tab
2. Right-click action button, click Format AutoShape on shortcut menu, click Colors and Lines tab
3. Press ALT+O, press O
4. In Voice Command mode, say "Format, AutoShape, Colors and Lines"

The slide master action button is filled with the color light purple. The fill color now is set to this color. The next step is to position the action button precisely in a desired location on the slide master.

Displaying Guides and Positioning the Action Button

Earlier in this project you used the PowerPoint grid and guides to align the WordArt text object on Slide 1. The guides will help you position the action button on the slide master. The steps on the next page will display the guides and align the action button.

To Display Guides and Position the Action Button

1. **With the slide master visible, right-click anywhere in the blue area of the slide except the title text or body text placeholders or the action button. Click Grid and Guides on the shortcut menu.**
2. **When the Grid and Guides dialog box displays, click Display drawing guides on screen in the Guide settings area and then click the OK button.**
3. **Point to the horizontal guide anywhere in the gray area outside of the slide. Click and then drag the guide to 2.20 inches below center. If necessary, drag the vertical guide to 4.50 inches left of center.**
4. **Drag the action button until the top edge snaps to the horizontal guide and the left edge snaps to the vertical guide.**
5. **Right-click the slide master anywhere in the blue area of the slide except the title text or body text placeholders or the action button. Click Grid and Guides on the shortcut menu.**
6. **When the Grid and Guides dialog box displays, click Display drawing guides on screen in the Guide settings area.**
7. **Click the OK button.**

The action button is positioned in the lower-left corner of the slide (Figure 4-73). The guides are hidden.

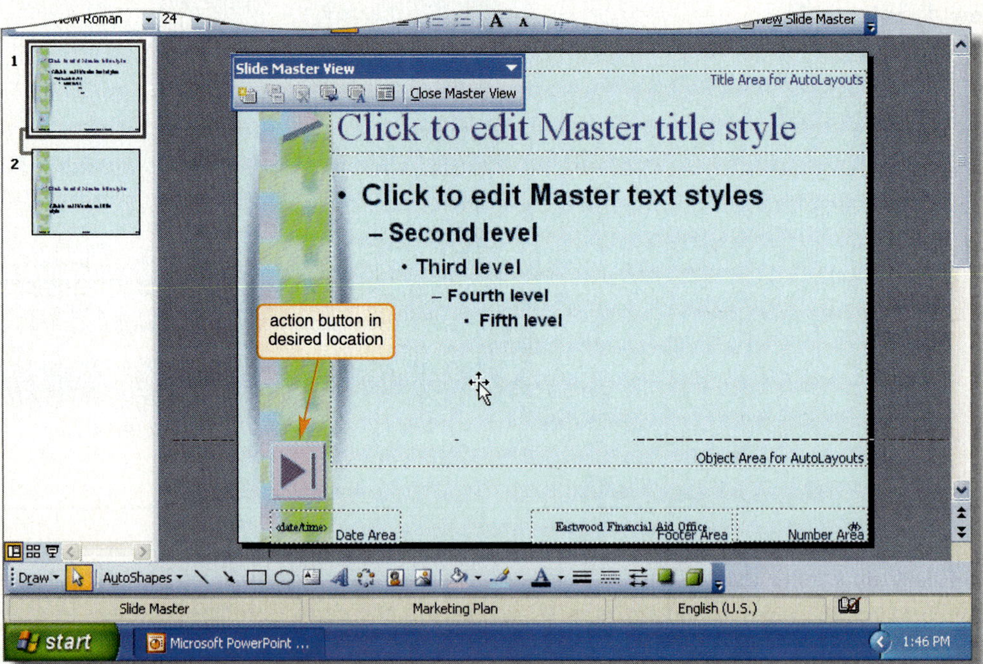

FIGURE 4-73

The action button displays in the desired location.

Rotating the Action Button

The Marketing Plan design template has a vertical purple and green stripe on the left side of the slide. Near the top of this stripe is a triangle positioned on an angle with one end pointing toward the upper-left corner of the slide. To add variety to your presentation, you want to balance the visual element of the stripe by rotating the action button so one end points toward the lower-right slide corner. Many PowerPoint objects can be rotated, including AutoShapes, pictures, and WordArt. The objects can be rotated in two ways. To rotate the object to any angle, drag the green rotate handle on the object in the direction you want it to rotate. The following steps describe how to rotate the action button on the slide master.

To Rotate the Action Button

1

- **With the slide master active, click the action button to select it.**
- **Drag the rotate handle on the action button to the right approximately 45 degrees.**

The action button turns toward the lower-right corner of the slide (Figure 4-74).

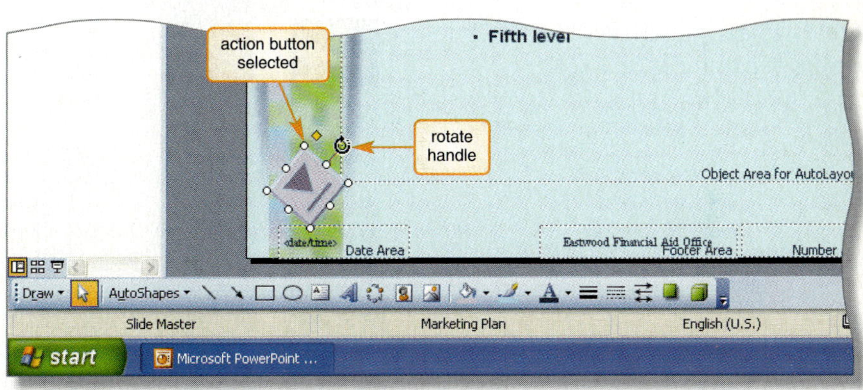

FIGURE 4-74

2

- **Click outside the rotate handle.**

The action button rotation is set (Figure 4-75).

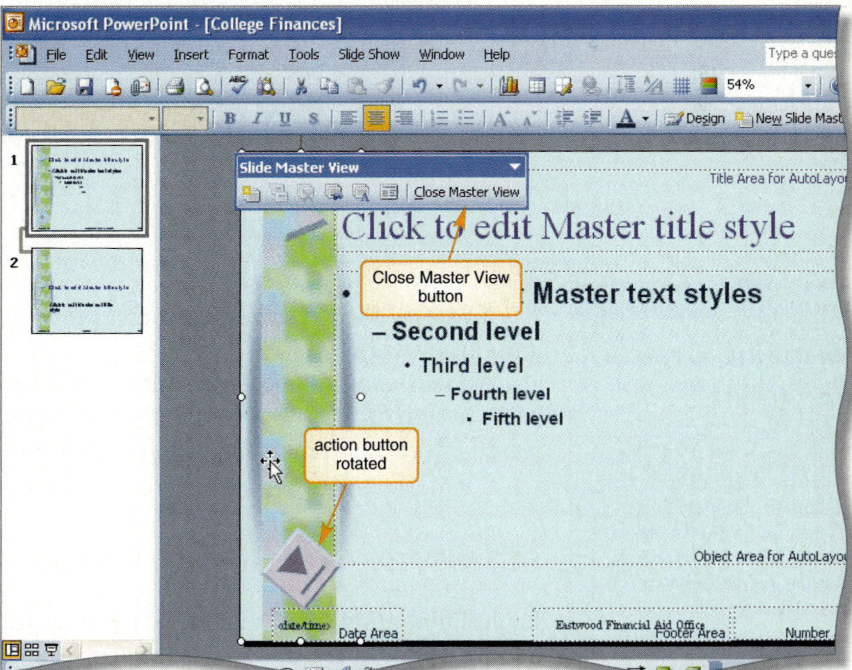

FIGURE 4-75

Other Ways

1. Click Draw button on the Drawing toolbar, point to Rotate or Flip, click Rotate Left 90° or Rotate Right 90°

Closing Master View

Now that all the changes to the slide master are complete, you can exit master view and return to normal view. All slides in the presentation have a new color scheme, a revised footer has been added to Slide 1, and an action button has been added to Slides 2 through 5. The following step closes master view.

To Close Master View

1

• **Click the Close Master View button on the Slide Master View toolbar.**

Slide 4 displays with the new color scheme and action button (Figure 4-76).

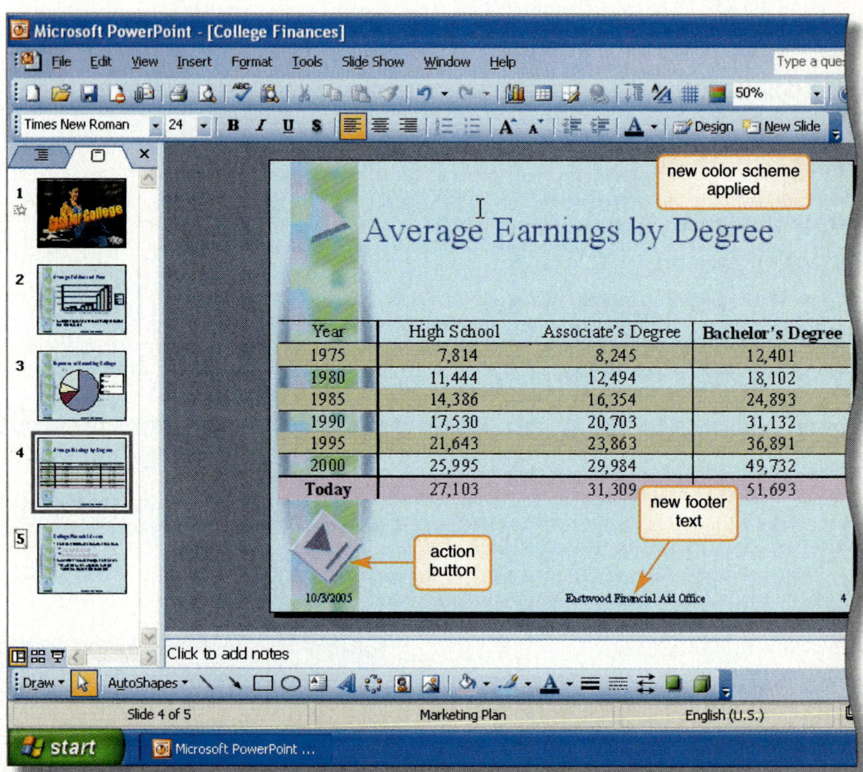

FIGURE 4-76

More About

Rotating Objects

Rotating objects on your slides can create an interesting effect. Once you select the AutoShape, picture, or WordArt object, you can rotate the object 90 degrees to the left or to the right by clicking the Draw button on the Drawing toolbar, pointing to Rotate or Flip, and then clicking Rotate Left or Rotate Right. If you press the SHIFT key while dragging the rotate handle, you will constrain the object's rotation to 15-degree angles.

You now should save your presentation because you have done a substantial amount of work.

All text and graphical elements have been added to the five slides in the presentation. You now will modify the presentation format by adding transition and sound effects and rehearsing the presentation timing.

Modifying the Presentation Format

PowerPoint allows you to control the way you advance from one slide to another by adding a **slide transition**. The AutoContent Wizard added animations to the slides, but it did not apply a slide transition. Some animation schemes include transitions, but if the one you select does not or if you want to change the transition, PowerPoint allows you to apply this effect using the Slide Transition task pane. A slide transition can be applied to a single slide, a group of slides, or an entire presentation.

The second modification you will make is to rehearse the slide timing. When you **rehearse timings**, you start the slide show in **rehearsal mode** and then specify the number of seconds you want each slide to display on the screen when you run the slide show.

Adding a Slide Transition Effect to a Slide Show

PowerPoint has more than 50 unique slide transition effects, and you can vary the speed of each in a presentation. The name of the slide transition characterizes the visual effect that is displayed. For example, the slide transition effect, Split Vertical Out, displays the next slide by covering the previous slide with two vertical boxes moving from the center of the screen until the two boxes reach the left and right edges of the screen. The effect is similar to opening draw drapes over a window.

PowerPoint requires you to select at least one slide before applying slide transition effects. In this presentation, you apply slide transition effects to all slides except the title slide. Because Slide 5 already is selected, you must select Slides 2, 3, and 4. The quickest method of selecting these slides is by using the SHIFT+click technique you used to delete slides in this project.

The slide show includes the **Shape Diamond slide transition effect** between slides. That is, all slides begin stacked on top of one another, like a deck of cards. As you click the mouse button to view the next slide, the new slide enters the screen by starting at the center of the slide and opening up in a circle to the edges.

The following steps apply the Shape Diamond slide transition effect to the College Finances presentation.

More About

Delivering Presentations

If you want to be a better public speaker, consider joining Toastmasters International. This non-profit organization has helped more than three million people lose their fears of public speaking, become better listeners, and advance in their careers. Toastmasters members meet frequently and practice various types of public speaking, including giving prepared and impromptu speeches, conducting meetings, and giving and receiving constructive feedback. To learn more about this organization and to find a local chapter near you, visit the PowerPoint 2003 More About Web page (scsite.com/ppt2003/more) and click Delivering.

To Add a Slide Transition Effect to a Slide Show

1

- **Click Slide 5 on the Slides tab.**
- **Press and hold down the SHIFT key and then click Slide 2.**
- **Release the SHIFT key.**

Slides 2 through 5 are selected, as indicated by the heavy border around each slide.

2

- **Point to Slide 2 and right-click.**
- **Point to Slide Transition on the shortcut menu (Figure 4-77).**

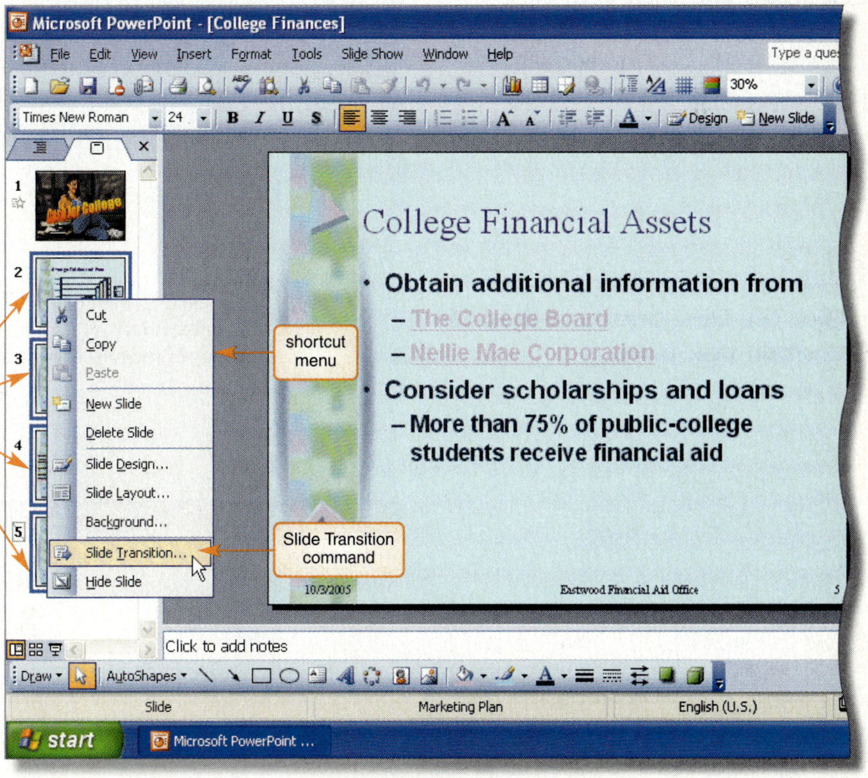

FIGURE 4-77

3

- **Click Slide Transition.**
- **When the Slide Transition task pane is displayed, click the down scroll arrow in the Apply to selected slides list until Shape Diamond is displayed.**
- **Click Shape Diamond.**

The Slide Transition task pane is displayed (Figure 4-78). The Apply to selected slides list displays available slide transition effects. The effect is previewed in the slide pane because the AutoPreview check box is checked. To see the preview again, click the Play button. To preview the effect on all slides in the presentation, click the Slide Show button.

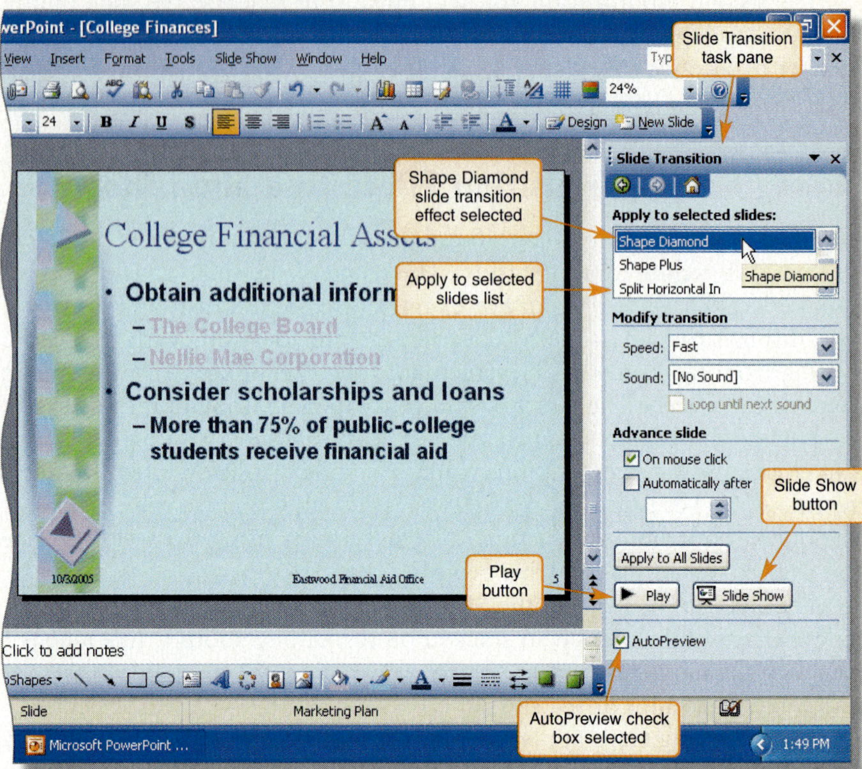

FIGURE 4-78

4

- **Click the Modify Transition Speed box arrow and then click Slow.**

The effect is previewed again in the slide pane. Slow is displayed in the Modify Transition Speed box (Figure 4-79). You can select a transition speed of Slow, Medium, or Fast.

5

- **Click the Close button in the Slide Transition task pane.**

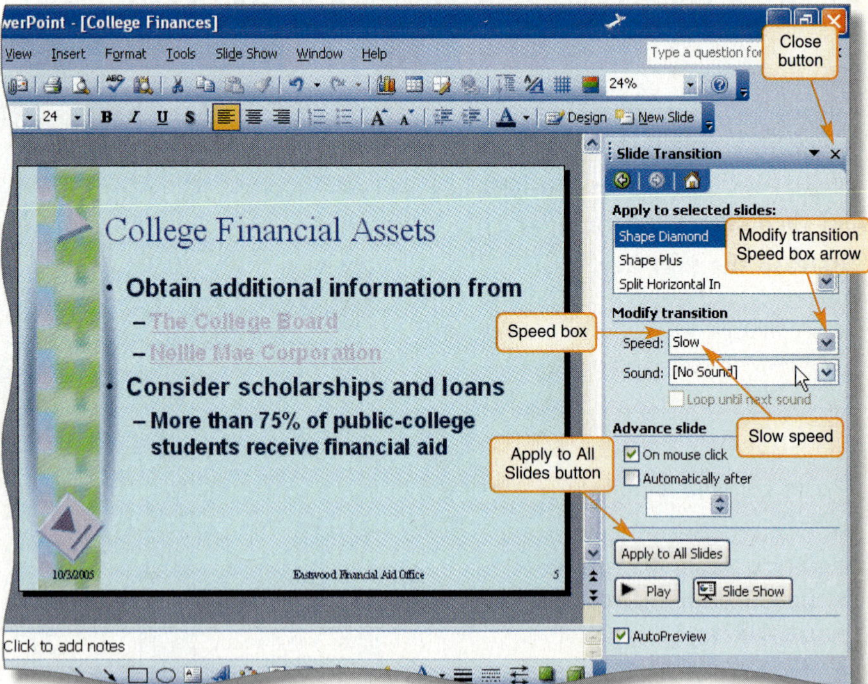

FIGURE 4-79

To apply slide transition effects to every slide in the presentation, right-click a slide, click Slide Transition on the shortcut menu, choose the desired slide transition effect, and then click the Apply to All Slides button in the Slide Transition task pane. To remove slide transition effects, select the slides to which slide transition effects are applied, click the up scroll arrow in the Apply to selected slides list until No Transition is displayed, and then click No Transition.

The Shape Diamond slide transition effect has been applied to the presentation. You should save the slide show again. The next step in creating this slide show is to set timings for the slide show.

Other Ways

1. Select slides, on Slide Show menu click Slide Transition, select desired transition, select desired transition speed, click Close button
2. Select slides, press ALT+D, press T, press arrow keys to select desired transition, press ENTER, press arrows keys to select desired transition speed, click Close button
3. In Voice Command mode, say "Slide Show, Slide Transition"

Rehearsing Timings

In previous slide shows, you clicked to advance from one slide to the next. Because all slide components have been added to the five slides in the presentation, you now can set the time each slide is displayed on the screen. You can set these times in two ways. One method is to specify each slide's display time manually in the Slide Transition task pane. The second method is to use PowerPoint's **rehearsal feature**, which allows you to advance through the slides at your own pace, and the amount of time you view each slide is recorded. You will use the second technique in this project.

When you begin rehearsing a presentation, the Rehearsal toolbar is displayed. The **Rehearsal toolbar** contains buttons that allow you to start, pause, and repeat viewing the slides in the slide show and to view the times for each slide and the elapsed time. Table 4-4 describes the buttons on the Rehearsal toolbar.

Table 4-4 Rehearsal Toolbar Buttons

BUTTON	BUTTON NAME	DESCRIPTION
	Next	Displays the next slide or next animated element on the slide.
	Pause	Stops the timer. Click the Next or Pause button to resume timing.
0:00:19	Slide Time	Indicates the length of time a slide has displayed. You can enter a slide time directly in the Slide Time box.
	Repeat	Clears the Slide Time box and resets the timer to 0:00.
0:00:19	Elapsed Time	Indicates slide show total time.

Table 4-5 indicates the desired timings for the five slides in the College Finances presentation. Slide 1 is displayed and the effect plays for 40 seconds. Slide 5 has the two hyperlinks, so you need to allow time to view the Web sites if you decide to display that slide.

Table 4-5 Slide Rehearsal Timings

SLIDE NUMBER	DISPLAY TIME	ELAPSED TIME
1	0:00	0:40
2	0:20	1:00
3	0:20	1:20
4	0:20	1:40
5	0:50	2:30

The following steps add slide timings to the slide show.

To Rehearse Timings

1

- **Click Slide Show on the menu bar and then click Rehearse Timings.**
- **Point to the Next button on the Rehearsal toolbar.**

Slide 1 is displayed and the Marketing Music sound effect plays (Figure 4-80).

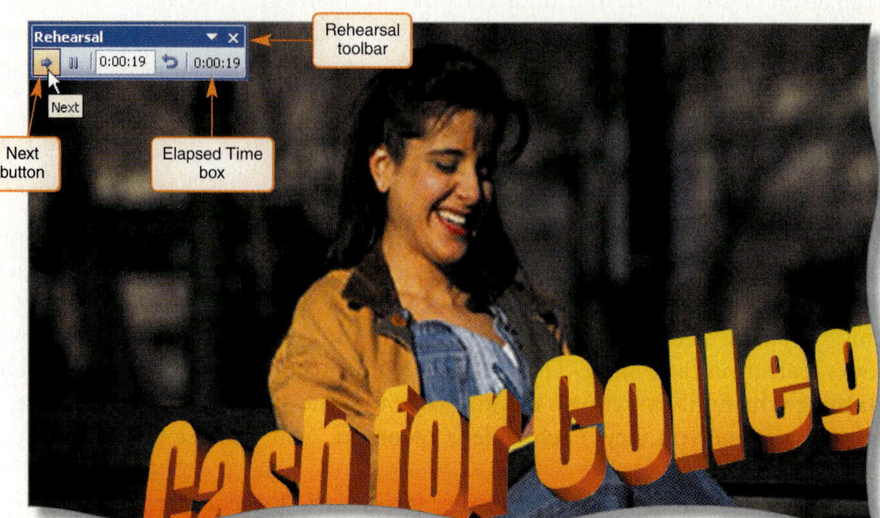

FIGURE 4-80

2

- **When the Elapsed Time box displays 0:40, click the Next button.**

Slide 2 is displayed.

3

- **When the Elapsed Time box displays 1:00, click the Next button to display Slide 3.**
- **When the Elapsed Time box displays 1:20, click the Next button to display Slide 4.**
- **When the Elapsed Time box displays 1:40, press H to display Slide 5.**
- **When the Elapsed Time box displays 2:30, click the Next button to display the black slide.**
- **Point to the Yes button in the Microsoft Office PowerPoint dialog box.**

The Microsoft Office PowerPoint dialog box displays the total time and asks if you want to keep the new slide timings with a total elapsed time of 0:02:30 (Figure 4-81).

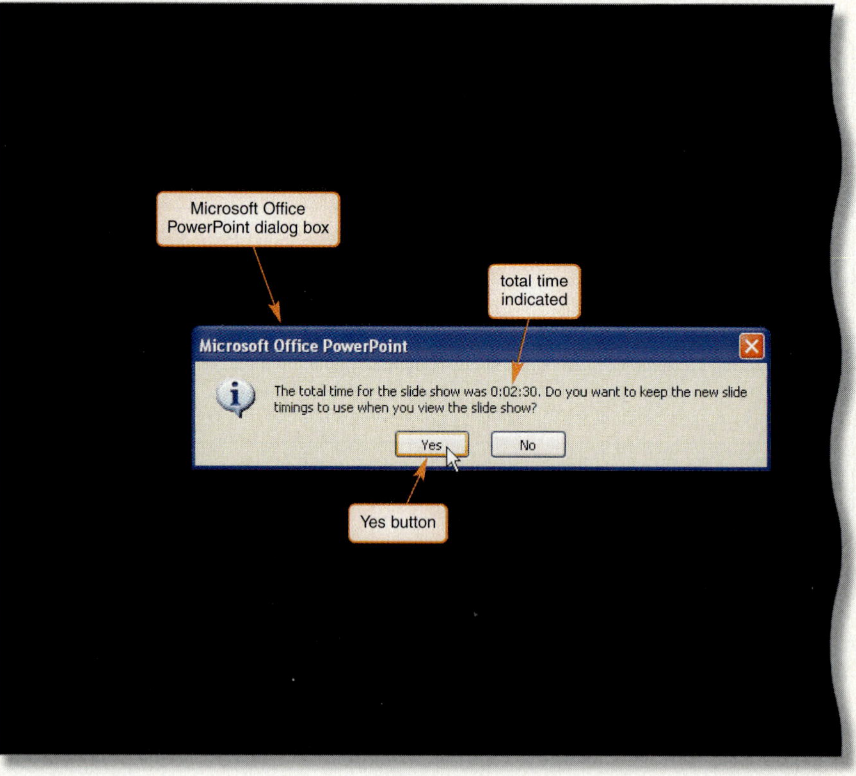

FIGURE 4-81

4

• **Click the Yes button.**

Each slide's timing is displayed in the lower-left corner in slide sorter view (Figure 4-82).

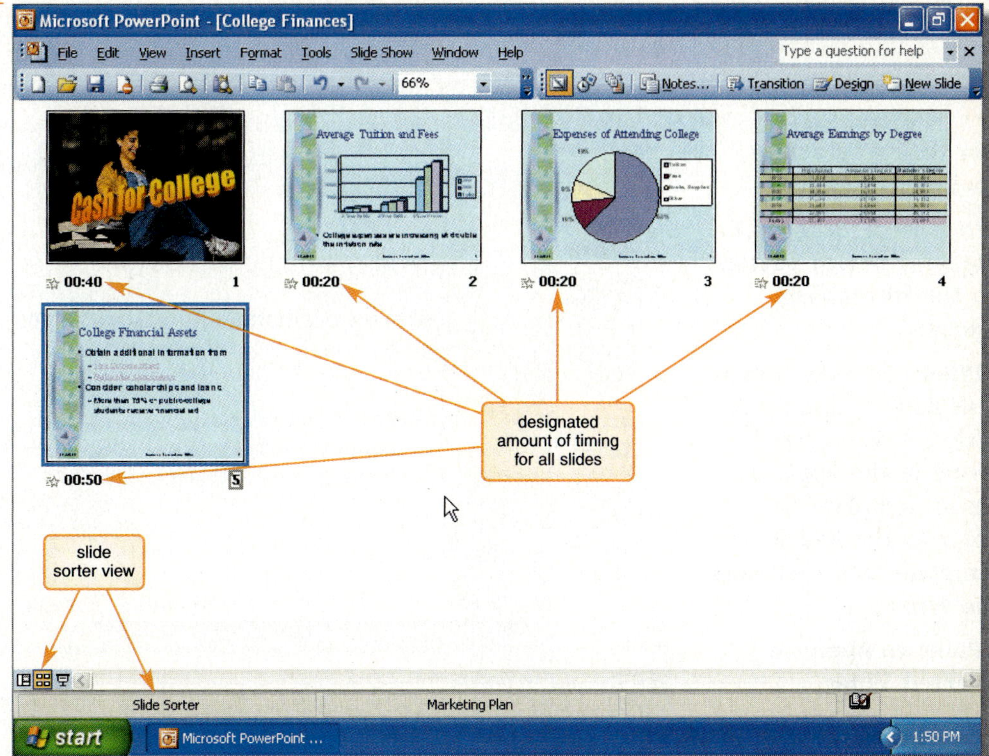

FIGURE 4-82

Other Ways

1. Press ALT+D, press R
2. In Voice Command mode, say "Slide Show, Rehearse Timings"

The College Finances slide timing is complete. The presentation will run two minutes and thirty seconds.

Replacing the Slide Master

To add more variety to the presentation, you want to apply more than one design template. This feature is referred to as support for multiple masters. Each design template inserts a title and slide master automatically into the presentation, so more than one set of Slide-Title master pairs is displayed in Slide Master view. The steps on the next page describe how to apply a second design template to the College Finances presentation.

To Replace the Slide Master

1

- **In slide sorter view, double-click Slide 5.**
- **In normal view, click the Slide Design button on the Formatting toolbar.**
- **When the Slide Design task pane is displayed, click the down scroll arrow in the Apply a design template list, point to the Radial template, and then click the arrow.**
- **Point to Apply to Selected Slides.**

Radial is the desired design template for Slide 5 (Figure 4-83). If the Radial template is not displayed in the Apply a design template list, click the Additional Design Templates template to install additional templates or see your instructor.

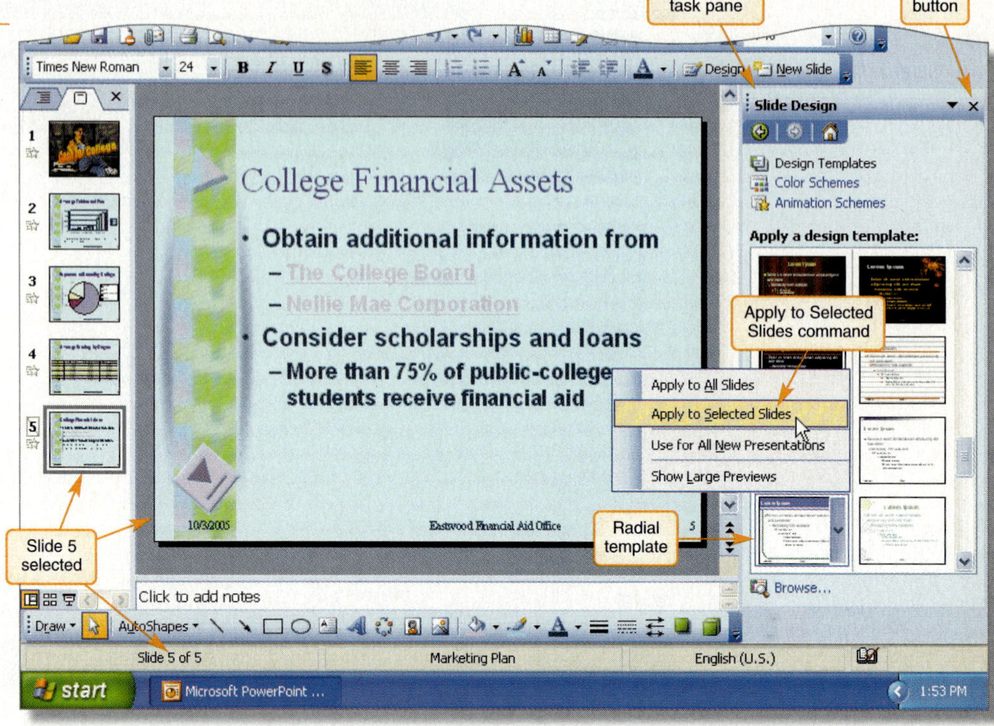

FIGURE 4-83

2

- **Click Apply to Selected Slides.**
- **Click the Close button in the Slide Design task pane.**

Slide 5 is displayed with the Radial design template (Figure 4-84).

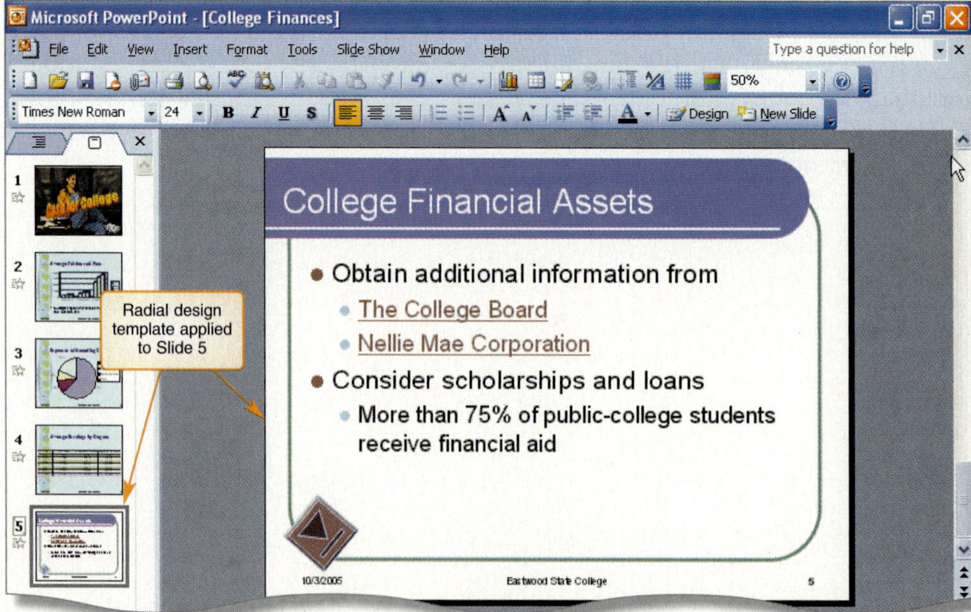

FIGURE 4-84

Slides 1 through 4 in the presentation have the Marketing Plan design template, and Slide 5 has the Radial design template. You should save these changes by clicking the Save button on the Formatting toolbar.

Adding Notes and Printing Speaker Notes

Slides and handouts usually are printed to distribute to audience members. These printouts also are helpful to speakers so they can write notes that will guide them through a presentation. As you create slides, you may find material you want to state verbally and do not want to include on the slide. You can type and format notes in the **notes pane** as you work in normal view and then print this information as **notes pages**. Notes pages print with a small image of the slide at the top and the comments below the slide. Charts, tables, and pictures added to the notes pane also print on these pages. You can make changes to the **notes master** if you want to alter the default settings, such as the font or the position of page elements, such as the slide area and notes area.

> *More About*
>
> **Modifying Page Setup**
>
> The slide size can be customized for printing. If you want a slide to print in a precise size, click Page Setup on the File menu and then click the desired option in the Slides sized for box. If you click Custom, you can enter the desired measurements in the Width and Height text boxes. While all slides in the presentation will print in this one orientation, you can specify other setups for printing an outline, handouts, and notes pages.

Adding Notes

In this project, comments are added to Slides 2, 4, and 5. After adding comments, you can print a set of speaker notes. The following steps add text to the notes pane on these slides and then print the notes.

To Add Notes

1

- **With Slide 5 displaying, click the notes pane and then type** `More than $90 billion in financial aid is available in the form of grants, loans, and jobs.`

The **notes** *provide supplementary information for a speaker at a presentation (Figure 4-85)*

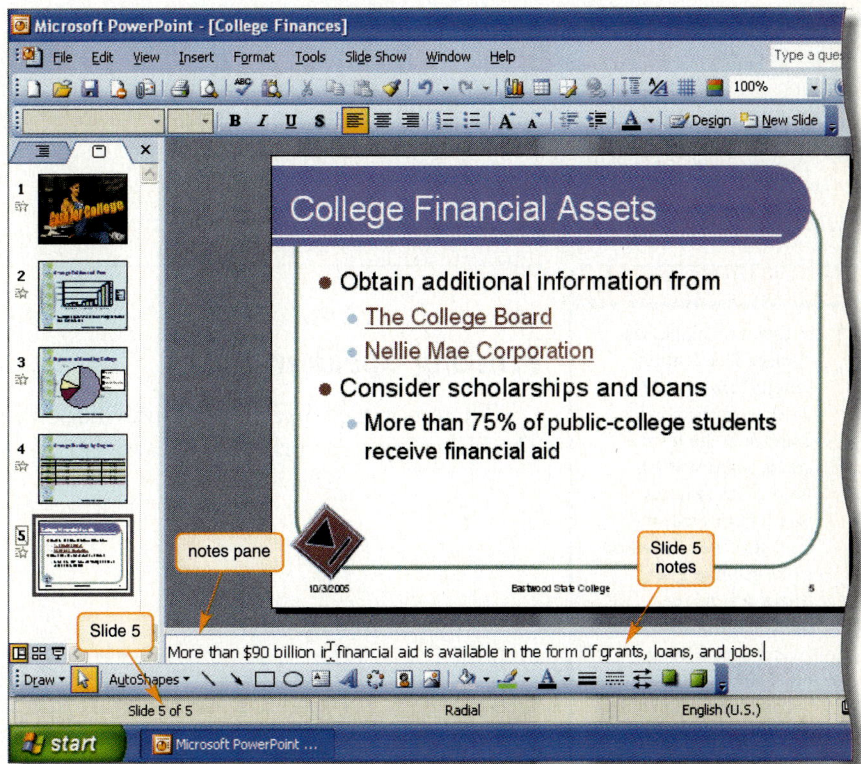

FIGURE 4-85

2

- **Click the Previous Slide button to display Slide 4.**
- **Click the notes pane and then type** `Most graduates state that their increased earnings make their bachelor's degree a worthwhile investment.`

3

- **Click the Previous Slide button two times to display Slide 2.**
- **Click the notes pane and then type** `Every year it becomes increasingly difficult for students to afford attending college. Many students use their credit cards to fund their educations.`

Only the last line of these notes is displayed (Figure 4–86). Dragging the splitter bar up enlarges the notes pane. Clicking the notes pane scroll arrows allows you to view all of the text.

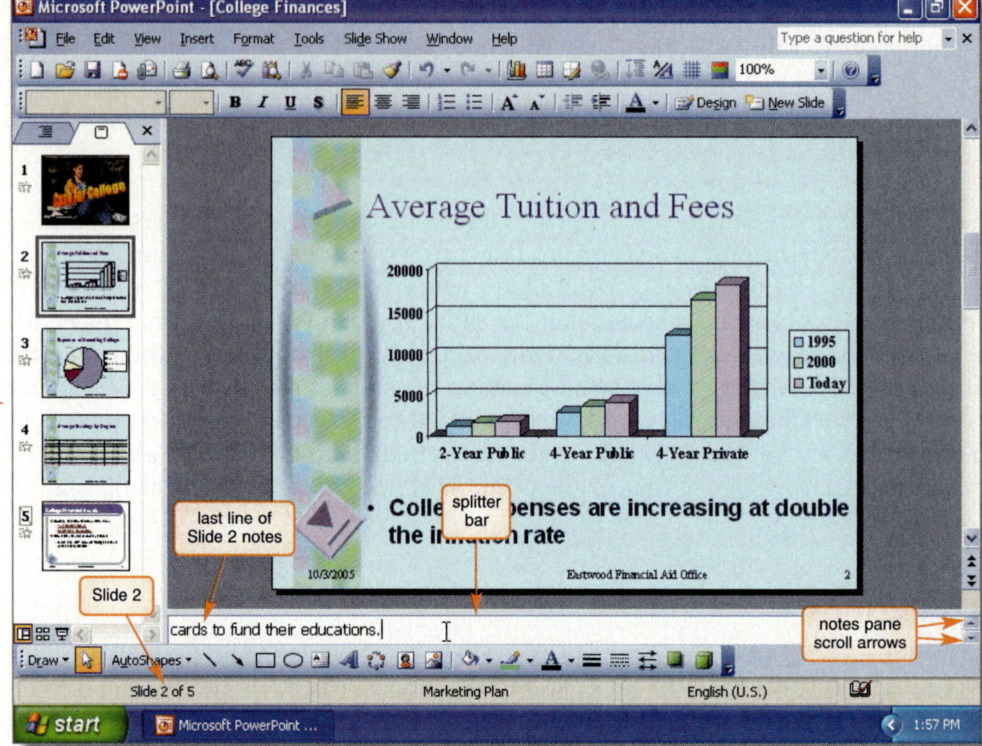

FIGURE 4-86

Other Ways

1. In Dictation mode, say "[select Slide 5 notes pane], More than $90 billion in financial aid is available in the form of grants, loans, and jobs., [select Slide 4 notes pane], Most graduates state that their increased earnings make their bachelor's degree a worthwhile investment., [select Slide 2 notes pane], Every year it becomes increasingly difficult for students to afford attending college. Many students use their credit cards to fund their educations."

Printing Speaker Notes

These notes give additional information that supplements the text on the slides. The following steps print the speaker notes.

To Print Speaker Notes

1

- **Click File on the menu bar and then click Print.**
- **When the Print dialog box is displayed, click the Print what box arrow and then click Notes Pages.**

The Print dialog box is displayed (Figure 4-87). Notes Pages appears highlighted in the Print what box.

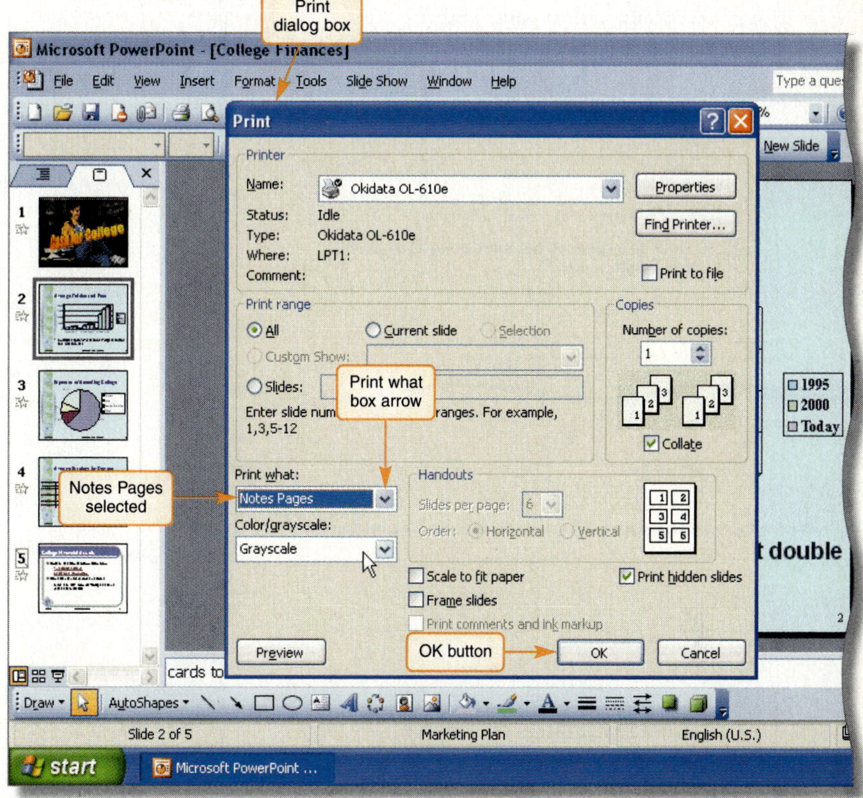

FIGURE 4-87

2

- **Click the OK button.**

PowerPoint displays the five notes pages (Figure 4-88). The notes appear on Slides 2, 4, and 5.

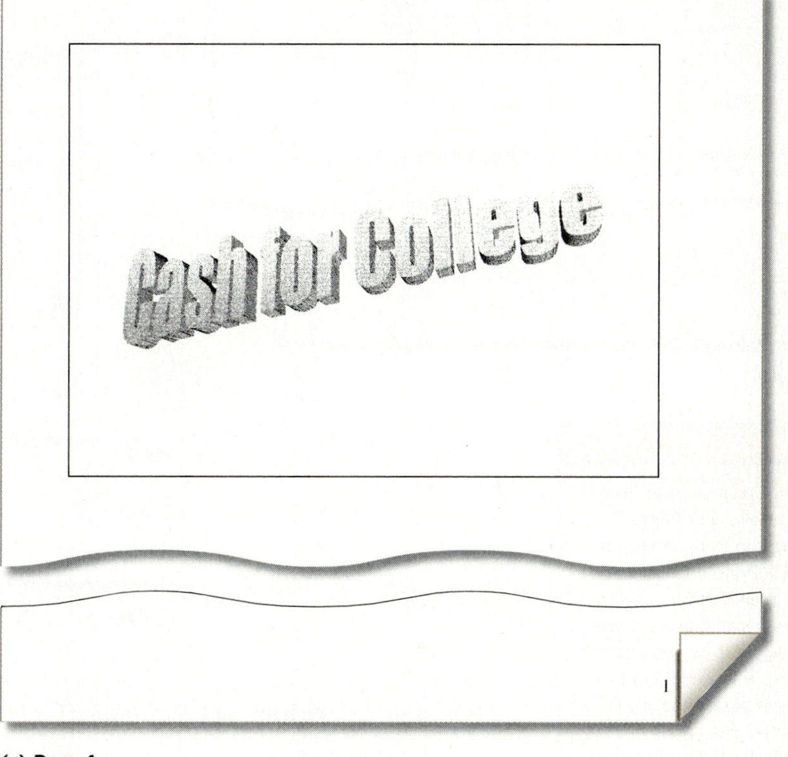

(a) Page 1

FIGURE 4-88

(continued)

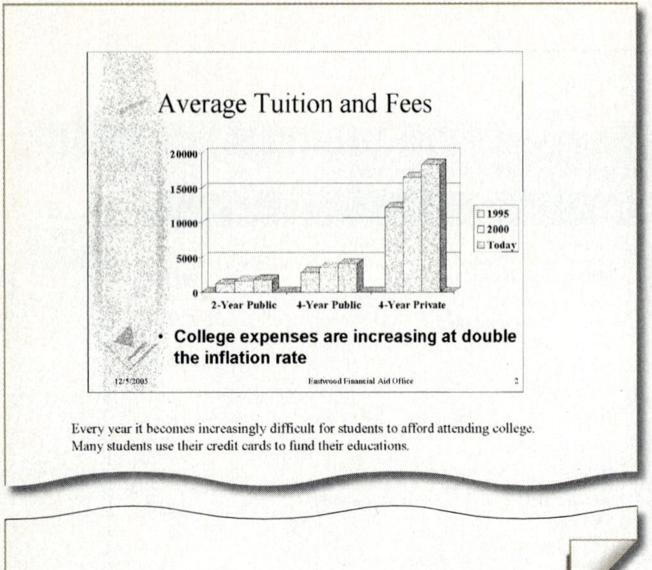

(b) Page 2

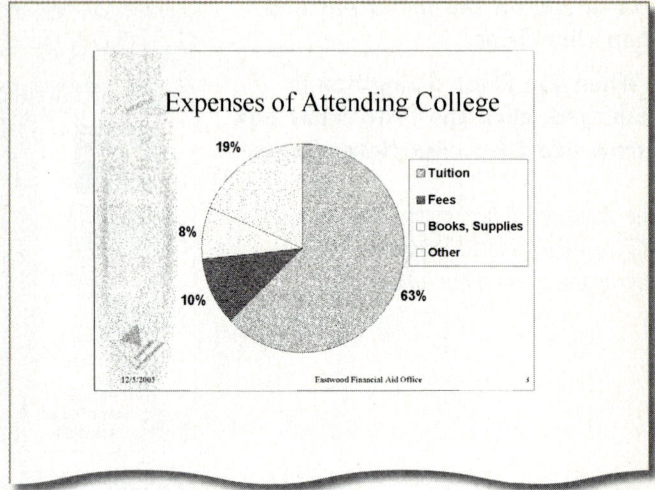

(c) Page 3

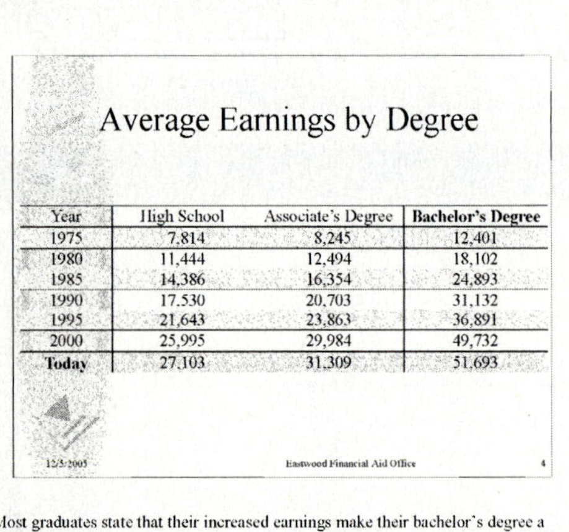

Average Earnings by Degree

Year	High School	Associate's Degree	Bachelor's Degree
1975	7,814	8,245	12,401
1980	11,444	12,494	18,102
1985	14,386	16,354	24,893
1990	17,530	20,703	31,132
1995	21,643	23,863	36,891
2000	25,995	29,984	49,732
Today	27,103	31,309	51,693

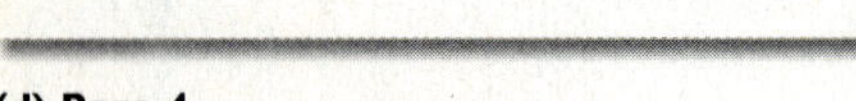

(d) Page 4

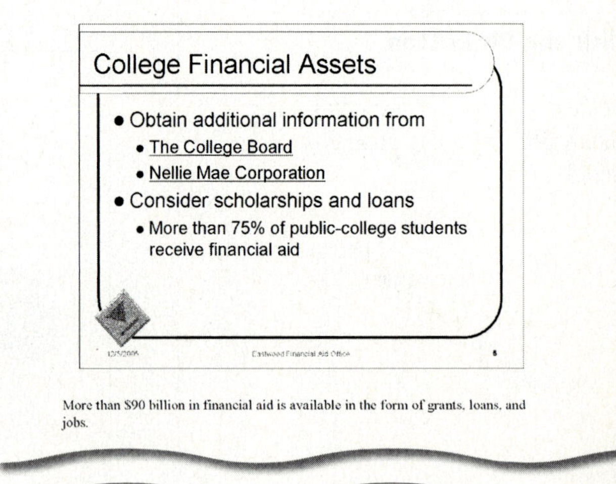

(e) Page 5

FIGURE 4-88 *(continued)*

Other Ways

1. On File menu click Print Preview, click Notes Pages in Print What list, click Print button on Print Preview toolbar
2. Press ALT+F, press P, press TAB, press W, press DOWN ARROW key until Notes Pages is selected, press ENTER, press ENTER
3. In Voice Command mode, say "File, Print, Print What, Notes Pages, OK"

Saving the Presentation in Rich Text Format

The presentation is complete. You now should spell check and then save it again by clicking the Spelling and Save buttons, respectively, on the Standard toolbar. So you can import the text into a Word document or another word processing package, you will save the presentation in **Rich Text Format (.rtf)**. When you save the file as an .rtf outline, you lose any graphics, such as the Word table and Excel worksheet. The following steps save the presentation as an .rtf outline.

More About

Page Orientation

Once you change the page orientation for slides or for the outline, handouts, and notes pages, you may discover that your text placeholders or other slide objects are not proportional or no longer look balanced on the slide. If this occurs, consider changing the shape or placement of these slide elements on each slide. If the change needs to be made on every slide, make the modifications on the slide master.

To Save the Presentation in Rich Text Format

1

- **Click File on the menu bar and then click Save As.**

2

- **When the Save As dialog box is displayed, click the Save as type box arrow, scroll down, and then click Outline/RTF.**

You can save the presentation in a variety of formats (Figure 4-89).

3

- **Click the Save button.**

PowerPoint saves the text of the presentation with the file name College Finances.rtf. If no more space remains on your Data Disk, insert another floppy disk.

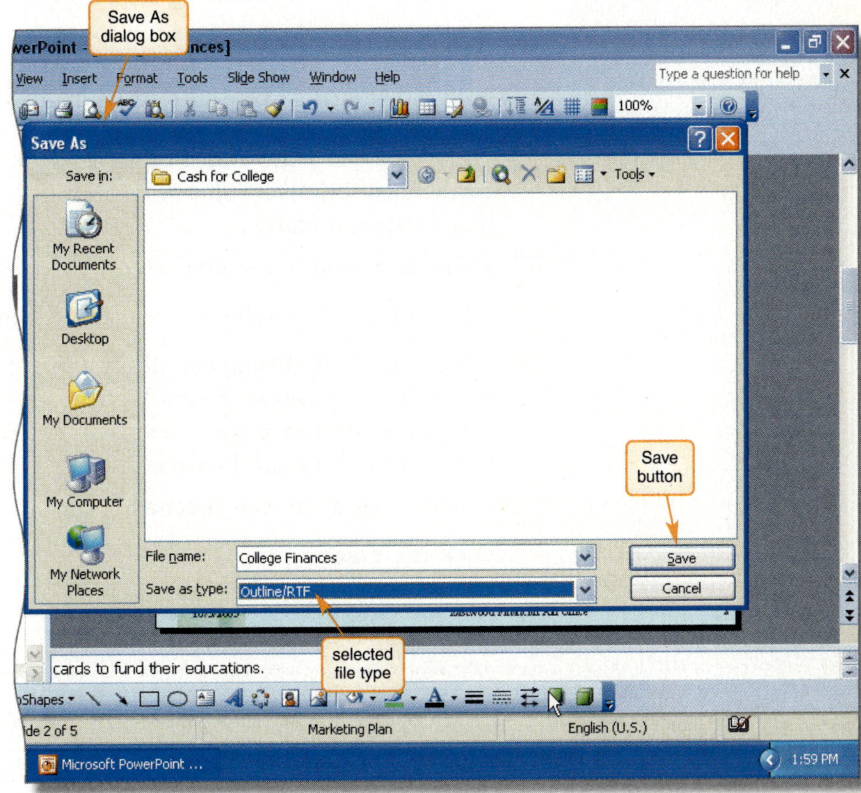

FIGURE 4-89

Other Ways

1. Press ALT+F, press A, press ALT+T, press DOWN ARROW key, press ENTER, press ENTER
2. In Voice Command mode, say "File, Save As, Save as type, Outline RTF, Save"

More About

Sending to Microsoft Word

When you send your PowerPoint slides to Microsoft Word, they are visible in the word processing document. To send the slides, point to Send To on the File menu and then click Microsoft Office Word. Select the desired page layout, and then click either the Paste or Paste link option button in the Add slides to Microsoft Office Word document area. Click Paste if you want to embed the slides; click Paste link if you want to link the slides to the Word document so they will be updated in the Word document when you edit them in PowerPoint.

Running a Slide Show with Hyperlinks and an Action Button

The College Finances presentation contains a variety of useful features that provide value to an audience. The hyperlinks on Slide 5 show useful Web sites that give current information on finding cash to finance a college education. In addition, the action button allows a presenter to jump to Slide 5 while Slides 2, 3, or 4 are being displayed. If an audience member asks a question or if the presenter needs to answer specific questions regarding financial aid, the information on Slide 5 can be accessed immediately by clicking the action button.

Running a Slide Show with Hyperlinks to the Internet

Running a slide show that contains hyperlinks is the same as running any other slide show. When a presentation contains hyperlinks and you are connected to the Internet, you can click the hyperlink text to command your default browser to locate the hyperlink file. The following steps run the College Finances presentation.

To Run the Slide Show with Hyperlinks to the Internet

1. **Click Slide 1 on the Slides tab. Click the Slide Show button at the lower-left corner of the PowerPoint window. Slide 1 is displayed and the sound effect plays automatically.**
2. **Slides 2, 3, and 4 are displayed according to the slide timings.**
3. **When Slide 4 is displayed, press the H key.**
4. **When Slide 5 is displayed, click the first hyperlink to start your browser and view The College Board Web page. If necessary, maximize the Web page window when the page is displayed. Click the Close button on the Web page title bar to stop the browser.**
5. **Repeat Step 3 for the second hyperlink.**
6. **Click the black slide.**

Slide 1 is displayed in normal view.

More About

Black Slides

A black slide may help an audience focus on the speaker. To create this slide, click the New Slide button on the Standard toolbar, select the Blank slide layout, click Format on the menu bar, click Background, click the Background fill box arrow, and then click the color black.

Running a Slide Show with an Action Button

Once you have run the presentation and have seen all slides display, you should run the presentation again to use the action button. When you click the action button in the College Finances slide show, PowerPoint will display Slide 5 because you hyperlinked the button to the last slide in the presentation. When Slide 5 is displayed and you view the information and Web sites, you want to return to one of the other slides in the presentation. Jumping to particular slides in a presentation is called **navigating**. PowerPoint provides a set of keyboard shortcuts to help you navigate to various slides during the slide show. These navigational features are listed in Table 4-6.

Table 4-6 Navigation Shortcut Keys

KEYBOARD SHORTCUT	PURPOSE
N Click SPACEBAR RIGHT ARROW DOWN ARROW ENTER PAGE DOWN	Advance to the next slide
P BACKSPACE LEFT ARROW UP ARROW PAGE UP	Return to the previous slide
Number followed by ENTER	Go to a specific slide
B PERIOD	Display a black screen Return to slide show from a black screen
W COMMA	Display a white screen Return to slide show from a white screen
ESC CTRL+BREAK HYPHEN	End a slide show

When running a slide show, you can press the F1 key to see a list of these keyboard controls. The following steps describe how the action button can be used to enhance a slide show being displayed in front of an audience.

To Run the Slide Show with an Action Button

1. **If necessary, click Slide 1 on the Slides tab. Click the Slide Show button at the lower-left corner of the PowerPoint window.**
2. **When Slide 3 is displayed, click the action button.**
3. **When Slide 5 is displayed, type the number 3 and then press the ENTER key to return to Slide 3.**

More About

The PowerPoint Help System

Need Help? It is no further than the Type a question for help box on the menu bar in the upper-right corner of the window. Click the box that contains the text, Type a question for help (Figure 4-89 on page PPT 289), type `help`, and then press the ENTER key. PowerPoint responds with a list of topics you can click to learn about obtaining help on any PowerPoint-related topic. To find out what is new in PowerPoint 2003, type `what is new in PowerPoint` in the Type a question for help box.

Delivering and Navigating a Presentation Using the Slide Show Toolbar

When you begin running a slide show and move the mouse pointer, the Slide Show toolbar is displayed. The **Slide Show toolbar** contains buttons that allow you to navigate to the next side or previous slide, mark up the current slide, or change the current display. When you move the mouse, the toolbar is displayed in the lower-left corner of the slide; it disappears after the mouse has not been moved for three seconds. Table 4-7 describes the buttons on the Slide Show toolbar.

Table 4-7 Slide Show Toolbar Buttons

BUTTON	DESCRIPTION	FUNCTION
	previous slide	Previous slide or previous animated element on the slide
	pointer arrow	Shortcut menu for arrows, pens, and highlighters
	slide show options	Shortcut menu for slide navigation and screen displays
	next slide	Next slide or next animated element on the slide

You click the arrow buttons on either end of the toolbar to navigate backward or forward through the slide show. The pointer arrow button has a variety of functions, most often to add **ink** notes or drawings to your presentation to emphasize aspects of slides or make handwritten notes. This feature is available in all views except Slide Sorter view. To highlight items on a slide in Slide Show view, you would follow these steps.

To Highlight Items on a Slide

1. **If the Slide Show toolbar is not visible, rest the mouse pointer on the slide or click Options on the Tools menu, click the View tab and then click Show popup toolbar.**
2. **On the Slide Show toolbar, click the pointer arrow and then click Highlighter.**
3. **Move the mouse to highlight any area of the slide.**

Instead of the Highlighter, you also can click Ballpoint Pen and Felt Tip Pen to draw or write notes on the slides. To change the color of ink during the presentation, you would perform the following step.

To Change Ink Color

1. **Click the pointer arrow, point to Ink Color, and the select the desired color.**

When the presentation ends, PowerPoint will prompt you to keep or discard the ink annotations.

To hide the mouse pointer and Slide Show toolbar during the slide show, you would perform the following step.

To Hide the Mouse Pointer and Slide Show Toolbar

1 **Click the pointer arrow on the Slide Show toolbar, point to Arrow Options, and then click Hidden.**

By default, the mouse pointer and toolbar are set at Automatic, which means they are hidden after three seconds of no movement. After you hide the mouse pointer and toolbar, they remain hidden until you choose one of the other commands on the Pointer Options submenu. They are displayed again when you move the mouse.

To keep the mouse pointer and toolbar displayed at all times during a slide show, you would perform the following step.

To Constantly Display the Mouse Pointer and Slide Show Toolbar

1 **Click the pointer arrow on the Slide Show toolbar, point to Arrow Options, and then click Visible.**

When you click the slide show options button on the Slide Show toolbar, PowerPoint displays the Popup menu that appears when you right-click a slide in slide sorter view. This menu is described on pages PPT 48 – 50.

The College Finances presentation now is complete. If you made any changes to your presentation since your last save, you now should save it again before quitting PowerPoint.

Project Summary

Project 4 started by using the AutoContent Wizard to generate some text and graphics using the Marketing Plan design template. After adding a picture to the title slide background, you created a WordArt title and added a sound effect to that slide. Next, you used Microsoft Graph to create a chart and then inserted an Excel chart and added a Word table. You then created a slide containing hyperlinks to Web sites containing additional financial aid information. You then customized presentation elements by changing the color scheme, modifying the footer, and adding an action button. You used the Thesaurus to change the slide wording. After adding and modifying the slide elements, you added slide transitions, rehearsed timings, and inserted a second slide master. To assist the individual who is presenting the slide show, you added notes to the slides and printed speaker notes. Finally, you saved the presentation in Rich Text Format and then ran the slide show to display the hyperlinks.

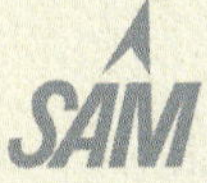

If you have a SAM user profile, you may have access to hands-on instruction, practice, and assessment of the skills covered in this project. Log in to your SAM account and go to your assignments page to see what your instructor has assigned.

What You Should Know

Having completed this project, you should be able to perform the tasks below. The tasks are listed in the same order they were presented in this project. For a list of the buttons, menus, toolbars, and commands introduced in this project, see the Quick Reference Summary at the back of this book and refer to the Page Number column.

1. Start and Customize a New Presentation (PPT 228)
2. Use the AutoContent Wizard (PPT 229)
3. Create a Folder and Save a Presentation (PPT 232)
4. Add a Picture to Create a Custom Background (PPT 232)
5. Delete the Title and Subtitle Text Placeholders (PPT 234)
6. Select a WordArt Style (PPT 236)
7. Enter the WordArt Text (PPT 237)
8. Change the WordArt Height and Width (PPT 239)
9. Display the Grid and Guides and Position the WordArt Object (PPT 241)
10. Hide Guides (PPT 243)
11. Add a Sound Effect (PPT 243)
12. Delete Slides (PPT 245)
13. Display the Next Slide and Edit the Title and Bulleted List Text (PPT 247)
14. Change the Slide Layout and Position the Text Placeholder (PPT 248)
15. Insert a Chart and Replace the Sample Data (PPT 249)
16. Display the Next Slide, Edit the Title Text, and Delete the Text Placeholder (PPT 252)
17. Insert an Excel Chart (PPT 253)
18. Scale and Move an Excel Chart (PPT 256)
19. Display the Next Slide, Edit the Title Text, and Change the Slide Layout (PPT 257)
20. Insert a Word Table (PPT 258)
21. Scale and Move a Word Table (PPT 259)
22. Display the Next Slide and Edit the Text (PPT 260)
23. Add a Hyperlink to a Slide (PPT 261)
24. Add the Remaining Hyperlink to a Slide (PPT 262)
25. Hide a Slide (PPT 264)
26. Find Text (PPT 265)
27. Find and Replace Text (PPT 265)
28. Find a Word and Use the Thesaurus (PPT 266)
29. Find a Second Synonym (PPT 268)
30. Change the Presentation Template Color Scheme (PPT 269)
31. Modify the Footer on the Slide Master (PPT 271)
32. Add an Action Button and an Action Setting (PPT 272)
33. Scale an Action Button (PPT 274)
34. Add a Fill Color to the Action Button (PPT 275)
35. Display Guides and Position the Action Button (PPT 276)
36. Rotate the Action Button (PPT 277)
37. Close Master View (PPT 278)
38. Add a Slide Transition Effect to a Slide Show (PPT 279)
39. Rehearse Timings (PPT 282)
40. Replace the Slide Master (PPT 284)
41. Add Notes (PPT 285)
42. Print Speaker Notes (PPT 287)
43. Save the Presentation in Rich Text Format (PPT 289)
44. Run the Slide Show with Hyperlinks to the Internet (PPT 290)
45. Run the Slide Show with an Action Button (PPT 291)
46. Highlight Items on a Slide (PPT 292)
47. Change Ink Color (PPT 292)
48. Hide the Mouse Pointer and Slide Show Toolbar (PPT 293)
49. Constantly Display the Mouse Pointer and Slide Show Toolbar (PPT 293)

Learn It Online

Instructions: To complete the Learn It Online exercises, start your browser, click the Address bar, and then enter the Web address scsite.com/ppt2003/learn. When the PowerPoint 2003 Learn It Online page is displayed, follow the instructions in the exercises below. Each exercise has instructions for printing your results, either for your own records or for submission to your instructor.

1 Project Reinforcement TF, MC, and SA

Below PowerPoint Project 4, click the Project Reinforcement link. Print the quiz by clicking Print on the File menu for each page. Answer each question.

2 Flash Cards

Below PowerPoint Project 4, click the Flash Cards link and read the instructions. Type 20 (or a number specified by your instructor) in the Number of playing cards text box, type your name in the Enter your Name text box, and then click the Flip Card button. When the flash card is displayed, read the question and then click the ANSWER box arrow to select an answer. Flip through Flash Cards. If your score is 15 (75%) correct or greater, click Print on the File menu to print your results. If your score is less than 15 (75%) correct, then redo this exercise by clicking the Replay button.

3 Practice Test

Below PowerPoint Project 4, click the Practice Test link. Answer each question, enter your first and last name at the bottom of the page, and then click the Grade Test button. When the graded practice test is displayed on your screen, click Print on the File menu to print a hard copy. Continue to take practice tests until you score 80% or better.

4 Who Wants To Be a Computer Genius?

Below PowerPoint Project 4, click the Computer Genius link. Read the instructions, enter your first and last name at the bottom of the page, and then click the PLAY button. When your score is displayed, click the PRINT RESULTS link to print a hard copy.

5 Wheel of Terms

Below PowerPoint Project 4, click the Wheel of Terms link. Read the instructions, and then enter your first and last name and your school name. Click the PLAY button. When your score is displayed, right-click the score and then click Print on the shortcut menu to print a hard copy.

6 Crossword Puzzle Challenge

Below PowerPoint Project 4, click the Crossword Puzzle Challenge link. Read the instructions, and then enter your first and last name. Click the SUBMIT button. Work the crossword puzzle. When you are finished, click the Submit button. When the crossword puzzle is redisplayed, click the Print Puzzle button to print a hard copy.

7 Tips and Tricks

Below PowerPoint Project 4, click the Tips and Tricks link. Click a topic that pertains to Project 4. Right-click the information and then click Print on the shortcut menu. Construct a brief example of what the information relates to in PowerPoint to confirm you understand how to use the tip or trick.

8 Newsgroups

Below PowerPoint Project 4, click the Newsgroups link. Click a topic that pertains to Project 4. Print three comments.

9 Expanding Your Horizons

Below PowerPoint Project 4, click the Articles for Microsoft PowerPoint link. Click a topic that pertains to Project 4. Print the information. Construct a brief example of what the information relates to in PowerPoint to confirm you understand the contents of the article.

10 Search Sleuth

Below PowerPoint Project 4, click the Search Sleuth link. To search for a term that pertains to this project, select a term below the Project 4 title and then use the Google search engine at google.com (or any major search engine) to display and print two Web pages that present information on the term.

11 PowerPoint Online Training

Below PowerPoint Project 4, click the PowerPoint Online Training link. When your browser displays the Microsoft Office Online Web page, click the PowerPoint link. Click one of the PowerPoint courses that covers one or more of the objectives listed at the beginning of the project on page PPT 226. Print the first page of the course before stepping through it.

12 Office Marketplace

Below PowerPoint Project 4, click the Office Marketplace link. When your browser displays the Microsoft Office Online Web page, click the Office Marketplace link. Click a topic that relates to PowerPoint. Print the first page.

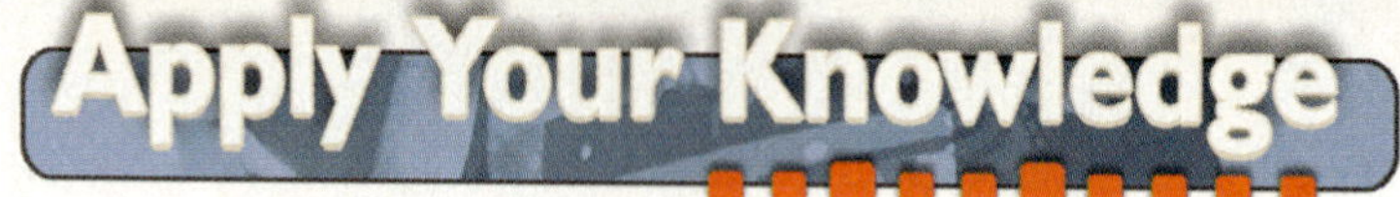

1 Seattle Fish Facts

Instructions: Start PowerPoint. Open the presentation Apply 4-1 Fish on the Data Disk. See the inside back cover of this book for instructions for downloading the Data Disk or see your instructor for information on accessing the clips and files required for this book. The two slides in the presentation give information on fish, with the background of The Seattle Aquarium on Slide 1 for interest. Make the following changes to the slides so they appear as shown in Figure 4-90.

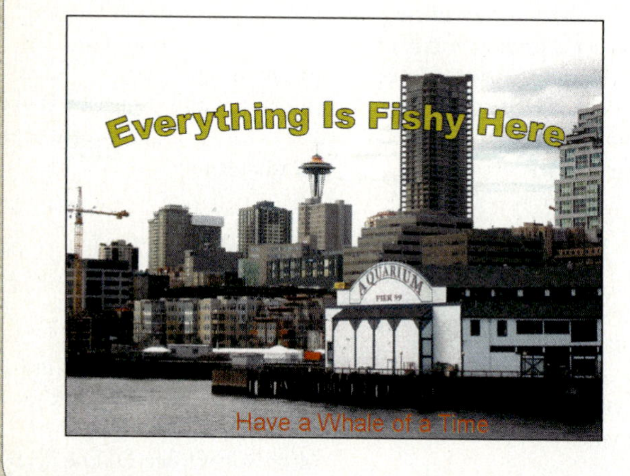

(a) Slide 1

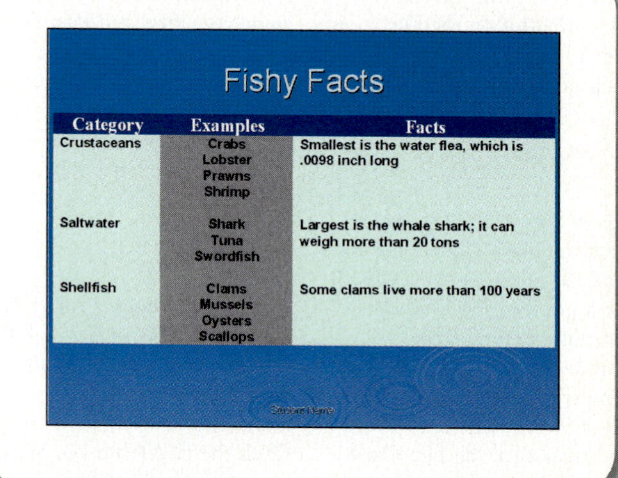

(b) Slide 2

FIGURE 4-90

Create a new folder with the name, Fish. Save the presentation with the file name, Apply 4-1 Seattle, in the new folder.

On Slide 1, apply the Network design template to the Title Slide slide layout and change the color scheme to the scheme in row 5, column 1. Add the picture, Seattle, from the Data Disk to the Slide 1 background and omit the background graphics from the master. Move the subtitle text placeholder down to the bottom of the slide. Change the subtitle text color to red (color 6 in the palette of available colors).

Delete the title text placeholder. Create the WordArt Object by selecting the WordArt style in row 1, column 3. Scale the WordArt height and width to 130 %. Change the WordArt object color by clicking the Fill Color button arrow on the Drawing toolbar and then clicking the color gold (color 5 in the palette of available colors). Drag the WordArt object to the position shown in Figure 4-90a.

Create a hyperlink for the WordArt object with a Seattle visitor's Web site. To create this hyperlink, select the WordArt object, click the Insert Hyperlink button on the Formatting toolbar, and then type `www.seeseattle.org` in the Address text box when the Insert Hyperlink dialog box is displayed. Click the OK button.

In the Slide 1 notes pane, type `Seattle is a scenic waterfront city with views of the Olympic and Cascade Mountains.`

Apply Your Knowledge

Using the Slide master, add your name to the Slide 2 Footer Area. On Slide 2, apply the Ripple design template. Insert the Word table, Fish Facts, from the Data Disk. Scale the table to 160 % and then center the table under the title text placeholder.

In the Slide 2 notes pane, type `The Seattle Aquarium features a Pacific coral reef, a salmon ladder, sea otters, and other fish and mammals.`

Apply the Fade Smoothly slide transition effect to both slides with the Slow transition speed and the Breeze sound.

Save the presentation again and then run the slide show. Mark up the slides using the highlighter and orange ink and keep the ink annotations. Print speaker notes and then hand in the hard copies to your instructor.

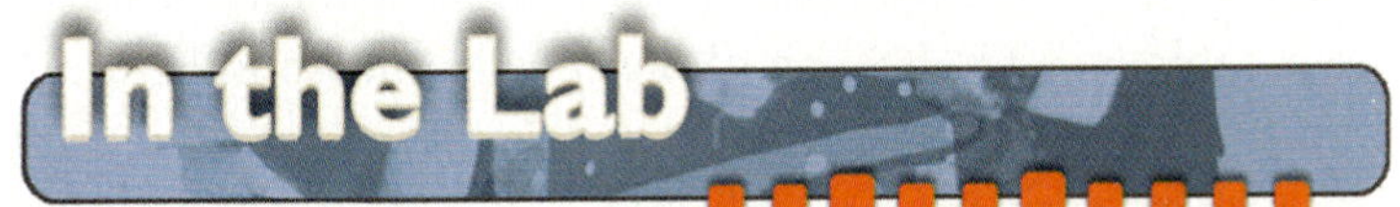

1 Credit Card Debt

Problem: The College Finances presentation in the project explores the costs of attending college and finding monetary support for meeting the expenses. The notes on Slide 2 indicate that many students use credit cards to fund their college bills. While credit cards are convenient and generally easily accessible, they can become a burden when the balance exceeds household income. Credit card debt has risen dramatically in recent years as unemployment has increased and college expenses have increased more quickly than inflation rates. Your campus credit union offers services for students and staff and also offers a credit card. The manager, Danny Dollars, wants to emphasize that the near-record level of debt compared to disposable income is reaching dangerous levels for many students. He has surveyed the credit union members and found that the average amount of debt per household has risen for both undergraduate and graduate students in the past 15 years. The statistics from his survey are summarized in Table 4-8.

Table 4-8 Debt Percent Per Household

	15 YEARS AGO	10 YEARS AGO	5 YEARS AGO	TODAY
Undergraduate Students	52.3	67.3	74.2	81.2
Graduate Students	63.4	76.8	81.2	87.3

You have a part-time job as a teller, and Danny has asked you to help him with seminars he is scheduling with incoming students. You have agreed to create a PowerPoint presentation to accompany his lectures and to run on a computer in the credit union office. Danny wants to approve the title slide before you work on the entire project, and you agree to create the title slide and slide showing the debt percent chart. The title slide contains a WordArt Object and a picture as the background. You create the slides shown in Figures 4-91a and 4-91b on pages PPT 298 and PPT 299.

(continued)

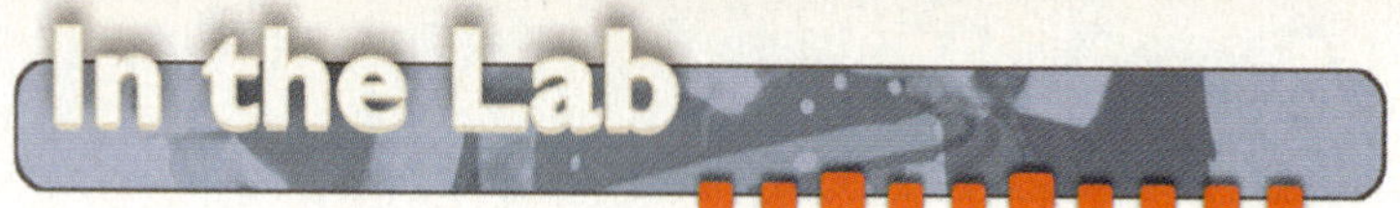

Credit Card Debt *(continued)*

Instructions: Perform the following tasks:

1. Start PowerPoint, open a new presentation, and apply the Slit design template. Change the color scheme to the gray scheme in row 4, column 2. Add the ATM picture from the Data Disk to the Slide 1 background and omit the background graphics from the master.
2. On Slide 1, delete the subtitle text placeholder. Create the WordArt element shown in Figure 4-91a. Use the WordArt style in row 3, column 1. Change the WordArt height to 2.5". Display the grid and guides and then position the object above the hand as shown in Figure 4-91a.
3. Type and then italicize the title text, change the font to Century Schoolbook, decrease the font size to 48, and change the font color to green (color 8 in the palette of available colors).
4. Drag the middle sizing handle on the top edge of the title text placeholder down to the top edge of the title text. Drag the title text placeholder to the bottom of the slide as shown in Figure 4-91a.
5. Insert a new slide and apply the Title and Content slide layout. Type `Debt Percent Per Household` in the title text placeholder. Add a chart using the data in Table 4-8 on the previous page. Scale the chart to 110 % and position the chart as shown in Figure 4-91b.
6. Add the Cover Right-Down slide transition effect to both slides. Modify the transition speed to Medium.
7. In the Slide 1 notes pane, type `Use your charge card in emergencies and shop with cash.` In the Slide 2 notes pane, type `One of your classmates had $207,000 in credit card debt before graduation by charging tuition, books, rent, and educational expenses.`
8. Save the presentation with the file name, Lab 4-1 Credit Card.
9. Display and print speaker notes. Close the presentation. Hand in the hard copy to your instructor.

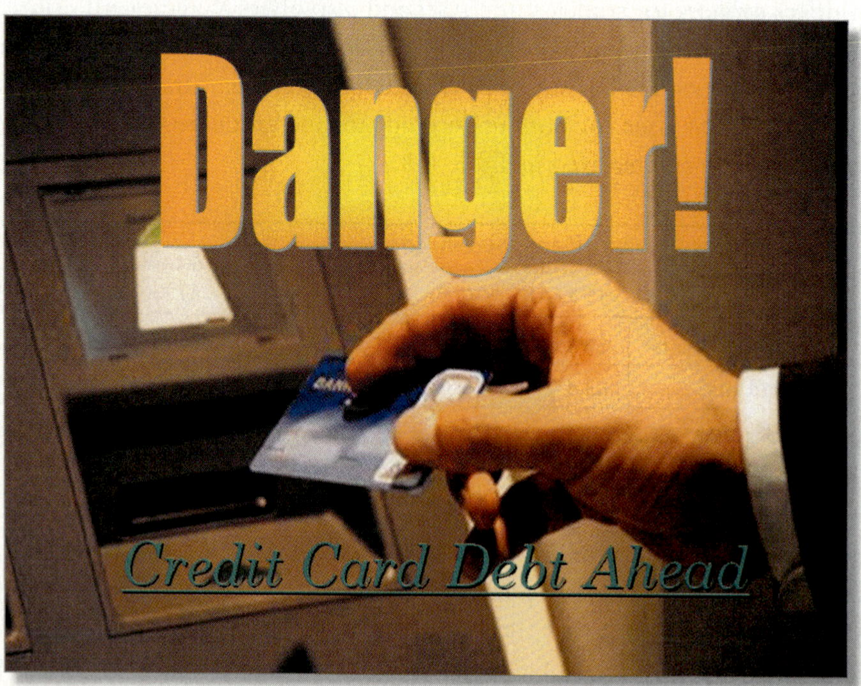

FIGURE 4-91a

In the Lab

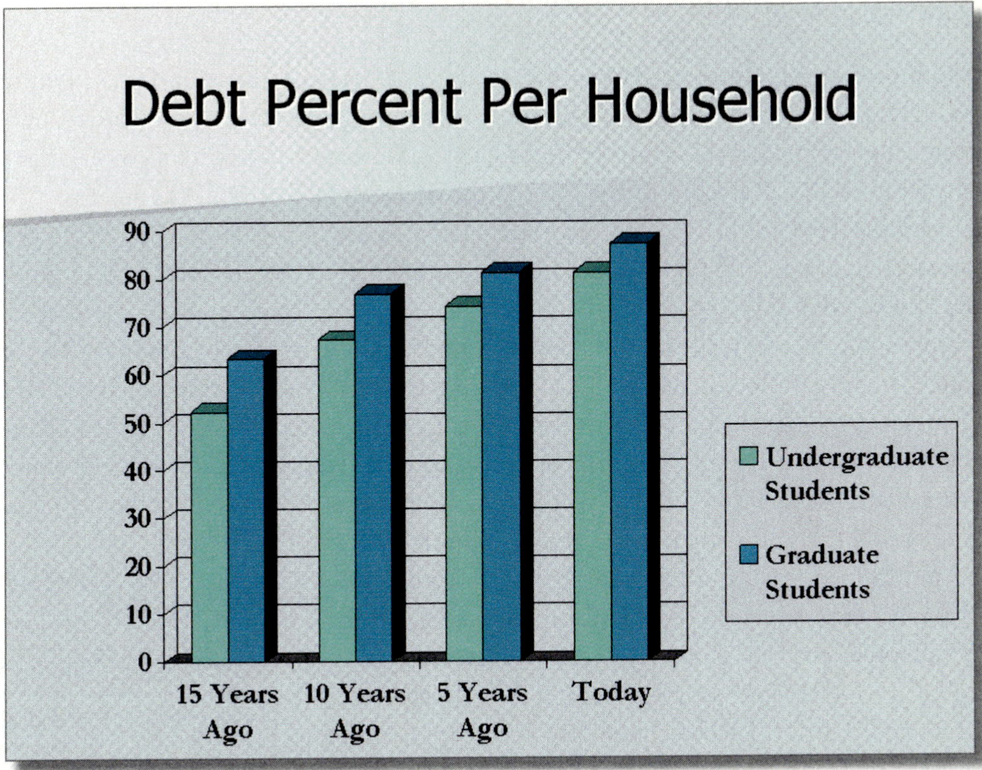

FIGURE 4-91b

2 Campus Job Fair

Problem: Every spring the Placement Office at your campus sponsors a job fair for upcoming graduates. This year the placement director wants to add interest to the event by showing a PowerPoint presentation with interesting information about the world of work. You have been asked to create this slide show that will run on a computer at a registration table on the day of the job fair. The slide show will focus on workplace facts and figures. It will include WordArt on the title slide and a chart showing the percentage of jobs in the healthcare field.

Instructions: Perform the following tasks:

1. Open a new presentation and use the AutoContent Wizard to generate content for the on-screen presentation. Use the Product/Services Overview presentation type in the Sales / Marketing category. When the Presentation options panel is displayed in the AutoContent Wizard, type `Northlake College Job Fair` as the presentation title and your name as the footer text. Include only the date last updated in the footer.
2. On Slide 1, modify the title text, Northlake College Job Fair, by changing the font to Bookman Old Style and italicizing and centering the text.
3. Delete the Your Logo Here placeholder in the upper-left corner and replace it with the WordArt object shown in Figure 4-92a on page PPT 301. Create this object using the WordArt style in row 5, column 1. Scale the WordArt object to 125 %.

(continued)

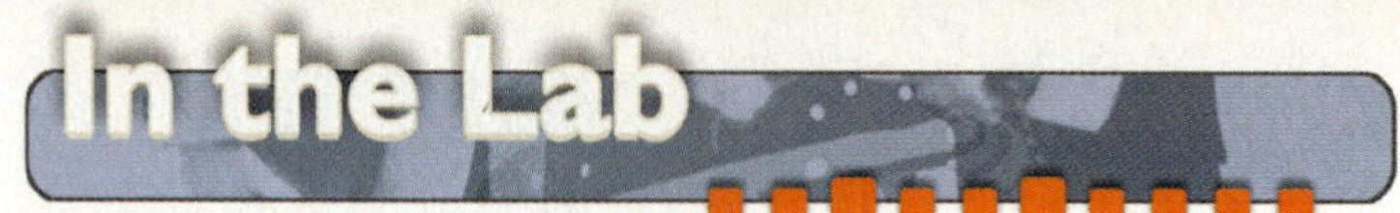

Campus Job Fair *(continued)*

4. Replace the subtitle text with the text shown in Figure 4-92a. Increase the subtitle text font size to 60 and bold the text. Change the font color to dark brown (color 6 in the palette of available colors).
5. Insert the sound file, Happy Urban, from the Data Disk and instruct PowerPoint to play the sound automatically. Drag the speaker icon off the slide to the lower-right corner of the screen.
6. On Slide 2, Overview, replace the bulleted text with the text shown in Figure 4-92b. Change the title text font to Bookman Old Style. Bold the title and bulleted text. Change the color scheme only for this slide to the scheme in row 2, column 1.
7. On Slide 3, replace the title text, Features & Benefits, with the title text shown in Figure 4-92c. Bold this text and change the font to Bookman Old Style. Delete the bulleted text, change the slide layout to Title Only, and then insert the Excel chart, Health Employment.xls, from the Data Disk. Scale this chart to 175 %, display the grid and guides, and position it as shown in Figure 4-92c. Insert the sound file, Heartbeat, from your Data Disk and instruct PowerPoint to play the sound automatically. Drag the speaker icon off the slide to the lower-right corner of the screen. If desired, delete the bullets.
8. On Slide 4, Applications, enter the title text shown in Figure 4-92d. Change the title text font to Bookman Old Style. Bold the text. Apply the Title and Content slide layout. If desired, delete the bullets.
9. Add a chart using the data in Table 4-9. Dr. Scholl's and the American Podiatry Association compiled these figures. Scale the chart to 105 % and position the chart as shown in Figure 4-91d.
10. Delete Slides 5, 6, and 7.
11. Use the Slide master to change the first-level paragraph bullet to a bull's eye, which is part of the Wingdings font. Increase the bullet size to 110 percent of text and change the color to black (color 2 in the palette of available colors).
12. Apply the Faded zoom animation scheme to all slides; the Cover Left-Down slide transition effect to Slides 2, 3, and 4; and the Fade Smoothly slide transition effect to Slide 1.
13. Use the Thesaurus to find a synonym for the word, positions.
14. Hide Slide 3.
15. Create a new folder with the name, Northlake College. Save the presentation with the file name, Lab 4-2 Job Fair, in the new folder. Save the presentation as a Rich Text Format outline and then send the presentation to Microsoft Word.
16. Run the Job Fair presentation. Hide Slide2. Run the presentation again displaying all stock. Mark up the slides using the Ballpoint Pen and blue ink and keep the ink annotations.
17. Print the slides as a handout with two slides on one page.

Table 4-9 Walking Professionals

PROFESSION	MILES WALKED YEARLY
Police Officer	1,632
Letter Carrier	1,056
TV Reporter	1,008
Nurse	942
Doctor	840

In the Lab

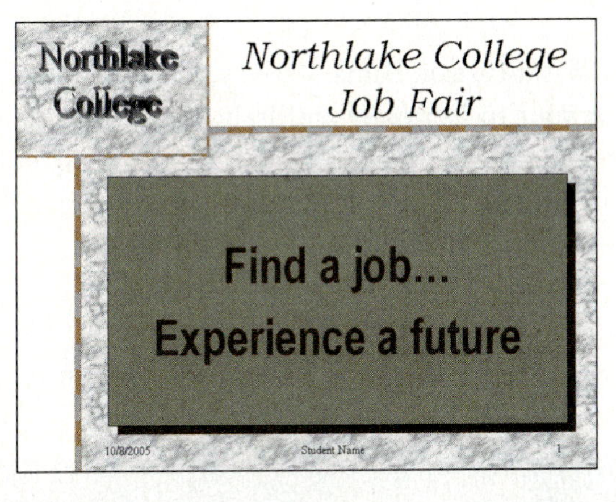

(a) Slide 1

Overview

- More than 500 employers
  - Searching for qualified graduates in fields from aviation to zoology
- Full- and part-time positions available
  - Permanent and seasonal job openings

10/8/2005 Student Name 2

(b) Slide 2

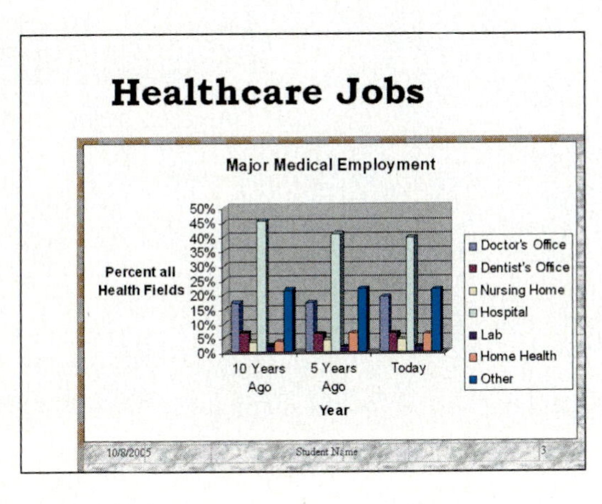

(c) Slide 3

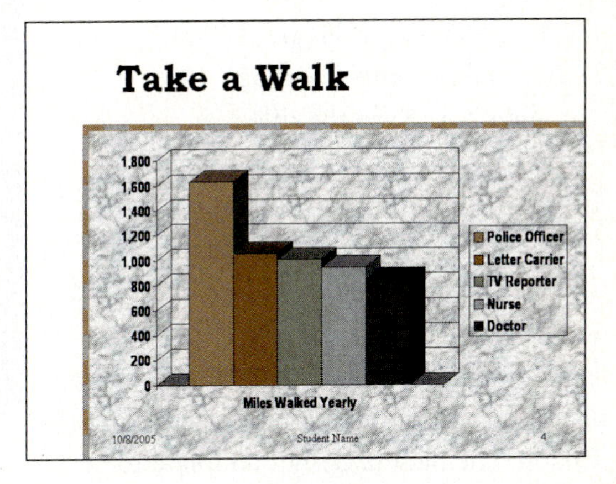

(d) Slide 4

FIGURE 4-92

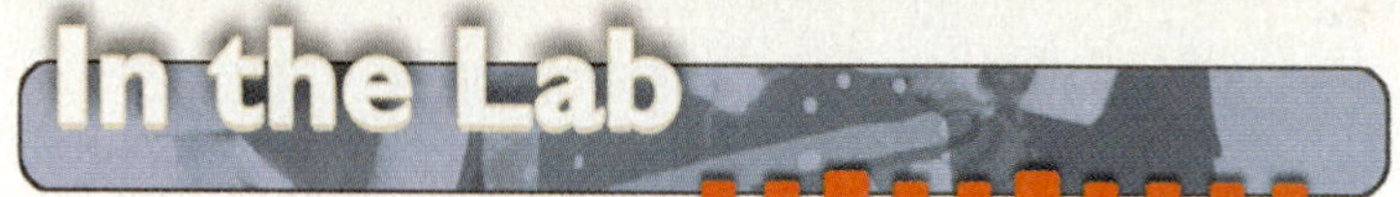

3 U Travel 2 Travel Agency's European Tour

Problem: You work for the local travel agency, U Travel 2. Your supervisor, Annie Airway, has asked you to make a presentation to community groups to promote the newest tour to Germany and Italy. You decide to create a PowerPoint slide show to accompany your presentation and use the AutoContent Wizard to help you develop the key ideas for the slides. You create the presentation shown in Figures 4-93a through 4-93d.

Instructions: Perform the following tasks:

1. Create a new presentation, and use the AutoContent Wizard to generate content for the on-screen presentation. Use the Project Overview presentation type in the Project category. Include the date and slide number in the footer. Enter your name as the footer text.
2. On Slide 1, type the title and subtitle text shown in Figure 4-93a. Insert WordArt with the text, Book Now!, using the WordArt style in row 5, column 3. Scale the WordArt height and width to 215 %. Display the grid and guides, and position the art as shown in Figure 4-93a.
3. Delete Slides 3 and 6 through 11.
4. On Slide 2, replace the title text, Project Goals, with the text shown in Figure 4-93b. Italicize and bold this text. Delete the text placeholder. Change the slide layout to Title only. Insert the Word table, Travel Program, from the Data Disk. Scale the table to 205 % and center the table under the title text placeholder.
5. Change the Slide 2 design template to Echo and then change the color scheme to the scheme in row 5, column 2.
6. Insert an Information action button to the right of the Day 1 highlight table text, Explore Heidelberg Castle. Hyperlink the button to Slide 3 (Next Slide). Play the Wind sound when the mouse is clicked. Change the action button fill color to blue (color 7 in the palette of available colors) and scale it to 35 %.

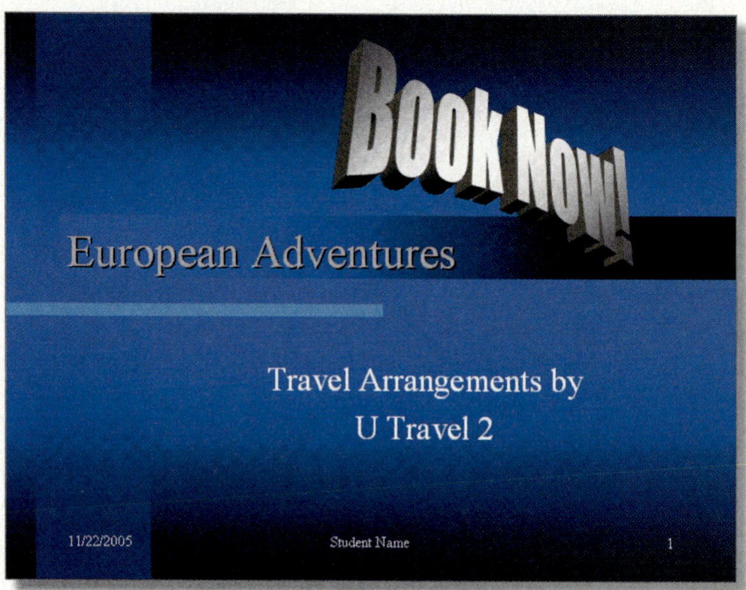

FIGURE 4-93a

Tour Highlights

Day	City	Highlight
1	Heidelberg	Explore Schloss Castle
2	Munich	Two-hour walking tour
3	Munich	Visit Nymphenburg Palace
4	Venice	Tour Piazza San Marco
5	Venice	Gondola ride on Grand Canal
6	Lucerne	View medieval prosperity
7	Lucerne	Boat trip to Mt. Pilatus

2 Student Name 11/22/2005

FIGURE 4-93b

In the Lab

7. Insert an Information action button to the right of the Day 4 highlight table text, Tour Piazza San Marco. Hyperlink the button to Slide 4 (Last Slide). Play the Arrow sound when the mouse is clicked. Change the action button fill color to blue (color 7 in the palette of available colors) and scale it to 35 %.
8. On Slide 3, replace the title text with the title text, Historic Heidelberg, and then italicize and bold this text and change the font color to red (color 7 in the palette of available colors). Change the slide layout to Title, Text, and Content and replace the bulleted text with the text shown in Figure 4-93c. Insert the Heidelberg picture from the Data Disk, scale it to 25 %, display the grid and guides, and move it to the location shown in the figure. Create a hyperlink for the word, Heidelberg, with the URL, www.heidelberg.de.
9. Create a hyperlink for the Heidelberg picture to Slide 2 by selecting the picture and clicking the Insert Hyperlink button. When the Insert Hyperlink dialog box is displayed, click the Place in This Document button in the Link to list, click the 2. Tour Highlights slide title in the Select a place in this document list, and then click the OK button.
10. On Slide 4, replace the title text with the title text, Venice Vistas, and then italicize and bold this text and change the font color to red (color 7 in the palette of available colors). Change the slide layout to Title, Content, and Text and replace the bulleted text with the text shown in Figure 4-93d. Insert the Venice picture from the Data Disk, display the grid and guides, and move it to the location shown in the figure. Create a hyperlink for the word, Venice, with the URL, www.doge.it.

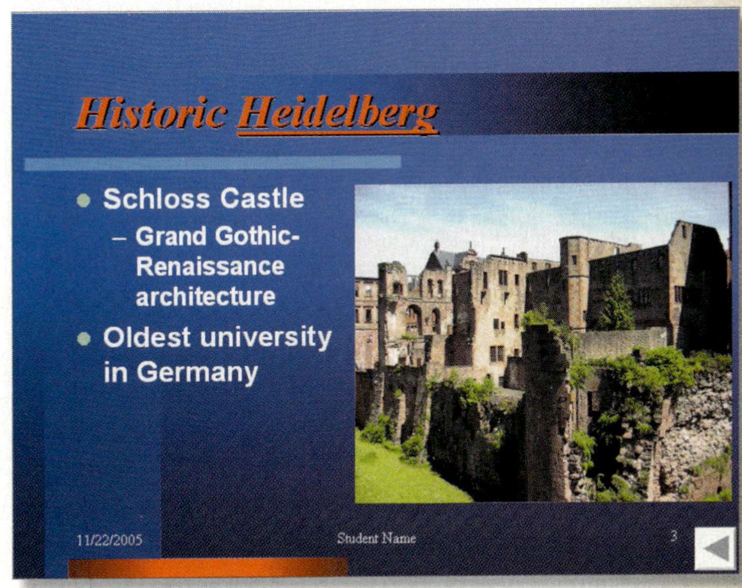

FIGURE 4-93c

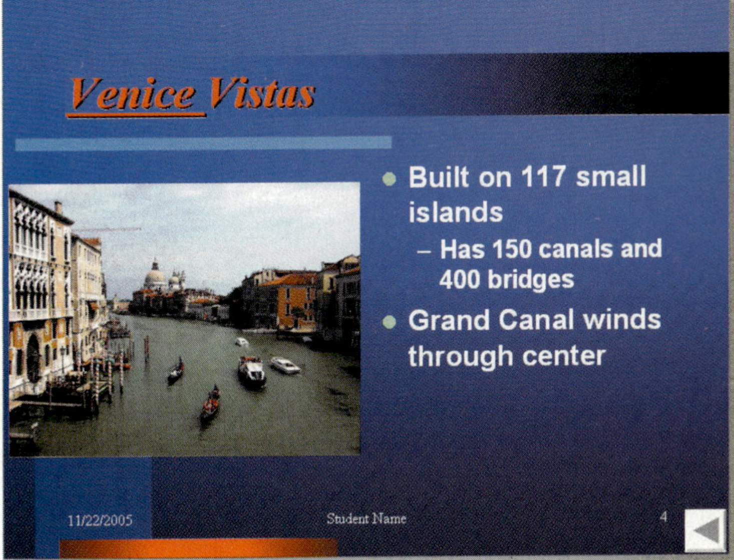

FIGURE 4-93d

(continued)

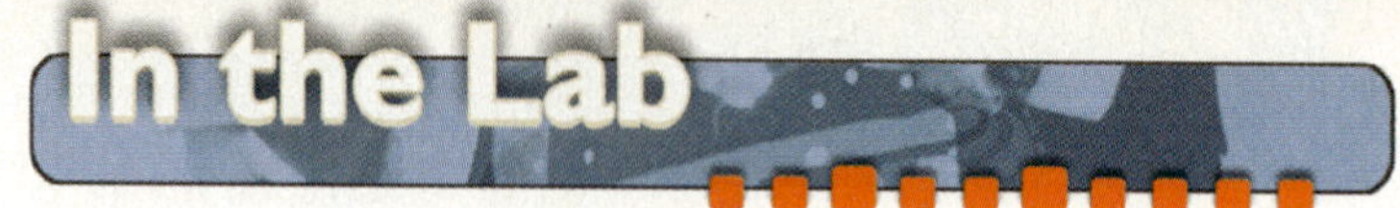

U Travel 2 Travel Agency's European Tour *(continued)*

11. On both Slide 3 and Slide 4, insert a Back or Previous action button in the lower-right corner of the slide. Hyperlink the button to Slide 2 by clicking the Hyperlink to arrow in the Action Settings dialog box, scrolling down and then clicking Slide, clicking 2. Tour Highlights in the Hyperlink to Slide dialog box, and then clicking the OK button. Change the action button fill color to white (color 2 in the row of available colors) and scale it to 50 %.
12. Apply the Comb Horizontal slide transition effect to Slides 2, 3, and 4. Modify the transition speed to Slow. Hide Slide 2.
13. Use the Thesaurus to find a synonym for the word, winds.
14. Rehearse timings for the slide show. Have Slide 1 display for 30 seconds, Slide 2 for 40 seconds, Slide 3 for 20 seconds, and Slide 4 for 20 seconds.
15. In the Slide 2 notes pane, type `Tour price includes airfare, hotels, admission to all attractions, and guided tours.` In the Slide 3 notes pane, type `This city blends old-world charm and modern-day excitement. Scholoss Castle's half-demolished state adds to its picturesque and romantic appeal.` In the Slide 4 notes pane, type `The Piazza and Basilica di San Marco are the undisputed symbols of the city. A gondola ride represents the classic romantic Venice.`
16. Run the presentation. Hide Slide 2. Run the presentation again displaying Slide 2 and using all hyperlinks.
17. Create a folder with the name, Europe. Save the presentation with the file name, Lab 4-3 Europe. Save the presentation as a Rich Text Format outline and then send the presentation to Microsoft Word. Print speaker notes. Change the page setup so that the pages print in landscape orientation, and print the presentation as a handout. Quit PowerPoint.

Cases and Places

The difficulty of these case studies varies:
■ are the least difficult and ■■ are more difficult. The last exercise is a group exercise.

Note: Remember to use the 7×7 rule as you design the presentations: a maximum of seven words on a line and a maximum of seven lines on one slide.

1 ■ Bicycling is an excellent method of achieving a low-impact cardiovascular workout while viewing the scenic outdoors. Pedaling for one hour on a flat road burns approximately 50 calories. Nearly 60 million people ride their bikes at least once a year, and 15 million bikers ride at least once weekly. Obviously the basic piece of equipment is an appropriate bike, and the key is finding the best bike for the rider's budget and recreational needs. Bikes can be grouped into three categories: comfort, fitness, and road. Comfort bikes are best suited for short rides. They cost approximately $300, have wide tires and a large seat, and weigh about 30 pounds. A rider sits upright because the handlebars are curved upwards. Fitness bikes range from $600 to $900 and are good for long, invigorating rides. The seat and tires are narrow and the handlebars are straight, so the rider's torso is slightly forward. They weigh between 22 and 29 pounds. Devoted riders prefer road bikes, which weigh less than 22 pounds. The downward-curving handlebars, thin tires, and narrow seat enhance aerodynamics. You work at Bobby's Bodacious Bikes, which carries a wide variety of bikes. Customers often have many questions about the styles and models of bikes, so you decide to simplify their purchasing decisions by developing a slide show. You start by designing a title slide that captures the spirit of biking. Modify the template color scheme and default font. Use a picture as the background on Slide 1 and add a WordArt element. Create a Word table that organizes the information in the categories of comfort, fitness, and road bikes. Use the Thesaurus to change at least 2 words. Enhance the presentation by adding sound clips and slide transition effects.

2 ■ Internet dating services were practically nonexistent in 1997 but now are the fastest growing segment of the industry. Many online services users formerly placed personal ads in newspapers, which once were the largest segment of the industry. While some of the online dating companies claim that 75 percent of their members have found a date by using the sites, some independent analysts claim that as many as 30 percent of the people who register misrepresent their age, weight, or marital status. Likewise, traditional independent dating services also are experiencing an increase in business. Sole proprietors with home-based offices run many of these operations, and their customers often have six-figure salaries. The Office of Student Activities at your college is considering starting a matchmaking program, and the director has surveyed students to see what dating services they have used throughout the years. Table 4-10 lists the survey results.

Table 4-10 Dating Services

	1995	1998	2001	2004
Independent	120	105	90	231
Newspaper	480	360	290	210
Internet	—	16	270	315

One of the requirements in your sociology class is to write a research paper and then give an oral report on your findings. You decide to study the dating services industry and want to prepare a PowerPoint presentation explaining the major concepts. Using the techniques introduced in this project, create a short slide show. Use the statistics in Table 4-10 to add a chart to one slide. Include WordArt on the title slide, sound effects, and transition effects. When you run the presentation, use pens and highlighters for emphasis, and then keep the ink annotations. Add action buttons to jump to the first slide when you are displaying Slide 3 and to jump to Slide 4 when you are displaying Slide 2. Format the action buttons with shadows and bold lines. Use the Thesaurus to change at least 2 words.

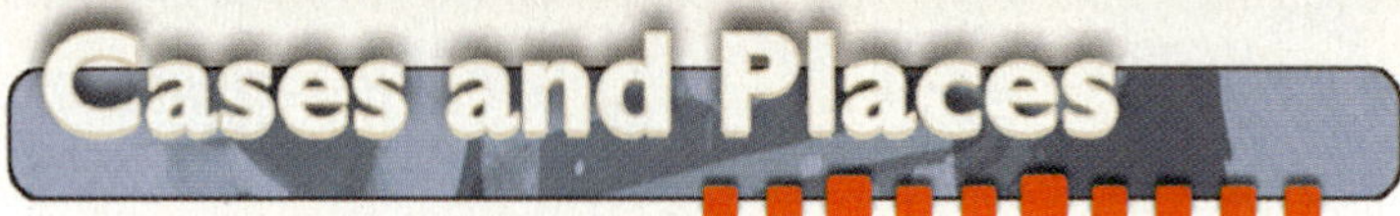

Cases and Places

The difficulty of these case studies varies:
■ are the least difficult and ■■ are more difficult. The last exercise is a group exercise.

3 ■■ Copyrights are given to authors and other people who create original works, such as books, photographs, and music. These legal protections prevent having third parties reproduce the works without the copyright holders' consent. Only copyright holders can reproduce their copyrighted works. Copyrights last for a specific number of years depending on when the works were created. If the work was created and published on or after January 1, 1987, the copyright begins when the work was created and endures for the life of the creator plus 50 years after the creator's death. If the work was created prior to January 1, 1978, it is protected for 28 years with an option to renew the copyright for another 47 years. The copy center at your college wants to prepare a slide show and handouts emphasizing these copyright rules in an effort to prevent students and staff from photocopying copyrighted works. You decide to develop a slide show to run at the front counter. Prepare a short presentation aimed at encouraging customers to follow the copyright guidelines. Include a chart showing the length of time a copyright lasts. The title slide should include WordArt for visual appeal. Hide 1 slide. The final slide should have hyperlinks to copyright information on the United States Copyright Office and The Bureau of National Affairs, Inc. Web sites.

4 ■■ Energy bars have found their way into many athletes' workout bags. Recently, Americans spent more than $1.4 million on these bars, which range in price from $1 to more than $2.50 each. The bars have various nutritional elements, including protein, carbohydrates, soy, and fiber. Visit your local sporting goods or nutrition store and compare the ingredients in five different energy bars. Compare price, serving size, calories, protein, carbohydrates, fat, saturated fat, fiber, and sugars. Then read articles or search the Internet to find nutrition experts' reviews and opinions of these bars' nutritional quality. Develop a PowerPoint slide show reporting your findings. Include a chart comparing the energy bars. Enhance the presentation by adding slide transition effects, an animation scheme, and timings. Include hyperlinks to three of the bars' Web sites. Add speaker notes to the slides and print these notes.

5 ■■ **Working Together** Hybrid cars use both an electric motor and a small gas engine. They are environmentally friendly because they get approximately 50 miles per gallon and have low emissions. Compared with a base model four-door car, they cost about $5,000 more, but their upkeep costs are about equal. Have each member of your team visit or telephone several local car dealers to obtain information about a particular hybrid car and its competitors. Gather data about:

1) Sticker price
2) Rebates
3) Required and recommended maintenance
4) Gas mileage
5) Estimated expenses for five years
6) Insurance rates
7) Horsepower

After coordinating the data, create a presentation with at least one slide showcasing each vehicle. Summarize your findings in a Word table. As a group, critique each slide. Enhance the presentation by modifying the slide background, adding clips, applying animation schemes and transition effects, and rehearsing timings. Include hyperlinks to three Web sites. Add speaker notes to the slides and print these notes. Hand in a hard copy of the final presentation.

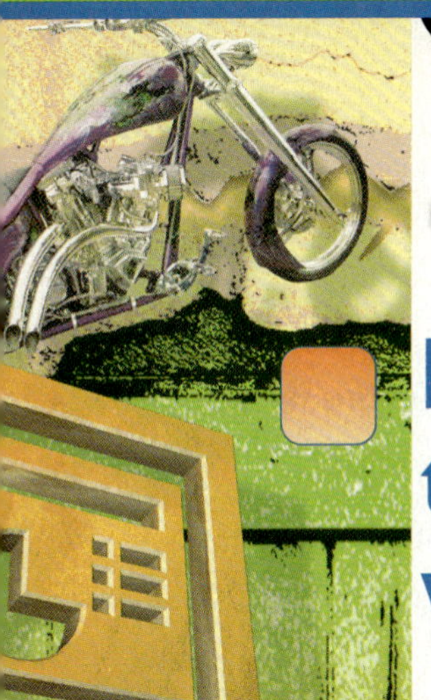

MICROSOFT Office PowerPoint 2003

Delivering Presentations to and Collaborating with Workgroups

CASE PERSPECTIVE

Motorcycle sales have been climbing steadily in recent years as riders yearn for the adventure and freedom offered by this form of transportation. With this popularity, however, has come an increase in the number of motorcyclists' accidents. In an effort to promote motorcycle safety, the local motorcycle dealer is planning to present a series of seminars. John Jamison, the owner of Cycles Unlimited, wants to offer workshops on riding and street skills. The speaker at the seminars will be Andy Andreessen, who is an experienced motorcycle rider and instructor.

John has asked you to help him develop a PowerPoint presentation that gives an overview of the seminars. He would like you to develop the presentation and then deliver it to Andy and two members of his staff for review. You set up a review cycle so Andy and two members of his staff can comment on your presentation. When you have incorporated their comments in your final document, you will schedule and deliver an online broadcast to these three reviewers.

In addition, John wants to put this PowerPoint presentation on a compact disc to take to speaking engagements in the community. You agree to help by using PowerPoint's Package for CD feature, which includes the Microsoft Office PowerPoint Viewer so the packaged presentation can run on any computer that does not have PowerPoint installed.

As you read through this Collaboration Feature, you will learn how to develop a review cycle to track, accept, and reject changes in a presentation; add, edit, and delete comments in a presentation; and compare and merge presentations. In addition, you will learn how to prepare the presentation for a remote delivery by scheduling and defining settings for online broadcasts and packaging the presentation to a folder for storage on a compact disc.

Objectives

You will have mastered the material in this project when you can:

- Merge slide shows
- Insert, review, accept, and reject comments
- Schedule and deliver online broadcasts
- Save presentations using the Package for CD option

Introduction

The phrase, the whole is greater than the sum of its parts, certainly can apply to a PowerPoint slide show. Often presentations are enhanced when individuals collaborate to fine-tune text, visuals, and design elements on the slides. PowerPoint offers an effective method of sending presentations for review and for sharing comments. A **review cycle** occurs when a slide show author e-mails a file to multiple reviewers so they can make comments and changes to their copies of the slides and then return the file to the author. If the author uses Microsoft Outlook to send the presentation for review, this e-mail program automatically **tracks changes** to the file by displaying who made the changes and comments.

Another method of collaborating with colleagues is by broadcasting the presentation over the Web. **Presentation broadcasting** delivers the slide show to remote audiences who are on the same intranet or are using the Internet. An **intranet** is an internal network that applies Internet technologies and is used to distribute company information to employees.

More About

Embedding Fonts

Four base fonts are included with Microsoft Windows: Arial, Courier New, Symbol, and Times New Roman. In addition, 20 other fonts are included with Office XP. They include Bookman Old Style, Comic Sans MS, Tahoma, and Verdana. For a list of these fonts, type `embedding fonts` in the Type a question for help box and then click the About embedding fonts link. To learn more about fonts, visit the PowerPoint 2003 More About Web page (`scsite.com/ppt2003/more`) and click Fonts.

PowerPoint file sizes often are much larger than those produced by other Microsoft Office programs, such as Word and Excel. Presentations with embedded pictures and video easily can grow beyond the 1.44 MB capacity of floppy disks. The large file size may present difficulties if you need to transport your presentation to show on another computer. One solution to this file size limitation is to use PowerPoint's **Package for CD** option. This element saves all the components of a presentation so it can be delivered on a computer other than the one on which it was created. Linked documents and multimedia files automatically are included in this packaged file, but they can be excluded if desired. The feature can embed any TrueType font that is included in Windows; however, it cannot embed other TrueType fonts that have built-in copyright restrictions.

Part 1: Workgroup Collaboration Using a Review Cycle

The slide show consists of four slides that provide guidelines for motorcycle riders and motorists. Topics address clothing for comfort and safety, factors leading to accidents, and riding and driving advice. The presentation uses a picture, clips, and WordArt to add visual interest. Figures 1a through 1d show the four original slides, and Figures 1e through 1h show slides that were modified after receiving comments from three people who reviewed the original slide show.

ORIGINAL PRESENTATION

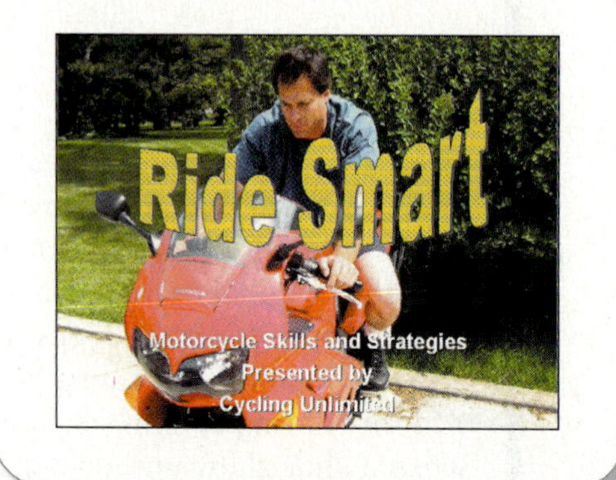

(a) Slide 1

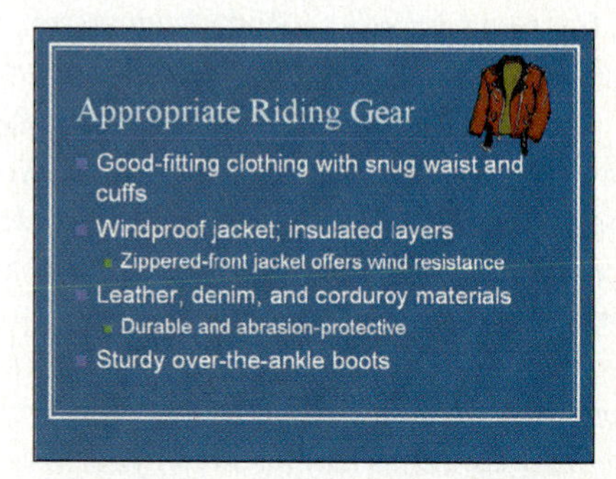

(b) Slide 2

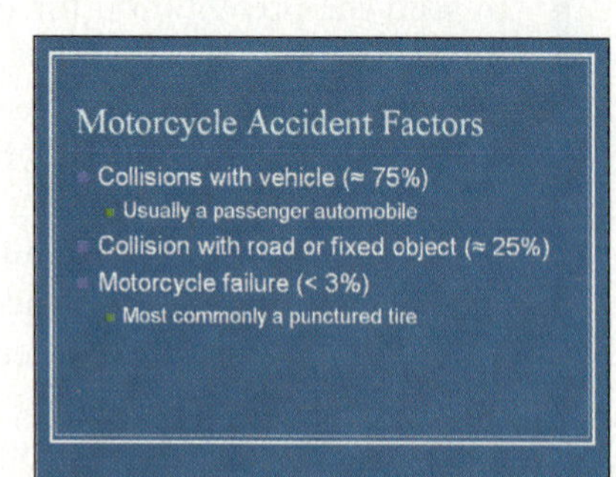

(c) Slide 3

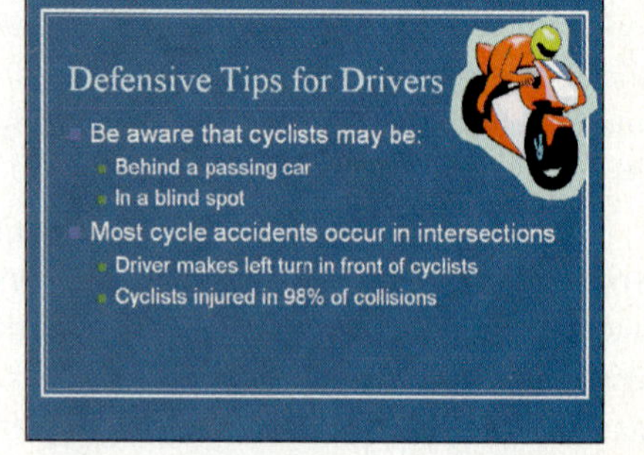

(d) Slide 4

FIGURE 1

REVISED PRESENTATION

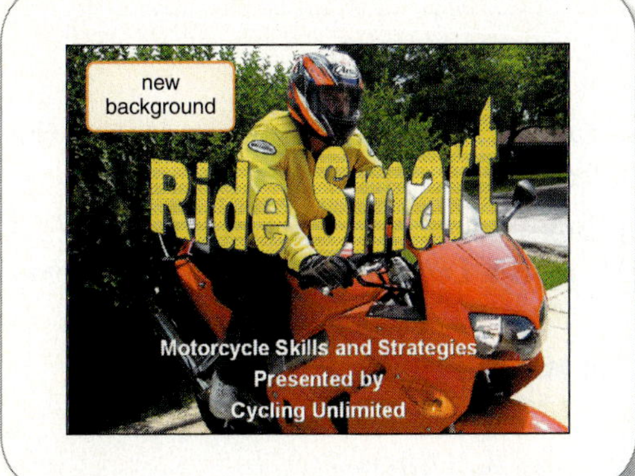

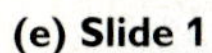

(e) Slide 1

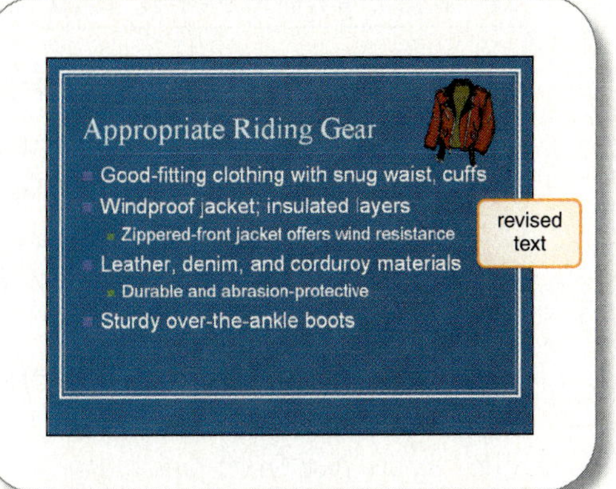

(f) Slide 2

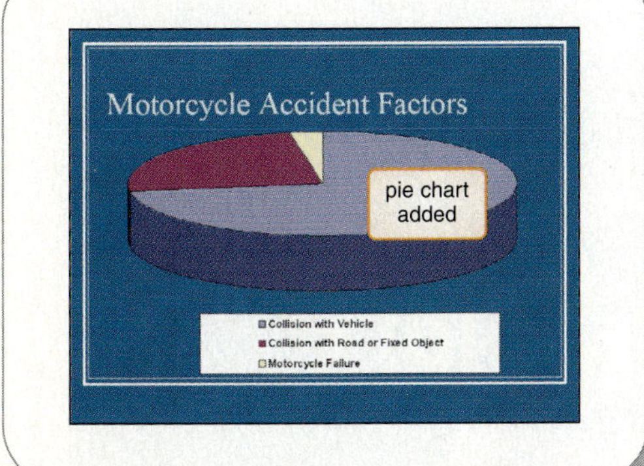

(g) Slide 3

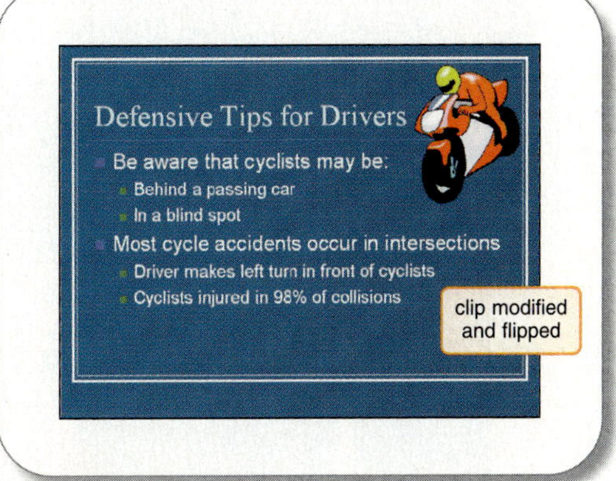

(h) Slide 4

FIGURE 1 *(continued)*

To avoid reading notes and changes made on printouts of a presentation, you can send the PowerPoint file to reviewers using Microsoft Outlook or any other 32-bit e-mail program that is compatible with the Messaging Application Programming Interface (MAPI), a network or Microsoft Exchange server, or a disk. Reviewers can edit the file using any version of PowerPoint.

The review cycle consists of inserting a comment on a slide, sending the presentation to reviewers, receiving the edited file, and evaluating the reviewers' suggestions by accepting and rejecting each comment using the Revisions task pane and Reviewing toolbar.

> *More About*
>
> **Linked Files**
>
> Linked files and graphics must be included in the attachment or embedded in the presentation if you want your reviewers to examine the entire slide show.

Starting PowerPoint and Opening a File

The steps on the next page illustrate how to start PowerPoint and open the presentation, Ride Smart, from the Data Disk. See the inside back cover for instructions for downloading the Data Disk or see your instructor for information about accessing the files required for this book.

To Start PowerPoint and Open a Presentation

1. **Insert your Data Disk into drive A.**
2. **Click the Start button on the Windows taskbar, point to All Programs on the Start menu, and then click Open Office Document.**
3. **When the Open Office Document dialog box is displayed, click the Look in box arrow and then click 3½ Floppy (A:) in the Look in list. Double-click the file name, Ride Smart.**
4. **If the Language bar is displayed, click its Minimize button.**

Slide 1 of the Ride Smart presentation is displayed in normal view (Figure 2).

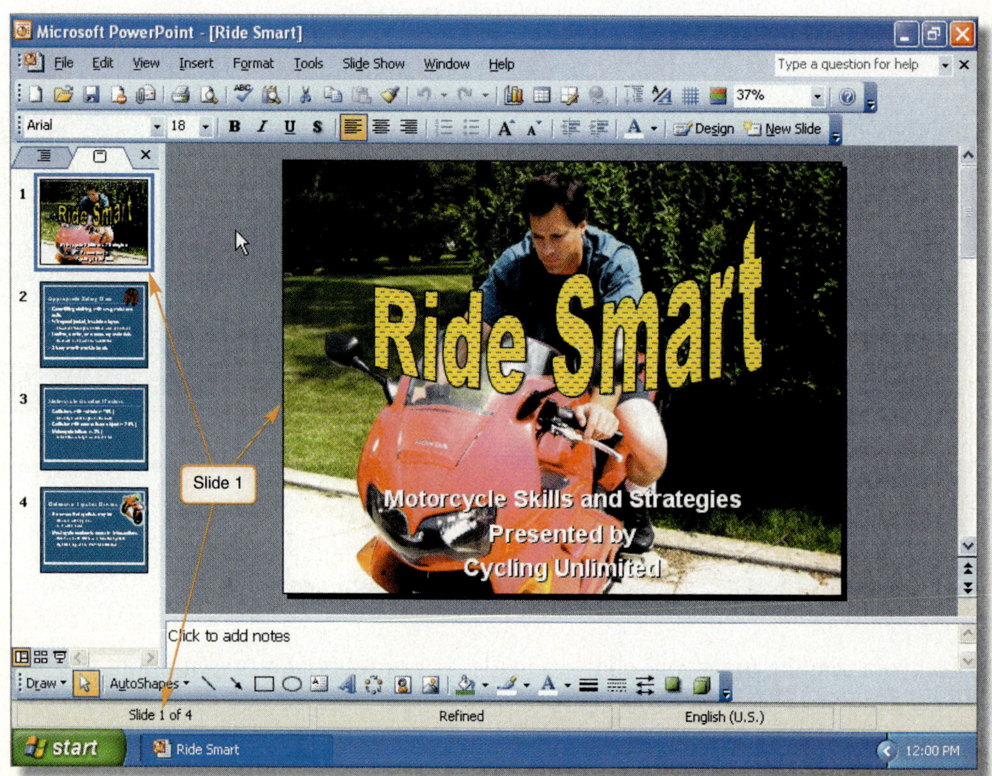

FIGURE 2

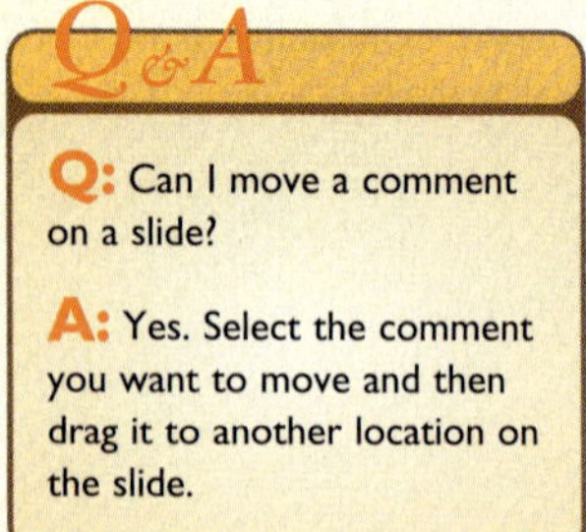

Q&A
Q: Can I move a comment on a slide?
A: Yes. Select the comment you want to move and then drag it to another location on the slide.

Displaying the Reviewing Toolbar and Inserting a Comment

To prepare a presentation for review, you might want to insert a comment containing information for the reviewers. A **comment** is a description that normally does not display as part of the slide show. The comment can be used to clarify information that may be difficult to understand, to pose questions, or to communicate suggestions. The first step in the review cycle for this project is to display the Reviewing toolbar and then insert a comment on Slide 1 asking the reviewers to express their opinions openly.

One method of inserting a comment is by clicking the Insert Comment button on the Reviewing toolbar. This toolbar is shown in Figure 4 on page PPT 312, and the buttons are described in Table 1.

Table 1 Buttons on the Reviewing Toolbar

BUTTON	BUTTON NAME	DESCRIPTION
	Show/Hide Markup	Displays comments on slides. It is activated when the first comment is entered.
Reviewers...	Reviewers	Displays the user names for all presentation reviewers.
	Previous Item	Selects the previous comment.
	Next Item	Selects the next comment.
	Apply	Incorporates the change into the presentation. Also applies all changes to the current slide or presentation.
	Unapply	Reverses the change made to the document. Also reverses all changes made to the current slide or presentation.
	Insert Comment	Adds a comment to a slide.
	Edit Comment	Changes the comment text.
	Delete Comment	Deletes a comment from a slide.
End Review...	End Review	Stops the reviewing process. All unapplied changes are lost.
	Revisions Pane	Displays or hides the Revisions task pane.
	Toolbar Options	Allow you to select the particular buttons you want to display on the toolbar.

The steps on the next page show how to display this toolbar and insert a comment on Slide 1.

To Display the Reviewing Toolbar and Insert a Comment

1

- **Click View on the menu bar and then point to Toolbars.**
- **Point to Reviewing on the Toolbars submenu.**

The View menu and Toolbars submenu are displayed (Figure 3).

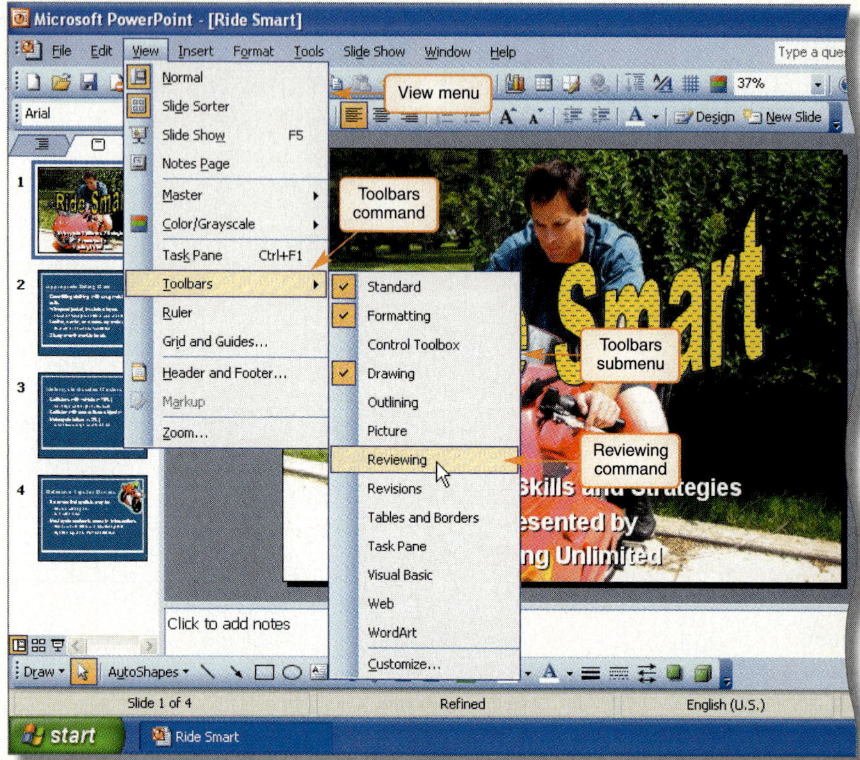

FIGURE 3

2

- **Click Reviewing.**
- **Click the Insert Comment button on the Reviewing toolbar.**

The Reviewing toolbar is displayed, and PowerPoint opens a **comment box** *at the top of the slide (Figure 4). The presentation author's name is John Jamison, and his initials are JJ. The initials reflect the name that was entered when Microsoft Office 2003 was installed. Your author's initials may differ from those in this figure. PowerPoint adds a small rectangle, called a* **comment marker**, *to the upper-left corner of the slide. The number, 1, following the author's initials indicates the comment is the first comment made by this reviewer.*

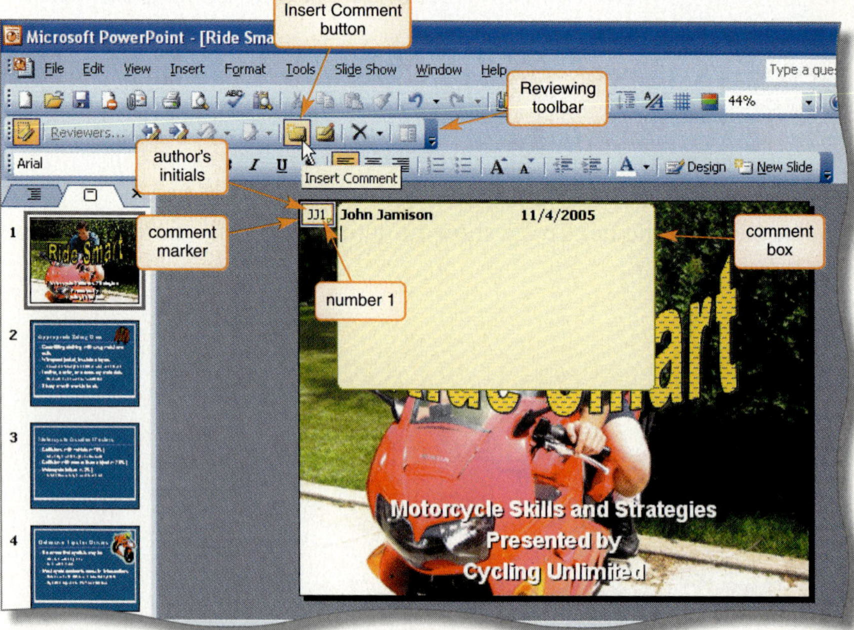

FIGURE 4

3

• **Type** `Please review this presentation and make suggestions about the art and text. Thanks.` **in the comment box.**

The author's name, date, and comment are displayed in the comment box (Figure 5).

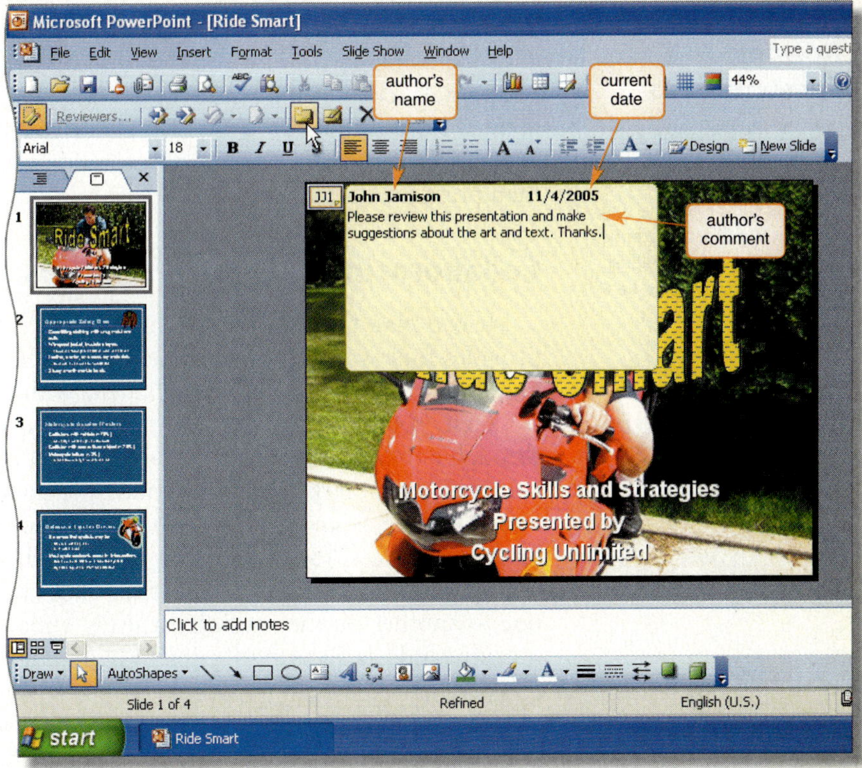

FIGURE 5

4

• **Click anywhere outside the comment box and then click the Save button on the Standard toolbar to save the presentation.**

*Clicking outside the comment box hides the text and **locks in** the comment. Your initials and the comment number are displayed (Figure 6).*

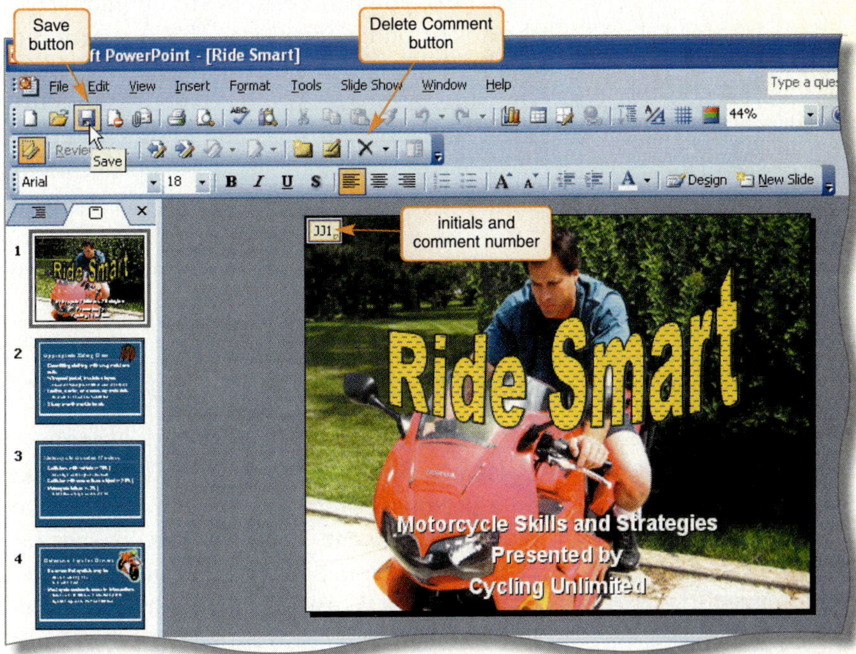

FIGURE 6

Other Ways

1. On Insert menu click Comment
2. Press ALT+I, press M
3. In Voice Command mode, say "Insert, Comment"

More About

Routing Presentations

Options for deadlines, deliveries, and status checks are available when you prepare a presentation for routing. The Add Routing Slip dialog box allow you to select whether the presentation should be sent to all the recipients simultaneously or if they should receive it sequentially in the order you specify. Reviewers make changes and insert comments using any version of PowerPoint. The presentation eventually returns to you.

When PowerPoint closes the comment box, the comment disappears from the screen. If you want to redisplay the comment, point to the comment marker. You can drag the comment to move its position on the slide. To change the reviewer's name and initials, click Tools on the menu bar, click Options, click the General tab, and then edit the Name and Initials fields. If you want to delete a comment, click the Delete Comment button on the Reviewing toolbar or click the comment marker and then press the DELETE key.

Collaborating with Workgroups

If you plan to have others edit your slide show or suggest changes, PowerPoint provides four ways to collaborate with others. **Collaborating** means working together in cooperation on a document with other PowerPoint users.

First, you can **distribute** your slide show to others, physically on a disk or through e-mail using the Send To command on the File menu. With the Send To command, you may choose to embed the document as part of the e-mail message or attach the file as an e-mail attachment, which allows recipients of the e-mail message to open the file if the application is installed on their systems.

Second, you can **route** your slide show to a list of people who pass it along from one to another on the routing list using e-mail. The Send To command on the File menu includes a Routing Recipient command. You specify e-mail addresses, the subject, and the message in the **routing slip**, which is similar to an e-mail message. PowerPoint creates the e-mail message with routing instructions and reminds people who open the document to pass it along to the next person in the routing list when they are finished.

Third, you can **collaborate** interactively with other people through discussion threads or online meetings. The integration of **NetMeeting** with Microsoft Office 2003 allows you to share and exchange files with people at different locations. When you start an online meeting from within PowerPoint, NetMeeting automatically starts in the background and allows you to share the contents of your file(s).

Fourth, you can collaborate by sharing the slide show. **Sharing** means more than simply giving another user a copy of your file. Sharing implies that multiple people can work independently on the same slide show simultaneously.

With any of the collaboration choices, you should keep track of the changes that others make to your slide show.

More About

Using NetMeeting

Collaborate with and receive feedback from other people simultaneously as you complete your presentation. Microsoft has integrated its Office and NetMeeting programs so a number of people can view a presentation and share the contents of a file. You can schedule the meeting in advance by using Microsoft Outlook or start an impromptu online meeting from within an active PowerPoint presentation. If your colleagues are available and they decide to accept your invitation, the online meeting begins. They can use such tools as a whiteboard, video, and audio to present their opinions and comments. To learn more about NetMeeting, visit the PowerPoint 2003 More About Web page (`scsite.com/ppt2003/more`) and click NetMeeting.

Distributing the Slide Show for Review

The next step is to send the slide show to Andy Andreessen and two of his assistants, Brianna Brooke and Christi Clarke. If you are completing this project on a personal computer, you will be prompted to choose the e-mail addresses of the recipients. You can use the recipients specified in the steps in this project, or you can substitute the e-mail addresses shown with e-mail addresses from your address book or class. Your return e-mail contact information must be valid to round trip the file back to yourself. The term **round trip** refers to sending a document to recipients and then receiving it back at some point in time.

The following steps illustrate how to distribute the presentation for review.

To Send the Presentation for Review

1

- **Click File on the menu bar, point to Send To, and then point to Mail Recipient (for Review).**

The File menu and Send To submenu are displayed (Figure 7).

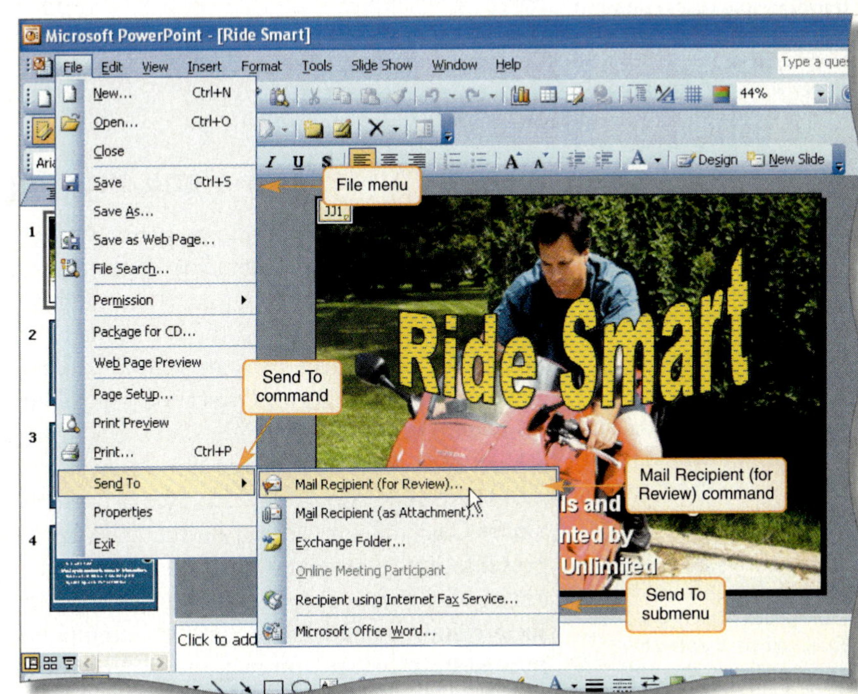

FIGURE 7

2

- **Click Mail Recipient (for Review).**
- **If the Choose Profile dialog box is displayed, choose your user profile and then click the OK button. If the Office Assistant is displayed, click No thanks.**
- **When the e-mail Message window is displayed, type** Andy_Andreessen@hotmail.com; Brianna_Brooke@hotmail.com; Christi_Clarke@hotmail.com **in the To text box.**

PowerPoint displays the e-mail Message window (Figure 8). If you are working on a networked system, see your instructor or network administrator for the correct e-mail account to use.

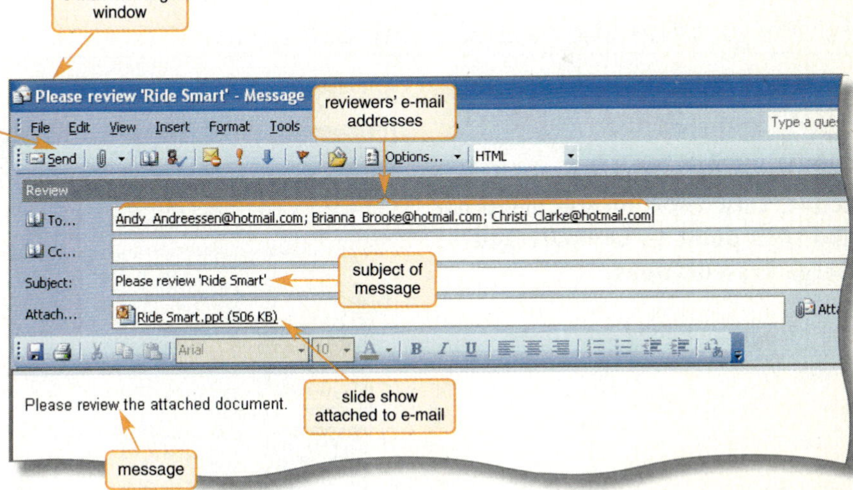

FIGURE 8

3

- **Click the Send button on the Standard toolbar.**

The e-mail with the attached presentation is sent to the three reviewers.

Other Ways

1. Press ALT+F, press D, press C, enter addresses, press ALT+S
2. In Voice Command mode, say "File, Send To, Mail Recipient for Review, [type addresses], Send"

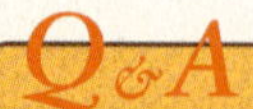

Q: Can I change the text of a comment?

A: Yes. Double-click the comment, type your changes, and then click outside the comment box. You also can change another reviewer's comment in the same manner. You will become the author of that comment, and your initials then will display in the comment box.

More About

Print Preview Options

The Options button on the Print Preview toolbar allows you to adjust print preview options. For example, clicking the Color/Grayscale command shows how the slides will print on a black and white printer. The Frame Slides command adds a border around each slide, and the Scale to Fit Paper command enlarges or reduces the slide image to fill the paper.

Each of the reviewers opens the presentation and makes comments and suggestions about the presentation. Andy Andreessen's comments include changes to the Slide 1 background and a suggestion about the clip on Slide 4. Brianna Brooke's comments suggest a change to the text on Slide 2 to make the presentation conform to the 7 × 7 rule and recommend a slide transition on each slide. Christi Clarke's comments discuss repositioning the clip on Slide 2 and replacing the figures on Slide 3 with a chart. All the reviewers make the proposed changes to the presentation. The next section describes how you will merge these files and review the suggestions.

Merging Slide Shows and Printing Comments

PowerPoint keeps a **change history** with each shared slide show. The slide show owner reviews each presentation comment and then makes a decision about whether to accept the suggested change. After the reviewers commented on the Ride Smart presentation, they changed the file name to include their last names and then e-mailed the revised file back to you. If you and your reviewers use Microsoft Outlook as your e-mail program, PowerPoint automatically combines the reviewed presentations with your original slide show. If you used another e-mail program, a server, or a hard disk, you must merge the reviewers' files with your original.

Three slide shows — Ride Smart-Andreessen, Ride Smart-Brooke, and Ride Smart-Clarke — are stored on the Data Disk. As the owner of the original presentation, you review their comments and modifications and make decisions about whether to accept these suggestions. In this Collaboration Feature, you will see a printout of each slide and the comments each reviewer has made about the presentation before you begin to accept and reject each suggestion.

PowerPoint can print these slides and comments on individual pages. The following steps use this slide show to illustrate printing these suggestions.

To Merge Slide Shows and Print Comments

1

- **With the Ride Smart presentation active, click Tools on the menu bar and then point to Compare and Merge Presentations.**

The Tools menu is displayed (Figure 9).

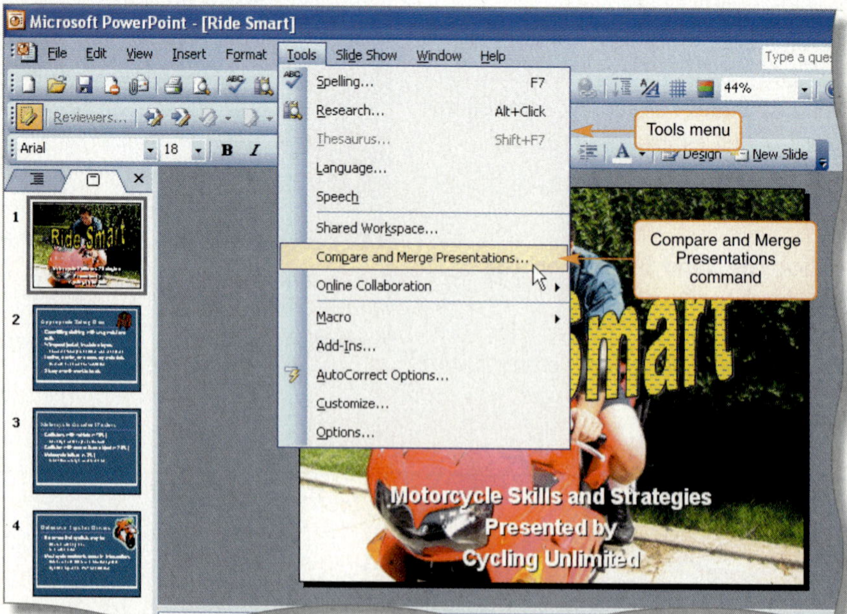

FIGURE 9

2

- **Click Compare and Merge Presentations.**
- **If necessary, when the Choose Files to Merge with Current Presentation dialog box is displayed, click the Look in box arrow and then click 3½ Floppy (A:).**
- **Click Ride Smart-Andreessen.**
- **Press the CTRL key, click Ride Smart-Brooke and Ride Smart-Clarke.**
- **Release the CTRL key.**

The Choose Files to Merge with Current Presentation dialog box is displayed (Figure 10). The files displayed on your computer may vary. The three selected files contain comments and revisions from the three reviewers. The steps instructed you to select the files to merge in the order they were sent to the reviewers, but you can merge files in any order.

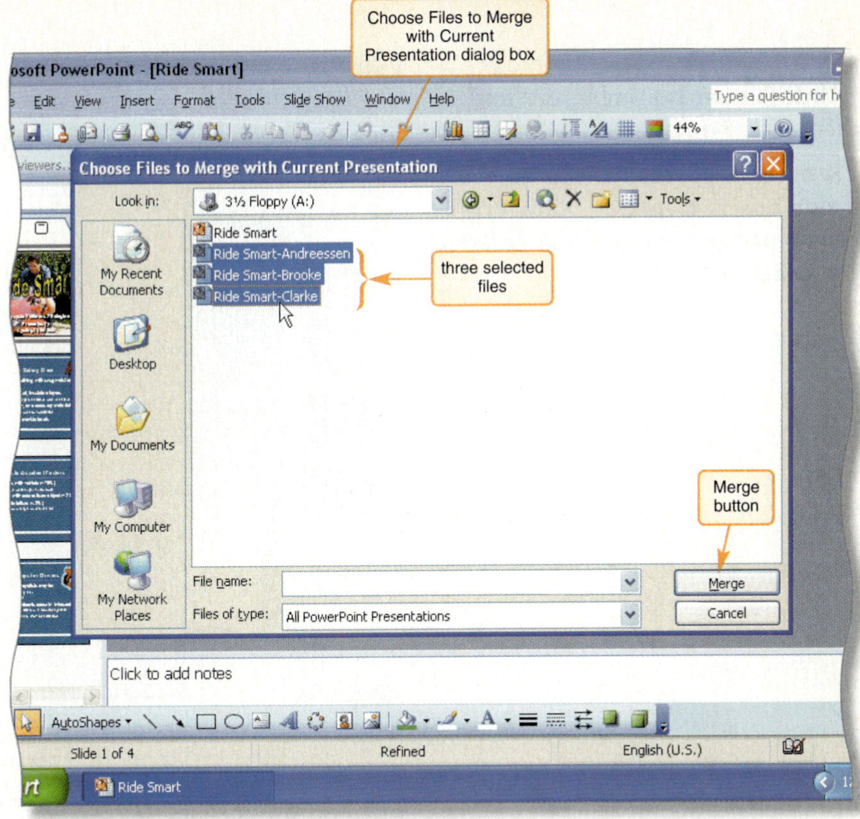

FIGURE 10

3

- **Click the Merge button.**
- **If a Microsoft Office PowerPoint dialog box is displayed asking if you want to browse your presentation, click the Continue button. If a Microsoft Office PowerPoint dialog box is displayed asking if you want to merge these changes with your original presentation, click the Yes button.**

The Revisions task pane is displayed (Figure 11). Each reviewer's comments in the Slide changes area are marked in a distinct color, which helps identify the author of each suggestion. The order of the comments in the list depends on the order in which the files were merged with the original presentation. PowerPoint may display your comments in a different sequence.

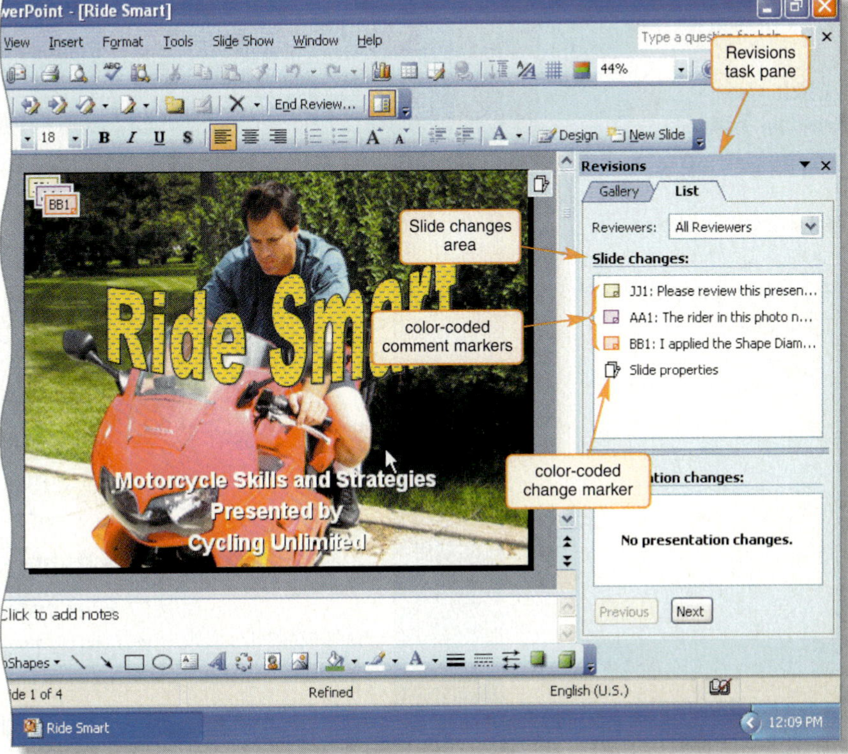

FIGURE 11

4

- **Click File on the menu bar and then click Print.**
- **If necessary, when the Print dialog box is displayed, click Print comments and ink markup to select the check box.**

The Print dialog box is displayed (Figure 12).

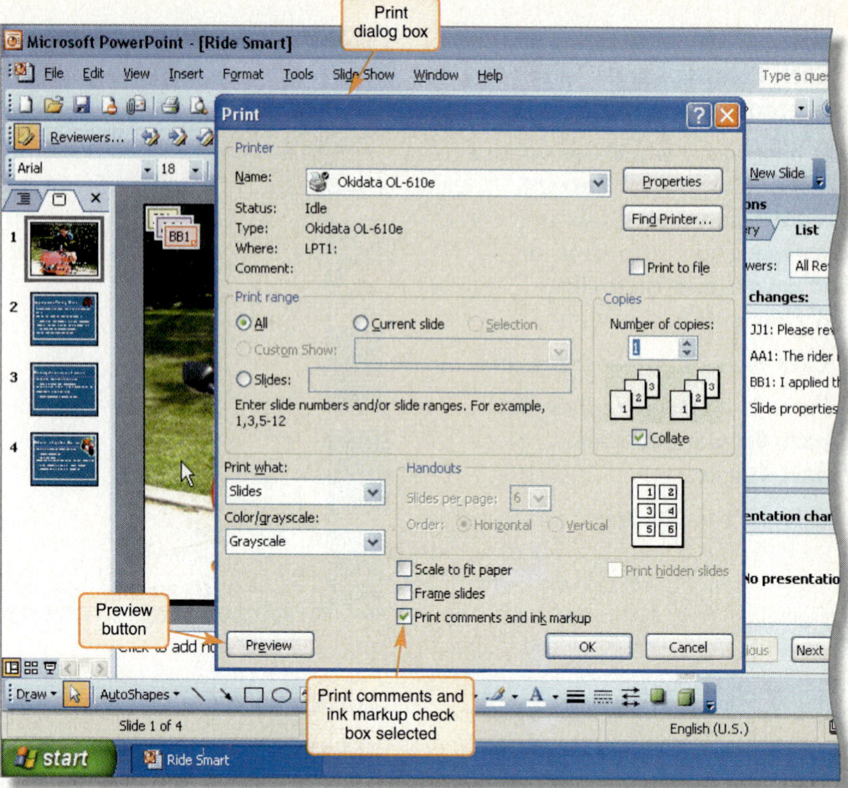

FIGURE 12

5

- **Click the Preview button.**

Slide 1 is displayed in the Print Preview window (Figure 13). To preview each of the eight pages, click the Next Page button.

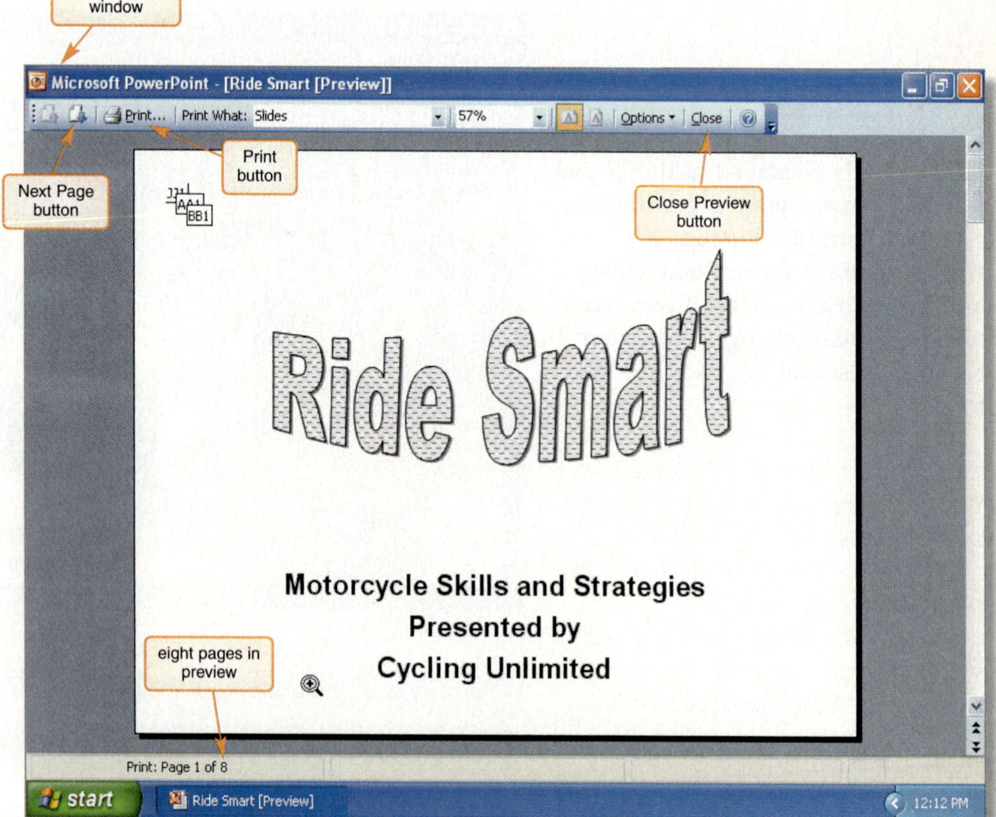

FIGURE 13

6

- **Click the Print button.**
- **Click the OK button.**

The four slides and four comment pages print, as shown in Figure 14.

7

- **Click the Close Preview button.**

The Close Preview button closes the Print Preview window. PowerPoint returns to normal view.

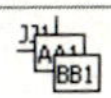

Ride Smart

Motorcycle Skills and Strategies
Presented by
Cycling Unlimited

(a) page 1

Slide 1

JJ1	Please review this presentation and make suggestions about the art and text. Thanks. John Jamison, 11/4/2005
AA1	The rider in this photo needs appropriate riding gear for safety and comfort. I recommend you substitute this slide. Andy Andreessen, 11/1/2005
BB1	I applied the Shape Diamond transition effect to all slides in the presentation. Brianna Brooke, 11/2/2005

(b) page 2

Appropriate Riding Gear

BB2

- Good-fitting clothing with snug waist and cuffs
- Windproof jacket; insulated layers
  - Zippered-front jacket offers wind resistance
- Leather, denim, and corduroy materials
  - Durable and abrasion-protective
- Sturdy over-the-ankle boots

CC1

(c) page 3

Slide 2

CC1	I moved the leather jacket clip to the bottom of the slide and then enlarged it. I think it looks good in this corner. Christi Clarke, 11/3/2005
BB2	I changed the first first-level paragraph by deleting the word, and, and adding a comma. The slide now follows the 7 x 7 rule. Brianna Brooke, 11/2/2005

(d) page 4

FIGURE 14

CC2

Motorcycle Accident Factors

- Collisions with vehicle (≈ 75%)
  - Usually a passenger automobile
- Collision with road or fixed object (≈ 25%)
- Motorcycle failure (< 3%)
  - Most commonly a punctured tire

(e) page 5

Slide 3

CC2 The figures on your slide would have more impact if they were depicted in a chart.
Christi Clarke, 11/3/2005

(f) page 6

AA2

Defensive Tips for Drivers

- Be aware that cyclists may be:
  - Behind a passing car
  - In a blind spot
- Most cycle accidents occur in intersections
  - Driver makes left turn in front of cyclists
  - Cyclists injured in 98% of collisions

(g) page 7

Slide 4

AA2 The blue background around the motorcycle clip is distracting, so I deleted it. Also, the cyclist should be facing into the slide to direct the audience members' interest toward the text. I flipped the clip horizontally for you.
Andy Andreessen, 11/1/2005

(h) page 8

FIGURE 14 *(continued)*

Other Ways

1. In Voice Command mode, say "Tools, Compare and Merge Presentations, [select file names], Merge, Continue, File, Print, Include comment pages, Preview, Print, Close"

The eight printouts show each of the four slides and the comments each reviewer made about the slides. These pages are helpful to reference as you evaluate the reviewers' suggestions and changes.

Reviewing, Accepting, and Rejecting Comments

The Revisions task pane and Reviewing toolbar help you review each comment and then decide whether to accept the change or delete the suggestion. Color-coded comment and change markers are displayed in the Revisions task pane. The following steps show how to view each reviewer's comments for each slide in the presentation.

More About

Print Preview in Grayscale

The Grayscale mode displays slides with some of the background switched to white. This modified grayscale sometimes creates a more readable printed version than you would see with color printed in true grayscale. To view a slide in true grayscale while using print preview, point to the Color/Grayscale command on the Options menu and then click Color.

To Review and Accept Comments on Slide 1

1

- **With Slide 1 displaying, click the JJ1 comment marker on the List tab in the Revisions task pane.**
- **Point to the Delete Comment button on the Reviewing toolbar.**

The JJ1 comment box is displayed (Figure 15). The presentation author's name is John Jamison, and his initials are JJ. The initials in your comment box and color of your comment marker may vary. The comment marker indicates the first comment inserted before sending the presentation to the reviewers. Clicking the comment marker displays the comment.

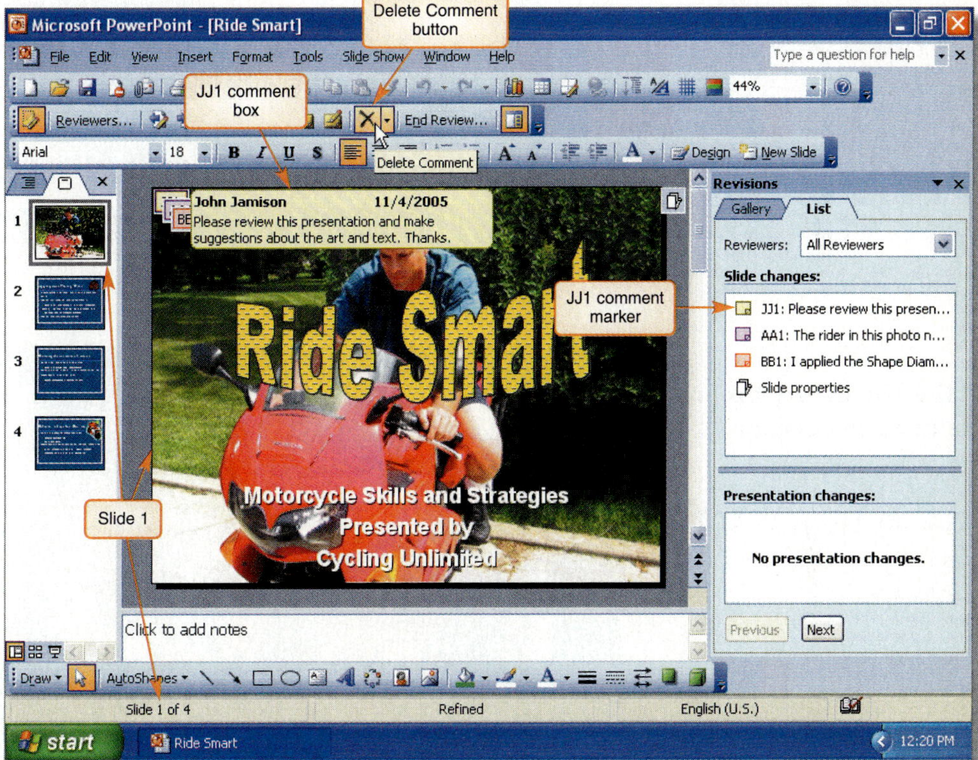

FIGURE 15

2

- **Click the Delete Comment button on the Reviewing toolbar.**
- **Click the AA1 comment marker on the List tab in the Revisions task pane.**

John Jamison's comment is deleted from Slide 1 (Figure 16). Andy Andreessen's first comment regarding substituting a background photo is displayed. The Slide properties change marker is blank, which indicates you have not applied any changes to the slide.

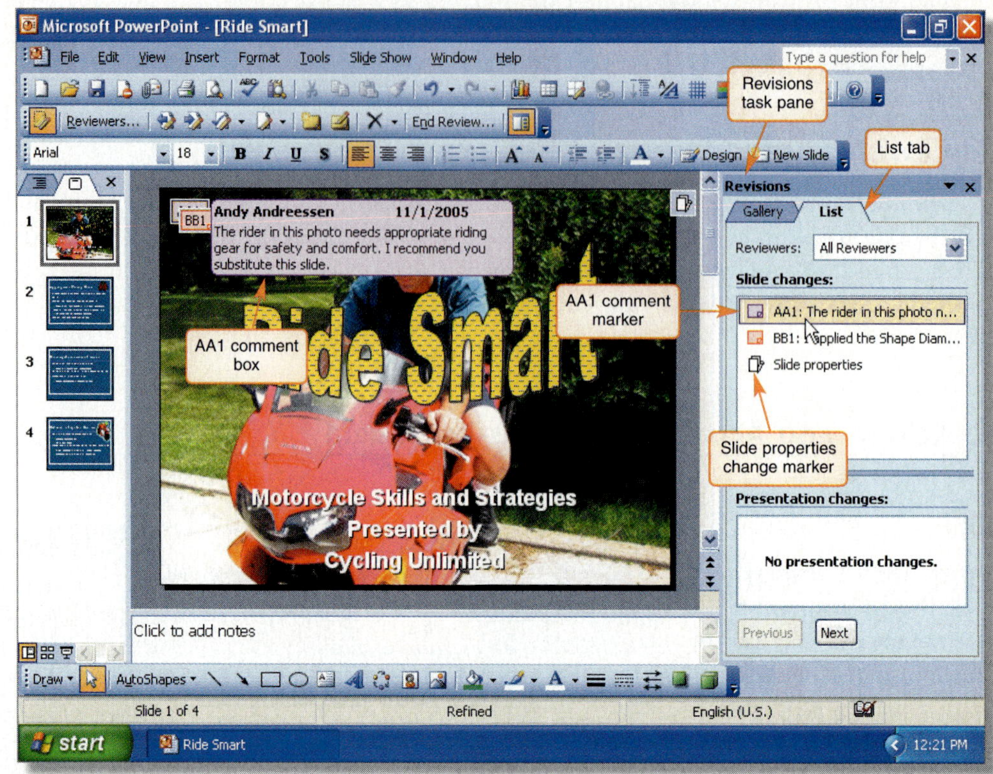

FIGURE 16

3

- **Click the Gallery tab in the Revisions task pane.**

The Gallery tab is displayed (Figure 17). The original Slide 1 does not have an appropriately dressed rider.

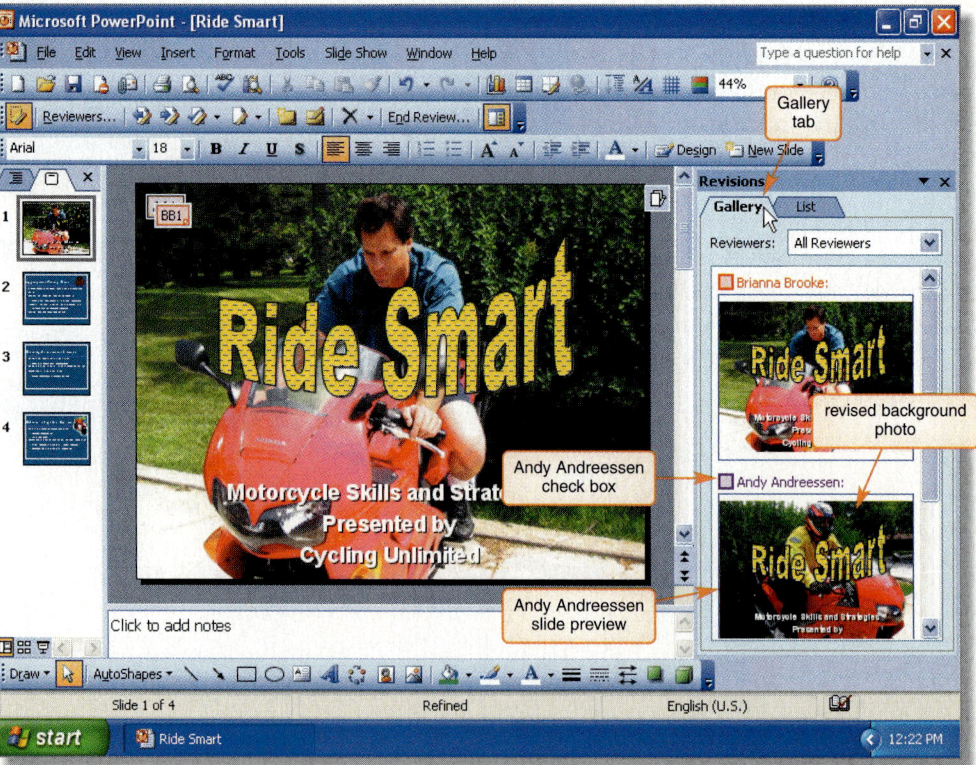

FIGURE 17

4

- **Click the Andy Andreessen check box above the Andy Andreessen slide preview.**

Slide 1 is displayed with the new background (Figure 18). Clicking the check box above the Andy Andreessen slide preview applies the revised slide he added to the presentation. You can accept the slide change by clicking the check box, clicking the slide preview, or clicking the Apply button on the Reviewing toolbar.

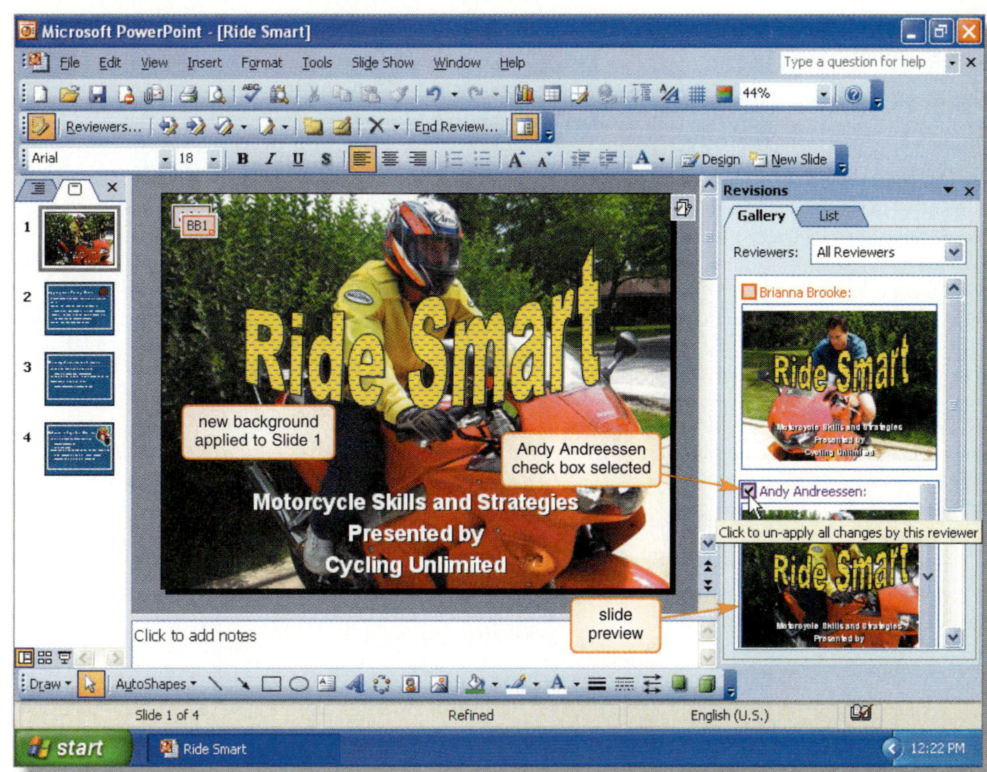

FIGURE 18

5

- **Click the List tab and then click the Delete Comment button on the Reviewing toolbar.**
- **Click the red BB1 comment marker.**

The Andy Andreessen change marker is deleted and the first Brianna Brooke comment is displayed (Figure 19).

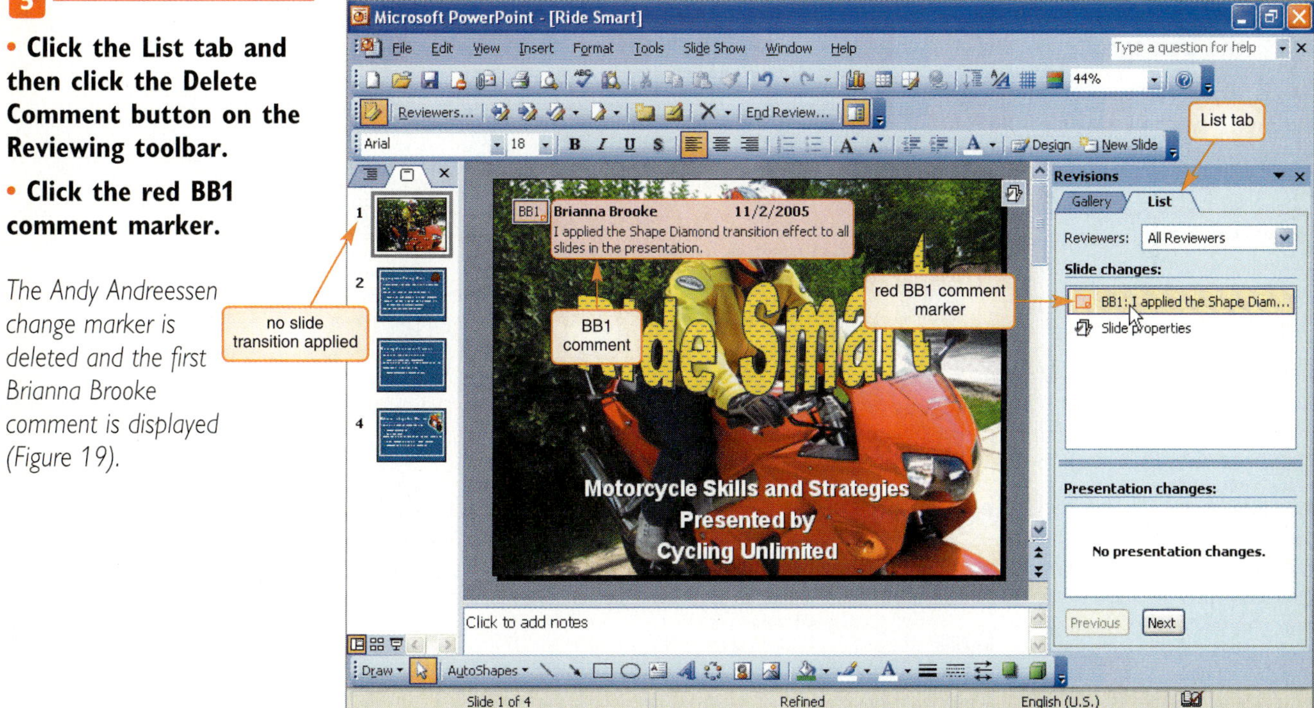

FIGURE 19

6

- **Click the Gallery tab.**
- **Click the Brianna Brooke check box above the Andy Andreessen slide preview.**

The Shape Diamond slide transition is applied to Slide 1 (Figure 20).

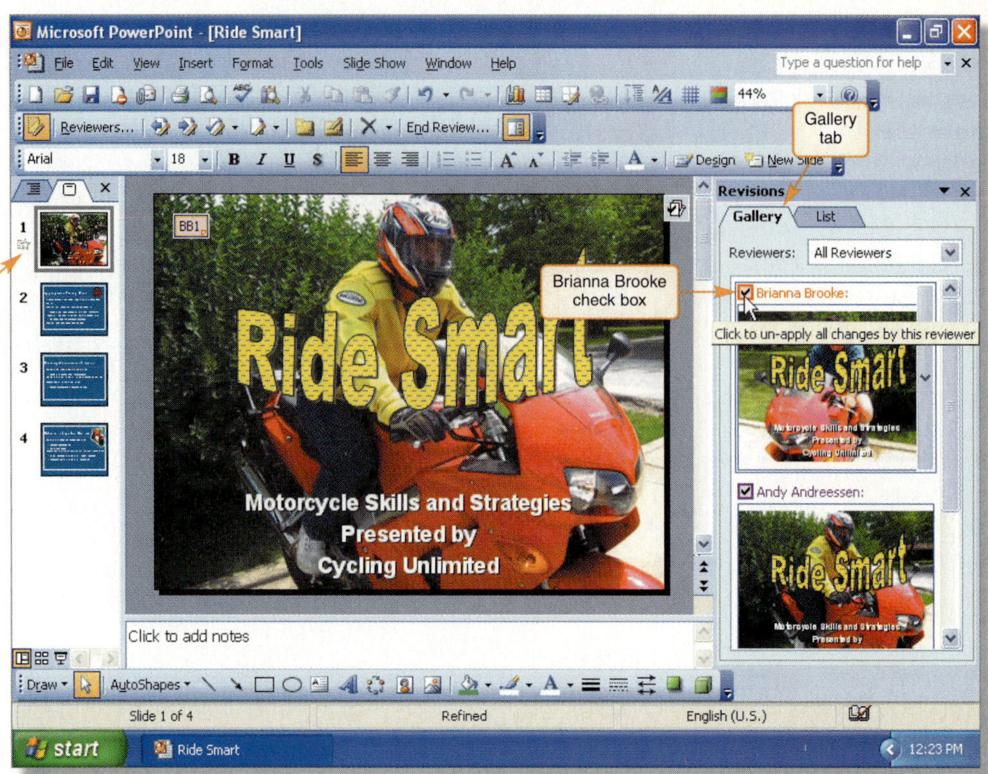

FIGURE 20

7

- **Click the List tab.**
- **Click the Delete Comment button on the Reviewing toolbar.**
- **Click the Slide properties change marker.**

Brianna Brooke's first comment is deleted from Slide 1. The checks indicate the changes you have applied (Figure 21). If you decide to unapply one or both of the Slide 1 changes, click the check boxes. A check mark is displayed in the Slide properties change marker, which indicates you have applied at least one change to the slide.

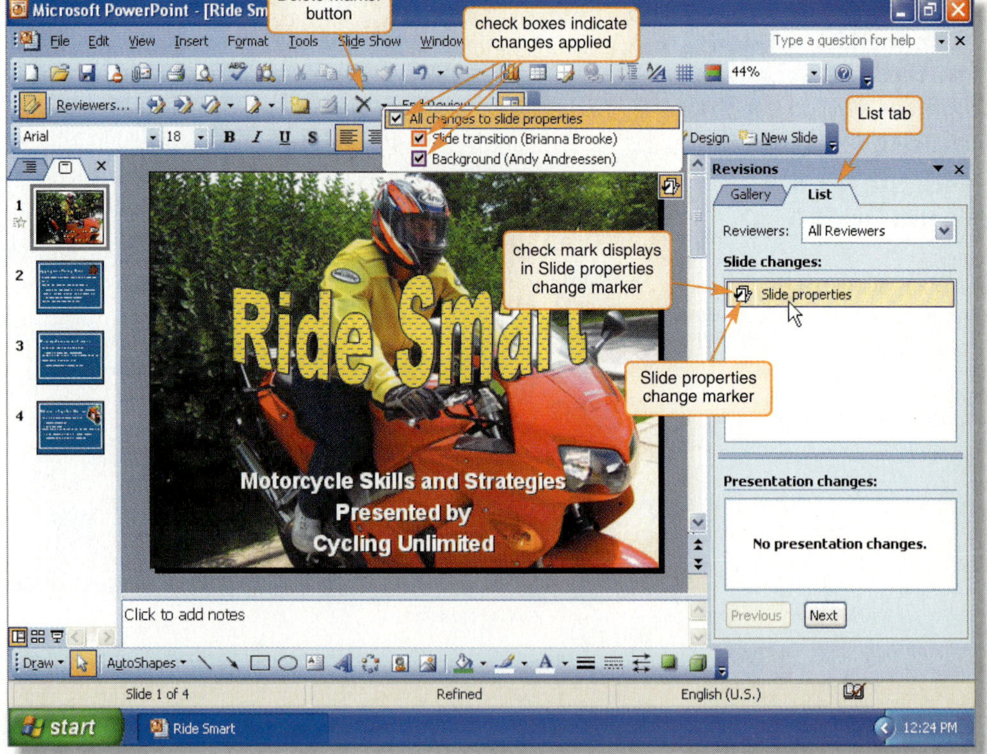

FIGURE 21

8

- **Click the Delete Marker button on the Reviewing toolbar.**

The new background and slide transition effect changes remain (Figure 22). The message in the Slide changes area in the Revisions task pane indicates that no more changes from the reviewers are available for Slide 1 and that the next comments are on Slide 2.

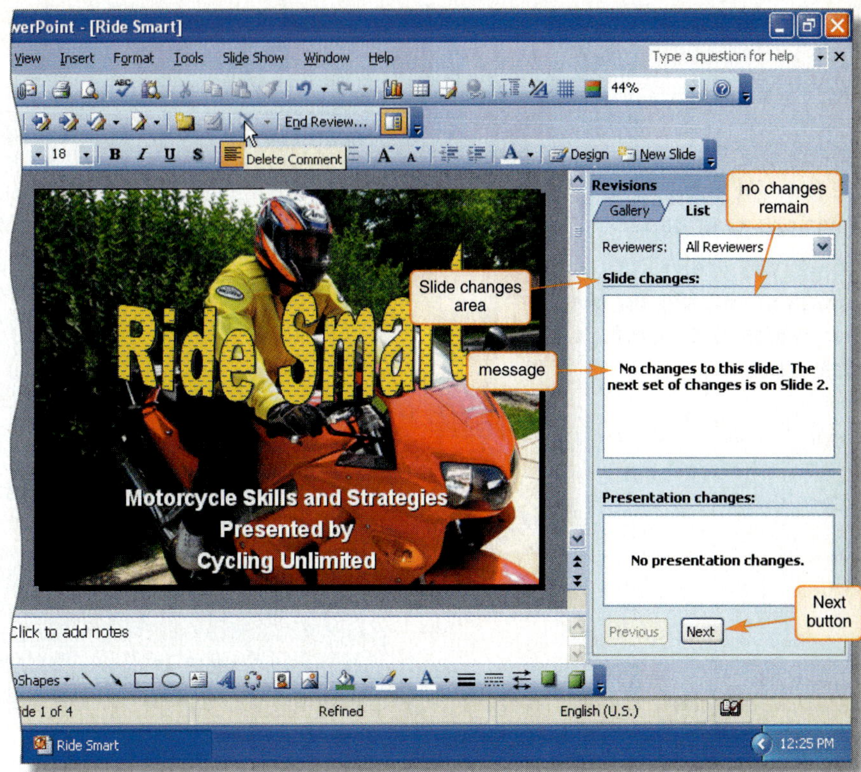

FIGURE 22

All the desired changes from the reviewers have been made to Slide 1. You now can review additional suggestions on the remaining slides in the slide show.

Reviewing, Accepting, and Rejecting Comments on Slides 2, 3, and 4

The three reviewers have made suggestions regarding the text and clip art on the next three slides. The steps on the next page illustrate how to review and accept comments on Slide 2.

More About

Personal Information

The three reviewers' names and initials display in the Revisions Pane. You may, however, not want your personal information displayed in a comment or macro or saved in a presentation. This information includes your name, initials, and company. To remove this information, click Tools on the menu bar and then click Options. When the Options dialog box displays, click the Security tab. In the Privacy options area, click Remove personal information from this file on save.

To Review and Accept or Reject Comments on Slide 2

1

- **Click the Next button on the List tab in the Revisions task pane.**
- **Click the green CC1 comment marker on the List tab in the Revisions task pane.**

The first Christi Clarke comment is displayed on Slide 2 (Figure 23).

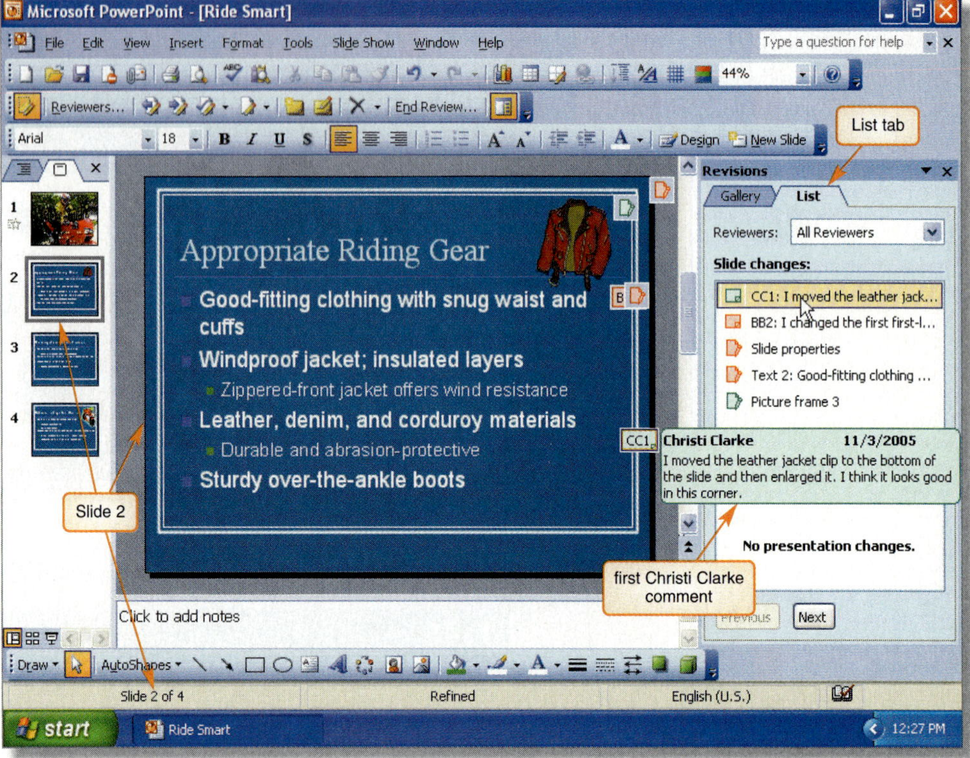

FIGURE 23

2

- **Click the Delete Comment button.**
- **Click the red BB2 comment marker.**

The Christi Clarke comment is deleted from Slide 2 and the second Brianna Brooke comment is displayed (Figure 24).

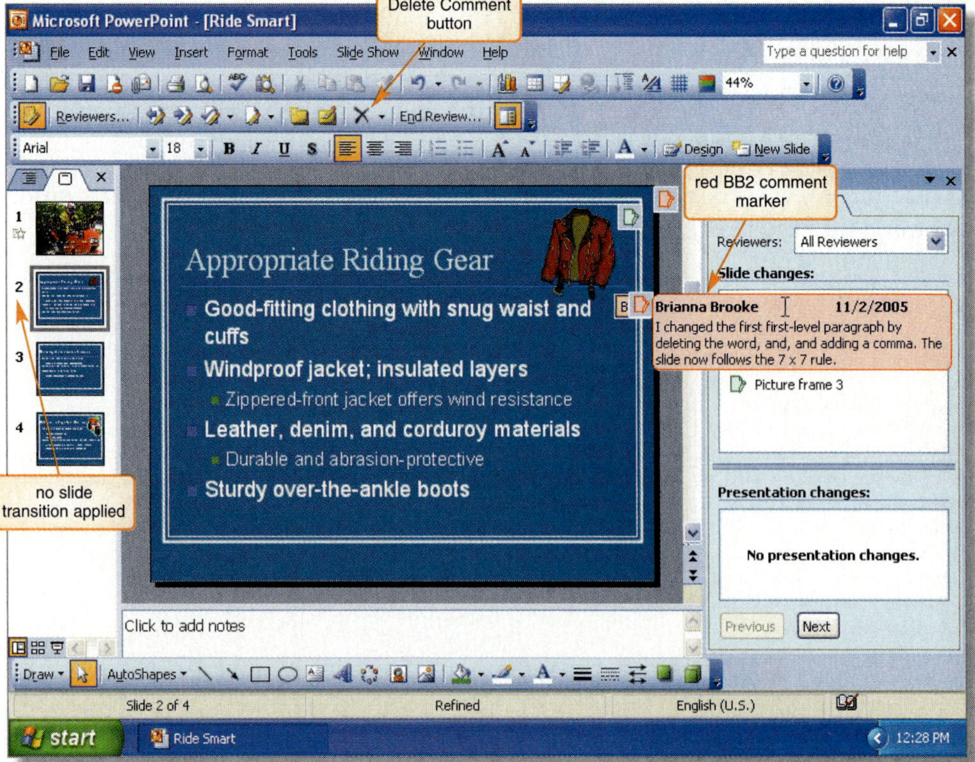

FIGURE 24

3

- **Click the Gallery tab.**
- **Click the Brianna Brooke check box above the Brianna Brooke slide preview.**

The Brianna Brooke revision is made to the first line of bulleted text in Slide 2 (Figure 25). The revision is displayed on the slide preview and on Slide 2. The first Brianna Brooke comment suggested and then applied a slide transition to all slides in the presentation. Clicking the check box accepts the changes. The animation icon indicates the Shape Diamond transition effect is applied to the slide.

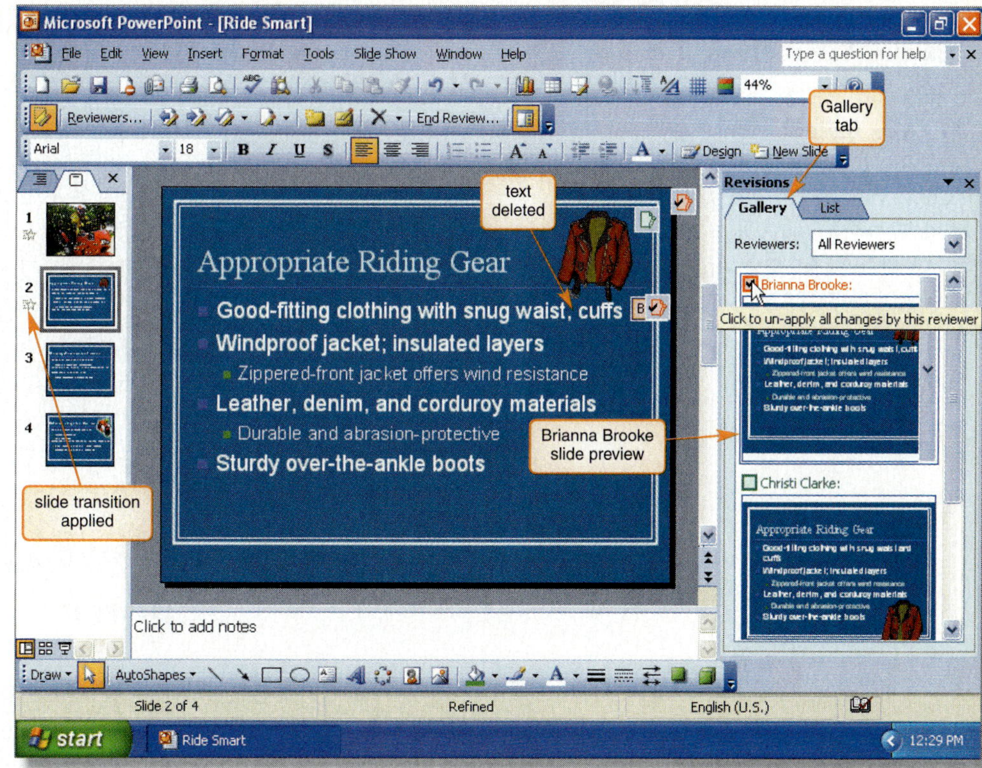

FIGURE 25

4

- **Click the List tab.**
- **Click the Delete Comment marker.**
- **Click the Slide properties change marker and then click the Delete Marker button.**
- **Click the Text 2 change marker and then click the Delete Marker button.**

All of the Brianna Brooke changes have been made to the slide (Figure 26).

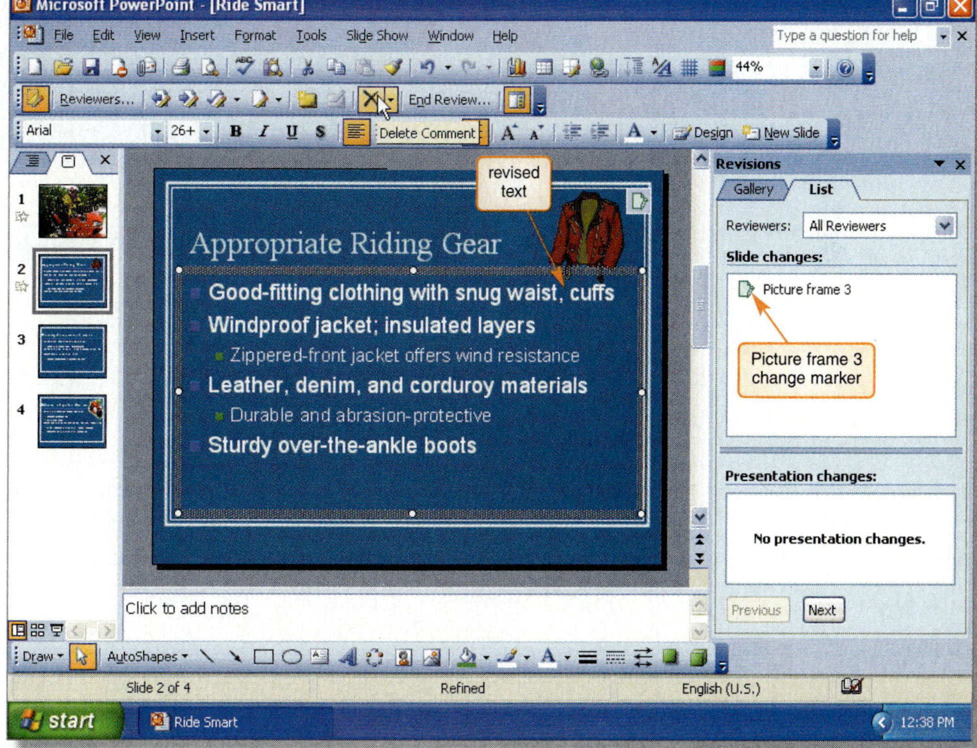

FIGURE 26

5

- **Click the Picture frame 3 change marker.**
- **Click the Gallery tab.**

The Christi Clarke slide modification to move and enlarge the leather jacket clip is displayed in the slide preview (Figure 27). If the Picture toolbar opens, click the Close button on the toolbar.

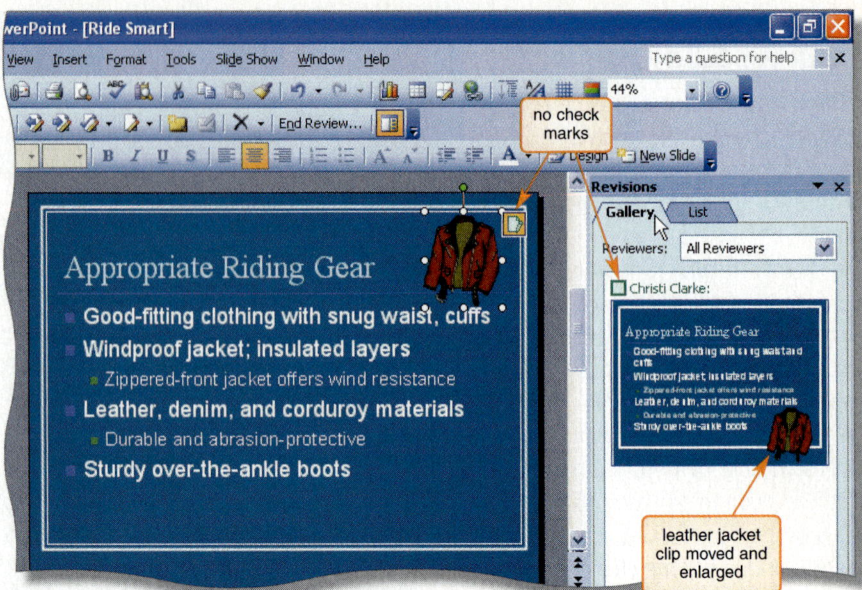

FIGURE 27

6

- **Click the List tab.**
- **Click the Delete Marker button.**

The message in the Slide changes area in the Revisions task pane indicates that no more changes from the reviewers are available for Slide 2 and that the next comments are on Slide 3 (Figure 28).

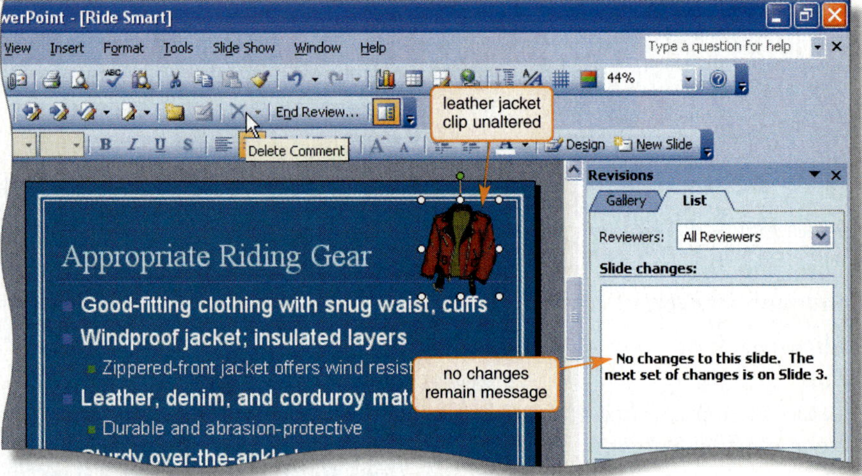

FIGURE 28

All the desired changes from the reviewers have been made to Slide 2. You accepted all the changes except moving the leather jacket to the lower-right corner of the slide. You now can review additional suggestions for the two remaining slides. The following steps illustrate how to review the comments on Slides 3 and 4 of the presentation using the instructions in Table 2.

To Review and Accept Comments on Slides 3 and 4

1. **Click the Next button on the List tab in the Revisions task pane.**
2. **Be certain to delete each comment marker or change marker after you have performed the action in Table 2.**
3. **Review the additional comments in the slide show and perform the actions indicated in Table 2.**

4 **When you have reviewed all the comments, click the Close button in the Revisions task pane.**

5 **Save the Ride Smart presentation.**

6 **Run the Ride Smart presentation to see the modifications.**

7 **If the Reviewing toolbar is displayed, hide it by clicking View on the menu bar, pointing to Toolbars, and then clicking Reviewing on the Toolbars submenu.**

The process of reviewing and accepting the changes to the slide show is complete. The Ride Smart presentation has been updated with suggestions from the three reviewers (Figure 29). You may need to use a second disk to save the file.

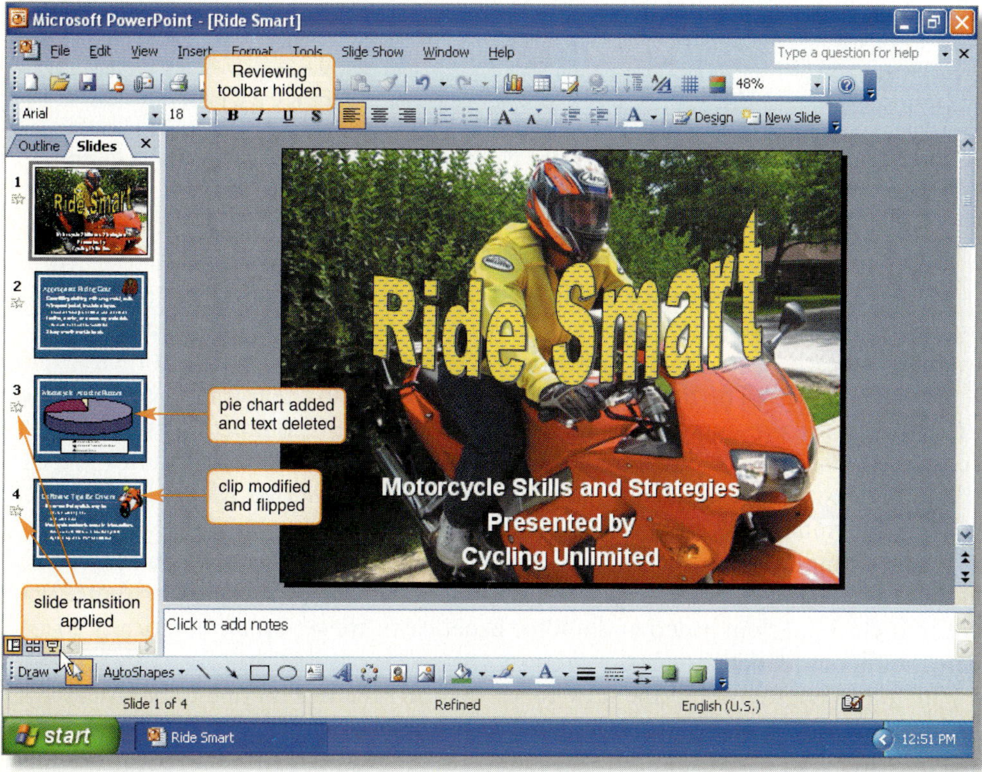

FIGURE 29

Table 2 Changes for Slides 3 and 4

SLIDE NUMBER	COMMENT MARKER	CHANGE MARKER	ACTION
3	CC2		Read and then delete the comment.
		Slide properties	Apply only the Brianna Brooke slide transition.
		Object 2	Apply the Christi Clarke Inserted Object.
		Text 2	Apply the Christi Clarke Deleted Text 3.
4	AA2		Read and then delete the comment.
		Slide properties	Apply the Brianna Brooke slide transition.
		Group 3	Apply the Andy Andreessen Inserted Group.
		Picture frame 3	Apply the change to delete Picture frame 3.

These changes complete the Ride Smart slide show. The next step is to schedule and deliver this presentation as a broadcast to remote audiences.

Part 2: Scheduling and Delivering Online Broadcasts

> *More About*
>
> **Zoom**
>
> Zooming in or out on a slide helps you view details and align text precisely. To use the zoom feature in the Outline tab or the Slides tab or for the slide displayed in the slide pane, click the area you want to view, click the arrow next to the Zoom box on the Standard toolbar, and then click the desired magnification. When you use zoom for the slide pane, click Fit to redisplay the entire slide.

PowerPoint's **broadcasting feature** allows remote viewers to see live performances of presentations. While saving slide shows as Web pages creates static versions of presentations, **delivering** broadcasts actually allows presenters to give presentations and include their voices and video.

Note: If you plan to step through this project on a computer, then you first need to confirm that the Online Broadcast command is available on the Slide Show menu on your computer. If the Online Broadcast command is available, then you can proceed with the project. If the Online Broadcast command is not available on the Slide Show menu, then you must download this feature from the Microsoft Office Online Web site. To display the Microsoft Office Online home page, click Microsoft Office Online on the Help menu. For additional information, enter `Online Broadcast` in the Type a question for help box or see your instructor for download instructions.

Windows Media Services or a third-party Windows Media Services provider must be used if a presentation is broadcast to more than 10 computers, and the files must be placed on a shared network server for viewers to access via their Internet connections. The file location must be specified in the form of \\servername\sharename\. If the presentation includes video, Microsoft recommends using Windows Media Services. Prepare to deliver the broadcast about 30 minutes prior to the broadcast time so you can upload the file to the Windows Media Server and send e-mail reminder messages to your audience.

When setting up a broadcast, you must decide when to schedule it, whether you will record and save the broadcast for airing at a later date, and what attributes you want to include, such as video and audio. Broadcasts are set up automatically to include audio and video streams.

The following steps describe how to set up and schedule an online broadcast, which requires a connection to a network or to the Internet.

To Set Up and Schedule an Online Broadcast

1

- **Click Slide Show on the menu bar, point to Online Broadcast, and then point to Schedule a Live Broadcast.**

The Slide Show menu and Online Broadcast submenu are displayed (Figure 30).

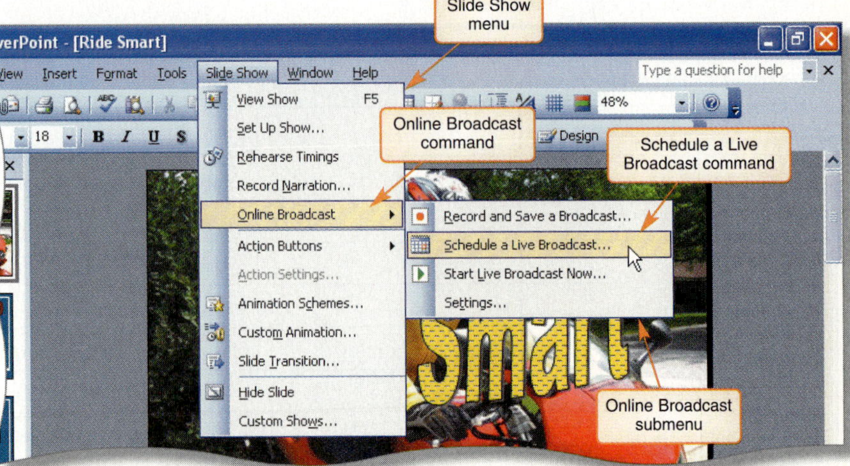

FIGURE 30

2

- **Click Schedule a Live Broadcast on the Online Broadcast submenu.**
- **When the Schedule Presentation Broadcast dialog box is displayed, click the Description text box and then type** `This presentation will inform motorcyclists and automobile drivers about defensive techniques to reduce the occurrence and severity of motorcycle accidents.`
- **Select the current name in the Speaker text box, and then type** `Andy Andreessen` **as the speaker name.**
- **If necessary, type a semicolon and your name in the Keywords text box.**
- **Delete any text in the Copyright and Email text boxes.**

The Schedule Presentation Broadcast dialog box is displayed as shown (Figure 31). The information in the text boxes will be displayed in the e-mail message sent to audience members.

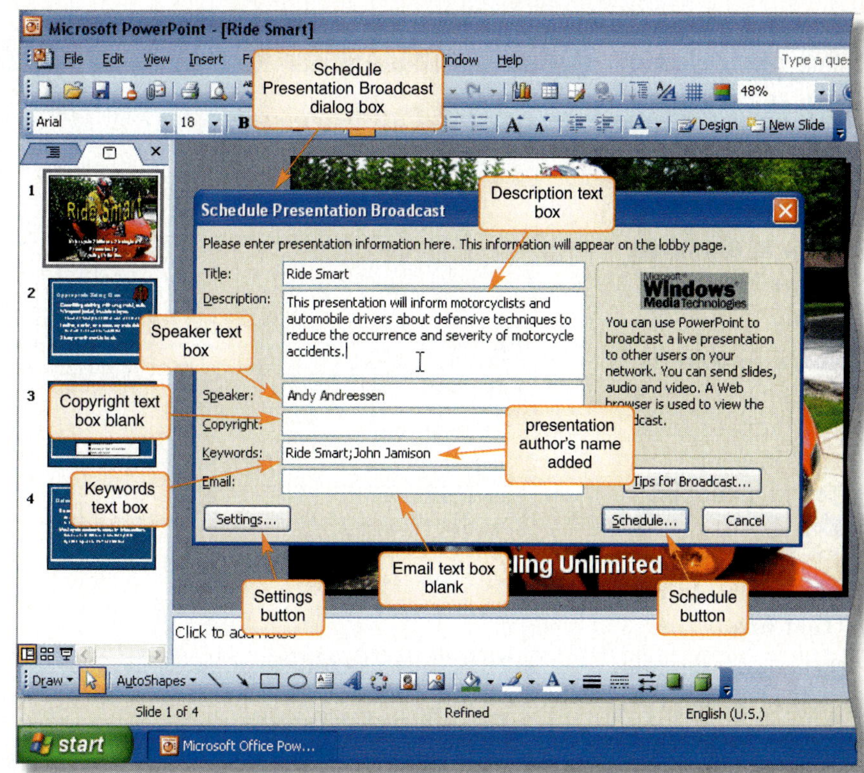

FIGURE 31

3

- **Click the Settings button.**
- **If necessary, when the Broadcast Settings dialog box is displayed, click None in the Audio/Video area on the Presenter tab.**
- **If necessary, click Display speaker notes with the presentation in the Presentation options area to remove the check mark.**
- **Ask your instructor where the broadcast files will be stored on your computer network, and then, in the Save broadcast files in text box, enter the location where these broadcast files will be stored by typing the location or browsing to the file.**

This presentation does not have audio or video components or speaker notes (Figure 32).

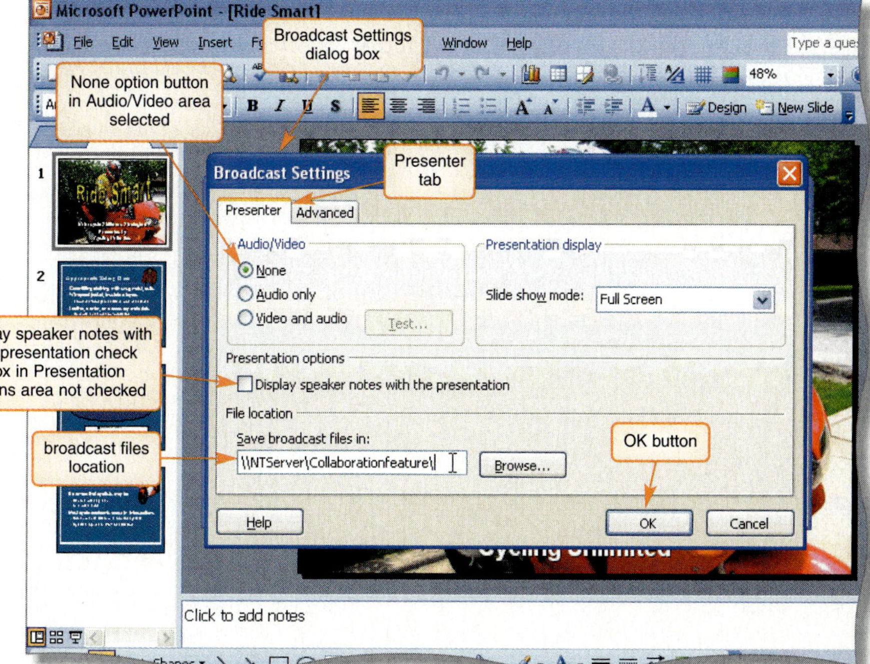

FIGURE 32

4

- **Click the OK button.**
- **Click the Schedule button.**
- **When the Ride Smart - Meeting window is displayed, click the Maximize button.**
- **On the Appointment tab, type** `Andy_Andreessen@hotmail.com; Brianna_Brooke@hotmail.com; Christi_Clarke@hotmail.com` **in the To text box.**
- **Click the Start time date box arrow, click the right arrow at the top of the calendar until the desired month is displayed, and then click the desired date.**
- **Click the Start time time box arrow and then click the desired time in the list.**

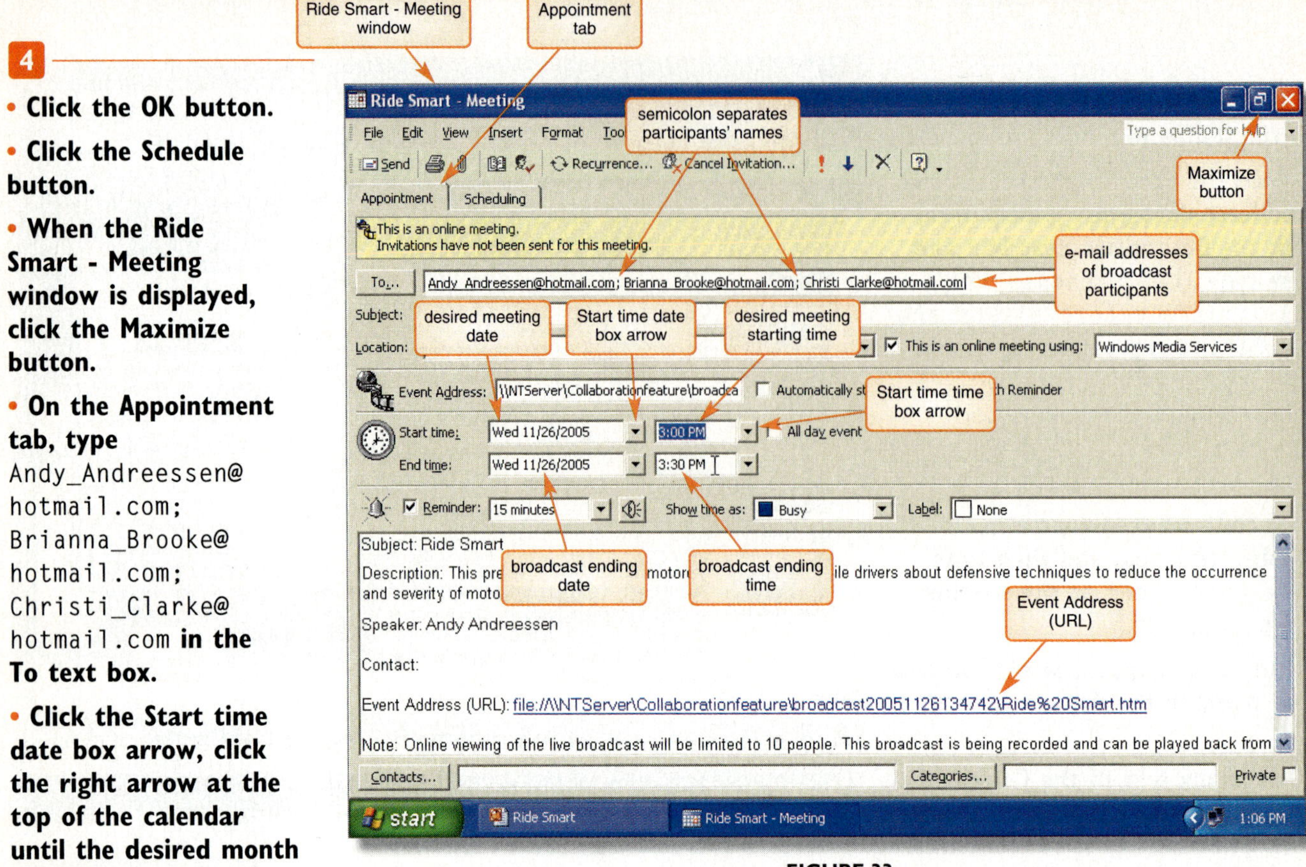

FIGURE 33

You may need to click a blinking Ride Smart - Meeting button on the taskbar to open the window. The Ride Smart - Meeting window is displayed as shown (Figure 33). Semicolons or commas can separate recipients' names. Sending the e-mail notifies the three reviewers that the broadcast has been scheduled for a particular date and time and can be viewed at the Event Address (URL) listed in the message. Meetings are scheduled automatically for 30 minutes on the same date.

5

- **Click the Send button on the Standard toolbar.**
- **When the Microsoft Office PowerPoint dialog box is displayed indicating the broadcast has been scheduled successfully and the broadcast settings have been saved, point to the OK button.**

The message indicates the broadcast settings have been saved in your Ride Smart file (Figure 34).

6

- **Click the OK button.**

Andy Andreessen, Brianna Brooke, and Christi Clarke will receive an e-mail message indicating that the Ride Smart broadcast has been scheduled.

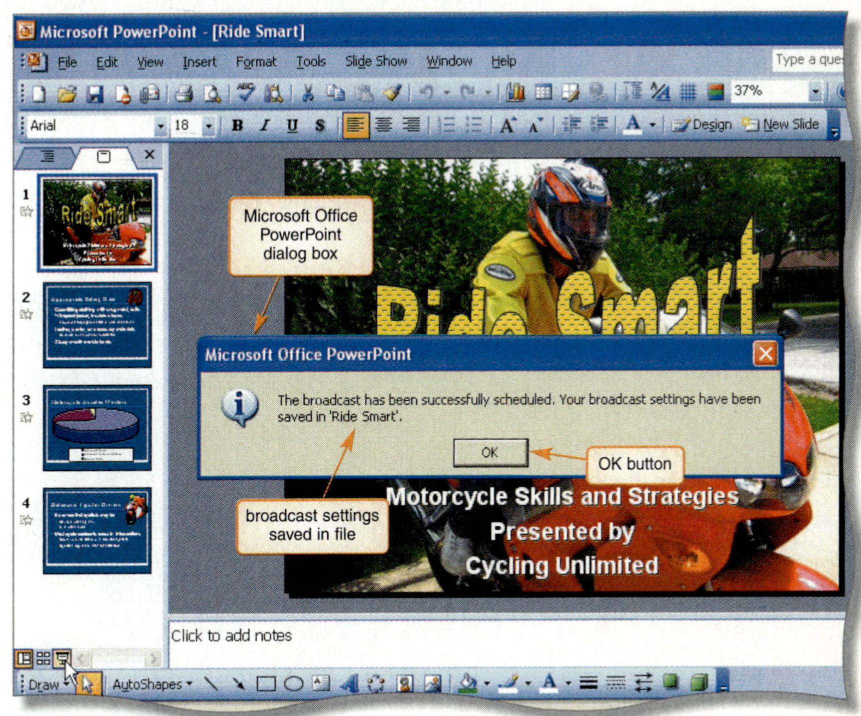

FIGURE 34

Other Ways

1. Press ALT+D, press O, press S
2. In Voice Command mode, say "Slide Show, Online Broadcast, Schedule a Live Broadcast"

The presentation has been set up and scheduled. When you are ready to begin the broadcast, click Slide Show on the menu bar, point to Online Broadcast, and then click Start Live Broadcast Now on the Online Broadcast submenu. When the Live Presentation Broadcast dialog box is displayed, click the Ride Smart broadcast and then click the Broadcast button. Andy Andreessen, Brianna Brooke, and Christi Clarke can view the slides by launching their Internet browsers and typing the link listed in their e-mail message invitations.

Broadcasting is one method of sharing a presentation with viewers. The next part of this project prepares the Ride Smart presentation so you can present the slide show with audience members at remote locations.

Part 3: Saving the Presentation Using the Package for CD Option

If your computer has compact disc (CD) burning hardware, the Package for CD option will copy a PowerPoint presentation and linked files onto a CD. Two types of CDs can be used: recordable (CD-R) and rewritable (CD-RW). If the CD-RW has existing content, these files will be overwritten. The PowerPoint Viewer is included so you can show the presentation on another computer that has Microsoft Windows but does not have PowerPoint installed. The **PowerPoint Viewer** also allows users to view presentations created with PowerPoint 2002, 2000, and 97.

More About

The PowerPoint Viewer

The PowerPoint Viewer is installed by default when Microsoft Office 2003 is installed. In addition, it is available for download from the Microsoft Office Online Web site. It supports opening presentations created using Microsoft PowerPoint 97 and later.

The Package for CD dialog box allows you to select the presentation files to copy, linking and embedding options, whether to add the Viewer, and passwords to open and modify the files. The following steps show how to save a presentation and related files to a CD using the Package for CD feature.

To Package a Presentation for Storage on a Compact Disc

1

- **Insert a CD-RW or a blank CD-R into your CD drive.**
- **With the Ride Smart presentation active, click File on the menu bar and then point to Package for CD.**

The File menu is displayed (Figure 35).

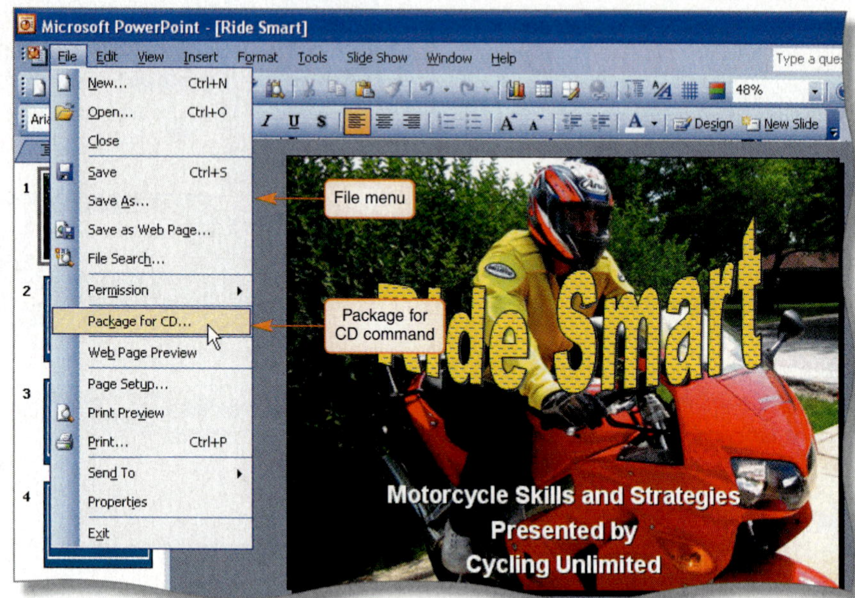

FIGURE 35

2

- **Click Package for CD.**

When the Package for CD dialog box is displayed, type `Collaboration` **in the Name the CD text box.**

PresentationCD is the default CD name. Ride Smart is the file that PowerPoint will copy to the CD (Figure 36). If desired, you can click the Add Files button to save additional files. You also can click the Options button if you do not want to include the PowerPoint Viewer and linked files, if you want to embed TrueType fonts, or if you want to use passwords to open or modify the files. You can click the Close button to exit the Package for CD dialog box.

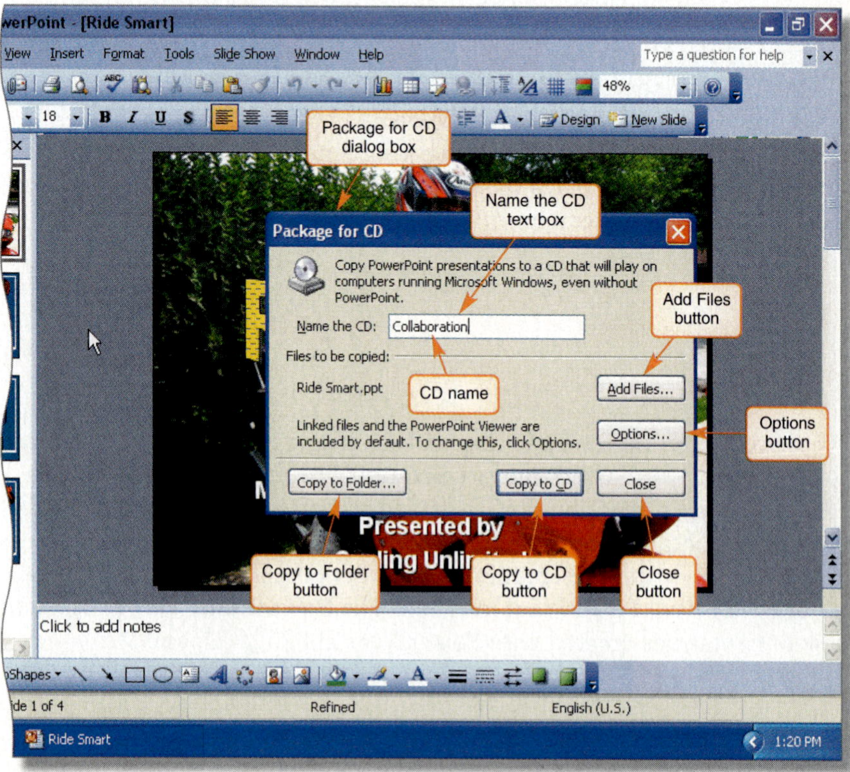

FIGURE 36

3

- **Click the Copy to CD button.**

PowerPoint packages the presentation files and displays status messages of which files are being added to the package. When all files have been copied successfully to the CD, PowerPoint displays a message asking if you want to copy the same files to another CD (Figure 37).

4

- **Click the No button in the Microsoft Office PowerPoint dialog box.**
- **Click the Close button in the Package for CD dialog box.**

PowerPoint closes the Package for CD dialog box and displays the Ride Smart presentation in normal view.

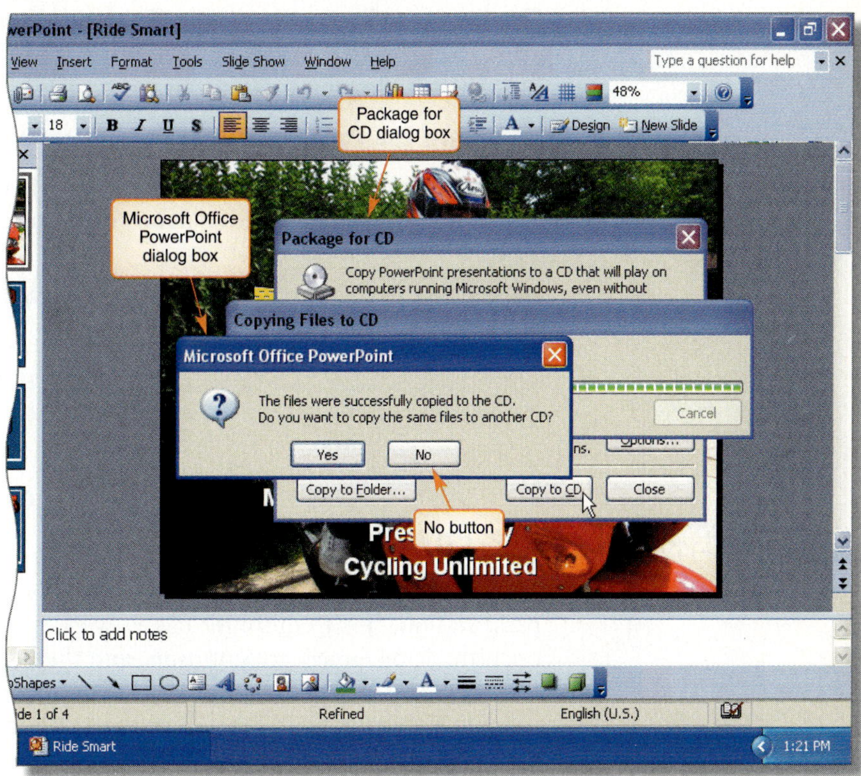

FIGURE 37

Other Ways

1. Press ALT+F, press K, type CD name, press ALT+C
2. In Voice Command mode, say "File, Package for CD"

The Package for CD feature saves the presentation and related files on your CD. You now are ready to transport the presentation to a remote site.

Copying a Presentation Package to a Folder

The Package for CD option also allows you to save the presentation and related files to a folder on your computer or a network. If you do not include the viewer, the feature also allows you to save the files to a folder on a floppy disk. You then can use CD burning software to transfer these files to a CD. The steps on the next page describe how to copy the presentation and viewer to a folder on your computer.

More About

Passwords

You can protect your slide content on CDs by using passwords on all packaged presentations. The passwords specify whether a user can look at or modify a file. In addition, you can add Information Rights Management to files that require more security. Only users with Office PowerPoint 2003 or later can view presentations protected by Information Rights Management, and these files cannot be viewed in the PowerPoint viewer.

To Copy a Presentation Package to a Folder

1. **Click Package for CD on the File menu.**
2. **When the Package for CD dialog box is displayed, click Copy to Folder.**
3. **When the Copy to Folder dialog box is displayed, type the desired name for the folder in the Folder name text box and the desired folder location in the Location text box.**
4. **Click the OK button in the Copy to Folder dialog box.**
5. **Click the Close button in the Package for CD dialog box.**

PowerPoint saves the presentation in a folder on the CD.

Viewing a Packaged Presentation Using the PowerPoint Viewer

When you arrive at a remote location, you will need to open the packed presentation. If the computer has PowerPoint installed, you can start PowerPoint, open the Ride Smart presentation, and then click the Slide Show button. If PowerPoint is not installed or if you simply want to run the presentation, the following steps explain how to run the presentation using the PowerPoint Viewer.

To View a Packaged Presentation Using the PowerPoint Viewer

1. **Insert your Collaboration CD in the CD drive. Right-click the Start button on the taskbar and then click Open on the shortcut menu.**
2. **Click the Up button on the Standard Buttons toolbar until the My Computer window is displayed. Double-click the Collaboration CD drive icon.**

PowerPoint opens the Ride Smart presentation and runs the slide show.

This project is complete. You now should close the Ride Smart presentation.

Closing the Presentation

The following step illustrates how to close the presentation but leave PowerPoint running.

To Close the Presentation

1. **Click File on the menu bar and then click Close on the File menu.**

PowerPoint closes the Ride Smart presentation.

Other Ways

1. Press ALT+F, press C
2. In Voice Command mode, say "File, Close"

Collaboration Feature Summary

This Collaboration Feature demonstrated three methods of sharing a presentation with others. In Part 1, you set up a review cycle and sent the presentation for review. In Part 2, you learned to set up and schedule an online broadcast. In Part 3, you learned to use the Package for CD feature to save and transport files.

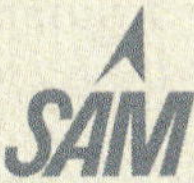

If you have a SAM user profile, you may have access to hands-on instruction, practice, and assessment of the skills covered in this project. Log in to your SAM account and go to your assignments page to see what your instructor has assigned.

What You Should Know

Having completed this project, you should be able to perform the tasks below. The tasks are listed in the same order they were presented in this project. For a list of the buttons, menus, toolbars, and commands introduced in this project, see the Quick Reference Summary at the back of this book and refer to the Page Number column.

1. Start PowerPoint and Open a Presentation (PPT 310)
2. Display the Reviewing Toolbar and Insert a Comment (PPT 312)
3. Send the Presentation for Review (PPT 315)
4. Merge Slide Shows and Print Comments (PPT 316)
5. Review and Accept Comments on Slide 1 (PPT 321)
6. Review and Accept or Reject Comments on Slide 2 (PPT 326)
7. Review and Accept Comments on Slides 3 and 4 (PPT 328)
8. Set Up and Schedule an Online Broadcast (PPT 330)
9. Package a Presentation for Storage on a Compact Disc (PPT 334)
10. Copy a Presentation Package to a Folder (PPT 336)
11. View a Packaged Presentation Using the PowerPoint Viewer (PPT 336)
12. Close the Presentation (PPT 336)

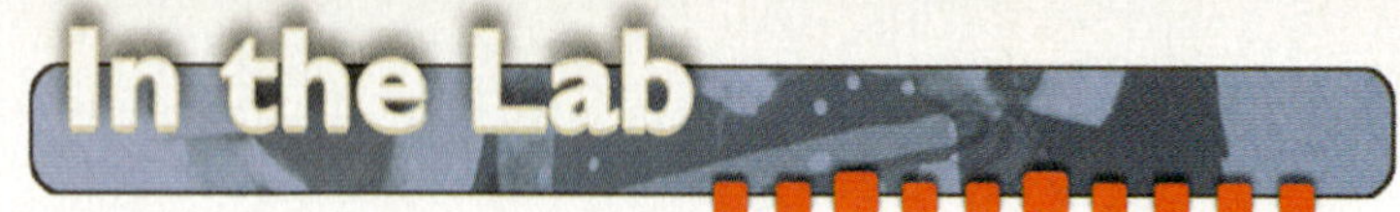

1 Reviewing and Accepting Comments, Scheduling a Broadcast, and Using the Package for CD Option

Problem: Your geology class is studying the Rocky Mountains. Your instructor has asked students to prepare a report on one aspect of this topic, and you have decided to prepare a PowerPoint presentation on the tundra that exists in Rocky Mountain National Park (RMNP). You visited RMNP this past summer and have several photographs you can insert in your slide show. You prepare the Rocky Mountain Tundra presentation, which is shown in Figures 38a through 38d, and then ask your professor and your lab partner to review the slide show and to send you comments. You create the final presentation shown in Figures 38e through 38h on page PPT 340. In addition, your professor wants you to broadcast the revised presentation to students enrolled in another section of the class. She also requests that you use the Package for CD feature to transfer the presentation so she can run the slide show on computers in the Geology Lab.

Instructions: Perform the following tasks:

1. Open the presentation, Lab CF-1 Rocky Mountain Tundra, from the Data Disk. The slides are shown in Figures 38a through 38d.
2. Merge the instructor's revised file, Rocky Mountain Tundra-Professor Jackson, and your lab partner's file, Rocky Mountain Tundra-Beth, on the Data Disk. Preview the slides and then increase the Zoom percent to 150% to view the tundra on Slide 1. Print the slides and the comments.
3. Accept all transitions and template changes throughout the presentation.
4. On Slide 1, accept all the changes and delete the markers.
5. On Slide 2, reject Jackson's clip art and accept Beth's photo and delete the markers.
6. On Slide 3, accept Jackson's changes and reject Beth's editing change and delete the markers.
7. On Slide 4, accept all changes and delete the markers.
8. Schedule the broadcast for October 28 at 10:00 a.m. Invite your instructor to the broadcast.
9. Save the presentation with the file name, Lab CF-1 New Rocky Mountain Tundra. Print handouts with two slides per page.
10. Save the presentation using the Package for CD feature. Do not embed TrueType fonts, and do not include the Viewer.
11. Close the presentation. Hand in the printouts of the original slides, the comments, and the handouts of the revised slides and the CD containing the presentation to your instructor.

In the Lab

ORIGINAL PRESENTATION

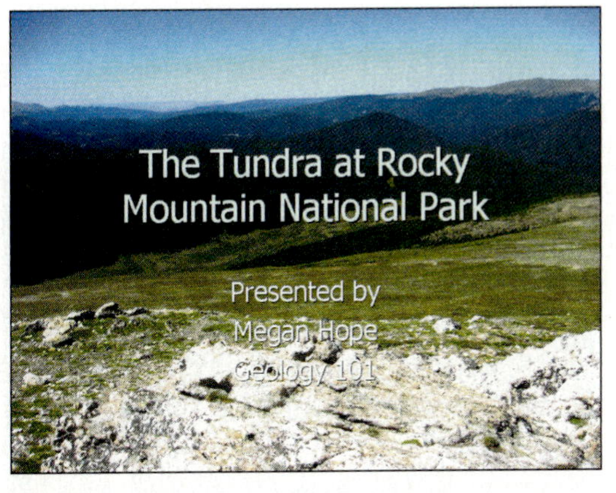

The Tundra at Rocky Mountain National Park
Presented by
Megan Hope
Geology 101

(a) Slide 1

Defining a Tundra

- Treeless area
- Permanently frozen subsoil
- Low-growing vegetation
- Generally found in arctic regions

(b) Slide 2

Seeing the RMNP Tundra

- Unique area south of the Arctic Circle
- Old Fall River Road cuts through area
  - Open only during summer
  - Old one-way gravel road
  - 15 m.p.h. speed limit

(c) Slide 3

RMNP Tundra Facts

- Footsteps damage fragile vegetation
- Cache la Poudre river flows 1,600 feet below
  - Snowmelt causes fast-flowing waters
  - Temperatures less than 50 degrees

(d) Slide 4

FIGURE 38

(continued)

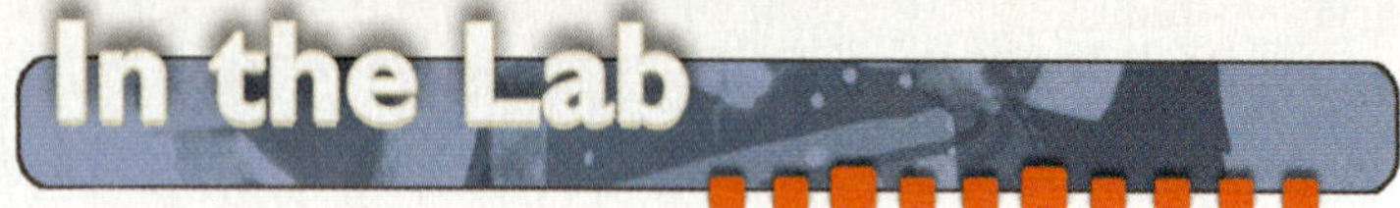

Reviewing and Accepting Comments, Scheduling a Broadcast, and Using the Package for CD Option *(continued)*

REVISED PRESENTATION

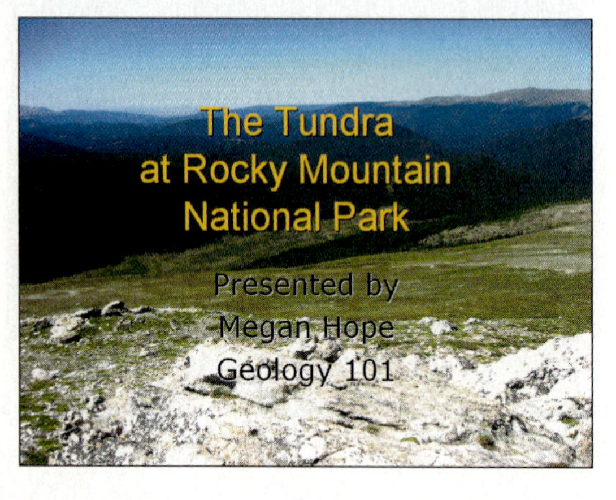

(e) Slide 1

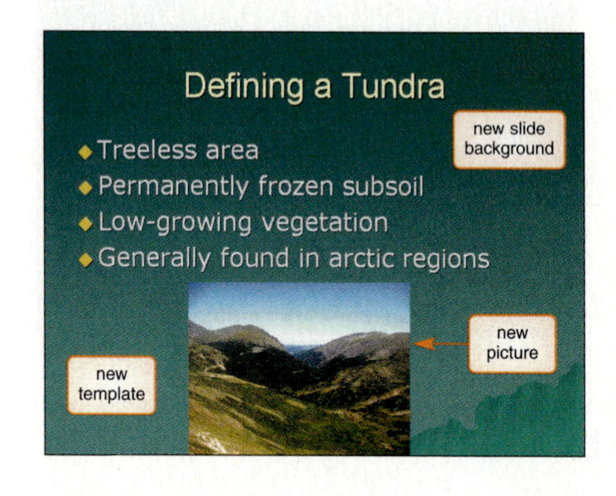

(f) Slide 2

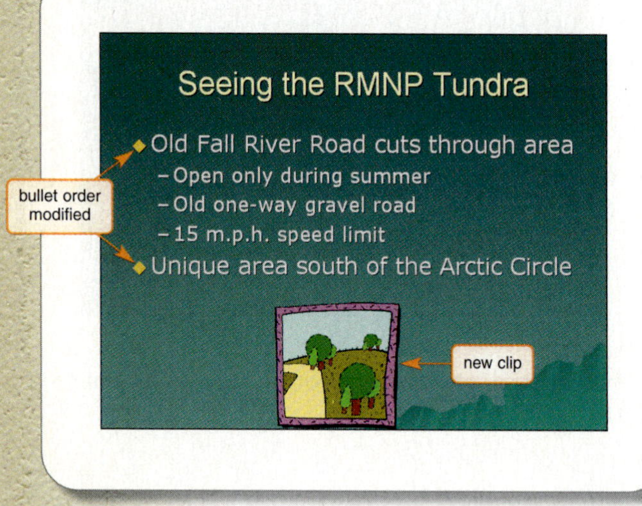

(g) Slide 3

RMNP Tundra Facts

- Footsteps damage fragile vegetation
- Cache la Poudre river flows 1,600 feet below
  - Snowmelt causes fast-flowing waters
  - Temperatures less than 50 degrees

new picture

(h) Slide 4

FIGURE 38 *(continued)*

In the Lab

2 Reviewing a Presentation and Saving Changes Using the Package for CD Option

Problem: Jessica Cantero successfully has shown the Nutrition and Fitness slide show you created for her in Project 2 to several groups of students at your college. She has made a few changes to the presentation and has e-mailed you her revised file, Lab CF-2 Nutrition and Fitness-Cantero. She informs you that she would like to present the slide show at the local health food store and at the library. Both of these locations have computers, so she would like to transport the slide show on a CD and install it on the computers at these sites instead of taking her notebook computer to these events. You agree to make her suggested changes to the presentation and to help her by using the Package for CD feature to transfer the slide show. Create the final presentation shown in Figures 39a through 39e.

Instructions: Perform the following tasks:

1. Open the Nutrition and Fitness presentation shown in Figures 2-1a through 2-1e on page PPT 83. (If you did not complete Project 2, see your instructor for a copy of the presentation.)
2. Merge the Lab CF-2 Nutrition and Fitness-Cantero file on your Data Disk. Print the slides and her comments. Accept all of Jessica's changes except the clip art change on Slide 5 and the animation settings. Delete the markers.
3. Create a new folder with the name, Revised Nutrition and Fitness. Save the presentation with the file name, Lab CF-2 Nutrition and Fitness Revised. Preview the slides, and then print Notes Pages.
4. Save the file using the Package for CD option. Include the linked files and embed TrueType fonts.
5. Close the presentation. Hand in the printouts of the original slides, the comments, and the Notes Pages and the CD containing the presentation to your instructor.

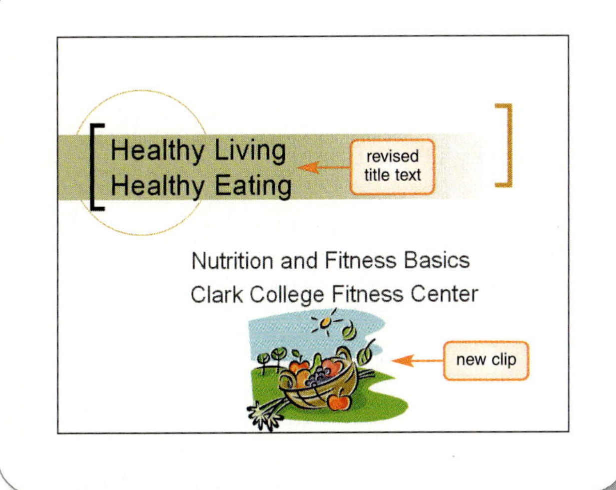

(a) Slide 1

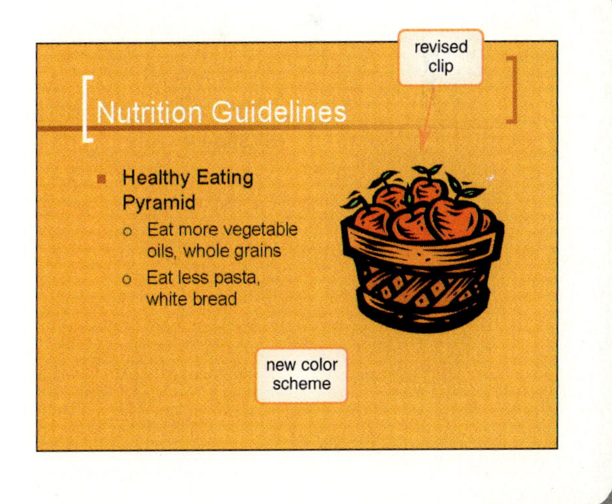

(b) Slide 2

FIGURE 39

(continued)

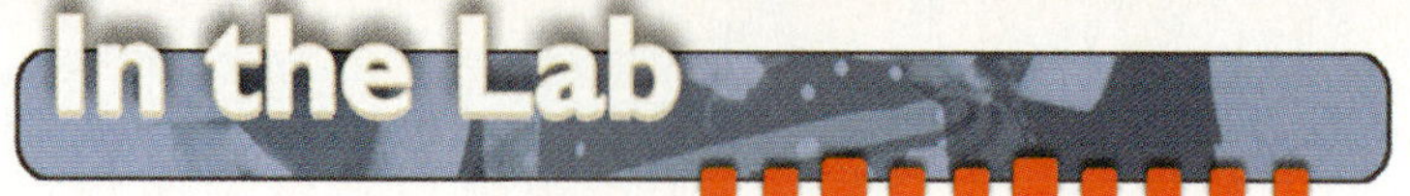

Reviewing a Presentation and Saving Changes Using the Package for CD Option *(continued)*

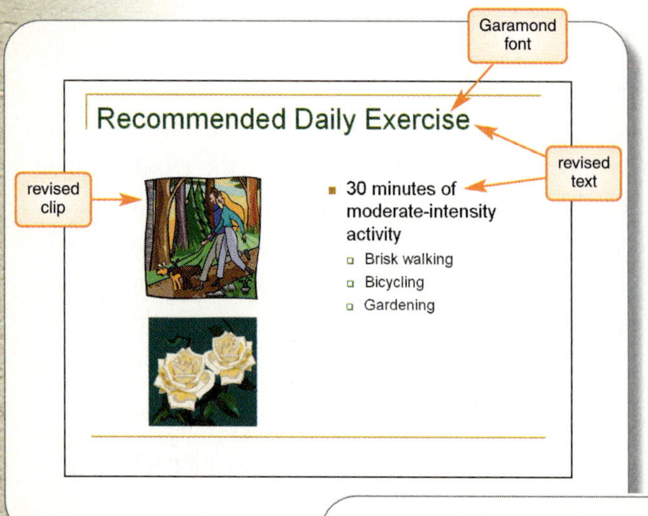

(c) Slide 3

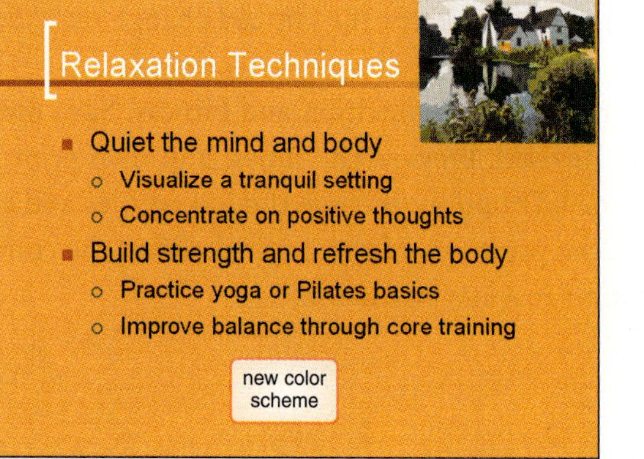

(d) Slide 4

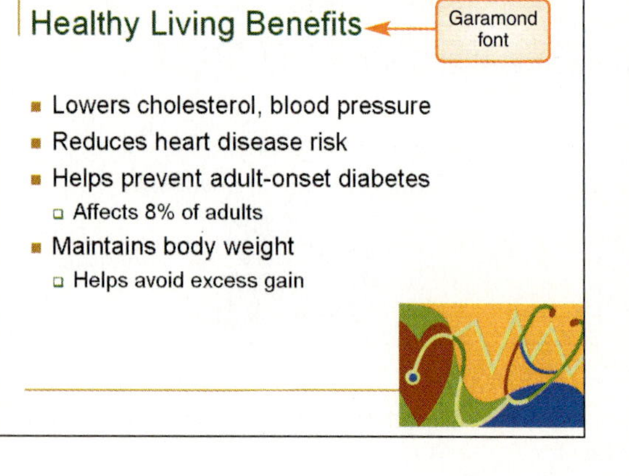

(e) Slide 5

FIGURE 39 *(continued)*

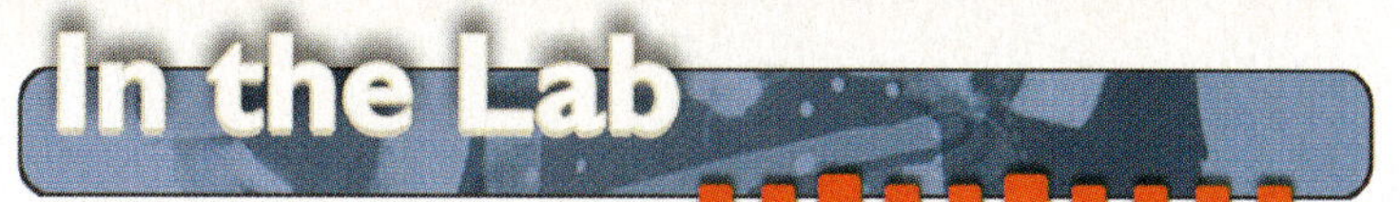

3 Broadcasting a Presentation and Reviewing Comments

Problem: After viewing the College Finances presentation in Project 4, you decide to create a similar presentation highlighting specific financial aid guidelines and policies at your college. You create the slide show and decide to solicit comments regarding the presentation from your professors, friends, classmates, or family members. You ask your network administrator or instructor to upload this file to a shared folder on your school's Web server.

Instructions: Perform the following tasks:

1. Invite two people and your instructor to view the online broadcast. Schedule the broadcast for 2:00 p.m. next Tuesday or a day and time that is convenient for the three invitees.
2. Insert a comment on Slide 1 of the presentation. Send the presentation to two professors, friends, classmates, or family members. Ask the reviewers to make comments and changes to the presentation and have them send their files back to you.
3. Merge their files with your original presentation. Preview the slides, and then preview them in Grayscale mode. Print the slides and their comments.
4. Review their comments and accept or reject their suggestions. Create a new folder with the name, Finances Broadcast. Save the presentation with the file name, Lab CF-3 Financial Aid. Print the revised slides.
5. Close the presentation. Hand in the printed original slides, comments, and revised slides to your instructor.

MICROSOFT

Office Outlook 2003

Schedule Management and Instant Messaging Using Outlook

PROJECT

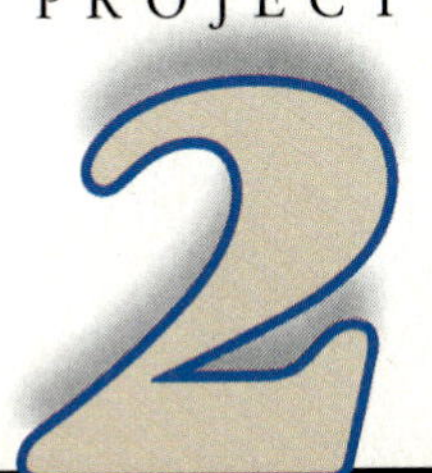

CASE PERSPECTIVE

Maria Rosado is a student-athlete at Woodland Community College. Her busy schedule includes classes, working part-time in the registrar's office, as well as being captain of the Woodland Community College High Flyers championship women's basketball team. As a busy college student, she is concerned about scheduling her school and work activities so they do not interfere with her basketball games and practice schedule. As captain, she is responsible for scheduling team meetings and she would like a simple way to plan future team meetings. She recently read an article about Outlook and thinks it would be the perfect tool to maintain her personal schedule and help with planning team meetings. She also read that she could use instant messaging with Outlook, and knows how easy it would be to communicate with team members and co-workers using this Outlook feature. She is unfamiliar with Outlook, however, and needs some direction.

You work part-time at the Help desk in the school's computer lab and are quite familiar with Outlook and its features. Maria has visited the Help desk requesting that you help her set up her calendar. She would like to use Outlook to schedule her classes, practices, games, work schedule, and other events. She read that Outlook allows you to create a single calendar event and set a weekly recurrence pattern, which will help her with this task. Maria feels that having her time scheduled should help her coordinate her school activities and her extracurricular activities more efficiently. She also would like for you to show her how to set up a team meeting, including inviting attendees and organizing any resources she may need. Finally, Maria would like you to help her set up instant messaging using Outlook. With your help, she can accomplish this goal.

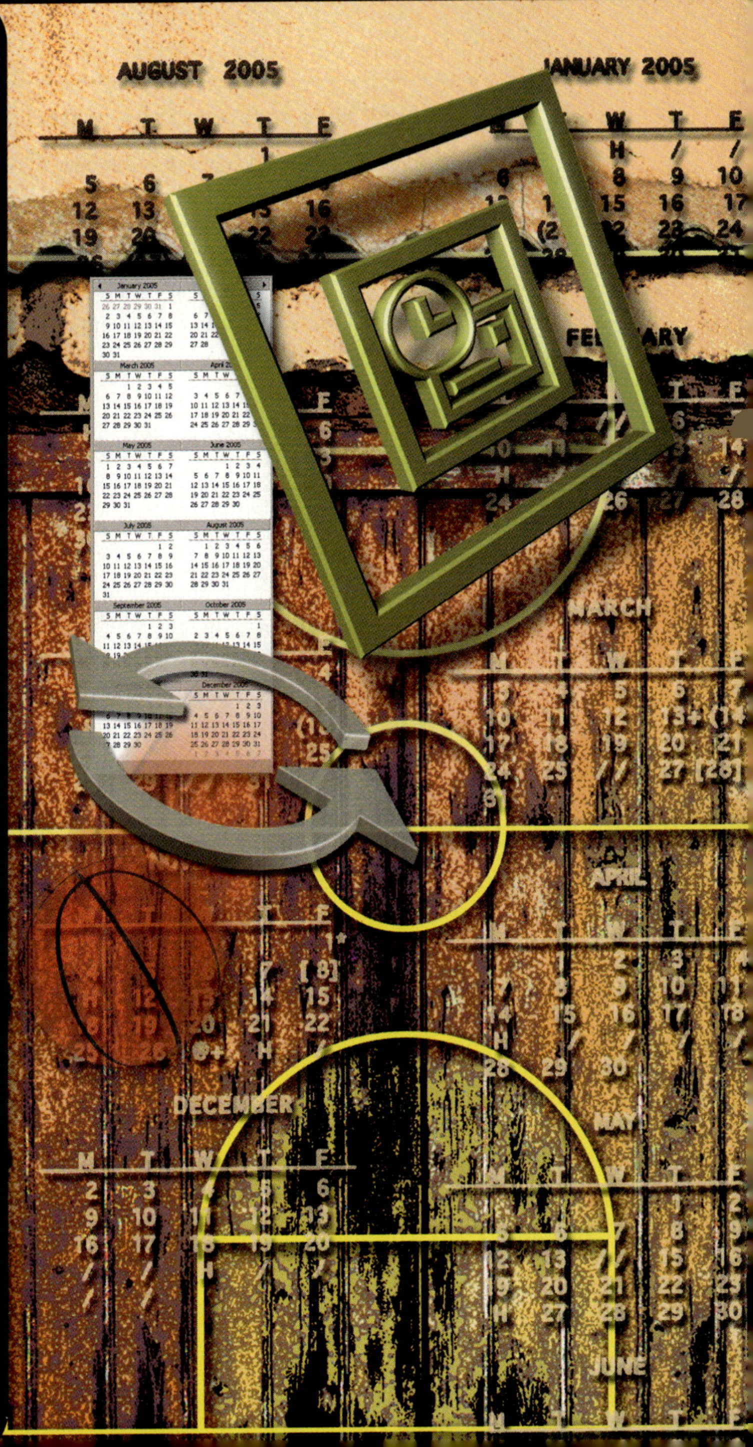

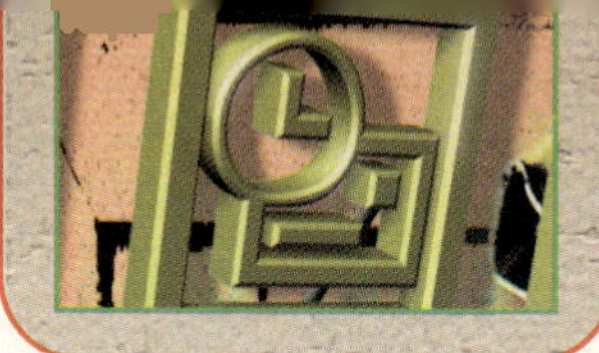

MICROSOFT Office Outlook 2003

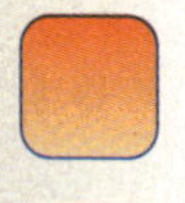

Schedule Management and Instant Messaging Using Outlook

PROJECT 2

Objectives

You will have mastered the material in this project when you can:

- Start Outlook and open the Calendar folder
- Describe the components of the Calendar - Microsoft Outlook window and understand the elements of the Outlook Navigation Pane
- Enter, move, and edit one-time and recurring appointments
- Create an event
- Display the calendar in Day, Work Week, Week, and Month views
- Create and customize a task list and move it to a new folder
- Import, export, and delete personal subfolders
- Delegate tasks
- Schedule a meeting
- Customize the calendar
- Print the calendar in Daily Style, Weekly Style, and Monthly Style
- Enable and start instant messaging in Outlook
- Add an instant messaging address in the contact list
- Send an instant message and send a file with instant messaging

Introduction

Whether you are CEO of a major company or president of an extracurricular activity group in school, Outlook has all the features you need for scheduling and managing appointments, meetings, and tasks (top of Figure 2-1). Using Outlook's Calendar component, managers can schedule meetings and appointments, and assign tasks for the other members of the group and even keep track of meeting attendance and task progression. Outlook also allows you to store miscellaneous information using Notes.

In addition to the contact related capabilities, Outlook is a great tool for scheduling and managing your own time. Most individuals have multiple appointments to keep and tasks to accomplish in a day, week, or month. Outlook assists in maintaining a full schedule such as this, organizing the information in a structured, readable manner.

Outlook also has an instant messaging feature (bottom of Figure 2-1) that works in conjunction with Windows Messenger or MSN Messenger. This allows you to communicate instantaneously with people in your contact list who also use one of these instant messenger services.

OUTLOOK CALENDAR

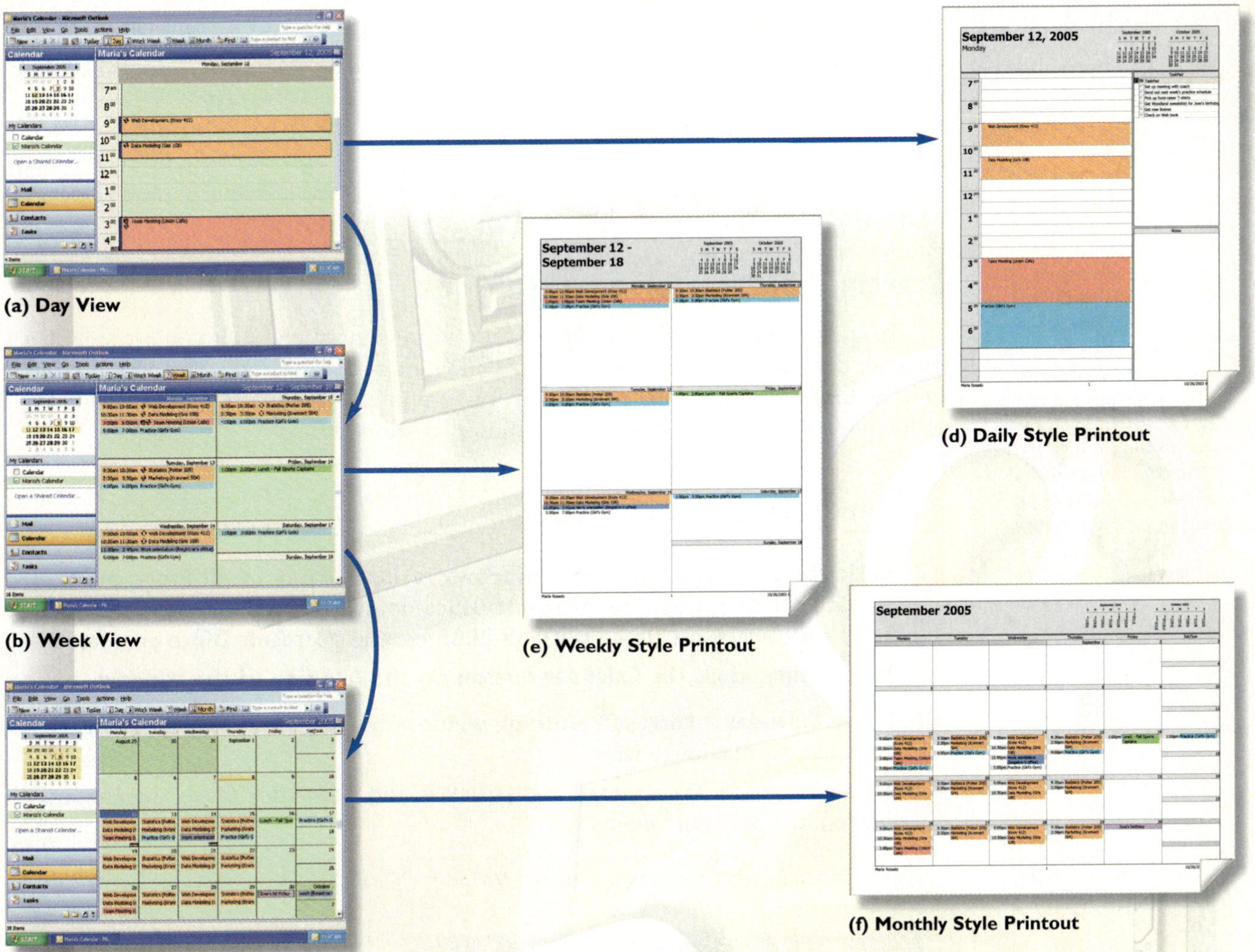

(a) Day View

(b) Week View

(c) Month View

(d) Daily Style Printout

(e) Weekly Style Printout

(f) Monthly Style Printout

INSTANT MESSAGING VIA OUTLOOK

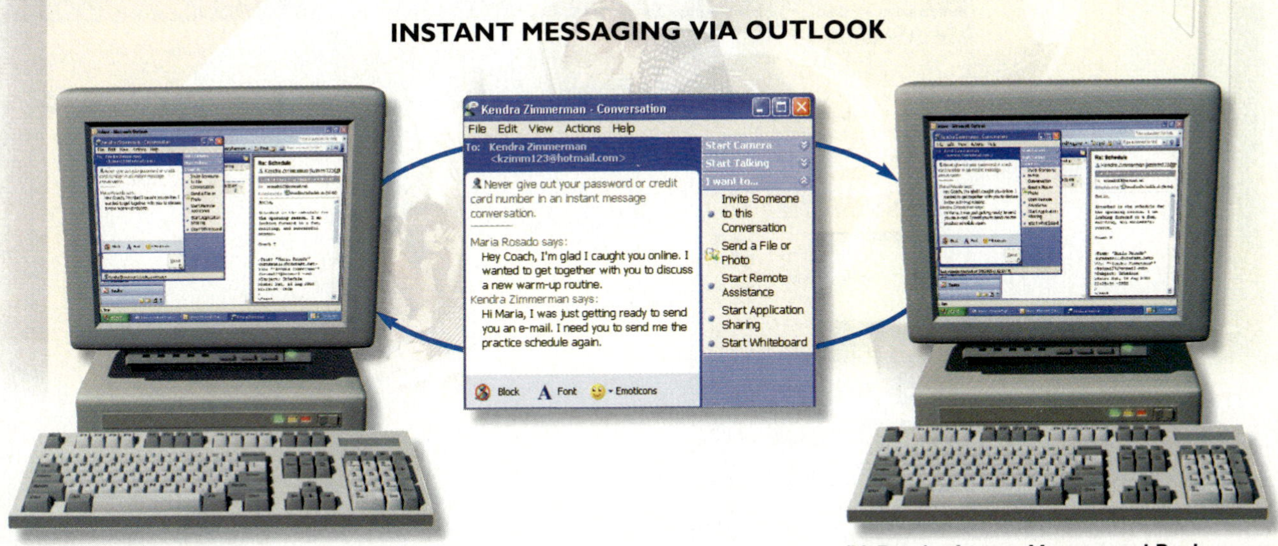

(g) Send Instant Message

(h) Receive Instant Message and Reply

FIGURE 2-1

Project Two — Personal Information Manager

In Project 2, the basic features of Outlook are illustrated while creating a calendar of classes, work schedules, and extra-curricular activities for Maria Rosado. Scheduling meetings is illustrated. In addition to creating the calendar, the project shows how to print it in three views: Day, Week, and Month. Figures 2-1d, 2-1e, and 2-1f on the previous page show the resulting printouts. The project also shows how to create a task list and delegate those tasks. Finally, the project presents using Windows Messenger with Outlook.

More About

The Outlook 2003 Help System

Need Help? It is no further than the Type a question for help box on the menu bar in the upper-right corner of the window. Click the box that contains the text, Type a question for help (Figure 2-2 on the previous page), type `help`, and then press the ENTER key. Outlook responds with a list of topics you can click to learn about obtaining help on any Outlook -related topic. To find out what is new in Outlook 2003, type `what is new in Outlook` in the Type a question for help box.

Starting and Customizing Outlook

To start and customize Outlook, Windows must be running. If you are stepping through this project on a computer and you want your screen to agree with the figures in this book, then you should set your computer's resolution to 800 × 600. The following steps start Outlook and customize its window.

To Start and Customize Outlook

1. **Click the Start button on the Windows taskbar, point to All Programs on the Start menu, point to Microsoft Office on the All Programs submenu, and then click Microsoft Office Outlook 2003 on the Microsoft Office submenu.**
2. **If necessary, click the Calendar button on the left side of the window.**
3. **If the Calendar - Microsoft Outlook window is not maximized, double-click its title bar to maximize it.**
4. **If the Language bar appears, right-click it and then click Close the Language bar on the shortcut menu.**

Outlook is started and displays the Calendar - Microsoft Outlook window as shown in Figure 2-2.

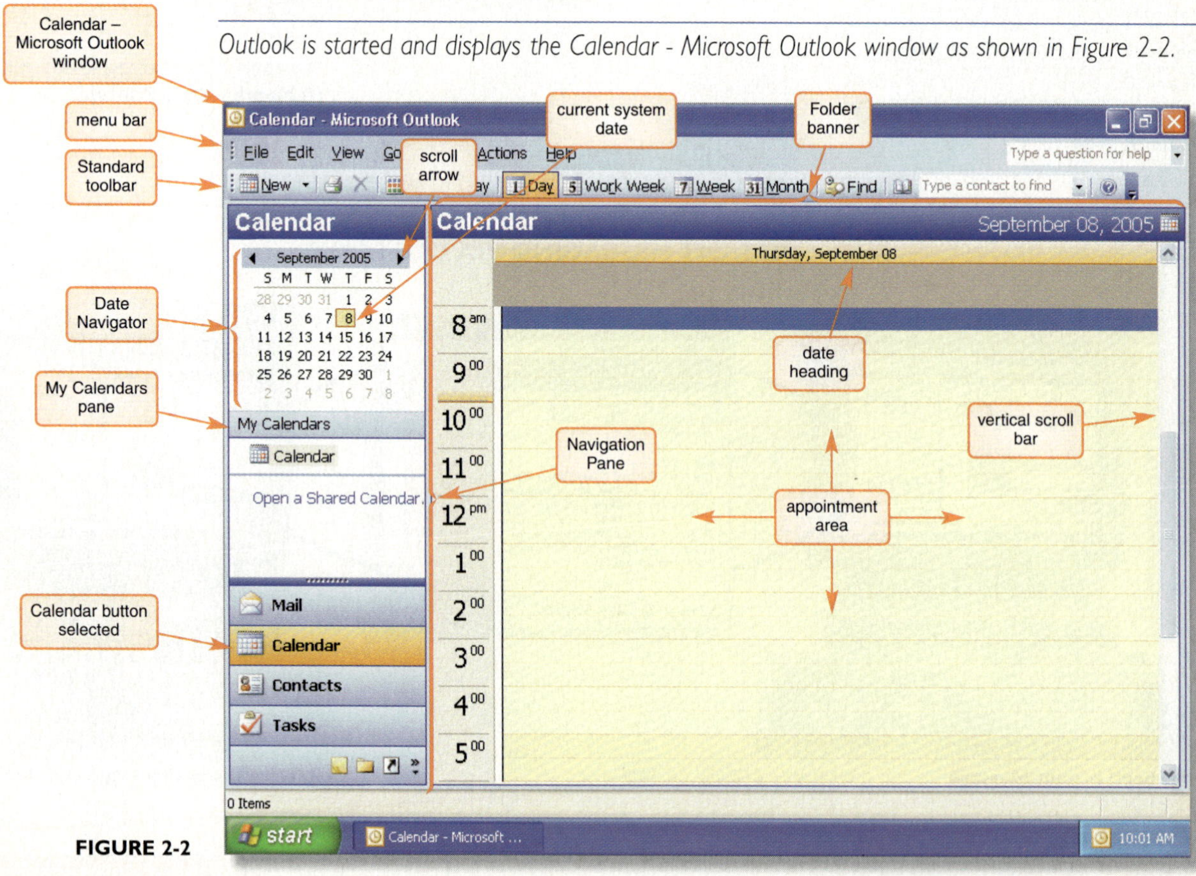

FIGURE 2-2

The Calendar - Microsoft Outlook Window

The **Calendar - Microsoft Outlook window** (Figure 2-2) includes a variety of features to help you work efficiently. It contains many elements similar to the windows in other Office applications, as well as some that are unique to Outlook. The main elements of the Calendar window are the Navigation Pane, the Standard toolbar, and the appointment area. The following paragraphs explain some of the features of the Calendar window.

FOLDER BANNER The **Folder banner** (Figure 2-2) is the horizontal bar just below the Standard toolbar. An icon for the active folder, the name of the active folder, and the selected date display in the Folder banner.

NAVIGATION PANE The **Navigation Pane** (Figure 2-2) includes two sets of buttons and two panes: the Date Navigator pane and My Calendars pane. The **Date Navigator** includes a calendar for the current month and scroll arrows. When you click the scroll arrows to move to a new date, Calendar displays the name of the month, week, or day in the current view in the appointment area. The current system date has a square around it in the Date Navigator. Dates displayed in bold in the Date Navigator indicate days on which an item is scheduled.

Below the Date Navigator, the My Calendars pane includes a list of available calendars on your computer. In this pane, you can select a single calendar to view, or view other calendars side-by-side with your calendar.

On the lower portion of the Navigation Pane are two groups of buttons (Figure 2-3). The first group of buttons are shortcuts representing the standard items that are part of Microsoft Outlook: Mail, Calendar, Contacts, and Tasks. The second group of buttons are shortcuts to other functions of Outlook: Notes, Folder List, Shortcuts, and Configure buttons. When you click a shortcut, Outlook opens the corresponding folder. The function performed when you click each folder is illustrated in Figure 2-3.

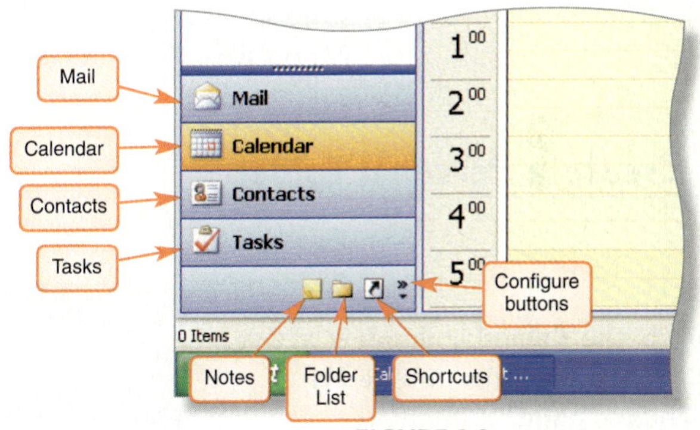

FIGURE 2-3

APPOINTMENT AREA The **appointment area** (Figure 2-2) contains a date heading and, under the date heading, time slots for the current view. The date currently selected in the Date Navigator appears in the date heading. By default, workday time slots are set from 8:00 a.m. to 5:00 p.m. in one hour increments. Time slots outside this period are shaded. A vertical scroll bar allows backward or forward movement through the time slots.

Scheduled items, such as appointments, meetings, or events, display in the appointment area. An **appointment** is an activity that does not involve other resources or people. The term **resources** refers to meeting rooms, audio visual equipment, and other items that may be used with an appointment or in a meeting. Resources are discussed in more detail later in this project. A **meeting**, by contrast, is an appointment to which other resources or people are invited. Outlook's Calendar can be used to schedule several people to attend a meeting or only one person to attend an appointment (such as a class). An **event** is an activity that lasts 24 hours or longer, such as a seminar, birthday, or vacation. Scheduled events do not occupy time slots in the appointment area; instead, they display in a banner below the date heading.

STANDARD TOOLBAR Figure 2-4 shows the Standard toolbar in the Calendar window. The button names indicate their functions. Each button can be clicked to perform a frequently used task, such as creating a new appointment, printing, or changing the current view.

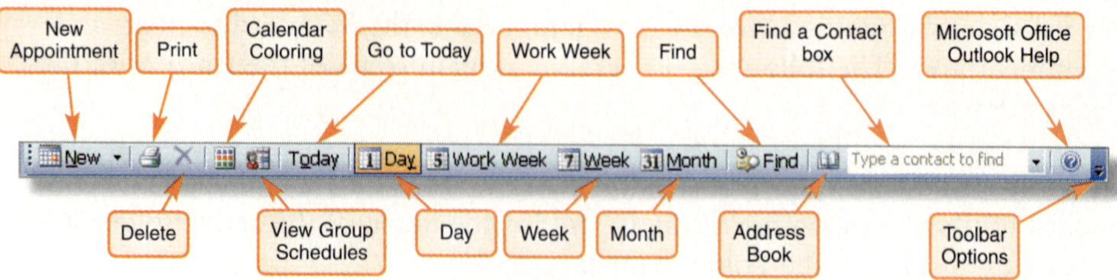

FIGURE 2-4

Creating a Personal Folder

If you were the only person using Outlook on a computer, you could enter appointments and events directly into the main Calendar folder, creating a daily, weekly, and monthly schedule. In many office and school situations, however, several people share one computer and therefore need to create separate folders in which to store appointments and events. The following steps create a personal folder for Maria Rosado.

To Create a Personal Folder

1

- **With the Calendar window active, right-click Calendar in the My Calendars pane.**

Outlook displays the Calendar shortcut menu (Figure 2-5).

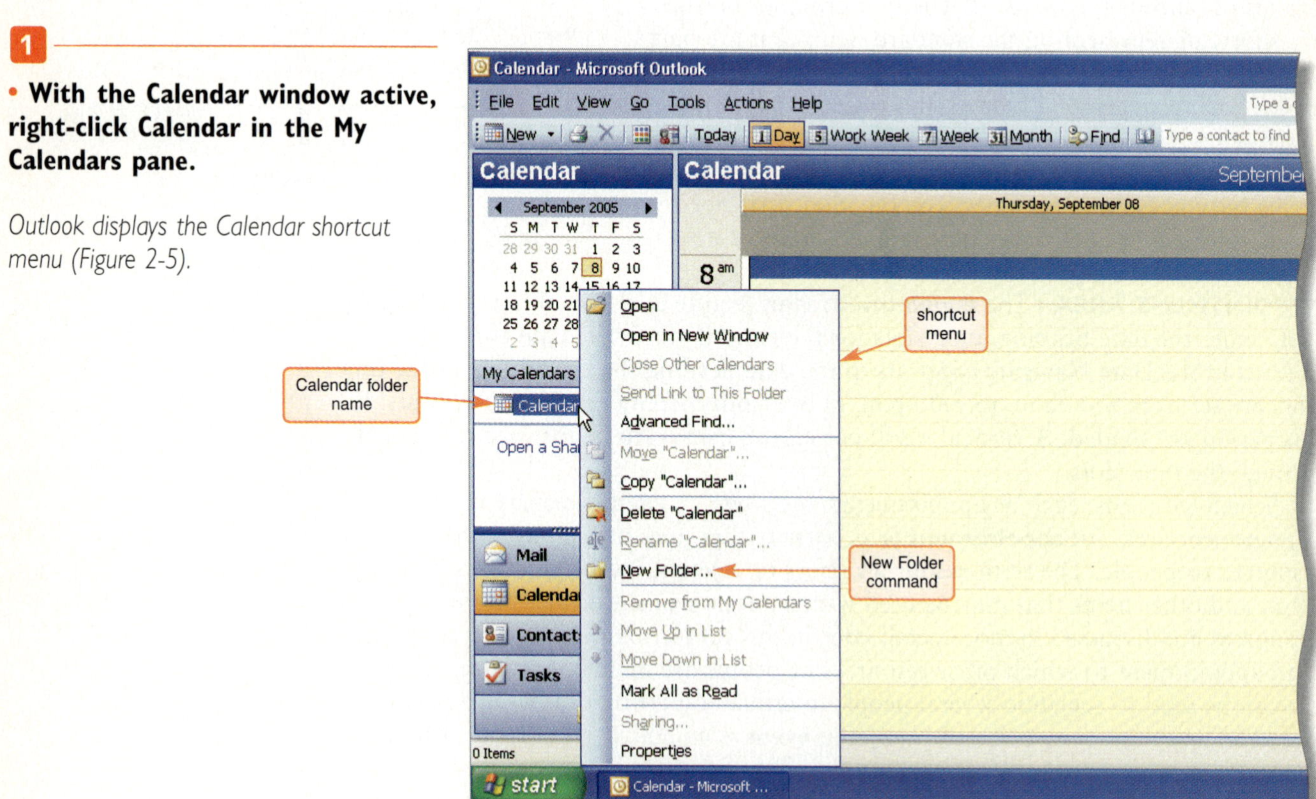

FIGURE 2-5

2

- **Click New Folder on the Calendar shortcut menu.**
- **When Outlook displays the Create New Folder dialog box, type** `Maria's Calendar` **in the Name text box.**
- **Select Calendar Items in the Folder contains text box.**
- **Click Calendar in the Select where to place the folder list box.**

The new folder, Maria's Calendar, becomes a subfolder of the Calendar folder (Figure 2-6). Maria's Calendar appears in the Name text box.

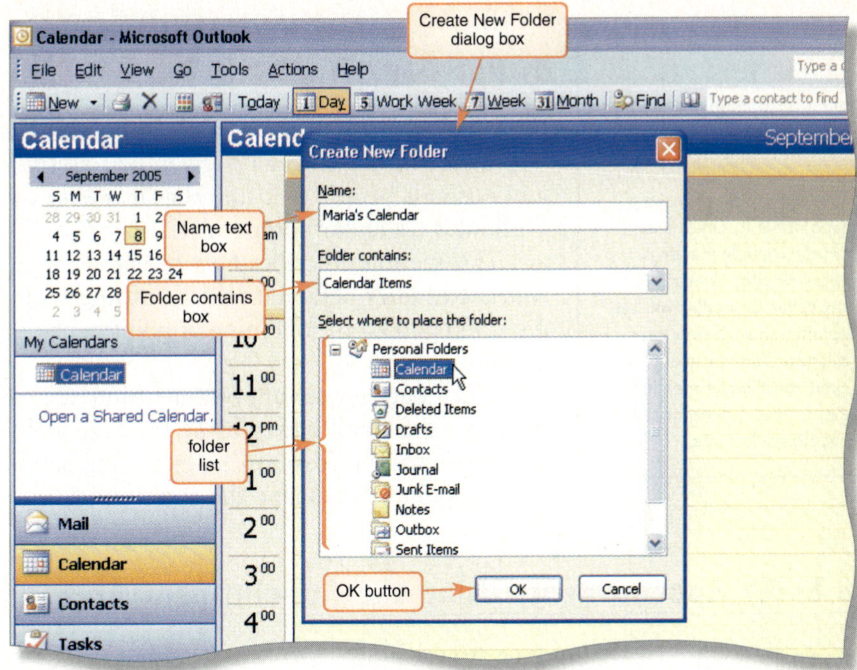

FIGURE 2-6

3

- **Click the OK button.**
- **Click the check box next to Maria's Calendar in the My Calendars list. Click the check box next to Calendar to remove the existing check mark.**

Outlook displays a list of available folders in the My Calendars pane and displays an empty appointment area (Figure 2-7).

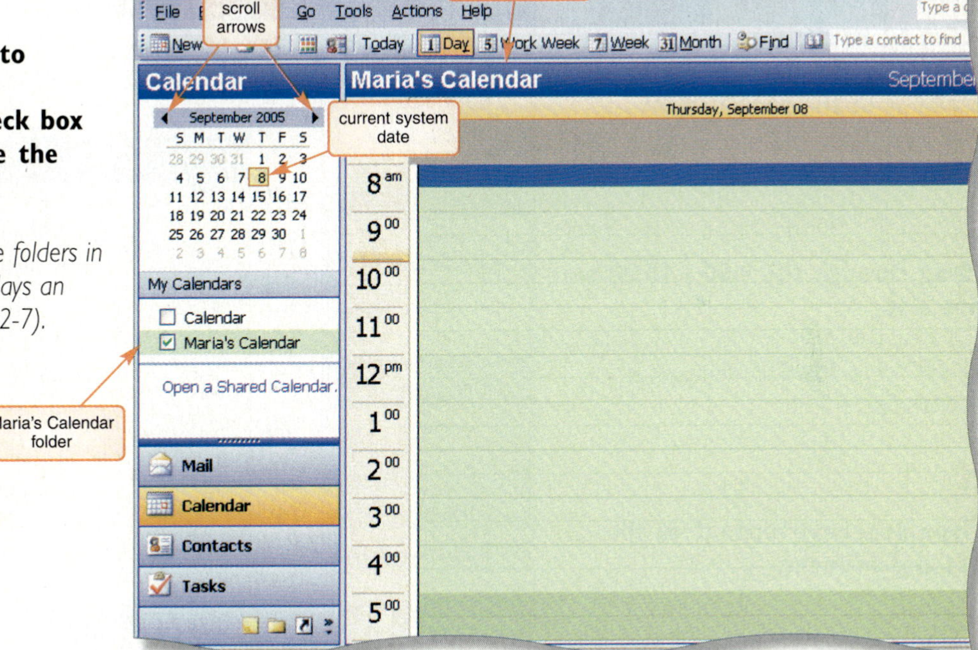

FIGURE 2-7

Figure 2-7 shows the default view for Calendar. If this view does not appear on your computer, click View on the menu bar, point to Arrange By, point to Current View, and then make sure the Day/Week/Month option is selected.

Other Ways

1. On File menu point to Folder, click New Folder on Folder submenu
2. Press CTRL+SHIFT+E
3. In Voice Command mode, say "File, New Folder"

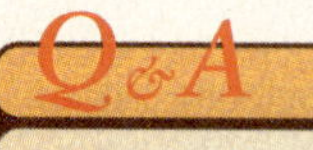

Q: Can I access other users' calendars?

A: Yes. Other users can give you access to their calendars. This allows you to make appointments, check free times, schedule meetings, check or copy contacts, or any other tasks that you can accomplish with your own calendar. This is useful if you need to schedule meetings or events that depend on other people's schedules.

Entering Appointments Using the Appointment Area

Calendar allows you to schedule appointments, meetings, and events for yourself as well as for others who have given permission to open their personal folders. Students and business people will find that it is easy to schedule resources and people with Outlook's Calendar component.

This section describes how to enter appointments, or in this case, classes into Maria Rosado's personal folder, starting with classes for September 12, 2005. Work days and games are one-time appointments; classes and team meetings are recurring appointments.

When entering an appointment into a time slot that is not visible in the current view, use the scroll bar to bring the time slot into view. Once you enter an appointment, you can perform ordinary editing actions. The following steps show how to enter appointments using the appointment area.

To Enter Appointments Using the Appointment Area

1

- **If necessary, click the scroll arrows in the Date Navigator to display September 2005.**
- **Click 12 in the September calendar in the Date Navigator to display it in the appointment area.**

2

- **Drag through the 9:00 - 10:00 am time slot.**

The 9:00 am - 10:00 am time slot is selected (Figure 2-8).

3

- **Type** `Web Development` **as the first appointment.**

As you begin typing, the selected time slot changes to a text box with blue top and bottom borders.

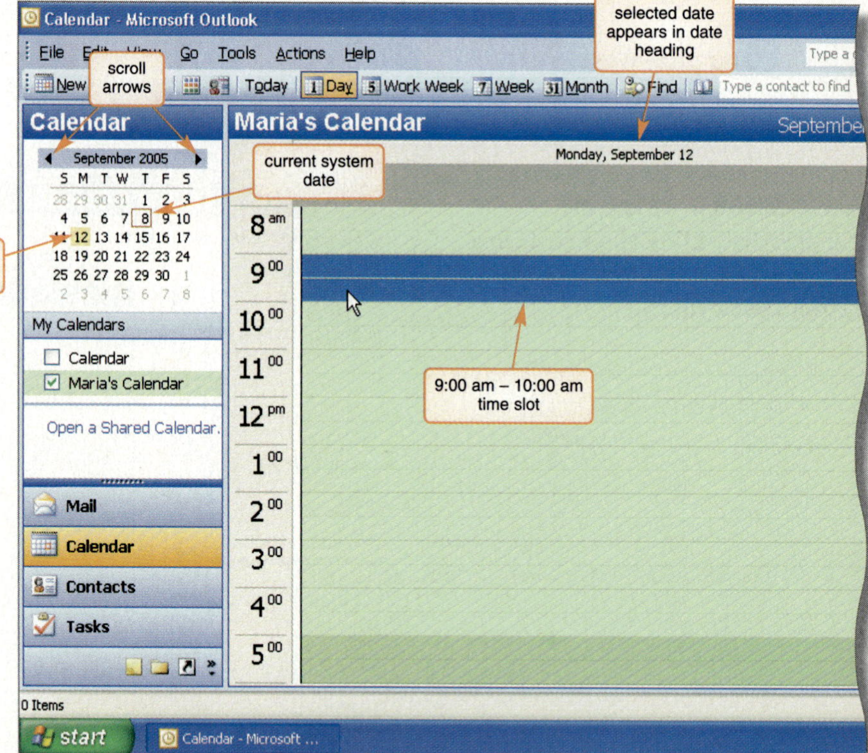

FIGURE 2-8

4

- **Drag through the 10:30 am - 11:30 am time slot.**
- **Type** `Data Modeling` **as the second appointment.**

5

• **Drag through the 12 pm - 1:00 pm time slot.**

• **Type** `Lunch - Fall Sports Captains` **as the third appointment and then press the ENTER key.**

The three appointments display in the appointment area (Figure 2-9).

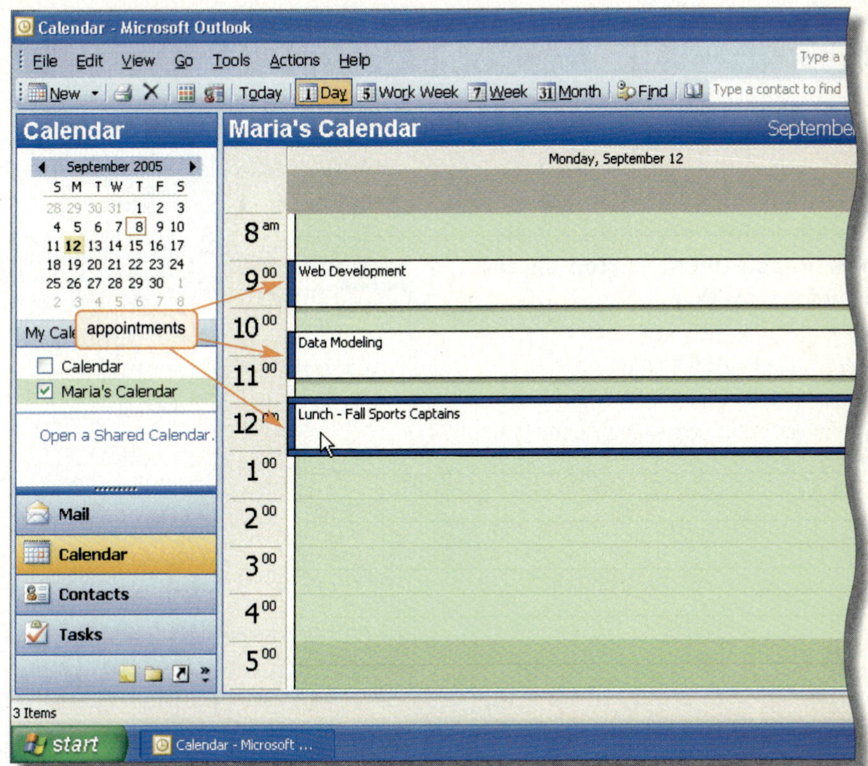

FIGURE 2-9

If you make a mistake while typing and notice the error before clicking outside the appointment time slot or pressing the ENTER key, use the BACKSPACE key to erase all the characters back to and including the error. To cancel the entire entry before clicking outside the appointment time slot or pressing the ENTER key, press the ESC key. If you discover an error in an appointment after clicking outside the appointment or pressing the ENTER key, click the appointment and retype the entry. Later in this project, additional editing techniques are discussed.

Entering Appointments Using the Appointment Window

You can enter appointments either by typing them directly into the appointment area as shown in the previous section, or you can enter them using the **Appointment window**. Using the Appointment window is a slightly more involved process, but it allows the specification of more details about the appointment. The steps on the next page describe how to enter an appointment at 3:00 p.m. to 5:00 p.m. using the appointment window.

More About

Appointments

Appointments can be designated as busy, free, tentative, or out of office. The Private check box in the Appointment window allows you to designate as private any appointments, tasks, meetings, or contacts. The private designation prevents viewing by other users with access to your calendar. Private calendar elements are identified with a key symbol.

To Enter and Save Appointments Using the Appointment Window

1

- **Drag through the 3:00 pm - 5:00 pm time slot and then click the New Appointment button on the Standard toolbar.**

The Untitled - Appointment window opens with the insertion point in the Subject text box in the Appointment sheet (Figure 2-10).

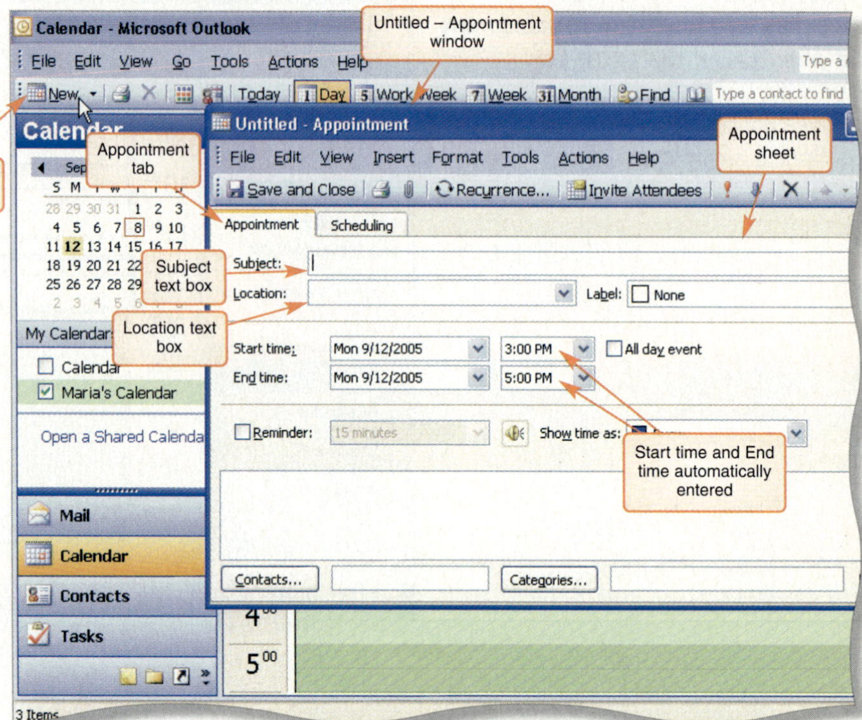

FIGURE 2-10

2

- **Type** `Team meeting` **in the Subject text box and then press the TAB key to move the insertion point to the Location text box.**
- **Type** `Union Cafe` **in the Location text box.**

Both the subject and location of the appointment appear in the appropriate text boxes. Once typed, the appointment subject appears on the Team Meeting - Appointment window title bar and on the taskbar (Figure 2-11).

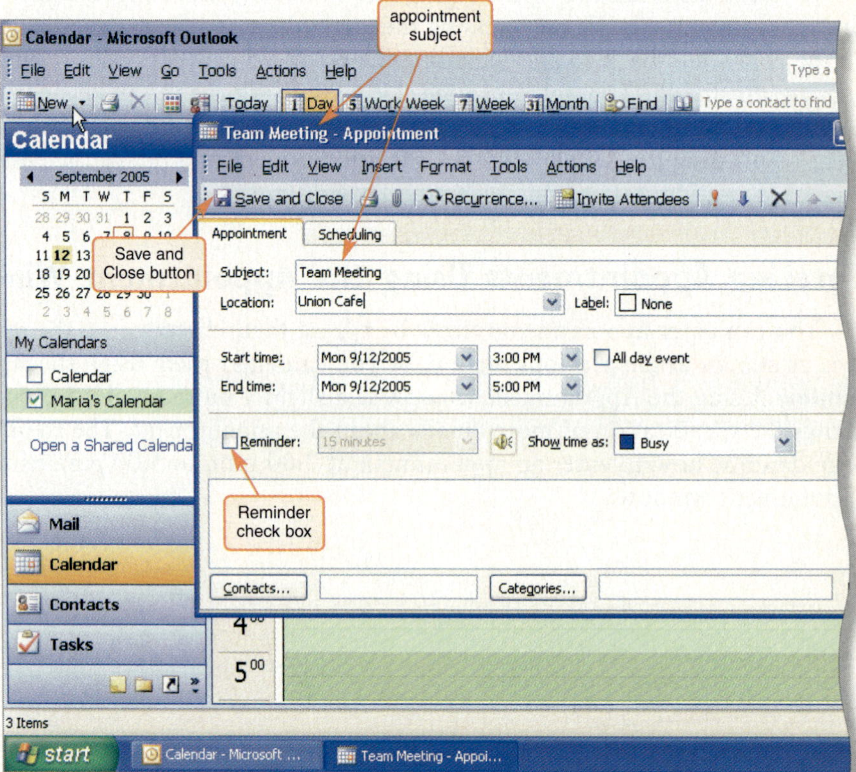

FIGURE 2-11

3

• **Click the Save and Close button on the Standard toolbar.**

Outlook saves the appointment and closes the Appointment window. The schedule for Monday, September 12 appears in the appointment area with the four new appointments entered (Figure 2-12).

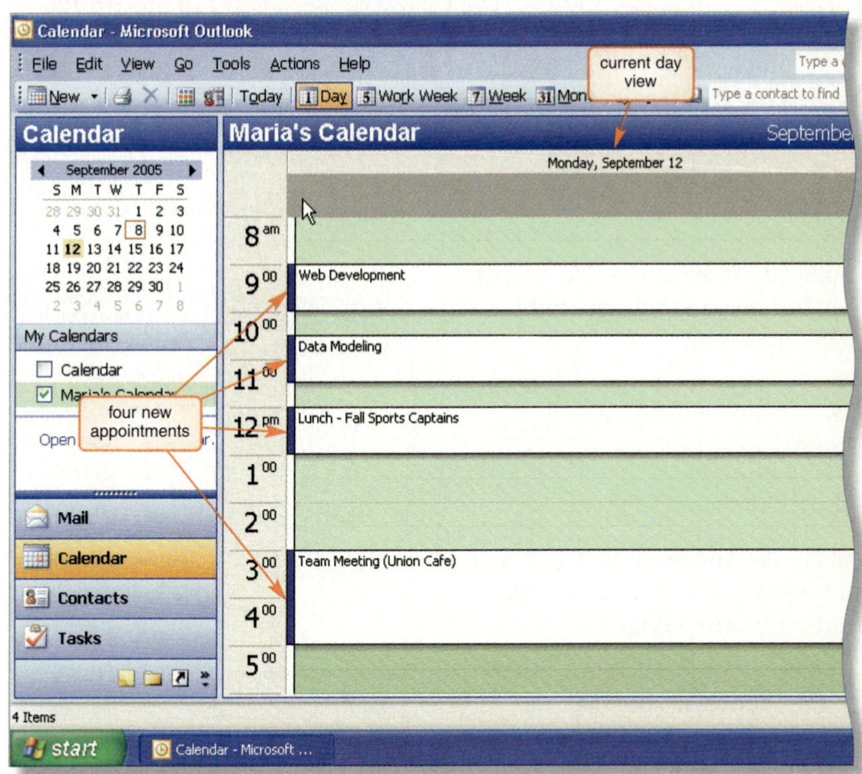

FIGURE 2-12

Other Ways

1. Double-click time slot, enter appointment
2. On Actions menu click New Appointment
3. Right-click time slot, click New Appointment on shortcut menu
4. Press CTRL+N
5. Press ALT+A, type O
6. In Voice Command mode, say "Actions, New Appointment"

The Reminder check box (Figure 2-11) can be checked to instruct your computer to play a reminder sound before an appointment time. A bell icon, called the **Reminder symbol**, appears next to appointments with reminders.

Press the TAB key to move through the fields in the Appointment window (Figure 2-11), or click any text or list box to make a change. Normal editing techniques also can be used to make changes.

Recurring Appointments

Many appointments are **recurring**, or occur at regular intervals. For example, a class held every Monday and Wednesday from 9:00 a.m. to 10:00 a.m. is a recurring appointment. In this project, Maria Rosado's college classes and team meetings occur at regular, weekly intervals. Typing these recurring appointments for each occurrence would be very time-consuming. By designating an appointment as recurring, the appointment needs to be added only once and then recurrence is specified for the days on which it occurs. Table 2-1 lists Maria's recurring appointments.

Table 2-1 Recurring Appointments

TIME	APPOINTMENT	OCCURRENCE
9:00 am - 10:00 am	Web Development (Knoy 412)	Every Monday and Wednesday (30 times)
10:30 am - 11:30 am	Data Modeling (Gris 108)	Every Monday and Wednesday (30 times)
3:00 pm - 5:00 pm	Team Meeting (Union Cafe)	Every other Monday (15 times)

The following steps enter the recurring appointments.

To Enter Recurring Appointments

1

- **With Monday, September 12, 2005 displayed, double-click the words Web Development in the 9:00 – 10:00 time slot.**

The Web Development - Appointment window opens.

2

- **Click the Location text box and then type** `Knoy 412` **to set the location of the class.**
- **Point to the Recurrence button on the Standard toolbar.**

The symbol on the Recurrence button (Figure 2-13) will become the Recurrence symbol that appears beside the appointment in the appointment area.

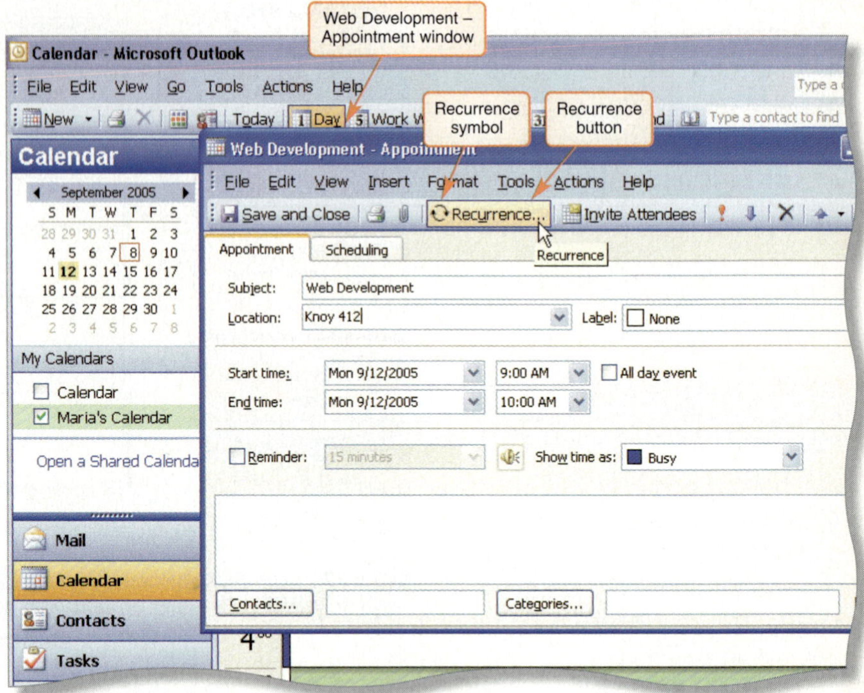

FIGURE 2-13

3

- **Click the Recurrence button.**
- **When the Appointment Recurrence dialog box is displayed, click the Wednesday check box to select the days this appointment will recur.**
- **Click End after in the Range of recurrence area, double-click the End after text box, and then type** `30` **as the number of occurrences.**

Outlook displays the Appointment Recurrence dialog box (Figure 2-14). The Web Development appointment is set to recur on Mondays (selected as the default) and Wednesday (selected in the step) and end after 30 occurrences.

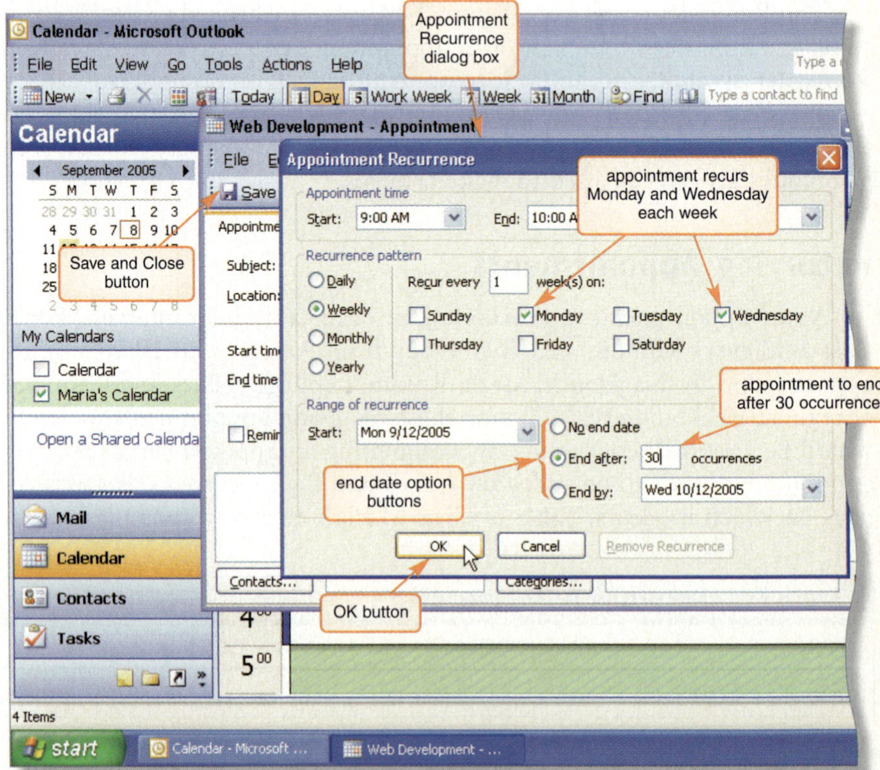

FIGURE 2-14

4

- **Click the OK button.**
- **Click the Save and Close button on the Standard toolbar in the Web Development - Appointment window.**

5

- **Repeat Steps 1 through 4 to make the Data Modeling and Team Meeting appointments recurring. Refer to Table 2-1 on page OUT 75 for the location, range, and ending dates.**

The Monday, September 12 schedule is complete (Figure 2-15). A Recurrence symbol appears beside each recurring appointment.

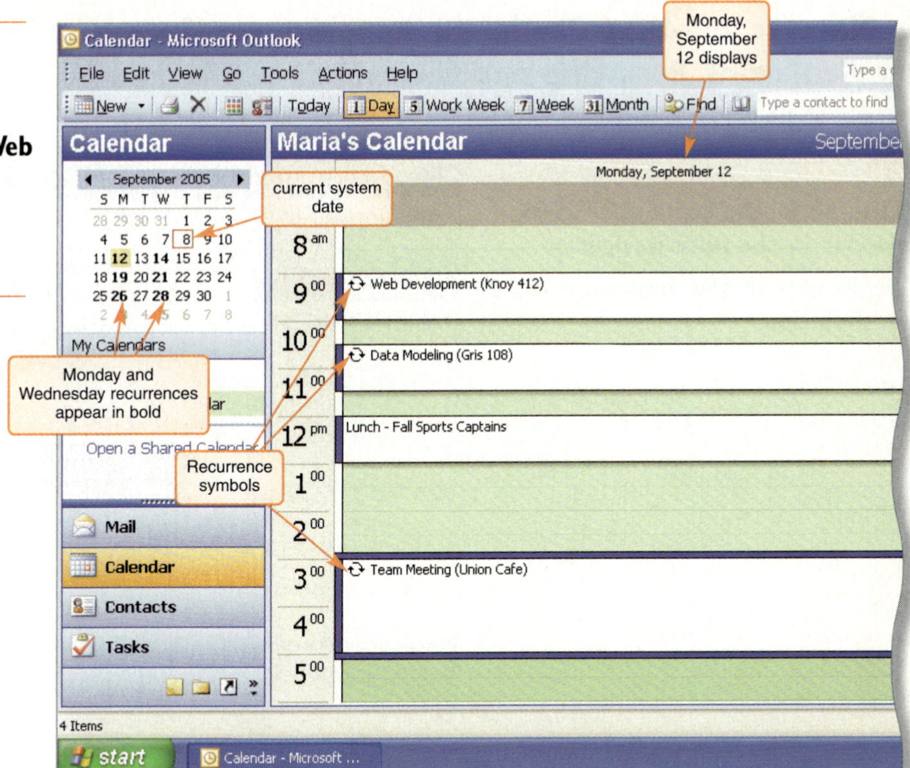

FIGURE 2-15

The Date Navigator serves several purposes when creating appointments. Recurring appointments are assigned to their appropriate dates automatically. After an appointment is assigned to a date, it appears bold in the Date Navigator (Figure 2-15). You can change these features using the Customize Current View command on the Current View submenu of the Arrange By menu accessed by clicking View on the menu bar.

The Date Navigator also allows easy movement and display of a specific date in the appointment area. This allows appointment to be entered on that date.

More About

The Recurrence Symbol

The Recurrence symbol can be applied to appointments, events, meetings, and tasks. Double-click the item to open its dialog box and then click the Recurrence button.

Moving to the Next Day in Calendar and Entering the Remaining Recurring Appointments

With the Monday schedule entered, the next step is to move to the next day in the appointment area and complete the recurring appointments for every Tuesday and Thursday using the appointment information in Table 2-2. Because the recurring appointments start on Tuesday, Tuesday must be displayed in the appointment area. The steps on the next page show how to move to the next day using the Date Navigator and then enter the remaining recurring appointments.

Table 2-2 Additional Recurring Appointments

TIME	APPOINTMENT	OCCURRENCE
9:30 am - 10:30 am	Statistics (Potter 205)	Every Tuesday and Thursday (30 times)
2:30 pm - 3:30 pm	Marketing (Krannert 504)	Every Tuesday and Thursday (30 times)

To Move to the Next Day in the Appointment Area, and Enter the Remaining Recurring Appointments

1

- **Click 13 in the September 2005 calendar in the Date Navigator.**
- **Drag through the 9:30 am - 10:30 am time slot.**

Tuesday, September 13 appears in the appointment area (Figure 2-16).

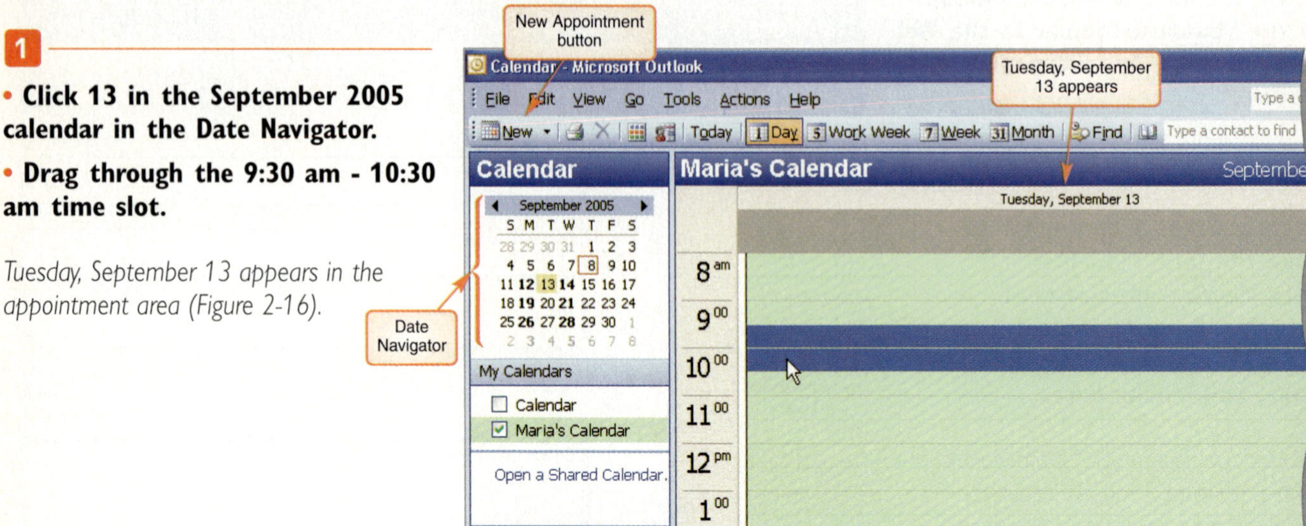

FIGURE 2-16

2

- **Click the New Appointment button on the Standard toolbar.**

3

- **Enter the recurring appointments provided in Table 2-2 on the previous page.**
- **Click the Save and Close button in the Appointment window.**

The appointments for Tuesday, September 13 are displayed (Figure 2-17). These appointments are scheduled to recur on Tuesdays and Thursdays and appear in bold on the calendar in the Date Navigator.

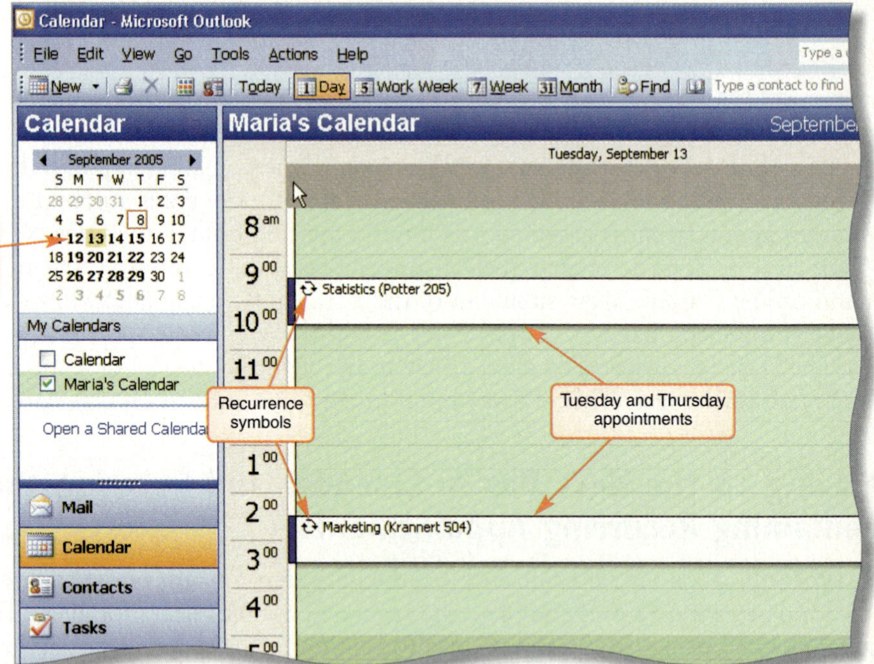

FIGURE 2-17

Other Ways

1. On Actions menu click New Recurring Appointment
2. Press ALT+A, type A
3. In Voice Command Mode, say "Actions, New Recurring Appointment"

Daily, weekly, monthly, or yearly recurrence patterns are possible in the Appointment Recurrence options. Outlook also provides three options for the range of recurrence. Appointments can recur every week or choice of weeks for one or multiple days. An appointment can be set to occur a certain number of times or up to a certain date. If the recurring appointment is ongoing, such as office hours, you can select the No end date option button (Figure 2-14 on page OUT 76).An appointment can be set as recurring when it first is entered, or, if you decide to make a one-time appointment recurring later, double-click the appointment and then click the Recurrence button. You can edit recurring appointments to add new days, omit certain days, or change other recurrence details. Editing recurring appointments is covered in more detail later in this project.

More About

Moving a Recurring Appointment

If a recurring appointment is moved, only the selected instance of the appointment is moved. If all instances of an appointment need to be moved, open the appointment, click Recurrence on the Appointment menu, and then change the recurrence pattern.

Using Natural Language Phrases to Enter Appointment Dates and Times

In the steps just completed, dates and times were entered in the Appointment window using standard numeric entries. Outlook's **AutoDate function**, however, provides the capability of specifying appointment dates and times using **natural language phrases**. For example, you can type phrases such as, next Tuesday, two weeks from yesterday, or midnight, and Outlook will calculate the correct date and/or time.

This example schedules working at the registrar's office next Wednesday, September 14, 2005 from noon to 2:45 p.m., and one week from Saturday on September 24, 2005 from 8:00 a.m. to noon. The following steps describe how to enter the date and time for the work schedule using natural language phrases.

Note: If you are stepping through this project on a computer, then you should set your system clock to September 8, 2005 or the steps in the next section will not work properly.

To Enter Appointment Dates and Times Using Natural Language Phrases

1

- **With Tuesday, September 13 displayed in the appointment area, click the New Appointment button on the Standard toolbar.**

2

- **Type** `Work orientation` **in the Subject text box and then press the TAB key.**
- **Type** `Registrar's office` **in the Location text box and then press the TAB key twice.**
- **Type** `next Wednesday` **in the Start time date box for the date.**

The appointment information is entered in the Appointment window. Next Wednesday is entered in the Start time date box (Figure 2-18).

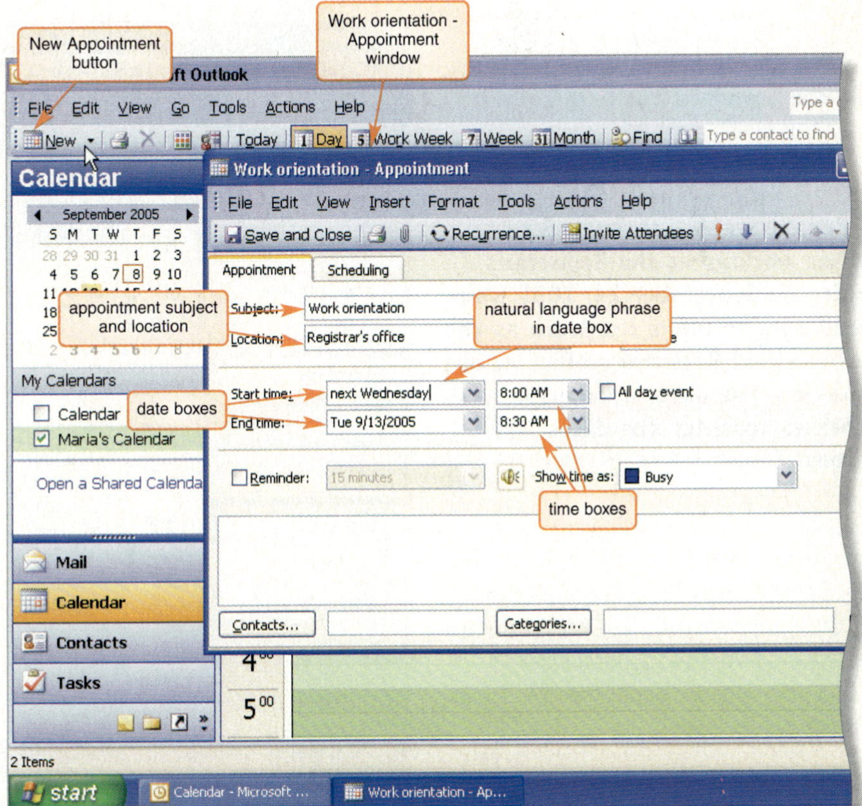

FIGURE 2-18

- **Press the TAB key.**
- **Type** noon **in the Start time box.**
- **Press the TAB key twice.**

Outlook automatically converts the phrase, this Wednesday, into the date, Wed 9/14/2005, in both the Start time date and End time date boxes. It also converts the word, noon, into 12:00 PM in the time box (Figure 2-19).

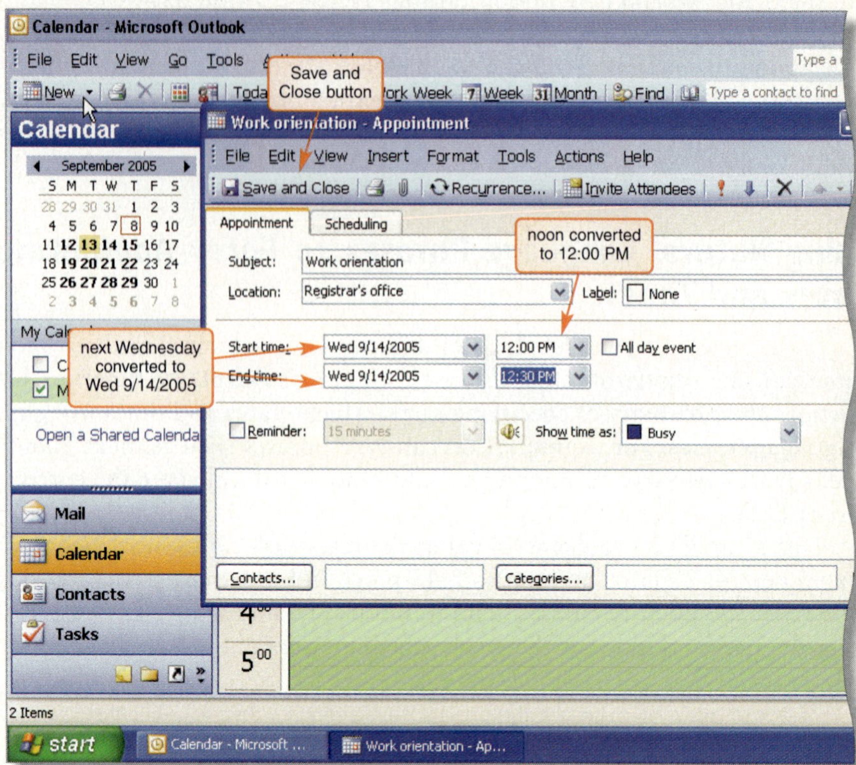

FIGURE 2-19

- **Type** two forty five **in the End time time box and then press the ENTER key.**

Outlook automatically converts the words, two forty five, to 2:45 PM and sets the appointment end time for 2:45 PM. Outlook sets appointments for 30 minutes unless you enter a new end time or drag through a longer time slot in the appointment area before clicking the New Appointment button or changing the default setting.

5

- **Click the Save and Close button on the Standard toolbar.**

6

- **Repeat Steps 1 through 5 to enter working at the Registrar's office on September 24, 2005 from 8:00 a.m. to noon. Use work as the subject and Registrar's office as the location. Use natural language phrases to enter the dates and times.**

Outlook closes the Appointment window and Tuesday, September 13 appears in the appointment area. The Work orientation and work appointments are added to the calendar on Wednesday, September 14, 2005, and Saturday, September 24, 2005 (Figure 2-20).

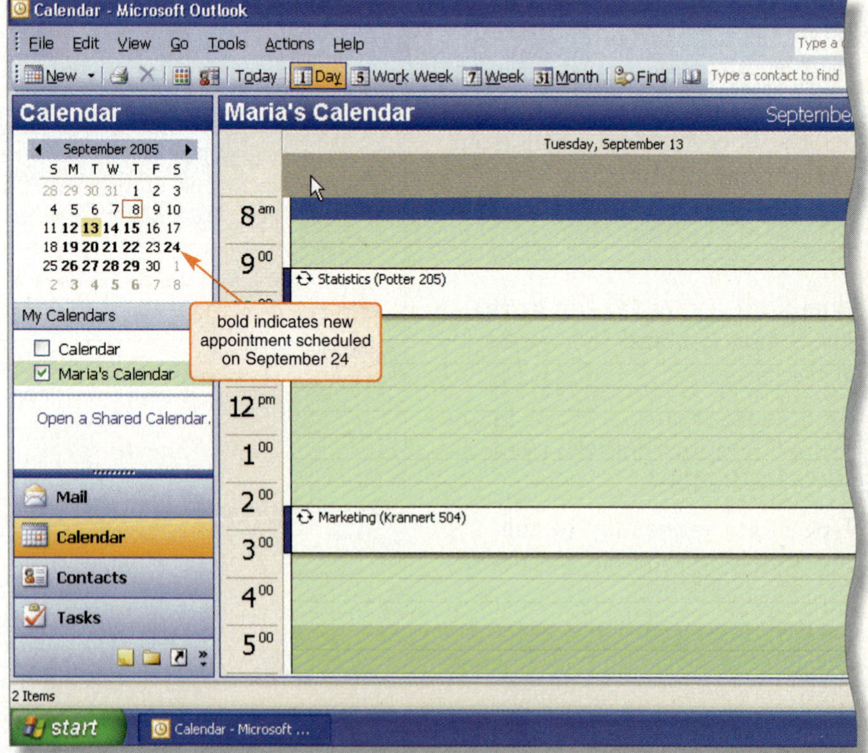

FIGURE 2-20

In addition to these natural language phrases, Outlook can convert abbreviations and ordinal numbers into complete words and dates. For example, you can type Feb instead of February or the first of September instead of 9/1. Outlook's Calendar application also will convert words such as yesterday, tomorrow, and the names of holidays that occur only once each year, such as Valentine's Day. Table 2-3 lists various AutoDate options.

Table 2-3 AutoDate Options

CATEGORY	EXAMPLES
Dates Spelled Out	• July twenty-third, March 29th, first of December • this Fri, next Sat, two days from now • three weeks ago, next week • one month from today
Times Spelled Out	• noon, midnight • nine o'clock a.m., five twenty • 7 pm
Descriptions of Times and Dates	• now • yesterday, today, tomorrow • next, last • ago, before, after, ending, following • for, from, that, this, till, through, until
Holidays	• Cinco de Mayo • Christmas, Christmas Day, Christmas Eve • Halloween • Independence Day • New Year's Day, New Year's Eve • St. Patrick's Day • Valentine's Day • Veterans Day

Entering the Remaining One-Time Appointments

Table 2-4 contains the current week's practice schedule along with the game schedule for the first two months of the upcoming season. The following steps show how to enter the remaining one-time appointments.

Table 2-4 Additional One-Time Appointments

DATE	TIME	APPOINTMENT	LOCATION
9/12/2005	5:00 p.m. - 7:00 p.m.	Practice	Girl's Gym
9/13/2005	4:00 p.m. - 6:00 p.m.	Practice	Girl's Gym
9/14/2005	5:00 p.m. - 7:00 p.m.	Practice	Girl's Gym
9/15/2005	4:00 p.m. - 6:00 p.m.	Practice	Girl's Gym
9/17/2005	1:00 p.m. - 3:00 p.m.	Practice	Girl's Gym
10/7/2005	7:30 p.m. - 9:30 p.m.	Game	City Arena
10/8/2005	5:00 p.m. - 7:00 p.m.	Game	City Arena
10/15/2005	6:30 p.m. - 8:30 p.m.	Game	Willowcreek
10/21/2005	6:30 p.m. - 8:30 p.m.	Game	Woodland Arena
10/29/2005	7:00 p.m. - 9:00 p.m.	Game	Woodland Arena
11/10/2005	5:30 p.m. - 7:30 p.m.	Game	Saint Stevens
11/19/2005	3:00 p.m. - 5:00 p.m.	Game	Tri-State

To Enter the Remaining One-Time Appointments

1. **With the Calendar window active, click September 12, 2005 in the Date Navigator.**
2. **Click the New Appointment button on the Standard toolbar.**
3. **Type `Practice` in the Subject text box, and then press the TAB key.**
4. **Type `Girl's Gym` in the Location text box, and then press the TAB key three times.**
5. **Type `5 pm` in the Start time time box, press the TAB key two times, and then type `7 pm` in the End time time box.**
6. **Click the Save and Close button on the Standard toolbar.**
7. **Using techniques demonstrated in this project, repeat Steps 1 through 6 to enter the remaining one-time appointments in Table 2-4.**

Editing Appointments

Because schedules often need to be rearranged, Outlook provides several ways of editing appointments. Edit the subject and location of an appointment by clicking the appointment and editing the information directly in the appointment area, or double-click the appointment and make corrections using the Appointment window. All occurrences in a series of recurring appointments can be changed, or a single occurrence can be altered.

Deleting Appointments

Appointments sometimes are canceled and must be deleted from the schedule. For example, the schedule created thus far in this project contains an appointment on Thursday, November 24, 2005. Because November 24 is Thanksgiving Day, however, no classes will meet and the scheduled appointment needs to be deleted. The following steps describe how to delete an appointment from the calendar.

To Delete an Appointment

1

- **Click the scroll arrows in the Date Navigator to display November 2005.**
- **Click 24 in the November 2005 calendar.**
- **Click the first appointment to be deleted, Statistics, and then point to the Delete button on the Standard toolbar.**

Thursday, November 24 appears at the top of the appointment area (Figure 2-21). The blue top and bottom borders indicate the Statistics appointment is selected.

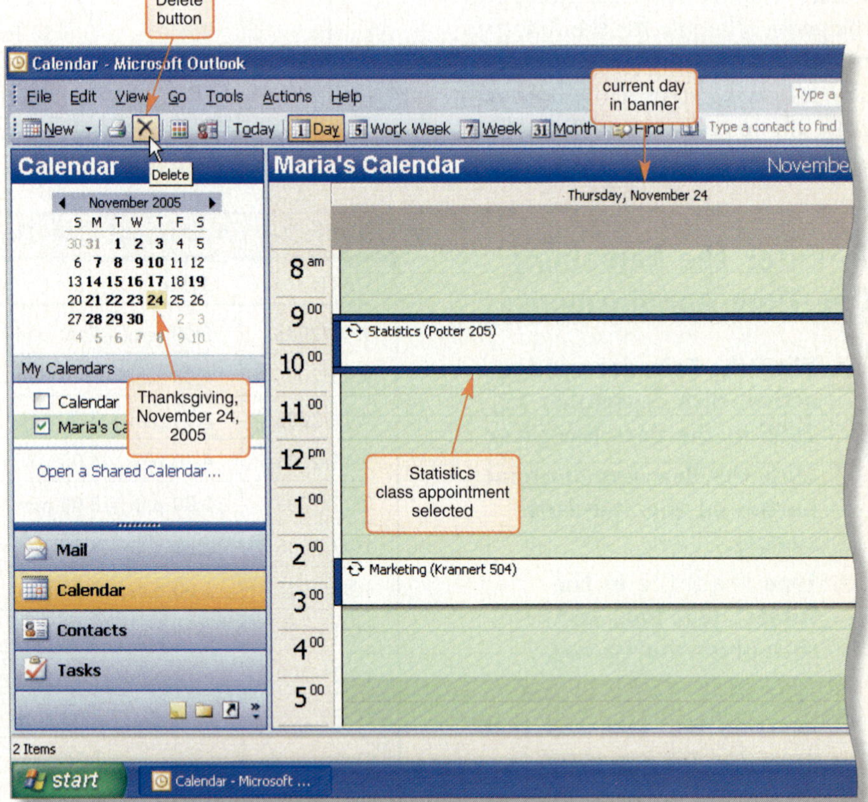

FIGURE 2-21

2

• **Click the Delete button.**

Because the appointment selected is a recurring appointment, Outlook displays a Confirm Delete dialog box providing the option of deleting all occurrences of the recurring appointment or just this one (Figure 2-22). The Delete this occurrence option button is selected by default.

3

• **Click the OK button.**

The Statistics appointment is deleted from Thursday, November 24, 2005. All other occurrences of the appointment remain in the schedule.

4

• **Repeat Steps 1 through 3 to delete the Marketing appointment from Thursday, November 24, 2005.**

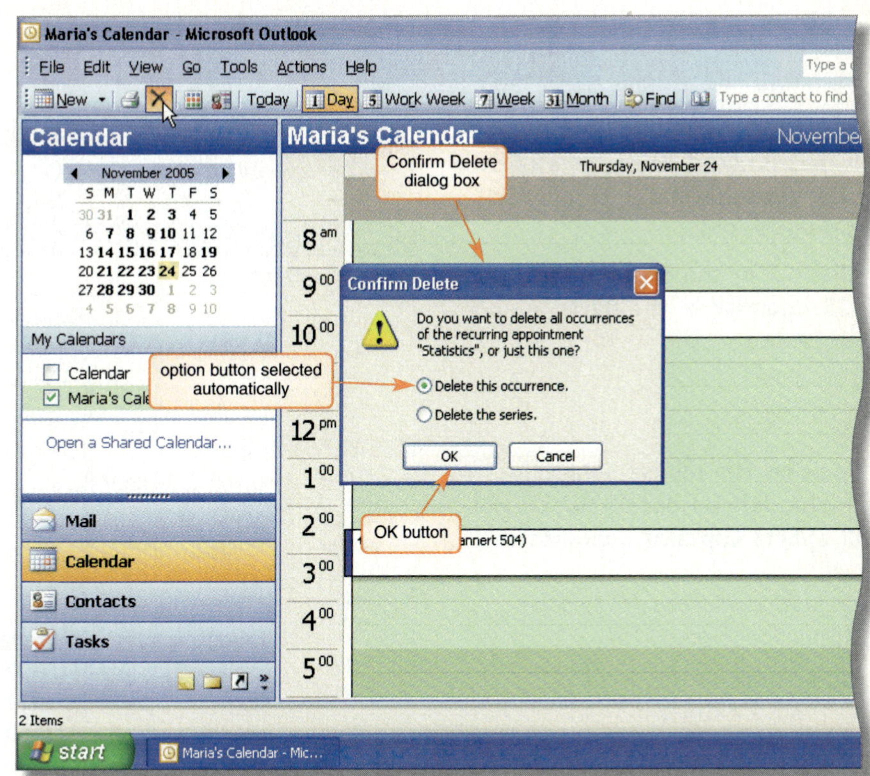

FIGURE 2-22

Other Ways

1. Right-click appointment to be deleted, click Delete on shortcut menu
2. Click blue border of appointment, press Delete

Appointments also can be deleted using the DELETE key. First, select the entire appointment by clicking the blue left border and then press the DELETE key. If the entire appointment is not selected, pressing the DELETE key (or the BACKSPACE key) will not delete the entry; it will delete only individual characters of the appointment subject. Even if all the characters are deleted, the time slot remains active and any symbols remain in place.

Moving Appointments to a New Time

Outlook also provides several ways to move appointments. Suppose for instance, that some team captains cannot make if for lunch at noon on Monday, September 12, 2005. The appointment needs to be rescheduled to 1:00 p.m. to 2:00 p.m. Instead of deleting and then retyping the appointment, simply drag it to the new time slot. The steps on the next page describe how to move an appointment to a new time.

More About

Editing Appointments

If you cannot remember the details about a specific appointment, you easily can check it. Click Tools on the menu bar, point to Find, and then click Advanced Find to locate the appointment in question. In the Look for box, click Appointments and Meetings. You then may search for any word or subject.

To Move an Appointment to a New Time

1

- **If necessary, click the scroll arrow in the Date Navigator to display September 2005.**
- **Click 12 in the September 2005 calendar in the Date Navigator.**

2

- **Position the mouse pointer on the blue left border of the Lunch - Fall Sports Captains appointment.**

The mouse pointer changes to a four-headed arrow (Figure 2-23).

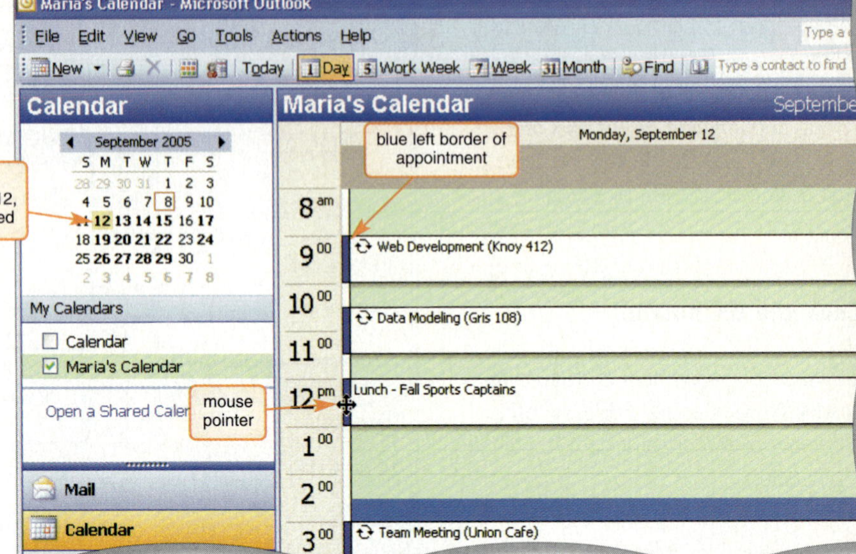

FIGURE 2-23

3

- **Drag the appointment down to the 1:00 pm - 2:00 pm time slot. Do not release the mouse button.**

*As the appointment is dragged, the mouse pointer changes to a pointer with a small dotted box below it, called the **drag icon**.*

4

- **Release the mouse button to drop the appointment in the new time slot.**

The appointment is placed in the 1:00 pm - 2:00 pm time slot (Figure 2-24). Outlook automatically allows adequate time for the moved appointment, in this case, one hour.

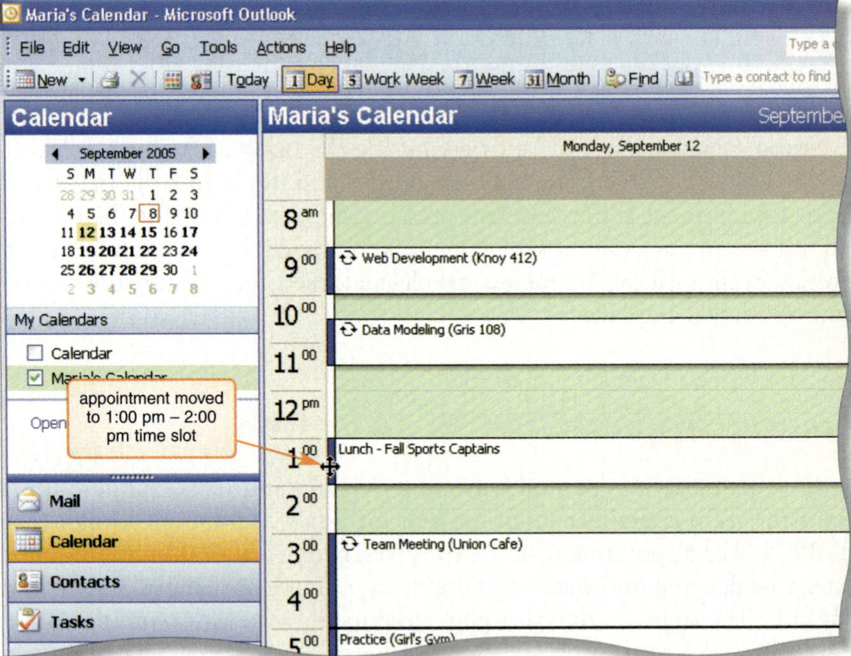

FIGURE 2-24

Other Ways

1. Double-click appointment, edit date in Start date date box in Appointment window
2. Click left border of appointment, press CTRL+X, click new date in Date Navigator, click new time slot in appointment

An appointment can be moved to a new time using the Appointment window, as well. Simply type a different time in the Start time or End time time boxes or click one of the time box arrows and select a different time in the list. Natural language phrases also can be used in the time box, which Outlook converts to the appropriate times.

Moving Appointments to a New Date

If an appointment is being moved to a new date but remaining in the same time slot, simply drag the appointment to the new date in the Date Navigator. Using this method allows the movement of an appointment quickly and easily to a new date, as shown in the following steps.

To Move an Appointment to a New Date

1

- **Click 12 in the September 2005 calendar in the Date Navigator.**
- **Click the blue left border of the Lunch - Fall Sports Captains appointment to select it.**
- **Drag the appointment from the appointment area to the 16 in the September 2005 calendar. Do not release the mouse button.**

Dragging outside the appointment area causes the mouse pointer to change to the drag icon. A black border appears around the 16 in the September 2005 calendar in the Date Navigator (Figure 2-25).

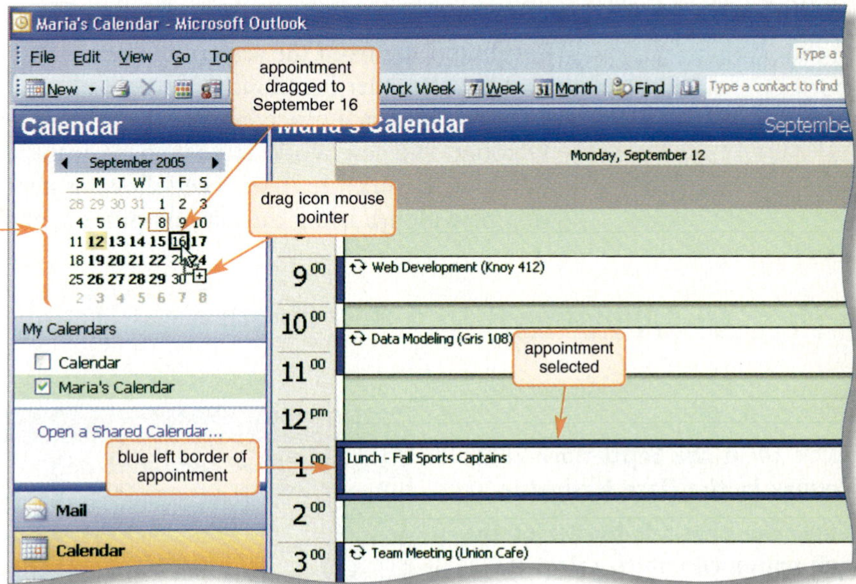

FIGURE 2-25

2

- **Release the mouse button.**

The appointment moves from Monday, September 12, 2005 to Friday, September 16, 2005 (Figure 2-26).

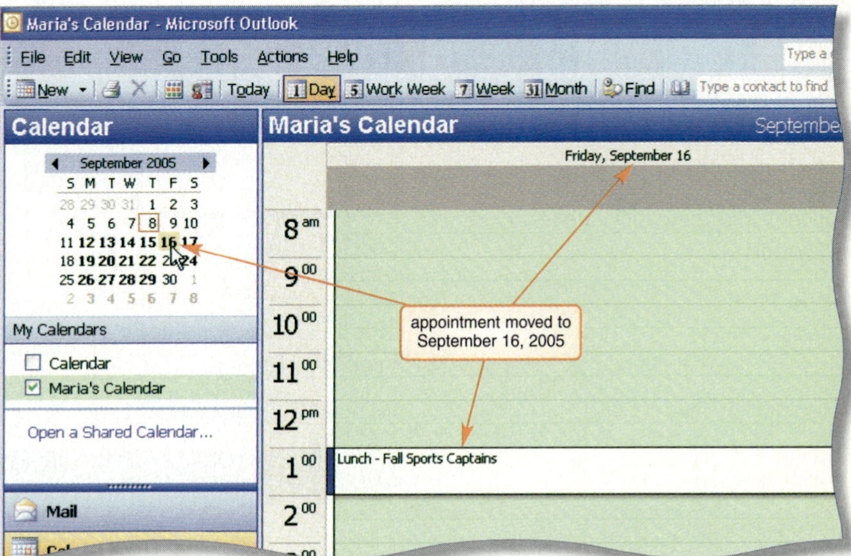

FIGURE 2-26

Outlook provides several ways to move appointments to new dates in addition to the drag and drop method used in the previous steps. Appointments can be moved to new dates by making changes in the Appointment window or by using the cut and paste method.

More About

Moving Appointments

To send an appointment to a coworker or classmate, right-click the appointment and click Forward on the shortcut menu.

Moving an Appointment to a New Month

If an appointment is being moved to a month not displayed in the Date Navigator, it cannot be dragged to a date not displayed. In this case, cutting and pasting the appointment to a new date can be used.

When you cut an item in most other Office 2003 applications, the item that you cut disappears from the screen. In Outlook, the item remains on the screen until it is pasted to another location.

The registrar's office has decided to reschedule the Saturday time slot to a date in October. The new work date is moved from Saturday, September 24, 2005 to Saturday, October 1, 2005. The following steps describe how to move an appointment to a new month using the cut and paste method.

To Move an Appointment to a New Month

1

- **Click 24 in the September 2005 calendar in the Date Navigator.**
- **Click the blue left border of the work appointment to select it.**
- **Click Edit on the menu bar.**

The Edit menu appears (Figure 2-27).

2

- **Click Cut on the Edit menu.**

The appointment is copied to the Office Clipboard, and the appointment remains on the screen.

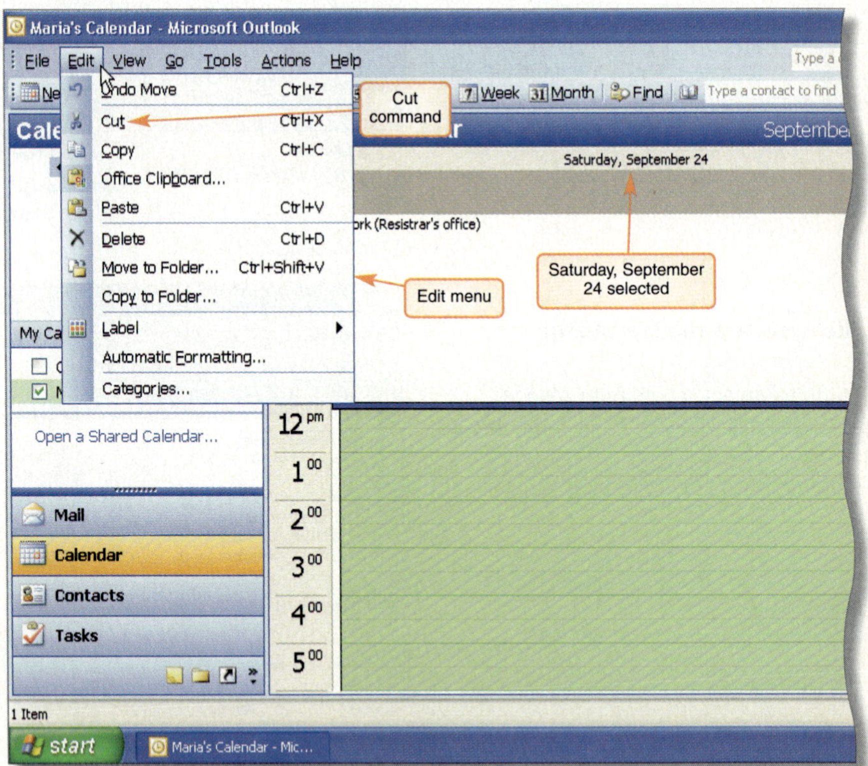

FIGURE 2-27

3

- **Click the right scroll arrow in the Date Navigator to display October 2005.**
- **Click 1 in the October 2005 calendar in the Date Navigator.**

Outlook displays Saturday, October 1 in the appointment area. The 8:00 am - 12:00 pm time slot is automatically selected (Figure 2-28) because this was the size of the time slot cut from September 24, 2005.

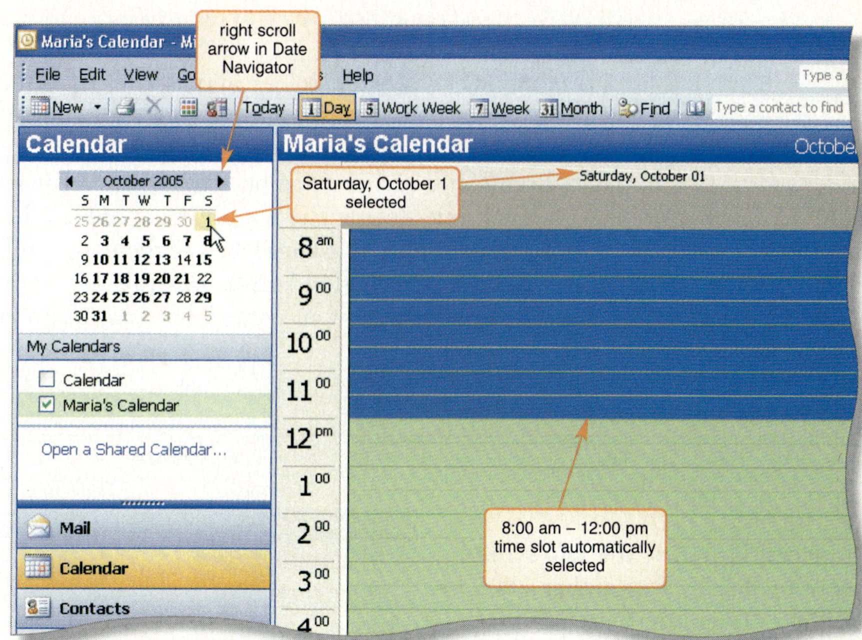

FIGURE 2-28

4

- **Click Edit on the menu bar and then click Paste.**

The appointment now appears in the 8:00 am - 12:00 pm time slot in the appointment area for Saturday, October 1 (Figure 2-29).

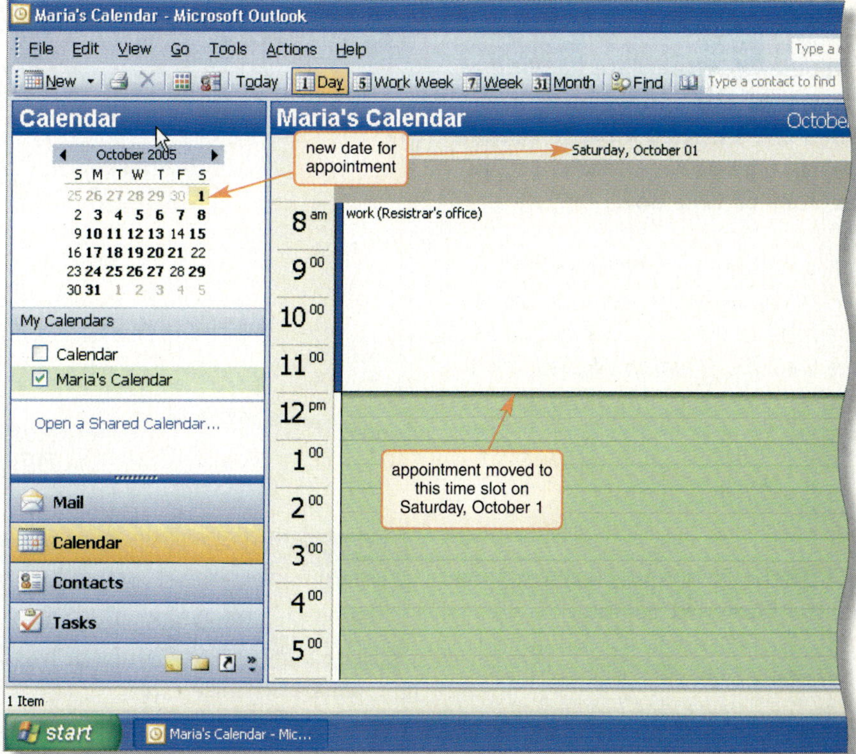

FIGURE 2-29

Either the drag-and-drop method or the cut and paste method is available for appointment movement. Regardless of the method, the results are the same. An appointment can be moved to a different time on the same day, to a different day, or an entirely different month.

Creating an Event

Outlook's Calendar folder allows you to keep track of important events. **Events** are activities that last 24 hours or longer. Examples of events include birthdays, conferences, weddings, vacations, holidays, and so on and can be one-time or recurring. Events differ from appointments in one primary way — they do not display in individual time slots in the appointment area. When an event is scheduled, its description appears in a small **banner** below the date heading. The details of the event can be indicated as time that is free, busy, or out of the office during the event. The following steps show how to enter a birthday as an event.

To Create an Event

1

- **If necessary, click the left scroll arrow to display September 2005 in the Date Navigator. Click 30 in the September 2005 calendar in the Date Navigator.**

2

- **Double-click the date heading at the top of the appointment area. When the Untitled - Event window opens, type** `Jose's birthday` **in the Subject text box.**

Outlook displays the Untitled - Event window (Figure 2-30). Double-clicking the date heading allows all day events to be scheduled. The All day event check box thus is selected by default. The Show time as box indicates Free.

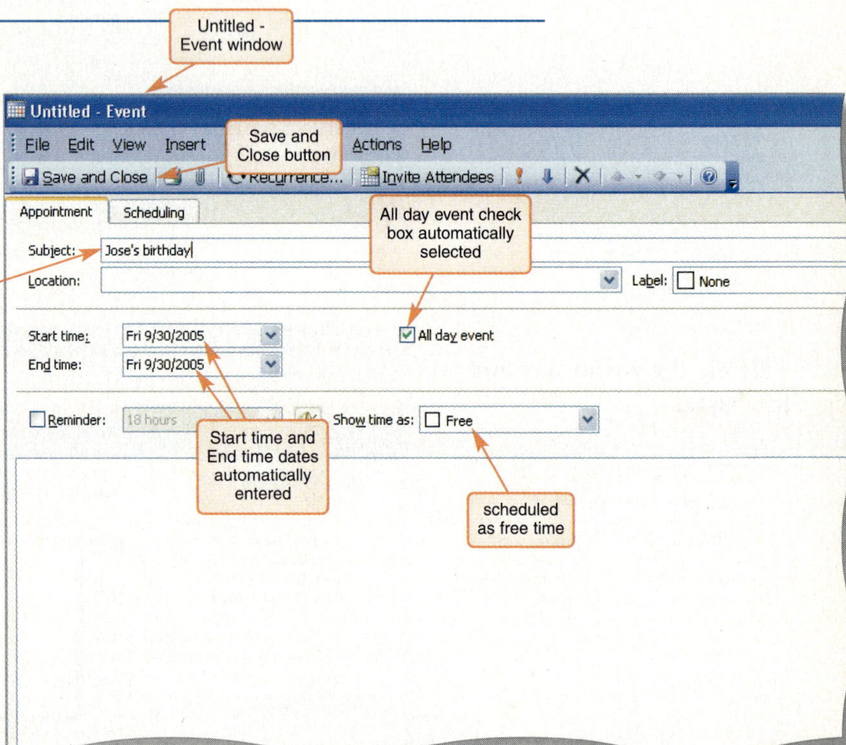

FIGURE 2-30

3

- **Click the Save and Close button on the Standard toolbar.**

The Event subject appears in a banner below the date heading (Figure 2-31).

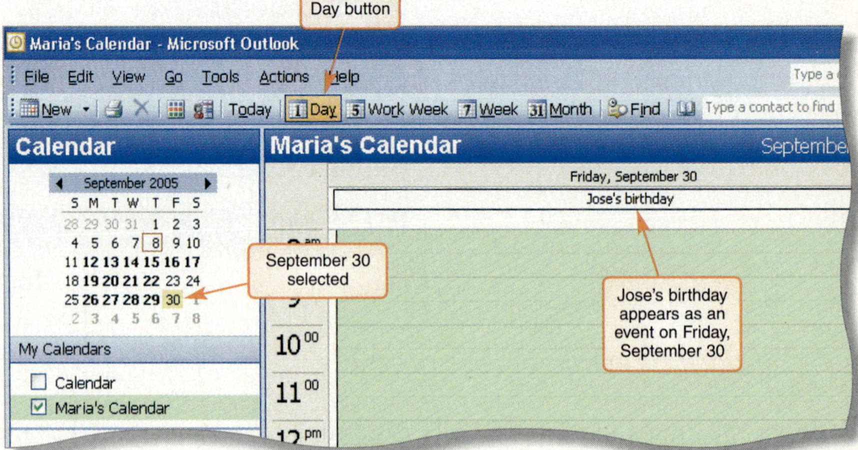

FIGURE 2-31

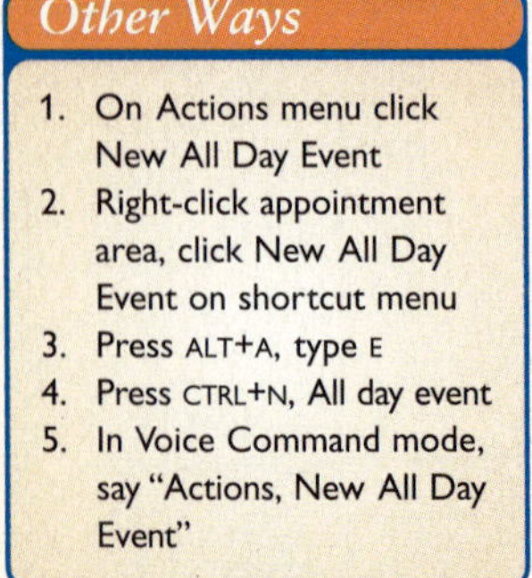

Other Ways

1. On Actions menu click New All Day Event
2. Right-click appointment area, click New All Day Event on shortcut menu
3. Press ALT+A, type E
4. Press CTRL+N, All day event
5. In Voice Command mode, say "Actions, New All Day Event"

You could use the same steps to enter holidays as annual events; however, Outlook has a folder of typical holidays for various countries that can be added to your calendar automatically. To do this, click Options on the Tools menu. Click Calendar Options, and then click Add Holidays in the Calendar Option sheet.

More About

Locations

As appointments or events are entered with specific locations, the locations automatically are accumulated in a list. To access this list, open the appointment and click the Location box arrow. Frequently used locations can be selected from this list, thereby saving typing time.

Displaying the Calendar in Week and Month Views

The default view type of the Calendar folder is the Day/Week/Month view. While in **Day/Week/Month view**, Outlook can display calendars in four different views: Day, Work Week, Week, and Month. So far in this project, you have used only the Day view, which is indicated by the selected Day button on the Standard toolbar (Figure 2-31).

Now that the schedule is complete, it also can be displayed in Week or Month view. Although the screen appears quite differently in Week and Month views, the same tasks can be performed as in Day view: appointments and events can be added, edited, or deleted, and reminders can be set or removed.

Work Week View

The **Work Week view** shows five work days (Monday through Friday) in columnar style. The advantage of displaying a calendar in this view is the ability to see how many appointments are scheduled for the Monday through Friday time frame, eliminating the weekends. The following step changes the Calendar view to Work Week view.

Other Ways

1. On View menu click Work Week
2. Press ALT+V, type R
3. In Voice Command mode, say "Work Week"

To Change to Work Week View

1

- **Click Tuesday, September 13 in the Date Navigator.**
- **Click the Work Week button on the Standard toolbar.**
- **If necessary, scroll up in the appointment area until the 8:00 am time slot appears.**

The calendar is displayed in Work Week view (Figure 2-32). Notice that September 12 through September 16 all are highlighted in the Date Navigator.

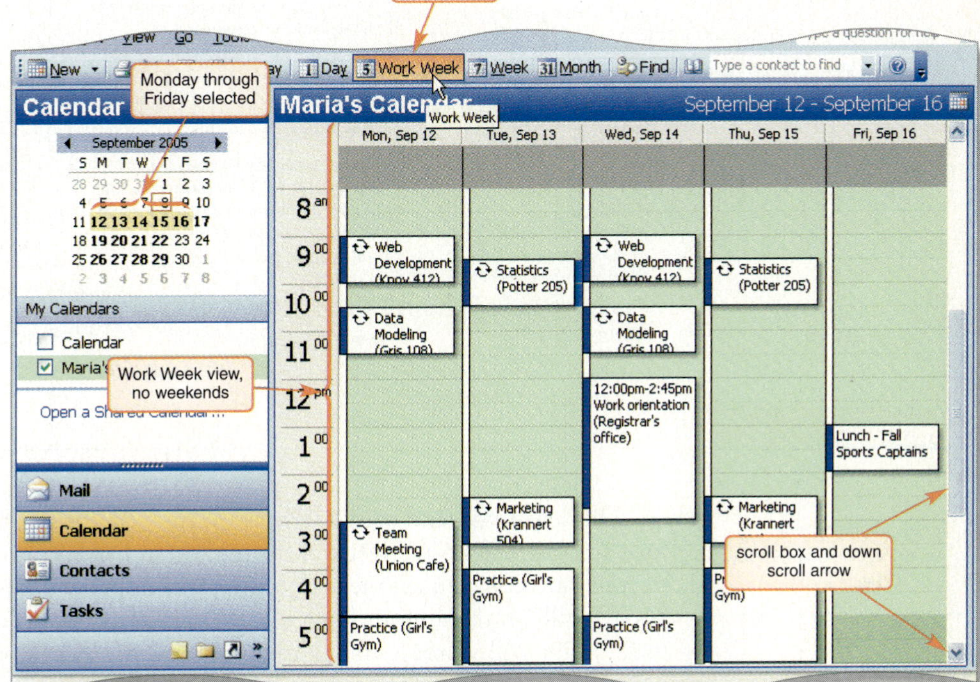

FIGURE 2-32

> *More About*
>
> **Holidays and Observances**
>
> For more information about holidays and observances, visit the Outlook 2003 More About Web page (scsite.com/out2003/more) and click Calendar.

The scroll box and scroll arrows on the vertical scroll bar allow backward or forward movement within the selected week. An individual appointment can be selected by double-clicking it. As shown in Figure 2-32 on the previous page, some appointments may be too long to display horizontally in the appointment area. Dragging the border of the appointment area to the right will increase its width so that more of the appointment text appears.

Week View

The advantage of displaying a calendar in **Week view** is to see how many appointments are scheduled for any given week. In Week view, the seven days of the selected week display in the appointment area. The five days of the work week (Monday through Friday) display in individual frames, while Saturday and Sunday share a single frame. The following step describes how to display the calendar in Week view.

To Change to Week View

1

- **Click the Week button on the Standard toolbar.**

The calendar appears in Week view (Figure 2-33).

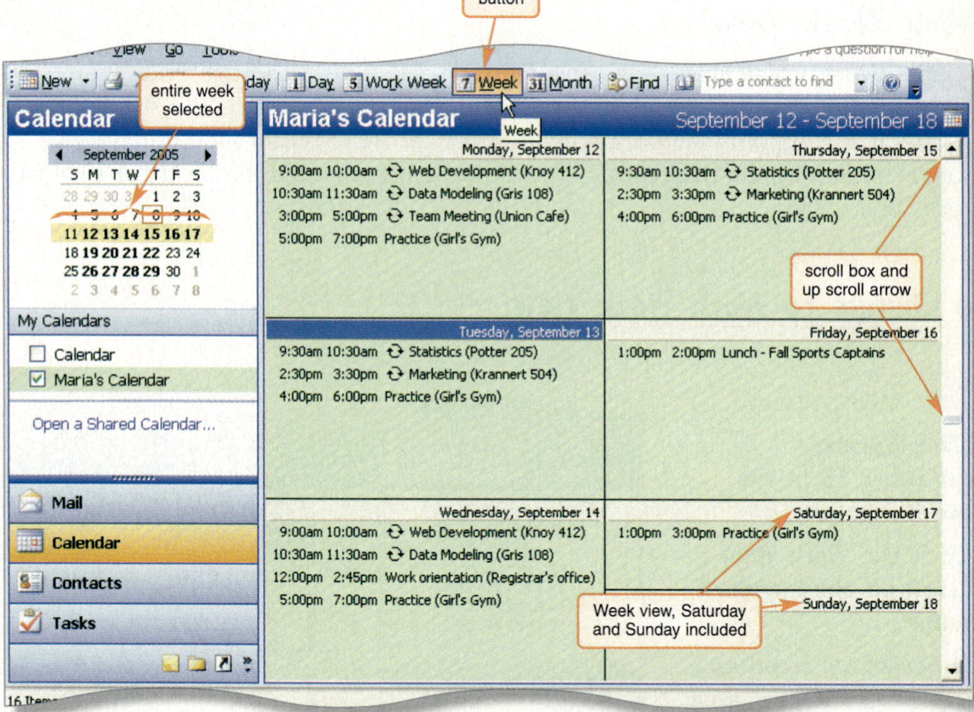

FIGURE 2-33

> *Other Ways*
>
> 1. On View menu click Week
> 2. Press ALT+V, type W
> 3. In Voice Command mode, say "Week"

The scroll box and scroll arrows on the vertical scroll bar allow backward or forward movement one week at a time. As in Day view, double-click an appointment to view and edit appointment details. Some appointments may be too long to display horizontally in the appointment area. Dragging the border of the appointment area to the right will increase its width so that more of the appointment descriptions display. If a day contains too many items to display vertically, Outlook will display a down arrow in the lower-right corner of the day frame. Clicking the down arrow returns the calendar to Day view so you can view the rest of the appointments for the day.

Month View

The **Month view** resembles a standard monthly calendar page and displays a schedule for an entire month. Appointments are listed in each date frame in the calendar. The following steps illustrate how to display the calendar in Month view.

To Change to Month View

1

• **Click the Month button on the Standard toolbar.**

Outlook displays the calendar in Month view (Figure 2-34).

2

• **Click the Day button to return to Day view.**

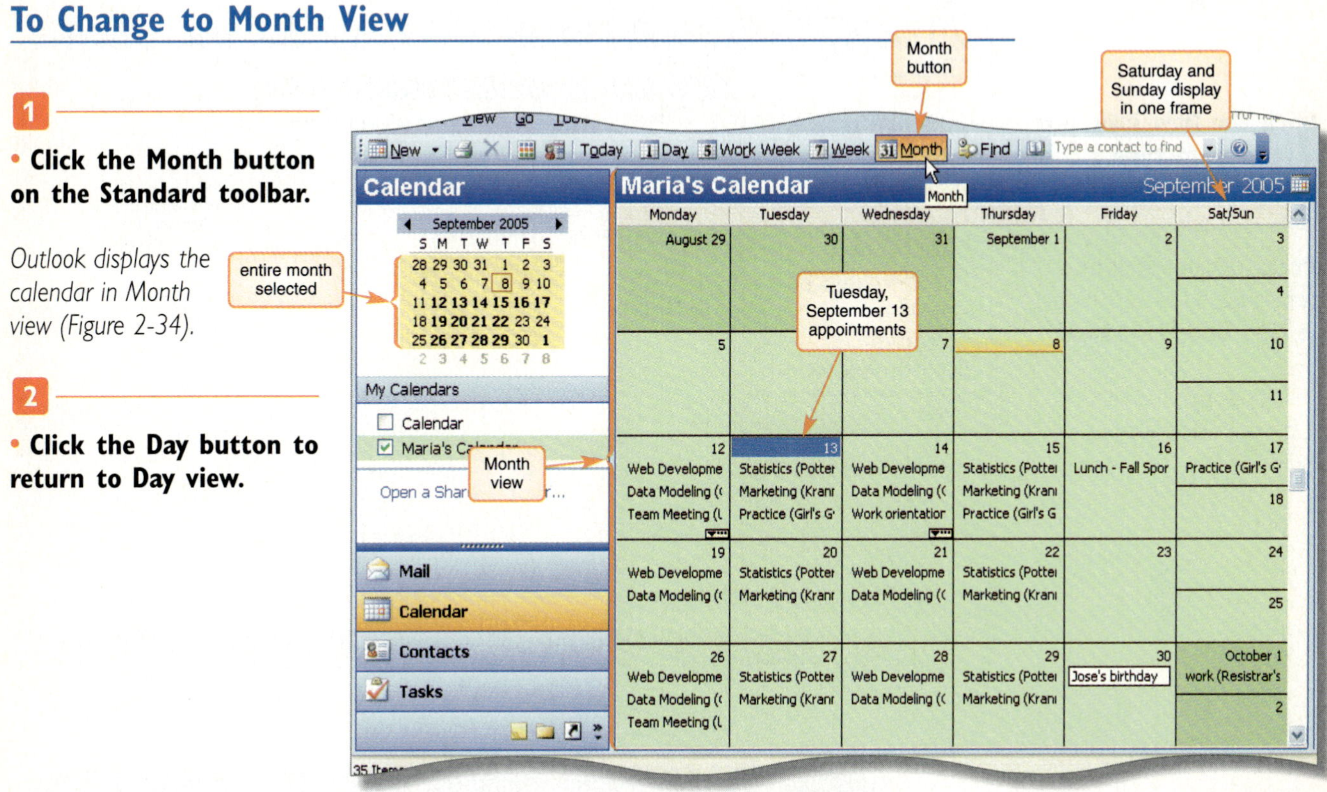

FIGURE 2-34

> ***Other Ways***
>
> 1. On View menu click Month
> 2. Press ALT+V, type M
> 3. In Voice Command mode, say "Month"

Use the vertical scroll box and scroll arrows on the vertical scroll bar to move the Month view forward and backward one week at a time. As you drag the scroll box, Outlook displays the first day of the week in a ScreenTip beside the scroll box. As with Day and Week views, you can add, edit, or delete appointments in Month view. Because the appointments are abbreviated considerably in Month view, however, it is easier to switch back to Day view to make changes.

Using Tasks to Create a Task List

With the daily appointments organized, you can use Tasks to organize the many duties and projects for each day. Tasks allows creation of a **task list** of items that need to be tracked through completion. **Tasks** can be simple to do items, daily reminders, assignments with due dates, or business responsibilities. In this project, Table 2-5 contains tasks that occur once and will be later made into group tasks, assigned, or forwarded. The steps on the next page show how to create a task list.

Table 2-5 Task List

TASK	DUE DATE
Check on Web book	9/14/2005
Get new license	9/30/2005
Pick up fund-raiser T-shirts	9/9/2005
Send out next week's practice schedule	9/11/2005
Set up meeting with Coach	9/11/2005

To Create a Task List

1

- **Click the Tasks button in the Navigation Pane.**

2

- **Click the New Task text box and then type** `Check on Web book` **as the first task.**
- **Press the TAB key and then type** `9/11/2005` **in the Due Date text box.**

Outlook displays the Tasks - Microsoft Outlook window (Figure 2-35).

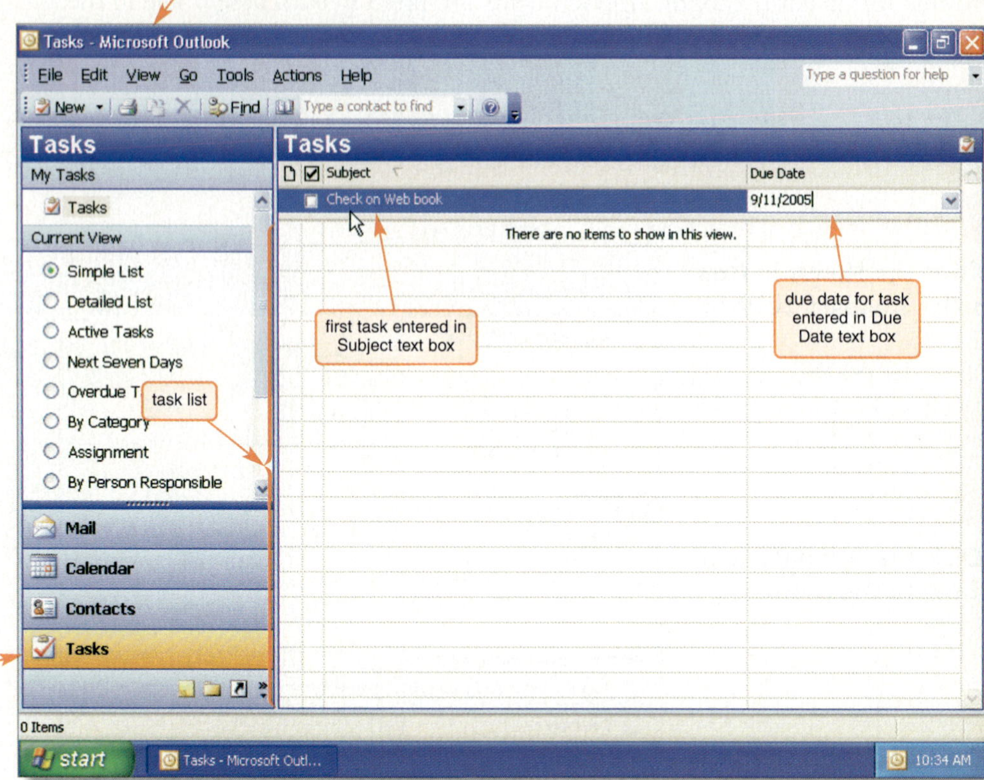

FIGURE 2-35

3

- **Press the ENTER key.**
- **Repeat Steps 1 and 2 to enter the remaining tasks in Table 2-5 on the previous page.**

The task icon appears to the right of each task. As each task is entered, the previous task moves down the list.

4

- **Click outside the task list.**

The Task window is displayed with all the tasks entered in the task list as shown in Figure 2-36.

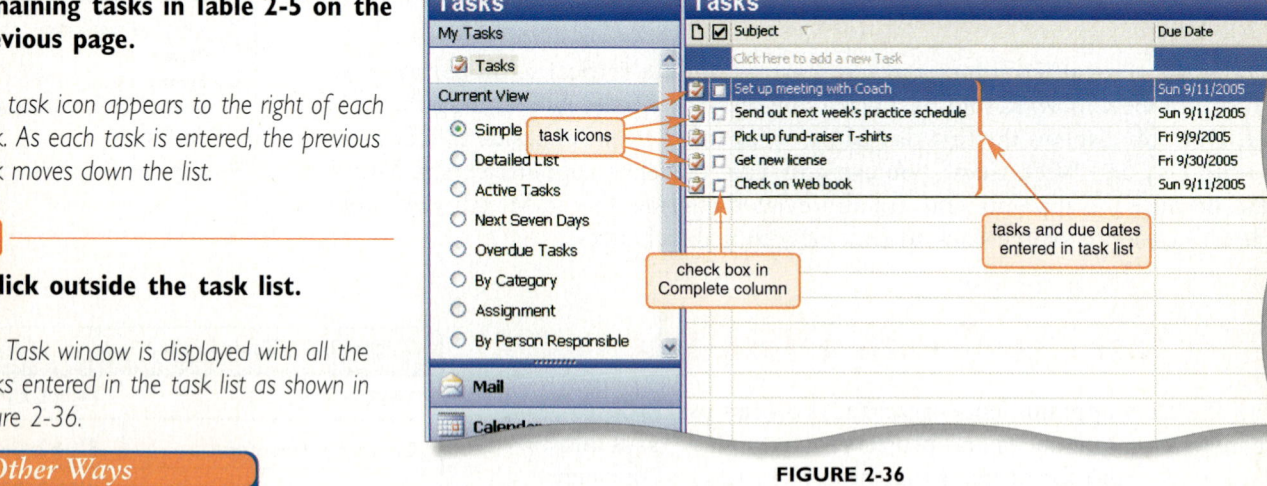

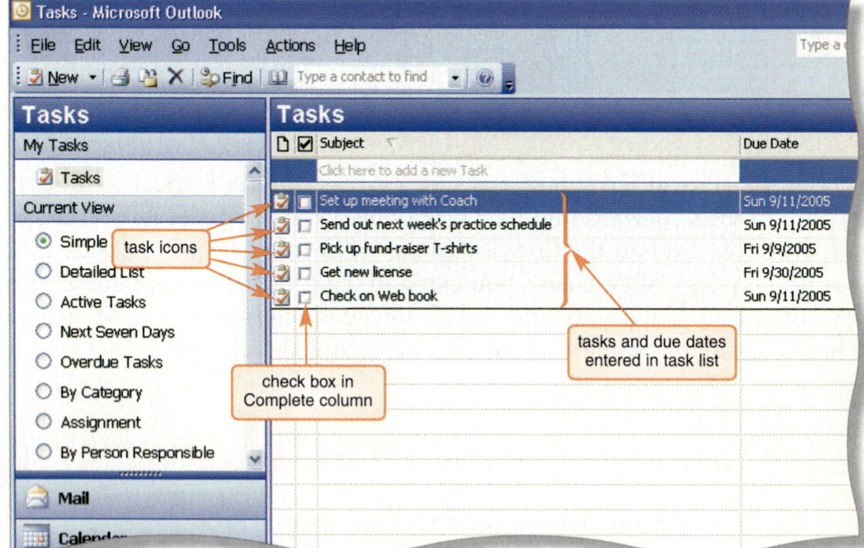

FIGURE 2-36

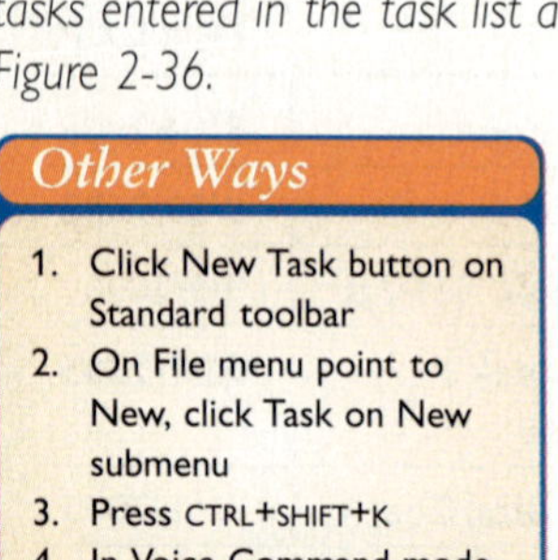

Other Ways

1. Click New Task button on Standard toolbar
2. On File menu point to New, click Task on New submenu
3. Press CTRL+SHIFT+K
4. In Voice Command mode, say "New Task"

To add details to tasks, such as start dates, status, and priority, double-click a task in the task list to open a Task window.

When a task is complete, click the check box in the Sort by: Complete column to the left of the task's subject. A check mark called a **Completed icon** will appear in the Complete column and a line will be placed through the task indicating it is complete. To delete a task entirely from the task list, select the task and then click the Delete button on Standard toolbar.

If you have many tasks on various days, or if you delegate tasks, it is advisable to create a personal Tasks folder for your task list. This also is true if you are working in a lab situation or on a shared computer.

More About

Tasks

You can add a task to your Outlook task list from within Word. This is helpful if you have a Word document that must be reviewed, and you want a reminder to do so.

Exporting, Deleting, and Importing Subfolders

The calendar is now ready to be saved on a floppy disk. Saving your work on a floppy disk allows you to take your schedule to another computer.

With many application software packages, a single file, such as a letter or spreadsheet, can be saved directly on a floppy disk. With Outlook, however, each appointment, task, or contact is a file in itself. Thus, rather than saving numerous individual files, Outlook uses an **Import and Export Wizard** to guide you through the process of saving an entire subfolder. Transferring a subfolder to a floppy disk is called **exporting**. Moving a subfolder back to a computer is called **importing**. Subfolders can be imported and exported from any Outlook application. Outlook then saves the subfolder on a floppy disk, adding the extension **.pst**.

More About

Editing Tasks

You can drag a task from the Task list to the Calendar button in the Navigation Pane, thereby making the task an appointment.

Exporting Subfolders

The following steps show how to export Maria's Calendar subfolder to a floppy disk.

To Export a Subfolder to a Floppy Disk

1

- **Insert a floppy disk in drive A.**
- **Click File on the menu bar and then click Import and Export.**

2

- **When the Import and Export Wizard dialog box is displayed, click Export to a file in the Choose an action to perform list.**

Outlook displays the Import and Export Wizard dialog box (Figure 2-37). Using this Wizard allows you to perform one of six import and export options available with Outlook.

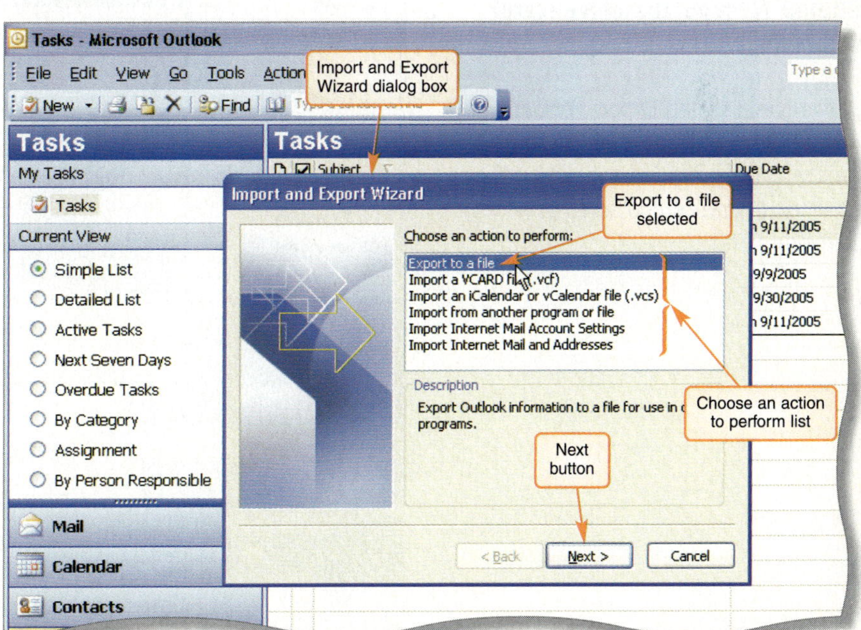

FIGURE 2-37

3

- **Click the Next button.**
- **In the Export to a File dialog box, click Personal Folder File (.pst) and then click the Next button.**
- **If necessary, click the plus sign (+) to the left of the Calendar icon in the Select a folder to export from list.**
- **Click Maria's Calendar.**

Outlook displays the Export Personal Folders dialog box (Figure 2-38). The Maria's Calendar subfolder is selected as the folder from which to export.

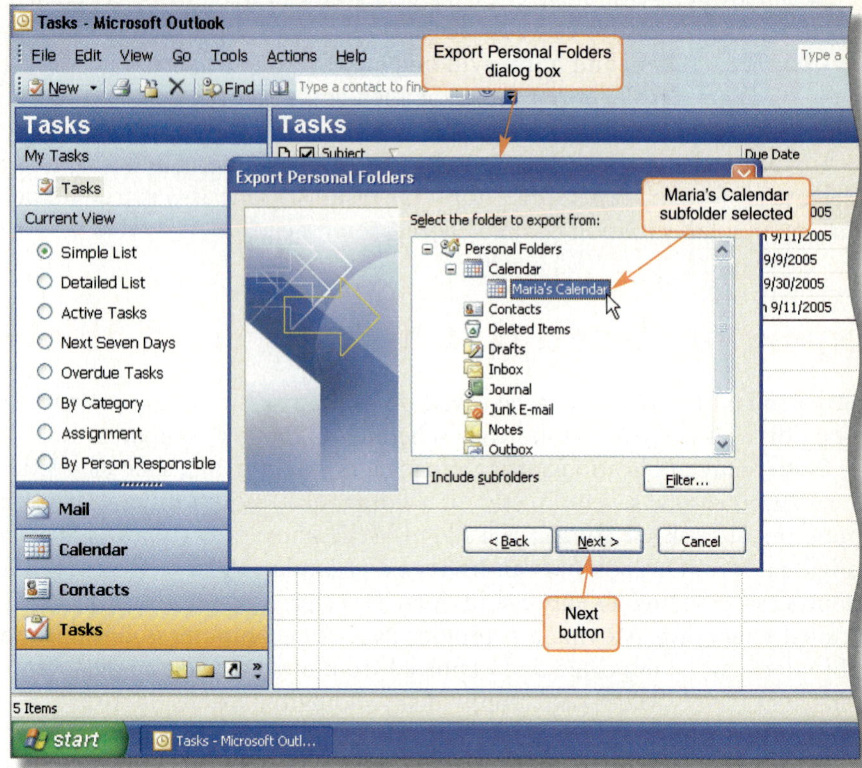

FIGURE 2-38

4

- **Click the Next button.**
- **Type** `a:\Maria's Calendar.pst` **in the Save exported file as text box. (If your floppy drive is not labeled A, type the drive letter accordingly.)**

Outlook displays the Export Personal Folders dialog box with the new subfolder name (Figure 2-39). The subfolder will be exported to drive A and saved as Maria's Calendar.

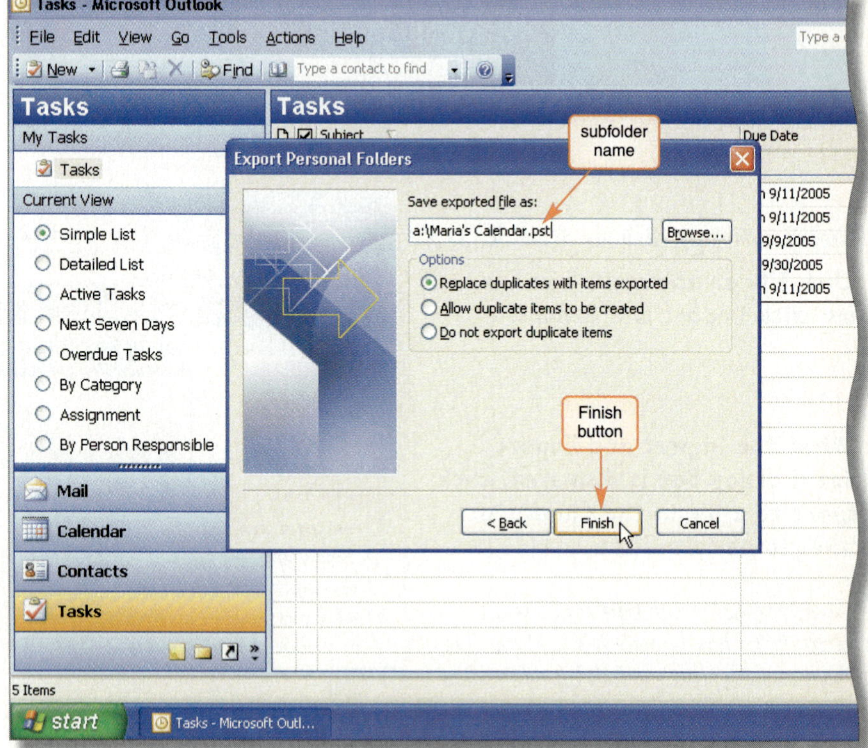

FIGURE 2-39

5

- **Click the Finish button.**

Outlook displays the Create Microsoft Personal Folders dialog box (Figure 2-40) as the folder is exported. The subfolder is saved on the floppy disk.

6

- **Click the OK button.**

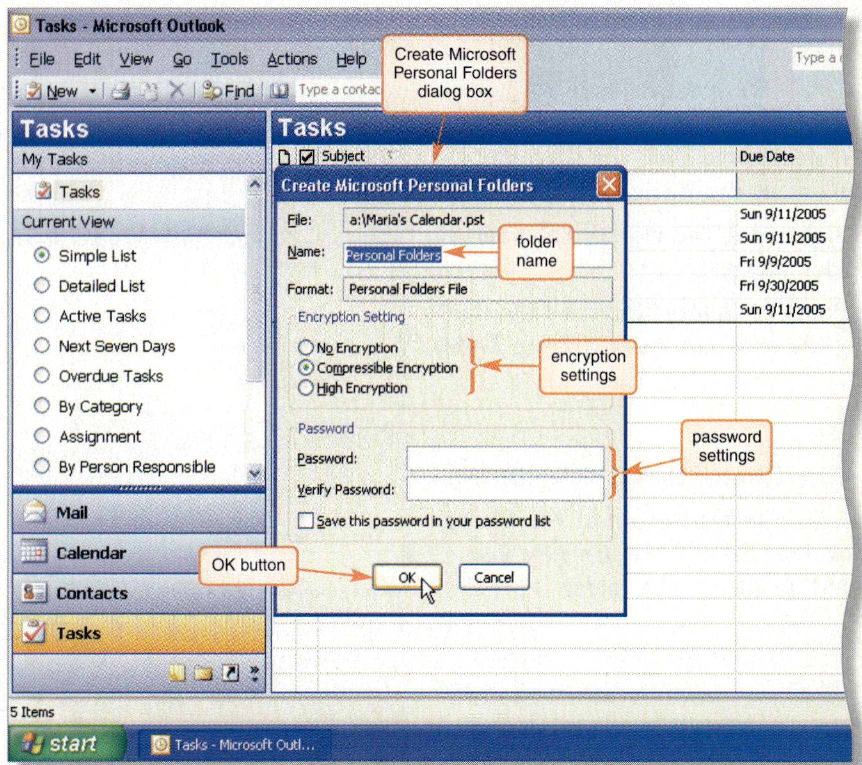

FIGURE 2-40

To export a folder, you do not have to have that particular Outlook application open. For example, if you were to export a Contact subfolder, the Contact window would not have to be open. Instead, when the Export Personal Folders dialog box is displayed, click the plus sign (+) next to the Contacts icon and then click the appropriate subfolder.

Subfolders can be exported to a personal folder file, which can be viewed only in Outlook or saved as another file type, such as a text file, which then can be imported into other programs. Importing and exporting folders allows Outlook items to be shared easily. For example, a company Calendar subfolder may be imported to publicize a company meeting, a group Contacts subfolder may be imported to make information about the people who work on a project available to every one, or a team Tasks subfolder may be imported to help everyone track work on a project.

> *More About*
>
> **Saving**
>
> All appointments, events, meetings, and tasks are saved as separate files on your disk. As such, they can be edited, moved, copied, or deleted. These items can be saved as a group using the Import and Export Wizard on the File menu.

Deleting Subfolders

The Maria's Calendar subfolder now has been exported onto a floppy disk. A copy of it is still present on the hard disk of your computer, however, and appears in Outlook's Folder List. To delete a subfolder from the computer entirely, use the Delete command. The steps on the next page illustrate how to delete a personal subfolder.

To Delete a Personal Subfolder

1

- **If necessary, click the Calendar button in the Navigation Pane.**
- **Right-click the Maria's Calendar folder banner.**
- **Point to Delete "Maria's Calendar" on the shortcut menu (Figure 2-41).**

2

- **Click Delete "Maria's Calendar".**
- **Click the Yes button in the dialog box that asks if you are sure you want to delete the folder.**

The Maria's Calendar folder no longer appears.

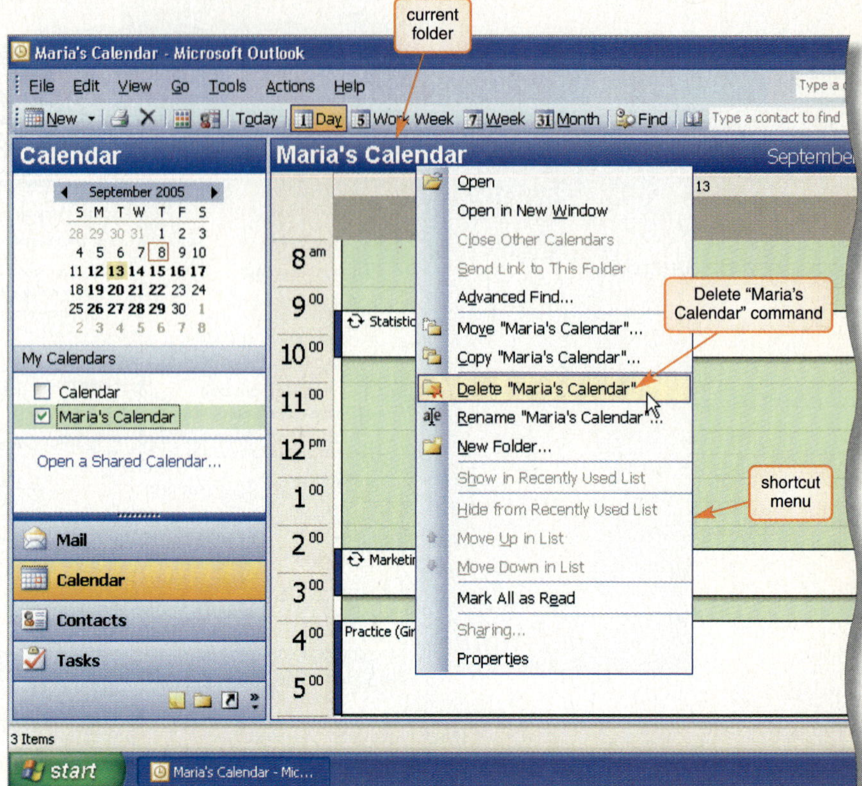

FIGURE 2-41

Other Ways

1. On File menu point to Folders, click Delete on Folders submenu
2. Press ALT+F, press F, press D
3. In Voice Command mode, say "File, Folders, Delete"

Outlook sends the deleted subfolder to a special folder in the Folder List called **Deleted Items**. If you accidentally delete a subfolder without first exporting it to a floppy disk, you still can open the subfolder by double-clicking it in the Deleted Items folder in the Folder List. To display the subfolder, you may need to click the plus sign (+) next to the Deleted Items folder.

Once a subfolder is no longer needed, right-click the subfolder in the Deleted Items folder in the Folder List and then click Delete on the shortcut menu. Deleting a subfolder from the Deleted Items folder permanently removes it from the hard disk. You can delete only subfolders; Outlook's main component folders, such as Calendar, Mail, and Contacts, cannot be deleted.

Thus far, a schedule and a task list have been created and the schedule has been exported to a personal subfolder on a floppy disk. Once a subfolder is created and exported, often it will need to be imported, or retrieved, from the disk. For example, you might want to revise office hours, add exam dates to the schedule, or use the schedule on a different computer. To do so, the schedule must be imported from the subfolder on the floppy disk.

Importing Subfolders

Earlier, the Calendar subfolder containing appointment and event files was exported to a floppy disk. The following steps illustrate how to import the same Calendar subfolder from the floppy disk. To import a subfolder, Outlook must be running. Any type of subfolder then can be imported from any application within Outlook. The following steps import a subfolder.

To Import a Subfolder

1

- **Insert the floppy disk containing the calendar in drive A.**
- **If necessary, click the Calendar button in the Navigation Pane.**

2

- **Click File on the menu bar and then click Import and Export.**
- **When the Import and Export Wizard dialog box is displayed, click Import from another program or file and then click the Next button.**
- **When the Import a File dialog box is displayed, click Personal Folder File (.pst) and then click the Next button.**

3

- **In the Import Personal Folders dialog box, type `a:\Maria's Calendar.pst` in the File to Import text box or click the Browse button to access the floppy drive and select the Maria's Calendar subfolder.**

The drive, subfolder name, and extension for the subfolder display in the File to import text box (Figure 2-42).

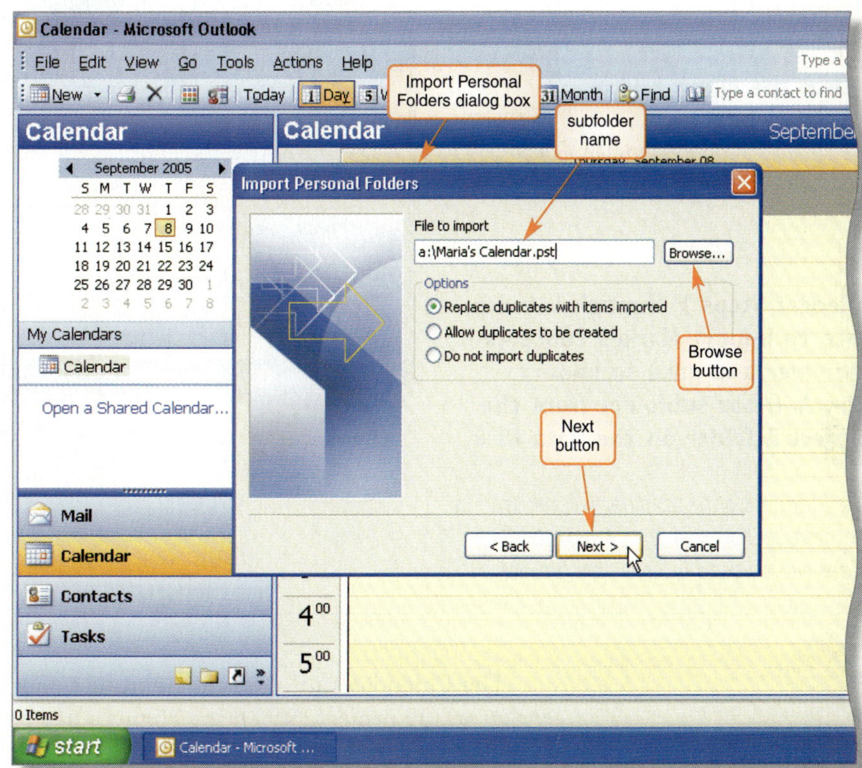

FIGURE 2-42

4

- **Click the Next button.**
- **When the Import Personal Folders dialog box is displayed, click Calendar in the Select the folder to import from list.**

In the Import Personal folders dialog box, you can choose the Outlook folder to import from (Figure 2-43).

5

- **Click the Finish button.**

The subfolder is imported into Outlook as a subfolder of Calendar.

6

- **Repeat Steps 1 through 5 twice, once to import Maria's Contacts subfolder and once to import Maria's Inbox subfolder from the Project 2 folder on the Data Disk.**

The Maria's Contacts folder will be used in the next section and the Maria's Inbox folder will be used later in this project.

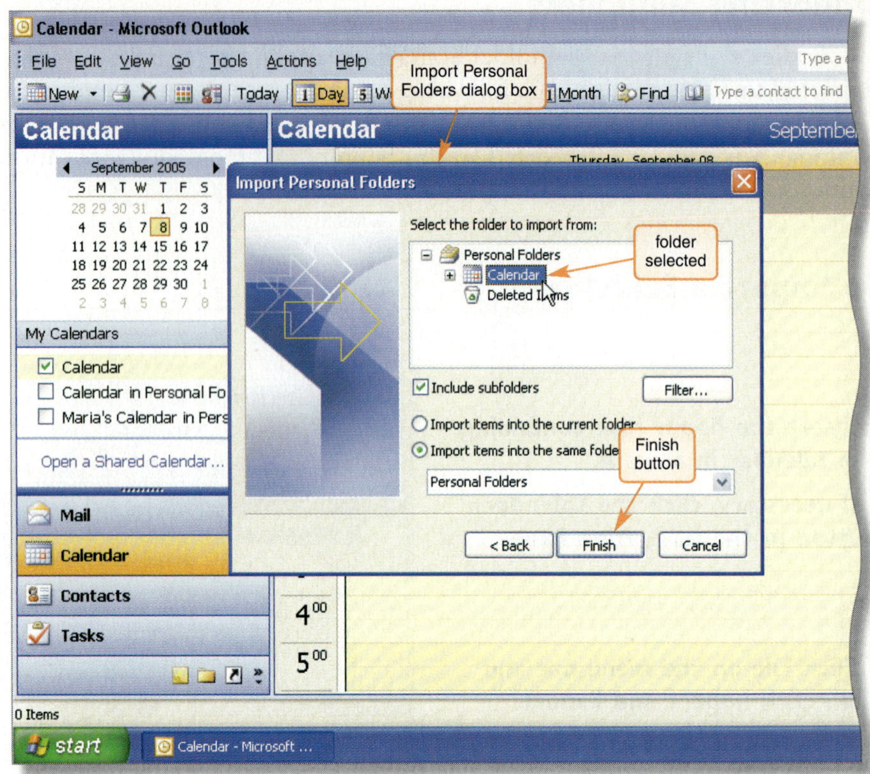

FIGURE 2-43

The Calendar subfolder now can be opened, edited, and printed as described earlier in the project. When the changes are complete, the subfolder again can be exported and deleted from the hard disk. In addition to Outlook subfolders, Outlook's Import and Export Wizard allows the import of a Personal Address Book with contact names, addresses and telephone numbers, or existing information to be brought in from other programs, such as Microsoft Mail or Schedule +.

> *More About*
>
> **Importing**
>
> Other contact information can be imported through the Import and Export Wizard on the File menu. This wizard allows you to copy information that was created and saved in other applications to Outlook.

Meeting and Task Management Using Outlook

If you are a person in charge of an organization or group, you are likely to encounter times when you will have to schedule meetings and delegate, or assign, tasks to other members of the group. Using your contact list, Outlook allows you easily to perform these functions. The following sections illustrate how to assign tasks and schedule meetings with individuals in the Maria's Contacts list.

Assigning Tasks

Sometimes, a person's personal schedule becomes so busy that it is necessary to assign certain tasks to other individuals. Using the task list, Outlook allows you to assign any task to any individual in your contact list. Using the task list previously created in this project and the imported Maria's Contacts contact list, the following steps show how to assign a task to an individual in the Maria's Contacts contact list.

To Assign a Task to Another Person

1

- **Click the Contacts button in the Navigation pane and then click Maria's Contacts in the My Contacts list.**
- **If necessary, click the Tasks button in the Navigation Pane.**
- **Double-click the Pick up fund-raiser T-shirts task.**
- **When the Pick up fund-raiser T-shirts - Task window is displayed, double-click the title bar to maximize the window.**

Outlook displays the Pick up fund-raiser T-shirts - Task window (Figure 2-44).

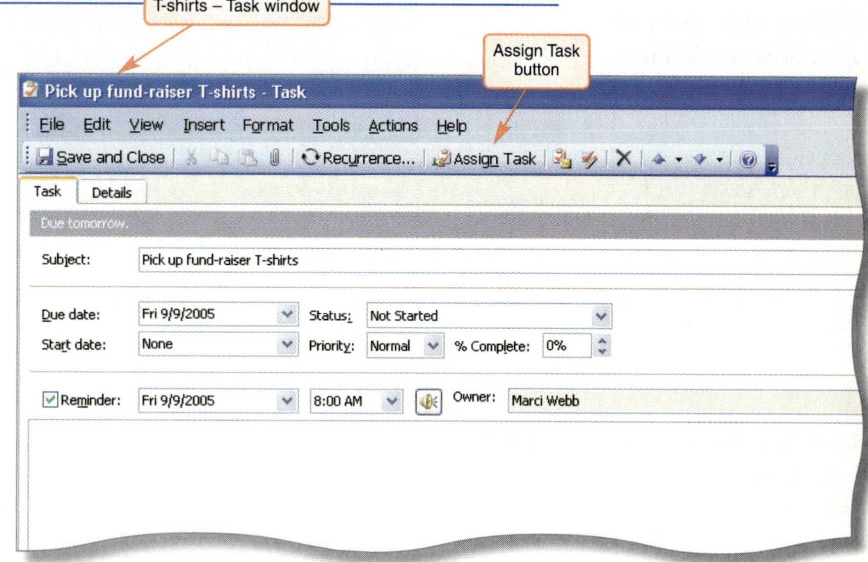

FIGURE 2-44

2

- **Click the Assign Task button on the Standard toolbar.**
- **Type** `Patti Sabol` **in the To text box.**

The Pick up fund-raiser T-shirts - Task window changes into a window similar to an e-mail message window. Patti Sabol is entered as the recipient for this task (Figure 2-45).

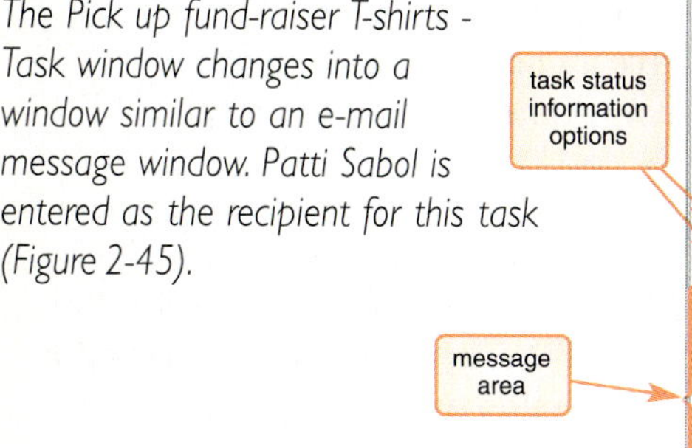

FIGURE 2-45

3

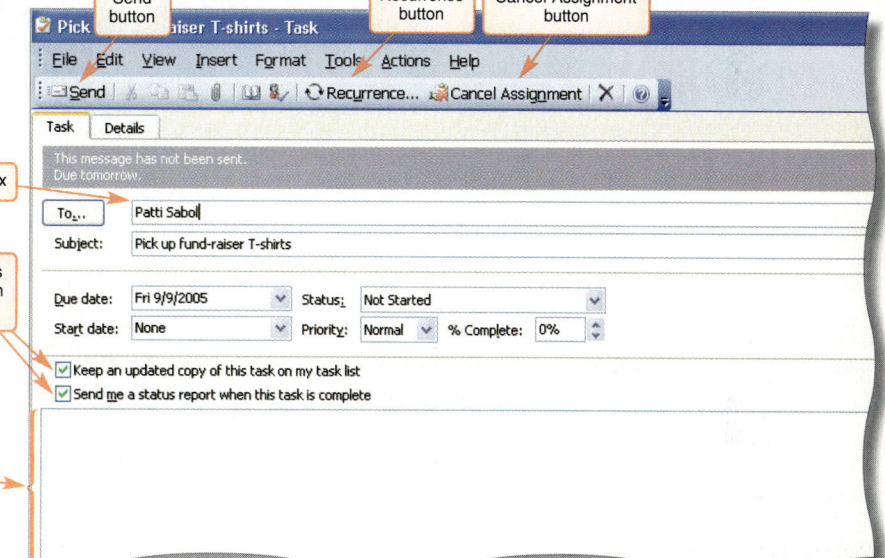

- **Click the Send button on the Standard toolbar.**
- **If necessary, click the OK button when the Microsoft Office Outlook dialog box appears.**

Outlook closes the Pick up fund-raiser T-shirts - Task window, stores the task request in the Outbox folder while it e-mails the request, moves the request to the Sent Items folder, and displays the Tasks - Microsoft Outlook window (Figure 2-46).

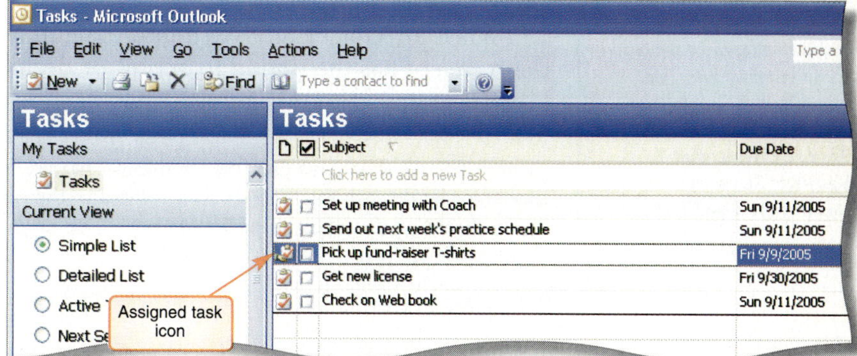

FIGURE 2-46

4

• **Double-click the Pick up fund-raiser T-shirts task.**

Outlook displays the Pick up fund-raiser T-shirts - Task window. Outlook has added an information bar indicating you are waiting for a response from the recipient (Figure 2-47).

5

• **Click the Close button on the Pick up fund-raiser T-shirts - Task window.**

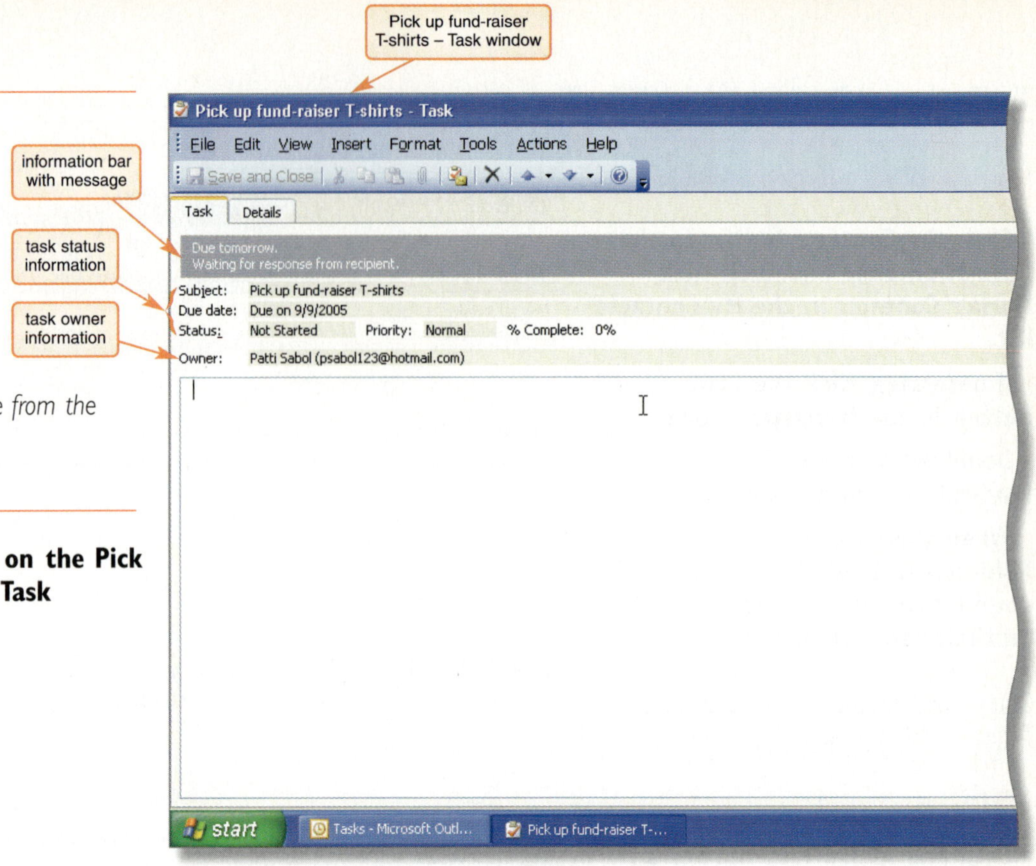

Pick up fund-raiser T-shirts – Task window

information bar with message

task status information

task owner information

FIGURE 2-47

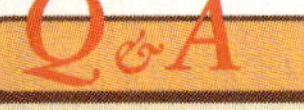

Q: Can I assign a task to more than one person at a time?

A: Yes, Outlook does allow you to assign a task to more than one person at a time; however, in order to have Outlook keep you up to date on the progress of the task, you must divide the work into separate tasks, and then assign each task individually. For example, if you wanted to assign a research project to three researchers, you would have to create three separate tasks named Research: Researcher 1, Research: Researcher 2, and Research: Researcher 3.

The information bar shown in Figure 2-47 indicates that the sender is waiting on a response from the recipient. Until you receive an acceptance from the task recipient, you are still the owner of the task. That means that you are responsible for its progression.

Along with the task information, Outlook provides you with an area to type a message with your task assignment (Figure 2-45 on the previous page). Two check boxes are included: Keep an updated copy of this task on my task list, and Send me a status report when this task is complete (Figure 2-45). These boxes are checked by default. These boxes allow you to see the task progression as the recipient updates the task in their task list.

Accepting a Task Assignment

When a recipient receives a task assignment, it appears in his or her Inbox. Then, the recipient has the option to accept or decline the task. The following steps show how to accept a task assignment.

Note: The steps on page OUT 101 and OUT 102 are for demonstration purposes only. Thus, if you are stepping through this project on a computer, then you must have someone send you a task request so it displays in the Inbox as shown in Figure 2-48 on the next page.

To Accept a Task Assignment

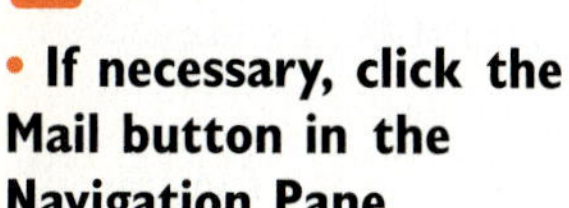

- **If necessary, click the Mail button in the Navigation Pane.**
- **Click the plus sign (+) next to the Inbox folder in the All Mail Folders list, and then select the Maria's Inbox folder.**
- **Click the Juanita Rosado Task Request to highlight it.**

Outlook displays the Inbox folder with the task request highlighted (Figure 2-48). All the information for the request appears in the Reading Pane along with the Accept and Decline buttons.

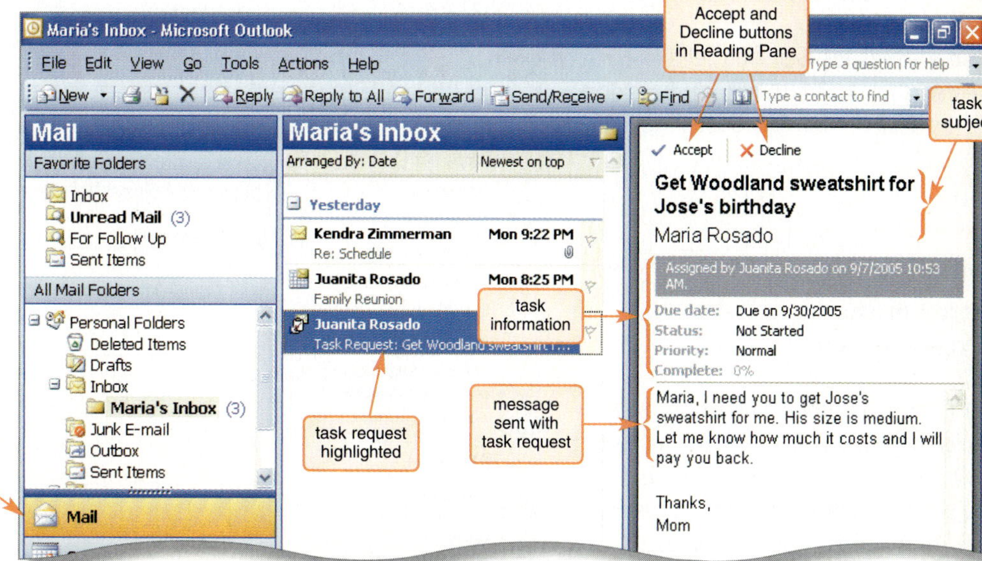

FIGURE 2-48

- **Double-click the Task Request message heading to open it.**

Outlook opens the Get Woodland sweatshirt for Jose's birthday - Task window (Figure 2-49).

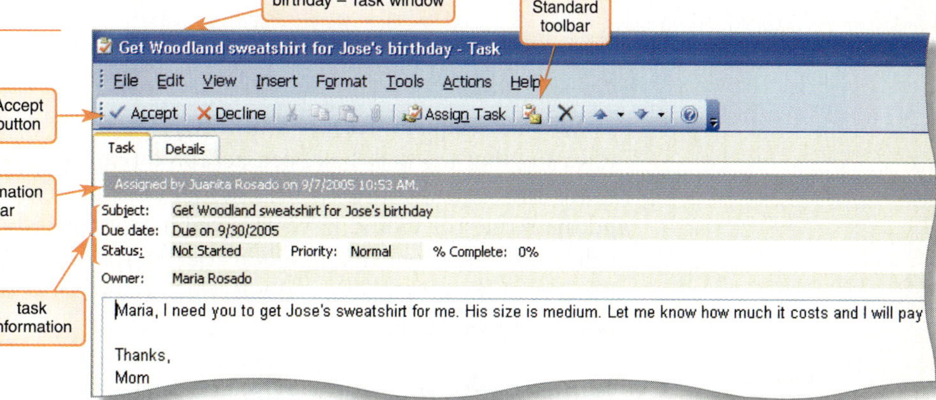

FIGURE 2-49

- **Click the Accept button on the Standard toolbar.**

Outlook displays the Accepting Task dialog box (Figure 2-50).

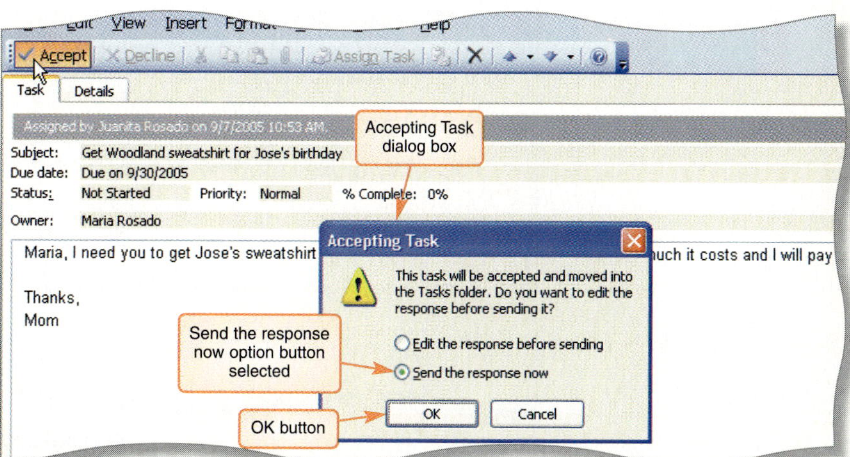

FIGURE 2-50

4

• **Click Send the response now, and then click the OK button.**

Outlook closes the Get Woodland sweatshirt for Jose's birthday - Task window and the Inbox - Microsoft Outlook window appears.

5

• **Click the Task button in the Navigation Pane.**

The Tasks - Microsoft Outlook window is displayed (Figure 2-51). The task request has been removed from the Inbox folder and placed in the Tasks folder as a new task. An Accepted Task icon appears to the left of the Get Woodland sweatshirt for Jose's birthday task.

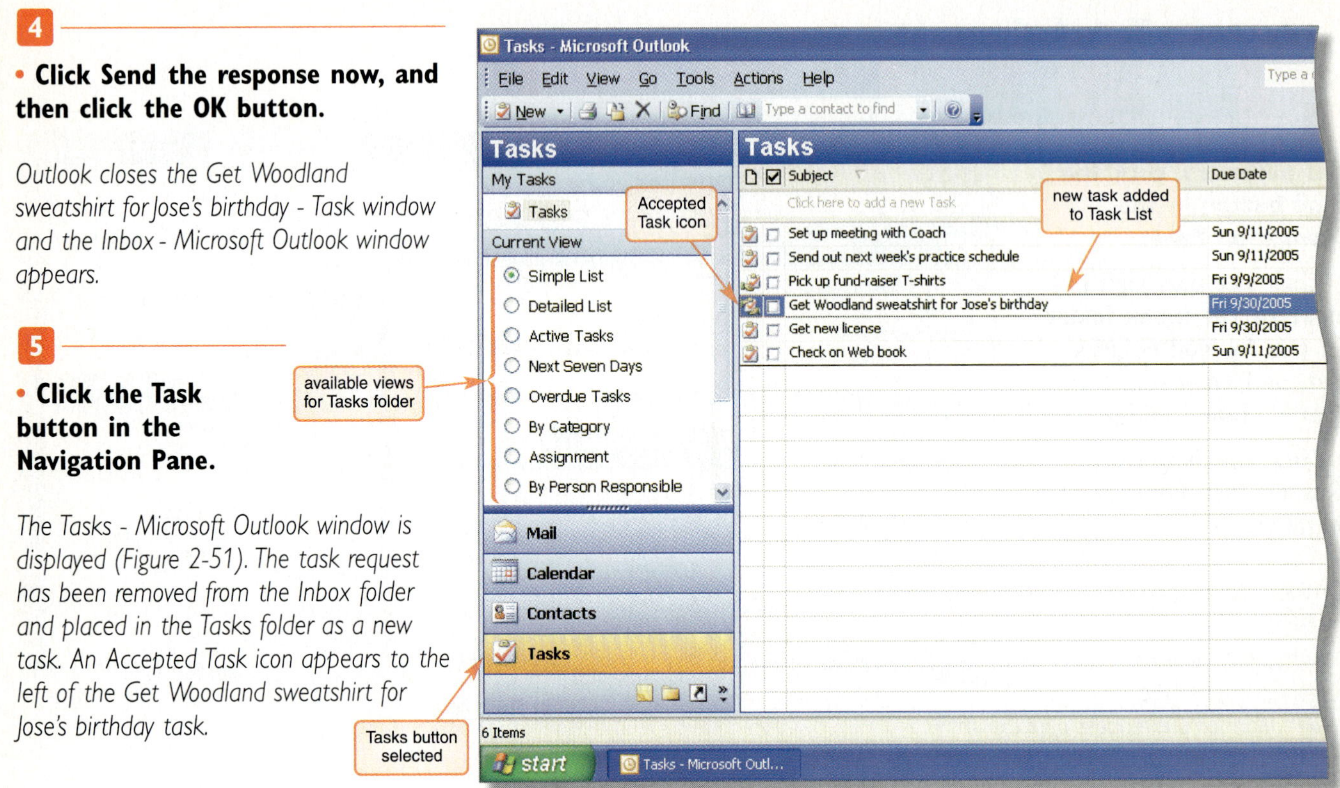

FIGURE 2-51

When a recipient accepts a task request, the requestor receives a message indicating that the task has been accepted (Figure 2-52). If the recipient had chosen to decline the task, the task request would have been moved to the Deleted Items folder, and the requestor would have received a message indicating that the request was declined. In the event that someone declines a task request, the requester can either take on that task by clicking the Return to Task List button, or attempt to assign the task to someone else.

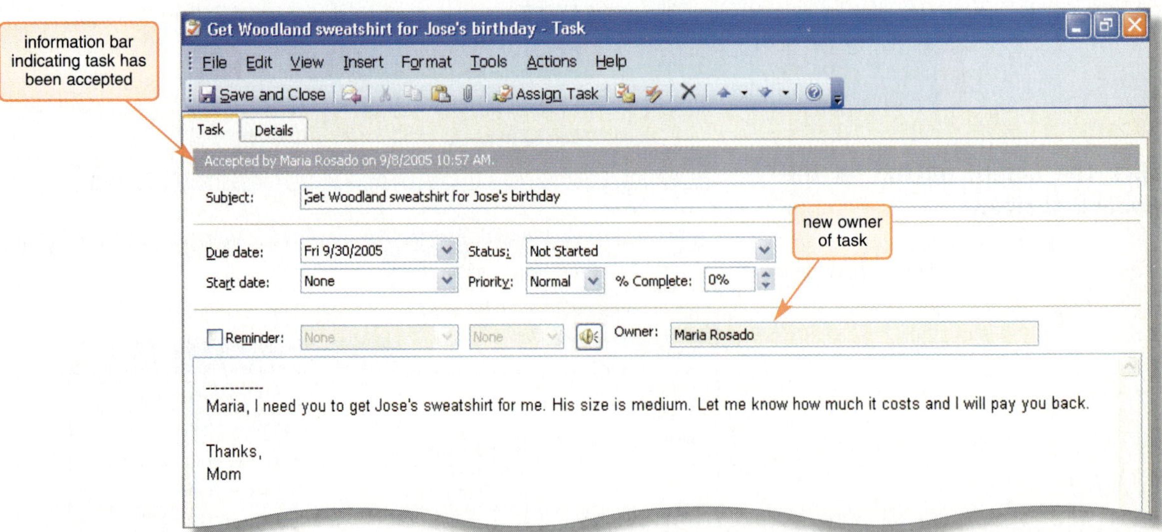

FIGURE 2-52

Customizing the Tasks Window and Moving Tasks to a Personal Folder

The default view for the task list is shown in Figure 2-51. This view contains the Task icon, the completed task check box, the task description, and the due date. Outlook allows to you add or delete columns, or **fields**, so you can display only the information that you want to view. To modify the current view of the task list, you would follow these steps.

To Add or Delete Fields in a View

1. On the View menu, point to Arrange By, point to Current View, and then click Customize Current View on the Current View submenu.
2. When the Customize View: Simple List dialog box is displayed, click the Fields button.
3. To add a new field, select a field in the Available fields list, and then click the Add button.
4. To delete a field, select a field in the Show these fields in this order list, and then click the Remove button.
5. When you are finished customizing the view, click the OK buttons in both open dialog boxes.

More About

Updating Tasks

To send a status report for a task on which you are working, open the task. On the Actions menu, click Send Status Report. If the task was assigned to you, the person who sent the task request automatically will be added to the update list.

For the same reason you created a separate folder for calendar items, you may want to create a separate folder for tasks and move the current task list to that folder. The following steps describe how to create a personal tasks folder and move the current task list to that folder.

To Move Tasks to a New Personal Folder

1. With the Tasks window active, right-click the Tasks title bar above the task list.
2. Click New folder on the shortcut menu.
3. When the Create New Folder dialog box is displayed, type Maria's Tasks in the Name text box and select Tasks in the select where to place the folder list. Click the OK button.
4. Click the first task in the task list, then, while holding the shift key, click the last task in the task list to select all the tasks in the task list.
5. Right-click the task list. Click Move to Folder on the shortcut menu.
6. When the Move Items dialog box is displayed, select Maria's Tasks in the Move the selected items to the folder list. Click the OK button.

More About

Tasks

You can customize the Calendar window to include the task list. When you export the Calendar folder, however, the task list is not included. The task list is kept in the Tasks folder and is kept separate from the Calendar folder.

Scheduling a Meeting with Outlook

Earlier in this project an appointment was added for a team meeting. Outlook allows you to invite multiple attendees to a meeting by sending a single invitation. The sections on the next page will show how to invite attendees and schedule resources for that meeting.

To Invite Attendees to a Meeting

1

- **With the Calendar window active, click September 12 in the Date Navigator.**
- **Double-click the Team Meeting appointment to open the Team Meeting - Recurring Appointment window.**
- **When the Open Recurring Item dialog box is displayed, click Open this occurrence, and then click the OK button.**
- **Double-click the title bar to maximize the window.**
- **Click the Scheduling tab.**

Outlook opens the Team Meeting - Recurring Appointment window (Figure 2-53).

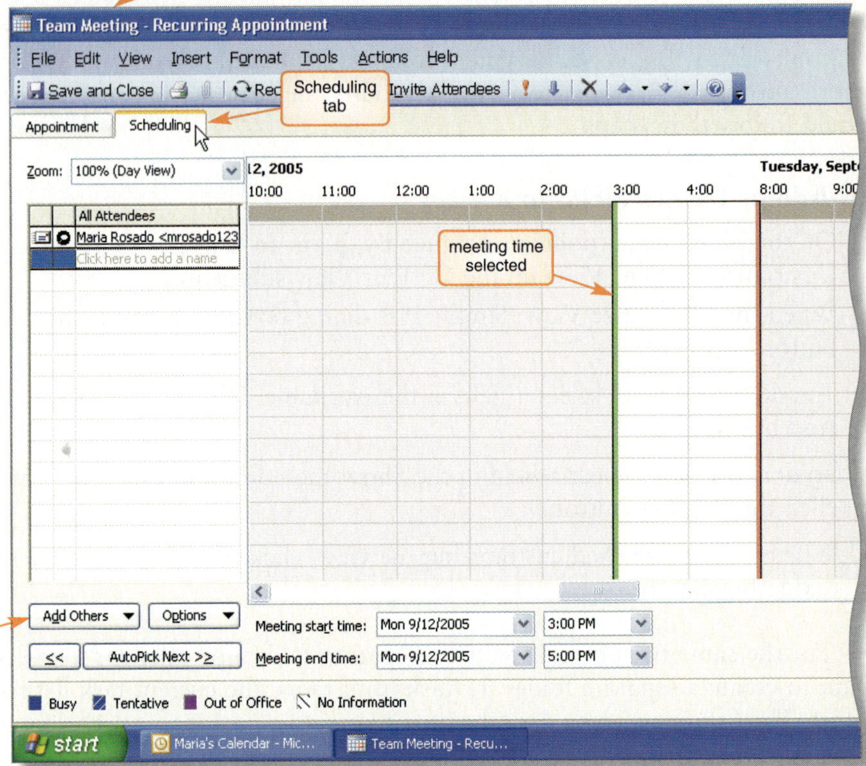

FIGURE 2-53

2

- **Click the Add Others button, and then click Add From Address Book.**

Outlook displays the Select Attendees and Resources dialog box (Figure 2-54).

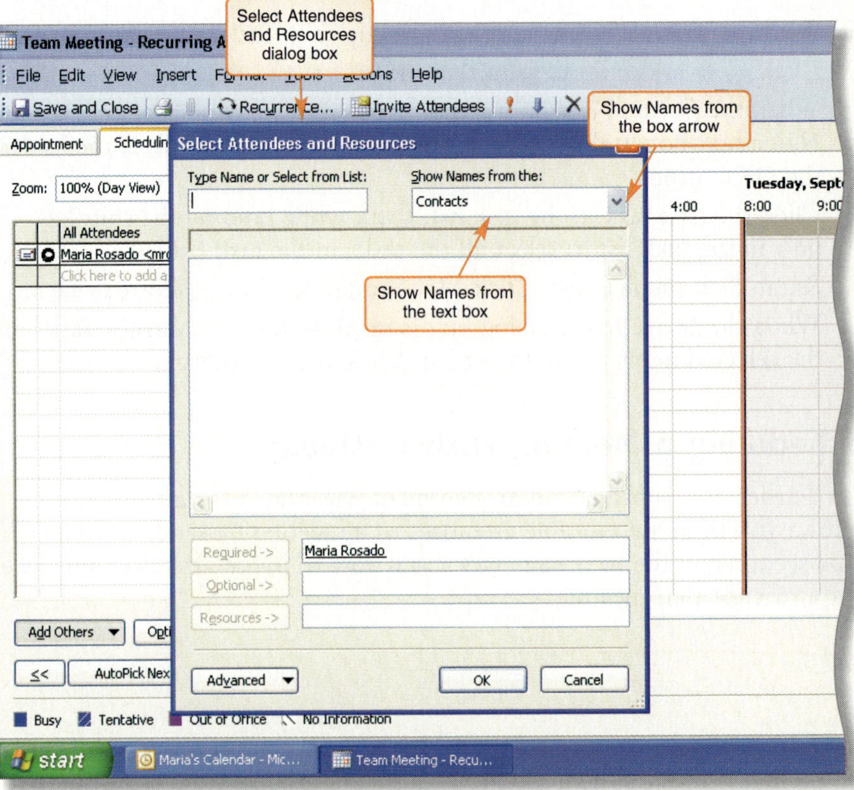

FIGURE 2-54

3

- **Click the Show Names from the box arrow, and then click Maria's Contacts.**
- **While holding the SHIFT key, click Susan Hadley to select the entire list.**
- **Click the Required button.**

The selected names from the contact list are added to the Required text box (Figure 2-55).

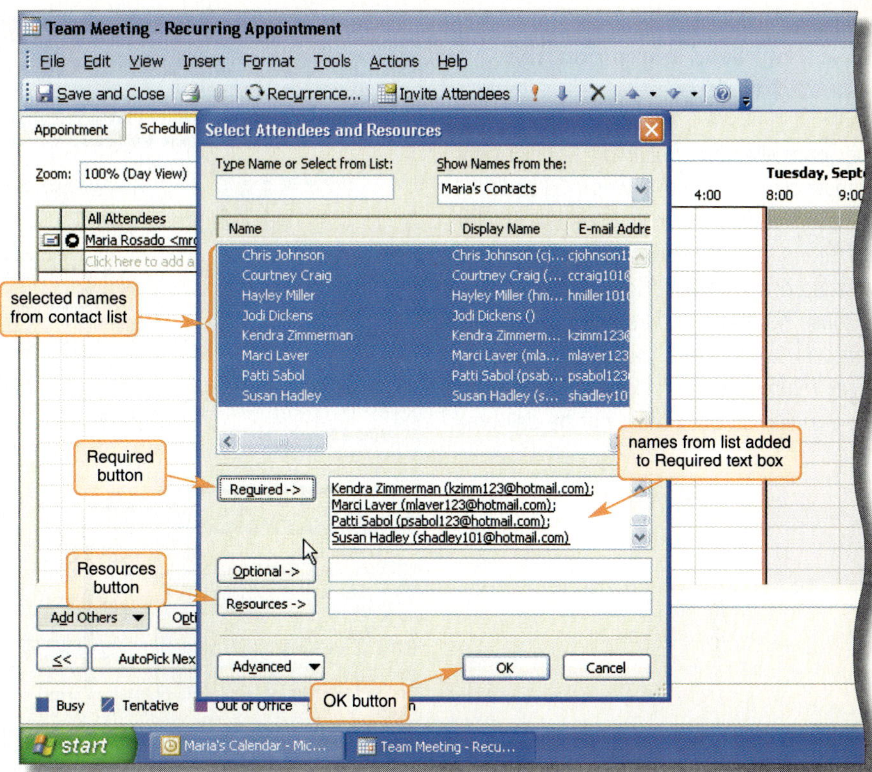

FIGURE 2-55

4

- **Click the OK button.**
- **If the Microsoft Office Internet Free/Busy dialog box displays, click the Cancel button.**

The Select Attendees and Resources dialog box closes and the Team Meeting - Recurring Appointment window is displayed with selected attendees in the All Attendees list (Figure 2-56).

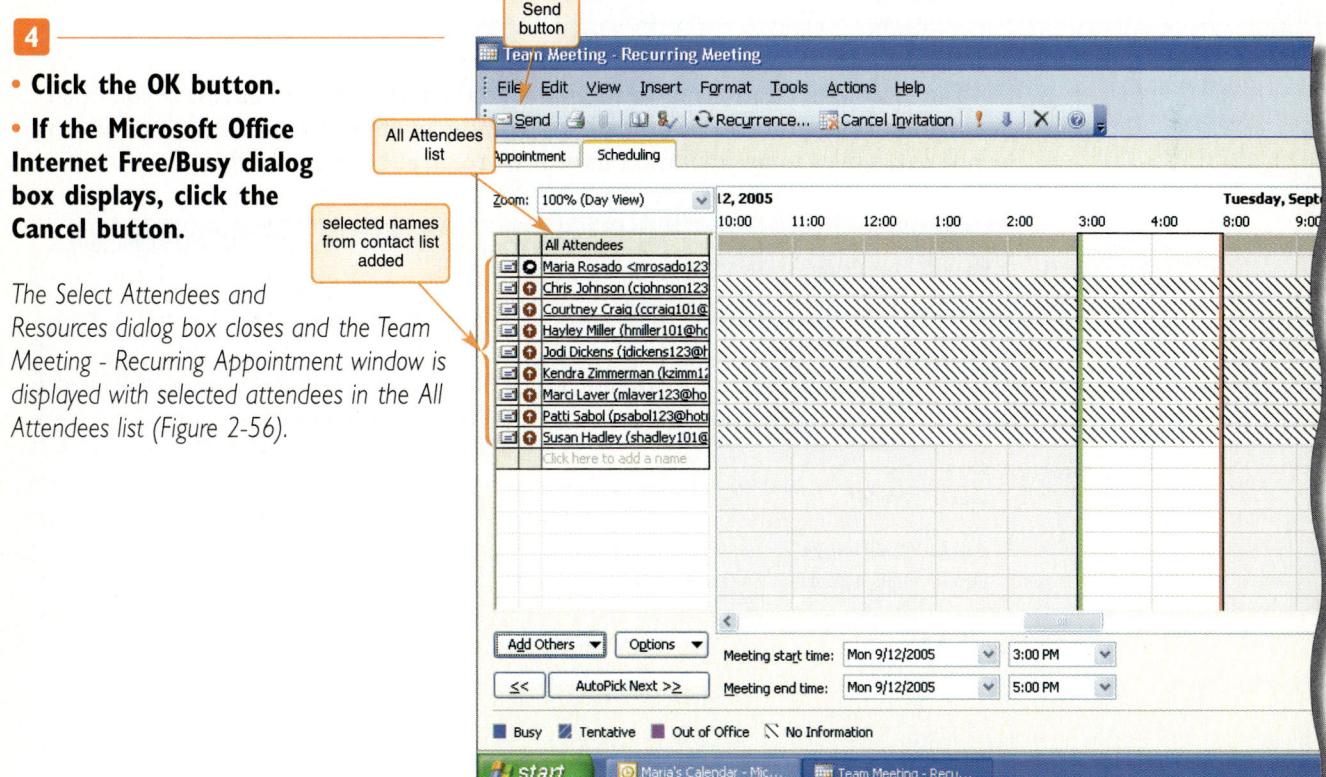

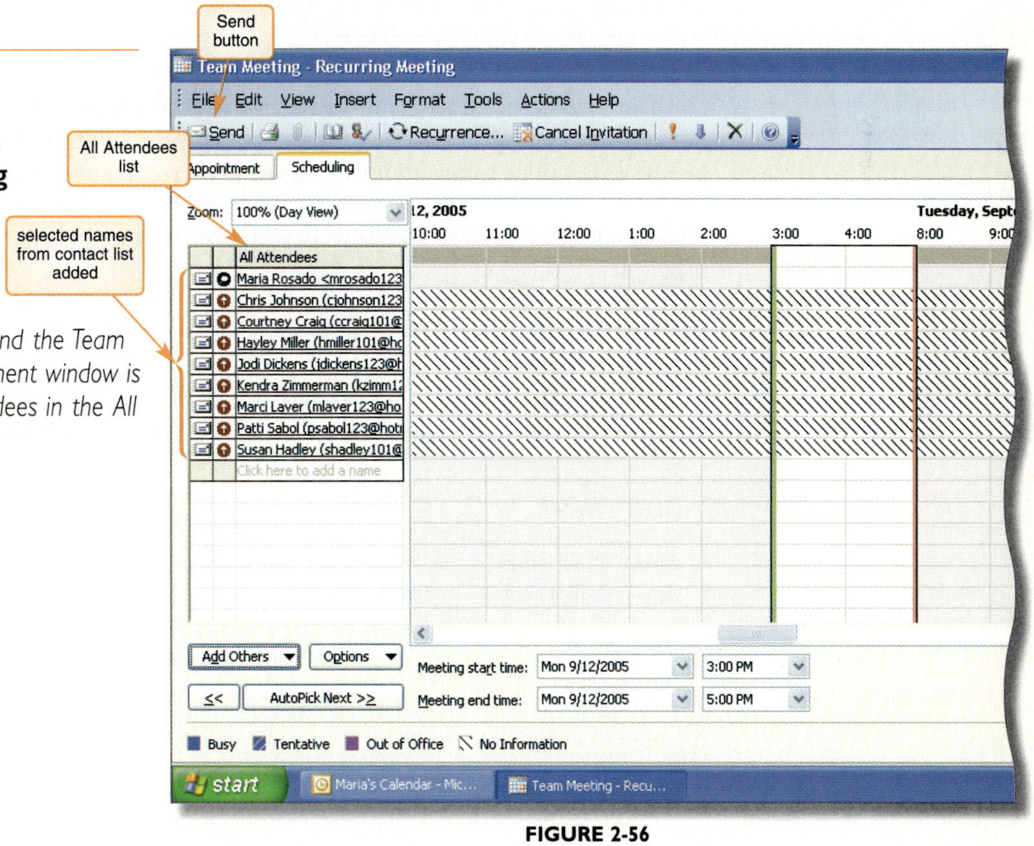

Send button

All Attendees list

selected names from contact list added

FIGURE 2-56

5

• **Click the Send button on the Standard toolbar.**

The Team Meeting -Recurring Appointment window closes and the Maria's Calendar - Microsoft Outlook window is displayed with a meeting icon displaying next to the Team Meeting appointment (Figure 2-57). Because the e-mail addresses in Maria's Contacts are fictitious, you may get messages returned to your inbox indicating that the e-mail messages could not be delivered.

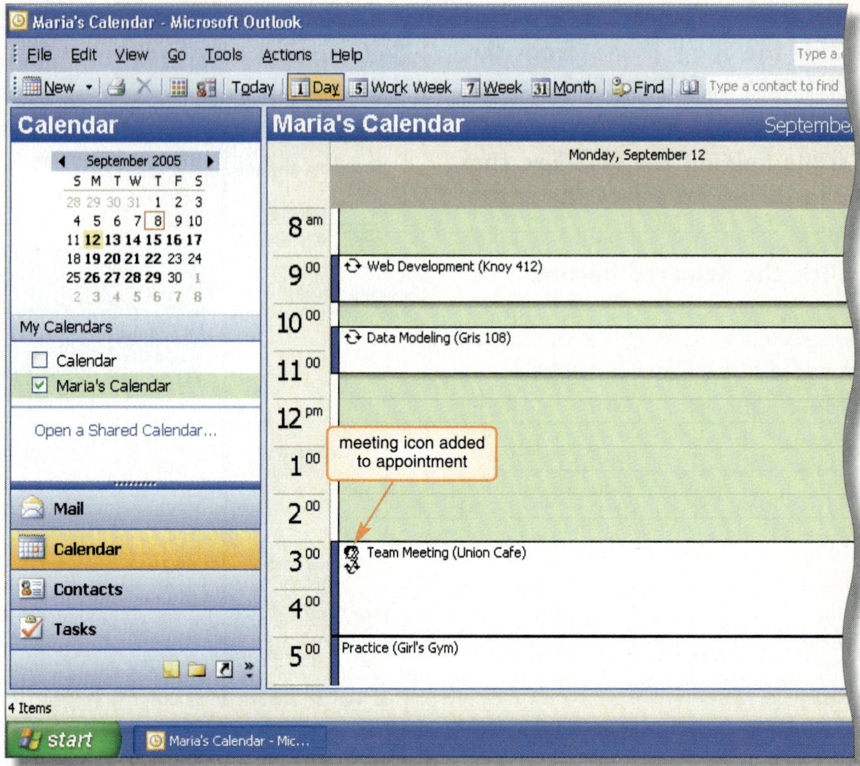

FIGURE 2-57

The meeting invitations have been sent to the respective attendees. If you open the appointment, you will be able to see who the invitation was sent to and whether or not any replies to an invitation have been received (Figure 2-58).

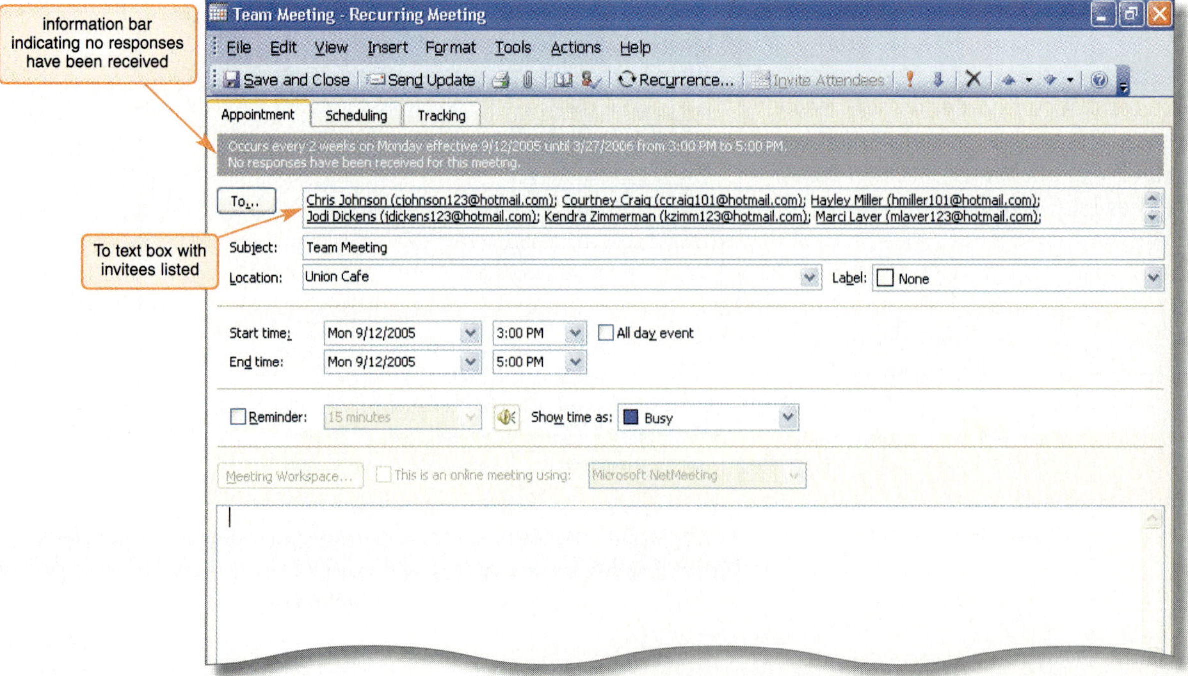

FIGURE 2-58

Scheduling Resources

If you use a Microsoft Exchange server e-mail account, you are able to schedule resources for your meetings in addition to inviting attendees. Resources are items necessary to run your meeting, such as the meeting room where you plan to hold your meeting, or an overhead projector you may want to use for a presentation.

Resources are set up on the server by an individual in the organization. If the resource is available at the time of the meeting, it will accept the invitation automatically, if not, the resource will decline the invitation automatically.

Accepting and Declining Meeting Requests

Once a meeting request has been received, you have to decide to accept it or decline it. A meeting request will appear in your Inbox similar to the one shown in Figure 2-59. Outlook allows you to choose from four responses: Accept, Tentative, Decline, or Propose New Time. The steps on the next page show how to accept a meeting request.

More About

Meeting Workspace

Microsoft Outlook and SharePoint Services offer Meeting Workspace to help you plan your meeting more efficiently. A Meeting Workspace is a Web site for centralizing all the information required for one or more meetings. To learn more about Meeting Workspace, visit the Outlook 2003 More About Web page (scsite.com/out2003/more) and click Meetings.

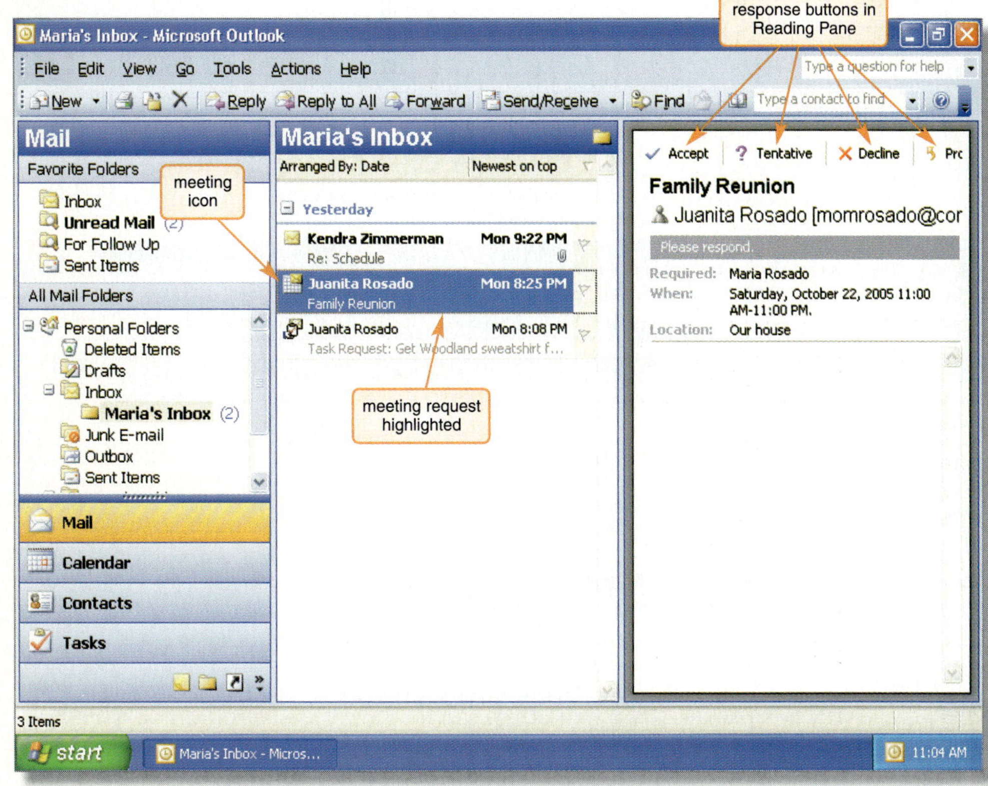

FIGURE 2-59

To Accept a Meeting Request

1

- **If necessary, click the Mail button in the Navigation Pane.**

Outlook displays the Inbox folder with the meeting request selected (Figure 2-60). All the information for the request appears in the Reading Pane along with the Accept, Tentative, Decline, and Propose New Time buttons.

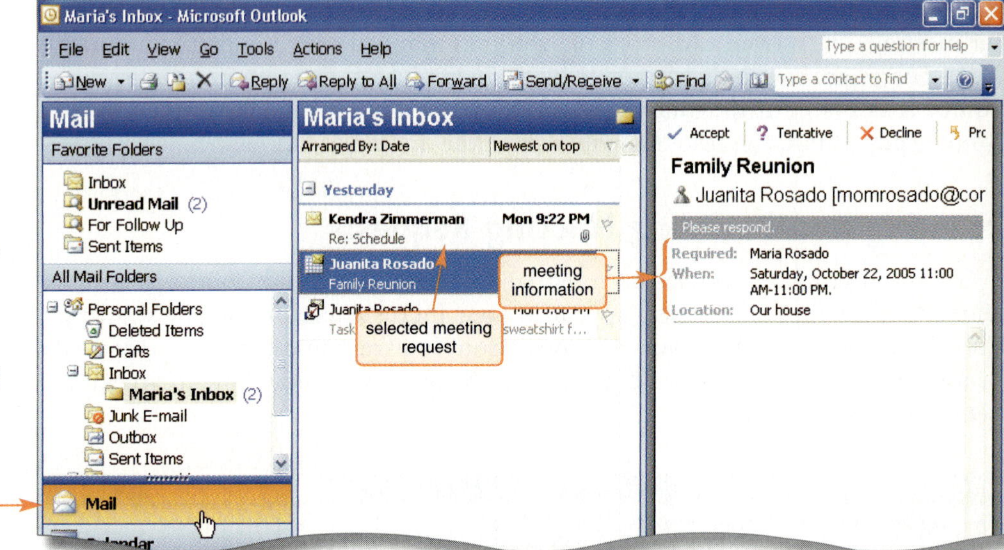

FIGURE 2-60

2

- **Double-click the Family Reunion message heading to open it.**

Outlook opens the Family Reunion - Meeting window (Figure 2-61).

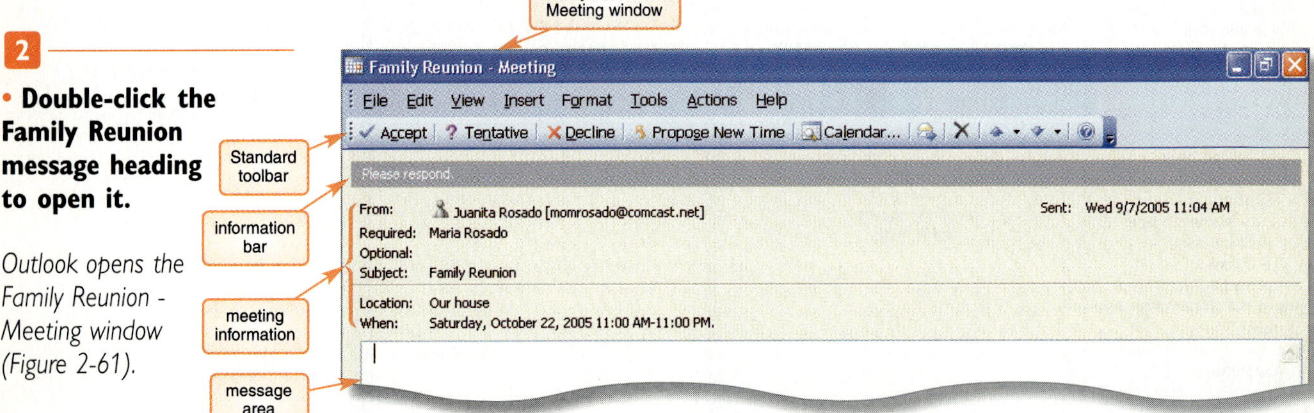

FIGURE 2-61

3

- **Click the Accept button on the Standard toolbar.**

Outlook displays the Microsoft Office Outlook dialog box (Figure 2-62).

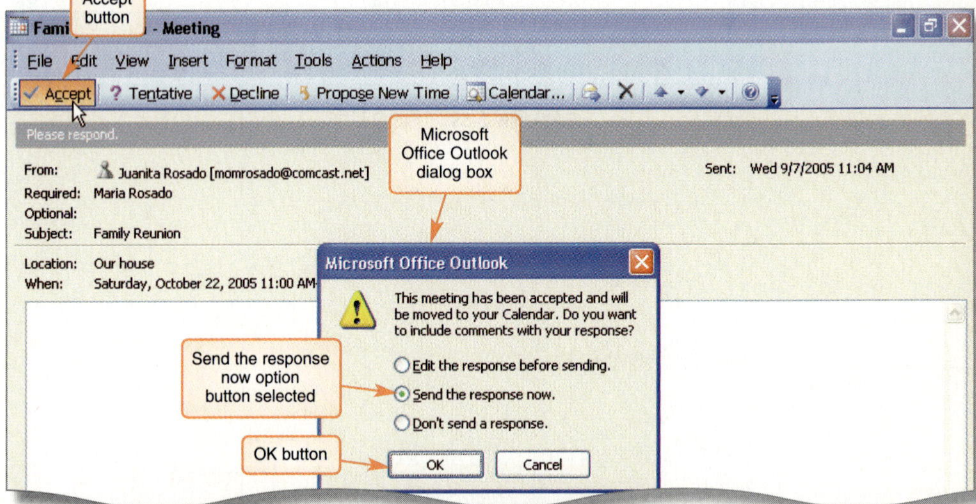

FIGURE 2-62

4

• **Click Send the response now, and then click the OK button.**

Outlook closes the Family Reunion - Meeting window and displays the Inbox - Microsoft Outlook window.

5

• **Click the Calendar button in the Navigation Pane.**

• **Click the right scroll arrow in the Date Navigator so the October 2005 calendar appears.**

• **Click October 22 in the Date Navigator.**

The Calendar - Microsoft Outlook window is displayed (Figure 2-63). The meeting request has been removed from the Inbox folder and placed in the Calendar folder as a new meeting. Outlook may send the meeting request to the default Calendar folder because the invitation was sent to someone other than the current user. To view the new meeting click the Calendar box in the My Calendars pane.

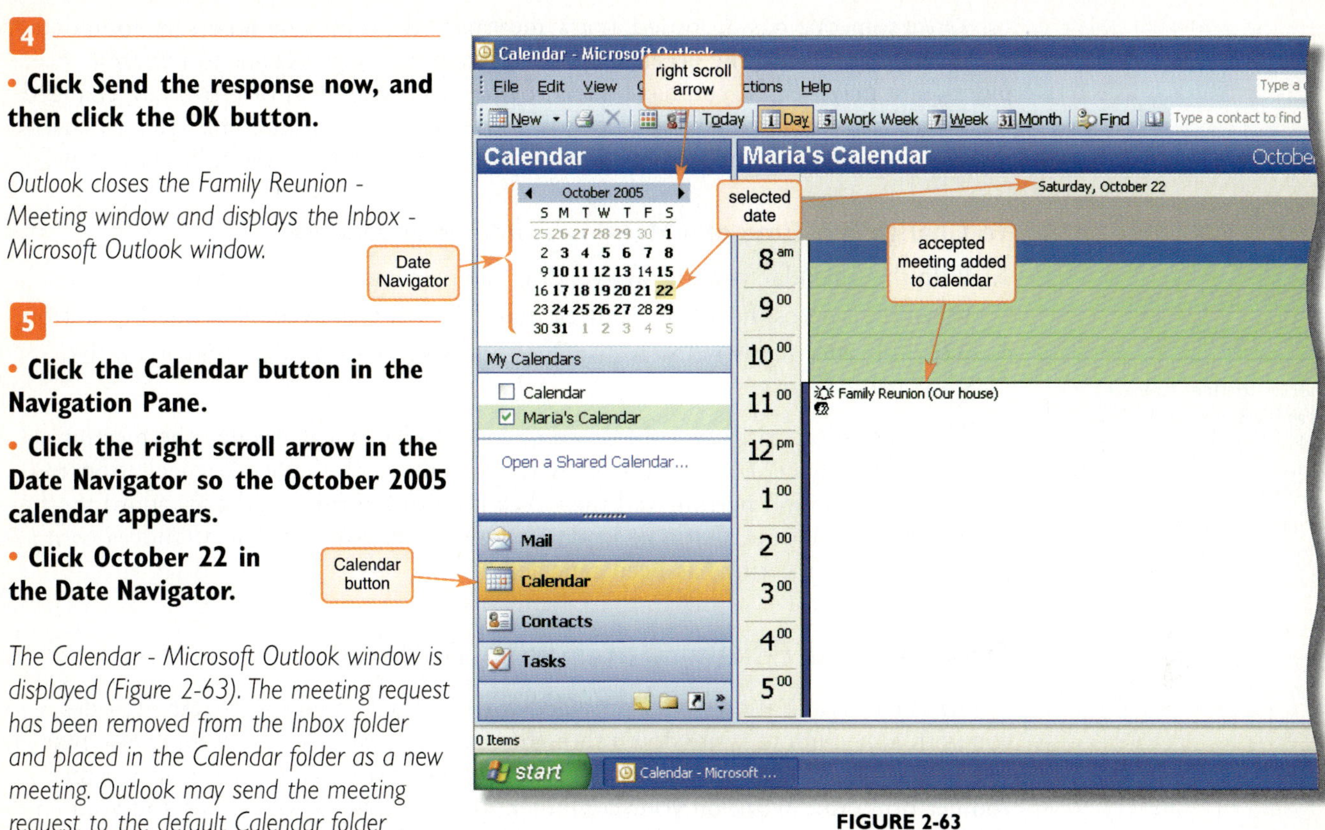

FIGURE 2-63

When a meeting request is accepted, the meeting organizer receives a message indicating that the request has been accepted. If the meeting request is declined, the request is moved to the Deleted Items folder, and the meeting organizer receives a message indicating that the request was declined.

Proposing New Meeting Times

One of the available responses to a meeting request is to propose a new time. When you click the Propose a New Time button, Outlook allows you to send a response to the meeting organizer indicating that you tentatively accept the request, but propose the meeting be held at a different time. To propose a new time for a meeting, you would perform the following steps.

To Propose a New Meeting Time

1. Double-click the appropriate meeting request to open the request.
2. Click the Propose New Time button on the Standard toolbar.
3. When the Propose New Time dialog box is displayed, drag through the time slot that you want to propose, or enter the appropriate information in the Meeting start time and Meeting end time time boxes.
4. Click the Propose Time button.
5. When the New Time Proposed - Meeting Response window is displayed, click the Send button.

Once someone has proposed a new meeting time, it may be necessary to update the meeting request to the other potential attendees. Other reasons to update a meeting request may be that you have added or removed attendees or resources, changed the meeting to a recurring series, or moved the meeting to a different date. To change the time of a meeting and send an update, you would perform the following steps.

More About

Meeting Times

If you use Windows SharePoint Services and have access to other attendees' calendars, use the AutoPick Next button in the Scheduling sheet of the Meeting window to find the next available free time for all attendees.

To Change the Time of a Meeting and Send an Update

1. With the Calendar window active, drag the meeting to its new time.
2. When the Microsoft Office Outlook dialog box is displayed, click the Yes button.
3. When the Meeting window is displayed, click the Send Update button on the Standard toolbar.

If the situation arises that the meeting needs to be canceled, open the meeting window, click Cancel Meeting on the Actions menu, click the Send cancellation and delete meeting option button, and then click the Send button on the Standard toolbar of the meeting window. Outlook sends a high priority e-mail to the attendees with a message that the meeting has been canceled.

Creating and Editing Notes with Outlook

Another organizational tool provided with Outlook is Notes. **Notes** provides you with a medium to write down thoughts, ideas, questions, or anything else that you might write down on a sticky note or note pad. Notes can remain open while you perform other work on your computer. You can add to your notes and your changes are saved automatically. Notes can be color coded per your personal specifications. For example, a blue note may be an issue that you want to bring to the attention of your boss, a green note may be an idea you want to pass along to a coworker, and so on. The following steps show how to create and edit a note.

To Create and Edit a Note

1

• **Click the Notes button in the Navigation Pane.**

• **Click the New Note button on the Standard toolbar.**

Outlook displays the Untitled - Notes window (Figure 2-64).

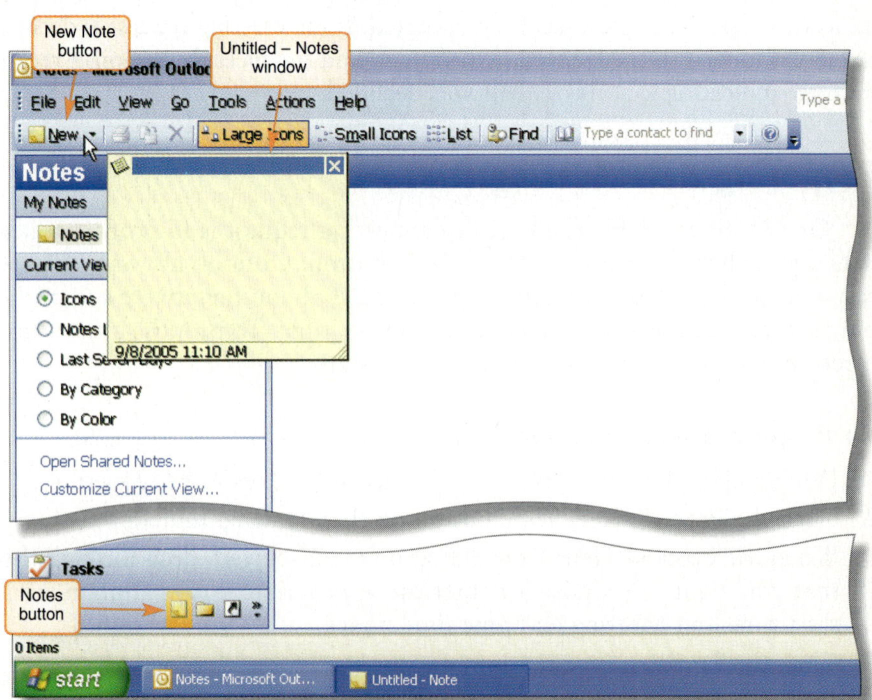

FIGURE 2-64

2

• **Type** `Talk about new warm-up routine with Coach` **as the entry.**

• **Point to the Close button.**

The text appears in the Untitled - Notes window (Figure 2-65).

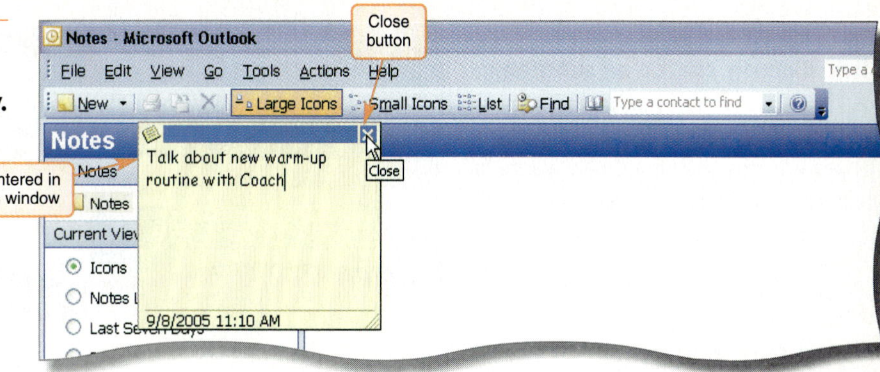

FIGURE 2-65

3

• **Click the Close button.**

Outlook closes the Untitled - Notes window and the note appears in the Notes folder (Figure 2-66).

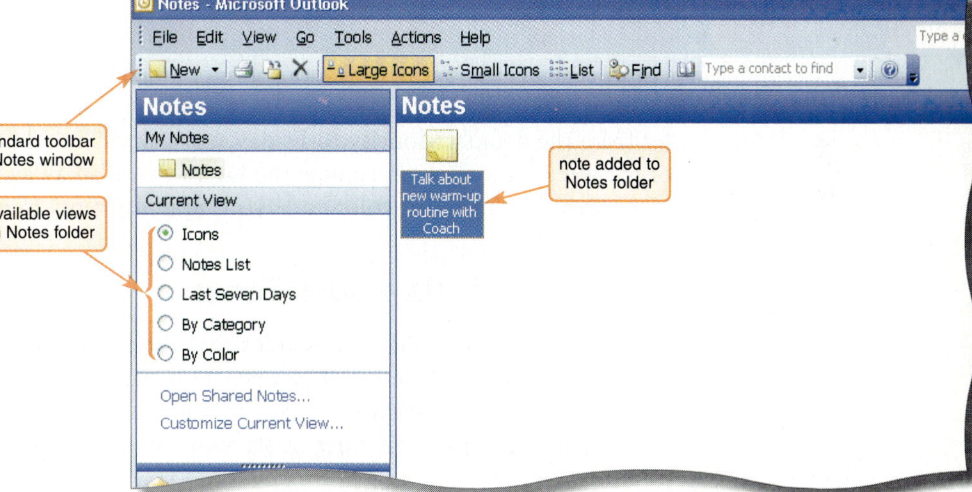

FIGURE 2-66

4

• **Right-click the note and then point to Color on the shortcut menu.**

Outlook displays the Color submenu (Figure 2-67).

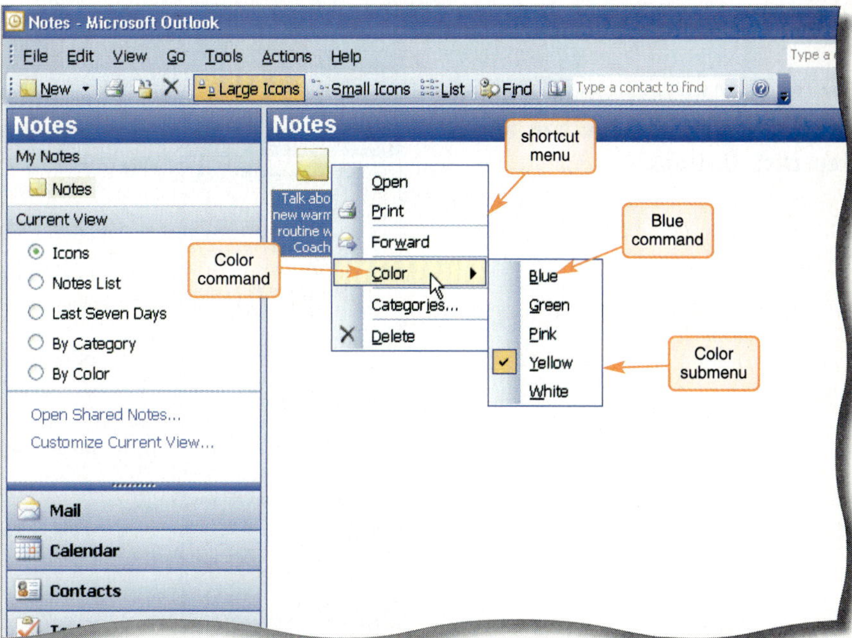

FIGURE 2-67

5

- **Click Blue on the Color submenu.**

The Notes - Microsoft Outlook window is displayed with the Talk about new warm-up routine with Coach note colored blue (Figure 2-68).

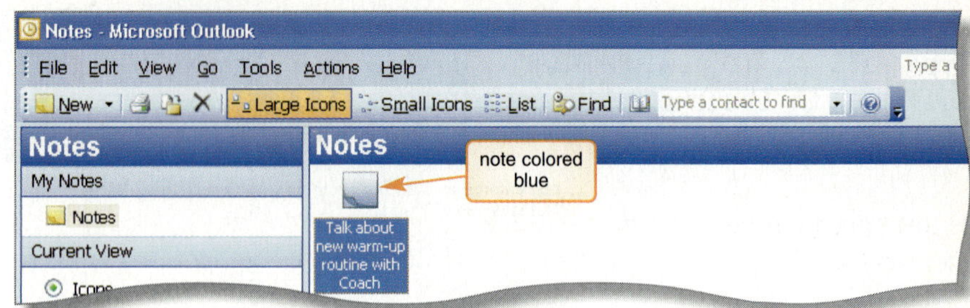

FIGURE 2-68

Other Ways

1. Click Note icon in Notes window, point to Color, click color on Color submenu

Customize Calendar Settings

Outlook provides you with several options to change the appearance of the Calendar window. You can customize your work week by selecting the days you work if they differ from the default Monday to Friday work week. In addition to customizing the days of the week, you also can change the hours that display as work hours in the appointment area. You also can color code your appointments to make them easier to view.

Setting Work Days and Times

Some people may have schedules that differ from the standard Monday through Friday work week. Whether it is a six-days-per-week schedule or a four-days-per-week schedule, Outlook allows you to select the days that display in your calendar. The following steps show how to set work week options.

To Set Work Week Options

1

- **With the Calendar window active, click Tools on the menu bar, and then click Options.**

Outlook displays the Options dialog box (Figure 2-69).

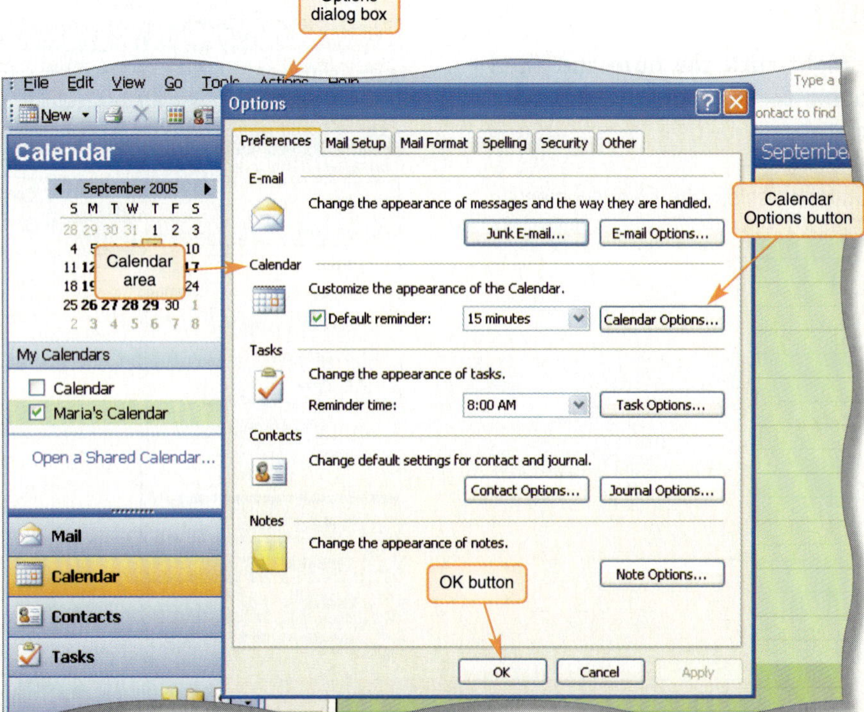

FIGURE 2-69

2

- **Click the Calendar Options button.**

Outlook displays the Calendar Options dialog box (Figure 2-70).

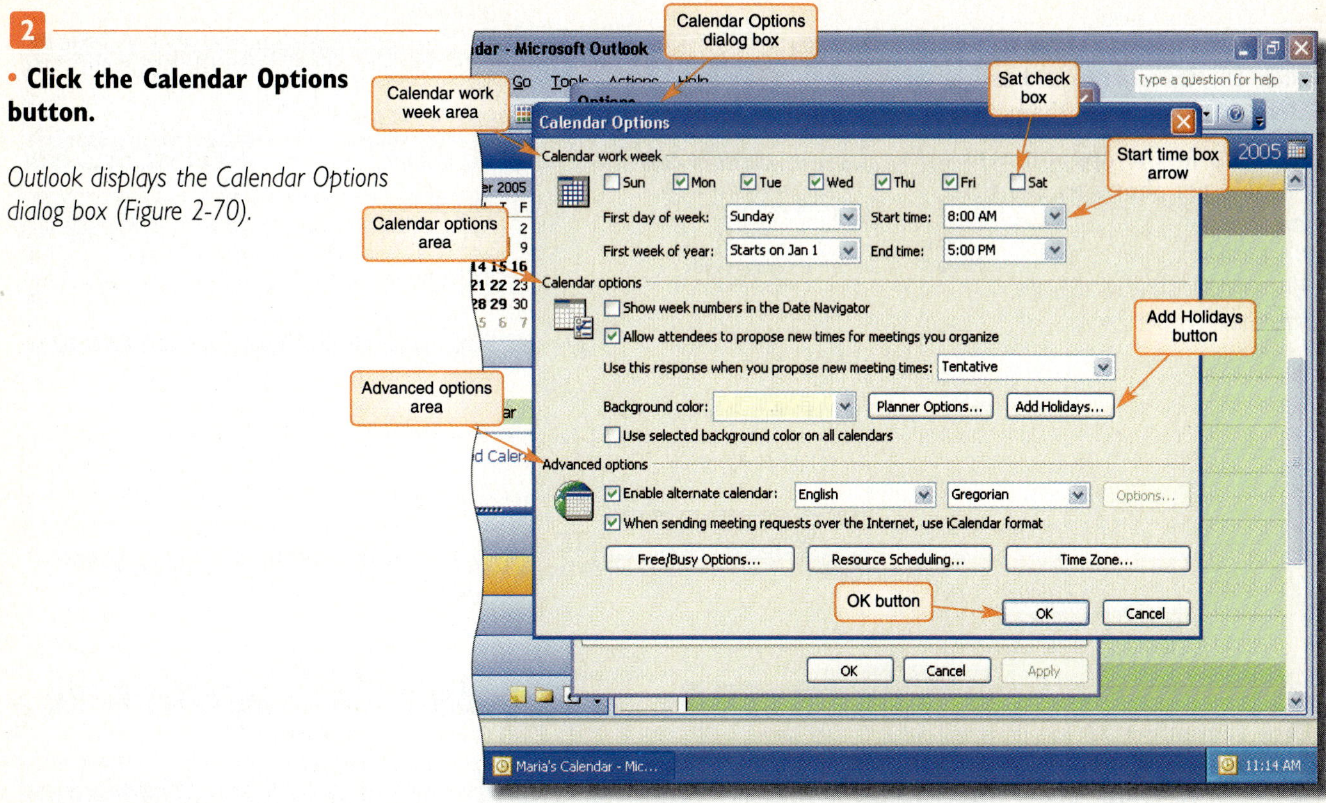

FIGURE 2-70

3

- **In the Calendar work week area, click the Sat check box.**
- **Click the Start time box arrow and then select 7:00 AM as the new start time.**

The work week has been changed to a six-day week with the start time changed to 7:00 AM (Figure 2-71).

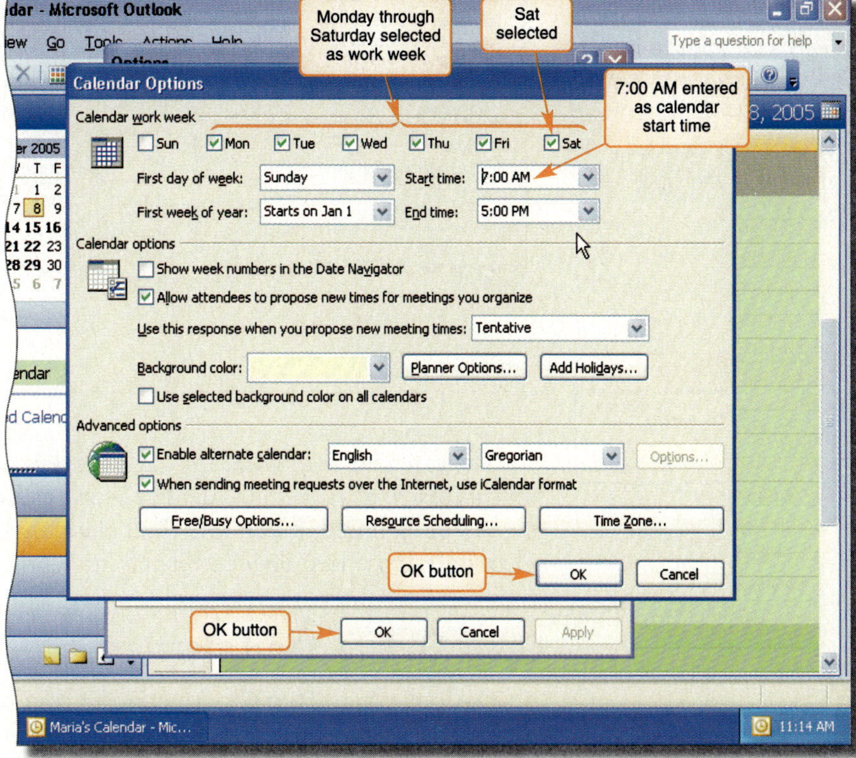

FIGURE 2-71

4

- **Click the OK button in both open dialog boxes to close them.**
- **Scroll up in the Appointment area so that 6 am shows as the first time slot.**

7:00 no longer is included in the shaded area (Figure 2-72).

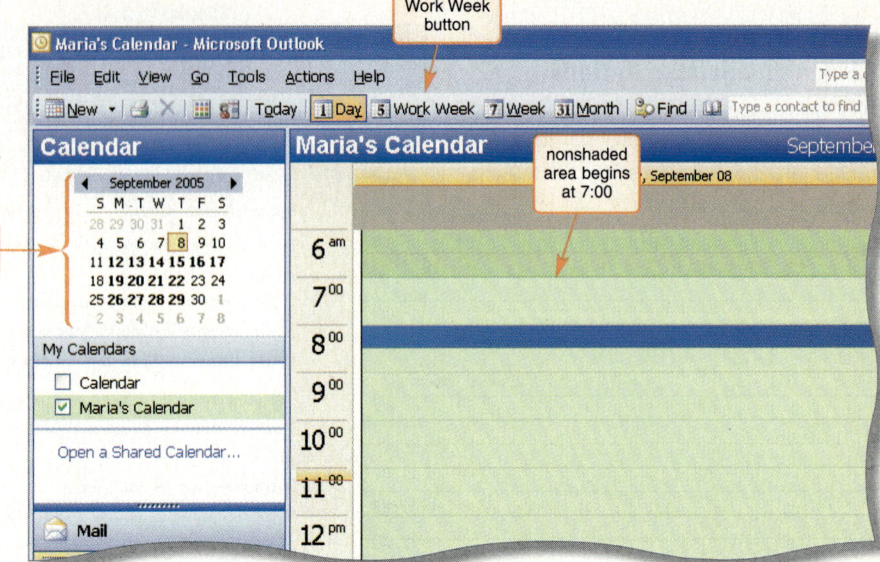

FIGURE 2-72

5

- **Click September 12 in the Date Navigator.**
- **Click the Work Week button on the Standard toolbar.**

Saturday now appears in Work Week view as an active work day (Figure 2-73). Notice that Saturday also is included in the shaded bar in the Date Navigator.

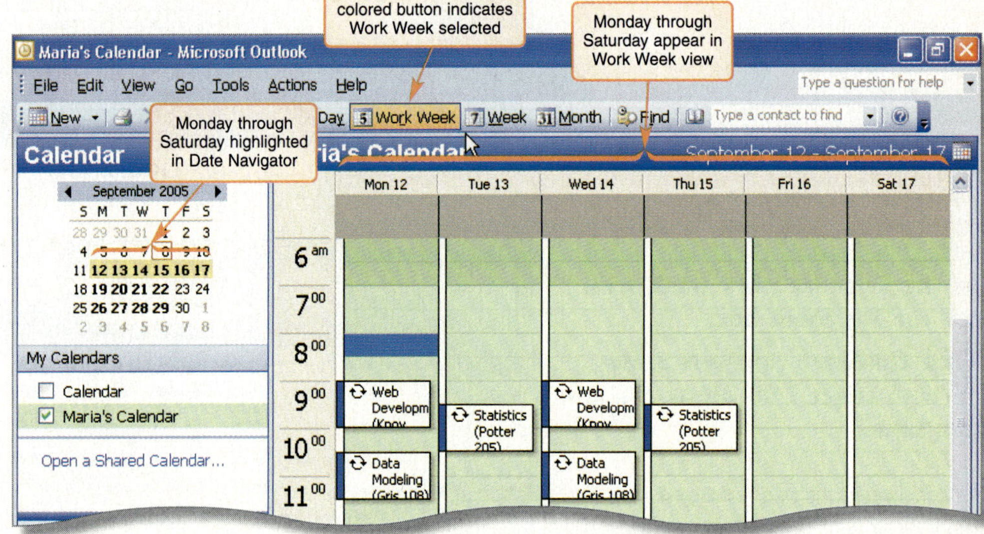

FIGURE 2-73

Other Ways

1. Press ALT+T, press O, press C

The calendar is now set up for a six-day work week. You also can select nonsuccessive days in the Calendar work week area (Figure 2-70 on the previous page). For example, if you only had class on Tuesday's and Thursday's, you could select only those two days to display in Work Week view.

Color Coding the Calendar

Outlook offers 10 colors to choose from to color appointments and meetings. For example, you can color your class schedule one color, your work schedule another color, and your extracurricular activities yet another color. Outlook has default labels for the colors that can be changed to fit your needs. The following steps show how to color code the Maria's Calendar calendar and edit the calendar labels.

To Color Code the Calendar and Edit Calendar Labels

1

- **With the Calendar window active, click the Month button on the Standard toolbar to display the calendar in Month view.**
- **Click the Calendar Coloring button on the Standard toolbar.**

Outlook displays the Calendar Coloring menu (Figure 2-74). The color options are not available because an appointment has not been selected.

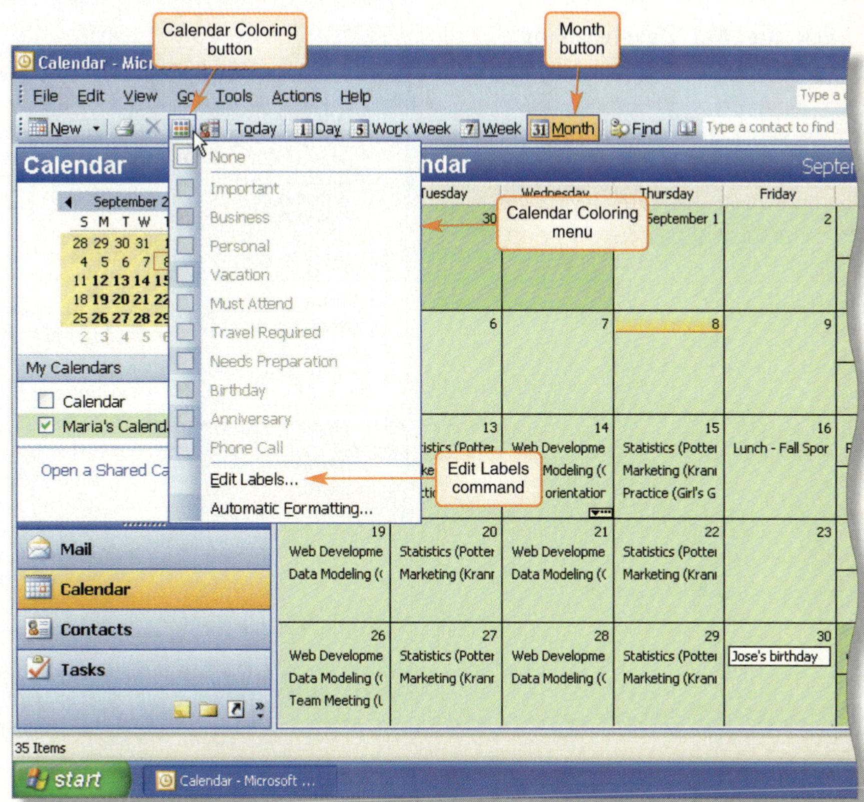

FIGURE 2-74

2

- **Click Edit Labels on the Calendar Coloring menu.**
- **Triple click the Business entry in the second text box in the Edit Calendar Labels dialog box and type** `Work` **as the entry.**
- **Press the TAB key three times, and then type** `Class` **in place of the Must Attend entry.**
- **Press the TAB key once, and then type** `Practice` **in place of the Travel Required entry.**

Outlook displays the Edit Calendar Labels dialog box (Figure 2-75). The three labels have been changed.

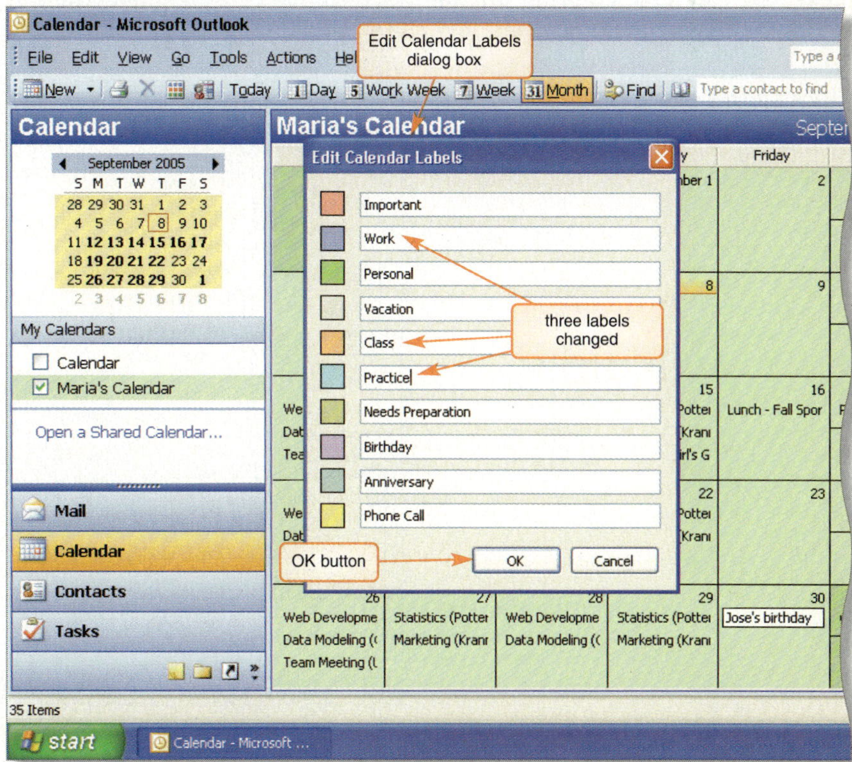

FIGURE 2-75

3

- **Click the OK button.**
- **Click the Web Development appointment on September 12th.**

Outlook closes the Edit Calendar Labels dialog box and displays the calendar in Month view with the Web Development appointment on September 12 selected (Figure 2-76).

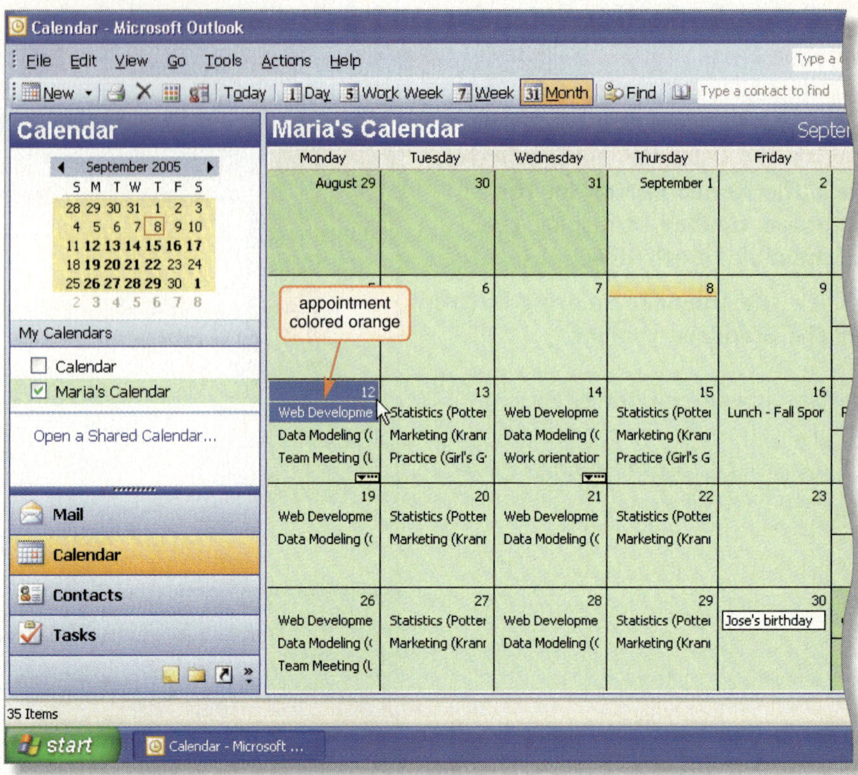

FIGURE 2-76

4

- **Click the Calendar Coloring button on the Standard toolbar.**

Outlook displays the Calendar Coloring menu (Figure 2-77). The color options are now available.

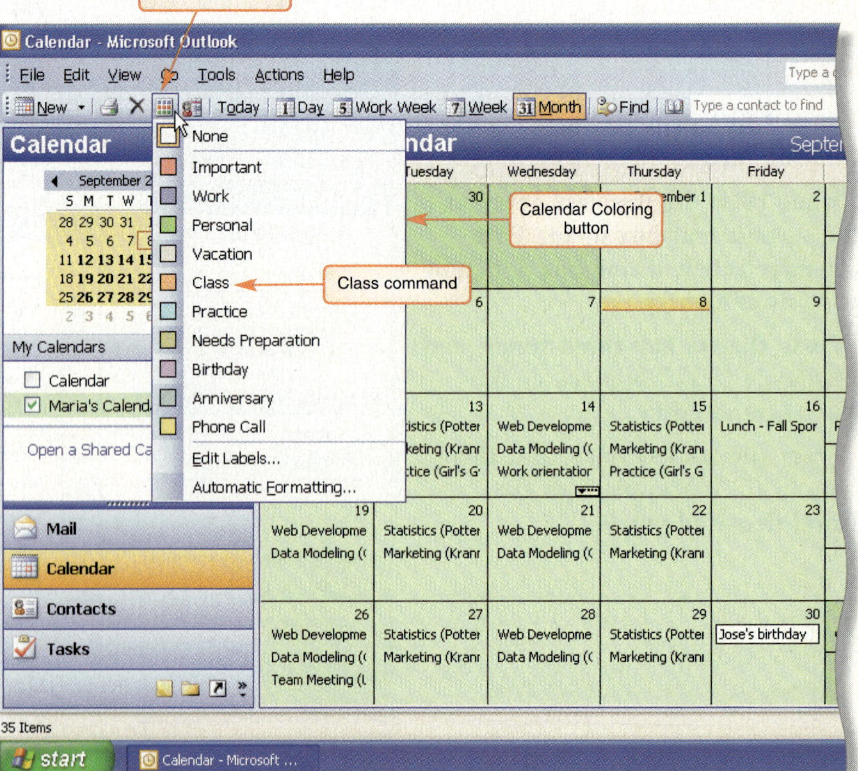

FIGURE 2-77

5

• **Click Class on the Calendar Coloring menu.**

The Maria's Calendar - Microsoft Outlook window is displayed with all occurrences of the Web Development appointment color coded orange (Figure 2-78).

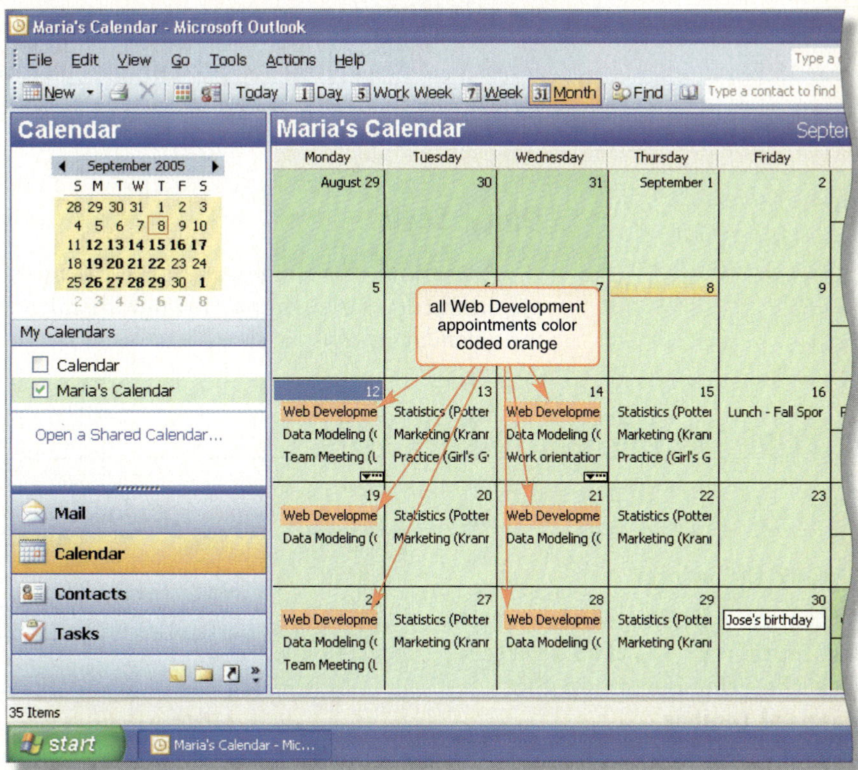

FIGURE 2-78

6

• **Repeat Steps 3 through 5 to color code the remaining recurring appointments in the calendar. Select Important as the label and color for the Team Meeting recurring appointment.**

The Maria's Calendar - Microsoft Outlook window is displayed with the recurring appointments color coded (Figure 2-79).

7

• **Using the methods described in Steps 1 through 5, color code the remaining items in the calendar.**

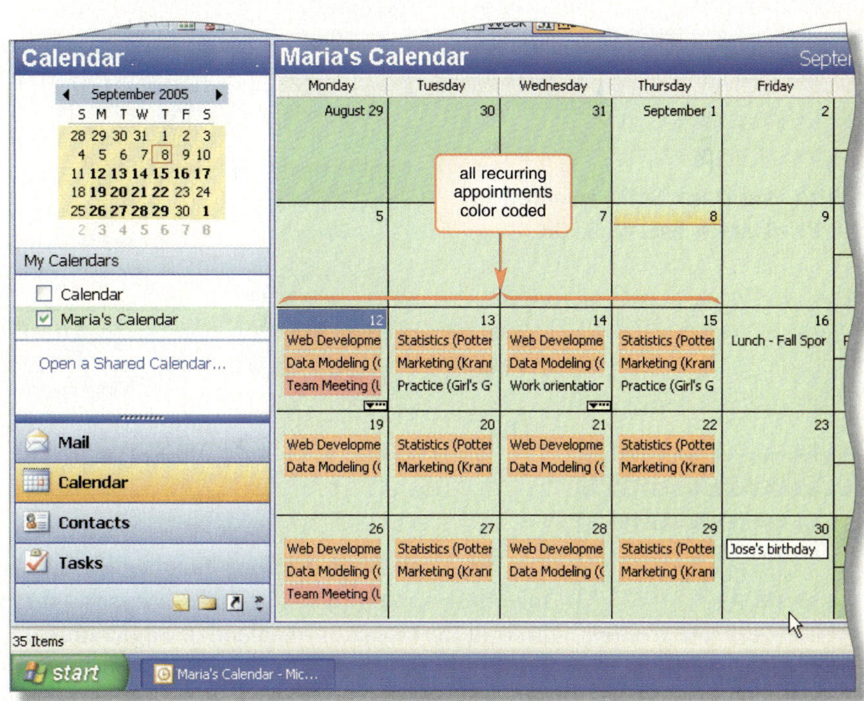

FIGURE 2-79

The calendar is now color coded. When the calendar is opened, the user will be able to differentiate between the various types of appointments.

Printing a Calendar

All or part of a calendar can be printed in a number of different layouts, or **print styles**. The following section describes how to print the calendar in Daily, Weekly, and Monthly Styles.

Daily Style

A printout of a single day of the calendar, called **Daily Style**, shows the day's appointments, tasks, and a two-month calendar. The steps below show how to print the calendar in Daily Style.

To Print the Calendar in Daily Style

1

- **Ready the printer.**
- **With the Calendar window active and September 12, 2005 selected, click the Print button on the Standard toolbar.**

Outlook displays the Print dialog box (Figure 2-80). Because the Appointment window was in Day view when the Print button was clicked, Daily Style is selected in the Print style list by default.

2

- **With the Daily Style selected in the Print style list, click OK.**

The daily schedule of appointments for Monday, September 12, 2005 prints on the printer. The printout should display as shown in Figure 2-1d on page OUT 67.

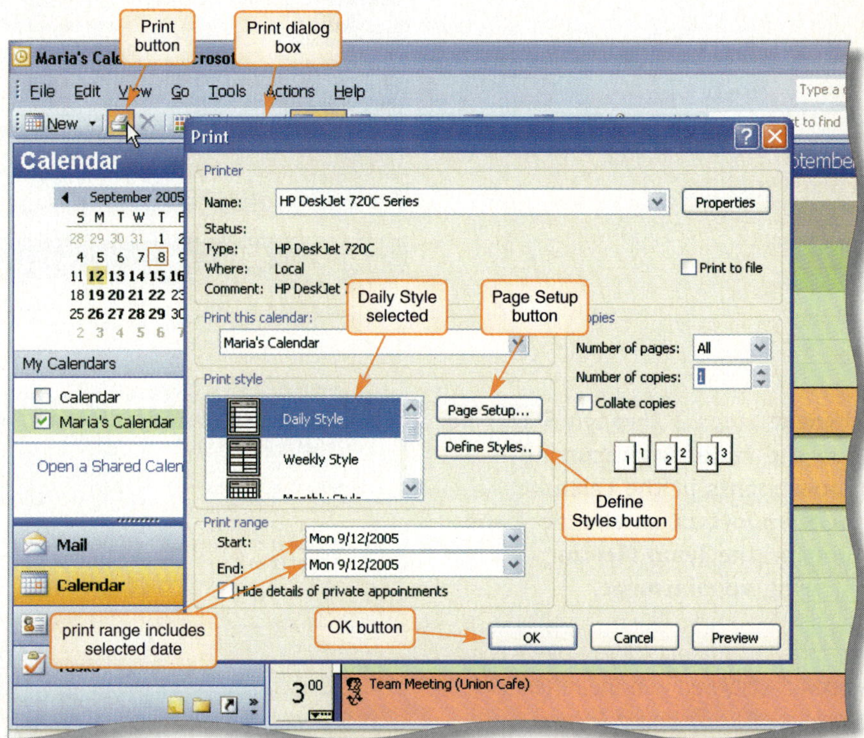

FIGURE 2-80

Other Ways

1. On File menu click Print
2. Press CTRL+P
3. In Voice Command mode, say "File, Print"

The Daily Style printout includes features from the Day view of the Calendar, including appointments, events, tasks, and notes. Dates with appointments print in bold in the two-month calendar. Page numbers and current system dates display at the bottom of the page. The Page Setup button in the Print dialog box allows style modifications to include or omit various features, including the TaskPad and the Notes area. Specific time ranges also can be printed rather than the default 7:00 AM to 6:00 PM.

Weekly Style

Printing a calendar in Weekly Style can be accomplished through the Print button on the Standard toolbar while viewing the calendar in Week view, or by selecting the Weekly Style in the Print dialog box, as explained in the following step.

To Print the Calendar in Weekly Style

1 **Ready the printer. Click the Print button on the Standard toolbar. Click Weekly Style in the Print style list and then click the OK button.**

The calendar for the week of Monday, September 12, 2005 through Sunday, September 18, 2005 prints on the printer as shown in Figure 2-1e on page OUT 67.

Monthly Style

The following step prints the calendar in Monthly Style.

To Print the Calendar in Monthly Style

1 **Ready the printer. Click the Print button on the Standard toolbar. Click Monthly Style in the Print Style list and then click the OK button.**

The calendar for the month of September prints on the printer as shown in Figure 2-1f on page OUT 67.

Selecting Monthly Style prints the calendar in landscape orientation. Some appointments are truncated due to the lack of space. The Monthly Style of printout is intended to show the larger picture rather than the detail of a Daily Style printout.

Another useful print style is **Tri-fold Style**, which prints a daily appointment list, a task list, and a calendar for the week. To save styles and setups, use the **Define Styles button** in the Print dialog box.

More About

Printing

The margins, page orientation, or paper size can be changed in the Page Setup dialog box. To access the Page Setup dialog box, click the Page Setup button in the Print dialog box (Figure 2-80).

Printing the Task List

To print only the task list, first open the Task folder. The following steps describe how to print the task list by itself.

To Print the Task List

1 **Click the Tasks button in the Navigation Pane to display the task list.**

2 **Click the Print button on the Standard toolbar. When the Print dialog box is displayed, click the OK button.**

The task list prints (Figure 2-81).

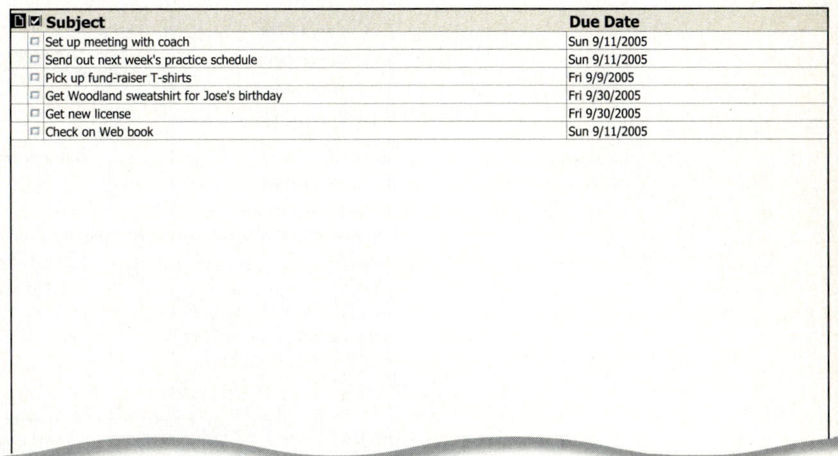

Subject	Due Date
Set up meeting with coach	Sun 9/11/2005
Send out next week's practice schedule	Sun 9/11/2005
Pick up fund-raiser T-shirts	Fri 9/9/2005
Get Woodland sweatshirt for Jose's birthday	Fri 9/30/2005
Get new license	Fri 9/30/2005
Check on Web book	Sun 9/11/2005

FIGURE 2-81

Archiving Items

Outlook has a built-in feature called **AutoArchive** that helps manage Outlook folders. AutoArchive is on by default and can be scheduled to run automatically. AutoArchive searches Outlook folders for items that are used infrequently, and items of which the content is no longer valid (a completed task, and old meeting, etc.). AutoArchive can be set up either to delete expired items permanently, and/or move old items to a special archive file. When AutoArchive is run for the first time, Outlook automatically creates this archive file. Outlook also creates an Archive Folders folder in the Folder List. The Archive Folders maintains the existing folder structure in the Folder List. AutoArchive does not delete any folders from a folder list even if they are empty. If you decide that you want to move archived items back to their original folders, you can use the Import Export wizard to move the items back to the original folder or any folder you specify.

Customizing AutoArchive

Outlook allows you to change how AutoArchive works. The default settings, or global settings, of AutoArchive are set to archive all folders except the Contacts folder. You also can have **per-folder settings** that will override the global settings. With per-folder settings you can have different archive settings for different folders. The following steps show how to change the default settings for AutoArchive.

To Change the Default Settings for AutoArchive

1

- **Click Tools on the menu bar, and then click Options.**
- **When the Options dialog box is displayed, click the Other tab.**

Outlook displays the Options dialog box (Figure 2-82).

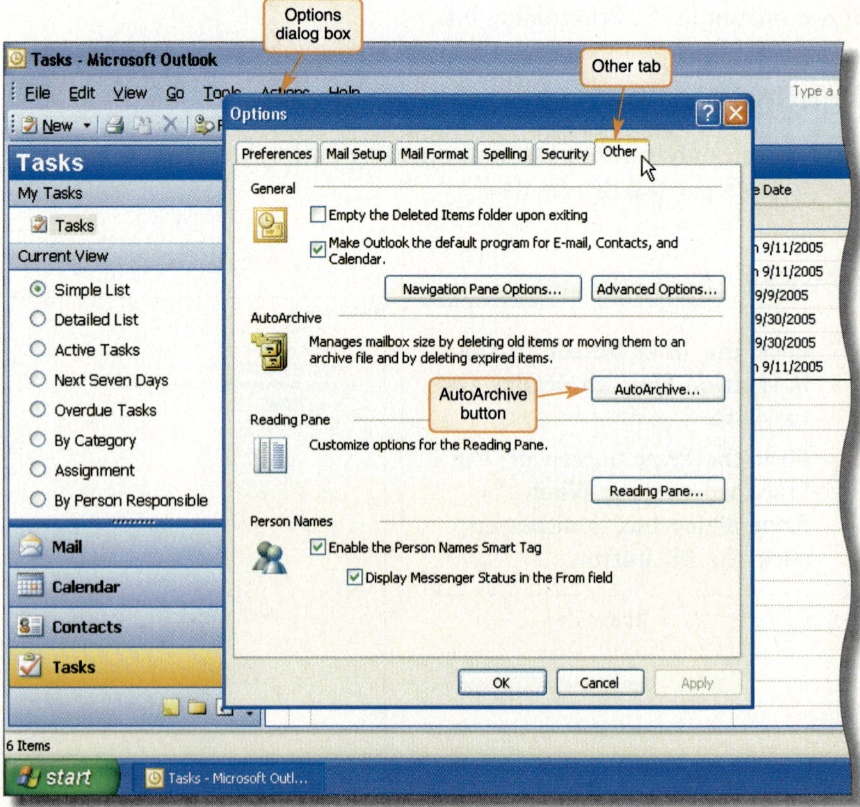

FIGURE 2-82

2

• **Click the AutoArchive button.**

Outlook displays the AutoArchive dialog box (Figure 2-83).

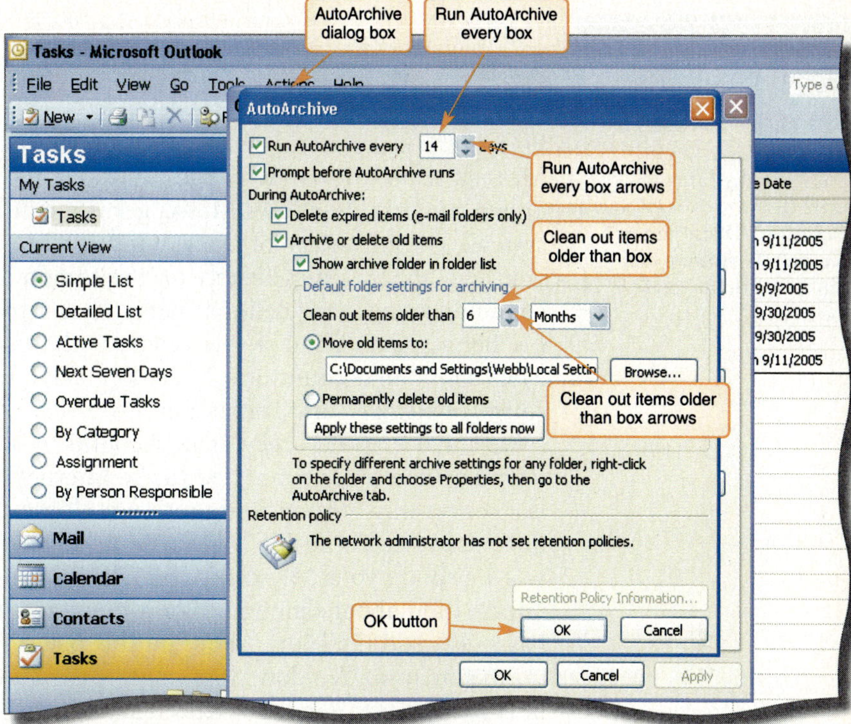

FIGURE 2-83

3

• **If necessary, click the Run AutoArchive every check box.**

• **Change the Run AutoArchive every box to 10 by clicking the down arrow.**

• **Change the Clean out items older than box to 8 by clicking the up arrow.**

The default settings have been changed and are ready to be applied (Figure 2-84).

4

• **Click the OK button in both open dialog boxes.**

Outlook closes the two dialog boxes. AutoArchive is now set to run every 10 days, and any items older than 8 months will be cleaned out.

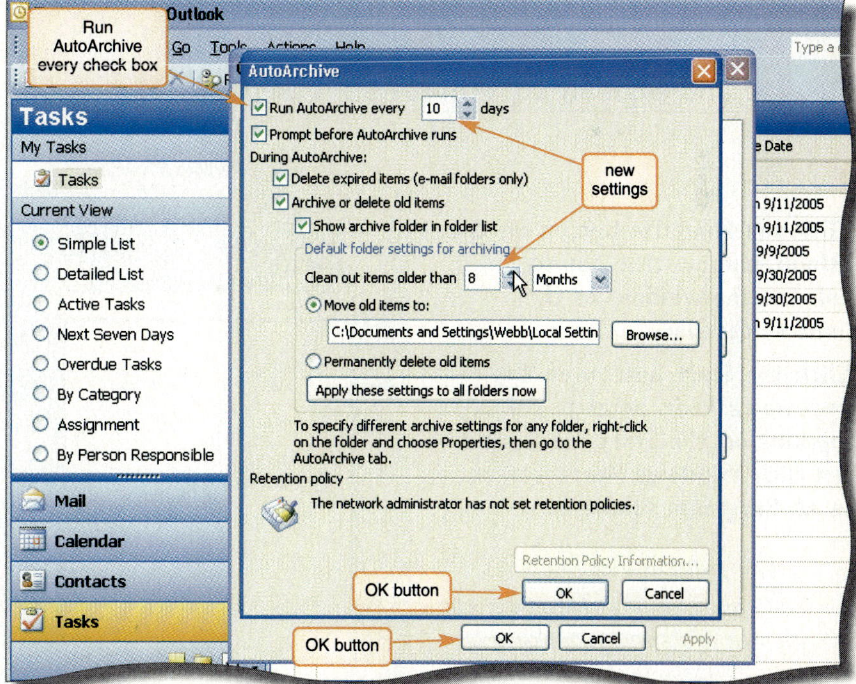

FIGURE 2-84

Other Ways

1. Press ALT+T, press O

The global settings have been changed so AutoArchive runs every 10 days and will clean out items older than 8 months.

To change the archive settings for an individual folder, right-click the folder, click Properties on the shortcut menu, and then click the AutoArchive tab.

More About

.NET Passports

.NET Passports are available for children ages 12 and under who live in the United States and use MSN Messenger. A Kids Passport requires the signature of a parent or guardian to use the service.

Using Windows Messenger and Instant Messaging with Outlook

One of the more useful communication tools available with Outlook is Windows Messenger. **Windows Messenger** allows you to communicate instantly with your online contacts. Windows Messenger is included with the Windows XP operating system. The advantage of using Windows Messenger over e-mail is that the message you send appears immediately on the computer of the person with whom you are communicating, provided that person has signed in to Windows Messenger.

Before using Window Messenger with Outlook, a contact first must have an MSN Hotmail account or a Microsoft .NET Passport and have Windows Messenger software installed and running on his or her computer. **MSN Hotmail** is a Microsoft service that provides free e-mail accounts to allow you to read your e-mail messages from any computer connected to the Internet. The **Microsoft .NET Passport** service is a secure way for you to sign in to multiple Web sites using just one user name and one password. As an MSN Hotmail user, your MSN Hotmail sign-in name and password also are your Microsoft .NET Passport user name and password. For more information about signing up for a free MSN Hotmail account or Microsoft .NET Passport, read the More About on this page.

Before using Windows Messenger with Outlook, you must enable instant messaging in Outlook, start Windows Messenger, and sign in to the .NET Messenger service using your sign-in name and password. The following steps illustrate how to sign in and enter the password for Maria Rosado. The following steps start Windows Messenger and sign in to the .NET Messenger Service using your sign-in name and password.

To Start and Sign In to Windows Messenger

1

- **Click the Minimize button on the Outlook window title bar to minimize the window to the Windows taskbar.**
- **Click the Start button on the Windows taskbar, point to All Programs on the Start menu, and then click Windows Messenger on the All Programs submenu.**

The Windows Messenger window is displayed (Figure 2-85). The Messenger icon and Click here to sign in link display in an area below the menu bar.

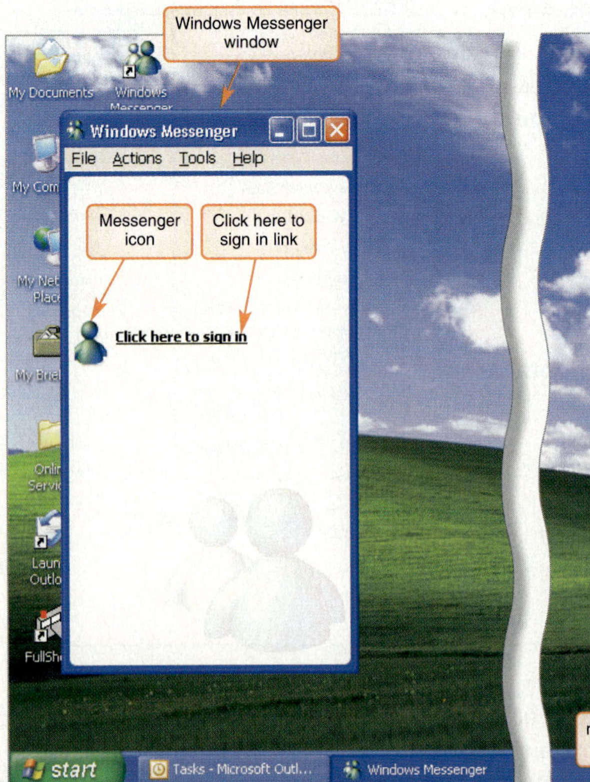

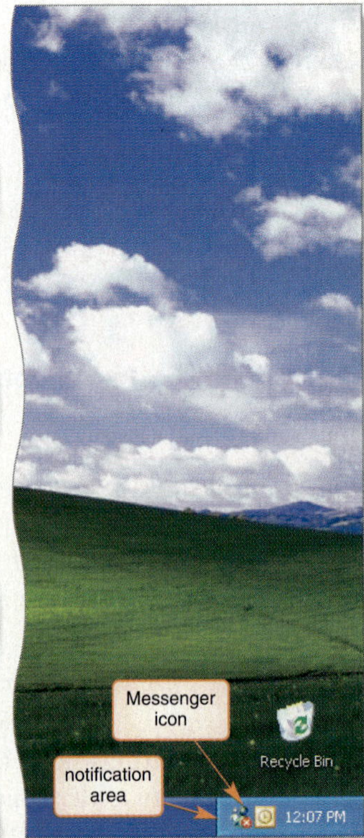

FIGURE 2-85

2

- **Click the Click here to sign in link.**
- **When the Connect to Messaging Services dialog box is displayed, click the .NET Messaging Service box, and then click the OK button.**
- **Type your e-mail address and password in the appropriate text boxes in the .NET Messenger Service dialog box.**

Messenger displays the .NET Messenger Service dialog box (Figure 2-86). The dialog box contains the E-mail address text box containing your e-mail address, Password text box containing your password, Sign me in automatically check box, Get a .NET Passport link, and Help link.

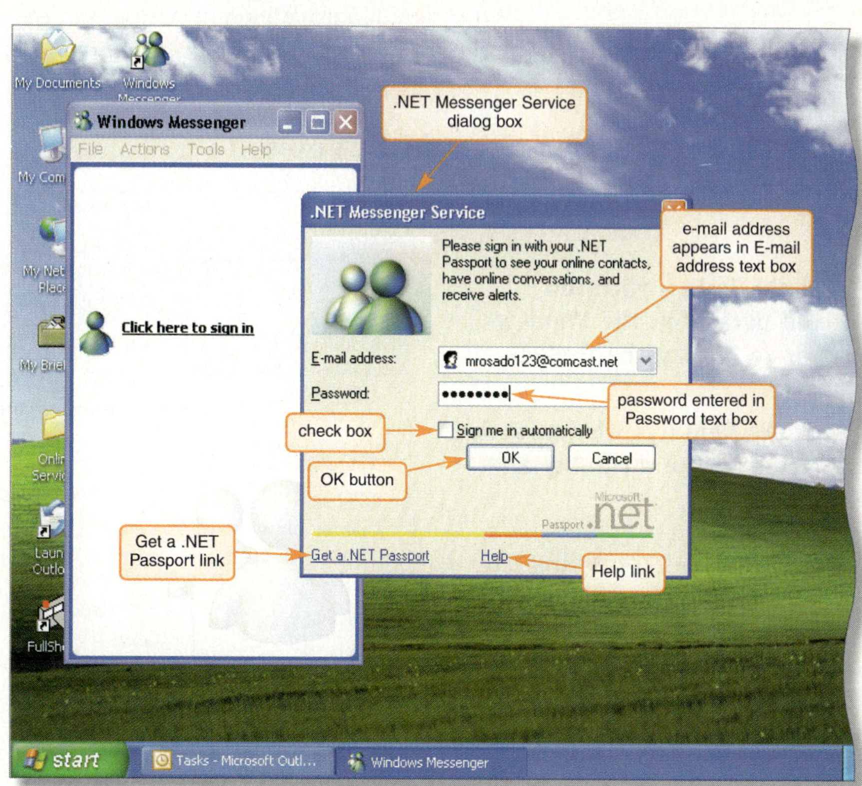

FIGURE 2-86

3

- **Click the OK button.**

The .NET Messenger Service dialog box closes, you are signed in to the .NET Messenger Service, and the contents of the Windows Messenger window change (Figure 2-87). The Windows Messenger window contains a menu bar, three tabs along the left side of the window, and the My Status sheet.

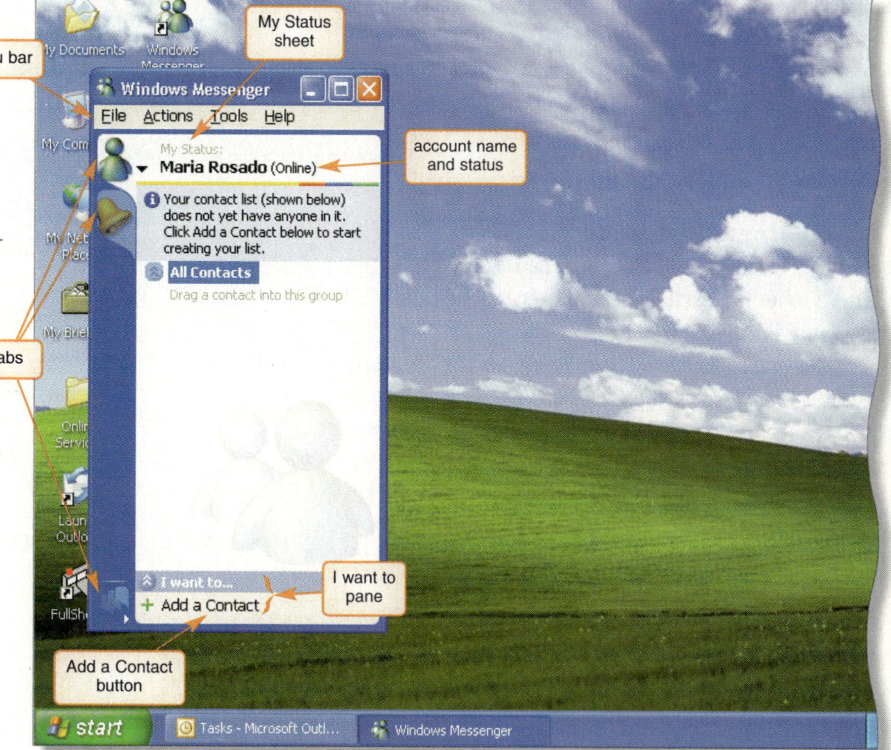

FIGURE 2-87

Other Ways

1. Double-click Messenger icon in status area

After signing into Windows Messenger, the next step is to enable instant messaging in Outlook. The steps below illustrate how to enable instant messaging in Outlook.

To Enable Instant Messaging in Outlook

1

- **Click the Tasks - Microsoft Outlook button on the Windows taskbar to display the Outlook window.**
- **With the Contacts window active, click Tools on the menu bar and click Options.**

Outlook displays the Options dialog box (Figure 2-88).

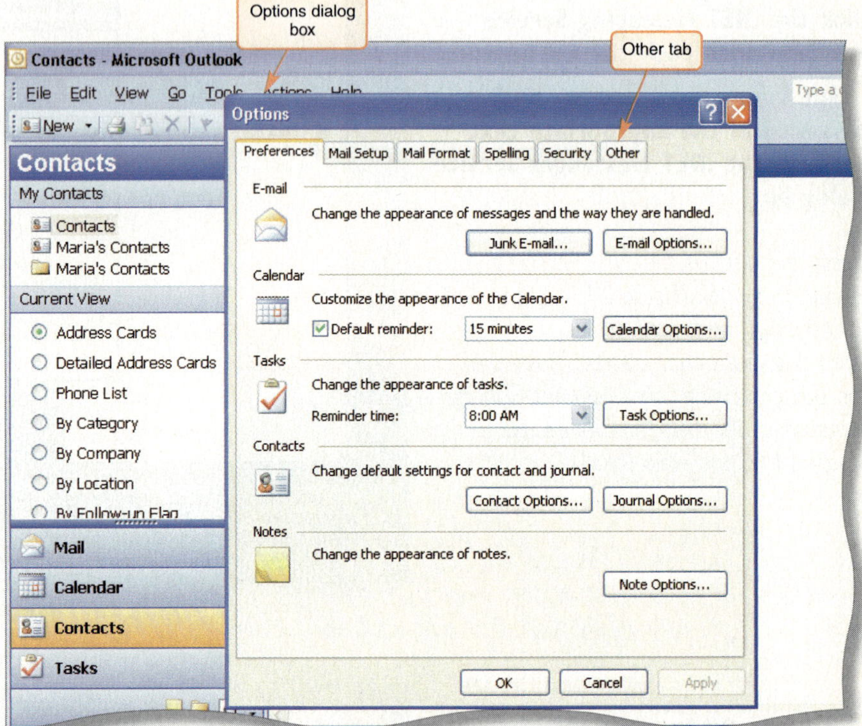

FIGURE 2-88

2

- **Click the Other tab.**
- **In the Other sheet, click the two boxes in the Person Names area to place a check mark in each box as shown in Figure 2-89.**

The Other sheet is activated. A check mark appears in the Enable the Person Names Smart Tag check box and the Display Messenger Status in the From field check box (Figure 2-89).

3

- **Click the OK button.**
- **Minimize the Outlook window.**

Outlook closes the Options dialog box and minimizes the Outlook window to the taskbar.

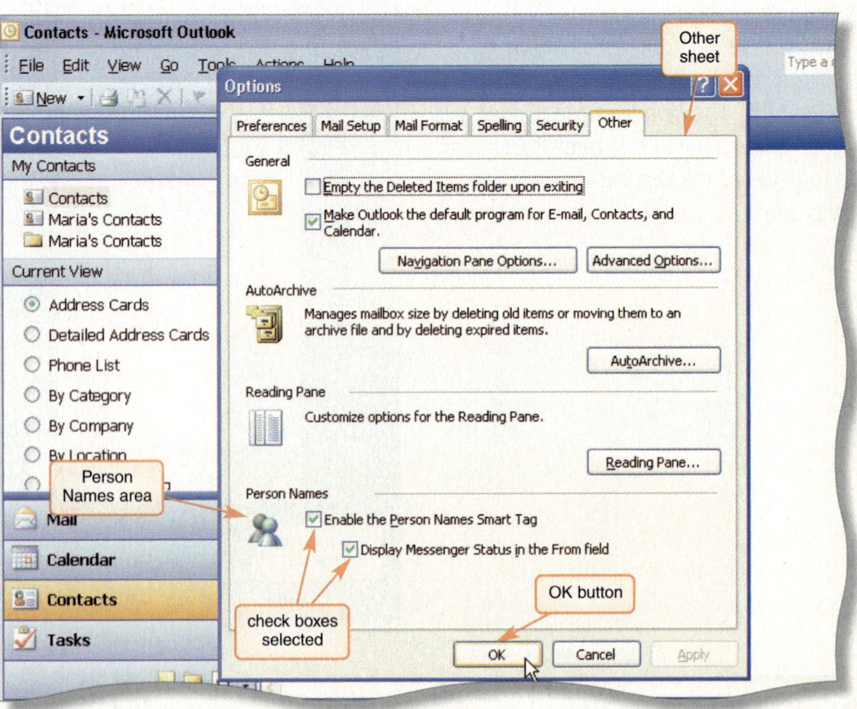

FIGURE 2-89

Clicking the Sign me in automatically check box (Figure 2-86 on page OUT 123) allows you to sign-in automatically each time you start Windows Messenger. Clicking the Get a .NET Passport link allows you to obtain a Microsoft .NET passport.

The My Status sheet in Figure 2-87 on page OUT 123 contains the Windows Messenger account name (Maria Rosado), account status (Online), and a message indicating that the contact list does not have anyone in it.

Adding a Contact to the Messenger Contact List

To use Windows Messenger with Outlook, contacts must be entered in the Messenger contact list, and the contact's Instant Messaging (IM) address must be entered in the Outlook contacts list. Table 2-6 contains the IM addresses for the contacts in the Maria's Contacts contact list.

Table 2-6 IM Addresses

CONTACT NAME	IM ADDRESS
Courtney Craig	ccraig101@hotmail.com
Jodi Dickens	jdickens123@hotmail.com
Susan Hadley	shadley101@hotmail.com
Chris Johnson	cjohnson123@hotmail.com
Marci Laver	mlaver123@hotmail.com
Hayley Miller	hmiller123@hotmail.com
Patti Sabol	psabol123@hotmail.com
Kendra Zimmerman	kzimm123@hotmail.com

After starting Windows Messenger, you can add a contact to the contact list if you know the e-mail address or Windows Messenger sign-in name of the contact. A contact must have an MSN Hotmail account or a Microsoft .NET Passport and have the Windows Messenger or MSN Messenger software installed on their computer. If you try to add a contact that does not meet these requirements, you are given the chance to send the contact an e-mail invitation that explains how to get a passport and download the Windows Messenger or MSN Messenger software.

To simplify the process of adding a contact to the contact list, Windows Messenger allows you to use the Add a Contact wizard. The **Add a Contact wizard** assists you in adding a contact to the contact list. The steps on the next page show how to add a contact to the Messenger contact list using the e-mail addresses listed in Table 2-6.

More About

Instant Messaging

For more information about instant messaging, visit the Outlook 2003 More About Web page (scsite.com/out2003/more) and then click Instant Messaging.

To Add a Contact to the Messenger Contact List

1

- **Click Add a Contact in the Windows Messenger window (Figure 2-87 on page OUT 123).**
- **When the Add a Contact dialog box is displayed, point to the Next button.**

Windows Messenger starts the Add a Contact wizard and displays the Add a Contact dialog box (Figure 2-90). The dialog box contains a question, two option buttons, a message, and the Next button. The By e-mail address or sign-in name option button is selected.

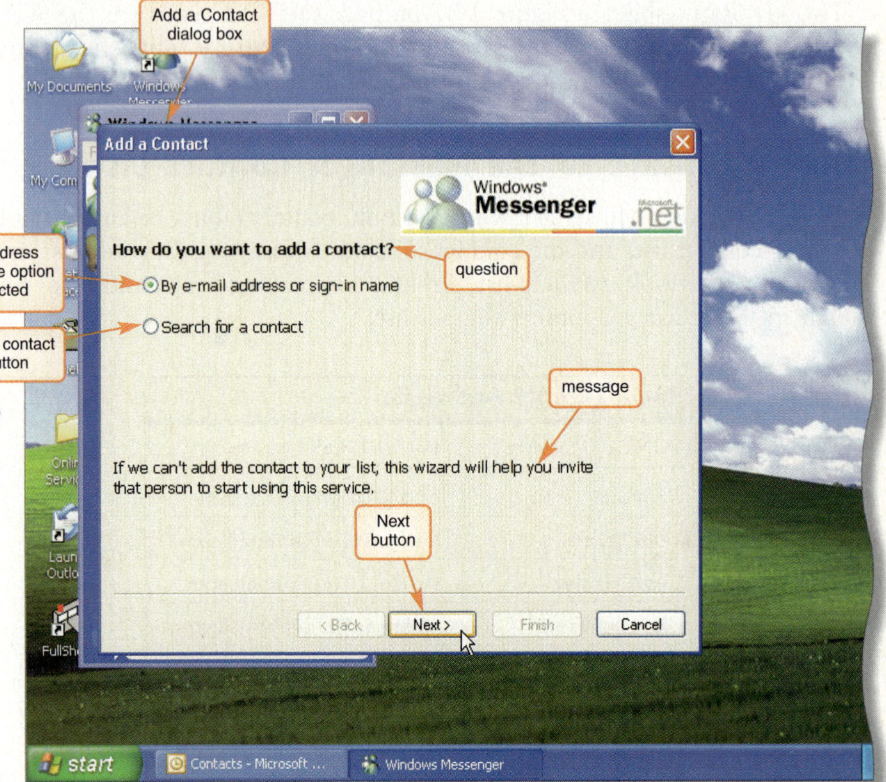

FIGURE 2-90

2

- **Click the Next button.**
- **Type** `ccraig101@hotmail.com` **in the text box.**

The contents of the Add a Contact dialog box change (Figure 2-91). The ccraig101@hotmail.com e-mail address appears in the text box.

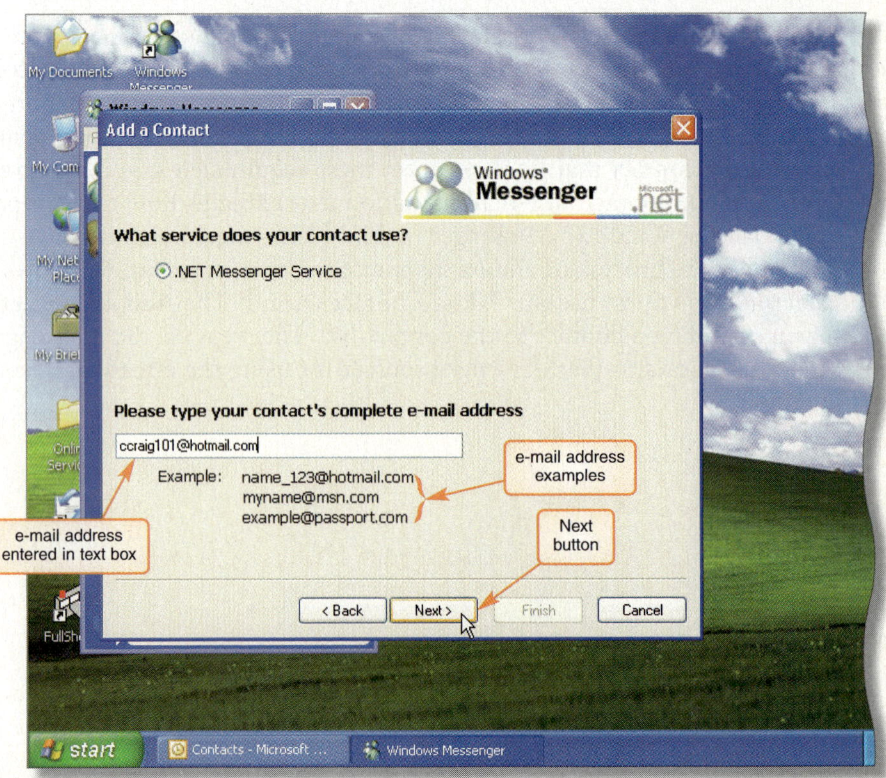

FIGURE 2-91

3

• **Click the Next button.**

The contents of the Add a Contact dialog box change (Figure 2-92). The dialog box contains a message indicating (Courtney Craig) was successfully added to the contact list.

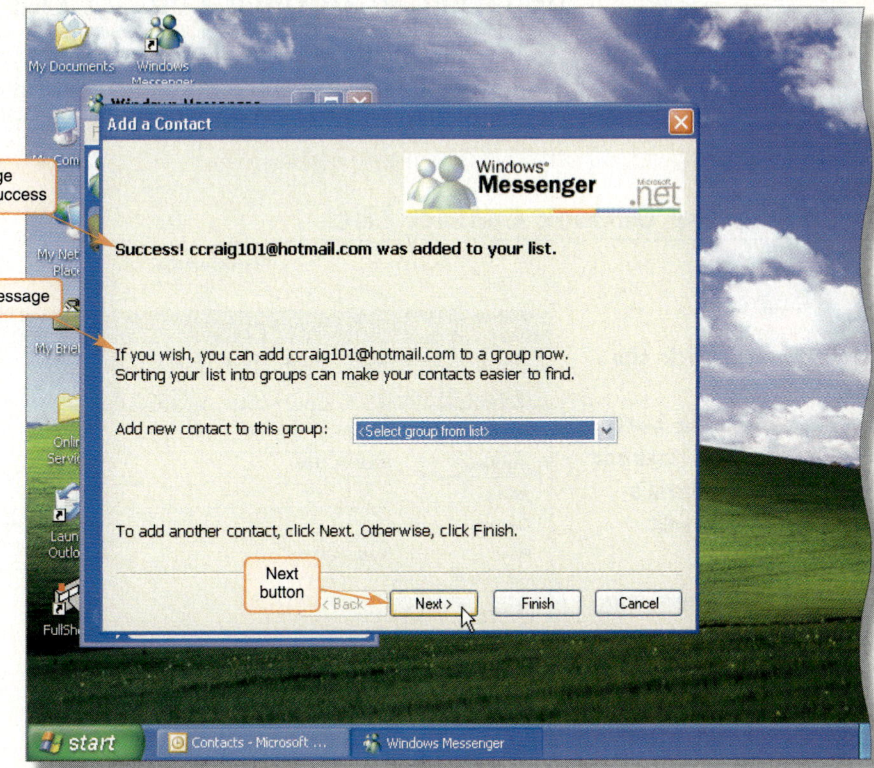

FIGURE 2-92

4

• **Click the Next button two times to advance to the first Add a Contact dialog box (see Figure 2-90).**

5

• **Repeat Steps 2 through 4 to enter the remaining contacts in Table 2-6 on page OUT 125.**

• **After you have added the Kendra Zimmerman entry, click Finish button in the dialog box with the You're done! Message.**

The Add a Contact wizard closes, the contacts from Table 2-6 are added to the contact list (Figure 2-93).

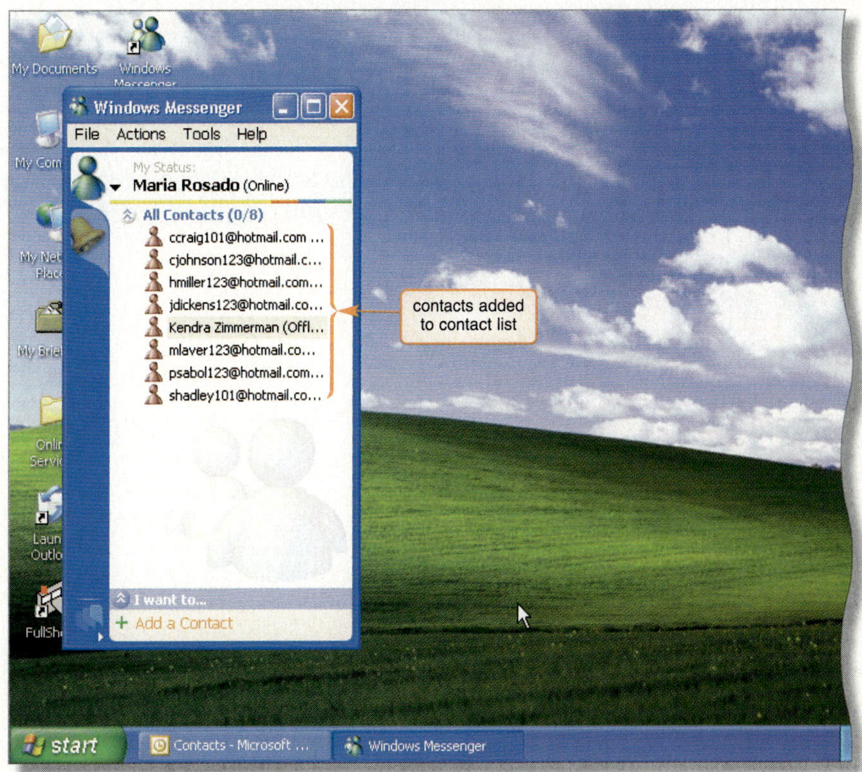

FIGURE 2-93

Updating an Outlook Contact List

To complete the process of setting up instant messaging with Outlook, the contact list must be updated with the IM addresses of the contacts listed in Table 2-6 on page OUT 125. The following steps show how to update the Maria's Contacts contact list.

To Update the Outlook Contact List

1

- **If necessary, click the Maria's Contacts - Microsoft Outlook button on the Windows taskbar to display the Maria's Contacts - Microsoft Outlook window.**
- **Double-click the Craig, Courtney entry to open the Courtney Craig - Contact window.**

Outlook opens the Courtney Craig - Contact window (Figure 2-94).

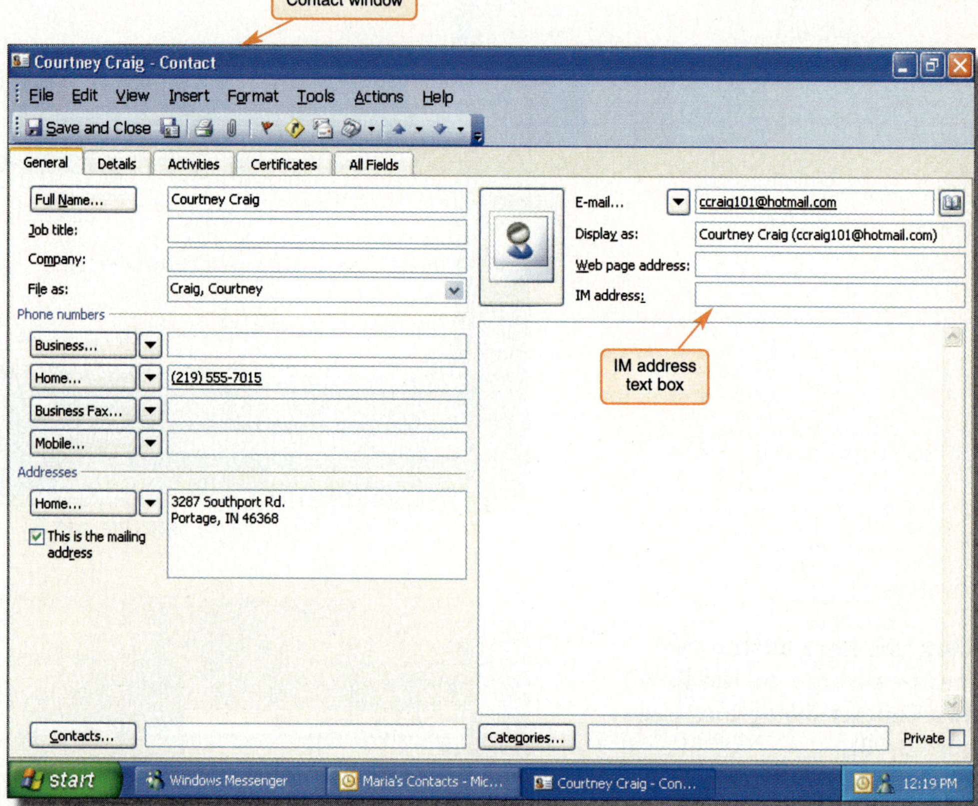

FIGURE 2-94

2

- **Click the IM address text box.**
- **Type** `ccraig101@hotmail.com` **as the IM address.**

The IM address for Courtney Craig is entered in the appropriate text box (Figure 2-95).

3

- **Click the Save and Close button on the Standard toolbar.**

4

- **Repeat Steps 1 through 3 to add the remaining IM addresses from Table 2-6 to the Maria's Contacts contact list.**

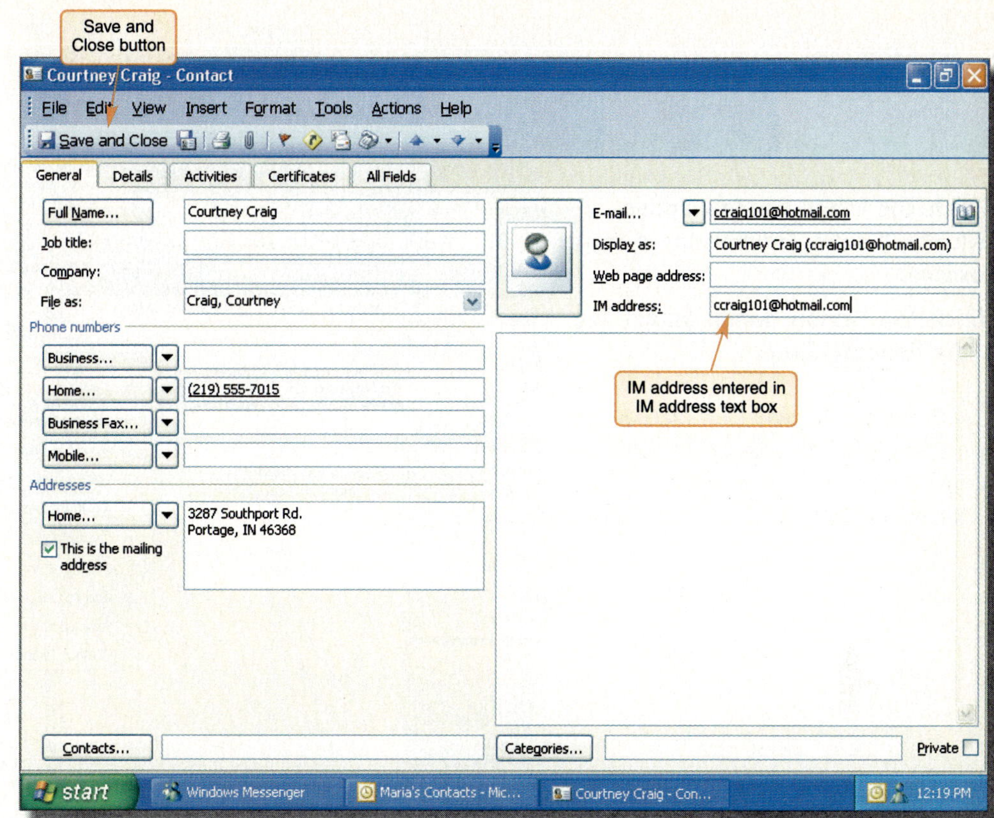

FIGURE 2-95

Communicating Using Outlook and Windows Messenger

To use Windows Messenger with Outlook, the person with whom you want to communicate must be online, and, for this project, must have an e-mail message in an Outlook folder. Using Outlook, when you open an e-mail message from an individual or view the message in the Reading Pane, the Person Names Smart Tag is shown next to the sender's name. Placing the mouse pointer over the Person Names Smart Tag will show a ScreenTip indicating the person's online status. The steps on the next page show how to send an instant message to someone you know is online.

Note: The steps that begin on the next page are for demonstration purposes only. Thus, if you are stepping through this project on a computer, then you must have someone with an Instant Messenger address send you an e-mail so it displays in the Inbox as shown in Figure 2-96 on the next page.

More About

The Person Name Smart Tag

The Person Name Smart Tag can indicate online status for any person whose instant messaging e-mail address you have added to your instant messaging contact list. The Person Name Smart Tag also shows online status for individuals using the Exchange Instant Messaging Service or SIP Communications Service, even if they are not in your contact list.

To Send an Instant Message

1

- **With the Inbox window active, click the Kendra Zimmerman e-mail message.**
- **Click the Person Names Smart Tag in the Reading Pane.**

Outlook displays the Smart Tag menu (Figure 2-96). The message at the top of the menu indicates that Kendra Zimmerman is online.

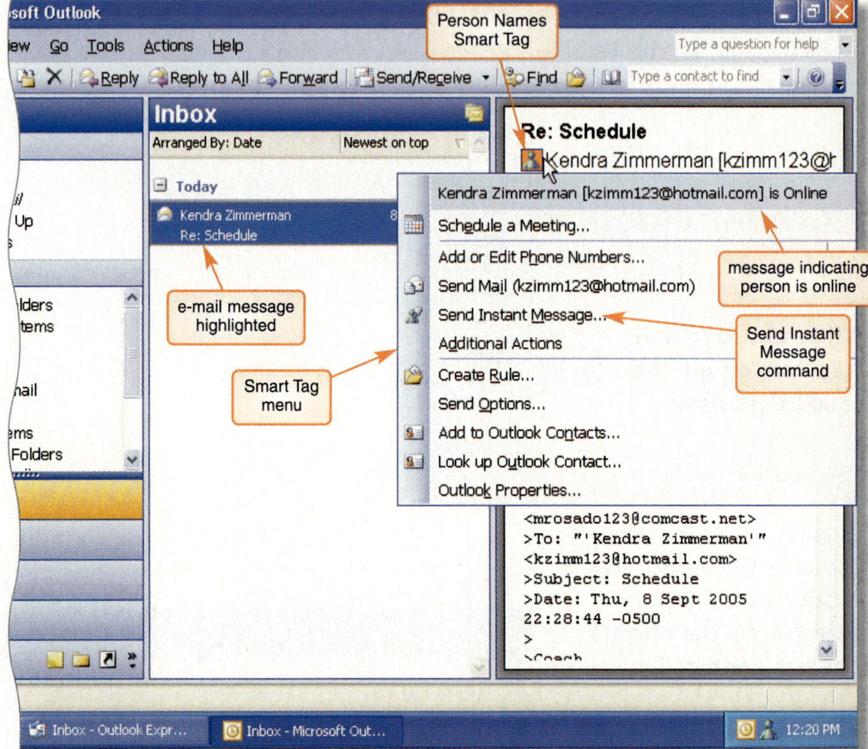

FIGURE 2-96

2

- **Click Send Instant Message on the Smart Tag menu.**

Outlook displays the Kendra Zimmerman - Conversation window (Figure 2-97).

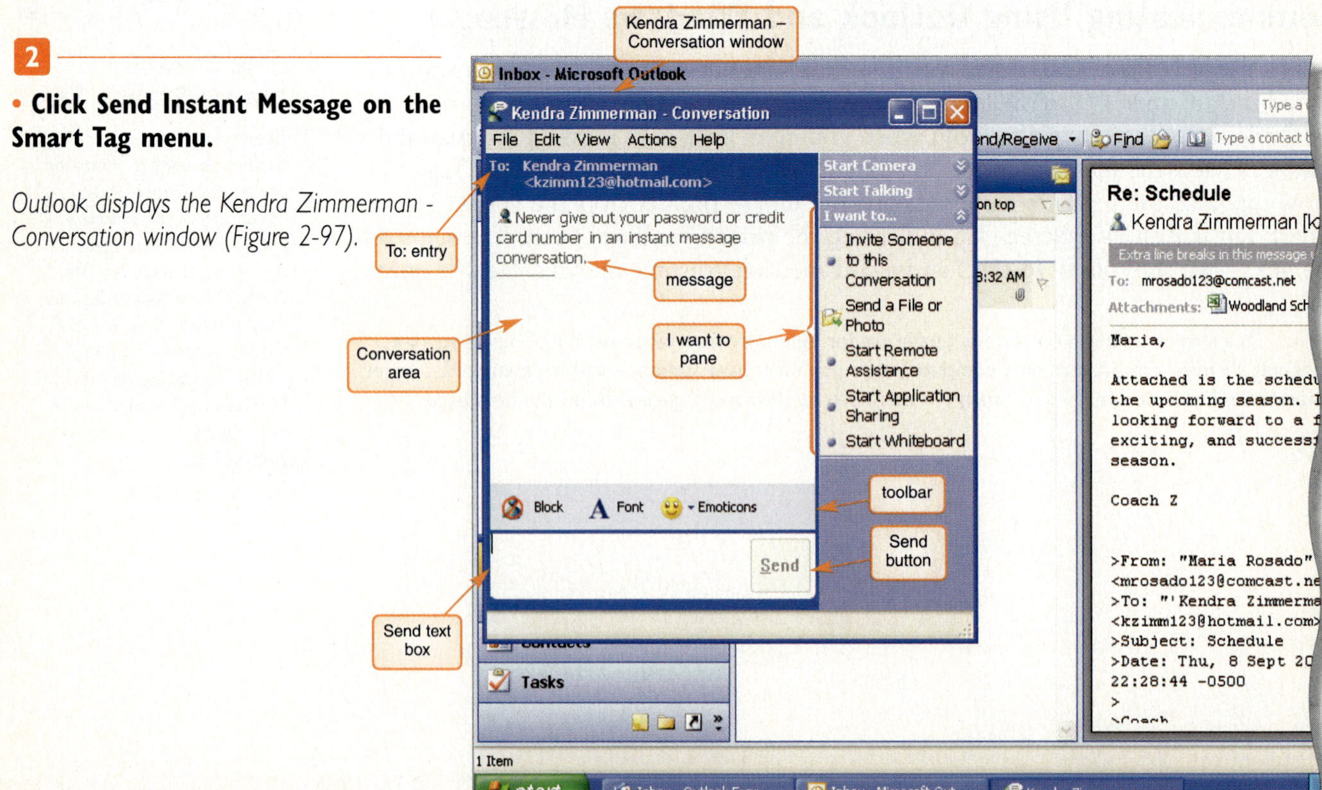

FIGURE 2-97

3

• **Type** Hey Coach, I'm glad I caught you online. I wanted to get together with you to discuss a new warm-up routine. **in the Send text box, and then click the Send button.**

Windows Messenger removes the message from the text box, displays the sender's name and message in the Conversation area, and displays the status of the receiver at the bottom of the Conversation window (Figure 2-98). The status indicates that Kendra Zimmerman is typing a message.

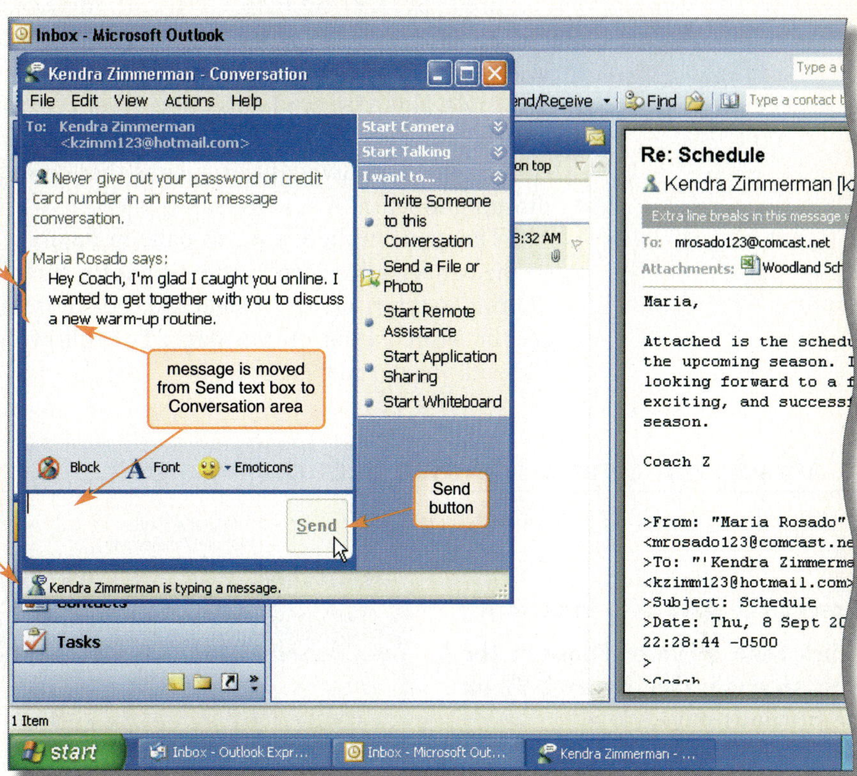

FIGURE 2-98

4

• **The receiver of the message (Kendra Zimmerman) types and sends a response.**

Windows Messenger displays the receiver's name (Kendra Zimmerman) and message in the Conversation area and changes the message at the bottom of the Conversation window to indicate the date and time the message was received (Figure 2-99).

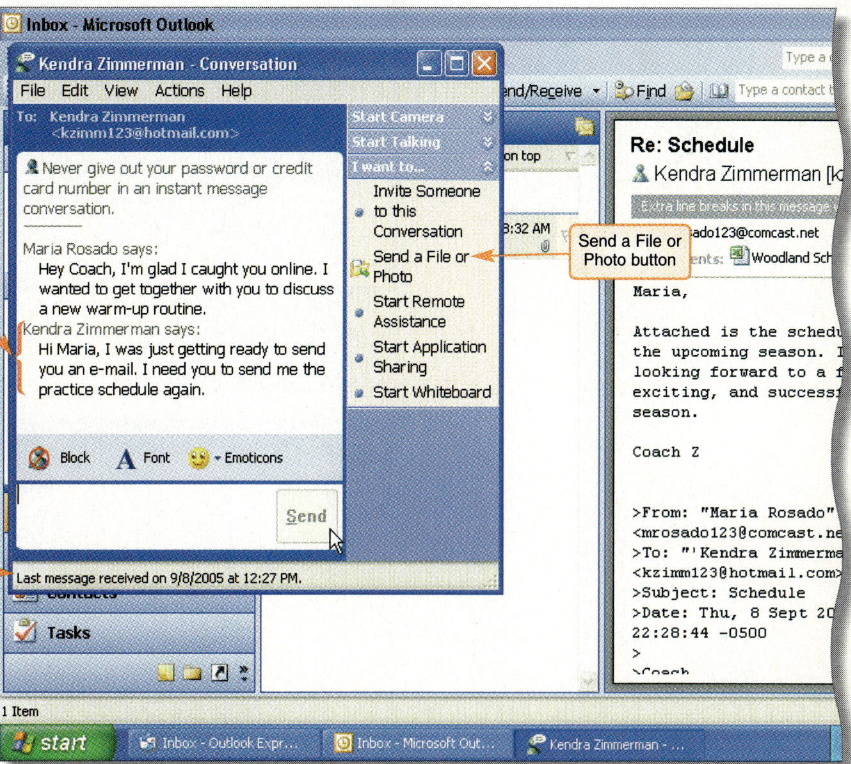

FIGURE 2-99

In Figure 2-97 on page OUT 130, three buttons appear on the toolbar. The Block button allows you to block a contact. The contact will not be able to see your name in his or her contact list or contact you. The Font button allows you to select a font, font style, font size, and apply special effects to the text in a message. The Emoticons button allows you to insert icons in a message that convey an emotion or a feeling. Among the icons available are icons that convey happiness, surprise, confusion, and disappointment.

The items in the I want to pane in Figure 2-97 allow you to invite another person to the conversation, send a file or photo, start Remote Assistance, start Application Sharing, or start using Whiteboard. For more information on the latter three items, see the More About on this page. The following steps show how to attach and send a file with instant messaging.

To Attach and Send a File with Instant Messaging

1

- **Insert the Data Disk in drive A.**
- **Click Send a File or Photo in the I want to pane. (See Figure 2-99 on the previous page.)**

Outlook displays the Send a File to Kendra Zimmerman dialog box (Figure 2-100).

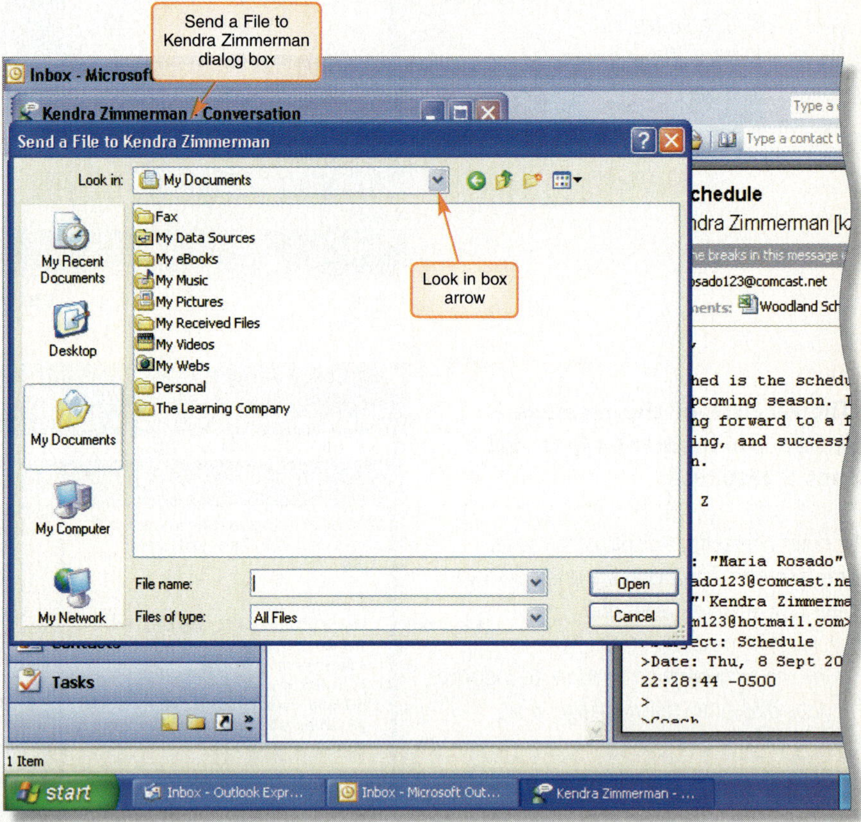

FIGURE 2-100

2

- **Click the Look in box arrow and then click 3½ Floppy (A:).**
- **Click Updated Practice Schedule in the Send a File to Kendra Zimmerman dialog box.**

The Updated Practice Schedule file is highlighted (Figure 2-101).

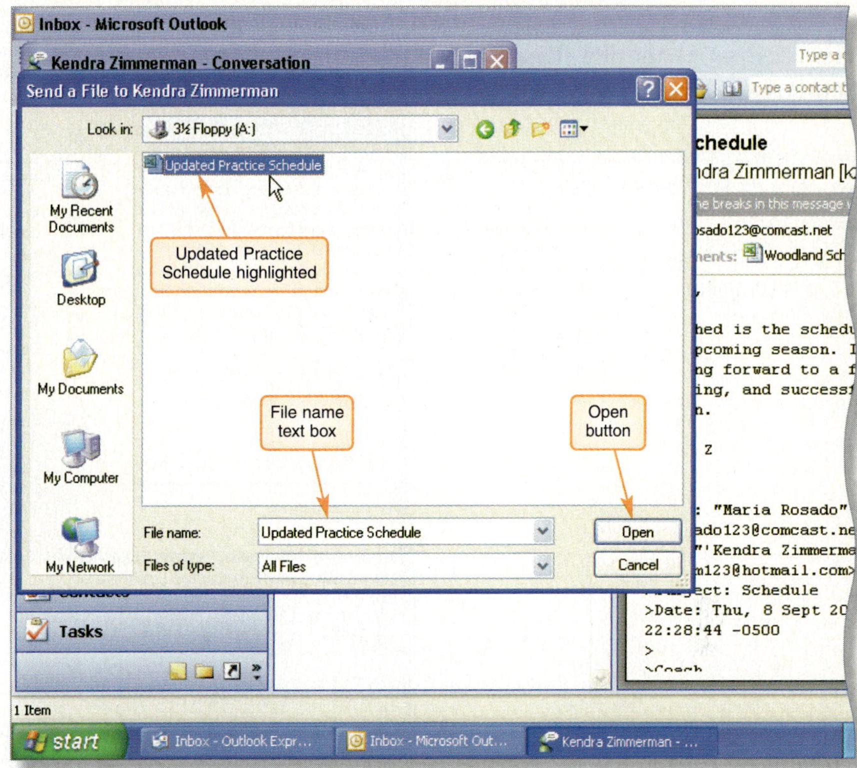

FIGURE 2-101

3

- **Click the Open button in the Send a File to Kendra Zimmerman dialog box.**

The Send a File to Kendra Zimmerman dialog box closes and a message appears in the Conversation area of the Kendra Zimmerman - Conversation window, indicating that you are waiting for the receiver to accept the file (Figure 2-102).

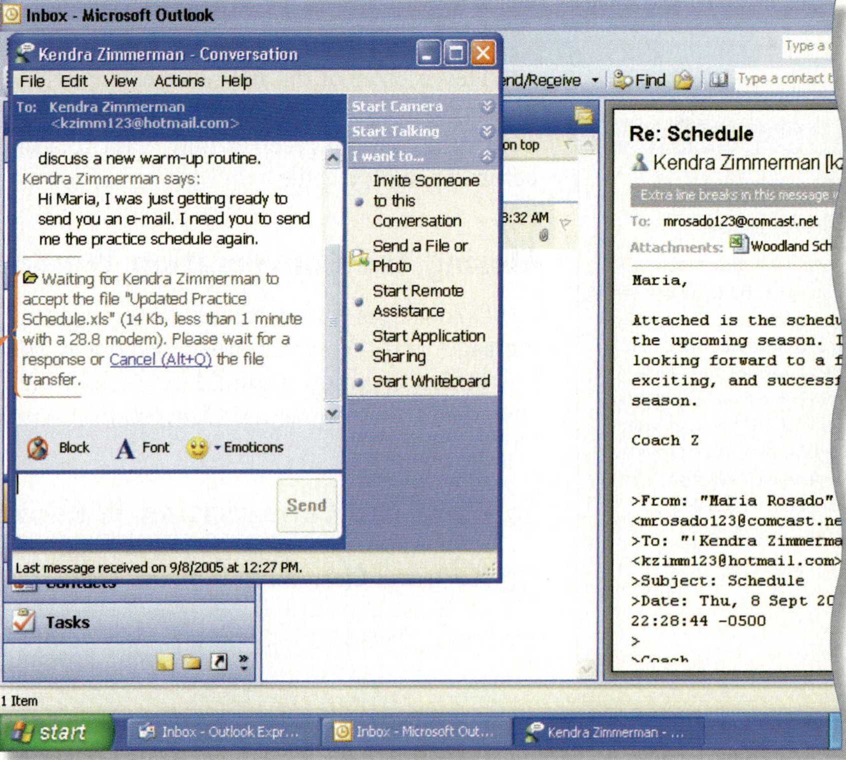

FIGURE 2-102

4

• **The receiver of the file (Kendra Zimmerman) has accepted the file.**

Two messages appear in the Conversation area: (1) indicating the file has been accepted, and (2) indicating the transfer of the file is complete (Figure 2-103).

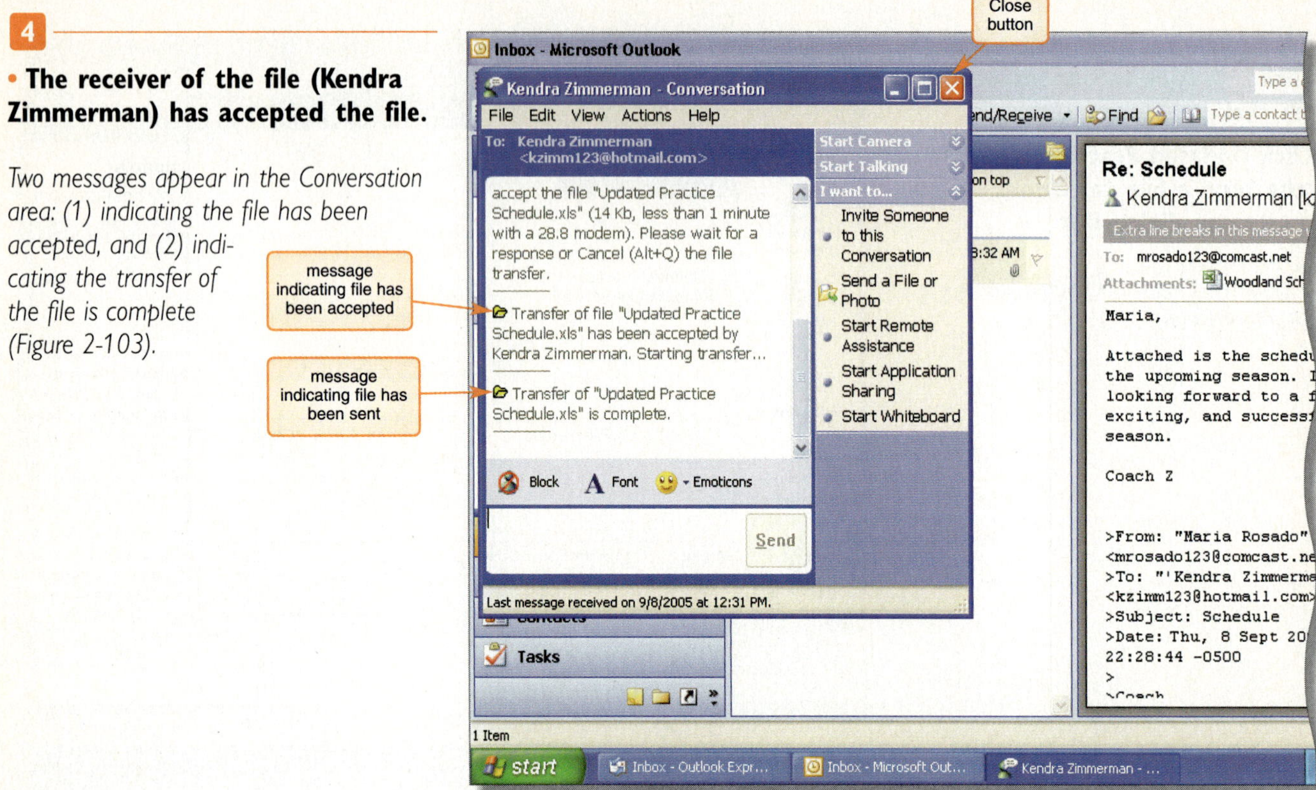

FIGURE 2-103

The receiver of the file receives a message indicating he or she has received the file successfully. The message contains a link with the location of the file along with a warning that the receiver may want to scan the file with a virus-scanning program before opening the file.

> *More About*
>
> **The Quick Reference**
>
> For a table that lists how to complete the tasks covered in this book using the mouse, menu, shortcut menu, and keyboard, see the Quick Reference Summary at the back of this book, or visit the Outlook 2003 Quick Reference Web page (scsite.com/out2003/qr).

Closing the Conversation Window

Participants can continue conversing in this manner, reading each others messages and then typing their responses. When the conversation is complete, the Conversation window should be closed to end the conversation. The following step describes how to close the Conversation window.

To Close the Conversation Window

1 **Click the Close button in the Conversation window.**

The Kendra Zimmerman - Conversation window closes.

Quitting Outlook

With the project complete, the final step is to close the Outlook program and return to the Windows desktop. The following step describes how to quit Outlook.

To Quit Outlook

1 **Click the Close button on the Outlook title bar.**

Outlook closes, and the Windows desktop is displayed.

More About

Microsoft Certification

Microsoft Office Certification provides an opportunity for you to obtain a valuable industry credential — proof that you have the Outlook skills required by employers. For more information, see Appendix E or visit the Outlook 2003 Certification Web page (scsite.com/out2003/cert).

Project Summary

In this project, you learned to use Outlook to create a personal schedule, organize meetings, and create a task list. You learned how to enter appointments, create recurring appointments, move appointments to new dates, schedule events, and view and print your calendar in different views and print styles. You created a task list, assigned tasks, and accepted a task assignment. You learned how to invite attendees and schedule resources for a meeting, accept a meeting request, and propose and change the time of a meeting. You also learned how to color code and label your calendar to make it easier to view. You created and edited notes. You exported your personal subfolder to a floppy disk and later imported subfolders for further updating. You also learned about using AutoArchive and customizing AutoArchive settings. Finally, you learned how to enable and sign into Windows Messenger through Outlook, added contacts to the contact list, and sent an instant message including sending a file through instant messaging.

What You Should Know

Having completed this project, you should be able to perform the tasks below. The tasks are listed in the same order they were presented in this project. For a list of buttons, menus, toolbars, and commands introduced in this project, see the Quick Reference Summary at the back of this book and refer to the Page Number column.

1. Start and Customize Outlook (OUT 68)
2. Create a Personal Folder (OUT 70)
3. Enter Appointments Using the Appointment Area (OUT 72)
4. Enter and Save Appointments Using the Appointment Window (OUT 74)
5. Enter Recurring Appointments (OUT 76)
6. Move to the Next Day in the Appointment Area and Enter the Remaining Recurring Appointments (OUT 78)
7. Enter Appointment Dates and Times Using Natural Language Phrases (OUT 79)
8. Enter the Remaining One-Time Appointments (OUT 81)
9. Delete an Appointment (OUT 82)
10. Move an Appointment to a New Time (OUT 84)
11. Move an Appointment to a New Date (OUT 85)
12. Move an Appointment to a New Month (OUT 86)
13. Create an Event (OUT 88)
14. Change to Work Week View (OUT 89)
15. Change to Week View (OUT 90)
16. Change to Month View (OUT 91)
17. Create a Task List (OUT 92)
18. Export Subfolders to a Floppy Disk (OUT 93)
19. Delete a Personal Subfolder (OUT 96)
20. Import a Subfolder (OUT 97)
21. Assign a Task (OUT 99)
22. Accept a Task Assignment (OUT 101)
23. Add or Delete Fields in a View (OUT 103)
24. Move Tasks to a New Personal Folder (OUT 103)
25. Invite Attendees to a Meeting (OUT 104)
26. Accept a Meeting Request (OUT 108)

27. Propose a New Meeting Time (OUT 109)
28. Change the Time of a Meeting and Send an Update (OUT 110)
29. Create and Edit a Note (OUT 110)
30. Set Work Week Options (OUT 112)
31. Color Code the Calendar and Edit Calendar Labels (OUT 115)
32. Print the Calendar in Daily Style (OUT 118)
33. Print the Calendar in Weekly Style (OUT 119)
34. Print the Calendar in Monthly Style (OUT 119)
35. Print the Task List (OUT 119)
36. Change the Default Settings for AutoArchive (OUT 120)
37. Start and Sign In to Windows Messenger (OUT 122)
38. Enable Instant Messaging in Outlook (OUT 124)
39. Add a Contact to the Messenger Contact List (OUT 126)
40. Update the Outlook Contact List (OUT 128)
41. Send an Instant Message (OUT 130)
42. Attach and Send a File with Instant Messaging (OUT 132)
43. Close the Conversation Window (OUT 134)
44. Quit Outlook (OUT 135)

Learn It Online

Instructions: To complete the Learn It Online exercises, start your browser, click the Address bar, and then enter the Web address scsite.com/out2003/learn. When the Outlook 2003 Learn It Online page is displayed, follow the instructions in the exercises below. Each exercise has instructions for printing your results, either for your own records or for submission to your instructor.

1 Project Reinforcement TF, MC, and SA

Below Outlook Project 2, click the Project Reinforcement link. Print the quiz by clicking Print on the File menu for each page. Answer each question.

2 Flash Cards

Below Outlook Project 2, click the Flash Cards link and read the instructions. Type 20 (or a number specified by your instructor) in the Number of playing cards text box, type your name in the Enter your Name text box, and then click the Flip Card button. When the flash card is displayed, read the question and then click the ANSWER box arrow to select an answer. Flip through Flash Cards. If your score is 15 (75%) correct or greater, click Print on the File menu to print your results. If your score is less than 15 (75%) correct, then redo this exercise by clicking the Replay button.

3 Practice Test

Below Outlook Project 2, click the Practice Test link. Answer each question, enter your first and last name at the bottom of the page, and then click the Grade Test button. When the graded practice test is displayed on your screen, click Print on the File menu to print a hard copy. Continue to take practice tests until you score 80% or better.

4 Who Wants To Be a Computer Genius?

Below Outlook Project 2, click the Computer Genius link. Read the instructions, enter your first and last name at the bottom of the page, and then click the PLAY button. When your score is displayed, click the PRINT RESULTS link to print a hard copy.

5 Wheel of Terms

Below Outlook Project 2, click the Wheel of Terms link. Read the instructions, and then enter your first and last name and your school name. Click the PLAY button. When your score is displayed, right-click the score and then click Print on the shortcut menu to print a hard copy.

6 Crossword Puzzle Challenge

Below Outlook Project 2, click the Crossword Puzzle Challenge link. Read the instructions, and then enter your first and last name. Click the SUBMIT button. Work the crossword puzzle. When you are finished, click the Submit button. When the crossword puzzle is redisplayed, click the Print Puzzle button to print a hard copy.

7 Tips and Tricks

Below Outlook Project 2, click the Tips and Tricks link. Click a topic that pertains to Project 2. Right-click the information and then click Print on the shortcut menu. Construct a brief example of what the information relates to in Outlook to confirm you understand how to use the tip or trick.

8 Newsgroups

Below Outlook Project 2, click the Newsgroups link. Click a topic that pertains to Project 2. Print three comments.

9 Expanding Your Horizons

Below Outlook Project 2, click the Articles for Microsoft Outlook link. Click a topic that pertains to Project 2. Print the information. Construct a brief example of what the information relates to in Outlook to confirm you understand the contents of the article.

10 Search Sleuth

Below Outlook Project 2, click the Search Sleuth link. To search for a term that pertains to this project, select a term below the Project 2 title and then use the Google search engine at google.com (or any major search engine) to display and print two Web pages that present information on the term.

11 Outlook Online Training

Below Outlook Project 2, click the Outlook Online Training link. When your browser displays the Microsoft Office Online Web page, click the Outlook link. Click one of the Outlook courses that covers one or more of the objectives listed at the beginning of the project on page OUT 66. Print the first page of the course before stepping through it.

12 Office Marketplace

Below Outlook Project 2, click the Office Marketplace link. When your browser displays the Microsoft Office Online Web page, click the Office Marketplace link. Click a topic that relates to Outlook. Print the first page.

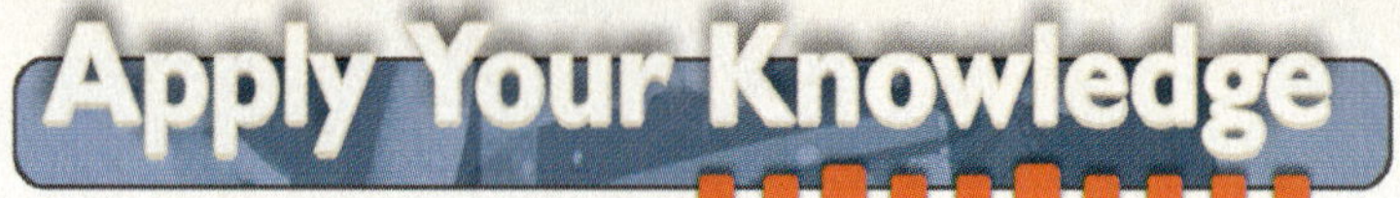

1 Creating a Schedule

Instructions Part 1: Start Outlook. Create a Calendar folder using your name as the name of the new folder. Create a schedule using the information in Table 2-7. Use the Options command on the Tools menu to set up the calendar for a six-day work week with hours from 7:00 AM to 6:00 PM. Color code the schedule using the following labels: School, Work, and Personal. This calendar is for the fall semester that begins Monday, August 22, 2005, and ends Friday, December 16, 2005. When the calendar is complete, print the calendar in Month view and submit to your instructor.

Table 2-7 Appointment Information

APPOINTMENT	LABEL	DAYS	TIME	OCCURRENCES
Operating Systems	School	M, W	7:30 am - 9:00 am	30
Supervision	School	M, W	11:30 am - 1:00 pm	30
Accounting	School	T, Th	7:00 pm - 8:30 pm	30
Work (Open)	Work	T, Th, Sa	7:00 am - 3:30 pm	August 23 August 25 August 27
Dentist Appointment	Personal	W	4:00 pm - 5:00 pm	August 24
Work (Close)	Work	T, Th, Sa	9:00 am - 6:00 pm	August 30 September 1 September 3
Labor Day 5k Run	Personal	S	8:30 am - 10:00 am	September 4
Accounting Study Lab	School	W	3:00 pm - 4:00 pm	Every other Wednesday for 15 occurrences

Instructions Part 2: Use the Microsoft Office Outlook Help system to learn more about the Calendar Options dialog box shown in Figure 2-70 on page OUT 113. Write a report summarizing all the options available in the Calendar Options dialog box.

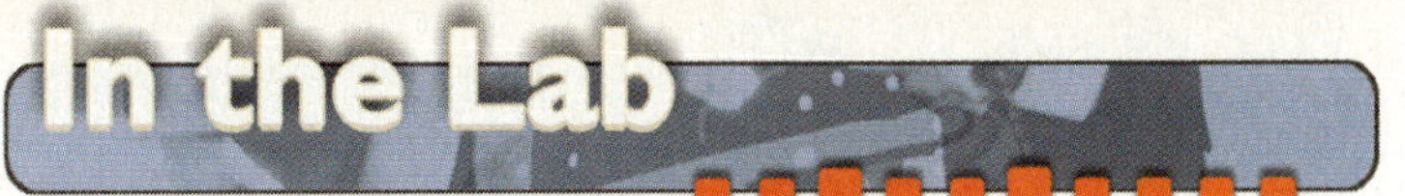

1 Planning a Meeting

Problem: You are the project manager for a large government project. The project involves working with individuals from county, state, and federal offices. With the project start date approaching, you need to organize a meeting to get all the required signatures on your contract.

Instructions Part 1: Perform the following tasks.

1. Import the Lab 2-1 Contacts folder into Outlook (Figure 2-104).

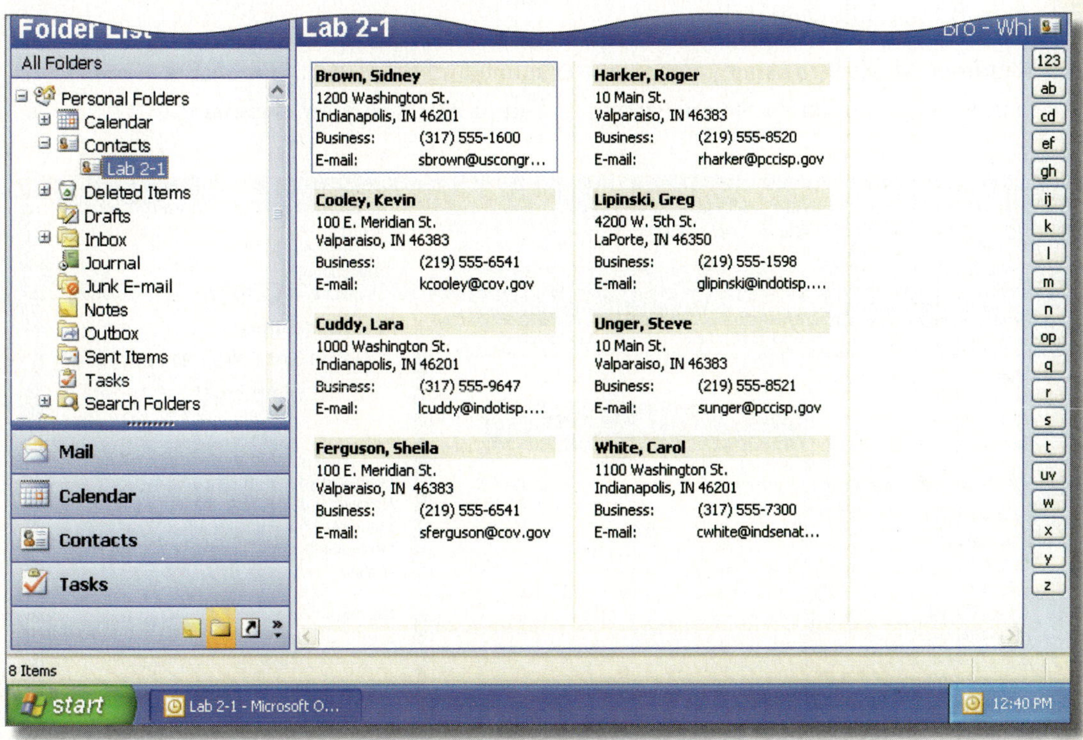

FIGURE 2-104

2. Organize a meeting for Wednesday, November 9, 2005 from 9:00 a.m. until noon inviting only those contacts that hold a county, state, or federal office.
3. Submit a printout of the meeting to your instructor.
4. Change the date and time of the meeting from November 9, 2005 to November 11, 2005 from 1:00 p.m. until 3:00 p.m.
5. Send out an updated meeting invitation.
6. Submit a printout of the updated meeting to your instructor.
7. You have just found out that your presence is required elsewhere on the meeting date. Cancel the meeting using the Cancel Meeting command on the Actions menu.

Instructions Part 2: Use the Outlook Help system to obtain information on scheduling resources. Write a one-page report describing how scheduling resources works. If your instructor has set up resources for you to access, schedule a room and an audio visual device for the meeting described in Part 1.

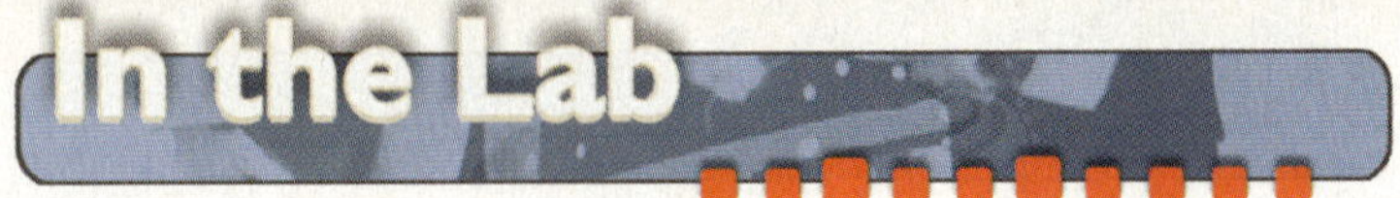

2 Using Windows Messenger with Outlook

Problem: You are preparing for an important meeting and need a file updated by a coworker in another department. You do not have that individual's information in your contact list, however. You leave a message on her voice mail about the file and she e-mails you requesting that you send the file to her. Because you have only a short time before the meeting begins, you decide to use Windows Messenger with Outlook to communicate and send the file to your coworker. *Note:* To use instant messaging, you should complete this exercise with a classmate.

Instructions: Perform the following tasks.

1. Sign in to Windows Messenger using your own user name and password.
2. Send an e-mail message similar to the one shown in Figure 2-105 to your classmate.

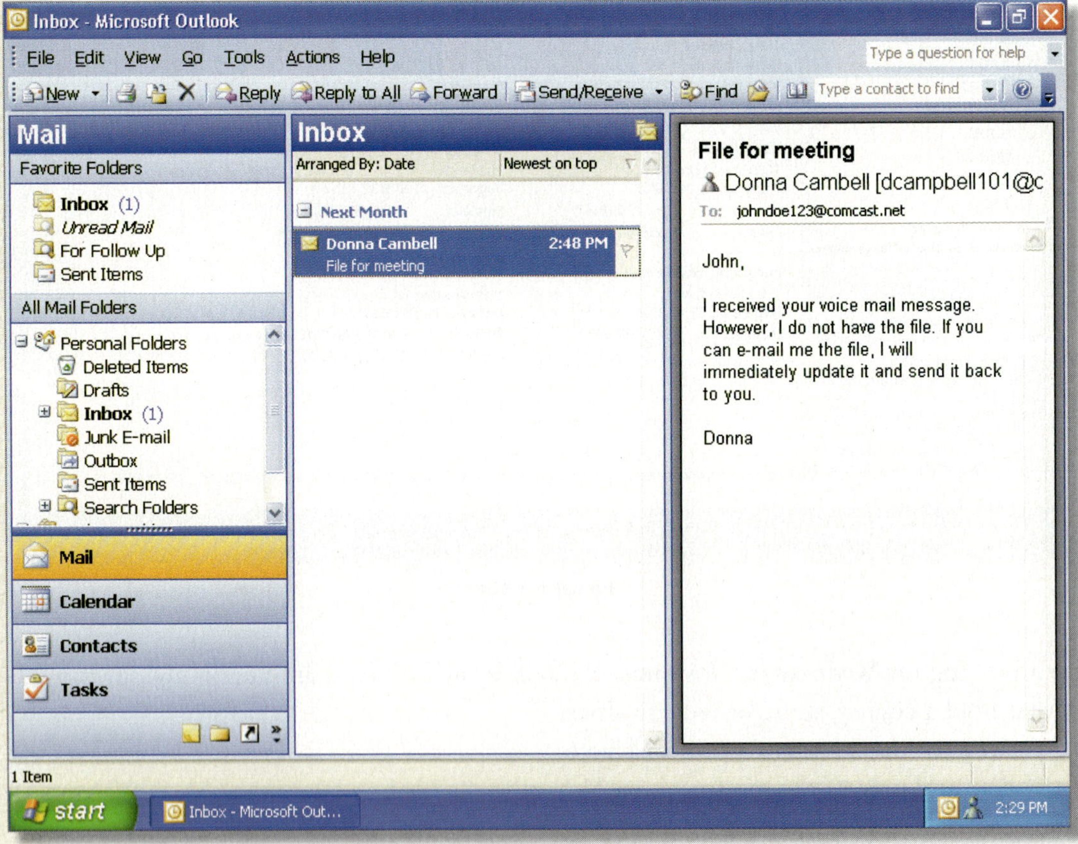

FIGURE 2-105

3. Add the sender to your Windows Messenger and Outlook contact lists. Be sure to include her instant message address in Outlook.
4. Insert the Data Disk into drive A on your computer.
5. Send an instant message indicating that you will send the file using Windows Messenger.
6. Send the Quarterly Report file from the Data Disk to the sender.

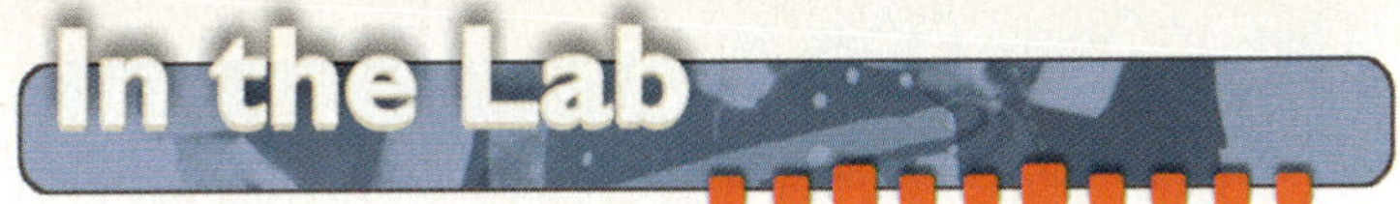

7. When you receive the file, open the file and submit a printout with your name and the name of the person you completed the exercise with to your instructor.
8. Sign out of Windows Messenger and close all open windows.

3 Creating a Calendar and a Task List

Problem: You are the owner of a small hardware store. Your company has experienced rapid growth during the last several months, and with spring approaching, you need to change to regular from seasonal stock. As the owner, you also have administrative duties to perform, such as staff meetings, payroll, advertising, and sales campaigns. To make your schedule even more hectic, you coach your child's spring baseball team on Wednesday nights from 5:00 p.m. to 6:30 p.m., and Saturday's from 12:00 p.m. to 2:00 p.m. at Community Little League Fields. You need to create a schedule of appointments as well as a task list to help you keep track of your various jobs and responsibilities each day.

Instructions Part 1: Perform the following tasks.

1. Create a personal Calendar subfolder named A-1 Hardware.
2. Change the start time of the calendar to 7:00 am.
3. Enter the appointments in the calendar, using the information listed in Table 2-8.

Table 2-8 Appointment Information

DESCRIPTION	DATE	TIME
Staff meeting	Every Monday from March 6, 2006 - April 24, 2006	7:00 am - 8:00 am
Meeting to prepare Winter Closeout Sale	March 1, 2006	8:30 am - 10:30 am
Enter payroll	Every Thursday	4:00 pm - 5:00 pm
Ryan's birthday	March 21, 2006	
Conference call with Karen and Bob	March 14, 2006	9:00 am - 10:00 am
Meet with plumbing supplier	March 16, 2006	1:00 pm - 2:00 pm
Lunch with Ruth	March 29, 2006	12:00 pm - 1:00 pm

4. Create a task list containing the following tasks:
   a. Call Kyle to confirm plumbing supplier's visit.
   b. Schedule meeting to discuss spring and summer sales goals.
   c. Call to check lawn fertilizer delivery.
   d. Clear out snow blowers to make room for lawn mowers.
   e. Replace snow shovels with lawn and garden tools.
5. Print the calendar for the month of March and submit to your instructor.

(continued)

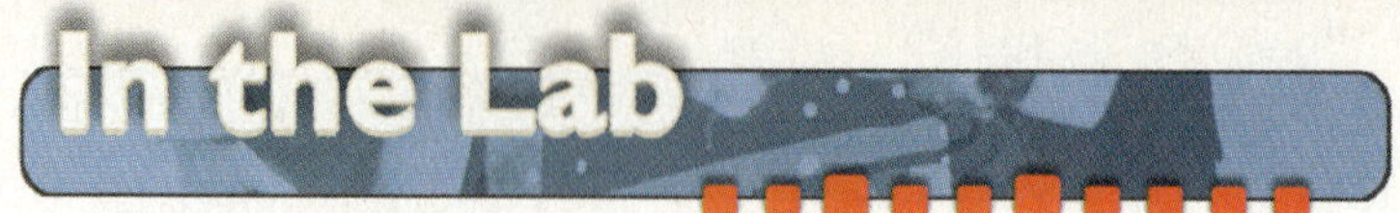

Creating a Calendar and a Task List *(continued)*

This part of the exercise requires that you work as a team with two classmates.

Instructions Part 2: With the growth of your hardware store, you have been able to hire a manager and assistant manager. Perform the following tasks.

1. Add the due dates in Table 2-9 to the tasks created in Part 1.
2. Using the tasks created in Part 1, assign the tasks per Table 2-9. Obtain and use the e-mail addresses of two classmates for Manager and Assistant Manager.
3. Have the classmate representing the Manager accept one task and decline one task, and the classmate representing the Assistant Manager accept one task and decline one task.
4. Modify the current view of the task list to include the Owner field using the Customize Current View command accessed by pointing to Arrange By on the View menu, then pointing to Current View on the Arrange By submenu.
5. Print the modified task list and submit to your instructor.
6. Create a personal Tasks subfolder called A-1 Tasks and move the task list you just created to the new subfolder.
7. Export both the personal subfolders created in this exercise to a floppy disk, archive the files, and then delete them from the hard disk.
8. Close all open windows.

Table 2-9 Task Information

TASKS FROM PART 1	ASSIGNMENT	DUE DATE
Call Kyle to confirm plumbing supplier's visit	Manager	March 15, 2006
Call to check lawn fertilizer delivery	Manager	March 10, 2006
Clear out snow blowers to make room for lawn mowers	Assistant Manager	March 30, 2006
Replace snow shovels with lawn and garden tools	Assistant Manager	March 20, 2006

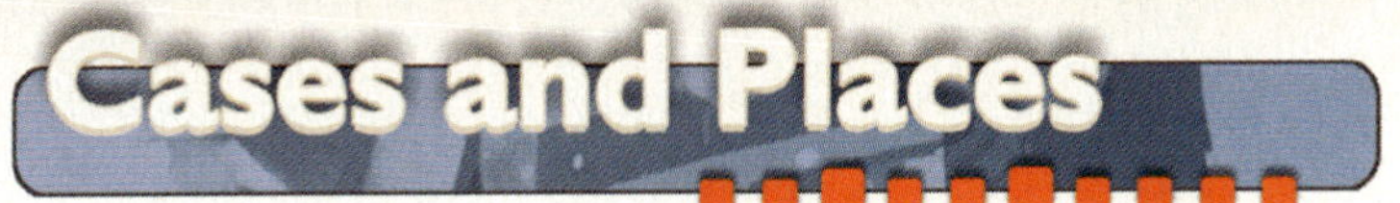

Cases and Places

The difficulty of these case studies varies:
■ are the least difficult and ■■ are more difficult. The last exercise is a group exercise.

1 ■ Create a personal schedule for the next month. Include any work and class time, together with study time. You also can include any extracurricular activities in which you participate. Use recurring appointments when possible. All day activities should be scheduled as events. Color code the calendar as necessary. Print the calendar in Monthly Style and submit to your instructor.

2 ■ At work, you are in charge of scheduling for the month of May. Create a schedule of work times for four employees. Josh works Mondays, Wednesdays, and Fridays from 9:00 a.m. to 5:00 p.m. Julie works Tuesdays, Thursdays, and Saturdays from 9:00 a.m. to 5:00 p.m. Javier works from 12:00 p.m. until 9:00 p.m. on Mondays, Wednesdays, and Fridays. Claire completes the schedule working from 12:00 p.m. until 9:00 p.m. on Tuesdays, Thursdays, and Saturdays. Set the calendar so reflect a six day work week with hours ranging from 9:00 a.m. to 9:00 p.m. Print the calendar in Monthly Style and submit to your instructor.

3 ■ Create journal entries from your personal schedule for the past week. Comment on activities in which you participated and tasks that you accomplished. Write when the activity started and ended. Note the problems (if any) associated with the activity. When commenting on completed tasks, include notes about results of having completed it. Specify what would have happened had the task not been completed when it was. Write a brief summary of your journal and submit to your instructor.

4 ■■ Use the natural language phrase option in the Start time date box to create a list of events for the year. Create a new calendar that contains the following holidays: New Year's Day, Valentine's Day, St. Patrick's Day, Independence Day, Halloween, Veteran's Day, Christmas Eve, Christmas Day, and New Year's Eve. For the last four holidays, indicate that you will be out of the office all day. Also, add events for several family or friend birthdays or anniversaries, using the natural language phrase option. For instance, schedule these events by utilizing the phrase, two weeks from today (or something similar) as a start date. Try different phrase options to schedule these events. Color code the events to separate birthdays from anniversaries, etc. Select two months to print in Monthly Style and submit them to your instructor.

5 ■■ **Working Together** Choose a member of your team to organize a meeting. The organizer will send out meeting invitations to each group member using Outlook. Each member either should accept the meeting time or decline the meeting time and propose a new meeting time based on their individual schedules using Outlook. Use a combination of e-mail and Windows Messenger with Outlook to discuss proposed meeting times with the organizer. Each team member should print out the appointment and hand it in to the instructor.

MICROSOFT
Office 2003

Integration Case Studies

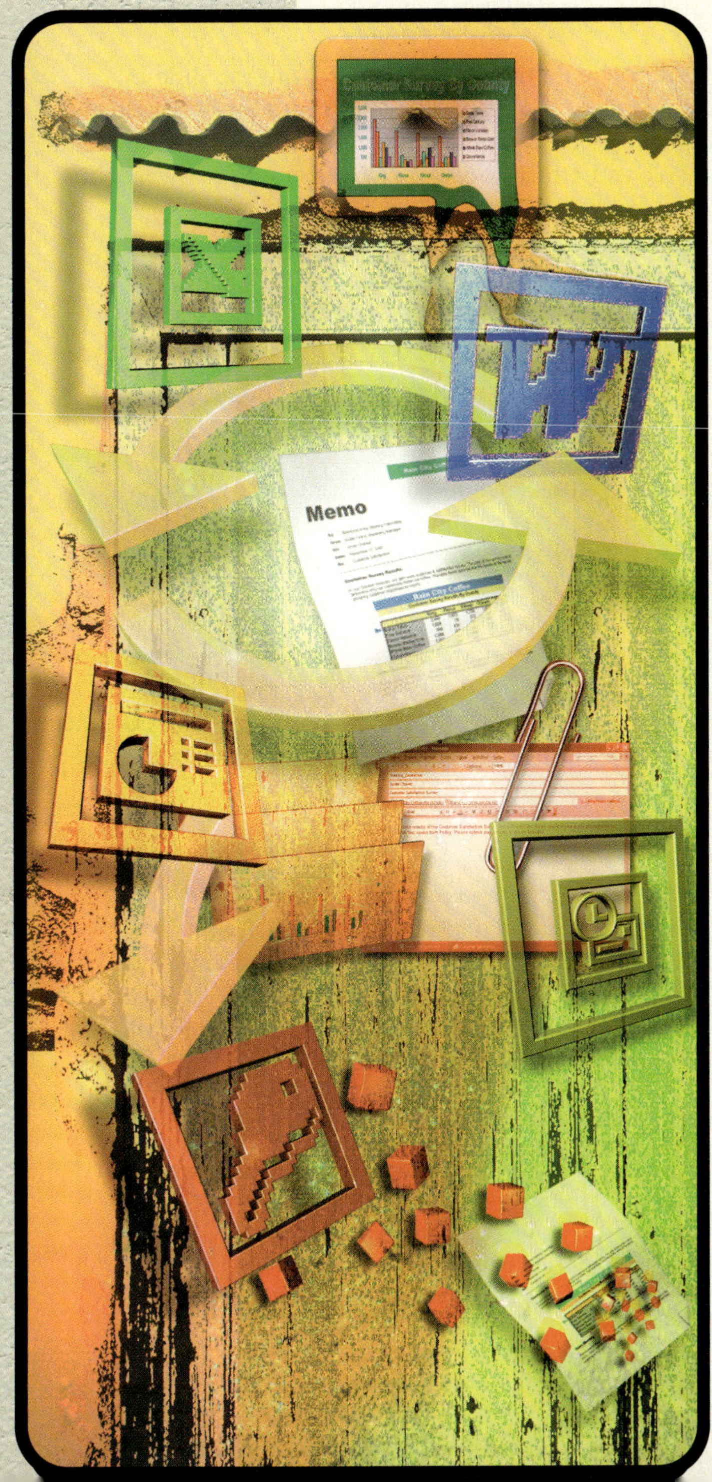

Introduction

In these case studies, you will use the concepts and techniques presented in the projects and Integration Features in this book to integrate all of the Office 2003 applications. The first case study requires that you link an existing Excel worksheet into a Word document, embed an Excel chart into a PowerPoint presentation, and then insert (attach) the Word document and PowerPoint presentation to an e-mail message using Outlook. The second case study requires you to use an existing Access database table as the data source for a Word form letter; it also requires you to use WordArt to create the letterhead for the form letter. In the third case study, you will create an Access database table and then convert the table twice, first to a Word document and second to an Excel worksheet. You then will convert the Word document to an Excel worksheet and vice versa. The files for the first and second case studies are provided on the Data Disk for this textbook. See the inside back cover for instructions for obtaining the Data Disk.

1 Integrating Excel, Word, PowerPoint, and Outlook

Problem: Rain City Coffee enclosed a survey along with its October invoices in order to collect data on customer satisfaction. Susan Herns, a marketing manager at Rain City, has received the completed surveys and summarized the results in an Excel worksheet. She also has charted the results using Excel. The worksheet and corresponding charts are saved in a workbook named Rain City Coffee.

Susan would like to schedule a meeting to discuss the survey results with the steering committee of Rain City Coffee. She plans to send an e-mail message to the committee to schedule the meeting and ask for comments and suggestions. To ensure that the committee can review the results before the meeting, Susan will attach two documents to the e-mail message: (1) a memo that includes the Excel worksheet summarizing the survey results, and (2) a PowerPoint slide that includes the Excel chart depicting the survey results.

As Susan's assistant, you are to create the memo in Word and the slide in PowerPoint. Susan wants you to embed the Excel worksheet into the Word document and the Excel chart into the PowerPoint slide. Finally, she wants you to create an e-mail message using Outlook and attach the Word document and PowerPoint slide.

Part 1: Reviewing the Excel Workbook

Instructions: Open the Rain City Coffee workbook shown in Figures 1a and 1b from the Data Disk. Before you begin creating the memo and slide, familiarize yourself with their contents. Print each sheet of the workbook.

Part 2: Creating a Memorandum in Word with an Embedded Excel Worksheet

Instructions: Create a memorandum to schedule the meeting with the steering committee, as shown in Figure 1d. After typing the text in the memo, embed the Customer Survey Results By County worksheet from the Excel workbook into the memo.

Leave the Excel workbook open and start Word. Use the Professional Memo template to create the memo. Modify the template text so that the memo matches Figure 1d. Next, embed the Customer Survey Results By County worksheet into the memo. (Do not type the worksheet; rather, embed it from Excel.) Save the document using the file name, Rain City Coffee. Print the memorandum with the embedded worksheet.

Part 3: Creating a Slide in PowerPoint with an Embedded Excel Chart

Instructions: Create a slide (Figure 1c) to be used in the presentation to the board of directors.

Leave the Excel workbook open and start PowerPoint. Select a blank slide for the slide's layout and use a background color as shown in Figure 1c. Use WordArt to create the title. Embed the Customer Survey Results By County chart into the slide. Save the presentation using the file name, Rain City Coffee.

Part 4: Attaching the Files to an E-Mail Message

Instructions: Using Outlook, create the e-mail message (Figure 1e) and attach the Word document and PowerPoint slide to the e-mail message. Print the e-mail message.

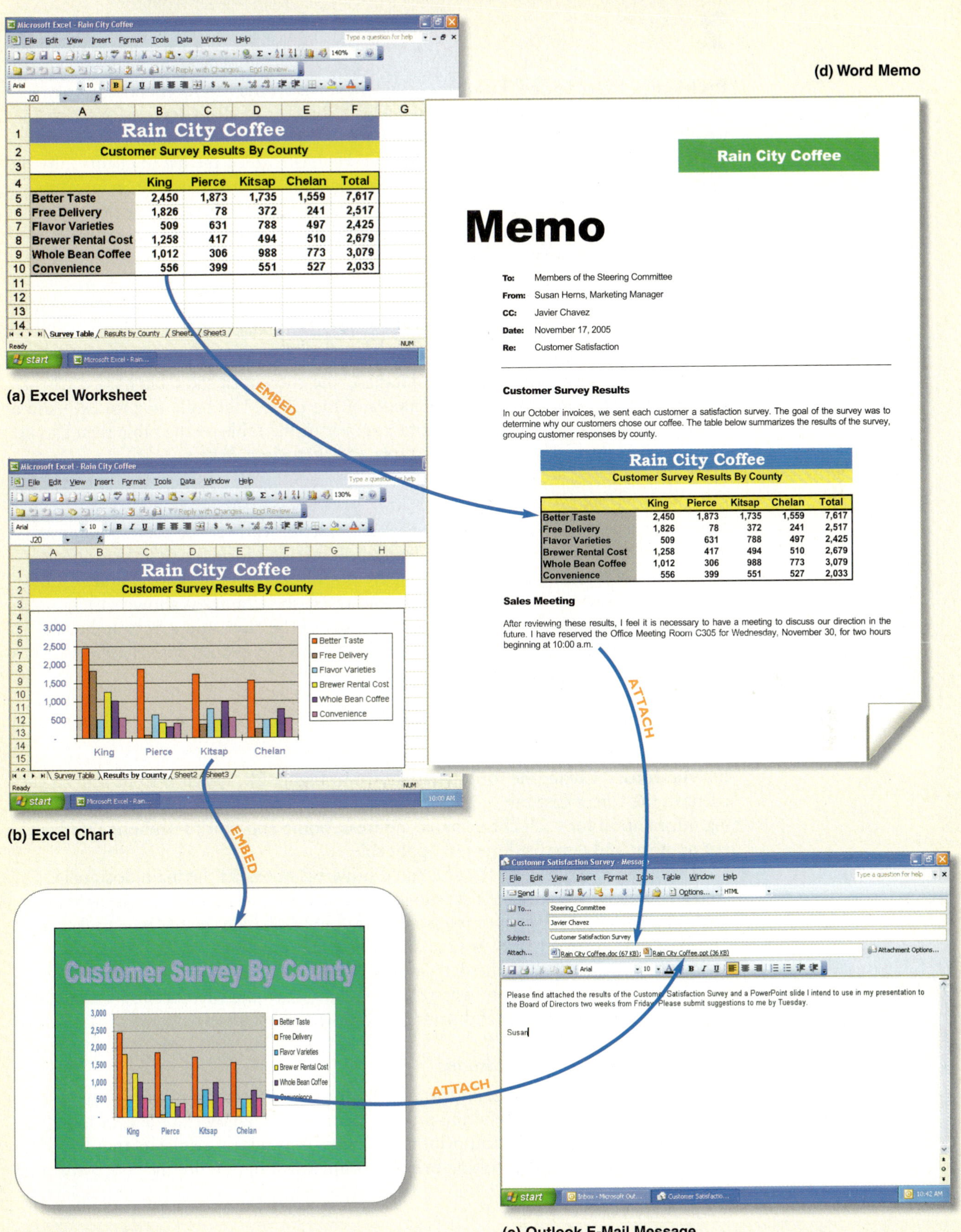

	King	Pierce	Kitsap	Chelan	Total
Better Taste	2,450	1,873	1,735	1,559	7,617
Free Delivery	1,826	78	372	241	2,517
Flavor Varieties	509	631	788	497	2,425
Brewer Rental Cost	1,258	417	494	510	2,679
Whole Bean Coffee	1,012	306	988	773	3,079
Convenience	556	399	551	527	2,033

(a) Excel Worksheet

(b) Excel Chart

(c) PowerPoint Slide

(d) Word Memo

(e) Outlook E-Mail Message

FIGURE 1

2 Integrating Word, WordArt, and Access

Problem: Every spring, Eastlake Swim Club sends letters to its clients to verify the Club's internal records. In the past, the Club's director of client services, Nathan Kennedy, has used Word to type these letters to each client individually. This year, he wants to automate the process even further. He has entered the list of clients into an Access table (Figure 2a), which is saved in a database named Eastlake Swim Club. He has asked you to prepare a form letter to be sent to all clients using the Access database table as a data source. He also would like you to develop a creative letterhead for Eastlake Swim Club that can be used on all its business correspondence. The completed form letter, with letterhead, is shown in Figure 2b.

Part 1: *Reviewing and Maintaining the Access Database Table*

Instructions: The database table is in a file named Eastlake Swim Club, which is located on the Data Disk. Open the database and then open the table named Client List. Familiarize yourself with the contents of the Client List table (Figure 2a). Add a record that contains information about yourself to the table — the table then should contain six records. Print the revised table and then close Access.

Part 2: *Creating the Letterhead*

Instructions: Your first task is to develop the letterhead for the correspondence. Start Word and then display the header area. Insert and format a WordArt object, using the text, Eastlake, as shown in Figure 2b. Insert the swimming clip art to the right of the WordArt object. Reposition and resize the clip art as shown in Figure 2b. Finally, enter the telephone number and address of the club, add a bottom border, and color it dark green. When you are finished with the header, save the file as Eastlake Letterhead and print a copy.

Part 3: *Creating the Form Letter Using an Access Database Table as the Data Source*

Instructions: Create the form letter shown in Figure 2b, which is to be sent to each client in the Client List table. The form letter is to verify the accuracy of the following information for each client: name, address, home and work telephone numbers, fax number, and e-mail address, if applicable.

Using the Eastlake Letterhead created in Part 2 above as the main document, create a form letter using the text shown in Figure 2b and the Access database table as the data source. When specifying the data source, change the file type to Access Databases in the Select Data Source dialog box and then locate and click Eastlake Swim Club as the name of the data source. When you are finished with the main document, save the document using the file name, Eastlake Membership Update, and then print it. Finally, merge and print the form letters for the six records.

Part 4: *Setting Query Conditions*

Instructions: Merge and print form letters for only those clients with a home area code of 253. On the resulting printed form letters, handwrite the condition you specified. Next, merge and print form letters for only those clients that have e-mail addresses. On the resulting printed form letters, handwrite the condition you specified.

ID	Title	First Name	Last Name	Address1	Address2	City	State	ZIP code	Home Phone	Work Phone	Fax Number	Email Address
1	Mr.	Michael	Shank	517 Howard Ave.		Seattle	WA	98101-	(206) 555-9123	(206) 555-6712	(206) 555-3125	
2	Dr.	Jerad	DeRolf	2510 81st St.		Seattle	WA	98105-	(206) 555-8282	(206) 555-4523	(206) 555-1111	DeRolf@isp.net
3	Ms.	Hannah	Cameron	312 Douglas St.	Apt. 4A	Seattle	WA	98110-	(253) 555-3102	(253) 555-9087		Cutie@isp.com
4	Mr.	Ray	Lykins	4699 Green Ave.		Seattle	WA	98105-	(206) 555-5209	(206) 555-1523	(206) 555-6653	
5	Mrs.	Marsha	Steiger	P.O. Box 1812	Apt. 16	Seattle	WA	98101-	(253) 555-2192	(253) 555-6666	(253) 555-8897	M_Steiger@isp.edu

(a) Access Table

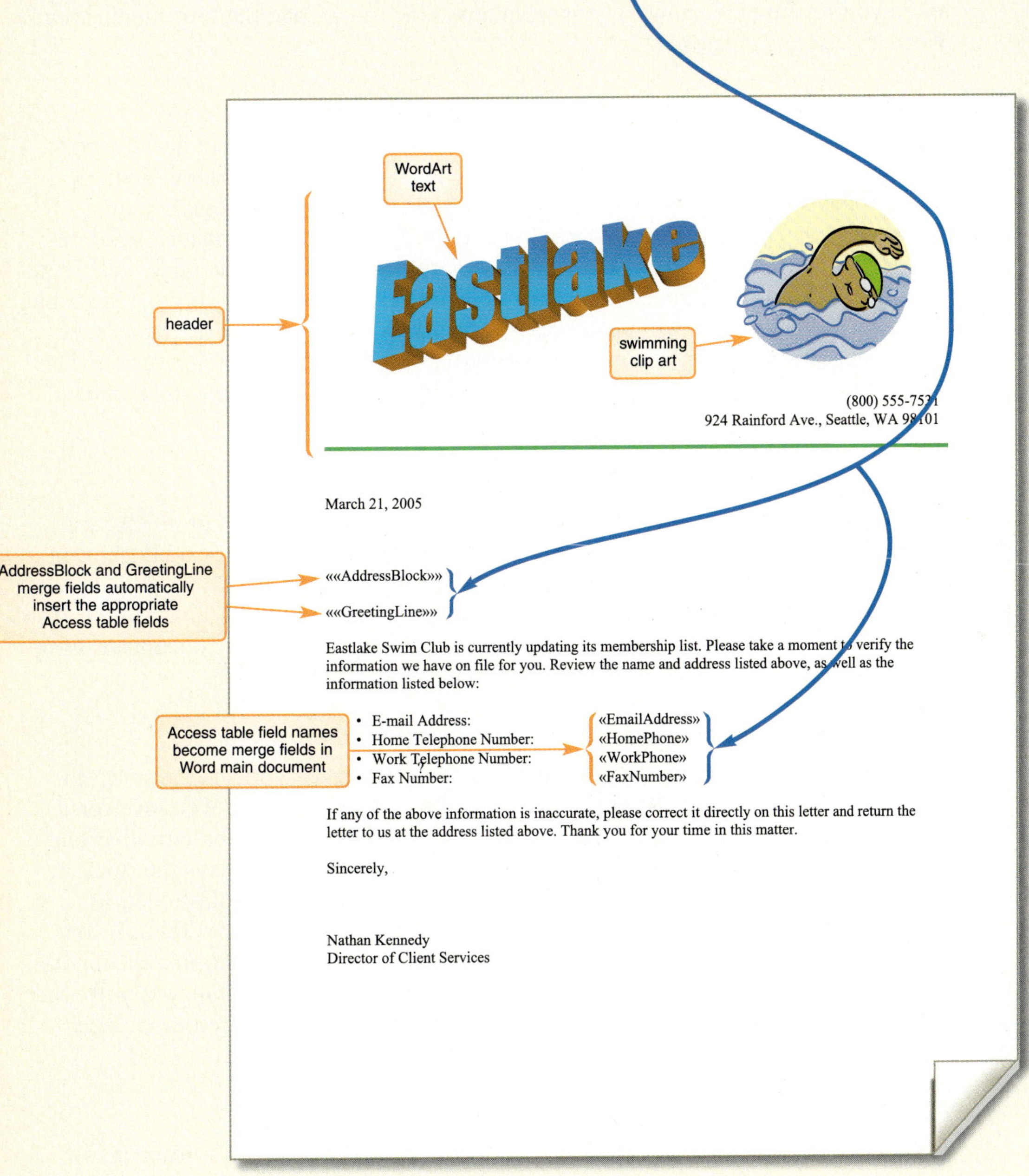
WordArt text
header
swimming clip art
AddressBlock and GreetingLine merge fields automatically insert the appropriate Access table fields
Access table field names become merge fields in Word main document

Eastlake

(800) 555-7531
924 Rainford Ave., Seattle, WA 98101

March 21, 2005

«AddressBlock»

«GreetingLine»

Eastlake Swim Club is currently updating its membership list. Please take a moment to verify the information we have on file for you. Review the name and address listed above, as well as the information listed below:

- E-mail Address: «EmailAddress»
- Home Telephone Number: «HomePhone»
- Work Telephone Number: «WorkPhone»
- Fax Number: «FaxNumber»

If any of the above information is inaccurate, please correct it directly on this letter and return the letter to us at the address listed above. Thank you for your time in this matter.

Sincerely,

Nathan Kennedy
Director of Client Services

(b) Word Document

FIGURE 2

3 Integrating Access into Word and Excel

Problem: The owner of Web Investors, Inc., Jackie Garfield, would like to work with the daily stock records. The problem is that the records are stored in an Access database table (Figure 3a) and Jackie is unfamiliar with Access. Instead, she wants to work with the records in both Word and Excel. Thus, she has asked you to convert the Access table to both a Word document and an Excel worksheet. She also has asked you to show her how to convert in any direction among the three applications, Word, Excel, and Access.

Part 1: Creating the Access Table and Entering the Data

Instructions: Design and create the Access database table that contains the stock information. The field names for the table are as follows: Stock Symbol, Today's High, Today's Low, Today's Close, 52-Week High, and 52-Week Low. Obtain a recent copy of *The Wall Street Journal* or use the Internet to obtain stock information for five different stocks. Enter the information as records in the table you create. The Access screen in Figure 3a shows sample data entered in the Web Portfolio table. The actual data you use will be different. When you finish creating the table, save the database using the file name, Web Investors. Print the Access table. Turn in *The Wall Street Journal* pages or printouts of the Web pages you used for stock quotes along with the Access table.

Part 2: Converting an Access Table to a Word Document

Instructions: Convert the Web Portfolio table to a Word table. With the Access table selected in the Web Investors: Database window, click the OfficeLinks button arrow on the Database toolbar and then click Publish It with MS Word. When the Word document window displays the stock information as a Word table, format it so that it is readable and professional, as shown in Figure 3b. Save the document using the file name, Web Portfolio. Print the resulting Word table.

Part 3: Converting an Access Table to an Excel Worksheet

Instructions: Convert the Web Portfolio table to an Excel worksheet. Return to the Access database table. With the Access table highlighted in the Web Investors: Database window, click the OfficeLinks button arrow on the Database toolbar and then click Analyze It with MS Excel. When the Excel window displays the stock information as a worksheet, format it so that it is readable and professional, as shown in Figure 3c. Save the workbook using the file name, Web Portfolio. Below the table, add two rows that use Excel's statistical functions to determine the highest and lowest values for each of the numeric columns in the table. (***Note:*** you will need to format the stock quotes as numbers rather than text.) Print the resulting Excel worksheet.

Part 4: Converting among Word, Excel, and Access

Instructions: Use the techniques described earlier in this book to convert in any direction among Word, Excel, and Access. For example, open the Excel workbook Web Portfolio and convert it to Word. Next, convert the workbook to Access. Do the same for the Word document Web Portfolio. Print each of the four files created.

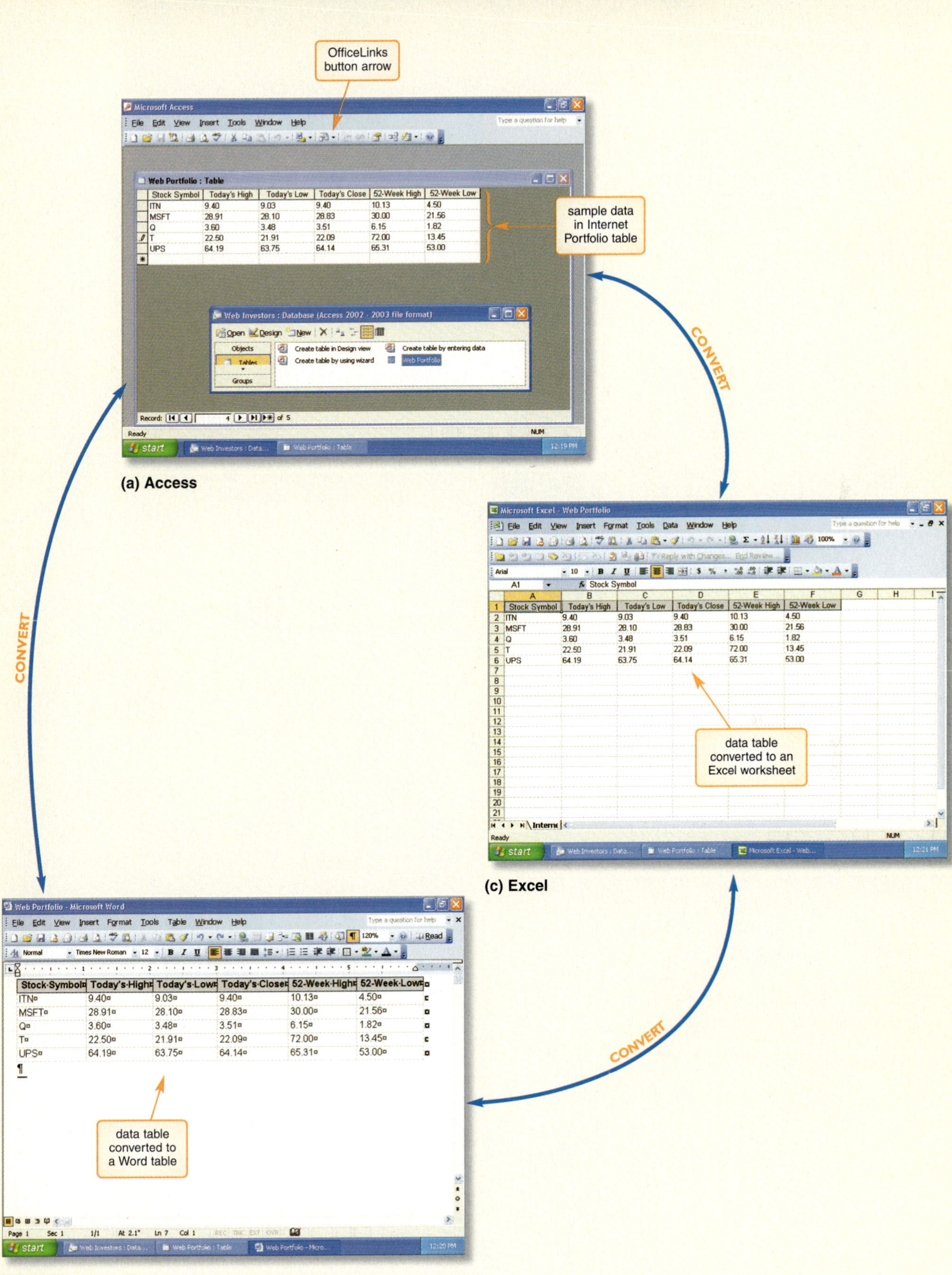

(a) Access

(c) Excel

(b) Word

FIGURE 3

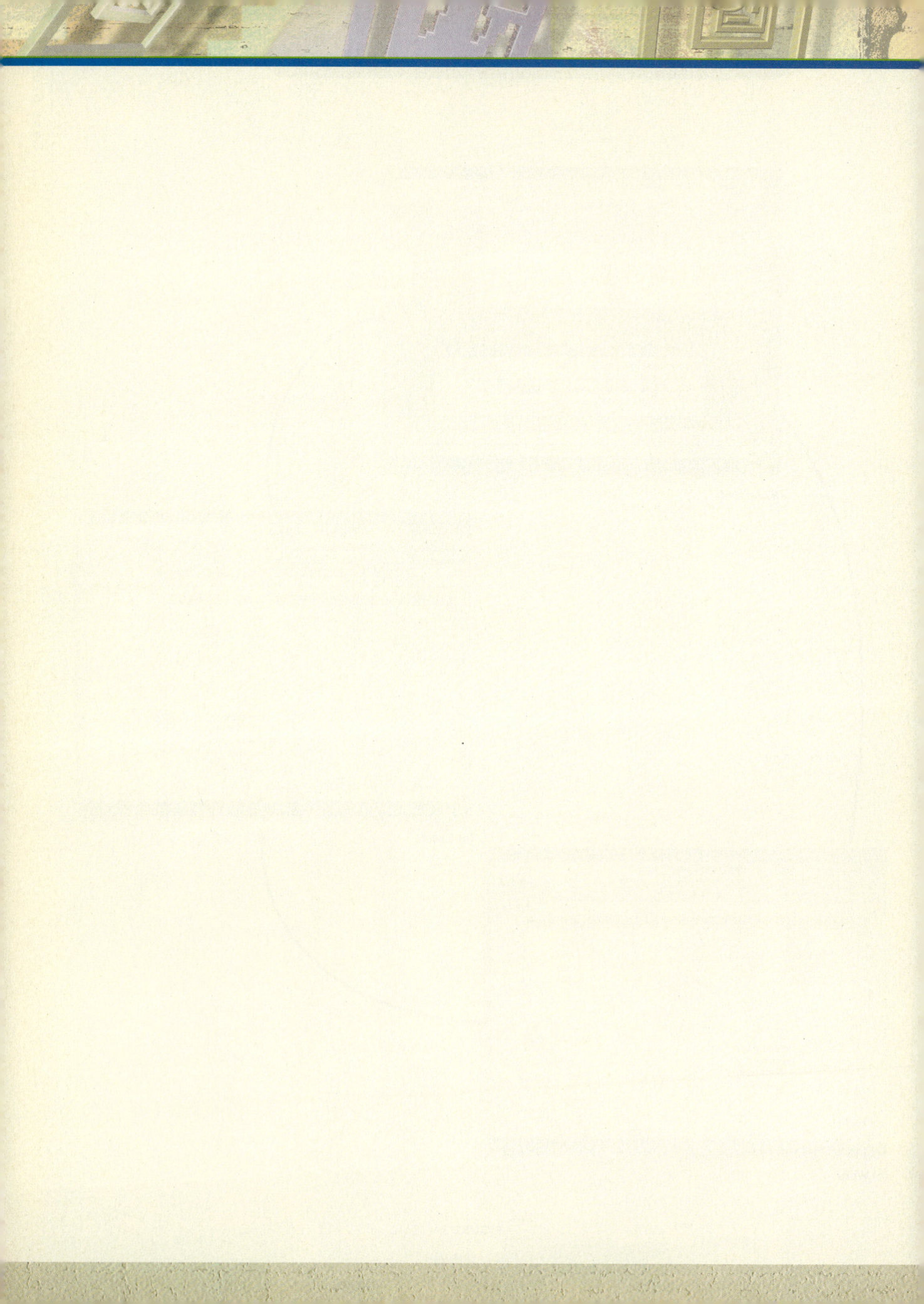

Appendix A

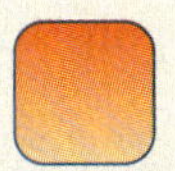

Microsoft Office Help System

Using the Microsoft Office Help System

This appendix shows you how to use the Microsoft Office Help system. At anytime while you are using one of the Microsoft Office 2003 applications, you can interact with its Help system and display information on any topic associated with the application. To illustrate the use of the Office Help system, you will use the Microsoft Word application in this appendix. The Help systems in other Office applications respond in a similar fashion.

As shown in Figure A-1, five methods for accessing Word's Help system are available:

1. Microsoft Office Word Help button on the Standard toolbar
2. Microsoft Office Word Help command on the Help menu
3. Function key F1 on the keyboard
4. Type a question for help box on the menu bar
5. Office Assistant

1 MICROSOFT OFFICE WORD HELP BUTTON ON STANDARD TOOLBAR

2 MICROSOFT OFFICE WORD HELP COMMAND ON HELP MENU

3 FUNCTION KEY F1 ON KEYBOARD

4 TYPE A QUESTION FOR HELP BOX ON MENU BAR

5 OFFICE ASSISTANT

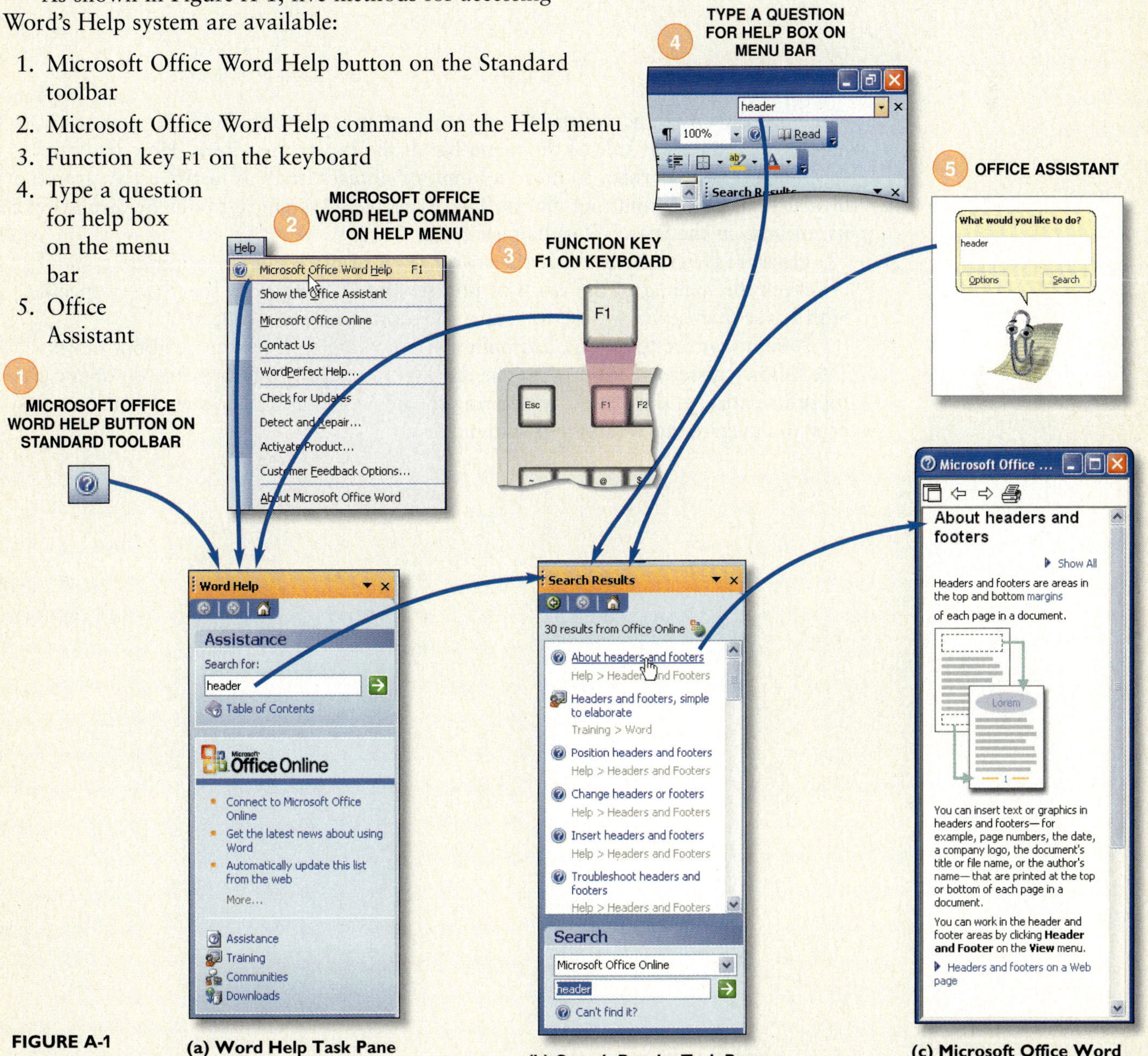

FIGURE A-1

(a) Word Help Task Pane

(b) Search Results Task Pane

(c) Microsoft Office Word Help Window

All five methods result in the Word Help system displaying a task pane on the right side of the Word window. The first three methods cause the **Word Help task pane** to display (Figure A-1a on the previous page). This task pane includes a Search text box in which you can enter a word or phrase on which you want help. Once you enter the word or phrase, the Word Help system displays the Search Results task pane (Figure A-1b on the previous page). With the Search Results task pane displayed, you can select specific Help topics.

As shown in Figure A-1, methods 4 and 5 bypass the Word Help task pane and display the **Search Results task pane** (Figure A-1b) with a list of links that pertain to the selected topic. Thus, any of the five methods for accessing the Word Help system results in displaying the Search Results task pane. Once the Word Help system displays this task pane, you can choose links that relate to the word or phrase on which you searched. In Figure A-1, for example, header was the searched topic (About headers and footers), which resulted in the Word Help system displaying the Microsoft Office Word Help window with information about headers and footers (Figure A-1c on the previous page).

Navigating the Word Help System

The quickest way to access the Word Help system is through the Type a question for help box on the right side of the menu bar at the top of the screen. Here you can type words, such as ruler, font, or column, or phrases, such as justify a paragraph, or how do I display formatting marks. The Word Help system responds by displaying a list of links in the Search Results task pane.

Here are two tips regarding the words or phrases you enter to initiate a search: (1) check the spelling of the word or phrase; and (2) keep your search very specific, with fewer than seven words, to return the most accurate results.

Assume for the following example that you want to know more about tables. The following steps show how to use the Type a question for help box to obtain useful information about tables by entering the keyword table. The steps also show you how to navigate the Word Help system.

To Obtain Help Using the Type a Question for Help Box

1

- **Click the Type a question for help box on the right side of the menu bar, type `table`, and then press the ENTER key (Figure A-2).**

The Word Help system displays the Search Results task pane on the right side of the window. The Search Results task pane contains a list of 30 links (Figure A-2). If you do not find what you are looking for, you can modify or refine the search in the Search area at the bottom of the task pane. The topics displayed in your Search Results task pane may be different.

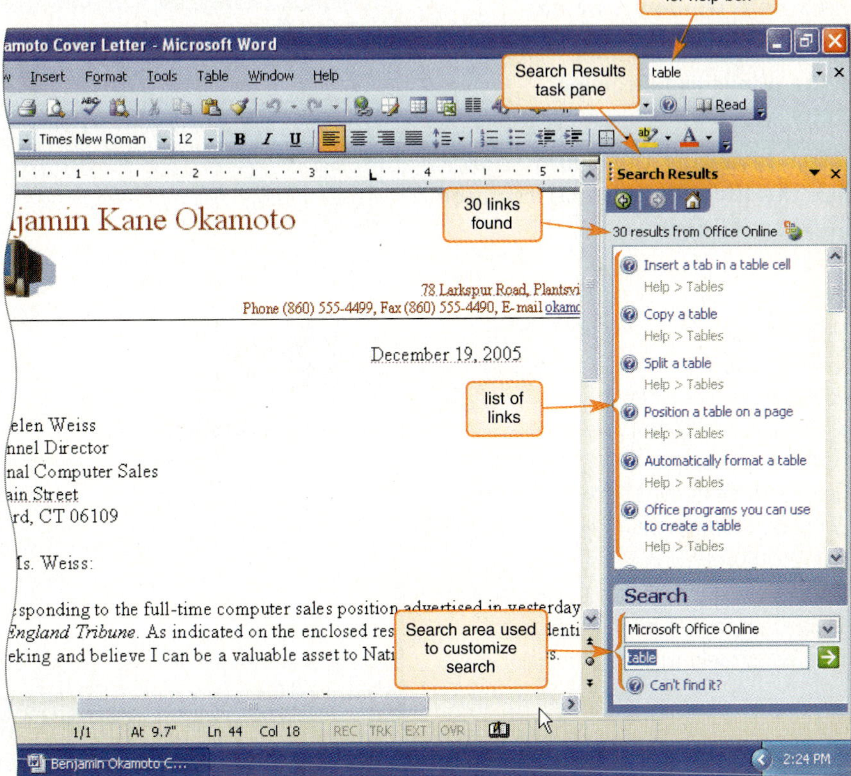

FIGURE A-2

2

Scroll down the list of links in the Search Results task pane and then click the About tables link.

- **When Word displays the Microsoft Office Help Word window, click its Auto Tile button in the upper-left corner of the window (Figure A-4 on the next page), if necessary, to tile the windows.**

Word displays the Microsoft Office Word Help window with the desired information about tables (Figure A-3). With the Microsoft Office Word Help window and Microsoft Word window tiled, you can read the information in one window and complete the task in the other window.

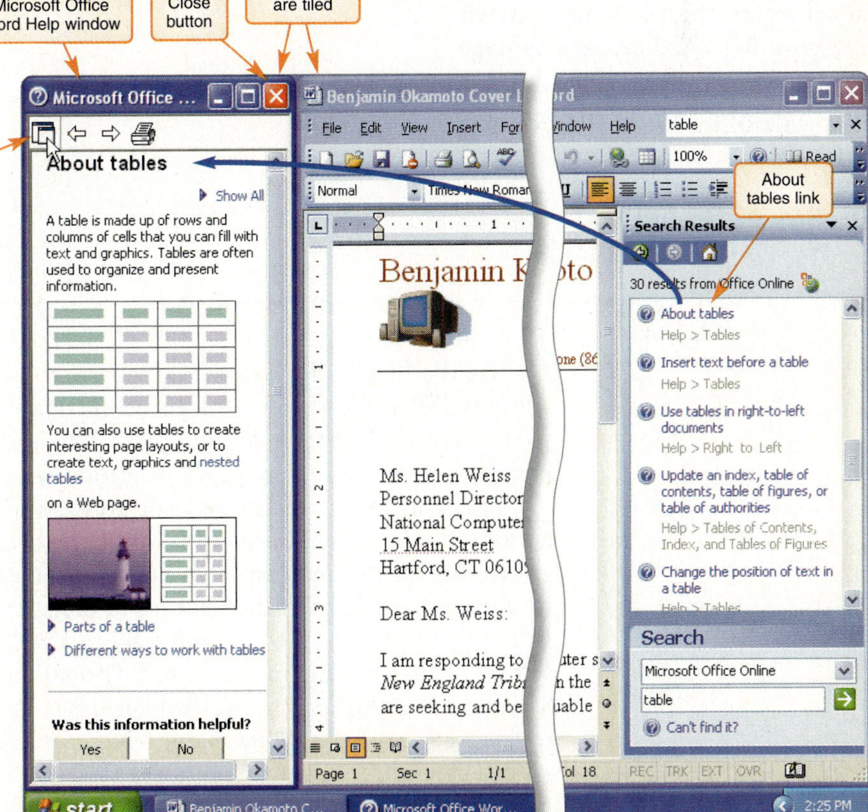

FIGURE A-3

3

• **Double-click the Microsoft Office Word Help window title bar.**

• **Click the Show All link in the upper-right corner of the window.**

• **After reviewing the information, click the Hide All link that replaced the Show All link.**

The Microsoft Office Word Help window is maximized so it fills the entire screen (Figure A-4). If you are connected to the Internet, you can give Microsoft your opinion as to whether the information was helpful by clicking the Yes or No button at the bottom of the page. The Show All link expands the coverage of information and the Hide all link condenses the information displayed on the topic in the Microsoft Office Word Help window.

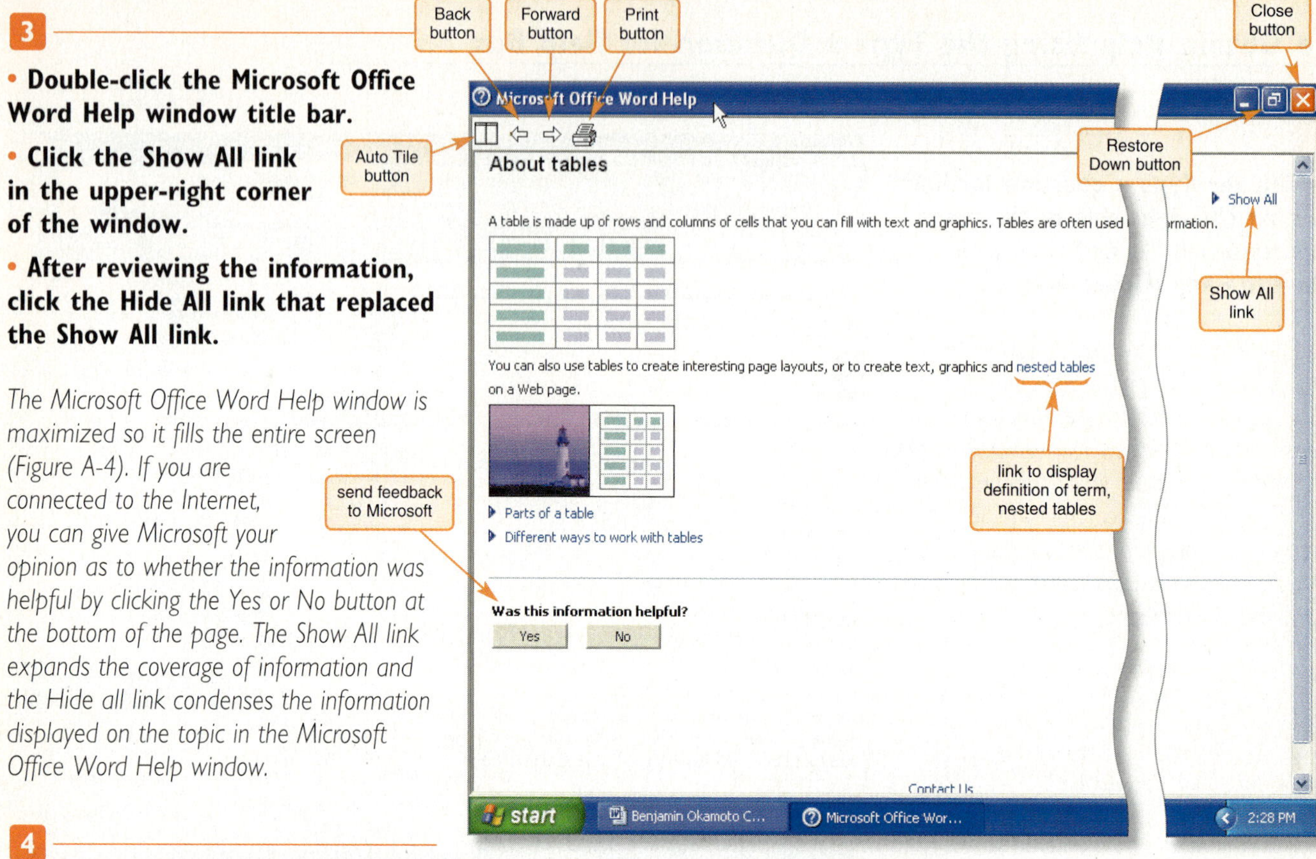

FIGURE A-4

4

• **Click the Restore Down button on the right side of the Microsoft Office Word Help window title bar to return to the tiled state shown in Figure A-3 on the previous page.**

• **Click the Close button on the Microsoft Office Word Help window title bar.**

The Microsoft Office Word Help window is closed and the Word document is active.

Use the four buttons in the upper-left corner of the Microsoft Office Word Help window (Figure A-4) to tile or untile, navigate through the Help system, or print the contents of the window. As you click links in the Search Results task pane, the Word Help system displays new pages of information. The Word Help System remembers the links you visited and allows you to redisplay the pages visited during a session by clicking the Back and Forward buttons (Figure A-4).

If none of the links presents the information you want, you can refine the search by entering another word or phrase in the Search text box in the Search Results task pane (Figure A-2 on the previous page). If you have access to the Web, then the scope is global for the initial search. **Global** means all of the categories listed in the Search box of the Search area in Figure A-2 are searched. For example, you can, restrict the scope to **Offline Help,** which results in a search of related links only on your hard disk.

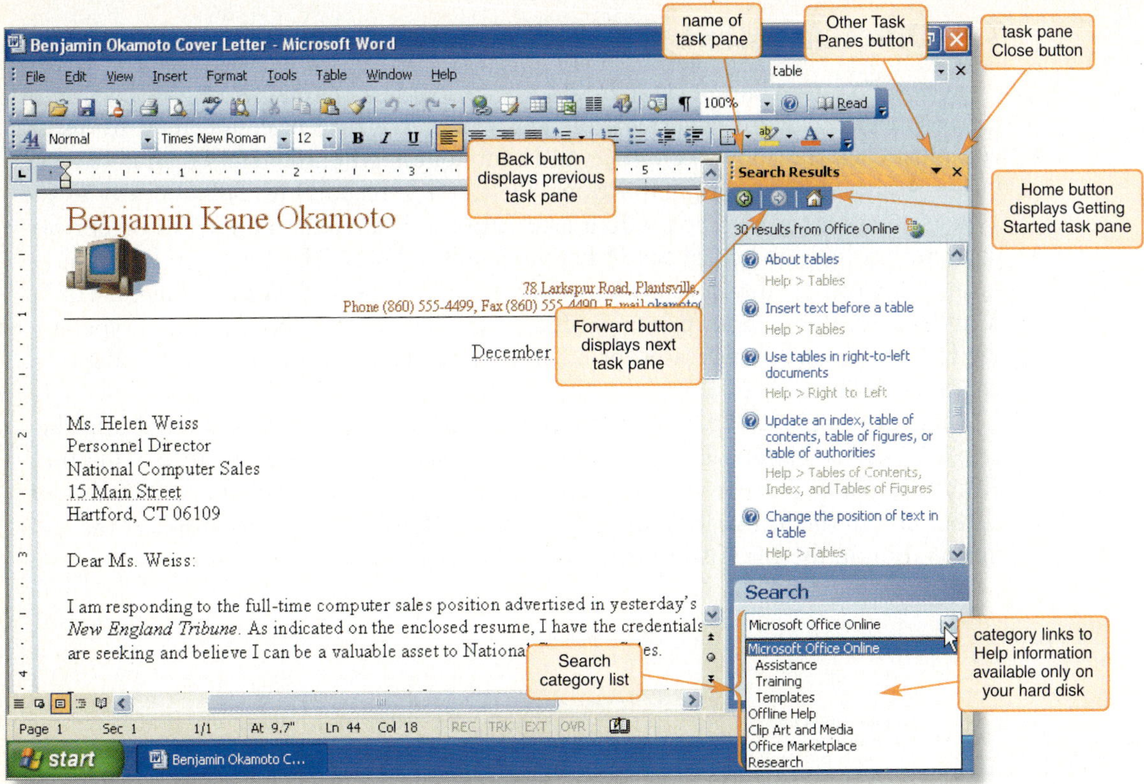

FIGURE A-5

Figure A-5 shows several additional features of the Search Results task pane. The Other Task Panes button and Close button on the Search Results task pane title bar allow you to display other task panes and close the Search Results task pane. The three buttons below the Search Results task pane title bar allow you to navigate between task panes (Back button and Forward button) and display the Getting Started task pane (Home button).

As you enter words and phrases in the Type a question for help box, the Word Help system adds them to the Type a question for help list. To display the list of previously typed words and phrases, click the Type a question for help box arrow (Figure A-6).

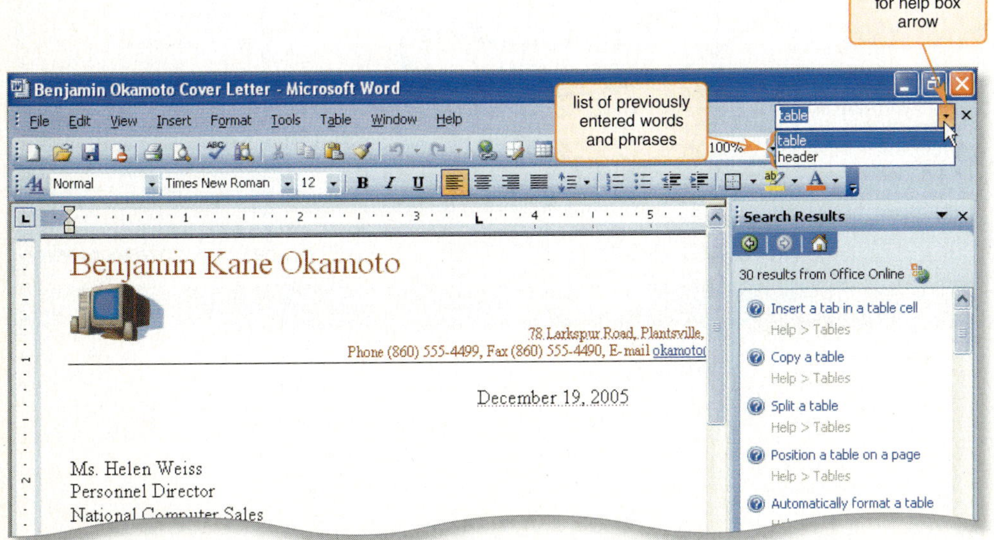

FIGURE A-6

The Office Assistant

The **Office Assistant** is an icon (middle of Figure A-7) that Word displays in the Microsoft Office Word window while you work. For the Office Assistant to display, you must click the Show the Office Assistant command on the Help menu. The Office Assistant has multiple functions. First, it will respond in the same way as the Type a question for help box with a list of topics that relate to the word or phrase you enter in the text box in the Office Assistant balloon. The entry can be in the form of a word or phrase as if you were talking to a person. For example, if you want to learn more about printing a file, in the balloon text box, you can type any of the following words or phrases: print, print a document, how do I print a file, or anything similar.

In the example in Figure A-7, the phrase, print a document, is entered into the Office Assistant balloon text box. The Office Assistant responds by displaying the Search Results task pane with a list of links from which you can choose. Once you click a link in the Search Results task pane, the Word Help system displays the information in the Microsoft Office Word Help window (Figure A-7).

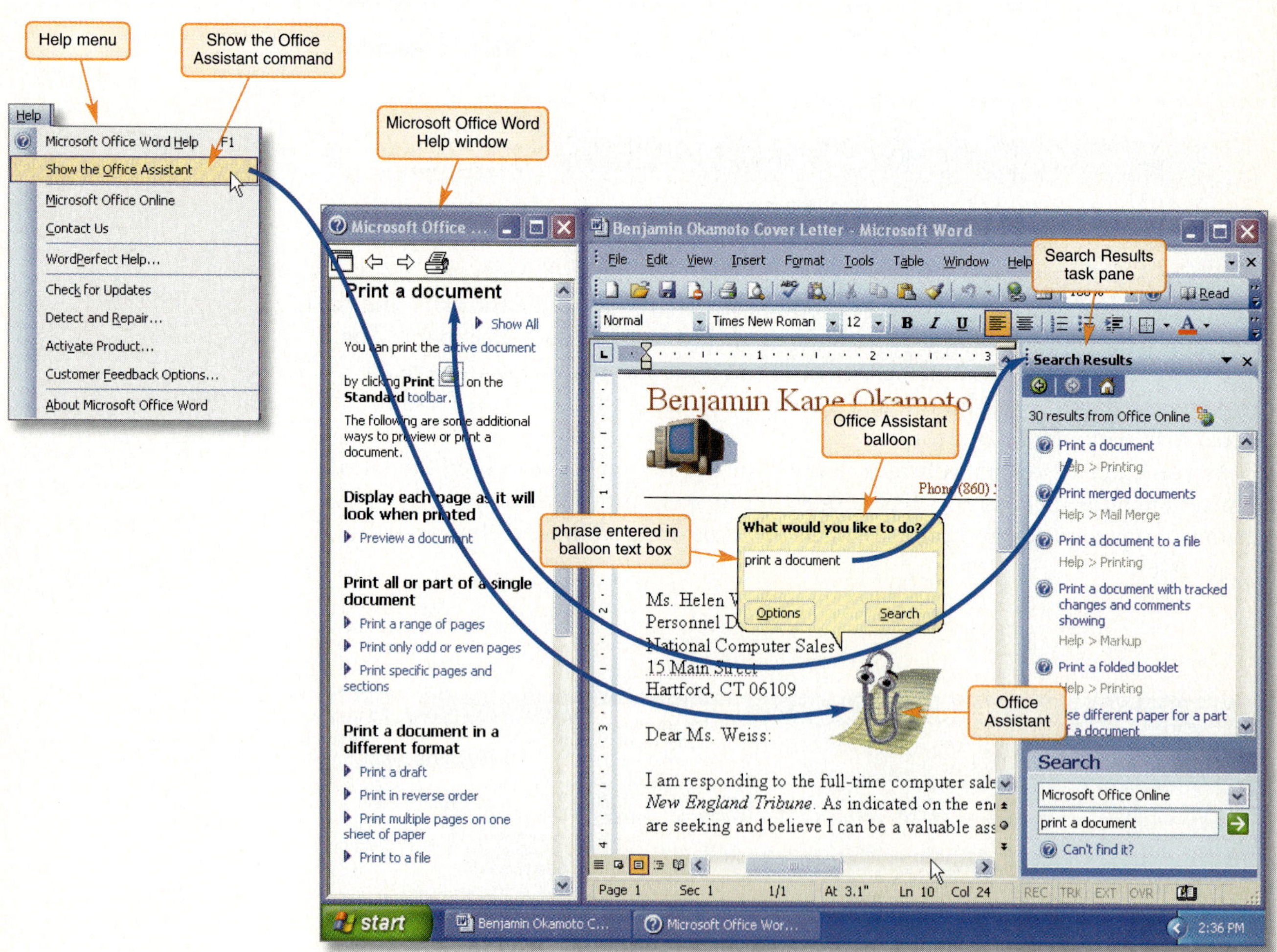

FIGURE A-7

In addition, the Office Assistant monitors your work and accumulates tips during a session on how you might increase your productivity and efficiency. The accumulation of tips must be enabled. You enable the accumulation of tips by right-clicking the Office Assistant, clicking Options on the shortcut menu, and then selecting the types of tips you want accumulated. You can view the tips at anytime. The accumulated tips appear when you activate the Office Assistant balloon. Also, if at anytime you see a light bulb above the Office Assistant, click it to display the most recent tip. If the Office Assistant is hidden, then the light bulb shows on the Microsoft Office Word Help button on the Standard toolbar.

You hide the Office Assistant by invoking the Hide the Office Assistant command on the Help menu or by right-clicking the Office Assistant and then clicking Hide on the shortcut menu. The Hide the Office Assistant command shows on the Help menu only when the Office Assistant is active in the Word window. If the Office Assistant begins showing up on your screen without you instructing it to show, then right-click the Office Assistant, click Options on the shortcut menu, click the Use the Office Assistant check box to remove the check mark, and then click the OK button.

If the Office Assistant is active in the Word window, then Word displays all program and system messages in the Office Assistant balloon.

You may or may not want the Office Assistant to display on the screen at all times. As indicated earlier, you can hide it and then show it later through the Help menu. For more information about the Office Assistant, type `office assistant` in the Type a question for help box and then click the links in the Search Results task pane.

Question Mark Button in Dialog Boxes and Help Icon in Task Panes

You use the Question Mark button with dialog boxes. It is located in the upper-right corner on the title bar of the dialog boxes, next to the Close button. For example, in Figure A-8 on the next page, the Print dialog box appears on the screen. If you click the Question Mark button in the upper-right corner of the dialog box, the Microsoft Office Word Help window is displayed and provides information about the options in the Print dialog box.

Some task panes include a Help icon. It can be located in various places within the task pane. For example, in the Clip Art task pane shown in Figure A-8, the Help icon appears at the bottom of the task pane and the Tips for finding clips link appears to the right of the Help icon. When you click the link, the Microsoft Office Word Help window is displayed and provides tips for finding clip art.

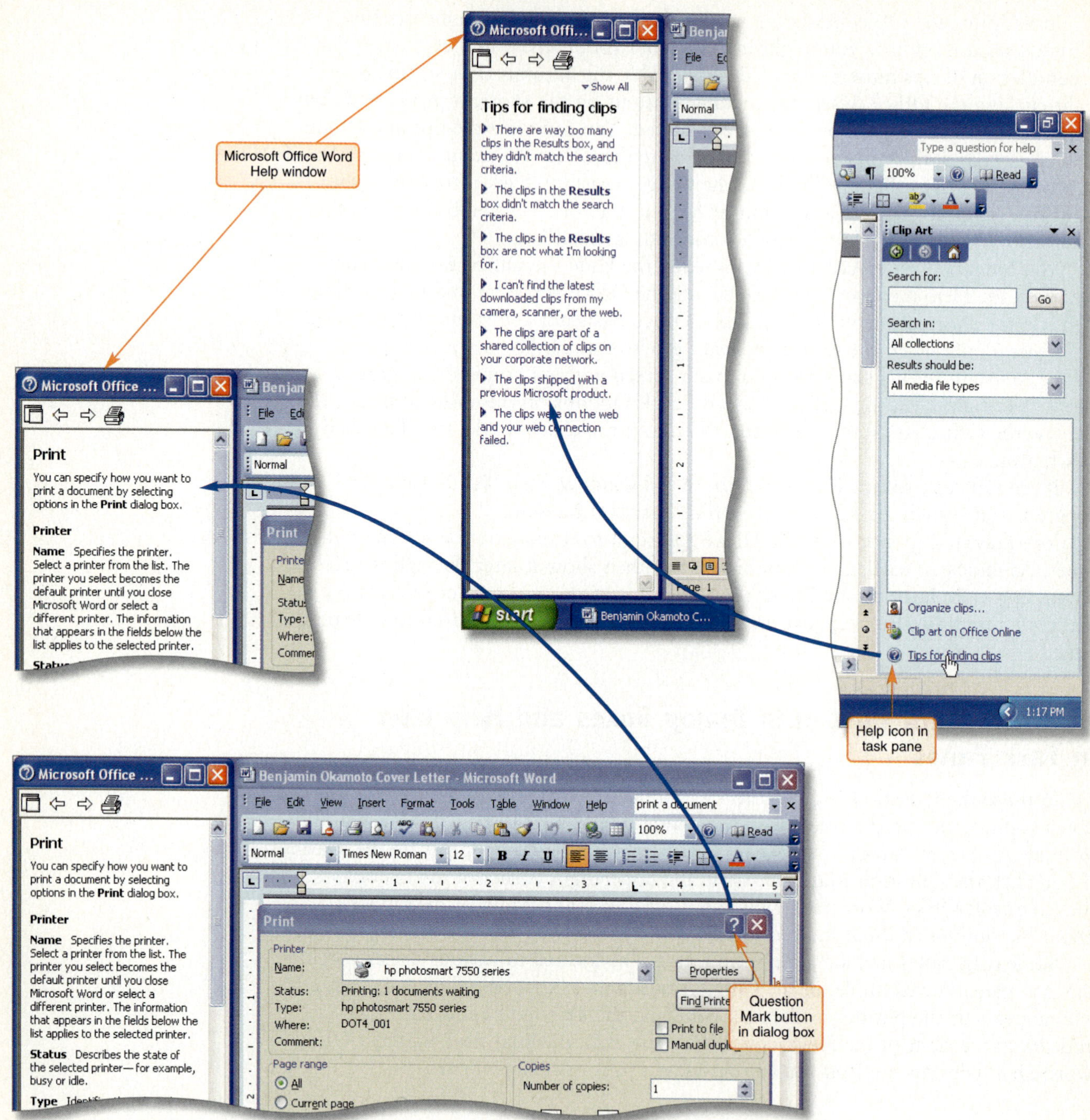

FIGURE A-8

Other Help Commands on the Help Menu

Thus far, this appendix has discussed the first two commands on the Help menu: (1) the Microsoft Office Word Help command (Figure A-1 on page APP 1) and (2) the Show the Office Assistant command (Figure A-7 on page APP 6). Several additional commands are available on the Help menu as shown in Figure A-9. Table A-1 summarizes these commands.

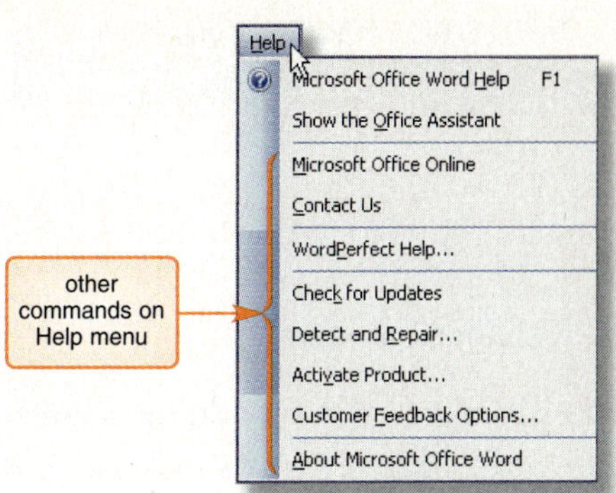

FIGURE A-9

Table A-1 Summary of Other Help Commands on the Help Menu

COMMAND ON HELP MENU	FUNCTION
Microsoft Office Online	Activates the browser, which displays the Microsoft Office Online Home page. The Microsoft Office Online Home page contains links that can improve Office productivity.
Contact Us	Activates the browser, which displays Microsoft contact information and a list of useful links.
WordPerfect Help	Displays the Help for WordPerfect Users dialog box, which includes information about carrying out commands in Word.
Check for Updates	Activates the browser, which displays a list of updates to Office 2003. These updates can be downloaded and installed to improve the efficiency of Office or to fix an error in one or more of the Office applications.
Detect and Repair	Detects and repairs errors in the Word program.
Activate Product	Activates Word if it has not already been activated.
Customer Feedback Options	Gives or denies Microsoft permission to collect anonymous information about the hardware.
About Microsoft Office Word	Displays the About Microsoft Word dialog box. The dialog box lists the owner of the software and the product identification. You need to know the product identification if you call Microsoft for assistance. The three buttons below the OK button are the System Info button, Tech Support button, and Disabled Items button. The System Info button displays system information, including hardware resources, components, software environment, and applications. The Tech Support button displays technical assistance information. The Disabled Items button displays a list of disabled items that prevents Word from functioning properly.

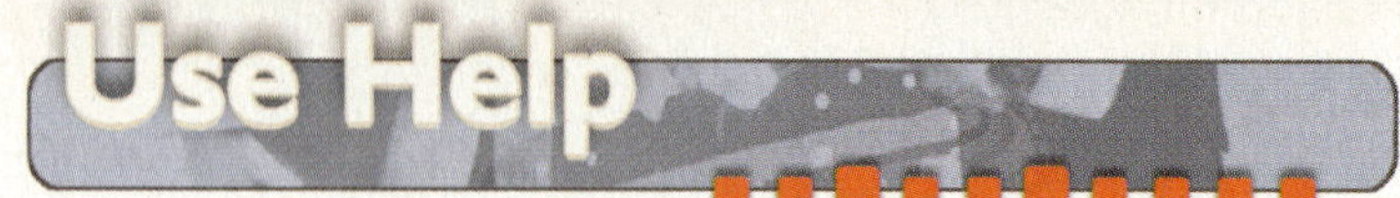

1 Using the Type a Question for Help Box

Instructions: Perform the following tasks using the Word Help system.

1. Use the Type a question for help box on the menu bar to get help on adding a bullet.
2. Click Add bullets or numbering in the list of links in the Search Results task pane. If necessary, tile the windows. Double-click the Microsoft Office Word Help window title bar to maximize it. Click the Show All link. Read and print the information. At the top of the printout, write down the number of links the Word Help system found.
3. Click the Restore Down button on the Microsoft Office Word Help title bar to restore the Microsoft Office Word Help window.
4. One at a time, click two additional links in the Search Results task pane and print the information. Hand in the printouts to your instructor. Use the Back and Forward buttons to return to the original page.
5. Use the Type a question for help box to search for information on adjusting line spacing. Click the Adjust line or paragraph spacing link in the Search Results task pane. Maximize the Microsoft Office Word Help window. Read and print the contents of the window. One at a time, click the links on the page and print the contents of the window. Close the Microsoft Office Word Help window.
6. For each of the following words and phrases, click one link in the Search Results task pane, click the Show All link, and then print the page: page zoom; date; print preview; office clipboard; word count; and themes.

2 Expanding on the Word Help System Basics

Instructions: Use the Word Help system to understand the topics better and answer the questions listed below. Answer the questions on your own paper, or hand in the printed Help information to your instructor.

1. Show the Office Assistant. Right-click the Office Assistant and then click Animate! on the shortcut menu. Repeat invoking the Animate! command to see various animations.
2. Right-click the Office Assistant, click Options on the shortcut menu, click the Reset my tips button, and then click the OK button. If necessary, repeatedly click the Office Assistant and then click off the Office Assistant until a light bulb appears above the Office Assistant. When you see the light bulb, it indicates that the Office Assistant has a tip to share with you.
3. Use the Office Assistant to find help on undoing. Click the Undo mistakes link and then print the contents of the Microsoft Office Word Help window. Close the window. Hand in the printouts to your instructor. Hide the Office Assistant.
4. Press the F1 key. Search for information on Help. Click the first two links in the Search Results task pane. Read and print the information for both links.
5. Display the Help menu. One at a time, click the Microsoft Office Online, Contact Us, and Check for Updates commands. Print the contents of each Internet Explorer window that displays and then close the window. Hand in the printouts to your instructor.
6. Click About Microsoft Office Word on the Help menu. Click the Tech Support button, print the contents of the Microsoft Office Word Help window, and then close the window. Click the System Info button. If necessary, click the plus sign to the left of Components in the System Summary list to display the Components category. Click CD-ROM and then print the information. Click Display and then print the information. Hand in the printouts to your instructor.

Appendix B

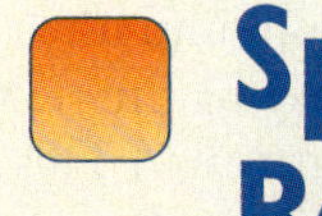

Speech and Handwriting Recognition and Speech Playback

Introduction

This appendix discusses the Office capability that allows users to create and modify worksheets using its alternative input technologies available through **text services**. Office provides a variety of text services, which enable you to speak commands and enter text in an application. The most common text service is the keyboard. Other text services include speech recognition and handwriting recognition.

The Language Bar

The **Language bar** allows you to use text services in the Office applications. You can utilize the Language bar in one of three states: (1) in a restored state as a floating toolbar in the Word window (Figure B-1a or Figure B-1b if Text Labels are enabled); (2) in a minimized state docked next to the notification area on the Windows taskbar (Figure B-1c); or (3) hidden (temporarily closed and out of the way). If the Language bar is hidden, you can activate it by right-clicking the Windows taskbar, pointing to Toolbars on the shortcut menu (Figure B-1d), and then clicking Language bar on the Toolbars submenu. If you want to close the Language bar, right-click the Language bar and then click Close the Language bar on the shortcut menu (Figure B-1e).

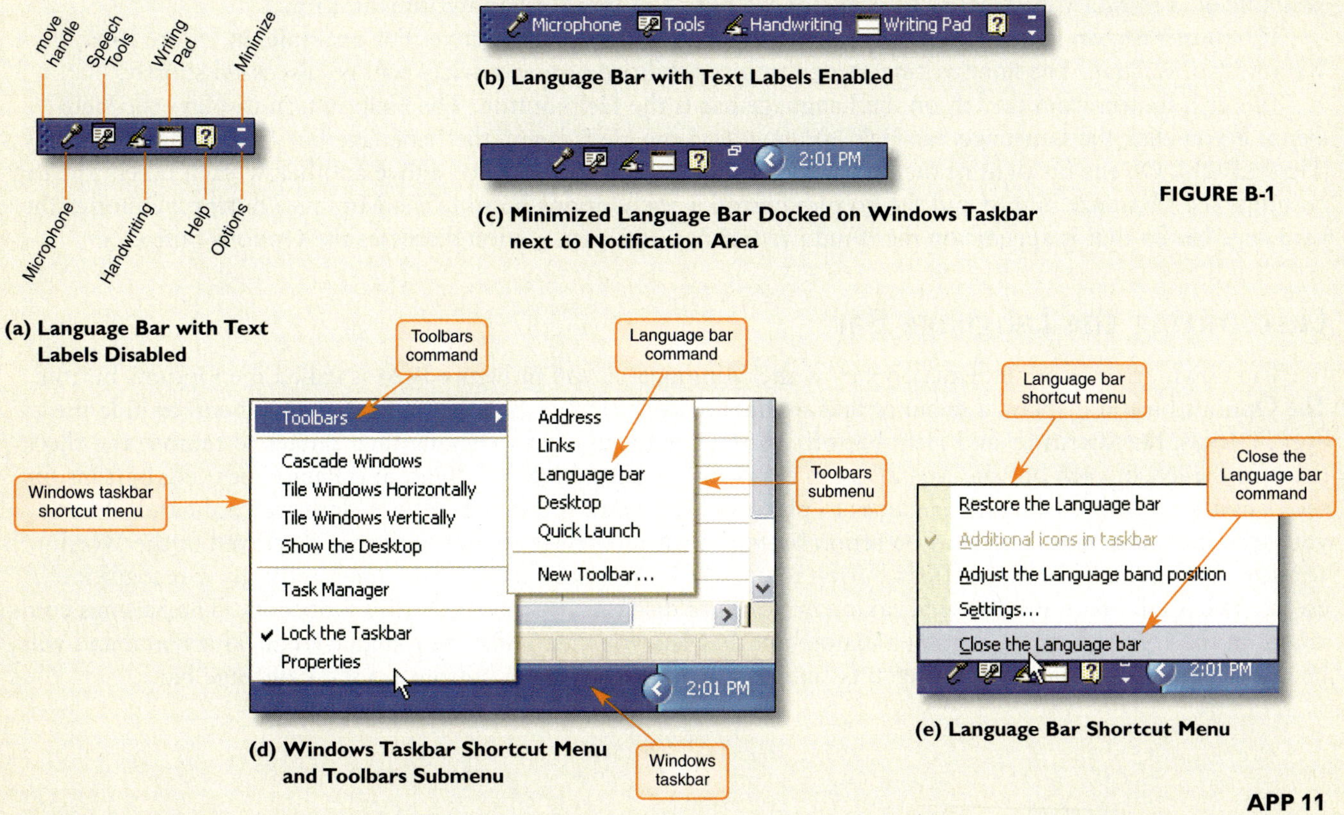

move handle
Speech Tools
Writing Pad
Minimize
Microphone
Handwriting
Help
Options

(a) Language Bar with Text Labels Disabled

Microphone Tools Handwriting Writing Pad

(b) Language Bar with Text Labels Enabled

2:01 PM

(c) Minimized Language Bar Docked on Windows Taskbar next to Notification Area

FIGURE B-1

Toolbars command
Language bar command
Windows taskbar shortcut menu
Toolbars submenu
Windows taskbar
Toolbars
Cascade Windows
Tile Windows Horizontally
Tile Windows Vertically
Show the Desktop
Task Manager
Lock the Taskbar
Properties
Address
Links
Language bar
Desktop
Quick Launch
New Toolbar...
2:01 PM

(d) Windows Taskbar Shortcut Menu and Toolbars Submenu

Language bar shortcut menu
Close the Language bar command
Restore the Language bar
Additional icons in taskbar
Adjust the Language band position
Settings...
Close the Language bar
2:01 PM

(e) Language Bar Shortcut Menu

When Windows was installed on your computer, the installer specified a default language. For example, most users in the United States select English (United States) as the default language. You can add more than 90 additional languages and varying dialects such as Basque, English (Zimbabwe), French (France), French (Canada), German (Germany), German (Austria), and Swahili. With multiple languages available, you can switch from one language to another while working in Word. If you change the language or dialect, then text services may change the functions of the keys on the keyboard, adjust speech recognition, and alter handwriting recognition. If a second language is activated, then a Language icon appears immediately to the right of the move handle on the Language bar and the language name is displayed on the Word status bar. This appendix assumes that English (United States) is the only language installed. Thus, the Language icon does not appear in the examples in Figure B-1 on the previous page.

Buttons on the Language Bar

The Language bar shown in Figure B-2a contains seven buttons. The number of buttons on your Language bar may be different. These buttons are used to select the language, customize the Language bar, control the microphone, control handwriting, and obtain help.

The first button on the left is the Microphone button, which enables and disables the microphone. When the microphone is enabled, text services adds two buttons and a balloon to the Language bar (Figure B-2b). These additional buttons and the balloon will be discussed shortly.

The second button from the left is the Speech Tools button. The Speech Tools button displays a menu of commands (Figure B-2c) that allow you to scan the current document looking for words to add to the speech recognition dictionary; hide or show the balloon on the Language bar; train the Speech Recognition service so that it can interpret your voice better; add and delete specific words to and from its dictionary, such as names and other words not understood easily; and change the user profile so more than one person can use the microphone on the same computer.

The third button from the left on the Language bar is the Handwriting button. The Handwriting button displays the Handwriting menu (Figure B-2d), which lets you choose the Writing Pad (Figure B-2e), Write Anywhere (Figure B-2f), or the on-screen keyboard (Figure B-2g). The On-Screen Symbol Keyboard command on the Handwriting menu displays an on-screen keyboard that allows you to enter special symbols that are not available on a standard keyboard. You can choose only one form of handwriting at a time.

The fourth button indicates which one of the handwriting forms is active. For example, in Figure B-2a, the Writing Pad is active. The handwriting recognition capabilities of text services will be discussed shortly.

The fifth button from the left on the Language bar is the Help button. The Help button displays the Help menu. If you click the Language Bar Help command on the Help menu, the Language Bar Help window appears (Figure B-2h). On the far right of the Language bar are two buttons stacked above and below each other. The top button is the Minimize button and the bottom button is the Options button. The Minimize button minimizes the Language bar so that it appears on the Windows taskbar. The next section discusses the Options button.

Customizing the Language Bar

The down arrow icon immediately below the Minimize button in Figure B-2a is called the Options button. The Options button displays a menu of text services options (Figure B-2i). You can use this menu to hide the Speech Tools, Handwriting, and Help buttons on the Language bar by clicking their names to remove the check mark to the left of each button. You also can show the Correction, Speak Text, and Pause Speaking buttons on the Language bar by clicking their names to place a check mark to the left of the respective command. When you select text and then click the Correction button, a list of correction alternatives is displayed in the Word window. You can use the Corrections button to correct both speech recognition and handwriting recognition errors. The Speak Text and Pause Speaking buttons are discussed at the end of this Appendix. The Settings command on the Options menu displays a dialog box that lets you customize the Language bar. This command will be discussed shortly. The Restore Defaults command redisplays hidden buttons on the Language bar.

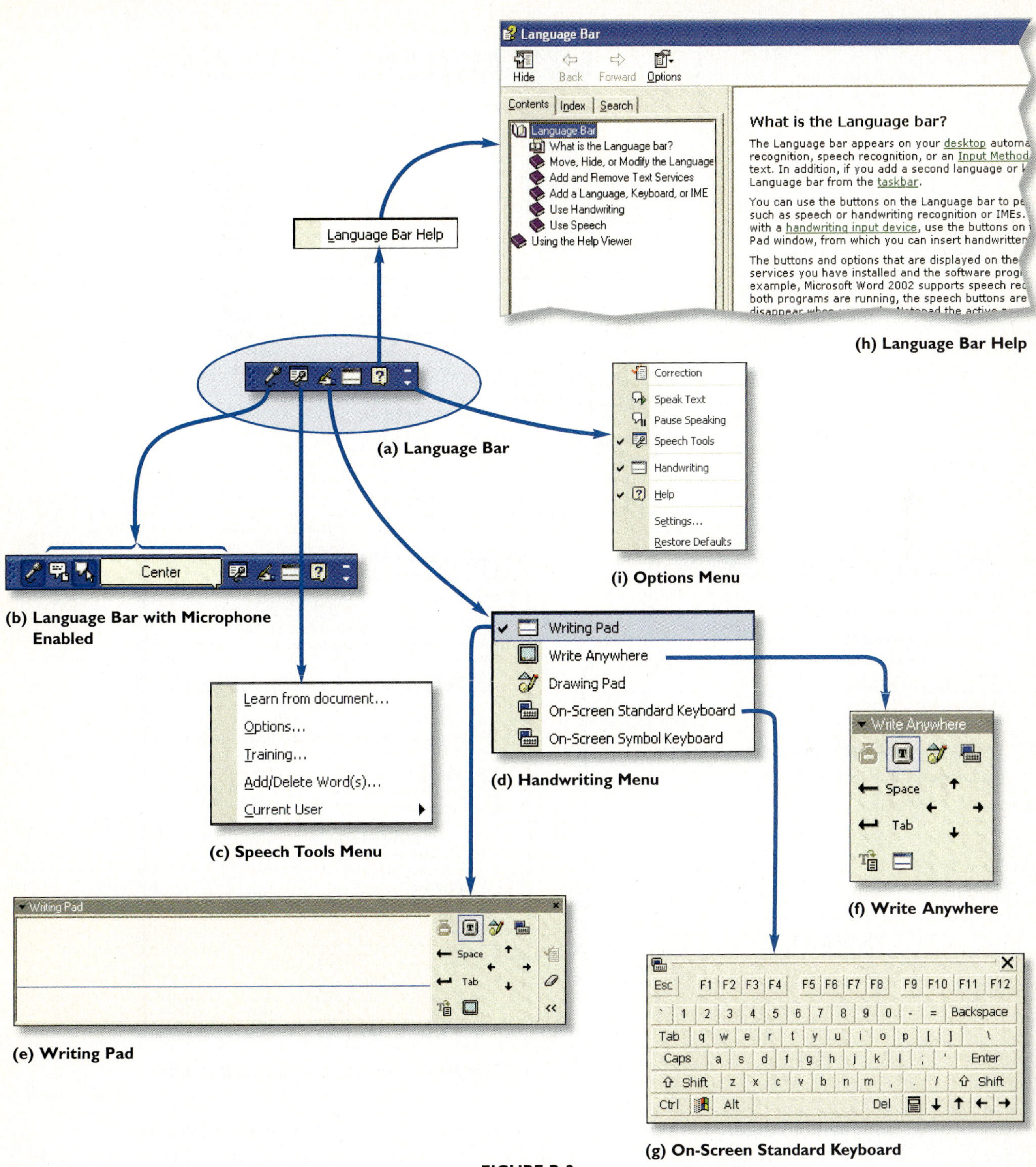

FIGURE B-2

If you right-click the Language bar, a shortcut menu appears (Figure B-3a on the next page). This shortcut menu lets you further customize the Language bar. The Minimize command on the shortcut menu docks the Language bar on the Windows taskbar. The Transparency command in Figure B-3a toggles the Language bar between being solid and transparent. You can see through a transparent Language bar (Figure B-3b). The Text Labels command toggles on text labels on the Language bar (Figure B-3c) and off (Figure B-3b). The Vertical command displays the Language bar vertically on the screen (Figure B-3d).

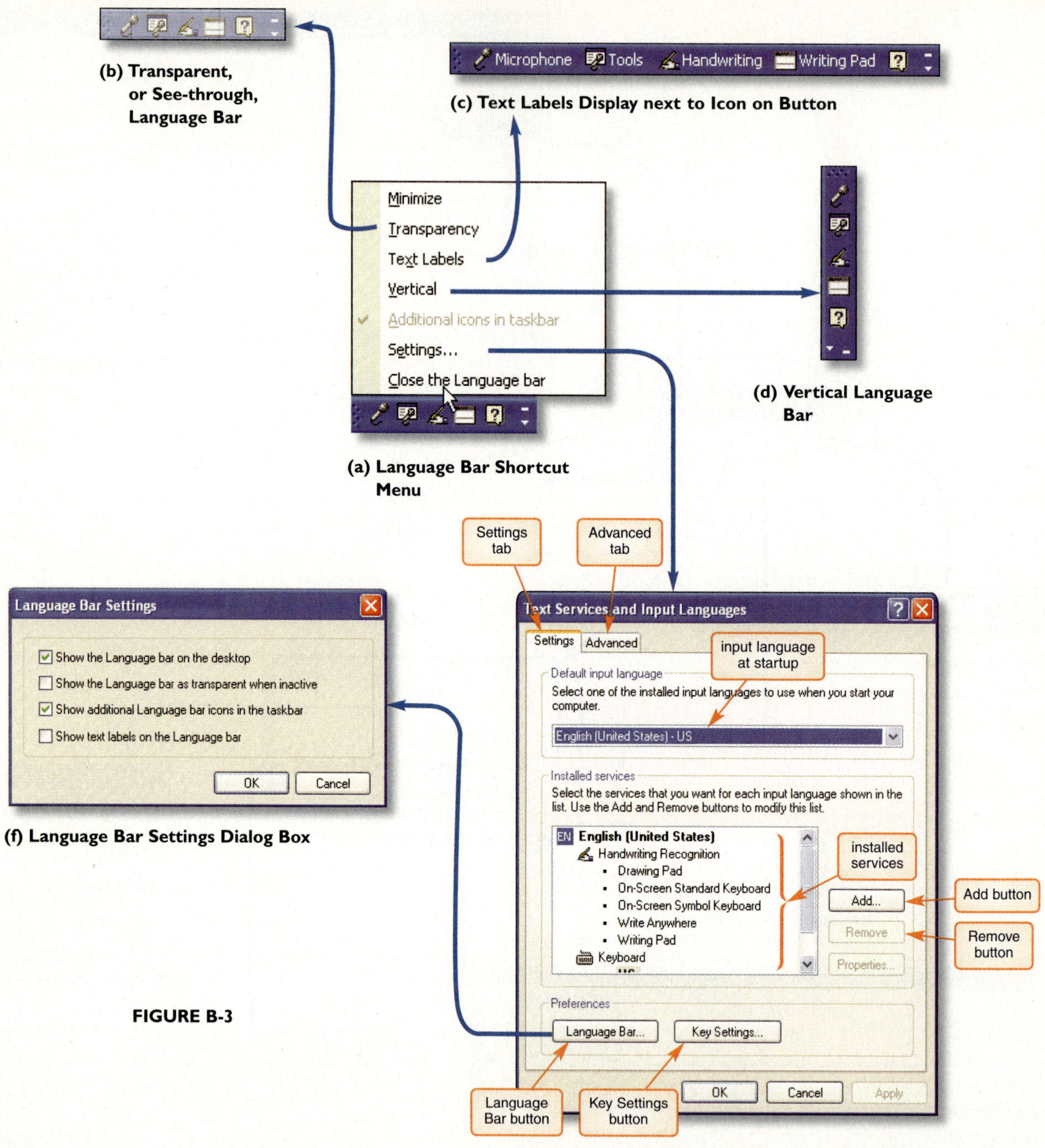

(b) Transparent, or See-through, Language Bar

(c) Text Labels Display next to Icon on Button

(d) Vertical Language Bar

(a) Language Bar Shortcut Menu

(f) Language Bar Settings Dialog Box

(e) Text Services and Input Languages Dialog Box

FIGURE B-3

The Settings command in Figure B-3a displays the Text Services and Input Languages dialog box (Figure B-3e). The Text Services and Input Languages dialog box allows you to add additonal languages, add and remove text services, modify keys on the keyboard, modify the Language bar, and extend support of advanced text services to all programs, including Notepad and other programs that normally do not support text services (through the Advanced tab). If you want to remove any one of the services in the Installed services list, select the service, and then click the Remove button. If you want to add a service, click the Add button. The Key Settings button allows you to modify the keyboard. If you click the Language Bar button in the Text Services and Input Languages dialog box, the Language Bar Settings dialog box appears (Figure B-3f). This dialog box contains Language bar options, some of which are the same as the commands on the Language bar shortcut menu shown in Figure B-3a.

The Close the Language bar command on the shortcut menu shown in Figure B-3a closes or hides the Language bar. If you close the Language bar and want to redisplay it, see Figure B-1d on page APP 11.

Speech Recognition

The **Speech Recognition service** available with Office enables your computer to recognize human speech through a microphone. The microphone has two modes: dictation and voice command (Figure B-4). You switch between the two modes by clicking the Dictation button and the Voice Command button on the Language bar. These buttons appear only when you turn on Speech Recognition by clicking the Microphone button on the Language bar (Figure B-5a on the next page). If you are using the Microphone button for the very first time in Word, it will require that you check your microphone settings and step through voice training before activating the Speech Recognition service.

The Dictation button places the microphone in Dictation mode. In **Dictation mode**, whatever you speak is entered as text at the location of the insertion point. The Voice Command button places the microphone in Voice Command mode. In **Voice Command mode**, whatever you speak is interpreted as a command. If you want to turn off the microphone, click the Microphone button on the Language bar or in Voice Command mode say, "Mic off" (pronounced mike off). It is important to remember that minimizing the Language bar does not turn off the microphone.

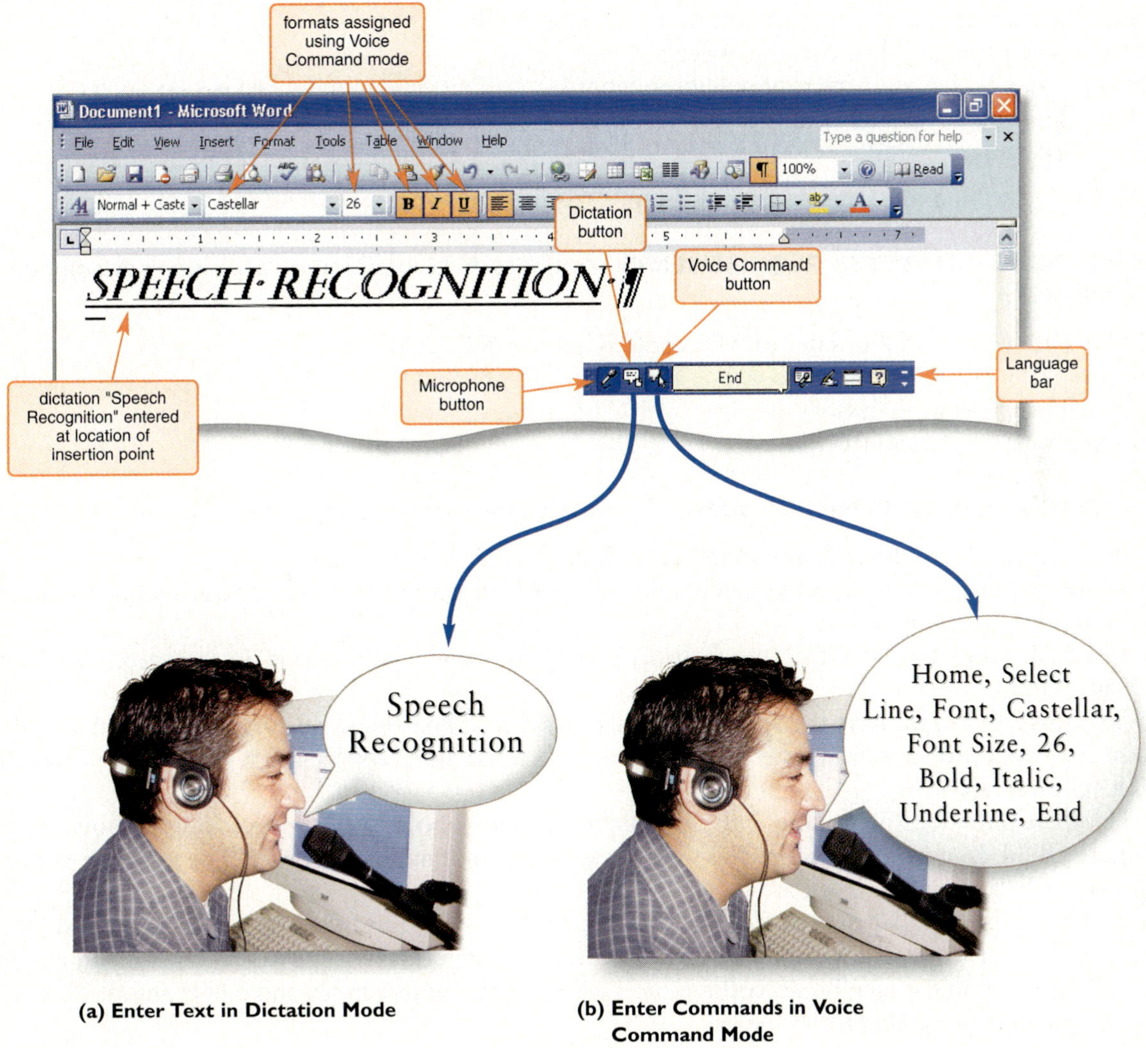

(a) Enter Text in Dictation Mode

(b) Enter Commands in Voice Command Mode

FIGURE B-4

The Language bar speech message balloon shown in Figure B-5b displays messages that may offer help or hints. In Voice Command mode, the name of the last recognized command you said appears. If you use the mouse or keyboard instead of the microphone, a message will appear in the Language bar speech message balloon indicating the word you could say. In Dictation mode, the message, Dictating, usually appears. The Speech Recognition service, however, will display messages to inform you that you are talking too soft, too loud, too fast, or to ask you to repeat what you said by displaying, What was that?

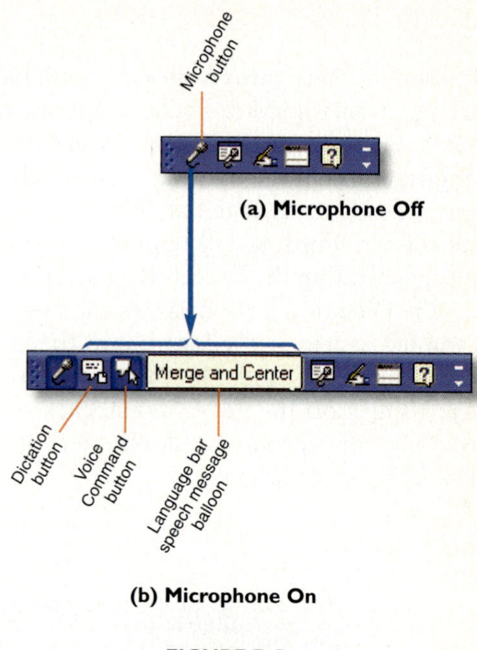

FIGURE B-5

Getting Started with Speech Recognition

For the microphone to function properly, you should follow these steps:

1. Make sure your computer meets the minimum requirements.
2. Start Word. Activate Speech Recognition by clicking Tools on the menu bar and then clicking Speech.
3. Set up and position your microphone, preferably a close-talk headset with gain adjustment support.
4. Train Speech Recognition.

The following sections describe these steps in more detail.

SPEECH RECOGNITION SYSTEM REQUIREMENTS For Speech Recognition to work on your computer, it needs the following:

1. Microsoft Windows 98 or later or Microsoft Windows NT 4.0 or later
2. At least 128 MB RAM
3. 400 MHz or faster processor
4. Microphone and sound card

SETUP AND POSITION YOUR MICROPHONE Set up your microphone as follows:

1. Connect your microphone to the sound card in the back of the computer.
2. Position the microphone approximately one inch out from and to the side of your mouth. Position it so you are not breathing into it.
3. On the Language bar, click the Speech Tools button and then click Options on the Speech Tools menu (Figure B-6a).
4. When text services displays the Speech input settings dialog box (Figure B-6b), click the Advanced Speech button. When text services displays the Speech Properties dialog box (Figure B-6c), click the Speech Recognition tab.
5. Click the Configure Microphone button. Follow the Microphone Wizard directions as shown in Figures B-6d, B-6e, and B-6f. The Next button will remain dimmed in Figure B-6e until the volume meter consistently stays in the green area.
6. If someone else installed Speech Recognition, click the New button in the Speech Properties dialog box and enter your name. Click the Train Profile button and step through the Voice Training dialog boxes. The Voice Training dialog boxes will require that you enter your gender and age group. It then will step you through voice training.

You can adjust the microphone further by clicking the Settings button in the Speech Properties dialog box (Figure B-6c). The Settings button displays the Recognition Profile Settings dialog box that allows you to adjust the pronunciation sensitivity and accuracy versus recognition response time.

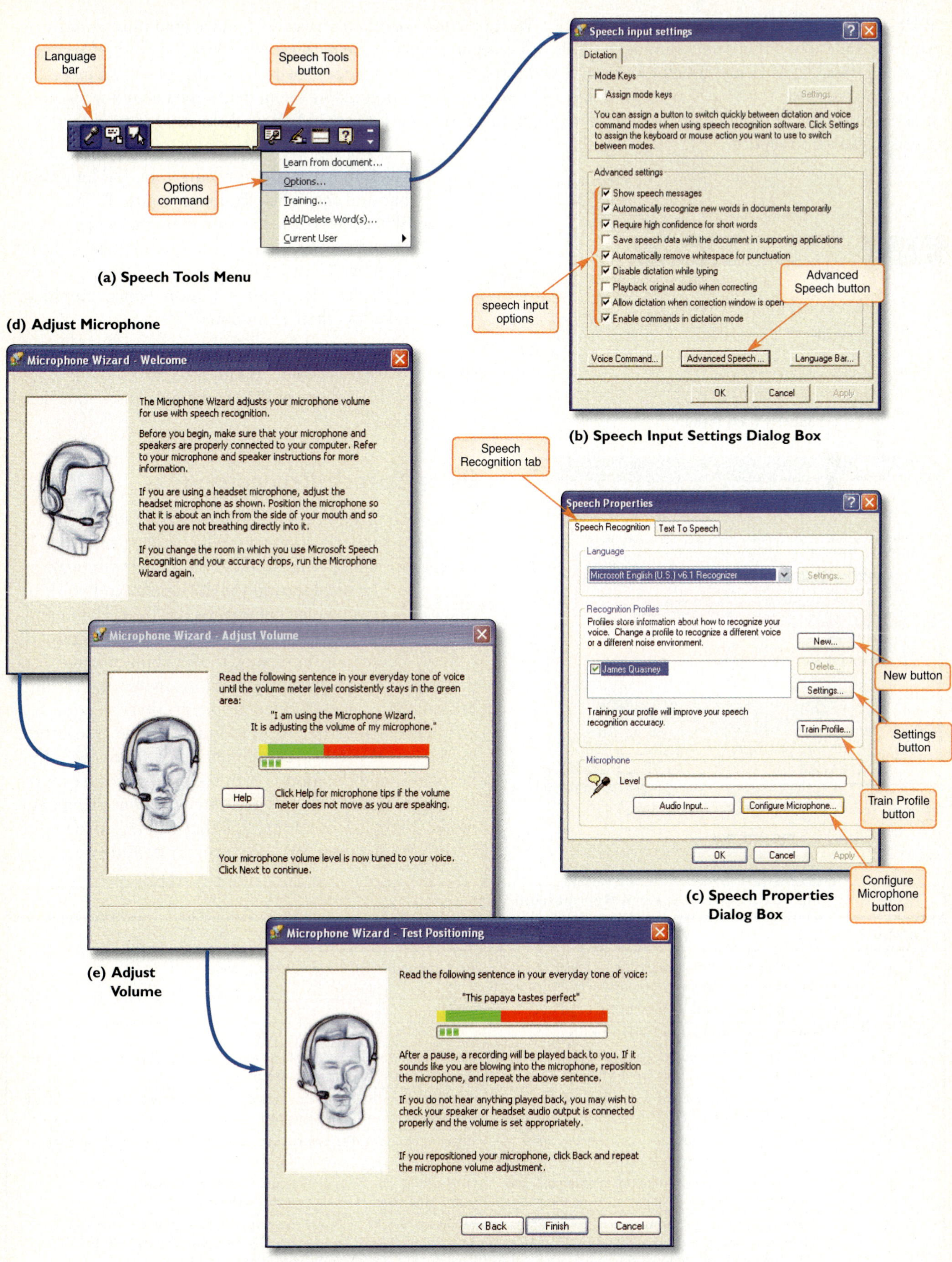

Language bar
Speech Tools button
Learn from document...
Options...
Training...
Add/Delete Word(s)...
Current User
Options command
(a) Speech Tools Menu
Speech input settings
Dictation
Mode Keys
Assign mode keys
Settings...
You can assign a button to switch quickly between dictation and voice command modes when using speech recognition software. Click Settings to assign the keyboard or mouse action you want to use to switch between modes.
Advanced settings
Show speech messages
Automatically recognize new words in documents temporarily
Require high confidence for short words
Save speech data with the document in supporting applications
Automatically remove whitespace for punctuation
Disable dictation while typing
Playback original audio when correcting
Allow dictation when correction window is open
Enable commands in dictation mode
speech input options
Advanced Speech button
Voice Command...
Advanced Speech ...
Language Bar...
OK
Cancel
Apply
(b) Speech Input Settings Dialog Box
(d) Adjust Microphone
Microphone Wizard - Welcome
The Microphone Wizard adjusts your microphone volume for use with speech recognition.
Before you begin, make sure that your microphone and speakers are properly connected to your computer. Refer to your microphone and speaker instructions for more information.
If you are using a headset microphone, adjust the headset microphone as shown. Position the microphone so that it is about an inch from the side of your mouth and so that you are not breathing directly into it.
If you change the room in which you use Microsoft Speech Recognition and your accuracy drops, run the Microphone Wizard again.
Speech Recognition tab
Speech Properties
Speech Recognition
Text To Speech
Language
Microsoft English (U.S.) v6.1 Recognizer
Settings...
Recognition Profiles
Profiles store information about how to recognize your voice. Change a profile to recognize a different voice or a different noise environment.
New...
James Quasney
Delete...
Settings...
Training your profile will improve your speech recognition accuracy.
Train Profile...
Microphone
Level
Audio Input...
Configure Microphone...
OK
Cancel
Apply
New button
Settings button
Train Profile button
Configure Microphone button
(c) Speech Properties Dialog Box
Microphone Wizard - Adjust Volume
Read the following sentence in your everyday tone of voice until the volume meter level consistently stays in the green area:
"I am using the Microphone Wizard.
It is adjusting the volume of my microphone."
Help
Click Help for microphone tips if the volume meter does not move as you are speaking.
Your microphone volume level is now tuned to your voice. Click Next to continue.
(e) Adjust Volume
Microphone Wizard - Test Positioning
Read the following sentence in your everyday tone of voice:
"This papaya tastes perfect"
After a pause, a recording will be played back to you. If it sounds like you are blowing into the microphone, reposition the microphone, and repeat the above sentence.
If you do not hear anything played back, you may wish to check your speaker or headset audio output is connected properly and the volume is set appropriately.
If you repositioned your microphone, click Back and repeat the microphone volume adjustment.
< Back
Finish
Cancel
(f) Test Microphone

FIGURE B-6

TRAIN THE SPEECH RECOGNITION SERVICE The Speech Recognition service will understand most commands and some dictation without any training at all. It will recognize much more of what you speak, however, if you take the time to train it. After one training session, it will recognize 85 to 90 percent of your words. As you do more training, accuracy will rise to 95 percent. If you feel that too many mistakes are being made, then continue to train the service. The more training you do, the more accurately it will work for you. Follow these steps to train the Speech Recognition service:

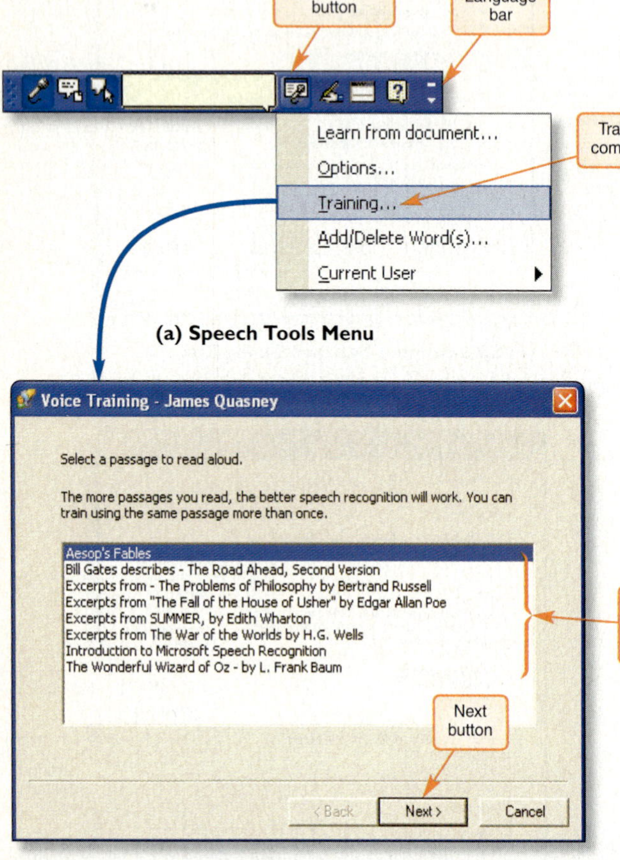

(a) Speech Tools Menu

(b) Voice Training Dialog Box

FIGURE B-7

1. Click the Speech Tools button on the Language bar and then click Training (Figure B-7a).
2. When the Voice Training dialog box appears (Figure B-7b), click one of the sessions and then click the Next button.
3. Complete the training session, which should take less than 15 minutes.

If you are serious about using a microphone to speak to your computer, you need to take the time to go through at least three of the eight training sessions listed in Figure B-7b.

Using Speech Recognition

Speech recognition lets you enter text into a document similarly to speaking into a tape recorder. Instead of typing, you can dictate text that you want to be displayed in the document, and you can issue voice commands. In Voice Command mode, you can speak menu names, commands on menus, toolbar button names, and dialog box option buttons, check boxes, list boxes, and button names. Speech recognition, however, is not a completely hands-free form of input. Speech recognition works best if you use a combination of your voice, the keyboard, and the mouse. You soon will discover that Dictation mode is far less accurate than Voice Command mode. Table B-1 lists some tips that will improve the Speech Recognition service's accuracy considerably.

Table B-1 Tips to Improve Speech Recognition

NUMBER	TIP
1	The microphone hears everything. Though the Speech Recognition service filters out background noise, it is recommended that you work in a quiet environment.
2	Try not to move the microphone around once it is adjusted.
3	Speak in a steady tone and speak clearly.
4	In Dictation mode, do not pause between words. A phrase is easier to interpret than a word. Sounding out syllables in a word will make it more difficult for the Speech Recognition service to interpret what you are saying.
5	If you speak too loudly or too softly, it makes it difficult for the Speech Recognition service to interpret what you said. Check the Language bar speech message balloon for an indication that you may be speaking too loudly or too softly.
6	If you experience problems after training, adjust the recognition options that control accuracy and rejection by clicking the Settings button shown in Figure B-6c on the previous page.
7	When you are finished using the microphone, turn it off by clicking the Microphone button on the Language bar or in Voice Command mode, say "Mic off." Leaving the microphone on is the same as leaning on the keyboard.
8	If the Speech Recognition service is having difficulty with unusual words, then add the words to its dictionary by using the Learn from document and Add/Delete Word(s) commands on the Speech Tools menu (Figure B-8a). The last names of individuals and the names of companies are good examples of the types of words you should add to the dictionary.
9	Training will improve accuracy; practice will improve confidence.

The last command on the Speech Tools menu is the Current User command (Figure B-8a). The Current User command is useful for multiple users who share a computer. It allows them to configure their own individual profiles, and then switch between users as they use the computer.

For additional information about the Speech Recognition service, enter `speech recognition` in the Type a question for help box on the menu bar.

(a) Speech Tools Menu

(b) Add/Delete Word(s) Dialog Box

FIGURE B-8

Handwriting Recognition

Using the Office **Handwriting Recognition service**, you can enter text and numbers into Word by writing instead of typing. You can write using a special handwriting device that connects to your computer or you can write on the screen using your mouse. Four basic methods of handwriting are available by clicking the Handwriting button on the Language bar: Writing Pad; Write Anywhere; Drawing Pad; and On-Screen Keyboard. Although the on-screen keyboard does not involve handwriting recognition, it is part of the Handwriting menu and, therefore, will be discussed in this section.

If your Language bar does not include the Handwriting button, then for installation instructions, enter `install handwriting recognition` in the Type a question for help box on the menu bar.

Writing Pad

To display the Writing Pad, click the Handwriting button on the Language bar and then click Writing Pad (Figure B-9). The **Writing Pad** resembles a notepad with one or more lines on which you can use freehand to print or write in cursive. With the Text button enabled, you can form letters on the line by moving the mouse while holding down the mouse button. To the right of the notepad is a rectangular toolbar. Use the buttons on this toolbar to adjust the Writing Pad, select cells, and activate other handwriting applications.

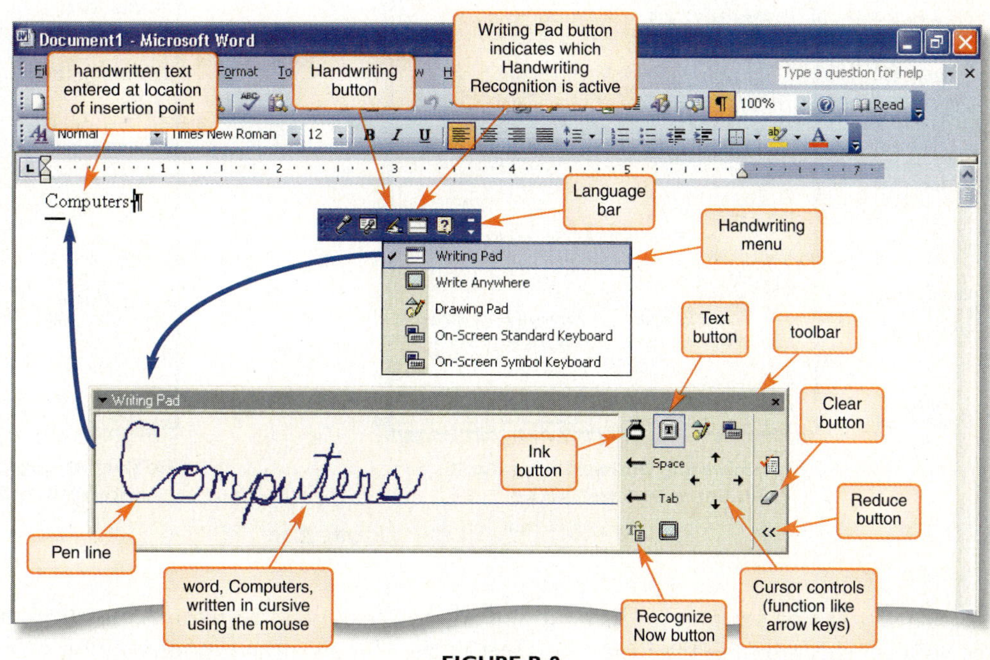

FIGURE B-9

Consider the example in Figure B-9 on the previous page. With the insertion point at the top of the document, the word, Computers, is written in cursive on the **Pen line** in the Writing Pad. As soon as the word is complete, the Handwriting Recognition service automatically converts the handwriting to typed characters and inserts the text at the location of the insertion point. With the Ink button enabled, instead of the Text button, the text is inserted in handwritten form in the document.

You can customize the Writing Pad by clicking the Options button on the left side of the Writing Pad title bar and then clicking the Options command (Figure B-10a). Invoking the Options command causes the Handwriting Options dialog box to be displayed. The Handwriting Options dialog box contains two sheets: Common and Writing Pad. The Common sheet lets you change the pen color and pen width, adjust recognition, and customize the toolbar area of the Writing Pad. The Writing Pad sheet allows you to change the background color and the number of lines that are displayed in the Writing Pad. Both sheets contain a Restore Default button to restore the settings to what they were when the software was installed initially.

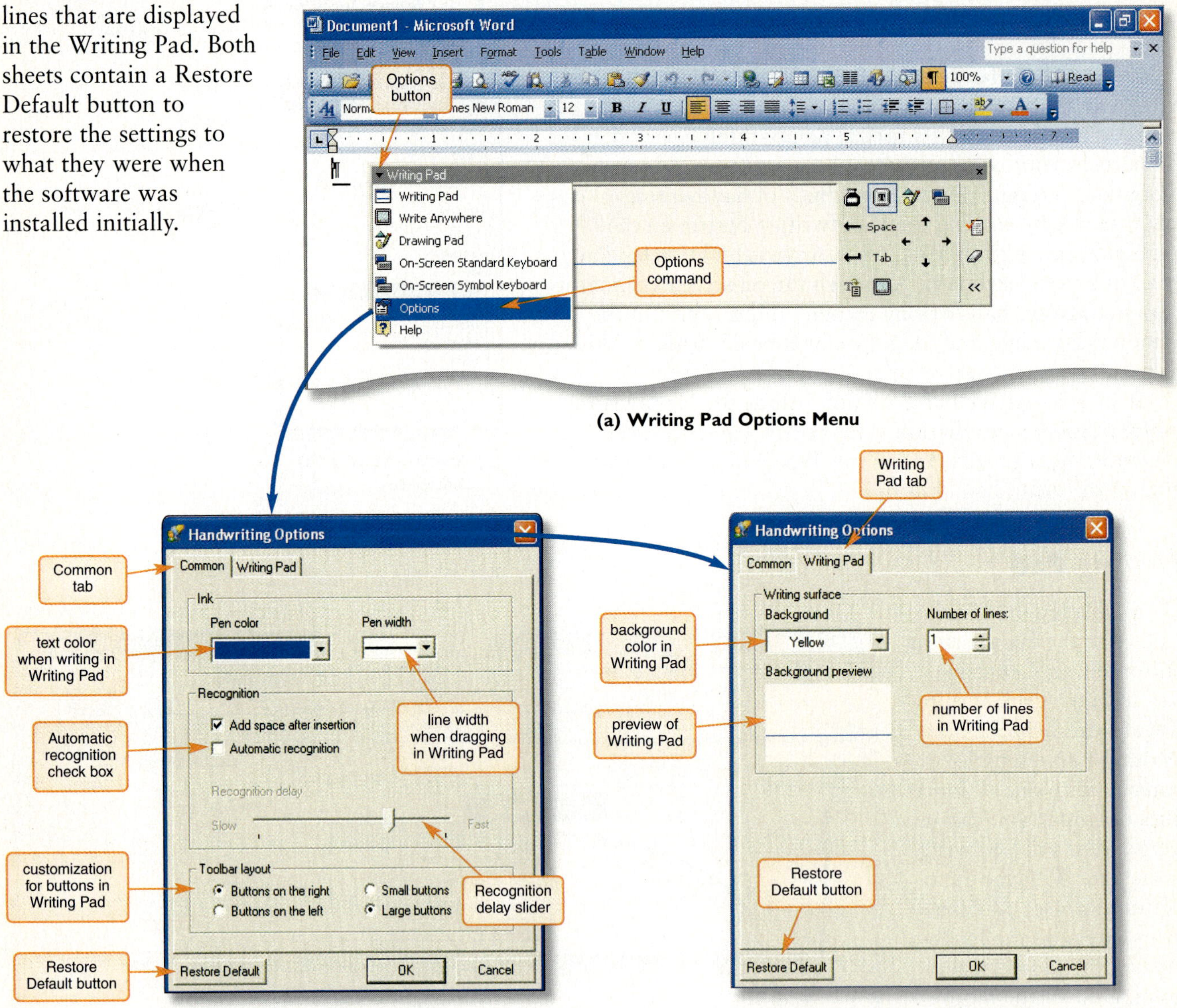

(a) Writing Pad Options Menu

(b) Handwriting Options Dialog Box with Common Sheet Active

(c) Handwriting Options Dialog Box with Writing Pad Sheet Active

FIGURE B-10

When you first start using the Writing Pad, you may want to remove the check mark from the Automatic recognition check box in the Common sheet in the Handwriting Options dialog box (Figure B-10b). With the check mark removed, the Handwriting Recognition service will not interpret what you write in the Writing Pad until you click the Recognize Now button on the toolbar (Figure B-9 on the previous page). This allows you to pause and adjust your writing.

The best way to learn how to use the Writing Pad is to practice with it. Also, for more information, enter `handwriting recognition` in the Type a question for help box on the menu bar.

Write Anywhere

Rather than use Writing Pad, you can write anywhere on the screen by invoking the Write Anywhere command on the Handwriting menu (Figure B-11) that appears when you click the Handwriting button on the Language bar. In this case, the entire window is your writing pad.

In Figure B-11, the word, `Report`, is written in cursive using the mouse button. Shortly after the word is written, the Handwriting Recognition service interprets it, assigns it to the location of the insertion point, and erases what was written.

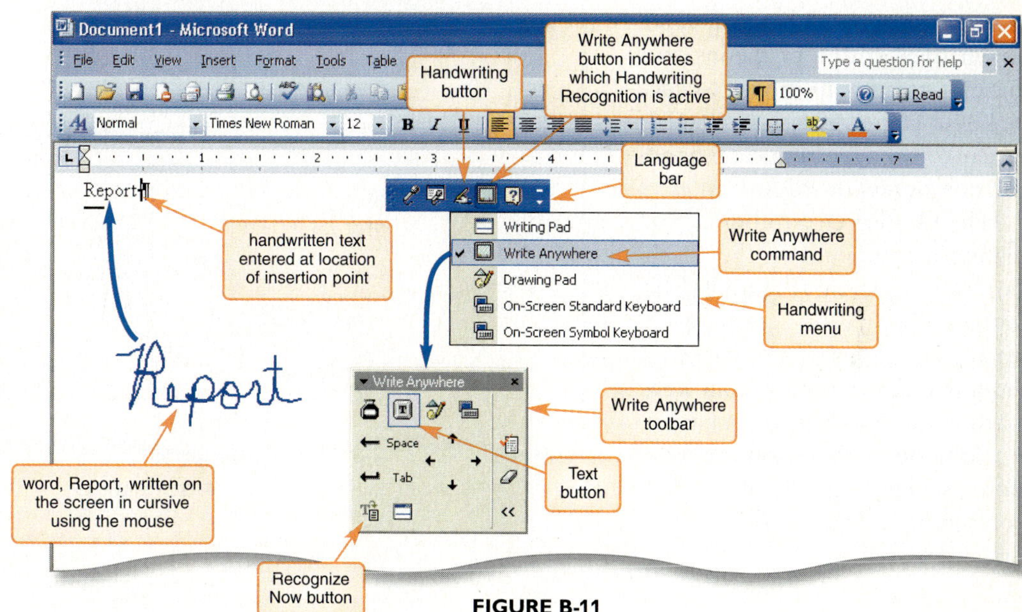

FIGURE B-11

It is recommended that when you first start using the Write Anywhere service that you remove the check mark from the Automatic recognition check box in the Common sheet in the Handwriting Options dialog box (Figure B-10b). With the check mark removed, the Handwriting Recognition service will not interpret what you write on the screen until you click the Recognize Now button on the toolbar (Figure B-11).

Write Anywhere is more difficult to use than the Writing Pad, because when you click the mouse button, Word may interpret the action as moving the insertion point rather than starting to write. For this reason, it is recommended that you use the Writing Pad.

Drawing Pad

With the Drawing Pad, you can insert a freehand drawing or sketch in a Word document. To display the Drawing Pad, click the Handwriting button on the Language bar and then click Drawing Pad (Figure B-12). Create a drawing by dragging the mouse in the Drawing Pad. In Figure B-12, the mouse was used to draw a tic-tac-toe game. When you click the Insert Drawing button on the Drawing Pad toolbar, Word inserts the drawing in the document at the location of the insertion point. Other buttons on the toolbar allow you to erase a drawing, erase your last drawing stroke, copy the drawing to the Office Clipboard, or activate the Writing Pad.

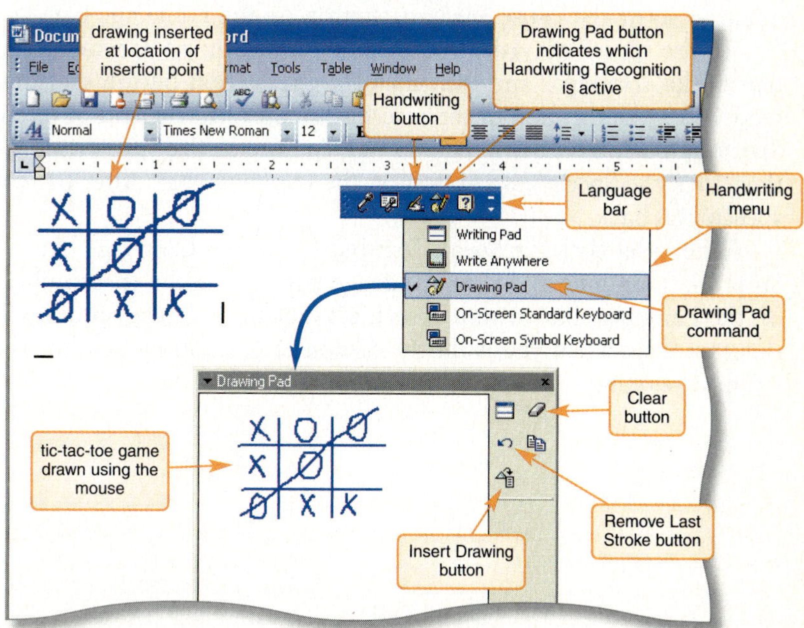

FIGURE B-12

The best way to learn how to use the Drawing Pad is to practice with it. Also, for more information, enter `drawing pad` in the Type a question for help box on the menu bar.

On-Screen Keyboard

The On-Screen Standard Keyboard command on the Handwriting menu (Figure B-13) displays an on-screen keyboard. The **on-screen keyboard** lets you enter data at the location of the insertion point by using your mouse to click the keys. The on-screen keyboard is similar to the type found on hand-held computers or PDAs.

The On-Screen Symbol Keyboard command on the Handwriting menu (Figure B-13) displays a special on-screen keyboard that allows you to enter symbols that are not on your keyboard, as well as Unicode characters. **Unicode characters** use a coding scheme capable of representing all the world's current languages.

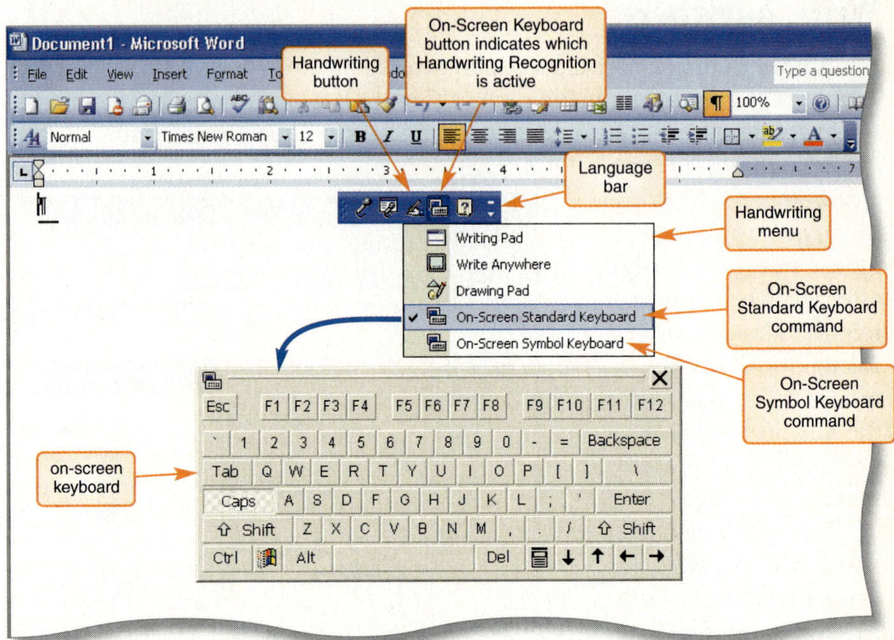

FIGURE B-13

Speech Playback

Using **speech playback**, you can have your computer read back the text in a document. Word provides two buttons for speech playback: Speak Text and Pause Speaking. To show the Speak Text button on the Language bar, click the Options button on the Language bar (Figure B-14) and then click Speak Text on the Options menu. Similarly, click the Options button on the Language bar and then click Pause Speaking on the Options menu to show the Pause Speaking button on the Language bar.

To use speech playback, position the insertion point where you want the computer to start reading back the text in the document and then click the Speak Text button on the Language bar (Figure B-14). The computer reads from the location of the insertion point until the end of the document or until you click the Pause Speaking button on the Language bar. An alternative is to select the text you want the computer to read and then click the Speak Text button on the Language bar. After the computer reads back the selected text, it stops speech playback.

When you click the Speak Text button on the Language bar, it changes to a Stop Speaking button. Click the Stop Speaking button on the Language bar to stop the speech playback. If you click the Pause Speaking button on the Language bar to stop speech playback, the Pause Speaking button changes to a Resume Speaking button that you click when you want the computer to continue reading the document from the location at which it stopped reading.

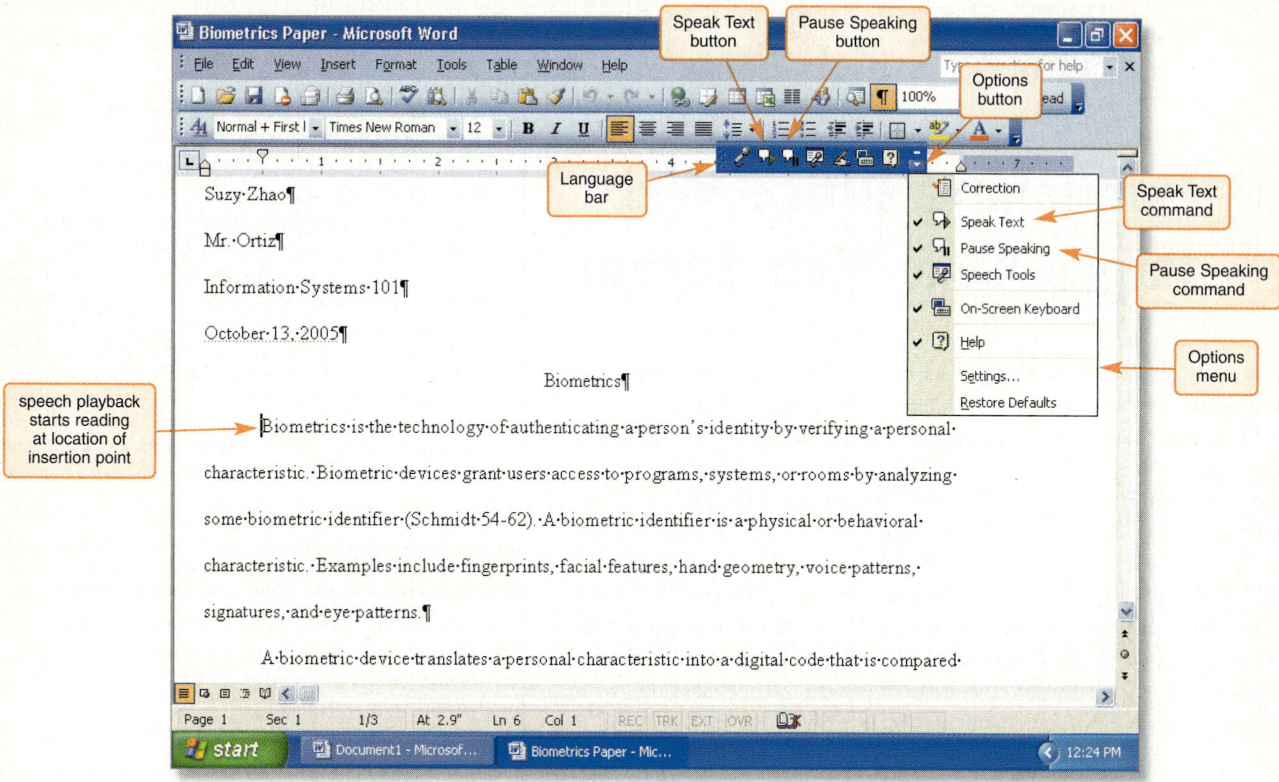

FIGURE B-14

Customizing Speech Playback

You can customize speech playback through the Speech Properties dialog box. Click the Speech Tools button on the Language bar and then click Options on the Speech Tools menu (Figure B-6a on page APP 17). When text services displays the Speech input settings dialog box (Figure B-6b), click the Advanced Speech button. When text services displays the Speech Properties dialog box, click the Text To Speech tab (Figure B-15). The Text To Speech sheet has two areas: Voice selection and Voice speed. The Voice selection area lets you choose between two male voices and one female voice. You can click the Preview Voice button to hear a sample of the voice. The Voice speed area contains a slider. Drag the slider to slow down or speed up the pace of the speaking voice.

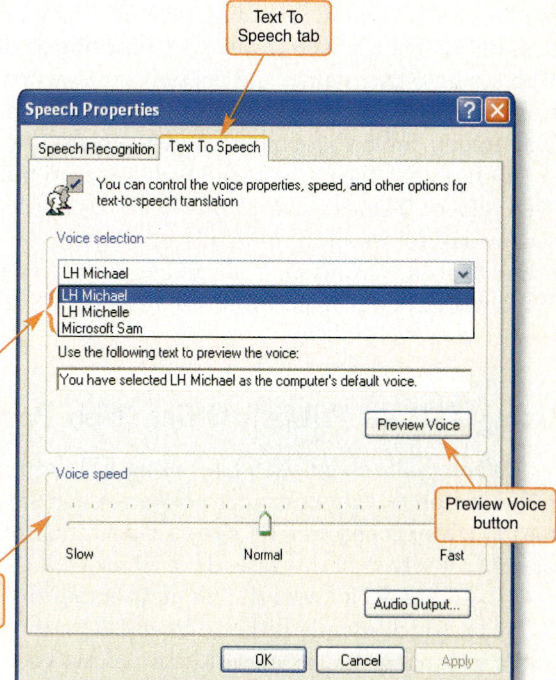

FIGURE B-15

Appendix C

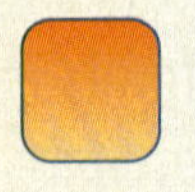

Publishing Office Web Pages to a Web Server

With the Office applications, you use the Save as Web Page command on the File menu to save the Web page to a Web server using one of two techniques: Web folders or File Transfer Protocol. A **Web folder** is an Office shortcut to a Web server. **File Transfer Protocol** (**FTP**) is an Internet standard that allows computers to exchange files with other computers on the Internet.

You should contact your network system administrator or technical support staff at your ISP to determine if their Web server supports Web folders, FTP, or both, and to obtain necessary permissions to access the Web server. If you decide to publish Web pages using a Web folder, you must have the Office Server Extensions (OSE) installed on your computer.

Using Web Folders to Publish Office Web Pages

When publishing to a Web folder, someone first must create the Web folder before you can save to it. If you are granted permission to create a Web folder, you must obtain the URL of the Web server, a user name, and possibly a password that allows you to access the Web server. You also must decide on a name for the Web folder. Table C-1 explains how to create a Web folder.

Office adds the name of the Web folder to the list of current Web folders. You can save to this folder, open files in the folder, rename the folder, or perform any operations you would to a folder on your hard disk. You can use your Office program or Windows Explorer to access this folder. Table C-2 explains how to save to a Web folder.

Using FTP to Publish Office Web Pages

When publishing a Web page using FTP, you first must add the FTP location to your computer before you can save to it. An FTP location, also called an **FTP site**, is a collection of files that reside on an FTP server. In this case, the FTP server is the Web server.

To add an FTP location, you must obtain the name of the FTP site, which usually is the address (URL) of the FTP server, and a user name and a password that allows you to access the FTP server. You save and open the Web pages on the FTP server using the name of the FTP site. Table C-3 explains how to add an FTP site.

Office adds the name of the FTP site to the FTP locations list in the Save As and Open dialog boxes. You can open and save files using this list. Table C-4 explains how to save to an FTP location.

Table C-1 Creating a Web Folder

1. Click File on the menu bar and then click Save As (or Open).
2. When the Save As dialog box (or Open dialog box) appears, click My Network Places on the My Places bar, and then click the Create New Folder button on the toolbar.
3. When the Add Network Place Wizard dialog box appears, click the Next button. If necessary, click Choose another network location. Click the Next button. Click the View some examples link, type the Internet or network address, and then click the Next button. Click Log on anonymously to deselect the check box, type your user name in the User name text box, and then click the Next button. Enter the name you want to call this network place and then click the Next button. Click the Finish button.

Table C-2 Saving to a Web Folder

1. Click File on the menu bar and then click Save As.
2. When the Save As dialog box appears, type the Web page file name in the File name text box. Do not press the ENTER key.
3. Click My Network Places on the My Places bar.
4. Double-click the Web folder name in the Save in list.
5. If the Enter Network Password dialog box appears, type the user name and password in the respective text boxes and then click the OK button.
6. Click the Save button in the Save As dialog box.

Table C-3 Adding an FTP Location

1. Click File on the menu bar and then click Save As (or Open).
2. In the Save As dialog box, click the Save in box arrow and then click Add/Modify FTP Locations in the Save in list; or in the Open dialog box, click the Look in box arrow and then click Add/Modify FTP Locations in the Look in list.
3. When the Add/Modify FTP Locations dialog box appears, type the name of the FTP site in the Name of FTP site text box. If the site allows anonymous logon, click Anonymous in the Log on as area; if you have a user name for the site, click User in the Log on as area and then enter the user name. Enter the password in the Password text box. Click the OK button.
4. Close the Save As or the Open dialog box.

Table C-4 Saving to an FTP Location

1. Click File on the menu bar and then click Save As.
2. When the Save As dialog box appears, type the Web page file name in the File name text box. Do not press the ENTER key.
3. Click the Save in box arrow and then click FTP Locations.
4. Double-click the name of the FTP site to which you wish to save.
5. When the FTP Log On dialog box appears, enter your user name and password and then click the OK button.
6. Click the Save button in the Save As dialog box.

Appendix D

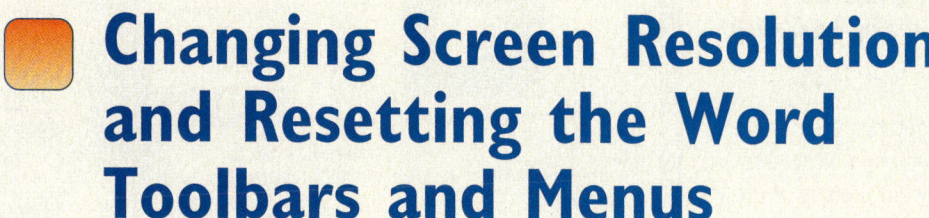

Changing Screen Resolution and Resetting the Word Toolbars and Menus

This appendix explains how to change your screen resolution in Windows to the resolution used in this book. It also describes how to reset the Word toolbars and menus to their installation settings.

Changing Screen Resolution

The **screen resolution** indicates the number of pixels (dots) that your computer uses to display the letters, numbers, graphics, and background you see on your screen. The screen resolution usually is stated as the product of two numbers, such as 800 × 600 (pronounced 800 by 600). An 800 x 600 screen resolution results in a display of 800 distinct pixels on each of 600 lines, or about 480,000 pixels. The figures in this book were created using a screen resolution of 800 × 600.

The screen resolutions most commonly used today are 800 × 600 and 1024 x 768, although some Office specialists operate their computers at a much higher screen resolution, such as 2048 x 1536. The following steps show how to change the screen resolution from 1024 × 768 to 800 × 600.

To Change the Screen Resolution

1

- **If necessary, minimize all applications so that the Windows desktop appears.**
- **Right-click the Windows desktop.**

Windows displays the Windows desktop shortcut menu (Figure D-1).

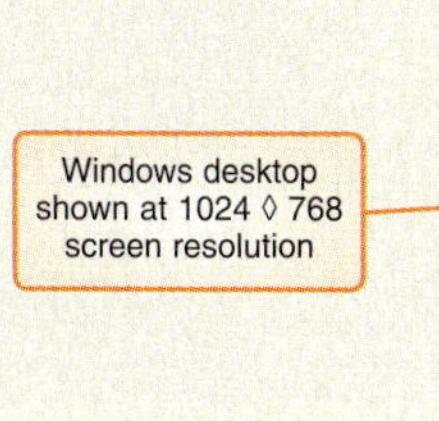

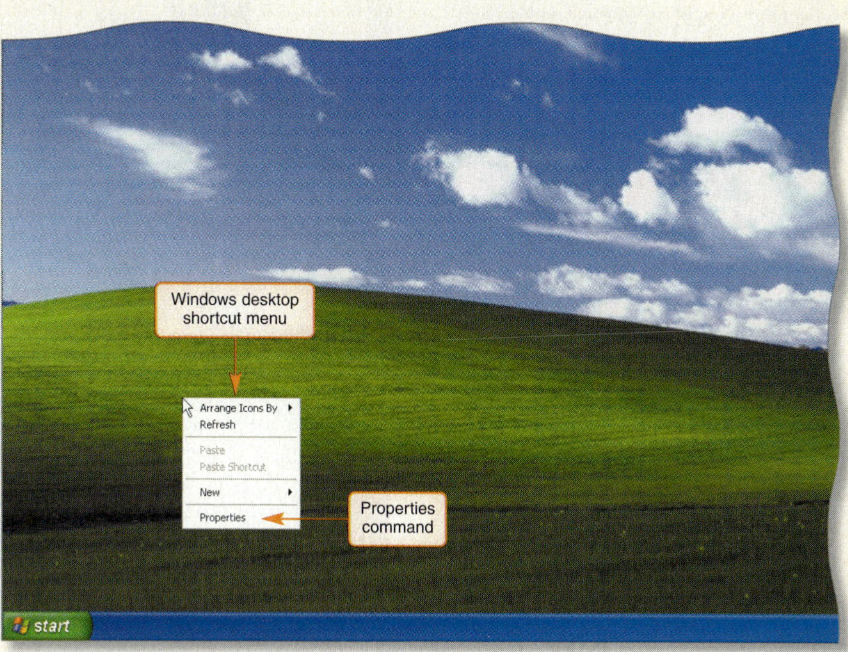

FIGURE D-1

2

• **Click Properties on the shortcut menu.**

• **When Windows displays the Display Properties dialog box, click the Settings tab.**

Windows displays the Settings sheet in the Display Properties dialog box (Figure D-2). The Settings sheet shows a preview of the Windows desktop using the current screen resolution (1024 x 768). The Settings sheet also shows the screen resolution and the color quality settings.

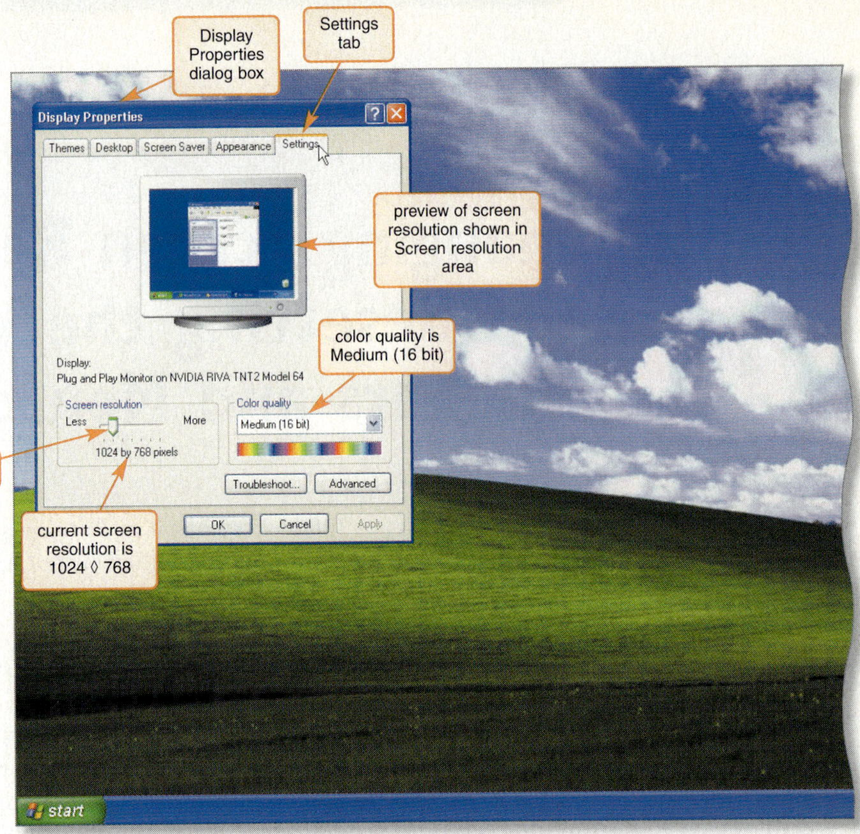

FIGURE D-2

3

• **Drag the slider in the Screen resolution area to the left so that the screen resolution changes to 800 x 600.**

The screen resolution in the Screen resolution area changes to 800 × 600 (Figure D-3). The Settings sheet shows a preview of the Windows desktop using the new screen resolution (800 × 600).

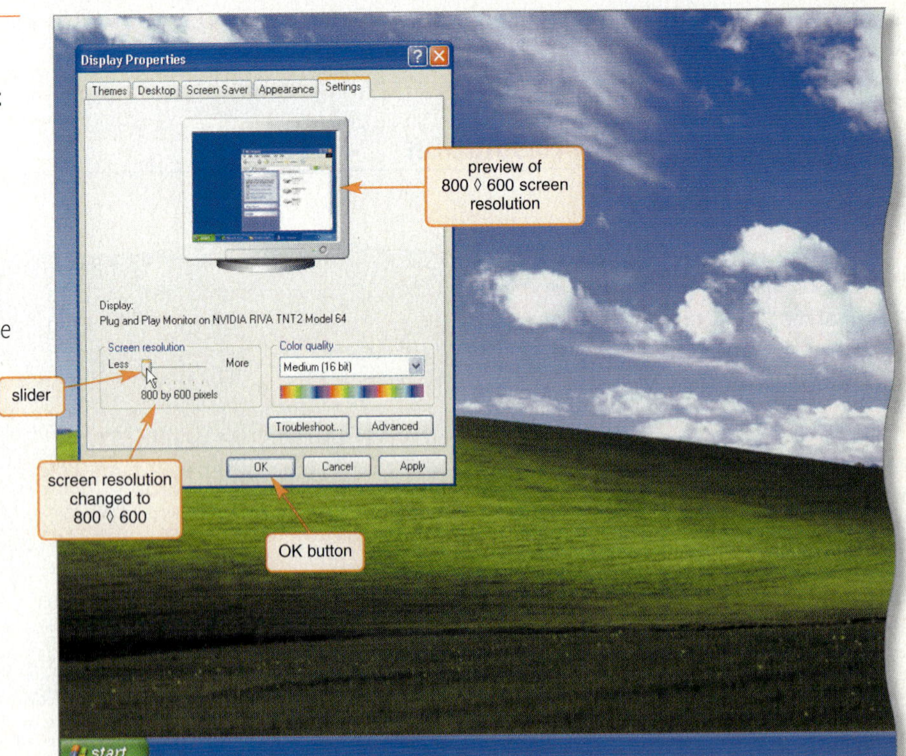

FIGURE D-3

4

- **Click the OK button.**
- **If Windows displays the Monitor Settings dialog box, click the Yes button.**

Windows changes the screen resolution from 1024 × 768 to 800 × 600 (Figure D-4).

800 ◊ 600 screen resolution

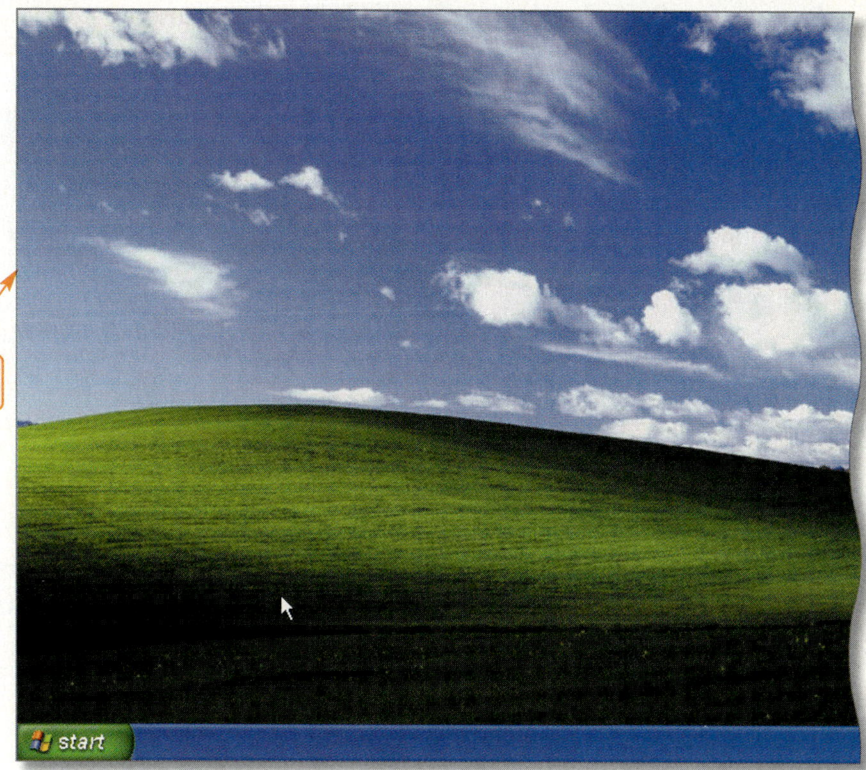

FIGURE D-4

As shown in the previous steps, as you decrease the screen resolution, Windows displays less information on your screen, but the information increases in size. The reverse also is true: as you increase the screen resolution, Windows displays more information on your screen, but the information decreases in size.

Resetting the Word Toolbars and Menus

Word customization capabilities allow you to create custom toolbars by adding and deleting buttons and personalize menus based on their usage. Each time you start Word, the toolbars and menus are displayed using the same settings as the last time you used it. The figures in this book were created with the Word toolbars and menus set to the original, or installation, settings.

Resetting the Standard and Formatting Toolbars

The steps on the next page show how to reset the Standard and Formatting toolbars.

To Reset the Standard and Formatting Toolbars

1

- **Start Word.**
- **Click the Toolbar Options button on the Standard toolbar and then point to Add or Remove Buttons on the Toolbar Options menu.**

Word displays the Toolbar Options menu and the Add or Remove Buttons submenu (Figure D-5).

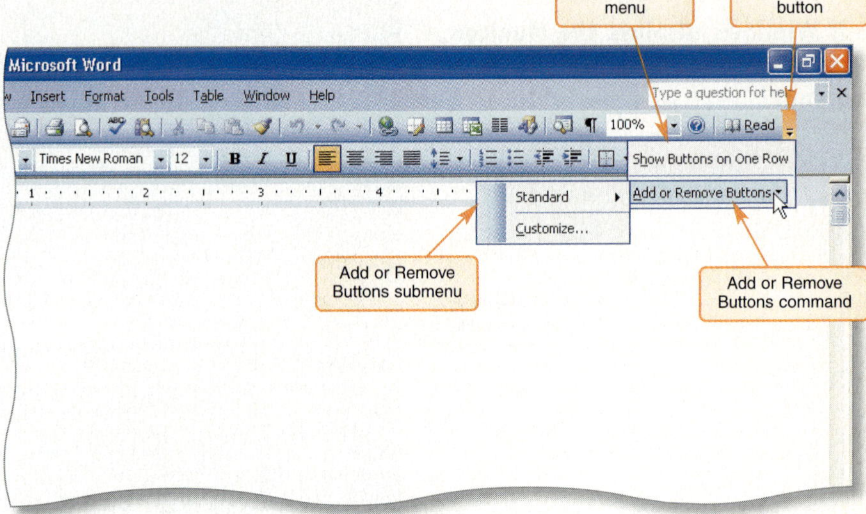

FIGURE D-5

2

- **Point to Standard on the Add or Remove Buttons submenu.**
- **When Word displays the Standard submenu, scroll down and then point to Reset Toolbar.**

The Standard submenu indicates the buttons and boxes that are displayed on the Standard toolbar (Figure D-6). To remove a button from the Standard toolbar, click a button name with a check mark to the left of the name to remove the check mark.

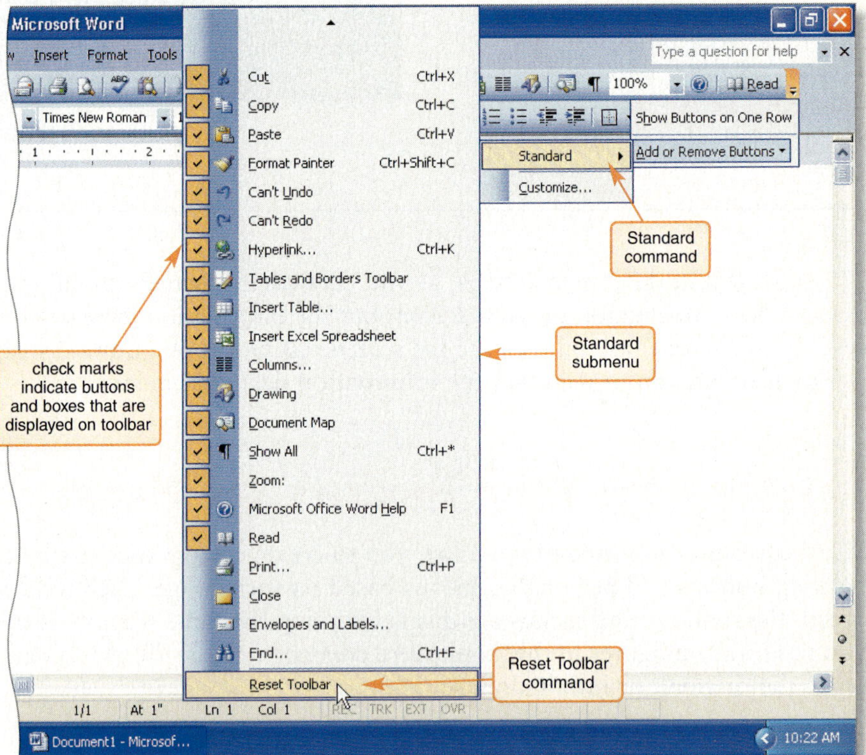

FIGURE D-6

3

- **Click Reset Toolbar.**
- **If a Microsoft Word dialog box is displayed, click the Yes button.**

Word resets the Standard toolbar to its original settings.

4

- **Reset the Formatting toolbar by following Steps 1 through 3 and replacing any reference to the Standard toolbar with the Formatting toolbar.**

Not only can you use the Standard submenu shown in Figure D-6 to reset the Standard toolbar to its original settings, but you also can use it to customize the Standard toolbar by adding and deleting buttons. To add or delete buttons, click the button name on the Standard submenu to add or remove the check mark. Buttons with a check mark to the left currently are displayed on the Standard toolbar; buttons without a check mark are not displayed on the Standard toolbar. You can complete the same tasks for the Formatting toolbar, using the Formatting submenu to add and delete buttons from the Formatting toolbar.

Other Ways

1. On View menu point to Toolbars, click Customize on Toolbars submenu, click Toolbars tab, click toolbar name, click Reset button, click OK button, click Close button
2. Right-click toolbar, click Customize on shortcut menu, click Toolbars tab, click toolbar name, click Reset button, click OK button, click Close button
3. In Voice Command mode, say "View, Toolbars, Customize, Toolbars, [desired toolbar name], Reset, OK, Close"

Resetting the Word Menus

The following steps show how to reset the Word menus to their original settings.

To Reset the Word Menus

1

- **Click the Toolbar Options button on the Standard toolbar and then point to Add or Remove Buttons on the Toolbar Options menu.**

Word displays the Toolbar Options menu and the Add or Remove Buttons submenu (Figure D-7).

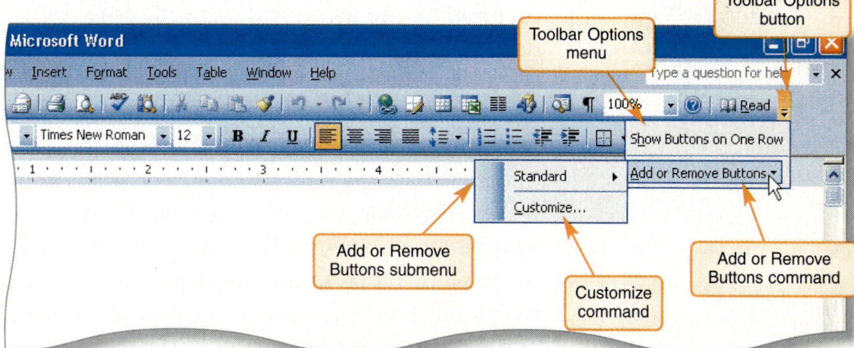

FIGURE D-7

2

- **Click Customize on the Add or Remove Buttons submenu.**
- **When Word displays the Customize dialog box, click the Options tab.**

The Customize dialog box contains three sheets used for customizing the Word toolbars and menus (Figure D-8).

3

- **Click the Reset menu and toolbar usage data button.**
- **When Word displays the Microsoft Word dialog box, click the Yes button.**
- **Click the Close button in the Customize dialog box.**

Word resets the menus to the original settings.

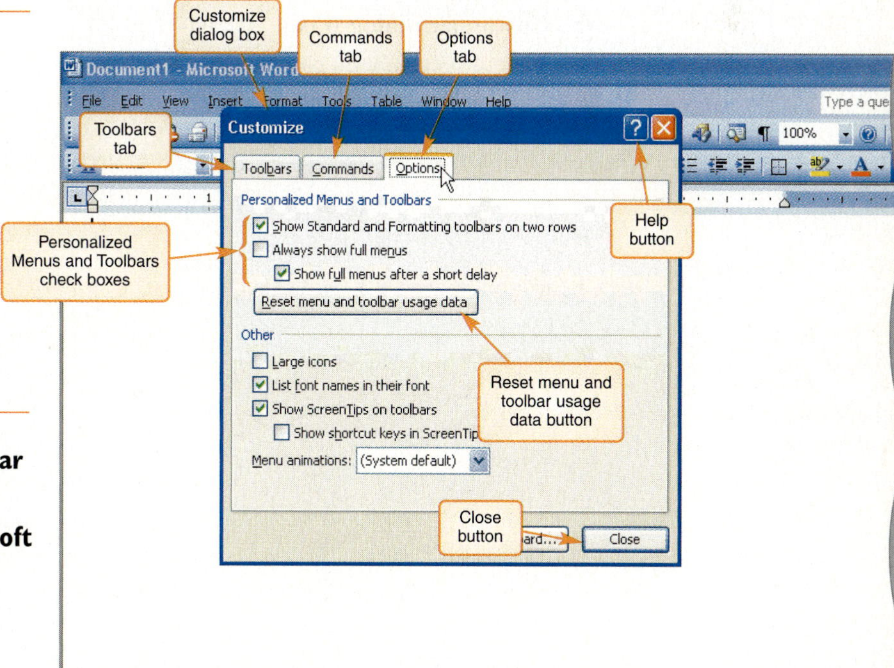

FIGURE D-8

Other Ways

1. On View menu point to Toolbars, click Customize on Toolbars submenu, click Options tab, click Reset menu and toolbar usage data button, click Yes button, click Close button
2. Right-click toolbar, click Customize on shortcut menu, click Options tab, click Reset menu and toolbar usage data button, click Yes button, click Close button
3. In Voice Command mode, say "View, Toolbars, Customize, Options, Reset menu and toolbar usage data, Yes, Close"

Using the Options sheet in the Customize dialog box, as shown in Figure D-8 on the previous page, you can select options to personalize menus and toolbars. For example, you can select or deselect a check mark that instructs Word to display the Standard and Formatting toolbars on two rows. You also can select whether Word always displays full menus or displays short menus followed by full menus, after a short delay. Other options available on the Options sheet including settings to instruct Word to display toolbars with large icons; to use the appropriate font to display font names in the Font list; and to display a ScreenTip when a user points to a toolbar button. Clicking the Help button in the upper-right corner of the Customize dialog box displays Help topics that will assist you in customizing toolbars and menus.

Using the Commands sheet in the Customize dialog box, you can add buttons to toolbars and commands to menus. Recall that the menu bar at the top of the Word window is a special toolbar. To add buttons to a toolbar, click a category name in the Categories list and then drag the command name in the Commands list to a toolbar. To add commands to a menu, click a category name in the Categories list, drag the command name in the Commands list to a menu name on the menu bar, and then, when the menu is displayed, drag the command to the desired location in the list of menu commands.

Using the Toolbars sheet in the Customize dialog box, you can add new toolbars and reset existing toolbars and the menu. To add a new toolbar, click the New button, enter a toolbar name in the New Toolbar dialog box, and then click the OK button. Once the new toolbar is created, you can use the Commands sheet to add or remove buttons, as you would with any other toolbar. If you add one or more buttons to an existing toolbar and want to reset the toolbar to its original settings, click the toolbar name in the Toolbars list so a check mark is displayed to the left of the name and then click the Reset button. If you add commands to one or more menus and want to reset the menus to their default settings, click Menu Bar in the Toolbars list on the Toolbars sheet so a check mark is displayed to the left of the name and then click the Reset button. When you have finished, click the Close button to close the Customize dialog box.

Appendix E

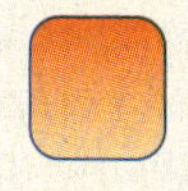

Microsoft Office Specialist Certification

What Is Microsoft Office Specialist Certification?

Microsoft Office Specialist certification provides a framework for measuring your proficiency with the Microsoft Office 2003 applications, such as Microsoft Office Word 2003, Microsoft Office Excel 2003, Microsoft Office Access 2003, Microsoft Office PowerPoint 2003, and Microsoft Office Outlook 2003. The levels of certification are described in Table E-1.

Table E-1 Levels of Microsoft Office Specialist Certification

LEVEL	DESCRIPTION	REQUIREMENTS	CREDENTIAL AWARDED
Microsoft Office Specialist	Indicates that you have an understanding of the basic features in a specific Microsoft Office 2003 application	Pass any ONE of the following: Microsoft Office Word 2003 Microsoft Office Excel 2003 Microsoft Office Access 2003 Microsoft Office PowerPoint 2003 Microsoft Office Outlook 2003	Candidates will be awarded one certificate for each of the Specialist-level exams they have passed: Microsoft Office Word 2003 Microsoft Office Excel 2003 Microsoft Office Access 2003 Microsoft Office PowerPoint 2003 Microsoft Office Outlook 2003
Microsoft Office Expert	Indicates that you have an understanding of the advanced features in a specific Microsoft Office 2003 application	Pass any ONE of the following: Microsoft Office Word 2003 Expert Microsoft Office Excel 2003 Expert	Candidates will be awarded one certificate for each of the Expert-level exams they have passed: Microsoft Office Word 2003 Expert Microsoft Office Excel 2003 Expert
Microsoft Office Master	Indicates that you have a comprehensive understanding of the features of four of the five primary Microsoft Office 2003 applications	Pass the following: Microsoft Office Word 2003 Expert Microsoft Office Excel 2003 Expert Microsoft Office PowerPoint 2003 And pass ONE of the following: Microsoft Office Access 2003 or Microsoft Office Outlook 2003	Candidates will be awarded the Microsoft Office Master certificate for fulfilling the requirements.

Why Should You Be Certified?

Being Microsoft Office certified provides a valuable industry credential — proof that you have the Office 2003 applications skills required by employers. By passing one or more Microsoft Office Specialist certification exams, you demonstrate your proficiency in a given Office 2003 application to employers. With more than 400 million people in 175 nations and 70 languages using Office applications, Microsoft is targeting Office 2003 certification to a wide variety of companies. These companies include temporary employment agencies that want to prove the expertise of their workers, large corporations looking for a way to measure the skill set of employees, and training companies and educational institutions seeking Microsoft Office 2003 teachers with appropriate credentials.

The Microsoft Office Specialist Certification Exams

You pay $50 to $100 each time you take an exam, whether you pass or fail. The fee varies among testing centers. The **Microsoft Office Expert** exams, which you can take up to 60 minutes to complete, consist of between 40 and 60 tasks that you perform on a personal computer in a simulated environment. The tasks require you to use the application just as you would in doing your job. The **Microsoft Office Specialist** exams contain fewer tasks, and you will have slightly less time to complete them. The tasks you will perform differ on the two types of exams. After passing designated Expert and Specialist exams, candidates are awarded the **Microsoft Office Master** certificate (see the requirements in Table E-1 on the previous page).

How to Prepare for the Microsoft Office Specialist Certification Exams

The Shelly Cashman Series offers several Microsoft-approved textbooks that cover the required objectives of the Microsoft Office Specialist certification exams. For a listing of the textbooks, visit the Shelly Cashman Series Microsoft Office Specialist Center at scsite.com/winoff2003/cert. Click the link Shelly Cashman Series Microsoft Office 2003-Approved Microsoft Office Textbooks (Figure E-1). After using any of the books listed in an instructor-led course, you should be prepared to take the indicated Microsoft Office Specialist certification exam.

How to Find an Authorized Testing Center

To locate a testing center, call 1-800-933-4493 in North America, or visit the Shelly Cashman Series Microsoft Office Specialist Center at scsite.com/winoff2003/cert. Click the link Locate an Authorized Testing Center Near You (Figure E-1). At this Web site, you can look for testing centers around the world.

Shelly Cashman Series Microsoft Office Specialist Center

The Shelly Cashman Series Microsoft Office Specialist Center (Figure E-1) lists more than 15 Web sites you can visit to obtain additional information about certification. The Web page (scsite.com/winoff2003/cert) includes links to general information about certification, choosing an application for certification, preparing for the certification exam, and taking and passing the certification exam.

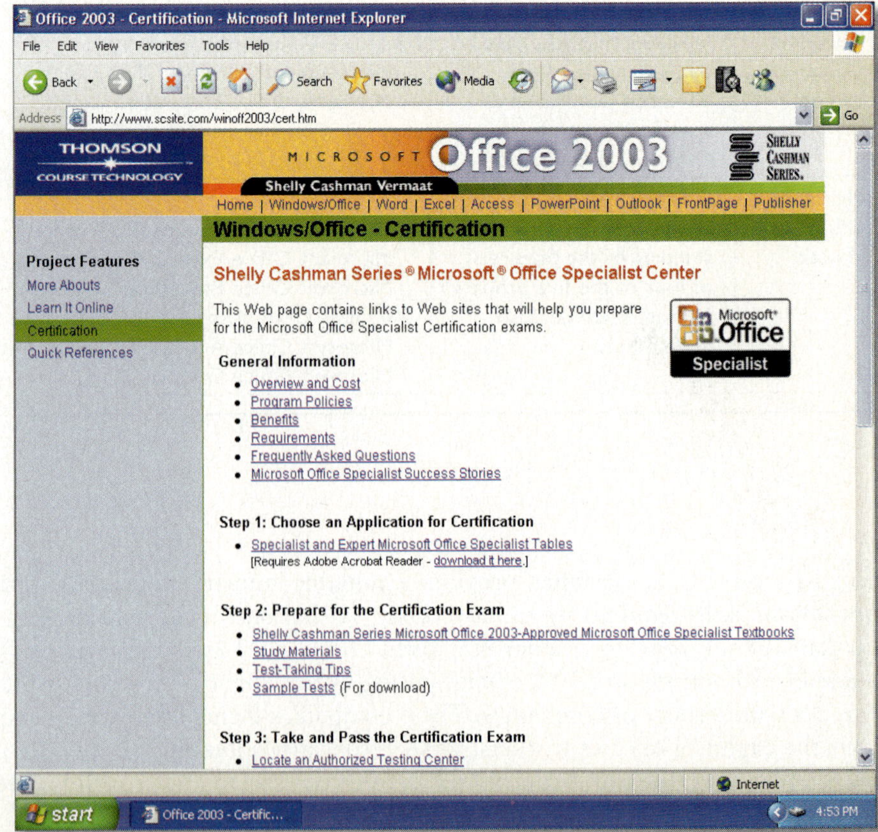

FIGURE E-1

Microsoft Office Specialist Certification Map

The tables on the following pages list the skills sets and activities you should be familiar with if you plan to take one of the Microsoft Office Specialist certification examinations. Each activity is accompanied by page numbers on which the activity is illustrated and page numbers on which the activity is part of an exercise.

Microsoft Office Word 2003

The Word portion of *Microsoft Office 2003: Introductory Concepts and Techniques* (ISBN 0-619-25574-9 or 0-619-20057-X or 0-619-25558-7 or 0-619-20024-3) and *Microsoft Office 2003: Advanced Concepts and Techniques* (ISBN 0-619-20025-1 or 0-619-20026-X) used in combination in a two-sequence course has been approved by Microsoft as courseware for specialist-level certification. Table E-2 lists the specialist-level examination skill sets, activities, page numbers where the activities are demonstrated, and page numbers where the activities can be practiced.

Table E-3 lists the expert-level examination skill sets, activities, page numbers where the activities are demonstrated, and page numbers where the activities can be practiced. **POST-ADV** means that the activity is demonstrated in the companion textbook *Microsoft Office 2003: Post Advanced Concepts and Techniques* (ISBN 0-619-20027-8).

Table E-2 Specialist-Level Skill Sets, Activities, and Locations in Book for Microsoft Office Word 2003

SKILL SET	SKILL BEING MEASURED	SKILL DEMONSTRATED IN BOOK	SKILL EXERCISE IN BOOK
I. Creating Content	A. Insert and edit text, symbols and special characters	WD 18-20, WD 22-25, WD 27, WD 57, WD 58-59, WD 83, WD 107, WD 112-114, WD 118-120, WD 125, WD 152, WD 154-157, WD 166-172, WD 180, WD 245, WD 360-361, WD 390-391, WD 418-419, WD 427-428	WD 65 (Apply Your Knowledge Steps 2-4), WD 67 (In the Lab 1 Step 3), WD 69 (In the Lab 2 Step 3), WD 70 (In the Lab 3 Step 1), WD 78 (Cases and Places 1-3), WD 129 (Apply Your Knowledge Steps 1, 7-8, 10), WD 131 (In the Lab 1 Steps 8-9), WD 133 (In the Lab 2 Part 1 Steps 3b, 4, Part 2 Step 1), WD 134 (In the Lab 3 Steps 2-3), WD 136 (Cases and Places 5), WD 199 (In the Lab 1 Steps 1-2), WD 202 (Cases and Places 5), WD 293 (In the Lab 3 Step 3a), WD 368 (In the Lab 1 Step 10), WD 371 (In the Lab 2 Step 11), WD 450-451 (In the Lab 1 Steps 2-6), WD 451-452 (In the Lab 2 Steps 2-6), WD 453 (In the Lab 3 Step 2)
	B. Insert frequently used pre-defined text	WD 84 (2nd paragraph), WD 89-90, WD 91-93, WD 177-179, WD 181-182	WD 129 (Apply Your Knowledge Step 10), WD 134 (In the Lab 3 Step 1), WD 135 (Cases and Places 1), WD 200 (In the Lab 2 Step 2)
	C. Navigate to specific content	WD 110-112, WD 116-117, WD 246	WD 129 (Apply Your Knowledge Step 6), WD 131 (In the Lab 1 Step 11), WD 133 (In the Lab 2 Part 2 Steps 2, 4), WD 456 (Cases and Places 5)
	D. Insert, position and size graphics	WD 46-50, WD 230-231, WD 304-311, WD 383-387, WD 393-396, WD 411-415	WD 60 (In the Lab 2 Steps 12-13), WD 65 (Apply Your Knowledge Step 15), WD 68 (In the Lab 1 Steps 13-14), WD 70 (In the Lab 3 Steps 6-7), WD 289 (In the Lab 1 Step 1), WD 291 (In the Lab 2 Step 1), WD 293 (In the Lab 3 Step 1), WD 367 (In the Lab 1 Step 2), WD 369 (In the Lab 2 Step 2), WD 374 (Cases and Places 1), WD 451 (In the Lab 2 Steps 2, 8), WD 454 (In the Lab 3 Step 6), WD 455-456 (Cases and Places 2-5)
	E. Create and modify diagrams and charts	WD 258-264, WD 421-431	WD 291 (In the Lab 2 Step 3b), WD 294 (In the Lab 3 Step 7), WD 295-296 (Cases and Places 2-5), WD 451 (In the Lab 2 Step 10), WD 455 (Cases and Places 4)
	F. Locate, select and insert supporting information	WD 118, WD 124, WD 125	WD 129 (Apply Your Knowledge Step 13), WD 134 (In the Lab 3 Step 3), WD 135 (Cases and Places 2-4)
II. Organizing Content	A. Insert and modify tables	WD 150-151, WD 182-187, WD 250-256, WD 272-280, WD 355, WD 357, WD 358	WD 198 (Apply Your Knowledge Steps 4-13), WD 200 (In the Lab 2 Step 2), WD 200 (In the Lab 3 Step 2), WD 287 (Apply Your Knowledge Steps 1-15), WD 290 (In the Lab 1 Step 3a), WD 291-292 (In the Lab 2 Step 3a), WD 293-294 (In the Lab 3 Steps 3c, 3e, 6), WD 295 (Cases and Places 1), WD 368 (In the Lab 1 Step 9), WD 370 (In the Lab 2 Step 10), WD 373 (In the Lab 3 Step 7)

Table E-2 Specialist-Level Skill Sets, Activities, and Locations in Book for Microsoft Office Word 2003 *(continued)*

SKILL SET	SKILL BEING MEASURED	SKILL DEMONSTRATED IN BOOK	SKILL EXERCISE IN BOOK
	B. Create bulleted lists, numbered lists and outlines	WD 153-154, WD 156, WD 187-189, WD 270-271, WD 329-331, WD 458-461	WD 70 (In the Lab 1 Step 5), WD 72 (Cases and Places 4), WD 199 (In the Lab 1), WD 200 (In the Lab 2), WD 200 (In the Lab 3 Step 2), WD 202 (Cases and Places 5), WD 290 (In the Lab 1 Step 3b), WD 291 (In the Lab 2 Step 3c), WD 293 (In the Lab 3 Step 3d), WD 295-296 (Cases and Places 2-5), WD 369-370 (In the Lab 2 Step 5), WD 374 (Cases and Places 1), WD 479 (In the Lab 1 Step 1)
	C. Insert and modify hyperlinks	WD 108, WD 122, WD 174, WD 207, WD 212-213	WD 131 (In the Lab 1 Step 8), WD 133 (In the Lab 2 Step 3b), WD 200 (In the Lab 2 Step 2), WD 216 (In the Lab 2 Steps 2, 4)
III. Formatting Content	A. Format text	WD 17, WD 34-36, WD 40-42, WD 44, WD 87, WD 117, WD 161, WD 173, WD 213, WD 221, WD 226-228, WD 265-269, WD 332, WD 403-404, WD 436-438, WD 459-460	WD 65 (Apply Your Knowledge Steps 5-6, 8-13), WD 67-68 (In the Lab 1 Steps 1, 5, 8-11), WD 68-69 (In the Lab 2 Steps 1, 5, 8-10), WD 70 (In the Lab 3 Steps 1, 3-4), WD 71 (Cases and Places 3), WD 72 (Cases and Places 4), WD 129 (Apply Your Knowledge Steps 2, 9), WD 198 (Apply Your Knowledge Steps 3, 9), WD 200 (In the Lab 2 Step 2), WD 288 (Apply Your Knowledge Step 19), WD 289 (In the Lab 1 Steps 1-2), WD 290 (In the Lab 1 Steps 2, 3c), WD 291 (In the Lab 2 Steps 1, 3c), WD 293 (In the Lab 3 Steps 1-2, 3e, 6e), WD 370 (In the Lab 2 Step 5), WD 449 (Apply Your Knowledge Steps 5-6), WD 455 (Cases and Places 1), WD 456 (Cases and Places 5), WD 479 (In the Lab 1 Step 1)
	B. Format paragraphs	WD 37-38, WD 79-80, WD 82-83, WD 86-89, WD 104-105, WD 163-165, WD 172-173, WD 176-177, WD 221-223, WD 223-225, WD 280, WD 312-313, WD 329-331, WD 388-390, WD 401, WD 409-410, WD 413	WD 65 (Apply Your Knowledge Steps 7, 14), WD 67 (In the Lab 1 Steps 6-7, 12), WD 69 (In the Lab 2 Steps 6-7, 11), WD 129 (Apply Your Knowledge Steps 3-4), WD 131 (In the Lab 1 Steps 3, 5-8), WD 133 (In the Lab 2 Part 1 Steps 1-3, Part 2 Step 2), WD 134 (In the Lab 3), WD 135-136 (Cases and Places 1-5), WD 198 (Apply Your Knowledge Steps 1-2), WD 199-200 (In the Lab 2 Step 2), WD 289 (In the Lab 1 Steps 1-2), WD 291 (In the Lab 2 Step 1-2), WD 293 (In the Lab Step 1), WD 368 (In the Lab 1 Step 3), WD 369-370 (In the Lab 2 Steps 3, 5), WD 449 (Apply Your Knowledge Step 1), WD 450-451 (In the Lab 1 Steps 2, 6, 8), WD 453-454 (In the Lab 3 Steps 2, 5, 9), WD 455 (Cases and Places 2-4)
	C. Apply and format columns	WD 398-400, WD 406, WD 409-410, WD 415-417, WD 420	WD 449 (Apply Your Knowledge Steps 2-4), WD 450-451 (In the Lab 1 Steps 3-4, 6-7), WD 451-452 (In the Lab 2 Steps 3-4, 6-7), WD 453-454 (In the Lab 3 Steps 3-5, 8-9), WD 455-456 (Cases and Places 1-5)
	D. Insert and modify content in headers and footers	WD 81-84, WD 246-249	WD 129 (Apply Your Knowledge Step 10), WD 131 (In the Lab 1 Step 4), WD 133 (In the Lab 2 Part 1 Step 1, Part 3 Step 2), WD 134 (In the Lab 3 Step 1), WD 135-136 (Cases and Places 1-5), WD 293-294 (In the Lab 3 Steps 8-9, 11), WD 295-296 (Cases and Places 2-5)
	E. Modify document layout and page setup	WD 77-79, WD 103, WD 235-237, WD 244, WD 356, WD 399, WD 404-405, WD 406	WD 131 (In the Lab 1 Steps 2, 7), WD 133 (In the Lab 2 Part 1 Steps 1-2, Part 3 Step 2), WD 134 (In the Lab 3), WD 135-136 (Cases and Places 1-5), WD 289 (In the Lab 1 Step 2), WD 291 (In the Lab 2 Step 2), WD 293-294 (In the Lab 3 Steps 2, 3b), WD 368 (In the Lab 1 Step 9), WD 370 (In the Lab 2 Step 10), WD 375-376 (Cases and Places 2-5), WD 449 (Apply Your Knowledge Steps 2-3), WD 451 (In the Lab 1 Steps 3, 7), WD 452 (In the Lab 2 Steps 3, 7), WD 453 (In the Lab 3 Steps 3, 8), WD 456-457 (Cases and Places 1-5)
IV. Collaborating	A. Circulate documents for review	WD 123, WD 461-462	WD 134 (In the Lab 3 Step 5), WD 479 (In the Lab 1 Step 3), WD 480 (In the Lab 2 Step 6)
	B. Compare and merge documents	WD 473-475	WD 480 (In the Lab 2 Steps 5-6), WD 480 (In the Lab 3)
	C. Insert, view and edit comments	WD 463-466	WD 480 (In the Lab 2 Steps 2-4), WD 480 (In the Lab 3)
	D. Track, accept and reject proposed changes	WD 466-471	WD 480 (In the Lab 2 Steps 3-6), WD 480 (In the Lab 3)
V. Formatting and Managing Documents	A. Create new documents using templates	WD 142-148, WD 175, WD 302-304	WD 199 (In the Lab 1 Steps 1-2), WD 201-202 (Cases and Places 1-5), WD 367 (In the Lab 1 Step 1), WD 369 (In the Lab 2 Step 1), WD 372 (In the Lab 3 Step 2)

Table E-2 Specialist-Level Skill Sets, Activities, and Locations in Book for Microsoft Office Word 2003

SKILL SET	SKILL BEING MEASURED	SKILL DEMONSTRATED IN BOOK	SKILL EXERCISE IN BOOK
	B. Review and modify document properties	WD 100-101, WD 102, WD 193-194	WD 131 (In the Lab 1 Step 12), WD 133 (In the Lab 2 Part 1 Step 7, Part 2 Step 6, Part 3 Step 5), WD 134 (In the Lab 3 Step 4), WD 200 (In the Lab 2 Steps 3, 6)
	C. Organize documents using file folders	WD 313, WD 344	WD 366 (Apply Your Knowledge Steps 3, 11), WD 368 (In the Lab 1 Steps 4-5, 8, 14), WD 370-371 (In the Lab 2 Steps 4-5, 8-9, 12, 15), WD 372-373 (In the Lab 3 Step 3), WD 374-376 (Cases and Places 1-5)
	D. Save documents in appropriate formats for different uses	WD 30, WD 205, WD 206, WD 240	WD 216 (In the Lab 1 Steps 2, 5-6), WD 216 (In the Lab 2 Step 2)
	E. Print documents, envelopes and labels	WD 53, WD 190-191, WD 241, WD 345-350, WD 350-351, WD 472	WD 65 (Apply Your Knowledge Step 17), WD 68 (In the Lab 1 Step 16), WD 69 (In the Lab 2, Step 15), WD 70 (In the Lab 3 Step 9), WD 131 (In the Lab 1 Step 12), WD 200 (In the Lab 2 Step 7), WD 200 (In the Lab 3 Step 3), WD 368 (In the Lab 1 Step 8), WD 370-371 (In the Lab 2 Steps 8-9), WD 479 (In the Lab 1 Step 1)
	F. Preview documents and Web pages	WD 52, WD 158-159, WD 208-209	WD 70 (In the Lab 3 Step 7), WD 199 (In the Lab 1 Step 5), WD 200 (In the Lab 2 Step 5), WD 216 (In the Lab 1 Step 3), WD 216 (In the Lab 2 Step 5), WD 290 (In the Lab 1 Step 4), WD 292 (In the Lab 2 Step 4), WD 294 (In the Lab 3 Step 14)
	G. Change and organize document views and windows	WD 9, WD 20-21, WD 77, WD 148-149, WD 169-170, WD 172, WD 220, WD 232, WD 282-284, WD 312, WD 361, WD 422, WD 426, WD 34-435, WD 441-444, WD 459, WD 472, WD 407-408	WD 67 (In the Lab 1 Step 2), WD 68 (In the Lab 2 Step 2), WD 71-72 (Cases and Places 1-5), WD 133 (In the Lab 2 Part 3 Step 1), WD 135-136 (Cases and Places 1-5), WD 199 (In the Lab 1 Step 2), WD 288 (Apply Your Knowledge Step 18), WD 289 (In the Lab 1), WD 294 (In the Lab 3 Step 15), WD 368 (In the Lab 1 Steps 3, 10), WD 369 (In the Lab 2 Step 3), WD 371 (In the Lab 2 Step 11), WD 449 (Apply Your Knowledge Steps 11-13), WD 450-451 (In the Lab 1), WD 451-452 (In the Lab 2), WD 452 (In the Lab 2 Step 13), WD 454 (In the Lab 3 Step 11), WD 455 (Cases and Places 1), WD 456 (Cases and Places 5), WD 479 (In the Lab 1 Step 1),

Table E-3 Expert-Level Skill Sets, Activities, and Locations in Book for Microsoft Office Word 2003

SKILL SET	SKILL BEING MEASURED	SKILL DEMONSTRATED IN BOOK	SKILL EXERCISE IN BOOK
I. Formatting Content	A. Create custom styles for text, tables and lists	WD 96-98, WD 267-269, **POST-ADV**	WD 133 (In the Lab 2 Part 1 Step 2, Part 2 Step 2), WD 135-136 (Cases and Places 2-5), WD 290 (In the Lab 1 Step 3c), WD 291 (In the Lab 2 Step 3c), WD 293-294 (In the Lab 3 Steps 3e, 6e), **POST-ADV**
	B. Control pagination	WD 103, WD 154-155, WD 236, WD 244, **POST-ADV**	WD 131 (In the Lab 1 Step 7), WD 133 (In the Lab 2 Part 1 Step 2, Part 3 Step 2), WD 134 (In the Lab 3 Step 1), WD 135-136 (Cases and Places 1-5), WD 199 (In the Lab 1 Step 2), WD 289 (In the Lab 1 Step 2), WD 291 (In the Lab 2 Step 2), WD 293 (In the Lab 3 Steps 2, 3b, 5), **POST-ADV**
	C. Format, position and resize graphics using advanced layout features	WD 49-51, WD 231, WD 310, WD 393-394, WD 396, WD 426, WD 427, **POST-ADV**	WD 69 (In the Lab 2 Step 13), WD 70 (In the Lab 3 Step 7), WD 199-200 (In the Lab 2 Step 1), WD 201 (Cases and Places 1), WD 289 (In the Lab 1 Step 1), WD 291 (In the Lab 2 Step 1), WD 293 (In the Lab 3 Step 1), WD 367 (In the Lab 1 Step 2), WD 369 (In the Lab 2 Step 2), WD 451-452 (In the Lab 2 Steps 2, 10), WD 453-454 (In the Lab 3 Step 6), WD 455 (Cases and Places 2), WD 455 (Cases and Places 2, 4), **POST-ADV**
	D. Insert and modify objects	WD 304-311, WD 383-387, WD 411-415, WD 421-431, **POST-ADV**	WD 367 (In the Lab 1 Step 2), WD 369 (In the Lab 2 Step 2), WD 450-451 (In the Lab 1 Steps 2, 8), WD 451-452 (In the Lab 2 Steps 2, 10), WD 453-454 (In the Lab 3 Steps 2, 6), WD 455-456 (Cases and Places 2-5), **POST-ADV**

Table E-3 Expert-Level Skill Sets, Activities, and Locations in Book for Microsoft Office Word 2003 *(continued)*

SKILL SET	SKILL BEING MEASURED	SKILL DEMONSTRATED IN BOOK	SKILL EXERCISE IN BOOK
	E. Create and modify diagrams and charts using data from other sources	POST-ADV	POST-ADV
II. Organizing Content	A. Sort content in lists and tables	WD 109-110, WD 342, WD 359, POST-ADV	WD 133 (In the Lab 2 Part 1 Step 3), WD 134 (In the Lab 3 Step 1), WD 135-136 (Cases and Places 1-5), WD 366 (Apply Your Knowledge Step 6), WD 368 (In the Lab 1 Step 12), WD 371 (In the Lab 2 Step 13), WD 374 (Cases and Places 1), POST-ADV
	B. Perform calculations in tables	WD 254	WD 198 (Apply Your Knowledge Step 7), WD 288 (Apply Your Knowledge Steps 9-10), WD 290 (In the Lab 1 Step 3a), WD 293 (In the Lab 3 Step 3c)
	C. Modify table formats	WD 177-178, WD 251-253, WD 274-275, WD 276-277, WD 279-280, WD 322-329, WD 358, POST-ADV	WD 200 (In the Lab 2 Step 2), WD 287 (Apply Your Knowledge Steps 1, 4-7, 11-14), WD 289-290 (In the Lab 1 Step 3a), WD 291 (In the Lab 2 Step 3a), WD 293 (In the Lab 3 Step 3c), WD 366 (Apply Your Knowledge Step 2), WD 367-368 (In the Lab 1 Steps 4-5, 8-9), WD 369-370 (In the Lab 2 Steps 4-5, 8-10), WD 370 (In the Lab 2 Step 10), WD 372-373 (In the Lab 3 Steps 1, 3-4, 7), WD 374-375 (Cases and Places 1-4), POST-ADV
	D. Summarize document content using automated tools	POST-ADV	POST-ADV
	E. Use automated tools for document navigation	POST-ADV	POST-ADV
	F. Merge letters with other data sources	WD 301-304, WD 314-329, WD 335-345	WD 366 (Apply Your Knowledge Steps 4-8), WD 367-368 (In the Lab 1 Steps 1-7), WD 369-370 (In the Lab 2 Steps 1-7), WD 372-373 (In the Lab 3 Steps 1-6), WD 374-375 (Cases and Places 1-4)
	G. Merge labels with other data sources	WD 345-351	WD 368 (In the Lab 1 Step 8), WD 370 (In the Lab 2 Step 8), WD 374-375 (Cases and Places 1-4)
	H. Structure documents using XML	POST-ADV	POST-ADV
III. Formatting Documents	A. Create and modify forms	POST-ADV	POST-ADV
	B. Create and modify document background	WD 207-208, WD 280-281, WD 438-440, POST-ADV	WD 216 (In the Lab 2 Steps 2-3), WD 294 (In the Lab 3 Step 10), WD 295-296 (Cases and Places 2-5), WD 449 (Apply Your Knowledge Steps 7-8), WD 456 (Cases and Places 5), POST-ADV
	C. Create and modify document indexes and tables	POST-ADV	POST-ADV
	D. Insert and modify endnotes, footnotes, captions, and cross-references	WD 93-99, POST-ADV	WD 131 (In the Lab 1 Step 7), WD 133 (In the Lab 2 Part 1 Step 2, Part 2 Steps 3-4, Part 3 Steps 1-3), WD 134 (In the Lab 3 Step 1), WD 135-136 (Cases and Places 1-5), POST-ADV
	E. Create and manage master documents and subdocuments	POST-ADV	POST-ADV
IV. Collaborating	A. Modify track changes options	WD 471 (last paragraph on page), WD 472-473	WD 480 (In the Lab 3)
	B. Publish and edit Web documents	WD 205-215, Appendix C	WD 216 (In the Lab 1 Steps 2-5), WD 216 (In the Lab 2 Steps 2-7)
	C. Manage document versions	POST-ADV	POST-ADV
	D. Protect and restrict forms and documents	POST-ADV	POST-ADV
	E. Attach digital signatures to documents	POST-ADV	POST-ADV
	F. Customize document properties	POST-ADV	POST-ADV
V. Customizing Word	A. Create, edit, and run macros	POST-ADV	POST-ADV
	B. Customize menus and toolbars	POST-ADV	POST-ADV
	C. Modify Word default settings	WD 121, WD 229, POST-ADV	WD 136 (Cases and Places 5), WD 296 (Cases and Places 5), POST-ADV

Microsoft Office Excel 2003

The Excel portion of *Microsoft Office 2003: Introductory Concepts and Techniques* (ISBN 0-619-25574-9 or 0-619-20057-X or 0-619-25558-7 or 0-619-20024-3) and *Microsoft Office 2003: Advanced Concepts and Techniques* (ISBN 0-619-20025-1 or 0-619-20026-X) used in combination in a two-sequence course has been approved by Microsoft as courseware for specialist-level certification. Table E-4 lists the specialist-level examination skill sets, activities, page numbers where the activities are demonstrated, and page numbers where the activities can be practiced.

Table E-5 lists the expert-level examination skill sets, activities, page numbers where the activities are demonstrated, and page numbers where the activities can be practiced. **POST-ADV** means that the activity is demonstrated in the companion textbook *Microsoft Office 2003: Post Advanced Concepts and Techniques* (ISBN 0-619-20027-8).

Table E-4 Specialist-Level Skill Sets, Activities, and Locations in Book for Microsoft Office Excel 2003

SKILL SET	SKILL BEING MEASURED	SKILL DEMONSTRATED IN BOOK	SKILL EXERCISE IN BOOK
I. Creating Data and Content	A. Enter and edit cell content	EX 16-23, EX 50-53, EX 72-88, EX 151-154, EX 259, EX 269, EX 385, EX 386	EX 57 (Apply Your Knowledge 1), EX 58-64 (In the Lab 1-3, Cases and Places 1-5), EX 212 (In the Lab 1 Step 2), EX 298 (In the Lab 1 Step 6), EX 299 (In the Lab 1 Part 2 Step 4), EX 301 (In the Lab 3 Step 7)
	B. Navigate to specific cell content	EX 36-37, EX 252, EX 285-287, EX 443-446	EX 57 (Apply Your Knowledge 1), EX 58-64 (In the Lab 1-3, Cases and Places 1-5), EX 455 (Apply Your Knowledge 1 Step 5), EX 460 (In the Lab 2 Part 3)
	C. Locate, select and insert supporting information	EX 402-403, EX 430-432	EX 455 (Apply Your Knowledge 1 Step 5), EX 457 (In the Lab 1 Step 8)
	D. Insert, position, and size graphics	EX 278-280, EX 424-426	EX 303 (In the Lab 3 Step 10), EX 456 (In the Lab 1 Step 5), EX 459 (In the Lab 2 Step 5)
II. Analyzing Data	A. Filter lists using AutoFilter	EX 346-350	EX 373 (In the Lab 2 Part 3), EX 377 (Cases and Places 3)
	B. Sort lists	EX 333-338	EX 370 (In the Lab 1 Part 3), EX 372 (In the Lab 2 Part 1), EX 377 (Cases and Places 2)
	C. Insert and modify formulas	EX 72-77, EX 79-80, EX 80-87, EX 168-172, EX 173-175, EX 253-255, EX 268-270	EX 62 (In the Lab Part 3), EX 130 (In the Lab 1 Part 1), EX 130 (In the Lab 1 Part 1), EX 133 (In the Lab 1 Part 1 Steps 2, 4), EX 135 (In the Lab 2 Part 1 Steps 3, 5), EX 140-143 (Cases and Places 1-5), EX 211 (Apply Your Knowledge 1 Steps 5-8), EX 212 (In the Lab 1 Part 1), EX 217 (In the Lab 2 Part 1), EX 220 (In the Lab 3 Part 1 Step 11), EX 301 (In the Lab 2 Step 4), EX 303 (In the Lab 3 Step 7), EX 455 (Apply Your Knowledge 1 Part 1 Step 2)
	D. Use statistical, date and time, financial, and logical functions	EX 23-24, EX 26-27, EX 80-87, EX 165-167, EX 170-172, EX 254-255, EX 268-270, EX 386-387	EX 59 (In the Lab 1 Step 2), EX 59 (In the Lab 2 Step 2), EX 130 (Apply Your Knowledge 1 Part 1), EX 133 (In the Lab 1 Part 1 Step 4), EX 135 (In the Lab 2 Part 1 Step 5), EX 212 (In the Lab 1 Part 1 Step 1), EX 216 (In the Lab 2 Part 1 Step 1), EX 296 (Apply Your Knowledge 1 Step 3), EX 303 (In the Lab 3 Step 4)
	E. Create, modify, and position diagrams and charts based on worksheet data	EX 38-41, EX 187-199, EX 419-428	EX 59 (In the Lab 1 Step 6), EX 60 (In the Lab 2 Step 5), EX 62 (In the Lab 3 Part 2), EX 214 (In the Lab 1 Part 2), EX 217 (In the Lab 2 Part 2), EX 459 (In the Lab 2 Step 5), EX 463 (Cases and Places 3)
III. Formatting Data and Content	A. Apply and modify cell formats	EX 28-36, EX 90-110, EX 177-186, EX 250, EX 262-263, EX 273-275, EX 315, EX 383, EX 391-402	EX 59 (In the Lab 1 Step 5), EX 60 (In the Lab 2 Step 5), EX 61 (In the Lab 3 Part 1), EX 63-64 (Cases and Places 1-5), EX 131 (Apply Your Knowledge 1), EX 133 (In the Lab 1 Steps 6-8), EX 135 (In the Lab 2 Part 1 Steps 6-9), EX 140-143 (Cases and Places 1-5), EX 214 (In the Lab 1 Step 8), EX 217 (In the Lab 2 Steps 8-10)
	B. Apply and modify cell styles	EX 398-401	EX 456 (In the Lab 1 Step 2), EX 464 (Cases and Places 4)

Table E-4 Specialist-Level Skill Sets, Activities, and Locations in Book for Microsoft Office Excel 2003 *(continued)*

SKILL SET	SKILL BEING MEASURED	SKILL DEMONSTRATED IN BOOK	SKILL EXERCISE IN BOOK
	C. Modify row and column formats	EX 32-33, EX 91-94, EX 96-97, EX 107-111, EX 155-156, EX 159-162, EX 290, EX 312-313, EX 324	EX 59 (In the Lab 1 Step 4), EX 60 (In the Lab 2 Step 3), EX 133 (In the Lab 1 Steps 6-7), EX 135 (In the Lab 3 Step 1), EX 135 (In the Lab 2 Step 6), EX 212 (In the Lab 1 Step 4), EX 216 (In the Lab 2 Steps 3 and 4), EX 219 (In the Lab 3 Steps 1-3), EX 296 (Apply Your Knowledge 1 Step 9), EX 298 (In the Lab 1 Step 14), EX 301 (In the Lab 2 Step 14), EX 303 (In the Lab 3 Step 19), EX 369 (In the Lab 1 Part 1), EX 375 (In the Lab 3 Part 1 Step 1), EX 376 (In the Lab 3 Part 2), EX 480 (In the Lab 2 Step 2)
	D. Format worksheets	EX 28-37, EX 124, EX 197-199, EX 290-291	EX 135 (In the Lab 2 Step 10), EX 137-139 (In the Lab 3 Parts 1-4), EX 214 (In the Lab 1 Part 2), EX 217 (In the Lab 2 Step 11), EX 298 (In the Lab 1 Step 14), EX 301 (In the Lab 2 Step 14), EX 303 (In the Lab 3 Step 19)
IV. Collaborating	A. Insert, view and edit comments	EX 428-430, EX 432	EX 456-457 (In the Lab 1 Steps 3, 7), EX 459 (In the Lab 2 Step 6)
V. Managing Workbooks	A. Create new workbooks from templates	EX 404-406	EX 457 (In the Lab 1 Step 8, EX 458 (In the Lab 2 Step 1)
	B. Insert, delete and move cells	EX 24-27, EX 157-159, EX 161-162, EX 174-175, EX 271-272, EX 351, EX 407-408, EX 415-419, EX 469-470	EX 62 (In the Lab 3 Part 3), EX 212 (In the Lab 1 Step 7), EX 216 (In the Lab 2 Step 6), EX 221 (In the Lab 3 Steps 1-3), EX 480 (In the Lab 1 Step 2 and In the Lab 2 Step 2), EX 459 (In the Lab 2 Steps 2, 4)
	C. Create and modify hyperlinks	EX 278-282	EX 303 (In the Lab 3 Step 10)
	D. Organize worksheets	EX 197-199, EX 312, EX 406-407, EX 422	EX 214 (In the Lab 1 Part 2), EX 217 (In the Lab 2 Step 11), EX 369 (In the Lab 1 Part 1), EX 375 (In the Lab 3 Part 1 Step 1), EX 456 (Apply Your Knowledge 1 Step 1), EX 459 (In the Lab 1 Step 2), EX 463-464 (Cases and Places 2-3, 5)
	E. Preview data in other views	EX 113-116, EX 228-230, EX 436, EX 442	EX 133 (In the Lab 1 Step 10), EX 137 (In the Lab 3 Part 2), EX 138 (In the Lab 2 Part 3), EX 239 (In the Lab 1 Part 1 Step 1), EX 240 (In the Lab 2 Part 1 Step 1), EX 459 (In the Lab 2 Part 2)
	F. Customize Window layout	EX 163-164, EX 175-176, EX 202-207, EX 243, EX 291-292, EX 449	EX 215 (In the Lab 1 Part 3), EX 216-217 (In the Lab 2 Steps 2, 11, 14), EX 219-220 (In the Lab 3 Steps 6, 17), EX 298 (In the Lab 1 Step 14), EX 301 (In the Lab 2 Step 14), EX 303 (In the Lab 3 Step 19), EX 456 (Apply Your Knowledge 1 Part 2)
	G. Setup pages for printing	EX 113-116, EX 283-287, EX 432-437, EX 439-443	EX 131 (Apply Your Knowledge 1), EX 133 (In the Lab 1 Step 11), EX 137 (In the Lab 3 Part 1), EX 296 (Apply Your Knowledge 1 Step 6), EX 298 (In the Lab 1 Step 10), EX 299 (In the Lab 1 Step 9), EX 301 (In the Lab 3 Step 9), EX 303 (In the Lab 3 Step 14), EX 455 (Apply Your Knowledge 1 Step 4), EX 456 (In the Lab 1 Step 5), EX 459 (In the Lab 2 Part 2), EX 462 (In the Lab 3 Step 6)
	H. Print data	EX 113-120, EX 282-287, EX 437-439	EX 296 (Apply Your Knowledge 1 Step 6), EX 298 (In the Lab 1 Step 14), EX 459 (In the Lab 2 Steps 7-8)
	I. Organize workbooks using file folders	EX 230-232	EX 240 (In the Lab 3)
	J. Save data in appropriate formats for different uses	EX 228-238, EX 361-364	EX 239 (In the Lab 1 Parts 1-2), EX 240 (In the Lab 2 Parts 1-2), EX 370 (In the Lab 1 Part 5)

Table E-5 Expert-Level Skill Sets, Activities, and Locations in Book for Microsoft Office Excel 2003

SKILL SET	SKILL BEING MEASURED	SKILL DEMONSTRATED IN BOOK	SKILL EXERCISE IN BOOK
I. Organizing and Analyzing Data	A. Use subtotals	EX 338-342	EX 370 (In the Lab 1 Part 4), EX 377 (Cases and Places 2)
	B. Define and apply advanced filters	EX 350-356	EX 373-374 (In the Lab 2 Part 4), EX 376 (In the Lab 3 Part 6)
	C. Group and outline data	EX 340-342	EX 373-374 (In the Lab 2 Part 4), EX 376 (In the Lab 3 Part 6)
	D. Use data validation	EX 315-318, **POST-ADV**	EX 369 (In the Lab 1 Part 1), EX 375 (In the Lab 3 Part 1 Step 1), **POST-ADV**
	E. Create and modify list ranges	EX 311-327	EX 369 (In the Lab 1 Part 1), EX 375 (In the Lab 3 Part 1)
	F. Add, show, close, edit, merge and summarize scenarios	**POST-ADV**	**POST-ADV**
	G. Perform data analysis using automated tools	EX 204-208, EX 256-265, **POST-ADV**	EX 215 (In the Lab 1 Part 3), EX 218 (In the Lab 2 Part 3), EX 221 (In the Lab 3 Part 2), EX 223-224 (Cases and Places 3-5), EX 296 (Apply Your Knowledge Step 4), EX 298 (In the Lab 1 Step 6, Part 2), EX 301 (In the Lab 2 Step 7), **POST-ADV**
	H. Create PivotTable and PivotChart reports	**POST-ADV**	**POST-ADV**
	I. Use Lookup and Reference functions	EX 323-327	EX 375 (In the Lab 3 Part 1 Step 3), EX 377 (Cases and Places 4)
	J. Use Database functions	EX 358-359	EX 374 (In the Lab 2 Part 5), EX 377 (Cases and Places 4)
	K. Trace formula precedents, dependents and errors	**POST-ADV**	**POST-ADV**
	L. Locate invalid data and formulas	EX 89-90, EX 292-294, **POST-ADV**	EX 131 (Apply Your Knowledge 1 Part 1), EX 297 (In the Lab 1 Part 1 Step 4), EX 302 (In the Lab 3, Step 5), **POST-ADV**
	M. Watch and evaluate formulas	**POST-ADV**	**POST-ADV**
	N. Define, modify and use named ranges	EX 251-252- EX 255, EX 285-287, EX 351, EX 354	EX 296 (Apply Your Knowledge 1 Step 6), EX 297 (In the Lab 1 Step 4), EX 301 (In the Lab 2 Step 4)
	O. Structure workbooks using XML	**POST-ADV**	**POST-ADV**
II. Formatting Data and Content	A. Create and modify custom data formats	EX 395-398	EX 456 (In the Lab 1 Step 2)
	B. Use conditional formatting	EX 103-106, EX 263-266	EX 133 (In the Lab 1 Step 8), EX 135 (In the Lab 2 Step 8), EX 298 (In the Lab 1 Step7),
	C. Format and resize graphics	EX 278-280	EX 303 (In the Lab 3, Step 17)
	D. Format charts and diagrams	EX 192-198, EX 422-428	EX 214 (In the Lab 1, Part 2), EX 217-218, (In the Lab 2 Part 2), EX 459 (In the Lab 2 Step 5)
III. Collaborating	A. Protect cells, worksheets, and workbooks	EX 286-289, **POST-ADV**	EX 296 (Apply Your Knowledge 1 Steps 7, 9), EX 298-299 (In the Lab 1 Part 1 Steps 12, 14, Part 2 Step 8), EX 301 (In the Lab 2 Steps 10, 14), EX 303 (In the Lab 3 Steps 12 and 16), **POST-ADV**
	B. Apply workbook security settings	**POST-ADV**	**POST-ADV**
	C. Share workbooks	**POST-ADV**	**POST-ADV**
	D. Merge workbooks	**POST-ADV**	**POST-ADV**
	E. Track, accept, and reject changes to workbooks	**POST-ADV**	**POST-ADV**
IV. Managing Data and Workbooks	A. Import data to Excel	EX 120-123, **POST-ADV**	EX 136-139 (In the Lab 3), EX 143 (Cases and Places 5), EX 460-462 (In the Lab 3), **POST-ADV**
	B. Export data from Excel	**POST-ADV**	**POST-ADV**
	C. Publish and edit Web worksheets and workbooks	EX 225-239, **POST-ADV**	EX 239 (In the Lab 1), EX 240 (In the Lab 2), **POST-ADV**
	D. Create and edit templates	EX 382-410	EX 456-457 (In the Lab 1), EX 458-459 (In the Lab 2), EX 462-464 (Cases and Places 1-3, 5)
	E. Consolidate data	EX 414-419	EX 459 (In the Lab 2 Step 4), EX 460-462 (In the Lab 3), EX 462-464 (Cases and Places 1-3, 5)
	F. Define and modify workbook properties	**POST-ADV**	**POST-ADV**

Table E-5 Expert-Level Skill Sets, Activities, and Locations in Book for Microsoft Office Excel 2003 *(continued)*

SKILL SET	SKILL BEING MEASURED	SKILL DEMONSTRATED IN BOOK	SKILL EXERCISE IN BOOK
V. Customizing Excel	A. Customize toolbars and menus	**POST-ADV**	**POST-ADV**
	B. Create, edit, and run macros	**POST-ADV**	**POST-ADV**
	C. Modify Excel default settings	EX 390-391, EX 400, EX 406	EX 457 (In the Lab 1 Steps 6, 9-10)

Microsoft Office Access 2003

The Access portion of *Microsoft Office 2003: Introductory Concepts and Techniques* (ISBN 0-619-25574-9 or 0-619-20057-X or 0-619-25558-7 or 0-619-20024-3) and *Microsoft Office 2003: Advanced Concepts and Techniques* (ISBN 0-619-20025-1 or 0-619-20026-X) used in combination in a two-sequence course has been approved by Microsoft as courseware for specialist-level certification. Table E-6 lists the specialist-level examination skill sets, activities, page numbers where the activities are demonstrated, and page numbers where the activities can be practiced. There is no expert-level examination for Microsoft Office Access 2003.

Table E-6 Specialist-Level Skill Sets, Activities, and Locations in Book for Microsoft Office Access 2003

SKILL SET	SKILL BEING MEASURED	SKILL DEMONSTRATED IN BOOK	SKILL EXERCISE IN BOOK
I. Structuring Databases	A. Create Access databases	AC 10	AC 56-64 (In The Lab 1-3, Cases and Places 1-5)
	B. Create and modify tables	AC 15, AC 159, AC 127-130	AC 63 (Cases and Places 3), AC 171 (Cases and Places 3), AC 167-172 (All Exercises)
	C. Define and modify field types	AC 130, AC 147	AC 169 (In The Lab 2 Step 5f, In The Lab 3 Part 1), AC 172 (Cases and Places 5)
	D. Modify field properties	AC 127-128, AC 140-144, AC 160, AC 263, AC 265	AC 167-172 (All Exercises), AC 304 (Apply Your Knowledge, Steps 1, 3), AC 312 (Cases and Places 3)
	E. Create and modify one-to-many relationships	AC 151, AC 342	AC 171-172 (Cases and Places 1-4), AC 374 (Cases and Places 2)
	F. Enforce referential integrity	AC 152, AC 342	AC 167 (Apply Your Knowledge Step 17), AC 169 (In The Lab 1 Step 13), AC 170 (In The Lab 2 Step 11), AC 170 (In The Lab 3 Part 3), AC 171-172 (Cases and Places 1-4), AC 374-376 (All Cases and Places)
	G. Create and modify queries	AC 34, AC 37, AC 104, AC 154	AC 55 (Apply Your Knowledge Steps 3-6), AC 60 (In The Lab 2 Step 2), AC 62 (In The Lab Part 3), AC 63-64 (Cases and Places 3-4), AC 109 (Apply Your Knowledge Step 8), AC 111 (In The Lab 2 Step 12), AC 112 (Cases and Places 5), AC 172 (Cases and Places 4), AC 171 (Cases and Places 3), AC 172 (Cases and Places 5), AC 376 (Cases and Places 5)
	H. Create forms	AC 38, AC 228, AC 274	AC 57 (In The Lab 1 Step 8), AC 61 (In the Lab 3 Part 1), AC 64 (Cases and Places 4), AC 249-256 (All Exercises), AC 304-312 (All Exercises)
	I. Add and modify form controls and properties	AC 227, AC 232, AC 235, AC 237, AC 241, AC 286, AC 288	AC 249-256 (All Exercises)
	J. Create reports	AC 43, AC 198, AC 217	AC 55-64 (All Exercises)
	K. Add and modify report control properties	AC 209	AC 249-256 (All Exercises)
	L. Create a data access page	AC 380	AC 398 (In The Lab 1)
II. Entering Data	A. Enter, edit and delete records	AC 23, AC 28, AC 116, AC 119, AC 125	AC 54-64 (All Exercises), AC 167-172 (All Exercises)
	B. Find and move among records	AC 27	AC 55 (Apply Your Knowledge Step 1), AC 57 (In The Lab 1 Step 9), AC 60 (In The Lab 2 Step 3), AC 62 (In The Lab 3 Part 2)
	C. Import data to Access	AC 176-180	AC 191 (In The Lab 1)

Table E-6 Specialist-Level Skill Sets, Activities, and Locations in Book for Microsoft Office Access 2003

SKILL SET	SKILL BEING MEASURED	SKILL DEMONSTRATED IN BOOK	SKILL EXERCISE IN BOOK
III. Organizing Data	A. Create and modify calculated fields and aggregate functions	AC 96-97, AC 99-103	AC 110 (In The Lab 1 Step 11), AC 111 (In The Lab 3 Part 3), AC 112 (Cases and Places 3), AC 110 (In The Lab 1 Steps 12, 13), AC 111 (In The Lab 2 Step 11, In The Lab 3 Part 3), AC 112 (Cases and Places 1-4)
	B. Modify form layout	AC 211, AC 216	AC 254 (In The Lab 3), AC 256 (Cases and Places 5)
	C. Modify report layout and page setup	AC 30-31, AC 212, AC 222	AC 170 (In The Lab 3 Parts 2-3), AC 254 (In The Lab 3), AC 256 (Cases and Places 5)
	D. Format datasheets	AC 131-135	AC 171 (Cases and Places 2)
	E. Sort records	AC 86-89, AC 155, AC 205, AC 240	AC 167 (Apply Your Knowledge Step 15), AC 171-172 (Cases and Places 2, 4), AC 256 (Cases and Places 5)
	F. Filter records	AC 121, AC 123	AC 167 (Apply Your Knowledge Step 13), AC 169 (In The Lab 2 Step 9)
IV. Managing Databases	A. Identify object dependencies	AC 299	AC 312 (Cases and Places 5)
	B. View objects and object data in other views	AC 23, AC 29-31, AC 42, AC 202, AC 208, AC 347, AC 354, AC 384	AC 54-64 (All Exercises), AC 170 (In The Lab 3), AC 366 (Apply Your Knowledge), AC 368-373 (In The Lab 1-3), AC 376 (Cases and Places 5)
	C. Print database objects and data	AC 29-31, AC 47, AC 72, AC 242	AC 54-64 (All Exercises, AC 109-112 (All Exercises), AC 249-256 (All Exercises), AC 304-312 (All Exercises)
	D. Export data from Access	AC 181, AC 183, AC 184, AC 185-187	AC 192 (In The Lab 2)
	E. Back up a database	AC 162-163	AC 167 (Apply Your Knowledge Step 18), AC 170 (In The Lab 2 Step 12), AC 171 (Cases and Places 1-2)
	F. Compact and repair databases	AC 163-164	AC 169 (In The Lab 1 Step 14), AC 170 (In The Lab 2 Step 12), AC 171 (Cases and Places 1-2)

Microsoft Office PowerPoint 2003

The PowerPoint portion of *Microsoft Office 2003: Introductory Concepts and Techniques* (ISBN 0-619-25574-9 or 0-619-20057-X or 0-619-25558-7 or 0-619-20024-3) and *Microsoft Office 2003: Advanced Concepts and Techniques* (ISBN 0-619-20025-1 or 0-619-20026-X) used in combination in a two-sequence course has been approved by Microsoft as courseware for specialist-level certification. Table E-7 lists the specialist-level examination skill sets, activities, page numbers where the activities are demonstrated, and page numbers where the activities can be practiced. There is no expert-level examination for Microsoft Office PowerPoint 2003.

Table E-7 Specialist-Level Skill Sets, Activities, and Locations in Book for Microsoft Office PowerPoint 2003

SKILL SET	SKILL BEING MEASURED	SKILL DEMONSTRATED IN BOOK	SKILL EXERCISE IN BOOK
I. Creating Content	A. Create new presentations from templates	PPT 18-43, PPT 85-111, PPT 163-210, PPT 228-231	PPT 69-71 (In the Lab 1 Steps 1-3), PPT 132-133 (In the Lab 1 Steps 1-4), PPT 297-298 (In the Lab 1 Step 1), PPT 299-301 (In the Lab 2 Steps 1-10), PPT 302-303 (In the Lab 3 Steps 1-11)
	B. Insert and edit text-based content	PPT 20-24, PPT 31-42, PPT 53-56, PPT 88-94, PPT 165-167, PPT 247, PPT 257, PPT 260, PPT 266-268	PPT 69-71 (In the Lab 1 Steps 2-4), PPT 72-73 (In the Lab 2 Step 4), PPT 74-77 (In the Lab 3 Part 1 Step 2, Part 2 Step 6), PPT 132-134 (In the Lab 1 Steps 2-4), PPT 218-219 (In the Lab 2 Step 1), PPT 220-221 (In the Lab 3 Step 1), PPT 222 (Cases and Places 3), PPT 299-301 (In the Lab 2 Steps 4, 6-8, 13), PPT 302-304 (In the Lab 3 Step 14), PPT 305 (Cases and Places 1 and 2)

Table E-7 Specialist-Level Skill Sets, Activities, and Locations in Book for Microsoft Office PowerPoint 2003 *(continued)*

SKILL SET	SKILL BEING MEASURED	SKILL DEMONSTRATED IN BOOK	SKILL EXERCISE IN BOOK
	C. Insert tables, charts and diagrams	PPT 190-195, PPT 195-207, PPT 246-251	PPT 218-219 (In the Lab 2 Steps 5-6), PPT 220-221 (In the Lab 3 Steps 5-6), PPT 222-223 (Cases and Places 1-2, 4), PPT 305-306 (Cases and Places 2-4), PPT 297-298 (In the Lab 1 Step 5), PPT 299-301 (In the Lab 2 Step 9)
	D. Insert pictures, shapes and graphics	PPT 99-106, PPT 170-172, PPT 175-177	PPT 132-134 (In the Lab 1 Steps 2-3, 5-6), PPT 134-135 (In the Lab 2 Steps 2-5), PPT 217 (In the Lab 1 Steps 3, 5), PPT 297-298 (In the Lab 1 Step 2), PPT 299-301 (In the Lab 2 Step 3), PPT 302-303 (In the Lab 3 Step 2)
	E. Insert objects	PPT 243-244, PPT 251-255, PPT 256-258	PPT 296-297 (Apply Your Knowledge 1 Step 6), PPT 299-301 (In the Lab 2 Steps 5, 7), PPT 302-303 (In the Lab 3 Steps 4, 9, 11)
II. Formatting Content	A. Format text-based content	PPT 23-27, PPT 173-175, PPT 186-190, PPT 193-195	PPT 69-71 (In the Lab 1 Step 2), PPT 72-73 (In the Lab 2 Step 2), PPT 217 (In the Lab 1 Step 2), PPT 220-221 (In the Lab 3 Step 3), PPT 297-298 (In the Lab 1 Step 3), PPT 299-301 (In the Lab 2 Steps 2, 4, 11), PPT 302-304 (In the Lab 3 Steps 9, 11)
	B. Format pictures, shapes and graphics	PPT 108-111, PPT 116-119, PPT 178-184, PPT 239-240, PPT 255-256, PPT 258-259, PPT 274-278	PPT 132-134 (In the Lab 1 Steps 2-3, 5-6), PPT 132-134 (In the Lab 1 Steps 2, 5-6), PPT 134-135 (In the Lab 2 Steps 2-5, 8), PPT 136-137 (In the Lab 3 Steps 2-5), PPT 216 (Apply Your Knowledge 1 Step 2), PPT 217 (In the Lab 1 Step 7), PPT 220-221 (In the Lab 3 Steps 6, 8), PPT 296-297 (Apply Your Knowledge 1 Step 6), PPT 302-304 (In the Lab 3 Step 12)
	C. Format slides	PPT 17-20, PPT 85, PPT 144, PPT 97-99, PPT 169-172, PPT 207-208, PPT 232-233, PPT 248, PPT 285, PPT 289	PPT 69-71 (In the Lab 1 Step 1), PPT 131-132 (Apply Your Knowledge 1 Steps 3, 5), PPT 132-134 (In the Lab 1 Steps 3, 5-6), PPT 134-135 (In the Lab 2 Step 1), PPT 217 (In the Lab 1 Step 1), PPT 218-219 (In the Lab 2 Steps 5-6), PPT 220-221 (In the Lab 3 Step 3), PPT 297-298 (In the Lab 1 Step 1), PPT 299-301 (In the Lab 2 Steps 6-8), PPT 302-304 (In the Lab 3 Steps 5, 18)
	D. Apply animation schemes	PPT 114-116, PPT 210	PPT 131-132 (Apply Your Knowledge 1 Step 6), PPT 136-137 (In the Lab 3 Step 7), PPT 218-219 (In the Lab 2 Step 9), PPT 299-300 (In the Lab 2 Step 12), PPT 302-304 (In the Lab 3 Step 13)
	E. Apply slide transitions	PPT 278-281	PPT 296-297 (Apply Your Knowledge 1 Step 8), PPT 297-298 (In the Lab 1 Step 6), PPT 299-301 (In the Lab 2 Step 12)
	F. Customize slide templates	PPT 268-270	PPT 296-297 (Apply Your Knowledge 1 Step 2), PPT 297-298 (In the Lab 1 Step 1), PPT 299-301 (In the Lab 2 Step 1), PPT 305 (Cases and Places 1)
	G. Work with masters	PPT 112-113, PPT 184-190, PPT 223-236, PPT 248, PPT 252, PPT 257, PPT 270-278, PPT 283-285	PPT 132-134 (In the Lab 1 Step 7), PPT 134-135 (In the Lab 2 Step 6), PPT 136-137 (In the Lab 3 Step 6), PPT 218-219 (In the Lab 2 Step 7), PPT 220-221 (In the Lab 3 Step 7), PPT 223 (Cases and Places 4), PPT 296-297 (Apply Your Knowledge 1 Steps 2-3, 6), PPT 297-298 (In the Lab 1 Steps 2, 4), PPT 299-301 (In the Lab 2 Steps 1, 3, 11)
III. Collaborating	A. Track, accept and reject changes in a presentation	PPT 314-316; PPT 321-329	PPT 338-340 (In the Lab 1 Steps 3-7), PPT 341-342 (In the Lab 2 Step 2), PPT 343 (In the Lab 3 Step 4)
	B. Add, edit and delete comments in a presentation	PPT 310-314, PPT 321-329	PPT 338-340 (In the Lab 1 Steps 2-7), PPT 341-342 (In the Lab 2 Step 2), PPT 343 (In the Lab 3 Steps 2, 4)
	C. Compare and merge presentations	PPT 316-317	PPT 338-340 (In the Lab 1 Step 2), PPT 341-342 (In the Lab 2 Step 2), PPT 343 (In the Lab 3 Step 3)
IV. Managing and Delivering Presentations	A. Organize a presentation	PPT 30-31, PPT 89-97, PPT 209-210, PPT 240-243, PPT 245, PPT 261-263, PPT 275-276, PPT 285-286, PPT 330	PPT 69-71 (In the Lab 1 Step 3), PPT 132-134 (In the Lab 1 Steps 3-4), PPT 218-219 (In the Lab 2 Step 4), PPT 220-221 (In the Lab 3 Step 4), PPT 296-297 (Apply Your Knowledge 1 Step 4), PPT 297-298 (In the Lab 1 Steps 2, 5, 7), PPT 299-301 (In the Lab 2 Steps 7, 9-10), PPT 302-304 (In the Lab 3 Steps 2, 6-7, 9-12, 16), PPT 306 (Cases and Places 3-5), PPT 338-340 (In the Lab 1 Step 2)

Table E-7 Specialist-Level Skill Sets, Activities, and Locations in Book for Microsoft Office PowerPoint 2003

SKILL SET	SKILL BEING MEASURED	SKILL DEMONSTRATED IN BOOK	SKILL EXERCISE IN BOOK
	B. Set up slide shows for delivery	PPT 212-213, PPT 263-265, PPT 272-278	PPT 218-219 (In the Lab 2 Step 11), PPT 220-221 (In the Lab 3 Step 10), PPT 222-223 (Cases and Places 2, 5), PPT 299-301 (In the Lab 2 Step 14), PPT 302-304 (In the Lab 3 Steps 6-7, 11, 13), PPT 305-306 (Cases and Places 2-3)
	C. Rehearse timing	PPT 281-283	PPT 302-304 (In the Lab 3 Step 15), PPT 306 (Cases and Places 4-5)
	D. Deliver presentations	PPT 46-50, PPT 292-293	PPT 74-77 (In the Lab 3 Part 1 Step 2, Part 2 Step 6), PPT 296-297 (Apply Your Knowledge 1 Step 9), PPT 299-301 (In the Lab 2 Step 16), PPT 302-304 (In the Lab 3 Step 17), PPT 305 (Cases and Places 1-2)
	E. Prepare presentations for remote delivery	PPT 333-335	PPT 338-340 (In the Lab 1 Step 10), PPT 341-342 (In the Lab 2 Steps 3-4)
	F. Save and publish presentations	PPT 146-149, PPT 154-157, PPT 231-232, PPT 336, Appendix C	PPT 158 (In the Lab 1 Steps 2-3, 6), PPT 158 (In the Lab 2 Steps 2-3, 8), PPT 159 (In the Lab 3 Steps 2-3), PPT 299-301 (In the Lab 2 Step 15), PPT 341-342 (In the Lab 2 Step 3), PPT 343 (In the Lab 3 Step 4)
	G. Print slides, outlines, handouts, and speaker notes	PPT 56-59, PPT 60-61, PPT 122-126, PPT 211, PPT 286-288, PPT 316-321	PPT 69-71 (In the Lab 1 Step 7), PPT 72-73 (In the Lab 2 Steps 6-8), PPT 158 (In the Lab 1 Step 7), PPT 296-297 (Apply Your Knowledge 1 Step 9), PPT 297-298 (In the Lab 1 Step 9), PPT 299-301 (In the Lab 2 Step 17), PPT 302-304 (In the Lab 3 Step 18), PPT 338-340 (In the Lab 1 Steps 2, 9), PPT 341-342 (In the Lab 2 Steps 2-3), PPT 343 (In the Lab 3 Step 3)
	H. Export a presentation to another Microsoft Office program	PPT 289	PPT 299-301 (In the Lab 2 Step 15), PPT 302-304 (In the Lab 3 Step 18)

Microsoft Office Outlook 2003

The Outlook portion of *Microsoft Office 2003: Introductory Concepts and Techniques* (ISBN 0-619-25574-9 or 0-619-20057-X or 0-619-25558-7 or 0-619-20024-3) and *Microsoft Office 2003: Advanced Concepts and Techniques* (ISBN 0-619-20025-1 or 0-619-20026-X) used in combination in a two-sequence course has been approved by Microsoft as courseware for specialist-level certification. Table E-8 lists the specialist-level examination skill sets, activities, page numbers where the activities are demonstrated, and page numbers where the activities can be practiced. There is no expert-level examination for Microsoft Office Outlook 2003.

Table E-8 Specialist-Level Skill Sets, Activities, and Locations in Book for Microsoft Office Outlook 2003

SKILL SET	SKILL BEING MEASURED	SKILL DEMONSTRATED IN BOOK	SKILL EXERCISE IN BOOK
I. Messaging	A. Originate and respond to e-mail and instant messages	OUT 13-16, OUT 23-25, OUT 51-53, OUT 129-131	OUT 62 (In the Lab 1 Part 2 Step 1), OUT 63 (In the Lab 3 Part 2), OUT 64 (Cases and Places 3), OUT 140 (In the Lab 2 Steps 3, 6), OUT 141 (In the Lab 2 Step 7), OUT 143 (Cases and Places 5)
	B. Attach files to items	OUT 27 -29, OUT 132-134	OUT 62 (In the Lab 1 Part 2 Step 3), OUT 141 (In the Lab 2 Steps 7-8)
	C. Create and modify a personal signature for messages	OUT 19-23	OUT 63 (In the Lab 3 Part 1, Part 3 Step 4)
	D. Modify e-mail message settings and delivery options	OUT 15, OUT 29-31, OUT 34-38	OUT 62 (In the Lab 1 Part 2 Steps 2, 4-5, In the Lab 2), OUT 63 (In the Lab 3 Part 2)
	E. Create and edit contacts	OUT 41-44, OUT 125-127, OUT 128-129	OUT 61 (Apply Your Knowledge 1), OUT 64 (Cases and Places 1-5), OUT 140 (In the Lab 2 Step 4)
	F. Accept, decline, and delegate tasks	OUT 98-102	OUT 142 (In the Lab 3 Part 2)

Table E-8 Specialist-Level Skill Sets, Activities, and Locations in Book for Microsoft Office Outlook 2003 *(continued)*

SKILL SET	SKILL BEING MEASURED	SKILL DEMONSTRATED IN BOOK	SKILL EXERCISE IN BOOK
II. Scheduling	A. Create and modify appointments, meetings, and events	OUT 72-77, OUT 79-81, OUT 88-89, OUT 103-107	OUT 138 (Apply Your Knowledge 1 Part 1), OUT 139 (In the Lab 1 Part 1 Step 2, Part 2), OUT 141 (In the Lab 3 Part 1 Step 3), OUT 143 (Cases and Places 1, 4-5)
	B. Update, cancel, and respond to meeting requests	OUT 107-110	OUT 139 (In the Lab 1 Part 1 Steps 4-5, 7), OUT 143 (Cases and Places 5)
	C. Customize Calendar settings	OUT 112-117	OUT 138 (Apply Your Knowledge 1 Parts 1-2), OUT 141 (In the Lab 3 Part 1 Step 2), OUT 143 (Cases and Places 1-2)
	D. Create, modify, and assign tasks	OUT 91-93, OUT 98-100	OUT 141 (In the Lab 3 Part 1 Step 4), OUT 142 (In the Lab 3 Part 2)
III. Organizing	A. Create and modify distribution lists	OUT 53-56	OUT 61 (Apply Your Knowledge 1 and In the Lab 1 Part 1)
	B. Link contacts to other items	OUT 58	OUT 64 (Cases and Places 3)
	C. Create and modify notes	OUT 110-112	OUT 143 (Cases and Places 3)
	D. Organize items	OUT 31-34, OUT 44-48, OUT 103, OUT 114-117	OUT 61 (Apply Your Knowledge 1), OUT 62 (In the Lab 2), OUT 64 (Cases and Places 3, 5), OUT 138 (Apply Your Knowledge 1), OUT 142 (In the Lab 3 Part 2 Step 4), OUT 143 (Cases and Places 1)
	E. Organize items using folders	OUT 39-41, OUT 70-71, OUT 95-96, OUT 103, OUT 120-121	OUT 61 (Apply Your Knowledge 1 Part 1), OUT 64 (Cases and Places 4), OUT 138 (Apply Your Knowledge Part 1), OUT 141 (In the Lab 3 Part 1 Step 1), OUT 142 (In the Lab 3 Part 2 Steps 6-7)
	F. Search for items	OUT 38, OUT 46-47	OUT 63 (In the Lab 3 Part 3 Step 2), OUT 64 (Cases and Places 2)
	G. Save items in different file formats	OUT 56-58	OUT 62 (In the Lab 1 Part 3)
	H. Assign items to categories	OUT 47-49	OUT 64 (Cases and Places 4)
	I. Preview and print items	OUT 12, OUT 49-50, OUT 118-119	OUT 61-62 (Apply Your Knowledge 1 and In the Lab 1 Part 1, Part 2 Step 6), OUT 63 (In the Lab 3 Part 1, Part 2, Part 3 Step 5), OUT 64 (Cases and Places 1-5), OUT 138 (Apply Your Knowledge 1 Part 1), OUT 139 (In the Lab 1 Part 1 Step 6, Part 2), OUT 141 (In the Lab 2 Step 8, In the Lab 3 Part 1 Step 5), OUT 142 (In the Lab 3 Part 2 Step 5), OUT 143 (Cases and Places 1-5)

Index

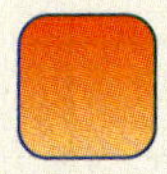

Quick Reference Summary

In the Microsoft Office 2003 applications, you can accomplish a task in a number of ways. The following five tables (one each for Microsoft Office Word 2003, Microsoft Office Excel 2003, Microsoft Office Access 2003, Microsoft Office PowerPoint 2003, and Microsoft Office Outlook 2003) provide a quick reference. The first column identifies the task. The second column indicates the page number on which the task is discussed in the book. The subsequent four columns list the different ways the task in column one can be carried out. You can invoke the commands listed in the MOUSE, MENU BAR, and SHORTCUT MENU columns using Voice commands.

Table 1 Microsoft Office Word 2003 Quick Reference Summary

TASK	PAGE NUMBER	MOUSE	MENU BAR	SHORTCUT MENU	KEYBOARD SHORTCUT
1.5 Line Spacing	WD 87	Line Spacing button arrow on Formatting toolbar	Format | Paragraph | Indents and Spacing tab	Paragraph | Indents and Spacing tab	CTRL+5
Animate Text	WD 437		Format | Font | Text Effects tab	Font | Text Effects tab	
Arrange All Open Documents	WD 443		Window | Arrange All		
AutoCorrect Entry, Create	WD 91		Tools | AutoCorrect Options | AutoCorrect tab		
AutoCorrect Options	WD 90	AutoCorrect Options button			
AutoShape, Add Text	WD 308			Add Text	
AutoShape, Format	WD 307	Double-click inside AutoShape	Format | AutoShape	Format AutoShape	
AutoShape, Insert	WD 306	AutoShapes button on Drawing toolbar	Insert | Picture | AutoShapes		
AutoText Entry, Create	WD 179		Insert | AutoText | New		ALT+F3
AutoText Entry, Insert	WD 181		Insert | AutoText		Type entry, then F3
Background Color, Change	WD 438		Format | Background		
Blank Line Above Paragraph	WD 87		Format | Paragraph | Indents and Spacing tab	Paragraph | Indents and Spacing tab	CTRL+0 (zero)
Bold	WD 44	Bold button on Formatting toolbar	Format | Font | Font tab	Font | Font tab	CTRL+B
Border, Bottom	WD 172	Border button arrow on Formatting toolbar	Format | Borders and Shading | Borders tab		
Border, Page	WD 433		Format | Borders and Shading | Page Border tab	Borders and Shading | Page Border tab	
Bulleted List	WD 187	Bullets button on Formatting toolbar	Format | Bullets and Numbering | Bulleted tab	Bullets and Numbering | Bulleted tab	* and then space followed by text, then ENTER
Capitalize Letters	WD 87		Format | Font | Font tab	Font | Font tab	CTRL+SHIFT+A
Case of Letters	WD 87				SHIFT+F3
Center	WD 38	Center button on Formatting toolbar	Format | Paragraph | Indents and Spacing tab	Paragraph | Indents and Spacing tab	CTRL+E
Center Vertically	WD 233		File | Page Setup | Layout tab		
Character Formatting, Remove	WD 87		Format | Font | Font tab	Font | Font tab	CTRL+SPACEBAR
Character Spacing, Modify	WD 227		Format | Font | Character Spacing tab	Font | Character Spacing tab	
Character Style, Apply	WD 269	Style box arrow on Formatting toolbar	Format | Styles and Formatting		
Character Style, Create	WD 268	Styles and Formatting button on Formatting toolbar	Format | Styles and Formatting		

Table 1 Microsoft Office Word 2003 Quick Reference Summary *(continued)*

TASK	PAGE NUMBER	MOUSE	MENU BAR	SHORTCUT MENU	KEYBOARD SHORTCUT
Chart, Change Chart Type	WD 262		Chart | Chart Type	Right-click chart, Chart Type	
Chart, Move Legend	WD 261		Select legend, Format | Selected Legend | Placement tab	Right-click legend, Format Legend | Placement tab	
Chart, Resize	WD 262	Drag sizing handles			
Chart Table	WD 259		Insert | Picture | Chart		
Clip Art, Insert	WD 46		Insert | Picture | Clip Art		
Clip Art, Insert from Web	WD 230		Insert | Picture | Clip Art		
Clipboard Task Pane, Display	WD 169	Double-click Office Clipboard icon in tray	Edit | Office Clipboard		
Close All Open Documents	WD 362		SHIFT+File | Close All		
Close Document	WD 59	Close button on menu bar	File | Close		CTRL+W
Color Characters	WD 161	Font Color button arrow on Formatting toolbar	Format | Font | Font tab	Font | Font tab	
Column Break, Insert	WD 406		Insert | Break		CTRL+SHIFT+ENTER
Columns	WD 400	Columns button on Standard toolbar	Format | Columns		
Columns, Balance	WD 420		Insert | Break		
Column, Delete	WD 250		Table | Delete | Columns	Delete Columns	
Columns, Format	WD 416		Format | Columns		
Comment, Insert	WD 463	New Comment button on Reviewing toolbar	Insert | Comment		
Compare and Merge Documents	WD 473		Tools | Compare and Merge Documents		
Copy (Collect Items)	WD 166	Copy button on Standard toolbar	Edit | Copy	Copy	CTRL+C
Count Words	WD 100	Recount button on Word Count toolbar	Tools | Word Count		
Custom Dictionary	WD 121		Tools | Options | Spelling and Grammar tab		
Cut Text	WD 245	Cut button on Standard toolbar	Select text, Edit | Cut	Select Text | Cut	Select text, CTRL+X
Data Source, Type New	WD 315	Mail Merge Recipients button on Mail Merge toolbar	Tools | Letters and Mailings | Mail Merge		
Date, Insert	WD 177		Insert | Date and Time		
Default Font Settings, Modify	WD 229		Format | Font	Font	
Delete (Cut) Text	WD 59	Cut button on Standard toolbar	Edit | Cut	Cut	CTRL+X or DELETE
Demote List Item	WD 189	Decrease Indent button on Formatting toolbar			
Diagram, Add Segments	WD 423	Insert Shape button on Diagram toolbar		Insert Shape	
Diagram, AutoFormat	WD 425	AutoFormat button on Diagram toolbar			
Diagram, Insert	WD 421	Insert Diagram or Organization Chart button on Drawing toolbar	Insert | Diagram		
Display Two Documents Side by Side	WD 443		Window | Compare Side by Side		
Distribute Columns Evenly	WD 275	Distribute Columns Evenly button on Tables and Borders toolbar	Table | AutoFit | Distribute Columns Evenly		
Distribute Rows Evenly	WD 274	Distribute Rows Evenly button on Tables and Borders toolbar	Table | AutoFit | Distribute Rows Evenly		
Document Summary, Modify	WD 193		File | Properties | Summary tab		
Document Window, Open New	WD 160	New Blank document button on Standard toolbar		File | New | Blank document	CTRL+N

Table 1 Microsoft Office Word 2003 Quick Reference Summary

TASK	PAGE NUMBER	MOUSE	MENU BAR	SHORTCUT MENU	KEYBOARD SHORTCUT
Double-Space Text	WD 80	Line Spacing button on Formatting toolbar	Format | Paragraph | Indents and Spacing tab	Paragraph | Indents and Spacing tab	CTRL+2
Double Strikethrough Characters	WD 229		Format | Font | Font tab	Font | Font tab	
Double-Underline	WD 87		Format | Font | Font tab	Font | Font tab	CTRL+SHIFT+D
Drawing Canvas, Format	WD 311	Double-click edge of drawing canvas	Format | Drawing Canvas	Format Drawing Canvas	
Drawing Canvas, Insert	WD 305		Insert | Picture | New Drawing		
Drawing Canvas, Resize	WD 310	Drag sizing handles	Format | Drawing Canvas | Size tab	Format Drawing Canvas | Size tab	
Drawing Grid	WD 395	Draw button on Drawing toolbar			
Drop Cap	WD 403		Format | Drop Cap		
Edit Field	WD 322			Edit Field	
E-Mail Document	WD 123	E-mail button on Standard toolbar	File | Send To | Mail Recipient		
E-Mail Document, as Attachment	WD 123		File | Send To | Mail Recipient (as Attachment)		
E-mail Document, for Review	WD 462		File | Send To | Mail Recipient (for Review)		
Emboss, Characters	WD 229		Format | Font | Font tab	Font | Font tab	
Engrave, Characters	WD 229		Format | Font | Font tab	Font | Font tab	
Envelope, Address	WD 190		Tools | Letters and Mailings | Envelopes and Labels | Envelopes tab		
Field Code, Display	WD 335		Tools | Options | View tab	Toggle Field Codes	ALT+F9
Field Codes, Print	WD 336		Tools | Options | Print tab		
File Properties, Display	WD 194	Views button arrow in Open dialog box			
Find	WD 117	Select Browse Object button on vertical scroll bar	Edit | Find		CTRL+F
Find a Format	WD 266	Select Browse Object button on vertical scroll bar	Edit | Find | Format button		CTRL+F
Find and Replace	WD 116	Double-click status bar to left of status indicators	Edit | Replace		CTRL+H
First-Line Indent	WD 88	Drag First Line Indent marker on ruler	Format | Paragraph | Indents and Spacing tab	Paragraph | Indents and Spacing tab	
Folder, Create	WD 313		File | Save As | Create New Folder button		CTRL+F12 | Create New Folder button
Folder, Rename	WD 344			In Open dialog box, right-click folder | Rename	In Open dialog box, select folder, F2
Font	WD 36	Font box arrow on Formatting toolbar	Format | Font | Font tab	Font | Font tab	CTRL+SHIFT+F
Font Size	WD 17	Font Size box arrow on Formatting toolbar	Format | Font | Font tab	Font | Font tab	CTRL+SHIFT+P
Footer	WD 249	Switch Between Header and Footer button on Header and Footer toolbar	View | Header and Footer		
Footnote, Create	WD 94		Insert | Reference | Footnote		
Footnote, Delete	WD 99	Delete note reference mark in document window			
Footnote, Edit	WD 99	Double-click note reference mark in document window	View | Footnotes		
Footnotes to Endnotes, Convert	WD 99		Insert | Reference | Footnote		
Format Characters, Font Dialog Box	WD 227		Format | Font | Font tab	Font | Font tab	
Format Painter	WD 427	Format Painter button on Standard toolbar			

Table 1 Microsoft Office Word 2003 Quick Reference Summary *(continued)*

TASK	PAGE NUMBER	MOUSE	MENU BAR	SHORTCUT MENU	KEYBOARD SHORTCUT
Formatting, Clear	WD 173	Styles and Formatting button on Formatting toolbar or Style box arrow on Formatting toolbar			CTRL+SPACEBAR; CTRL+Q
Formatting Marks	WD 21	Show/Hide ¶ button on Standard toolbar	Tools | Options | View tab		CTRL+SHIFT+*
Frame, New	WD 210	desired button on Frames toolbar			
Frame Properties, Modify	WD 214	Frame Properties button on Frames toolbar	Format | Frames | Frame Properties	Frame Properties	
Frames Page, Create	WD 210		Format | Frames | New Frames Page		
Full Menu	WD 13	Double-click menu name	Click menu name, wait few seconds		
Full Screen View	WD 407		View | Full Screen		
Go To	WD 111, WD 246	Select Browse Object button on vertical scroll bar	Edit | Go To		CTRL+G
Graph, Exit and Return to Word	WD 263	Click anywhere outside chart			
Graphic, Brighten	WD 396	More Brightness button on Picture toolbar	Format | Picture	Format Picture	
Graphic, Darken	WD 396	Less Brightness button on Picture toolbar	Format | Picture	Format Picture	
Graphic, Flip	WD 394	Draw button on Drawing toolbar			
Graphic, Format as Floating	WD 393	Text Wrapping button on Picture toolbar	Format | Picture | Layout tab	Format Picture | Layout tab	
GreetingLine Merge Field, Edit	WD 323			Edit Greeting Line	
Hanging Indent, Create	WD 105	Drag Hanging Indent marker on ruler	Format | Paragraph | Indents and Spacing tab	Paragraph | Indents and Spacing tab	CTRL+T
Hanging Indent, Remove	WD 87	Drag Hanging Indent marker on ruler	Format | Paragraph | Indents and Spacing tab	Paragraph | Indents and Spacing tab	CTRL+SHIFT+T
Header, Different from Previous	WD 247		View | Header and Footer		
Header, Display	WD 81		View | Header and Footer		
Help	WD 60 and Appendix A	Microsoft Office Word Help button on Standard toolbar	Help | Microsoft Office Word Help		F1
Hidden Text	WD 360		Format | Font | Font tab	Font | Font tab	
Hidden Text, Hide/Show	WD 361	Show/Hide ¶ button on Standard toolbar			CTRL+SHIFT+*
Highlight Text	WD 213, WD 436	Highlight button on Formatting toolbar			
HTML Source	WD 206		View | HTML Source		
Hyperlink, Convert to Regular Text	WD 174	AutoCorrect Options button | Undo Hyperlink		Remove Hyperlink	CTRL+Z
Hyperlink, Create	WD 108, WD 212	Insert Hyperlink button on Standard toolbar		Hyperlink	Web address then ENTER or SPACEBAR
Hyperlink, Edit	WD 207	Insert Hyperlink button on Standard toolbar		Hyperlink	CTRL+K
IF Field, Insert	WD 327	Insert Word Field button on Mail Merge toolbar	Insert | Field		
Indent, Decrease	WD 87	Decrease Indent button on Formatting toolbar	Format | Paragraph | Indents and Spacing tab	Paragraph | Indents and Spacing tab	CTRL+SHIFT+M
Indent, Increase	WD 87	Increase Indent button on Formatting toolbar	Format | Paragraph | Indents and Spacing tab	Paragraph | Indents and Spacing tab	CTRL+M
Insert File	WD 238		Insert | File		
Italicize	WD 41	Italic button on Formatting toolbar	Format | Font | Font tab	Font | Font tab	CTRL+I
Justify Paragraph	WD 401	Justify button on Formatting toolbar	Format | Paragraph | Indents and Spacing tab	Paragraph | Indents and Spacing tab	CTRL+J
Language Bar, Close	WD 16			Right-click Language bar, click Close the Language bar	

Table 1 Microsoft Office Word 2003 Quick Reference Summary

TASK	PAGE NUMBER	MOUSE	MENU BAR	SHORTCUT MENU	KEYBOARD SHORTCUT
Last Editing Location	WD 239				SHIFT+F5
Leader Characters	WD 164		Format | Tabs		
Left-Align	WD 86	Align Left button on Formatting toolbar	Format | Paragraph | Indents and Spacing tab	Paragraph | Indents and Spacing tab	CTRL+L
Line Break, Enter	WD 154				SHIFT+ENTER
Link Copied Item	WD 418		Edit | Paste Special		
List Item, Demote	WD 331	Increase Indent button on Formatting toolbar			SHIFT+TAB
List Item, Promote	WD 331	Decrease Indent button on Formatting toolbar			TAB
Mail Merge Fields, Insert	WD 325	Insert Merge Fields button on Mail Merge toolbar			
Mail Merge to New Document Window	WD 356	Merge to New Document button on Mail Merge toolbar			
Mail Merge, Directory	WD 353	Main document setup button on Mail Merge toolbar	Tools | Letters and Mailings | Mail Merge		
Mail Merge, Envelopes	WD 351	Main document setup button on Mail Merge toolbar	Tools | Letters and Mailings | Mail Merge		
Mail Merge, Mailing Labels	WD 345	Main document setup button on Mail Merge toolbar	Tools | Letters and Mailings | Mail Merge		
Mail Merge, Select Records	WD 339	Mail Merge Recipients button on Mail Merge toolbar			
Mail Merge, Sort Data Records	WD 342	Mail Merge Recipients button on Mail Merge toolbar			
Mail Merge to Printer	WD 338	Merge to Printer button on Mail Merge toolbar			
Mail Merged Data, View	WD 343	View Merged Data button on Mail Merge toolbar			
Mailing Label, Address	WD 191		Tools | Letters and Mailings | Envelopes and Labels | Labels tab		
Margins	WD 78	In print layout view, drag margin boundary on ruler	File | Page Setup | Margins tab		
Menus and Toolbars, Reset	Appendix D	Toolbar Options button on toolbar | Add or Remove Buttons | Customize | Options tab	View | Toolbars | Customize | Options tab		
Move Selected Text	WD 113	Drag and drop	Edit | Cut; Edit | Paste	Cut; Paste	CTRL+X; CTRL+V
Nonbreaking Hyphen	WD 180		Insert | Symbol | Special Characters tab		CTRL+SHIFT+HYPHEN
Nonbreaking Space	WD 180		Insert | Symbol | Special Characters tab		CTRL+SHIFT+SPACEBAR
Note Pane, Close	WD 99	Close button in note pane			
Numbered List	WD 189	Numbering button on Formatting toolbar	Format | Bullets and Numbering | Numbered tab	Bullets and Numbering | Numbered tab	1. and then space followed by text, then ENTER
Open Document	WD 55	Open button on Standard toolbar	File | Open		CTRL+O
Outline, Create	WD 459	Outline View button on horizontal scroll bar	View | Outline		
Outline Numbered List	WD 329		Format | Bullets and Numbering | Outline Numbered tab	Bullets and Numbering | Outline Numbered tab	
Outline, on Characters	WD 229		Format | Font | Font tab	Font | Font tab	
Page Alignment	WD 237		File | Page Setup | Layout tab		
Page Break	WD 103		Insert | Break		CTRL+ENTER
Page Break, Delete	WD 244	Cut button on Standard toolbar	Select page break, Edit | Cut	Select page break, Cut	Select page break, DELETE
Page Numbers, Insert	WD 83	Insert Page Number button on Header and Footer toolbar	Insert | Page Numbers		
Page Numbers, Modify	WD 248	Format Page Number button on Header and Footer toolbar	Insert | Page Numbers | Format button		
Page Orientation	WD 356		File | Page Setup | Margins tab		

Table 1 Microsoft Office Word 2003 Quick Reference Summary *(continued)*

TASK	PAGE NUMBER	MOUSE	MENU BAR	SHORTCUT MENU	KEYBOARD SHORTCUT
Paragraph, Change Format	WD 312	Click link in Reveal Formatting task pane	Format | Paragraph | Indents and Spacing tab	Paragraph | Indents and Spacing tab	
Paragraph Formatting, Remove	WD 87		Format | Paragraph | Indents and Spacing tab	Paragraph | Indents and Spacing tab	CTRL+Q
Paragraph Style, Apply	WD 332	Style box arrow on Formatting toolbar	Format | Styles and Formatting		
Paste	WD 170	Paste button on Standard toolbar or click icon in Office Clipboard gallery in Office Clipboard task pane	Edit | Paste	Paste	CTRL+V
Paste Options, Display Menu	WD 115	Paste Options button			
Pattern Fill Effect	WD 439		Format | Background | Fill Effects button		
Picture Bullets	WD 270		Format | Bullets and Numbering | Bulleted tab	Bullets and Numbering | Bulleted tab	
Print Document	WD 53	Print button on Standard toolbar	File | Print		CTRL+P
Print Preview	WD 158	Print Preview button on Standard toolbar	File | Print Preview		CTRL+F2
Print Specific Pages	WD 241		File | Print		CTRL+P
Promote List Item	WD 189	Increase Indent button on Formatting toolbar			
Propagate Labels	WD 350	Propagate Labels button on Mail Merge toolbar	Tools | Letters and Mailings | Mail Merge		
Quit Word	WD 54	Close button on title bar	File | Exit		ALT+F4
Reading Layout	WD 443	Read button on Standard toolbar	View | Reading Layout		ALT+R
Redo Action	WD 39	Redo button on Standard toolbar	Edit | Redo		
Research Task Pane, Display and Use	WD 124	ALT+click word in document	Tools | Research		
Research Task Pane, Insert text from	WD 125			Right-click selected text in task pane, click Copy; right-click location to paste in document, click Paste	Select text in task pane, CTRL+C; click location to paste in document, CTRL+V
Repeat Command	WD 39		Edit | Repeat		
Resize Graphic	WD 50	Drag sizing handle	Format | Picture | Size tab	Format Picture | Size tab	
Resize Graphic, Format Picture Dialog Box	WD 231	Double-click graphic	Format | Picture | Size tab	Format Picture | Size tab	
Restore Graphic	WD 51	Format Picture button on Picture toolbar	Format | Picture | Size tab	Format Picture | Size tab	
Resume Wizard	WD 142		File | New | General Templates | Other Documents tab		
Reveal Formatting	WD 283		Format | Reveal Formatting		SHIFT+F1
Reviewer Ink Colors, Change	WD 472		Tools | Options | Track Changes tab		
Right-Align	WD 37	Align Right button on Formatting toolbar	Format | Paragraph | Indents and Spacing tab	Paragraph | Indents and Spacing tab	CTRL+R
Ruler, Show or Hide	WD 11		View | Ruler		
Save, All Open Documents	WD 363		SHIFT + File | Save All		
Save as Web Page	WD 205		File | Save as Web Page		
Save Document - Different File Format	WD 206		File | Save As		
Save Document - New Name	WD 52		File | Save As		F12
Save Document - Same Name	WD 52	Save button on Standard toolbar	File | Save		CTRL+S
Save New Document	WD 28	Save button on Standard toolbar	File | Save		CTRL+S

Table 1 Microsoft Office Word 2003 Quick Reference Summary

TASK	PAGE NUMBER	MOUSE	MENU BAR	SHORTCUT MENU	KEYBOARD SHORTCUT
Section Break, Continuous	WD 399		Insert | Break		
Section Break, Next Page	WD 236		Insert | Break		
Select Document	WD 113	Point to left and triple-click	Edit | Select All		CTRL+A
Select Graphic	WD 49	Click graphic			
Select Group of Words	WD 43	Drag through words			CTRL+SHIFT+RIGHT ARROW
Select Line	WD 40	Point to left of line and click			SHIFT+DOWN ARROW
Select Multiple Paragraphs	WD 33	Point to left of first paragraph and drag down			CTRL+SHIFT+DOWN ARROW
Select Nonadjacent Text	WD 257				CTRL, while selecting additional text
Select Paragraph	WD 113	Triple-click paragraph			
Select Sentence	WD 112	CTRL+click sentence			CTRL+SHIFT+RIGHT ARROW
Select Word	WD 58	Double-click word			CTRL+SHIFT+RIGHT ARROW
Send Outline to PowerPoint	WD 476		File | Send To | Microsoft Office PowerPoint		
Shade Paragraph	WD 224, WD 413	Shading Color button on Tables and Borders toolbar	Format | Borders and Shading | Shading tab	Borders and Shading | Shading tab	
Shadow, on Characters	WD 229		Format | Font | Font tab	Font | Font tab	
Single-Space Text	WD 275	Line Spacing button arrow on Formatting toolbar	Format | Paragraph | Indents and Spacing tab	Paragraph | Indents and Spacing tab	CTRL+1
Small Uppercase Letters	WD 87		Format | Font | Font tab	Font | Font tab	CTRL+SHIFT+K
Smart Tag Actions, Display Menu	WD 192	Point to smart tag indicator, click Smart Tag Actions button			
Sort Paragraphs	WD 109		Table | Sort		
Spelling and Grammar Check At Once	WD 119	Spelling and Grammar button on Standard toolbar	Tools | Spelling and Grammar	Spelling	F7
Spelling Check as You Type	WD 26	Double-click Spelling and Grammar Status icon on status bar		Right-click flagged word, click correct word on shortcut menu	
Split Window	WD 441	Split box on vertical scroll bar	Window | Split		
Strikethrough, characters	WD 229		Format | Font | Font tab	Font | Font tab	
Style, Modify	WD 96	Styles and Formatting button on Formatting toolbar	Format | Styles and Formatting		
Styles and Formatting Task Pane, Display	WD 152	Styles and Formatting button on Formatting toolbar	View | Task Pane		
Subscript	WD 87		Format | Font | Font tab	Font | Font tab	CTRL+=
Superscript	WD 87		Format | Font | Font tab	Font | Font tab	CTRL+SHIFT+PLUS SIGN
Switch to Open Document	WD 166	Program button on taskbar	Window | document name		ALT+TAB
Symbol, Insert	WD 390		Insert | Symbol		ALT+0 (zero) then ANSI code on numeric keypad
Synonym	WD 118		Tools | Language | Thesaurus	Synonyms | desired word	SHIFT+F7
Tab Stops, Set	WD 164	Click location on ruler	Format | Tabs		
Table, Align Cell Contents	WD 279	Align button arrow on Tables and Borders toolbar	Table | Table Properties | Cell tab	Table Properties | Cell tab	
Table, AutoFormat	WD 187, WD 255	Table AutoFormat button on Tables and Borders toolbar	Table | Table AutoFormat		
Table, Convert Text	WD 355		Table | Convert | Text to Table		
Table, Draw	WD 272	Draw Table button on Tables and Borders toolbar	Table | Draw Table		
Table, Erase Lines	WD 274	Eraser button on Tables and Borders toolbar			

Table 1 Microsoft Office Word 2003 Quick Reference Summary *(continued)*

TASK	PAGE NUMBER	MOUSE	MENU BAR	SHORTCUT MENU	KEYBOARD SHORTCUT
Table, Fit Columns to Table Contents	WD 185	Double-click column boundary	Table | AutoFit | AutoFit to Contents	AutoFit | AutoFit to Contents	
Table, Insert Empty	WD 183	Insert Table button on Standard toolbar	Table | Insert | Table		
Table, Insert Row	WD 184		Table | Insert | Rows Above/Below	Right-click selected row; Insert Rows	TAB from lower-right cell
Table, Merge cells	WD 251	Merge Cells button on Tables and Borders toolbar	Select cells, Table | Merge Cells	Right-click selected cells, Merge Cells	
Table, Modify Properties	WD 258		Table | Table Properties	Table Properties	
Table, Resize Column	WD 186, WD 251	Drag column boundary	Table | Table Properties | Column tab	Table Properties | Column tab	
Table, Right-Align Cell Contents	WD 256	Align Right button on Formatting toolbar	Format | Paragraph | Indents and Spacing tab		CTRL+R
Table, Rotate Cell Text	WD 276	Change Text Direction button on Tables and Borders toolbar	Format | Text Direction	Text Direction	
Table, Row Height	WD 278	Drag row border	Table | Table Properties | Row tab	Table Properties | Row tab	
Table, Select	WD 186	Click table move handle	Table | Select | Table		ALT+5 (on numeric keypad)
Table, Select Cell	WD 186	Click left edge of cell			Press TAB
Table, Select Column	WD 186	Click top border of column			
Table, Select Multiple Cells	WD 186	Drag through cells			
Table, Select Row	WD 186	Click to left of row			
Table, Shade Cells	WD 277	Shading Color button arrow on Tables and Borders toolbar	Format | Borders and Shading | Shading tab	Borders and Shading | Shading tab	
Table, Sort	WD 359	Sort Ascending button on Tables and Borders toolbar	Table | Sort		
Table, Split Cells	WD 253	Split Cells button on Tables and Borders toolbar	Select cells, Table | Split Cells	Right-click selected cells, Split Cells	
Table, Sum a Column	WD 254	AutoSum button on Tables and Borders toolbar	Table | Formula		
Task Pane, Close	WD 10	Close button on task pane	View | Task Pane		
Task Pane, Display Different	WD 10	Other Task Panes button on task pane			
Template, Open	WD 175		File | New | On my computer		
Template, Use	WD 302		File | New | On my computer		
Text Box, Format	WD 412	Double-click text box	Format | Text Box	Format Text Box	
Text Box, Insert	WD 411	Text Box button on Drawing toolbar	Insert | Text Box		
Theme, Apply	WD 208		Format | Theme		
Toolbar, Dock	WD 82	Double-click toolbar title bar			
Toolbar, Float	WD 82	Drag toolbar move handle			
Toolbar, Show Entire	WD 14	Double-click move handle on toolbar	Tools | Customize | Options tab		
Track Changes	WD 467	Double-click TRK indicator on status bar	Tools | Track Changes		CTRL+SHIFT+E
Tracked Changes, Review	WD 469	Show button or Next button on Reviewing toolbar			
Underline	WD 42	Underline button on Formatting toolbar	Format | Font | Font tab	Font | Font tab	CTRL+U
Underline Words, not Spaces	WD 87		Format | Font | Font tab	Font | Font tab	CTRL+SHIFT+W
Undo Command or Action	WD 39	Undo button on Standard toolbar	Edit | Undo		CTRL+Z
User Information, Change	WD 194		Tools | Options | User Information tab		

Table 1 Microsoft Office Word 2003 Quick Reference Summary

TASK	PAGE NUMBER	MOUSE	MENU BAR	SHORTCUT MENU	KEYBOARD SHORTCUT
Vertical Rule	WD 409		Format | Borders and Shading | Borders tab		
Watermark	WD 281		Format | Background | Printed Watermark		
Web Page Frame, Resize	WD 211	Drag frame border	Format | Frames | Frame Properties | Frame tab		
Web Page, Preview	WD 209		File | Web Page Preview		
White Space, Hide or Show	WD 149	Hide or Show White Space button	Tools | Options | View tab		
WordArt Drawing Object, Format	WD 384	Format WordArt button on WordArt toolbar	Format | WordArt	Format WordArt	
WordArt Drawing Object, Insert	WD 383	Insert WordArt button on Drawing toolbar	Insert | Picture | WordArt		
WordArt Drawing Object, Shape	WD 387	WordArt Shape button on WordArt toolbar			
Wrap Text Around Graphic	WD 394, WD 427	Text Wrapping button Picture or Diagram toolbar	Format | Picture or Diagram | Layout tab	Format Picture or Format Diagram | Layout tab	
Zoom	WD 21	Zoom box arrow on Formatting toolbar	View | Zoom		
Zoom Text Width	WD 169	Zoom box arrow on Formatting toolbar	View | Zoom		
Zoom Two Pages	WD 435	Zoom box arrow on Formatting toolbar	View | Zoom		

Table 2 Microsoft Office Excel 2003 Quick Reference Summary

TASK	PAGE NUMBER	MOUSE	MENU BAR	SHORTCUT MENU	KEYBOARD SHORTCUT
Advanced Filter	EX 351		Data | Filter | Advanced Filter		ALT+D | F | A
Arrow, Add	EX 427	Arrow button on Drawing toolbar			
AutoFilter	EX 346		Data | Filter | AutoFilter		ALT+D | F | F
AutoFormat	EX 34		Format | AutoFormat		ALT+O | A
AutoSum	EX 23	AutoSum button on Standard toolbar	Insert | Function		ALT+= (equal)
Bold	EX 30	Bold button on Formatting toolbar	Format | Cells | Font tab	Format Cells | Font tab	CTRL+B
Borders	EX 96	Borders button on Formatting toolbar	Format | Cells | Border tab	Format Cells | Border tab	CTRL+1 | B
Center	EX 97	Center button on Formatting toolbar	Format | Cells | Alignment tab	Format Cells | Alignment tab	CTRL+1 | A
Center Across Columns	EX 33, EX 312	Merge and Center button on Formatting toolbar	Format | Cells | Alignment tab	Format Cells | Alignment tab	CTRL+1 | A
Chart	EX 39	Chart Wizard button on Standard toolbar	Insert | Chart		F11
Clear Cell	EX 52	Drag fill handle back	Edit | Clear | All	Clear Contents	DELETE
Close All Workbooks	EX 452		SHIFT+File | Close All		SHIFT+ALT+F | C
Close Workbook	EX 46	Close button on menu bar or workbook Control-menu icon	File | Close		CTRL+W
Color Background	EX 94	Fill Color button on Formatting toolbar	Format | Cells | Patterns tab	Format Cells | Patterns tab	CTRL+1 | P
Color Tab	EX 198			Tab Color	
Column Width	EX 107	Drag column heading boundary	Format | Column | Width	Column Width	ALT+O | C | W
Comma Style Format	EX 108	Comma Style button on Formatting toolbar	Format | Cells | Number tab | Accounting	Format Cells | Number tab | Accounting	CTRL+1 | N
Comment	EX 428		Insert | Comment	Insert Comment	ALT+I | M
Conditional Formatting	EX 104, EX 263		Format | Conditional Formatting		ALT+O | D

Table 2 Microsoft Office Excel 2003 Quick Reference Summary *(continued)*

TASK	PAGE NUMBER	MOUSE	MENU BAR	SHORTCUT MENU	KEYBOARD SHORTCUT
Copy and Paste	EX 157	Copy button and Paste button on Standard toolbar	Edit | Copy; Edit | Paste	Copy to copy; Paste to paste	CTRL+C; CTRL+V
Custom Formats	EX 395		Format | Cells | Number tab | Custom	Format Cells | Number tab | Custom	ALT+O | E | N
Currency Style Format	EX 98	Currency Style button on Formatting toolbar	Format | Cells | Number tab | Currency	Format Cells | Number | Currency	CTRL+1 | N
Cut	EX 159	Cut button on Standard toolbar	Edit | Cut	Cut	CTRL+X
Data Form	EX 318		Data | Form		ALT+D | O
Data Table	EX 261		Data | Table		ALT+D | T
Date	EX 166	Insert Function box on formula bar	Insert | Function		CTRL+SEMICOLON
Decimal Place, Decrease	EX 100	Decrease Decimal button on Formatting toolbar	Format | Cells | Number tab | Currency	Format Cells | Number tab | Currency	CTRL+1 | N
Decimal Place, Increase	EX 99	Increase Decimal button on Formatting toolbar	Format | Cells | Number tab | Currency	Format Cells | Number tab | Currency	CTRL+1 | N
Delete Rows or Columns	EX 161		Edit | Delete	Delete	
Draft Quality	EX 283		File | Page Setup | Sheet tab		ALT+F | U | S
Drop Shadow	EX 184	Shadow Style button on Drawing toolbar			
Embed a Clip Art	EX 277		Insert | Picture | Clip Art		ALT+I | P | C
E-Mail from Excel	EX 125	E-mail button on Standard toolbar	File | Send To | Mail Recipient		ALT+F | D | A
File Management	EX 232		File | Save; right-click file name	ALT+F | A, right-click file name	
Find	EX 443		Edit | Find		CTRL+F
Fit to Print	EX 118		File | Page Setup | Page tab		ALT+F | U | P
Folder, New	EX 232		File | Save As		ALT+F | A
Font Color	EX 32	Font Color button on Formatting toolbar	Format | Cells | Font tab	Format Cells | Font tab	CTRL+1 | F
Font Size	EX 31	Font Size box arrow on Formatting toolbar	Format | Cells | Font tab	Format Cells | Font tab	CTRL+1 | F
Font Type	EX 29	Font box arrow on Formatting toolbar	Format | Cells | Font tab	Format Cells | Font tab	CTRL+1 | F
Footer	EX 432		File | Page Setup | Header/Footer tab		ALT+F | U | H
Format Graphic	EX 280	Button on Picture toolbar	Format | Picture	Format Picture	ALT+O | I
Formula Assistance	EX 83	Insert Function box on formula bar	Insert | Function		CTRL+A after you type function name
Formula Checker	EX 292		Tools | Error Checking		ALT+T | K
Formulas Version	EX 118		Tools | Options | View tab | Formulas		CTRL+ACCENT MARK
Freeze Worksheet Titles	EX 163		Window | Freeze Panes		ALT+W | F
Full Screen	EX 11		View | Full Screen		ALT+V | U
Function	EX 81	Insert Function box on formula bar	Insert | Function		SHIFT+F3
Go To	EX 37	Click cell	Edit | Go To		F5
Goal Seek	EX 206		Tools | Goal Seek		ALT+T | G
Gridlines	EX 283		File | Page Setup | Sheet tab		ALT+F | U | S
Header	EX 432		File | Page Setup | Header/Footer tab		ALT+F | U | H
Help	EX 53 and Appendix A	Microsoft Excel Help button on Standard toolbar	Help | Microsoft Excel Help		F1
Hide Column	EX 109, EX 289	Drag column heading boundary	Format | Column | Hide	Hide	CTRL+0 (zero) to hide CTRL+SHIFT+RIGHT PARENTHESIS to display
Hide Row	EX 111, EX 289	Drag row heading boundary	Format | Row | Hide	Hide	CTRL+9 to hide CTRL+ SHIFT+LEFT PARENTHESIS to display
Hide Sheet	EX 289		Format | Sheet | Hide		ALT+O | H | H
Hide Workbook	EX 290		Window | Hide		ALT+W | H

Table 2 Microsoft Office Excel 2003 Quick Reference Summary

TASK	PAGE NUMBER	MOUSE	MENU BAR	SHORTCUT MENU	KEYBOARD SHORTCUT
Hyperlink	EX 277	Insert Hyperlink on Standard toolbar	Insert | Hyperlink	Hyperlink	CTRL+K
In-Cell Editing	EX 50	Double-click cell			F2
Insert Rows or Columns	EX 160		Insert | Rows or Insert | Columns	Insert	ALT+I | R or C
Italicize	EX 186	Italicize button on Formatting toolbar	Format | Cells | Font tab	Format Cells | Font tab	CTRL+I
Language Bar	EX 15 and Appendix B	Language Indicator button in tray	Tools | Speech | Speech Recognition		ALT+T | H | H
Link	EX 469		Edit | Paste Special		ALT+E | S
Link Update	EX 452		Edit | Links		ALT+E | K
List	EX 313		Data | List | Create List		ALT+D | I | C
Margins	EX 433		File | Page Setup | Margins		ALT+F | U | M
Merge Cells	EX 33	Merge and Center button on Formatting toolbar	Format | Cells | Alignment tab	Format Cells | Font tab | Alignment tab	ALT+O | E | A
Move Cells	EX 159	Point to border and drag	Edit | Cut; Edit | Paste	Cut; Paste	CTRL+X; CTRL+V
Name Cells	EX 37, EX 257, EX 284	Click Name box in formula bar and type name	Insert | Name | Create or Insert | Name | Define		ALT+I | N | D
New Workbook	EX 53	New button on Standard toolbar	File | New		CTRL+N
Open Workbook	EX 47	Open button on Standard toolbar	File | Open		CTRL+O
Outline a Range	EX 248	Borders button on Formatting toolbar	Format | Cells | Border tab	Format Cells | Border tab	CTRL+1 | B
Outline a Worksheet	EX 342		Data | Group and Outline		ALT+D | G | A
Page Break	EX 439		Insert | Page Break		ALT+I | B
Page Break, Remove	EX 439		Insert | Remove Page Break		ALT+I | B
Percent Style Format	EX 103	Percent Style button on Formatting toolbar	Format | Cells | Number tab | Percentage	Format Cells | Number tab | Percentage	CTRL+1 | N
Preview Worksheet	EX 114	Print Preview button on Standard toolbar	File | Print Preview		ALT+F | V
Print Area, Clear	EX 284		File | Print Area | Clear Print Area		ALT+F | T | C
Print Area, Set	EX 283		File | Print Area | Set Print Area		ALT+F | T | S
Print Row and Column Headings	EX 283		File | Page Setup | Sheet tab		ALT+F | U | S
Print Row and Column Titles	EX 283		File | Page Setup | Sheet tab		ALT+F | U | S
Print Worksheet	EX 113	Print button on Standard toolbar	File | Print		CTRL+P
Protect Worksheet	EX 286		Tools | Protection | Protect Sheet		ALT+T | P | P
Quit Excel	EX 46	Close button on title bar	File | Exit		ALT+F4
Range Finder	EX 89	Double-click cell			
Redo	EX 52	Redo button on Standard toolbar	Edit | Redo		ALT+E | R
Remove Splits	EX 204	Double-click split bar	Window | Split		ALT+W | S
Rename Sheet Tab	EX 198	Double-click sheet tab		Rename	
Replace	EX 445		Edit | Replace		CTRL+H
Research	EX 430	Research button on Standard toolbar	Tools | Research		ALT+click cell
Resolution	Appendix D			Right-click desktop, Properties | Settings	
Rotate Text	EX 151		Format | Cells | Alignment tab	Format Cells | Alignment tab	ALT+O | E | A
Row Height	EX 110	Drag row heading boundary	Format | Row | Height	Row Height	ALT+O | R | E
Save as Web Page	EX 230		File | Save as Web Page		ALT+F | G
Save Workbook – Different Format	EX 361		File | Save As		ALT+F | A
Save Workbook – New Name	EX 42		File | Save As		ALT+F | A
Save Workbook – Same Name	EX 89	Save button on Standard toolbar	File | Save		CTRL+S

Table 2 Microsoft Office Excel 2003 Quick Reference Summary *(continued)*

TASK	PAGE NUMBER	MOUSE	MENU BAR	SHORTCUT MENU	KEYBOARD SHORTCUT
Search for File	EX 447	Click Search button on Standard toolbar	File | Search		ALT+F | H
Select All of Worksheet	EX 53	Select All button on worksheet			CTRL+A
Select Cell	EX 16	Click cell			Use arrow keys
Select Multiple Sheets	EX 200	CTRL+click tab or SHIFT+click tab		Select All Sheets	
Series	EX 151, EX 386	Drag fill handle	Edit | Fill | Series		ALT+E | I | S
Shortcut Menu	EX 92	Right-click object			SHIFT+F10
Sort	EX 333	Click Sort Ascending or Sort Decending button on Standard toolbar	Data | Sort		ALT+D | S
Spell Check	EX 112	Spelling button on Standard toolbar	Tools | Spelling		F7
Split Cell	EX 33	Merge and Center button on Formatting toolbar	Format | Cells | Alignment tab	Format Cells | Alignment tab	ALT+O | E | A
Split Window into Panes	EX 203	Drag vertical or horizontal split box	Window | Split		ALT+W | S
Stock Quotes	EX 121, EX 460		Data | Import External Data | Import Data		ALT+D | D | D
Style, Add	EX 399		Format | Style | Add button		ALT+O | S
Style, Apply	EX 400		Format | Style		ALT+O | S
Subtotals	EX 338		Data | Subtotals		ALT+D | B
Subtotals, Remove	EX 342		Data | Subtotals | Remove All button		ALT+D | B | R
Synonym	EX 402	Research button on Standard toolbar	Tools | Research		ALT+click cell
Task Pane	EX 8		View | Task Pane		ALT+V | K
Text Box, Add	EX 427	Text Box button on Drawing toolbar			
Toolbar, Dock	EX 182	Drag toolbar to dock			
Toolbar, Reset	Appendix D	Toolbar Options, Add or Remove Buttons, Customize, Toolbars		Customize | Toolbars	ALT+V | T | C | B
Toolbar, Show Entire	EX 13	Double-click move handle			
Toolbar, Show or Hide	EX 182	Right-click toolbar, click toolbar name	View | Toolbars		ALT+V | T
Underline	EX 187	Underline button on Formatting toolbar	Format | Cells | Font tab	Format Cells | Font tab	CTRL+U
Undo	EX 51	Undo button on Standard toolbar	Edit | Undo		CTRL+Z
Unfreeze Worksheet Titles	EX 176		Windows | Unfreeze Panes		ALT+W | F
Unhide Column	EX 109	Drag column heading boundary to left	Format | Column | Unhide	Unhide	ALT+O | C | U
Unhide Row	EX 111	Drag row heading boundary down	Format | Row | Unhide	Unhide	ALT+O | R | U
Unhide Sheet	EX 289				
Unhide Workbook	EX 290				
Unlock Cells	EX 286		Format | Cells | Protection tab	Format Cells | Protection tab	CTRL+1 | SHIFT+P
Unprotect Worksheet	EX 289		Tools | Protection | Unprotect Sheet		ALT+T | P | P
Web Page Preview	EX 228		File | Web Page Preview		ALT+F | B
WordArt	EX 423	Insert WordArt button on Drawing toolbar	Insert | Picture | WordArt		ALT+I | P | W
Workspace File	EX 449		File | Save Workspace		ALT+F | W
Zoom	EX 201	Zoom box on Standard toolbar	View | Zoom		ALT+V | Z

Table 3 Microsoft Office Access 2003 Quick Reference Summary

TASK	PAGE NUMBER	MOUSE	MENU BAR	SHORTCUT MENU	KEYBOARD SHORTCUT
Add Combo Box	AC 235, AC 237	Combo Box tool			
Add Drop Areas	AC 360		View | Drop Areas		
Add Field	AC 129	Insert Rows button	Insert | Rows	Insert Rows	INSERT
Add Group of Records	AC 139	Query Type button arrow | Append Query	Query | Append Query	Query Type | Append Query	
Add Label	AC 241	Label tool			
Add Record	AC 23, AC 116	New Record button	Insert | New Record		
Add Switchboard Item	AC 334, AC 336	New button			
Add Switchboard Page	AC 332	New button			
Add Table to Query	AC 92	Show Table button	Query | Show Table	Show Table	
Add Text Box	AC 232	Text Box tool			
Advanced Filter/Sort	AC 124		Records | Filter | Advanced Filter Sort		
Align Controls	AC 212		Format | Align	Align	
Apply Filter	AC 121, AC 123	Filter By Selection or Filter By Form button	Records | Filter		
Calculate Statistics	AC 100	Totals button	View | Totals	Totals	
Change Chart Type	AC 356	Chart Type button	PivotChart | Chart Type	Chart Type	
Change Group of Records	AC 136	Query Type button arrow | Update Query	Query | Update Query	Query Type | Update Query	
Change Margins	AC 222	Setup	File | Page Setup | Margins tab	Page Setup	
Change PivotChart Organization	AC 358	By Row/By Column button	PivotChart | By Row/By Column		
Change Property	AC 215, AC 243	Properties button	View | Properties	Properties	F4
Change Tab Order	AC 295		View | Tab Order	Tab Order	
Clear Query	AC 75		Edit | Clear Grid		
Close Database	AC 26	Close Window button	File | Close		
Close Form	AC 39	Close Window button	File | Close		
Close Query	AC 73	Close Window button	File | Close		
Close Table	AC 21	Close Window button	File | Close		
Collapse Subdatasheet	AC 153	Expand indicator (-)			
Compact a Database	AC 163		Tools | Database Utilities | Compact and Repair		
Create Calculated Field	AC 96			Zoom	SHIFT+F2
Create Data Access Page	AC 380	New Object button arrow | Page	Insert | Page		
Create Database	AC 10	New button	File | New		CTRL+N
Create Form	AC 38, AC 228	New Object button arrow | AutoForm	Insert | AutoForm		
Create Index	AC 161	Indexes button	View | Indexes		
Create Input Mask	AC 263	Input Mask property box			
Create Lookup Wizard Field	AC 147	Text arrow | Lookup Wizard			
Create Macro	AC 317	New Object button arrow | Macro	Insert | Macro		
Create PivotChart	AC 347	View button arrow | PivotChart View	View | PivotChart View	PivotChart View	
Create PivotTable	AC 355	View button arrow | PivotTable View	View | PivotTable View	PivotTable View	
Create PivotTable in Data Access Page	AC 390	Office PivotTable tool	Insert | Office PivotTable		
Create Query	AC 68	New Object button arrow | Query	Insert | Query		
Create Report	AC 43	New Object button arrow | Report	Insert | Report		

Table 3 Microsoft Office Access 2003 Quick Reference Summary *(continued)*

TASK	PAGE NUMBER	MOUSE	MENU BAR	SHORTCUT MENU	KEYBOARD SHORTCUT
Create Snapshot	AC 184		File | Export, select SNP as file type	Export, select SNP as file type	
Create Switchboard	AC 330		Tools | Database Utilities | Switchboard Manager		
Create Table	AC 17	Tables object | Create table in Design view or Create table by using wizard	Insert | Table		
Crosstab Query	AC 104	New Object button arrow | Query	Insert | Query		
Default Value	AC 142	Default Value property box			
Delete Field	AC 130	Delete Rows button	Edit | Delete	Delete Rows	DELETE
Delete Group of Records	AC 138	Query Type button arrow | Delete Query	Query | Delete Query	Query Type | Delete Query	
Delete Record	AC 125	Delete Record button	Edit | Delete Record	Delete Record	DELETE
Exclude Duplicates	AC 87	Properties button	View | Properties | Unique Values Only	Properties | Unique Values Only	
Exclude Field from Query Results	AC 78	Show check box			
Expand Subdatasheet	AC 153	Expand indicator (+)			
Export Data Using Drag and Drop	AC 183	Drag object to desired application			
Export Data Using Export Command	AC 183		File | Export	Export	
Field Size	AC 19, AC 127	Field Size property box			
Field Type	AC 20	Data Type box arrow | appropriate type			Appropriate letter
Filter Records	AC 121, AC 123	Filter By Selection or Filter By Form button	Records | Filter		
Font in Datasheet	AC 133		Format | Font	Font	
Format	AC 144	Format property box			
Format a Calculated Field	AC 98	Properties button	View | Properties	Properties	
Format Datasheet	AC 134		Format | Datasheet	Datasheet	
Group Data Access Page	AC 386	Group by Table button			
Group in Query	AC 103	Totals button	View | Totals		
Import	AC 177		File | Get External Data | Import	Import	
Include All Fields in Query	AC 78	Double-click asterisk in field list			
Include Field in Query	AC 71	Double-click field in field list			
Join Properties	AC 94		View | Join Properties	Join Properties	
Key Field	AC 19	Primary Key button	Edit | Primary Key	Primary Key	
Link	AC 180		File | Get External Data | Link Tables	Link Tables	
Modify Switchboard Page	AC 333, AC 335	Edit button			
Move Control	AC 230	Drag control			
Move to Design View	AC 291	View button	View | Design View	Design View	
Move to First Record	AC 27	First Record button			CTRL+UP ARROW
Move to Last Record	AC 27	Last Record button			CTRL+DOWN ARROW
Move to Next Record	AC 27	Next Record button			DOWN ARROW
Move to Previous Record	AC 27	Previous Record button			UP ARROW
Open Database	AC 26	Open button	File | Open		CTRL+O
Open Form	AC 116	Forms object | Open button		Open	Use ARROW keys to move highlight to name, then press ENTER key

Table 3 Microsoft Office Access 2003 Quick Reference Summary

TASK	PAGE NUMBER	MOUSE	MENU BAR	SHORTCUT MENU	KEYBOARD SHORTCUT
Open Table	AC 26	Tables object | Open button		Open	Use ARROW keys to move highlight to name, then press ENTER key
Preview Table	AC 30	Print Preview button	File | Print Preview	Print Preview	
Print Relationships	AC 151		File | Print Relationships		
Print Report	AC 47	Print button	File | Print	Print	CTRL+P
Print Results of Query	AC 72	Print button	File | Print	Print	CTRL+P
Print Table	AC 30	Print button	File | Print	Print	CTRL+P
Quit Access	AC 50	Close button	File | Exit		ALT+F4
Relationships (Referential Integrity)	AC 150	Relationships button	Tools | Relationships		
Remove Control	AC 222	Cut button	Edit | Cut	Cut	DELETE
Remove Filter	AC 122	Remove Filter button	Records | Remove Filter/Sort		
Resize Column	AC 131, AC 268	Drag right boundary of field selector	Format | Column Width	Column Width	
Resize Control	AC 282	Drag sizing handle			
Resize Row	AC 268	Drag lower boundary of row selector	Format | Row Height	Row Height	
Resize Section	AC 224	Drag section boundary			
Restructure Table	AC 126	Tables object | Design button		Design View	
Return to Select Query Window	AC 72	View button arrow	View | Design View		
Run Query	AC 71	Run button	Query | Run		
Save Form	AC 39	Save button	File | Save		CTRL+S
Save PivotChart as Data Access Page	AC 395		File | Save As		
Save Query	AC 80	Save button	File | Save		CTRL+S
Save Table	AC 21	Save button	File | Save		CTRL+S
Search for Record	AC 117	Find button	Edit | Find		CTRL+F
Select Fields for Report	AC 44	Add Field button or Add All Fields button			
Show Legend	AC 355	Show Legend button	PivotChart | Show Legend		
Simple Query Wizard	AC 34	New Object button arrow | Query	Insert | Query		
Sort and Group in Report	AC 205	Sorting and Grouping button	View | Sorting and Grouping	Sorting and Grouping	
Sort Data in Query	AC 86	Sort row | Sort row arrow | type of sort			
Sort Records	AC 155	Sort Ascending or Sort Descending button	Records | Sort | Sort Ascending or Sort Descending	Sort Ascending or Sort Descending	
Switch Between Form and Datasheet Views	AC 41, AC 120	View button arrow	View | Datasheet View		
Top-Values Query	AC 89	Top Values button	View | Properties	Properties	
Update Hyperlink Field	AC 271	Insert Hyperlink	Insert | Hyperlink	Hyperlink | Edit Hyperlink	CTRL+K
Update OLE Field	AC 269		Insert | Object	Insert Object	
Use AND Criterion	AC 84				Place criteria on same line
Use OR Criterion	AC 85				Place criteria on separate lines
Validation Rule	AC 141	Validation Rule property box			
Validation Text	AC 141	Validation Text property box			
View Object Dependencies	AC 299		View | Object Dependencies		

Table 4 Microsoft Office PowerPoint 2003 Quick Reference Summary

TASK	PAGE NUMBER	MOUSE	MENU BAR	SHORTCUT MENU	KEYBOARD SHORTCUT
Animate Text	PPT 114		Slide Show | Custom Animation | Add Effect button		ALT+D | M
Black Slide, End Show	PPT 42		Tools | Options | End with black slide		ALT+T | O | E
Check Spelling	PPT 54	Spelling button on Standard toolbar	Tools | Spelling		F7
Clip Art, Add Animation Effects	PPT 117		Slide Show | Custom Animation		ALT+D | M
Clip Art, Change Size	PPT 109	Format Picture button on Picture toolbar | Size tab	Format | Picture | Size tab	Format Picture | Size tab	ALT+O | I | Size tab
Clip Art, Insert	PPT 101, PPT 104	Insert Clip Art button on Drawing toolbar	Insert | Picture | Clip Art		ALT+I | P | C
Clip Art, Move	PPT 108	Drag			
Delete Text	PPT 56	Cut button on Standard toolbar	Edit | Cut	Cut	CTRL+X or BACKSPACE or DELETE
Demote a Paragraph on Outline tab	PPT 90	Demote button on Outlining toolbar			TAB or ALT+SHIFT+RIGHT ARROW
Design Template	PPT 18	Slide Design button on Formatting toolbar	Format | Slide Design	Slide Design	ALT+O | D
Display a Presentation in Black and White	PPT 57	Color/Grayscale button on Standard toolbar	View | Color/Grayscale | Pure Black and White		ALT+V | C | U
Edit Web Page through Browser	PPT 152	Edit button on Internet Explorer Standard Buttons toolbar	File on browser menu bar | Edit with Microsoft PowerPoint in browser window		ALT+F | D in browser window
E-Mail from PowerPoint	PPT 127	E-mail button on Standard toolbar	File | Send To | Mail Recipient		ALT+F | D | A
End Slide Show	PPT 50			End Show	ESC
Font	PPT 24	Font box arrow on Formatting toolbar	Format | Font	Font	ALT+O | F
Font Color	PPT 24	Font Color button arrow on Formatting toolbar, desired color	Format | Font	Font | Color	ALT+O | F | ALT+C | DOWN ARROW
Font Size, Decrease	PPT 27	Decrease Font Size button on Formatting toolbar	Format | Font	Font | Size	CTRL+SHIFT+LEFT CARET (<)
Font Size, Increase	PPT 25	Increase Font Size button on Formatting toolbar	Format | Font	Font | Size	CTRL+SHIFT+RIGHT CARET (>)
Header and Footer, Add to Outline Page	PPT 112		View | Header and Footer | Notes and Handouts tab		ALT+V | H | Notes and Handouts tab
Help	PPT 62 and Appendix A	Microsoft PowerPoint Help button on Standard toolbar	Help | Microsoft PowerPoint Help		F1
Italicize	PPT 24	Italic button on Formatting toolbar	Format | Font | Font style	Font | Font style	CTRL+I
Language Bar	PPT 16 and Appendix B	Language Indicator button in tray	Tools | Speech | Speech Recognition		ALT+T | H | H
Move a Paragraph Down	PPT 87	Move Down button on Outlining toolbar			ALT+SHIFT+DOWN ARROW
Move a Paragraph Up	PPT 87	Move Up button on Outlining toolbar			ALT+SHIFT+UP ARROW
New Slide	PPT 30	New Slide button on Formatting toolbar	Insert | New Slide		CTRL+M
Next Slide	PPT 45	Next Slide button on vertical scroll bar			PAGE DOWN
Normal View	PPT 96	Normal View button at lower-left PowerPoint window	View | Normal		ALT+V | N
Open Presentation	PPT 52	Open button on Standard toolbar	File | Open		CTRL+O
Paragraph Indent, Decrease	PPT 37	Decrease Indent button on Formatting toolbar			SHIFT+TAB or ALT+SHIFT+LEFT ARROW
Paragraph Indent, Increase	PPT 36	Increase Indent button on Formatting toolbar			TAB or ALT+SHIFT+RIGHT ARROW
Preview Presentation as Web Page	PPT 144		File | Web Page Preview		ALT+F | B

Table 4 Microsoft Office PowerPoint 2003 Quick Reference Summary

TASK	PAGE NUMBER	MOUSE	MENU BAR	SHORTCUT MENU	KEYBOARD SHORTCUT
Previous Slide	PPT 45	Previous Slide button on vertical scroll bar			PAGE UP
Print a Presentation	PPT 60	Print button on Standard toolbar	File | Print		CTRL+P
Print an Outline	PPT 122		File | Print | Print what box arrow | Outline View		CTRL+P | TAB | TAB | DOWN ARROW | Outline View
Promote a Paragraph on Outline tab	PPT 89	Promote button on Outlining toolbar			SHIFT+TAB or ALT+ SHIFT+LEFT ARROW
Publish a Presentation	PPT 154		File | Save as Web Page | Publish | Publish		ALT+F | G | ALT+P | ALT+P
Quit PowerPoint	PPT 50	Close button on title bar or double-click control icon on title bar	File | Exit		ALT+F4 or CTRL+Q
Redo Action	PPT 22	Redo button on Standard toolbar	Edit | Redo		CTRL+Y or ALT+E | R
Save a Presentation	PPT 27	Save button on Standard toolbar	File | Save		CTRL+S
Save as Web Page	PPT 147		File | Save as Web Page		ALT+F | G
Slide Layout	PPT 98		Format | Slide Layout	Slide Layout	ALT+O | L
Slide Show View	PPT 47	Slide Show button at lower-left PowerPoint window	View | Slide Show		F5 or ALT+V | W
Slide Sorter View	PPT 95	Slide Sorter View button at lower-left PowerPoint window	View | Slide Sorter		ALT+V | D
Spelling Check	PPT 54	Spelling button on Standard toolbar	Tools | Spelling	Spelling	F7
Task Pane	PPT 11		View | Task Pane		ALT+V | K
Toolbar, Reset	Appendix D	Toolbar Options button on toolbar, Add or Remove Buttons, Customize, Toolbars tab		Customize | Toolbars tab	ALT+V | T | C | B
Toolbar, Show Entire	PPT 9	Double-click move handle			
Undo Action	PPT 22	Undo button on Standard toolbar	Edit | Undo		CTRL+Z or ALT+E | U
Web Page, Preview	PPT 144		File | Web Page Preview		ALT+F | B
Zoom Percentage, Increase	PPT 44	Zoom Box arrow on Standard toolbar	View | Zoom		ALT+V | Z

Table 5 Microsoft Office Outlook 2003 Quick Reference Summary

TASK	PAGE NUMBER	MOUSE	MENU BAR	SHORTCUT MENU	KEYBOARD SHORTCUT
Accept Meeting Request	OUT 108	Accept button on Standard toolbar in Meeting window	Actions | Accept	Accept	ALT+C
Accept Task Assignment	OUT 101	Accept button on Standard toolbar in Task window		Actions | Accept	Accept ALT+C
Address E-Mail Message	OUT 51	To button in Mail window			CTRL+SHIFT+B
Assign Task	OUT 99	Assign Task button on Standard toolbar in Task window	Actions | Assign Task	Assign Task	ALT+N
Attach File to E-Mail Message	OUT 28	Insert File button on Standard toolbar in Message window	Insert | File		ALT+I, L
Change to Day View	OUT 91	Day button on Standard toolbar	View | Day		ALT+V, Y
Change to Month View	OUT 91	Month button on Standard toolbar	View | Month		ALT+V, M
Change to Week View	OUT 90	Week button on Standard toolbar	View | Week		ALT+V, K
Change to Work Week View	OUT 89	Work Week button on Standard toolbar	View | Work Week		ALT+V, R
Color Code Calendar	OUT 115	Calendar Coloring button on Standard toolbar	Edit | Label	Label	ALT+E, L
Compose E-Mail Message	OUT 24	New button on Standard toolbar	File | New | Mail Message		CTRL+N
Create a Note	OUT 110	New button on Standard toolbar	Actions | New Note	New Note	CTRL+SHIFT+N

Table 5 Microsoft Office Outlook 2003 Quick Reference Summary *(continued)*

TASK	PAGE NUMBER	MOUSE	MENU BAR	SHORTCUT MENU	KEYBOARD SHORTCUT
Create a Task	OUT 92	New button on Standard toolbar			CTRL+SHIFT+K
Create an Event	OUT 88	New button on Standard toolbar	Actions | New All Day Event	New All Day Event	CTRL+N | ALT+A, N
Create Contact List	OUT 42	New button on Standard toolbar	Actions | New Contact	New Contact	CTRL+N | ALT+A, N
Create Distribution List	OUT 54	New button on Standard toolbar	File | New | Distribution List		CTRL+SHIFT+L
Create E-Mail Signature	OUT 20		Tools | Options		ALT+T, O
Create Personal Folder	OUT 40		File | New | Folder	New Folder	CTRL+SHIFT+E
Create Subfolder	OUT 70		File | New | Folder	New Folder	CTRL+SHIFT+E
Create View Filter	OUT 32		View | Arrange By	Custom	ALT+V, A, M
Delete an Appointment	OUT 82	Delete button on Standard toolbar	Edit | Delete	Delete	CTRL+D
Delete E-Mail Message	OUT 17	Delete button on Standard toolbar	Edit | Delete	Delete	CTRL+D
Delete Folder	OUT 96	Delete button on Standard toolbar	File | Folder | Delete	Delete	ALT+F, F, D
Display Contacts in a Category	OUT 49	Find button on Standard toolbar	Tools | Find		CTRL+E
Enter Appointments	OUT 74	New button on Standard toolbar	Actions | New Appointment	New Appointment	CTRL+SHIFT+A | ALT+A, O
Find a Contact	OUT 46	Find button on Standard toolbar	Tools | Find		CTRL+E
Flag E-Mail Messages	OUT 30		Actions | Follow Up	Follow Up	ALT+A, U
Forward E-Mail Message	OUT 16	Forward button on Standard toolbar	Actions | Forward	Forward	ALT+W
Import/Export Folders	OUT 93		File | Import and Export		ALT+F, T
Invite Attendees to Meeting	OUT 104	Add Others button in Appointment window	Actions | Invite Attendees		ALT+N
Move an Appointment	OUT 86		Edit | Cut | Edit | Paste		CTRL+X | CTRL+V
Move to Next Day	OUT 78		Go | Go to Date	Go to Date	CTRL+G
Open Calendar	OUT 68		Go | Calendar		
Open E-Mail Message	OUT 11		File | Open	Open	ALT+F, O
Organize Contacts	OUT 48		Tools | Organize		ALT+T, Z
Print Calendar	OUT 118	Print button on Standard toolbar	File | Print		CTRL+P
Print Contact List	OUT 50	Print button on Standard toolbar	File | Print		CTRL+P
Print E-Mail Message	OUT 12	Print button on Standard toolbar	File | Print		CTRL+P
Print Task List	OUT 119	Print button on Standard toolbar	File | Print		CTRL+P
Propose New Meeting Time	OUT 109	Propose New Time button on Standard toolbar in Meeting window	Actions | Propose New Time	Propose New Time	ALT+A, S
Recurring Appointments	OUT 76	Recurrence button on Standard toolbar in Appointment window	Actions | New Recurring Appointment	New Recurring Appointment	ALT+A, A
Reply to E-Mail Message	OUT 13	Reply button on Standard toolbar	Actions | Reply	Reply	ALT+R
Save Contact List as Text File	OUT 56		File | Save As		ALT+F, A
Send E-Mail Message	OUT 29	Send button on Standard toolbar	File | Send To		ALT+S
Send Instant Message	OUT 130		Actions | New Instant Message		ALT+A, S
Send Meeting Update	OUT 110	Send Update button on Standard toolbar in Meeting window			ALT+D
Set Message Delivery Options	OUT 34	Options button on Mail toolbar in Message window			ALT+P
Set Message Importance and Sensitivity	OUT 34	Options button on Mail toolbar in Message window			ALT+P
Sort E-Mail Messages	OUT 31		View | Arrange By		ALT+V, A